# Yard & Garden Tractor

SERVICE MANUAL ■ 1ST EDITION

PRIMEDIA Information Data Products
P.O. Box 12901 ■ Overland Park, KS 66282-2901
Phone: 800-262-1954 Fax: 800-633-6219
www.primediabooks.com

Library of Congress Catalog Card Number 92-70701



June, 2002
December, 2004

Cover photo courtesy of:
Cub Cadet Corp.

# Yard & Garden Tractor

*SERVICE MANUAL ■ 1ST EDITION*

***Tractor Manufacturers:***

- Allis-Chalmers
- Ariens
- Baron
- Bolens
- Broadmoor
- Case/Ingersoll
- Cub Cadet
- Jim Dandy
- John Deere
- Deutz-Allis
- Engineering Products Co.
- Ford
- Gilson
- Gravely
- Homesteader
- Honda
- International Harvester
- Jacobsen
- Kubota
- Landlord
- Lawn Ranger
- MTD
- Murray
- Power King
- Raider
- Serf
- Simplicity
- Snapper
- Sovereign
- Special
- Speedex
- Western Auto
- Wheel Horse
- White
- Wizard
- Work Horse
- Yard-Man
- Yeoman

***Engine Manufacturers:***

- Briggs & Stratton
- Honda
- Kawasaki
- Kohler
- Kubota
- Onan
- Tecumseh
- Wisconsin

**Publisher** Shawn Etheridge

**EDITORIAL**

***Editor***
Mike Hall

***Technical Writers***
Ben Evridge
Rodney J. Rom

***Editorial Production Manager***
Dylan Goodwin

***Senior Production Editor***
Greg Araujo

***Production Editors***
Holly Messinger
Darin Watson

***Associate Production Editors***
Susan Hartington
Julie Jantzer-Ward
Justin Marciniak

***Technical Illustrators***
Matt Hall
Bob Meyer

**MARKETING/SALES AND ADMINISTRATION**

***Associate Publisher***
Vickie Martin

***Marketing Director***
Rod Cain

***Manager, Promotions and Packaging***
Elda Starke

***Advertising & Promotions Coordinator***
Melissa Abbott

***Marketing Coordinator***
Chris Gregory

***Art Director***
Chris Paxton

***Associate Art Director***
Jennifer Knight

***Sales Managers***
Dutch Sadler, Marine
Matt Tusken, Motorcycles

***Business Manager***
Ron Rogers

***Customer Service Manager***
Terri Cannon

***Customer Service Representatives***
Shawna Davis
Courtney Hollars
Susan Kohlmeyer
April LeBlond
Jennifer Lassiter
Luis Lebron

***Warehouse & Inventory Manager***
Leah Hicks

**PRIMEDIA**
Business Magazines & Media
P.O. Box 12901, Overland Park, KS 66282-2901 • 800-262-1954 • 913-967-1719

***The following books and guides are published by PRIMEDIA Business Directories & Books.***

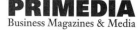

**More information available at *primediabooks.com***

# CONTENTS

## GENERAL

## GASOLINE ENGINE FUNDAMENTALS SECTION



## TRACTOR SERVICE SECTION



## TRANSAXLE SERVICE SECTION



## GEAR TRANSMISSION SERVICE SECTION

# CONTENTS (Cont.)

## REDUCTION GEAR AND DIFFERENTIAL SERVICE SECTION



## HYDROSTATIC TRANSMISSION SERVICE SECTION



## ENGINE SERVICE SECTION



# Dual Dimensions

**This service manual provides specifications in both the U.S. Customary and Metric (SI) systems of measurement. The first specification is given in the measuring system perceived by us to be the preferred system when servicing a particular component. The second specification (given in parentheses) is the converted measurement. For instance, the specification "0.011 inch (0.28 mm)" indicates that we feel the preferred measurement, in this instance, is the U.S. measurement system and the metric equivalent of 0.011 inch is 0.28 mm.**

# FUNDAMENTALS SECTION

## ENGINE FUNDAMENTALS

### OPERATING PRINCIPLES

The one, two or four cylinder engines used to power riding lawn mowers, garden tractors, pumps, generators, welders, mixers, windrowers, hay balers and many other items of power equipment in use today are basically similar. All are technically known as "Internal Combustion Reciprocating Engines."

The source of power is heat formed by burning a combustible mixture of petroleum products and air. In a reciprocating engine, this burning takes place in a closed cylinder containing a piston. Expansion resulting from the heat of combustion applies pressure on the piston to turn a shaft by means of a crank and connecting rod.

The fuel-air mixture may be ignited by means of an electric spark (Otto Cycle Engine) or by heat formed from compression of air in the engine cylinder (Diesel Cycle Engine). The complete series of events which must take place in order for the engine to run occurs in two revolutions of the crankshaft (four strokes of the piston in cylinder) and is referred to as a "Four-Stroke Cycle Engine."

**OTTO CYCLE.** In a spark ignited engine, a series of five events is required in order for the engine to provide power. This series of events is called the "Cycle" (for "Work Cycle" ) and is repeated in each cylinder of the engine as long as work is being done. This series of events which comprise the "Cycle" is as follows:

1. The mixture of fuel and air is pushed into the cylinder by atmospheric pressure when the pressure within the engine cylinder is reduced by the piston moving downward in the cylinder.
2. The mixture of fuel and air is compressed by the piston moving upward in the cylinder.
3. The compressed fuel-air mixture is ignited by a timed electric spark.
4. The burning fuel-air mixture expands, forcing the piston downward in the cylinder thus converting the chemical energy generated by combustion into mechanical power.
5. The gaseous products formed by the burned fuel-air mixture are exhausted from the cylinder so a new "Cycle" can begin.

The above described five events which comprise the work cycle of an engine are commonly referred to as (1), INTAKE; (2), COMPRESSION; (3), IGNITION; (4), EXPANSION (POWER); and (5), EXHAUST.

**DIESEL CYCLE.** The Diesel Cycle differs from the Otto Cycle in that air alone is drawn into the cylinder during the intake period. The air is heated from being compressed by the piston moving upward in the cylinder then a finely atomized charge of fuel is injected into the cylinder where it mixes with the air and is ignited by the heat of the compressed air. In order to create sufficient heat to ignite the injected fuel, an engine operating on the Diesel Cycle must compress the air to a much greater degree than an engine operating on the Otto Cycle where the fuel-air mixture is ignited by an electric spark. The power and exhaust events of the Diesel Cycle are similar to the power and exhaust events of the Otto Cycle.

**FOUR-STROKE CYCLE.** In a four-stroke cycle engine operating on the Otto Cycle (spark ignition), the five events of the cycle take place in four strokes of the piston, or in two revolutions of the engine crankshaft. Thus, a power stroke occurs only on alternate downward strokes of the piston.

In view "A" of Fig. 1-1, the piston is on the first downward stroke of the cycle. The mechanically operated intake valve has opened the intake port and, as the downward movement of the piston has reduced the air pressure in the cylinder to below atmospheric pressure, air is forced through the carburetor, where fuel is mixed with the air, and into the cylinder through the open intake port. The intake valve remains open and the fuel-air mixture continues to flow into the cylinder until the piston reaches the bottom of its downward stroke. As the piston starts on its first upward stroke, the mechanically operated intake valve closes and, since the exhaust valve is closed, the fuel-air mixture is compressed as in view "B".

Just before the piston reaches the top of its first upward stroke, a spark at the spark plug electrodes ignites the compressed fuel-air mixture. As the engine crankshaft turns past top center, the burning fuel-air mixture expands rapidly and forces the piston downward on its power stroke as shown in view "C". As the piston reaches the bottom of the power stroke, the mechanically operated exhaust valve starts to open and as the pressure of the burned fuel-air mixture is higher than atmospheric pressure, it starts to flow out the open exhaust port. As the engine crankshaft turns past bottom center, the exhaust valve is almost completely open and remains open dur-

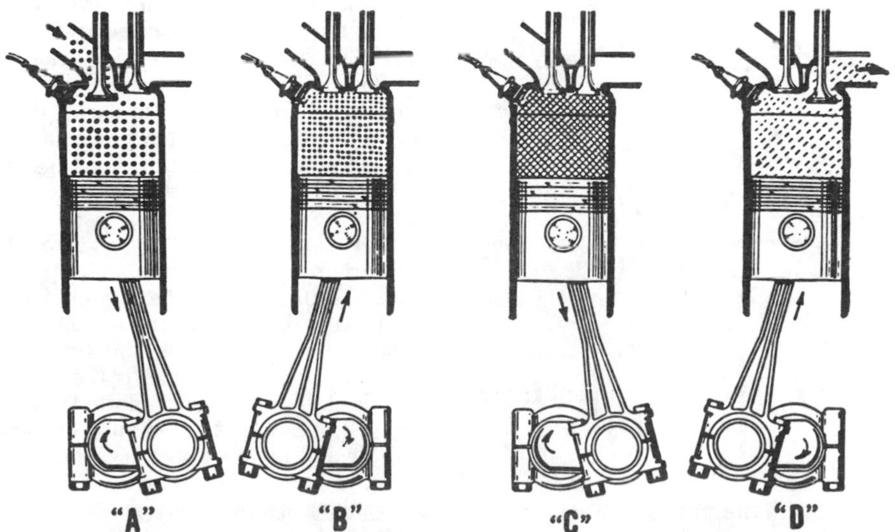


*Fig. 1-1 — Schematic diagram of four-stroke cycle engine operating on the Otto (spark ignition) cycle. In view "A", piston is on first downward (intake) stroke and atmospheric pressure is forcing fuel-air mixture from carburetor into cylinder through the open intake valve. In view "B", both valves are closed and piston is on its first upward stroke compressing the fuel-air mixture in cylinder. In view "C", spark across electrodes of spark plug has ignited fuel-air mixture and heat of combustion rapidly expands the burning gaseous mixture forcing the piston on its second downward (expansion or power) stroke. In view "D", exhaust valve is open and piston on its second upward (exhaust) stroke forces the burned mixture from cylinder. A new cycle then starts as in view "A".*

ing the upward stroke of the piston as shown in view "D". Upward movement of the piston pushes the remaining burned fuel-air mixture out of the exhaust port. Just before the piston reaches the top of its second upward or exhaust stroke, the intake valve opens and the exhaust valve closes. The cycle is completed as the crankshaft turns past top center and a new cycle begins as the piston starts downward as shown in view "A".

In a four-stroke cycle engine operating on the Diesel Cycle, the sequence of events of the cycle is similar to that described for operation on the Otto Cycle, but with the following exceptions: On the intake stroke, air only is taken into the cylinder. On the compression stroke, the air is highly compressed which raises the temperature of the air. Just before the piston reaches top dead center, fuel is injected into the cylinder and is ignited by the heated, compressed air. The remainder of the cycle is similar to that of the Otto Cycle.

# CARBURETOR FUNDAMENTALS

## OPERATING PRINCIPLES

Function of the carburetor on a spark-ignition engine is to atomize the fuel and mix the atomized fuel in proper proportions with air flowing to the engine intake port or intake manifold. Carburetors used on engines that are to be operated at constant speeds and under even loads are of simple design since they only have to mix fuel and air in a relatively constant ratio. On engines operating at varying speeds and loads, the carburetors must be more complex because different fuel-air mixtures are required to meet the varying demands of the engine.

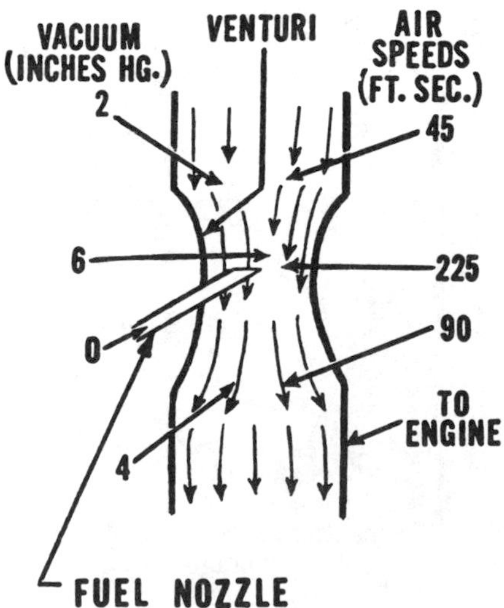


*Fig. 2-1—Drawing illustrating the venturi principle upon which carburetor design is based. Figures at left are inches of mercury vacuum and those at right are air speeds in feet per second that are typical of conditions found in a carburetor operating at wide open throttle. Zero vacuum in fuel nozzle corresponds to atmospheric pressure.*

**FUEL-AIR MIXTURE RATIO REQUIREMENTS.** To meet the demands of an engine being operated at varying speeds and loads, the carburetor must mix fuel and air at different mixture ratios. Fuel-air mixture ratios required for different operating conditions are approximately as follows:

| | Fuel | Air |
|---|---|---|
| Starting, cold weather | 1 lb. | 7 lbs. |
| Accelerating | 1 lb. | 9 lbs. |
| Idling (no load) | 1 lb. | 11 lbs. |
| Part open throttle | 1 lb. | 15 lbs. |
| Full load, open throttle | 1 lb. | 13 lbs. |

**BASIC DESIGN.** Carburetor design is based on the venturi principle which simply means that a gas or liquid flowing through a necked-down section (venturi) in a passage undergoes an increase in velocity (speed) and a decrease in pressure as compared to the velocity and pressure in full size sections of the passage. The principle is illustrated in Fig. 2-1, which shows air passing through a carburetor venturi. The figures given for air speeds and vacuum are approximate for a typical wide-open throttle operating condition. Due to low pressure (high vacuum) in the venturi, fuel is forced out through the fuel nozzle by the atmospheric pressure (0 vacuum) on the fuel; as fuel is emitted from the nozzle, it is atomized by the high velocity air flow and mixes with the air.

In Fig. 2-2, the carburetor choke plate and throttle plate are shown in relation to the venturi. Downward pointing arrows indicate air flow through the carburetor.

At cranking speeds, air flows through the carburetor venturi at a slow speed; thus, the pressure in the venturi does not usually decrease to the extent that atmospheric pressure on the fuel will force fuel from the nozzle. If the choke plate is closed as shown by dotted line in Fig. 2-2, air cannot enter into the carburetor and pressure in the carburetor decreases greatly as the engine is turned at cranking speed. Fuel can then flow from the fuel nozzle. In manufacturing the carburetor choke plate or disc, a small hole or notch is cut in the plate so that some air can flow through the plate when it is in closed position to provide air for the starting fuel-air mixture. In some instances, after starting a cold engine, it is advantageous to leave the choke plate in a partly closed position as the restriction of air flow will decrease the air pressure in carburetor venturi, thus causing more fuel to flow from the nozzle, resulting in a richer fuel-air mixture. The choke plate or disc should be in fully open position for normal engine operation.

If, after the engine has been started, the throttle plate is in wide-open position as shown by the solid line in Fig. 2-2, the engine can obtain enough fuel and air to run at dangerously high speeds. Thus, the throttle plate or disc must be partly closed as shown by the dotted lines to control engine speed. At no load, the engine requires very little air and fuel to run at its rated speed and the throttle must be moved on toward the closed position as shown by the dash lines. As more load is placed on the engine, more fuel and air are required for the engine to operate at its rated speed and throttle must be moved closer to the wide open position as shown by the solid line. When the engine is required to develop maximum power or speed the throttle must be in the wide open position.

Although some carburetors may be as simple as the basic design just described, most engines require more complex design features to provide variable fuel-air mixture ratios for different operating conditions. These design features will be described in the following paragraph.

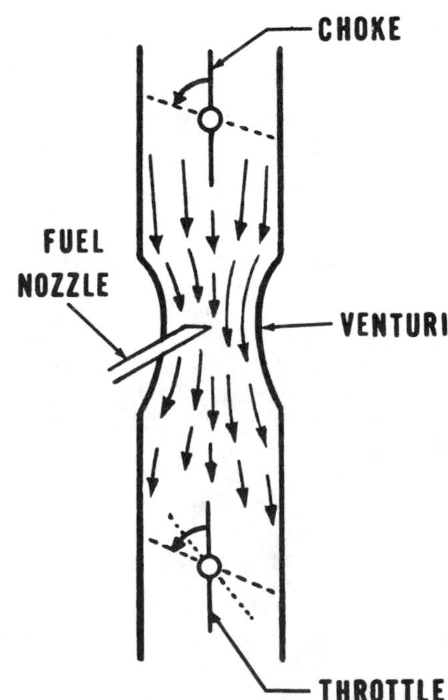


*Fig. 2-2—Drawing showing basic carburetor design. Text explains operation of the choke and throttle valves. In some carburetors, a primer pump may be used instead of the choke valve to provide fuel for the starting fuel-air mixture.*

### CARBURETOR TYPE

Carburetors are the float type and are either of the downshaft or side draft design. The following paragraph describes the features and operating principles of the float type carburetor.

**FLOAT TYPE CARBURETOR.** The principle of float type carburetor operation is illustrated in Fig. 2-3. Fuel is delivered at inlet (I) by gravity with fuel tank placed above carburetor, or by a fuel lift pump when tank is located below carburetor inlet. Fuel flows into the open inlet valve (V) until fuel level (L) in bowl lifts float against fuel valve needle and closes the valve. As fuel is emitted from the nozzle (N) when engine is running, fuel level will drop, lowering the float and allowing valve to open so fuel will enter the carburetor to meet the requirements of the engine.

In Fig. 2-4, a cut-away view of a well known make of float type carburetor is shown. Atmospheric pressure is maintained in fuel bowl through passage (20) which opens into carburetor air horn ahead of the choke plate (21). Fuel level is maintained at just below level of opening (O) in nozzle (22) by float (19) actuating inlet valve needle (8). Float height can be adjusted by bending float tang (5).

When starting a cold engine, it is necessary to close the choke plate (21) as shown by dotted lines so as to lower the air pressure in carburetor venturi (18) as engine is cranked. Then, fuel will flow up through nozzle (22) and will be emitted from openings (O) in nozzle. When an engine is hot, it will start on a leaner fuel-air mixture than when cold and may start without the choke plate being closed.

When engine is running at slow idle speed (throttle plate nearly closed as indicated by dotted lines in Fig. 2-4), air pressure above the throttle plate is low and atmospheric pressure in fuel bowl forces fuel up through the nozzle and out through orifice in seat (14) where it mixes with air passing the throttle plate. The idle fuel mixture is adjustable by turning needle (15) in or out as required. Idle speed is adjustable by turning the throttle stop screw (not shown) in or out to control amount of air passing the throttle plate.

When throttle plate is opened to increase engine speed, velocity of air flow through venturi (18) increases, air pressure at venturi decreases and fuel will flow from openings (O) in nozzle instead of through orifice in idle seat (14). When engine is running at high speed, pressure in nozzle (22) is less than at vent (12) opening in carburetor throat above venturi. Thus, air will enter vent and travel down the vent into the nozzle and mix with the fuel in the nozzle. This is referred to as air bleeding and is illustrated in Fig. 2-5.

Many different designs of float type carburetors will be found when servicing the different makes and models of engines. Reference should be made to the engine repair section of this manual for adjustment and overhaul specifications. Refer to carburetor servicing paragraphs in fundamentals sections for service hints.

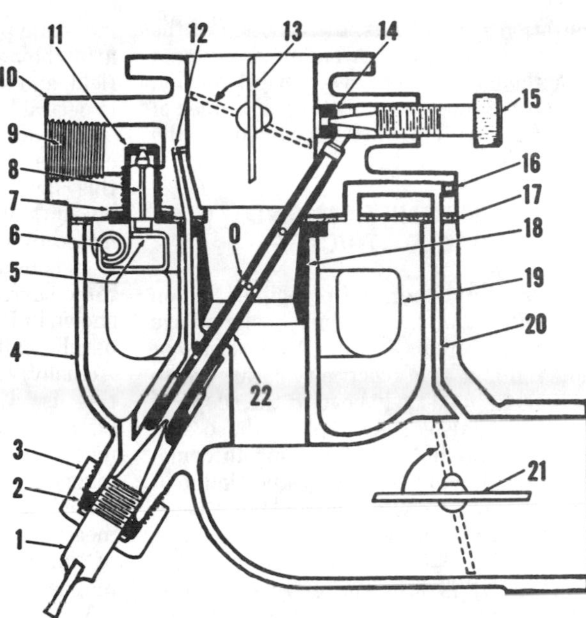


*Fig. 2-4—Cross-sectional drawing of float type carburetor used on some engines.*

0. Orifice
1. Main fuel needle
2. Packing
3. Packing nut
4. Carburetor bowl
5. Float tang
6. Float hinge pin
7. Gasket
8. Inlet valve
9. Fuel inlet
10. Carburetor body
11. Inlet valve seat
12. Vent
13. Throttle plate
14. Idle orifice
15. Idle fuel needle
16. Plug
17. Gasket
18. Venturi
19. Float
20. Fuel bowl vent
21. Choke
22. Fuel nozzle

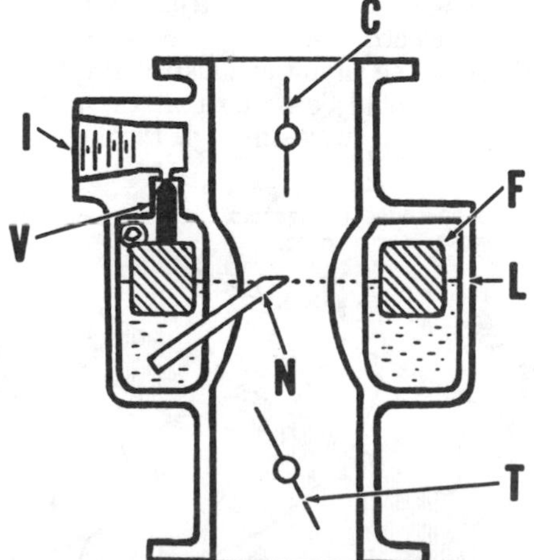


*Fig. 2-3—Drawing showing basic float type carburetor design. Fuel must be delivered under pressure either by gravity or by use of fuel pump, to the carburetor fuel inlet (I). Fuel level (L) operates float (F) to open and close inlet valve (V) to control amount of fuel entering carburetor. Also shown are the fuel nozzle (N), throttle (T) and choke (C).*

*Fig. 2-5—Illustration of air bleed principle explained in text.*

# IGNITION SYSTEM FUNDAMENTALS

The ignition system provides a properly timed surge of extremely high voltage electrical energy which flows across the spark plug electrode gap to create the ignition spark. Engines may be equipped with either a magneto or battery ignition system. A magneto ignition system generates electrical energy, intensifies (transforms) this electrical energy to the extremely high voltage required and delivers this electrical energy at the proper time for the ignition spark. In a battery ignition system, a storage battery is used as a source of electrical energy and the system transforms the relatively low electrical voltage from the battery into the high voltage required and delivers the high voltage at proper time for the ignition spark. Thus, the function of the two systems is somewhat similar except for the basic source of electrical energy. The fundamental operating principles of ignition systems are explained in the following paragraphs.

## MAGNETISM AND ELECTRICITY

The fundamental principles upon which ignition systems are designed are presented in this section. As the study of magnetism and electricity is an entire scientific field, it is beyond the scope of this manual to fully explore these subjects. However, the following information will impart a working knowledge of basic principles which should be of value in servicing engines.

**MAGNETISM.** The effects of magnetism can be shown easily while the theory of magnetism is too complex to be presented here. The effects of magnetism were discovered many years ago when fragments of iron ore were found to attract each other and also attract other pieces of iron. Further, it was found that when suspended in air, one end of the iron ore fragment would always point in the direction of the North Star. The end of the iron ore fragment pointing north was called the "north pole" and the opposite end the "south pole." By stroking a piece of steel with a "natural magnet," as these iron ore fragments were called, it was found that the magnetic properties of the natural magnet could be transferred or "induced" into the steel.

Steel which will retain magnetic properties for an extended period of time after being subjected to a strong magnetic field are called "permanent magnets;" iron or steel that loses such magnetic properties soon after being subjected to a magnetic field are called "temporary magnets." Soft iron will lose magnetic properties almost immediately after being removed from a magnetic field, and so is used where this property is desirable.

The area affected by a magnet is called a "field of force." The extent of this field of force is related to the strength of the magnet and can be determined by use of a compass. In practice, it is common to illustrate the field of force surrounding a magnet by lines as shown in Fig. 3-1 and the field of force is usually called "lines of force" or "flux." Actually, there are no "lines;" however, this is a convenient method of illustrating the presence of the invisible magnetic forces and if a certain magnetic force is defined as a "line of force," then all magnetic forces may be measured by comparison. The number of "lines of force" making up a strong magnetic field is enormous.

Most materials when placed in a magnetic field are not attracted by the magnet, do not change the magnitude or direction of the magnetic field, and so are called "non-magnetic materials." Materials such as iron, cobalt, nickel or their alloys, when placed in a magnetic field will concentrate the field of force and hence are magnetic conductors or "magnetic materials." There are no materials known in which magnetic fields will not penetrate and magnetic lines of force can be deflected only by magnetic materials or by another magnetic field.

Alnico, an alloy containing aluminum, nickel and cobalt, retains magnetic properties for a very long period of time after being subjected to a strong magnetic field and is extensively used as a permanent magnet. Soft iron, which loses magnetic properties quickly, is used to concentrate magnetic fields as in Fig. 3-1.

**ELECTRICITY.** Electricity, like magnetism, is an invisible physical force whose effects may be more readily explained than the theory of what electricity consists of. All of us are familiar with the property of electricity to produce light, heat and mechanical power. What must be explained for the purpose of understanding ignition system operation is the inter-relationship of magnetism and electricity and how the ignition spark is produced.

Electrical current may be defined as a flow of energy in a conductor which, in some ways, may be compared to flow of water in a pipe. For electricity to flow, there must be a pressure (voltage) and a complete circuit (closed path) through which the electrical energy may return, a comparison being a water pump and a pipe that receives water from the outlet (pressure) side of the pump and returns the water to the inlet side of the pump. An electrical circuit may be completed by electricity flowing through the earth (ground), or through the metal framework of an engine or other equipment ("grounded" or "ground" connections). Usually, air is an insulator through which electrical energy will not flow. However if the force (voltage) becomes great, the resistance of air to the flow of electricity is broken down and a current will flow, releasing energy in the form of a spark. By high voltage electricity breaking down the resistance of the air gap between the spark plug electrodes, the ignition spark is formed.

**ELECTRO-MAGNETIC INDUCTION.** The principle of electro-magnetic induction is as follows: When a wire (conductor) is moved through a field of magnetic force so as to cut across the lines of force (flux), a potential voltage or electromotive force (emf) is induced in the wire. If the wire is a part of a completed electrical circuit, current will flow through the circuit as illustrated in Fig. 3-2. It should be noted that the movement of the wire through the lines of

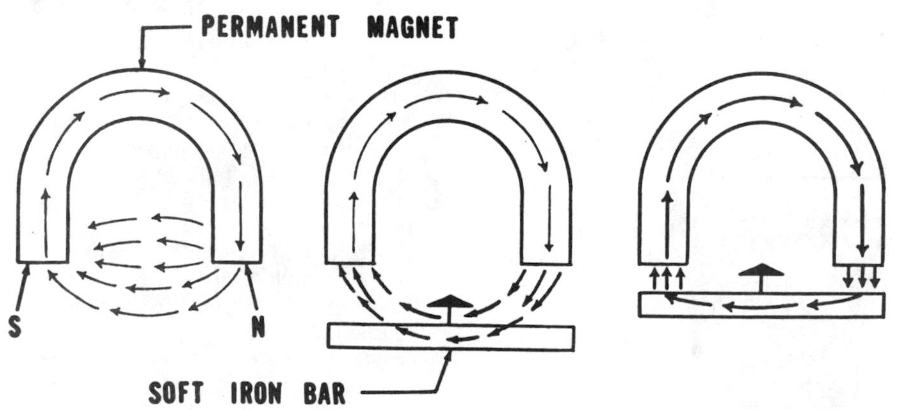


*Fig. 3-1 — In left view, field of force of permanent magnet is illustrated by arrows showing direction of magnetic force from north pole (N) to south pole (S). In center view, lines of magnetic force are being attracted by soft iron bar that is being moved into the magnetic field. In right view, the soft iron bar has been moved close to the magnet and the field of magnetic force is concentrated within the bar.*

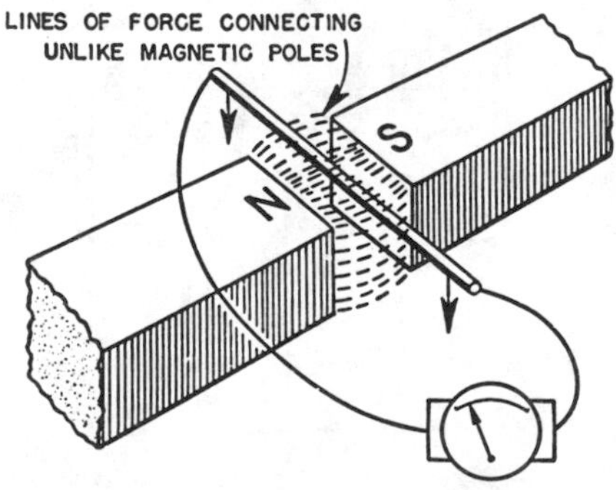


*Fig. 3-2 — When a conductor is moved through a magnetic field so as to cut across lines of force, a potential voltage will be induced in the conductor. If the conductor is a part of a completed electrical circuit, current will flow through the circuit indicated by the gage.*

magnetic force is a relative motion; that is, if the lines of force of a moving magnetic field cut across a wire, this will also induce an emf to the wire.

The direction of an induced current is related to the direction of magnetic force and also to the direction of movement of the wire through the lines of force, or flux. The voltage of an induced current is related to the strength, or concentration of lines of force, of the magnetic field and to the rate of speed at which the wire is moved through the flux. If a length of wire is wound into a coil and a section of the coil is moved through magnetic lines of force, the voltage induced will be proportional to the number of turns of wire in the coil.

**ELECTRICAL MAGNETIC FIELDS.** When a current is flowing in a wire, a magnetic field is present around the wire as illustrated in Fig. 3-3. The direction of lines of force of this magnetic field is related to the direction of current in the wire. This is known as the left hand rule and is stated as follows: If a wire carrying a current is grasped in the left hand with thumb pointing in direction electrons are moving, the curved fingers will point the direction of lines of magnetic force (flux) encircling the wire.

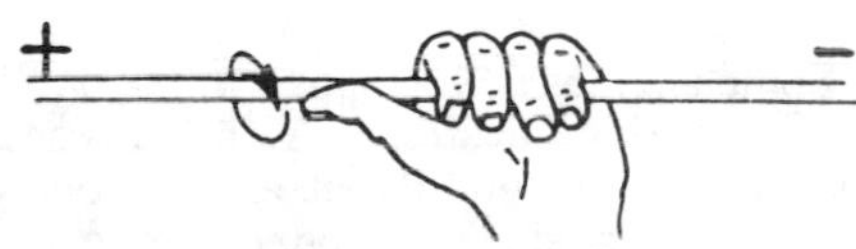


*Fig. 3-3—A magnetic field surrounds a wire carrying an electrical current. The direction of magnetic force is indicated by the left hand rule; that is, if thumb of left hand points in direction that electrical current is flowing in conductor, fingers of the left hand will indicate direction of magnetic force.*

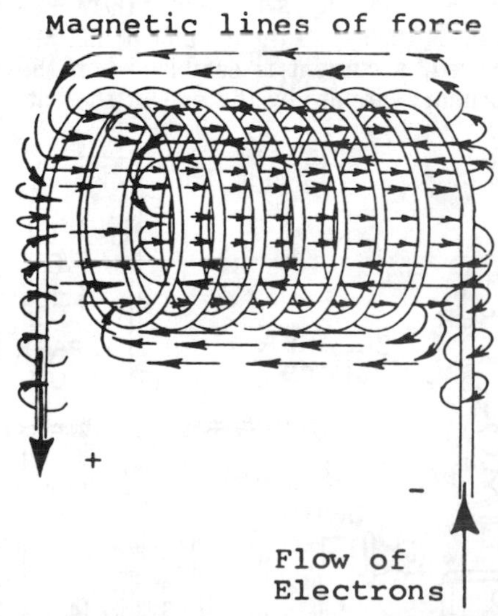


*Fig. 3-4—When a wire is wound in a coil, the magnetic force created by a current in the wire will tend to converge in a single strong magnetic field as illustrated. If the loops of the coil are wound closely together, there is little tendency for lines of force to surround individual loops of the coil.*

**NOTE: The currently used electron theory explains the movement of electrons from negative to positive. Be sure to use the LEFT HAND RULE with the thumb pointing the direction electrons are moving (toward positive end of a conductor).**

If a current is flowing in a wire that is wound into a coil, the magnetic flux surrounding the wire converge to form a stronger magnetic field as shown in Fig. 3-4. If the coils of wire are very close together, there is little tendency for magnetic flux to surround individual loops of the coil and a strong magnetic field will surround the entire coil. The strength of this field will vary with the current flowing through the coil.

**STEP-UP TRANSFORMERS (IGNITION COILS).** In both battery and magneto ignition systems, it is necessary to step-up, or transform, a relatively low primary voltage to the 15,000 to 20,000 volts required for the ignition spark. This is done by means of an ignition coil which utilizes the interrelationship of magnetism and electricity as explained in preceding paragraphs.

Basic ignition coil design is shown in Fig. 3-5. The coil consists of two separate coils of wire which are called the primary coil winding and the secondary coil winding, or simply the primary winding and secondary winding. The primary winding as indicated by the heavy, black line is of larger diameter wire and has a smaller number of turns when compared to the secondary winding indicated by the light line.

A current passing through the primary winding creates a magnetic field (as indicated by the "lines of force") and this field, concentrated by the soft iron core, surrounds both the primary and secondary windings. If the primary winding current is suddenly interrupted, the magnetic field will collapse and the lines of force will cut through the coil windings. The resulting induced voltage in the secondary winding is greater than the voltage of the current that was flowing in the primary winding and is related to the number of turns of wire in each winding. Thus:

$$\text{Induced secondary voltage} = \text{primary voltage} \times \frac{\text{No. of turns in secondary winding}}{\text{No. of turns in primary winding}}$$

For example, if the primary winding of an ignition coil contained 100 turns of wire and the secondary winding contained 10,000 turns of wire, a current having an emf of 200 volts flowing in the primary winding, when suddenly interrupted, would result in an emf of:

$$200 \text{ Volts} \times \frac{10{,}000 \text{ turns of wire}}{100 \text{ turns of wire}} = 20{,}000 \text{ volts}$$

SELF-INDUCTANCE. It should be noted the collapsing magnetic field resulting from interrupted current in the primary winding will also induce a current in the primary winding. This effect is termed "self-inductance." This self-induced current is such as to oppose any interruption of current in the primary winding, slowing the collapse of the magnetic field and reducing the efficiency of the coil. The self-induced primary current flowing across the slightly open breaker switch, or contact

*Fig. 3-5—Drawing showing principles of ignition coil operation. A current in primary winding will establish a magentic field surrounding both the primary and secondary windings and the field will be concentrated by the iron core. When primary current is interrupted, the magnetic field will "collapse" and the lines of force wil cut the coil windings inducing a very high voltage in the secondary winding.*

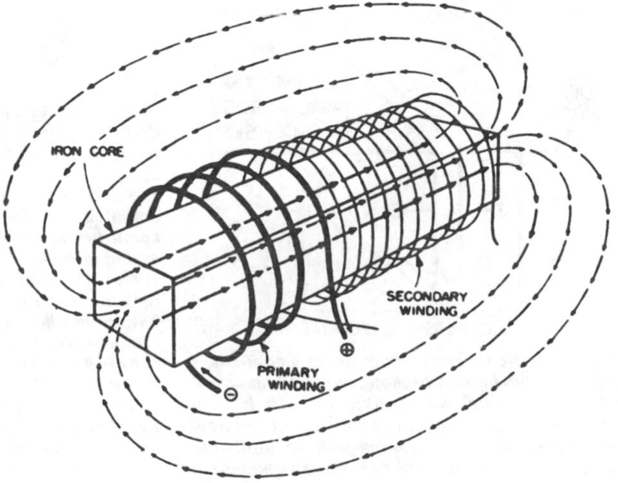

points, will damage the contact surfaces due to the resulting spark.

To momentarily absorb, then stop the flow of current across the contact points, a capacitor or, as commonly called, a condenser is connected in parallel with the contact points. A simple condenser is shown in Fig. 3-6; however, the capacity of such a condenser to absorb current (capacitance) is limited by the small surface area of the plates. To increase capacity to absorb current, the condenser used in ignition systems is constructed as shown in Fig. 3-9.

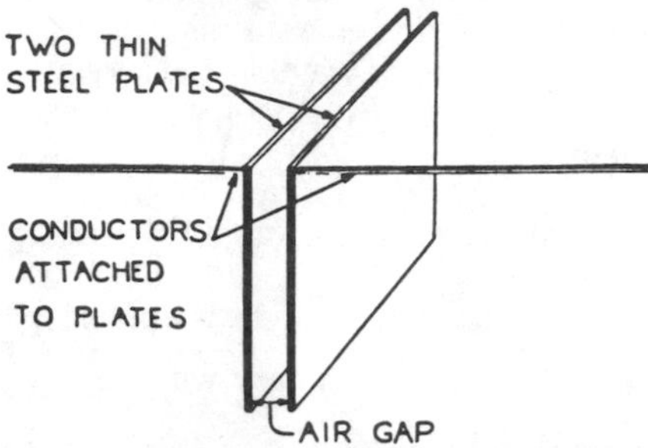


***Fig. 3-6—Drawing showing construction of a simple condenser. Capacity of such a condenser to absorb current is limited due to the relatively small surface area. Also, there is a tendency for current to arc across the air gap. Refer to Fig. 3-9 for construction of typical ignition system condenser.***

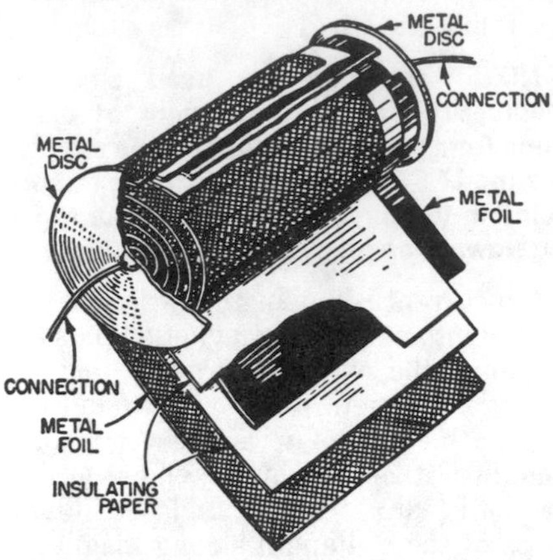


***Fig. 3-9—Drawing showing construction of typical ignition system condenser. Two layers of metal foil, insulated from each other with paper, are rolled tightly together and a metal disc contacts each layer, or strip of foil. Usually, one disc is grounded through the condenser shell.***

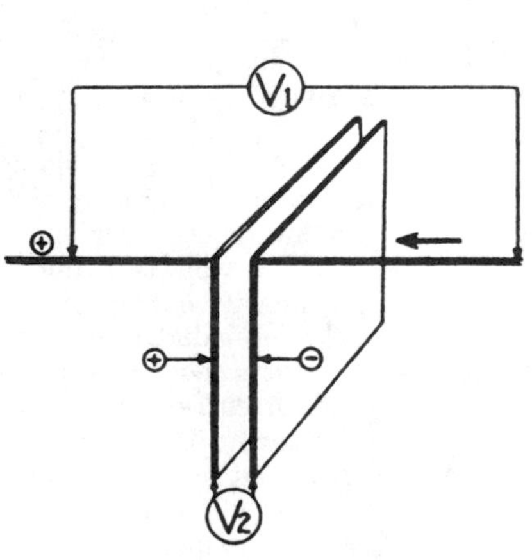


***Fig. 3-7—A condenser in an electrical circuit will absorb electrons until opposing voltage (V2) is built up across condenser plates which is equal to the voltage (V1) of the electrical current.***

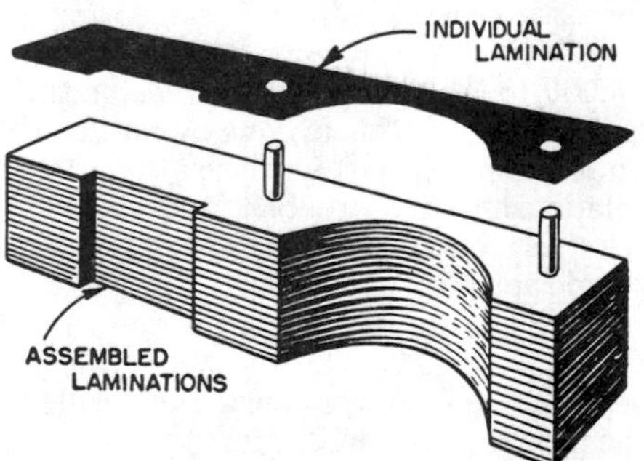


***Fig. 3-10—To prevent formation of "eddy currents" within soft iron cores used to concentrate magnetic fields, core is assembled of plates or "laminations" that are insulated from each other. In a solid iron core, there is a tendency for counteracting magnetic forces to build up from stray currents induced in the core.***

EDDY CURRENTS. It has been found that when a solid soft iron bar is used as a core for an ignition coil, stray electrical currents are formed in the core. These stray, or "eddy currents," create opposing magnetic forces causing the core to become hot and also decrease efficiency of the coil. As a means of preventing excessive formation of eddy currents within the core, or other magnetic field carrying parts of a magneto, a laminated plate construction as shown in Fig. 3-10 is used instead of solid material. The plates, or laminations, are insulated from each other by a natural oxide coating formed on the plate surfaces or by coating the plates with varnish. The cores of some ignition coils are constructed of soft iron wire instead of plates and each wire is insulated by a varnish coating. This type construction serves the same purpose as laminated plates.

## BATTERY IGNITION SYSTEMS

Some engines are equipped with a battery ignition system. A schematic diagram of a typical battery ignition system for a single cylinder engine is shown in Fig. 3-11. Designs of battery ignition systems may vary, especially as to location of breaker points and method for actuating the points; however, all operate on the same basic principles.

**BATTERY IGNITION SYSTEM PRINCIPLES.** Refer to the schematic diagram in Fig. 3-11. When the timer cam is turned so the contact points are closed, a current is established in the primary circuit by the emf of the bat-

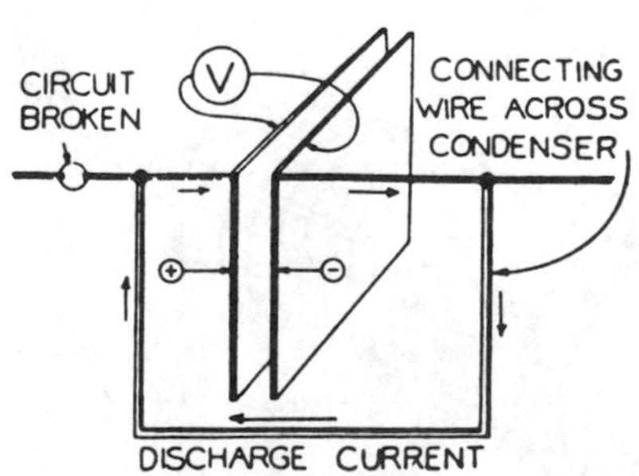


***Fig. 3-8—When a circuit containing a condenser is interrupted (circuit broken), the condenser will retain a potential voltage (V). If a wire is connected across the condenser, a current will flow in reverse direction of charging current until condenser is discharged (voltage across condenser plates is zero).***

***Fig. 3-11—Schematic diagram of typical battery ignition system used on single cylinder engine. On unit shown, breaker points are actuated by timer cam; on some units, points may be actuated by cam on engine camshaft. Refer to Fig. 3-12 for cut-away view of typical battery ignition coil. In this Fig., primary coil winding is shown as heavy black line (outside coil loops) and secondary winding is shown by lighter line (inside coil loops).***

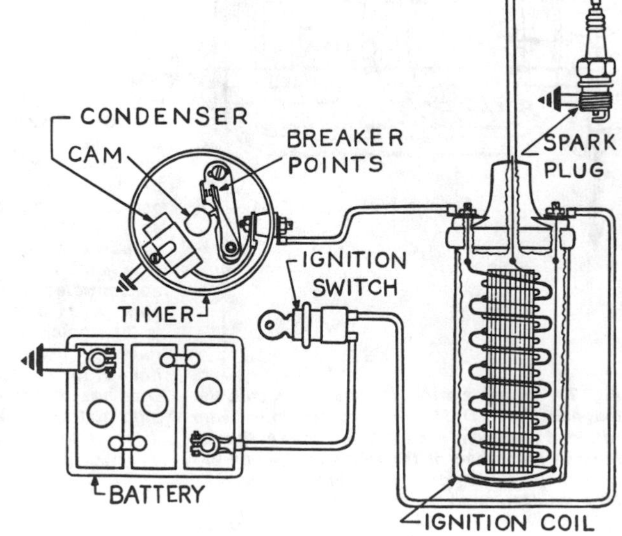

tery. This current flowing through the primary winding of the ignition coil establishes a magnetic field concentrated in the core laminations and surrounding the windings. A cut-away view of a typical ignition coil is shown in Fig. 3-12. At the proper time for the ignition spark, contact points are opened by the timer cam and primary ignition circuit is interrupted. The condenser, wired in parallel with breaker contact points between timer terminal and ground, absorbs self-induced current in the primary circuit for an instant and brings the flow of current to a quick, controlled stop. The magnetic field surrounding the coil rapidly cuts the primary and secondary windings creating an emf as high as 250 volts in the primary winding and up to 25,000 volts in the secondary winding. Current absorbed by the condenser is discharged as breaker points close, grounding the condenser lead wire.

Due to resistance of the primary winding, a certain period of time is required for maximum primary current flow after breaker contact points are closed. At high engine speeds, points remain closed for smaller interval of time, hence primary current does not build up to maximum and secondary voltage is somewhat less than at low engine speed. However, coil design is such that the minimum voltage available at high engine speed exceeds the normal maximum voltage required for ignition spark.

## MAGNETO IGNITION SYSTEMS

By utilizing principles of magnetism and electricity as outlined in previous paragraphs, a magneto generates an electrical current of relatively low voltage, then transforms this voltage into the extremely high voltage necessary to produce ignition spark. This surge of high voltage is timed to create the ignition spark and ignite the compressed fuel-air mixture in the engine cylinder at the proper time in the Otto cycle as described in the paragraphs on fundamentals of engine operation principles.

Two different types of magnetos are used on air-cooled engines and, for discussion in this section of the manual, will be classified as "flywheel type magnetos" and "self-contained unit type magnetos."

### Flywheel Type Magnetos

The term "flywheel type magneto" is derived from the fact that the engine flywheel carries the permanent magnets and is the magneto rotor. In some

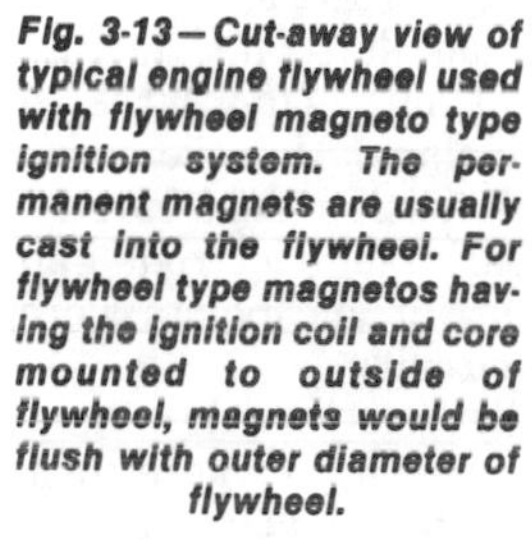

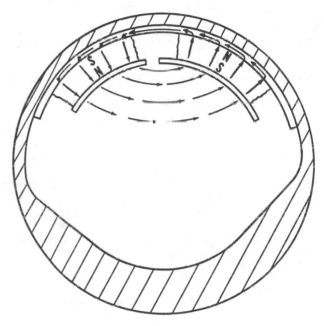

*Fig. 3-13—Cut-away view of typical engine flywheel used with flywheel magneto type ignition system. The permanent magnets are usually cast into the flywheel. For flywheel type magnetos having the ignition coil and core mounted to outside of flywheel, magnets would be flush with outer diameter of flywheel.*

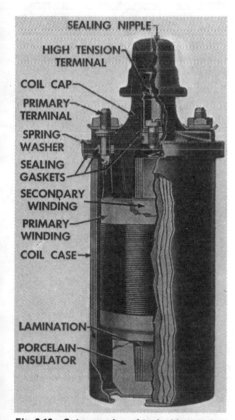

*Fig. 3-12—Cut-away view of typical battery ignition system coil. Primary winding consists of approximately 200-250 turns (loops) of heavier wire; secondary winding consists of several thousand turns of fine wire. Laminations concentrate magnetic lines of force and increase efficiency of the coil.*

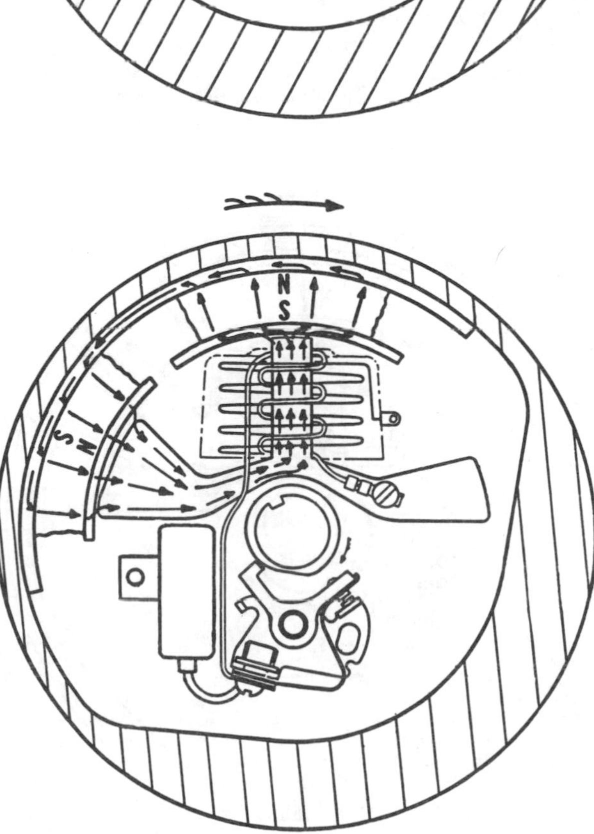

*Fig. 3-14—View showing flywheel turned to a position so lines of force of the permanent magnets are concentrated in the left and center core legs and are interlocking the coil windings.*

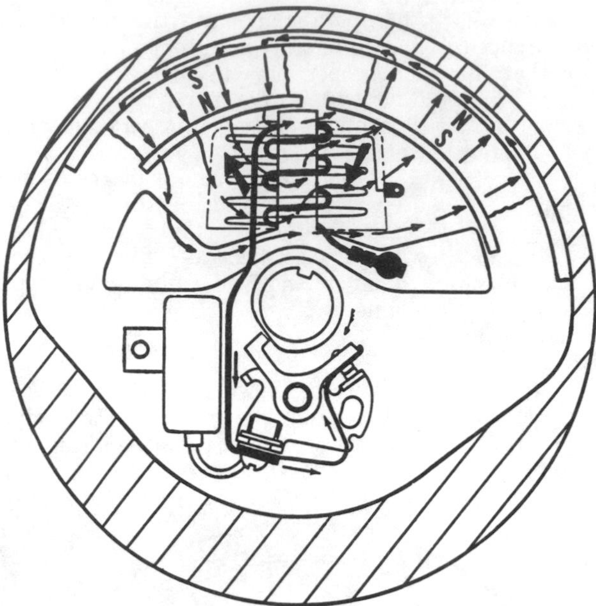

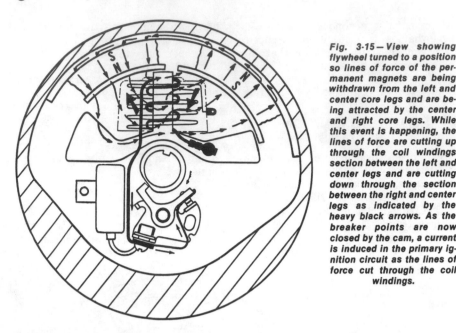

*Fig. 3-15—View showing flywheel turned to a position so lines of force of the permanent magnets are being withdrawn from the left and center core legs and are being attracted by the center and right core legs. While this event is happening, the lines of force are cutting up through the coil windings section between the left and center legs and are cutting down through the section between the right and center legs as indicated by the heavy black arrows. As the breaker points are now closed by the cam, a current is induced in the primary ignition circuit as the lines of force cut through the coil windings.*

similar systems, magneto rotor is mounted on engine crankshaft as is the flywheel, but is a part separate from flywheel.

**FLYWHEEL MAGNETO OPERATING PRINCIPLES.** In Fig. 3-13, a cross-sectional view of a typical engine flywheel (magneto rotor) is shown. The arrows indicate lines of force (flux) of the permanent magnets carried by the flywheel. As indicated by arrows, direction of force of magnetic field is from north pole (N) of left magnet to south pole (S) of right magnet.

Figs. 3-14, 3-15, 3-16 and 3-17 illustrate operational cycle of flywheel type magneto. In Fig. 3-14, flywheel magnets have moved to a position over left and center legs of armature (ignition coil) core. As magnets moved into this position, their magnetic field was attracted by armature core as illustrated in Fig. 3-1 and a potential voltage (emf) was induced in coil windings. However, this emf was not sufficient to cause current to flow across spark plug electrode gap in high tension circuit and points were open in primary circuit.

In Fig. 3-15, flywheel magnets have moved to a new position to where their magnetic field is being attracted by center and right legs of armature core, and is being withdrawn from left and center legs. As indicated by heavy black arrows, lines of force are cutting up through the section of coil windings between left and center legs of armature and are cutting down through coil windings section between center and right legs. If the left hand rule, as explained in a previous paragraph, is applied to the lines of force cutting through the coil sections, it is seen that the resulting emf induced in the primary circuit will cause a current to flow through primary windings and breaker points which have now been closed by action of the cam.

At the instant movement of lines of force cutting through coil winding sections is at maximum rate, maximum flow of current is obtained in primary circuit. At this time, cam opens breaker points interrupting primary circuit and, for an instant, flow of current is absorbed by condenser as illustrated in Fig. 3-16. An emf is also induced in secondary coil windings, but voltage is not sufficient to cause current to flow across spark plug gap.

Flow of current in primary windings creates a strong electromagnetic field surrounding coil windings and up through center leg of armature core as shown in Fig. 3-17. As breaker points were opened by the cam, interrupting primary circuit, magnetic field starts to collapse cutting coil windings as indicated by heavy black arrows. The emf induced in primary circuit would be sufficient to cause a flow of current across opening breaker points were it not for condenser absorbing flow of current and bringing it to a controlled stop. This allows electromagnetic field to collapse at such a rapid rate to induce a very high voltage in coil high tension or secondary windings. This voltage, in order of

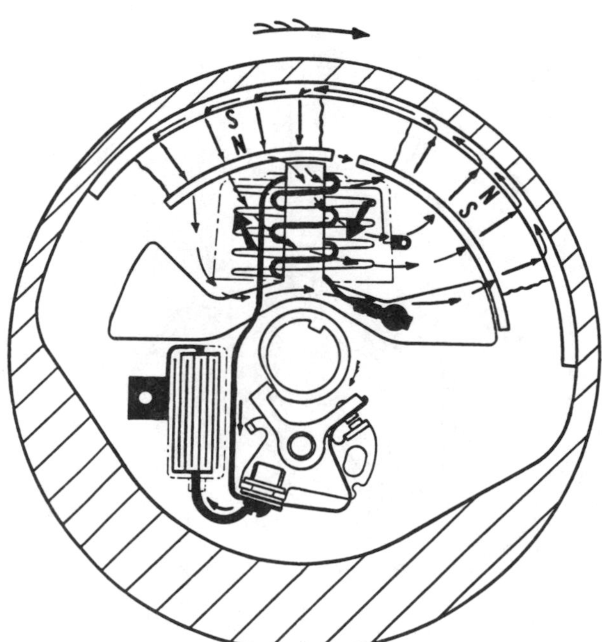


*Fig. 3-16—The flywheel magnets have now turned slightly past the position shown in Fig. 3-15 and the rate of movement of lines of magnetic force cutting through the coil windings is at the maximum. At this instant, the breaker points are opened by the cam and flow of current in the primary circuit is being absorbed by the condenser, bringing the flow of current to a quick, controlled stop. Refer now to Fig. 3-17.*

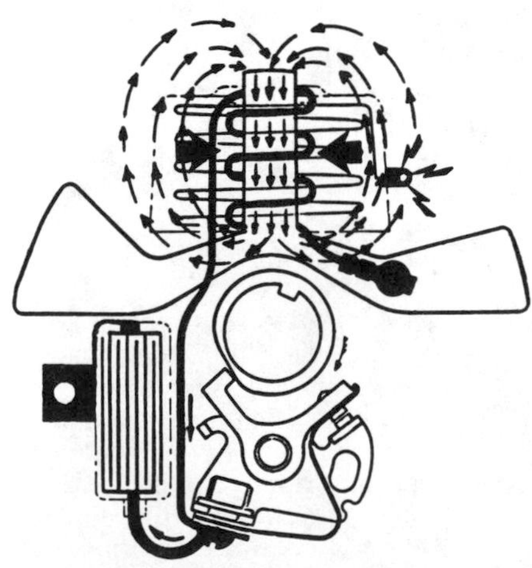

*Fig. 3-17—View showing magneto ignition coil, condenser and breaker points at same instant as illustrated in Fig. 3-16; however, arrows shown above illustrate lines of force of the electromagnetic field established by current in primary coil windings rather than the lines of force of the permanent magnets. As the current in the primary circuit ceases to flow, the electromagnetic field collapses rapidly, cutting the coil windings as indicated by heavy arrows and inducing a very high voltage in the secondary coil winding resulting in the ignition spark.*

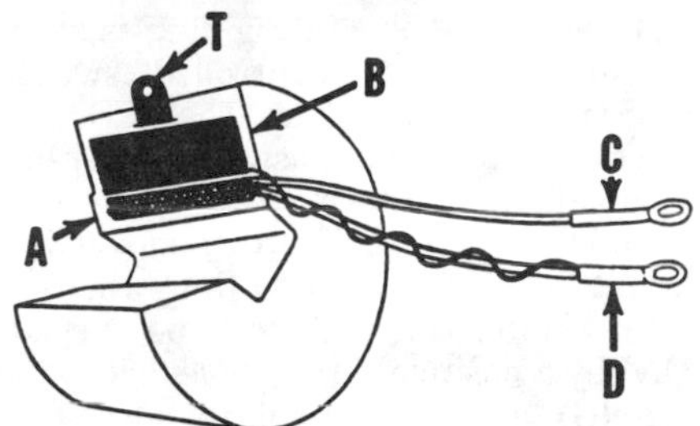


Fig. 3-18—Drawing showing construction of a typical flywheel magneto ignition coil. Primary winding (A) consists of about 200 turns of wire. Secondary winding (B) consists of several thousand turns of fine wire. Coil primary and secondary ground connection is (D); primary connection to breaker point and condenser terminal is (C); and coil secondary (high tension) terminal is (T).

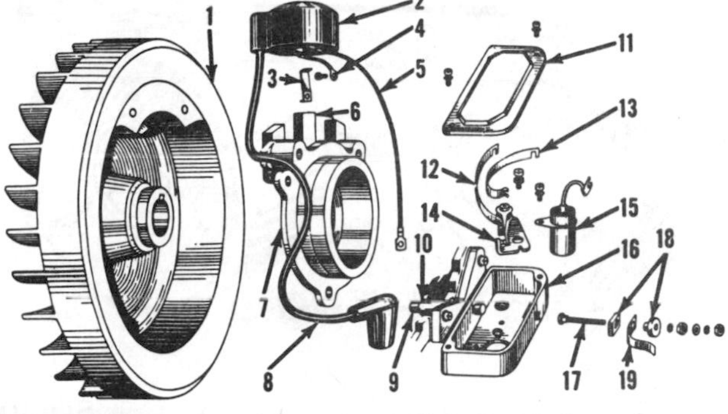

Fig. 3-19—Exploded view of a typical flywheel type magneto used on single cylinder engines in which the breaker points (14) are actuated by a cam on engine camshaft. Push rod (9) rides against cam to open and close points. In this type unit an ignition spark is produced only on alternate revolutions of the flywheel as the camshaft turns at one-half engine speed.

1. Flywheel
2. Ignition coil
3. Coil clamps
4. Coil ground lead
5. Breaker point lead
6. Armature core laminations
7. Crankshaft bearing RETAINER
8. High tension lead
9. Push rod
10. Bushing
11. Breaker box cover
12. Point lead strap
13. Breaker point spring
14. Breaker point assy.
15. Condenser
16. Breaker box
17. Terminal bolt
18. Insulators
19. Grounding (stop) spring

15,000 to 25,000 volts, is sufficient to break down resistance of air gap between spark plug electrodes and a current will flow across gap. This creates ignition spark which ignites compressed fuel-air mixture in engine cylinder.

## Self-Contained Unit Type Magnetos

Some four-stroke cycle engines are equipped with a magneto which is a self-contained unit as shown in Fig. 3-20. This type magneto is driven from engine timing gears via a gear or coupling. All components of the magneto are enclosed in one housing and magneto can be removed from engine as a unit.

**UNIT TYPE MAGNETO OPERATING PRINCIPLES.** In Fig. 3-21, a schematic diagram of a unit type magneto is shown. Magneto rotor is driven through an impulse coupling (shown at right side of illustration). Function of impulse coupling is to increase rotating speed of rotor, thereby increasing magneto efficiency, at engine cranking speeds.

A typical impulse coupling for a single cylinder engine magneto is shown in Fig. 3-22. When engine is turned at cranking speed, coupling hub pawl engages a stop pin in magneto housing as engine piston is coming up on compression stroke. This stops rotation of coupling hub assembly and magneto rotor. A spring within coupling shell (see Fig. 3-23) connects shell and coupling hub; as engine continues to turn, spring winds up until pawl kickoff contacts pawl and disengages it from stop pin. This occurs at the time an ignition spark is required to ignite compressed fuel-air mixture in engine cylinder. As pawl is released, spring connecting coupling shell and hub unwinds and rapidly spins magneto rotor.

Magneto rotor (see Fig. 3-21) carries permanent magnets. As rotor turns, alternating position of magnets, lines of force of magnets are attracted, then withdrawn from laminations. In Fig. 3-21, arrows show magnetic field concentrated within laminations, or armature core. Slightly further rotation of magnetic rotor will place magnets to where laminations will have greater attraction for opposite poles of magnets. At this instant, lines of force as indicated by arrows will suddenly be withdrawn and an opposing field of force will be established in laminations. Due to this rapid movement of lines of force, a current will be induced in primary magneto circuit as coil windings are cut by lines of force. At instant maximum current is induced in primary windings, breaker points are opened by a cam on magnetic rotor shaft interrupting primary circuit. The lines of magnetic force established by primary current (refer to Fig. 3-5) will cut through secondary windings at such a

Fig. 3-20—Some engines are equipped with a unit type magneto having all components enclosed in a single housing (H). Magneto is removable as a unit after removing retaining nuts (N). Stop button (B) grounds out primary magneto circuit to stop engine. Timing window is (W).

rapid rate to induce a very high voltage in secondary (or high tension) circuit. This voltage will break down resistance

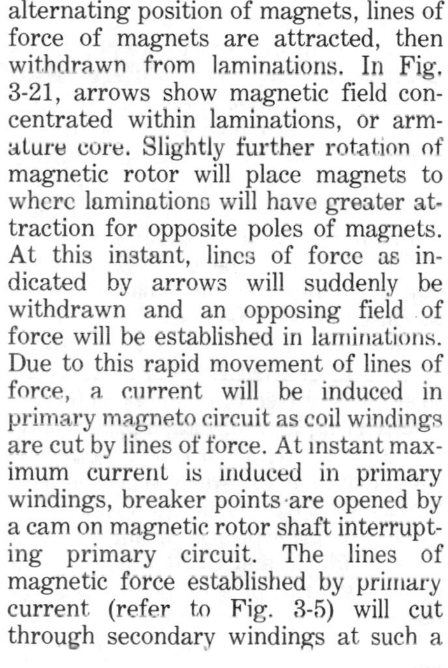

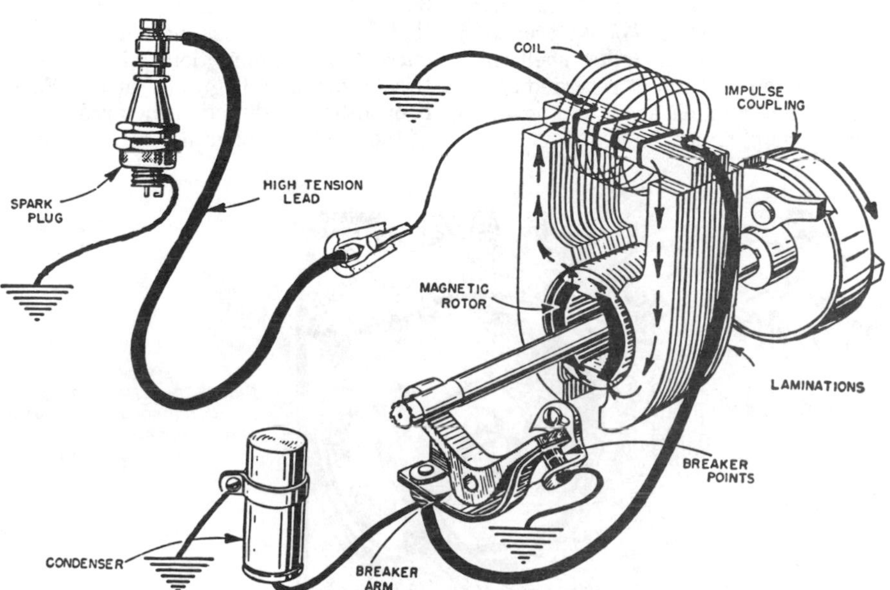


Fig. 3-21—Schematic diagram of typical unit type magneto for single cylinder engine. Refer to Figs. 3-22, 3-23 and 3-24 for views showing construction of impulse couplings.

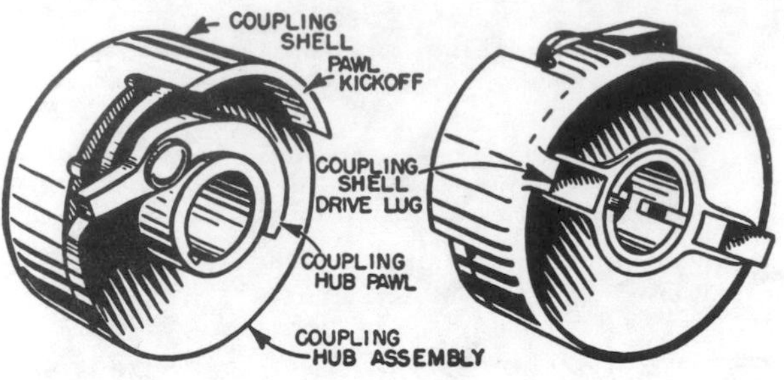


*Fig. 3-22—Views of typical impulse coupling for magneto driven by engine shaft with slotted drive connection. Coupling drive spring is shown in Fig. 3-23. Refer to Fig. 3-24 for view of combination magneto drive gear and impulse coupling used on some magnetos.*

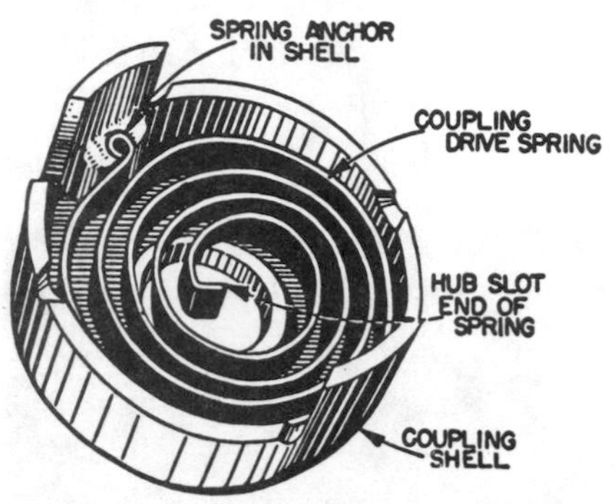


*Fig. 3-23—View showing impulse coupling shell and drive spring removed from coupling hub assembly. Refer to Fig. 3-22 for views of assembled unit.*

of spark plug electrode gap and a spark across electrodes will result.

At engine operating speeds, centrifugal force will hold impulse coupling hub pawl (See Fig. 3-22) in a position so it cannot engage stop pin in magneto housing and magnetic rotor will be driven through spring (Fig. 3-23) connecting coupling shell to coupling hub. The impulse coupling retards ignition spark, at cranking speeds, as engine piston travels closer to top dead center while magnetic rotor is held stationary by pawl and stop pin. The difference in degrees of impulse coupling shell rotation between position of retarded spark and normal running spark is known as impulse coupling lag angle.

## SOLID STATE IGNITION SYSTEM

**BREAKERLESS MAGNETO SYSTEM.** Solid state (breakerless) magneto ignition system operates somewhat on the same basic principles as conventional type flywheel magneto previously described. The main difference is breaker contact points are replaced by a solid state electronic Gate Controlled Switch (GCS) which has no moving parts. Since, in a conventional system breaker points are closed over a longer period of crankshaft rotation than is the "GCS", a diode has been added to the circuit to provide the same characteristics as closed breaker points.

BREAKERLESS MAGNETO OPERATING PRINCIPLES. The same basic principles for electro-magnetic induction of electricity and formation of magnetic fields by electrical current as outlined for conventional flywheel type magneto also apply to the solid state magneto. Therefore principles of different components (diode and GCS) will complete operating principles of the solid state magneto.

The diode is represented in wiring diagrams by the symbol shown in Fig. 3-25. The diode is an electronic device that will permit passage of electrical current in one direction only. In electrical schematic diagrams, current flow is opposite the direction the arrow part of the symbol is pointing.

The symbol shown in Fig. 3-26 is used to represent gate controlled switch (GCS) in wiring diagrams. The GCS acts as a switch to permit passage of current from cathode (C) terminal to anode (A) terminal when in "ON" state and will not permit electric current to flow when in "OFF" state. The GCS can be turned "ON" by a positive surge of electricity at gage (G) terminal and will remain "ON" as long as current remains positive at gate terminal or as long as current is flowing through GCS from cathode (C) terminal to anode (A) terminal.

The basic components and wiring diagram for solid state breakerless magneto are shown schematically in Fig. 3-27. In Fig. 3-28, magneto rotor (flywheel) is turning and ignition coil magnets have just moved into position so their lines of force are cutting ignition coil windings and producing a negative surge of current in primary windings. The diode allows current to flow opposite to the direction of diode symbol arrow and action is same as conventional magneto with breaker points closed. As rotor (flywheel) continues to turn as shown in Fig. 3-29, direction of magnetic flux lines will reverse in armature center leg. Direction of current will change in primary coil circuit and previously conducting diode will be shut off. At this point, neither diode is conducting. As voltage begins to build up as rotor continues to turn, condenser acts

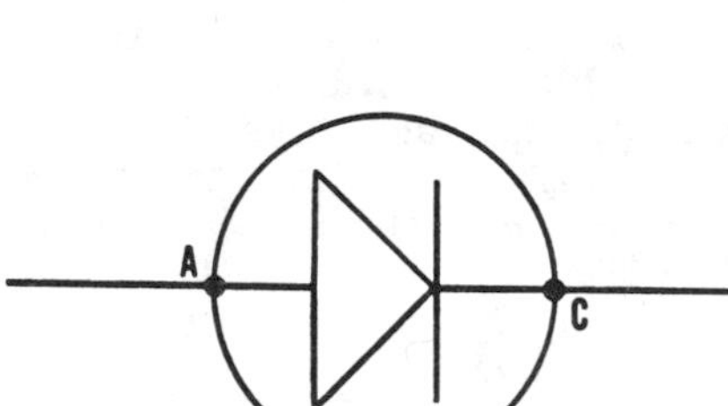


*Fig. 3-25—In a diagram of an electrical circuit, the diode is represented by the symbol shown above. The diode will allow current to flow in one direction only, from cathode (C) to anode (A).*

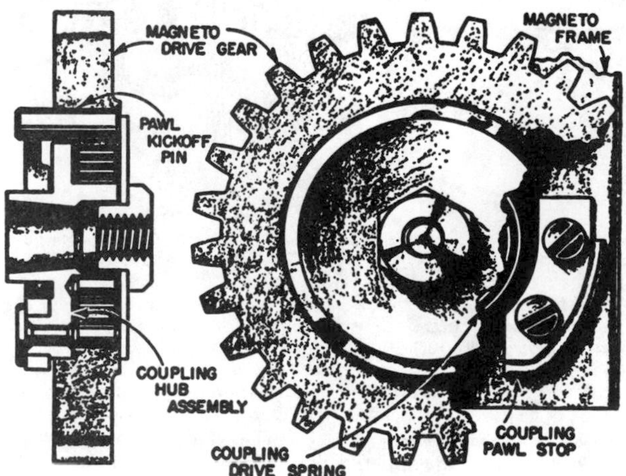


*Fig. 3-24—Views of combination magneto drive gear and impulse coupling used on some magnetos.*

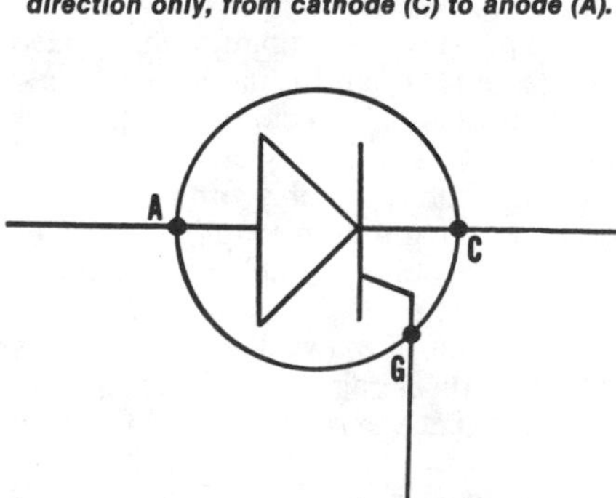


*Fig. 3-26—The symbol used for a Gate Controlled Switch (GCS) in an electrical diagram is shown above. The GCS will permit current to flow from cathode (C) to anode (A) when "turned on" by a positive electrical charge at gate (G) terminal.*

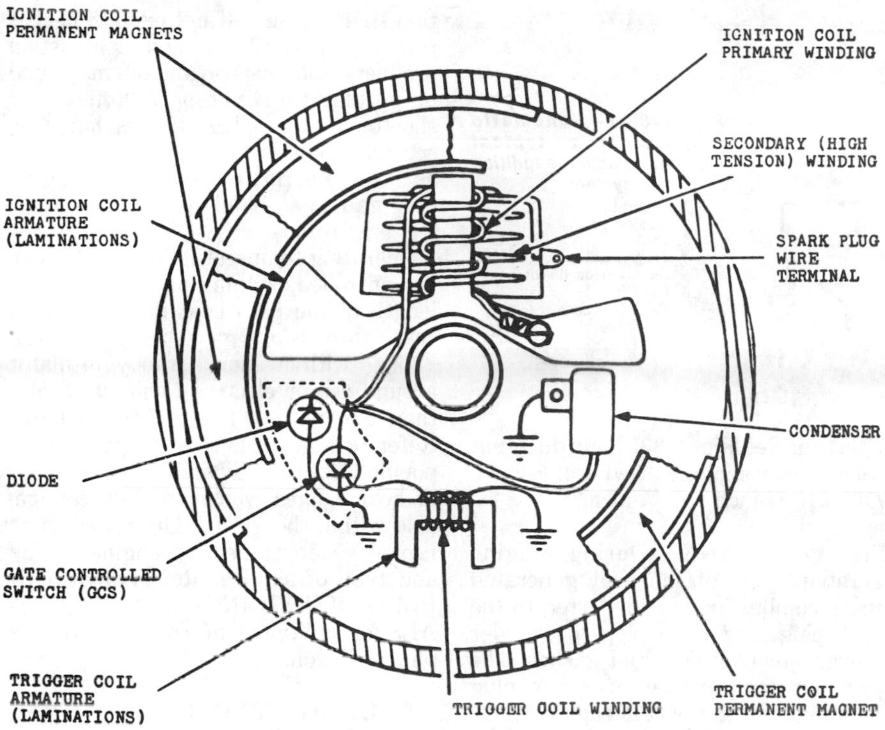

IGNITION COIL PERMANENT MAGNETS
IGNITION COIL PRIMARY WINDING
SECONDARY (HIGH TENSION) WINDING
IGNITION COIL ARMATURE (LAMINATIONS)
SPARK PLUG WIRE TERMINAL
CONDENSER
DIODE
GATE CONTROLLED SWITCH (GCS)
TRIGGER COIL ARMATURE (LAMINATIONS)
TRIGGER COIL WINDING
TRIGGER COIL PERMANENT MAGNET

***Fig. 3-27—Schematic diagram of typical breakerless magneto ignition system. Refer to Figs. 3-28, 3-29 and 3-30 for schematic views of operating cycle.***

as a buffer to prevent excessive voltage build up at GCS before it is triggered.

When rotor reaches approximate position shown in Fig. 3-30, maximum flux density has been achieved in center leg of armature. At this time the GCS is triggered. Triggering is accomplished by triggering coil armature moving into field of a permanent magnet which induces a positive voltage on the gate of GCS. Primary coil current flow results in the formation of an electromagnetic field around primary coil which induces a voltage of sufficient potential in secondary coil windings to "fire" spark plug.

When rotor (flywheel) has moved magnets past armature, GCS will cease to conduct and revert to "OFF" state until it is triggered. The condenser will discharge during time GCS was conducting.

**CAPACITOR DISCHARGE SYSTEM.** Capacitor discharge (CD) ignition system uses a permanent magnet rotor (flywheel) to induce a current in a coil, but unlike conventional flywheel magneto and solid state breakerless magneto described previously, current is stored in a capacitor (condenser). Then, stored current is discharged through a transformer coil to create ignition spark. Refer to Fig. 3-31 for a schematic of a typical capacitor discharge ignition system.

CAPACITOR DISCHARGE OPERATING PRINCIPLES. As permanent flywheel magnets pass by input generating coil (1–Fig. 3-31), current produced charges capacitor (6). Only half of the generated current passes through diode (3) to charge capacitor. Reverse current is blocked by diode (3) but passes through Zener diode (2) to complete reverse circuit. Zener diode (2) also limits maximum voltage of forward current. As flywheel continues to turn and magnets pass trigger coil (4), a small amount of electrical current is generated. This current opens gate controlled switch (5) allowing capacitor to discharge through pulse transformer (7). The rapid voltage rise in transformer primary coil induces a high voltage secondary current which forms ignition spark when it jumps spark plug gap.

## THE SPARK PLUG

In any spark ignition engine, the spark plug (See Fig. 3-32) provides means for igniting compressed fuel-air mixture in

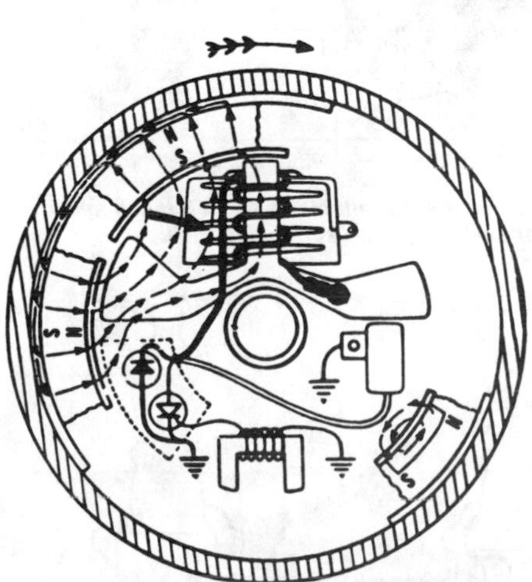


***Fig. 3-28—View showing flywheel of breakerless magneto system at instant of rotation where lines of force of ignition coil magnets are being drawn into left and center legs of magneto armature. The diode (see Fig. 3-25) acts as a closed set of breaker points in completing the primary ignition circuit at this time.***

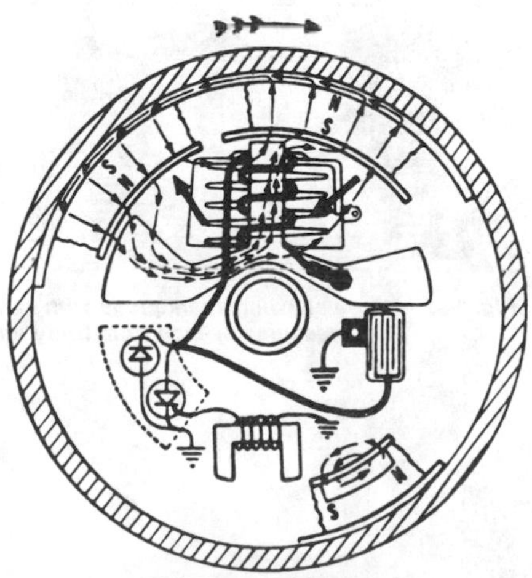


***Fig. 3-29—Flywheel is turning to point where magnetic flux lines through armature center leg will reverse direction and current through primary coil circuit will reverse. As current reverses, diode which was previously conducting will shut off and there will be no current. When magnetic flux lines have reversed in armature center leg, voltage potential will again build up, but since GCS is in "OFF" state, no current will flow. To prevent excessive voltage build up, the condenser acts as a buffer.***

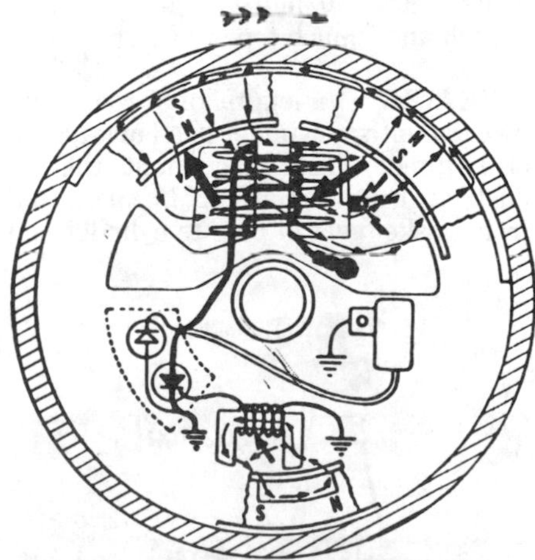


***Fig. 3-30—With flywheel in the approximate position shown, maximum voltage potential is present in windings of primary coil. At this time the triggering coil armature has moved into the field of a permanent magnet and a positive voltage is induced on the gate of the GCS. The GCS is triggered and primary coil current flows resulting in the formation of an electromagnetic field around the primary coil which induces a voltage of sufficient potential in the secondary windings to "fire" the spark plug.***

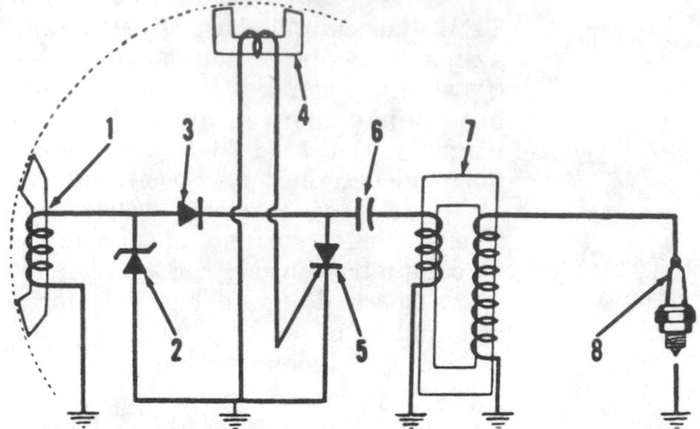

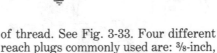

Fig. 3-31 — Schematic diagram of a typical capacitor discharge ignition system.

1. Generating coil
2. Zener diode
3. Diode
4. Trigger coil
5. Gate controlled switch
6. Capacitor
7. Pulse transformer (coil)
8. Spark plug

cylinder. Before an electric charge can move across an air gap, intervening air must be charged with electricity, or ionized. If spark plug is properly gapped and system is not shorted, not more than 7,000 volts may be required to initiate a spark. Higher voltage is required as spark plug warms up, or if compression pressures or distance of air gap is increased. Compression pressures are highest at full throttle and relatively slow engine speeds, therefore, high voltage requirements or a lack of available secondary voltage most often shows up as a miss during maximum acceleration from a slow engine speed.

There are many different types and sizes of spark plugs which are designed for a number of specific requirements.

**THREAD SIZE.** The threaded, shell portion of the spark plug and the attaching hole in cylinder are manufactured to meet certain industry established standards. The diameter is referred to as "Thread Size." Those commonly used are: 10 mm, 14 mm, 18 mm, 7/8-inch and 1/2-inch pipe.

**REACH.** The length of thread, and thread depth in cylinder head or wall are also standardized throughout the industry. This dimension is measured from gasket seat of plug to cylinder end of thread. See Fig. 3-33. Four different reach plugs commonly used are: 3/8-inch, 7/16-inch, 1/2-inch and 3/4-inch.

**HEAT RANGE.** During engine operation, part of the heat generated during combustion is transferred to the spark plug, and from plug to cylinder through steel threads and gasket. The operating temperature of spark plug plays an important part in engine operation. If too much heat is retained by plug, fuel-air mixture may be ignited by contact with heated surface before ignition spark occurs. If not enough heat is retained, partially burned combustion products (soot, carbon and oil) may build up on plug tip resulting in "fouling" or shorting out of plug. If this happens, secondary current is dissipated uselessly as it is generated instead of bridging plug gap as a useful spark, and engine will misfire.

Operating temperature of plug tip can be controlled, within limits, by altering length of the path heat must follow to reach threads and gasket of plug. Thus, a plug with a short, stubby insulator around center electrode will run cooler than one with a long, slim insulator. Refer to Fig. 3-34. Most plugs in more popular sizes are available in a number of heat ranges which are interchangeable within the group. The proper heat range is determined by engine design and type of service. Refer to SPARK PLUG SERVICING FUNDAMENTALS for additional information on spark plug selection.

**SPECIAL TYPES.** Sometimes, engine design features or operating conditions call for special plug types designed for a particular purpose.

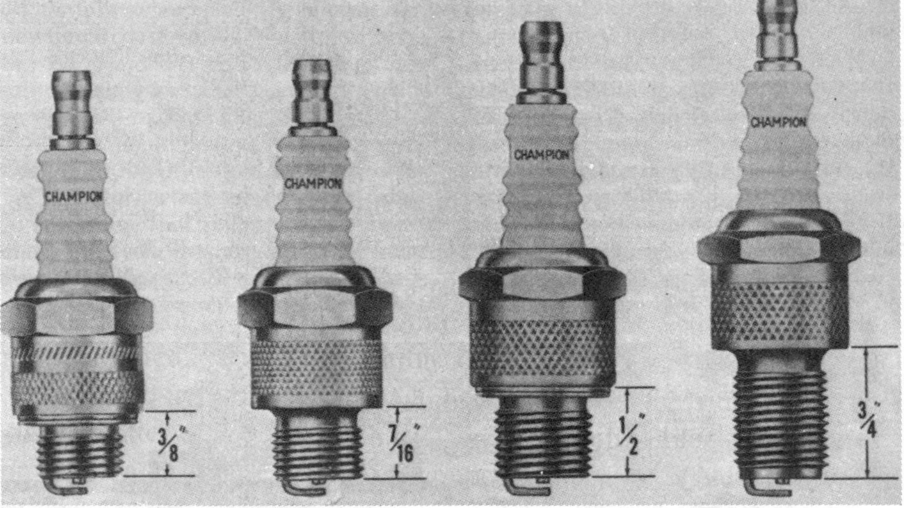


*Fig. 3-33 — Views showing spark plugs with various "reaches" available. A 3/8-inch reach spark plug measures 3/8-inch from firing end of shell to gasket surface of shell.*

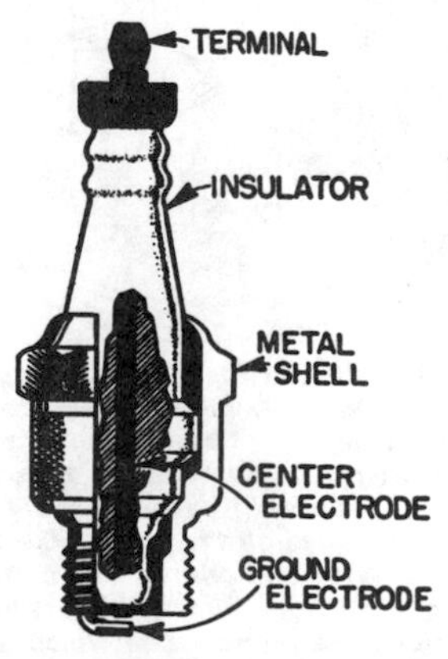


*Fig. 3-32 — Cross-sectional drawing of spark plug showing construction and nomenclature.*

*Fig. 3-34 — Spark plug tip temperature is controlled by the length of the path heat must travel to reach cooling surface of the engine cylinder head.*

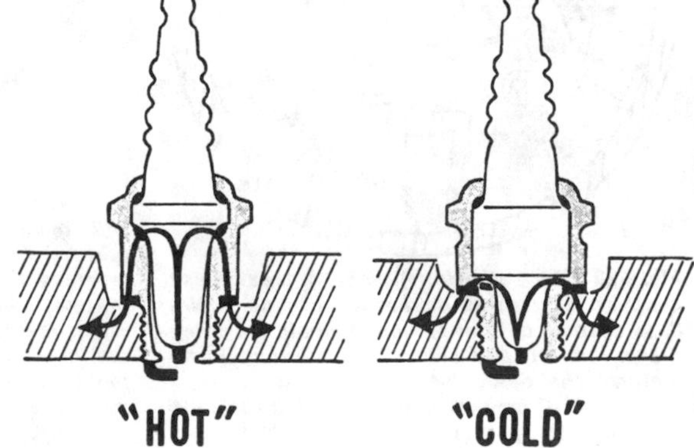

# ENGINE POWER AND TORQUE RATINGS

The following paragraphs discuss terms used in expressing engine horsepower and torque ratings and explains methods for determining different ratings. Some engine repair shops are now equipped with a dynamometer for measuring engine torque and/or horsepower and the mechanic should be familiar with terms, methods of measurement and how actual power developed by an engine can vary under different conditions.

## GLOSSARY OF TERMS

**FORCE.** Force is an action against an object that tends to move the object from a state of rest, or to accelerate movement of an object. For use in calculating torque or horsepower, force is measured in pounds.

**WORK.** When a force moves an object from a state of rest, or accelerates movement of an object, work is done. Work is measured by multiplying force applied by distance force moves object, or:

$$\text{work} = \text{force} \times \text{distance}.$$

Thus, if a force of 50 pounds moved an object 50 feet, work done would equal 50 pounds times 50 feet, or 2500 pounds-feet (or as it is usually expressed, 2500 foot-pounds).

**POWER.** Power is the rate at which work is done; thus, if:

$$\text{work} = \text{force} \times \text{distance},$$

then:

$$\text{power} = \frac{\text{force} \times \text{distance}}{\text{time}}$$

From the above formula, it is seen that power must increase if time in which work is done decreases.

**HORSEPOWER:** Horsepower is a unit of measurement of power. Many years ago, James Watt, a Scotsman noted as inventor of the steam engine, evaluated one horsepower as being equal to doing 33,000 foot-pounds of work in one minute. This evaluation has been universally accepted since that time. Thus, the formula for determining horsepower is:

$$\text{horsepower} = \frac{\text{pounds} \times \text{feet}}{33{,}000 \times \text{minutes}}$$

Horsepower (hp.) ratings are sometimes converted to kilowatt (kW) ratings by using the following formula:

$$\text{kW} = \text{hp.} \times 0.745\,699\,9$$

When referring to engine horsepower ratings, one usually finds the rating expressed as brake horsepower or rated horsepower, or sometimes as both.

BRAKE HORSEPOWER. Brake horsepower is the maximum horsepower available from an engine as determined by use of a dynamometer, and is usually stated as maximum observed brake horsepower or as corrected brake horsepower. As will be noted in a later paragraph, observed brake horsepower of a specific engine will vary under different conditions of temperature and atmospheric pressure. Corrected brake horsepower is a rating calculated from observed brake horsepower and is a means of comparing engines tested at varying conditions. The method for calculating corrected brake horsepower will be explained in a later paragraph.

RATED HORSEPOWER. An engine being operated under a load equal to the maximum horsepower available (brake horsepower) will not have reserve power for overloads and is subject to damage from overheating and rapid wear. Therefore, when an engine is being selected for a particular load, the engine's brake horsepower rating should be in excess of the expected normal operating load. Usually, it is recommended that the engine not be operated in excess of 80% of the engine maximum brake horsepower rating; thus, the "rated horsepower" of an engine is usually equal to 80% of maximum horsepower the engine will develop.

**TORQUE.** In many engine specifications, a "torque rating" is given. Engine torque can be defined simply as the turning effort exerted by the engine output shaft when under load.

Torque ratings are sometimes converted to newton-meters (N·m) by using the following formula:

$$\text{N·m} = \text{foot pounds of torque} \times 1.355\,818$$

It is possible to calculate engine horsepower being developed by measuring torque being developed and engine output speed. Refer to the following paragraphs.

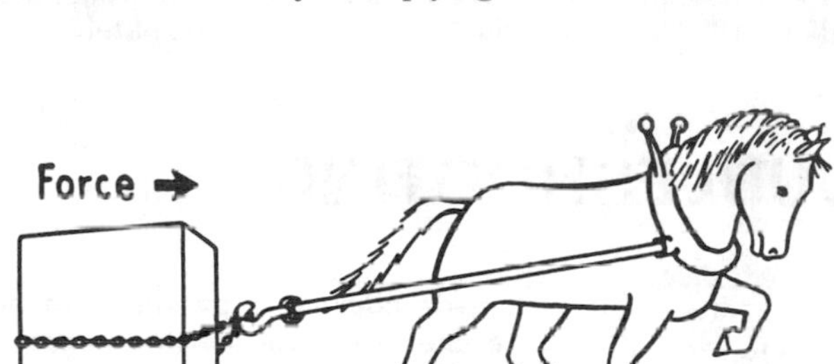


*Fig. 4-1—A force, measured in pounds, is defined as an action tending to move an object or to accelerate movement of an object.*

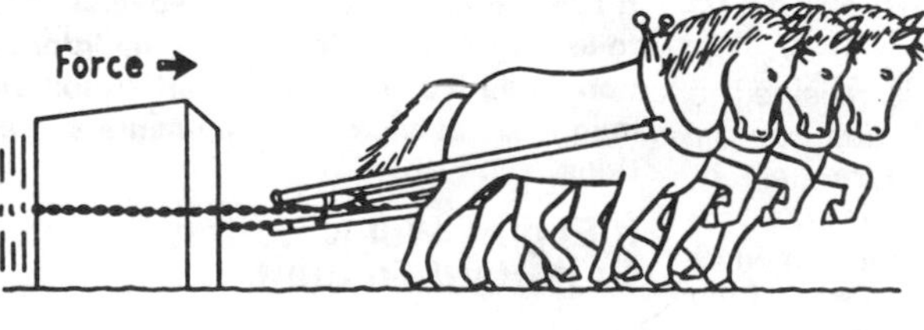


*Fig. 4-2—If a force moves an object from a state of rest or accelerates movement of an object, then work is done.*

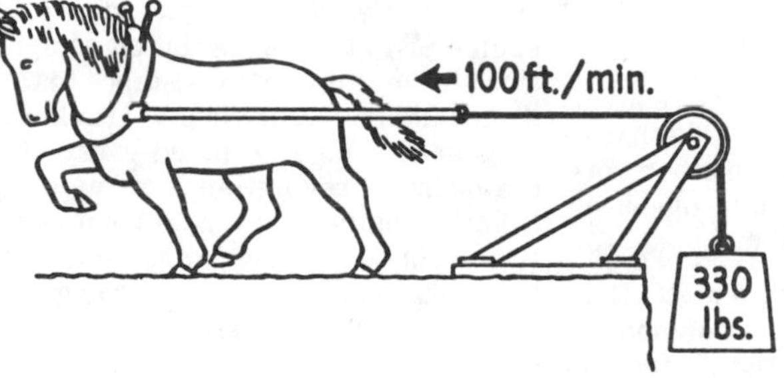


*Fig. 4-3—This horse is doing 33,000 foot-pounds of work in one minute, or one horsepower.*

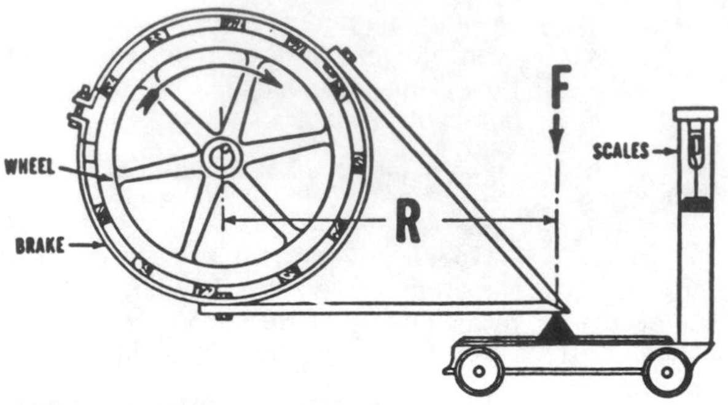


*Fig. 4-4—Diagram showing a prony brake on which the torque being developed by an engine can be measured. By also knowing the rpm of the engine output shaft, engine horsepower can be calculated.*

## MEASURING ENGINE TORQUE AND HORSEPOWER

**PRONY BRAKE.** The prony brake is the most simple means of testing engine performance. Refer to diagram in Fig. 4-4. A torque arm is attached to a brake on wheel mounted on engine output shaft. The torque arm, as the brake is applied, exerts a force (F) on scales. Engine torque is computed by multiplying force (F) times length of torque arm radius (R), or:

$$\text{engine torque} = F \times R.$$

If, for example, torque arm radius (R) is 2 feet and force (F) being exerted by torque arm on scales is 6 pounds, engine torque would be 2 feet×6 pounds, or 12 foot-pounds.

To calculate engine horsepower being developed by use of the prony brake, we must also count revolutions of engine output shaft for a specific length of time. In formula for calculating horsepower:

$$\text{horsepower} = \frac{\text{feet} \times \text{pounds}}{33{,}000 \times \text{minutes}}$$

Feet in formula will equal circumference transcribed by torque arm radius multiplied by number of engine output shaft revolutions. Thus:

$$\text{feet} = 2 \times 3.14 \times \text{radius} \times \text{revoultions}.$$

Pounds in formula will equal force (F) of torque arm. If, for example, force (F) is 6 pounds, torque arm radius is 2 feet and engine output shaft speed is 3300 revolutions per minute, then:

$$\text{horsepower} = \frac{2 \times 3.14 \times 2 \times 3300 \times 6}{33{,}000 \times 1}$$

or,

$$\text{horsepower} \times 7.54$$

**DYNAMOMETERS.** Some commercial dynamometers for testing small engines are now available, although the cost may be prohibitive for all but larger repair shops. Usually, these dynamometers have a hydraulic loading device and scales indicating engine speed and load; horsepower is then calculated by use of a slide rule type instrument.

## HOW ENGINE HORSEPOWER OUTPUT VARIES

Engine efficiency will vary with the amount of air taken into the cylinder on each intake stroke. Thus, air density has a considerable effect on horsepower output of a specific engine. As air density varies with both temperature and atmospheric pressure, any change in air temperature, barometric pressure, or elevation will cause a variance in observed engine horsepower. As a general rule, engine horsepower will:

A. Decrease approximately 3% for each 1000 foot increase above 1000 ft. elevation;

B. Decrease approximately 3% for each 1 inch drop in barometric pressure; or,

C. Decrease approximately 1% for each 10° rise in temperature (Fahrenheit).

Thus, to fairly compare observed horsepower readings, observed readings should be corrected to standard temperature and atmospheric pressure conditions of 60°F., and 29.92 inches of mercury. The correction formula specified by the Society of Automotive Engineers is somewhat involved; however for practical purposes, the general rules stated above can be used to approximate corrected brake horsepower of an engine when observed maximum brake horsepower is known.

For example, suppose the engine horsepower of 7.54 as found by use of the prony brake was observed at an altitude of 3000 feet and at a temperature of 100°F. At standard atmospheric pressure and temperature conditions, we could expect an increase of 4% due to temperature (100° −60° x 1% per 10°) and an increase of 6% due to altitude (3000 ft.-1000 ft.x3% per 1000 ft.) or a total increase of 10%. Thus, corrected maximum horsepower from this engine would be approximately 7.54 + .75, or approximately 8.25 horsepower.

# TROUBLESHOOTING

When servicing an engine to correct a specific complaint, such as engine will not start, is hard to start, etc., a logical step-by-step procedure should be followed to determine cause of trouble before performing any service work. This procedure is "TROUBLESHOOTING."

Of course, if an engine is received in your shop for a normal tune up or specific repair work is requested, troubleshooting procedure is not required and work should be performed as requested. It is wise, however, to fully check the engine before repairs are made and recommend any additional repairs or adjustments necessary to ensure proper engine performance.

The following procedures, as related to a specific complaint or trouble, have proven to be a satisfactory method for quickly determining cause of trouble in a number of engine repair shops.

**NOTE: It is not suggested the troubleshooting procedure as outlined in following paragraphs be strictly adhered to at all times. In many instances, customer's comments on when trouble was encountered will indicate cause of trouble. Also, the mechanic will soon develop a diagnostic technique that can only come with experience. In addition to the general troubleshooting procedure, reader should also refer to special notes following this section and to the information included in engine, carburetor and magneto servicing fundamentals sections.**

### If Engine Will Not Start—Or Is Hard To Start

1. If engine is equipped with a rope or crank starter, turn engine slowly. As engine piston is coming up on compression stroke, a definite resistance to turning should be felt on rope or crank. This resistance should be noted every other crankshaft revolution on a single cylinder engine, on every revolution of a two cylinder engine and on every ½-revolution of a four cylinder engine. If correct cranking resistance is noted, engine compression can be considered as not the cause of trouble at this time.

**NOTE: Compression gages for gasoline engines are available and are of value in troubleshooting engine service problems.**

Where available from engine manufacturer, specifications will be given for engine compression pressure in engine service sections of this manual. On engines having electric starters, remove spark plug and check engine compression with gage; if gage is not available, hold thumb so spark plug hole is partly covered. An alternating blowing and suction action should be noted as engine is cranked.

If very little or no compression is noted, refer to appropriate engine repair section for repair of engine. If check indicates engine is developing compression, proceed to step 2.

2. Remove spark plug wire and hold wire terminal about ⅛-inch (3.18 mm) away from cylinder (on wires having rubber spark plug boot, insert a small screw or bolt in terminal).

**NOTE: A test plug with ⅛-inch (3.18 mm) gap is available or a test plug can be made by adjusting the electrode gap of a new spark plug to 0.125 inch (3.18 mm).**

While cranking engine, a bright blue spark should snap across the ⅛-inch (3.18 mm) gap. If spark is weak or yellow, or if no spark occurs while cranking engine, refer to IGNITION SYSTEM SERVICE FUNDAMENTALS for information on appropriate type system.

If spark is satisfactory, remove and inspect spark plug. Refer to SPARK PLUG SERVICE FUNDAMENTALS. If in doubt about spark plug condition, install a new plug.

**NOTE: Before installing plug, make certain electrode gap is set to proper dimension shown in engine repair section of this manual. Refer also to Fig. 5-1.**

If ignition spark is satisfactory and engine will not start with new plug, proceed with step 3.

3. If engine compression and ignition spark are adequate, trouble within the fuel system should be suspected. Remove and clean or renew air cleaner or cleaner element. Check fuel tank (Fig. 5-2) and make certain it is full of fresh fuel as prescribed by engine manufacturer. If equipped with a fuel shut-off valve, make certain valve is open.

If engine is equipped with remote throttle controls that also operate carburetor choke plate, check to be certain that when controls are placed in choke position, carburetor choke plate is fully closed. If not, adjust control linkage so choke will fully close; then, try to start engine. If engine does not start after several turns, remove air cleaner assembly; carburetor throat should be wet with gasoline. If not, check for reason fuel is not getting to carburetor. On models with gravity feed from fuel tank to carburetor (fuel tank above carburetor), disconnect fuel line at carburetor to see that fuel is flowing through the line. If no fuel is flowing, remove and clean fuel tank, fuel line and any fuel filters or shut-off valve.

On models having a fuel pump separate from carburetor, remove fuel line at carburetor and crank engine through several turns; fuel should spurt from open line. If not, disconnect fuel line from tank to fuel pump at pump connection. If fuel will not run from open line, remove and clean fuel tank, line and if so equipped, fuel filter and/or shut-off valve. If fuel runs from open line, remove and overhaul or renew the fuel pump.

After making sure clean, fresh fuel is available at carburetor, again try to start engine. If engine will not start, refer to recommended initial adjustments for carburetor in appropriate engine repair section of this manual and adjust carburetor idle and/or main fuel needles.

If engine will not start when compression and ignition test within specifications and clean, fresh fuel is available to carburetor, remove and clean or overhaul carburetor as outlined in CARBURETOR SERVICING FUNDAMENTALS section of this manual.

4. The preceding troubleshooting techniques are based on the fact that to run, an engine must develop compression, have an ignition spark and receive proper fuel-air mixture. In some instances, there are other factors involved. Refer to special notes following this section for service hints on finding common causes of engine trouble that may not be discovered in normal troubleshooting procedure.

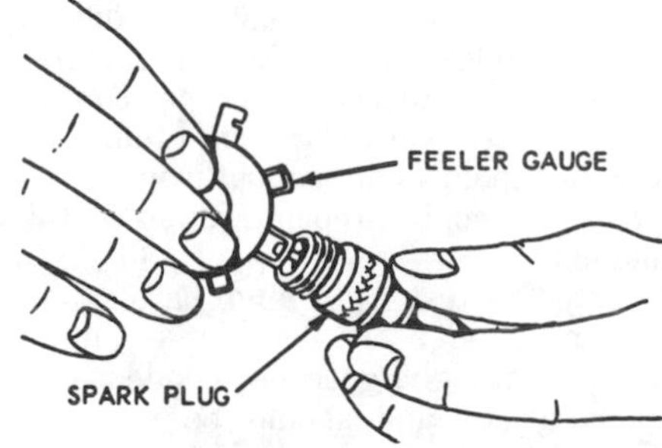


*Fig. 5-1 — Be sure to check spark plug electrode gap with proper size feeler gage and adjust gap to specification recommended by manufacturer.*

## If Engine Starts, Then Stops

This complaint is usually due to fuel starvation, but may be caused by a faulty ignition system. Recommended troubleshooting procedure is as follows:

1. Remove and inspect fuel tank cap; on all engines, fuel tank is vented through breather in fuel tank cap so air can enter tank as fuel is used. If engine stops after running several minutes, a clogged breather should be suspected. On some engines, it is possible to let engine run with fuel tank cap removed and if this permits engine to run without stopping, clean or renew cap.

**CAUTION: Be sure to observe safety precautions before attempting to run engine without fuel tank cap in place. If there is any danger of fuel being spilled on engine or spark entering open tank, do not attempt to run engine without fuel tank cap in place. If in doubt, try a new cap.**

2. If clogged breather in fuel tank cap is eliminated as cause of trouble, a partially clogged fuel filter or fuel line should be suspected. Remove and clean fuel tank and line and if so equipped, clean fuel shut-off valve and/or fuel tank filter. On some engines, a screen or felt type fuel filter is located in carburetor fuel inlet; refer to engine repair section for appropriate engine make and model for carburetor construction.

3. After cleaning fuel tank, line, filters, etc., if trouble is still encountered, a sticking or faulty carburetor inlet needle valve or float may be cause of trouble. Remove, disassemble and clean carburetor using data in engine repair section and in CARBURETOR SERVICE FUNDAMENTALS as a guide.

4. If fuel system is eliminated as cause of trouble by performing procedure outlined in steps 1, 2 and 3, check magneto or battery ignition coil on tester if such equipment is available. If not, check for ignition spark immediately after engine stops.

*Fig. 5-2 — Condensation can cause water and rust to form in fuel tank even though only clean fuel has been poured into tank.*

## Ignition Service

Renew coil, condenser and breaker points if no spark is noted. Also, check for engine compression immediately after engine stops; trouble may be caused by sticking intake or exhaust valve or cam followers (tappets). If no or little compression is noted immediately after engine stops, refer to ENGINE SERVICE FUNDAMENTALS section and to engine repair data in appropriate engine repair section of this manual.

## Engine Overheats

When air cooled engines overheat, check for:

1. Air inlet screen in blower housing plugged with grass, leaves, dirt or other debris.
2. Remove blower housing and shields and check for dirt or debris accumulated on or between cooling fins on cylinder.
3. Missing or bent shields on blower housing. (Never attempt to operate an air cooled engine without all shields and blower housing in place.)
4. A too lean main fuel-air adjustment of carburetor.
5. Improper ignition spark timing. Check breaker point gap, and on engine with unit type magneto, check magneto to engine timing. On battery ignition units with timer or distributor, check for breaker points opening at proper time.
6. Engines being operated under loads in excess of rated engine horsepower or at extremely high ambient (surrounding) air temperatures may overheat.

## Engine Surges When Running

Trouble with an engine surging is usually caused by improper carburetor adjustment or improper governor adjustment.

1. Refer to CARBURETOR paragraphs in appropriate engine repair section and adjust carburetor as outlined.
2. If adjusting carburetor did not correct surging condition, refer to GOVERNOR paragraph and adjust governor linkage.
3. If any wear is noted in governor linkage and adjusting linkage did not correct problem, renew worn linkage parts.
4. If trouble is still not corrected, remove and clean or overhaul carburetor as necessary. Also check for any possible air leaks between the carburetor to engine gaskets or air inlet elbow gaskets.

## Special Notes on Engine Troubleshooting

**ENGINES WITH COMPRESSION RELEASE.** Several different makes of four-stroke cycle engines now have a compression release that reduces compression pressure at cranking speeds, thus making it easier to crank the engine. Most models having this feature will develop full compression when turned in a reverse direction. Refer to the appropriate engine repair section in this manual for detailed information concerning compression release used on different makes and models.

# IGNITION SYSTEM SERVICE

The fundamentals of servicing ignition systems are outlined in the following paragraphs. Refer to appropriate heading for type ignition system being inspected or overhauled.

## BATTERY IGNITION SERVICE FUNDAMENTALS

Usually all components are readily accessible and while use of test instruments is sometimes desirable, condition of the system can be determined by simple checks. Refer to following paragraphs.

**GENERAL CONDITION CHECK.** Remove spark plug wire and if terminal is rubber covered, insert small screw or bolt in terminal. Hold uncovered end of terminal or bolt inserted in terminal about 1/8-inch (3.18 mm) away from engine or connect spark plug wire to test plug. Crank engine while observing gap between spark plug wire terminal and engine; if a bright blue spark snaps across gap, condition of system can be considered satisfactory. However, ignition timing may have to be adjusted. Refer to timing procedure in appropriate engine repair section.

**VOLTAGE, WIRING AND SWITCH CHECK.** If no spark, or a weak yellow-orange spark occurred when checking system as outlined in preceding paragraph, proceed with following checks:

Test battery condition with hydrometer or voltmeter. If check indicates a dead cell, renew battery; recharge battery if a discharged condition is indicated.

**NOTE: On models with electric starter or starter-generator unit, battery can be assumed in satisfactory condition if the starter cranks the engine freely.**

If battery checks within specifications, but starter unit will not turn engine, a faulty starter unit is indicated and ignition trouble may be caused by excessive current draw of such a unit. If battery and starting unit, if so equipped, are in satisfactory condition, proceed as follows:

Remove battery lead wire from ignition coil and connect a test light of same voltage as battery between disconnected lead wire and engine ground. Light should go on when ignition switch is in "off" position. If not, renew switch and/or wiring and recheck for satisfactory spark. If switch and wiring are functioning properly, but no spark is obtained, proceed as follows:

**BREAKER POINTS AND CONDENSER.** Remove breaker box cover and, using small screwdriver, separate and inspect breaker points. If burned or deeply pitted, renew breaker points and condenser. If point contacts are clean to grayish in color and are only slightly pitted, proceed as follows: Disconnect condenser and ignition coil lead wires from breaker point terminal and connect a test light and battery between terminal and engine ground. Light should go on when points are closed and should go out when points are open. If light fails to go out when points are open, breaker arm insulation is defective and breaker points must be renewed. If light does not go on when points are in closed position, clean or renew breaker points. In some instances, new breaker point contact surfaces may have an oily or wax coating or have foreign material between the surfaces so proper contact is prevented. Check ignition timing and breaker point gap as outlined in appropriate engine repair section of this manual.

Connect test light and battery between condenser lead and engine ground; if light goes on, condenser is shorted out and should be renewed. Capacity of condenser can be checked if test instrument is available. It is usually good practice to renew condenser whenever new breaker points are being installed if tester is not available.

**IGNITION COIL.** If a coil tester is available, condition of coil can be checked. However, if tester is not available, a reasonably satisfactory performance test can be made as follows:

Disconnect high tension wire from spark plug. Turn engine so cam has allowed breaker points to close. With ignition switch on, open and close points with small screwdriver while holding high tension lead about 1/8 to 1/4-inch (3.18 to 6.35 mm) away from engine ground. A bright blue spark should snap across gap between spark plug wire and ground each time points are opened. If no spark occurs, or spark is weak and yellow-orange, renewal of ignition coil is indicated.

Sometimes, an ignition coil may perform satisfactorily when cold, but fail after engine has run for some time and coil is hot. Check coil when hot if this condition is indicated.

## FLYWHEEL MAGNETO SERVICE FUNDAMENTALS

In servicing a flywheel magneto ignition system, the mechanic is concerned with troubleshooting, service adjustments and testing magneto components. The following paragraphs outline basic steps in servicing a flywheel type magneto. Refer to appropriate engine section for adjustment and test specifications for a particular engine.

### Troubleshooting

If engine will not start and malfunction of ignition system is suspected, make the following checks to find cause of trouble.

Check to be sure ignition switch (if so equipped) is in "On" or "Run" position and the insulation on wire leading to ignition switch is in good condition. Switch can be checked with timing and test light as shown in Fig. 5-3. Disconnect lead from switch and attach one clip of test light to switch terminal and remaining clip to engine. Light should go on when switch is in "Off" or "Stop" position, and should go off when switch is in "On" or "Run" position.

Inspect high tension (spark plug) wire for worn spots in insulation or breaks in wire. Frayed or worn insulation can be repaired temporarily with plastic electrician's tape.

If no defects are noted in ignition switch or ignition wires, remove and inspect spark plug as outlined in SPARK PLUG SERVICING section. If spark plug is fouled or is in questionable condition, connect a spark plug of known quality to high tension wire, ground base of spark plug to engine and turn engine rapidly with starter. If spark across electrode gap of spark plug is a bright blue, magneto can be considered in satisfactory condition.

**NOTE: Some engine manufacturers specify a certain type spark plug and a specific test gap. Refer to appropriate engine service section; if no specific spark plug type or electrode gap is recommended for test purposes, use spark plug type and electrode gap recommended for engine make and model.**

If spark across gap of test plug is weak or orange colored, or no spark occurs as engine is cranked, magneto should be serviced as outlined in the following paragraphs.

### Magneto Adjustments

**BREAKER CONTACT POINTS.** Adjustment of breaker contact points affects both ignition timing and magneto edge gap. Therefore, breaker contact point gap should be carefully adjusted according to engine manufacturer's specifications. Before adjusting breaker contact gap, inspect contact points and renew if condition of contact surfaces is questionable. It is sometimes desirable to check condition of points as follows: Disconnect condenser and primary coil leads from breaker point terminal. Attach one clip of test light (See Fig. 5-3) to breaker point terminal and remaining clip of test light to magneto ground.

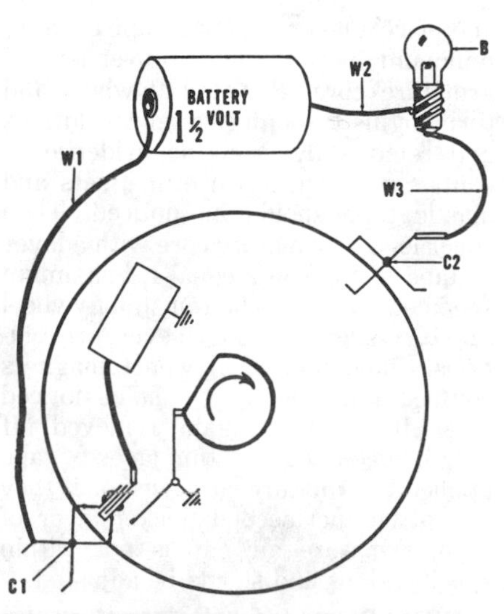

*Fig. 5-3—Drawing showing a simple test lamp for checking ignition timing and/or breaker point opening.*

B. 1½ volt bulb
C1. Spring clamp
C2. Spring clamp
W1. Wire
W2. Wire
W3. Wire

Light should be out when contact points are open and should go on when engine is turned to close breaker contact points. If light stays on when points are open, insulation of breaker contact arm is defective. If light does not go on when points are closed, contact surfaces are dirty, oily or are burned.

Adjust breaker point gap as follows unless manufacturer specifies adjusting breaker gap to obtain correct ignition timing. First, turn engine so points are closed to be sure contact surfaces are in alignment and seat squarely. Then, turn engine so breaker point opening is maximum and adjust breaker gap to manufacturer's specification. A wire type feeler gage is recommended for checking and adjusting the breaker contact gap. Be sure to recheck gap after tightening breaker point base retaining screws.

**IGNITION TIMING.** On some engines, ignition timing is nonadjustable and a certain breaker point gap is specified. On other engines, timing is adjustable by changing position of magneto stator plate with a specified breaker point gap or by simply varying breaker point gap to obtain correct timing. Ignition timing is usually specified either in degrees of engine (crankshaft) rotation or in piston travel before piston reaches top dead center position. In some instances, a specification is given for ignition timing even though timing may be nonadjustable; if a check reveals timing is incorrect on these engines, it is an indication of incorrect breaker point adjustment or excessive wear of breaker cam. Also, on some engines, it may indicate a wrong breaker cam has been installed or cam has been installed in a reversed position on engine crankshaft.

Some engines may have a timing mark or flywheel locating pin to locate flywheel at proper position for ignition spark to occur (breaker points begin to

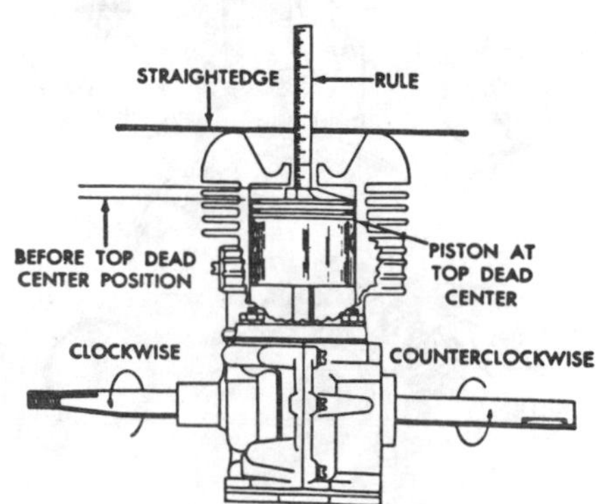


*Fig. 5-4—On some engines, it will be necessary to measure piston travel with rule, dial indicator or special timing gage when adjusting or checking ignition timing.*

open). If not, it will be necessary to measure piston travel as illustrated in Fig. 5-4 or install a degree indicating device on engine crankshaft.

A timing light as shown in Fig. 5-3 is a valuable aid in checking or adjusting engine timing. After disconnecting ignition coil lead from breaker point terminal, connect leads of timing light as shown. If timing is adjustable by moving magneto stator plate, be sure breaker point gap is adjusted as specified. Then, to check timing, slowly turn engine in normal direction of rotation past point at which ignition spark should occur. Timing light should be on, then go out (breaker points open) just as correct timing location is passed. If not, turn engine to proper timing location and adjust timing by relocating magneto stator plate or varying breaker contact gap as specified by engine manufacturer. Loosen screws retaining stator plate or breaker points and adjust position of stator plate or points so points are closed (timing light is on). Then, slowly move adjustment until timing light goes out (points open) and tighten retaining screws. Recheck timing to be sure adjustment is correct.

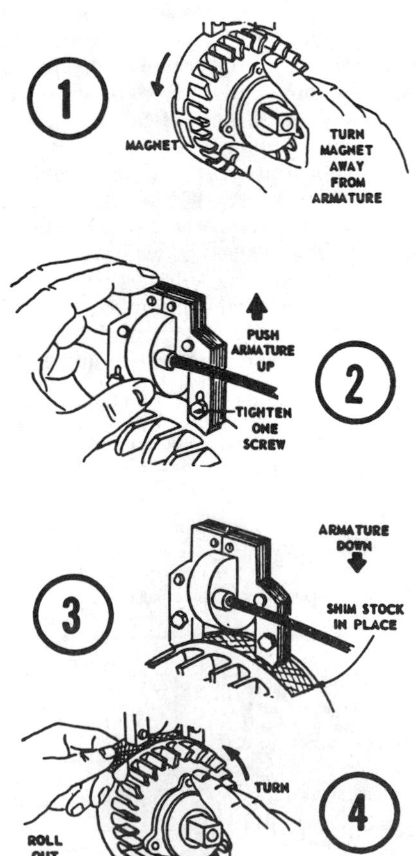


*Fig. 5-5—Views showing adjustment of armature air gap when armature is located outside flywheel. Refer to Fig. 5-6 for engines having armature located inside flywheel.*

**ARMATURE AIR GAP.** To fully concentrate magnetic field of flywheel magnets within armature core, it is necessary that flywheel magnets pass as closely to armature core as possible without danger of metal to metal contact. Clearance between flywheel magnets and legs of armature core is called armature air gap.

On magnetos where armature and high tension coil are located outside of the flywheel rim, adjustment of armature air gap is made as follows: Turn engine so flywheel magnets are located directly under legs of armature core and check clearance between armature core and flywheel magnets. If measured clearance is not within manufacturers specifications, loosen armature core mounting screws and place shims of thickness equal to minimum air gap specification between magnets and armature core (Fig. 5-5). The magnets will pull armature core against shim stocks. Tighten armature core mounting screws, remove shim stock and turn engine through several revolutions to be sure flywheel does not contact armature core.

Where armature core is located under or behind flywheel, the following methods may be used to check and adjust armature air gap: On some engines, slots or openings are provided in flywheel through which armature air gap can be checked. Some engine manufacturers provide a cutaway flywheel that can be installed temporarily for checking armature air gap. A test flywheel can be made out of a discarded flywheel (See Fig. 5-6), or out of a new flywheel if service volume on a particular engine warrants such expenditure. Another method of checking armature air gap is to remove flywheel and place a layer of plastic tape equal to minimum specified air gap over legs of armature core. Reinstall flywheel and turn engine through several revolutions and remove flywheel; no evidence of contact between flywheel magnets and plastic tape should be noticed. Then cover legs of armature core with a layer of tape of thickness equal to maximum specified air gap; then, reinstall flywheel and turn engine through several revolutions. Indication of flywheel magnets contacting plastic tape should be noticed after flywheel is again removed. If magnets contact first thin layer of tape applied to armature core legs, or if they do not contact second thicker layer of tape, armature air gap is not within specifications and should be adjusted.

**NOTE: Before loosening armature core mounting screws, scribe a mark on mounting plate against edge of armature core so that adjustment of air gap can be gaged.**

In some instances it may be necessary to slightly enlarge armature core mounting holes before proper air gap adjustment can be made.

**MAGNETO EDGE GAP.** The point of maximum acceleration of movement of flywheel magnetic field through high tension coil (and therefore, the point of maximum current induced in primary coil windings) occurs when trailing edge of flywheel magnet is slightly past left hand leg of armature core. The exact point of maximum primary current is determined by using electrical measuring devices, distance between trailing edge of flywheel magnet and leg of armature core at this point is measured and becomes a service specification. This distance, which is stated either in thousandths of an inch or in degrees of flywheel rotation, is called the Edge Gap or "E" Gap.

For maximum strength of ignition spark, breaker points should just start to open when flywheel magnets are at specified edge gap position. Usually, edge gap is nonadjustable and will be maintained at proper dimension if contact breaker points are adjusted to recommended gap and correct breaker cam is installed. However, magneto edge gap can change (and spark intensity thereby reduced) due to the following:

a. Flywheel drive key sheared
b. Flywheel drive key worn (loose)
c. Keyway in flywheel or crankshaft worn (oversized)
d. Loose flywheel retaining nut which can also cause any above listed difficulty
e. Excessive wear on breaker cam
f. Breaker cam loose on crankshaft
g. Excessive wear on breaker point rubbing block or push rod so points cannot be properly adjusted.

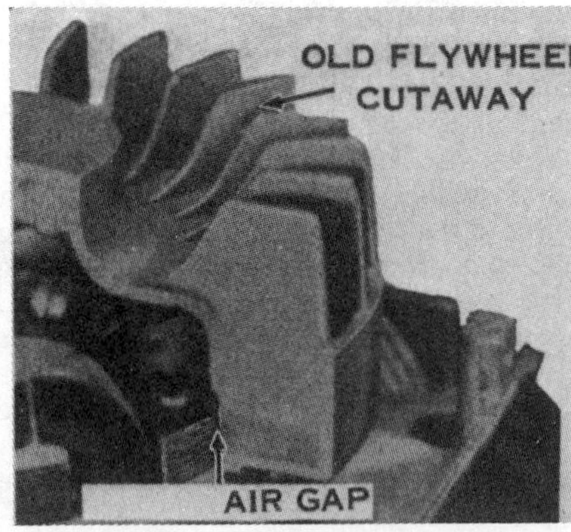


*Fig. 5-6—Where armature core is located inside flywheel, check armature gap by using a cutaway flywheel unless other method is provided by manufacturer; refer to appropriate engine repair section. Where possible, an old discarded flywheel should be used to cut-away section for checking armature gap.*

## Unit Type Magneto Service Fundamentals

Improper functioning of carburetor, spark plug or other components often causes difficulties that are thought to be an improperly functioning magneto. Since a brief inspection will often locate other causes for engine malfunction, it is recommended one be certain magneto is at fault before opening magneto housing. Magneto malfunction can easily be determined by simple tests as outlined in following paragraph.

## Troubleshooting

With a properly adjusted spark plug in good condition, ignition spark should be strong enough to bridge a short gap in addition to actual spark plug gap. With engine running, hold end of spark plug wire not more than 1/16-inch (1.59 mm) away from spark plug terminal. Engine should not misfire.

To test magneto spark if engine will not start, remove ignition wire from magneto end cap socket. Bend a short piece of wire so when it is inserted in end cap socket, other end is about ⅛-inch (3.18 mm) from engine casting. Crank engine slowly and observe gap between wire and engine, a strong blue spark should jump gap the instant impulse coupling trips. If a strong spark is observed, it is recommended magneto be eliminated as source of engine difficulty and spark plug, ignition wire and terminals be thoroughly inspected.

If, when cranking engine, impulse coupling does not trip, magneto must be removed from engine and coupling overhauled or renewed. It should be noted that if impulse coupling will not trip, a weak spark will occur.

## Magneto Adjustments and Service

**BREAKER POINTS.** Breaker points are accessible for service after removing magneto housing end cap. Examine point contact surfaces for pitting or pyramiding (transfer of metal from one surface to the other); a small tungsten file or fine stone may be used to resurface points. Badly worn of badly pitted points should be renewed. After points are resurfaced or renewed, check breaker point gap with rotor turned so points are opened maximum distance. Refer to MAGNETO paragraph in appropriate engine repair section for point gap specifications.

When installing magneto end cap, both end cap and housing mating surfaces should be thoroughly cleaned and a new gasket be installed.

**CONDENSER.** Condenser used in unit type magneto is similar to that used in other ignition systems. Refer to MAGNETO paragraph in appropriate engine repair section for condenser test specifications. Usually, a new condenser should be installed whenever breaker points are being renewed.

**COIL.** The ignition coil can be tested without removing the coil from housing. Instructions provided with coil tester should have coil test specifications listed.

**ROTOR.** Usually, service on magneto rotor is limited to renewal of bushings or bearings, if damaged. Check to be sure rotor turns freely and does not drag or have excessive end play.

**MAGNETO INSTALLATION.** When installing a unit type magneto on an engine, refer to MAGNETO paragraph in appropriate engine repair section for magneto to engine timing information.

## SOLID STATE IGNITION SERVICE FUNDAMENTALS

Because of differences in solid state ignition construction, it is impractical to outline a general procedure for solid state ignition service. Refer to specific engine section for testing, overhaul notes and timing of solid state ignition systems.

## SPARK PLUG SERVICING

**ELECTRODE GAP.** Spark plug electrode gap should be adjusted by bending the ground electrode. Refer to Fig. 5-7. Recommended gap is listed in SPARK PLUG paragraph in appropriate engine repair section of this manual.

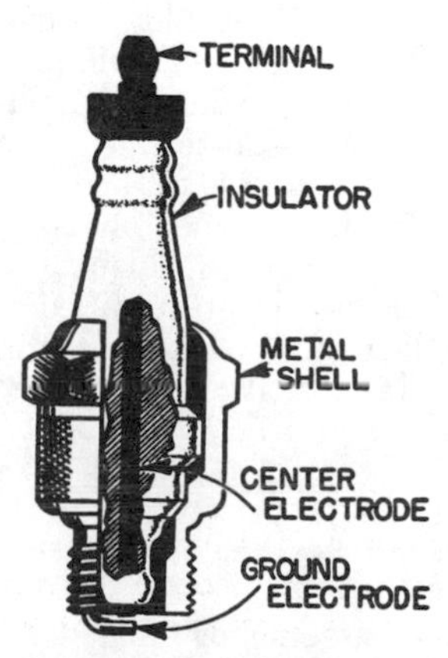


*Fig. 5-7—Cross-sectional drawing of spark plug showing construction and nomenclature.*

*Fig. 5-8—Normal plug appearance in four-stroke cycle engine. Insulator is light tan to gray in color and electrodes are not burned. Renew plug at regular intervals as recommended by engine manufacturer.*

*Fig. 5-9—Appearance of spark plug indicating cold fouling. Causing of cold fouling may be use of a too-cold plug, excessive idling or light loads, carburetor choke out of adjustment, defective spark plug wire or boot, carburetor adjusted too "rich" or low engine compression.*

*Fig. 5-10—Appearance of spark plug indicating wet fouling; a wet, black oily film is over entire firing end of plug. Cause may be oil getting by worn valve guides, worn oil rings or plugged breather or breather valve in tappet chamber.*

*Fig. 5-11—Appearance of spark plug indicating overheating. Check for plugged cooling fins, bent or damaged blower housing, engine being operated without all shields in place or other causes of engine overheating. Also can be caused by too lean a fuel-air mixture or spark plug not tightened properly.*

**CLEANING AND ELECTRODE CONDITIONING.** Spark plugs are most usually cleaned by abrasive action commonly referred to as "sand blasting." Actually, ordinary sand is not used, but a special abrasive which is nonconductive to electricity even when melted, thus the abrasive cannot short out plug current. Extreme care should be used in cleaning plugs after sand blasting, however, as any particles of abrasive left on plug may cause damage to piston rings, piston or cylinder walls. Some engine manufacturers recommend spark plug be renewed rather than cleaned because of possible engine damage from cleaning abrasives.

After plug is cleaned by abrasive, and before gap is set, electrode surfaces between grounded and insulated electrodes should be cleaned and returned as nearly as possible to original shape by filing with a point file. Failure to properly dress electrodes can result in high secondary voltage requirements, and misfire of the plug.

**PLUG APPEARANCE DIAGNOSIS.** Appearance of a spark plug will be altered by use, and an examination of plug tip can contribute useful information which may assist in obtaining better spark plug life. Figs. 5-8 through 5-11 are provided by Champion Spark Plug Company to illustrate typical observed conditions. Listed in captions are probable causes and suggested corrective measures.

# CARBURETOR SERVICING FUNDAMENTALS

The bulk of carburetor service consists of cleaning, inspection and adjustment. After considerable service it may become necessary to overhaul the carburetor and renew worn parts to restore original operating efficiency. Although carburetor condition affects engine operating economy and power, ignition and engine compression must also be considered to determine and correct causes of poor performance.

Before dismantling carburetor for cleaning or overhaul, clean all external surfaces and remove accumulated dirt and grease. Refer to appropriate engine repair section for carburetor exploded or cross-sectional views. Dismantle carburetor and note any discrepancies to assure correction during overhaul. Thoroughly clean all parts and inspect for damage or wear. Wash jets and passages and blow clear with clean, dry compressed air. Do not use a drill or wire to clean jets as possible enlargement of calibrated holes will disturb operating balance. Measurement of jets to determine extent of wear is difficult and new parts are usually installed to assure satisfactory results.

Carburetor manufacturers provide for many of their models an assortment of gaskets and other parts usually needed to do a correct job of cleaning and overhaul. These assortments are usually catalogued as Gasket Kits and Overhaul Kits respectively.

On float type carburetors, inspect float pin and needle valve for wear and renew if necessary. Check metal floats for leaks and where a dual type float is installed, check alignment of float sections. Check cork floats for loss of protective coating and absorption of fuel.

**NOTE: Do not attempt to recoat cork floats with shellac or varnish or to resolder leaky metal floats. Renew part if defective.**

Check fit of throttle and choke valve shafts. Excessive clearance will cause improper valve plate seating and will permit dust or grit to be drawn into engine. Air leaks at throttle shaft bores due to wear will upset carburetor calibration and contribute to uneven engine operation. Rebush valve shaft holes where necessary and renew dust seals. If rebushing is not possible, renew body part supporting shaft. Inspect throttle and choke valve plates for proper installation and condition.

Power or idle adjustment needles must not be worn or grooved. Check condition of needle seal packing or "O" ring and renew packing or "O" ring if necessary.

Reinstall or renew jets, using correct size listed for specific model. Adjust power and idle settings as described for specific carburetors in engine service section of manual.

It is important that carburetor bore at idle discharge ports and in vicinity of throttle valve be free of deposits. A partially restricted idle port will produce a "flat spot" between idle and mid-range rpm. This is because the restriction makes it necessary to open throttle wider than the designed opening to obtain proper idle speed. Opening throttle wider than the design specified amount will uncover more of the port than was intended in calibration of carburetor. As a result an insufficient amount of the port will be available as a reserve to cover transition period (idle to the mid-range rpm) when the high speed system begins to function.

When reassembling float type carburetors, be sure float position is properly adjusted. Refer to CARBURETOR paragraph in appropriate engine repair section for float level adjustment specifications.

# ENGINE SERVICE

## DISASSEMBLY AND ASSEMBLY

Special techniques must be developed in repair of engines of aluminum alloy or magnesium alloy construction. Soft threads in aluminum or magnesium castings are often damaged by carelessness in overtightening fasteners or in attempting to loosen or remove seized fasteners. Manufacturer's recommended torque values for tightening screw fasteners should be followed closely.

**NOTE: If damaged threads are encountered, refer to following paragraph, "REPAIRING DAMAGED THREADS."**

A given amount of heat applied to aluminum or magnesium will cause it to expand a greater amount than will steel under similar conditions. Because of different expansion characteristics, heat is usually recommended for easy installation of bearings, pins, etc., in aluminum or magnesium castings. Sometimes, heat can be used to free parts that are seized or where an interference fit is used. Heat, therefore, becomes a service tool and the application of heat one of the required service techniques. An open flame is not usually advised because it destroys paint and other protective coatings and because a uniform and controlled temperature with open flame is difficult to obtain. Methods commonly used are heating in oil or water, with a heat lamp, electric hot plate, electric hot air gun, or in an oven or kiln. The use of water or oil gives a fairly accurate temperature control but is somewhat limited as to the size and type of part that can be handled. Thermal crayons are available which can be used to determine temperature of a heated part. These crayons melt when the part reaches a specified temperature, and a number of crayons for different temperatures are available. Temperature indicating crayons are usually available at welding equipment supply houses.

Use only specified gaskets when reassembling, and use an approved gasket cement or sealing compound unless otherwise stated. Seal all exposed threads and repaint or retouch with an approved paint.

## REPAIRING DAMAGED THREADS

Damaged threads in castings can be renewed by use of thread repair kits which are recommended by a number of equipment and engine manufacturers. Use of thread repair kits is not difficult, but instructions must be carefully followed. Refer to Figs. 5-12 through 5-15 which illustrate the use of Heli-Coil thread repair kits that are manufactured by the Heli-coil Corporation, Danbury, Connecticut.

Heli-Coil thread repair kits are available through parts departments of most engine and equipment manufacturers; thread inserts are available in all National Coarse (USS) sizes from #4 to 1½ inch and National Fine (SAE) sizes from #6 to 1½ inch. Also, sizes for repairing 14 mm and 18 mm spark plug ports are available.

## VALVE SERVICE FUNDAMENTALS

When overhauling engines, obtaining proper valve sealing is of primary importance. The following paragraphs cover fundamentals of servicing intake and exhaust valves, valve seats and valve guides.

**REMOVING AND INSTALLING VALVES.** A valve spring compressor, one type of which is shown in Fig. 5-16, is a valuable aid in removing and installing intake and exhaust valves. This tool is used to hold spring compressed while removing or installing pin, collars or retainer from valve stem. Refer to Fig. 5-17 for views showing some of the different methods of retaining valve spring to valve stem.

**VALVE REFACING.** If valve face (See Fig. 5-18) is slightly worn, burned or pitted, valve can usually be refaced providing proper equipment is available. Many shops will usually renew valves, however, rather than invest in somewhat costly valve refacing tools.

Before attempting to reface a valve, refer to specifications in appropriate engine repair section for valve face angle. On some engines, manufacturer recommends grinding the valve face to an angle of ½° to 1° less than that of the valve seat. Refer to Fig. 5-19. Also, nominal valve face angle may be either 30° or 45°.

After valve is refaced, check thickness of valve "margin" (See Fig. 5-18). If margin is less than manufacturer's minimum specification (refer to specifications in appropriate engine repair section), or is less than one-half the margin of a new valve, renew valve. Valves having excessive material removed in refacing operation will not give satisfactory service.

When refacing or renewing a valve, the seat should also be reconditioned, or in engines where valve seat is renewable, a new seat should be installed. Refer to following paragraph "RESEATING OR RENEWING VALVE SEATS." Then, the seating surfaces should be lapped in using a fine valve grinding compound.

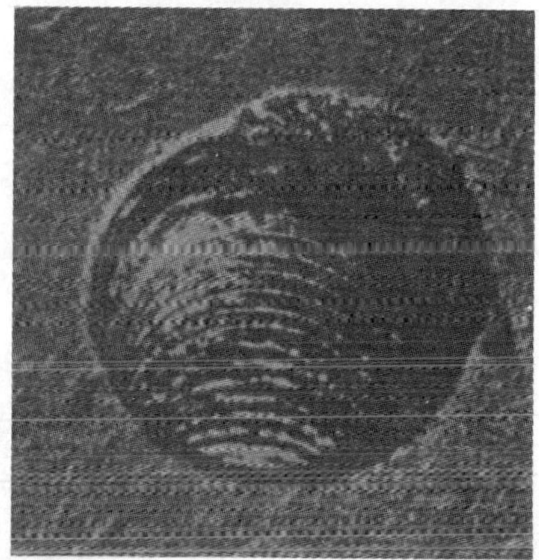

*Fig. 5-12—Damaged threads in casting before repair. Refer to Figs. 5-13, 5-14 and 5-15 for steps in installing thread insert. (Series of photos provided by Heli-Coil Corp., Danbury, Conn.)*

*Fig. 5-14—Special drill taps are provided in thread repair kit for threading drilled hole to correct size for outside of thread insert. A standard tap cannot be used.*

*Fig. 5-13—First step in repairing damaged threads is to drill out old threads using exact size drill recommended in instructions provided with thread repair kit. Drill all the way through an open hole or all the way to bottom of blind hole, making sure hole is straight and that centerline of hole is not moved in drilling process.*

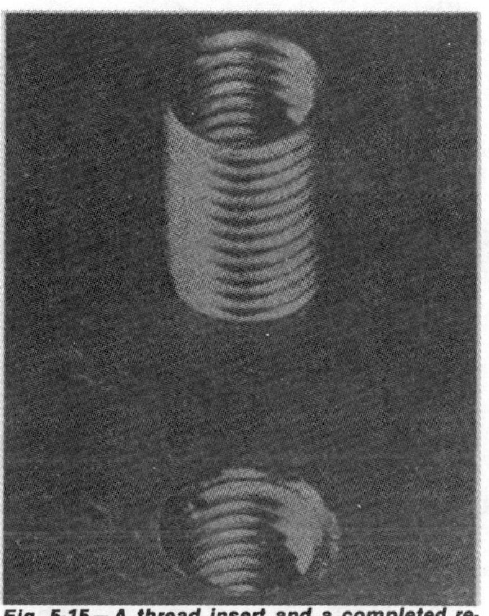

*Fig. 5-15—A thread insert and a completed repair are shown above. Special tools are provided in thread repair kit for installation of thread insert.*

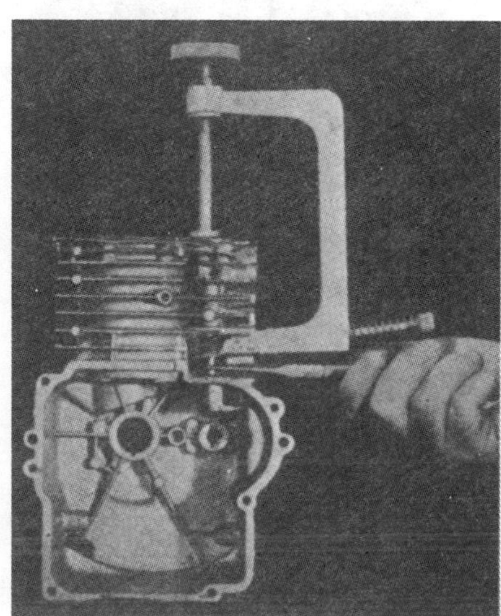

*Fig. 5-16—View showing one type of valve spring compressor being used to remove keeper. (Block is cut-away to show valve spring.)*

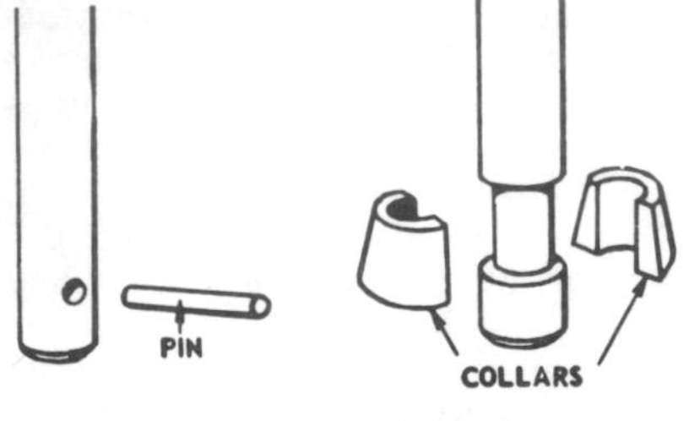


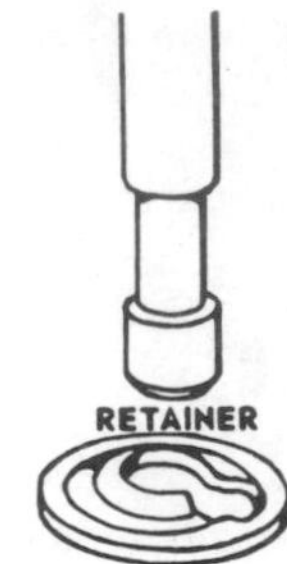


*Fig. 5-17—Drawing showing three types of valve spring keepers used.*

**RESEATING OR RENEWING VALVE SEATS.** On engines having valve seat machined in cylinder block casting, seat can be reconditioned by using a correct angle seat grinding stone or valve seat cutter. When reconditioning valve seat, care should be taken that only enough material is removed to provide a good seating on valve contact surface. The width of seat should then be measured (See Fig. 5-20) and if width exceeds manufacturer's maximum specifications, seat should be narrowed by using one stone or cutter with an angle 15° greater than valve seat angle and a second stone or cutter with an angle 15° less than seat angle. When narrowing seat, coat seat lightly with Prussian blue and check where seat contacts valve face by inserting valve in guide and rotating valve lightly against seat. Seat should contact approximate center of valve face. By using only narrow angle seat narrowing stone or cutter, seat contact will be moved towards outer edge of valve face.

On engines having renewable valve seats, refer to appropriate engine repair section in this manual for recommended method of removing old seat and installing new seat. Refer to Fig. 5-21 for one method of installing new valve seats. Seats are retained in cylinder block bore by an interference fit; that is, seat is slightly larger than bore in block. It sometimes occurs that valve seat will become loose in bore, especially on engines with aluminum crankcase. Some manufacturers provide oversize valve seat inserts (insert O.D. larger than standard part) so that if standard size insert fits loosely, bore can be cut oversize and a new insert be tightly installed. After installing valve seat insert in engines of aluminum construction, metal around seat should be peened as shown in Fig. 5-22. Where a loose insert is encountered and an oversize insert is not available, loose insert can usually be tightened by centerpunching cylinder block material at three equally spaced points around insert, then peening completely around insert as shown in Fig. 5-22.

For some engines with cast iron cylinder blocks, a service valve seat insert is available for reconditioning valve

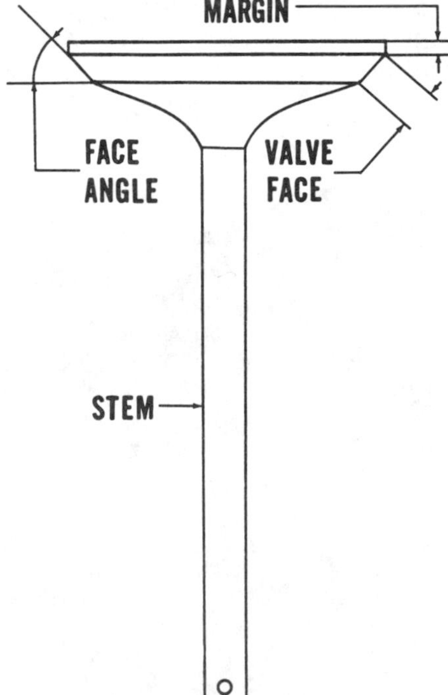


*Fig. 5-18—Drawing showing typical four-stroke cycle engine valve. Face angle is usually 30° or 45°. On some engines, valve face is ground to an angle of ½ or 1 degree less than seat angle.*

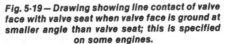

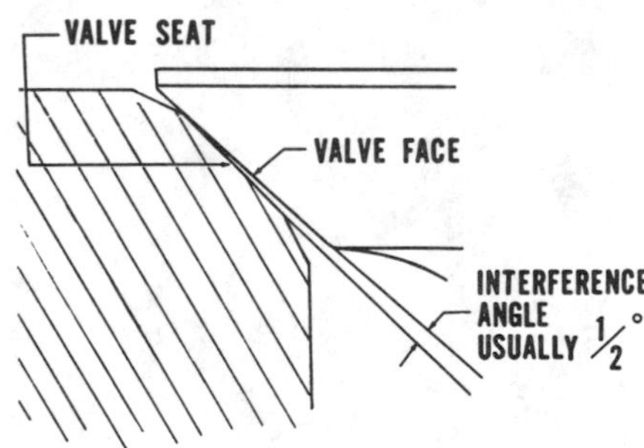


*Fig. 5-19—Drawing showing line contact of valve face with valve seat when valve face is ground at smaller angle than valve seat; this is specified on some engines.*

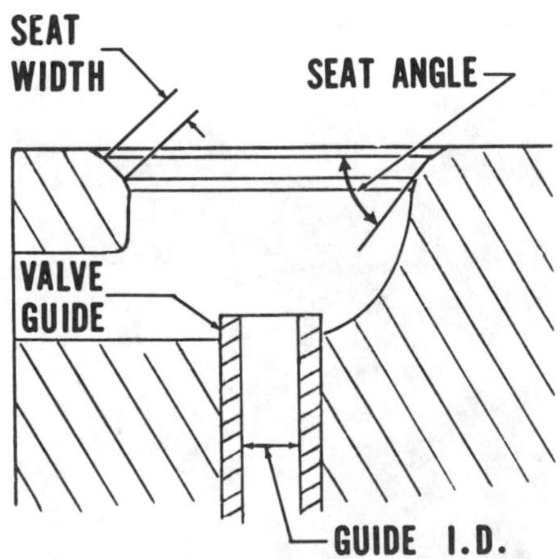


*Fig. 5-20—Cross-sectional drawing of typical valve seat and valve guide as used on some engines. Valve guide may be integral part of cylinder block; on some models so constructed, valve guide I.D. may be reamed out and an oversize valve stem installed. On other models, a service guide may be installed after counterboring cylinder block.*

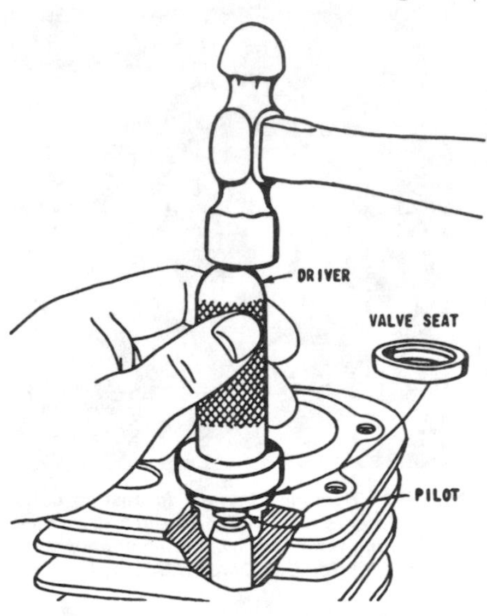


*Fig. 5-21—View showing one method used to install valve seat insert. Refer to appropriate engine repair section for manufacturer's recommended method.*

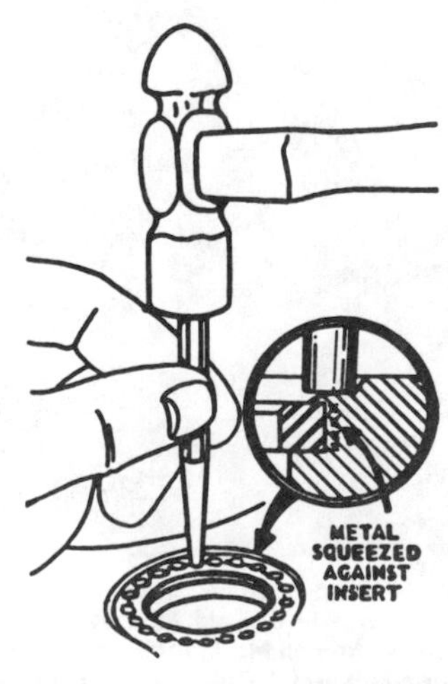


*Fig. 5-22—It is usually recommended that on aluminum block engines, metal be peened around valve seat insert after insert is installed.*

seat, and is installed by counterboring cylinder block to specified dimensions, then driving insert into place. Refer to appropriate engine repair section in this manual for information on availability and installation of service valve seat inserts for cast iron engines.

## INSTALLING OVERSIZE PISTON AND RINGS

Some engine manufacturers have oversize piston and ring sets available for use in repairing engines in which cylinder bore is excessively worn and standard size piston and rings cannot be used. If care and approved procedure are used in boring the cylinder oversize, installation of an oversize piston and ring set should result in a highly satisfactory overhaul.

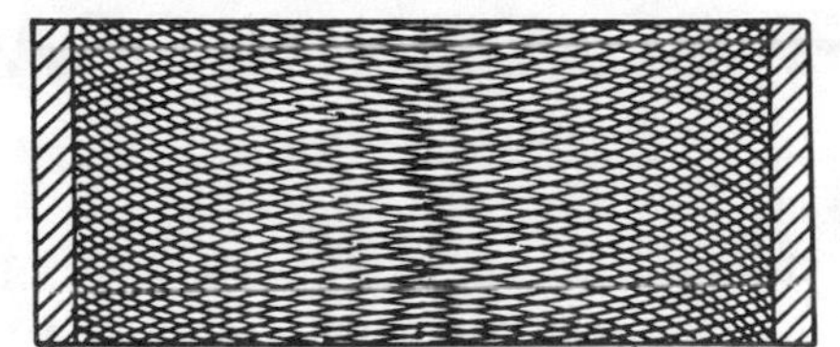

*Fig. 5-23—A cross-hatch pattern as shown should be obtained when honing cylinder. Pattern is obtained by moving hone up and down cylinder bore as it is being turned by slow speed electric drill.*

Cylinder bore may be oversized by using either a boring bar or a hone; however, if a boring bar is used, it is usually recommended cylinder bore be finished with a hone. Refer to Fig. 5-23.

Where oversize piston and rings are available, it will be so noted in appropriate engine repair section of this manual. Also, the standard bore diameter will also be given. Before attempting to rebore or hone the cylinder to oversize, carefully measure the cylinder bore to be sure standard size piston and rings will not fit within tolerance. Also, it may be possible cylinder is excessively worn or damaged and reboring or honing to largest oversize will not clean up worn or scored surface.

# OFF-SEASON STORAGE

A proper storage procedure can extend the life of equipment by preventing damage when the equipment is not used. Exact procedures for storing depend on the type of equipment, length of storage, time of year stored and storage location. To obtain satisfactory results, equipment storage must be coordinated with a regular maintenance program. The following outline lists procedures applicable for extended storage of most powered equipment.

## ENTERING INTO STORAGE

Drain old oil from all regularly serviced compartments such as engine crankcase, gearboxes, chain cases, etc., while oil is warm. Refill with new approved oil to the level recommended by the equipment manufacturer.

Clean and dry all exterior surfaces. Remove all accumulated dirt and repair any damaged surface. Paint exposed surfaces to prevent rust.

Clean all cooling air passages and straighten, repair or renew any part which would interfere with normal air flow. Remove shrouds and deflectors necessary to inspect and clean all cooling air passages. Clean all grease, oil, dirt, leaves, etc., from all cooling system components.

Lubricate all normally serviced surfaces with approved oil or grease. If equipped with grease fittings, attempt to purge old grease from joint.

Inspect for worn or broken parts. Make necessary adjustments and repair all damage. Tighten all loose hardware.

Fuel should be either drained or treated with an approved stabilizer. All fuel should be drained from tank, filters, lines, pumps and carburetor unless specifically discouraged by manufacturer. Do not add fuel stabilizer to any fuel containing alcohol. Fuel containing alcohol will separate if permitted to sit for long and internal parts may be extensively damaged by corrosion. Some manufacturers recommend coating inside of tank with a small amount of oil to deter rusting in tank. Filters should be serviced initially and water traps should be serviced regularly while in storage.

Install new filter elements. Some filters can be cleaned and serviced, but most should be installed new at this time.

Pour a small amount (usually 1 tablespoon) of oil into each cylinder of engine through spark plug hole. Crank engine with starter about 12 revolutions to distribute oil, then install spark plugs and reconnect spark plug wires.

Install protective caps at ends of all disconnected lines. Seal openings of exhaust, air intake, engine dipstick and crankcase breather tube.

Loosen all drive belts and remove pressure from friction drive components. Inspect and note condition of drive belts. If condition is questionable, a new belt should be installed when removing equipment from storage.

Support all mounted assemblies, removing weight from lift arms and hydraulic systems (of models so equipped). Retract all hydraulic cylinders, if possible. Coat exposed parts of cylinder rods and other exposed machined surfaces with grease to prevent rust.

Remove battery and store in a cool, dry place. Do not permit battery to freeze and maintain fully charged, checking approximately every 30 days.

Block the equipment to remove all weight from tires. Wheels and tires should be stored in a cool, dark, dry location away from operating electrical equipment.

Store the equipment in a dry protected place. If necessary to store outside, cover equipment to prevent entrance of water, but do not seal tightly. Sealing may cause condensation and accelerate rusting.

## REMOVING FROM STORAGE

Check for obvious damage to covering and equipment and repair as necessary.

Install tires and wheels. Inflate tires with correct amount of air. Remove any blocks used during storage.

Charge battery, then install in equipment making sure that battery is properly retained. Clean battery cables and battery posts, then attach cables to battery terminals.

Remove covers from exhaust, air intake, engine dipstick and crankcase breather tube. Remove any protective caps from lines disconnected during disassembly. Be sure ends are clean, then reconnect lines.

Check all filters. Install new filters, or clean and service existing filters as required.

Adjust all drive belts and friction drive components to correct tension as recommended by the manufacturer. New belts should be installed if condition is questionable.

Fill fuel tank with correct type of fuel. Check for leaks. Gaskets may dry up or carburetor needle valve may stick during storage. Repair any problems before attempting to start. Drain water traps and check condition of fuel filters.

Lubricate all surfaces normally lubricated with oil or grease. Check cooling passages for restrictions such as insect, bird or animal nests. Check oil in all compartments such as engine crankcase, gearboxes, chain cases, etc., for proper level. Evidence of too much oil may indicate water settled below oil. Drain oil if contamination is suspected or if time of storage exceeds recommended time change interval. Fill to proper level with correct type of oil.

# SERVICE SHOP TOOL BUYERS' GUIDE

This listing of service shop tools is solely for the convenience of users of the manual and does not imply endorsement or approval by Intertec Publishing Corporation of the tools and equipment listed. The listing is in response to many requests for information on sources for purchasing special tools and equipment. Every attempt has been made to make the listing as complete as possible at time of publication and each entry is made from the latest material available.

Special engine service tools such as drivers, pullers, gages, etc., which are available from the engine manufacturer are not listed in this section of the manual. Where a special service tool is listed in the engine service section of this manual, the tool is available from the central parts or service distributors listed at the end of most engine service sections, or from the manufacturer.

**NOTE TO MANUFACTURERS AND NATIONAL SALES DISTRIBUTORS OF ENGINE SERVICE TOOLS AND RELATED SERVICE EQUIPMENT. To obtain either a new listing for your products, or to change or add to an existing listing, write to Intertec Publishing Corporation, Book Division, P.O. Box 12901, Overland Park, KS 66282-2901.**

## Engine Service Tools

**Ammco Tools, Inc.**
Wacker Park
North Chicago, Illinois 60064
Valve spring compressor, torque wrenches, cylinder hones, ridge reamers, piston ring compressors, piston ring expanders.

**Bloom, Inc.**
Highway 939 West
Independence, Iowa 50644
Engine repair stand with crankshaft straightening attachment.

**Brush Research Mfg.Co., Inc.**
4642 East Floral Drive
Los Angeles, California 90022
Cylinder hones.

**E-Z Lok**
P.O. Box 2069
Gardena, California 90247
Thread repair insert kits.

**Fairchild Fastener Group**
3000 W. Lomita Blvd.
Torrance, California 90505
Thread repair insert kits (Keenserts) and installation tools.

**Foley-Belsaw Company**
**Outdoor Power Equipment Parts Div.**
6301 Equitable Road
P.O. Box 419593
Kansas City, Missouri 64141
Crankshaft straightener and repair stand, valve refacer, valve seat grinder, parts washer, cylinder hone, ridge reamer, piston ring expander and compressor, flywheel puller, torque wrench.

**Frederick Manufacturing Corp.**
4840 E. 12th Street
Kansas City, Missouri 64127
Piston groove cleaner, compression tester, piston ring expander and compressor, valve spring compressor, valve seat grinder, valve refacer, cylinder hone, flywheel puller, flywheel wrench, flywheel holder, starter spring rewinder, condenser pliers.

**Heli-Coil**
Shelter Rock Lane
Danbury, Connecticut 06810
Thread repair kits, thread inserts, installation tools.

**K-D Tools**
3575 Hempland Road
Lancaster, Pennsylvania 17604
Thread repair kits, valve spring compressors, reamers, micrometers, dial indicators, calipers.

**Keystone Reamer & Tool Co.**
South Front Street
P.O. Box 308
Millersburg, Pennsylvania 17061
Valve seat cutter and pilots, reamers, screw extractors, taps and dies.

**Ki-Sol Corporation**
100 Larkin Williams Ind. Ct.
Fenton, Missouri 63026
Cylinder hone, ridge reamer, ring compressor, ring expander, ring groove cleaner, torque wrenches, valve spring compressor, valve refacing equipment.

**K-Line Industries, Inc.**
315 Garden Avenue
Holland, Michigan 49424
Cylinder hone, ridge reamer, ring compressor, valve guide tools, valve spring compressor, reamers.

**K.O. Lee Company**
200 South Harrison
P.O. Box 1416
Aberdeen, South Dakota 57402

**Kwik-Way Mfg. Co.**
500 57th Street
Marion, Iowa 52302
Cylinder boring equipment, valve facing equipment, valve seat grinding equipment.

**Lisle Corporation**
807 East Main
Clarinda, Iowa 51632
Cylinder hones, ridge reamers, ring compressors, valve spring compressors.

**Microdot, Inc.**
P.O. Box 3001
Fullerton, California 92634
Thread repair insert kits.

**Mighty Midget Mfg. Co.,**
**Div. of Kansas City Screw Thread Co.**
2908 E. Truman Road
Kansas City, Missouri 64127
Crankshaft straightener.

**Neway Manufacturing, Inc.**
1013 N. Shiawassee
Corunna, Michigan 48817
Valve seat cutters.

**OTC**
655 Eisenhower Drive
Owatonna, Minnesota 55060
Valve tools, spark plug tools, piston ring tools, cylinder hones.

**Power Lawnmower Parts, Inc.**
1920 Lyell Avenue
P.O. Box 60860
Rochester, New York 14606-0860
Flywheel pullers, starter wrench, flywheel holder, gasket cutter tool, gasket scraper tool, crankshaft cleaning tool, ridge reamer, valve spring compressor, valve seat cutters, thread repair kits, valve lifter, piston ring expander.

**Precision Manufacturing & Sales, Co., Inc.**
2140 Range Road
Clearwater, Florida 34625
Cylinder boring equipment, measuring instruments, valve equipment, hones, hand tools, test equipment, threading tools, presses, parts washers, milling machines, lathes, drill presses, glass beading machines, dynos, safety equipment.

**Sioux Tools, Inc.**
2901 Floyd Blvd.
P.O. Box 507
Sioux City, Iowa 51102
Valve refacing and seat grinding equipment.

**Sunnen Product Company**
7910 Manchester Avenue
St. Louis, Missouri 63143
Cylinder hones, rod reconditioning, valve guide reconditioning.

## Test Equipment and Gages

**AW Dynamometer, Inc.**
P.O. Box 428
Colfax, Illinois 61728
Engine test dynamometer.

**B.C. Ames Company**
131 Lexington
Waltham, Massachusetts 02254
Micrometers, dial gages, calipers.

**Dixson, Inc.**
287 27 Road
Grand Junction, Colorado 81503
Tachometer, compression gage, timing light.

**Foley-Belsaw Company**
**Outdoor Power Equipment Parts Div.**
6301 Equitable Road
P.O. Box 419593
Kansas City, Missouri 64141
Cylinder gage, amp/volt testers, condenser and coil tester, magneto tester, ignition testers, tachometers, spark testers, compression gages, timing lights and gages, micrometers and calipers, carburetor testers, vacuum gages.

**Frederick Manufacturing Corp.**
4840 E. 12th Street
Kansas City, Missouri 64127
Ignition tester, tachometer, compression gage.

**Graham-Lee Electronics, Inc.**
4220 Central Avenue N.E.
Minneapolis, Minnesota 55421
Coil and condenser tester.

**K-D Tools**
3575 Hempland Road
Lancaster, Pennsylvania 17604
Diode tester and installation tools, compression gage, timing light, timing gages.

**Ki-Sol Corporation**
100 Larkin Williams Ind. Ct.
Fenton, Missouri 63026
Micrometers, telescoping gages, compression gages, cylinder gages.

**K-Line Industries, Inc.**
315 Garden Avenue
Holland, Michigan 49424
Compression gage, leakdown tester, micrometers, dial gages.

**Merc-O-Tronic Instruments Corporation**
215 Branch Street
Almont, Michigan 48003
Igition analyzers for conventional, solid-state and magneto systems, electric tachometers, electronic tachometer and dwell meter, power timing lights, ohmmeters, compression gages, mechanical timing devices.

**OTC**
655 Eisenhower Drive
Owatonna, Minnesota 55060
Feeler gages, hydraulic test gages.

**Power Lawnmower Parts, Inc.**
1920 Lyell Avenue
P.O. Box 60860
Rochester, New York 14606-0860
Compression gage, cylinder gage, magneto tester, compression gage, condenser and coil tester.

**Prestolite Electronic Div.**
**An Allied Company**
4 Seagate
Toledo, Ohio 43691
Magneto test plug.

**Simpson Electric Company**
853 Dundee Avenue
Elgin, Illinois 60120
Electrical and electronic test equipment.

**L.S. Starrett Company**
121 Crescent St.
Athol, Massachusetts 01331
Micrometers, dial gages, bore gages, feeler gages.

**Stevens Instrument Company**
P.O. Box 193
Waukegan, Illinois 60079
Ignition analyzers, timing lights, volt-ohm meter, tachometer, spark checkers, CD ignition testers.

**Stewart-Warner Corporation**
580 Slawin Ct.
Mt. Prospect, Illinois 60056
Compression gage, ignition tachometer, timing light ignition analyzer.

## Shop Tools and Equipment

**AC Delco Division**
**General Motors Corp.**
3031 W. Grand Blvd.
P.O. Box 33115
Detroit, Michigan 48232
Spark plug tools.

**Black & Decker Mfg. Co.**
626 Hanover Pike
Hampstead, Maryland 21074
Electric power tools.

**Champion Pneumatic Machinery Co.**
1301 N. Euclid Avenue
Princeton, Illinois 61356
Air compressors.

**Champion Spark Plug Company**
P.O. Box 910
Toledo, Ohio 43661
Spark plug cleaning and testing equipment, gap tools and wrenches.

**Chicago Pneumatic Tool Co.**
2200 Bleecker St.
Utica, New York 13501
Air impact wrenches, air hammers, air drills and grinders, nut runners, speed ratchets.

**Cooper Tools**
P.O. Box 728
Apex, North Carolina 27502
Chain type engine hoists and utility slings.

**E-Z Lok**
P.O. Box 2069
Gardena, California 90247
Thread repair insert kits.

**Fairchild Fastener Group**
3000 W. Lomita Blvd.
Torrance, California 90505
Thread repair insert kits (Keenserts) and installation tools.

**Foley-Belsaw Company**
**Outdoor Power Equipment Parts Div.**
6301 Equitable Road
P.O. Box 419593
Kansas City, Missouri 64141
Torque wrenches, parts washers, micrometers and calipers.

**Frederick Manufacturing Corp.**
4840 E. 12th Street

Kansas City, Missouri 64127
Torque wrenches, gear pullers.

**G&H Products, Inc.**
P.O. Box 770
St. Paris, Ohio 43027
Equipment lifts.

**General Scientific Equipment Co.**
525 Spring Garden St.
Philadelphia, Pennsylvania 19122
Safety equipment.

**Graymills Corporation**
3705 N. Lincoln Avenue
Chicago, Illinois 60613
Parts washing equipment.

**Heli-Coil**
Shelter Rock Lane
Danbury, Connecticut 06810
Thread repair kits, thread inserts, installation tools.

**Ingersoll-Rand**
253 E. Washington Avenue
Washington, New Jersey 07882
Air and electric impact wrenches, electric drills and screwdrivers.

**Jaw Manufacturing Co.**
39 Mulberry St.
P.O. Box 213
Reading, Pennsylvania 19603
Files for repair or renewal of damaged threads, rethreader dies, flexible shaft drivers and extensions, screw extractors, impact drivers.

**Jenny Division of Homestead Ind., Inc.**
700 Second Avenue
Coraopolis, Pennsylvania 15108
Steam cleaning equipment, pressure washing equipment.

**K-Line Industries, Inc.**
315 Garden Avenue
Holland, Michigan 49424
Pullers, crack detectors, gloves, aprons, eyewear.

**Keystone Reamer & Tool Co.**
South Front Street
P.O. Box 308
Millersburg, Pennsylvania 17061
Adjustable reamers, twist drills, taps, dies.

**Microdot, Inc.**
P.O. Box 3001
Fullerton, California 92634
Thread repair insert kits.

**OTC**
655 Eisenhower Drive
Owatonna, Minnesota 55060
Bearing and gear pullers, hydraulic shop presses.

**Power Lawnmower Parts, Inc.**
1920 Lyell Avenue
P.O. Box 60860
Rochester, New York 14606-0860
Flywheel pullers, starter wrench.

**Shure Manufacturing Corp.**
1601 S. Hanley Road
St. Louis, Missouri 63144
Steel shop benches, desks, engine overhaul stand.

**Sioux Tools, Inc.**
2901 Floyd Blvd.
P.O. Box 507
Sioux City, Iowa 51102
Air and electric impact tools, drills, grinders.

**Sturtevant Richmont**
3203 N. Wolf Rd.
Franklin Park, Illinois 60131
Torque wrenches, torque multipliers, torque analyzers.

## Mechanic's Hand Tools

**Channellock, Inc.**
1306 South Main St.
P.O. Box 519
Meadville, Pennsylvania 16335

**John H. Graham & Company**
P.O. Box 739
Oradell, New Jersey 07649

**Jaw Manufacturing Co.**
39 Mulberry St.
P.O. Box 213
Reading, Pennsylvania 19603

**K-D Tools**
3575 Hempland Road
Lancaster, Pennsylvania 17604

**K-Line Industries, Inc.**
315 Garden Avenue
Holland, Michigan 49424

**OTC**
655 Eisenhower Drive
Owatonna, Minnesota 55060

**Snap-On Tools**
2801 80th Street
Kenosha, Wisconsin 53140

**Triangle Corporation-Tool Division**
P.O. Box 1807
Orangeburg, South Carolina 29115

## Shop Supplies (Chemicals, Metallurgy Products, Seals, Sealers, Common Parts Items, etc.).

**Clayton Manufacturing Co.**
4213 N. Temple City Blvd.
El Monte, California 91731
Steam cleaning compounds and solvents.

**E-Z Lok**
P.O. Box 2069
Gardena, California 90247
Thread repair insert kits.

**Eutectic + Castolin**
40-40 172nd Street
Flushing, New York 11358
Specialized repair and maintenance welding alloys.

**Fairchild Fastener Group**
3000 W. Lomita Blvd.
Torrance, California 90505
Thread repair insert kits (Keensserts) and installation tools.

**Foley-Belsaw Company**
**Outdoor Power Equipment Parts Div.**
6301 Equitable Road
P.O. Box 419593
Kansas City, Missouri 64141
Parts washers, cylinder head rethreaders, micrometers, calipers, gasket material, nylon rope, oil and grease products, bolt, nut, washer and spring assortments.

**Frederick Manufacturing Corp.**
4840 E. 12th Street
Kansas City, Missouri 64127
Thread repair kits.

**Graymills Corporation**
3705 N. Lincoln Avenue
Chicago, Illinois 60613
Parts cleaning fluids.

**Heli-Coil**
Shelter Rock Lane
Danbury, Connecticut 06810
Thread repair kits, thread inserts, installation tools.

**K-Line Industries, Inc.**
315 Garden Avenue
Holland, Michigan 49424
Machining lubricants, solvents, cleaning solutions.

**Loctite Corporation**
705 North Mountain Road
Newington, Connecticut 06111
Compounds for locking threads, retaining bearings and securing machine parts; sealants and adhesives.

**Microdot, Inc.**
P.O. Box 3001
Fullerton, California 92634
Thread repair insert kits.

**Permatex Industrial**
30 Tower Lane

Avon Park South
Avon, Connecticut 06001
Cleaning chemicals, gasket sealers, pipe sealants, adhesives, lubricants, thread locking and forming compounds.

**Power Lawnmower Parts, Inc.**
1920 Lyell Avenue
P.O. Box 60860
Rochester, New York 14606-0860
Grinding compound paste, gas tank sealer stick, shop aprons, eyewear.

**Radiator Specialty Co.**
1900 Wilkinson Blvd.
Charlotte, North Carolina 28208
Cleaning chemicals (Gunk) and solder seal.

---

# ARIENS

## CONDENSED SPECIFICATIONS

| | MODELS | | | | |
|---|---|---|---|---|---|
| | 13989, 13990 | 13948, 913002, 913003 | GT12 | GT14 | GT16 |
| Engine Make | Tecumseh | B&S | Kohler | Kohler | Kohler |
| Model | VH70 | 191707 | K301S | K321S | K341S |
| Bore | 2¾ in. (69.8 mm) | 3 in. (76.2 mm) | 3⅜ in. (85.7 mm) | 3½ in. (88.9 mm) | 3¾ in. (95.2 mm) |
| Stroke | 2-17/32 in. (64.3 mm) | 2¾ in. (69.8 mm) | 3¼ in. (82.5 mm) | 3¼ in. (82.5 mm) | 3¼ in. (82.5 mm) |
| Piston Displacement | 15.0 cu. in. (246 cc) | 19.44 cu. in. (319 cc) | 29.07 cu. in. (476 cc) | 31.27 cu. in. (512 cc) | 35.89 cu. in. (588 cc) |
| Horsepower | 7 | 8 | 12 | 14 | 16 |
| Slow Idle Speed – Rpm | 1800 | 1750 | 1800 | 1800 | 1800 |
| High Idle Speed (No Load) – Rpm | 3750 | 4000 | Note 2 | Note 3 | Note 4 |
| Crankcase Oil Capacity | 1½ pints (0.7L) | 2¼ pints (1L) | 4 pints (1.9L) | 4 pints (1.9L) | 4 pints (1.9L) |
| Weight – | | | | | |
| Above 32°F (0°C) | | | SAE 30 | | |
| 0°F (–18°C) to 32°F (0°C) | | | SAE 10W | | |
| Below 0°F (–18°C) | | | SAE 5W-20 | | |
| Transmission Oil Capacity | 2 pints (0.9L) | 2 pints (0.9L) | 7 pints (3.3L) | 7 pints (3.3L) | 7 pints (3.3L) |
| Weight | SAE 90 EP | SAE 90 EP | | SAE 10W-30 | |

| | MODELS | | | | |
|---|---|---|---|---|---|
| | S-8 Gear | S-8 Hydro | S-10 Gear | S-12 Hydro | S-14 Gear |
| Engine Make | B&S | B&S | Kohler | Kohler | Kohler |
| Model | 191707 | 191707 | K241S | K301S | K321S |
| Bore | 3 in. (76.2 mm) | 3 in. (76.2 mm) | 3¼ in. (82.5 mm) | 3⅜ in. (85.7 mm) | 3½ in. (88.9 mm) |
| Stroke | 2¾ in. (69.8 mm) | 2¾ in. (69.8 mm) | 2⅞ in. (73.0 mm) | 3¼ in. (82.5 mm) | 3¼ in. 82.5 mm) |
| Piston Displacement | 19.44 cu. in. (319 cc) | 19.44 cu. in. (319 cc) | 23.9 cu. in. (392 cc) | 29.07 cu. in. (476 cc) | 31.27 cu. in. (512 cc) |
| Horsepower | 8 | 8 | 10 | 12 | 14 |
| Slow Idle Speed – Rpm | 1750 | 1750 | 1600 | 1600 | 1600 |
| High Idle Speed (No Load) – Rpm | 3500 | 3500 | Note 1 | Note 2 | Note 3 |
| Crankcase Oil Capacity | 2¼ pints (1L) | 2¼ pints (1L) | 4 pints (1.9L) | 4 pints (1.9L) | 4 pints (1.9L) |
| Weight – | | | | | |
| Above 32°F (0°C) | | | SAE 30 | | |
| 0°F (–18°C) to 32°F (0°C) | | | SAE 10W | | |
| Below 0°F (–18°C) | | | SAE 5W-20 | | |
| Transmission Oil Capacity | 2¾ pints (1.3L) | .......... | 4 pints (1.9L) | 7 pints (3.3L) | 4 pints (1.9L) |
| Weight | SAE 90 EP | ATF Type "A" | SAE 90 EP | SAE 10W-30 | SAE 90 EP |
| Differential Oil Capacity | .......... | 2 pints | .......... | .......... | .......... |
| Weight | .......... | SAE 90 EP | .......... | .......... | .......... |

| | MODELS | | | | |
|---|---|---|---|---|---|
| | S-14 Hydro | S-16 Hydro | YT8 | YT10 | YT11 |
| Engine Make | Kohler | Kohler | Tecumseh | Tecumseh | B&S |
| Model | K321S | K321S | VM80 | TVM220 | 252707 |
| Bore | 3½ in. (88.9 mm) | 3¾ in. (95.2 mm) | 3-5/16 in. (84.2 mm) | 3-5/16 in. (84.2 mm) | 3-7/16 in. (87.3 mm) |
| Stroke | 3¼ in. (82.5 mm) | 3¼ in. (82.5 mm) | 2¾ in. (69.8 mm) | 2-17/32 in. (64.31 mm) | 2⅝ in. (66.7 mm) |
| Piston Displacement | 31.27 cu. in. (512 cc) | 35.89 cu. in. (588 cc) | 23.75 cu. in. (389 cc) | 21.82 cu. in. (358 cc) | 24.36 cu. in. (399 cc) |
| Horsepower | 14 | 16 | 8 | 10 | 11 |
| Slow Idle Speed – Rpm | 1600 | 1600 | 1800 | 1800 | 1800 |
| High Idle Speed (No Load) – Rpm | Note 3 | Note 4 | 3250 | 3250 | 3250 |
| Crankcase Oil Capacity | 4 pints (1.9L) | 4 pints (1.9L) | 2 pints (0.9L) | 2 pints (0.9L) | 3 pints (0.9L) |
| Weight – | | | | | |
| Above 32°F (0°C) | | | SAE 30 | | |
| 0°F (–18°C) to 32°F (0°C) | | | SAE 10W | | |
| Below 0°F (–18°C) | | | SAE 5W-20 | | |
| Transmission Oil Capacity | 7 pints (3.3L) | 7 pints (3.3L) | 24 oz. (710mL) | 24 oz. (710mL) | 24 oz. (710mL) |
| Weight | SAE 10W-30 | SAE 10W-30 | Lithium Grease | Lithium Grease | Lithium Grease |

NOTE 1: Engine S.N. 7541007 and below – 3600 rpm; S.N. 7541008 and above – 3250 rpm.
NOTE 2: Engine S.N. 8173991 and below – 3600 rpm; S.N. 8173992 and above – 3250 rpm.
NOTE 3: Engine S.N. 8117916 and below – 3600 rpm; S.N. 8117917 and above – 3250 rpm.
NOTE 4: Engine S.N. 8119833 and below – 3600 rpm; S.N. 8119834 and above – 3250 rpm.

# FRONT AXLE AND STEERING SYSTEM

## AXLE MAIN MEMBER

### Models 13948, 13989, 13990, 913002, 913003

To remove axle main member (1 – Fig. A1), first disconnect steering drag link (6) from steering arm (7). Support front end of tractor with a hoist or jack and remove axle pivot bolt (17). Raise front of tractor and roll front axle assembly from tractor. Inspect pivot bolt bushing (19) and bolt and renew if necessary.

### Models S-8G And S-8H

To remove front axle, disconnect tie rod ends (4 – Fig. A2) from steering spindles. Detach drag link (1) from link (3), unbolt link clamps (2) and remove link (3). Support front of tractor, unscrew pivot pin retaining bolt and withdraw pivot pin (18). Raise front of tractor and roll front axle assembly along with mower bracket (19) away from tractor.

### Models S-10G, S-12H, S-14G, S-14H, S-16H, GT12, GT14, GT16

Front axle is supported by pto drive housing tube. To remove front axle, remove any pto driven accessories from pto drive shaft and disconnect drag link from steering arm (4 – Fig. A3). Unscrew bolts securing pto drive housing to frame bracket. Support front of tractor and withdraw pto drive towards front of tractor until axle is clear of pto drive shaft. Raise front of tractor and roll front axle assembly away from tractor.

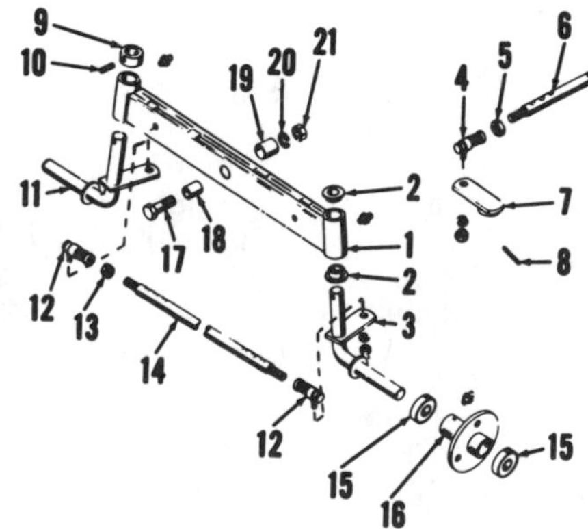


*Fig. A1 – Exploded view of front axle main member assembly used on Models 13948, 13989, 13990, 913002 and 913003.*

1. Main member
2. Bushing
3. Steering spindle L.H.
4. Ball joint
5. Nut
6. Drag link
7. Steering arm
8. Roll pin
9. Collar
10. Roll pin
11. Steering spindle R.H.
12. Ball joint
13. Nut
14. Tie rod
15. Ball bearing
16. Wheel hub
17. Pivot bolt
18. Spacer
19. Bushing
20. Lockwasher
21. Nut

### Models YT8, YT10, YT11

To remove axle main member (10 – Fig. A4), disconnect tie rod ends at steering spindles (11 and 15). Support front of tractor, remove axle pivot bolt and roll axle assembly away from tractor.

## TIE ROD

### Models 13948, 13989, 13990, 913002, 913003

The adjustment tie rod (14 – Fig. A1) can be removed after first removing nuts securing ball joint ends to steering arms. To adjust front wheel toe-in, remove tie rod, loosen locknuts and turn ball joint ends in or out as required to obtain ⅛-inch (3 mm) toe-in.

### Models S-8G And S-8H

These models are equipped with individual tie rods from tie rod connecting link (3 – Fig. A2) to steering spindles. To adjust toe-in, turn steering wheel until rear edge of connecting link (3) is perpendicular to tractor frame. Loosen jam nuts on tie rods and detach ends of tie rods from steering spindles. Adjust length of tie rods and attach to steering spindles. Desired toe-in is 1/16 to 1/8-inch (1.5-3 mm). Repeat procedure until desired toe-in is obtained and tighten jam nuts.

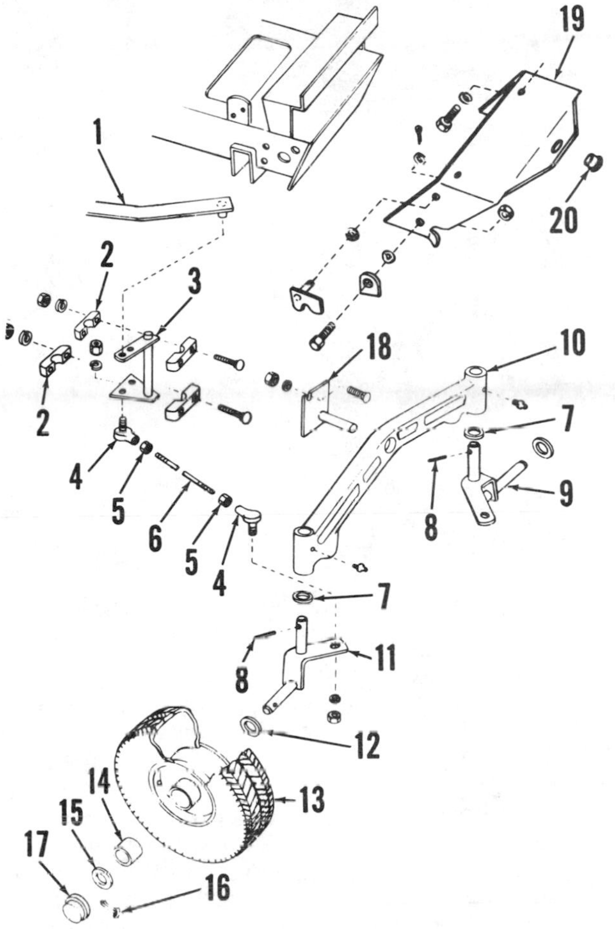

### Models S-10G, S-12H, S-14G, S-14H, S-16H, GT12, GT14, GT16

The adjustable tie rod (14–Fig. A3) can be removed after first removing nuts securing ball joint ends (12) to steering spindle arms. To adjust front wheel toe-in, loosen locknuts (13), then rotate tie rod as required to obtain 1/8-inch (3 mm) toe-in. Tighten locknuts.

### Models YT8, YT10, YT11

These models are equipped with individual tie rods connecting steering pivot (7–Fig. A4) to steering spindles (11 and 15). To adjust toe-in, disconnect tie rods at steering spindles. Loosen locknuts and turn ball joint ends in or out until 1/8 to 1/4-inch (1.5-3 mm) toe-in is obtained.

## STEERING SPINDLES

### All Models

Spindles on all models are retained by a pin in upper end of spindle, except on Models S-10G, S-12H, S-14G, S-14H, S-16H, GT12, GT14 and GT16 which have right spindle retained by steering arm (4–Fig. A3). To remove spindles, support front of tractor and remove wheels. Disconnect tie rod and drag link. On Models S-10G, S-12H, S-14G, S-14H, S-16H, GT12, GT14 and GT16, unscrew clamp bolt in steering arm. On all models, drive roll pins out of upper end of spindle and remove spindle from axle.

All models except Model S-8 are equipped with renewable spindle bushings. Reassemble by reversing disassembly procedure. Lubricate with multipurpose grease.

## STEERING GEAR

### Models 13948, 13989, 13990, 913002, 913003

**R&R AND OVERHAUL.** To remove steering gear, first remove hood and disconnect drag link from steering arm (18–Fig. A5). Unscrew nut (10) at end of cross shaft (13). Drive roll pin (11) out of quadrant gear (12) and shaft and remove gear and shaft. Drive out roll pin (5) to remove pinion gear (8).

Inspect bushings and renew as needed. Lubricate bushings and gear teeth with light coat of multi-purpose grease. To reassemble, reverse removal procedure making sure wheels are in straight ahead position when pinion gear (8) is centered in quadrant gear (12).

*Fig. A2—Exploded view of Model S-8G or Model S-8H front axle assembly.*

1. Drag link
2. Clamp
3. Steering link
4. Tie rod end
5. Nut
6. Tie rod
7. Washer
8. Pin
9. Steering spindle L.H.
10. Front axle main member
11. Steering spindle R.H.
12. Washer
13. Wheel
14. Bushing
15. Washer
16. Cotter pin
17. Grease cap

### Models S-8G, S-8H, YT8, YT10, YT11

**R&R AND OVERHAUL.** To remove steering gear, first drive out roll pin retaining steering wheel to shaft and remove steering wheel. Raise hood, disconnect wires from ignition switch, remove throttle lever knob and detach dash panel from tractor. Unscrew sector gear clamp bolts (14–Fig. A6). Disconnect drag link (17) from steering arm (19) and remove cotter pin (5) from shaft (6). Remove cotter pin from steering arm (19), then drive shaft down out of sector gear (15). Drive roll pin (8) out of pinion gear (7) and withdraw steering shaft, pinion gear and sector gear.

Inspect bushings for wear or other damage and renew as necessary. Reassemble by reversing removal procedure making sure wheels are in straight ahead position and pinion gear is centered in sector gear. Lubricate bushings

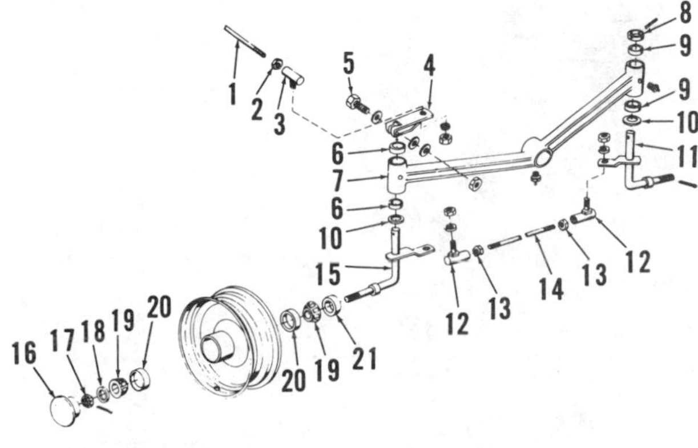

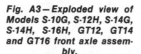

*Fig. A3—Exploded view of Models S-10G, S-12H, S-14G, S-14H, S-16H, GT12, GT14 and GT16 front axle assembly.*

1. Drag link
2. Nut
3. Ball joint
4. Steering arm
5. Bolt
6. Bushing
7. Front axle
8. Collar
9. Bushing
10. Washer
11. Steering spindle L.H.
12. Ball joint
13. Nut
14. Tie rod
15. Steering spindle R.H.
16. Grease cap
17. Castle nut
18. Washer
19. Bearing
20. Bearing cup
21. Seal

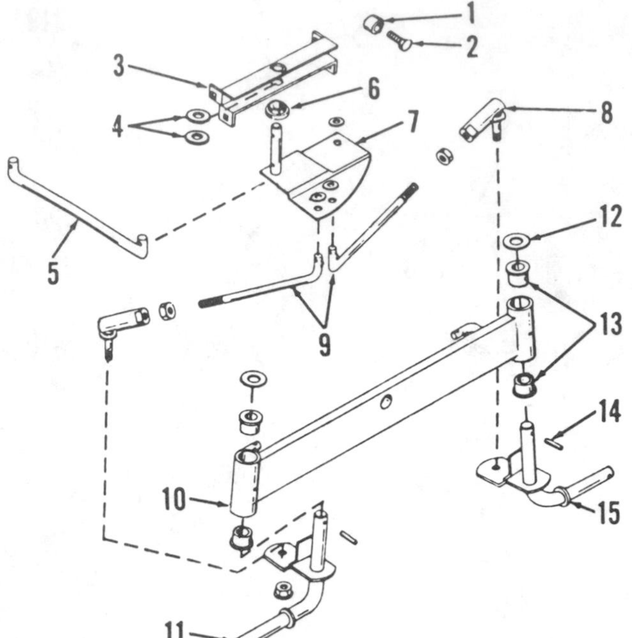

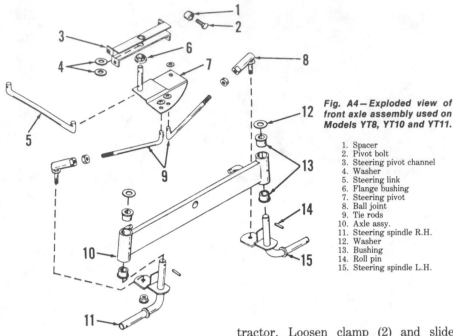

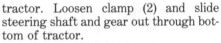

*Fig. A4—Exploded view of front axle assembly used on Models YT8, YT10 and YT11.*

1. Spacer
2. Pivot bolt
3. Steering pivot channel
4. Washer
5. Steering link
6. Flange bushing
7. Steering pivot
8. Ball joint
9. Tie rods
10. Axle assy.
11. Steering spindle R.H.
12. Washer
13. Bushing
14. Roll pin
15. Steering spindle L.H.

and gears with light coat of multi-purpose grease.

### Models S-10G, S-12H, S-14G, S-14H, S-16H, GT12, GT14, GT16

**R&R AND OVERHAUL.** To remove steering gear, first remove steering wheel retaining nut and steering wheel. Remove steering arm (5–Fig. A7) from steering gear shaft, and unbolt and remove steering gear bracket (4). Raise front of tractor to allow steering gear and shaft to be removed from bottom of tractor. Loosen clamp (2) and slide steering shaft and gear out through bottom of tractor.

To disassemble steering gear, remove lever and shaft assembly (11–Fig. A8). Remove bearing adjuster plug (17) and bump steering cam (15) out of steering tube (4). Steering cam (15) is not available separately; if renewal is necessary, complete steering gear assembly must be replaced. Inspect bearings and races for wear or other damage and renew if necessary.

When reassembling unit, bearing adjuster plug (17) should be tightened to remove all end play; but, cam (15) must still rotate freely. Install lever and shaft assembly (11), seal (8), retainer (9), washer (7) and one nut (6). Be sure cam follower (10) engages steering cam (15) but does not bind when making following adjustment. Tighten adjusting nut (6) until there is 0.100 inch (2.54 mm) clearance between steering shaft plate (11) and gasket retainer (9), then install jam nut (5) to lock in position. Locate cam in mid-position (half way between full right and full left turn). Tighten cam follower screw (10) finger tight and secure with jam nut (12). Steering cam must turn from full right to full left turn without binding. Lubricate with approximately ¼-pound (120mL) of multi-purpose grease.

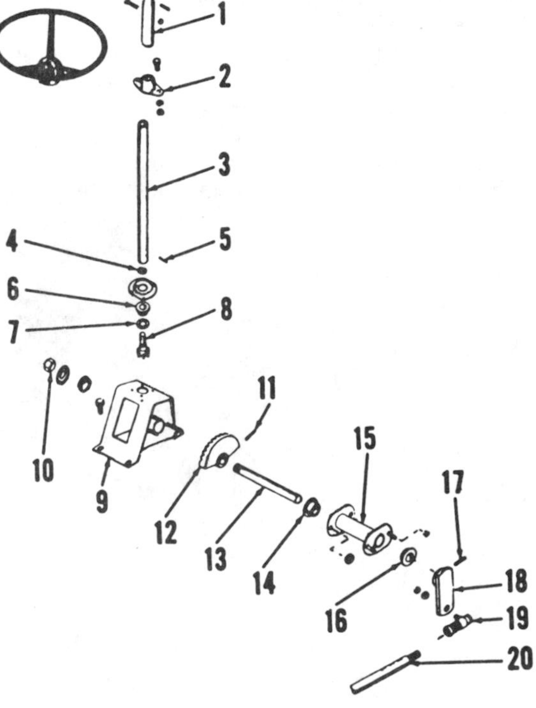


*Fig. A5—Exploded view of steering gear assembly used on Models 13948, 13989, 13990, 913002 and 913003.*

1. Shaft extension
2. Bearing
3. Steering shaft
4. Wave washer
5. Roll pin
6. Bushing
7. Washer
8. Pinion gear
9. Bracket
10. Nut
11. Pin
12. Quadrant gear
13. Cross shaft
14. Bushing
15. Support
16. Bushing
17. Pin
18. Lever
19. Ball joint
20. Drag link

# ENGINE

## REMOVE AND REINSTALL

### Models 13948, 13989, 13990, 913002, 913003

To remove engine, remove hood and on electric start models, disconnect battery cables and starter wire. On Model 13990, disconnect three prong ignition wire connector. On other models, disconnect ignition wires at engine. Disconnect carburetor choke and throttle cables. Close fuel valve beneath fuel tank and disconnect fuel line at carburetor. Release belt tension and remove engine drive belt. Unbolt engine mounting bolts and lift engine from tractor.

To reinstall engine, reverse removal procedure.

### Models S-8G, S-8H, YT8, YT10, YT11

The engine may be removed by using following procedure: Tilt hood forward, disconnect fuel line and remove fuel tank and tank bracket. Disconnect battery cables, ignition and starter wires and throttle cable. Remove drive belts from engine pulleys and remove pulleys. Unscrew engine mounting bolts and remove engine.

### Models S-10G, S-12H, S-14G, S-14H, S-16H, GT12, GT14, GT16

To remove engine, disconnect wires to headlights and remove hood, heat duct, grille and side panels from front of tractor. Hood, grille and side panels can be removed as a unit. Remove pto belts and disconnect wire to pto clutch at front of engine. Disconnect battery cables and electrical wires to engine. Disconnect choke and throttle cables from engine. Detach fuel line from carburetor. Unscrew drive coupling screws and engine mounting bolts. Using a suitable hoist, lift engine towards front and remove engine.

## OVERHAUL

### All Models

Engine make and model are listed at the beginning of this section. To overhaul engine components and accessories, refer to Briggs & Stratton, Kohler or Tecumseh sections of this manual.

# CLUTCH

### Models 13948, 13989, 13990, 913002, 913003

**OPERATION.** The clutch is a belt idler type that is spring loaded. Two belts are used between right angle drive pulley (21–Fig. A9) and transmission pulley (7). A Hi-Lo speed range is provided by positioning clutch idler pulley (2) on desired drive belt (5 or 8). The clutch idler is positioned by moving control rod (18) on left side of tractor in or out.

**ADJUSTMENT.** The clutch idler pulley is spring loaded and does not require adjustment. Renew drive belts if excessively worn. To renew drive belts, remove frame top cover in front of seat, then remove front belt cover (22–Fig. A9. Remove rear hitch and rear belt cover (6). Depress clutch to release belt tension and remove drive belts.

### Model S-8G

**OPERATION.** Refer to Fig. A10 for drawing illustrating belt drive used on Model S-8G. Refer to Fig. A 11 for exploded view of belt drive components. Depressing clutch-brake pedal will pull spring loaded pulley (11–Fig. A10) away from transmission drive belt thereby allowing belt to slip. Spring loaded pulley (11) will tighten belt when clutch-brake pedal is released.

**ADJUSTMENT.** Clutch free travel is adjusted by turning adjusting nuts (A–Fig. A12) until there is 3/16-inch (5 mm) movement before bolt (B) contacts front of slot in clutching link when clutch-brake pedal is depressed.

Transmission belt drive idler must be adjusted if belt slips or idler spring no longer pulls against idler with clutch-brake pedal released. To adjust belt idler, loosen bolt (A–Fig. A13) and move idler shaft in idler hole to increase tension on belt and spring. Position belt guide approximately 1/8-inch (3 mm) from belt and tighten bolt (A). Belt guide (B) should be approximately 1/8-inch (3 mm) away from transmission belt where belt enters transmission pulley. Loosen bolt (C) to reposition belt guide. Check operation of belt by depressing and releasing clutch-brake pedal. Adjustment of transmission belt idler may affect clutch free travel which should be rechecked.

Intermediate shaft drive belt tension must be adjusted if belt slips or idler bracket shown in Fig. A14 contacts stop bolt. Adjust belt tension by loosening bolts (A) and bolts at right end of shaft and move shaft rearward to increase belt tension. Keep shaft parallel to rear of tractor frame and move shaft rear-

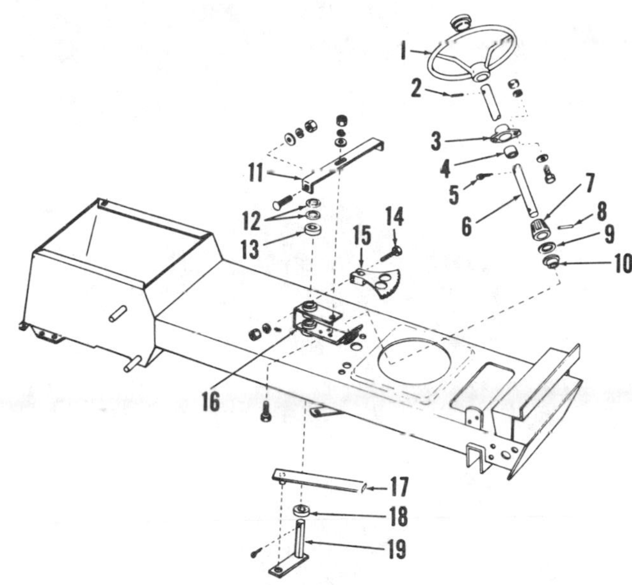


*Fig. A6—Exploded view of steering mechanism used on Models S-8G, S-8H, YT8, YT10 and YT11.*

1. Steering wheel
2. Spring pin
3. Flange bearing
4. Spacer
5. Cotter pin
6. Steering shaft
7. Pinion gear
8. Pin
9. Washer
10. Bushing
11. Bracket
12. Washer
13. Bushing
14. Bolt
15. Sector gear
16. Steering bracket
17. Drag link
18. Bushing
19. Steering arm

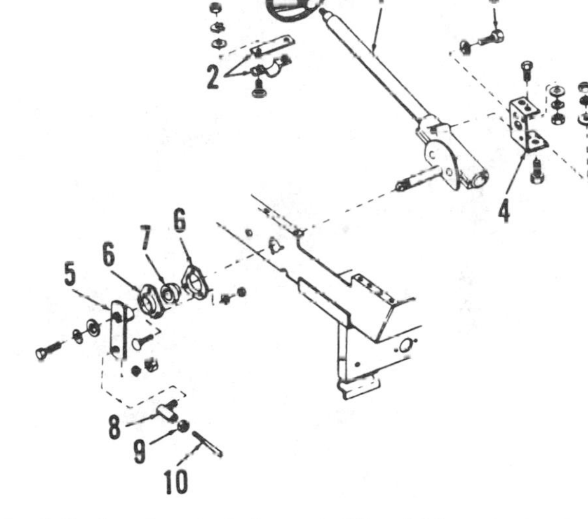


*Fig. A7—Exploded view of steering mechanism used on Models S-10G, S-12H, S-14G, S-14H, S-16H, GT12, GT14 and GT16. See Fig. A8 for exploded view of steering gear assembly (1).*

1. Steering gear & shaft
2. Clamp
3. Cap screw
4. Bracket
5. Steering arm
6. Bearing flange
7. Bearing & collar
8. Ball joint
9. Nut
10. Drag link

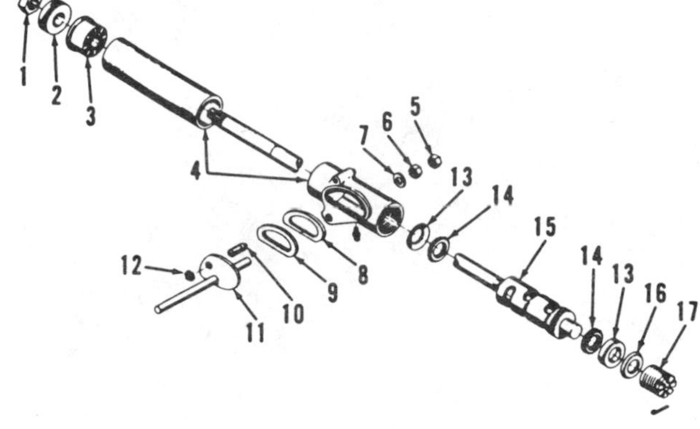


*Fig. A8—Exploded view of steering gear assembly used on Models S-10G, S-12H, S-14G, S-14H, S-16H, GT12, GT14 and GT16.*

1. Nut
2. Dust seal
3. Bearing
4. Housing
5. Jam nut
6. Nut
7. Washer
8. Oil seal
9. Seal retainer
10. Cam follower screw
11. Lever
12. Nut
13. Bearing race
14. Bearing
15. Steering cam & shaft
16. Belleville washer
17. Adjusting plug

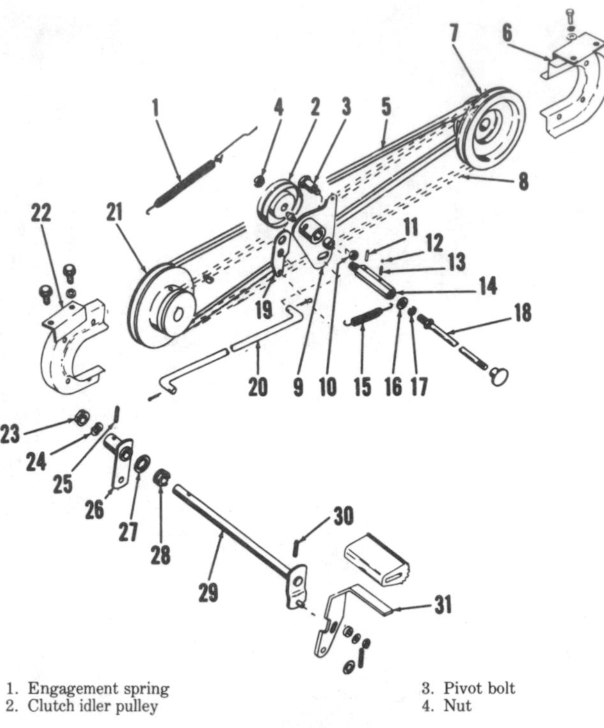


**Fig. A9—View of early clutch system. Move rod (18) in or out to position clutch idler pulley on desired drive belt for Hi or Lo range speeds. Clutch pedal must be depressed before moving rod.**

1. Engagement spring
2. Clutch idler pulley
3. Pivot bolt
4. Nut
5. Hi-range drive belt
6. Rear belt cover
7. Transmission pulley
8. Lo-range drive belt
9. Plate
10. Nut
11. Roll pin
12. Ball
13. Spring
14. Shift rod
15. Spring
16. Washer
17. Lockwasher
18. Control rod
19. Lever
20. Clutch rod
21. Right angle drive pulley
22. Front belt cover
23. Bushing
24. Wave washer
25. Roll pin
26. Lever
27. Washer
28. Bushing
29. Shaft
30. Roll pin
31. Clutch pedal

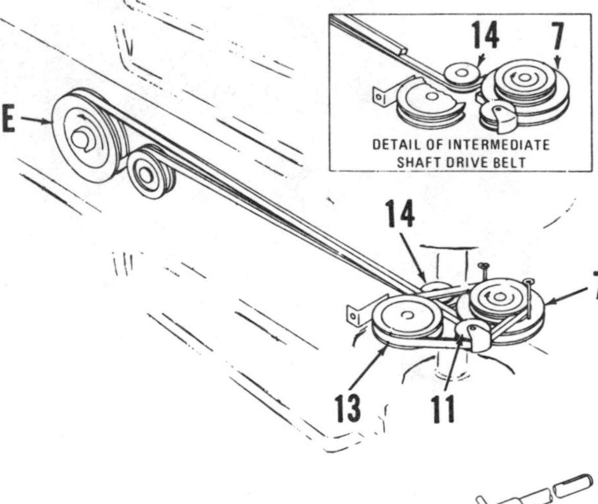


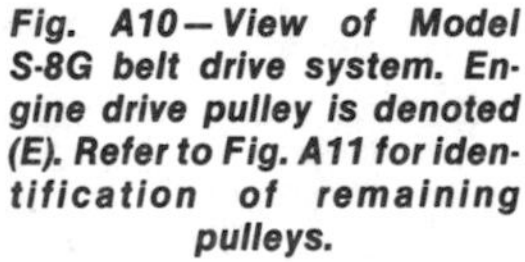

**Fig. A10—View of Model S-8G belt drive system. Engine drive pulley is denoted (E). Refer to Fig. A11 for identification of remaining pulleys.**

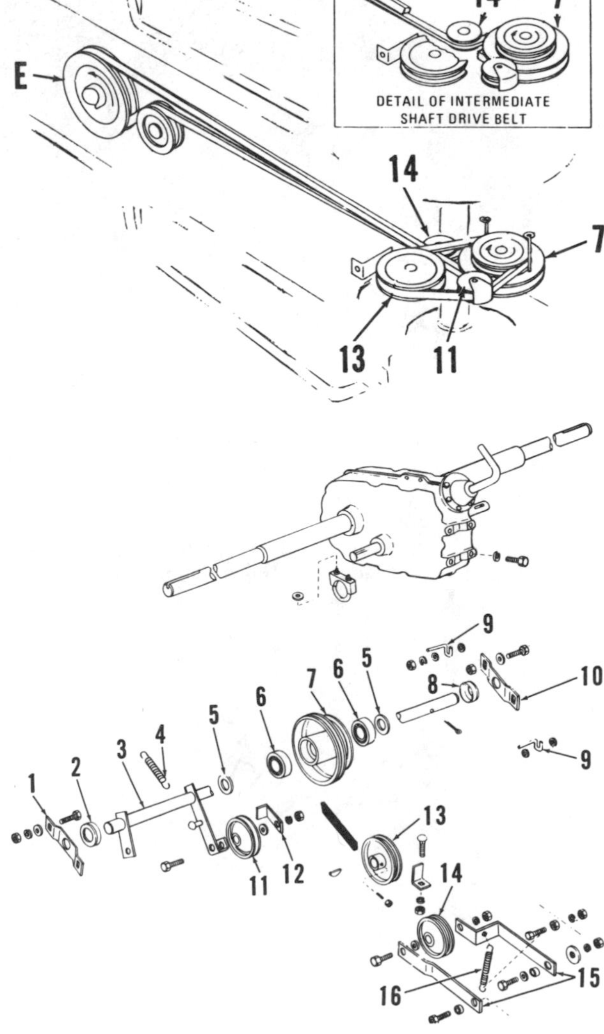


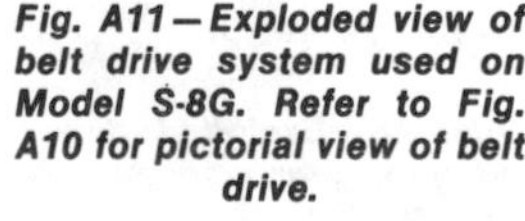

**Fig. A11—Exploded view of belt drive system used on Model S-8G. Refer to Fig. A10 for pictorial view of belt drive.**

1. Support
2. Nylon bearing
3. Idler pivot
4. Spring
5. Spacer
6. Bearing
7. Intermediate pulley
8. Nylon bearing
9. Belt guide
10. Support
11. Clutch pulley
12. Belt guide
13. Transmission pulley
14. Idler pulley
15. Idler bracket
16. Spring

ward until front edge of idler bracket is flush with plate (C). Shaft must be parallel to rear of tractor frame to within 1/16-inch (1.5 mm). Locate belt guides (D and E) approximately ⅛-inch (3 mm) away from transmission drive belt and tighten bolts (A). Recheck clutch free play.

### Models YT8, YT10, YT11

**OPERATION.** The clutch is a spring loaded belt idler type. The drive belt is used to transfer power from crankshaft pulley to jackshaft and a traction belt transfers power from jackshaft to transaxle pulley. The spring loaded clutch idler (11–Fig. A15) applies tension on drive belt.

**ADJUSTMENT.** The clutch idler pulley is spring loaded and does not require adjustment. Renew drive belts if excessively worn. To renew traction belt (4–Fig. A15), lift rear deck assembly and rotate belt guards away from transaxle pulley and clutch arm. Depress clutch pedal and remove belt.

To renew drive belt, lift rear deck and remove traction belt. Disconnect spring (16–Fig. A15) from clutch arm (19). Disconnect main idler spring (13) from frame. Disconnect pto linkage and remove three cap screws mounting pto spindle to frame. Raise assembly about ½-inch (13 mm) and tip pulleys toward center of tractor. Note path of belt and remove belt. Reinstall belts by reversing removal procedures.

## BRAKE

### Models 13948, 13989, 13990, 913002, 913003

**ADJUSTMENT.** Brake adjustment is accomplished by turning hex nut (11–Fig. A16) at end of brake band rod. Turning nut clockwise will increase brake band tension while turning nut counter-clockwise will release tension. Brake should be adjusted so braking action begins when brake pedal is depressed one inch.

After adjusting brake band, loosen rear brake rod jam nut (Fig. A17) and depress brake pedal. Be sure pedal does not bottom against foot rest. Turn rear brake rod adjusting nut until brake lock clears tab by 1/16 to ⅛-inch (1.5-3 mm). Retighten jam nut. Turn front brake rod adjusting nut so brake pedal is at least 3/16-inch (5 mm) away from foot rest when fully depressed.

### Models S-8G And S-8H

**ADJUSTMENT.** Depress clutch-brake pedal on Model S-8G or brake

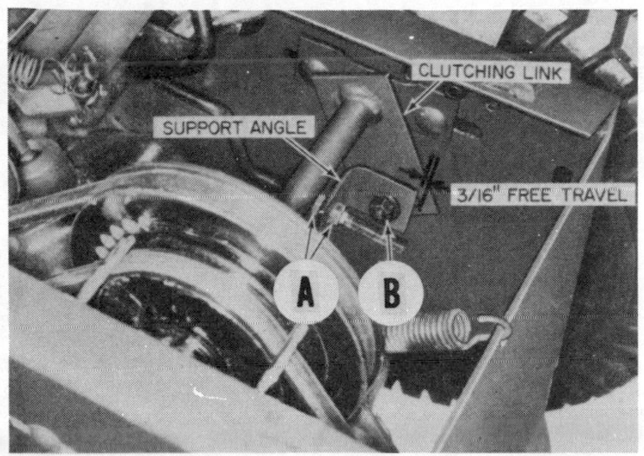


*Fig. A12—View of Model S-8G clutch mechanism. Refer to text for clutch free travel adjustment.*

*Fig. A13—View of Model S-8G clutch idler and belt pulleys. Refer to text for adjustment.*

pedal on Model S-8H and engage brake lock. Tighten nuts (B–Fig. A19) until spring is compressed to 1¾ inches (45 mm). Nuts (B) must be at least 1/16-inch (1.5 mm) away from support during this portion of adjustment. Release brake lock and allow brake or clutch-brake pedal to return to normal position against stop. Turn nuts (C) to obtain a spring length of 1-15/16 inches (49 mm) for S-8G models or 2⅛ inches (54 mm) for S-8H models. Clutch free travel may require adjustment after brake is adjusted and should be checked as outlined in CLUTCH section.

## Models S-10G And S-14G

**ADJUSTMENT.** Braking is provided by drum-type brakes located on outer axle ends. Brakes should be adjusted when pedal can be depressed over two inches.

To adjust brakes, raise and support rear of tractor, then remove rear wheels. Insert screw-driver through slot provided in brake drum and turn star washer (Fig. A20) until brake locks; then, back star washer off one turn. Reinstall wheels.

## Models S-12H, S-14H, S-16H, GT12, GT14, GT16

**ADJUSTMENT.** Dynamic braking is provided by moving hydrostatic transmission control lever to neutral position. All models are equipped with a neutral return pedal which will return transmission to neutral for emergency braking when depressed. Some models are also equipped with wheel brakes located on rear axles to prevent tractor from rolling when transmission is in neutral. All models utilize a park-lock pin which engages reduction gear in differential housing to provide positive braking when tractor is parked.

The overcenter latch pin (4–Fig. A21) prevents accidental engagement of park-lock pin (3) through a combination of slots in pivot plate and frame plate. For proper operation, overcenter latch should be actuated when control lever is moved approximately ½-⅔ of its travel in "PARK-START" slot and park-lock

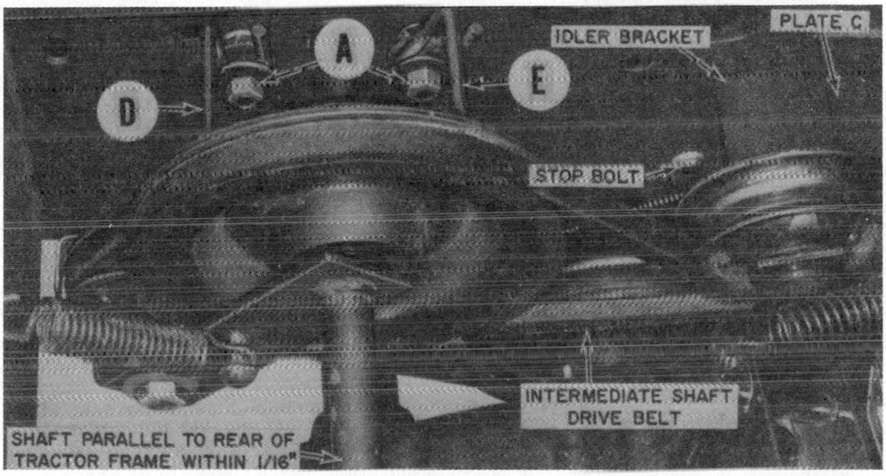

*Fig. A14—View of Model S-8G belt drive. Refer to text for intermediate belt adjustment.*

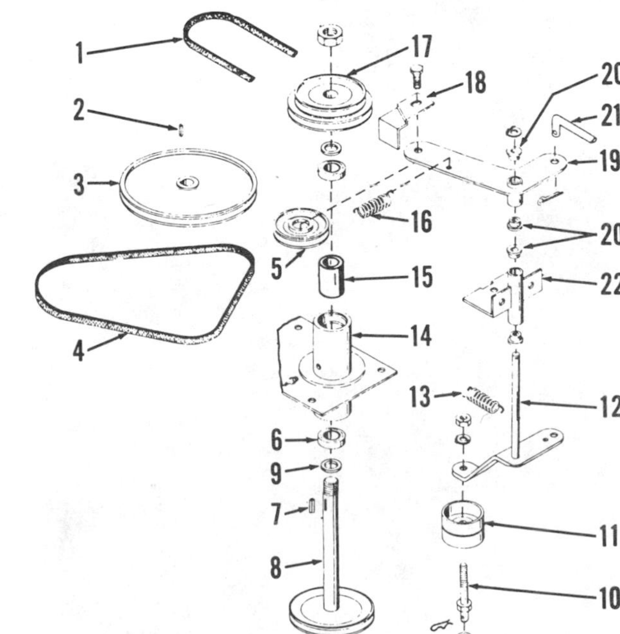


*Fig. A15—Exploded view of belt drive system used on Models YT8 and YT11.*

1. Main drive belt
2. Key
3. Transaxle pulley
4. Traction belt
5. Idler pulley
6. Bearing
7. Key
8. Jackshaft spindle
9. Washer
10. Idler mounting bolt
11. Clutch idler pulley
12. Idler arm
13. Drive spring
14. Spindle housing
15. Spacer
16. Spring
17. Pulley
18. Belt retainer
19. Clutch arm
20. Bushing
21. Clutch rod
22. Idler pivot

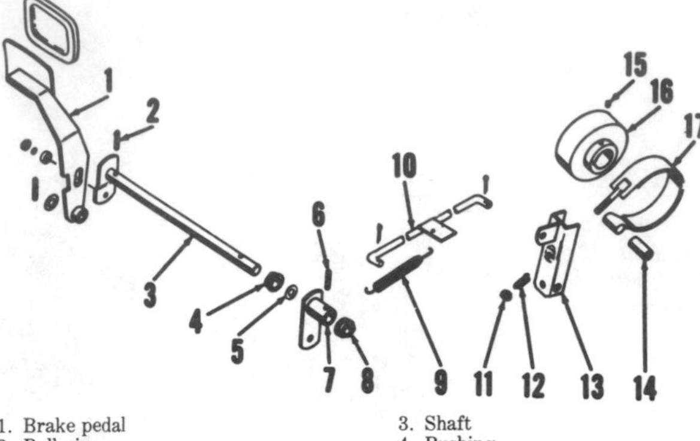

Fig. A16—Exploded view of brake assembly used on Models 13948, 13989, 13990, 913002 and 913003.

1. Brake pedal
2. Roll pin
3. Shaft
4. Bushing
5. Washer
6. Roll pin
7. Lever
8. Bushing
9. Spring
10. Brake rod
11. Nut
12. Spring
13. Bracket
14. Spacer
15. Set screw
16. Brake drum
17. Brake band

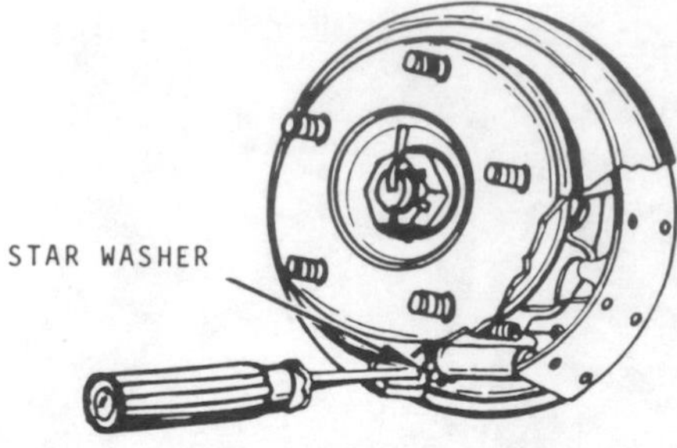


Fig. A20—Drum-type brakes, located on axle ends, are used on some early models. Refer to text.

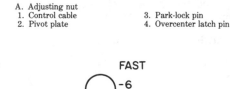

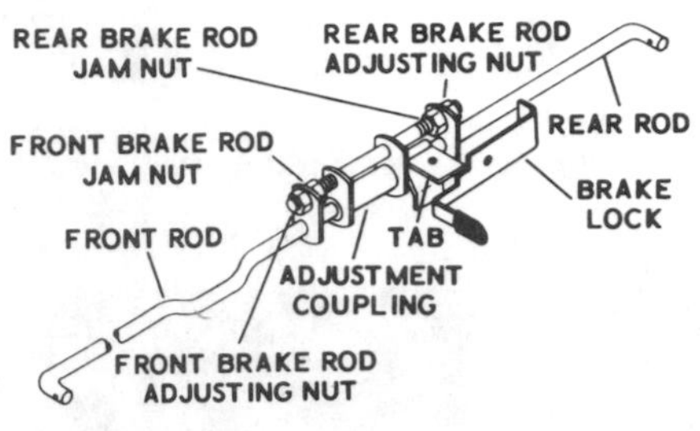


Fig. A17—View of brake rod assembly used on Models 13948, 13989, 13990, 913002 and 913003. Refer to text for adjustment procedure.

pin engaged after 3/4 of lever travel. Refer to Fig. A22. Overcenter latch pin will "click" when actuated.

Overcenter latch pin actuation is adjusted by turning nuts (A–Fig. A21) to move cable housing until desired operation of latch pin is obtained. Tightening or loosening nut (A–Fig. A23) will adjust park-lock brake to hold control lever at rear of "PARK-START" slot when starting tractor engine.

The tractor wheel brakes (models so equipped) require adjustment if brake pedal can be depressed more than two

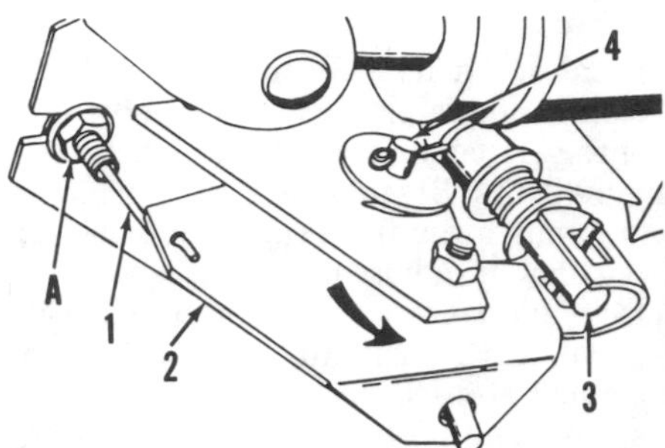

Fig. A21—View of parking brake mechanism on Models S-12H, S-14H, S-16H, GT12, GT14 and GT16. Refer to text for adjustment.

A. Adjusting nut
1. Control cable
2. Pivot plate
3. Park-lock pin
4. Overcenter latch pin

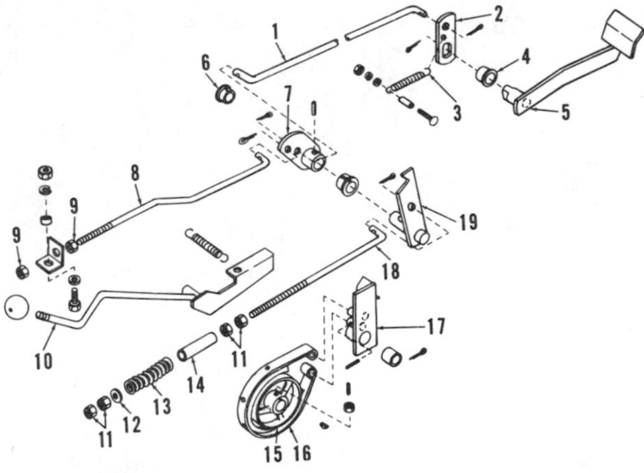
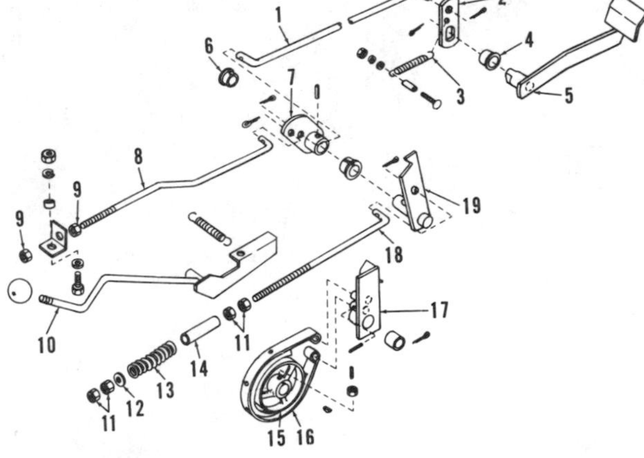

Fig. A18—Exploded view of brake mechanism used on Models S-8G and S-8H. Clutch rod is used only on Model S-8G.

1. Clutch-brake rod
2. Lever
3. Spring
4. Bushing
5. Clutch-brake pedal
6. Bushing
7. Clutch arm
8. Clutch rod
9. Nut
10. Parking brake lever

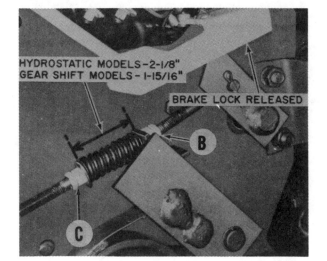

Fig. A19—Brake on Models S-8G and S-8H is adjusted by turning nuts (C and B). Refer to text.

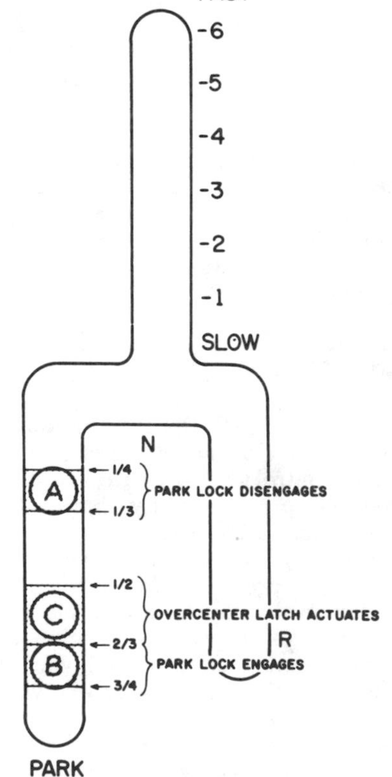


Fig. A22—View of gear shift pattern showing positions of parking brake engagement and disengagement on Models S-12H, S-14H, S-16H, GT12, GT14 and GT16.

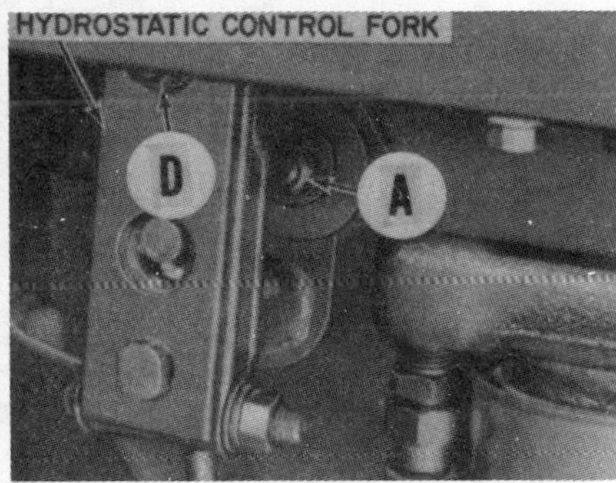


*Fig. A23 – View of hydrostatic shift control fork.*

inches. To adjust brakes, proceed as follows: Raise and support rear of tractor so wheels are free to turn. Open transmission free-wheeling valves, located on top of transmission, by rotating cam up. On models equipped with disc-type brakes, tighten brake adjusting nuts (Fig. A24) evenly until brake just starts to drag, then back each nut off 1/8-turn. Adjust brake on opposite wheel using same procedure. On models equipped with drum-type brakes, remove wheel and insert screwdriver in slot provided in brake drum (Fig. A20). Adjust star washer until brake locks, then back washer off one turn. Adjust brake on opposite wheel using same procedure.

### Models YT8, YT10, YT11

**ADJUSTMENT.** All models are equipped with a caliper-disc brake located on lower right side of transaxle assembly. To adjust brake, position tractor on level surface and place shifter lever in neutral. Adjust set screw (3–Fig. A25) in brake jaw assembly (4) until brake starts to lock with pedal up; then, back set screw off 1/2-turn counter-clockwise.

Tension on brake pedal is adjustable. If pedal does not return or feels loose, adjust nut on end of brake rod just inside frame next to parking brake slot. Tighten nut until spring is 1 1/4 inches (32 mm) long.

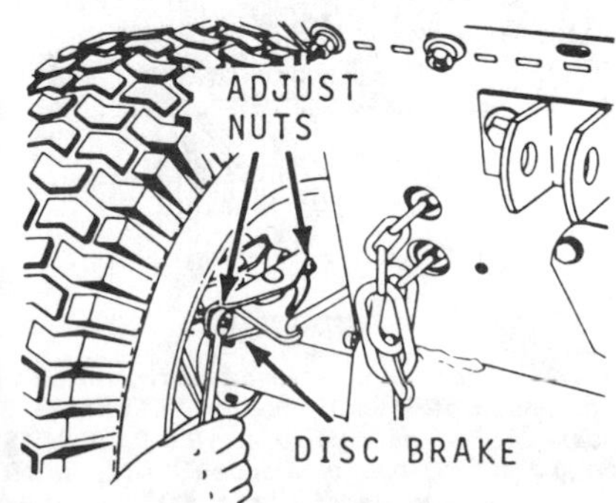


*Fig. A24 – View of typical caliper-disc brake used on some models. Adjust nuts as shown until brake begins to drag, then back nuts off 1/8-turn.*

*Fig. A25 – Models YT8, YT10 and YT11 are equipped with a caliper-disc brake located on lower right side of transaxle.*

1. Brake rod
2. Disc
3. Adjusting screw
4. Brake jaw assy.

# RIGHT ANGLE DRIVE

### All Models So Equipped

**R&R AND OVERHAUL.** To remove right angle drive unit, release idler pulley tension and slide engine drive belt off of lower right angle drive pulley. Remove lower pulley from right angle drive. Remove frame cover in front of seat and remove front belt cover. Depress clutch and remove drive belts from upper pulley of right angle drive. Remove right angle drive and pulley from tractor then remove pulley from right angle drive shaft.

To disassemble right angle drive unit, remove cover (1–Fig. A26), gasket (2) and lubricant. Unbolt and remove seal retainer (13) with oil seal (14) and gasket (12). Withdraw output shaft (10) with bearing (11). Remove output gear (9). Remove oil seal (17) and snap ring (16). Drive input shaft (6) with gear (4) and bearing (5) out cover opening of case (7). Bearings (8 and 15) can now be removed from case. Remove snap ring (3) and remove drive gear (4) and bearing (5) from input shaft. Remove bearing (11) from output shaft (10).

Clean and inspect all parts and renew any showing excessive wear or other damage. Reassemble by reversing disassembly procedure and fill unit with 4 ounces (120mL) of Moly EP lithium grease.

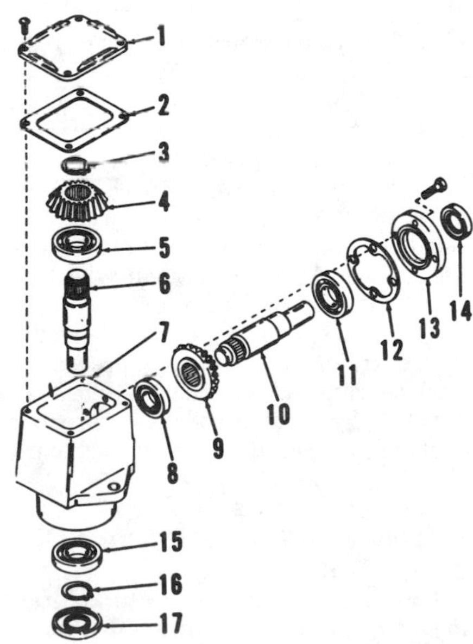


*Fig. A26 – Exploded view of typical right angle drive used on some models.*

1. Cover
2. Gasket
3. Snap ring
4. Input gear
5. Bearing
6. Input shaft
7. Case
8. Bearing
9. Output gear
10. Output shaft
11. Bearing
12. Gasket
13. Seal retainer
14. Oil seal
15. Bearing
16. Snap ring
17. Oil seal

# PTO DRIVE

### Models 13948, 13989, 13990, 913002, 913003

Pto clutch tension is adjusted by turning two nuts located on pto clutch rod under dash. Turning nut (N–Fig. A27) clockwise will increase tension. Refer to Fig. A27 for correct dimensions with clutch engaged.

### Models S-8G And S-8H

Pto control mechanism should be adjusted if pto slips or rear nuts (B–Fig. A28) contact pivot block (P). Engage pto and tighten nuts (C) until spring length (D) is 2 5/8 inches (67 mm). It may be necessary to turn nuts (B) away from pivot block (P) so they are not in contact with pivot block when measuring spring length. With pto clutch disengaged, turn nuts (B) to obtain 1/4-inch (6 mm) clear-

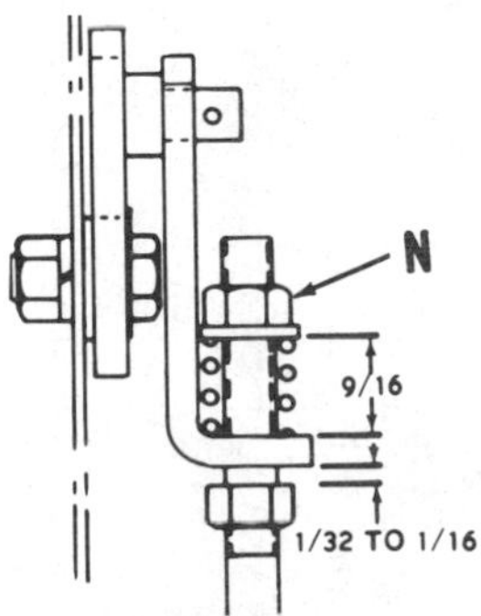


*Fig. A27 – Adjust pto clutch tension on Models 13948, 13989, 13990, 913002 and 913003 by turning nuts on clutch rod to obtain dimensions shown above. Turning nut (N) clockwise increases tension.*

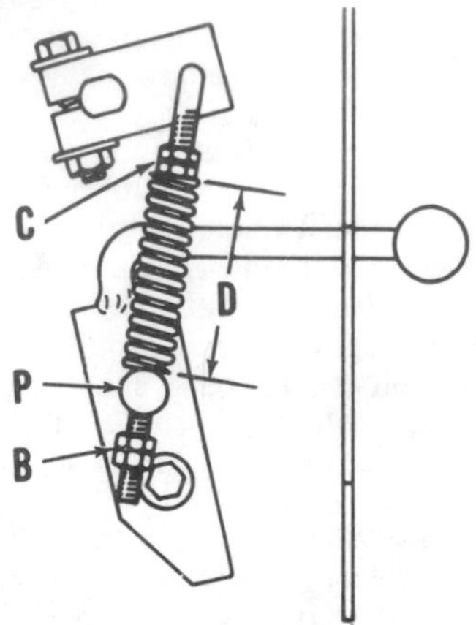


Fig. A28—View of Model S-8G or S-8H pto control lever in engaged position. See text.

ance (M) between control lever and rear of lever slot as shown in Fig. A29.

## Models GT12, GT14, GT16

Models GT12, GT14 and GT16 are equipped with an electro-magnetic clutch mounted on engine crankshaft. The pto shaft (12–Fig. A30) rides in bearings and a tube (18), which also supports front axle assembly. Belt tension is automatically adjusted by spring loaded idler pulley (5).

To disassemble electro-magnetic clutch, unbolt and remove brake flange (7). Remove cap screw (9) and spacer (8); then, using a suitable puller, remove clutch pulley (6) and rotor (3). Unbolt and remove field assembly (1).

Field, rotor and armature are not available separately. If renewal is necessary complete clutch must be renewed. When reassembling clutch, check clearance "A" between rotor and armature. Add or remove shims (4) as required to obtain 0.060-0.125 inch (1.524-3.175 mm) clearance. Complete reassembly in reverse of disassembly. Tighten retaining cap screw (8) to 25 ft.-lbs. (34 N·m) torque.

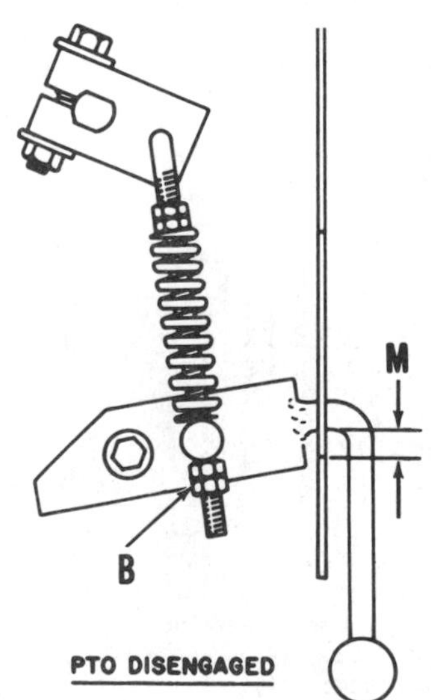


Fig. A29—View of Model S-8G or S-8H pto control lever in disengaged position. See text.

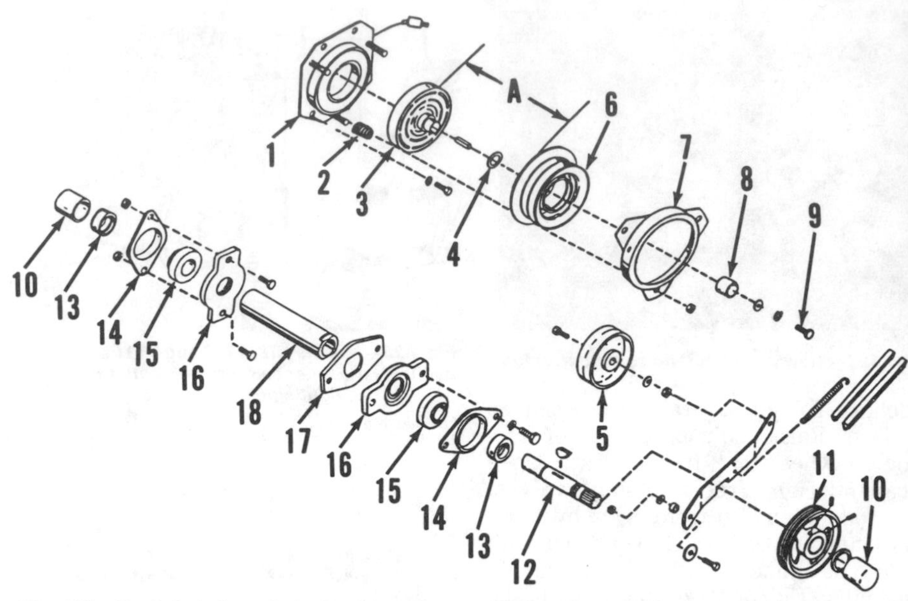


Fig. A30—Exploded view of electro-magnetic pto clutch and pto shaft assembly used on Models GT12, GT14 and GT16.

1. Field assy.
2. Spring
3. Rotor assy.
4. Shim
5. Idler pulley
6. Drive pulley
7. Brake flange
8. Spacer
9. Retainer screw
10. Rubber cover
11. Driven pulley
12. Pto shaft
13. Locking collar
14. Flangettes
15. Bearing
16. Flange
17. Anti-pivot plate
18. Tube

Adjust clutch as follows: With clutch disengaged, check clearance (C–Fig. A31) using a feeler gage through four slots (1) in brake flange. Clearance must be 0.010-0.015 inch (0.254-0.381 mm); tighten or loosen brake flange mounting nuts (5) to obtain correct gap.

To disassemble pto drive shaft assembly, remove shaft covers (10–Fig. A30), belts, pto pulley (11) and bearing lock collars (13). Support front of tractor and unbolt bearing flanges, then withdraw shaft, bearings and tube.

Reassemble pto drive shaft assembly by reversing disassembly procedure. Lock bearing locking collars (13) to bearings (15) by turning collars in direction of shaft rotation, then lock collars to pto shaft (12) with set screws.

## Models S-10G, S-12H, S-14G, S-14H, S-16H

An electro-magnetic pto clutch, mounted on engine crankshaft, is used on these models. The pto shaft (1–Fig. A32) rides in bearings in pto housing (3) which also supports front axle assembly. Belt tension is automatically adjusted by spring loaded idler pulley (7).

To remove electro-magnetic clutch, remove retaining screw (17) and spacer (15), then pull rotor assembly (14) off crankshaft. Unbolt and remove field assembly (13). Field and rotor are not available separately; if renewal is necessary, complete clutch must be replaced.

Reinstall clutch in reverse of disassembly procedure. Tighten studs retain-

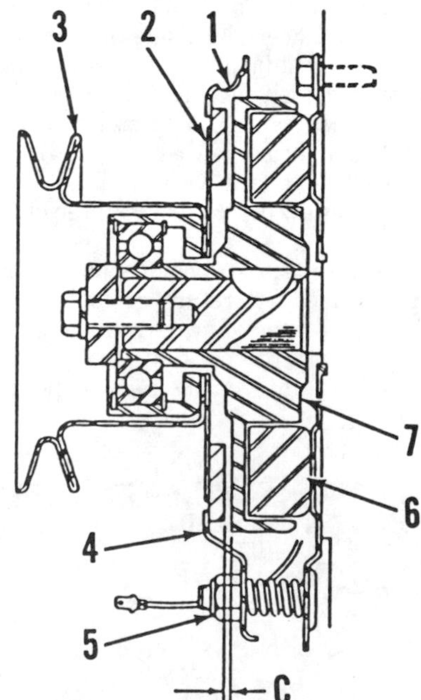


Fig. A31—Cross-sectional view of typical electro-magnetic pto clutch used on "S" and "GT" models. Adjust nuts (5) to provide 0.010-0.015 inch (0.254-0.381 mm) clearance (C) with clutch disengaged. Refer to text.

1. Adjustment slot (4)
2. Armature-brake assy.
3. Pulley
4. Brake flange
5. Locknut
6. Field assy.
7. Rotor assy.

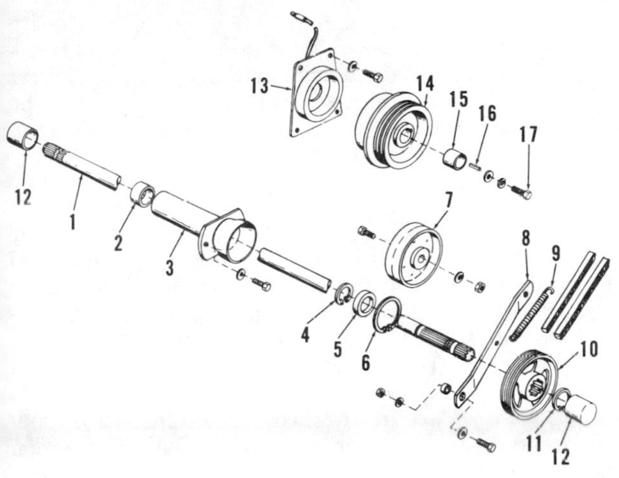

Fig. A32—Exploded view of pto clutch and shaft assembly used on Models S-10G, S-12H, S-14G, S-14H and S-16H. Pto housing (3) supports front axle.

1. Pto shaft
2. Needle bearing
3. Housing
4. Snap ring
5. Bearing
6. Snap ring
7. Idler pulley
8. Idler arm
9. Spring
10. Driven pulley
11. Snap ring
12. Cover
13. Electric clutch field
14. Clutch & drive pulley
15. Sleeve
16. Key
17. Cap screw

ing field assembly to 30 ft.-lbs. (41 N·m). Tighten cap screw retaining rotor-armature assembly to 25 ft.-lbs. (34 N·m). When reinstalling brake flange (4–Fig. A31), adjust locknuts (5) to provide 0.010-0.015 inch (0.254-0.381 mm) gap (C) with clutch disengaged. Gap can be checked by inserting feeler gage through four slots (1) in brake flange.

To disassemble pto shaft, remove covers (12–Fig. A32), belts and pulley (10). Support front of tractor and remove cap screws retaining pto housing (3) to frame bracket, then withdraw pto drive towards front of tractor. Remove snap rings, shaft and bearings. Reassemble unit by reversing removal procedure.

### Models YT8, YT10, YT11

All models are equipped with a spring loaded idler pto clutch. No adjustment is required. If belt slips, renew belt or idler spring.

# HYDROSTATIC TRANSMISSION

## EATON

### Model S-8H

**DRIVE RELEASE.** The tractor may be moved short distances with engine stopped by rotating cam arm shown in Fig. A34 rearward to force free wheeling valve rod down into transmission. Opening free-wheeling valve relieves oil pressure in transmission and rear wheels are free to turn. The free-wheeling cam arm must be returned to its forward position to operate tractor with engine running.

**LUBRICATION.** Type of oil recommended for hydrostatic transmission used on Models S-8H is Type "A" ATF. Oil level is indicated on oil reservoir tank next to transmission and should indicate reservoir is half full. Care should be used when filling reservoir to prevent contamination of fluid.

If air enters transmission fluid, system must be bled to remove air using following procedure: Unscrew nut from left end of free-wheeling cam shaft and move shaft to right until cam is clear of free-wheeling valve as shown in Fig. A35. Clean dirt and debris from free-wheeling valve and reservoir. Loosen nut (B) and unscrew free-wheeling valve rod (C). Do not allow dirt or other foreign material to enter transmission. Remove reservoir fill cap and add Type "A" ATF until reservoir is half full. Raise rear of tractor, start engine and run engine at slow idle speed. Move speed control lever to forward and reverse positions until oil appears at free-wheeling valve hole. Stop engine and screw rod (C) into transmission and tighten nut (B) to 30 in.-lbs. (3 N·m). Be careful not to damage "O" rings in transmission. Install cam assembly and screw nuts on left end of shaft to position cam in center of free-wheeling rod. Recheck oil level in reservoir and fill with fluid until half full.

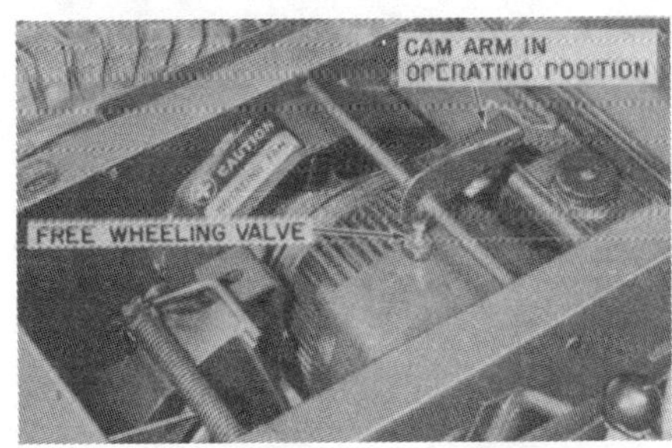


Fig. A34—View showing location of free-wheeling valve and cam on Model S-8H.

**ADJUSTMENT.** Model S-8H is equipped with a neutral-brake pedal on right side of tractor which returns transmission to neutral when pedal is depressed. To adjust neutral-brake pedal, place transmission shift lever in "PARK-START" (neutral) slot of shift quadrant and loosen bolt (A–Fig. A37). Depress pedal and apply brake lock. Tighten bolt (A). Check operation by placing shift lever in forward position and depress pedal. Shift lever should return to "PARK-START". Repeat check with shift lever in reverse position. Do not move shift lever and depress neutral-brake pedal simultaneously as control linkage may be bent or mis-adjusted.

Tractor wheels should not move when transmission shift lever is in "PARK-START" (neutral) position. If tractor creeps in neutral, proceed as follows: Adjust neutral-brake pedal as previously outlined. Place shift lever in "PARK-START" (neutral) position and note position of bolt (B–Fig. A37) in control cam. Centerline of bolt head should be aligned with timing mark. If bolt and mark are not aligned, loosen bolt (C) and move control cam up or down to align centerline of bolt head (B) with timing mark. Tighten bolt (C). Support rear of tractor so rear tires can rotate without touching ground. Start engine and run at full throttle. Loosen bolt (B) slightly and with a screwdriver inserted in slots (S) of pintle lever and friction plate, pivot pintle left or right until rear tires stop turning. Tighten bolt (B).

Friction brake shown in Fig. A37 may be adjusted by turning nut (D) to increase friction against friction plate and maintain speed settings of shift lever.

Fig. A35—Cam assembly on Model S-8H must be moved as shown to remove free-wheeling valve so transmission can be bled.

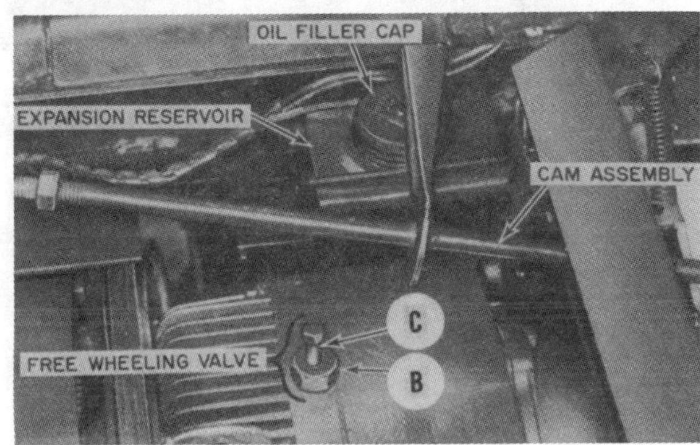

**REMOVE AND REINSTALL.** To remove hydrostatic transmission, remove outer fan shield attached to frame. Unscrew cap screw and remove fan, drive pulley and drive belt. Unscrew free-wheeling cam shaft nuts and remove cam assembly shown in Fig. A34. Disconnect shift linkage from transmission shift shaft. Disconnect oil line from reservoir to transmission and remove reservoir. Plug all openings in oil line and transmission to prevent contamination. Unscrew cap screws securing transmission to differential, move transmission to left and lift transmission out of tractor.

Reinstall by reversing removal procedure. Bleed air from system and adjust linkage as previously outlined.

**OVERHAUL.** Model S-8H is equipped with an Eaton Model 6 hydrostatic transmission. Refer to Eaton Model 6 section in HYDROSTATIC TRANSMISSION SERVICE section for overhaul procedure.

## VICKERS

### All Models So Equipped

**DRIVE RELEASE.** Free-wheeling valve located on left side of transmission and shown in Fig. A40 may be depressed to move tractor with engine stopped. Depressing free-wheeling valve relieves oil pressure and allows motor to turn.

**LUBRICATION.** The hydrostatic transmission, differential and hydraulic system, if so equipped, use a common oil reservoir in the differential housing. Recommended oil is SAE 10W-30 detergent type automotive engine oil having API classification SE. Maintain oil level at lowest edge of filler pipe threads with tractor on level ground. Capacity is approximately 7 pints (3.3L). Oil filter located under control console should be changed after every 500 hours of operation or every two years.

**ADJUSTMENT.** Transmission shift linkage must be adjusted if tractor creeps or moves forward or rearward when shift lever is in neutral slot.

Fine adjustment of transmission control linkage may cure creeping problem. To perform fine adjustment, raise and support rear of tractor so rear wheels are free to turn. Place transmission control lever in "PARK-START" position and raise rear deck. Start engine and move control lever to neutral slot. Increase engine speed to approximately full throttle. Loosen clamp bolt (B – Fig. A41) until cam follower is free to rotate and turn eccentric in either direction as required to stop rear wheel rotation. Retighten clamp bolt (B). Check adjustment by moving shift control lever into forward and reverse positions and back to neutral. Rear wheels should not turn with shift control lever in neutral.

If fine adjustment of cam follower eccentric does not stop rear wheel rotation in neutral, or if shift linkage has been disassembled, it will be necessary to use the following procedure for neutral adjustment: Raise and support rear of tractor so rear wheels are free to turn. Move shift control lever to "PARK-START" position and raise rear deck.

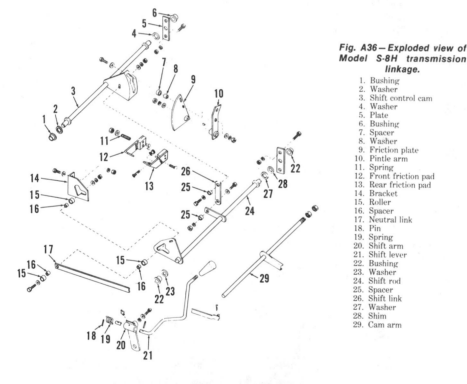

*Fig. A36 – Exploded view of Model S-8H transmission linkage.*

1. Bushing
2. Washer
3. Shift control cam
4. Washer
5. Plate
6. Bushing
7. Spacer
8. Washer
9. Friction plate
10. Pintle arm
11. Spring
12. Front friction pad
13. Rear friction pad
14. Bracket
15. Roller
16. Spacer
17. Neutral link
18. Pin
19. Spring
20. Shift arm
21. Shift lever
22. Bushing
23. Washer
24. Shift rod
25. Spacer
26. Shift link
27. Washer
28. Shim
29. Cam arm

*Fig. A37 – View of shift mechanism adjustment points on Model S-8H. Refer to text.*

*Fig. A40 – View showing location of free-wheeling valve (V) on models equipped with Vickers transmission. Knob must be pushed in to move tractor with engine stopped.*

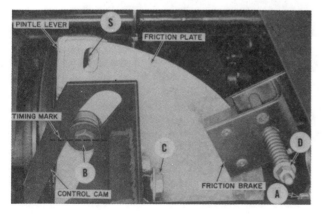

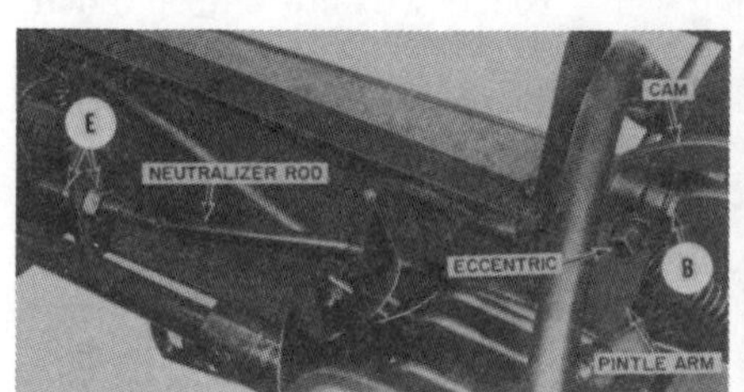


*Fig. A41 – View of shift mechanism used on models equipped with Vickers transmission.*

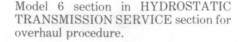

Loosen clamp bolt (B–Fig. A42) and rotate eccentric until cam follower roller is in lowest portion of neutral section in cam slot as shown in Fig. A42. Neutral section of cam slot is portion of cam slot which will not move pintle arm when cam is moved up and down. Retighten clamp bolt (B). Move shift control lever to position cam follower roller in middle of neutral section of cam slot. Loosen pintle arm clamp bolts (A–Fig. A42) so pintle shaft can slip in pintle arm. Move shift control lever to "PARK-START" position and start engine. Operate engine between ⅔ and full throttle speed. Transmission will seek its neutral position. Stop engine and check to be sure cam roller is still in center of neutral section in cam slot. Carefully tighten pintle arm clamp bolts (A) to 30-35 ft.-lbs. (41-47 N·m). Cam or pintle arm must not be disturbed when tightening bolts. Loosen shift control fork bolt (D–Fig. A43). Hold cam to prevent movement of cam follower roller in cam slot and move control fork until it is aligned with neutral slot in control shift pattern. Tighten bolt (D).

If necessary, additional fine adjustment can now be made by adjusting eccentric roller using procedure previously outlined.

The shift lever fork slides between two friction plates which can be adjusted to increase or decrease friction as desired. The friction plates are held together by two screws and springs. There should be sufficient spring pressure on friction plates to hold control lever at any selected setting. Raise rear deck and insert a screwdriver through access holes in left side of control console to adjust screws.

*Fig. A43 – View of hydrostatic shift control fork. Adjust park lock brake at "A." Loosen bolt "D" to adjust neutral position of control fork.*

If neutral return pedal does not shift hydrostatic control lever to neutral position from either forward or reverse position when pedal is depressed, adjust length of neutralizer rod by means of nuts (E–Fig. A41).

**REMOVE AND REINSTALL.** To remove hydrostatic transmission, mark and disconnect hydraulic hoses. Plug or cap openings to prevent entrance of dirt or other foreign material. Remove plate directly above drive shaft and disconnect drive shaft rear coupler. Detach coupler half from transmission input shaft. Remove pintle arm from transmission. Unbolt and remove supporting brace between crossmember and transmission. Unbolt transmission and lift transmission from tractor. Drain lubricant and clean exterior of transmission.

Reinstall hydrostatic transmission by reversing removal procedure. Fill reduction drive and differential housing to proper level with SAE 10W-30 oil. Refer to LUBRICATION paragraph.

**OVERHAUL.** A Vickers Model T66Z hydrostatic transmission is used. Refer to Vickers Model T66 section in HYDROSTATIC TRANSMISSION SERVICE section for overhaul procedure.

## SUNDSTRAND

### All Models So Equipped

**LUBRICATION.** The hydrostatic transmission shares a common reservoir in gear reduction and differential unit. Recommended oil is SAE 10W-30 engine oil having API classification SE. If ambient temperature is above 80°F (27°C) and tractor will be in heavy load conditions, change transmission oil to SAE 30. Maintain oil level at top of filler plug pipe elbow (3–Fig. A50). Check oil level with tractor on level surface and engine running at fast idle. Care should

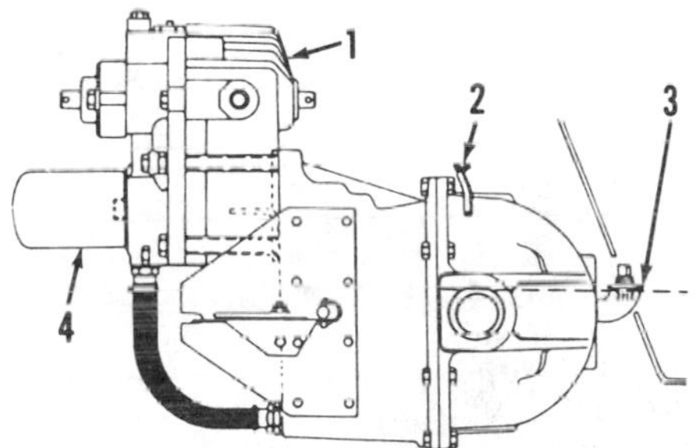


*Fig. A50 – Recommended transmission oil is SAE 10W-30 engine oil for models equipped with Sundstrand hydrostatic transmission. Fill to top of filler plug pipe elbow (3).*

1. Hydrostatic transmission
2. Breather
3. Oil level & filler plug
4. Oil filter

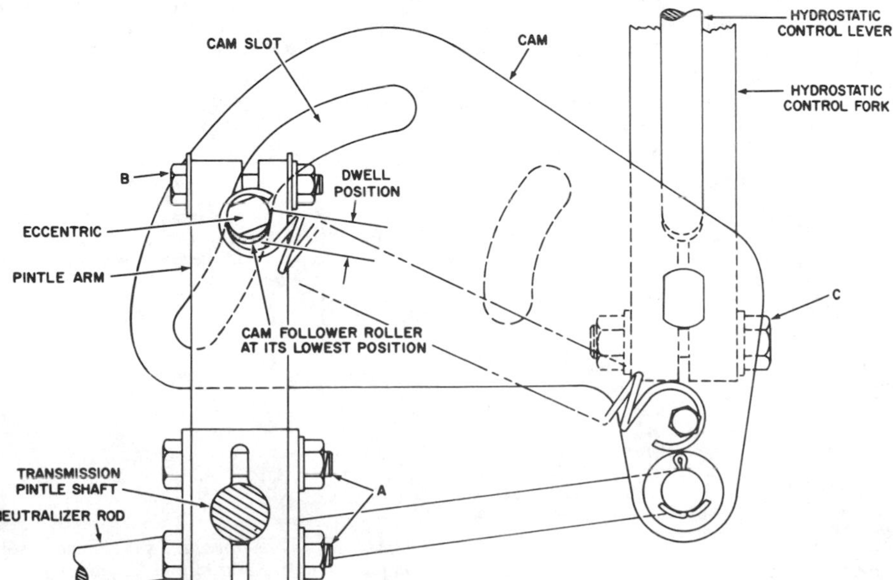


*Fig. A42 – Diagram of typical shift mechanism used on models equipped with Vickers transmission. Refer to text for adjustment.*

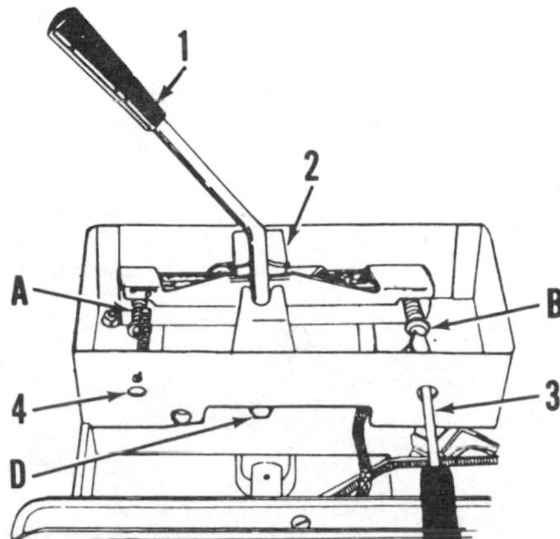


*Fig. A51 – View of control lever friction adjustment screws (A and B). Top of console is removed for ease of viewing.*

1. Control lever
2. Control fork
3. Screwdriver
4. Access holes

be used when filling reservoir to prevent contamination of fluid. The oil and oil filter (4) should be changed every 500 hours of operation or once a year, whichever comes first. Be sure transmission breather (2) is not plugged.

**ADJUSTMENT.** If tractor creeps when hydrostatic control lever is in neutral slot, shift linkage must be adjusted.

Proper friction adjustment on control lever is necessary for proper operation. Control lever friction plates must be adjusted so control lever (1 – Fig. A51) will remain at any selected setting under normal operating conditions. Friction plate spring pressure is adjusted by tightening screws at "A" and "B." Raise rear deck and insert screwdriver through access holes (4) as shown. Friction plates must remain parallel, check and adjust screws evenly. If tractor has a tendency to speed up, tighten screw "A" slightly more than "B." If tractor slows down, tighten screw "B" slightly more than "A."

EARLY MODELS. To adjust control linkage, proceed as follows: Raise and support rear of tractor so wheels are free to turn. Start engine and place control lever in neutral position. With engine speed at full throttle, loosen clamp bolt (B – Fig. A52) and turn eccentric as required until rear wheels stop turning. Retighten clamp bolt (B). Check adjustment by moving lever into forward and reverse positions and back to neutral. Wheels should not turn with shift lever in neutral.

If fine adjustment of cam follower eccentric does not stop rear wheel rotation in neutral, or if shift linkage has been disassembled, it will be necessary to use following procedure for neutral adjustment: Raise and support rear of tractor so wheels are free to turn. Loosen clamp bolt (B – Fig. A52) and turn eccentric until flats on eccentric are parallel with cam slot as shown, then retighten clamp bolt. Move cam to align cam follower roller with cam dwell center mark. Loosen pintle lever clamp bolt (A) so pintle shaft can rotate freely in pintle lever. Start engine and place control lever in neutral position. Move pintle lever as required until wheels stop turning. Be sure cam follower roller is still aligned with cam dwell center mark, then shut off engine. Carefully tighten bolt (A) making sure cam or pintle lever position is not disturbed. Loosen adjusting nuts on shift rod and neutralizer rod, then depress neutralizer pedal. Make sure cam follower roller is aligned with cam dwell center mark, and adjust nuts snug against neutralizer plate. Loosen shift control fork bolt (D – Fig. A51). Hold cam to prevent movement of cam follower roller in cam slot and move control fork until it is aligned with neutral slot in control console. Retighten nut (D).

If wheels still creep when in neutral, loosen clamp bolt (B – Fig. A52) and adjust eccentric roller until wheels stop. Retighten clamp bolt (B).

LATE MODELS. To adjust control linkage, proceed as follows: Raise and support rear of tractor so wheels are free to turn. Remove floor plate, then disconnect shift rod yoke (2 – Fig. A53) from neutralizer rod (3). If shift lever does not return to neutral position when neutral return pedal is depressed, adjust length of neutralizer rod using adjusting nuts (4). Loosen locking nut (1 – Fig. A54) so eccentric (2) can be turned with a wrench. Start engine and move shift lever to neutral position. With engine running at full throttle, adjust eccentric until wheels stop turning and tighten locking nut. Shut off engine and adjust shift rod yoke until shift rod (7) is centered in slot in transmission lever (6).

**REMOVE AND REINSTALL.** To remove hydrostatic transmission, first disconnect battery and drain lubricant. Remove rear deck and fuel tank. Disconnect drive shaft rear coupler and remove coupler half from transmission input shaft. Disconnect hydraulic hoses and plug or cap all openings to prevent entrance of dirt. Disconnect control linkage from transmission. Unbolt transmission and remove from rear axle differential assembly.

Reinstall hydrostatic unit in reverse of removal. Fill reservoir with clean 10W-30 engine oil. Prime transmission by removing implement relief valve, located on top of unit between directional valves, and pour in one pint (0.5L) of 10W-30 oil. Reinstall relief valve but do not tighten valve plug. Start engine and run until oil runs past threads of plug, then tighten plug.

**OVERHAUL.** A Sundstrand Series 15 "U" type hydrostatic transmission is used. Refer to Sundstrand Series 15 "U" Type section in HYDROSTATIC TRANSMISSION SERVICE section for overhaul procedure.

# TRANSAXLE

## LUBRICATION

### All Models

Models 13948, 13989, 13990, 913002, 913003 and S-8 are equipped with Peerless 1200 series transaxle. Models

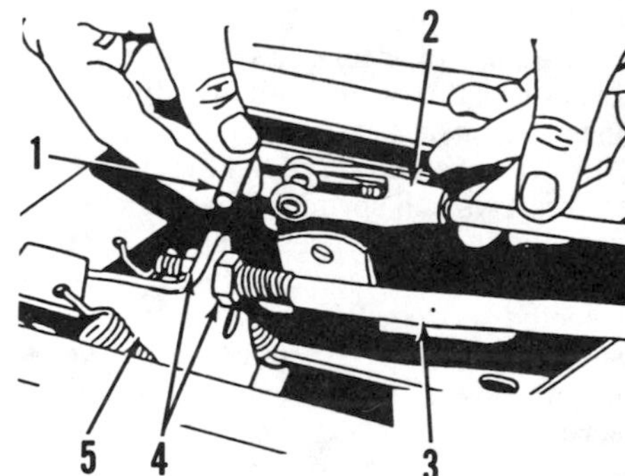


*Fig. A53 – To adjust hydrostatic shift linkage on late models, shift rod (2) must be disconnected from neutralizer rod (3). Refer to text.*

1. Pin
2. Shift rod
3. Neutralizer rod
4. Adjusting nuts
5. Neutralizer plate

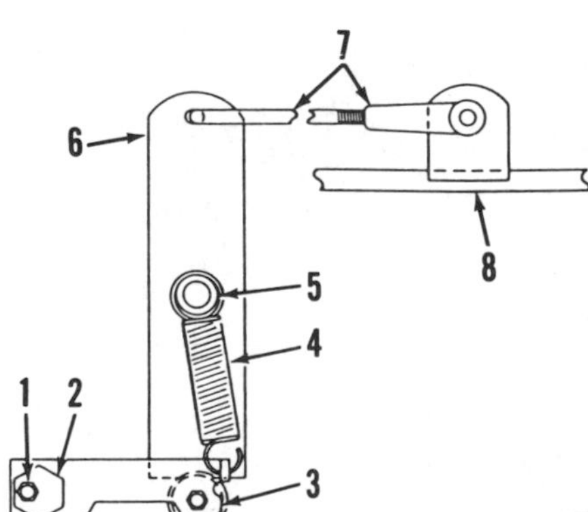


*Fig. A54 – View of hydrostatic shift linkage used on late models. Refer to text for adjustment.*

1. Locking nut
2. Eccentric
3. Bearing
4. Spring
5. Pintle arm
6. Pintle lever
7. Shift rod & yoke
8. Neutralizer rod

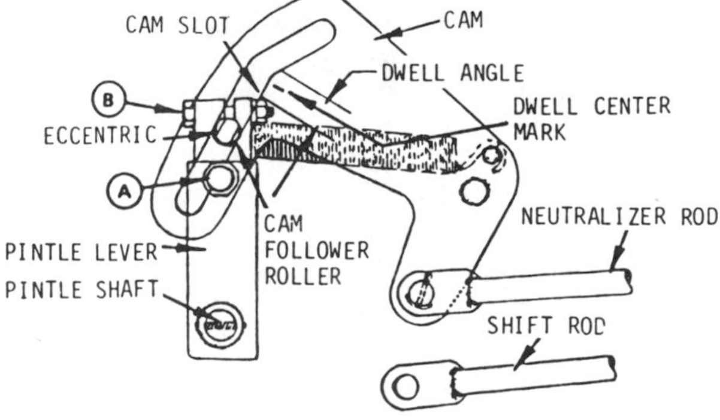


*Fig. A52 – Diagram of typical mechanism used on early models equipped with hydrostatic transmission. Refer to text for adjustment.*

S-10G and S-14G are equipped with Peerless 2300 series transaxle. Models YT8, YT10 and YT11 are equipped with Foote Model 4000-5 transaxle. Refer to CONDENSED SPECIFICATIONS at the beginning of this section for transaxle lubricating fluid type and capacity for model being serviced.

### REMOVE AND REINSTALL

#### Model S-8G

To remove transaxle, remove brake band and shift linkage. Remove transaxle drive belt. Unscrew two front mounting cap screws. Support rear of tractor and unscrew axle retaining "U" bolts. Raise rear of tractor and roll transaxle away from tractor.

To reinstall transaxle, reverse removal procedure.

#### Models YT8, YT10, YT11

To remove transaxle, raise rear deck and remove traction belt. Remove shift lever knob and place transmission in neutral. Disconnect and remove range selector lever linkage. Disconnect brake linkage. Remove rear hitch plate and support tractor under frame. Use a floor jack to support front of transmission. Remove four cap screws from transaxle mount and "U" bolts from axle housing. Roll transaxle away from tractor. Remove rear wheels, clean case and place on bench.

To reinstall transaxle, reverse removal procedure.

#### All Other Models So Equipped

To remove transaxle, remove rear hitch plate from rear of frame and frame top cover in front of seat. Remove rear drive belt cover, depress clutch and remove drive belts from transaxle pulley. Disconnect brake rod from brake band. Unscrew transaxle retaining cap screws located beneath seat. Support rear of tractor and remove retaining axle brackets. Roll transaxle assembly from tractor. Remove input pulley, brake assembly and wheels and hubs from transaxle.

To reinstall transaxle, reverse removal procedure.

### OVERHAUL

#### All Models

Models 13948, 13989, 13990, 913002, 913003 and S-8 are equipped with a Peerless 1200 series transaxle. Models S-10G and S-14G are equipped with a Peerless 2300 series transaxle. Models YT8, YT10 and YT11 are equipped with a Foote Model 4000-5 transaxle. Refer to the appropriate Peerless or Foote section in TRANSAXLE SERVICE section for overhaul procedure.

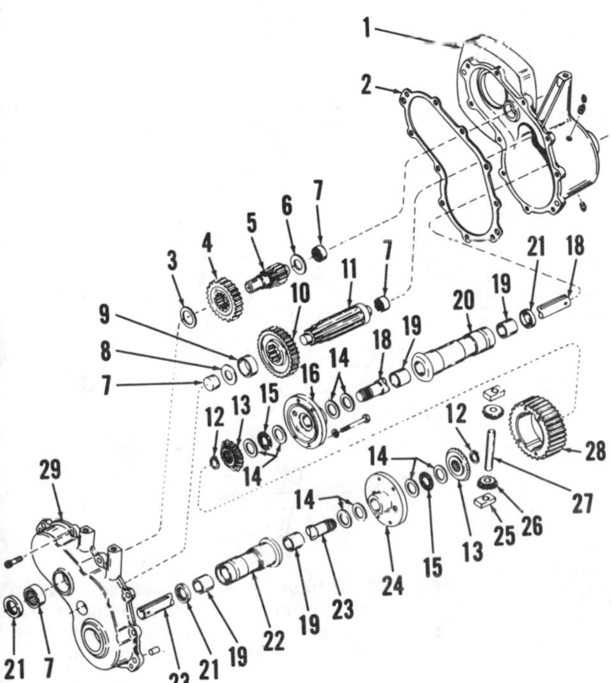

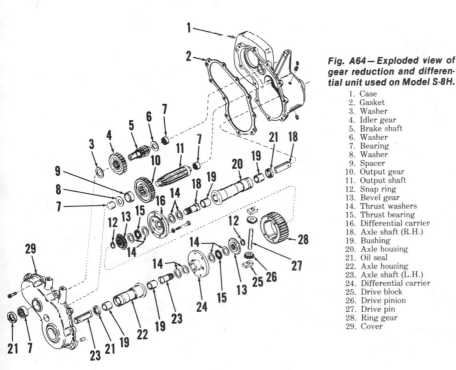

***Fig. A64 — Exploded view of gear reduction and differential unit used on Model S-8H.***

1. Case
2. Gasket
3. Washer
4. Idler gear
5. Brake shaft
6. Washer
7. Bearing
8. Washer
9. Spacer
10. Output gear
11. Output shaft
12. Snap ring
13. Bevel gear
14. Thrust washers
15. Thrust bearing
16. Differential carrier
18. Axle shaft (R.H.)
19. Bushing
20. Axle housing
21. Oil seal
22. Axle housing
23. Axle shaft (L.H.)
24. Differential carrier
25. Drive block
26. Drive pinion
27. Drive pin
28. Ring gear
29. Cover

## REDUCTION GEARS AND DIFFERENTIAL

#### Model S-8H

**R&R AND OVERHAUL.** Model S-8 Hydro is equipped with a Peerless Model 1309 reduction gear and differential unit. To remove rear axle assembly, remove hydrostatic transmission as previously outlined. Unscrew front mounting screws and axle "U" bolts. Raise rear of tractor and roll rear end assembly away from tractor.

Remove wheel and hub assemblies from axles. Remove brake disc from brake shaft. Clean axle shafts and remove any burrs on shafts. Unscrew cap screws and drive out dowel pins in cover (29 – Fig. A64). Lift cover off case and axle shaft. Withdraw brake shaft (5), input gear (4) and thrust washers (3 and 6) from case. Remove output shaft (11), output gear (10), spacer (9), thrust washer (8) and differential assembly from case. Axle shaft housings (20 and 22) must be pressed from case and cover.

To disassemble differential, unscrew four cap screws and separate axle shaft and carriage assemblies from ring gear (28). Drive blocks (25), bevel pinion gears (26) and drive pin (27) can now be removed from ring gear. Remove snap rings (12) and slide axle shafts (18 and 23) from axle gears (13) and carriages (16 and 24).

Clean and inspect all parts and renew any parts damaged or excessively worn. When installing needle bearings, press bearings in from inside of case or cover until bearings are 0.015-0.020 inch (0.381-0.508 mm) below thrust surfaces. Be sure heads of differential cap screws and right axle shaft (18) are installed in right carriage housing (16). Right axle shaft is installed through case (1). Tighten differential cap screws to 7 ft.-lbs. (9 N•m) and cover cap screws to 10 ft.-lbs. (14 N•m). Differential assembly and output shaft (11) must be installed in case at same time. Remainder of assembly is reverse of disassembly procedure. Fill unit with approximately two pints (0.9L) of SAE 90 EP gear lube.

#### Models S-12H, S-14H, S-16H, GT12, GT14, GT16

**R&R AND OVERHAUL.** To remove gear reduction and differential unit, remove hydrostatic transmission as outlined in previous paragraph and proceed as follows: Detach parking pawl assembly from housing and disconnect brake control rods. Support rear of tractor and unbolt axle brackets from frame. Roll unit forward until oil filter pipe is clear of rear hitch plate, raise tractor and roll assembly rearward from tractor.

To disassemble unit, drain lubricant from housing, then remove wheels and hubs (1–Fig. A65) from axles (6). Unbolt axle bearing retainer and withdraw axle and bearing assemblies from rear housing (7). Unbolt and separate front and rear housings (23 and 7). Be sure differential bearing caps are marked for correct reassembly as they are matched to front housing. Unbolt and remove bearing caps, then pry differential assembly out of housing. Drive a pointed punch through pinion shaft expansion plug (20) and pry plug out of housing. Remove snap ring (19) and shim (18) from end of pinion shaft. Remove side cover (25) and place a screwdriver blade under edge of reduction gear (24) to prevent gear from binding, then press pinion gear (13) out of housing and remove outer bearing (21), spacer (17) and reduction gear (24). Press pinion shaft out of inner bearing (14). Press bearing cups (15 and 22) out of housing.

To disassemble differential, drive lock pin (2) out of pinion shaft (3) as shown in Fig. A66; then, drive pinion shaft (3) from housing. Rotate pinion gears (27–Fig. A65) 90 degrees to openings in differential case and remove pinion gears (27), side gears (28) and thrust washers (26 and 29). To remove differential case bearings (9), use a suitable puller inserting puller jaws into indentations provided in differential case. Remove cap screws securing ring gear (12) to case, then drive ring gear off case using a hammer and wood block.

Clean and inspect all parts and renew any parts damaged or excessively worn.

Reassemble in reverse of disassembly procedure. When installing inner bearing cup (15) in original housing (23), reuse original shim pack (16). If housing (23) is being renewed, determine proper shim pack as follows: Install bearing cup (15) in housing without shims. Press bearing cone (14) on pinion shaft and position shaft and bearing in housing. Using a depth measuring tool similar to one shown in Fig. A67, measure distance from bottom of bearing cradles to pinion gear surface. Subtract measured dimension from 1.2097 and difference will be required shim pack thickness. Remove inner bearing cup, install required shim pack and reinstall cup into housing.

Position pinion gear, reduction gear (chamfered side of splines towards pinion gear) and spacer in housing. Press outer bearing cone onto pinion shaft until a slight drag is felt when gear is turned by hand, then install thickest shim (18–Fig. A65) possible which will still allow installation of snap ring (19). Use sealer when installing expansion plug (20) and side cover (25).

Position ring gear (12) on differential case (11) and pull gear into place by tightening retaining cap screws evenly. Final torque on cap screws should be 50-55 ft.-lbs. (68-75 N·m).

Press bearing cones (9) on original differential case (11) using original shims (10). If differential case is being renewed, install 0.020 inch shim pack under each bearing. Position differential assembly in front housing with ring gear facing same side as reduction gear cover. Install bearing caps in their original positions and tighten cap screws to 40-45 ft.-lbs. (54-61 N·m).

Using a dial indicator, check for proper ring gear to pinion backlash of 0.003-0.007 inch (0.076-0.178 mm). If necessary, adjust backlash by moving shims (10) from one side to the other until correct backlash is obtained. To check gear teeth contact pattern, paint teeth with gear pattern compound, then rotate pinion while applying light load to ring gear. Compare contact area on teeth with patterns illustrated in Fig. A68 and correct if necessary. Desired tooth contact pattern on ring gear is shown at "A." To move toe pattern "B" towards heel, shim ring gear away from pinion, within 0.003-0.007 inch (0.076-0.178 mm) backlash limits. To move heel pattern "C" towards toe, shim ring gear closer to pinion, within backlash limits. If pattern is low "D", remove shims located under pinion inner bearing

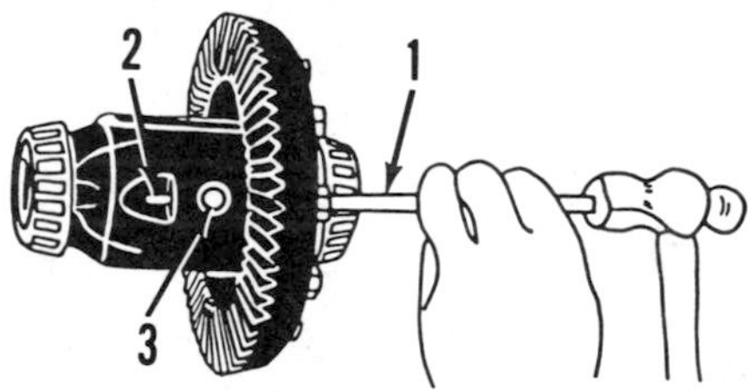


***Fig. A66—To disassemble differential, use a long, thin punch (1) to drive retaining pin (2) out of pinion shaft (3), then drive pinion shaft out of differential case.***

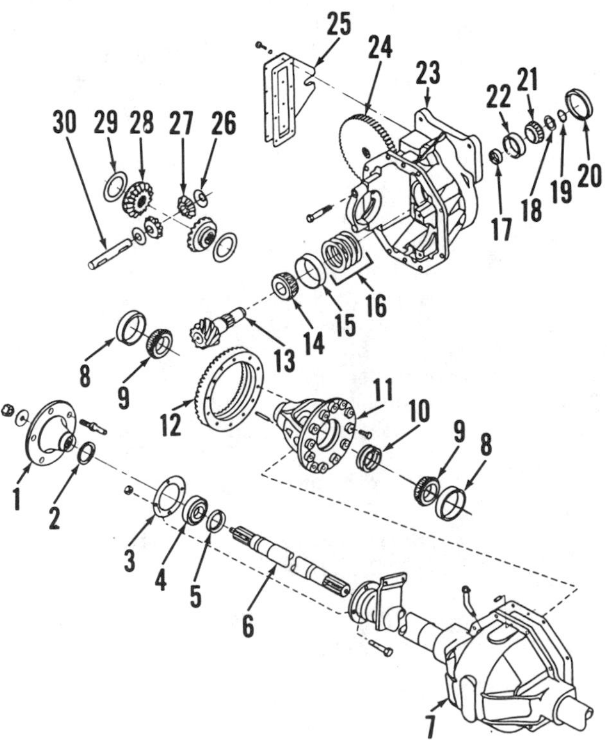


***Fig. A65—Exploded view of gear reduction, differential and rear axle unit used on Models S-12H, S-14H, S-16H, GT12, GT14 and GT16.***

1. Hub
2. Felt seal
3. Retainer
4. Axle bearing
5. Oil seal
6. Axle
7. Rear housing
8. Bearing cup
9. Bearing cone
10. Shims
11. Differential case
12. Ring gear
13. Pinion gear
14. Bearing cone (inner)
15. Bearing cup (inner)
16. Shims
17. Spacer
18. Shim
19. Snap ring
20. Expansion plug
21. Bearing cone (outer)
22. Bearing cup (outer)
23. Front housing
24. Reduction gear
25. Cover
26. Thrust washer (2)
27. Pinion gear (2)
28. Side gear (2)
29. Thrust washer (2)
30. Pinion shaft

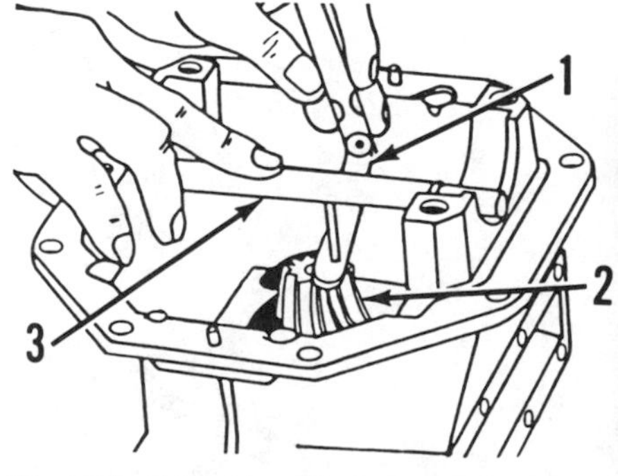


***Fig. A67—If front housing is renewed, measure from bottom of bearing cradles to pinion gear surface as shown to determine pinion shaft shim pack thickness. Refer to text.***

1. Feeler gage
2. Pinion shaft
3. Depth measuring tool

cup. If pattern is high "E", increase shim pack under pinion inner bearing cup.

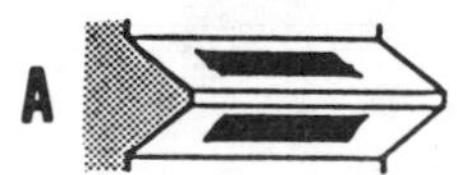


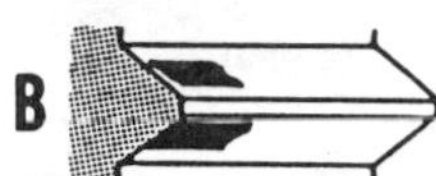


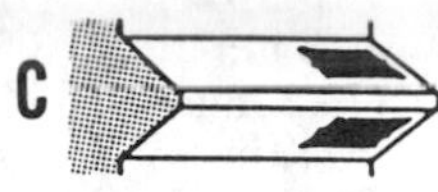


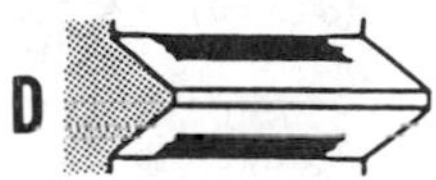


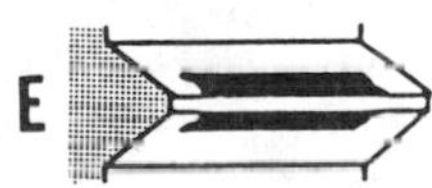


*Fig. A68—Illustration of typical gear teeth contact patterns encountered when checking ring gear and pinion. "A" pattern desired; "B" too close to toe; "C" too close to heel; "D" contact too low; "E" contact too high. Refer to text and correct as necessary.*

Assemble front housing to rear housing and tighten retaining screws to 18-23 ft.-lbs. (24-32 N·m).

# HYDRAULIC LIFT

## All Models So Equipped

**OPERATION.** The hydrostatic transmission charge pump supplies oil flow to operate hydraulic lift cylinder. Oil flow is controlled by a hand operated control valve with four positions: Up, Hold, Down and Float. Hydraulic system pressure should be 500-800 psi (3448-5516 kPa) at full engine rpm.

**CYLINDER OVERHAUL.** To disassemble cylinder, first remove adapter fittings from cylinder body (8–Fig. A69), then remove rod cap (2) from body. Withdraw piston rod (4) and piston (5) from body. Unscrew retaining screw (7) to remove piston from rod.

Inspect cylinder body, piston and rod for scoring or other damage and renew as needed. Renew all "O" ring seals. Coat all parts with clean oil when reassembling.

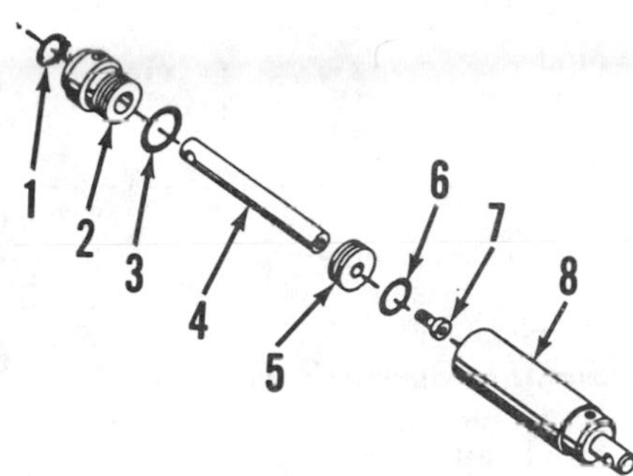


*Fig. A69—Exploded view of hydraulic lift cylinder used on models so equipped.*

1. "O" ring
2. Rod cap
3. "O" ring
4. Piston rod
5. Piston
6. "O" ring
7. Cap screw
8. Cylinder body

# BOLENS

## CONDENSED SPECIFICATIONS

| | MODELS | | | | | |
|---|---|---|---|---|---|---|
| | **730** | **733** | **736** | **G9, 853** | **LT8, G8** | **G10*** |
| Engine Make | B&S | B&S | B&S | B&S | B&S | Tecumseh |
| Model | 170702 | 170701 | 170701 | 190401 | 191707 | HH100 |
| Bore | 3 in. (76.2 mm) | 3 in. (76.2 mm) | 3 in. (76.2 mm) | 3 in. (76.2 mm) | 3 in. (76.2 mm) | 3-5/16 in. (84.1 mm) |
| Stroke | 2-3/8 in. (60.3 mm) | 2-3/8 in. (60.3 mm) | 2-3/8 in. (60.3 mm) | 2-3/4 in. (69.8 mm) | 2-3/4 in. (69.8 mm) | 2-3/4 in. (69.8 mm) |
| Piston Displacement | 16.79 cu. in. (275 cc) | 16.79 cu. in. (275 cc) | 16.79 cu. in. (275 cc) | 19.44 cu. in. (319 cc) | 19.44 cu. in. (319 cc) | 23.7 cu. in. (389 cc) |
| Horsepower | 7 | 7 | 7 | 8 | 8 | 10 |
| Slow Idle Speed – Rpm | 1750 | 1750 | 1750 | 1750 | 1750 | 1200 |
| High Idle Speed (No Load) – Rpm. | 3600 | 3600 | 3600 | 3600 | 3600 | 3600 |
| Full Load Speed – Rpm | 3250 | 3250 | 3250 | 3250 | 3250 | 3250 |
| Crankcase Oil Capacity | 2-1/4 pints (1L) | 2-1/4 pints (1L) | 2-1/4 pints (1L) | 2-3/4 pints (1.3L) | 2-1/4 pints (1L) | 3 pints (1.4L) |
| Weight – | | | | | | |
| Above 32°F (0°C) | SAE 30 | | | | | |
| 0°F (−18°C) to 32°F (0°C) | SAE 10W-30 | | | | | |
| Below 0°F (−18°C) | SAE 5W-20 | | | | | |
| Transmission Oil Capacity | 3 pints (1.4L) | 3 pints (1.4L) | .......... | 5 pints (2.4L) | 1-1/2 pints (0.7L) | 5 pints (2.4L) |
| Weight | SAE 90 EP | SAE 90 EP | Type "A" | SAE 90 EP | SAE 90 EP | SAE 90 EP |

*Early Model G10 with S.N.0100101-029999 uses a Tecumseh HH100 engine.
Late Model G10 beginning with S.N.0300101 uses a B&S 251417 engine.

---

| | MODELS | | | | | |
|---|---|---|---|---|---|---|
| | **1053, 1054** | **G11** | **G11XL** | **H11XL** | **LT11** | **1225, 1256** |
| Engine Make | Wisconsin | B&S | B&S | B&S | B&S | Wisconsin |
| Model | TR-10D | 252417 | 253417 | 253417 | 252707 | TRA-12D |
| Bore | 3-1/8 in. (79.3 mm) | 3-7/16 in. (87.3 mm) | 3-7/16 in. (87.3 mm) | 3-7/16 in. (87.3 mm) | 3-7/16 in. (87.3 mm) | 3-1/2 in. (88.9 mm) |
| Stroke | 2-5/8 in. (66.7 mm) | 2-5/8 in. (66.7 mm) | 2-5/8 in. (66.7 mm) | 2-5/8 in. (66.7 mm) | 2-5/8 in. (66.7 mm) | 2-7/8 in. (73.0 mm) |
| Piston Displacement | 20.2 cu. in. (331 cc) | 24.36 cu. in. (399 cc) | 24.36 cu. in. (399 cc) | 24.36 cu. in. (399 cc) | 24.36 cu. in. (399 cc) | 27.66 cu. in. (453 cc) |
| Horsepower | 10 | 11 | 11 | 11 | 11 | 12 |
| Slow Idle Speed – Rpm | 1000 | 1750 | 1750 | 1750 | 1750 | 1000 |
| High Idle Speed (No Load) – Rpm. | 3800 | 3600 | 3600 | 3600 | 3600 | 3860 |
| Full Load Speed – Rpm | 3450 | 3300 | 3300 | 3300 | 3300 | 3600 |
| Crankcase Oil Capacity | 2 pints (0.9L) | 3 pints (1.4L) | 3 pints (1.4L) | 3 pints (1.4L) | 3 pints (1.4L) | 2 pints (0.9L) |
| Weight – | | | | | | |
| Above 32°F (0°C) | SAE 30 | | | | | |
| 0°F (−18°C) to 32°F (0°C) | SAE 10W-30 | | | | | |
| Below 0°F (−18°C) | SAE 5W-20 | | | | | |
| Transmission Oil Capacity | 5 pints (2.4L) | 5 pints (2.4L) | 3 pints (1.4L) | 16 pints (7.6L) | 1-1/2 pints (0.7L) | .......... |
| Weight | SAE 90 EP | SAE 90 EP | SAE 90 EP | ** | SAE 90 EP | Type "A" |

MODELS

| | 1254 | G12,1253 | G12XL | H12XL | 1257 |
|---|---|---|---|---|---|
| Engine Make | Wisconsin | Tecumseh | Tecumseh | Tecumseh | Tecumseh |
| Model | TRA-12D | HH120 | OH120 | OH120 | HH120 |
| Bore | 3½ in. (88.9 mm) | 3½ in. (88.9 mm) | 3⅛ in. (79.3 mm) | 3⅛ in. (79.3 mm) | 3½ in. (88.9 mm) |
| Stroke | 2⅞ in. (73.0 mm) | 2⅞ in. (73.0 mm) | 2¾ in. (69.8 mm) | 2¾ in. (69.8 mm) | 2⅞ in. (73.0 mm) |
| Piston Displacement | 27.66 cu. in. (453 cc) | 27.66 cu. in. (453 cc) | 21.1 cu. in. (346 cc) | 21.1 cu. in. (346 cc) | 27.66 cu. in. (453 cc) |
| Horsepower | 12 | 12 | 12 | 12 | 12 |
| Slow Idle Speed – Rpm | 1000 | 1200 | 1200 | 1200 | 1200 |
| High Idle Speed (No Load) – Rpm | 3860 | 3600 | 3600 | 3600 | 3600 |
| Full Load Speed-Rpm | 3600 | 3200 | 3200 | 3200 | 3200 |
| Crankcase Oil Capacity | 2 pints (0.9L) | 3 pints (1.4L) | 3 pints (1.4L) | 3 pints (1.4L) | 3 pints (1.4L) |
| Weight – | | | | | |
| Above 32°F (0°C) | SAE 30 | SAE 30 | SAE 30 | SAE 30 | SAE 30 |
| 0°F (–18°C) to 32°F (0°C) | SAE 10W-30 | SAE 10W-30 | SAE 10W-30 | SAE 10W-30 | SAE 10W-30 |
| Below 0°F (–18°C) | SAE 5W-20 | SAE 5W-20 | SAE 5W-20 | SAE 5W-20 | SAE 5W-20 |
| Transmission Oil Capacity | 5 pints (2.4L) | 5 pints (2.4L) | 3 pints (1.4L) | 16 pints (7.6L) | ......... |
| Weight | SAE 90 EP | SAE 90 EP | SAE 90 EP | ** | Type "A" |

MODELS

| | 1455, 1476, 1477 | G14 | G14XL | H14 | H14XL |
|---|---|---|---|---|---|
| Engine Make | Wisconsin | Tecumseh | Tecumseh | Tecumseh | Tecumseh |
| Model | S-14D | HH140 | OH140 | HH140 | OH140 |
| Bore | 3¾ in. (95.2 mm) | 3-5/16 in. (84.1 mm) | 3-5/16 in. (84.1 mm) | 3-5/16 in. (84.1 mm) | 3-5/16 in. (84.1 mm) |
| Stroke | 3 in. (76.2 mm) | 2¾ in. (69.8 mm) | 2¾ in. (69.8 mm) | 2¾ in. (69.8 mm) | 2¾ in. (69.8 mm) |
| Piston Displacement | 33.1 cu. in. (542 cc) | 23.75 cu. in. (389 cc) | 23.75 cu. in. (389 cc) | 23.75 cu. in. (389 cc) | 23.75 cu. in. (389 cc) |
| Horsepower | 14 | 14 | 14 | 14 | 14 |
| Slow Idle Speed-Rpm | 1000 | 1200 | 1200 | 1200 | 1200 |
| High Idle Speed (No Load) – Rpm | 3680 | 3600 | 3600 | 3600 | 3600 |
| Full Load Speed – Rpm | 3400 | 3200 | 3200 | 3200 | 3200 |
| Crankcase Oil Capacity | 4 pints (1.9L) | 3 pints (1.4L) | 3 pints (1.4L) | 3 pints (1.4L) | 3 pints (1.4L) |
| Weight – | | | | | |
| Above 32°F (0°C) | SAE 30 | SAE 30 | SAE 30 | SAE 30 | SAE 30 |
| 0°F (–18°C) to 32°F (0°C) | SAE 10W-30 | SAE 10W-30 | SAE 10W-30 | SAE 10W-30 | SAE 10W-30 |
| Below 0°F (–18°C) | SAE 5W-20 | SAE 5W-20 | SAE 5W-20 | SAE 5W-20 | SAE 5W-20 |
| Transmission Oil Capacity | 20 pints (9.5L) | 5 pints (2.4L) | 3 pints (1.4L) | 20 pints (9.5L) | 16 pints (7.6L) |
| Weight | Type "A" | SAE 90 EP | SAE 90 EP | Type "A" | ** |

| | MODELS | | | | |
|---|---|---|---|---|---|
| | 1556 | G16XL | H16 | H16XL | QS16 |
| Engine Make | Tecumseh | Tecumseh | Tecumseh | Tecumseh | Kohler |
| Model | HH150 | OH160 | HH160 | OH160 | K341 |
| Bore | 3½ in. (88.9 mm) | 3½ in. (88.9 mm) | 3½ in. (88.9 mm) | 3½ in. (88.9 mm) | 3¾ in. (95.2 mm) |
| Stroke | 2⅞ in. (73.0 mm) | 2⅞ in. (73.0 mm) | 2⅞ in. (73.0 mm) | 2⅞ in. (73.0 mm) | 3¼ in. (82.5 mm) |
| Piston Displacement | 27.66 cu. in. (453 cc) | 27.66 cu. in. (453 cc) | 27.66 cu. in. (453 cc) | 27.66 cu. in. (453 cc) | 35.89 cu. in. (588 cc) |
| Horsepower | 15 | 16 | 16 | 16 | 16 |
| Slow Idle Speed – Rpm | 1200 | 1200 | 1200 | 1200 | 2350 |
| High Idle Speed (No Load) – Rpm | 3600 | 3600 | 3600 | 3600 | 3600 |
| Full Load Speed – Rpm | 3200 | 3200 | 3200 | 3200 | 3400 |
| Crankcase Oil Capacity | 3 pints (1.4L) | 3 pints (1.4L) | 3 pints (1.4L) | 3 pints (1.4L) | 4 pints (1.9L) |
| Weight – | | | | | |
| Above 32°F (0°C) | SAE 30 | | | | |
| 0°F (–18°C) to 32°F (0°C) | SAE 10W-30 | | | | |
| Below 0°F (–18°C) | SAE 5W-20 | | | | |
| Transmission Oil Capacity | 20 pints (9.5L) | 3 pints (1.4L) | 20 pints (9.5L) | 16 pints (7.6L) | 20 pints (9.5L) |
| Weight | Type "A" | SAE 90 EP | Type "A" | ** | Type "F" |

**Refer to HYDROSTATIC DRIVE UNIT paragraphs for recommended transmission oil.

# FRONT AXLE AND STEERING SYSTEM

## AXLE MAIN MEMBER

### Models G8-LT8-LT11

The axle main member (16 – Fig. B1) is mounted directly to front main frame and pivots on bolt (18). To remove front axle assembly, disconnect drag link (15) from steering arm. Using a suitable jack or hoist, raise front of tractor. Remove pivot bolt and roll front axle assembly from tractor.

### Models 730-733-736

To remove front axle main member, place pto control lever in disengaged position and remove pto drive belt from groove of pto driven pulley shown in Fig. B3. Disconnect drag link from steering arm (14 – Fig. B2). Support front of tractor. Remove pto pulley retaining cap screw (S – Fig. B3) and axle pivot bolt and nut (N). Let pto pulley drop down on its spindle far enough for axle to be lowered and removed from tractor. Renew pivot bushing and bolt if excessive wear is indicated.

### Models G9-G10-G11-G12-G14-H14-H16-1053-1054-1225-1253-1254-1256-1257-1556

The axle main member (11 – Fig. B4) is mounted in axle support (7) and pivots on pin (6). To remove front axle assembly, first unbolt and remove pto support from front axle support (7). Disconnect drag link ball joint end (12) from steering spindle arm (10). Support front of tractor using a jack or hoist, and after removing roll pin, drive pivot pin (6) forward out of axle support. Raise front of tractor and roll front axle assembly from under tractor.

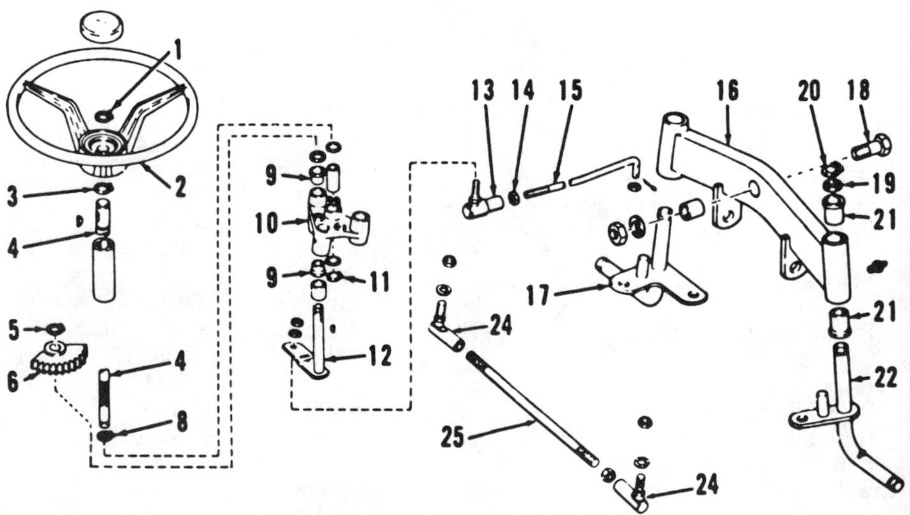


*Fig. B1 – Exploded view of front axle and steering assembly used on Model G8. Models LT8 and LT11 are similar.*

1. Snap ring
2. Steering wheel
3. Snap ring
4. Shaft
5. Snap ring
6. Quadrant gear
8. Snap ring
9. Bushing
10. Steering support
11. Snap ring
12. Steering arm
13. Ball joint
14. Jam nut
15. Drag link
16. Axle main member
17. Steering spindle L.H.
18. Pivot bolt
19. Washer
20. Snap ring
21. Bushing
22. Steering spindle R.H.
24. Ball joint ends
25. Tie rod

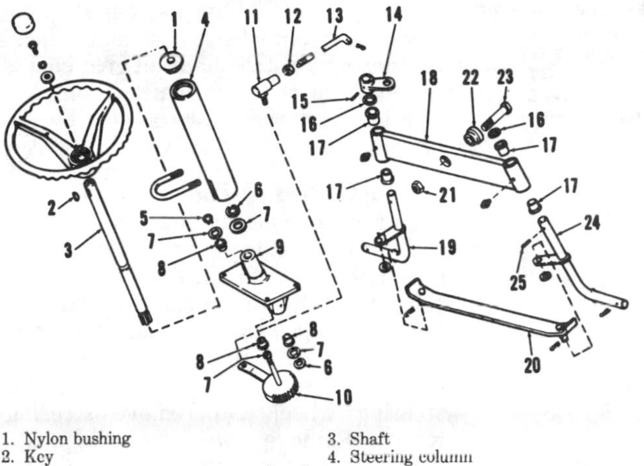

1. Nylon bushing
2. Key
3. Shaft
4. Steering column

***Fig. B2—Exploded view of front axle and steering gear assemblies used on Models 730, 733 and 736.***

5. Snap ring
6. Snap ring
7. Washer
8. Bushing
9. Steering support
10. Quadrant gear
11. Ball joint
12. Jam nut
13. Drag link
14. Steering arm
15. Pin
16. Washer
17. Bushing
18. Axle main member
19. Steering spindle L.H.
20. Tie rod
21. Nut
22. Bushing
23. Pivot bolt
24. Steering spindle R.H.
25. Pin

***Fig. B3—On Models 730, 733 and 736, unscrew cap screw (S) and allow pto pulley to drop down enough so axle can be removed after removing pivot bolt nut (N).***

## Models G11XL-G12XL-G14XL-G16XL-H11XL-H12XL-H14XL-H16XL

The front axle assembly (25–Fig. B5) is mounted in axle support (16) and pivots on bolt (21). To remove axle assembly, unbolt and remove pto idler pulley assembly from front axle support (16). Disconnect drag link (27) from steering arm (26). Support front of tractor with jack or hoist. Remove pivot bolt and axle support mounting bolt. Remove axle support and roll axle assembly away from tractor.

## Models 1455-1476-1477

To remove front axle assembly, first release and remove pto drive belts. Disconnect ball joint (12–Fig. B6) at forward end of drag link from right hand steering arm (16). Raise and support front of tractor under frame rails so pivot pin (17) can be removed, then raise front of tractor so axle assembly will clear and can be rolled forward from under frame. If heavy wear is evident, renew pivot pin (17) and its bushings (19).

## Model QS16

Axle main member (13–Fig. B7) pivots on pin (6) supported by axle bolster (5). To remove, disconnect forward end of drag link (15) from left steering arm (14). When tractor has been raised and blocked up safely, remove roll pin from pivot pin (6). Push pin out to rear, lower axle and roll forward from under tractor. Axle pivot parts are unbushed. Severe wear will call for renewal.

# TIE ROD

## Models 730-733-736

Removal of tie rod is self-evident after inspection of unit. Toe-in is not adjustable on these models. Tie rod ends should be inspected for wear and repaired as necessary to retain original wheel alignment.

## All Other Models

The adjustable tie rod can be removed after first removing nuts securing ball joint ends to steering arms. To adjust front wheel toe-in, loosen locknuts and turn ball joint ends in or out as required to obtain 1/8 to 3/8-inch (3-9 mm) toe-in.

# STEERING SPINDLES

## Models G8-LT8-LT11

To remove steering spindles, support tractor under axle main member and remove front wheels. Disconnect drag link from left steering spindle. Remove tie rod. Remove snap rings (20–Fig. B1) retaining steering spindles and remove steering spindles.

## Models 730-733-736

To remove steering spindles, first support tractor under axle main member and remove front wheels. Disconnect drag link at steering arm (14–Fig. B2), remove tie rod (20), drive out roll pin (15) and remove steering arm (14). Left hand steering spindle may now be removed. Drive out roll pin (25) and remove right hand steering spindle (24).

## Models G9-G10-G11-G12-G14-H14-H16-1053-1054-1225-1254-1256-1257-1556

To remove steering spindles (10 and 14–Fig. B4), block up under axle main member and remove front wheels. Disconnect drag link ball joint end from

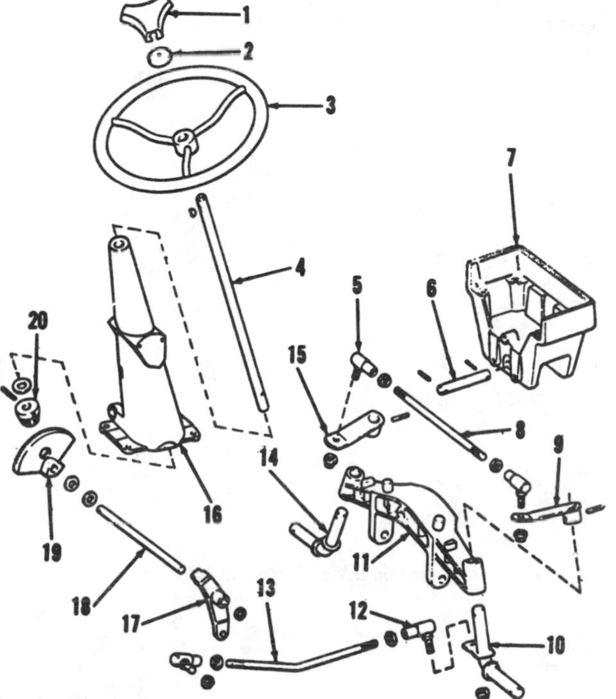

***Fig. B4—Exploded view of typical front axle and steering system used on Models G9, G10, G11, G12, G14, H14, H16, 1053, 1054, 1225, 1253, 1254, 1256, 1257 and 1556.***

1. Cover
2. Washer
3. Steering wheel
4. Steering shaft
5. Tie rod end
6. Pivot pin
7. Axle support
8. Tie rod
9. Steering arm R.H.
10. Steering spindle R.H.
11. Axle main member
12. Drag link end
13. Drag link
14. Steering spindle L.H.
15. Steering arm L.H.
16. Steering support
17. Quadrant arm
18. Cross shaft
19. Quadrant gear
20. Pinion gear

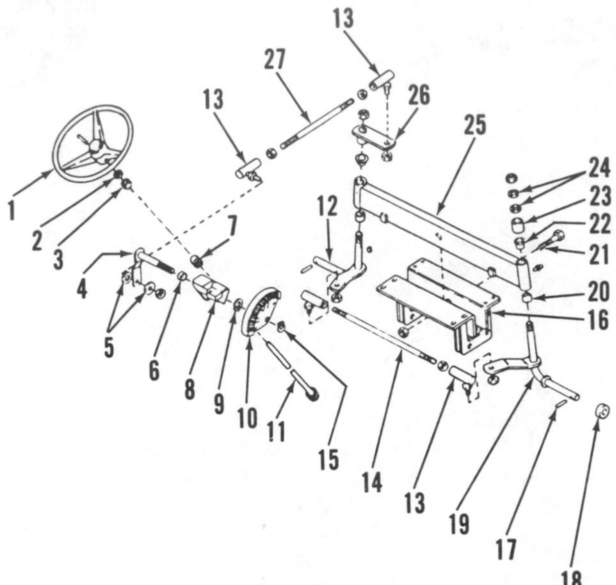


*Fig. B5—Exploded view of front axle and steering system used on Models G11XL, G12XL, G14XL, G16XL, H11XL, H12XL, H14XL and H16XL.*

1. Steering wheel
2. Washer
3. Bearing
4. Steering arm
5. Spacers
6. Spacer
7. Flange bushing
8. Support bracket
9. Shim
10. Sector gear
11. Steering shaft assy.
12. Spindle L.H.
13. Ball joint ends
14. Tie rod
15. Snap ring
16. Axle support
17. Roll pin
18. Wheel bearing
19. Spindle R.H.
20. Bronze bearing
21. Pivot bolt
22. Flange bushing
23. Hub
24. Flat washers
25. Axle main member
26. Steering arm
27. Drag link

steering spindle arm. Drive out roll pins securing tie rod steering arms (9 and 15) to steering spindles. Bump spindles downward out of steering arms and axle main member.

## Models G11XL-G12XL-G14XL-G16XL-H11XL-H12XL-H14XL-H16XL

To remove steering spindles, support front axle assembly and remove front wheels. Disconnect drag link (27–Fig. B5) and remove tie rod (14). Remove locknut and spindle arm (26). Left hand spindle can now be removed. Remove locknut, flat washers, steering hub (23), and withdraw right hand spindle. Check flange bearings (22) and bronze bearings (20) for excessive wear and renew as necessary.

## Models 1455-1476-1477

To remove either steering spindle from these models, block up under front axle and remove wheel with bearings and seals from spindle. Disconnect tie rod (11–Fig. B6) and drag link (13). Remove clamp bolt from steering arm (14 or 16) and pull steering arm from spindle (24). Remove key and lower steering spindle out of axle end. Clean and inspect bearing parts (20 through 23) making necessary renewal as called for by wear or damage. Lubricate spindle bearings and wheel bearings with multi-purpose grease (Bolens 16020) during reassembly and recheck toe-in before returning to service.

## Model QS16

To remove steering spindles, raise and block under front axle for wheel removal. With this design, removal of drag link and tie rod from steering arms is optional. Steering spindle (9–Fig. B7) can be separated from steering arm (7) after backing out cap screw at top. Remove Woodruff key after lifting off steering arm and lower steering spindle from axle. Inspect, clean and lubricate all bearing parts. Renew parts as necessary.

# STEERING GEAR

## Models G8-LT8-LT11

To remove steering gear, disconnect drag link from steering arm (12–Fig. B1). Remove quadrant gear snap ring (5) and remove quadrant gear (6) and steering arm (12). Remove snap ring (1) or roll pin and lift off steering wheel. Remove snap rings (8 and 11) and withdraw steering shaft (4). Check steering support bushings (9) for wear and renew if necessary.

During reassembly, position steering wheel and front wheels in straight ahead position and install quadrant gear so it is centered on steering shaft pinion. Adjust left and right turn angles by adjusting ball joint end (13) on drag link.

## Models 730-733-736

To remove steering gear, first disconnect drag link from arm of quadrant gear (10–Fig. B2). Remove left engine side panel. Remove quadrant gear retaining snap ring (5) and withdraw quadrant gear (10) from underside of tractor. Unscrew cap screw retaining steering wheel and remove steering wheel. Remove two snap rings (6) holding steering shaft in support (9) and remove steering shaft (3). It may be necessary to remove or deflect drive belt for access to lower snap ring.

Check bushings for wear and renew if necessary. During reassembly, position steering wheel and front wheels in straight ahead position. Install quadrant gear (10) so it is centered on pinion of steering shaft. Drag link can be adjusted to provide equal left and right turn angles by adjusting drag link end (11).

## Models G9-G10-G11-G12-G14-H14-H16-1053-1054-1225-1254-1256-1257-1556

The steering gear used is a pinion and quadrant gear type. To remove steering gear, first disconnect rear drag link ball joint end from quadrant arm (17–Fig. B4). Remove foot rest from left side of tractor and remove pins from cross shaft (18). Using a long thin punch, drive cross shaft towards left side of tractor and remove steering arm and quadrant gear (19). Drive roll pin from pinion gear (20) and withdraw steering shaft (4) from steering support (16).

When reassembling, minor wear in

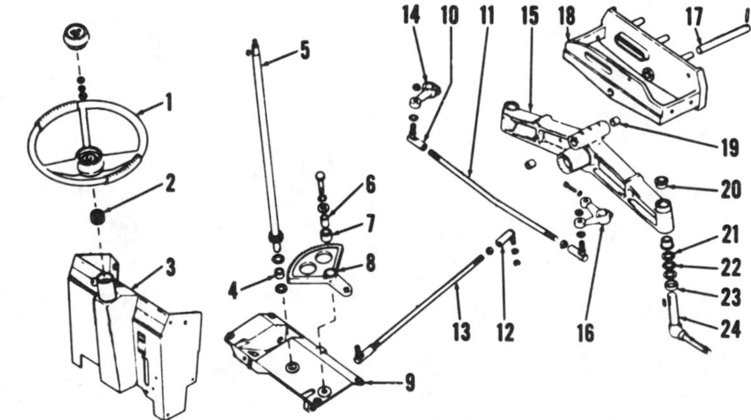


*Fig. B6—Exploded view of front axle and steering system used on Models 1455, 1476 and 1477.*

1. Steering wheel
2. Bearing
3. Steering column
4. Bushing
5. Steering shaft
6. Spacer
7. Bushing
8. Quadrant gear
9. Steering support
10. Tie rod end
11. Tie rod
12. Drag link end
13. Drag link
14. Steering arm L.H.
15. Axle main member
16. Steering arm R.H.
17. Pivot pin
18. Axle support
19. Pivot bushing
20. Flange bearing
21. Thrust race
22. Thrust bearing
23. Dust seal
24. Steering spindle

teeth of tapered pinion and gear sector can be compensated for by use of more or thicker spacer washers. Do not mesh too tight; just eliminate looseness.

When reinstalling steering gear, place front wheels in straight ahead position and then center quadrant gear on pinion. The drag link (13) can be lengthened or shortened as required so front wheels will have equal angle for left and right turns.

### Models G11XL-G12XL-G14XL-G16XL-H11XL-H12XL-H14XL-H16XL

To remove steering gear, disconnect drag link from steering arm (4–Fig. B5). Remove snap ring (15) from steering arm (4). Keep track of all shims and their locations during disassembly. Remove steering arm shaft, shims and quadrant gear. Remove roll pin from steering wheel and withdraw steering shaft from bottom side of tractor. It may be necessary to tap steering shaft down until flange bushing is pushed out of steering support (8).

Check bushings and gears for wear and renew as necessary. Reassemble steering gear by reversing disassembly procedure. If pinion and quadrant gears do not engage fully, adjust shims between quadrant gear and steering support. Adjust drag link as required to have equal turning angle on right or left turns.

### Models 1455-1476-1477

To remove steering gear, disconnect rear ball joint of drag link (13–Fig. B6) from lever portion of quadrant gear (8). Remove logo plate from center of steering wheel followed by retaining nut and washers so steering wheel can be pulled off steering shaft (5). Take care not to lose Woodruff key from tapered portion of shaft. Remove cotter key from lower end of steering shaft (5) below support plate (9) so shaft can be lifted up to disengage its pinion from quadrant (8) and clear of support plate. Tip shaft and column so shaft can be lowered out of tube down past rear edge of support plate (9) and out from under tractor. Take care not to damage self-aligning bearing (2) and protect bronze bushing (4) from dirt. Back out pivot bolt and remove quadrant gear (8).

Thoroughly clean and inspect gears and bushings for wear and damage. All parts are serviced for individual renewal as needed.

When reinstalling, set steering wheel and tractor front wheels in straight ahead position and reinstall quadrant gear (8) properly centered on steering pinion of shaft (5). Engine oil is specified as correct lubricant for steering shaft, bushings and drag link ends.

Steering radius stops which limit right and left movement of quadrant gear are fitted in right side frame rail. Be sure adjusters (square-head set screws) are set to limit turning radius to prevent wheel interference with under-tractor attachments and locknuts are secure.

When drag link is being reconnected to lever arm portion of quadrant gear, its overall length should be measured. On Models 1455, 1476 and 1477, this length should be 24-9/16 inches (623.9 mm). Adjust as needed.

### Model QS16

To remove steering gear assembly, first remove logo cap from hub of steering wheel, back off retainer nut and remove wheel. Remove Woodruff key from tapered portion of upper shaft assembly (4–Fig. B7). Disconnect ball joint (23) from pitman arm (22) to separate drag link. Remove nut from inboard end of sector shaft (16) and bump shaft out of steering sector (17). Then, while holding sector in one hand, grasp pitman arm (22) and pull shaft clear of steering support casting (20) with pitman arm attached. If shaft (16) is to be renewed, remove pitman arm (22).

To remove upper and lower steering shafts (4 and 18), remove retaining rings (1) from each shaft so shafts can be separated at swivel coupling at lower end of upper shaft. Take care not to lose Woodruff key. Remove lower shaft (18) with pinion from under tractor.

Clean and inspect shaft bearings (3 and 19). Renew as necessary. If bushings (21) require renewal, unbolt and remove steering support (20) for set up in a shop press to drive old bushings out and press new ones into bushing bores.

Lubricate during reassembly. Set front wheels straight ahead and center quadrant gear on pinion. Then, adjust length of drag link by its threaded ends to equalize turning radius each way from centered position of steering wheel.

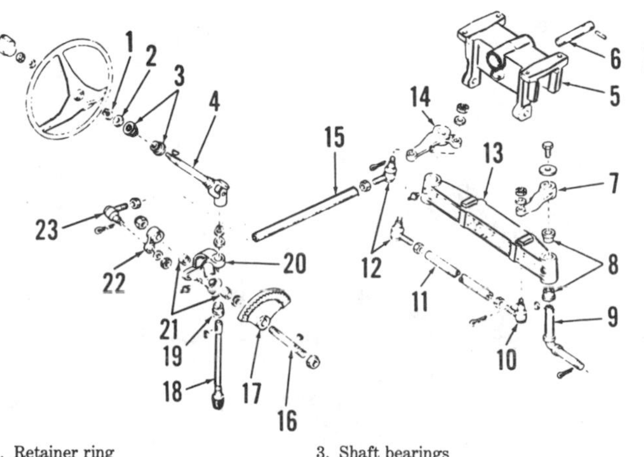

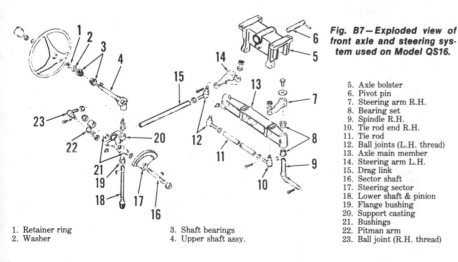

*Fig. B7—Exploded view of front axle and steering system used on Model QS16.*

1. Retainer ring
2. Washer
3. Shaft bearings
4. Upper shaft assy.
5. Axle bolster
6. Pivot pin
7. Steering arm R.H.
8. Bearing set
9. Spindle R.H.
10. Tie rod end R.H.
11. Tie rod
12. Ball joints (L.H. thread)
13. Axle main member
14. Steering arm L.H.
15. Drag link
16. Sector shaft
17. Steering sector
18. Lower shaft & pinion
19. Flange bushing
20. Support casting
21. Bushings
22. Pitman arm
23. Ball joint (R.H. thread)

# ENGINE

## REMOVE AND REINSTALL

### Models G8-LT8-LT11

To remove engine, detach drive belts from engine pulley and remove pulley from engine crankshaft. Tilt engine hood forward and disconnect battery cables, starter and alternator or starter-generator wires, ignition wires, choke and throttle cables. Close fuel valve under fuel tank and disconnect fuel line. Unscrew engine mount bolts and lift engine from tractor.

### Models 730-733-736

Before removing engine, remove drive belts from engine drive pulley, then remove engine drive pulley. Unscrew retaining screws and remove hood. Disconnect battery cables and remove battery. Disconnect starter-generator wires, ignition wires, choke and throttle cables. Close fuel valve under fuel tank and disconnect fuel line. Unscrew engine mount bolts; move engine towards rear so engine clears fuel tank, then lift engine from tractor.

### Models G9-G10-G11-G12-G14-H14-H16-1053-1054-1225-1254-1256-1257-1556

To remove engine, raise hood and disconnect hood stop rod. Remove cap screws securing hood and grille hinge to tractor frame and lift off hood and grille assembly. Disconnect battery cables, wires from starter-generator, ignition wire and choke and throttle control cables. Release belt tension and remove drive belt or belts. Remove pto belt guide and with pto lever in neutral position, remove pto belt or belts. Unbolt engine, slide it forward and lift it from tractor frame.

To reinstall engine, reverse removal procedure.

### Models G11XL-G12XL-G14XL-G16XL-H11XL-H12XL-H14XL-H16XL

To remove engine, remove hood and side panels. Disconnect battery cables, starter, alternator and ignition wires. Disconnect choke and throttle cables. Close fuel tank shut-off valve and disconnect fuel line at filter. Remove drive shaft bolts at engine. Disconnect pto clutch wire. Scribe a line on front engine supports along frame for ease in reinstalling engine. Remove engine mount bolts and lift engine out.

Reinstall engine by reversing removal procedure. Align scribed lines (made during removal) on engine front supports with frame, then install front mounting bolts. Insert proper engine mount spacers to obtain specified clearance between frame and bottom surface of engine support. On Models G11XL and H11XL, clearance should be 3/16 to ¼-inch (5-6 mm), and on all other models 7/16 to ½-inch (11-13 mm).

**NOTE: Front and rear rubber engine mounts are not interchangeable. The rear mounts are softer than front mounts; press down on center of mounts to identify for correct installation.**

When reinstalling drive shaft, make sure drive hub on hydrostatic models is 5/16-inch (8 mm) from face of transmission. On gear drive models, hub on right angle gear box should be bottomed against end of shaft splines.

### Models 1455-1476-1477

To remove engine, proceed in this sequence: Disconnect battery cables. Remove bolt and set screw at forward end of drive shaft. Disconnect headlight wiring then unlatch and unbolt hood at hinge and stop arm for removal. Close shut off valve under fuel tank and disconnect fuel line. Remove support bolts from gas tank-battery platform and lift out as an assembly. Identify and remove carburetor control cables and interfering wiring from engine, then unbolt engine mounts. Release and remove pto belts from engine pulley. For security, attach hoist to engine, then slip engine forward to disengage from drive shaft and lift engine out of frame. Reverse these steps to reinstall.

### Model QS16

To remove engine, open hood, loosen three screws at bottom of each side panel and release two quarter-turn fasteners at top of each panel for removal. Disconnect headlight wiring connector plugs and hood lanyard from muffler support and hood can be lifted off and set aside.

Disconnect battery cables and remove battery clamp so battery can be removed. Shut off fuel valve at tank and remove line at carburetor or at fuel filter. Disconnect control cables at carburetor. Release and remove pto drive belts. Remove cable from starter motor, uncouple leads to regulator/rectifier and disconnect orange primary lead at ignition coil. Separate rear of engine crankshaft from driveshaft by removing through-bolt and Woodruff key (when used). When bolts are removed from engine mounts, engine can be raised, shifted forward and lifted clear of engine compartment.

Reinstall engine by reversal of this order, taking care that battery connection is not made until just before replacing engine hood and grille assembly.

## OVERHAUL

### All Models

Engine make and model are listed at the beginning of this section. To overhaul engine components and accessories, refer to appropriate engine sections of this manual.

# DRIVE BELTS

## REMOVE AND REINSTALL

### Models G8-LT8-LT11

To remove drive belt (15–Fig. B8), move clutch idler pulley away from belt and remove belt from engine pulley. Slide belt off transmission pulley (16). Place transmission end of drive belt through gear shift lever slot in floor of tractor. Move belt over end of gear shift lever and pull belt back through floor and remove from tractor.

### Models G9-G10-G11-G12

To remove drive belt, depress clutch-brake pedal and slip belt from engine and drive shaft pulleys. When renewing drive belt, make certain idler pulley (5–Fig. B9) is in outside hole of idler control arm (4).

### Models G11XL-G12XL-G14XL-G16XL

To remove drive belt (B–Fig. B10), loosen belt guides. Depress clutch pedal, remove idler pulley and slip belt from transaxle and gear box pulleys. After installing new belt, adjust belt guides to clearances as follows: Idler pulley belt guide (G) ⅛-inch (3 mm), transaxle pulley (H) 3/32-inch (2 mm) and gear box pulley (F) 1/16-inch (1.5 mm) clearance.

### Models 730-733-736

To remove drive belts, unbolt idler support (29–Fig. B11), move idler pulleys away from drive belts and slide drive belts off pulleys. When installing new drive belt, be sure idler pulley is working against drive belt.

### Models 853-1053-1054-1253-1254-G14

To remove drive belts, refer to Fig. B12 or B13 and remove belt guide on models so equipped. On Model 853, place speed range lever between high and low range. This will position belt tightener between high and low range belts and remove belt tension. On all other models, tie idler pulley away from belts with wire. Unscrew nut from front end of drive shaft and remove washers. Remove four cap screws holding drive shaft support to mounting plate and remove support by sliding forward. Drive belts may now be removed. Install drive belts by reversing removal procedure.

### Models 1225-1256-1257-1556-H14-H16

To remove drive belts, pull idler pulley away from drive belts. Loosen belt guide retaining bolts and move belt guides

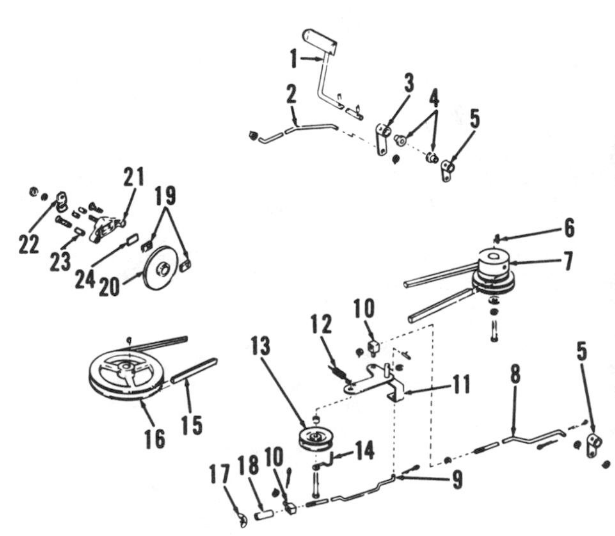


***Fig. B8—Exploded view of clutch-brake assembly used on Models G8, LT8 and LT11.***

1. Clutch-brake pedal
2. Brake lock assy.
3. Brake lock arm
4. Nylon bushing
5. Brake arm
6. Key
7. Crankshaft pulley
8. Clutch rod
9. Brake rod
10. Pivot blocks
11. Idler arm assy.
12. Spring
13. Idler pulley
14. Belt guard
15. Drive belt
16. Transaxle pulley
17. Wing nut
18. Spacer
19. Brake pads
20. Brake disc
21. Brake pad holder
22. Lever
23. Spacer
24. Plate

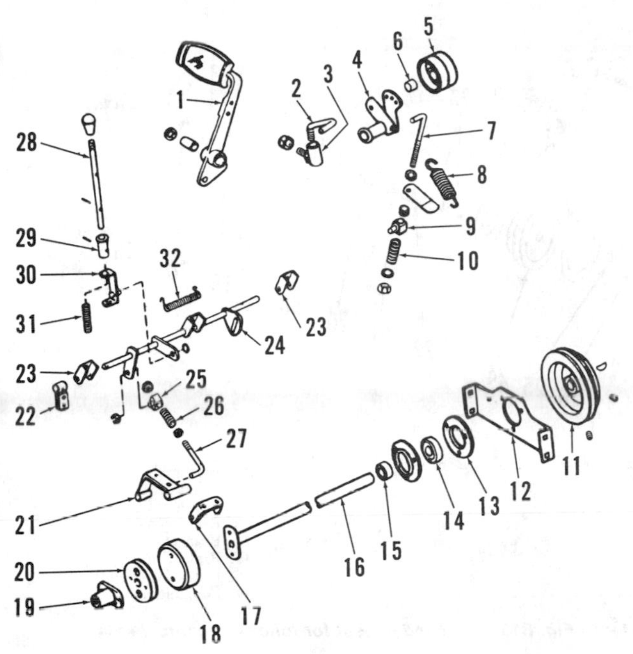

*Fig. B9 — Exploded view of clutch-brake system used on Models G9, G10, G11 and G12.*

1. Clutch-brake pedal
2. Clutch rod
3. Ball joint end
4. Idler arm
5. Clutch idler pulley
6. Spacer
7. Brake rod
8. Clutch spring
9. Pivot block
10. Spring
11. Drive shaft pulley
12. Bearing support
13. Bearing retainer
14. Bearing
15. Collar
16. Drive shaft
17. Bracket
18. Brake drum
19. Coupling flange
20. Coupling
21. Brake shoe (drive shaft)
22. Brake shoe (transmission)
23. Brackets
24. Brake shaft
25. Pivot block
26. Spring
27. Brake rod
28. Park brake lever
29. Brake lock
30. Pivot
31. Spring
32. Torsion spring

away from drive belts. Slip drive belts off driven pulley then off drive pulley and remove through bottom of tractor.

# CLUTCH

## ADJUSTMENT

### Models G9-G10-G11-G12

The clutch on these models is belt idler type. The only adjustment consists of changing belt tension. To increase belt tension, move idler pulley (5 – Fig. B9) from outside hole to center hole in idler control arm (4).

### Models 853-1053-1054-1253-1254-G14

A double-plate, disc type clutch is used on these models. Refer to Fig. B12 or B13. A pedal on left side of tractor operates clutch and also activates service brake.

Clutch should be disengaged when clutch pedal is approximately 2/3 depressed. If not, adjust nuts (A and B – Fig. B14) on clutch rod (5) until clutch disengages properly and pedal has approximately ½-inch (13 mm) free travel.

The clutch brake plate (3 – Fig. B14), used on all models except Model 853, mechanically stops rotation of drive shaft when clutch is disengaged to prevent gear clash when shifting gears. With clutch in fully engaged position, there should be 3/32-inch (2.4 mm) clearance "C" between rear clutch flange (2) and brake plate friction surface. To adjust, move brackets (27 – Fig. B13) forward or back in slotted holes provided in brackets. Lubricate splined area of drive shaft to insure free movement of rear clutch flange.

On Model 853, brake drum (45 – Fig. B12) and brake shoe (43) are used to stop drive shaft when clutch is disengaged. Refer to BRAKES section for adjustment procedure.

**NOTE: After clutch adjustment is completed, be sure switch actuator (14 – Fig. B13) engages interlock switch (11) correctly. Switch should begin to actuate with pedal at halfway point. Adjust by repositioning bracket (12) in its mounting slots.**

### All Other Models (So Equipped)

On models having a spring loaded clutch idler pulley, adjustment is not necessary. Renew drive belt or idler spring when idler pulley does not take up drive belt slack and slippage occurs.

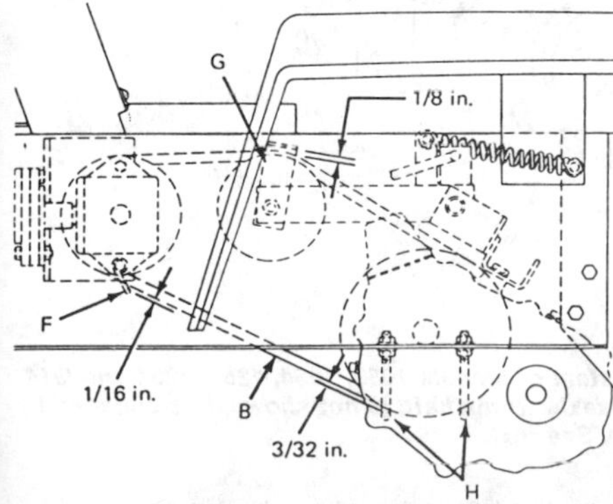


*Fig. B10 — Models G11XL, G12XL, G14XL and G16XL use a spring loaded idler pulley for main drive clutch. Adjust belt guides to clearances shown.*

B. Drive belt
F. Gear box belt guide
G. Idler pulley belt guide
H. Transaxle belt guides

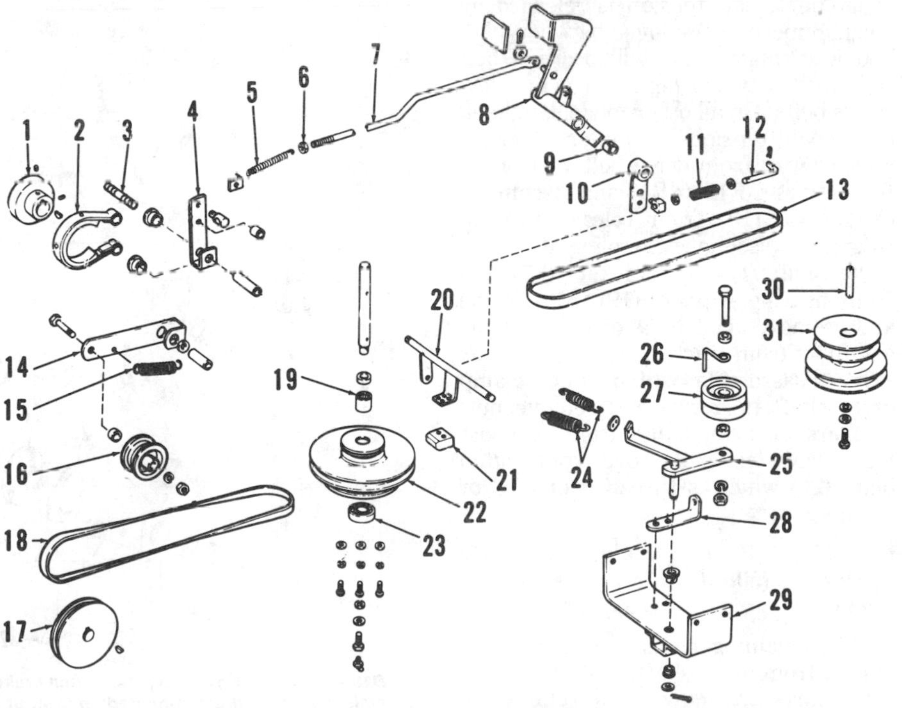

*Fig. B11 — Exploded view of clutch-brake system used on Models 730 and 733. Model 736 uses same clutch system. Refer to text for 736 brake system.*

1. Brake drum
2. Brake band
3. Stud
4. Brake arm
5. Spring
6. Adjusting nut
7. Brake rod
8. Clutch-brake pedal
9. Bushing
10. Lever
11. Spring
12. Brake rod
13. Drive belt
14. Lever
15. Spring
16. Idler pulley
17. Transmission pulley
18. Drive belt
19. Bearing
20. Shaft
21. Pulley brake pad
22. Pulley
23. Bearings
24. Springs
25. Clutch arm
26. Belt guide
27. Clutch pulley
28. Spring mount
29. Mount plate
30. Key
31. Engine pulley

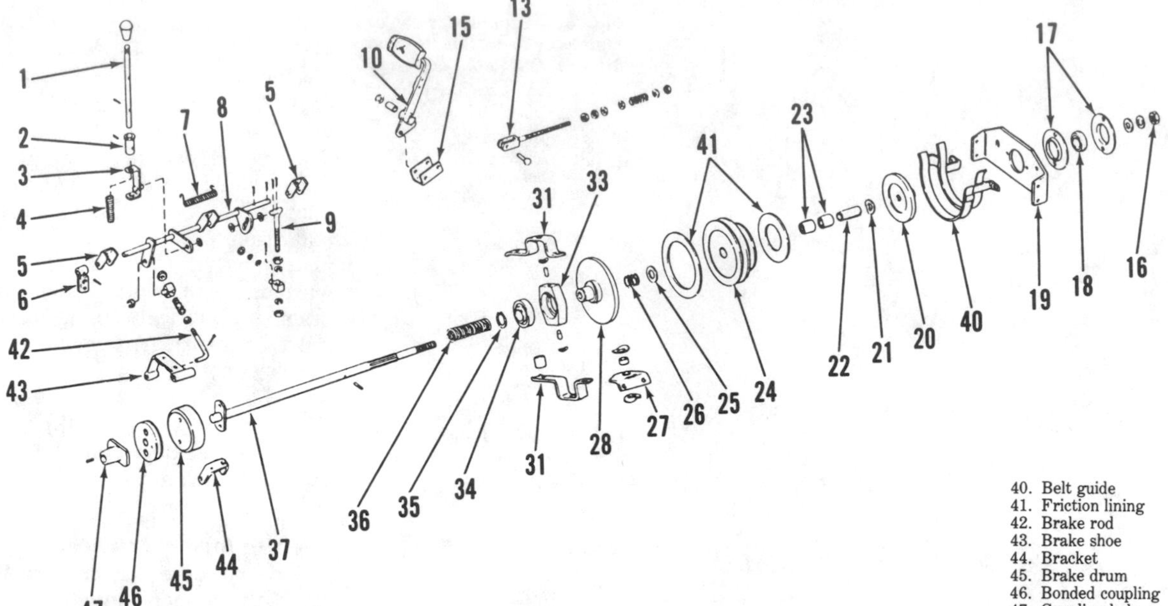

40. Belt guide
41. Friction lining
42. Brake rod
43. Brake shoe
44. Bracket
45. Brake drum
46. Bonded coupling
47. Coupling hub

*Fig. B12—Exploded view of clutch-brake system used on Model 853. Refer to Fig. B13 for legend except for following components.*

## R&R AND OVERHAUL

### Models 853-1053-1054-1253-1254-G14

To remove clutch assembly, first release drive belt tension. On models equipped with 2-speed drive belt arrangement, belt tension is released by placing speed range lever between high and low range. This will position belt tightener between high range and low range belts. On all other models, unhook drive belt tension spring or tie idler pulley away from drive belt with wire. Refer to Fig. B12 or B13 and disconnect clutch rod (13) from release bearing yoke (31). Disconnect coupling at rear of drive shaft. Unbolt brackets (27) and front bearing support (19) from frame and remove clutch and drive shaft assembly from tractor.

To disassemble clutch unit, clamp drive shaft in a vise and remove nut, washers, bearing and front support from drive shaft. Remove front clutch plate (20) which is threaded on end of drive shaft.

**CAUTION: Remove this plate carefully as all parts following it are under tension from clutch pressure spring (36).**

The remaining parts can now be removed from drive shaft.

All parts are individually renewable. To renew drive pulley clutch facings, first remove old friction lining and clean each side of pulley (24). Cement new friction linings to pulley and place front and rear clutch flanges (20 and 28) on top of friction linings. Firmly clamp together pulley and flange assembly and place in oven, preheated to 400°F (200°C), for a minimum of 15 minutes.

Reassembly procedure is reverse of disassembly. Reinstall assembly on tractor and, on Model 853, adjust drive belt tension by moving bearing support (19) up or down on mounting bracket until desired tension is obtained. Drive belt tension is correct when belt tightener pulley moves 2 inches (50 mm) from disengaged position to full engaged position. Other models require no drive belt adjustment since a spring loaded belt tightener is used. Adjust clutch as previously outlined.

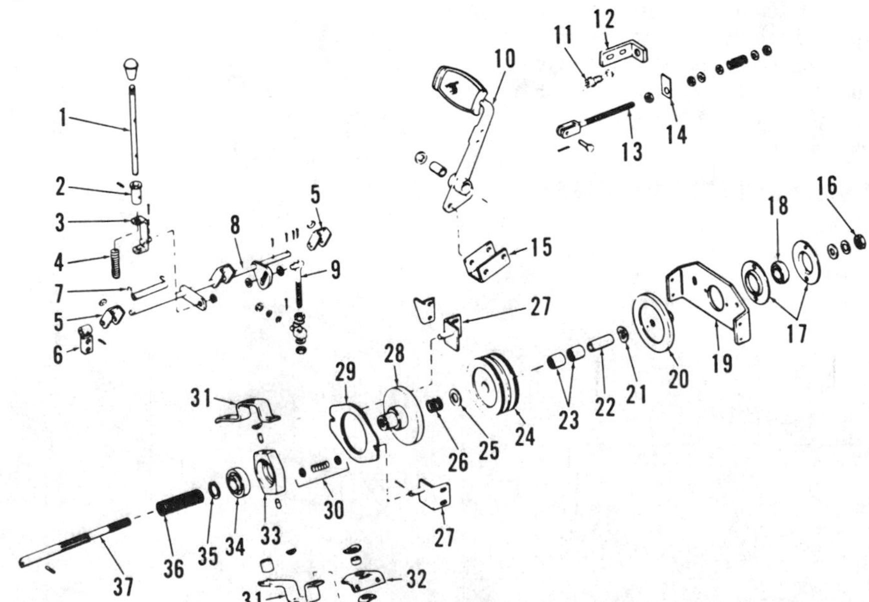

*Fig. B13—Exploded view of typical clutch-brake system of Models 1053, 1054, 1253, 1254 and G14. Transmission brake drum, mounted on front of transaxle wormshaft, is not shown. It is engaged by brake shoe (6). See text.*

1. Parking brake lever
2. Brake lock
3. Lever pivot
4. Spring
5. Bracket (2)
6. Brake shoe
7. Torsion spring
8. Brake shaft
9. Brake rod
10. Clutch-brake pedal
11. Interlock switch
12. Switch bracket
13. Clutch rod
14. Switch actuator
15. Link
16. Locking nut
17. Bearing flanges
18. Bearing
19. Bearing support
20. Clutch flange-front
21. Bowed washer
22. Spacer
23. Needle bearings (2)
24. Sheave & facing
25. Thrust race
26. Spring
27. Bracket assy. (2)
28. Clutch flange (rear)
29. Brake plate
30. Spring/washer set (2)
31. Bearing yoke halves
32. Bracket
33. Bearing retainer
34. Release bearing
35. Retainer
36. Spring
37. Drive shaft

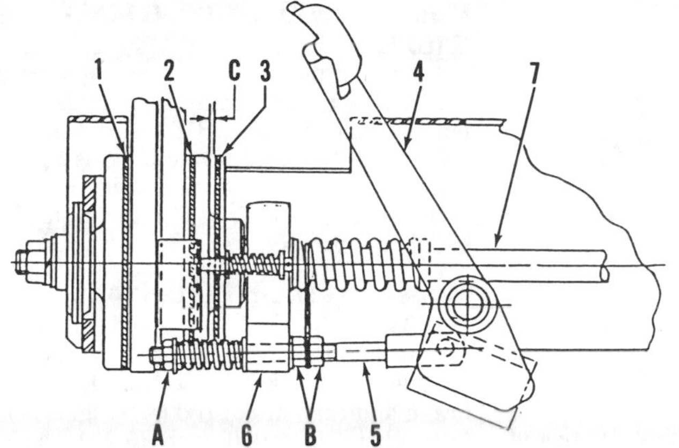


*Fig. B14—View of double plate, disc type clutch used on Models 1053, 1054, 1253, 1254 and G14. Model 853 is similar except brake plate (3) is not used. Refer to text for adjustment procedure.*

A. Adjusting nut
B. Adjusting nuts
C. 3/32-inch (2.4 mm) clearance
1. Front clutch flange
2. Rear clutch flange
3. Brake plate
4. Clutch-brake pedal
5. Clutch rod
6. Yoke
7. Drive shaft

# BRAKES

## ADJUSTMENT

### Models G8-LT8-LT11

A disc type brake is used on these models. To adjust brake, turn wing nut (17–Fig. B8) at end of brake control rod. Adjust brake so it is not effective before clutch is disengaged. If brake cannot be adjusted to give full braking action, renew brake pads.

### Models G9-G10-G11-G12

To adjust brakes, refer to Fig. B9 and depress clutch-brake pedal (1) until clutch is disengaged. Then, adjust nuts, moving pivot block (9) on brake rod (7), until brake shoe (22) is tight against brake drum on transaxle wormshaft. The brake on drive shaft can now be adjusted by moving pivot block (25) on brake rod (27) so brake shoe (21) will contact drive shaft brake drum (18) immediately after clutch is disengaged.

### Models 730-733

A band type brake is used on these models. To adjust brake, turn adjusting nut (6–Fig. B11) on brake rod (7) so brake band is tight on drum when clutch-brake pedal is fully depressed. Brake band should not drag on drum until clutch is disengaged by clutch-brake pedal.

### Model 736

Model 736 is equipped with a disc brake as shown in Fig. B15. To adjust brake, turn adjusting nut (5) so brake pads will be tight against disc when brake pedal is depressed. Be sure brake pads do not drag against disc when brake pedal is not applied.

### Model 853

To adjust main brake, located on transaxle wormshaft, refer to Fig. B12 and depress clutch-brake pedal until clutch is disengaged. Adjust nuts, moving pivot block on brake rod (9), until brake shoe (6) is tight against brake drum on transaxle wormshaft. The brake on drive shaft (37) can now be adjusted by moving pivot block on brake rod (42) until brake shoe (43) contacts brake drum (45) immediately after clutch is completely disengaged.

### Models 1053-1054-1253-1254-G14

To adjust drive shaft brake, loosen nuts and move brackets (27–Fig. B13) to obtain 3/32-inch (2 mm) gap between lining on brake plate (29) and rear clutch plate (28) with clutch engaged. Retighten nuts on brackets. Then adjust nuts, moving pivot block on brake rod (9), until brake shoe (6) contacts brake drum on transaxle immediately after clutch is completely disengaged. Brake must be fully applied when pedal (10) is depressed to within one inch of pedal stop.

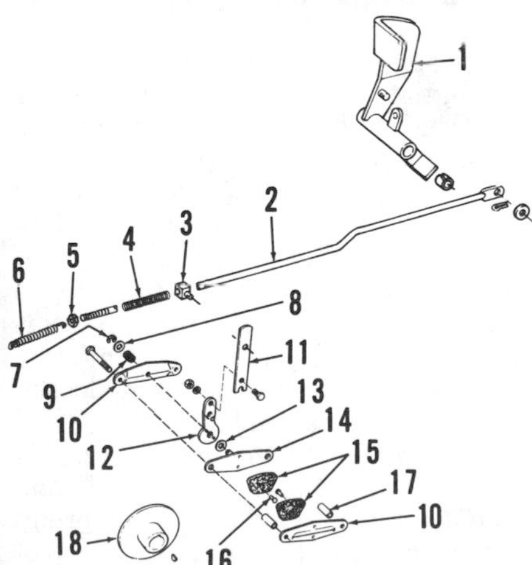


*Fig. B15—Exploded view of Model 736 brake system. Refer to Fig. B11 for clutch mechanism.*

1. Clutch-brake pedal
2. Brake rod
3. Pivot block
4. Spring
5. Adjusting nut
6. Spring
7. Snap ring
8. Washer
9. Spring
10. Carrier
11. Brake arm
12. Cam arm
13. Washer
14. Caliper
15. Brake pads
16. Rivet
17. Spacer
18. Brake disc

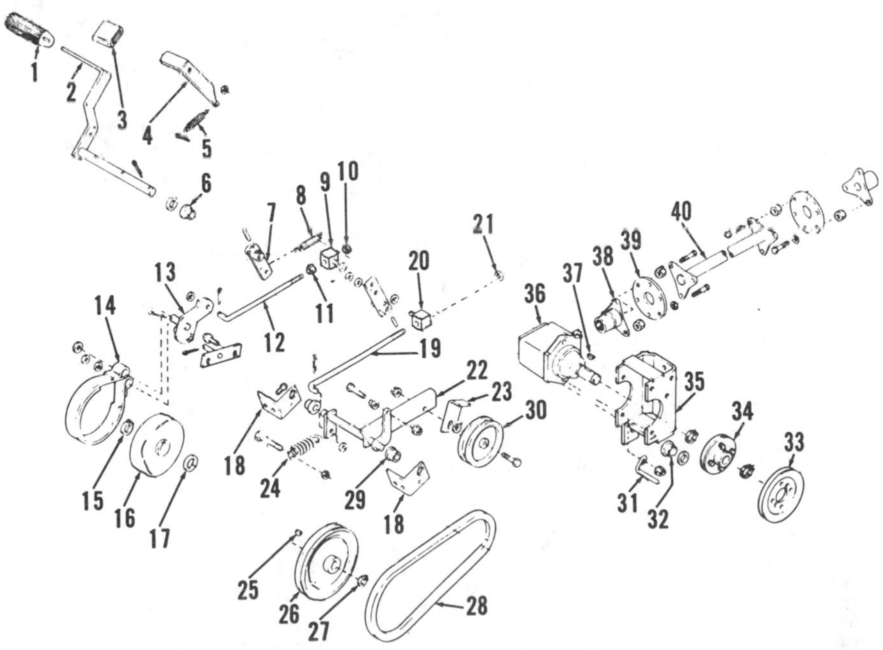

*Fig. B16—Exploded view of clutch and brake system used on Models G11XL, G12XL, G14XL and G16XL.*

1. Pedal pad
2. L.H. pedal assy.
3. Grip
4. Brake lock
5. Spring
6. Bushing
7. Control arm
8. Spring
9. Pivot block
10. Locknut
11. Adjusting nut
12. Brake rod
13. Brake arm assy.
14. Brake band
15. Snap ring
16. Brake drum
17. Thrust washer
18. Idler arm support
19. Clutch rod
20. Pivot block
21. Locknut
22. Idler shaft assy.
23. Belt guide
24. Spring
25. Key
26. Transaxle pulley
27. Snap ring
28. Drive belt
29. Bushing
30. Idler pulley
31. Belt guide
32. Bushing
33. Pulley
34. Hub assy.
35. Gear box support
36. Gear box assy.
37. Key
38. Hub
39. Coupling disc
40. Drive shaft

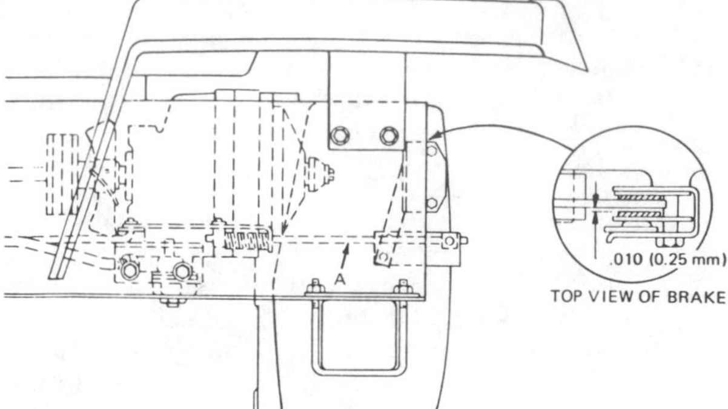


*Fig. B17—To adjust brake on Models H11XL, H12XL, H14XL and H16XL, turn brake rod (A) until there is 0.010 inch (0.254 mm) between brake disc and pad.*

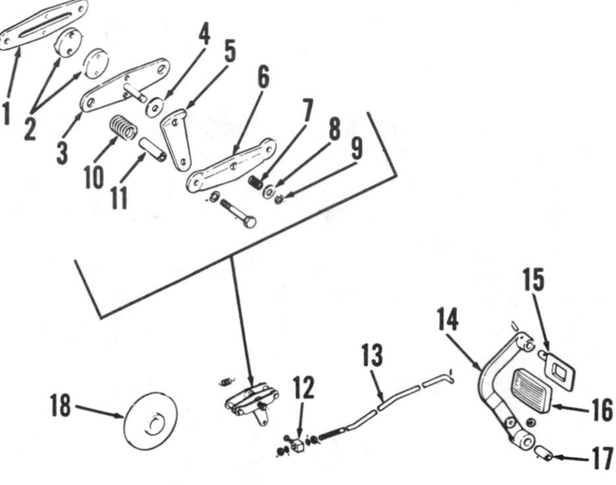

*Fig. B18—Exploded view of typical disc brake assembly used on Models 1256, 1257, 1455, 1476, 1477, 1556, H14 and H16. On some models, actuating linkage may be different from that shown.*

1. Carrier (inner)
2. Brake pads
3. Carrier (outer)
4. Washer
5. Cam
6. Cam actuator
7. Spring
8. Washer
9. Snap ring
10. Spring
11. Spacer
12. Pivot block
13. Brake rod
14. Brake arm
15. Brake pedal
16. Pad
17. Spacer
18. Brake disc

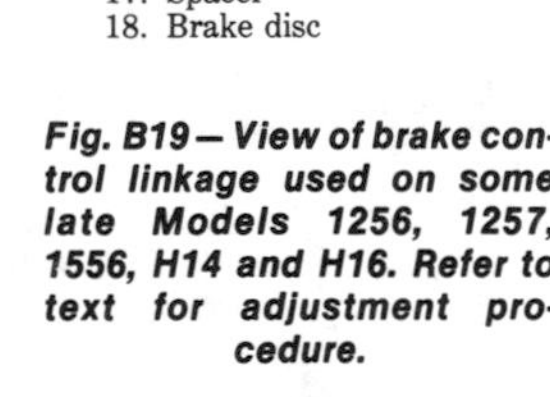

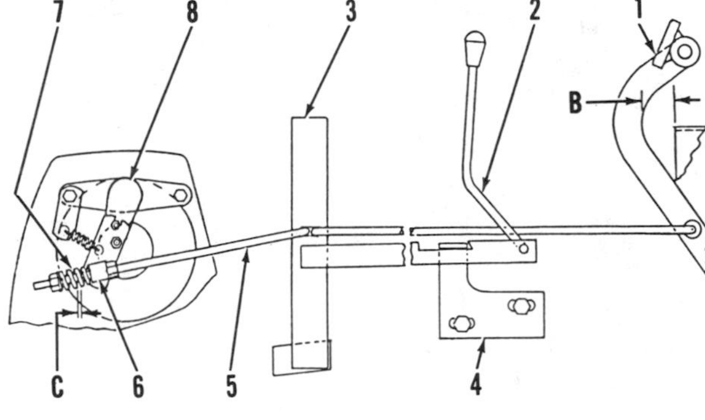

*Fig. B19—View of brake control linkage used on some late Models 1256, 1257, 1556, H14 and H16. Refer to text for adjustment procedure.*

B. 1/2-5/8-inch (13-16 mm)
C. 0.010 inch (0.254 mm) clearance
1. Brake pedal
2. Park brake lever
3. Brake arm
4. Park brake stop
5. Brake rod
6. Pivot block
7. Spring
8. Disc brake assy.

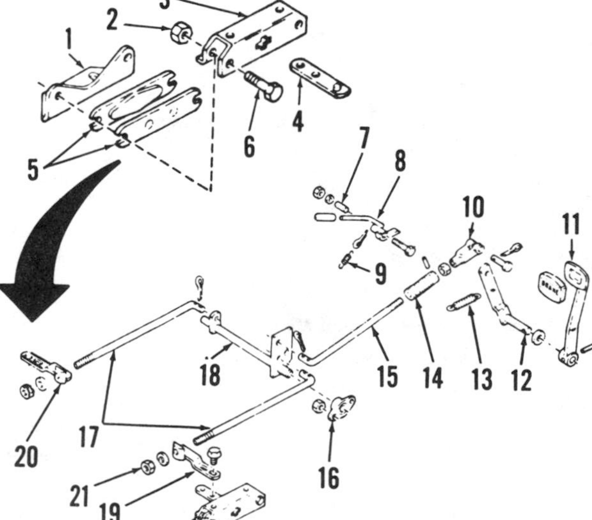

*Fig. B20—Exploded view of brake system used on Model QS16.*

1. Brake support
2. Locknut
3. Bracket
4. Lever
5. Pad plates
6. Bolt
7. Spacer
8. Latch
9. Extension spring
10. Clevis
11. Pedal
12. Brake arm
13. Return spring
14. Ratchet
15. Adjusting rod
16. Flange bearing
17. Brake rods (2)
18. Transfer shaft
19. Arm extension R.H.
20. Arm extension L.H.
21. Locknut
22. Brake assy. R.H.

## Models G11XL-G12XL-G14XL-G16XL

A band type brake is used on these models. To adjust brake, turn adjusting nuts (10 and 11–Fig. B16) to reposition pivot block (9) until brake band is tight on drum when pedal is depressed. Brake band should not drag on drum until pedal is depressed.

## Models H11XL-H12XL-H14XL-H16XL

A disc type brake is used on these models. To adjust brake, release parking brake and turn brake rod (A–Fig. B17) until there is 0.010 inch (0.254 mm) clearance between brake disc and pad. When brake pedal is fully released, brake disc must turn freely.

## Models 1256-1257-1455-1476-1477-1556-H14-H16

These hydrostatic drive models are equipped with a mechanically actuated caliper disc brake with its single disc fixed to input pinion shaft of tractor's reduction gear and differential unit. See Fig. B18. Some minor differences in linkages occur among models, but service is identical. Actual function of disc brake is to serve as a parking brake or when towing or pushing tractor in free-wheeling. Dynamic braking of hydrostatic transmission is service brake for these models.

Before adjusting disc brake it is advisable to inspect brake caliper assembly for damaged spacers, springs or cam levers and to renew badly worn pads or carriers. With brake rod disconnected, brake assembly is easily unbolted from axle housing for disassembly and necessary parts renewal. All parts are serviced.

Basic adjustment calls for setting linkage length to limit pedal travel. On early models, adjust operating length of brake control rod (13–Fig. B18) to obtain a maximum of 1½ inch (38 mm) free pedal travel before brake engagement. On late models, engage parking brake, then adjust parking brake stop (4–Fig. B19) to provide ½ to 5/8-inch (13-16 mm) clearance (B) between pedal and pedal stop. With pedal in "Park" position, loosen front adjusting nut on brake rod (5) and tighten rear nut to compress spring (7) until there is a 0.010 inch (0.254 mm) gap (C) between middle coils of spring. Turn front adjusting nut up to pivot block (6), then back off ½-turn.

## Model QS16

On Model QS16, brake discs are mounted on axle shafts just inboard of wheel hubs. See Fig. B20 for exploded view of parts and typical linkage.

Brake pad clearance is checked and adjusted as shown in Fig. B21. When

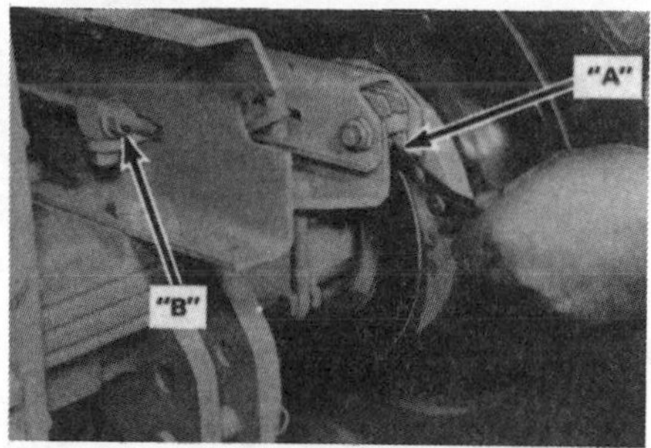


**Fig. B21 — When adjusting brake on Model QS16, clearance at "A" must never exceed 0.010 inch (0.254 mm). Adjust at locknut "B" with parking brake released.**

measurement between pad face and disc at point "A" exceeds 0.010 inch (0.254 mm) with brake pedal relaxed, adjust brake by turning nut "B" as required. If pads are in serviceable condition, acceptable clearance from disc surface may be from 0 to 0.010 inch (0-0.254 mm), **equal** on both axles. If brake pads are worn to excess, remove brake rod (17 – Fig. B20) from brake arm (19 or 20) and unbolt brake assembly from tractor axle housing for removal. With one pad retainer bolt (6) removed, pads (5) can be removed for renewal.

# PTO DRIVE

## Models 730-733-736-G8-LT8-LT11

Pto clutch uses a spring loaded idler. No adjustment is required. If belt slips, renew belt or idler spring. Bearings in pto drive pulley are renewable.

## Models G11XL-G12XL-G14XL-G16XL-H11XL-H12XL-H14XL-H16XL

**ADJUSTMENT.** All models are equipped with an electro-magnetic clutch mounted on engine crankshaft. Belt tension is controlled by adjustable idler pulleys. To adjust belt tension, proceed as follows:

On early models, turn adjuster knob (1 – Fig. B22) until indicator wire (A) is between adjustment lines on side of idler support. On late models, turn adjuster knob (1 – Fig. B23) until indicators (B) are even with one another. On all models, both idlers should be in line after adjustment is completed.

The only adjustment necessary on pto clutch is clutch-brake clearance (C – Fig. B24) which should be 0.010 to 0.015 (0.254-0.381 mm) with clutch disengaged. Check clearance at four slots (1) provided in brake flange (4) using a feeler gage. If necessary, adjust brake flange locknuts (5) to obtain specified clearance at each slot.

**TESTING.** If clutch does not engage, check the following: Check voltage at clutch lead which should be 10 volts minimum. Clutch coil resistance should be between 3.0 and 2.3 ohms. A reading outside these values indicates a faulty coil. Current draw should be 4.17 amps. Individual components of clutch are not serviced separately; renew as complete unit if necessary.

**REMOVE AND REINSTALL.** Disconnect battery ground cable, then remove hood, side panels and front frame cross plate. Slip belt off pulley. Disconnect electrical connector. Remove locknuts retaining brake flange (4 – Fig. B24) and withdraw flange and springs. Unscrew mounting cap screw from crankshaft and remove pulley and armature assembly (2) and rotor assembly (7). Unbolt and remove coil assembly (6).

Reinstall in reverse order of removal. On models equipped with Briggs and Stratton engines, be sure spacers (8 – Fig. B24) are installed at coil mounting cap screws and on crankshaft as shown. Tighten rotor retaining cap screw to 25 ft.-lbs. (34 N · m) torque. Adjust brake as previously outlined.

## Models QS16

**ADJUSTMENT.** To adjust pto actuating linkage and brake shoe proceed as follows: Loosen control cable bracket retaining screws located on left side of console, then move bracket down in slots to increase tension on belts. To adjust pto brake, loosen cap screws (4 – Fig. B25) and move brake shoe (3) in slots to obtain 0.012 inch (0.305 mm) clearance between brake shoe and rim of drive pulley.

**REMOVE AND REINSTALL.** To remove pto drive belts, first remove hood. Place pto control lever in "On" position and remove brake shoe pivot pin (2 – Fig. B25). Move control lever to "Off" position and disconnect springs (5 and 6). Slip belts off pulleys and reinstall new belts by reversing removal procedure. Adjust as previously outlined.

## Models 1455-1476-1477

**ADJUSTMENT.** To adjust pto control linkage, disconnect control rod (3 – Fig. B26) from pto lever (1). Adjust position of clevis yoke (4) on control rod until desired belt tension is obtained. With

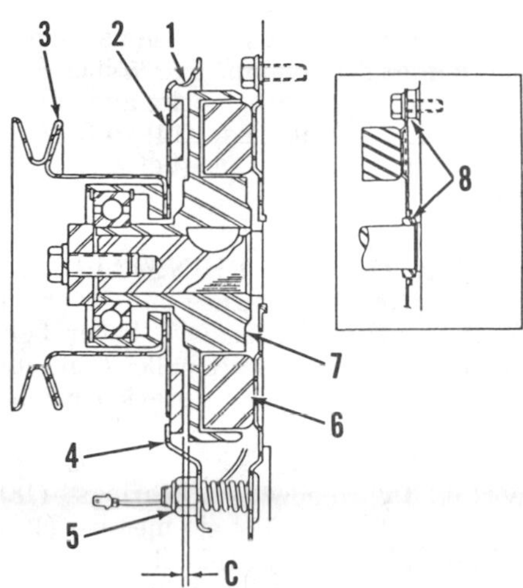


**Fig. B24 — An electro-magnetic pto clutch is used on all "XL" models. Spacers (8) are used only on tractors with a Briggs & Stratton engine. Four slots (1) are provided in brake flange (4) to check clutch-brake clearance (C). Refer to text.**

C. 0.010-0.015-inch (0.254-0.381 mm) clearance
1. Adjustment slot (4)
2. Armature/brake assy.
3. Drive pulley
4. Brake flange
5. Locknut (4)
6. Coil assy.
7. Rotor assy.
8. Spacers

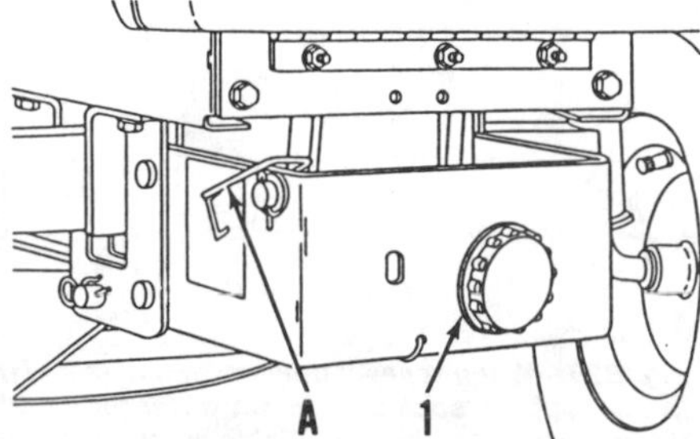


**Fig. B22 — To adjust pto belt tension on early "XL" models, turn adjuster knob (1) until indicator wire (A) is between adjustment lines on side of idler support.**

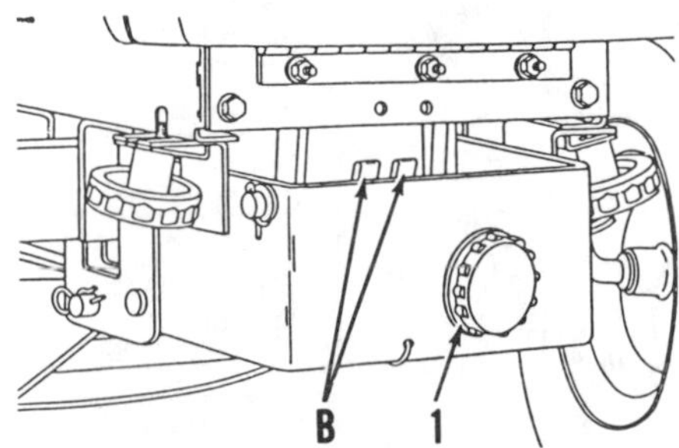


**Fig. B23 — On late "XL" models, turn adjuster knob (1) until indicators (B) are parallel to adjust pto belt to correct tension.**

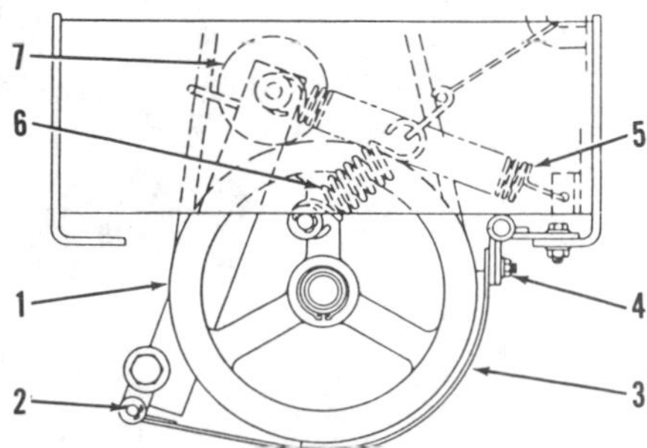


**Fig. B25 — View of pto driven pulley and idler used on Model QS16. Adjust brake shoe (3) to provide 0.012 inch (0.305 mm) clearance between shoe and rim of pulley.**

1. Pto pulley
2. Pin
3. Belt guide & brake shoe assy.
4. Nut (2)
5. Idler spring
6. Extension spring
7. Idler pulley

pto lever in "On" position, adjust upper belt guide (7) to obtain 1/8 to 1/4-inch (3-6 mm) clearance between belts and guide. Adjust lower belt guide (14) to 3/32 to 1/8-inch (2-3 mm) clearance between belts and guide.

**REMOVE AND REINSTALL.** To renew drive belts, place pto lever in "Off" position and remove lower belt guide. Slip old belts off pulleys and install new belts; adjust as previously outlined.

The pto shaft (17–Fig. B26) is supported by renewable bearings (18) located in front axle main member (19). The pto idler pulley (6) is also equipped with a renewable ball bearing.

### All Other Models

**ADJUSTMENT.** To adjust pto drive belts, loosen three cap screws securing pto support (7–Fig. B27) to front axle support (12). Raise or lower pto support to obtain desired belt tension. Check adjustment of lower belt guide; there should be 1/8-inch (3 mm) clearance between pulley and guide when pto is engaged.

On some late models, a pto brake is used. To adjust brake, place pto lever in disengaged position. Adjust lower nut (2–Fig. B28) until bowed washer (1) is fully compressed. Adjust upper nut (5) to obtain 1/16-inch (1.5 mm) gap ("G") as shown. Pulley must stop within five seconds; if not, readjust nut (2) to provide more braking pressure.

**REMOVE AND REINSTALL.** To renew pto belts, place belt idlers in disengaged position. Loosen or remove belt guides as necessary. Slip old belts off pulleys and install new belts. Adjust as previously outlined.

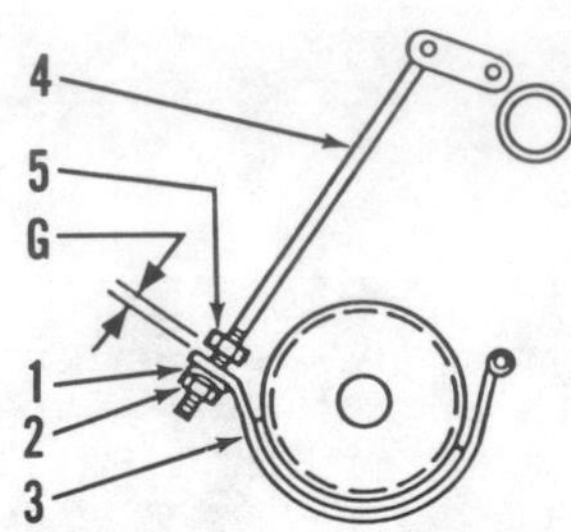


***Fig. B28—On models so equipped, adjust pto brake so pulley stops within five seconds. Refer to text.***

1. Bowed washer
2. Lower nut
3. Brake band
4. Control rod
5. Upper nut
G. 1/16-inch (1.5 mm) gap

The pto shaft (2–Fig. B29) is supported by renewable bearings (3 and 4) located in pto support housing (5). When reassembling pto shaft assembly, soak nylon washer-seal (1) in hot water, 140-160°F (60-70°C), for about five minutes to make seal pliable before installation. After reassembly is complete, lubricate through fitting in housing with multi-purpose grease.

# INTERLOCK SWITCHES

For safety reasons, many models of these tractors are furnished with interlock switches which are usually wired in series with ignition and starting circuits to insure that parking brakes are applied, tractor drive is in neutral and pto controls are in their disengaged position. All such safety switches are covered here because their adjustment for proper operation concerns simultaneous adjustment of other mechanical systems as brakes and transmission linkages.

**IMPORTANT NOTE: If tractor cannot be started, the occasional failure of one of these switches may be misjudged as the failure of another working circuit such as that of starter solenoid, ignition switch or**

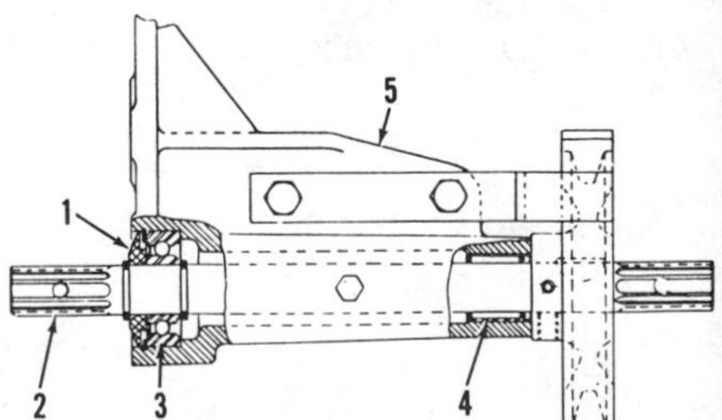


***Fig. B29—When renewing nylon washer-seal (1) in pto support, soak seal in hot water for about five minutes to make seal pliable before installation.***

1. Nylon washer-seal
2. Pto shaft
3. Ball bearing
4. Needle bearing
5. Pto support

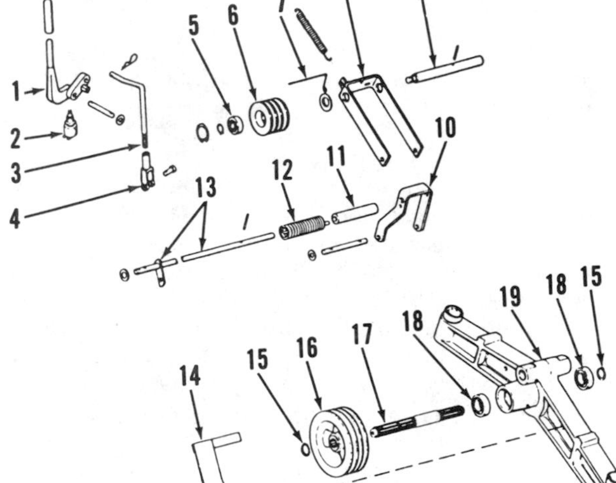

***Fig. B26—Exploded view of pto control linkage used on Models 1455, 1476 and 1477. Pto shaft (17) is supported by renewable bearings (18) located in front axle main member (19).***

1. Pto lever
2. Interlock switch
3. Control rod
4. Clevis yoke
5. Bearing
6. Idler pulley
7. Belt guide
8. Idler shaft bracket
9. Idler shaft
10. Control arm
11. Sleeve
12. Torsion spring
13. Control shaft
14. Belt guide
15. Snap ring
16. Pto pulley
17. Pto shaft
18. Bearings
19. Axle main member

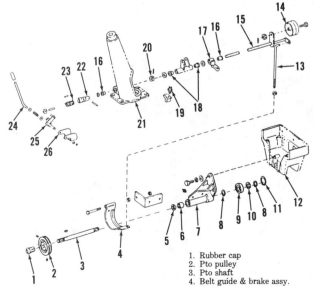

***Fig. B27—Exploded view of typical pto shaft assembly and control linkage used on Models G9, G10, G11, G12, G14, H14, 1054, 1225, 1253, 1254, 1256, 1257 and 1556. Some early models are not equipped with interlock switch (19) or brake band (4).***

1. Rubber cap
2. Pto pulley
3. Pto shaft
4. Belt guide & brake assy.
5. Seal
6. Needle bearing
7. Pto support
8. Snap rings
9. Ball bearing
10. Nylon washer-seal
11. Snap ring
12. Axle support
13. Control rod
14. Idler pulley
15. Control shaft
16. Nylon bearings
17. Shaft support
18. Flanged bushings
19. Interlock switch
20. Switch actuator cam
21. Steering support
22. Pivot arm
23. Spring
24. Control lever
25. Control pivot
26. Support bracket

**ignition coil. If all interlock switches are in correct adjustment, they can be tested very quickly for operating condition by use of an inexpensive self-powered test light. To make such a test, first disconnect battery ground cable to prevent accidental short circuit which might damage solid state ignition or rectifier-regulator as used on recent production engines. Then, isolate switch terminals at connector. With test light connected across interlock switch leads or terminals, manually operate switch and check for clean "ON" and "OFF" action. If continuity through closed switch is at all doubtful, it should be renewed.**

## ADJUSTMENT

### Models G8-LT8-LT11-736

These models have interlock switches operated by clutch-brake pedal and pto actuating linkage. Some late models also use an interlock switch located under operator's seat. Be sure switches are being engaged properly by movement of clutch-brake pedal, pto lever and seat. Check continuity if starting problems are encountered.

### Models G9-G10-G11-G12-G14-1054-1254

All models use two interlock switches, and some models are also equipped with a third switch actuated by sitting on operator's seat.

Pto switch is operated by a cam (2–Fig. B30) located on pto control shaft. With pto lever in "OFF" position, flat of cam should be in vertical position as shown and actuator spring (3) should just contact switch button. Check switch operation and adjust as necessary.

The clutch-brake pedal interlock switch (4–Fig. B31) should begin to close when pedal is halfway depressed. To adjust, move switch mounting bracket so actuator spring (3) contacts switch (4) properly.

On models equipped with seat interlock switch (2–Fig. B32), be sure switch is activated when seat is depressed.

### Models 1225-1256-1257-1556-H14-H16

These models use two interlock switches connected in series with start terminal of ignition key switch and switch terminal of starter solenoid.

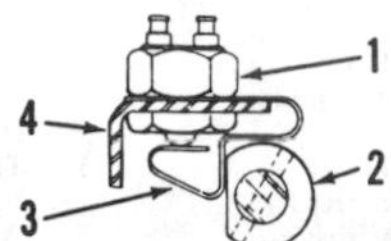


*Fig. B30—View of interlock switch, actuator spring and pto linkage cam used on Models G9, G10, G11, G12, G14, 1054 and 1254.*

1. Interlock switch
2. Pto cam
3. Actuator spring
4. Transmission cover

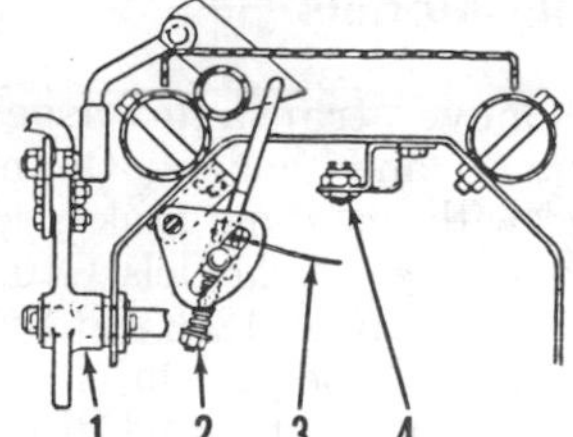


*Fig. B31—View of typical parking brake interlock switch used on Models G9, G10, G11, G12, G14, 1054 and 1254.*

1. Clutch-brake pedal
2. Brake rod
3. Actuating spring
4. Interlock switch

One switch is operated by a cam located on pto control shaft. To adjust switch, move pto lever to "OFF" position. Refer to Fig. B33 and set clearance of 1/64 to 3/64-inch (0.4-1.2 mm) between switch button and cam by loosening mounting cap screws (A) and shifting switch bracket (B) up or down in its slots.

The brake interlock switch (B–Fig. B34) is actuated by a cam located on park brake control rod on early models. To adjust, place park lock lever in "Park" position and loosen switch bracket cap screws (A). Move bracket (B) in or out to obtain 1/64 to 3/64-inch (0.4-1.2 mm) clearance between switch and cam. On some late models, switch is actuated by parking brake linkage as shown in Fig. B35. This switch requires no adjustment; however, it should be tested if doubtful.

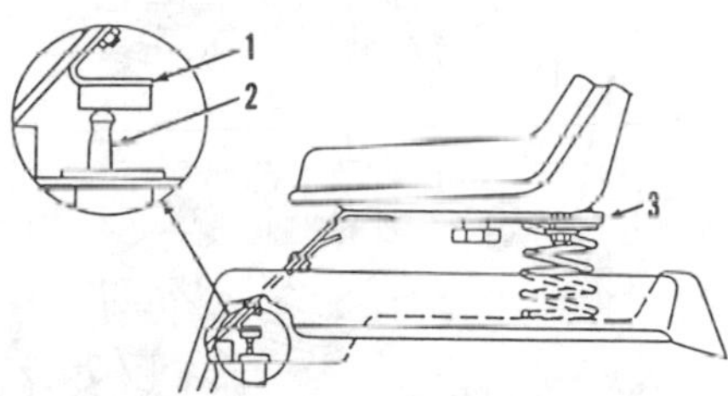


*Fig. B32—View of seat interlock switch location typical of all models so equipped.*

1. Actuating bracket
2. Interlock switch
3. Seat support

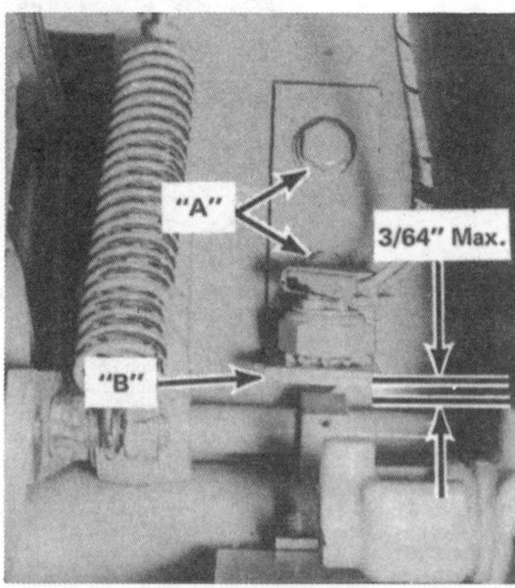


*Fig. B33—View of pto interlock switch used on Models 1225, 1256, 1257, 1556, H14 and H16. With pto OFF, loosen cap screws "A" and shift mounting bracket "B" to set required clearance from cam.*

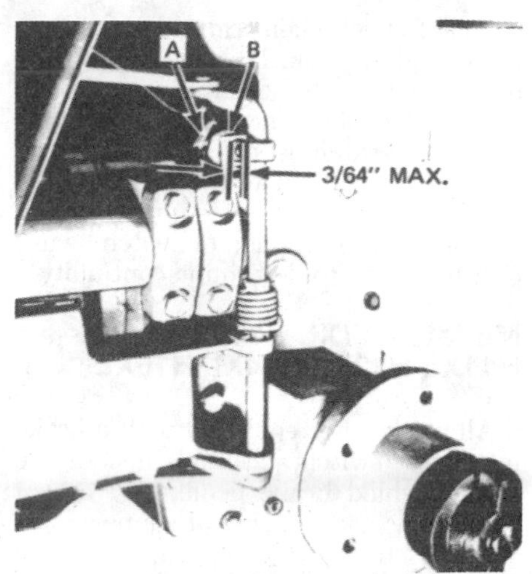


*Fig. B34—On some early model hydrostatic drive tractors, brake interlock switch is activated by a cam on park brake control rod.*

### Models 1455-1476-1477

On these tractors, two interlock switches are used. One is mounted on reduction gear housing cover behind hydrostatic unit and is engaged by the

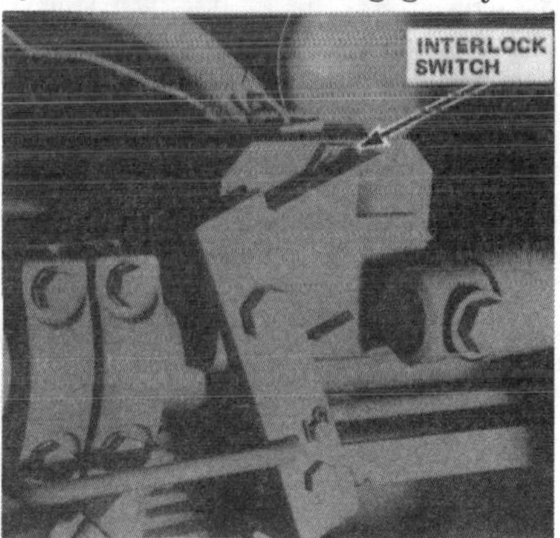


*Fig. B35—On some late model hydrostatic drive tractors, brake interlock switch is activated when brake pedal is depressed. Switch requires no adjustment.*

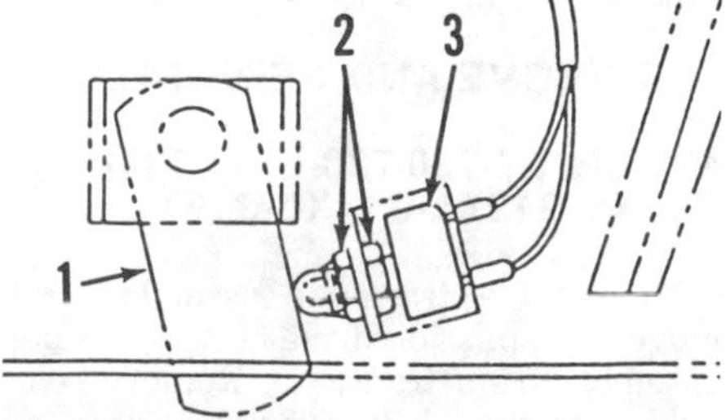


*Fig. B36—On "XL" models, brake interlock switch is actuated by brake control arm (1) when brake pedal is depressed.*

1. Brake control arm
2. Adjusting nuts
3. Interlock switch

oil relief spool when transmission is set in neutral or park. It is not adjustable, but should be checked for continuity if starting trouble is encountered. Another interlock switch is engaged by movement of pto control lever to "OFF" position. Be sure contact is made and if necessary, check action of switch by use of a test light to determine continuity.

### Models G11XL-G12XL-G14XL-H11XL-H12XL-H14XL-H16XL

All models are equipped with a brake interlock switch, located inside the frame behind brake pedal, and a seat switch, located under seat support.

When brake is applied, interlock switch button (3 – Fig. B36) should be depressed approximately 3/32 inch (2 mm). To adjust, loosen nuts (2) and move switch forward or back as required.

The seat switch should be activated when back edge of seat support is depressed 5/8 inch (16 mm). Loosen and move bracket (1 – Fig. B32) to obtain proper switch adjustment.

### Model QS16

Two microswitches, one on parking brake rod, another on pto control serve as safety interlocks on this model. They are spring-actuated and nonadjustable.

If brake interlock should be disconnected, be sure its spring clip is reinstalled at a mid-point on brake rod between ratchet and threaded portion.

Test for continuity if a tractor starting problem develops.

# TRANSAXLE

## LUBRICATION

### All Models

Refer to CONDENSED SPECIFICATIONS at the beginning of this section for transaxle lubricating fluid type and capacity for model being serviced.

## REMOVE AND REINSTALL

### Models G8-730-733-LT8-LT11-G11XL-G12XL-G14XL-G16XL

To remove transaxle assembly, remove transmission drive belt and brake assembly from transaxle. Remove rear axle retaining bolts, support rear of tractor and roll transaxle assembly from tractor.

To reinstall transaxle, reverse removal procedure.

### All Other Models

To remove transaxle assembly, remove seat and fenders. On models equipped with disc type brake, remove brake assembly. On Models G10, G12, G14, 853, 1053, 1054, 1253 and 1254, remove park brake lever. On all models, support rear of tractor and disconnect drive shaft. Unbolt retaining bolts and roll transaxle assembly from tractor.

To reinstall transaxle, reverse removal procedure.

## OVERHAUL

### All Models

Models G8, LT8 and LT11 are equipped with a Peerless 600 series transaxle. Models 730 and 733 are equipped with a



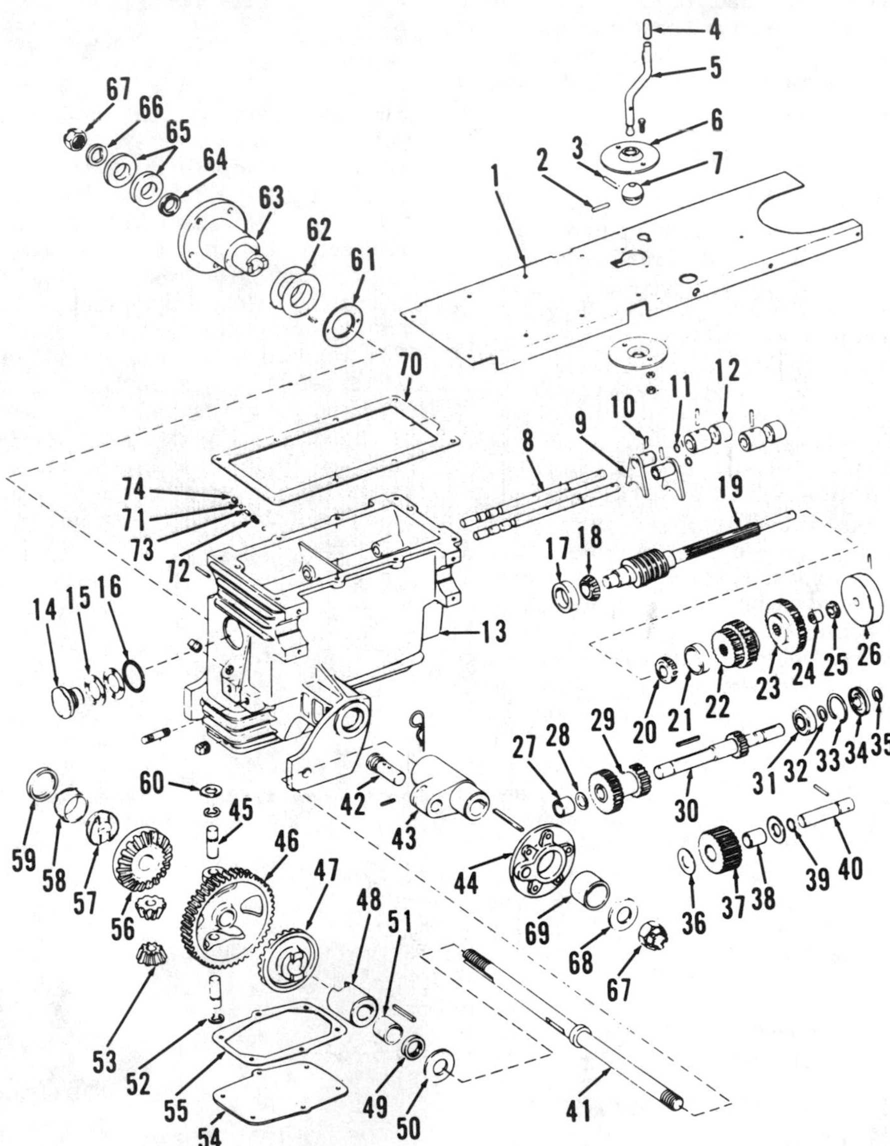


*Fig. B41 — Exploded view of transaxle assembly used on Models G9, G10, G11 and 853.*

1. Transaxle cover
2. Dowel pin
3. Drive pin
4. Knob
5. Shift lever
6. Retainer
7. Pivot ball
8. Shifter rail
9. Shifter fork
10. Roll pin
11. Seal ring
12. Connector
13. Transaxle case
14. Bearing retainer cap
15. Shim
16. "O" ring
17. Bearing cup
18. Bearing cone
19. Wormshaft
20. Bearing cone
21. Bearing cup
22. Second & third sliding gear
23. First & reverse sliding gear
24. Bearing
25. Oil seal
26. Brake drum
27. Bearing
28. Snap ring
29. Cluster gear
30. Input shaft
31. Ball bearing
32. Snap ring
33. Retainer ring
34. Oil seal
35. Snap ring
36. Thrust washer
37. Reverse idler gear
38. Bushing
39. Seal ring
40. Idler shaft
41. Axle shaft
42. Free-wheeling pin
43. Hub drive coupling
44. Hub (R.H.)
45. Differential pinion shaft
46. Wormwheel
47. Side gear (R.H.)
48. Side gear drive
49. Oil seal
50. Thrust bearing
51. Bushing
52. Snap ring
53. Differential pinion gear
54. Bottom cover
55. Gasket
56. Side gear (L.H.)
57. Side gear coupling
58. Bushing
59. Oil seal
60. Washer
61. Thrust bearing
62. Shim
63. Wheel hub
64. Oil seal
65. Thrust bearing
66. Special washer
67. Axle nut
68. Washer
69. Bearing
70. Gasket
71. Ball
72. Spring
73. Pin
74. Set screw

Peerless 1200 series transaxle. Models G11XL, G12XL, G14XL and G16XL are equipped with a Peerless 2300 series transaxle with a limited-slip differential. Models G9, G10, G11 and 853 are equipped with a three-speed transaxle manufactured for Bolens. Models G12, G14, 1053, 1054 and 1254 are equipped with a three-speed transaxle plus a Hi-Lo range contained within the transaxle case manufactured for Bolens. On models equipped with a Peerless transaxle, refer to the appropriate Peerless section in TRANSAXLE SERVICE section for overhaul procedure. On all other models, refer to the following paragraphs for transaxle overhaul procedure.

## Models G9-G10-G11-853

After removing transaxle assembly, remove rear wheels and unbolt and re-

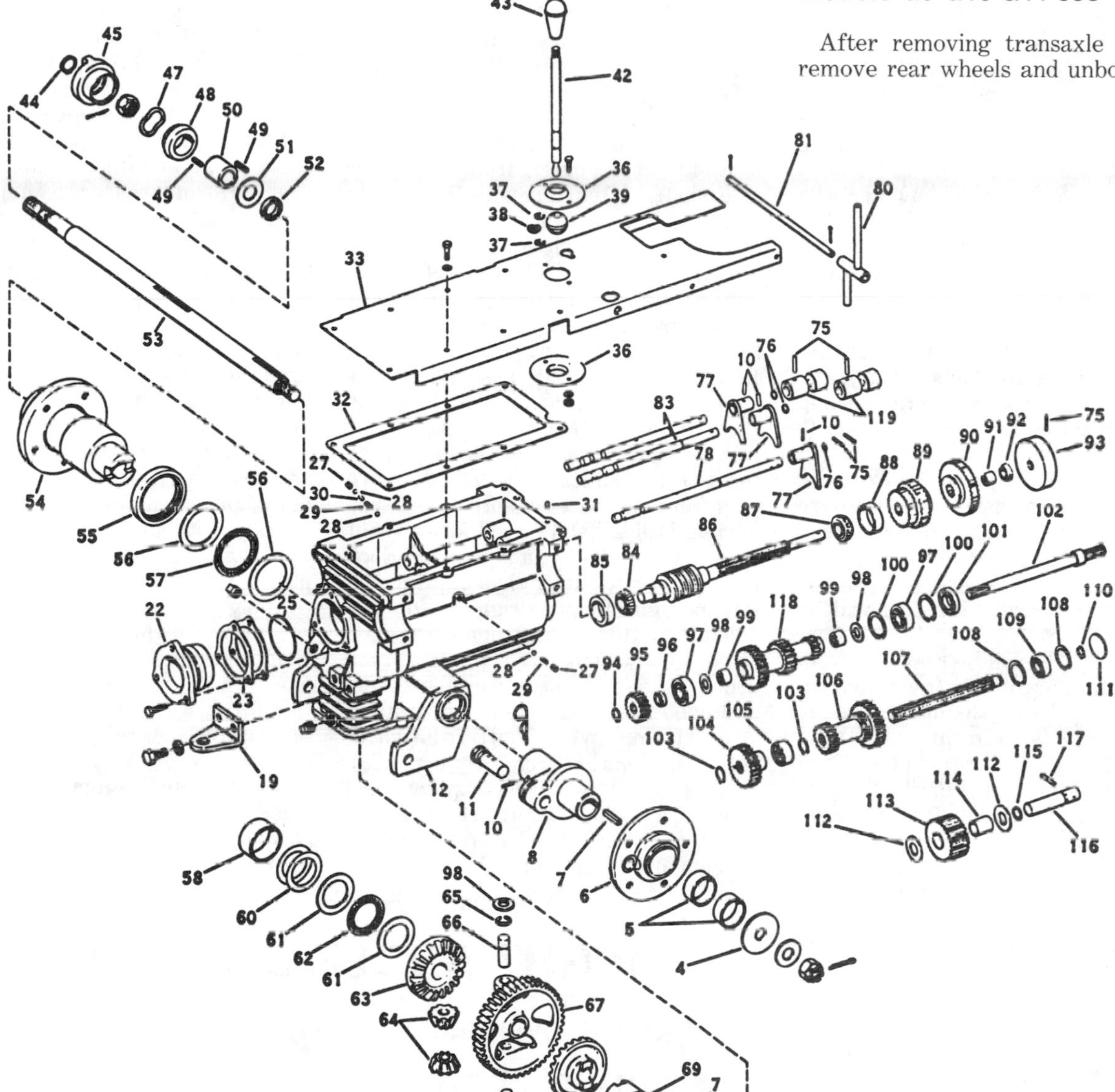

*Fig. B42 — Exploded view of transaxle assembly used on Models G12, G14, 1053, 1054, 1253 and 1254.*

4. Thrust washer
5. Bushing
6. Hub (R.H.)
7. Key
8. Hub drive coupling
10. Roll pin
11. Free-wheeling pin
12. Transaxle case
15. Bottom cover
16. Gasket
19. Hitch plate
22. Bearing retainer cap
23. Shim
25. "O" ring
27. Plug
28. Detent ball
29. Spring
30. Interlock pin
31. Breather
32. Gasket
33. Transaxle cover
36. Retainer
37. Snap ring
38. Seal ring
39. Pivot ball
42. Shift lever
43. Knob
44. Snap ring
45. Handwheel
47. Spring washer (4 used)
48. "Posi-Traction--cone
49. Key
50. Cone drive hub
51. Washer
52. Oil seal
53. Axle shaft
54. Hub (L.H.)
55. Oil seal
56. Thrust washer
57. Thrust bearing
58. Bushing
60. Shim
61. Thrust washer
62. Thrust bearing
63. Side gear (L.H.)
64. Differential pinion gear
65. Snap ring
66. Differential pinion shaft
67. Wormwheel
68. Side gear (R.H.)
69. Side gear drive hub
70. Set screw
71. Lock wire
72. Bearing
73. Bearing
74. Washer
75. Roll pin
76. Seal ring
77. Shifter fork
78. Range shifter rail
80. Range shift lever
81. Cross shaft
83. Shifter rails
84. Bearing cone
86. Wormshaft
87. Bearing cone
88. Bearing cup
89. Second & third sliding gear
90. First & reverse sliding gear
91. Bearing
92. Oil seal
93. Brake drum
94. Snap ring
95. Input gear
96. Spacer
97. Ball bearing
98. Washer
99. Bearing
100. Retainer ring
101. Oil seal
102. Input shaft
103. Snap ring
104. Input driven gear
105. Bearing
106. Hi-Lo range gear
107. Splined shaft
108. Retainer ring
109. Ball bearing
110. Snap ring
111. Expansion plug
112. Thrust washer
113. Reverse idler gear
114. Bushing
115. Seal ring
116. Idler shaft
117. Roll pin
118. Cluster gear

move top cover assembly (1 – Fig. B41). Remove cotter pin and castellated nut from left end of axle shaft. Then, drive out 3/16 inch shearproof pin located next to right side gear drive hub (48). Move axle shaft to the right until side gear drive hub key can be removed. Remove left wheel hub (63), shims (62) and thrust washer (61). Unbolt and remove transaxle bottom cover (54), then withdraw axle shaft from right side of case while holding differential and wormwheel assembly. Remove differential and side gears through bottom opening of case.

To remove shifter rails (8) and forks (9), first drive out roll pins holding forks to rails. After removing plug from interlock pin bore on left side of case, pull left shifter rail forward out of case.

**NOTE: Hold hand over interlock pin bore to catch detent balls, spring and interlock pin. Remove right shifter rail and lift out both shifter forks.**

Drive out roll pin and remove brake drum (26) from wormshaft (19). Remove cap screws from bearing retaining cap (14) and bump wormshaft out rear of case. Bearing retainer cap (14), shims (15) and rear bearing cup (17) will be removed from rear of case and sliding gears (22 and 23) will be removed from inside of case as wormshaft is removed. Remove drive shaft coupling flange, key and snap ring, pry out front seal (34) and remove bearing retainer ring (33). Bump input shaft (30) forward until ball bearing (31) is free of case. Remove snap ring (28) from rear of input shaft, withdraw input shaft and lift cluster gear (29) from inside of case. Drive out roll pin securing reverse idler shaft in case and remove shaft (40), reverse idler gear (37) and thrust washers.

Reassemble unit by reversing disassembly procedure, and making the following adjustments. When reinstalling wormshaft, add or remove shims (15) as required to obtain 0.004-0.008 inch (0.120-0.203 mm) end play. After reassembling differential and axle shaft in case, adjust left axle nut tight enough so differential will operate without binding. Then, adjust right axle nut to obtain minimum end play but do not bind axle.

Aply a light coat of Prussian Blue to several teeth on wormwheel (46). Rotate wormshaft and check wear pattern on painted wormwheel teeth (area where blue is removed). If pattern is not centered on wormwheel, add or remove shims (62) at left hub as required to center pattern.

**NOTE: One 0.005 inch (0.127 mm) shim equals approximately 1/16 inch (1.59 mm) shift of wormwheel wear pattern.**

Readjust differential and axle end play as outlined before.

### Models G12-G14-1053-1054-1253-1254

Remove transaxle unit, then remove rear wheels. Unbolt and remove bottom cover (15 – Fig. B42) and top cover assembly (33). Remove snap ring (44), adjusting handwheel (45), cotter pin, castellated nut, four spring washers (47), "Posi-Traction" drive cone (48), cone drive hub (50) and two straight keys (49), in this order, from left end of axle shaft. After removing set screw (70) from side gear drive hub (69), move axle shaft to the right until drive hub key can be removed. Remove left wheel hub (54) and while holding wormwheel and differential assembly, withdraw axle shaft (53) from right side of case. Remove differential assembly, side gears, thrust bearings and shims through bottom opening of case.

Drive out roll pins securing shifter forks (77) to shifter rails (83). Remove plug from interlock pin bore on left side of case. Pull left shifter rail forward out of case while holding hand over interlock pin bore to catch detent balls, spring and interlock pin. Remove right shifter rail and lift shifter forks from wormshaft sliding gears. Remove roll pin and brake drum (93) from front of wormshaft (86) and unbolt bearing retainer at rear of case. Bump wormshaft rearward, removing bearing retainer cap (22), shims (23), rear bearing cup (85) and sliding gears (89 and 90) as shaft is withdrawn from case. Remove roll pin from range shifter fork and rail and remove plug, spring and detent ball from right side of case. Withdraw range shifter rail (78) and lift out shifter fork. Remove expansion plug (111) and bearing retainer ring (108) from front of case and remove snap ring and gear (104) from splined shaft (107). Bump splined shaft forward until bearing is free from case. Remove snap ring from rear of splined shaft, withdraw shaft and lift Hi-Lo range sliding gear (106) from case. Pry oil seal (101) from case and remove bearing retainer ring (100). Remove snap ring, input gear (95) and spacer from input shaft (102) and then, remove cluster gear (118) and washers as input shaft is withdrawn from case. Drive roll pin from idler shaft and remove idler shaft (116), reverse idler gear (113) and thrust washers.

Reassembly procedure is reverse of disassembly. When reinstalling wormshaft, add or remove shims (23) at bearing retainer cap to obtain 0.004-0.008 inch (0.102-0.203 mm) wormshaft end play. After reassembling differential and axle shaft in case, adjust left axle nut tight enough so differential will operate without binding. Then, adjust right axle nut to obtain minimum end play but do not bind axle.

Apply a light coat of Prussian Blue to several wormwheel teeth. Rotate wormshaft and check wear pattern on painted wormwheel teeth (area where blue is removed). If wear pattern is not centered on wormwheel, add or remove shims (60) as required to center pattern. One 0.005 inch (0.127 mm) shim will shift wear pattern approximately 1/16 inch (1.59 mm). Readjust differential and axle end play as previously outlined.

# RIGHT ANGLE DRIVE UNIT

## R&R AND OVERHAUL

### Models G11XL-G12XL-G14XL-G16XL

To remove right angle drive unit, remove idler pulley and slide drive belt off right angle drive pulley. Remove pulley from right angle drive. Remove frame

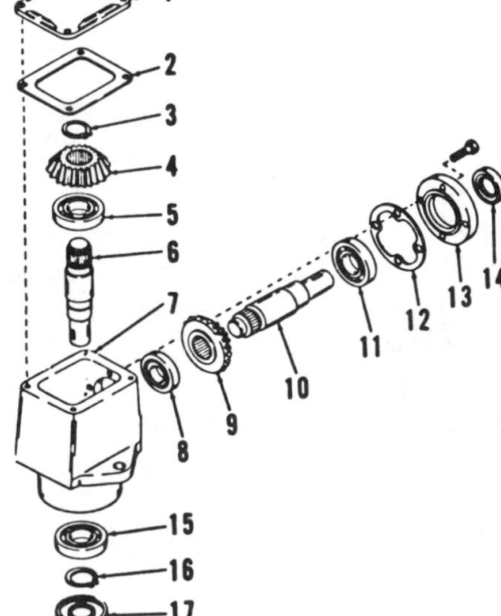


*Fig. B44 – Exploded view of right angle drive used on Models G11XL, G12XL, G14XL and G16XL.*

1. Cover
2. Gasket
3. Snap ring
4. Input gear
5. Bearing
6. Input shaft
7. Case
8. Bearing
9. Output gear
10. Output shaft
11. Bearing
12. Gasket
13. Seal retainer
14. Oil seal
15. Bearing
16. Snap ring
17. Oil seal

cover in front of seat and remove front belt cover. Remove right angle drive from tractor.

To disassemble right angle drive unit, remove cover (1–Fig. B44), gasket (2) and lubricant. Unbolt and remove seal retainer (13) with oil seal (14) and gasket (12). Withdraw output shaft (10) with bearing (11). Remove output gear (9). Remove oil seal (17) and snap ring (16). Drive input shaft (6) with gear (4) and bearing (5) out the cover opening of case (7). Bearings (8 and 15) can now be removed from case. Remove snap ring (3) and remove drive gear (4) and bearing (5) from input shaft. Remove bearing (11) from output shaft (10).

Clean and inspect all parts and renew any showing excessive wear or other damage. Reassemble by reversing disassembly procedure and fill unit with 4 ounces (120 mL) of Moly EP lithium grease.

# HYDROSTATIC TRANSMISSION

## LUBRICATION

### Model 736

The manufacturer recommends that oil in reservoir be renewed once a year when operating under normal conditions. If tractor is operated frequently in extremely dusty conditions, renew oil in reservoir once each month. To renew oil, disconnect oil line at reservoir. Plug line to prevent entrance of dirt and oil loss from transmission. Remove, clean and dry reservoir, then reassemble on tractor. Fill reservoir at "FULL" mark on dipstick using Bolens #171-9650 hydraulic oil or Type "A" automatic transmission fluid.

### Models 1225-1256-1257-1556-H14-H16-H11XL-H12XL-H14XL-H16XL

Maintain hydraulic oil level at "FULL" mark on reservoir dipstick. Use Bolens #171-9650 hydraulic oil or Type "A" automatic transmission fluid on all models except "XL" models. On "XL" models, recommended oil is as follows: If tractor is used under constant heavy load conditions in hot weather, use SAE 30 oil with API classification, SC, SD or SE. Under normal load conditions and temperatures above 20° F (−7°C), use SAE 20 oil with API classification SC, SD or SE. When temperatures are 20° F (−7°C) and below, use Type "F" automatic transmission fluid.

The hydraulic oil and oil filter should be renewed each 250 hours of operation or once a year under normal operating conditions, or more often if operating under constant heavy load conditions or extremely dusty conditions.

### Models 1455-1476-1477

The manufacturer recommends renewing hydraulic oil filter and transmission oil each 300 hours of operation or once each year. The capacity of reduction gear and differential housing (also hydraulic reservoir) is 10 quarts (9.5 L). Fill only with Bolens #171-9650 hydraulic oil or Type "A" automatic transmission fluid.

### Model QS16

Weekly or 25 hour checks are recommended for transmission fluid with filter changes at 200 hour intervals. Recommended oil is Type "F" automatic transmission fluid. Approximate capacity is 20 pints (9.5 L). Always change transmission fluid when discolored or contaminated.

## LINKAGE ADJUSTMENT

### Model 736

To adjust hydrostatic drive linkage, block up rear wheels so they do not touch ground. Start engine with travel pedal in neutral position. Rear wheels should not rotate. If wheels rotate, loosen nut (A–Fig. B49) and cap screw (B). Move bracket (C) either forward or backward until rear wheels stop turning. Retighten nut (A) and cap screw (B) and recheck adjustment of travel pedal.

### Models 1225-1256-1257

Before making neutral adjustment, be sure parking pawl engages transmission drive gear when selector lever is placed in PARK position. With transmission in PARK position, differential should be locked. If differential is not locked, proceed as follows: Remove clevis pin (A–Fig. B50). Turn adjusting block (B) to lengthen stud (C) until pawl (D) correctly engages transmission gear (E).

**NOTE: Do not turn pawl (D) as mesh between pawl and transmission gear will be misaligned.**

To accomplish neutral adjustment, first raise and support rear of tractor so wheels are off ground. Refer to Fig. B51 and loosen cap screws (A). Start engine; if wheels rotate forward, move bracket (B) forward until wheels stop and noise in hydrostatic transmission ceases. If wheels rotate in reverse, tap bracket (B) towards rear. Retighten cap screws (A).

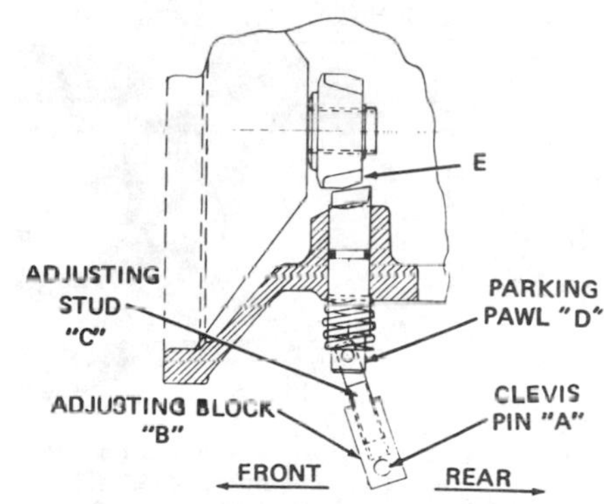


*Fig. B50—View of parking pawl and transmission gear on Models 1225, 1256 and 1257. Refer to text for parking pawl adjustment.*

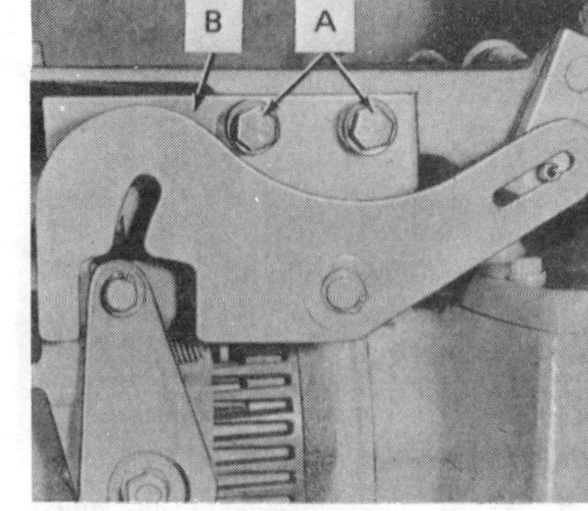


*Fig. B51—View of hydrostatic control cam assembly used on Models 1225, 1256 and 1257.*

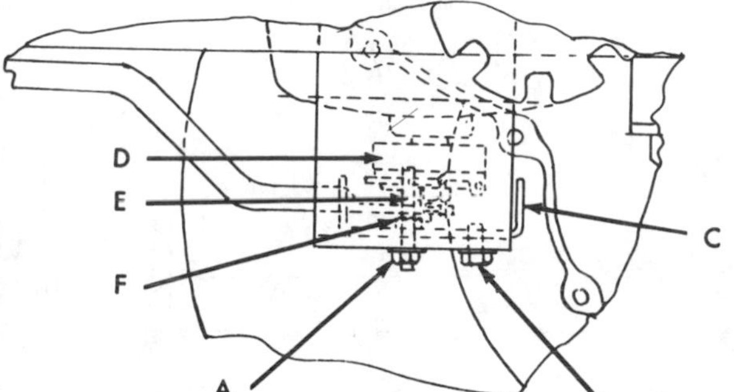


*Fig. B49—View of neutral adjustment points on Model 736. Refer to text for procedure.*

A. Nut
B. Cap screw
C. Bracket
D. Control arm
E. Stud
F. Nut

## Models 1455-1476-1477

Hydrostatic linkage for Eaton Model 12 transmission used on these models is adjusted as follows:

With selector lever in DRIVE position, all linkages should move freely. Loosen two jam nuts on control rod away from swivel block, then place selector lever in PARK position. See Fig. B52. Parking pawl should be fully meshed in bull gear. Push spool of unloader assembly back into PARK detent position. (Front detent groove inside casting.) Adjust two jam nuts up against swivel block (3). Place selector lever in NEUTRAL position. Push tractor forward and backward to be sure tractor free-wheels freely in this position. Place selector lever in DRIVE and activate travel pedal. Check to see that pin in transaxle control linkage moves freely into upper and lower slot of interlock plate. If interference is evident, readjust jam nuts to eliminate interlock-slot pin interference.

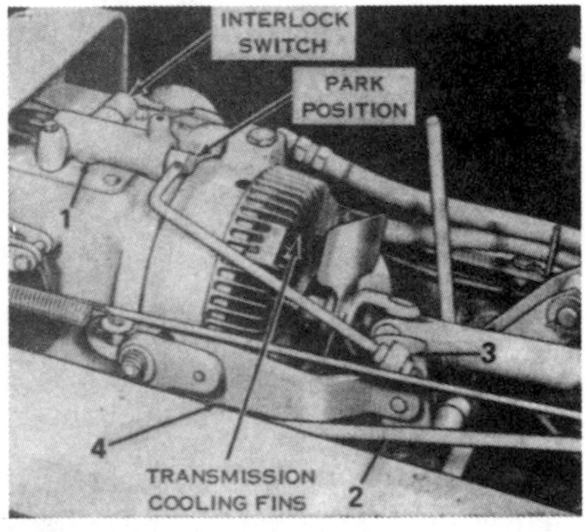


***Fig. B52—View of adjustment points on Eaton Model 12 transmission in Models 1455, 1476 and 1477. Note location of interlock switch. See adjustment procedure in text.***

1. Unloader valve (oil relief) assy.
2. Parking pawl link rod
3. Swivel block
4. Interlock plate

## Models 1556-H14-H16

When tractor "creeps" either forward or back in neutral, then neutral control of hydrostatic unit (Model 10) requires adjustment. Be sure transmission fluid level is correct before undertaking adjustment, then proceed as follows:

With engine turned off, release parking brake, set travel pedal in full reverse and check under right side of tractor to determine if pin ("A"–Fig. B53) is snug in corner "B" of locking lever "C." If not, loosen cap screw "D" and shift locking lever "C" until pin is in position shown. Tighten cap screw.

Now, raise and block under rear of tractor so drive wheels are clear and start engine, setting throttle for one-quarter speed, control pedal in neutral. Refer to Fig. B53 and slightly loosen cap screws "E" which hold adjusting bracket "G" through elongated holes to control support "H." Hold neutral arms "F" in contact with pin "K", then shift adjusting bracket "G" forward if creep is in forward direction, or back if creeping is to the rear until wheel rotation and hydrostatic noise stops.

**NOTE: Edge of adjustment bracket "G" must be kept parallel to edge of control support "H."**

**IMPORTANT: Pin "A" must enter slot "J" of locking lever "C" without contacting sides of slot. If contact is made, loosen cap screw "D" and readjust until pin "A" travels length of slot "J" freely. Be sure to retighten cap screw "D."**

## Models H11XL-H12XL-H14XL-H16XL

To adjust hydrostatic drive linkage, block up rear of tractor so rear wheels clear ground. Start engine with travel pedal in neutral position. If rear wheels creep, loosen cap screws (A–Fig. B54) and move support plate (1) forward if wheels rotate forward or toward rear of tractor if wheels rotate in reverse. Secure support plate when wheels stop rotating. Stop engine and lock brake. Loosen jam nuts (B) and move rod (4) until pin lightly contacts slot (C) of neutral plate.

## Model QS16

To perform linkage neutral adjustment on tractor equipped with Sundstrand hydrostatic unit, proceed as follows:

Remove seat and fender assemblies. Be sure free-wheeling valve on left side of unit is closed, and fluid level is correct. Jack up tractor and block securely under axle so rear wheels are clear. With travel pedal in neutral, start engine and release parking brake. Refer to Fig. B55 and loosen nuts "B" at rear end of rod "C." If wheels creep in forward direction, shorten rod "C" working length by tightening outer nut until rotation stops. If creep is to rear, increase length of rod "C" by tightening inner nut until backward rotation is halted. Tighten both sides securely, then check performance.

### REMOVE AND REINSTALL

## Model 736

To remove hydrostatic transmission, disconnect hydraulic reservoir hose and remove reservoir. Plug openings to prevent entrance of dirt into system. Unbolt and remove seat and fenders. Remove backplate or hitch assembly from frame. Remove disc brake assembly. Unbolt and remove fan screen and cooling fan. Disconnect control rod from lever on hydrostatic transmission. Remove drive belt and transmission input pulley. Support tractor frame, remove cap screws from top of frame and "U" bolt from axle supports. Roll reduction gear and differential assembly with hydrostatic transmission rearward

***Fig. B53—View of transmission linkage adjustment to eliminate creeping in neutral on Models 1556, H14 and H16. Refer to text for procedure.***

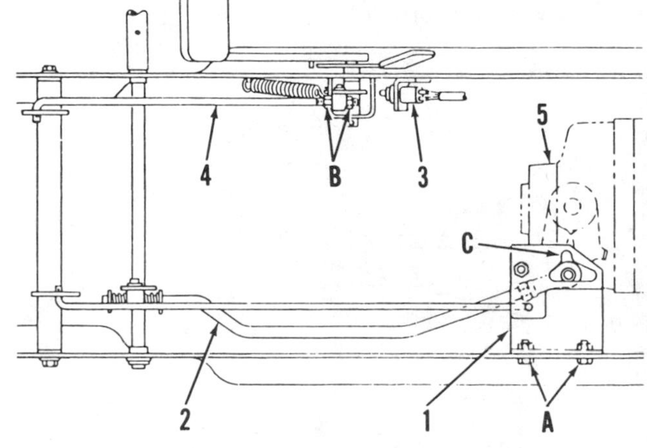


***Fig. B54—View showing adjustment points for hydrostatic drive Models H11XL, H12XL, H14XL and H16XL. Refer to text for details.***

A. Cap screws
B. Nuts
C. Slot
1. Support plate
2. Speed control rod
3. Interlock switch
4. Brake rod
5. Hydrostatic unit

from tractor. Place unit on left wheel and tire (right axle pointing upward). Remove right rear wheel, then unbolt and remove hydrostatic transmission.

Reinstall hydrostatic transmission by reversing removal procedure. Use new mounting gasket and tighten four hydrostatic transmission mounting cap screws to 200 in.-lbs. (22.6 N·m). Fill hydraulic reservoir to dipstick full mark with approved fluid. Fill reduction gear and differential housing to level plug opening with SAE 90 EP gear oil. Check and adjust linkage as necessary.

### Models 1225-1256-1257-1556-H14-H16-H11XL-H12XL-H14XL-H16XL

To remove hydrostatic transmission from these models, first unbolt and remove seat and fender assemblies. Disconnect and remove hydraulic fluid reservoir hose and reservoir (if so equipped) along with all auxiliary hydraulic hoses. Plug or cap all openings as soon as disconnect is made. Disconnect disc brake linkage and remove brake assembly. Disconnect hydrostatic control rod from control linkage, but do not remove control arm from control shaft until later.

**NOTE: Be sure all hydraulic assembly parts and hoses are adequately identified to eliminate error in reinstallation.**

Raise and support rear of tractor frame and disconnect drive shaft. On all models except "XL" models, place scribe marks on frame tubes and reduction gear housing to aid realignment during reassembly. On "XL" models, scribe a line on left hand frame rail at rear edge of quadrant support plate. When reinstalling transaxle, plate must be parallel with frame. On all models, remove retaining screws and clamps and roll assembly rearward from tractor frame.

Remove control arm and levers from control shaft using suitable puller. Do not attempt to pry or drive control arm off shaft, as internal damage can occur. Rotate reduction drive housing so input shaft of hydrostatic transmission points upward and block securely; transmission can now be unbolted and lifted off.

Reinstall transmission on reduction and differential housing, using a new gasket, and tighten cap screws to 20 ft.-lbs. (27 N·m). Reinstall assembly on tractor by reversing removal procedure. Fill hydraulic reservoir to dipstick full mark with approved hydraulic fluid. Operate engine at 1/3 throttle and shift hydrostatic drive to forward and reverse several times to purge air from system. Recheck fluid level and adjust linkage as necessary.

### Models 1455-1476-1477

To remove hydrostatic transmission from tractors in this model group, first, drain automatic transmission fluid (ATF) from reservoir. Remove seat and fender asemblies which includes deck assembly forward of operator's seat. Support rear of tractor under frame rails, disconnect and remove brake control linkage. Disconnect and remove transmission control linkages. Remove hoses for hydraulic system (if so equipped) and tape or otherwise protect open lines or connection fittings. Be sure to identify removed items for ease of reassembly. Remove oil filter, then unbolt attaching bolts so entire assembly can be rolled rearward away from tractor frame.

Tip transmission back and rest on a six inch (15.2 cm) block. Remove hydraulic oil lines. Remove control arm from hydrostatic control shaft using a suitable puller. Do not pry or drive control arm off shaft, as internal damage can occur. Unbolt and lift off hydrostatic transmission.

Reinstall hydrostatic transmission by reversing removal steps. Refill unit with Type "F" automatic transmission oil. Adjust linkage as needed.

### Model QS16

To remove hydrostatic transmission begin by unbolting and removing seat and fender assemblies.

**NOTE: If service to hydrostatic assembly only is intended, it is not necessary to remove rear axle and reduction gear housing. If removal of rear axle will be required, see REDUCTION AND DIFFERENTIAL section following.**

Drain and discard fluid from transaxle. At forward end of drive shaft, loosen set screw and remove bolt which attaches front universal joint to engine crankshaft so drive shaft can slide forward for removal from input shaft of hydrostatic unit. Uncouple and remove hydraulic lines from top of pump section housing. This will require removal of forward ends of these lines at hydraulic control valve so lines are not damaged. Tape over or cap openings. Uncouple external pickup tube from pump section and at front of reduction gear housing just under hydrostatic motor section. Leave elbow fittings in place after plugging or capping against dirt entry. Remove fluid filter from under pump section. Remove cap screw holding mounting tab for neutral adjustment rod (see Fig. B55) so rod can be disengaged and removed. Drive out roll pin which holds control linkage on control shaft and remove linkage assembly. Remove mounting cap screws and lift out hydrostatic transmission.

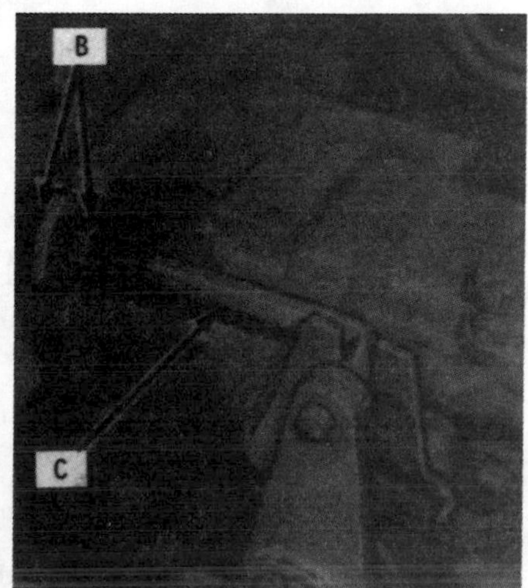


*Fig. B55—Linkage neutral adjustment of Sundstrand hydrostatic unit on Model QS16 is made by changing length of rod "C" by shifting nuts "B." Refer to text.*

To reinstall hydrostatic transmission, the reverse of preceding steps applies with these additional steps and cautions:

Be sure filter mount (stud tube) is securely staked so as not to turn when filter is installed. Use grease to hold gasket in place on motor end flange, then use three **shorter** cap screws to mount hydrostatic unit against reduction gear housing, leaving **longer** cap screw for attaching neutral adjustment rod tab. Tighten all cap screws to 31 ft.-lbs. (42 N·m). When drive shaft is reinstalled, check for 1/8 inch (3 mm) clearance between drive shaft end and pump input shaft. Loosen engine mounts to adjust, if necessary. Fill new filter with Type "F" automatic transmission fluid and screw on hand tight. Use about 8 quarts (7.5 L) of new fluid to charge reduction gear housing. Loosen pickup tube at pump (front) end and retighten when fluid appears at fitting. Remove spark plug and crank engine for 15-20 seconds to fill unit with fluid, then reinstall spark plug. Start engine and operate at low throttle engaging hydraulic lift lever so lift system will fill with fluid. Block up rear axle and perform linkage neutral adjustment as previously covered. Check fluid level on dipstick and top off to level mark.

## OVERHAUL

### All Models

Model 736 is equipped with an Eaton Model 6 hydrostatic transmission.

Models 1225, 1256, 1257, 1556, H14 and H16 are equipped with an Eaton Model 10 hydrostatic transmission. Models H11XL, H12XL, H14XL and H16XL are equipped with an Eaton Model 11 hydrostatic transmission. Models 1455, 1476 and 1477 are equipped with an Eaton Model 12 hydrostatic transmission. Model QS16 is equipped with a Sundstrand Series 15 "In-Line" type hydrostatic transmission. Refer to the appropriate Eaton or Sundstrand section in HYDROSTATIC TRANSMISSION SERVICE section for overhaul procedure.

# REDUCTION GEARS AND DIFFERENTIAL

## REMOVE AND REINSTALL

### Model 736

To remove reduction gear and differential assembly, disconnect hydraulic reservoir hose and remove reservoir. Plug openings to prevent entrance of dirt into system. Unbolt and remove seat and fenders. Remove backplate or hitch assembly from frame. Remove disc brake assembly. Unbolt and remove fan screen and cooling fan. Disconnect control rod from lever on hydrostatic transmission. Remove drive belt and transmission input pulley. Support tractor frame, remove cap screws from top of frame and "U" bolt from axle supports. Roll reduction gear and differential assembly with hydrostatic transmission rearward from tractor. Place unit on left wheel and tire (right axle pointing upward). Remove right rear wheel, then unbolt and remove hydrostatic transmission.

Reinstall transaxle unit by reversing removal procedure. Use new mounting gasket and tighten four hydrostatic transmission mounting cap screws to 200 in.-lbs. (22.6 N·m). Fill hydraulic reservoir to dipstick full mark with approved fluid. Fill reduction gear and differential housing to level plug opening with SAE 90 EP gear oil. Check and adjust linkage as necessary.

### Models 1225-1256-1257-H11XL-H12XL-H14XL-H16XL

To remove reduction gear and differential assembly, first unbolt and remove seat and fender assemblies. Disconnect and remove hydraulic fluid reservoir hose and reservoir (if so equipped) along with all auxiliary hydraulic hoses. Plug or cap all openings immediately. Identify hoses to ensure correct reassembly. Disconnect brake linkage and remove disc brake assembly. Disconnect speed control linkage. On "XL" models, scribe a line on left hand frame rail at rear edge of quadrant support plate, then unbolt plate. On all other models, put scribe marks on frame tubes and reduction gear housing to aid realignment during reassembly. On all models, remove retaining screws and clamps and roll assembly rearward from tractor. Hydrostatic transmission can now be separated from reduction drive housing.

Reinstall unit on tractor by reversing removal procedure. Tighten hydrostatic retaining screws to 20 ft.-lbs. (27 N·m). Fill hydraulic reservoir with approved hydraulic fluid. Operate engine at ⅓-throttle and shift hydrostatic transmission to forward and reverse several times to purge air from system. Recheck fluid level and adjust linkage as required.

### Models 1455-1476-1477

To remove axle-differential assembly from tractors in this model group, first, drain transmission fluid from reservoir. Remove seat and fender assemblies which includes deck assembly forward of operator's seat. Support rear of tractor under frame rails, disconnect and remove brake control linkage. Disconnect and remove transmission control linkages. Remove hoses for hydraulic system (if so equipped) and tape or otherwise protect open lines or connection fittings. Be sure to identify removed items for ease of reassembly. Remove oil filter, then unbolt attaching bolts so entire assembly can be rolled rearward away from tractor frame.

Reverse this order to reinstall.

### Models 1556-H14-H16

To remove rear axle, final drive and transmission unit from these tractors, disengage pto and drain axle housing oil reservoir by removing plug at bottom of side cover beneath left axle housing. Remove tractor seat, fender assembly and fender support. Disconnect and cap off hydraulic lines, storage tank, filter and lift system, taking measures to protect against dirt. Disconnect and remove hydrostatic controls at hydrostatic control shaft (under tractor) and uncouple and remove brake assembly from rear axle housing. Place solid supports beneath tractor frame rails (tubes) and unbolt frame clamps from sides of axle housing. It may be desirable to remove fan guard. Check for clearance, and roll complete drive assembly to the rear, carefully disengaging drive shaft splines from input shaft of hydrostatic transmission. Do not force.

Reinstallation is performed in reverse of this sequence, followed by renewal of lubricant. Perform necessary adjustments.

### Model QS16

To remove axle and final drive, drain oil from reservoir in housing. Drain plug is located at front of housing just below oil filter. Remove seat and fender assemblies, then disconnect transmission control linkage. Disconnect hydraulic lines from fittings above charge pump, protect from dirt, loosen or remove at hydraulic control valve and set aside. Remove set screw from front universal joint, slip drive shaft forward and disengage from hydrostatic input shaft. Disconnect brake linkage inside frame rails, and note that disc brake assembly will be released from its mount on axle when "U" bolts are removed. Support rear of tractor under frame, then remove cap screws which hold frame rails to axle housing followed by cap screws in transmission support, so entire drive assembly can be rolled rearward.

Reverse this order for reinstallation, replenish transmission fluid and perform necessary adjustments.

## OVERHAUL

### Model 736

Remove reduction gear and differential assembly and hydrostatic transmission from tractor. Separate hydrostatic transmission from reduction gear and differential housing. Drain lubricant from differential housing and remove brake disc from brake shaft.

To overhaul gear reduction and differential unit, refer to exploded view in Fig. B66. Clean axle shafts and remove any burrs on shafts. Unscrew cap screws and drive out dowel pins in cover. Lift cover off case and axle shaft. Remove brake shaft (5), idler gear (4) and thrust washers (3 and 6) from case. Withdraw output shaft (11), output gear (10), spacer (9), thrust washer (8) and differential assembly from case. Axle shaft housings (20 and 22) must be pressed from case and cover.

To disassemble differential, unscrew four cap screws (17) and separate axle shaft and carriage assemblies from ring gear (28). Drive blocks (25), bevel pinion gears (26) and drive pin (27) can now be removed from ring gear. Remove snap rings (12) and slide axle shafts (18 and 23) from axle gears (13) and carriages (16 and 24).

Clean and inspect all parts and renew any parts damaged or excessively worn. When installing needle bearings, press bearings in from inside of case or cover until bearings are 0.015-0.020 inch (0.381-0.508 mm) below thrust surfaces. Be sure heads of differential cap screws (17) and left axle shaft (18) are installed in left carriage housing (16). Left axle shaft is installed through case (1). Tighten differential cap screws to 7 ft.-lbs. (9 N·m) and cover cap screws to 10 ft.-lbs. (14 N·m). Differential assembly and output shaft (11) must be installed in case at same time. Remainder of assembly is reverse of disassembly procedure.

After assembly is completed, fill transmission reservoir to full mark on dipstick with Bolens #171-9650 hydraulic oil or Type "A" automatic transmission fluid. Fill reduction and differential housing to level plug with SAE 90 EP gear lube.

## Models 1225-1256-1257-1556-H14-H16

Remove reduction gear and differential assembly and hydrostatic transmission from tractor. Remove hydrostatic control plate from left side and separate hydrostatic transmission from reduction gear and differential housing. Drain lubricant from differential housing and remove brake disc from brake shaft.

To overhaul gear reduction and differential unit, remove outer snap ring, adjusting handwheel (33–Fig. B67), spring washers (34), inner snap ring, shim (35), "Posi-Traction" drive cone (36), coupling (37) and keys (38) from left end of axle. Remove left wheel hub (41), then remove cover (23) from case (8). Remove right hub nut (13) and right wheel hub (11). Withdraw axle (1) and differential components. Input shaft components (16 through 20) can now be removed.

Clean and inspect all components for damage or excessive wear. When reassembling differential, shims (5) are used to position right side gear with drive pinions (29) and also are used to adjust axle end play. Change number or size of shims (5) to obtain an end play of 0.002-0.014 inch (0.051-0.356 mm). Install left wheel hub (41), seal (40), thrust washer (39), coupling (37), cone (36) and snap ring (32). Push inward on left end of axle shaft and measure distance between coupling (37) and snap ring (32). Install shims (35) as required to reduce the gap to 0.002-0.016 inch (0.051-0.406 mm). To assemble gear reduction and differential unit, reverse disassembly procedure.

After assembly is completed, fill transmission reservoir to full mark on dipstick with Bolens #171-9650 hydraulic oil or Type "A" automatic transmission fluid. Fill reduction and differential housing to level plug with SAE 90 EP gear lube.

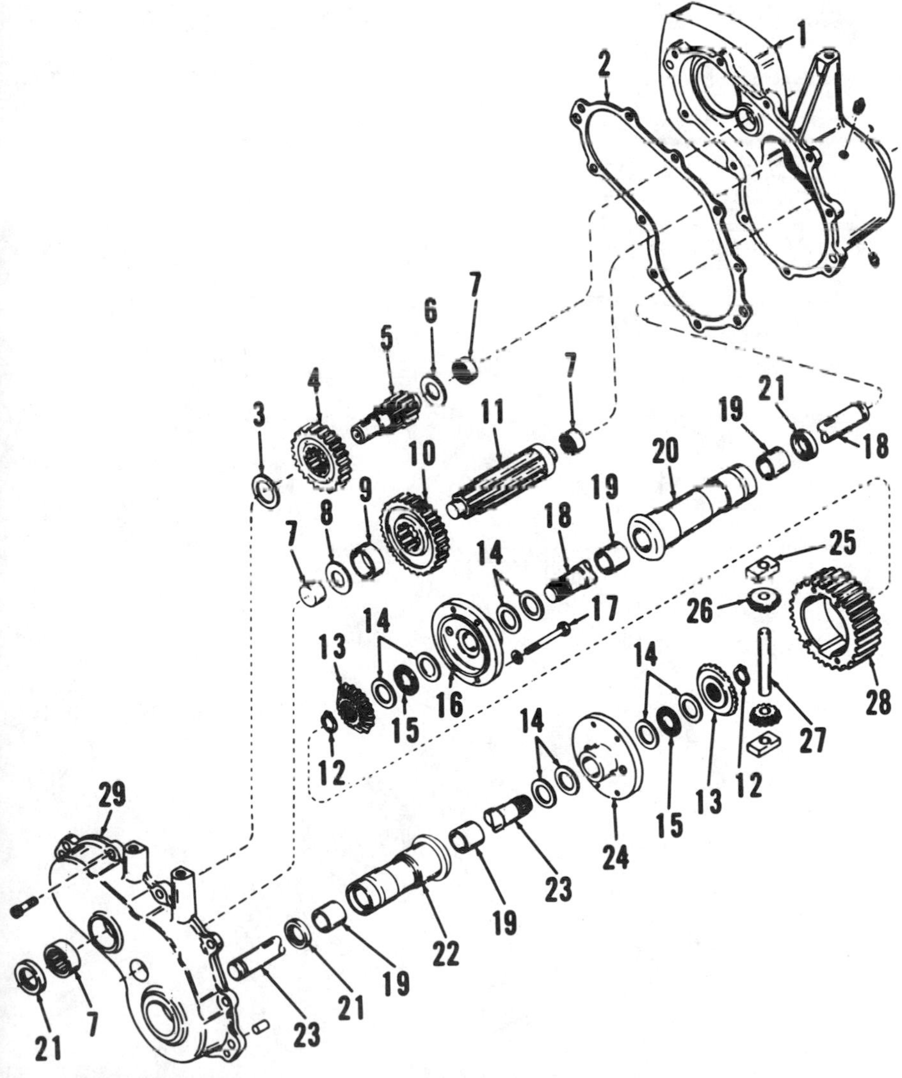


*Fig. B66—Exploded view of gear reduction and differential unit used on Model 736.*

1. Case
2. Gasket
3. Washer
4. Idler gear
5. Brake shaft
6. Washer
7. Bearing
8. Washer
9. Spacer
10. Output gear
11. Output shaft
12. Snap ring
13. Bevel gear
14. Thrust washers
15. Thrust bearing
16. Differential carrier
17. Bolt
18. Axle shaft (R.H.)
19. Bushing
20. Axle housing
21. Oil seal
22. Axle housing
23. Axle shaft (L.H.)
24. Differential carrier
25. Drive block
26. Drive pinion gear
27. Drive pin
28. Ring gear
29. Cover

## Models H11XL-H12XL-H14XL-H16XL

Remove reduction gear and differential assembly and hydrostatic transmission from tractor. Separate hydrostatic transmission from reduction gear and drain differential housing. Remove brake disc assembly.

To overhaul reduction gear and differential, unbolt and remove right hand transaxle cover (9–Fig. B68). Remove cluster gear assembly (14) and pinion shaft (5). Make sure thrust races (6) and bearing (7) stay with shaft (5). Unbolt and remove left hand cover (33). Lift differential assembly from housing.

To disassemble differential, unscrew four cap screws and separate ring gear (24), carrier (23) and cover (17). Remove snap ring (21), pinion shaft (22) and bevel pinion gears (20). Remove snap rings (19) and slide axles (18) out of axle gears and differential carrier assembly (17 and 23).

Clean and inspect all parts and renew any parts damaged or excessively worn. When installing needle bearings inside covers, press pinion shaft bearings (2 and 8), cluster gear bearings (12) and axle housing bearings (10 and 32) 1/32 to 1/16 inch (0.8-1.5 mm) below machined surface. Press inner axle bearings to ¼ inch (6 mm) below machined surface. Reassemble differential and tighten cap screws to 25 to 30 ft.-lbs. (34-41 N·m). Install differential assembly and side covers and check axle end play. End play should be a minimum of 0.005-0.020 inch (0.127-0.508 mm) and is adjusted by changing shim (25). Reassemble gear reduction and differential unit and torque side cover cap screws to 30 ft.-lbs. (41 N·m).

After assembly is completed, reinstall assembly on tractor and fill with automatic transmission fluid Type "F" approximately 8 quarts (7.5 L). Adjust linkage as necessary.

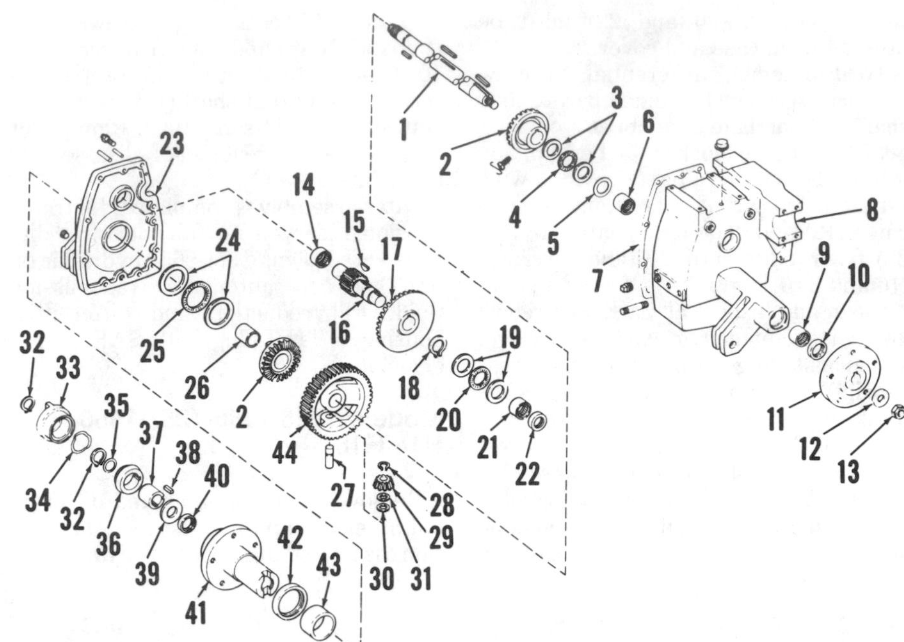

***Fig. B67—Exploded view of gear reduction and differential unit on Models 1225, 1256, 1257, 1556, H14 and H16.***

1. Axle shaft
2. Side gear
3. Thrust washers
4. Thrust bearing
5. Shim
6. Bearing
7. Gasket
8. Case
9. Bearing
10. Oil seal
11. Wheel hub
12. Washer
13. Nut
14. Bearing
15. Key
16. Pinion shaft
17. Bevel gear
18. Snap ring
19. Thrust washers
20. Thrust bearing
21. Bearing
22. Oil seal
23. Cover
24. Thrust washers
25. Thrust bearing
26. Bearing
27. Drive pin
28. Snap ring
29. Drive pinion
30. Thrust washer
31. Thrust washer
32. Snap ring
33. Adjusting handwheel
34. Spring washer
35. Shim
36. Cone
37. Coupling
38. Key
39. Thrust washer
40. Oil seal
41. Wheel hub
42. Oil seal
43. Bearing
44. Ring gear

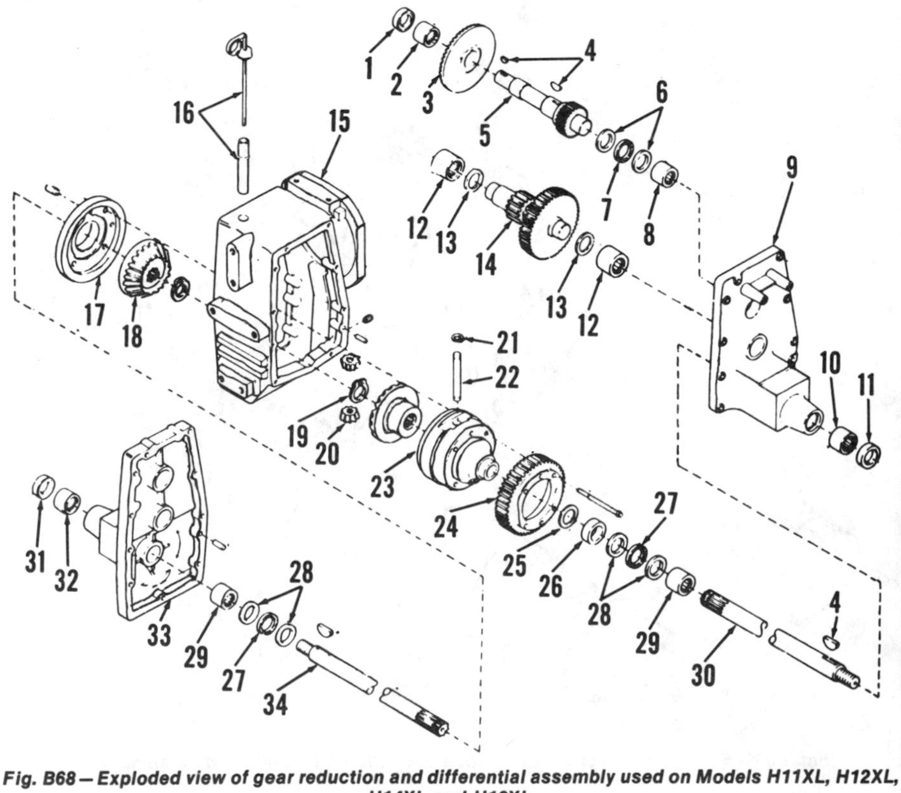

## Models 1455-1476-1477

After removing hydrostatic drive and differential assembly, remove wheels, hubs and drive keys from axles. Using a ⅜ inch Allen wrench, remove oil filter stud (10–Fig. B69). Unbolt and remove unloader assembly and cover (2). Remove bearing flange (55), brake shaft (58) and coupler (52). Remove locating bolt (12), then remove hydrostatic unit from transaxle housing.

To disassemble reduction gears and differential, unbolt and remove axle housing (26). Slide differential assembly from transaxle housing (51) and lay it aside for later disassembly. Remove bowed "E" ring (47) and while holding bull gear (48), withdraw intermediate shaft (50) and spacer (49) from housing. Lift out bull gear.

Remove six cap screws (34) from differential assembly and separate axle assemblies from ring gear (37). Remove floating pinion shaft (43), pinion gears (41) and thrust washers (40) from ring gear. Side gears (39), shims (38) and covers (36 and 44) can be removed from axle shafts after first removing retaining rings (42).

Remove bushing (20) with parking pawl (24) from transaxle housing.

Inspect all parts and renew any showing excessive wear or other damage. When renewing needle bearings, press new bearings beyond machined casting

***Fig. B68—Exploded view of gear reduction and differential assembly used on Models H11XL, H12XL, H14XL and H16XL.***

1. Oil seal
2. Needle bearing
3. Bevel gear
4. Key
5. Pinion shaft
6. Thrust race
7. Thrust bearing
8. Needle bearing
9. Transaxle cover (R.H.)
10. Bearing
11. Oil seal
12. Needle bearing
13. Thrust race
14. Cluster gear assy.
15. Transaxle housing
16. Dipstick assy.
17. Differential cover
18. Axle gear
19. Snap ring
20. Pinion gear
21. Snap ring
22. Pinion shaft
23. Carrier
24. Ring gear
25. Shim
26. Spacer
27. Thrust bearing
28. Thrust race
29. Needle bearing
30. Axle (R.H.)
31. Oil seal
32. Bearing
33. Transaxle cover (L.H.)
34. Axle (L.H.)

surface as follows: Axle bearings (32) 0.040 inch (1.016 mm) below machined surface; needle bearings (28) 0.005-0.030 inch (0.127-0.762 mm) below machined surface; intermediate shaft needle bearing (46) 0.005-0.020 inch (0.127-0.508 mm) below machined surface.

Reassemble differential, keeping the following points in mind: Right hand axle shaft (45) is more than 2 inches (50 mm) longer than left axle shaft (35), and cover (44) with threaded bolt holes must be assembled on right hand axle shaft. After bolting differential assembly together, support differential on end cover (44) only with axle shaft (45) pointing downward. Insert a feeler gage between shim (38) and end cover (36) through one of the end cover slots, to measure clearance. Add or remove shims as required to obtain a clearance of 0.001-0.007 inch (0.025-0.178 mm). This will provide proper differential bevel gear backlash.

Renew all "O" rings, gaskets and oil seals and reassemble transaxle by reversing disassembly procedure.

Reinstall assembly on tractor; fill with Bolens #171-9650 hydraulic oil or Type "A" automatic transmission fluid and adjust linkage as necessary.

## Model QS16

After removing rear axle assembly with hydrostatic drive unit, thoroughly clean entire unit to eliminate possibility of dirt entering system when hydrostatic unit is separated.

Remove plug (9–Fig. B70) to drain fluid from system, then four mounting cap screws so hydrostatic unit can be lifted off and set aside. Continue disassembly by removal of right hand drive wheel, hub, brake disc rotor and Woodruff key (10). Back out cap screws (33) and remove right hand housing and axle sleeve (34) by sliding carefully from axle (19). Entire reduction gear set, cluster gear (8), pinion shaft (5) and input bevel gear (4) can be slipped together from housing (3). Watch for thrust races (7) during removal. Remove left side cover (25) after wheel, hub and brake disc are removed, then both axles (11 and 19) and complete bull gear (16) assembly can be removed.

Carefully inspect all thrust races (7) and thrust bearings (30) for undue wear,

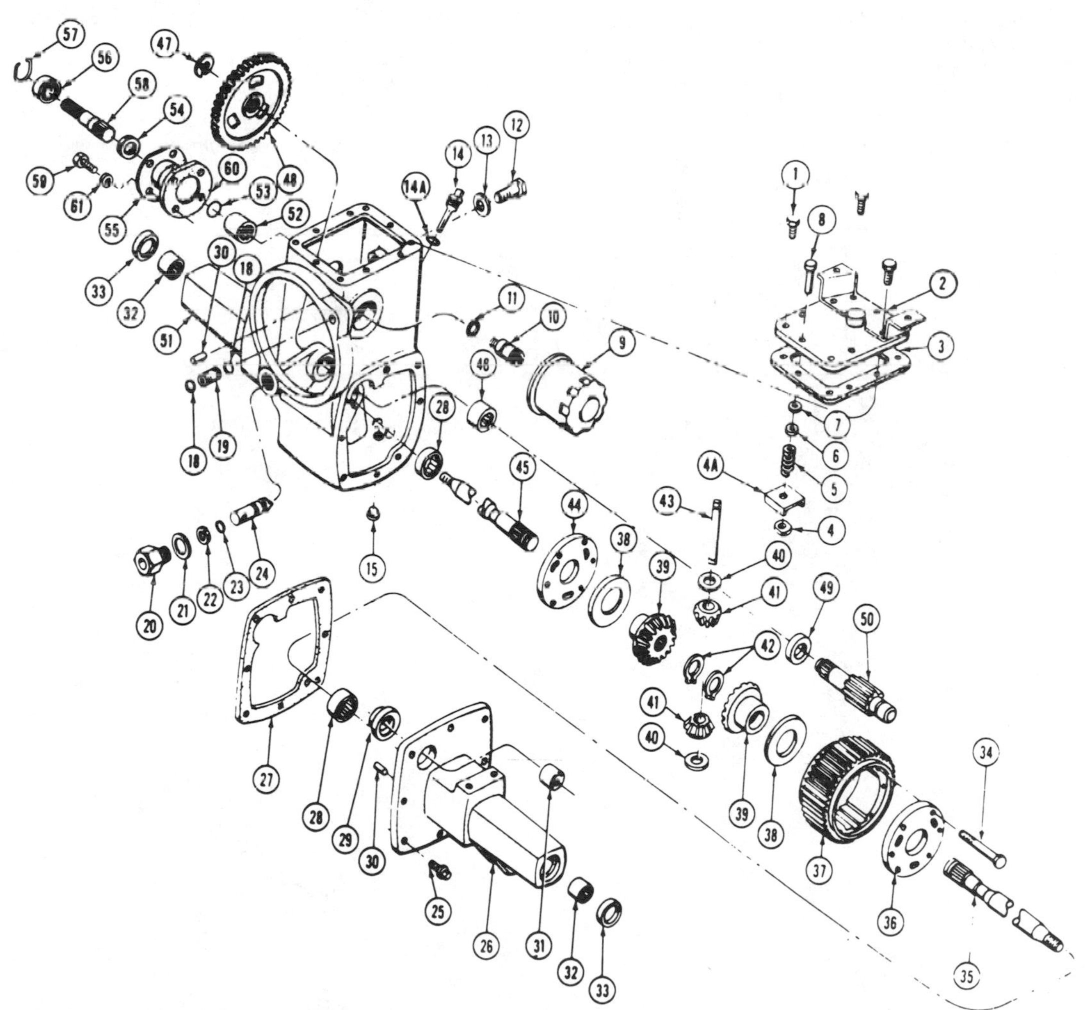

*Fig. B69—Exploded view of axle, reduction gear and differential unit used on Models 1455, 1476 and 1477.*

1. Cap screw
2. Cover
3. Gasket
4. Speed nut
4A. Deflector
5. Spring
6. Washer
7. Gasket
8. Unloader button
9. Oil filter
10. Filter stud
11. "O" ring
12. Locating bolt
13. Seal washer
14. Dipstick
14A. "O" ring
15. Drain plug
18. "O" rings
19. Tube
20. Bushing
21. Seal washer
22. Quad ring
23. "O" ring
24. Parking pawl
25. Cap screw
26. Axle housing
27. Gasket
28. Needle bearing
29. Spacer
30. Dowel
31. Needle bearing
32. Needle bearing
33. Oil seal
34. Cap screw
35. Axle shaft (L.H.)
36. Cover (L.H.)
37. Ring gear
38. Shim
39. Side gears
40. Thrust washers
41. Pinion gears
42. Retaining rings
43. Shaft
44. Cover (R.H.)
54. Axle (R.H.)
46. Needle bearing
47. Bowed "E" ring
48. Bull gear
49. Spacer
50. Intermediate shaft
51. Transaxle housing
52. Coupling
53. Snap ring
54. Oil seal
55. Bearing flange
56. Ball bearing
57. Snap ring
58. Brake shaft
59. Cap screw
60. Gasket
61. Seal washer

galling or other damage. Remove axle seals (23) and remove and check condition of axle needle bearings (24). Renew bearings as needed, installing so they are seated from 1/32 to 1/16 inch (0.8-1.5 mm) past counterbore for axle seal. Always renew seals when axle is disassembled for any reason. Be sure to use a properly fitted seal driver.

Carefully check condition of all needle bearings (24, 27 and 28) in side housings; renew if at all doubtful. Press new bearings, identification side out, with a fitted drive to a point 1/32 to 1/16 inch (0.8-1.5 mm) below machined surface.

If there is evidence of damage or excessive wear in axle-differential assembly, remove four cap screws (20) so axle and bull gear carriers (12 and 18) can be removed. Side bevel gears (13) can be removed from axles (11 and 19) after snap rings (14) are removed. Check condition of pinion gears (15) and pinion shaft (17) and renew as needed.

**NOTE: When renewing any gears, be sure part numbers are properly checked out; ratios may differ.**

To reassemble final drive when overhaul is complete, begin with bull gear-differential and axles. When carrier side plates (12 and 18) are set in place, cap screws (20) should be tightened to 30 ft.-lbs. (41 N·m) in even cross-sequence. Rotation should be free with no perceptible binding or roughness between pinions and side gears. Minimum of 0.010 inch (0.254 mm) alxe end play is essential. Side gear should have 0.004 inch (0.102 mm) minimum clearance with bull gear carriers (12 and 18). Axle shaft end play is most easily checked by measuring between inner end of spacer (31) and carrier side plate (18) when axle is partially reassembled. Use a feeler gage, and add or remove shims to hold within limits of 0.005-0.030 inch (0.127-0.762 mm).

Backlash between all gear sets is 0.004-0.010 inch (0.102-0.254 mm).

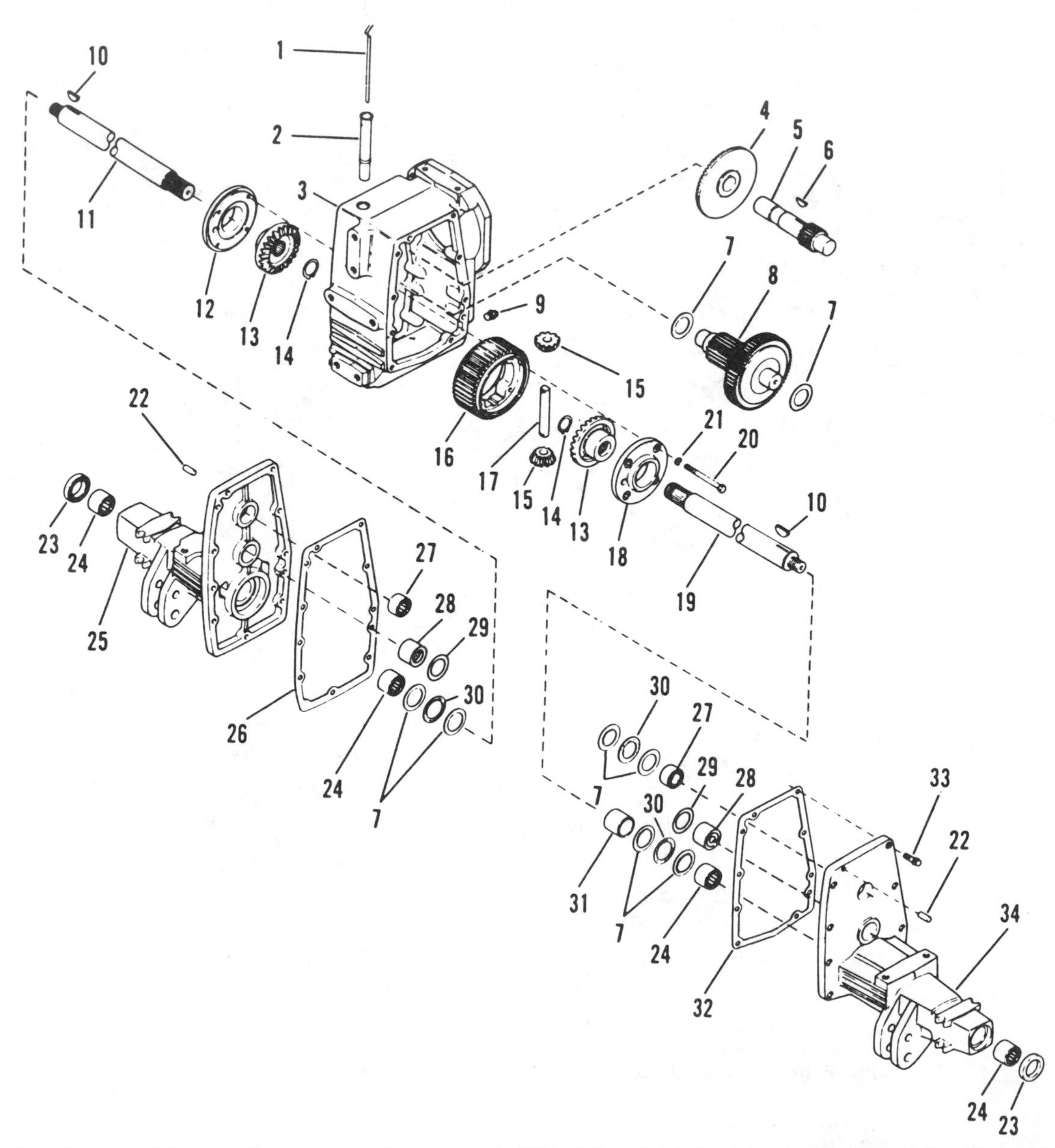

***Fig. B70—Exploded view of final drive-reduction gear and differential used with Sundstrand hydrostatic unit on Model QS16.***

1. Dipstick
2. Fill pipe
3. Housing
4. Input bevel gear
5. Pinion shaft
6. Woodruff key
7. Thrust race (8)
8. Cluster gear
9. Plug
10. Woodruff key (2)
11. Axle (L.H.)
12. Bull gear carrier (L.H.)
13. Side gear (2)
14. Snap ring (2)
15. Pinion gear
16. Bull gear
17. Pinion shaft
18. Bull gear carrier (R.H.)
19. Axle (R.H.)
20. Cap screw (4)
21. Lockwasher
22. Dowel pin (4)
23. Oil seal (2)
24. Needle bearing (4)
25. Housing cover (L.H.)
26. Cover gasket
27. Nedle bearing
28. Needle bearing
29. Shim(s)
30. Thrust bearing (3)
31. Spacer
32. Cover gasket
33. Cap screw (17)
34. Housing cover (R.H.)

Check after gears are reinstalled in case. Use new side gaskets (26 and 32). Check side clearance of cluster gear (8) between thrust washer (7) and right hand side cover. Add or remove shims (29) if not within 0.005-0.030 inch (0.127-0.762 mm) limit. Remove right hand cover to do so. When assembly is completed, torque cover cap screws to 30 ft.-lbs. (41 N·m).

Check entire reduction gear assembly for freedom of rotation before remounting hydrostatic unit. Refill axle housing with specified fluid and reassemble to tractor frame. Test and perform required adjustments.

# HYDRAULIC SYSTEM

## All Models So Equipped

**TESTING.** Hydraulic lift system pressure is provided by charge and auxiliary hydraulic pump located in hydrostatic transmission. Hydraulic lift pressure should be 450-500 psi (3100-3447 kPa) on all models except QS16, which should be 550-800 psi (3792-5516 kPa).

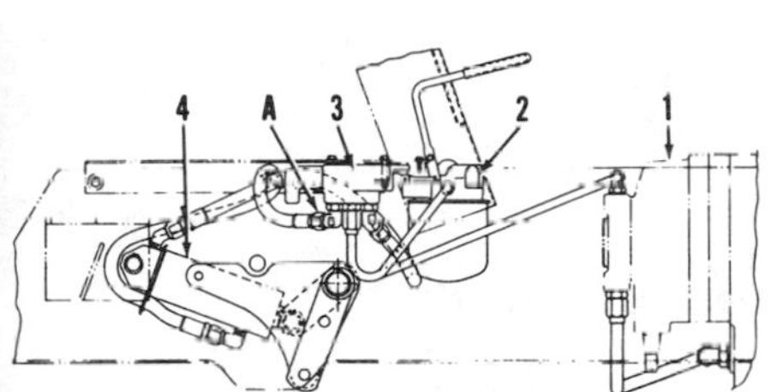


***Fig. B71 — On models so equipped, hydrostatic charge pump supplies hydraulic lift system pressure. To check pressure, install a 1000 psi (7000 kPa) pressure gage in hydraulic line "A" using a tee fitting. Refer to text.***

1. Hydrostatic transmission
2. Oil filter
3. Control valve
4. Hydraulic cylinder

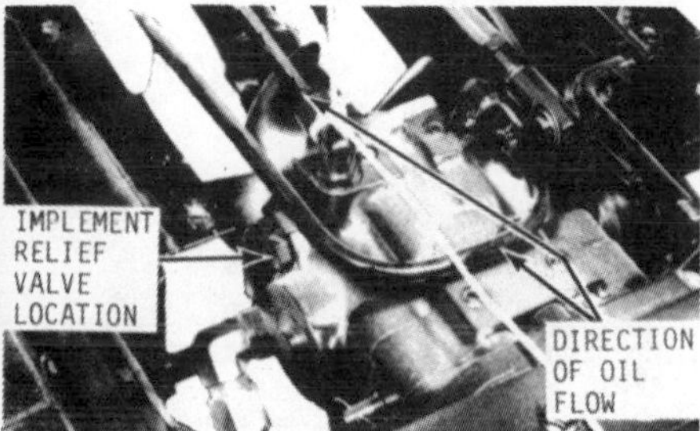


***Fig. B72 — On Model QS16, implement relief valve is located behind plug as shown. Shims are available to adjust pressure.***

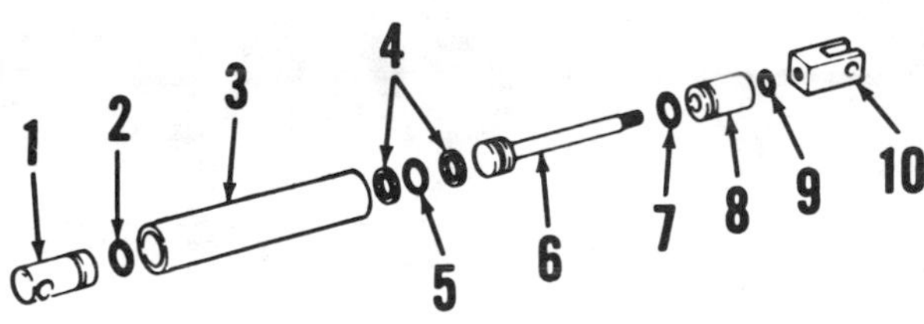


***Fig. B73 — Exploded view of early style hydraulic cylinder used on some models.***

1. Cylinder head
2. "O" ring
3. Cylinder tube
4. Washers
5. "O" ring
6. Piston & rod
7. "O" ring
8. Gland
9. "O" ring
10. Clevis

To check pressure on all models, proceed as follows: Using a tee fitting, install a 1000 psi (7000 kPa) pressure gage in hydraulic line (A – Fig. B71) between control valve (3) and lift cylinder (4). With oil at operating temperature and engine running at full rpm, move control lever until cylinder reaches end of its travel and observe pressure reading.

If pressure is low, check the following:

1. System low on oil.
2. Plugged hydraulic filter.
3. Hydraulic valve or cylinder leaking internally.
4. Malfunctioning implement relief valve.
5. Charge pump defective.

On Model QS16, shims are available to increase implement relief valve pressure setting. See Fig. B72. One 0.012 inch shim will increase pressure approximately 50 psi (345 kPa).

### HYDRAULIC CYLINDER

## All Models So Equipped

To remove piston rod assembly from cylinder, elbow hose fittings must first be removed from cylinder tube. Refer to appropriate Fig. B73 or B74. Then, remove cylinder gland (8) from cylinder tube and withdraw piston rod assembly from cylinder.

Inspect piston and cylinder for wear, scoring or other damage and renew as necessary. Renew all "O" rings and ring washers. Coat all "O" rings with grease to prevent damage during reassembly.

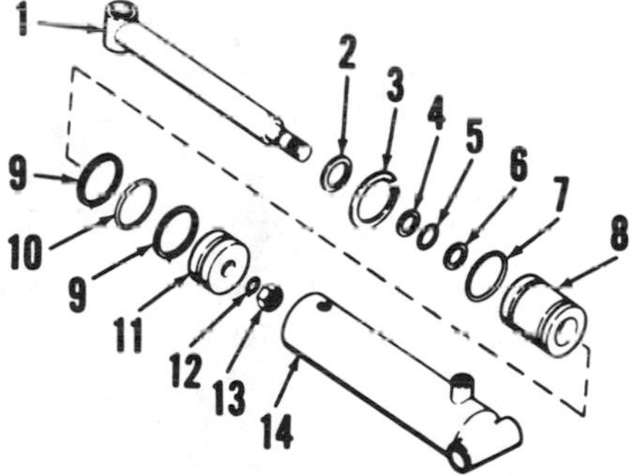


***Fig. B74 — Exploded view of late style hydraulic cylinder used on some models.***

1. Piston rod
2. Seal
3. Snap ring
4. Washer
5. "O" ring
6. Washer
7. "O" ring
8. Gland
9. Washer
10. "O" ring
11. Piston
12. Washer
13. Nut
14. Cylinder

### CONTROL VALVE

## All Models So Equipped

To remove spool (7 – Fig. B75) from valve body (5), remove screw from end of spool, detent assembly and centering spring and guides. Withdraw spool from lever end of valve body.

If spool or valve body is damaged, renew complete valve assembly. Install new lip seal rings (6) onto spool with lip opening towards inside of spool. Coat seal rings with grease and reinstall spool into valve body from lever end.

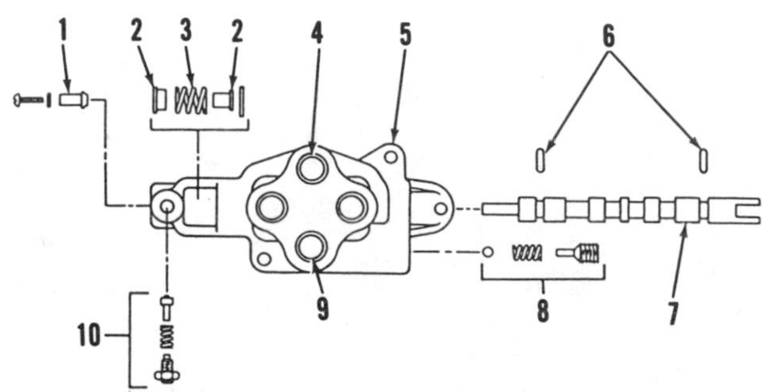

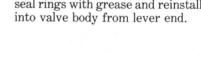

***Fig. B75 — Exploded view of typical hydraulic lift control valve. When renewing lip seals (6), lip opening goes towards inside of spool (7).***

1. Detent ramp
2. Spring guides
3. Centering spring
4. Outlet
5. Valve body
6. Lip seals
7. Valve spool
8. Relief valve assy.
9. Inlet
10. Detent assy.

# CASE/INGERSOLL

## CONDENSED SPECIFICATIONS

| | MODELS | | | | |
|---|---|---|---|---|---|
| | 107 | 108 | 110 | 117 | 118 |
| Engine Make | Tecumseh | B&S | B&S | Tecumseh | B&S |
| Model | V70 | 190707 | 251707 | V70 | 190707 |
| Bore | 2¾ in. (69.8 mm) | 3 in. (76.2 mm) | 3-7/16 in. (87.3 mm) | 2¾ in. (69.8 mm) | 3 in. (76.2 mm) |
| Stroke | 2-17/32 in. (64.3 mm) | 2¾ in. (69.8 mm) | 2⅝ in. (66.7 mm) | 2-17/32 in. (64.3 mm) | 2¾ in. (69.8 mm) |
| Piston Displacement | 15 cu. in. (246 cc) | 19.44 cu. in. (319 cc) | 24.36 cu. in. (399 cc) | 15 cu. in. (246 cc) | 19.44 cu. in. (319 cc) |
| Horsepower | 7 | 8 | 10 | 7 | 8 |
| Slow Idle Speed – Rpm | 1000 | 1750 | 1750 | 1000 | 1750 |
| High Idle Speed (No Load) – Rpm | 3600 | 3600 | 3600 | 3600 | 3600 |
| Full Load Speed – Rpm | 3500 | 3500 | 3500 | 3500 | 3500 |
| Crankcase Oil Capacity | 1½ pints (0.7L) | 2¼ pints (1L) | 2¼ pints (1L) | 1½ pints (0.7L) | 2¼ pints (1L) |
| Weight – | | | | | |
| Above 32°F (0°C) | SAE 30 | | | | |
| 0°F (–18°C) to 32°F (0°C) | SAE 10W-30 | | | | |
| Below 0°F (–18°C) | SAE 5W-20 | | | | |
| Transmission Oil Capacity | 2 pints (0.9L) | 2 pints (0.9L) | 2 pints (0.9L) | .......... | .......... |
| Weight | SAE 90 EP | SAE 90 EP | SAE 90 EP | Type "A" | Type "A" |
| Differential Oil Capacity | .......... | .......... | .......... | 2¾ pints (1.3L) | 2¾ pints (1.3L) |

| | MODELS | | | |
|---|---|---|---|---|
| | 210 | 220 | 222, 442 | 224, 444 |
| Engine Make | Kohler | Kohler | Kohler | Kohler |
| Model | K241A | K241A | K301A | K321A |
| Bore | 3¼ in. (82.5 mm) | 3¼ in. (82.5 mm) | 3⅜ in. (85.7 mm) | 3½ in. (88.9 mm) |
| Stroke | 2⅞ in. (73.0 mm) | 2⅞ in. (73.0 mm) | 3¼ in. (82.5 mm) | 3¼ in. (82.5 mm) |
| Piston Displacement | 23.9 cu. in. (392 cc) | 23.9 cu. in. (392 cc) | 29.07 cu. in. (476 cc) | 31.27 cu. in. (512 cc) |
| Horsepower | 10 | 10 | 12 | 14 |
| Slow Idle Speed – Rpm | 1000 | 1000 | 1000 | 1000 |
| High Idle Speed (No Load) – Rpm | 3600 | 3600 | 3600 | 3600 |
| Full Load Speed – Rpm | 3500 | 3400 | 3400 | 3500 |
| Crankcase Oil Capacity | 3 pints (1.4L) | 3 pints (1.4L) | 3 pints (1.4L) | 4 pints (1.9L) |
| Weight – | | | | |
| Above 32°F (0°C) | SAE 30 | | | |
| 0°F (–18°C) to 32°F (0°C) | SAE 10W-30 | | | |
| Below 0°F (–18°C) | SAE 5W-20 | | | |
| Transmission Oil Capacity | 3 pints (1.4L) | 10 pints (4.7L) | 10 pints (4.7L) | 10 pints (4.7L) |
| Weight – | | | | |
| Above 32°F (0°C) | SAE 90 EP | SAE 20W-40 | SAE 20W-40 | SAE 20W-40 |
| Below 32°F (0°C) | SAE 90 EP | SAE 5W-20 | SAE 5W-20 | SAE 5W-20 |
| Differential Oil Capacity | .......... | 6 pints (2.8L) | 6 pints (2.8L) | 6 pints (2.8L) |
| Weight | .......... | SAE 90 EP | SAE 90 EP | SAE 90 EP |

# FRONT AXLE AND STEERING SYSTEM

## AXLE MAIN MEMBER

### All Models

The axle main member is mounted to main frame and pivots on a pivot pin on all models. To remove axle assembly, refer to Figs. C1 or C2, then disconnect drag link from steering arm on Models 107, 108, 110, 117 and 118 or from right steering spindle on all other models. Using a suitable jack under main frame, raise front of tractor until weight is removed from front wheels. Remove pivot pin, then raise front of tractor to clear axle main member. Roll front axle assembly forward from tractor.

## TIE ROD

### All Models

The tie rod used on all models is adjustable and front wheel toe-in is adjusted as follows: Disconnect tie rod ball joints (5–Fig. C1 or 10 and 12–Fig. C2) from steering spindles, loosen locknuts, and turn tie rod ends in or out as required. The correct toe-in is 1/8 to 1/4-inch (3-6 mm) measured as shown in Fig. C3.

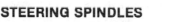

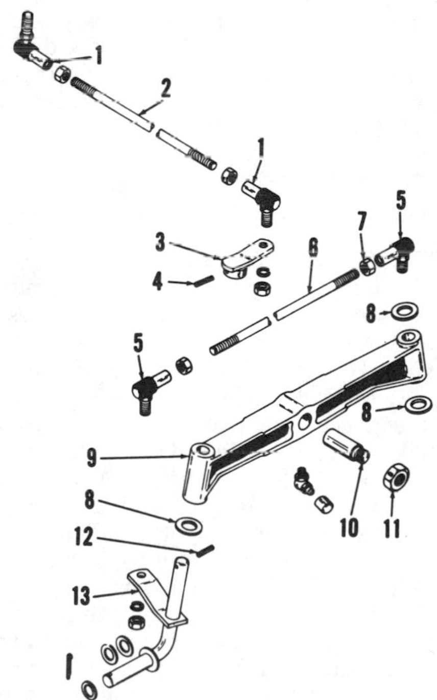

*Fig. C1—Exploded view of axle main member assembly used on Models 107, 108, 110, 117 and 118.*

1. Ball joint
2. Drag link
3. Steering arm
4. Roll pin
5. Ball joint
6. Tie rod
7. Locknut
8. Washer
9. Axle main member
10. Pivot pin
11. Nut
12. Roll pin
13. Steering spindle

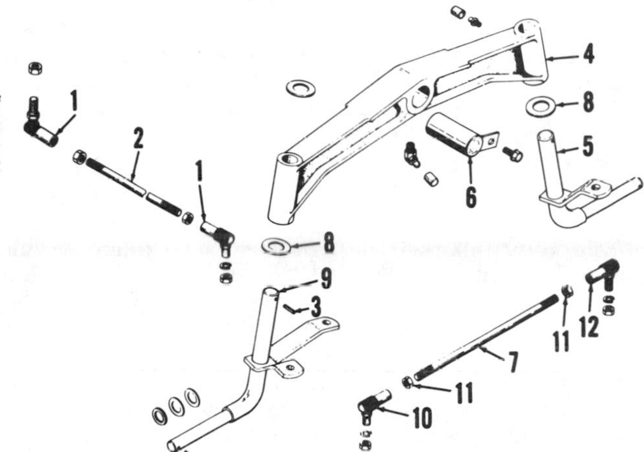

*Fig. C2—Exploded view of front axle and components used on Model 442. Models 210, 220, 222, 224 and 444 are similar.*

1. Ball joint
2. Drag link
3. Roll pin
4. Axle main member
5. Steering spindle L.H.
6. Pivot pin
7. Tie rod
8. Thrust washer
9. Steering spindle R.H.
10. Ball joint
11. Locknut
12. Ball joint

## STEERING SPINDLES

### All Models

To remove steering spindles, block up under axle main member and remove front wheels. Disconnect drag link from right steering arm on Models 107, 108, 110, 117 and 118, or from right steering spindle on other models and remove tie rod. Remove cotter pins and washers, retaining rings or roll pins from top of steering spindles and lower steering spindles out of axle main member.

## STEERING GEAR

### Models 107-108-110-117-118

**R&R AND OVERHAUL.** Refer to Fig. C4 and remove steering wheel retaining nut (1), steering wheel and key (4). Disconnect drag link from quadrant gear (7). Using a suitable jack or hoist, raise front of tractor. Unscrew cap screws retaining pivot pin (8) and remove pin and quadrant gear (7). Withdraw steering shaft (3) through bottom of tractor. Remove and inspect bushings (2) for excessive wear.

Reinstall by reversing removal procedure. Position quadrant gear arm at a

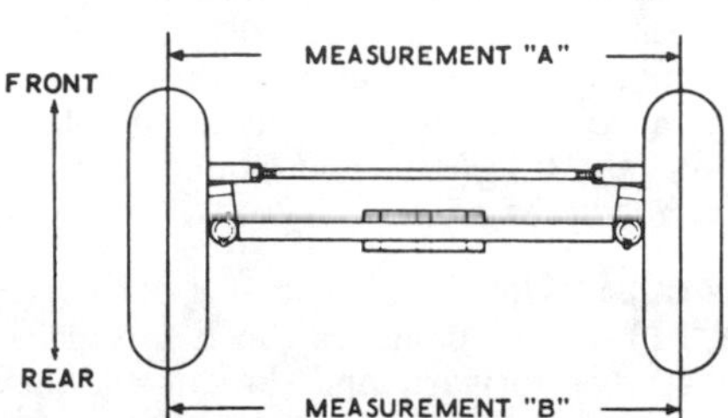


*Fig. C3—Toe-in measurement "A" should be 1/8 to 1/4-inch (3-6 mm) less than measurement "B" with both measurements taken at hub height.*

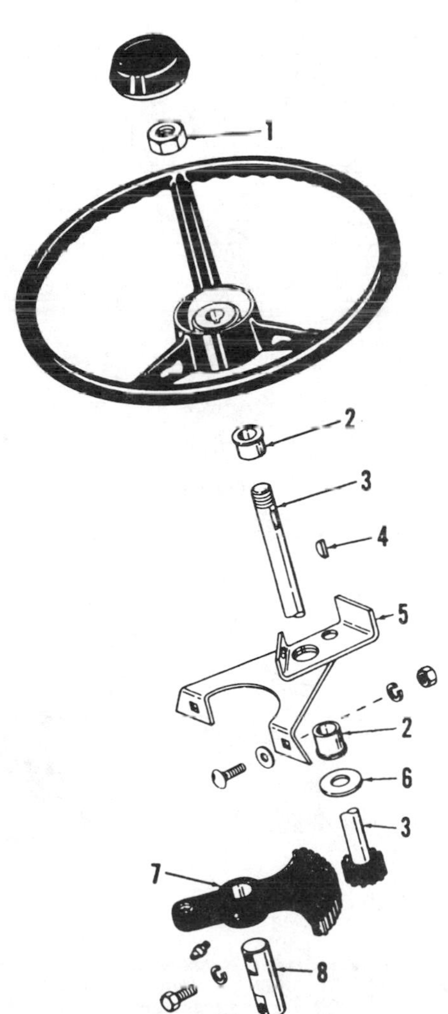

*Fig. C4—Exploded view of steering gear assembly used on Models 107, 108, 110, 117 and 118.*

1. Nut
2. Bushing
3. Steering shaft & pinion
4. Key
5. Bracket
6. Washer
7. Quadrant gear
8. Steering pin

90 degree angle to drag link with front wheels in straight ahead position and connect drag link.

### Models 210-220-222-224-442-444

**R&R AND OVERHAUL.** Refer to Fig. C5 or C6 and remove steering wheel retaining nut and steering wheel (1). On late Models 220, 222, 442 and 444 and all 224 tractors, remove key (17 – Fig. C6) and tube (16). On all models, raise front of tractor using a suitable jack or hoist and disconnect drag link from quadrant gear (11 – Fig. C5 or C6). Remove cap screw (15), lockwasher (14), washer (13), quadrant gear (11) and shims (10 and 12). Shims (10 and 12) should be kept in the order they are removed to aid in reassembly. On early Models 210, 220, 222, 442 and 444, unseat retaining ring (4 – Fig. C5) from its groove, then on all models withdraw steering shaft and pinion (3 – Fig. C5 or C6) from steering support (7) and from underside of tractor. Remove nylon bushing (2) from steering column. Unbolt and remove steering support (7). Remove locknut (6), then unscrew stub shaft (9) from support.

Clean and inspect all parts and renew any showing excessive wear or other damage. To reassemble, reverse disassembly procedure. On early Models 210, 220, 222, 442 and 444 steering shaft (3 – Fig. C5) end play is controlled by washers (5 and 8) and retaining ring (4). On late production models and all 224 tractors, tighten steering wheel retaining nut to remove excessive end play of steering shaft (3). Shims (10 – Fig. C5 or C6) are used to adjust gear backlash between quadrant gear (11) and steering shaft pinion. Adjust gear backlash by repositioning shims (10) from upper to lower side of quadrant gear (11) to decrease backlash or from lower to upper side of quadrant gear to increase backlash. Backlash should be minimal without causing binding of gears. Gears should be lubricated with good quality multi-purpose grease after every 50 hours of operation.

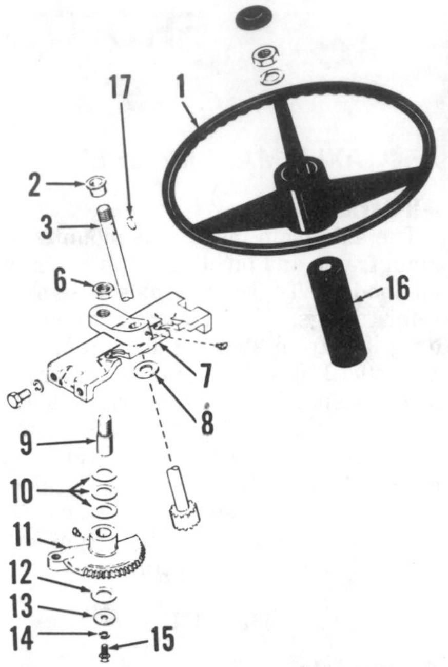

*Fig. C6 – Exploded view of steering gear assembly used on late production 220, 222, 442 and 444 tractors and all 224 tractors.*

1. Steering wheel
2. Nylon bushing
3. Steering shaft & pinion
6. Locknut
7. Steering support
8. Washer
9. Stub shaft
10. Shims
11. Quadrant gear
12. Shim
13. Washer
14. Lockwasher
15. Cap screw
16. Tube
17. Key

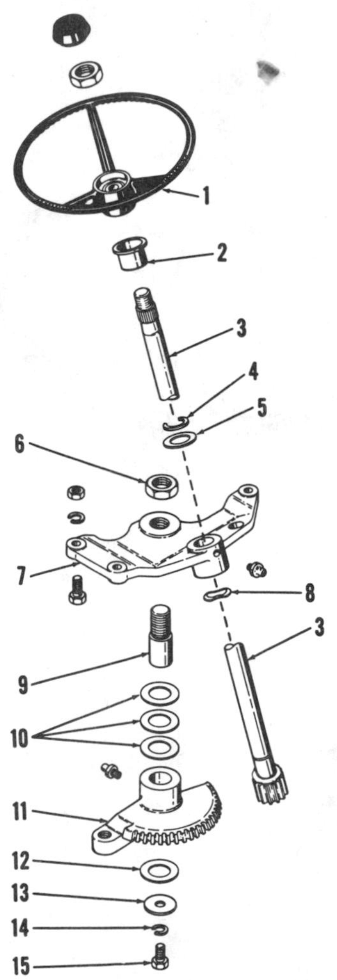


*Fig. C5 – Exploded view of steering gear assembly used on Model 210 and early production 220, 222, 442 and 444 tractors.*

1. Steering wheel
2. Bushing
3. Steering shaft & pinion
4. Retainer ring
5. Washer
6. Nut
7. Support plate
8. Wave washer
9. Steering pin
10. Shims
11. Quadrant gear
12. Shim
13. Washer
14. Lockwasher
15. Cap screw

# ENGINE

## REMOVE AND REINSTALL

### Models 107-117

To remove engine, remove hood and grille and disconnect battery cables. Disconnect fuel line, starter generator wires, ignition wire and choke and throttle control cables. Detach drive belts from engine drive pulley. Unscrew mounting bolts and lift engine from tractor.

To reinstall engine, reverse removal procedure.

### Models 108-110-118

To remove engine, tilt hood and grille assembly forward, disconnect battery cables and remove battery. Disconnect starter cable, alternator wire and magneto ground wire. Disconnect fuel line and choke and throttle control cable. Remove belts from engine drive pulley. Remove four engine mounting plate bolts and lift engine and mounting plate from tractor.

### Model 210

To remove engine, tilt hood and grille assembly forward and disconnect battery cables, starter-generator wires and ignition wire. Disconnect headlight wire, choke and throttle control cables and fuel line. Unbolt and remove belt guard, then remove belt from engine drive pulley. Disconnect pto clutch linkage. Remove four engine mount cap screws and lift engine and mounting plates from tractor.

Reinstall engine assembly by reversing removal procedure.

### Models 220-222-224-442-444

To remove engine, tilt hood and grille forward. Disconnect battery cables, starter-generator wires and ignition wire. Disconnect headlight wires and pull through hole in engine plate. Disconnect choke and throttle cables and fuel line. Disconnect pto clutch control rod (models so equipped). Disconnect hydraulic line at oil tank and drain oil tank. Disconnect hydraulic line leading to oil cooler. Unscrew mounting bolts securing bracket holding oil tank and oil cooler and remove as an assembly. On late production 220, 222 and 442 tractors and all 224 and 444 tractors, drain engine crankcase and remove drain tube. Disconnect oil lines from hydraulic pump, unbolt engine and lift engine and pump from tractor frame.

To reinstall engine, reverse removal procedure. Be sure crankcase and hydraulic reservoir are refilled and hydraulic hoses are properly connected before starting engine.

### OVERHAUL

Engine make and model are listed at the beginning of this section. To overhaul engine components and accessories, refer to Briggs & Stratton, Kohler and Tecumseh sections of this manual.

# CLUTCH AND BRAKE

## Model 107

The clutch and brake mechanisms are actuated by clutch-brake pedal on right side of tractor. Refer to Fig. C7 for an exploded view of clutch and brake assemblies. Clutch is spring loaded and does not require adjustment. To adjust brake, turn adjusting nuts (11 – Fig. C7) so brake will engage when clutch is disengaged.

## Model 108-110

A belt idler type clutch and a disc brake are used on these tractors. The clutch idler is spring loaded and does not require adjustment. Refer to Fig. C8 for exploded view of clutch and brake assemblies. To adjust brake, disconnect eye-bolt (15) from actuating lever (23). Adjust nuts (24) until free movement at top of actuating lever does not exceed ½-inch (13 mm), then reconnect eye-bolt. Adjust nut (13) on brake rod so brake will engage when clutch is fully disengaged.

## Model 117

A clutch is not used on Model 117 tractors. The control arm of hydrostatic transmission has a natural tendency to return to neutral position when there is no tension against arm. To prevent control arm from working into neutral position when speed control lever is released, a plate attached to control arm is held by a friction button on the end of brake control rod. Refer to Fig. C9. When brake is applied, the plate is released and transmission control arm is allowed to move into neutral position.

To adjust brake, turn adjusting nuts (13) to provide sufficient braking action. After adjusting brake, adjustment of neutral linkage should be checked.

## Model 118

The belt idler clutch is operated by clutch-brake pedal on right side of tractor. As pedal is depressed, pin on clutch-brake pedal rotates pivot plate (8 – Fig. C10) and clutch idler (7) to release tension on drive belt (2). As pedal is further depressed, brake band (16) is drawn tight on brake drum (13). Adjust brake by turning nut (14) on brake rod. Make certain clutch is fully disengaged before brake is applied.

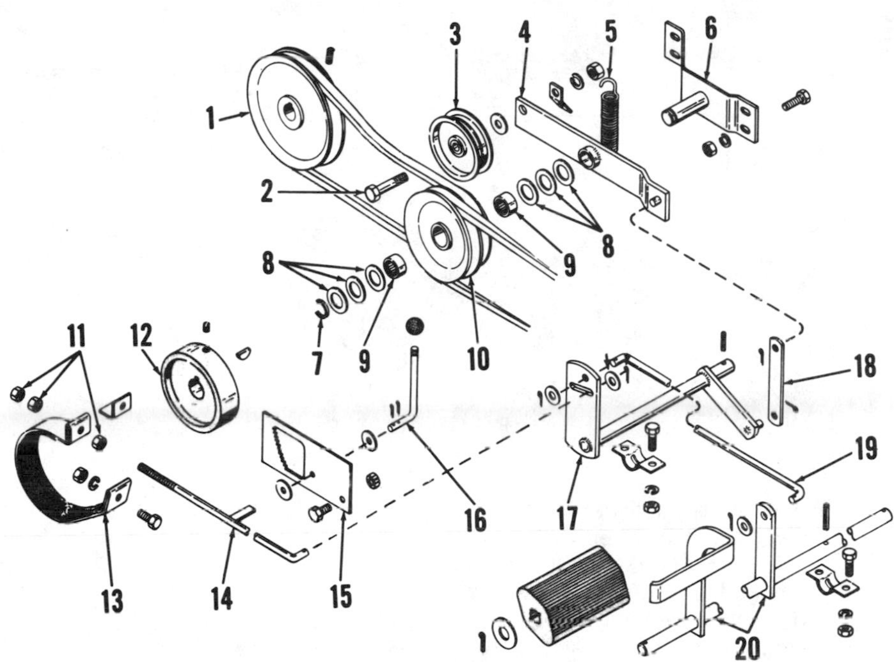

*Fig. C7 – View showing clutch and brake assemblies on Model 107.*

1. Transmission pulley
2. Bolt
3. Clutch idler pulley
4. Lever
5. Spring
6. Jackshaft
7. Snap ring
8. Washers
9. Bearing
10. Jackshaft pulley
11. Nuts
12. Brake drum
13. Brake band
14. Brake rod
15. Parking brake bracket
16. Parking brake lever
17. Lever
18. Idler arm
19. Clutch-brake rod
20. Pedal & shaft

## Model 210

The belt idler clutch is operated by clutch-brake pedal on left side of tractor. To adjust clutch, loosen locknut (8 – Fig.

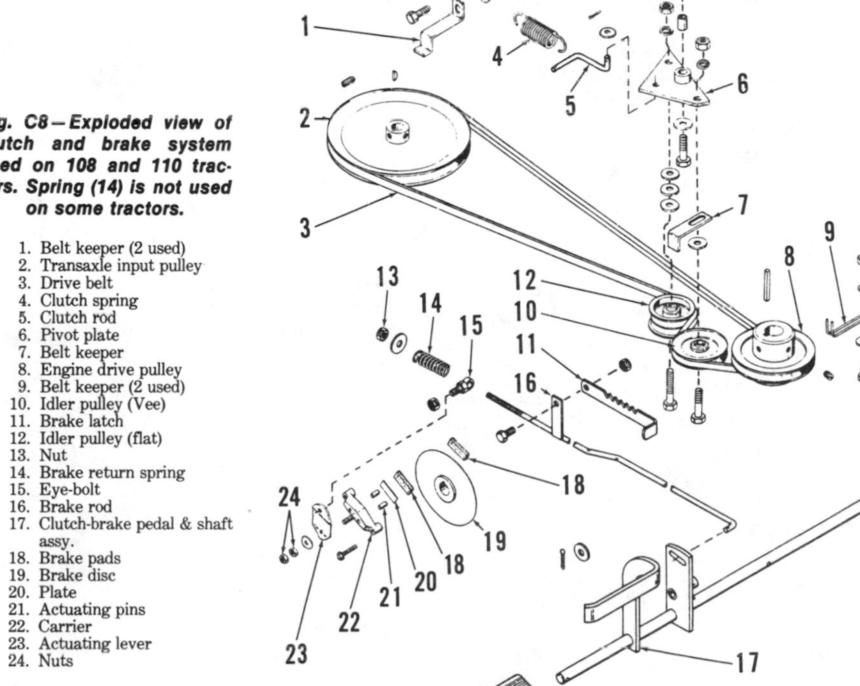

*Fig. C8 – Exploded view of clutch and brake system used on 108 and 110 tractors. Spring (14) is not used on some tractors.*

1. Belt keeper (2 used)
2. Transaxle input pulley
3. Drive belt
4. Clutch spring
5. Clutch rod
6. Pivot plate
7. Belt keeper
8. Engine drive pulley
9. Belt keeper (2 used)
10. Idler pulley (Vee)
11. Brake latch
12. Idler pulley (flat)
13. Nut
14. Brake return spring
15. Eye-bolt
16. Brake rod
17. Clutch-brake pedal & shaft assy.
18. Brake pads
19. Brake disc
20. Plate
21. Actuating pins
22. Carrier
23. Actuating lever
24. Nuts

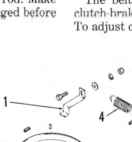

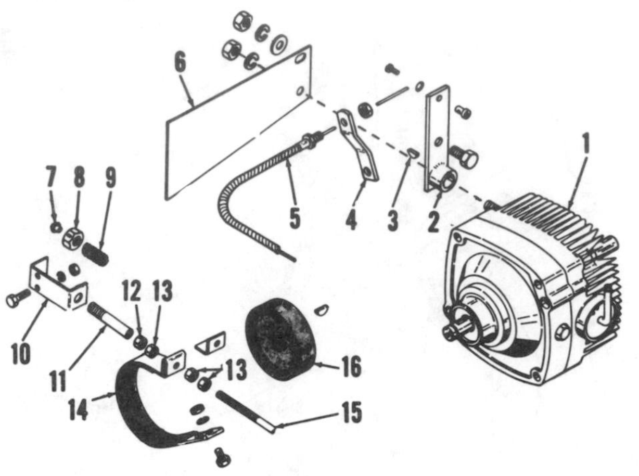


*Fig. C9—View showing brake and transmission friction plate on Model 117.*

1. Transmission
2. Control arm
3. Key
4. Cable bracket
5. Speed control cable
6. Friction plate
7. Friction button
8. Nut
9. Spring
10. Bracket
11. Rod extension
12. Locknut
13. Adjusting nuts
14. Brake band
15. Brake rod
16. Brake drum

C11) and rotate turnbuckle (7) as necessary until a clearance of 1/8-inch (3 mm) is obtained between brake latch pin on pedal arm and instrument tower side panel. Tighten locknut.

To adjust brake, turn adjusting nuts (1) on brake link (9) so clutch will fully disengage before brake is applied. With pedal in normal (up) position, compressed length of brake spring (2) should be approximately 1¼ inches (32 mm).

### Models 220-222-224-442-444

To adjust brake on early production 220, 222, 442 and 444 tractors, refer to Fig. C12. Remove clevis pin (8) and turn clevis (9) until there is sufficient braking action when brake pedal is depressed. Do not over-adjust brake. When brake pedal is depressed, there must be enough brake pedal travel for neutral return spring attached to brake pedal to return speed control lever to neutral.

Later production 220, 222, 442 and 444 models, and all 224 tractors are equipped with band type brake shown in Fig. C13. To adjust brake, first adjust brake linkage mounting nuts to obtain 0.010-0.015 inch (0.254-0.381 mm) clearance between washers and brake arms. Disconnect brake rod clevis from vertical link. Place range transmission in neutral position. Tighten band adjusting nut until tractor cannot be moved manually, then back nut off 1½ turns. Hold brake vertical link in vertical position and push it rearward until all slack is removed from linkage. With brake pedal in full release (up) position, adjust clevis on linkage rod until holes in clevis are aligned with hole in vertical link. Install clevis pin.

# DRIVE BELTS

## REMOVE AND REINSTALL

### Model 107

To remove front drive belt, remove pto drive belt from engine pulley. Move spring loaded idler away from front drive belt and slide drive belt off engine pulley and jackshaft pulley (10–Fig. C7). To remove rear drive belt, remove front drive belt as previously outlined, disengage clutch and slide rear drive belt off jackshaft pulley (10) and transmission pulley (1).

### Model 108-110

To remove drive belt (3–Fig. C8), depress clutch-brake pedal and lock in this position with brake latch (11). Loosen retaining bolts and move belt keepers (1, 7 and 9) away from belt. Remove drive belt from pulleys.

Install new drive belt, making certain belt is positioned around idlers (10 and 12) as shown in Fig. C8. Adjust all belt keepers to 1/16-inch (1.5 mm) from belt when clutch-brake pedal is in normal (up) position. Belt keeper (7) should be positioned halfway between points where belt enters and leaves Vee idler pulley (10).

### Model 117

To remove drive belt, first remove pto drive belt from engine pulley. Move spring loaded idler away from front of drive belt and slide drive belt off engine pulley and transmission pulley.

Install new drive belt by reversing removal procedure.

### Model 118

To remove drive belt (2–Fig. C10), first tilt hood forward and remove battery. Loosen retaining nuts and move belt keepers (4, 6 and 12) away from belt. Remove pto drive belt from engine pulley (5). Depress clutch-brake pedal and engage brake latch (10). Remove drive belt.

Using Fig. C10 as a guide, install new belt on pulleys as shown. Install pto drive belt on engine pulley. Release clutch-brake pedal. Adjust all belt keepers to 1/16-inch (1.5 mm) clearance from belt when pedal is in normal (up) position. Belt keeper (4) should be positioned halfway between points where belt enters and leaves Vee idler pulley (7). Reinstall battery.

### Model 210

To remove primary drive belt (20–Fig. C11), loosen retaining nut and move belt keeper (17) away from belt. Unbolt bearing flanges (25) from frame and move jackshaft assembly to the right and downward. Remove primary drive belt. Install new belt by reversing removal procedure. Adjust belt keeper (17) so there is a clearance of 1/16-inch (1.5 mm) between keeper and belt. Keeper should be centered between points where belt enters and leaves idler pulley (16).

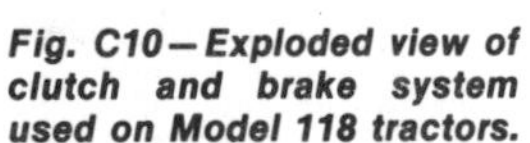

*Fig. C10—Exploded view of clutch and brake system used on Model 118 tractors.*

1. Transmission input pulley
2. Drive belt
3. Flat idler (frame)
4. Belt keeper
5. Engine drive pulley
6. Belt keeper
7. Clutch idler
8. Pivot plate
9. Clutch spring
10. Brake latch
11. Flat idler
12. Belt keeper
13. Brake drum
14. Nut
15. Spring
16. Brake band
17. Brake rod
18. Clutch-brake pedal & shaft assy.

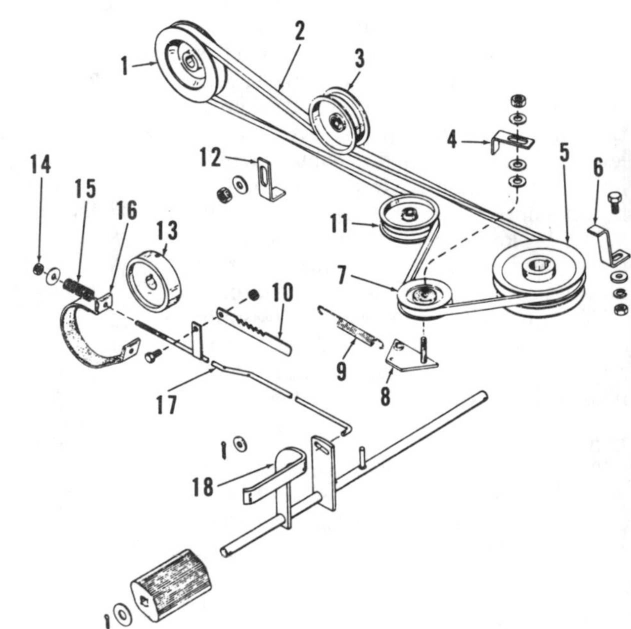

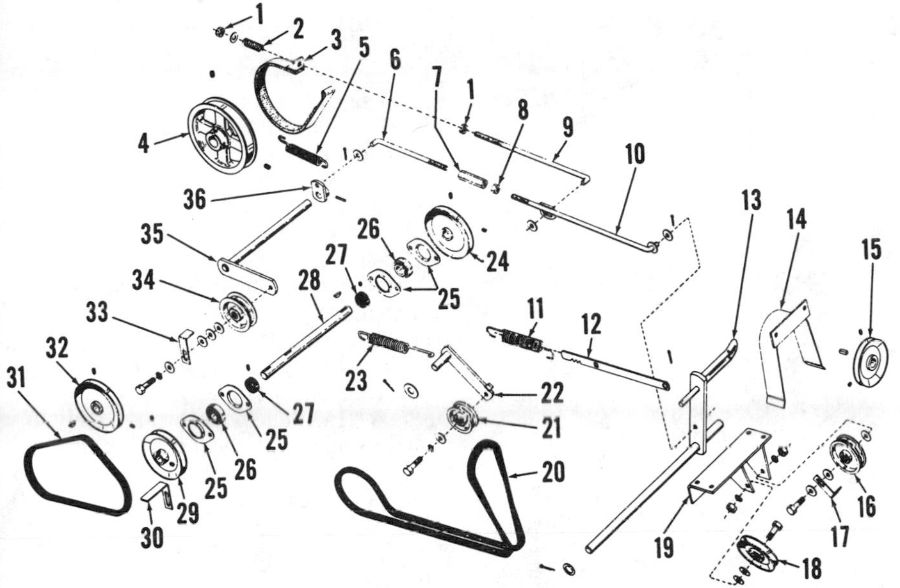

*Fig. C11—Exploded view of clutch and brake system used on Model 210 tractors.*

1. Brake adjusting nuts
2. Spring
3. Brake band
4. Brake drum
5. Clutch spring
6. Clutch link
7. Turnbuckle
8. Locknut
9. Brake link
10. Clutch-brake rod
11. Return spring
12. Brake latch
13. Clutch-brake pedal & shaft assy.
14. Belt guard
15. Engine drive pulley
16. Flat idler
17. Belt keeper
18. Vee idler
19. Bracket
20. Primary drive belt
21. Idler pulley
22. Idler arm
23. Spring
24. Pulley
25. Bearing flanges
26. Bearing
27. Lock collar
28. Jackshaft
29. Pulley
30. Belt keeper
31. Transaxle drive belt
32. Transaxle input pulley
33. Belt keeper
34. Clutch idler pulley
35. Clutch idler shaft
36. Arm

To remove transaxle drive belt (31–Fig. C11), loosen belt keepers (30 and 33) and move them away from belt. Depress clutch-brake pedal and remove belt. Install new belt over pulleys and release pedal. Adjust belt keepers so there is a clearance of 1/16-inch (1.5 mm) between keepers and belt. Position keeper (33) so it is centered above clutch idler pulley (34) when clutch-brake pedal is depressed. Adjust clutch and brake linkage as necessary.

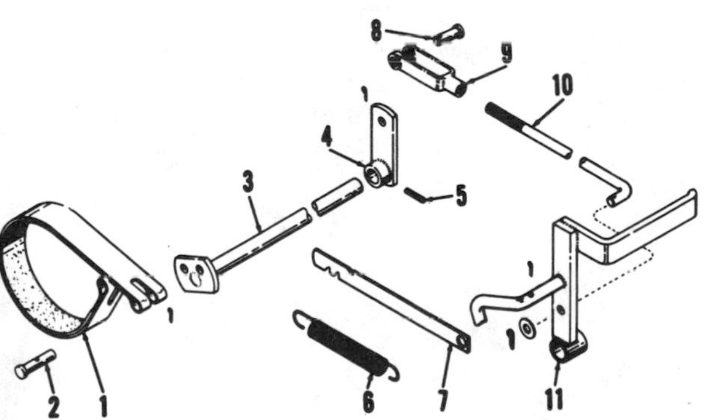

*Fig. C12—Exploded view of brake assembly used on early production Models 220, 222, 442 and 444. Parking brake arrangement may differ on earlier models.*

1. Brake band
2. Pin
3. Shaft
4. Arm
5. Roll pin
6. Spring
7. Parking brake latch
8. Pin
9. Clevis
10. Brake rod
11. Brake pedal

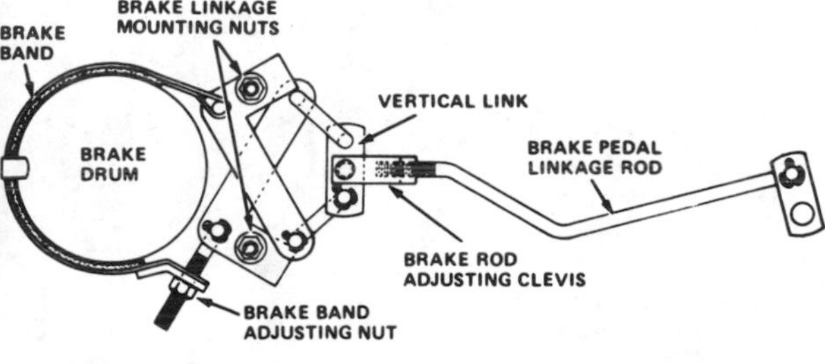


*Fig. C13—Brake assembly used on late production 220, 222, 442 and 444 tractors and all 224 tractors.*

# CASE/INGERSOLL HYDRAULIC DRIVE

Models 220, 222, 224, 442 and 444 are equipped with a hydraulic drive system. To service system and its components, refer to following paragraphs.

## OPERATION

### Models 220-222-224-442-444

The three main components of hydraulic drive are hydraulic pump, control valve and hydraulic motor. The hydraulic pump draws oil from the reservoir located at front of tractor behind oil cooler. Oil is pumped to the drive control valve and when control valve is in neutral, oil passes through the valve and to the oil cooler. After flowing through the oil cooler, oil is returned to reservoir. If control valve is in forward or reverse position, oil is directed to hydraulic motor. This causes motor shaft to rotate which in turn drives range transmission input gear. Oil returning from the motor, flows through control valve, through oil cooler and to reservoir. When control lever is returned to neutral position, oil flow between valve and motor stops which stops rotation of motor shaft providing a dynamic braking action to stop tractor.

## OIL FLOW AND PRESSURE CHECK

### Models 220-222-224-442-444

To check oil flow and system pressure, install a "Hydra Sleuth," "Flo-Rater" or equivalent tester as shown in Fig. C14. Remove hydraulic lines from control valve to hydraulic motor and plug control valve ports, Close shut-off valve in line and fully open load valve on tester. Start and operate engine at 3600 rpm until hydraulic oil temperature is approximately 120°F (50°C). Check and record flow at 0 pressure. Slowly close tester load valve until pressure gage reading is 1000 psi (6895 kPa) and note flow reading. This flow reading must not be more than 25 percent less than previously recorded 0 pressure flow reading. If pump output flow drops more than 25 percent, pump is worn and must be overhauled or renewed.

If pump output flow drop is less than 25%, record flow at 1000 psi (6895 kPa) and continue tests. Fully open shut-off valve in line and load valve on tester. With engine still operating at 3600 rpm, move control lever in full forward or reverse position. Slowly close load valve on tester until pressure gage reading is

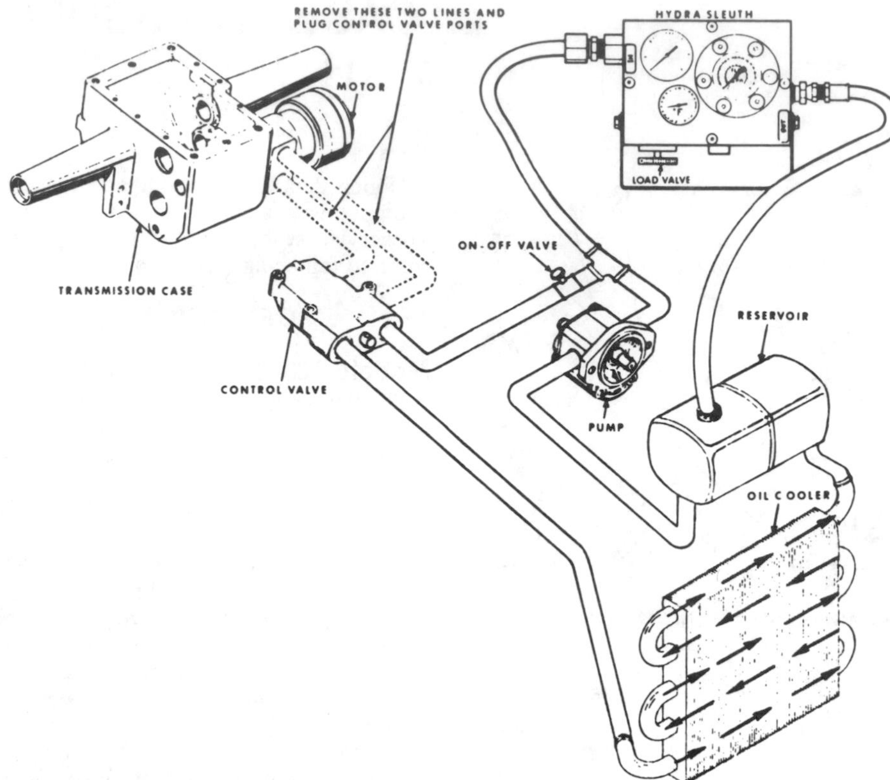


***Fig. C14—View showing "Hydra Sleuth" tester installed to check flow and pressure of hydraulic drive system on Models 220, 222, 224, 442 and 444.***

1000 psi (6895 kPa) and note flow reading. This reading must not exceed ½-gpm (1.9L/min.) less than previously recorded pump gpm flow at 1000 psi (6895 kPa). If control valve internal leakage is more than ½-gpm (1.9L/min.), check and adjust relief valve pressure.

To check relief valve pressure, close load valve on tester and note pressure gage reading. The relief valve should open between 1850-2000 psi (12755-13790 kPa) on Models 220, 222 and 442. On Models 224 and 444, relief valve opening pressure should be 2050-2150 psi (14135-14825 kPa). On all models, turn adjusting plug (1–Fig. C15 or 8–Fig. C16) in to increase pressure or out to decrease pressure as required. Recheck control valve for internal leakage.

If control valve leakage still exceeds ½-gpm (1.9L/min.), valve body is excessively worn or cracked and valve must be renewed.

Remove test equipment and install original lines. If pump and control valve check out good and adequate tractor performance cannot be obtained, remove hydraulic motor and overhaul or renew motor.

## CONTROL VALVE

### Models 220-222-224-442-444

Early Models 220, 222, 442 and 444 tractors were equipped with a single-spool Dukes drive control valve (Fig. C15). Later production models and all 224 tractors are equipped with Dukes control valve shown in Fig. C16. Spool (3), detent assembly (11 through 18) and secondary (lift) relief valve assembly (19 through 23) are not used on models not equipped with hydraulic lift.

**R&R CONTROL VALVE.** To remove control valve, first drain hydraulic reservoir. Disconnect control lever linkage and hydraulic lines. Unbolt and remove control valve assembly. Plug hydraulic line openings to prevent dirt from entering system.

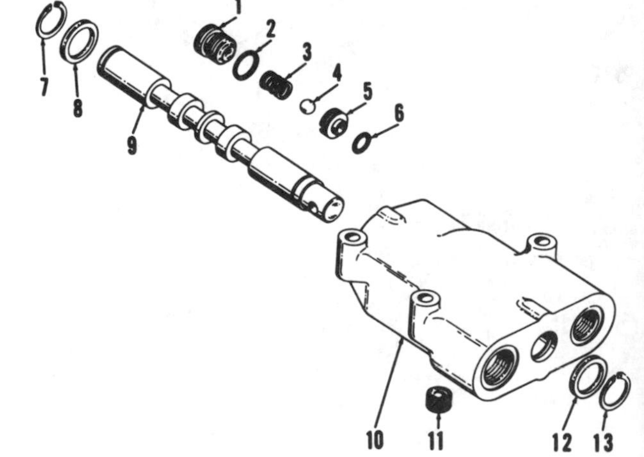


***Fig. C15—Exploded view of Dukes single-spool control valve used on early production 220, 222, 442 and 444 tractors.***

1. Adjusting plug
2. "O" ring
3. Spring
4. Ball
5. Ball seat
6. "O" ring
7. Snap ring
8. Quad ring
9. Spool
10. Body
11. Plug
12. Quad ring
13. Snap ring

**OVERHAUL (EARLY DUKES).** To disassemble control valve, refer to exploded view in Fig. C15 and remove snap rings (7 and 13) from ends of spool (9) and withdraw spool from body. Remove quad rings at both ends of spool bore in body. Unscrew relief spring adjusting plug (1) and remove spring (3) and ball (4). Unscrew relief ball seat (5) and remove "O" ring (6).

Inspect components and renew any which are excessively worn. To reinstall spool (9), quad rings and snap rings, install quad ring (12) in spool bore. Insert spool (9) from back end of body as shown in Fig. C15. Pull spool through body until rear end of spool just clears rear quad ring groove in spool bore and install quad ring (8). Install front snap ring (13) on spool and carefully push spool into body and through rear quad ring (8). Install rear snap ring (7).

After installing control valve in tractor, check relief valve opening pressure and adjust as necessary.

**OVERHAUL (LATE DUKES).** To disassemble control valve, refer to Fig. C16 and proceed as follows: Remove snap rings (1) and withdraw travel spool (2).

**NOTE: Some models, without hydraulic lift, are not equipped with lift spool (3), detent assembly (11 through 18) and secondary relief valve assembly (19 through 23).**

On valves with two spools, remove plugs (18), springs (17) and detent balls (16), then unbolt and remove detent cover (15), withdraw lift spool assembly from valve body (5). Detent stem (14), spacer (13), centering spring (12) and washer (11) can now be removed. Unscrew cap (10) and remove gasket (9), adjusting screw (8), spring (7) and main relief ball (6). Place body (5) on a bench so drain plug (24) is pointing upward. Remove cap (19), gasket (20), adjusting screw (21), spring (22) and secondary relief ball (23). Remove "O" rings (4) from valve body.

Clean and inspect all parts and renew any showing excessive wear or other damage. When installing relief valves, turn about ½ of adjusting screw threads into the valve. Install new "O" ring seals (4) in grooves in front end of valve body. Lubricate seals and insert spools (2 and 3) into correct bores at rear (relief valve) end of valve body. Push spools forward through front seals until rear seal grooves in bores are exposed. Install and lubricate rear seal rings, then move spools back to normal centered position. Install snap rings on travel spool (2) and using "Loctite" on detent stem threads, install washer (11), centering spring (12), spacer (13) and detent stem (14) on lift spool (3). Install detent cover (15), balls (16), springs (17) and plugs (18).

After installing control valve on tractor, adjust main relief valve pressure as previously outlined and secondary relief valve pressure to 575 psi (3965 kPa).

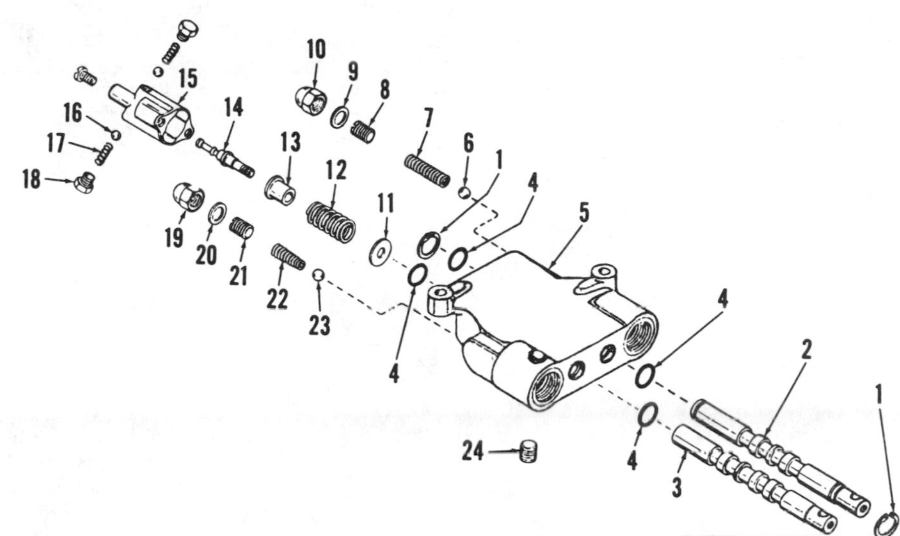

***Fig. C16 — Exploded view of Dukes two-spool control valve used on late production 220, 222, 442 and 444 tractors and all 224 tractors. Spool (3) and items (11 through 23) are used only on models equipped with hydraulic lift.***

1. Snap rings
2. Travel spool
3. Lift spool
4. "O" rings
5. Valve body
6. Main relief ball
7. Main relief spring
8. Adjusting screw
9. Gasket
10. Cap
11. Washer
12. Centering spring
13. Spacer
14. Detent stem
15. Detent cover
16. Detent ball
17. Spring
18. Plug
19. Cap
20. Gasket
21. Adjusting screw
22. Secondary relief spring
23. Secondary relief ball
24. Drain plug

## HYDRAULIC PUMP

### Models 220-222-224-442-444

Wooster, Cessna and Borg-Warner hydraulic pumps have been used on these tractors. Refer to Figs. C17, C18 and C19 for identification and to following paragraphs for service procedures.

**R&R PUMP.** To remove hydraulic pump, drain hydraulic oil and disconnect hydraulic lines from pump. Cap or plug openings to prevent dirt from entering system. On tractors prior to S.N. 9646800, unbolt and remove side panels. Then, unbolt and remove pump and support assembly from side of tractor. On tractors with S.N. 9646800 and later, remove battery and battery tray. Unbolt and remove pump and support assembly from above.

On all models, mark position of coupling on pump shaft for aid in reassembly. Loosen set screw and remove coupling half from pump. Unbolt and remove pump from support.

Reinstall pump by reversing removal procedure. Make certain hydraulic reservoir is refilled before starting engine.

**OVERHAUL (WOOSTER).** To disassemble pump, refer to Fig. C17 and clamp flange of front cover (11) in a vise.

**CAUTION: Do not clamp on pump body.**

Scribe a line across pump covers and body for aid in reassembly. Remove cap screws from rear cover (1) and remove rear cover and seal ring (2). Remove pump body (3) with bearings (4 and 7), driven gear (5) and drive gear (6). Withdraw bearings and gears from pump body. Remove brass pressure seal (8), rubber spacer (9), seal ring (10) and oil seal (12) from front cover.

Clean and inspect all parts and renew any that are excessively worn or otherwise damaged. When reassembling, renew all seals and lubricate all internal parts with clean oil. Install drive gear shaft carefully to prevent damage to lip of oil seal (12). Tighten four pump cap screws evenly to a torque of 28-32 ft.-lbs. (38-43 N·m).

**OVERHAUL (CESSNA).** To disassemble pump, refer to Fig. C18 and scribe a line across covers (1 and 11) and

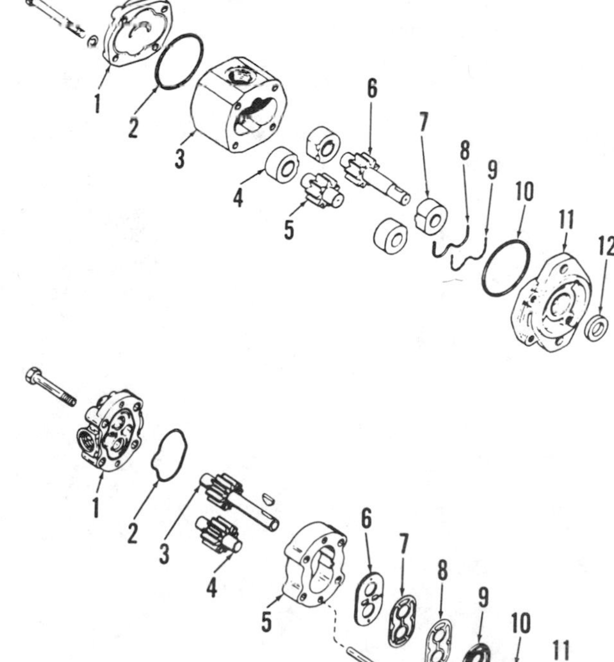

***Fig. C17 — Exploded view of Wooster hydraulic drive pump used on some early model tractors equipped with Case/Ingersoll hydraulic drive.***

1. Rear cover
2. Seal ring
3. Pump body
4. Bearing
5. Driven gear
6. Drive gear
7. Bearing
8. Pressure seal
9. Rubber spacer
10. Seal ring
11. Front cover
12. Oil seal

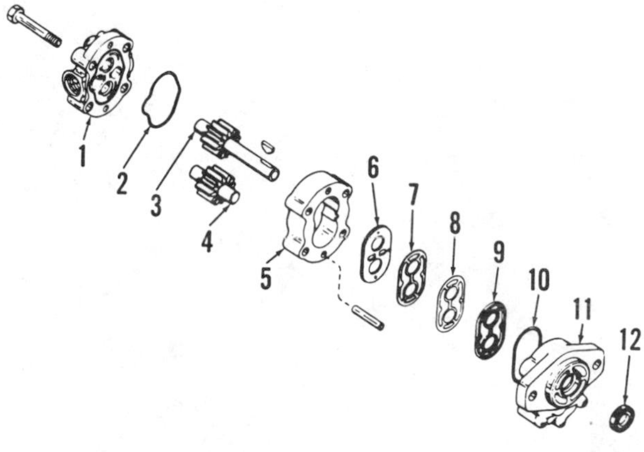

***Fig. C18 — Exploded view of hydraulic pump similar to Cessna hydraulic pump used on some late production tractors equipped with Case/Ingersoll hydraulic drive.***

1. Rear cover
2. Seal ring
3. Drive gear
4. Driven gear
5. Pump body
6. Diaphragm
7. Back-up gasket
8. Protector gasket
9. Diaphragm seal
10. Seal ring
11. Front cover
12. Oil seal

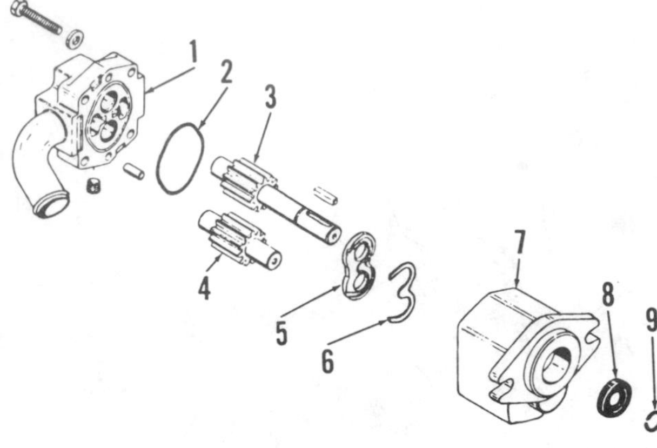

*Fig. C19—Exploded view of typical Borg-Warner hydraulic pump used on some late production tractors equipped with Case/Ingersoll hydraulic drive.*

1. Rear cover assy.
2. Seal ring
3. Drive gear
4. Driven gear
5. Wear plate
6. Pressure seal
7. Pump body
8. Oil seal
9. Snap ring

body (5) for aid in reassembly. Remove cap screws from rear cover (1) and separate rear cover and seal ring (2) from pump body. Withdraw driven gear (4) and drive gear (3). Separate body (5) from front cover (11). Note position of small pressure vent hole in diaphragm (6), gaskets (7 and 8) and diaphragm seal (9) and place a mark on adjacent area on cover. Remove diaphragm, gaskets, diaphragm seal and seal ring (10) from cover. Inspect shaft oil seal (12) and if removal is necessary, heat front cover (11) to approximately 250°F (120°C). Then, pull oil seal straight out of cover.

Clean and inspect all parts and renew any showing excessive wear or other damage. When reassembling, renew all seals, gaskets and diaphragm. Install diaphragm seal (9) with open "V" side first in cover (11) and small pressure vent hole adjacent to previously affixed mark on cover. Install gaskets (7 and 8) and diaphragm (6) aligning pressure vent holes with hole in diaphragm seal. Bronze side of diaphragm must face gears. Lubricate internal parts with clean oil. Make certain scribe marks on covers (1 and 11) and pump body (5) are aligned. Install and tighten cover cap screws to a torque of 24-26 ft.-lbs. (33-35 N·m).

**OVERHAUL (BORG-WARNER).** To disassemble pump, refer to Fig. C19 and scribe a line across cover (1) and pump body (7) for aid in reassembly. Remove cap screws from rear cover and separate cover from pump body. Remove seal ring (2) and snap ring (9), then withdraw driven gear (4) and driving gear (3). Remove wear plate (5) and pressure seal (6). To remove oil seal (8), heat pump body to approximately 250°F (120°C), then pull oil seal straight out of cover.

Clean and inspect all parts and renew any showing excessive wear or other damage. When reassembling, lubricate internal parts with clean oil. Press new oil seal (8) in cover until seal is 0.188 inch (4.78 mm) below flush with end of bore. Install pressure seal (6) in wear plate (5). Install wear plate assembly in body (7). Carefully install drive gear (3) so lip of oil seal is not damaged. Install driven gear (4) with long end of shaft in body. Place new seal ring (2) in groove in cover (1), install cover assembly and align scribe marks. Install cap screws and tighten them to a torque of 24-26 ft.-lbs. (33-35 N·m). Place snap ring (9) in its groove on shaft.

## HYDRAULIC MOTOR

### Models 220-222-224-442-444

**REMOVE AND REINSTALL.** To remove hydraulic motor, place range transmission shift lever in neutral position. Block up under tractor frame and place a rolling floor jack under range transmission and differential housing. Unbolt and remove fenders, seat and seat support. Disconnect hydraulic lines from hydraulic drive motor and plug or cap all openings. Remove cap screws securing range transmission and differential assembly to tractor frame and roll assembly rearward from tractor. Drain lubricant from transmission and differential housing, then unbolt and remove top cover. Remove left rear wheel. Unbolt hydraulic drive motor, hold range transmission sliding gear and withdraw drive motor. Let sliding gear rest in bottom of transmission housing.

When reinstalling hydraulic drive motor, use new "O" ring on motor housing. Hold range transmission sliding gear in position (shift fork between gears) and insert motor output shaft through housing and gear. Apply "Loctite" to cap screw threads and tighten motor retaining cap screws to a torque of 110-125 ft.-lbs. (149-169 N·m). The balance of installation is reverse of removal procedure. Fill transmission and differential housing to level plug opening with SAE 90 EP gear oil. Capacity is approximately 6 pints (2.8L). Fill hydraulic reservoir with new oil using SAE 5W-20 for temperatures below 32°F (0°C) or SAE 20W-40 for temperatures above 32°F (0°C). Use oil with API classification of SC, SD or SE.

### Early Models 220-222

**OVERHAUL HYDRAULIC MOTOR.** These models are equipped with a hydraulic motor as shown in Fig. C20. Before disassembling motor, mark a line across surface of gerotor housing (18), spacer plate (15) and body (10). Also mark port side of mounting flange (1) and mark a line across front end of spool (7) bore and mounting flange (1) bore. These marks will aid in reassembly.

Unscrew cap screws (24) and remove end cap (22), "O" ring (21) and spacer (13). Remove rotor (19), rollers (20) and housing (18) as a unit. Remove "O" ring (17) and unscrew cap screws (16). Remove spacer plate (15), "O" ring (14) and drive coupling (12). Remove retaining cap screws and separate mounting flange (1) from body by tapping lightly on flange with a leather mallet. Remove washer (2), quad ring (4), "O" ring (5) and thrust washer (6) from flange (1). Withdraw spool (7) from body and drive pin (9) from body.

Inspect all parts for scratches, scoring and excessive wear. Spool (7) and body (10) are available only as an assembly. End cap (22) and spacer plate (15) may be polished but should not be grooved. Check thickness of housing (18), rotor (19) and rollers (20). Thickness of rotor and rollers must be within 0.002 inch (0.051 mm) of housing thickness. If dif-

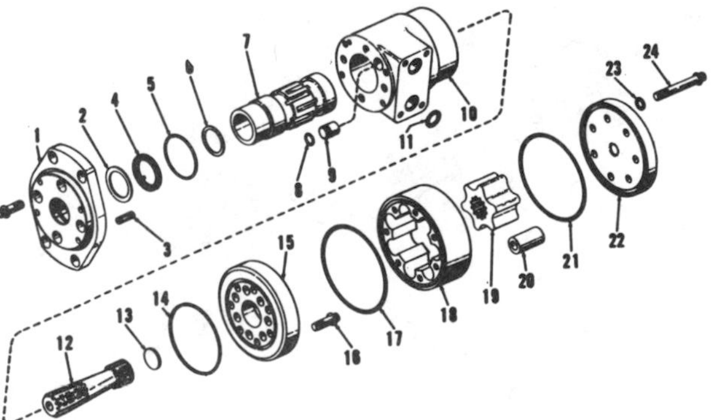

*Fig. C20—Exploded view of hydraulic motor used on early Models 220 and 222.*

1. Mounting flange
2. Washer
3. Roll pin
4. Quad ring
5. "O" ring
6. Thrust washer
7. Spool
8. "O" ring
9. Pin
10. Body
11. "O" ring
12. Drive coupling
13. Spacer
14. "O" ring
15. Spacer plate
16. Cap screw
17. "O" ring
18. Gerotor housing
19. Rotor
20. Roller
21. "O" ring
22. End cap
23. Washer
24. Cap screw

ference in thickness is greater than 0.002 inch (0.051 mm), housing (18), rotor (19) and rollers (20) must be renewed as an assembly. Seals and washers are available as an overhaul kit.

To assemble motor, install plug (9) so "O" ring end is to outside. Install components (2 through 6) in mounting flange (1) and install flange on body so marked side is on side of body ports. Tap mounting flange onto body and tighten cap screws evenly to 215 in.-lbs. (24 N·m). Make certain roll pins (3) do not protrude beyond face of mounting flange. Slide spool (7) into body (10) until it bottoms on thrust washer (6) in flange. Align marks on spool (7) and mounting flange (1). Install "O" rings (14 and 17) on spacer plate (15). Install spacer plate on body (10) so smaller "O" ring (14) is adjacent to body and marks are aligned. Secure plate with cap screws (16) and tighten to 175 in.-lbs. (19 N·m). Slide drive coupling (12), longer splined end first, through spacer plate and into spool. Install rotor, rollers and housing assembly with marks aligned. Stand motor on its mounting flange and install spacer (13) and end cap (22). Tighten cap screws (24) evenly to 175 in.-lbs. (19 N·m).

If no alignment marks were made during disassembly, or if new parts are used, it may be necessary to realign gerotor assembly to obtain proper motor operation. Reinstall motor and refill reservoir. Start engine and move control lever in forward position. Tractor should move forward; however, if tractor moves rearward with control lever in forward position, hydraulic motor is not properly aligned. To correct this condition, remove end cap (22) from motor. Index mark gerotor housing (18) to spacer plate (15) and rotor (19) to a spline on drive coupling (12). Slide rotor and housing assembly off drive coupling and rotate assembly one coupling tooth in either direction, then slide rotor back on drive coupling. Reinstall end cap (22) using new washers (23) and tighten cap screws evenly to 175 in.-lbs. (19 N·m). Recheck for correct operation.

## Late Models 220-222 and All Models 224-442-444

**OVERHAUL HYDRAULIC MOTOR.** To disassemble hydraulic drive motor, clamp motor body port boss in a padded jaw vise with output shaft pointing downward. Remove seven cap screws (24–Fig. C21) and remove end cover (23), seal ring (22), commutator (19) and commutator ring (18). Remove sleeve (21), manifold (17) and manifold plate (16). Lift drive link (11), wear plate (12), rotor (13), rollers (14) and stator (15) off body (5). Remove output shaft (10), then remove snap ring (1), spacer (2), shim (3) and oil seal (4). Remove seal ring (9). Do not remove needle bearing (8), thrust bearing (7) or thrust washer (6) from body (5) as these parts are not serviced separately.

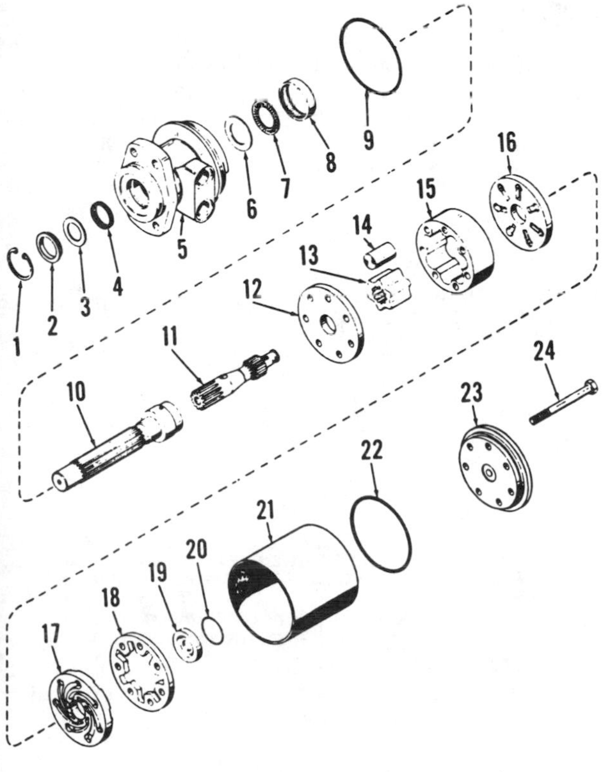

Clean and inspect all parts for excessive wear or other damage and renew as necessary. A seal ring and seal kit (items 2, 3, 4, 9, 20 and 22) is available for resealing motor. To reassemble motor, clamp body port boss in a padded vise with seven tapped holes upward. Insert shaft (10) and drive link (11). Install new seal ring (9) in groove on body (5). Place stator (15) on wear plate (12) and install rotor and rollers (13 and 14) with counterbore in rotor facing upward. Place wear plate and rotor assembly over drive link and onto body.

**NOTE: Two cap screws, 3/8 x 4½ inches with heads removed, can be used to align bolt holes in body (5) with holes in wear plate (12), stator (15), manifold plate (16), manifold (17), commutator plate (18) and end cover (23).**

Install manifold plate (16) with slots toward rotor. Install manifold (17) with swirl grooves toward rotor and diamond shaped holes upward. Place commutator ring (18) and commutator (19) on manifold with bronze ring groove facing upward. Place bronze seal ring (20) into groove with rubber side downward. Lubricate seal ring (9) and install sleeve (21) over assembled components. Install new seal ring (22) on end cover (23), lubricate seal ring and install end cover. Remove line up bolts and install seven cap screws (24). Tighten cap screws evenly to 50 ft.-lbs. (68 N·m).

Remove motor from vise and place it on bench with output shaft pointing upward. Lubricate and install new oil seal (4), shim (3), spacer (2) and snap ring (1). Lubricate motor by pouring new oil in one port and rotating output shaft until oil is expelled from other port.

***Fig. C21—Exploded view of Ross hydraulic drive motor used on late Models 220 and 222 and all Models 224, 442 and 444.***

1. Snap ring
2. Spacer
3. Shim washer (0.10 in.)
4. Oil seal
5. Body
6. Thrust washer
7. Thrust bearing
8. Needle bearing
9. Seal ring
10. Output shaft
11. Drive link
12. Wear plate
13. Rotor
14. Roller (6)
15. Stator
16. Manifold plate
17. Manifold
18. Commutator ring
19. Commutator
20. Seal ring
21. Sleeve
22. Seal ring
23. End cover
24. Cap screw (7)

# HYDROSTATIC TRANSMISSION

### LUBRICATION

## Models 117-118

Both models are equipped with an Eaton Model 6 hydrostatic transmission. Approximate fluid capacity is 2¾ pints (1.3 L) of Type "A" automatic transmission fluid.

### NEUTRAL ADJUSTMENT

## Model 117

The control arm of hydrostatic transmission used on Model 117 tractors has a natural tendency to return to neutral position when there is no tension against control arm. To prevent control arm

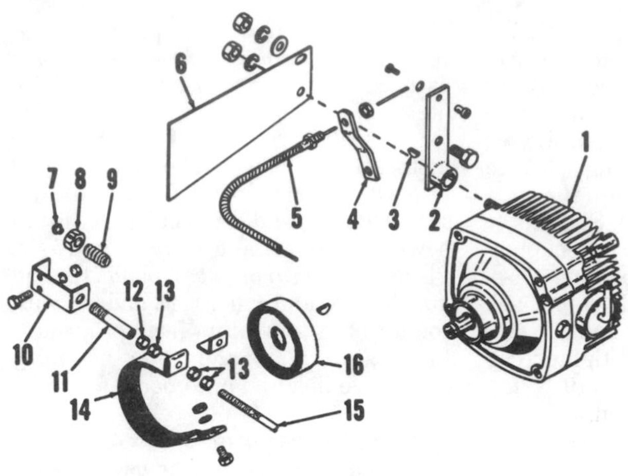


*Fig. C23—View showing brake, transmission linkage and friction plate used on Model 117 tractors.*

1. Transmission
2. Control arm
3. Key
4. Cable bracket
5. Speed control cable
6. Friction plate
7. Friction button
8. Nut
9. Spring
10. Bracket
11. Rod extension
12. Locknut
13. Adjusting nuts
14. Brake band
15. Brake rod
16. Brake drum

from working into neutral position under normal operation, a plate attached to control arm is held by a friction button on end of brake control rod. Refer to Fig. C23. When brake is applied, plate is released and transmission control arm is allowed to move to neutral position.

To adjust neutral linkage, loosen locknut (12–Fig. C23) and turn control rod extension (11) to increase or decrease friction between button (7) and plate (6). There should be sufficient friction to prevent transmission control arm from self-neutralizing when speed control lever is released, but speed control lever should not be difficult to move. Turn nut (8) to adjust spring tension on control rod so it will return to original position when brake is disengaged.

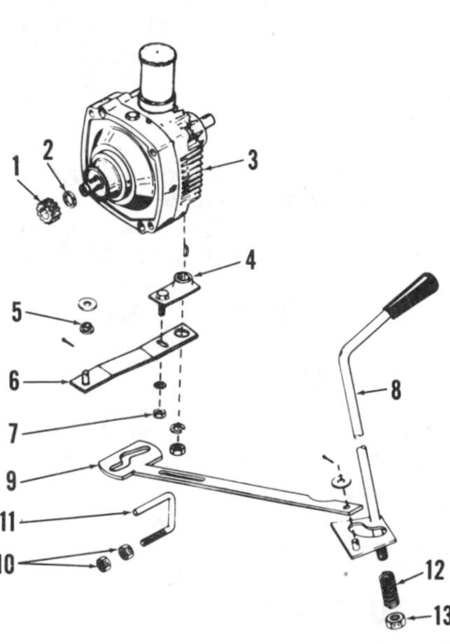


*Fig. C24—Exploded view of transmission shift linkage used on Model 118 tractors.*

1. Transmission output gear
2. Spacer
3. Transmission
4. Control arm
5. Cam follower pin bushing
6. Control link
7. Adjusting nut
8. Travel control lever
9. Control cam
10. Adjusting nuts
11. "U" bolt
12. Spring
13. Nut

Adjust brake as necessary, then recheck adjustment of neutral linkage.

## Model 118

To adjust neutral position of transmission linkage on Model 118 tractors, refer to Fig. C24 and proceed as follows: Place travel control lever (8) in neutral detent position. At this time, cam follower pin on control link (6) should be centered in S-slot of control cam (9) as shown in Fig. C25. If not, adjust nuts (10–Fig. C24) to move "U" bolt (11) as shown in Fig. C26 until follower pin is centered in S-slot. Block up under rear of tractor so rear wheels are free to turn. With travel control lever in neutral detent position, start engine and operate at approximately half throttle. Rear wheels should remain stationary. If wheels rotate forward or rearward, loosen nut (7–Fig. C24) and while keeping cam follower pin on control link (6) centered in S-slot as shown in Fig. C25, move control arm (4–Fig. C24) as required to stop rotation of wheels. Retighten nut (7). Move travel control lever through forward and reverse drive ranges and recheck neutral adjustment.

## REMOVE AND REINSTALL

## Models 117-118

To remove hydraulic transmission, tilt seat and fender assembly forward and drain lubricant from gear reduction and differential housing.

On Model 117, disconnect control cable from transmission and detach friction plate from control arm of transmission. Remove oil expansion reservoir and mounting plate.

On Model 118, disconnect control cam from control link. Oil expansion reservoir can be removed if desired by rotating it in a clockwise direction.

**CAUTION: If oil expansion reservoir is removed, precautions should be taken to prevent entrance of dirt or other foreign material into transmission.**

On either model, unbolt and remove screen and cooling fan. Remove drive belt from input pulley. Unbolt transmission from gear reduction housing and lift hydraulic transmission from tractor.

Before disassembling transmission, thoroughly clean exterior of unit. Remove venting plug, invert assembly and drain fluid from unit.

Reinstall hydrostatic transmission by reversing removal procedure. Check and adjust linkage for neutral position as required. Fill reservoir 1/3 full with transmission fluid.

## OVERHAUL

## Models 117-118

Both models are equipped with an Eaton Model 6 hydrostatic transmission. Refer to Eaton Model 6 section in HYDROSTATIC TRANSMISSION SERVICE section for overhaul procedure.

*Fig. C25—View showing correct neutral position of cam follower pin in S-slot of control cam on Model 118.*

CAM FOLLOWER SHOULD BE IN THIS POSITION WHEN TRAVEL CONTROL LEVER IS IN NEUTRAL.

TRAVEL CONTROL CAM

CAM FOLLOWER

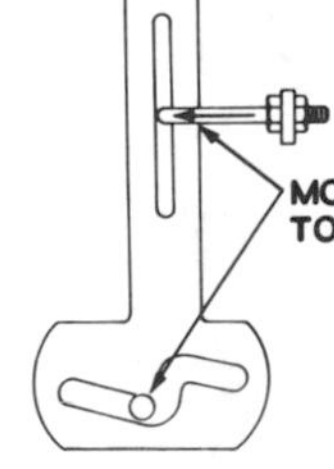

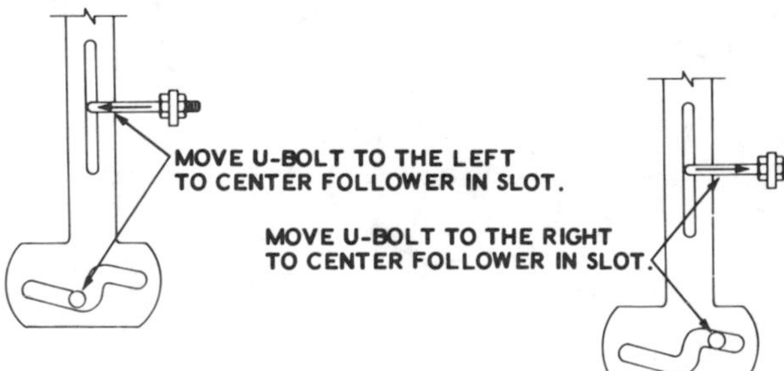


*Fig. C26—Procedure for adjusting control cam neutral position on Model 118.*

# TRANSAXLE

## LUBRICATION

### Models 107-108-110-210

Model 107 is equipped with a Peerless 1200 series transaxle. Approximate capacity is 2 pints (0.9 L) of SAE 90 EP gear lubricant. Lubricant is added through gear shift opening.

Models 108 and 110 are equipped with a Peerless 600 series transaxle. Approximate capacity is 2 pints (0.9 L) of SAE 90 EP gear lubricant. Lubricant is added through gear shift opening.

Model 210 is equipped with a Peerless 2300 series transaxle. Approximate capacity is 3 pints (1.4 L) of SAE 90 EP gear lubricant. Lubricant is added through gear shift opening.

## REMOVE AND REINSTALL

### Models 107-108-110-210

On Models 107, 108 and 110, disconnect brake linkage, depress clutch-brake pedal and remove drive belt from transaxle input pulley. On Model 210, unbolt and remove belt guard. Disconnect brake linkage, depress clutch-brake pedal and remove drive belt from transaxle input pulley. On all models, support tractor under frame and remove shift lever knob. Unbolt transaxle from frame, raise rear of tractor and remove transaxle assembly.

Reinstall transaxle by reversing removal procedure. Adjust clutch and brake linkage as required.

## OVERHAUL

### Models 107-108-110-210

Model 107 is equipped with a Peerless 1200 series transaxle. Models 108 and 110 are equipped with a Peerless 600 series transaxle. Model 210 is equipped with a Peerless 2300 series transaxle. Refer to the appropriate Peerless section in TRANSAXLE SERVICE section for overhaul procedure.

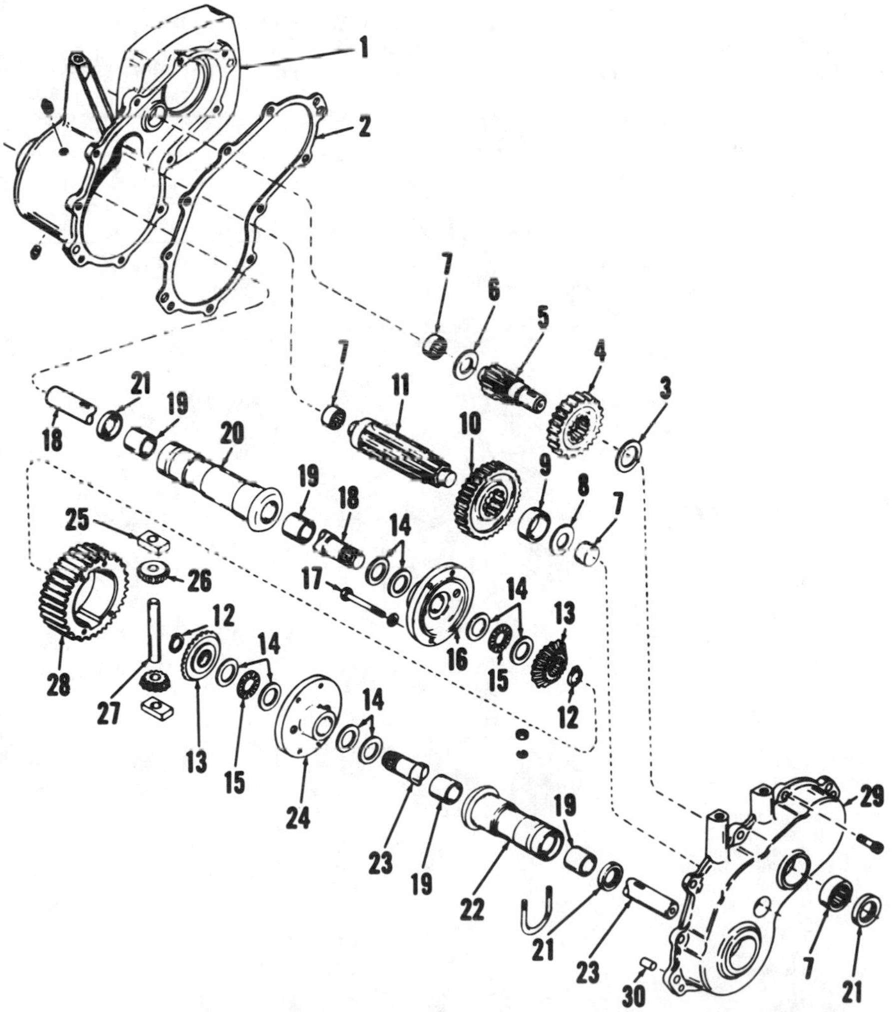

# REDUCTION GEARS AND DIFFERENTIAL

### Models 117-118

**REMOVE AND REINSTALL.** To remove reduction gears and differential assembly, tilt seat and fender assembly forward and drain lubricant from reduction and differential housing.

On Model 117, remove oil expansion reservoir and mounting plate. Plug opening to prevent dirt or other foreign material from entering hydrostatic drive unit. Disconnect control cable and detach friction plate from control arm of transmission.

On Model 118, disconnect control cam from control link on hydrostatic transmission.

On either model, unbolt and remove screen and cooling fan. Remove drive belt from input pulley, then disconnect and remove brake assembly. Support rear of tractor and unbolt reduction drive and differential assembly from tractor frame. Raise rear of tractor and remove assembly.

To reinstall reduction drive and differential assembly, reverse removal procedure. Refill reduction drive and differential housing with 2¾ pints (1.3 L) of SAE 90 EP gear oil. Fill transmission oil expansion reservoir ⅓ full with Type "A" automatic transmission fluid. Adjust control linkage and brake as required.

### Models 117-118

**OVERHAUL.** With reduction drive and differential assembly removed as outlined in preceding paragraph, unbolt and remove hydrostatic transmission and rear wheel and hub assemblies. Clean axle shafts and remove any rust or burrs. Place unit in a vise with left axle shaft pointing downward. Remove cap screws and drive dowel pins out of cover. Lift cover (29 – Fig. C34) off case and axle shaft. Withdraw brake shaft

*Fig. C34 – Exploded view of Peerless Model 1305 reduction gear and differential unit used on Models 117 and 118.*

1. Case
2. Gasket
3. Washer
4. Idler gear
5. Brake shaft
6. Washer
7. Bearing
8. Washer
9. Spacer
10. Output gear
11. Output shaft
12. Snap ring
13. Bevel gear
14. Thrust washers
15. Thrust bearing
16. Differential carrier
17. Cap screw
18. Axle shaft (L.H.)
19. Bushing
20. Axle housing
21. Oil seal
22. Axle housing
23. Axle shaft (R.H.)
24. Differential carrier
25. Drive block
26. Drive pinion gear
27. Drive pin
28. Ring gear
29. Cover
30. Dowel pin

(5), idler gear (4) and thrust washers (3 and 6) from case. Remove output shaft (11), output gear (10), spacer (9) and thrust washer (8), then remove differential and axle shaft assembly. Axle shaft housings (20 and 22) can be pressed from case and cover.

To disassemble differential, remove four cap screws (17) and separate axle shaft and carrier assemblies from ring gear (28). Drive blocks (25), bevel pinion gears (26) and drive pin (27) can now be removed from ring gear. Remove snap rings (12) and slide axle shafts (18 and 23) from axle gears (13) and carriers (16 and 24).

Clean and inspect all parts and renew any showing excessive wear or other damage. When installing needle bearings, press bearings in from inside of case or cover until bearings are 0.015-0.020 inch (0.381-0.508 mm) below thrust surfaces. Be sure heads of differential cap screws (17) and left axle shaft (18) are installed in left carrier (16). Tighten differential cap screws to 7 ft.-lbs. (9 N·m) and cover-to-case cap screws to 10 ft.-lbs. (14 N·m). Differential assembly and output shaft (11) must be installed in case at the same time. Remainder of assembly is reverse of disassembly procedure.

Reinstall by reversing removal procedure. Transmission and differential oil should be renewed each 500 hours of operation or once each year. Use SAE 90 EP gear oil. Capacity is approximately 6 pints (2.8 L).

**OVERHAUL.** To disassemble range transmission and differential assembly, drain lubricant, then remove top cover and rear wheels. Place a large drive punch against inside end of brake shaft (38 – Fig. C35) and hit drift sharply with a hammer. This will dislodge retaining ring (5) from its groove in brake shaft. Remove retaining ring and brake idler gear (4) as brake shaft is withdrawn. Unbolt hydraulic drive motor (30), hold sliding gear (14) and remove drive motor, input shaft and sliding gear. On early production models, input shaft is separate from drive motor. Unseat retaining rings (15), withdraw shift rod (31) and remove shift fork (16). Remove "C" rings (18) from inner end of axle shafts (27 and 40), withdraw axle shafts and lift out differential assembly with spacer (9) and thrust washers (10 and 24). Remove locknuts (11) and bolts (26), then remove low speed ring gear (12) and high speed ring gear (23). Separate differential case halves (13 and 22) and remove drive pin (21) with roll pin (7), thrust washers (19), pinion gears (20) and axle gears (17). Remove oil seals (28, 33 and 37). Remove plug (34) and needle bearing (35). If necessary, remove brake shaft bushings (6 and 36) and axle shaft flanged bushings (8, 25 and 29). New bushings must be reamed after installation.

Clean and inspect all parts and renew any showing excessive wear or other damage. If brake shaft bushings were removed, press new bushings into position, then ream inner bushing (6) to 1.004-1.005 inches (25.502-25.527 mm) and outer bushing (36) to 1.192-1.193 inches (30.277-30.302 mm). If axle shaft bushings were removed, install inner bushings (8 and 25) with oil groove downward, then install outer bushings (29). Ream all four axle bushings to 1.876-1.877 inches (47.650-47.675 mm). Reassemble differential and ring gears. Use new locknuts (11) and tighten them to 50 ft.-lbs. (68 N·m). Use new oil seals (28, 33 and 37), new gasket (2) and new "O" ring on drive motor flange. Use 0.015 inch thick spacers (9) as required to adjust differential unit side play until side play is 0.005-0.030 inch (0.127-0.762 mm). When installing drive motor, apply a suitable thread locking solution on cap screw threads and tighten cap screws to 110-125 ft.-lbs. (150-169 N·m). Fill transmission and differential housing to level plug opening with SAE 90 EP gear oil. Capacity is approximately 6 pints (2.8 L).

# RANGE TRANSMISSION AND DIFFERENTIAL

## Models 220-222-224-442-444

A two-speed range transmission is used on all models. The range transmission and differential are contained in one case. The transmission shift lever has three positions; High, Neutral and Low. When transmission is in neutral, tractor can be moved manually.

**REMOVE AND REINSTALL.** To remove range transmission and differential assembly, place shift lever in neutral position. Block up under tractor frame and place a rolling floor jack under transmission and differential housing. Unbolt and remove fenders, seat and seat support. Disconnect brake rod and remove brake band. Disconnect hydraulic lines from hydraulic drive motor and plug or cap all openings to prevent entrance of dirt or other foreign material. Remove cap screws securing transmission and differential assembly to tractor frame and roll assembly rearward from tractor.

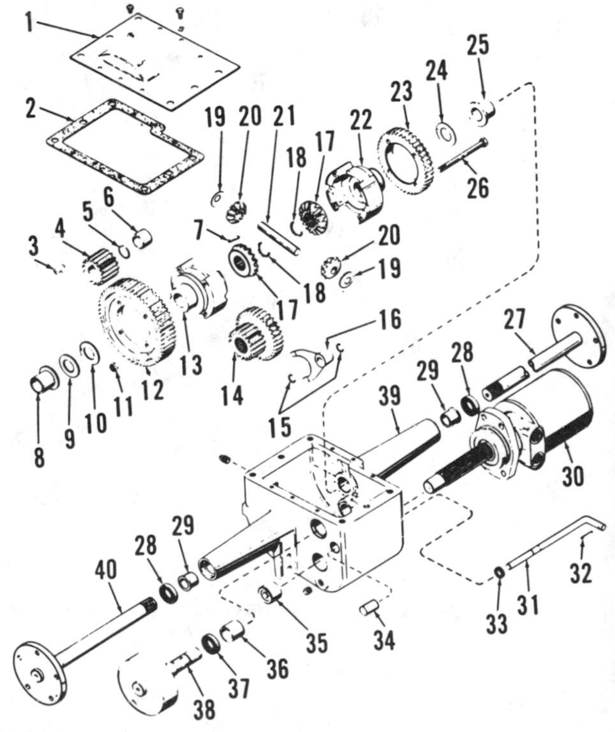


***Fig. C35 — Exploded view of range transmission and differential used on Models 220, 222, 224, 442 and 444. On early production units, input shaft is separate from drive motor (30).***

1. Cover
2. Gasket
3. Key
4. Brake idler gear
5. Retaining ring
6. Bushing
7. Roll pin
8. Flanged bushing
9. Spacer
10. Thrust washer
11. Locknut (4)
12. Low speed ring gear
13. Differential case half
14. Hi-Lo sliding gear
15. Retaining rings
16. Shift fork
17. Axle gears
18. "C" rings
19. Thrust washers
20. Bevel pinion gears
21. Drive pin
22. Differential case half
23. High speed ring gear
24. Thrust washer
25. Flanged bushing
26. Bolt (4)
27. Axle shaft (L.H.)
28. Oil seal (2)
29. Flanged bushing (2)
30. Drive motor
31. Shift rod
32. Roll pin
33. Oil seal
34. Plug
35. Needle bearing
36. Bushing
37. Oil seal
38. Brake drum & shaft
39. Transmission & differential housing
40. Axle shaft (R.H.)

# PTO CLUTCH

Models 210, 220, 222, 224, 442 and 444 may be equipped with a dry disc pto clutch shown in Fig. C36 or C37.

## Model 210

**R&R AND OVERHAUL.** To remove pto clutch, tilt hood forward and disconnect pto control rod from cam actuator lever (3 – Fig. C36). Remove left hand thread cap screw (2), hub spacer (8), Belleville springs (7), spacer (9), outer cam (5) with bearing (6) and cam actuator lever (3) as an assembly. Remove retaining ring (21), inner cam (16) with bearing (15), shim and spacer pack (14 and 9), pulley (12) with bearing (13) and friction disc (11). Spacers (9) and springs (10) can now be removed. Remove two machine screws (20) and lift off clutch plate (19) and grass screen (18). Unbolt and remove drive hub (17).

Clean and inspect all parts and renew any showing excessive wear or other damage. Install drive hub (17) and tighten four cap screws to 35-40 ft.-lbs. (47-54 N·m). Place screen (18) and clutch plate (19) on drive hub and tighten machine screws securely. Fit two springs (10), one spacer (9), two springs (10), one spacer (9) and two springs (10), one spacer (9), in this sequence on drive hub. Place friction disc (11) over shoulder of clutch pulley (12), then place both on drive hub. Install original shim and spacer pack (14 and 9). Measure diameter of cam (16) at each side of lever notches. One side will measure about 3 inches (76 mm) and the other about 2⅞ inches (73 mm). Install cam and bearing (16 and 15) on drive hub with shorter side of cam downward and install retaining ring (21). Place washer, hub spacer (8), Belleville springs (7) and spacer (9) on left hand thread cap screw (2). Position outer cam (5) with bearing (6) so longer diameter between notches is downward. Install cam actuating lever (3) in notches of inner cam (16), then install outer cam assembly. Tighten cap screw (2) to 35-40 ft.-lbs. (47-54 N·m).

With clutch disengaged, measure friction disc clearance using two feeler gages 180 degrees apart. Clearance should measure 0.015-0.025 inch (0.381-0.635 mm). To increase clearance, remove shims (14) or to decrease clearance, add shims (14) as required.

**NOTE: If clutch will not disengage, check for incorrect assembly of cams. When correctly installed, facing notches on inner and outer cams are out of alignment when clutch is engaged or disengaged.**

## Models 220-222-224-442-444

**R&R AND OVERHAUL.** To remove pto clutch, remove tractor hood and unbolt oil cooler supports from frame. Rotate oil cooler assembly ahead for access to clutch. Disconnect pto control rod from cam actuator lever (3 – Fig. C37). Remove left hand thread cap screw (2), fan (1), hub spacer (9), Belleville springs (8), outer cam (5) with bearing (6) and cam actuator (3) as an assembly. Remove washer (4), inner cam (16) with bearing (15), spacer and shim pack (7 and 14), pulley (12) with bearing (13) and friction disc (11). Spacers (7) and springs (10) can now be removed. Remove two machine screws (20) and lift off clutch plate (19) and grass screen (18). Unbolt and remove drive hub (17).

Clean and inspect all parts and renew any showing excessive wear or other damage. Check friction disc for glaze and wear. If friction surface is glazed or if friction disc thickness measures less than ⅛ inch (3 mm), renew friction disc. Sealed bearings (6, 13 and 15) must rotate freely and quietly.

Install drive hub (17) and tighten four cap screws to 35-40 ft.-lbs. (47-54 N·m). Place screen (18) and clutch plate (19) on drive hub and tighten machine screws (20) securely. Install springs (10) and spacers (7) in same sequence as original assembly. Place friction disc (11) over shoulder of clutch pulley (12), then place

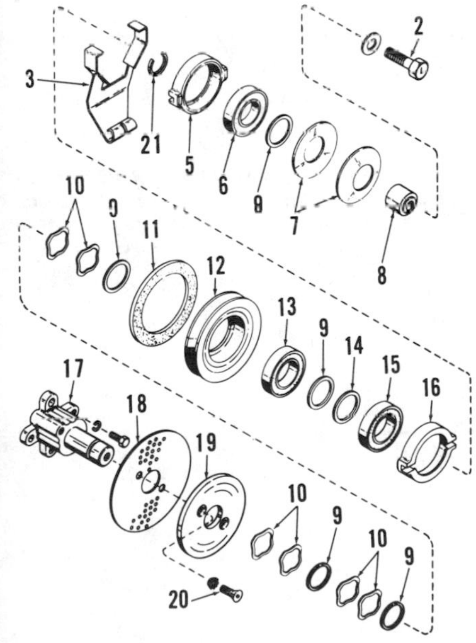


*Fig. C36 – Exploded view of power take-off clutch used on Model 210 tractors.*

2. Cap screw (L.H. thread)
3. Cam actuator lever
5. Outer cam
6. Bearing
7. Belleville springs
8. Hub spacer
9. Spacers (0.050 in.)
10. Springs
11. Friction disc
12. Clutch pulley
13. Bearing
14. Shim (0.010 in.)
15. Bearing
16. Inner cam
17. Drive hub
18. Grass screen
19. Clutch plate
20. Machine screw (2 used)
21. Retaining ring

*Fig. C37 – Exploded view of typical pto clutch used on Models 220, 222, 224, 442 and 444.*

1. Fan
2. Cap screw (L.H. thread)
3. Cam actuator lever
4. Washer
5. Outer cam
6. Bearing
7. Spacer (0.050 in.)
8. Belleville springs
9. Hub spacer
10. Springs
11. Friction disc
12. Clutch pulley
13. Bearing
14. Shim (0.010 in.)
15. Bearing
16. Inner cam
17. Drive hub
18. Grass screen
19. Clutch plate
20. Machine screw (2)

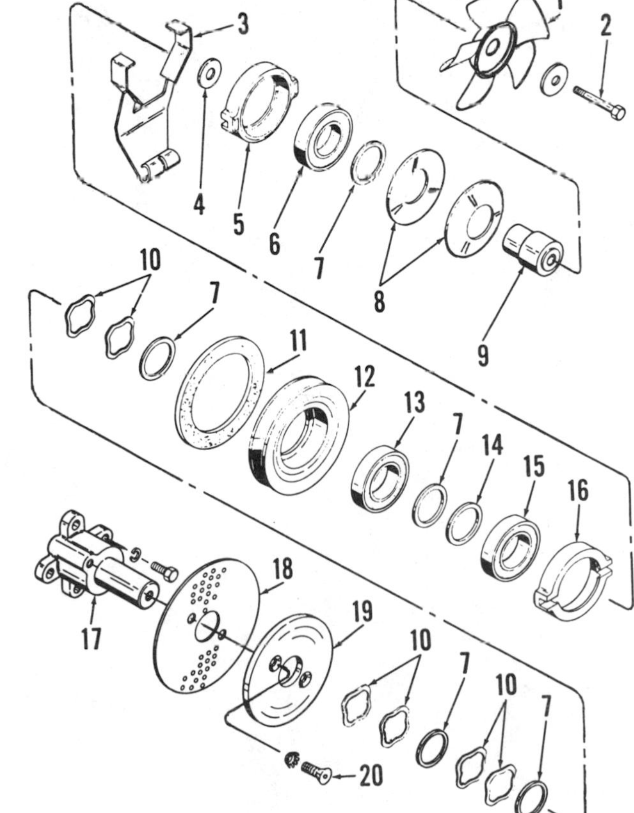

both on drive hub. Install original spacer and shim pack (7 and 14). Measure diameter of inner cam (16) at each side of lever notches. One side will measure about 3 inches (76 mm) and other about 2⅝ inches (73 mm). Install cam and bearing assembly (15 and 16) with shorter side of cam downward, on drive hub. Place washer, fan (1), hub spacer (9) and Belleville springs (8) on left hand thread cap screw (2). Position outer cam (5) with bearing (6) and washer (4) on hub spacer (9) so longer diameter of cam between notches is downward. Install cam actuating lever (3) in notches of inner cam (16), then install outer cam assembly (1 through 9). Tighten cap screw (2) to 35-40 ft.-lbs. (47-54 N·m).

With clutch disengaged, measure friction disc clearance using two feeler gages 180 degrees apart. Clearance should measure 0.015-0.025 inch (0.381-0.635 mm). To increase clearance, remove shims (14) or to decrease clearance, add shims (14) as required.

**NOTE: If clutch will not disengage, check for incorrect assembly of cams (5 and 16). When correctly installed, facing notches on inner and outer cams are out of alignment when clutch is engaged or disengaged.**

Bolt oil cooler supports to tractor frame and install hood.

# HYDRAULIC LIFT

## All Models So Equipped

The hydraulic lift system pressure is provided by hydraulic drive pump. The control valve used is two-spool Dukes valve shown in Fig. C16. Refer to appropriate paragraphs in HYDRAULIC TRANSMISSION section for service procedure on pump and control valve.

### LIFT CYLINDER

**REMOVE AND REINSTALL.** With lift cylinder in retracted position, disconnect the two hoses. Unpin and remove cylinder assembly.

Reinstall cylinder by reversing removal procedure. Operate cylinder to full extended and retracted position several times. Then, with cylinder in retracted position, check oil level in hydraulic reservoir. Add oil as necessary. Use SAE 5W-20 oil if temperature is below 32°F (0°C) or SAE 20W-40 oil if temperature is above 32°F (0°C).

**OVERHAUL (F30).** Remove street elbows from cylinder tube (8 – Fig. C38) and drain cylinder. Pull outward on clevis (1) and remove rod guide (2) and rod and piston assembly. Unscrew clevis from rod (5), then remove guide (2). Remove cylinder head (10) from tube (8). Remove and discard all "O" rings and back-up rings.

Clean and inspect all parts and renew any showing excessive wear, scoring or other damage. When reassembling, renew all "O" rings and back-up rings and lubricate internal parts with SAE 20W oil. Apply a suitable thread locking solution on threads of rod (5) and tighten clevis securely. Use pipe thread sealer or Teflon tape on threads and install two street elbows.

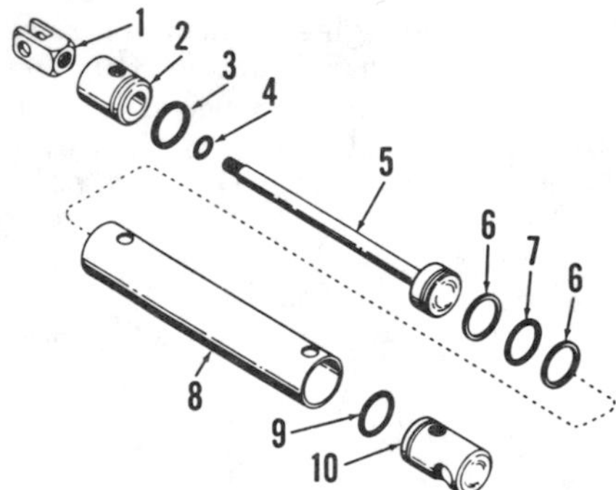


***Fig. C38 – Exploded view of Model F30 hydraulic lift cylinder used on some tractors.***

1. Clevis
2. Rod guide
3. "O" ring
4. "O" ring
5. Rod & piston
6. Back-up rings
7. "O" ring
8. Tube
9. "O" ring
10. Cylinder head

**OVERHAUL (H30 or J30).** Drain oil from cylinder and disassemble as follows: Clean all paint and/or rust from inside base end of cylinder tube (3 – Fig. C39). Push piston and rod assembly and end plate (7 or 8) out of cylinder tube. Remove "O" ring (5) from piston, "O" ring (6) from end plate (7 or 8) and wiper seal (1) and "O" ring (2) from cylinder tube.

Clean and inspect all parts and renew any showing excessive wear, scoring or other damage. When reassembling, renew wiper seal and "O" rings which are available in a seal kit. Lubricate wiper seal and all "O" rings and use caution not to damage "O" rings during reassembly. Install end plate (7 or 8) just far enough to permit installation of cylinder mounting pin.

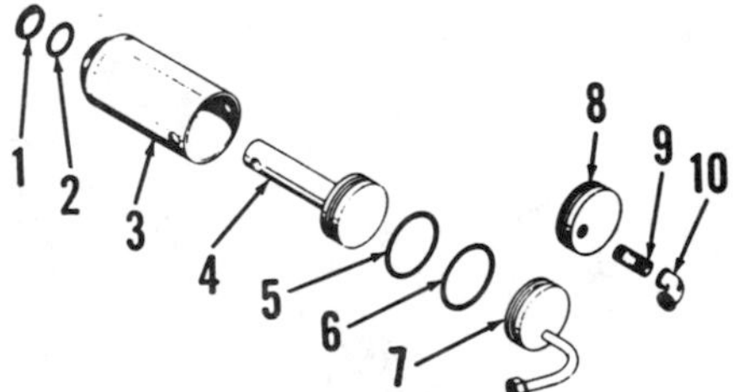


***Fig. C39 – Exploded view of Model H30 or J30 hydraulic lift cylinder used on some tractors. Items 8, 9 and 10 are used on H30 cylinder.***

1. Wiper seal
2. "O" ring
3. Cylinder tube
4. Rod & piston
5. "O" ring
6. "O" ring
7. End plate (J30)
8. End plate (H30)
9. Pip nipple
10. Pipe elbow

# CUB CADET

## CONDENSED SPECIFICATIONS

| | MODELS | | | |
|---|---|---|---|---|
| | **72, 73** | **86** | **104, 106, 108** | **105, 107, 109** |
| Engine Make | Kohler | Kohler | Kohler | Kohler |
| Model | K161 | K181 | K241A | K241A |
| Bore | 2 7/8 in. (73 mm) | 2 15/16 in. (74.6 mm) | 3 1/4 in. (82.5 mm) | 3 1/4 in. (82.5 mm) |
| Stroke | 2 1/2 in. (63.5 mm) | 2 3/4 in. (69.8 mm) | 2 7/8 in. (73 mm) | 2 7/8 in. (73 mm) |
| Displacement | 16.22 cu. in. (266 cc) | 18.6 cu. in. (305 cc) | 23.9 cu. in. (392 cc) | 29.07 cu. in. (392 cc) |
| Rated power | 7 hp (5.2 kW) | 8 hp (5.9 kW) | 10 hp (7.4 kW) | 10 hp (7.4 kW) |
| Slow Idle Speed—Rpm | 1000 | 1000 | 1000 | 1000 |
| High Idle Speed (No-Load)—Rpm | 3780 | 3780 | 3800 | 3800 |
| Crankcase Oil Capacity | 2 1/2 pts. (1.2 L) | 2 1/2 pts. (1.2 L) | 3 pts. (1.4 L) | 3 pts. (1.4 L) |
| Transmission Oil Capacity | 7 pts. (3.3 L) | 7 pts. (3.3 L) | 7 pts. (3.3 L) | 14 pts. (6.6 L) |
| Transmission Type | Gear | Gear | Gear | Hydro |

| | MODELS | | | |
|---|---|---|---|---|
| | **124, 126, 128** | **125, 127, 129** | **80, 282** | **81, 182 (Early)** |
| Engine Make | Kohler | Kohler | B&S | B&S |
| Model | K301A | K301A | 191707 | 191707 |
| Bore | 3 3/8 in. (85.7 mm) | 3 3/8 in. (85.7 mm) | 3 in. (76.2 mm) | 3 in. (76.2 mm) |
| Stroke | 3 1/4 in. (82.5 mm) | 3 1/4 in. (82.5 mm) | 2 3/4 in. (69.8 mm) | 2 3/4 in. (69.8 mm) |
| Displacement | 29.07 cu. in. (476 cc) | 29.07 cu. in. (476 cc) | 19.44 cu. in. (319 cc) | 19.44 cu. in. (319 cc) |
| Rated Power | 12 hp (8.9 kW) | 12 hp (8.9 kW) | 8 hp (5.9 kW) | 8 hp (5.9 kW) |
| Slow Idle Speed—Rpm | 1000 | 1000 | 1800 | 1800 |
| High Idle Speed (No-Load)—Rpm | 3800 | 3800 | 3500 | 3500 |
| Crankcase Oil Capacity | 3 pts. (1.4 L) | 3 pts. (1.4 L) | 3 pts. (1.4 L) | 3 pts. (1.4 L) |
| Transmission Oil Capacity | 7 pts. (3.3 L) | 14 pts. (6.6 L) | * | 2 3/4 pts. (1.3 L) |
| Transmission Type | Gear | Hydro | Hydro | Gear |

*Reduction gear and differential capacity is 2 3/4 pints (1.3 L). Hydrostatic transmission capacity is 1 1/2 pints (0.7 L).

| | MODELS | |
|---|---|---|
| | **182 (Late)** | **111, 382 (Early)** |
| Engine Make | B&S | B&S |
| Model | 191707 | 252707 |
| Bore | 3 in. (76.2 mm) | 3 7/16 in. (87.3 mm) |
| Stroke | 2 3/4 in. (69.8 mm) | 2 5/8 in. (66.7 mm) |
| Displacement | 19.44 cu. in. (319 cc) | 24.36 cu. in. (399 cc) |
| Rated Power | 8 hp (5.9 kW) | 11 hp (8.2 kW) |
| Slow Idle Speed—Rpm | 1800 | 1800 |
| High Idle Speed (No-Load)—Rpm | 3500 | 3500 |
| Crankcase Oil Capacity | 3 pts. (1.4 L) | 3 pts. (1.4 L) |
| Transmission Oil Capacity | 24 oz. (710 mL) | 2 3/4 pts. (1.3 L) |
| Transmission Type | Gear | Gear |

# CONDENSED SPECIFICATIONS

| | MODELS | | | |
|---|---|---|---|---|
| | **382 (Late)** | **382H** | **482, 1100** | **147, 149** |
| Engine Make | B&S | B&S | B&S | Kohler |
| Model | 252707 | 252707 | 253707 | K341 |
| Bore | $3^7/_{16}$ in. (87.3 mm) | $3^7/_{16}$ in. (87.3 mm) | $3^7/_{16}$ in. (87.3 mm) | $3^1/_2$ in. (88.9 mm) |
| Stroke | $2^5/_8$ in. (66.7 mm) | $2^5/_8$ in. (66.7 mm) | $2^5/_8$ in. (66.7 mm) | $3^1/_4$ in. (82.5 mm) |
| Displacement | 24.36 cu. in. (399 cc) | 24.36 cu. in. (399 cc) | 24.36 cu. in. (399 cc) | 31.27 cu. in. (512 cc) |
| Rated Power | 11 hp (8.2 kW) | 11 hp (8.2 kW) | 11 hp (8.2 kW) | 14 hp (10.4 kW) |
| Slow Idle Speed—Rpm | 1800 | 1800 | 1750 | 1000 |
| High Idle Speed (No-Load)—Rpm | 3500 | 3500 | 3600 | 3800 |
| Crankcase Oil Capacity | 3 pts. (1.4 L) | 3 pts. (1.4 L) | 3 pts. (1.4 L) | 3 pts. (1.4 L) |
| Transmission Oil Capacity | 24 oz. (710 mL) | ** | 4 pts. (1.9 L) | 14 pts. (6.6 L) |
| Transmission Type | Gear | Hydro | Gear | Hydro |

**Reduction gear and differential capacity is $2^3/_4$ pints (1.3 L). Hydrostatic transmission capacity is $1^1/_2$ pints (0.7 L).

| | MODELS | | | |
|---|---|---|---|---|
| | **169** | **800** | **1000** | **1015** |
| Engine Make | Kohler | Kohler | Kohler | B&S |
| Model | K341 | K181QS | K241AQS | 251707 |
| Bore | $3^3/_4$ in. (95.2 mm) | $2^{15}/_{16}$ in. (74.6 mm) | $3^1/_4$ in. (82.5 mm) | $3^7/_{16}$ in. (87.3 mm) |
| Stroke | $3^1/_4$ in. (82.5 mm) | $2^3/_4$ in. (69.8 mm) | $2^7/_8$ in. (73.0 mm) | $2^5/_8$ in. (66.7 mm) |
| Displacement | 35.90 cu. in. (588 cc) | 18.63 cu. in. (305 cc) | 23.9 cu. in. (392 cc) | 24.36 cu. in. (399 cc) |
| Rated power | 16 hp (11.9 kW) | 8 hp (5.9 kW) | 10 hp (7.4 kW) | 10 hp (7.4 kW) |
| Slow Idle Speed—Rpm | 1000 | 1800 | 1800 | 1750 |
| High Idle Speed (No-Load)—Rpm | 3600 | 3600 | 3600 | 3400 |
| Crankcase Oil Capacity | 3 pts. (1.4 L) | $2^1/_2$ pts. (1.2 L) | 3 pts. (1.4 L) | 3 pts. (1.4 L) |
| Transmission Oil Capacity | 14 pts. (6.6 L) | $2^1/_2$ pts. (1.2 L) | 3 pts. (1.4 L) | 30 oz. (887 mL) |
| Transmission Type | Hydro | Gear | Gear | Gear |

| | MODELS | | | |
|---|---|---|---|---|
| | **1020** | **1200** | **1204** | **1210, 1211** |
| Engine Make | B&S | Kohler | Kohler | Kohler |
| Model | 251707 | K301AQS | K301 | K301 |
| Bore | $3^7/_{16}$ in. (87.3 mm) | $3^3/_8$ in. (85.7 mm) | $3^3/_8$ in. (85.7 mm) | $3^3/_8$ in. (85.7 mm) |
| Stroke | $2^5/_8$ in. (66.7 mm) | $3^1/_4$ in. (82.5 mm) | $3^1/_4$ in. (82.5 mm) | $3^1/_4$ in. (82.5 mm) |
| Displacement | 24.36 cu. in. (399 cc) | 29.07 cu. in. (476 cc) | 29.07 cu. in. (476 cc) | 29.07 cu. in. (476 cc) |
| Rated power | 10 hp (7.4 kW) | 12 hp (8.9 kW) | 12 hp (8.9 kW) | 12 hp (8.9 kW) |
| Slow Idle Speed—Rpm | 1750 | 1800 | 1800 | 1800 |
| High Idle Speed (No-Load)—Rpm | 3400 | 3600 | 3600 | 3600 |
| Crankcase Oil Capacity | 3 pts. (1.4 L) | 3 pts. (1.4 L) | 3 pts. (1.4 L) | 3 pts. (1.4 L) |
| Transmission Oil Capacity | *** | 7 pts. (3.3 L) | 4 pts. (1.9 L) | 14 pts. (6.6 L) |
| Transmission Type | Hydro | Gear | Gear | Hydro |

***Refer to HYDROSTATIC TRANSMISSION section.

# CONDENSED SPECIFICATIONS

| | MODELS | | | |
|---|---|---|---|---|
| | 1215 | 1220 | 1250 | 1315 |
| Engine Make | B&S | B&S | Kohler | Kohler |
| Model | 281707 | 281707 | K301AQS | CV125S |
| Bore | 3 7/16 in. (87.3 mm) | 3 7/16 in. (87.3 mm) | 3 3/8 in. (85.7 mm) | 3 7/16 in. (87.1 mm) |
| Stroke | 3 1/16 in. (77.7 mm) | 3 1/16 in. (77.7 mm) | 3 1/4 in. (82.5 mm) | 2 5/8 in. (67 mm) |
| Displacement | 28.4 cu. in. (465 cc) | 28.4 cu. in. (465 cc) | 29.07 cu. in. (476 cc) | 24.29 cu. in. (398 cc) |
| Rated power | 12 hp (8.9 kW) | 12 hp (8.9 kW) | 12 hp (8.9 kW) | 12.5 hp (9.3 kW) |
| Slow Idle Speed—Rpm | 1750 | 1750 | 1800 | 1800 |
| High Idle Speed (No-Load)—Rpm | 3400 | 3400 | 3600 | 3400 |
| Crankcase Oil Capacity | 3 pts. (1.4 L) | 3 pts. (1.4 L) | 3 pts. (1.4 L) | 4 pts. (1.9 L) |
| Transmission Oil Capacity | 30 oz. (887 mL) | *** | 14 pts. (6.6 L) | 30 oz. (887 mL) |
| Transmission Type | Gear | Hydro | Hydro | Gear |

***Refer to HYDROSTATIC TRANSMISSION section.

| | MODELS | | | |
|---|---|---|---|---|
| | 1320 | 1405 | 1450 | 1650 |
| Engine Make | Kohler | Kohler | Kohler | Kohler |
| Model | CV125S | CV14S | K321AQS | K341AQS |
| Bore | 3 7/16 in. (87.1 mm) | 3 7/16 in. (87.1 mm) | 3 1/2 in. (88.9 mm) | 3 3/4 in. (95.2 mm) |
| Stroke | 2 5/8 in. (67 mm) | 2 5/8 in. (67 mm) | 3 1/4 in. (82.5 mm) | 3 1/4 in. (82.5 mm) |
| Displacement | 24.29 cu. in. (398 cc) | 24.29 cu. in. (398 cc) | 31.27 cu. in. (512 cc) | 35.90 cu. in. (588 cc) |
| Rated power | 12.5 hp (9.3 kW) | 14 hp (10.4 kW) | 14 hp (10.4 kW) | 16 hp (11.9 kW) |
| Slow Idle Speed—Rpm | 1800 | 1800 | 1800 | 1800 |
| High Idle Speed (No-Load)—Rpm | 3400 | 3400 | 3600 | 3600 |
| Crankcase Oil Capacity | 4 pts. (1.9 L) | 4 pts. (1.9 L) | 3 pts. (1.4 L) | 3 pts. (1.4 L) |
| Transmission Oil Capacity | 30 oz. (887 mL) | 30 oz. (887 mL) | 14 pts. (6.6 L) | 14 pts. (6.6 L) |
| Transmission Type | Gear | Gear | Hydro | Hydro |

# FRONT AXLE SYSTEM

### AXLE MAIN MEMBER

#### All Models

The front axle main member is mounted directly on the main frame and pivots on center mounting pivot pin or bushing. Refer to Figs. CC1, CC2, CC3 and CC4. The pivot pin or bushing is retained by a nut on Models 80, 81, 111, 182, 282, 382 and 482, by a bolt on Models 1015, 1020, 1204, 1210, 1211, 1215, 1220, 1315, 1320 and 1405, and by a spring pin on all other models.

To remove front axle main member assembly, raise front of tractor and re-

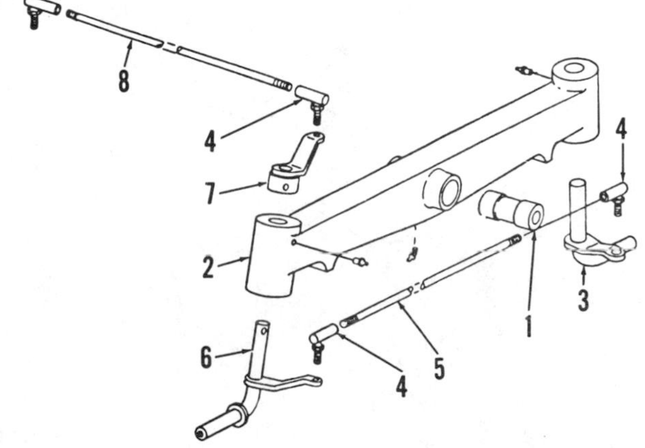


***Fig. CC1—Exploded view of front axle assembly used on Models 80, 81, 111, 182, 282 and 382.***

1. Pivot bushing
2. Axle main member
3. Steering spindle R.H.
4. Tie rod ball joint end
5. Tie rod
6. Steering spindle L.H.
7. Drag link arm
8. Drag link

Illustrations courtesy Cub Cadet Corp.

move front wheels. Disconnect steering drag link from drag link arm or steering spindle. Remove axle pivot pin, bushing or bolt and lower front axle assembly from tractor.

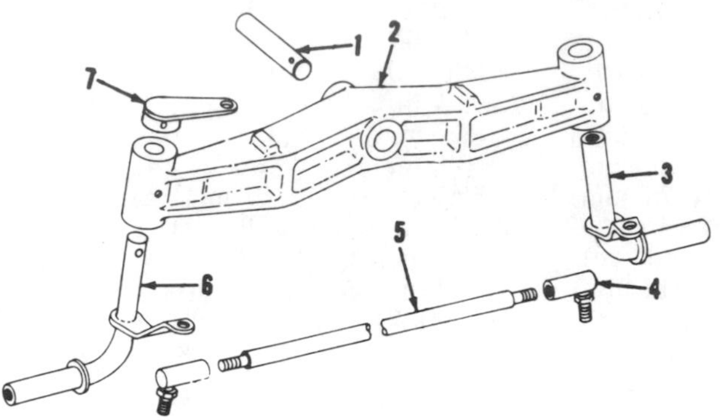


*Fig. CC2—Exploded view of front axle assembly used on Models 72, 73, 104, 105, 106, 107, 124, 125, 126, 127 and 147.*

1. Pivot pin
2. Axle main member
3. Steering spindle R.H.
4. Tie rod ball joint end
5. Tie rod
6. Steering spindle L.H.
7. Drag link arm

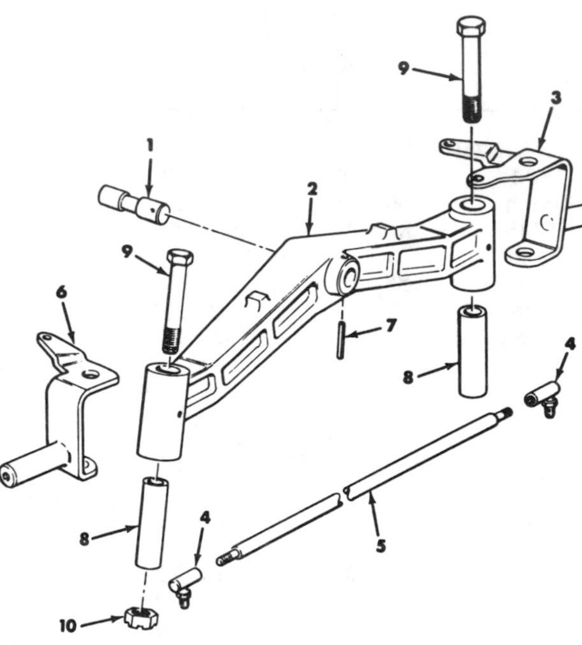


*Fig. CC3—Exploded view of typical front axle assembly used on Models 86, 108, 109, 128, 129, 149, 169, 482, 800, 1000, 1100, 1200, 1204, 1210, 1211, 1250, 1450 and 1650. Some models use a pivot bolt instead of pin (1).*

1. Pivot pin
2. Axle main member
3. Steering spindle L.H.
4. Tie rod ball joint end
5. Tie rod
6. Steering spindle R.H.
7. Retaining pin
8. Spacer
9. Steering spindle bolt
10. Nut

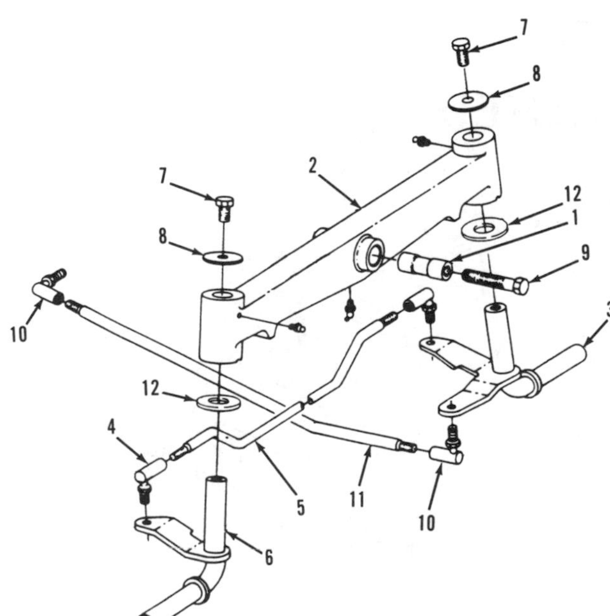

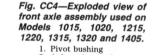

*Fig. CC4—Exploded view of front axle assembly used on Models 1015, 1020, 1215, 1220, 1315, 1320 and 1405.*

1. Pivot bushing
2. Axle main member
3. Left spindle
4. Tie rod end
5. Tie rod
6. Right spindle
7. Cap screw
8. Washer
9. Bolt
10. Drag link end
11. Drag link
12. Thrust washers

To reinstall axle main member, reverse the removal procedure. Lubricate pivot pin with multipurpose grease. On models equipped with axle adjustment bolts (B—Fig. CC5), adjust each bolt until head of bolt contacts axle main member, then tighten jam nut.

## TIE ROD

### All Models

Tie rod ball joint ends (4—Fig. CC1, CC2, CC3 or CC4) are not adjustable and should be renewed if excessively worn.

Front wheels should toe-in $^1/_{16}$ to $^1/_8$ inch (1.5-3 mm). To adjust toe-in, disconnect one tie rod ball joint from steering spindle. Loosen ball joint locknuts and turn tie rod in or out as necessary. Note that some tie rods (5—Fig. CC4) have a bend in the center for clearance and bend must face downward when tie rod is installed.

## STEERING SPINDLES

### Models 86-108-109-128-129-149-169-482-800-1000-1100-1200-1204-1210-1211-1250-1450-1650

To remove steering spindles (3 and 6—Fig. CC3), support front of tractor and remove front wheels. Disconnect drag link and tie rod ends from steering spindles. Remove nuts (10) and steering spindle bolts (9). Remove steering spindles and spacers (8) from axle main member.

Inspect spindles, wheels and bearings for excessive wear and renew as necessary. When reassembling, tighten nuts (10) to 80 ft.-lbs. (108 N·m). Lubricate with multipurpose grease.

### All Other Models

To remove steering spindles (3 and 6—Fig. CC1, CC2 or CC4), first raise and support front of tractor. Remove front wheels. Disconnect drag link and tie rod from steering spindles. Remove pins and/or cap screws from top of steering

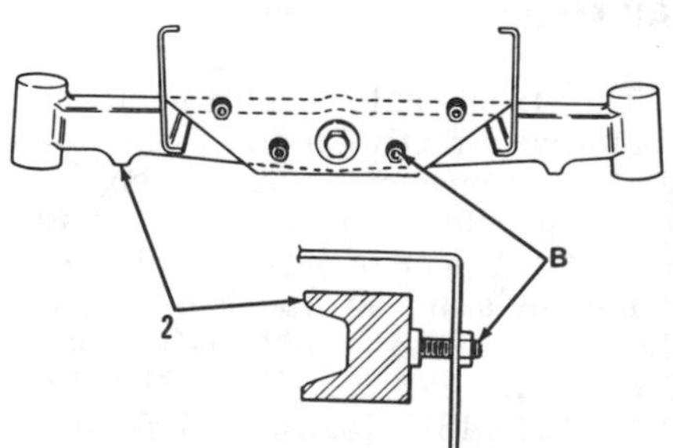


*Fig. CC5—On models equipped with axle adjustment bolts, the head of both bolts (B) must contact axle main member (2).*



Illustrations courtesy Cub Cadet Corp.

spindles and lower spindles from axle main member.

Inspect spindles, axle, wheels and bearings for excessive wear and renew as necessary. When reassembling spindles, tighten retaining cap screws (if equipped) to 33-37 ft.-lbs. (45-50 N·m). Lubricate with multipurpose grease.

## STEERING GEAR

### Models 80-81-111-182-282-382

**R&R AND OVERHAUL.** To remove steering gear, first disconnect and remove battery. Disconnect pto rod, spring and ignition switch. Remove solenoid mounting bolts and lay solenoid on frame. Disconnect throttle cable and fuel line at carburetor. Remove steering arm cover and disconnect drag link. Drive roll pin out of bottom of steering wheel and lift wheel off. Remove steering column tower. Remove cotter pin and washer from steering shaft and lift shaft out. Remove pivot bolt from steering gear assembly and slide gear rearward out of frame.

Inspect nylon bearing (5—Fig. CC6) and bushing (6) for wear or damage. Check for broken or worn gear teeth, bent shafts or stripped threads. Renew damaged or worn parts as necessary.

To renew steering shaft bushing, carefully break old bushing with a chisel and remove bushing. Heat new bushing in boiling water for five minutes to make it flexible. Position bushing in a socket and drive it in with a wooden or rubber mallet.

Reassemble and install by reversing removal procedure. Apply "Lubriplate" or equivalent grease liberally to gear assembly, bearings and shaft.

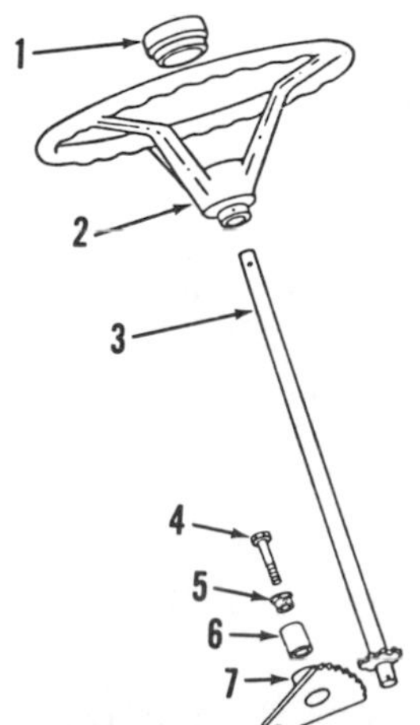

*Fig. CC6—Exploded view of steering unit used on Models 80, 81, 111, 182, 282 and 382.*

1. Steering wheel cap
2. Steering wheel
3. Steering shaft assy.
4. Pivot bolt
5. Bearing
6. Drag link bushing
7. Steering gear assy.

### Models 1204-1210-1211

**R&R AND OVERHAUL.** To remove steering gear, first remove steering wheel center cover. Remove nut (7—Fig. CC7) and use a suitable puller to remove steering wheel. Disconnect drag link at steering arm plate (14). Remove mounting bolts retaining steering gear housing and tube. Lower steering gear housing and tube assembly through the control panel and out of tractor.

To disassemble, clamp steering arm plate (14—Fig. CC7) in a vise and remove nut (11) and jam nut (12). Separate housing and tube assembly (4) from steering arm plate. Remove cotter pin (21) and adjustment plug (20). Remove steering shaft and cam assembly (8) and bearings from housing and tube assembly.

During reassembly, coat the cam, bearing balls and races with lithium base grease. Install steering shaft and cam, balls and races into housing and tube assembly. Make certain that races enter housing squarely and are not cocked. Thread adjustment plug (20) into housing until end play of cam is removed but shaft still turns freely. Insert cotter pin (21) into nearest hole in adjustment plug.

Fill housing with lithium base grease. Loosen jam nut (12) and back cam adjustment bolt (13) out two turns. Install seal (16), retainer (15) and steering arm plate (14). Install the washer and nut (11). Tighten the nut until there is 3/32 inch (2.4 mm) clearance between steering arm plate and housing (Fig. CC8). Install a jam nut against nut (11—Fig. CC7) and tighten jam nut to 40 ft.-lbs. (54 N·m). Lubricate at fitting (17) until grease begins to appear between steering arm plate (14) and housing. Center steering cam by rotating steering shaft halfway between full right and full left turn. Turn cam adjustment bolt (13) inward to eliminate backlash, then tighten jam nut (12) to 40 ft.-lbs. (54 N·m). Steering shaft should rotate smoothly with minimum backlash.

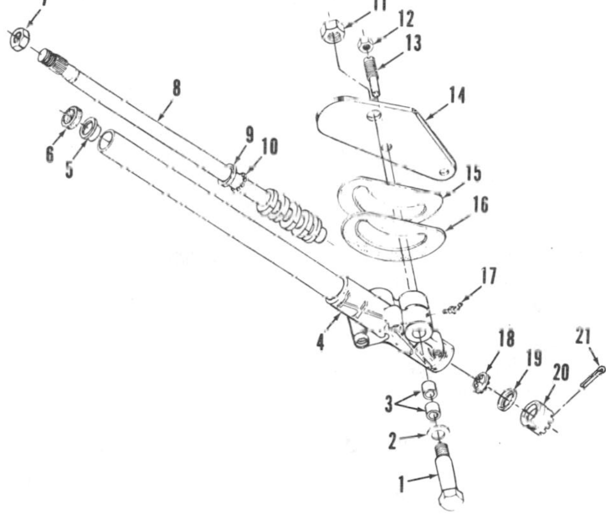

*Fig. CC7—Exploded view of steering shaft and gear assembly used on Models 1204, 1210 and 1211.*

1. Pivot bolt
2. Washer
3. Bushings
4. Housing & tube assy.
5. Bearing
6. Seal
7. Nut
8. Steering shaft & cam
9. Bearing race
10. Bearing
11. Nut
12. Jam nut
13. Cam adjustment bolt
14. Steering arm plate
15. Seal retainer
16. Seal
17. Grease fitting
18. Bearing & retainer
19. Bearing race
20. Adjustment plug
21. Cotter pin

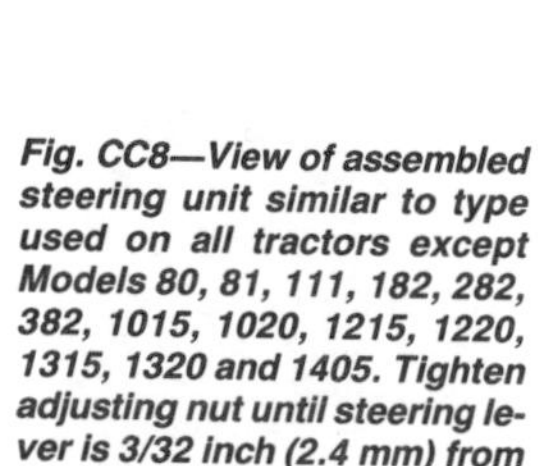

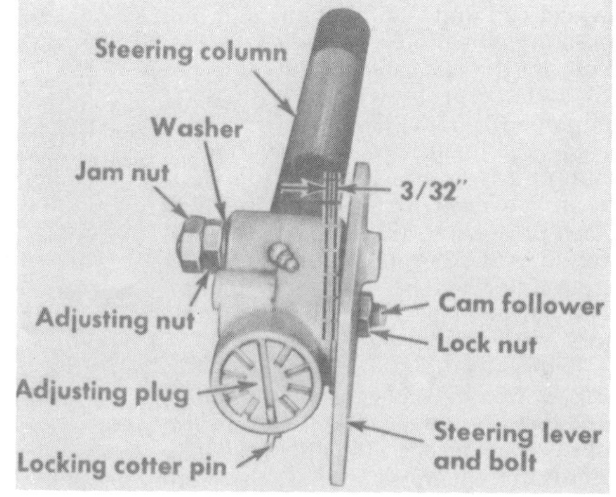


*Fig. CC8—View of assembled steering unit similar to type used on all tractors except Models 80, 81, 111, 182, 282, 382, 1015, 1020, 1215, 1220, 1315, 1320 and 1405. Tighten adjusting nut until steering lever is 3/32 inch (2.4 mm) from housing.*

### Models 72-73-86-104-105-106-107-108-109-124-125-126-127-128-129-147-149-169-482-800-1000-1100-1200-1250-1450-1650

**R&R AND OVERHAUL.** To remove steering gear, first remove steering wheel, felt seal, retainer, bearing and bearing retainer from upper end of steering column. Disconnect drag link rear ball joint from steering gear lever (11—Fig. CC9). Remove the two cap screws securing steering unit to frame cross member, then lower unit and remove from under side of tractor.

To disassemble, remove lever and bolt assembly (11—Fig. CC9). Remove cam bearing adjuster plug (8) and bump steering cam assembly (15) out of steering column. Remove bearings (6) and bearing races (7).

When reassembling unit, cam bearing adjuster plug (8) should be tightened to remove all end play, but cam must still rotate freely. Stake adjuster plug or install cotter pin to prevent it from working loose. Install lever and bolt assembly (11). Install copper washer (5) and adjusting nut. Tighten adjusting nut until steering lever is $^{3}/_{32}$ inch (2.4 mm) from cam housing. See Fig. CC8. Tighten jam nut to 40 ft.-lbs. (54 N·m). To adjust cam follower (14—Fig. CC9), locate cam in mid-position (halfway between full right and full left turn). Turn cam follower screw in until zero backlash is obtained and secure with locknut. Steering cam should turn from a full left to full right turn without binding. Lubricate steering gear with multipurpose grease.

### Models 1015-1020-1215-1220-1315-1320-1405

**R&R AND OVERHAUL.** To remove steering gear assembly, first disconnect battery cables. On Models 1215 and 1220, remove battery. On Models 1015, 1020, 1315 and 1320, remove the fuel tank. On all models, remove steering wheel cap and retaining nut and pull steering wheel off steering shaft. Disconnect throttle cable, choke cable, pto electric clutch wire harness (if equipped), engine ground wire, starter cable and main wire harness. Remove nuts or screws attaching steering shaft bearing to dash. Remove nuts attaching dash pedestal to frame and lift pedestal up over steering shaft. Disconnect drag link from steering arm. Remove bolts attaching steering box to frame and remove steering gear assembly.

To disassemble steering gear, refer to Fig. CC10 and remove cap (10), nut (9) and bolt (8). Remove nut (19) from end of steering arm shaft (5), disengage snap ring (22) from groove in shaft and withdraw shaft and bevel gear (21) from steering box (11). Remove nut (18) and pull steering wheel shaft out of steering box and pinion gear (16).

Inspect bushings for wear or damage and renew as necessary. Check for broken gear teeth or bent shafts and renew parts as necessary. To reassemble, reverse the disassembly procedure. Turn adjusting bolt (8—Fig. CC10) to obtain minimum amount of backlash between bevel gear and pinion gear, while still allowing steering wheel shaft to turn freely. Install steering gear assembly. With front wheels in straight ahead position, pinion gear must be in the center of bevel gear.

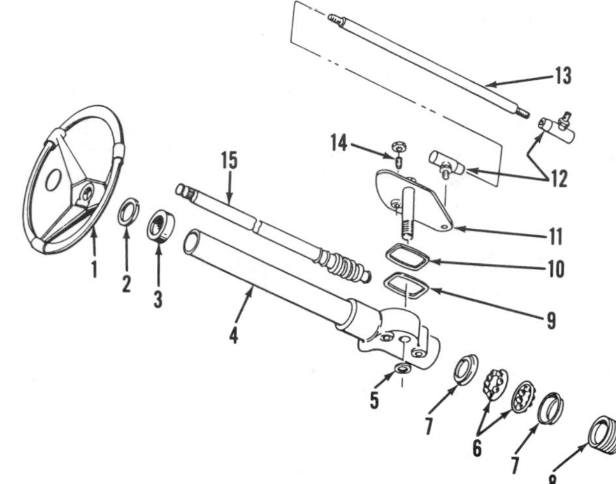


*Fig. CC9—Exploded view of typical steering unit used on Models 72, 73, 86, 104, 105, 106, 107, 108, 109, 124, 125, 126, 127, 128, 129, 147, 149, 169, 482, 800, 1000, 1100, 1200, 1250, 1450 and 1650.*

1. Steering wheel
2. Seal
3. Column bearing
4. Steering column
5. Copper washer
6. Retainer & ball assy.
7. Bearing race
8. Adjusting plug
9. Seal
10. Retainer
11. Lever & ball assy.
12. Drag link ends
13. Drag link
14. Cam follower stud
15. Steering cam

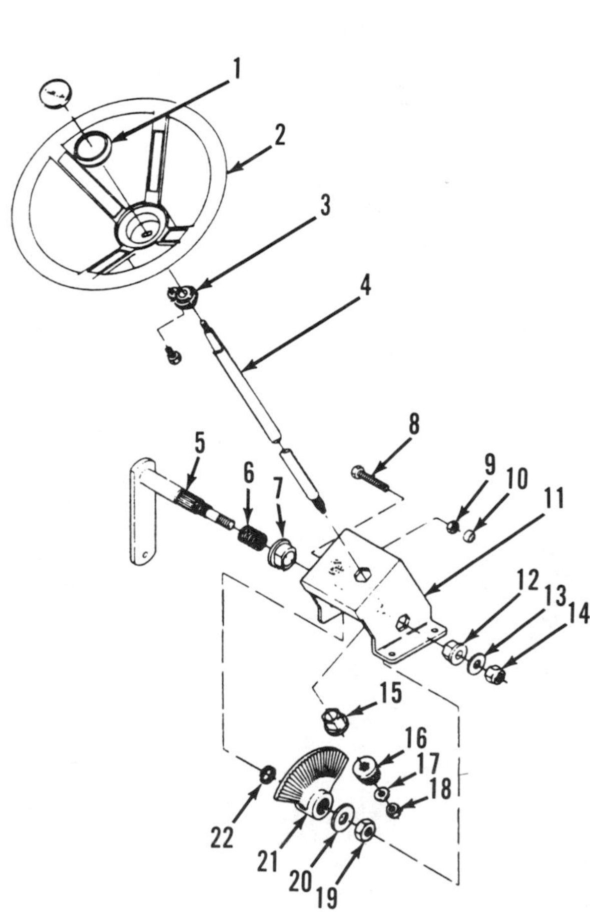


*Fig. CC10—Exploded view of steering gear assembly used on Models 1015, 1020, 1215, 1220, 1315, 1320 and 1405.*

1. Steering wheel cap
2. Steering wheel
3. Column bearing
4. Steering shaft
5. Steering arm shaft
6. Spring
7. Flange bushing
8. Cap screw
9. Jam nut
10. Cap
11. Steering box
12. Flange bushing
13. Thrust washer
14. Locknut
15. Flange bushing
16. Pinion gear
17. Thrust washer
18. Locknut
19. Jam nut
20. Thrust washer
21. Bevel gear
22. Snap ring

## ENGINE

### REMOVE AND REINSTALL

### Models 80-81-111-182-282-382

To remove engine, first remove grille and hood assemblies. Disconnect battery cables, starter, charging and control



Illustrations courtesy Cub Cadet Corp.

module wires. Shut off fuel at fuel tank, disconnect fuel line at carburetor and remove fuel tank. Disconnect choke and throttle cables. Work mower drive and main drive belts free of engine pulley and idler pulley. Remove engine mounting bolts and lift engine out of frame.

Reinstall engine by reversing removal procedure.

### Models 72-73-86-104-105-106-107-108-109-124-125-126-127-128-129-147-149-169

To remove engine, first disconnect battery cable. On models equipped with firewall mounted fuel tank, shut off fuel and remove fuel tank and panel extension as an assembly. On all models, disconnect and remove front pto linkage. Remove grille and hood assembly. Disconnect generator-starter wires and ignition wires. Disconnect choke and throttle cables. Raise front of tractor and remove the four engine mounting bolts. Slide engine forward and lift from frame using a suitable hoist.

Reinstall engine in reverse order of removal.

### Models 1204-1210-1211

To remove engine, raise hood and unhook side panel extension spring, flat washer and wing nut on each side. Remove the two side panels. Close fuel shut-off valve located on the bottom left side of fuel tank and disconnect fuel line at fuel tank. Remove the two hex nuts and flat washers and remove fuel tank. Disconnect the four headlight wires at headlights and separate headlight wiring harness from grille. Remove the four bolts and lockwashers retaining grille and hood to front of frame and remove hood and grille assembly. Remove bolts on each side of pedestal and gas tank straps. Disconnect all electrical connections at engine and starter. Remove air cleaner cover and disconnect throttle and choke cables. Remove bolt on right side retaining heat shield and remove heat shield. Remove ground wire and wiring harness from left heat shield. Remove screw on bottom of coupling guard (attached to heat shield) and lift heat shield and coupling guard out of tractor. Remove drive pin at drive shaft coupling at rear of engine. Remove the two nuts securing coupling to flexible disc and slide coupling and disc back on drive shaft. Remove the two bolts retaining the self-aligning bearing on engine at drive shaft. Remove the four engine mounting bolts and remove engine from tractor.

Reinstall engine by reversing removal procedure.

### Models 1015-1020-1215-1220-1315-1320-1405

To remove engine, disconnect and remove the battery. Disconnect the two extension springs from bottom of the grille. Loosen grille pivot bracket retaining bolts on each side of grille. Remove pivot bracket bolts from one side only and pull grille and hood off the pivot brackets. Disconnect choke cable and throttle cable. Disconnect fuel line from fuel pump. Disconnect ground wire, main wiring harness and starter cable at the engine. On Models 1215 and 1220, disconnect wire to electric clutch. Raise front of tractor and unbolt and remove electric clutch, engine pulley and belt guard, crankshaft spacer and drive belt idler pulley. On all other models, remove engine pulley and drive belt idler pulley. On all models, remove four engine mounting bolts and lift engine from frame using a suitable hoist.

Reinstall engine by reversing removal procedure while noting the following special instructions: Be sure that the four spacers are located between engine and frame. When installing engine belt guard mounting plate, be sure that welded bolts on plate face downward (away from tractor frame). Hub side of idler pulley must face upward (toward tractor frame).

### Models 482-800-1000-1100-1200-1250-1450-1650

To remove engine, first disconnect battery ground cable. Disconnect headlight wiring and remove grille housing, hood and side panels. Disconnect starter wires, charging wires, electric clutch wires, ignition wires and ground wires. Remove air filter assembly, then disconnect choke and throttle linkage. Shut off fuel at tank, disconnect fuel line from carburetor and remove fuel tank and supports. Remove engine mounting bolts (on some models, front of tractor must be raised for access to front bolts). On models so equipped, disconnect flexible drive coupler (3—Fig. CC12) from rear of engine. On all models, slide engine forward and use a suitable hoist to lift engine from frame.

Reinstall by reversing removal procedure.

*Fig. CC12—On some hydrostatic transmission models, a flexible drive coupler (3) is used. Remove cap screws (2) to disconnect. Model 1100 is shown; other models are similar.*

## OVERHAUL

### All Models

Engine make and model are listed at the beginning of this section. To overhaul engine components and accessories, refer to Kohler or Briggs & Stratton section of this manual.

# CLUTCH

A spring-loaded, dry disc type clutch is used on Models 72, 73, 86, 104, 106, 108, 124, 126, 128, 800, 1000 and 1200. On all other gear drive models, a spring-loaded, belt idler type clutch is used.

### Models 72-73-86-104-106-108-124-126-128-800-1000-1200

**ADJUSTMENT.** To maintain correct clearance of 0.050 inch (1.27 mm) between clutch release bearing and clutch release lever, clutch pedal must have a free travel (measured at pedal return stop) of approximately 9/32 inch (7 mm) on Models 86, 108, 128, 800, 1000 and 1200 or 3/16 inch (5 mm) on Models 72, 73, 104, 106, 124 and 126. It is necessary to adjust the linkage when free travel measurement becomes less than the required 3/16 or 9/32 inch (5 mm or 7 mm). To adjust linkage, turn adjusting nut (2—Fig. CC13) on front end of clutch re-

*Fig. CC13—Underside view of Model 1000 brake and clutch control linkage. Other models so equipped are similar.*

1. Clutch release lever
2. Adjusting nut
3. Release rod
4. Safety start switch
5. Brake rods

Illustrations courtesy Cub Cadet Corp.

lease rod in or out as required to obtain proper free travel.

**R&R AND OVERHAUL.** Complete service of clutch, clutch shaft, loading spring, release bearing and cushion spring will require moving engine forward. To remove clutch assembly, proceed as follows:

Remove frame cover and clutch shield. On Models 800, 1000 and 1200, disconnect flex coupling from rear of clutch shaft. On all other models, drive roll pins out of rear coupling and slide coupling forward on clutch shaft. On models equipped with electric lift cylinder, remove cylinder and mounting bracket. On all models, remove release lever pivot pin (2—Fig. CC14) and hanger bracket (1), and disconnect clutch release rod from pedal arm. Remove engine mounting bolts, then slide engine forward far enough to clear clutch parts. The complete clutch can now be removed from tractor.

Using a suitable press and slotted washer, compress clutch loading spring (Fig. CC15) and remove coiled spring pin, then release spring tension. Remove spring pins from pressure plates and withdraw clutch shaft from remaining parts. Refer to Fig. CC16 or Fig. CC17 for exploded view of clutch assembly.

Inspect clutch disc for wear and for elongated holes from drive plate pins. Inspect slotted hub of rear pressure plate; if slots are cupped, renew pressure plate. Inspect remaining parts for wear or other damage and renew as needed.

Reassemble by reversing disassembly procedure. On Models 800, 1000 and 1200, one drive plate pin (7—Fig. CC14) is longer than the other two. Drive disc spring (6) should be installed on the longest pin. Be sure steel ball spacer (3—Fig. CC17) is in place when reassembling rear flex coupling. Adjust clutch linkage as previously outlined.

*Fig. CC14—View of typical main drive clutch used on some gear drive models.*

1. Hanger bracket
2. Pivot pin
3. Driving disc
4. Drive plate
5. Pressure plate assy.
6. Drive disc spring
7. Drive pin

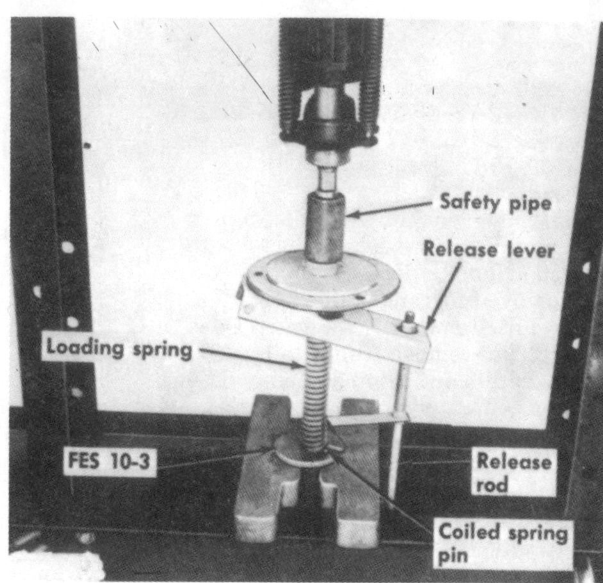


*Fig. CC15—View showing clutch loading spring compressed for coiled spring pin removal. Refer to text for details.*

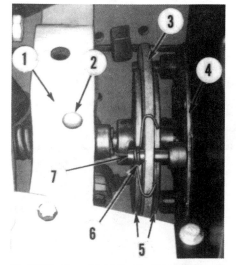

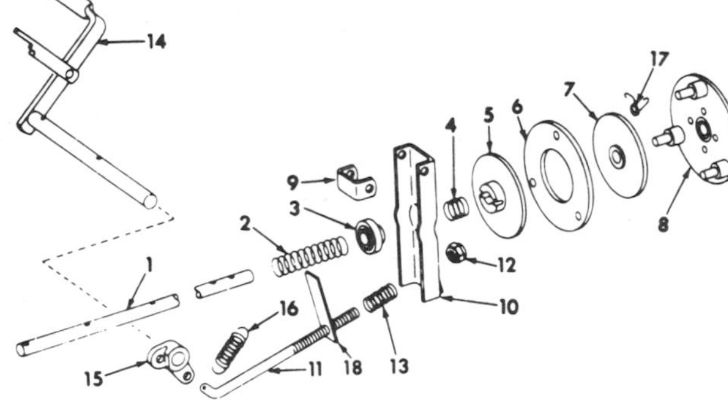

*Fig. CC16—Exploded view of clutch assembly used on early models equipped disc type clutch.*

1. Clutch shaft
2. Loading spring
3. Release bearing
4. Cushion spring
5. Pressure plate
6. Clutch disc
7. Pressure plate
8. Clutch drive plate
9. Bracket
10. Release lever
11. Rod
12. Adjusting nut
13. Spring
14. Pedal assy.
15. Clutch & brake arm
16. Pedal return spring
17. Anti-chatter spring (3)
18. Safety switch lever

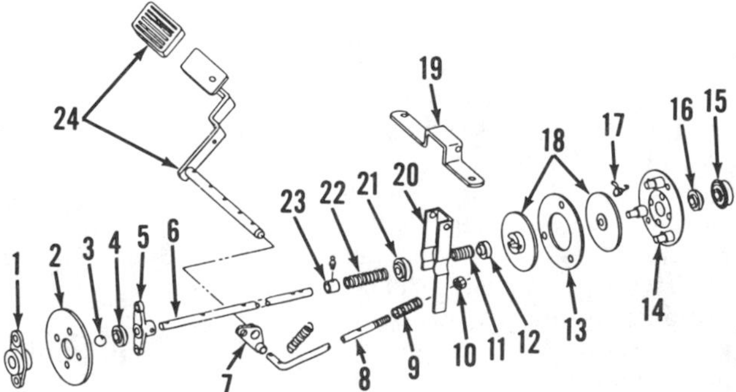

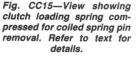

*Fig. CC17—Exploded view of clutch assembly used on late models equipped with a disc type clutch. Items 15, 16 and 23 are used on tractors with serial number 612808 and after.*

1. Drive shaft coupling
2. Flex disc
3. Ball
4. Bushing
5. Coupling arm
6. Clutch shaft
7. Clutch & brake arm
8. Clutch release rod
9. Spring
10. Adjusting nut
11. Teasing spring
12. Spacer
13. Clutch disc
14. Drive plate
15. Pilot hub
16. Bushing
17. Anti-chatter spring (3)
18. Pressure plates
19. Clutch lever hanger
20. Release lever
21. Throwout bearing
22. Loading spring
23. Lubricating bushing
24. Pressure plates



Illustrations courtesy Cub Cadet Corp.

# BRAKES

## Models 72-73-104-105-124-125-800-1000-1200-1250-1450-1650 (Internal)

**REMOVE AND REINSTALL.** The brake on these models is located in the reduction gear housing. To remove brake disc linings, it is necessary to detach transmission and reduction gear housing from frame as follows: Remove fenders, seat and seat support. Drive out pin from clutch shaft rear coupling or unbolt flexible coupling if so equipped. Disconnect brake rod. Support rear of frame and remove cap screws securing frame to transmission and reduction gear housings. Push down on drawbar and pull rearward on transmission. Roll rear assembly away from frame.

On gear drive models, support transmission housing and drain transmission lubricant. Remove brake adjuster screw, pivot pin, brake lever, push rod and ball from housing. Refer to Figs. CC18 and CC19. Remove reduction drive front cover, reduction gear retaining cap screw and reduction gear. The brake disc, linings and retainer can then be removed.

On hydrostatic drive models, differential, bevel pinion shaft and constant mesh gear (Fig. CC20) must be removed. Refer to DIFFERENTIAL AND REDUCTION GEAR paragraphs for procedure. After removing constant mesh gear, remove rear brake lining from housing recess and push front lining and retainer forward out of housing.

Reassemble by reversing disassembly procedure.

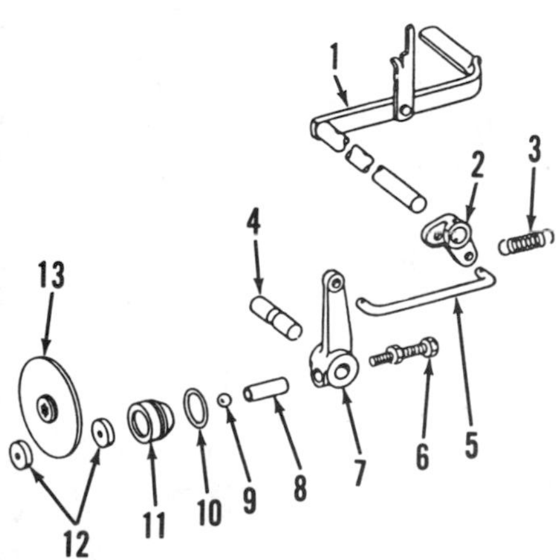


*Fig. CC18—Exploded view of internal brake assembly used on some models.*

1. Clutch & brake pedal
2. Pedal arm
3. Return spring
4. Pivot pin
5. Brake rod
6. Adjusting screw
7. Brake lever
8. Push rod
9. Ball
10. "O" ring
11. Lining retainer
12. Brake linings
13. Brake disc

**ADJUSTMENT.** To adjust brake on gear drive models, turn adjusting screw (6—Fig. CC18) in or out as required to obtain correct pedal travel. Brake should start to engage with pedal depressed to within $1^5/_{16}$ inches (33 mm) from pedal stop. Brake must be fully engaged when pedal is depressed to within $^3/_4$ inch (19 mm) from pedal stop.

To adjust brake on hydrostatic drive models, support rear of tractor so rear wheels can turn freely. With brake pedal in up position, tighten brake lever adjusting screw (S—Fig. CC21) until finger tight. Depress and release brake pedal, then retighten adjusting screw finger tight and secure with jam nut (N). Brake must be fully engaged before brake pedal contacts the pedal stop, but must not drag when pedal is in up position.

## Models 86-106-107-108-109-126-127-128-129-147-149-169-800-1000-1200-1210-1211-1250-1450-1650 (External)

The brakes on these models are mechanically actuated and located at the end of both rear axles. The brakes are disc type with brake pads contacting a disc attached to wheel hub and axle. To disassemble, remove wheels and disconnect brake rod (9—Fig. CC22) from cam lever (11). Remove the two bolts attaching brake assembly to mounting bracket (13). Inspect parts for excessive wear and renew as necessary.

**ADJUSTMENT.** To adjust brakes, support rear of tractor so rear wheels can rotate freely. Adjust brakes by turning jam nuts at end of each brake rod

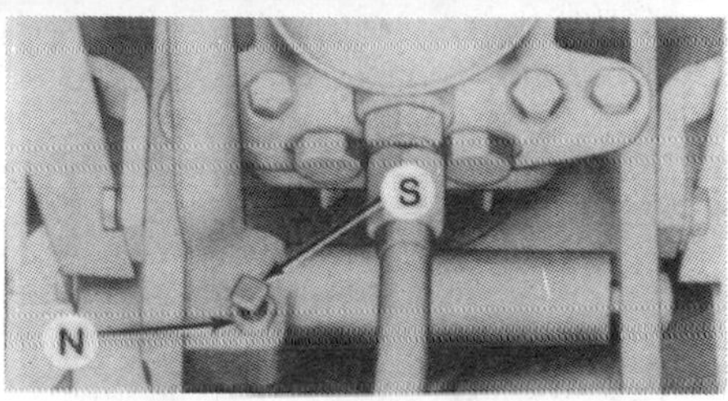


*Fig. CC21—View showing location of brake lever adjusting screw (S) on hydrostatic models equipped with internal brake assembly.*

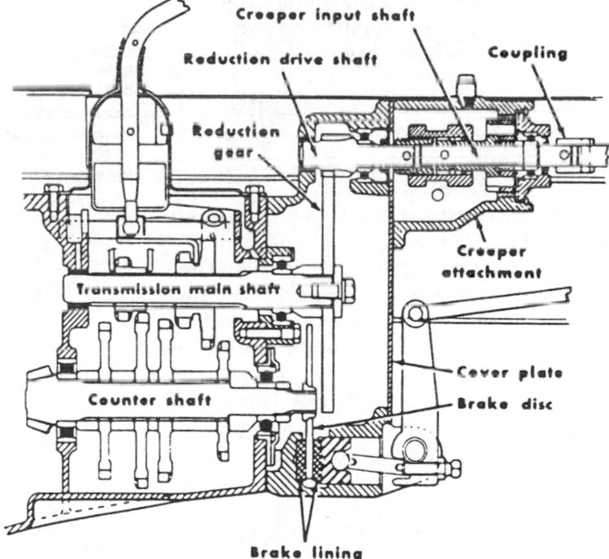


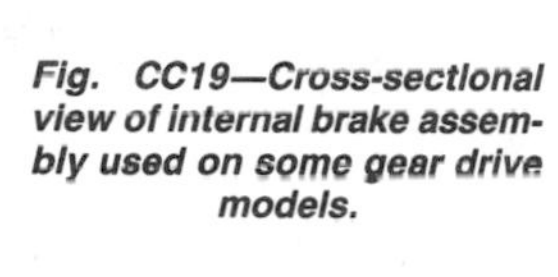

*Fig. CC19—Cross-sectional view of internal brake assembly used on some gear drive models.*

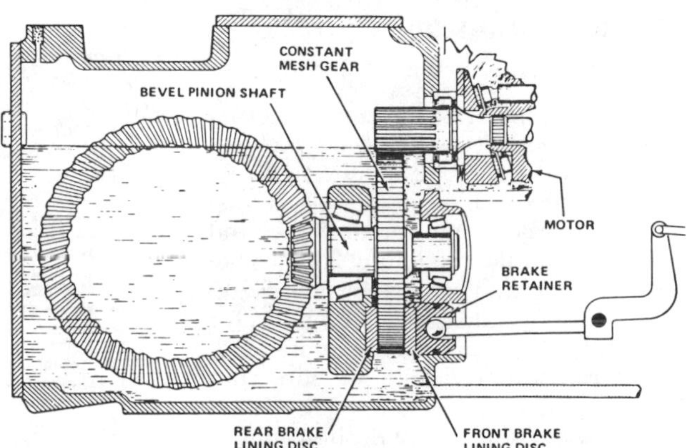


*Fig. CC20—Cross-sectional view of internal brake assembly used on some hydrostatic drive models.*

Illustrations courtesy Cub Cadet Corp.

(9—Fig. CC22). Brakes must not engage before pedal is within maximum distance above pedal stop of $1\frac{11}{16}$ inches (43 mm) on Models 107, 127 and 147 or $1\frac{1}{4}$ inches (32 mm) on all other models. On all models, brakes should be fully engaged when pedal is depressed to a point $\frac{3}{4}$ inch (19 mm) above pedal stop.

Brakes must have equal stopping action at both wheels. With rear wheels supported off the ground, start engine and operate in third gear on gear drive models or in forward position on hydrostatic transmission models. Apply brakes. If one wheel stops sooner than other wheel, adjust brake rod on wheel that does not stop until both wheels stop simultaneously.

### Models 80-81-111-182 (Early)-282-382 (Early)-482-1100-1204

The brakes on these models are mechanically actuated and are externally mounted on left side of transaxle. The brakes are disc type with brake pads contacting a disc attached to brake shaft of transaxle. To disassemble, remove left rear wheel, fender and foot support. Remove brake control rod adjusting nut. Unbolt and remove brake assembly. See Fig. CC23. Inspect all parts for excessive wear and renew as necessary.

**ADJUSTMENT.** To adjust brake, pedal should be in raised position. Move actuator cam (10—Fig. CC23) forward until brake pads contacts disc. Adjust brake rod nut to allow a clearance of $\frac{1}{4}$ inch (6 mm) between adjusting nut and actuating cam on Models 80, 81, 111, 182, 282 and 382. On Models 482, 1100 and 1204, turn adjusting nut to obtain $\frac{1}{4}$ inch (6 mm) clearance between brake rod spacer and actuating cam.

To check adjustment, put tractor in gear (with engine off) and attempt to push it while slowly depressing clutch-brake pedal. Brake should start to apply as clutch disengages. There should be no neutral zone between brake and clutch action. Readjust as necessary.

### Models 182 (Late)-382 (Late)-1015-1020-1215-1220-1315-1320-1405

The disc type brake on these tractors is located on left side of the transaxle on Models 182 and 382 and on right side of transaxle on all other models. To disassemble brake, remove rear wheel and disconnect brake rod spring from brake lever. Unbolt and remove brake assembly from transaxle. Inspect all parts for excessive wear and renew as needed. When reinstalling brake, be sure that hub side of brake disc (3—Fig. CC24) faces away from transaxle housing.

**ADJUSTMENT.** To adjust brake, pedal should be in released position. Loosen jam nut and turn adjusting nut (8—Fig. CC24) in until brake disc (3) is locked. Then, back off adjusting nut $\frac{1}{4}$ turn and tighten jam nut. Recheck braking action.

# DRIVE BELTS

### Models 80-81-111-182 (Early)-282-382 (Early)

**REMOVE AND REINSTALL.** There is no adjustment for drive belts. When belt becomes worn or stretched to a point where slippage occurs, belt must be renewed.

To renew drive belt, disconnect spark plug wire and remove mower if so equipped. Refer to Fig. CC26 and disconnect mower drive belt idler from mower clutch arm. Push up on drive idler to relieve belt tension, then work drive belt off intermediate drive pulley and transmission pulley. After removing transmission belt, crankshaft main drive belt can be removed. Install new belts by reversing removal procedure.

### Models (Late) 182-382

**REMOVE AND REINSTALL.** A spring-loaded belt idler type clutch is used on these tractors. No adjustment

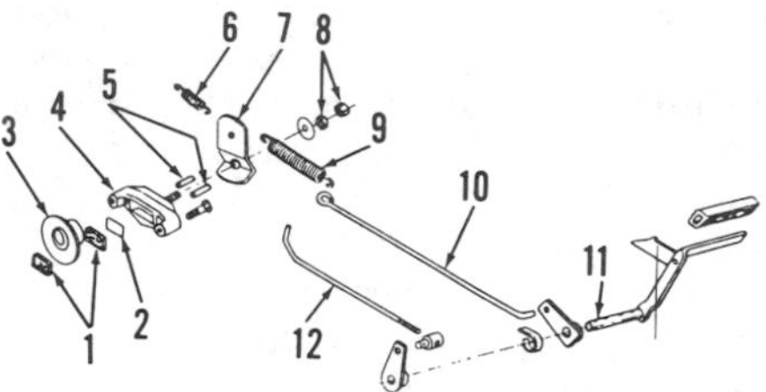


***Fig. CC24—Exploded view of disc brake assembly and control linkage used on late Model 182 and 382 tractors equipped with 5-speed transaxle. Brake used on Models 1015, 1020, 1215, 1220, 1315, 1320 and 1405 is similar.***

1. Brake pads
2. Back-up plate
3. Brake disc
4. Holder
5. Pins
6. Return spring
7. Brake lever
8. Locknuts
9. Tension spring
10. Brake rod
11. Clutch-brake pedal
12. Clutch rod

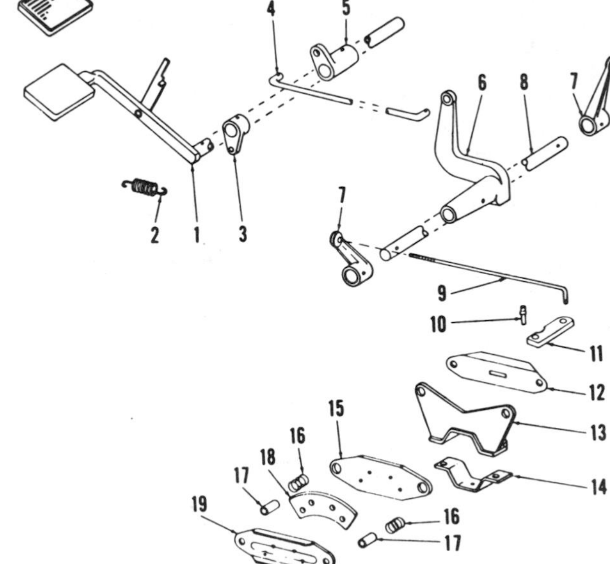


***Fig. CC22—Exploded view of typical external type disc brake assembly used on some models. Brake caliper assemblies are located at end of both rear axles. Neutral return arm (3) is used only on hydrostatic models.***

1. Brake & clutch pedal
2. Return spring
3. Neutral return arm
4. Brake rod
5. Rod lever
6. Brake lever
7. Brake arm
8. Pivot shaft
9. Brake rod
10. Pin
11. Cam lever
12. Cam plate
13. Bracket
14. Flange
15. Carrier
16. Spring
17. Bushing
18. Brake pad (2)
19. Carrier

***Fig. CC23—Exploded view of external single caliper disc brake assembly used on some models equipped with transaxle.***

1. Pad
2. Brake & clutch pedal
3. Brake rod lever
4. Clutch spring
5. Brake lever
6. Extension spring
7. Brake rod
8. Brake disc & hub assy.
9. Key
10. Cam
11. Actuator plate
12. Compression spring
13. Thrust washer
14. Retaining ring
15. Bushing
16. Thrust washer
17. Stud plate
18. Return spring
19. Rib plate assy.

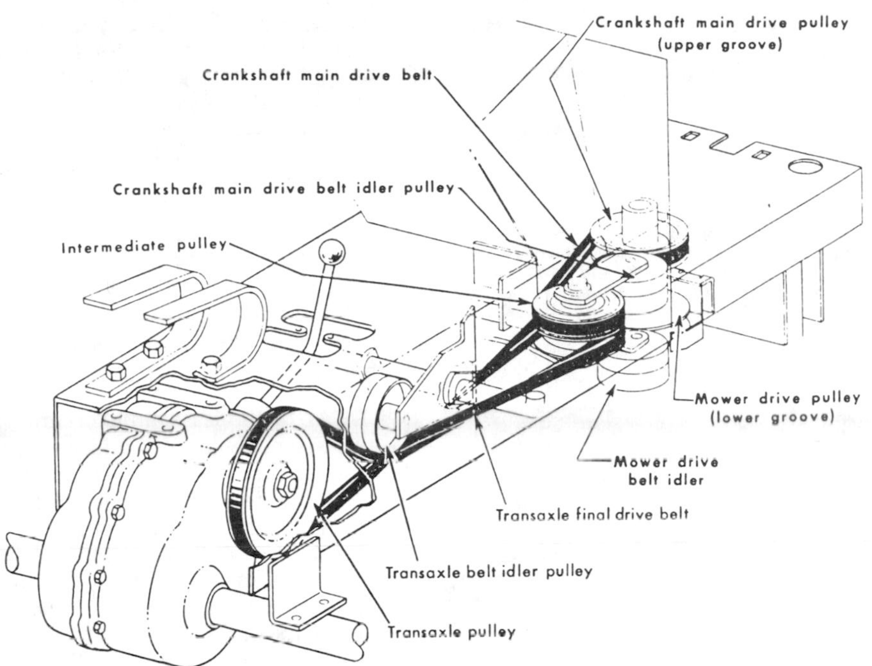


*Fig. CC26—Basic drive belt installation diagram for Models 81, 111, and early 182 and 382 tractors. There is no adjustment for drive belt. Drive belt installation on Models 80 and 282 is similar.*

is required. If belt slips due to excessive wear or stretching, renew belt.

To renew drive belt, remove engine pulley belt guard (10—Fig. CC27). Unbolt and remove idler pulley (7). Remove shift lever (1). Remove retaining screws and move transaxle belt guard (13) out of the way. Remove belt from engine pulley and lift belt up and over transaxle pulley.

Reinstall belt by reversing removal procedure.

## Models 482-1100-1204

**REMOVE AND REINSTALL.** The drive belt is factory preset and requires no adjustment. When belt becomes worn or stretched to a point where slippage occurs, a new belt should be installed.

To renew drive belt, disconnect battery. Remove drawbar assembly and center frame cover. Depress brake pedal and lock in lowest position. Loosen bolts securing drive belt guides (5—Fig. CC28). Remove idler pulley (4) and two bolts securing right angle drive (3) to cross member. Rotate right angle drive downward and remove drive belt. When installing new belt, adjust drive belt guides to gap of $^1/_8$ to $^3/_{16}$ inch (3-5 mm) between belt and guides.

## Models 1015-1020-1215-1220-1315-1320-1405

**REMOVE AND REINSTALL.** A spring-loaded belt idler type clutch is used on these tractors. No adjustment is required. If belt slips due to excessive wear or stretching, renew belt.

To renew drive belt, first remove mower from tractor. If equipped with electric pto clutch, unbolt and remove clutch assembly. Loosen cap screws retaining the pulley belt guards and swing guards out of the way. Remove the idler pulley, and on hydrostatic drive models remove fan from transaxle pulley. Slide belt over transaxle input pulley and remove belt. Install new belt by reversing removal procedure.

# RIGHT ANGLE DRIVE UNIT

## Models 482-1100-1204

**R&R AND OVERHAUL.** To remove right angle drive unit, remove center frame cover and depress clutch-brake pedal. Drive roll pin from rear half of flexible coupler. Remove mounting bolts and work unit free of drive belt.

To disassemble right angle drive unit, remove cover (1—Fig. CC29) and drain lubricant from gear case. Remove output pulley, seal retainer (13) and bearing (11). Using a brass drift, tap down on output gear (9) while pulling up on output shaft. Continue until shaft is free of inner bearing. Remove oil seal (17) and snap ring (16), then withdraw input shaft (6) with bearing (5) and gear (4). Bearing (8 and 15) can now be removed.

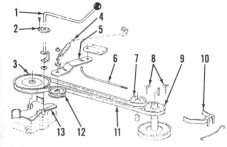

*Fig. CC27—Exploded view of drive belt and clutch idler used on late Models 182 and 382 equipped with 5-speed transaxle.*

1. Shift lever
2. Bushing
3. Transaxle pulley
4. Idler spring
5. Clutch bracket
6. Clutch rod
7. Idler pulley
8. Belt guides
9. Engine pulley
10. Belt guide
11. Drive belt
12. Clutch idler pulley
13. Belt keeper

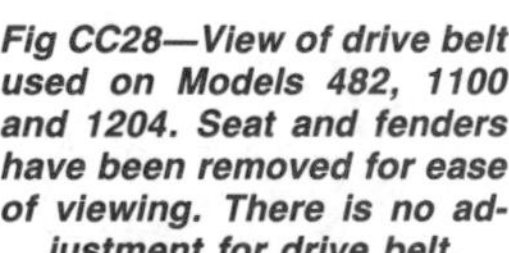

*Fig CC28—View of drive belt used on Models 482, 1100 and 1204. Seat and fenders have been removed for ease of viewing. There is no adjustment for drive belt.*

1. Mounting bolts
2. Cross support
3. Right angle drive
4. Idler pulley
5. Drive belt guides
6. Input pulley

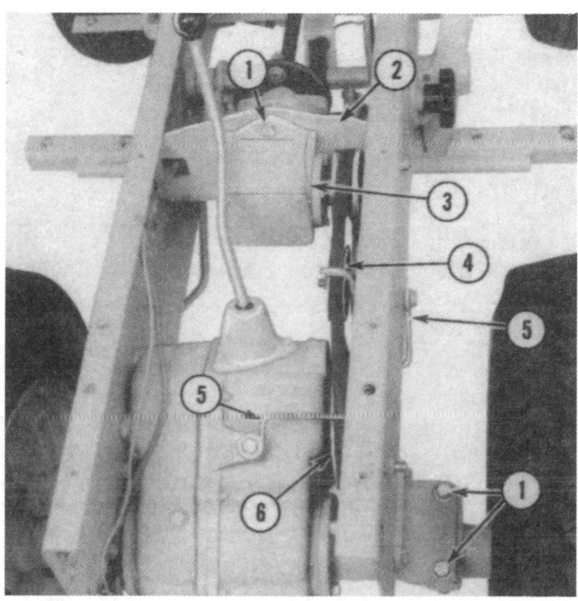

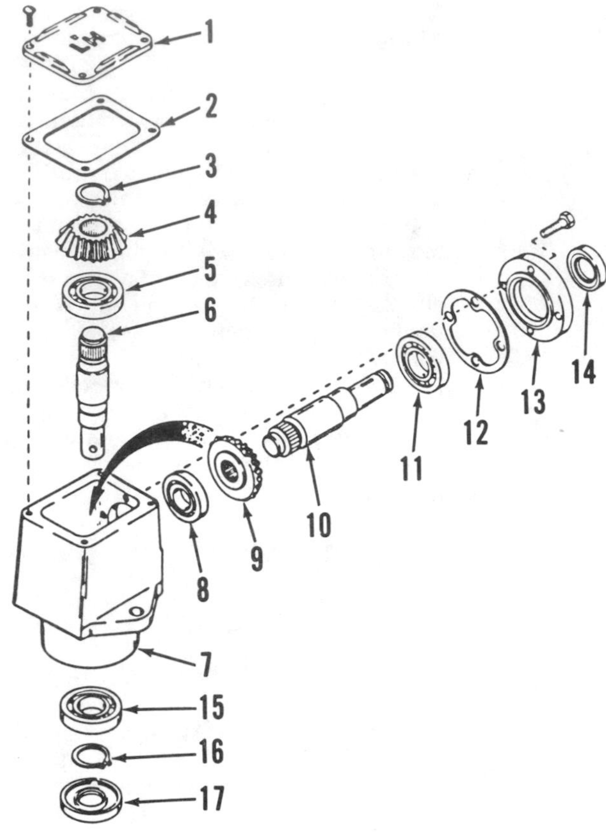


*Fig. CC29—Exploded view of right angle drive unit used on Models 482 and 1100. Unit used on Model 1204 is similar.*

1. Cover
2. Gasket
3. Snap ring
4. Input gear
5. Bearing
6. Input shaft
7. Case
8. Bearing
9. Output gear
10. Output shaft
11. Bearing
12. Gasket
13. Seal retainer
14. Oil seal
15. Bearing
16. Snap ring
17. Oil seal

Remove snap ring (3), input gear (4) and bearing (5) from input shaft.

Clean and inspect all parts and renew any showing excessive wear or damage. Reassemble unit by reversing disassembly procedure and fill unit with 4 ounces (118 mL) of lithium base grease.

# 2-SPEED CREEPER DRIVE

A 2-speed creeper drive is available for some gear drive models. The creeper drive is mounted to the front of reduction drive. A speed selection lever allows shifting to standard (direct drive) speed or creeper (4 to 1 underdrive) speed as desired.

**CAUTION: Do not attempt to shift creeper drive while engine clutch is engaged or while tractor is in motion.**

## All Models So Equipped

**REMOVE AND REINSTALL.** On Models 86, 108, 128, 800, 1000 and 1200, remove creeper drive shift lever knob, then unbolt and remove frame cover. Drive both roll pins from drive shaft rear coupling and slide coupling forward on shaft. Drain creeper drive unit. Unbolt and remove unit.

**NOTE: Drive shaft will have to be moved slightly to the side to allow unit to slide off splined driven coupling (3—Fig. CC30).**

On all other models, disconnect battery cables and remove fenders and seat support as necessary. Drive a wooden wedge between front axle and frame on each side to prevent tractor from tipping. Remove creeper drive shift lever knob and breather. Disconnect front brake rod and drive out drive shaft coupling rear pin. Support tractor frame, then remove mounting bolts and roll transmission and differential assembly rearward from tractor. Drain creeper drive unit. Unbolt unit and remove from reduction drive coupling (3—Fig. CC30).

On all models, reinstall creeper drive unit and reassemble tractor by reversing removal and disassembly procedures. Fill creeper drive unit to level plug opening with Cub Cadet Hydraulic/Transmission fluid or equivalent lubricant.

**OVERHAUL.** To disassemble creeper drive unit, remove snap ring (22—Fig. CC30) and withdraw shaft (14) with retainer (20), bearing (17), planet carrier and gears (12 and 13) and direct drive coupling (4). Drive out coiled spring pin securing direct drive coupling (4) to shaft and remove coupling. Slide planet carrier, gears and thrust washer from input shaft. Remove snap ring (16) and withdraw shaft and bearing from retainer (20). Bearing (17) can be pressed from shaft after snap ring (18) is removed. Remove oil seal (21) from bearing retainer.

To remove shifter assembly, drive shift poppet pin from shift lever shaft and remove poppet (10) and spacer (11). Move shift lever toward rear of housing and remove shift collar (2) from yoke (1). Drive pin from shift yoke and shaft, then withdraw shift lever shaft from yoke and housing. Remove "O" rings (7).

Clean and inspect all parts and renew any showing excessive wear or other damage. Use new oil seal (21) and "O" rings (7 and 19) when reassembling. Using Figs. CC30, CC31 and CC32 as a guide, reassemble creeper drive unit by reversing disassembly procedure.

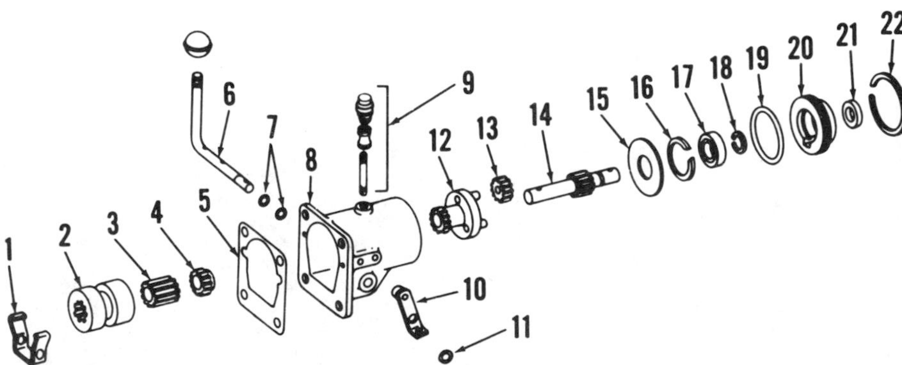


*Fig. CC30—Exploded view of 2-speed creeper drive unit used on some gear drive models. Driven coupling (3) is pinned to reduction drive shaft.*

1. Shift yoke
2. Shift collar
3. Driven coupling
4. Direct drive coupling
5. Gasket
6. Shift lever
7. "O" rings
8. Housing
9. Breather assy.
10. Shift poppet
11. Spacer
12. Planet carrier
13. Planet gear (3 used)
14. Input shaft
15. Thrust washer
16. Snap ring
17. Ball bearing
18. Snap ring
19. "O" ring
20. Bearing retainer
21. Oil seal
22. Snap ring



Illustrations courtesy Cub Cadet Corp.

# REDUCTION DRIVE

### Models 72-73-86-104-106-108-124-126-128-800-1000-1200

**R&R AND OVERHAUL.** To remove reduction drive, first split tractor as follows: On all models, disconnect battery cables and on models with battery under the seat, remove battery. On all models except Model 73, remove fenders and seat support. On Models 86, 108, 128, 800, 1000 and 1200, remove frame cover. On all models, drive a wooden wedge between front axle and frame on each side to prevent tractor from tipping. Disconnect brake rod from brake lever. Disconnect clutch shaft rear coupler. Note that models with rear flexible coupling have a steel ball spacer located in coupling to properly locate clutch shaft. On models equipped with three-point hitch, remove lift lever and attaching plate. On models where necessary, remove creeper drive and transmission shift lever knobs. On all models, support tractor frame, remove mounting bolts and roll transmission and differential assembly rearward from tractor.

Drain oil and remove creeper drive unit if so equipped. Drain oil from transmission and differential housing. Remove brake cross shaft and levers, then unbolt and remove reduction drive front cover. Using a suitable puller, remove reduction shaft (12—Fig. CC33) with bearing (6) and oil seal (9). Unbolt and remove reduction driven gear (2) and spacer (1). Remove cap screws securing reduction housing (5) to transmission and remove housing. Press needle bearing (11) out rear side of housing.

When reassembling, press needle bearing (11) into housing until flush with rear surface. Renew copper sealing washers on housing mounting lower cap screws, and tighten mounting cap screws to 80 ft.-lbs. (108 N·m). Tighten reduction gear retaining screw to 55 ft.-lbs. (75 N·m). Recouple tractor in reverse order of splitting procedure.

### Models 105-107-109-125-127-129-147-169-1210-1211-1250-1450-1650

The constant mesh reduction gear on these hydrostatic drive models is located between bevel pinion shaft mounting bearings. To remove reduction gear, refer to DIFFERENTIAL AND REDUCTION GEAR section.

### Models 80-282-382H-1020-1220-1320

The reduction gears on these hydrostatic drive models are contained in reduction drive and differential unit. For service procedures, refer to DIFFERENTIAL AND REDUCTION GEAR section.

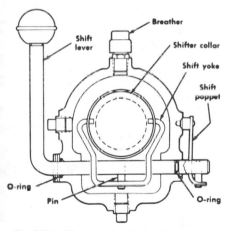

*Fig. CC31—Cross-sectional view of creeper drive shifting components.*

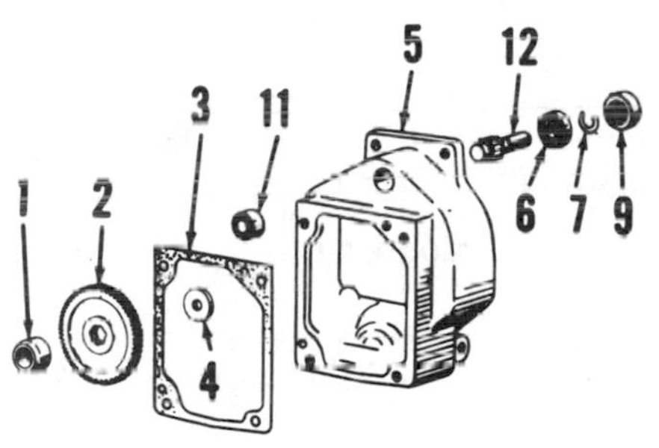

*Fig. CC33—Exploded view of reduction gear drive used on Models 72, 73, 86, 104, 106, 124, 126, 128, 800, 1000 and 1200.*

1. Reduction gear spacer
2. Driven reduction gear
3. Gasket
4. Retainer
5. Reduction housing
6. Front bearing
7. Snap ring
9. Oil seal
11. Rear bearing
12. Reduction shaft

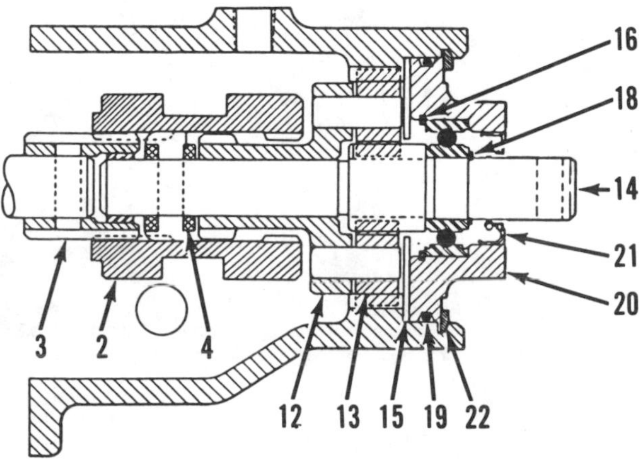

*Fig. CC32—Cross-sectional side view of creeper drive assembly with shifter collar in direct drive position. Refer to Fig. CC31 legend for identification of parts.*

# TRANSAXLE

## LUBRICATION

### All Models So Equipped

Models 81, 111, and early 182 and 382 are equipped with a Peerless 1200 series transaxle. Transaxle fluid capacity is approximately 2¾ pints (1.3 L) of SAE 90 EP gear lube.

Late Models 182 and 382 are equipped with a Peerless 800 series transaxle. Transaxle fluid capacity is approximately 24 ounces (710 mL) of Bentonite grease.

Models 482, 1100 and 1204 are equipped with a Peerless 2300 series transaxle. Transaxle fluid capacity is approximately 4 pints (1.9 L) of SAE 90 EP gear lube.

Models 1015, 1215, 1315 and 1405 are equipped with a Peerless 920 series transaxle. Transaxle fluid capacity is 30 ounces (887 mL) of Bentonite grease.

## REMOVE AND REINSTALL

### Models 81-111-(Early) 182-382

Disconnect transaxle drive belt. Raise rear of tractor and support under axle housing. Remove rear wheels, drive keys and spacers. Remove left fender and foot support. Remove brake mounting bolts and brake caliper assembly, brake disc and key. Remove drawbar assembly and gear shift knob. Unbolt transaxle housing from frame and slide frame slightly to the left to clear brake shaft. Carefully raise frame off transaxle.

Reinstall by reversing removal procedure.

### Models (Late) 182-382

Raise and support rear of tractor. Place wooden wedge between front axle and frame on both sides to prevent tractor from tipping. Slip drive belt off transaxle pulley. Disconnect brake linkage. Remove drawbar assembly and gear shift knob. Unbolt transaxle housing from support brackets and separate transaxle from frame. Unbolt and remove brake pad holder and brake disc. Remove rear wheel assemblies.

Reinstall by reversing removal procedure.

### Models 482-1100-1200

Disconnect and remove battery. Remove fenders, foot platforms and center frame cover. Drive a block of wood between front axle and frame on both sides to prevent tractor from tipping. Loosen drive belt guide bolts and depress clutch-brake pedal to its lowest position. Work drive belt off transaxle input pulley. Remove brake mounting bolts and brake assembly. Support rear of tractor, then remove mounting bolts and roll transaxle assembly from tractor.

Reinstall by reversing removal procedure.

### Models 1015-1215-1315-1405

Disconnect battery cables and remove the battery. Disconnect seat safety switch and remove seat and seat bracket. Remove center panel and fenders. Disconnect fuel line and remove fuel tank. Remove belt keeper from top of transaxle housing. Depress clutch/brake pedal and engage parking brake lever. Disconnect shift linkage at transaxle. Remove belt fixed idler pulley and work drive belt off transaxle pulley. Release clutch/brake pedal and disconnect brake rod spring from brake lever. Raise and support rear of tractor. Place wood wedge between front axle and frame on both sides to prevent tractor from tipping. Remove drawbar hitch plate. Remove U-bolts attaching transaxle to frame and roll transaxle out from under rear of tractor.

To reinstall, reverse the removal procedure.

## OVERHAUL

### All Models

Refer to appropriate TRANSAXLE SERVICE section in this manual for overhaul procedure.

# HYDROSTATIC TRANSMISSION

## LUBRICATION

### Models 105-107-109-125-127-129-147-149-169-1210-1211-1250-1450-1650

These models are equipped with Sundstrand hydrostatic transmission. Manufacturer recommends renewing oil filter and oil in hydrostatic transmission after each 150 hours of operation or once a year, whichever comes first. Refill system with 14 pints (6.6 L) of Cub Cadet Transmission Hydraulic Fluid or equivalent lubricant.

### Models 80-282-382H

These models are equipped with an Eaton Model 6 hydrostatic transmission. Periodically check fluid level and maintain level at full mark on reservoir. Transmission fluid capacity is approximately 1½ pints (0.7 L) of Cub Cadet Transmission Hydraulic Fluid or equivalent lubricant.

### Models 1020-1220-1320

These models are equipped with a Hydro-Gear Model BDU-10S hydrostatic transmission. Periodically check fluid level and maintain level at full mark on reservoir. Recommended transmission fluid is Cub Cadet Transmission Hydraulic Fluid or equivalent lubricant.

## LINKAGE ADJUSTMENT

### Models 105-107-109-125-127-129-147-149-169-1210-1211-1250-1450-1650

If tractor creeps with control lever in neutral position, control linkage must be adjusted. Before adjusting linkage, make certain that foot brake is properly adjusted, then proceed as follows:

Control lever friction adjustment should be checked and adjusted first. A pull of approximately 10 pounds (5 kg) should be required to move lever in either direction. On Models 105 and 125, tighten adjusting nut (18—Fig. CC34) as required to obtain desired lever friction. On Models 107, 127 and 147, tighten adjusting nut, located on friction adjusting shaft (10—Fig. CC35), as necessary. On Models 109, 129, 149 (serial number 426000 and after) and 169, friction adjusting nut is located on lower end of control shaft (14—Fig. CC36). On Models

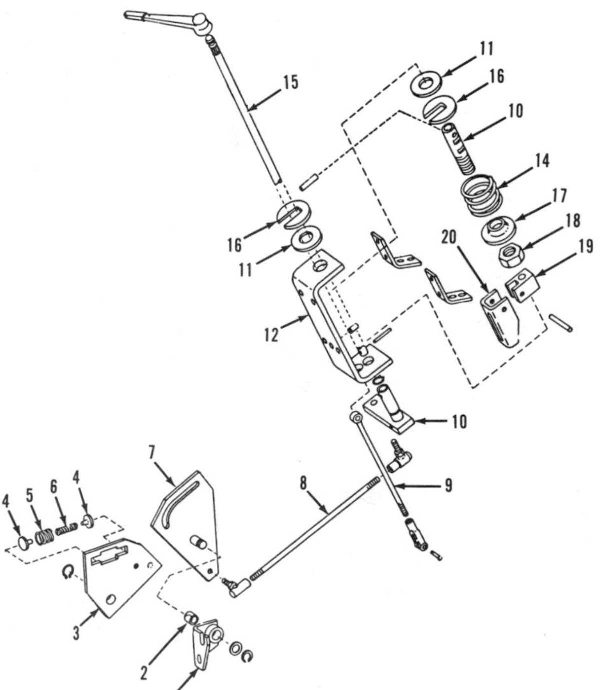


***Fig. CC34—Exploded view of hydrostatic transmission control linkage used on Models 105 and 125.***

1. Cam pivot bracket
2. Pivot bushing
3. Damper spring plate
4. Damper spring guide pins
5. Damper spring (heavy)
6. Damper spring (light)
7. Speed control cam
8. Speed control rod
9. Neutral return rod
10. Friction adjusting shaft
11. Friction discs
12. Support bracket
14. Friction spring
15. Control lever
16. Spring retainers
17. Spring guide
18. Locknut
19. Speed control centering cam swivel
20. Centering cam channel

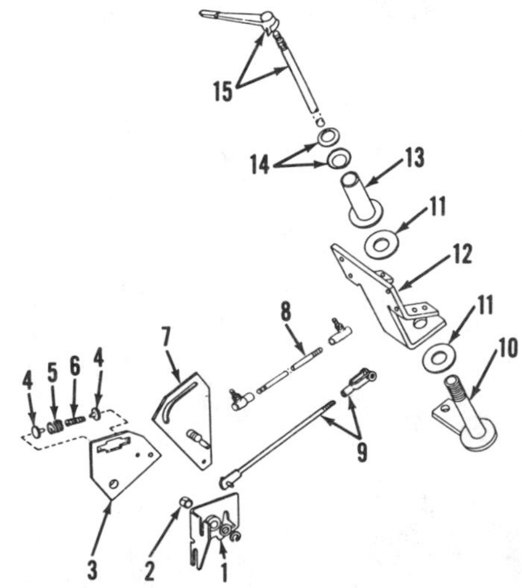


***Fig. CC35—Exploded view of hydrostatic transmission control linkage used on Models 107, 127 and 147. Refer to Fig. CC34 legend for items 1 through 9.***

10. Friction adjusting shaft
11. Friction discs
12. Support bracket
13. Friction collar
14. Belleville washers
15. Control rod & handle



Illustrations courtesy Cub Cadet Corp.

1210, 1211, 1250, 1450 and 1650, adjust lever friction by tightening locknut that secures control handle (14—Fig. CC37) to control bracket (12) as required.

To adjust control linkage neutral position, first remove seat and fender assembly on Models 105, 107, 125, 127 and 147; on all other models, remove frame cover. On all models, raise and securely block rear of tractor so rear wheels are off the ground and block front wheels so tractor cannot move. Loosen cam bracket (1—Fig. CC34, CC35, CC36 or CC37) mounting screws, then start engine and operate at half throttle. Move speed control lever to forward position, then fully depress brake pedal and lock in place. Adjust cam bracket upward or downward until wheels stop turning and any excessive noise or vibration in transmission is eliminated, then tighten cam bracket cap screws.

With brake pedal fully depressed, neutral return rod (9) should not touch end of slot in speed control cam (7). If rod touches, disconnect clevis end of rod from brake cross shaft and adjust as needed. Release the brake pedal and move control lever to forward position, then fully depress brake pedal and release it. Speed control lever should return to neutral position and wheels should stop turning. If control lever does not return to neutral position, adjust length of speed control rod (8—Fig. CC34, CC35, CC36 or CC37) until speed control lever is in neutral position when brake pedal is depressed.

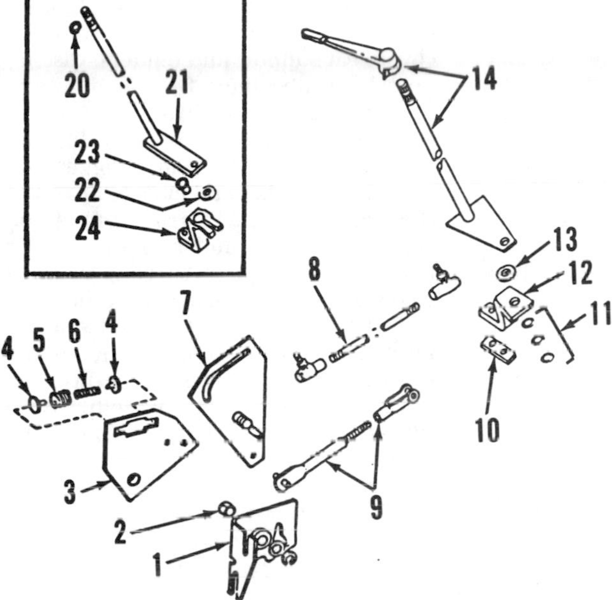


*Fig. CC36—Exploded view of hydrostatic transmission control linkage used on Models 109, 129, 149 and 169. Items 20 through 24 (inset) are used on Models 109, 129 and 149 prior to serial number 426000. Items 10 through 14 are used on late Models 109, 129 and 149 and on all 169 models. Refer to Fig. CC34 legend for items 1 through 9.*

10. Support shim
11. Belleville washers
12. Control shaft support
13. Friction disc
14. Control shaft & handle
20. Retaining ring
21. Control shaft
22. Spacer
23. Friction bushing
24. Control shaft support

## Models 80-282-382H

Raise rear wheels off the ground and support rear frame securely. Adjust friction nut on linkage to obtain an 8-10 pound (3.5-4.5 kg) effort at speed control lever. Start and run engine at full throttle. With speed control lever in neutral position, rear wheels should not turn. Adjust turnbuckle on control linkage rod (14—Fig. CC38) if wheels creep.

**CAUTION: Stop engine before making adjustment to linkage.**

## Models 1020-1220-1320

A pull of approximately 10 pounds (5 kg) should be required to move speed control lever (10—Fig. CC39). Tighten

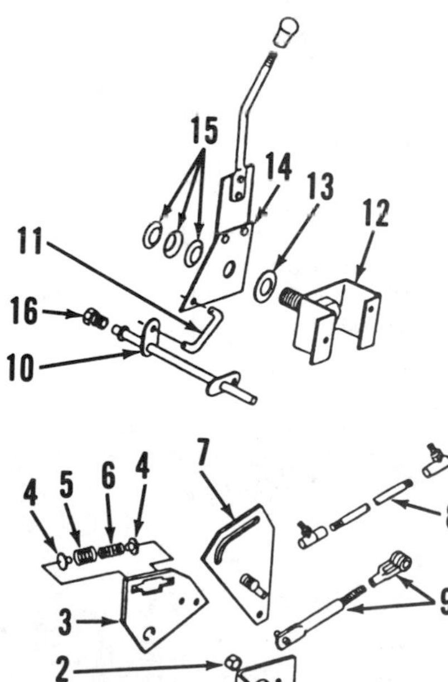


*Fig. CC37—Exploded view of hydrostatic transmission control linkage used on Models 1210, 1211, 1250, 1450 and 1650. Refer to Fig. CC34 legend for items 1 through 9.*

10. Control rockshaft
11. Connecting link
12. Control bracket
13. Friction washer
14. Control handle
15. Belleville washers
16. Rockshaft bearing

*Fig. CC38—View of drive belts and hydrostatic transmission used on Models 80, 282 and 382H tractors.*

1. Main drive belt idler
2. Mower pulley
3. Mower drive belt idler
4. Main drive pulley
5. Intermediate drive pulley
6. Main drive belt
7. Final drive belt
8. Idler pulley
9. Hydrostatic pulley
10. Gear reduction unit
11. Brake adjusting nut
12. Hydrostatic transmission
13. Fan
14. Hydrostatic speed control rod

friction adjusting nuts (11) on speed control lever shaft as necessary.

Raise rear wheels off the ground and support rear frame securely. Start engine and move speed control lever to neutral "N" position. If rear wheels turn with control lever in neutral, shut off engine and adjust linkage as follows: If tractor creeps forward, loosen jam nuts (1—Fig. CC39) and turn adjuster stud (2) counterclockwise until wheels stop turning. If tractor creeps rearward, turn adjuster clockwise.

## REMOVE AND REINSTALL

### Models 105-107-125-127-147

To remove hydrostatic transmission and differential assembly, first disconnect battery cables. Remove seat, seat support, fenders and air deflector. Disconnect control rod ball joint (5—Fig. CC40) from speed control cam (4). Disconnect neutral return rod (1), front brake rod (9) and drive shaft coupling. Drive wooden wedge between front axle and frame on each side to prevent tractor from tipping. Raise and support rear of tractor. Support differential case with a rolling floor jack to prevent unit from tilting forward. Unbolt assembly from main frame, place release lever in release position and roll assembly rearward from tractor.

Reinstall assembly by reversing removal procedure. Adjust brakes and hydrostatic control linkage as necessary.

### Models 109-129-149-169-1210-1211-1250-1450-1650

If desired, hydrostatic transmission can be removed from tractor without removing differential assembly. Disconnect battery cables and remove frame cover. Disconnect hydraulic lines from hydrostatic unit to hydraulic lift valve if so equipped. Drive out dowel pin from front of drive shaft at engine drive plate hub. Unbolt and remove drive shaft coupling disc (3—Fig. CC41), then remove drive shaft. Disconnect front brake rod (1). Drain oil from differential housing and disconnect transmission suction line. Remove cam bracket mounting bolts (7) and move cam bracket and linkage up out of the way. Unbolt hydrostatic transmission from differential housing and remove unit through top opening in frame.

Reinstall hydrostatic transmission by reversing removal procedure. Adjust brakes and control linkage as necessary.

To remove hydrostatic transmission and differential as an assembly, first remove battery. Unbolt and remove frame cover seat support and fenders. Disconnect hydraulic lines from hydrostatic unit to hydraulic lift valve if so equipped. Disconnect drive shaft flexible coupling. Unbolt cam bracket and move cam bracket and linkage up out of the way. Disconnect front brake rod from cross shaft and rear brake rods from brake calipers. Drive a wooden wedge between front axle and frame on each side to prevent tractor from tipping. Raise and support rear of tractor. Place a rolling floor jack under differential housing to prevent assembly from tilting forward. Unbolt differential housing from main frame and roll assembly rearward from tractor.

Reinstall transmission and differential assembly by reversing removal procedure. Adjust brakes and control linkage as necessary.

### Models 80-282-382H

To remove hydrostatic transmission, raise and support rear of tractor. Remove rear wheels, left fender, foot support and drawbar. Remove brake caliper and disc. Disconnect transmission speed control rod. Pull belt idler pulley (8—Fig. CC38) away from drive belt to release tension on belt and remove belt from transmission input pulley. Support differential housing with a suitable jack.

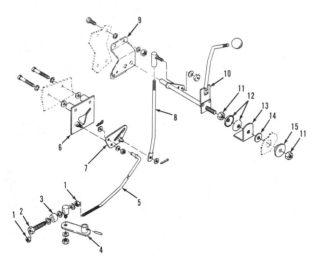

***Fig. CC39—Exploded view of hydrostatic transmission control linkage used on Models 1020, 1220 and 1320.***

1. Nuts
2. Adjustment stud
3. Rubber washer
4. Control arm
5. Hydrostatic control rod
6. Cam plate
7. Cam lever
8. Control rod
9. Support bracket
10. Control lever
11. Jam nuts
12. Belleville washers
13. Friction bracket
14. Friction washer
15. Shoulder spacer

***Fig. CC40—Bottom view of hydrostatic transmission showing location of brake and transmission control linkage typical of Models 105, 107, 125, 127 and 147. Rear brake rods (7) are not used on Models 105 and 125.***

1. Neutral return rod
2. Speed control rod
3. Jam nut
4. Control cam
5. Ball joint
6. Brake adjusting nuts
7. Brake rods (rear)
8. Brake lever
9. Brake rod (front)
10. Brake pedal cross shaft

***Fig. CC41—Top view of hydrostatic transmission used on Models 109, 129, 149, 169, 1210, 1211, 1250, 1450 and 1650. Unit can be removed from tractor without removing differential. Refer to text.***

1. Brake rod
2. Drive shaft
3. Flexible disc
4. Roll pin
5. Coupling arm
6. Alignment mark
7. Cam bracket cap screw

Remove differential housing mounting bolts and axle housing U-bolts and remove transmission and differential assembly from tractor. Drain oil from unit, then unbolt and separate hydrostatic transmission from differential.

Reinstall transmission by reversing removal procedure. Adjust brakes and control linkage as necessary.

### Models 1020-1220-1320

To remove hydrostatic unit, raise and support rear of tractor. Disconnect brake control rod and transmission speed control rod. Remove knob from dump valve rod. Remove drive belt from transmission input pulley. Remove transmission mounting bolts and axle housing U-bolts. Roll transmission assembly rearward from tractor. Unbolt and separate hydrostatic unit from differential housing. Note that couplings on hydrostatic input and output shafts are held in place with Loctite. It may be necessary to heat couplings and use a puller to remove couplings from shafts.

Reinstall transmission by reversing removal procedure. If drive couplings were removed from input and output shafts, use Loctite 609 to bond couplings to shafts and allow to cure for 24 hours before operating unit. Adjust brake linkage and speed control linkage as necessary.

## OVERHAUL

### All Models

Models 105, 107, 109, 125, 127, 129, 149, 169, 1210, 1211, 1250, 1450 and 1650 are equipped with a Sundstrand 15 series "U" type hydrostatic transmission. Models 80, 282 and 382H are equipped with an Eaton Model 6 hydrostatic transmission. Models 1020, 1220 and 1320 are equipped with a Hydro-Gear BDU-10S series hydrostatic transmission. Refer to the appropriate Eaton, Hydro-Gear or Sundstrand section in HYDROSTATIC TRANSMISSION SERVICE section for overhaul procedure.

# TRANSMISSION AND DIFFERENTIAL

## R&R AND OVERHAUL

### Models 72-73-86-104-106-108-124-126-128-800-1000-1200

Remove transmission and differential housing from tractor and remove reduction drive unit as outlined in previous paragraphs, then proceed as follows:

Remove rear axles and carriers as in AXLE SHAFTS paragraphs. Remove shift lever and transmission top cover assembly. Remove shifter fork retaining cap screws and rotate shifter rails to unseat poppet balls. Slide rails forward out of shifter forks and case.

**CAUTION: Insert a small punch into poppet bores to prevent poppet balls from flying out when shift rails are being removed.**

Remove cap screws from mainshaft bearing retainer (9—Fig. CC42) and bump mainshaft (7 or 32) and bearing forward and out of case. The first and reverse and second and third sliding gears will be removed as shaft is withdrawn from case. Remove cap screw from reverse idler shaft (3) and remove shaft and reverse idler gear (2). Before removing countershaft (10), differential unit must be removed from housing.

To remove differential unit, remove right and left differential bearing cages. Identify number and thickness of shims removed from each side for aid in reassembly. Turn differential unit as shown in Fig. CC43 and remove unit from housing.

Remove countershaft nut and bump shaft rearward out of transmission as gears and spacers are removed. Note sequence of spacers and gears for reassembly. See Fig. CC44. Remove countershaft front bearing, retainer and shims. Identify shims for reassembly.

To disassemble differential, remove differential lock pin (12—Fig. CC45) and drive out pinion shaft (11). Rotate side gears 90 degrees and remove pinion gears and side gears.

When reassembling, differential bearings should be adjusted to obtain a preload of 1 to 8 pounds (0.5-3.6 kg) pull on a spring scale as shown in Fig. CC46. Preload is adjusted by adding or removing shims (B—Fig. CC45) behind differential bearing cages (2).

*Fig. CC43—The differential unit must be turned to position shown to remove unit from housing.*

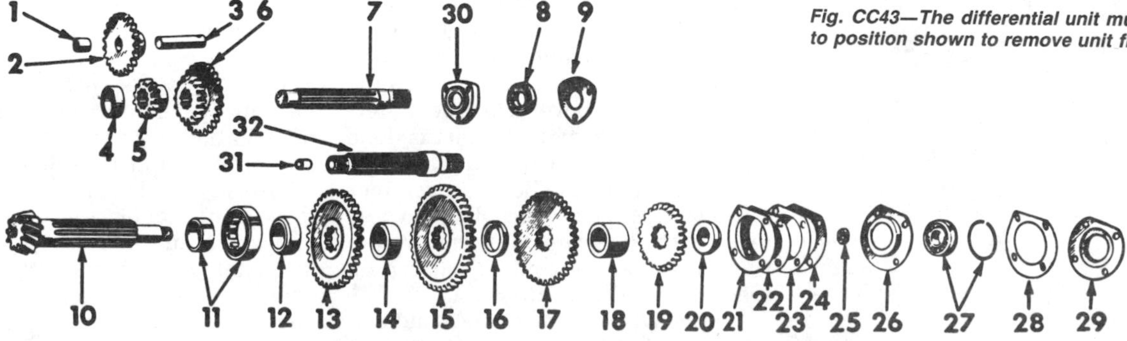


*Fig. CC42—Exploded view of transmission gears and shafts used on Models 72, 73, 104, 106, 108, 124, 126, 128, 800, 1000 and 1200. Mainshaft (32) is used on models equipped with transmission driven power take-off.*

1. Bushing
2. Reverse idler gear
3. Reverse idler shaft
4. Bearing
5. First & reverse sliding gear
6. Second & third sliding gear
7. Mainshaft
8. Bearing
9. Bearing retainer
10. Countershaft (bevel pinion)
11. Bearing
12. Spacer
13. Reverse gear
14. Spacer
15. First speed gear
16. Spacer
17. Second speed gear
18. Spacer
19. Third speed gear
20. Spacer
21. Shim
22. Shim
23. Shim
24. Shim
25. Nut
26. Bearing retainer
27. Bearing
28. Gasket
29. Bearing retainer
30. Bearing cage
31. Bushing
32. Mainshaft

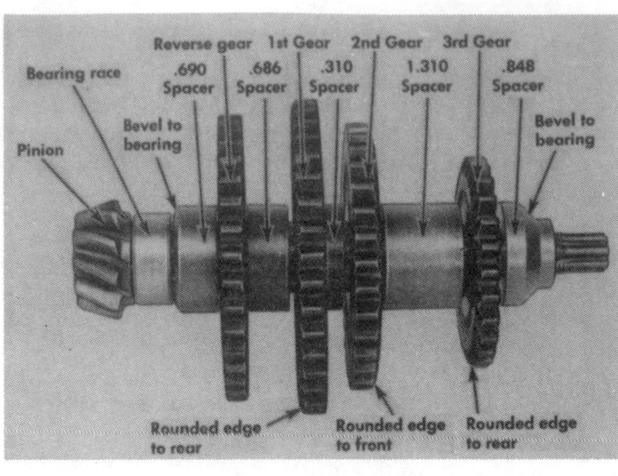


*Fig. CC44—View showing correct installation of gears and spacers on countershaft (bevel pinion).*

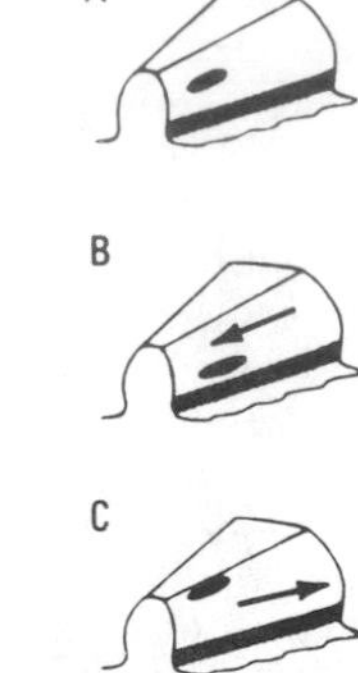


*Fig. CC47—Bevel pinion tooth contact pattern is correct at "A," too low at "B" and too high at "C."*

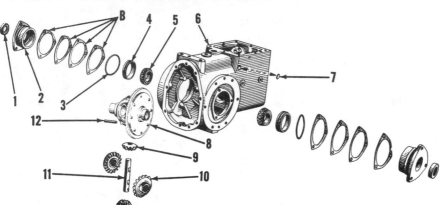

*Fig. CC45—Exploded view of differential assembly used on Models 72, 73, 86, 104, 106, 108, 124, 126, 128, 800, 1000 and 1200.*

B. Shims
1. Oil seal
2. Differential bearing cage
3. "O" ring
4. Bearing cup
5. Bearing cone
6. Transmission/ differential case
7. Expansion plug
8. Ring gear & differential housing
9. Pinion gear
10. Side gear
11. Pinion shaft
12. Pinion shaft lock pin

*Fig. CC46—Differential bearing preload is correct when a steady pull of 1 to 8 pounds (0.5-3.6 kg) on a spring scale is required to rotate differential assembly as shown.*

Check backlash between differential ring gear and pinion gear and adjust to 0.003-0.005 inch (0.076-0.127 mm) by moving shim or shims (B—Fig. CC45) from behind one differential bearing cage to the other bearing cage. Do not add or subtract shims from total shim pack thickness as this would affect previously adjusted differential bearing preload.

Adjustment of bevel pinion (countershaft) for proper tooth contact is done by adding or removing shims behind countershaft front bearing retainer (26—Fig. CC42). Paint bevel pinion gear teeth with Prussian Blue, then rotate ring gear. Observe contact pattern on tooth surfaces. Refer to Fig. CC47. The area of heaviest contact will be indicated by coating being removed at such points. On the actual pinion, areas shown in black on the illustration will be bright.

The correct tooth contact pattern is shown at "A" in Fig. CC47. If pattern is too low as "B," remove shims as necessary to correct pattern. If pattern is too high as "C," add shims to correct pattern.

Reassembly of remainder of transmission and differential is reverse of disassembly.

# DIFFERENTIAL AND REDUCTION GEAR

## R&R AND OVERHAUL

### Models 105-107-109-125-127-129-147-149-169-1210-1211-1250-1450-1650

Remove hydrostatic drive and differential assembly as previously outlined in HYDROSTATIC TRANSMISSION section. Remove rear cover (33—Fig. CC48) and drain lubricant. Remove hydrostatic drive unit from differential housing. Working through rear cover opening, remove "C" type snap rings from inner end of rear axle shafts. Unbolt axle carriers from differential housing, then remove axle shaft and axle carrier assemblies.

Unbolt and remove differential carrier bearing cages (1) and shim packs (2). Keep shim packs with each cage and identify cages for each side. Turn differential unit as shown in Fig. CC43 and remove unit from housing.

To disassemble differential unit, remove shaft retaining pin (35—Fig. CC48) and drive out shaft (32). Rotate side gears 90 degrees and remove pinion gears (30) and side gears (31). Bearing cones (4) can now be renewed if necessary.

Remove expansion plug (20) and snap ring (21). Then, using a brass drift and hammer, drive bevel pinion shaft (29) rearward out of bearing cone (22) and reduction gear (8). Remove snap ring (25) and bearing cone (28) from bevel pinion shaft. Remove top cover (6) and gasket (7), then lift out reduction gear (8). Bearing cups (23 and 27) can now be removed from housing. Remove shim pack (26) and identify for aid in reassembly.

Clean and inspect all parts and renew any showing excessive wear or other damage.

Reassemble differential unit by reversing disassembly procedure. Install differential unit and bolt bearing cages (1) with shim packs (2) to housing. Using a cord and spring scale as shown in Fig. CC46, check carrier bearing preload. Add or remove shims (2—Fig. CC48) until a steady pull of 1 to 8 pounds (0.5-3.6 kg) is required to rotate differential unit. With preload adjusted, unbolt and remove bearing cages and shim packs, keeping shim packs with the cages from later reassembly. Remove differential unit and set it aside.

If a new bevel pinion shaft (29—Fig. CC48), differential housing (24) or bearing cup and cone (27 and 28) are installed, select shim pack (26) as follows: Add the number stamped on housing (24), located just left of breather plug (5), to the number stamped on end of bevel pinion shaft (29). The sum of these two numbers plus 0.015 inch (0.38 mm) will be correct thickness shim pack (26). Install shim pack, then press bearing cup (27) in until it bottoms against shims. Install bearing cone (28) and snap ring (25) on bevel pinion shaft (29). Press bearing cup (23) in until it is seated against the shoulder. Then, install bevel pinion shaft assembly and reduction gear (8). Support gear end of bevel pinion shaft with a wood block and press bearing cone (22) onto pinion shaft.

**CAUTION: Use extreme care when installing this bearing. Press bearing cone onto shaft only to the point where shaft has a zero end play and zero rolling torque. Remove assembly from press and check shaft end play several times during installation of bearing cone to prevent preloading the pinion bearing.**

Using a feeler gage, measure distance between bearing cone (22) and front edge of snap ring groove on front end of pinion shaft. This distance minus 0.003 inch (0.076 mm) will determine correct thickness snap ring (21) to be installed. Snap rings are available in various thicknesses. After correct snap ring is installed, tap bevel pinion shaft rearward to seat bearing cone (22) against snap ring. Install a new expansion plug (20).

Reinstall differential unit and carrier bearing cages (1) with shim packs (2). Check backlash between ring gear and bevel pinion. The correct backlash is 0.003-0.005 inch (0.076-0.127 mm). Adjust backlash, if necessary, by moving a shim or shims (2—Fig. CC48) from behind one differential carrier (1) to the other differential carrier. Do not increase or decrease total shim thickness as this would change the previously adjusted bearing preload.

To check ring gear and bevel pinion tooth contact pattern, apply a light coat of Prussian Blue to bevel pinion teeth. Rotate ring gear and observe contact pattern on pinion teeth. Refer to Fig. CC47. The desired tooth contact pattern is shown at "A." If it is necessary to adjust tooth contact pattern, add or remove shims at shim pack (26—Fig. CC48) as required. If tooth contact pattern is too low as shown at ("B"—Fig. CC47), add shims to correct the pattern. If pattern is too high as "C," remove shims to correct the pattern.

Reinstall hydrostatic drive unit and axle shaft and axle carrier assemblies. Install assembly on tractor by reversing removal procedure. Fill hydrostatic transmission and differential housing with 14 pints (6.6 L) of Cub Cadet Transmission Hydraulic Fluid or equivalent lubricant. Adjust brakes and control linkage as necessary.

## Models 80-282-382H

To remove reduction gear and differential unit, first remove hydrostatic transmission and reduction gear assembly as previously outlined in HYDROSTATIC TRANSMISSION section. Separate hydrostatic unit from reduction gear housing.

A Peerless 1300 series reduction gear and differential unit is used on these models. Refer to Peerless section in REDUCTION GEAR AND DIFFERENTIAL SERVICE section for overhaul procedure.

Reinstall transaxle assembly and refill unit with approximately $2^{3}/_{4}$ pints (1.3 L) of SAE 90 EP gear lubricant.

## Models 1020-1220-1320

Remove hydrostatic drive unit and transaxle as previously outlined in HYDROSTATIC TRANSMISSION section. Separate hydrostatic unit from transaxle housing. Note that hydrostatic input and output shafts are coupled to transaxle shafts with two sets of couplers which are retained on the shafts with Loctite. It may be necessary to heat couplers and use a suitable puller to remove couplers from shafts. Remove wheel and hub assemblies from axles.

A Hydro-Gear 210-1010S transaxle is used on these models. Refer to Hydro-Gear section in REDUCTION GEAR AND DIFFERENTIAL SERVICE section for overhaul procedure.

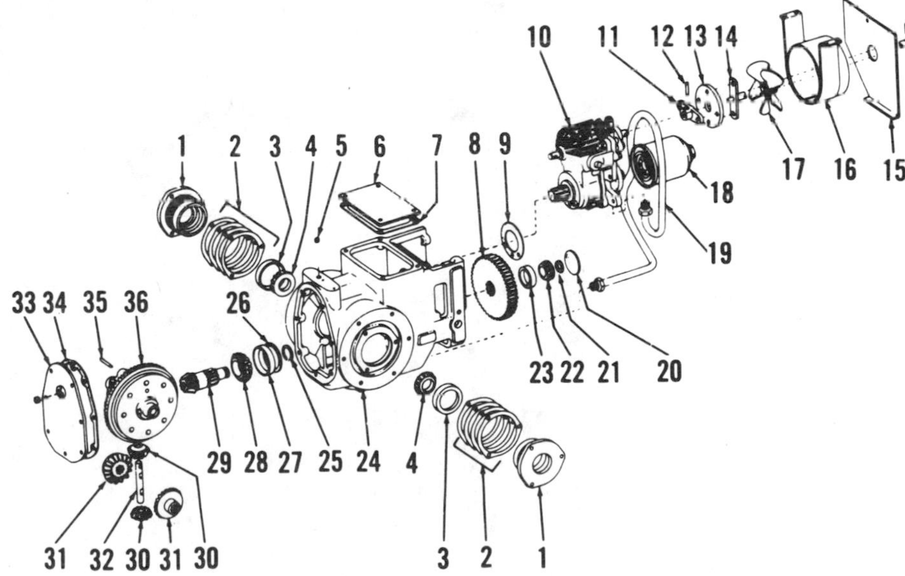


*Fig. CC48—Exploded view of typical differential assembly and related parts used on hydrostatic transmission Models 105, 107, 109, 125, 127, 129, 147, 149, 169, 1210, 1211, 1250, 1450 and 1650.*

1. Differential bearing cage
2. Shims
3. Bearing cup
4. Bearing cone
5. Breather plug
6. Top cover
7. Gasket
8. Reduction gear
9. Gasket
10. Hydrostatic unit
11. Drive coupling half
12. Roll pin
13. Drive coupling disc
14. Drive shaft
15. Air baffle plate
16. Fan shroud
17. Fan
18. Oil filter
19. Suction tube
20. Expansion plug
21. Snap ring
22. Bearing cone
23. Bearing cup
24. Differential housing
25. Snap ring
26. Shim pack
27. Bearing cup
28. Bearing cone
29. Bevel pinion shaft
30. Differential pinion
31. Differential side gear
32. Shaft
33. Rear cover
34. Gasket
35. Pin
36. Ring gear

Illustrations courtesy Cub Cadet Corp.

Reinstall couplings using Loctite 609 to bond couplings to shafts. Allow Loctite to cure for 24 hours before operating unit. Assemble hydrostatic unit on reduction gear housing and tighten mounting bolts to 80-120 in.-lbs. (9.0-13.6 N·m).

# AXLE SHAFTS

### Models 72-73-86-104-105-106-107-108-109-124-125-126-127-128-129-147-149-169-800-1000-1200-1210-1211-1250-1450-1650

The axle carriers (4—Fig. CC55) do not have to be removed to remove axle shafts (1). To remove axles, first drain oil from differential housing. Support rear of tractor and remove rear wheels. Remove brake assembly from axle housing on models so equipped. Remove rear cover from differential housing. Remove "C" type snap rings (6) from inner ends of axles, then slide axles out of carriers. Oil seal (2) and bearing (3) or bushing may be removed from housings using a suitable puller.

To remove axle carriers from differential housing, remove cap screws attaching axle carrier to differential housing. Raise tractor frame to clear axle carriers and withdraw carriers.

Axle bushing on Model 73 must be pressed into position with oil groove at the bottom. On all other models, install needle bearing until flush with outer edge of its bore. Oil seal must be installed with lip toward bushing or bearing.

# FRONT PTO CLUTCH

### ELECTRIC CLUTCH (Horizontal Crankshaft)

### All Models So Equipped

**R&R AND OVERHAUL.** If clutch fails to engage, check for minimum of 10 volts at clutch wire with pto switch in ON position. If there is no voltage, check for blown fuse, faulty wiring or switch. Clutch field coil should draw 3.5-4.0 amperes. A reading outside this range indicates a faulty field coil.

To remove clutch, first remove hood side panels. Remove grille housing and hood as an assembly. Disconnect clutch wire. Remove pto brake flange (4—Fig. CC56), retaining bolt (3), washer (2) and spacer (1). Use a suitable puller to remove clutch rotor assembly (Fig. CC57) from crankshaft. Remove stud bolts to remove field coil if necessary.

Renewal of field coil, rotor assembly and/or rotor bearing is the only service available on electric clutch.

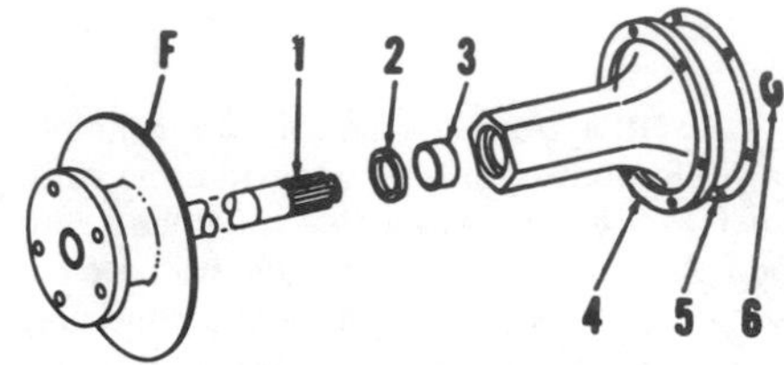


*Fig. CC55—Exploded view of axle and carrier used on some models. Brake disc (F) is used on models equipped with external, axle mounted disc brakes. Models 72 and 73 use a bushing instead of needle bearing (3).*

1. Axle
2. Oil seal
3. Needle bearing
4. Axle carrier
5. Gasket
6. "C" ring retainer
7. Brake disc

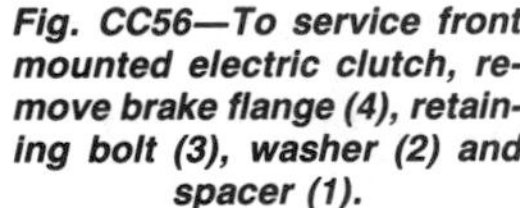

*Fig. CC56—To service front mounted electric clutch, remove brake flange (4), retaining bolt (3), washer (2) and spacer (1).*

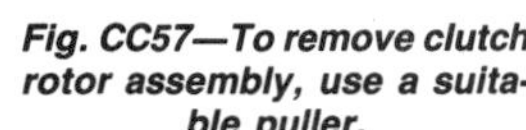

*Fig. CC57—To remove clutch rotor assembly, use a suitable puller.*

*Fig. CC58—Check clearance between driven disc and driving hub using a feeler gage at three evenly spaced locations. The gap should be 0.060-0.090 inch (1.524-2.286 mm). Refer to text for details.*

**NOTE: There may be factory installed shims between driving hub and driven disc bearing. Be sure shims are in place during reassembly to assure proper braking action.**

Before reassembling clutch, measure clearance between driven disc and driven hub using a feeler gage (Fig. CC58) at three evenly spaced locations. This gap should be 0.060-0.090 inch (1.52-2.28 mm), and is adjusted by adding or subtracting shims as required on driving hub.

**NOTE: Some late production models do not require shims. The air gap is permanently set. This clutch in unpainted, the early production clutch (shims required) is painted black.**

Assemble clutch by reversing disassembly procedure. Adjust clutch as follows: Disengage clutch and check clearance between driven disc and driving hub by placing a feeler gage in the four slots in brake flange (Fig. CC59). The gap should be 0.010 inch (0.25 mm) at each position. Tighten or loosen brake flange mounting nuts (1) to obtain correct air gap.

### ELECTRIC CLUTCH (Vertical Crankshaft)

### Models 1215-1220

**R&R AND OVERHAUL.** If pto clutch fails to engage, perform the following checks: With key switch on (engine off), there should be battery voltage at terminal 5 (red wire) of pto switch. If not, check for faulty wire or key switch. Move pto switch to engaged position, there should be voltage at terminals 3 (black wire), 4 (brown wire) and 5 of pto switch. If not, switch is faulty. Clutch coil resistance should be 2.4-3.4 ohms. Clutch coil current draw should be 3.5-4.0 amperes.

To remove pto clutch, disconnect wire to clutch. Remove clutch retaining bolt and withdraw clutch from engine crankshaft. Remove stud nuts (2—Fig. CC60) to separate armature (4) and rotor (5) from field coil (6).

To reinstall clutch, reverse the removal procedure. Adjust clutch as follows: With pto switch OFF, insert feeler gage through each of the three slots (S—Fig. CC61) in armature housing and measure air gap between armature and rotor. Air gap should be 0.010-0.025 inch (0.25-0.63 mm) and is adjusted by tightening or loosening the three stud nuts (2).

When pto clutch has been renewed, clutch and brake friction surfaces should be burnished as follows: Run engine at $^1/_2$ throttle and engage and disengage the clutch five times (10 seconds on and 10 seconds off). Increase engine speed to $^3/_4$ throttle and engage and disengage clutch five times.

### MECHANICAL CLUTCH

### All Models So Equipped

**R&R AND OVERHAUL.** To remove front pto clutch, first remove grille and on some early models, remove grille support. Disconnect pto linkage and move clutch release shaft out of the way. Remove jam set screws from each of the three holes in clutch pulley housing. See Fig. CC62. Withdraw clutch assembly from tractor. Bearing and collar will remain on engine crankshaft as shown in Fig. CC63. To remove bearing (2), loosen lock collar set screw (1) and turn collar (5) in opposite direction of crankshaft rotation, then pull bearing and collar off crankshaft.

Remove three jam nuts (1—Fig. CC64). Loosen three clutch finger screws (1—

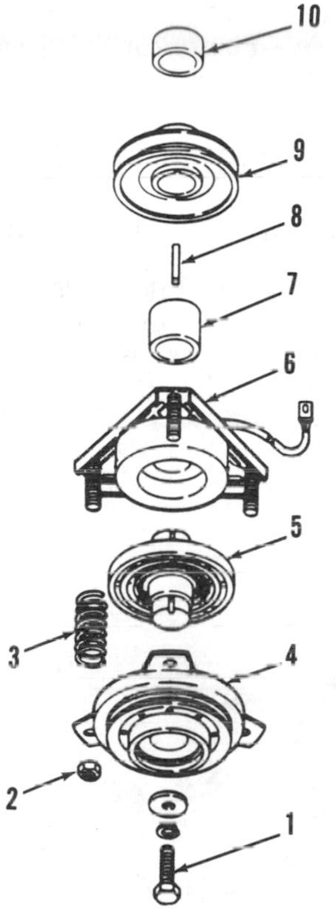


*Fig. CC60—Exploded view of electric pto clutch used on Models 1215 and 1220.*

1. Retaining bolt
2. Nut (3)
3. Spring (3)
4. Armature
5. Rotor
6. Coil assy.
7. Bushing
8. Key
9. Engine pulley
10. Spacer

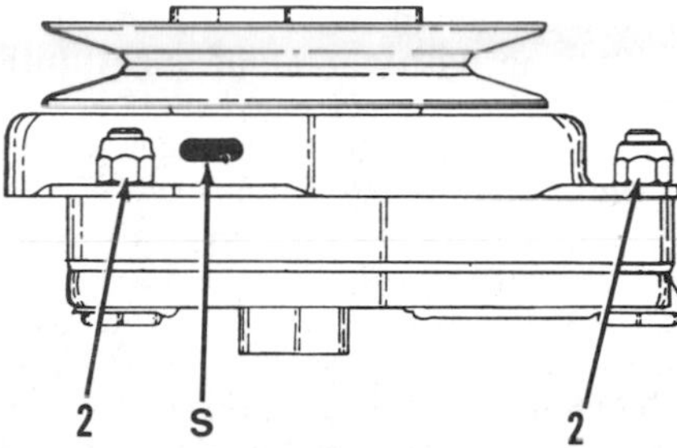


*Fig. CC61—Check air gap setting between armature and rotor using a feeler gage at the three slots (S) in cover. Specified gap is 0.010-0.025 inch (0.25-0.63 mm). Tighten or loosen mounting nuts (2) to obtain desired gap.*

*Fig. CC62—Remove jam set screw and lock set screws from each of the three holes (1), then withdraw front pto clutch.*

*Fig. CC59—Check clearance between driven disc and driving hub by inserting feeler gage in the four slots in brake flange. Gap should be 0.010 inch (0.25 mm) at each position. Tighten or loosen brake flange mounting nuts (1) to obtain clearance.*

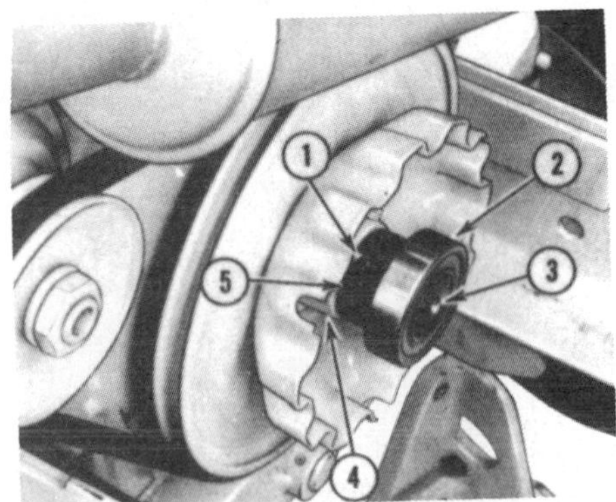


*Fig. CC63—Front pto clutch bearing and collar on engine crankshaft. To lock collar (5) to bearing (2), turn collar in direction of crankshaft rotation.*

Fig. CC65) evenly and remove pressure plate, friction disc and three compression springs. Fingers (4), thrust button (2) and pressure springs (3) can now be removed.

Clean and inspect all parts for excessive wear or other damage. A clutch service kit consisting of a friction disc, pressure springs and anti-chatter springs is available.

Reassemble by reversing disassembly procedure and adjust finger screws as follows: Install gage (1—Fig. CC66), which is furnished in clutch service kit, in position shown. Tighten finger screws (2) (in line with center of gage) until ends of gage contact machined surface of pulley; adjust other two finger screws in same manner. Recheck each of the three positions with the gage to make certain all three adjustments are equal. Install jam nuts (1—Fig. CC64) and tighten to 72-84 in.-lbs. (8.2-9.5 N·m).

If bearing (2—Fig. CC63) was removed, install bearing flush with end of crankshaft. Turn lock collar (5) in direction of crankshaft rotation to lock bearing to crankshaft. Align set screw holes in clutch pulley housing with slots in drive pulley cup as shown in Fig. CC67 and slide clutch assembly part way on bearing. Equally space and install three anti-chatter springs as shown in Fig. CC67. Push clutch assembly the rest of the way on bearing. Install three cone point (1/2 inch long) set screws and tighten to 60-72 in.-lbs. (6.8-8.1 N·m). Install and tighten flat point (1/4 inch long) set screws to 72-84 in.-lbs. (8.1-9.5 N·m).

Reconnect pto clutch linkage and adjust as follows: With pto clutch hand lever fully forward (disengaged), adjust control rod turnbuckle to obtain a clearance of 1/64 to 3/64 inch (0.4-1.2 mm) between wear button on linkage arm and thrust button on clutch.

# REAR PTO UNIT

## Gear Drive Models So Equipped

A rear pto unit (Fig. CC68) is available on some gear drive models. The pto is driven by the transmission input shaft. A shift clutch (11) locks splines on pto shaft directly to splines on rear of transmission input shaft. Clutch/brake pedal must be depressed and tractor motion stopped before engaging pto.

To remove pto unit, remove seven cap screws from retainer (2). Pull shaft and retainer assembly rearward allowing shift clutch (11) to disengage from shift lever shaft (12 or 30).

Disassemble removed unit as follows: Loosen set screw in clutch (11) and slide clutch from shaft (6). Remove retaining ring (10) and shield (9), then withdraw shaft and bearing from retainer (2). Remove snap ring (8) and press shaft from bearing (7). Remove oil seal (1) from retainer. If shift lever shaft (12 or 30) is excessively worn, remove exterior linkage and remove shaft from inside differential housing.

Clean and inspect all parts and renew any showing excessive wear or other damage. Reassemble by reversing disassembly procedure. Tighten set screw in clutch (11) only enough to prevent clutch from traveling beyond stops on the cut-a-way spline on shaft. Clutch must slide freely from stop to stop. Oil seal (1) should be installed with lip to inside.

Using new gasket (3), insert pto shaft through hole in differential rear cover (4) and engage pin on shift lever shaft

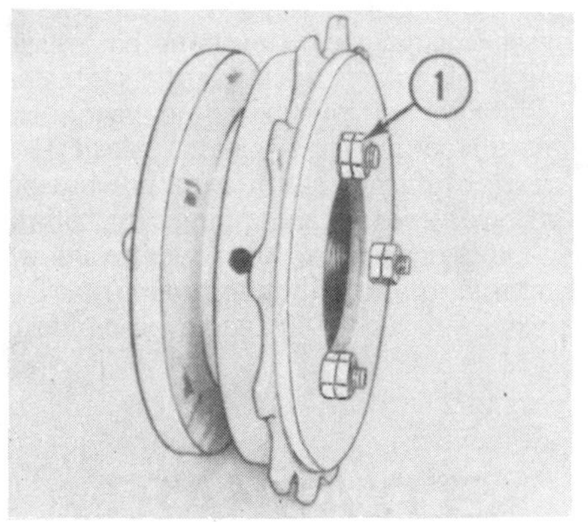


*Fig. CC64—Jam nuts (1) are used to lock clutch finger adjusting screws.*

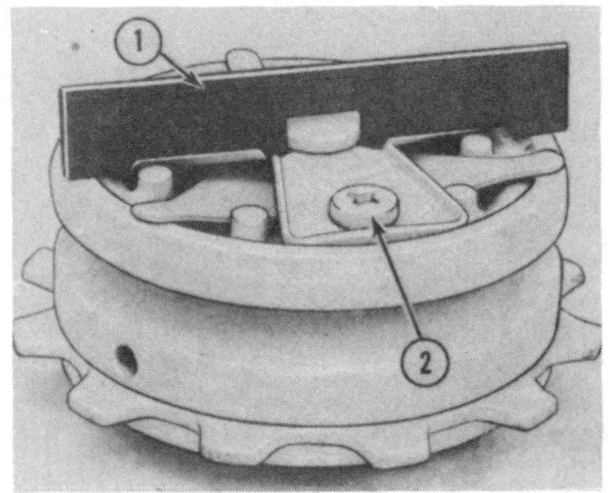


*Fig. CC66—With gage (1) in position shown, adjust finger screw (2) as outlined in text. Adjust other two fingers in same manner.*

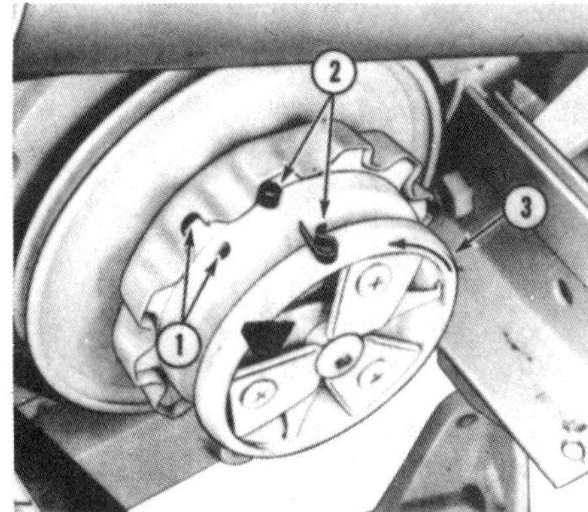

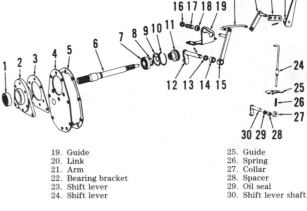

*Fig. CC67—When installing front pto clutch, align set screw holes with slots (1) and position anti-chatter springs (2) in relation to normal direction of clutch pulley rotation (3) as shown.*

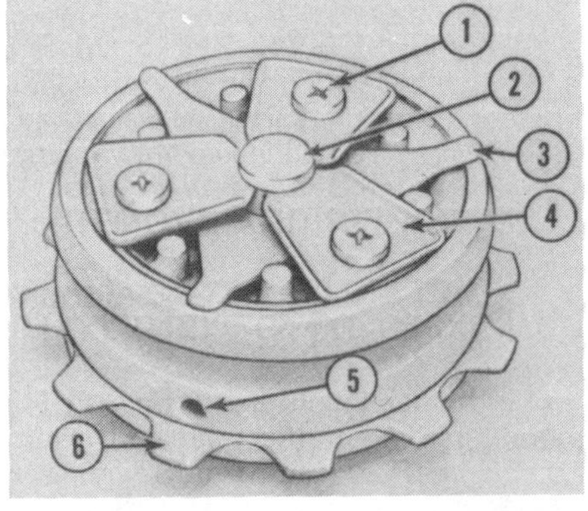


*Fig. CC65—Front pto clutch assembly. Set screw holes (5) must be centered on lugs of clutch disc (6).*

1. Finger screws
2. Thrust button
3. Pressure springs
4. Clutch finer
5. Set screw hole
6. Clutch disc

*Fig. CC68—Exploded view of rear pto assembly used on some gear drive models. Shift linkage (24 through 30) is used on Models 72 and 73. Linkage (12 through 23) is used on other models.*

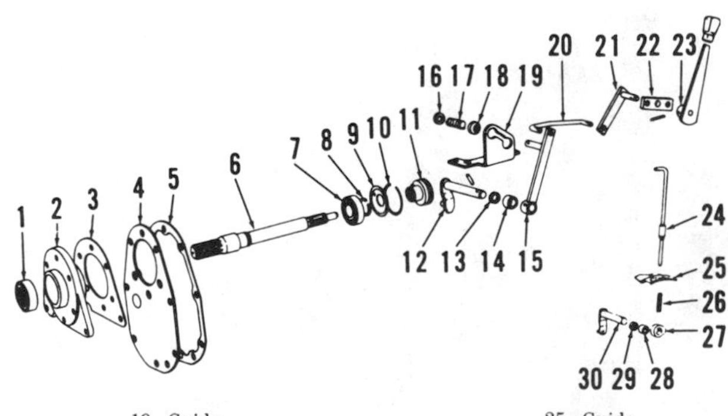


1. Oil seal
2. Retainer
3. Gasket
4. Differential cover
5. Gasket
6. Pto shaft
7. Bearing
8. Snap ring
9. Shield
10. Retaining ring
11. Shift clutch
12. Shift lever shaft
13. Oil seal
14. Spacer
15. Lever
16. Washer
17. Spring
18. Poppet
19. Guide
20. Link
21. Arm
22. Bearing bracket
23. Shift lever
24. Shift lever
25. Guide
26. Spring
27. Collar
28. Spacer
29. Oil seal
30. Shift lever shaft



Illustrations courtesy Cub Cadet Corp.

in groove in shift clutch. Move assembly forward and insert pilot end of shaft (11) in rear end of transmission input shaft. Bolt assembly in position.

# ELECTRIC LIFT

## All Models So Equipped

A self-contained electric lift unit (Fig. CC69) is available on some models. To remove lift unit, first disconnect battery cables. On some models, frame cover and side panel extensions must be removed. On all models, disconnect electrical connector at motor, remove two attaching pins and lift assembly from tractor.

To disassemble unit, remove two screws through motor and pry motor and drive coupling from adapter.

**CAUTION: Do not let end plates separate from motor body.**

If motor or drive coupling is to be renewed, drive out pin (7—Fig. CC70) and separate coupling (5) from motor (6). Motor is serviced only as an assembly. Remove brake springs (3) and brake cam (4) from pinion shaft (2). Remove four screws and lift off adapter (1). Pull pinion shaft (2) and bearing from housing, remove retaining ring and press bearing from pinion shaft. Loosen set screw (26—Fig. CC69) and unscrew housing (14) from outer tube (24). Remove bushing screws (21), pull clevis assembly (22) from translating tube (19) and withdraw lift screw and translating tube assembly from outer tube. Oil seal (20) and guide bushing (30) can now be removed from outer tube. Drive out pin (7—Fig. CC71) and remove spiroid gear (6), bearing (5) and washer (4) from lift screw (3). Remove lift screw (2—Fig. CC72), drive both pins (4) inward and remove lifting nut (1) from translating tube (5). Drive stop pin (3) from lift screw. To disassemble clevis and slip clutch assembly, remove self-locking nut and slide Belleville washers, thrust washers and bushing from clevis.

Clean and inspect all parts and renew any showing excessive wear or other damage. Reassemble by reversing disassembly procedure, keeping the following points in mind: Belleville washers (1—Fig. CC73) and thrust washers (2) must be installed as shown on each side of slip clutch bushing. Tighten self-locking nut (1—Fig. CC74) on slip clutch and clevis to 25-30 in.-lbs. (2.8-3.4 N·m). Stop pin (3—Fig. CC72) should be installed so equal amount of pin extends from each side of lift screw (2). Lubricate internal parts with lithium base

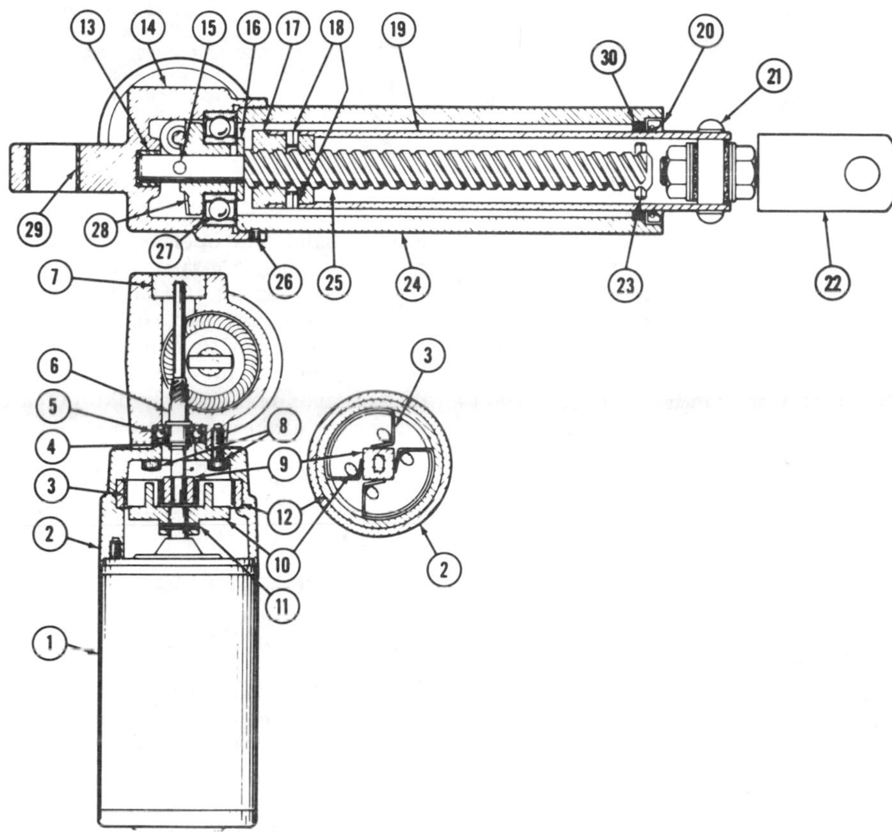

*Fig. CC69—Sectional view of electric lift unit used on some models.*

1. Motor
2. Adapter
3. Brake springs
4. Retaining ring
5. Pinion bearing
6. Pinion shaft
7. Pinion bushing
8. "Tap tite" screws
9. Brake cam
10. Drive coupling
11. Spring pin
12. Liner insert
13. Bushing
14. Housing
15. Drive pin
16. Washer
17. Lifting nut
18. Pins
19. Translating tube
20. Oil seal
21. Bushing screws
22. Clevis assy.
23. Stop pin
24. Outer tube
25. Lift screw
26. Set screw
27. Load bearing
28. Spiroid gear
29. Bushing
30. Guide bushing

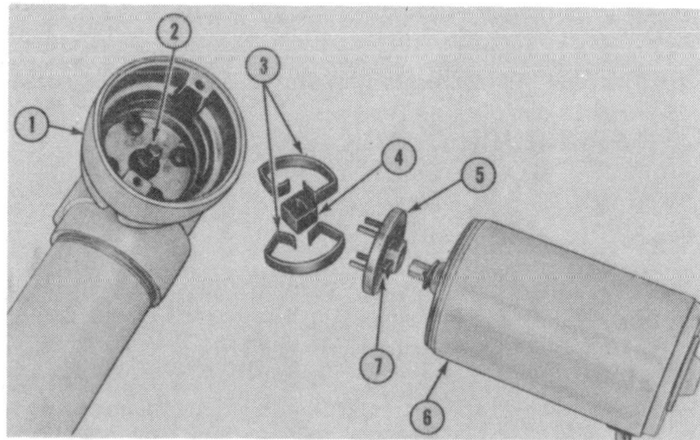

*Fig. CC70—View showing motor, drive coupling and brake assembly removed from lift unit.*

1. Adapter
2. Pinion shaft
3. Brake springs
4. Brake cam
5. Drive coupling
6. Motor
7. Spring pin

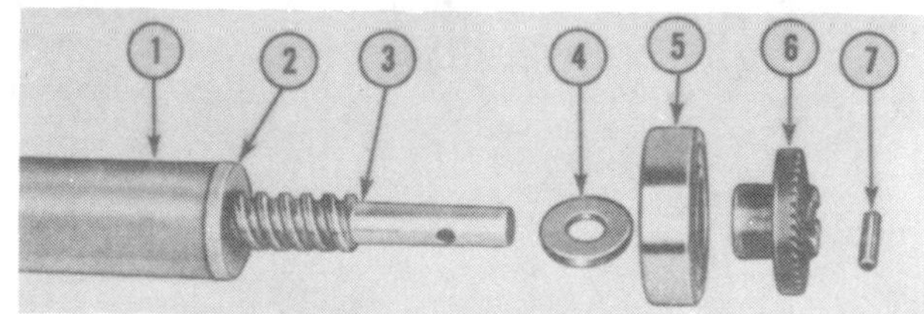

*Fig. CC71—Spiroid gear, load bearing and washer are removed from lift screw after removing drive pin.*

1. Translating tube
2. Lifting nut
3. Lift screw
4. Washer
5. Load bearing
6. Spiroid gear
7. Drive pin

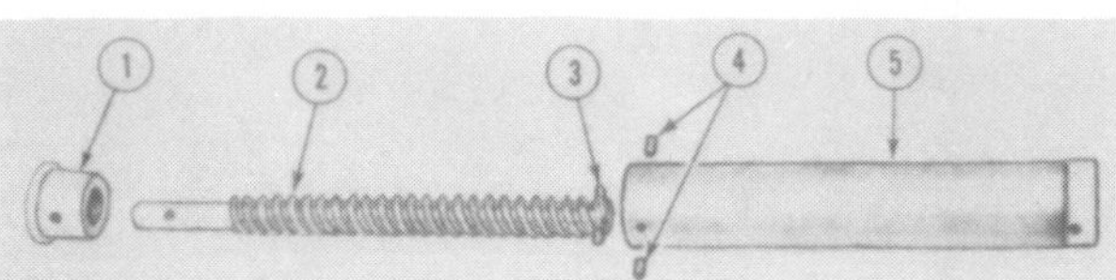

Fig. CC72—Remove lift screw, drive both pins (4) inward and remove lifting nut.
1. Lifting nut
2. Lift screw
3. Stop pin
4. Pins
5. Translating tube

grease. Install new oil seal (20—Fig. CC69) with lip towards inside.

Reinstall lift unit on tractor and adjust slip clutch as follows: Attach an implement to tractor hitch, start engine and hold lift switch in raise position. The lift unit should raise implement without slipping, but must rotate freely at the fully raised position. A slight slip on engagement of the load is permissible, but once load is moving slippage should not occur until maximum travel is reached. If slippage is excessive, tighten adjusting nut (3—Fig. CC74) in increments of 1/8 turn to correct slip clutch setting.

# HYDRAULIC LIFT

## OPERATION

### All Models So Equipped

The hydrostatic drive charge pump furnishes fluid to the hydraulic lift system. On models equipped with hydraulic lift, charge pump relief valve is located on right side of transmission center housing under plug (4—Fig. CC75). The hydraulic lift system relief valve is located on top of center housing under plug (2). Lift pressure is regulated by lift relief valve at 500-625 psi (3450-4310 kPa). The single spool control valve is used to direct pressurized fluid to double-acting lift cylinder.

## PRESSURE CHECK AND ADJUSTMENT

### All Models So Equipped

To check hydraulic lift pressure, install a 1000 psi (7000 kPa) test gage in pressure test port as shown in Fig. CC76. Start engine and operate at approximately 2/3 full engine rpm. With lift control valve in neutral, test gage should indicate charge pressure of 70-120 psi (485-825 kPa). With control valve in raise position and lift cylinder at the end of its stroke, test gage should indicate maximum lift pressure of 500-625 psi (3450-4310 kPa). If lift pressure is not within specified range, remove lift pressure relief valve and add or remove spring shims as required.

## CONTROL VALVE

### All Models So Equipped

**R&R AND OVERHAUL.** To remove hydraulic lift control valve, make certain any mounted equipment is in fully lowered position. Shut off fuel, then unbolt and remove fuel tank and side panels as an assembly. Identify and disconnect hydraulic lines from valve. Disconnect control lever link, then unbolt and remove valve assembly.

To disassemble control valve, refer to Fig. CC77 and remove end cap (10). Withdraw spool assembly. Rear "O" ring (12) and bushing (9) will be removed with spool assembly. Unscrew shoulder bolt (7) and separate washers (13), spacer (8) and centering spring (11) from spool (5). Remove front "O" ring from spool bore. Unscrew plug (2) and remove "O" ring (3), spring (4) and lift check valve (1).

Clean and inspect all parts for excessive wear or other damage. If spool (5) or valve body (6) is scored or otherwise

Fig. CC76—Install pressure gage in center housing test port to check lift pressure.

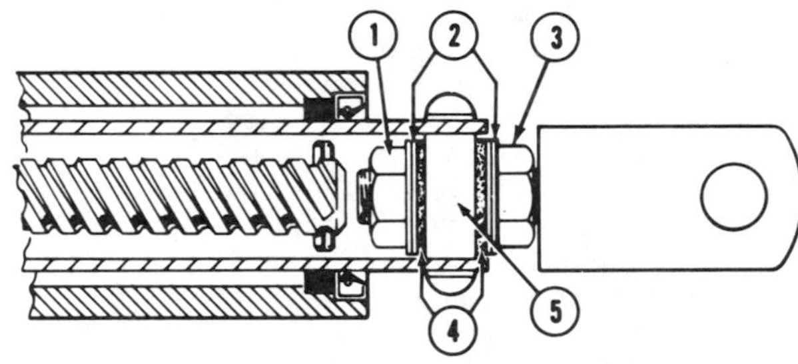

Fig. CC74—Sectional view showing installation of slip clutch and clevis assembly.
1. Self-locking nut
2. Belleville washer
3. Adjusting nut
4. Thrust washers
5. Bushing

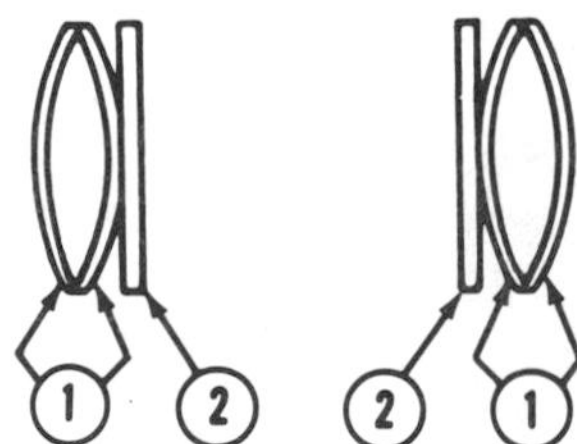

Fig. CC73—Belleville washers (1) and thrust washer (2) must be installed as shown on each side of slip clutch bushing.

Fig. CC75—On models equipped with hydraulic lift, hydrostatic charge relief valve is located on right side of transmission center housing and lift relief valve is located on top of center housing.
1. Check valves
2. Hydraulic lift relief valve
3. Lift pressure test port
4. Charge relief valve



Illustrations courtesy Cub Cadet Corp.

damaged, renew complete control valve assembly as spool and body are not serviced separately.

When reassembling, use new "O" rings and lubricate all parts with clean hydraulic fluid. Apply Loctite 242 on threads of shoulder bolt (7), and install washers, spacer and centering spring on spool. Tighten shoulder bolt to 60-90 in.-lbs. (7-10 N·m). Install "O" rings (12), bushing (9) and spool assembly. Tighten end cap (10) to 20-25 ft-lbs. (27-34 N·m). Install lift check valve (1), spring (4), "O" ring (3) and plug (2).

Reinstall control valve by reversing removal procedure. Start engine and operate at approximately 2/3 full throttle speed. Cycle lift cylinder several times to expel air from system and check for leaks. Check fluid level in differential housing and fill to proper level with hydraulic fluid.

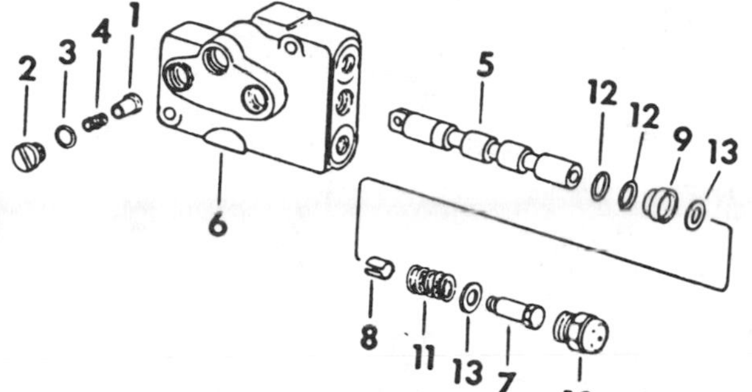


*Fig. CC77—Exploded view of hydraulic lift control valve.*

1. Lift check valve
2. Plug
3. "O" ring
4. Spring
5. Spool
6. Valve body
7. Shoulder bolt
8. Spacer
9. Bushing
10. End cap
11. Centering spring
12. "O" rings
13. Washers

### HYDRAULIC LIFT CYLINDER

#### All Models So Equipped

Service on lift cylinder is limited to renewal of hoses, fittings and fitting "O" rings or renewal of complete cylinder assembly. Parts for cylinder are not serviced separately.

# ELECTRICAL WIRING DIAGRAMS

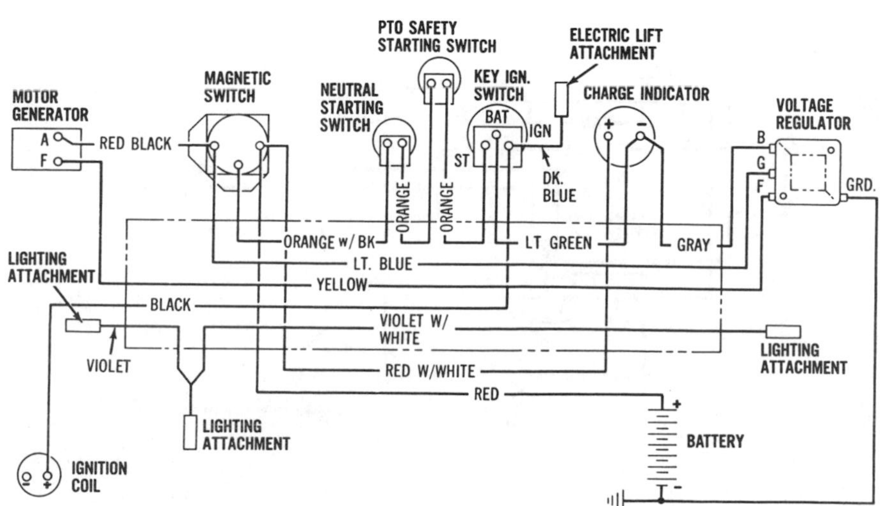


*Fig. CC80—Electrical wiring diagram for Models 86, 108, 109, 128, 129, 149 and 169.*

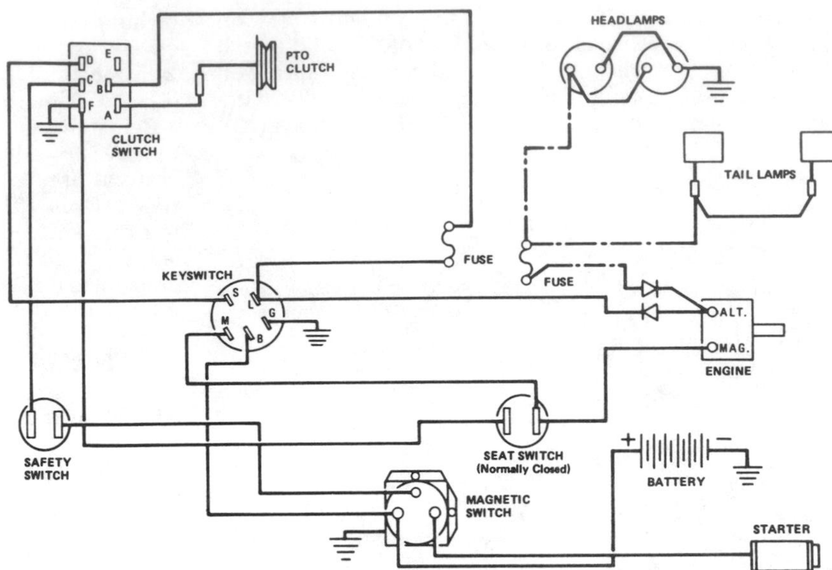


*Fig. CC81—Electrical wiring diagram for Model 482.*

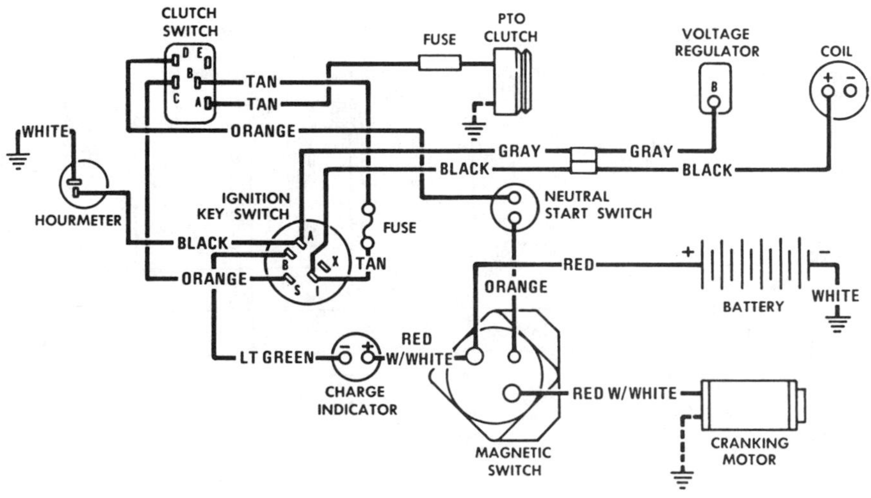


*Fig. CC82—Electrical wiring diagram for Models 800, 1000, 1200, 1250, 1450 and 1650.*



Illustrations courtesy Cub Cadet Corp.

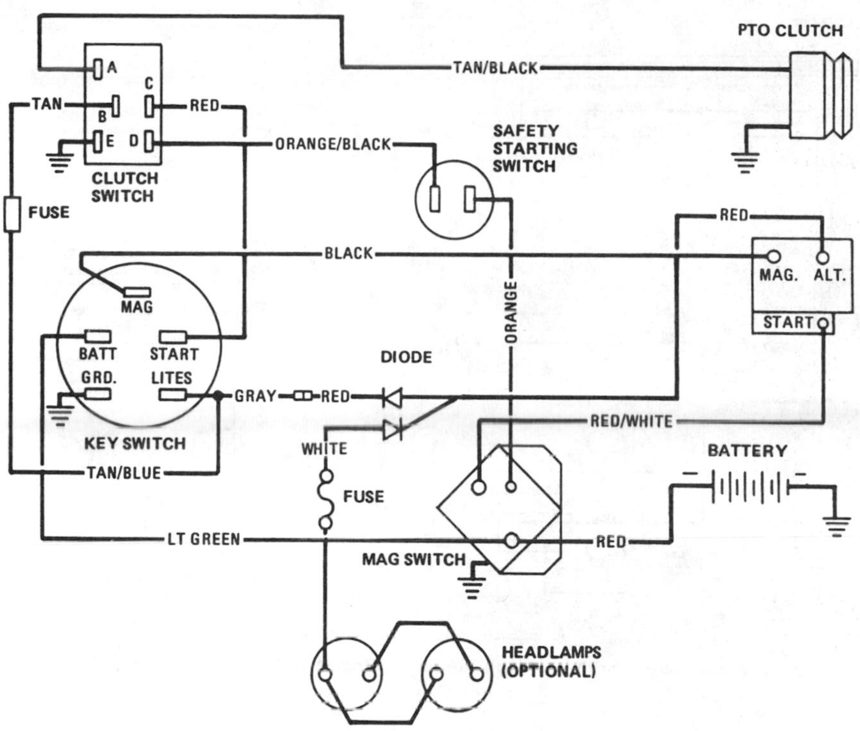


*Fig. CC83—Electrical wiring diagram for Model 1100.*

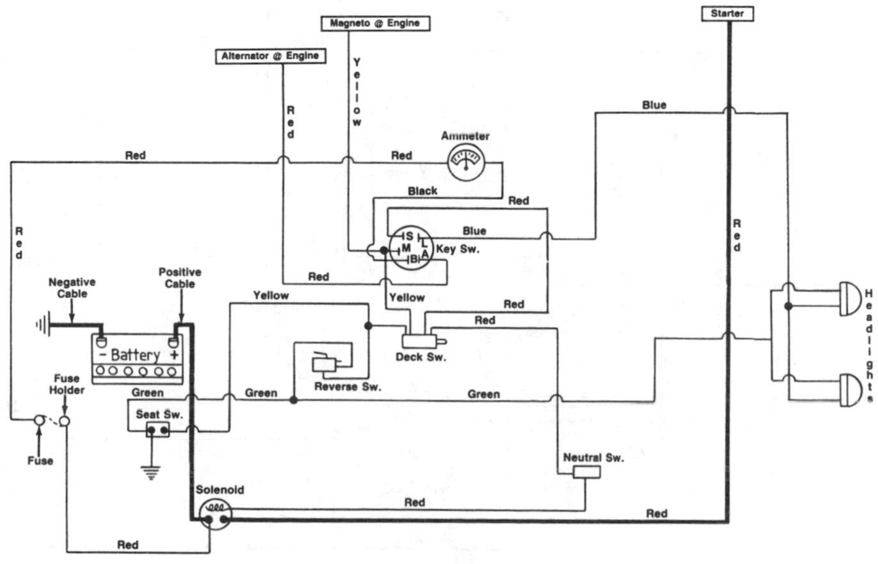


*Fig. CC84—Electrical wiring diagram for Models 1015, 1020, 1315 and 1320.*

Illustrations courtesy Cub Cadet Corp.

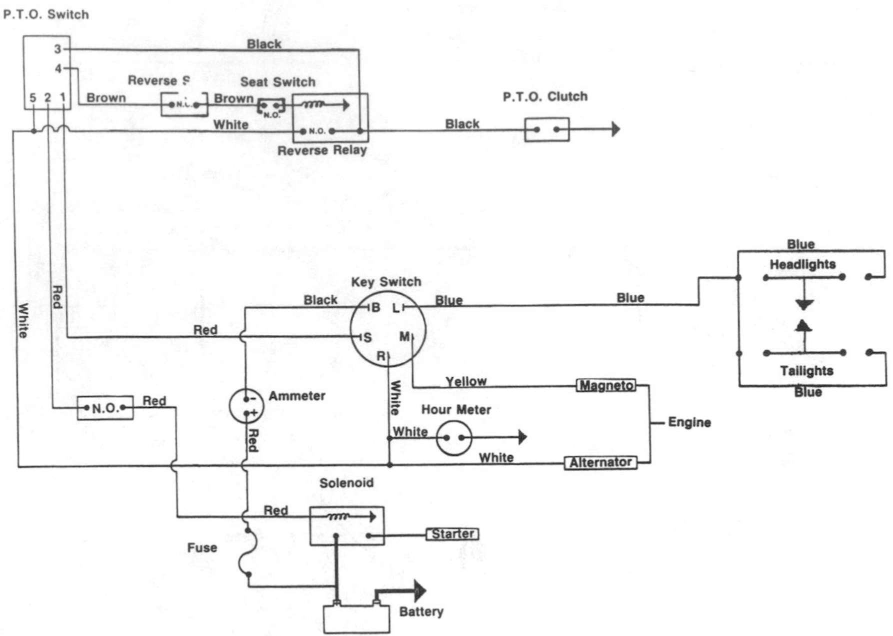


*Fig. CC85—Electrical wiring diagram for Models 1204, 1210 and 1211.*

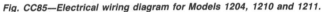

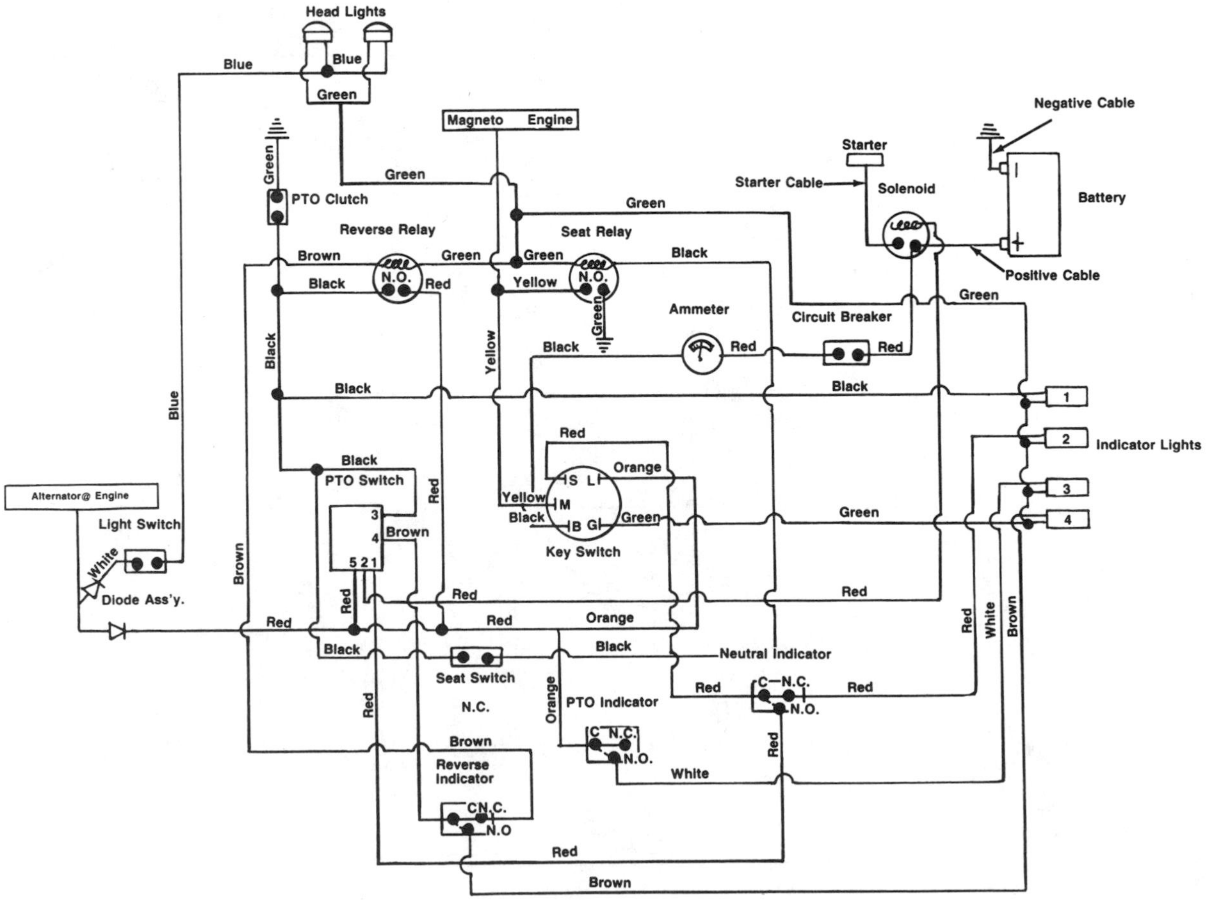

---

Head Lights
Blue
Blue
Green
Magneto Engine
Negative Cable
Green
PTO Clutch
Green
Starter
Starter Cable
Solenoid
Battery
Green
Reverse Relay
Seat Relay
Brown
Green
Green
Black
Positive Cable
Black
N.O.
Red
Yellow
N.O.
Green
Black
Yellow
Green
Ammeter
Circuit Breaker
Black
Red
Red
Black
Black
1
Blue
Red
2
Indicator Lights
Black
Orange
PTO Switch
Red
S L
3
Alternator@ Engine
Yellow
M
Black
B G
Green
Green
4
Light Switch
Brown
Key Switch
White
Brown
Diode Ass'y.
Red
Red
Red
Red
Red
Orange
Red
White
Brown
Black
Black
Neutral Indicator
Seat Switch
Red
C—N.C.
Red
N.O.
N.C.
PTO Indicator
Red
Orange
C N.C.
N.O.
Brown
Red
White
Reverse Indicator
C N.C.
N.O
Red
Brown

*Fig. CC86—Electrical wiring diagram for Models 1215 and 1220 with serial number 107,999 and below.*



Illustrations courtesy Cub Cadet Corp.

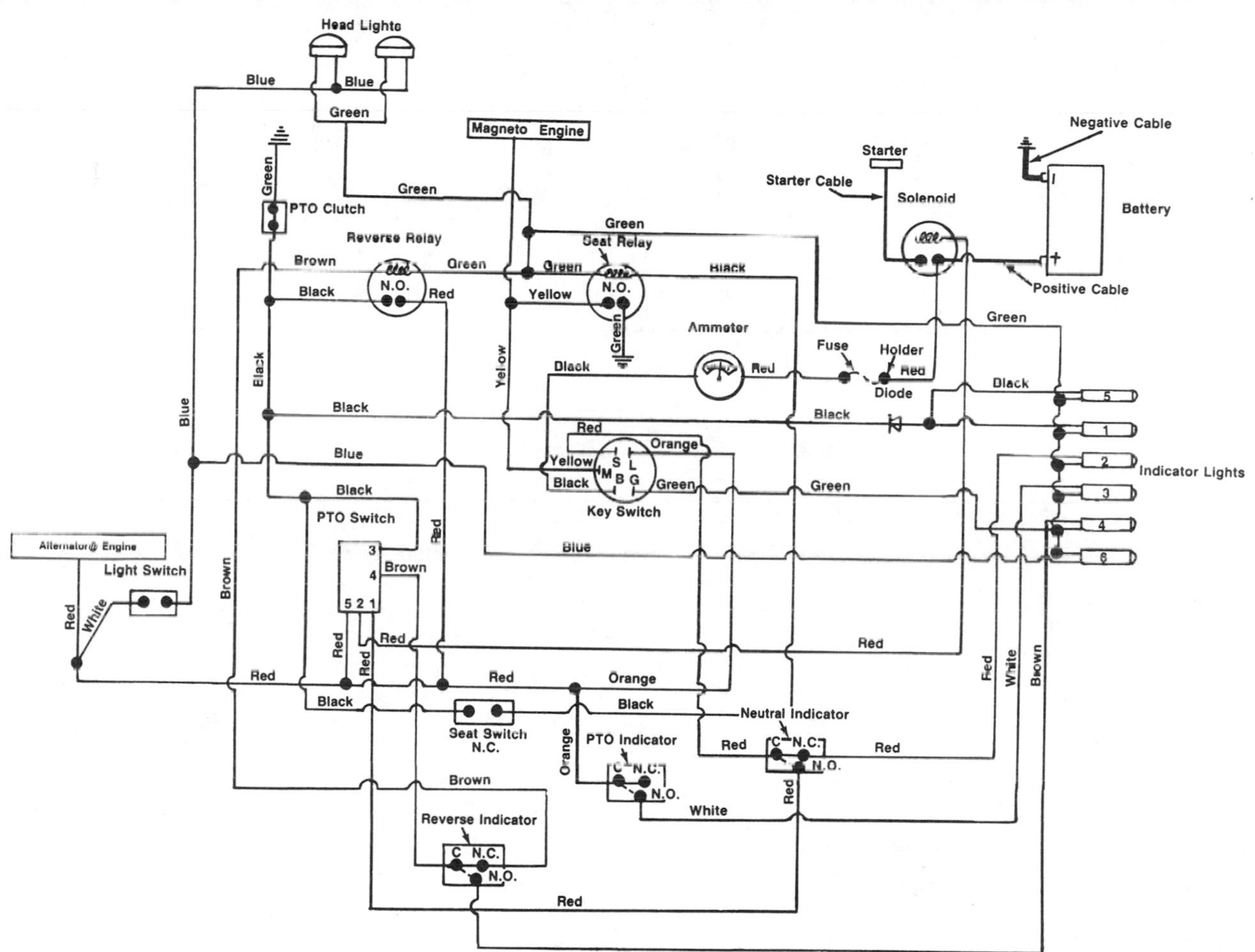


*Fig. CC87—Electrical wiring diagram for Models 1215 and 1220 with serial number 108,000 and above.*

Illustrations courtesy Cub Cadet Corp.

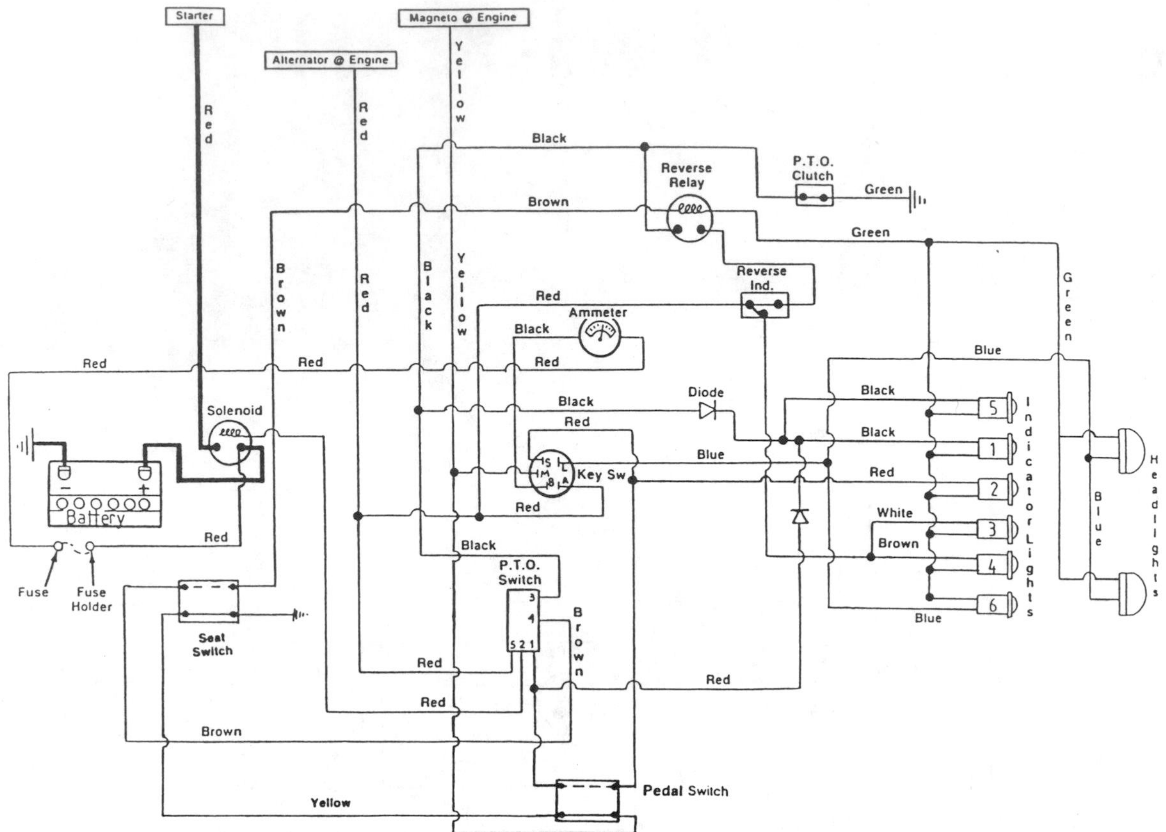


*Fig. CC88—Electrical wiring diagram for Model 1405.*



Illustrations courtesy Cub Cadet Corp.

# JOHN DEERE

## CONDENSED SPECIFICATIONS

| | MODELS | | | |
|---|---|---|---|---|
| | 60 | 70 | 100 | 108 |
| Engine Make | Tecumseh | Tecumseh | B&S | B&S |
| Model | VH60 | VH70 | 190707 | 191707 |
| Bore | 2-5/8 in. (66.7 mm) | 2-3/4 in. (69.8 mm) | 3 in. (76.2 mm) | 3 in. (76.2 mm) |
| Stroke | 2-1/2 in. (63.5 mm) | 2-17/32 in. (64.3 mm) | 2-3/4 in. (69.8 mm) | 2-3/4 in. (69.8 mm) |
| Piston Displacement | 13.5 cu.in. (221 cc) | 15.0 cu.in. (246 cc) | 19.44 cu.in. (319 cc) | 19.44 cu.in. (319 cc) |
| Rated Power | 6 hp (4.5 kW) | 7 hp (5.2 kW) | 8 hp (5.9 kW) | 8 hp (5.9 kW) |
| Slow Idle Speed—Rpm | 1500 | 1700 | 1900 | 1750 |
| High Idle Speed (No-Load)—Rpm | 3600 | 3600 | 3600 | 3500 |
| Crankcase Oil Capacity | 1-1/2 pts. (0.7 L) | 1-1/2 pts. (0.7 L) | 2-1/4 pts. (1.1 L) | 2-1/4 pts. (1.1 L) |
| Transmission Oil Capacity | 3 pts. (1.4 L) | 3 pts. (1.4 L) | 3 pts. (1.4 L) | 24 ozs. (710 mL) |
| Weight | SAE 90 | SAE 90 | SAE 90 | Grease |

| | MODELS | | | |
|---|---|---|---|---|
| | 110 | 110 | 110 | 111 |
| Engine Make | Kohler | Kohler | Kohler | B&S |
| Model | K161S | K181S | K241AS | 252707 |
| Bore | 2-7/8 in. (73.0 mm) | 2-15/16 in. (74.6 mm) | 3-1/4 in. (82.5 mm) | 3-7/16 in. (87.3 mm) |
| Stroke | 2-1/2 in. (63.5 mm) | 2-3/4 in. (69.8 mm) | 2-7/8 in. (73.0 mm) | 2-5/8 in. (66.7 mm) |
| Piston Displacement | 16.22 cu.in. | 18.6 cu.in. | 23.9 cu.in. | 24.4 cu.in. |
| Rated Power | 7 hp (5.2 kW) | 8 hp (5.9 kW) | 10 hp (7.4 kW) | 11 hp (8.2 kW) |
| Slow Idle Speed—Rpm | 1800 | 1800 | 1200 | 1750 |
| High Idle Speed (No-Load)—Rpm | 3800 | 3800 | 3800 | 3500 |
| Crankcase Oil Capacity | 2-1/2 pts. (1.2 L) | 2-1/2 pts. (1.2 L) | 3 pts. (1.4 L) | 3 pts. (1.4 L) |
| Transmission Oil Capacity | 2 pts. (0.9 L) | 3 pts. (1.4 L) | 3-1/2 pts. (1.6 L) | 24 ozs. (710 mL) |
| Weight | SAE 90 | SAE 90 | SAE 90 | Grease |

| | MODELS | | | |
|---|---|---|---|---|
| | 112 | 112 | 112 | 120 |
| Engine Make | Tecumseh | Kohler | Kohler | Kohler |
| Model | HH100 | K241AS | K301AS | K301AS |
| Bore | 3-5/16 in. (84.1 mm) | 3-1/4 in. (82.5 mm) | 3-3/8 in. (85.7 mm) | 3-3/8 in. (85.7 mm) |
| Stroke | 2-3/4 in. (69.8 mm) | 2-7/8 in. (73.0 mm) | 3-1/4 in. (82.5 mm) | 3-1/4 in. (82.5 mm) |
| Piston | 23.7 cu.in. (388 cc) | 23.9 cu.in. (392 cc) | 29.07 cu.in. (476 cc) | 29.07 cu.in. (476 cc) |
| Rated Power | 10 hp (7.4 kW) | 10 hp (7.4 kW) | 12 hp (8.9 kW) | 12 hp (8.9 kW) |
| Slow Idle Speed—Rpm | 1700 | 1200 | 1200 | 1200 |
| High Idle Speed (No-Load)—Rpm | 3800 | 3800 | 3800 | 3800 |
| Crankcase Oil Capacity | 2-1/2 pts. (1.2 L) | 3 pts. (1.4 L) | 3 pts. (1.4 L) | 3 pts. (1.4 L) |
| Transmission Oil Capacity | 3 pts. (1.4 L) | 3-1/2 pts. (1.6 L) | 3-1/2 pts. (1.6 L) | 10 pts. (4.7 L) |
| Weight | SAE 90 | SAE 90 | SAE 90 | ATF "F" |

# CONDENSED SPECIFICATIONS

| | MODELS | | | |
|---|---|---|---|---|
| | 130 | 140 | 160 | 165 |
| Engine Make | Kawasaki | Kohler | Kawasaki | Kawasaki |
| Model | FC290V | K321AS | FB460V | FB460V |
| Bore | 3.07 in. (78 mm) | 3-1/2 in. (88.9 mm) | 3.5 in. (89 mm) | 3.5 in. (89 mm) |
| Stroke | 2.36 in. (60 mm) | 3-1/4 in. (82.5 mm) | 2.91 in. (74 mm) | 2.91 in. (74 mm) |
| Piston Displacement | 17.5 cu.in. (286 cc) | 31.27 cu.in. (512 cc) | 28.1 cu.in. (460 cc) | 28.1 cu.in. (460 cc) |
| Rated Power | 9 hp (6.7 kW) | 14 hp (10.4 kW) | 12.5 hp (9.3 kW) | 12.5 hp (9.3 kW) |
| Slow Idle Speed—Rpm | 1400 | 1200 | 1400 | 1400 |
| High Idle Speed (No-Load)—Rpm | 3350 | 3800 | 3350 | 3350 |
| Crankcase Oil Capacity | 2-1/4 pts. (1.1 L) | 3 pts. (1.4 L) | 3 pts.* (1.4 L) | 3 pts.* (1.4 L) |
| Transmission Oil Capacity | 30 ozs. (887 mL) | 10 pts. (4.7 L) | 30 ozs. (887 mL) | 1.5 pts. (0.7 L) |
| Weight | SAE 90 | ATF "F" | SAE 90 | SAE 30 |
| Differential Oil Capacity | ..... | ..... | ..... | 1.5 pts. (0.7 L) |
| Weight | ..... | ..... | ..... | SAE 90 |

*Add 0.8 pint (0.4 L) with filter change.

---

| | MODELS | | | |
|---|---|---|---|---|
| | 175 | 180 | 185 | 200 |
| Engine Make | Kawasaki | Kawasaki | Kawasaki | Kohler |
| Model | FC420V | FC540V | FC540V | K181QS |
| Bore | 3.5 in. (89 mm) | 3.5 in. (89 mm) | 3.5 in. (89 mm) | 2-15/16 in. (74.6 mm) |
| Stroke | 2.68 in. (68 mm) | 3.39 in. (86 mm) | 3.39 in. (86 mm) | 2-3/4 in. (69.8 mm) |
| Piston Displacement | 25.8 cu.in. (423 cc) | 32.6 cu.in. (535 cc) | 32.6 cu.in. (535 cc) | 18.6 cu.in. (305 cc) |
| Power Rating | 14 hp (10.4 kW) | 17 hp (12.7 kW) | 17 hp (12.7 kW) | 8 hp (5.9 kW) |
| Slow Idle Speed—Rpm | 1400 | 1400 | 1400 | 1700 |
| High Idle Speed (No-Load)—Rpm | 3350 | 3350 | 3350 | 3500 |
| Crankcase Oil Capacity | 2-3/4 pts.* (1.3 L) | 3-1/2 pts.* (1.6 L) | 3-1/2 pts.* (1.6 L) | 2-1/2 pts. (1.2 L) |
| Transmission Oil Capacity | 1-1/2 pts. (0.7 L) | 36 ozs. (1065 mL) | See Text | 3-1/2 pts. (1.6 L) |
| Weight | SAE 30 | Grease | See Text | SAE 90 |
| Differential Oil Capacity | 1-1/2 pts. (0.7 L) | ..... | See Text | ..... |
| Weight | SAE 90 | | See Text | |

*Add 0.8 pint (0.4 L) with filter change.

# CONDENSED SPECIFICATIONS

| | MODELS | | | |
|---|---|---|---|---|
| | 208 | 210 | 212 | 214 |
| Engine Make | Kohler | Kohler | Kohler | Kohler |
| Model | K181S | K241QS | K301AQS | K321AQS |
| Bore | 2-15/16 in. | 3-1/4 in. | 3-3/8 in. | 3-1/2 in. |
| | (74.6 mm) | (82.5 mm) | (85.7 mm) | (88.9 mm) |
| Stroke | 2-3/4 in. | 2-7/8 in. | 3-1/4 in. | 3-1/4 in. |
| | (69.8 mm) | (73.0 mm) | (82.5 mm) | (82.5 mm) |
| Piston Displacement | 18.6 cu.in. | 23.9 cu.in. | 29.1 cu.in. | 31.27 cu.in. |
| | (305 cc) | (392 cc) | (477 cc) | (512 cc) |
| Rated Power | 8 hp | 10 hp | 12 hp | 14 hp |
| | (5.9 kW) | (7.4 kW) | (8.9 kW) | (10.4 kW) |
| Slow Idle Speed—Rpm | 1700 | 1700 | 1700 | 1700 |
| High Idle Speed (No-Load)—Rpm | 3500 | 3500 | 3500 | 3500 |
| Crankcase Oil Capacity | 2-1/2 pts. | 3 pts. | 3 pts. | 3 pts. |
| | (1.2 L) | (1.4 L) | (1.4 L) | (1.4 L) |
| Transmission Oil Capacity | 3-1/2 pts. | 3-1/2 pts. | 3-1/2 pts. | 3-1/2 pts. |
| | (1.6 L) | (1.6 L) | (1.6 L) | (1.6 L) |
| Weight | SAE 90 | SAE 90 | SAE 90 | SAE 90 |

| | MODELS | | |
|---|---|---|---|
| | 216 | 300 | 312 |
| Engine Make | Kohler | Kohler | Kohler |
| Model | K341AQS | K341AQS | K301AQS |
| Bore | 3-3/4 in. | 3-3/4 in. | 3-3/8 in. |
| | (95.2 mm) | (95.2 mm) | (85.7 mm) |
| Stroke | 3-1/4 in. | 3-1/4 in. | 3-1/4 in. |
| | (82.5 mm) | (82.5 mm) | (82.5 mm) |
| Piston Displacement | 35.90 cu. in. | 35.90 cu. in. | 29.07 cu. in. |
| | (588 cc) | (588 cc) | (476 cc) |
| Rated Power | 16 hp | 16 hp | 12 hp |
| | (11.9 kW) | (11.9 kW) | (8.9 kW) |
| Slow Idle Speed—Rpm | 1700 | 2000 | 2400 |
| High Idle Speed (No-Load)—Rpm | 3500 | 3500 | 3500 |
| Crankcase Oil Capacity | 3 pts. | 3 pts. | 3 pts. |
| | (1.4 L) | (1.4 L) | (1.4 L) |
| Transmission Oil Capacity | 3-1/2 pts. | 10 pts. | 10 pts. |
| | (1.6 L) | (4.7 L) | (4.7 L) |
| Weight | SAE 90 | ATF "F" | ATF "F" |

| | MODELS | |
|---|---|---|
| | 314 | 316 |
| Engine Make | Kohler | Kohler |
| Model | K321AQS | K341AQS |
| Bore | 3-1/2 in. | 3-3/4 in. |
| | (88.9 mm) | (95.2 mm) |
| Stroke | 3-1/4 in. | 3-1/4 in. |
| | (82.5 mm) | (82.5 mm) |
| Piston Displacement | 31.27 cu. in. | 35.90 cu. in. |
| | (512 cc) | (588 cc) |
| Rated Power | 14 hp | 16 hp |
| | (10.4 kW) | (11.9 kW) |
| Slow Idle Speed—Rpm | 2000 | 2000 |
| High Idle Speed (No-Load)—Rpm | 3500 | 3500 |
| Crankcase Oil Capacity | 3 pts. | 3 pts. |
| | (1.4 L) | (1.4 L) |
| Transmission Oil Capacity | 10 pts. | 10 pts. |
| | (4.7 L) | (4.7 L) |
| Weight | ATF "F" | ATF "F" |

# FRONT AXLE SYSTEM

## AXLE MAIN MEMBER

### Models 108-111-130-160-165-175-180-185

To remove front axle assembly, first remove hood, muffler and muffler guard. Remove electric pto clutch on models so equipped. Raise and support front of tractor. Disconnect drag link (3) and tie rod (9) from steering spindles. Remove cap screws retaining axle rear pivot anchor (8—Fig. JD1). Turn pivot anchors onto axle pivot shaft and lower axle from tractor.

Inspect axle pivot shaft and anchors for wear and renew as necessary. To reinstall axle, reverse the removal procedure.

### All Other Models

To remove front axle assembly, refer to appropriate Fig. JD2 through JD6. Disconnect tie rod ends and drag link (models so equipped) from steering spindles. Raise and support front of tractor. Remove axle pivot bolt and lower axle from tractor.

Inspect axle pivot bushings (if used) and pivot bolt for wear and renew if necessary. To reinstall axle, reverse the removal procedure.

## TIE RODS

### All Models

Refer to Figs. JD1 through JD6 and note that tie rod ball joint ends are renewable on some models, while on other models tie rods and ball joints are integral and must be renewed as an assembly.

Front wheel toe-in is adjustable on late Models 110 and 112, all Models 120 and 140, and 200 series and 300 series tractors. Recommended toe-in is $^{3}/_{16}$ inch (5 mm). See Fig. JD7. To adjust toe-in, loosen ball joint end jam nuts and turn tie rod(s) as necessary. On models with two tie rods, be sure to adjust length of both tie rods equally.

## STEERING SPINDLES

### All Models

To remove steering spindles, raise and support front of tractor and remove front wheels. Refer to appropriate Fig. JD1 through JD6 and disconnect tie rod(s) and drag link from spindles as necessary. Drive out roll pins or remove snap rings retaining spindles in axle, then lower spindles from axle main member.

On models so equipped, inspect spindle bushings for excessive wear and renew as necessary. New bushings must be reamed after installation to obtain desired spindle-to-bushing clearance.

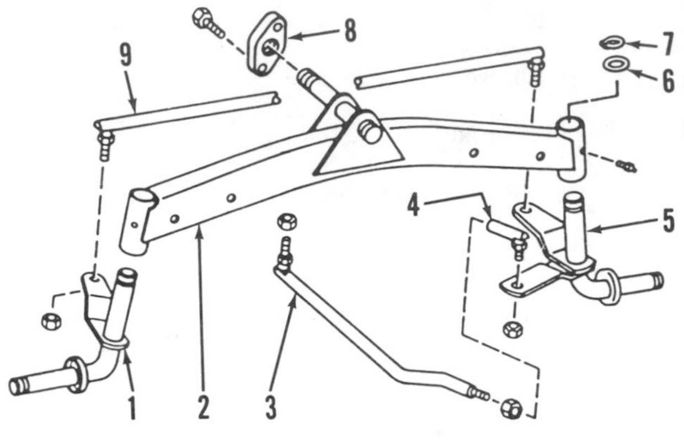


***Fig. JD1—Exploded view of front axle assembly used on Models 108, 111, 130, 160, 165, 175, 180 and 185.***

1. Steering spindle R.H.
2. Axle main member
3. Drag link
4. Ball joint
5. Steering spindle L.H.
6. Washer
7. Snap ring
8. Pivot pin anchor
9. Tie rod

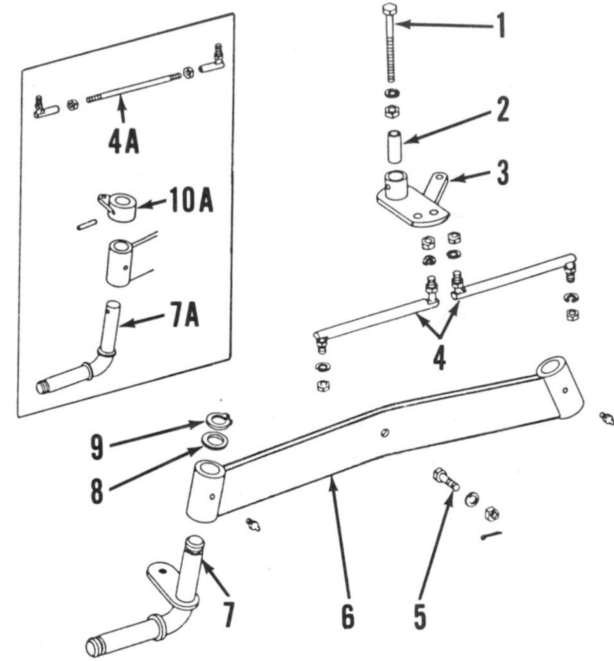


***Fig. JD2—Exploded view of front axle assembly used on Models 60, 70 and 100. Adjustable tie rod (4A), spindle (7A) and spindle arm (10A) shown in inset were used on some early tractors.***

1. Cap screw
2. Bearing
3. Steering arm
4. Tie rods
5. Pivot bolt
6. Axle main member
7. Steering spindle
8. Washer
9. Snap ring

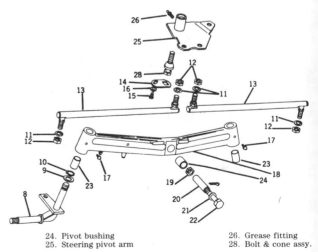

***Fig. JD3—Exploded view of typical front axle assembly used on Model 110 prior to 1973 and Model 112 prior to 1972. Tie rod is adjustable on some models and steering spindle is retained by a collar on early models.***

8. Steering spindle
9. Washer
10. Snap ring
11. Lockwasher
12. Nut
13. Tie rod
14. Lock plate
15. Self-tapping screw
16. Washer
17. Grease fitting
18. Axle main member
19. Nut
20. Pivot bearing
21. Washer
22. Pivot bolt
23. Spindle bushing
24. Pivot bushing
25. Steering pivot arm
26. Grease fitting
28. Bolt & cone assy.

### STEERING CONE ADJUSTMENT

#### Models 110 (Early)-112 (Early)-120-140-300-312-316

Steering arm (25—Fig. JD3 or 1—Fig. JD5) should turn freely through entire steering range. If steering arm turns hard or is too loose, remove bolt and cone assembly (28 or 2). Clean and lubricate cone and arm, then reinstall bolt and cone. With tie rods and drag link disconnected, tighten bolt until slight drag is felt when turning steering arm by hand and all end play has been removed. Install lock plate (14 or 5) over bolt and reconnect tie rods and drag link.

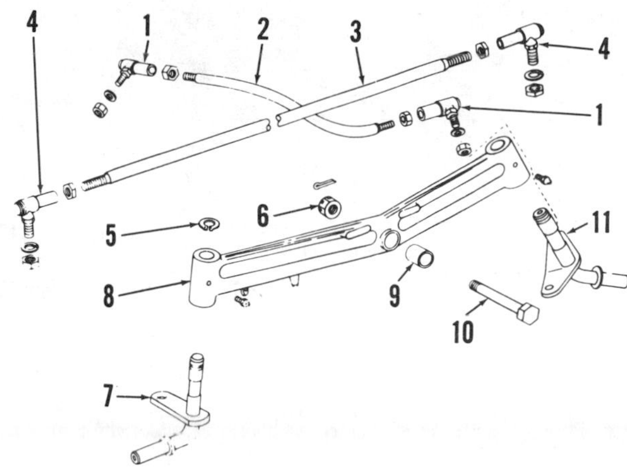


*Fig. JD4—Exploded view of front axle assembly used on Model 110 after 1972, Model 112 after 1971 and all 200 series tractors.*

1. Ball joint
2. Drag link
3. Tie rod
4. Ball joint
5. Snap ring
6. Nut
7. Steering spindle R.H.
8. Axle
9. Bushing
10. Pivot bolt
11. Steering spindle L.H.

## STEERING GEAR

### REMOVE AND REINSTALL

#### Model 60

To remove steering gear, first remove cap screw (15—Fig. JD8) and withdraw steering wheel and upper shaft (11). Disconnect drag link (22) from lever arm (19). Unbolt housing (5) from frame and remove steering gear assembly from underside of tractor.

#### Models 70-100

To remove steering gear, remove steering wheel using a suitable puller. Disconnect drag link from lever arm (19—Fig. JD9). Remove three mounting bolts and remove steering gear assembly from underside of tractor.

#### Models 108-111

To remove steering gear assembly, remove pin (3—Fig. JD10) and lift steering wheel off shaft. Raise hood and remove battery and battery base. Remove nuts and bolts retaining steering shaft support bearing (2) and instrument panel. Disconnect instrument panel electrical wires and throttle control cable, then slide instrument panel off steering shaft. Remove bolts, spacers (5), washers, clamp plates (6) and steering wheel shaft. Disconnect drag link from sector arm (17). Remove support bracket bolts and gear case mounting bolts, then lower gear case assembly from tractor.

#### Models 130-160-165-175-180-185

To remove steering gear assembly, remove bolt (3—Fig. JD11) and lift steering wheel off shaft. Raise the hood, disconnect battery cables and remove battery. Disconnect all wires from dash.

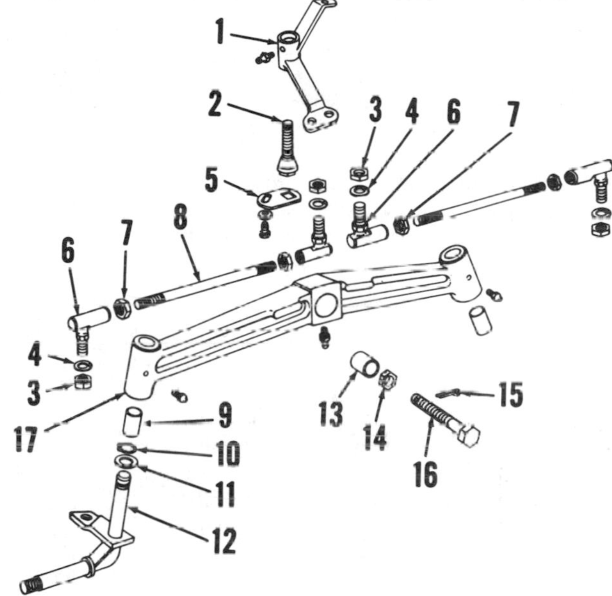


*Fig. JD5—Exploded view of front axle assembly used on Models 120 and 140. Axle assembly used on Models 300, 312 and 316 is similar except spindle bushings (9) are not used.*

1. Steering arm
2. Bolt & cone assy.
3. Nut
4. Lockwasher
5. Lock plate
6. Ball joint
7. Jam nut
8. Tie rod
9. Bushing
10. Snap ring
11. Washer
12. Steering spindle
13. Bushing
14. Nut
15. Cotter pin
16. Pivot bolt
17. Axle

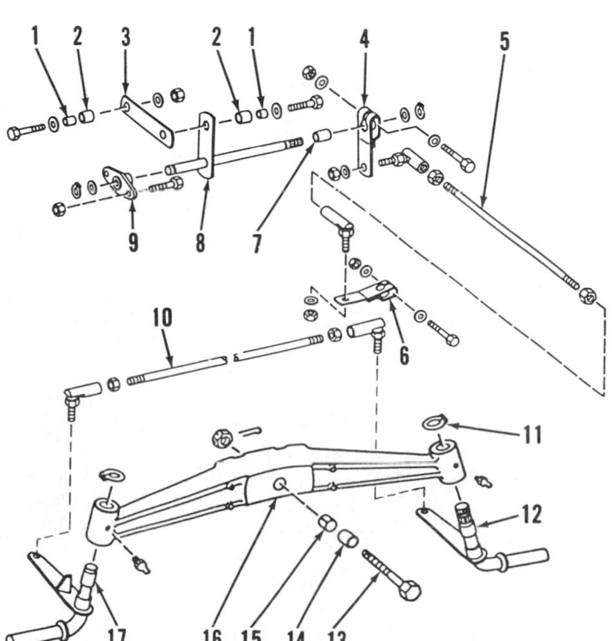

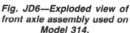

*Fig. JD6—Exploded view of front axle assembly used on Model 314.*

1. Bushing
2. Bearing
3. Link
4. Steering arm (rear)
5. Drag link
6. Steering arm (front)
7. Bushing
8. Pivot shaft
9. Bearing
10. Tie rod
11. Snap ring
12. Steering spindle L.H.
13. Pivot bolt
14. Bushing
15. Spacer
16. Axle main member
17. Steering spindle R.H.

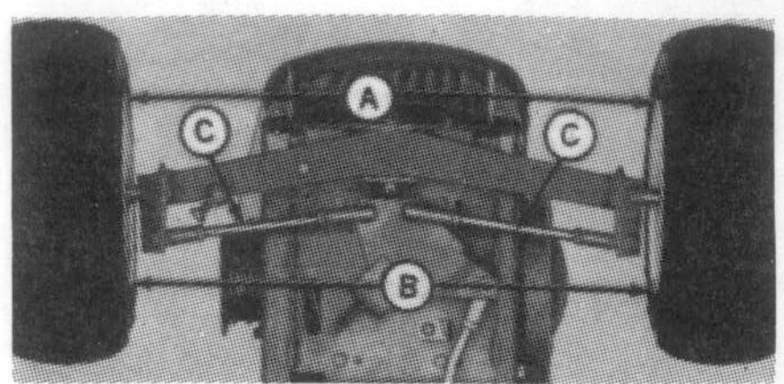


*Fig. JD7—On models equipped with adjustable tie rods (C), toe-in is correct when distance (A) is 3/16 inch (5 mm) less than distance (B).*

Disconnect throttle control cable. Remove nuts retaining dash panel and lift dash off steering shaft. Remove cotter pins (5 and 10). Drive steering shaft (4) up through pinion gear (11) and remove gear, bearings (2 and 8), washers (7), spring (6) and steering shaft.

Disconnect drag link from sector shaft (20). Remove shaft support (17) retaining nuts, then unbolt and remove sector gear support (12) and sector gear (15) assembly.

To reinstall steering gear assembly, reverse the disassembly procedure while noting the following special instructions. Be sure that mark on sector gear (15) is aligned with mark on sector shaft (20). When installing pinion gear, make sure that mark (A—Fig. JD12) on pinion gear is aligned with mark (B) on sector gear. With dots aligned, front wheels should be in straight ahead position. If not, disconnect drag link from steering spindle and move wheels to straight ahead position. Adjust length of drag link so that ball joint end fits into steering spindle without moving front wheels. Reconnect drag link to spindle.

### All Other Models

To remove steering gear unit, pry emblem out of steering wheel and remove nut. Using a suitable puller, remove steering wheel. Disconnect drag link rear ball joint from lever arm (19—Fig. JD9). Remove battery, then remove clamp securing steering column to pedestal. Unbolt steering unit from frame, slide steering column down out of dash and remove steering gear assembly from underside of tractor.

## OVERHAUL

### Models 108-111

After removing steering gear case, remove gear case bolts and separate case by tapping lightly with a plastic hammer. Remove washers, gears and keys. Slide shafts out of case halves and support bracket.

Inspect bearing (16—Fig. JD10) for wear or looseness. Check leather disc (8) for deterioration. Inspect pinion shaft (9), sector shaft (17), pinion gear (12) and sector gear (13) for wear, damage or cracks.

To reassemble, reverse the disassembly procedure. Apply multipurpose grease on bearings and steering gear teeth.

### Models 130-160-165-175-180-185

To disassemble steering gear, remove cotter pins (16—Fig. JD11), washers (14), spring (13) and support (12) from sector shaft (20). Mark the sector gear and shaft to ensure correct alignment when reassembling, then remove bearing (8), washer (9) and gear (15) from shaft. Remove support (17) and bearing (19) from sector shaft.

Inspect bearings, springs, steering shaft, sector shaft and steering gears for wear or other damage and renew as necessary.

When reassembling, be sure that marks on sector gear and shaft are aligned.

### All Other Models

After removing steering gear assembly, remove lever arm and bolt (19—Fig. JD8 or JD9). Remove adjusting plug (1)

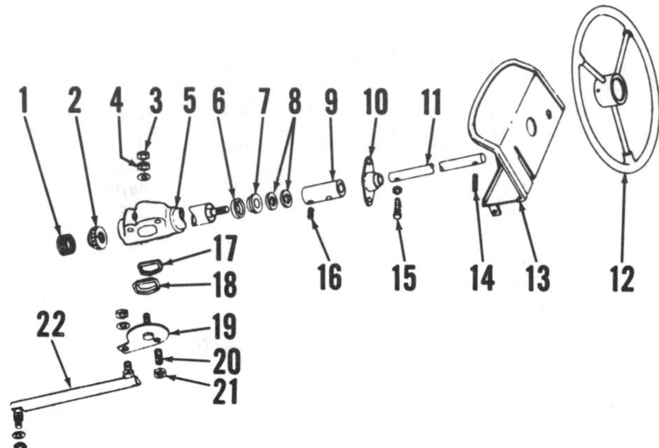

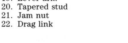

*Fig. JD8—Exploded view of steering gear used on Model 60.*

1. Adjusting plug
2. Bearing
3. Jam nut
4. Adjusting nut
5. Housing & shaft assy.
6. Bearing retainer
7. Bearing
8. Felt washers
9. Sleeve coupling
10. Upper shaft bearing
11. Upper steering shaft
12. Steering wheel
13. Dash panel
14. Groove pin
15. Cap screw
16. Set screw
17. Lever arm seal
18. Seal retainer
19. Lever arm
20. Tapered stud
21. Jam nut
22. Drag link

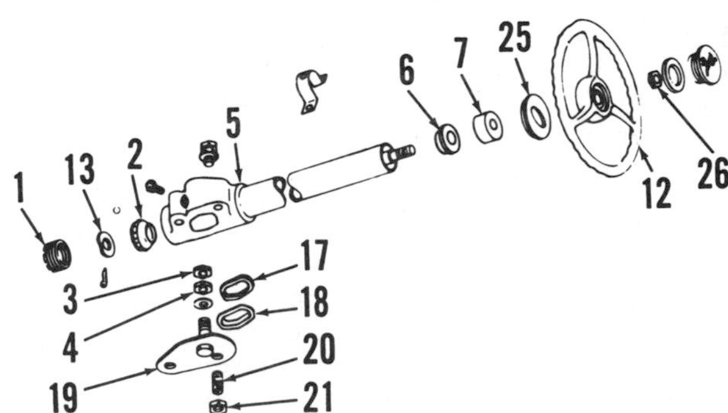

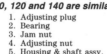

*Fig. JD9—Exploded view of steering gear used on 200 and 300 series tractors and Model 112. Models 70, 100, 110, 120 and 140 are similar.*

1. Adjusting plug
2. Bearing
3. Jam nut
4. Adjusting nut
5. Housing & shaft assy.
6. Bearing
7. Seal
12. Steering wheel
13. Spring washer
17. Lever arm seal
18. Seal retainer
19. Lever arm
20. Tapered stud
21. Jam nut
25. Grommet
26. Nut

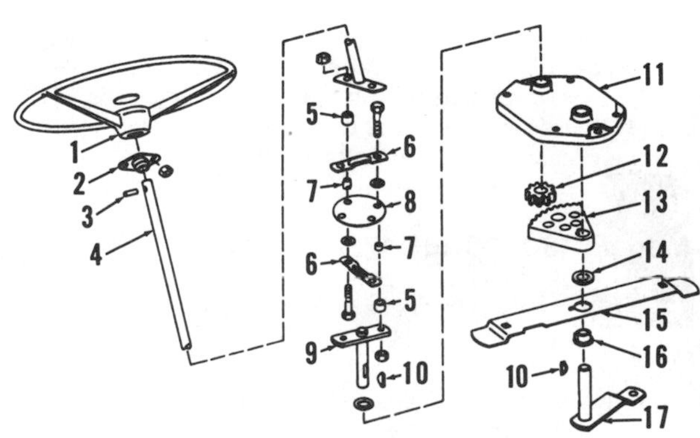

*Fig. JD10—Exploded view of steering gear used on Models 108 and 111.*

1. Steering wheel
2. Bearing
3. Pin
4. Steering shaft
5. Spacer (4 used)
6. "O" ring
7. Bushing (4 used)
8. Disc
9. Lower shaft
10. Key
11. Case assy.
12. Pinion gear
13. Sector gear
14. Washer
15. Support
16. Bearing
17. Lever arm

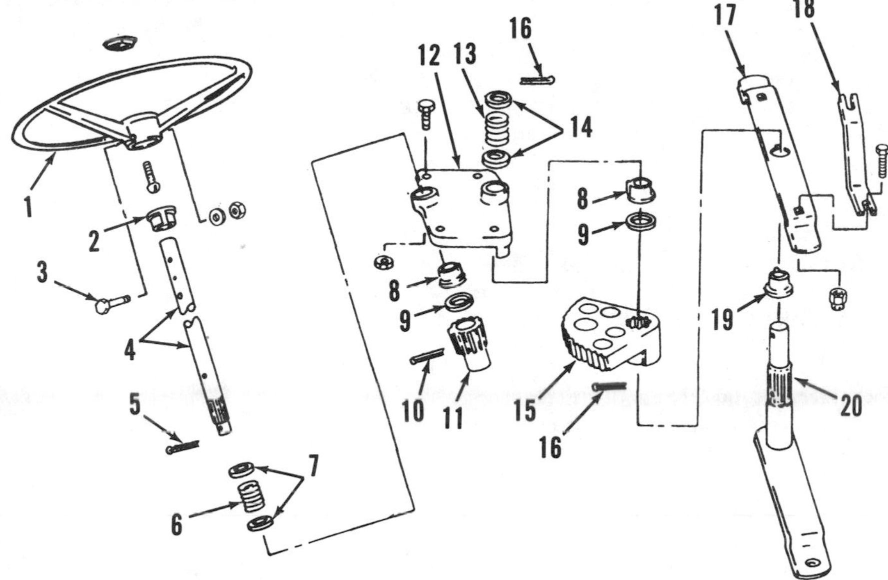


*Fig. JD11—Exploded view of steering gear used on Models 130, 160, 165, 175, 180 and 185.*

1. Steering wheel
2. Bushing
3. Bolt
4. Steering shaft
5. Cotter pin
6. Spring
7. Washers
8. Bushing
9. Washer
10. Cotter pin
11. Pinion gear
12. Support
13. Spring
14. Washers
15. Sector gear
16. Cotter pin
17. Sector shaft support
18. Strap
19. Bushing
20. Sector shaft

and bump worm shaft and bearing out of housing (5). Check all parts for excessive wear and renew as necessary.

When reassembling, install worm shaft and bearings in housing, then tighten adjusting plug (1) to remove all end play. The worm shaft must still rotate freely. Install cotter pin to prevent adjusting plug from working loose. Install lever arm and bolt assembly (19), seal (17) and seal retainer (18). Loosen jam nut (21) and turn tapered stud (20) out two turns. Tighten adjusting nut (4) on lever arm bolt to remove end play of bolt. At this time, distance between lever arm and housing should be $^{1}/_{16}$ to $^{3}/_{32}$ inch (1.5-2.5 mm). Tighten jam nut (3) to 22-25 ft.-lbs. (30-34 N·m) torque. Set lever arm in center position (half way between full right and full left turn). Turn tapered stud (20) in to remove all backlash. Tighten jam nut to a torque of 40 ft.-lbs. (54 N·m).

When properly adjusted, a slight drag can be detected as lever arm passes mid-position each time unit is turned through full steering range. Lubricate steering unit with approximately $^{1}/_{4}$ pound (120 mL) multipurpose grease.

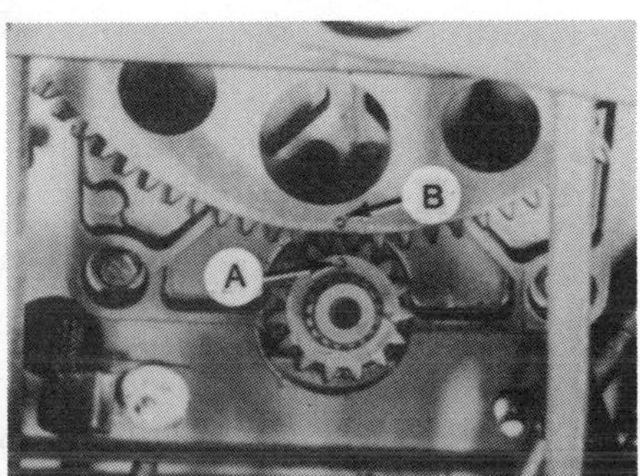


*Fig. JD12—When assembling steering gears on Models 130, 160, 165, 175, 180 and 185, make sure that dot (A) on pinion gear is aligned with dot (B) on sector gear.*

# ENGINE

## REMOVE AND REINSTALL

### Models 60-70

To remove engine, disconnect fuel line, then unbolt and remove hood, grille and fuel tank. Disconnect battery ground cable, starting motor cable, choke-throttle control cable and wires from rectifier panel. Detach spring from primary idler to relieve tension on primary belt. Remove spring locking pin and disconnect pto clutch arm. Slip primary drive belt from engine pulley. Unbolt engine from frame and lift engine from tractor.

To reinstall engine, reverse removal procedure.

### Models 100-110-112

To remove engine, first remove grille, hood, grille cowls and engine shields. Disconnect battery ground cable, flexible fuel line at tank connection, ignition wire from coil and wires from starter-generator. Remove fuel tank. Disconnect choke and throttle control cables from engine. Detach pto linkage and wires on electric pto if so equipped. Remove pto unit. Remove drive belts as outlined in DRIVE BELTS section. Unbolt engine from frame and lift engine assembly from tractor.

To reinstall engine, reverse removal procedure.

### Models 108-111

To remove engine, remove hood assembly. Disconnect battery cables, engine wiring and throttle cable. Remove fuel line at carburetor and drain fuel tank. Mark position of front bumper, then remove bumper. Remove muffler and exhaust pipe. Detach pto linkage and wires on electric pto if so equipped. Remove pto unit. Remove drive belt as outlined in DRIVE BELTS section. Remove crankshaft pulley and key. Unbolt engine and rotate engine to free oil drain while lifting engine out.

### Models 120-140

To remove engine, remove hood and grille as a unit. Disconnect fuel line and remove fuel tank. Disconnect battery cables, ignition wires and starter-generator wires. Remove battery and battery base. Disconnect choke and throttle cables. Remove two cap screws to free drive shaft from clutch cone. Remove engine mounting cap screws and lift engine from tractor.

To reinstall engine, reverse removal procedure.

### Models 130-160-165-175-180-185

To remove engine, first remove hood, muffler and pedestal shroud. Disconnect battery ground cable. Close fuel shut-off valve and disconnect fuel line. Disconnect throttle control cable. Disconnect ground wire, starter wires and ignition wires from engine. Remove electric pto clutch. Relieve tension on traction drive belt and remove belt from drive pulley. Remove drive pulley and key from engine crankshaft. Remove engine mounting cap screws, rotate engine to clear oil drain hole in frame and lift engine from tractor.

To reinstall engine, reverse the removal procedure. Apply an anti-seize lubricant to crankshaft before installing drive pulley. Tighten pto clutch mounting cap screw to 45 ft.-lbs. (56 N·m).

### Models 200-208-210-212-214-216

To remove engine, remove grille, hood and side panels. Disconnect battery cables, engine wiring harness and starter lead. Shut off fuel at tank and disconnect fuel line at fuel pump. Remove air cleaner assembly and disconnect throttle and choke cables. Disconnect pto linkage and remove clutch. Remove crankshaft pulley bolt, depress clutch and slide pulley and belt off end of crankshaft. Remove engine mounting bolts and lift engine from tractor.

To reinstall engine, reverse the removal procedure.

### Models 300-312-314-316

To remove engine, remove grille, hood and hood support. Remove air cleaner assembly. Shut off fuel at tank and disconnect fuel line at fuel pump. Disconnect throttle cable and choke cable. Disconnect battery cables, engine wiring harness, starter cable and electric pto clutch wire. Disconnect drive shaft at rear of engine. Remove engine mounting bolts and lift engine from frame using suitable hoist.

To reinstall engine, reverse the removal procedure.

## OVERHAUL

### All Models

Engine make and model are listed at the beginning of this section. To overhaul engine components and accessories, refer to appropriate Briggs & Stratton, Kawasaki, Kohler or Tecumseh section of this manual.

# CLUTCH AND BRAKE

### Models 60-70-100

**OPERATION.** The clutch and brake are operated by a clutch-brake pedal on left side of tractor, except on later models which have separate pedals. When pedal is depressed, clutch idler (11—Fig. JD13 or JD14) releases tension on secondary drive belt and allows countershaft pulley (15) to turn freely within secondary belt. As belt tension is released, brake band (2—Fig. JD15 or JD15A) is pulled tight on brake drum and tractor motion is stopped. Model 60 tractors with serial numbers prior to 20001 were equipped with step sheaves on countershaft and transaxle which provide a high-low speed range.

**ADJUSTMENT.** Clutch idler pulley is spring loaded, but requires adjustment on models with clutch-brake pedal when secondary belt idler pulley drops low enough to strike lower belt guide as clutch-brake pedal is depressed. To make adjustment, turn adjusting nut on brake linkage (early Model 60) or on brake band (2—Fig. JD15) until idler does not strike guide. Depress clutch-brake pedal and make certain clutch idler releases secondary belt tension before brake is applied.

**CAUTION: Over-tightening brake adjustment can cause simultaneous braking and driving action which can seriously damage transaxle unit.**

On later Model 70 and all 100 tractors with separate brake and clutch pedals, brake is adjusted by removing spring pin

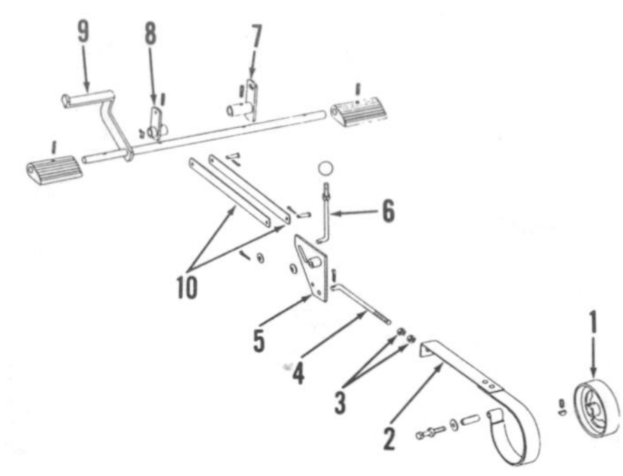


*Fig. JD15—Exploded view of typical brake linkage used on Models 60 and early 70 tractors (prior to S.N. 50001).*

1. Brake drum
2. Brake band
3. Adjusting nuts
4. Brake rod
5. Pivot plate
6. Parking brake lever
7. Clutch arm
8. Brake arm
9. Clutch-brake pedal
10. Brake straps

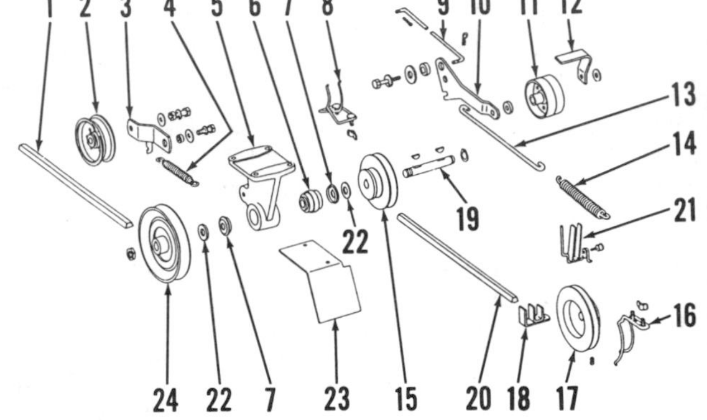


*Fig. JD13—Exploded view of clutch assembly used on early Model 60 tractors (prior to S.N. 20001). Countershaft sheave (15) is equipped with renewable bearing (6).*

1. Primary belt
2. Front idler
3. Idler arm
4. Idler spring
5. Countershaft support
6. Bearing assy.
7. Seal
8. Belt guide (front)
9. Clutch rod
10. Clutch idler arm
11. Clutch idler
12. Belt guide
13. Link
14. Idler spring
15. Countershaft sheave
16. Belt guide (rear)
17. Transaxle sheave
18. Belt guide (lower)
19. Countershaft
20. Secondary belt
21. Belt guide (upper)
22. Washer
23. Shield
24. Driven pulley

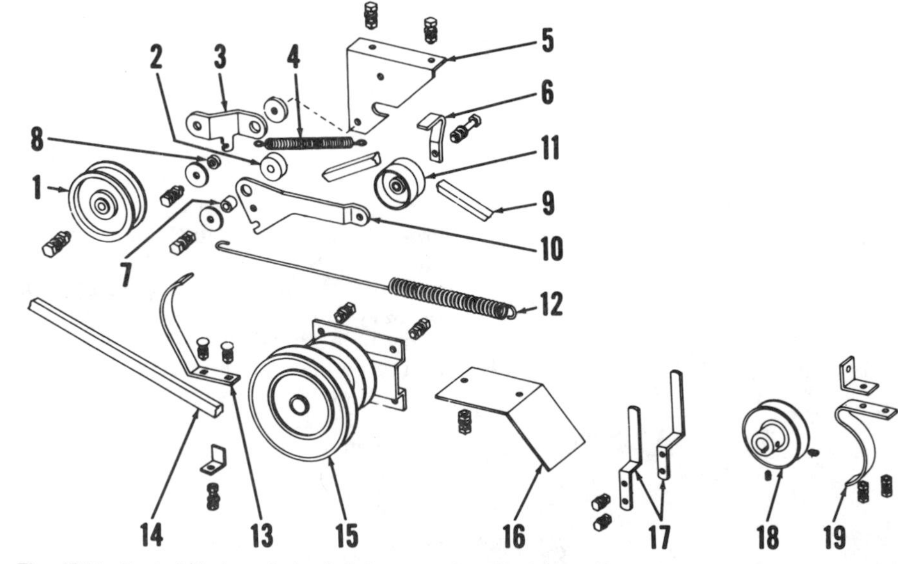


*Fig. JD14—Exploded view of clutch linkage used on Models 60 (S.N. 20001 and after), 70 and 100.*

1. Idler pulley
2. Spacer
3. Arm
4. Spring
5. Bracket
6. Belt guide
7. Bearing
8. Bearing
9. Secondary drive belt
10. Clutch idler arm
11. Idler pulley
12. Spring
13. Belt guide
14. Primary drive belt
15. Counter sheave assy.
16. Belt guard
17. Belt guides
18. Transmission drive pulley
19. Belt guide

and turning brake rod (5—Fig. JD15A) into brake strap (4) to tighten brake.

## Models 108-111-130-160-180

**OPERATION.** The clutch and brake are operated by separate pedals. When clutch pedal is depressed, bellcrank assembly (8—Fig. JD16) pivots and loosens drive belt from drive pulleys stopping forward or reverse movement.

**ADJUSTMENT.** To adjust clutch, stop engine and put transmission in gear. Loosen center nut on front idler pulley (7—Fig. JD16). Turn adjusting bolt (20) in or out until there is 3.7 inches (94 mm) between inside of frame and inner surface of flat idler (5). Adjust belt guide (21) to provide $^{3}/_{16}$ inch (5 mm) clearance between guide and belt.

To adjust brake, first be sure that parking brake is not engaged. Use a feeler gage to measure clearance between brake pad and brake disc. Clearance should be 0.020 inch (0.50 mm). Turn adjusting nut on brake lever (13—Fig. JD17) to obtain clearance.

**R&R AND OVERHAUL.** Raise and support rear of tractor and remove right rear wheel. Disconnect brake rod (12—Fig. JD17) from brake lever (13). Unbolt and remove caliper assembly (14). Withdraw brake disc (17) and inner brake pad from transaxle.

Inspect parts and renew as necessary. Reassemble in reverse of disassembly procedure and adjust as outlined in ADJUSTMENT paragraph.

## Model 120

**OPERATION.** Model 120 is equipped with a cone type clutch and automotive type drum brake. See Figs. JD18 and JD20. The clutch and brake are actuated by clutch-brake pedal on left side of tractor. As pedal is depressed to engage brake, a neutral cam attached to pedal linkage returns hydrostatic transmission to neutral.

**ADJUSTMENT.** To check clutch adjustment, measure clearance between clutch throw-out arm (7—Fig. JD18) and throw-out bearing (11) with clutch-brake pedal in engaged (up) position. Clearance should be $^{1}/_{32}$ to $^{1}/_{16}$ inch (0.8-1.5 mm) as shown in Fig. JD19. To make clutch adjustment, remove battery and base. Loosen nut and move adjusting bolt as shown in Fig. JD20 until correct adjustment is obtained. Retighten nut securely.

To adjust brake, remove clip and pin at end of brake rod and turn clevis. Brake should be adjusted so brake is engaged when clutch-brake pedal is fully

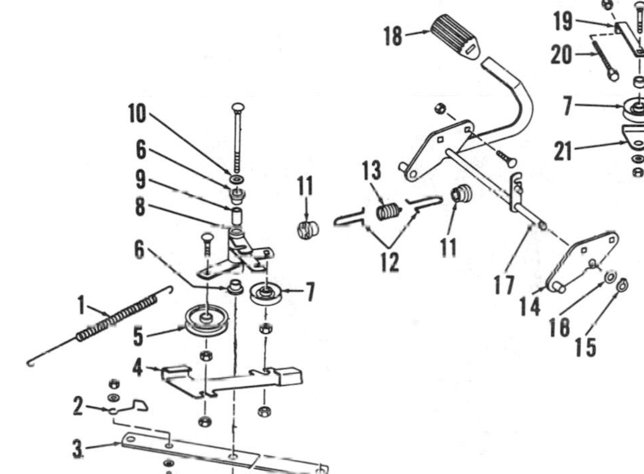

*Fig. JD16—Exploded view of clutch and bellcrank assembly used on Models 108 an 111. Clutch and bellcrank assembly used on Models 130, 160 and 180 is similar.*

1. Spring
2. Belt guide
3. Support
4. Belt guard
5. Flat idler pulley
6. Bushing
7. "V" idler pulley
8. Bellcrank
9. Bushing
10. Washer
11. Cap
12. Link
13. Spring
14. Mounting bracket
15. Snap ring
16. Washer
17. Clutch shaft
18. Pad
19. Adjusting link
20. Adjusting bolt
21. Belt guard

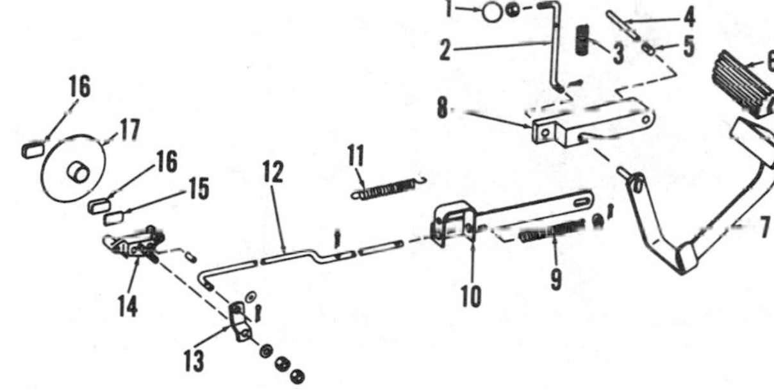

*Fig. JD17—Exploded view of brake linkage used on Models 108 and 111.*

1. Knob
2. Parking brake rod
3. Spring
4. Pin
5. Spacer
6. Pad
7. Brake pedal assy.
8. Latch
9. Spring
10. Strap
11. Spring
12. Brake rod
13. Brake lever
14. Caliper
15. Plate
16. Brake pads
17. Rotor

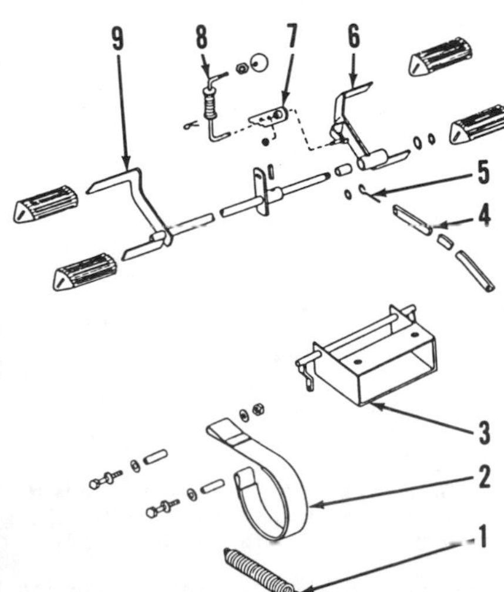

*Fig. JD15A—Exploded view of brake linkage used on late Model 70 (after S.N.50000) and Model 100.*

1. Return spring
2. Brake band
3. Pedestal & brake rod
4. Brake strap
5. Brake rod
6. Brake pedal
7. Locking pawl
8. Parking brake lever
9. Clutch pedal

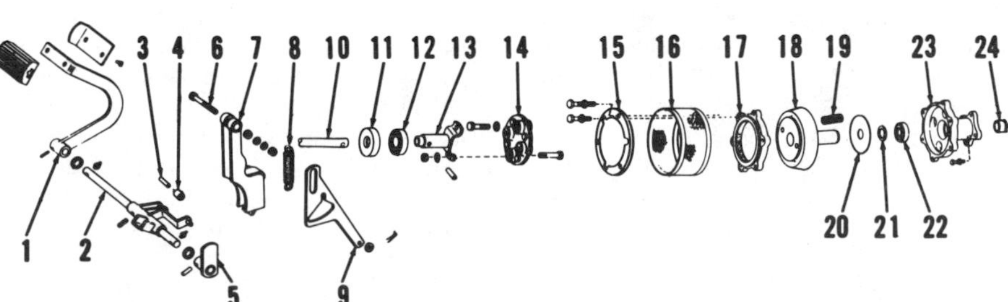

*Fig. JD18—Exploded view of clutch assembly used on Models 120 and 140.*

1. Clutch pedal
2. Shaft
3. Spring pin
4. Roller
5. Brake arm
6. Pivot bolt
7. Clutch arm
8. Spring
9. Transmission neutral arm
10. Drive shaft
11. Bearing cap
12. Bearing
13. Drive hub
14. Front hub
15. Screen cap
16. Screen
17. Clutch cup
18. Clutch cone & shaft
19. Spring (4 used)
20. Large washer
21. Small washer
22. Bearing
23. Drive hub
24. Bushing

depressed, but brake should not engage before clutch is disengaged.

**R&R AND OVERHAUL CLUTCH.** To remove clutch, remove engine as previously outlined and remove clutch assembly. Clutch throw-out bearing may also be serviced at this time. Inspect components for excessive wear or damage. Uneven wear of clutch cup lining (17—Fig. JD18) may indicate excessive clearance between clutch cone shaft and bushing (24). Adequately support drive hub (23) to prevent cracking when pressing against bushing (24). Bronze bushing inside diameter is 1.004 inches (25.5 mm) while bushing outside diameter is 1.254 inches (31.85 mm). Outside diameter of clutch cone shaft is 0.999 inch (25. 37 mm). Clutch springs should test 64-71 pounds (280-316 N) when compressed to a length of 1.125 inches (28 mm).

To reassemble clutch, reverse disassembly procedure. When installing bushing (24) in drive hub, refer to Fig. JD21 for bushing location. Tighten drive hub-to-flywheel cap screws to 20 ft.-lbs. (27 N·m). Install $1^{3}/_{4}$ inch cap screws spaced evenly in clutch cup (17—Fig. JD18) to pull cup and drive hub together. Install end cap (15) and screen (16) using $1^{1}/_{4}$ inch cap screws. Tighten all cup cap screws to 20 ft.-lbs. (27 N·m). Adjust clutch as outlined in ADJUSTMENT paragraph.

**R&R AND OVERHAUL BRAKES.** Model 120 is equipped with a drum and shoe type brake. To disassemble brake, support rear of tractor and remove wheel. Remove wheel hub (17—Fig. JD22) and using a suitable puller, remove brake drum (16). Remainder of disassembly is self-evident after inspection of assembly.

Renew any components showing excessive wear. Be sure wheel hub seal and back plate (11) are properly aligned on axle housing flange before tightening back plate retaining nuts to 15 ft.-lbs. (20 N·m). After assembly, adjust brake as previously outlined.

*Fig. JD19—Bottom view showing correct clutch adjustment on Models 120 and 140.*

*Fig. JD20—To adjust clutch action on Models 120 and 140, loosen nut and move adjusting bolt (6—Fig. JD18). Refer to text for details.*

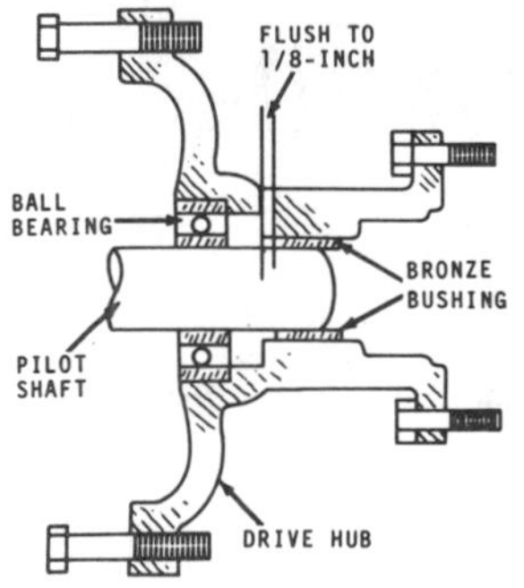


*Fig. JD21—Press bearing (24—Fig. JD18) into drive hub (23) until bushing is seated as shown in above drawing.*

## Model 140

**OPERATION.** Model 140-H1 tractors with S.N. 10001 through 38000 and Model 140-H3 tractors with S.N. 30001 through 46883 are equipped with a cone type engine disconnect clutch. The clutch is operated by a foot pedal on left side of tractor. See Fig. JD18.

Model 140 tractors with S.N. 10001 through 30000 are equipped with disc brakes at each rear wheel. Brakes are operated by individual pedals which can be locked together. Model 140-H1 tractors with S.N. 30001 through 38000 and S.N. 46604 and later and Model 140-H3 tractors with S.N. 30001 and later are equipped with automotive type drum and shoe brakes at each rear wheel. Brakes are operated by individual brake pedals which can be locked together. Model 140-H1 tractors with S.N. 38001 through 46603 are equipped with a single automotive type drum and shoe brake located at right rear wheel. Brake is operated by brake-neutral return pedal on left side of tractor.

**CLUTCH ADJUSTMENT.** To check clutch adjustment, measure clearance between clutch release arm (7—Fig. JD18) and release bearing retainer (11) with clutch pedal in engaged (up) position. Clearance should be $^{1}/_{32}$ to $^{1}/_{16}$ inch (0.8-1.5 mm). See Fig. JD19. To adjust clearance, remove battery and battery base plate. Loosen nut and move adjusting bolt as shown in Fig. JD20 until correct adjustment is obtained. Tighten nut securely.

**BRAKE ADJUSTMENT.** To adjust disc brakes on Model 140 with S.N. 10001 through 30000, support rear of tractor so rear wheels are free to turn. Open free-wheeling valve on transmission. Loosen locknuts (12—Fig. JD23), remove pin (9) from clevis (11) on both brakes. Adjust clevis on right brake rod (14) until a slight drag is felt when rotating wheel (brake rod reconnected). Then, back off clevis just enough to remove all drag. Reconnect brake rod and tighten locknut. Repeat procedure on left brake. Brakes should be adjusted equally so both brakes will be applied simultaneously when pedals are locked together.

To adjust brake on Model 140 with S.N. 38001 through 46603, first disconnect clevis (3—Fig. JD22) from brake arm (8). Pull top of brake arm forward. Brake should be applied when brake arm is in vertical position. If not, loosen clamp (9) and readjust position of brake arm on cam (12). Tighten clamp. Adjust clevis (3) on brake rod (7) so brake will be applied immediately after brake-neutral return pedal has moved hydrostatic control to neutral position.

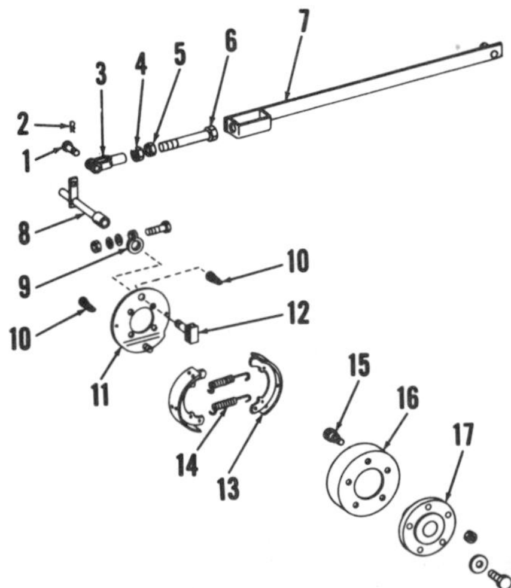


*Fig. JD22—Exploded view of typical drum and shoe brake assembly used on Model 120. Brake assembly used on Model 140 (S.N. 30001 and later) is similar.*

1. Pin
2. Clip
3. Clevis
4. Adjusting nut
5. Locknut
6. Bolt
7. Brake rod
8. Brake arm
9. Clamp
10. Spring
11. Back plate
12. Cam
13. Brake shoe
14. Return spring
15. Wheel stud
16. Brake drum
17. Wheel hub

On all other Model 140 tractors equipped with drum and shoe brakes at both rear wheels, adjust brakes as follows: First disconnect clevis (3—Fig. JD22) from brake arm (8) on each brake. Pull top of brake arms forward. Brakes should be applied when brake arms are in vertical position. If not, loosen clamp (9) and readjust position of brake arms on cam (12). Lock brake pedals together. Adjust clevis (3) on each brake rod (7) until both brakes are fully applied when pedals are depressed to a point where park lock will engage in second notch.

**R&R AND OVERHAUL.** To remove clutch, first remove engine and clutch assembly as outlined in ENGINE paragraph. Unbolt and remove ring and screen (15 and 16—Fig. JD18), then remove four cap screws securing drive hub (23) to engine flywheel. Lift clutch assembly from engine. Unbolt clutch cap (17) and separate clutch cone (18), four springs (19), washer (20) and spacer (21) from drive hub (23). To remove clutch release bearing (12), drive out roll pin and remove drive yoke (13) from drive shaft (10). Remove bearing from yoke.

Clean and inspect all parts and renew any showing excessive wear or other damage. Uneven wear of clutch cup lining may indicate excessive clearance between clutch cone shaft and bushing (24). Adequately support drive hub (23) and press ball bearing (22) and bushing (24) from hub. Bushing inside diameter is 1.004 inches (25.5 mm) and outside diameter is 1.254 inches (31.85 mm). Outside diameter of clutch cone shaft is 0.999 inch (25.37 mm). Clutch springs should test 64-71 pounds (280-316 N) when compressed to a length of $1\frac{1}{8}$ inches (28 mm).

To reassemble clutch, reverse disassembly procedure. When installing bushing (24) in drive hub (23), refer to Fig. JD21 for bushing location. Tighten drive hub to flywheel cap screws to a torque of 20 ft.-lbs. (27 N·m). Install three evenly spaced $1\frac{3}{4}$ inch long cap screws in clutch cup (17—Fig. JD18) to pull cup and drive hub together. Then, install ring (15) and screen (16) using $1\frac{1}{4}$ inch long cap screws. Tighten all clutch cup cap screws to 20 ft.-lbs. (27 N·m).

With engine and clutch assembly reinstalled, adjust clutch as required.

**OVERHAUL (DISC BRAKE).** To disassemble brakes, support rear of tractor and remove rear wheels. Disconnect clevis (11—Fig. JD23) from actuating cam (10). Remove cap screws (7), then remove cam plate (1), cam (10), brake pads (3 and 6), spacers (2) and springs (5).

Clean and inspect all parts and renew any showing excessive wear or other damage. Thickness of new brake pads is ¼ inch (6.35 mm). Pads should be renewed when worn to a thickness of 1/8 inch (3.2 mm) or less. If disc (4) is damaged, use a suitable puller to remove wheel hub, then unbolt disc from hub.

When reassembling, tighten disc retaining cap screws to a torque of 10 ft.-lbs. (14 N·m) and wheel hub retaining nut to 250 in.-lbs. (28 N·m). Adjust brakes as required.

## Models 165-175-185 (Prior to S.N. 475000)

**OPERATION.** These tractors are equipped with hydrostatic drive and do not use an engine disconnect clutch. A disc type brake is located on left side of rear axle housing. As brake pedal is depressed, the brake is actuated and the hydrostatic transmission control linkage is returned to neutral position.

**ADJUSTMENT.** To adjust brakes, first make sure park brake is not engaged. Use a feeler gage to measure clearance between brake pad and brake disc. Clearance should be 0.020 inch (0.50 mm). Turn adjusting nut (10—Fig. JD24) on brake lever (11) to obtain correct clearance.

**R&R AND OVERHAUL.** Raise and support rear of tractor and remove left rear wheel. Disconnect brake rod (9—Fig. JD24). Remove retaining cap screws and withdraw brake holder (15), plate (16) and outer brake pad (17). Slide brake disc (18) against frame and remove inner brake pad. To remove brake disc, rear axle housing must be lowered to provide clearance disc removal.

Inspect parts and renew as necessary. Reassemble in reverse of disassembly procedure. Adjust brake as outlined in ADJUSTMENT paragraph.

## Model 185 (S.N. 147000 and After)

**OPERATION.** The brake assembly is mounted internally in the rear axle housing. As brake pedal is depressed, the brake is applied, the hydrostatic transmission control linkage is returned

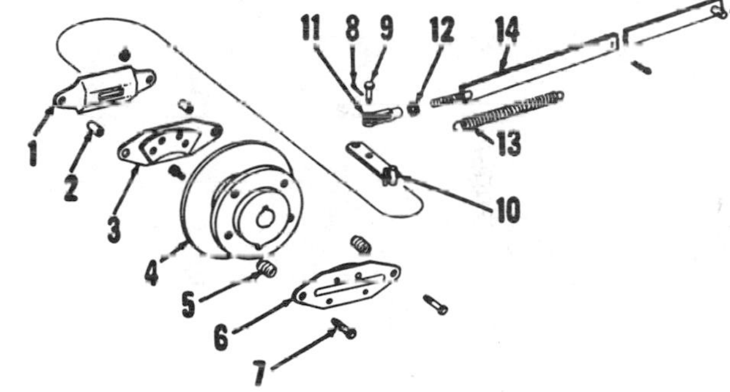


*Fig. JD23—Exploded view of disc brake assembly used on Model 140 tractors with S.N. 10001 through 30000. Disc brakes are used on both rear wheels.*

1. Cam plate
2. Spacer
3. Brake pad (inner)
4. Disc & hub
5. Spring
6. Brake pad (outer)
7. Cap screw
8. Clip
9. Pin
10. Actuating cam
11. Clevis
12. Locknut
13. Spring
14. Brake rod

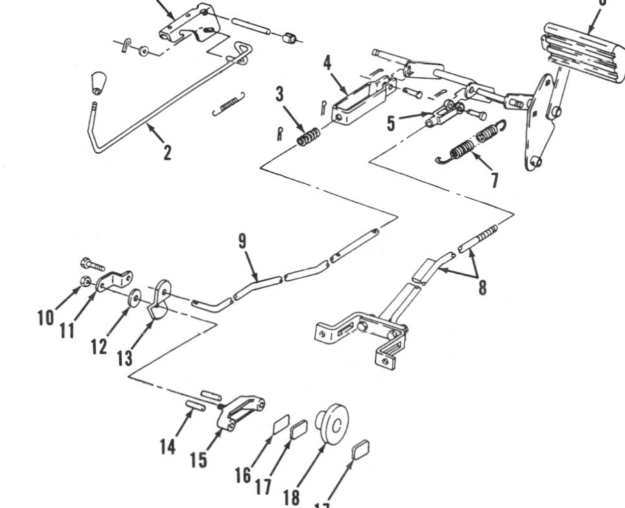


*Fig. JD24—Exploded view of brake linkage and neutral return linkage used on Models 165, 175 and 185 (prior to S.N. 475001).*

1. Park brake latch
2. Park brake rod
3. Spring
4. Yoke
5. Yoke
6. Brake pedal
7. Return spring
8. Neutral return linkage
9. Brake rod
10. Adjusting nut
11. Bracket
12. Washer
13. Brake lever
14. Brake actuator pins
15. Brake holder
16. Plate
17. Brake pads
18. Brake disc

to neutral position and the bellcrank assembly (5—Fig. JD26) pivots and loosens drive belt from drive pulley.

**ADJUSTMENT.** There is no adjustment required for drive belt bellcrank assembly or for the transmission brake.

**OVERHAUL.** Removal and installation of brake components are covered in DIFFERENTIAL service section.

## Model 208

**OPERATION.** The clutch and brake are operated by separate pedals. When clutch pedal is depressed, clutch pulley releases tension on secondary belt and allows drive pulley to turn free within the belt. As brake pedal is depressed, brake band is pulled tight on brake drum and tractor motion is stopped.

**ADJUSTMENT.** Clutch idler pulley is spring loaded and requires no adjustment. To adjust brake, disconnect brake rod clevis from brake shaft. Turn clevis on brake rod as necessary to tighten brake. Test operation on level surface at slow speed. Brake is properly adjusted if strong resistance is encountered when pedal is depressed approximately one inch (25 mm) from deck.

**R&R AND OVERHAUL.** Raise and support rear of tractor. Remove left rear wheel. Remove pin attaching brake arm to brake band link. Remove brake band bracket mounting cap screws through two access holes in left side of frame. Slip brake band off the brake pulley. To remove brake pulley, remove pulley set screw and use a suitable puller to remove pulley from transaxle brake shaft.

To reinstall, reverse the removal procedure.

## Models 300-312-314-316

**OPERATION.** These tractors are equipped with hydrostatic drive and do not use an engine disconnect clutch. Individual drum type brakes, located at each rear wheel, are used on all models. On Models 300 and 316, separate brake pedals are used for each rear wheel. On Models 312 and 314, a single brake pedal is used to actuate both brakes simultaneously.

**ADJUSTMENT.** To adjust brakes, remove pin (1—Fig. JD27) and turn yoke (2) to lengthen or shorten brake link (4). Adjust brakes so both rear wheels are locked when brake pedal or pedals are engaged in second notch of parking brake latch.

**R&R AND OVERHAUL.** Raise and support rear of tractor and remove rear wheels. Remove hub retaining nut (8—Fig. JD27) and pull brake drum (5) us-

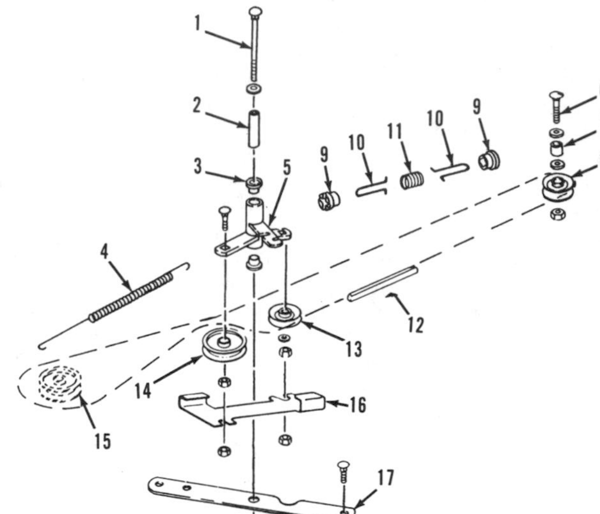

***Fig. JD26—Exploded view of clutch and bellcrank assembly used on Model 185 (S.N. 475001 and later).***

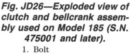

1. Bolt
2. Bushing
3. Bushing
4. Spring
5. Bellcrank
6. Bolt
7. Spacer
8. Pulley
9. Cap
10. Link
11. Spring
12. Drive belt
13. Idler pulley
14. Idler pulley
15. Pulley
16. Belt guard
17. Support

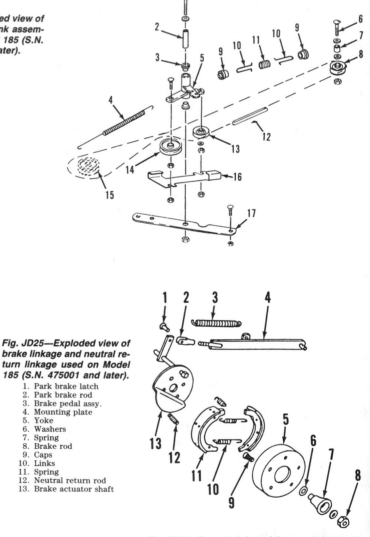

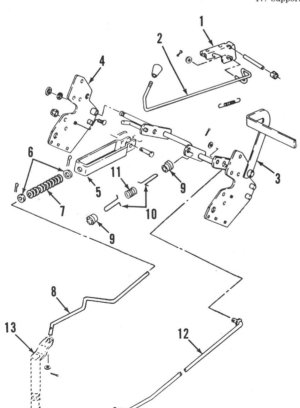

***Fig. JD25—Exploded view of brake linkage and neutral return linkage used on Model 185 (S.N. 475001 and later).***

1. Park brake latch
2. Park brake rod
3. Brake pedal assy.
4. Mounting plate
5. Yoke
6. Washers
7. Spring
8. Brake rod
9. Caps
10. Links
11. Spring
12. Neutral return rod
13. Brake actuator shaft

***Fig. JD27—Exploded view of drum and shoe brake assembly used on Models 300, 312, 314 and 316.***

1. Pin
2. Yoke
3. Return spring
4. Brake link
5. Brake drum
6. Felt seal
7. Hub
8. Retaining nut
9. Wheel stud
10. Return springs
11. Brake shoes
12. Hold-down springs
13. Back plate

ing a suitable puller. Disconnect springs (10 and 12) and remove brake shoes (11).

Inspect all parts for excessive wear or other damage and renew as necessary. Reassemble in reverse order of disassembly. Tighten hub retaining nut to 35-40 ft.-lbs. (47-54 N·m). Adjust brakes as previously outlined.

# CLUTCH, BRAKE AND VARIABLE DRIVE

## Models 110-112-200-210-212-214-216

**OPERATION.** A variable pulley, belt drive system is used on all 110, 112, 200, 210, 212, 214 and 216 models. On early models, clutch and brake are actuated by one pedal while clutch and brake on later models are operated by separate pedals. Depressing clutch pedal will move variator pulleys forward and release tension on primary drive belt, thereby allowing engine pulley to turn free on belt. Fully depressing clutch-brake pedal on early models will actuate rear brake.

## Models 110 and 112 Prior to S.N. 100,001

**ADJUSTMENT.** If tractor will not operate with variable speed control lever in notch 1 (rear position on quadrant), refer to Fig. JD28 and adjust linkage as follows:

Remove inspection plate from adjusting hole in pedestal and remove pin (B). Move variable speed lever to notch 5 on quadrant. Remove brake rod pin (D). Disconnect and ground spark plug wire, then crank engine several revolutions with starter. Measure distance (F) between footrest and clutch-brake arm. This distance should be 1/2 inch (13 mm). If not, insert a tapered punch or narrow screwdriver until distance (F) is exactly 1/2 inch (13 mm). Hold link (A) to top of slot and turn clevis up or down as required until pin (B) can be easily inserted. Secure pin (B) with spring locking pin and install inspection plate. Install pin (D) temporarily and while cranking engine several times with starter, move variable speed control lever to notch 1 (slow position). Depress clutch-brake pedal as far as possible and measure distance between footrest and clutch-brake pedal. This distance should be 3/4 inch (19 mm). If clearance is more or less than 3/4 inch (19 mm), adjust brake rod (G) until proper clearance is obtained. Secure pin (D) with spring locking pin and connect spark plug wire.

## Models 110 and 112 After S.N. 100,000

**ADJUSTMENT.** Models 110 and 112 after S.N. 100,000 are equipped with variable drive system shown in Fig. JD29. Some models have a clutch-brake pedal, while later models have separate clutch and brake pedals.

If tractor will not operate with variable drive lever in slow position (rear notch), clutch or clutch-brake pedal must be adjusted. Place variable drive lever in third notch from front. Remove adjusting hole plug from right side of console and loosen adjusting screw (3—Fig. JD29) as shown in Fig. JD31. Disconnect and ground spark plug wire. Turn engine several revolutions with electric starter until clutch or clutch-brake pedal comes up as high as it will go. Center the adjusting screw (3—Fig. JD29) in adjusting hole and tighten the adjusting screw. Check tractor operation. If tractor does not operate at slow speed after clutch adjustment, primary drive belt is stretched and must be renewed.

Brake adjustment is accomplished by disconnecting clevis in brake linkage and turning clevis to effectively lengthen or shorten brake rod. On models with a clutch-brake pedal, distance between pedal and foot rest should not be less than 3/4 inch (19 mm) with pedal fully

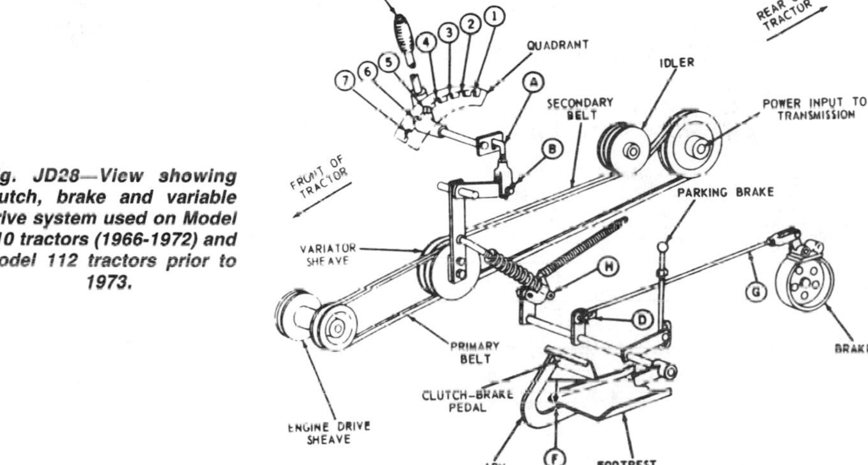


*Fig. JD28—View showing clutch, brake and variable drive system used on Model 110 tractors (1966-1972) and Model 112 tractors prior to 1973.*

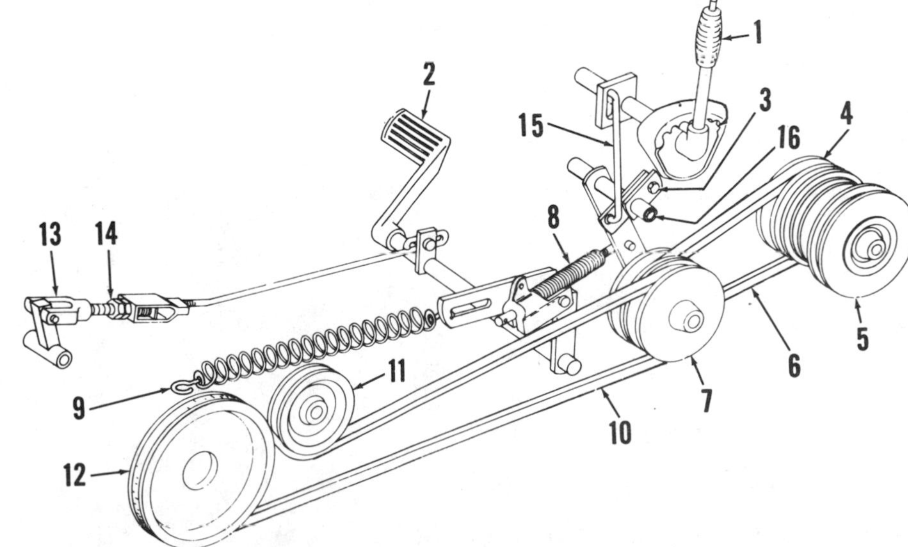

*Fig. JD29—View of variable drive used on Models 110 and 112 after S.N. 100,000. Later models have separate clutch and brake pedals.*

1. Drive lever
2. Clutch-brake pedal
3. Adjusting screw
4. Engine pulley
5. Pto pulley
6. Primary drive belt
7. Variable pulley
8. Clutch override
9. Spring
10. Secondary drive belt
11. Idler pulley
12. Transaxle pulley
13. Brake yoke
14. Locknut
15. Link
16. Cap screw

depressed. Parking brake engagement should be possible on all models after brake adjustment.

On models with a clutch-brake pedal, a clutch override unit (8—Fig. JD29) is provided to ensure braking action when pedal is depressed. To adjust clutch override, place variable drive lever in front notch in quadrant and measure distance between end of pedal and foot rest as shown in Fig. JD32. If pedal distance is greater than 7 to 8 inches (178-203 mm) with pedal released, clutch override must be adjusted. Turn adjusting screw in clutch override unit as shown in Fig. JD33 by inserting a suitable tool into hole in adjusting screw. Turn screw counterclockwise to obtain desired pedal height.

Belt guide clearance for primary belt on variator pulley should be $^{1}/_{16}$ to $^{1}/_{8}$ inch (1.5-3 mm) to prevent primary belt from jumping off pulley when clutch-brake or clutch pedal is depressed.

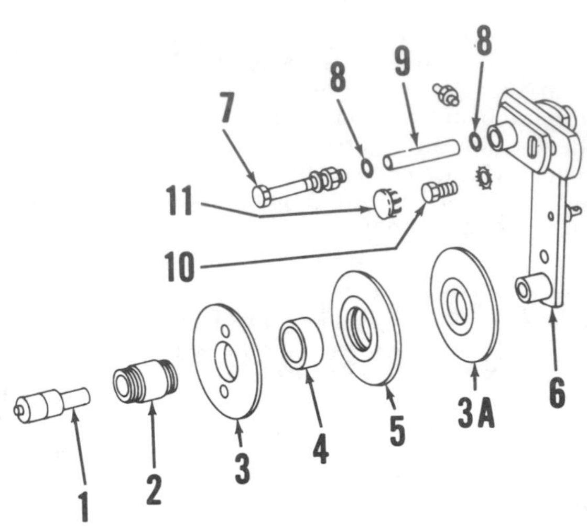


*Fig. JD30—Exploded view of variable drive pulley and control lever.*

1. Bearing & shaft
2. Hub
3. Outer flange
3A. Outer flange
4. Bearing
5. Movable flange
6. Lever
7. Cap screw
8. "O" ring
9. Ferrule
10. Adjusting screw
11. Plug

## Models 200-210-212-214-216

**ADJUSTMENT.** To adjust brake on tractors with S.N. 30001-95000, remove pin from clevis on brake rod (6—Fig. JD34 or 4—Fig. JD35) and turn clevis as necessary to position brake pedal arm in first notch of parking brake ratchet.

To adjust brake on tractors after S.N. 95000, disconnect clutch-brake strap (2—Fig. JD36) and turn strap into clevis to tighten brake. Brake is properly adjusted when strong resistance is encountered as clutch-brake pedal is depressed to within approximately one inch (25 mm) from deck.

If tractor will not operate in slow speed position, clutch pedal must be adjusted. Place variable drive lever in third notch from front. Remove button plug from adjusting hole in right side of console and loosen cap screw one to two turns. Disconnect and ground spark plug wire, then crank engine with starter until clutch pedal raises as high as it will go. Push down on cap screw to remove slack in linkage and retighten screw. Check tractor operation. If tractor does not operate at slow speed after adjustment, primary belt is stretched and must be renewed.

Adjust variator spring (13—Fig. JD36) to obtain desired load sensing characteristics as follows: To increase load sensitivity, loosen spring tension by lengthening eyebolt. Increasing spring tension (shortening eyebolt) will reduce load sensitivity.

## All Models

**OVERHAUL BRAKE.** Raise and support rear of tractor. Remove left rear wheel. Remove pin connecting brake arm to brake band link. Remove brake band bracket mounting cap screws through two access holes in left side of frame. Slip brake band off the brake pulley. To remove brake pulley, remove pulley set screw and use a suitable puller to remove pulley from transaxle brake shaft.

To reinstall, reverse the removal procedure.

**OVERHAUL VARIABLE DRIVE.** To remove variable drive pulley, remove secondary belt from pulley and depress clutch-brake or clutch pedal. Loosen primary belt guide screw so primary belt can be removed from variable drive pulley. Disconnect variable drive spring. Disconnect clutch override, on models so equipped, from pulley lever. Remove battery and battery base. Disconnect speed control link at lower end. Unscrew pivot cap screw (7—Fig. JD30) and remove variable drive pulley from bottom of tractor by passing pivot end of assembly through notch in frame.

Variable pulley outer flanges (3 and 3A—Fig. JD30) are threaded on hub (2). Unscrew flange (3) counterclockwise by inserting a suitable tool in holes in flange. Remove movable flange (5).

*Fig. JD31—View showing location of adjusting screw (3—Fig. JD29) to adjust variable drive.*

*Fig. JD32—Clutch-brake pedal on late Models 110 and 112 that are so equipped should have 3/4 inch (19 mm) clearance between pedal and foot rest when pedal is fully depressed. Pedal height should not be greater than 7-8 inches (178-203 mm). See Fig. JD33.*

*Fig. JD33—Adjust clutch override as outlined in text to obtain 7-8 inches (178-203 mm) pedal height as shown in Fig. JD32.*

Press against outer race of bearing (1) to separate bearing and lever (6) from pulley assembly. Unscrew outer flange (3A) from hub, using same procedure used when removing flange (3).

Inspect components for excessive wear and damage. Movable flange bearing (4) and flange (5) are available only as a unit. Bearing (4) is self-lubricating and no attempt should be made to lubricate bearing. Note following dimensions:

Movable flange bearing (4)—
  Inside diameter . . . 2.0015-2.0025 in. (50.838-50.863 mm)

Hub (2)—
  Inside diameter . . . . . 1.179-1.180 in. (29.95-29.97 mm)
  Outside diameter . . . 1.999-2.001 in. (50.78-50.82 mm)

Bearing (1)—
  Outside diameter . . 1.1806-1.1811 in. (29.987-30.000 mm)

Bearing shaft (1)—
  Outside diameter . 0.6240-0.6255 in. (15.850-15.888 mm)

Lever (6) shaft
  bearing bore . . . . . 0.6262-0.6267 in. (15.905-15.918 mm)

When assembling variable drive pulley unit, note the following: Press bearing (1—Fig. JD30) into hub (2) until bearing is flush with outer surface of flange (3A). Press lever (6) on bearing shaft (1) so end of shaft is flush with outer edge of lever. Stake threads three or four places after outer flanges (3 and 3A) are installed on hub (2). Be sure that "O" rings (8) are not dislodged during installation of assembly on tractor.

# DRIVE BELTS

## REMOVE AND REINSTALL

### Models 60-70-100

To remove primary belt, first detach primary idler spring (Fig. JD37). Remove spring locking pin and disconnect pto clutch arm. Slip belt out of sheaves. When installing new primary belt, make certain belt is turned and positioned exactly as shown in Fig. JD37. A reverse twist of belt will result in reverse tractor travel and possible transaxle damage. After primary belt is installed, disconnect and ground spark plug wire and slowly turn engine with recoil starter while checking belt travel direction.

To remove secondary (range) belt on early Model 60, remove thumb screws and pivot tractor seat and fender assembly rearward. Loosen wing nuts on tractor frame (top and bottom) and slide belt guides to rear of slotted holes. Remove thumb screw and belt guide forks between clutch idler and transaxle input pulley. Depress clutch-brake pedal and lock in down position. Remove belt from sheaves.

To remove secondary drive belt on late Model 60 and Models 70 and 100, depress clutch-brake pedal and set parking brake. Remove seat and fender unit. Loosen cap screws and slide rear belt guide out of the way. See Fig. JD38. Remove front belt guide, unhook front idler arm spring and remove primary belt from rear pulley. Unhook rear idler arm spring, loosen cap screws on rear idler mount and remove secondary belt. When reinstalling belt guides, there should be approximately 1/16 inch (1.5 mm) clearance between guide and belt.

When installing secondary belt, reverse the removal procedure. The belt may be installed in either Hi-range or Lo-range set of grooves on early Model 60. (Hi-range grooves are the outside set.) Install belt guides in their original positions. Adjust brake as previously outlined. Lower seat assembly and install thumb screws.

### Models 108-111

To remove drive belt, engage pto lever. Loosen idler pulley center bolt and

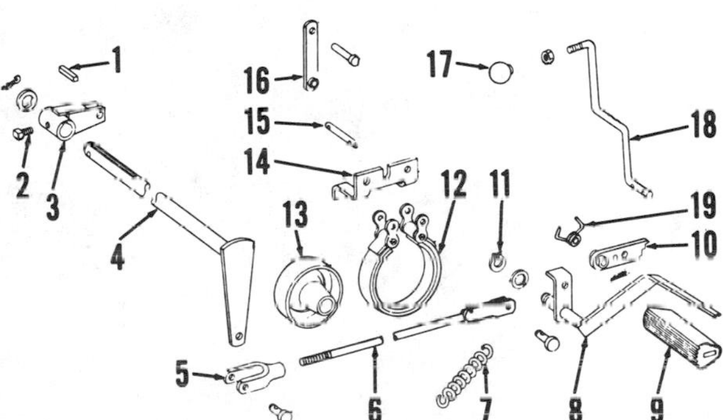

*Fig. JD34—Exploded view of brake mechanism used on Models 200, 210, 212 and 214 with S.N. 30001-55000.*

1. Key
2. Set screw
3. Arm
4. Brake shaft
5. Clevis
6. Brake rod
7. Spring
8. Brake pedal assy.
9. Pad
10. Ratchet
11. Snap ring
12. Brake band
13. Brake drum
14. Bracket
15. Pin
16. Link
17. Knob
18. Parking brake rod
19. Spring

*JD35—Exploded view of brake linkage used on Models 200, 210, 212 and 214 with S.N. 55001-95000. Model 208 is similar.*

1. Bearing
2. Brake shaft
3. Clevis
4. Brake rod
5. Spring
6. Pad
7. Brake pedal
8. Spring
9. Ratchet
10. Brake pedal shaft
11. Snap ring
12. Brake band
13. Brake drum
14. Bracket
15. Spacers
16. Link
17. Knob
18. Parking brake rod

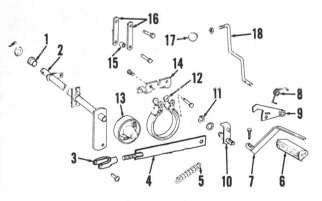

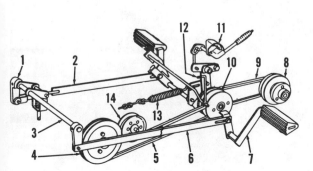

*Fig. JD36—View showing clutch, brake and variable drive system used on Models 210, 212, 214 and 216 with S.N. 95001 and later.*

1. Brake arm
2. Clutch-brake strap
3. Brake shaft
4. Transaxle pulley
5. Secondary drive belt
6. Brake pedal straps
7. Brake pedal
8. Crankshaft pulley
9. Primary drive belt
10. Variator pulley
11. Variable speed control assy.
12. Parking brake rod
13. Variator spring
14. Idler pulley

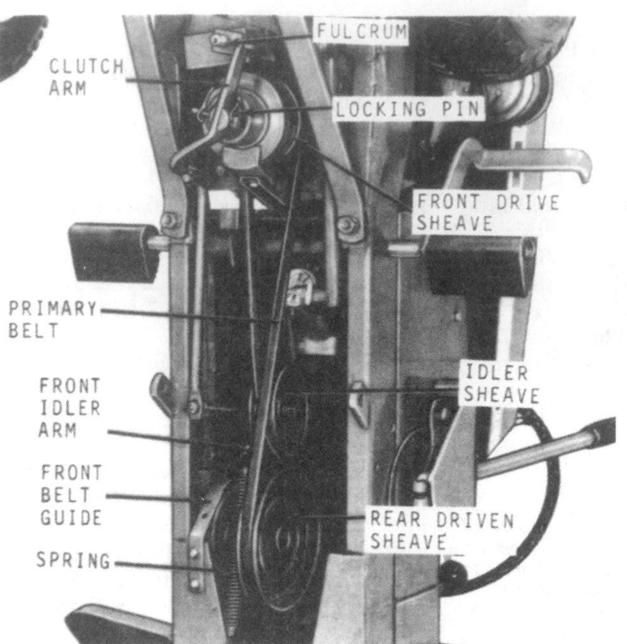


*Fig. JD37—Underside view of primary drive belt on Models 60, 70 and 100. Be sure belt is installed as shown. A reverse twist of belt will result in reverse tractor travel.*

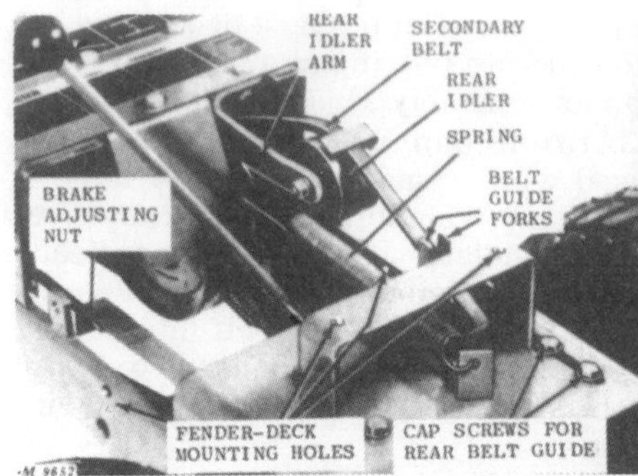


*Fig. JD38-View of secondary drive belt on late Model 60 and Models 70 and 100.*

belt tightener bolt, then move pulley and guard away from belt. Disconnect drag link from steering arm. Remove steering support mounting bolts and turn support parallel with belt. Remove clutch idler pulley belt guard. Depress clutch pedal and remove belt.

Reinstall drive belt by reversing removal procedure. Adjust belt tension as follows: With clutch engaged (pedal up), loosen nut ("C"—Fig. JD39) on idler ("B") and turn adjusting bolt ("A") to obtain 3.7 inches (94 mm) clearance between flat idler and inside of frame. Adjust belt guide to $^{3}/_{16}$ inch (5 mm) clearance from belt and tighten idler nut.

## Models 110-112

If excessive belt stretching allows secondary belt idler to rub on lower belt strand, additional belt tension can be obtained by moving transaxle rearward to second set of mounting holes in frame. If tractor still does not move when variable speed lever is in notch 1, renew primary belt.

To remove primary belt, first remove secondary belt as follows: Block up secondary idler to remove belt tension. See Fig. JD40. Unbolt transaxle input pulley, slide pulley off hub and remove secondary belt. Remove engine muffler, belt guard, primary belt guide and pto on models so equipped. Depress clutch-brake pedal and lock in down position to hold variator forward. Lift primary belt off variator and engine sheaves.

Reinstall belts by reversing removal procedure. If a new secondary belt is being installed, transaxle must be in front mounting position. After renewing belts, readjust linkage as previously outlined.

## Models 130-160-180-185 (After S.N. 475000)

To remove drive belt, first remove mower from tractor. Disconnect wiring harness from electric pto clutch, then unbolt and remove pto clutch. On all models except 185, loosen adjusting idler retaining nut. Remove steering support mounting cap screws and turn steering support so it is parallel to drive belt. Disconnect steering drag link from steering shaft arm. Remove belt guide (2—Fig. JD41) from clutch idler pulleys. Remove bolts attaching clutch support (1) to frame and turn support so it is parallel with drive belt (3). Depress clutch pedal and slip drive belt out of pulleys.

To reinstall drive belt, reverse the removal procedure. On all tractors except Model 185, slide belt adjusting idler in its mounting slot until clearance of 3.7 inches (94 mm) is obtained between flat idler and inside of frame as shown in Fig. JD42. Tighten nut on adjusting idler. Tighten pto clutch mounting cap screw to 45 ft.-lbs. (56 N·m).

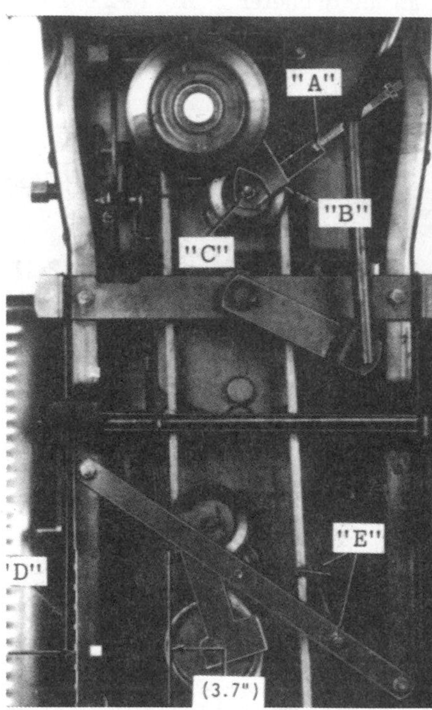


*Fig. JD39—Underside view of drive belt on Models 108 and 111. Belt tension is adjusted by turning bolt "A." Refer to text for procedure.*

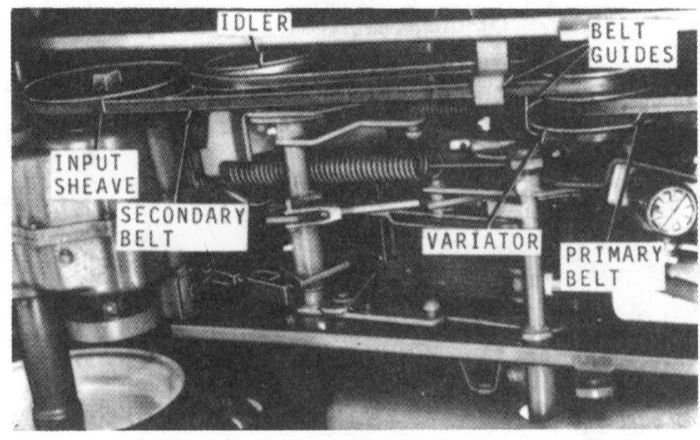


*Fig. JD40—Underside view of drive belts on Models 110 and 112. Models 200, 210, 212, 214 and 216 are similar.*

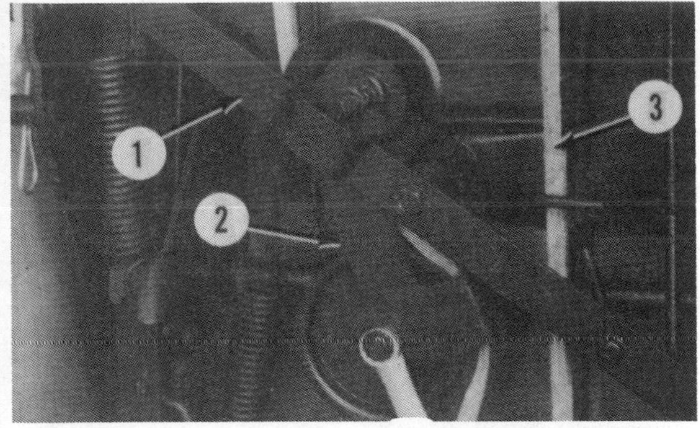


*Fig. JD41—Underside view of traction drive belt clutch idler assembly used on Models 130, 160, 180 and 185 (S.N. 475001 and later.)*
1. Clutch support
2. Belt guide
3. Drive belt

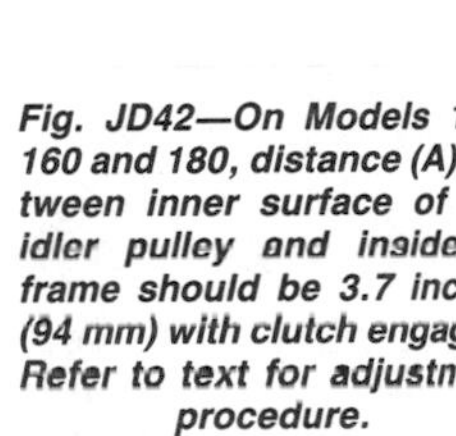
*Fig. JD42—On Models 130, 160 and 180, distance (A) between inner surface of flat idler pulley and inside of frame should be 3.7 inches (94 mm) with clutch engaged. Refer to text for adjustment procedure.*

## Models 165-175-185 (Prior to S.N. 475001)

To remove drive belt, first remove mower from tractor. Disconnect electrical leads from pto clutch, then unbolt and remove pto clutch. Remove steering support mounting bolts and turn support (2—Fig. JD43) so that it is parallel with drive belt (3). Disconnect drag link from steering shaft arm. Disconnect transmission neutral return rod (1) from brake cross shaft. Push against spring loaded belt idler to relieve spring tension or disconnect spring, then remove drive belt from pulleys.

To reinstall drive belt, reverse the removal procedure. No adjustment is required on the spring loaded idler pulley assembly. Tighten pto clutch mounting cap screw to 45 ft.-lbs. (56 N·m).

## Models 200-210-212-214-216

To remove primary belt, remove right hand side panel. Disconnect pto linkage and remove pto clutch pulley. Move variable speed control lever forward. Push up on secondary belt idler and remove secondary belt from variator pulley. See Fig. JD40. Loosen primary belt guide at variator, depress clutch pedal and remove primary belt.

To remove secondary belt, move variable speed control lever forward. Push up on idler pulley and slip belt off variator pulley. Depress clutch pedal to allow belt to pass brake pedal shaft. Remove transaxle pulley cap screws and slide pulley off hub to provide clearance for belt removal.

Reinstall belts by reversing removal procedure. After renewing belts, readjust variator and brake as previously outlined.

## Model 208

To remove secondary belt, push up on secondary idler pulley and slip belt off clutch pulley. Depress clutch pedal to allow belt to pass brake pedal shaft. Loosen transaxle pulley cap screws and slide pulley far enough off hub to remove belt.

To remove primary belt, disconnect pto linkage and remove pto clutch pulley. Push up on secondary belt idler and slip secondary belt off clutch pulley. Loosen belt guide, depress clutch pedal and remove belt. Reinstall new belt by reversing removal procedure.

# MANUAL PTO CLUTCH

Models 60, 70, 100, 110, 112, 200, 208, 210, 212, 214 and 216 may be equipped with a cone type manual pto clutch. The pto pulley is supported on engine crankshaft by two roller bearings and is forced against clutch cone on engine

*Fig. JD43—Underside view of traction drive belt on Models 165, 175 and 185 (prior to S.N. 475001).*
1. Neutral return rod
2. Steering support
3. Drive belt

pulley by pto clutch linkage. Disengaging pto clutch slides pto pulley from clutch cone and against a brake shoe which stops pto pulley rotation.

## ADJUSTMENT

### Models 60-70-100

To adjust pto clutch linkage, first engage clutch. Clutch arm (4—Fig. JD45) should be parallel to frame. If not, remove locking pin, lower the arm and turn fulcrum bolt (5) in or out. Slowly engage and disengage clutch. When clutch cone contacts clutch cup, clutch arm (4) should have raised $^{1}/_{2}$ inch (13 mm). Turn adjusting nuts (1) clockwise to increase or turn counterclockwise to decrease arm movement. With pto engaged, there should be $^{1}/_{16}$ inch (1.5 mm) clearance (B) between clutch cone and brake shoe (7). Loosen cap screw retaining brake and adjust position of brake shoe to obtain clearance.

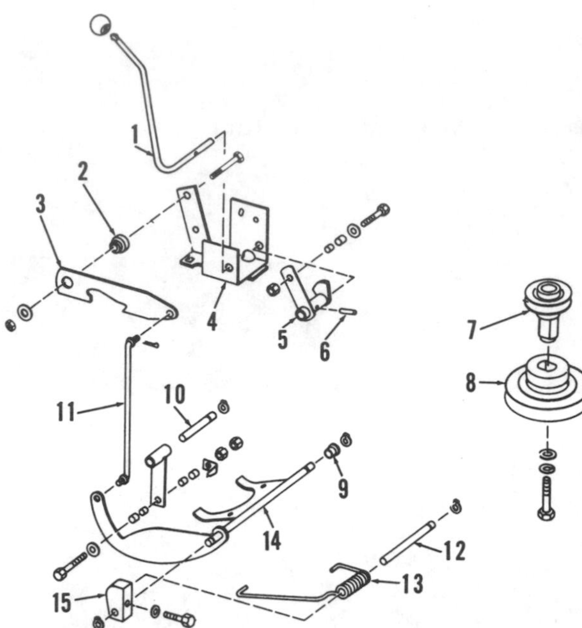


***Fig. JD46—Exploded view of manual pto linkage used on Models 108 and 111.***

1. Pto lever
2. Pivot
3. Arm
4. Pivot bracket
5. Follower
6. Pin
7. Crankshaft pulley
8. Pto pulley
9. Bearing
10. Shaft
11. Link
12. Shaft
13. Return spring
14. Actuator
15. Bearing

### Models 108-111

To adjust clutch linkage, engage pto lever. Loosen cap screw and slide block (15—Fig. JD46) back and forth to center clutch fork. There should be approximately $^{1}/_{16}$ inch (1.5 mm) clearance between fork and cone on each side.

### Model 110 Prior to 1973

To adjust pto clutch linkage on these tractors, refer to Fig. JD47 and turn inner nut (B) until there is $1^{5}/_{16}$ inches (33 mm) clearance between nut and inner beginning of threads. Turn outer nut (A) to provide $^{5}/_{8}$ inch (16 mm) clearance between nut and outer end of link (C). There must be a gap of at least $^{3}/_{8}$ to $^{3}/_{4}$ inch (10-19 mm) between end of clutch arm and channel as shown in Fig. JD47 when pto linkage is actuated. On early models it may be necessary to lower fulcrum bolt (Fig. JD48) in tractor frame by slotting mounting holes in frame to obtain desired $^{3}/_{8}$ to $^{3}/_{4}$ inch (10-19 mm) clearance.

Free travel of pto control lever in instrument panel should be approximately $^{1}/_{2}$ total travel of lever. To obtain desired free travel, screw fulcrum bolt shown in Fig. JD48 in or out. There should be approximately $^{1}/_{16}$ inch (1.5 mm) clearance between brake shoe and pto pulley when pto is engaged. To adjust brake shoe clearance, loosen brake shoe mounting screw and move brake shoe.

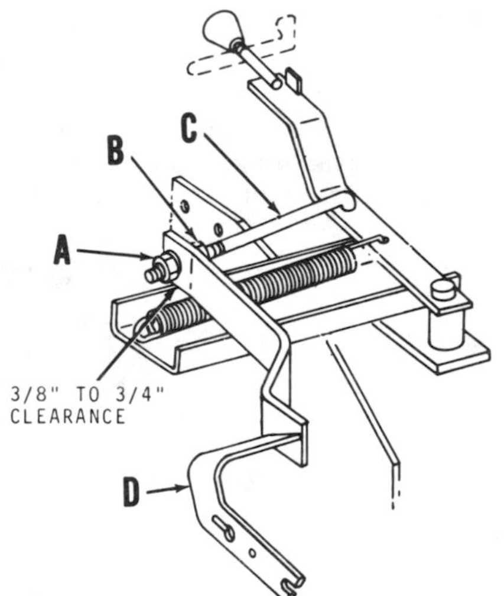


***Fig. JD47—View of manual pto clutch linkage used on Models 110 and 112 prior to 1974 equipped with 8 hp Kohler engine. Refer to text for adjustment.***

A. Outer nut
B. Inner nut
C. Link
D. Clutch arm

### All 1973 Model 110 and 1974 Model 110 With 8 hp Engine

To adjust clutch linkage, move pto clutch lever to disengaged position (down). Adjust location of jam nuts (6—Fig. JD49) to provide $^{1}/_{8}$ inch (3 mm) clearance between spring pin (7) and cam lever (14) when control lever is in engaged position (up).

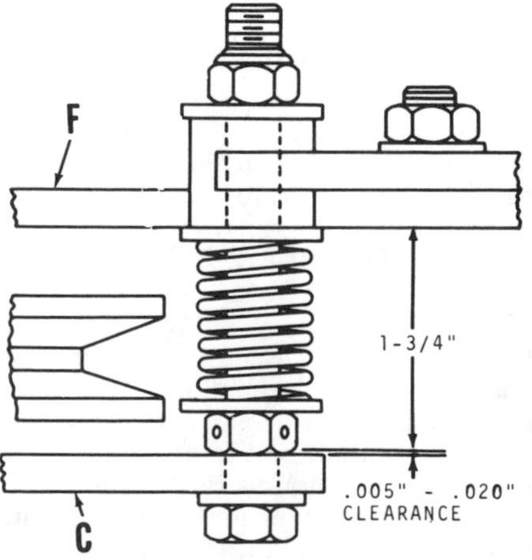


***Fig. JD48—Refer to text to adjust travel of pto control lever on Models 110 and 112. Initial adjustment of fulcrum bolt in frame (F) and clutch arm (C) is shown.***

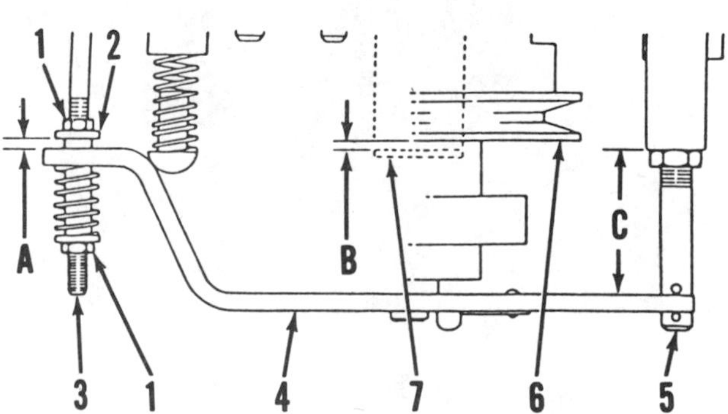


***Fig. JD45—View of manual pto control linkage used on Models 110 and 112 after 1973 equipped with a Kohler engine. Other models so equipped are similar. Refer to text for adjustment.***

1. Adjusting nuts
2. Washer
3. Clutch rod
4. Clutch arm
5. Fulcrum bolt
6. Pulley
7. Clutch brake

There should be approximately $\frac{1}{16}$ inch (1.5 mm) clearance between brake shoe and pto pulley when pto is engaged. To adjust brake shoe clearance, loosen brake shoe mounting screw and move brake shoe.

### Models 110 and 112 After 1973 Except 8 hp

Refer to Fig. JD45 and adjust fulcrum bolt (5) length (C) to $2\frac{1}{2}$ inches (63.5 mm). Engage pto and adjust position of nuts (1) to obtain $\frac{5}{32}$ inch (4 mm) gap (A) between washer (2) and clutch arm (4) as shown. Clutch arm should be close to parallel with pto pulley. If necessary, screw fulcrum bolt in or out to correct angle of clutch arm but be sure to retain $\frac{5}{32}$ inch (4 mm) gap between washer and clutch arm. With pto engaged, there should be $\frac{1}{32}$ inch (1 mm) clearance (B) between pulley (6) and brake shoe (7). Loosen cap screw retaining brake and adjust position of brake shoe to obtain desired clearance.

### Models 200-208-210-212-214-216

To adjust pto clutch linkage, first adjust length (C) of fulcrum bolt (5—Fig. JD45) to a setting of $2\frac{1}{2}$ inches (63.5 mm). With clutch engaged, adjust nuts (1) to obtain $\frac{5}{32}$ inch (4 mm) gap (A) between clutch arm (4) and washer (2) on models prior to S.N. 80001. On tractors with S.N. 80001 and after, gap (A) should be $\frac{3}{32}$ inch (2 mm). On all models, clutch arm (4) should be approximately parallel with pulley. If necessary, readjust fulcrum bolt (5) to obtain correct angle of clutch arm. With pto engaged, there should be $\frac{1}{32}$ inch (1 mm) clearance (B) between pulley (6) and brake shoe (7). Loosen retaining screw and reposition brake as necessary.

## OVERHAUL

### All Models So Equipped

Refer to exploded view in Fig. JD50 of manual pto clutch used on Models 110, 112, 200, 208, 210, 212, 214 and 216. To disassemble, loosen clutch brake shoe (15) to allow clutch cup (6) to be removed. Remove cap screw (10) and withdraw bearing inner race (13) and clutch cone (14) from engine crankshaft. Remove snap ring (2) and clutch arm pivot (1) from clutch cup. Remove snap ring (7), then press out needle bearings (8) and oil seal (9).

To reassemble, reverse the disassembly procedure. Refer to Fig. JD51 or JD52 and locate needle bearings and seal as shown. Seal lip should be to-

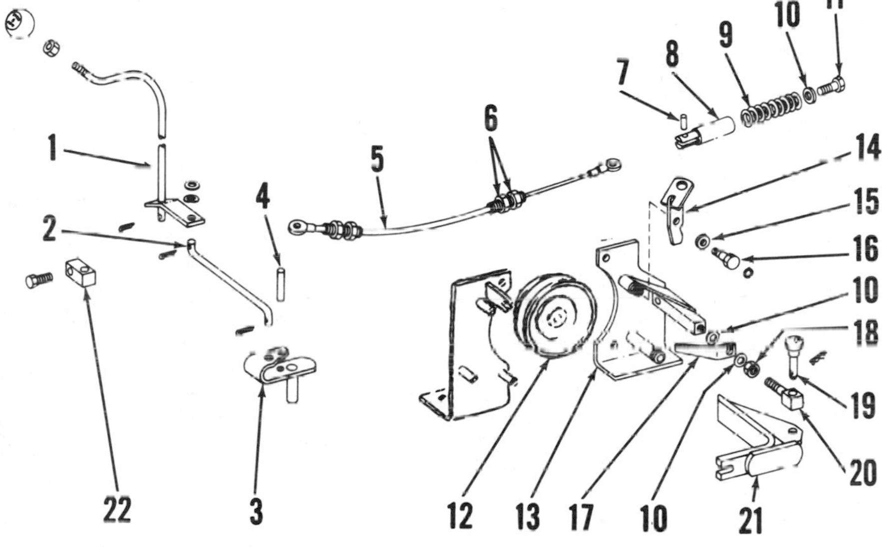


*Fig. JD49—Exploded view of pto clutch linkage used on 1973 Models 110 and 112 and 1974 Model 110 with 8 hp engine.*

1. Handle
2. Link
3. Pivot bracket
4. Spring pin
5. Cable
6. Adjusting nuts
7. Spring pin
8. Spring rod
9. Spring
10. Washer
11. Cap screw
12. Pto clutch
13. Bracket
14. Cam lever
15. Spring washer
16. Shoulder bolt
17. Spring
18. Nut
19. Pin
20. Pivot bolt
21. Clutch lever
22. Pivot block

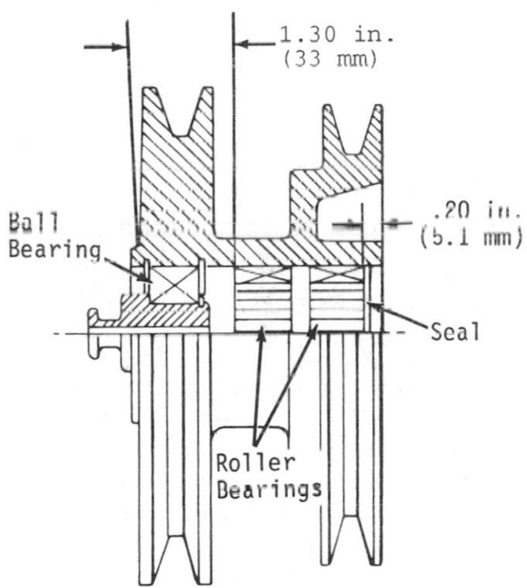

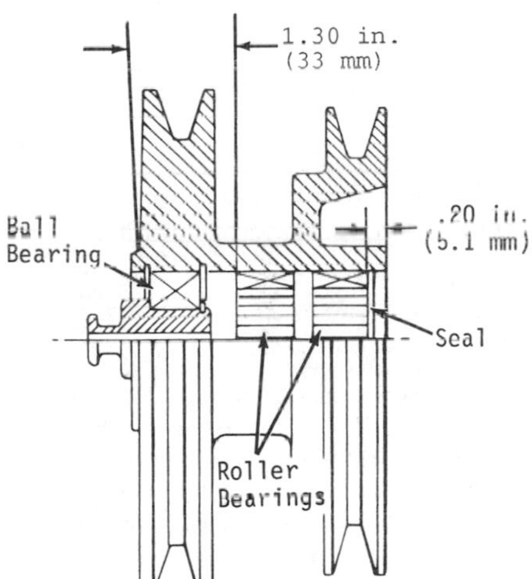

*Fig. JD51—Install bearings and seat (S) on models with inset clutch cone as shown above.*

*Fig. JD50—Exploded view of typical manual pto clutch used on Models 110, 112, 200, 208, 210, 212, 214 and 216.*

1. Clutch actuator pivot
2. Snap ring
3. Bearing
4. Snap ring
5. Pulley
6. Clutch cup & pulley
7. Snap ring
8. Bearings
9. Oil seal
10. Cap screw
11. Snap ring
12. Washer
13. Bearing inner race
14. Engine pulley & clutch cone
15. Brake

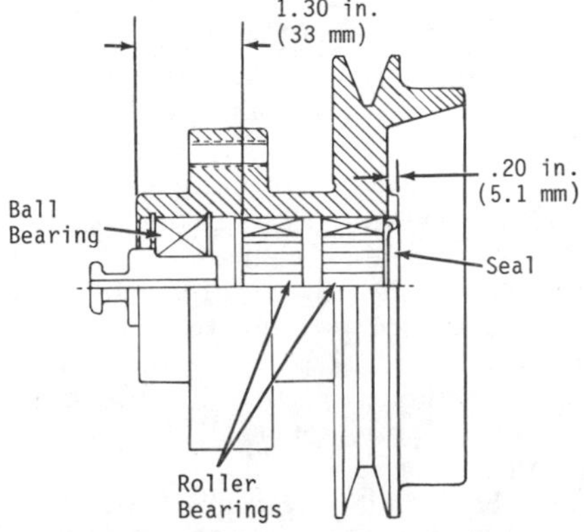


*Fig. JD52—Install bearings and seal (S) on models with clutch cone outboard as shown above.*

ward engine. Pack bearings with high temperature grease.

Some 110 and 112 models prior to 1971 were not equipped with pto clutch arm fulcrum bolt shown in Fig. JD48. This bolt assembly is available as a kit and should be installed to dimensions shown in Fig. JD48 on models lacking this bolt.

# ELECTRIC PTO CLUTCH

## All Models So Equipped

Some later Models 108, 111, and 112 and Models 120, 130, 140, 160, 165, 175, 180, 185, 300, 312, 314 and 316 are equipped with an electric pto clutch.

**TESTING.** Use the following procedure for locating pto malfunction. Turn ignition switch to "ON" position and actuate pto switch. If clutch does not engage, disconnect wiring connector at clutch and use a 12-volt test lamp to check continuity of wire coming from pto switch. If lamp lights, pto is either defective or wiring connector at clutch field coil is faulty. To check pto field coil, remove clutch from tractor. Ground field coil frame and energize coil lead wire with known 12-volt source. Hold a suitable piece of metal next to coil and note if metal is attracted. If metal is not attracted to coil, renew field coil assembly.

**ADJUSTMENT.** Pto clutch must be adjusted if clutch has been disassembled or if operation becomes erratic. With clutch disengaged, insert a feeler gage through slots in clutch plate and measure clearance between clutch rotor and armature. There should be 0.015 inch (0.38 mm) clearance between armature and clutch rotor at each of the slots in clutch plate. To adjust, tighten or loosen clutch adjusting nuts (6—Fig. JD53 or JD54) to obtain correct clearance.

**R&R AND OVERHAUL.** To remove pto clutch, disconnect electrical wires and remove clutch retaining bolt. Remove clutch assembly from crankshaft. Use a plastic hammer to tap and loosen clutch from crankshaft if necessary.

To disassemble Ogura clutch (Fig. JD53), remove adjusting nuts (6). Support armature housing (8) and press bearing collar (5) out of armature assembly. Remove snap ring (11) and press bearing (10) and spacer (9) from armature housing.

To disassemble Warner clutch (Fig. JD54), remove adjusting nuts (6) and separate armature (8) and rotor (7) from field coil housing (3). Press bearing (10) from armature if necessary.

Inspect bearings for wear or damage. Inspect for broken or distorted springs (4). Check contact surfaces of rotor and armature for scored or worn condition. Renew parts as necessary.

To reassemble either type clutch, reverse the disassembly procedure.

Apply anti-seize lubricant to crankshaft before reinstalling clutch assembly. Tighten clutch retaining cap screw to 45 ft.-lbs. (56 N·m). Adjust clutch as previously outlined.

# TRANSAXLE

## REMOVE AND REINSTALL

### Models 60-70

To remove transaxle unit, first unbolt and remove seat and fender assembly. Disconnect clutch idler spring and brake rod. Loosen wing nuts on tractor frame (top and bottom) and slide belt guides to rear of slotted holes. Remove secondary belt from transaxle input sheave. Unbolt and remove rear hitch plate. Place a block under front of transaxle unit to prevent it from tilting forward. Remove axle support clamps and cap screws securing transaxle to frame. Using a jack or hoist, raise tractor frame and remove transaxle assembly.

When reinstalling unit, reverse removal procedure and check brake adjustment as previously outlined.

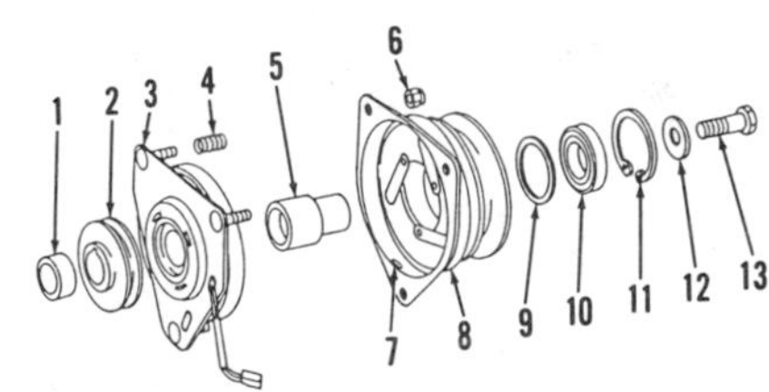


*Fig. JD53—Exploded view of Ogura electric pto clutch used on some tractors.*

1. Collar
2. Pulley
3. Field coil & rotor assy.
4. Spring (3)
5. Bearing collar
6. Adjusting nut (3)
7. Adjustment slot (3)
8. Armature & pulley assy.
9. Spacer
10. Bearing
11. Snap ring
12. Washer
13. Retaining screw

### Model 100

To remove transaxle, unbolt and remove fender-deck assembly. Disconnect clutch idler spring. Remove rear belt guide and hitch plate. Depress rear idler and remove drive belt from transaxle pulley. Remove screw, washers and nut to disconnect brake band. Place jack stands under frame. Remove shift lever knob. Remove transaxle mounting bolts and roll unit rearward.

When reinstalling unit, reverse removal procedure and check clutch and brake adjustments as previously outlined.

### Models 108-111

To remove transaxle, securely block up rear of tractor and place shift lever in neutral. Disconnect brake rod from brake arm. Depress clutch pedal and remove drive belt from transaxle pulley. Disconnect shift arm from transaxle and neutral start switch. Place a floor jack under transaxle. Remove transaxle support bolts and "U" bolts. Lower the transaxle from the frame. Remove rear wheel and hub assemblies.

To reinstall transaxle, reverse the removal procedure. Check clutch and brake adjustments as previously outlined.

### Models 110-112-200-206-210-212-214-216

To remove transaxle assembly, first disconnect neutral start switch wires,

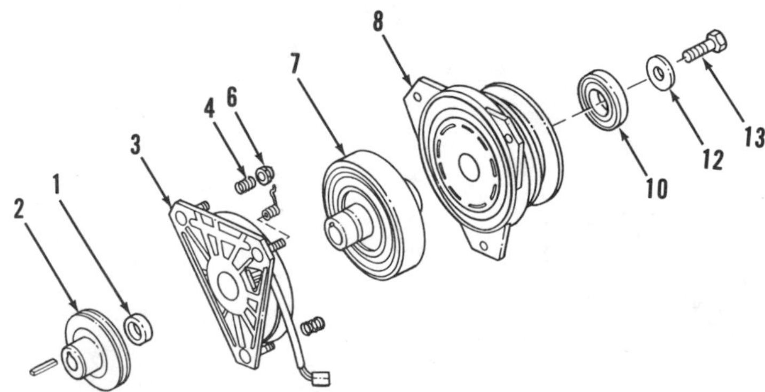


*Fig. JD54—Exploded view of Warner electric pto clutch used on some tractors.*

1. Collar
2. Pulley
3. Field coil
4. Springs
6. Adjusting nut
7. Rotor
8. Armature & pulley assy.
10. Bearing
12. Washer
13. Retaining screw

then remove seat and fenders. Remove secondary belt idler spring and brake linkage.

**CAUTION: On Models 200, 210, 212, 214 and 216, idler spring tension is severe. Place speed control in "Fast" position, then carefully remove spring.**

Unscrew cap screws from transaxle input sheave. Slide sheave off hub and remove secondary belt. Remove shift lever knob and on all 4-speed models remove shift lever quadrant. Place a block under front of transaxle unit to prevent it from tilting forward and block up rear of tractor frame. Remove remaining cap screws securing transaxle support and hitch plate to frame. Roll transaxle assembly away from tractor.

When reinstalling unit, reverse removal procedure and adjust variable drive and brake linkage as previously outlined.

### Models 130-160-180

To remove transaxle, first remove mower. Raise and support rear of tractor. Depress clutch pedal and slip traction drive belt off transaxle drive pulley. Disconnect brake control rod from disc brake lever. Disconnect neutral start switch wire located on top of transaxle. Disconnect transaxle shift arm. Remove bolts attaching hitch plate to frame, then roll transaxle rearward from tractor.

To reinstall, reverse the removal procedure. Adjust traction drive belt, brakes and shift linkage as necessary.

## OVERHAUL

### All Models So Equipped

Models 60, 70 and 100 are equipped with a Peerless 1200 series transaxle. Model 110, prior to S.N. 15001, is equipped with a Peerless 2000 series transaxle. Model 110, after S.N. 15000, and Models 112, 200, 208, 210, 212, 214 and 216 are equipped with a Peerless 2300 series transaxle. Models 130, 160 and 180 are equipped with a Peerless 800 series transaxle. On all models, refer to the appropriate PEERLESS SERVICE section in this manual for overhaul procedure. Model 112 tractors with hydraulic lift are equipped with a limited-slip differential and use components shown in Fig. JD55.

# HYDROSTATIC TRANSMISSION

## LUBRICATION

### Model 140 S.N. 10001-30000

It is recommended that transmission oil filter be renewed after every 100 hours of operation, and oil in transmission be renewed after every 500 hours of operation. Transmission and differential have a common oil reservoir. To drain fluid, remove drain plug. Recommended lubricant is John Deere All-Weather Hydraulic Fluid or Type "F" automatic transmission fluid.

### Models 120-300-312-314-316-140 S.N. 30001 and Later

It is recommended that transmission oil filter be renewed after every 100 hours of operation, and oil in transmission be renewed after every 500 hours of operation. Transmission and differential have a common oil reservoir. To drain fluid, disconnect transmission-to-differential cooling tube at bottom of differential.

Oil capacity is approximately 10 pints (4.7 L). Recommended lubricant is John Deere All-Weather Hydraulic Fluid or Type "F" automatic transmission fluid.

### Models 165-175-185 Prior to S.N. 475001

Transmission oil level should be checked when oil is cold. Park tractor on level surface and raise the seat. Clean area around oil fill tube, then remove filler tube cap. Oil level should be just above screen in reservoir, or 5½ inches (140 mm) from top of fill tube. If oil level is low, add oil to bring level just above screen. Recommended oil is SAE 30 engine oil with API classification of SE, CC or CD. Capacity is approximately 1.5 pints (0.7 L).

**NOTE: DO NOT drain or change transmission oil while tractor is covered by manufacturer's warranty, otherwise warranty will be void.**

To refill hydrostatic transmission with oil after unit has been serviced, remove oil reservoir cap and vent plug from top of transmission housing. Fill reservoir with SAE 30 engine oil until oil flows from vent hole. Rotate both input and output shafts several revolutions to purge air from system, then add oil to reservoir until oil again flows from vent hole. Install and tighten vent plug. Continue to refill reservoir until oil is at cold level FULL mark on units with a dipstick, or until oil is 5½ inches (140 mm) below top of reservoir on units without a dipstick.

### Model 185 S.N. 475001 and After

Transmission oil level should be checked when oil is cold. Park tractor on level surface and look under right fender to see oil reservoir. Oil should be up to OIL LEVEL line on reservoir. If not, raise seat and clean around oil reservoir cap. Remove cap and fill to proper level with SAE 10W-30 engine oil with API classification of SE, CC or CD. Capacity is approximately 28.7 fluid ounces (850 cc).

**NOTE: DO NOT drain or change transmission oil while tractor is covered by manufacturer's warranty, otherwise the warranty will be void.**

To refill hydrostatic transmission with oil and bleed air from system after unit has been serviced, proceed as follows: Fill oil reservoir to FULL line. Raise and support rear of tractor so rear wheels are off the ground. Start engine and run at idle speed for about three minutes. Then, move transmission control lever to full forward for 10 seconds, return lever to neutral for five seconds, push tow

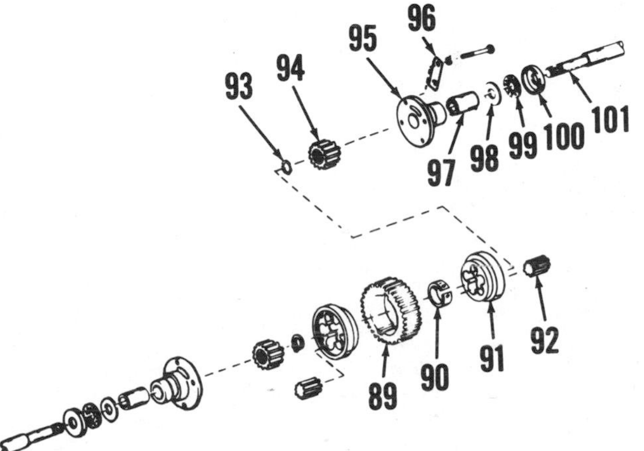

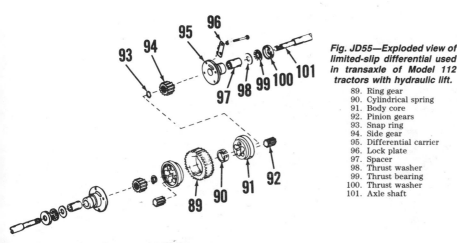

*Fig. JD55—Exploded view of limited-slip differential used in transaxle of Model 112 tractors with hydraulic lift.*

89. Ring gear
90. Cylindrical spring
91. Body core
92. Pinion gears
93. Snap ring
94. Side gear
95. Differential carrier
96. Lock plate
97. Spacer
98. Thrust washer
99. Thrust bearing
100. Thrust washer
101. Axle shaft

(bleed valve) for two seconds, move lever to full forward for 15 seconds and stop engine. Fill reservoir to FULL line. Start engine and run at idle speed. Place transmission control lever in neutral position for 10 seconds, then move lever to full forward for 10 seconds and return lever to neutral. Stop engine and fill reservoir to FULL line.

## LINKAGE ADJUSTMENT

### Model 140 S.N. 10001-30000

A free-wheeling valve is located on the transmission beneath tractor seat. Opening the valve allows transmission oil to recirculate through the motor, bypassing the pump. This allows manual movement of tractor. Free-wheeling valve must be fully closed for full power to be transmitted to rear wheels.

If tractor creeps with control lever in neutral position, linkage adjustment is necessary. Remove fender-deck assembly and block up under tractor frame so one rear wheel is off the ground. Close free-wheeling valve, release parking brake and place transmission control lever in neutral position. Remove ball joint end (11—Fig. JD58) of control rod from cam (8). Move cam so cam roller (9) is aligned with neutral marks on cam. Holding cam in this position, adjust ball joint of control rod so it will drop into hole of cam and secure with locknut.

Start engine and run at idle speed. Being careful not to contact transmission fan, loosen locknut and turn eccentric nut (6) clockwise and counterclockwise to center nut at point where rear wheel will not creep in either direction. Tighten locknut.

With engine running and tractor blocked up, check control lever travel from neutral to forward and neutral to reverse at point where rear wheel just begins to creep. Distances should be equal. To adjust control lever neutral position, disconnect control rod ball joint (11) from control cam and turn ball joint as necessary. Recheck control lever movement.

### Models 120-140 S.N. 30001 and Later

A free-wheeling valve knob is located beneath the seat. When valve knob is turned clockwise, both check valves are held open and oil is allowed to recirculate through hydraulic motor while bypassing the pump. This allows manual movement of tractor. Free-wheeling valve knob must be turned fully counterclockwise for full power to be transmitted to rear wheels.

If tractor creeps with control lever in neutral position, linkage adjustment is necessary. Remove fender-deck assembly and block up under tractor frame so one rear wheel is off the ground. Be sure free-wheeling valve is closed. Release parking brake and place hydrostatic control lever in neutral position. Remove control rod ball joint (9—Fig. JD59) from control cam (5). Align cam roller (8) with neutral mark "N" on cam. Note that cam is stepped and when roller is on step, edge of roller will be aligned with neutral mark. Hold cam in neutral position and adjust control rod ball joint until it aligns with hole in cam. Install ball joint retaining nut and lockwasher and tighten jam nut.

Start engine and run at idle. Being careful not to contact transmission fan, loosen locknut (7) and turn eccentric nut (6) clockwise and counterclockwise to center nut at point where rear wheel will not creep in either direction. Tighten locknut (7).

With engine running and tractor blocked up, check control lever travel from neutral to forward and from neutral to reverse at point rear wheel just begins to creep. Distances should be equal. To adjust control lever neutral position, disconnect control rod ball joint (9) from control cam and turn ball joint as necessary. Recheck control lever movement.

### Models 165-175-185 Prior to S.N. 475001

If tractor creeps when brake pedal is fully depressed, neutral return linkage should be adjusted as follows: Raise and support rear of tractor so rear wheels are off the ground. Move hydrostatic control lever to neutral position. Disconnect brake rod from disc brake lever. Disconnect transmission control rod ball joint (J—Fig. JD60) from hydrostatic control lever (L). Engage parking brake and start engine. Loosen jam nut and turn adjusting bolt (B) until rear wheels stop turning. Tighten jam nut.

Disengage park brake and move hydrostatic control arm (A) to the rear as far as it will go. There should be 0.030-0.100 inch (0.7-2.5 mm) clearance (C) between adjusting bolt and control arm. If not, disconnect neutral return rod yoke from brake cross shaft and turn yoke as necessary to obtain correct clearance.

Reconnect neutral return linkage and brake linkage. Engage park brake. Loosen jam nut on hydrostatic control rod ball joint (J) and turn joint as required so that it slips into hole in hydrostatic control lever (L).

If hydrostatic control lever will not stay in position when released or if lever is hard to move, tighten or loosen adjusting nut on linkage compression spring (Fig. JD61).

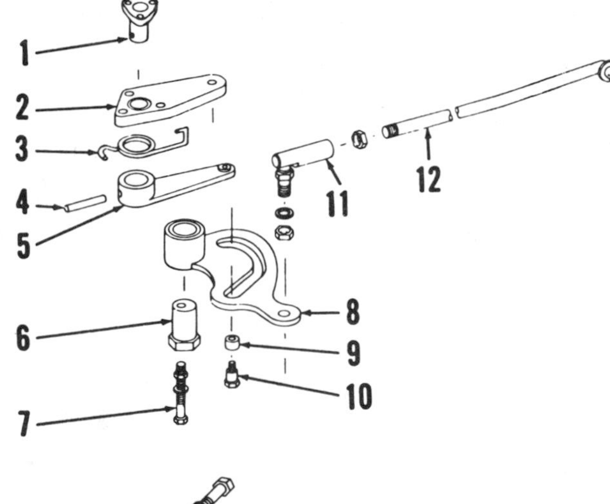


**Fig. JD58—Exploded view of transmission control linkage used on Model 140 tractors with S.N 10001 through 30000.**
1. Trunnion shaft
2. Trunnion plate
3. Cam spring
4. Roll pin
5. Swashplate arm
6. Eccentric
7. Cap screw
8. Control cam
9. Cam roller
10. Shoulder bolt
11. Ball joint end
12. Control rod

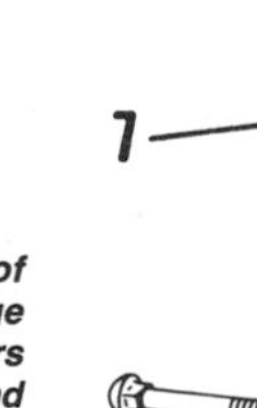

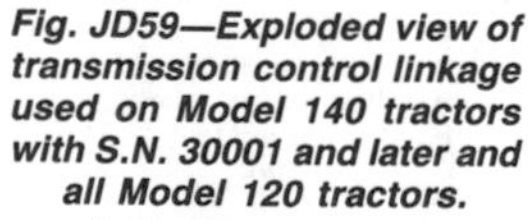

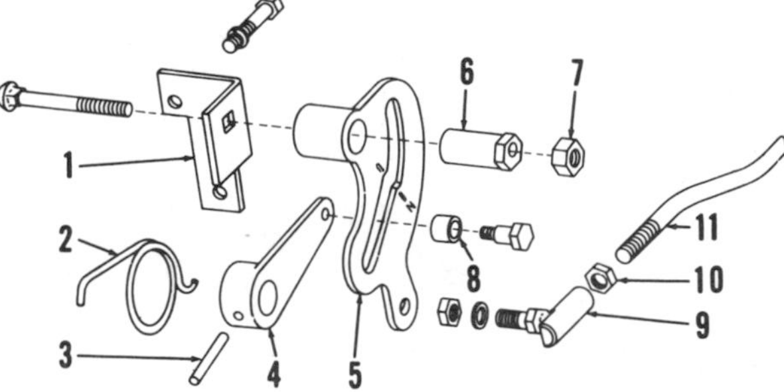


**Fig. JD59—Exploded view of transmission control linkage used on Model 140 tractors with S.N. 30001 and later and all Model 120 tractors.**
1. Bracket
2. Spring
3. Pin
4. Control arm
5. Control cam
6. Eccentric
7. Nut
8. Cam roller
9. Ball joint end
10. Locknut
11. Control rod

### Model 185 S.N. 475001 and Later

If tractor creeps when brake pedal is fully depressed, neutral return linkage should be adjusted as follows: Raise and support rear of tractor so rear wheels are off the ground. Move hydrostatic control lever to neutral position. Loosen cam pivot nut (1—Fig. JD62) and engage park brake. Move the cam (2) so roller (3) is centered in "V" of cam. Hold cam against roller and tighten retaining nut. Loosen jam nuts (6) on hydrostatic control link (5). Start engine and turn link until rear wheel stop turning, then tighten jam nuts.

Operate transmission in forward and reverse and apply brake and release. Rear wheels must stop turning when brake is applied and released. If wheels continue to turn, readjust linkage as needed.

If hydrostatic control lever will not stay in position when released or if lever is hard to move, tighten or loosen linkage compression spring adjusting screw (Fig. JD61) as necessary.

### Models 300-312-314-316

A free-wheeling valve knob is located beneath the seat. When valve knob is turned clockwise, both check valves are held open and oil is allowed to recirculate through hydraulic motor while bypassing the pump. This allows manual movement of tractor. Free-wheeling valve knob must be turned fully counterclockwise for full power to be transmitted to rear wheels.

To adjust hydrostatic control linkage, first raise and securely block rear of tractor so one rear wheel is free to turn. With transmission control lever in neutral position, remove pin (6—Fig. JD63) from clevis and move control arm (7) until roller (8) seats in control arm detent.

Start engine and run at idle speed. Being careful not to contact transmission fan, loosen locknut (2) and turn eccentric (3) until raised wheel stops turning. Tighten locknut. Loosen jam nut (1) and turn clevis (4) until pin (6) can be installed, then retighten jam nut.

A slight drag should be felt when moving hydrostatic control lever. To adjust control linkage friction brake, refer to Fig. JD64 and turn adjusting nut (1) to tighten or loosen linkage brake (2) as required.

## TESTING

### Models 120-140-300-312-314-316

To check implement circuit hydraulic pressure, install a 0-1000 psi (0-7000 kPa) pressure gage at front hydraulic outlet (if so equipped) or tee into hydraulic line going to lift cylinder. Operate hydraulic control lever to direct oil flow to pressure gage. With engine at full throttle, pressure should be between 500 and 600 psi (3447-4137 kPa). If necessary, shims are available to increase implement relief valve spring pressure.

To check transmission charge circuit pressure, remove pipe plug from top of transmission and install a 0-300 psi (0-2000 kPa) pressure gage using a 1/8 inch pipe adapter as shown in Fig. JD65. At half throttle, charge pressure should be 75-110 psi (517-758 kPa).

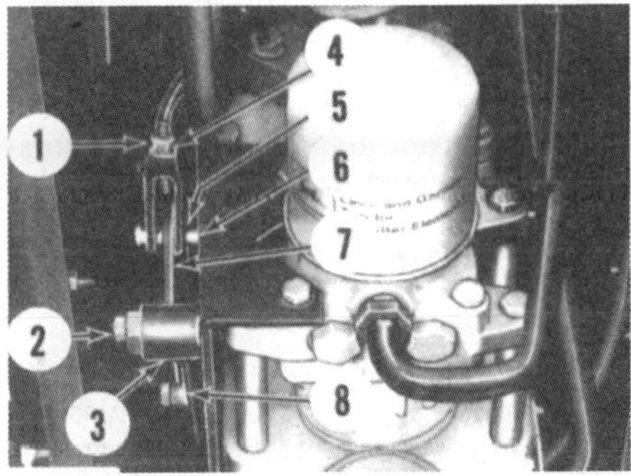


*Fig. JD63—Underside view of hydrostatic control linkage used on Models 300, 312, 314 and 316.*

1. Jam nut
2. Locknut
3. Eccentric
4. Clevis
5. Cotter pin
6. Pin
7. Control arm
8. Roller

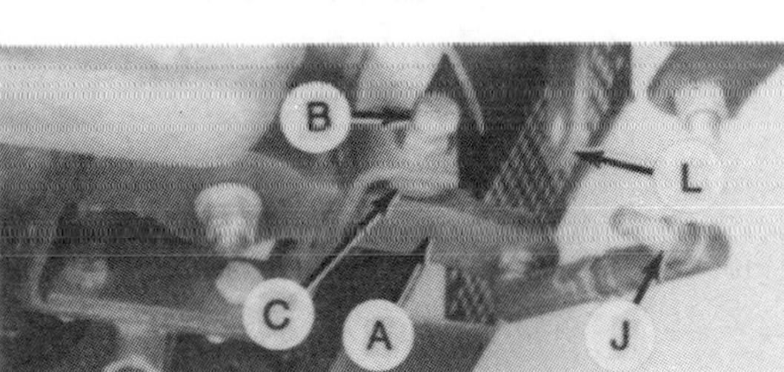


*Fig. JD60—Underside view of hydrostatic transmission control linkage used on Models 165, 175 and 185 (prior to S.N. 475001).*

A. Control arm
B. Adjusting screw
J. Control link ball joint
L. Control lever

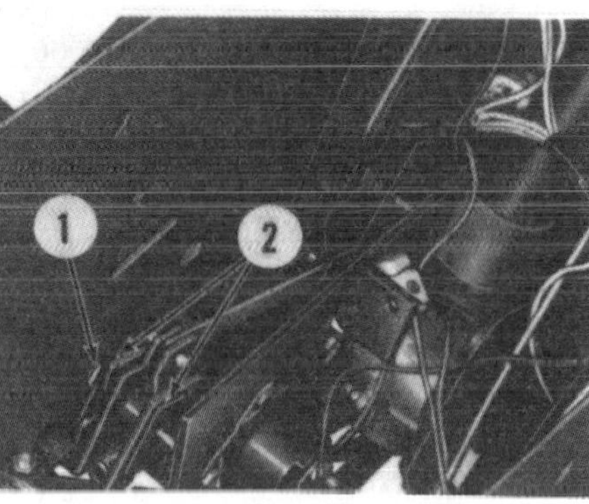


*Fig. JD64—On Models 300, 312, 314 and 316, adjust nut (1) to tighten or loosen hydrostatic control linkage brake (2) until a slight drag is felt when moving control lever.*

*Fig. JD61—To adjust hydrostatic control lever friction adjustment, turn nut (2) to compress spring (1) until control lever will hold in position.*

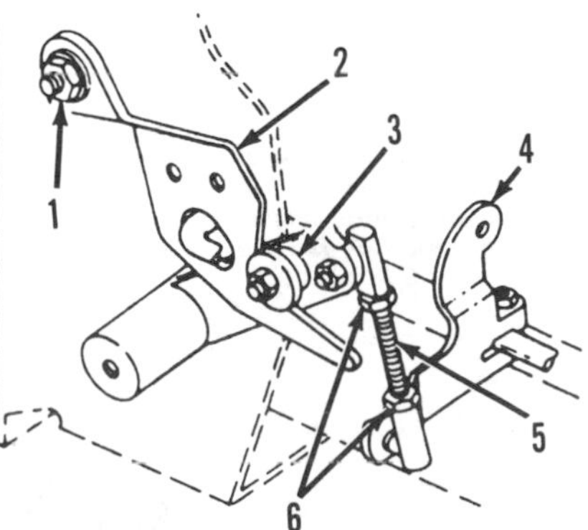


*Fig. JD62—Refer to text for adjustment of hydrostatic control linkage used on Model 185 (S.N. 475001 and later).*

1. Nut
2. Cam
3. Roller
4. Control arm
5. Control link
6. Jam nuts

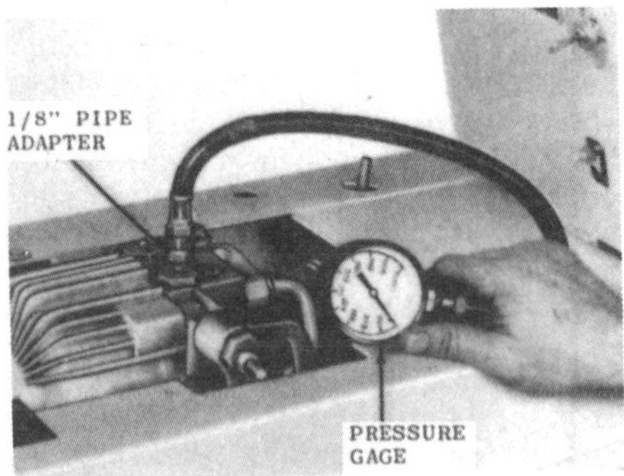


*Fig. JD65—To check hydrostatic transmission charge pressure on Models 120, 140, 300, 312, 314 and 316, remove pipe plug from top of transmission and install pressure gage using 1/8 inch pipe adapter as shown. Refer to text.*

If pressures are low, check for low transmission oil level, plugged oil filter, defective relief valves, defective charge pump or internal damage to transmission.

Transmission does not have to be removed to service check valves, relief valves or charge pump (except Model 140 S.N. 10000-30001). If a transmission internal problem is suspected, remove and cut open hydraulic filter before removing and disassembling transmission. Check for metal chips or other contamination in the filter which might indicate cause of problem. Brass and steel chips in the oil usually indicate transmission internal damage.

## REMOVE AND REINSTALL

### Models 120-140

To remove hydrostatic transmission, first remove fender and deck assembly. Disconnect drive shaft at rear flex coupling. Remove transmission fan shield and fan. Disconnect pto shaft extension if so equipped. Disconnect transmission control rod at control cam. Disconnect brake rods at brake lever. Disconnect hydraulic oil lines and unscrew hitch plate cap screws. Support rear of tractor. On early Model 140 tractors (S.N. 10001-30001), remove hitch plate and unscrew axle housing mounting bolts. On all other models, unscrew transmission bracket cap screws. Support rear of tractor, then roll transmission and differential assembly from rear of tractor. Disconnect oil intake tube to transmission. Transmission may now be removed from differential.

To reinstall transmission, reverse the removal procedure.

### Models 165-175-185 Prior to S.N. 475001

To remove hydrostatic transmission, first remove mower. Raise and support rear of tractor. Drain lubricant from differential housing. Remove mower height knob, park brake knob and transmission tow valve knob. Disconnect seat safety switch. Unbolt and remove pedestal shroud and platform. Shut off fuel and remove fuel tank. Remove transmission cooling fan shield. Disconnect transmission control rod ball joint (8—Fig. JD66) from transmission control arm (11). Remove control arm retaining nut and remove control arm and key from transmission. Disconnect brake control rod from brake lever. Remove three cap screws and two "U" bolts attaching differential housing to frame and lower differential and transmission assembly. Remove traction drive belt from transmission pulley, then remove differential and transmission from tractor. Remove transmission mounting cap screws and separate transmission from differential housing.

To reinstall transmission, reverse the removal procedure. Refill transmission with SAE 30 engine oil and refill differential housing with SAE 90 gear lubricant. Adjust transmission linkage as previously outlined.

### Model 185 S.N. 475001 and Later

To remove hydrostatic transmission, first remove mower. Raise and support rear of tractor. Disconnect transmission tow valve linkage. Disconnect oil reservoir hose. Disconnect transmission control rod ball joint from transmission control arm. Disconnect neutral return control rod. Disconnect brake control rod from brake cam shaft. Remove traction drive belt from transmission pulley. Remove bolts attaching hitch plate to frame, then roll differential and transmission assembly rearward from tractor. Drain oil from differential housing and hydrostatic transmission. Remove transmission cooling fan and drive pulley. Remove transmission mounting cap screws and separate transmission from differential housing.

Install hydrostatic transmission assembly. Reinstall transaxle assembly in tractor and refill differential housing to level plug opening with SAE 10W-30 engine oil. Refill hydrostatic reservoir with SAE 10W-30 engine oil and bleed air from system as previously outlined in hydrostatic transmission LUBRICATION paragraph.

### Models 300-312-314-316

To remove hydrostatic transmission, first remove fender and deck assembly and fuel tank. Drain fluid from gear reduction housing and disconnect hydraulic oil lines. Disconnect drive shaft at rear flex coupling. Disconnect control linkage at control cam, then unbolt and remove cam arm and mounting bracket. Remove six cap screws securing transmission to gear reduction housing and remove transmission through bottom of frame.

## OVERHAUL

### All Models

Model 140 with S.N. 10001 through 30000 is equipped with a right angle drive Sundstrand hydrostatic transmission. Models 120, 140 (S.N. 30001 and later), 300, 312, 314 and 316 are equipped with a "U" type Sundstrand hydrostatic transmission. Models 165, 175 and 185 (S.N. prior to 475001) are equipped with an Eaton Model 7 hydrostatic transmission. Model 185 (S.N. 475001 and later) are equipped with a Hydro-Gear BDU series hydrostatic transmission. Refer to appropriate Eaton, Hydro-Gear or Sundstrand section in HYDROSTATIC TRANSMISSION SERVICE section for overhaul procedure.

# DIFFERENTIAL AND REDUCTION GEARS

## REMOVE AND REINSTALL

### Models 120-140-300-312-314-316

To remove differential, first raise and support rear of tractor frame. Remove

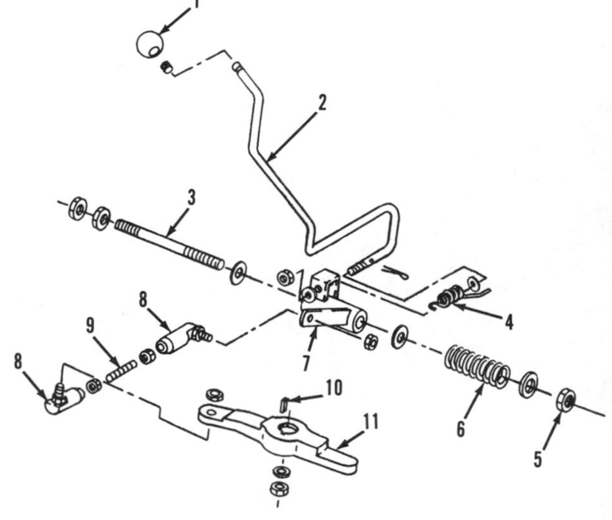


***Fig. JD66—Exploded view of hydrostatic transmission shift lever and control linkage used on Models 165, 175 and 185 (prior to S.N. 475001).***

1. Knob
2. Shift lever
3. Stud
4. Torsion spring
5. Nut
6. Friction spring
7. Pivot
8. Ball joint ends
9. Control link
10. Key
11. Control arm

fender and deck assembly. Disconnect drive shaft at rear flex coupling. Remove transmission fan shield and fan. Disconnect pto shaft extension if so equipped. Disconnect transmission control linkage at control cam and disconnect brake rod at brake lever. Drain fluid from differential housing and disconnect hydraulic oil lines. On early Model 140 (S.N. 10001-30000), remove hitch plate. On all models, support front of transmission with a floor jack, then remove transmission and axle mounting cap screws. Roll transmission and differential assembly rearward from tractor. Unbolt and remove transmission from differential housing. Cap or plug all hydraulic fittings to prevent entry of dirt.

Reinstall by reversing the removal procedure.

### Models 165-175-185 Prior to S.N. 475001

To remove differential assembly, first remove mower. Raise and support rear of tractor. Drain lubricant from differential housing. Remove rear wheels. Remove mower height knob, park brake knob and transmission tow valve knob. Unbolt and remove pedestal shroud and platform. Shut off fuel and remove fuel tank. Remove transmission cooling fan shield. Disconnect transmission control rod ball joint from transmission control arm. Remove control arm retaining nut and remove arm and key from transmission. Disconnect brake control rod from brake lever. Remove three cap screws and two "U" bolts attaching differential housing to frame and lower differential and transmission assembly. Remove traction drive belt from transmission pulley, then remove differential and transmission from tractor. Remove transmission mounting cap screws and separate transmission from differential housing.

To reinstall differential unit, reverse the removal procedure. Refill differential housing with SAE 90 gear lubricant until lubricant level is just below oil fill/check plug opening. Adjust transmission linkage as previously outlined.

### Model 185 S.N. 475001 and Later

To remove differential assembly, first remove mower. Raise and support rear of tractor. Disconnect transmission tow valve linkage. Disconnect oil reservoir hose. Disconnect transmission control rod ball joint from transmission control arm. Disconnect neutral return control rod. Disconnect brake control rod from brake cam shaft. Remove traction drive belt from transmission pulley. Remove bolts attaching hitch plate to frame and roll differential and transmission assembly from tractor. Drain oil from differential housing and hydrostatic transmission. Remove transmission cooling fan and drive pulley. Remove transmission mounting cap screws and separate transmission from differential housing.

Install hydrostatic transmission assembly. Reinstall transaxle assembly in tractor and refill differential housing to level plug opening with SAE 10W-30 engine oil. Refill hydrostatic reservoir with SAE 10W-30 engine oil and bleed air from system as previously outlined in hydrostatic transmission LUBRICATION paragraph.

## OVERHAUL

### Model 140 S.N. 10001-30000

To disassemble differential, unscrew retaining screws and separate axle housing (1 and 21—Fig. JD69), being careful not to lose rollers of uncaged bearings used in housing of early models. Remove clips securing oil tube in left axle housing (1) and remove tube. Remove countershaft gear (3) and differential assembly. Drive out spring pin (5), then pinion shaft (12). Disassembly of remainder of differential is self-evident with inspection of unit.

Inspect components for damage or excessive wear. Check oil tubes for bends or cracks or the possibility of rubbing against gears. Minimum countershaft (3) journal outside diameter is 0.990 inch (25.15 mm). Minimum pinion shaft (12) outside diameter is 0.682 inch (17.32 mm). Minimum differential case (4) outer journal outside diameter is 1.874 inch (47.60 mm).

When installing ring gear (13) on differential case (4), tighten three opposite screws until gear is pulled up tightly on case, then tighten all screws to 50 ft.-lbs. (68 N·m). On early models with uncaged roller bearings, be sure bearing rollers stay in place during reassembly. Tighten axle housing cap screws to 20 ft.-lbs. (27 N·m). Oil filter should be changed when differential is overhauled to prevent contaminated oil from damaging transmission.

### Models 140 (S.N. 30000 and Later)-120-300-312-314-316

To disassemble differential unit, first remove cap screw and washer from center of each wheel hub. Use a suitable puller to remove wheel hubs. Remove brake and back plate assembly. Remove seal retainers (6—Fig. JD70) and bearing retainers (8), then withdraw axles (11) and bearings from differential housing. Unscrew cap screws and separate front housing (28) from rear housing (2). Mark differential case bearing caps to aid in reassembly, then remove caps. Remove differential case (15) from housing. It may be necessary to pry case from housing using two wooden han-

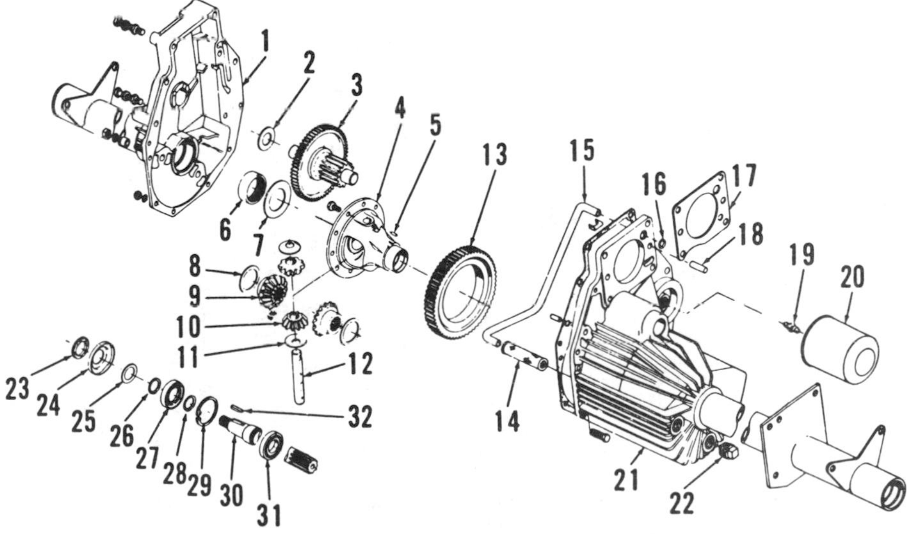


*Fig. JD69—Exploded view of differential assembly used on Model 140 tractors with S.N. 10001-30000.*

1. Housing L.H.
2. Thrust washer (2)
3. Gear & countershaft
4. Differential case
5. Pinion shaft retaining pin
6. Bearing
7. Thrust washer
8. Thrust washer
9. Side gear
10. Pinion gear
11. Thrust washer
12. Pinion gear shaft
13. Ring gear
14. Oil strainer
15. Oil suction pipe
16. "O" ring
17. Gasket
18. Dowel pin
19. Oil filter fitting
20. Oil filter
21. Housing R.H.
22. Plug
23. Felt seal
24. Bearing retainer
25. Shim
26. Snap ring
27. Bearing
28. Snap ring
29. Snap ring
30. Axle shaft
31. Oil seal
32. Key

dles. Drive pinion pin (16) out of pinion shaft (19) and drive pinion shaft from differential case (15). Remove pinion gears (18) and thrust washers (17). Remove side gears (20) and thrust washers (21). If bearing renewal is required, pull case bearings (13) from case. Unscrew cap screws and drive ring gear (22) off case.

To remove pinion and spur gears, remove expansion plug (34) from front differential housing. Remove snap ring (33) and shim (32). Press pinion gear (23) out of housing. Before applying pressure to pinion shaft, remove side cover of housing and insert ¹/₈ inch (3 mm) steel spacer or suitable screwdriver blade under edge of spur gear (27) as shown in Fig. JD71. This will prevent spur gear from cocking and possibly cracking differential housing. Catch pinion gear after it is pressed free. Spur gear (27—Fig. JD70), spacer (29) and outer pinion bearing may now be removed. Press pinion gear out of bearing cone (24). Remove bearing cups (25 and 30) and shim (26) from housing.

Clean and inspect all parts for excessive wear or damage and renew as required.

To reassemble, reverse the disassembly procedure. If new pinion gear (23), front housing (28) or bearing cups are installed, select correct shim pack (26) as follows: Install pinion gear with bearing cup and cone in housing without shims. Position tool JDST-10 in bearing cradles as shown in Fig. JD72 and measure distance between tool depth pin and face of pinion gear. Measured distance will be thickness of shim pack (26—Fig. JD70) to be installed. Remove pinion gear, bearing cone and cup and install correct thickness shims. Press outer pinion bearing (31) on pinion gear shaft (23) until there is a slight drag felt when pinion is turned by hand. Install thickest shim (32) which will allow installation of snap ring (33).

If differential case (15) is renewed, install a 0.020 inch (0.50 mm) shim pack (14) under each differential bearing (13). If differential case is not renewed, reinstall shims which were removed during disassembly. Tighten ring gear cap screws to a torque of 50-55 ft.-lbs. (68-75 N·m). Be sure to install bearing caps in their original positions. Tighten bearing cap retaining screws to 40-45 ft.-lbs. (54-61 N·m).

Gear backlash between ring and pinion gears should be 0.003-0.007 inch (0.076-0.178 mm). Transfer shims (14) from one side of differential case to the other until correct backlash is obtained. As a final check of ring gear and pinion adjustment, paint ring gear with a suitable gear pattern compound such as Prussian Blue and check mesh position of gear teeth. Adjust size or number of shims (14 or 26) to obtain correct mesh pattern as shown in Fig. JD73.

Reinstall axle and brake assemblies. Fill differential housing with 10 pints (4.7 L) of John Deere Hy-Gard transmission and hydraulic fluid or Type F automatic transmission fluid. Adjust clutch, brake and hydrostatic control linkage as required.

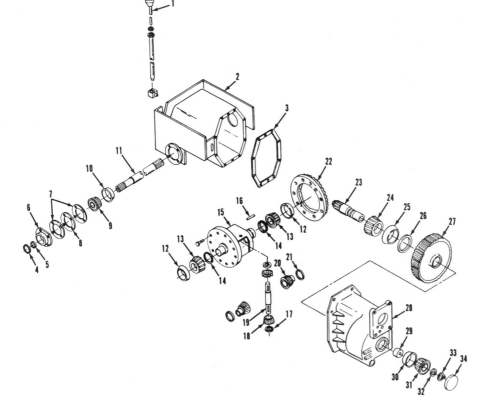

*Fig. JD71—Spur gear (27) should be supported as shown to prevent housing damage when pressing out pinion gear shaft.*

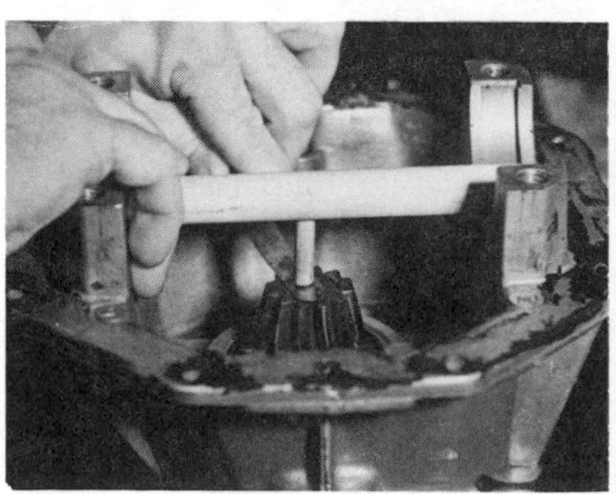

*Fig. JD72—To determine thickness of pinion gear shim pack, measure as shown and refer to text.*

*Fig. JD70—Exploded view of typical differential assembly used on Late Model 140 tractors (S.N. 30001 and later) and all Models 120, 300, 312, 314 and 316.*

1. Dipstick
2. Rear housing & mounting bracket
3. Gasket
4. Felt seal
5. "O" ring
6. Seal retainer
7. Gaskets
8. Bearing retainer
9. Bearing cone
10. Bearing cup
11. Axle shaft
12. Bearing cup
13. Bearing cone
14. Shims
15. Case
16. Pin
17. Thrust washer
18. Pinion gear
19. Pinion shaft
20. Side gear
21. Thrust washer
22. Ring gear
23. Drive pinion gear & shaft
24. Bearing cone
25. Bearing cup
26. Shims
27. Spur gear
28. Front housing
29. Spacer
30. Bearing cup
31. Bearing cone
32. Shim
33. Snap ring
34. Expansion plug

## Models 165-175-185 Prior to S.N. 475001

To disassemble differential, first unbolt and remove hydrostatic transmission from differential housing. Remove disc brake assembly. Clean axle shafts and remove any burrs from shafts. Unscrew cap screws and drive out dowel pins in cover (29—Fig. JD75). Lift cover off case (1) and axle shaft. Withdraw brake shaft (5), idler gear (4) and thrust washers (3 and 6) from case. Remove output shaft (11), output gear (10), spacer (9), thrust washer (8) and differential assembly from case. Unscrew four cap screws (17) and separate axle shafts (18 and 23) and differential carriers (16 and 24) from ring gear (28). Pinion blocks (25), bevel pinion gears (26) and shaft (27) can now be removed from ring gear. Remove snap rings (12) and slide axle shafts from axle gears (13) and carriers (16 and 24).

Clean and inspect all parts and renew any parts that are damaged or excessively worn. Lubricate all parts with SAE 90 oil during reassembly.

When installing needle bearings, press bearings in from inside of case or cover until bearings are 0.015-0.020 inch (0.38-0.51 mm) below thrust surfaces. Be sure heads of differential cap screws (17) and right axle shaft (18) are installed in right carrier housing (16). Right axle shaft is installed through case (1). Tighten differential carrier cap screws to 84 in.-lbs. (9.5 N·m) and differential case cap screws to 97 in.-lbs. (11 N·m). Install hydrostatic transmission on differential case. Refill differential housing with 1.5 pints (0.7 L) of SAE 90 oil.

## Model 185 S.N. 475001 and Later

To disassemble differential, first unbolt and remove hydrostatic transmission from differential housing. Unbolt and remove cover (23—Fig. JD76) with idler gear (25) and shaft (28). Remove drive gear assembly (30, 31 and 32) and brake assembly (33 through 41). Unbolt and remove axle housings with axles from differential housing. Unbolt and remove bearing retainer (15) with counter gear (20) and bevel pinion shaft (12). Remove differential assembly from housing. Remove differential case cap screws (8) and separate differential components (1 through 6).

Inspect all parts for excessive wear or damage. Refer to the following wear tolerance specifications:

Idler gear (25) ID . . . . . 0.827-0.828 in. (21.01-21.03 mm)
Idler shaft (28) OD . . . . 0.668-0.669 in. (16.99-17.00 mm)

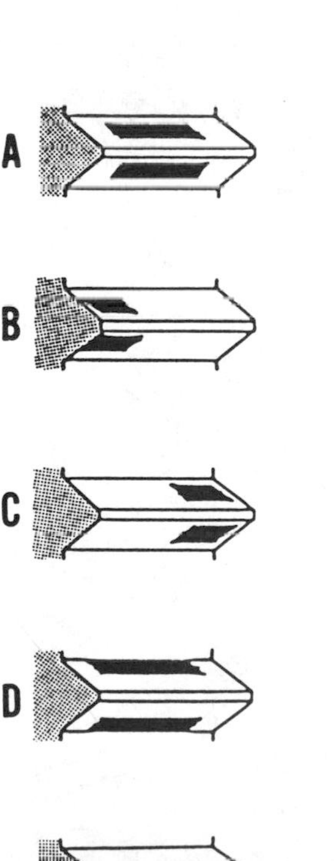

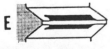

*Fig. JD73—Illustration of typical gear teeth contact patterns encountered when checking ring gear and pinion. "A" pattern is desired; "B" too close to toe; "C" too close to heel; "D" contact too low; "E" contact too high.*

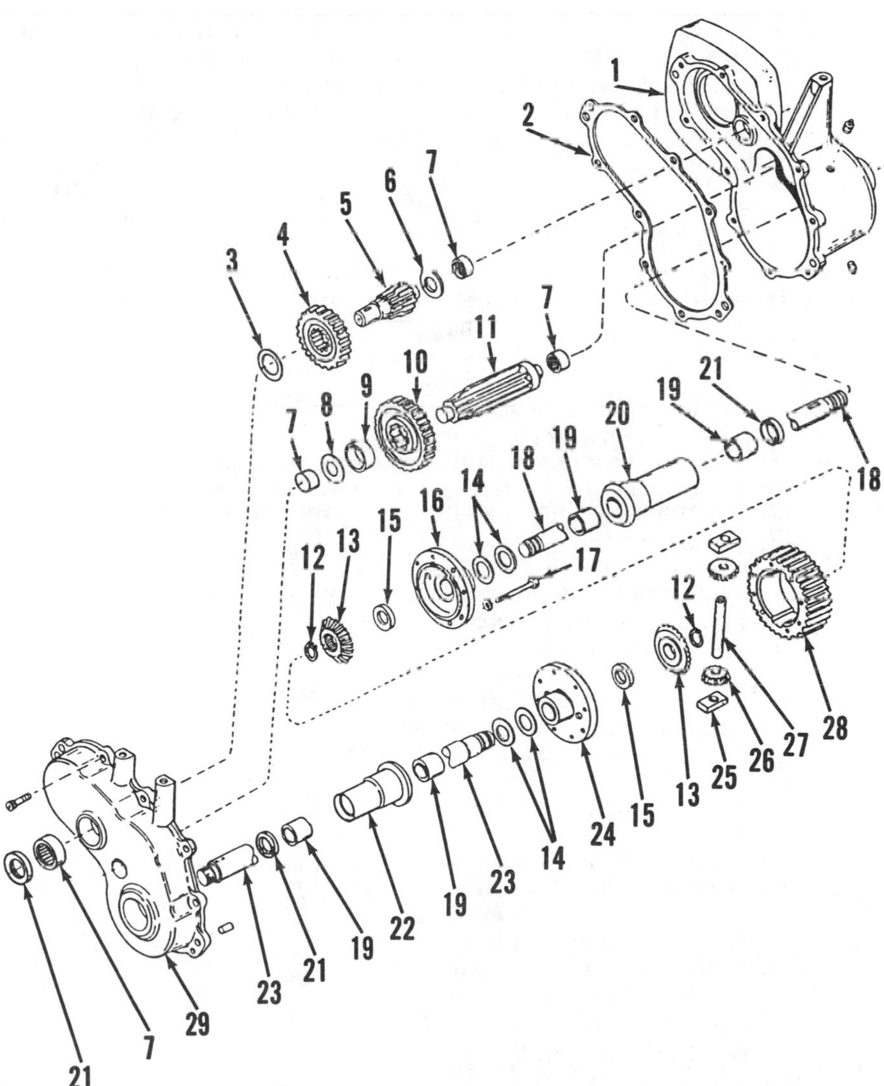

*Fig. JD75—Exploded view of Peerless Model 1319 gear reduction and differential unit used on Models 165, 175 and 185 (prior to S.N. 475001).*

1. Case
2. Gasket
3. Washer
4. Idler gear
5. Brake shaft
6. Washer
7. Bearing
8. Washer
9. Spacer
10. Output gear
11. Output shaft
12. Snap ring
13. Side gears
14. Thrust washers
15. Thrust bearing
16. Differential carrier
17. Bolt
18. Axle shaft R.H.
19. Bushing
20. Axle housing
21. Oil seal
22. Axle housing
23. Axle shaft L.H.
24. Differential carrier
25. Drive block
26. Pinion
27. Pinion shaft
28. Ring gear
29. Cover

Counter gear (20) ID . . 0.788-0.789 in. (20.01-20.03 mm)
Bevel pinion shaft (12) OD . . . . . . . . . . . . 0.787-0.788 in. (20.00-20.02 mm)
Brake lever shaft (33) OD . . . . . . . . . . . . 0.786-0.789 in. (19.97-20.03 mm)
Brake lever bore ID in cover (23) . . . . . 0.791-0.795 in. (20.10-20.20 mm)
Brake lever bore ID in housing (11) . . . 0.789-0.790 in. (20.05-20.08 mm)
Differential pinion shaft (4) OD . . . . . . . . 0.549-0.550 in. (13.97-13.98 mm)
Differential pinion gear (5) ID . . . . . . . . . 0.552-0.553 in. (14.03-14.05 mm)

To reassemble, reverse the disassembly procedure. Apply Loctite 242 to threads of differential case cap screws (8) and tighten to 230 in.-lbs. (26 N·m). Position differential assembly in the housing.

**NOTE: Ring gear and bevel pinion gear backlash must be checked after bevel pinion drive assembly and axles are installed. Install items (13, 20 and 21) after checking backlash.**

Assemble bevel pinion drive assembly, except key (13), counter gear (20) and bearing (21), in bearing retainer (15). Note that new differential housing (11) has untapped bolt holes. If differential housing is renewed, tighten bearing retainer cap screws to 260 in.-lbs. (29 N·m); if original housing is reused, tighten cap screws to 220 in.-lbs. (25 N·m). Install left and right axle assemblies. Tighten axle housing mounting cap screws to 260 in.-lbs. (29 N·m) if differential housing was renewed, or 220 in.-lbs. (25 N·m) if original housing was reused.

Check and adjust ring gear to bevel pinion gear backlash as follows: Position a dial indicator on housing so indicator pointer is against edge of keyway in bevel pinion shaft. Hold axle and differential assembly from moving, then move bevel pinion shaft back and forth and measure ring gear to bevel pinion gear backlash at pinion shaft keyway. Specified backlash is 0.006-0.012 inch (0.15-0.30 mm). To adjust backlash, add or remove shims (11—Fig. JD81) from left axle shim pack.

When gear backlash is properly adjusted, install key (13—Fig. JD76), counter gear (20) and bearing (21) on bevel pinion shaft (12). Install brake assembly and drive gear assembly (30 through 41). Assemble idler gear (25) and shaft (28) assembly in cover (23). Apply suitable liquid gasket maker to mating surfaces of differential housing and cover. Tighten cover retaining cap screws to 260 in.-lbs. (29 N·m) if differential housing was renewed, or 220 in.-lbs. (25 N·m) if original housing is reused.

Install hydrostatic transmission assembly. Reinstall transaxle assembly in tractor and refill housing to level plug opening with SAE 10W-30 engine oil. Refill hydrostatic reservoir with SAE 10W-30 engine oil and bleed air from system as previously outlined in hydrostatic transmission LUBRICATION paragraph.

# AXLE SHAFTS

## Model 140 S.N. 10001-30000

Axles, seals, bearings and hubs can be serviced without removing differential assembly. To remove axle, block under tractor and remove rear wheel, brake and wheel hub. With a suitable size chisel, cut or drive off bearing retainer (24—Fig. JD69). Note in Figs. JD77 and JD78 the difference between outer axle assemblies. On Model 140 tractors with S.N. 10001 through 14750 shown in Fig. JD77, axle may be withdrawn from axle housing by pulling outward. On Model 140 tractors with S.N. 14751 through 30000, remove outer snap ring (5—Fig. JD78) before pulling axle assembly from

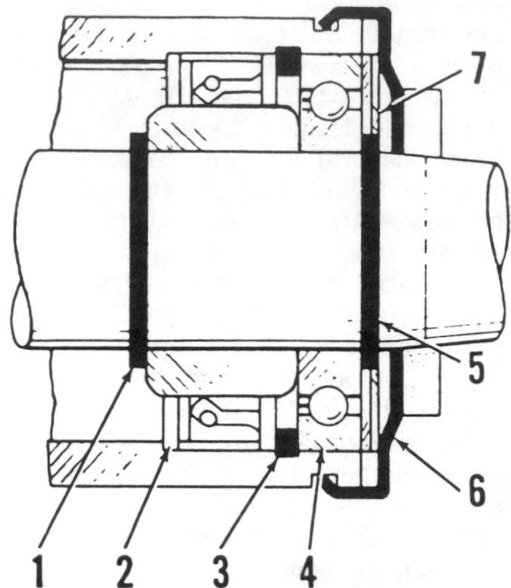


*Fig. JD77—Cross-sectional view of rear axle outer bearing seal and retainer installation on Model 140 with S.N. 10001 through 14750.*

1. Snap ring
2. Oil seal
3. Snap ring
4. Bearing
5. Snap ring
6. Retainer
7. Metal spacers

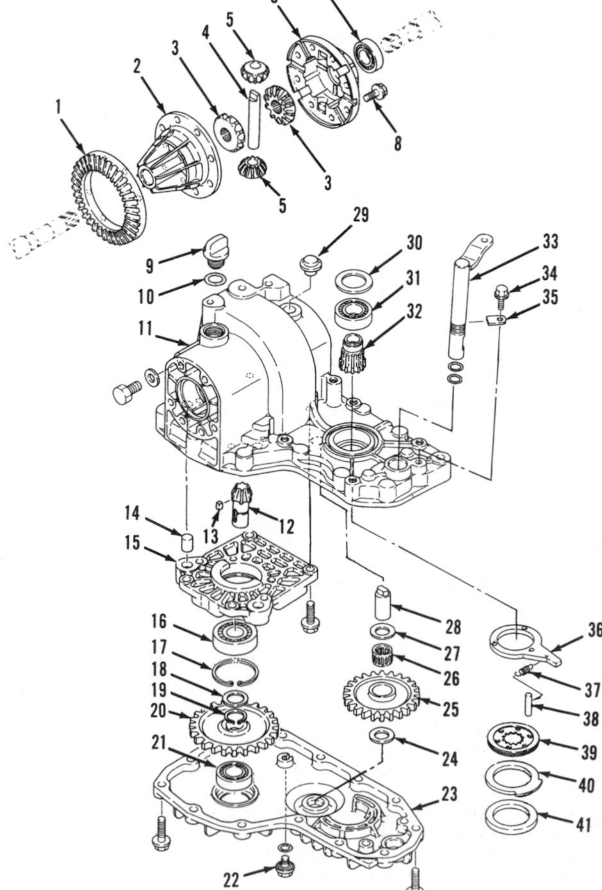

*Fig. JD76—Exploded view of gear reduction and differential unit used on Model 185 (S.N. 475001 and later).*

1. Bevel ring gear
2. Differential case
3. Axle side gears
4. Pinion shaft
5. Pinion
6. Differential case
7. Bearing
8. Cap screw
9. Oil filler cap
10. "O" ring
11. Differential housing
12. Bevel pinion gear
13. Key
14. Dowel
15. Bearing retainer
16. Bearing
17. Snap ring
18. Thrust washer
19. Snap ring
20. Counter gear
21. Bearing
22. Plug
23. Cover
24. Thrust washer
25. Idler gear
26. Needle bearing
27. Thrust washer
28. Idler shaft
29. Bleed valve
30. Spacer
31. Bearing
32. Motor drive gear
33. Brake cam shaft
34. Cap screw
35. Plate
36. Brake actuator
37. Spring
38. Pin
39. Brake disc
40. Plate
41. Spacer

axle housing. Press bearing off axle after removing snap ring (26—Fig. JD69). Remove snap ring from axle tube and remove oil seal.

Inspect components for damage or excessive wear. To reassemble, reverse the disassembly procedure. Early models (S.N. 10001-14750) have metal spacers (7—Fig. JD77) between retainer and bearing. Retainer (6) on early models must be crimped into groove around axle tube after installation.

### Models 140 S.N. 30001 and Later-120-300-312-314-316

Axles, seals, bearings and hubs can be serviced without removing differential assembly. To remove axle, block up tractor under frame and remove rear wheel. Unscrew cap screw and remove washer from center of wheel hub, then use a suitable puller to remove wheel hub. Remove brake and back plate assembly (Fig. JD79). Remove seal retainer (6—Fig. JD70), gaskets (7) and bearing retainer (8). Withdraw axle (11) and bearing (9).

**NOTE: A ring (R—Fig. JD80) is epoxyed to bearing cup (C) to prevent bearing cone (B) from separating from bearing cup. If ring separates from bearing cup when bearing cone is removed, bearing cup must be removed separately. Press bearing cone off axle shaft.**

To reassemble axle, reverse the disassembly procedure. Assemble bearing cone, bearing cup and ring on axle before installing axle. Cement ring to bearing cup as shown in Fig. JD80 using an epoxy adhesive. If bearing protrudes slightly, use more than one gasket between end of axle tube and bearing retainer. Make sure hub seal is aligned with axle, then tighten back plate retaining nuts to 15 ft.-lbs. (29 N·m).

### Models 165-175-185 Prior to S. N. 475001

Differential housing must be disassembled to service axle shafts and bearings on these tractors. Refer to REDUCTION GEARS AND DIFFERENTIAL paragraphs for overhaul procedure.

### Model 185 S.N. 475001 and Later

Axles, seal, bearings and hubs can be serviced without removing differential housing from tractor. To remove axle assemble, block up tractor under frame and remove rear wheel. Unbolt and remove rear axle housing from differential housing.

To disassemble, remove snap ring (9—Fig. JD81) and pull axle shaft (1 or 14) out of axle housing (5 or 13). Pry oil seal (2) out of housing. Remove snap ring (3) and drive needle bearing (4) from housing as required.

To reassemble, reverse the disassembly procedure. Tighten axle housing mounting cap screws to 220 in.-lbs. (25 N·m).

# HYDRAULIC SYSTEM

### All Models So Equipped

**OPERATION.** Some Model 110, 112, 210, 212, 214 and 216 tractors are equipped with a hydraulic lift system. The hydraulic system is pressure fed by a gear type pump driven by the tractor engine. Hydraulic fluid is directed by an open center spool control valve to a double-acting cylinder.

Models 120, 140, 300, 312, 314 and 316 are equipped with an open center hydraulic system which uses hydraulic pressure supplied by the hydrostatic transmission charge pump. A double-acting cylinder rotates a rockshaft to raise and lower implements. Some models are equipped with quick-disconnect auxiliary outlets to allow remote cylinder operation.

**NOTE: Hydraulic system components should be cleaned before disconnecting hydraulic lines or disassembling components. Open fittings should be capped to prevent dirt from entering system.**

Type "F" automatic transmission fluid or John Deere Hy-Gard transmission fluid should be used in hydraulic system on all models.

## HYDRAULIC PUMP

### Models 110-112-210-212-214-216 So Equipped

Two pump configurations have been used on Models 110 and 112. One type has oil reservoir in line with pump drive shaft while the other type has oil reservoir at a 90 degree angle to pump drive shaft. Hydraulic pump used on 200 series tractors (Fig. JD84) uses a remote mounted reservoir. Overhaul of these hydraulic pumps is similar.

Remove oil reservoir from pump and scribe a line across pump body (1—Fig. JD83), gear body (16) and front plate (27). Unscrew four cap screws and tap

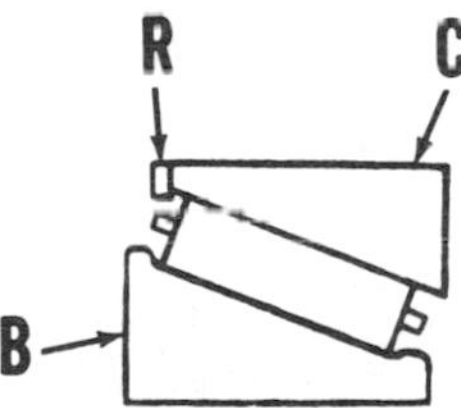


*Fig. JD80—Axle bearing cone (B) is retained in cup (C) by ring (R) which is epoxyed to edge of cup on Models 120, 140 and 300 series tractors.*

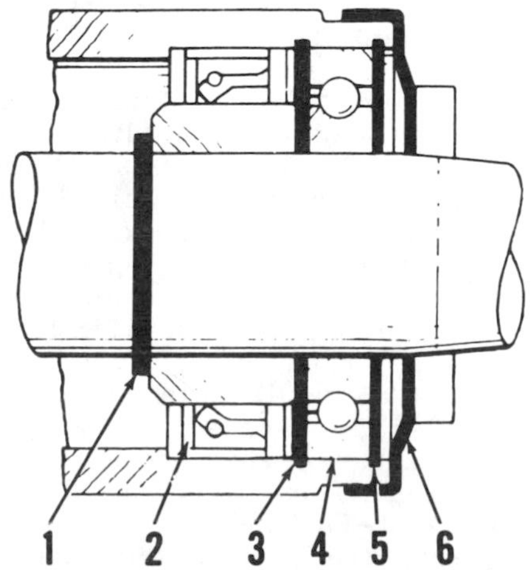


*Fig. JD78—Cross-sectional view of rear axle outer bearing, seal and retainer installation on Model 140 with S.N. 14751 through 30000.*

1. Snap ring
2. Oil seal
3. Snap ring
4. Bearing
5. Snap ring
6. Retainer

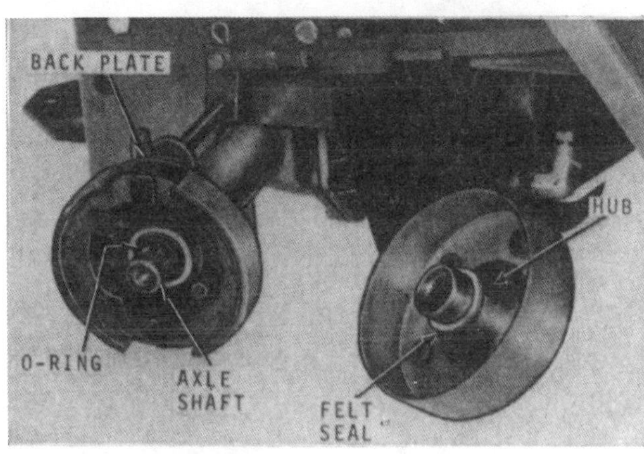


*Fig. JD79—Wheel hub and brake drum removed from Model 140 tractor with S.N. 30001 and later. Models 120, 300, 312, 314 and 316 are similar. Remove brake and back plate assembly, then withdraw axle shaft and bearing assembly.*

against front plate (27) to separate front plate, gear body (16) and pump body (1). Remove diaphragm (21), heat shield (22), gasket (23) and seal (24) from front plate (27) being careful not to damage surface of plate. Check depth of relief valve seat (2) in pump body. Seat should be renewed if depth is not 1.776-1.786 inches (45.11-45.36 mm) or if seat is loose. Loosen valve seat by applying heat to pump body. Use Loctite retaining compound when installing new seat.

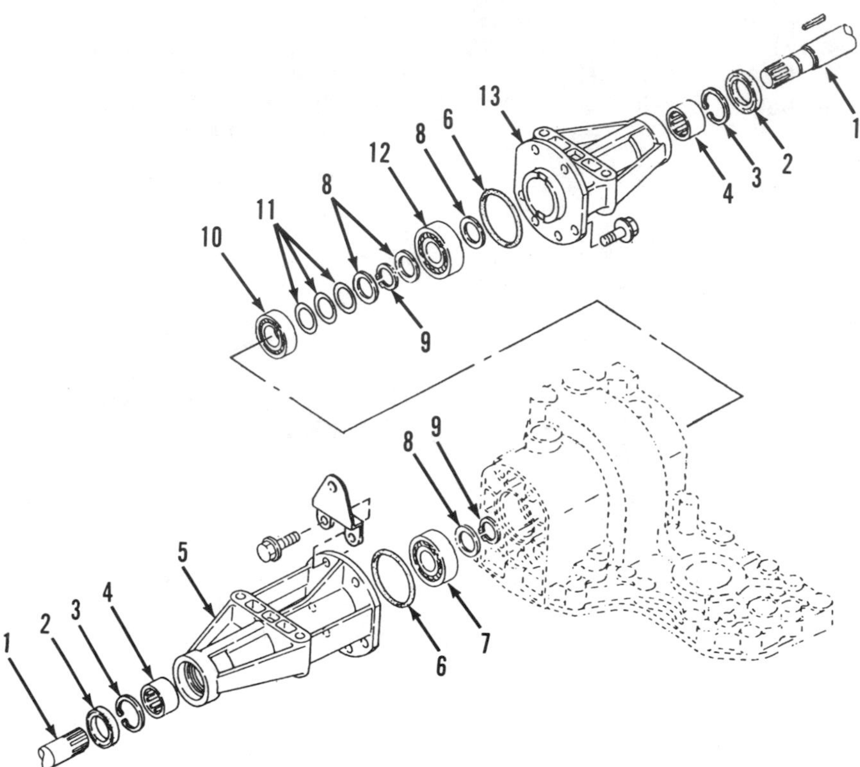

*Fig. JD81—Exploded view of rear axle assembly used on Model 185 (S.N. 475001 and later).*

1. Axle R.H.
2. Seal
3. Snap ring
4. Bearing
5. Axle housing
6. "O" ring
7. Bearing
8. Washer
9. Snap ring
10. Bearing
11. Shims
12. Bearing
13. Axle housing
14. Axle L.H.

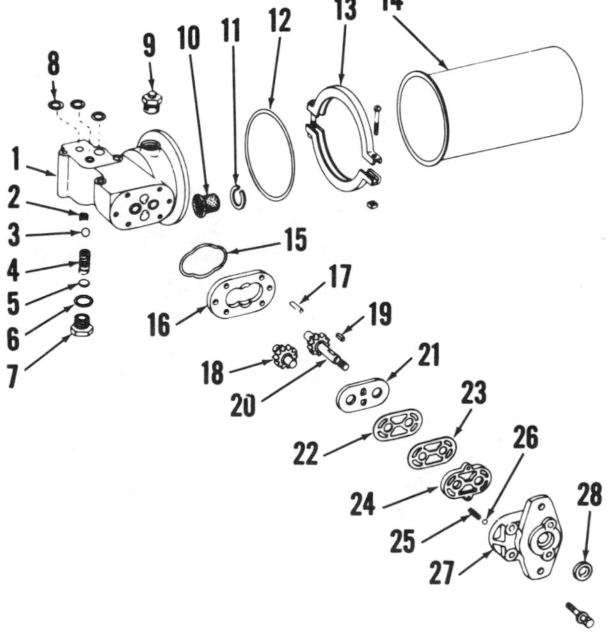

*Fig. JD83—Exploded view of right angle hydraulic lift pump used on some tractors. In-line type hydraulic pump is similar.*

1. Pump body
2. Relief valve seat
3. Ball
4. Valve spring
5. Shim
6. "O" ring
7. Plug
8. "O" ring
9. Vent plug
10. Filter
11. Snap ring
12. "O" ring
13. Clamp
14. Reservoir
15. "O" ring
16. Gear body
17. Dowel pin
18. Driven gear
19. Key
20. Drive gear
21. Diaphragm
22. Heat shield
23. Gasket
24. Seal
25. Spring
26. Check ball
27. Front plate
28. Seal

Clean and inspect components for excessive wear and damage. Pump gears should be renewed as a unit. Small scratches and a wear pattern may be present on pump body but should not exceed 0.0015 inch (0.038 mm).

Install a new diaphragm (21) with seal (24), gasket (23) and heat shield (22). Seal (24) must be installed in front plate with "V" groove of seal facing front plate. Place diaphragm (21) in front plate with bronze face up. Diaphragm must fit inside raised edge of seal (24). Lubricate gears and shafts with clean oil before assembly and apply a light coat of gasket sealer to machined surfaces of body (16). Complete assembly of pump being sure to align scribed line across front plate (27), body (16) and pump body. Tighten front plate cap screws to 190-210 in.-lbs. (22-23 N·m).

Some models are equipped with a relief valve spring (4) which provides 1500 psi (10340 kPa). Manufacturer recommends that relief valve spring H31256H be installed which reduces system pressure to 800 psi (5515 kPa) if 1500 psi (10340 kPa) is excessive. Shims (5) are available for adjusting relief valve opening pressure.

Hydraulic pump used on 200 series tractors have maximum output of 4 gallons (15 L) per minute at 500-600 psi (3450-4135 kPa).

### Models 120-140-300-312-314-316

The hydrostatic transmission charge pump is the power supply for hydraulic system on these models. For testing and overhaul procedures, refer to HYDROSTATIC TRANSMISSION section.

## CONTROL VALVE

### Models 110-112-210-212-214-216 So Equipped

Refer to Figs. JD85, JD86 and JD87 for exploded view of control valves which are used. Hydraulic lines should be marked to aid in reassembly. Drive cross pin out of end of spool being careful not to bend spool. Remove cap (1—Fig. JD85) and snap ring (3) to remove spool (11) on control valve shown in Fig. JD85. Remove spool on control valves shown in Fig. JD86 and JD87 after unscrewing plug (8—Fig. JD86 or 3—Fig. JD87). Note that heat must be applied to bolt end of spool before unscrewing bolt (2—Fig. JD85 or 4—Fig. JD87).

Inspect spool, housing and components of control valve. Spool and housing must be renewed as a unit. Renew weak or broken springs. Renew all "O" rings and lubricate "O" rings in housing with oil before installing spool. Be careful not to cut "O" rings when installing spool. Apply Loctite 242 on threads of bolt (2—Fig. JD85 or 4—Fig. JD87) and tighten bolt to 60-65 in.-lbs. (6.8-7.3 N·m). Tighten control valve to pump body cap screws to 7-10 ft.-lbs. (9-14 N·m).

## Model 120

Model 120 is equipped with a single spool control valve. To service control valve, refer to exploded views in Figs. JD88 or JD89. Spool and valve assembly may be removed after removing end cap or plug. If spool or valve bore is damaged, entire valve must be renewed. If spool screw (2) was removed, use Loctite 242 on screw threads when reassembling. Tighten spool end cap or plug so cap or plug is snug, but spool will still turn without binding.

## Model 140

Three types of control valves have been used. The single spool control valve provides one controllable hydrau-

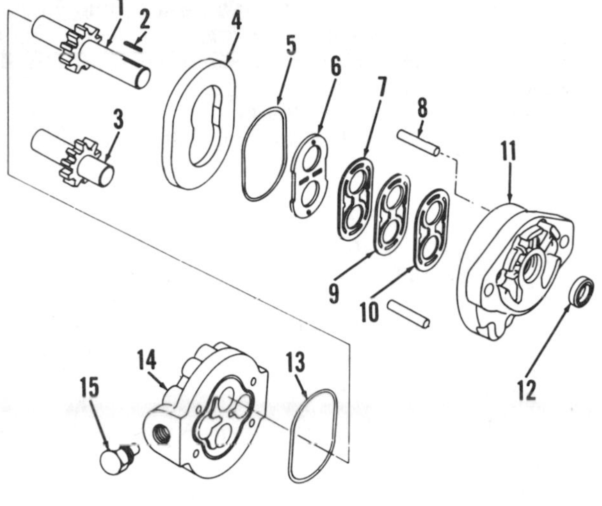


*Fig. JD84—Exploded view of hydraulic pump used on 200 series tractors.*

1. Drive gear
2. Key
3. Driven gear
4. Center section
5. "O" ring
6. Wear plate
7. Heat shield
8. Pin
9. Gasket
10. "V" seal
11. Front cover
12. Seal
13. "O" ring
14. Back cover
15. Relief valve

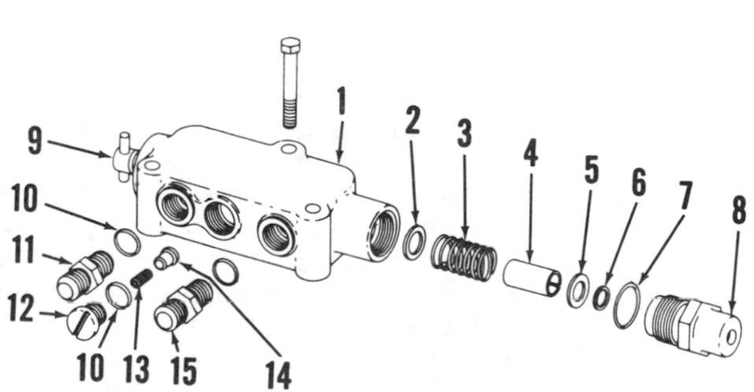


*Fig. JD85—Exploded view of control valve used on in-line hydraulic pump.*

1. Cap
2. Bolt
3. Snap ring
4. Washer
5. Spring
6. Spacer
7. Washer
8. "O" ring
9. "O" rings
10. Valve body
11. Spool
12. Lift check plunger
13. Spring
14. "O" ring
15. Plug
16. Cylinder

*Fig. JD86—Exploded view of control valve used on right angle hydraulic pump.*

1. Valve body
2. Washer
3. Spring
4. Spacer
5. Washer
6. Snap ring
7. "O" ring
8. Plug
9. Spool
10. "O" ring
11. Fitting
12. Plug
13. Spring
14. Lift check plunger
15. Fitting

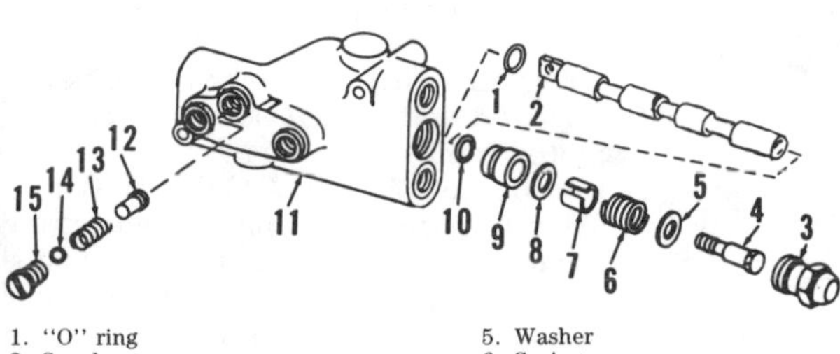


*Fig. JD87—Exploded view of hydraulic lift control valve used on 200 series tractors. Control valve used on Model 314 (S.N. 95001 and later) is similar except a retaining ring is used in place of screw (4) to retain centering spring (6).*

1. "O" ring
2. Spool
3. Cap
4. Screw
5. Washer
6. Spring
7. Spacer
8. Washer
9. Bushing
10. "O" ring
11. Valve body
12. Detent plunger
13. Spring
14. "O" ring
15. Plug

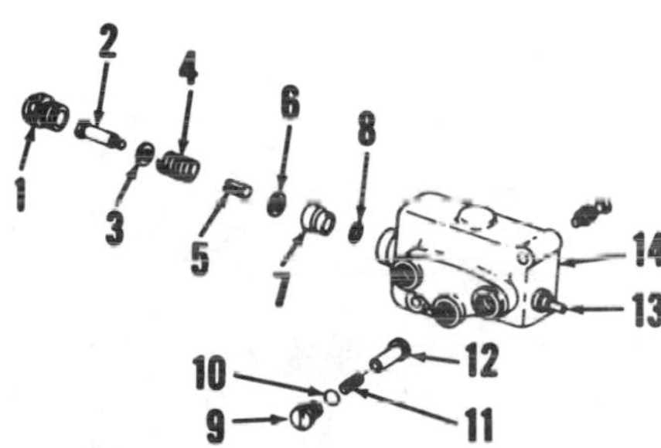


*Fig. JD88—Exploded view of control valve used on early Model 120 tractors and Model 140-H1 tractors (S.N. 10001 through 30000).*

1. End plug
2. Spool screw
3. Washer
4. Spring
5. Bushing
6. Washer
7. Bushing
8. "O" ring
9. Plug
10. "O" ring
11. Spring
12. Check valve
13. Spool
14. Valve body

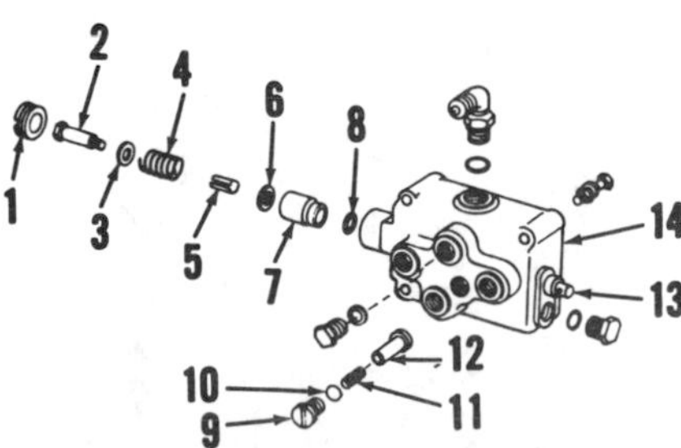


*Fig. JD89—Exploded view of control valve used on late Model 120 tractors, Model 140-H1 tractors (S.N. 30001 and later) and Model 312 tractors.*

1. End cap
2. Spool screw
3. Washer
4. Spring
5. Bushing
6. Washer
7. Bushing
8. "O" ring
9. Plug
10. "O" ring
11. Spring
12. Check valve
13. Spool
14. Body

lic circuit. Using a three spool control valve provides three controllable hydraulic circuits.

To service control valve, refer to exploded views in Figs. JD88, JD89 or JD90. Spool assembly may be removed after removing end cap. Be careful when removing end cap from float detent screw so balls (17—Fig. JD90) are not lost. Spools should not be interchanged on three spool control valves. If spool or valve bore is damaged, entire valve must be renewed.

When reassembling control valve, note that on three spool control valves a 1¼ inch (32 mm) spring is used with float detent screw and a 1 inch (25 mm) spring is used with other spool screws. Use Loctite 242 on threads of all spool screws. Tighten spool end cap or plug so cap or plug is snug, but spool will still turn without binding.

## Models 300-316

A two spool control valve is used on these models providing two controllable hydraulic circuits. One spool is equipped with a detent to provide a "float" position.

To service control valve, refer to exploded view in Fig. JD91. Spool assemblies can be removed after removing end caps (1) from valve body.

**NOTE: When removing float spool cap (longest cap), place a cloth over cap to catch spring-loaded detent balls (2) as cap is removed.**

Spools are select fitted and should not be interchanged in bores. If spool or valve bores are worn or damaged, complete valve must be renewed.

When reassembling valve, renew all "O" rings (7, 10 and 11) and lubricate with clean oil before installing spools. Note that centering springs (5 and 12) are of different lengths and that a spacer (13) is installed between washers (4) on spool without detent. Apply Loctite to threads of spool screws (3). Tighten end caps until snug making sure spools turn without binding.

## Models 312-314

A single spool control valve is used on Models 312 and 314. Refer to appropriate Fig. JD87 or JD89 for exploded view of valves used. Spool assembly can be removed after removing end cap. If spool or valve bore is worn or damaged, complete valve must be renewed.

When reassembling valve, renew all "O" rings and lubricate all parts with clean oil before assembly. Apply Loctite 242 to threads of spool screw and tighten to 5-8 ft.-lbs. (7-11 N·m). Tighten end cap snug, but be sure spool turns without binding.

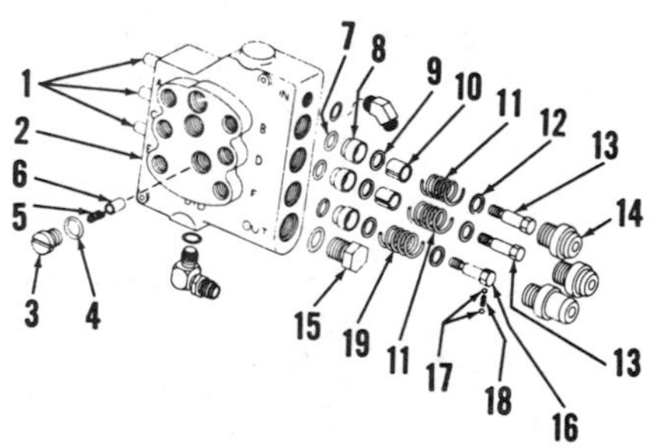


***Fig. JD90—Exploded view of control valve used on Model 140-H3 tractors (S.N. 30001 and later).***

1. Spools
2. Body
3. Plug
4. "O" ring
5. Spring
6. Check valve
7. "O" ring
8. Bushing
9. Washer
10. Bushing
11. Spring (1 in.)
12. Washer
13. Spool screw
14. End cap
15. Plug
16. Float detent screw
17. Balls
18. Spring
19. Spring (1-1/4 in.)

## HYDRAULIC CYLINDER

## All Models So Equipped

A double-acting hydraulic cylinder is used on all models to raise or lower tractor rockshaft. Hydraulic cylinder is a welded assembly and is not serviceable. Renew cylinder assembly as a unit if malfunction occurs.

To test cylinder for internal leakage, proceed as follows: Fully retract cylinder, then disconnect return hose (going to end of cylinder opposite rod end) from control valve. Place open end of hose in a container. With engine running, actuate control lever to retract cylinder. Oil leaking past piston seal ring will be indicated by a continuous flow of oil from open end of cylinder hose.

## ELECTRIC LIFT

## Models 110-112-200-208-210-212-214-216 So Equipped

An electric lift system is available for these models. The lift system consists of lifting linkage, lift actuator, a reversible electric motor, raising and lowering solenoids and a lift switch. Refer to appropriate wiring diagram in Fig. JD92 or JD93 and exploded view of motor and lift actuator in Fig. JD94.

**TESTING.** To determine if electric lift malfunction is electrical or mechanical, disconnect wire coupler at electric motor and connect leads from a 12-volt test light or voltmeter into coupler leads from electrical system. Turn ignition switch on and actuate lift switch to "UP" and "DOWN" positions. If voltmeter or test light indicates voltage is present in both positions, then malfunction is in motor, lift actuator or mechanical linkage. If voltage is not present, use schematic in Fig. JD92 or JD93 and trouble-shoot electrical system.

If previous test indicates a malfunction in electric lift motor, lift actuator or mechanical linkage, inspect linkage for possible binding or obstructions in linkage. To check motor, remove motor and connect leads of motor to battery posts of tractor battery; motor shaft should rotate freely. Reverse motor leads to battery; motor shaft should rotate freely in opposite direction. Renew motor if it fails to operate satisfactorily in both directions. If motor operates satisfactorily, disassemble lift actuator and renew components as necessary.

**OVERHAUL.** To service lift actuator, remove two through-bolts and remove motor from gear housing. Remove motor adapter (5—Fig. JD94). Pry spacer (4) out of gear housing and withdraw brake spring (3), if so equipped. Do not attempt to remove worm gear from gear housing (1). Gear and housing must be renewed as a complete unit. Remove retaining screws and separate cover tube

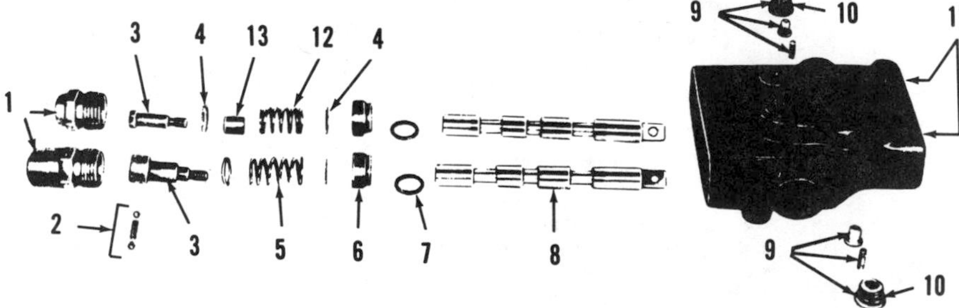

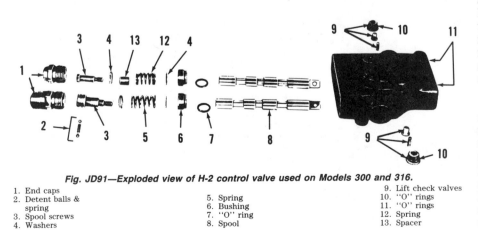

***Fig. JD91—Exploded view of H-2 control valve used on Models 300 and 316.***

1. End caps
2. Detent balls & spring
3. Spool screws
4. Washers
5. Spring
6. Bushing
7. "O" ring
8. Spool
9. Lift check valves
10. "O" rings
11. "O" rings
12. Spring
13. Spacer

(9) with actuator assembly from gear housing (1), then pull cover tube off actuator. Drive out pin (14) and remove thrust washers and bearings, gear and bearing support from actuator (16). If actuator is damaged, complete actuator assembly must be renewed.

When reassembling, lubricate gears and bearings with multipurpose grease. Install brake spring (3) into gear housing with drive shaft arm between prongs of spring, if so equipped. Be sure that spring coils are positioned in recess and that spring rotates freely. When installing motor, be sure that spring ends are located within fork legs of motor shaft bracket.

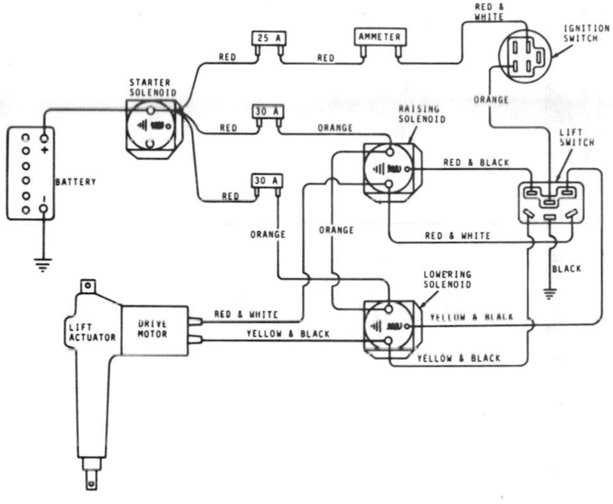


***Fig. JD92—Typical wiring schematic of electric lift system used on some Model 110 and 112 tractors.***

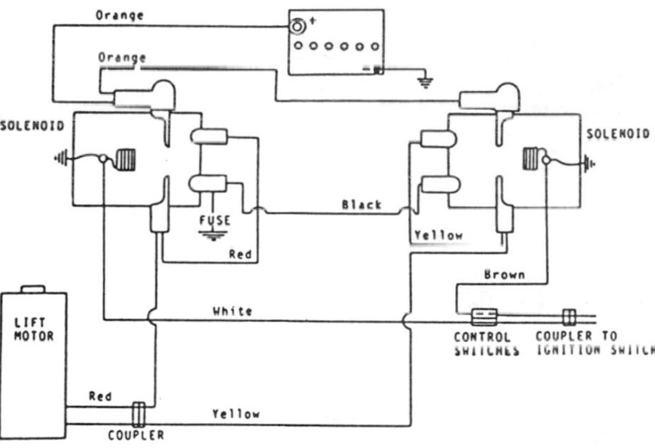


***Fig. JD93—Wiring schematic of electric lift system used on some Model 200, 208, 210, 212, 214 and 216 tractors.***

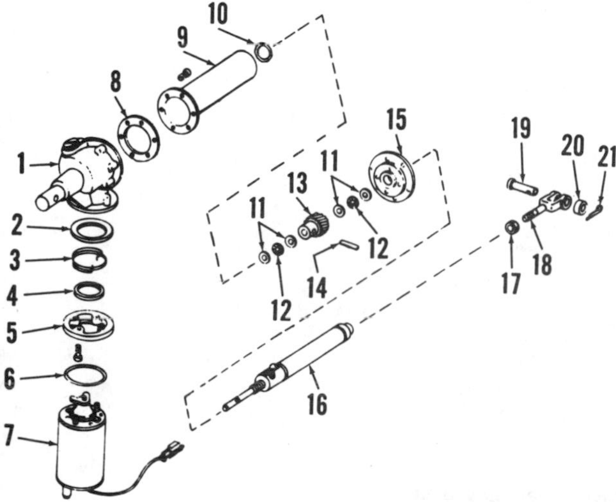


***Fig. JD94—Exploded view of typical electric lift motor and actuator.***

1. Gear housing
2. Gasket
3. Brake spring
4. Spacer
5. Adapter
6. "O" ring
7. Motor
8. Gasket
9. Tube cover
10. "O" ring
11. Thrust washer
12. Thrust bearing
13. Gear
14. Pin
15. Bearing support
16. Actuator
17. Locknut
18. Yoke
19. Pin
20. Spacer
21. Cotter pin

**ADJUSTMENT.** On Models 110 and 112, it may be necessary to adjust reach of lift actuator rod (16—Fig. JD94) if mower deck contacts drag link. Loosen locknut (17) and turn rod to obtain 1/4 to 3/8 inch (6-10 mm) clearance between mower deck and drag link.

On Models 200, 208, 210, 212, 214 and 216, cam and control switches must be adjusted as follows: On models equipped with an adjustable cam (3—Fig. JD95), there must be a three inch (76 mm) radius (R) from center of pivot shaft (2) to outer diameter of cam (3). Remove cam and arm assembly from left side of pedestal and install special tool JDM-65 (1) as shown. Loosen cap screws (4) and adjust edges of cam to edges of tool. Tighten cap screws and reinstall cam assembly. On models with one-piece cam and arm assembly, cam adjustment is not required; however, cam side play (A—Fig. JD96) must not exceed 1/6 inch (1.5 mm). If side play is excessive, add shim washers (1). There should be two spacers (4) located between switches (3) as shown in Fig. JD96. If not, install spacer kit AM36200. On all models, switches must close when on raised surface of cam. If switches do not close properly, loosen retaining nuts and move switches toward cam as required. Both switches should be open at center of cam.

# SAFETY INTERLOCK SWITCHES

## All Models

All models are equipped with transmission and pto neutral-start interlock switches. Some models are also equipped with a seat interlock switch.

On models equipped with electric pto clutch, pto switch must be in "OFF" po-

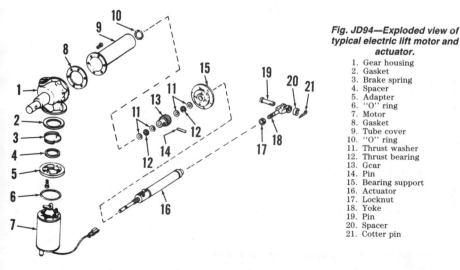

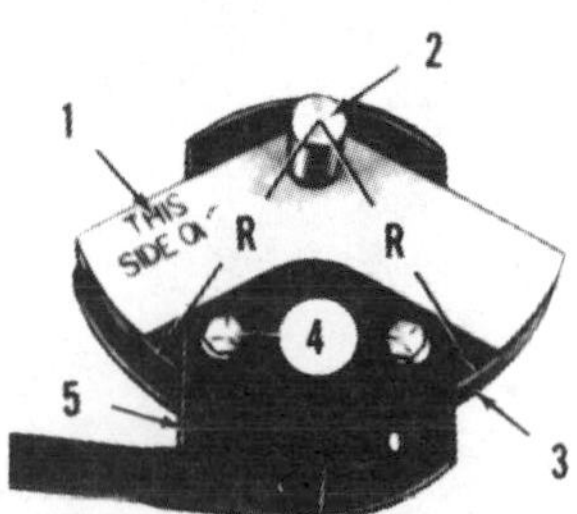


***Fig. JD95—Electric lift models equipped with adjustable cam assembly, a 3 inch (76 mm) radius (R) must be maintained from center of pivot shaft to outer edge of cam. To ensure accurate adjustment, use JDM-65 special tool as shown.***

1. JDM-65 tool
2. Pivot shaft
3. Cam
4. Cap screws
5. Arm

sition to activate pto neutral-start switch. Safety switch is not adjustable and must be renewed if testing indicates switch failure.

On models equipped with manual pto clutch, neutral-start switch is closed when control lever is placed in disengaged position. If necessary, loosen switch mounting screws and adjust for proper operation. Be careful not to bottom out switch plunger to prevent damage to switch.

All models are equipped with a transmission neutral-start switch. To adjust switch, loosen mounting screws or nuts and move switch until it closes when transmission shift lever is placed in neutral position. On hydrostatic transmission models, switch should close when hydrostatic control lever is placed in neutral position or when brake pedal is fully depressed. To prevent damage to switch, be sure switch is not bottomed out after adjustment.

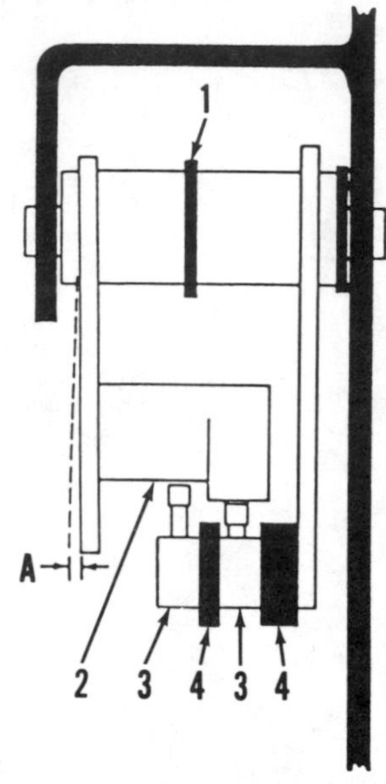


***Fig. JD96—On electric lift models equipped with one-piece cam and arm assembly, cam arm side play (A) must not exceed 1/16 inch (1.5 mm). Add shims (1) as necessary. Two spacers must be installed between switches as shown. Refer to text.***

1. Shim washer
2. Cam
3. Switches
4. Spacers

# WIRING SCHEMATICS

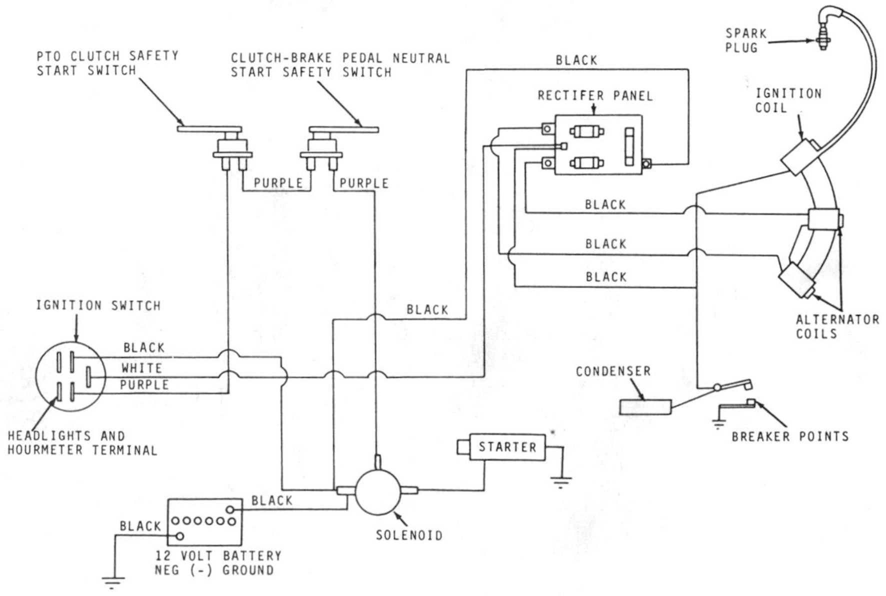


***Fig. JD100—Electrical wiring diagram for Models 60 and 70.***

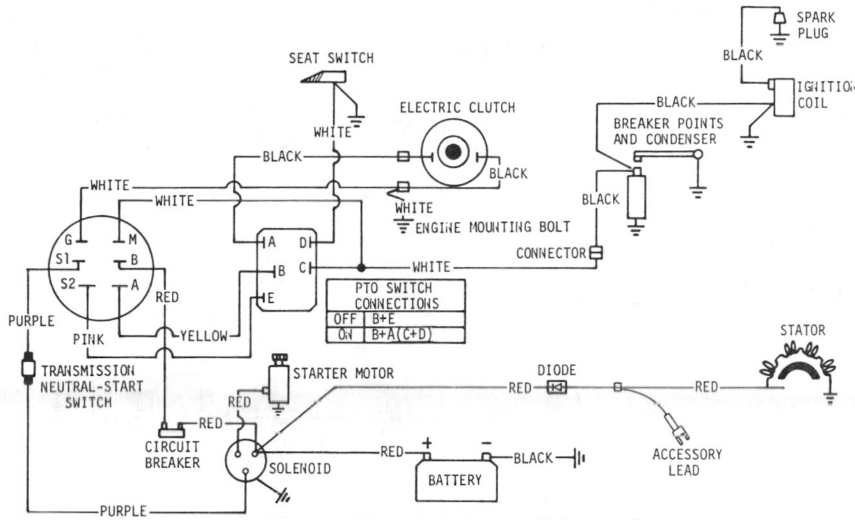


***Fig. JD101—Electrical wiring diagram for Models 108 and 111 tractors (S.N. 95001-120000).***

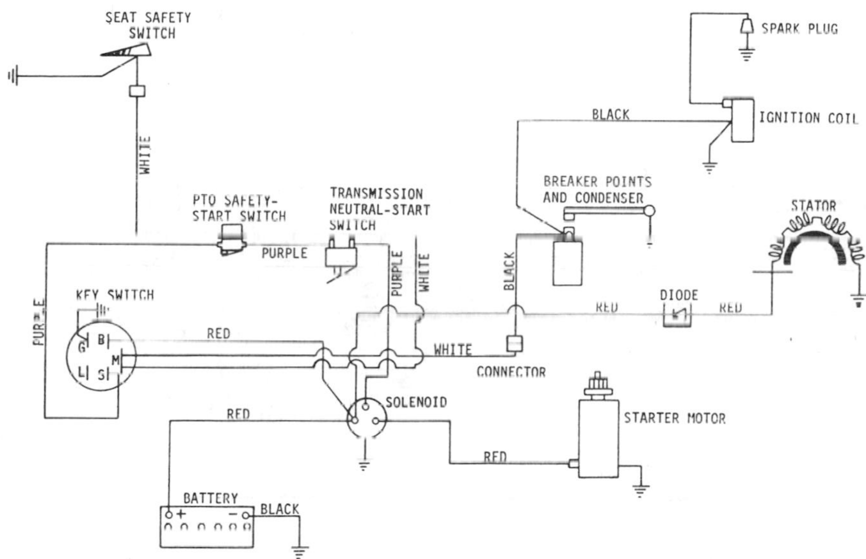


***Fig. JD102—Electrical wiring diagram for Models 108 and 111 tractors (S.N. 120001 and later).***

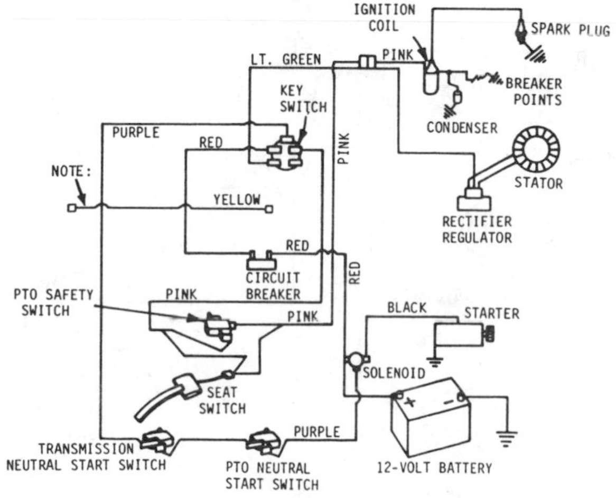


***Fig. JD103—Electrical wiring diagram for Model 208.***

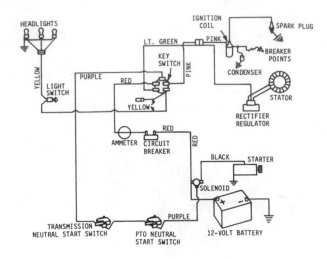

*Fig. JD104—Electrical wiring diagram for Models 200, 210, 212 and 214 tractors (S.N. 30001-70000).*

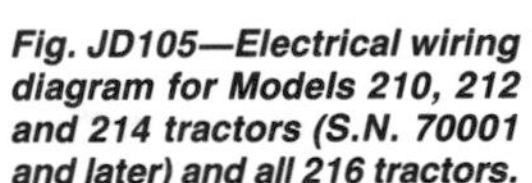

*Fig. JD105—Electrical wiring diagram for Models 210, 212 and 214 tractors (S.N. 70001 and later) and all 216 tractors.*

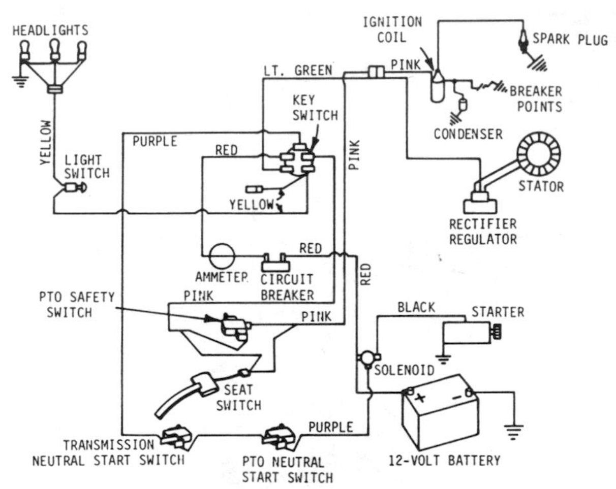


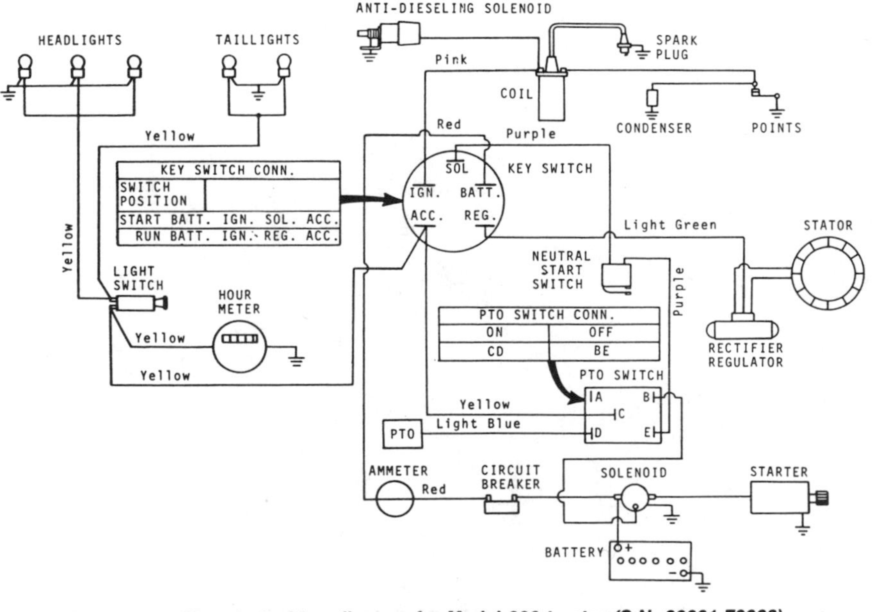


*Fig. JD106—Electrical wiring diagram for Model 300 tractor (S.N. 30001-70000).*

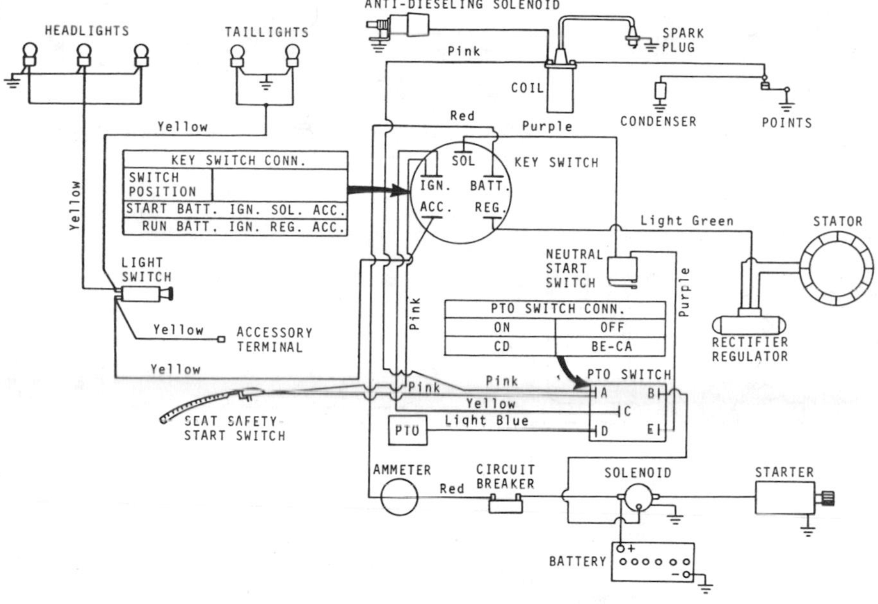


*Fig. JD107—Electrical wiring diagram for Model 300 tractor (S.N. 70001-80000) and all 316 tractors.*

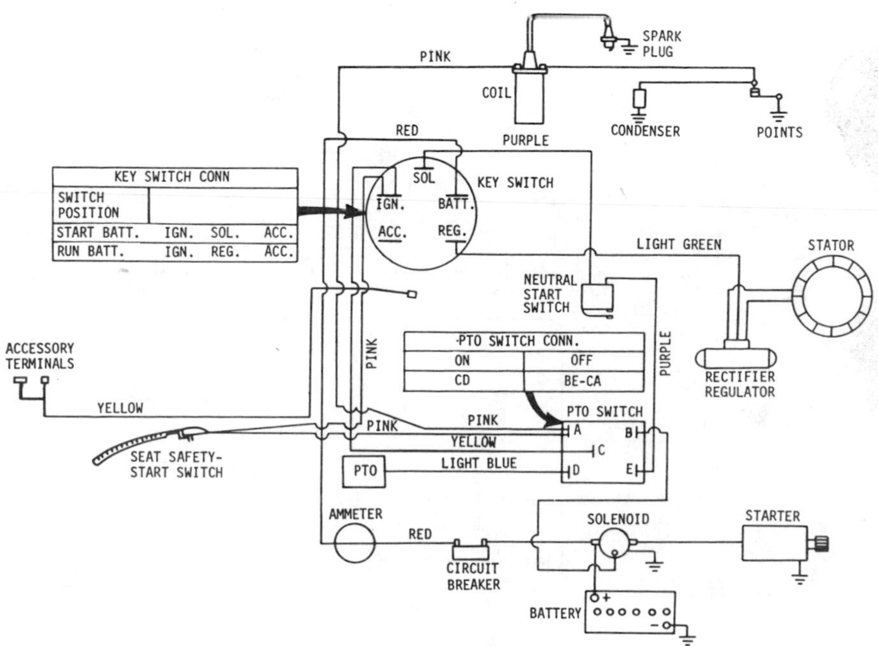


*Fig. JD108—Electrical wiring diagram for Models 312 and 314.*

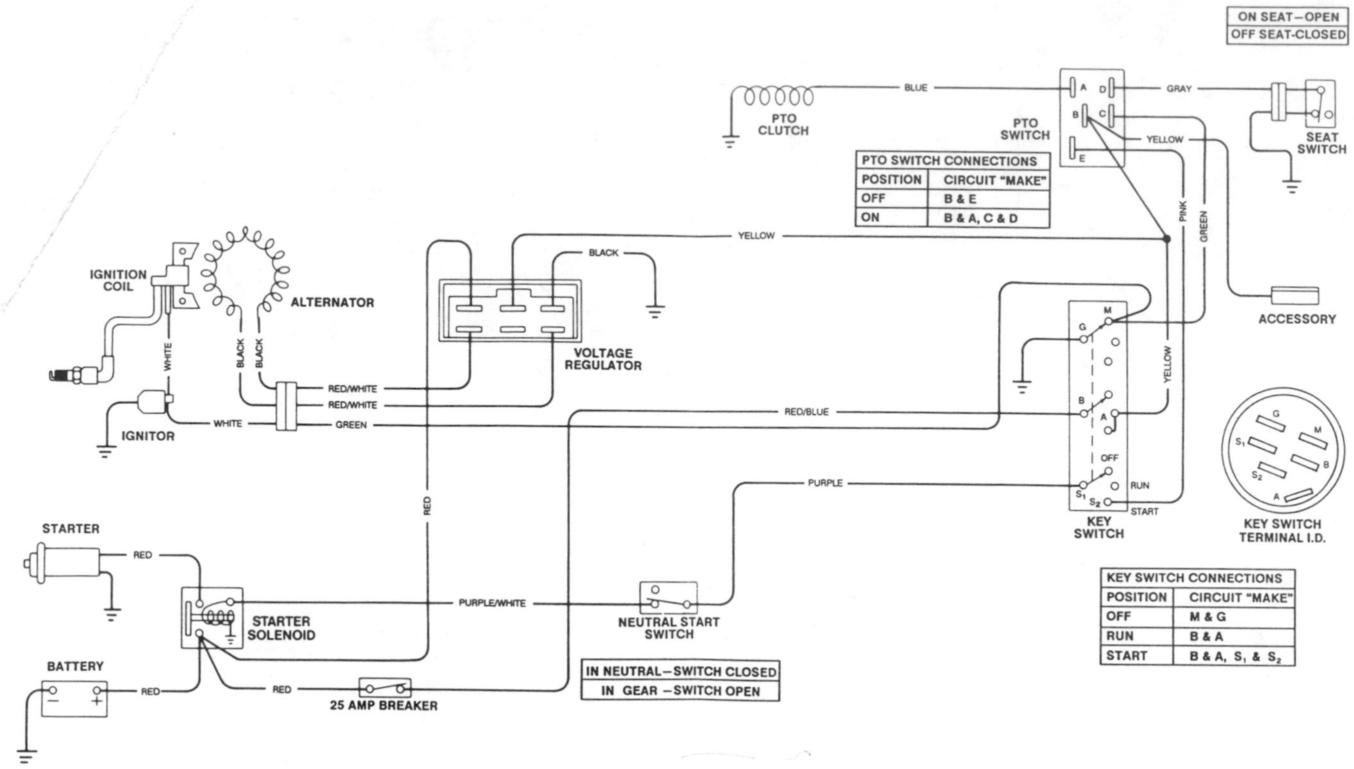


*Fig. JD109—Electrical wiring diagram for Model 130 (prior to S.N. 423870).*

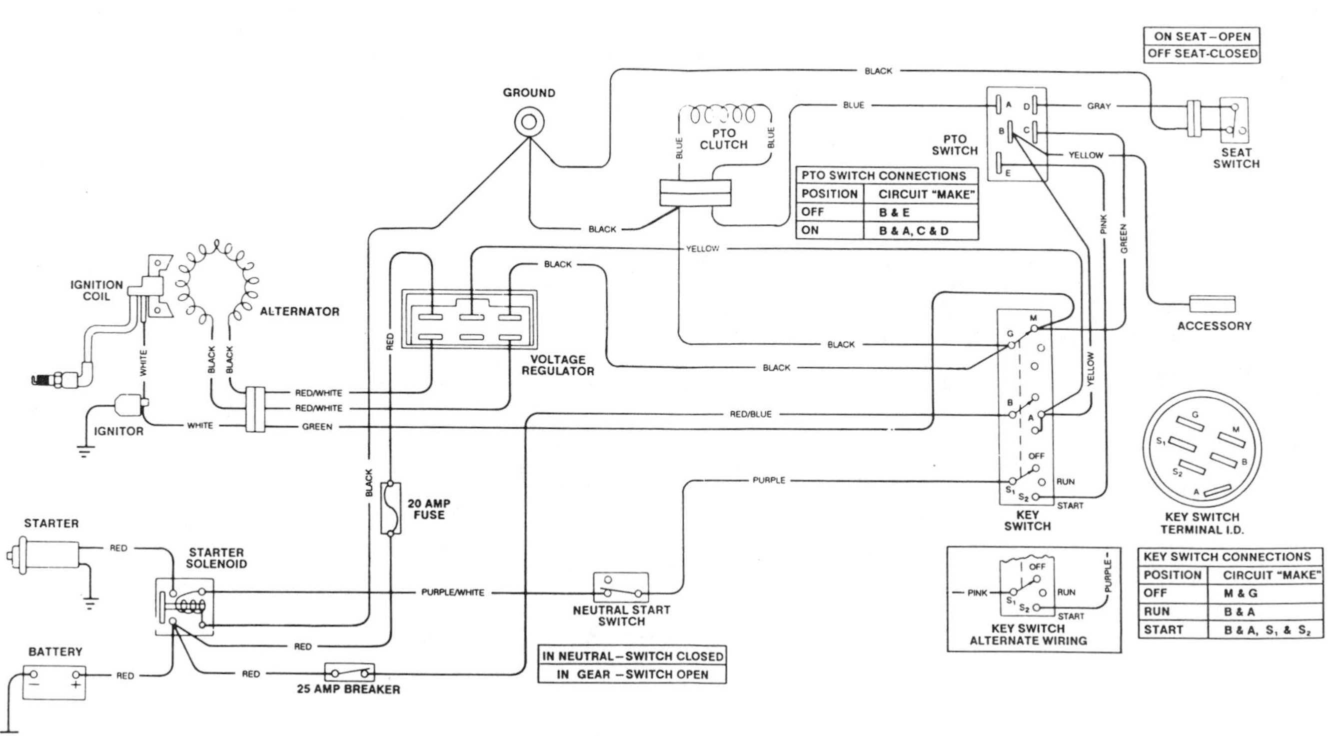


*Fig. JD110—Electrical wiring diagram for Model 130 (S.N. 423870 and later).*

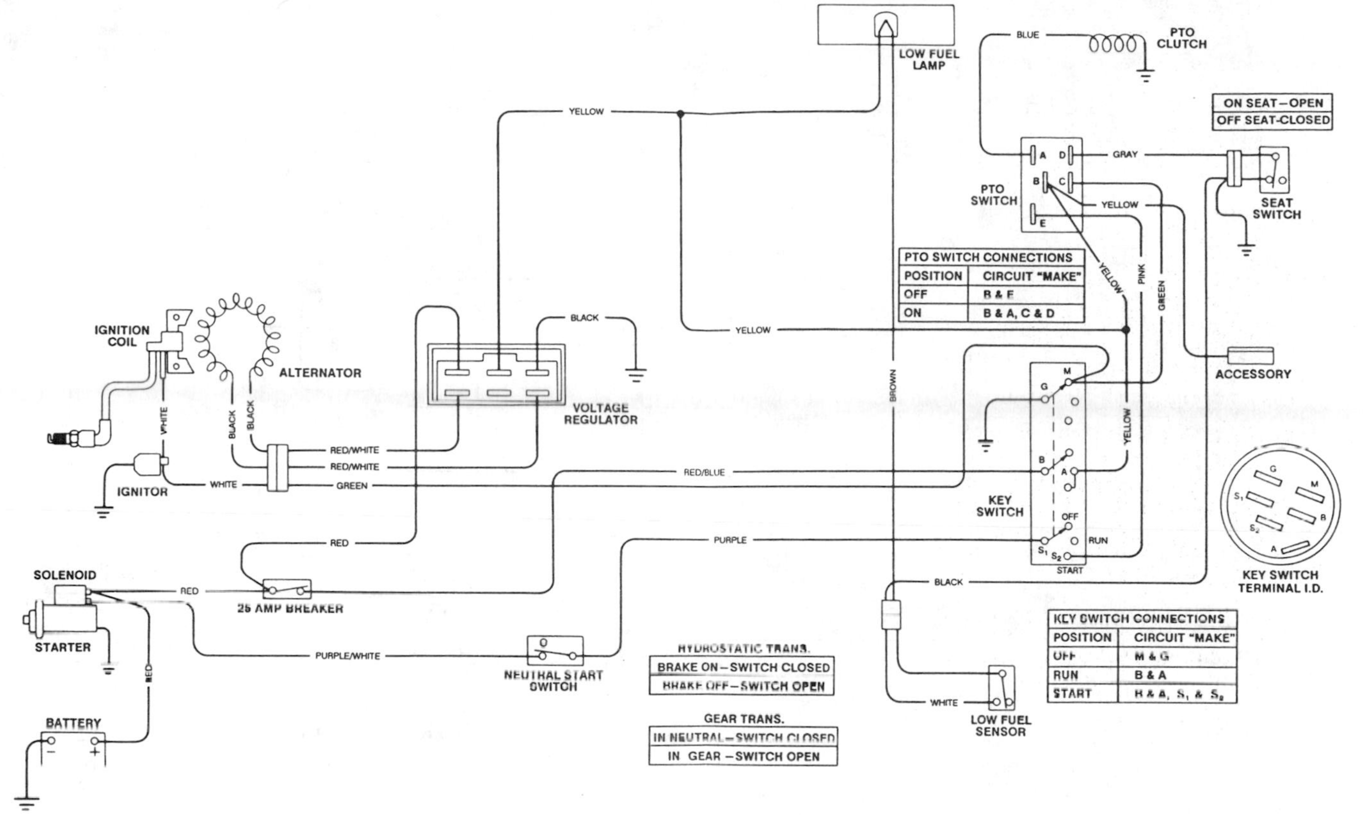

| PTO SWITCH CONNECTIONS | |
|---|---|
| POSITION | CIRCUIT "MAKE" |
| OFF | B & E |
| ON | B & A, C & D |

| ON SEAT–OPEN |
|---|
| OFF SEAT–CLOSED |

| KEY SWITCH CONNECTIONS | |
|---|---|
| POSITION | CIRCUIT "MAKE" |
| OFF | M & G |
| RUN | B & A |
| START | B & A, $S_1$ & $S_2$ |

| HYDROSTATIC TRANS. |
|---|
| BRAKE ON–SWITCH CLOSED |
| BRAKE OFF–SWITCH OPEN |

| GEAR TRANS. |
|---|
| IN NEUTRAL–SWITCH CLOSED |
| IN GEAR–SWITCH OPEN |

*Fig. JD111—Electrical wiring diagram for Models 160 (prior to S.N. 428431) and 165 (prior to S.N. 425969).*

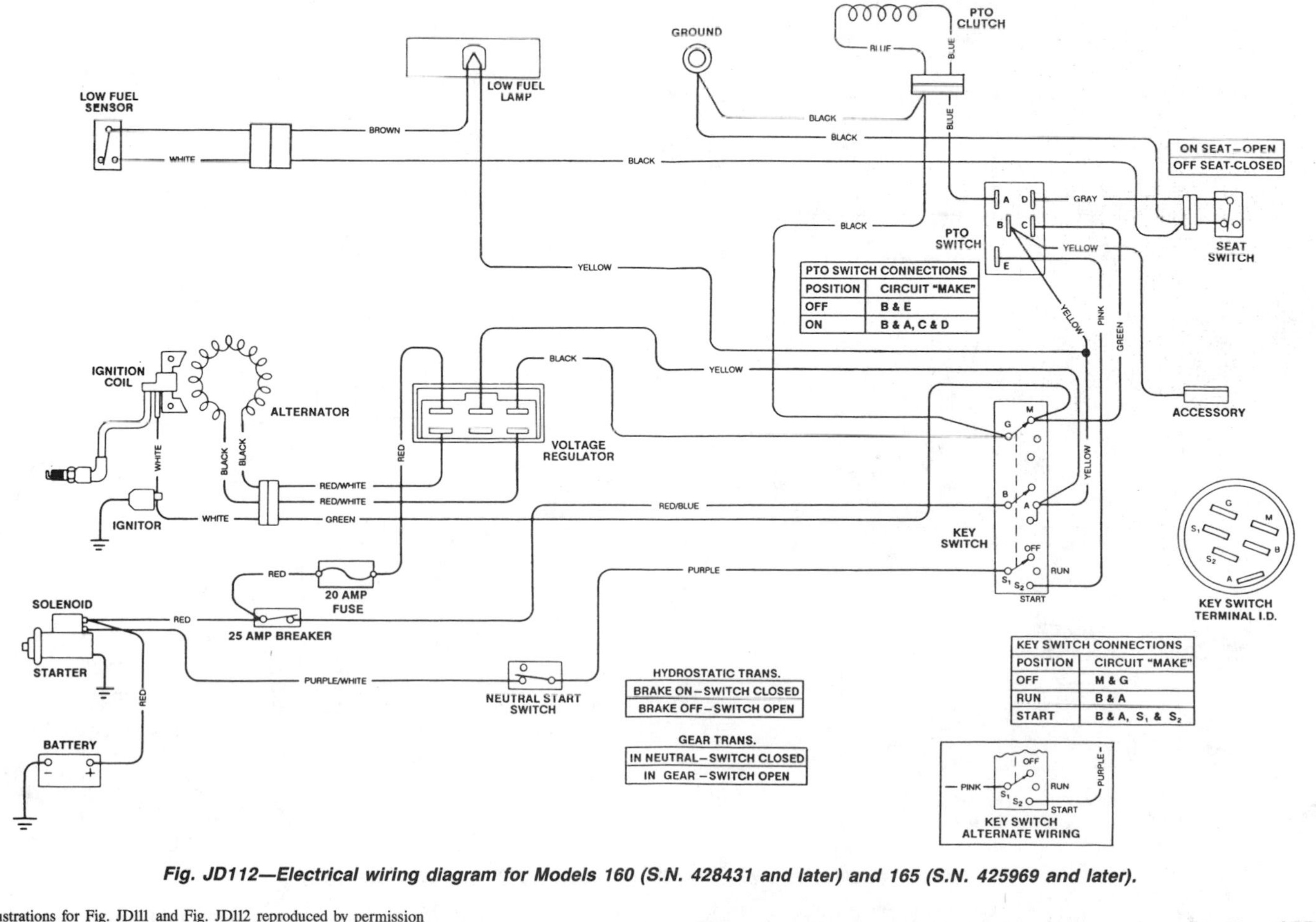

| ON SEAT–OPEN |
|---|
| OFF SEAT–CLOSED |

| PTO SWITCH CONNECTIONS | |
|---|---|
| POSITION | CIRCUIT "MAKE" |
| OFF | B & E |
| ON | B & A, C & D |

| KEY SWITCH CONNECTIONS | |
|---|---|
| POSITION | CIRCUIT "MAKE" |
| OFF | M & G |
| RUN | B & A |
| START | B & A, $S_1$ & $S_2$ |

| HYDROSTATIC TRANS. |
|---|
| BRAKE ON–SWITCH CLOSED |
| BRAKE OFF–SWITCH OPEN |

| GEAR TRANS. |
|---|
| IN NEUTRAL–SWITCH CLOSED |
| IN GEAR–SWITCH OPEN |

KEY SWITCH ALTERNATE WIRING

*Fig. JD112—Electrical wiring diagram for Models 160 (S.N. 428431 and later) and 165 (S.N. 425969 and later).*

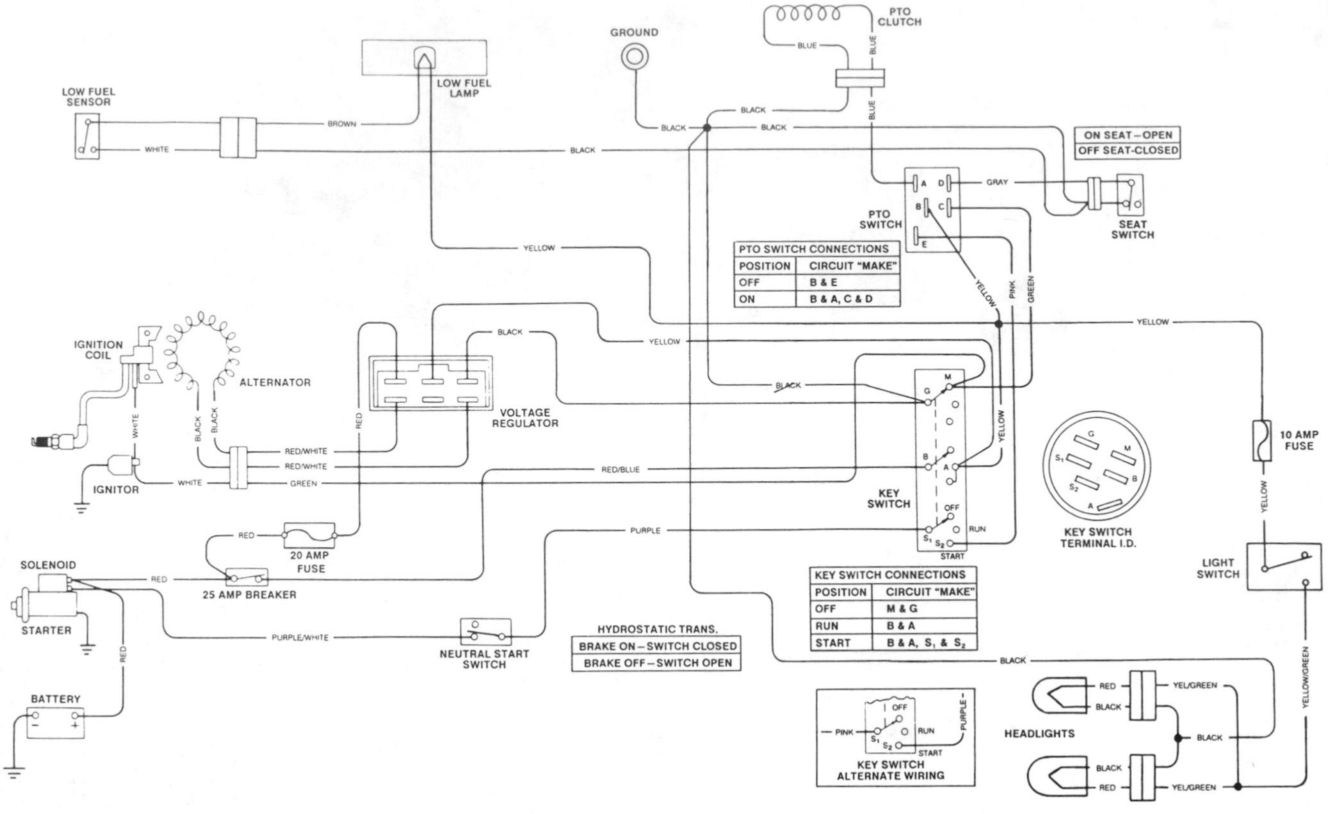

| ON SEAT–OPEN |
|---|
| OFF SEAT–CLOSED |

| PTO SWITCH CONNECTIONS | |
|---|---|
| POSITION | CIRCUIT "MAKE" |
| OFF | B & E |
| ON | B & A, C & D |

| KEY SWITCH CONNECTIONS | |
|---|---|
| POSITION | CIRCUIT "MAKE" |
| OFF | M & G |
| RUN | B & A |
| START | B & A, $S_1$ & $S_2$ |

| HYDROSTATIC TRANS. |
|---|
| BRAKE ON–SWITCH CLOSED |
| BRAKE OFF–SWITCH OPEN |

KEY SWITCH ALTERNATE WIRING

*Fig. JD113—Electrical wiring diagram for Model 175 (prior to S.N. 475001).*

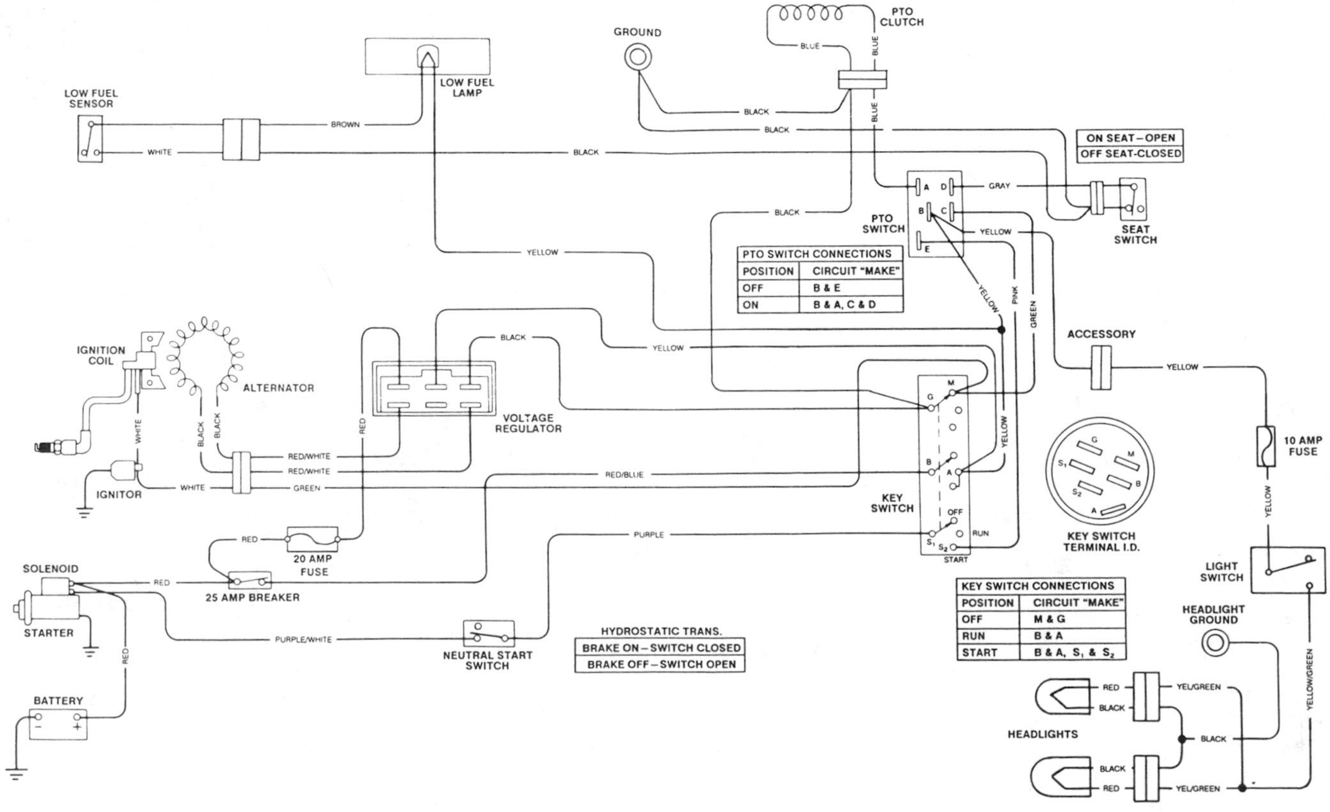

| ON SEAT–OPEN |
|---|
| OFF SEAT–CLOSED |

| PTO SWITCH CONNECTIONS | |
|---|---|
| POSITION | CIRCUIT "MAKE" |
| OFF | B & E |
| ON | B & A, C & D |

| KEY SWITCH CONNECTIONS | |
|---|---|
| POSITION | CIRCUIT "MAKE" |
| OFF | M & G |
| RUN | B & A |
| START | B & A, $S_1$ & $S_2$ |

| HYDROSTATIC TRANS. |
|---|
| BRAKE ON–SWITCH CLOSED |
| BRAKE OFF–SWITCH OPEN |

*Fig. JD114—Electrical wiring diagram for Model 175 (S.N. 475001 and later).*

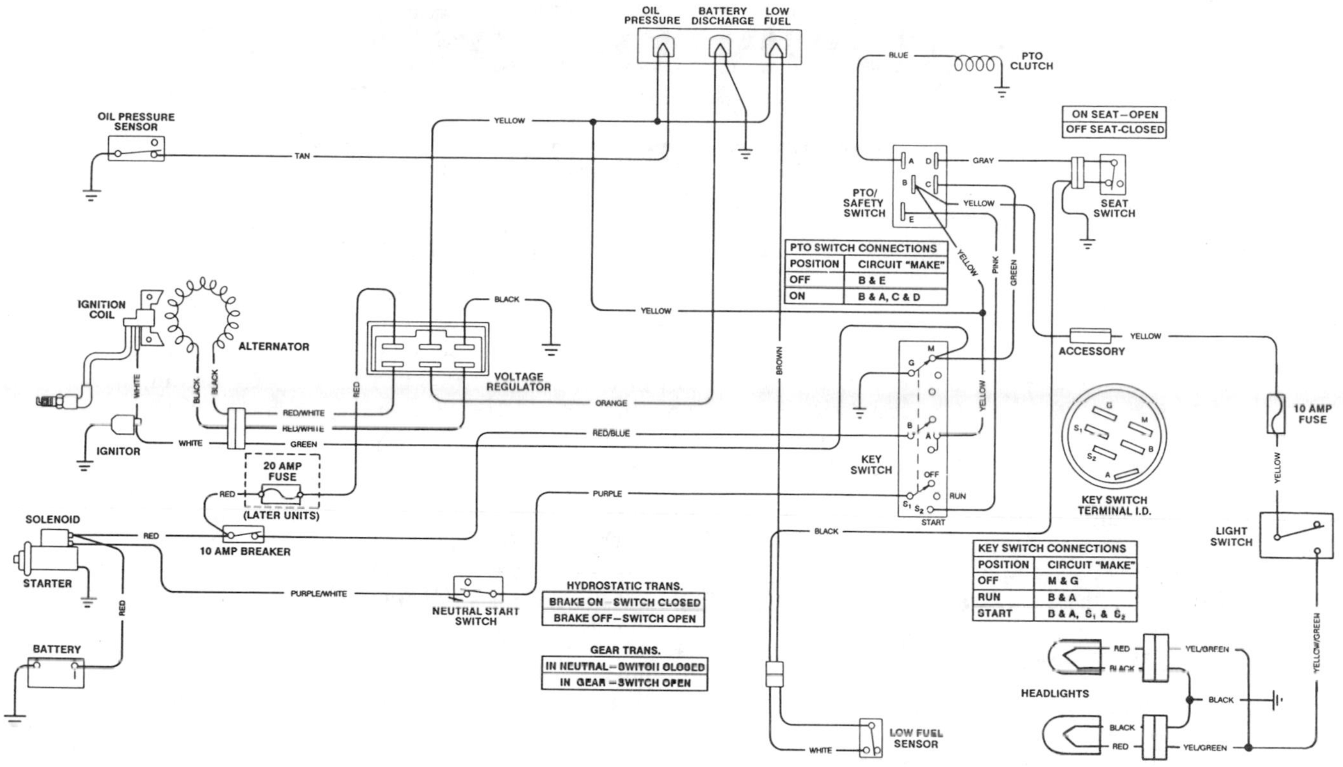


*Fig. JD115—Electrical wiring diagram for Models 180 and 185 (prior to S.N. 475001).*

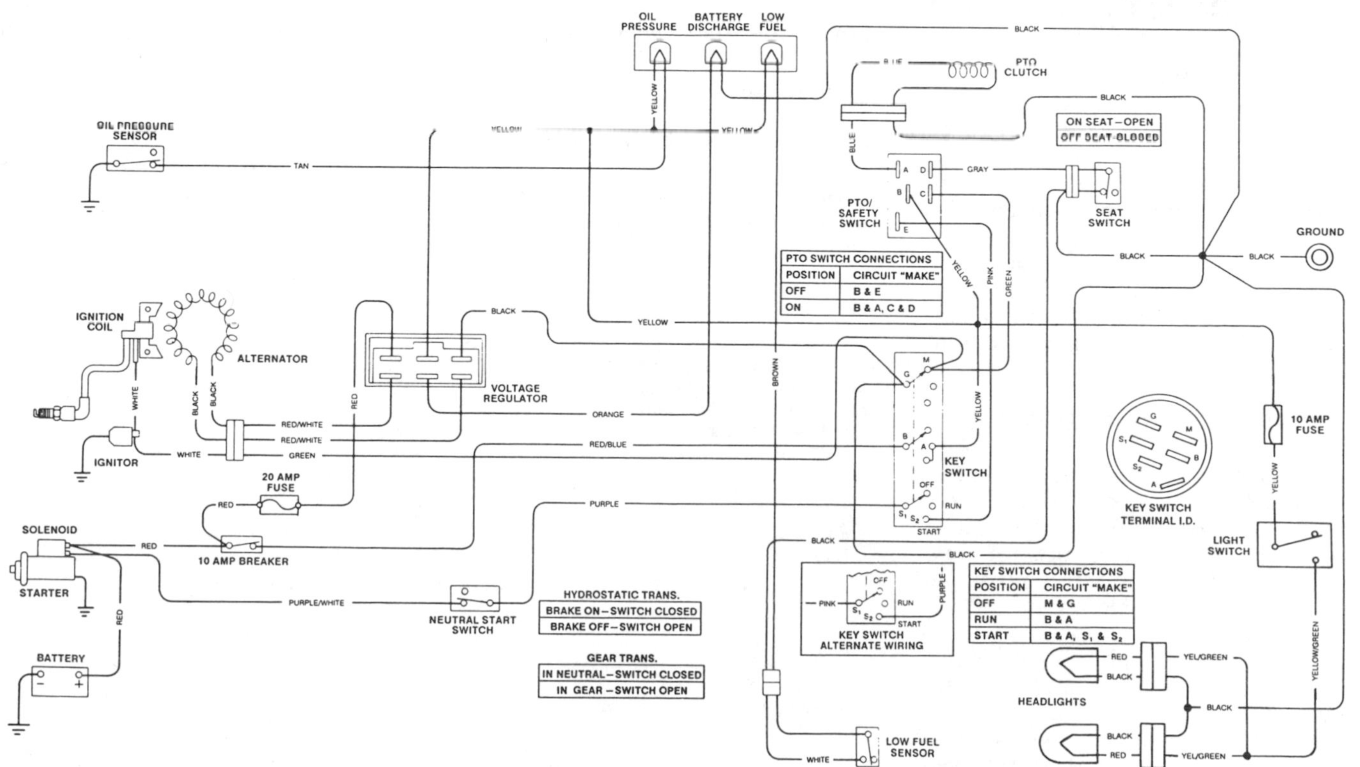


*Fig. JD116—Electrical wiring diagram for Models 180 and 185 (S.N. 475001 and later).*

# JOHN DEERE

## CONDENSED SPECIFICATIONS

| | MODELS | | |
|---|---|---|---|
| | 240 | 260 | 265 |
| Engine Make | Kawasaki | Kawasaki | Kawasaki |
| Model | FC420V | FC540V | FC540V |
| Bore | 89 mm (3.5 in.) | 89 mm (3.5 in.) | 89 mm (3.5 in.) |
| Stroke | 68 mm (2.68 in.) | 86 mm (3.38 in.) | 86 mm (3.38 in.) |
| Displacement | 423 cc (25.8 cu. in.) | 535 cc (32.6 cu. in.) | 535 cc (32.6 cu. in.) |
| Power Rating | 10.4 kW (14 hp) | 12.6 kW (17 hp) | 12.6 kW (17 hp) |
| Slow Idle Speed—Rpm | | 1400 rpm | |
| High Idle Speed (No-Load)—Rpm | | 3350 rpm | |
| Capacities— | | | |
| Crankcase | 1.3 L* (2.8 pts.) | 1.6 L* (3.4 pts.) | 1.6 L* (3.4 pts.) |
| Transmission | See Text | See Text | 2.5 L (2.6 qts.) |
| Fuel Tank | | 11.4 L (3.0 gals.) | |

*Add 0.4 L (0.8 pt.) with filter change.

# FRONT AXLE AND STEERING SYSTEM

### MAINTENANCE

The front wheel spindles should be lubricated after every 50 hours of operation. Jack up front axle so wheels are suspended and apply grease to spindles through grease fitting at each end of axle. One or two shots from a hand-held grease gun should be sufficient. Use a good quality, lithium based grease. Check for looseness and binding in front axle components.

### R&R AXLE MAIN MEMBER

Raise and support front of tractor. Disconnect drag link end (14—Fig. JD201) from steering arm (13). Using a suitable jack, support axle assembly. Unscrew pivot pin nut (1). Unscrew pivot pin mounting screws and lower axle assembly out of tractor.

Inspect components for excessive wear and damage. Bushings in axle are renewable.

When reinstalling axle, tighten pivot pin nut (1) until axle end play is removed but axle still pivots freely.

### TIE ROD AND TOE-IN

The tie rod (11—Fig. JD201) is equipped with renewable ends that are not interchangeable.

Front wheel toe-in should be 3-6 mm (1/8 to 1/4 in.). Adjust toe-in by altering tie rod length.

### STEERING SPINDLES

Raise and support side to be serviced. Remove wheel and tire. Disconnect tie rod end, and if needed, drag link end. If removing right spindle (7—Fig. JD201), detach snap ring securing top of spindle and withdraw spindle from axle. If removing left spindle (17), mark end of spindle and steering arm (13) so arm can be returned to original position. Remove clamp bolt, remove steering arm and withdraw spindle from axle.

Inspect components for excessive wear and damage. Renewable bushings (5) are located in axle.

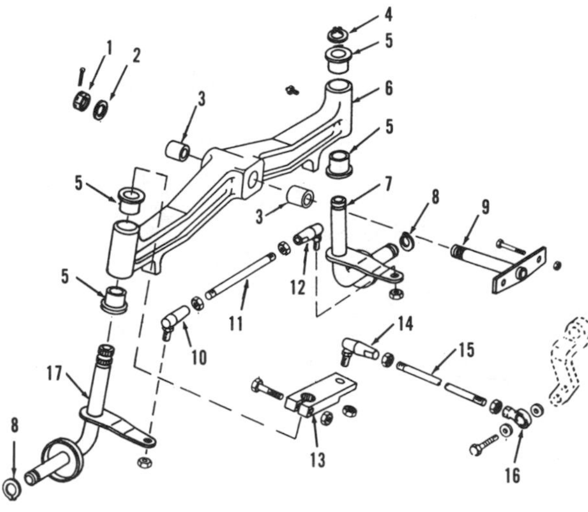


*Fig. JD201—Exploded view of front axle assembly. Note that rod ends (12 and 14) have left-hand threads.*

1. Slotted nut
2. Washer
3. Bushing
4. Snap ring
5. Bushing
6. Axle main member
7. Spindle R.H.
8. Snap ring
9. Pivot
10. Tie rod end
11. Tie rod
12. Tie rod end
13. Steering arm
14. Drag link end
15. Drag link
16. Drag link end
17. Spindle L.H.

### DRAG LINK

A drag link with adjustable ends is located between steering arm and pitman arm. Adjust length of drag link so equal turns of steering wheel are required to reach full left and right turn from neutral position.

Steering effort and response can be adjusted by changing the connecting point of drag link in pitman arm. Connecting drag link to lower hole in pitman arm will provide quick steering response when tractor is not heavily loaded. Connecting drag link to upper hole in pitman arm will provide reduced steering effort when tractor is equipped with heavy loads on front axle, but steering response will be slower because more turns of steering wheel will be required to turn the front wheels.

### FRONT WHEEL BEARINGS

Front wheel bearings are sealed and should not require lubrication. Wheel bearings are a press fit in wheel hub.

### STEERING GEAR

**R&R AND OVERHAUL.** Detach drag link from pitman arm. Scribe match marks on pitman arm and end of pitman shaft, then remove pitman arm. Raise hood and remove lower pedestal panel. Disconnect steering column shaft from gearbox shaft. Unscrew fasteners securing gearbox and remove gearbox.

The steering gear is a recirculating ball type. Refer to Fig. JD202 for an exploded view of gearbox. To disassemble, remove side cover (3) and end cover (18) and withdraw pitman shaft (7) and wormshaft assembly (15). The wormshaft is available only as an assembly and no attempt should be made to disassemble the unit.

When assembling gearbox, perform the following adjustments: Back out adjusting screw (6) until it stops. Turn wormshaft (15) in (clockwise) until stopped, then turn back one-half turn. Install needed shims (17) so rolling torque when turning steering shaft is 0.4 N·m (3.5 in.-lbs.). Install thickest shim (5) allowed when assembling unit and make sure pitman shaft (7) is centered on ball nut when nut is at midpoint of travel. Turn adjusting screw (6) so steering shaft rolling torque increases to 1.1 N·m (9.5 in.-lbs.), then tighten locknut (1) while holding adjusting screw in place.

Gearbox oil capacity is 170 mL (6 oz.). Recommended oil is SAE 90 gear oil rated GL-5. After installation, check oil level by removing check plug. Oil level should be 25 mm (1 in.) below top of plug hole.



# ENGINE

### LUBRICATION

Check oil level before operation and after every four hours of operation. Determine oil level by resting dipstick on top of dipstick tube; do not screw in.

Manufacturer recommends oil with API classification SE or SF. Use SAE 30 oil for temperatures above 32°F (0°C); use SAE 10W-30 oil for temperatures between -4°F (-20°C) and 86°F (30°C); SAE 5W-30 may be used between 50°F (10°C) and -31°F (-35°C).

Change oil and filter after first five hours of operation and then after every 100 hours of operation, or more frequently if operation is severe. On Model 240 without oil filter, change engine oil after every 50 hours of operation.

### REMOVE AND REINSTALL

To remove engine, first remove hood, muffler and pedestal shroud. Disconnect battery ground cable. Close fuel shut-off valve and disconnect fuel line. Disconnect throttle control cable. Disconnect ground wire, starter wires and ignition wires from engine. Remove electric pto clutch. Relieve tension on traction drive belt and remove belt from drive pulley. Remove drive pulley and key from engine crankshaft. Remove engine mounting cap screws and lift engine from tractor.

To reinstall engine, reverse the removal procedure. Apply an anti-seize lubricant to crankshaft before installing drive pulley. Tighten pto clutch mounting cap screw to 56 N·m (45 ft.-lbs.).

### OVERHAUL

Engine make and models are listed at the beginning of this section. To overhaul engine components and accessories, refer to Kawasaki engine section in this manual.

# CLUTCH AND TRACTION DRIVE BELT

### Models 240-260

**ADJUSTMENT.** When the clutch pedal (1—Fig. JD203) is depressed, bellcrank assembly (18) pivots and loosens drive belt (2) from drive pulleys, stopping forward or reverse movement of tractor. At the same time that clutch is disengaged, the transmission interlock linkage (which is connected to clutch pedal shaft) moves the interlock arm (13) to unlock the shifter fork and allow a shift to be made.

To adjust clutch, stop engine and release clutch pedal. Loosen nut on front idler pulley (6). Move front idler pulley until clutch pedal spring (7) is 54 mm (2 in.) long. On some models, bellcrank idler pulley (9) can also be adjusted to make up for belt stretch.

**R&R DRIVE BELT.** To remove traction drive belt (2—Fig. JD203), first remove mower deck. Disconnect wiring harness from electric pto clutch, then unbolt and remove pto clutch. Remove adjusting idler pulley (6) and belt guide (3). Remove remaining belt guides (5, 8, 15, 17 and 20) as necessary. Depress clutch to relieve spring tension or disconnect spring (10), then slip belt out of pulleys.

To reinstall belt, reverse the removal procedure. Adjust belt tension as previously outlined.

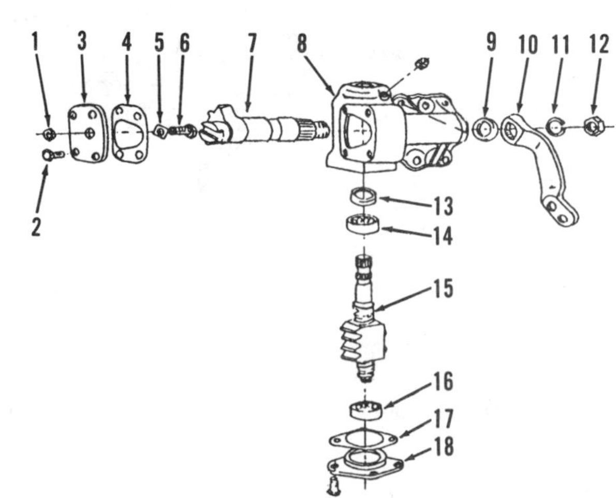


*Fig. JD202—Exploded view of steering gearbox.*
1. Nut
2. Screw
3. Cover
4. Gasket
5. Shim
6. Adjuster
7. Pitman shaft
8. Gearbox
9. Seal
10. Pitman arm
11. Lockwasher
12. Nut
13. Seal
14. Bearing
15. Shaft & nut assy.
16. Bearing
17. Shim
18. Cover

## Model 265

The hydrostatic power train used on Model 265 uses a spring-loaded idler pulley and belt drive system as shown in Fig. JD204. The belt tension is held constant by spring (8) and no adjustment is required. If belt slippage occurs due to wear or belt stretch, renew drive belt.

**R&R DRIVE BELT.** To remove traction drive belt, first remove mower deck. Disconnect electrical wiring from pto clutch, then unbolt and remove pto clutch. Remove belt guides as necessary. Disconnect belt tension spring or move idler pulley pivot to relieve spring tension on belt, then slip belt out of pulleys.

To reinstall belt, reverse the removal procedure.

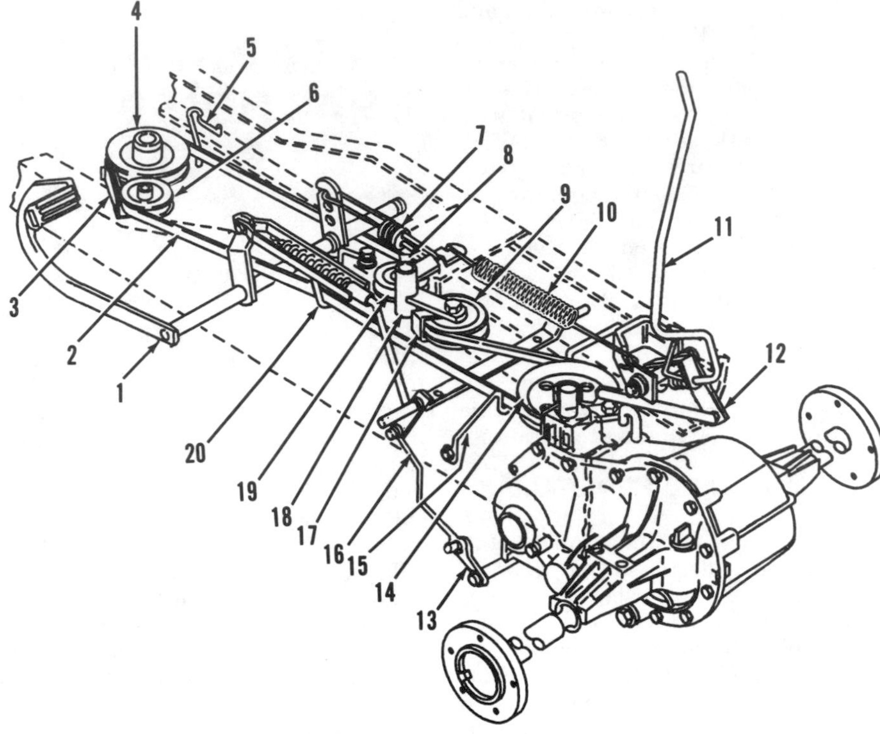


***Fig. JD203—View showing power train components on gear drive Models 240 and 260.***

1. Clutch pedal
2. Traction drive belt
3. Belt guide
4. Engine pulley
5. Belt guide
6. Belt tension idler pulley
7. Clutch pedal spring
8. Belt guide
9. Bellcrank idler
10. Belt tension spring
11. Shift lever
12. Shift linkage
13. Shift interlock arm
14. Transaxle pulley
15. Belt guide
16. Interlock linkage
17. Belt guide
18. Clutch bellcrank
19. Bellcrank idler
20. Belt guide

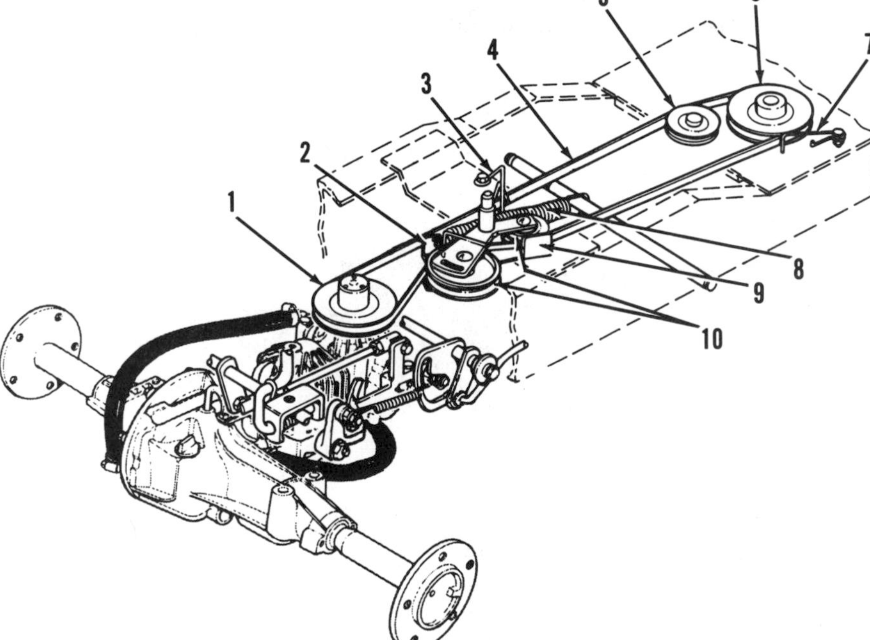


***Fig. JD204—View showing power train components on hydrostatic drive Model 265.***

1. Transmission pulley
2. Belt guide
3. Belt guide
4. Traction drive belt
5. Belt idler
6. Engine pulley
7. Belt guide
8. Belt tension spring
9. Belt guide
10. Bellcrank idlers

# BRAKES

The shoe and drum type brake is located on right side of differential housing on Models 240 and 260 and on left side of differential housing on Model 265.

### ADJUSTMENT

Refer to Fig. JD207 for an exploded view of clutch and brake linkage used on Models 240 and 260. No adjustment of brake is required on these tractors.

To adjust brake on Model 265, place parking brake in locked position. Measure gap between washer (W—Fig. JD205) and spring retainer (R). Gap should be 8-14 mm (0.31-0.55 in.), if not, loosen nut (N) and turn nut (T). Retighten nut (N).

### R&R BRAKES

Refer to Fig. JD206 for an exploded view of brake assembly. To disassemble, detach rod from brake arm and remove screws securing cover (6). Remove spring (4) and brake shoes (3). Remove snap ring (2) and withdraw brake drum (1).

Inspect components for excessive wear and damage. On Models 240 and

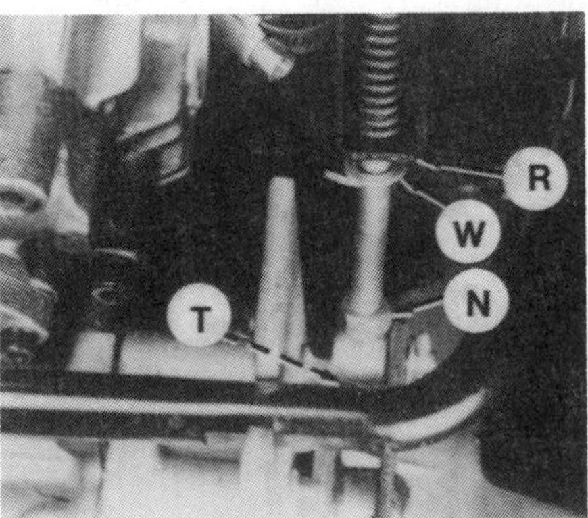


***Fig. JD205—Gap between washer (W) and spring retainer (R) on brake rod should be 8-14 mm (0.31-0.55 in.), if not, loosen nut (N) and turn nut (T). Retighten nut (N).***

260, brake lever shaft (7—Fig. JD206) diameter should be 19.95-20.00 mm (0.785-0.787 in.). Shaft bore in cover (6) should be 20.02-20.05 mm (0.788-0.789 in.). Maximum allowable shaft to cover clearance is 0.5 mm (0.020 in.).

On Model 265, brake arm shaft (7) diameter should be 17.96-18.00 mm (0.707-0.709 in.). Shaft bore in cover (6) should be 18.02-18.04 mm (0.709-0.710 in.). Maximum allowable shaft to bore clearance is 0.5 mm (0.020 in.).

To reinstall brake, reverse removal procedure. Install spring (4) so open portion is toward brake arm. Apply grease to brake arm shaft. While tightening cover screws, push brake arm forward so brake shoes will contact drum thereby centering cover. Tighten cover screws to 24 N·m (18 ft.-lbs.) if holes are threaded, or to 29 N·m (22 ft.-lbs.) on new cases with untapped holes. Adjust brake as outlined in previous section.

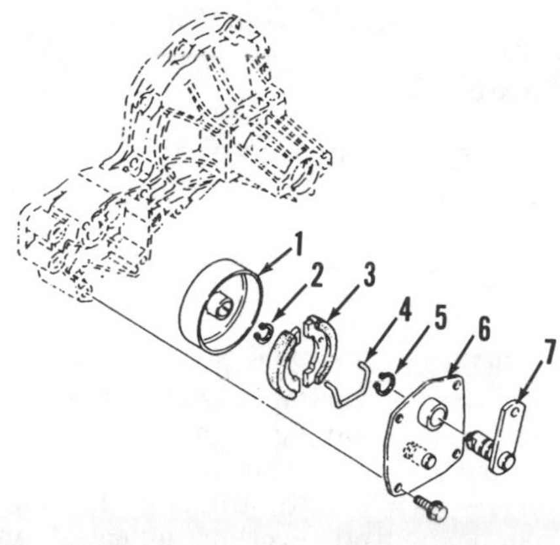


*Fig. JD206—Exploded view of brake assembly typical of all models.*

1. Drum
2. Snap ring
3. Brake shoes
4. Spring
5. Snap ring
6. Cover
7. Arm

neutral, then disconnect shift rod from transaxle shift arm. Disconnect brake control rod and transaxle interlock control rod. Depress clutch pedal and remove drive belt from transaxle pulley. Remove transaxle mounting bolts and lower transaxle from tractor.

To reinstall, reverse removal procedure.

## OVERHAUL

### Models 240-260

Models 240 and 260 are equipped with a TUFF TORQ transaxle manufactured by Kanzaki. Refer to Kanzaki section in TRANSAXLE SERVICE section for overhaul procedure.

# TRANSAXLE

## LUBRICATION

### Models 240-260

Check transaxle oil level after every 25 hours of operation. Oil level should be maintained at top mark on dipstick, which is located at rear of transaxle. Add oil as necessary.

**NOTE: Two different lubricants have been used in production of transaxle. Check color of oil to determine correct oil to use. If oil is honey colored, use John Deere GL-5 gear lubricant or equivalent. If oil is red, use John Deere All-Weather Hydrostatic fluid or type "F" automatic transmission fluid. DO NOT mix oil.**

## SHIFT LEVER NEUTRAL ADJUSTMENT

### Models 240-260

Move transmission shift lever to neutral and shut off engine. If shift lever is not positioned in neutral notch in deck quadrant slot, adjust shift lever as follows: Loosen nut (3—Fig. JD207) and turn nut (4) forward to move lever forward in quadrant slot or turn nut rearward to move lever rearward. Hold nut (4) and tighten nut (3).

## REMOVE AND REINSTALL

### Models 240-260

To remove transaxle, securely block up rear of tractor. Place shift lever in

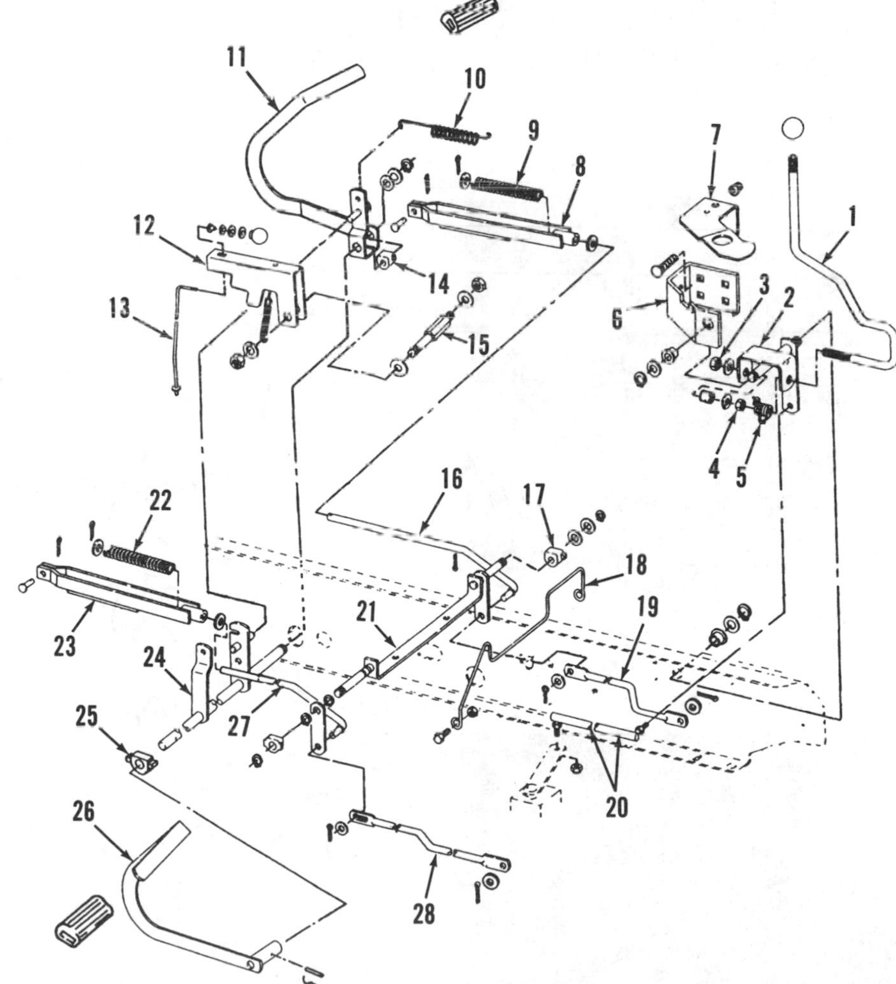


*Fig. JD207—Exploded view of clutch, brake and shift linkage used on Models 240 and 260.*

1. Shift lever
2. Shift bracket
3. Nut
4. Nut
5. Torsion spring
6. Bracket
7. Support
8. Spring retainer
9. Brake compression spring
10. Return spring
11. Brake pedal
12. Park brake latch
13. Brake rod
14. Bearing
15. Stud
16. Brake rod
17. Bearing
18. Belt guide
19. Brake rod
20. Shift rod
21. Brake shaft
22. Clutch compression spring
23. Spring retainer
24. Clutch shaft
25. Bearing
26. Clutch pedal
27. Interlock rod
28. Interlock rod

# HYDROSTATIC TRANSMISSION

## LUBRICATION

### Model 265

Check transmission fluid level after every 25 hours of operation. Fluid level should be maintained at top mark on dipstick attached to fill plug (P—Fig. JD208). Fluid level should be checked when transmission is warm. Be sure tractor is on level surface and engine is stopped when checking.

Transmission fluid and filter should be changed after first 50 hours of operation and then every 250 hours of operation thereafter. Partially fill new filter with oil before installing.

Recommended fluid is John Deere All-Weather Hydrostatic Fluid or good quality type "F" automatic transmission fluid.

Oil capacity is approximately 2.5 L (2.6 qts.).

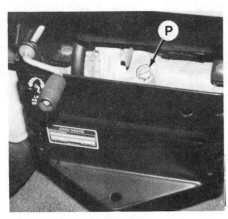

*Fig. JD208—View showing location of transmission fill plug (P).*

*Fig. JD209—Adjust hydrostatic control lever friction by rotating nut (N) so force required to move control lever is 22-36 N (5-8 lbs.).*

## ADJUSTMENTS

### Model 265

**CONTROL LEVER FRICTION.** Force required to move hydrostatic control lever should be 22-36 N (5-8 lbs.). Adjust control lever friction by rotating nut (N—Fig. JD209).

**NEUTRAL POSITION.** Securely support rear of tractor so rear wheels are off ground. Run engine at fast throttle setting and move transmission control lever so wheels stop turning (this may not be neutral position indicated on shift panel). Stop engine.

Loosen eccentric retaining screw (18—Fig. JD210) and rotate eccentric (14—Fig. JD210 and JD211) so roller (12) is centered in notch of control arm (11). Loosen nut (19—Fig. JD210). Engage parking brake. Turn eccentric (7) so roller (20) is centered in slot of cam (6), then retighten nut (19). Being certain roller (12) is centered in notch of control arm (11), turn nuts (21) so shift control lever is centered in neutral notch of shift panel. Run engine and check adjustments. Shift lever should return to neutral when brake is depressed and rear wheels should not turn when shift lever is in neutral.

## PRESSURE TEST

**CHARGE PUMP PRESSURE TEST.** To check charge pump pressure, first start and run engine at fast idle until transmission oil is warm. Stop engine and install a 0-150 psi (0-1000 kPa) pressure gage in either port (P—Fig. JD212) located in front of transmission. Move transmission control lever to neutral, run engine at slow idle and check pressure.

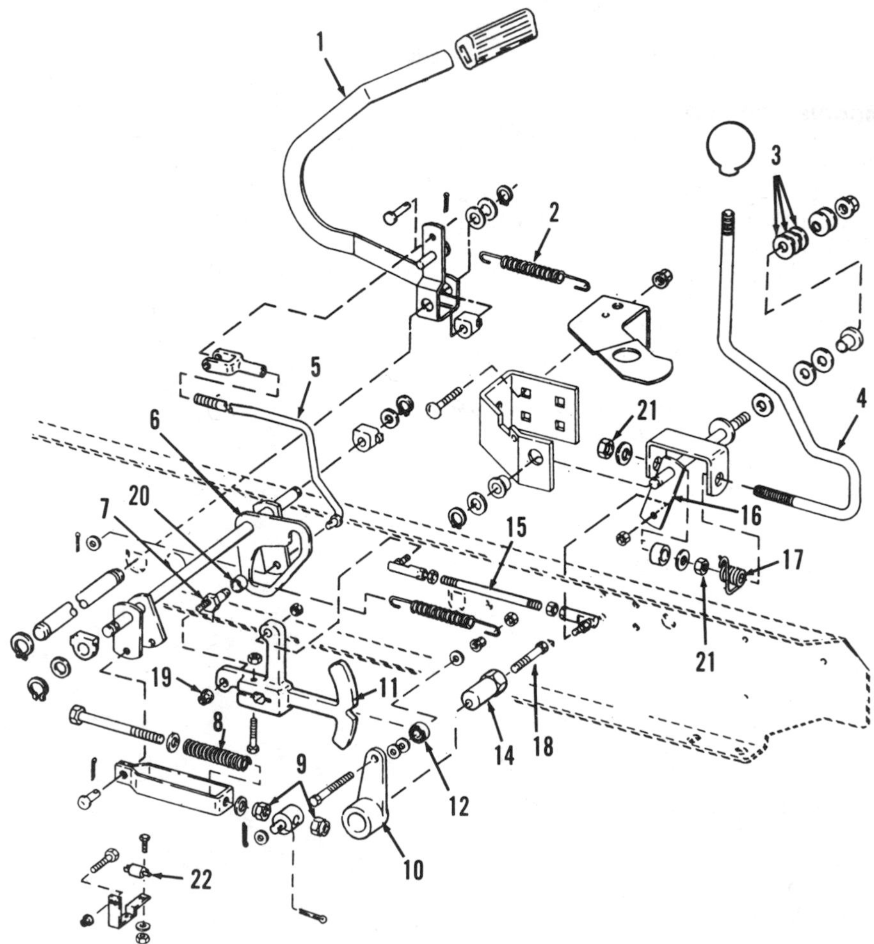


*Fig. JD210—Exploded view of transmission control linkage.*

1. Pedal
2. Spring
3. Spring washers
4. Shift lever
5. Control rod
6. Cam plate
7. Eccentric
8. Spring
9. Nuts
10. Control lever
11. Control arm
12. Roller
14. Eccentric
15. Rod
16. Lever
17. Spring
18. Screw
19. Nut
20. Roller
21. Nut
22. Neutral switch

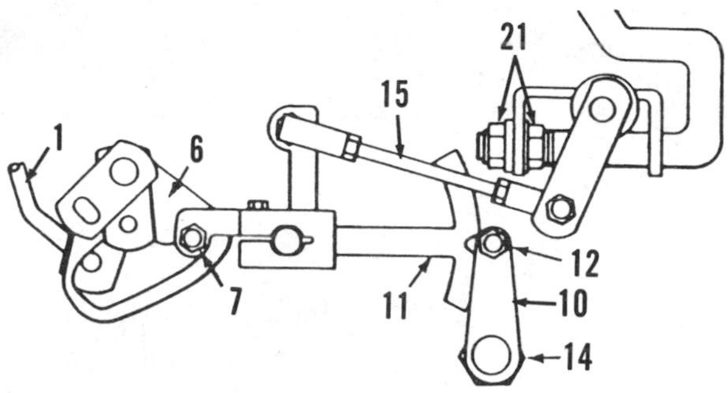


Fig. JD211—Drawing of transmission control mechanism. Refer to text for adjustment.

Fig. JD212—Connect a suitable pressure gage to either port (P) to check hydraulic pressure. See text.

**NOTE: Transmission must be in neutral and wheels must not rotate. Do not move transmission control lever out of neutral as pressure will increase and may damage pressure gage.**

Charge pump pressure must be 193-490 kPa (28-71 psi). If low, be sure transmission filter and charge pump relief valve are in good condition. Relief valve pressure is not adjustable.

### REMOVE AND REINSTALL

#### Model 265

To remove transmission, securely block up rear of tractor. Disconnect hydrostatic transmission control linkage and brake control linkage. Disconnect traction drive belt tension spring or move belt idler pulley pivot to relieve tension on belt, then slip belt out of transmission pulley. Remove transaxle mounting nuts and bolts and lower transaxle assembly from tractor.

Drain oil from transaxle housing. Disconnect hydrostatic transmission suction and return hoses. Unbolt and remove hydrostatic transmission from transaxle housing.

To reinstall, reverse the removal procedure.

### OVERHAUL

#### Model 265

A Hydro-Gear Model BDU-21L hydrostatic transmission is used on Model 265. Refer to Hydro-Gear section in HYDROSTATIC TRANSMISSION SERVICE section for overhaul procedure.

## DIFFERENTIAL AND REDUCTION GEARS

### R&R AND OVERHAUL

#### Model 265

Remove differential housing and transmission assembly from tractor as outlined in TRANSMISSION section. Separate hydrostatic transmission from differential unit. Remove wheels and brake components. To reinstall unit, reverse the removal procedure.

Model 265 is equipped with a Kanzaki reduction gear and differential unit. Refer to Kanzaki section in REDUCTION GEAR AND DIFFERENTIAL SERVICE section for overhaul procedure.

## POWER TAKE-OFF

#### All Models

**TESTING.** Use the following procedure for locating pto malfunction. Turn ignition switch to "ON" position and actuate pto switch. If clutch does not engage, disconnect wiring connector at clutch and use a 12-volt test lamp to check continuity of wire coming from pto switch. If lamp lights, pto is either defective or wiring connector at clutch field coil is faulty. To check pto field coil, remove clutch from tractor. Ground field coil frame and energize coil lead wire with known 12-volt source. Hold a suitable piece of metal next to coil and note if metal is attracted. If metal is not attracted to coil, renew field coil assembly.

**ADJUSTMENT.** Pto clutch must be adjusted if clutch has been disassembled or if operation becomes erratic. With clutch disengaged, insert a feeler gage through slots in clutch plate and measure clearance between clutch rotor and armature as shown in Fig. JD214. There should be clearance of 0.38-0.64 mm (0.015-0.025 in.) on Warner clutch, or 0.30-0.51 mm (0.012-0.020 in.) on Ogura clutch at each of the slots in clutch plate. To adjust, tighten or loosen clutch adjusting nuts (N) to obtain correct clearance.

**R&R AND OVERHAUL.** To remove pto clutch, disconnect electrical wires and remove clutch retaining bolt. Remove clutch assembly from crankshaft. Use a plastic hammer to tap and loosen clutch from crankshaft if necessary.

To disassemble Ogura clutch (Fig. JD215), remove adjusting nuts (7). Support armature housing (6) and press bearing collar (5) out of armature assembly. Remove snap ring (10) and press bearing (9) and spacer (8) from armature housing.

To disassemble Warner clutch (Fig. JD216), remove adjusting nuts (4) and separate armature and rotor from field coil housing.

Inspect bearings for wear or damage. Inspect for broken or distorted springs. Check contact surfaces of rotor and ar-

Fig. JD214—Adjust pto clutch by turning each of the three adjusting nuts (N) until clearance between rotor and armature is 0.41 mm (0.016 in.).

mature for scored or worn condition. Renew parts or clutch assembly as necessary.

To reassemble either type clutch, reverse the disassembly procedure.

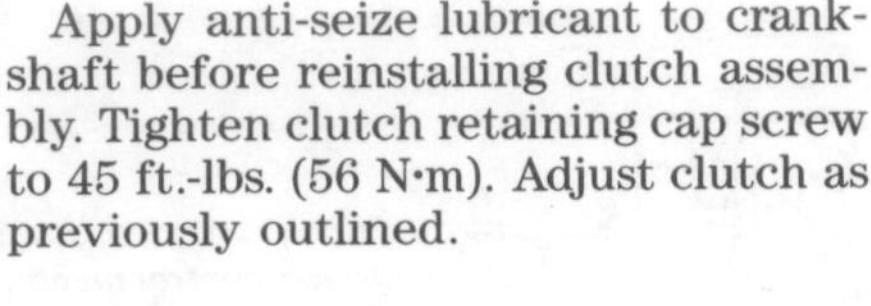

Apply anti-seize lubricant to crankshaft before reinstalling clutch assembly. Tighten clutch retaining cap screw to 45 ft.-lbs. (56 N·m). Adjust clutch as previously outlined.

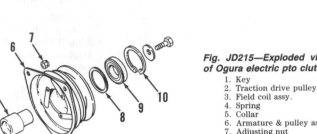

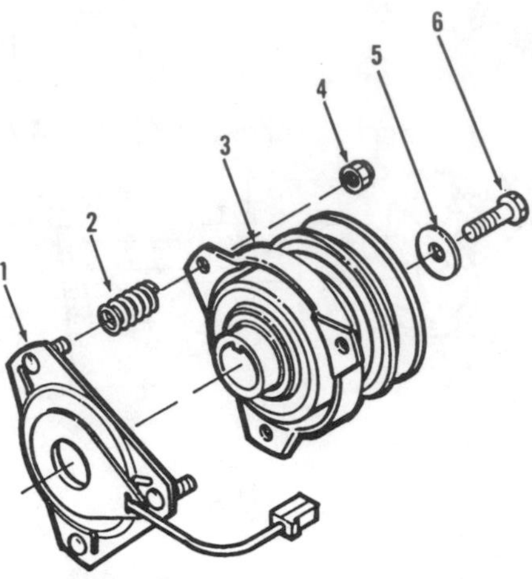


*Fig. JD216—Exploded view of Warner electric pto clutch.*

1. Field coil assy.
2. Spring
3. Armature & rotor assy.
4. Adjusting nut
5. Washer
6. Cap screw

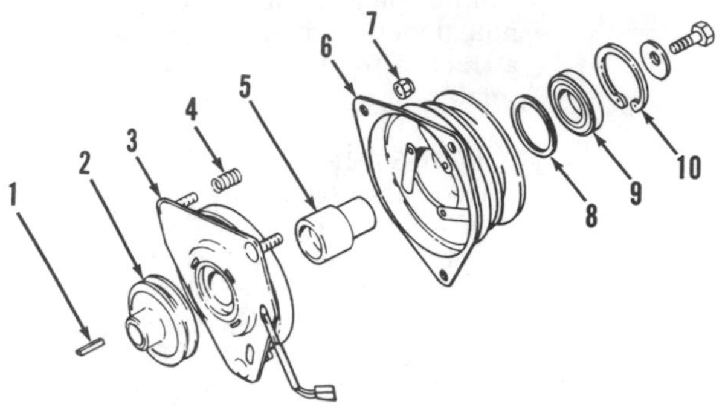


*Fig. JD215—Exploded view of Ogura electric pto clutch.*

1. Key
2. Traction drive pulley
3. Field coil assy.
4. Spring
5. Collar
6. Armature & pulley assy.
7. Adjusting nut
8. Spacer
9. Bearing
10. Snap ring

# WIRING SCHEMATICS

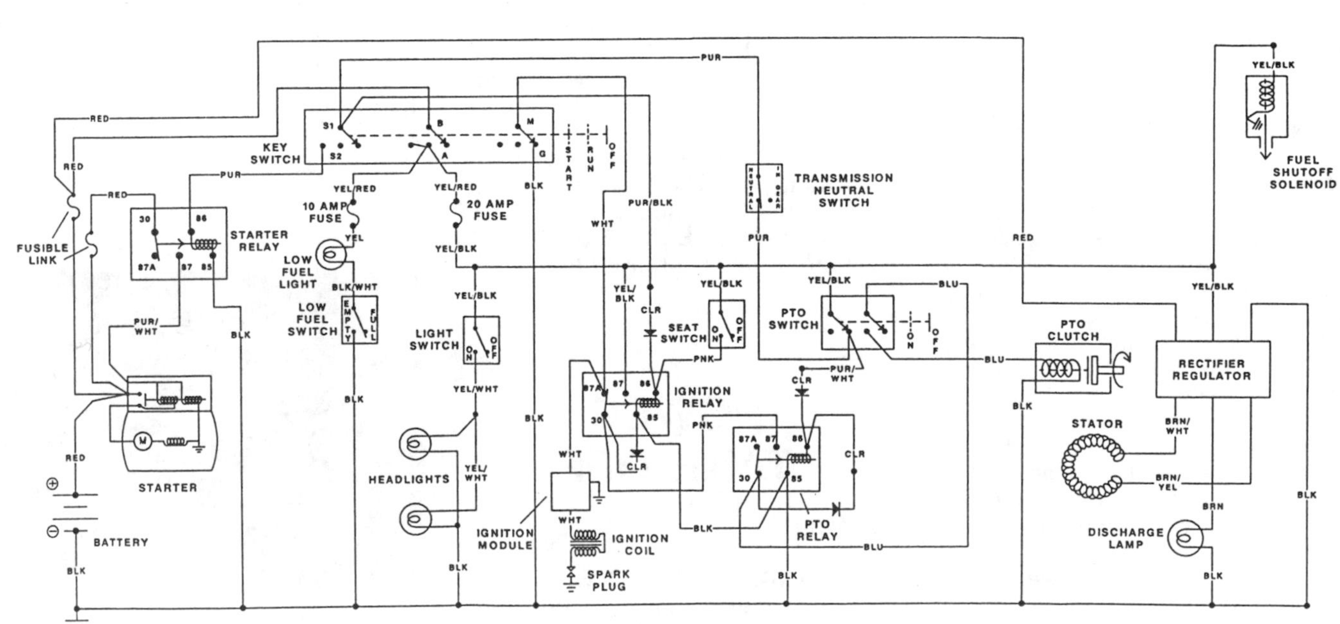


*Fig. JD217—Electrical system schematic for Model 240.*

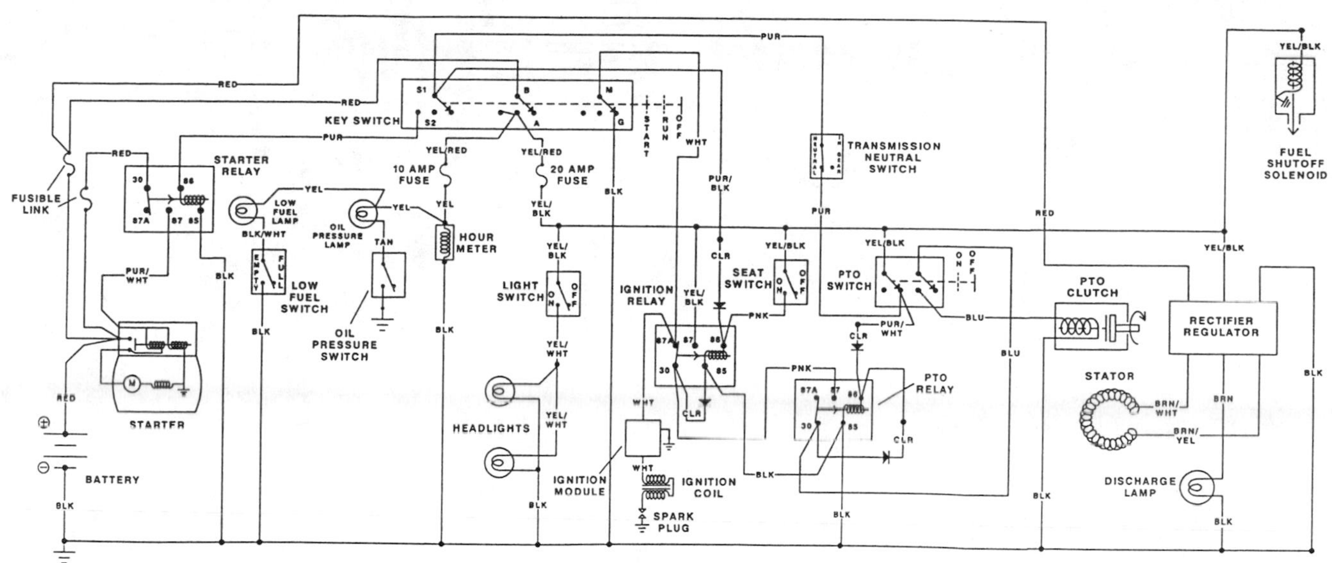


*Fig. JD218—Electrical system schematic for Models 260 and 265.*

---

# JOHN DEERE

## CONDENSED SPECIFICATIONS

| | MODELS | |
|---|---|---|
| | STX30 | STX38 |
| Engine Make | Kohler | Kohler |
| Model | CV12.5S-1216 | CV12.5S-1215 |
| Bore | 87 mm (3.425 in.) | 87 mm (3.425 in.) |
| Stroke | 67 mm (2.638 in.) | 67 mm (2.638 in.) |
| Displacement | 398 cc (24.3 cu. in.) | 398 cc (24.3 cu. in.) |
| Rated Power | 6.7 kW (9 hp) | 9.3 kW (12.5 hp) |
| Slow Idle Speed—Rpm | 1350 | 1350 |
| High Idle Speed (No-Load)—Rpm | 3350 | 3350 |
| Capacities— | | |
| Crankcase w/Filter | 1.9 L (2 qts.) | 1.9 L (2 qts.) |
| Fuel Tank | 4.7 L (1.25 gals.) | 4.7 L (1.25 gals.) |

## FRONT AXLE SYSTEM

### AXLE MAIN MEMBER

#### All Models

**REMOVE AND REINSTALL.** To remove front axle assembly, raise and support front of tractor. Remove front wheels. Disconnect stabilizer arms from axle. Disconnect tie rods from spindles. Unbolt and remove muffler. Remove axle pivot bolt (10—Fig. JD250) and lower axle assembly (8) from tractor. Remove hub cap (1), snap ring (2) and wheel hubs (4) from axle spindles.

Inspect axle bushing (9) and pivot bolt (10) for excessive wear and renew as necessary. Steering spindles (11) are not serviced separately. Axle assembly must be renewed if spindles or axle are excessively worn or damaged. Check wheel bearings (3) and wheel hub (4) for wear or damage and renew as required.

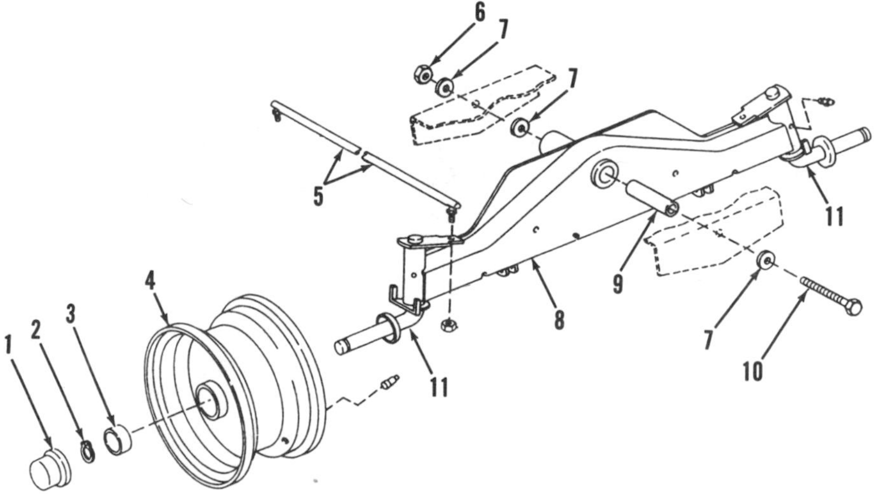


*Fig. JD250—Exploded view of front axle assembly. Spindles (11) are not renewable.*

1. Cap
2. Snap ring
3. Bearing
4. Wheel hub
5. Tie rod
6. Nut
7. Washers
8. Axle main member
9. Pivot bushing
10. Pivot bolt
11. Spindles

To install axle assembly, reverse the removal procedure. Tighten axle pivot bolt to 54 N·m (40 ft.-lbs.). Tighten tie rod retaining nuts to 22 N·m (16 ft.-lbs.).

## STEERING GEAR

#### All Models

**REMOVE AND REINSTALL.** Remove bolt (2—Fig. JD251) and steering wheel (1) from steering shaft. Shut off fuel and disconnect fuel line at the filter. Disconnect throttle control cable at engine. Remove dash retaining screws and remove dash and fuel tank. Disconnect tie rods from steering sector gear (14). Remove upper cotter pin (6) and washers (3, 4 and 5) from steering shaft (7). Push shaft down until pinion gear (9) is accessible and remove cotter pin (8), washers (10) and pinion gear.

**NOTE: Washers (10), if used, are not interchangeable with other washers on steering shaft. Later production tractors do not use washers (10).**

Pull steering shaft (7) up through console. Remove snap ring (11) and washers (12), then withdraw sector gear (14).

Inspect gears and shafts for excessive wear or damage and renew as required.

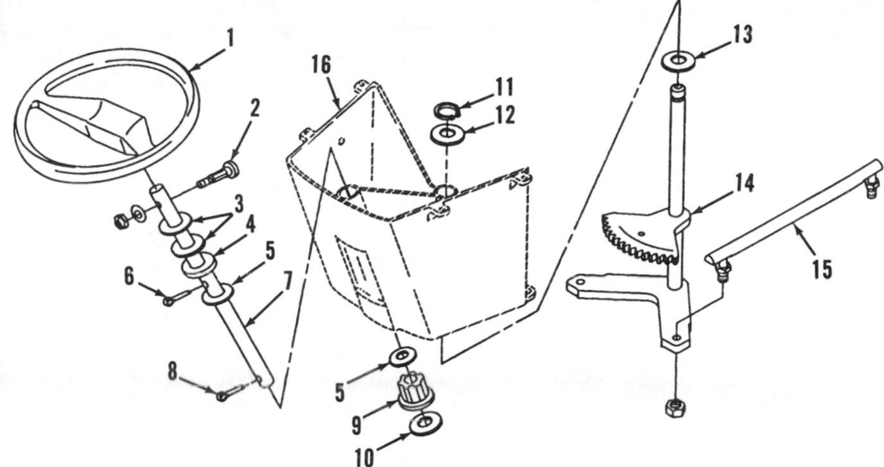


*Fig. JD251—Exploded view of steering gear assembly. Washers (10) are not used on some tractors.*

1. Steering wheel
2. Retaining bolt
3. Washers
4. Washer
5. Washer
6. Cotter pin
7. Steering shaft
8. Cotter pin
9. Pinion gear
10. Washer
11. Snap ring
12. Washer
13. Washer
14. Sector gear & shaft
15. Tie rod (2 used)

Inspect four bushings located in steering console (16) and renew if excessively worn.

When reinstalling steering gears, adjust quantity of washers on top and bottom of sector gear shaft and steering shaft to obtain minimum amount of backlash without binding. When installing pinion gear (9—Fig. JD252), align dot (D) on gear with notch (N) on steering shaft. Tighten tie rod retaining nuts to 22 N·m (16 ft.-lbs.).

# ENGINE

## All Models

**REMOVE AND REINSTALL.** To remove engine, first disconnect battery ground cable. Raise hood and disconnect springs from hood brackets, then lower hood and move forward to remove hood from tractor. Shut off fuel and disconnect fuel line from engine. Disconnect throttle control cable. Disconnect starter wires and ignition wires. Remove heat shield and muffler. Slip mower drive belt off pto clutch. Disconnect pto clutch wire harness, remove clutch retaining bolt and remove clutch from crankshaft. Remove traction drive pulley and key from crankshaft. Remove engine mounting cap screws and lift engine from tractor.

To reinstall engine, reverse the removal procedure. Tighten engine mounting cap screws to 32 N·m (24 ft.-lbs.). Apply anti-seize compound to crankshaft, then install drive pulley and pto clutch assembly. Tighten pto clutch cap screw to 73 N·m (54 ft.-lbs.).

**OVERHAUL.** Engine make and model are listed at the beginning of this section. To overhaul engine components and accessories, refer to Kohler section of this manual.

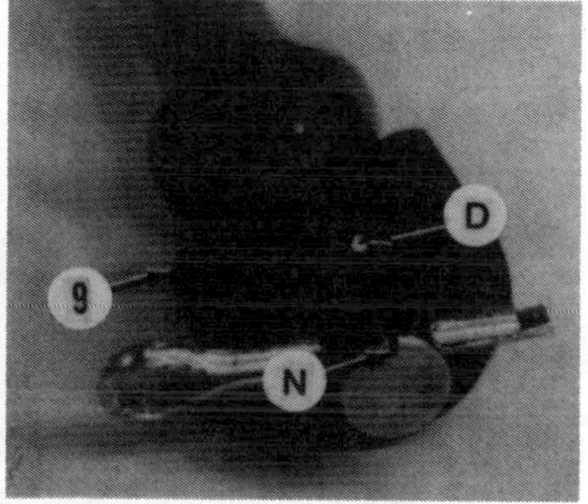


*Fig. JD252—Dimple (D) on pinion gear (9) should be aligned with notch (N) in end of steering shaft.*



# CLUTCH AND TRACTION DRIVE BELT

All models are equipped with a spring-loaded belt idler type clutch. When clutch pedal is depressed, clutch arm (6—Fig. JD253) moves idler pulley (7) to loosen drive belt from drive pulleys, stopping forward or reverse movement.

**R&R DRIVE BELT.** To remove traction drive belt (11—Fig. JD253), first remove pto clutch from engine crankshaft. Disconnect tie rods from steering arm. Remove belt guides (9 and 14) from idler pulleys. Disconnect spring (6—Fig. JD254) and remove park brake rod (4). Remove drive pulley (3—Fig. JD253) from engine crankshaft, then slip belt out of transaxle pulley and remove from tractor.

To install belt, reverse the removal procedure. Apply anti-seize compound to crankshaft before installing drive pulley and pto clutch.

To adjust belt tension, engage park brake. Move adjusting pulley (8—Fig. JD253) to remove all slack from belt and tighten pulley retaining bolt. Release park brake. Length of clutch release spring (17) should be 47 mm (1.85 in.) if belt is properly adjusted. Repeat adjustment procedure if necessary.

**R&R CLUTCH ARM.** To remove clutch arm (6—Fig. JD253), engage park brake and remove belt guide (14) and clutch idler pulley (7). Release park

*Fig. JD253—Exploded view of traction drive belt, pulleys and belt guides.*

1. Idler pulley
2. Spacer
3. Engine drive pulley
4. Belt guide
5. Belt tension spring
6. Clutch arm
7. Clutch pulley
8. Adjusting idler pulley
9. Belt guide
10. Transaxle pulley
11. Traction drive belt
12. Belt guide
13. Belt guide
14. Belt guide
15. Bushing
16. Link
17. Clutch compression spring
18. Belt guide

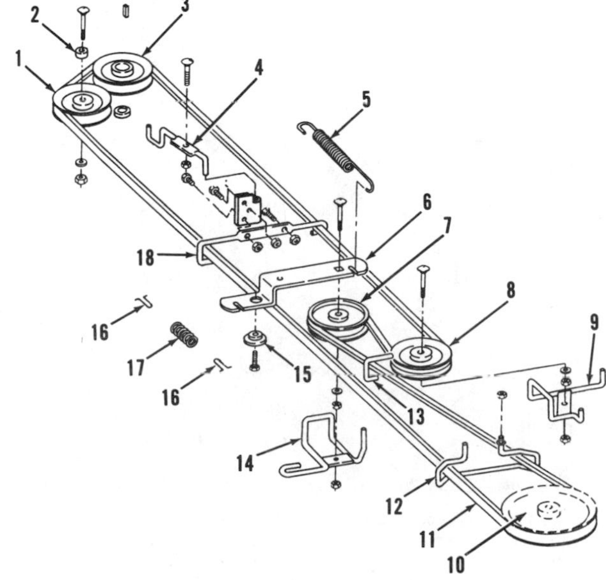

brake and disconnect spring (5) from clutch arm. Remove mounting cap screw, bushing (15) and arm (6) from tractor.

To reinstall, reverse the removal procedure. Apply Loctite 242 to threads of clutch arm mounting cap screw and tighten to 34 N·m (25 ft.-lbs.).

# BRAKE

## All Models

**ADJUSTMENT.** To adjust brake, first make sure park brake is disengaged. Use a feeler gage to measure clearance between brake disc and pad as shown in Fig. JD255. Clearance should be 0.5 mm (0.020 in.). Turn nut (N) to obtain correct clearance.

**REMOVE AND REINSTALL.** To remove brake assembly, raise and support rear of tractor. Remove right rear wheel. Disconnect brake rod from brake lever (6—Fig. JD256). Remove brake mounting cap screws and withdraw brake holder (4), disc (2) and pads (1).

To reinstall brake, reverse the removal procedure. Adjust brake as previously outlined.

# TRANSAXLE

## All Models

**LUBRICATION.** The transaxle is filled at the factory with SAE 90 GL5 gear lubricant and does not require periodic checking of lubricant level. If an oil leak develops, leak should be repaired and unit refilled with gear lubricant. Transaxle capacity is approximately 1.3 L (44 oz.).

Transaxle rear axle bearings should be lubricated with multipurpose grease after every 25 hours of operation. A grease fitting is located on each side of transaxle housing.

**REMOVE AND REINSTALL.** To remove transaxle, raise and support rear of tractor. Remove rear wheels. Remove belt guide from adjusting pulley (8—Fig. JD253) and move pulley forward to loosen traction drive belt. Remove drive belt from transaxle pulley. Disconnect transaxle shift linkage and brake linkage. Disconnect wiring from safety start switch located on top of transaxle. Remove cap screws attaching transaxle to frame and lower transaxle from tractor.

To reinstall transaxle, reverse the removal procedure. Adjust drive belt tension as previously outlined.

**OVERHAUL.** A Peerless Model 930 transaxle is used on all models. Refer to Peerless section in TRANSAXLE SERVICE section for overhaul procedure.

# PTO CLUTCH

## All Models

**ADJUSTMENT.** Clutch should be adjusted if clutch has been disassembled or if operation becomes erratic. With clutch disengaged, insert a feeler gage through slot in clutch plate (Fig. JD257) and measure clearance between clutch rotor and armature. Clearance should be 0.41 mm (0.016 in.). To adjust, tighten adjusting nut (B) next to slot until feeler gage (A) just begins to bind. Do not overtighten. Repeat adjustment at each of the slots in clutch plate.

**TESTING.** Use the following procedure for locating pto malfunction. Turn ignition switch to "ON" position and actuate pto switch. If clutch does not engage, disconnect wiring connector at field coil and use a 12-volt test lamp to check continuity of wire coming from pto switch. If lamp lights, pto is either defective or wiring connection at clutch field coil is poor.

To check field coil, remove clutch from tractor. Ground field coil frame and energize coil lead wire with 12-volt battery. Hold a suitable piece of metal adjacent to coil and note if metal is at-

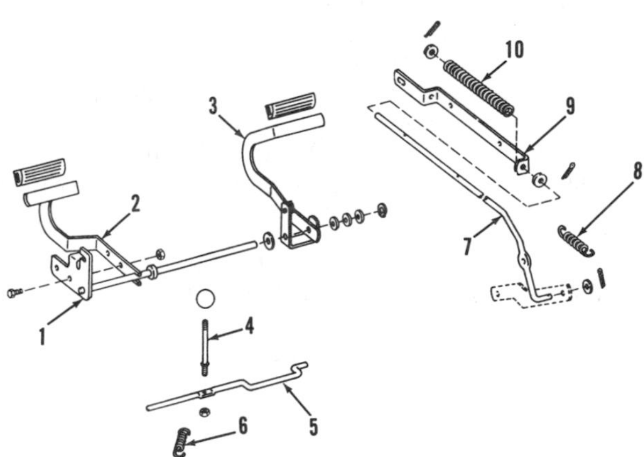

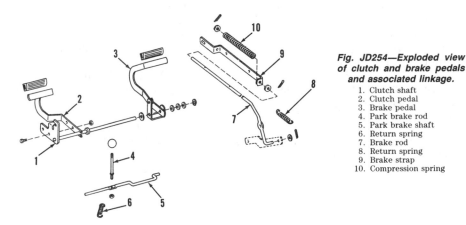

*Fig. JD254—Exploded view of clutch and brake pedals and associated linkage.*
1. Clutch shaft
2. Clutch pedal
3. Brake pedal
4. Park brake rod
5. Park brake shaft
6. Return spring
7. Brake rod
8. Return spring
9. Brake strap
10. Compression spring

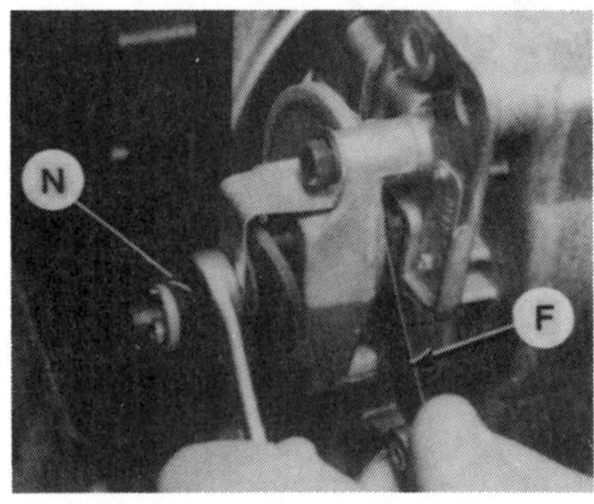


*Fig. JD255—Clearance between brake disc and brake pad should be 0.5 mm (0.020 in.) with brake disengaged. Turn nut (N) to adjust.*

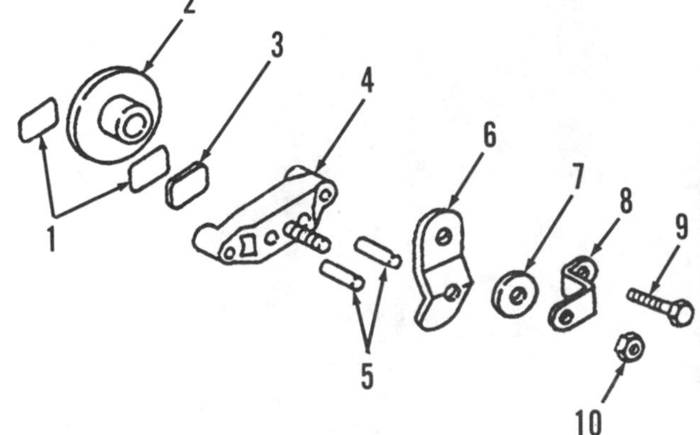


*Fig. JD256—Exploded view of disc brake assembly.*
1. Brake pads
2. Brake disc
3. Back plate
4. Brake holder
5. Actuating pins
6. Brake lever
7. Washer
8. Bracket
9. Cap screw
10. Adjusting nut

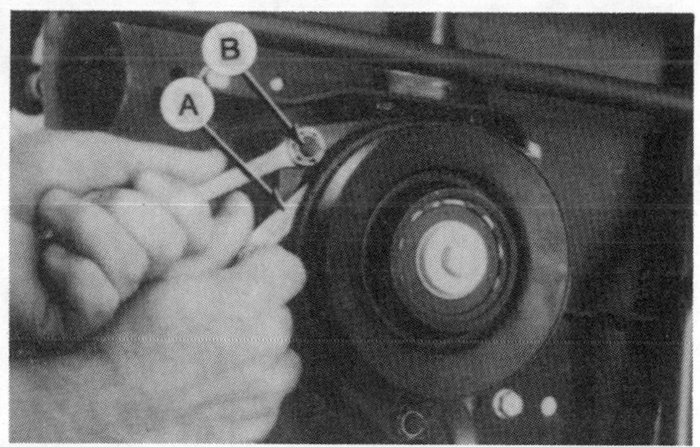


Fig. JD257—Use a feeler gage (A) to measure clearance between pto clutch rotor and armature. Turn nuts (B) to adjust clearance. Refer to text.

To disassemble clutch, remove three nuts (7—Fig. JD258) and separate armature assembly (9), rotor (8) and field coil (5).

Inspect bearings in field housing and armature for wear or damage and renew bearings or housing assemblies as necessary. Inspect contact surfaces of rotor and armature for scoring, grooves or other damage and renew as needed.

Apply anti-seize compound on crankshaft before reinstalling clutch. Install clutch and tighten retaining cap screw to 73 N·m (54 ft.-lbs.). Adjust clutch as previously outlined.

tracted. If metal is not attracted, renew field coil assembly.

**R&R AND OVERHAUL.** To remove pto clutch, move mower deck to lowest position and move mower belt tension lever to release position. Disconnect clutch wire harness connector. Slip drive belt out of clutch pulley. Hold the clutch assembly and remove retaining cap screw. Remove clutch assembly from crankshaft.

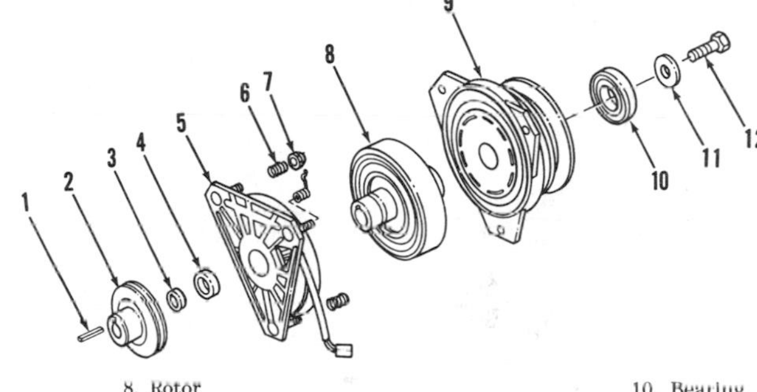


*Fig. JD258—Exploded view of Warner electric pto clutch used on early production models. Clutch used on later models is similar except that collar (4) is not used and bearing (10) is not available separately.*

1. Key
2. Pulley
3. Hub
4. Spacer
5. Coil assy.
6. Spring
7. Nut
8. Rotor
9. Armature & pulley assy.
10. Bearing
11. Washer
12. Cap screw

# WIRING SCHEMATIC

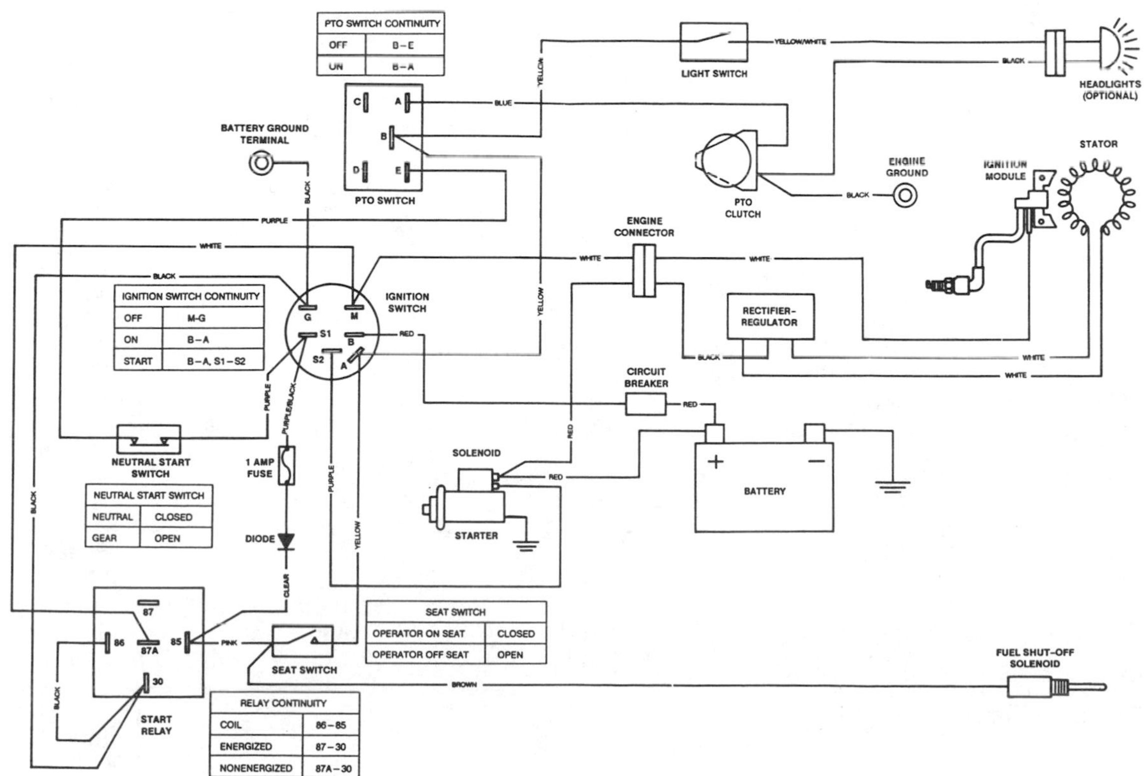


*Fig. JD260—Wiring schematic typical of all models.*

# DEUTZ-ALLIS

## CONDENSED SPECIFICATIONS

| | MODELS | | |
|---|---|---|---|
| | **B206, Homesteader 6** | **Homesteader 7** | **B208, Homesteader 8** |
| Engine Make | B&S | B&S | B&S |
| Model | 146707 | 170702 | 190701 |
| Bore | 2-2/4 in. (69.8 mm) | 3 in. (76.2 mm) | 3 in. (76.2 mm) |
| Stroke | 2-3/8 in. (60.3 mm) | 2-3/8 in. (60.3 mm) | 2-3/4 in. (69.8 mm) |
| Displacement | 14.11 cu. in. (231 cc) | 16.79 cu. in. (275 cc) | 19.44 cu. in. (318 cc) |
| Rated Power | 6 hp (4.5 kW) | 7 hp (5.2 kW) | 8 hp (6.0 kW) |
| Slow Idle Speed—Rpm | 1750 | 1750 | 1750 |
| High Idle Speed (No-Load)—Rpm | 3600 | 3600 | 3600 |
| Crankcase Oil Capacity | 2-1/4 pints (1 L) | 2-1/4 pints (1 L) | 2-1/4 pints (1 L) |
| Weight— | | | |
| Above 32°F (0°C) | | SAE 30 | |
| 0°F (-18°C) to 32°F (0°C) | | SAE 10W-30 | |
| Below 0°F (-18°C) | | SAE 5W-20 | |
| Transmission Oil Capacity | 1-1/2 pints (0.7 L) | 1-1/2 pints (0.7 L) | 1-1/2 pints (0.7 L) |
| Weight | SAE 90 EP | SAE 90 EP | SAE 90 EP |

| | MODELS | | |
|---|---|---|---|
| | **B210** | **B212** | **HB212** |
| Engine Make | B&S | B&S | B&S |
| Model | 243431 | 300421 | 300421 |
| Bore | 3-1/16 in. (77.8 mm) | 3-7/16 in. (87.3 mm) | 3-7/16 in. (87.3 mm) |
| Stroke | 3-1/4 in. (82.5 mm) | 3-1/4 in. (82.5 mm) | 3-1/4 in. (82.5 mm) |
| Displacement | 23.94 cu. in. (392 cc) | 30.16 cu. in. (494 cc) | 30.16 cu. in. (494 cc) |
| Rated Power | 10 hp (7.5 kW) | 12 hp (8.9 kW) | 12 hp (8.9 kW) |
| Slow Idle Speed—Rpm | 1750 | 1750 | 1750 |
| High Idle Speed (No-Load)—Rpm | 3600 | 3600 | 3600 |
| Crankcase Oil Capacity | 4 pints (1.9 L) | 4 pints (1.9 L) | 4 pints (1.9 L) |
| Weight— | | | |
| Above 32°F (0°C) | | SAE 30 | |
| 0°F (-18°C) to 32°F (0°C) | | SAE 10W-30 | |
| Below 0°F (-18°C) | | SAE 5W-20 | |
| Transmission Oil Capacity | 3 pints (1.4 L) | 3 pints (1.4 L) | 3-1/2 pints (1.6 L) |
| Weight | SAE 90 EP | SAE 90EP | Power Fluid 821 |
| Bevel Gear Housing Oil Capacity | 1 pint (0.5 L) | 1 pint (0.5 L) | 1 pint (0.5 L) |
| Weight | | SAE 90 EP | |
| Gear Reduction Housing Oil Capacity | ...... | ...... | 3 pints (1.4 L) |
| Weight | ...... | ...... | SAE 90 EP |

# CONDENSED SPECIFICATIONS

| | MODELS | | |
|---|---|---|---|
| | 310, 310D | 312, 312D | 312H |
| Engine Make | Kohler | Kohler | Kohler |
| Model | K241S | K301S | K301S |
| Bore | 3-1/4 in. (82.5 mm) | 3-3/8 in. (85.7 mm) | 3-3/8 in. (85.7 mm) |
| Stroke | 2-7/8 in. (73.0 mm) | 3-1/4 in. (82.5 mm) | 3-1/4 in. (82.5 mm) |
| Displacement | 23.9 cu. in. (392 cc) | 29.07 cu. in. (476 cc) | 29.07 cu. in. (476 cc) |
| Rated Power | 10 hp (7.5 kW) | 12 hp (8.9 kW) | 12 hp (8.9 kW) |
| Slow Idle Speed—Rpm | 1750 | 1750 | 1750 |
| High Idle Speed (No-Load)—Rpm | 3600 | 3600 | 3600 |
| Crankcase Oil Capacity | 4 pints (1.9 L) | 4 pints (1.9 L) | 4 pints (1.9 L) |
| Weight— | | | |
| Above 32°F (0°C) | | SAE 30 | |
| 0°F (-18°C) to 32°F (0°C) | | SAE 10W-30 | |
| Below 0°F (-18°C) | | SAE 5W-20 | |
| Transmission Oil Capacity | 1 pint (0.5 L) | 1 pint (0.5 L) | 3-1/2 pints (1.6 L) |
| Weight | SAE 90 EP | SAE 90 EP | Power Fluid 821 |
| Bevel Gear Housing Oil Capacity | 1 pint (0.5 L) | 1 pint (0.5 L) | 1 pint (0.5 L) |
| Weight | | SAE 90 EP | |
| Gear Reduction Housing | | | |
| Oil Capacity | ...... | ...... | 3 pints (1.4 L) |
| Weight | ...... | ...... | |

| | MODELS | | |
|---|---|---|---|
| | 314, 314D | 314H | 410, 410S |
| Engine Make | Kohler | Kohler | Kohler |
| Model | K321S | K321S | K241S |
| Bore | 3-1/2 in. (88.9 mm) | 3-1/2 in. (88.9 mm) | 3-1/4 in. (82.5 mm) |
| Stroke | 3-1/4 in. (82.5 mm) | 3-1/4 in. (82.5 mm) | 2-7/8 in. (73.0 mm) |
| Displacement | 31.27 cu. in. (512 cc) | 31.27 cu. in. (512 cc) | 23.9 cu. in. (392 cc) |
| Rated Power | 14 hp (10.4 kW) | 14 hp (10.4 kW) | 10 hp (7.5 kW) |
| Slow Idle Speed—Rpm | 1750 | 1750 | 1700 |
| High Idle Speed (No-Load)—Rpm | 3600 | 3600 | 3600 |
| Crankcase Oil Capacity | 4 pints (1.9 L) | 4 pints (1.9 l) | 4 pints (1.9 L) |
| Weight— | | | |
| Above 32°F (0°C) | | SAE 30 | |
| 0°F (-18°C) to 32°F (0°C) | | SAE 10W-30 | |
| Below 0°F (-18°C) | | SAE 5W-30 | |
| Transmission Oil Capacity | 1 pint (0.5 L) | 3-1/2 pints (1.6 L) | 3 pints (1.4 L) |
| Weight | SAE 90 EP | Power Fluid 821 | SAE 90 EP |
| Bevel Gear Housing Oil Capacity | 1 pint (0.5 L) | 1 pint (0.5 L) | 1 pint (0.5 L) |
| Weight | | SAE 90 EP | |
| Gear Reduction Housing | | | |
| Oil Capacity | ...... | 3 pints (1.4 L) | ...... |
| Weight | ...... | SAE 90 EP | ...... |

# CONDENSED SPECIFICATIONS

| | MODELS | | |
|---|---|---|---|
| | **414S** | **416H** | **416S** |
| Engine Make | Kohler | Kohler | Kohler |
| Model | K321S | K341S | K341S |
| Bore | 3-1/2 in. (88.9 mm) | 3-3/4 in. (95.2 mm) | 3-3/4 in. (95.2 mm) |
| Stroke | 3-1/4 in. (82.5 mm) | 3-1/4 in. (82.5 mm) | 3-1/4 in. (82.5 mm) |
| Displacement | 31.27 cu. in. (512 cc) | 35.89 cu. in. (588 cc) | 35.89 cu. in. (588 cc) |
| Rated Power | 14 hp (10.4 kW) | 16 hp (11.9 kW) | 16 hp (11.9 kW) |
| Slow Idle Speed—Rpm | 1700 | 1700 | 1700 |
| High Idle Speed (No-Load)—Rpm | 3600 | 3600 | 3600 |
| Crankcase Oil Capacity | 4 pints (1.9 L) | 4 pints (1.9 L) | 4 pints (1.9 L) |
| Weight— | | | |
| Above 32°F (0°C) | | SAE 30 | |
| 0°F (-18°C) to 32°F (0°C) | | SAE 10W-30 | |
| Below 0°F (-18°C) | | SAE 5W-20 | |
| Transmission Oil Capacity | 3 pints (1.4 L) | 3 pints (1.4 L) | 3-1/2 pints (1.6 L) |
| Weight | SAE 90 EP | SAE 90 EP | Power Fluid 821 |
| Bevel Gear Housing Oil Capacity | 1 pint (0.5 L) | 1 pint (0.5 L) | 1 pint (0.5 L) |
| Weight | | SAE 90 EP | |

| | MODELS | | |
|---|---|---|---|
| | **608** | **608LT** | **608LTD** |
| Engine Make | B&S | B&S | B&S |
| Model | 191707 | 191707 | 191707 |
| Bore | 3 in. (76.2 mm) | 3 in. (76.2 mm) | 3 in. (76.2 mm) |
| Stroke | 2-3/4 in. (69.8 mm) | 2-3/4 in. (69.8 mm) | 2-3/4 in. (69.8 mm) |
| Displacement | 19.44 cu. in. (318 cc) | 19.44 cu. in. (318 cc) | 19.44 cu. in. (318 cc) |
| Rated Power | 8 hp (6.0 kW) | 8 hp (6.0 kW) | 8 hp (6.0 KW) |
| Slow Idle Speed—Rpm | 1800 | 1800 | 1750 |
| High Idle Speed (No-Load)—Rpm | 3600 | 3600 | 3600 |
| Crankcase Oil Capacity | 2-1/4 pints (1 L) | 2-1/4 pints (1 L) | 2-1/4 pints (1 L) |
| Weight— | | | |
| Above 32°F (0°C) | | SAE 30 | |
| 0°F (-18°C) to 32°F (0°C) | | SAE 10W-30 | |
| Below 0°F (-18°C) | | SAE 5W-20 | |
| Transmission Oil Capacity | 3-1/2 pints (1.6 L) | 1-1/2 pints (0.7 L) | 30 ounces (887 mL) |
| Weight | SAE 90 EP | SAE 90 EP | Bentonite Grease |

# CONDENSED SPECIFICATIONS

| | MODELS | | |
|---|---|---|---|
| | 610 | 611LT | 611LTD |
| Engine Make | B&S | B&S | B&S |
| Model | 251707 | 252707 | 252707 |
| Bore | 3-7/16 in. (87.3 mm) | 3-7/16 in. (87.3 mm) | 3-7/16 in. (87.3 mm) |
| Stroke | 2-5/8 in. (66.7 mm) | 2-5/8 in. (66.7 mm) | 2-5/8 in. (66.7 mm) |
| Displacement | 24.36 cu. in. (399 cc) | 24.36 cu. in. (399 cc) | 24.36 cu. in. (399 cc) |
| Rated Power | 11 hp (8.2 kW) | 11 hp (8.2 kW) | 11 hp (8.2 kW) |
| Slow Idle Speed—Rpm | 1750 | 1750 | 1750 |
| High Idle Speed (No-Load)—Rpm | 3600 | 3600 | 3600 |
| Crankcase Oil Capacity | 2-3/4 pints (1.3 L) | 3 pints (1.4 L) | 3 pints (1.4 L) |
| Weight— | | | |
| Above 32°F (0°C) | | SAE 30 | |
| 0°F (-18°C) to 32°F (0°C) | | SAE 10W-30 | |
| Below 0°F (-18°C) | | SAE 5W-20 | |
| Transmission Oil Capacity | 3-1/2 pints (1.6 L) | 1-1/2 pints (0.7 L) | 30 ounces (887 mL) |
| Weight | SAE 90 EP | SAE 90 EP | Bentonite Grease |

| | MODELS | |
|---|---|---|
| | 611H | 710 (3 spd.), 710 (6 spd.) |
| Engine Make | B&S | Kohler |
| Model | 252707 | K241S |
| Bore | 3-7/16 in. (87.3 mm) | 3-1/4 in. (82.5 mm) |
| Stroke | 2-5/8 in. (66.7 mm) | 2-7/8 in. (73.0 mm) |
| Displacement | 24.36 cu. in. (399 cc) | 23.9 cu. in. (392 cc) |
| Rated Power | 11 hp (8.2 kW) | 10 hp (7.5 kW) |
| Slow Idle Speed—Rpm | 1750 | 1700 |
| High Idle Speed (No-Load)—Rpm | 3600 | 3600 |
| Crankcase Oil Capacity | 3 pints (1.4 L) | 4 pints (1.9 L) |
| Weight— | | |
| Above 32°F (0°C) | SAE 30 | |
| 0°F (-18°C) to 32°F (0°C) | SAE 10W-30 | |
| Below 0°F (-18°C) | SAE 5W-20 | |
| Transmission Oil Capacity | * | 4-1/2 pints (2.1 L) |
| Weight | Power Fluid 821 | SAE 90 EP |
| Bevel Gear Housing Oil Capacity | ...... | 1 pint (0.5 L) |
| Weight | ...... | SAE 90 EP |

*Refer to hydrostatic transmission REMOVE AND REINSTALL section.

# CONDENSED SPECIFICATIONS

| | MODELS | |
|---|---|---|
| | **712S** | **712H** |
| Engine Make | Kohler | Kohler |
| Model | K301S | K301S |
| Bore | 3-3/8 in. (85.7 mm) | 3-3/8 in. (85.7 mm) |
| Stroke | 3-1/4 in. (82.5 mm) | 3-1/4 in. (82.5 mm) |
| Displacement | 29.07 cu. in. (476 cc) | 29.07 cu. in. (476 cc) |
| Rated Power | 12 hp (8.9 kW) | 12 hp (8.9 kW) |
| Slow Idle Speed—Rpm | 1700 | 1700 |
| High Idle Speed (No-Load)—Rpm | 3600 | 3600 |
| Crankcase Oil Capacity | 4 pints (1.9 L) | 4 pints (1.9 L) |
| Weight— | | |
| Above 32°F (0°C) | SAE 30 | SAE 30 |
| 0°F (-18°C) to 32°F (0°C) | SAE 10W-30 | SAE 10W-30 |
| Below 0°F (-18°C) | SAE 5W-20 | SAE 5W-20 |
| Transmission Oil Capacity | 4-1/2 pints (2.1 L) | 6 pints (2.8 L) |
| Weight | SAE 90 EP | Power Fluid 821 |
| Bevel Gear Housing Oil Capacity | 1 pint (0.5 L) | 1 pint (0.5 L) |
| Weight | SAE 90 EP | SAE 90 EP |

| | | MODELS | |
|---|---|---|---|
| | **716 (6 spd.)** | **716H** | **716H*** |
| Engine Make | Kohler | Kohler | B&S |
| Model | K341S | K341S | 326437 |
| Bore | 3-3/4 in. (95.2 mm) | 3-3/4 in. (95.2 mm) | 3-9/16 in. (90.5 mm) |
| Stroke | 3-1/4 in. (82.5 mm) | 3-1/4 in. (82.5 mm) | 3-1/4 in. (82.5 mm) |
| Displacement | 35.89 cu. in. (588 cc) | 35.89 cu. in. (588 cc) | 32.4 cu. in. (531 cc) |
| Rated Power | 16 hp (11.9 kW) | 16 hp (11.9 kW) | 16 hp (11.9 kW) |
| Slow Idle Speed—Rpm | 1700 | 1700 | 1700 |
| High Idle Speed (No-Load)—Rpm | 3600 | 3600 | 3600 |
| Crankcase Oil Capacity | 4 pints (1.9 L) | 4 pints (1.9 L) | 4 pints (1.9 L) |
| Weight— | | | |
| Above 32°F (0°C) | SAE 30 | SAE 30 | SAE 30 |
| 0°F (-18°C) to 32°F (0°C) | SAE 10W-30 | SAE 10W-30 | SAE 10W-30 |
| Below 0°F (-18°C) | SAE 5W-20 | SAE 5W-20 | SAE 5W-20 |
| Transmission Oil Capacity | 4-1/2 pints (2.1 L) | 6 pints (2.8 L) | 6 pints (2.8 L) |
| Weight | SAE 90 EP | Power Fluid 821 | Power Fluid 821 |
| Bevel Gear Housing Oil Capacity | 1 pint (0.5 L) | 1 pint (0.5 L) | 1 pint (0.5 L) |
| Weight | SAE 90 EP | SAE 90 EP | SAE 90 EP |
| Gear Reduction Housing Oil Capacity | ...... | 3 pints (1.4 L) | 3 pints (1.4 L) |
| Weight | ...... | SAE 90 EP | SAE 90 EP |

*Tractors with S.N. 16902115465 through 16902116155.

# CONDENSED SPECIFICATIONS

| | MODELS | | |
|---|---|---|---|
| | 808GT | 810GT | 811GT |
| Engine Make | B&S | B&S | B&S |
| Model | 191707 | 251707 | 252707 |
| Bore | 3 in. (76.2 mm) | 3-7/16 in. (87.3 mm) | 3-7/16 in. (87.3 mm) |
| Stroke | 2-3/4 in. (69.8 mm) | 2-5/8 in. (66.7 mm) | 2-5/8 in. (66.7 mm) |
| Displacement | 19.44 cu. in. (318 cc) | 24.36 cu. in. (399 cc) | 24.36 cu. in. (399 cc) |
| Rated Power | 8 hp (6.0 kW) | 10 hp (7.5 kW) | 11 hp (8.2 kW) |
| Slow Idle Speed—Rpm | 1750 | 1750 | 1750 |
| High Idle Speed (No-Load)—Rpm | 3600 | 3600 | 3600 |
| Crankcase Oil Capacity | 2-1/4 pints (1 L) | 3 pints (1.4 L) | 3 pints (1.4 L) |
| Weight— | | | |
| Above 32°F (0°C) | | SAE 30 | |
| 0°F (-18°C) to 32°F (0°C) | | SAE 10W-30 | |
| Below 0°F (-18°C) | | SAE 5W-20 | |
| Transmission Oil Capacity | 3-1/2 pints (1.6 L) | 3-1/2 pints (1.6 L) | 3-1/2 pints (1.6 L) |
| Weight | | SAE 90 EP | |

| | MODELS | | |
|---|---|---|---|
| | T-811 | 912 (6 spd.) | 912H |
| Engine Make | B&S | Kohler | Kohler |
| Model | 252707 | K301S | K301S |
| Bore | 3-7/16 in. (87.3 mm) | 3-3/8 in. (85.7 mm) | 3-3/8 in. (85.7 mm) |
| Stroke | 2-5/8 in. (66.7 mm) | 3-1/4 in. (82.5 mm) | 3-1/4 in. (82.5 mm) |
| Displacement | 24.36 cu. in. (399 cc) | 29.07 cu. in. (476 cc) | 29.07 cu. in. (476 cc) |
| Rated Power | 11 hp (8.2 kW) | 12 hp (8.9 kW) | 12 hp (8.9 kW) |
| Slow Idle Speed—Rpm | 1750 | 1500 | 1500 |
| High Idle Speed (No-Load)—Rpm | 3600 | 3600 | 3600 |
| Crankcase Oil Capacity | 3 pints (1.4 L) | 4 pints (1.9 L) | 4 pints (1.9 L) |
| Weight— | | | |
| Above 32°F (0°C) | | SAE 30 | |
| 0°F (-18°C) to 32°F (0°C) | | SAE 10W-30 | |
| Below 0°F (-18°C) | | SAE 5W-20 | |
| Transmission Oil Capacity | 3-1/2 pints (1.6 L) | 4-1/2 pints (2.1 L) | 6 pints (2.8 L) |
| Weight | | Power Fluid 821 | |
| Bevel Gear Housing Oil Capacity | ...... | 1 pint (0.5 L) | 1 pint (0.5 L) |
| Weight | ...... | SAE 90 EP | SAE 90 EP |

# CONDENSED SPECIFICATIONS

| | MODELS | | |
|---|---|---|---|
| | 912H | 914H | 914S |
| Engine Make | Kohler | Kohler | Kohler |
| Model | K301S | K321S | K321S |
| Bore | 3-3/8 in. (85.7 mm) | 3-1/2 in. (88.9 mm) | 3-1/2 in. (88.9 mm) |
| Stroke | 3-1/4 in. (82.5 mm) | 3-1/4 in. (82.5 mm) | 3-1/4 in. (82.5 mm) |
| Displacement | 29.07 cu. in. (476 cc) | 31.27 cu. in. (512 cc) | 31.27 cu. in. (512 cc) |
| Rated Power | 12 hp (8.9 kW) | 14 hp (10.4 kW) | 14 hp (10.4 kW) |
| Slow Idle Speed—Rpm | 1500 | 1500 | 1500 |
| High Idle Speed (No-Load)—Rpm | 3600 | 3600 | 3600 |
| Crankcase Oil Capacity | 4 pints (1.9 L) | 4 pints (1.9 L) | 4 pints (1.9 L) |
| Weight— | | | |
| Above 32°F (0°C) | | SAE 30 | |
| 0°F (-18°C) to 32°F (0°C) | | SAE 10W-30 | |
| Below 0°F (-18°C) | | SAE 5W-20 | |
| Transmission Oil Capacity | 6 pints (2.8 L) | 4-1/2 pints (2.1 L) | 6 pints (2.8 L) |
| Weight | | Power Fluid 821 | |
| Bevel Gear Housing Oil Capacity | 1 pint (0.5 L) | 1 pint (0.5 L) | 1 pint (0.5 L) |
| Weight | | Power Fluid 821 | |

| | MODELS | | |
|---|---|---|---|
| | 916H | 1914 | 1916 |
| Engine Make | Kohler | Kohler | Kohler |
| Model | K341S | M14 | M16 |
| Bore | 3-3/4 in. (95.2 mm) | 3-1/2 in. (88.9 mm) | 3-11/16 in. (95.25 mm) |
| Stroke | 3-1/4 in. (82.5 mm) | 3-1/4 in. (82.5 mm) | 3-1/4 in. (82.5 mm) |
| Displacement | 35.89 cu. in. (588 cc) | 31.2 cu. in. (512 cc) | 35.9 cu. in. (588 cc) |
| Rated Power | 16 hp (11.9 kW) | 14 hp (10.4 kW) | 16 hp (11.9 kW) |
| Slow Idle Speed—Rpm | 1500 | 1200 | 1200 |
| High Idle Speed (No-Load)—Rpm | 3600 | 3600 | 3600 |
| Crankcase Oil Capacity | 4 pints (1.9 L) | 4 pints (1.9 L) | 4 pints (1.9 L) |
| Weight— | | | |
| Above 32°F (0°C) | | SAE 30 | |
| 0°F (-18°C) to 32°F (0°C) | | SAE 10W-30 | |
| Below 0°F (-18°C) | | SAE 5W-20 | |
| Transmission Oil Capacity | 4-1/2 pints (2.1 L) | 6 quarts (5.7 L) | 6 quarts (5.7 L) |
| Weight | SAE 90 EP | Type F ATF | Type F ATF |
| Bevel Gear Housing Oil Capacity | 1 pint (0.5 L) | ...... | ...... |
| Weight | SAE 90 EP | ...... | ...... |

# FRONT AXLE SYSTEM

## AXLE MAIN MEMBER

### Models B206-Homesteader 6-Homesteader 7

The front axle main member (1—Fig. DA1) is supported by a pivot bolt in tractor frame. To remove front axle assembly, support front of tractor and disconnect drag link from steering arm (2). Remove pivot bolt (5) and roll front axle assembly away from tractor.

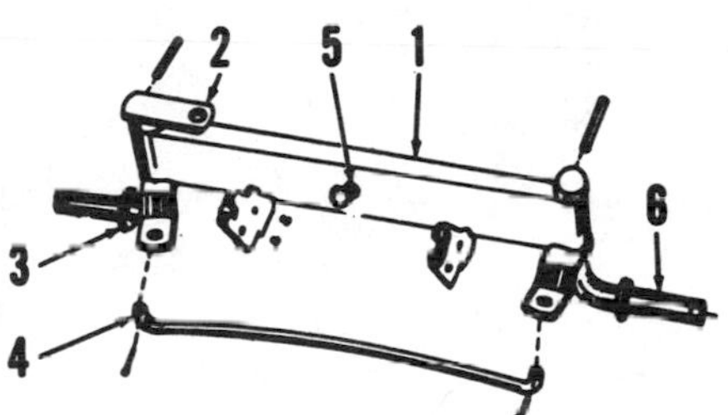


*Fig. DA1—Exploded view of front axle assembly used on Models B206, Homesteader 6 and Homesteader 7.*

1. Main axle member
2. Steering arm
3. Steering spindle L.H.
4. Tie rod
5. Pivot bolt
6. Steering spindle R.H.

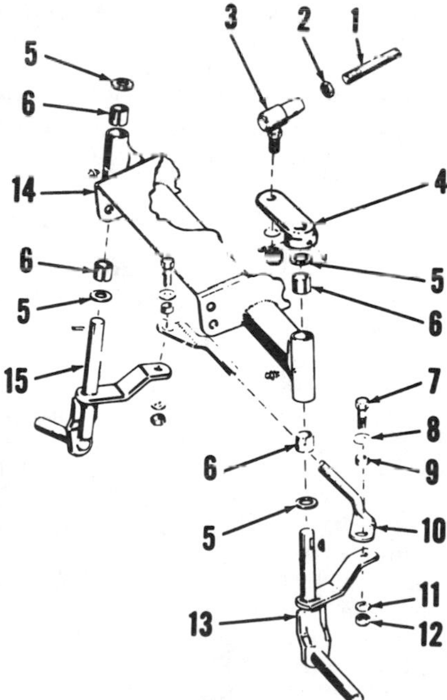


*Fig. DA2—Exploded view of front axle assembly used on Models B208, 608, 610 and Homesteader 8.*

1. Drag link
2. Locknut
3. Ball joint
4. Steering arm
5. Washer
6. Bushing
7. Bolt
8. Washer
9. Spacer
10. Tie rod
11. Washer
12. Nut
13. Steering spindle L.H.
14. Axle & frame assy.
15. Steering spindle R.H.

### Models B208-Homesteader 8-608-610

The front axle main member (14—Fig. DA2) is welded to tractor frame. Renewal of frame assembly is necessary if axle cannot be repaired.

### Models 310-310D-312-312D-312H-314-314D-314H

Axle main member (12—Fig. DA3) is mounted on main frame and pivots on pin (10). To remove front axle assembly, support front of tractor frame and disconnect tie rods from steering spindle arms. Remove pivot bolt (10) and roll axle assembly from tractor.

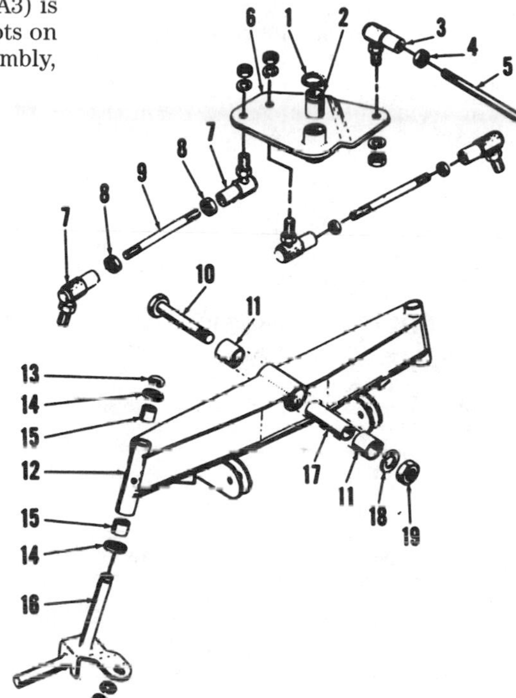


*Fig. DA3—Exploded view of front axle and steering plate assembly used on Models 310, 310D, 312, 312D, 312H, 314, 314D and 314H.*

1. Snap ring
2. Bushing
3. Ball joint
4. Locknut
5. Drag link
6. Steering plate
7. Ball joint
8. Locknut
9. Tie rod
10. Pivot bolt
11. Bushing
12. Axle main member
13. "E" ring
14. Washer
15. Bushing
16. Steering spindle
17. Sleeve
18. Lockwasher
19. Nut

### Models 410-410S-414S-416S-416H

Axle main member (12—Fig. DA4) is mounted in main frame and pivots on

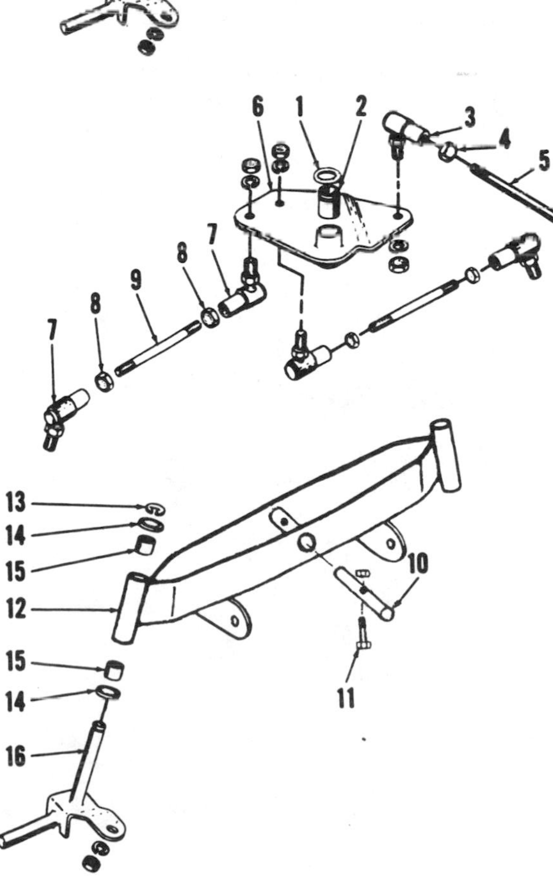


*Fig. DA4—Exploded view of front axle and steering plate assembly used on Models 410, 410S, 414S, 416S and 416H.*

1. Snap ring
2. Bushing
3. Ball joint
4. Locknut
5. Drag link
6. Steering plate
7. Ball joint
8. Locknut
9. Tie rod
10. Pivot pin
11. Bolt
12. Axle main member
13. "E" ring
14. Washer
15. Bushing
16. Steering spindle

Illustrations courtesy Deutz-Allis Corp.

pin (10). To remove front axle assembly, disconnect tie rod ball joint ends (7) from steering spindle arms. Remove retaining bolt (11) and using a jack under frame behind axle, support front of tractor. Drive out pivot pin (10), raise front of tractor and roll axle assembly from tractor.

### Models 608LT-608LTD-611H-611LT-611LTD-808GT-810GT-811GT-T811

The axle main member and stabilizer is a welded assembly (6—Fig. DA5). The unit pivots on a center mounting bolt (2) at the front and a flange bearing at the rear of stabilizer. To remove front axle assembly, raise front of tractor and block securely. Disconnect drag link from steering arm (9). Remove center mounting bolt (2) and pull axle assembly forward out of rear flange bearing.

### Models B210-B212-HB212-700 Series-900 Series

The axle main member and stabilizer assembly (12—Fig. DA6) is a welded assembly. The unit pivots on a center mounting bolt (38) at the front and in frame angle at rear of stabilizer. To remove front axle assembly, disconnect drag link ball joint end (16) from steering arm (15). Raise front of tractor and remove pivot bolt (38) and spacer (13) from center of axle. Lower front of axle and pull forward to slide stabilizer out of frame angle. The frame angle is bolted to main frame and can be renewed if stabilizer pivot hole is excessively worn.

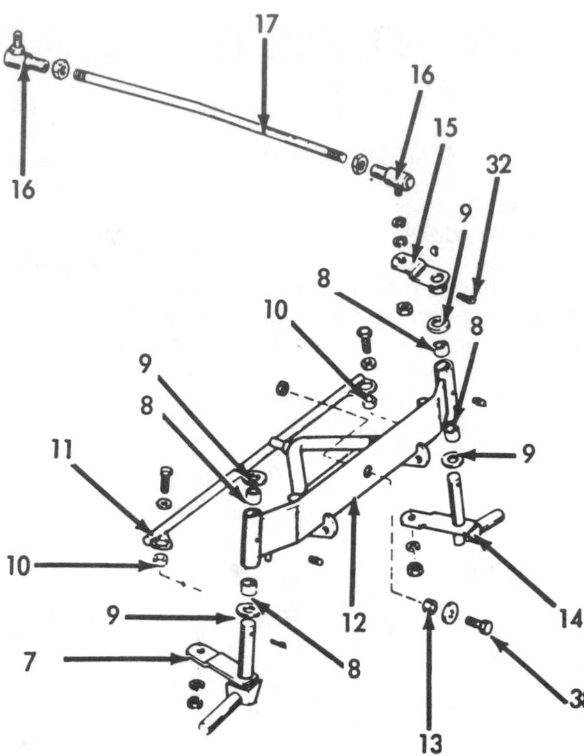


***Fig. DA6—Exploded view of front axle assembly used on Models B210, B212, HB212, 700 Series and 900 Series tractors.***

7. Steering spindle R.H.
8. Steering spindle bearings
9. Washers
10. Tie rod spacers
11. Tie rod
12. Axle main member
13. Pivot bolt spacer
14. Steering spindle L.H.
15. Steering arm
16. Drag link ends
17. Drag link
32. Set screw
38. Axle pivot pin

### Models 1914-1916

On these tractors, axle main member (15—Fig. DA7) is stationary, and axle spindle housings (7 and 21) pivot on pins (23). To remove axle main member (15), support front of tractor and remove hood. Detach drag link from steering arm (3). Remove guard for front pto. Push against belt idler and detach pto belts. Unscrew bolts (B—Fig. DA8) retaining pto bearing support, then pull pto shaft and housing assembly forward out of axle and frame. Unscrew bolts securing pivot pins (23—Fig. DA7) and drive out pins toward front of tractor. Support axle assembly, remove bolt (10) and lower axle away from tractor.

Inspect components for excessive wear and damage. Reinstall by reversing removal procedure. Tighten bolt (10) to 90-120 ft.-lbs. (122-163 N·m). Lubricate pivot pins by injecting grease through grease fittings.

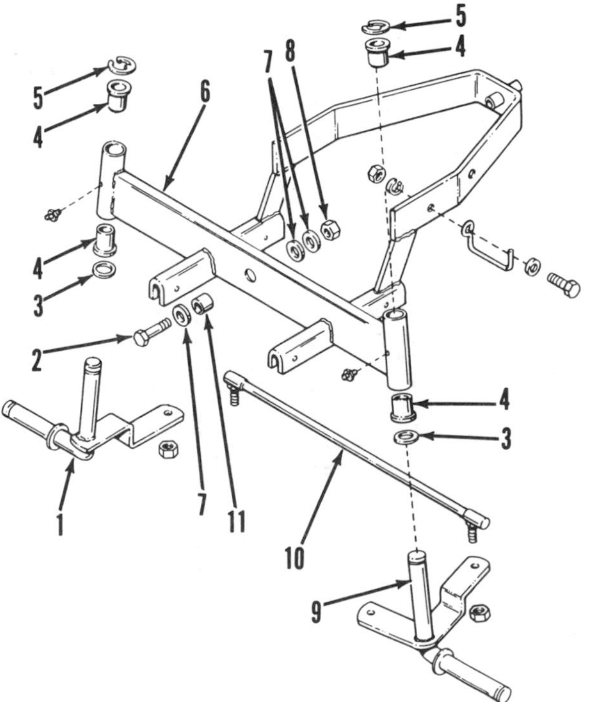


***Fig. DA5—Exploded view of front axle assembly used on Models 608LT, 608LTD, 611H, 611LT, 611LTD, 808GT, 810GT, 811GT and T811. Some models use a washer and straight bushing in place of flanged bushing (4).***

1. Spindle
2. Front pivot bolt
3. Washer
4. Bushings
5. Retaining ring
6. Main member
7. Washers
8. Nut
9. Spindle
10. Tie rod
11. Spacer

## TIE ROD

### Models 310-310D-312-312D-312H-314-314D-314H-410-410S-414S-416S-416H

Dual tie rods are used on these models. Length of tie rods is adjustable and should be adjusted so there is approximately 1/8 inch (3 mm) front wheel toe-in. To adjust toe-in, disconnect ball joints from steering spindles, loosen locknuts and turn tie rod ball joints in or out as required. Be sure that both tie rods are adjusted to equal length.

### Models 608LT-608LTD-611H-611LT-611LTD-808GT-810GT-811GT-T811

A single, adjustable tie rod (10—Fig. DA5) is used on early style axles. Renew tie rod if ball joint ends are excessively worn. On later style axles, tie rod is not adjustable.

To adjust toe-in on early style axles, disconnect one of the tie rod ball joints from steering spindles. Loosen ball joint



Illustrations courtesy Deutz-Allis Corp.

jam nuts and turn ball joints in or out as required. Toe-in should be $^{1}/_{16}$ to $^{1}/_{8}$ inch (1.5-3.0 mm). Toe-in is not adjustable on later style axles equipped with nonadjustable tie rod.

## Models 1914-1916

A single tie rod (2—Fig. DA7) is used on these models. Renew tie rod if ball joint ends (1) are excessively worn.

Front wheel toe-in should be $^{1}/_{2}$ to $^{3}/_{4}$ inch (13-19 mm). To adjust, loosen ball joint jam nuts and turn tie rod in or out to obtain desired toe-in. Tie rod thread length should be equal at both ball joints. Hold ball joint with a wrench when tightening jam nuts to prevent ball joint socket and ball stud from being forced together and possibly damaging the ball joint.

## All Other Models

The tie rod is not adjustable and can be removed after disconnecting tie rod from steering spindles.

# STEERING SPINDLES

## Models B206-Homesteader 6-Homesteader 7

To remove steering spindles (3 and 6—Fig. DA1), raise and support front of tractor and remove front wheels. Disconnect tie rod (4) from spindles and drag link from steering arm (2). Drive out pin holding steering arm, remove the arm and lower left spindle out of axle. Remove retaining pin and lower right spindle out of axle.

## Models B206-608-610-Homesteader 8

To remove steering spindles (13 and 15—Fig. DA2), raise and support front of tractor and remove front wheels. Disconnect tie rod (10) from spindles. Remove set screw retaining steering arm (4) to left spindle (13) and remove the arm. Remove key from spindle and lower spindle out of axle. Remove retaining pin and lower right spindle (15) out of axle.

Axle is equipped with renewable spindle bushings (6). Lubricate with multipurpose lithium base grease.

## Models 310-310D-312-312D-312H-314-314D-314H-410-410S-414S-416H-416S

To remove steering spindles (16—Fig. DA3 or DA4), support front of tractor and remove front wheels. Disconnect tie rod ends from spindles. Remove "E" ring (13) from top of spindle and lower spindle out of axle main member.

All models are equipped with renewable spindle bushings (15). Lubricate with multipurpose lithium base grease.

## Models 608LT-608LTD-611H-611LT-808GT-810GT-811GT-T811

To remove steering spindles (1 and 9—Fig. DA5), support front of tractor and

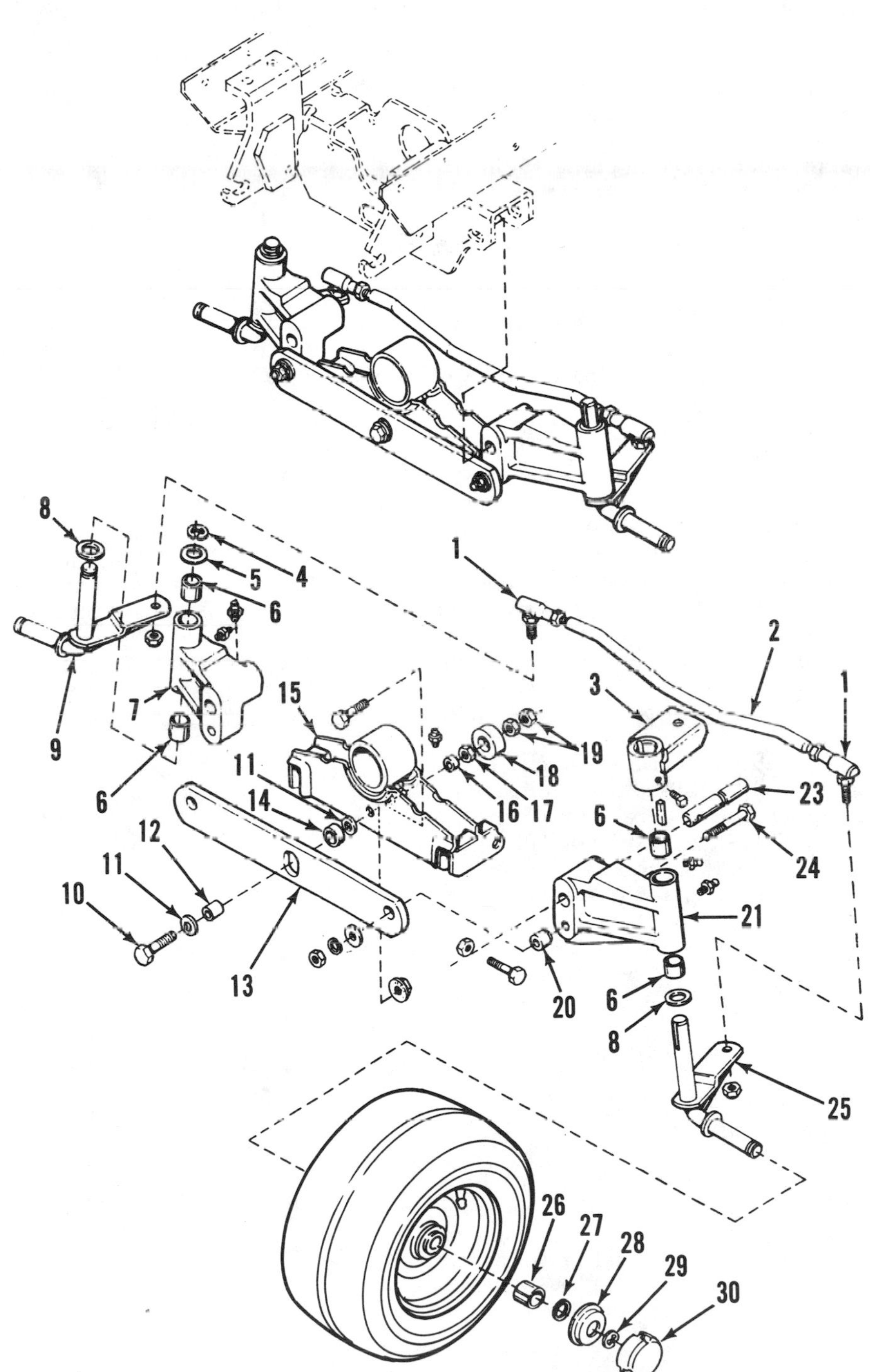


*Fig. DA7—Exploded view of front axle assembly used on Models 1914 and 1916.*

1. Tie rod end
2. Tie rod
3. Steering arm
4. "E" ring
5. Washer
6. Bushing
7. Axle pivot R.H.
8. Washer
9. Spindle R.H.
10. Cap screw
11. Washer
12. Spacer
13. Axle link
14. Spacer
15. Axle main member
16. Spacer
17. Nut
18. Retainer
19. Jam nuts
20. Spacer
21. Axle pivot L.H.
23. Pivot pin
24. Cap screw
25. Spindle L.H.
26. Bushing
27. Shim washer
28. Retainer
29. "E" ring
30. Hub cap

remove front wheels. Disconnect tie rod (10) from spindles. Remove "E" rings (5) from top of spindles and lower spindle out of axle main member.

All models are equipped with renewable spindle bushings (4). Lubricate with multipurpose lithium base grease.

*Fig. DA8—Remove bolts (B) so pto shaft and support assembly can be removed on Models 1914, 1916.*

### Models B210-B212-HB212-700 Series-900 Series

To remove steering spindles (7 and 14—Fig. DA6), support front of tractor and remove front wheels. Disconnect tie rod (11) from spindles. Remove set screw (32) retaining steering arm (15) to left spindle (14). Remove steering arm and key, then lower left spindle out of axle main member. Remove retaining pin from right spindle (7) and lower spindle from axle.

All models are equipped with renewable spindle bushings (8). Lubricate with multipurpose lithium base grease.

### Models 1914-1916

To remove spindle (9 or 25—Fig. DA7), support front of tractor and remove wheel. Detach tie rod (2) from spindle. On right spindle (9), remove "E" ring (4) and slide spindle out of axle end. To remove left spindle (25), loosen set screws and pull steering arm (3) off spindle. Remove key and slide spindle out of axle end.

Bushings (6) are renewable. Tighten tie rod ends to 45-60 ft.-lbs. (61-81 N·m). Tighten steering arm set screws to 13-19 ft.-lbs. (18-25 N·m). When installing front wheels, install shim washers (27) as required so wheel hub side play is 1/32 inch (0.8 mm). Lubricate spindles and wheel hubs with multipurpose lithium base grease.

# STEERING GEAR

## R&R AND OVERHAUL

### Models B206-Homesteader 6-Homesteader 7

These tractors are equipped with a steering arm at the end of steering column which transfers steering motion using two drag links and a pivot arm to steering spindle arm. Disassembly is self-evident upon inspection.

### Models B210-B212-HB212

To remove steering gear, remove hood, side panels and battery. Disconnect electrical wires from voltage regulator and remove fuel tank. Loosen set screw and remove steering wheel and key. Unbolt and remove dash assembly. Remove collar from steering shaft, then unbolt and remove battery support. Disconnect "U" joint (3—Fig. DA9) from gear and yoke assembly (5), and remove steering shaft. Disconnect the rear drag link ball joint from steering arm (10). Remove nut and washers from steering arm shaft and remove steering gear (8) as steering arm and shaft is withdrawn. Remove nut, lockwasher and set screw from lower end of eccentric pin (4), then withdraw eccentric pin with gear and yoke assembly (5). Unbolt and remove steering bracket (7).

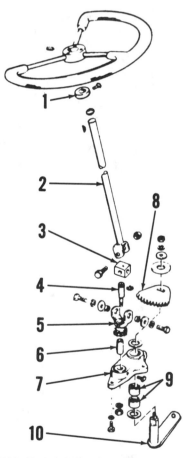

*Fig. DA9—Exploded view of steering gear used on Models B210, B212 and HB212.*

1. Collar
2. Steering shaft
3. "U" joint
4. Eccentric pin
5. Gear & yoke assy.
6. Bushing
7. Steering bracket
8. Steering gear
9. Needle bearings
10. Steering arm & shaft

Check needle bearings (9) and bushing (6) and renew as necessary.

When reassembling, lubricate needle bearings, bushing and gear teeth with multipurpose grease. Before attaching drag link or assembling "U" joint, adjust gear backlash as follows: With eccentric pin nut and set screw loose, rotate eccentric pin to obtain a minimum backlash between gears. Tighten nut and set screw, then rotate gears to make certain gears do not bind. If binding condition exists, increase backlash slightly.

Complete balance of reassembly by reversing disassembly procedure.

### Models B208-Homesteader 8-608-610

To remove steering gear, first remove hood and steering wheel. Disconnect ignition wire and choke and throttle cables. Unbolt and lift off dash assembly and upper steering shaft support. Raise front of tractor and disconnect drag link (17—Fig. DA10) from steering gear (16). Unbolt and remove steering gear. Remove nut securing steering pinion (12) to frame and remove upper steering shaft, "U" joint and steering pinion.

Inspect bushings, steering gears and steering shaft "U" joint for excessive wear and renew as necessary.

When reassembling steering unit, move steering gear (16) closer to steering pinion (12) as necessary to remove excessive steering wheel play. To reassemble, reverse disassembly procedure.

### Models 310-310D-312-312D-312H-314-314H-410-410S-414S-416S-416H

To remove steering gear, first remove steering wheel and loosen clamp bolts at instrument panel. Disconnect drag link from steering gear arm and remove bolts securing steering gear housing (5—Fig. DA11) to frame. Raise front of tractor and lower steering gear and shaft out underside of tractor.

To disassemble steering gear, remove nuts (9), steering lever (15) with follower stud (16), seal retainer (17) and seal (18). Remove plug (12) and withdraw steering shaft and worm (10), bearings (6 and 7) and Belleville washer (11).

When reassembling steering gear, tighten plug (12) to 10-14 ft.-lbs. (14-19 N·m). Check to see that steering shaft turns freely after plug is installed. Loosen locknut (14) and back out follower stud (16) two turns, then install lever and bolt assembly (15) with seal (18) and retainer (17). Adjust nuts (9) so seal (18) is in full contact with housing (5), but do not compress seal. Locate steering lever in mid-position (half way between full left and full right turn). Turn follower stud (16) in to obtain zero backlash and tighten locknut (14). Steering shaft must turn from full right to full left turn position without binding. Lubricate unit with approximately 1/4 pound (120 mL) of multipurpose grease.

## Models 608LT-608LTD-611H-611LT-611LTD-808GT-810GT-811GT-T811

To remove steering gear, raise hood and disconnect battery cables. Drain fuel tank and disconnect throttle cable from carburetor. Remove the steering wheel. Unbolt and remove upper dash and fuel tank. Disconnect electrical wires from engine. Unbolt and remove shift panel and lower dash. On early Models 608LT and 611LT, remove steering support (5—Fig. DA12). Late models are not equipped with support. On all models, disconnect drag link (14) from steering rod (12). Unbolt and remove steering plate (16) and steering shaft (8).

Remove base plate (11), sector gear (10) and steering rod (8) as an assembly. To remove sector gear, remove two set screws and use a suitable puller or press to force steering rod from gear.

Inspect bushings in base plate and steering plate for wear or damage and renew as necessary.

When reassembling sector gear and steering rod, install key with rounded end towards bent end of steering rod. Press rod into steering gear until end of rod is approximately 1/4 inch (6 mm) above face of gear hub. Be sure that beveled end of spacer (6) is toward steering shaft gear (8). Complete reassembly by reversing disassembly procedure.

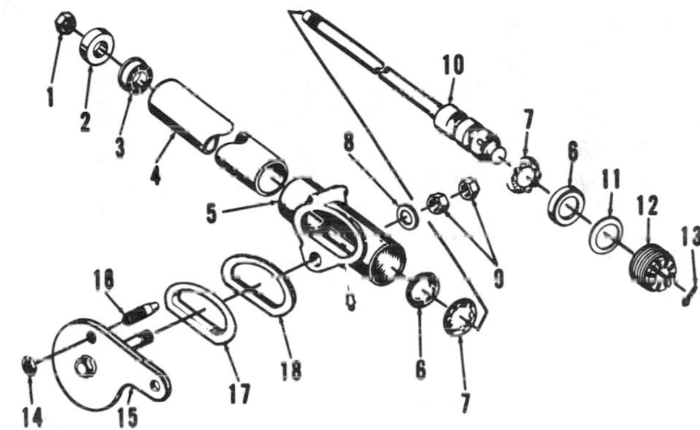

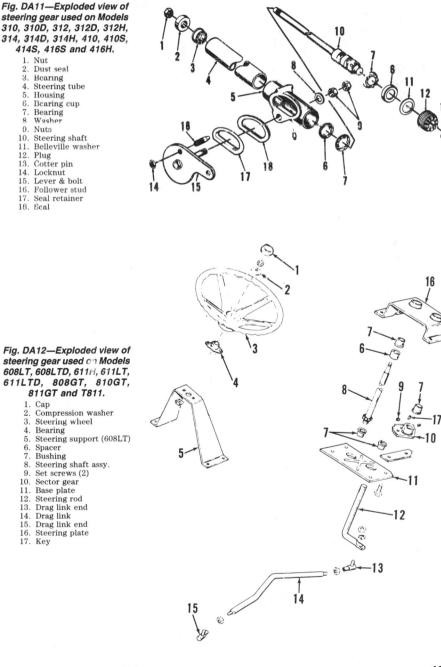

*Fig. DA11—Exploded view of steering gear used on Models 310, 310D, 312, 312D, 312H, 314, 314D, 314H, 410, 410S, 414S, 416S and 416H.*

1. Nut
2. Dust seal
3. Bearing
4. Steering tube
5. Housing
6. Bearing cup
7. Bearing
8. Washer
9. Nuts
10. Steering shaft
11. Belleville washer
12. Plug
13. Cotter pin
14. Locknut
15. Lever & bolt
16. Follower stud
17. Seal retainer
18. Seal

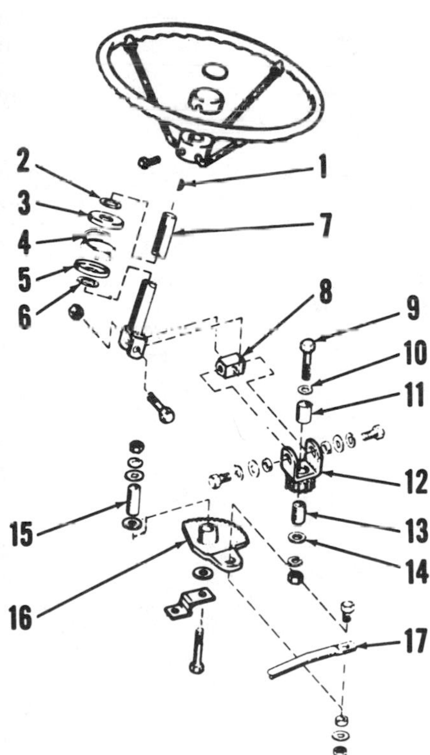


*Fig. DA10—Exploded view of steering gear used on Models B208, 608, 610 and Homesteader 8.*

1. Key
2. Washer
3. Cup
4. Spring
5. Cup
6. Washer
7. Steering shaft
8. "U" joint
9. Bolt
10. Washer
11. Spacer
12. Gear & yoke assy.
13. Bushing
14. Washer
15. Sleeve
16. Quadrant gear
17. Drag link

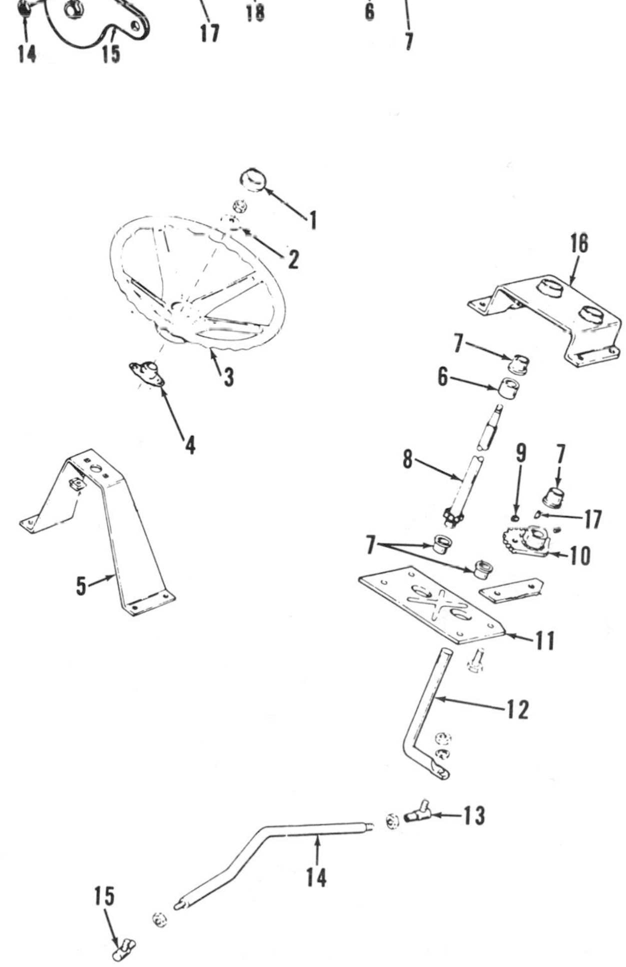


*Fig. DA12—Exploded view of steering gear used on Models 608LT, 608LTD, 611H, 611LT, 611LTD, 808GT, 810GT, 811GT and T811.*

1. Cap
2. Compression washer
3. Steering wheel
4. Bearing
5. Steering support (608LT)
6. Spacer
7. Bushing
8. Steering shaft assy.
9. Set screws (2)
10. Sector gear
11. Base plate
12. Steering rod
13. Drag link end
14. Drag link
15. Drag link end
16. Steering plate
17. Key

## Models 710 (3 spd.)-710 (6 spd.)-712H-712S-716 (6 spd.)-912 (6 spd.)-912H-914H-914S-916H

To remove steering gear, remove battery and steering wheel. Disconnect drag link from steering arm (13—Fig. DA13) and turn steering arm to allow access to mounting bolts. Remove mounting bolts and move steering gear assembly forward until casting lug clears edge of frame opening, then lower assembly from tractor.

To disassemble steering gear, clamp support casting in a vise and remove locknut (B—Fig. DA14) and washer. Use a plastic mallet to remove steering arm from bevel drive gear and casting. Position steering shaft in a vise. Remove retaining ring (10) and use a piece of hardwood to drive pinion gear off shaft. Remove key from shaft and slide shaft out of bushing. Loosen locknuts (14) and remove adjusting cap screws (A), adjusting plate (6) and bushing (7). Use a bearing puller to remove needle bearings from support casting.

During reassembly, press needle bearings into each end of bore with end of bearing marked "Torrington" facing outward. The bearing at gear end must be $^1/_8$ inch (3 mm) below surface of casting. The bearing at steering arm end must fit flush with casting. Install bushing (7—Fig. DA14) and adjusting plate assembly, and tighten adjusting plate cap screws (A) until about $^1/_{64}$ inch (0.4 mm) of bushing is above casting surface.

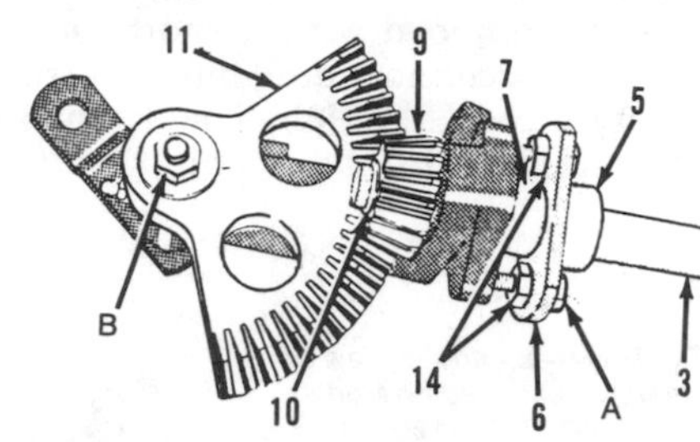


*Fig. DA14—View of steering gear assembly removed from tractor. Refer to text for disassembly procedure.*

A. Adjusting cap screws
B. Locknut & flat washer
3. Steering shaft
5. Set collar
6. Steering plate
7. Bushing
9. Pinion
10. "E" ring
11. Bevel gear
14. Locknuts

## Models 1914-1916

To service steering gear assembly, remove hood, air plenum and battery. Remove dash side panels and tunnel cover. Remove steering wheel nut (1—Fig. DA15) and pull steering wheel from steering shaft (7) using a suitable puller. Remove snap ring (10) from lower end of steering shaft, raise shaft until clear of support plate (14) and withdraw shaft from bottom of tractor. Note that some early model tractors use a two-piece steering shaft. Disconnect drag link end (31) from steering arm (29). Unbolt and remove steering gear assembly from tractor.

Remove bevel gear (19) and steering arm (29) from steering arm shaft (24). Remove snap rings (27) and withdraw steering arm shaft from gear housing (21). Remove snap ring (18), bevel pinion (17), thrust washer (16) and steering gear and shaft (11) from housing.

Bushings (4, 15 and 22) are renewable. Renew thrust washers (8 and 16) as necessary if steering shaft end play is excessive.

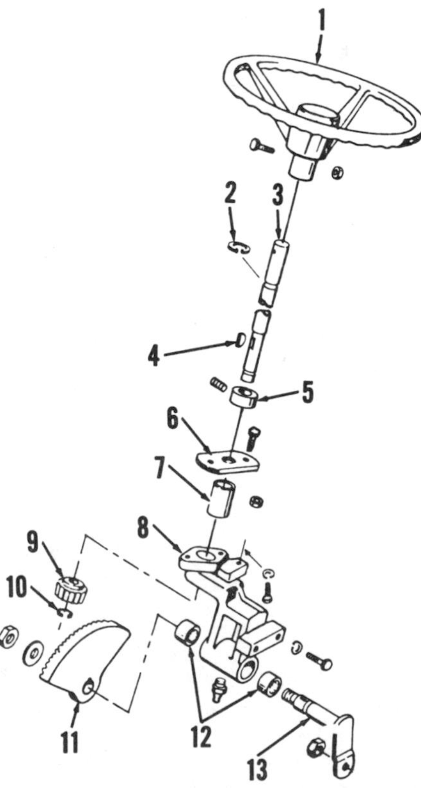


*Fig. DA13—Exploded view of steering gear used on Models 710 (3 spd.), 710 (6 spd.), 712H, 712S, 716 (6 spd.), 716H, 912 (6 spd.), 912H, 914S, 914H and 916H.*

1. Steering wheel
2. Retaining ring
3. Steering shaft
4. Key
5. Set collar
6. Steering plate
7. Bushing
8. Casting
9. Pinion
10. "E" ring
11. Bevel gear
12. Needle bearings
13. Steering arm assy.

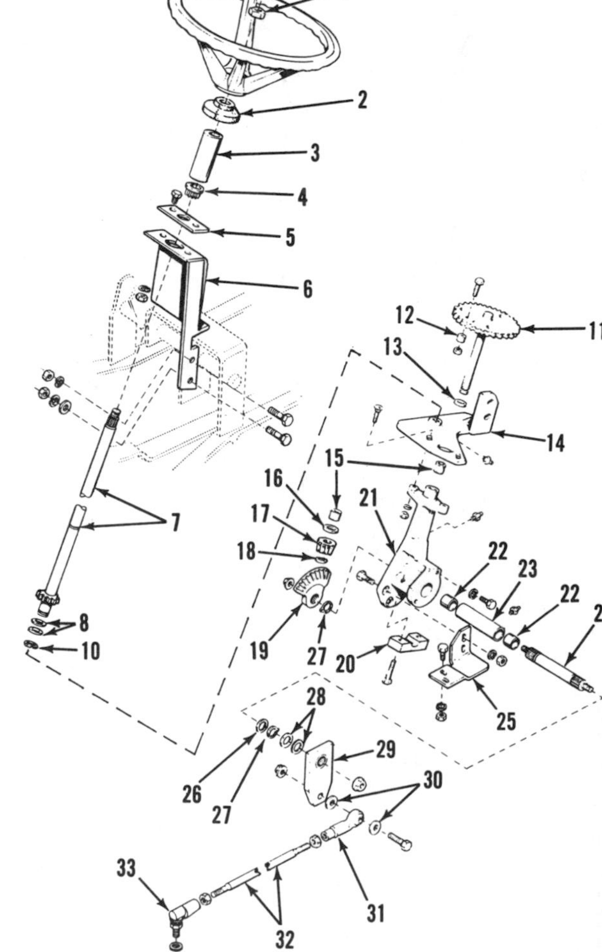


*Fig. DA15—Exploded view of steering gear assembly used on Models 1914 and 1916.*

1. Nut
2. Boot
3. Tube
4. Bushing
5. Retainer plate
6. Support bracket
7. Steering shaft
8. Thrust washers
10. Retaining ring
11. Gear & shaft
12. Spacer
13. Curved washer
14. Support plate
15. Bushings
16. Thrust washer
17. Pinion gear
18. Retaining ring
19. Sector gear
20. Clamp
21. Steering gear housing
22. Bushings
23. Tube
24. Sector shaft
25. Bracket
26. Washer
27. Snap ring
28. Washers
29. Steering arm
30. Washers
31. Ball joint
32. Drag link
33. Ball joint



Illustrations courtesy Deutz-Allis Corp.

When assembling, note the following: Pinion gear (17) must be centered on bevel gear (19) when front wheels are pointing straight ahead. Apply Loctite to nut securing bevel gear (19) to shaft and tighten to 35-40 ft.-lbs. (47-54 N·m). Apply Loctite to screws securing clamp (20) and tighten to 25-30 ft.-lbs. (34-40 N·m). Apply Loctite to nut securing steering arm (29) to shaft and tighten to 35-40 ft.-lbs. (47-54 N·m). Tighten bolt securing drag link end (31) to 45-60 ft.-lbs. (62-81 N·m).

# ENGINE

## REMOVE AND REINSTALL

### Models B206-B208-Homesteader 6-Homesteader 7-Homesteader 8

To remove engine on Model B206, loosen two hood hold-down knobs and tilt hood forward. On Models Homesteader 6 and Homesteader 7, unlatch rear of hood and tilt hood forward. Remove hood on Models B208 and Homesteader 8. On all models, disconnect ignition wire, fuel line, choke cable and throttle cable. Remove drive belt from engine pulley on underside of tractor. Remove engine pulley. Remove engine mounting bolts and lift engine from tractor frame.

To reinstall engine, reverse removal procedure.

### Models B210-B212-HB212

Engine removal requires removal of hood, grille, grille support and dash. Disconnect battery and ignition wire and remove battery. Slide flexible fuel line off tank connection, then remove fuel tank. Remove wires from starter-generator and disconnect choke and throttle control cables from engine. Remove engine oil drain pipe. Disconnect drive shaft front coupling and remove bolts securing engine to frame. Slide engine forward and lift it out of frame.

### Models 310-310D-312-312D-312H-314-314D-314H-410-410S-414S-416H-416S

To remove engine, remove hood and front grille assembly, supporting brace and engine shield. Remove front pto drive belt. Disconnect battery cables and ignition wires. Disconnect throttle and choke cables. Disconnect fuel line at fuel pump. Disconnect drive shaft coupling at rear of engine. Remove engine mounting bolts. If engine cannot be moved to the side far enough to clear oil drain pipe, then drain engine oil and remove oil drain pipe. Lift engine from tractor.

### Models 608-610

To remove engine, first remove hood and disconnect battery cables. Remove grille assembly and grille support. Disconnect throttle cable, choke cable and fuel line at engine. Mark wires for reassembly, then disconnect electrical connections at regulator and generator. Remove regulator and generator from engine. Remove drive belts and pulleys from engine crankshaft. Remove engine mounting bolts and lift engine from tractor.

### Models 608LT-608LTD-611H-611LT-611LTD

To remove engine, tilt hood assembly forward and remove front engine brace. Disconnect battery ground cable. Remove fuel line at carburetor and drain fuel tank. Disconnect throttle cable. Mark all wires for reassembly, then disconnect engine ground wire, charging circuit wires and starter wires. Remove drive belt from engine pulley.

**NOTE: Early model tractors have a small hole in frame for crankshaft, requiring removal of engine pulley prior to removing engine. Late models have a larger hole in frame, allowing engine to be removed without removing pulley.**

On early models (small frame hole), remove cap screw retaining engine pulley and use a suitable puller to remove pulley from crankshaft. It may be necessary to tap pulley with a soft hammer to aid in removal. On all models, remove engine mounting bolts and lift engine from tractor.

### Models 710 (3 spd.)-710 (6 spd.)-712H-712S-716 (6 spd.)-716H-912 (6 spd.)-912H-914H-914S-916H

To remove engine, remove hood and front grille assembly. Disconnect fuel line from fuel pump and plug hose or drain fuel tank. Disconnect battery ground cable, all electrical wires, choke cable and throttle cable from engine. Remove flywheel to drive shaft cap screws. Remove four engine mounting bolts and lift engine from tractor.

### Models 808GT-810GT-811GT-T811

To remove engine, disconnect battery ground cable from battery. Remove fuel line at carburetor and drain fuel tank. Disconnect throttle cable, choke cable, engine ground wire, charging circuit wires and starter wires. On 810GT tractors, remove muffler assembly. On all models, remove four engine mounting bolts and lift engine from tractor.

### Models 1914-1916

To remove engine, disconnect battery ground cable and remove hood. Remove dash side panels. Disconnect all interfering electrical wires. Disconnect fuel line and remove air cleaner. Detach throttle and choke cables. Remove pto guard and detach pto drive belts. Loosen screws securing engine to engine plate and slide engine forward so drive shaft separates from transmission input shaft. Remove engine mounting bolts, lift engine toward front of tractor, detach drive shaft and remove engine.

Reinstall by reversing removal procedure.

## OVERHAUL

Engine make and model are listed at the beginning of this section. To overhaul engine components and accessories, refer to appropriate Briggs & Stratton or Kohler sections of this manual.

# CLUTCH

## ADJUSTMENT

### Models B206-Homesteader 6-Homesteader 7

To adjust clutch linkage, clutch-brake pedal must be in clutch engaged position. Insert an Allen wrench through opening in right side of frame and loosen set screw in collar (6—Fig. DA16). Position collar so it is $^1/_8$ inch (3 mm) from angle clip (8) and tighten set screw.

### Model B208

To adjust clutch, clutch-brake pedal must be in clutch engaged position. Refer to Fig. DA17. Compression spring on clutch rod should be compressed about $^3/_4$ inch (19 mm). To adjust, loosen set screw in collar (B) and move collar to obtain correct length of spring. Turn adjusting nut (C) at end of clutch rod to adjust movement of clutch idler pulley against drive belt. Clutch idler pulley should release drive belt when clutch-brake pedal is depressed.

### Model Homesteader 8

With foot pedal up (clutch engaged position), adjust clutch rod outer set collar (2—Fig. DA18) to obtain $^5/_8$ inch (16 mm) clearance between collar and clutch rod guide. Then depress foot pedal all the way and adjust inner set collar (4) so clutch rod spring (3) is just free to rotate on rod.

## Models B210-B212-310-310D-312-312D-314-314D

With clutch-brake pedal in clutch engaged position, refer to Fig. DA19 and adjust control rod locknuts (L) so there is $^{7}/_{8}$ inch (22 mm) clearance (C) between locknuts and idler pulley pivot arm rod guide (G) with variable speed lever in "LOW" speed position.

## Model HB212

To adjust clutch, clutch-brake pedal must be in clutch engaged position. Turn adjusting nuts (8—Fig. DA20) so there is $^{1}/_{8}$ inch (3 mm) clearance between adjusting nuts and closest end of rod guide (7).

## Models 312H-314H-416H

With clutch-brake pedal in clutch engaged position, there should be $^{5}/_{8}$ inch (16 mm) clearance between closest nut (13—Fig. DA21) and end of rod guide (14). Turn locknuts if necessary to obtain correct spacing.

## Model 410

To adjust clutch idler linkage, first make certain brake linkage is properly adjusted as outlined in "BRAKE" adjustment paragraph. Then, with clutch brake pedal in clutch engaged position, adjust jam nuts so there is $^{1}/_{2}$ inch (13 mm) clearance between jam nuts and clutch rod guide. See Fig. DA22.

## Models 410S-414S-416S

To adjust clutch idler linkage, first make certain brake linkage is properly adjusted as outlined in appropriate "BRAKE" adjustment paragraph. Then, with clutch-brake pedal in clutch engaged position, refer to Fig. DA23 and adjust jam nuts on clutch rod to obtain a clearance of $^{3}/_{4}$ inch (19 mm) between jam nuts and clutch rod guide.

## Models 608-610

With foot pedal up (clutch engaged position), adjust clutch rod locknut (Fig. DA24) to obtain $^{3}/_{8}$ inch (9.5 mm) clearance between nut and clutch rod guide. Then, depress foot pedal all the way and adjust inner set collar until clutch rod spring is just free to rotate on rod.

**NOTE: Some early models use set collars in place of locknuts, but adjustment procedure is the same.**

## Models 608LT-611LT

To adjust clutch, pedal must be in engaged (up) position and idler pulley tight against drive belt. On early models, adjust set collar (Fig. DA25) on clutch rod until clutch rod spring length is $2^{1}/_{4}$ inches (57 mm). Note that collar can be relocated more easily if foot pedal is depressed, but $2^{1}/_{4}$ inches (57 mm) dimension must be measured with clutch fully engaged. With clutch rod spring correctly set, adjust jam nuts at end of clutch rod to obtain $^{3}/_{8}$ inch (9.5 mm) clearance between rod guide and nuts as shown in Fig. DA25.

On late models, be sure that foot pedal is released (up) and idler pulley is tight against drive belt. Adjust nuts at front of clutch rod to obtain $^{1}/_{2}$ inch (13 mm) clearance (Fig. DA26) between adjustment nut and rod guide. Then, fully depress clutch-brake pedal, loosen

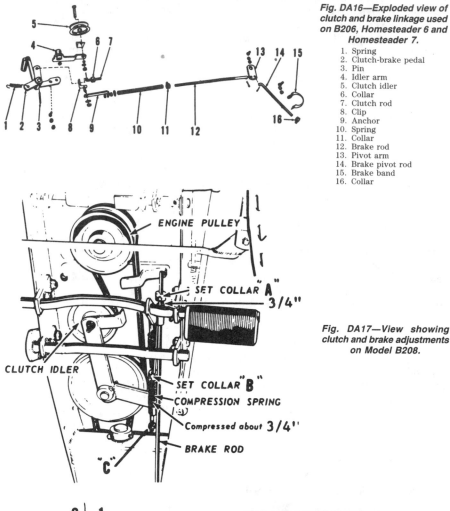

*Fig. DA16—Exploded view of clutch and brake linkage used on B206, Homesteader 6 and Homesteader 7.*

1. Spring
2. Clutch-brake pedal
3. Pin
4. Idler arm
5. Clutch idler
6. Collar
7. Clutch rod
8. Clip
9. Anchor
10. Spring
11. Collar
12. Brake rod
13. Pivot arm
14. Brake pivot rod
15. Brake band
16. Collar

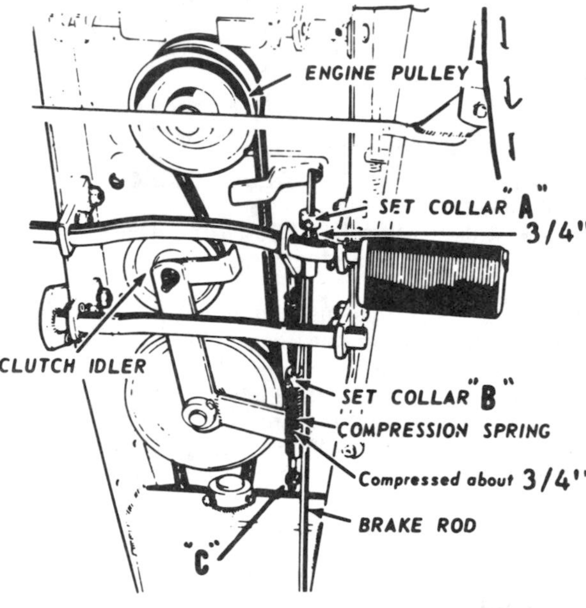


*Fig. DA17—View showing clutch and brake adjustments on Model B208.*

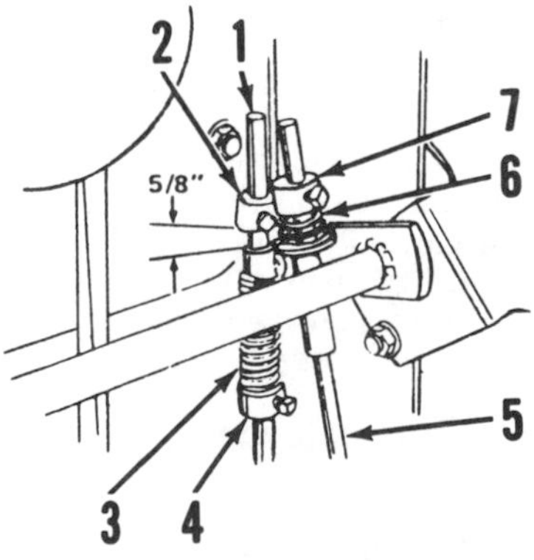


*Fig. DA18—View showing clutch and brake adjustment points on Homesteader 8 tractor.*

1. Clutch rod
2. Outer collar
3. Clutch spring
4. Inner collar
5. Brake rod
6. Tapered spring
7. Collar

*Fig. DA19—View showing clutch rod adjustment on models with variable speed drive. Distance (C) between rod guide (G) and rod nuts (L) should be 7/8 inch (22 mm).*



Illustrations courtesy Deutz-Allis Corp.

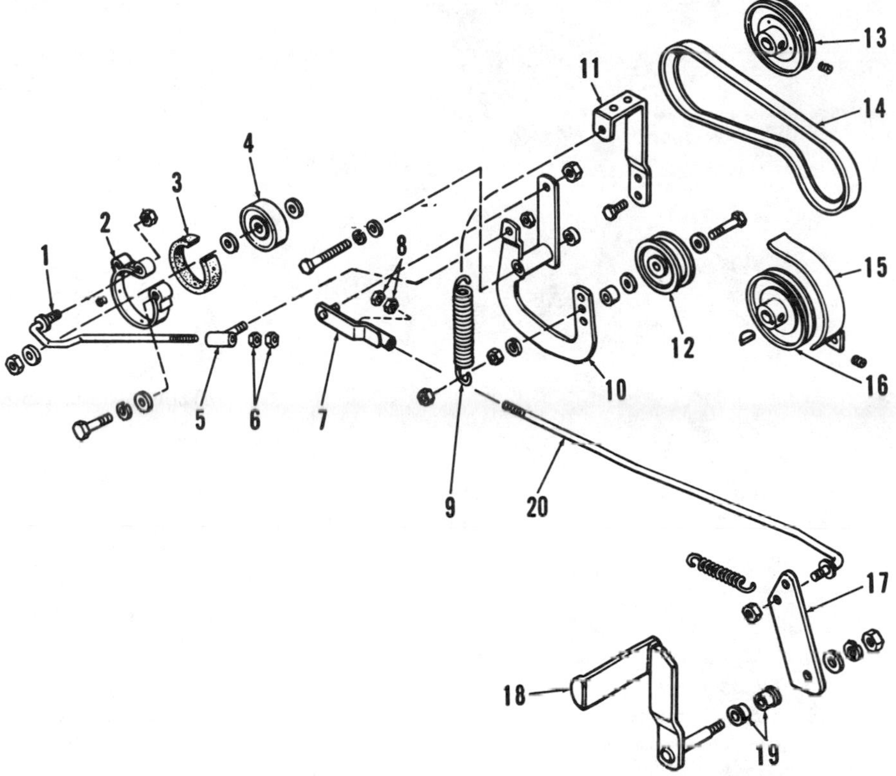


*Fig. DA20—Exploded view of clutch and brake assemblies used on Model HB212.*

1. Brake rod
2. Brake band
3. Brake lining
4. Brake drum
5. Rod guide
6. Adjusting nuts
7. Clutch rod guide
8. Adjusting nuts
9. Spring
10. Clutch-brake arm
11. Bracket
12. Clutch idler pulley
13. Transmission pulley
14. Drive belt
15. Belt guard
16. Bevel gear pulley
17. Arm
18. Clutch-brake pedal
19. Bushings
20. Clutch-brake rod

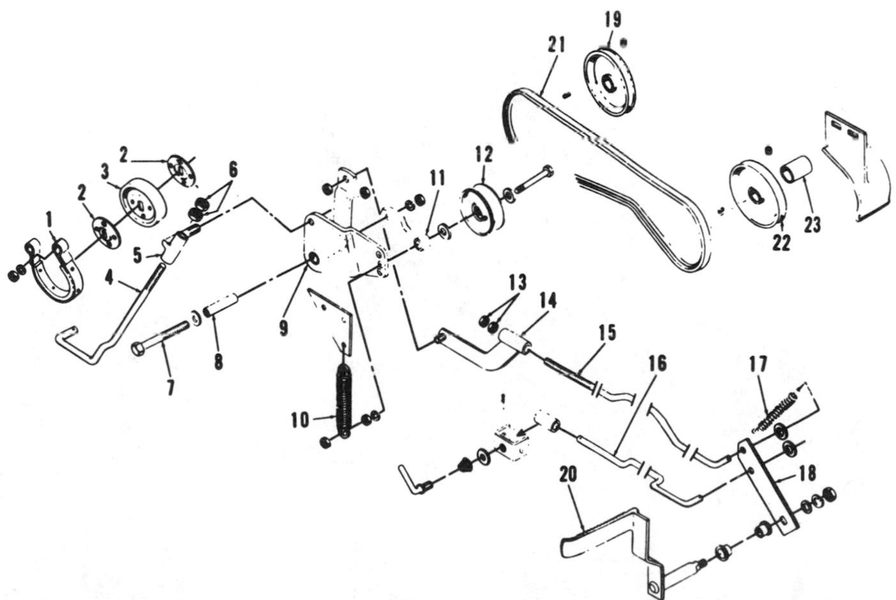


*Fig. DA21—Exploded view of clutch and brake assemblies used on Models 312H, 314H and 416H.*

1. Brake band
2. Washers
3. Brake drum
4. Brake rod
5. Rod guide
6. Adjusting nuts
7. Pivot bolt
8. Bushing
9. Clutch-brake arm
10. Spring
11. Bushing
12. Clutch idler pulley
13. Adjusting nuts
14. Rod guide
15. Clutch-brake rod
16. Parking brake rod
17. Spring
18. Arm
19. Transmission pulley
20. Clutch-brake pedal
21. Drive belt
22. Bevel gear pulley
23. Bushing

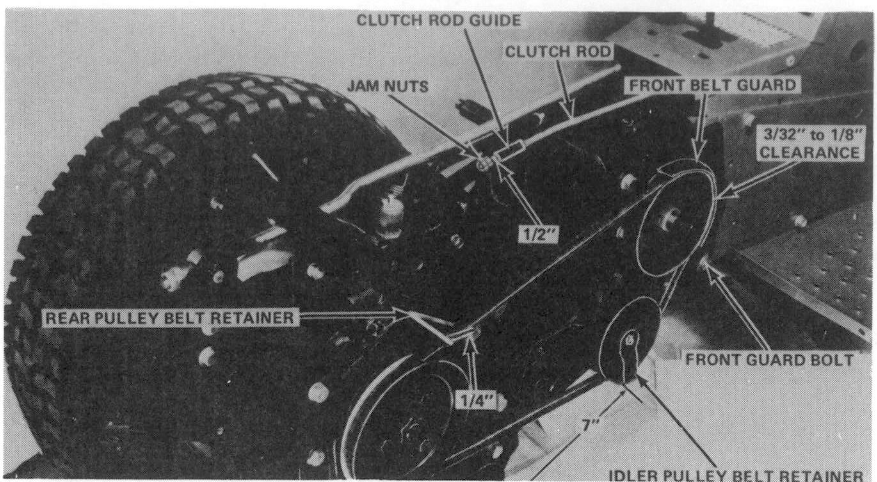


*Fig. DA22—View showing clutch rod adjustment on Model 410 tractors. Distance between rod guide and jam nuts should be ½ inch (13 mm). Note positions of belt guard and belt retainers.*

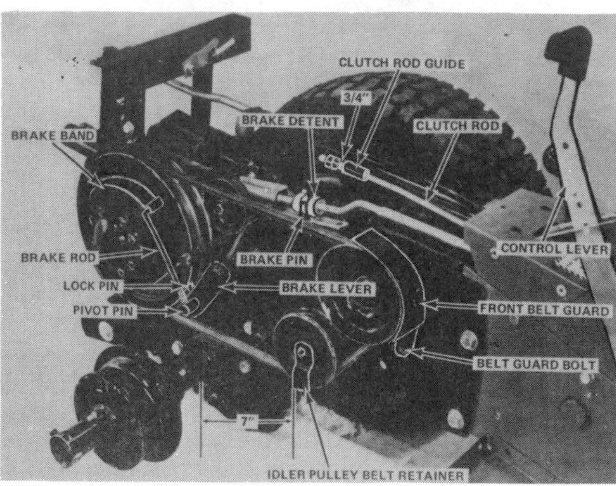


*Fig. DA23—View of clutch idler linkage adjustment points on Models 410S, 414S and 416S tractors. Distance between rod guide and jam nuts should be ¾ inch (19 mm).*

collar set screw and move collar against clutch rod spring until spring is compressed $^1/_2$ inch (13 mm). Tighten set screw and check clutch operation.

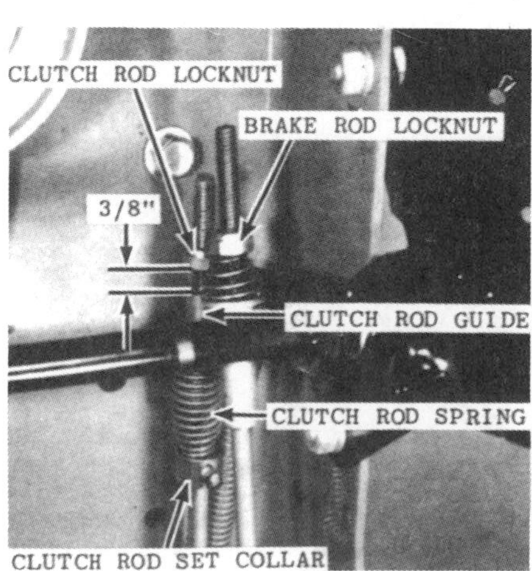


*Fig. DA24—View of brake and clutch linkage used on Models 608 and 610. Early models are slightly different but adjustment procedure is basically the same.*

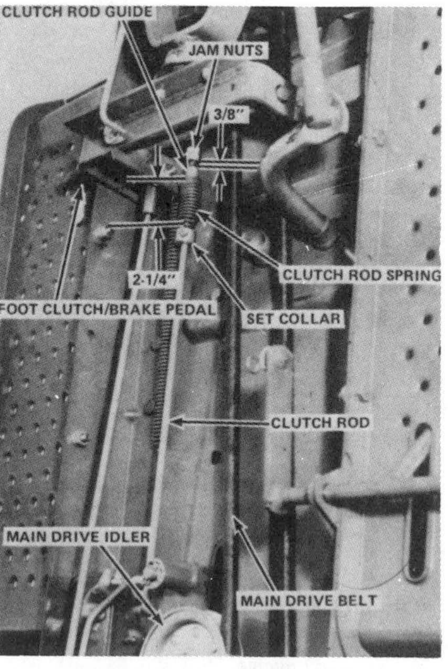


*Fig. DA25—View showing clutch rod adjustment on early Models 608LT and 611LT. Distance between rod guide and jam nuts should be 3/8 inch (10 mm). Refer to text for details.*

## Models 608LTD-611LTD

Due to a change of design of front axle support, there are two different clutch adjustment procedures. If tractor has a $^3/_4$ inch (19 mm) hole in axle support as shown at location "F" (Fig. DA27), adjust clutch as follows: Be sure that clutch pedal is in engaged (up) position and idler pulley is tight against drive belt. Adjust nut (2—Fig. DA27) at front of clutch rod (1) to obtain $^7/_8$ to 1 inch (22-25 mm) clearance between nut and rod guide (3). Fully depress and lock clutch-brake pedal. Loosen set screw in collar (4) and move collar against clutch rod spring, located between collar and rod guide (3), until spring is compressed $^1/_4$ to $^3/_8$ inch (6-9 mm). Tighten collar set screw and check clutch operation.

If tractor does not have a $^3/_4$ inch (19 mm) hole in axle support, adjust clutch as follows: Be sure that clutch pedal is in engaged (up) position and idler pulley is tight against drive belt. Adjust nut (2—Fig. DA28) at front of clutch rod (1) so gap between nut and rod guide (3) is $^9/_{16}$ to $^5/_8$ inch (14-15 mm). Fully depress and lock clutch-brake pedal. Loosen set screw in collar (4) and move collar against clutch rod spring, located between collar and rod guide (3), until spring is compressed $^7/_{16}$ to $^9/_{16}$ inch (11-14 mm). Tighten collar set screw and check clutch operation.

## Models 710 (3 spd.)-710 (6 spd.)-712H-712S-716 (6 spd.)-716H-912 (6 spd.)-912H-914H-914S-916H

With clutch-brake pedal in engaged (up) position, turn adjusting nuts (Fig. DA29) until clearance (A) between front nut and clutch rod guide is $^3/_8$ inch (9.5 mm) on Models 710 (3 spd.), 710 (6 spd.) and 912 (6 spd.), or $^1/_4$ inch (6 mm) on all other models.

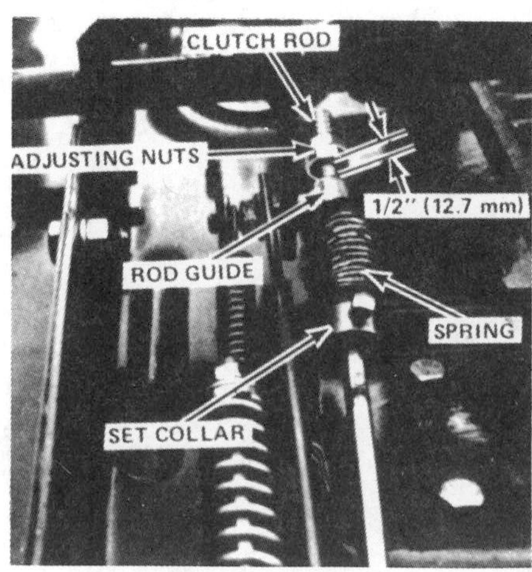


*Fig. DA26—Clutch rod adjustment points on late Models 608LT and 611LT.*

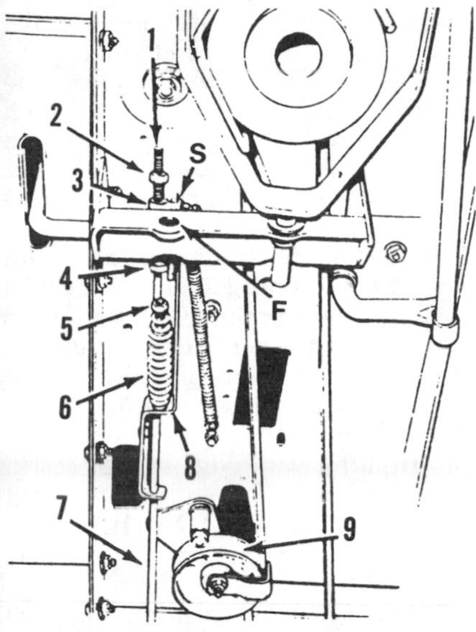


Fig. DA27—View of brake and clutch linkage used on Models 608LTD and 611LTD that have a ¾ inch (19 mm) hole (F) in front axle support. Refer to text for adjustment procedure.

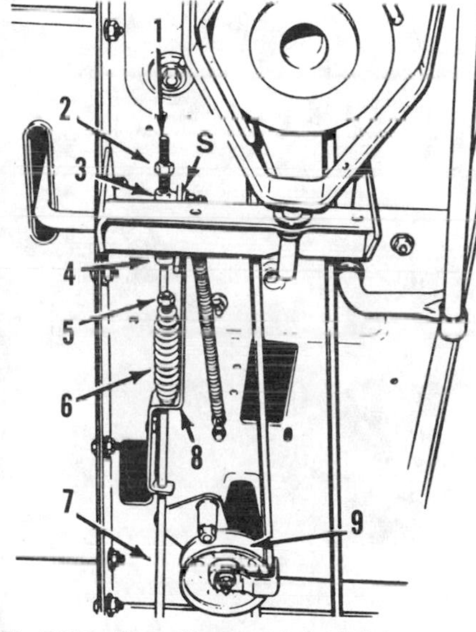


Fig. DA28—View of brake and clutch linkage used on Models 608LTD and 611LTD that do not have a ¾ inch (19 mm) hole in front axle support. Refer to text for adjustment procedure.

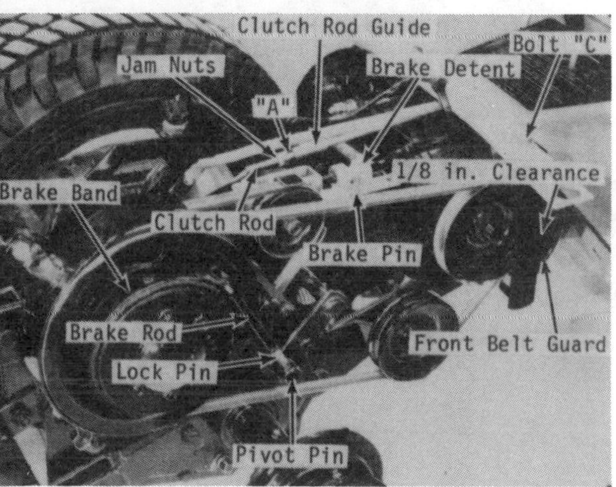


Fig. DA29—View of clutch rod adjustment on 700 and 900 Series tractors. Tractor equipped with shuttle clutch is shown; other models are similar.

## Models 808GT-810GT-811GT

To adjust clutch idler linkage, first make certain that brake linkage is properly adjusted as outlined in appropriate "BRAKE" adjustment paragraph. On all models, be sure that clutch-brake pedal is in engaged (up) position when adjusting linkage. On early models, press idler pulley against drive belt to remove slack in belt. Measure gap between adjusting nut (A—Fig. DA30) and clutch rod guide (C). Gap should be $^7/_{16}$ to $^9/_{16}$ inch (11-14 mm) as shown. Adjust nut (A) as required to obtain desired gap.

To adjust clutch rod spring tension, fully depress pedal and engage parking brake. Clutch rod spring (B) should be compressed $^7/_{16}$ to $^1/_2$ inch (11-13 mm). If not, loosen set screw and move collar (D) to compress spring to recommended distance.

On late models, distance between set collar (D—Fig. DA31) and rod guide (B) should be $^1/_2$ to $^5/_8$ inch (13-16 mm) with pedal in engaged position., Adjust by loosening set screw (E) and moving collar to obtain correct measurement.

## Models T811

On Model T811, variable speed control and clutch are adjusted together. Place speed control lever up in full speed position, then loosen shoulder bolt (4—Fig. DA32). With transmission in neutral, start engine, depress clutch pedal, set parking brake and stop engine. Unlatch parking brake and allow pedal to come up slowly, then measure distance from pedal shaft to forward edge of foot rest. Distance should be 5$^1/_2$ inches (140 mm). If not, adjust nut (2—Fig. DA33) toward spring to increase measurement or loosen nut to decrease measurement. Place speed control lever down in low speed position, then pull upper handle (1—Fig. DA32) only upward and hold to lock lever in position. Push bar (3) down and tighten shoulder bolt.

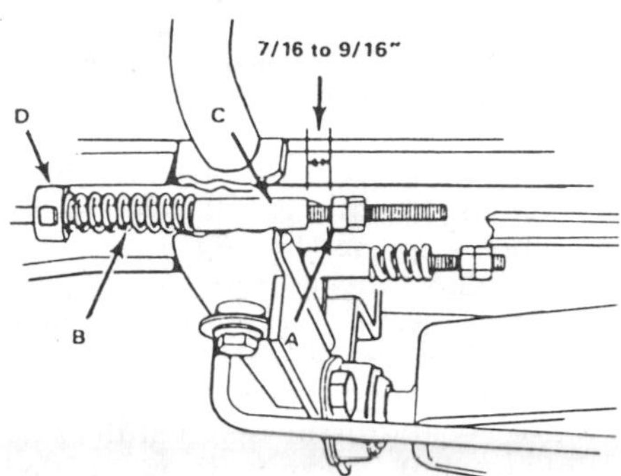


Fig. DA30—Clutch adjustment point for early Models 808GT, 810GT and 811GT. Refer to text for details.

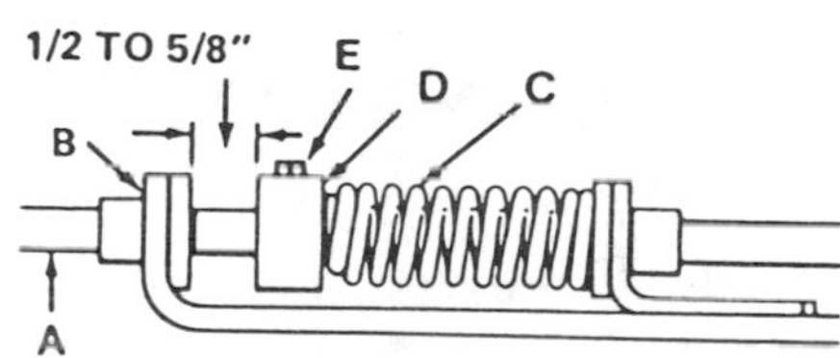


Fig. DA31—Clutch adjustment point for late Models 808GT and 811GT.

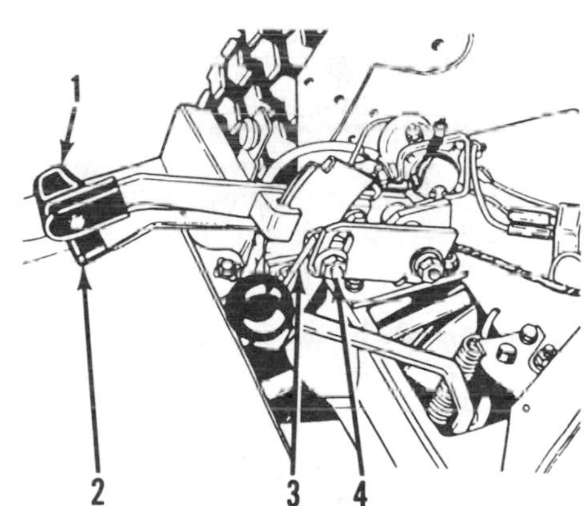


Fig. DA32—View of variable speed control linkage used on Model T811.

1. Control lever
2. Handle
3. Bar
4. Shoulder bolt

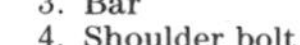

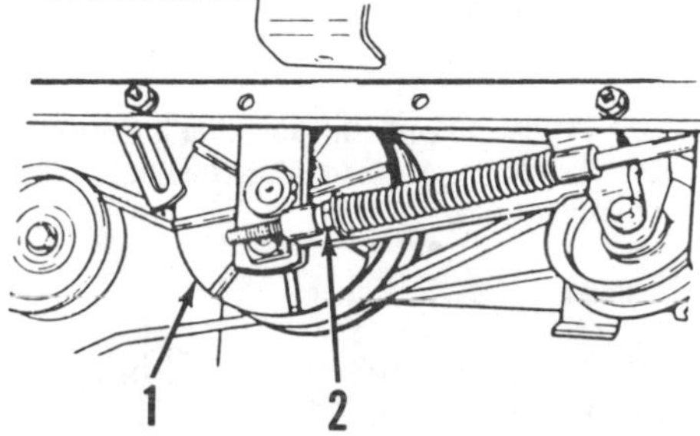


Fig. DA33—Variable speed pulley (1) and clutch rod used on Model T811. Adjusting nut (2) is used to adjust clutch. Refer to text.

# BRAKE

## ADJUSTMENT

### Models B206-Homesteader 6-Homesteader 7

To adjust brake, position clutch-brake pedal in clutch engaged position and compress spring (10—Fig. DA16) to a length of $5^1/_2$ inches (140 mm). Position collar (11) against spring and tighten set screw. Position collar (16) on brake rod (14) so brake is engaged when clutch-brake pedal is depressed, but does not drag on drum when pedal is released.

### Model B208

To adjust brake, depress clutch-brake pedal until brake is fully engaged, then lock parking brake and release clutch-brake pedal. Adjust set collar (A—Fig. DA17) so it is $^3/_4$ inch (19 mm) from rod guide.

### Model Homesteader 8

To adjust brake, foot pedal must be in release (up) position. Position brake rod set collar (7—Fig. DA18) against tapered spring (6) making sure spring is not compressed. Fully depress foot pedal. On early models (prior to S.N. 26401001), pedal should stop $1^1/_4$ inches (32 mm) from pedal stop stud. On late models (S.N. 26401001 and after), pedal should stop $2^1/_2$ inches (63 mm) from front edge of foot rest. Adjust set collar (7) as necessary to obtain desired measurement.

### Models B210-B212-310-310D-312-312D-314-314D

Adjust brake by first checking clutch adjustment as outlined in "CLUTCH" adjustment paragraph. Tighten adjusting nuts on brake band assembly until drive belt on variable speed pulley creeps when engine is running and clutch-brake pedal is depressed. Then, loosen brake adjusting nuts gradually until creeping motion of drive belt stops when engine is running and pedal is depressed.

**CAUTION: To prevent possible injury, engine should be stopped while turning brake adjusting nuts.**

### Models HB212-312H-314H

Brake should be adjusted so brake is fully engaged when clutch-brake pedal is depressed. With hydrostatic control lever in neutral position, turn brake adjusting nuts (6—Fig. DA20 or DA21) until brake band is tight against brake drum. With clutch-brake pedal released, brake band should not drag against brake drum.

### Models 410-410S-414S-416S

To adjust brake, refer to Fig. DA34. Adjust jam nuts on brake rod until forward edge of clutch arm is $^5/_8$ inch (16 mm) from rear corner of bevel gear housing when clutch-brake pedal is firmly depressed. Make certain that clutch idler releases belt tension properly before brake is applied.

### Model 416H

To adjust brake, refer to Fig. DA35. Loosen jam nut at front of parking brake rod, then turn handle and rod end until brake is tight against fender. With parking brake engaged and foot pedal released, adjust nuts on foot brake rod to provide $^1/_2$ inch (13 mm) clearance between nuts and brake rod guide.

### Models 608-610

To adjust brake, first loosen jam nut on parking brake rod and turn rod end until brake is tight when park brake handle is in upright position. Then, with parking brake engaged and foot pedal released, adjust brake rod locknut until it just contacts tapered coil spring (Fig. DA24). Depress foot pedal fully and adjust locknut as necessary until forward edge of foot pedal stops $2^1/_2$ inches (63 mm) from forward edge of foot rest.

### Models 608LT-608LTD-611LT-611LTD

With foot pedal in released (up) position, adjust brake as follows: On all models, push brake cam lever (Fig. DA36) forward by hand to remove slack

*Fig. DA34—View showing brake adjustment on Models 410, 410S, 414S and 416S. Refer to text for adjusting procedure.*

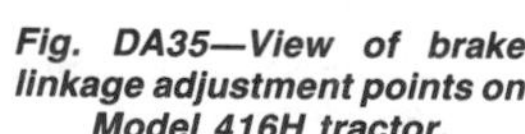
*Fig. DA35—View of brake linkage adjustment points on Model 416H tractor.*

Illustrations courtesy Deutz-Allis Corp.

in linkage and measure gap between rear of brake cam lever and cam lever stop with a feeler gage. Gap should be 1/8 inch (3 mm). If necessary, loosen jam nut and tighten adjusting nut on brake cam lever stud to decrease gap or loosen adjusting nut to increase gap.

Adjust brake rod springs as follows: On early models, hold foot brake rod (Fig. DA37) forward to remove slack. Adjust jam nuts on front of brake rod to obtain clearance of 5/8 to 3/4 inch (16-19 mm) between nuts and spring. Adjust nuts on rear of hand brake rod to just hold spring against rod guide without moving brake arm away from stop. For final adjustment check, apply brake and measure length of brake rod springs. Springs must not be less than 7/8 inch (22 mm) and not more than 15/16 inch (24 mm) long. Readjust jam nuts if necessary to bring springs within limits.

On late models, push brake rod guide (8—Fig. DA38) forward so mounting cap screw is at rear of slot (S) in rod guide. Then, adjust jam nuts (5) until brake rod spring (6) is just free to turn on brake rod (7).

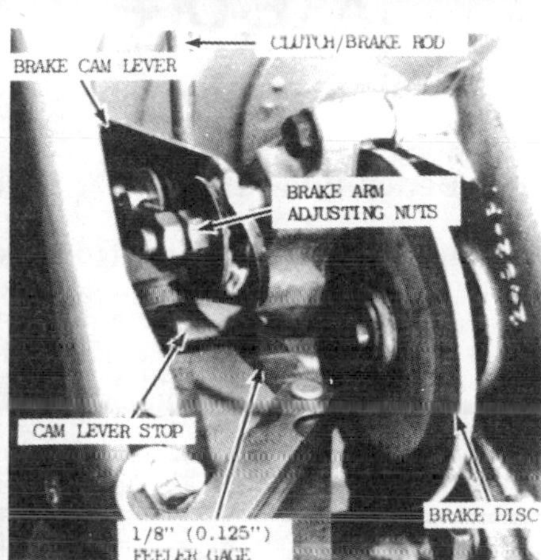


**Fig. DA36—View of caliper-disc brake used on Models 608LT and 611LT.**

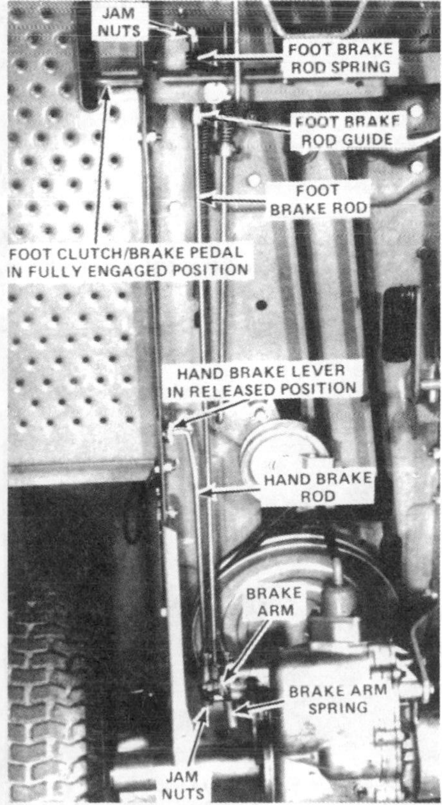


**Fig. DA37—Underside view of brake linkage used on early Models 608LT and 611LT.**

## Model 611H

With brake pedal in released (up) position, measure clearance between brake disc and pad with a feeler gage. Clearance should be 0.010 inch (0.25 mm). If necessary, loosen jam nut on brake cam stud and tighten or loosen inner nut to obtain desired clearance.

With brake rod guide (3—Fig. DA39) moved rearward as far as slot will allow, brake spring (2) should be snug against adjusting nut (1), but spring should still be just free to turn on brake rod (4).

## Models 710 (3 spd.)-712S-914S

To adjust brake, turn jam nuts on rear end of brake rod until front edge of clutch arm (Fig. DA40) is 5/8 inch (16 mm) from lift cable guide when pedal is fully depressed and brake is locked. When parking brake lever is pulled upward against fender, brake should be locked. If not, loosen jam nut on parking brake rod and turn brake lever and rod end until parking brake operation is correct.

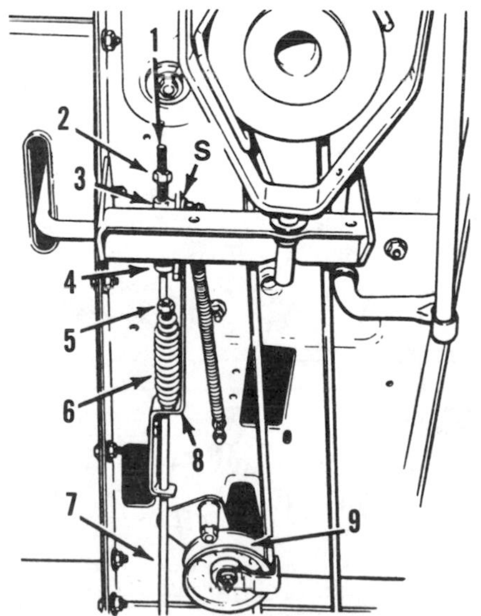


**Fig. DA38—Underside view of brake linkage used on Models 608LTD and 611LTD.**

1. Clutch rod
2. Nut
3. Clutch rod guide
4. Set collar
5. Nut
6. Spring
7. Brake rod
8. Brake rod guide
9. Idler pulley

## Models 712H-716H-912H-914H-916H

To adjust brake, loosen jam nut on front end of parking brake rod (Fig. DA41) and turn handle and rod end until parking brake is tight when brake handle is against fender in brake lock position. With parking brake engaged and foot pedal released, adjust jam nuts on front of brake rod to obtain 3/4 inch (19 mm) clearance between jam nut and rod guide.

## Models 716 (6 spd.)-912 (6 spd.)

To adjust brake, depress pedal and move dual range lever until cam lever (Fig. DA42) is under gate finger. Insert 0.030 inch (0.76 mm) feeler gage between lever and finger, then release pedal so spring pressure will hold gage

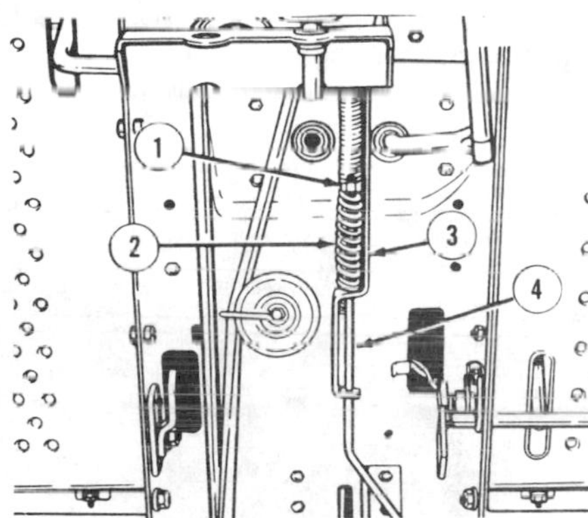


**Fig. DA39—Underside view of brake linkage used on Model 611H.**

1. Adjusting nut
2. Spring
3. Rod guide
4. Brake rod

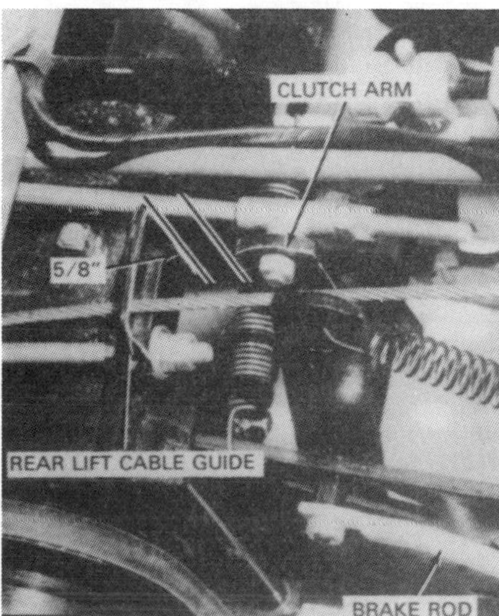


**Fig. DA40—View showing brake adjustment on Models 710 (3 spd.), 712S and 914S. Refer to text for adjusting procedure.**

Illustrations courtesy Deutz-Allis Corp.

in place. Loosen jam nut on front end of parking brake rod and turn lever and rod end until tension is felt when moving lever into engaged position. Retighten jam nut. With parking brake engaged, turn jam nut on rear of brake rod until front nut just contacts brake band, then turn an additional 1/3 turn.

### Models 808GT-810GT-811GT

To adjust brake on early models, release parking brake and push brake rod (A—Fig. DA43) forward to seat brake band on drum. The gap between nut (B) and spring (D) should be 7/16 to 9/16 inch (11-14 mm). If not, adjust nut (B) as required and lock in place with nut (C).

To adjust brake on late models, release parking brake and push brake rod (1—Fig. DA44) up slightly. Measure gap (C) between spacer (3) and brake band (2), which should be 9/16 to 11/16 inch (14-17 mm). Adjust nut (4) to obtain correct measurement.

**CAUTION: A minimum of two threads must extend through nut.**

### Model T811

To adjust brake, place transmission in neutral and start engine. Move variable speed control lever to full speed position and shut off engine. Shift transmission into gear without depressing clutch-brake pedal. Pull forward on brake band (2—Fig. DA44) to remove slack, then measure gap (C) between spacer (3) and brake band which should be 5/8 to 3/4 inch (16-19 mm). Adjust nut (4) if necessary to obtain correct measurement.

### Models 1914-1916

Raise and support rear of tractor. Remove rubber plug from brake backing plate. Insert brake adjusting tool or screwdriver through brake adjustment slot in backing plate and turn adjustment wheel until it is difficult to rotate tire and wheel by hand. (Turning adjusting wheel downward tightens the brake.) Depress brake pedal firmly to seat shoes, then release pedal. Back adjuster wheel off until just a slight drag is felt when rotating tire and wheel by hand. Adjust opposite side in the same manner making certain left and right pedal height is equal.

Apply both brakes and set parking brake so tractor will not move. Measure compressed length of brake rod spring (Fig. DA45), which should be 1 5/8 inches (41.3 mm). Loosen outer nut and turn inner nut as necessary to obtain correct dimension. Tighten outer nut against inner nut. Repeat spring tension adjustment on opposite brake rod.

# POWER TAKE-OFF

## CLUTCH ADJUSTMENT

### All Models Except 700 Series-900 Series-1914-1916

A spring-loaded idler is used to apply tension to pto belt. Correct belt tension is maintained by adjusting length of idler tension spring. Tension of idler pulley against drive belt should be sufficient to drive implement without belt slippage. Excessive tension will cause premature failure of belts and pulley bearings.

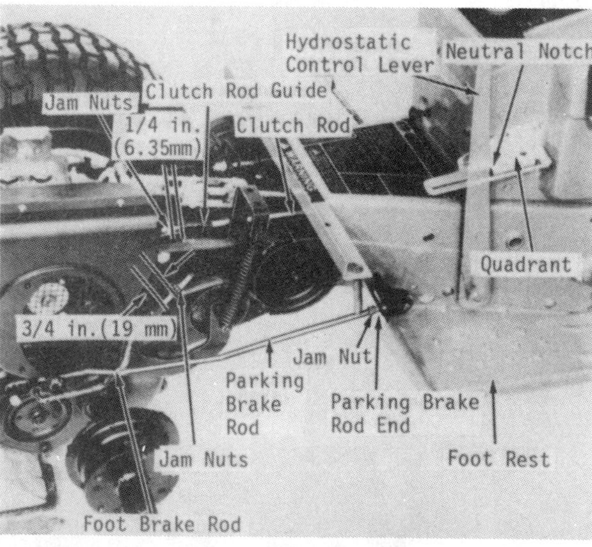


*Fig. DA41—View showing clutch and brake rod adjustments for Models 712H, 716H, 912H, 914H and 916H.*

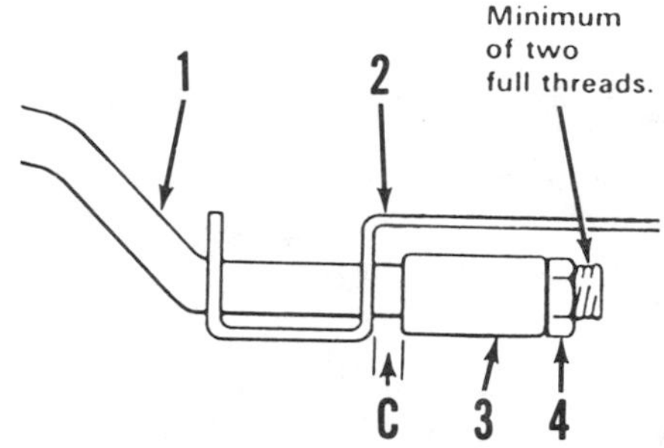


*Fig. DA44—On late Models 808GT and 811GT and all Model T811 tractors, adjust nut (4) to obtain specified gap at (C) when adjusting brake. Refer to text for details.*

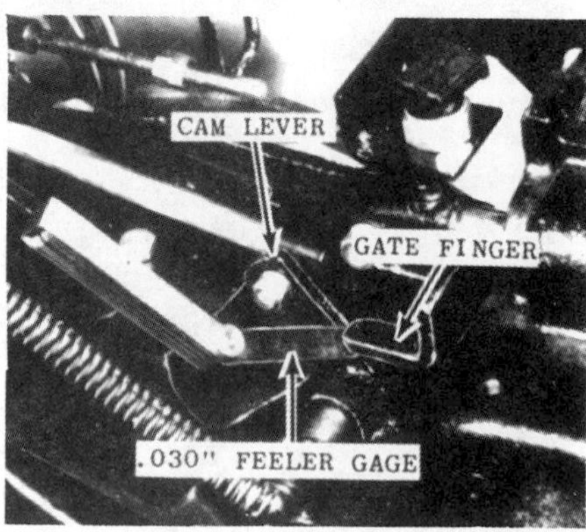


*Fig. DA42—On 716 (6 spd.) and 912 (6 spd.) tractors, insert 0.030 inch (0.76 mm) feeler gage between cam lever and gate finger when adjusting brakes.*

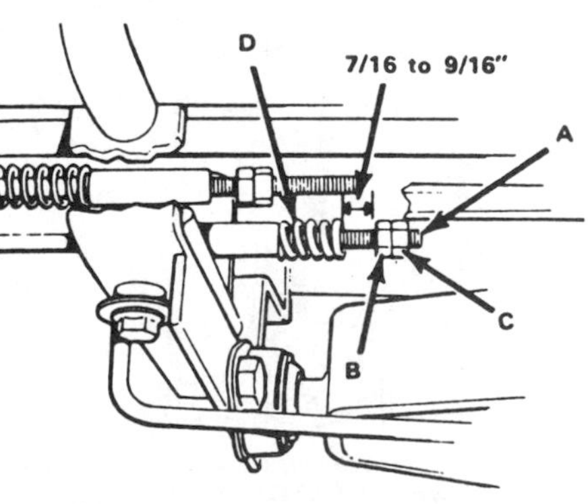


*Fig. DA43—Brake rod adjustment point for early Models 808GT, 810GT and 811GT. Distance between rod spring and jam nuts should be 7/16 to 9/16 inch (11-14 mm). Refer to text for details.*

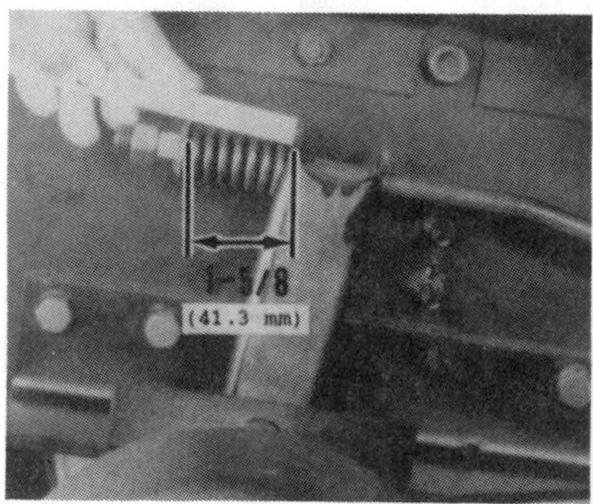


*Fig. DA45—On Models 1914 and 1916, brake rod spring length should be 1-5/8 inches (41.3 mm) with parking brake set. Turn nuts on end of brake rod to adjust spring length as necessary.*



Illustrations courtesy Deutz-Allis Corp.

## Models 710-712-716-912-914-916

All models use a mechanical, friction-type pto clutch. Belt tension is adjusted by changing position of idler pulley. Pto clutch is properly adjusted when clutch pulley (Fig. DA46) moves away from clutch cone, as shown at "B," a distance of 1/8 inch (3 mm) on Models 710, 712 and 716 or 1/16 inch (1.5 mm) on Models 912, 914 and 916 when clutch is disengaged. Turn adjusting nuts "A" on pto clutch rod clockwise to increase pulley travel or counterclockwise to decrease travel.

## Models 1914-1916

An electrically actuated pto clutch is used on these models. To adjust pto clutch, first remove the hood. Check clearance between armature and rotor using a feeler gage at the three slots (S—Fig. DA47) provided in the armature cover. Turn each of the adjusting nuts (N) as necessary until clearance between armature and rotor is 0.015-0.020 inch (0.4-0.5 mm) at each of the three slots. Do not overtighten nuts. Operate clutch several times and recheck clearance.

Pto belt tension is controlled by spring-loaded idler and is not adjustable. Renew belt if worn to the point that slippage occurs.

*Fig. DA46—View of pto clutch used on Models 710, 712, 716, 912, 914 and 916. Adjust clutch to obtain dimension "B," 1/8 inch (3 mm) on 700 Series tractors or 1/16 inch (1.5 mm) on 900 Series tractors.*

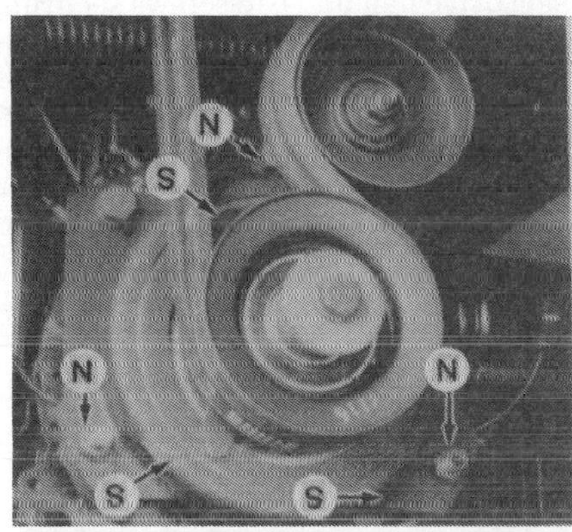


*Fig. DA47—On Models 1914 and 1916, insert a feeler gage into each of the three slots (S) in armature cover to measure clearance between armature and rotor. Adjust nuts (N) as necessary to obtain clearance of 0.015-0.020 inch (0.4-0.5 mm) at each of the three slots.*

## Models 710-712-716-912-914-916

**R&R AND OVERHAUL CLUTCH.** Remove drive belt from pto pulley. Remove retaining nut (15—Fig. DA48) and withdraw clutch plate (14). Protect threads on pto shaft and pry key out of shaft keyway.

**CAUTION: Pto pulley is spring loaded. Install a C-clamp as shown in Fig. DA49 to compress spring and hold pulley before attempting to remove pulley retaining ring.**

Compress pulley internal spring with a C-clamp (Fig. DA49) as shown, then remove retaining ring. Remove pivot assembly retaining screws. Slowly release clamp and remove pto clutch assembly. Remove cotter pin retaining idler pivot to right side plate, then withdraw idler assembly.

Check pto shaft runout at outer retaining ring groove with a dial indicator. If runout exceeds 0.010 inch (0.25 mm), shaft should be renewed or straightened. Refer to BEVEL GEARS paragraphs. Inspect all parts for excessive wear or other damage and renew as necessary.

Reassemble in reverse order of disassembly procedure. Be sure bearing (11—Fig. DA48) is installed with locking groove facing outward. If clutch plate retaining nut (15) is 3/4 inch, tighten to 70 ft.-lbs. (95 N·m). If 1/2 inch nut is used, tighten to 50 ft.-lbs. (68 N·m). Adjust clutch as previously outlined.

## Models 1914-1916

**R&R AND OVERHAUL PTO CLUTCH AND DRIVE SHAFT.** The pto clutch (Fig. DA50) is located on front of the engine and pto shaft assembly is located in the front frame support. To remove clutch or drive shaft, remove hood and pto guard. Push against belt idler and detach pto belts. Remove clutch retaining cap screw (10) and nuts (N). Pull armature (1) and rotor (2) off crank-

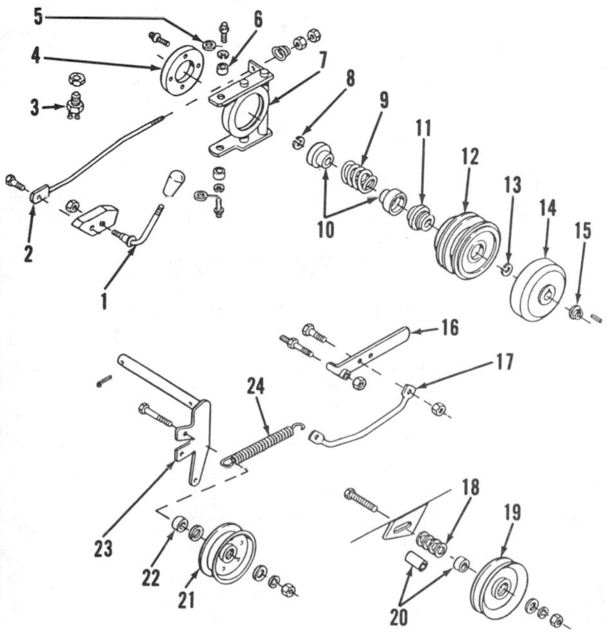


*Fig. DA48—Exploded view of pto clutch and idler pulley assembly used on 700 and 900 Series tractors.*

1. Clutch control handle
2. Control rod
3. Interlock switch
4. Brake disc
5. Spring washer
6. Spacer (2)
7. Pivot assy.
8. Retaining ring
9. Spring
10. Spring guides
11. Bearing
12. Pulley
13. Retaining ring
14. Clutch plate
15. Retaining nut
16. Tensioning lever
17. Tension rod
18. Washers (4)
19. Rear idler pulley
20. Spacers
21. Front idler pulley
22. Spacer
23. Pivot arm
24. Tension spring

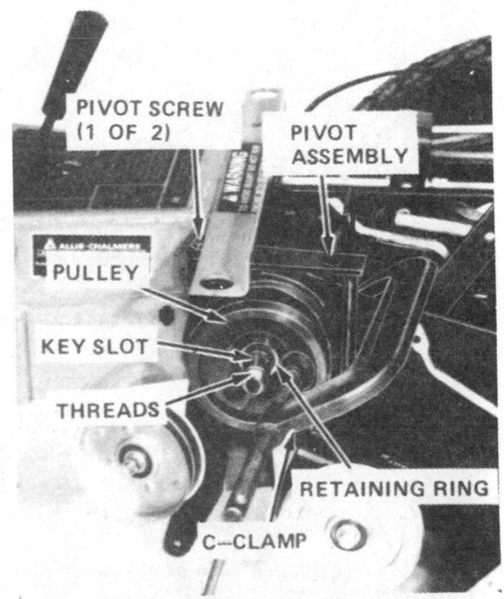


*Fig. DA49—When disassembling pto clutch on 700 and 900 Series tractors, compress pulley internal spring with a C-clamp as shown, then remove retaining ring and slowly release spring pressure.*

shaft. Unbolt and remove field coil assembly if necessary. Unscrew bolts retaining pto bearing support (19) to frame and withdraw pto shaft assembly.

Maximum allowable pto shaft end play is 1/8 inch (3.2 mm). If end play is excessive, inspect shaft (18) and bearings (17 and 20) and renew as necessary.

To disassemble pto shaft, remove snap rings (15) and press shaft (18) and bearings out of bearing support.

Bearings are a press fit on shaft and in housing (19). Bearings must contact inner snap rings (15). Install rear bearing (20) on shaft, pressing against bearing inner race. Then press shaft and bearing assembly into housing, pressing against bearing outer race. Install remaining bearing (17) onto shaft and into housing, pressing against bearing inner and outer races while supporting rear end of shaft and outer race of rear bearing. Bearings are sealed and no periodic lubrication is required.

To reinstall pto shaft assembly and clutch assembly, reverse the removal procedure. Tighten clutch adjusting nuts (N) until clearance between armature and rotor is 0.015-0.020 inch (0.4-0.5 mm). Clearance can be measured at each of the three slots provided in armature using a feeler gage.

# BEVEL GEARS

## REMOVE AND REINSTALL

### Models B210-B212

To remove bevel gear unit, first remove dash and top frame cover. Remove seat and fender assembly. Support tractor under main frame just ahead of bevel gear housing. Disconnect brake linkage, clutch-brake rod and transmission shift rod. On variable speed drive models, disconnect fork from transmission pulley. Remove pto drive belt on models so equipped. Remove transmission drive belt and cap screws securing transmission to side plate. Roll transmission rearward away from tractor. Disconnect drive shaft and remove drive shaft flange from bevel gear shaft. Remove cap screws securing bevel gear housing to frame and lift off bevel gear assembly.

### Models HB212

To remove bevel gear drive unit, first remove steering wheel, dash assembly and top frame cover. Remove seat deck and fender assembly. Support tractor under main frame just ahead of bevel gear housing and also under gear reduction housing. Remove left rear wheel and hub assembly. Remove bevel gear pto belt pulley and disconnect pto tension spring. Unbolt belt guard and remove drive belt and pulley from right end of bevel gear shaft. Disconnect drive shaft coupling from right end of bevel gear shaft. Disconnect drive shaft coupling from bevel gear input shaft. Unbolt and remove left side plate. Remove remaining cap screws securing bevel gear unit to frame, then lift unit from tractor.

Reinstall bevel gear unit by reversing removal procedure. Adjust clutch and brake linkage as necessary.

### Models 310-312-314-410-414-416

To remove bevel drive unit, first unbolt and remove seat deck and fender assembly. Raise and support tractor main frame just ahead of bevel gear housing. Remove left rear wheel and hub assembly. On models so equipped, remove bevel gear pto belt pulley and disconnect pto tension spring. On variable drive models, disconnect fork from drive pulley on right end of bevel gear shaft, then remove belt and pulley. On all other models, unbolt belt guard, then remove drive belt and bevel gear pulley. On all models, unbolt and remove left side plate. Disconnect drive shaft rear coupling from bevel gear input shaft. Unbolt and remove bevel gear unit from tractor.

When reinstalling bevel gear unit, install sufficient thickness of shims on right side so shims extend 0.010-0.015 inch (0.25-0.38 mm) past outside machined surface of gear case. Reinstall unit by reversing removal procedure.

### Models 710-712-716-912-914-916

To remove bevel gear unit, the complete drive unit, pulleys and belts must first be removed. Refer to appropriate transmission section for removal procedure. Refer to POWER TAKE-OFF paragraphs and remove pto clutch assembly and idler pulley assembly. Remove pulley from right side of bevel gear unit. Disconnect drive shaft from bevel gear input shaft. Remove cap screws securing gear box to side plates. Pull side plates apart and withdraw bevel gear unit.

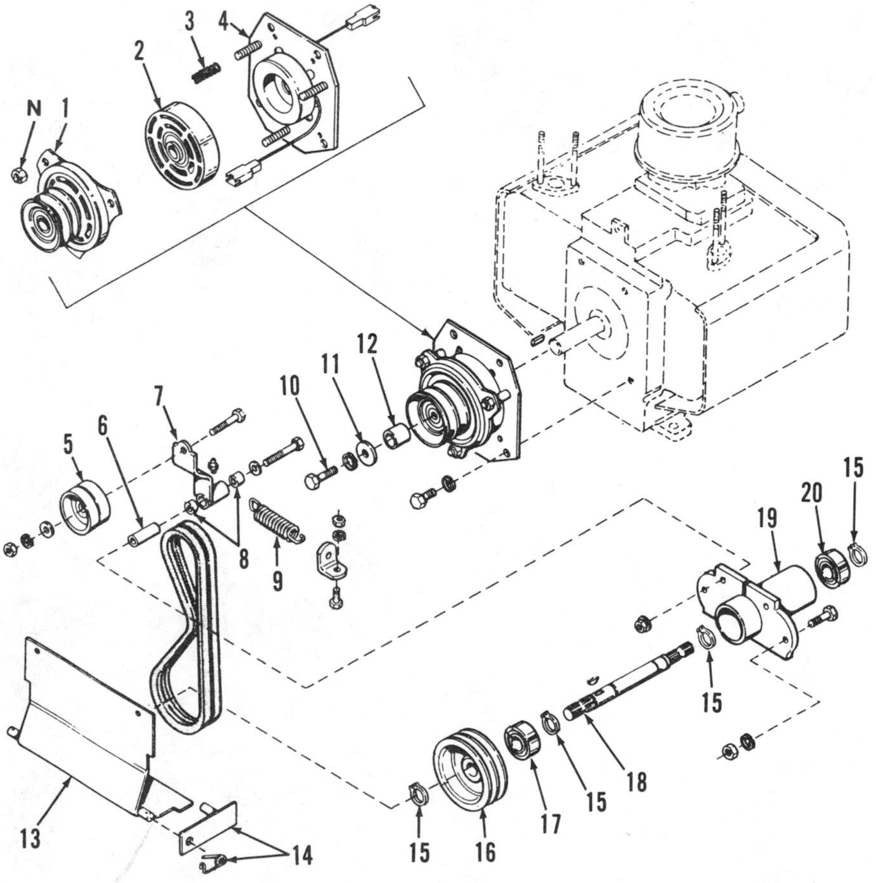

*Fig. DA50—Exploded view of pto clutch and shaft assembly used on Models 1914 and 1916.*

1. Armature
2. Rotor
3. Springs
4. Field
5. Pulley
6. Spacer
7. Idler arm
8. Bushings
9. Spring
10. Cap screw
11. Washer
12. Spacer
13. Pto guard
14. Clip pin & link
15. Snap ring
16. Pto drive pulley
17. Bearing
18. Pto shaft
19. Bearing support
20. Bearing



Illustrations courtesy Deutz-Allis Corp.

Reinstall bevel gear unit in reverse order of removal.

### OVERHAUL

### All Models So Equipped

To disassemble bevel gear unit, remove housing cover (11—Fig. DA51) and drain lubricant. Drive output shaft (16) to the left until key is free of bevel gear (18). Remove key and disengage snap ring (17) from groove in shaft. Remove bevel gear and snap ring as shaft is withdrawn from housing. Remove cap screw and bearing clamp plate (14), then bump input shaft assembly rearward out of housing. Remove cap screw (12) and washers (13) and withdraw bevel gear (10) and bearing (9) from input shaft (7). Bearings (5, 20 and 22) and oil seals (3, 19 and 23) can now be removed from housing (21).

Clean and inspect all parts and renew any showing excessive wear or other damage. Using new oil seals and gasket, reassemble by reversing disassembly procedure. Be sure to install washers (13) with concave side facing head of cap screw (12); tighten cap screw to 27 ft.-lbs. (37 N•m). Fill unit to level plug or bottom of dipstick with recommended oil.

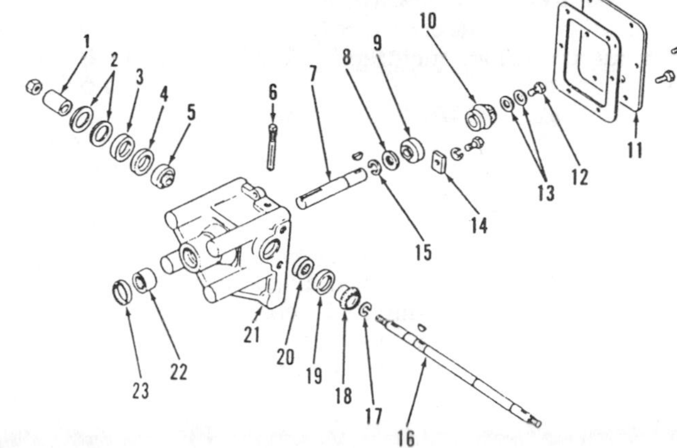


*Fig. DA51—Exploded view of bevel gear drive unit used on some models. Spacer (4) and oil level dipstick (6) are not used on some models.*

1. Spacer
2. Shims
3. Oil seal
4. Spacer
5. Bearing
6. Dipstick
7. Input shaft
8. Washer
9. Bearing
10. Bevel gear (drive)
11. Cover
12. Cap screw
13. Washers
14. Clamp plate
15. Retaining ring
16. Output shaft
17. Retaining ring
18. Bevel gear (driven)
19. Oil seal
20. Bearing
21. Housing
22. Bearing
23. Oil seal

# SHUTTLE DRIVE

### Models 410S-414S-416S-712S-914S

A forward-reverse shuttle drive is used on these models. The transaxles used on these models are equipped with four forward gears. The shuttle drive control lever, located on right side of tractor, has three positions: forward, neutral and reverse. This allows tractor to be driven in forward or reverse direction in any of the four transaxle gears. Transaxle gears can be shifted when shuttle drive control lever is in neutral position or when clutch-brake pedal is depressed. When shuttle drive control lever is in neutral position, a brake pad is applied against transaxle input shaft pulley. This stops input shaft from turning to facilitate gear shifting.

**ADJUSTMENT.** To adjust shuttle drive linkage, either unbolt and remove seat deck and fender assembly or tilt seat forward, lift out tool tray, support rear of tractor and remove right rear wheel. Place shuttle drive control lever in neutral position and adjust transmission safety interlock switch (3—Fig. DA52) so carriage head bolt contacts and closes switch. Be sure bolt head does not touch switch when shift lever is engaged in any of the four gears.

Refer to Fig. DA53 and loosen set screw in brake detent (5), then slide detent forward or rearward as required to center detent groove on brake pin (4). Tighten set screw. Move control lever to full forward position. Loosen locknut on pulley brake pad stud and adjust brake pad (1—Fig. DA52) to obtain 1/8 inch (3 mm) clearance (A) between brake pad and forward drive pulley flange (2) as shown. Tighten locknut.

Place control lever in neutral position and loosen set screw in set collar (2—Fig. DA53). Move rod guide (7) forward until slack is removed from forward drive belt (1). Hold rod guide forward, then move set collar and spring (8) forward and tighten screw in set collar. Move control lever to full forward drive position and measure distance between rear of set collar and rear leg of rod guide. This distance should be 1/8 inch (3 mm) as shown in Fig. DA53. If not, relocate set collar to obtain this dimension.

Place control lever in neutral position. Refer to Fig. DA54, then unpin and remove swivel (A) from hole (B). Rotate until reverse drive brake band (C) is snug on shuttle planetary carrier when swivel is reconnected in hole (B).

*Fig. DA52—On models equipped with shuttle drive, adjust transmission interlock switch (3) so carriage head bolt contacts and closes switch when control lever is placed in neutral position. Adjust brake pad (1) to provide 1/8 inch (3 mm) clearance (A) in forward drive position.*

A. 1/8 in. (3 mm) clearance
1. Brake pad
2. Drive pulley
3. Interlock switch

Reassemble tractor and test operation of shuttle drive. If operation is unsatisfactory, refer to the following problems and their possible causes:

**A. Will not pull forward with full power.**

Caused by: Incorrect adjustment of set collar (Fig. DA53) resulting in low tension on forward drive belt.

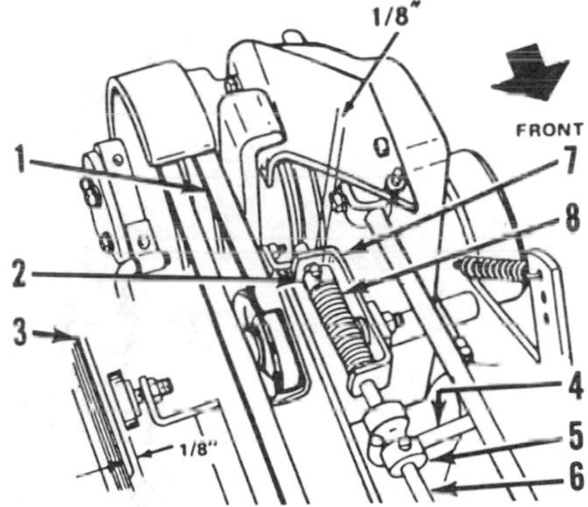


*Fig. DA53—With shuttle control in forward drive position, adjust control rod set collar (2) to provide 1/8 inch (3 mm) gap as shown.*

1. Forward drive belt
2. Set collar
3. Drive pulley & brake pad
4. Brake pin
5. Brake detent spool
6. Shuttle control rod
7. Rod guide
8. Spring

*Fig. DA54—With shuttle control lever in neutral position, adjust swivel (A) until reverse brake band (C) is snug when swivel is reconnected in hole (B).*

**B. Tractor creeps forward when control lever is in neutral position.**

Caused by: Too much tension on forward drive belt.

**C. Will not pull with full power in reverse.**

Caused by: Reverse drive brake band (C—Fig. DA54) adjustment too loose.

**D. Tractor creeps rearward when control lever is in neutral position.**

Caused by: Reverse drive brake band (C—Fig. DA54) adjustment too tight.

**E. Cannot shift gears without grinding when shuttle control lever is in neutral position.**

Caused by: Brake detent (5—Fig. DA53) not positioned correctly or clearance of brake pad (Fig. DA52) not adjusted properly.

**R&R AND OVERHAUL.** To remove forward-reverse shuttle drive unit, support rear of tractor and remove right rear wheel. Disconnect and remove reverse drive planetary brake (23 through 26—Fig. DA55). Remove drive belts (28 and 29). Using a screwdriver, pry cap (5) from planetary cover (6). Remove nut (7) and gear (8). Carefully withdraw planetary assembly.

To disassemble unit, remove nuts from bolts (14) and planetary shafts (3). Remove cover (6), seal ring (9) and bearing (10). Needle bearings (1), planetary pinions (2), sleeves (4) and planetary carrier (11) can now be removed. Remove gear (15), seal ring (16), bearing (17), seal ring (18), pulley (19), inner race (20), thrust washer (21) and forward drive pulley half (22) from transaxle input shaft.

Clean all parts and renew any showing excessive wear or other damage. Using new seal rings, reassemble by reversing disassembly procedure. Tighten nuts

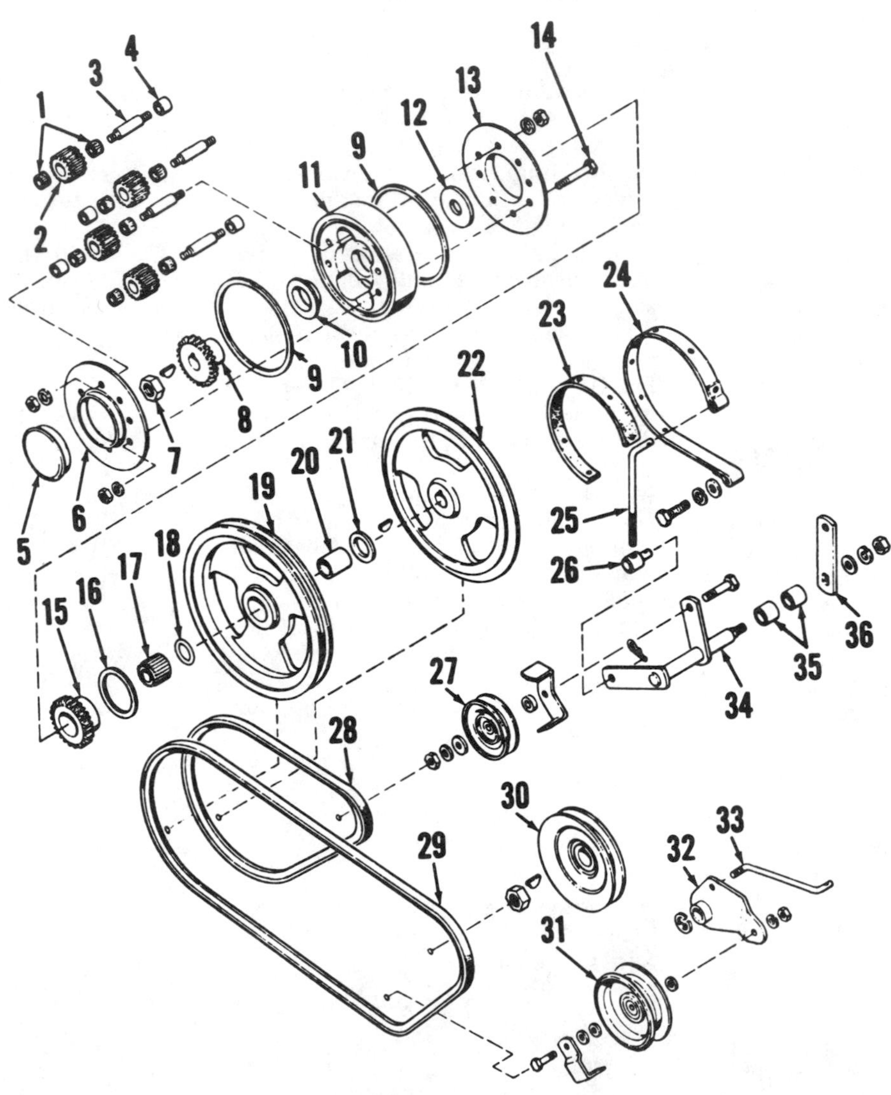


*Fig. DA55—Exploded view of forward-reverse shuttle drive unit used on Models 410S, 414S, 416S, 712S and 914S.*

1. Needle bearings
2. Planetary pinions
3. Planetary shafts
4. Sleeves
5. End cap
6. Cover (outer)
7. Nut
8. Gear
9. Seal ring
10. Flange bearing
11. Planetary carrier
12. Thrust washer
13. Cover (inner)
14. Through-bolts (4 used)
15. Gear
16. Seal
17. Roller bearing
18. Seal ring
19. Pulley
20. Inner race
21. Thrust washer
22. Forward drive pulley half
23. Brake lining
24. Reverse drive brake band
25. Rod
26. Swivel
27. Forward drive idler pulley
28. Forward drive belt
29. Main drive belt
30. Pulley (bevel gear driven)
31. Clutch idler pulley
32. Idler arm
33. Clutch link
34. Shuttle drive lever & shaft assy.
35. Bushings
36. Lever

on through-bolts (14) and planetary shaft (3) to torque of 12-15 ft.-lbs. (16-20 N·m). Tighten planetary retaining nut (7) to torque of 75 ft.-lbs. (102 N·m). Pack unit with multipurpose lithium base grease.

# VARIABLE SPEED PULLEY

## Models B210-B212-310-310D-312-312D-314-314D

**ADJUSTMENT.** Do not attempt to move variable speed control lever when engine is stopped or when clutch-brake pedal is depressed. Place variable speed control lever in "HIGH" position and remove drive belt and guards. Loosen attaching bolt or ball joint locknut between control rod (4—Fig. DA56) and rocker arm (17), then push rocker arm as far forward as possible so inside hubs of drive pulley sheaves (13 and 14) make contact. Retighten rocker arm bolt or nut. Reinstall drive belt and guards.

With control lever in "HIGH" position, clearance should be $^3/_{16}$ inch (5 mm) between drive belt and front guard. Move variable speed control lever to "LOW" position. Front edge of idler pulley belt stop (19) should be $9^1/_4$ inches (235 mm) from outer surface of rear axle tube. To make adjustment, loosen nut which retains idler pulley. With control lever in "LOW" position, top of drive belt should be approximately $^1/_8$ inch (3 mm) below rim of driven pulley halves (24 and 26). Make belt adjustment by turning turnbuckle.

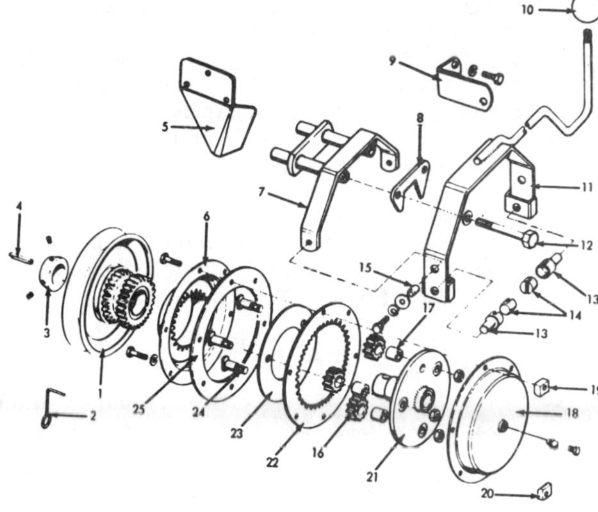

***Fig. DA57—Exploded view of Hi-Lo Range pulley assembly used on some models.***

1. Pulley assy.
2. Belt stop
3. Collar
4. Key
5. Guard
6. Cover (inner)
7. Support
8. Shift stop
9. Shift rod support
10. Knob
11. Shift fork
12. Cap screw
13. Pivots
14. Pivot bearings
15. Spacers
16. Pinions
17. Needle bearings
18. Cover (outer)
19. Special nut
20. Special nut
21. Spider assy.
22. Ring gear
23. Spider plate
24. Spider bolts
25. Shift ring

**R&R AND OVERHAUL.** To remove variable pulley assembly, first support right rear axle and remove right rear wheel. Remove drive belt guards and drive belt. Remove drive pulley retaining nut (16—Fig. DA56) and withdraw drive pulley assembly. Disconnect control rod (4) from rocker arm (17) and remove rocker arm by unscrewing retaining nut. Unscrew bolt holding driven pulley fork (30) and remove driven pulley fork, connecting bolts and turnbuckle (18), and drive pulley arm (9). Unscrew retaining nut (31) and remove driven pulley assembly.

Inspect assembly for damaged or excessively worn components. Be sure that pulley sheaves are straight and run true. After reassembly, check adjustment as outlined in preceding paragraph.

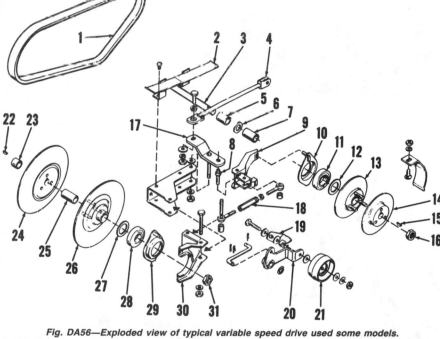

***Fig. DA56—Exploded view of typical variable speed drive used some models.***

1. Drive belt
2. Belt guard
3. Bevel gear shaft
4. Control rod
5. Spacer
6. Washer
7. Spacer
8. Rod
9. Fork
10. Bearing retainer
11. Ball bearing
12. Retainer
13. Movable pulley sheave
14. Fixed pulley sheave
15. Key
16. Nut
17. Lever
18. Turnbuckle
19. Belt guide
20. Idler arm
21. Clutch idler pulley
22. Key
23. Spacer
24. Fixed pulley sheave
25. Spacer
26. Movable pulley sheave
27. Retainer
28. Ball bearing
29. Bearing retainer
30. Fork
31. Nut

# HI-LO RANGE PULLEY

The Hi-Lo two-speed transmission input pulley is used on some early models to provide lower ground speeds without altering pto rpm. When shifted to low range, ground speeds will be reduced to approximately $^1/_3$ of standard (high range) ground speeds.

## All Models So Equipped

**R&R AND OVERHAUL.** To remove two-speed pulley assembly, first unbolt shift rod support (9—Fig. DA57). Then, unbolt and remove shift support and shift fork assembly. Loosen set screws in collar (3) and withdraw Hi-Lo pulley assembly.

To disassemble unit, remove six cap screws from outer edge of covers.

**NOTE: Mark location of special nuts (19 and 20) for aid in reassembly.**

Separate covers (6 and 18) and remove shaft ring (25) and reduction gear assembly. Remove spider bolts (24), pinions (16) and needle bearings (17).

Check all parts for excessive wear and renew as necessary. When reassembling, lubricate with multipurpose lithium base grease. Reinstall assembly by reversing removal procedure.

# DUAL RANGE 6 SPEED

The dual range 6 speed tractors have 3 forward gears and one reverse with a dual range pulley system. To select Hi or Lo range, tractor must be stopped and clutch-brake pedal fully depressed. Move range lever forward for Hi or backward for Lo.

## Models 710 (6 spd.)-716 (6 spd.)-912 (6 spd.)

**PULLEY AND BELT RENEWAL.** To renew pulleys or belts, remove front belt guard. However, idler pulley can be renewed without removal of belt guards and belts. Depress clutch-brake pedal and remove belt from pulley. Remove locknut and pulley. Remove cotter pin from pulley brake rod (3—Fig. DA58). Do not remove brake rod from rear belt guard unless it is to be renewed. Remove rear belt guard and pulley brake rod assembly. To renew drive pulleys, remove center nut and pulleys from bevel gear box cross shaft. To renew driven pulleys, remove three cap screws, spacers (11) and pulleys. The driven pulley hub (9) is keyed on input shaft and is removed by removing locknut on input shaft. Reinstall assembly by reversing removal procedure.

**ADJUSTMENTS.** Adjust rear belt guard to obtain $^1/_8$ inch (3 mm) clearance between guard and edge of pulley. To adjust idler pulley height, depress clutch-brake pedal, move range lever to Hi range and release pedal. With outside belt resting on front and rear belt guards, adjust idler pulley so there is a minimum of $^1/_8$ inch (3 mm) clearance between outside belt and pulley. To adjust pulley brake, engage clutch-brake pedal and move range lever to Hi or Lo range. Set coil length of rear spring (Fig. DA59) to $1^3/_8$ inches (35 mm). Set front spring compressed length of $1^3/_4$ inches (45 mm) between jam nut and rod guide. If drive belt slips under load, move idler spring into next higher hole of lever pivot (5—Fig. DA58) to increase belt tension.

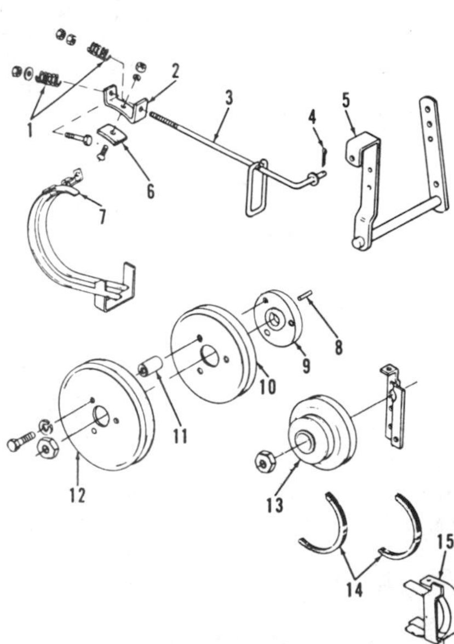


*Fig. DA58—Exploded view of dual range pulley system used on Models 710 (6 spd.), 716 (6 spd.) and 912 (6 spd.)*

1. Spring
2. Pulley brake strap
3. Brake rod assy.
4. Cotter pin
5. Lever pivot assy.
6. Brake pad
7. Rear belt guard
8. Key
9. Pulley hub
10. Pulley
11. Spacer (3 used)
12. Pulley
13. Drive pulley
14. Drive belts
15. Front belt guard

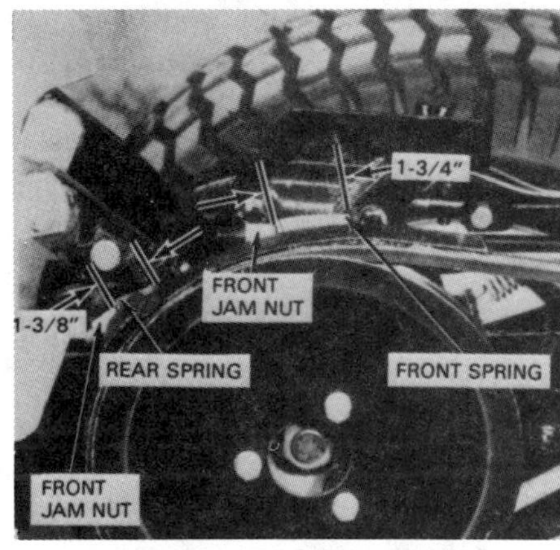


*Fig. DA59—Pulley brake adjustment points on Models 710 (6 spd.), 716 (6 spd.) and 912 (6 spd.). Refer to text for adjustment procedure.*

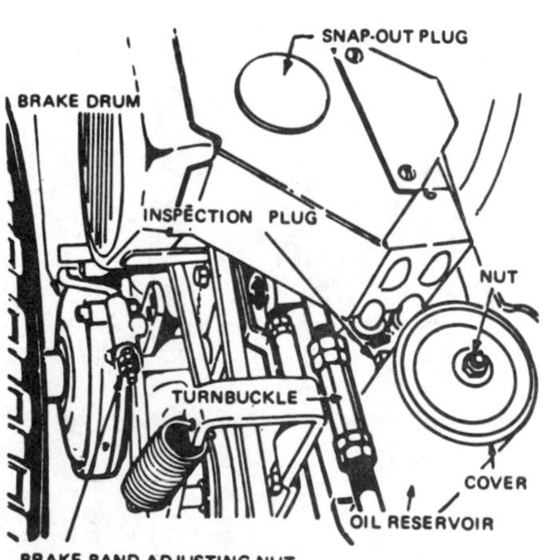


*Fig. DA60—View of hydrostatic control linkage adjustment points on Models HB212, 312H, 314H and 416H. Refer to text.*

# HYDROSTATIC TRANSMISSION

A Vickers T66 hydrostatic drive unit is used on Models HB212, 312H, 314H and 416H; an Eaton Model 7 hydrostatic transmission is used on Model 611H; a Sundstrand Series 15 "U" type hydrostatic transmission is used on all other models.

### ADJUSTMENT

## Models HB212-312H-314H-416H

To adjust hydrostatic control linkage, block up under rear of tractor so wheels do not touch the ground. Start engine and operate at $^1/_3$ full speed. With clutch engaged, move hydrostatic control lever to forward position, then into neutral position. Rear wheels should not rotate when control lever is in neutral position. If wheels continue to turn, loosen locknuts at both ends of turnbuckle on control rod shown in Fig. DA60. Turn turnbuckle as required until wheels stop turning when control lever is in neutral position. Tighten locknuts and recheck adjustment.

## Model 611H

If tractor creeps forward or backward when hydrostatic control lever is in neutral position, adjust hydrostatic control linkage as follows: Sit on tractor seat and start engine. Move hydrostatic control lever to position where tractor does not creep and there is least amount of noise coming from hydrostatic unit. Stop the engine, but do not move control lever. The control lever quadrant has slotted mounting holes. Loosen mounting screws and move quadrant so control lever is positioned in neutral notch. Tighten quadrant screws. Start engine, move control lever to forward position, then back to neutral slot and check for correct neutral.

If transmission control lever is too hard to move or will not stay in position, loosen set screws (2—Fig. DA61), if so equipped, and loosen or tighten adjusting nut (3) as necessary.

To adjust transmission engagement lever (located under the seat), first move lever to forward position. Check the clearance (C—Fig. DA61) between the end of transmission engagement valve



Illustrations courtesy Deutz-Allis Corp.

plunger and the fitting. Clearance should be 0.060-0.125 inch (1.5-3.2 mm). To adjust, loosen engagement lever bracket (1) screws and move bracket to obtain recommended clearance. Retighten bracket retaining screws.

### Models 712H-716H-912H-914H-916H

To adjust hydrostatic control linkage, park tractor on level ground, shift control lever to neutral notch and set parking brake. Raise seat deck and check centering mark on hydrostatic control cam (Fig. DA62). If mark is not centered, loosen bolt (A) and move control cam in hydrostatic control strap until mark is centered. Lower seat deck, start engine and release parking brake. If tractor still creeps in neutral, note direction and reset parking brake and shut off engine. Loosen jam nut (B) on cam pivot shaft. If tractor creep was in reverse, turn adjusting nut (C) $^{1}/_{8}$ to $^{1}/_{4}$ turn clockwise (viewed from right side). If creep was forward, turn adjusting nut $^{1}/_{8}$ to $^{1}/_{4}$ turn counterclockwise. Tighten jam nut and recheck adjustment.

### Models 1914-1916

If tractor moves when control lever is in neutral position, remove right side dash panel, then raise and securely support rear of tractor so wheels are off ground. Engage parking brake. Loosen nuts (1, 2 and 3—Fig. DA63). Position speed control lever in full rear location and tighten nut (1). Disengage parking brake and move speed control lever to neutral. Run engine at full throttle, move speed control lever forward so wheels rotate then move lever rearward until wheels stop turning. Stop engine and engage parking brake (nut 3 must be loose). As brake is applied cam plate (5) will drop down. Align spacer (4) on nut (3), then tighten nut (3) without moving the linkage. Loosen nut (1) and move speed control lever to neutral. Tighten nuts (1 and 2). Check operation.

## REMOVE AND REINSTALL

### Models HB212-312H-314H-416H

To remove hydrostatic transmission, first disconnect battery ground cable. remove seat and fender assembly. Remove fender support braces and oil cooler support bracket. Disconnect transmission control rod. Remove drive belt from transmission pulley. Drain lubricant from transmission oil reservoir and disconnect transmission oil lines. Remove oil cooler fan, shroud and oil cooler assembly. See Fig. DA64. Remove cap screws securing transmission to gear reduction housing and remove transmission.

To reinstall transmission, reverse removal procedure. Use following procedure to refill transmission with oil: Before installing transmission in tractor, fill pump and motor with Power Fluid 821 or equivalent lubricant through case drain opening. With transmission and cooling system installed and oil lines connected, position hydrostatic control lever in neutral position and fill reservoir with oil to correct level. Disconnect engine coil wire, and at short intervals crank engine with starter. Recheck and add oil if necessary to oil reservoir. Connect engine coil wire and run engine at idle speed. Recheck oil level. Make several short runs at a slow speed in for-

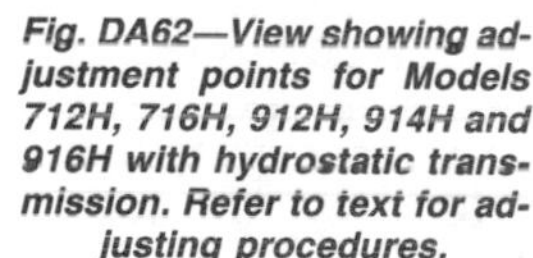
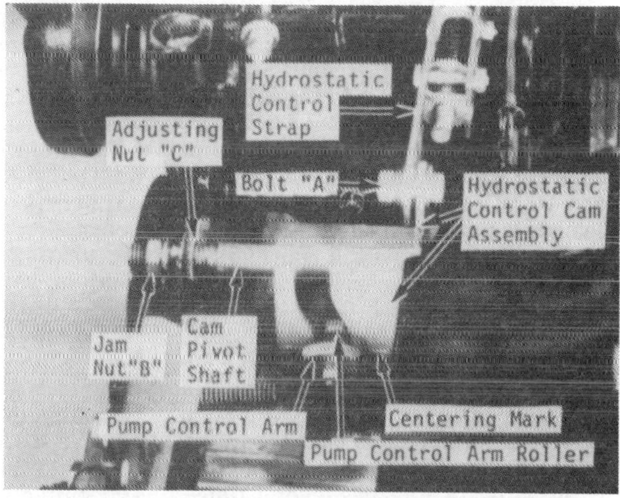


*Fig. DA62—View showing adjustment points for Models 712H, 716H, 912H, 914H and 916H with hydrostatic transmission. Refer to text for adjusting procedures.*

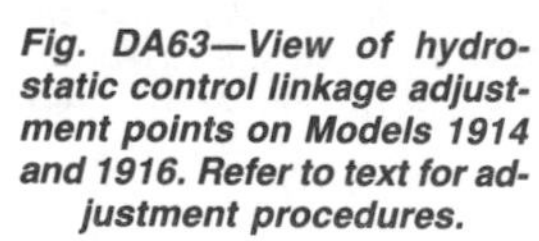
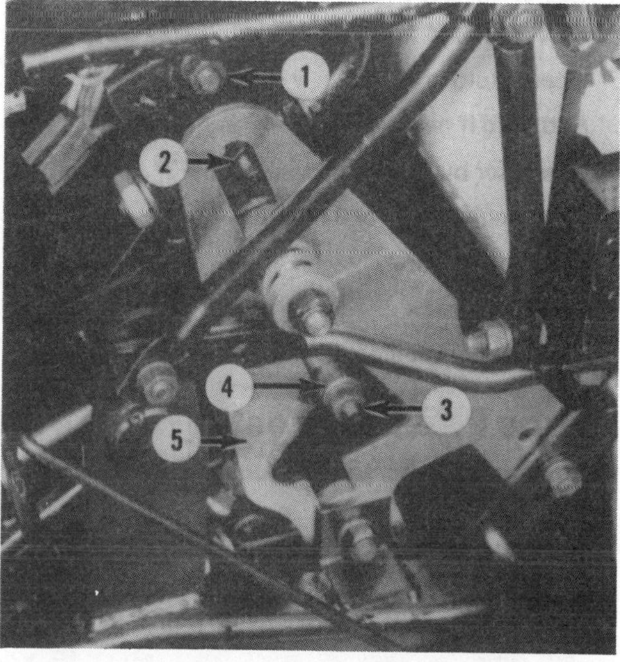


*Fig. DA63—View of hydrostatic control linkage adjustment points on Models 1914 and 1916. Refer to text for adjustment procedures.*

1. Nut
2. Nut
3. Nut
4. Spacer
5. Cam lever

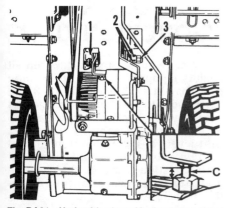

*Fig. DA61—Underside view of hydrostatic control linkage used on Model 611H. Refer to text for adjustment procedure.*

Illustrations courtesy Deutz-Allis Corp.

ward and in reverse and recheck oil level. Transmission oil should now be purged of air.

### Model 611H

To remove hydrostatic transmission, first remove mower deck. Remove battery and seat deck. Remove cap from oil reservoir and remove drain plug from bottom of hydrostatic housing and drain oil. Remove oil reservoir, noting that reservoir has left-hand threads. Raise and support rear of tractor or lift front of tractor with a hoist attached to front axle so rear wheels are clear of the ground. Remove cooling fan from hydrostatic input shaft. Unbolt and remove belt stop from hydrostatic unit, then remove belt from hydrostatic input pulley. Remove remaining two cap screws attaching hydrostatic unit to transaxle housing, then move hydrostatic unit away from transaxle.

To reinstall hydrostatic transmission, reverse the removal procedure. Tighten the cap screws attaching hydrostatic transmission to transaxle housing to 20 ft.-lbs. (27 N·m). Fill hydrostatic unit with Power Fluid 821 or equivalent lubricant using the following procedure: Remove vent plug from top of hydrostatic transmission body. Fill transmission with fluid through reservoir until fluid flows from vent plug hole. Rotate input and output shafts to purge air from transmission, fill reservoir with fluid until fluid again appears at vent hole and reinstall vent plug. Fill reservoir with fluid to "cold" oil level mark. Start engine and run at low speed. Operate unit in forward and reverse several times, then check fluid level in reservoir and fill as necessary.

### Models 712H-716H-912H-914H-916H

To remove hydrostatic transmission, remove seat and fender assembly. Support left rear side of tractor and remove left rear wheel. Remove transmission fan, shroud and deflector. Loosen and remove drive belt, input pulley and fan. Disconnect pump control arm spring. Remove bolt, control arm roller and nut. Remove oil filter and drain lubricant from reduction gear housing. Disconnect hydraulic hoses at oil filter assembly. Remove mounting bolts and slide transmission out of gear case.

To reinstall transmission, reverse the removal procedure. Use following procedure to refill and prime transmission. While holding relief valve up, add recommended oil until oil is visible in filler tube. Remove and ground spark plug wire. Raise rear wheels off the ground, set speed control lever halfway forward and crank engine. When wheels start to move, stop cranking. Reconnect spark plug wire, start and run tractor for about two minutes. Stop engine and hold relief valve in up position. Add oil until oil is within 1/8 inch (3 mm) of top of filler tube. Recheck oil level after 5 hours operation.

### Models 1914-1916

To remove hydrostatic transmission, remove pto guard and detach pto drive belts. Loosen screws securing engine to engine plate and slide engine forward so drive shaft separates from transmission input shaft. Remove seat, fuel tank and tunnel cover. Disconnect lower transmission hose and drain transmission oil. Detach hydraulic lines from transmission. Remove control damper and disconnect control linkage. Remove screws securing transmission to transaxle and remove transmission.

To reinstall transmission, reverse removal procedure. Tighten transmission mounting screws to 25-30 ft.-lbs. (34-41 N·m). Refill transmission with Type F automatic transmission fluid, then prime transmission as follows: Raise and support rear of tractor so rear wheels are off the ground. Remove spark plug, reconnect wire to spark plug and ground plug to engine. Move speed control lever to full forward position, then crank engine with starter until rear wheels begin to move. System is now primed. Check fluid level and reinstall spark plug.

## OVERHAUL

### Models HB212-312H-314H-416H

All models are equipped with a Vickers Model T66 hydrostatic transmission. Refer to Vickers Model T66 section in HYDROSTATIC TRANSMISSION SERVICE section for overhaul procedure.

### Model 611H

Model 611H is equipped with an Eaton Model 7 hydrostatic transmission. Refer to Eaton Model 7 section in HYDROSTATIC TRANSMISSION SERVICE section for overhaul procedure.

### Models 712H-716H-912H-914H-916H-1914-1916

All models are equipped with a Sundstrand Series 15 "U" type hydrostatic transmission. Refer to Sundstrand Series 15 "U" section in HYDROSTATIC TRANSMISSION SERVICE section for overhaul procedure.

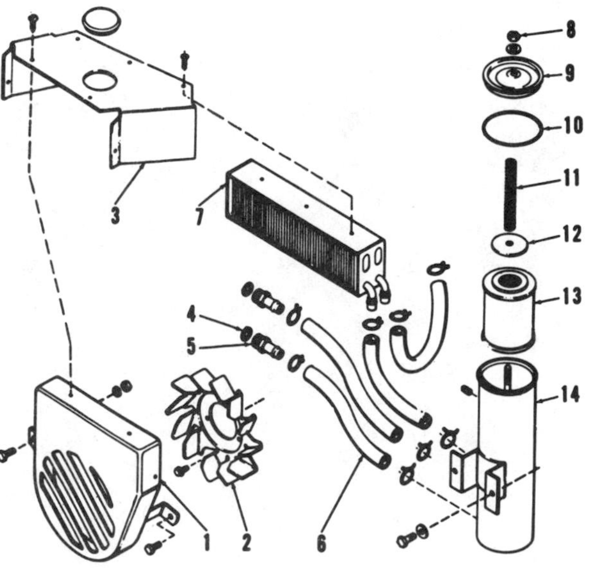


*Fig. DA64—Exploded view of hydrostatic cooling system and oil reservoir used on Models HB212, 312H, 314H and 416H.*

1. Fan housing
2. Fan
3. Shroud
4. "O" ring
5. Fitting
6. Hydraulic hose
7. Oil cooler
8. Nut
9. Cover
10. "O" ring
11. Spring
12. Washer
13. Oil filter
14. Oil reservoir

# GEAR REDUCTION UNIT

A gear reduction unit is used on all models equipped with a hydrostatic transmission. On Models HB212, 312H, 314H and 416H, a sliding drive gear is used in gear reduction unit so the tractor may be moved manually. When gear shift lever (4—Fig. DA66) is in vertical position, drive gear (21) will be engaged with reduction gear (43). To disengage gears, turn shift lever away from reduction housing.

**CAUTION: Tractor brakes are inoperative when shift lever is in disengaged position.**



Illustrations courtesy Deutz-Allis Corp.

### Models HB212-312H-314H-416H-712H-716H-912H-914H-916H

**REMOVE AND REINSTALL.** To remove gear reduction unit, support tractor under main frame just ahead of bevel gear housing. Remove seat deck and fender assembly. Drain reduction unit housing. Remove rear wheels, hubs, differential assembly and axle shaft. Remove bevel gear pto belt pulley and disconnect pto tension spring. Support gear reduction housing and remove left side plate. Drain hydrostatic transmission reservoir (models so equipped), disconnect oil lines and control rod, then unbolt and remove reservoir, oil cooler, shroud and cooler fan (models so equipped). Unbolt and remove hydrostatic transmission and brake band. Remove cap screws securing gear reduction unit to right side plate and lift unit from tractor.

Reinstall by reversing removal procedure. On Models HB212, 312H, 314H and 416H, fill reduction unit to level plug opening with SAE 90 EP gear oil and fill hydrostatic reservoir with Power Fluid 821 or equivalent lubricant. On all other models, reduction gear housing also serves as reservoir for hydrostatic transmission. Refill with Power Fluid 821 or equivalent.

**OVERHAUL.** To disassemble gear reduction unit, remove brake drum and clean all paint, burrs and rust from keyed end of axle tube (37—Fig. DA66). Unbolt and remove cover (40) from case (17). Remove washer (27) and first reduction gear (23). Remove snap ring (14), then withdraw output gear and axle tube assembly (41 through 45). On Models HB212, 312H, 314H and 416H, loosen set screw (46) and remove as a unit the shift fork and rail assembly (7 through 10). On all models, remove brake shaft assembly (18 through 22). Use caution when removing shift rail (10) from shift fork (9) as poppet ball and spring (7 and 8) will be released. Loosen locknut (5), remove shifter stem (6) and withdraw shift lever (4). Oil seals and needle bearings can now be removed from case and cover as required.

Reassemble in reverse order of disassembly procedure. When renewing bearings, always press against end stamped with manufacturers name or number. Press bearings into housing until 1/8 inch (3 mm) below inside machined surface of housing. Axle tube bearings (16 and 35) should be pressed in until outside edge of bearing is flush with outside edge of small bore in housing.

### Model 611H

**REMOVE AND REINSTALL.** Hydrostatic transmission and gear reduction are removed as a unit. Support rear of

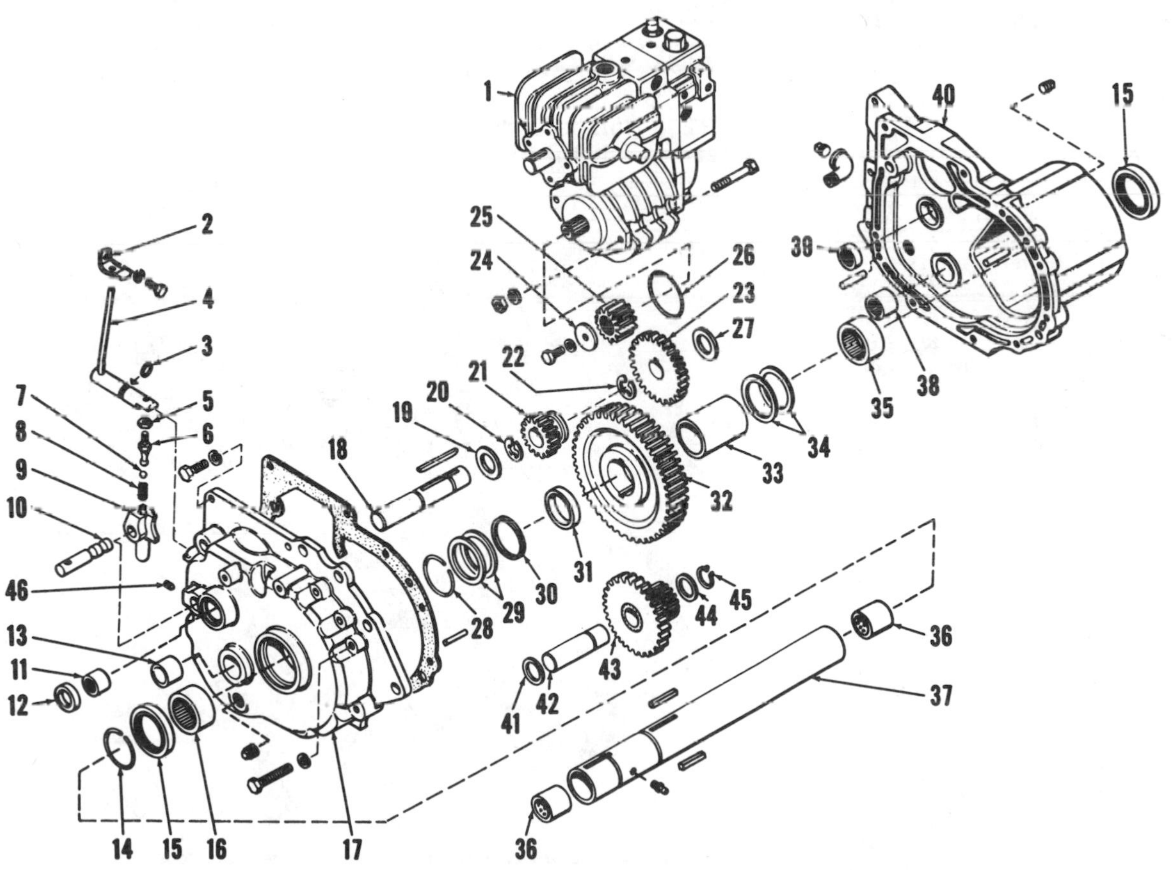


*Fig. DA66—Exploded view of gear reduction unit used on Models HB212, 312H, 314H and 416H. Gear reduction unit used on Models 712H, 716H, 912H, 914H and 916H is similar except that shift assembly (2 through 10) and sliding gear (21) are not used.*

1. Hydrostatic transmission
2. Lever latch
3. "O" ring
4. Gear shift lever
5. Nut
6. Shift stem
7. Ball
8. Spring
9. Shift fork
10. Shift rail
11. Bearing
12. Oil seal
13. Bearing
14. Snap ring
15. Oil seal
16. Bearing
17. Case
18. Brake shaft
19. Washer
20. "E" ring
21. Sliding gear
22. "E" ring
23. Gear
24. Washer
25. Input gear
26. "O" ring
27. Washer
28. Snap ring
29. Washers
30. Washer
31. Spacer
32. Ring gear
33. Spacer
34. Washers
35. Bearing
36. Bushing
37. Axle tube
38. Bearing
39. Bearing
40. Cover
41. Washer
42. Shaft
43. Pinion & gear
44. Washer
45. Snap ring
46. Set screw

Illustrations courtesy Deutz-Allis Corp.

tractor and remove rear wheels. Remove drive belt from transmission pulley. Detach control rod from transmission control arm. Detach brake rod and return spring. Unscrew gear reduction housing mounting screws in floor pan. Support unit, remove axle mounting "U" bolts and lower unit out of tractor. Drain oil from gear reduction housing. Unscrew transmission mounting screws and separate transmission from gear reduction housing.

Refill gear housing with SAE 90 EP gear oil before attaching hydrostatic transmission to gear housing. To reinstall transmission and gear reduction unit, reverse removal procedure. Tighten transmission mounting screws to 20 ft.-lbs. (27 N·m). Tighten gear reduction housing-to-floor pan mounting screws to 20 ft.-lbs. (27 N·m).

**OVERHAUL.** A Peerless 1300 series reduction gear and differential unit is used on Model 611H. Refer to Peerless section in REDUCTION GEAR AND DIFFERENTIAL SERVICE section for overhaul procedure.

### Models 1914-1916

**REMOVE AND REINSTALL.** To remove hydrostatic transmission and gear reduction housing as a unit, proceed as follows: Remove tunnel cover and upper and lower side panels on left side. Disconnect rear wiring harness. Disconnect fuel line and detach line from oil cooler bulkhead. Detach fender supports and footrest supports from frame. Remove seat, fender and fuel tank assembly. Drain oil from gear reduction housing and remove fill tube. Remove 90 degree elbow on bottom of transmission. Detach brake and control linkage. Disconnect hoses and tubing from front of transmission. Support rear of tractor and gear reduction housing, unscrew fasteners securing reduction housing to frame and lower drive unit. Roll drive unit away from tractor.

Separate hydrostatic transmission from gear reduction housing while noting location of spacers. Remove wheels and brackets.

Reverse removal procedure for installation. Tighten rear axle mounting screws to 40-50 ft.-lbs. (54-68 N·m). Tighten drawbar mounting screws to 100 ft.-lbs. (136 N·m). Tighten axle nuts to 75-110 ft.-lbs. (102-150 N·m). Tighten screws securing front of gear reduction housing to crossmember to 40-50 ft.-lbs. (54-68 N·m). Tighten transmission to gear reduction screws to 25-30 ft.-lbs. (34-41 N·m).

**OVERHAUL.** To disassemble reduction gear and differential assembly, remove hitch plate and the six bolts securing each axle housing to differential housing. Separate differential housing and axle housings. Remove cap screws and separate case cover (12—Fig. DA68) from case (33). Remove countershaft (7) and gear assemblies, intermediate shaft (18) and gear assemblies, output shaft (27) and gear (26), and ring gear (37) and differential assembly. Remove cap screw (44) and disassemble differential as needed.

Inspect all parts for wear, looseness and damage and renew as needed. When renewing needle bearings in cover (12) or case (33), drive bearings in until they are 0.015-0.020 inch (0.38-0.50 mm) below thrust surfaces of cover and case.

Reassemble by reversing disassembly procedure. Renew all gaskets and seals. Apply Loctite 242 to cap screws (44) and tighten to 7-10 ft.-lbs. (10-13 N·m). Tighten housing cover cap screws to 20 ft.-lbs. (27 N·m).

# TRANSAXLE

### Models B206-Homesteader 6-Homesteader 7-608LT-611LT

**REMOVE AND REINSTALL.** To remove transaxle, support rear of tractor and remove drive belt from transaxle input pulley. Disconnect brake linkage from transaxle. Remove rear wheels and remove gear shift knob. Remove cap screws securing transaxle to frame brackets. Remove axle mounting "U" bolts. Remove transaxle from tractor by tilting transaxle so shift lever passes through frame and brake drum clears brake band.

To reinstall transaxle, reverse removal procedure.

**OVERHAUL.** All models are equipped with a Peerless 600 Series transaxle. Refer to Peerless Series 600 section in TRANSAXLE SERVICE section for overhaul procedure.

### Models B208-Homesteader 8

**REMOVE AND REINSTALL.** To remove transaxle, remove drive belt from transaxle pulley and remove brake band. Remove gear shift lever knob. Support rear of tractor frame and remove axle "U" bolts. Roll transaxle away from tractor.

To reinstall transaxle, reverse removal procedure.

**OVERHAUL.** All Models are equipped with a Peerless 1200 Series transaxle.

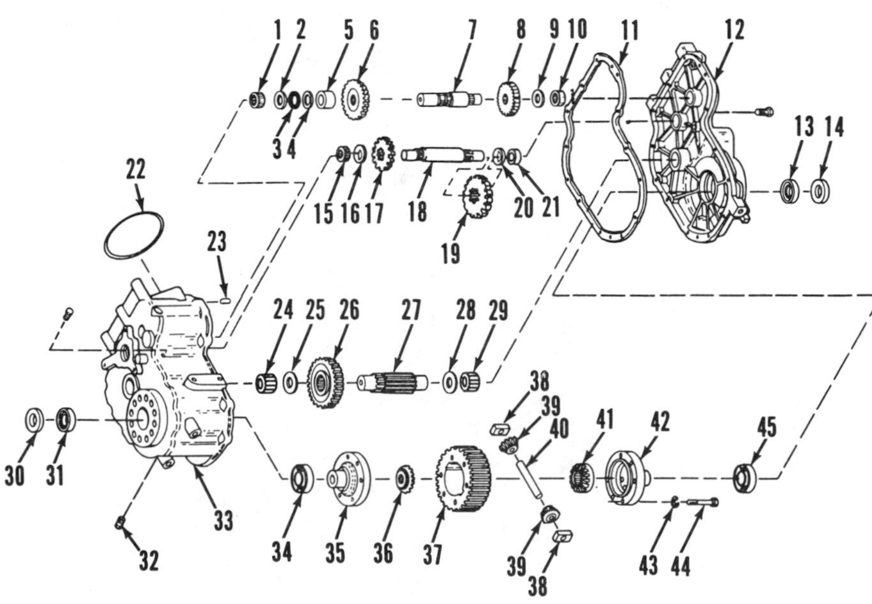

*Fig. DA68—Exploded view of gear reduction unit used on Models 1914 and 1916.*

1. Bearing
2. Thrust washer
3. Thrust bearing
4. Thrust washer
5. Spacer
6. Bevel gear
7. Countershaft
8. Spur gear
9. Thrust washer
10. Bearing
11. Gasket
12. Cover
13. Seal
14. Washer
15. Bearing
16. Thrust bearing
17. Spur gear (17 T)
18. Intermediate shaft
19. Intermediate gear (27 T)
20. Thrust washer
21. Bearing
22. "O" ring
23. Dowel pin
24. Bearing
25. Thrust washer
26. Output gear (33 T)
27. Output shaft
28. Thrust washer
29. Bearing
30. Washer
31. Seal
32. Drain plug
33. Case
34. Bearing
35. Differential carrier
36. Axle gear
37. Ring gear
38. Pinion blocks
39. Pinion gears
40. Cross shaft
41. Axle gear
42. Differential carrier
43. Washer
44. Bolt
45. Bearing



Illustrations courtesy Deutz-Allis Corp.

Refer to Peerless Series 1200 section in TRANSAXLE SERVICE section for overhaul procedure.

### Models 608-610-808GT-810GT-811GT-T811

**REMOVE AND REINSTALL.** To remove transaxle, remove seat and fender assembly. Disconnect brake rod from brake band and disconnect clutch rod from idler bracket. Remove drive belt and transaxle pulley. Unbolt and remove shift lever assembly. On Models 608 and 610, loosen set screws on set collar and slide transaxle rearward until it is free. On all other models, remove "U" bolt clamp from right axle and remove frame support and transaxle support bolts. Lower transaxle and slide it clear of tractor.

To reinstall transaxle, reverse removal procedure.

**OVERHAUL.** All models are equipped with a 3-speed transaxle manufactured by Simplicity Manufacturing Company. Refer to Simplicity 3-Speed section in TRANSAXLE SERVICE section for overhaul procedure.

### Models 608LTD-611LTD

**REMOVE AND REINSTALL.** To remove transaxle, support rear of tractor and remove rear wheels. Disconnect transmission interlock switch. Disconnect brake rod and return spring from brake lever. Disconnect shift links. Remove drive belt from transaxle pulley. Support transaxle and remove cap screws attaching transaxle to side supports. Tilt transaxle forward so pulley clears frame and slide to the left to clear right axle shaft from side support. Remove transaxle from tractor.

To reinstall transaxle, reverse removal procedure. Coat axle shafts with anti-seize lubricant. Install washers and spacers on axle shafts with longer spacer on right axle. Install wheels and secure with E-rings, making sure that tang on E-ring is not aligned with shaft keyway.

**OVERHAUL.** All Models are equipped with a 5-speed Peerless 800 Series transaxle. Refer to Peerless Series 800 section in TRANSAXLE SERVICE section for overhaul procedure.

# GEAR TRANSMISSION

### All Models So Equipped

**REMOVE AND REINSTALL.** The gear transmission used on tractors equipped with forward-reverse shuttle drive is equipped with four forward gears. Reverse gear is not required in this transmission since reverse drive, in any gear, is provided by forward-reverse shuttle drive unit. The transmission used on other gear drive models has three forward gears and one reverse. The differential is located on right rear wheel hub on all models.

To remove transmission, raise rear of tractor so rear wheels are off the ground. Support tractor under the frame just ahead of bevel gear housing. Remove seat deck and fender assembly and disconnect brake linkage and transmission shift rod. Remove rear wheels, hubs, differential assembly and axle shaft. Remove forward-reverse shuttle drive unit on models so equipped. On other models, remove transmission input pulley. Then, on all models, place a jack or blocks under transmission housing. Unbolt transmission from side plates and lift unit from tractor.

To reinstall transmission, reverse removal procedure.

**OVERHAUL.** All models are equipped with a 3-speed or 4-speed transmission manufactured by Simplicity Manufacturing Company. Refer to Simplicity 3-Speed and 4-Speed With Shuttle Drive section in GEAR TRANSMISSION SERVICE section for overhaul procedure.

# DIFFERENTIAL

### All Models So Equipped

**R&R AND OVERHAUL.** To remove differential, block up rear of tractor and remove rear wheels. Remove set screws from left hub and remove hub and key. Loosen set screws and remove set collar and washers from axle on left side of transmission. Remove right hub, differential and axle assembly. It may be necessary to tap on the edge of differential hub to remove it from axle tube.

To disassemble differential, remove set collar from right end of axle shaft. Remove bolts from outer edge of differential case. Remove nuts from inner row of cap screws and separate case halves, leaving cap screws in position to stabilize pinions, spacers and washers (or springs). Identify all parts to aid in reassembly. The rest of disassembly is evident upon inspection of unit and reference to Fig. DA69 or DA70.

When reinstalling assembled unit, make sure that axle and differential are properly seated so seal between differential and wheel hub is compressed. The axle is held in this position by the set collar on axle shaft at left side of transmission case.

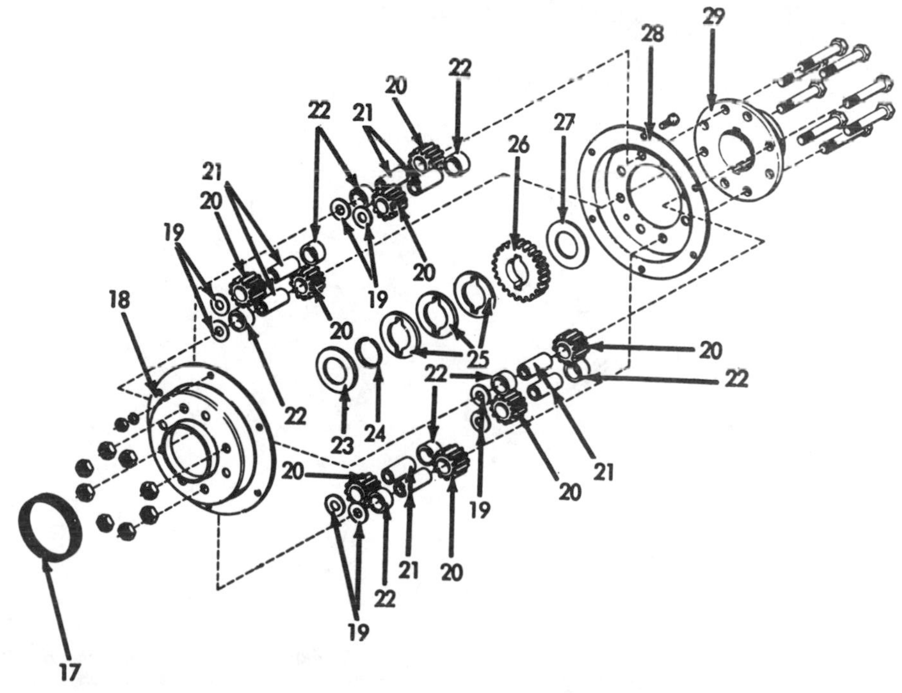


*Fig. DA69—Exploded view of early differential unit with right differential gear and hub and axle shaft removed.*

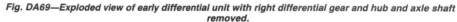

17. Seal
18. Differential cover R.H.
19. Washers
20. Pinions
21. Spindles
22. Spacers
23. Washers
24. Snap ring
25. Axle washers
26. Differential gear L.H.
27. Washer
28. Differential cover L.H.
29. Differential carrier

Illustrations courtesy Deutz-Allis Corp.

**TRACTION ADJUSTMENT.** Some models are equipped with controlled traction adjusters shown in Fig. DA71. Adjustment of traction differential is made by tightening cap screws (2) within right rear wheel hub to 20 ft.-lbs. (27 N·m).

**NOTE: Under torque will allow excessive wheel slippage and over torque will cause hard steering due to lack of differential action.**

# ELECTRIC LIFT

## All Models So Equipped

**OVERHAUL.** To disassemble electric lift unit, remove cap screws securing electric motor (4—Fig. DA72) to gear case (3) and withdraw motor. Motor is serviced as a complete unit. To remove tube assembly, remove cap screw (7) from gear case and withdraw tube (9) with a rotating motion. On late models, screw and brake assembly (12) and tube (9) are serviced as an assembly. On early models, screw assembly is serviced separately and can be removed by removing four retaining screws (8), then pull inner tube (13) and screw (12) out of outer tube.

To disassemble gear case, unbolt and remove end cover (1) and withdraw intermediate gear assembly (2). Remove outer tube (9) and screw assembly (12). Then, using a suitable punch, drive the brake drive pin (6) out of clutch gear shaft (5). Using C-clamps or vise grips, compress Belleville washers (Fig. DA73) and remove snap ring from clutch gear shaft. Disassemble clutch gear assembly and inspect for excessive wear or other damage. Renew complete assembly if service is required.

Reassemble by reversing removal procedure. Lubricate with multipurpose grease.

# HYDRAULIC SYSTEM

## Models 912H-914H-916H-1914-1916

The hydrostatic drive unit supplies pressurized oil for the hydraulic lift system. Refer to HYDROSTATIC TRANSMISSION SERVICE section for service information for hydrostatic drive unit.

**CHARGE PUMP PRESSURE TEST.** To check charge pressure, remove tunnel cover. Remove pipe plug from top of hydrostatic housing and install a 0-300 psi (0-2000 kPa) dampened pressure gage or a gage with snubber in port (P—Fig. DA75). Start and run engine at fast idle. Charge pump pressure should be 90-180 psi (620-1240 kPa). If low, be sure transmission filter and charge pump relief valve are in good condition. Charge relief valve pressure setting is adjustable using shims.

**LIFT SYSTEM PRESSURE TEST.** To check lift system pressure, install a 0-1000 psi (0-7000 kPa) pressure gage in hydrostatic housing test port (P—Fig. DA75) as outlined in CHARGE PUMP

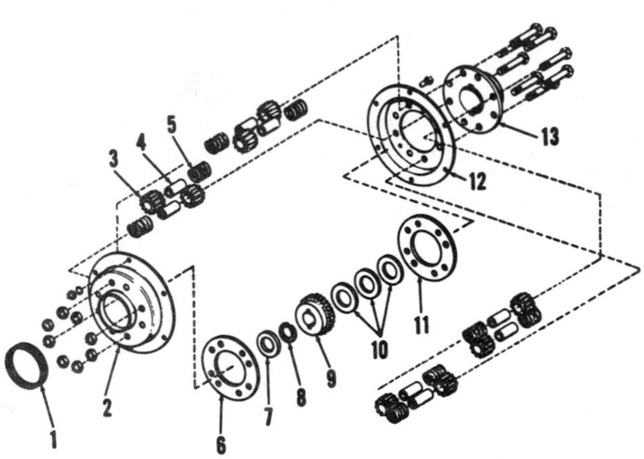

*Fig. DA70—Exploded view of late type differential assembly. Early type does not use spacer plates (6 and 11) and has a spacer in place of spring (5).*

1. Seal
2. Differential cover R.H.
3. Pinion
4. Spindle
5. Spring
6. Spacer plate
7. Axle washer
8. Snap ring
9. Differential gear
10. Axle washers
11. Spacer plate
12. Differential cover L.H.
13. Carrier

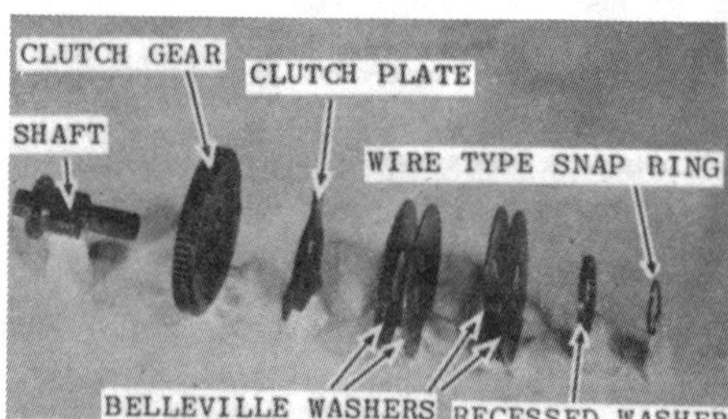


*Fig. DA73—Exploded view of electric lift overload clutch and gear assembly. Note position of Belleville washers when disassembling clutch. Only three Belleville washers are used in some clutches.*

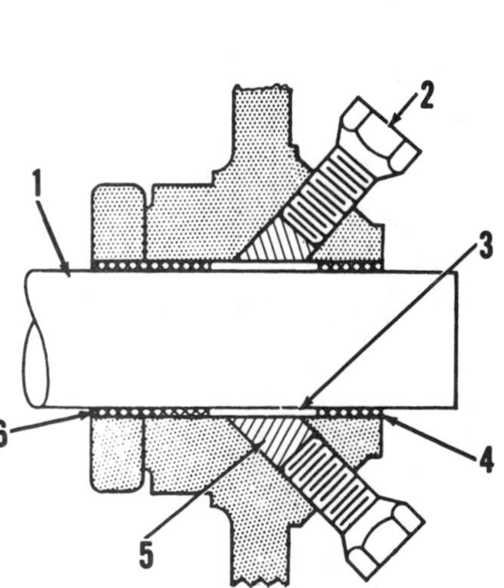

*Fig. DA71—Cross-sectional view of right rear wheel hub showing controlled traction adjusters.*

1. Axle shaft
2. Adjusting screws
3. Nylon bearing
4. Bushing
5. Nylon plug
6. Bushing

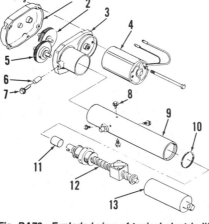

*Fig. DA72—Exploded view of typical electric lift assembly used on some models.*

1. Cover
2. Intermediate gear
3. Housing
4. Motor
5. Clutch gear assy.
6. Drive pin
7. Cap screw
8. Cap screw
9. Outer tube
10. Seal ring
11. Sleeve
12. Screw & brake assy.
13. Inner tube

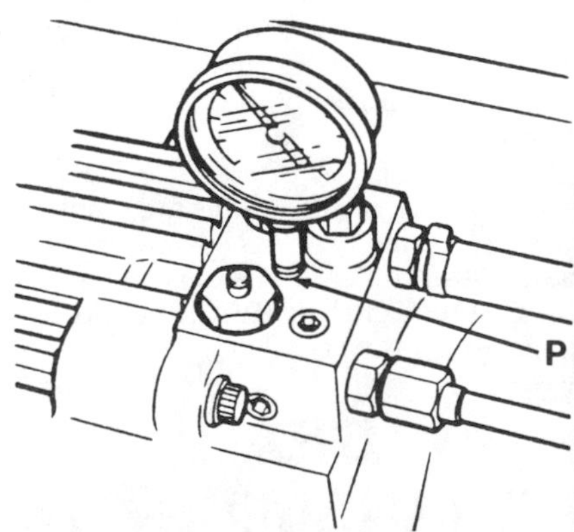


*Fig. DA75—To check charge pressure or implement lift pressure on Models 912H, 914H, 916H, 1914 and 1916, remove plug from top of hydrostatic housing and install a pressure gage in test port (P). Refer to text.*



Illustrations courtesy Deutz-Allis Corp.

PRESSURE TEST. Start and run engine at fast idle. Operate lift control lever to fully extend lift cylinder and obtain system relief pressure reading. System pressure should be 700-900 psi (4830-6205 kPa). If low, be sure transmission filter and implement relief valve are in good condition. Implement relief valve pressure setting is adjustable using shims.

**CONTROL VALVE.** Before removing control valve from tractor, mark all hydraulic lines to assure correct installation during reassembly. Remove upper dash panel from left side of tractor. Disconnect hydraulic hoses from valve and cap all openings. Disconnect control linkage from valve spool. Remove retaining bolts and remove valve assembly.

Refer to Fig. DA76, DA77 or DA78 for an exploded view of control valve. Prior to disassembly, thoroughly clean outside of valve housing. Disassemble valve and inspect all parts for wear and damage. Renew all "O" rings. Valve spool and body are a select fit and complete valve assembly must be renewed if either is excessively worn or damaged.

Reassemble by reversing disassembly procedure. Lubricate all internal components with hydraulic oil prior to assembly.

**HYDRAULIC CYLINDER.** Hydraulic cylinder is a welded assembly and no service parts are available. Renew cylinder if internal or external leakage is apparent.

To check cylinder for internal leakage, start engine and fully extend cylinder. Stop engine and disconnect front hose of cylinder from control valve. Place end of hose in a container. Start engine and move lift control lever to extend cylinder. A small amount of oil may initially flow from open end of hose, then oil flow should stop. If oil flow continues, renew cylinder.

To remove cylinder, remove tunnel cover and upper dash panel from right side of tractor. Clean outside of cylinder and hydraulic hoses, then disconnect hose from front of cylinder. Cap openings to prevent entry of dirt in system. Remove retainer clips and pins retaining cylinder. Disconnect hose from rear of cylinder and remove cylinder from tractor.

To install cylinder, reverse the removal procedure. Fully extend and retract cylinder several times to purge air from system.

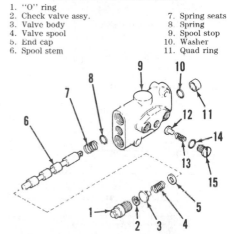

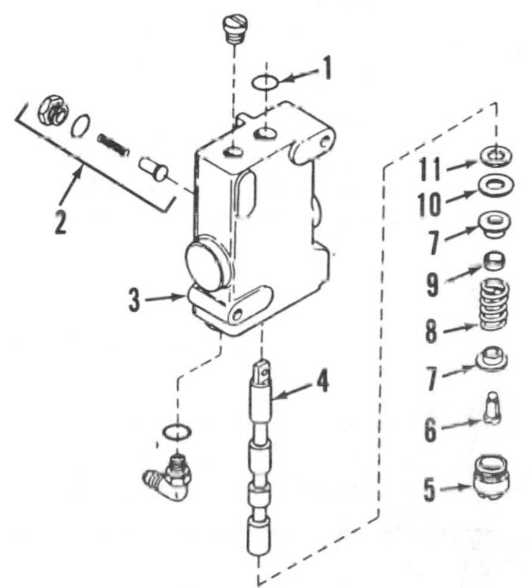


*Fig. DA76—Exploded view of CESSNA lift control valve used on some models equipped with hydraulic lift.*

1. "O" rings
2. Check valve assy.
3. Valve body
4. Valve spool
5. Bushing
6. End cap
7. Retaining ring
8. Washer
9. Spring
10. Spool
11. Washers

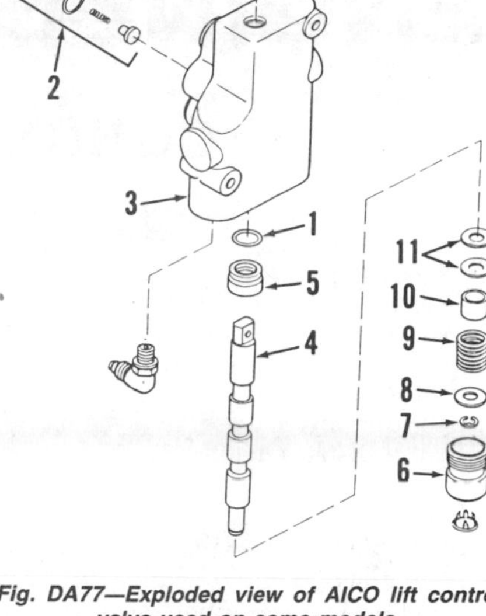


*Fig. DA77—Exploded view of AICO lift control valve used on some models.*

1. "O" ring
2. Check valve assy.
3. Valve body
4. Valve spool
5. End cap
6. Spool stem
7. Spring seats
8. Spring
9. Spool stop
10. Washer
11. Quad ring

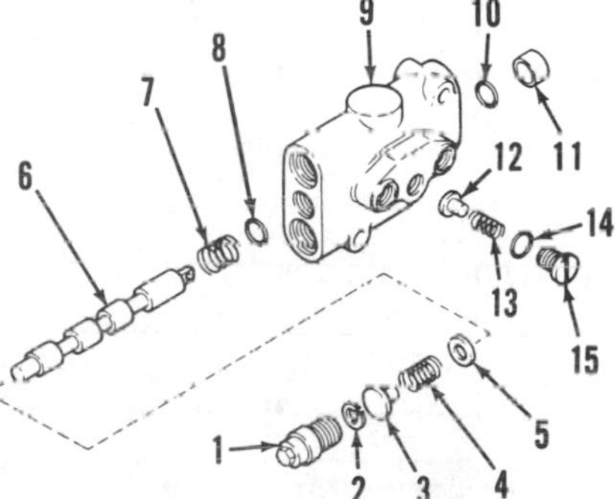


*Fig. DA78—Exploded view lift control valve used on Models 1914 and 1916.*

1. Plug
2. Snap ring
3. Spacer
4. Spring
5. Washer
6. Valve spool
7. Spring
8. "O" ring
9. Body
10. "O" ring
11. Wiper
12. Lift check valve
13. Spring
14. "O" ring
15. Plug

Illustrations courtesy Deutz-Allis Corp.

# ENGINEERING PRODUCTS CO.

## CONDENSED SPECIFICATIONS

| | Jim Dandy | | | Special |
|---|---|---|---|---|
| Engine Make | B&S | B&S | Kohler | Kohler |
| Model | 23DFB | 243431 | K321 | K331 |
| Bore | 3 in. (76.2 mm) | 3-1/16 in. (77.8 m) | 3½ in. (88.9 mm) | 3⅝ in. (92.1 mm) |
| Stroke | 3¼ in. (82.5 mm) | 3¼ in. (82.5 mm) | 3¼ in. (82.5 mm) | 3¼ in. (82.5 mm) |
| Piston Displacement | 22.97 cu in. (376 cc) | 23.94 cu. in. (392 cc) | 31.27 cu. in. (512 cc) | 33.6 cu. in. (551 cc) |
| Horsepower | 9 | 10 | 14 | 12.5 |
| Slow Idle Speed – Rpm | 1200 | 1200 | 1000 | 1000 |
| High Idle Speed (No Load) – Rpm | 3600 | 3600 | 3600 | 3600 |
| Full Load Speed – Rpm | 3300 | 3300 | 3300 | 3300 |
| Crankcase Oil Capacity | 4 pints (1.9L) | 4 pints (1.9L) | 4 pints (1.9L) | 6 pints (2.8L) |
| Weight – | | | | |
| Above 32°F (0°C) | SAE 30 | | | |
| 0°F (–18°C) to 32°F (0°C) | SAE 10W | | | |
| Below 0°F (–18°C) | SAE 5W-20 | | | |
| Transmission Oil Capacity | ½ pint (0.2L) | | | |
| Weight | EP 80-90 | | | |
| Final Drive Oil Capacity | ¾ pint (0.3L) | ¾ pint (0.3L) | ¾ pint (0.3L) | 1½ pint (0.7L) |
| Weight | EP 80-90 | | | |
| Differential Oil Capacity | 2 pints (0.9L) | | | |
| Weight | EP 80-90 | | | |

| | Power King | | | 1612 |
|---|---|---|---|---|
| Engine Make | Kohler | Kohler | Kohler | Kohler |
| Model | K241 | K301 | K321 | K301 |
| Bore | 3¼ in. (82.5 mm) | 3⅜ in. (85.7 mm) | 3½ in. (88.9 mm) | 3⅜ in. (85.7 mm) |
| Stroke | 2⅞ in. (73.0 mm) | 3¼ in. (82.5 mm) | 3¼ in. (82.5 mm) | 3½ in. (88.9 mm) |
| Piston Displacement | 23.9 cu. in. (392 cc) | 29.07 cu. in. (476 cc) | 31.27 cu. in. (512 cc) | 29.07 cu. in. (476 cc) |
| Horsepower | 10 | 12 | 14 | 12 |
| Slow Idle Speed – Rpm | 1000 | 1000 | 1000 | 1000 |
| High Idle Speed (No Load) – Rpm | 3600 | 3600 | 3600 | 3600 |
| Full Load Speed – Rpm | 3300 | 3300 | 3300 | 3300 |
| Crankcase Oil Capacity | 5 pints (2.3L) | 5 pints (2.3L) | 4 pints (1.9L) | 4 pints (1.9L) |
| Weight – | | | | |
| Above 32°F (0°C) | SAE 30 | | | |
| 0°F (–18°C) to 32°F (0°C) | SAE 10W | | | |
| Below 0°F (–18°C) | SAE 5W-20 | | | |
| Transmission Oil Capacity | ½ pint (0.2L) | | | |
| Weight | EP 80-90 | | | |
| Final Drive Oil Capacity | 1½ pints (0.7L) | | | ¾ pint (0.3L) |
| Weight | EP 80-90 | | | |
| Differential Oil Capacity | 2 pints (0.9L) | | | |
| Weight | EP 80-90 | | | |

| | Power King | | | |
|---|---|---|---|---|
| | 1614 | 1616 | 2414 | 2416 |
| Engine Make | Kohler | B&S | Kohler | B&S |
| Model | K321 | 326437 | K321 | 326437 |
| Bore | 3½ in. (88.9 mm) | 3-9/16 in. (90.5 mm) | 3½ in. (88.9 mm) | 3-9/16 in. (90.5 mm) |
| Stroke | 3¼ in. (82.5 mm) | 3¼ in. (82.5 mm) | 3¼ in. (82.5 mm) | 3¼ in. (82.5 mm) |
| Piston Displacement | 31.27 cu. in. (512 cc) | 32.4 cu. in. (531 cc) | 31.27 cu. in. (512 cc) | 32.4 cu. in. (531 cc) |
| Horsepower | 14 | 16 | 14 | 16 |
| Slow Idle Speed – Rpm | 1000 | 1200 | 1000 | 1200 |
| High Idle Speed (No Load) – Rpm | 3600 | 3600 | 3600 | 3600 |
| Full Load Speed – Rpm | 3300 | 3300 | 3300 | 3300 |
| Crankcase Oil Capacity | 4 pints (1.9L) | | | |
| Weight – | | | | |
| Above 32°F (0°C) | SAE 30 | | | |
| 0°F (–18°C) to 32°F (0°C) | SAE 10W | | | |
| Below 0°F (–18°C) | SAE 5W-20 | | | |
| Transmission Oil Capacity | ½ pint (0.2L) | | | |
| Weight | EP 80-90 | | | |
| Final Drive Oil Capacity | 1½ pints (0.7L) | | | |
| Weight | EP 80-90 | | | |
| Differential Oil Capacity | 2 pints (0.9L) | | | |
| Weight | EP 80-90 | | | |

# FRONT AXLE AND STEERING SYSTEM

## AXLE MAIN MEMBER

### All Models

The axle main member (4 – Fig. E1) is mounted to the main frame and pivots on stud (15). To remove front axle assembly, disconnect drag link from arm on steering spindle. Remove nut from front of pivot stud (15). Block up under front of tractor frame and move axle assembly forward off pivot stud. The two needle bearings (3) can now be removed from axle main member center bore.

## TIE ROD

### All Models

The tie rod (2 – Fig. E1) is adjustable on all models and front wheel toe-in should be adjusted to ⅛-inch (3 mm). Removal of tie rod is evident after examination of unit and reference to Fig. E1.

## STEERING SPINDLES

### All Models

To remove steering spindles (8 and 16 – Fig. E1), support axle main member and remove front wheels. Disconnect drag link from left steering spindle. Remove steering arms (5) and keys from top of steering spindles and lower steering spindles down out of axle main member. Bushings (6) and bearings (7) can now be removed. Axle shaft (9) is removable from steering spindle.

## STEERING GEAR

### All Models

**REMOVE AND REINSTALL.** To remove steering gear assembly, first remove steering arm from steering unit. Unbolt steering gear from frame and lift steering gear assembly from tractor. To reinstall unit, reverse removal procedure.

### Early Models

**OVERHAUL.** To disassemble removed steering gear, remove steering wheel (2 – Fig. E2), clamp (8) and slide jacket assembly from steering shaft. Unbolt and remove side cover (16) and

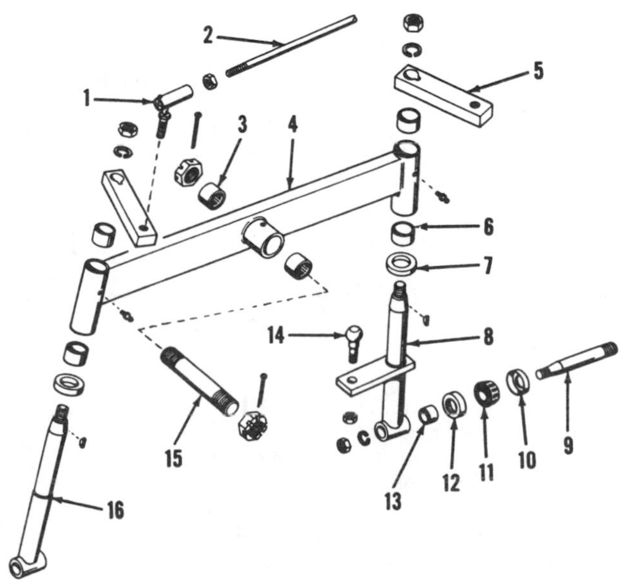


*Fig. E1 – Exploded view of typical front axle assembly.*

1. Tie rod end
2. Tie rod
3. Pivot bearing
4. Axle main member
5. Steering arm
6. Bushing
7. Load bearing
8. L.H. steering spindle
9. Axle shaft
10. Bearing cup
11. Bearing cone
12. Oil seal
13. Spacer
14. Ball stud
15. Axle pivot stud
16. R.H. steering spindle

Illustrations courtesy Engineering Products Co.

withdraw levershaft assembly (18). Remove cap screws securing upper cover (9) to steering gear housing (20) and withdraw steering shaft assembly. The balance of disassembly is evident after examination of unit and reference to Fig. E2.

When reassembling, add or remove shims (10) to adjust steering shaft bearings. Steering shaft (14) should rotate freely with zero end play. Shims are available in 0.002, 0.003 and 0.010 inch thicknesses. Using a new gasket (17), install levershaft assembly and side cover. Loosen locknut and turn adjuster screw (15) to adjust the levershaft to cam backlash. Turn steering shaft from full left to full right turn to make certain unit has zero end play but does not bind when passing mid-position. To complete assembly, install jacket and bearing assembly and steering wheel. Fill steering gear to level plug with EP80-90 gear lubricant.

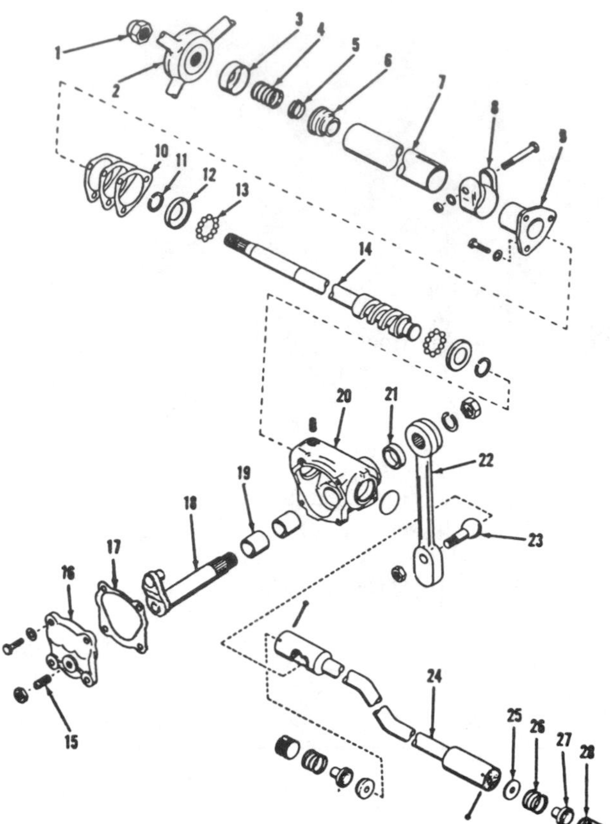

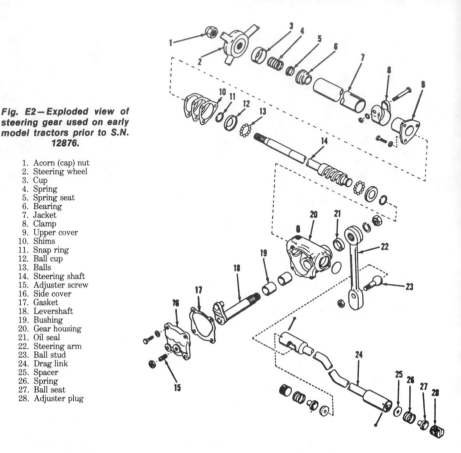

***Fig. E2—Exploded view of steering gear used on early model tractors prior to S.N. 12876.***

1. Acorn (cap) nut
2. Steering wheel
3. Cup
4. Spring
5. Spring seat
6. Bearing
7. Jacket
8. Clamp
9. Upper cover
10. Shims
11. Snap ring
12. Ball cup
13. Balls
14. Steering shaft
15. Adjuster screw
16. Side cover
17. Gasket
18. Levershaft
19. Bushing
20. Gear housing
21. Oil seal
22. Steering arm
23. Ball stud
24. Drag link
25. Spacer
26. Spring
27. Ball seat
28. Adjuster plug

### Late Models

**OVERHAUL.** To disassemble removed steering gear, first remove steering wheel. Then, unbolt and remove side cover assembly (2–Fig. E3) and withdraw levershaft (4). Remove locknut (18), lock ring (17) and adjuster plug (16). Steering shaft (13) and bearings can now be removed. Upper shaft bearing (7) can be removed from housing tube and renewed if necessary.

When reassembling, install new oil seal (9) with lip to inside. With upper shaft bearing in place, install steering shaft and bearings. Tighten adjuster plug (16) until shaft rotates freely with zero end play. Secure adjuster plug with lock ring and locknut. Install levershaft and side cover with new gasket (3). Locate levershaft in mid-position (half way between full right and full left turn). Turn adjusting screw (1) in until zero backlash is obtained and tighten locknut. Steering shaft should turn from full left to full right turn without binding. Fill steering gear housing to level plug with EP80-90 gear lubricant.

# ENGINE

### All Models

**REMOVE AND REINSTALL.** To remove engine, first shut off fuel at fuel tank and disconnect fuel line from engine. Remove hood and grille assembly. On electric start models, disconnect battery cables, starter and generator wires and other electrical wiring as needed. On all models, disconnect ignition wire, choke and throttle control cables from engine. Working through openings in clutch housing, remove cap screws securing engine to clutch housing; remove all set screws, located at bottom of belt groove, securing flywheel to engine crankshaft. Unbolt engine from mounting bracket, slide engine forward while prying rearward on flywheel until engine shaft is clear of flywheel, then lift engine from tractor.

Reinstall engine by reversing removal procedure.

**OVERHAUL.** Engine make and model are listed at beginning of section. To overhaul engine components and accessories, refer to Briggs & Stratton or Kohler sections of this manual.

# CLUTCH

The clutch used on all models is a 6½ inch (165 mm), dry disc, spring loaded type.

### All Models

**R&R AND OVERHAUL.** To remove clutch assembly, separate flywheel housing from clutch housing as follows: Shut off fuel at fuel tank and disconnect fuel line from engine. Remove hood and grille assembly. On electric start models, disconnect battery cables, starter and generator wires. If equipped with hydraulic lift, disconnect hydraulic hoses from hydraulic pump. On all models, disconnect choke and throttle control

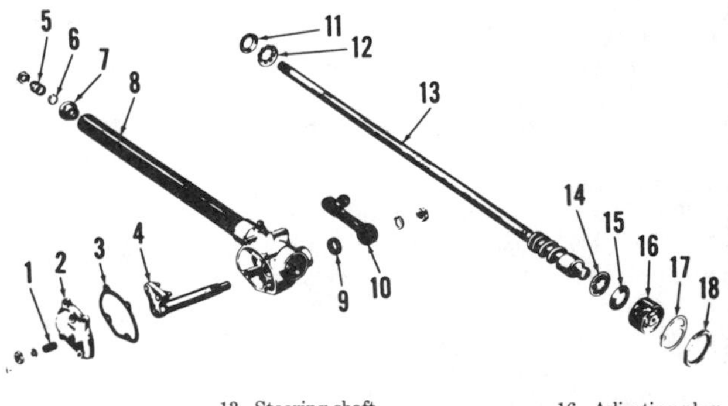

***Fig. E3—Exploded view of typical late model steering gear assembly. Locknut (18) differs in later production, and spring (5) and spring seat (6) are not used.***

1. Adjuster screw
2. Side cover
3. Gasket
4. Levershaft
5. Spring
6. Spring seat
7. Jacket tube bearing
8. Housing & tube assy.
9. Seal
10. Steering arm
11. Ball cup
12. Balls
13. Steering shaft
14. Balls
15. Ball cup
16. Adjusting plug
17. Lockwasher
18. Locknut



Illustrations courtesy Engineering Products Co.

cables and electrical wiring as necessary. Remove cap screws securing flywheel housing to clutch housing. Unbolt engine from mounting bracket; slide engine forward to clear clutch shaft, then lift engine from tractor.

Unbolt and remove clutch assembly from flywheel (2 – Fig. E4). If necessary to remove flywheel, be sure to remove all set screws, located at bottom of pulley groove, before pulling flywheel off engine shaft. Renew seal (15) and pilot bearing (16) in flywheel if necessary.

Clutch disc lining consists of 8 segments (4 thick and 4 thin). When relining clutch disc (4), the 4 thick segments (3) must be installed on flywheel side of disc. Ball type clutch release bearing (13) can be inspected and renewed, if necessary, at this time.

Before reinstalling clutch assembly on flywheel, lubricate clutch shaft pilot bearing (16). Align clutch and clutch shaft splines by turning engine front pulley, then complete reassembly by reversing removal procedure.

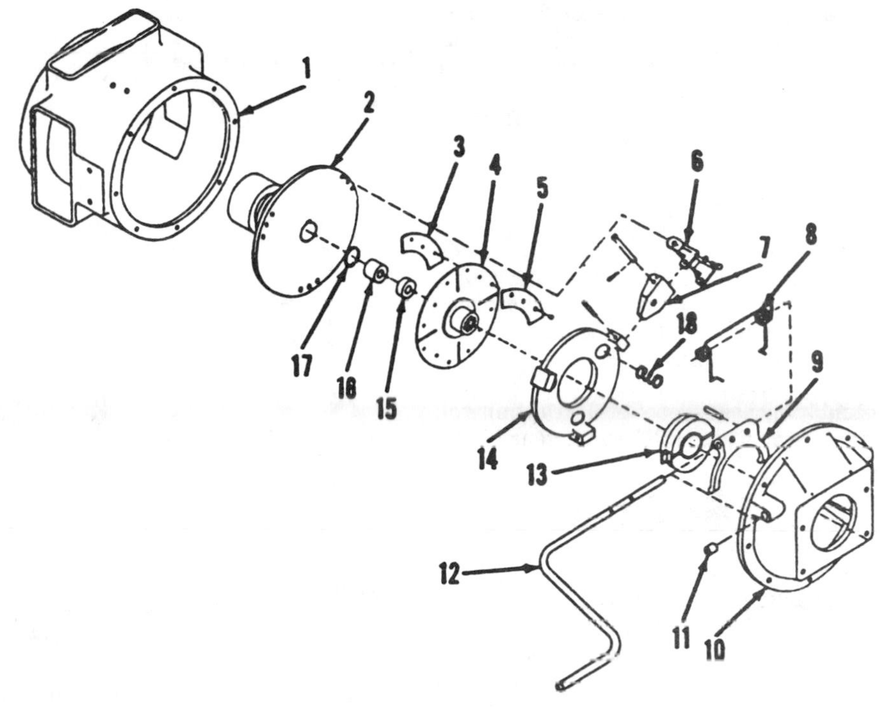

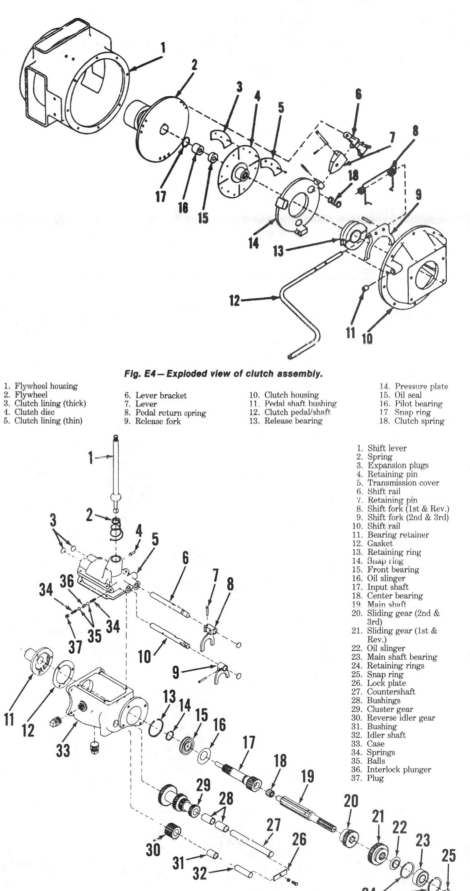

*Fig. E4 – Exploded view of clutch assembly.*

1. Flywheel housing
2. Flywheel
3. Clutch lining (thick)
4. Clutch disc
5. Clutch lining (thin)
6. Lever bracket
7. Lever
8. Pedal return spring
9. Release fork
10. Clutch housing
11. Pedal shaft bushing
12. Clutch pedal/shaft
13. Release bearing
14. Pressure plate
15. Oil seal
16. Pilot bearing
17. Snap ring
18. Clutch spring

# TRANSMISSION

The automotive type transmission has 3 forward gears and 1 reverse. An optional tandem transmission, mounted behind regular transmission, is availabe on some models to provide 6 forward speeds and 3 reverse speeds. Tandem transmission is an exact duplicate of regular transmission.

## All Models

**REMOVE AND REINSTALL.** To remove transmission, first separate clutch housing from flywheel housing as outlined in CLUTCH paragraph. Unbolt and remove clutch housing from front of transmission case. Remove cap screws securing front of drive shaft tube to rear of transmission case. Slide transmission forward to disconnect drive shaft splines and remove transmission from tractor.

**OVERHAUL.** Unbolt and remove transmission top cover and shift control assembly. Remove cap screws from input shaft bearing retainer (11 – Fig. E5) and withdraw input shaft (17) and bearing assembly.

**NOTE: Watch for center bearing (18), consisting of 13 rollers, as they can fall into lower part of transmission case as input shaft is removed.**

Remove snap ring retaining main shaft bearing (23) in case and bump shaft out of case. Sliding gears (20 and 21) will be removed as main shaft (19) is withdrawn. Unbolt and remove lock

1. Shift lever
2. Spring
3. Expansion plugs
4. Retaining pin
5. Transmission cover
6. Shift rail
7. Retaining pin
8. Shift fork (1st & Rev.)
9. Shift fork (2nd & 3rd)
10. Shift rail
11. Bearing retainer
12. Gasket
13. Retaining ring
14. Snap ring
15. Front bearing
16. Oil slinger
17. Input shaft
18. Center bearing
19. Main shaft
20. Sliding gear (2nd & 3rd)
21. Sliding gear (1st & Rev.)
22. Oil slinger
23. Main shaft bearing
24. Retaining rings
25. Snap ring
26. Lock plate
27. Countershaft
28. Bushings
29. Cluster gear
30. Reverse idler gear
31. Bushing
32. Idler shaft
33. Case
34. Springs
35. Balls
36. Interlock plunger
37. Plug

*Fig. E5 – Exploded view of transmission. Tandem transmission, when furnished for extra gear reduction, is identical except for shape of shift lever.*

plate (26) retaining idler shaft (32) and countershaft (27) in transmission case. Remove idler shaft and reverse idler gear (30) and countershaft and cluster gear (29). Drive pins from shift forks and remove expansion plugs from top cover. Remove second and third shift rail (10) and fork (9) and then, first and reverse shift rail (6) and fork (8). A poppet spring and ball are located outside each rail and an interlock plunger (36) is positioned between rails. Further disassembly procedure is evident after examination of unit.

Reassemble in reverse order of disassembly procedure. Refill transmission with ½-pint (0.2L) EP80-90 gear oil.

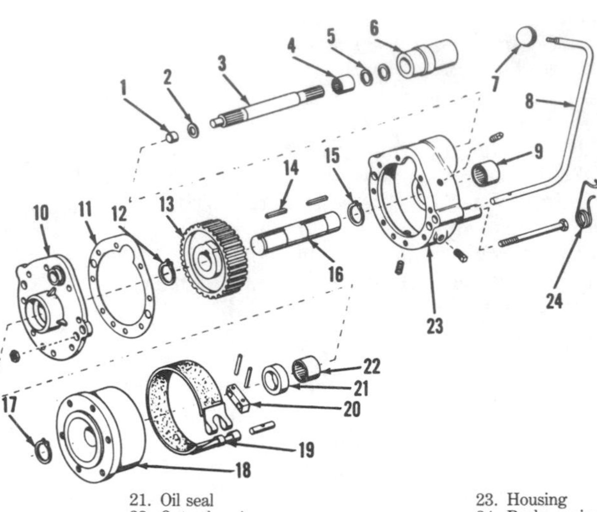

***Fig. E6—Exploded view of early style (L.H.) brake assembly used on early Jim Dandy models. See Fig. E8 for newer design.***

1. Needle bearing
2. Washer
3. Pinion shaft
4. Needle bearing
5. Oil seal
6. Axle tube
7. Lever knob
8. Hand lever
9. Inner bearing
10. Cover
11. Gasket
12. Snap ring
13. Drive (bull) gear
14. Key
15. Snap ring
16. Axle shaft
17. Snap ring
18. Hub & brake drum
19. Brake band
20. Brake cam
21. Oil seal
22. Outer bearing
23. Housing
24. Brake spring

# BRAKE

The brakes are band on drum type and are individually operated. Four different styles of brakes have been used as shown in Figs. E6, E8, E9 and E11. Early models tractors were equipped with hand brake levers located on left and right sides of tractor. Late production tractors are equipped with two brake pedals on right side of tractor.

## Jim Dandy and 1612 Models

**REMOVE AND REINSTALL.** To remove brakes from Jim Dandy tractors prior to S.N. 16834, block up under rear of main frame and remove rear wheels. Drive pins from brake cams (20–Fig. E6) and slide pins and brake lever from bands. Expand bands (19) and remove from drums (18). The drums are integral with wheel hubs. The drums can be removed after first removing snap rings from axle outer ends. Reinstall by reversing removal procedure. On models equipped with foot pedals, adjust linkage (Fig. E7) to equalize pedal height.

On all Model 1612 and Jim Dandy models beginning with production S.N. 16834, brake drum is no longer integral with wheel hub and is mounted outboard of final drive housing on an extension of pinion shaft (24–Fig. E8). Compare Figs. E6 and E8 to identify changes. Service procedures are not greatly altered.

## Power King Models and Special

**REMOVE AND REINSTALL.** To remove brakes from tractors prior to S.N. 52590, support rear of main frame and remove rear wheels. On models having foot brakes, disconnect pedal linkage at rear axle. Unbolt brake housing (2–Fig. E9) from final drive housing and lift off brake assembly. Drive out pin (3) and remove cap screws securing bands (6) inside housings. Brake drums (7), located on final drive pinion shafts (13), can be removed after first removing set screws. Reinstall by reversing removal procedure. Equalize pedal height on models with foot brakes by adjusting threaded clevises on brake links (Fig. E10).

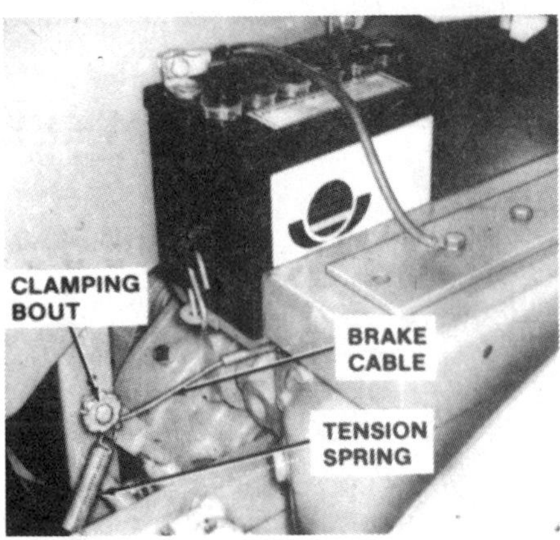


***Fig. E7—Adjust brake cable length to equalize pedal height on Model 1612 and late Jim Dandy models equipped with foot pedal operated brakes.***

On models beginning with S.N. 52590, brake housing (2–Fig. E9) is no longer used and operating linkage is different. Refer to Figs. E11 and E12. Service procedure is similar to early models as outlined above.

To adjust brake pedal spring tension, turn adjusting nut (5–Fig. E12) to compress or release spring (4). To adjust brake band, loosen jam nut (6) and turn adjusting nut (8) to reposition transfer block (7); turning adjusting nut clockwise tightens brake band around brake drum. Whenever transfer block is moved, stop bolt (10) must be moved an equal distance.

# FINAL DRIVE

## Jim Dandy-1612

**REMOVE AND REINSTALL.** After removing brakes as previously outlined, place a jack or blocks under differential housing. Remove cap screws securing final drive to main frame. Pull straight

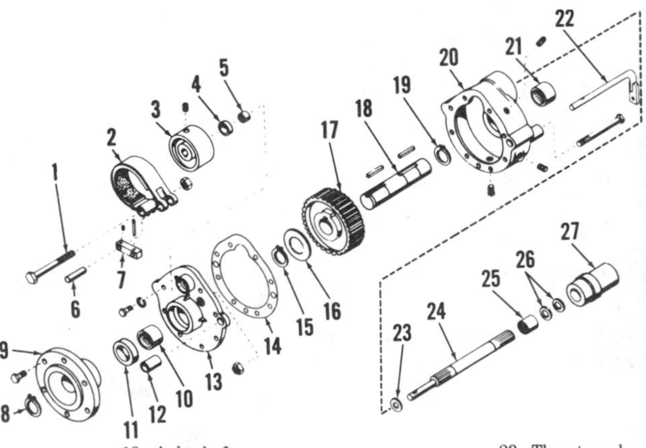

***Fig. E8—Exploded view of up-to-date design brake and final drive assembly for Jim Dandy and 1612 models. Note that drum (3) is no longer part of hub (9) and that lever (22) is part of pedal linkage (not hand operated as before).***

1. Band anchor bolt
2. Brake band
3. Brake drum
4. Seal
5. Pinion bearing
6. Cam pin
7. Brake cam
8. Snap ring
9. Hub
10. Outer bearing
11. Oil seal
12. Spacer
13. Cover
14. Gasket
15. Outer snap ring
16. Thrust washer
17. Bull gear
18. Axle shaft
19. Inner snap ring
20. Housing
21. Inner bearing
22. Brake lever
23. Thrust washer
24. Pinion shaft
25. Shaft bearing
26. Bearing seals
27. Axle tube



Illustrations courtesy Engineering Products Co.

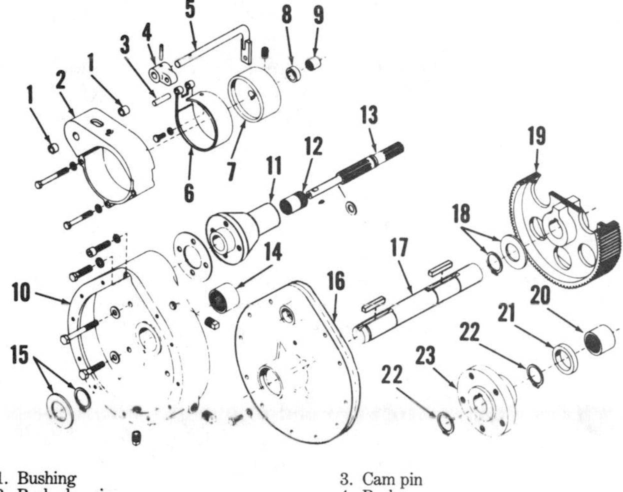

1. Bushing
2. Brake housing
3. Cam pin
4. Brake cam

*Fig. E9—Exploded view of brake and final drive for Power King models prior to S.N. 52590. Brake lever (5) connects to pedal linkage. See Fig. E11 for latest design.*

5. Brake lever
6. Brake band
7. Brake drum
8. Shaft seal
9. Pinion bearing
10. Final drive housing
11. Pinion tube
12. Bearing & seal
13. Pinion shaft
14. Axle inner bearing
15. Thrust washer & snap ring
16. Final drive cover
17. Axle shaft
18. Thrust washer & snap ring
19. Bull gear
20. Axle outer bearing
21. Oil seal
22. Snap ring (2)
23. Wheel hub

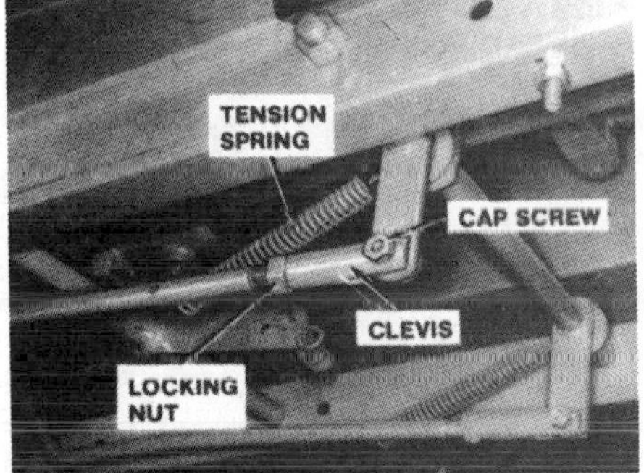


*Fig. E10—Equalize brake pedal height by adjusting threaded clevises on brake links.*

out on final drive and remove assembly from tractor. Unbolt and remove final drive cover (10–Fig. E6) or (13–Fig. E8) and then remove drive gear (bull gear) and axle shaft. If final drive pinion shaft was not removed with final drive housing, it can be withdrawn from differential at this time.

Reinstall final drive by reversing removal procedure and refill each final drive with ¾-pint (0.3L) of EP80-90 gear lubricant.

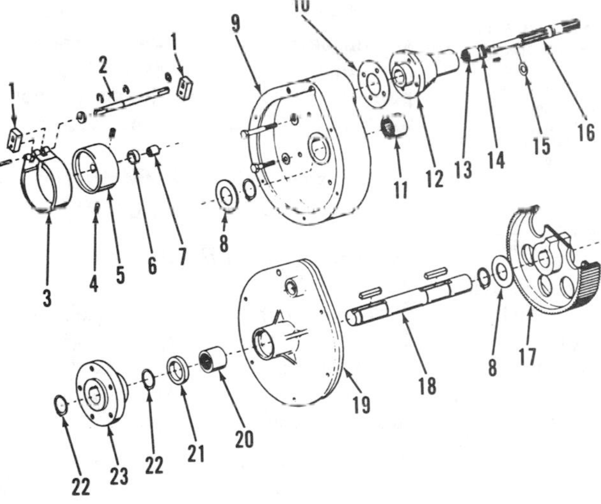

*Fig. E11—Exploded view of latest style brakes and final drive assembly used on Power King models with S.N. 52590 and after.*

1. Brake cams
2. Brake shaft
3. Brake band
4. Set screw
5. Brake drum
6. Seal
7. Bearing
8. Thrust washers
9. Final drive housing
10. Gasket
11. Axle inner bearing
12. Bearing housing
13. Bearing
14. Seal
15. Thrust washer
16. Pinion shaft
17. Bull gear
18. Axle
19. Cover
20. Axle outer bearing
21. Seal
22. Snap rings
23. Wheel hub

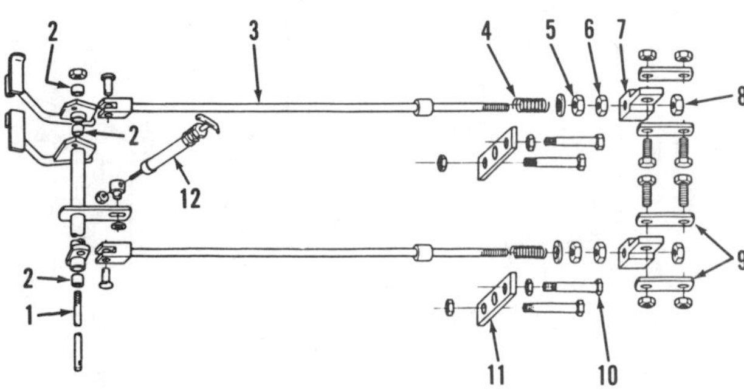

*Fig. E12—Exploded view of brake control linkage used on Power King models with S.N. 52590 and after.*

1. Brake pedal shaft
2. Bushings
3. Brake link
4. Return spring
5. Adjusting nut
6. Jam nut
7. Brake transfer block
8. Adjusting nut
9. Transfer straps
10. Stop bolt
11. Support bracket
12. Park brake control

### Power King Models and Special

**REMOVE AND REINSTALL.** To remove final drives, first remove brakes as covered in preceding text. Remove snap ring, wheel hub and key from axle shaft. Unbolt and remove final drive cover (16–Fig. E9 or E11) followed by drive (bull) gear (19) and axle shaft (17). Support differential housing using a jack or blocks. Remove cap screws securing final drive housing (10) to tractor main frame and pull final drive housing straight out from differential housing. Final drive pinion shaft (13) can now be removed. Further disassembly procedures are apparent after examination of unit.

Reinstall final drive by reversing removal procedure, and refill each final drive housing with 1½ pints (0.7L) of EP80-90 gear lubricant.

# DIFFERENTIAL

### All Models

**REMOVE AND REINSTALL.** To remove differential assembly, first remove brakes and final drives as outlined in preceding sections. Then, unbolt and remove seat and bracket assembly. Remove cap screws which secure differential housing to drive shaft tube. Move differential assembly rearward to disconnect drive shaft splines, then lift differential from tractor. To reinstall, reverse sequence of these operations.

**OVERHAUL.** To disassemble removed differential assembly, unbolt and remove rear cover (22–Fig. E13). Remove cap screws which hold bearing retainer clamps (21) and lift out ring gear and differential case assembly with side bearings (19 and 20).

**IMPORTANT NOTE: Observe number and placement of adjusting shims (18) which will be needed in reassembly. In current production, side bearing adjusting shims are placed between bearing cone and differential case.**

Continue disassembly by removal of lock pin and differential pinion shaft (28) followed by thrust block (31). Rotate differential side gears and remove pinion gears (30), side gears (27) and thrust washers (26 and 29). After removing nut (5) from bevel pinion (17), bump pinion rearward out of differential housing. Oil baffle (6), slinger (7), bearing cone (8), shims (10) and spacer (13) will be removed with bevel pinion. Bevel pinion bearing cups (9 and 15) and shim pack (14) can now be removed from differential housing (12).

When reassembling, adjust bevel pin-

Illustrations courtesy Engineering Products Co.

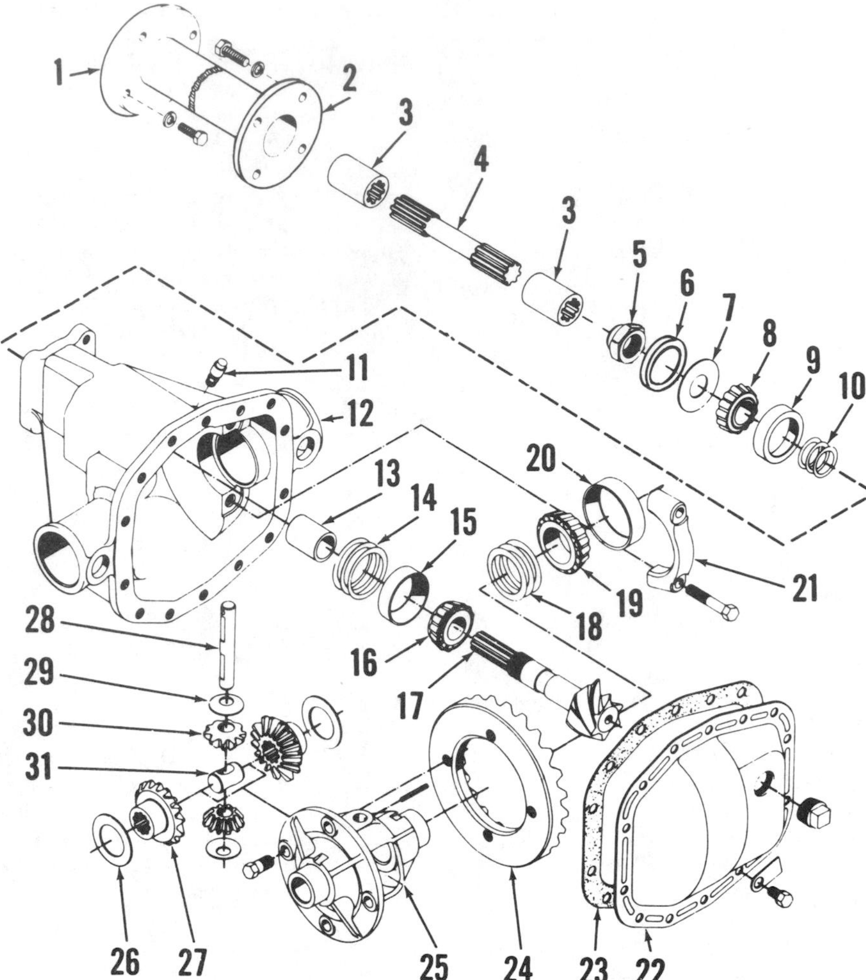

*Fig. E13—Exploded view of typical Dana differential used on all models. Principal change made in recent production is in design of drive shaft (4). Oil baffle (6) is not used on late models.*

1. Gasket
2. Shaft tube
3. Coupling
4. Drive shaft
5. Pinion nut
6. Oil baffle
7. Oil slinger
8. Bearing cone
9. Bearing cup
10. Shim pack
11. Breather
12. Housing
13. Spacer
14. Shim pack
15. Bearing cup
16. Bearing cone
17. Pinion
18. Shim pack
19. Bearing cone
20. Bearing cup
21. Bearing cap
22. Rear cover
23. Gasket
24. Ring gear
25. Differential case
26. Thrust washer
27. Side gear
28. Pinion shaft
29. Thrust washer
30. Differential pinion
31. Thrust block

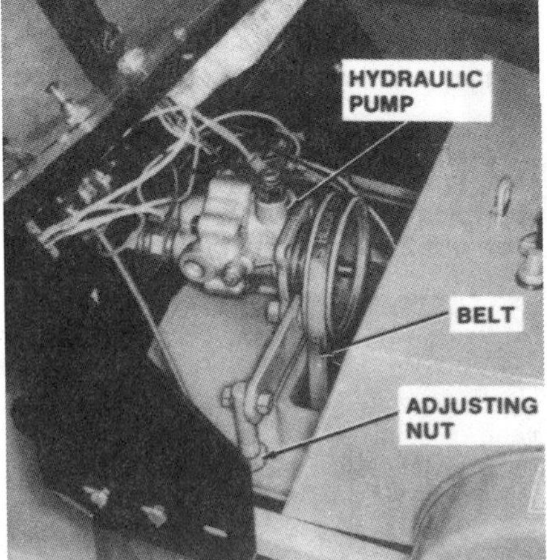


*Fig. E14—Hydraulic pump, on models so equipped, is mounted on top of flywheel housing. When adjusting drive belt tension, do not overtighten.*

ion bearings by adding or removing shims (10) until pinion will revolve freely with zero end play. Install ring gear and differential case assembly with shim packs (18) made up to eliminate differential case side play. Check backlash between ring gear and pinion and adjust to approximately 0.005 inch (0.127 mm) by shifting shims (18) from one side of differential case to the other. After these adjustments are made, apply a thin coat of red lead or Prussian Blue to ring gear teeth. Then rotate gears and check tooth contact pattern by observing how coloring has been rubbed off ring gear teeth. A correct pattern is one which is well centered. If pattern is too high, move shims as necessary from forward pinion bearing position to rear bearing location. If pattern is too low on gear teeth, move shims from rear pinion bearing to forward end of pinion shaft. After pattern is confirmed as correct, it will be necessary to readjust backlash in the gearset. To complete reassembly, reverse disassembly procedure. Refill differential with two pints (0.9L) of EP80-90 gear oil.

# HYDRAULIC LIFT

### All Models So Equipped

Some models are equipped with a hydraulic lift system. A gear type hydraulic pump is belt driven from a pulley on engine crankshaft. Hydraulic oil or automatic transmission fluid (Dexron) should be used in hydraulic system. Capacity is approximately five quarts (4.7L). Fluid should be 1½ inches (38 mm) below top of reservoir tank with hydraulic cylinder fully retracted.

**NOTE: Hydraulic system components should be cleaned before disconnecting hydraulic lines or disassembling components. Open fittings should be capped to prevent dirt from entering system.**

## HYDRAULIC PUMP AND DRIVE BELT

### All Models So Equipped

Service parts are not available for hydraulic pump. If service is necessary, renew pump as a complete unit.

Pump drive belt tension is adjusted by adjusting position of nut (Fig. E14) on

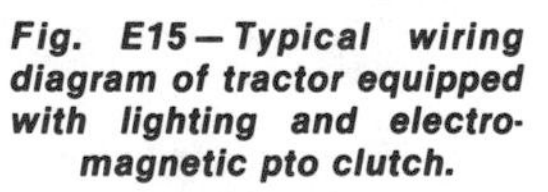

*Fig. E15—Typical wiring diagram of tractor equipped with lighting and electromagnetic pto clutch.*

1. Battery
2. Solenoid
3. Starter
4. Rectifier
5. Headlights
6. Light switch
7. Magnetic clutch (pto)
8. Clutch switch
9. Seat switch
10. To ignition coil
11. Ignition switch
12. Fuse

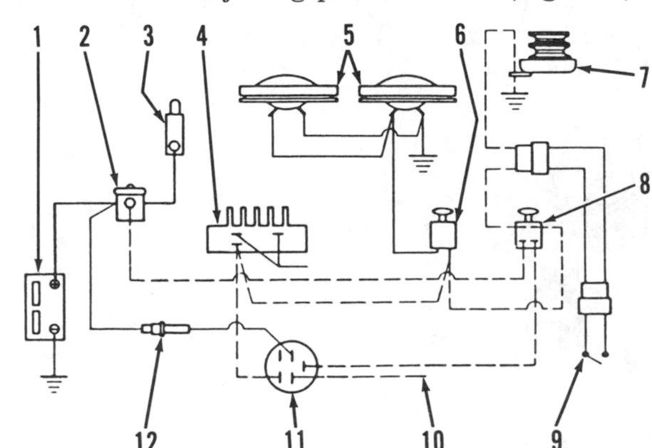



Illustrations courtesy Engineering Products Co.

tensioning rod. Tension is correct if belt doesn't slip when system is under load; do not overtighten.

To renew drive belt, engine must be pulled forward to disengage crankshaft from flywheel. Unbolt engine from mounting bracket and clutch housing. Remove all set screws, located at bottom of pulley groove, securing flywheel to engine shaft. Pull engine forward while prying rearward on flywheel until shaft is separated from flywheel. Install new belt and recouple engine to flywheel. Adjust belt tension as previously outlined.

## HYDRAULIC CONTROL VALVE

### All Models So Equipped

A single spool, four way valve is used with raise, lower, hold and float positions. A relief valve located in valve body limits system pressure to 1000 psi (6895 kPa). Valve spool and body must be renewed as a unit.

## HYDRAULIC CYLINDER

### All Models So Equipped

A cylinder repair kit is available to renew packing and "O" rings. To disassemble cylinder, remove snap ring from ram end of cylinder and withdraw end cap and ram from cylinder tube. Be sure to clean all parts thoroughly and lubricate packing and "O" rings with clean hydraulic oil when reassembling.

# FORD

## CONDENSED SPECIFICATIONS

| | GEAR DRIVE MODELS | | | |
|---|---|---|---|---|
| | **LT75** | **LT80** | **LT8** | **LT100, LT110** |
| Engine Make | B&S | Kohler | B&S | B&S |
| Model | 170702 | K181S | 190000 | 252707 |
| Bore | 3 in. (76.2 mm) | 2-15/16 in. (74.6 mm) | 3 in. (76.2 mm) | 3-7/16 in. (87.3 mm) |
| Stroke | 2-3/8 in. | 2-3/4 in. | 2-3/4 in. | 2-5/8 in. |
| Piston Displacement | 16.79 cu. in. (275 cc) | 18.6 cu. in. (305 cc) | 19.44 cu. in. (319 cc) | 24.36 cu. in. (399 cc) |
| Rated Power | 7 hp (5.2 kW) | 8 hp (5.9 kW) | 8 hp (5.9 kW) | 11 hp (8.2 kW) |
| Slow Idle Speed—Rpm | 1750 | 1000 | 1750 | 1750 |
| High Idle Speed (No-Load)—Rpm | 3600 | 3800 | 3600 | 3600 |
| Capacities— | | | | |
| Crankcase | 2-1/4 pts. (1 L) | 2-1/4 pts. (1 L) | 2-3/4 pts. (1.3 L) | 2-1/2 pts. (1.2 L) |
| Transmission | 1-1/2 pts. (0.7 L) | 1-1/2 pts. (0.7 L) | * | 1-1/2 pts. (0.7 L) |
| Weight | SAE 90 | SAE 90 | | SAE 90 |

*Refer to LUBRICATION under TRANSAXLE paragraphs.

---

| | GEAR DRIVE MODELS | | | |
|---|---|---|---|---|
| | **LT11** | **LT12** | **LGT100** | **LGT120** |
| Engine Make | B&S | B&S | Kohler | Kohler |
| Model | 250000 | 281707 | K241S | K301S |
| Bore | 3-7/16 in. (87.3 mm) | 3-7/16 in. (87.3 mm) | 3-1/4 in. (82.5 mm) | 3-3/8 in. (85.7 mm) |
| Stroke | 2-5/8 in. (66.7 mm) | 3-1/16 in. (77.7 mm) | 2-7/8 in. (73.0 mm) | 3-1/4 in. (82.5 mm) |
| Piston Displacement | 24.36 cu. in. (399 cc) | 28.42 cu. in. (465 cc) | 23.9 cu. in. (392 cc) | 29.07 cu. in. (476 cc) |
| Rated Power | 11 hp (8.2 kW) | 12 hp (8.9 kW) | 10 hp (7.4 kW) | 12 hp (8.9 kW) |
| Slow Idle Speed—Rpm | 1750 | 1750 | 1000 | 1000 |
| High Idle Speed (No-Load)—Rpm | 3600 | 3600 | 3600 | 3600 |
| Capacities— | | | | |
| Crankcase | 2-1/2 pts. (1.2 L) | 3 pts. (1.4 L) | 3 pts. (1.4 L) | 3 pts. (1.4 L) |
| Transmission | * | * | 4 pts. (1.9 L) | 4 pts. (1.9 L) |
| Weight | | | SAE 90 EP | SAE 90 EP |

*Refer to LUBRICATION under HYDROSTATIC TRANSMISSION paragraphs.

# CONDENSED SPECIFICATIONS

| | GEAR DRIVE MODELS |
|---|---|
| | LGT14 |
| Engine Make | Kohler |
| Model | M14 |
| Bore | 3-1/2 in. (88.9 mm) |
| Stroke | 3-1/4 in. (82.55 mm) |
| Piston Displacement | 31.27 cu. in. (512 cc) |
| Rated Power | 14 hp (10.4 kW) |
| Slow Idle Speed—Rpm | 1200 |
| High Idle Speed-(No-Load)—Rpm | 3400 |
| Capacities— | |
| Crankcase w/Filter | 4 pts. (1.9 L) |
| Transmission | 1-1/2 pts. (0.7 L) |
| Weight | SAE 90 EP |

| | HYDROSTATIC TRANSMISSION MODELS | | |
|---|---|---|---|
| | LT85 | LT11H | LT12H |
| Engine Make | B&S | B&S | B&S |
| Model | 191707 | 250000 | 281707 |
| Bore | 3 in. (76.2 mm) | 3-7/16 in. (87.3 mm) | 3-7/16 in. (87.3 mm) |
| Stroke | 2-3/4 in. (69.8 mm) | 2-5/8 in. (66.7 mm) | 3-1/16 in. (77.7 mm) |
| Piston Displacement | 19.44 cu.in. (319 cc) | 24.36 cu. in. (399 cc) | 28.4 cu. in. (465 cc) |
| Rated Power | 8 hp (5.9 kW) | 11 hp (8.2 kW) | 12 hp (8.9 kW) |
| Slow Idle Speed—Rpm | 1750 | 1750 | 1750 |
| High Idle Speed (No-Load)—Rpm | 3600 | 3600 | 3600 |
| Capacities— | | | |
| Crankcase | 2-3/4 pts. (1.3 L) | 2-1/2 pts. (1.2 L) | 3 pts. (1.4 L) |
| Transmission | * | * | * |

*Refer to LUBRICATION under HYDROSTATIC TRANSMISSION paragraphs.

| | HYDROSTATIC TRANSMISSION MODELS | | |
|---|---|---|---|
| | LGT12H | LGT125 | LGT14H |
| Engine Make | Kohler | Kohler | Kohler |
| Model | M12 | K341AS | M14 |
| Bore | 3-3/8 in. (85.7 mm) | 3-3/8 in. (85.7 mm) | 3-1/2 in. (88.9 mm) |
| Stroke | 3-1/4 in. (85.5 mm) | 3-1/4 in. (85.5 mm) | 3-1/4 in. (85.5 mm) |
| Piston Displacement | 29.07 cu. in. (476 cc) | 29.07 cu. in. (476 cc) | 31.27 cu. in. (512 cc) |
| Rated Power | 12 hp (8.9 kW) | 12 hp (8.9 kW) | 14 hp (10.4 kW) |
| Slow Idle Speed—Rpm | 1200 | 1000 | 1200 |
| High Idle Speed (No-Load)—Rpm | 3400 | 3600 | 3400 |
| Capacities— | | | |
| Crankcase | 4 pts. (1.9 L) | 3 pts. (1.4 L) | 4 pts. (1.9 L) |
| Transmission | * | * | * |

*Refer to LUBRICATION under HYDROSTATIC TRANSMISSION paragraphs.

# CONDENSED SPECIFICATIONS

| | HYDROSTATIC TRANSMISSION MODELS | | |
|---|---|---|---|
| | LGT140 | LGT145 | LGT165 |
| Engine Make | Kohler | Kohler | Kohler |
| Model | K321S | K321AS | K341S |
| Bore | 3-1/2 in. (88.9 mm) | 3-1/2 in. (88.9 mm) | 3-3/4 in. (95.2 mm) |
| Stroke | 3-1/4 in. (85.5 mm) | 3-1/4 in. (85.5 mm) | 3-1/4 in. (85.5 mm) |
| Piston Displacement | 31.27 cu. in. (512 cc) | 31.27 cu. in. (512 cc) | 35.89 cu. in. (588 cc) |
| Rated Power | 14 hp (10.4 kW) | 14 hp (10.4 kW) | 16 hp (11.9 kW) |
| Slow Idle Speed—Rpm | 1000 | 1000 | 1000 |
| High Idle Speed (No-Load)—Rpm | 3600 | 3600 | 3600 |
| Capacities— | | | |
| Crankcase | 4 pts. (1.9 L) | 3 pts. (1.4 L) | 3 pts. (1.4 L) |
| Transmission | * | * | * |

*Refer to LUBRICATION under HYDROSTATIC TRANSMISSION paragraphs.

# FRONT AXLE AND STEERING SYSTEM

## AXLE MAIN MEMBER

### All Models Except LT8-LT11-LT11H-LT12-LT12H-LGT12H-LGT14-LGT14H

Axle main member is center mounted to the frame and pivots on a bolt or pin riding in a tube or bushings. Refer to Figs. F1, F2 or F3 for an exploded view of front axle assembly. To remove front axle assembly, detach implement lift bars if so equipped. Raise and support front of tractor. Disconnect drag link ball joint from steering arm. Remove axle pivot bolt or pin and roll axle assembly from tractor.

Inspect axle pivot bushings and pivot bolt or pin for excessive wear and renew as necessary. Lubricate with multipurpose lithium base grease.

To reinstall axle assembly, reverse the removal procedure.

### Models LT8-LT11-LT11H-LT12-LT12H-LGT12H-LGT14-LGT14H

Axle main member is center mounted to the frame and pivots on a bolt (4—Fig. F4 or F5). To remove front axle assembly, first remove mower from tractor. Raise and support front of tractor. Disconnect drag link from left spindle steering arm. Loosen (do not remove) two rear cap screws attaching axle rear pivot bracket to frame, and remove the two front cap screws from pivot bracket. Remove axle pivot bolt, then pull axle assembly down and forward to remove from tractor.

Inspect axle pivot bushings (if used) and pivot bolt for excessive wear and renew as necessary. Lubricate with multipurpose lithium base grease.

## TIE ROD AND DRAG LINK

### All Models

Front wheel toe-in should be 1/8 to 1/4 inch (3-6 mm). To check toe-in, measure distance between front tires at front and rear of tires as shown in Fig. F6. To adjust tie rod for correct front wheel toe-in, disconnect tie rod from one of the steering spindles. Loosen locknuts and turn tie rod ends in or out as required to obtain recommended toe-in.

Turn steering wheel to full left turn. Left spindle should hit axle stop before steering gear reaches full left turn stop tab. To adjust steering stop, disconnect drag link from pitman arm and loosen drag link end jam nut. Move axle so left spindle is against axle stop. Turn steering wheel full left turn, then turn wheel approximately 1 inch (25 mm) clockwise. Adjust rod end on drag link until drag link can be easily connected to steering pitman arm. Retighten drag link end jam nut.

## STEERING SPINDLES

### All Models

To remove steering spindles, refer to Fig. F1, F2, F3, F4 or F5. Raise and support front of tractor, then remove front wheels. Disconnect tie rod and drag link from spindle steering arms. On all models except LGT12H, LGT14 and

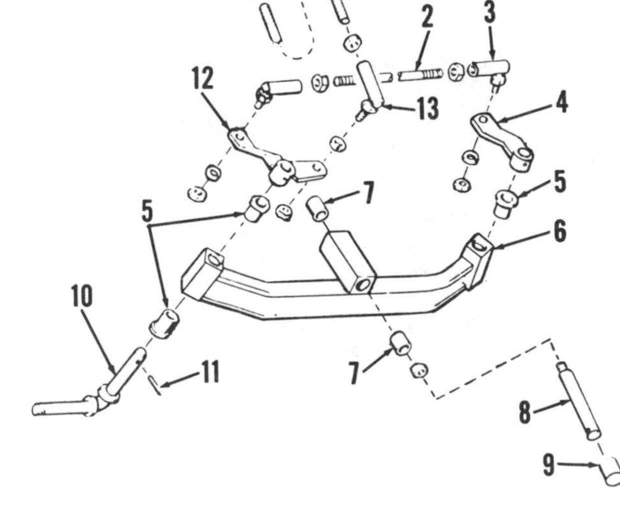


*Fig. F1—Exploded view of front axle assembly used on Models LT75, LT80, LT85, LT100 and LT110.*

1. Drag link
2. Tie rod
3. Ball joint
4. Tie rod arm
5. Bushing
6. Axle main member
7. Bushing
8. Pivot bolt
9. Cap
10. Steering spindle
11. Pin
12. Steering arm
13. Ball joint



Illustrations courtesy Ford New Holland, Inc.

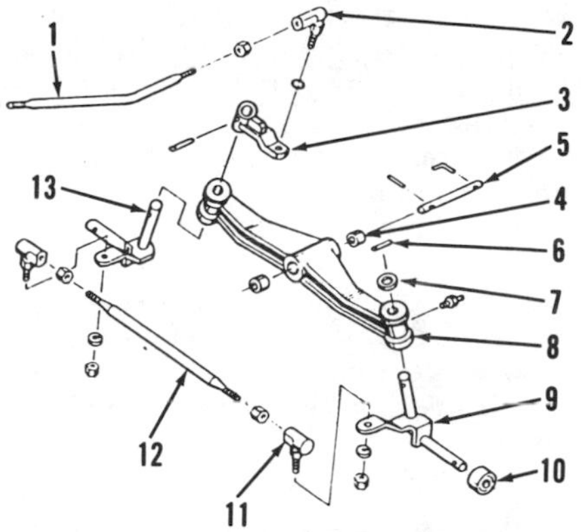

***Fig. F2—Exploded view of front axle assembly used on Models LGT100, LGT120, LGT125, LGT145 and LGT165.***

1. Drag link
2. Ball joint
3. Steering arm
4. Bushing (2)
5. Pivot pin
6. Roll pin
7. Washer
8. Axle main member
9. Steering spindle R.H.
10. Wheel bearing
11. Ball joint
12. Tie rod
13. Steering spindle L.H.

LGT14H, drive out roll pins and remove steering arms from spindles, then lower spindles from axle. On Models LGT12H, LGT14 and LGT14H, remove spindle king pins (8—Fig. F5) and remove spindles from axle.

Inspect spindles and spindle bushings (if so equipped) for excessive wear and renew as necessary. Reinstall by reversing removal procedure. Lubricate with multipurpose lithium base grease.

## STEERING GEAR

### Models LT75-LT80-LT85-LT100-LT110

**R&R AND OVERHAUL.** To remove steering gear, remove hood, disconnect battery cables and remove battery. Disconnect drag link from steering arm (12—Fig. F7). Remove steering wheel. Drive out pin and remove pinion gear (11). Withdraw steering shaft (4). Remove steering arm and then remove quadrant gear and shaft assembly (9).

To reassemble, reverse disassembly procedure. Adjust thrust spacer (15) to eliminate excessive gear backlash, but be sure gears do not bind when turning. Lubricate steering gears with light coat of multipurpose grease.

### Models LT8-LT11-LT12

**R&R AND OVERHAUL.** To remove steering gear, raise and secure hood. Disconnect battery cables and remove battery. Remove cotter pin (12—Fig. F8) and remove spacer (13). Loosen but do not remove the nuts from the two lower bearing retaining bolts (14). Compress bellows (5) to expose bolt (3). Remove bolt (3) and lift steering wheel (2), bellows cap (4) and bellows (5) off steering shaft (11). Disconnect drag link end (8) from steering sector shaft. Remove spring clip and clevis pin connecting end

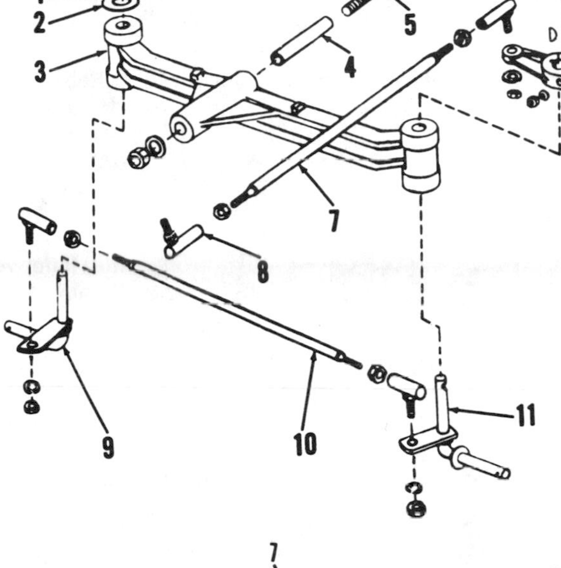

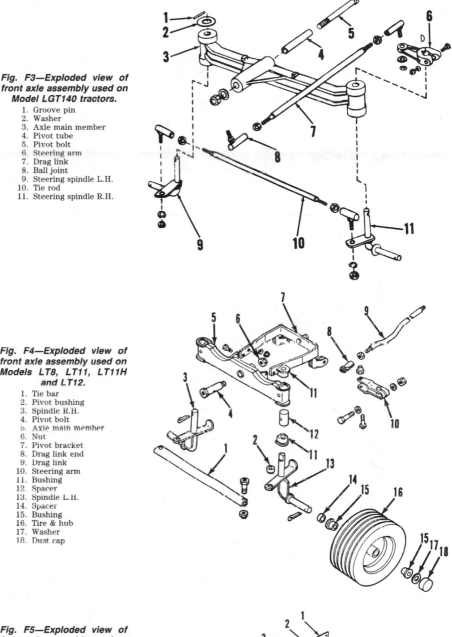

***Fig. F3—Exploded view of front axle assembly used on Model LGT140 tractors.***

1. Groove pin
2. Washer
3. Axle main member
4. Pivot tube
5. Pivot bolt
6. Steering arm
7. Drag link
8. Ball joint
9. Steering spindle L.H.
10. Tie rod
11. Steering spindle R.H.

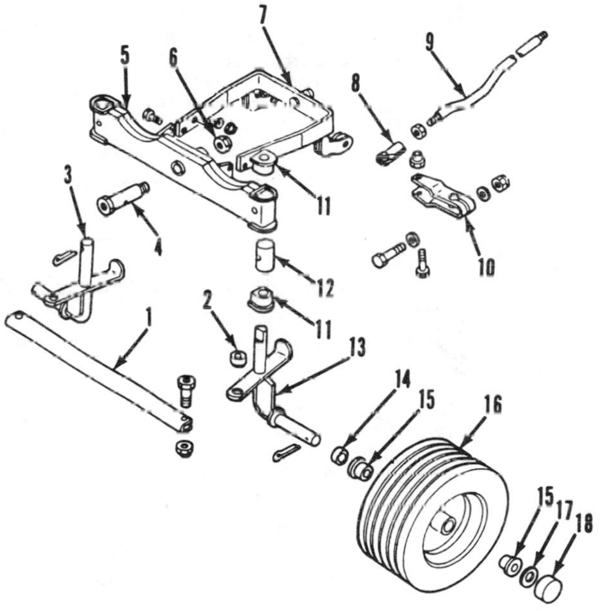

***Fig. F4—Exploded view of front axle assembly used on Models LT8, LT11, LT11H and LT12.***

1. Tie bar
2. Pivot bushing
3. Spindle R.H.
4. Pivot bolt
5. Axle main member
6. Nut
7. Pivot bracket
8. Drag link end
9. Drag link
10. Steering arm
11. Bushing
12. Spacer
13. Spindle L.H.
14. Spacer
15. Bushing
16. Tire & hub
17. Washer
18. Dust cap

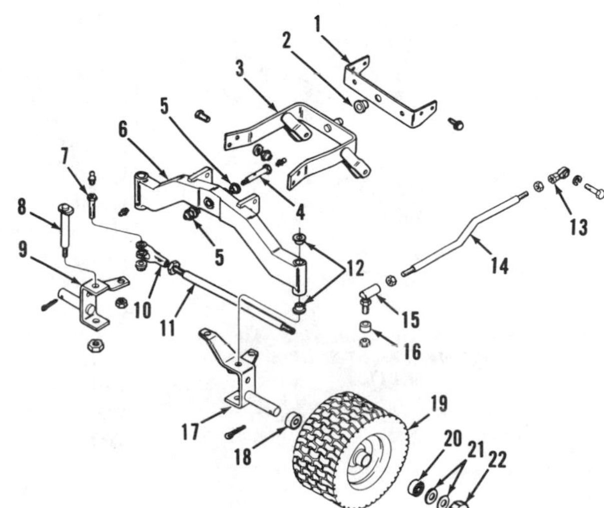

***Fig. F5—Exploded view of front axle assembly used on Models LGT12H, LGT14 and LGT14H.***

1. Rear pivot bracket
2. Bushing
3. Axle pivot support
4. Pivot bolt
5. Bushings
6. Axle main member
7. Tie rod cap screw
8. King pin
9. Spindle R.H.
10. Tie rod end
11. Tie rod
12. Bushings
13. Drag link end
14. Drag link
15. Ball joint end
16. Spacer
17. Spindle L.H.
18. Bearing (sealed)
19. Wheel
20. Bearing (unsealed)
21. Washer
22. Hub cap

of speed control rod to speed control bellcrank (gear selector lever at transaxle). Remove parking brake knob, jam nut and washers. Push brake link in and allow to drop down as far as possible. Remove slotted machine screw and remove pto lever "T" handle knobs. Remove the two cap screws retaining pto support bracket at bottom side of steering and pto crossmember, then work pto lever assembly out from behind the crossmember. Remove "E" clip (10) and carefully work plastic split bushing and steering sector out of crossmember. Remove bushing from steering sector. Locating tab on bushing should be aligned with slot in crossmember.

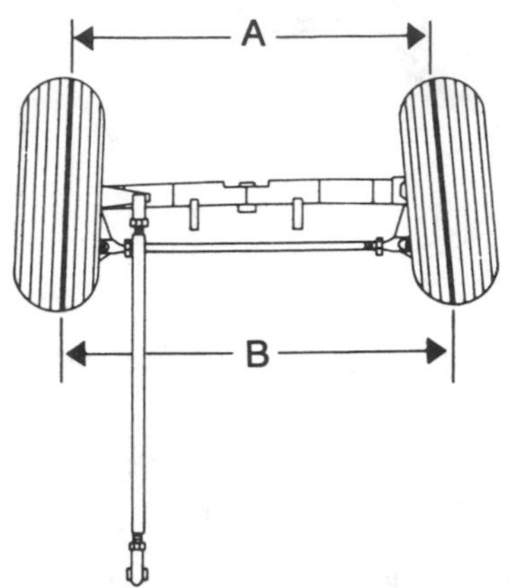


*Fig. F6—To check front wheel toe-in, measure distance (A) between front of tires and distance (B) between rear of tires at the same height. Distance (A) should be 1/8 to ¼ inch (3-6 mm) less than distance (B). Refer to text for adjustment procedure.*

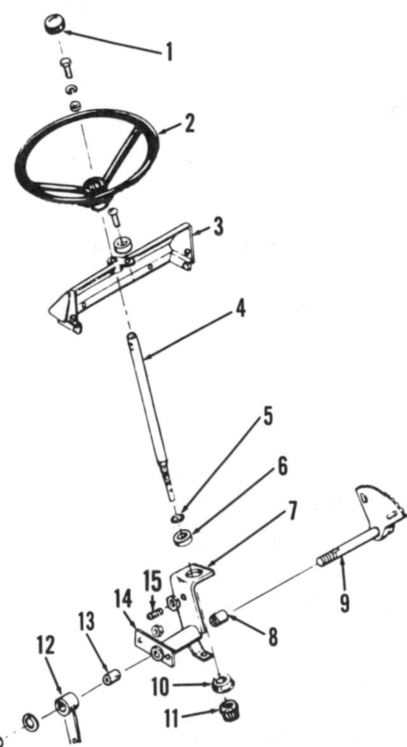


*Fig. F7—Exploded view of steering gear assembly used on Models LT75, LT80, LT85, LT100 and LT110.*

1. Cap
2. Steering wheel
3. Instrument panel
4. Steering shaft
5. "O" ring
6. Seal
7. Support assy.
8. Pivot bushing
9. Quadrant gear & shaft
10. Bearing
11. Pinion gear
12. Arm
13. Bushing
14. Shaft support
15. Thrust spacer

Remove the four cap screws retaining steering and pto support crossmember between frame. Rotate crossmember 90 degrees and work crossmember off of steering gear sector arm. Carefully drive top bushing on steering gear sector arm upward until unseated from frame saddle. Remove the throttle control knob. Remove the two screws attaching throttle control to instrument panel and work throttle control out slot in instrument panel. Remove necessary nuts and wire connections and remove ammeter from instrument panel. Remove the eight self-tapping screws along bottom side edges of instrument panel shroud and the two bolts (6) retaining upper bearing. Pivot front of instrument panel upward (note location of any electrical connections which may become disconnected) and lift panel off steering shaft. Pull steering shaft out of lower bearing. Remove lower bearing as required. Carefully remove steering sector assembly up out of frame.

When reinstalling steering assembly, liberally grease gear teeth with multipurpose lithium base grease. Steering wheel spokes should be centered with the centerline of tractor when front wheels are in the straight forward position. Gear mesh is controlled by position of lower bearing (15), and gears should mesh evenly and smoothly. Tighten bearing flange retaining bolts to 10-15 ft.-lbs. (13-20 N·m). Steering wheel play of $1^1/_2$ inches (38 mm), measured at outside diameter of steering wheel, is considered excessive and indicates need to adjust gear mesh or renew worn parts.

## Model LT11H-LT12H

**R&R AND OVERHAUL.** Raise and secure hood. Disconnect battery cables and remove battery. Remove cotter pin (12—Fig. F8) and remove spacer (13). Loosen but do not remove the nuts from the two lower bearing retaining bolts (14). Compress bellows (5) to expose bolt (3). Remove bolt (3) and lift steering wheel (2), bellows cap (4) and bellows (5) off steering shaft (11).

Turn steering wheel all the way to the right and disconnect drag link end (8). Remove the cap screw, locknut and washer holding steering arm to steering gear sector shaft, then pull steering arm off of shaft. Remove the key and spacer from steering gear sector shaft. Remove the throttle control knob. Remove the two screws attaching throttle control to instrument panel and work throttle out slot in instrument panel. Remove necessary nuts and wire connections and remove ammeter. Remove the two cap screws retaining upper bearing to instrument panel shroud. Remove the eight self-tapping screws from bottom side edges of instrument panel shroud. Lift front of instrument panel upward and over steering shaft and remove panel. Pull steering shaft out of lower bearing to remove. Push steering gear sector assembly up and out of hole in frame.

When reinstalling steering assembly, lubricate gear teeth with multipurpose lithium base grease. Steering wheel spokes should be centered with the centerline of tractor when front wheels are in the straight forward position. Gear mesh is controlled by lower bearing (15) position, and gears should mesh evenly and smoothly. Tighten bearing flange retaining bolts to 10-15 ft.-lbs. (13-20 N·m).

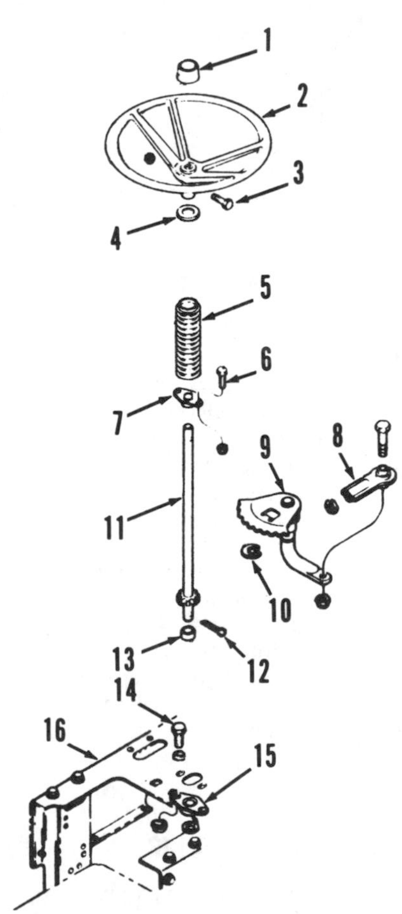


*Fig. F8—Exploded view of steering column used on Models LT8, LT11 LT11H and LT12.*

1. Cap
2. Steering wheel
3. Bolt
4. Retaining cap
5. Bellows
6. Bolt
7. Upper bearing
8. Drag link end
9. Steering sector
10. "E" clip
11. Steering shaft & gear
12. Cotter pin
13. Spacer
14. Bolt
15. Lower bearing
16. Frame



Illustrations courtesy Ford New Holland, Inc.

Steering wheel free play of $1^1/_2$ inches (38 mm), measured at outside diameter of steering wheel, is considered excessive and indicates need to adjust gear mesh or renew worn parts.

### Models LGT12H-LGT14-LGT14H

**R&R AND OVERHAUL.** Raise hood, disconnect battery cables and remove battery. On tractors equipped with adjustable height steering wheel, compress steering shaft bellows (6—Fig. F9) to expose steering shaft. Remove cap screw attaching sleeve (5) to steering shaft (8) and lift steering wheel (3), adapter (4), sleeve and bellows off steering shaft. On tractors with single height steering wheel, remove steering wheel cap (1) and unscrew cap screw (2) attaching steering wheel to steering shaft (8). Lift steering wheel and bellows (6) off steering shaft.

On all models, disconnect throttle and choke control cables from engine. Drain fuel and remove fuel tank. Remove screws attaching instrument panel to frame. Remove bolts attaching steering shaft upper bearing (7) to instrument panel. On hydrostatic drive tractors, remove "T" handle knob from traction drive lever. On all models, pull choke cable out from underneath steering mechanism while lifting instrument panel over steering shaft.

Disconnect drag link rod end from steering pitman arm (16). Remove four screws attaching steering mechanism to support channel (20). Remove retaining screw from pinion support brace (19), then lift steering mechanism from tractor.

To disassemble steering mechanism, remove nut (17) and separate pitman arm (16) from steering rod (10). Drive out spring pin (13) and withdraw steering shaft (8) from pinion gear (14). Inspect bushings (12 and 15) and renew as required. Check condition of sector gear (16) and pinion gear (14) teeth.

To reassemble and install steering mechanism, reverse disassembly and removal procedures. Do not tighten steering rod nut (17) until after unit is installed in tractor. Lubricate steering gear teeth with multipurpose lithium base grease. Lubricate bushings with SAE 30 engine oil. Be sure that choke cable is routed under steering mechanism when reinstalling assembly. Adjust gear mesh and steering wheel free play as follows:

There should be approximately 1 inch (25 mm) steering wheel free play, measured at outer diameter of steering wheel. To adjust, pull upward on steering wheel shaft to remove end play, then tighten steering rod nut (17) through hole in left side of instrument panel to obtain desired free play. Loosen nut to increase free play if steering is too tight.

On models with adjustable height steering wheel, install cap screw attaching sleeve (5) to steering shaft (8) through lowest hole in sleeve for HIGH steering wheel position, or through highest hole in sleeve for LOW steering wheel position.

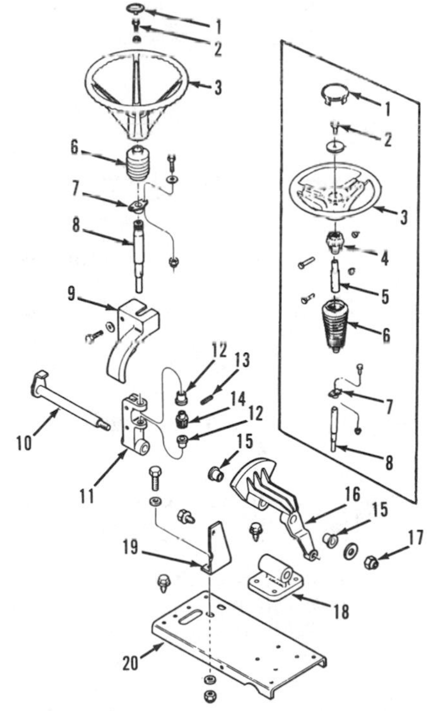

*Fig. F9—Exploded view of steering gear assembly used on Models LGT12H, LGT14 and LGT14H. Items shown in inset are used on tractors equipped with adjustable height steering wheel.*

1. Cap
2. Cap screw
3. Steering wheel
4. Adapter
5. Sleeve
6. Bellows
7. Bearing
8. Steering shaft
9. Cover
10. Sector shaft
11. Pinion support
12. Bushings
13. Roll pin
14. Pinion gear
15. Bushing
16. Sector gear & pitman arm assy.
17. Adjusting nut
18. Sector support
19. Pinion support
20. Steering support channel

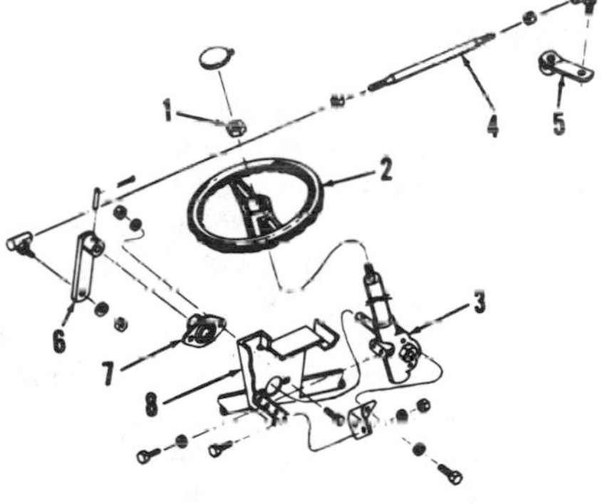

*Fig. F10—Exploded view of typical steering assembly used on Models LGT100, LGT120, LGT125, LGT145 and LGT165. Refer to Fig. F11 for exploded view of steering gear (3).*

1. Nut
2. Steering wheel
3. Steering gear assy.
4. Drag link
5. Steering arm
6. Steering lever
7. Bearing
8. Console

### Models LGT100-LGT120-LGT125-LGT145-LGT165

**R&R AND OVERHAUL.** To remove steering gear, first remove drive shaft and implements attached to underside of tractor which block steering gear removal. Remove hood. Drive out retaining pin to remove steering lever (6—Fig. F10) from steering gear (3) shaft. Unscrew steering wheel retaining nut (1) and pull steering wheel off steering shaft. Unscrew mounting bolts and remove steering gear out bottom of tractor.

To disassemble steering gear, unbolt and remove lever and shaft assembly (11—Fig. F11). Remove cam bearing adjuster plug (17), then bump steering cam assembly (15) out of steering column. Remove and inspect bearings and races.

To reassemble, reverse the disassembly procedure. After unit is assembled, tighten cam adjuster plug (17) until end play is removed from steering shaft (15), but shaft and cam must still rotate freely. Install cotter pin to prevent plug (17) from moving. Tighten inner nut (6) until steering lever (11) is $^3/_{32}$ inch (2.4 mm) from housing. Tighten jam nut (5) against nut (6). To adjust steering wheel free play, locate cam in mid-position (halfway between full right and full left

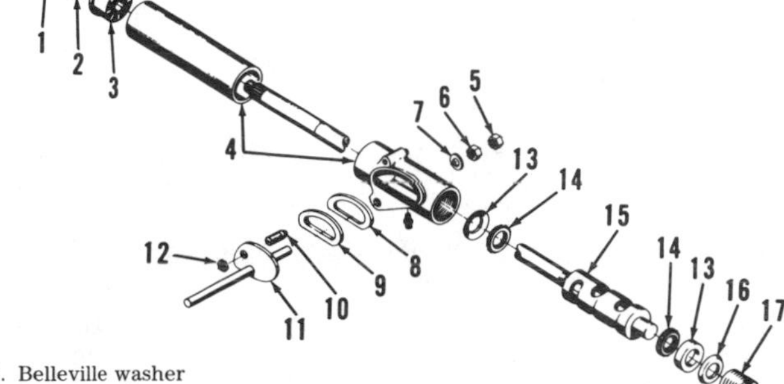

*Fig. F11—Exploded view of steering gear assembly used on Models LGT100, LGT120, LGT125, LGT145 and LGT165.*

1. Nut
2. Dust seal
3. Bearing
4. Housing
5. Jam nut
6. Adjusting nut
7. Washer
8. Seal
9. Seal retainer
10. Cam follower screw
11. Lever & shaft
12. Locknut
13. Bearing race
14. Bearing
15. Steering cam & shaft
16. Belleville washer
17. Adjusting plug

turn) and turn cam follower screw (10) in until zero backlash is obtained. Tighten locknut (12) to hold screw in position. Steering shaft should turn from lock-to-lock without binding. If steering binds, readjust cam follower screw (10). Lubricate steering gear through fitting on housing with multipurpose grease.

### Model LGT140

**R&R AND OVERHAUL.** To remove steering gear, first remove steering wheel (1—Fig. F12). Raise tractor hood and loosen set screw in collar (3). Using a jack or hoist, raise front of tractor. Disconnect drag link ball joint from quadrant arm and remove retaining ring (8) and washer (7) from quadrant shaft (5). Quadrant shaft can now be withdrawn from bushings (6) located in main frame.

Unbolt steering shaft support (10) from tractor frame and rotate support so it can be removed through frame opening. Steering shaft and pinion gear (4) can be lowered through frame opening and removed from underside of tractor. Bushings (2, 6 and 9) can now be renewed if excessive wear is evident.

Reassembly is reverse of disassembly procedure. Steering wheel play can be adjusted as follows: Loosen two bolts securing steering shaft support (10) to frame. Move support toward quadrant gear and tighten bolts. This adjustment moves pinion gear on steering shaft closer to quadrant gear, reducing backlash. Lubricate gear teeth and bushings with light coat of multipurpose grease.

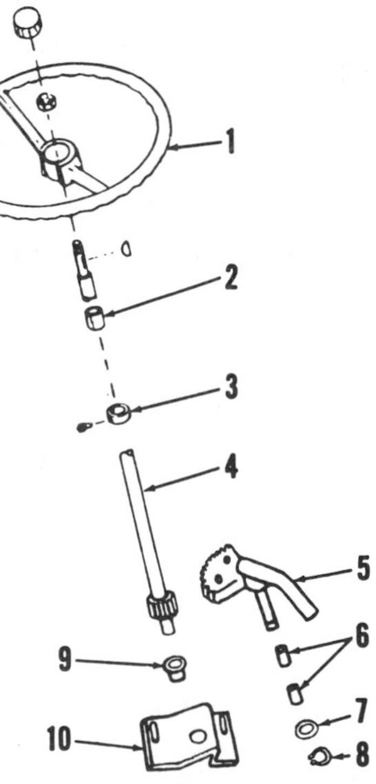

*Fig. F12—Exploded view of steering gear used on Model LGT140 tractors.*

1. Steering wheel
2. Shaft upper bushing
3. Collar
4. Steering shaft
5. Quadrant
6. Bushings
7. Washer
8. Retaining rings
9. Shaft lower bushing
10. Shaft support

# ENGINE

## LUBRICATION

### All Models

Engine oil should be changed after every 50 hours of operation. Drain oil from crankcase while engine is warm. Refill engine with recommended oil to FULL mark on dipstick. DO NOT overfill. When checking oil level, dipstick cap should be bottomed against top of oil fill tube.

Use a high quality detergent oil with API classification SF. Straight weight SAE 30 oil is recommended for use in temperatures above 32°F (0°C). Multiviscosity SAE 10W-30 oil is recommended for use when temperatures will be below 32°F (0°C). If multiviscosity oil is used in temperatures above 32°F (0°C), increased oil consumption may occur and more frequent oil changes are required.

## REMOVE AND REINSTALL

### Models LT75-LT85

To remove engine, remove tractor hood and shut off fuel valve under tank. Disconnect hose from carburetor inlet fitting. Disconnect throttle cable, battery cables, ignition wire and starter solenoid lead between starter and solenoid. Disconnect black wire and yellow wire at rectifier. Disconnect pto clutch actuator rod at front end of tractor. Remove pto drive belt. Remove tractor rear cover and rear belt guide, then remove main drive belt by depressing clutch pedal so tension is released on belt. Remove pulley from engine crankshaft. Remove engine mounting bolts and lift engine from tractor.

Reinstall engine by reversing removal procedure.

### Model LT80

To remove engine, first remove ground cable from battery. Disconnect fuel line from tank. Disconnect choke and throttle control cables from engine. Identify and disconnect ignition wires and wires from starter-generator. Unbolt and remove starter-generator. Remove left foot rest and drive belt rear guard. Remove attachment drive clutch control handle and remove thumb screw from attachment clutch housing bracket. Unbolt and remove front belt guard. Depress clutch-brake pedal and lock in down position with park brake. Remove engine mounting bolts. Remove drive belt from engine pulley and lift engine from tractor.

Reinstall by reversing removal procedure. Adjust drive belt as outlined in CLUTCH AND BRAKE section.

### Models LT8-LT11-LT12

To remove engine, first remove mower deck from tractor. Loosen (do not remove) cap screws retaining left and right transaxle pulley belt guides to frame and swing belt guides away from pulley. Remove belt guide from upper engine pulley. Depress clutch-brake pedal and set parking brake. Work drive belt off transaxle pulley and engine pulley. Disconnect the green headlight wire at connector clipped to right side of engine shroud. Remove hood retaining cable, hood hinge pin and hood. Disconnect battery cables. Identify and disconnect all necessary electrical wiring from engine. Disconnect throttle cable and choke cable from engine. Disconnect fuel line at fuel filter. Turn steering wheel until front wheels are as far right as possible. Remove the four cap screws retaining engine to engine base assembly, then lift engine from tractor.

Reinstall engine by reversing removal procedure.

### Model LT11H

To remove engine, first remove mower deck from tractor. Lift seat pan and loosen (do not remove) traction drive brake adjustment jam nut on top, right side of frame to allow primary traction drive belt to be worked off bottom of inner jackshaft pulley. Remove belt from upper engine pulley. Disconnect green headlight wire at connector clipped to right side of engine shroud. Remove hood retaining cable, hood hinge pin and hood. Disconnect battery cables. Identify and disconnect all necessary electrical wiring from engine. Disconnect throttle cable from engine. Disconnect fuel line at fuel filter. Remove the four cap screws retaining engine to engine base assembly, then lift engine from tractor.

Reinstall engine by reversing removal procedure. Adjust traction drive belt as outlined in DRIVE BELT paragraphs.

### Model LT12H

To remove engine, first remove mower deck from tractor. Work the primary traction drive belt off engine pulley. Remove hood retaining cable, hinge pin and hood. Disconnect battery cables. Identify and disconnect all necessary



Illustrations courtesy Ford New Holland, Inc.

electrical wiring from engine. Disconnect throttle cable from engine. Disconnect fuel line at carburetor. Remove cap screws attaching engine to engine base assembly and lift engine from tractor.

Reinstall engine by reversing removal procedure.

### Models LGT12H-LGT14-LGT14H

To remove engine, raise hood and disconnect green wire at connector at left corner of hood. Disconnect hood retaining cable, remove hood hinge pin and remove hood from tractor. Disconnect battery ground cable. Identify and disconnect electrical wiring to engine, starter and electric pto clutch. Disconnect fuel line at fuel filter. Disconnect throttle and choke control cables from engine. Remove U-bolt securing exhaust pipe to frame. On gear drive tractors, loosen two set screws on rear of drive shaft. On hydrostatic drive tractors, remove long set screw through notch in transmission cooling fan hub and loosen short set screw on rear of drive shaft. On all models, pry drive shaft forward to separate rear universal joint from gear box or transmission input shaft.

**NOTE: Drive shaft is a balanced assembly and must be reassembled the same way that it is removed. Scribe match marks on universal joints and drive shaft to ensure correct reassembly.**

Pull drive shaft out of front universal joint. Remove four cap screws attaching engine to mounting brackets. Lift engine from tractor.

To reinstall engine, reverse the removal procedure. Be sure that spacers are installed between engine mounting base and isolator brackets, and that ground strap is attached to left front cap screw. Align match marks on drive shaft and universal joints. Make certain that foam gasket attached to baffle plate is tight against engine shroud. If necessary, adjust baffle forward until foam gasket seals against engine shroud.

### Models LT100-LT110-LGT100-LGT120

To remove engine, first remove mower deck from tractor. Remove ground cable from battery. Disconnect fuel line from tank, then unbolt and remove fuel tank assembly. Identify and disconnect ignition wires and starter-generator wires. Remove starter-generator belt guard and starter-generator assembly. Disconnect choke and throttle control cables. Unbolt and remove foot rest and drive belt rear guard. Remove pto drive clutch control handle and remove thumb screws from pto clutch housing bracket. Rotate housing to separate from bracket. Unbolt and remove front belt guard. Fully depress clutch-brake pedal and lock park brake to hold pedal down. Unbolt engine from tractor frame, remove drive belt from engine pulley and lift engine from tractor.

Reinstall by reversing removal procedure and adjust drive belt as outlined in CLUTCH AND BRAKE section.

### Model LGT125-LGT145-LGT165

To remove engine, remove hood and disconnect battery cables, ignition wires and starter wires. Disconnect pto clutch wires and pto belt on models so equipped. Detach choke and throttle rods and remove drive shaft shield. Disconnect drive shaft. Drain engine oil, unscrew engine mounting bolts on underside of oil pan and lift engine out of tractor.

To install engine, reverse removal procedure. Refill engine with recommended lubricant.

### Model LGT140

To remove engine, raise hood and disconnect battery cables. Disconnect fuel line, then unbolt and remove fuel tank assembly. Identify and disconnect ignition wires and wires from starter-generator. Unbolt and remove belt guard and starter-generator assembly. Disconnect choke and throttle control cables. Remove left foot rest and drive belt rear guard. Disconnect pto clutch wires. Pull clutch cover rod outward, rotate cover and remove assembly from engine. Depress clutch-brake pedal and remove transmission drive belt from engine pulley. Remove engine mounting bolts and lift engine from tractor.

Reinstall engine by reversing removal procedure.

## OVERHAUL

### All Models

Engine make and model are listed at the beginning of this section. To overhaul engine components and accessories, refer to Briggs & Stratton and Kohler sections of this manual.

# CLUTCH AND BRAKE

### Models LT75-LT85

**ADJUSTMENT.** The clutch idler pulley is spring loaded and does not require adjustment. Drive belt should be inspected for excessive wear or stretching which may result in clutch slippage.

Brake should be adjusted so brake is not engaged until clutch is disengaged. To adjust brake, turn adjusting nut (1—Fig. F13) until correct brake action is obtained.

### Models LT80-LT100-LT110-LGT100-LGT120-LGT140

**ADJUSTMENT.** To adjust clutch and brake linkage, first remove left foot rest and drive belt rear guard. With clutch-brake pedal in upper (clutch engaged) position, measure distance between inner sides of drive belt directly over clutch idler pulley as shown in Fig. F14. This distance must be $1^{7}/_{8}$ to $2^{1}/_{8}$ inches (48-54 mm). If not, loosen engine mounting bolts and move engine forward or rearward as required until proper dimension "A" is obtained.

Depress clutch-brake pedal until brake band is tight on brake drum and lock park brake. Measure distance (dimension "B"—Fig. F15) between flange of clutch idler pulley to lower edge of frame. This distance must be 1 to $1^{1}/_{4}$ inches (25-32 mm). If not, release brake lock and on Model LGT140, adjust nut on front of brake rod until dimension "B" is correct. On all other models, disconnect brake rod retainer from brake arm as shown in Fig. F16 and adjust retainer on brake rod to obtain correct dimension "B."

Reinstall belt guard and foot rest.

### Models LT8-LT11-LT12

**ADJUSTMENT.** The clutch idler pulley is spring loaded and does not require adjustment. If belt slippage occurs, drive belt should be inspected for excessive wear or stretching and renewed as required.

To adjust brake, fully depress brake pedal and set parking brake. Spring on brake rod (Fig. F17) should be compressed to $2^{1}/_{4}$ inches (57 mm). Adjust by turning locknut. With spring correctly adjusted, depress brake pedal and try to push tractor in forward. If brake does not stop rear wheels, release brake pedal and loosen jam nut at brake lever. Tighten inner adjustment nut until rear wheels cannot be turned when pedal is depressed. Rear wheels should be free to turn with brake pedal in up position. If brake pad drags against brake disc when pedal is up, loosen adjusting nut slightly. Hold adjusting nut and tighten jam nut against it. If correct brake adjustment cannot be obtained, renew brake pads.

**OVERHAUL.** To renew brake pads, raise and support rear of tractor. Re-

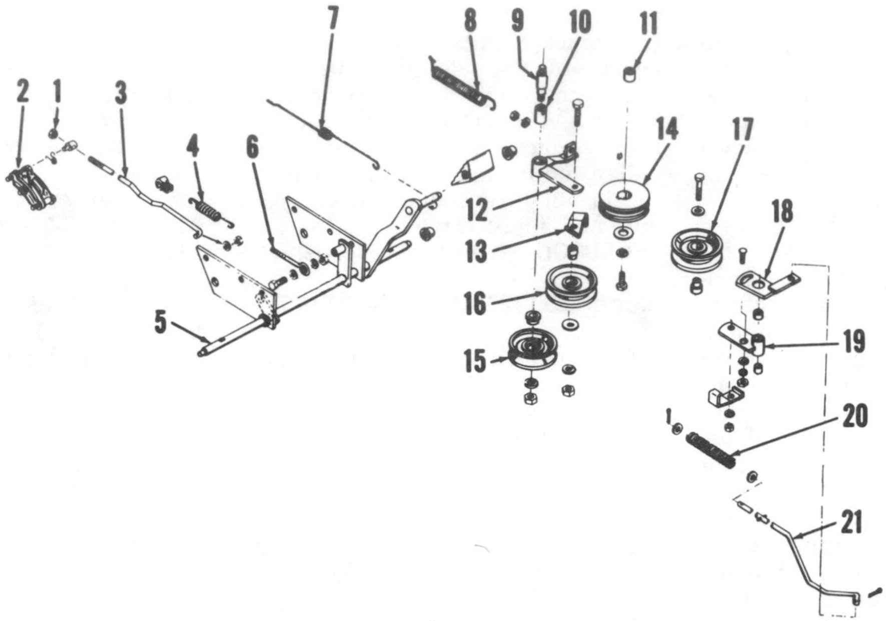


*Fig. F13—Exploded view of clutch and brake assembly used on Models LT75 and LT85. Brake adjusting nut is at opposite end of control rod (3) on Model LT85.*

1. Adjusting nut
2. Brake assy.
3. Brake rod
4. Spring
5. Pedal & shaft
6. Idler arm link
7. Pedal return spring
8. Spring
9. Idler shaft
10. Bushing
11. Spacer
12. Clutch idler arm
13. Belt retainer
14. Engine pulley
15. Idler pulley
16. Clutch idler pulley
17. Pto idler pulley
18. Pto lever
19. Pivot lever
20. Spring
21. Pto control rod

*Fig. F14—On Models LT80, LT100, LT110, LGT100, LGT120 and LGT140, clutch adjustment is correct when dimension "A" is 1-7/8 to 2-1/8 inches (48-54 mm) with clutch engaged.*

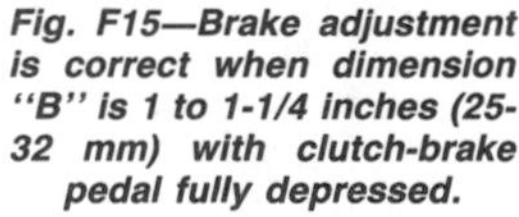

*Fig. F15—Brake adjustment is correct when dimension "B" is 1 to 1-1/4 inches (25-32 mm) with clutch-brake pedal fully depressed.*



Illustrations courtesy Ford New Holland, Inc.

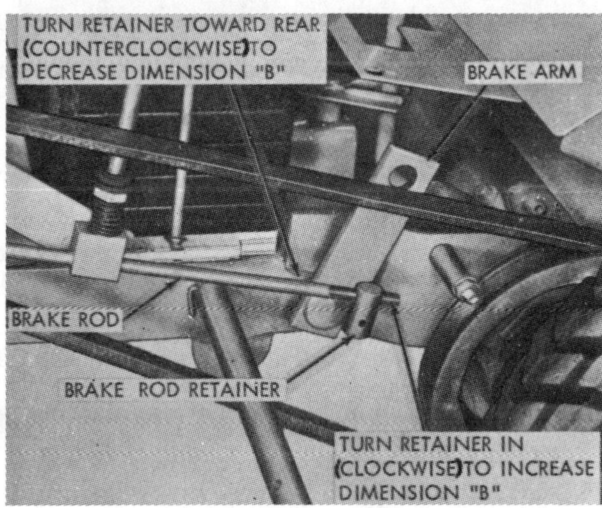


*Fig. F16—View showing location and method of brake adjustment. On Model LGT140, adjustment nut is on front of brake rod. Refer to text.*

move "E" ring from axle and remove right rear wheel and tire assembly. Disconnect brake rod from brake lever. Remove two screws retaining brake pad holder (5—Fig. F18) to transaxle case. Remove outer brake pad, back-up plate (2) and actuator pins (4) from holder. Withdraw brake disc (3) from transaxle shaft and remove inner brake pad.

Reassembly is reverse of disassembly. Adjust brake as previously outlined.

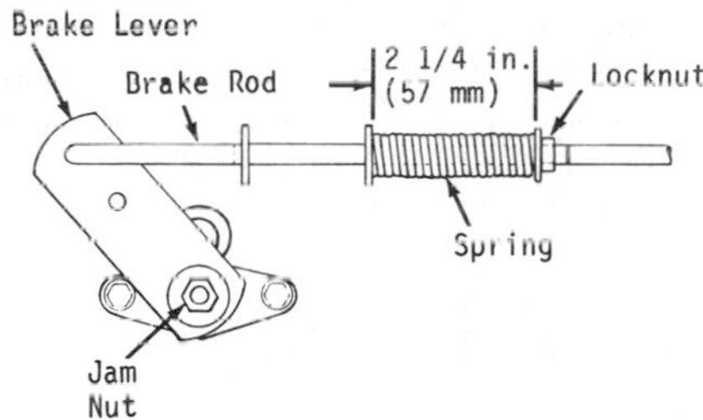


*Fig. F17—With brake pedal fully depressed, brake spring should measure 2-1/4 inches (57 mm) on Models LT8, LT11 and LT12. Refer to text.*

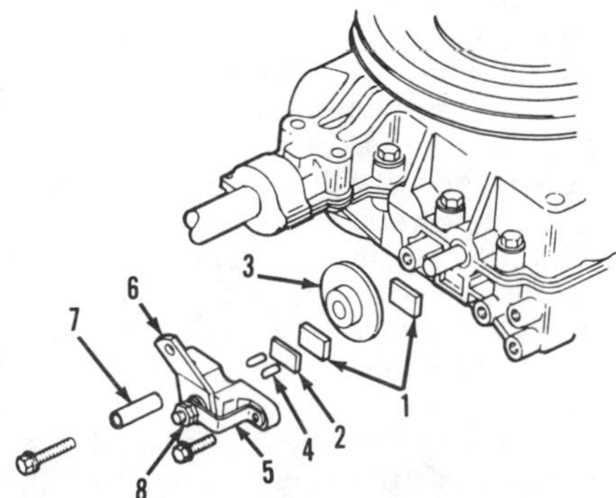

*Fig. F18—Exploded view of disc brake assembly used on Models LT8, LT11 and LT12.*

1. Brake pads
2. Back plate
3. Brake disc
4. Actuating pins
5. Brake pad holder
6. Brake lever
7. Spacer
8. Adjusting nuts

## Models LT11H

**ADJUSTMENT.** Clutch-brake pedal is designed to return hydrostatic transmission control lever to neutral position when depressed. If tractor creeps forward or backward after pedal is fully depressed, adjust linkage as outlined under ADJUSTMENT in the following HYDROSTATIC TRANSMISSION paragraphs.

To adjust brake, first adjust brake rod locknut to dimension shown in Fig. F19. Depress brake pedal and set park brake. Loosen jam nut and tighten brake adjustment nut (Fig. F19) until brake pads are tight against brake disc. Hold adjustment nut and tighten jam nut.

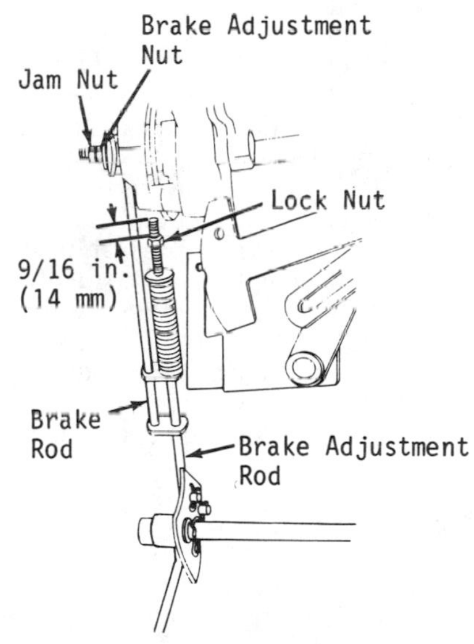


*Fig. F19—Locknut on brake adjustment rod must be located 9/16 inch (14 mm) from rod end. Refer to text.*

**OVERHAUL.** To renew brake pads, raise and support rear of tractor. Remove "E" ring from axle and remove right rear wheel. Disconnect brake rod from brake lever. Remove two screws attaching brake caliper to differential case and withdraw brake assembly.

Inspect all parts for excessive wear and renew as required. Reassembly is reverse of disassembly procedure. Adjust brake as previously outlined.

## Model LGT14

**ADJUSTMENT.** The clutch idler pulley is spring loaded and does not require adjustment. If slippage occurs, drive belt should be inspected for excessive wear or stretching and renewed as necessary.

To adjust brake, depress clutch-brake pedal and set parking brake. Brake rod spring (Fig. F20) should be compressed to length of $2^1/_2$ inches (63.5 mm). To adjust spring length, turn brake rod nut as necessary. With brake pedal depressed, try to push tractor forward. If brake does not stop rear wheels from turning, release brake and remove cotter pin (Fig. F20) from brake adjusting nut. Turn nut clockwise to tighten brake pads against brake disc. Clearance between outer brake pad and brake disc should be 0.015 inch (0.38 mm) with brake pedal released. Depress brake pedal and push tractor forward. If brake does not perform properly, brake pads should be renewed.

**OVERHAUL.** To renew brake pads, raise and support rear of tractor. Remove left rear wheel. Disconnect brake control rod from brake lever. Remove

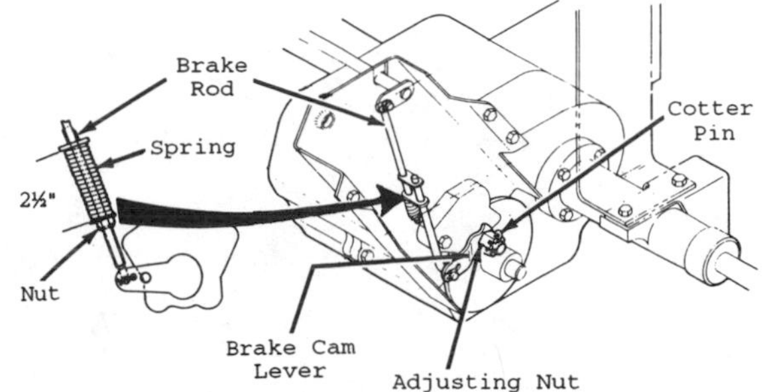


*Fig. F20—On Model LGT14, brake rod spring should be compressed to length of 2-1/2 inches (63.5 mm) when clutch-brake pedal is fully depressed. Refer to text for adjustment procedure.*

cap screws securing brake assembly to transaxle (Fig. F20A). Be sure to note position of flat and tube type spacers located on inside of brake. Pull brake disc off brake shaft and remove inner brake pad from transaxle housing.

Inspect all parts for excessive wear and renew as necessary. To reassemble, reverse the disassembly procedure. Adjust brake as previously outlined.

### Model LGT14H

**ADJUSTMENT.** Clutch-brake pedal is designed to return hydrostatic transmission control lever to neutral position when depressed. If tractor creeps forward or backward after pedal is fully depressed, adjust linkage as outlined under ADJUSTMENT in the following HYDROSTATIC TRANSMISSION paragraphs.

To adjust brake, depress clutch-brake pedal and set park brake. Remove cotter pin from castle nut (2—Fig. F21) and turn nut clockwise until brake pads are tight against brake disc. Reinstall cotter pin and check brake operation. Make sure brake does not drag when clutch-brake pedal is in up position.

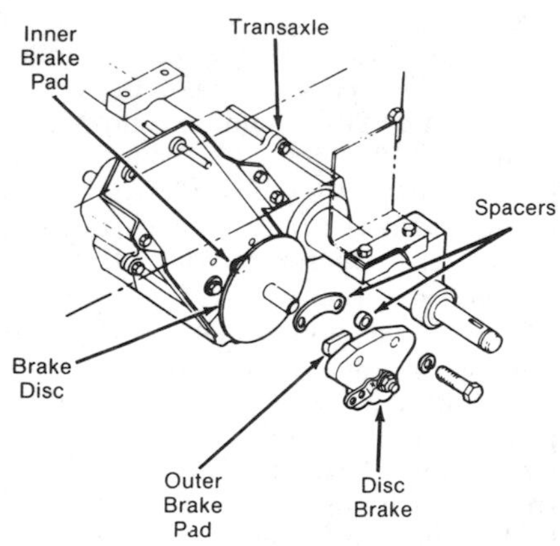


*Fig. F20A—Exploded view of brake assembly used on Model LGT14.*

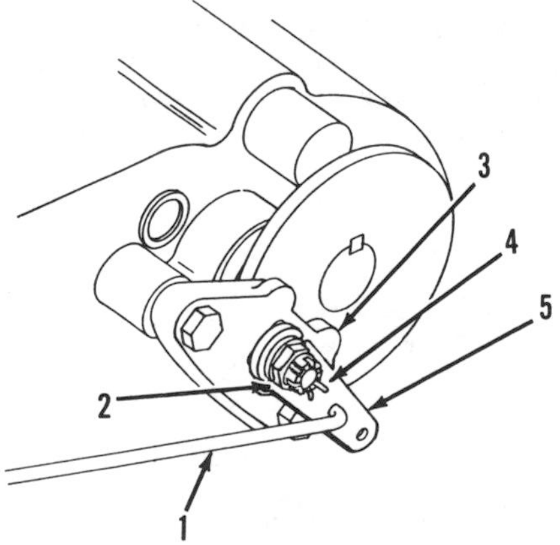


*Fig. F21—View of disc brake assembly used on Models LGT12H and LGT14H. Refer to text for adjustment procedure.*

**OVERHAUL.** To renew brake pads, raise and support rear of tractor. Remove left rear wheel. Disconnect brake rod from brake lever. Remove brake mounting bolts and remove brake assembly.

Inspect all parts for excessive wear and renew as necessary. Reassembly is reverse of disassembly procedure. Adjust brake as previously outlined.

### Models LGT125-LGT145-LGT165

**ADJUSTMENT.** These models are not equipped with a clutch. A band type brake operates against a drum attached to a shaft extending from differential unit. Refer to Fig. F22 and turn jam nut (B) and adjusting nut (A) until desired brake adjustment is obtained. Be sure brake does not drag when brake pedal is released.

# DRIVE BELT

### Model LT75

**REMOVE AND REINSTALL.** To remove transaxle drive belt, remove cover plate at rear of tractor. Depress clutch-brake pedal and set parking brake. Remove pto drive belt from lower groove of engine pulley and transaxle drive belt from upper groove. Work belt free from belt guides and idler pulleys. Remove belt from transmission input pulley. Move belt up through shift lever opening then over end of shift lever and back down through shift lever opening. Remove belt from tractor.

Install belt by reversing removal procedure. Be sure belt is not twisted and not riding on any belt guides with clutch-brake pedal released. No adjustment is required to the spring loaded belt idler pulley.

### Model LT85

**REMOVE AND REINSTALL.** To remove primary drive belt, fully depress clutch-brake pedal and set parking brake. Remove belt from right angle drive pulley. Remove pto drive belt from lower groove of engine pulley and primary drive belt from upper groove. Work drive belt free from idler pulleys and belt guides and remove from tractor.

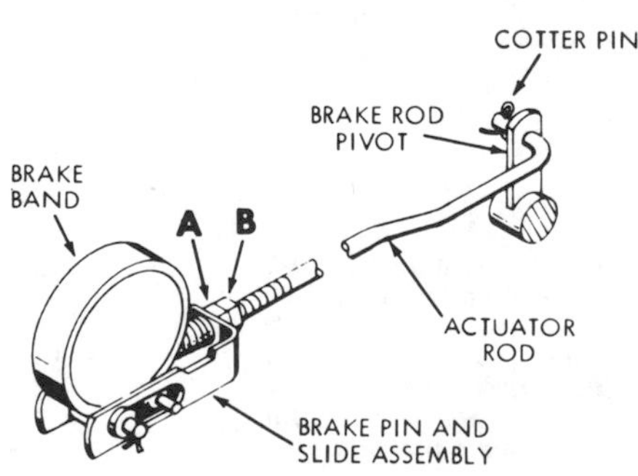


*Fig. F22—View of brake assembly used on Models LGT125, LGT145 and LGT165. Adjust brake by turning adjusting nut (A) and jam nut (B).*

To install primary drive belt, reverse removal procedure. Be sure belt is not twisted and not riding on any belt guides when clutch is engaged.

To remove secondary drive belt, remove seat and fender assembly. Release spring tension on idler pulley and remove drive belt between right angle drive and transaxle. Reverse removal procedure to reinstall belt.

There is no adjustment required for either belt.

### Models LT8-LT11-LT12

**REMOVE AND REINSTALL.** To remove transaxle drive belt, first remove mower deck. Depress clutch-brake pedal and set parking brake. Note position of belt guides (Fig. F23), then remove cap screws retaining flat idler pulley (4) and "V" idler pulley (2) to clutch pivot bracket (1). Disconnect speed control rod clevis or gear select lever (as equipped) at transaxle. Loosen (do not remove) left and right transaxle belt guides (13) and swing them out of the way. Remove belt guide (8) from engine upper drive pulley (6), then slip traction drive belt down and off both engine pulleys and through lower belt guide (9).

When installing new belt, guides must be positioned $^{1}/_{8}$ inch (3 mm) from belt and pulley when belt is tight. The spring loaded clutch idler pulleys do not require adjustment.

### Model LT11H

**REMOVE AND REINSTALL.** To remove primary drive belt, first remove mower deck. Lift fender and seat support up and loosen primary drive belt adjustment nuts (Fig. F24). Work belt (3—Fig. F25) off bottom of inner jackshaft pulley, then remove belt from engine pulley and through belt guide.

Install primary drive belt by reversing removal procedure. Belt tension should be adjusted using the primary belt adjusting nuts so that light pressure on belt at a point midway between engine pulley and jackshaft pulley deflects belt 1 inch (25 mm).

Secondary drive belt (1—Fig. F25) can be removed after primary belt has been removed. Pull spring loaded idler down to loosen belt. Remove belt from outer jackshaft pulley (2) and transmission pulley. Work belt between the flexible fan blades and fan guard to remove.

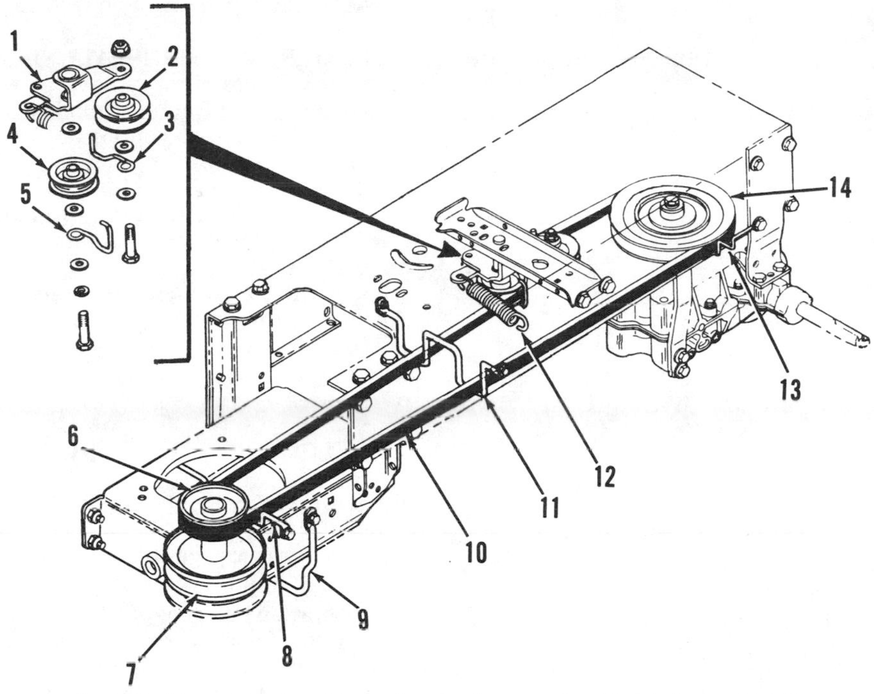

Fig. F23—View of traction drive belt and pulleys used on Models LT8 and LT11.

1. Clutch pivot bracket
2. V-idler pulley
3. Belt guide
4. Flat idler pulley
5. Belt guide
6. Engine pulley (traction drive)
7. Engine pulley (pto)
8. Belt retainer, upper
9. Belt retainer, lower
10. Traction belt
11. Belt guide
12. Idler spring
13. Belt guide
14. Transaxle pulley

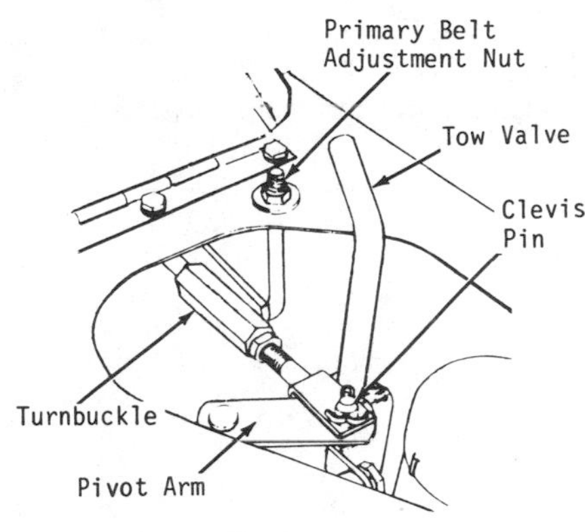

Fig. F24—View showing location of primary drive belt adjustment nuts on Model LT11H.

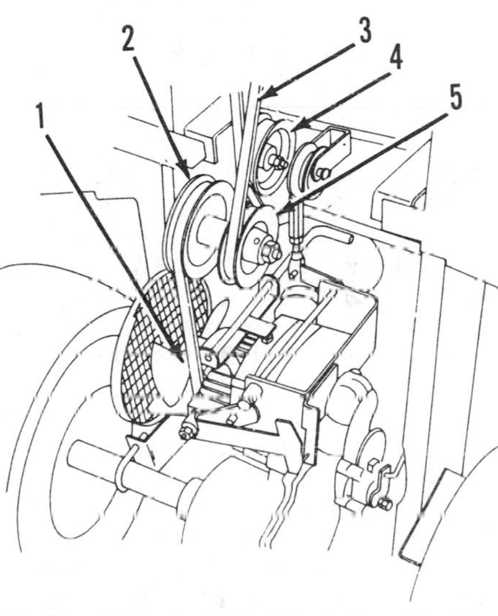

Fig. F25—View of traction drive belts and pulleys used on Model LT11H.

1. Secondary drive belt
2. Jackshaft outer pulley
3. Primary drive belt
4. Flat idler pulley
5. Jackshaft inner pulley

Install secondary drive belt by reversing removal procedure. No adjustment of spring loaded idler is required.

## Model LT12H

**REMOVE AND REINSTALL.** To remove primary drive belt (2—Fig. F25A), first remove mower deck. Work the belt off the engine pulley (1) while turning engine pulley clockwise by hand. Remove belt from jackshaft pulley (7), then pull belt forward through belt guide.

To install primary drive belt, reverse the removal procedure. No adjustment of belt tension is required.

Secondary drive belt (3) can be removed after primary belt has been removed. Pull spring loaded idler (6) to relieve tension on belt. Remove belt from jackshaft pulley and transmission pulley. Work belt around the fan blades and remove from tractor.

To install secondary belt, reverse the removal procedure. Be sure that spring loaded idler pulley (6) is positioned on back side of belt. No adjustment of idler is required.

## Model LGT14

**REMOVE AND REINSTALL.** To remove traction drive belt (4—Fig. F26), first remove nut attaching V-idler pulley (11) to idler arm (7). Depress clutch-brake pedal and set parking brake. Slide V-idler pulley off shaft until belt is clear of belt guide (6). Remove belt retaining flat idler pulley (5) and remove pulley and belt guide (12). Remove belt from right angle gear box pulley and transaxle pulley.

To install new belt, reverse the removal procedure. Be sure that flat

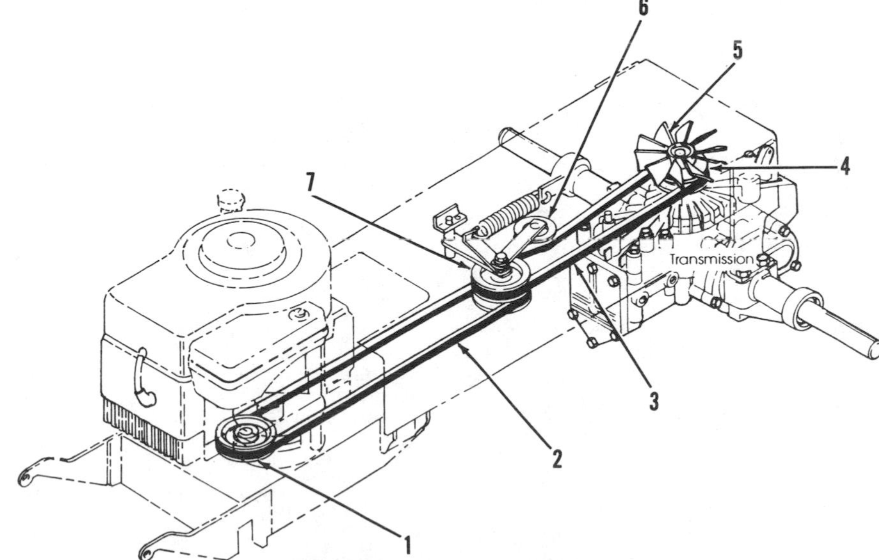

Fig. F25A—View of traction drive belts and pulleys used on Model LT12H.

1. Engine pulley
2. Primary traction belt
3. Secondary traction belt
4. Transmission drive pulley
5. Fan
6. Spring loaded idler
7. Jackshaft pulley

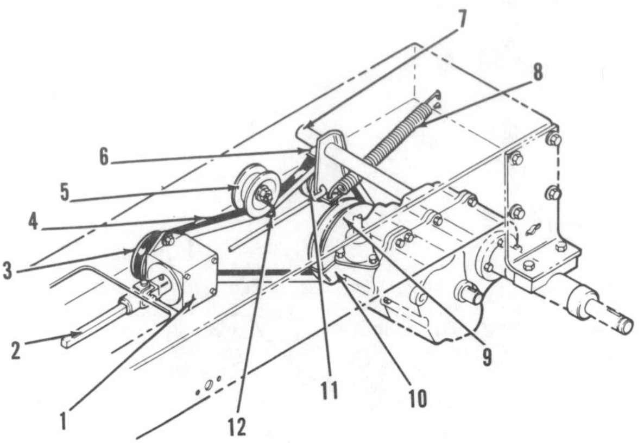


*Fig. F26—View of traction drive belt used on Model LGT14.*

1. Angle gear box
2. Drive shaft
3. Pulley
4. Traction drive belt
5. Flat idler pulley
6. Belt guide
7. Movable idler arm
8. Spring
9. Transaxle pulley
10. Belt guide
11. V-idler pulley
12. Belt guide

side of belt runs under flat idler pulley. The spring loaded idler does not require any adjustment.

## Models LT80-LT100-LT110-LGT100-LGT120-LGT140

**REMOVE AND REINSTALL.** To remove transaxle drive belt, remove left foot rest and rear belt guard. On later models, remove electric pto clutch from engine crankshaft as outlined in ELECTRIC PTO CLUTCH section. On early models, remove pto drive clutch control handle and remove thumb screw from clutch housing bracket. Rotate housing to separate it from bracket. On all models, unbolt and remove front belt guard. Fully depress clutch-brake pedal and lock park brake. Loosen setscrew in transaxle input pulley and slide pulley out on shaft so belt will clear upper and lower belt retainers. Remove drive belt from input pulley first and then from engine drive pulley.

To install new belt, reverse removal procedure. Adjust clutch and brake as previously outlined.

### DRIVE SHAFT

## Models LGT12H-LGT14-LGT14H

**REMOVE AND REINSTALL.** To remove drive shaft, first remove mower deck from under tractor.

**NOTE: Drive shaft is a balanced assembly and must be reassembled the same as it was removed. Scribe match marks on universal joints and drive shaft prior to removal to ensure correct reassembly.**

On gear drive tractors, loosen two setscrews in rear universal joint (Fig. F27). On hydrostatic drive tractors, remove one long setscrew from rear universal joint through notch in fan hub and loosen short setscrew in rear universal joint. On all models, pry drive shaft forward until rear universal joint is free from gear box or transmission input shaft. Pull drive shaft out of front universal joint and remove from tractor. Unbolt and remove front universal joint from engine.

If drive shaft is worn or damaged, renew drive shaft as an assembly. To reinstall drive shaft, reverse removal procedure making sure that match marks on universal joints and shaft are aligned.

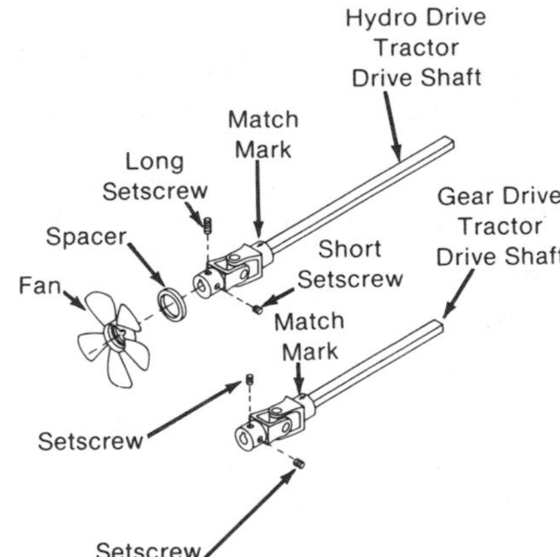


*Fig. F27—View of drive shaft (upper) used on Models LGT12H and LGT14H and drive shaft (lower) used on Model LGT14. Note that drive shafts are balanced assemblies and must be reassembled in same position as removed.*

## Models LGT125-LGT145-LGT165

**REMOVE AND REINSTALL.** To remove drive shaft, first remove mower deck from under tractor. Unbolt drive shaft front and rear couplings (6 and 1—Fig. F28). Loosen setscrew (7) in front coupling and slide coupling forward on engine crankshaft. Remove flexible coupling discs (3), then remove drive shaft (4).

Inspect drive shaft for bending and flexible discs for excessive wear or damage and renew as necessary. Reinstall drive shaft by reversing removal procedure.

### ELECTRIC PTO CLUTCH

## All Models So Equipped

**ADJUSTMENT.** Clutch should be adjusted if clutch has been disassembled or if operation becomes erratic. Remove front grille for access to clutch. With clutch disengaged, insert a feeler gage through slot in clutch plate (Fig. F30) and measure clearance between clutch rotor and armature. Clearance should be 0.012 inch (0.30 mm). To adjust, tighten the adjusting nut next to the slot until feeler gage just begins to bind. Do not overtighten. Repeat adjustment at each of the slots in clutch plate. All slots must be adjusted equally.

**TESTING.** Use the following procedure for locating pto malfunction. Turn ignition switch to "ON" position and actuate pto switch. If clutch does not engage, disconnect wiring connector at field coil and use a 12-volt test lamp to check continuity of wire coming from pto switch. If lamp lights, pto is either defective or wiring connection at clutch field coil is poor.

To check field coil, disconnect clutch wire harness connector. Using an ohmmeter set to low scale, connect one probe to clutch field coil wire and other probe to clutch flange. Normal resis-

*Fig. F28—Exploded view of drive shaft assembly used on Models LGT125, LGT145 and LGT165.*

1. Transmission coupling
2. Bearing
3. Flexible coupling discs
4. Drive shaft
5. Bushing
6. Engine coupling
7. Setscrew

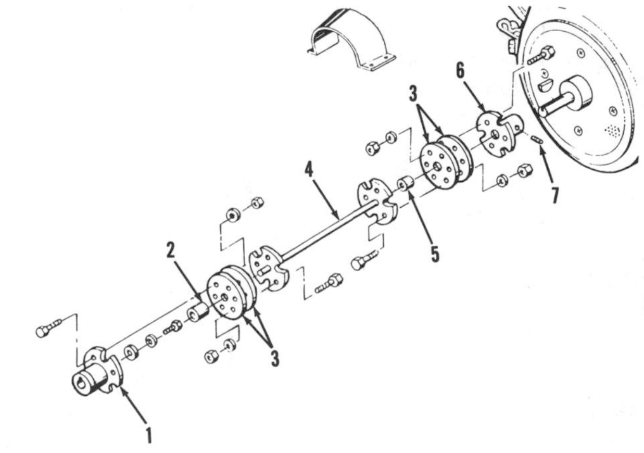




Illustrations courtesy Ford New Holland, Inc.

tance reading is 2.05-2.77 ohms. A reading outside this range indicates field coil is faulty and unit should be renewed.

**REMOVE AND REINSTALL.** To remove pto clutch, first remove front grille. Disconnect clutch wire at the connector. Slip drive belt out of clutch pulley. Hold the clutch assembly and remove retaining cap screw, square bearing washer and spacer from front of clutch. Remove cap screws attaching field coil housing to engine, then pull clutch assembly off crankshaft.

Inspect bearings in field housing and armature for wear or damage. Inspect contact surfaces of rotor and armature for scoring, grooves or other damage. Renew clutch unit as required.

Apply anti-seize compound on crankshaft before reinstalling clutch. Install clutch and tighten retaining cap screw to 50 ft.-lbs. (68 N·m). Adjust clutch as previously outlined. If a new clutch is installed, burnish clutch friction surfaces as follows: Start engine and run at full speed. Turn pto ON and Off six times, allowing mower to come to a complete stop between On-Off cycles. Recheck armature-to-rotor air gap as previously outlined.

# RIGHT ANGLE DRIVE UNIT

## Model LGT14

**REMOVE AND REINSTALL.** To remove right angle drive unit, remove mower deck from under tractor. Remove drive shaft and traction drive belt as previously outlined. Remove gear box mounting cap screws. Rotate gear box until belt pulley faces rear of tractor, then work gear box rearward, down and out of frame.

To reinstall gear box, reverse the removal procedure. Be sure that drive shaft is reassembled the same way it was removed.

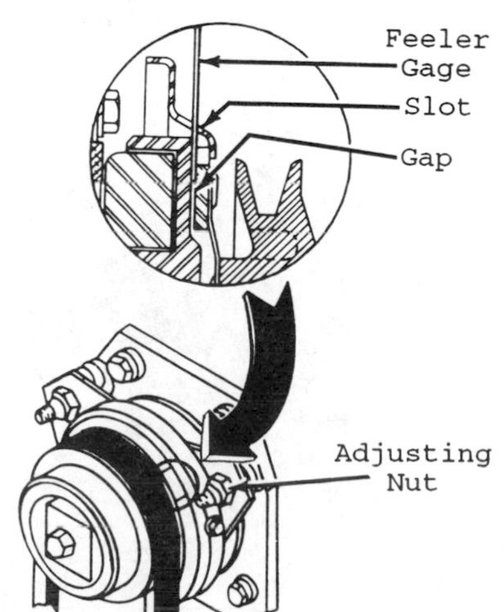


*Fig. F30—Clearance between electric pto clutch armature and rotor can be checked by inserting a feeler gage through access slot in clutch housing. Refer to text for adjustment procedure.*

## Models LT85-LGT100-LGT120

**REMOVE AND REINSTALL.** To remove right angle drive unit, remove seat and fender assembly. Remove drive belts from right angle drive pulleys as previously outlined. Remove lower drive pulley, unscrew drive unit mounting bolts and remove gear box from tractor.

To reinstall, reverse the removal procedure.

## All Models

**OVERHAUL.** To disassemble right angle drive unit, remove cover (1—Fig. F31) and drain lubricant from gear box. Unbolt and remove seal retainer (13) with oil seal (14) and gasket (12). Withdraw output shaft (10) with bearing (11). Remove snap ring (18) and output gear (9). Remove oil seal (17) and snap ring (16). Drive input shaft (6) with gear (4) and bearing (5) out cover opening of case (7). Bearings (8 and 15) can now be removed from case. Remove snap ring (3) and remove drive gear (4) and bearing (5) from input shaft. Remove bearing (11) from output shaft (10).

Clean and inspect all parts and renew any showing excessive wear or other damage. Reassemble by reversing disassembly procedure. Refill unit with 4 ounces (120 mL) of Moly EP lithium base grease.

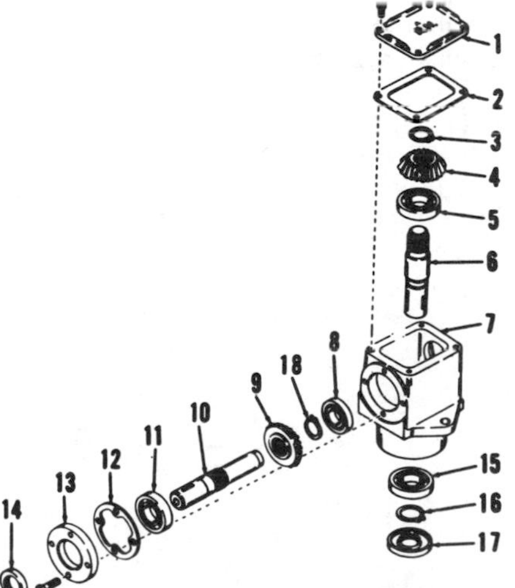


*Fig. F31—Exploded view of right angle drive unit used on Models LT85, LGT14, LGT100 and LGT120.*

1. Cover
2. Gasket
3. Snap ring
4. Input gear
5. Bearing
6. Input shaft
7. Case
8. Bearing
9. Output gear
10. Output shaft
11. Bearing
12. Gasket
13. Seal retainer
14. Oil seal
15. Bearing
16. Snap ring
17. Oil seal
18. Snap ring

# TRANSAXLE

### LUBRICATION

## All Models So Equipped

Models LT75, LT80, LT100 AND LT110 are equipped with a Peerless 600 series transaxle. Manufacturer recommends filling transaxle with $1^1/_2$ pints (0.7 L) of SAE 90 EP gear lubricant. Models LT8, LT11 and LT12 are equipped with a Peerless 800 series transaxle. Transaxle is filled at the factory with 30 ounces (0.9 L) of lithium base grease. Models LGT14, LGT100 and LGT120 are equipped with a Peerless 2300 series transaxle. Manufacturer recommends filling transaxle with 4 pints (1.9 L) of SAE 90 EP gear lubricant.

### REMOVE AND REINSTALL

## Model LT75

To remove transaxle, remove drive belt and disconnect gearshift lever spring. Position shift lever in neutral and remove shift knob. Remove rear cover at rear of tractor and remove transaxle pulley belt guide. Raise and support rear of tractor. Unscrew transaxle retaining bolts and remove transaxle from tractor.

To reinstall transaxle, reverse the removal procedure.

## Models LT8-LT11-LT12

Remove traction drive belt as outlined in previous DRIVE BELT paragraphs. Disconnect gear selector lever at transaxle. Disconnect brake control rod at brake lever. Raise and support rear of tractor. Remove cap screws attaching axle mounting brackets to frame. Roll transaxle assembly rearward from tractor.

To reinstall transaxle, reverse the removal procedure.

## Models LGT14

To remove transaxle, first remove mower deck from under tractor. Raise and support rear of tractor. Remove shift lever knob. Remove both rear wheels. Disconnect brake control rod from brake lever. Unbolt and remove disc brake assembly from transaxle. Lower rear of tractor until transaxle housing rests on the floor. Remove two bolts on each side attaching axle housings to mounting brackets. Remove one cap screw on left side attaching brake support plate to transaxle housing. Remove drive belt from transaxle pulley, lift rear of tractor and pull transaxle away from tractor.

To reinstall transaxle, reverse the removal procedure.

### Models LT80-LT100-LT110-LGT100-LGT120

To remove transaxle assembly, first remove both foot rests, drive belt rear guard and brake guard. Unbolt and remove seat and fender assembly. Disconnect brake linkage. Loosen set screw in input pulley, depress clutch-brake pedal, slide input pulley out on shaft and remove drive belt. Remove drawbar hitch from rear of main frame. Raise rear of tractor and support main frame in front of transaxle. Place a rolling floor jack under transaxle. Unbolt transaxle from main frame and roll transaxle away from tractor.

Reinstall transaxle assembly by reversing removal procedure. Adjust drive belt and brake as previously outlined.

### OVERHAUL

### All Models So Equipped

Models LT75, LT80, LT100 and LT110 are equipped with a Peerless 600 series transaxle. Models LT8, LT11 and LT12 are equipped with a Peerless 800 series transaxle. Models LGT14, LGT100 and LGT120 are equipped with a Peerless 2300 series transaxle. Refer to appropriate Peerless section in TRANSAXLE SERVICE section for overhaul procedure.

# HYDROSTATIC TRANSMISSION

### LUBRICATION

### Models LT11H

Hydrostatic transmission is separate from differential unit, and transmission uses different fluid than the differential unit.

To check transmission fluid level, raise seat and remove cap from filler tube on top of transmission (Fig. F32). Reservoir filler tube is marked for both hot and cold oil level. To fill unit, remove filler cap and bleed plug and add SAE 20 detergent oil through filler tube until oil level is at top of air bleed plug opening. Install plug and continue to add oil through filler tube until oil is at "cold" level line on filler tube. Capacity is approximately $1^1/_4$ pints (0.6 L).

Differential unit oil level should be at lower edge of oil level plug opening (Fig. F32). Manufacturer recommends SAE 90 EP gear lubricant. Approximate capacity is $2^3/_4$ pints (1.3 L).

### Model LT12H

The hydrostatic transmission and transaxle unit share a common oil reservoir. Oil level should be checked with transmission hot and engine stopped. Raise tractor hood and clean dirt from reservoir cover. Remove cover and check oil level in reservoir (Fig. F33). If oil level is low, add SAE 20 detergent oil as necessary.

### Model LT85

The hydrostatic transmission on Model LT85 is lubricated by oil contained in transmission reservoir. Reservoir should be filled with tractor level, until oil reaches lower lip of reservoir as shown in Fig. F34. Recommended lubricant is Ford M-2C41-A fluid or equivalent.

### Model LGT12H-LGT14H

The hydrostatic transmission and gear reduction unit share a common oil reservoir. Oil level should be checked with engine stopped. Raise seat support and clean around plug and dipstick (Fig. F35). Remove dipstick and check oil level. Maintain level within $^1/_4$ inch (6 mm) of "FULL" mark. If necessary, add SAE 20 detergent oil at dipstick plug opening to bring fluid to correct level. Transmission oil capacity is approximately 6 quarts (5.7 L).

Transmission oil filter should be changed after the first 25 hours of operation and every 100 hours of operation thereafter. Spin-on type oil filter is located under right side of tractor frame.

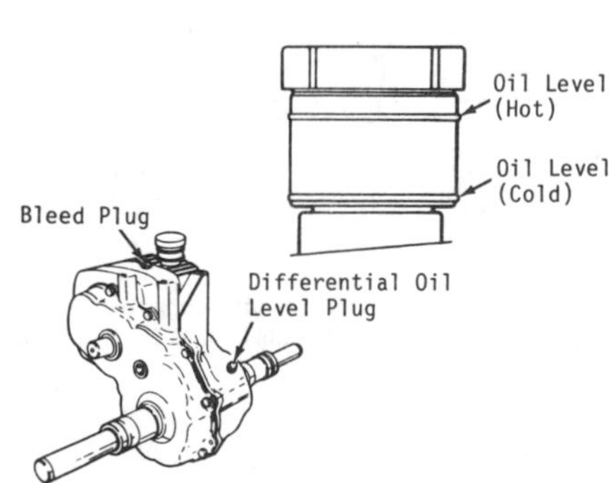


*Fig. F32—On Model LT11H, refer to text for procedures to obtain correct transmission and differential oil levels.*

### Models LGT125-LGT145-LGT165

The hydrostatic transmission shares a common reservoir with differential unit. Fill differential through fill plug opening (F—Fig. F36) until oil reaches level of plug (L). Recommended transmission oil for all models is Ford M-2C41-A or equivalent.

Transmission oil is routed through an external oil filter (9—Fig. F37). Manu-

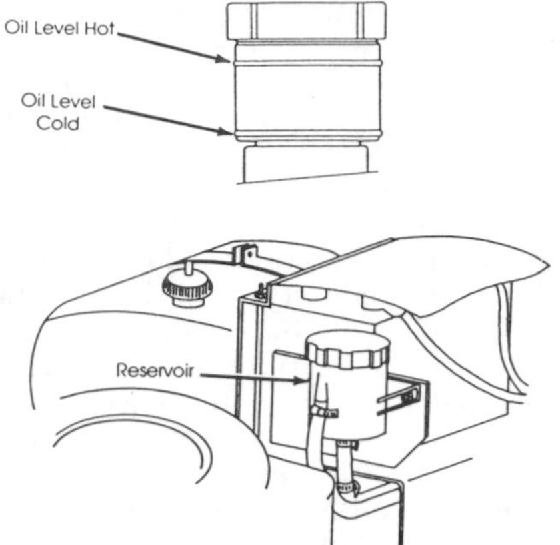


*Fig. F33—Transmission oil level can be checked at the oil reservoir. "Hot" and "Cold" oil level marks are indicated on the reservoir.*

*Fig. F34—Fill hydrostatic transmission reservoir and differential housing on Model LT85 to levels shown by dotted lines. Refer to text.*

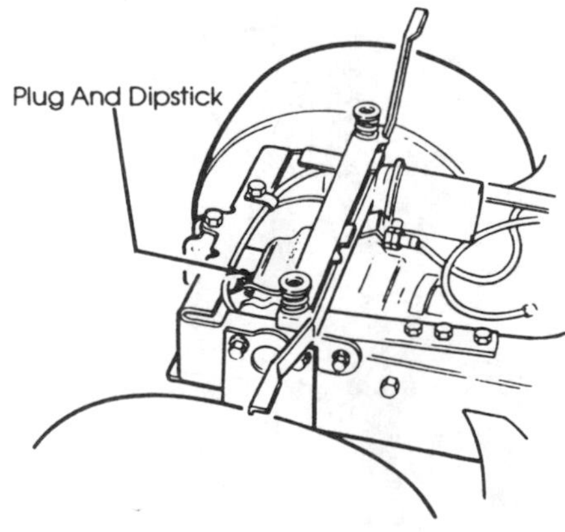


*Fig. F35—On Models LGT12H and LGT14H, transmission oil fill plug and dipstick are located at rear of differential housing. Transmission and differential share common reservoir.*

facturer recommends renewing filter after first 10 hours of operation and every 100 hours of operation thereafter.

## LINKAGE ADJUSTMENT

### Model LT11H (Early Models)

To check transmission neutral adjustment, start tractor and allow to reach operating temperature. Move drive control lever to forward, then depress clutch-brake pedal. Repeat test in reverse direction. When clutch-brake pedal is depressed, drive lever should return to neutral position and all forward or reverse motion should stop. If not, adjust linkage as follows:

Position tractor on level surface. Block front wheels and raise and support left rear wheel off the ground. Disconnect brake rod at parking brake ratchet assembly. Loosen bolts retaining neutral finger spring and bracket (Fig. F38).

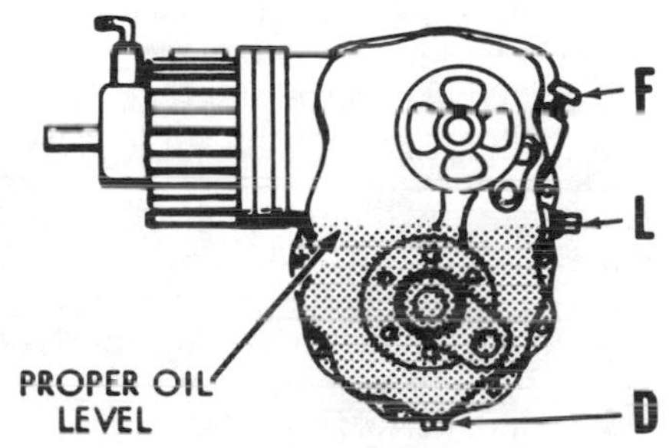


*Fig. F36—Fill differential housing on Models LGT125, LGT145 and LGT165 through fill hole (F) until oil reaches level of plug hole (L). Drain oil by removing drain plug (D).*

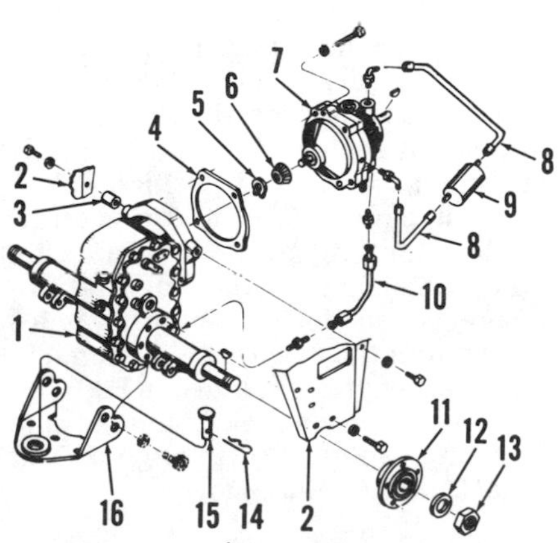


*Fig. F37—View of hydrostatic transmission and gear reduction unit on Models LGT125, LGT145 and LGT165.*

1. Gear reduction & differential
2. Frame
3. Spacer
4. Gasket
5. Snap ring
6. Pinion gear
7. Hydrostatic transmission
8. Hydraulic line
9. Filter
10. Suction hydraulic line
11. Axle flange
12. Lockwasher
13. Nut
14. Hairpin cotter
15. Clevis pin
16. Hitch plate

Place drive lever in forward position, then fully depress clutch-brake pedal and set parking brake latch. This will set drive lever in neutral position. Do Not move this lever again during adjustment procedure.

Disconnect seat restraint cable and raise fender and seat support. Disconnect control rod clevis from pivot arm (Fig. F39). Lower seat support and start engine. Move control arm in conjunction with neutral finger spring and bracket forward or backward until left rear wheel stops turning. Make certain that finger is in control arm notch as shown in inset of Fig. F38. Tighten bolts to secure bracket and neutral pivot spring in this position. Stop engine. Loosen jam nut on turnbuckle (Fig. F39) and turn turnbuckle as required to align hole in clevis with hole in pivot arm. Do Not move pivot arm to align holes or allow neutral finger spring to slip from notch. With holes aligned, insert clevis pin and secure with cotter pin. Tighten jam nut on turnbuckle. Start engine and recheck neutral lever adjustment.

### Model LT11H (Late Models)

To check transmission neutral adjustment, drive tractor forward with throttle set in fast position. Depress clutch-brake pedal all the way down, then release pedal. Repeat test in reverse direction. If tractor creeps in either direction after clutch-brake pedal is released, adjust control linkage as follows:

Position tractor on a level surface and block front wheels to prevent tractor from rolling. Raise and support left rear wheel off the ground. Disconnect brake cable clevis from brake lever. Depress clutch-brake pedal and set parking brake latch. Loosen pivot bracket retaining cap screw (Fig. F40). Start engine and run at full speed. Insert screwdriver into pivot bracket adjustment slot. If rear wheel rotates forward, turn screwdriver counterclockwise until wheel stops turning. If wheel rotates in reverse direction, turn screwdriver clockwise until wheel stops turning. Stop engine and tighten pivot bracket retaining screw to secure adjustment. Start engine and recheck transmission neutral adjustment.

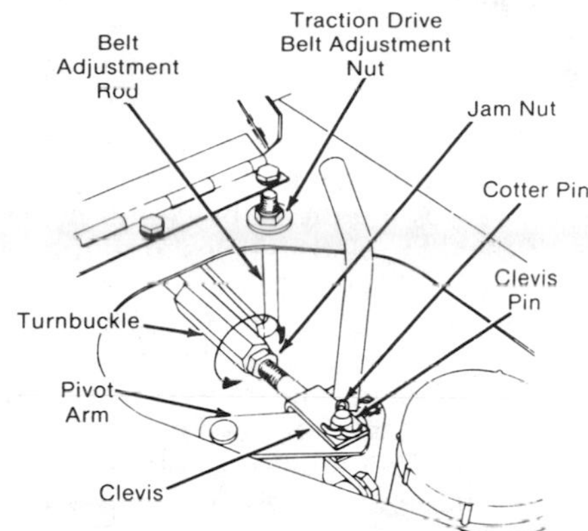


*Fig. F39—View of hydrostatic control linkage used on early Model LT11H.*

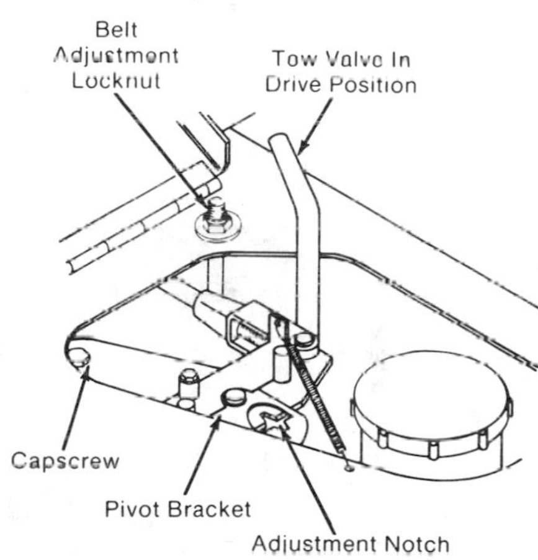


*Fig. F40—View of hydrostatic control linkage used on late Model LT11H. Insert screwdriver into adjustment notch and turn to adjust neutral setting. Refer to text.*

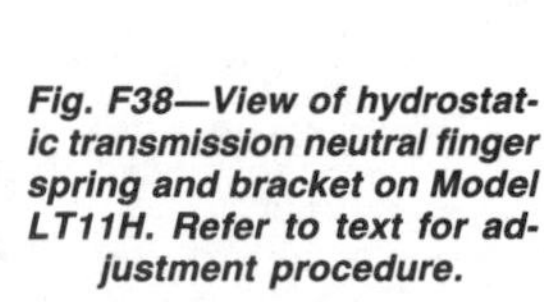

*Fig. F38—View of hydrostatic transmission neutral finger spring and bracket on Model LT11H. Refer to text for adjustment procedure.*

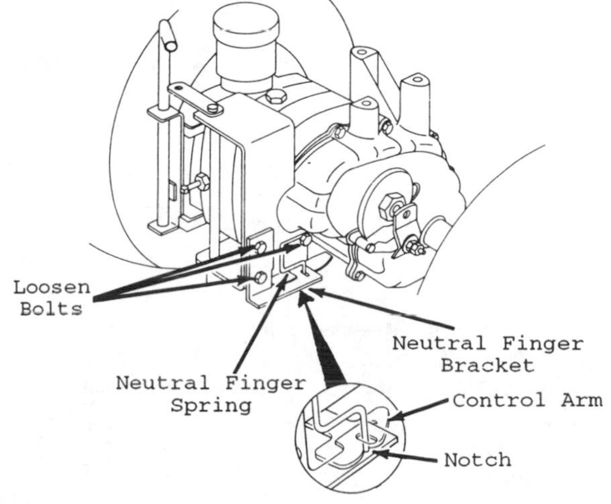

## Model LT12H

To check transmission neutral adjustment, depress foot control pedal (1—Fig. F41) to drive tractor forward. Depress brake pedal (2) all the way down, then release pedal. Repeat test in reverse. If tractor creeps in either direction after pedal is released, adjust control linkage as follows:

Position tractor on a level surface and block front wheels to prevent tractor from rolling. Raise and support rear of tractor so rear wheels are off the ground. Loosen neutral lock pivot bracket (18) mounting bolts and move the bracket in slotted holes until transmission is in neutral position.

To adjust speed control pedal linkage, fully depress pedal (1), then release pedal. Loosen speed control rod clamp (16) and adjust length of speed control rods (15 and 17) as required to place transmission in neutral. Tighten clamp screw and check for proper operation. Repeat adjustment if necessary.

## Model LT85

To adjust hydrostatic transmission linkage, remove cover screen at rear of tractor. Refer to Fig. F42 and turn adjusting nuts on speed control rod where it is attached to speed control arm. Moving adjusting nuts toward front of tractor will increase forward speed, while turning nuts in opposite direction will increase reverse speed.

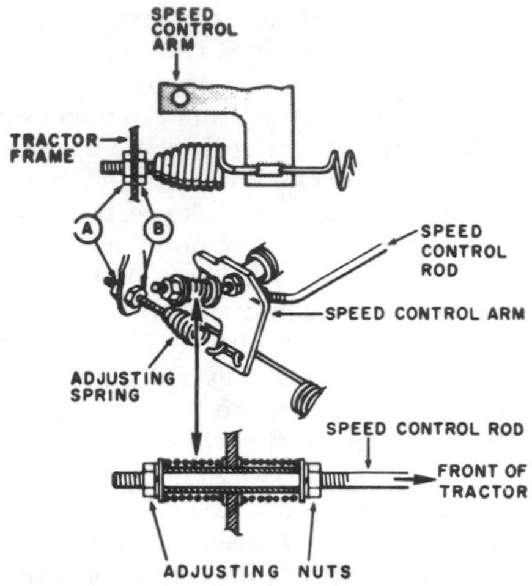


*Fig. F42—Views of speed control arm and adjusting nuts on Model LT85 hydrostatic transmission. Refer to text for adjustment procedure.*

If tractor creeps forward or reverse when linkage is in neutral, adjust linkage as follows: Raise and support rear of tractor so rear wheels are off the ground. Place speed control lever in neutral position and start engine. Turn adjusting nuts (A and B—Fig. F42) to increase or decrease spring tension against speed control arm until rear wheels stop turning. Secure adjusting nuts when neutral position is obtained.

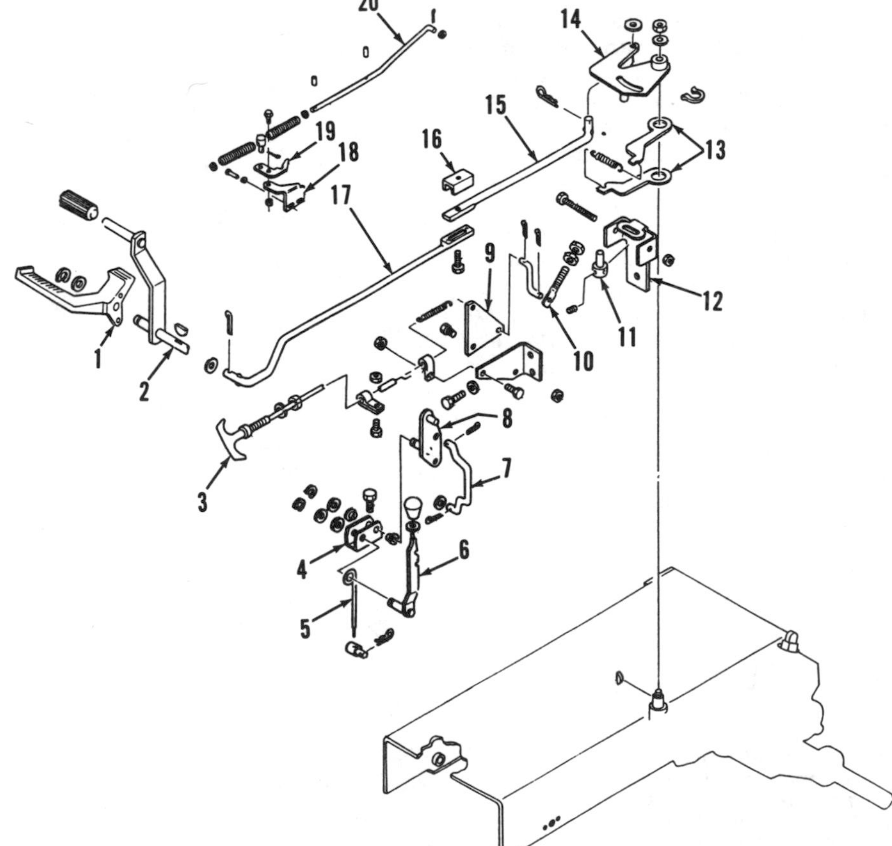


*Fig. F41—View of hydrostatic control linkage used on Model LT12H.*

1. Speed control foot pedal
2. Brake pedal
3. Tow valve cable
4. Pivot bracket
5. Cruise release rod
6. Cruise release lever
7. Speed control link
8. Speed control arm
9. Pivot lever
10. Tow valve link
11. Neutral trunnion
12. Trunnion support
13. Neutral straps
14. Transmission control assy.
15. Speed control rear rod
16. Clamp
17. Speed control front rod
18. Lock bracket
19. Neutral control lock
20. Neutral lock rod

## Model LGT12H-LGT14H (Dash Mounted Drive Lever)

To check transmission neutral adjustment, drive tractor forward with throttle set in fast position. Depress clutch-brake pedal all the way down, then release pedal. Repeat test in reverse direction. If tractor creeps in either direction after clutch-brake pedal is released, adjust control linkage as follows:

Position tractor on level surface. Block front wheels to prevent rolling and block up rear of tractor so left rear wheel is off the ground. Be sure transaxle range control lever is in "HI" position. Disconnect brake control rod from brake lever. Loosen (do not remove) bolts retaining neutral finger spring and neutral finger bracket to left side of frame. Move drive control lever to forward position, then depress brake-clutch pedal and set parking brake latch. This will set drive lever in neutral position. Loosen jam nuts on control rod turnbuckle. Turnbuckle is located under right side of frame just ahead of rear wheel. Start engine and slowly turn turnbuckle (clockwise or counterclockwise) until rear wheel stops turning. Make sure that drive lever remains in neutral position on instrument panel while adjusting turnbuckle. Stop engine, hold turnbuckle and tighten jam nuts. Slide neutral finger bracket in slotted mounting holes until neutral finger spring is centered in control arm notch as shown in Fig. F43. Tighten neutral bracket and spring mounting bolts. Start engine and recheck neutral adjustment.

## Model LGT14H (Foot Pedal Control)

To check transmission neutral adjustment, drive tractor forward with throttle set in fast position. Depress clutch-brake pedal all the way down, then release pedal. Repeat test in reverse direction. If tractor creeps in either direction after clutch-brake pedal is released, adjust control linkage as follows:

Position tractor on level surface. Block front wheels to prevent rolling and block up rear of tractor so left rear wheel is off the ground. Be sure transaxle range control lever is in "HI" position. Disconnect brake control cable from brake lever. Depress clutch-brake pedal and set parking brake. Loosen (do not remove) pivot bracket cap screw (2—Fig. F44). Start engine and insert a screwdriver blade into adjustor notch (3) of pivot bracket. If rear wheel rotates forward, turn screwdriver clockwise until wheel stops turning. If wheel rotates in reverse direction, turn screwdriver counterclockwise until wheel stops turning. Stop engine and tighten pivot bracket cap screw to secure adjustment.

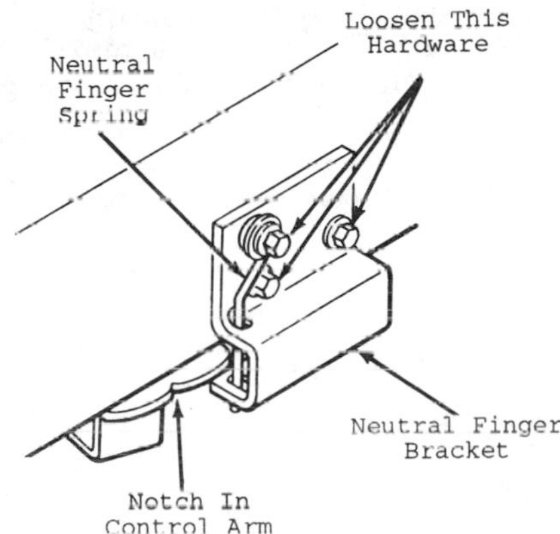


*Fig. F43—View of hydrostatic transmission neutral finger spring and bracket on Models LGT12H and LGT14H. Refer to text for adjustment procedure.*

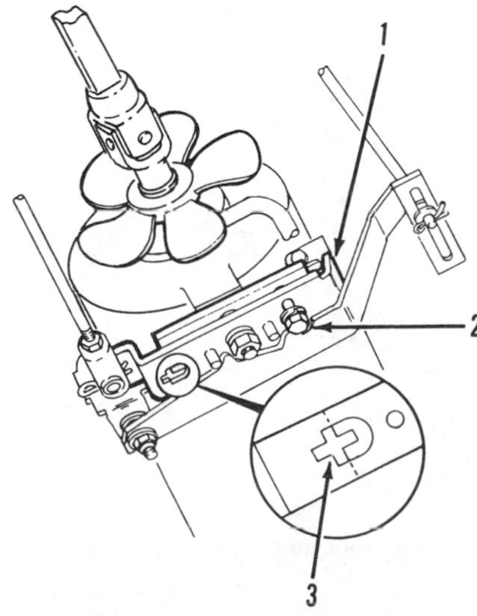


*Fig. F44—View of hydrostatic control linkage on Models LGT12H and LGT14H. Insert screwdriver into slot (3) and turn to adjust neutral setting. Refer to text.*

Start engine and run at fast speed. Depress forward drive pedal, then release pedal; rear wheel must come to complete stop. If not, repeat adjustment procedure.

## Models LGT125-LGT145-LGT165

Tractor should not move either forward or backward when transmission control lever is in "Neutral" position. If tractor will not remain stationary with control lever in neutral position, transmission linkage must be adjusted as follows:

Raise rear of tractor so rear wheels may rotate freely. Be sure tractor is blocked to prevent rolling. Refer to Fig. F45 and loosen nuts (A) and (B). Turn stud (C) toward rear of tractor if tractor creeps forward, or toward front of tractor if tractor creeps rearward. Tighten nuts (A) and (B), start engine and check transmission operation.

## Model LGT140

If tractor creeps in either direction when transmission control lever is in "Neutral" position, adjust control lever linkage as follows:

Block up rear of tractor to allow both rear wheels to rotate freely. Fully depress clutch-brake pedal and apply park brake lock. Loosen set screw on side of Drive-No Drive control knob and remove knob. Unbolt and remove seat and seat support. Remove hairpin cotter from ball joint rod (Fig. F46). Slide ball joint rod from control arm and remove bushing. Locate neutral position of transmission speed arm by moving speed arm up and down until a clicking sound is heard as arm locks in neutral notch. Move speed control lever to its neutral lock position. Start tractor engine and make sure that rear wheels do not rotate. Loosen locknut on ball joint and turn rod in or out of ball joint until rod end and bushing can be inserted into hole in control arm. Install hairpin cotter and tighten locknut on ball joint. Reinstall seat support, seat and Drive-No Drive knob.

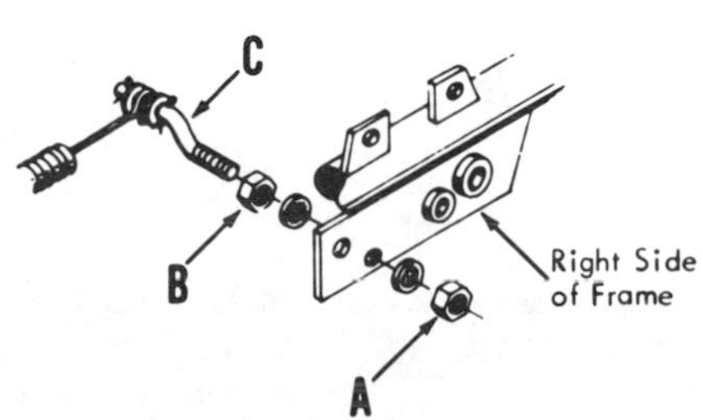


*Fig. F45—Loosen nuts (A and B) and turn stud (C) as indicated in text to adjust transmission linkage on Models LGT125, LGT145 and LGT165.*

## REMOVE AND REINSTALL

## Model LT11H

To remove hydrostatic transmission and differential assembly, remove mower deck from tractor. Raise and support rear of tractor. Remove right rear wheel. Remove the three cap screws retaining transmission fan guard. Remove fan guard and fan, then reinstall the three cap screws to maintain torque bracket alignment. Disconnect shift lever clevis (Fig. F39) from control linkage pivot arm. Remove rear hitch plate from between main frame. Pull spring loaded idler pulley down and work secondary drive belt off transmission input pulley and idler pulley. Disconnect brake control rod at brake lever. Reinstall right rear wheel. Remove the two locknuts on left and right "U" bolts retaining axle housings to support brackets. Support transmission and remove the three cap screws retaining differential to torque bracket. Raise rear of tractor and roll transmission/differential assembly away from tractor. Remove four cap screws retaining transmission to differential and separate transmission from differential.

Reinstall transmission by reversing the removal procedure. Transmission should be filled with approximately $1^1/_4$ pints (0.6 L) of SAE 20 detergent oil. Differential should be filled with approximately $2^3/_4$ pints (1.3 L) of SAE 90 EP gear oil. Adjust hydrostatic control linkage as previously outlined.

## Model LT12H

To remove hydrostatic transmission and transaxle assembly, first remove mower deck from tractor. Remove primary and secondary drive belts as previously outlined. Disconnect brake control linkage and transmission control linkage. Disconnect and remove reservoir oil lines from transmission. Remove cap

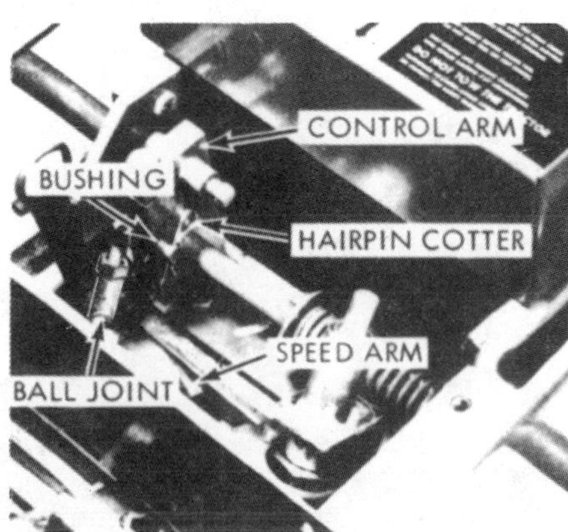


*Fig. F46—View showing location of hydrostatic transmission control linkage adjustment on Model LGT140.*

Illustrations courtesy Ford New Holland, Inc.

screws attaching transmission to main frame. Support transmission assembly with a jack to prevent tipping, then raise rear of tractor until clear of transmission and move to one side.

To reinstall transmission, reverse the removal procedure.

## Model LT85

To remove hydrostatic transmission, remove seat and fender assembly. Remove transmission drive belt by releasing spring tension against idler pulley. Remove cover at rear of tractor and disconnect speed control rod shown in Fig. F42 from speed control arm. Disconnect springs from speed control arm. Remove brake assembly from brake disc. Support rear of tractor, unscrew axle mounting bolts and remove transmission and differential from tractor. Drain lubricant from differential and separate transmission from differential.

To reinstall transmission, reverse the removal procedure.

## LGT12H-LGT14H

To remove hydrostatic transmission, first remove mower deck from tractor. Raise and support rear of tractor. Remove long set screw through notch in transmission cooling fan from rear of drive shaft. Loosen short set screw in drive shaft, then push drive shaft forward until rear universal joint is free of transmission input shaft.

On models with dash mounted speed control lever, disconnect speed control rod (10—Fig. F47) from transmission control arm (12). Disconnect and remove brake rod from tractor. Remove three screws attaching neutral finger spring (14) and bracket (13) to left side of main frame.

On models with foot pedal speed control, disconnect brake cable (4—Fig. F48) from brake lever. Disconnect rear speed control rod (11) from transmission control arm (12). Disconnect neutral return rod (6) from neutral return lever (13).

On all models, unbolt and remove rear wheels. Lower tractor until transaxle rests on the floor. Raise the seat and disconnect hydraulic hose from top of charge pump. Remove cap screw attaching hydraulic hose clamp to main frame. Support front of transmission to prevent tipping, then remove cap screws attaching transaxle to main frame. Raise rear of tractor up far enough to disconnect hydraulic return hose from transmission. Raise rear of tractor to clear transmission and move to one side. Rotate transaxle until transmission faces upward. Disconnect oil inlet tube at charge pump and transaxle housing. Remove four cap screws attaching transmission to transaxle and remove transmission assembly.

To reinstall transmission, reverse the removal procedure while noting the following special instructions: When lowering main frame over transaxle, be sure to align Hi/Lo range control shaft stud on right side of transaxle into slotted hole of Hi-Lo shift lever. Install long

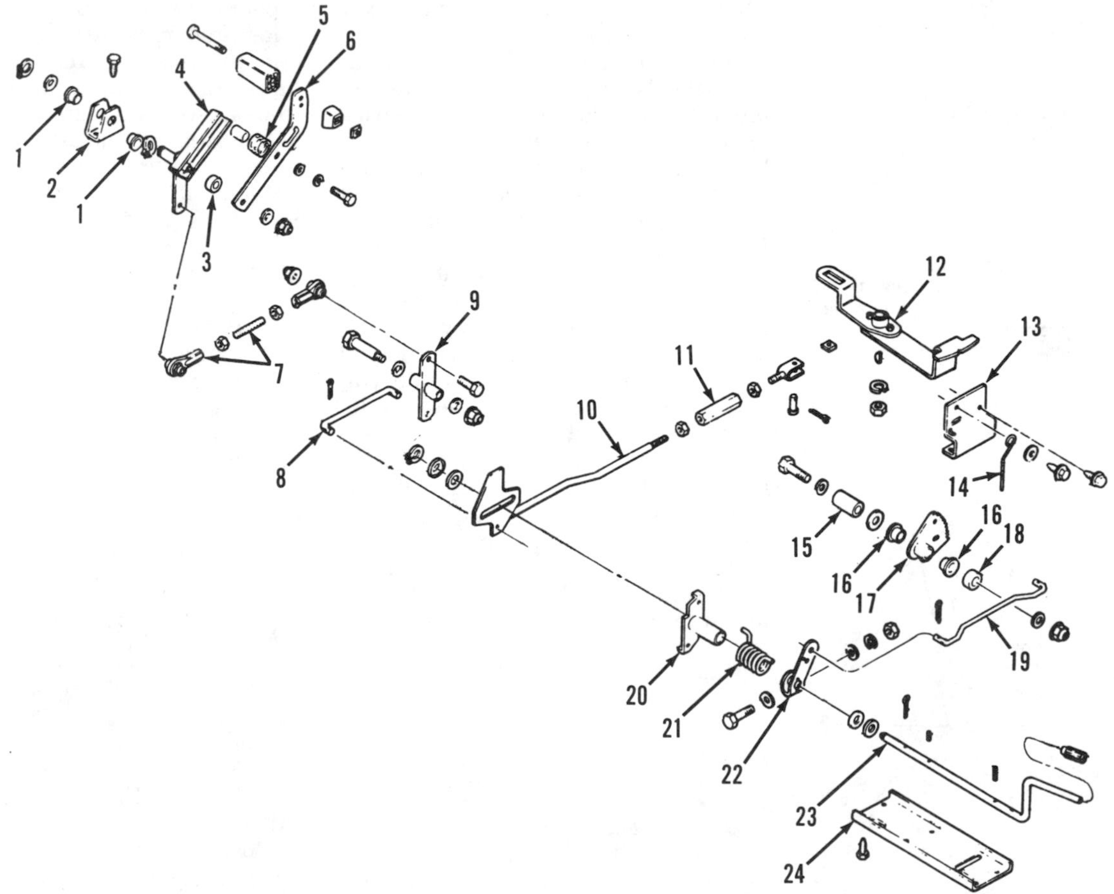


*Fig. F47—Exploded view of transmission control linkage used on Models LGT12H and LGT14H equipped with dash mounted drive control lever.*

1. Bushing
2. Pivot bracket
3. Rubber bushing
4. Speed control lever
5. Friction spring
6. Speed control handle
7. Speed control rod
8. Speed control link
9. Speed control bellcrank
10. Drive control rod
11. Turnbuckle
12. Transmission control lever
13. Neutral finger guide
14. Neutral finger spring
15. Sleeve
16. Bushing
17. Park brake ratchet
18. Spacer
19. Park brake link
20. Neutral return lever
21. Neutral return spring
22. Brake arm
23. Clutch/brake pedal
24. Support plate



Illustrations courtesy Ford New Holland, Inc.

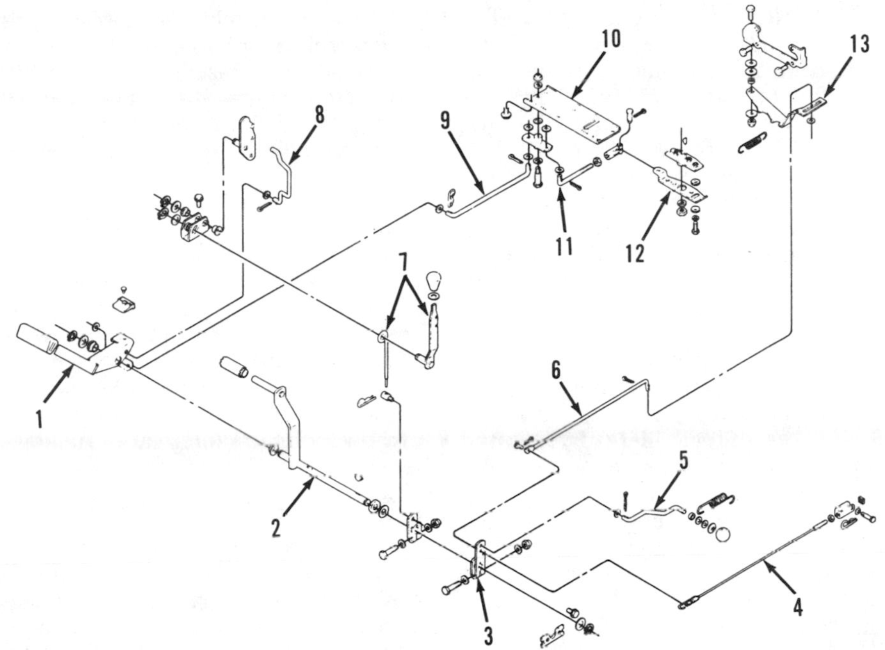

Fig. F48—Exploded view of transmission control linkage used on Models LGT12H and LGT14H equipped with foot pedal drive control.

1. Forward/reverse pedal
2. Clutch/brake pedal
3. Brake arm
4. Brake cable
5. Park brake link
6. Neutral return rod
7. Speed control release lever
8. Speed control link
9. Speed control rod
10. Support plate
11. Speed control rod
12. Transmission control lever
13. Neutral return lever

spacer (Fig. F49) first on left side of transaxle, install cap screw through spacer and tighten to pull transaxle to the left to make installation of right spacer easier. Insert short spacer (Fig. 49) on right side of transaxle. Refill transmission with SAE 20 detergent oil. Adjust transmission control linkage as previously outlined.

## Models LGT125-LGT145-LGT165

To remove hydrostatic transmission, remove pedals (16 and 17—Fig. F50) from transmission control lever (15) and brake control lever (18). Detach reverse pedal (19) from transmission lever (15). Unscrew speed range lever (12) and parking brake shaft (7) knobs. Remove rear seat and fender assembly from tractor frame. Disconnect hydraulic hoses to transmission and detach control lever (23) from transmission control shaft. Plug openings in transmission and hoses to prevent entry of dirt. Remove drive shaft as previously outlined. Unscrew transmission mounting bolts and remove transmission.

To reinstall transmission, reverse the removal procedure.

## Model LGT140

To remove hydrostatic drive unit, place a rolling floor jack under reduction-differential housing and raise and support rear of tractor. Remove rear wheels. Remove battery cover and battery. Loosen set screw in Drive-No Drive knob and remove knob. Unbolt and remove seat assembly with seat support. Remove left foot rest and drive belt rear guard. Depress clutch pedal and remove drive belt. Disconnect and remove brake rear linkage and brake band. Disconnect transmission control linkage at ball joint link. Unbolt and remove hydrostatic drive unit and reduction drive and differential assembly from tractor.

Remove three attaching cap screws and lift hydrostatic unit from reduction and differential assembly.

Reinstall hydrostatic unit by reversing the removal procedure. Adjust brake and clutch control linkage as outlined in BRAKE AND CLUTCH section. Adjust transmission control linkage as previously outlined.

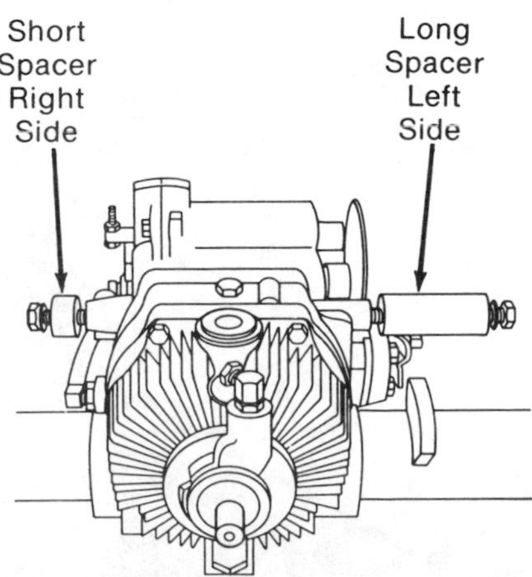


Fig. F49—On Models LGT12H and LGT14H, spacers are used on two of the transaxle mounting bolts to center transaxle between main frame.

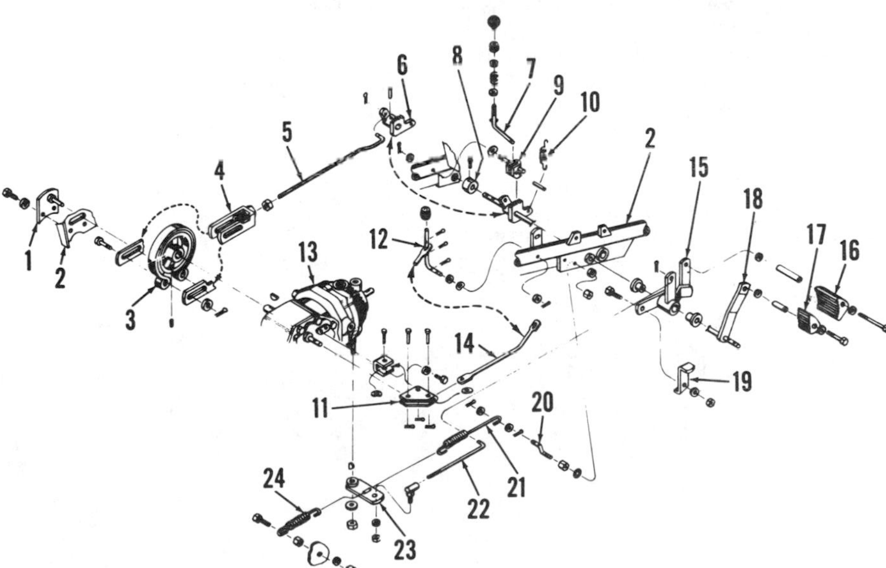

Fig. F50—Exploded view of transmission and brake control linkage used on Models LGT125, LGT145 and LGT165.

1. Brake mount
2. Frame
3. Brake band & drum
4. Bracket
5. Brake rod
6. Brake arm & sector
7. Parking brake
8. Collar
9. Parking brake pawl
10. Spring
11. Bellcrank
12. Dual range selector
13. Transmission assy.
14. Dual range rod
15. Transmission control levers
16. Forward pedal
17. Brake pedal
18. Brake lever
19. Reverse pedal
20. Stud
21. Spring
22. Transmission control rod
23. Transmission control arm
24. Spring

### OVERHAUL

#### All Models So Equipped

Models LT11H and LT85 are equipped with an Eaton Model 6 hydrostatic transmission. Model LT12H is equipped with Eaton 750 series hydrostatic transmission. Models LGT12H and LGT14H are equipped with an Eaton Model 11 hydrostatic transmission. Models LGT125, LGT145 and LGT165 are equipped with an Eaton Model 10 hydrostatic transmission. Model LGT140 is equipped with a Sundstrand "Hydrogear" type hydrostatic transmission. Refer to appropriate Eaton or Sundstrand section in HYDROSTATIC TRANSMISSION SERVICE section for overhaul procedure.

# REDUCTION GEARS AND DIFFERENTIAL

### R&R AND OVERHAUL

#### Models LT11H-LT85-LGT12H-LGT14H-LGT125-LGT140-LGT145-LGT165

Removal of reduction gear and differential unit is outlined in hydrostatic transmission REMOVE AND REINSTALL section.

Models LT11H and LT85 are equipped with Peerless 1300 series reduction gear and differential unit. Models LGT12H, LGT14H, LGT125, LGT145 and LGT165 are equipped with a Peerless 2500 series dual-range gear reduction and differential unit. Model LGT140 is equipped with a Peerless 2400 series gear reduction and differential unit. Refer to appropriate Peerless section in REDUCTION GEAR AND DIFFERENTIAL SERVICE section for overhaul procedure.

# HYDRAULIC LIFT

#### All Models So Equipped

**OPERATION.** The hydraulic implement lift receives hydraulic power supply from hydrostatic transmission charge pump. A single spool, open center control valve directs fluid to a double-acting hydraulic cylinder. The control valve is equipped with an adjustable relief valve that limits system pressure at approximately 600 psi (4137 kPa). Seal repair kits are only service parts available for control valve and hydraulic cylinder.

**TESTING.** When checking relief valve pressure setting, hydraulic fluid must be at normal operating temperature. Shut off engine and relieve hydraulic pressure in system. Using a 1/4 inch tee fitting, install a 0-1000 psi (0-7000 kPa) pressure gage in piston end of hydraulic cylinder (Fig. F51).

Start engine and operate at full speed. Operate hydraulic control valve lever to move piston to end of its stroke and observe pressure gage reading. On Models LGT12H and LGT14H, pressure should be 750-850 psi (5170-5860 kPa). On all other models, pressure should be approximately 600 psi (4137 kPa). If necessary, adjust system relief valve, located in lift control valve, to obtain desired system pressure. If specified operating pressure cannot be obtained, check the following: Low hydraulic fluid level, hydraulic filter plugged, defective relief valve, restriction in hydraulic line, charge pump worn.

### CONTROL VALVE

#### Models LGT12H-LGT14H

**R&R AND OVERHAUL.** A single spool open center control valve equipped with an integral pressure relief valve is used. Refer to Fig. F52 for exploded view of control valve assembly.

To remove control valve, raise seat and tag control valve hoses to ensure proper reassembly. Disconnect hydraulic hoses from valve. Disconnect control linkage from valve spool. Remove valve mounting bolts and remove valve assembly.

Clean outside of valve prior to disassembly. Remove screw (1—Fig. F52) from end of valve spool (8) and withdraw spool from valve body. Remove washers (3), spacer (4) and spring (5). Unscrew adjusting screw (9) while counting the number of turns required to remove screw from body. Remove relief valve spring (10) and ball (11).

Inspect all parts for wear or damage. Renew all seals. Valve body (6) and spool (7) are matched parts and must be renewed as an assembly if either part is worn or damaged.

Coat all parts with clean oil during reassembly. Thread relief valve adjusting screw (9) into body the same amount of turns as required for removal. Reinstall valve assembly and adjust pressure setting as outlined in TESTING paragraph.

#### All Other Models So Equipped

**R&R AND OVERHAUL.** A single spool, open center control valve equipped with an integral pressure relief valve is used. Refer to Fig. F53 for an exploded view of relief valve assembly.

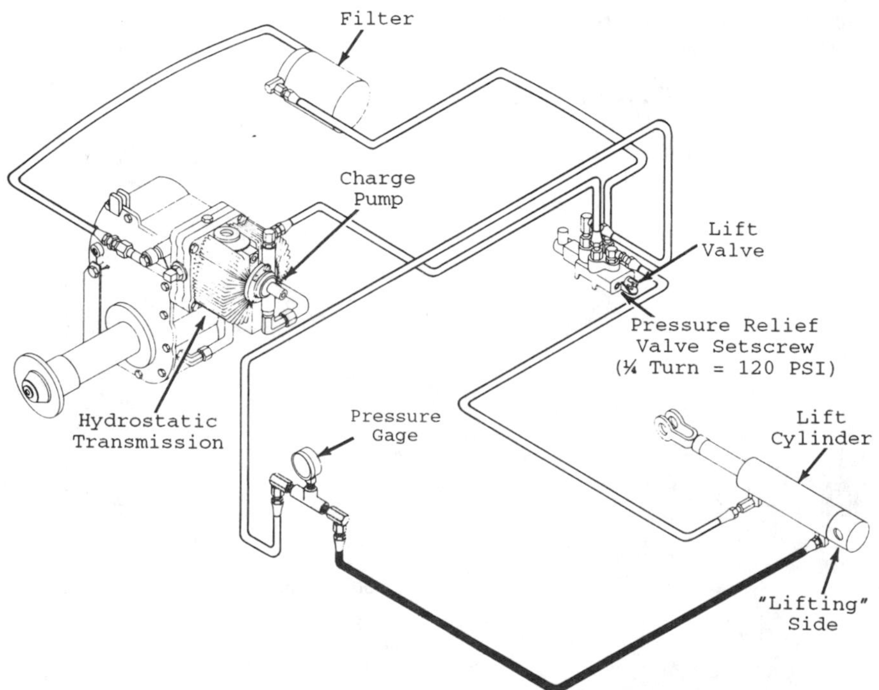


*Fig. F51—A hydraulic lift system is available on some models. To check lift system relief pressure, install a pressure gage in the line between lift control valve and piston side of cylinder. Refer to text for details.*



Illustrations courtesy Ford New Holland, Inc.

To remove valve, raise hood and remove side panels and battery. Clean exterior of valve, then tag all hydraulic lines to ensure proper reassembly. Disconnect hydraulic lines from valve, disconnect lift control linkage and remove valve from tractor. Plug all openings to prevent entry of dirt.

To disassemble valve, remove end cap (18—Fig. F53) and withdraw spool assembly from valve body. Remove acorn nut (1), loosen jam nut (3) and remove relief valve assembly.

Clean and inspect all parts for wear or other damage. Complete valve assembly must be renewed if any parts other than seals require service.

Coat all parts with clean oil and use new "O" rings during reassembly. Thread relief valve adjusting screw (4) into body approximately ¼ inch (6 mm) for initial setting. Reinstall valve assembly and adjust pressure setting as outlined in TESTING paragraph.

## HYDRAULIC CYLINDER

### All Models So Equipped

To check cylinder seals for internal leakage, first fully extend piston rod. Disconnect hydraulic hose from rod end of cylinder. Start engine and operate lift control valve to extend rod. There may be an initial flow of oil out open cylinder port, then oil flow should stop. If oil continues to flow from cylinder port, cylinder piston seal is faulty.

Before removing lift cylinder, remove attachment from tractor. Disconnect hydraulic lines from cylinder and plug all openings. Remove cotter pins and slide cylinder off mounting pins.

To disassemble cylinder, first remove hydraulic fitting from rod end of cylinder. On Models LGT12H and LGT14H, pull rod (7—Fig. F54), rod guide (9) and piston (5) out of cylinder. On all other models, remove snap ring (7—Fig. F55) from end of cylinder. Pull rod (13), rod guide (11) and piston (3) out of cylinder. On all models, remove piston from rod and remove and discard all seals.

**NOTE: Do not clamp rod or piston in a vise. Be careful not to scratch or mar rod.**

Inspect rod, piston and cylinder bore for wear or other damage and renew as necessary. Renew all "O" rings and back-up rings.

Coat parts with clean oil during reassembly. Be careful not to twist or cut "O" rings when assembling. Align tapped port in rod guide with hole in cylinder tube.

Reinstall cylinder on tractor and check hydraulic oil level. Start engine and cycle cylinder several times to purge air from cylinder.

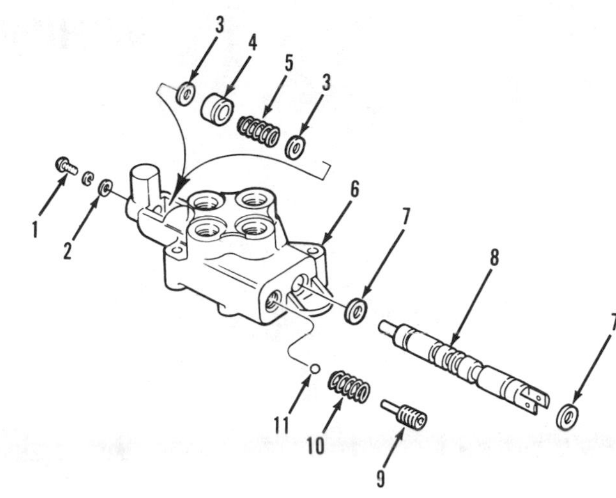

***Fig. F52—Exploded view of lift control valve used on Models LGT12H and LGT14H.***

1. Screw
2. Washer
3. Washers
4. Spacer
5. Centering spring
6. Valve body
7. Seals
8. Spool
9. Adjusting screw
10. Relief valve spring
11. Relief valve ball

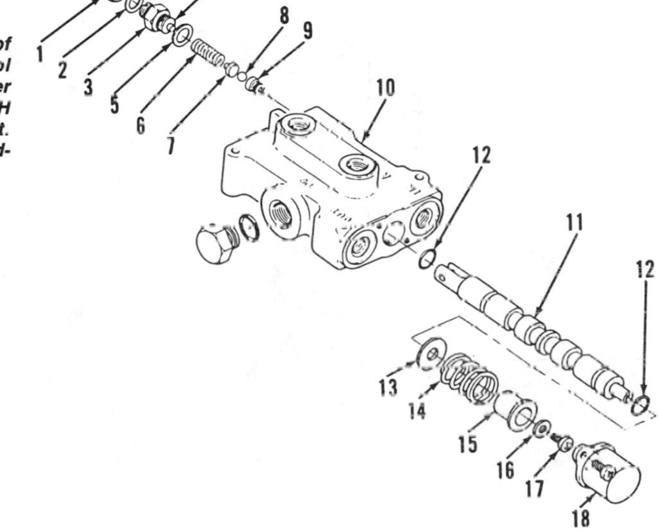

***Fig. F53—Exploded view of typical hydraulic control valve used on models other than LGT12H and LGT14H equipped with hydraulic lift. Pressure relief valve is adjustable. Refer to text.***

1. Nut
2. Washer
3. Jam nut
4. Adjusting screw
5. Washer
6. Spring
7. Ball retainer
8. Ball
9. Seat
10. Valve body
11. Spool
12. "O" rings
13. Washer
14. Centering spring
15. Cup
16. Washer
17. Screw
18. End cap

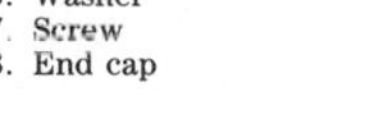

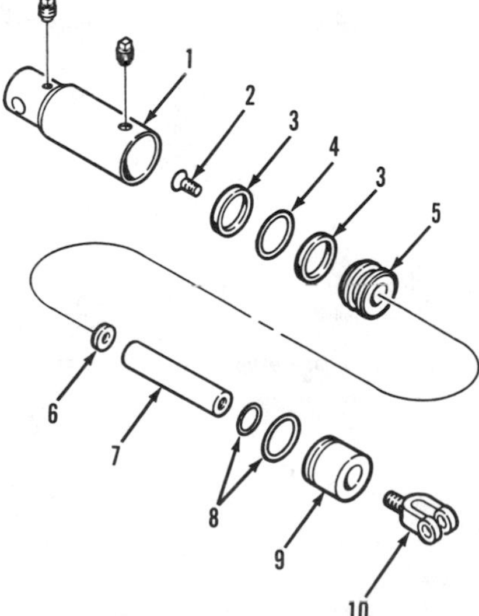

***Fig. F54—Exploded view of hydraulic lift cylinder used on Models LGT12H and LGT14H.***

1. Cylinder tube
2. Screw
3. Back-up rings
4. "O" ring
5. Piston
6. Rubber disc
7. Piston rod
8. "O" rings
9. Rod guide
10. Clevis

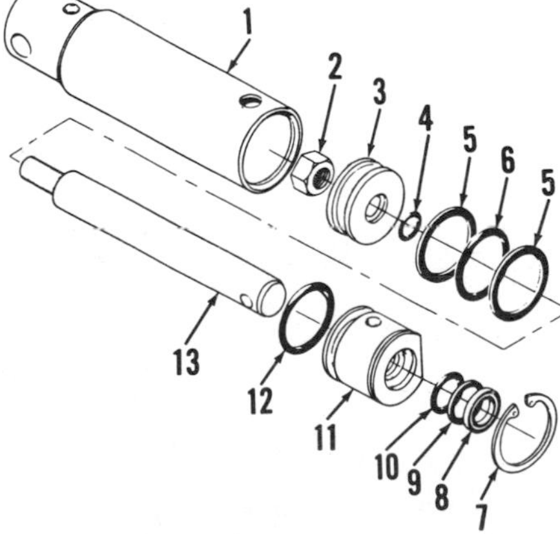

***Fig. F55—Exploded view of typical hydraulic lift cylinder used models other than LGT12H and LGT14H.***

1. Cylinder tube
2. Nut
3. Piston
4. "O" ring
5. Back-up rings
6. "O" ring
7. Snap ring
8. Seal
9. Back-up ring
10. "O" ring
11. Rod guide
12. "O" ring
13. Piston rod

# WIRING DIAGRAMS

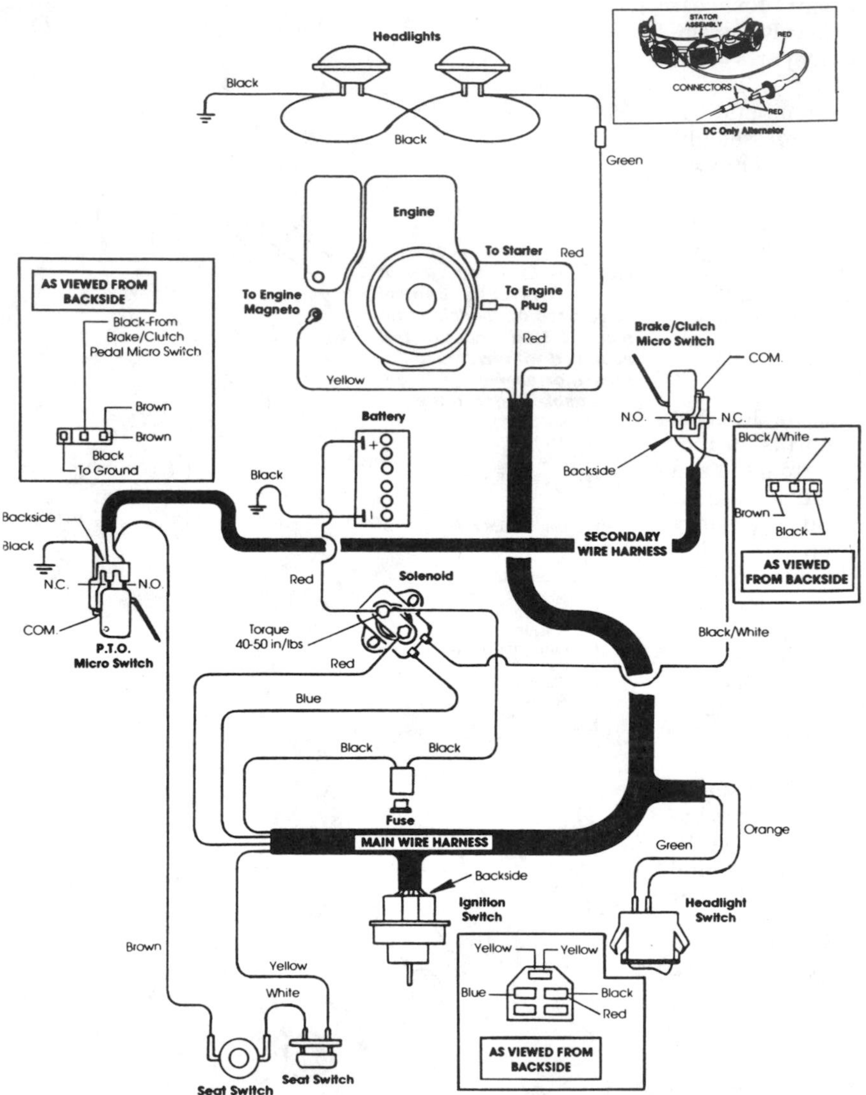


*Fig. F60—Electrical wiring schematic for Model LT8.*



Illustrations courtesy Ford New Holland, Inc.

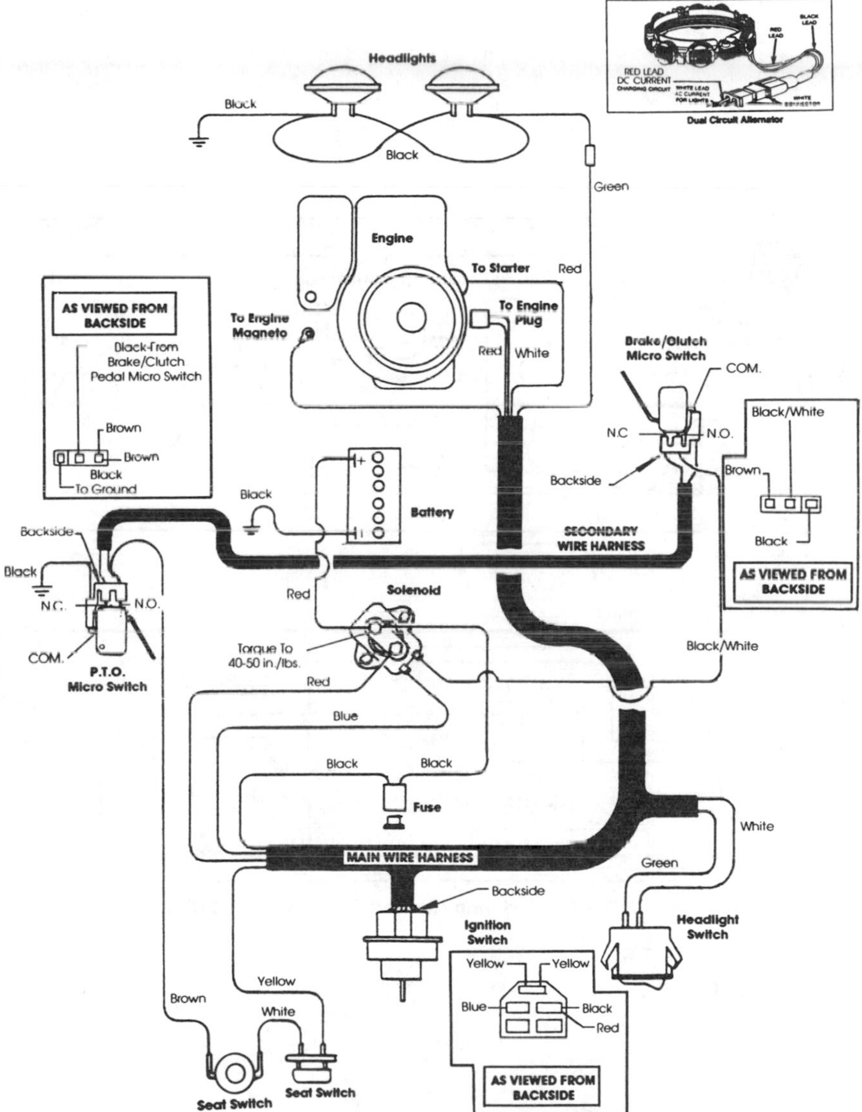


*Fig. F61—Electrical wiring schematic for Model LT12.*

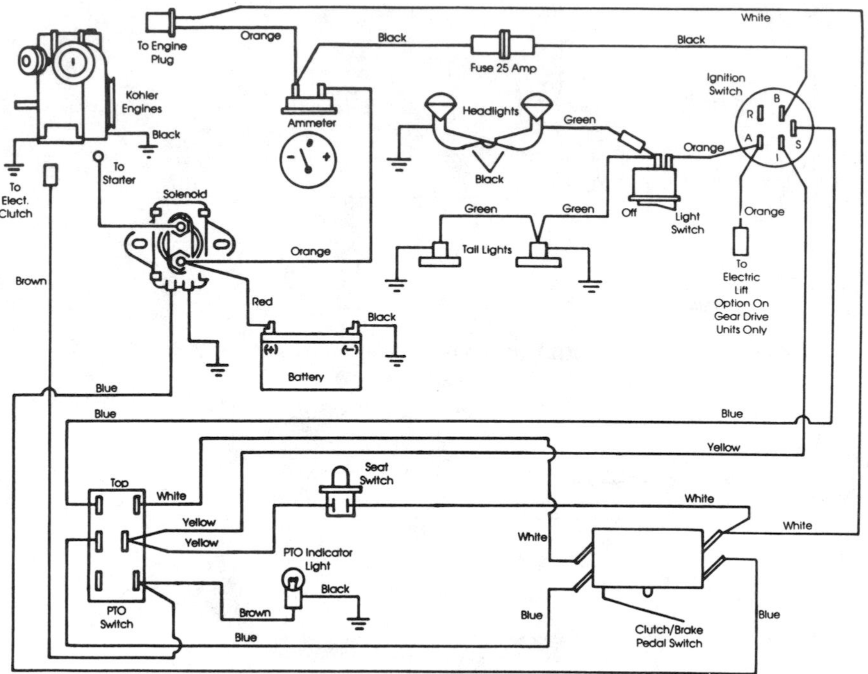


*Fig. F62—Electrical wiring schematic for Model LGT12H.*



Illustrations courtesy Ford New Holland, Inc.

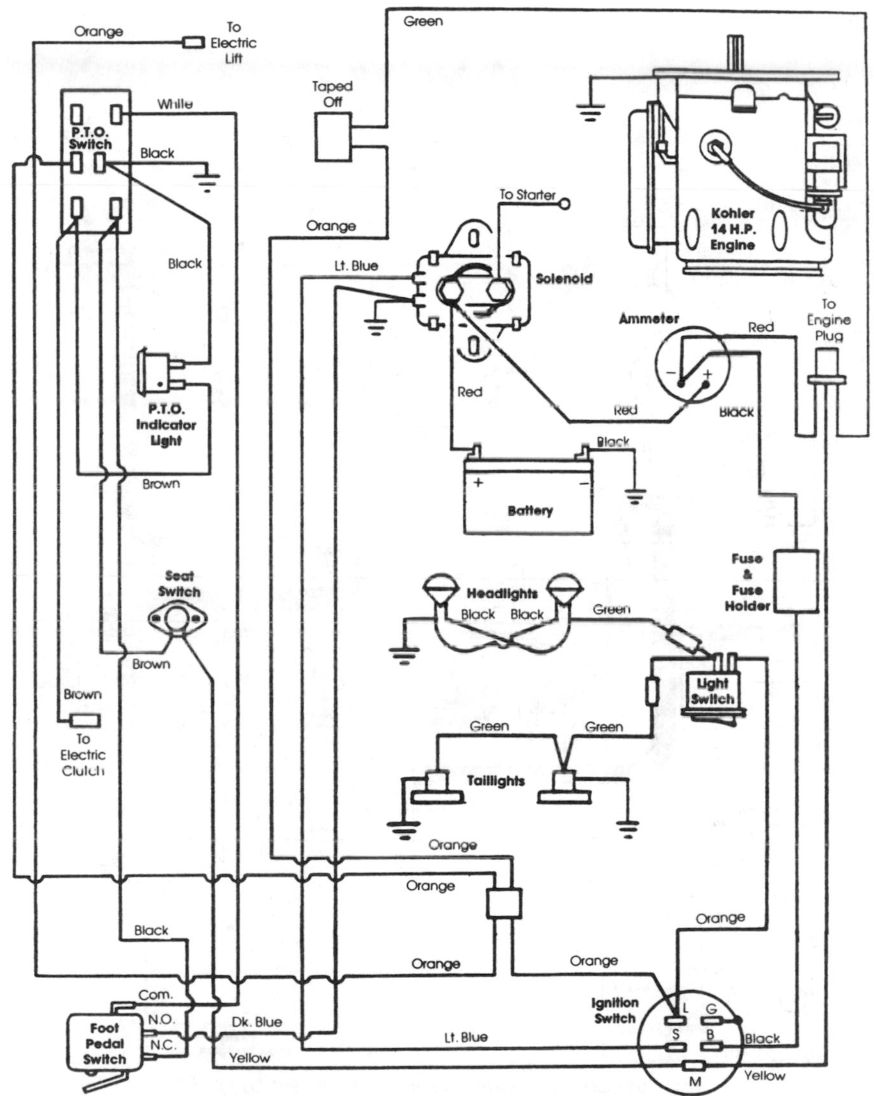


*Fig. F63—Electrical wiring schematic for Model LGT14.*

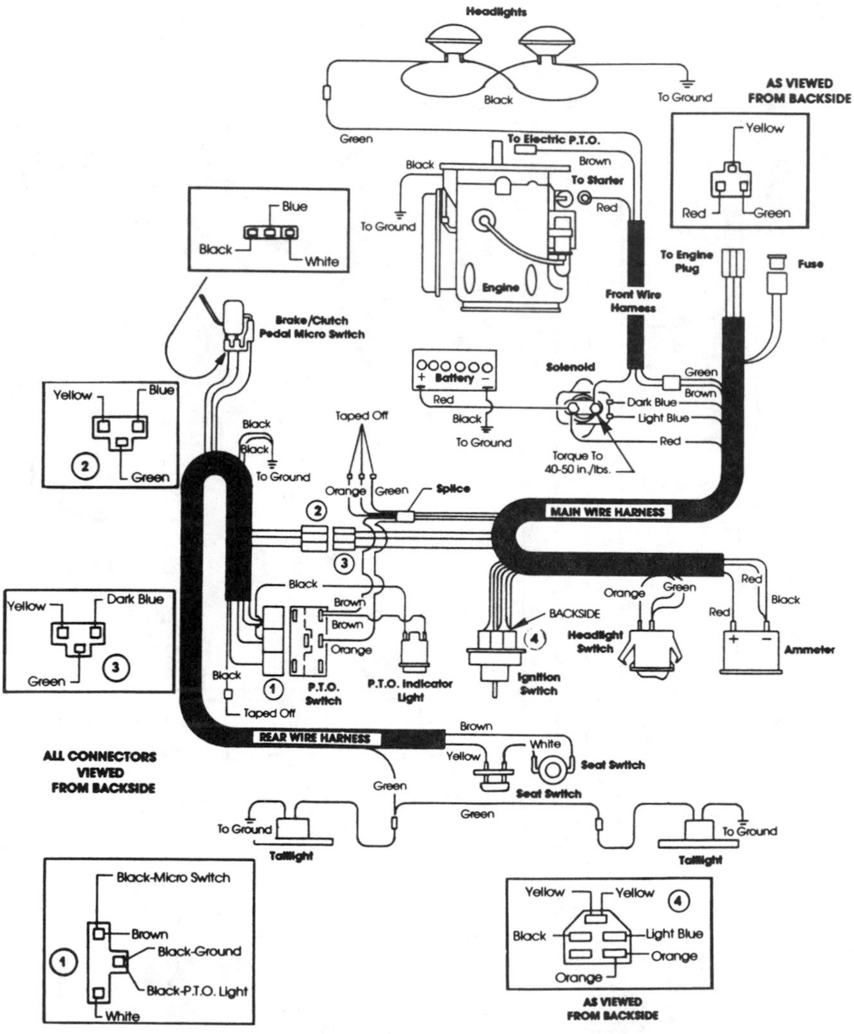


*Fig. F64—Electrical wiring schematic for Model LGT14H.*



Illustrations courtesy Ford New Holland, Inc.

# GILSON BROTHERS CO.

## CONDENSED SPECIFICATIONS

| | MODELS | | | | |
|---|---|---|---|---|---|
| | 754, 769 | 755 | 768 | 770, 771 | 772, 775 |
| Engine Make | B&S | B&S | B&S | B&S | B&S |
| Model | 243434 | 320424 | 190705 | 300424 | 170705 |
| Bore | 3-1/16 in. (77.8 mm) | 3-9/16 in. (90.5 mm) | 3 in. (76.2 mm) | 3-7/16 in. (87.3 mm) | 3 in. (76.2 mm) |
| Stroke | 3¼ in. (82.5 mm) | 3¼ in. (82.5 mm) | 2¾ in. (69.8 mm) | 3¼ in. (82.5 mm) | 2⅜ in. (60.3 mm) |
| Piston Displacement | 23.94 cu. in. (392 cc) | 32.4 cu. in. (531 cc) | 19.44 cu. in. (319 cc) | 30.16 cu. in. (494 cc) | 16.79 cu. in. (275 cc) |
| Horsepower | 10 | 14 | 8 | 12 | 7 |
| Slow Idle Speed – Rpm | 1000 | 1000 | 1750 | 1000 | 1750 |
| High Idle Speed (No Load) – Rpm | 3600 | 3600 | 3600 | 3600 | 3600 |
| Full Load Speed – Rpm | 3240 | 3240 | 3000 | 3240 | 3000 |
| Crankcase Oil Capacity | 4 pints (1.9L) | 4 pints (1.9L) | 2¼ pints (1L) | 4 pints (1.9L) | 2¼ pints (1L) |
| Weight – | | | | | |
| Above 32°F (0°C) | | | SAE 30 | | |
| 0°F (−18°C) to 32°F (0°C) | | | SAE 10W | | |
| Below 0°F (−18°C) | | | SAE 5W-20 | | |
| Transmission Oil Capacity | 4 pints (1.9L) | 4 pints (1.9L) | 1½ pints (0.7L) | 4 pints (1.9L) | 1½ pints (0.7L) |
| Weight | | | SAE 90 EP | | |

| | MODELS | | | | |
|---|---|---|---|---|---|
| | 773, 776 | 774, 867 | 780 | 52072, 52080 | 52073, 52081 |
| Engine Make | B&S | B&S | Kohler | B&S | B&S |
| Model | 170702 | 320424 | K181S | 190707 | 252707 |
| Bore | 3 in. (76.2 mm) | 3-9/16 in. (90.5 mm) | 2-5/16 in. (58.7 mm) | 3 in. (76.2 mm) | 3-7/16 in. (87.3 mm) |
| Stroke | 2⅜ in. (60.3 mm) | 3¼ in. (82.5 mm) | 2¾ in. (69.8 mm) | 2¾ in. (69.8 mm) | 2⅝ in. (66.7 mm) |
| Piston Displacement | 16.79 cu. in. (275 cc) | 32.4 cu. in. (531 cc) | 18.6 cu. in. (305 cc) | 19.44 cu. in. (319 cc) | 24.36 cu. in. (399 cc) |
| Horsepower | 7 | 14 | 8 | 8 | 11 |
| Slow Idle Speed – Rpm | 1750 | 1000 | 1200 | 1000 | 1000 |
| High Idle Speed (No Load) – Rpm | 3600 | 3600 | 3600 | 3600 | 3600 |
| Full Load Speed – Rpm | 3000 | 3240 | 3240 | 3240 | 3240 |
| Crankcase Oil Capacity | 2¼ pints (1L) | 4 pints (1.9L) | 2½ pints (1.2L) | 2¼ pints (1L) | 2½ pints (1.2L) |
| Weight – | | | | | |
| Above 32°F (0°C) | | | SAE 30 | | |
| 0°F (−18°C) to 32°F (0°C) | | | SAE 10W | | |
| Below 0°F (−18°C) | | | SAE 5W-20 | | |
| Transmission Oil Capacity | 1½ pints (0.7L) | 8 pints (3.8L) | 3 pints (1.4L) | 24 oz. (710mL) | 24 oz. (710mL) |
| Weight | SAE 90 EP | ATF "A" | SAE 90 EP | EP Lithium Grease | EP Lithium Grease |

| | MODELS | | | |
|---|---|---|---|---|
| | **52082, 52083** | **52112** | **52113** | **52117, 52122** |
| Engine Make | B&S | B&S | B&S | B&S |
| Model | 252707 | 252707 | 190707 | 252707 |
| Bore | 3-7/16 in. (87.3 mm) | 3-7/16 in. (87.3 mm) | 3 in. (76.2 mm) | 3-7/16 in. (87.3 mm) |
| Stroke | 2⅝ in. (66.7 mm) | 2⅝ in. (66.7 mm) | 2¾ in. (69.8 mm) | 2⅝ in. (66.7 mm) |
| Piston Displacement | 24.36 cu. in. (399 cc) | 24.36 cu. in. (399 cc) | 19.44 cu. in. (319 cc) | 24.36 cu. in. (399 cc) |
| Horsepower | 11 | 11 | 8 | 11 |
| Slow Idle Speed – Rpm | 1000 | 1000 | 1000 | 1000 |
| High Idle Speed (No Load) – Rpm | 3600 | 3600 | 3600 | 3600 |
| Full Load Speed – Rpm | 3240 | 3240 | 3240 | 3240 |
| Crankcase Oil Capacity | 2½ pints (1.2 L) | 2½ pints (1.2 L) | 2¼ pints (1 L) | 2½ pints (1.2 L) |
| Weight – | | | | |
| Above 32°F (0°C) | SAE 30 | | | |
| 0°F (−18°C) to 32°F (0°C) | SAE 10W | | | |
| Below 0°F (−18°C) | SAE 5W-20 | | | |
| Transmission Oil Capacity | 24 oz. (710 mL) | 22 oz. (651 mL) | 24 oz. (710 mL) | 24 oz. (710 mL) |
| Weight | EP Lithium Grease | EP Lithium Grease | EP Lithium Grease | EP Lithium Grease |

| | MODELS | | | |
|---|---|---|---|---|
| | **53000, 53005** | **53001, 53006** | **53002** | **53003, 53004** |
| Engine Make | B&S | B&S | B&S | B&S |
| Model | 243434 | 320424 | 300424 | 320424 |
| Bore | 3-1/16 in. (77.8 mm) | 3-9/16 in. (90.5 mm) | 3-7/16 in. (87.3 mm) | 3-9/16 in. (90.5 mm) |
| Stroke | 3¼ in. (82.5 mm) | 3¼ in. (82.5 mm) | 3¼ in. (82.5 mm) | 3¼ in. (82.5 mm) |
| Piston Displacement | 23.94 cu. in. (392 cc) | 32.4 cu. in. (531 cc) | 30.16 cu. in. (494 cc) | 32.4 cu. in. (531 cc) |
| Horsepower | 10 | 14 | 12 | 14 |
| Slow Idle Speed – Rpm | 1000 | 1000 | 1000 | 1000 |
| High Idle Speed (No Load) – Rpm | 3600 | 3600 | 3600 | 3600 |
| Full Load Speed – Rpm | 3240 | 3240 | 3240 | 3240 |
| Crankcase Oil Capacity | 4 pints (1.9 L) | 4 pints (1.9 L) | 4 pints (1.9 L) | 4 pints (1.9 L) |
| Weight – | | | | |
| Above 32°F (0°C) | SAE 30 | | | |
| 0°F (−18°C) to 32°F (0°C) | SAE 10W | | | |
| Below 0°F (−18°C) | SAE 5W-20 | | | |
| Transmission Oil Capacity | 4 pints (1.9 L) | 4 pints (1.9 L) | 4 pints (1.9 L) | 8 pints (3.8 L) |
| Weight | SAE 90 EP | SAE 90 EP | SAE 90 EP | AFT "A" |

| | MODELS | | | | |
|---|---|---|---|---|---|
| | **53008, 53009** | **53010** | **53019, 53021** | **53020, 53022** | **53023** |
| Engine Make | B&S | B&S | B&S | B&S | B&S |
| Model | 325434 | 325434 | 326437 | 326437 | 243434 |
| Bore | 3-9/16 in. (90.5 mm) | 3-9/16 in. (90.5 mm) | 3-9/16 in. (90.5 mm) | 3-9/16 in. (90.5 mm) | 3-1/16 in. (77.8 mm) |
| Stroke | 3¼ in. (82.5 mm) | 3¼ in. (82.5 mm) | 3¼ in. (82.5 mm) | 3¼ in. (82.5 mm) | 3¼ in. (82.5 mm) |
| Piston Displacement | 32.4 cu. in. (531 cc) | 32.4 cu. in. (531 cc) | 32.4 cu. in. (531 cc) | 32.4 cu. in. (531 cc) | 23.94 cu. in. (392 cc) |
| Horsepower | 15 | 15 | 16 | 16 | 10 |
| Slow Idle Speed – Rpm | 1000 | 1000 | 1000 | 1000 | 1000 |
| High Idle Speed (No Load) – Rpm | 3600 | 3600 | 3600 | 3600 | 3600 |
| Full Load Speed – Rpm | 3240 | 3240 | 3240 | 3240 | 3240 |

| | MODELS (Cont.) | | | | |
|---|---|---|---|---|---|
| | 53008, 53009 | 53010 | 53019, 53021 | 53020, 53022 | 53023 |
| Crankcase Oil Capacity | 4 pints (1.9 L) | | | | |
| Weight– | | | | | |
| Above 32°F (0°C) | SAE 30 | | | | |
| 0°F (−18°C) to 32°F (0°C) | SAE 10W | | | | |
| Below 0°F (−18°C) | SAE 5W-20 | | | | |
| Transmission Oil Capacity | 4 pints (1.9 L) | 8 pints (3.8 L) | 4 pints (1.9 L) | 8 pints (3.8 L) | 4 pints (1.9 L) |
| Weight | SAE 90 EP | ATF "A" | SAE 90 EP | ATF "A" | SAE 90 EP |

| | MODELS | | | | |
|---|---|---|---|---|---|
| | 53024, 53025, 53026 | 53027, 53028 | 53030, 53031, 53032 | 53033, 53034 | 53038, 53039 |
| Engine Make | B&S | B&S | B&S | B&S | B&S |
| Model | 326437 | 326437 | 326437 | 251707 | 252707 |
| Bore | 3-9/16 in. (90.5 mm) | 3-9/16 in. (90.5 mm) | 3-9/16 in. (90.5 mm) | 3-7/16 in. (87.3 mm) | 3-7/16 in. (87.3 mm) |
| Stroke | 3¼ in. (82.5 mm) | 3¼ in. (82.5 mm) | 3¼ in. (82.5 mm) | 2⅝ in. (66.7 mm) | 2⅝ in. (66.7 mm) |
| Piston Displacement | 32.4 cu. in. (531 cc) | 32.4 cu. in. (531 cc) | 32.4 cu. in. (531 cc) | 24.36 cu. in. (399 cc) | 24.36 cu. in. (399 cc) |
| Horsepower | 16 | 16 | 16 | 10 | 11 |
| Slow Idle Speed – Rpm | 1000 | 1000 | 1000 | 1000 | 1000 |
| High Idle Speed (No Load) – Rpm | 3600 | 3600 | 3600 | 3600 | 3600 |
| Full Load Speed – Rpm | 3240 | 3240 | 3240 | 3240 | 3240 |
| Crankcase Oil Capacity | 4 pints (1.9 L) | 4 pints (1.9 L) | 4 pints (1.9 L) | 2½ pints (1.2 L) | 2½ pints (1.2 L) |
| Weight– | | | | | |
| Above 32°F (0°C) | SAE 30 | | | | |
| 0°F (−18°C) to 32°F (0°C) | SAE 10W | | | | |
| Below 0°F (−18°C) | SAE 5W-20 | | | | |
| Transmission Oil Capacity | 4 pints (1.9 L) | 10 pints (4.7 L) | 4 pints (1.9 L) | 4 pints (1.9 L) | 4 pints (1.9 L) |
| Weight | SAE 90 EP | * | SAE 90 EP | SAE 90 EP | SAE 90 EP |

*Refer to LUBRICATION under HYDROSTATIC TRANSMISSION paragraphs.

# FRONT AXLE AND STEERING SYSTEM

## AXLE MAIN MEMBER

### Models 768-772-773-775-776

To remove axle main member (4 – Fig. G1), disconnect drag link (2) from steering arm (3). Support front of tractor and remove pivot pin (5). Raise front of tractor to clear axle and roll front axle assembly from tractor.

### Models 754-755-780-53000-53001-53008

To remove axle main member (2 – Fig. G2), disconnect drag link from steering arm (3). Support front of tractor and remove pivot bolts from axle and stabilizer. Raise front of tractor slightly and roll front axle assembly from tractor. Unbolt stabilizer (1) from axle main member. Renew pivot bushings (4 and 8) as necessary.

### Models 769-770-771-774-867-53002-53003-53004-53005-53006-53009-53010

To remove axle main member (7 – Fig. G3), disconnect drag link from steering

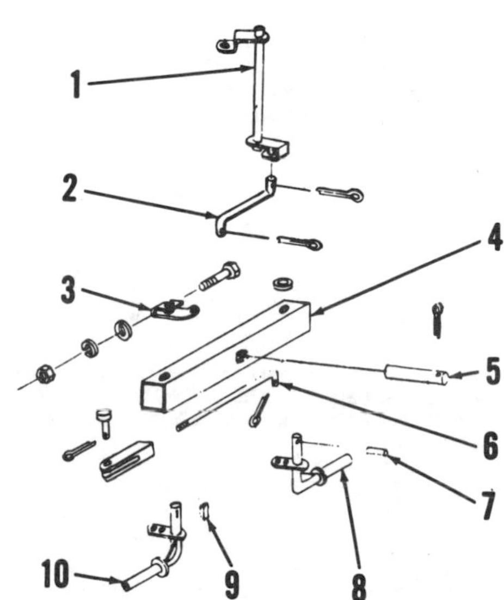


*Fig. G1 – Exploded view of front axle assembly used on Models 768, 772, 773, 775 and 776.*

1. Steering shaft
2. Drag link
3. Steering arm
4. Axle main member
5. Pivot pin
6. Tie rod
7. Roll pin
8. Steering spindle (L.H.)
9. Key
10. Steering spindle (R.H.)

spindle arm. Support front of tractor, loosen set screw (9) and remove pivot pin (8). Raise front of tractor to clear axle and roll axle assembly from tractor.

### Models 52072-52073-52080-52081-52082-52083-52112-52113-52117-52122-53033-53034-53038-53039

To remove axle main member (14–Fig. G4 or G5), support front of tractor and disconnect mower (if so equipped) from axle pivot bracket. Disconnect drag link (21) from steering arm (22). Remove axle pivot bolt (16) and roll front axle away from tractor.

Inspect pivot bolt and pivot bushings and renew as necessary. Reinstall axle by reversing removal procedure.

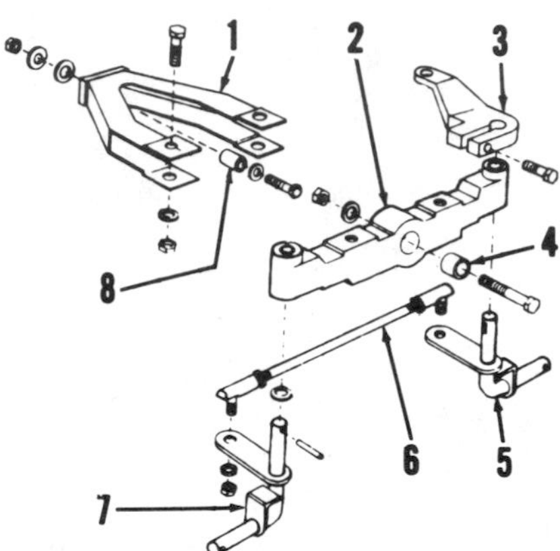

***Fig. G2—Exploded view of front axle assembly used on Models 754, 755, 780, 53000, 53001 and 53008.***

1. Axle stabilizer
2. Axle main member
3. Steering arm
4. Pivot bushing
5. Steering spindle (L.H.)
6. Tie rod
7. Steering spindle (R.H.)
8. Spacer bushing

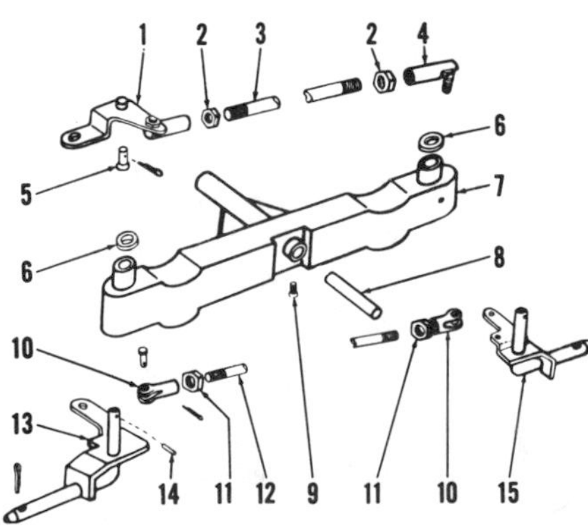

***Fig. G3—Exploded view of front axle assembly used on Models 769, 770, 771, 774, 867, 53002, 53003, 53004, 53005, 53006, 53009 and 53010.***

1. Bellcrank
2. Nut
3. Drag link
4. Ball joint
5. Swivel pin
6. Washer
7. Axle main member
8. Pivot pin
9. Set screw
10. Clevis
11. Nut
12. Tie rod
13. Steering spindle (R.H.)
14. Roll pin
15. Steering spindle (L.H.)

### Models 53019-53020-53021-53022-53023-53024-53025-53026-53027-53028-53030-53031-53032

To remove axle main member (6–Fig. G6), first support front of tractor. Disconnect drag link from steering spindle arm. Loosen set screw (10) and remove pivot pin (8), then raise front of tractor to clear axle and roll axle assembly away from tractor.

## TIE RODS

### All Models

Removal of tie rod is evident after examination of unit and reference to Figs. G1 through G6. To adjust front wheel toe-in on models equipped with adjustable tie rods, disconnect tie rod ends from steering spindle arms, loosen jam nuts and turn ends in or out as required. Toe-in should be 1/8 inch (3 mm) measured as shown in Fig. G7.

## STEERING SPINDLES

### Models 768-772-773-775-776

To remove steering spindles (8 and 10–Fig. G1), support front of tractor and remove front wheels. Disconnect drag link (2) and tie rod (6). Remove steering arm (3), key (9) and right steering spindle (10). Drive out roll pin (7) and remove left steering spindle (8).

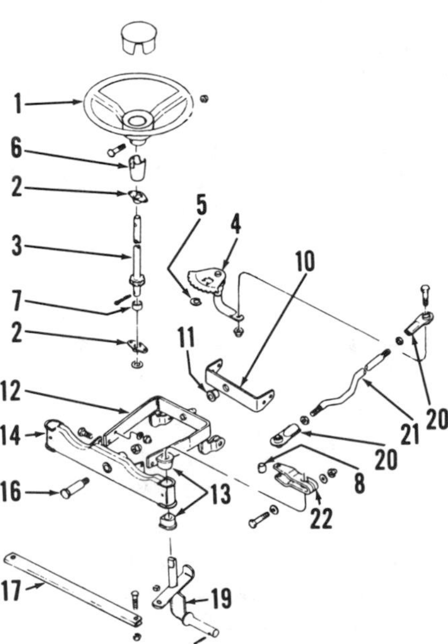

***Fig. G4—Exploded view of front axle and steering gear assembly used on Models 52072, 52073, 52080, 52081, 52082, 52083, 52112, 52113, 52117 and 52122.***

1. Steering wheel
2. Bearings
3. Steering shaft
4. Quadrant gear
5. "E" ring
6. Sleeve
7. Spacer
8. Spacer
10. Axle pivot bracket
11. Bushing
12. Axle bracket
13. Spindle bushing
14. Axle main member
16. Pivot bolt
17. Tie bar
19. Steering spindle (L.H.)
20. Ball joints
21. Drag link
22. Steering arm

### Models 754-755-780-53000-53001-53008

To remove steering spindles (5 and 7–Fig. G2), support front of tractor and remove front wheels. Disconnect drag link and tie rod. Remove steering arm (3), key and left steering spindle (5). Drive out roll pin and remove right steering spindle (7).

Reassemble by reversing removal procedure. Lubricate with multipurpose grease.

### Models 769-770-771-774-867-53002-53003-53004-53005-53006-53009-53010

To remove steering spindles (13 and 15–Fig. G3), support front of tractor and remove front wheels. Disconnect

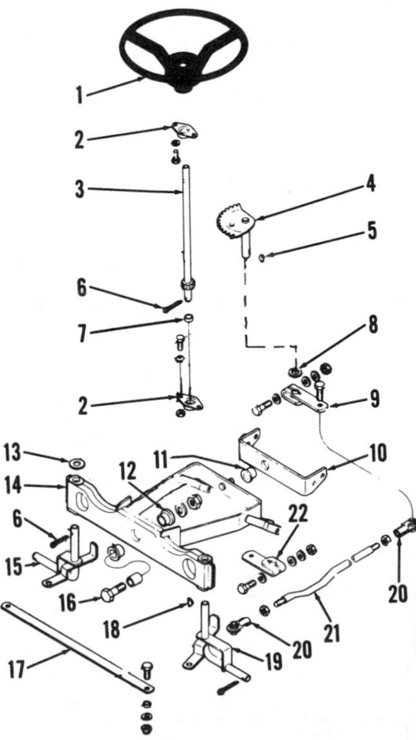

***Fig. G5—Exploded view of front axle and steering gear assemblies used on Models 53033, 53034, 53038 and 53039.***

1. Steering wheel
2. Bearing
3. Steering shaft
4. Quadrant gear
5. Key
6. Cotter pin
7. Spacer
8. Spacer
9. Steering arm
10. Axle pivot bracket
11. Bearing
12. Axle pivot bushing
13. Flat washer
14. Axle assy.
15. Steering spindle (R.H.)
16. Pivot bolt
17. Tie bar
18. Key
19. Steering spindle (L.H.)
20. Ball joint
21. Drag link
22. Steering arm

drag link and tie rod from spindle arms. Drive out roll pins and remove steering spindles.

Inspect parts for excessive wear or other damage and renew as necessary. Lubricate with multipurpose lithium base grease.

### Models 52072-52073-52080-52081-52082-52083-52112-52113-52117-52122-53033-53034-53038-53039

To remove steering spindles (15 and 19–Fig. G4 or G5), support front of tractor and remove front wheels. Disconnect tie bar (17) and drag link (21) from spindle arms. Loosen clamp bolt and remove steering arm (22) and left steering spindle (19). Remove cotter key and lower right steering spindle from axle.

Inspect all parts for excessive wear or other damage. Some models are equipped with renewable spindle bushings. Lubricate with multipurpose lithium base grease.

### Models 53019-53020-53021-53022-53023-53024-53025-53026-53027-53028-53030-53031-53032

To remove steering spindles (7 and 12–Fig. G6), support front of tractor and remove front wheels. Disconnect drag link and tie rod from spindle arms. Drive out roll pins and lower spindles from axle.

Clean and inspect parts for excessive wear. All models are equipped with renewable spindle bushings (5). Lubricate with multipurpose lithium base grease.

## STEERING GEAR

### Models 768-772-773-775-776

Remove hood for access to steering gear. Drive out roll pin (3–Fig. G8) and remove steering wheel. Disconnect drag link (7) from arm on quadrant gear (6). Unbolt and remove quadrant gear. Remove bolt (8) and steering shaft (2), then withdraw pinion gear (5).

### Models 754-755-780-53000-53001-53008

To remove steering gear, refer to Fig. G9 and disconnect drag link (7) from quadrant shaft (8). Remove nuts (10 and 11), drive out roll pin (6) and withdraw shaft (8). Remove quadrant gear (5). Drive out roll pins (13) and remove steering wheel (1) and pinion gear (4). Unbolt flange bearing (2) and remove steering shaft (3) and bracket (12). Support (9) can now be unbolted and removed if necessary.

Reassembly is reverse of disassembly procedure. To adjust steering gear play, loosen locknut (11) and turn adjusting nut (10) until steering wheel turns freely with minimum of play. Tighten locknut (11). Lubricate steering mechanism at grease fittings with multipurpose grease and apply light coat of grease to steering gears. Apply SAE 30 oil at oil hole in steering support (9).

### Models 52072-52073-52080-52081-52082-52083-52112-52113-52117-52122

To remove steering gear, remove steering wheel. Remove cotter pin from bottom of steering shaft (3–Fig. G4). Unbolt shaft upper bearing and withdraw steering shaft assembly. Disconnect drag link (21) from quadrant gear (4), remove "E" ring (5) and withdraw gear.

Inspect bearings and gears for wear and renew as necessary. Reassemble by reversing disassembly procedure. Lubricate bearings and gears with multipurpose grease.

To adjust steering gear mesh, loosen lower flange bearing mounting bolts and move steering shaft (3) towards steering gear (4). When gears mesh smoothly and evenly, tighten mounting bolts.

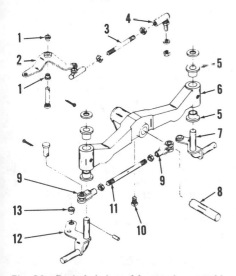

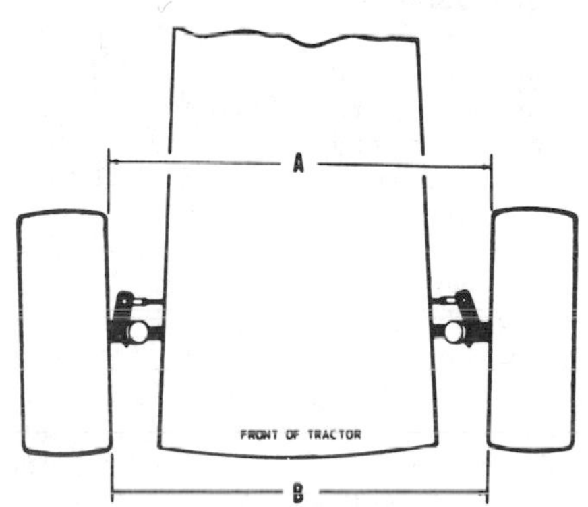


*Fig. G7—Toe-in is correct when distance "B" is 1/8 inch (3 mm) less than distance "A" with both measurements taken at hub height.*

*Fig. G6—Exploded view of front axle assembly used on Models 53019, 53020, 53021 and 53022. Models 53023, 53024, 53025, 53026, 53027, 53028, 53030, 53031 and 53032 are similar.*

1. Bushings
2. Bellcrank
3. Drag link
4. Ball joint end
5. Flanged bushings
6. Axle main member
7. Steering spindle (L.H.)
8. Pivot pin
9. Clevis
10. Set screw
11. Tie rod
12. Steering spindle (R.H.)
13. Bushing

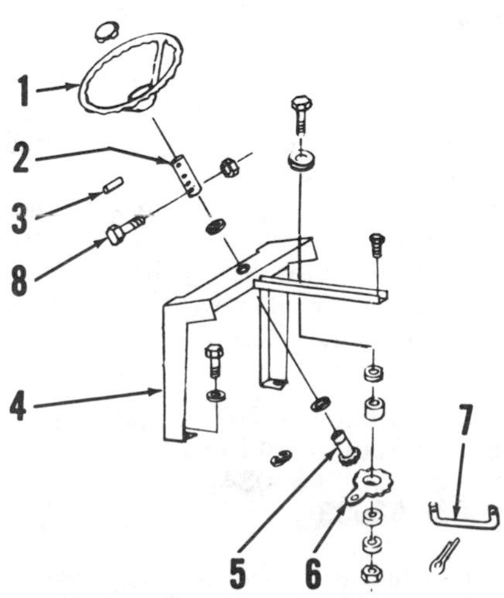


*Fig. G8—Exploded view of steering gear assembly used on Models 768, 772, 773, 775 and 776.*

1. Steering wheel
2. Steering shaft
3. Roll pin
4. Frame
5. Pinion
6. Quadrant gear
7. Drag link
8. Bolt

*Fig. G9—Exploded view of steering gear assembly used on Models 754, 755, 780, 53000, 53001 and 53008.*

1. Steering wheel
2. Flange bearing
3. Steering shaft
4. Pinion gear
5. Quadrant gear
6. Roll pin
7. Drag link
8. Quadrant shaft & arm
9. Support
10. Adjusting nut
11. Locknut
12. Bracket
13. Roll pins

### Models 53033-53034-53038-53039

To remove steering gear, first remove steering wheel. Remove cotter pin from bottom of steering shaft (3–Fig. G5), unbolt shaft upper bearing flange and withdraw steering shaft. Disconnect steering arm (9) from quadrant gear (4) and withdraw gear.

Inspect bearings and gears for wear and renew as necessary. Reassemble by reversing disassembly procedure. Lubricate bearings and gears with multipurpose grease.

To adjust steering gear mesh, loosen lower flange bearing mounting screws and move steering shaft (3) towards steering gear (4). When gears mesh smoothly and evenly, tighten bearing mounting screws.

### All Other Models

Remove steering gear by first disconnecting drag link end (20–Fig. G10) from quadrant gear (11). Remove nuts (18 and 19) and unbolt supports (14) from frame. Lower the assembly and withdraw shaft (13). Spacer (17), quadrant gear (11) and bushing (12) can be removed as shaft is withdrawn. Drive out roll pin (10) and remove pinion gear (9) and bracket (16) with bushings (8). Remove cap screw (1) and steering wheel (2), then unbolt bearing (4) and remove shaft (7) and bearing assembly. To reassemble, reverse disassembly procedure.

To adjust steering gear play, loosen set screw (15) and locknut (19). Turn adjusting nut (18) until steering wheel turns freely with a minimum of play. Retighten locknut (19) and set screw (15). Lubricate steering mechanism with light coat of SAE 30 oil.

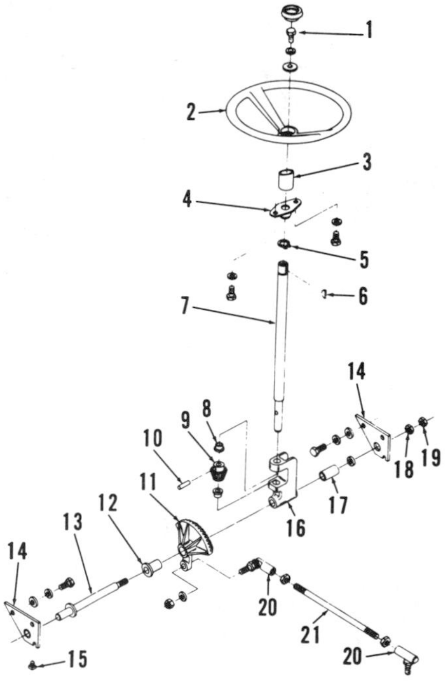

*Fig. G10—Exploded view of typical steering gear assembly used on some models.*

1. Cap screw
2. Steering wheel
3. Sleeve
4. Flange bearing
5. Snap ring
6. Key
7. Steering shaft
8. Bushing
9. Pinion gear
10. Roll pin
11. Quadrant gear
12. Bushing
13. Shaft
14. Support
15. Set screw
16. Bracket
17. Spacer
18. Adjusting nut
19. Locknut
20. Ball joint ends
21. Drag link

# ENGINE

## REMOVE AND REINSTALL

### Models 754-755-780-53000-53001-53008

To remove engine assembly, loosen hood locks and tilt hood forward. On electric start models, disconnect battery cables and remove battery. Disconnect wires from starter-generator and ignition coil or magneto. On all models, disconnect throttle and choke control cables. Unbolt and remove belt guard from right side of engine. Remove engine draw bolt from front of tractor frame, then remove engine mounting bolts. Remove drive belts from engine and lift engine from tractor.

Reinstall engine by reversing removal procedure. Adjust engine drive belts as follows: Tighten engine drive belts and move engine forward to tighten belts. Make certain engine drive pulley and pulley on jackshaft are aligned, then tighten engine mounting bolts.

### Models 768-772-773-775-776

To remove engine assembly, unbolt and remove hood. Disconnect and remove battery on electric start models. Disconnect starter-generator and ignition wires. Detach throttle and choke control cable from engine. Remove drive belts from engine drive pulley on underside of tractor. Remove engine mounting bolts and lift engine from tractor.

### Models 52072-52073-52080-52081-52082-52083-52113-52117-52122-53033-53034-53038-53039

To remove engine assembly, remove hood assembly and disconnect battery cables. Lift fender and seat support and turn belt adjusting nut on top of frame counterclockwise 1/2 to 1 1/2 turns. Remove main drive belt and crankshaft pulley. Disconnect electrical wiring, throttle and choke cables. Shut off fuel valve and disconnect fuel line at carburetor. Remove engine mounting bolts and lift engine from tractor. To reinstall engine, reverse removal procedure. Adjust drive belt as required.

### All Other Models

To remove engine assembly, unfasten and tilt hood forward. Disconnect battery cables and remove battery. Disconnect starter-generator and ignition wires. Unbolt drive shaft coupler from rear of engine. Disconnect pto control rod from front pto assembly. Remove pto drive belt. Disconnect throttle and choke cables. Drain engine oil. Unbolt engine from engine base (oil pan) and lift engine from tractor.

**NOTE: Engine base is bolted to side and bottom of frame rails and is the front axle support. To remove engine base, support tractor frame, remove front axle pivot pin, then unbolt and remove base.**

When reinstalling engine, use new engine base gasket and refill with correct engine oil.

## OVERHAUL

### All Models

Engine make and model are listed at the beginning of this section. To overhaul engine components and accessories, refer to Briggs & Stratton and Kohler sections of this manual.

# CLUTCH AND BRAKE

The clutch used on all gear drive models is belt idler type and is operated by clutch-brake pedal. When pedal is depressed, clutch idler tension is removed from transaxle drive belt. This allows clutch drive pulley to turn free within transaxle drive belt. At this time, brake band is drawn tight on brakedrum, or caliper brake is tightened on brake disc, stopping tractor motion.

Models 774, 867, 52112, 53003, 53004 53010, 53020, 53022, 53027 and 53028 are equipped with a hydrostatic transmission. When pedal on left side of tractor is depressed, drive control linkage is moved to neutral position and hydrostatic transmission dynamically brakes tractor. A mechanical parking brake is also provided.

## ADJUSTMENT

### Models 754-755-780-53000-53001-53008

The clutch idler is spring loaded and requires no adjustment. The clutch-brake pedal (23–Fig. G11) can be adjusted by loosening bolt (21) and moving pedal on adjusting plate (22). When desired pedal position is obtained, tighten bolt (21).

Adjust brake by turning adjusting nut (4) on rear of brake rod (15). Depress clutch-brake pedal and check to see that brake band (5) does not tighten on brake drum (3) until clutch idler tension is removed from transaxle drive belts.

### Models 768-772-773-775-776

To adjust clutch, refer to Fig. G12. Remove spring clip and clevis pin from clutch rod clevis. Turn clevis to adjust clutch action. Brake rod should not contact rear of slot in frame when clutch-brake pedal is depressed. Drive belt should be renewed if adjustment will not prevent contact between rod and rear of slot.

To adjust brake, first check clutch adjustment. Turn adjusting nut shown in Fig. G13. Brake should engage when clutch-brake pedal is depressed but should not drag when clutch is engaged.

### Models 774-867-52112-53003-53004-53010-53020-53027-53028

These models use a hydrostatic transmission and are not equipped with an engine disconnect clutch. Refer to the following HYDROSTATIC TRANSMISSION section for adjustment of control linkage.

On Models 53027 and 53028, a caliper-disc type brake, located on left side of transaxle, is used. To adjust brake, move speed control lever to "Fast" position. Depress neutral-brake pedal until

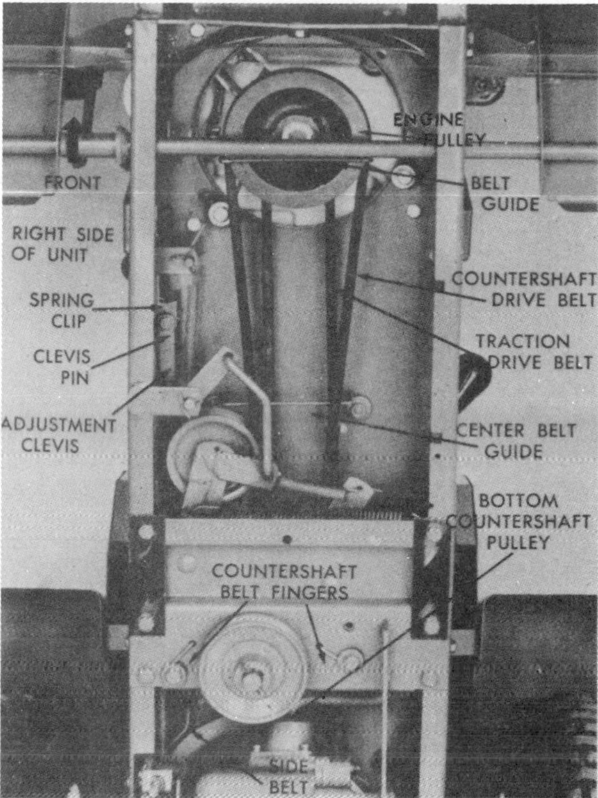


*Fig. G12—Bottom view of Models 768, 772, 773, 775 and 776. For clutch adjustment procedure, refer to text.*

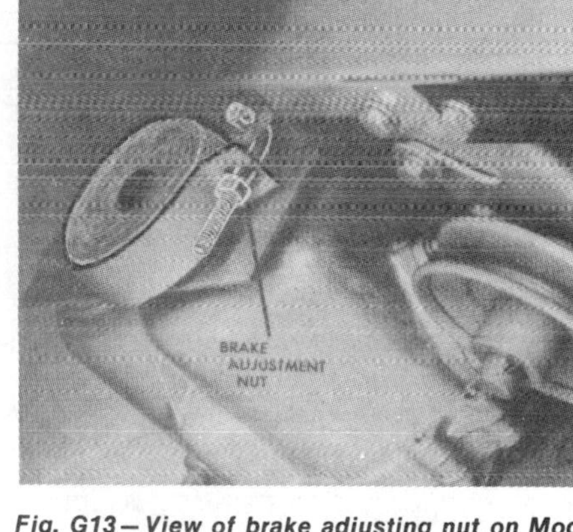


*Fig. G13—View of brake adjusting nut on Models 768, 772, 773, 775 and 776.*

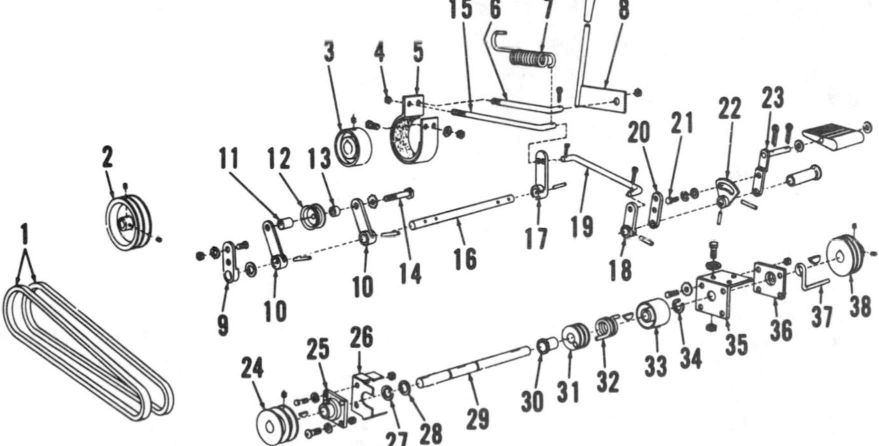

*Fig. G11—Exploded view of clutch-brake system used on Models 754, 755, 780, 53000, 53001 and 53008.*

1. Transaxle belts
2. Transaxle input pulley
3. Brake drum
4. Adjusting nut
5. Brake band
6. Park brake rod
7. Clutch tension spring
8. Park brake lever
9. Bracket
10. Idler arm
11. Bushing
12. Idler
13. Spacer
14. Bolt
15. Brake rod
16. Shaft
17. Clutch-brake lever
18. Arm
19. Clutch-brake rod
20. Bracket
21. Bolt
22. Adjusting plate
23. Clutch-brake pedal
24. Jackshaft input pulley
25. Bearing assy.
26. Belt guide
27. Snap ring
28. Washer
29. Jackshaft
30. Bearing
31. Clutch drive pulley
32. Torsion spring
33. Spring drive sleeve
34. Snap ring
35. Bracket
36. Bearing assy.
37. Belt guide
38. Pto pulley

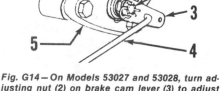

*Fig. G14—On Models 53027 and 53028, turn adjusting nut (2) on brake cam lever (3) to adjust brake.*

1. Brake disc
2. Adjusting nut
3. Cam lever
4. Brake link
5. Caliper assy.

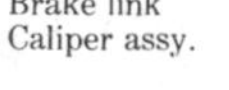

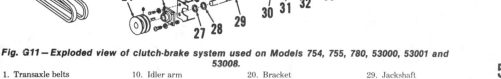

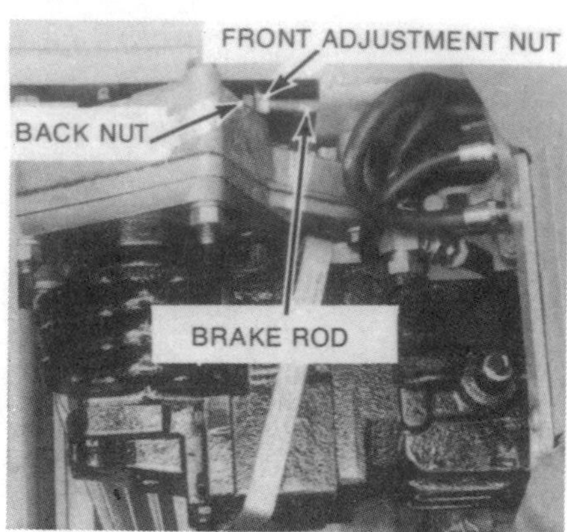


*Fig. G15—View of brake linkage adjustment point on Models 774, 867, 53003, 53004, 53010, 53020 and 53022.*

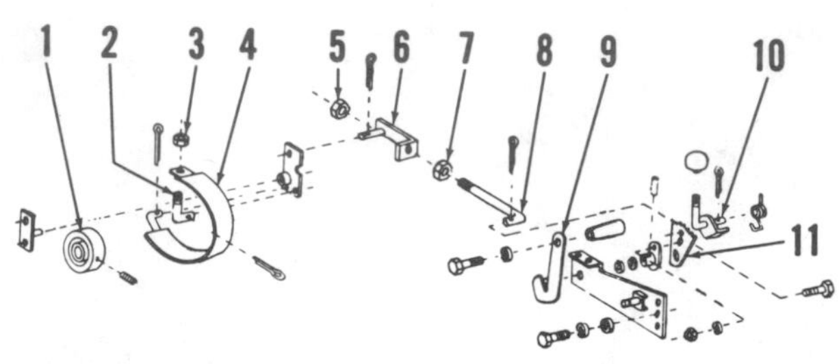

*Fig. G16—Exploded view of typical parking brake linkage used on hydrostatic drive models equipped with drum type brake.*

1. Brake drum
2. Rod
3. Nut
4. Brake band
5. Adjusting nut
6. Link
7. Adjusting nut
8. Rod
9. Parking brake lever
10. Parking brake latch
11. Ratchet

speed control lever returns to neutral position, then turn adjusting nut (2–Fig. G14) on disc brake clockwise until brake pads contact brake disc.

A drum type brake, located on left side of transaxle, is used on all other models. To adjust brake, raise seat and loosen front adjustment nut (Fig. G15) and turn rear nut to shorten brake linkage rod. When adjustment is correct, tighten front nut against linkage. If additional adjustment is required, tighten locknut (3–Fig. G16) on brake band rod (2) until brake is locked when park brake handle is ½ inch (13 mm) from end of slot.

### Models 769-770-771-53002-53005-53006-53009-53019-53021-53023-53024-53025-53026-53030-53031-53032

The clutch mechansim is spring loaded and does not require adjustment. Drive belt should be inspected for fraying, cracking or excessive wear and renewed as necessary. Check for clutch idler tension against drive belt. There should be no belt slippage when clutch pedal is in up position. If drive belt slips, check for faulty clutch tension spring or for excessive wear or stretching of drive belt.

Brake adjustment is accomplished by turning adjusting nut (Fig. G17) on rod at brake band. Adjust brake so brake band does not contact brake drum until clutch idler tension is removed from transaxle drive belt.

### Models 52072-52073-52080-52081-52082-52083-52113-52117-52122

The clutch pivot bracket (1–Fig. G18) is spring loaded and does not require adjustment. There should be no belt slippage when clutch-brake pedal is in up position. If drive belt slips, check for faulty clutch tension spring and be sure pivot bracket is pivoting freely. Check belt for excessive wear or stretching and renew as necessary.

Disc type brake is located on right side of transaxle. To adjust brake, turn adjusting nuts (Fig. G19) clockwise to tighten brake pads against brake disc. Do not overtighten.

### Models 52112-53033-53034-53038-53039

To adjust main drive belt, lift rear fender and seat support assembly. Loosen locknut on underside of frame (Fig. G20). Turn nut on top of frame clockwise to tighten or counterclockwise to loosen. To check belt tension, press downward approximately at mid-point of belt. The belt should move 1 inch (25 mm).

The final drive belt requires no adjustment. The belt is adjusted by a spring loaded idler pulley. Check idler arm to be sure it pivots freely and provides tension.

To adjust brake, remove cotter pin from brake adjusting nut. Turn nut clockwise to tighten brake pad and compensate for wear (Fig. G21). Slight drag is permitted.

# DRIVE BELTS

## REMOVE AND REINSTALL

### Models 754-755-780-53000-53001-53008

To remove transaxle drive belts (1–Fig. G11), first unbolt and remove belt

*Fig. G17—View of drum type brake, located on side of transaxle, used on some models.*

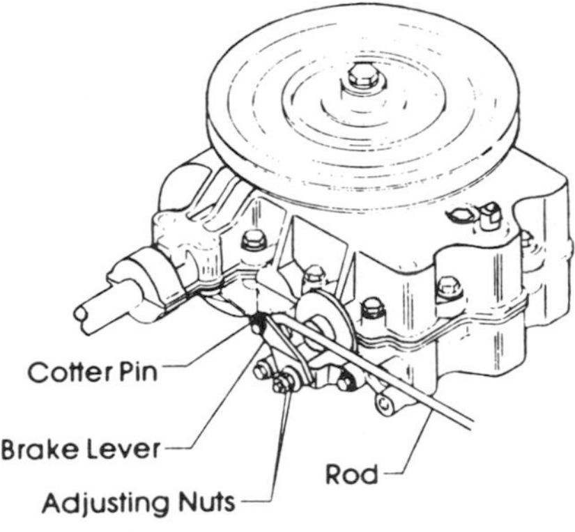


*Fig. G19—Disc type brake is located on right side of transaxle on Models 52072, 52073, 52080, 52081, 52082, 52083, 52113, 52117 and 52122.*

*Fig. G18—View of traction drive belt and spring loaded clutch idler used on Models 52072, 52073, 52080, 52081, 52082, 52083, 52113, 52117 and 52122.*

1. Pivot bracket
2. Belt finger
3. V-idler pulley
4. Transaxle pulley
5. Belt finger
6. Flat idler pulley
7. Tension spring
8. Traction belt
9. Lower belt retainer
10. Upper belt retainer
11. Engine pulley

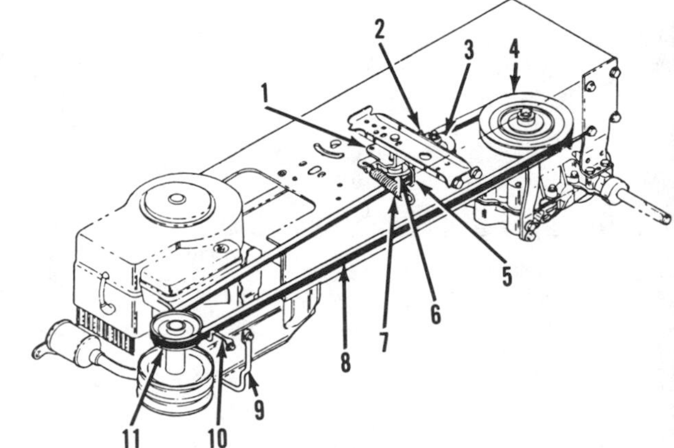

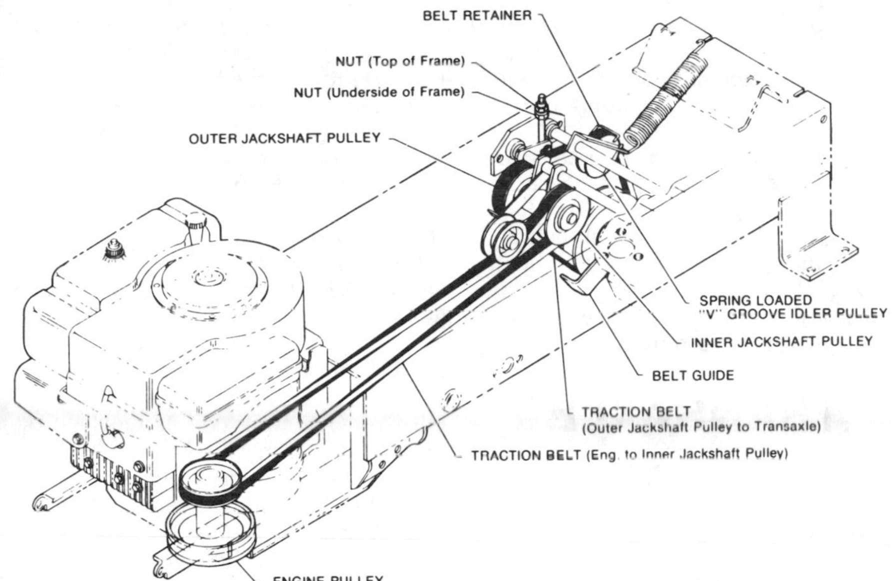


*Fig. G20—View of traction drive belts and adjustment points on Models 52112, 53033, 53034, 53038 and 53039.*

guide from around transaxle input pulley (2). Remove cotter pin from left end of shaft (16). Remove bolt (14), then lift out idler (12) with spacer (13) and bushing (11). Slide shaft (16) to the left. Unbolt bracket (35) from tractor frame. Remove belts over end of shaft assemblies.

The transaxle drive belts are serviced only as a matched set and both belts should be renewed at the same time. Install new belts by reversing removal procedure. Adjust clutch-brake pedal position and brake linkage as necessary.

## Models 768-772-773-775-776

If tractor must be tipped to reach underside of tractor, remove seat, rear shroud assembly and battery. Remove engine pulley belt guide (Fig. G12) and remove countershaft drive belt from engine pulley. Loosen rear belt guide bolt and side belt guide bolts and slide belt guides away from belt. Remove traction drive belt.

To reinstall drive belt, reverse removal procedure. Position rear and side belt guides so there is 1/16 to 1/8 inch (1.5-3 mm) clearance between belt and guide.

## Model 769-770-771-53002-53005-53006-53009-53019-53021-53024-53025-53026-53032 (With Variable Speed)

These models are equipped with an upper pulley which drives the traction drive belt and has a movable flange. Flange position is changed by moving variable speed control lever. As flange position is changed, radius that traction drive belt follows is altered, thereby changing drive ratio. To remove traction drive belt, remove belt guide around transaxle driven pulley and loosen retaining bolt of upper belt finger and move belt finger away from belt. Move variable speed control lever rearward to slow position. Spread flanges of drive pulley and remove belt. Push flanges of pulley together so belt can be moved between pulley and control cam as shown in Fig. G22. Remove traction drive belt. When installing traction drive belt, position belt guide and belt finger so there is 1/16 inch (1.5 mm) clearance between guide or finger and belt.

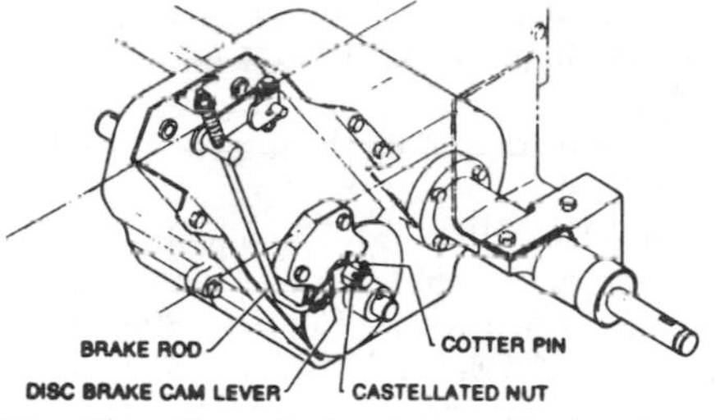


*Fig. G21—View of disc brake adjustment on Models 53033, 53034, 53038 and 53039. Model 52112 is similar.*

## Models 769-770-771-53002-53005-53006-53009-53019-53021-53023-53024-53025-53026-53030-53031-53032 (Without Variable Speed)

To remove traction drive belt, refer to Fig. G23, remove rear belt guide bolt and loosen front guide bolt. Move belt guide away from belt. Loosen belt finger bolt, move finger upward and remove traction drive belt. When installing traction drive belt, position belt guide and belt finger so there is 1/16 inch (1.5 mm) clearance between guide or finger and the belt.

## Models 52072-52073-52080-52081-52082-52083-52113-52117-52122

To remove traction drive belt, first remove any attachments mounted under tractor. Set parking brake, then remove flat idler pulley (6–Fig. G18) and V-idler pulley (3) from pivot bracket (1). Disconnect shift rod from transmission shift lever. Remove upper belt retainer (10), then slip belt off pulleys and remove from tractor.

Install new belt by reversing removal procedure. Belt finger (5) should point directly at left side of frame and belt finger (2) should point directly at right side of frame.

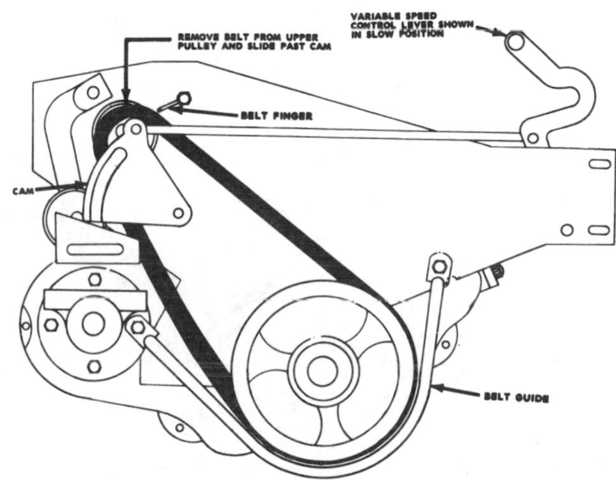


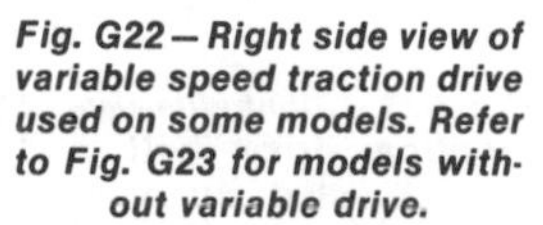

*Fig. G22—Right side view of variable speed traction drive used on some models. Refer to Fig. G23 for models without variable drive.*

### Models 52112-53033-53034-53038-53039

To remove main drive belt, lift rear fender and seat support assembly and refer to Fig. G20. Loosen belt tension adjusting nut. **Do not remove.** Remove engine pulley belt cover. Work belt off inner jackshaft pulley and engine pulley. Install new belt by reversing removal procedure.

To remove final drive belt, depress foot pedal and set parking brake. Loosen "V" groove idler pulley and remove belt. Reassemble by reversing disassembly procedure and adjust belt retainer. With belt engaged, there must be 1/16 to 1/8 inch (1.5-3 mm) clearance between retainer and belt.

**CAUTION: All belt guards must be in place before operating tractor.**

# RIGHT ANGLE DRIVE

### Models 769-770-771-53002-53005-53006-53009-53019-53021-53023-53024-53025-53026-53030-53031-53032

**R&R AND OVERHAUL.** To remove right angle drive unit, raise seat assembly and unbolt drive shaft rear coupling. Remove traction drive belt from pulley, then loosen set screws and remove pulley assembly. Unbolt and remove right angle drive from tractor.

To disassemble unit, remove cover (1–Fig. G24) and gasket (2). Unbolt and remove retainer (13) with oil seal (14) and gasket (12). Withdraw output shaft (10) and bearing (11), then remove driven gear (9) through cover opening. Remove oil seal (17) and snap ring (16). Push input shaft (6), bearing (5) and drive gear (4) out through cover opening. Gear and bearing can be removed from input shaft after first removing snap ring (3). To remove bearing (8), either tap outside of housing (7) behind bearing with a mallet or apply heat to housing.

Clean and inspect all parts and renew any showing excessive wear or other damage. Reassemble by reversing disassembly procedure. Use new oil seals and gaskets and fill unit half full with multipurpose lithium base grease.

Reinstall right angle drive unit on tractor by reversing removal procedure.

# TRANSAXLE

## LUBRICATION

### All Models

Model 780 is equipped with a Peerless 1700 series transaxle. Approximate capacity is 3 pints (3.8 L) of SAE 90 EP gear lubricant.

Models 768, 772, 773, 775 and 776 are equipped with a Peerless 600 series transaxle. Approximate capacity is 1½ pints (0.7 L) of SAE 90 EP gear lubricant.

Models 754, 755, 769, 770, 771, 53000, 53001, 53002, 53006, 53008, 53009, 53019, 53021, 53023, 53024, 53025, 53026, 53030, 53031, 53032, 53033, 53034, 53038 and 53039 are equipped with a Peerless 2300 series transaxle. Approximate capacity is 4 pints (1.9 L) of SAE 90 EP gear lubricant. Gear lubricant is added through shift lever opening.

Models 52072, 52073, 52080, 52081, 52082, 52083, 52113, 52117 and 52122 are equipped with a Peerless 800 series transaxle. Transaxle is filled at factory with 1½ pints (0.7 L) of lithium base grease.

## REMOVE AND REINSTALL

### Models 768-772-773-775-776

To remove transaxle assembly, first remove seat, rear shroud assembly and battery. Loosen belt guide bolts and slide belt guides away from belt. Remove traction drive belt from transaxle input pulley. Disconnect brake linkage. Remove cap screws retaining transaxle to frame and remove "U" bolts securing axle housings to frame. Raise rear of tractor and remove transaxle assembly from tractor.

Reinstall by reversing removal procedure. Adjust clutch and brake linkage as required.

### All Other Models So Equipped

To remove transaxle assembly, first unbolt and remove belt guide from around transaxle input pulley. Depress clutch-brake pedal and remove traction drive belt from transaxle input pulley. Disconnect brake linkage and remove brake band (models so equipped). Place a floor jack under transaxle to prevent unit from tipping forward. Block up under frame, unbolt transaxle from frame, raise rear of frame and roll transaxle rearward from tractor.

To reinstall transaxle, reverse removal procedure.

## OVERHAUL

### All Models

Model 780 is equipped with a Peerless 1700 series transaxle. Models 768, 772, 773, 775 and 776 are equipped with a Peerless 600 series transaxle. Models

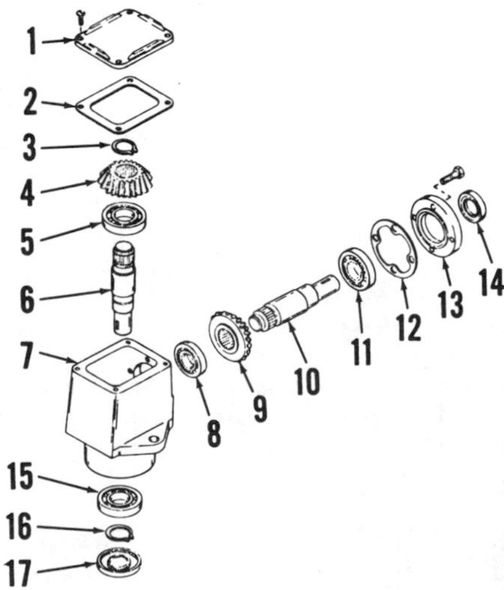

*Fig. G24—Exploded view of right angle drive unit used on models so equipped.*

1. Cover
2. Gasket
3. Snap ring
4. Drive gear
5. Bearing
6. Input shaft
7. Housing
8. Bearing
9. Driven gear
10. Output shaft
11. Bearing
12. Gasket
13. Retainer
14. Oil seal
15. Bearing
16. Snap ring
17. Oil seal

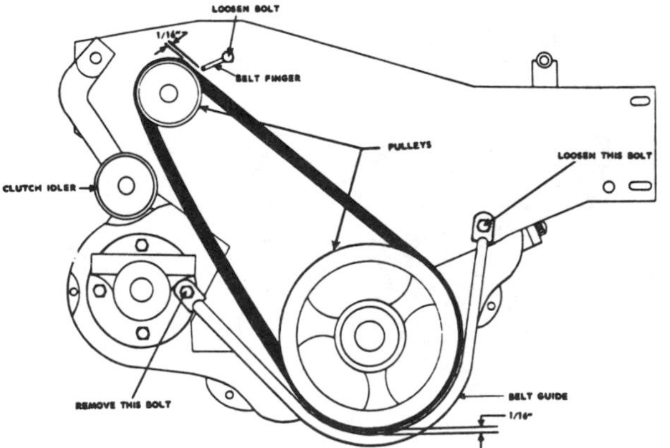


*Fig. G23—Right side view of traction drive belt and pulleys used on models without variable speed.*

754, 755, 769, 770, 771, 53000, 53001, 53002, 53006, 53008, 53009, 53019, 53021, 53023, 53024, 53025, 53026, 53030, 53031, 53032, 53033, 53034, 53038 and 53039 are equipped with a Peerless 2300 series transaxle. Models 52072, 52073, 52080, 52081, 52082, 52083, 52113, 52117 and 52122 are equipped with a Peerless 800 series transaxle.

On all models, refer to the appropriate Peerless section in TRANSAXLE SERVICE section for overhaul procedure.

# HYDROSTATIC TRANSMISSION

## LUBRICATION

### Models 774-867-53003-53004-53010-53020-53022

Models 774, 867, 53003, 53004, 53010, 53020 and 53022 are equipped with a Vickers T66 hydrostatic transmission. Recommended oil is Type "A" automatic transmission fluid. The oil should be changed and filter renewed if there is any evidence of oil contamination or if hydrostatic unti is disassembled. Capacity is approximately 8 pints (3 L).

### Models 52112

Model 52112 is equipped with an Eaton Model 6 hydrostatic transmission. Hydrostatic transmission is separate from differential unit and transmission uses different fluid than the gear reduction unit. Transmission fluid level should be at the appropriate level line marked on reservoir filler tube when unit is hot or cold.

### Models 53027-53028

Models 53027 and 53028 are equipped with Eaton Model 10 hydrostatic transmission. The hydrostatic transmission shares a common reservoir with reduction drive and differential unit. Reservoir may be filled at factory with either Type "A" automatic transmission fluid or SAE 20W SE rated engine oil. If transmission fluid is being renewed, completely drain system and refill with SAE 20W engine oil rated SE. Reservoir capacity is approximately 10 pints (4.7 L).

**NOTE: If adding oil to system, do not intermix the two types of fluid.**

Transmission oil is routed through an external oil filter. Manufacturer recommends renewing filter after first 50 hours of operation and every 250 hours thereafter.

## ADJUSTMENT

### Models 774-867-53003-53004-53010-53020-53022

To adjust hydrostatic transmission control linkage, block up under rear of tractor so both rear wheels are free to rotate. Start engine and move transmission control lever to reverse and forward positions, then depress neutral pedal. Wheels should stop turning. If wheels turn when neutral pedal is fully depressed, stop engine. Remove cotter pin (Fig. G34), loosen locknut and rotate turnbuckle one notch at a time as required. If wheels are rotating rearward, rotate turnbuckle to lengthen control rod or if wheels were turning forward, shorten control rod. After each ¼-turn (1 notch) adjustment, start engine and recheck neutral return position. When adjustment is correct, install cotter pin and tighten locknut.

If unable to stop wheels from turning with turnbuckle adjustment, remove spring clip, loosen locknut and remove clevis pin. Rotate clevis ½-turn at a time as required. If wheels turn rearward, lengthen control rod or if wheels turn forward, shorten rod. When adjustment is correct, install spring clip and tighten locknut.

### Models 52112-53027-53028

If tractor creeps either forward or backward with neutral-brake pedal depressed, control linkage should be adjusted. Transmission should be at operating temperature before checking or adjusting transmission.

**CAUTION: Do not attempt to adjust linkage while engine is running.**

Raise and securely block rear of tractor so rear wheels may rotate freely. Refer to Fig. G40 and loosen jam nuts (1). Turn turnbuckle (3) 1/6-turn clockwise (lengthens rod) if tractor creeps backward or counterclockwise if tractor creeps forward. Recheck transmission operation and repeat adjustment procedure as needed. If fine adjustment does not correct creeping, additional adjustment may be obtained as follows: Disconnect clevis (6) from transmission control arm (4) and turn clevis ½-turn counterclockwise (lengthens rod) if tractor creeps backward or clockwise if tractor creeps forward. Check operation and repeat adjustment as required. If tractor begins to creep in opposite direction, make final adjustment with turnbuckle as previously outlined.

If ground speed control lever does not stay in position under load, tighten linkage friction spring to increase tension on control lever. Do not overtighten to the point that depressing neutral-brake pedal will not return control linkage to neutral.

## REMOVE AND REINSTALL

### Models 774-867-53003-53004-53010-53020-53022

To remove hydrostatic transmission, remove seat pan and shift plate from top of frame. Thoroughly clean transmission and surrounding area to prevent entrance of dirt or other foreign material

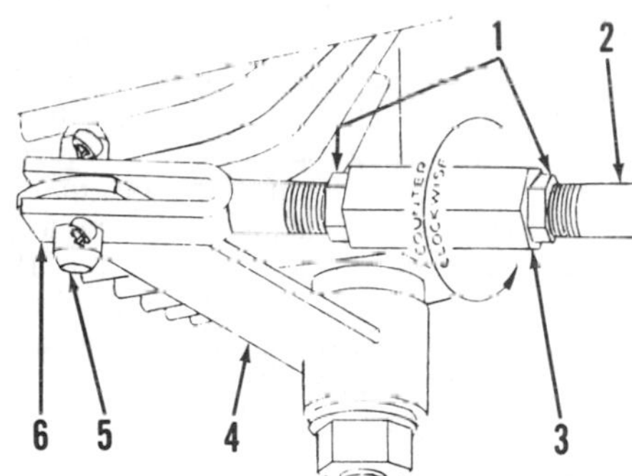


*Fig. G40 — View of hydrostatic transmission control linkage. Refer to text for adjustment procedure.*

1. Jam nuts
2. Control rod
3. Turnbuckle
4. Control arm
5. Pin
6. Clevis

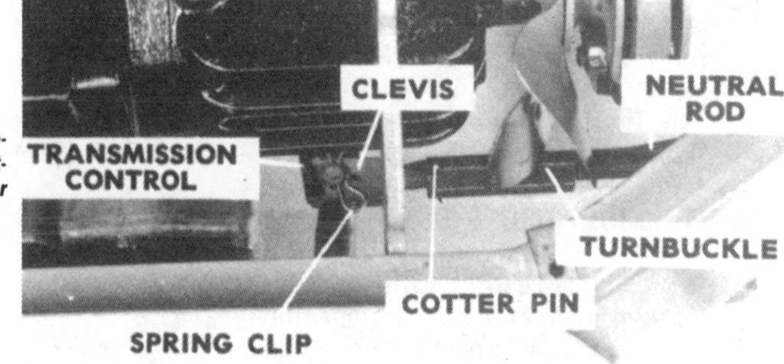


*Fig. G34 — View of hydrostatic control rod adjustment points. Refer to text for procedure.*

into system. Disconnect oil lines from transmission and plug or cap openings. Remove control rod clevis pin and loosen set screws in drive shaft rear coupling. Unbolt transmission from reduction drive and differential housing. Move transmission toward right side of tractor, hold unit level and pry input shaft out of drive shaft coupling hub. Tilt front end of transmission downward and lift assembly from tractor.

When reinstalling transmission, renew mounting gasket and reverse removal procedure. Fill reduction drive and differential housing to level plug opening with Type "A" automatic transmission fluid. Start engine and operate at low idle speed for about one minute. Recheck fluid level and add as needed. Start engine and operate at approximately half throttle. Make several short runs forward and rearward at low speed. Stop engine, check for external leakage, then recheck fluid level and add as needed. Check control linkage and adjust as necessary.

### Model 52112

To remove transmission and differential assembly, raise and support right wheel of tractor off the ground. Remove right wheel assembly. Remove the three cap screws retaining fan guard. Remove fan guard and fan, then reinstall the three cap screws to maintain torque bracket alignment. Temporarily reinstall right wheel. Disconnect shift lever clevis at transmission. Remove rear hitch plate from between main frame. Pull spring loaded idler pulley down and work secondary drive belt off transmission input pulley and idler pulley. Disconnect brake adjustment rod at brake lever. Remove the two locknuts on left and right "U" bolts retaining axle housings to support brackets. Support transmission, then remove the three cap screws retaining differential assembly to torque bracket. Raise and support rear main frame and pull differential/transmission assembly out and away from tractor. Remove tire and wheel assemblies. Remove the four cap screws retaining transmission to differential and separate assemblies.

Reinstall transmission/differential assembly by reversing removal procedure. Transmission should be filled with approximately 22 ounces (651 mL) of SAE 20 detergent oil. Differential should be filled with approximately 2¾ pints (1.3 L) of SAE 90 EP gear oil.

### Models 53027-53028

To remove hydrostatic transmission, first remove seat and fender assembly and shift plate. Disconnect brake return spring and rear brake link at parking brake ratchet. Disconnect transmission control rod clevis from control lever. Loosen set screws and slide fan hub towards transmission and disconnect drive shaft coupling from transmission input shaft. Drain transmission fluid, then identify and disconnect hydraulic hoses to transmission. Plug all openings to prevent entry of dirt. Support transmission to prevent tipping, then remove transaxle mounting bolts. Raise and move rear of frame away from transmission assembly. Remove fan assembly and disconnect intake hose and filter hose from transmission. Unbolt and remove hydrostatic transmission from transaxle.

Reinstall by reversing removal procedure. Renew hydraulic filter and transmission oil. Adjust control linkage as previously outlined.

## OVERHAUL

### All Models

Models 774, 867, 53003, 53004, 53010, 53020 and 53022 are equipped with a Vickers Model T66 hydrostatic transmission. Model 52112 is equipped with an Eaton Model 6 hydrostatic transmission. Models 53027 and 53028 are equipped with an Eaton Model 10 hydrostatic transmission.

On all models, refer to appropriate Eaton or Vickers section in HYDROSTATIC TRANSMISSION SERVICE section for overhaul procedure.

# REDUCTION DRIVE AND DIFFERENTIAL

### Models 774-867-53003-53004-53010-53020-53022

**R&R AND OVERHAUL.** To remove reduction drive and differential unit, first remove hydrostatic transmission as outlined previously. Drain fluid from reduction drive and differential unit. Attach a hoist to rear seat bracket to support tractor. Disconnect brake rod from ratchet. Remove "U" bolts from axle tubes and unbolt unit from frame. Raise rear of tractor frame and roll assembly rearward from tractor.

Remove oil filter, brake drum and rear wheels. Remove nuts (19–Fig. G44), washers (20) and rear wheel hubs. Slide dust seals (21) from axle shafts, then us-

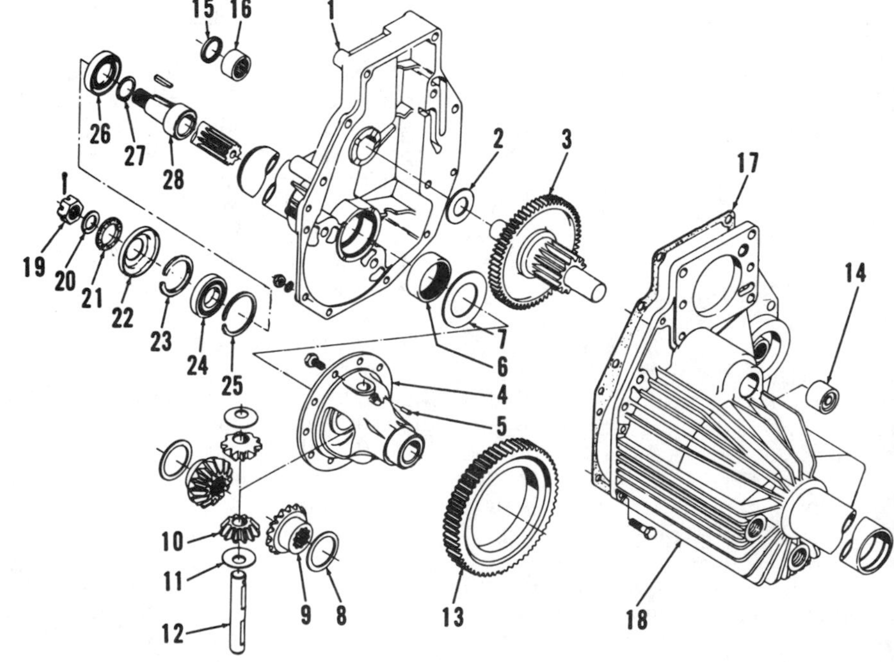


*Fig. G44—Exploded view of reduction drive and differential unit used on Models 774, 867, 53003, 53004, 53010, 53020 and 53022.*

1. Left housing
2. Thrust washer
3. Reduction gear & countershaft
4. Differential case
5. Pin
6. Bearing
7. Thrust washer
8. Thrust washer
9. Side gear
10. Bevel pinion
11. Thrust washer
12. Differential pinion shaft
13. Ring gear
14. Needle bearing
15. Oil seal
16. Needle bearing
17. Gasket
18. Right housing
19. Nut
20. Washer
21. Seal
22. Bearing retainer
23. Snap ring
24. Bearing
25. Snap ring
26. Oil seal
27. Snap ring
28. Axle shaft

ing a hammer and chisel, remove bearing retainers (22). Remove snap rings (23) and withdraw axle shafts (28) with bearings (24). Oil seals (26) can be removed after removing snap rings (25).

Place reduction drive and differential assembly in a vise with left axle tube pointing downward. Remove housing bolts and drive out two alignment spring pins. Lift off right housing (18). Remove differential and ring gear assembly, then remove reduction gear and countershaft (3). Do not lose the four thrust washers (2 and 7). Drive out pin (5), then drive out differential pinion shaft (12). Rotate side gears (9) until bevel pinions (10) and thrust washers (11) can be removed from case (4), then remove side gears (9) and thrust washers (8). Remove ten retaining cap screws and using a hammer and wooden block, drive ring gear (13) from case (4). Oil seal (15) and needle bearings (6, 14 and 16) can now be removed.

Clean and inspect all parts and renew any showing excessive wear or other damage. Reassemble by reversing disassembly procedure. When installing ring gear (13) on case (4), tighten three opposite cap screws until gear is pulled up tightly on case, then tighten all cap screws to a torque of 50 ft.-lbs. (68 N•m). Renew all seals and gaskets. Install oil seals (2 – Fig. G45) in axle tubes with lip to the inside, then install snap ring (3). Pack axle bearings (4) with high grade multipurpose grease and carefully install axle shaft and bearing assemblies. Install snap ring (5), pack new retainers (6) with multipurpose grease and install retainers.

After unit is installed on tractor and hydrostatic transmission is installed, renew fluid filter and install new Type "A" automatic transmission fluid. Capacity is approximately 8 pints (3.8 L).

## Model 52112

**R&R AND OVERHAUL.** To remove reduction gear and differential unit, refer to the previous REMOVE AND REINSTALL paragraphs in HYDROSTATIC TRANSMISSION section and remove hydrostatic transmission and differential as a complete assembly. Remove wheel and hub assemblies from axles. Drain differential lubricant and separate transmission from differential. Remove brake disc from brake shaft. Clean axle shafts and remove any burrs on shafts. Unscrew cap screws and drive out dowel pins in cover (29 – Fig. G46). Lift cover off case and axle shaft. Withdraw brake shaft (5), idler gear (4) and thrust washers (3 and 6) from case. Remove output shaft (11), output gear (10), spacer (9), thrust washer (8) and differential assembly from case. Axle shaft housings (20 and 22) must be pressed from case to cover.

To disassemble differential, unscrew four cap screws (17) and separate axle shaft and carriage assemblies from ring gear (28). Drive blocks (25), bevel pinion gears (26) and drive pin (27) can now be removed from ring gear. Remove snap rings (12) and slide axle shafts (18 and 23) from axle gears (13) and carriages (16 and 24).

Clean and inspect all parts and renew any parts damaged or excessively worn. When installing needle bearings, press bearings in from inside of case or cover until bearings are 0.015-0.020 inch

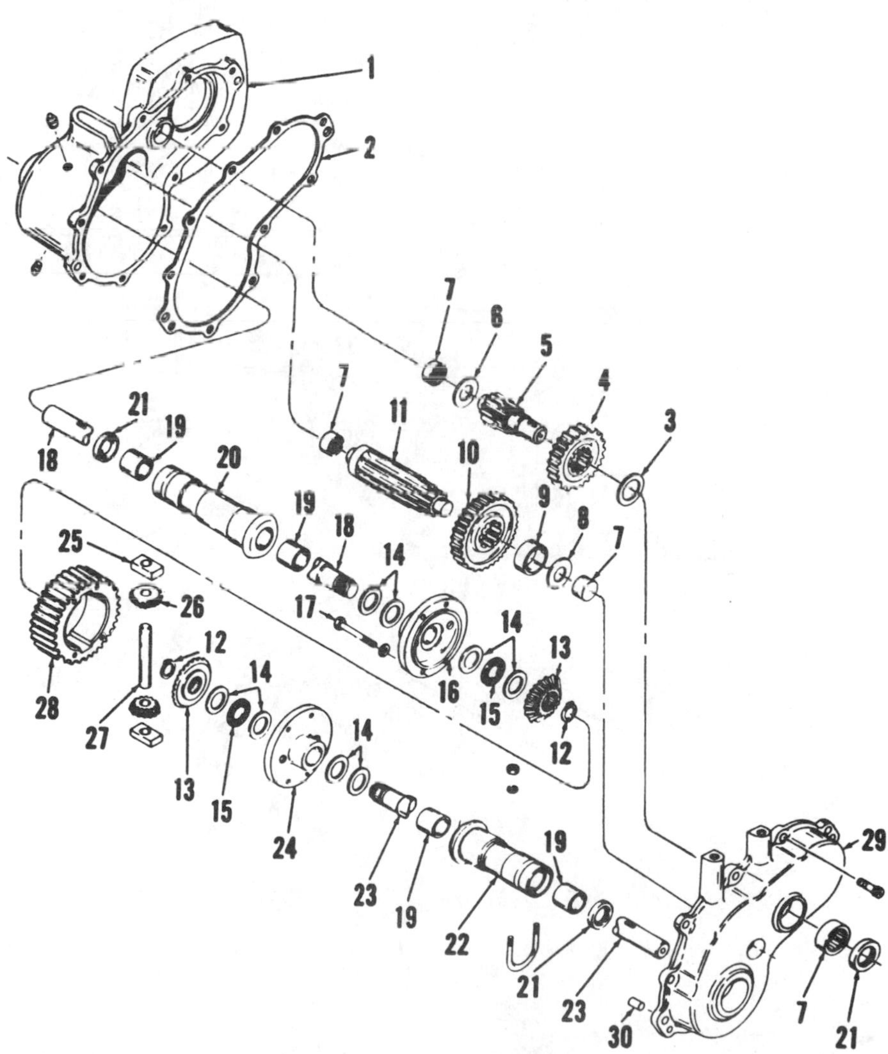


*Fig. G46 — Exploded view of gear reduction and differential unit used on Model 52112.*

1. Case
2. Gasket
3. Washer
4. Idler gear
5. Brake shaft
6. Washer
7. Bearing
8. Washer
9. Spacer
10. Output gear
11. Output shaft
12. Snap ring
13. Side gears
14. Thrust washers
15. Thrust bearing
16. Differential carrier
17. Bolt
18. Axle shaft (L.H.)
19. Bushing
20. Axle housing
21. Oil seal
22. Axle housing
23. Axle shaft (R.H.)
24. Differential carrier
25. Drive block
26. Drive pinion
27. Drive pin
28. Ring gear
29. Cover
30. Dowel pin

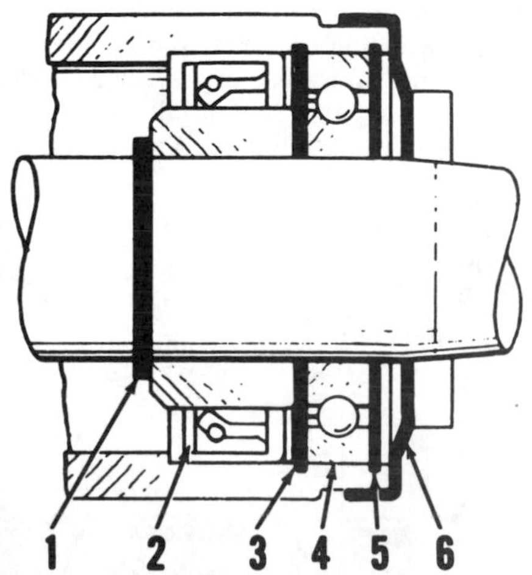


*Fig. G45 — Sectional view of axle outer bearing and oil seal installation on Models 774, 867, 53003, 53004, 53010, 53020 and 53022.*

1. Snap ring
2. Oil seal
3. Snap ring
4. Ball bearing
5. Snap ring
6. Retainer

(0.381-0.508 mm) below thrust surfaces. Be sure heads of differential cap screws (17) and left axle shaft (18) are installed in left carriage housing (16). Left axle shaft is installed through case (1). Tighten differential cap screws to 7 ft.-lbs. (9 N·m) and cover cap screws to 10 ft.-lbs. (14 N·m). Differential assembly and output shaft (11) must be installed in case at same time. Remainder of assembly is reverse of disassembly procedure. After installation, fill reduction gear and differential assembly with 2¾ pints (1.3 L) of SAE 90 EP gear oil.

## Models 53027-53028

**R&R AND OVERHAUL.** Models 53027 and 53028 are equipped with a dual range gear reduction assembly which drives through a limited slip differential. Remove gear reduction and differential unit and separate hydrostatic transmission from unit as previously outlined in HYDROSTATIC TRANSMISSION section. Remove wheels and clean exterior of unit.

To disassemble, remove axle housings (15–Fig. G47). Position unit with cover up, then remove cover (13). Lift out differential assembly and axles (40 through 54). Remove output shaft (36), gear (35) and thrust washers (34). Unscrew set screw (2) and remove spring (3) and ball (4). Remove brake shaft (32), sliding gear (33) and shift fork (10) and rod (8). Remove input shaft and gear components (18 through 25).

To disassemble differential assembly, remove cap screws (53) and remove differential carriers (41 and 52) and axles from ring gear assembly. Remove snap ring to separate axle gear, carrier and axle. Remove pinions (47) and separate body cores (45 and 48) from ring gear (46).

Inspect components for damage or excessive wear. To reassemble unit, reverse disassembly procedure. Check movement of shift rod when tightening set screw (2). Install gears (22 and 25) so bevels of gears face together as shown in Fig. G48. Install carrier cap screws (53–Fig. G47) so head of cap screw is on side of shorter carrier (52). Do not rotate axle housings after housing has been pressed tight against seal (11) as seal may be cut.

Fill unit with SAE 20W engine oil with API rating SE and allow oil to seep past roller bearings into axle housings. Recheck oil level and add oil to correct level at check plug opening in case.

Install unit in tractor by reversing removal procedure. Adjust brake linkage.

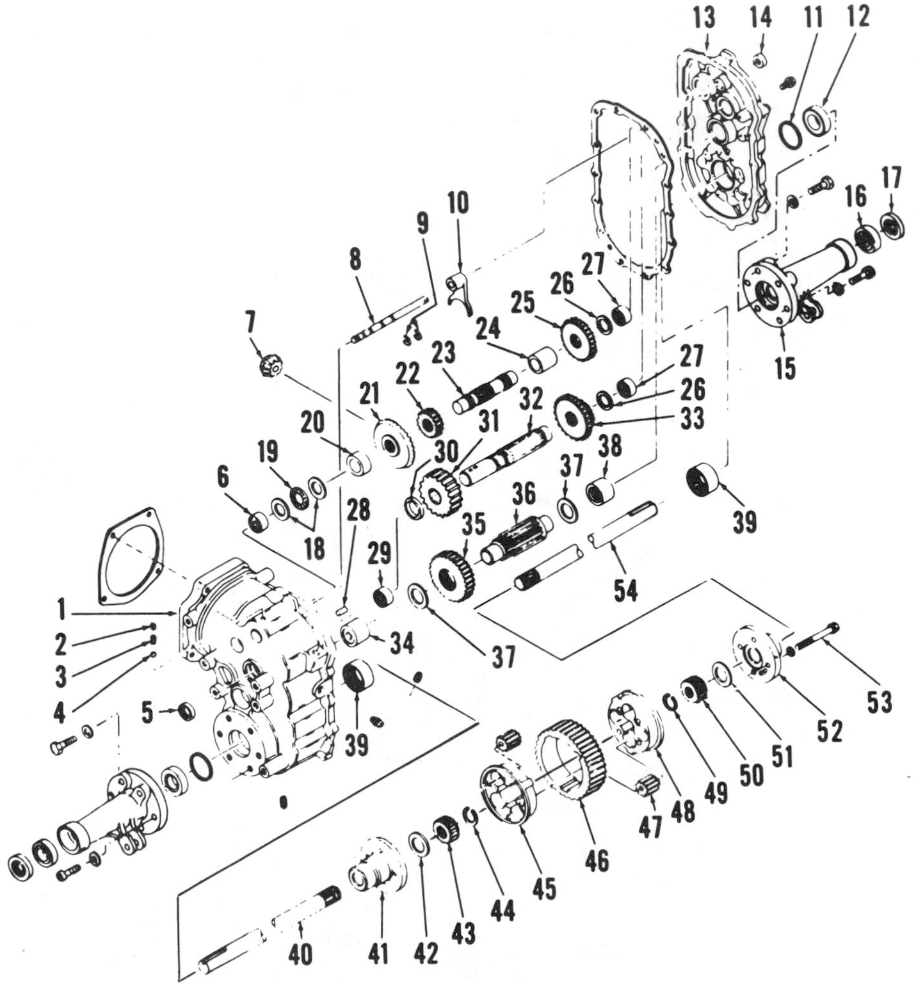

*Fig. G47–Exploded view of dual range reduction drive and differential assembly used on Models 53027 and 53028.*

1. Case
2. Set screw
3. Spring
4. Ball
5. Seal
6. Needle bearing
7. Transmission output gear
8. Shift rail
9. Snap rings
10. Shift fork
11. Quad ring
12. Tapered roller bearing
13. Cover
14. Seal
15. Axle housing
16. Ball bearing
17. Seal
18. Thrust washers
19. Thrust bearing
20. Spacer
21. Bevel gear
22. Gear (low range)
23. Shaft
24. Spacer
25. Gear (high range)
26. Thrust washer
27. Needle bearing
28. Dowel pin
29. Needle bearing
30. Spacer
31. Gear (17T)
32. Brake shaft
33. Sliding gears
34. Needle bearing
35. Gear (33T)
36. Output shaft
37. Thrust washer
38. Needle bearing
39. Needle bearing
40. Axle shaft (L.H.)
41. Differential carrier (L.H.)
42. Thrust washer
43. Axle gear
44. Snap ring
45. Body core
46. Ring gear
47. Pinion gears (8)
48. Body core
49. Snap ring
50. Axle gear
51. Thrust washer
52. Differential carrier (R.H.)
53. Cap screw
54. Axle shaft (R.H.)

# HYDRAULIC SYSTEM

On hydrostatic drive models equipped with hydraulic lift, hydraulic system pressure is provided by charge and auxiliary hydraulic pump located in hydrostatic transmission. Refer to appropriate HYDROSTATIC TRANSMISSION SERVICE section for schematic drawing of hydraulic system and service procedures covering charge pump. Hydraulic control valve directs fluid to lift cylinder.

On gear drive models equipped with hydraulic lift, a self-contained hydraulic unit, consisting of a gear pump, control valve and oil reservoir, is used along with a companion hydraulic cylinder. The hydraulic pump is belt driven.

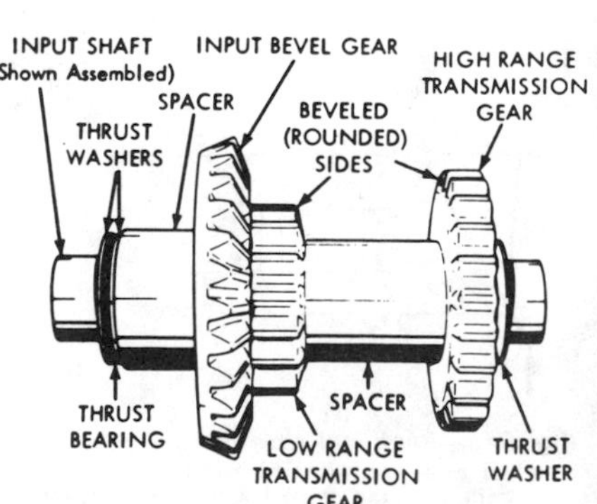


*Fig. G48–View of reduction drive input shaft and gears. Note position of bevels on gears.*

**NOTE: On some models, hydraulic system may be filled at factory with either Type "A" (red) automatic transmission fluid or SAE 20W (honey color) "SE" rated engine oil. Do not intermix the two type fluids.**

## TESTING

### Hydrostatic Drive Models So Equipped

Hydraulic lift maximum pressure should be 800 psi (5516 kPa) on Models 53027 and 53028. System pressure is regulated by a pressure relief valve located in lift control valve. On all other models, maximum lift pressure should be 500 psi (3447 kPa). Pressure is regulated by auxiliary circuit relief valve located in hydrostatic transmission center section.

To check pressure on all models, proceed as follows: Using a tee fitting, install a 1000 psi (7000 kPa) pressure gage in hydraulic line between control valve and lift cylinder on "lifting" side of cylinder. With oil at operating temperature and engine running at full rpm, actuate control lever until cylinder reaches end of its travel and observe pressure reading. On Models 53027 and 53028, relief valve setting can be adjusted by turning relief valve set screw located in end of control valve – 1/4-turn equals approximately 120 psi (827 kPa).

If pressure is low, check the following:

1. System low on oil.
2. Plugged hydraulic filter.
3. Malfunctioning implement relief valve.
4. Hydraulic valve or cylinder leaking internally.
5. Charge pump defective.

### Gear Drive Models So Equipped

Hydraulic life system maximum pressure should be 500 psi (3447 kPa). Pressure is regulated by a relief valve (17 – Fig. G49) located in hydraulic unit valve body.

To check lift system pressure, install a 1000 psi (7000 kPa) pressure gage in hydraulic line between hydraulic unit and "lifting" side of cylinder using a tee fitting. With oil at operating temperature and engine running at full rpm, actuate control lever to move cylinder to end of its travel and observe pressure reading. If pressure is low, check the following:

1. System low on oil.
2. Malfunctioning pressure relief valve.
3. Hydraulic cylinder leaking internally.
4. Pump or control valve defective.

## HYDRAULIC PUMP

### Hydrostatic Drive Models So Equipped

On hydrostatic drive models, hydrostatic transmission charge pump is power source for hydraulic system. Refer to appropriate HYDROSTATIC TRANSMISSION SERVICE section for charge pump service procedures.

### Gear Drive Models So Equipped

To disassemble hydraulic unit, first thoroughly clean exterior of unit and refer to Fig. G49. Remove filler plug (19) and drain fluid from reservoir. Unscrew retaining nut (23) and remove reservoir (20). Remove pump cover (12) and withdraw drive gear (15), idler gear (13) and idler shaft (16). Remove pressure relief valve assembly (17). Remove snap ring (1) and withdraw spool valve (6).

Inspect all parts for excessive wear or other damage. If spool or body is worn or damaged, it is recommended that complete hydraulic unit be renewed. Reassemble unit by reversing disassembly procedure. Reinstall unit on tractor and adjust drive belt tension so belt deflects 1/8 to 1/4-inch (3-6 mm) midway between pulleys under finger pressure.

## CONTROL VALVE

### Gear Drive Models So Equipped

On gear drive models, refer to HYDRAULIC PUMP paragraphs for service procedure covering control unit and pump assembly.

### Hydrostatic Drive Models So Equipped

Before beginning disassembly of valve, thoroughly clean exterior of valve. Remove screw (1 – Fig. G50) from end of spool (7), then pull spool out con-

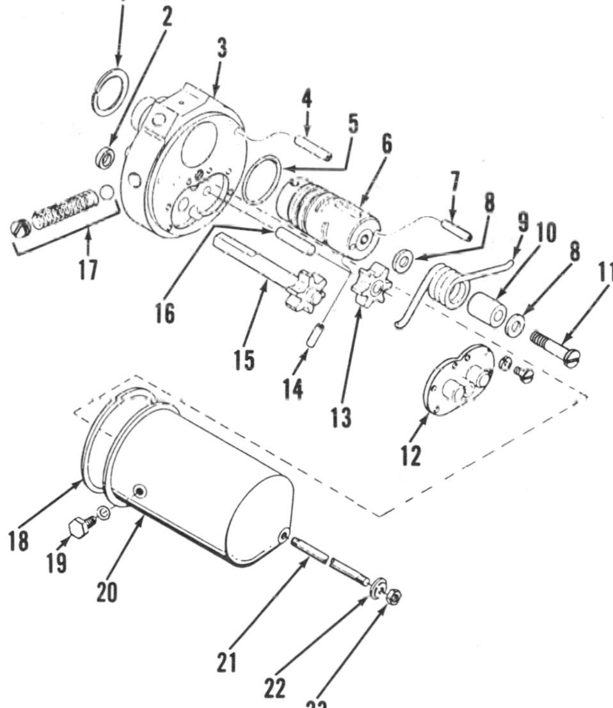


***Fig. G49 — Exploded view of self-contained hydraulic unit used on gear drive model tractors equipped with hydraulic lift.***

1. Snap ring
2. Oil seal
3. Body
4. Roll pin (3/16 x 1-1/2 in.)
5. "O" ring
6. Spool valve
7. Roll pin (5/32 x 1-1/4 in.)
8. Washers
9. Centering spring
10. Sleeve
11. Retaining screw
12. Pump cover
13. Idler gear
14. Roll pin (5/32 x 7/8 in.)
15. Drive gear
16. Idler shaft
17. Relief valve assy.
18. Gasket
19. Plug
20. Reservoir
21. Stud
22. Special washer
23. Nut

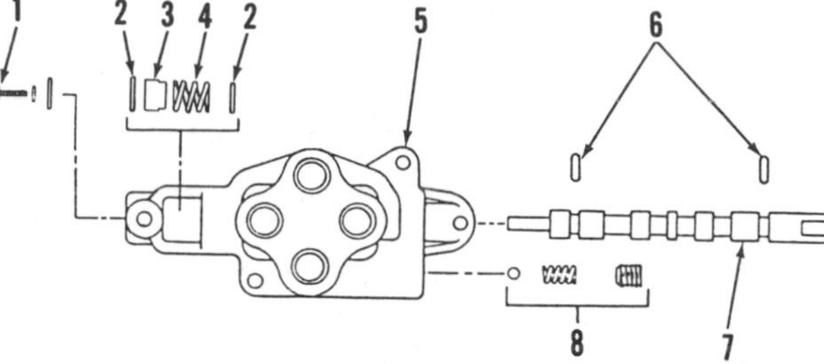


***Fig. G50 — Exploded view of typical hydraulic lift control valve used on hydrostatic drive model tractors. Open side of lip seals (6) goes towards center of spool.***

1. Screw
2. Washers
3. Spacer
4. Centering spring
5. Valve body
6. Lip seals
7. Valve spool
8. Relief valve assy.

trol lever end of valve body. Remove washers (2), spacer (3) and centering spring (4). Unscrew set screw and remove relief valve spring and ball (8).

Inspect parts for wear or other damage. If spool or body is damaged, complete valve assembly must be renewed. Install new seals (6) over each end of spool with open "V" side of seals facing each other. Coat all parts with clean oil and reassemble by reversing disassembly procedure. Be sure end of spool moves through centering spring and washers easily. Reinstall valve assembly and check and adjust relief valve setting as outlined in TESTING paragraph.

### HYDRAULIC CYLINDER

### All Models So Equipped

To disassemble hydraulic cylinder, first thoroughly clean outside of cylinder and refer to Fig. G51. Note positions of hose fittings, then remove fittings from cylinder body. Remove head (1), guide (8) and piston assembly (6) from tube (3).

Clean and inspect parts and renew as needed. Renew all "O" rings and back-up washers. Coat all parts with clean oil prior to reassembly. Be sure "O" rings are not cut or twisted when reassembling.

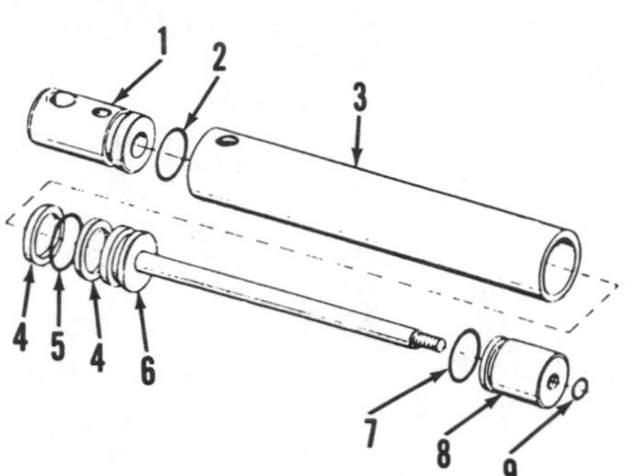


***Fig. G51—Exploded view of typical hydraulic cylinder used on all models equipped with hydraulic lift.***

1. Head
2. "O" ring
3. Tube
4. Back-up washers
5. "O" ring
6. Piston assy
7. "O" ring
8. Guide
9. "O" ring

## SAFETY INTERLOCK SWITCHES

### All Models So Equipped

Some models are equipped with an interlock system which will allow engine to start only if clutch-brake or neutral-brake pedal is fully depressed. On later models, pto lever must also be in disengaged position or held in START position before engine will start.

If engine will not start with controls in correct position, check the following: Check interlock switches to be sure contact is made when controls are moved to starting position. If interlock switches are not being actuated, readjust as necessary. Check for broken or disconnected wires. Use a test light to check continuity and repair as needed.

**CAUTION: Being able to start engine without moving pto control to disengaged or start position and/or fully depressing foot pedal is dangerous and should be corrected immediately.**

# GRAVELY

## CONDENSED SPECIFICATIONS

| | MODELS | | | | |
|---|---|---|---|---|---|
| | **408** | **424** | **424** | **430** | **430** |
| Engine Make | Kohler | Kohler | Onan | Kohler | Onan |
| Model | K181 | K241 | NB | K301 | NB |
| Bore | 2-15/16 in. (74.6 mm) | 3¼ in. (82.5 mm) | 3-9/16 in. (90.5 mm) | 3⅜ in. (85.7 mm) | 3-9/16 in. (90.5 mm) |
| Stroke | 2¾ in. (69.8 mm) | 2⅞ in. (73.0 mm) | 3 in. (76.2 mm) | 3¼ in. (82.5 mm) | 3 in. (76.2 mm) |
| Piston Displacement | 18.6 cu. in. (305 cc) | 23.9 cu. in. (392 cc) | 30.0 cu. in. (492 cc) | 29.07 cu. in. (476 cc) | 30.0 cu. in. (492 cc) |
| Horsepower | 8 | 10 | 10 | 12 | 12 |
| Slow Idle Speed – Rpm | 1000 | 1200 | 1000 | 1200 | 1000 |
| High Idle Speed (No Load) – Rpm | 3800 | 3600 | 3600 | 3600 | 3600 |
| Crankcase Oil Capacity | 2½ pints (1.2L) | 5 pints (2.4L) | 4 pints (1.9L) | 5 pints (2.4L) | 4 pints (1.9L) |
| Transmission Oil Capacity | 6 pints (2.8L) | 10 pints (4.7L) | 10 pints (4.7L) | 10 pints (4.7L) | 10 pints (4.7L) |
| Weight | | | SAE 90 EP | | |

| | MODELS | | | | |
|---|---|---|---|---|---|
| | **432** | **810** | **812** | **814** | **816S** |
| Engine Make | Kohler | Kohler | Kohler | Kohler | B&S |
| Model | K321 | K241 | K301 | K321 | 326437 |
| Bore | 3½ in. (88.9 mm) | 3¼ in. (82.5 mm) | 3⅜ in. (85.7 mm) | 3½ in. (88.9 mm) | 3-9/16 in. (90.5 mm) |
| Stroke | 3¼ in. (82.5 mm) | 2⅞ in. (73.0 mm) | 3¼ in. (82.5 mm) | 3¼ in. (82.5 mm) | 3¼ in. (82.5 mm) |
| Piston Displacement | 31.27 cu. in. (512 cc) | 23.9 cu. in. (392 cc) | 29.07 cu. in. (476 cc) | 31.27 cu. in. (512 cc) | 32.4 cu. in. (531 cc) |
| Horsepower | 14 | 10 | 12 | 14 | 16 |
| Slow Idle Speed – Rpm | 1200 | 1200 | 1200 | 1200 | 1200 |
| High Idle Speed (No Load) – Rpm | 3600 | 3600 | 3600 | 3600 | 3600 |
| Crankcase Oil Capacity | 5 pints (2.4L) | 5 pints (2.4L) | 5 pints (2.4L) | 5 pints (2.4L) | 4 pints (1.9L) |
| Transmission Oil Capacity | 10 pints (4.7L) | 12 pints (5.7L) | 12 pints (5.7L) | 12 pints (5.7L) | 12 pints (5.7L) |
| Weight | SAE 90 EP | | SAE 30 | | |

# CONDENSED SPECIFICATIONS

| | MODELS | | | |
|---|---|---|---|---|
| | 8102 | 8120, 8121 | 8122, 8123 | 8163B |
| Engine Make | Kohler | Kohler | Kohler | B&S |
| Model | K241 | K301 | K301 | 326437 |
| Bore | 3¼ in. (82.5 mm) | 3⅜ in. (85.7 mm) | 3⅜ in. (85.7 mm) | 3-9/16 in. (90.5 mm) |
| Stroke | 2⅞ in. (73.0 mm) | 3¼ in. (82.5 mm) | 3¼ in. (82.5 mm) | 3¼ in. (82.5 mm) |
| Piston Displacement | 23.9 cu. in. (392 cc) | 29.07 cu. in. (476 cc) | 29.07 cu. in. (476 cc) | 32.4 cu. in. (531 cc) |
| Horsepower | 10 | 12 | 12 | 16 |
| Slow Idle Speed – Rpm | 1200 | 1200 | 1200 | 1200 |
| Crankcase Oil Capacity | 5 pints (2.4L) | 5 pints (2.4L) | 5 pints (2.4L) | 4 pints (1.9L) |
| Transmission Oil Capacity | 12 pints (5.7L) | | | |
| Weight | SAE 30 | | | |

| | MODELS | | | |
|---|---|---|---|---|
| | 1232G, 1238G | 1232H | 1238H | 1238H |
| Engine Make | B&S | B&S | B&S | Kawasaki |
| Model | 281707 | 281707 | 281707 | FB460V |
| Bore | 3.44 in. (87.3 mm) | 3.44 in. (87.3 mm) | 3.44. (87.3 mm) | 89 mm (3.50 in.) |
| Stroke | 3.06 in. (77.7 mm) | 3.06 in. (77.7 mm) | 3.06 in. (77.7 mm) | 74 mm (2.91 in.) |
| Piston Displacement | 28.4 cu. in. (465 cc) | 28.4 cu. in. (465 cc) | 28.4 cu. in. (465 cc) | 460 cc (28.1 cu. in.) |
| Rated Power | 12 hp (8.9 kW) | 12 hp (8.9 kW) | 12 hp (8.9 kW) | 12.5 hp (9.3 kW) |
| Slow Idle Speed—Rpm | 1200 | 1200 | 1200 | 1200 |
| High Idle Speed (No-Load)—Rpm | 3300 | 3300 | 3300 | 3300 |
| Capacities— | | | | |
| Crankcase | 3 pts. (1.4 L) | 3 pts. (1.4 L) | 3 pts. (1.4 L) | 3 pts. (1.4 L) |
| Transmission | 24 oz. (0.7 L) | 4.8 pts. (2.3 L) | 4.8 pts. (2.3 L) | 4.8 pts. (2.3 L) |
| Weight | Grease | SAE 20W-20 | SAE 20W-20 | SAE 20W-20 |

| | MODELS | |
|---|---|---|
| | GEM 12.5 | GEM 14 |
| Engine Make | Kohler | Kohler |
| Model | CV12.5 | CV14 |
| Bore | 3.43 in. (87 mm) | 3.43 in. (87 mm) |
| Stroke | 2.64 in. (67 mm) | 2.64 in. (67 mm) |
| Piston Displacement | 24.3 cu. in. (398 cc) | 24.3 cu. in. (398 cc) |
| Rated Power | 12.5 hp (9.3 kW) | 14 hp (10.5 kW) |
| Slow Idle Speed—Rpm | 1200 | 1200 |
| High Idle Speed (No-Load)—Rpm | 3600 | 3600 |
| Capacities— | | |
| Crankcase | 4 pints (1.9 L) | 4 pints (1.9 L) |
| Transmission | 6 quarts (5.7 L) | 6 quarts (5.7 L) |
| Weight | SAE 20W-20 | SAE 20W-20 |



Illustrations courtesy Gravely International, Inc.

# FRONT AXLE AND STEERING SYSTEM

## FRONT AXLE MAIN MEMBER

### Model 408

The axle main member (5—Fig. GR1) is mounted directly to front of main frame and pivots on pin (6). To remove front axle main member, disconnect tie rods (4) from steering spindles (1 and 7). Support front of tractor and remove pivot pin (6). Raise front of tractor and roll axle assembly away from tractor.

Reinstall axle by reversing removal procedure. Lubricate with multipurpose grease.

### Models 424-430-432—Early Models 810-812-814

The axle main member (1—Fig. GR2 or GR3) is mounted directly to front of main frame and pivots on pin (5). To remove front axle main member, disconnect tie rod (2) ends from steering arms (3). Support front of tractor, remove pivot pin (5) and roll axle assembly from tractor.

Inspect parts for wear or other damage and renew as necessary. Reassembly is reverse of removal procedure. Lubricate pivot pin with multipurpose grease.

### Models 816S-8102-8121-8122-8123-8163B—Late Models 810-812-814

The axle main member (15—Fig. GR8) is mounted directly to main frame and pivots on bolt (17). To remove front axle, disconnect tie rod ends (13) from steering arms (8). Support front of tractor, remove pivot bolt (17) and roll axle assembly from tractor.

Reinstall axle by reversing removal procedure. Lubricate with multipurpose grease.

### Models 1232G-1232H-1238G-1238H-GEM 12.5-GEM 14

The axle main member (12—Fig. GR4) is center mounted directly to main frame and pivots on bolt (1). To remove front axle, disconnect tie rod ends from spindles (14). Support front of tractor and remove front wheels. Remove pivot bolt (1) and lower axle from tractor.

Reinstall axle by reversing removal procedure. Lubricate with multipurpose grease.

## TIE RODS AND TOE-IN

### Models 408-424-430-432—Early Models 810-812-814

The tie rods are nonadjustable. If ball joints are excessively worn, renew tie rod assemblies. Front wheel toe-in is not adjustable on these models.

### Models 816S-8102-8120-8121-8122-8123-8163B—Late Models 810-812-814

Front wheel toe-in of 0 to $^{3}/_{4}$ inch (0-19 mm) is recommended. Measure toe-in at wheel hub height at front and back of tires. To adjust toe-in, first check which wheel is excessively toed in or out. Disconnect tie rod ball joint (13—Fig. GR8) from steering arm (18) and turn tie rod ends as necessary to obtain desired toe-in. Renew ball joints that are excessively worn.

### Models 1232G-1232H-1238G-1238H-GEM 12.5-GEM 14

Front wheel toe-in of $^{1}/_{16}$ to $^{1}/_{8}$ inch (1.6-3.2 mm) is recommended. To check toe-in, measure distance between front wheels at wheel hub height at front and back of wheels. Front of wheels should be closer together (toed in) than rear of wheels.

To adjust toe-in, loosen tie rod jam nuts and turn each tie rod (9—Fig. GR4) an equal amount clockwise to decrease toe-in or counterclockwise to increase toe-in. Renew tie rod ball joints that are excessively worn.

## STEERING SPINDLES

### Model 408

To remove steering spindles (1 and 7—Fig. GR1), support front of tractor and remove wheels. Disconnect tie rods from steering spindles. Remove "E" ring (3) and lower steering spindles out of axle.

Lubricate with multipurpose grease and reassemble in reverse of removal.

### Models 424-430-432—Early Models 810-812-814

To remove steering spindles (4—Fig. GR2 or GR3), support front of tractor and remove wheels. Disconnect tie rods from steering arms (3). Unscrew clamp bolt or retaining nut and remove steering arm. Lower steering spindle out of axle.

Inspect for excessive wear or other damage and renew as required. Lubricate with multipurpose grease.

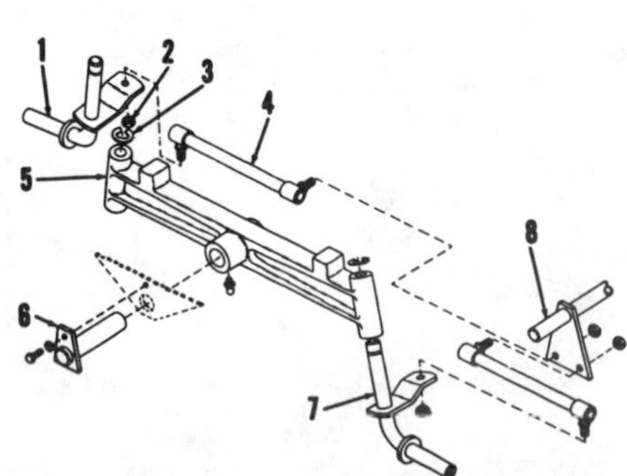


*Fig. GR1—Exploded view of front axle assembly used on Model 408.*

1. Steering spindle, R.H.
2. Nut
3. "E" ring
4. Tie rod
5. Axle main member
6. Pivot pin
7. Steering spindle, L.H.
8. Steering shaft

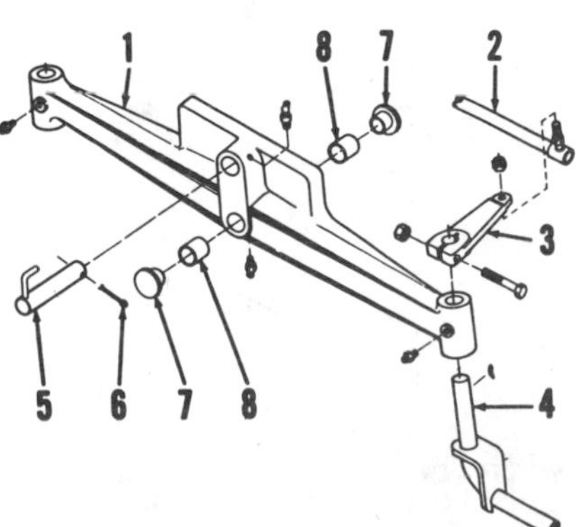


*Fig. GR2—Exploded view of front axle assembly used on Models 424, 430 and 432.*

1. Axle main member
2. Tie rod
3. Steering arm
4. Steering spindle
5. Pivot pin
6. Cotter pin
7. Plug
8. Pto shaft bushing

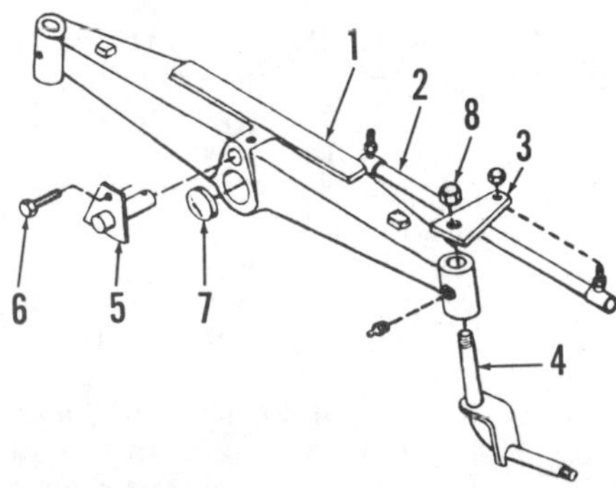


*Fig. GR3—Exploded view of front axle assembly used on early Models 810, 812 and 814.*

1. Axle main member
2. Tie rod
3. Steering arm
4. Steering spindle
5. Pivot pin
6. Cap screw
7. Plug
8. Nut

### Models 816S-8102-8120-8121-8122-8123-8163B—Late Models 810-812-814

To remove steering spindles (19—Fig. GR8), support front of tractor and remove wheels. Disconnect tie rods from spindle arms (18) and remove locknut securing arms to spindles. Slide steering arms off splines and withdraw spindles form axle.

Steering spindles are interchangeable. Lubricate with multipurpose grease.

### Models 1232G-1232H-1238G-1238H-GEM 12.5-GEM 14

To remove steering spindles (13—Fig. GR4), raise and support front of tractor. Remove front wheels. Disconnect tie rod ends from spindles. Drive out spring pin (14) and lower spindle from axle.

Inspect spindles and bushings (11) for excessive wear and renew as necessary. Lubricate with multipurpose grease. Reinstall spindle by reversing removal procedure.

## STEERING GEAR

### Model 408

To remove steering assembly, disconnect tie rods from steering plate. Remove bolts from bracket (8—Fig. GR5), then lower bracket, quadrant gear (10) and shaft from tractor. Remove steering shaft nut (1) and remove steering wheel. Remove key and "E" ring (3). Loosen set screw (5) and lower steering shaft (6) out of tractor.

Reassembly is reverse of disassembly procedure. Adjust mesh of quadrant gear (10) to steering shaft gear by adding or removing washers (7). Lubricate with multipurpose grease at fitting on bracket (8) and apply thin layer of grease on teeth of steering gears.

### Models 424-430-432—Early Models 810-812-814

**EXPOSED STEERING GEAR.** Early 424, 430 and 432 models are equipped with an exposed steering gear system as shown in Fig. GR6.

To remove quadrant steering gear, disconnect tie rod ends from gear and remove cotter pin holding pivot pin. Remove pivot pin and slide gear out of tractor. To remove steering shaft, remove steering wheel and snap ring. Remove cotter pin holding shaft in frame cross member. Raise shaft up out of frame cross member, then lower shaft out of tractor.

Reassemble steering gear assembly in reverse order of disassembly. Lubricate quadrant gear at grease fitting with multipurpose grease and apply thin layer of grease on gear teeth.

**ENCLOSED STEERING GEAR.** Early Models 810, 812 and 814 and later Models 424, 430 and 432 are equipped with an enclosed steering gear system. See Fig. GR7.

To remove steering gear assembly, remove hood, fuel tank and battery. Remove steering wheel and "E" ring (3) from steering shaft (5). Disconnect tie rod ends from steering arm (13) and remove bolts securing gear box to frame. Lower gear box and steering shaft down through frame and out of tractor.

To disassemble unit, remove steering arm (13) and mounting plate. Remove "E" ring (8) and withdraw quadrant gear (10). Remove "E" ring (6) and spacer (7) and withdraw steering shaft. On Models 810, 812 and 814, pinion gear may be removed from steering shaft.

Clean and inspect all parts for excessive wear or other damage and renew as necessary. Reassemble in reverse order of disassembly. Pack housing with multipurpose grease before reinstalling mounting plate.

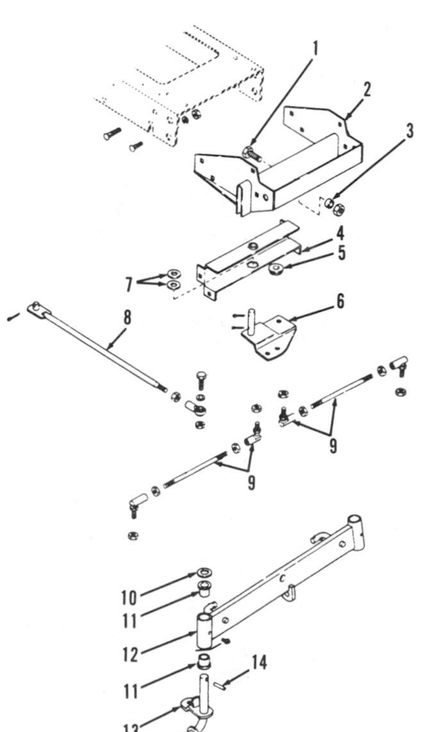


*Fig. GR4—Exploded view of front axle assembly used on Models 1232G-1232H-1238G-1238H.*

1. Pivot bolt
2. Axle support
3. Spacer
4. Steering pivot channel
5. Flange bushing
6. Steering pivot
7. Washers
8. Drag link
9. Tie rods
10. Washer
11. Flange bushings
12. Axle main member
13. Spindle
14. Spring pin

### Models 816S-8102-8120-8121-8122-8123-8163B—Late Models 810-812-814

These tractors are equipped with rack and pinion steering as shown in Fig. GR9.

To remove steering shaft (4—Fig. GR8), remove steering wheel, bushing (2) and retainer ring (3). Remove steering shaft nut (12) and withdraw shaft. Disconnect tie rod ends from steering arms (8). Unbolt and remove steering arms, rack (5) and bearing support (10).

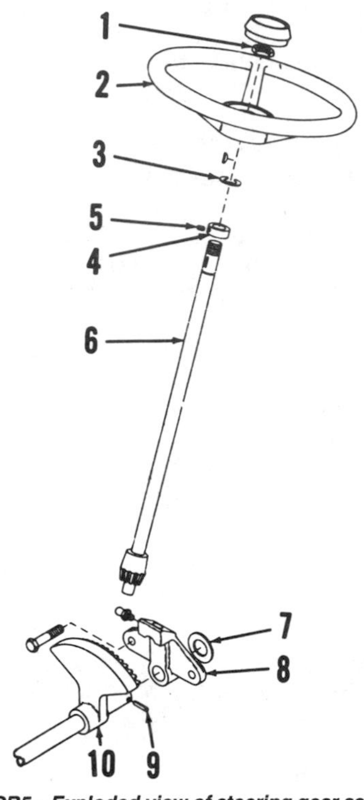


*Fig. GR5—Exploded view of steering gear assembly used on Model 408.*

1. Nut
2. Steering wheel
3. "E" ring
4. Collar
5. Set screw
6. Steering shaft
7. Washer
8. Bracket
9. Pin
10. Quadrant gear & shaft

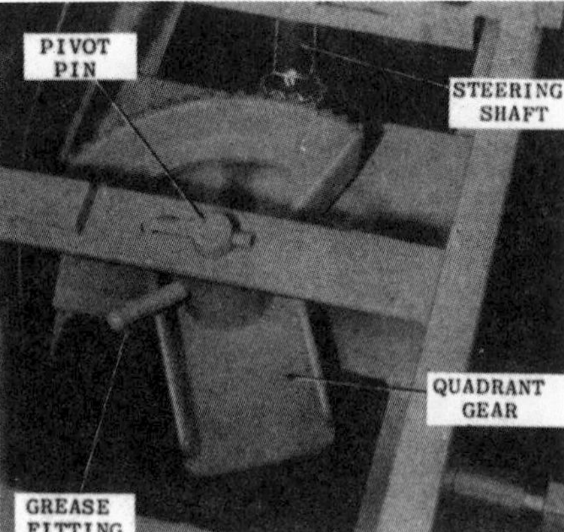


*Fig. GR6—View of exposed steering gear system used on early Models 424, 430 and 432.*

Reassembly is reverse of disassembly procedure. Be sure that front wheels are positioned straight ahead when installing steering shaft (4). Tighten adjusting nuts (26) to obtain desired gear mesh, then tighten locknuts (27) to secure adjustment. Lubricate with multipurpose grease.

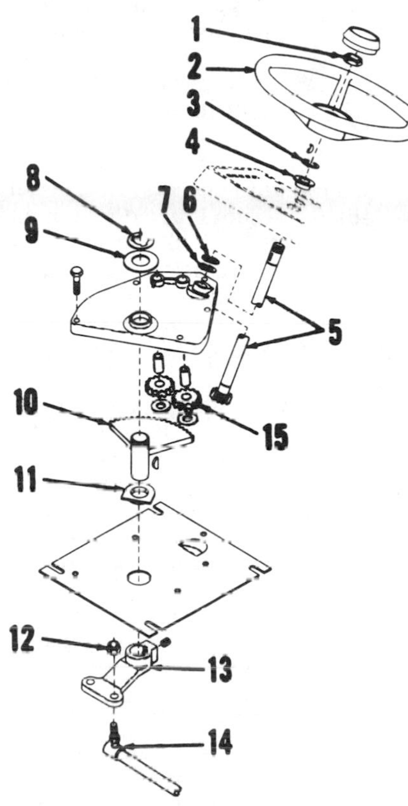


Fig. GR7—Exploded view of enclosed steering gear assembly used on late Models 424, 430 and 432 tractors and early Models 810, 812 and 814 tractors.

1. Nut
2. Steering wheel
3. "E" ring
4. Bushing
5. Steering shaft & pinion
6. "E" ring
7. Washer
8. "E" ring
9. Washer
10. Quadrant gear
11. Bushing
12. Nut
13. Steering arm
14. Tie rod
15. Spur gears

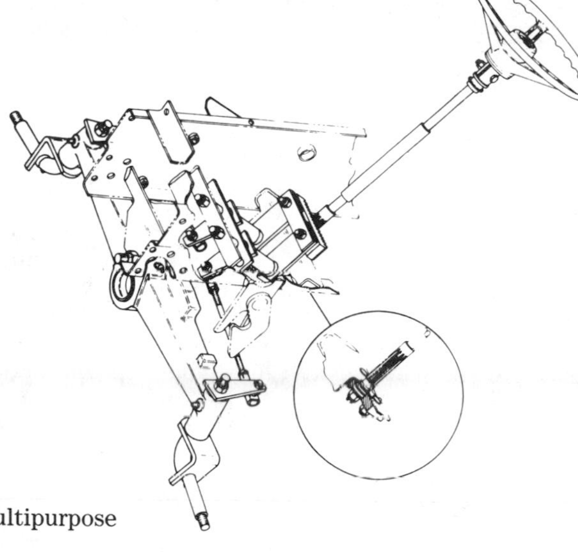

Fig. GR9—View of front axle and steering assembly used on 8000 series tractors and late Model 810, 812, 814 and 816S tractors.

## Models 1232G-1232H-1238G-1238H-GEM 12.5-GEM 14

To remove steering gear assembly, disconnect fuel line and remove fuel tank. Remove bolts attaching steering shaft flange bearing (2—Fig. GR10) to instrument panel. Drive spring pin (6) out of pinion gear (7) and withdraw steering wheel (1) and shaft (5) from tractor. Disconnect drag link from steering arm (18). Remove cotter pin (17) from steering arm shaft. Remove clamp bolts (10) from sector gear (9), then pull steering arm out of sector gear and remove gear from support (14).

To remove steering pivot (6—Fig. GR4), disconnect tie rods (9) and drag link (8) from pivot. Remove cotter pins from pivot shaft and withdraw pivot, washers (7) and flange bushing (5) from steering pivot channel (4).

Inspect bearings (2, 8 and 13—Fig. GR10) for wear or damage and renew as necessary. Check pinion gear and sector gear teeth for wear or damage. Lubricate gear teeth with multipurpose grease prior to reassembly.

Reassembly is reverse of disassembly procedure.

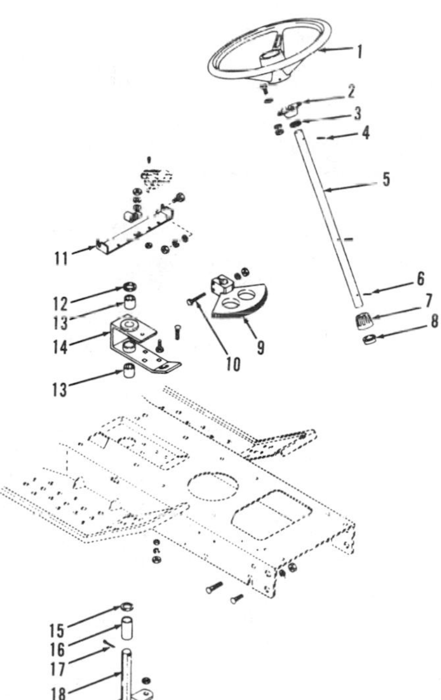


Fig. GR10—Exploded view of steering gear assembly used on Models 1232G, 1232H, 1238G and 1238H. Steering gear assembly used on GEM (Gravely Estate Mower) tractor is similar.

1. Steering wheel
2. Flange bearing
3. Washer
4. Spring pin
5. Steering shaft
6. Pin
7. Pinion gear
8. Bearing
9. Sector gear
10. Clamp bolt
11. Support bracket
12. Washer
13. Bushings
14. Steering support
15. Washer
16. Spacer
17. Cotter pin
18. Steering arm

Fig. GR8—Exploded view of front axle and steering assembly used on late Model 810, 812, 814, 816S and 8000 series tractors.

1. Steering wheel
2. Bushing
3. Retainer ring
4. Steering shaft
5. Rack
6. Rack bushings
7. Flange bearing
8. Steering arm
9. Pivot sleeve
10. Bearing support
11. Bearing
12. Locknut
13. Ball joint
14. Tie rod
15. Axle main member
16. Axle pivot tube
17. Pivot bolt
18. Spindle arms
19. Steering spindle L.H.
20. Caps
21. Steering spindle R.H.
22. Locknut
23. Adjustment plate
24. Thrust washer
25. Strap
26. Adjusting nut
27. Locknut

Illustrations courtesy Gravely International, Inc.

# ENGINE

## REMOVE AND REINSTALL

### Model 408

To remove engine, remove hood and grille assembly. Remove ground cable from battery and remove belt guard. Disconnect choke and throttle control cables. Disconnect starter cable from starter. Disconnect wiring harness at connector under fuel tank. Slip drive belts off engine drive pulley. Remove engine mounting bolts and lift engine out of tractor.

To reinstall engine, reverse removal procedure.

### Models 1232G-1232H-1238G-1238H

To remove engine, first remove mower deck from tractor. Remove hood and grille assembly. Remove ground cable from battery. Disconnect throttle control cable from engine. Disconnect fuel line. Disconnect wires from starter. Disconnect engine wiring harness connector. Move belt idler to relieve tension on drive belt and slip belt off engine pulley. Remove engine mounting bolts and lift engine out of tractor.

To reinstall engine, reverse removal procedure.

### Models GEM 12.5-GEM 14

To remove engine, first remove mower deck from tractor. Remove hood and grille assembly. Disconnect ground cable from battery. Disconnect throttle control cable from engine. Disconnect fuel line. Disconnect wires from starter and engine wiring harness. Disconnect springs from jackshaft drive belt idler arm and transmission drive belt idler arm. Disconnect electrical wire to electric pto clutch. Unbolt and remove electric clutch torque arm, then remove belt from pto clutch. Remove center bolt from pto clutch and remove clutch assembly. Remove transmission drive belt from engine pulley. Remove engine mounting bolts and lift engine from tractor.

To reinstall engine, reverse the removal procedure.

### All Other Models

To remove engine, remove seat and fender assembly and drain transmission oil. Detach ground cable from battery. Disconnect fuel line, choke and throttle cables and starter cable. Disconnect wiring harness connector and remove rear hitch. Use a suitable hoist to support engine. Remove engine mounting bolts and lift engine from tractor.

Refer to Fig. GR11 and remove transmission input gear, thrust bearing and engine adapter. When reassembling, renew "O" ring seal.

## OVERHAUL

### All Models

Engine make and model are listed at the beginning of this section. To overhaul engine, refer to appropriate engine service section in this manual.

*Fig. GR11—View of typical engine adapter plate, transmission input gear, key, "O" ring and thrust bearing used on some models. Use suitable gear puller to remove input gear.*

# CLUTCH AND BRAKES

### Model 408

A belt idler type clutch is used on Model 408 tractor. To adjust clutch, depress clutch pedal and turn adjusting nuts (8—Fig. GR12) until top of belt idler pulley (11) is level with bottom of transmission pulley.

To adjust brake, turn adjusting nuts (6) on brake rod until desired brake action is obtained. Be sure brake does not engage before clutch is disengaged, but there should be sufficient braking action with pedal fully depressed.

### Models 424-430-432

Clutch is mounted integrally with transmission; refer to transmission section for servicing. To accomplish clutch adjustment, turn adjusting nuts on Hi-Lo and Forward-Reverse control rods so springs are nearly compressed as control lever is locked into position. Adjustment must be made for each lever position. If clutch slippage still occurs after adjustment is made, refer to transmission section and inspect clutch assembly.

Models 424, 430 and 432 are equipped with band type brakes at each rear wheel. The brakes operate independently of each other. Brake action is ad-

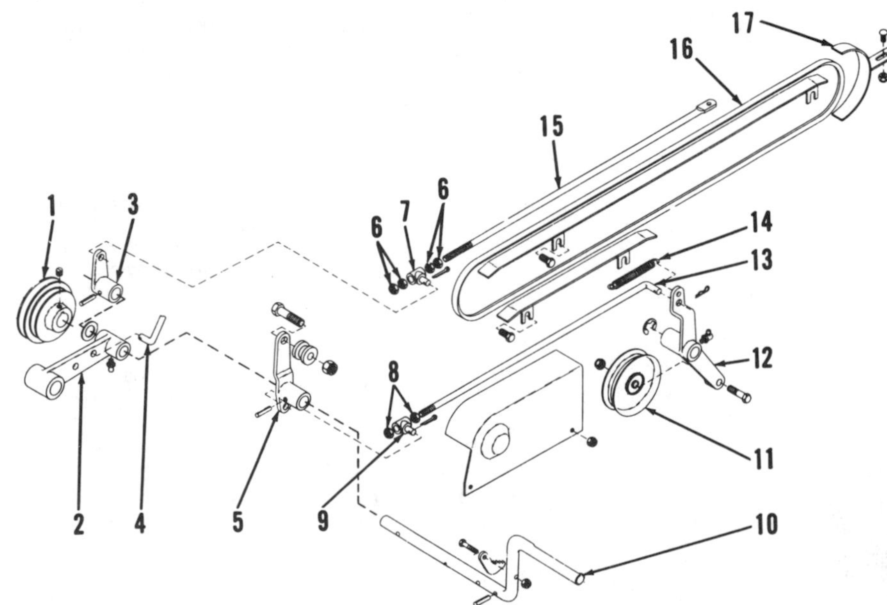


*Fig. GR12—Exploded view of clutch-brake system used on Model 408.*

1. Engine pulley
2. Pto arm
3. Brake lever
4. Pto rod
5. Clutch arm
6. Adjusting nuts
7. Trunnion
8. Adjusting nuts
9. Trunnion
10. Clutch-brake pedal
11. Clutch pulley
12. Clutch lever
13. Clutch rod
14. Spring
15. Brake rod
16. Drive belt
17. Belt guard

justed by turning nut (N—Fig. GR13) on brake band stud.

### Models 810-812-814-816S-8102-8120-8121-8122-8123-8163B

Clutches for forward and reverse speeds are mounted at sides of transmission; forward clutch on right side, reverse clutch on left side. Clutch action is adjusted by placing forward-reverse lever in neutral position and disconnecting clutch rods (4—Fig. GR14). Loosen or tighten nuts (1) until there is 0.020-0.030 inch (0.51-0.76 mm) gap between clutch discs (2). Be sure that forward-reverse lever is in vertical position. Adjust length of clutch rods by turning rods in yoke (5) until rod can be connected to clutch cam (3) without disturbing position of cam or forward-reverse lever.

All models have as standard equipment a band type brake (6) mounted on transmission shaft. Adjust brake by turning brake rod (8) in yoke. Be sure that brake linkage cam (7) returns the direction control clutches to neutral position before brake begins to apply.

Individual rear wheel drum brakes are available as a kit for some models. Adjust each brake by disconnecting clevis (2—Fig. GR15) from brake arm (1) and turning clevis on brake rod until desired brake action is obtained.

### Models 1232G-1238G

A spring loaded belt idler type clutch is used on all models. The clutch is operated by a foot pedal and no adjustment of clutch is required. If slippage occurs, inspect drive belt for excessive wear or stretching and renew as necessary.

Refer to Fig. GR18 for exploded view of clutch linkage and jackshaft drive assembly. To replace primary drive belt, first remove mower or front mounted attachment from tractor. Disconnect spring (5) from traction clutch idler arm (11). Disconnect pto actuating rod (21) from pto idler arm (7), then disconnect spring (12) from idler arm. Loosen cap screws retaining jackshaft housing (16) to transaxle mount. Disconnect tension spring from primary drive belt idler

*Fig. GR13—Brake action on Models 424, 430 and 432 is adjusted by turning nut (N).*

*Fig. GR14—View of right side of Model 810 transmission showing forward-reverse clutch and transmission brake. Other 800 and 8000 series tractors are similar.*

1. Adjusting nuts
2. Clutch discs
3. Clutch cam
4. Clutch rod
5. Yoke
6. Transmission brake
7. Brake cam
8. Brake rod

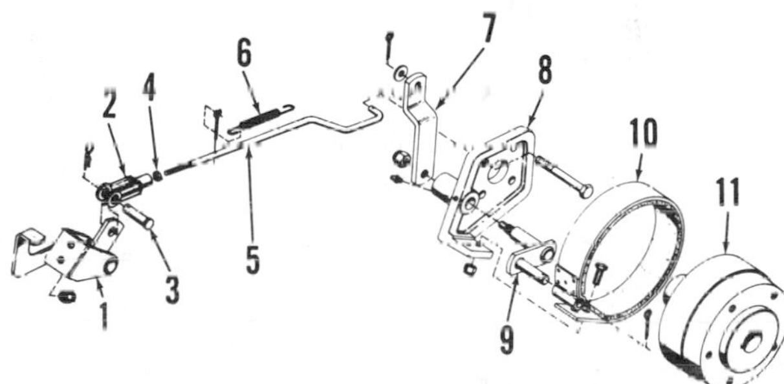


*Fig. GR15—Exploded view of rear wheel band type brake available as a kit for some models. Right side brake is similar.*

1. Brake arm
2. Clevis
3. Pin
4. Jam nut
5. Brake rod
6. Spring
7. Brake lever
8. Mounting plate
9. Actuating arm
10. Brake band
11. Drum

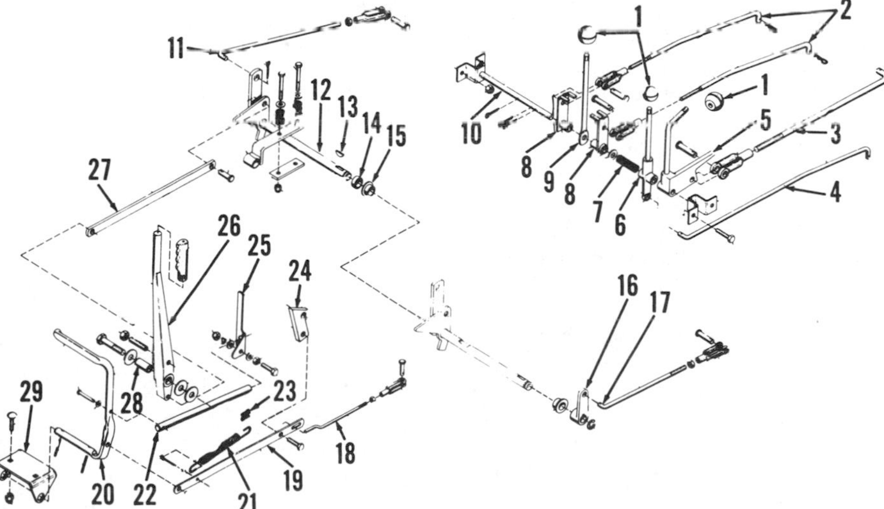


*Fig. GR16—Exploded view of clutch and brake linkage used on 8000 series and late Model 810, 812, 814 and 816S tractors.*

1. Knob
2. Shifting rod
3. Pto rod
4. Two-speed rod
5. Pto control assy.
6. Two-speed control
7. Spring
8. Shifter arm
9. Shift lever
10. Cross shaft
11. Forward clutch rod
12. Clutch shaft bracket
13. Key
14. Spacer
15. Bushing
16. Reverse clutch arm
17. Reverse clutch rod
18. Link
19. Link
20. Brake pedal
21. Spring
22. Parking brake rod
23. Clip
24. Brake cam
25. Parking brake bracket
26. Forward-reverse lever
27. Shifter link
28. Bushing
29. Brake pedal bracket

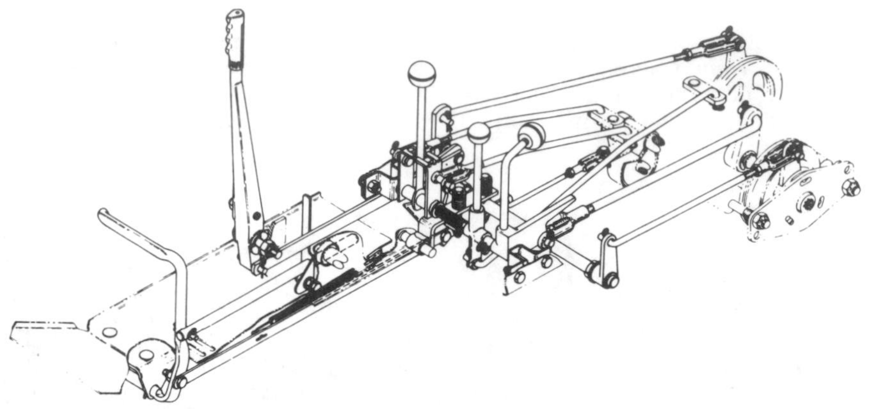

*Fig. GR17—View of transmission and brake linkage used on 8000 series and late Model 810, 812, 814 and 816S tractors.*

arm, then remove belt from engine pulley. Rotate pto idler (7) until hairpin at top of idler pivot shaft can be removed. Lower idler assembly until pivot shaft is free from traction clutch idler arm (11). Slide drive belt between upper and lower idler arms and remove from tractor. To reinstall belt, reverse removal procedure.

To replace transaxle drive belt, loosen belt guide retaining cap screws and move guides away from belt. Depress clutch pedal to relieve tension on belt and work belt off pulleys. Install new belt by reversing removal procedure. Adjust belt guides to provide $^1/_{16}$ to $^1/_8$ inch (1.6-3.2 mm) clearance between belt and guides.

Models 1232-G and 1238-G are equipped with a disc type brake mounted on right side of transaxle housing (Fig. GR19). To adjust brake, position tractor on a level surface and place gear shift lever in neutral so tractor can be pushed by hand to check brake action. With brake pedal released, turn setscrew (6) in brake pad holder clockwise until brake just starts to lock. Then, turn setscrew counterclockwise $^1/_2$ turn. Push tractor by hand to check brake action and to make sure that brake pads (2 and 3) do not drag on brake disc (9) when brake is released.

To renew brake pads, disconnect brake rod from brake lever (7—Fig. GR19). Remove shoulder bolt (8) and withdraw lever, brake jaw (5) and outer brake pad (3). Remove brake disc (9) from transaxle shaft and remove inner brake pad (2) and spring (1) from transaxle housing. To reassemble, reverse disassembly procedure. Adjust brake as previously outlined.

## Models 1232H-1238H

A spring loaded belt idler type clutch is used on all models. The clutch is operated by a hand lever (1—Fig. GR20) and no adjustment is required. If slippage occurs, inspect drive belt for excessive wear or stretching and renew as necessary.

To replace main drive belt, first remove mower deck or front mounted equipment from tractor. Disconnect clutch control lever (1—Fig. GR20) from idler arm (11). Disconnect main idler pulley tension spring from frame, then remove drive belt from engine pulley. Remove belt from jackshaft pulley and remove from tractor. Install new belt in reverse order of removal.

To replace traction drive belt, first remove main drive belt as outlined above. Loosen belt guide retaining screws and move belt guides away from belt. Move idler arm (11) to relieve spring tension on drive belt, then work belt off jackshaft and transmission pulleys. Install

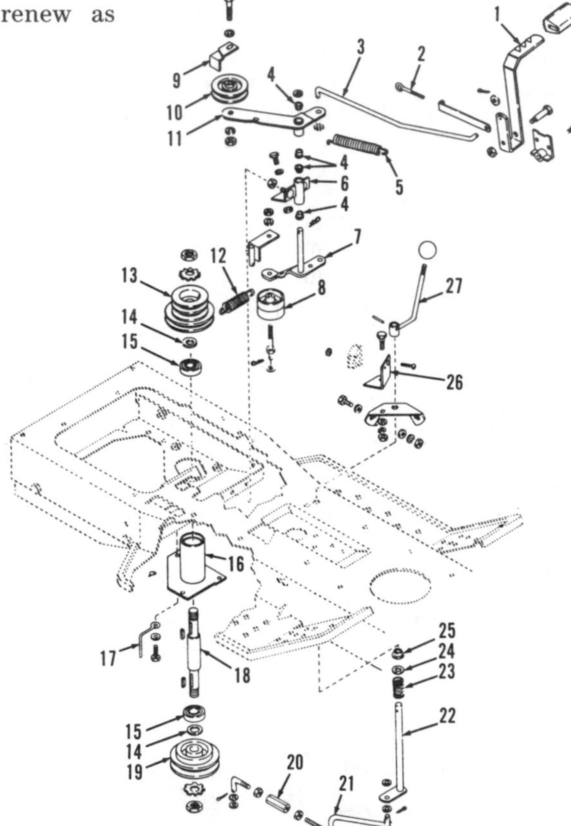

*Fig. GR18—Exploded view of spring loaded belt idler clutch used on Models 1232G and 1238G.*

1. Clutch pedal
2. Eyebolt
3. Clutch rod
4. Flange bushings
5. Tension spring
6. Idler pivot
7. Idler arm
8. Idler
9. Belt guide
10. Idler pulley
11. Idler arm
12. Spring
13. Double groove pulley
14. Washer
15. Bearing
16. Spindle housing
17. Belt guide
18. Jackshaft
19. Jackshaft pulley
20. Turnbuckle
21. Idler link
22. Pto lever
23. Spring
24. Washer
25. Flange bushing
26. Safety switch bracket
27. Pto lever

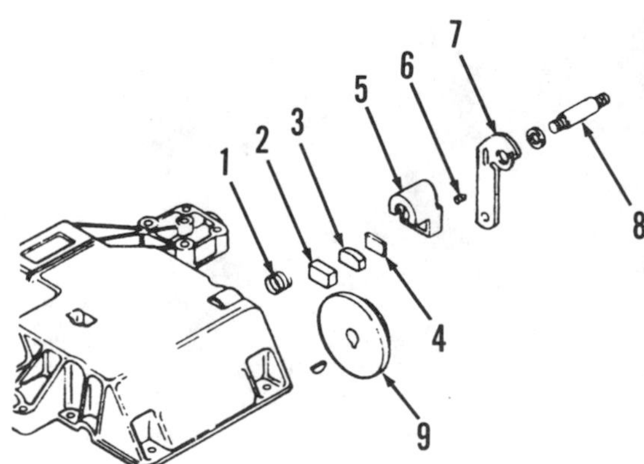

*Fig. GR19—Exploded view of disc brake assembly used on Models 1232G and 1238G.*

1. Spring
2. Brake pad, inner
3. Brake pad, outer
4. Back-up plate
5. Brake jaw assy.
6. Setscrew
7. Brake actuating lever
8. Shoulder bolt

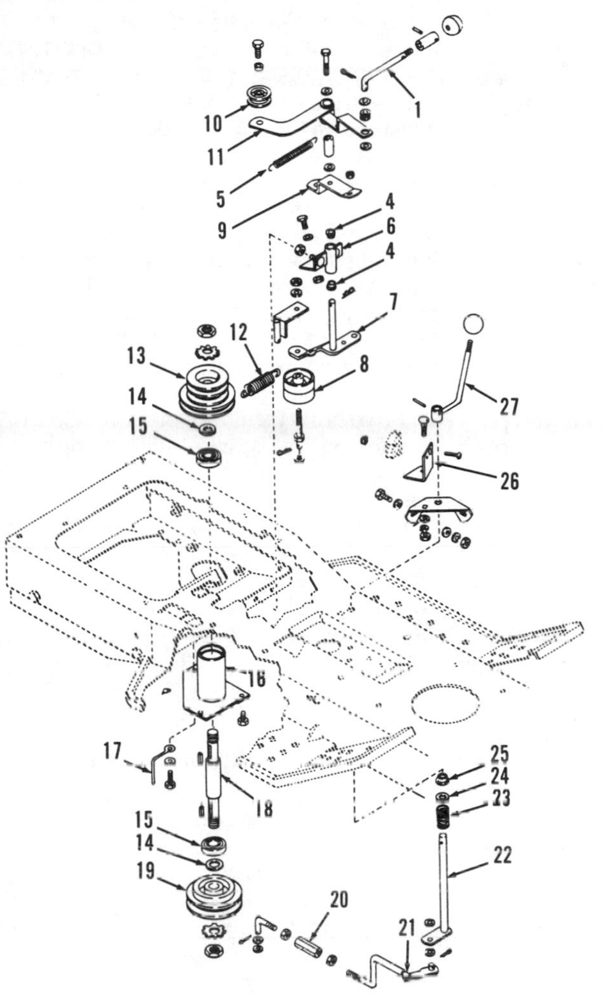


*Fig. GR20—Exploded view of spring loaded belt idler clutch used on Models 1232H and 1238H.*

1. Clutch handle
4. Flange bushings
6. Pivot bracket
7. Idler arm
8. Idler
9. Idler bracket
10. Idler pulley
11. Clutch arm
12. Spring
13. Double groove pulley
14. Washer
15. Bearing
16. Spindle housing
17. Belt guide
18. Jackshaft
19. Jackshaft pulley
20. Turnbuckle
21. Idler link
22. Pto lever
23. Spring
24. Washer
25. Flange bushing
26. Safety switch bracket
27. Pto lever

new belt and adjust belt fingers to provide $^1/_{16}$ to $^1/_8$ inch (1.6-3.2 mm) clearance between belt and fingers.

Models 1232-H and 1238-H are equipped with a disc type brake located inside the transmission unit. When brake pedal is depressed, hydrostatic transmission control linkage is returned to neutral position and then brake is applied. To adjust parking brake, depress brake pedal and measure gap (G—Fig. GR21) between clutch rod collar (2) and rod pivot (1). Gap should be $^1/_{16}$ inch (1.6 mm). To adjust gap, loosen jam nut at brake clevis pivot (4) and turn pivot bolt (3) until recommended gap between rod collar and pivot is obtained. Release parking brake, then depress brake pedal and recheck for proper gap. Refer to HYDROSTATIC TRANSMISSION SERVICE section for brake repair procedures.

## Models GEM 12.5-GEM 14

A spring loaded belt idler is used on all tractors and no adjustment is required. If slippage occurs, inspect drive belt for excessive wear or stretching and renew as necessary.

To replace transmission drive belt, remove mower deck from tractor. Disconnect springs from jackshaft drive belt idler arm and transmission drive belt idler arm. Disconnect electrical wire to pto clutch. Unbolt and remove torque arm from pto clutch, then slip belt off pto clutch pulley. Remove center bolt from pto clutch and remove clutch assembly. Slip transmission drive belt off engine pulley and then transmission pulley. Install new belt in reverse order of removal.

GEM tractors are equipped with a disc type brake located inside the transmission unit. When brake pedal is depressed, hydrostatic transmission control linkage is returned to neutral position and then brake is applied. To adjust parking brake, depress brake pedal and set parking brake rod. Measure gap (G—Fig. GR21A) between clutch rod collar (1) and rod pivot (2). Gap should be $^1/_{16}$ inch (1.6 mm). To adjust gap, loosen jam nut at brake clevis pivot (4) and turn pivot bolt (5) until recommended gap between rod collar and pivot is obtained. Release parking brake, then depress brake pedal and recheck for proper gap. Refer to HYDROSTATIC TRANSMISSION SERVICE section for brake repair procedures.

# HYDROSTATIC TRANSMISSION

### LUBRICATION

## Models 1232H-1238H

The transaxle housing serves as a common reservoir for hydrostatic transmission and gear reduction unit. An expansion tank and dipstick are located at the rear of unit. To check oil level, raise rear deck and clean expansion tank cap, then remove cap and dipstick. When transmission is cold, oil level should be at mark indicated on dipstick. If low,

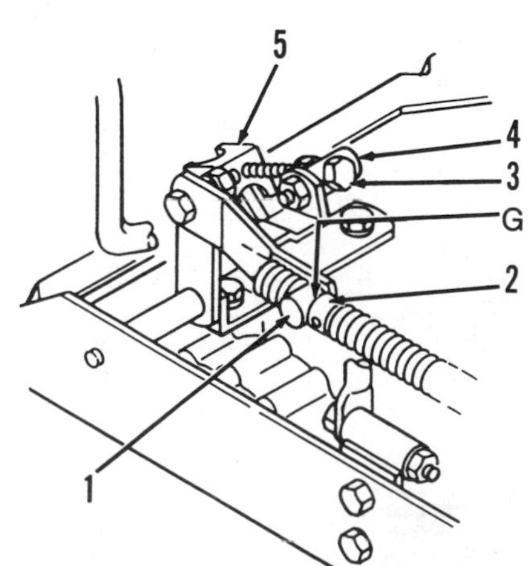


*Fig. GR21—View showing adjustment point for brake linkage on Models 1232H and 1238H. Refer to text for procedure.*

1. Pivot
2. Collar
3. Brake adjusting bolt
4. Pivot
5. Brake clevis

*Fig. GR21A—View showing adjustment point for brake linkage on GEM 12.5 and GEM 14 tractors. Refer to text for procedure.*

1. Washer
2. Pivot
3. Brake clevis
4. Pivot
5. Brake adjusting bolt

add SAE 20W-20 detergent oil. DO NOT use multiviscosity oil.

If oil appears to be milky or black, it is possible oil is contaminated with water or has been overheated and unit should be drained and refilled. Capacity is approximately 4.8 pints (2.3 L).

## Models GEM 12.5-GEM 14

The transaxle housing serves as a common reservoir for hydrostatic transmission and gear reduction unit. An oil expansion tank is located below the instrument panel, directly below the battery. To check oil level, raise hood and clean area around expansion tank cap/dipstick, then remove dipstick. When transmission is cold, oil level should be at mark indicated on dipstick. If low, add SAE 20W-20 oil. DO NOT use multiviscosity oil.

If oil appears to be milky or black, it is possible oil is contaminated with water or has been overheated and unit should be drained and refilled. Capacity is approximately 6 quarts (6.7 L).

The transmission oil filter should be changed after the first 10 hours of operation and after every 400 hours of operation thereafter or yearly, whichever comes first.

# ADJUSTMENT

## Models 1232H-1238H

If tractor continues to creep forward or rearward when shift control handle is moved to neutral position or when brake pedal is fully depressed then released, hydrostatic control linkage should be adjusted as follows:

Raise and support rear of tractor so rear wheels are off the ground. Remove rear wheels. Block front wheels to prevent tractor from rolling. Raise seat and seat deck and start engine. Loosen cap screw (25—Fig. GR22) and turn eccentric (26) until rear axles stop turning and pump whine stops. If neutral adjustment is correctly obtained, tighten eccentric cap screw being careful not to move eccentric.

If wheel creep or pump whine cannot be adjusted by turning eccentric, turn jam nuts (12) to move pivot (13) on control rod (14) until rear axles stop turning and whine stops. Readjust eccentric (26) so neutral arm bearing (24) is positioned in notch in speed control arm (11).

If speed control lever (1—Fig. GR22) will not remain in position when released, increase tension of control lever friction spring (18) by turning friction adjusting bolt (16) clockwise. If lever is too hard to move, turn friction adjusting bolt counterclockwise.

## Models GEM 12.5-GEM 14

If tractor creeps forward or backward with speed control lever in neutral position, control linkage should be adjusted as follows: Support rear of tractor and remove rear wheels. Loosen two bolts on bottom side of torque bracket (22—Fig. GR24) retaining cam follower pivot bracket (26). Start engine and operate at approximately 1/3 full throttle. Turn pivot bracket adjusting bolt (23) as necessary until axles stop turning and pump whine has stopped. Note that no more than 3 or 4 turns of adjusting bolt should be required to obtain neutral position. If neutral position is correctly obtained, tighten pivot bracket mounting bolts being careful not to disturb bracket adjustment. If unable to obtain neutral position by turning adjusting bolt, proceed with additional adjustment procedure outlined below.

Remove knob from speed control lever and remove rear deck from tractor. Remove fuel tank and use a suitable length of fuel line so tank can be connected to engine, but positioned in a remote location. Loosen the two bolts and nut that retain speed selector lever (4—Fig. GR23) to arm (7) and the two bolts that retain pivot bracket (26—Fig. GR24) to torque bracket (22). Depress brake pedal and check that ball bearing cam follower (17) is located in center of neutral cam (19). If not, adjust brake linkage as previously outlined in CLUTCH AND BRAKES section. Make sure that ball bearing (28) is located in detent of control arm (30). If not, loosen jam nuts (31) and adjust neutral arm (33) as necessary. Start engine and operate at about 1/3 full throttle. Depress brake pedal and adjust pivot bracket adjusting bolt (23) until rear axles do not creep and there is no pump whine. Be sure that cam follower bearing (28) remains in detent of control arm (30), readjust neutral arm (33) if necessary. Stop engine and tighten neutral arm jam nuts and two bolts retaining pivot bracket to torque bracket. Be careful not to disturb setting of control linkage when tightening fasteners.

Install fuel tank and rear deck. Hold speed selector lever (4—Fig. GR23) in neutral slot and tighten center nut and two bolts attaching lever to arm, being careful not to move inner arm (7). Center nut (1) should be tightened as necessary to obtain desired friction on control lever.

# REMOVE AND REINSTALL

## Models 1232H-1238H

To remove transaxle assembly, first remove mower deck from tractor. Disconnect hydraulic oil expansion tank hoses,

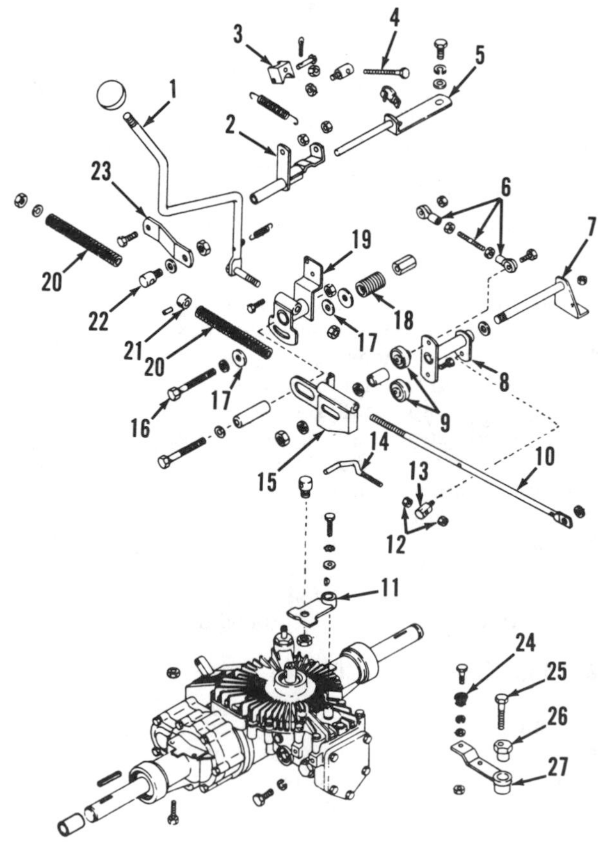

*Fig. GR22—Exploded view of hydrostatic transmission control linkage used on Models 1232H and 1238H.*

1. Shift lever
2. Brake tube
3. Brake clevis
4. Brake adjusting bolt
5. Brake bracket
6. Link
7. Brake pivot
8. Shift control arm
9. Ball bearings
10. Brake rod
11. Speed control arm
12. Jam nuts
13. Pivot
14. Speed control link
15. Brake bracket
16. Friction adjusting bolt
17. Friction washer
18. Compression spring
19. Shift bracket
20. Spring
21. Collar
22. Pivot
23. Brake link
24. Ball bearing
25. Cap screw
26. Eccentric
27. Neutral detent arm



Illustrations courtesy Gravely International, Inc.

then unbolt and remove drawbar and expansion tank from rear of frame. Disconnect brake control linkage. Slip primary drive belt off jackshaft pulley. Disconnect clutch control lever from clutch idler arm. Remove knob from transmission speed control lever. Raise and support rear of tractor. Remove cap screws attaching transaxle mounting plate to main frame and roll transaxle assembly from tractor. Remove transmission drive pulley and fan. Disconnect speed control link from transmission control arm. Remove cap screws attaching transaxle housing to mounting plate and separate transaxle from plate.

To reinstall transaxle, reverse the removal procedure.

### Models GEM 12.5-GEM 14

To remove transaxle assembly, first remove mower deck from tractor. Disconnect hydraulic oil expansion tank hoses from hydrostatic unit. Disconnect brake control linkage and speed control linkage. Remove jackshaft drive belt and transmission drive belt. Remove mounting bolts attaching transaxle assembly to frame. Support rear of tractor and remove transaxle from tractor.

To reinstall transaxle, reverse the removal procedure.

## OVERHAUL

### Models 1232H-1238H-GEM12.5-GEM 14

Models 1232H and 1238H are equipped with an Eaton 750 series hydrostatic transmission and transaxle assembly. GEM models are equipped with an Eaton 850 series hydrostatic transmission and transaxle assembly. Refer to Eaton section of HYDROSTATIC TRANSMISSION SERVICE service section for overhaul procedure.

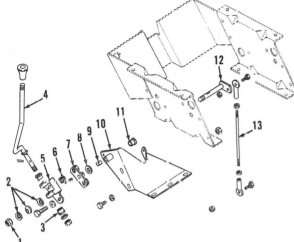

*Fig. GR23—Exploded view of hydrostatic transmission control linkage used on GEM tractors.*

1. Locknut
2. Belleville washers
3. Flange bushing
4. Shift lever
5. Outer arm
6. Spring
7. Inner arm
8. Washer
9. Bushing
10. Brace
11. Flange bushing
12. Shift arm
13. Shift rod

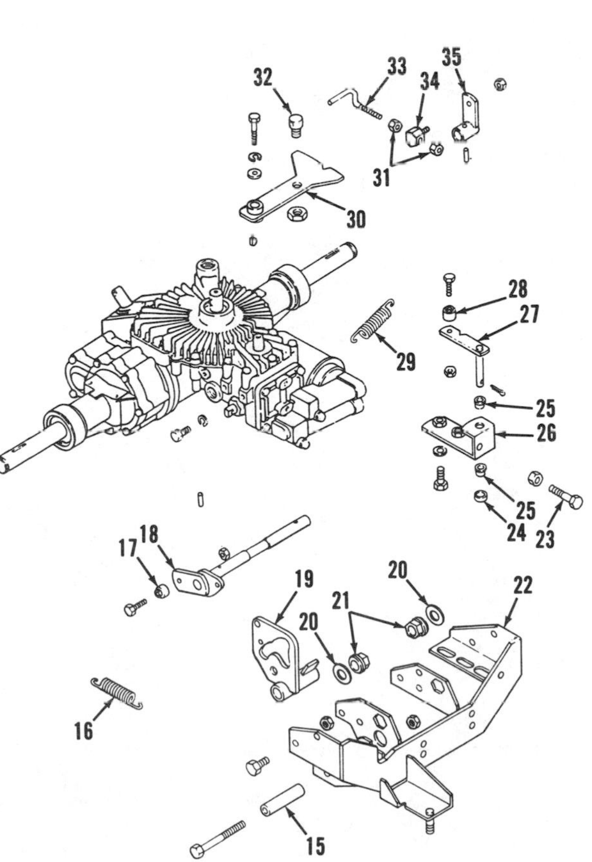


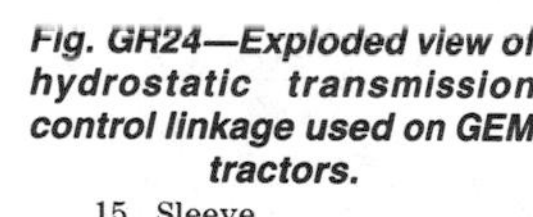

*Fig. GR24—Exploded view of hydrostatic transmission control linkage used on GEM tractors.*

15. Sleeve
16. Spring
17. Ball bearing
18. Cross shaft
19. Cam
20. Washer
21. Flange bushing
22. Torque bracket
23. Adjusting bolt
24. Bushing
25. Flange bushing
26. Pivot bracket
27. Neutral detent arm
28. Ball bearing
29. Spring
30. Speed control arm
31. Jam nuts
32. Pivot
33. Control link
34. Pivot
35. Control arm

# TRANSAXLE

## REMOVE AND REINSTALL

### Model 408

To remove transaxle, remove belt guard and remove drive belt from transaxle pulley. Disconnect brake rod and remove brake band assembly. Remove bracket holding transaxle to frame. Remove shift lever knob. Disconnect forward-reverse control rod from shift strap. Remove spring from frame. Remove clamps securing transaxle to tractor frame. Lift rear of tractor frame and roll transaxle away from tractor.

### Models 424-430-432

To remove transaxle, remove seat and rear fender assembly. Remove engine as previously outlined. Disconnect brake control rods at brakes. Disconnect lift attachment control rod and transaxle control rods. Disconnect attachment control rod at front end of transaxle. Support rear of tractor frame and remove transaxle retaining bolts and roll transaxle away from tractor.

### Models 810-812-814-816S-8102-8120-8121-8122-8123-8163B

To remove transaxle, remove engine as previously outlined. Detach hydraulic lines from pump and drain hydraulic reservoir on models equipped with hydraulic lift. Detach forward and reverse clutch rods from clutch cams (3—Fig. GR14) and two-speed rod from shifter arm. Remove shift rods from 1-3 and 2-4 shift arms. Remove pto rod from pto lever and lift rod from cross shaft. Detach brake rod from brake band and unscrew bolts securing cross shaft to transmission. Raise cross shaft up to clear transmission. Block rear wheels and support front of transaxle. Unscrew transaxle to frame mounting bolts and roll frame and forward section of tractor away from transaxle.

### Models 1232G-1238G

To remove transaxle, first remove mower deck from tractor. Unbolt and remove drawbar from rear of frame. Remove knobs from gear selector lever and range selector lever. Loosen transaxle belt guards and move them away from drive belt. Depress clutch pedal to relieve tension on belt and work belt off transaxle pulley. Slip primary drive belt off jackshaft pulley. Disconnect brake control rod and spring from brake lever. Raise and support rear of tractor. Remove cap screws attaching transaxle mounting plate to main frame and roll transaxle assembly rearward from tractor.

## OVERHAUL

### Model 408

To disassemble transaxle, first remove transaxle as previously outlined. Drain lubricant from transaxle. Remove brake drum, input pulley, rear hitch, shift lever (77—Fig. GR26) and rear wheels.

Position transaxle so left axle is down. Unscrew cover screws and lift cover (76) off case (43). Remove sliding gear (62), washer (61), shift fork (74) and shift rod (73). Remove shift rod (69), shift fork (68), sliding gear (63), shaft (64) and gear (66). Remove gear (6), shaft (7) and gear (8). Remove forward-reverse shift shaft (11), shift fork (12), sliding gear (15) and input shaft (16). Remove gears (26, 28 and 30) and shaft (29). Remove gears (48 and 50) and shaft (49). Remove gears (56, 58 and 60), shaft (57) and spacer (59). Remove "E" ring (35) from end of left axle and remove side gear (36) and differential assembly components (37 through 41). Remove washer (52), shaft (53) and gears (54 and 55). Remove axles from case and cover if necessary. Right axle and side gear (34) are retained in cover by "E" ring (35). Disassembly of differential is evident after inspection of unit. Note position of pinion gears (39).

Inspect all components and renew any parts showing damage or excessive wear. To reassemble transaxle, reverse disassembly procedure. When cover assembly is placed on case assembly, there will be approximately one inch (25 mm) gap between case and cover due to case dropping down on axle. Raise case to

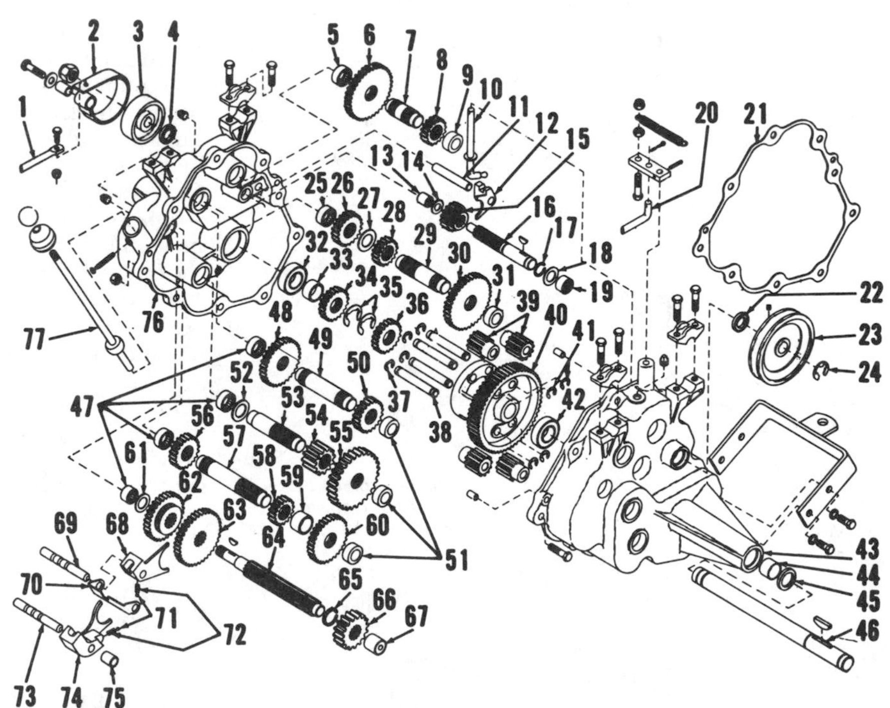


*Fig. GR26—Exploded view of transaxle used on Model 408.*

1. Brake rod
2. Brake band
3. Brake drum
4. Oil seal
5. Bearing
6. Gear
7. Shaft
8. Gear
9. Bearing
10. Forward-reverse shift lever
11. Shift shaft
12. Forward-reverse shift fork
13. Bearing
14. Thrust washer
15. Sliding gear
16. Input shaft
17. Snap ring
18. Thrust washer
19. Bearing
20. Forward-reverse shift rod
21. Gasket
22. Oil seal
23. Input pulley
24. "E" ring
25. Bearing
26. Gear
27. Thrust washer
28. Gear
29. Shaft
30. Gear
31. Bearing
32. Bearing
33. Spacer
34. Gear
35. "E" ring
36. Gear
37. "E" ring
38. Pinion pin
39. Pinion gears
40. Ring gear
41. "E" ring
42. Bearing
43. Case
44. Bushing
45. Oil seal
46. Axle shaft
47. Bearings
48. Gear
49. Shaft
50. Gear
51. Bearings
52. Thrust washer
53. Shaft
54. Gear
55. Gear
56. Gear
57. Shaft
58. Gear
59. Spacer
60. Gear
61. Thrust washer
62. Sliding gear (2nd-4th)
63. Sliding gear (1st-3rd)
64. Shaft
65. Snap ring
66. Gear
67. Bearing
68. Shift fork (1st-3rd)
69. Shift shaft
70. Shift stop
71. Shift balls
72. Springs
73. Shift shaft
74. Shift fork (2nd-4th)
75. Spacer
76. Cover
77. Shift lever



Illustrations courtesy Gravely International, Inc.

start bolts. Tighten bolts evenly. Fill transaxle with 6 pints (2.8 L) of SAE 90 EP gear oil.

## Models 424-430-432

To overhaul transaxle, first remove transaxle from tractor as previously outlined. To overhaul subassemblies, refer to following paragraphs.

**FORWARD-REVERSE SYSTEM.** The forward-reverse clutch and gears are housed in front part of transaxle. Remove advance housing (52—Fig. GR27) and rotate forward-reverse actuating shaft (2) so planetary system is released. Remove clutch and planetary components (45 through 50 and 25 through 36). Note that spacer plate bolts (25) have left hand threads.

Inspect components for damage or excessive wear. Inspect clutch cup (48) friction surfaces and renew cup if excessively worn. Inspect surfaces of reverse gear (49) and internal gear (47) and renew if excessively scored to prevent rapid wear of clutch cup.

To reassemble unit, reverse disassembly procedure. Orbit gears must be timed when installed. When orbit gears are meshed correctly with sun gear (34), small punch marks on orbit gears (31) will form an equilateral triangle.

**HIGH-LOW SYSTEM.** A high-low planetary gear set and clutch are located in rear of transaxle. To disassemble unit, rotate high-low actuating shaft (4—Fig. GR27) to release planetary system and remove components (5 through 22).

Inspect components for damage or excessive wear. Inspect clutch cup (7) friction surface and renew cup if excessively worn. Inspect clutch mating surface on clutch plate (12) and ring gear (8) and renew if excessively worn to prevent rapid wear to new clutch cup. To reassemble unit, reverse disassembly procedure.

**SWIFTAMATIC DIFFERENTIAL.** The Swiftamatic uses a two-speed axle with a differential assembly. To disassemble, unscrew retaining cap screws and remove right axle housing (33—Fig.

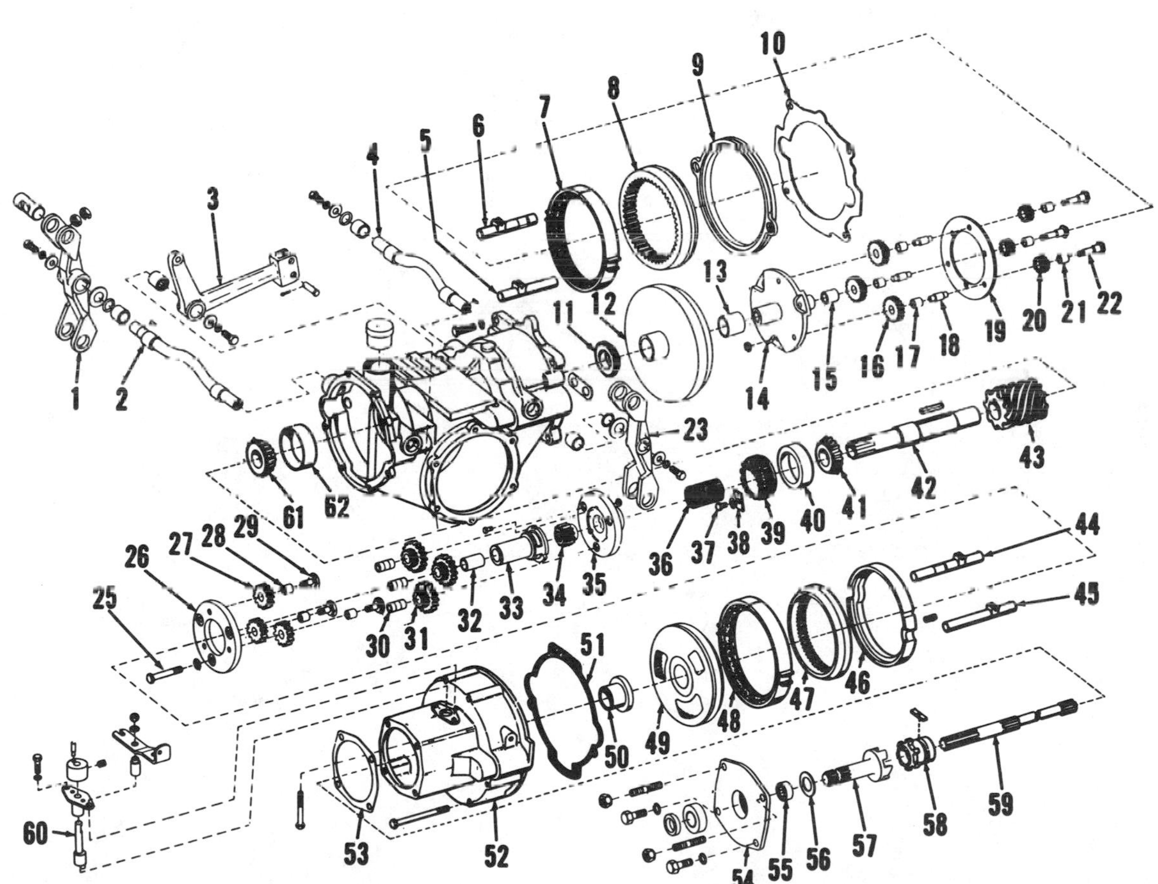

*Fig. GR27—Exploded view of transaxle used on Models 424, 430 and 432.*

1. Forward-reverse lever
2. Forward-reverse actuating shaft
3. Shift link
4. Hi-Lo actuating shaft
5. Clutch slide rod
6. Clutch slide rod
7. Clutch cup
8. Ring gear
9. Gear cup
10. Gasket
11. Thrust plate
12. Clutch plate
13. Bushing
14. Gear carrier
15. Bushing
16. Orbit gear
17. Bushing
18. Pin
19. Pin spacer
20. Orbit gear
21. Bushing
22. Pin
23. Hi-Lo lever
25. Bolt (L.H. thread)
26. Pin plate
27. Reverse idler gear
28. Bushing
29. Bolt
30. Pin
31. Orbit gear
32. Bearing
33. Quill
34. Sun gear
35. Pin plate
36. Spring
37. Screw
38. Lock plate
39. Bearing adjustment nut
40. Bearing cup
41. Bearing cone
42. Shaft
43. Worm gear
44. Clutch slide rod
45. Clutch slide rod
46. Gear cup
47. Internal gear
48. Clutch cup
49. Reverse gear
50. Thrust bushing
51. Gasket
52. Advance housing
53. Gasket
54. Cover
55. Bearing
56. Thrust washer
57. Pto output shaft
58. Pto clutch dog
59. Pto shaft
60. Pto actuating shaft
61. Bearing cone
62. Bearing cup

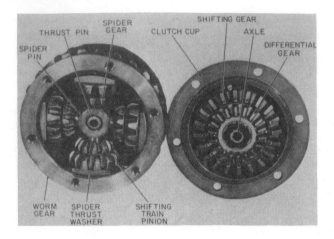

*Fig. GR28—View of differential assembly. All Models 424, 430 and 432 tractors are equipped with spider gear assembly shown in Fig. GR29.*

GR30). Check to see that stationary clutch (31) does not move in axle housing and that sliding clutch (29) will slide freely on splines of shifter gear (23).

To disassemble differential, remove left axle housing (1) and differential assembly components (5 through 28). Inspect ring gear (20) and worm gear (43—Fig. GR27). If renewal of worm gear is required, refer to FORWARD-REVERSE paragraph and remove forward-reverse assembly. Unscrew bearing nut (39) and withdraw worm gear and shaft assembly.

To reassemble differential and axle assemblies, reverse disassembly procedure. Tighten bearing nut (39—Fig. GR27) until end play is removed from worm gear shaft. Lock nut in place with screw and lock plate (38).

Note difference between early and late differential spider gear assemblies in Figs. GR29 and GR30. Early models with ring gear assembly shown in Fig. GR30 have only two pinion assemblies (13 through 18) and should be converted to late style by adding two additional pinion assemblies to pins of the drive pin (19) as shown in Fig. GR28. On early type differential assemblies, adjust gear mesh by installing pinion gear assembly components (13 through 18—Fig. GR30) in ring gear (20). Install gears (9 and 10) and carrier (6) on ring gear. Adjust size or number of shims (17) until gears have solid contact without wobble. Shims are available in sizes of 0.005 and 0.020 inch.

On all models, tighten differential carrier cap screws to 20 ft.-lbs. (27 N·m). To determine correct size and number of shims (2—Fig. GR30) to be installed, install reassembled differential assembly and place equal number and size of shims (2) with axle housing (1 and 33) and install axle housings. Secure axle housing with two cap screws and measure axle end play. End play should be approximately 0.020 inch (0.50 mm). Change number or size of shims (2) if necessary. Shim pack should be equal on both axle housings. Final tightening of axle housing cap screws should be to 45 ft.-lbs. (61 N·m) except for bottom cap screw on left axle housing which serves as oil drain and should be tightened securely. After assembly, fill transaxle with 10 pints (4.7 L) of SAE 90 EP gear oil.

## Models 810-812-814-816S-8102-8120-8121-8122-8123-8163B

To overhaul transmission, refer to previous section and remove transmission from frame. Remove clutch assembly on each side of transmission and remove keys from shafts. Turn transmission over onto left wheel and remove right wheel and hub. Remove brake assembly from right side and "E" ring (E—Fig. GR31) from pto shaft.

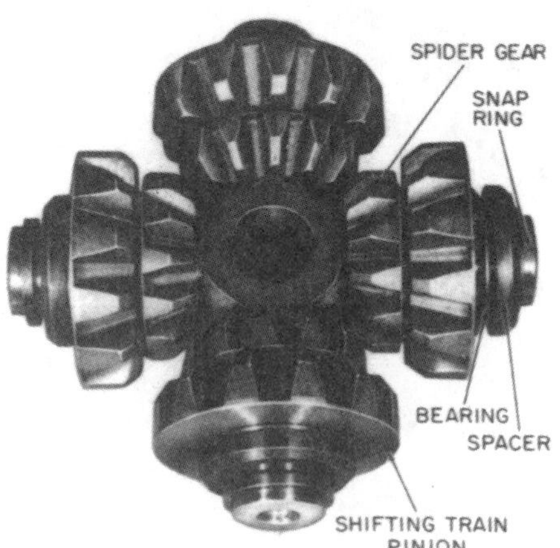


*Fig. GR29—View of spider gear assembly used on Models 424, 430 and 432.*

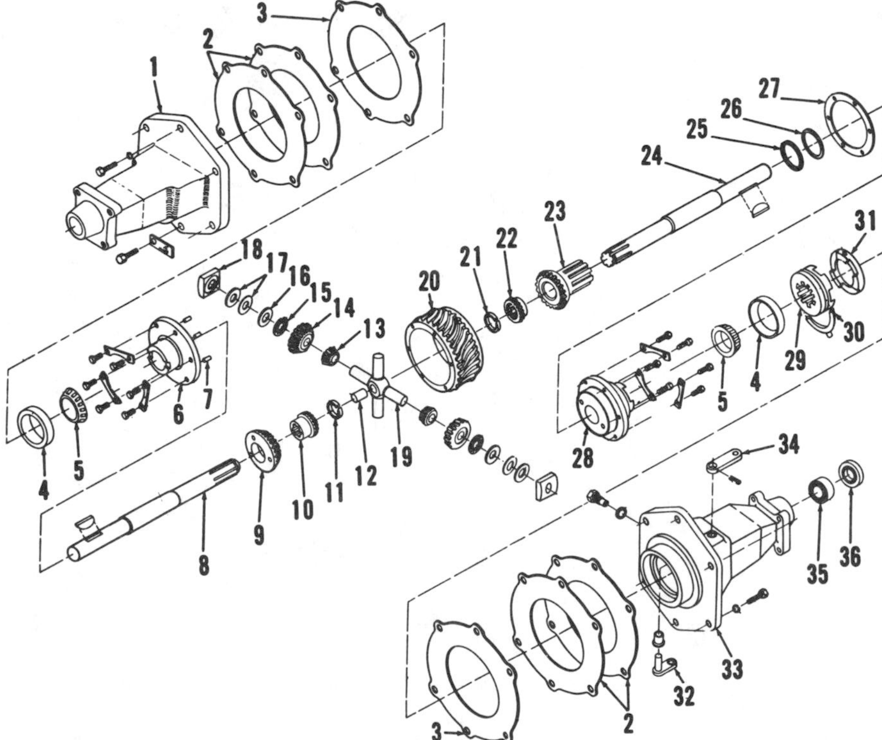

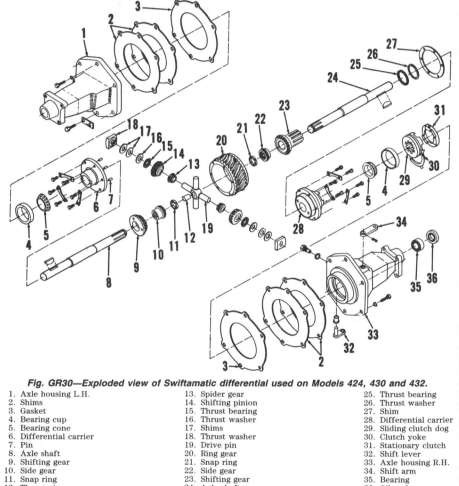

*Fig. GR30—Exploded view of Swiftamatic differential used on Models 424, 430 and 432.*

1. Axle housing L.H.
2. Shims
3. Gasket
4. Bearing cup
5. Bearing cone
6. Differential carrier
7. Pin
8. Axle shaft
9. Shifting gear
10. Side gear
11. Snap ring
12. Thrust pin
13. Spider gear
14. Shifting pinion
15. Thrust bearing
16. Thrust washer
17. Shims
18. Thrust washer
19. Drive pin
20. Ring gear
21. Snap ring
22. Side gear
23. Shifting gear
24. Axle shaft
25. Thrust bearing
26. Thrust washer
27. Shim
28. Differential carrier
29. Sliding clutch dog
30. Clutch yoke
31. Stationary clutch
32. Shift lever
33. Axle housing R.H.
34. Shift arm
35. Bearing
36. Oil seal

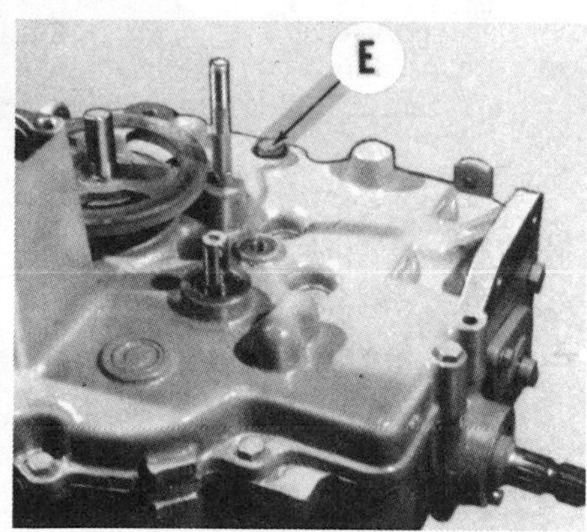


*Fig. GR31—"E" ring (E) must be removed to separate transmission cover from case.*

Clean dirt or paint from right axle and retainer, then remove right axle bearing retainer (2—Fig. GR32).

Unscrew cover screws and lift transmission cover (1) off case. Gear (19) should remain in bearing (15). Remove idler gear (6) and bearings. Remove plug (31—Fig. GR34), spring (32) and ball (33) and remove range shifter fork (23—Fig. GR32) along with Hi-Lo gear and shaft assembly (20 through 33). Remove gear (50) and pinion shaft (51) and slide gear (52) and shaft (54) out of sliding gears. Remove gears and shaft (60 through 64) assembly. Remove gear (65) then withdraw gears and shaft (43 through 48). Remove shaft (66) and gear (67). Unscrew plugs (62—Fig. GR34), remove shift detent balls and springs and remove shift forks (58—Fig. GR32) and gears (55 and 56) noting position of forks and gears. Note that interlock pin (66—Fig. GR34) may be dislodged. Remove reverse shaft (3—Fig. GR32), gears (8 and 13) and bearings.

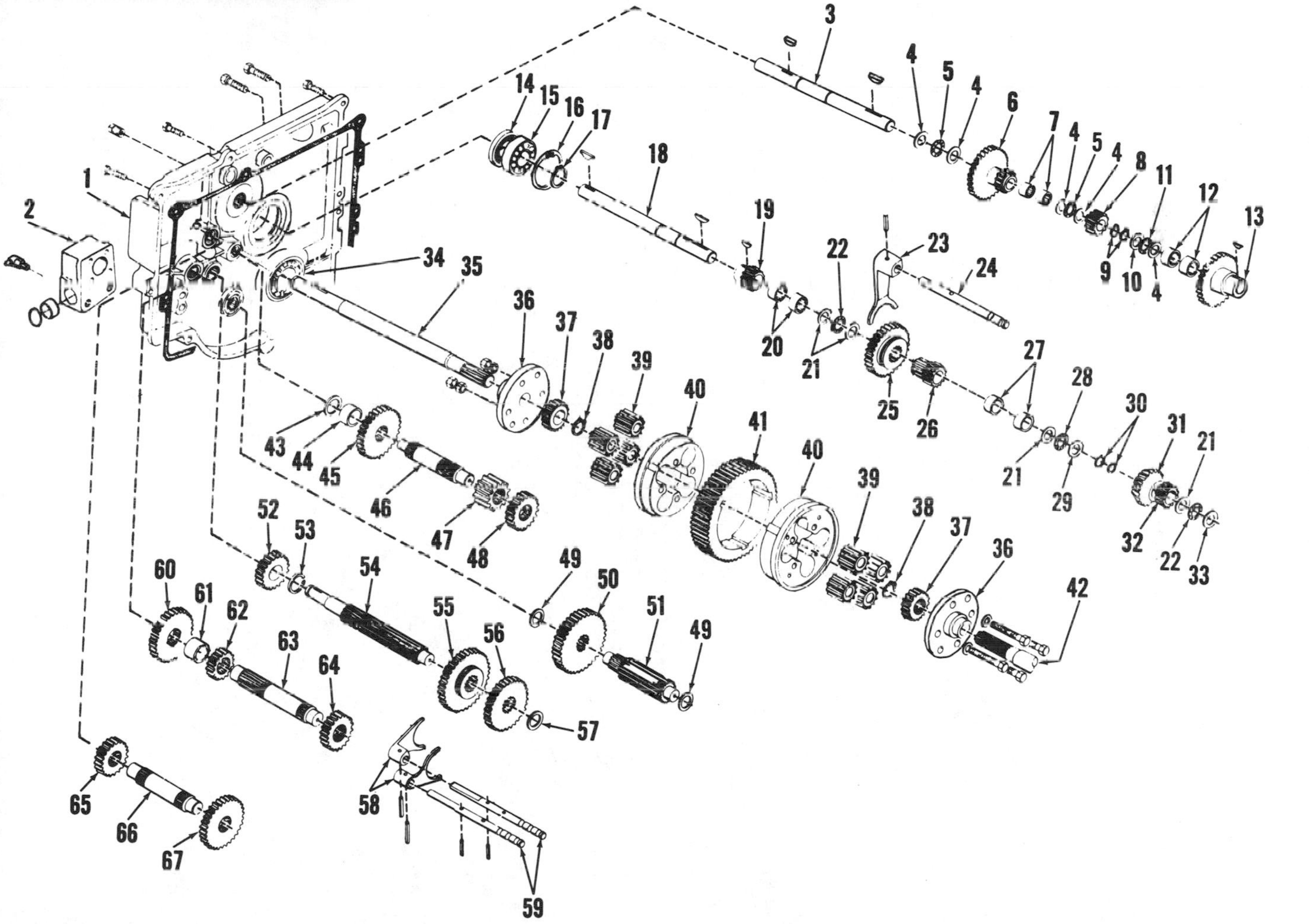

*Fig. GR32—Exploded view of transmission cover and shaft assemblies used on 800 and 8000 series tractors. Differential shown is used on early models. Refer also to Fig. GR33 and GR34.*

1. Cover
2. Right axle bearing retainer
3. Shaft
4. Bearing race (0.030 in.)
5. Thrust bearing
6. Idler gear
7. Needle bearing
8. Gear
9. Snap rings
10. Bearing race (0.090 in.)
11. Thrust bearing
12. Needle bearings
13. Reverse gear
14. Seal
15. Ball bearing
16. Snap ring
17. Snap ring
18. Shaft
19. Gear & bearing assy.
20. Needle bearing
21. Bearing race (0.030 in.)
22. Thrust bearing
23. Hi-Lo shift fork
24. Shift rod
25. Hi-Lo gear
26. Gear & bearing assy.
27. Needle bearing
28. Thrust bearing
29. Bearing race
30. Snap ring
31. Bevel gear
32. Gear
33. Bearing race (0.090 in.)
34. Ball bearing
35. Right axle shaft
36. End cap
37. Side gear
38. Snap ring
39. Pinion gears
40. Body core
41. Ring gear
42. Left axle shaft
43. Thrust washer
44. Spacer
45. Gear
46. Shaft
47. Gear
48. Gear
49. Thrust washer
50. Gear
51. Differential pinion
52. Gear
53. Snap ring
54. Shaft
55. Sliding gear
56. Sliding gear
57. Thrust washer (0.090 in.)
58. Shift forks
59. Shift rods
60. Gear
61. Spacer
62. Gear
63. Shaft
64. Gear
65. Gear
66. Shaft
67. Gear

Slide pto yoke shaft (9—Fig. GR34) through case and remove pto yoke (11). Remove bearing cap (59), snap ring (29) and pto shaft assembly (12 through 28). Disassemble pto assembly using exploded view in Fig. GR34 as a guide. Remove differential shown in Fig. GR32 or GR33.

Bevel gear differential shown in Fig. GR33 is used on tractors after S.N. 18930.

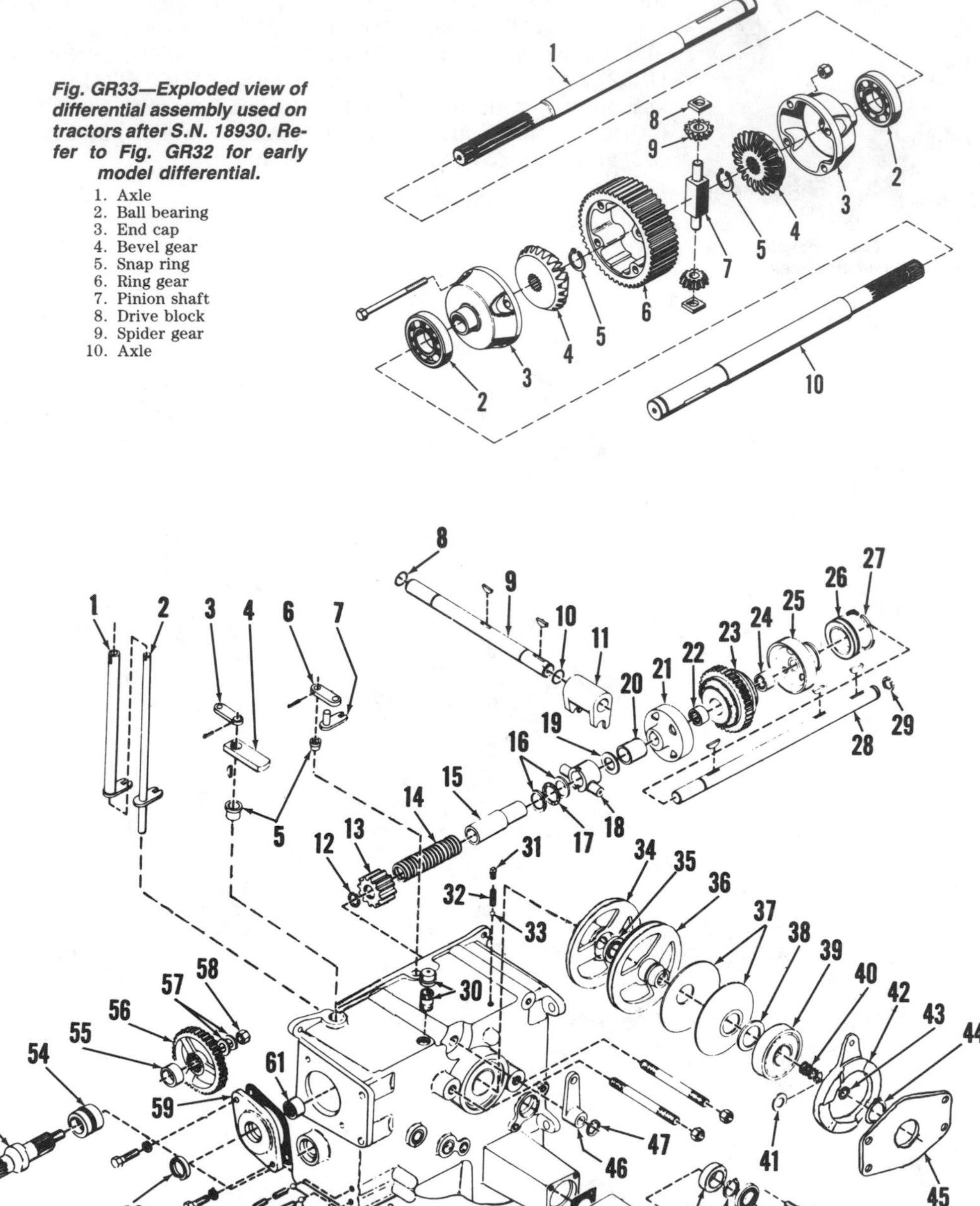

***Fig. GR33—Exploded view of differential assembly used on tractors after S.N. 18930. Refer to Fig. GR32 for early model differential.***

1. Axle
2. Ball bearing
3. End cap
4. Bevel gear
5. Snap ring
6. Ring gear
7. Pinion shaft
8. Drive block
9. Spider gear
10. Axle

***Fig. GR34—Exploded view of transmission case, pto shaft and clutch assemblies used on 800 and 8000 series tractors.***

1. Outer shift tube
2. Inner shift tube
3. Shift shaft shifter arm
4. Shift tube shifter arm
5. Bushing
6. Hi-Lo shift lever
7. Hi-Lo shift fork arm
8. "O" ring
9. Shaft
10. "O" ring
11. Pto yoke
12. Snap ring
13. Pto gear
14. Spring
15. Pto throwout
16. Bearing races
17. Thrust bearing
18. Pto shift collar
19. Thrust washer
20. Spacer
21. Clutch cup
22. Needle bearing
23. Clutch cone
24. Needle bearing
25. Clutch cup
26. Ball bearing
27. Snap ring
28. Pto shaft
29. Snap ring
30. Fill pipe & cup
31. Plug
32. Spring
33. Hi-Lo detent ball
34. Clutch hub
35. Oil seal
36. Clutch disc
37. Belleville spring
38. Shim
39. Ball bearing
40. Spring
41. Washer
42. Clutch arm
43. Snap ring
44. Snap ring
45. Clutch plate
46. Pto arm
47. Snap ring
48. Left axle bearing retainer
49. Ball bearing
50. Snap ring
51. Seal
52. Seal
53. Pto shaft
54. Bearing
55. Spacer
56. Pto gear
57. Washers
58. Locknut
59. Bearing cap
60. Seal
61. Bearing
62. Plug
63. Plug
64. Spring
65. Detent ball
66. Pin



Illustrations courtesy Gravely International, Inc.

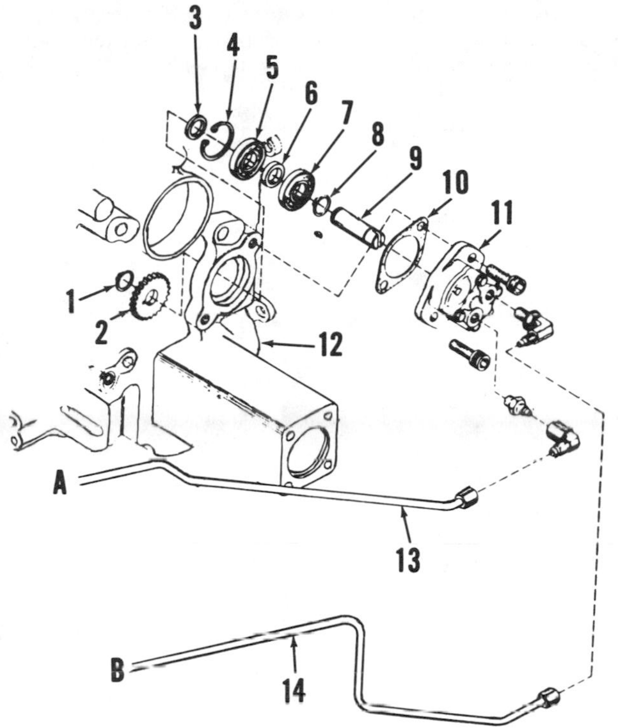

*Fig. GR35—Exploded view of hydraulic pump drive used on some models. Also refer to Fig. GR36.*

1. Snap ring
2. Pump gear
3. Spacer
4. Snap ring
5. Ball bearing
6. Spacer
7. Ball bearing
8. Snap ring
9. Shaft
10. Gasket
11. Hydraulic pump
12. Transmission case
13. Intake line
14. Pressure line

To disassemble clutch assembly, remove snap ring (43—Fig. GR34) and spring (40). Compress Belleville springs (37), remove snap ring (44) and separate clutch components.

To reassemble transmission, reverse disassembly procedure. Tighten differential bolts to 25-30 ft.-lbs. (34-41 N·m). Note location of 0.090 inch (2.28 mm) thick bearing races (10, 22 and 57—Fig. GR32) and 0.030 inch (0.76 mm) thick bearing races (4 and 21). Adjust clutch clearance to 0.030 inch (0.76 mm). Fill transmission with 12 pints (5.7 L) of SAE 30 engine oil.

### Models 1232G-1238G

Models 1232-G and 1238-G are equipped with a Foote 4000 series transaxle. Refer to Spicer (Foote) section in TRANSAXLE SERVICE SECTION in this manual for overhaul procedure.

# HYDRAULIC LIFT

## All Models So Equipped

Refer to Fig. GR35 for an exploded view of hydraulic pump drive used on models equipped with hydraulic lift. Remainder of hydraulic system is shown in Fig. GR36. Hydraulic pump is driven by gear (32—Fig. GR32) in transmission.

Recommended fluid for hydraulic system is Type "A" automatic transmission fluid. Capacity is 1-1/2 quarts (1.4 L) and may be checked with dipstick in reservoir (6—Fig. GR36). Fluid level should be maintained at "FULL" mark on dipstick.

*Fig. GR36—View of hydraulic lift system. Refer to Fig. GR35 for view of hydraulic pump drive.*

1. Control valve return
2. Valve-to-reservoir line
3. Hydraulic hose
4. Hydraulic hose
5. Cylinder
6. Reservoir
7. Lift lever
8. Pump intake line
9. Pump pressure line
10. Shaft
11. "E" ring

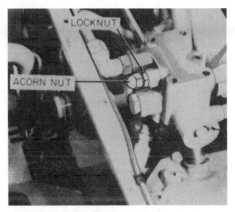

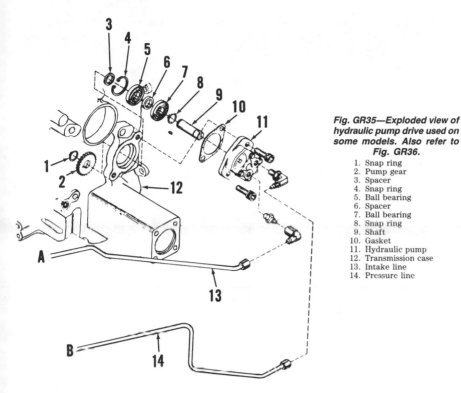

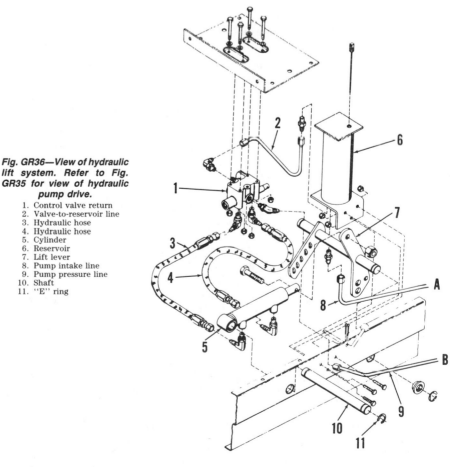

To check hydraulic system pressure, install a tee fitting in place of 90 degree elbow at "OUT" port of hydraulic pump. Connect hydraulic line to one side of tee and a pressure gage which reads at least 1500 psi (10,000 kPa) to other side of tee. Recheck hydraulic fluid level and add oil if necessary.

Start engine and accelerate to full throttle. Operate hydraulic lift. Pressure should read 950-1050 psi (6550-7240 kPa) when cylinder reaches limit in ei-

*Fig. GR37—Adjust hydraulic pressure by removing acorn nut, loosening locknut and turning screw covered by acorn nut.*

ther direction. If pressure is less than 950 psi (6550 kPa), remove acorn nut (Fig. GR37), loosen locknut and turn screw clockwise $^{1}/_{4}$ turn and recheck pressure. Do not set pressure higher than 1050 psi (7240 kpa). Pump or control valve is defective if pressure cannot be adjusted to specified relief setting.

# WIRING DIAGRAMS

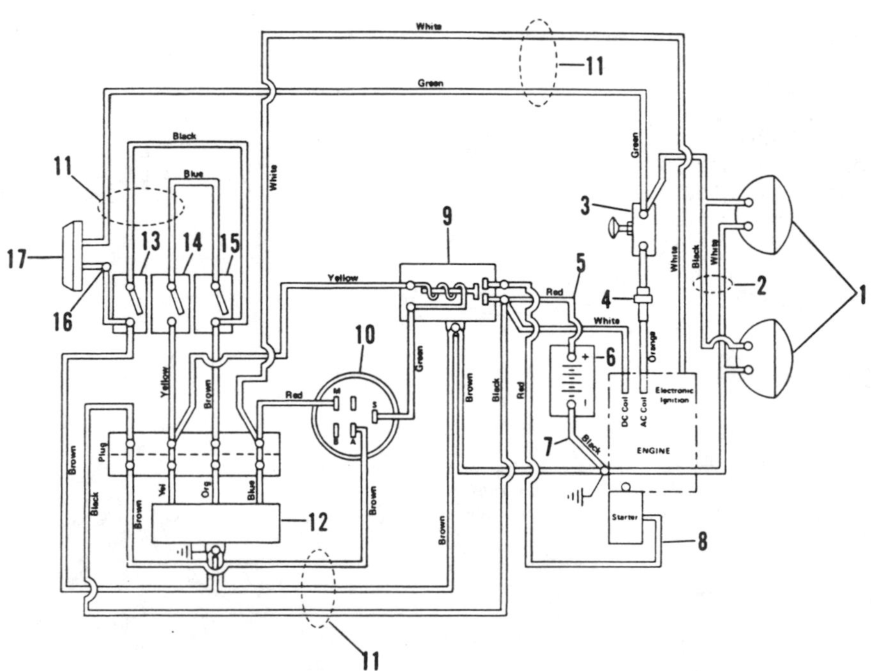


*Fig. GR40—Wiring diagram for 1200 series tractors equipped with Briggs & Stratton engine.*

1. Headlight
2. Wiring harness
3. Light switch
4. Fuse
5. Starter cable
6. Battery
7. Ground cable
8. Cable
9. Solenoid
10. Ignition switch
11. Wiring harness
12. Module
13. Seat switch
14. Interlock switch
15. Switch
16. Connector
17. Tail light

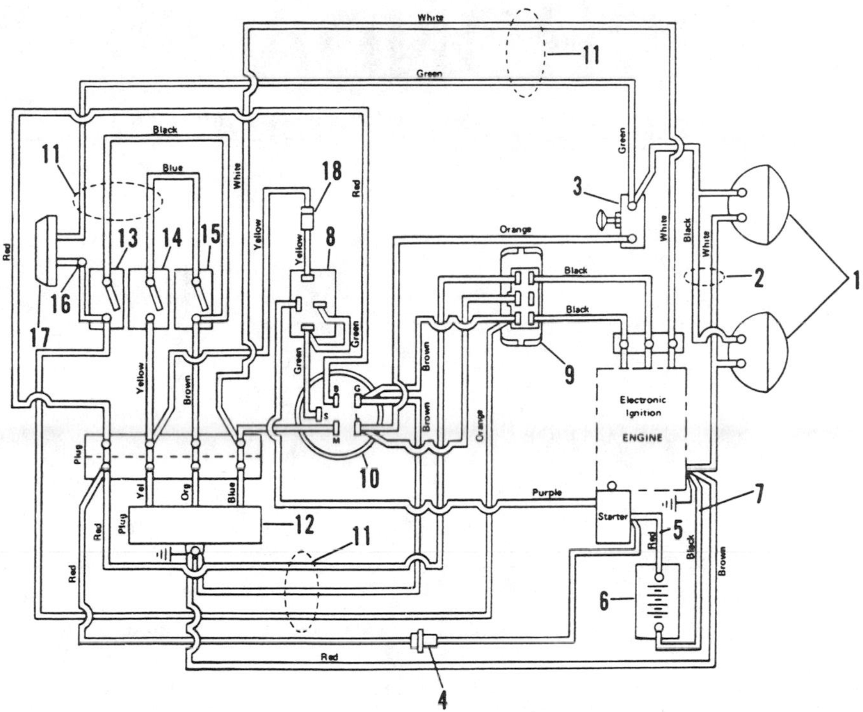


***Fig. GR41—Wiring diagram for 1238-H tractors equipped with Kawasaki engine.***

1. Headlight
2. Wiring harness
3. Light switch
4. Fuse
5. Starter cable
6. Battery
7. Ground cable
8. Relay
9. Regulator
10. Ignition switch
11. Wiring harness
12. Module
13. Seat switch
14. Interlock switch
15. Switch
16. Connector
17. Tail light

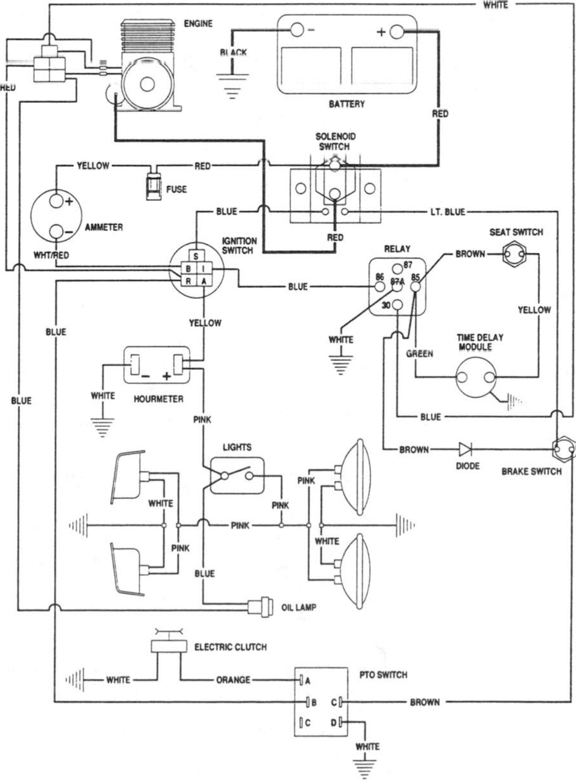


***Fig. GR42—Wiring diagram for Gravely Estate Mower (GEM) tractors.***

# HONDA

## CONDENSED SPECIFICATIONS

| | MODEL 3810 |
|---|---|
| Engine Make | Honda |
| Model | G400 |
| Bore | 86 mm (3.4 in.) |
| Stroke | 70 mm (2.8 in.) |
| Piston Displacement | 406 cc (24.9 cu. in.) |
| Horsepower | 10 |

| | MODEL (Cont.) 3810 |
|---|---|
| Slow Idle Speed | 2200 |
| Full Load Speed (Rpm) | 3600 |
| Crankcase Oil Capacity | 1.2 L (1.27 qt.) |
| Weight | SAE 10W-40 |
| Transaxle Oil Capacity | 2.4 L (2.54 qt.) |
| Weight | SAE 10W-40 |

## FRONT AXLE AND STEERING SYSTEM

### AXLE MAIN MEMBER

**REMOVE AND REINSTALL.** To remove axle main member (3–Fig. HN50), raise and support front of tractor. Disconnect outer drag link (8) end. Support main member and remove axle pivot bolt (9). Lower axle main member from main frame pivot point and roll axle out from under tractor.

When reinstalling axle main member, lubricate pivot bolt (9) with lithium base grease prior to installation.

### TIE ROD

The tie rod is equipped with threaded ends (4–Fig. HN50) at each end. Recommended toe-in is 3 mm (1/8 inch). Adjust length of tie rod by threading ends in or out as required.

### STEERING SPINDLES

**REMOVE AND REINSTALL.** To remove steering spindles, raise and support front of tractor. Remove left and right hub caps and remove cotter pins, castle nuts and flat washers. Remove tires, wheels and bearings. Disconnect tie rod ends at spindle to be removed.

To remove left spindle, remove clamp bolt (6–Fig. HN50) and spread steering lever (7) open to remove from spindle. Remove washer (5) and slide spindle down out of axle main member. Remove bushings (2) as required. When reinstalling spindle, align punch mark on spindle end with punch mark on steering lever (Fig. HN51).

To remove right steering spindle, remove snap ring (10–Fig. HN50) and slip spindle down out of axle main member. Renew bushings (2) as required.

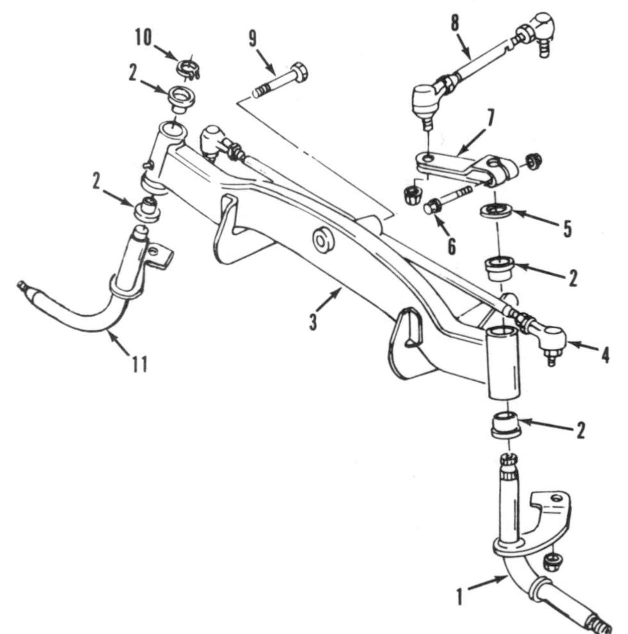

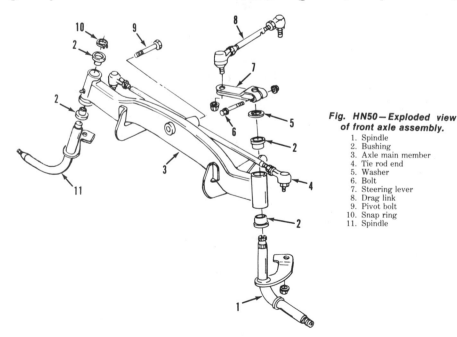

*Fig. HN50—Exploded view of front axle assembly.*
1. Spindle
2. Bushing
3. Axle main member
4. Tie rod end
5. Washer
6. Bolt
7. Steering lever
8. Drag link
9. Pivot bolt
10. Snap ring
11. Spindle

### STEERING GEAR

**R&R AND OVERHAUL.** To remove steering shaft and gear assembly, remove cover (1–Fig. HN52) and nut (2). Remove steering wheel (3) and flat washer (4). Disconnect drag link end at steering arm (15). Remove cap screws which retain steering plate (8). Remove the three cap screws retaining steering gear holder (17). Remove nut (11) and pull steering shaft (6) out of tractor. Remove gear (9) and washer (10). Remove steering gear (14) and washers (13 and 16). Renew bushings (5, 7 and 12) as required.

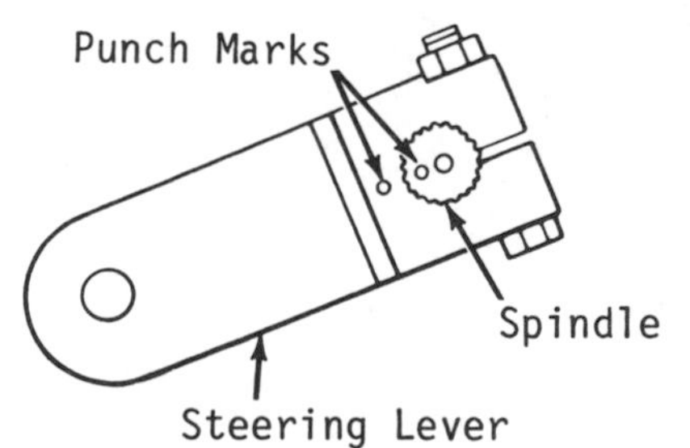


*Fig. HN51—When installing steering lever on spindle, align punch marks.*

Reverse removal procedure for reassembly. Make certain front wheels are straight ahead, larger opening in steering wheel is toward the top and steering gears are meshed in the center of gear (14) during reassembly. Tighten the three bolts retaining the steering gear holder (17) to 23-30 N·m (17-22 ft.-lbs.) and nuts (2 and 11) to 45-54 N·m (33-40 ft.-lbs.).

# ENGINE

**REMOVE AND REINSTALL.** Disconnect headlight wiring, remove hood restraint cable and hood retaining bolts and remove hood assembly. Disconnect negative and positive battery cables. Remove the front air shroud assembly. Disconnect the pto clutch cable at the clutch and remove attachment drive belt from pto pulley. Remove exhaust pipe, disconnect throttle cable and fuel line at carburetor. Disconnect all starter, charging coils, ignition wire and ground cables. Remove the four nuts retaining rubber engine mounts. Lift and slide engine from tractor disengaging drive shaft as engine is removed.

Reinstall by reversing removal procedure. Tighten exhaust pipe nuts to 18-24 N·m (13-18 ft.-lbs.). Make certain the lugs on rubber motor mounts are inserted into slots of mounting plates and tighten the four nuts retaining rubber motor mounts to 45-54 N·m (33-40 ft.-lbs.).

**OVERHAUL**

Model 3810 tractor is equipped with a Honda G400 engine. Refer to the Honda engine service section for overhaul procedure.

# DRIVE CLUTCH

**ADJUSTMENT.** To adjust drive clutch linkage, refer to ADJUSTMENT in BRAKE section. To check condition of drive clutch, place gear shift lever in second speed slot. Raise seat and remove the inspection hole cover. The indicator mark on the clutch lever should be between the two notches on the clutch housing (Fig. HN53). If indicator mark is past the red notch on the clutch housing, clutch disk must be renewed.

**R&R AND OVERHAUL (Early Style).** Remove drive shaft. Disconnect all clutch linkage. Remove damper hub (23 – Fig. HN54). Remove cap screw (18) and washer (17). Remove the three nuts retaining clutch assembly plate (2) bolted to transaxle input shaft and slide clutch assembly from shaft. Special clutch spring compressor (part 7960-750000A) is required to safely compress clutch spring (19) before nuts (22)

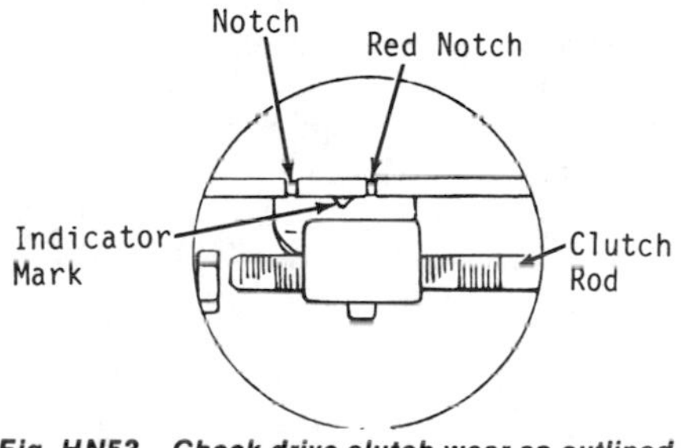


*Fig. HN53 – Check drive clutch wear as outlined in text.*

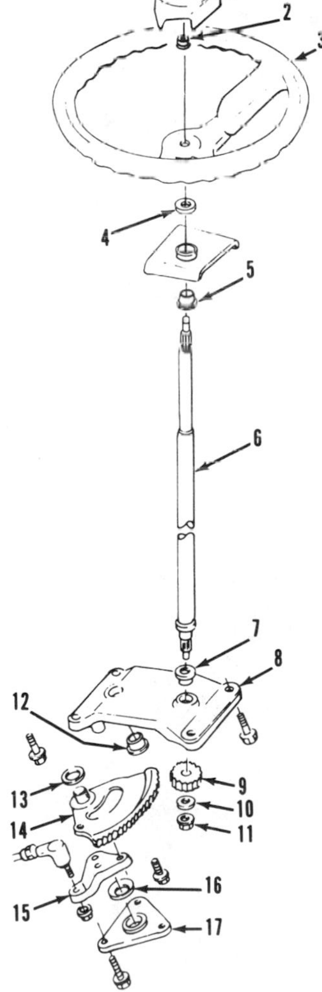


*Fig. HN52 – Exploded view of steering shaft and gears.*

1. Cover
2. Nut
3. Steering wheel
4. Flat washer
5. Bushing
6. Steering shaft
7. Bushing
8. Steering plate
9. Gear
10. Washer
11. Nut
12. Bushing
13. Washer
14. Gear
15. Steering arm
16. Washer
17. Steering gear holder

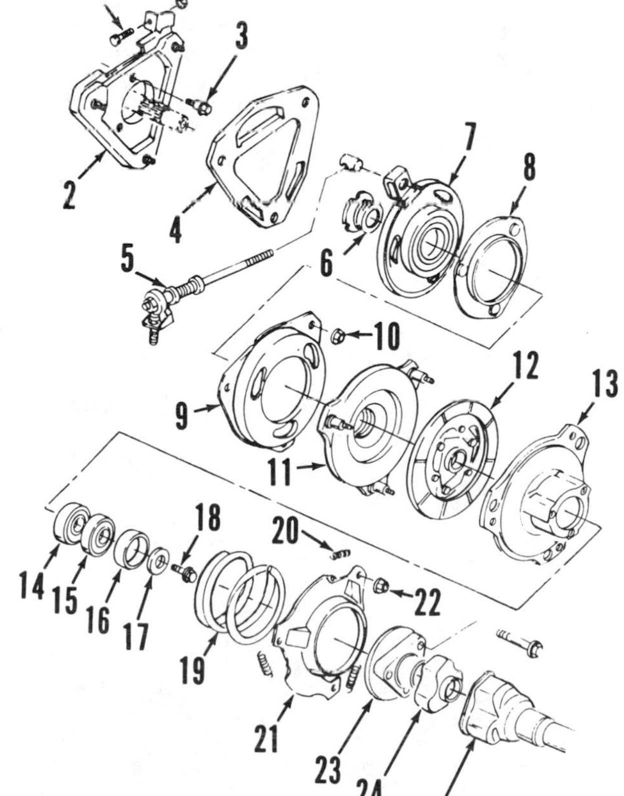


*Fig. HN54 – Exploded view of drive clutch assembly used on later models. Dust seal plate (4) and clutch setting springs (20) are not used on early models.*

1. Stop bolt
2. Clutch plate
3. Bolt
4. Dust seal plate
5. Clutch rod
6. Bearing lock nut
7. Ramp
8. Ball retainer
9. Rear clutch housing
10. Nut
11. Lifter plate
12. Clutch disc
13. Pressure plate
14. Bearing
15. Bearing
16. Collar
17. Washer
18. Cap screw
19. Spring
20. Clutch setting spring
21. Clutch cover
22. Nut
23. Damper hub
24. Damper
25. Drive shaft

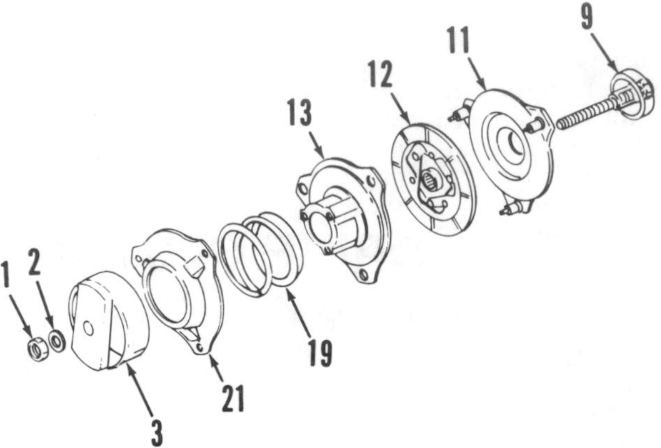


*Fig. HN55—Exploded view of spring loaded clutch pack with special spring compressor tool (part 07960-75000A).*

1. Nut
2. Washer
3. Special tool part
9. Special tool part
11. Lifter plate
12. Clutch disk
13. Pressure plate
19. Spring
21. Clutch cover

can be removed or installed (Fig. HN55). Old style nut (6–Fig. HN54) (left-hand thread) with 5 mm slots must be removed with a punch and hammer and renewed with a new nut with 6 mm slots for which tool (part 22583-750-003) is available to aid removal and installation.

Clean and inspect all parts. Thickness of clutch facing on disk (12) should be 5.9-6.1 mm (0.232-0.240 in.). If facing thickness is 3.9 mm (0.154 in.) or less, renew disk. Disk is installed with long side of splined hub toward lifter plate (11). Free length of spring (19) should be 58.2 mm (2.29 in.). If spring free length is 56.2 mm (2.213 in.) or less, renew spring. Nuts (22) retaining clutch spring are tightened to 10-13 N·m (88-115 in.-lbs.).

**R&R AND OVERHAUL. (Late Style).** Remove drive shaft. Disconnect all clutch linkage. Remove the three cap screws retaining damper hub (23–Fig. HN54) and remove hub. Remove cap screw (18) and washer (17). Remove the three nuts (10) and slide clutch assembly off of transaxle input shaft. Use special tool (part 07916-3710100) to remove left-hand thread bearing lock nut (6). Use special spring compressor tool (part 07960-750000A) to compress spring (19) in clutch pack (Fig. HN55). With tool compressing clutch pack, remove the three nuts (22–Fig. HN54). Slowly unscrew spring compressor tool and disassemble clutch pack.

Clean and inspect all parts. Thickness of clutch facing on disc (12) should be 5.9-6.1 mm (0.232-0.240 in.). If thickness is 3.9 mm (0.154 in.) or less, renew disc. Spring (19) free length should be 58.2 mm (2.29 in.). If free length is 56.2 mm (2.213 in.) or less, renew spring. When reassembling spring loaded clutch pack, refer to Fig. HN55 for assembly sequence. Align spring end with one of the three threaded studs on pressure plate (Fig. HN56). Install side of clutch disc (12–Fig. HN55) with long side of splined hub toward lifter plate (11). Tighten nuts (22 and 10–Fig. HN54) to 10-13 N·m (88-115 in.-lbs.). Tighten cap screw (18) to 24-30 N·m (18-22 ft.-lbs.). Make certain dust plate (4) is mounted on clutch plate (2) and that studs on clutch plate are through the holes in the dust plate.

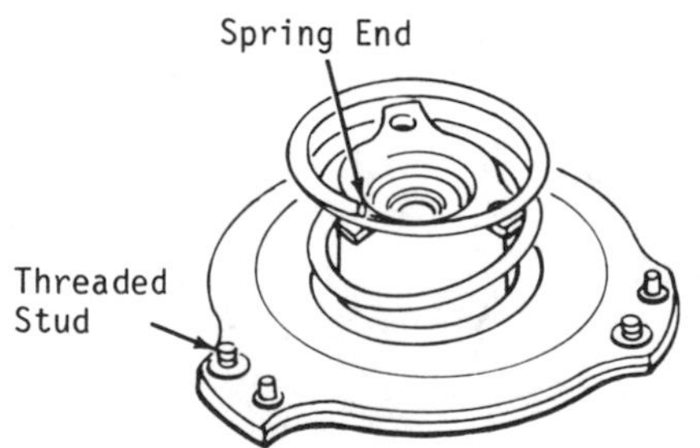


*Fig. HN56—Align end of clutch spring with threaded stud prior to assembly.*

# BRAKE

**ADJUSTMENT.** Depressing brake pedal disengages drive clutch and applies brake. Brake, clutch and shift linkage adjustments must be performed or checked in the following order. Brake pedal rod must be adjusted so there is no clearance between the end of operating rod and the front end of brake pedal slot when brake pedal is released (Fig. HN58). Loosen jam nut and turn adjusting nut to remove any clearance. Check brake pedal clutch cable free play by placing shift lever in second gear drive slot. Clutch arm link should have 0-0.5 mm (0.02 inch) free play. If adjustment is required, loosen locknuts and push clutch arm outward until shift lever contacts edge of gear plate slot. Reposition cable. Shift lever free play should be checked at this time. With shift lever in second gear slot, measure free movement of shift lever and inner (deepest) edge of slot. There should be 5-10 mm (0.2-0.4 in.) free play. Adjust by varying length of clutch rod (Fig. HN59). Hold the shift lever all the way to the left. Rod end of clutch arm should almost touch the stopper bolt (1–Fig. HN54). Rod end of clutch arm should be 11-12 mm (0.4-0.5 in.) from the head of stopper bolt when shift lever is allowed to return to the right side position.

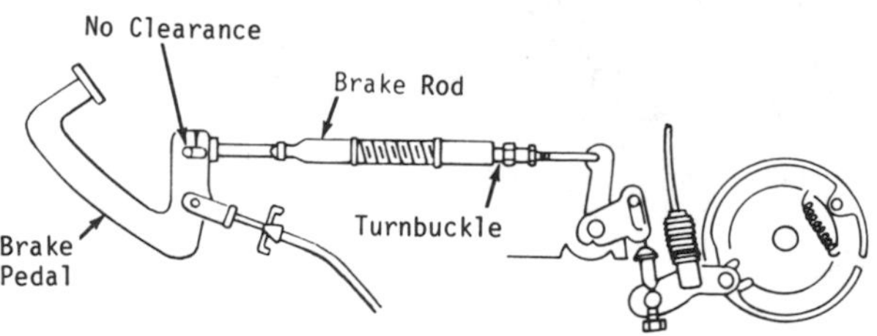


*Fig. HN58—Remove clearance by adjusting turnbuckle. Refer to text.*

**REMOVE AND REINSTALL BRAKE SHOES.** To check brake shoe wear, depress brake pedal and observe position of brake wear indicator located near brake assembly on transaxle (Fig. HN60). If indicator is near new limit point, renew brake shoes.

To remove brake shoes, remove the rear seat, rear fender and wire protec-

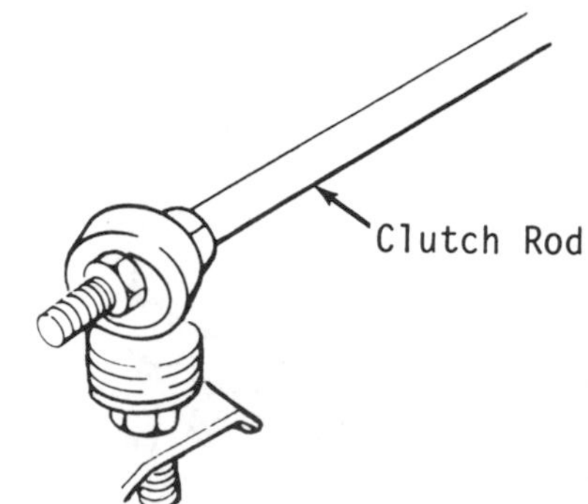


*Fig. HN59—Turn clutch rod to adjust length.*

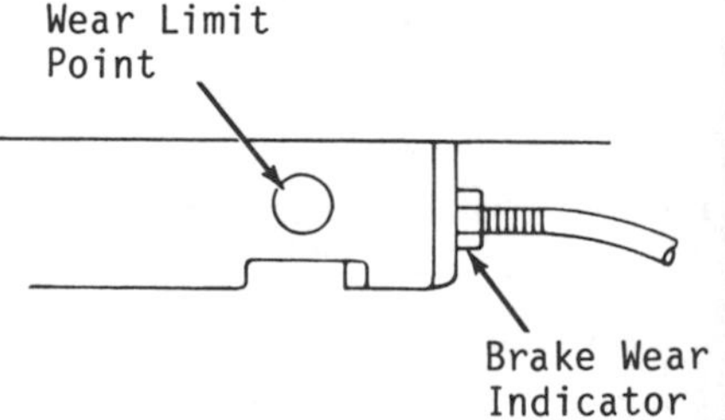


*Fig. HN60—Depress brake pedal and look at brake shoe wear indicator to determine if brake shoes should be renewed.*

tor. Drain transaxle housing. Remove cap screw (1–Fig. HN61), washer (2) and brake drum (3). Remove brake shoe spring (4) and brake shoes (5).

Clean and inspect all parts. Brake lining thickness should be 4.35-4.65 mm (0.171-0.183 in.). If lining thickness is 2.35 mm (0.093 in.) or less, renew brake shoe. If brake cam (6) is removed, reinstall in brake arm (11) so punch mark on cam is aligned with punch mark on brake arm. Refill transaxle with 2.4 L (2.54 qts.) of SAE 10W-40 oil.

# TRANSAXLE

**LUBRICATION.** Manufacturer recommends checking transaxle fluid level at 100 hour intervals of use. Transaxle fluid capacity is 2.4 L (2.54 qts.). Recommended lubricant is SAE 10W-30 oil.

**REMOVE AND REINSTALL.** Raise and support rear of tractor. Remove left and right wheel and tire assemblies. Remove drive shaft and drive clutch assembly. Disconnect shift rod at transaxle shift lever. Disconnect all necessary electrical connections. Remove fuel pump assembly. Disconnect brake rod at brake assembly. Support transaxle and remove the transaxle retaining bolts. Lower transaxle assembly out of frame and pull from under tractor.

Reinstall by reversing removal procedure. Refer to LUBRICATION to refill transaxle. Adjust all linkage as outlined under ADJUSTMENT in BRAKE section.

**OVERHAUL.** No service information available at time of publication.

# PTO

**PTO LEVER ADJUSTMENT.** Pto lever should have 3-5 mm (0.1-0.2 in.) free play. To adjust, loosen the jam nut at cable and bracket and turn the adjuster as required.

**DISASSEMBLY.** Refer to Fig. HN65 for an exploded view of components. Standard thickness for brake disc is 10.3-10.4 mm (0.406-0.409 in.). If thickness is 8.3 mm (0.327 in.) or less, renew brake disc (17) and friction disc (11). Standard thickness for friction disc (11) is 5.9-6.1 mm (0.232-0.240 in.). If thickness is 3.9 mm (0.154 in.) or less, renew friction disc (11) and brake disc (17). When installing friction disc (11), long side of splined hub is installed toward engine.

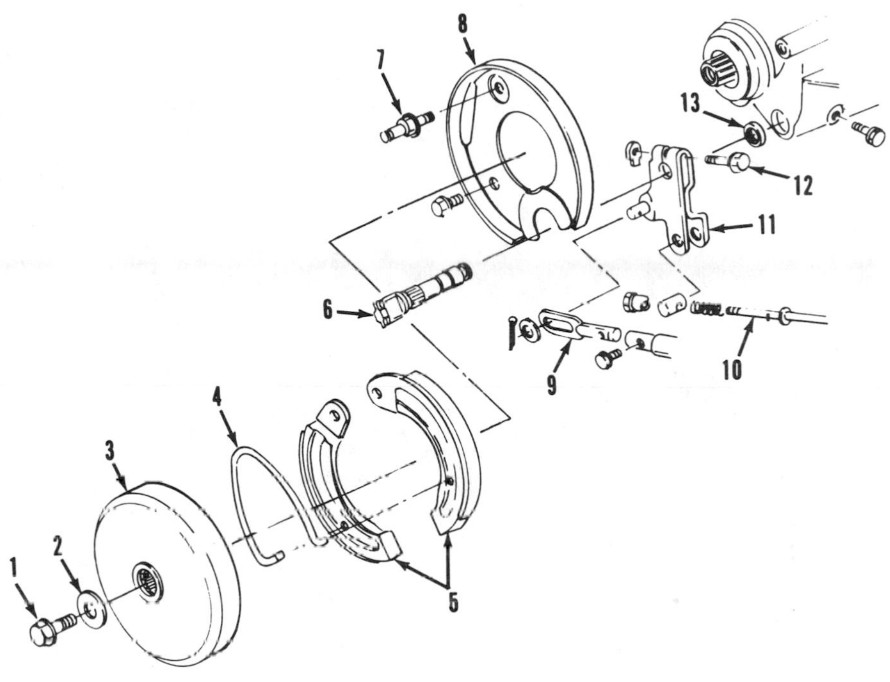

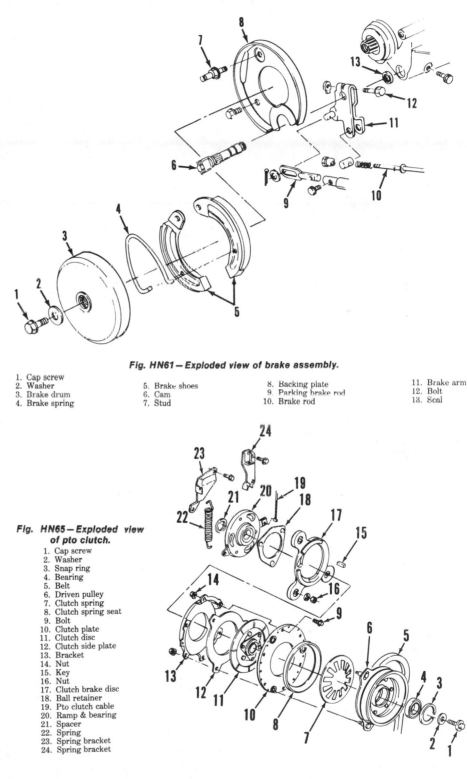

*Fig. HN61—Exploded view of brake assembly.*

1. Cap screw
2. Washer
3. Brake drum
4. Brake spring
5. Brake shoes
6. Cam
7. Stud
8. Backing plate
9. Parking brake rod
10. Brake rod
11. Brake arm
12. Bolt
13. Seal

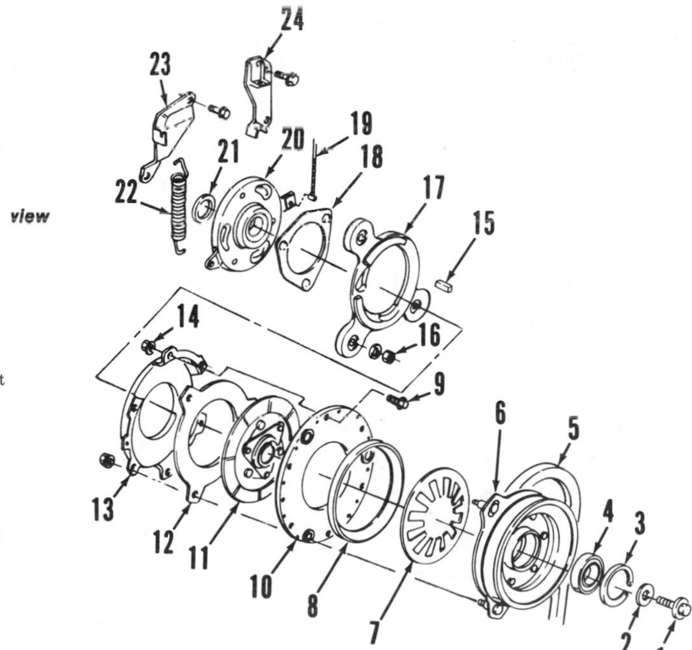


*Fig. HN65—Exploded view of pto clutch.*

1. Cap screw
2. Washer
3. Snap ring
4. Bearing
5. Belt
6. Driven pulley
7. Clutch spring
8. Clutch spring seat
9. Bolt
10. Clutch plate
11. Clutch disc
12. Clutch side plate
13. Bracket
14. Nut
15. Key
16. Nut
17. Clutch brake disc
18. Ball retainer
19. Pto clutch cable
20. Ramp & bearing
21. Spacer
22. Spring
23. Spring bracket
24. Spring bracket

# JACOBSEN

## CONDENSED SPECIFICATIONS

| | MODELS | | | | |
|---|---|---|---|---|---|
| | **LT700, LT750** | **LT700, LT710** | **LT750, LT760** | **LT80, LT860** | **LT885** |
| Engine Make | Tecumseh | B&S | B&S | B&S | B&S |
| Model | V70 | 170707 | 170707 | 191707 | 191707 |
| Bore | 2¾ in. (69.8 mm) | 3 in. (76.2 mm) | 3 in. (76.2 mm) | 3 in. (76.2 mm) | 3 in. (76.2 mm) |
| Stroke | 2-17/32 in. (64.3 mm) | 2⅜ in. (60.3 mm) | 2⅜ in. (60.3 mm) | 2¾ in. (69.8 mm) | 2¾ in. (69.8 mm) |
| Piston Displacement | 15.0 cu. in. (246 cc) | 16.79 cu. in. (275 cc) | 16.79 cu. in. (275 cc) | 19.44 cu. in. (319 cc) | 19.44 cu. in. (319 cc) |
| Horsepower | 7 | 7 | 7 | 8 | 8 |
| Slow Idle Speed – Rpm | 1800 | 1750 | 1750 | 1750 | 1750 |
| High Idle Speed (No Load) – Rpm | 3750 | 3600 | 3600 | 4000 | 4000 |
| Crankcase Oil Capacity | 1½ pints (0.7 L) | 2¼ pints (1 L) | 2¼ pints (1 L) | 2¼ pints (1 L) | 2¼ pints (1 L) |
| Transmission Oil Capacity | 1½ pints (0.7 L) | | | | * |
| Weight | SAE 90 EP | | | | Ford M-2C41-A |
| Differential Oil Capacity | .... | .... | .... | .... | 2¾ pints (1.3 L) |
| Weight | .... | .... | .... | .... | SAE 90 EP |

*Refer to Hydrostatic Transmission Lubrication paragraph.

| | MODELS | | | | |
|---|---|---|---|---|---|
| | **LT110** | **LT1060** | **800** | **1000** | **1200** |
| Engine Make | B&S | B&S | Kohler | Kohler | Kohler |
| Model | 251707 | 251707 | K181 | K241AQS | K301AQS |
| Bore | 3-7/16 in. (87.3 mm) | 3-7/16 in. (87.3 mm) | 2-15/16 in. (74.6 mm) | 3¼ in. (82.5 mm) | 3¼ in. (82.5 mm) |
| Stroke | 2⅝ in. (66.7 mm) | 2⅝ in. (66.7 mm) | 2¾ in. (69.8 mm) | 2⅞ in. (73.0 mm) | 3¼ in. (82.5 mm) |
| Piston Displacement | 24.36 cu. in. (399 cc) | 24.36 cu. in. (399 cc) | 18.6 cu. in. (305 cc) | 23.9 cu. in. (392 cc) | 29.07 cu. in. (476 cc) |
| Horsepower | 10 | 10 | 8 | 10 | 12 |
| Slow Idle Speed – Rpm | 1800 | 1800 | 1000 | 1000 | 1000 |
| High Idle Speed (No Load) – Rpm | 3600 | 3600 | 3600 | 3600 | 3600 |
| Crankcase Oil Capacity | 2½ pints (1.2 L) | 2½ pints (1.2 L) | 2½ pints (1.2 L) | 3 pints (1.4 L) | 3 pints (1.4 L) |
| Transmission Oil Capacity | 1½ pints (0.7 L) | 1½ pints (0.7 L) | 4 pints (1.9 L) | 4 pints (1.9 L) | 4 pints (1.9 L) |
| Weight | SAE 90 EP | | | | |

| | MODELS | | | | |
|---|---|---|---|---|---|
| | **1250** | **1450 (Early)** | **1450 (Late)** | **1650** | **GT10** |
| Engine Make | Kohler | Kohler | Kohler | Kohler | Kohler |
| Model | K301AQS | K321S | K321AQS | K341AQS | K241AS |
| Bore | 3⅜ in. (85.7 mm) | 3½ in. (88.9 mm) | 3½ in. (88.9 mm) | 3¾ in. (95.2 mm) | 3¼ in. (82.5 mm) |
| Stroke | 3¼ in. (82.5 mm) | 3¼ in. (82.5 mm) | 3¼ in. (82.5 mm) | 3¼ in. (82.5 mm) | 2⅞ in. (73.0 mm) |



Illustrations courtesy Jacobsen, Div. of Textron, Inc.

| | MODELS (Cont.) | | | | |
|---|---|---|---|---|---|
| | 1250 | 1450 (Early) | 1450 (Late) | 1650 | GT10 |
| Piston Displacement | 29.07 cu. in. (476 cc) | 31.27 cu. in. (512 cc) | 31.27 cu. in. (512 cc) | 35.89 cu. in. (588 cc) | 23.9 cu. in. (392 cc) |
| Horsepower | 12 | 14 | 14 | 16 | 10 |
| Slow Idle Speed – Rpm | 1000 | 1000 | 1000 | 1000 | 1000 |
| High Idle Speed (No Load) – Rpm | 3600 | 3600 | 3600 | 3600 | 3600 |
| Crankcase Oil Capacity | 3 pints (1.4 L) | 5 pints (2.4 L) | 3 pints (1.4 L) | 3 pints (1.4 L) | 4½ pints (2.1 L) |
| Transmission Oil Capacity | 8 pints (3.8 L) | * | 8 pints (3.8 L) | 8 pints (3.8 L) | 4 pints (1.9 L) |
| Weight | Ford M-2C41-A | * | Ford M-2C41-A | Ford M-2C41-A | SAE 90 EP |
| Differential Oil Capacity | .... | 2 pints (0.9L) | .... | .... | .... |
| Weight | .... | SAE 90 EP | .... | .... | .... |

*Refer to Hydrostatic Transmission Lubrication paragraph.

| | MODELS | | | |
|---|---|---|---|---|
| | GT12 | GT12H | GT14 | GT16 |
| Engine Make | Kohler | Kohler | Kohler | Kohler |
| Model | K301AS | K301AS | K321AS | K341AS |
| Bore | 3⅜ in. (85.7 mm) | 3⅜ in. (85.7 mm) | 3½ in. (88.9 mm) | 3¾ in. (95.2 mm) |
| Stroke | 3¼ in. (82.5 mm) | 3¼ in. (82.5 mm) | 3¼ in. (82.5 mm) | 3¼ in. (82.5 mm) |
| Piston Displacement | 29.07 cu. in. (476 cc) | 29.07 cu. in. (476 cc) | 31.27 cu. in. (512 cc) | 35.89 cu. in. (588 cc) |
| Horsepower | 12 | 12 | 14 | 16 |
| Slow Idle Speed – Rpm | 1000 | 1000 | 1000 | 1000 |
| High Idle Speed (No Load) – Rpm | 3600 | 3600 | 3600 | 3600 |
| Crankcase Oil Capacity | 4½ pints (2.1 L) | | | |
| Transmission Oil Capacity | 4 pints (1.9 L) | * | * | * |
| Weight | SAE 90 EP | Ford M-2C41-A | Ford M-2C41-A | Ford M-2C41-A |

*Refer to Hydrostatic Transmission Lubrication paragraph.

| | MODELS | | |
|---|---|---|---|
| | LT10 | LT12 | LTX8 |
| Engine Make | B&S | B&S | B&S |
| Model | 256707 | 281707 | 191707 |
| Bore | 3-7/16 in. (87.3 mm) | 3-7/16 in. (87.3 mm) | 3 in. (76.2 mm) |
| Stroke | 2-5/8 in. (66.7 mm) | 3-1/16 in. (77.7 mm) | 2-3/4 in. (69.8 mm) |
| Piston Displacement | 24.36 cu. in. (400 cc) | 28.4 cu. in. (465 cc) | 19.44 cu. in. (319 cc) |
| Rated Power | 10 hp (7.5 kW) | 12 hp (8.9 kW) | 8 hp (6.0 kW) |
| Slow Idle Speed—Rpm | 1750 | 1750 | 1750 |
| High Idle Speed (No-Load)—Rpm | 3600 | 3600 | 3600 |
| Crankcase Oil Capacity | 3 pints (1.4 L) | 3 pints (1.4 L) | 2-1/4 pints (1 L) |
| Transmission Oil Capacity | 24 ounces (710 mL) | | |
| Weight | Grease | | |

| | MODELS | | |
|---|---|---|---|
| | LTX11 | LTX12 | YT12 |
| Engine Make | B&S | B&S | B&S |
| Model | 253707 | 281707 | 281707 |
| Bore | 3-7/16 in. (87.3 mm) | 3-7/16 in. (87.3 mm) | 3-7/16 in. (87.3 mm) |
| Stroke | 2-5/8 in. (66.7 mm) | 3-1/16 in. (77.7 mm) | 3-1/16 in. (77.7 mm) |
| Piston Displacement | 24.36 cu. in. (400 cc) | 28.4 cu. in. (465 cc) | 28.4 cu. in. (465 cc) |
| Rated Power | 11 hp (8.2 kW) | 12 hp (8.9 kW) | 12 hp (8.9 kW) |
| Slow Idle Speed—Rpm | 1750 | 1750 | 1750 |
| High Idle Speed (No-Load)—Rpm | 3600 | 3600 | 3600 |
| Crankcase Oil Capacity | 2-1/2 pints (1.2 L) | 3 pints (1.4 L) | 3 pints (1.4 L) |
| Transmission Oil Capacity | | 24 ounces (710 mL) | |
| Weight | | Grease | |

# FRONT AXLE AND STEERING SYSTEM

## AXLE MAIN MEMBER

### All Models

Axle main member is center mounted to the main frame and pivots on a bolt or pin riding in bushings or in a pivot pin. Refer to Figs. J1, J2, J3 and J4 for an exploded view of front axle assembly.

To remove front axle, first detach implement lift bars if so equipped. Disconnect drag link ball joint end from steering arm. Raise front of tractor and support under main frame with suitable stands. Remove axle pivot pin or bolt, raise front of tractor until axle will clear main frame and roll axle assembly from under tractor.

Inspect pivot areas for excessive wear or damage. Axle pivot bushings (on models so equipped) are renewable. Lubricate axle pivot with multipurpose grease when reinstalling.

## TIE ROD

### All Models

Models LT10, LT12, LTX8, LTX11, LTX12 and YT12 are equipped with nonadjustable tie rods. All other models are equipped with adjustable type tie rods.

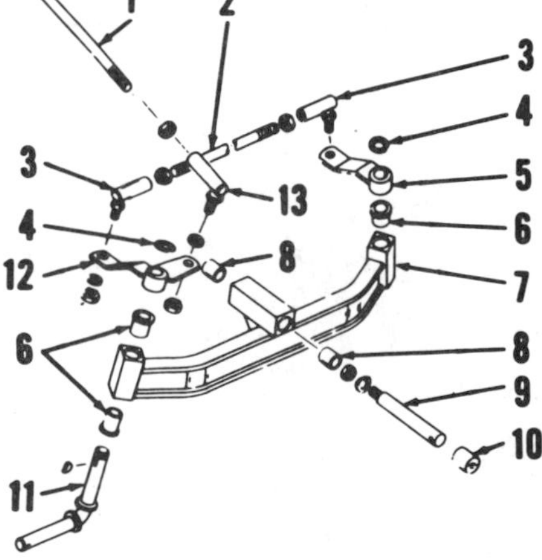

*Fig. J1—Exploded view of front axle main member assembly found on Models LT700, LT710, LT750, LT760, LT860, LT1060, LT80 and LT110.*

1. Drag link
2. Tie rod
3. Ball joints
4. Snap ring
5. Tie rod arm
6. Bushing
7. Axle main member
8. Bushing
9. Pivot bolt
10. Cap
11. Steering spindle
12. Steering arm

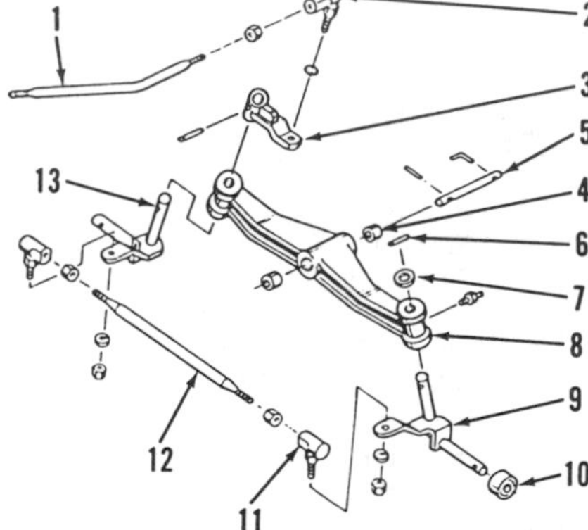

*Fig. J3—Exploded view of front axle assembly used on Models GT10, GT12, GT14, GT16, 1250, 1650 and late Models 1000, 1200 and 1450 tractors. Some models are not equipped with axle pivot bushings (4).*

1. Drag link
2. Ball joint
3. Steering arm
4. Bushing (2)
5. Pivot arm
6. Roll pin
7. Washer
8. Axle main member
9. Steering spindle R.H.
10. Wheel bearing
11. Ball joint
12. Tie rod
13. Steering spindle L.H.

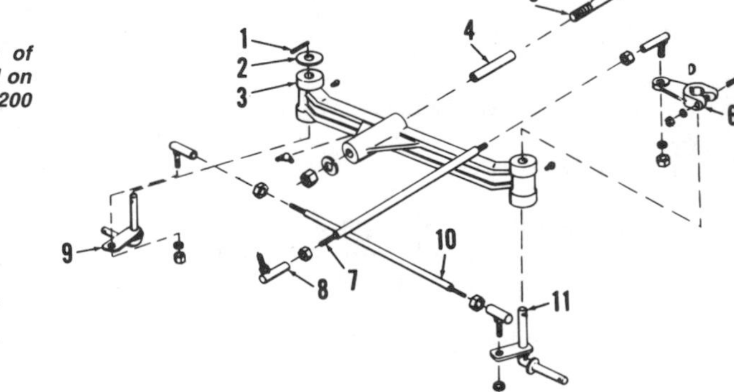

*Fig. J2—Exploded view of front axle assembly used on early Model 800, 1000, 1200 and 1450 tractors.*

1. Groove pin
2. Washer
3. Axle main member
4. Pivot tube
5. Pivot bolt
6. Steering arm
7. Drag link
8. Ball joint
9. Steering spindle L.H.
10. Tie rod
11. Steering spindle R.H.



Illustrations courtesy Jacobsen, Div. of Textron, Inc.

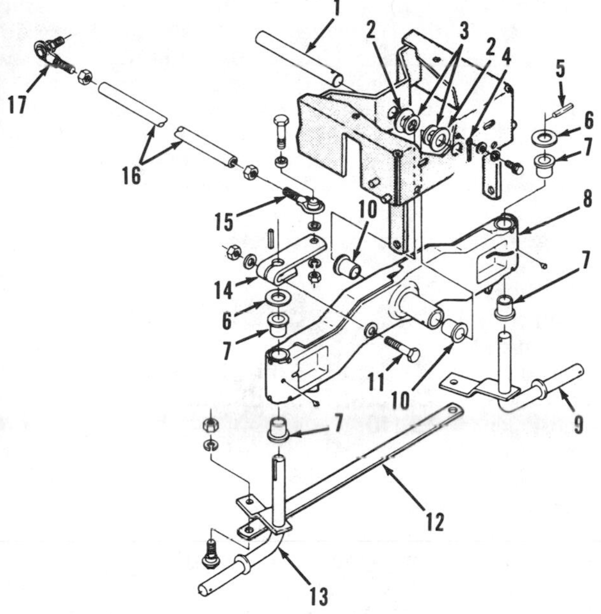

Fig. J4—Exploded view of front axle assembly used on Models LT10, LT12, LTX8, LTX11, LTX12 and YT12.

1. Pivot pin
2. Washers
3. Spacers
4. Cotter pin
5. Roll pin
6. Washer
7. Bushings
8. Axle main member
9. Steering spindle L.H.
10. Bushings
11. Clamp bolt
12. Tie rod
13. Steering spindle R.H.
14. Steering arm
15. Ball joint
16. Drag link
17. Ball joint

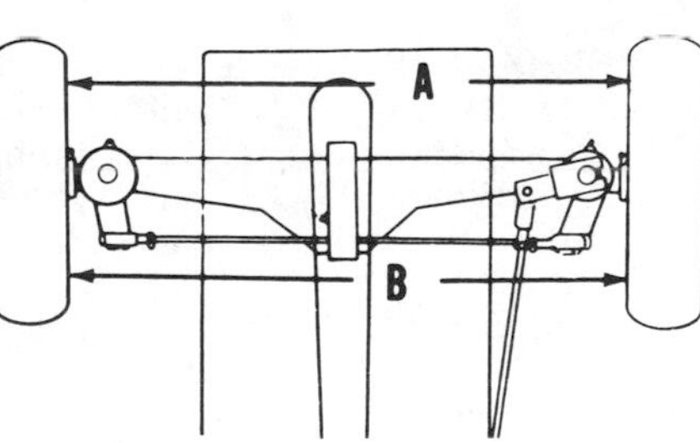


Fig. J5—Front wheel toe-in is correct when distance (A) is 1/8 to ¼ inch (3-6 mm) less than distance (B) when measured at hub height.

On models with adjustable tie rods, inspect tie rod ball joints for excessive wear and renew as required.

Front wheel toe-in (Fig. J5) should be 1/8 to 1/4 inch (3-6 mm). To adjust toe-in, disconnect tie rod from steering arm. Loosen locknuts and turn tie rod ends in or out as required to obtain desired toe-in.

## STEERING SPINDLES

### All Models

To remove steering spindles, refer to Figs. J1, J2, J3 or J4. Raise and support front of tractor. Remove front wheels. Disconnect tie rod and drag link ball joint ends from steering spindles and steering arm. Remove clamp bolt or roll pins, then remove steering arm and lower spindles from axle main member.

Some models are equipped with renewable spindle bushings (6—Fig. J1 and 7—Fig. J4). On all models, inspect spindles for excessive wear and renew as necessary. Lubricate spindles with multipurpose grease during reassembly.

## STEERING GEAR

### Models LT700-LT710-LT750-LT760-LT860-LT1060-LT885-LT80-LT110

**REMOVE AND REINSTALL.** To remove steering gear, remove hood, disconnect battery cables and remove battery. Disconnect drag link from steering arm (15—Fig. J6). Remove steering wheel. Drive out pin (5) and remove pinion gear (14). Withdraw steering shaft (4). Remove steering arm and then remove quadrant gear with attached cross-shaft.

To reassemble, reverse disassembly procedure. Adjust steering gear backlash with adjuster screw (10). Be sure gears do not bind when turning. Lubricate steering gears and bushings with a light coat of multipurpose grease.

### Models GT10-GT12-GT14-GT16-1250-1650 and Late Models 1000-1200-1450

**REMOVE AND REINSTALL.** To remove steering gear, remove hood, drive shaft and implements attached to underside of tractor which block steering gear removal. Drive out retaining pin to remove steering lever (6—Fig. J7) from steering gear (3) shaft. Unscrew steering wheel retaining nut (1) and remove steering wheel. Unscrew mounting bolts and remove steering gear out bottom of tractor. Refer to following paragraph for steering gear overhaul.

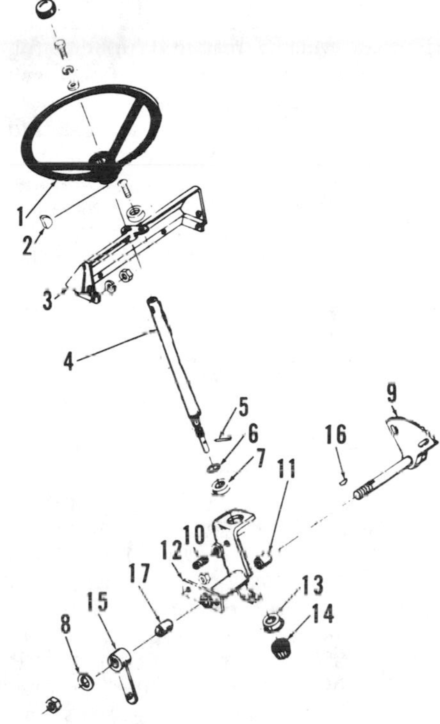

Fig. J6—Exploded view of steering gear assembly used on Models LT700, LT710, LT750, LT760, LT860, LT1060, LT885, LT80 and LT110.

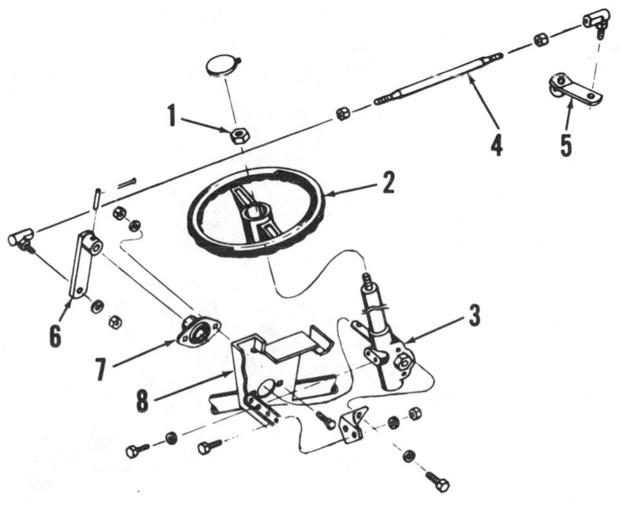

Fig. J7—Exploded view of steering assembly used on Models GT10, GT12, GT14, GT16, 1250, 1650 and late Models 1000, 1200 and 1450. Refer to Fig. J8 for exploded view of steering gear.

1. Nut
2. Steering wheel
3. Steering gear
4. Drag link
5. Steering arm
6. Steering lever
7. Bearing
8. Console

Illustrations courtesy Jacobsen, Div. of Textron, Inc.

**OVERHAUL.** Remove lever and bolt assembly (11—Fig. J8). Remove cam bearing adjuster plug (17) and bump steering cam assembly (15) out of steering column. Remove and inspect bearings and races.

After unit is reassembled, tighten cam adjuster plug until end play is removed from steering shaft (15), but shaft and cam can still rotate freely. Install cotter pin to prevent plug (17) from moving. Tighten inner nut (6) until steering lever (11) is $^{3}/_{32}$ inch (2.4 mm) from housing (4). Tighten jam nut (5) against nut (6). To adjust cam follower, locate cam in mid-position (halfway between full right and full left turn) and turn cam follower screw (10) in until zero backlash is obtained. Tighten locknut (12) to hold screw in position. Steering shaft should turn from lock-to-lock without binding. Lubricate gear through fitting on housing with multipurpose lithium base grease.

## Models (Early) 800-1000-1200-1450

**REMOVE AND REINSTALL.** To remove steering gear, first remove steering wheel (1—Fig. J9). Raise tractor hood and loosen set screw in collar (3). Using a jack or hoist, raise front of tractor. Disconnect drag link ball joint from quadrant arm and remove retaining ring (8) and washer (7) from quadrant shaft. Quadrant shaft can now be withdrawn from bushings (6) located in main frame. Unbolt steering shaft support (10) from tractor frame and rotate support so it can be removed from frame opening. Steering shaft and pinion gear (4) can be lowered through frame opening and removed from underside of tractor. Bushings (2, 6 and 9) can now be renewed if excessive wear is evident.

Reassembly is reverse of disassembly procedure. Steering wheel play can be adjusted as follows: Loosen two bolts securing steering shaft support (10) to frame. Move support toward quadrant gear and tighten bolts. This adjustment moves pinion gear on steering shaft closer to quadrant gear, reducing backlash. Lubricate gear with a light coat of multipurpose grease.

## Models LT10-LT12-LTX8-LTX11-LTX12-YT12

To remove steering gear, raise hood and disconnect battery ground cable. Remove bolts attaching steering shaft bearing (5—Fig. J10) to control tower (6). Remove nut (12) retaining pinion gear (11) to steering shaft (4), then withdraw shaft from control tower. Remove pinion gear and washer (10). Disconnect drag link ball joint from pitman arm (19). Remove nut (14) securing sector gear (13) and withdraw sector gear and pitman arm from steering support (20). Be careful not to lose ball (16) in end of gear spacer screw (17). Unbolt and remove steering support from frame (21) if necessary.

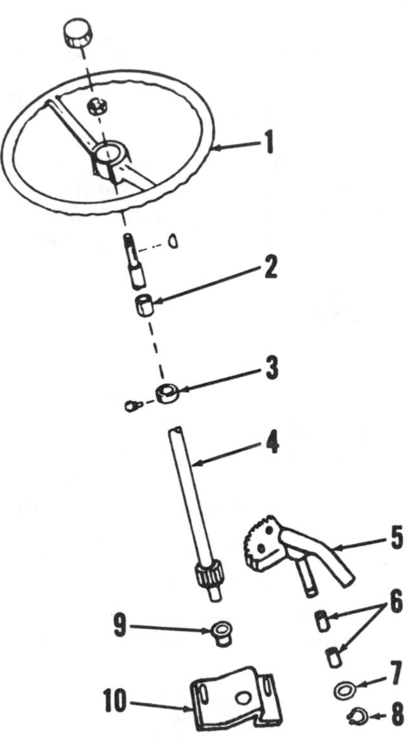


*Fig. J9—Exploded view of steering gear used on early Models 800, 1000, 1200 and 1450 tractors.*

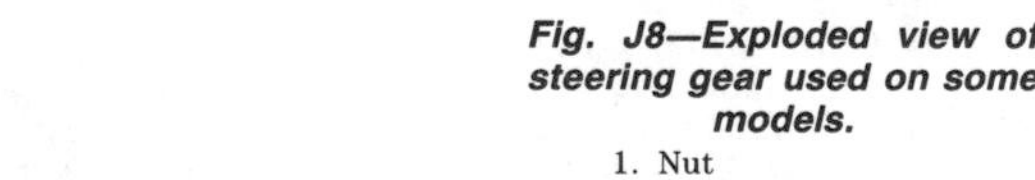

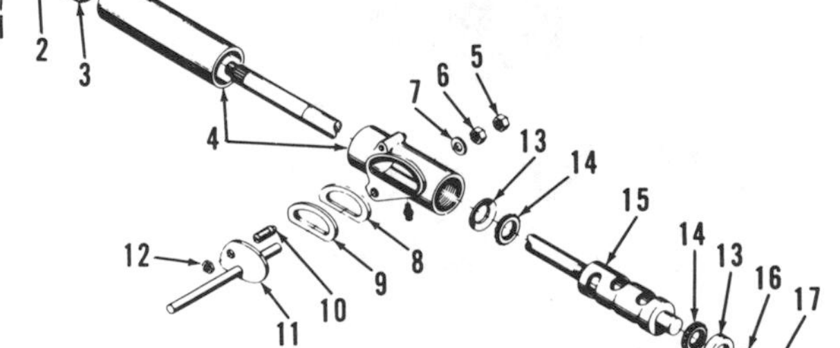


*Fig. J8—Exploded view of steering gear used on some models.*

1. Nut
2. Dust seal
3. Bearing
4. Housing
5. Jam nut
6. Nut
7. Washer
8. Oil seal
9. Seal retainer
10. Cam follower screw
11. Lever
12. Nut
13. Bearing race
14. Bearing
15. Steering cam & shaft
16. Belleville washer
17. Adjusting plug

Inspect all parts for excessive wear and damage and renew as necessary. To reassemble, reverse the disassembly procedure. Turn gear spacer screw (17) to adjust steering gear free play. Be sure gears do not bind when turning. Apply a light coat of multipurpose grease to teeth of sector gear and pinion gear. Lubricate steering shaft and pitman arm bearings with SAE 30 oil.

# ENGINE

## Models LT700-LT710-LT750-LT760-LT860-LT1060-LT885-LT80-LT110

To remove engine, remove tractor hood and shut off fuel valve under the tank. Pull hose from carburetor inlet fitting. Disconnect throttle cable, battery cables, ignition wire and starter solenoid. Disconnect black wire and yellow wire at rectifier. Disconnect pto clutch actuator rod at front end. Remove pto drive belt. Remove cover at rear of tractor and rear belt guide and remove main drive belt by depressing clutch pedal so tension is released on belt. Remove pulley from engine crankshaft. Unscrew mounting bolts and lift engine from tractor.

Reinstall by reversing the removal procedure.

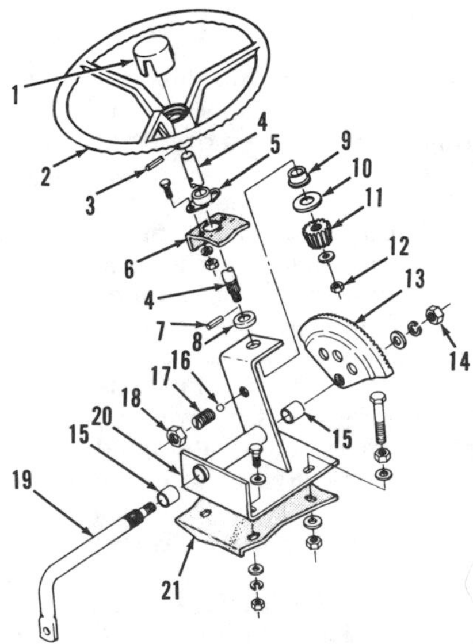


*Fig. J10—Exploded view of steering gear assembly used on Models LT10, LT12, LTX8, LTX11, LTX12 and YT12.*

1. Cap
2. Steering wheel
3. Roll pin
4. Steering shaft
5. Bearing
6. Control tower
7. Roll pin
8. Spacer
9. Bushing
10. Washer
11. Pinion gear
12. Nut
13. Steering sector gear
14. Nut
15. Bushing
16. Ball
17. Adjusting screw
18. Nut
19. Pitman arm
20. Steering gear support
21. Frame

### Models GT10-GT12-GT14-GT16-1250-1650 and Late Models 1000-1200-1450

To remove engine assembly, unbolt and remove hood assembly. Disconnect battery cables and remove battery. Disconnect ignition and starter wires. Disconnect choke cable and throttle linkage. Unbolt and remove grill support and drive shaft shield. Disconnect pto clutch wires. Unbolt drive shaft from coupling. Drain engine oil, unbolt engine from engine base (oil pan) and lift engine from tractor.

To reinstall engine, reverse the removal procedure. Fill oil pan with recommended engine oil.

### Models (Early) 800-1000-1200-1450

To remove engine assembly, raise hood and disconnect battery cables. Disconnect fuel line, then unbolt and remove fuel tank assembly. Identify and disconnect ignition wires and wires from starter-generator. Unbolt and remove belt guard and starter-generator assembly. Disconnect choke and throttle control cables. Remove left foot rest and drive belt rear guard. Disconnect pto clutch wires. Pull clutch cover rod outward, rotate cover and remove assembly from engine. Depress clutch-brake pedal and remove transmission drive belt from engine pulley. Unbolt and lift engine from tractor.

Reinstall by reversing the removal procedure. Adjust clutch and brake as required.

### Models LT10-LT12-LTX8-LTX11-LTX12-YT12

To remove engine, raise hood and disconnect battery cables. Remove mower deck from tractor. Shut off fuel and disconnect fuel line. Disconnect ignition and starter wires from engine. Disconnect throttle and choke control cables. Disconnect pto clutch wires and remove clutch retaining cap screw and slip clutch assembly off engine pulley. Depress clutch pedal to relieve tension on drive belt and remove belt from engine pulley. Remove engine pulley from crankshaft. Remove engine mounting bolts and lift engine from tractor.

To reinstall engine, reverse removal procedure. Tighten pto clutch retaining cap screw to 50 ft.-lbs. (68 N·m).

## OVERHAUL

### All Models

Engine make and model are listed at the beginning of this section. To overhaul engine components and accessories, refer to Briggs & Stratton, Kohler and Tecumseh sections of this manual.

# CLUTCH AND BRAKE

### Models LT700-LT710-LT750-LT760-LT860-LT1060-LT885-LT80-LT110

**ADJUSTMENT.** The clutch idler pulley is spring loaded and does not require adjustment. Drive belt should be inspected for excessive wear or stretching which may result in clutch slippage. Brake should be adjusted so brake is not engaged until clutch is disengaged. To adjust brake, turn adjusting nut (1—Fig. J11) until correct brake action is obtained.

### Models GT10-GT12

**ADJUSTMENT.** Clutch adjustment is accomplished as follows: Turn spring tension adjusting nut shown in Fig. J12 until there is sufficient spring tension on belt idler pulley to prevent belt slippage with clutch-brake pedal released. Do not overtighten adjusting nut. Adjust clutch actuating rod by turning adjusting nut (23—Fig. J13) to provide a gap of $^{1}/_{16}$ to $^{1}/_{8}$ inch (1.5-3 mm) between nut and trunnion (22) with clutch-brake pedal released.

Models GT10 and GT12 are equipped with a band type brake located adjacent to the transaxle. The brake is adjusted by disconnecting brake rod at brake arm (6—Fig. J13) and turning rod (9) to obtain desired brake operation. Be sure brake does not drag when clutch-brake pedal is released.

### Models GT12H-GT14-GT16-1250-1450 (Late)-1650

**ADJUSTMENT.** These models are not equipped with a clutch. A band type brake operates against a drum attached to a shaft extending from the differential unit. On Models GT12H, GT14 and GT16, refer to Fig. J15 and turn jam nut (B) and adjusting nut (A) until desired brake adjustment is obtained. Be sure brake does not drag when brake pedal is released. On Models 1250, 1450 and 1650, refer to Fig. J14 and loosen locknut (10) so adjusting nut (11) can be turned until correct pedal travel is obtained. Be sure brake does not drag when released.

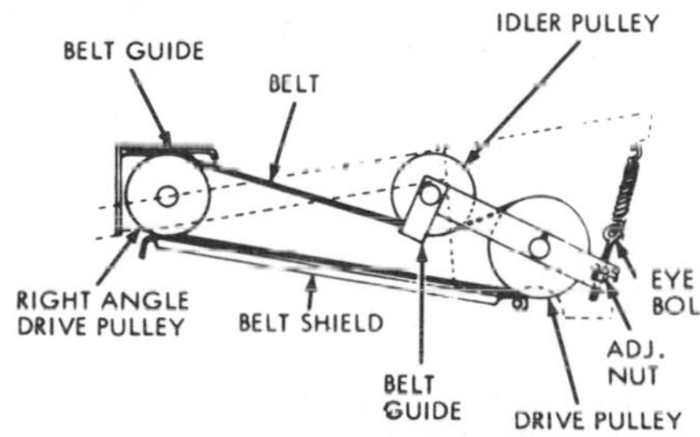

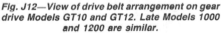

*Fig. J12—View of drive belt arrangement on gear drive Models GT10 and GT12. Late Models 1000 and 1200 are similar.*

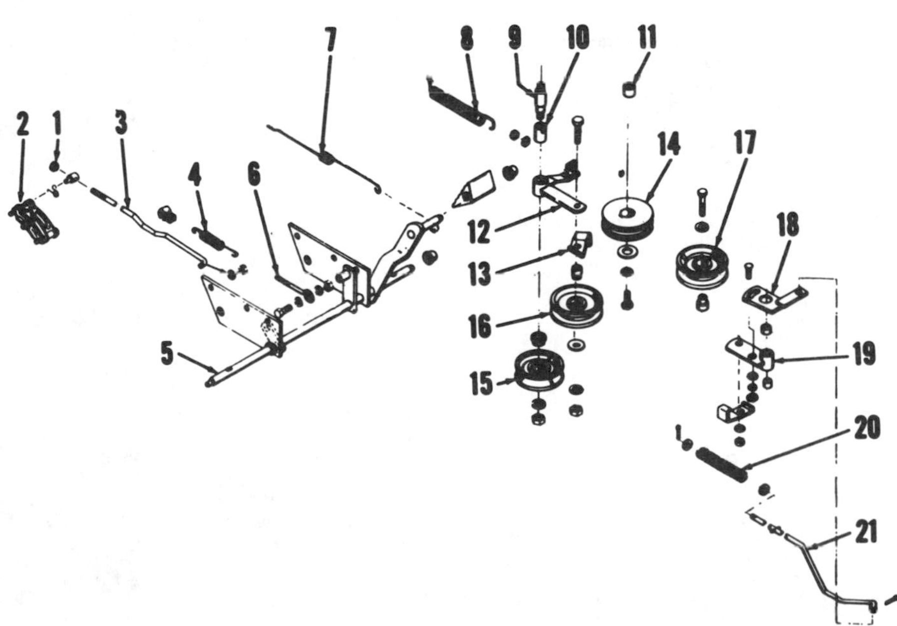


*Fig. J11—Exploded view of typical clutch and brake assembly found on Models LT700, LT710, LT750, LT760, LT860, LT1060, LT885, LT80 and LT110. Brake adjusting nut is at opposite end of brake rod (3) on Model LT885.*

## Models (Early) 800-1000-1200-1450

**ADJUSTMENT.** To adjust clutch and brake, remove left foot rest and drive belt rear guard. With clutch-brake pedal in clutch engaged (up) position, measure distance between inner side of drive belt directly over clutch idler pulley as shown in Fig. J16. This distance must be $1^7/_8$ to $2^1/_8$ inches (48-54 mm). If not, loosen engine mounting bolts and move engine forward or rearward as required until proper dimension "A" is obtained. Tighten engine mounting bolts.

Depress clutch-brake pedal until band is tight on brake drum, then engage park brake lock. Measure distance (dimension "B"—Fig. J17) between flange of clutch idler pulley and edge of frame. This distance must be 1 to $1^1/_4$ inches (25-32 mm). If not, release brake lock and adjust nut on front of brake rod until dimension "B" is correct. Reinstall belt guard and foot rest.

## Models (Late) 1000-1200

**ADJUSTMENT.** To adjust clutch, first turn spring tension adjusting nut shown in Fig. J12 until there is sufficient tension on belt idler pulley to prevent belt slippage. Do not overtighten adjusting nut. Adjust working length of clutch actuating rod (7—Fig. J13) by turning adjusting nuts so idler pulley disengages drive belt when clutch pedal is depressed approximately 2 inches (50 mm).

A band type brake is used on these models. Brake pedal travel should be about 3 to 4 inches (76-101 mm) before

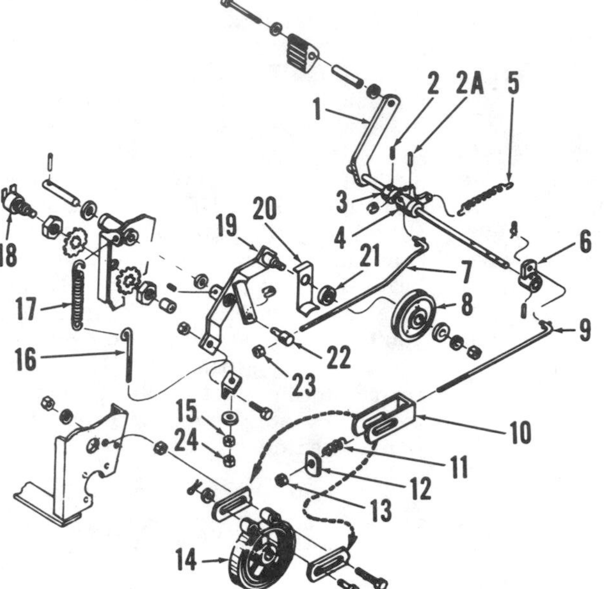


*Fig. J13—Exploded view of brake and clutch assembly on Models GT10 and GT12. Late Models 1000 and 1200 are similar.*

1. Clutch-brake pedal
2. Setscrew
2A. Pin
3. Collar
4. Parking brake sector
5. Spring
6. Brake arm
7. Clutch rod
8. Clutch idler pulley
9. Brake rod
10. Brake bracelet
11. Spring
12. Nut plate
13. Nut
14. Brake band & drum
15. Adjusting nut
16. Eye bolt
17. Spring
18. Safety start switch
19. Clutch pulley arm
20. Belt guide
21. Spacer
22. Trunnion
23. Nut
24. Jam nut

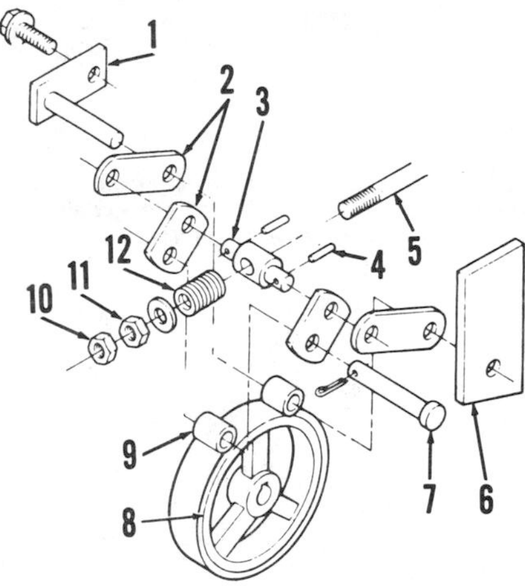


*Fig. J14—Exploded view of brake assembly used on Models 1250 and 1650. Late Models 1000, 1200 and 1450 are similar.*

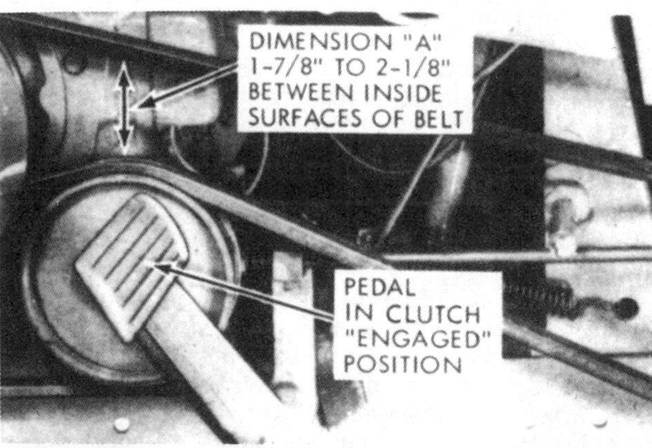


*Fig. J16—Clutch adjustment on early Models 800, 1000, 1200 and 1450 is correct when dimension "A" is 1-7/8 to 2-1/8 inches (48-54 mm) with clutch engaged. Refer to text.*

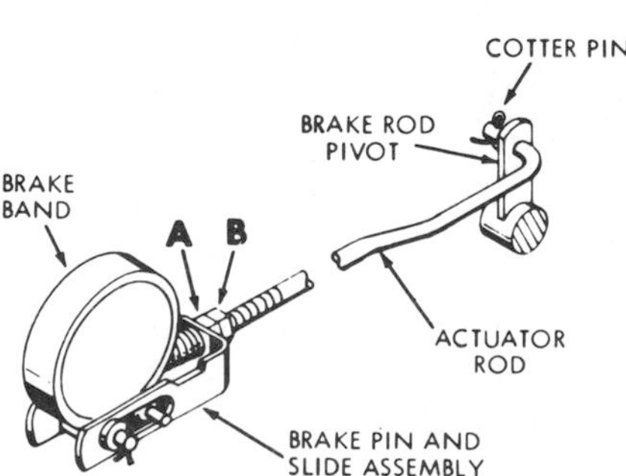


*Fig. J15—View of brake assembly used on Models GT12H, GT14 and GT16. Adjust brake by turning adjusting nut (A) and jam nut (B).*

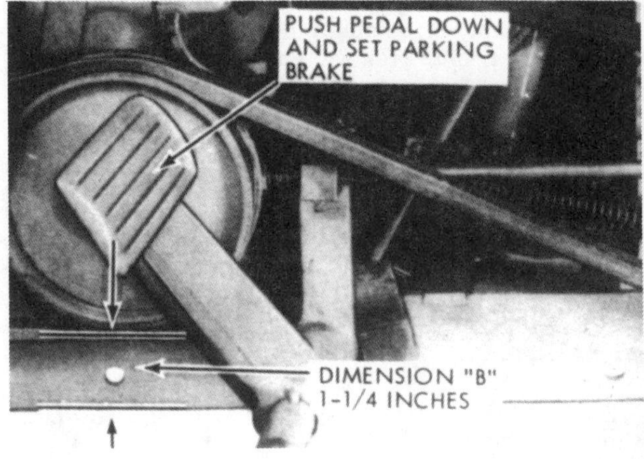


*Fig. J17—On early Models 800, 1000, 1200 and 1450 tractors, brake adjustment is correct when dimension "B" is 1 to 1-1/4 inches (25-32 mm) with clutch-brake pedal fully depressed. Refer to text.*



Illustrations courtesy Jacobsen, Div. of Textron, Inc.

brake applies. To adjust brake pedal travel, loosen locknut (10—Fig. J14) and turn adjusting nut (11) until correct travel is obtained. Be sure brake does not drag when brake pedal is released.

### Models LT10-LT12-LTX8-LTX11-LTX12-YT12

**ADJUSTMENT.** When clutch-brake pedal is depressed, clutch is disengaged and then brake is applied. The clutch idler pulleys (11 and 14—Fig. J18) are spring loaded and do not require adjustment. Traction drive belt should be inspected for excessive wear or stretching which may result in clutch slippage.

A disc type brake (6—Fig. J18) is mounted on right side of transaxle housing on all models. To adjust brake, release brake pedal and check that length of brake rod compression spring is $5^{7}/_{8}$ to $6^{1}/_{8}$ inch (149-156 mm). If not, turn adjusting nuts on brake rod to obtain specified spring length. Position tractor on a level surface and place gear shift lever in neutral so tractor can be pushed by hand to check brake action. With brake pedal released, turn setscrew (5—Fig. J19) in brake pad holder clockwise until brake just starts to lock. Then, turn setscrew counterclockwise $^{1}/_{2}$ turn. Push tractor by hand to check brake action and to make sure that brake pads (1) do not drag on brake disc (3) when brake is released.

# DRIVE BELT

### Models LT700-LT710-LT750-LT760-LT860-LT1060-LT80-LT110

**REMOVE AND REINSTALL.** To remove transaxle drive belt, remove cover plate at rear end of tractor. Depress clutch-brake pedal and set parking brake. Remove pto drive belt from lower groove of engine pulley and transaxle drive belt from upper groove. Work belt free from belt guides and idler pulleys. Remove belt from transmission input pulley. Move belt up through shift lever opening, then over end of shift lever and back down through shift lever opening. Remove belt from tractor.

Install belt by reversing removal procedure. Be sure belt is not twisted and not riding on any belt guides with clutch-brake pedal released.

### Model LT885

**REMOVE AND REINSTALL.** To remove primary drive belt, fully depress clutch-brake pedal and set parking brake. Remove belt from right angle drive pulley. Remove pto drive belt from lower groove of engine pulley and primary drive belt from upper groove. Work drive belt free from idler pulleys and belt guides and remove from tractor.

To install primary belt, reverse the removal procedure. Be sure belt is not twisted and is not riding on any belt guides when clutch is engaged.

To remove secondary belt, remove seat and fender assembly. Release spring tension on idler pulley and remove drive belt between right angle drive and transmission. Reverse the removal procedure to reinstall belt.

### Models GT10-GT12 and Late Models 1000-1200

**REMOVE AND REINSTALL.** Drive belt removal is accomplished as follows: Detach clutch idler spring (17—Fig. J13) and unscrew parking brake knob. Unscrew and remove panel surrounding gear shift lever. Remove belt guides adjacent to belt and remove belt. Install new belt by referring to Fig. J12. Check clutch action and readjust if necessary.

### Models (Early) 800-1000-1200-1450

**REMOVE AND REINSTALL.** To remove transmission drive belt, remove left foot rest and rear belt guard. On models with mechanical pto clutch, lift control handle from spring loaded stub shaft. On models with electric pto clutch, disconnect clutch wires, pull clutch cover rod outward and rotate cover downward. On all models, unbolt and remove front belt guard. Fully depress clutch-brake pedal and engage park brake lock. On hydrostatic drive models, loosen rear belt retainer and remove belt from pulleys. On gear drive models, loosen setscrew and slide transmission input pulley out on shaft until belt clears belt retainers. Then, remove belt from pulleys.

Install new belt by reversing the removal procedure. Adjust belt retainers to $^{1}/_{8}$ inch (3 mm) clearance from belt (clutch engaged). Adjust clutch and brake as necessary.

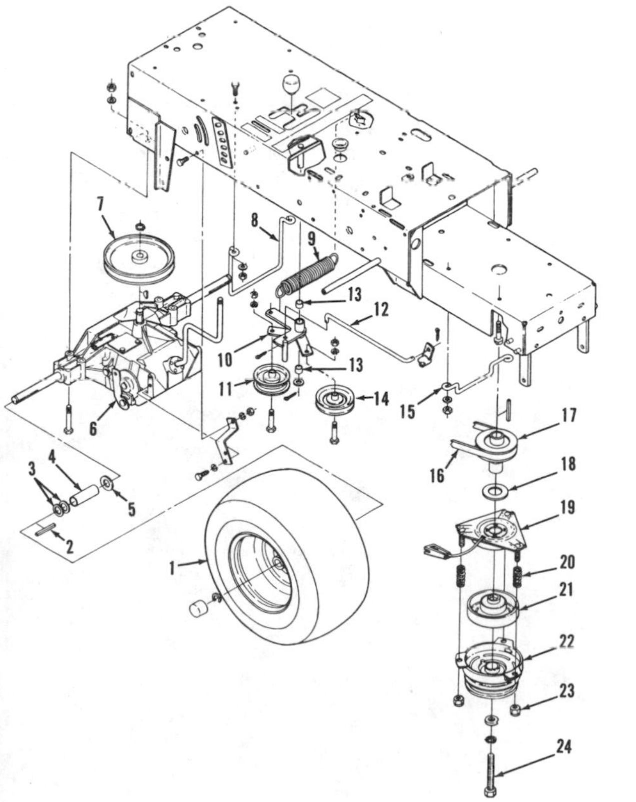

*Fig. J18—Exploded view of traction drive clutch idler pulleys and electric pto clutch assembly used on Models LT10, LT12, LTX8, LTX11, LTX12 and YT12.*

1. Rear wheel
2. Key
3. Spacers
4. Spacer
5. Washer
6. Disc brake assy.
7. Transaxle pulley
8. Belt guide
9. Traction clutch spring
10. Clutch bellcrank
11. Rear idler pulley
12. Clutch rod
13. Bushings
14. Front idler pulley
15. Belt guide
16. Traction drive belt
17. Engine pulley
18. Washer
19. Field coil assy.
20. Spring
21. Rotor
22. Armature & pulley assy.
23. Adjusting nut
24. Bolt

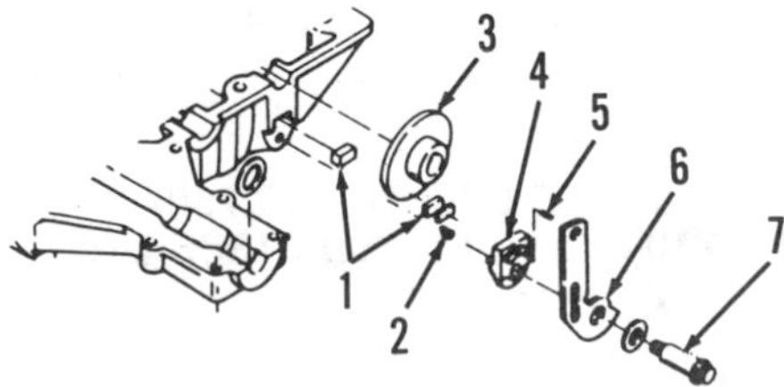


*Fig. J19—Exploded view of disc brake assembly used on Models LT10, LT12, LTX8, LTX11, LTX12 and YT12.*

1. Brake pads
2. Spring
3. Brake disc
4. Brake jaw
5. Setscrew
6. Brake lever
7. Shoulder bolt

Illustrations courtesy Jacobsen, Div. of Textron, Inc.

### Models LT10-LT12-LTX8-LTX11-LTX12-YT12

**REMOVE AND REINSTALL.** To remove transaxle drive belt, first remove mower deck from tractor. Depress clutch-brake pedal and set park brake latch. Remove hitch plate from rear of main frame. Work belt off transaxle pulley. Remove tie rod from front axle. Unbolt and remove pto clutch from engine crankshaft. Remove bolt attaching front idler pulley to idler bellcrank. Pull belt toward rear of tractor. Push belt up through opening in frame for shift lever, loop belt over top of shift lever and pull belt back down through shift lever opening in frame. Remove belt from tractor.

To install belt, reverse the removal procedure. Be sure that belt is not twisted and that back side of belt is against rear idler pulley. Tighten pto clutch retaining bolt to 50 ft.-lbs. (68 N·m).

## DRIVE SHAFT

### Models GT10-GT12-GT12H-GT14-GT16-1250-1650 and Late Models 1000-1200-1450

The drive shaft on Models GT10, GT12, 1000 and 1200 transfers power between engine and right angle drive, while drive shaft on all other models transfers power from engine directly to hydrostatic transmission. Drive shaft may be removed from bottom of tractor after removing bottom mounted implements which interfere with removal.

## PTO CLUTCH

### All Models So Equipped

Some models are equipped with an electric pto clutch. Pto clutch may be removed after disconnecting wires and unscrewing retaining cap screws in mounting flange and engine crankshaft. Individual service parts are available for some models, while on other models, clutch is available as a complete unit only.

### Models LT700-LT710-LT750-LT760-LT860-LT1060-LT885-LT80-LT110

**ADJUSTMENT.** Pto clutch should be adjusted if clutch has been disassembled or if operation becomes erratic. With clutch disengaged, insert a feeler gage through slot in clutch plate (Fig. J20) and measure clearance between clutch rotor and armature. Clearance should be 0.010 inch (0.25 mm). To adjust, tighten the adjusting nut next to the slot until feeler gage just begins to bind. Do not overtighten. Repeat adjustment at each of the slots in clutch plate. All slots must be adjusted equally.

**TESTING.** Use the following procedure for locating pto malfunction. Turn ignition switch to "ON" position and actuate pto switch. If clutch does not engage, disconnect wiring connector at field coil and use a 12-volt test lamp to check continuity of wire coming from pto switch. If lamp lights, pto is either defective or wiring connection at clutch field coil is poor.

### Models LT700-LT710-LT750-LT760-LT860-LT1060-LT885-LT80-LT110

**ADJUSTMENT.** Pto clutch adjustment is correct when resistance is felt as control lever is moved approximately $^{3}/_{4}$ inch (19 mm) from back edge of rear notch in control quadrant. To adjust pto clutch, first loosen adjustment lever bolt (Fig. J21). Position control lever approximately $^{3}/_{4}$ inch (19 mm) from back edge of rear notch in quadrant, then move idler until belt is snug in pulleys and idler. Tighten adjustment lever bolt and recheck for correct adjustment. Be sure belt stops in OFF position. If not, readjust as required increasing $^{3}/_{4}$ inch (19 mm) measurement by $^{1}/_{4}$ inch (6 mm) increments until belt stops in OFF position.

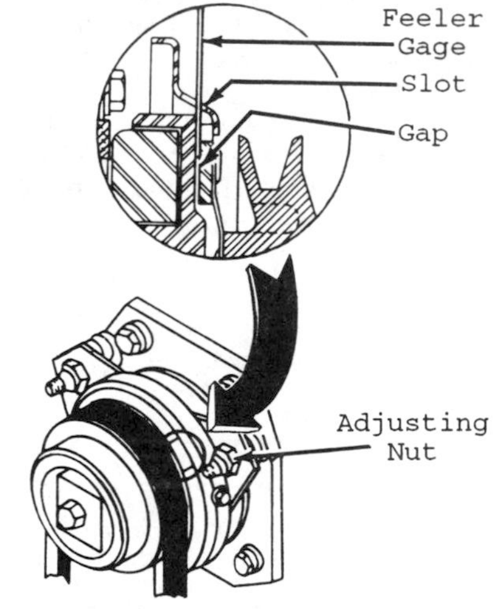


*Fig. J20—With pto clutch disengaged, clearance between rotor and armature should be 0.010 inch (0.25 mm). Refer to text for adjustment procedure.*

## RIGHT ANGLE DRIVE UNIT

### Model LT885

**REMOVE AND REINSTALL.** To remove right angle drive unit, remove seat and fender assembly. Remove drive belts from right angle drive pulleys as previously outlined. Remove lower drive pulley, unscrew drive unit mounting bolts and remove right angle drive unit.

### Models GT10-GT12 and Late Models 1000-1200

**REMOVE AND REINSTALL.** To remove right angle drive unit, remove drive belt and drive shaft as previously outlined. Remove drive shaft coupler from input shaft of right angle drive. Unscrew mounting bolts and remove right angle drive assembly.

### All Models

**OVERHAUL.** To disassemble right angle drive unit, remove cover (1—Fig. J22), gasket (2) and lubricant. Unbolt and remove seal retainer (13) with oil seal (14) and gasket (12). Withdraw output shaft (10) with bearing (11). Remove snap ring (18) and output gear (9). Re-

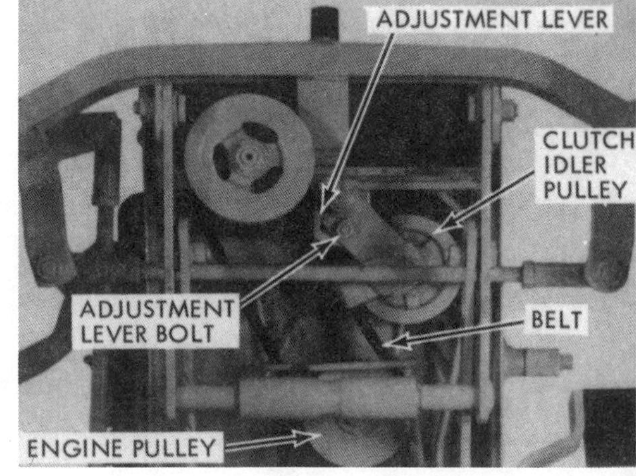


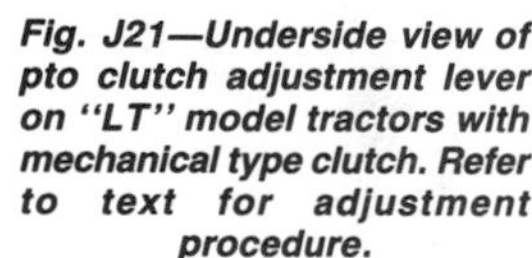
*Fig. J21—Underside view of pto clutch adjustment lever on "LT" model tractors with mechanical type clutch. Refer to text for adjustment procedure.*

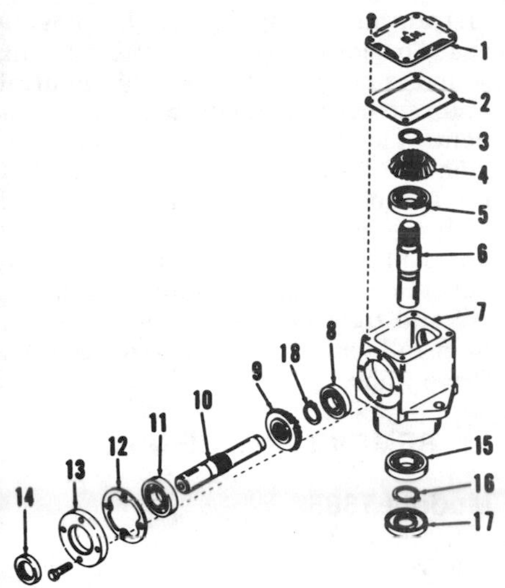


*Fig. J22—Exploded view of right angle drive unit used on Models LT885, GT10, GT12, 1000 and 1200.*

move oil seal (17) and snap ring (16). Drive input shaft (6) with gear (4) and bearing (5) out cover opening of case (7). Bearings (8 and 15) can now be removed from case. Remove snap ring (3) and remove drive gear (4) and bearing (11) from output shaft (10).

Clean and inspect all parts and renew any showing excessive wear or other damage. Reassemble by reversing disassembly procedure and fill unit with 4 ounces (120 mL) of Moly EP lithium base grease.

# TRANSAXLE

## Models LT700-LT710-LT750-LT760-LT860-LT1060-LT80-LT110

**LUBRICATION.** A Model 660A transaxle manufactured by Peerless Division of Tecumseh Products Company is used on LT80 and LT110 tractors. All other tractors use a Peerless Model 612A transaxle. All transaxles have three forward speeds and one reverse speed. Refer to the CONDENSED SPECIFICATIONS tables for transaxle fluid capacity.

**REMOVE AND REINSTALL.** To remove transaxle, remove drive belt as outlined previously and disconnect gearshift lever spring. Place transaxle in neutral and remove shift knob. Remove rear cover at rear of tractor and remove belt guide. Support rear of tractor using a suitable jack or hoist. Unscrew transaxle retaining bolts and move transaxle away from tractor.

**OVERHAUL.** All models are equipped with a Peerless 600 series transaxle. Refer to Peerless Series 600 section in TRANSAXLE service section of this book for overhaul procedure.

## Models GT10-GT12-800-1000-1200

**LUBRICATION.** Models GT10 and GT12 are equipped with a Peerless Model 2324 transaxle and Models 800, 1000 and 1200 use a Peerless Model 2306 transaxle. Both transaxles have four forward speeds and one reverse speed. Refer to the CONDENSED SPECIFICATIONS tables for transaxle fluid capacity and type.

**REMOVE AND REINSTALL.** To remove transaxle, detach drive belt as previously outlined. Remove brake drum assembly. Unscrew gear shift knob. Support rear of tractor and unscrew axle housing mounting bolts. Raise rear of tractor and roll transaxle assembly from tractor. Remove rear wheels.

To reinstall transaxle, reverse the removal procedure. Adjust drive belt and brake if necessary.

**OVERHAUL.** All models are equipped with a Peerless 2300 series transaxle. Refer to Peerless Series 2300 section in TRANSAXLE SERVICE section of this book for overhaul procedure.

## Models LT10-LT12-LTX8-LTX11-LTX12-YT12

**LUBRICATION.** All models are equipped with a Spicer (Foote) 4000 series transaxle. The transaxle is packed at the factory with 24 ounces (710 mL) of type "O" grease and should not require any maintenance unless disassembled for service.

**REMOVE AND REINSTALL.** To remove transaxle, unbolt and remove hitch plate from rear of main frame. Depress clutch-brake pedal and set park brake. Work drive belt off transaxle pulley. Disconnect brake control rod from brake lever. Remove knob from shift lever. Remove bolts attaching transaxle to frame. Raise rear of tractor and roll transaxle assembly rearward from tractor.

To reinstall transaxle, reverse the removal procedure.

**OVERHAUL.** All models are equipped with a Spicer (Foote) 4000 series transaxle. Refer to Spicer section in TRANSAXLE SERVICE section for overhaul procedure.

# HYDROSTATIC TRANSMISSION

### LUBRICATION

## All Models Except Early 1450

Hydrostatic transmission used on Model LT885 is lubricated by oil contained in transmission reservoir. Reservoir should be filled with tractor level until oil reaches lower lip of reservoir as shown in Fig J23. Hydrostatic transmission on all other models shares a common reservoir with differential unit. Fill differential through fill plug opening (F—Fig. J24) until oil reaches level of plug (L). Transmission oil used in all models should be Texaco Transhydral No. 2209, Ford M-2C41-A or equivalent.

Transmission oil on Models GT12H, GT14, GT16, 1250, 1450 and 1650 is routed through an external oil filter (9—Fig. J25). Jacobsen recommends renewing hydraulic filter after every 100 hours of operation. Additional filter renewal may be required if system is contaminated due to servicing or operation in extremely dusty conditions.

## Model 1450 (Early)

On early Model 145, transmission fluid is contained in an integral reservoir.

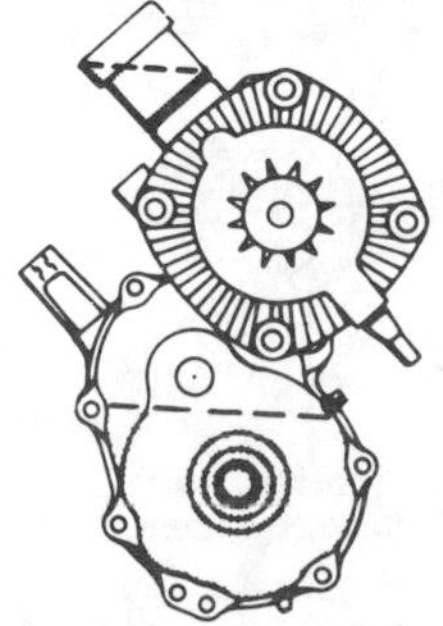

*Fig. J23—Fill hydrostatic transmission reservoir and differential on Model LT885 to levels shown by dotted lines. Refer to text and specifications for type of oil.*

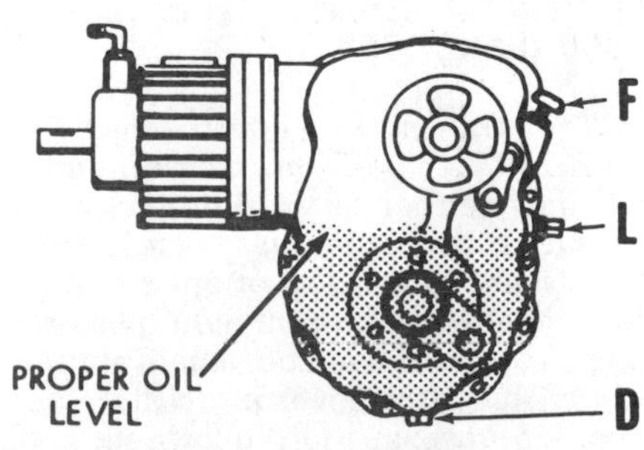


*Fig. J24—Fill rear end unit of Models GT12H, GT14, GT16, 1250, 1450 and 1650 through fill hole (F) until oil reaches level of plug hole (L). Drain oil by removing drain plug (D).*

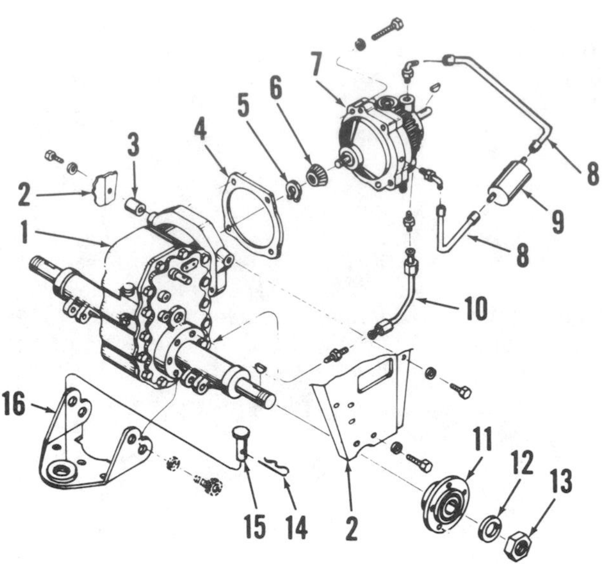

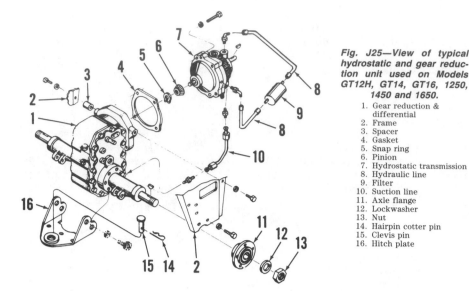

*Fig. J25—View of typical hydrostatic and gear reduction unit used on Models GT12H, GT14, GT16, 1250, 1450 and 1650.*

1. Gear reduction & differential
2. Frame
3. Spacer
4. Gasket
5. Snap ring
6. Pinion
7. Hydrostatic transmission
8. Hydraulic line
9. Filter
10. Suction line
11. Axle flange
12. Lockwasher
13. Nut
14. Hairpin cotter pin
15. Clevis pin
16. Hitch plate

Reservoir should be filled until oil level is ½ to 1 inch (13-25 mm) below bottom edge of filler hole located under tractor seat. Recommended oil is SAE 10W-30 detergent oil. The hydraulic filter, located within reservoir, should be changed if system becomes contaminated due to servicing or other means.

### LINKAGE ADJUSTMENT

#### Model LT885

To adjust hydrostatic transmission linkage, remove cover screen at rear of tractor. Refer to Fig. J26 and turn adjusting nuts on speed control rod where it is attached to speed control arm. Moving adjusting nuts toward front of tractor will increase forward speed while turning nuts in opposite direction will increase reverse speed.

If tractor creeps in neutral, block up tractor so rear wheels can rotate freely. Place speed control lever in neutral position and start engine. Turn adjusting nuts (A and B—Fig. J26) to increase or decrease spring tension against speed control arm until rear wheel remains stationary. Secure adjusting nuts when neutral position is found.

#### Models GT12H-GT14-GT16-1250-1450 (Late)-1650

When transmission control lever is in "NEUTRAL" position, tractor should not move either forward or backward. Be sure transmission has been warmed by at least 15 minutes of operation before checking transmission performance. If tractor will not remain stationary with control lever in "NEUTRAL" position, transmission linkage must be adjusted as follows:

Raise rear of tractor so rear wheels may rotate freely. Be sure tractor is blocked to prevent rolling. Refer to Fig. J27 and loosen nuts (A) and (B). Turn stud (C) toward rear of tractor if tractor creeps forward, or toward front of tractor if tractor creeps backward. Tighten nuts (A) and (B) and check transmission operation.

#### Model 1450 (Early)

If tractor creeps in either direction when control lever is in neutral position, adjust control lever linkage as follows: Jack up rear of tractor to allow both rear wheels to rotate freely. Fully depress clutch-brake pedal and apply park brake lock. Loosen set screw on side of Drive-No Drive control knob and remove knob. Unbolt and remove seat and seat apron. Remove hairpin cotter shown in Fig. J29 from ball joint rod. Slide ball joint rod from control arm and remove bushing. Locate neutral position of transmission speed arm by moving speed arm up and down until a clicking sound is heard as arm locks in neutral notch. Move speed control lever to its neutral lock position. Start tractor engine and make sure rear wheels do not rotate. Loosen locknut on ball joint and turn rod in or out of ball joint until rod end and bushing can be inserted into hole in control arm. Install hairpin cotter and tighten locknut on ball joint. Reinstall seat, seat apron and Drive-No Drive knob.

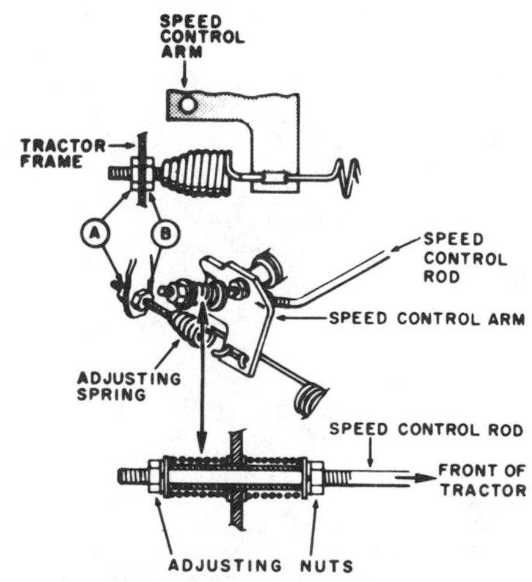


*Fig. J26—Views of speed control arm and adjusting nuts on Model LT885 hydrostatic transmission. Refer to text for adjustment.*

### REMOVE AND REINSTALL

#### Model LT885

To remove hydrostatic transmission, first remove seat and fender assembly. Remove cover at rear of tractor. Remove transmission drive belt by releasing spring tension against idler pulley. Disconnect speed control rod shown in Fig. J26 from speed control arm. Disconnect springs from speed control arm. Remove brake assembly from brake disc. Support rear of tractor, unscrew axle mounting bolts and remove transmission and differential from tractor. Drain lubricant from differential and separate transmission from differential housing.

To reinstall transmission, reverse removal procedure. Refill differential with 2¾ pints (1.3 L) of SAE 90 EP gear oil. Refill transmission reservoir to proper level as outlined in LUBRICATION section. Adjust speed control linkage and brake as previously outlined.

#### Models GT12H-GT14-GT16-1250-1450 (Late)-1650

To remove hydrostatic transmission, remove pedals on transmission (16 and 17—Fig. J28) and brake levers. Detach reverse pedal (19) from transmission lever (15). Unscrew speed range lever (12) and parking brake shaft (7) knobs. Remove seat and fender assembly from tractor frame. Disconnect hydraulic hoses to transmission and detach control lever (23) from transmission shaft.

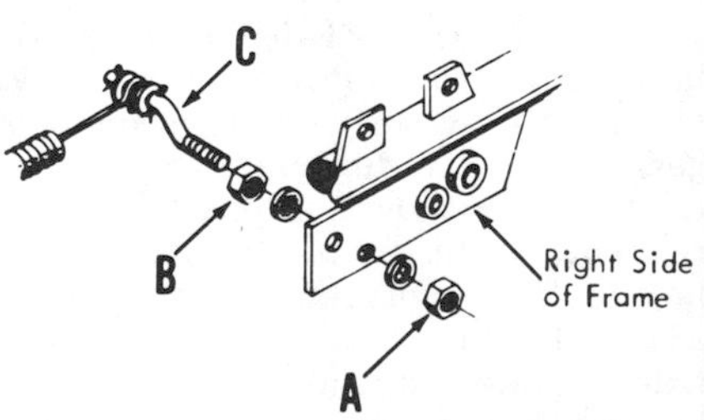


*Fig. J27—Loosen nuts (A and B) and turn stud (C) as indicated in text to adjust transmission linkage on Models GT12H, GT14, GT16, 1250, 1450 and 1650.*



Illustrations courtesy Jacobsen, Div. of Textron, Inc.

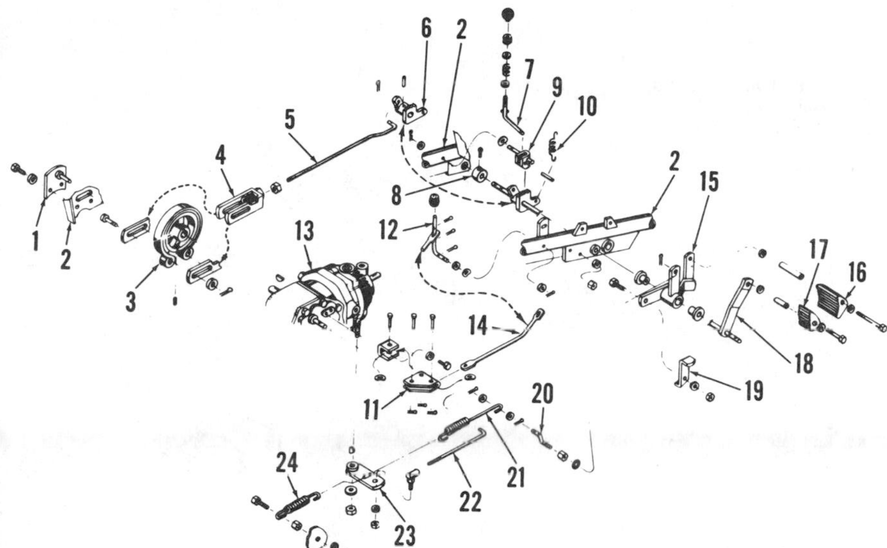

*Fig. J28—Exploded view of transmission and brake control linkage on Model GT12H. Other hydrostatic drive models are similar.*

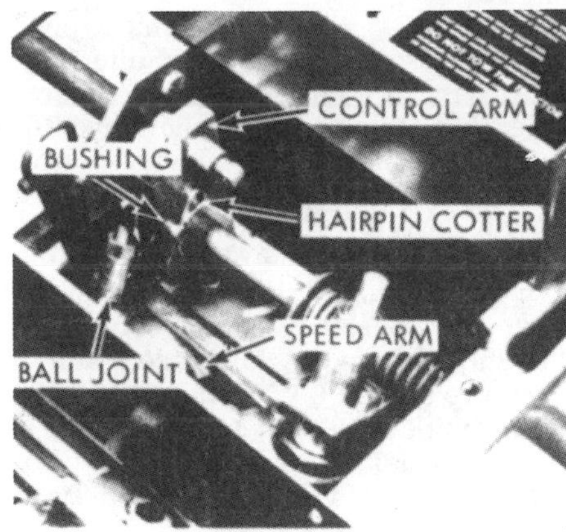

*Fig. J29—View showing location of hydrostatic transmission control linkage adjustment on early Model 1450.*

Plug openings in transmission and hoses to prevent entry of dirt. Remove drive shaft as previously outlined, unscrew mounting bolts and remove transmission.

To reinstall transmission, reverse removal procedure. Refill differential as indicated in LUBRICATION section.

### Model 1450 (Early)

To remove hydrostatic drive unit, place a rolling floor jack under reduction-differential housing and raise rear of tractor. Remove rear wheel assemblies. Remove battery cover and battery. Loosen set screw in drive-no drive knob and remove knob. Unbolt and remove seat assembly with seat apron. Remove left foot rest and drive belt rear guard. Depress clutch pedal and remove drive belt. Disconnect and remove brake rear linkage and brake band. Disconnect transmission control linkage at ball joint link. Unbolt and remove hydrostatic unit and differential assembly from tractor.

Remove three attaching cap screws and lift hydrostatic unit from reduction and differential assembly.

Remove unit by reversing removal procedure. Then, adjust brake and drive belt as outlined in CLUTCH AND BRAKE section and transmission control linkage as previously outlined.

## OVERHAUL

### All Models So Equipped

Model LT885 is equipped with an Eaton Model 6 hydrostatic transmission. Models GT12H, GT14 and GT16 are equipped with an Eaton Model 10 hydrostatic transmission. Models 1250, late 1450 and 1650 are equipped with an Eaton Model 11 hydrostatic transmission. Early Model 1450 is equipped with Sundstrand "Hydrogear" hydrostatic transmission. Refer to the appropriate Eaton or Sundstrand section in HYDROSTATIC TRANSMISSION SERVICE section of this book for overhaul procedure.

# REDUCTION GEARS AND DIFFERENTIAL

## REMOVE AND REINSTALL

### Models LT885-1450 (Early)

To remove reduction gear and differential unit, remove transmission and differential unit as previously outlined in HYDROSTATIC TRANSMISSION section. Remove wheel and hub assemblies from axles. Drain differential lubricant and separate transmission from differential. Remove brake disc from brake shaft.

To reinstall, reverse the removal procedure. Refill unit with SAE 90 EP gear oil. Adjust brake linkage and hydrostatic control linkage as necessary.

### Models GT12H-GT14-GT16-1250-1450 (Late)-1650

To remove gear reduction and differential unit, first remove hydrostatic transmission as previously outlined in HYDROSTATIC TRANSMISSION section. Drain oil from unit, remove brake assembly and detach dual-range shift linkage. Support rear of tractor and remove bolts securing reduction and differential unit to tractor frame. Raise rear of tractor and roll unit from tractor. Remove wheels and clean exterior of unit.

To reinstall, reverse the removal procedure. Refill unit with lubricant and adjust brake linkage and hydrostatic linkage as outlined in previous sections.

## OVERHAUL

### Models LT885-GT12H-GT14-GT16-1250-1450-1650

Model LT885 is equipped with a Peerless 1300 series reduction gear and differential unit. Models GT12H, GT14, GT16, 1250, 1450 (late) and 1650 are equipped with a Peerless 2500 series dual-range gear reduction and differential unit. Model 1450 (early) is equipped with a Peerless 2400 series gear reduction and differential unit. On all models, refer to appropriate Peerless section in REDUCTION GEAR AND DIFFERENTIAL SERVICE section for overhaul procedure.

# HYDRAULIC LIFT

### All Models So Equipped

**OPERATION.** Hydraulic pressure for lift circuit is provided by hydrostatic transmission charge pump. A single spool, open center control valve directs fluid to a double-acting hydraulic cylinder. The control valve is equipped with an adjustable relief valve which limits system pressure at approximately 500 psi (3447 kPa). Seal repair kits are the only service parts available for control valve and hydraulic cylinder.

**TESTING.** When checking relief valve pressure setting, hydraulic fluid must be at normal operating temperature. Shut off engine and relieve hydraulic pressure in system by moving control lever back and forth. Using a 1/4 inch tee fitting, install 0-1000 psi (0-7000 kPa) pressure gage in one of the hydraulic cylinder ports. With engine speed at high idle, operate hydraulic control lever and observe pressure gage reading. Pressure should be 500 psi (3447 kPa) with cylinder at end of its stroke. If necessary, adjust system relief valve, located in control valve, to obtain desired system pressure.

**NOTE: Two different designs of control valves have been used. On AICO valve, pressure setting is adjusted by adding or removing shims (3—Fig. J30). On VFP valve, turn adjusting screw (4—Fig. J31) in or out to adjust pressure setting.**

If 500 psi (3447 kPa) operating pressure cannot be attained, check the following: Low hydraulic fluid level, hydraulic filter plugged, defective relief valve, restriction in hydraulic line, charge pump worn.

**CONTROL VALVE.** A single spool, open center control valve equipped with an integral pressure relief valve is used. Refer to Fig. J30 or J31. Seal repair kit is only service part available.

To remove valve, raise hood and remove side panels and battery. Clean exterior of valve, then disconnect linkage and hydraulic lines. Plug all openings to prevent entry of dirt. Unbolt and remove valve.

To disassemble AICO valve, refer to Fig. J30 and remove end cap (20) and retainer (18). Withdraw spool assembly from valve body. Remove retaining ring (7) and washer (8), then remove back-up washers (9) and quad rings (10) from valve body. Remove relief valve assembly (1 through 6).

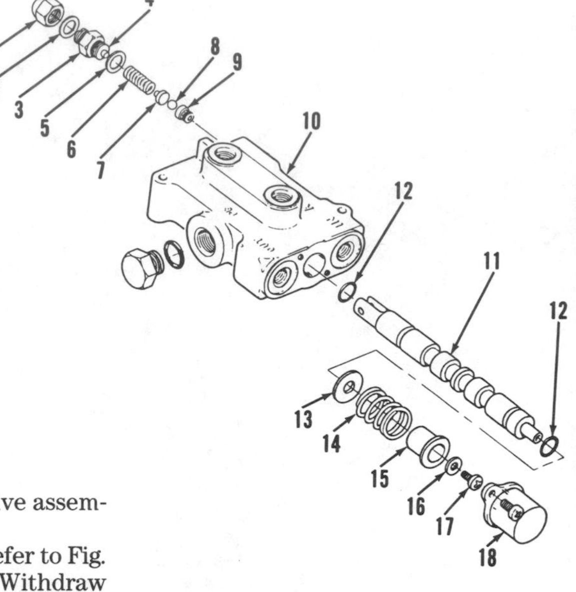

***Fig. J31—Exploded view of VFP hydraulic control valve used on some models.***

1. Acorn nut
2. Washer
3. Jam nut
4. Adjusting screw
5. Washer
6. Spring
7. Ball retainer
8. Ball
9. Seat
10. Valve body
11. Spool
12. "O" rings
13. Washer
14. Centering spring
15. Cup
16. Washer
17. Screw
18. End cap

To disassemble VFP valve, refer to Fig. J31 and remove end cap (18). Withdraw spool (11) from valve body. Unscrew acorn nut (1) and adjusting screw (4) and remove relief valve assembly.

Clean and inspect all parts for wear or other damage. Complete valve assembly must be renewed if service is necessary.

Reassemble valve using new seal rings. Coat all parts with clean hydraulic oil prior to assembly. On VFP valve, thread adjusting screw (4) into body approximately 1/4 inch (6 mm) for initial setting.

Reinstall valve and adjust pressure setting as outlined in TESTING paragraph.

**HYDRAULIC CYLINDER.** To remove lift cylinder, first retract cylinder then shut off engine and actuate control lever to relieve hydraulic pressure. Raise hood and remove side panels. Disconnect hydraulic lines and plug all openings. Remove cotter pins and slide cylinder off mounting pins.

To disassemble cylinder, remove hydraulic fitting and snap ring (7—Fig. J32) from rod end of cylinder. Drain fluid from cylinder and pull rod, rod guide and piston out of cylinder tube. Unscrew piston retaining nut and remove piston from rod.

**NOTE: Do not clamp rod or piston in a vise. Be careful not to scratch or mar rod.**

Seal repair kit is only service part available for cylinder repair. Inspect rod, piston and cylinder bore for excessive wear or other damage and renew as necessary. Coat all parts with hydraulic fluid prior to assembly.

Be sure "O" rings are not twisted or cut when reassembling. Align threaded port in rod guide (11) with hole in cylinder tube (1) prior to installation.

Reinstall cylinder and check hydraulic fluid level. Start engine and cycle cylinder several times to purge air from system.

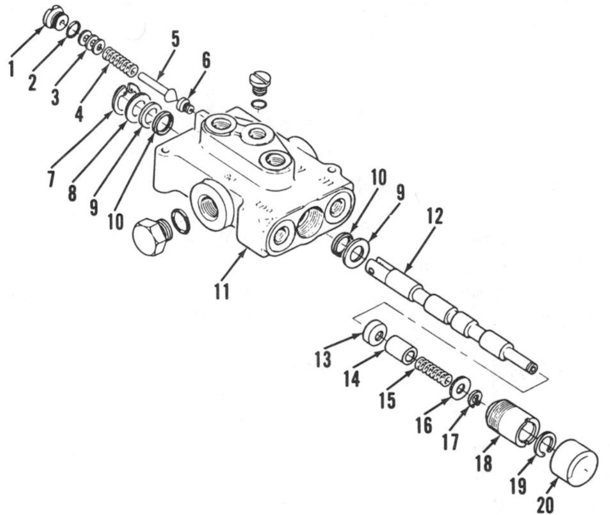

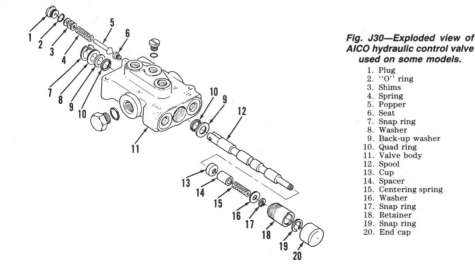

***Fig. J30—Exploded view of AICO hydraulic control valve used on some models.***

1. Plug
2. "O" ring
3. Shims
4. Spring
5. Popper
6. Seat
7. Snap ring
8. Washer
9. Back-up washer
10. Quad ring
11. Valve body
12. Spool
13. Cup
14. Spacer
15. Centering spring
16. Washer
17. Snap ring
18. Retainer
19. Snap ring
20. End cap

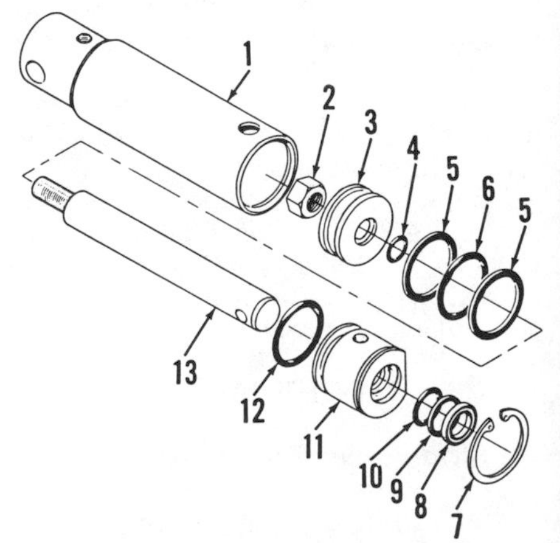

***Fig. J32—Exploded view of typical hydraulic lift cylinder used on some models.***

# KUBOTA

## CONDENSED SPECIFICATIONS

| | MODELS | |
|---|---|---|
| | T1400 | T1400H |
| Engine Make | Kubota | Kubota |
| Model | GH400V-L | GH400V-L |
| Bore | 84.2 mm (3.31 in.) | 84.2 mm (3.31 in.) |
| Stroke | 70 mm (2.76 in.) | 70 mm (2.76 in.) |
| Piston Displacement | 389 cc (23.7 cu. in.) | 389 cc (23.7 cu. in.) |
| Rated Power | 10.1 kW (13.5 hp) | 10.1 kW (13.5 hp) |
| Slow Idle Speed—Rpm | 1300 | 1300 |
| High Idle Speed (No-Load)—Rpm | 3350 | 3350 |
| Crankcase Oil Capacity | 1.4 L (1.5 qts.) | 1.4 L (1.5 qts.) |
| Transmission Oil Capacity | 2.6 L (2.7 qts.) | 0.57 L (0.6 qts.) |
| Weight | SAE 90 EP Gear Lube | SAE 10W-30 Engine Oil |
| Differential Oil Capacity | ....... | 1.8 L (1.9 qts.) |
| Weight | ....... | SAE 90 EP Gear Lube |

# FRONT AXLE AND STEERING SYSTEM

### AXLE MAIN MEMBER

#### All Models

**REMOVE AND REINSTALL.** To remove front axle assembly, first remove mower deck from tractor. Raise and support front of tractor. Remove drive belts from engine pulley, then unbolt and remove engine pulley. Disconnect drag link from spindle steering arm. Remove nut (5—Fig. K1), withdraw pivot bolt (9) and remove axle assembly from tractor.

Inspect axle (8), pivot tube (7) and pivot bolt for wear or damage and renew as necessary. Lubricate pivot tube with molybdenum disulfide grease. Reinstall axle by reversing removal procedure. Tighten axle retaining nut to 78-90 N·m (57-65 ft.-lbs.). Tighten drag link nut to 39-45 N·m (30-33 ft.-lbs.).

### TIE ROD AND TOE-IN

#### All Models

All models are equipped with an adjustable tie rod. Inspect tie rod ball joints for excessive wear and looseness and renew as needed.

To check front wheel toe-in, turn front wheels straight ahead and measure distance (A—Fig. K2) between front of tires and distance (B) between rear of tires. Distance (A) should be 0-5 mm (0-3/16 in.) less than distance (B). To ad-

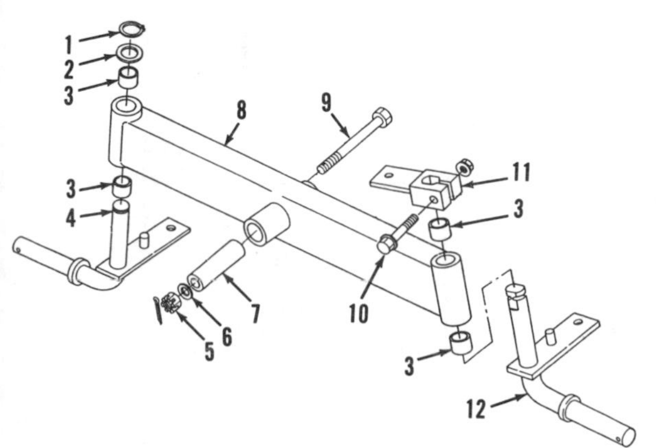


*Fig. K1—Exploded view of front axle assembly.*
1. Snap ring
2. Washer
3. Bushings
4. Spindle R.H.
5. Nut
6. Washer
7. Pivot tube
8. Axle main member
9. Pivot bolt
10. Clamp bolt
11. Steering arm
12. Spindle L.H.

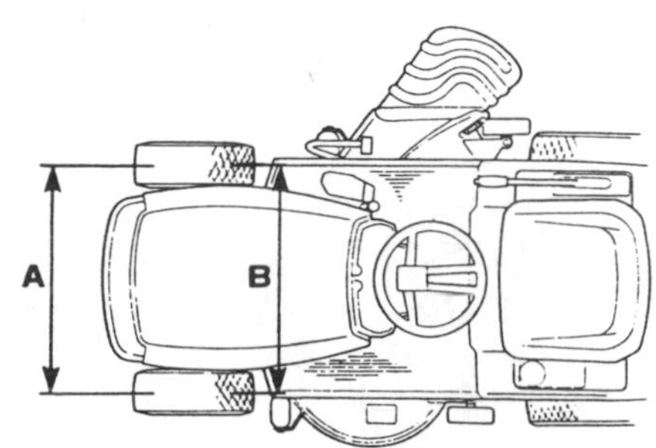


*Fig. K2—Front wheel toe-in should be 0-5 mm (0-3/16 in.). Refer to text for adjustment procedure.*

Illustrations courtesy Kubota Tractor Corp.

just, disconnect tie rod and change tie rod length as necessary. Tighten tie rod mounting nut to 24-27 N·m (18-20 ft.-lbs.).

### STEERING SPINDLES

#### All Models

**REMOVE AND REINSTALL.** To remove steering spindles (4 and 12—Fig. K1), raise and support front of tractor. Remove front wheels. Disconnect tie rod from spindles. Remove clamp bolt (10) from steering arm (11) on left spindle (12), then tap spindle out of steering arm and remove spindle from axle. Remove snap ring (1) from right spindle (4) and lower spindle from axle.

Inspect spindles and bushings for wear and renew as needed. Reinstall by reversing removal procedure. Tighten tie rod mounting nuts to 24-27 N·m (18-20 ft.-lbs.). Lubricate spindles with multipurpose grease.

### STEERING GEAR

#### All Models

**REMOVE AND REINSTALL.** To remove steering gears, first raise seat and disconnect battery cables. Disconnect fuel hose from fuel filter, remove fuel tank mounting screws and remove fuel tank. Disconnect air inlet pipe from air cleaner, remove air cleaner mounting screws and remove air cleaner. Remove steering wheel pad (1—Fig. K3) and unscrew steering wheel mounting nut (2). Pull steering wheel off steering shaft (5). Disconnect drag link from pitman arm. Unbolt and remove pitman arm (14) from sector gear shaft (9). Withdraw sector gear (9) from support (11). Remove cotter pin (8) from lower end of steering shaft (5). Remove instrument panel mounting screws, lift instrument panel up and remove steering shaft.

Inspect bushings and shafts for wear and renew as necessary. Check steering gear teeth for excessive wear or damage.

To reassemble, reverse removal procedure. Apply multipurpose grease to sector shaft bushings (10 and 12), steering shaft bushing (4) and steering gear teeth. Be sure to align match marks (M—Fig. K4) on pitman arm and sector gear shaft. Tighten pitman arm nut to 78-90 N·m (57-66 ft.-lbs.). Tighten drag link nut to 39-45 N·m (30-33 ft.-lbs.).

## ENGINE

#### All Models

**REMOVE AND REINSTALL.** To remove engine, raise seat and disconnect battery cables. Raise the hood and disconnect wiring connectors from head lights, ignition unit, charging coil and starter on right side of engine. On left side of engine, disconnect wiring connectors from fuel cut-off solenoid. Disconnect throttle control cable. Shut off fuel and disconnect fuel line from carburetor. Unbolt and remove fuel tank and air cleaner. On Model T1400, remove engine pulley belt guard. On all models, remove drive belts from engine pulley. Unscrew four engine mounting bolts and lift engine from tractor.

To reinstall engine, reverse removal procedure.

**OVERHAUL.** To overhaul engine components and accessories, refer to Kubota engine section of this manual.

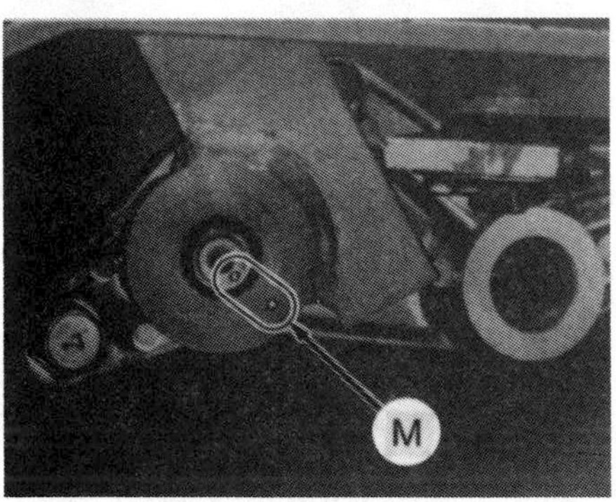


*Fig. K4—Match marks (M) on pitman arm and sector gear shaft must be aligned.*

## CLUTCH AND BRAKE

#### All Models

**ADJUSTMENT.** Clutch/brake pedal travel from released (up) position to fully depressed position should be 125-130 mm (4.92-5.12 in.) on Model T1400 and 70-80 mm (2.76-3.15 in.) on Model T1400H. To adjust pedal travel, loosen locknuts (2—Fig. K5) and turn adjusting screw (1) as necessary.

To adjust parking brake, depress brake pedal and lock it in place with a piece of wood. Loosen brake lock retainer mounting screws (3—Fig. K6), then pull park brake knob (1) to hook brake lock retainer (8) on stop (7) of brake pedal shaft. On Model T1400H, hook lock plate (5) on brake lock retainer (4). On all models, distance (L2—Fig. K7) between brake rod yoke (4) and end of brake rod (7) should be 25 mm (1 in.);

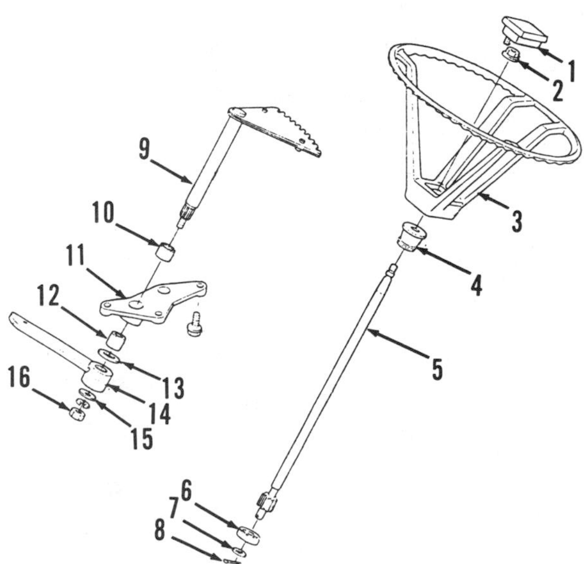

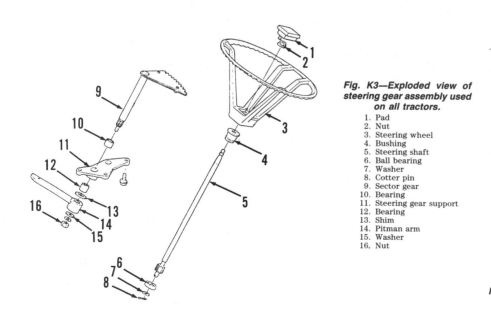

*Fig. K3—Exploded view of steering gear assembly used on all tractors.*

1. Pad
2. Nut
3. Steering wheel
4. Bushing
5. Steering shaft
6. Ball bearing
7. Washer
8. Cotter pin
9. Sector gear
10. Bearing
11. Steering gear support
12. Bearing
13. Shim
14. Pitman arm
15. Washer
16. Nut

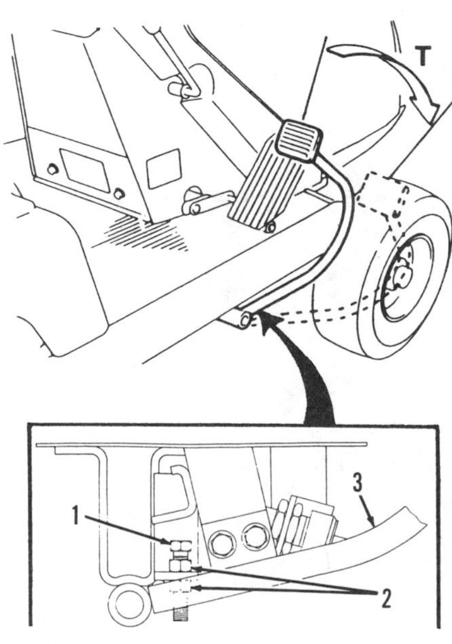


*Fig. K5—Brake pedal travel (T) is set by turning adjusting screw (1). Refer to text.*



Illustrations courtesy Kubota Tractor Corp.

if not, loosen jam nut (6) and turn brake rod (5) to adjust. Distance (L1) between end of brake rod and clevis pin (3) should be 1-2 mm (0.040-0.080 in.) on Model T1400 or 3-5 mm (0.120-0.200 in.) on Model T1400H. If measurement is not within specifications, loosen jam nuts (1) and turn turnbuckle (2) to adjust. After adjustment, tighten brake lock retainer mounting screws (3—Fig. K6).

On Model T1400H, depress brake pedal and measure pedal free travel. If free travel is not within range of 15-25 mm (0.6-1.0 in.), adjust turnbuckle (2—Fig. K7) to obtain desired free play.

On Model T1400, depress clutch/brake pedal and measure pedal travel necessary to engage brake. Travel should be within range of 80-90 mm (3.15-3.54 in.). If necessary, adjust turnbuckle (2—Fig. K7) to obtain desired pedal travel. Depress clutch/brake pedal and measure pedal travel necessary before clutch begins to disengage. Travel should be within range of 20-30 mm (0.79-1.18 in.). To adjust free travel, loosen jam nut (1—Fig. K8) and turn clutch rod turnbuckle (2) as necessary to obtain specified pedal travel. To check clutch disengagement position, raise and support rear of tractor so rear wheels are off the ground. Start engine and shift transmission to first speed. Push clutch/brake pedal down gradually and note when wheels stop turning. Measure distance that clutch/brake pedal traveled. Pedal travel required to engage brake must be greater than pedal travel required to disengage clutch. If not, repeat brake and clutch linkage adjustments.

**R&R AND OVERHAUL BRAKE.** The drum type brake is located on the left side of differential/axle housing. To remove brake assembly, disconnect brake rod from brake arm (8—Fig. K9). Unbolt and remove brake cover (7) with brake shoes (2), brake cam (5) and arm. Remove nut (9) and separate brake arm and cam from cover. Remove snap ring (4) and withdraw brake drum (1).

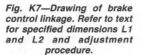

Inspect all parts for excessive wear. Renew brake shoes if thickness of shoes is less than 7.5 mm (0.295 in.). Renew brake drum if inside diameter exceeds 82.0 mm (3.228 in.).

To reinstall brake assembly, reverse removal procedure. Adjust brakes as outlined in ADJUSTMENT paragraph.

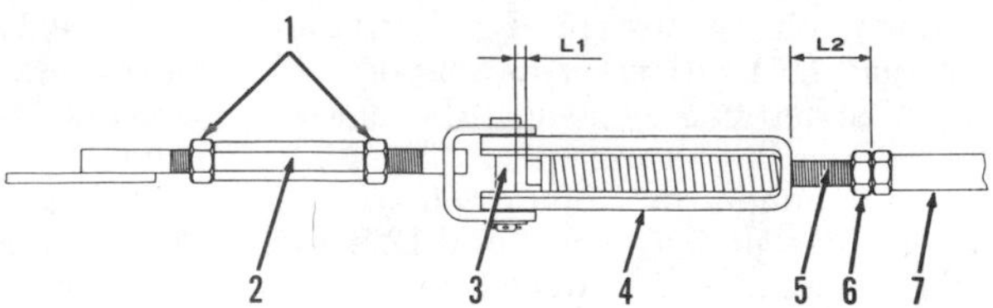


***Fig. K7—Drawing of brake control linkage. Refer to text for specified dimensions L1 and L2 and adjustment procedure.***
1. Jam nuts
2. Turnbuckle
3. Clevis pin
4. Clevis
5. Brake rod
6. Jam nut
7. Brake rod end

# SPEED VARIATOR

## Model T1400

**ADJUSTMENT.** The only adjustment necessary for the speed variator unit is maximum speed adjustment. To check maximum speed, raise and support rear of tractor so rear wheels are off the ground. Start engine and run at 3200 rpm. Shift gear shift lever to second speed position. Depress speed variator pedal all the way down and measure rear wheel revolutions per minute. If rear wheel rpm is not within specified range of 96 to 116 rpm, shut off engine, loosen locknut (2—Fig. K10) and turn speed change rod (1) to obtain desired wheel speed.

**NOTE: Initial setting length (L) of speed change rod (1) is 65-70 mm (2.56-2.76 in.).**

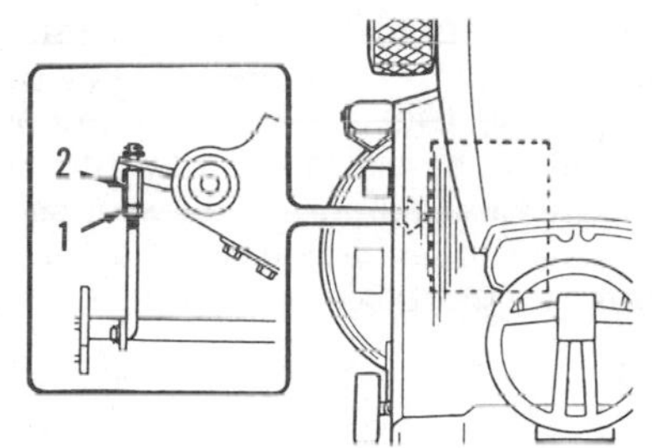


***Fig. K8—On Model T1400, clutch pedal free play is adjusted by turning clutch rod turnbuckle (2). Refer to text.***

**R&R AND OVERHAUL.** To remove speed variator, first remove mower deck from tractor. Raise and support front of tractor. Remove belt guard from engine pulley. Disconnect drag link from pitman arm, remove pitman arm nut and remove pitman arm from steering sector shaft. Disconnect belt pulley tension spring (7—Fig. K11) and spring (2). Disconnect speed change rod (3) and clutch rod (5). Remove snap ring retaining idler pulley arm (6) and remove arm and pulley. Remove speed variator belt guard. Remove drive belts between speed variator (4) and transmission and between speed variator and engine. Remove steering gear support mounting cap screws, then remove speed variator and steering gear support as an assembly.

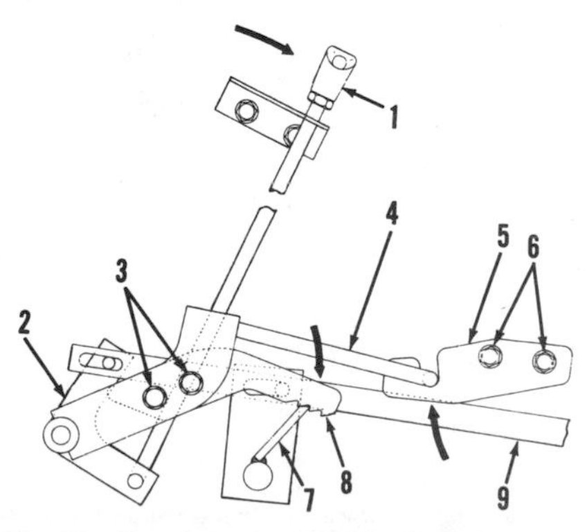


***Fig. K6—Drawing of parking brake linkage used on Model T1400H. Linkage used on Model T1400 is similar except brake lock (4) and lock plate (5) are not used.***
1. Parking brake knob
2. Parking brake arm
3. Mounting screws
4. Brake lock retainer
5. Lock plate
6. Mounting screws
7. Brake latch
8. Brake lock retainer
9. Brake rod

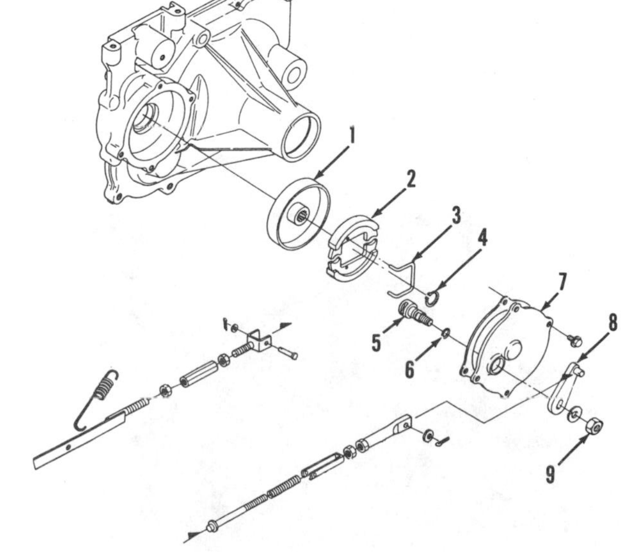


***Fig. K9—Exploded view of brake assembly used on all models.***
1. Brake drum
2. Brake shoes
3. Brake shoe spring
4. Snap ring
5. Brake cam
6. "O" ring
7. Brake cover
8. Brake arm
9. Nut

Remove snap ring (11—Fig. K12) and tap shaft (15) with steering support (16) out of speed change arm (14). Remove nut (10) and tap sheave shaft (1) out of speed change arm. Remove snap rings (6 and 13) and bearings (7 and 12) from speed change arm if necessary.

Inspect all parts for wear and renew as necessary. Inside diameter of movable sheave bushing (3) is 35.00-35.04 mm (1.378-1.379 in.) when new and maximum allowable diameter is 35.10 mm (1.382 in.).

To reassemble, reverse disassembly procedure. Apply light coat of grease to sheave bushing (3). Tighten sheave mounting nut (10) to 79-90 N·m (58-66 ft.-lbs.). Be sure to align match marks on pitman arm and steering sector shaft. Tighten pitman arm mounting nut to 79-90 N·m (58-66 ft.-lbs.) and drag link mounting nut to 39-45 N·m (29-33 ft.-lbs.). Check rear wheel speed and adjust speed change rod as necessary as outlined in ADJUSTMENT paragraph.

# HYDROSTATIC TRANSMISSION

## Model T1400H

**ADJUSTMENT.** To check and adjust maximum forward and maximum reverse speeds, raise and support rear of tractor so rear wheels are off the ground. Start engine and run at 3200 rpm. Move speed control pedal all the way in forward direction and measure rear wheel revolutions per minute, then move pedal all the way in reverse direction and measure rear wheel rpm. If wheel speed is not within specified range of 103-120 rpm in forward and 49-67 rpm in reverse, adjust foot pedal stop screws to obtain desired speed.

When speed control pedal is released, transmission should return to neutral and rear wheels should not creep either forward or reverse. If rear wheels continue to rotate, adjust as follows:

Raise and support rear of tractor. Remove rear wheels. Start engine and run at about 2500 rpm. Loosen cap screw securing eccentric shaft (11—Fig. K13), then rotate eccentric shaft until transmission is in neutral and axles stop turning. Tighten eccentric shaft cap screw, install rear wheels and check transmission operation.

**REMOVE AND REINSTALL.** To remove hydrostatic transmission, disconnect wiring connectors from seat safety interlock switch. Unbolt and remove seat and fender. Disconnect battery cables and remove battery. Drain lubricant from transaxle housing. Raise and support rear of tractor. Remove rear wheels. Disconnect brake control rod and speed change rod. Unbolt and remove transmission cooling fan, mounting flange and key from hydrostatic pump shaft. Unbolt and remove belt pulley and flange from transmission shaft. Support transmission assembly and unscrew transmission mounting bolts. Remove transmission and rear axle assembly from tractor. Disconnect return spring from hydrostatic control linkage. Remove hydrostatic transmission mounting nuts and separate hydrostatic unit from transaxle case.

To reinstall, reverse removal procedure. Adjust control linkage as previously outlined.

**OVERHAUL.** Model T1400H is equipped with a Hydro-Gear BDU-10 series hydrostatic transmission. Refer to Hydro-Gear section in HYDROSTATIC TRANSMISSION SERVICE section for overhaul procedure.

# REDUCTION GEARS AND DIFFERENTIAL

## Model T1400H

**R&R AND OVERHAUL.** To remove reduction gear and differential unit, refer to HYDROSTATIC TRANSMISSION section and separate hydrostatic unit from transaxle.

To disassemble transaxle, unbolt and remove neutral control arm and brake assembly from transaxle case. Remove transaxle case mounting screws, then separate transaxle case halves. Remove brake shaft assembly (2—Fig. K14), reduction gear shaft assembly (20) and the sprocket and differential assembly from transaxle case. Remove collar (9) and snap ring (11) from case. Tap bevel pinion shaft (18) assembly upward out of case. Remove differential mounting bolts and separate differential assembly (Fig. K15) from sprocket.

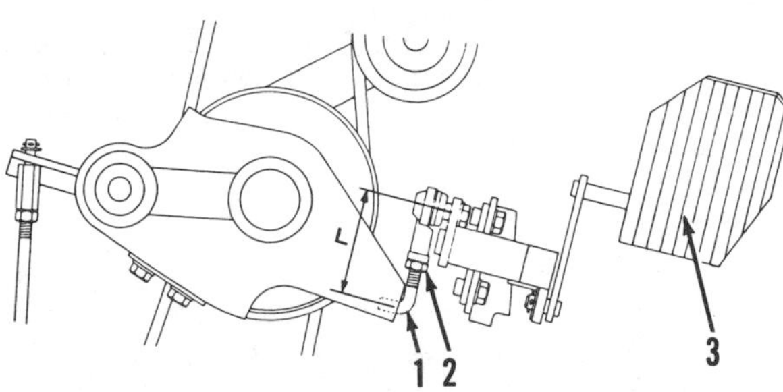


*Fig. K10—On Model T1400, maximum speed is adjusted by changing length of speed variator rod (1). Refer to text for procedure. Reference length (L) of rod is 65-70 mm (2.56-2.76 in.).*

*Fig. K11—Underside view of T1400 tractor.*

1. Engine pulley
2. Spring
3. Speed change rod
4. Speed variator assy.
5. Clutch rod
6. Belt tension idler arm
7. Tension spring

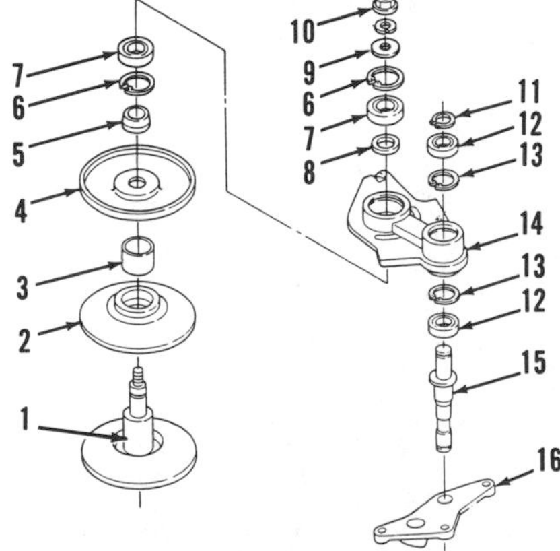


*Fig. K12—Exploded view of speed variator assembly used on Model T1400.*

1. Sheave shaft
2. Movable sheave
3. Bushing
4. Sheave
5. Collar
6. Snap ring
7. Ball bearing
8. Collar
9. Washer
10. Nut
11. Snap ring
12. Bearing
13. Snap ring
14. Speed change arm
15. Speed change shaft
16. Steering gear support



Illustrations courtesy Kubota Tractor Corp.

To reassemble, reverse the disassembly procedure. Tighten differential case mounting bolts to 48-56 N·m (36-41 ft.-lbs.). Backlash between bevel pinion shaft (18—Fig. K14) and bevel gear (3) should be 0.1-0.3 mm (0.004-0.012 in.). Change thickness of shims (12 and 16) as necessary to obtain desired backlash. Apply suitable liquid gasket to mating surface of transaxle case halves. Refill housing with Kubota hydrostatic transmission fluid or SAE 90 gear oil. Capacity is approximately 1.8 L (1.9 qts.).

# TRANSAXLE

## Model T1400

**REMOVE AND REINSTALL.** Drain lubricant from transaxle housing. Remove gear shift knob. Disconnect wiring connectors from seat safety switch, then unbolt and remove seat and fender. Disconnect battery cables and remove the battery. Remove drive pulley mounting screw and remove pulley from input shaft. Support rear of tractor and remove rear wheels. Disconnect brake control rod and shift rod from transaxle. Support transaxle, remove transaxle mounting bolts and separate transaxle from tractor.

To reinstall transaxle, reverse removal procedure.

**OVERHAUL.** To disassemble transmission, remove gear shift arm from shift lever. Remove brake cover, brake shoes and brake drum. Remove transaxle case mounting screws and separate case halves. Withdraw shift rod (30—Fig. K16) and shift fork (26) being careful not to lose detent spring (28) and ball (27). Remove main shaft (5) assembly and brake shaft (9) assembly. Remove countershaft (2) assembly and differential and drive sprocket assembly. Remove oil seal (23) and snap ring (22), then tap bevel pinion shaft (17) upward out of case. Remove differential mounting bolts and separate differential case (2—Fig. K15) from drive sprocket (1).

To reassemble transmission, reverse disassembly procedure. Tighten differential case mounting bolts to 48-56 N·m (36-41 ft.-lbs.). Backlash be-

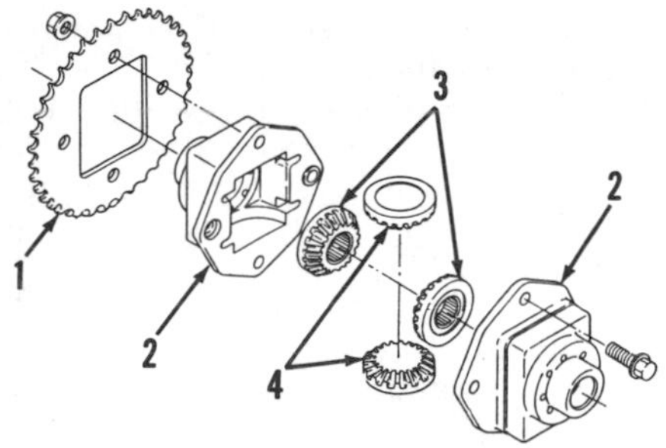


*Fig. K15—Exploded view of drive sprocket and differential assembly.*

1. Sprocket
2. Differential case
3. Differential side gears
4. Differential pinions

*Fig. K14—Exploded view of transaxle components used on Model T1400H.*

1. Bearing
2. Brake shaft
3. Bevel gear
4. Snap ring
5. Spacer
6. Gear
7. Bearing
8. Oil seal
9. Collar
10. Coupling
11. Snap ring
12. Shims
13. Snap ring
14. Ball bearing
15. Spacer
16. Shims
17. Ball bearing
18. Bevel pinion shaft
19. Bearing
20. Reduction gear shaft assy.
21. Chain
22. Bearing

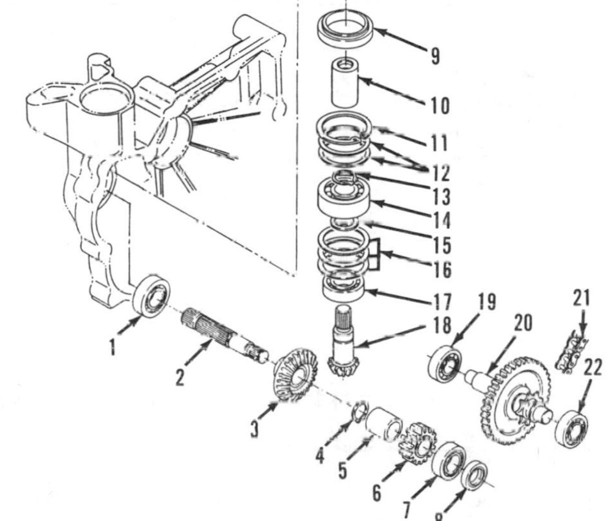


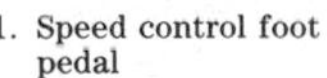

1. Speed control foot pedal
2. Pedal shaft
3. Brake lock
4. Spring
5. Speed change rod
6. Bushings
7. Speed change bellcrank
8. Control rod
9. Speed change arm
10. Ball bearing
11. Eccentric shaft
12. Bushing
13. Neutral arm
14. Transmission bypass lever
15. Support bracket
16. Spring

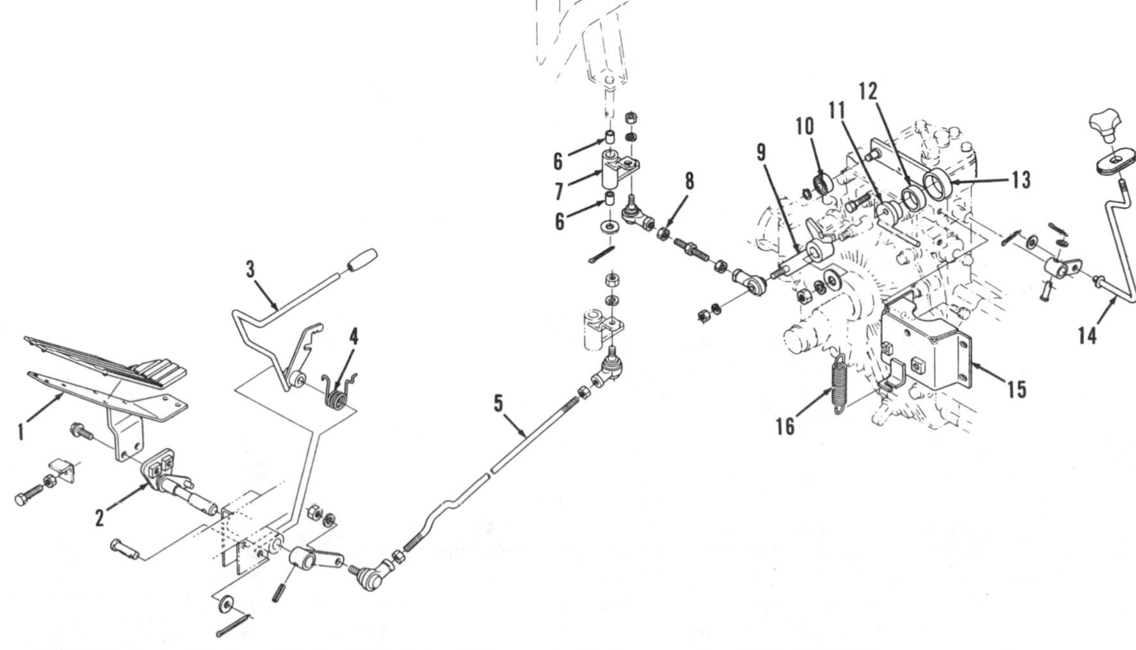


*Fig. K13—Exploded view of hydrostatic transmission control linkage used on Model T1400H.*

tween bevel pinion shaft (17—Fig. K16) and bevel gear (6) should be 0.15-0.40 mm (0.006-0.016 in.). Change thickness of shims (20) as necessary to obtain desired backlash. Apply suitable liquid gasket to mating surface of transaxle case halves.

Refill housing with Kubota hydrostatic transmission fluid or SAE 90 gear oil. Capacity is approximately 2.6 L (2.7 qts.).

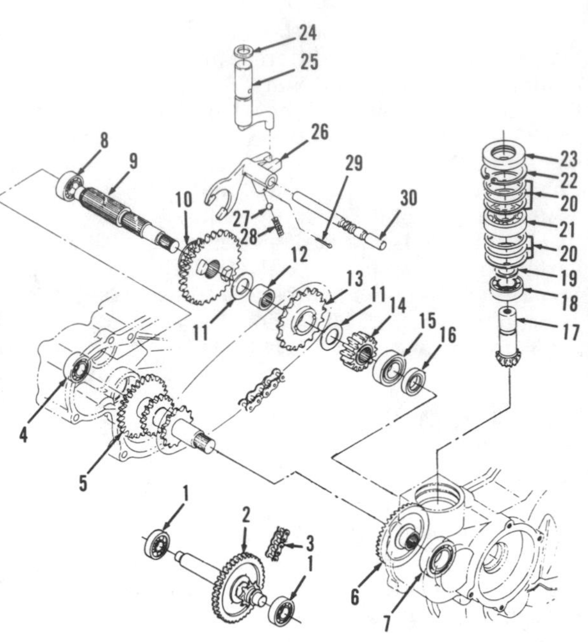

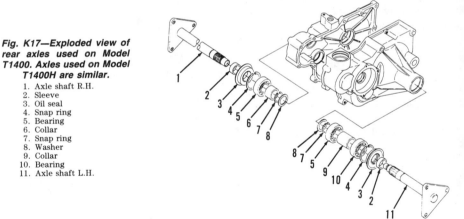

*Fig. K16—Exploded view of transaxle components used on Model T1400.*

1. Ball bearings
2. Reduction gear shaft
3. Chain
4. Ball bearing
5. Cluster gear shaft
6. Bevel gear
7. Ball bearing
8. Ball bearing
9. Brake shaft
10. Hi-Lo range gears
11. Thrust washer
12. Spline boss
13. Sprocket
14. Gear
15. Ball bearing
16. Oil seal
17. Bevel pinion shaft
18. Ball bearing
19. Spacer
20. Shims
21. Ball bearing
22. Snap ring
23. Oil seal
24. Oil seal
25. Shift lever
26. Shift fork
27. Detent ball
28. Spring
29. Cotter pin
30. Shift rod

# REAR AXLE

## All Models

**REMOVE AND REINSTALL.** To remove rear axles (1 and 11—Fig. K17), transaxle housing must be removed and disassembled as previously outlined.

Remove snap ring (7) from end of axle shaft and tap axle out of transaxle case. Remove oil seals (3) and bearings (5 and 10).

To reinstall axles, reverse removal procedure. Apply grease to lip of oil seals before installing axle shafts.

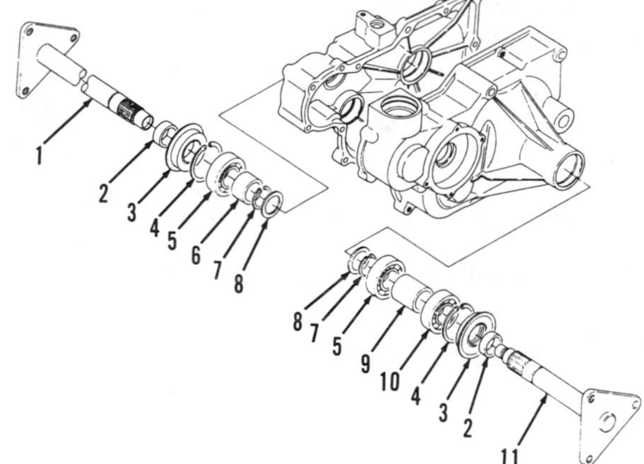

*Fig. K17—Exploded view of rear axles used on Model T1400. Axles used on Model T1400H are similar.*

1. Axle shaft R.H.
2. Sleeve
3. Oil seal
4. Snap ring
5. Bearing
6. Collar
7. Snap ring
8. Washer
9. Collar
10. Bearing
11. Axle shaft L.H.

# ELECTRICAL SYSTEM

## All Models

All models are equipped with a safety switch interlock system that prevents the engine from being started unless clutch/brake pedal is fully depressed, pto control lever is in neutral position and operator is seated in tractor seat. The clutch and pto switches are adjustable, the seat switch is not adjustable.

The clutch safety switch should indicate continuity when clutch pedal is fully depressed. There should not be continuity between switch leads when clutch pedal is released. The pto safety switch should indicate an open circuit when pto lever is in "ON" position. There should be continuity between switch leads when pto lever is in "OFF" position. The seat switch should indicate continuity between switch leads when switch is depressed. There should not be continuity when switch is released.

Clutch safety switch setting length (L—Fig. K18) between switch mounting plate (1) and tip of switch (2) should be 34-35 mm (1.34-1.38 in.) on Model T1400H or 37-38 mm (1.46-1.50 in.) on Model T1400. To adjust, turn switch mounting nuts (3) as necessary. Clutch safety switch is located on clutch pedal shaft support.

Pto safety switch setting length between switch mounting plate and tip of switch should be 39-41 mm (1.54-1.61 in.) with pto lever in "ON" position. To adjust, turn switch mounting nuts as necessary. The pto safety switch is located below the fuel tank on left side of tractor.

Refer to Kubota engine section for service procedures covering the starting system and charging system.

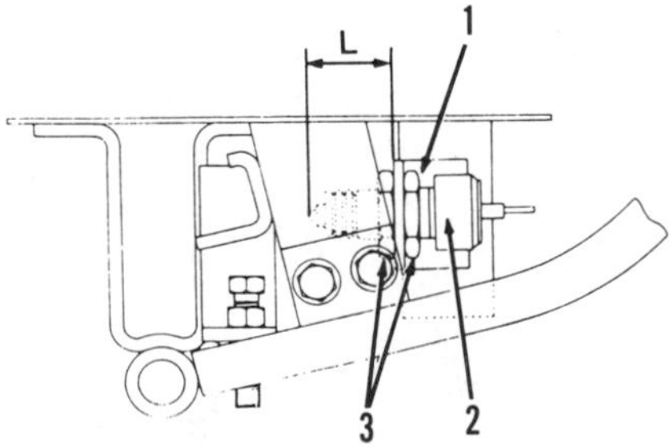


*Fig. K18—Distance (L) between safety switch mounting plate (1) and tip of switch (2) can be adjusted by turning switch mounting nuts (3). Refer to text for dimension (L).*



Illustrations courtesy Kubota Tractor Corp.

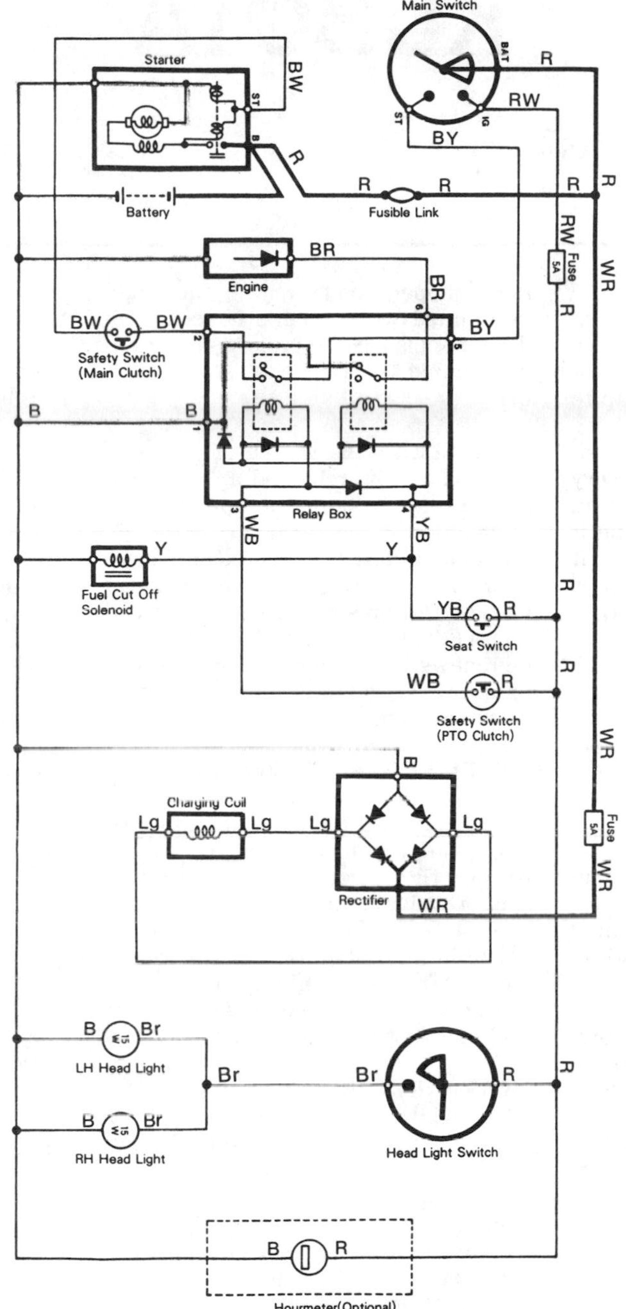


***Fig. K19—Tractor wiring schematic.***

B. Black
R. Red
Y. Yellow
Br. Brown
Lg. Light green
BR. Black/red
BW. Black/white
BY. Black/yellow
RW. Red/white
WB. White/black
WR. White/red
YB. Yellow/black

Illustrations courtesy Kubota Tractor Corp.

# KUBOTA

| Model | No. Cyls. | Bore | Stroke | Displacement | Horsepower |
|---|---|---|---|---|---|
| GH400V-L . . . . . . . . . . . . . . . | 1 | 84.2 mm (3.31 in.) | 70 mm (2.76 in.) | 389 cc (23.7 cu. in.) | 13.5 (10.1 kW) |

## MAINTENANCE

**SPARK PLUG.** Recommended spark plug is Nippon Denso W14FPR-UL 10 or NGK BPR4HA-10. Set electrode gap to 0.9-1.0 mm (0.035-0.039 in.).

Spark plug should be removed, cleaned and gap adjusted after every 100 hours of operation or once a year, whichever comes first. Renew plug if electrodes are burned and pitted or if porcelain is cracked. If frequent fouling is experienced, check for following conditions:

a. Carburetor setting too rich
b. Partially closed choke
c. Clogged air filter
d. Incorrect spark plug
e. Poor grade of gasoline
f. Too much oil in engine or crankcase breather restricted

**LUBRICATION.** Engine oil level should be checked prior to each operating interval. Oil should be maintained between reference marks on dipstick.

Use good quality oil with an API service classification SF. When temperature is below 15°C (59°F), SAE 20 or 10W-30 oil is recommended. When temperature is above 15°C (59°F), SAE 30 or 10W-30 oil is recommended.

Oil should be changed after the first 50 hours of operation and after each 100 hours of operation thereafter. Oil should be drained while engine is warm. Oil drain plug is located on left side of engine crankcase. Capacity is 1.4 L (1.5 qts.).

**AIR CLEANER.** The air cleaner element should be removed and cleaned after every 50 hours of operation or more often if operated in extremely dusty conditions. Use low pressure compressed air on inside of element to clean element. Air pressure should not exceed 30 psi (205 kPa). Filter element should be renewed if damaged or once yearly or after every sixth cleaning, whichever comes first.

**FUEL FILTER.** The fuel filter (Fig. K100) should be removed and cleaned after every 100 hours of operation or once yearly, whichever comes first. To remove filter element (2), close fuel shut-off valve (1) and unscrew sediment bowl (4) from filter base. Clean filter element in suitable solvent or renew element. After reassembling filter, open fuel shut-off valve and make sure that fuel does not leak.

**CARBURETOR.** A pilot jet (2—Fig. K101)) controls fuel-air mixture at idle speed and a fixed main jet controls fuel-air mixture at high speed. Initial adjustment of pilot jet screw is 1 to $1^1/_2$ turns open from lightly seated position. Main jet is not adjustable. Final adjustment of carburetor must be made with engine at normal operating temperature.

To adjust carburetor, proceed as follows: Start engine and set speed control lever at low speed position. Then, while holding carburetor throttle lever (1) against idle speed stop screw (3), turn stop screw to obtain lowest idle speed possible. Turn pilot jet screw (2) to obtain smoothest and highest idle speed possible. Turn idle speed stop screw as necessary to obtain idle speed of approximately 1250 rpm. Turn governor idling adjustment screw (10) to obtain specified idling speed of 1300 rpm.

To adjust choke, loosen choke rod retaining screw (8—Fig. K101). Move choke control lever (7) to the right and move choke rod retaining screw to the left in slotted hole, then tighten retaining screw in that position. Turn choke adjusting screw (12) until choke valve closes.

To disassemble carburetor, remove drain screw (3—Fig. K102) and drain fuel from float chamber. Remove fuel shut-off solenoid (1). Unscrew jet holder

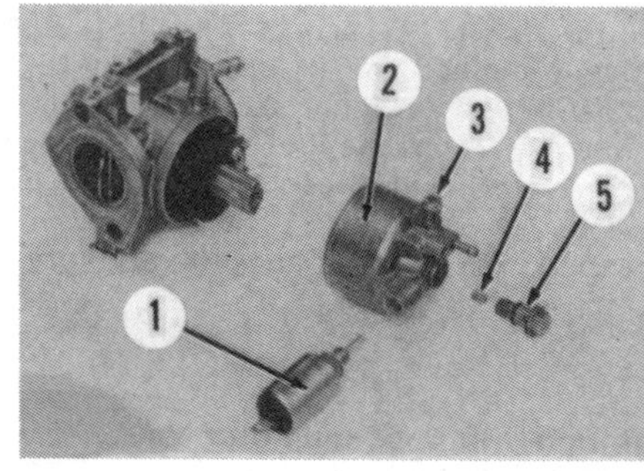


*Fig. K102—View of carburetor with float bowl removed.*

1. Fuel shut-off solenoid
2. Float bowl
3. Drain screw
4. Main jet
5. Main jet holder

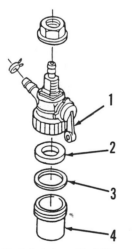

*Fig. K100—Exploded view of fuel filter assembly.*

1. Fuel shut-off valve
2. Filter element
3. Gasket
4. Fuel bowl

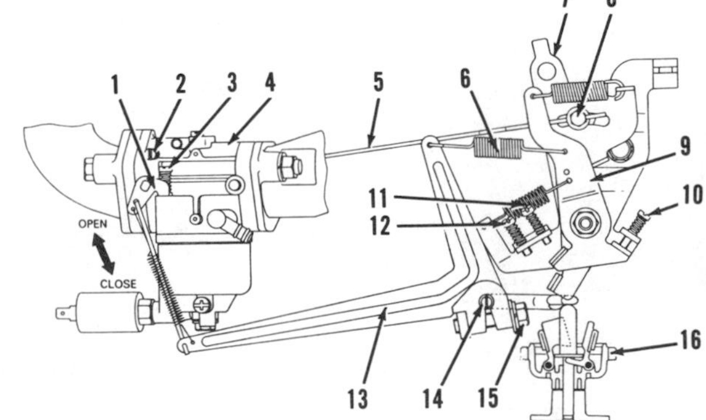


*Fig. K101—Adjustment points for carburetor and governor external linkage.*

1. Throttle shaft
2. Pilot screw
3. Idle speed screw
4. Carburetor
5. Choke rod
6. Governor spring
7. Speed control lever
8. Retaining screw
9. Speed control lever
10. Idle stop screw
11. High speed stop screw
12. Choke stop screw
13. Governor lever
14. Governor shaft
15. Clamp bolt
16. Governor flyweight assy.

(5) and remove float bowl (2) from carburetor body. Unscrew main jet (4) from jet holder. Withdraw float pin (7—Fig. K103) and remove float (9) and needle valve (6). Unscrew main nozzle (8) and pilot jet from carburetor body.

Clean all parts and internal passages using suitable solvent and compressed air. Do not use drills or wires to clean passages or jets as calibration of carburetor may be affected if passages or jets are enlarged. Use a 12-volt battery and jumper leads to check operation of fuel shut-off solenoid. Solenoid plunger should remain in retracted position while battery is connected to solenoid.

To reassemble carburetor, reverse the disassembly procedure. Tighten main nozzle to 1.96 N·m (17 in.-lbs.). Tighten jet holder to 7.85 N·m (69 in.-lbs.). Tighten fuel shut-off solenoid to 3.92 N·m (35 in.-lbs.).

**GOVERNOR.** A gear driven flyweight type governor assembly (16—Fig. K101) is located inside engine crankcase. To adjust governor external linkage, loosen governor lever clamp bolt (15). Move governor lever (13) by hand to fully open throttle valve (1). Use a screwdriver to turn governor lever shaft (14) clockwise as far as possible, then tighten governor lever clamp bolt. Start engine and move speed control lever to full speed position. Turn high speed adjusting screw (11) to obtain specified maximum no-load speed of 3350 rpm.

**IGNITION SYSTEM.** The engine is equipped with a transistor ignition system and regular maintenance is not required. Ignition timing is not adjustable. Ignition unit is located outside the flywheel. Clearance between ignition unit core and flywheel magnet should be 0.5 mm (0.020 in.).

To test ignition unit, remove cooling shroud. Disconnect connector between ignition unit and main switch, and high tension lead from spark plug. Measure primary coil resistance by connecting ohmmeter test leads (4—Fig. K104) across ignition unit primary wire (2) and core (1). Resistance should be approximately 1 ohm. Measure secondary coil resistance by connecting ohmmeter across high voltage lead (3) and core (1). Resistance should be approximately 9.5 ohms. Renew ignition unit if coil resistance is significantly higher or lower than specifications.

**CYLINDER HEAD AND COMBUSTION CHAMBER.** Standard compression pressure is 784-1078 kPa (114-156 psi). Excessive carbon build up on piston and cylinder head are indicated by higher than standard compression reading. A leaking cylinder head gasket, worn piston rings and cylinder bore or poorly seated valves are indicated by lower than standard compression reading.

**VALVE CLEARANCE ADJUSTMENT.** Clearance between valve stem and rocker arm should be checked and adjusted after every 300 hours of operation. Clearance must be checked with engine cold. Specified clearance is 0.08-0.12 mm (0.003-0.005 in.) for intake and exhaust.

Remove rocker arm cover. Remove spark plug, then rotate flywheel until piston is at top dead center on compression stroke. Insert feeler gage between end of valve stem and rocker arm to measure valve clearance. To adjust clearance, loosen rocker arm jam nut and turn adjusting screw as necessary (Fig. K105).

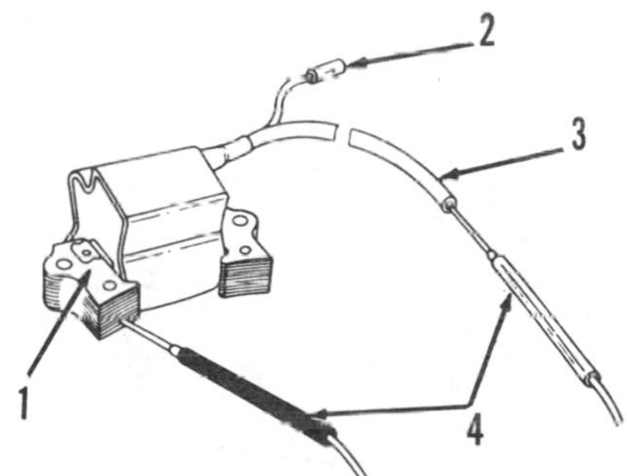


*Fig. K104—Test points for ignition coil. Refer to text for test procedure.*
1. Ignition coil
2. Primary wire
3. High tension wire
4. Ohmmeter test leads

## REPAIRS

**TIGHTENING TORQUES.** Recommended tightening torques are as follows:

Connecting rod bolts ...... 24-29 N·m (18-21 ft.-lbs.)
Cylinder head ........... 41-50 N·m (31-37 ft.-lbs.)
Crankcase cover .......... 14-19 N·m (10-14 ft.-lbs.)
Flywheel nut ........... 98-117 N·m (73-86 ft.-lbs.)
Spark plug .............. 10-24 N·m (8-18 ft.-lbs.)

**CYLINDER HEAD.** To remove cylinder head, first remove muffler cover, muffler, cylinder air shroud and flywheel cover. Disconnect governor linkage from carburetor, then unbolt and remove intake pipe and carburetor from cylinder head. Remove rocker arm cover. Unbolt and remove rocker arm assembly and push rods. Remove cylinder head mounting screws and remove cylinder head and gasket.

Remove snap rings (2—Fig. K106) and withdraw rocker arms (4) from rocker shafts (6). Identify parts so they can be reinstalled in their original positions. To avoid the possibility of valves contacting top of piston, loosen jam nuts (1) and turn adjusting screws (5) counterclockwise several turns before installing rocker arm assembly on cylinder head.

Compress valve springs and remove split retainers, spring retainers, springs and valves from cylinder head. Clean carbon from valve stems and cylinder head. Inspect all parts for wear or damage and renew as necessary. Valve face and seat angles are 45 degrees for intake

*Fig. K103—View of carburetor float assembly.*
6. Fuel needle valve
7. Pin
8. Main nozzle
9. Float

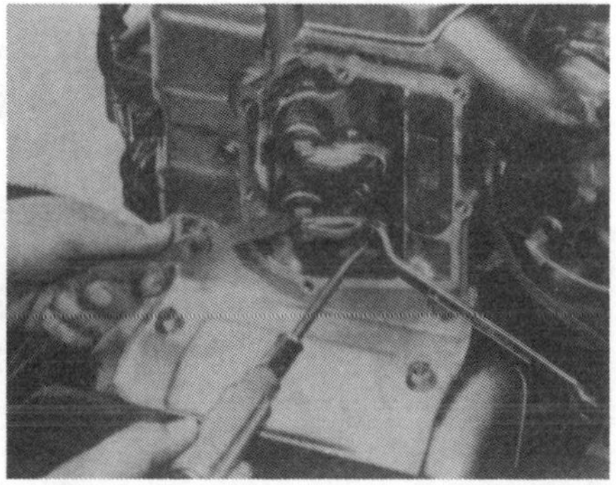

*Fig. K105—Adjusting valve clearance.*

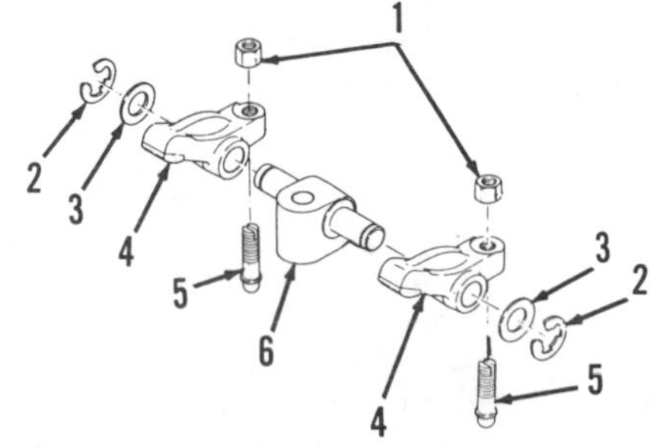


*Fig. K106—Exploded view of rocker arm assembly.*
1. Locknuts
2. Snap ring
3. Washer
4. Rocker arms
5. Adjusting screws
6. Rocker arm bracket

and exhaust. A 15 degree stone or cutter may be used to narrow valve seat if necessary.

Refer to the following specifications:

Rocker arm shaft
OD . . . . . . . . . . . . . 11.973-11.984 mm (0.4714-0.4718 in.)
Rocker arm ID . . . . 12.000-12.018 mm (0.4725-0.4731 in.)
Rocker arm-to-shaft clearance . . . . . . . . . 0.016-0.045 mm (0.0006-0.0018 in.)
Wear limit . . . . . . . . . . . . . 0.15 mm (0.006 in.)
Valve stem OD—
Intake . . . . . . . . . . . . 6.960-6.975 mm (0.2740-0.2746 in.)
Exhaust . . . . . . . . . . 7.940-7.960 mm (0.3126-0.3134 in.)
Valve guide ID—
Intake . . . . . . . . . . . . 7.000-7.015 mm (0.2756-0.2762 in.)
Exhaust . . . . . . . . . . . 8.000-8.015 in. (0.3150-0.3155 in.)
Valve stem-to-guide clearance—
Intake . . . . . . . . . . . . 0.025-0.055 mm (0.0010-0.0022 in.)
Wear limit . . . . . . . . . . . . . 0.10 mm (0.004 in.)
Exhaust . . . . . . . . . . 0.040-0.075 mm (0.0016-0.0029 in.)
Wear limit . . . . . . . . . . . . . 0.10 mm (0.004 in.)
Valve seat width—
Intake and exhaust . . . . . . . . 1.1 mm (0.044 in.)
Maximum allowable . . . . . . 1.7 mm (0.067 in.)
Valve spring free length . . . . . . . . . . . . . . 45.5-45.8 mm (1.791-1.803 in.)
Minimum allowable . . . . . 45.0 mm (1.772 in.)

Valve guides are renewable. Press old guide out toward top of cylinder head. Apply engine oil to new guide and use a suitable driver to press guide into cylinder head until stop ring on guide contacts cylinder head.

To reinstall cylinder head assembly, reverse the removal procedure. Make sure that washers (A—Fig. K107) are installed under the two cap screws indicated in Fig. K107. Tighten cylinder head screws (B) and flange screw (C) in three steps following tightening sequence shown in Fig. K107. Specified final torque for cap screws (B) is 41-50 N·m (31-37 ft.-lbs.) and for flange screw (C) is 18-23 N·m (13-17 ft.-lbs.). Adjust valve clearance as outlined in MAINTENANCE section.

**BALANCER SHAFTS.** Engine is equipped with two counter-rotating balancer shafts. To remove balancer shafts, unscrew crankcase cover screws and tap cover with a plastic mallet to separate cover (1—Fig. K108) from crankcase. Withdraw balancer shafts (3).

When installing balancer shafts, be sure to align alignment marks (A—Fig. K108A) on balancer gears (3) and crankshaft gear (2). When installing crankcase cover, be sure tang on oil pump shaft engages slot in end of balancer shaft. Tighten crankcase cover screws evenly to 14-19 N·m (10-14 ft.-lbs.).

**CONNECTING ROD.** Connecting rod rides directly on crankshaft journal. Connecting rod and piston are removed as an assembly after first removing cylinder head, crankcase cover, balancer gear shafts and connecting rod cap. Remove carbon or ring ridge (if present) from top of cylinder, then push piston and connecting rod out top of cylinder. Remove piston pin retaining rings and push pin out of piston and connecting rod.

Connecting rod small end inside diameter should be 20.015-20.025 mm (0.7880-0.7884 in.) and wear limit is 20.07 mm (0.790 in.). Connecting rod big end standard inside diameter should be 33.500-33.525 mm (1.3189-1.3199 in.). Crankpin standard outside diameter should be 33.475-33.485 mm (1.3179-1.3183 in.). Desired clearance between connecting rod big end and crankpin is 0.015-0.050 mm (0.0006-0.0020 in.), maximum allowable clearance is 0.10 mm (0.004 in.). Connecting rod is available with 0.25 and 0.50 mm undersize big end.

Measure side clearance of connecting rod on crankshaft using a feeler gage. Specified side clearance is 0.4-1.1 mm (0.016-0.043 in.). Connecting rod should be renewed if side clearance exceeds 1.5 mm (0.059 in.).

When assembling connecting rod to piston, arrow (2—Fig. K109) on piston crown must be aligned with machined surfaces (1) on connecting rod. Insert piston and connecting rod in cylinder so

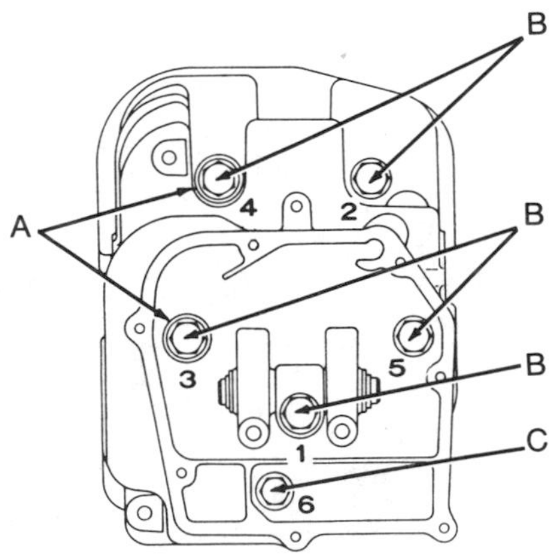

*Fig. K107—When tightening cylinder head bolts, follow sequence shown. Refer to text.*

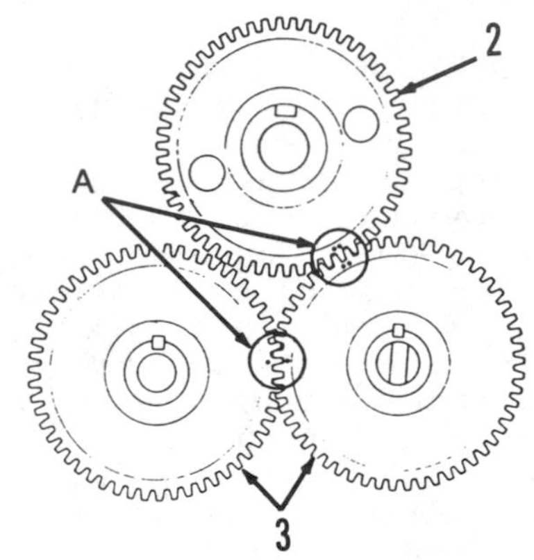

*Fig. K108A—Timing marks (A) on crankshaft gear (2) and balancer gears (3) must be aligned as shown.*

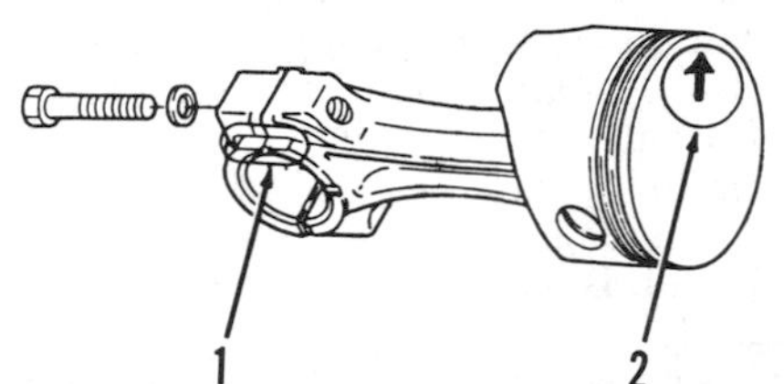

*Fig. K109—Assemble piston to connecting rod so arrow mark (2) on piston crown is aligned with machined surface (1) on connecting rod and cap.*

*Fig. K108—View of engine timing gears.*
1. Crankcase cover
2. Crankshaft
3. Balancer gears
4. Camshaft



Illustrations courtesy Kubota Tractor Corp.

Japanese character casting mark (M—Fig. K110) on connecting rod faces flywheel side of engine. Align machined marks (1—Fig. K109) on connecting rod and cap, apply engine oil to connecting rod screws and tighten evenly to 24-29 N·m (18-21 ft.-lbs.). Complete installation by reversing removal procedure.

**PISTON, PIN AND RINGS.** Piston and connecting rod are removed as an assembly. Refer to CONNECTING ROD section for removal and installation procedure.

After separating piston from connecting rod, remove piston rings and clean carbon and other deposits from piston surface and piston ring lands.

**CAUTION: Extreme care should be exercised when cleaning piston ring lands. Do not damage squared edges or widen piston ring grooves. If piston ring lands are damaged, piston must be renewed.**

Renew piston if skirt is scored, scratched or excessively worn. Measure piston skirt diameter at right angle to piston pin center line and 23 mm (0.91 in.) from lower edge of skirt. Skirt diameter should be 84.15-84.17 mm (3.3130-3.3138 in.) and wear limit is 84.05 mm (3.309 in.).

Piston pin bore in piston should be 19.995-20.003 mm (0.7872-0.7875 in.) and wear limit is 20.04 mm (0.7890 in.). Piston pin outside diameter should be 20.000-20.005 mm (0.7874-0.7876 in.) and wear limit is 19.96 mm (0.7858 in.).

Insert a new ring in piston ring groove and use a feeler gage to measure ring side clearance in piston ring grooves as shown in Fig. K111. Clearance should be 0.02-0.06 mm (0.0008-0.0024 in.). Renew piston if side clearance with a new ring exceeds 0.10 mm (0.004 in.).

Insert piston rings squarely into lower part (least worn part) of cylinder and use a feeler gage to measure ring end gap. Specified end gap for compression rings is 0.35-0.55 mm (0.014-0.022 in.). Specified end gap for oil ring is 0.20-0.70 mm (0.008-0.027 in.).

When assembling piston to connecting rod, be sure that arrow mark (2—Fig. K109) is aligned with machined surface (1) on connecting rod. When installing piston rings on piston, be sure that manufacturer's mark (M—Fig. 112) near ring end gap faces top of piston. Heat piston in hot oil or water for 10 to 15 minutes to facilitate installation of piston pin.

Lubricate piston and cylinder with engine oil prior to installing piston. Be sure that Japanese character casting mark (M—Fig. K110) on connecting rod faces flywheel side of engine. Stagger ring end gaps around piston as shown in Fig. K112. Insert piston into cylinder using a suitable ring compressor.

**CYLINDER, CRANKCASE, MAIN BEARINGS AND SEALS.** Cylinder and crankcase are an integral casting. Standard cylinder bore diameter is 84.200-84.225 mm (3.315-3.316 in.) and wear limit is 84.325 mm (3.320 in.). Cylinder may be bored or honed to fit oversize pistons. Pistons are available in oversizes of 0.25 and 0.50 mm.

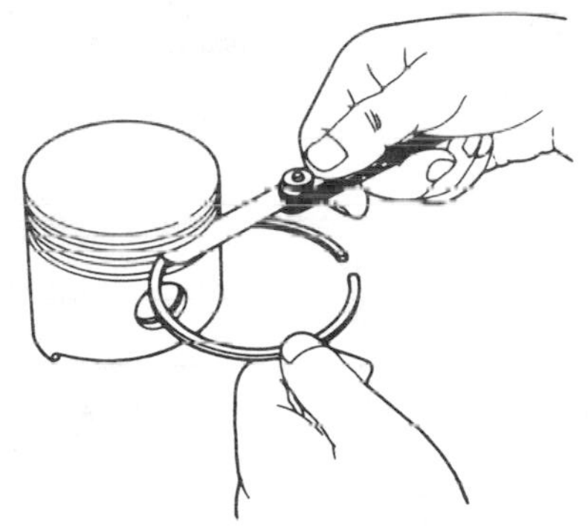

*Fig. K111—To check piston ring grooves for wear, insert new ring in groove and use a feeler gage measure side clearance. Refer to text for specifications.*

Main bearings are ball bearings. Bearings should be a light press fit in crankcase and crankcase cover.

Renew crankshaft seals if removed. Pack lip of seals with high temperature grease prior to installation.

**CRANKSHAFT.** Crankshaft can be removed from engine after removing all shrouds, flywheel, cylinder head, crankcase cover, balancer shafts, connecting rod and piston. Turn crankcase upside down so tappets fall away from camshaft, then withdraw crankshaft and camshaft together from crankcase.

Inspect crankshaft journals for wear, scratches or other damage. Crankpin may be reground to fit undersize connecting rod. Crankshaft main journals cannot be reground.

To reinstall crankshaft, reverse the removal procedure. Make certain that timing marks (T—Fig. K113) on crankshaft gear and camshaft gear are aligned, and that timing marks (A—Fig. K108A) on crankshaft gear and balancer gears are aligned.

Measure crankshaft end play using a dial indicator after crankcase cover is installed. Maximum allowable end play is 0.1 mm (0.004 in.). Adjust by adding or removing shims located on crankcase cover end of crankshaft.

**CAMSHAFT AND TAPPETS.** Camshaft is removed from engine at the same time as the crankshaft as outlined in CRANKSHAFT section above.

Inspect camshaft and tappets for wear, scoring, pitting or other damage and renew as necessary. Specified cam height for intake and exhaust is 34.685-34.715 mm (1.3656-1.3667 in.). Cam height wear limit is 34.5 mm (1.358 in.). When renewing camshaft, renew tappets also.

Reinstall camshaft and crankshaft, aligning timing marks (T—Fig. K113) on

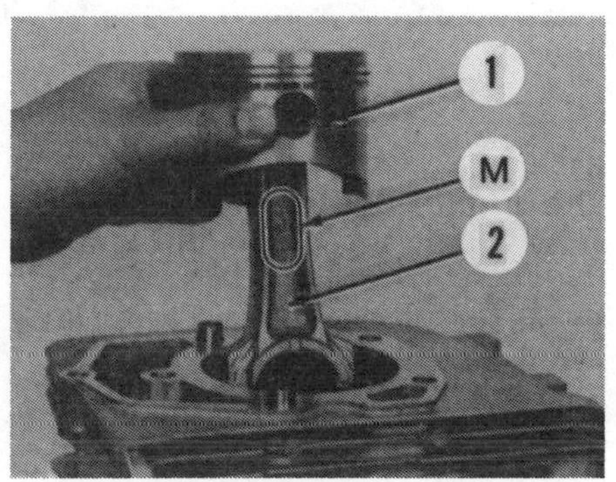


*Fig. K110—Install connecting rod and piston so casting mark (M) on connecting rod faces flywheel side of engine.*

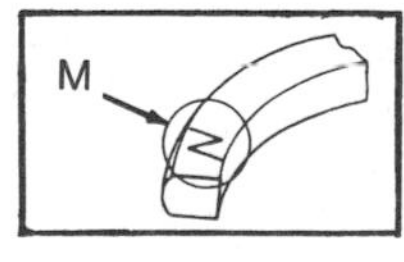


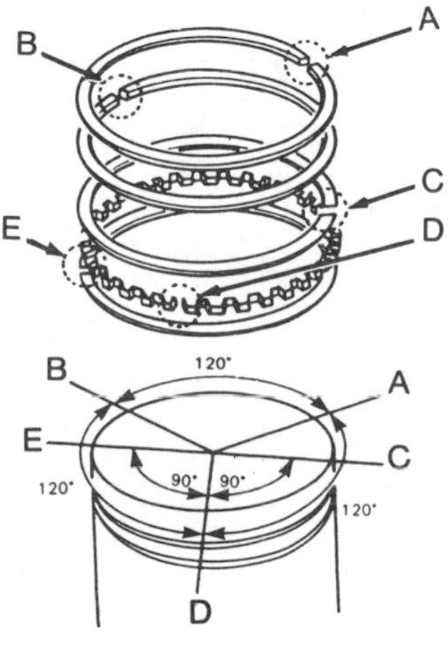


*Fig. K112—Drawing showing correct installation of piston rings. Refer to text for details.*

camshaft gear and crankshaft gear. Timing mark on camshaft gear is visible through hole in balancer drive gear.

Adjust valve clearance as outlined in MAINTENANCE section.

**OIL PUMP AND RELIEF VALVE.** The trochoid type oil pump is mounted on crankcase cover and driven by one of the balancer shafts. Pressurized oil is pumped through oil gallery in crankshaft to lubricate crankpin and connecting rod. A hole in the crankshaft allows excess oil to splash lubricate piston, cylinder wall and bearings.

To remove oil pump, unbolt and remove crankcase cover. Remove oil pump cover mounting screws, then push inner and outer rotors (2 and 3—Fig. K114) out of crankcase cover. Remove oil pressure regulator valve assembly from crankcase cover and inspect seating of valve poppet in cover.

Measure clearance between lobes of inner and outer rotors using a feeler gage. Specified clearance is 0.15 mm (0.006 in.) or less and wear limit is 0.20 mm (0.008 in.). Measure clearance between outer rotor and pump body using a feeler gage. Specified clearance is 0.130-0.223 mm (0.005-0.009 in.) and wear limit is 0.25 mm (0.010 in.). To measure pump rotor end clearance, place a strip of Plastigage on face of pump rotors and install pump assembly. Remove pump cover and measure width of Plastigage. Specified clearance is 0.02-0.06 mm (0.0008-0.0024 in.) and wear limit is 0.25 mm (0.010 in.). Renew pump assembly if any operating clearances exceed specified wear limits.

To reinstall oil pump, reverse the removal procedure. Make certain that tang of inner rotor engages slot in end of balancer shaft.

To check engine oil pressure, remove pipe plug from crankcase cover and install a suitable pressure gage and adapter in oil passage. With engine warm, measure oil pressure at idle speed and at maximum speed. Oil pressure should be 20 kPa (3 psi) or higher at idle speed and 98 kPa (14 psi) or higher at maximum speed. Minimum allowable oil pressure is 29 kPa (4 psi).

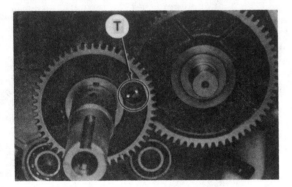

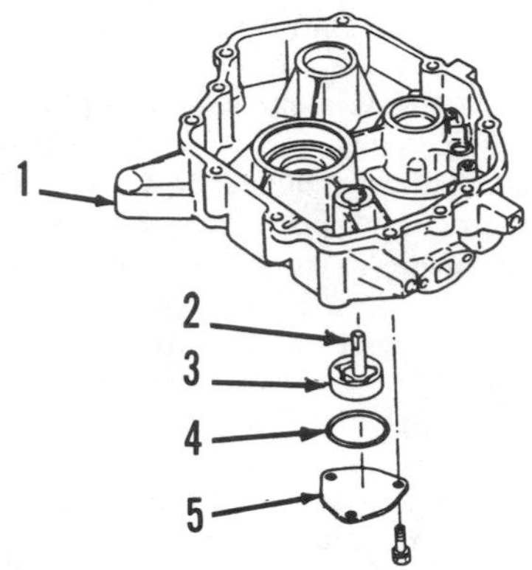


*Fig. K114—Engine oil pump is mounted in crankcase cover and driven by one of the balancer shafts.*

1. Crankcase cover
2. Inner rotor
3. Outer rotor
4. "O" ring
5. Pump cover

*Fig. K113—Timing marks (T) on crankshaft gear and camshaft gear must be aligned when installing crankshaft and camshaft.*

# KUBOTA

## SERVICING KUBOTA ACCESSORIES

### ELECTRIC STARTER

**TESTING.** Prior to removing starter motor for testing, check main switch and all wiring connectors for faulty connections.

To test starter motor, first remove starter from engine. Disconnect connecting lead from solenoid switch terminal. Connect a jumper lead from positive terminal of fully charged 12-volt battery to starter connecting lead. Momentarily connect jumper cable from battery negative terminal to starter motor housing (ground). If starter motor does not run, motor is faulty. If motor runs, solenoid switch may be faulty.

To check solenoid switch, connect a jumper lead from positive terminal of a 6-volt battery to "ST" terminal of solenoid. Connect jumper lead between negative terminal of battery to C terminal of solenoid. If plunger is pulled strongly inward, pull-in coil is good.

Connect jumper lead from positive terminal of 6-volt battery to "ST" terminal of solenoid. Connect jumper lead from negative terminal of battery to solenoid body. Push plunger in by hand, then release it. If plunger remains attracted inward in solenoid, hold-in coil is good.

Apply 12 volts between C terminal of solenoid and solenoid body. Push plunger inward by hand, then release it. If plunger is forced outward, solenoid coil is good.

**OVERHAUL.** To disassemble starter, disconnect connecting lead (15—Fig. K115) from solenoid switch (12). Unbolt and remove solenoid switch from starter motor. Remove through-bolts (22) and separate end frame (20), insulator (18), brush hôlder (16) and field coil yoke (13) from drive housing (3). Withdraw armature (10) with overrunning clutch (9) and drive lever (4) from drive housing.

Check armature for short or open circuit. Renew armature if there is continuity between commutator and armature coil wire, or between commutator and armature shaft. Renew armature if there is no continuity between commutator segments. Commutator outside diameter should be 28.0 mm (1.102 in.) and wear limit is 27.0 mm (1.063 in.). Commutator mica undercut depth should be 0.45-0.75 mm (0.018-0.029 in.) and wear limit is 0.20 mm (0.008 in.).

Clearance between armature shaft and bushings should be 0.02-0.07 mm (0.0008-0.0027 in.) and wear limit is 0.20 mm (0.008 in.).

There should be continuity between brush and field coil yoke assembly. Brush length when new is 10.0 mm (0.394 in.) and wear limit is 6.0 mm (0.236 in.).

Overrunning clutch pinion should rotate freely clockwise and should lock when rotated counterclockwise. Renew clutch assembly if pinion teeth are excessively worn or damaged.

To reassemble starter, reverse the disassembly procedure.

**CHARGING COIL AND RECTIFIER.** The flywheel must be removed from crankshaft to gain access to charging coil. To check coil, disconnect coil leads from rectifier and measure resistance between the two leads using an ohmmeter. Coil resistance should be approximately 0.33 ohms.

To check rectifier, disconnect rectifier wiring leads. Connect ohmmeter test leads to rectifier leads and check for resistance or infinity readings as indicated in Fig. K116. Reverse ohmmeter test lead connections and again check for resistance or infinity readings. If readings are not as indicated in Fig. K116, renew rectifier.

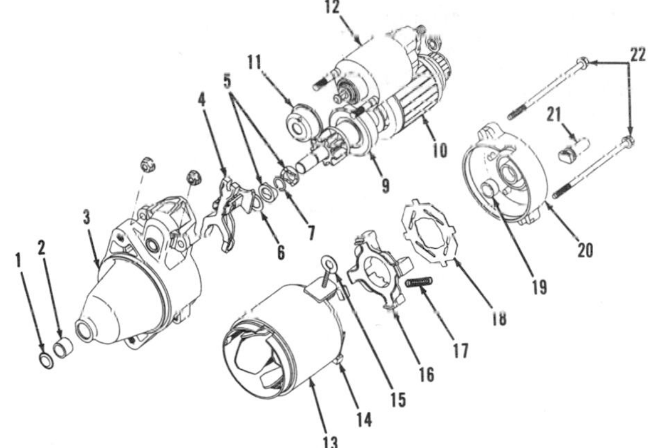

*Fig. K115—Exploded view of electric starter motor.*

1. Plug
2. Bushing
3. Drive housing
4. Drive lever
5. Pinion stop
6. Washer
7. Snap ring
9. Overrunning clutch
10. Armature
11. Gasket
12. Solenoid switch
13. Field coil yoke assy.
14. Brush
15. Connecting lead
16. Brush holder
17. Brush spring
18. Insulator
19. Bushing
20. End frame
21. Cover
22. Through-bolts

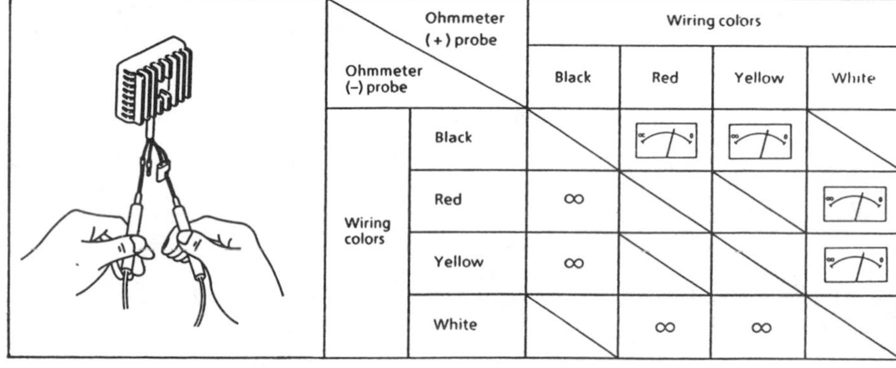

| Ohmmeter (−) probe \ Ohmmeter (+) probe — Wiring colors | Black | Red | Yellow | White |
|---|---|---|---|---|
| Black | | (meter) | (meter) | |
| Red | ∞ | | | (meter) |
| Yellow | ∞ | | | (meter) |
| White | | ∞ | ∞ | |

*Fig. K116—To test rectifier, use an ohmmeter to measure resistance between rectifier wires. Renew unit if resistance values are not as shown in chart.*

Illustrations courtesy Kubota Tractor Corp.

# MTD

## (Prior To 1988)

## CONDENSED SPECIFICATIONS

| | MODELS | | | |
|---|---|---|---|---|
| | 137-320<br>137-322<br>137-327 | 137-332<br>137-337 | 137-530<br>137-567<br>137-600 | 133-630A<br>133-632A |
| Engine Make | B&S | B&S | B&S | B&S |
| Model | 191701 | 252707 | 252707 | 190410 |
| Bore | 3 in.<br>(76.2 mm) | 3-7/16 in.<br>(87.3 mm) | 3-7/16 in.<br>(87.3 mm) | 3 in.<br>(76.2 mm) |
| Stroke | 2¾ in.<br>(69.8 mm) | 2⅝ in.<br>(66.7 mm) | 2⅝ in.<br>(66.7 mm) | 2¾ in.<br>(69.8 mm) |
| Piston Displacement | 19.44 cu. in.<br>(319 cc) | 24.36 cu. in.<br>(399 cc) | 24.37 cu. in.<br>(399 cc) | 19.44 cu. in.<br>(319 cc) |
| Horsepower | 8 | 11 | 11 | 8 |
| Slow Idle Speed – Rpm | 1200 | 1200 | 1200 | 1750 |
| High Idle Speed (No Load) – Rpm | 3600 | 3600 | 3600 | 3600 |
| Full Load Speed – Rpm | 3250 | 3250 | 3250 | 3250 |
| Crankcase Oil Capacity | 3 pints<br>(1.4 L) | 3 pints<br>(1.4 L) | 3 pints<br>1.4 L) | 2¾ pints<br>(1.3 L) |
| Weight – | | | | |
| Above 32°F (0°C) | SAE 30 | | | |
| 0°F (−18°C) to 32°F (0°C) | SAE 10W | | | |
| Below 0°F (−18°C) | SAE 5W-20 | | | |
| Transmission Oil Capacity | 10 oz.<br>(296 mL) | 10 oz.<br>(296 mL) | 10 oz.<br>(296 mL) | 24 oz.<br>(710 mL) |
| Weight | EP Lithium Grease | EP Lithium Grease | EP Lithium Grease | EP Lithium Grease |

| | MODELS | | | |
|---|---|---|---|---|
| | 133-638A<br>133-698A | 146-660A | 134-668A<br>134-669A | 146-672A |
| Engine Make | B&S | B&S | B&S | B&S |
| Model | 252707 | 190410 | 252707 | 251417 |
| Bore | 3-7/16 in.<br>(87.3 mm) | 3 in.<br>(76.2 mm) | 3-7/16 in.<br>(87.3 mm) | 3-7/16 in.<br>(87.3 mm) |
| Stroke | 2⅝ in.<br>(66.7 mm) | 2¾ in.<br>(69.8 mm) | 2⅝ in.<br>(66.7 mm) | 2⅝ in.<br>(66.7 mm) |
| Piston Displacement | 24.36 cu. in.<br>(399 cc) | 19.44 cu. in.<br>(319 cc) | 24.36 cu. in.<br>(399 cc) | 24.36 cu. in.<br>(399 cc) |
| Horsepower | 11 | 8 | 11 | 10 |
| Slow Idle Speed – Rpm | 1750 | 1750 | 1750 | 1750 |
| High Idle Speed (No Load) – Rpm | 3600 | 3600 | 3600 | 3600 |
| Full Load Speed – Rpm | 3250 | 3250 | 3250 | 3250 |
| Crankcase Oil Capacity | 3 pints<br>(1.4 L) | 3 pints<br>(1.4 L) | 3 pints<br>(1.4 L) | 3 pints<br>(1.4 L) |
| Weight – | | | | |
| Above 32°F (0°C) | SAE 30 | | | |
| 0°F (−18°C) to 32°F (0°C) | SAE 10W | | | |
| Below 0°F (−18°C) | SAE 5W-20 | | | |
| Transmission Oil Capacity | 24 oz.<br>(710 mL) | 3 pints<br>(1.4 L) | 24 oz.<br>(710 mL) | 3 pints<br>(1.4 L) |
| Weight | EP Lithium Grease | SAE 90 EP | EP Lithium Grease | SAE 90 EP |

# CONDENSED SPECIFICATIONS

| | MODELS | | | | |
|---|---|---|---|---|---|
| | 130-720A<br>132-730A | 130-760A<br>131-764A | 140-810A | 148-860A | 141-960 |
| Engine Make | B&S | B&S | B&S | B&S | B&S |
| Model | 252707 | 252707 | 252707 | 243431 | 320421 |
| Bore | 3-7/16 in.<br>(87.3 mm) | 3-7/16 in.<br>(87.3 mm) | 3-7/16 in.<br>(87.3 mm) | 3-1/16 in.<br>(77.8 mm) | 3-9/16 in.<br>(90.5 mm) |
| Stroke | 2⅝ in.<br>(66.7 mm) | 2⅝ in.<br>(66.7 mm) | 2⅝ in.<br>(66.7 mm) | 3¼ in.<br>(82.5 mm) | 3¼ in.<br>(82.5 mm) |
| Piston Displacement | 24.36 cu. in.<br>(399 cc) | 24.36 cu. in.<br>(399 cc) | 24.36 cu. in.<br>(399 cc) | 23.94 cu. in.<br>(392 cc) | 32.4 cu. in.<br>(531 cc) |
| Horsepower | 11 | 11 | 11 | 10 | 14 |
| Slow Idle Speed – Rpm | 1750 | 1750 | 1750 | 1200 | 1200 |
| High Idle Speed (No Load) – Rpm | 3600 | 3600 | 3600 | 3600 | 3600 |
| Full Load Speed – Rpm | 3250 | 3250 | 3250 | 3250 | 3250 |
| Crankcase Oil Capacity | 3 pints<br>(1.4 L) | 3 pints<br>(1.4 L) | 3 pints<br>(1.4 L) | 4 pints<br>(1.9 L) | 4 pints<br>(1.9 L) |
| Weight – | | | | | |
| Above 32°F (0°C) | | | SAE 30 | | |
| 0°F (−18°C) to 32°F (0°C) | | | SAE 10W | | |
| Below 0°F (−18°C) | | | SAE 5W-20 | | |
| Transmission Oil Capacity | 24 oz.<br>(710 mL) | ** | 4 pints<br>(1.9 L) | 4 pints<br>(1.9 L) | 4 pints<br>(1.9 L) |
| Weight | EP Lithium<br>Grease | ** | SAE 90 EP | SAE 90 EP | SAE 90 EP |
| Right Angle Drive Oil Capacity | .... | .... | .... | 6 oz.<br>(177 mL) | 6 oz.<br>(177 mL) |
| Weight | .... | .... | .... | EP Lithium<br>Grease | EP Lithium<br>Grease |
| Differential Oil Capacity | .... | 2¾ pints<br>(1.3 L) | .... | .... | .... |
| Weight | .... | SAE 90 EP | .... | .... | .... |

**Refer to Hydrostatic Transmission Lubrication section.

| | MODELS | | | | |
|---|---|---|---|---|---|
| | 142-960 | 144-960A | 141-990 | 142-990 | 141-990A |
| Engine Make | B&S | B&S | B&S | B&S | B&S |
| Model | 325431 | 326431 | 320427 | 325431 | 326431 |
| Bore | 3-9/16 in.<br>(90.5 mm) | 3-9/16 in.<br>(90.5 mm) | 3-9/16 in.<br>(90.5 mm) | 3-9/16 in.<br>(90.5 mm) | 3-9/16 in.<br>(90.5 mm) |
| Stroke | 3¼ in.<br>(82.5 mm) | 3¼ in.<br>(82.5 mm) | 3¼ in.<br>(82.5 mm) | 3¼ in.<br>(82.5 mm) | 3¼ in.<br>(82.5 mm) |
| Piston Displacement | 32.4 cu. in.<br>(531 cc) | 32.4 cu. in.<br>(531 cc) | 32.4 cu. in.<br>(531 cc) | 32.4 cu. in.<br>(531 cc) | 32.4 cu. in.<br>(531 cc) |
| Horsepower | 15 | 16 | 14 | 15 | 16 |
| Slow Idle Speed – Rpm | 1200 | 1200 | 1200 | 1200 | 1200 |
| High Idle Speed (No Load) – Rpm | 3600 | 3600 | 3600 | 3600 | 3600 |
| Full Load Speed – Rpm | 3250 | 3250 | 3250 | 3250 | 3250 |
| Crankcase Oil Capacity | | | 4 pints (1.9 L) | | |
| Weight – | | | | | |
| Above 32°F (0°C) | | | SAE 30 | | |
| 0°F (−18°C) to 32°F (0°C) | | | SAE 10W | | |
| Below 0°F (−18°C) | | | SAE 5W-20 | | |
| Transmission Oil Capacity | 4 pints<br>(1.9 L) | 4 pints<br>(1.9 L) | ** | ** | ** |
| Weight | SAE 90 EP | SAE 90 EP | ** | ** | ** |
| Right Angle Drive Oil Capacity | 6 oz.<br>(177 mL) | 6 oz.<br>(177 mL) | .... | .... | .... |
| Weight | EP Lithium<br>Grease | EP Lithium<br>Grease | .... | .... | .... |

**Refer to Hydrostatic Transmission Lubrication section.

# FRONT AXLE AND STEERING SYSTEM

## AXLE MAIN MEMBER

### Models 320-322-327-332-337-530-567-600-630A-632A-638A-668A-669A-698A

**REMOVE AND REINSTALL.** To remove axle main member (16–Fig. MT1), raise and support front of tractor and remove front wheels. Disconnect tie rod (14) from spindles (15). Unbolt steering arm (17) from left spindle and remove push cap (10) from right spindle, then withdraw spindles and bushings (11) from axle ends. Unbolt and separate axle from frame.

Reassemble by reversing removal procedure. Lubricate all bushings with SAE 30 oil.

### Models 660A-672A

**REMOVE AND REINSTALL.** To remove axle main member (4–Fig. MT2), disconnect tie rod outer ends from steering spindles (5 and 7). Raise and support front of tractor. Remove axle pivot bolt and roll axle assembly from tractor. Loosen set screws (2), remove collars (3) and remove steering spindles and wheels.

To reinstall axle, reverse removal procedure. Lubricate bushings with SAE 30 oil.

### Models 720A-730A-760A-764A-810A

**REMOVE AND REINSTALL.** To remove axle and main member (18–Fig. MT3), raise and support front of tractor. Disconnect drag link (12) from steering spindle (15). Remove axle pivot bolt (19) and lower axle from frame. Disconnect tie rod (16) from steering spindles. Remove dust cap and cotter pin from spindles, then remove steering spindles and wheels.

Reinstall axle by reversing removal procedure. Lubricate bushings with SAE 30 oil.

### Models 860A-960-960A-990-990A

**REMOVE AND REINSTALL.** To remove axle main member (5–Fig. MT4), disconnect drag link ball joint (10) from left steering spindle (11). Support tractor under main frame with a suitable jack. Remove axle pivot bolt (3), raise front of tractor and roll axle assembly away from tractor. Remove tie rod (8), loosen set screws (2) and remove collars (1). Withdraw steering spindles and wheels.

Inspect all parts for excessive wear and renew as necessary. Reinstall axle assembly and lubricate with multi-purpose grease.

## TIE RODS

### All Models

All models are equipped with adjustable tie rods. Refer to Figs. MT1 through MT4. Inspect ball joints for excessive wear and looseness and renew as needed.

To adjust front wheel toe-in, disconnect tie rod or rods from steering spindles. Loosen locknuts and adjust ball joints as required. Toe-in should be 1/8 inch (3 mm) measured as shown in Fig. MT5. On models with two tie rods, be sure to adjust both tie rods evenly.

## STEERING SPINDLES

### Models 320-322-327-332-337-530-567-600-630A-632A-638A-668A-669A-698A

**REMOVE AND REINSTALL.** To remove steering spindles, support front of tractor and remove front wheels. Disconnect drag link (20–Fig. MT1) and tie rod (14) from spindles. Remove push cap (10) from right spindle and steering arm (17) from left spindle, then withdraw spindles from axle.

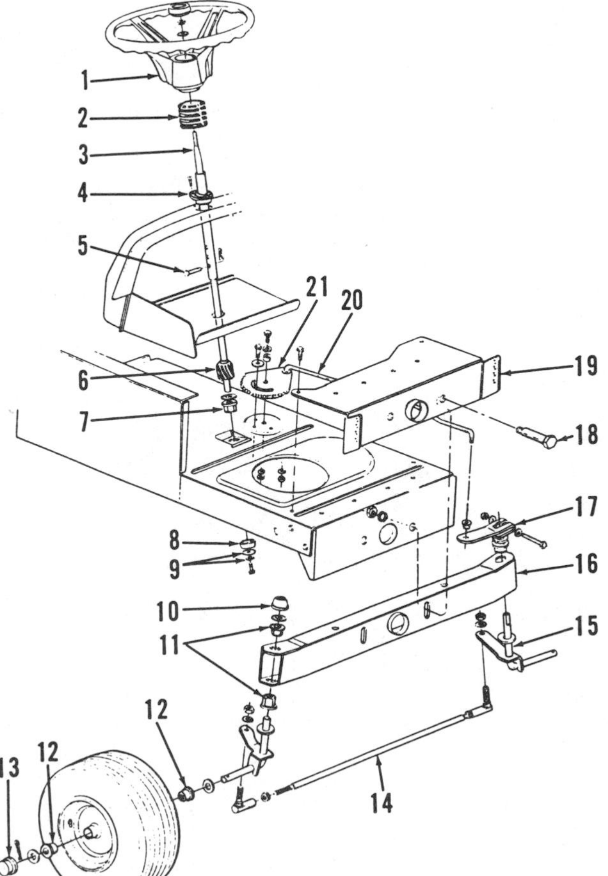

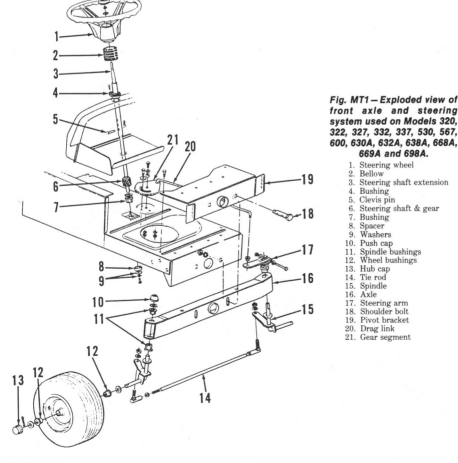

***Fig. MT1 — Exploded view of front axle and steering system used on Models 320, 322, 327, 332, 337, 530, 567, 600, 630A, 632A, 638A, 668A, 669A and 698A.***

1. Steering wheel
2. Bellow
3. Steering shaft extension
4. Bushing
5. Clevis pin
6. Steering shaft & gear
7. Bushing
8. Spacer
9. Washers
10. Push cap
11. Spindle bushings
12. Wheel bushings
13. Hub cap
14. Tie rod
15. Spindle
16. Axle
17. Steering arm
18. Shoulder bolt
19. Pivot bracket
20. Drag link
21. Gear segment

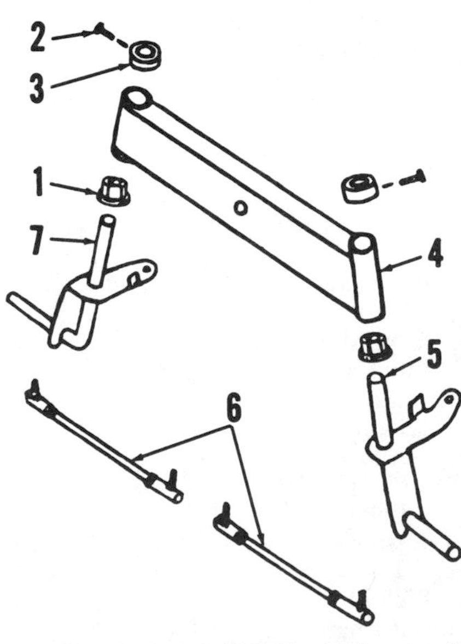

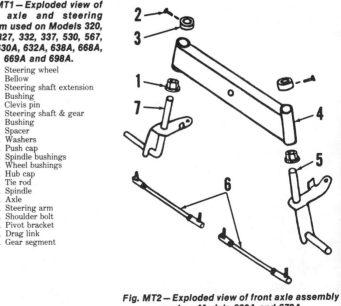

***Fig. MT2 — Exploded view of front axle assembly used on Models 660A and 672A.***

1. Flange bushing (4 used)
2. Set screw
3. Collar
4. Axle main member
5. Steering spindle (L.H.)
6. Tie rods
7. Steering spindle (R.H.)



Illustrations courtesy MTD Products, Inc.

Inspect spindles and bushings for wear and renew as needed. Reinstall by reversing removal procedure and lubricate with SAE 30 oil.

## Models 660A-672A

**REMOVE AND REINSTALL.** To remove steering spindles (5 and 7–Fig. MT2), support front of tractor and remove front wheels. Disconnect tie rod outer ends from spindle arms. Loosen set screw (2) and remove spindles and bushings (1) from axle ends.

Inspect parts for excessive wear and renew as required. To reinstall, reverse removal procedure. Lubricate with SAE 30 oil.

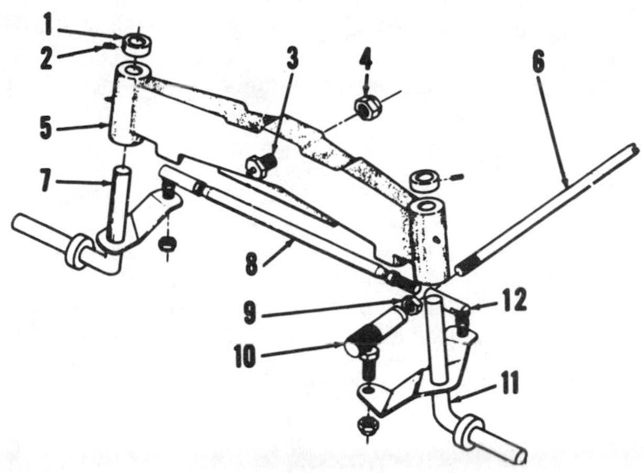

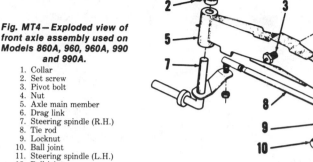

**Fig. MT4—Exploded view of front axle assembly used on Models 860A, 960, 960A, 990 and 990A.**

1. Collar
2. Set screw
3. Pivot bolt
4. Nut
5. Axle main member
6. Drag link
7. Steering spindle (R.H.)
8. Tie rod
9. Locknut
10. Ball joint
11. Steering spindle (L.H.)
12. Ball joint

## Models 720A-730A-760A-764A-810A

**REMOVE AND REINSTALL.** To remove steering spindles (15 and 17–Fig. MT3), raise and support front of tractor and remove wheels. Disconnect drag link (12) and tie rod (16) from spindle arms. Remove dust cover and cotter key from top of spindles, then withdraw spindles and bushings (13) from axle ends.

Reassemble by reversing removal procedure and lubricate with SAE 30 oil.

## Models 860A-960-960A-990-990A

**REMOVE AND REINSTALL.** To remove steering spindles (7 and 11–Fig. MT4), disconnect drag link ball joint (10) and tie rod (8) from spindle arms. Support front of tractor and remove front wheels. Loosen set screws (2), remove collars (1) and lower spindles from axle main member.

Inspect spindles and axle and renew as necessary. Lubricate with multi-purpose grease.

# STEERING GEAR

## Models 320-322-327-332-337-530-567-600-630A-632A-638A-668A-669A-698A

**REMOVE AND REINSTALL.** To remove steering gears, remove steering wheel cap, retaining nut and washer, then lift off steering wheel (1–Fig. MT1) and bellow (2). Disconnect battery cables. Remove clevis pin (5) and unbolt bushing (4), then withdraw shaft extension (3) and bushing. Disconnect drag link (20), then unbolt and remove gear segment (21). Remove retaining bolt from bottom of steering shaft (6) and withdraw washers (9), spacer (8), flange bushing (7) and steering shaft (6).

Inspect all parts for excessive wear or other damage and renew as needed. Reassemble by reversing removal procedure. Lubricate steering gears with multi-purpose lithium base grease and bushings with SAE 30 oil.

## Models 660A-672A

**REMOVE AND REINSTALL.** To remove steering gears, first disconnect tie rods from steering quadrant (13–Fig. MT6). Remove cap screw and washers from spacer (11) and the nut and Belleville washer from pivot bolt on bracket (12). Remove steering quadrant from tractor. Drive out roll pin (7), withdraw steering wheel and steering shaft assembly and remove pinion (9). Unbolt and remove bracket (10) with bushing (8). Remove cap (1), nut (2) and washer (3), then remove steering wheel (4) from steering shaft (6).

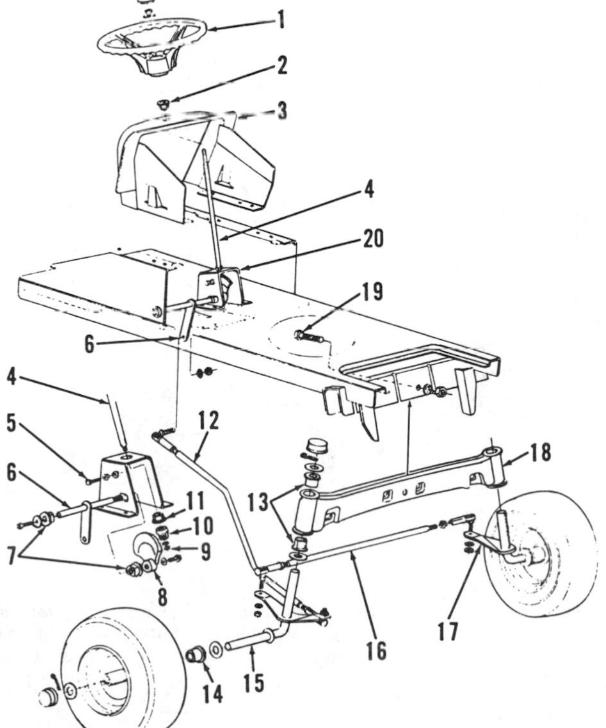


**Fig. MT3—Exploded view of front axle and steering system used on Model 720A, 730A, 760A, 764A and 810A tractors.**

1. Steering wheel
2. Bushing
3. Dash
4. Steering shaft
5. Adjusting screw
6. Steering arm
7. Bushings
8. Sector gear
9. Retaining nut
10. Pinion gear
11. Bushing
12. Drag link
13. Spindle bushings
14. Bushing
15. Spindle (R.H.)
16. Tie rod
17. Spindle (L.H.)
18. Axle main member
19. Pivot bolt
20. Steering gear housing

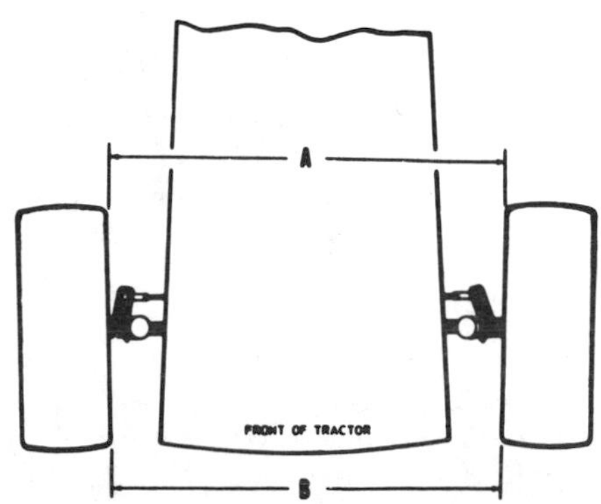


**Fig. MT5—Toe-in is correct when distance "B" is 1/8 inch (3 mm) less than distance "A" with both measurements taken at hub height.**

Reassemble by reversing disassembly procedure. Before bolting steering quadrant (13) in position, make certain steering wheel and front wheels are in straight ahead position. To adjust steering gear free play, loosen two mounting bolts in bracket (10). Move bracket forward to decrease free play, then tighten bracket mounting bolts.

Lubricate steering shaft bushings with SAE 30 oil and pinion gear and quadrant with multi-purpose grease.

### Models 720A-730A-760A-764A-810A

**REMOVE AND REINSTALL.** To remove steering gears, disconnect and remove battery and battery plate. Remove steering wheel and upper bushing (2–Fig. MT3). Disconnect drag link (12) from steering arm (6). Remove pivot bolt, washer and flange bushing (7) from steering arm (6). Remove four mounting bolts from steering support (20). Lift and rotate support to gain access to pinion gear (10). Remove pinion gear nut (9) and withdraw steering shaft (4). Unbolt and remove sector gear (8) from steering arm and shaft (6).

Reassemble by reversing removal procedure. Lubricate steering gears with light coat of multi-purpose grease and flange bushings with SAE 30 oil. Adjust backlash between steering gears by turning adjusting bolt (5) in or out, then tighten jam nut.

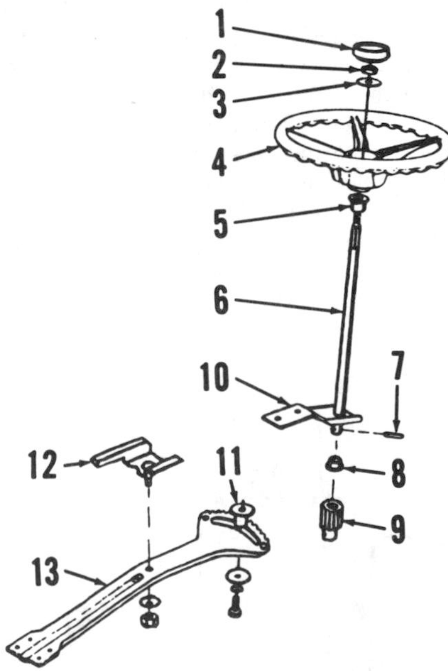


*Fig. MT6–Exploded view of steering gear assembly used on Models 660A and 672A.*

1. Cap
2. Nut
3. Wave washer
4. Steering wheel
5. Flange bushing
6. Steering shaft
7. Roll pin
8. Flange bushing
9. Pinion
10. Bracket
11. Spacer
12. Pivot bracket
13. Steering quadrant

### Models 860A-960-960A-990-990A

**REMOVE AND REINSTALL.** To remove steering gears, disconnect drag link (11–Fig. MT7 or MT8) from quadrant arm. On early models, loosen set screw in quadrant gear (10–Fig. MT7) and remove pivot shaft (9) and gear. Drive out roll pin (7), remove pinion gear (8) and withdraw steering shaft. On late models, remove pinion gear retaining nut and withdraw steering shaft (2–Fig. MT8) and pinion gear (6). Remove quadrant gear retaining nut and withdraw quadrant gear (7), pivot shaft (9) and bushings (10).

Reassemble by reversing removal procedure. On late models, adjust gear backlash by turning adjusting bolt (12–Fig. MT8) in or out as required. Lubricate with multi-purpose grease.

## ENGINE

### Models 320-322-327-332-337-530-567-600-630A-632A-638A-668A-669A-698A

**REMOVE AND REINSTALL.** To remove engine assembly, remove hood and grille support rods. Disconnect battery cables and electrical wiring from engine. Disconnect throttle and choke control cable. Disconnect fuel line. Remove engine pulley belt guard, then remove drive belt from pulley. Remove engine mounting cap screws and lift engine from tractor.

To reinstall engine, reverse removal procedure.

### Models 660A-672A

**REMOVE AND REINSTALL.** To remove engine assembly, unlatch rear of hood, then tilt hood and grille assembly forward. Disconnect battery cables and electrical wiring from engine. Disconnect throttle and choke control cable. Shut off fuel valve and disconnect fuel line. Remove brace from top of engine and muffler and belt guard from right side of engine. Remove belts from engine drive pulley. Remove engine mounting cap screws and lift engine from tractor.

To reinstall engine, reverse removal procedure.

### Models 720A-730A-760A-764A-810A

**REMOVE AND REINSTALL.** To remove engine assembly, remove hood and grille braces. Disconnect battery

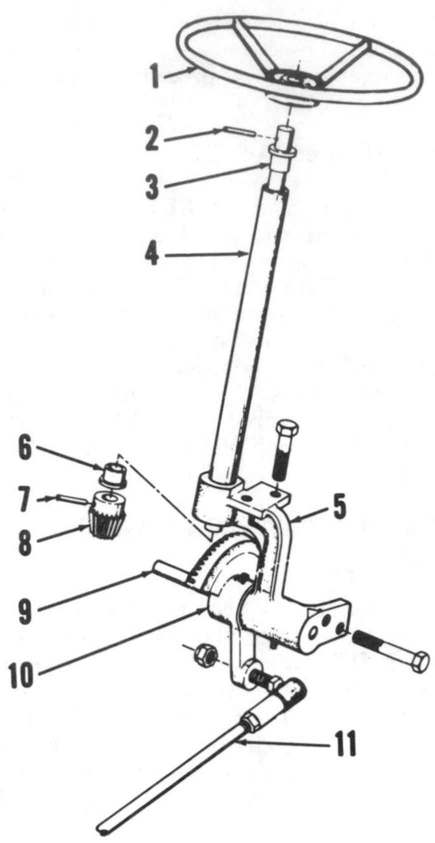


*Fig. MT7–Exploded view of steering gear assembly used on Models 860A. Models 960 and 990 are similar.*

1. Steering wheel
2. Roll pin
3. Bushing
4. Steering shaft
5. Steering support
6. Flange bushing
7. Roll pin
8. Pinion gear
9. Shaft
10. Quadrant gear
11. Drag link

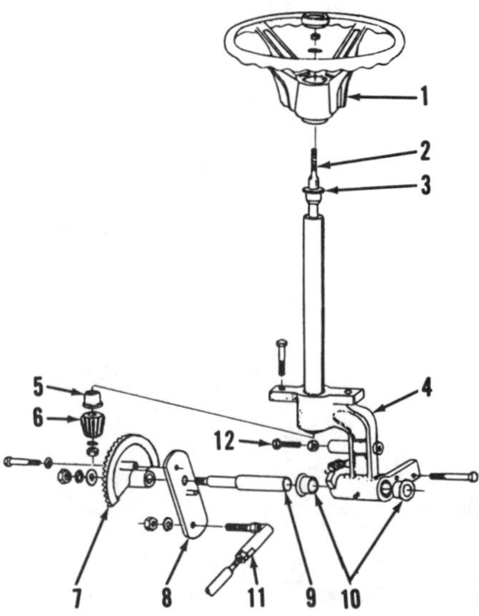


*Fig. MT8–Exploded view of steering gear assembly used on Model 990A.*

1. Steering wheel
2. Steering shaft
3. Bushing
4. Steering support
5. Bushing
6. Pinion gear
7. Quadrant gear
8. Steering arm
9. Pivot shaft
10. Bushings
11. Drag link
12. Adjusting bolt



Illustrations courtesy MTD Products, Inc.

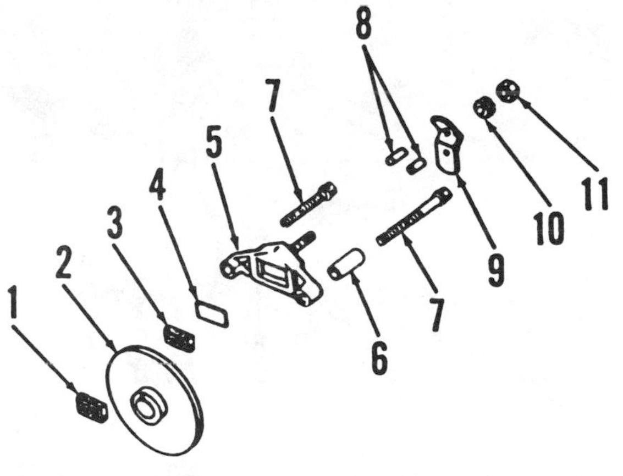


*Fig. MT9—Exploded view of typical disc brake assembly used on Models 630A, 632A, 638A, 668A, 669A, 698A, 720A and 730A. Models 320, 322, 327, 332, 337, 530, 567 and 600 are similar.*

1. Brake pad (inner)
2. Brake disc
3. Brake pad (outer)
4. Back-up plate
5. Carrier
6. Spacer
7. Cap screws
8. Dowel pins
9. Cam lever
10. Adjusting nut
11. Jam nut

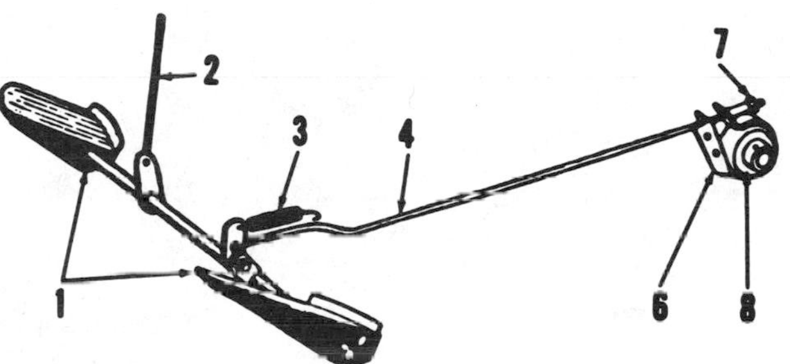


*Fig. MT10—View showing brake linkage and brake assembly used on Models 660A and 672A.*

1. Clutch-brake pedals
2. Clutch rod
3. Spring
4. Brake rod
6. Brake band
7. Adjusting nut
8. Brake drum

cables and engine electrical connections. Disconnect throttle and choke control cable. Remove drive belt from engine pulley. Remove engine mounting bolts and lift engine from tractor.

To reinstall engine, reverse removal procedure.

## Models 860A-960-960A

**REMOVE AND REINSTALL.** To remove engine assembly, remove hood and grille brace and disconnect battery cables. Unbolt right angle drive unit from frame, then move clutch and right angle drive assembly back from engine. Remove pto drive belts. Disconnect starter-generator wires, shut off fuel valve and disconnect fuel line. Disconnect throttle and choke control cables and remove muffler. Remove engine mounting bolts and lift engine from tractor.

To reinstall engine, reverse removal procedure. Adjust clutch and drive belt as necessary.

## Models 990-990A

**REMOVE AND REINSTALL.** To remove engine assembly, remove hood, grille brace and grille. Disconnect battery cables, starter wires and connectors at end of wiring harness. Disconnect fuel line and remove fuel tank and support bracket. Disconnect choke and throttle control cables. Loosen set screw in universal joint attached to engine crankshaft and drive out roll pin in opposite end of universal joint. Slide universal joint back on drive shaft. Remove lower pto belt guard and remove pto belts. Unbolt and lift engine from tractor.

Reinstall engine by reversing removal procedure.

## All Models

**OVERHAUL.** Engine make and model are listed at the beginning of this section. To overhaul engine components and accessories, refer to Briggs & Stratton section of this manual.

# CLUTCH AND BRAKE

## Models 320-322-327-332-337-530-567-600-630A-632A-638A-668A-669A-698A-720A-730A

**ADJUSTMENT.** The belt idler type clutch is spring loaded and does not require adjustment. If drive belt slips during normal operation due to excessive belt wear or stretching, renew drive belt.

To adjust disc brake, located on right side of transaxle, loosen jam nut (11–Fig. MT9) and turn adjusting nut (10) until disc is locked. Back off adjusting nut one complete turn and tighten jam nut.

**NOTE: When inside of cam lever (9–Fig. MT9) touches brake housing (5), brake pads (1 and 3) must be renewed.**

**R&R AND OVERHAUL BRAKE.** Disconnect brake linkage from cam lever. Unbolt and remove brake pad holder (5–Fig. MT9). Slide brake disc (2) off transaxle shaft and remove inner brake pad (1) from holder slot in transaxle housing.

Renew worn or damaged parts as necessary. Reassemble by reversing removal procedure and adjust as previously outlined.

## Models 660A-672A

**ADJUSTMENT.** A belt idler type clutch is used on these models. The clutch idler is spring loaded and does not require adjustment. However, angle of clutch-brake pedals (1–Fig. MT10) can be adjusted as follows: Remove cotter pin from lower end of clutch rod (2). Turn clutch rod in or out of ferrule as required until desired pedal angle is obtained.

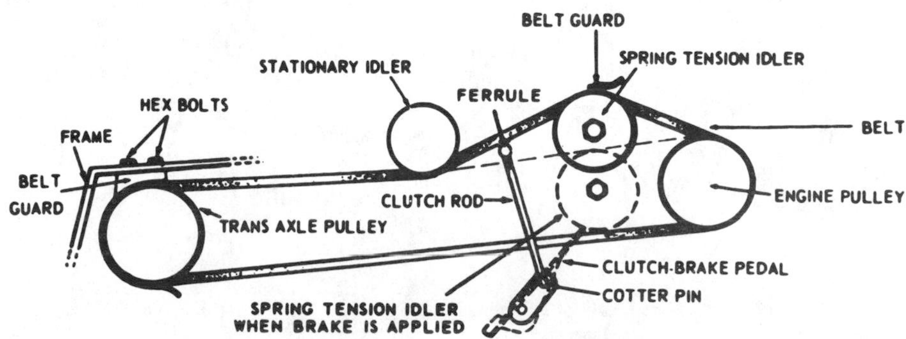


*Fig. MT11—Remove cotter pin and adjust length of clutch rod to adjust clutch-brake pedals to desired angle on Models 660A and 672A. Adjust brake linkage until tension idler is at disengaged position when brake is applied.*

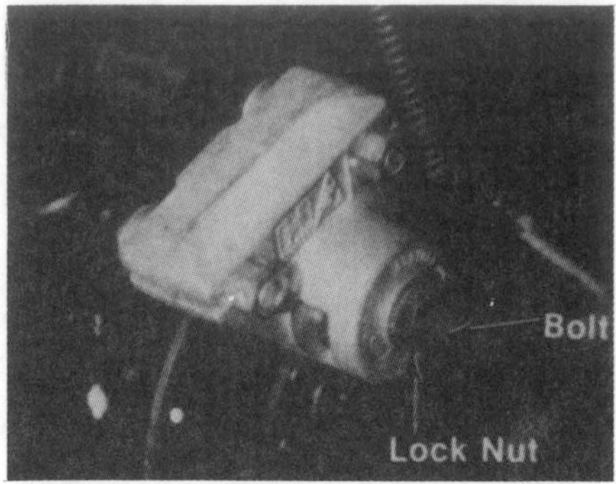


*Fig. MT12—To adjust disc brake on Models 760A, 764A and 810A, loosen locknut and turn center bolt all the way in. Then back bolt off one complete turn.*

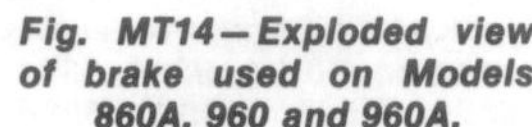

*Fig. MT14—Exploded view of brake used on Models 860A, 960 and 960A.*

1. Caliper & pad (inner)
2. Friction pad
3. Back-up disc
4. Caliper (outer)
5. Actuating pin
6. Spring
7. Cam lever
8. Washer
9. Adjusting nut
10. Spring (2 used)

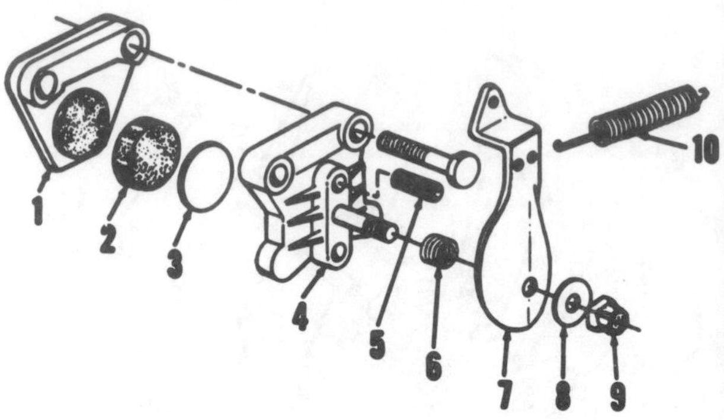


LEVELER SCREW
LOCK NUT
IDLER
PULLEY
A
TRANSMISSION PULLEY

*Fig. MT15—Adjust tension of transmission drive belt on Models 860A, 960 and 960A by turning leveler screw. Turning screw out increases belt tension. Belt should deflect approximately ½ inch (13 mm) "A" when 10 pound (44.5 N) force is applied.*

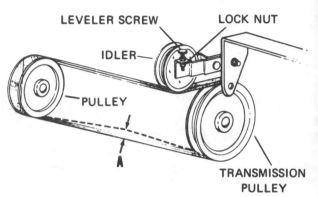

Adjust brake by turning adjusting nut (7) until top of spring tension idler is in disengaged position shown in Fig. MT11 when brake is applied. Brake service normally consists of renewing brake band (6–Fig. MT10).

## Models 760A-764A-810A

**ADJUSTMENT.** The clutch used on these models is spring loaded and does not require adjustment.

To adjust disc brake, loosen locknut (Fig. MT12) and turn adjusting bolt all the way in, then unscrew bolt one turn. Tighten locknut and check brake operation.

**R&R AND OVERHAUL BRAKE.** Disconnect tension spring and return spring from actuating lever. Unbolt and remove disc brake assembly from transaxle. Separate housings and remove brake pads.

Reinstall by reversing removal procedure and adjust brake as previously outlined.

## Models 860A-960-960A

**ADJUSTMENT.** The clutch used on these models is a spring loaded, double disc type and is operated by clutch pedal on left side of tractor. The clutch is adjusted by turning adjusting nut (15–Fig. MT13) at end of actuating chain (19). With clutch engaged, turn nut (15) until slack is removed from chain (19) and there is approximately 1/32 inch (1 mm) clearance between clutch arm (9) and bearing cover (10).

The brake is a disc type brake shown in Fig. MT14 and is operated by brake pedal on right side of tractor. To adjust brake, tighten nut (9) so tractor will stop when pedal is depressed but will still allow disc to turn free between brake pads when pedal is released.

To adjust tension of transmission drive belt, loosen locknut on belt idler leveler screw shown in Fig. MT15. Unscrewing leveler screw will increase belt tension. Belt deflection (A) should be ½ inch (13 mm) when 10 pounds (44.5 N) of force is applied midway between transmission input pulley and right angle drive pulley.

**R&R AND OVERHAUL CLUTCH.** To remove clutch assembly, disconnect clutch actuating rod and chain (19–Fig. MT13) from clutch arm (9). Remove clutch arm anchor bolt, then unbolt right angle drive bracket from frame. Move right angle drive and clutch assembly rearward and remove transmission drive belt from right angle drive pulley. Lift right angle drive and clutch assembly from tractor. Place right angle drive bracket in a vise and place a pair of "C" clamps as shown in Fig. MT16. Tighten clamps so pressure is relieved from upper pin (2), then drive out pin. Slowly release "C" clamps to relieve spring pressure. Remainder of disassembly is evident.

To reassemble clutch, reverse disassembly procedure. Adjust clutch and drive belt as outlined in preceding paragraph.

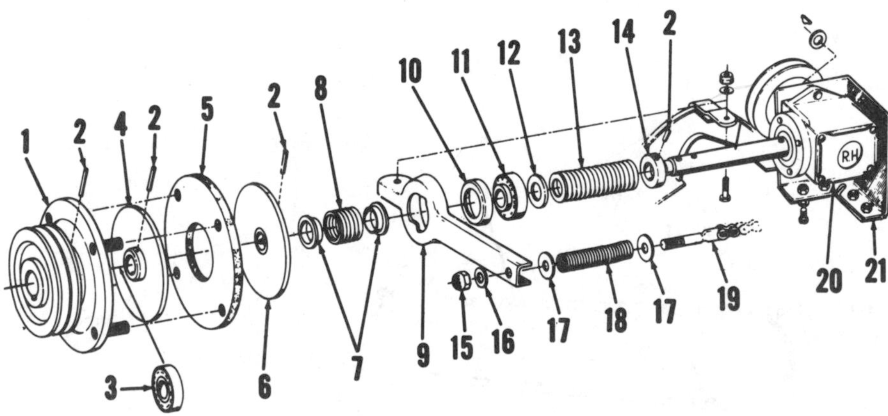

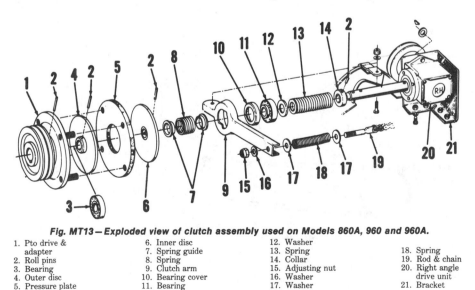

*Fig. MT13—Exploded view of clutch assembly used on Models 860A, 960 and 960A.*

1. Pto drive & adapter
2. Roll pins
3. Bearing
4. Outer disc
5. Pressure plate
6. Inner disc
7. Spring guide
8. Spring
9. Clutch arm
10. Bearing cover
11. Bearing
12. Washer
13. Spring
14. Collar
15. Adjusting nut
16. Washer
17. Washer
18. Spring
19. Rod & chain
20. Right angle drive unit
21. Bracket



Illustrations courtesy MTD Products, Inc.

**R&R AND OVERHAUL BRAKE.** Disconnect tension spring and return spring from cam lever (7–Fig. MT14). Unbolt and remove disc brake assembly.

Inspect and renew components as required. Reinstall brake assembly and adjust as previously outlined.

### Models 990-990A

**ADJUSTMENT.** These tractors are not equipped with a clutch. Brake pedal on right side of tractor actuates a disc brake on left side of reduction drive housing. As pedal is depressed, hydrostatic transmission control linkage is returned to neutral position. Refer to HYDROSTATIC TRANSMISSION section for neutral adjustment.

To adjust disc brake, tighten adjusting nut (15–Fig. MT17) until desired braking action is obtained. Be sure brake does not drag when brake pedal is released.

**R&R AND OVERHAUL BRAKE.** To remove brake, disconnect linkage from cam lever (16–Fig. MT17). Unbolt and remove housing (10), slide brake disc (8) off brake shaft and remove inner brake pad (7).

Inspect and renew parts as necessary. Reassemble brake by reversing removal procedure and adjust as previously outlined.

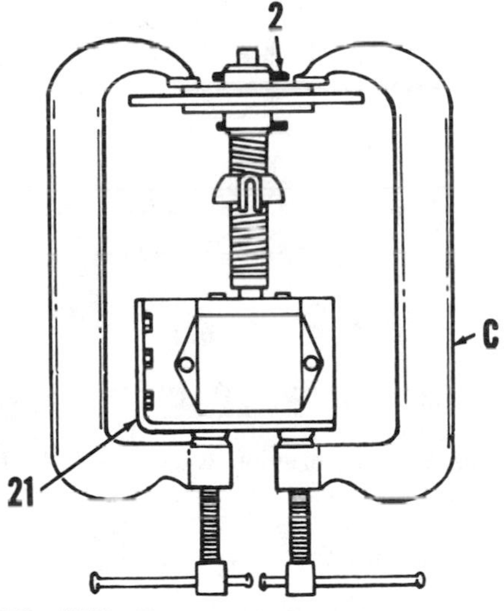


*Fig. MT16—To remove roll pin (2), tighten "C" clamps against outer disc and right angle drive bracket (21).*

## TRACTION DRIVE BELT

### Models 320-322-327-332-337

**R&R DRIVE BELTS.** To remove rear drive belt, start engine and place shift lever in neutral. Place speed control lever in high speed position and stop engine. Disconnect spark plug. Disconnect the large spring from transaxle support bracket (Fig. MT18). Spring puller (part 732-0571) is available to assist in removal of spring. Disconnect small spring from bolt on right side of frame and transaxle support bracket. Remove brake rod out of variable speed pulley bracket and loosen bolts which retain variable speed bracket to allow clearance to remove belts. Remove rear drive belt from around top of variable speed pulley. Remove belt from transaxle pulley and idler pulley.

To remove the front drive belt, remove the two self-tapping screws retaining engine pulley belt guard and remove belt guard. Remove drive belt from engine pulley and variable speed pulley.

Reinstall drive belts by reversing removal procedure.

### Models 530-567-600

**R&R DRIVE BELTS.** To remove rear drive belt, remove the two screws retaining transaxle cover. Unplug safety wire and remove cover. Push idler pulley toward right side of tractor and lift belt over idler pulley. Remove belt from variable speed pulley. Remove the two bolts retaining shift lever bracket to the frame on left side of tractor and swing bracket toward right so belt can be removed from transaxle pulley.

To remove front drive belt, first remove rear drive belt from idler pulley and variable speed pulley. Place lift lever in disengaged position. Remove the three cap screws (belt guides) from engine pulley belt guard. Remove the two bolts on each side of frame which retain engine pulley belt guard to frame. Slip engine pulley belt guard back and to the right to remove. Place clutch/brake pedal in park position. Push forward on variable speed pulley and lift belt off engine pulley. Release clutch/brake pedal. Work belt off variable speed pulley to remove.

Reverse removal procedure for reinstallation.

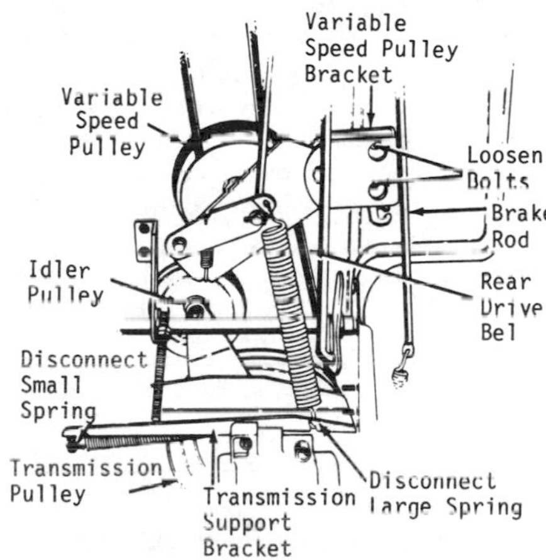


*Fig. MT18—View of drive belt and variable speed pulley arrangement used on Models 320, 322, 327, 332 and 337.*

*Fig. MT19—To remove drive belt on Models 720A and 730A, remove lower idler by taking center bolt out, unhook idler spring and swing idler plate out of the way.*

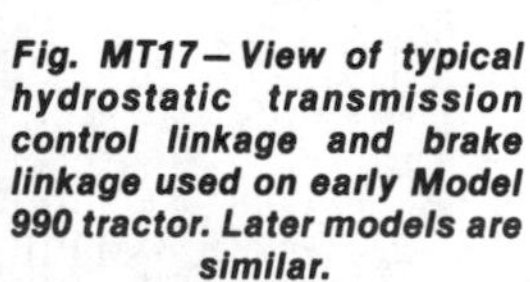

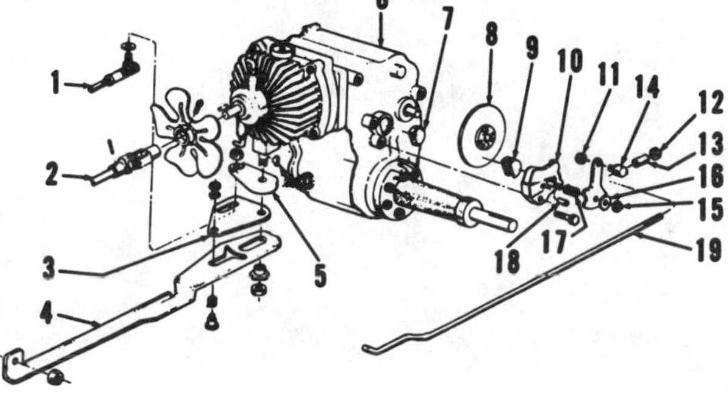

*Fig. MT17—View of typical hydrostatic transmission control linkage and brake linkage used on early Model 990 tractor. Later models are similar.*

1. Transmission control rod
2. Drive shaft & "U" joint
3. Control plate
4. Neutral return link
5. Control arm
6. Reduction drive unit
7. Brake pad (inner)
8. Brake disc
9. Brake pad (outer)
10. Brake housing
11. Nut
12. Adjusting nut
13. Spacer
14. Link
15. Adjusting nut
16. Cam lever
17. Spring
18. Pin (2 used)
19. Brake rod

### Models 630A-632A-638A-668A-669A-698A

**R&R DRIVE BELT.** To remove drive belt, first remove mower if so equipped. Remove engine pulley belt guard. Unbolt and remove idler pulley. Unbolt transaxle pulley belt guard and slide guard rearward. Unbolt and remove transaxle shift lever. Remove belt from engine pulley, then lift belt up and over transaxle pulley.

Install new belt by reversing removal procedure. Be sure back of belt is against idler pulley and belt is inside belt keepers.

### Models 660A-672A

**R&R DRIVE BELT.** To remove drive belt, first unbolt and remove belt guard from right side of engine. Remove pto drive belt if so equipped. Loosen bolt in center of spring tension idler and remove cap screw securing engine pulley to crankshaft. Slide pulleys out and remove drive belt from pulleys. Remove shoulder bolt or belt guard near transaxle input pulley and remove drive belt from tractor. Install new belt by reversing removal procedure. Adjust pedal angle and brake as required.

### Models 720A-730A

**R&R DRIVE BELT.** To remove drive belt, depress clutch pedal and set parking brake. Remove transaxle belt guard and slip belt from transaxle pulley. Remove lower idler by taking out center bolt (Fig. MT19). Unhook idler spring and swing idler plate out of the way. Remove cotter pin from clutch shaft and pull shaft from bracket (MT20). Remove upper idler pulley and shift rod cotter pin, then pull rod from bracket. Renew drive belt and reverse disassembly procedure to reassemble.

*Fig. MT20—To aid in drive belt renewal, remove cotter pin from clutch shaft and pull shaft from bracket.*

### Models 760A-764A-810A

**R&R DRIVE BELT.** To remove front drive belt, depress clutch-brake pedal and engage pedal lock. Unscrew belt guard retainer and swing guard towards front of tractor (Fig. MT21).

**NOTE: Observe twist in front belt. If new belt is installed backwards, tractor will run backwards.**

Loosen stop bolt behind jackshaft pulley (Fig. MT22) and pry pulley forward while slipping front belt off jackshaft pulley and engine pulley. Reverse procedure to install new belt.

*Fig. MT21—Unscrew belt guard and swing towards front of tractor.*

*Fig. MT22—To remove front drive belt on Models 760A, 764A and 810A, use a bar to pry pulley assembly forward and unhook belt from pulley.*

To remove rear drive belt on Models 760A and 764A, depress clutch-brake pedal and engage pedal lock. Remove belt guard pins (Fig. MT23) from jackshaft assembly. Remove idler pulley by removing center bolt. Remove hydrostatic pulley belt guard and loosen rear axle mounting bolts. Pry frame away from hydrostatic unit about 1/4 inch (6 mm) and remove belt from pulleys. Reverse procedure to install new belt.

To remove rear drive belt on Model 810A, depress clutch-brake pedal and engage pedal lock. Remove belt guard pins (Fig. MT23) from jackshaft assembly. Remove idler pulley by removing center bolt. Unbolt transaxle pulley and slide pulley and belt off. Reverse procedure to install a new belt.

### Models 860A-960-960A

**R&R DRIVE BELT.** To remove drive belt, turn leveler screw (Fig. MT15) in to release tension. Slip belt out of pulleys. Reverse procedure to install new belt. Unscrew leveler screw to increase belt tension. Belt should deflect 1/2 inch (13 mm) when 10 pounds (44.5 N) of force is applied midway between pulleys.

## RIGHT ANGLE DRIVE UNIT

### Models 860A-960-960A

**R&R AND OVERHAUL.** To remove right angle drive unit, remove clutch assembly as previously outlined, then separate clutch from right angle drive. Remove pulley and mounting bracket from drive unit.

*Fig. MT23—To remove rear clutch belt on Models 760A, 764A and 810A, remove belt guard pins and depress clutch-brake pedal.*



Illustrations courtesy MTD Products, Inc.

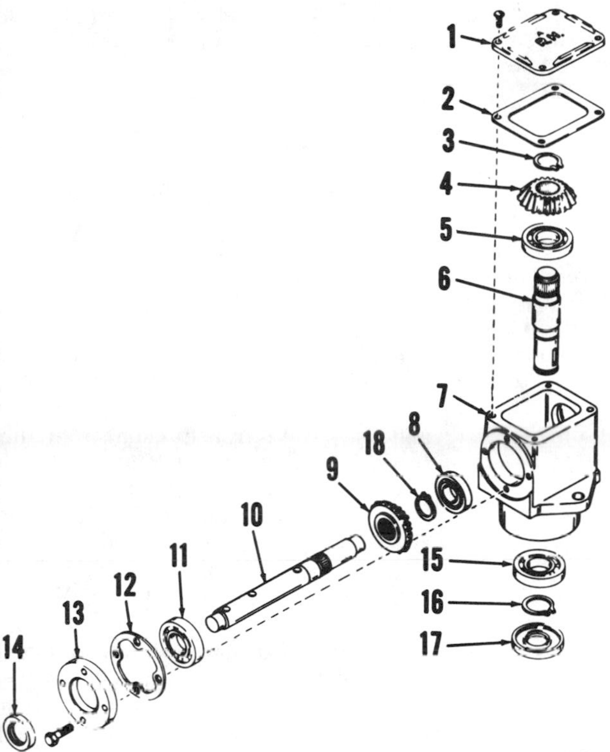

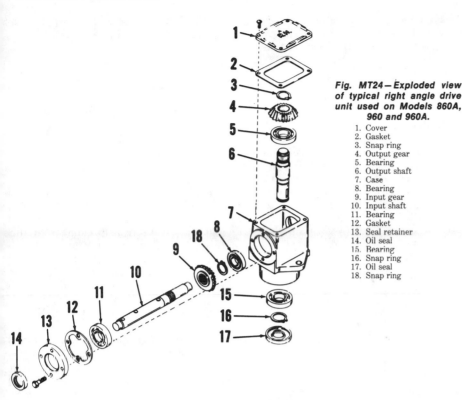

*Fig. MT24—Exploded view of typical right angle drive unit used on Models 860A, 960 and 960A.*

1. Cover
2. Gasket
3. Snap ring
4. Output gear
5. Bearing
6. Output shaft
7. Case
8. Bearing
9. Input gear
10. Input shaft
11. Bearing
12. Gasket
13. Seal retainer
14. Oil seal
15. Bearing
16. Snap ring
17. Oil seal
18. Snap ring

To disassemble right angle drive unit, remove cover (1–Fig. MT24) and gasket (2). Unbolt and remove seal retainer (13) with oil seal (14) and gasket (12). Unseat snap ring (18) from its groove in input shaft (10). Withdraw input shaft and bearing (11) and remove snap ring (18) and gear (9) through cover opening of case. Remove oil seal (17) and snap ring (16), then drive output shaft (6) with bearing (5) and gear (4) out through cover opening of case. Bearings (8 and 15) can now be removed from case. Remove snap ring (3), output gear (4) and bearing (5) from output shaft. Remove bearing (11) from input shaft.

Clean and inspect all parts and renew any showing excessive wear or other damage. Reassemble by reversing disassembly procedure and fill unit with 6 ounces (177 mL) of EP lithium grease.

# HYDROSTATIC TRANSMISSION

## LUBRICATION

### Models 760A-764A

The hydrostatic transmission is equipped with an integral reservoir. The reservoir is factory filled with SAE 20 engine oil and with SE rating.

If contamination is observed in reservoir tank or natural color of transmission fluid has changed (black or milky), fluid should be drained and renewed. To drain fluid, remove transmission from reduction gear housing, remove reservoir and vent plug from body. Turn unit upside down and allow to drain.

**NOTE: Reservoir tank has left hand threads.**

When refilling transmission, add oil until fluid overflows out vent hole in body. Then, reinstall vent plug and fill reservoir tank to COLD mark on tank.

### Models 990-990A

The Model 10 hydrostatic transmission shares a common reservoir with reduction drive and differential unit. Reservoir is factory filled with SAE 20 weight oil. When adding or renewing oil, use a high quality SAE 20 weight oil with SE rating. Reservoir capacity is approximately 10 pints (4.7 L).

Transmission oil is routed through an external oil filter located under left side of frame. Oil filter should be renewed after every 100 hours of operation or yearly, whichever comes first. Use Fram filter PH-16 or equivalent.

## LINKAGE ADJUSTMENT

### Models 760A-764A

If tractor moves when hydrostatic control lever is in neutral position, control linkage adjustment is needed. To adjust linkage, raise and block rear of tractor so both rear wheels are free to rotate. Place control lever in neutral position and loosen locknuts on connecting rod shown in Fig. MT26. State engine and release clutch pedal. Turn connecting rod until rear wheels stop turning. Shut off engine and tighten locknuts.

**CAUTION: Keep hands away from transmission cooling fan and drive belts during adjustment.**

### Models 990-990A

If tractor creeps forward or backward when control lever is in neutral position, hydrostatic control linkage adjustment is needed. To adjust control linkage, raise and securely block rear of tractor so rear wheels are free to rotate. Loosen nut (13–Fig. MT28) on brake rod (14) until brake is ineffective when pedal is fully depressed. Depress brake pedal and engage park lock. Control lever should be in neutral position. If not, adjust jam nuts (Fig. MT27) as required until control lever is in neutral position on quadrant.

Place reduction drive in low range, start engine and move transmission con-

*Fig. MT26—Underside view of hydrostatic transmission and control linkage rod on Models 760A and 764A.*

trol lever to forward drive position. Fully depress brake pedal, then release pedal. If rear wheels creep in either direction, refer to Fig. MT28 and loosen nut (6). Hold control plate (7) stationary and move control arm (8) until rear wheels stop turning. Tighten nut (6) and recheck adjustment. When neutral adjustment is complete, adjust brake linkage as required.

**CAUTION: Use extreme care not to get hands in transmission cooling fan during adjustment.**

If control lever has a tendency to return to neutral when tractor is under a hard pull, turn friction adjusting screw (Fig. MT27) in (clockwise) to increase lever friction. Be sure friction control is free of grease and oil.

### REMOVE AND REINSTALL

#### Models 760A-764A

To remove hydrostatic transmission, raise and block rear wheels. Depress clutch-brake pedal and remove idler pulley assembly. Remove seat and fender assemblies. Remove belt guide pin on pulley assembly and remove final drive belt. Disconnect transmission linkage at transmission and remove brake caliper assembly. Remove frame mounting bolt and axle housing retaining bolts, then remove transmission and differential assembly from tractor. Separate transmission from differential.

**CAUTION: If oil expansion reservoir is removed, precautions should be taken to prevent entrance of dirt or other foreign material into transmission. Reservoir tank has left hand threads.**

Reinstall transmission in tractor in reverse order of removal. Fill differential housing wiht 2¾ pints (1.3 L) of SAE 90 EP gear oil. Fill hydrostatic transmission reservoir with SAE 20 engine oil rated SE to level indicated on reservoir. Check and adjust linkage if necessary.

#### Models 990-990A

To remove hydrostatic transmission, remove fenders, seat and rear frame cover. Disconnect hydraulic hoses and plug or cap openings to prevent dirt from entering system. Drive out roll pin in rear universal joint and loosen set screw in cooling fan hub. Push universal joint forward on drive shaft and remove fan. Disconnect transmission control rod and neutral linkage from transmission. Unbolt and lift out the unit.

Reinstall unit in tractor by reversing removal procedure. Fill with recommended transmission fluid and adjust linkage as outlined in previous paragraphs.

### OVERHAUL

#### All Models

Models 760A and 764A are equipped with an Eaton Model 6 hydrostatic transmission. Models 990 and 990A are equipped with an Eaton Model 10 hydrostatic transmission. Refer to the appropriate Eaton section in HYDROSTATIC TRANSMISSION SERVICE section for overhaul procedure.

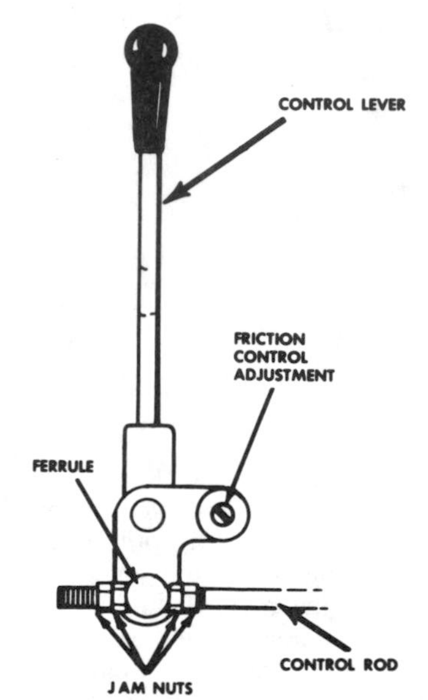


***Fig. MT27—Hydrostatic control lever position adjusting nuts. Note location of friction control adjustment screw.***

# REDUCTION GEARS AND DIFFERENTIAL

#### Models 760A-764A

**R&R AND OVERHAUL.** To remove reduction gear and differential unit, refer to hydrostatic transmission section and separate transmission from differential. Remove wheel and hub assemblies from axles. Remove park brake disc from brake shaft. Clean axle shafts and remove any burrs from shafts. Unscrew cap screws and drive out dowel pins in cover (29–Fig. MT33). Lift cover off case and axle shaft. Withdraw brake shaft (5), idler gear (4) and thrust washers (3 and 6) from case. Remove output shaft (11), output gear (10), spacer (9), thrust washer (8) and differential assembly from case. Axle shaft housings (20 and 22) must be pressed from case and cover.

To disassemble differential, unscrew cap screws (17) and separate axle shaft and carrier assemblies from ring gear (28). Drive blocks (25), bevel pinion gears (26) and drive pin (27) can now be removed from ring gear. Remove snap rings (12) and slide axle shafts (18 and 23) from axle gears (13) and carriers (16 and 24).

Clean and inspect all parts and renew any parts damaged or excessively worn. When installing needle bearings, press bearings in from inside of case or cover until bearings are 0.015-0.020 inch

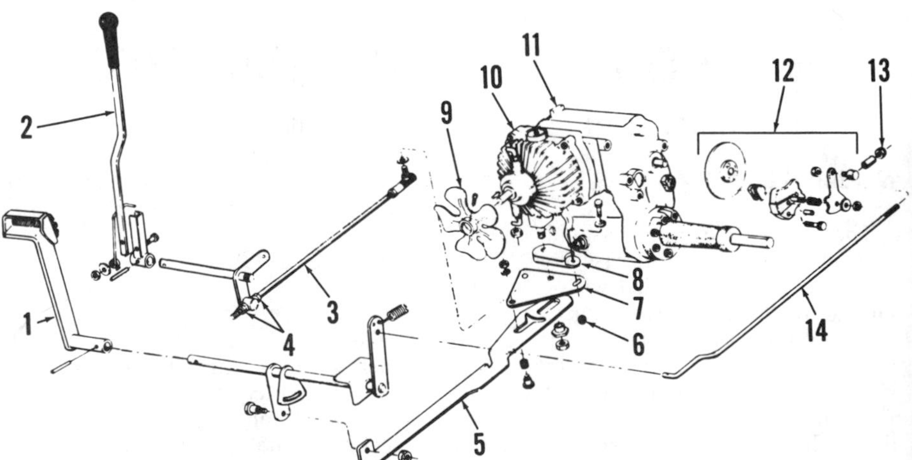


***Fig. MT28—Exploded view of hydrostatic control linkage, neutral return linkage and brake linkage used on 990 series tractors.***

1. Brake pedal
2. Control lever
3. Control rod
4. Adjusting nuts
5. Neutral return link
6. Adjusting nut
7. Control plate
8. Control arm
9. Cooling fan
10. Hydrostatic transmission
11. Gear reduction & differential unit
12. Disc brake assy.
13. Nut
14. Brake rod

(0.381-0.508 mm) below thrust surfaces. Be sure heads of differential cap screws (17) and right axle shaft (18) are installed in right carrier housing (16). Right axle shaft is installed through case (1). Tighten differential cap screws to 7 ft.-lbs. (9 N•m) and cover cap screws to 10 ft.-lbs. (14 N•m). Differential assembly and output shaft (11) must be installed in case at same time. Remainder of assembly is reverse of disassembly procedure. Refill differential unit with 2¾ pints (1.3 L) of SAE 90 EP gear oil.

### Models 990-990A

**R&R AND OVERHAUL.** To remove two-speed reduction drive and differential assembly, remove fenders, seat and rear frame cover. Disconnect hydraulic hoses and plug or cap openings to prevent dirt from entering system. Drive out roll pin in rear universal joint and loosen set screw in cooling fan. Push universal joint forward on drive shaft and remove cooling fan. Disconnect transmission control rod and neutral linkage from hydrostatic transmission, then disconnect brake rod. Support tractor frame, unbolt reduction drive and differential assembly from tractor, raise rear of frame and roll assembly rearward from tractor. Clean exterior of assembly, drain fluid and remove hydrostatic transmission. Remove disc brake assembly and rear wheel and hub assemblies.

To disassemble reduction drive and differential, remove axle housings (15–Fig. MT34). Position unit with cover (13) facing up, then unbolt and remove cover. Lift out differential and axle assembly (40 through 54). Remove output shaft (36), gear (35) and thrust washers (37). Unscrew set screw (2) and remove spring (3) and ball (4). Remove brake shaft (32), sliding gear (33), shift fork (10) and shift rail (8). Remove input shaft and gear components (18 through 26).

To disassemble differential, remove cap screws (53) and separate differential carriers (41 and 52) and axles from ring gear assembly. Remove snap rings (44 and 49) and separate axle gears (43 and 50), thrust washers (42 and 51) and axle shafts (40 and 54). Remove pinions (47) and separate body cores (45 and 48) from ring gear (46).

Inspect components for damage or excessive wear. To reassemble, reverse disassembly procedure. Check movement of shift rail when tightening set screw (2). Install gears (22 and 25) so bevels on gear teeth face together as shown in Fig. MT35. Install carrier cap screws (53–Fig. MT34) so heads of cap screws are on side of shorter carrier (52). Do not rotate axle housings after housings have been pressed tight against seals (11) as seals might be cut.

Install unit in tractor by reversing removal procedure. Fill with recommended transmission fluid and adjust linkage as outlined in previous paragraphs.

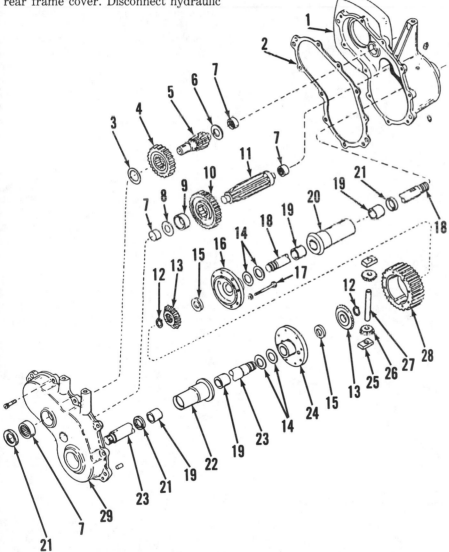

***Fig. MT33 – Exploded view of Peerless 1341 gear reduction and differential unit used on Models 760A and 764A.***

1. Case
2. Gasket
3. Washer
4. Idler gear
5. Brake shaft
6. Washer
7. Bearing
8. Washer
9. Spacer
10. Output gear
11. Output shaft
12. Snap ring
13. Side gears
14. Thrust washers
15. Thrust washer
16. Differential carrier
17. Bolt
18. Axle shaft (R.H.)
19. Bushing
20. Axle housing
21. Oil seal
22. Axle housing
23. Axle shaft (L.H.)
24. Differential carrier
25. Drive block
26. Drive pinion
27. Drive pin
28. Ring gear
29. Cover

# TRANSAXLE

## LUBRICATION

### Models 320-322-327-332-337-530-567-600

All models are equipped with MTD Model 717-0750A transaxle. Transaxle is lubricated and sealed at the factory with 10 ounces (296 mL) of EP lithium base grease.

### All Other Models

All models are equipped with a Peerless transaxle. Refer to the CONDENSED SPECIFICATIONS tables at the beginning of this service section for transaxle fluid capacity and fluid type for model being serviced.

## REMOVE AND REINSTALL

### Models 320-322-327-332-337-530-567-600

To remove transaxle assembly, first remove drive belts as outlined under

R&R DRIVE BELTS in TRACTION DRIVE BELT section. Disconnect all shift linkage and brake linkage at transaxle. Support rear of tractor and remove all bolts retaining transaxle to frame. Raise rear of tractor and roll transaxle assembly out from under tractor.

Reinstall by reversing removal procedure. Adjust disc brake as outlined under ADJUSTMENT in CLUTCH AND BRAKE section.

## Models 630A-632A-638A-668A-669A-720A-730A

To remove transaxle assembly, unbolt and remove seat plate and rear fenders. Support tractor main frame. Remove transaxle belt keeper assembly, then depress clutch-brake pedal and work drive belt off transaxle pulley. Disconnect shift linkage and brake linkage. Unbolt transaxle from support brackets and roll transaxle rearward away from tractor. Unbolt and remove brake pad holder and brake disc. Remove rear wheel and hub assemblies.

Reinstall transaxle by reversing removal procedure. Adjust brake linkage as required.

## Models 660A-672A-810A

To remove transaxle assembly, unbolt and remove rear frame cover. Remove shoulder bolt or belt guard near transaxle input pulley. Remove pulley retaining nut, depress clutch-brake pedal and slide belt and pulley from transaxle input shaft. Disconnect brake linkage and support tractor main frame. Remove transaxle mounting bolts, raise rear of tractor and roll transaxle assembly rearward from tractor. On Models 660A and 672A, unbolt and remove brake band and brake drum. On Model 810A, disconnect brake caliper and remove rotor assembly. Remove rear wheel and hub assemblies.

Reinstall transaxle by reversing removal procedure. Fill transaxle unit to level plug opening with SAE 90 EP gear oil. Adjust brake linkage as necessary.

## Models 860A-960-960A

To remove transaxle assembly, loosen locknut and turn idler leveler screw inward until drive belt can be removed from transaxle input pulley. Disconnect brake linkage and remove gear shift knob. Support tractor under main frame. Unbolt transaxle from tractor frame, raise rear of tractor and roll transaxle assembly rearward from tractor. Unbolt and remove disc brake assembly, transaxle input pulley and rear wheel and hub assemblies.

Reinstall transaxle by reversing removal procedure. Adjust brake, clutch and drive belt tension as required.

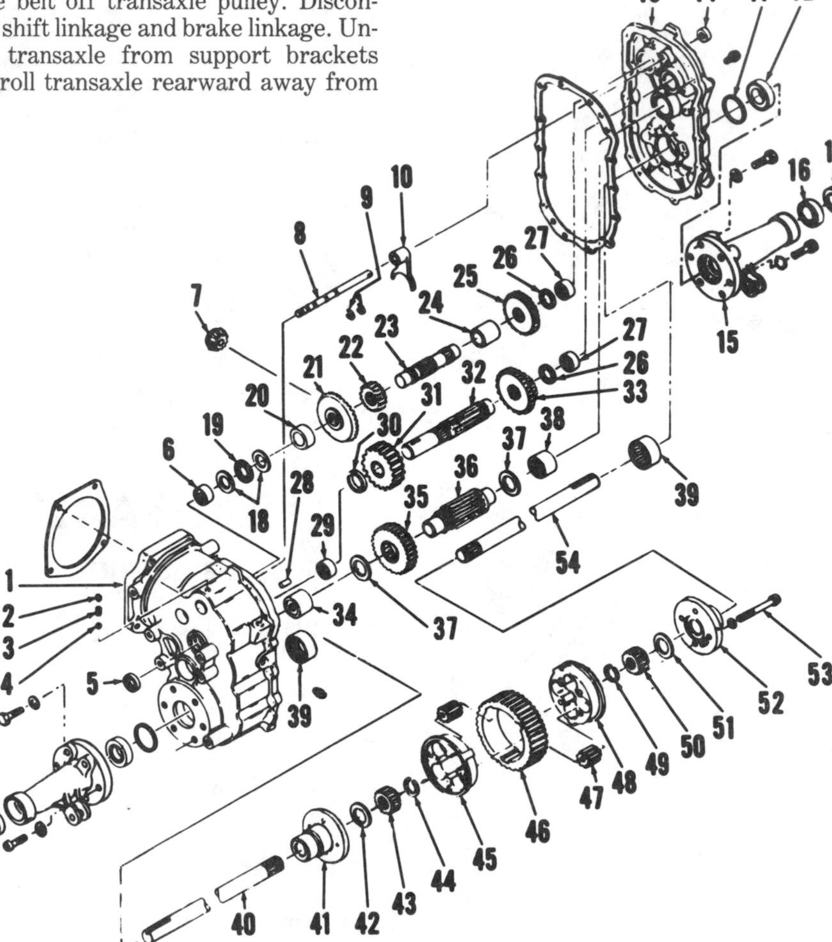

***Fig. MT34—Exploded view of Peerless Model 2503 2-speed reduction drive and differential assembly used on 990 and 990A tractors.***

1. Case
2. Set screw
3. Spring
4. Ball
5. Seal
6. Needle bearing
7. Transmission output gear
8. Shift rail
9. Snap rings
10. Shift fork
11. Quad ring
12. Tapered roller bearing
13. Cover
14. Seal
15. Axle housing
16. Ball bearing
17. Oil seal
18. Thrust washers
19. Thrust bearing
20. Spacer
21. Bevel gear
22. Gear (16T)
23. Shaft
24. Spacer
25. Gear (23T)
26. Thrust washer
27. Needle bearing
28. Dowel pin
29. Needle bearing
30. Spacer
31. Gear
32. Brake shaft
33. Sliding gear
34. Needle bearing
35. Output gear
36. Output shaft
37. Thrust washer
38. Needle bearing
39. Needle bearing
40. Axle (L.H.)
41. Differential carrier (L.H.)
42. Thrust washer
43. Axle gear
44. Snap ring
45. Body core
46. Ring gear
47. Pinion gears (8)
48. Body core
49. Snap ring
50. Axle gear
51. Thrust washer
52. Differential carrier (R.H.)
53. Cap screw
54. Axle (R.H.)

# OVERHAUL

## All Models

The transmission gears, shafts, differential and axle shafts are contained in one case. A MTD Model 717-0750A transaxle is used on Models 320, 322, 327, 332, 337, 530, 567 and 600. Peerless 800 series transaxle used on 630A, 632A, 638A, 668A, 669A, 720A and 730A tractors are equipped with 5 forward gears and 1 reverse. Peerless 1400 series transaxle used on 810A tractors and Peerless 1200 series transaxle used on 660A and 672A tractors are equipped with 3 forward gears and 1 reverse. Peerless 2300 series transaxle used on Models 860A, 960 and 960A tractors are equipped with 4 forward gears and 1 reverse. Refer to the appropriate MTD or Peerless section in TRANSAXLE SERVICE section for overhaul procedure.

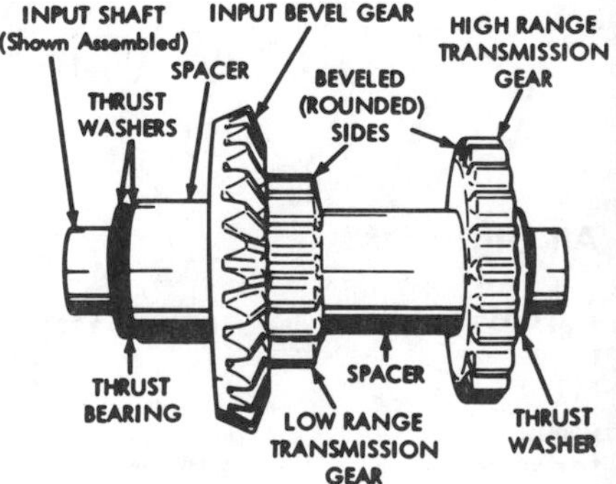


***Fig. MT35—View of input shaft and gears. Note position of bevels on gears.***

# MTD

## (1988 and Later)

## CONDENSED SPECIFICATIONS

Due to the numerous number of MTD models and the wide variety of engines installed, an accurate cross-reference and specification table is not available. Determine the manufacturer and model number of the engine being serviced and refer to the appropriate engine section in the rear of this manual for service information.

The following tractor models are covered in this section:

| | |
|---|---|
| 138-320 through 138-357 | 130-432 through 130-457 |
| 138-520 through 138-568 | 130-527 |
| 138-600 through 138-658 | 130-600 through 130-669 |
| 139-320 through 139-357 | 131-312 through 131-357 |
| 139-530 through 139-568 | 131-432 through 131-457 |
| 139-600 through 139-659 | 131-600 through 131-669 |
| 130-310 through 130-357 | |

# FRONT AXLE AND STEERING SYSTEM

### AXLE MAIN MEMBER

#### Models 130-527, 138-526, 138-528, 138-529

**REMOVE AND REINSTALL.** To remove axle main member (25—Fig. MT50), unbolt and remove hood and grille. Raise and support front of tractor frame and remove front wheels. Disconnect drag link end (22) at left spindle (24). Disconnect tie rod (23) from both spindles. Remove push nuts (17) and withdraw spindles (19 and 24) from axle. Support axle main member (25), remove bolt (16) and lower axle from tractor.

Reinstall by reversing removal procedure.

#### All Other Models

**REMOVE AND REINSTALL.** To remove axle main member (16—Fig. MT51), unbolt and remove hood and grille. Raise and support front of tractor and remove front wheels. Disconnect tie rod (18) from spindles (17 and 19). Remove push cap (22) from right

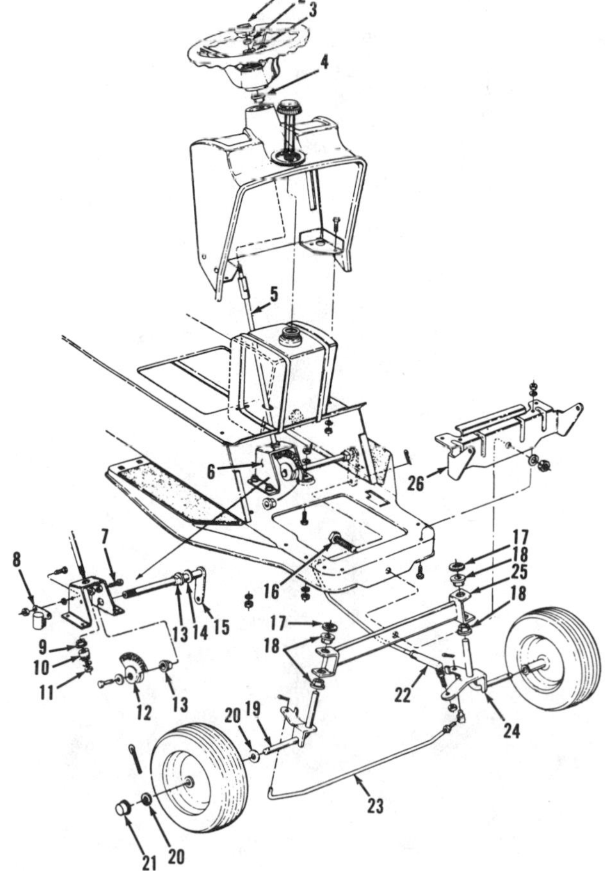

*Fig. MT50—Exploded view of front axle and steering gear assembly used on Models 130-527, 138-526, 138-528 and 138-529.*

1. Steering wheel cap
2. Nut
3. Belleville washer
4. Flange bushing
5. Steering shaft
6. Steering gear support
7. Adjusting screw
8. Solenoid
9. Flange bushing
10. Pinion gear
11. Nut
12. Sector gear
13. Flange bushing
14. Washer
15. Sector shaft & arm
16. Axle pivot bolt
17. Push nut
18. Flange bushings
19. Spindle R.H.
20. Washer
21. Hub cap
22. Drag link
23. Tie rod
24. Spindle L.H.
25. Axle main member
26. Axle pivot bracket

spindle (19) and lower spindle from axle. Disconnect drag link (9) from left spindle steering arm (14). Remove steering arm clamp bolt (15) and withdraw left spindle (17) from axle. Remove shoulder bolts (13), unbolt and remove axle pivot bracket (12) and separate axle from frame.

Reassemble by reversing removal procedure.

## TIE ROD AND TOE-IN

### All Models

All models are equipped with adjustable tie rod. Inspect ball joints for excessive wear and looseness and renew if needed.

Adjust length of tie rod to obtain front wheel toe-in of $^1/_8$ inch (3.2 mm). Secure tie rod ends with jam nuts.

## STEERING SPINDLES

### Models 130-527, 138-526, 138-528, 138-529

**REMOVE AND REINSTALL.** Raise and support front of tractor. Remove front wheels. Detach tie rod and drag link from steering spindle (24—Fig. MT50). Remove push caps (17) and lower spindles (19 and 24) out of axle main member. Inspect spindle bushings (18) and renew as necessary.

Reinstall by reversing removal procedure. Lubricate bushings with SAE 30 oil before installing spindles.

### All Other Models

**REMOVE AND REINSTALL.** Raise and support front of tractor. Remove front wheels. Detach drag link and tie rod from spindle arms. Remove steering arm clamp bolt (15—Fig. MT51) and lower left spindle (17) from axle. Remove push cap (22) and cotter pin from right spindle (19) and lower spindle from axle. Inspect spindle bushings (20) and wheel bushings (27) and renew as necessary.

Reinstall by reversing removal procedure. Lubricate bushings with SAE 30 oil before installing spindles.

## STEERING GEAR

### Models 130-527, 138-526, 138-528, 138-529

**REMOVE AND REINSTALL.** To remove steering gears, disconnect and remove battery and battery plate. Remove steering wheel and upper bushing (4—Fig. MT50). Remove retaining nut (11) from lower end of steering shaft and remove pinion gear (10) and bushing (9). Disconnect drag link (22) from steering arm (15). Remove retaining cap screw, Belleville washer and sector gear (12) from inner end of steering arm shaft (15). Withdraw steering arm shaft. Unbolt and remove steering gear support (6).

Reinstall by reversing removal procedure. Lubricate flange bushings with SAE 30 oil. Apply light coat of multipurpose grease to steering gear teeth. Adjust backlash between steering gears by turning adjusting bolt (7) in or out as necessary. Be sure gears turn smoothly without binding.

### All Other Models

**REMOVE AND REINSTALL.** To remove steering gears, disconnect battery cables. Remove steering wheel cap (1—Fig. MT51), retaining nut (2) and Belleville washer, then lift off steering wheel and bellow (3). Remove retaining screw from steering shaft flange bushing (4) and remove bushing from shaft. Disconnect drag link (9) from sector gear (8). Remove mounting bolt and shoulder bolt (6) from sector retainer plate (7) and withdraw sector gear. Remove retaining screw (24) from lower end of steering shaft (5) and remove steering shaft, thrust washer (10) and bushing (11).

Inspect all parts for excessive wear or damage and renew as necessary. Reinstall by reversing removal procedure. Lubricate flange bushings with SAE 30 oil. Apply light coat of multipurpose grease to teeth of steering gears.

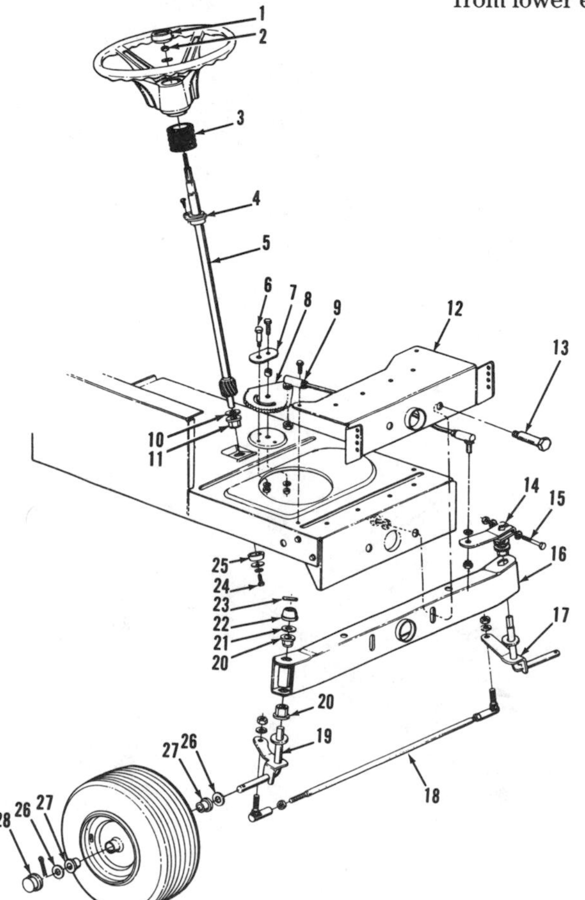


*Fig. MT51—Exploded view of front axle and steering system used on all other 500 series and 300, 400 and 600 series tractors.*

1. Steering wheel
2. Nut
3. Bellow
4. Flange bearing
5. Steering shaft
6. Shoulder bolt
7. Retainer plate
8. Sector gear
9. Drag link
10. Thrust washer
11. Flange bushing
12. Axle pivot bracket
13. Pivot stop bolt
14. Steering arm
15. Clamp bolt
16. Axle main member
17. Spindle L.H.
18. Tie rod
19. Spindle R.H.
20. Flange bushings
21. Washer
22. Push cap
23. Pin
24. Cap screw
25. Spacer
26. Washer
27. Wheel bearings
28. Hub cap

# ENGINE

### All Models

**REMOVE AND REINSTALL.** Remove hood, grille brace, or side panels, and grille. Disconnect battery cables, starter wires and all necessary electrical connections at engine. Disconnect fuel line. Disconnect choke and throttle control cables at engine. Remove drive belts from engine pulleys. Remove muffler heat shield, if so equipped. Remove engine mounting bolts and lift engine from tractor.

Reinstall by reversing removal procedure.

## OVERHAUL

### All Models

Refer to appropriate engine section in this manual for tune-up specifications, engine overhaul procedures and engine maintenance.

# CLUTCH AND BRAKE

## 300 Series and 400 Series Tractors

**ADJUSTMENT.** A continuously variable drive pulley is used on these models. Depressing the clutch-brake pedal part way disengages the clutch. Depressing pedal all the way down disengages the clutch and engages the disc brake.

To adjust clutch and speed control linkage, first adjust speed control lever linkage as follows: Push clutch-brake pedal forward until there is $^{1}/_{8}$ to $^{1}/_{4}$ inch (3.2-6.3 mm) clearance between stop (S—Fig. MT52) on brake rod (18) and variable speed pulley bracket (3) and hold pedal in this position. Position speed control shift lever (1) in parking brake position. Remove hairpin clip from speed control rod ferrule (F) and adjust ferrule on rod so lower end of rod (2) contacts rear end of slot in clutch/brake pedal cam (C). Reinstall hairpin clip.

Adjust speed control link (17—Fig. MT52) to obtain correct neutral adjustment as follows: Place transaxle shift lever in neutral position and start engine. Move speed control lever (1) to full speed position. Release clutch/brake pedal completely, then fully depress pedal and hold in this position. Shut off engine, and after engine completely stops, release clutch/brake pedal. Move speed control lever to first position. Disconnect speed control link (17) from variable speed torque bracket (14). Move clutch-brake pedal as far up as it will go. While holding pedal in this position, thread speed control link in or out of ferrule until rod lines up with hole in torque bracket. Install cotter pin to secure speed control link to torque bracket.

Disc brake is located on left side of transaxle. To adjust brake, remove cotter pin and adjust castle nut (1—Fig. MT53) so brake starts to engage when brake lever (2) is $^{1}/_{4}$ to $^{5}/_{16}$ inch (6.4-7.9 mm) away from axle housing. Make sure that brake does not drag when pedal is released.

## Models 130-527, 138-526, 138-528, 138-529

**ADJUSTMENT.** The clutch used on these models is a spring loaded, belt idler type and does not require adjustment. If drive belt (2—Fig. MT54) slips during normal operation due to excessive belt wear or stretching, renew drive belt.

To adjust disc brake, tighten nut (24—Fig. MT54) until brake pads lock differential sprocket, then loosen nut one turn. Check operation of brake and readjust as necessary.

## All Other 500 Series and 600 Series Tractors

**ADJUSTMENT.** A continuously variable drive pulley is used on these models. Depressing the clutch-brake pedal part way disengages the clutch. Depressing pedal all the way down disengages the clutch and engages the disc brake.

To adjust clutch and speed control linkage, first adjust speed control lever linkage as follows: Push clutch-brake pedal forward until the stop (Fig. MT55) on speed control rod contacts running board rod or slot in frame and hold pedal in this position. Position speed control shift lever in parking brake position. Remove hairpin clip from speed control rod ferrule and adjust ferrule on rod so it contacts rear end of slot in speed control lever cam. Reinstall hairpin clip.

Adjust speed control link (Fig. MT55) to obtain correct neutral adjustment as follows: Place transaxle shift lever in neutral position and start engine. Move speed control lever to full speed position. Release clutch/brake pedal completely, then fully depress pedal and hold in this position. Shut off engine, and after engine completely stops, release clutch/brake pedal. Move speed control lever to first position. Disconnect speed control link ferrule from clutch/brake pedal arm. Move clutch/brake pedal as far up as it will go. While holding pedal in this position, thread speed control link in or out of ferrule until ferrule lines up with hole in clutch/brake pedal arm. Install cotter pin to secure speed control link to pedal arm.

Disc brake is located on right side of transaxle. To adjust brake, remove cotter pin and adjust castle nut (1—Fig. MT53) so brake starts to engage when

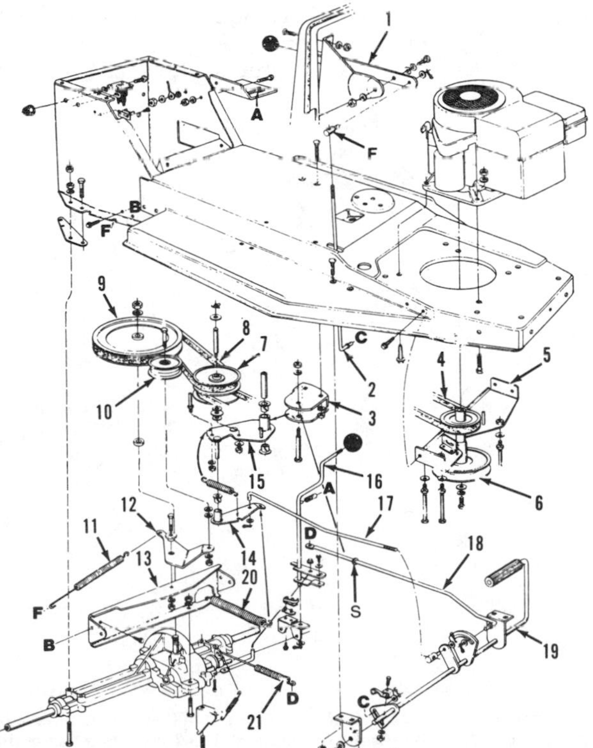

*Fig. MT52—Exploded view of variable speed drive system used on 300 and 400 series tractors.*

1. Speed control lever
2. Speed control rod
3. Variable pulley bracket
4. Front drive belt
5. Pulley guard
6. Engine pulley
7. Variable speed pulley assy.
8. Rear drive belt
9. Transaxle pulley
10. Idler pulley
11. Spring
12. Idler bracket
13. Transaxle support bracket
14. Variable speed torque bracket
15. Variable speed bracket
16. Shift rod
17. Speed control rod
18. Brake rod
19. Clutch/brake pedal
20. Tension spring
21. Brake spring

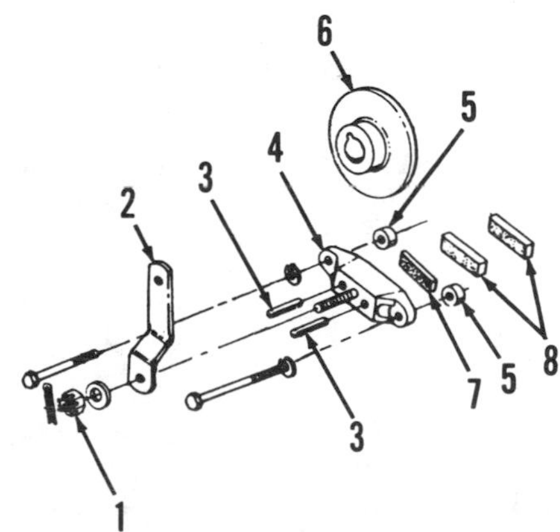

*Fig. MT53—Exploded view of disc brake typical of all models except 130-527, 138-526, 138-528 and 138-529.*

1. Adjusting nut
2. Brake lever
3. Actuating pins
4. Brake pad holder
5. Spacers
6. Brake disc
7. Back-up plate
8. Brake pads

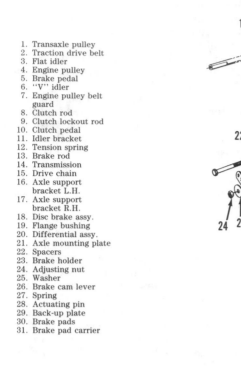

1. Transaxle pulley
2. Traction drive belt
3. Flat idler
4. Engine pulley
5. Brake pedal
6. "V" idler
7. Engine pulley belt guard
8. Clutch rod
9. Clutch lockout rod
10. Clutch pedal
11. Idler bracket
12. Tension spring
13. Brake rod
14. Transmission
15. Drive chain
16. Axle support bracket L.H.
17. Axle support bracket R.H.
18. Disc brake assy.
19. Flange bushing
20. Differential assy.
21. Axle mounting plate
22. Spacers
23. Brake holder
24. Adjusting nut
25. Washer
26. Brake cam lever
27. Spring
28. Actuating pin
29. Back-up plate
30. Brake pads
31. Brake pad carrier

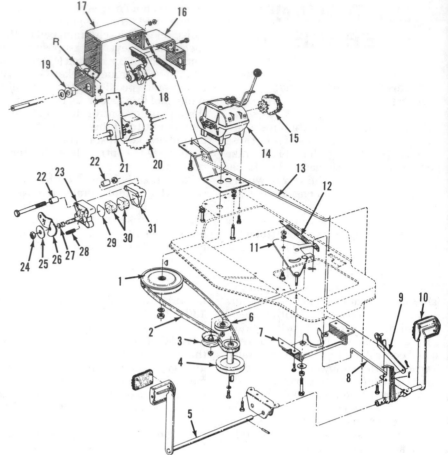

*Fig. MT54—Exploded view of traction drive system used on Models 130-527, 138-526, 136-528 and 138-529.*

brake lever (2) is ¼ to 5/16 inch (6.4-7.9 mm) away from axle housing. Make sure that brake does not drag when pedal is released.

# TRACTION DRIVE BELTS

## 300 Series and 400 Series Tractors

**R&R DRIVE BELTS.** To remove rear drive belt (8—Fig. MT52), first remove mower deck from underneath tractor. Start engine. Place shift lever in neutral and speed control lever in high speed position, then shut off engine. Disconnect tension spring (20) from transaxle support bracket (13). Note that a hole is provided in rear of frame for access to tension spring. Disconnect small spring (11) from right side of frame. Move brake rod (18) out of variable speed pulley bracket (3). Loosen, but do not remove, bolts securing variable speed pulley bracket. Work drive belt off top of variable speed pulley (7), then remove belt from transaxle pulley (9) and idler pulley (10). Reverse removal procedure to install new belt.

To remove front drive belt (4—Fig. MT52), first remove rear drive belt as outlined above. Unbolt and remove engine pulley belt guard (5). Slip drive belt off engine pulley and remove from variable speed pulley. Reverse removal

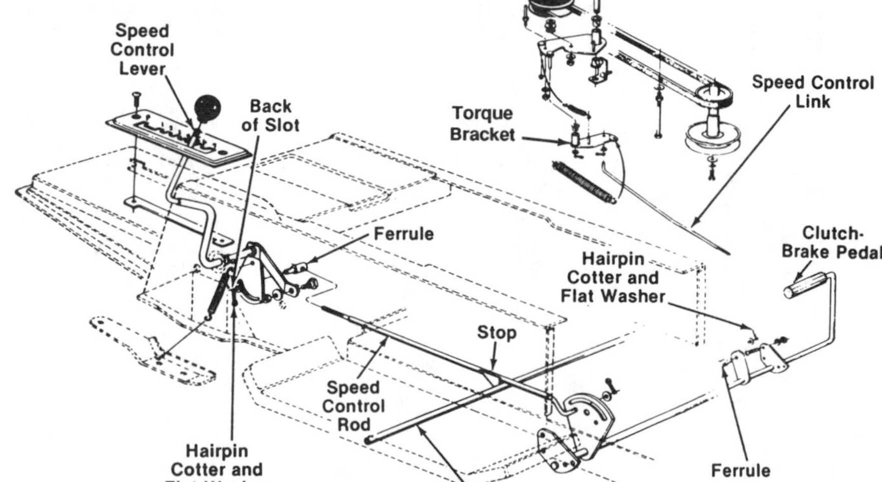


*Fig. MT55—Drawing of variable speed drive control linkage typical of 500 and 600 series tractors (except Models 130-527, 138-526, 138-528 and 138-529). Refer to text for speed control adjustment procedure.*



Illustrations courtesy MTD Products, Inc.

procedure to install new belt. Be sure that belt is not twisted and that it is positioned inside all belt guides.

### Models 130-527, 138-526, 138-528, 138-529

**R&R DRIVE BELT.** To remove traction drive belt (2—Fig. MT54), first remove mower deck from underneath tractor. Depress clutch pedal (10) and engage clutch lockout lever (9). Work drive belt off engine pulley (4) and transmission pulley (1) and remove from tractor. Reverse removal procedure to install new belt.

### All Other 500 Series and 600 Series Tractor

**R&R DRIVE BELTS.** To remove rear drive belt (4—Fig. MT56), remove shift lever cover from top of frame. Remove two bolts securing shift lever bracket to frame so belt can be removed between bracket and frame. Push idler pulley (3) away from belt to relieve belt tension and slip belt over the idler pulley. Remove belt from variable speed pulley (5) and transaxle pulley (2) and remove from tractor. Reverse removal procedure to install new belt.

To remove front drive belt (16—Fig. MT56), place clutch/brake pedal in park position. Remove rear belt from idler pulley and variable speed pulley as outlined above. Place mower deck lift lever in disengaged position. Remove engine pulley belt guides (18). Slip mower drive belt off engine pulley. Unbolt and remove engine pulley belt guard (19). Push variable speed pulley (5) to relieve tension on belt and work belt off engine pulley. Release clutch/brake pedal and remove belt from variable speed pulley. It may be helpful to remove belt guide (7) from pulley bracket (8). Reverse removal procedure to install new belt. Be sure that belt is not twisted and that it is positioned inside all belt guides.

# GEAR TRANSMISSION

### Models 130-527, 138-526, 138-528, 138-529

**LUBRICATION.** All models have transmission case packed with 12 ounces (355 mL) of EP lithium base grease at the factory and should not require additional lubrication.

**REMOVE AND REINSTALL.** To remove transmission (14—Fig. MT54), first remove transmission shift cover from rear frame. Disconnect battery cables and remove battery. Disconnect and remove chain (15) from transmission output sprocket. Depress clutch pedal and slip drive belt from transmission input pulley (1). Remove pulley retaining nut and withdraw pulley from transmission input shaft. Unscrew transmission mounting bolts and remove transmission from tractor.

To reinstall transmission, reverse removal procedure.

**OVERHAUL.** All models are equipped with a 700 series Peerless gear transmission. Refer to Peerless section in GEAR TRANSMISSION SERVICE section for overhaul procedure.

# DIFFERENTIAL

### Models 130-527, 138-526, 138-528, 138-529

**R&R AND OVERHAUL.** To remove differential (20—Fig. MT54), raise and support rear of tractor. Remove nut from chain adjuster rod, then disconnect drive chain (15). Disconnect brake control rod spring from brake lever (18). Unscrew axle support bracket mounting nuts and remove support brackets (16 and 17) with differential assembly from tractor. Remove rear wheels from axle shafts. Unbolt axle mounting plate (21) from axle support brackets and remove differential assembly from support brackets.

To disassemble, clean axles and remove any burrs. Unscrew differential carrier bolts and separate differential carrier housings (2—Fig. MT57). Remove drive pin (9), pinion gears (8) and thrust washers (7). Drive spring pins (6) out of side gears (5) and separate gears from axle shafts (4 and 11).

To reassemble differential, reverse disassembly procedure. Note that shorter axle (4) is installed on sprocket side of differential housing. Lubricate with 3 ounces (89 mL) of EP lithium base grease.

Reinstall differential by reversing removal procedure. Tighten nut on chain adjuster rod (R) to remove slack from drive chain before tightening axle support bracket mounting nuts.

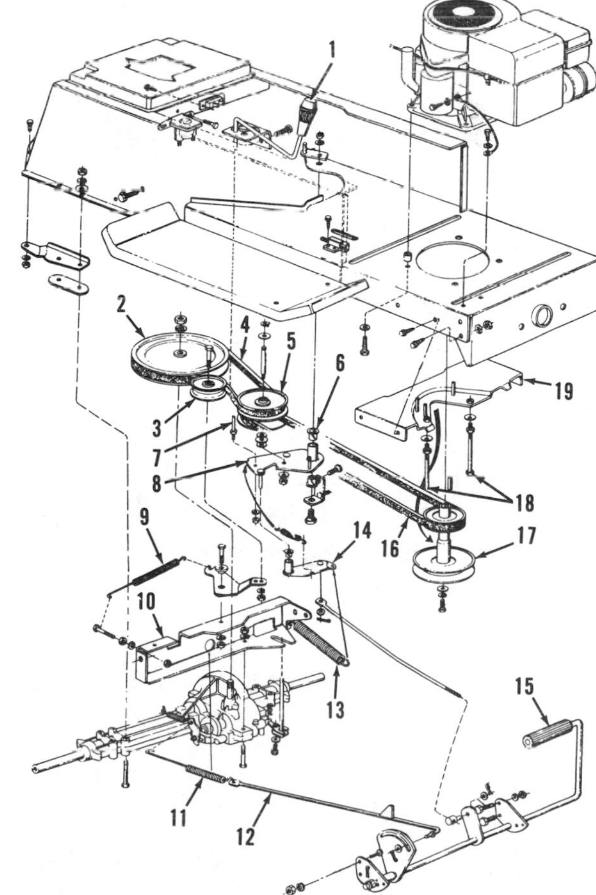

*Fig. MT56—Exploded view of variable drive control system typical of 500 and 600 series tractors (except Models 130-526, 138-526, 138-528 and 138-529).*

1. Shift lever
2. Transaxle pulley
3. Idler
4. Rear drive belt
5. Variable speed pulley assy.
6. Bushing
7. Belt guide
8. Variable speed bracket
9. Idler spring
10. Transaxle support bracket
11. Brake spring
12. Brake rod
13. Variable speed tension spring
14. Variable speed torque bracket
15. Clutch/brake pedal assy.
16. Front drive belt
17. Engine pulley
18. Belt guides
19. Engine pulley belt guard

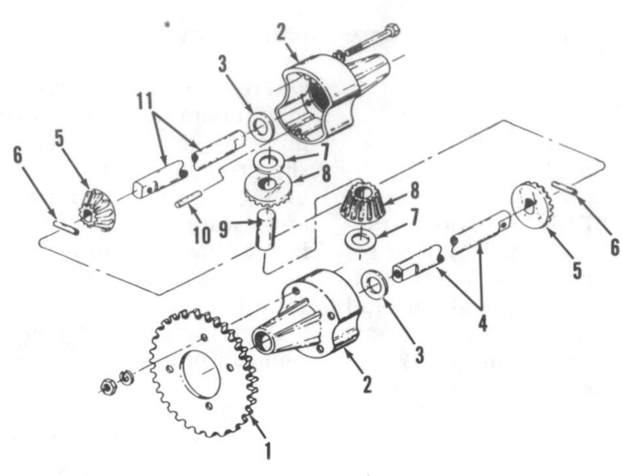


*Fig. MT57—Exploded view of differential assembly used on Models 130-527, 138-526, 138-528 and 138-529.*

1. Sprocket
2. Differential housing halves
3. Thrust washer
4. Axle shaft (short)
5. Side gears
6. Spring pin
7. Thrust washers
8. Pinion gears
9. Drive pin
10. Dowel pin
11. Axle shaft (long)

# TRANSAXLE

## All Models So Equipped

**LUBRICATION.** Transaxle used on 300, 400, 500 and 600 series tractors with variable speed drive system is lubricated with grease at factory and should not require additional lubrication. Capacity is 10 ounces (296 mL) of lithium based grease.

**REMOVE AND REINSTALL.** To remove transaxle assembly, first remove drive belt from transaxle pulley as previously outlined. Disconnect shift linkage and brake linkage at transaxle. Support rear of tractor and remove all fasteners securing transaxle to frame. Raise rear of tractor and roll transaxle assembly out from under tractor.

Reinstall by reversing removal procedure. Adjust brake as previously outlined.

**OVERHAUL.** All models are equipped with an MTD single speed transaxle. Refer to the MTD section in TRANSAXLE SERVICE section for overhaul procedure.

# WIRING DIAGRAMS

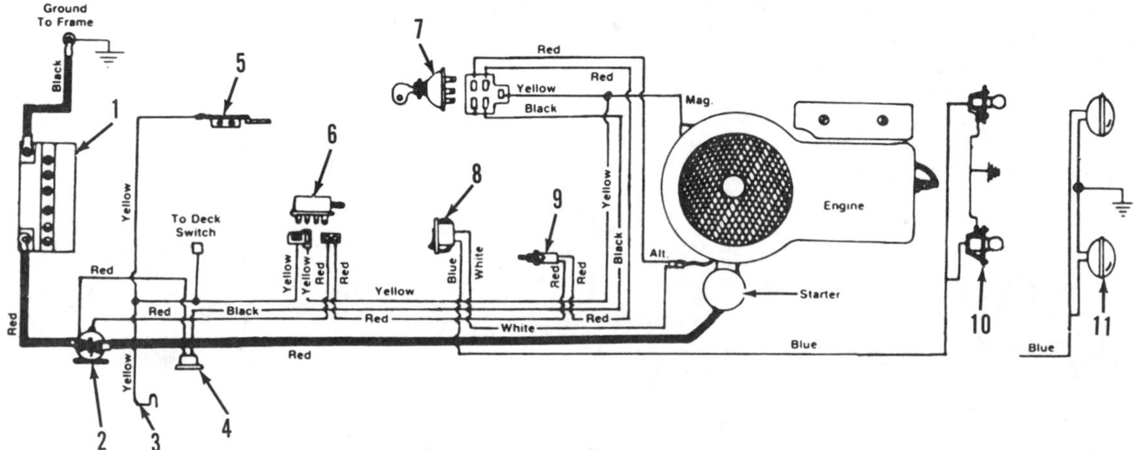


*Fig. MT60—Wiring diagram for Models 138-320 through 138-357 and 139-320 through 139-357.*

1. Battery
2. Solenoid
3. Seat switch
4. Circuit breaker
5. Spring switch
6. Safety switch
7. Ignition switch
8. Light switch
9. Safety switch
10. Headlight (square)
11. Headlight (round)

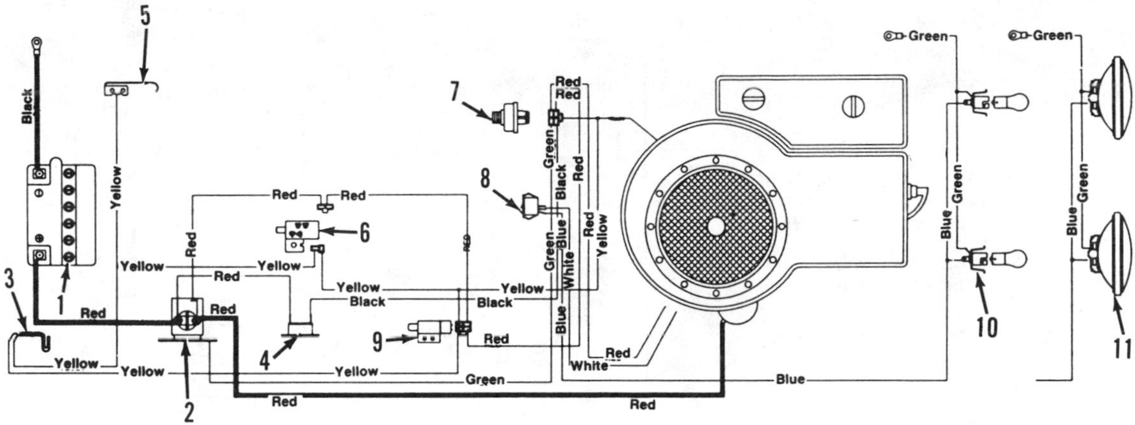


Fig. MT61—Wiring diagram for Models 130-310 through 130-357 and 131-310 through 131-357. Refer to Fig. MT60 for legend.

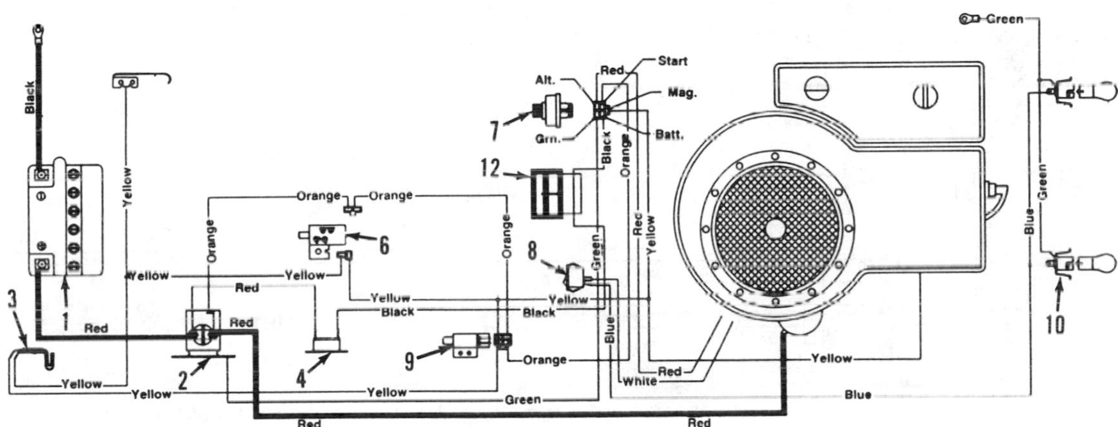

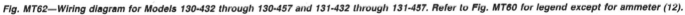

Fig. MT62—Wiring diagram for Models 130-432 through 130-457 and 131-432 through 131-457. Refer to Fig. MT60 for legend except for ammeter (12).

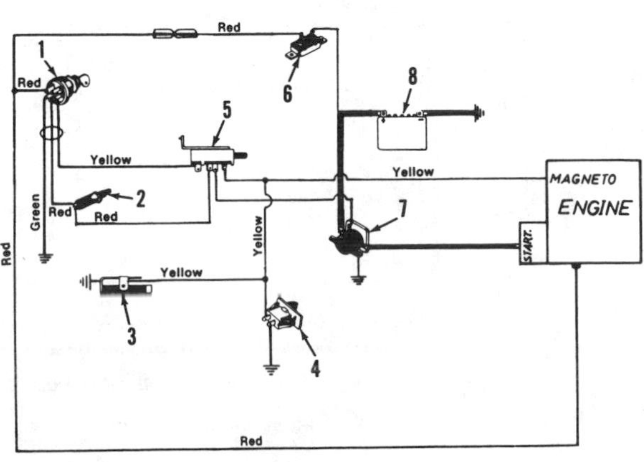

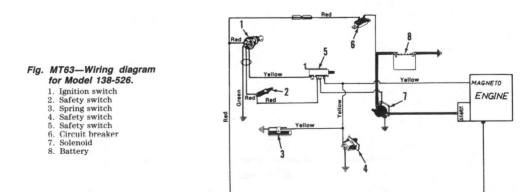

*Fig. MT63—Wiring diagram for Model 138-526.*

1. Ignition switch
2. Safety switch
3. Spring switch
4. Safety switch
5. Safety switch
6. Circuit breaker
7. Solenoid
8. Battery

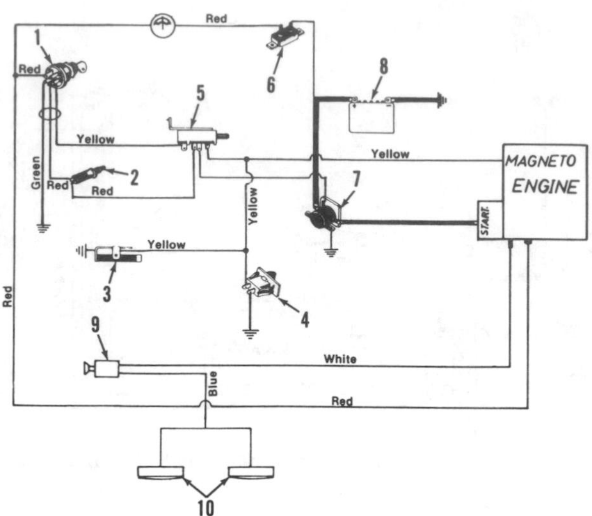

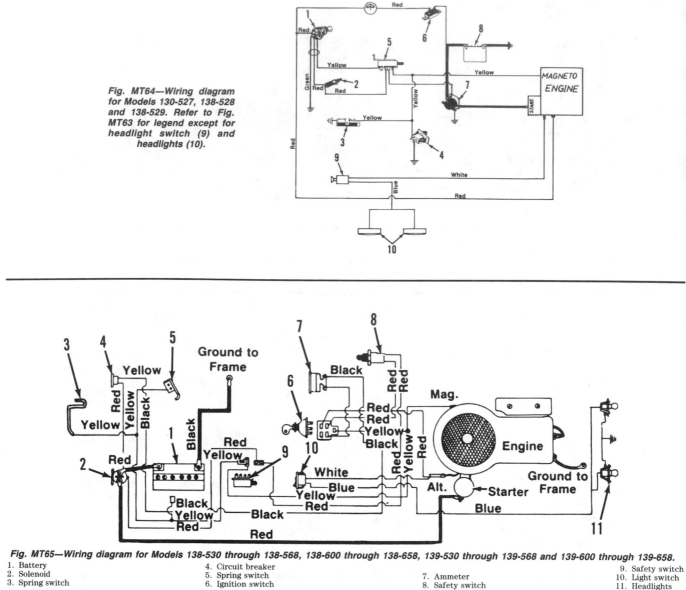

*Fig. MT64—Wiring diagram for Models 130-527, 138-528 and 138-529. Refer to Fig. MT63 for legend except for headlight switch (9) and headlights (10).*

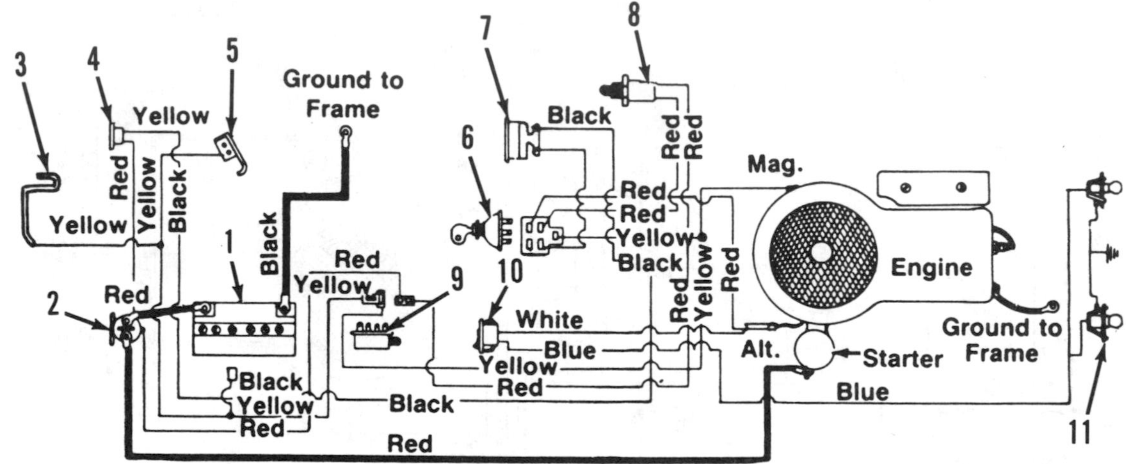


*Fig. MT65—Wiring diagram for Models 138-530 through 138-568, 138-600 through 138-658, 139-530 through 139-568 and 139-600 through 139-658.*

1. Battery
2. Solenoid
3. Spring switch
4. Circuit breaker
5. Spring switch
6. Ignition switch
7. Ammeter
8. Safety switch
9. Safety switch
10. Light switch
11. Headlights

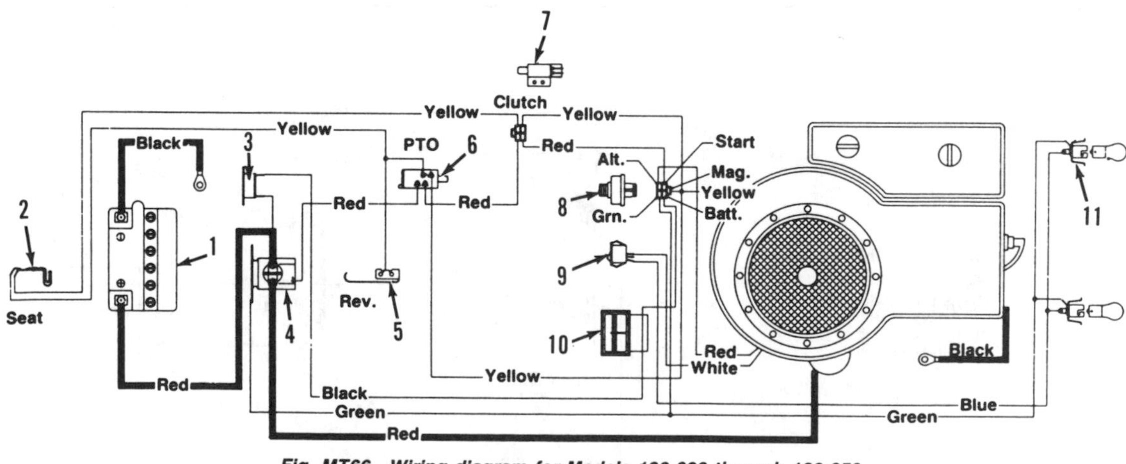


*Fig. MT66—Wiring diagram for Models 130-600 through 130-659.*

1. Battery
2. Safety switch
3. Circuit breaker
4. Solenoid
5. Safety switch
6. Safety switch
7. Safety switch
8. Ignition switch
9. Light switch
10. Ammeter
11. Headlights



Illustrations courtesy MTD Products, Inc.

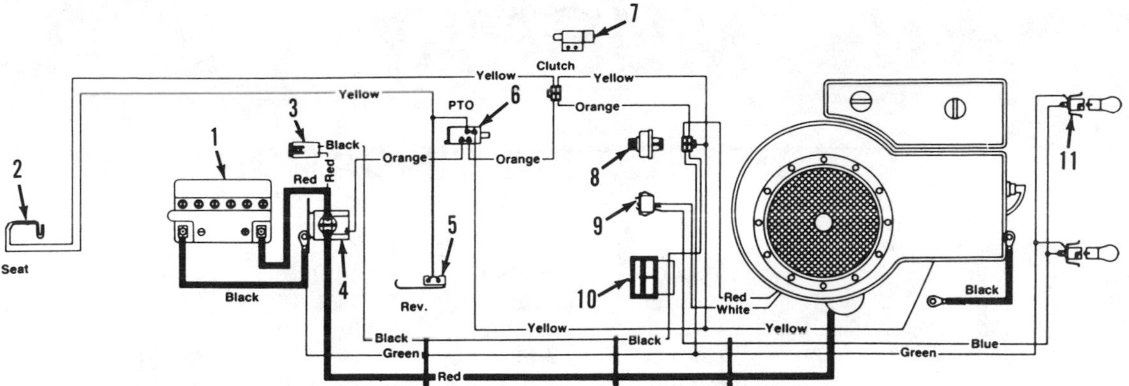


*Fig. MT67—Wiring diagram for Models 131-600 through 131-669. Refer to Fig. MT66 for legend.*

# MURRAY

## CONDENSED SPECIFICATION

| | MODEL | | | |
|---|---|---|---|---|
| | 38600 | 38608 | 40625 | 46620 |
| Engine Make | Tecumseh | B&S | B&S | B&S |
| Model | OVXL120 | 281707 | 286707 | 261707 |
| Bore | 3.31 in. (84.2 mm) | 3.44 in. (87.3 mm) | 3.44 in. (87.3 mm) | 3.43 in. (87 mm) |
| Stroke | 2.53 in. (64.3 mm) | 3.06 in. (77.7 mm) | 3.06 in. (77.7 mm) | 2.86 in. (73 mm) |
| Displacement | 21.8 cu. in. (357 cc) | 28.4 cu. in. (465 cc) | 28.4 cu. in. (465 cc) | 26.5 cu. in. (435 cc) |
| Power Rating | 12 hp (8.9 kW) | 12 hp (8.9 kW) | 12.5 hp (8.9 kW) | 14 hp (8.9 kW) |
| Slow Idle Speed Speed—Rpm | 1400 rpm | 1400 rpm | 1400 rpm | 1400 rpm |
| High Idle Speed (No-Load)—Rpm | 3600 rpm | 3600 rpm | 3600 rpm | 3600 rpm |
| Capacities— | | | | |
| Crankcase | 2 pts. (1 L) | 3 pts. (1.4 L) | 3 pts. (1.4 L) | 3 pts. (1.4 L) |
| Transaxle | 36 oz. (1065 mL) | 64 oz. (1892 mL) | 36 oz. (1065 mL) | 36 oz. (1065 mL) |

## FRONT AXLE AND STEERING SYSTEM

### AXLE MAIN MEMBER

#### All Models

**REMOVE AND REINSTALL.** To remove axle assembly, raise and support front of tractor. Disconnect drag link (13—Fig. M1) from spindle steering arm. Support axle main member (17) and unbolt and remove front axle support (16). Remove axle assembly from tractor.

Check axle main member pivot for excessive wear and renew as necessary. Reinstall by reversing the removal procedure. Lubricate axle pivot with engine oil.

### R&R STEERING SPINDLES

#### All Models

**REMOVE AND REINSTALL.** Raise and support front of tractor. Remove front tires and wheels. Detach tie rod (14—Fig. M1) from steering spindles (15 and 20). Disconnect drag link (13) from left steering spindle. Remove cotter pin and lower spindle from axle main member.

Renew bushings (18) and/or spindles as required. Reinstall by reversing the removal procedure. Lubricate spindle bushings with engine oil.

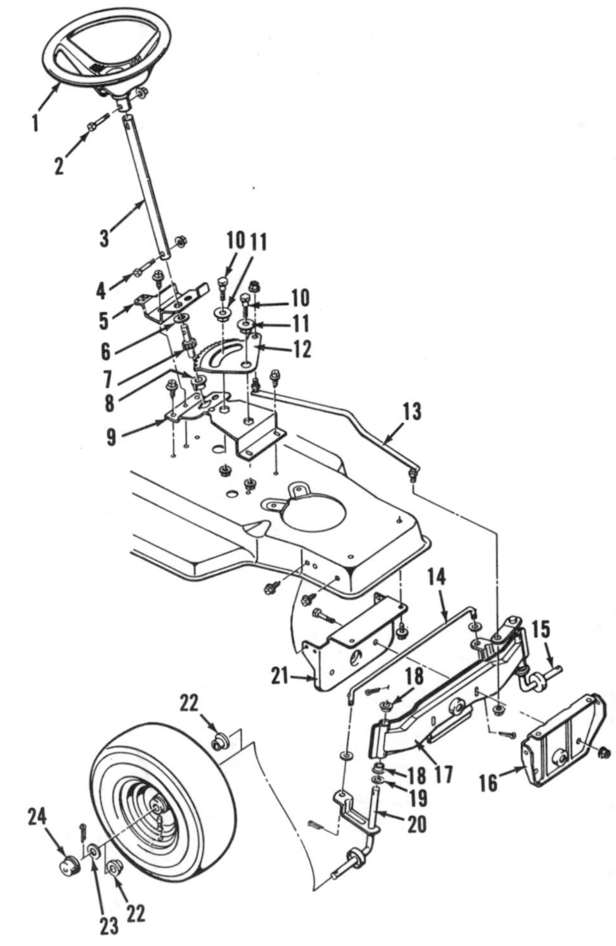


***Fig. M1—Exploded view of front axle assembly and steering gear used on all models.***

1. Steering wheel
2. Bolt
3. Steering shaft
4. Bolt
5. Steering gear bracket
6. Washer
7. Pinion gear
8. Bushing
9. Sector bracket
10. Shoulder bolt
11. Bearing
12. Sector gear
13. Drag link
14. Tie rod
15. Spindle L.H.
16. Axle front support
17. Axle main member
18. Bushing
19. Washer
20. Spindle R.H.
21. Axle rear support
22. Bushing
23. Washer
24. Hub cap

### R&R STEERING GEAR

#### All Models

**REMOVE AND REINSTALL.** Remove screws securing steering column bearing to control panel, remove bolt (4—Fig. M1) and pull steering wheel (1) and column (3) from control panel. Remove steering gear bracket (5) mounting screws and remove pinion gear (7) and bushing (8). Disconnect drag link (13) from steering sector gear (12). Remove shoulder bolts (10), bearings (11) and sector gear from sector bracket (9).

Reassemble by reversing disassembly procedure. Apply thin coat of grease to steering gear teeth.

## ENGINE

#### All Models

**REMOVE AND REINSTALL.** Remove hood assembly. Disconnect negative battery cable. Detach all interfering wires and cables. Disconnect fuel line. Remove muffler heat shield and muffler. Disengage drive belts from engine pulleys and remove pulleys. Unscrew engine mounting bolts and lift engine out of tractor.

Reinstall by reversing removal procedure.

**OVERHAUL.** Engine make and model are listed at the beginning of this section. For tuneup specifications, engine overhaul procedures and engine maintenance, refer to appropriate engine section in this manual.

## CLUTCH AND BRAKE

#### All Models

**ADJUSTMENT.** A belt idler type clutch is used on all models. To adjust clutch/brake pedal, disconnect clutch rod nut from lever assembly (Fig. M2). Turn adjustable nut to obtain $^3/_{16}$ inch (4.7 mm) clearance between clutch/brake pedal rod and end of slot in step plate (Fig. M2) when clutch rod is connected.

To adjust brake, push clutch/brake pedal completely forward and engage parking brake lock. Place shift lever in neutral position. Tighten hex nut (Fig. M3) until rear wheels are locked. Release brake and make certain wheels turn freely.

**R&R BRAKE PADS.** Disconnect brake rod at brake arm. Remove brake mounting cap screws and remove brake assembly from transaxle. Separate all parts.

Reinstall by reversing removal procedure. Adjust brakes as previously outlined.

## DRIVE BELT

#### Models 38600-38608

**REMOVE AND REINSTALL.** Remove mower deck from tractor. Depress clutch/brake pedal and set parking brake. Unbolt and remove idler pulley (15—Fig. M4). Loosen belt guides (1) around transaxle drive pulley (16). Remove belt from transaxle drive pulley and engine pulley, then push rear end of belt through shift lever hole and over shift lever as shown in Fig. M5. Pull belt under the shift lever and remove from under tractor.

Reinstall by reversing removal procedure. Be sure that belt is positioned inside all belt guides. Adjust clutch/brake pedal as outlined in clutch/brake ADJUSTMENT paragraph.

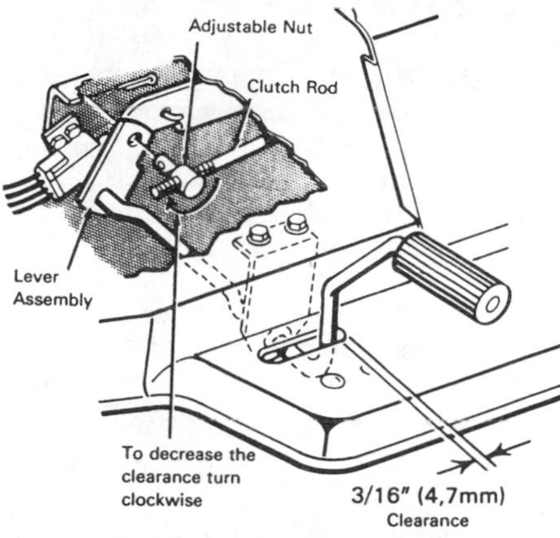

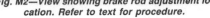

*Fig. M2—View showing brake rod adjustment location. Refer to text for procedure.*

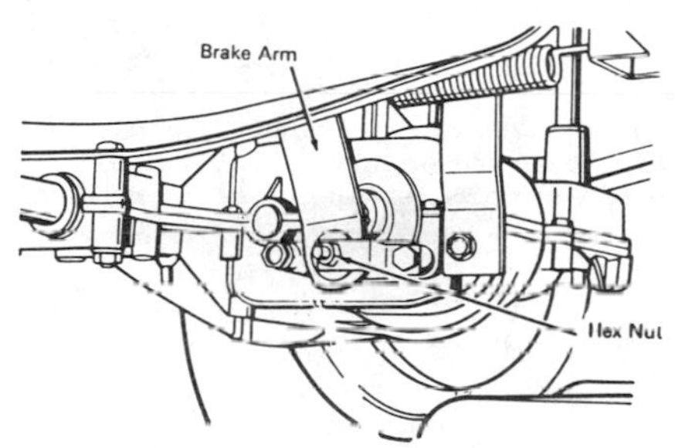


*Fig. M3—Adjust brake by turning brake arm nut as outlined in text.*

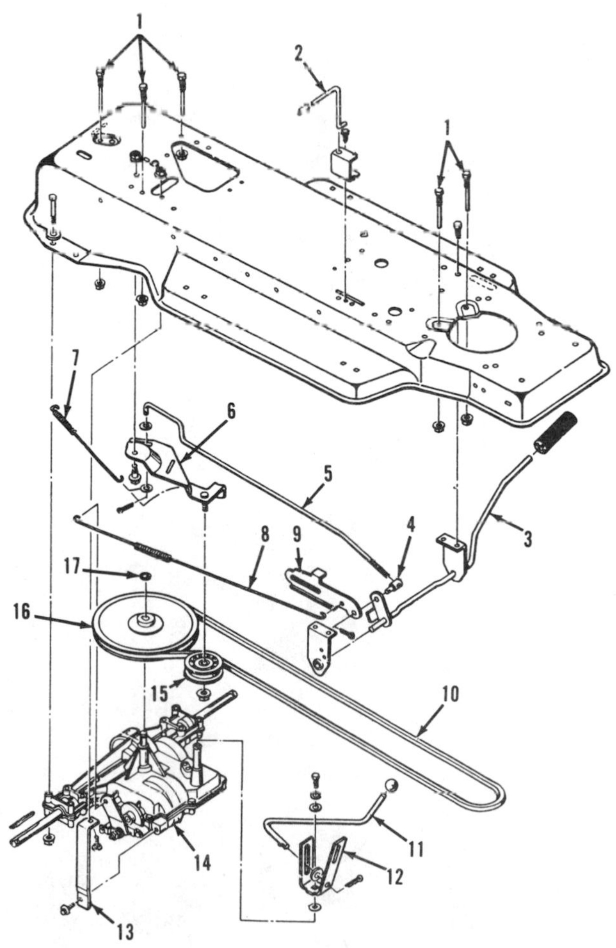


*Fig. M4—View of drive belt and spring-loaded, pivoting idler arrangement which provides traction clutch on Models 38600 and 38608.*

1. Belt guides
2. Park brake lever
3. Clutch/brake pedal
4. Adjustable nut
5. Clutch rod
6. Idler bracket
7. Tension spring
8. Brake rod
9. Park brake latch
10. Traction drive belt
11. Shift lever
12. Shift yoke
13. Support brace
14. Transaxle assy.
15. Idler pulley
16. Transaxle pulley
17. Snap ring

Illustrations courtesy Murray Ohio Mfg. Co.

### Models 40625-46620

**REMOVE AND REINSTALL.** Remove mower housing from tractor. Depress clutch/brake pedal and set parking brake. Unbolt and remove idler pulley (18—Fig. M6). Loosen belt guides (3) around transaxle drive pulley (17). Remove belt from transaxle pulley and engine pulley. Remove two screws from shift yoke support bracket (7—Fig. M7) and disconnect shift link (6) from shift lever (5). Remove drive belt from tractor.

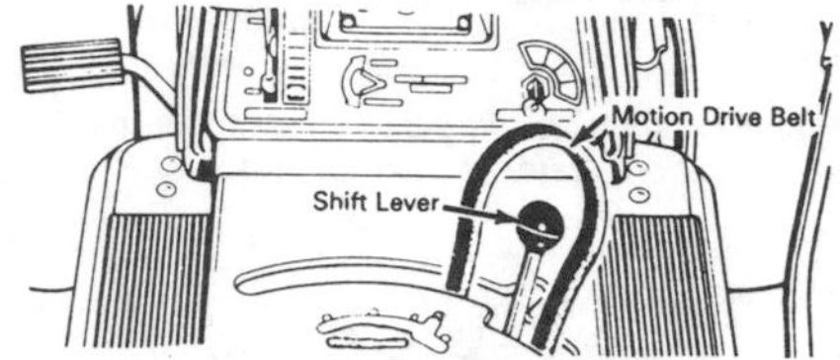


***Fig. M5—Drive belt on Models 38600 and 38608 must be pushed through gear shift lever opening and slipped over gear shift lever to remove. Refer to text.***

Reinstall drive belt by reversing removal procedure. Be sure that flat side of belt is against idler pulley and that belt is not twisted. Adjust clutch/brake pedal as outlined in clutch/brake ADJUSTMENT paragraph.

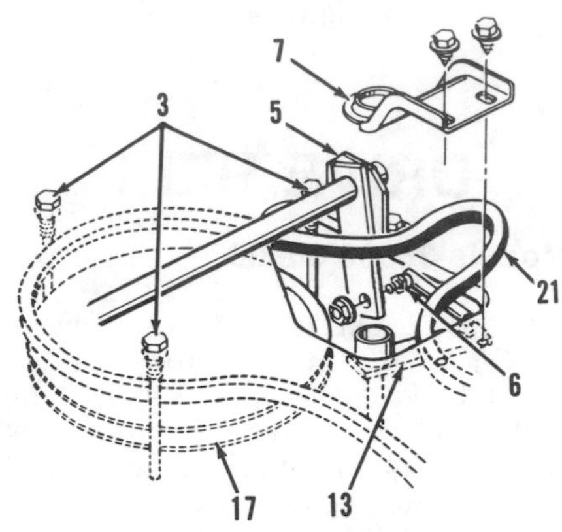


***Fig. M7—Support bracket (7) must be removed and shift link (6) must be disconnected in order to remove and install traction drive belt on Models 40625 and 46620. Refer to text.***

## TRANSAXLE

### All Models

**LUBRICATION.** The transaxle is packed with 36 ounces (1065 mL) of multipurpose, lithium base grease during manufacture and does not require periodic maintenance.

**REMOVE AND REINSTALL.** Remove mower deck from tractor. Raise and support rear of tractor. Disconnect brake rod from disc brake. Remove transaxle drive belt as outlined in DRIVE BELT section. On Models 38600 and 38608, remove knob from shift lever. On all models, remove bolts retaining transaxle to support bracket and tractor frame. Lift rear of frame and move transaxle rearward from tractor.

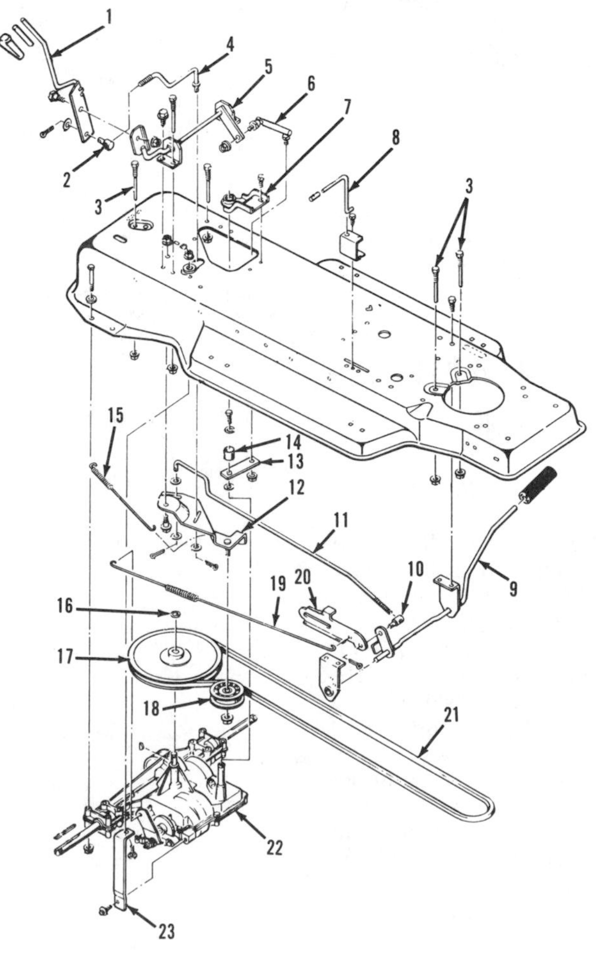

***Fig. M6—View of spring-loaded idler type drive clutch system used on Models 40625 and 46620.***

1. Shift lever
2. Adjustable nut
3. Belt guides
4. Clutch link
5. Shift arm
6. Shift link
7. Support bracket
8. Park brake lever
9. Clutch/brake pedal
10. Adjustable nut
11. Clutch rod
12. Idler bracket
13. Shift yoke
14. Support pilot
15. Tension spring
16. Snap ring
17. Transaxle pulley
18. Idler pulley
19. Brake rod
20. Park brake latch
21. Traction drive belt
22. Transaxle
23. Support brace



Illustrations courtesy Murray Ohio Mfg. Co.

Reinstall by reversing removal procedure.

**OVERHAUL.** These tractors may be equipped with a Peerless Series 920 or 930 transaxle, a Spicer 4360 series transaxle or a Spicer 4450 series transaxle. Refer to model number plate on transaxle housing to determine which transaxle is used, then refer to appropriate Peerless or Spicer section in TRANSAXLE SERVICE section for overhaul procedure.

# WIRING DIAGRAMS

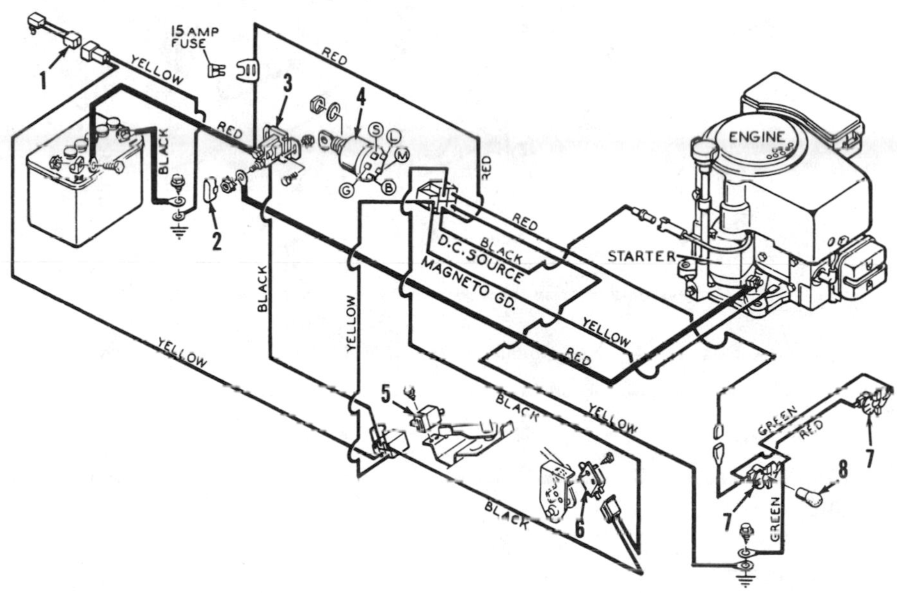


*Fig. M8—Wiring diagram for Model 38600.*

1. Seat safety switch
2. Cover
3. Solenoid
4. Ignition switch
5. Pto switch
6. Clutch safety switch
7. Light sockets
8. Light bulb

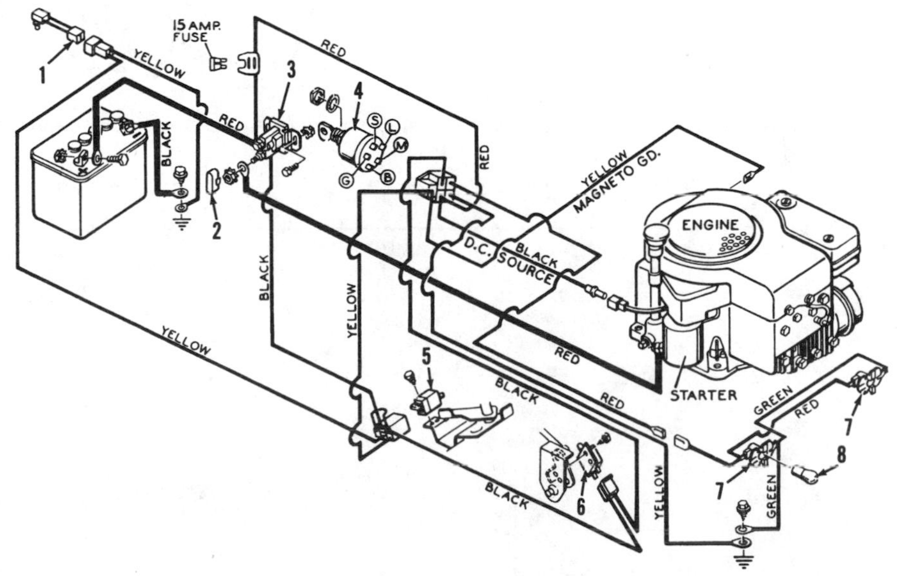


*Fig. M9—Wiring diagram for Model 38608. Refer to Fig. M8 for legend.*

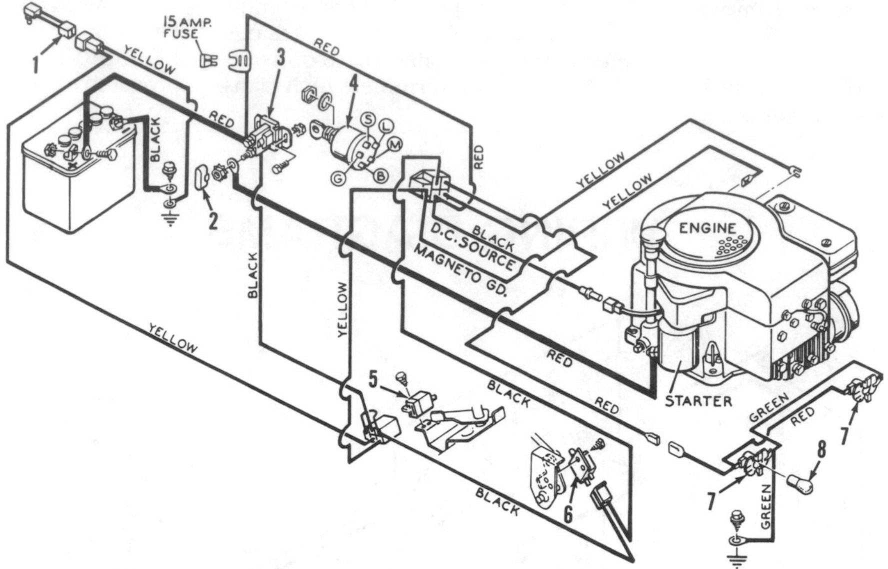


Fig. M10—Wiring diagram for Model 40625. Refer to Fig. M8 for legend.

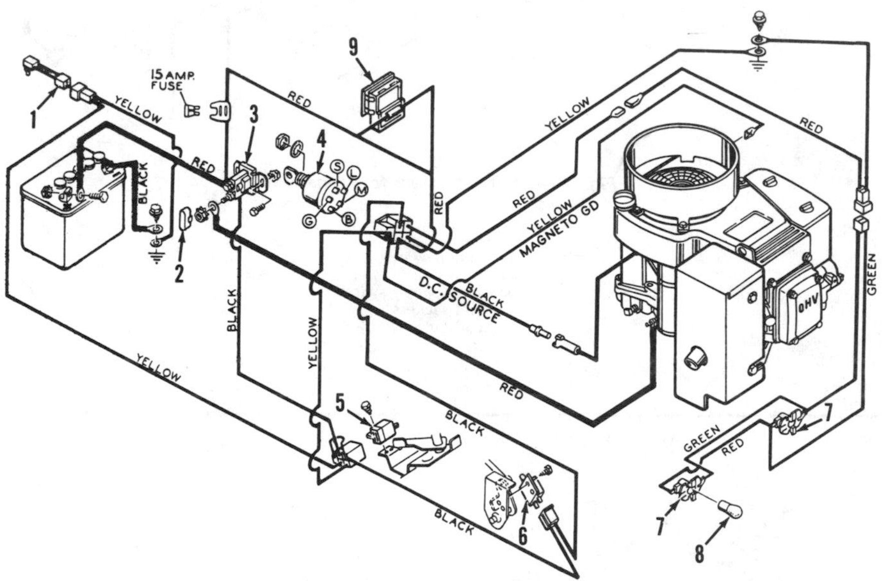


Fig. M11—Wiring diagram for Model 46620. Refer to Fig. M8 for legend except for ammeter (9).

# SIMPLICITY

## CONDENSED SPECIFICATIONS

| | MODELS | | | | |
|---|---|---|---|---|---|
| | **Broadmoor (1965)** | **Broadmoor 707** | **Broadmoor 717, 727** | **Broadmoor 728, 738** | **Serf 515, 525, 535** |
| Engine Make | B&S | B&S | B&S | B&S | B&S |
| Model | 142702 | 170402 | 171701 | 191701 | 130902 |
| Bore | 2¾ in. (69.8 mm) | 3 in. (76.2 mm) | 3 in. (76.2 mm) | 3 in. (76.2 mm) | 2-9/16 in. (65.1 mm) |
| Stroke | 2⅜ in. (60.3 mm) | 2⅜ in. (60.3 mm) | 2⅜ in. (60.3 mm) | 2¾ in. (69.8 mm) | 2-7/16 in. (61.9 mm) |
| Piston Displacement | 14.1 cu. in. (231 cc) | 16.79 cu. in. (275 cc) | 16.79 cu. in. (275 cc) | 19.44 cu. in. (319 cc) | 12.57 cu. in. (206 cc) |
| Horsepower | 6 | 7 | 7 | 8 | 5 |
| Slow Idle Speed – Rpm | 1800 | 1300 | 1300 | 1300 | 1300 |
| High Idle Speed (No-Load) – Rpm | 4000 | 3600 | 3600 | 3600 | 3600 |
| Full Load Speed – Rpm | 3600 | 3240 | 3240 | 3240 | 3240 |
| Crankcase Oil Capacity | 2¼ pints (1 L) | 2¾ pints (1.3 L) | 2¼ pints (1 L) | 2¼ pints (1 L) | 1¾ pints (0.8 L) |
| Weight – | | | | | |
| Above 32°F (0°C) | | | SAE 30 | | |
| 0°F (−8°C) to 32°F (0°C) | | | SAE 10W | | |
| Below 0°F (−18°C) | | | SAE 5W-20 | | |
| Transmission Oil Capacity | 2 pints (0.9 L) | 2 pints (0.9 L) | 2½ pints (1.2 L) | 3 pints (1.4 L) | 3 pints (1.4 L) |
| Weight | | | SAE 90 EP | | |
| Bevel Gear Housing Oil Capacity | .... | .... | .... | 1 pint (0.5 L) | 1 pint (0.5 L) |
| Weight | .... | .... | .... | SAE 90 EP | SAE 90 EP |

| | MODELS | | | | |
|---|---|---|---|---|---|
| | **Serf 535*** | **Yeoman 616** | **Yeoman 627, 637** | **Yeoman 648** | **Landlord (1965)** |
| Engine Make | B&S | B&S | B&S | B&S | B&S |
| Model | 130905 | 146702 | 170705 | 190707 | 23D |
| Bore | 2-9/16 in. (65.1 mm) | 2¾ in. (69.8 mm) | 3 in. (76.2 mm) | 3 in. (76.2 mm) | 3 in. (76.2 mm) |
| Stroke | 2-7/16 in. (61.9 mm) | 2⅜ in. (60.3 mm) | 2⅜ in. (60.3 mm) | 2¾ in. (69.8 mmm) | 3¼ in. (82.5 mm) |
| Piston Displacement | 12.57 cu. in. (206 cc) | 14.11 cu. in. (231 cc) | 16.79 cu. in. (275 cc) | 19.44 cu. in. (319 cc) | 22.97 cu. in. (376 cc) |
| Horsepower | 5 | 6 | 7 | 8 | 9 |
| Slow Idle Speed – Rpm | 1300 | 1300 | 1300 | 1300 | 1200 |
| High Idle Speed (No-Load) – Rpm | 3600 | 3600 | 3600 | 3600 | 3750 |
| Full Load Speed – Rpm | 3240 | 3240 | 3240 | 3240 | 3500 |
| Crankcase Oil Capacity | 1¾ pints (0.8 L) | 1¾ pints (0.8 L) | 2¼ pints (1 L) | 2¼ pints (1 L) | 4 pints (1.9 L) |
| Weight – | | | | | |
| Above 32°F (0°C) | | | SAE 30 | | |
| 0°F (−18C) to 32°F (0°C) | | | SAE 10W | | |
| Below 0°F (−18°C) | | | SAE 5W-20 | | |
| Transmission Oil Capacity | 2 pints (0.9L) | 2 pints (0.9L) | 2 pints (0.9L) | 2½ pints (1.2L) | 3 pints (1.4L) |
| Weight | | | SAE 90 EP | | |
| Bevel Gear Housing Oil Capacity | .... | .... | .... | .... | 1 pint (0.5 L) |
| Weight | .... | .... | .... | .... | SAE 90 EP |

*Electric start model.

| | MODELS | | | | |
|---|---|---|---|---|---|
| | **Landlord 2010, 2110, 2210** | **Landlord 3210V, 3310V** | **Landlord 3410, 3410S** | **Landlord 2012** | **Landlord 3310H, 3410H** |
| Engine Make | B&S | B&S | B&S | B&S | B&S |
| Model | 243431 | 243431 | 243431 | 300421 | 243431 |

| | MODELS (Cont.) | | | | |
|---|---|---|---|---|---|
| | **Landlord 2010, 2110, 2210** | **Landlord 3210V, 3310V** | **Landlord 3410, 3410S** | **Landlord 2012** | **Landlord 3310H, 3110H** |
| Bore | 3-1/16 in. (77.8 mm) | 3-1/16 in. (77.8 mm) | 3-1/16 in. (77.8 mm) | 3-1/16 in. (77.8 mm) | 3-1/16 in. (77.8 mm) |
| Stroke | 3¼ in. (82.5 mm) | 3¼ in. (82.5 mm) | 3¼ in. (82.5 mm) | 3¼ in. (82.5 mm) | 3¼ in. (82.5 mm) |
| Piston Displacement | 23.94 cu. in. (392 cc) | 23.94 cu. in. (392 cc) | 23.94 cu. in. (392 cc) | 30.16 cu. in. (494 cc) | 23.94 cu. in. (393 cc) |
| Horsepower | 10 | 10 | 10 | 12 | 10 |
| Slow Idle Speed – Rpm | 1200 | 1200 | 1200 | 1200 | 1200 |
| High Idle Speed (No-Load) – Rpm | 3600 | 3600 | 3600 | 3600 | 3600 |
| Full Load Speed – Rpm | 3240 | 3240 | 3240 | 3240 | 3240 |
| Crankcase Oil Capacity | | | 4 pints (1.9 L) | | |
| Weight – | | | | | |
| Above 32°F (0°C) | | | SAE 30 | | |
| 0°F (−18°C) to 32°F (0°C) | | | SAE 10W | | |
| Below 0°F (−18°C) | | | SAE 5W-20 | | |
| Transmission Oil Capacity | 3 pints (1.4 L) | 3 pints (1.4 L) | 3 pints (1.4 L) | 3 pints (1.4 L) | 3½ pints (1.6 L) |
| Weight | SAE 90 EP | SAE 90 EP | SAE 90 EP | SAE 90 EP | Dexron ATF |
| Bevel Gear Housing Oil Capacity | | | 1 pint (0.5 L) | | |
| Weight | | | SAE 90 EP | | |
| Reduction Housing Oil Capacity | .... | .... | .... | .... | 3 pints (1.4 L) |
| Weight | .... | .... | .... | .... | SAE 90 EP |

| | MODELS | | | | |
|---|---|---|---|---|---|
| | **Sovereign 3012, 3112V, 3212V** | **Sovereign 3112H, 3212H** | **Baron 3414S** | **Baron 3414H** | **Sovereign 3314V** |
| Engine Make | B&S | B&S | B&S | B&S | B&S |
| Model | 300421 | 300421 | 302434 | 302434 | 320421 |
| Bore | 3-7/16 in. (87.3 mm) | 3-7/16 in. (87.3 mm) | 3-7/16 in. (87.3 mm) | 3-7/16 in. (87.3 mm) | 3-9/16 in. (90.5 mm) |
| Stroke | 3¼ in. (82.5 mm) | 3¼ in. (82.5 mm) | 3¼ in. (82.5 mm) | 3¼ in. (82.5 mm) | 3¼ in. (82.5 mm) |
| Piston Displacement | 30.16 cu. in. (494 cc) | 30.16 cu. in. (494 cc) | 30.16 cu. in. (494 cc) | 30.16 cu. in. (494 cc) | 32.4 cu. in. (531 cc) |
| Horsepower | 12 | 12 | 13 | 13 | 14 |
| Slow Idle Speed – Rpm | 1200 | 1200 | 1200 | 1200 | 1200 |
| High Idle Speed (No-Load) – Rpm | 3600 | 3600 | 3600 | 3600 | 3600 |
| Full Load Speed – Rpm | 3240 | 3240 | 3240 | 3240 | 3240 |
| Crankcase Oil Capacity | | | 4 pints (1.9 L) | | |
| Weight – | | | | | |
| Above 32°F (0°C) | | | SAE 30 | | |
| 0°F (−18°C) to 32°F (0°C) | | | SAE 10W | | |
| Below 0°F (−18°C) | | | SAE 5W-20 | | |
| Transmission Oil Capacity | 2½ pints (1.2 L) | 3½ pints (1.6 L) | 3 pints (1.4 L) | 3½ pints (1.6 L) | 3 pints (1.4 L) |
| Weight | SAE 90 EP | Dexron ATF | SAE 90 EP | Dexron ATF | SAE 90 EP |
| Bevel Gear Housing Oil Capacity | | | 1 pint (0.5 L) | | |
| Weight | | | SAE 90 EP | | |
| Reduction Housing Oil Capacity | .... | 3 pints (1.4 L) | .... | 3 pints (1.4 L) | .... |
| Weight | .... | SAE 90 EP | .... | SAE 90 EP | .... |

| | MODELS | | | | |
|---|---|---|---|---|---|
| | **Sovereign 3314H** | **Sovereign 3415S** | **Sovereign 3415H** | **Sovereign 3416S** | **Sovereign 3416H** |
| Engine Make | B&S | B&S | B&S | B&S | B&S |
| Model | 320421 | 325431 | 325431 | 326430 | 326430 |
| Bore | 3-9/16 in. (90.5 mm) | 3-9/16 in. (90.5 mm) | 3-9/16 in. (90.5 mm) | 3-9/16 in. (90.5 mm) | 3-9/16 in. (90.5 mm) |
| Stroke | 3¼ in. (82.5 mm) | 3¼ in. (82.5 mm) | 3¼ in. (82.5 mm) | 3¼ in. (82.5 mm) | 3¼ in. (82.5 mm) |

MODELS (Cont.)

| | Sovereign 3314H | Sovereign 3415S | Sovereign 3415H | Sovereign 3416S | Sovereign 3416H |
|---|---|---|---|---|---|
| Piston Displacement | 32.4 cu. in. (531 cc) | 32.4 cu. in. (531 cc) | 32.4 cu. in. (531 cc) | 32.4 cu. in. (531 cc) | 32.4 cu. in. (531 cc) |
| Horsepower | 14 | 15 | 15 | 16 | 16 |
| Slow Idle Speed – Rpm | 1200 | 1200 | 1200 | 1200 | 1200 |
| High Idle Speed (No-Load) – Rpm | 3600 | 3600 | 3600 | 3600 | 3600 |
| Full Load Speed – Rpm | 3240 | 3240 | 3240 | 3240 | 3240 |
| Crankcase Oil Capacity | | | 4 pints (1.9 L) | | |
| Weight – | | | | | |
| Above 32°F (0°C) | | | SAE 30 | | |
| 0°F (–18°C) to 32°F (0°C) | | | SAE 10W | | |
| Below 0°F (–18°C) | | | SAE 5W-20 | | |
| Transmission Oil Capacity | 3½ pints (1.6 L) | 3 pints (1.4 L) | 3½ pints (1.6 L) | 3 pints (1.4 L) | 3½ pints (1.6 L) |
| Weight | Dexron ATF | SAE 90 EP | Dexron ATF | SAE 90 EP | Dexron ATF |
| Bevel Gear Housing Oil Capacity | | | 1 pint (0.5 L) | | |
| Weight | | | SAE 90 EP | | |
| Reduction Housing Oil Capacity | 3 pints (1.4 L) | .... | 3 pints (1.4 L) | .... | 3 pints (1.4 L) |
| Weight | SAE 90 EP | .... | SAE 90 EP | .... | SAE 90 EP |

MODELS

| | 4008, 4108 | 4111 | 4208 | 4211G |
|---|---|---|---|---|
| Engine Make | B&S | B&S | B&S | B&S |
| Model | 191707 | 252707 | 191707 | 252707 |
| Bore | 3.0 in. (76 mm) | 3.44 in. (87 mm) | 3.0 in. (76 mm) | 3.44 in. (87 mm) |
| Stroke | 2.75 in. (69 mm) | 2.62 in. (67 mm) | 2.75 in. (69 mm) | 2.62 in. (67 mm) |
| Piston Displacement | 19.4 cu. in. (319 cc) | 24.4 cu. in. (399 cc) | 19.4 cu. in. (319 cc) | 24.4 cu. in. (399 cc) |
| Horsepower | 8 | 11 | 8 | 11 |
| Slow Idle Speed – Rpm | 1750 | 1750 | 1750 | 1750 |
| High Idle Speed (No-Load) – Rpm | 3600 | 3600 | 3600 | 3600 |
| Full Load Speed – Rpm | 3400 | 3400 | 3400 | 3400 |
| Crankcase Oil Capacity | 2¼ pints (1.1 L) | 2½ pints (1.2 L) | 2¼ pints (1.1 L) | 2½ pints (1.2 L) |
| Weight – | | | | |
| Above 32°F (0°C) | | SAE 30 | | |
| 0°F (–18°C) to 32° F (0°C) | | SAE 10W | | |
| Below 0°F (–18°C) | | SAE 5W-20 | | |
| Transaxle Oil Capacity | 24 ounces (710 mL) | 24 ounces (710 mL) | * | * |
| Weight | SAE 90 EP | SAE 90 EP | * | * |

*Early Models 4208 and 4211G are equipped with a transaxle manufactured by Simplicity. Fluid capacity is 3 pints (1.4 L) of SAE 90 EP gear oil. Late Models 4208 and 4211G are equipped with a Peerless transaxle. Transaxle capacity is 30 ounces (888 mL) of EP lithium grease.

MODELS

| | 4211H | 5211G | 5211H | 6008, 6108 |
|---|---|---|---|---|
| Engine Make | B&S | B&S | B&S | B&S |
| Model | 252707 | 252707 | 252707 | 191707 |
| Bore | 3.44 in. (87 mm) | 3.44 in. (87 mm) | 3.44 in. (87 mm) | 3.0 in. (76 mm) |
| Stroke | 2.62 in. (67 mm) | 2.62 in. (67 mm) | 2.62 in. (67 mm) | 2.75 in. (69 mm) |
| Piston Displacement | 24.4 cu. in. (399 cc) | 24.4 cu. in. (399 cc) | 24.4 cu. in. (399 cc) | 19.4 cu. in. (319 cc) |
| Horsepower | 11 | 11 | 11 | 8 |
| Slow Idle Speed – Rpm | 1750 | 1750 | 1750 | 1750 |
| High Idle Speed (No-Load) – Rpm | 3600 | 3600 | 3600 | 3600 |
| Full Load Speed – Rpm | 3400 | 3400 | 3400 | 3400 |
| Crankcase Oil Capacity | 2½ pints (1.2 L) | 2½ pints (1.2 L) | 2½ pints (1.2 L) | 2¼ pints (1.1 L) |
| Weight – | | | | |
| Above 32°F (0°C) | | SAE 30 | | |
| 0°F (–18°C) to 32°F (0°C) | | SAE 10W | | |

| | MODELS (Cont.) | | | |
|---|---|---|---|---|
| | 4211H | 5211G | 5211H | 6008, 6108 |
| Below 0°F (−18°C) | SAE 5W-20 | | | |
| Transaxle Oil Capacity | 30 ounces (888 mL) | 30 ounces (888 mL) | 2¼ pints (1 L) | 3 pints (1.4 L) |
| Weight | Lithium Grease | Lithium Grease | Type A ATF | SAE 90 EP |

| | MODELS | | | |
|---|---|---|---|---|
| | 6010 | 6011 | 6111 | 7110 |
| Engine Make | B&S | B&S | B&S | Kohler |
| Model | 251707 | 252707 | 252707 | K241 |
| Bore | 3.44 in. (87 mm) | 3.44 in. (87 mm) | 3.44 in. (87 mm) | 3.25 in. (83 mm) |
| Stroke | 2.62 in. (67 mm) | 2.62 in. (67 mm) | 2.62 in. (67 mm) | 2.88 in. (73 mm) |
| Piston Displacement | 24.4 cu. in. (399 cc) | 24.4 cu. in. (399 cc) | 24.4 cu. in. (399 cc) | 23.9 cu. in. (392 cc) |
| Horsepower | 11 | 11 | 11 | 10 |
| Slow Idle Speed – Rpm | 1750 | 1750 | 1750 | 1750 |
| High Idle Speed (No-Load) – Rpm | 3600 | 3600 | 3600 | 3600 |
| Full Load Speed – Rpm | 3400 | 3400 | 3400 | 3400 |
| Crankcase Oil Capacity | 2½ pints (1.2 L) | 2½ pints (1.2 L) | 2½ pints (1.2 L) | 4 pints (1.9 L) |
| Weight – | | | | |
| Above 32°F (0°C) | SAE 30 | | | |
| 0°F (−18°C) to 32°F (0°C) | SAE 10W | | | |
| Below 0°F (−18°C) | SAE 5W-20 | | | |
| Transaxle Oil Capacity | 3 pints (1.4 L) | 3 pints (1.4 L) | 3 pints (1.4 L) | 3 pints (1.4 L) |
| Weight | SAE 90 EP | | | |

# FRONT AXLE SYSTEM

## AXLE MAIN MEMBER

### Broadmoor-Serf-Yeoman Models

The axle main member (3 – Fig. S1) and main frame is a welded assembly. Since front axle is rigid, pivot point is at rear of main frame and in front of transaxle unit.

### Landlord-Sovereign-Baron-7110 Models

The stabilizer and axle main member (3 – Fig. S2) is a welded assembly. The unit pivots on center mounting bolt and at rear of stabilizer. To remove the assembly, remove drag link ball joint end from steering arm (4) on left steering spindle. Raise front of tractor and remove cap screw (11) and spacer (12) from center of axle. Lower front of axle and pull forward to slide stabilizer pivot out of frame angle. The frame angle is bolted to main frame and can be renewed if stabilizer pivot hole is excessively worn.

### Series 4000-4100-4200-5200-6000-6100 Models

To remove axle main member (6 – Fig. S2A) assembly from tractor, support front of tractor and disconnect drag link at left spindle arm. Remove pivot bolt (2), pull axle assembly forward out of center pivot and remove axle. Renew spacer (11) and bolt (2) as necessary.

Reinstall by reversing removal procedure.

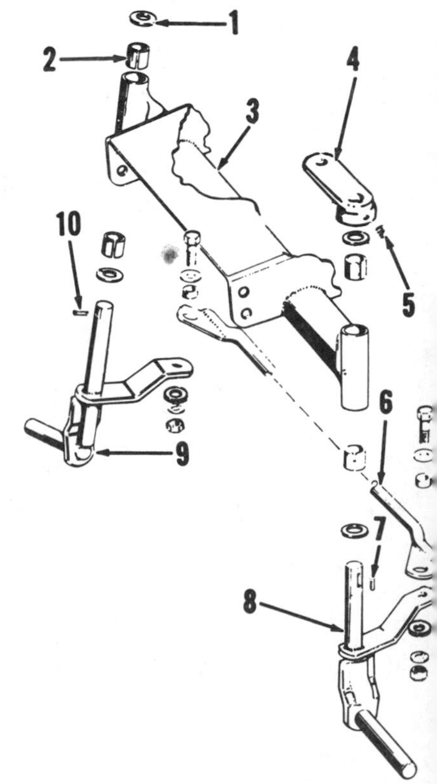


***Fig. S1 – Exploded view of front axle assembly used on Broadmoor, Serf and Yeoman models. Axle main member and frame is a welded assembly. On later models, right steering spindle is held with a retaining ring in place of roll pin (10).***

1. Washer
2. Steering spindle bearing
3. Axle main member
4. Steering arm
5. Set screw
6. Tie Rod
7. Key
8. Steering spindle (L.H.)
9. Steering spindle (R.H.)
10. Roll pin

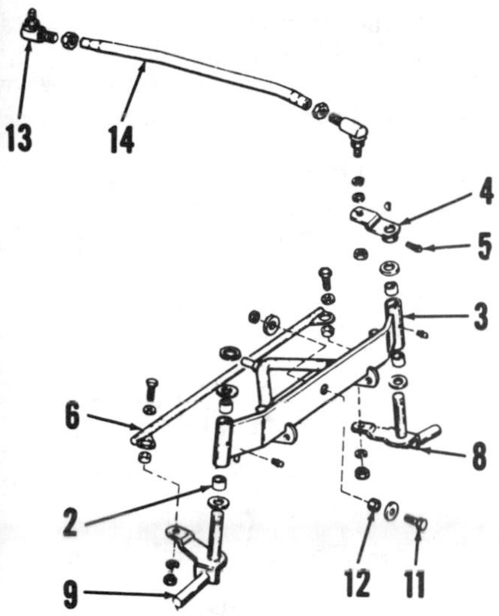

13 14 4 5 3 6 8 2 12 11 9

***Fig. S2—Exploded view of front axle assembly used on Landlord, Sovereign, Baron and 7110 tractors.***

2. Steering spindle bearing
3. Axle main member
4. Steering arm
5. Set screw
6. Tie rod
8. Steering spindle (L.H.)
9. Steering spindle (R.H.)
11. Axle pivot cap screw
12. Spacer
13. Ball joint end
14. Drag link

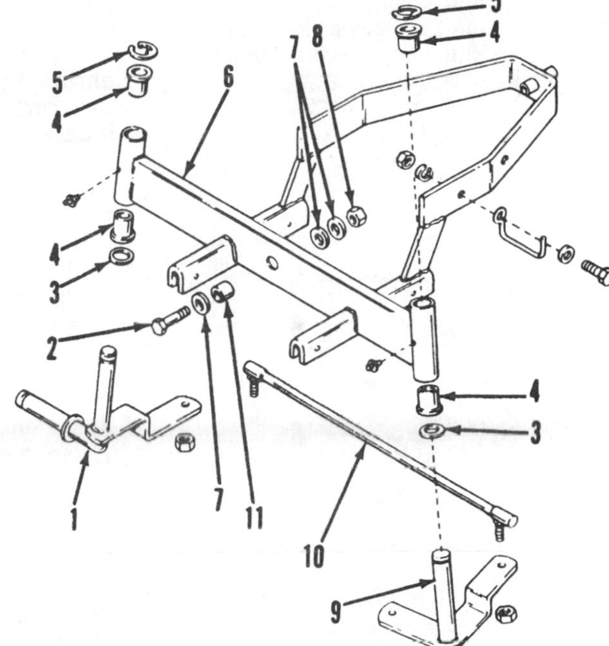


***Fig. S2A—Exploded view of front axle used on Series 4000, 4100, 4200, 5200, 6000 and 6100 models.***

1. Spindle
2. Front pivot bolt
3. Washer
4. Bushings
5. Retaining ring
6. Main member
7. Washers
8. Nut
9. Spindle
10. Tie rod
11. Spacer

### TIE ROD

#### All Models

Tie rod (6–Fig. S1 or S2) or (10–Fig. S2A) is nonadjustable and can be removed after removing bolts, washers and spacers securing tie rod to steering spindles.

### STEERING SPINDLES

#### Series 4000-4100-4200-5200-6000-6100 Models

To remove spindle (1 or 9–Fig. S2A), raise and support front of tractor. Remove front wheel and tire. Disconnect tie rod (10) from both sides and drag link from left side. Remove retaining ring (5) and remove spindle. Renew bushings (4), washers (3) and spindles (1 or 9) as necessary.

Reinstall by reversing removal procedure.

#### All Other Models

To remove steering spindles (8 and 9–Fig. S1 or S2), block up under front axle and remove front wheels. Disconnect tie rod from spindles. Loosen set screw (5) and remove steering arm (4) from left spindle. Lower spindle out of axle main member. Remove retaining pin or ring from top of right spindle and remove spindle. The four spindle bearings (2) (two in each end of axle main member) can be inspected and if necessary renewed at this time.

# STEERING GEAR

### R&R AND OVERHAUL

#### Serf Models

To remove steering shaft, remove hood and disconnect drag link (8–Fig. S3) from steering shaft (4). Remove steering wheel and disconnect throttle cable. Remove "E" ring (10) from lower end of steering shaft. Unbolt and lift dash, steering shaft and support from tractor. Remove retaining ring (2) and slide steering shaft out of steering support.

#### Broadmoor-Yeoman Models

To remove steering gear, first remove hood and steering wheel. Disconnect ignition wire and choke and throttle control cables. Unbolt and lift off dash assembly and upper steering shaft support. Raise front of tractor and disconnect drag link (5–Fig. S4) from steering gear (4). Unbolt and remove steering gear (4). Remove nut securing steering pinion to frame and withdraw upper steering shaft, "U" joint and steering pinion. Disassembly of "U" joint is evident after inspecting unit and reference to Fig. S4.

When reassembling steering units move steering gear (4) closer to steering pinion (8) to remove excessive steering wheel play. The remainder of assembly procedure is reverse of disassembly.

#### Landlord (1965) Model

To remove steering gear, place hood in raised position. Remove side panels and battery. Disconnect wires at starter-generator and ammeter to regulator wire at regulator. Loosen set screw and remove steering wheel. Unbolt and lift off dash assembly and lay same to left side of tractor. Slide flexible fuel line off tank connector. Remove cap screws securing tank support to main frame and lift off tank support and upper steering shaft support assembly. Disconnect rear drag link ball joint end from steering arm (7–Fig. S5). Loosen set screws and remove steering arm, Woodruff key and washer from steering gear shaft. The steering gear (5) can now be removed. Remove snap ring and washer from lower end of pinion gear shaft. Withdraw shaft assembly, with keyed on pinion gear, from bearing. The two steering gear bearings (6 and 9) can be removed from main frame after removing six attaching cap screws. Disassembly of "U" joint is evident after inspecting unit and reference to Fig. S5.

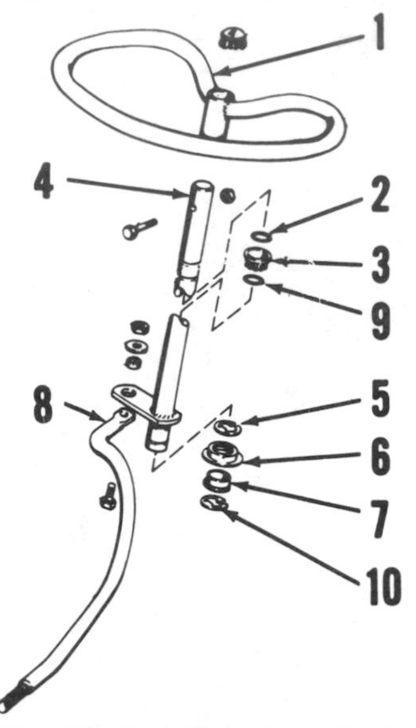

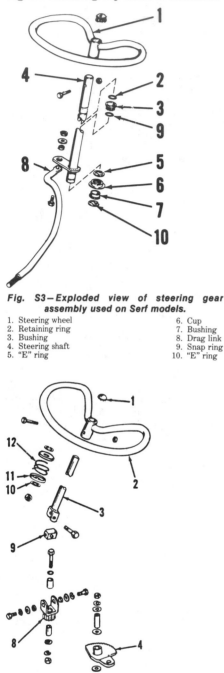

*Fig. S3—Exploded view of steering gear assembly used on Serf models.*

1. Steering wheel
2. Retaining ring
3. Bushing
4. Steering shaft
5. "E" ring
6. Cup
7. Bushing
8. Drag link
9. Snap ring
10. "E" ring

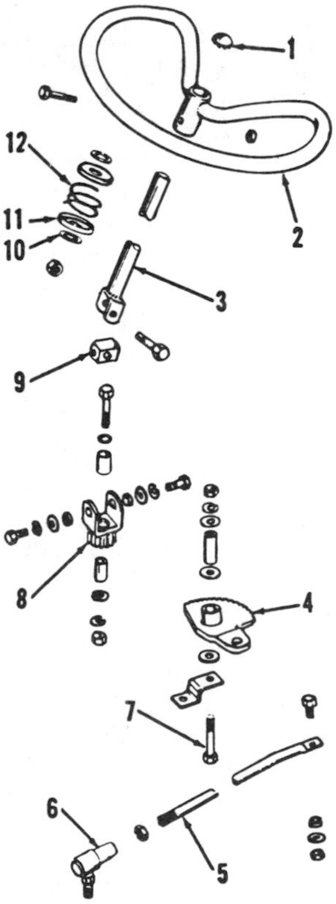

*Fig. 54—Exploded view of Broadmoor and Yeoman starting gear assembly. On later models, a flanged bushing is used in place of spring (12) and cups (11).*

1. Plug
2. Steering wheel
3. Upper steering shaft
4. Steering gear
5. Drag link
6. Ball joint end
7. Cap screw
8. Steering pinion
9. "U" joint
10. Washer
11. Spring cup
12. Spring

## Landlord (1966 Through 1970)—Sovereign Prior to 1971-7110 Models

To remove steering gear, remove hood, side panels and battery. Disconnect all interfering electrical wires and remove fuel tank. Loosen set screw and remove steering wheel and key. Unbolt and remove dash assembly and lay same to left side of tractor. Remove collar (1–Fig. S6) from steering shaft (2); then, unbolt and remove fuel tank and battery support. Disconnect "U" joint (3) from gear and yoke assembly (5) and remove steering shaft. Disconnect rear drag link ball joint from steering arm (10). Remove nut and washers from steering arm shaft and remove steering gear (8) as steering arm and shaft are withdrawn. Remove nut, lockwasher and set screw from lower end of eccentric pin (4) and withdraw eccentric pin with gear and yoke assembly (5). Unbolt and remove steering bracket (7).

Check needle bearings (9) and bushing (6) and renew as necessary.

When reassembling, lubricate needle bearings, bushing and gear teeth. Before attaching drag link, adjust gear backlash as follows: With eccentric pin nut and set screw loose, rotate eccentric pin to obtain minimum backlash between gears. Tighten nut and set screw, then rotate gears to make certain they do not bind. If binding condition exists, increase backlash slightly.

Complete balance of reassembly by reversing disassembly procedure.

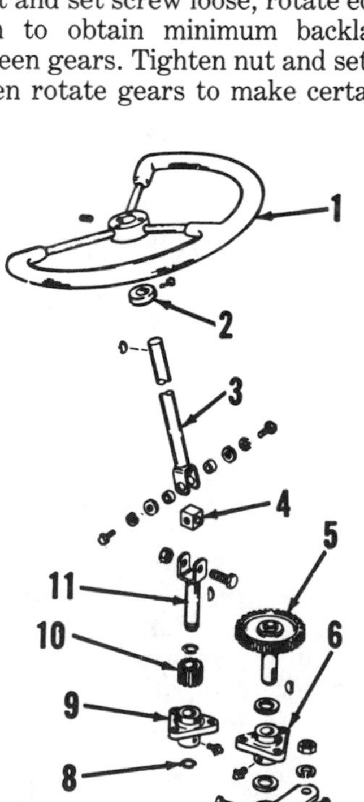


*Fig. S5—Exploded view of Landlord (1965) steering gear assembly*

1. Steering wheel
2. Set collar
3. Upper steering shaft
4. "U" joint
5. Steering gear
6. Bearing
7. Steering arm
8. Snap ring
9. Bearing
10. Steering pinion
11. Lower steering shaft

## Models 3310H-3310V-3314H-3314V-3410-3410H-3410S-3414H-3414S-3415H-3415S-3416H-3416S

To remove steering gear, tilt hood and grille assembly forward. Disconnect bat-

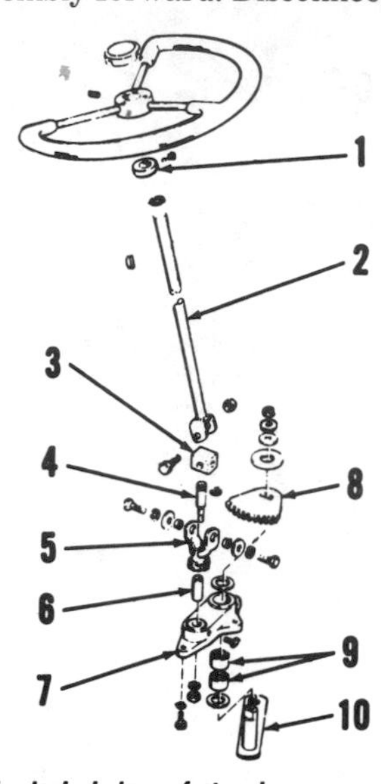


*Fig. S6—Exploded view of steering gear used on Landlord models (1966 through 1970), Sovereign models prior to 1971 and 7110 models.*

1. Collar
2. Steering shaft
3. "U" joint
4. Eccentric pin
5. Gear & yoke assy.
6. Bushing
7. Steering bracket
8. Steering gear
9. Needle bearings
10. Steering arm & shaf

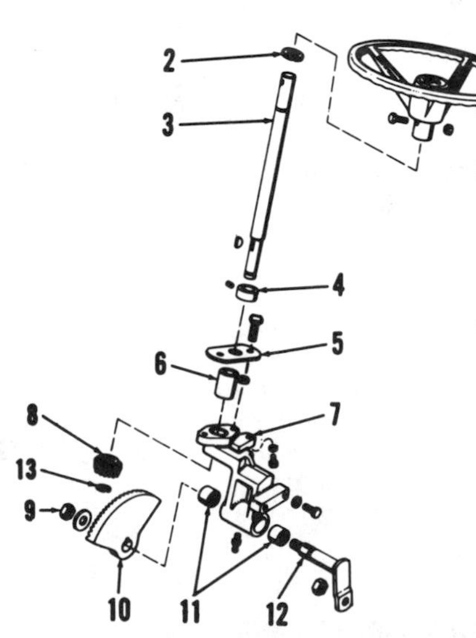


*Fig. S4—Exploded view of Broadmoor and Yeoman steering gear assembly. On later models, a flanged bushing is used in place of spring (12) and cups (11).*

1. Steering wheel
2. Snap ring
3. Steering shaft
4. Collar
5. Bracket
6. Bushing
7. Bracket
8. Pinion gear
9. Nut
10. Quadrant gea
11. Needle bearin
12. Steering arm
13. Snap ring

tery cables and remove battery. Remove steering wheel and loosen set screw in collar (4–Fig. S7). Remove snap ring (2) and pinion gear snap ring (13). Withdraw steering shaft and pinion gear. Remove retaining nut (9) and remove quadrant gear (10). To remove steering bracket (7), disconnect drag link from steering arm and remove bracket bolts. Needle bearings (11) may now be removed.

### Series 4000-4100-4200-5200-6000-6100 Models

To remove steering gear, remove steering wheel, upper dash, fuel tank and lower dash. Disconnect drag link (11–Fig. S7A) from steering rod (10). Unbolt and remove upper steering plate (6) and steering shaft (8). Remove lower plate (9) and steering rod (10).

Clean and inspect all parts. Renew bushings (5) as necessary.

To reassemble, install key (14) with rounded end toward bent end of steering rod (10) until top edge of gear is flush with end of key (14). Steering rod should extend approximately ¼ inch (6 mm) above steering gear. Install assembly on lower plate (9). Place spacer (7) on steering shaft (8) with bevel towards steering gear. Center steering gear on lower plate and install steering shaft so hole in shaft faces front and back.

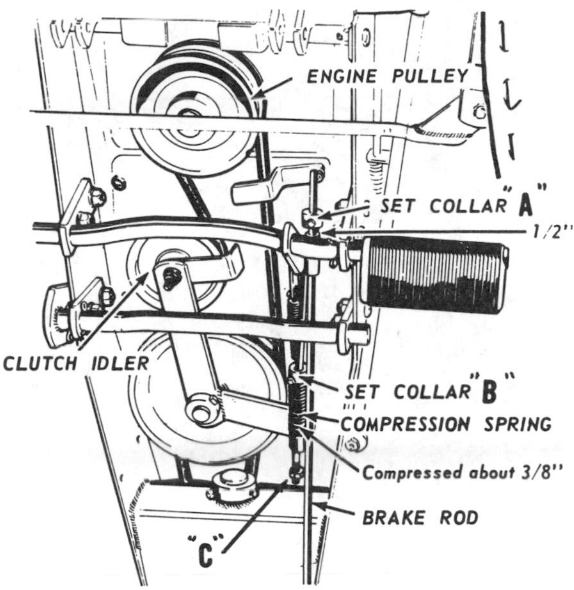


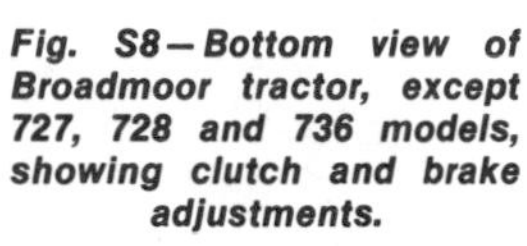
*Fig. S8—Bottom view of Broadmoor tractor, except 727, 728 and 736 models, showing clutch and brake adjustments.*

# ENGINE

## REMOVE AND REINSTALL

### Broadmoor-Serf-Yeoman Models

To remove engine, first remove hood. Disconnect ignition wire, flexible fuel line and choke and throttle control cables. Depress clutch-brake pedal and remove drive belt from engine pulley. Remove four engine mounting bolts and lift engine out of tractor frame.

To reinstall engine, reverse removal procedure.

### Landlord-Sovereign-Baron-7110 Models

To remove engine, first remove hood, grille and grille support. Disconnect battery ground cable and ignition wire. Slide flexible fuel line off tank shut-off valve. Disconnect wires from starter-generator and choke and throttle control cables from engine. Remove engine oil drain pipe on models so equipped. Unbolt drive shaft front coupling and remove four cap screws securing engine to frame. Slide engine forward and lift out of frame.

When reinstalling engine, tighten drive shaft coupling bolts to a torque of 20 ft.-lbs. (27 N•m).

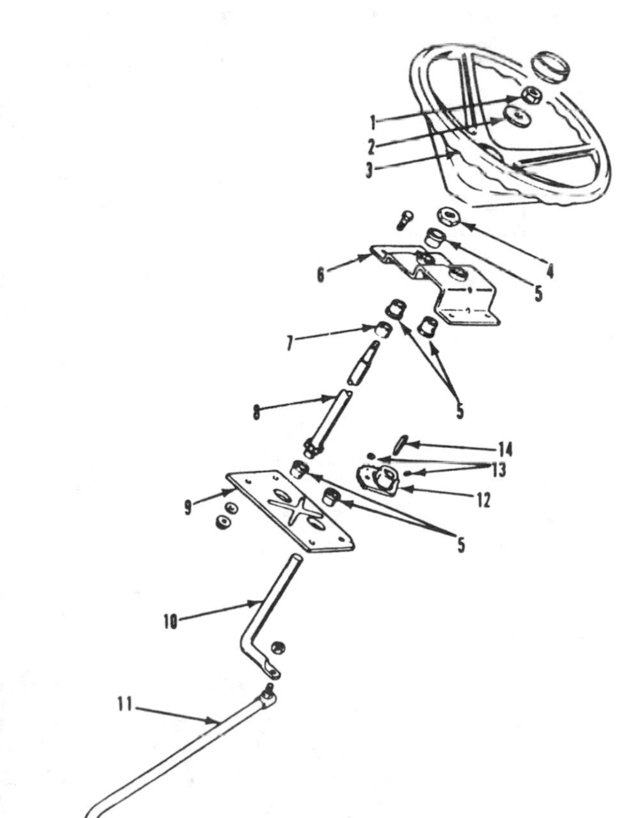


*Fig. S7A—Exploded view of steering shaft and mechanism used on 4000, 4100, 4200, 5200, 6000 and 6100 series models.*

1. Locknut
2. Washer
3. Steering wheel
4. Hex washer
5. Bushings
6. Upper steering plate
7. Spacer
8. Steering shaft
9. Lower steering plate
10. Steering rod
11. Drag link
12. Steering gear
13. Set screws
14. Key

### Series 4000-4100-4200-5200-6000-6100 Models

Disconnect battery ground cable. Disconnect fuel line at carburetor. Disconnect throttle and choke cables and all necessary electrical wiring. Remove drive belts. Remove engine mounting bolts and remove engine.

Reinstall by reversing removal procedure.

## OVERHAUL

### All Models

Engine make and model are listed at the beginning of this section. To overhaul engine components and accessories, refer to Briggs & Stratton and Kohler sections of this manual.

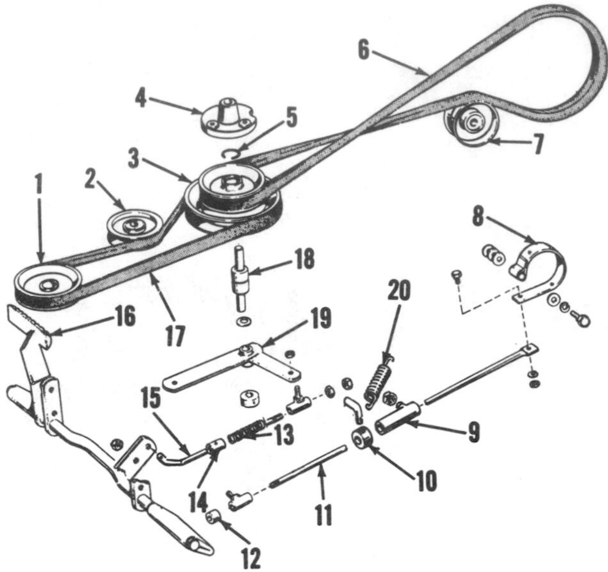

***Fig. S9—Exploded view of belt arrangement, clutch and brake system used on Broadmoor tractors except 727, 728 and 738 models.***

1. Engine drive pulley
2. Clutch idler pulley
3. Countershaft pulley
4. Countershaft hub
5. Snap ring
6. Transmission drive belt
7. Rear belt idler pulley
8. Brake band
9. Brake rod guide
10. Brake lock
11. Brake rod
12. Set collar
13. Clutch tension spring
14. Set collar
15. Clutch rod
16. Clutch-brake pedal
17. Engine drive belt
18. Countershaft & bearing
19. Idler lever
20. Brake spring

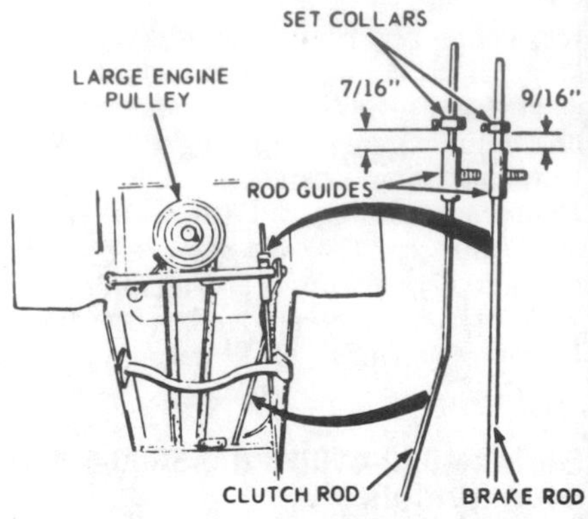


***Fig. S10—View of clutch and brake adjustments on Broadmoor 727, Serf 515 and 525 and Yeoman 616 and 627 models.***

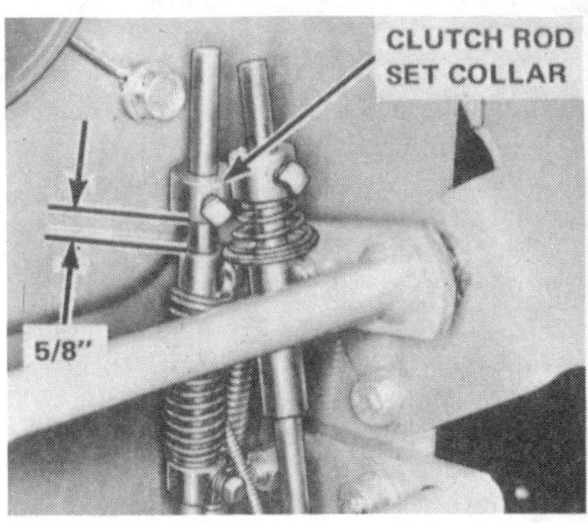


***Fig. S11—View of clutch rod adjustment on later Broadmoor, Serf and Yeoman models.***

# CLUTCH AND BRAKE

The clutch used on all models is a belt idler operated by clutch-brake pedal on right side of tractor. When clutch-brake pedal is depressed, idler tension is removed from drive belt, allowing drive pulley to turn free within belt. At this time, the brake rod which is also connected to clutch-brake pedal, tightens brake band on brake drum, stopping the tractor.

## ADJUSTMENT

### Broadmoor Models Except 727-728-738

With clutch-brake pedal released (clutch engaged), adjust set collar (B–Fig. S8) on clutch rod to compress spring about 3/8 inch (10 mm). Hold brake rod forward (band tight on drum) and with clutch still engaged, adjust set collar (A) on brake rod to obtain 1/2 inch (13 mm) clearance between set collar and brake rod guide. Slowly depress clutch-brake pedal and check to see that clutch idler is released when brake is applied. If not, adjust nut (C) on clutch rod to obtain proper action. Refer to Fig. S9 for exploded view of clutch-brake system.

### Broadmoor 727-Serf 515-525-Yeoman 616-627 Models

To adjust clutch and brake linkage, refer to Fig. S10. With clutch-brake pedal in up position, move set collars on clutch and brake rods until set collar on clutch rod is 7/16 inch (11 mm) from rod guide and set collar on brake rod is 9/16 inch (14 mm) from rod guide.

### Broadmoor 728-738-Serf 535-Yeoman 637-648-Early 4208-Early 4211G Models

To adjust clutch and brake linkage, refer to Fig. S11. With clutch-brake pedal in up position, adjust collar (13–Fig. S12) so it is against but not compressing spring (14). Depress clutch-brake pedal. Pedal should stop 2½ inches (64 mm) from front edge of foot rest. Release clutch-brake pedal and reposition collar (13) so correct pedal travel is obtained. With clutch-brake pedal in up position, distance between collar (8) and end of rod guide (9) should be 5/8 inch (16 mm) as shown in Fig. S11. Loosen set screw in collar and move collar to obtain correct measurement. Depress pedal all the way down and adjust position of collar (11–Fig. S12) so spring (10) is barely free to turn on clutch rod.

### Landlord (1965) Model

To adjust clutch and brake linkage, first tilt seat to the rear. Then, with clutch-brake pedal in normal position (clutch engaged), adjust nuts (A–Fig. S13) to give 3/4 inch (19 mm) clearance between rod guide (B) and nuts. Position set collar on clutch rod to compress spring 5/8 inch (16 mm). Recheck and if necessary readjust nuts (A) to clearance given above. When clutch pedal is operated, spring should be completely decompressed as locknuts (A) engage

***Fig. S12—Exploded view of clutch-brake linkage used on later Broadmoor, Serf and Yeoman models.***

1. Engine pulley
2. Drive belt
3. Clutch idler pulley
4. Idler bracket
5. Belt guide
6. Pto pulley
7. Clutch-brake pedal
8. Collar
9. Rod guide
10. Spring
11. Collar
12. Clutch rod
13. Collar
14. Spring
15. Washer
16. Rod guide
17. Brake rod
18. Parking brake collar
19. Spring
20. Rod guide
21. Brake band
22. Brake lining

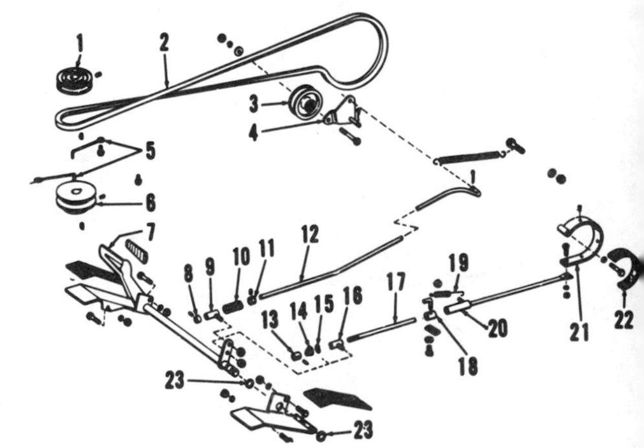

end of rod guide (B). Pull brake band up by hand so it is tight around brake drum. Adjust screw (C–Fig. S14) to obtain a clearance of ¾ inch (19 mm) between brake band and adjusting screw head. Depress clutch-brake pedal and check to see that idler pulley releases drive belt properly before brake is applied.

## Landlord Models 2010-2012-2110-2210

To adjust clutch idler and brake linkage, tilt seat rearward. With clutch-brake pedal in up position (clutch engaged), adjust locknuts on clutch rod to obtain 11/16 inch (17.5 mm) clearance between locknuts and rod guide as shown in Fig. S15. Refer to Fig. S16 and pull brake band up by hand until it is tight around brake drum. Adjust locknuts as required to obtain a clearance of 11/16 inch (17.5 mm) between brake band and locknuts as shown.

Depress clutch-brake pedal and check to see that clutch idler pulley releases belt tension properly before brake is applied.

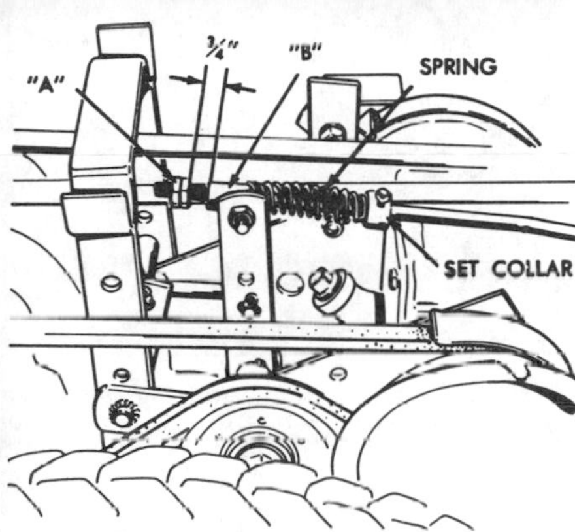


Fig. S13—View showing clutch adjustment on 1965 model Landlord tractor.

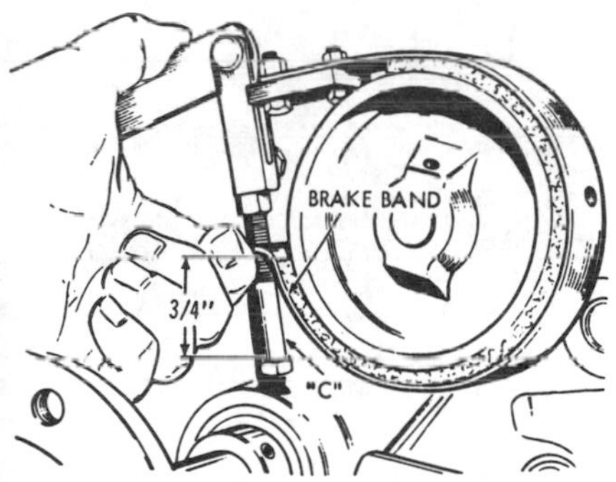


Fig. S14—Brake adjustment on 1965 model Landlord tractors is ¾ inch (19 mm), measured as shown.

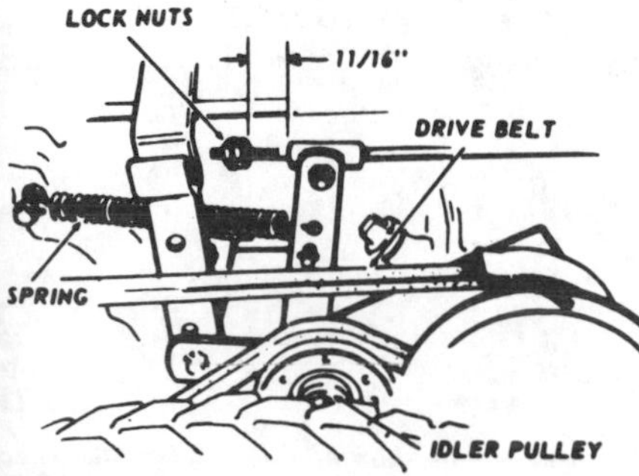


Fig. S15—On Landlord Models 2010 and 2012, adjust clutch rod locknuts to obtain 11/16 inch (17.5 mm) clearance as shown. Refer to text.

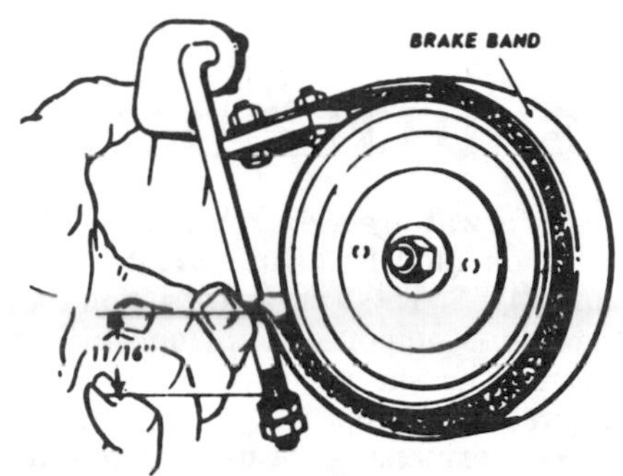


Fig. S16—The brake adjustment on Landlord models 2010 and 2012 is 11/16 inch (17.5 mm) measured as shown.

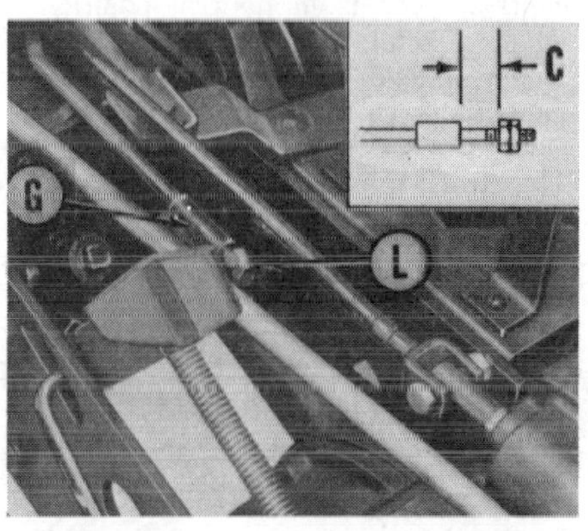


Fig. S17—View showing clutch rod adjustment on models with variable speed drive. Distance between rod guide "G" and rod nuts "L" should be ⅞ inch (22 mm) "C".

## Models 3012-3112V-3210V-3212V-3310V-3314V

Refer to Fig. S17 and adjust control rod locknuts (L) so there is ⅞ inch (22 mm) clearance between locknuts and rod guide (G) with variable speed lever in "LOW" speed position.

To adjust brake, check clutch adjustment as previously outlined. Tighten adjusting nuts (3–Fig. S18) on brake rod so drive belt on variable speed pulley creeps when engine is running and clutch-brake pedal is depressed. Loosen adjusting nuts gradually until creeping motion of drive belt stops when engine is running and clutch-brake pedal is depressed.

**CAUTION: To prevent possible injury, engine should be stopped while turning brake adjusting nuts.**

## Models 3112H-3212H-3310H-3314H-3410H-3414H-3415H-3416H

To adjust clutch, clutch-brake pedal must be in up position. Turn adjusting nuts (8–Fig. S19) so there is ⅛ inch (3 mm) clearance between adjusting nuts and closest end of rod guide (7).

To adjust brake, first be sure clutch is properly adjusted. Turn brake adjusting nuts (6–Fig. S19) so brake will operate when clutch-brake pedal is depressed

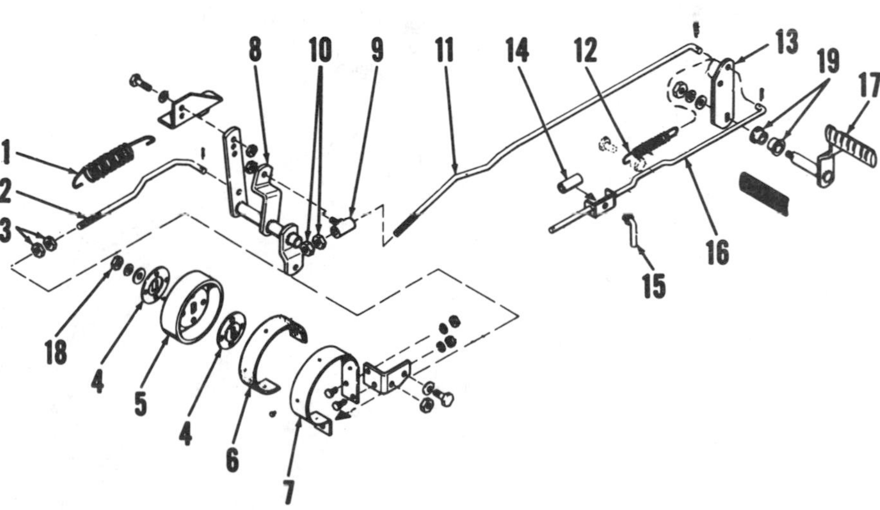


Fig. S18—Exploded view of clutch-brake linkage used on variable speed models.

1. Spring
2. Brake rod
3. Adjusting nuts
4. Washer
5. Brake drum
6. Brake lining
7. Brake band
8. Lever
9. Rod guide
10. Adjusting nuts
11. Clutch-brake rod
12. Spring
13. Lever
14. Spacer
15. Parking brake lock
16. Parking brake rod
17. Clutch-brake pedal
18. Nut
19. Bushing

but will not drag when clutch-brake pedal is released and clutch is engaged.

### Models 3410-3410S-3414S-3415S-3416S-7110

To adjust clutch idler linkage, tilt seat deck assembly rearward. With clutch-brake pedal in normal (clutch engaged) position, refer to Fig. S20 or S22 and adjust nuts (A) on clutch rod to obtain a clearance of 1/4 inch (6 mm) between adjusting nuts and rod guide.

To adjust foot brake, refer to Fig. S21 and back off adjusting nuts until foot brake is ineffective when pedal is fully depressed. Then, turn nut (A) clockwise, one turn at a time, until tractor will stop rolling backward satisfactorily when pedal is depressed. Secure adjusting nut (A) with locknut (B).

### Models 4008-4108-4111-Late 4208-Late 4211G-5211G-6008-6108-6010-6011-6111

Place transaxle in gear and release parking brake. Pull cam lever forward to remove slack. Refer to Fig. S23A and check gap between brake lever and stop. Gap should 1/8 inch (3 mm). To adjust, loosen jam nut at adjusting nut and turn adjusting nut as required to obtain correct gap. Tighten jam nut.

### Models 4211H-5211H

To adjust brake, release parking brake and check clearance between brake pad and brake disc. Correct clearance is 0.010 inch (0.254 mm). To adjust, tighten or loosen brake lever adjustment nut at brake caliper.

## SHUTTLE DRIVE

A forward-reverse shuttle drive is used on Models 3410S, 3414S, 3415S and 3416S. The transaxle used on these models is equipped with four forward gears. The shuttle drive control lever, located on right side of tractor, has three positions; forward, neutral and reverse. This allows tractor to be driven in forward or reverse direction in any of the four transaxle gears. Transaxle gears can be shifted when shuttle drive control lever is in neutral position or when clutch-brake pedal is depressed. When shuttle drive control lever is in neutral position, a brake is applied against transaxle input shaft pulley. This stops unput shaft from turning to facilitate gear shifting.

### Models 3410S-3414S-3415S-3416S

**ADJUSTMENT.** To adjust shuttle drive linkage, first tilt seat deck assembly rearward. Place shuttle drive control lever in neutral position. Refer to Fig. S22 and loosen set screw (B). Slide brake detent (C) forward or rearward as required to center detent groove on brake pin (D). Tighten set screw (B). Move control lever to forward position. Loosen nut (E–Fig. S23) and adjust brake pad (F) to obtain a 1/8 inch (3 mm)

*Fig. S20—View showing clutch rod adjustment on Landlord Model 3410. Distance between rod guide and nuts (A) should be 1/4 inch (6 mm).*

*Fig. S21—View showing location of brake adjusting nuts on Models 3410, 3410S, 3414S, 3415S and 3416S.*

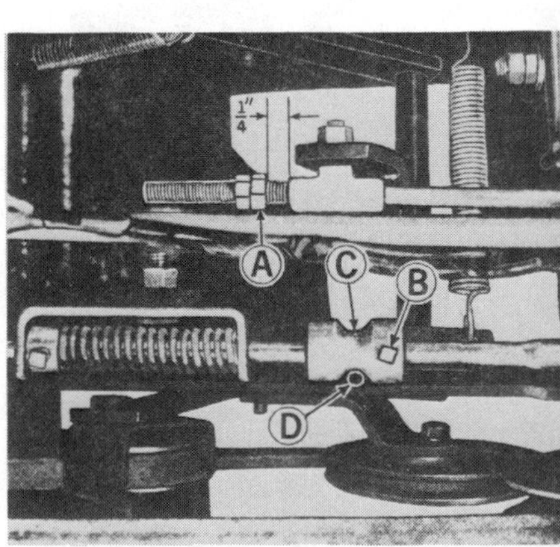


*Fig. S22—View showing clutch idler linkage adjustment and shuttle drive brake detent adjustment on Models 3410S, 3414S, 3415S and 3416S.*

A. Clutch adjusting nuts
B. Set screw
C. Brake detent
D. Brake pin

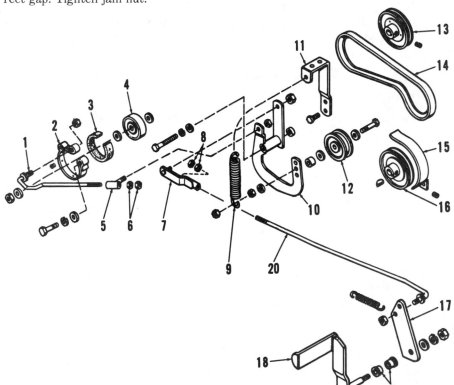

*Fig. S19—Exploded view of clutch-brake assembly used on Models 3112H, 3212H, 3310H, 3314H, 3410H, 3414H, 3415H and 3416H.*

1. Brake rod
2. Brake band
3. Brake lining
4. Brake drum
5. Rod guide
6. Adjusting nuts
7. Clutch rod guide
8. Adjusting nuts
9. Spring
10. Clutch-brake arm
11. Bracket
12. Clutch idler pulley
13. Transmission pulley
14. Drive belt
15. Belt guard
16. Bevel gear pulley
17. Arm
18. Clutch-brake pedal
19. Bushings
20. Clutch-brake rod

clearance between brake pad and input shaft pulley. Tighten nut (E).

Place control lever in neutral position and loosen set screw in collar (A – Fig. S23). Push rod guide assembly (B) forward until slack is removed from forward drive belt (C). Hold rod guide (B) forward and tighten collar set screw.

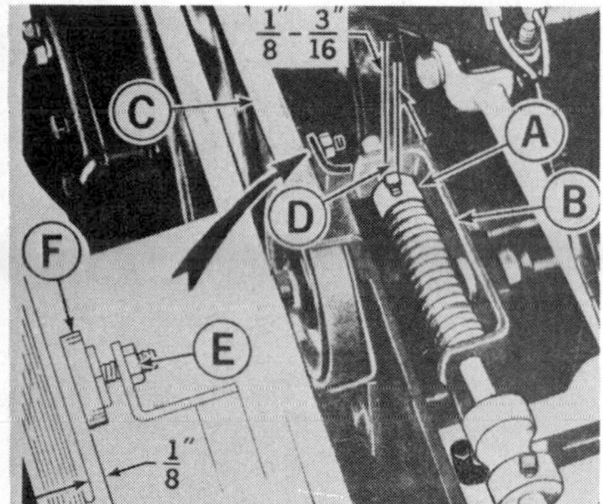


***Fig. S23 – Forward drive belt tension and neutral brake pad clearance adjustments on Models 3410S, 3414S, 3415S and 3416S.***

A. Collar
B. Rod guide
C. Forward drive belt
D. 1/8 to 3/16 inch (3-5 mm) distance
E. Locknut
F. Neutral brake pad

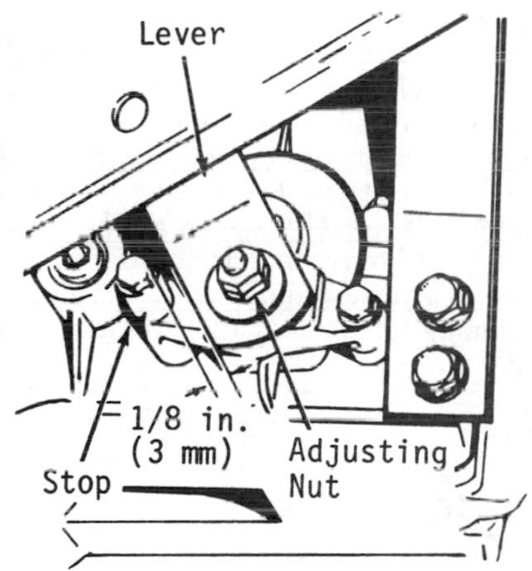


***Fig. S23A – With brake pedal released, there should be 1/8 inch (3 mm) gap between brake lever and stop.***

***Fig. S24 – On Models 3410S, 3414S, 3415S and 3416S, with shuttle control lever in neutral, adjust swivel (A) so reverse band (C) is snug when swivel is reconnected in hole (B).***

Move control lever to forward position and measure distance (D) between collar (A) and rod guide (B) which should be 1/8 to 3/16 inch (3-5 mm). If not, readjust position of collar (A) on linkage rod to obtain correct distance.

Place control lever in neutral position. Refer to Fig. S24, then unpin and remove swivel (A) from hole (B). Rotate swivel on rod until band (C) is snug on shuttle planetary carrier when swivel is reconnected in hole (B).

Test operation of shuttle drive. If operation is unsatisfactory, refer to the following problems and their possible causes:

A. Will not pull forward with full power.

Caused by: Incorrect adjustment of collar (A – Fig. S23) resulting in low tension on forward drive belt (C).

B. Tractor creeps forward when control lever is in neutral.

Caused by: Too much tension on forward drive belt (C – Fig. S23).

C. Will not pull with full power in reverse.

Caused by: Brake band (C – Fig. S24) adjustment too loose.

D. Tractor creeps rearward when control lever is in neutral.

Caused by: Brake band (C – Fig. S24) adjustment too tight.

E. Cannot shift gears without grinding when shuttle control lever is in neutral.

Caused by: Brake detent (C – Fig. S22) or clearance of brake pad (F – Fig. S23) not adjusted correctly.

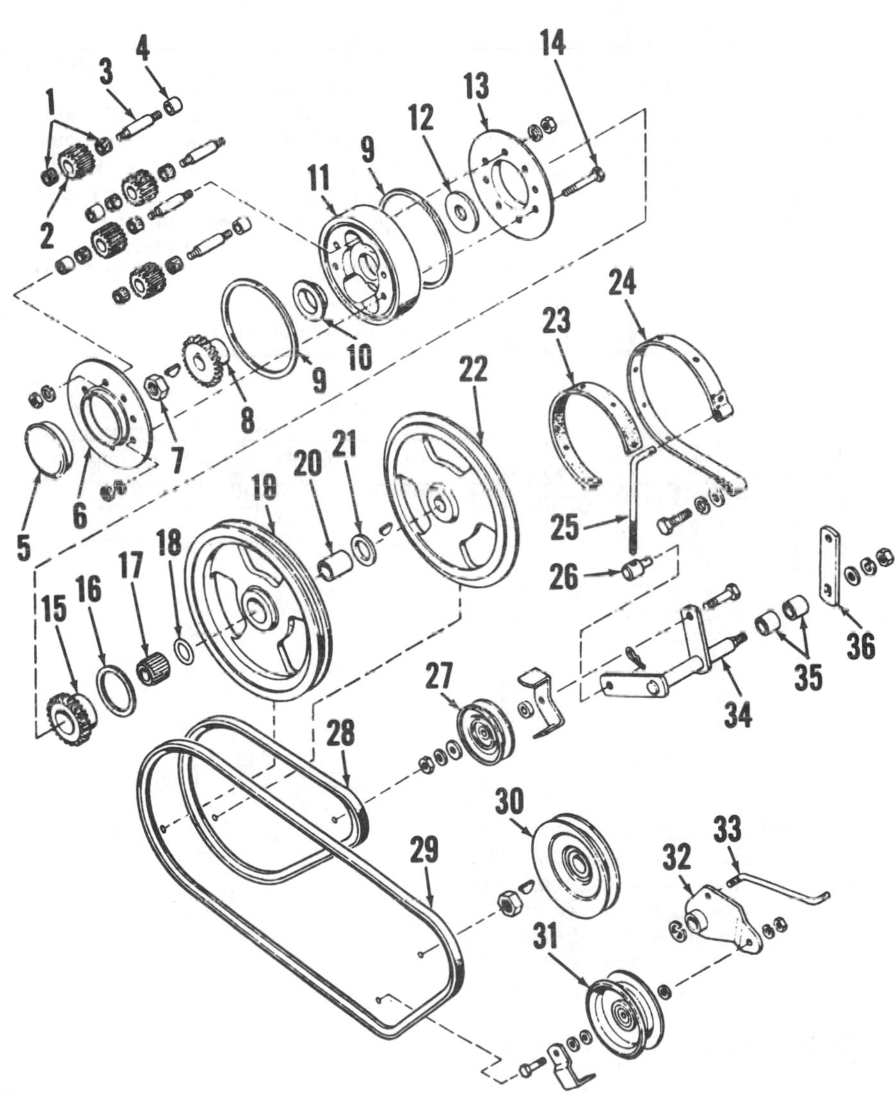


***Fig. S25 – Exploded view of forward-reverse shuttle drive unit used on Models 3410S, 3414S, 3415S and 3416S.***

1. Needle bearings
2. Planetary pinions
3. Planetary shafts
4. Sleeves
5. End cap
6. Cover
7. Nut
8. Gear
9. Seal ring
10. Flange bearing
11. Planetary carrier
12. Thrust washer
13. Cover
14. Through-bolts (4 used)
15. Gear
16. Seal ring
17. Roller bearing
18. Seal ring
19. Pulley
20. Inner race
21. Thrust washer
22. Half pulley
23. Brake lining
24. Reverse brake band
25. Rod
26. Swivel
27. Forward drive idler pulley
28. Forward drive belt
29. Main drive belt
30. Pulley (bevel gear driven)
31. Clutch idler pulley
32. Idler arm
33. Clutch link
34. Shuttle drive lever & shaft assy.
35. Bushings
36. Lever

### Models 3410S-3414S-3415S-3416S

**R&R AND OVERHAUL.** To remove forward-reverse shuttle drive unit, first disconnect and remove reverse drive planetary brake (23 through 26–Fig. S25). Remove drive belts (28 and 29). Using a screwdriver, pry cap (5) from planetary cover (6). Remove nut (7) and gear (8). Carefully withdraw planetary assembly.

To disassemble unit, remove nuts from bolts (14) and planetary shafts (3). Remove cover (6), seal ring (9) and bearing (10). Needle bearings (1), planetary pinions (2), sleeves (4) and planetary carrier (11) can now be removed. Remove gear (15), seal ring (16), bearing (17), seal ring (18), pulley (19), inner race (20) thrust washer (21) and half pulley (22) from transaxle input shaft.

Clean all parts and renew any showing excessive wear or other damage. Using new seal rings, reassemble by reversing disassembly procedure. Pack unit with EP lithium base grease. Adjust shuttle drive linkage as necessary.

# BEVEL GEARS

## REMOVE AND REINSTALL

### Models 3310V-3310H-3314V-3314H-3410-3410S-3410H-3414S-3414H-3415S-3415H-3416S-3416H

To remove bevel gear drive, support tractor under rear of main frame and under transaxle or gear reduction housing. Remove left rear wheel and hub. Remove bevel gear pto belt pulley and disconnect pto tension spring. Unbolt belt guard and remove drive belt from bevel gear drive pulley, then remove bevel gear pulley. Remove rear lift or other attachments secured to left side plate. Unbolt and remove left side plate. Disconnect drive shaft coupling from bevel gear input shaft. Unbolt and remove bevel gear unit from tractor.

Reinstall unit by reversing removal procedure. Adjust clutch and brake linkage as necessary.

### All Other Landlord & Sovereign Models

To remove bevel gear drive, first remove steering wheel, dash assembly and top frame cover as necessary, then proceed as follows: Support tractor under main frame just ahead of bevel gear housing and also under transaxle or gear reduction housing. Remove left rear wheel and hub assembly. On models so equipped, remove pto pulley from bevel gear shaft. Unbolt belt guard and remove drive belt and pulley from right side of bevel gear shaft. Disconnect drive shaft coupling from bevel gear input shaft. Unbolt and remove left side plate. Remove remaining cap screws securing bevel gear unit to frame and lift unit from tractor.

Reinstall bevel drive unit by reversing removal procedure. Adjust clutch and brake linkage as necessary.

## OVERHAUL

### All Models So Equipped

To disassemble bevel gear unit, drain lubricant and remove housing rear cover (4–Fig. S26) and gasket (5). Drive output shaft (9) to the left until key (8) is free of bevel gear (10). Remove key and disengage snap ring (11) from groove in shaft. Remove bevel gear (10) and snap ring as shaft is withdrawn from housing. Remove cap screw (13) and bearing clamp plate (14), then bump input shaft assembly rearward out of housing. Remove cap screw (6) and washers (7) and remove bevel gear (12) and bearing (15) from input shaft (19). Bearings (21, 23 and 26) and oil seals (20, 24 and 27) can now be removed.

Clean and inspect all parts and renew any showing excessive wear or other damage. Using new oil seals and gasket, reassemble by reversing disassembly procedure. Fill unit to level plug (1) or dipstick (22) with SAE 90 EP gear oil. Capacity is approximately one pint (0.5 L).

# VARIABLE SPEED PULLEY

### Models 3012-3112V-3210V-3212V-3310V-3314V

**OPERATION.** A variable speed belt and pulley system is used on Models 3012, 3112V, 3210V, 3212V, 3310V and 3314V. The sheaves of the pulleys are moved in or out by control linkage. Moving pulley sheaves changes effective diameter of the pulley and distance around pulleys drive belt must follow. This results in a change of drive ratio between the pulleys which may be varied to change tractor speed.

**ADJUSTMENT.** Do not attempt to move variable speed control lever when engine is stopped or clutch-brake pedal is depressed. Place variable speed control lever in "HIGH" position and remove drive belt and guards. Loosen attaching bolt between control rod (4–Fig. S27) and rocker arm (17) and push rocker arm as far forward as possible so inside hubs of drive pulley sheaves (13 and 14) make contact. Retighten rocker arm bolt. Reinstall drive belt and guards. With control lever in "HIGH" position, clearance should be 3/16 inch (5 mm) between drive belt and front guard. Move variable speed control lever to "LOW" position. Front edge of idler pulley belt stop (19) should be 8⅞ inches (225 mm) from outer surface of rear axle tube. To make adjustment, loosen nut retaining idler pulley (21). With control

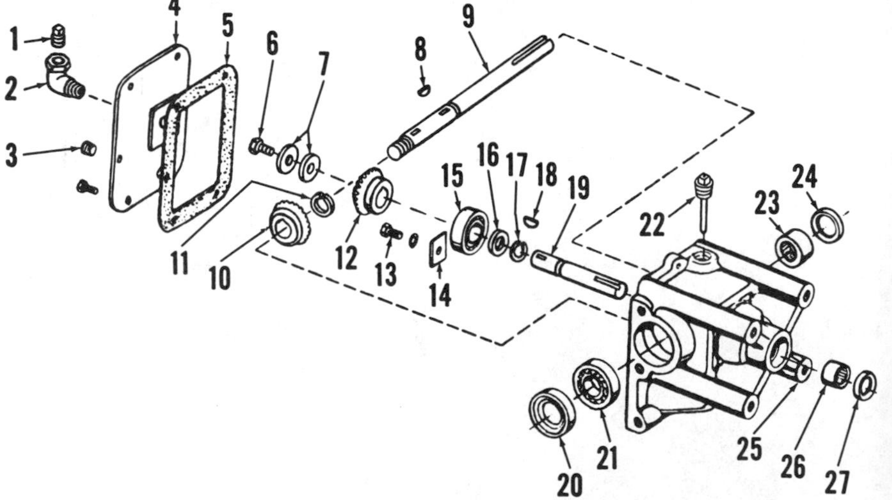


*Fig. S26—Exploded view of typical bevel gear unit used on Landlord, Baron and Sovereign tractors. Some units are equipped with oil level plug (1) and others have a dipstick on filler plug (22).*

1. Oil level plug
2. Elbow
3. Drain plug
4. Cover
5. Gasket
6. Cap screw
7. Compression washers
8. Key
9. Output shaft
10. Bevel driven gear
11. Snap ring
12. Bevel drive gear
13. Cap screw
14. Bearing clamp plate
15. Ball bearing
16. Washer
17. Snap ring
18. Key
19. Input shaft
20. Oil seal
21. Ball bearing
22. Dipstick
23. Needle bearing
24. Oil seal
25. Bevel gear housing
26. Needle bearing
27. Oil seal

lever in "LOW" position, top of drive belt should be approximately 1/8 inch (5 mm) below rim of drive pulley sheaves (24 and 26). Adjust position of belt by turning turnbuckle (18).

**R&R AND OVERHAUL.** To remove variable pulley assembly, first support right rear axle and remove right rear wheel. Remove drive belt guards and drive belt. Remove drive pulley retaining nut (16–Fig. S27) and withdraw drive pulley assembly. Disconnect control rod (4) from rocker arm (17) and remove rocker arm by unscrewing retaining nut. Unscrew bolt holding driven pulley fork (30) and remove driven pulley fork, connecting bolts and turnbuckle (18) and drive pulley arm (9). Unscrew retaining nut (31) and remove driven pulley assembly.

Inspect assembly for damage or excessively worn components. Be sure pulley sheaves are straight and run true. After reassembly, check adjustment as outlined in previous paragraph.

# HI-LO RANGE PULLEY

The Hi-Lo two speed transmission input pulley is used on some early models to provide slower ground speeds without altering pto rpm. When shifted to low range, ground speeds will be reduced to approximately 1/3 of standard (high range) ground speeds.

## Models So Equipped

**R&R AND OVERHAUL.** To remove two speed pulley assembly, first unbolt shift rod support (9–Fig. S28). Then, unbolt and remove shift support and shift fork assembly. Loosen set screws in collar (3) and withdraw Hi-Lo pulley assembly.

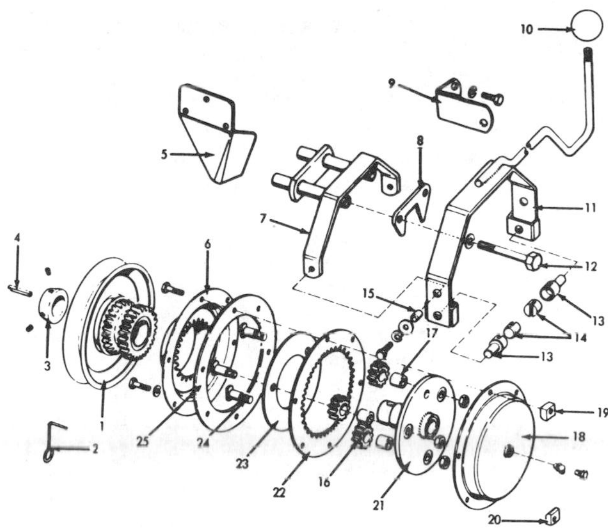

*Fig. S28—Exploded view of Hi-Lo Range pulley assembly.*

1. Pulley assy.
2. Belt stop
3. Collar
4. Key
5. Guard
6. Cover (inner)
7. Support
8. Shift stop
9. Shift rod support
10. Knob
11. Shift fork
12. Cap screw
13. Pivots
14. Pivot bearings
15. Spacers
16. Pinions
17. Needle bearings
18. Cover (outer)
19. Special nut (4)
20. Special nut (2)
21. Spider assy.
22. Ring gear
23. Spider plate
24. Spider bolts
25. Shift ring

To disassemble unit, remove six cap screws from outer edge of covers. Mark location of special nuts (19 and 20) for aid in reassembly. Separate covers and remove shift ring (25) and reduction gear assembly. Remove spider bolts (24), pinions (16) and needle bearings (17).

Check all parts for excessive wear and renew as necessary. When reassembling, lubricate with multi-purpose lithium base grease. Reinstall assembly by reversing removal procedure.

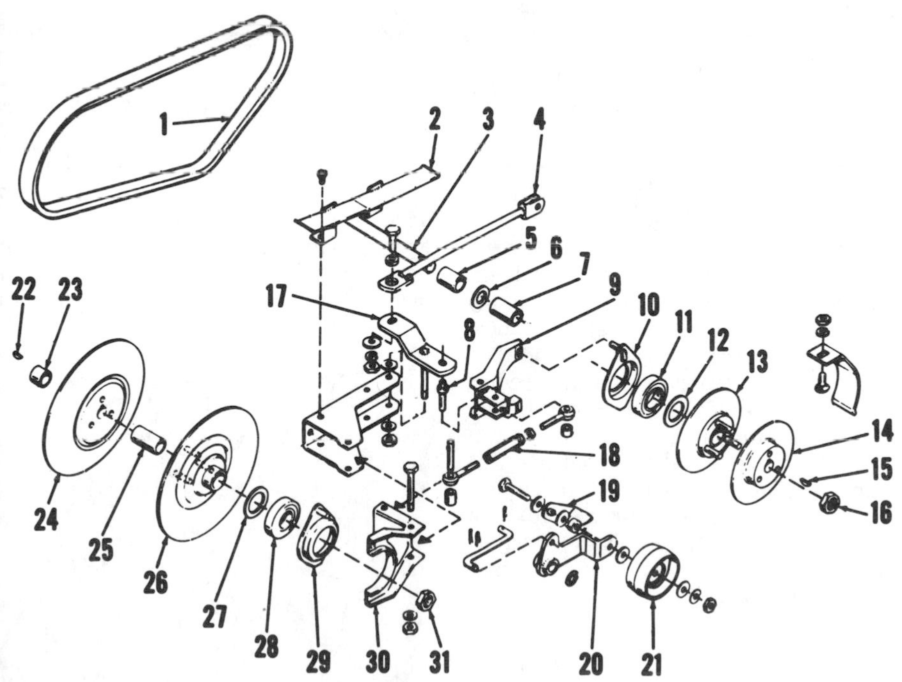

*Fig. S27—Exploded view of variable speed drive used on models so equipped.*

1. Drive belt
2. Belt guard
3. Bevel gear shaft
4. Control rod
5. Spacer
6. Washer
7. Spacer
8. Rod
9. Fork
10. Bearing retainer
11. Ball bearing
12. Retainer
13. Movable pulley sheave
14. Fixed pulley sheave
15. Key
16. Nut
17. Lever
18. Turnbuckle
19. Belt guide
20. Idler arm
21. Clutch idler pulley
22. Key
23. Spacer
24. Fixed pulley sheave
25. Spacer
26. Movable pulley sheave
27. Retainer
28. Ball bearing
29. Bearing retainer
30. Fork
31. Nut

# HYDROSTATIC TRANSMISSION

### LUBRICATION

#### All Hydrostatic Models Except Models 4211H And 5211H

These models are equipped with a Vickers Model T66 hydrostatic transmission. Refer to CONDENSED SPECIFICATIONS at the beginning of this section for fluid capacity and fluid type requirements.

#### Models 4211H-5211H

Models 4211H and 5211H are equipped with an Eaton hydrostatic transmission. Refer to CONDENSED SPECIFICATIONS at the beginning of this section for fluid capacity and fluid type requirements.

### ADJUSTMENT

#### All Hydrostatic Models Except Models 4211H And 5211H

To adjust hydrostatic control linkage, block up under rear of tractor so wheels do not touch ground. Start engine and operate at 1/3 full speed. With clutch engaged, move hydrostatic control lever to forward position then into neutral position. Rear wheels should not rotate when control lever is in neutral position. Loosen locknuts at both ends of turnbuckle on control rod shown in Fig. S29. Turn turnbuckle as required so wheels do not turn when control lever is in neutral position. Tighten locknuts and recheck adjustment.

### Models 4211H-5211H

If tractor creeps forward or backward with transmission lever in neutral notch, transmission lever must be adjusted. To adjust lever, start tractor and position lever so there is no creep forward or backward. Stop engine, raise seat deck and disconnect battery cables. Loosen the two screws retaining lever quadrant. Position lever quadrant so the lever is in the neutral notch. Tighten the two screws. Connect battery cables, lower seat deck and recheck adjustment.

## REMOVE AND REINSTALL

### All Hydrostatic Models Except Models 4211H-5211H

**REMOVE AND REINSTALL.** To remove hydrostatic transmission, first remove seat and fender assembly. Disconnect transmission control rod. Remove drive belt from transmission pulley. Drain lubricant from transmission oil reservoir and disconnect transmission oil lines. Remove oil cooler fan, shroud and oil cooler assembly. Remove cap screws securing transmission to gear reduction housing and remove transmission.

To reinstall transmission, reverse removal procedure. Use the following procedure to refill transmission with oil: Before installing transmission in tractor, fill pump and motor with recommended oil through case drain openings. With transmission and cooling system installed and oil lines connected, position hydrostatic control lever in neutral position and fill reservoir with oil to correct level. Disconnect engine coil wire and at short intervals turn engine over with starter. Recheck and add oil if necessary to oil reservoir. Connect engine coil wire and run engine at idle speed. Recheck oil level. Make several short runs at a slow speed in forward and in reverse and recheck oil level. Transmission oil should now be purged of air.

### Model 4211H

To remove hydrostatic transmission, first disconnect battery and drain fuel tank. Securely block tractor rear wheels to prevent tractor rolling and place 4 inch (101.6 mm) by 4 inch (101.6 mm) wooden blocks approximately 18 inches (45.7 cm) behind tractor. Use a suitable hoist to lift front of tractor until rear frame rests on blocks and wheels are clear of ground. Remove snap rings and slide wheels and spacers off axles. Remove drive belt at hydrostatic pulley and loop free end over engine pto pulley. Disconnect the transmission control lever at transmission. Disconnect all brake linkage at brake caliper. Remove the cap screws retaining transmission to floor pan. Support transmission and remove the two "U" bolts securing transmission and gear reduction unit to the frame. Lower unit out of tractor.

Reverse removal procedure for reinstallation. Tighten the three cap screws retaining transmission to floor pan to 20 ft.-lbs. (27 N•m). Adjust transmission control linkage and brake linkage as required.

### Model 5211H

To remove hydrostatic transmission, first disconnect battery and drain fuel tank. Securely block tractor rear wheels to prevent tractor rolling and place 4 inch (101.6 mm) by 4 inch (101.6 mm) wooden blocks approximately 18 inches (45.7 cm) behind tractor. Use a suitable hoist to lift front of tractor until rear frame rests on blocks and wheels are clear of ground. Remove snap rings and slide wheels and spacers off axles. Loosen cap screw in the center of transaxle input shaft and remove cooling fan. Remove the lower hydrostatic pump mounting bolt and loosen top bolt. Swing belt stop out of the way and remove belt from pulley. Disconnect control linkage at hydrostatic control arm. Disconnect all brake linkage at caliper. Remove the three cap screws retaining transmission to floor pan. Support transmission and remove the two "U" bolts securing transmission and reduction gear assembly to the frame. Lower unit out of tractor.

Reverse removal procedure for reinstallation. Tighten the three cap screws retaining transmission to floor pan to 20 ft.-lbs. (27 N•m). Adjust transmission control linkage and brake linkage as required.

## OVERHAUL

### All Models

All models except Models 4211H and 5211H are equipped with a Vickers Model T66 hydrostatic transmission. Models 4211H and 5211H are equipped with an Eaton Model 7 hydrostatic transmission. Refer to the appropriate Vickers or Eaton section in HYDROSTATIC TRANSMISSION SERVICE section for overhaul procedure.

# TRANSAXLE

## LUBRICATION

### All Models

Broadmoor, Serf and Yeoman models are equipped with a 2-speed or 3-speed transaxle manufactured by Simplicity. All other transaxle models are equipped with a Peerless transaxle. Refer to CONDENSED SPECIFICATIONS at the beginning of this section for fluid capacity and fluid type for model being serviced.

## REMOVE AND REINSTALL

### Broadmoor-Serf-Yeoman-6000-6108-6010-6011-6111-Early 4208-4211G Models

To remove transaxle, remove seat and fender assembly. Disconnect brake rod at brake band and remove drive belt from transaxle input pulley. Loosen set screws and remove set collar and washer from pivot shaft on side plate assembly. Roll transaxle assembly to the rear away from tractor.

Reinstall by reversing removal procedure.

### Late 4208-4211G And 5211G Models

To remove transaxle, remove seat deck, battery and drain fuel tank. Engage parking brake, place transaxle in gear and block rear wheels. Place a 4 inch (101.6 mm) by 4 inch (101.6 mm)

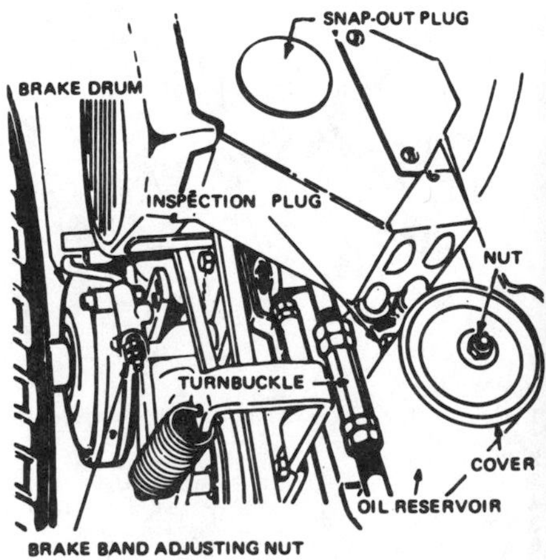


*Fig. S29—View of brake and hydrostatic adjustment points on hydrostatic models.*

block approximately 18 inches (45.7 cm) behind rear of tractor. Use a suitable hoist to raise front of tractor so rear frame support rests on block and tractor is in a vertical position. Disconnect all brake linkage at caliper. Disconnect shift linkage at transaxle. Remove drive belt from transaxle input pulley. Remove "E" clips, washers and wheel assemblies. Remove cap screws retaining left and right front support straps to transaxle. Remove cap screws retaining transaxle to right rear support plate. Support transaxle and remove cap screws retaining transaxle to left rear support plate. Tilt transaxle assembly forward so input pulley clears frame, then slide transaxle to the left to clear right axle shaft. remove transaxle.

Reinstall by reversing removal procedure.

### Models 4008-4108-4111

To remove transaxle, remove seat deck, battery and drain fuel tank. Engage parking brake, place transaxle in gear and block rear wheels. Place a 4 inch (101.6 mm) by 4 inch (101.6 mm) block approximately 18 inches (45.7 cm) behind rear of tractor. Use a suitable hoist to raise front of tractor so rear frame support rests on block and tractor is in a vertical position. Remove brake rod, parking brake rod guide (as equipped) and spring from cam lever. Place shift lever in neutral position and remove shift lever assembly. Remove drive belt from the transaxle pulley. Remove rear wheels. Remove torque strap from left side of transaxle and frame. Support transaxle assembly. Loosen "U" bolt nuts and remove left axle brace. Remove transaxle.

Reinstall by reversing removal procedure.

## OVERHAUL

### All Models

Broadmoor, Serf, Yeoman, 6008, 6108, 6010, 6011, 6111, early 4208 and early 4211G models are equipped with a Simplicity 2-speed or 3-speed transaxle. Late Models 4208 and 4211G and all 5211G models are equipped with a Peerless 800 series transaxle. Models 4008, 4108 and 4111 are equipped with a

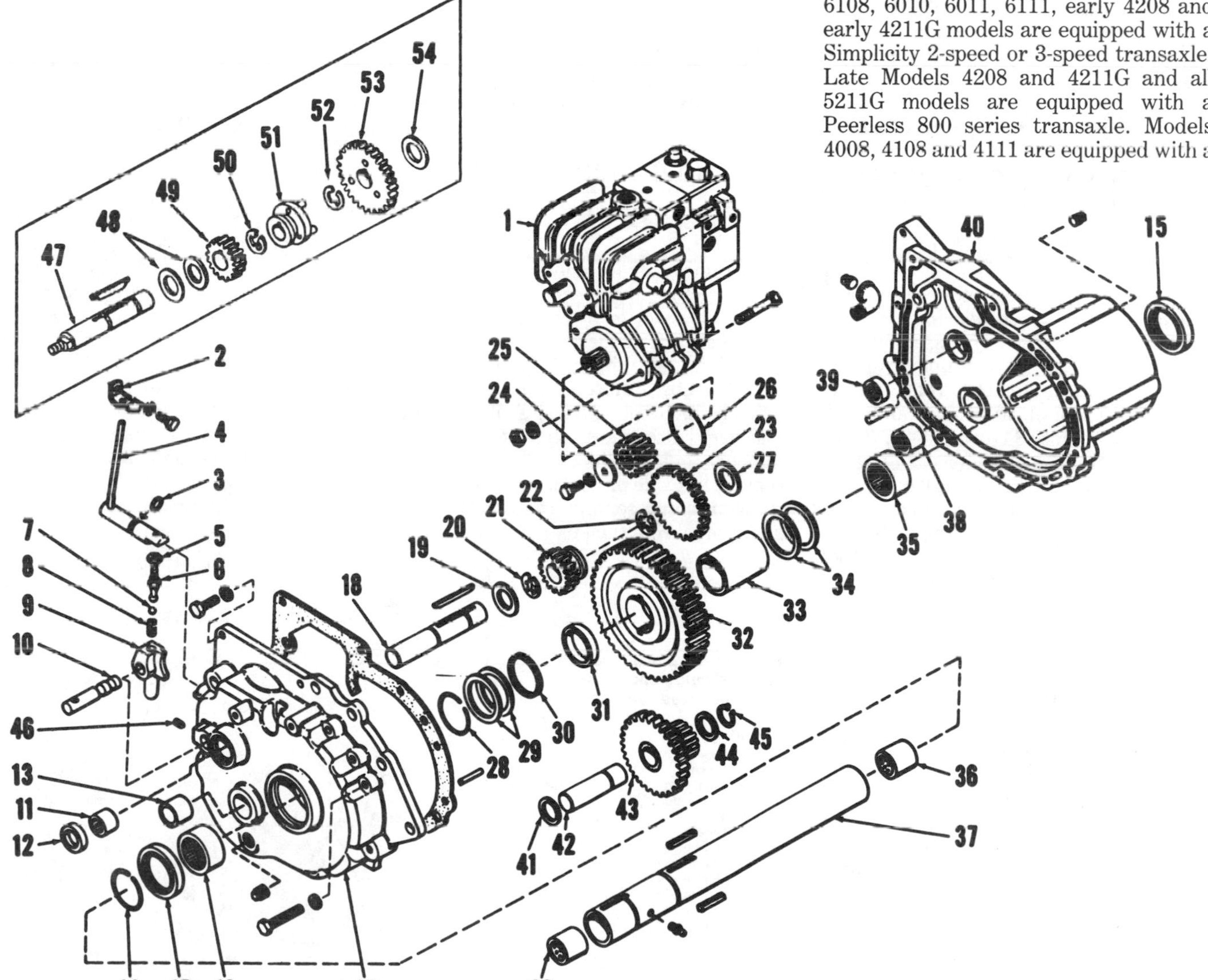


***Fig. S43—Exploded view of gear reduction unit used on models equipped with a hydrostatic transmission. Items (47 through 54) in inset are used on Models 3410H, 3414H, 3415H and 3416H.***

1. Hydrostatic transmission
2. Lever latch
3. "O" ring
4. Shift lever
5. Locknut
6. Shifter stem
7. Ball
8. Poppet spring
9. Shift fork
10. Shift rail
11. Needle bearing
12. Oil seal
13. Needle bearing
14. Snap ring
15. Oil seal
16. Needle bearing
17. Case
18. Brake shaft
19. Washer
20. "E" ring
21. Sliding gear
22. "E" ring
23. First reduction gear
24. Washer
25. Input gear
26. "O" ring
27. Washer
28. Snap ring
29. Washers
30. Washer
31. Spacer
32. Output gear
33. Spacer
34. Washer
35. Needle bearing
36. Bushing
37. Axle tube
38. Needle bearing
39. Needle bearing
40. Cover
41. Washer
42. Shaft
43. Second reduction gear
44. Washer
45. Snap ring
46. Set screw
47. Brake shaft
48. Washers
49. First reduction pinion
50. "E" ring
51. Sliding drive flange
52. "E" ring
53. First reduction gear
54. Washer

Peerless 600 series transaxle. Refer to the appropriate Simplicity or Peerless section in TRANSAXLE SERVICE section for overhaul procedure.

# GEAR TRANSMISSION

## LUBRICATION

### Landlord-Baron-Sovereign (Gear Drive)-7110 Models

These models are equipped with 3-speed or 4-speed gear transmissions manufactured by Simplicity. Refer to CONDENSED SPECIFICATIONS at the beginning of this section for fluid capacity and type for model being serviced.

## REMOVE AND REINSTALL

### Landlord-Baron-Sovereign (Gear Drive)-7110 Models

To remove transmission, raise rear of tractor to a point where rear wheels are free. Support tractor under frame just ahead of bevel gear housing. Remove seat deck and fenders assembly and disconnect brake linkage and transmission shift rod. Remove rear wheels, hubs, differential assembly and axle shaft. On Models 3410S, 3414S, 3415S and 3416S, remove forward-reverse shuttle drive unit. On all other models, remove transmission input pulley. On all models, place a suitable supporting fixture under transmission housing, then unbolt transmission from side plates and lift unit from tractor.

Reinstall by reversing removal procedure.

## OVERHAUL

### Landlord-Baron-Sovereign (Gear Drive-7110 Models

Transmission used on all models is a 3-speed or 4-speed gear transmission manufactured by Simplicity Manufacturing Corporation. Refer to Simplicity in GEAR TRANSMISSION SERVICE section for overhaul procedure.

# GEAR REDUCTION UNIT

A gear reduction unit is used on all models equipped with a hydrostatic transmission. On Models 3112H, 3212H, 3310H and 3314H, sliding drive gear (21 – Fig. S43) can be shifted to a neutral position so tractor may be moved manually.

**CAUTION: On these models, tractor brakes are inoperative when shift lever (4) is in disengaged position. When shift lever is in vertical (normal drive) position, drive gear (21) will be engaged with reduction gear (43).**

On Models 3410H, 3414H, 3415H and 3416H, reduction pinion (49) is in constant mesh with reduction gear (43) and tractor brakes are operative at all times. When shift lever (4) is moved from vertical (neutral) position to the right (normal drive position), pins on sliding drive flange (51) are engaged in holes in reduction gear (53).

Models 4211H and 5211H are equipped with gear reduction assembly shown in Fig. S44.

## REMOVE AND REINSTALL

### All Models Except 4211H-5211H

To remove gear reduction unit, support tractor under main frame just ahead of bevel gear housing. Remove seat deck and fenders assembly. Drain reduction unit housing. Remove rear wheels, hubs, differential assembly and axle shaft. Remove bevel gear pto belt pulley and disconnect pto tension spring. Support gear reduction housing and remove left side plate. Drain hydrostatic transmission reservoir. Disconnect lines and control rod, then unbolt and remove reservoir, oil cooler, shroud and cooler fan. Unbolt and remove hydrostatic transmission and brake band. Remove cap screws securing gear reduction unit to right side plate and lift unit from tractor.

Reinstall by reversing removal procedure. Fill reduction unit to level plug opening with SAE 90 EP gear oil. Fill hydrostatic reservoir with "Type A" automatic transmission fluid. Adjust brake and clutch idler linkage as required.

### Models 4211H-5211H

Reduction gear unit and hydrostatic drive transmission are removed as an assembly. Refer to REMOVE AND REINSTALL in the HYDROSTATIC TRANSMISSION section for removal procedure.

## OVERHAUL

### All Models Except 4211H-5211H

To disassemble gear reduction unit, remove brake drum and clean all paint, burrs and rust from keyed end of axle tube (37 – Fig. S43). Unbolt and remove cover (40) from case (17). Remove washer (27 or 54) and first reduction gear (23 or 53). Remove snap ring (14), then withdraw output gear and axle tube assembly (28 through 37). Remove second reduction gear and shaft assembly (41 through 45). Loosen set screw (46) and remove as a unit, shift fork and rail assembly (7 through 10) and brake shaft assembly (18 through

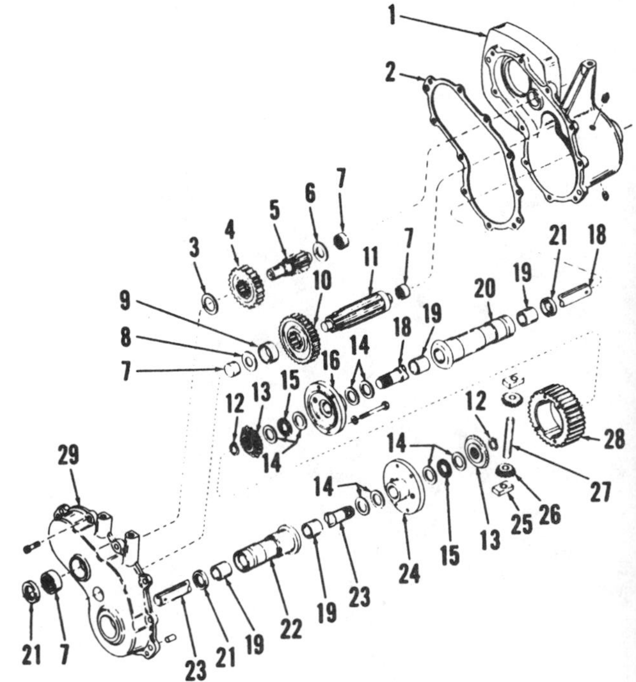


*Fig. S44 — Exploded view of gear reduction and differential unit used on Models 4211H and 5211H.*

1. Case
2. Gasket
3. Washer
4. Idler gear
5. Brake shaft
6. Washer
7. Bearing
8. Washer
9. Spacer
10. Output gear
11. Output shaft
12. Snap ring
13. Bevel gear
14. Thrust washers
15. Thrust bearing
16. Differential carrier
18. Axle shaft (R.H.)
19. Bushing
20. Axle housing
21. Oil seal
22. Axle housing
23. Axle shaft (L.H.)
24. Differential carrier
25. Drive block
26. Drive pinion
27. Drive pin
28. Ring gear
29. Cover

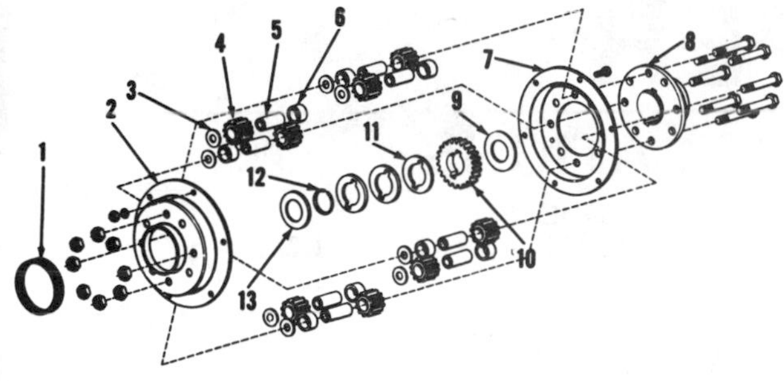

*Fig. S45—Exploded view of early Landlord or Sovereign differential unit with right differential gear, hub and axle shaft removed.*

1. Seal
2. Differential case (R.H.)
3. Washer
4. Pinion
5. Spindle
6. Spacer
7. Differential case (L.H.)
8. Carrier
9. Axle washer
10. Differential gear (L.H.)
11. Thrust washer
12. Axle washer

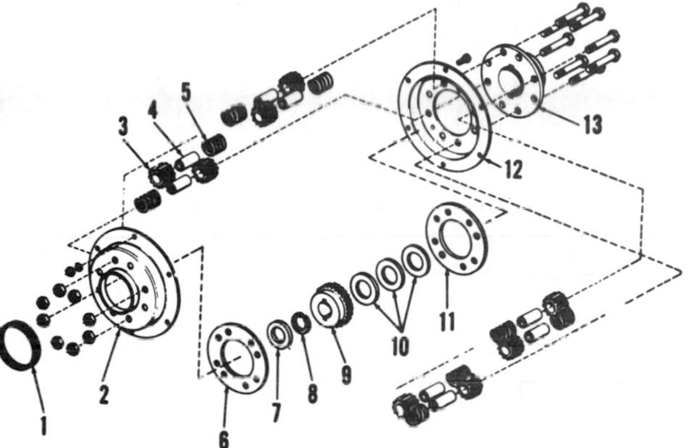

*Fig. S46—Exploded view of differential used on later Landlord and Sovereign and all Baron models. Early models do not use spacer plate (6) and have a spacer in place of springs (5).*

1. Seal
2. Differential cover (R.H.)
3. Pinion
4. Spindle
5. Spring
6. Ring spacer plate
7. Axle washer
8. Snap ring
9. Differential gear
10. Axle washer
11. Ring spacer plate
12. Differential cover (L.H.)
13. Carrier

22) or (47 through 52). Use caution when removing shift rail (10) from shift fork (9) as poppet ball and spring (7 and 8) will be released. Loosen locknut (5), remove shifter stem (6) and withdraw shift lever (4). Oil seals and needle bearings can now be removed from case and cover as required.

Clean and inspect all parts and renew any showing excessive wear or other damage. Using Fig. S43 as a guide, reassemble by reversing disassembly procedure.

### Models 4211H-5211H

To disassemble reduction gear, remove brake disc from brake shaft. Clean axle shafts and remove any burrs on shafts. Unscrew cap screws and drive out dowel pins in cover (29–Fig. S44). Lift cover off case and axle shaft. Withdraw brake shaft (5), idler gear (4) and thrust washers (3 and 6) from case. Remove output shaft (11), output gear (10), spacer (9), thrust washer (8) and differential assembly from case. Axle shaft housings (20 and 22) must be pressed from case and cover.

To disassemble differential, unscrew four cap screws and separate axle shaft and carriage assemblies from ring gear (28). Drive blocks (25), bevel pinion gears (26) and drive pin (27) can now be removed from ring gear. Remove snap rings (12) and slide axle shafts (18 and 23) from axle gears (13) and carriages (16 and 24).

Clean and inspect all parts and renew any parts damaged or excessively worn. When installing needle bearings, press bearings in from inside of case or cover until bearings are 0.015-0.020 (0.381-0.508 mm) below thrust surfaces. Be sure heads of differential cap screws and right axle shaft (18) are installed in right carriage housing (16). Right axle shaft is installed through case (1). Tighten differential cap screws to 7 ft.-lbs. (9 N•m) and cover cap screws to 10 ft.-lbs. (14 N•m). Differential assembly and output shaft (11) must be installed in case at same time. Remainder of assembly is reverse of disassembly procedure. Fill unit with approximately two pints (0.9 L) of SAE 90 EP gear lube.

# DIFFERENTIAL

### Landlord-Baron-Sovereign Models

**R&R AND OVERHAUL.** To remove differential assembly, block up rear of tractor and remove rear wheels. Loosen set screws, remove collar and withdraw right rear hub from axle shaft. Carefully remove differential assembly.

To disassemble differential, remove bolts from outer edge of differential case. Remove nuts from inner circle of cap screws and separate case halves, leaving cap screws in position to stabilize pinions, spacers and washers (or springs). Identify all parts for aid in reassembly. The balance of disassembly is evident after inspection of unit and reference to Figs. S45 and S46.

When reinstalling assembled unit, make sure axle and differential are properly seated so seal differential and right wheel hub is compressed. The axle is held in this position by set collar on axle shaft at left side of transmission. The differential is lubricated with multi-purpose grease through lubrication fitting on right rear hub.

**TRACTION ADJUSTMENT.** Some Landlord and Sovereign models are equipped with controlled traction adjusters. Adjustment of traction differential is made by tightening two cap screws in right rear wheel hub to 20 ft.-lbs. (27 N•m).

**NOTE: Under torque will allow excessive slippage and over torque will cause difficulty in steering due to lack of differential action.**

# SNAPPER

## CONDENSED SPECIFICATIONS

| | MODELS | | |
|---|---|---|---|
| | LT11 | LT12D | LT14H |
| Engine Make | B&S | B&S | Kohler |
| Model | 253417 | 280707 | CV14S |
| Bore | 3-7/16 in. (87.3 mm) | 3-7/16 in. (87.3 mm) | 3-7/16 in. (87 mm) |
| Stroke | 2-5/8 in. (66.7 mm) | 3-1/16 in. (77.7 mm) | 2-5/8 in. (67 mm) |
| Piston Displacement | 24.36 cu. in. (400 cc) | 28.4 cu. in. (465 cc) | 24.3 cu. in. (398 cc) |
| Horsepower | 11 (8.2 kW) | 12 (9.0 kW) | 14 (10.4 kW) |
| Slow Idle Speed—Rpm | 1200 | 1200 | 1200 |
| High Idle (No-Load)—Rpm | 3600 | 3600 | 3600 |
| Crankcase Oil Capacity | 3 pints (1.4 L) | 3 pints (1.4 L) | 4 pints (1.9 L) |
| Transmission Oil Capacity | | See Text | |

# FRONT AXLE AND STEERING SYSTEM

## MAINTENANCE

### All Models

The front wheel spindles and axle pivot pin should be lubricated after every 25 hours of operation. Jack up front axle so wheels are suspended and apply grease to spindles and axle through grease fittings. Use a good quality multipurpose grease. Check for looseness and binding in front axle components.

After 50 hours of operation, or twice each year, lubricate steering shaft bushings and sector gear bushings by injecting two shots of multipurpose grease through grease fittings.

## AXLE MAIN MEMBER

### Model LT11

**REMOVE AND REINSTALL.** Raise front of tractor and place support stands under frame to the rear of front axle. Disconnect drag link (26—Fig. SN1) at steering arm (28). Unscrew pivot bolt (36) and roll axle assembly away from tractor.

Remove pivot sleeve (38) and inspect components for excessive wear and damage. Bushings (37) in axle are renewable.

Reinstall axle and lubricate through grease fitting in axle main member until grease appears at bearings.

### Models LT12D-LT14H

**REMOVE AND REINSTALL.** Raise front of tractor and place support stands under frame to the rear of front axle. Remove the hood. Disconnect drag link (13—Fig. SN2) from steering arm (14). Remove front wheels. Unscrew axle pivot bolt (24), remove spacer (23) and lower axle main member (22) from frame.

Check axle pivot spacer, pivot bolt and axle for excessive wear and renew as necessary.

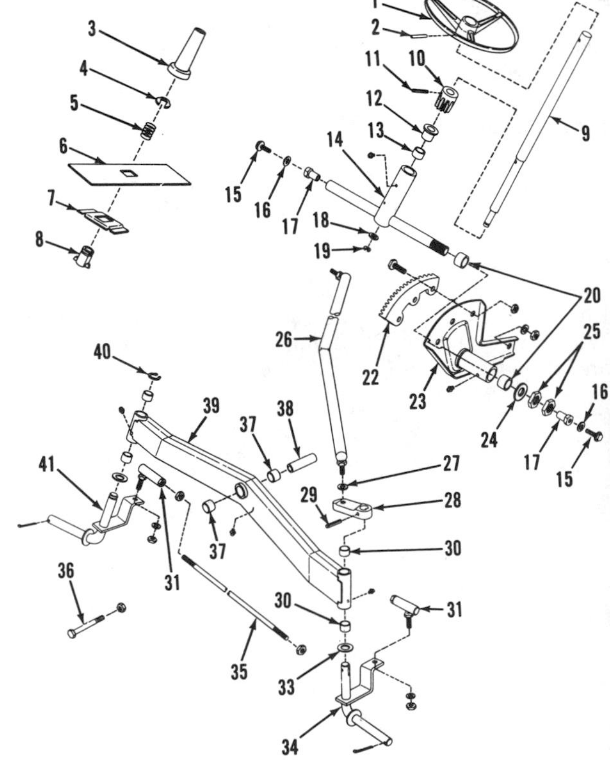

*Fig. SN1—Exploded view of front axle and steering gear assembly used on Model LT11.*

1. Steering wheel
2. Roll pin
3. Collar
4. Retainer
5. Spring
6. Cover
7. Riser
8. Bushing
9. Steering shaft
10. Pinion gear
11. Roll pin
12. Bushing
13. Bushing
14. Support
15. Screw
16. Lockwasher
17. Pivot
18. Washer
19. Snap ring
20. Bushing
22. Sector gear
23. Steering arm
24. Washer
25. Nuts
26. Drag link
27. Lockwasher
28. Steering arm
29. Roll pin
30. Bushing
31. Tie rod end
33. Thrust washer
34. Spindle
35. Tie rod
36. Pivot bolt
37. Bushings
38. Sleeve
39. Axle main member
40. Snap ring
41. Spindle



Illustrations courtesy Snapper Power Equipment.

To reinstall axle, reverse the removal procedure. Lubricate axle pivot with multipurpose grease.

## TIE ROD AND TOE-IN

### All Models

The tie rod (35—Fig. SN1 or 21—Fig. SN2) is equipped with renewable ball joint ends. Front wheel toe-in should be $^{3}/_{16}$ inch (4.8 mm). To check toe-in, park tractor on level surface with front wheels positioned straight ahead. Measure dimensions (A and B—Fig. SN3) at front and rear of tires at hub height. Dimension (A) should be $^{3}/_{16}$ inch (4.8 mm) less than dimension (B). To adjust toe-in, disconnect tie rod from one of the steering spindles. Loosen tie rod ball joint jam nuts and adjust length of tie rod as required to obtain specified toe-in.

## STEERING SPINDLES

### All Models

Raise and support front of tractor. Remove wheel and tire. Disconnect tie rod end, and if needed, drag link end. If removing right spindle (41—Fig. SN1 or 25—Fig. SN2), detach snap ring securing top of spindle and withdraw spindle from axle. If removing left spindle (34—Fig. SN1 or 19—Fig. SN2), drive out roll pin (29 or 15), then drive spindle down out of steering arm (28 or 14) and axle.

Inspect components for excessive wear and damage. Renewable bushings (30 or 17) are located in axle.

To reassemble, reverse the disassembly procedure. Lubricate bushings with multipurpose grease until grease is visible at the bushings.

## DRAG LINK

### All Models

A drag link (26—Fig. SN1 or 13—Fig. SN2) is located between steering arm and pitman arm. Inspect drag link ends for looseness and renew as necessary. Length of drag link is not adjustable on Model LT11. On Models LT12D and LT14H, length of drag link should be adjusted so front wheels turn equal distance in both directions when steering wheel is turned lock-to-lock.

## FRONT WHEEL BEARINGS

### All Models

To remove front wheel bushings, raise and support front of tractor. Remove dust cap from wheel hub and cotter pin from spindle end. Slide wheel hub assembly off spindle. Wheel bushings are a press fit in wheel hub. If bushings are loose in hub, renew or repair hub as necessary.

Lubricate bushings through grease fitting in wheel hub using a good quality multipurpose grease. Inject grease until visible around bushings.

## STEERING GEAR

### Model LT11

**R&R AND OVERHAUL.** To disassemble steering gear assembly, drive out pin (2—Fig. SN1) and remove steering wheel. Remove collar (3), retainer (4) and spring (5). Remove snap ring (19) and drive roll pin (11) out of steering gear (10). Pull steering shaft up until disengaged from support (14), then move shaft down out of dash panel. Detach drag link (26) from steering arm (23). Unscrew support screws (15) and remove support assembly (14) from bottom of tractor. Remainder of disassembly is evident after inspection of unit. Note that bushings are renewable.

Inspect components for damage and excessive wear. Reassemble by reversing disassembly procedure. Steering lock bushing (8) must be centered in dash panel and move freely before installing spring (5) and tightening screws (15). Move support (14) in slots in side panels to properly position bushing (8), then tighten screws (15). Lubricate with grease after assembly.

Adjust steering gear backlash as follows: To adjust sector gear backlash, loosen nuts (25—Fig. SN1). Tighten inner nut until backlash is removed but

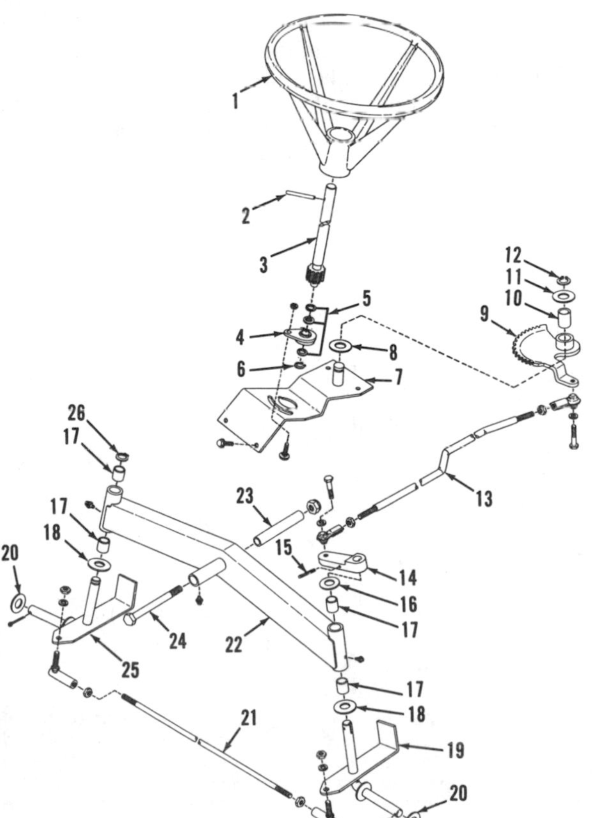


*Fig. SN2—Exploded view of front axle and steering gear assembly used on Models LT12D and LT14H.*

1. Steering wheel
2. Roll pin
3. Steering shaft
4. Steering adjuster
5. Shim washers
6. Snap ring
7. Steering support
8. Thrust washer
9. Sector gear
10. Bearing
11. Thrust washer
12. Snap ring
13. Drag link
14. Steering arm
15. Roll pin
16. Thrust washer
17. Bushings
18. Thrust washer
19. Spindle L.H.
20. Washer
21. Tie rod
22. Axle main member
23. Pivot spacer
24. Pivot bolt
25. Spindle R.H.
26. Snap ring

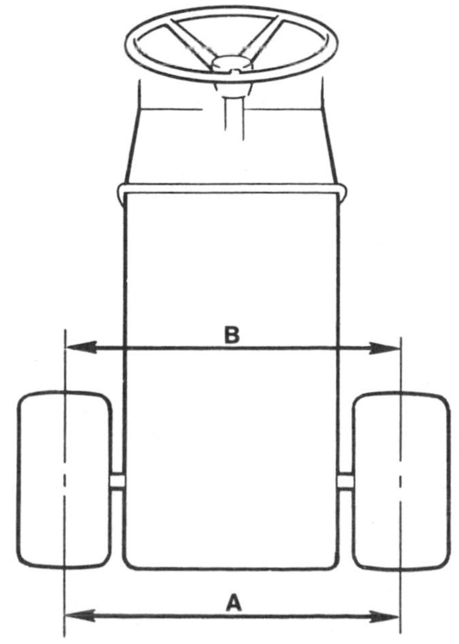


*Fig. SN3—Front wheel toe-in exists when distance (A) between front of tires is less than distance (B) between rear of tires.*

Illustrations courtesy Snapper Power Equipment.

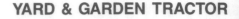

gears rotate without binding. Tighten outer nut against inner nut.

### Models LT12D-LT14H

**R&R AND OVERHAUL.** To remove steering gear assembly, first remove mower deck. Raise and support tractor high enough to allow work access underneath. Unhook latches at rear of hood, disconnect headlight wire and lift hood off front pivot pins. Disconnect drag link (13—Fig. SN2) from sector gear (9). Remove bolt securing steering adjuster (4), then rotate adjuster until steering shaft gear (3) is separated from sector gear teeth. Remove snap ring (12) and upper thrust washer (11) from sector gear and lift sector assembly off steering support stub shaft (7). Drive out roll pin (2) and remove steering wheel (1). Remove snap ring (6) from bottom of steering shaft, then use a brass drift to tap steering shaft upward until clear of steering adjuster (4). Rotate steering adjuster until adjuster locking tab aligns with notch in steering support, then lift and remove adjuster from steering support. Withdraw steering shaft downward through hole in steering support.

Inspect all parts for excessive wear and renew as required. To install steering gear assembly, reverse the removal procedure. Lubricate steering gear teeth with light coat of multipurpose grease.

Adjust steering gear "free play" as follows: Loosen steering adjuster carriage bolt (Fig. SN4). Move steering adjuster eccentric clockwise until free play is removed, but steering still turns freely without binding. Retighten steering adjuster carriage bolt.

## ENGINE

### Model LT11

To remove engine, remove hood and disconnect battery cables. Detach drive shaft from engine. Disconnect wiring to ignition coil, alternator, starter and electric pto clutch. Disconnect throttle control cable and choke cable at carburetor. Detach belt from pto pulley. Disconnect hose from fuel filter. Unscrew engine mounting screws and lift engine out of tractor.

Install engine by reversing removal procedure. Note that flat washers must be against flex disc when reinstalling drive shaft. Tighten drive shaft coupling set screws to 15 ft.-lbs. (20 N·m).

### Models LT12D-LT14H

To remove engine, first remove mower deck from tractor. Remove hood and disconnect battery cables. Disconnect wiring to ignition coil, alternator and starter. Disconnect throttle control cable and choke cable at carburetor. Detach fuel line at carburetor. Depress clutch-brake pedal and set park brake lever. Work traction drive belt off engine pulley. Remove engine mounting bolts and lift engine out of tractor.

Install engine by reversing removal procedure.

## BRAKE

### Model LT11

**ADJUSTMENT.** The brake/clutch pedal should engage the brake when the pedal is depressed into the lower portion of its travel. There should be approximately $^{3}/_{4}$ inch (19 mm) of free pedal travel between point where the clutch is disengaged and the brake is engaged.

To adjust brake engagement, remove cover plate from rear of frame. Move spacer ferrules (F—Fig. SN5) at end of brake cable. Placing ferrules between anchor (A) and lever (L) will cause earlier engagement.

To check adjustment, shut off engine and shift axle range selector lever to Hi or Lo. Attempt to roll tractor while slowly depressing clutch/brake pedal. There should be a place during the first half of pedal travel where clutch and brake are disengaged, allowing tractor to roll freely. Depressing pedal further should apply the brake.

**R&R AND OVERHAUL.** To disassemble brake, unbolt and remove pivot bracket (19—Fig. SN6). Detach brake cable (30) and remove pivot (21) and brake band (24) as and assembly. If necessary, unscrew retaining nut and remove brake drum (23).

Inspect components for excessive wear and damage. The brake band should be renewed if oil-soaked or worn to a thickness of $^{1}/_{16}$ inch (1.6 mm) or less.

Reassemble by reversing disassembly procedure. Check brake adjustment.

### Model LT12D

**ADJUSTMENT.** To adjust brake, loosen locknut and adjust brake cable housing toward rear of tractor to increase cable tension and braking action. See Fig. SN7.

After adjusting brake cable, check braking action as follows: Move speed selector lever to 6th speed position. Push tractor forward while slowly depressing clutch/brake pedal. There should be a place during the first half of pedal travel where the clutch is disengaged and brakes are not yet applied, allowing tractor to roll freely. Depressing pedal further should apply the brake. If not, repeat adjustment procedure.

### Model LT14H

**ADJUSTMENT.** Depressing the clutch-brake pedal returns hydrostatic control linkage to neutral, stopping forward or rearward motion, and applies the disc type brake.

To adjust brake, turn brake rod locknut (Fig. SN8) clockwise to tighten brakes or counterclockwise to loosen brakes. Clearance between brake disc and pad should be 0.010 inch (0.25 mm) with brake pedal in released (up) position. To adjust, remove cotter pin from brake lever castle nut (2—Fig. SN9) and tighten or loosen nut as necessary to obtain desired clearance.

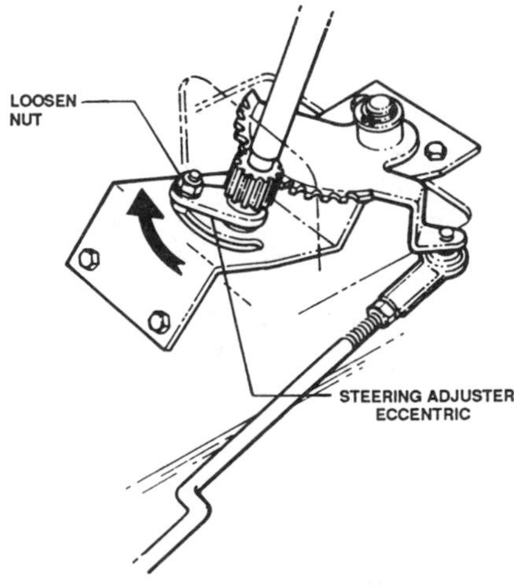


*Fig. SN4—Rotate steering adjuster eccentric to adjust steering free play on Models LT12D and LT14H.*

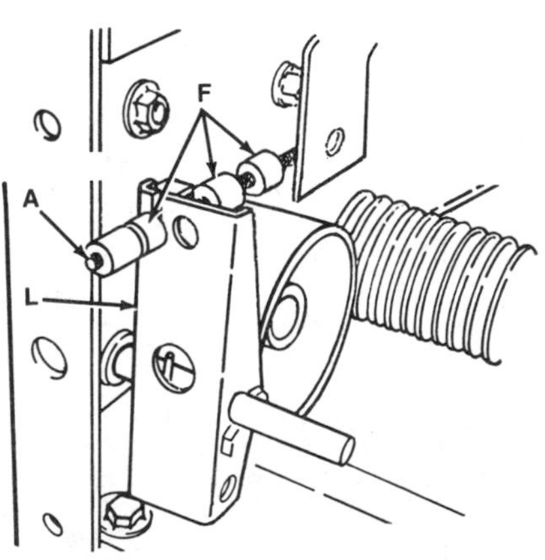


*Fig. SN5—To adjust brake engagement on Model LT11, detach brake cable from brake lever (L) and relocate spacer ferrules (F) as needed between anchor ferrule (A) and lever. Placing more ferrules between anchor and lever will result in earlier engagement.*

**R&R AND OVERHAUL.** To remove brake, disconnect brake linkage from brake lever (3—Fig. SN9). Remove mounting cap screws and withdraw brake holder (5). Remove brake disc (8) from transaxle shaft and remove inner brake pad (7) from transaxle housing.

Inspect all parts for excessive wear and renew as necessary. When installing brake, be sure back-up plate (6) is in place between brake holder (5) and brake pad (7). Be sure round end of actuator pins (4) is toward brake lever (3). Be sure brake disc is free of grease or oil.

# DRIVE BELT

## Models LT12D-LT14H

**REMOVE AND REINSTALL.** Raise the hood and disconnect spark plug wire to prevent accidental starting of engine. Remove rear cover plate from fenders. Depress clutch/brake pedal and engage park brake.

**NOTE: Although it is possible to remove and replace traction drive belt with mower attached, it is easier with mower removed.**

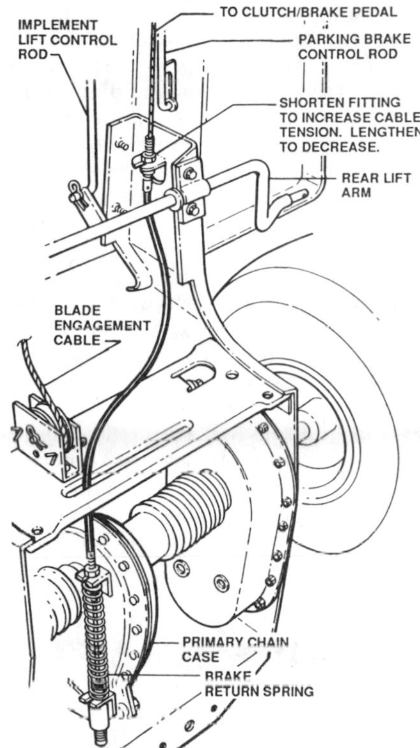


*Fig. SN7—View of brake control linkage used on Model LT12D. Refer to text for adjustment procedure.*

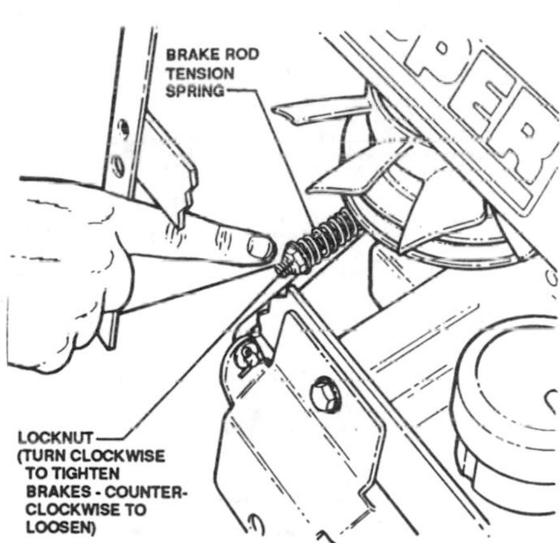


*Fig. SN8—On Model LT14H, turn brake rod locknut to adjust tension on brake rod spring.*

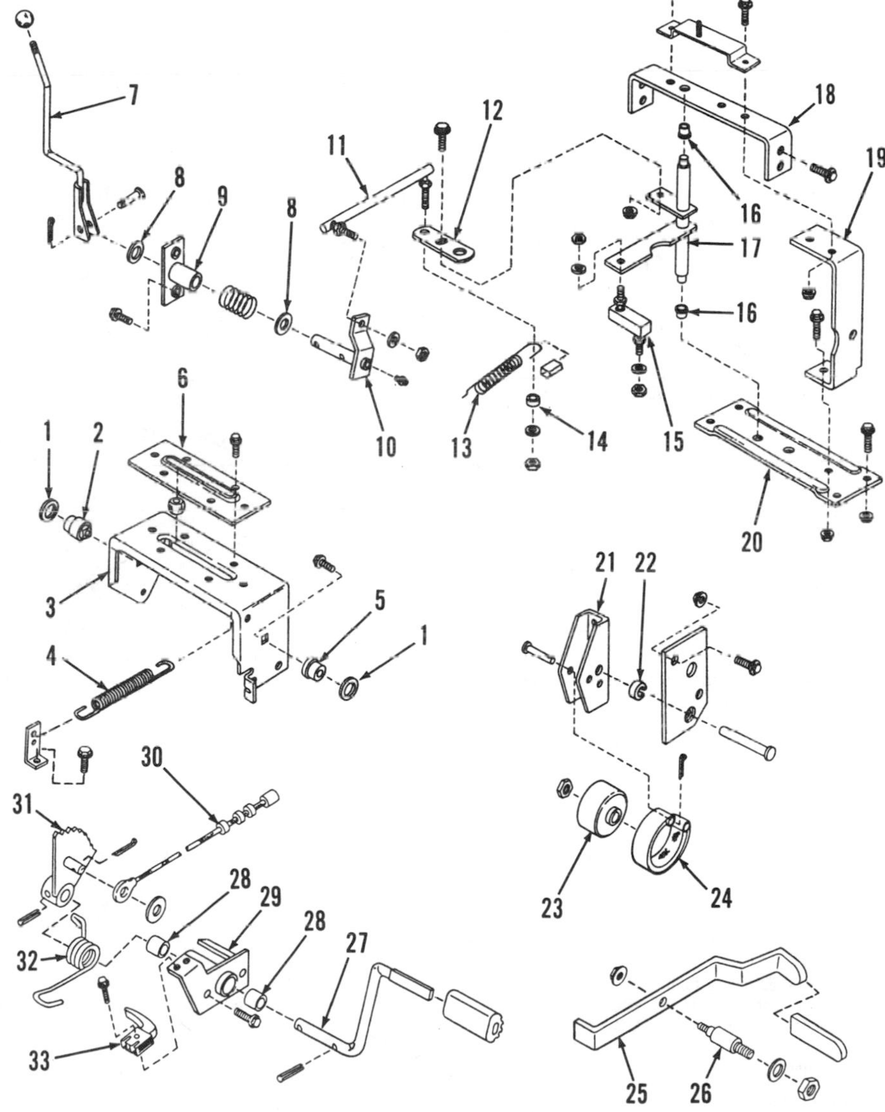

*Fig. SN6—Exploded view of brake and clutch mechanism used on Model LT11.*

1. Washer
2. Bushing
3. Clutch yoke
4. Spring
5. Bushing
6. Retainer plate
7. Shift shaft
8. Thrust washer
9. Shift pivot
10. Shift arm
11. Shift link
12. Shift arm
13. Spring
14. Roller
15. Shift link
16. Bushing
17. Shift arm
18. Bracket
19. Brake pivot bracket
20. Bracket
21. Brake pivot lever
22. Ring
23. Brake drum
24. Brake band
25. Park brake lever
26. Stub shaft
27. Clutch/brake pedal
28. Bushing
29. Pivot bracket
30. Cable
31. Parking brake ratchet
32. Spring
33. Clutch interlock switch

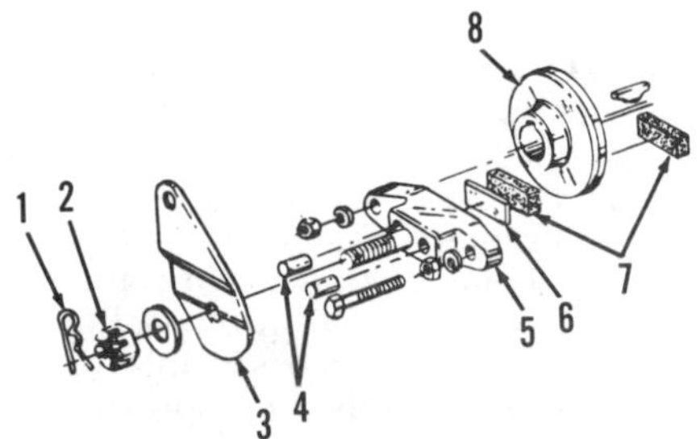

*Fig. SN9—Exploded view of disc type brake used on Model LT14H.*

1. Cotter pin
2. Nut
3. Brake lever
4. Actuating pins
5. Brake pad holder
6. Back-up plate
7. Brake pads
8. Brake disc

Remove mower deck from beneath tractor. Disconnect mower lift control rod from lift lever pivot. Disconnect spring from belt tension idler pulley. Work drive belt out of engine traction drive pulley and allow belt to remain on the hub between pulleys. Pull drive belt rearward and slip belt off transaxle drive pulley, then remove belt from tractor.

Place new belt around engine traction drive pulley. Route belt around outside of fixed idler pulley and inside of tension idler pulley. Be sure that belt is positioned above implement rear lift arm (Fig. SN10). On Model LT14H, twist rear of belt one half turn (180 degrees) to the left (counterclockwise) before installing belt on transaxle pulley (Fig. SN10A). Reconnect idler tension spring. Complete installation by reversing removal procedure.

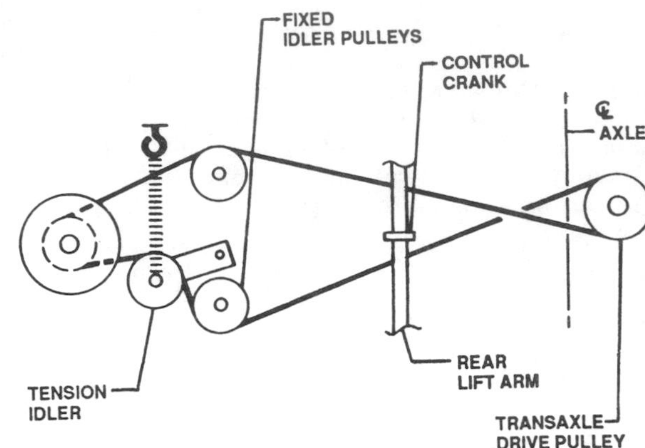


*Fig. SN10—Drawing showing traction drive belt routing for Model LT14H (viewed from underneath tractor). Model LT12D is similar except that only one fixed idler pulley is used and belt is not twisted at rear.*

# DRIVE SHAFT

## Model LT11

**REMOVE AND REINSTALL.** Remove console cover for access to drive shaft. Remove bolts that secure flex coupling discs (3—Fig. SN11) to engine output shaft and to drive disc hub (7). Slide drive shaft (6) out from between engine and drive disc hub.

To install drive shaft, reverse removal procedure. Apply light coat of grease to ends of drive shaft before installing hubs (4). Slide the hubs on the drive shaft to obtain desired shaft length, then tighten hub set screws to 15 ft.-lbs. (20 N·m).

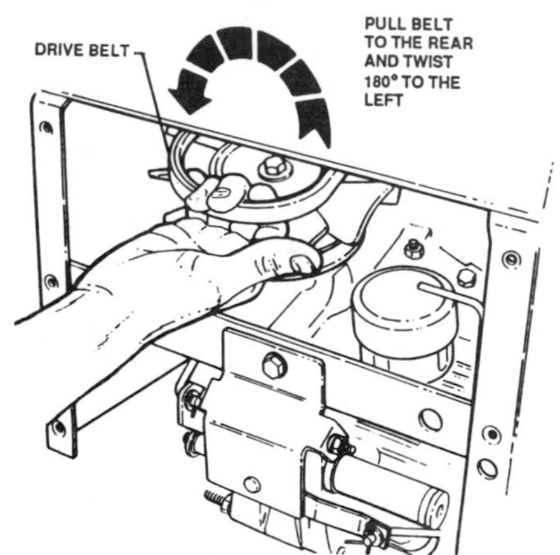


*Fig. SN10A—On Model LT14H, twist rear of drive belt one half turn counterclockwise before installing belt on transaxle drive pulley.*

# ELECTRIC POWER TAKE-OFF CLUTCH

## Model LT11

**TESTING.** To test clutch field coil for short or open circuits, disconnect wiring connector at clutch and connect ohmmeter positive test lead to coil terminal. Connect ohmmeter black test lead to engine ground. Field coil resistance should be 3.4-5.5K ohms. Renew clutch if coil resistance is infinite (open circuit) or excessively low (short circuit).

**ADJUSTMENT.** If clutch has been removed from tractor of if operation is erratic, clutch should be adjusted as follows:

Electric pto clutch should have 0.010 inch (0.25 mm) clearance between clutch rotor and armature with clutch disengaged. To check clearance, insert feeler gage in slots provided in clutch housing as shown in Fig. SN12. Adjust clearance by turning adjusting nuts (N) as necessary. Clearance must be the

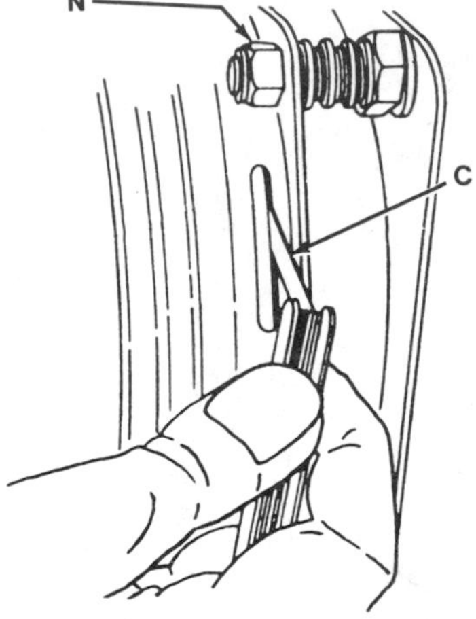


*Fig. SN12—To adjust pto clutch used on Model LT11, turn each adjusting nut (N) of pto clutch so clearance (C) between rotor and armature is 0.010 inch (0.025 mm).*

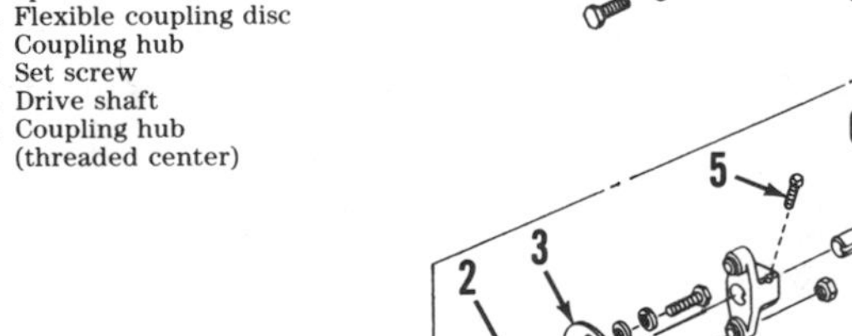

*Fig. SN11—Exploded view of drive shaft assembly used on Model LT11.*

1. Pto clutch assy.
2. Spacer
3. Flexible coupling disc
4. Coupling hub
5. Set screw
6. Drive shaft
7. Coupling hub (threaded center)

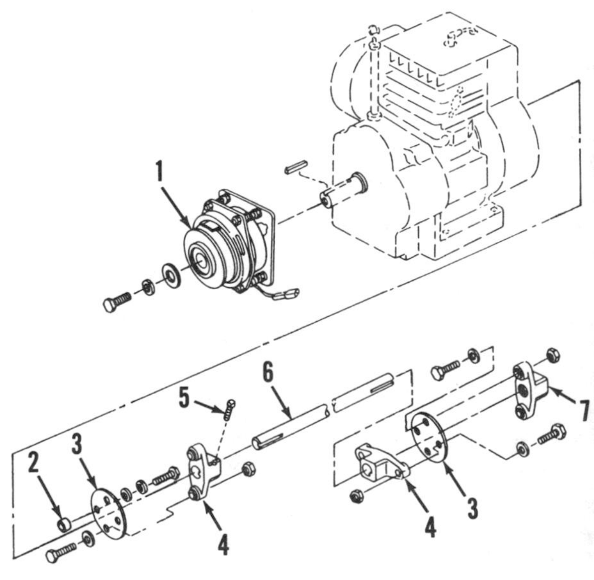




Illustrations courtesy Snapper Power Equipment.

same at each of the slots provided in clutch housing. Do not overtighten nuts. Operate clutch several times and recheck clearance.

**R&R AND OVERHAUL.** Clutch assembly (1—Fig. SN11) can be removed after removing center cap screw securing armature to engine crankshaft and four nuts (1—Fig. SN13) and shoulder bolts (3) securing clutch field coil (8) to engine block.

Inspect clutch components for excessive wear, scoring or other damage and renew as necessary. Install clutch and adjust clearance between rotor (7) and armature (6) as outlined in ADJUSTMENT paragraph.

If installing a new clutch, cycle clutch on and off several times at half throttle and then several times at full throttle to burnish clutch surfaces before returning tractor to regular service.

# TRACTION DRIVE CLUTCH

Models LT11 and LT12D are equipped with a clutch system that consists of a drive disc driven by the engine and a driven disc that transmits power to the transmission. The driven disc may be moved laterally against the drive disc to vary tractor speed. Depressing the brake/clutch pedal moves the driven disc away from the drive disc while applying the brake.

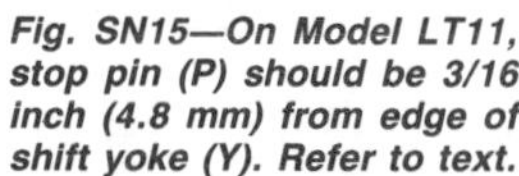

*Fig. SN15—On Model LT11, stop pin (P) should be 3/16 inch (4.8 mm) from edge of shift yoke (Y). Refer to text.*

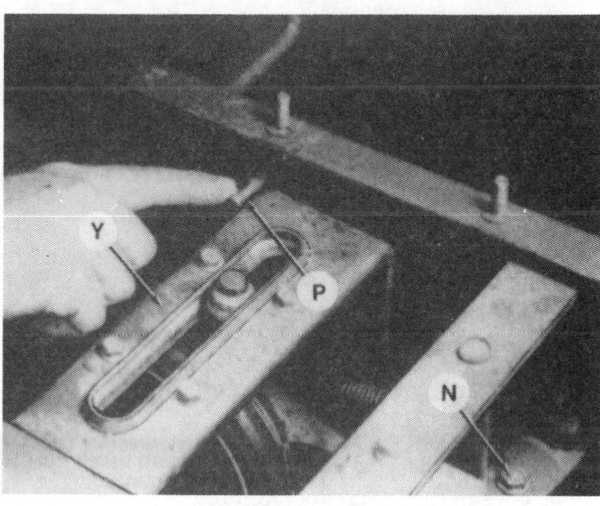


## Model LT11

**R&R AND OVERHAUL.** The driven disc (Fig. SN14) should be renewed if rubber is worn to a thickness of $^{1}/_{16}$ inch (1.6 mm) or less. To remove rubber disc, remove rear cover plate and seat support. Move shifter to neutral and unscrew nuts retaining disc to hub.

After installing new driven disc, check position of stop pin (P—Fig. SN15) which should be $^{3}/_{16}$ inch (4.8 mm) from edge of shift yoke (Y). The stop pin prevents metal-to-metal contact when rubber is excessively worn.

With driven disc in reverse position (right side of drive disc), center of driven disc should be $^{1}/_{16}$ inch (1.6 mm) below center of drive disc (see Fig. SN16). To obtain desired position, loosen screws securing bearing support (7—Fig. SN17) and relocate position of drive disc.

The shift handle should be located in neutral detent slot when driven disc is positioned in center of drive disc. If shift lever is not in neutral slot, loosen nut (N—Fig. SN15) and move shift arm to correctly position shift lever.

The drive disc (9—Fig. SN17) should be renewed if warped, excessively worn or damaged. Maximum allowable runout is 0.020 inch (0.51 mm). If drive disc must be removed, proceed as follows: Remove drive shaft. Unscrew spindle (5) from

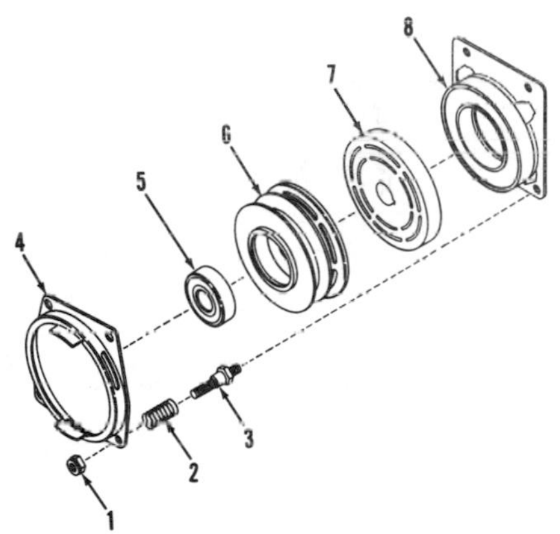


*Fig. SN13—Exploded view of pto electric clutch assembly used on Model LT11.*

1. Adjusting nut
2. Spring
3. Shoulder bolt
4. Brake cover
5. Bearing
6. Armature & pulley assy.
7. Rotor
8. Field coil

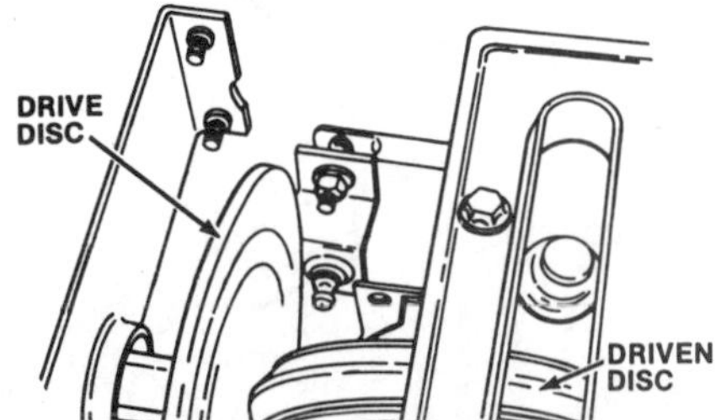


*Fig. SN14—View of transmission drive disc and driven disc used on Model LT11.*

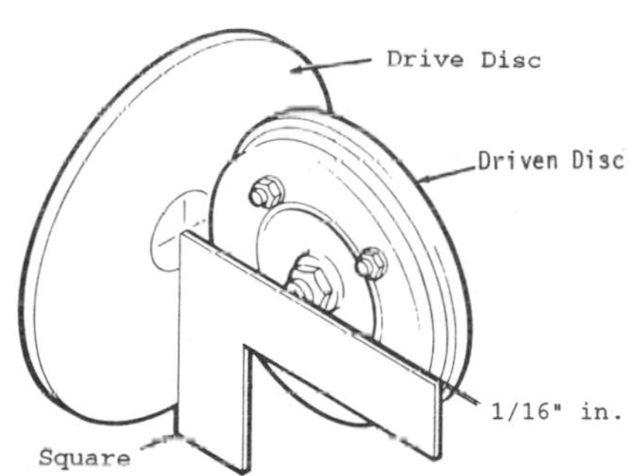


*Fig. SN16—With driven disc in reverse position (right side of drive disc), center of driven disc should be 1/16 inch (1.6 mm) below center of drive disc.*

*Fig. SN17—Exploded view of drive disc and shaft assembly used on Model LT11. Face of drive disc should be 2-3/16 inches (55.6 mm) from rear of support. Install shims (8) as needed.*

1. Coupler
2. Retainers
3. Tube
4. Bearings
5. Shaft
6. Spacers
7. Bearing support
8. Shim
9. Drive disc
10. Bearing
11. Button

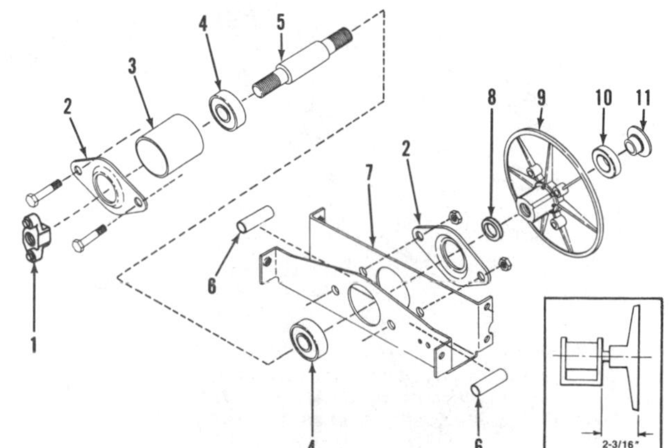


Illustrations courtesy Snapper Power Equipment.

disc (9) by turning coupler (1). Note that disc has left-hand threads. Unscrew coupler to remove front bearing. Coupler has left-hand threads. When assembling drive disc, install shims (8) as needed so face of disc is $2^{3}/_{16}$ inches (55.6 mm) from rear of support (7) as shown in Fig. SN17.

## Model LT12D

**ADJUSTMENT.** As driven disc wears, the clutch yoke must move farther up before driven disc contacts drive disc. Eventually, the yoke will contact the adjustable stop bolt (Fig. SN18) before driven disc engages drive disc, and tractor will have loss of pulling power.

To adjust clutch yoke to compensate for disc wear, first depress clutch/brake pedal and shift transmission lever to Neutral. Loosen jam nuts and turn stop bolt (Fig. SN18) about two turns clockwise. This will allow yoke to travel farther upward. To check clutch adjustment, lift driven disc up by hand and attempt to rotate it. If yoke is properly adjusted, the driven disc should contact drive disc and should not rotate.

To adjust shift detent, depress clutch pedal and move transmission shifter until primary clutch ball is in Neutral position in clutch yoke (Fig. SN18). Loosen bolt (2—Fig. SN19) attaching shift lever (5) to shift lever adjuster (4). Move shift lever adjuster until transmission shifter is positioned in Neutral notch of shift detent plate. Be sure that primary clutch ball is still in Neutral position in clutch yoke (Fig. SN18), then tighten shift lever adjuster bolt. Check for proper shifting and readjust if necessary.

**R&R AND OVERHAUL.** The driven disc should be renewed if rubber is worn to a thickness of $^{1}/_{16}$ inch (1.6 mm) or less. To remove rubber disc, remove rear cover plate from fenders. Move shifter to neutral, hold driven disc and unscrew nuts retaining disc to hub.

When installing new driven disc (2—Fig. SN20), be sure that fiber thrust washer (3) is centered over boss (B) on center of driven disc hub (1). If fiber washer is not free to "float" around boss on center of disc hub, it can cause clutch to bind.

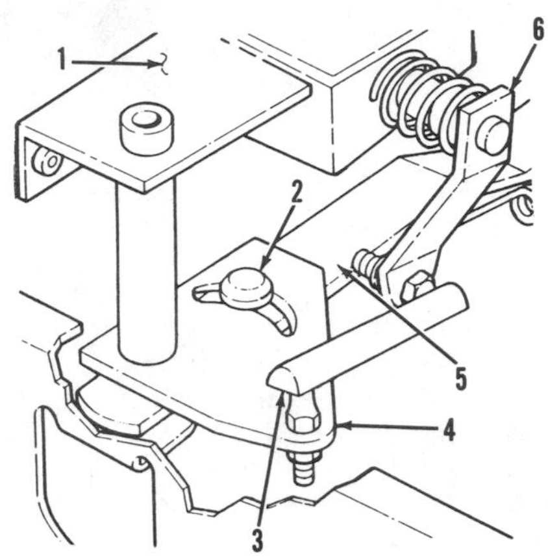

*Fig. SN19—Drawing of shift lever linkage used on Model LT12D. Refer to text for neutral adjustment procedure.*

1. Shift bracket
2. Bolt
3. Shift link
4. Shift lever adjuster
5. Shift lever
6. Shift arm

The drive disc (9—Fig. SN21) should be renewed if warped, excessively worn or damaged. Maximum allowable runout is 0.020 inch (0.51 mm). If drive disc must be removed, proceed as follows: Drive out roll pin and remove handle from transmission shifter lever. Remove rear cover. Disconnect wires to seat safety switch, then unbolt and remove fenders and seat. Unhook tension spring and reverse-assist spring (10) from clutch yoke (11). Disconnect clutch

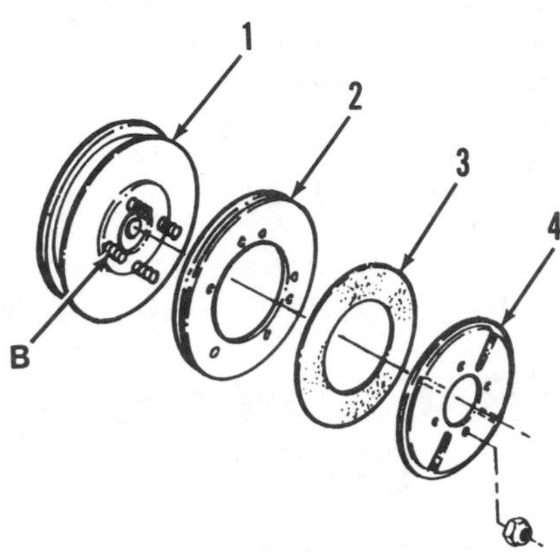


*Fig. SN20—Exploded view of driven disc assembly used on Model LT12D. When assembled, fiber washer (3) must be free to float around boss (B) on center of disc hub (1).*

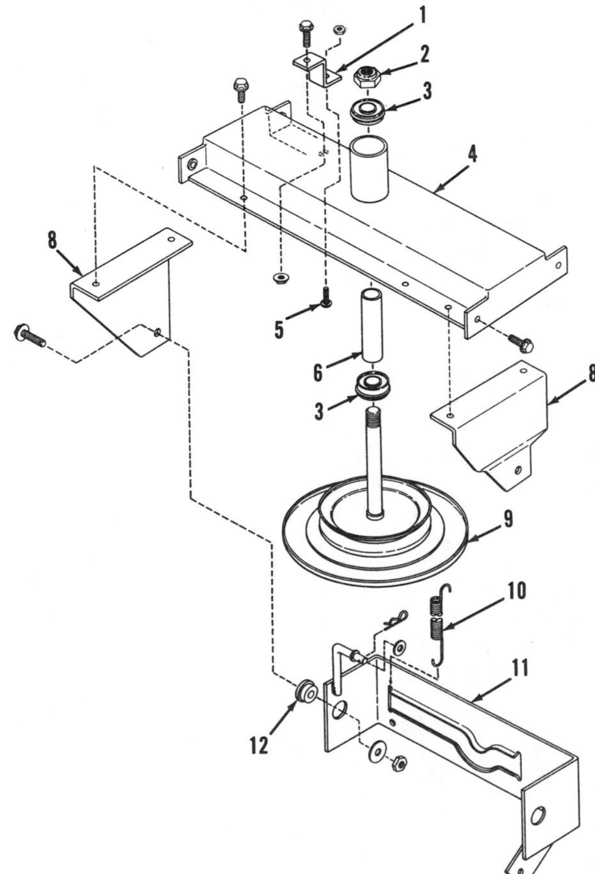

*Fig. SN21—Exploded view of drive disc and clutch yoke used on Model LT12D.*

1. Yoke stop bracket
2. Locknut
3. Bearings
4. Disc drive support
5. Yoke stop bolt
6. Spacer
8. Yoke pivot brackets
9. Drive disc assy.
10. Reverse helper spring
11. Clutch yoke
12. Yoke bearing

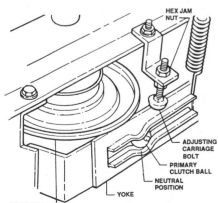

*Fig. SN18—If rubber on driven disc wears enough to cause loss of pulling power on Model LT12D, readjust yoke stop adjusting bolt as outlined in text.*



Illustrations courtesy Snapper Power Equipment.

rod from yoke arm. Loosen right-hand transmission support mounting bolts. Remove screws attaching drive disc support (4) to transmission supports. Move drive disc support to the rear until primary clutch ball is free of chain case shaft and withdraw drive disc support assembly from tractor. Remove clutch yoke and yoke pivot brackets from drive disc support. Remove locknut (2) and withdraw drive disc (9), bearings (3) and spacer (6) from support (4).

To install new drive disc, reverse removal procedure.

# PRIMARY CHAIN CASE

## Models LT11-LT12D

**LUBRICATION.** Check for presence of grease in chain case by removing plug (1—Fig. SN22). If lubricant is required, add 1 ounce of Snapper OO grease. Maximum capacity is 2 ounces. Excessive lubricant will result in leakage.

## Model LT11

**R&R AND OVERHAUL.** The primary chain case is accessible after removing transmission. To remove transmission, remove rear console panel, fenders and brake drum. Support rear of tractor and remove rear wheels. Unscrew locknut and drive tapered bolt out of right wheel hub and remove hub from axle. Remove set screws in lock collar on right axle, then use a punch to rotate lock collar in direction opposite of axle forward rotation and remove collar from axle. Remove cap screw from end of drive hex tube. Clean end of right axle shaft to ease removal of shaft through ball bearing. Loosen dust seal boot clamps on each end of hex tube. Detach lift hanger bracket on tractor underside which may interfere with transmission removal. Remove transmission retaining screws from tractor frame and withdraw transmission from tractor. Remove primary chain case from tractor.

To disassemble primary chain case, remove boots from each side. Unscrew locknut (14—Fig. SN22) and remove driven disc hub (13). Unscrew retaining screws and separate case halves (2 and 10). Remove input shaft (8), sprocket (6) and chain (9) as a unit.

Inspect components for damage and excessive wear. If bearing renewal is necessary, be sure to support area around bearing so case half is not distorted. Press bearings (7) into case until snap ring contacts case. Press needle bearings (4) into case from inside of case; press against lettered side of bearing. Hex hub (6) must slide freely on hex shaft.

When assembling chain case, install nylon thrust washers (5) so cupped side is toward hub (6). Install Belleville washers (12) with cupped side toward hub (13). Fill case with 2 ounces of Snapper OO grease.

## Model LT12D

**R&R AND OVERHAUL.** To remove primary chain case, raise and support rear of tractor. Remove rear cover, disconnect seat safety switch wires and unbolt and remove fenders and seat. Remove both rear wheels. Remove tapered bolt from right wheel hub and axle and remove wheel hub. Remove drive disc support assembly and clutch yoke as previously outlined in CLUTCH section. Remove cap screws retaining right-hand transmission support to right-hand transmission support extension. Loosen both boot clamps and slide boot away from right-hand transmission support and primary chain case. Remove right-hand transmission support. Disconnect shift link and brake lever from chain case. Slide chain case off end of hex drive tube.

To disassemble primary chain case, remove boots from each side. Unscrew locknut (18—Fig. SN23) and remove

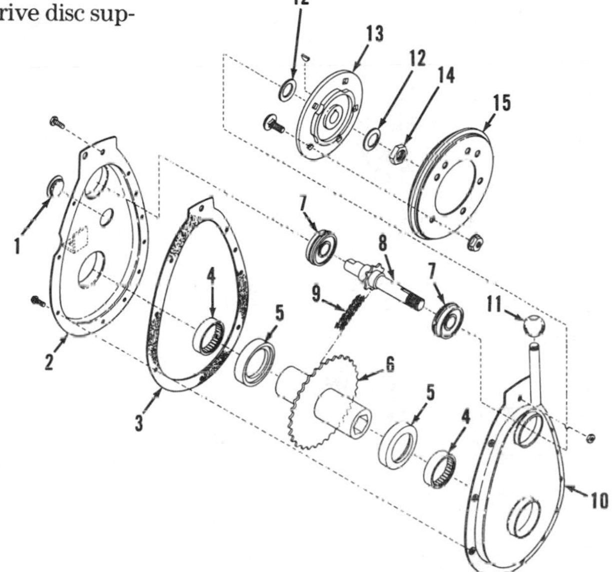

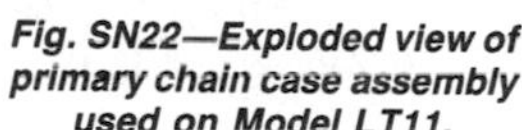

*Fig. SN22—Exploded view of primary chain case assembly used on Model LT11.*

1. Oil fill/check plug
2. Case cover
3. Gasket
4. Needle bearings
5. Nylon thrust washers
6. Hub & sprocket
7. Bearings
8. Input shaft & sprocket
9. Chain
10. Sprocket case
11. Clutch ball bushing
12. Belleville washers
13. Driven disc hub
14. Locknut
15. Driven disc

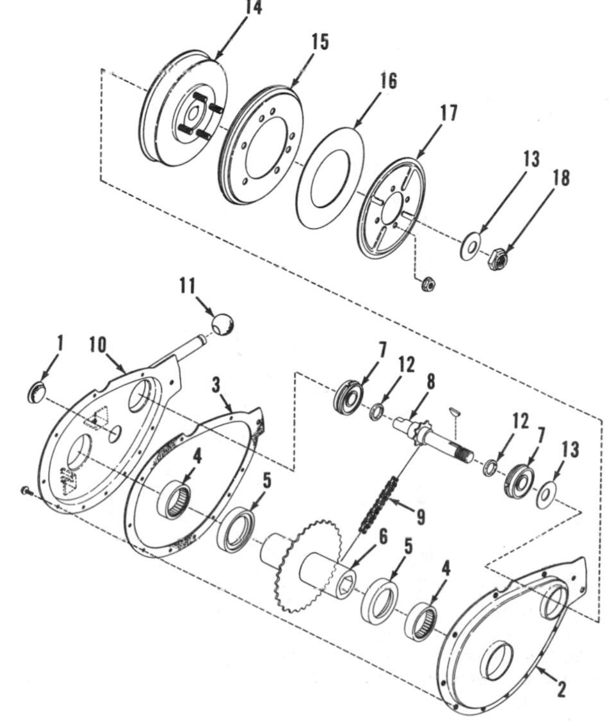

*Fig. SN23—Exploded view of primary chain case assembly used on Model LT12D.*

1. Oil level/check plug
2. Case cover
3. Gasket
4. Needle bearings
5. Nylon thrust washers
6. Hub & sprocket
7. Bearings
8. Input shaft & sprocket
9. Chain
10. Sprocket case
11. Clutch ball bushing
12. "O" rings
13. Belleville washers
14. Driven disc hub
15. Driven disc
16. Fiber thrust washer
17. Plate
18. Locknut

Illustrations courtesy Snapper Power Equipment.

driven disc hub (14). Unscrew retaining screws and separate case halves (2 and 10). Remove input shaft (8), sprocket (6) and chain (9) as a unit.

Inspect components for damage and excessive wear. If bearing renewal is necessary, be sure to support area around bearing so case half is not distorted. Press bearings (7) into case until snap ring contacts case. Press needle bearings (4) into case from inside of case; press against lettered side of bearing. Hex hub (6) must slide freely on hex shaft.

When assembling chain case, install nylon thrust washers (5) so cupped side is toward hub (6). Install Belleville washers (13) with cupped side toward hub (14). Fill case with 2 ounces of Snapper OO grease.

# GEAR TRANSMISSION

## Models LT11-LT12D

**LUBRICATION.** The oil level should be checked every season or after 100 hours of operation, whichever occurs first. Oil should be even with lower edge of plug opening (Fig. SN24). Add oil as needed through fill plug opening. Recommended oil is Snapper OO.

## Model LT11

**R&R AND OVERHAUL.** To remove transmission, remove rear console panel, fenders and brake drum. Support rear of tractor and remove rear wheels. Unscrew locknuts and drive tapered bolts from wheel hubs. Remove wheel hubs from axles. Remove set screws from lock collar on right axle. Use a punch to rotate lock collar in direction opposite of axle forward rotation and remove from axle. Remove boot clamp (31—Fig. SN25), dust seal (32), oil seal (33) and lock collar (34) from left axle. Remove cap screw (30) from end of drive hex tube (15). Clean ends of axles. Loosen dust seal boot clamps on each end of hex tube. Detach lift hanger bracket on tractor underside which may interfere with transmission removal. Remove transmission retaining screws from tractor frame and remove transmission from tractor.

To disassemble transmission, remove screws and nut securing cover (8—Fig. SN25) to transmission case and remove cover. Disassembly is evident after inspection of unit and referral to Fig. SN25 while noting the following: Note location of all thrust washers and shim washers as they are removed to ensure correct reassembly. Lift axle assembly (24), drive sprocket (13) and chain (23)

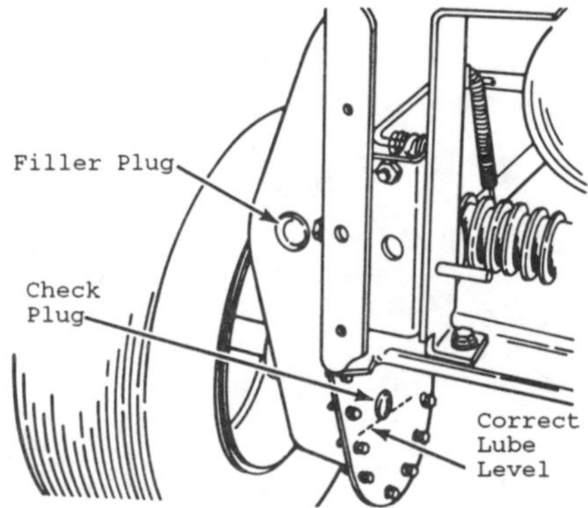


*Fig. SN24—Add oil to transmission as needed through fill plug opening so oil level is even with lower edge of check plug opening.*

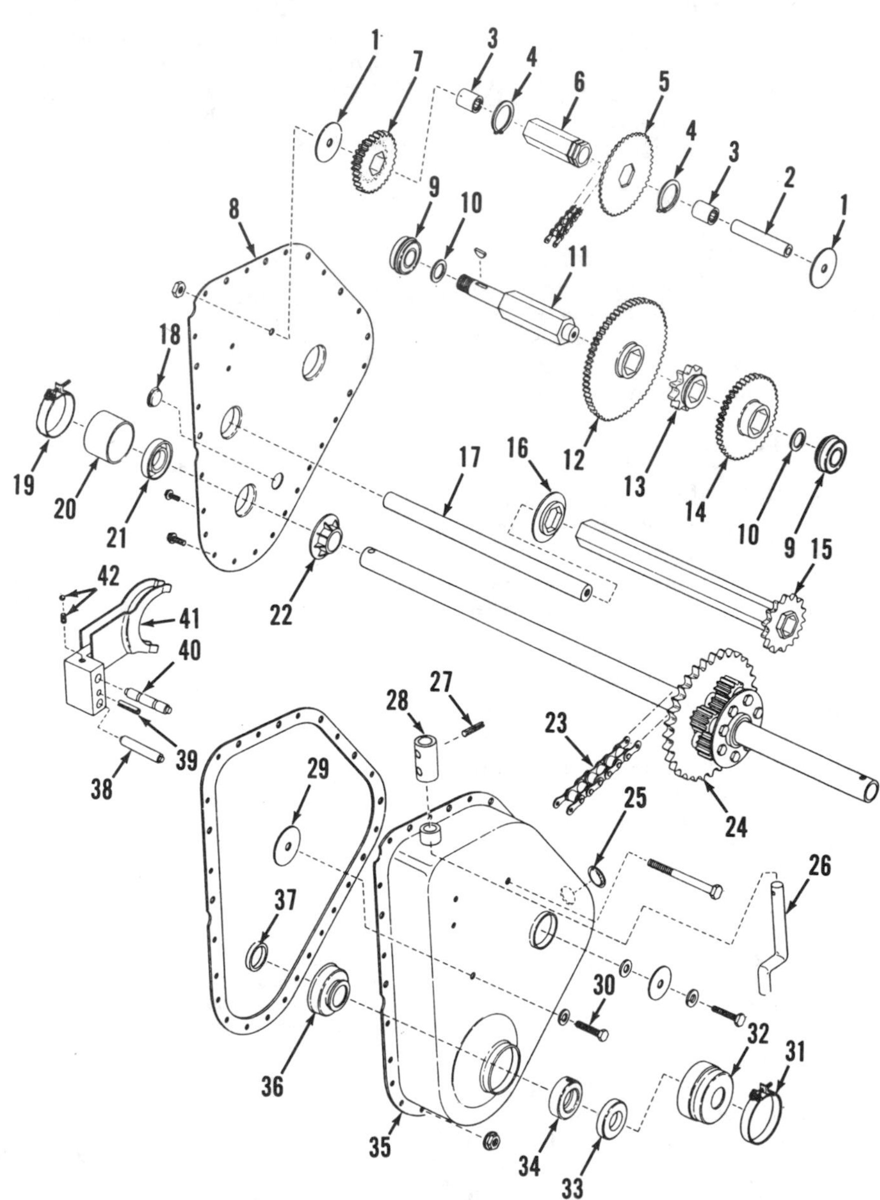

*Fig. SN25—Exploded view of transmission used on Model LT11.*

1. Thrust washer
2. Bearing race
3. Needle bearings
4. Snap ring
5. Sprocket
6. Hex tube
7. Cluster gear
8. Cover
9. Bearing
10. Shim washers
11. Third reduction shaft
12. Gear
13. Sprocket
14. Gear
15. Drive hex tube
16. Thrust washer
17. Drive tube support shaft
18. Oil level plug
19. Hose clamp
20. Seal cap
21. Oil seal
22. Special washer
23. Chain
24. Differential & axle assy.
25. Oil fill plug
26. Hi-Lo shift rod
27. Roll pin
28. Shift lever coupling
29. Thrust washer
30. Cap screw
31. Hose clamp
32. Dust seal cap
33. Oil seal
34. Lock collar
35. Transmission case
36. Bearing
37. Spacer
38. Shift guide pin
39. Roll pin
40. Detent guide pin
41. Shift fork
42. Detent ball & spring



Illustrations courtesy Snapper Power Equipment

out as an assembly. Shift fork (41) rides on guide pins (38 and 40) and must be pulled straight out. Lift hex shaft (15), drive chain and short hex tube (6) and sprocket (5) out as an assembly. Shaft (11) is retained by a screw at end of shaft. If shaft cannot be pulled out of bearing, reinstall screw and tap against it to dislodge shaft. If bearings must be removed, force bearings toward inside of case while supporting area around bearings so case will not be deformed.

Inspect shift fork assembly for wear or damage. Detent ball and spring (42) are located between roll pin (39) and detent pin (40). Renew shift fork if fingers are spread excessively.

Refer to Fig. SN26 for an exploded view of axle and differential assembly. Prior to disassembly note presence of alignment marks on sprocket (61) and differential plate (67). The eight misaligning thread type self-locking cap screws retaining differential plate and pinions (65) are intended to be used one time only; screws must be discarded and new screws must be installed. Discard spacers (66) if wear is indicated after comparing with a new spacer. Renew spacer (63) if worn. When assembling differential, alternate installation of gears (65) and spacers (66) so that a spacer is below one gear and above the next gear. Position plate (67) so match marks on sprocket and plate are aligned. Install new cap screws (68) and tighten to 18-25 ft.-lbs. (25-34 N·m).

Inspect transmission components for excessive wear and damage. Press needle bearings (3—Fig. SN25) into hex tube (6) until flush with tube ends. Press against lettered side of bearing. When installing new bearings in transmission case, press in from the inside. Reassemble by reversing disassembly procedure.

After installation, fill with oil through fill plug opening (Fig. SN24). Oil should be even with lower edge of plug opening. Recommended oil is Snapper OO.

## Model LT12D

**R&R AND OVERHAUL.** To remove transmission, first remove rear panel and disconnect seat safety switch wire. Unbolt and remove seat and fenders from tractor. Raise and support rear of tractor. Remove both rear wheels. Unscrew locknuts and drive tapered bolts from wheel hubs. Remove wheel hubs from axles. Remove drive disc support assembly as previously outlined in CLUTCH section. Remove bolts attaching left-hand transmission support to transmission support extension. Loosen boot clamp and slide boot away from left-hand transmission support. Withdraw transmission support, with transmission attached, as an assembly.

To disassemble transmission, remove retaining screws and nuts and separate left-hand transmission support (11—Fig. SN27) from transmission case (9). While holding hex drive tube (20) in place, pull differential and axle assembly out of the case. Remove chain (16), sprocket (15), gear (14) and spacer (18) from idler bolt (32). Withdraw hex drive tube (20).

Remove self-locking cap screws (26) from differential plate and discard; they cannot be reused. Lift plate (27) off bull gear (21) and remove pinion gears (28) and spacers (29). Remove axles (22 and 30) from bull gear.

Inspect all components for wear or damage and renew as necessary. The self-locking cap screws (26) are intended for use one time only and must be renewed whenever they are removed.

During reassembly, lubricate all bushings with Snapper OO grease. Insert long axle (22—Fig. SN27) and short axle (30) in bull gear (21) making certain nylon spacer (31) is positioned between the axle gears. Install pinion gears (28) and spacers (29) alternately so that a spacer is positioned below one gear and on top of the next gear (Fig. SN28). Install differential plate with new cap screws and tighten evenly to 18-25 ft.-lbs. (25-34 N·m). Install idler gear bolt (32—Fig. SN27), "O" ring (12) and cone washer (13) with edge of cone washer down over "O" ring. Install nylon hex washer (19) on hex shaft (20) with flange of washer toward hex shaft sprocket. Be sure that lubrication hole in gear (14) is clean. Assemble gear (14), sprocket (15), spacer (18), chain (16) and hex shaft (20) as a unit in case. Install metal thrust washer (5) on sprocket end of hex shaft with lip of washer toward the sprocket. Install cone washer (13) on idler bolt with edge of washer facing up, then install "O" ring (12) against the washer. Lubricate axle shafts, then insert long axle shaft into hex shaft. Install thrust washer (25) over end of short axle shaft.

Position left-hand support (11) on transmission case (9). Install nut on idler bolt (32), but do not tighten. Install two screws through end holes from case side to align case with support, install locknuts and tighten. Install and tighten eleven self-tapping screws. Tighten idler bolt nut to 18-20 ft.-lbs. (24-27 N·m).

Reinstall transmission by reversing removal procedure. Refill transmission case to proper level with Snapper OO grease.

# HYDROSTATIC DRIVE SYSTEM

## Model LT14H

**LUBRICATION.** Check level in oil reservoir at least twice each year (an access door is provided in fender rear cover plate). Do not allow any dirt or other foreign material to enter oil reservoir. Oil level should be checked when unit is cold and maintained at cold "Full Mark" indicated on reservoir (Fig. SN29). Recommended oil is SAE 20W motor oil.

**ADJUSTMENT.** Tractor should come to a complete stop when neutral return/brake pedal is fully depressed. If tractor continues to creep forward or rearward, adjust hydrostatic control linkage as follows:

Raise and support rear of tractor so rear wheels are free to turn. Remove rear cover from fenders. Start engine and move speed control lever to start wheel rotation in forward direction. Fully depress, then release neutral return/brake pedal and observe if wheels stop turning. If wheels continue to turn, shut off engine and loosen set screw (15—Fig. SN30) securing eccentric pin (11) to speed control arm (16).

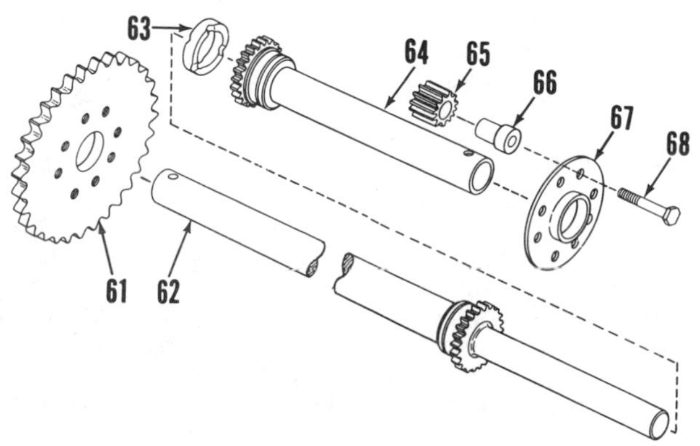

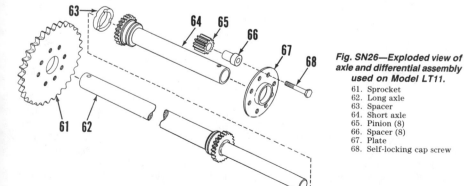

*Fig. SN26—Exploded view of axle and differential assembly used on Model LT11.*

61. Sprocket
62. Long axle
63. Spacer
64. Short axle
65. Pinion (8)
66. Spacer (8)
67. Plate
68. Self-locking cap screw

Illustrations courtesy Snapper Power Equipment.

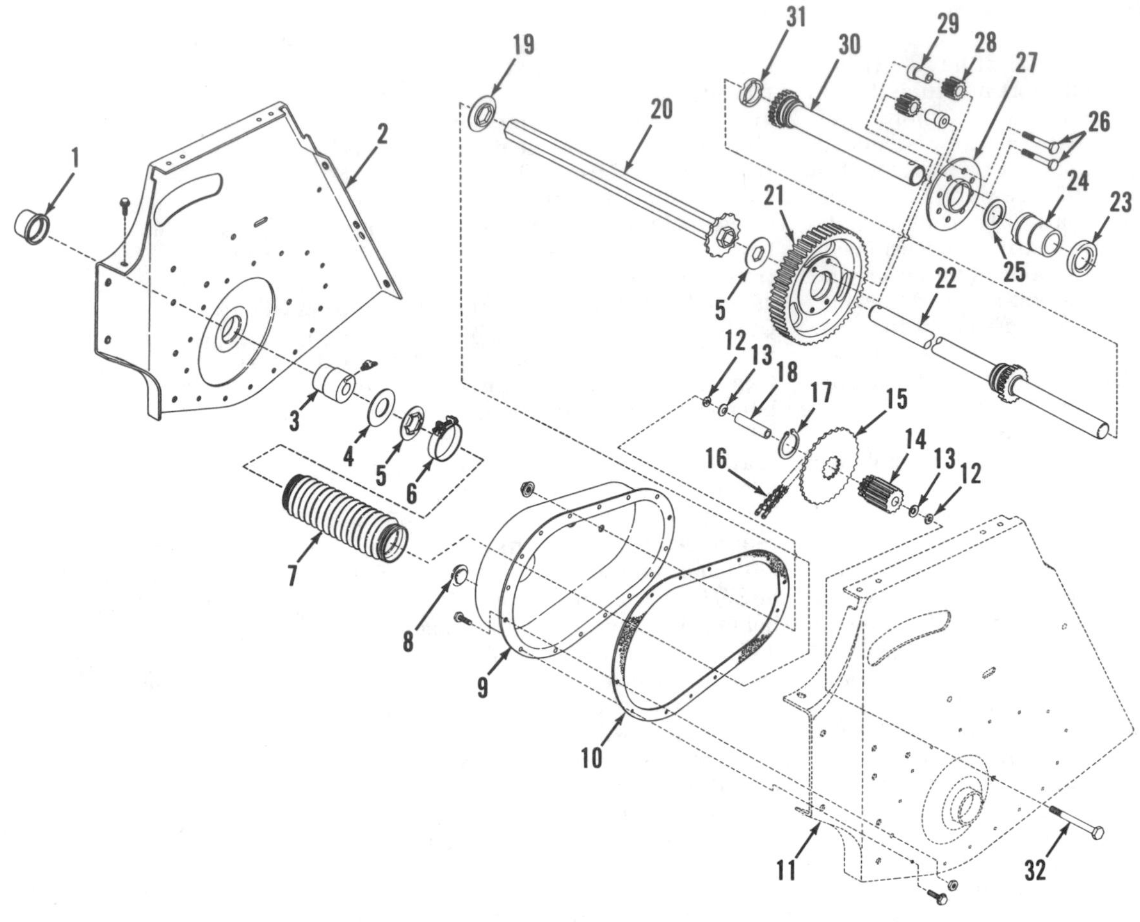


*Fig. SN27—Exploded view of transmission assembly used on Model LT12D.*

1. Dust cap
2. Transmission support R.H.
3. Axle bearing
4. Thrust washer
5. Thrust washer
6. Hose clamp
7. Oil seal boot
8. Oil fill/check plug
9. Transmission case
10. Gasket
11. Transmission support L.H.
12. "O" rings
13. Belleville washers
14. Gear
15. Sprocket
16. Chain
17. Snap ring
18. Spacer
19. Thrust washer
20. Hex drive tube
21. Bull gear
22. Axle shaft (long)
23. Oil seal
24. Axle bearing
25. Thrust washer
26. Special lock bolts
27. Differential plate
28. Pinion gears
29. Spacers
30. Axle shaft (short)
31. Nylon spacer

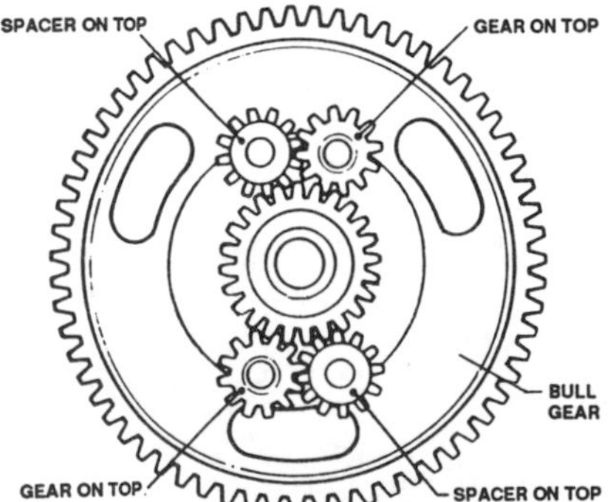


*Fig. SN28—Differential pinion gears and spacers must be assembled alternately with spacer above one gear and below next gear, and positioned diagonally as shown.*

**CAUTION: Do not attempt to adjust control linkage with engine running.**

Rotate eccentric pin to move speed control arm to neutral position. Tighten set screw (15), start engine and check tractor operation. If wheels continue to creep, repeat adjustment procedure.

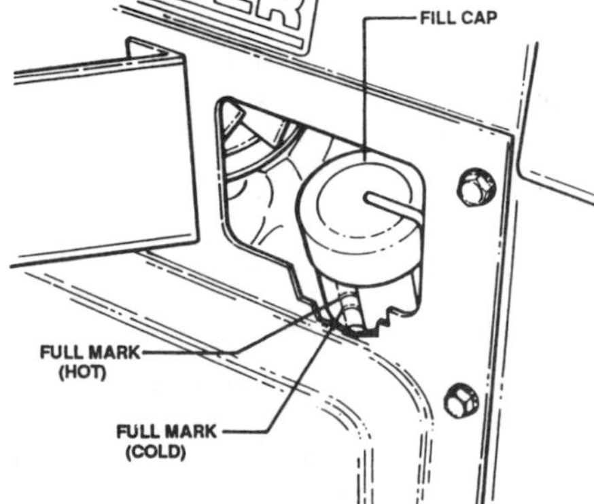


*Fig. SN29—Hydrostatic transmission filler cap is located behind access door in rear panel on Model LT14H.*

If speed control lever (1—Fig. SN30) will not remain in one position when released or if lever is hard to move, turn friction adjusting nut (5) to increase or decrease friction on lever bracket (2) as necessary.

**REMOVE AND REINSTALL.** To remove hydrostatic transmission, lower mower deck to lowest position. Remove rear cover from fenders. Disconnect traction drive belt idler spring, then work drive belt off transaxle drive pulley. Disconnect neutral return/brake cable (32—Fig. SN30). Disconnect speed control rod (10) from speed control arm. Remove cap screw attaching torque bracket (38) to rear support. Remove U-bolts attaching transaxle to side supports. Raise rear of tractor and roll transaxle and hydrostatic unit from under tractor. Remove cap screws securing hydrostatic unit (19) to transaxle housing and separate the two units. Note that hydrostatic transmission input and output shafts are coupled to transaxle shafts with two sets of couplers which are held in place by Loctite retaining compound. It may be necessary to heat couplers and use a puller to remove couplers from shafts.

To reinstall, reverse the removal procedure. Install drive couplers on transmission input and output shafts using Loctite 609 retaining compound. Apply Loctite 242 to threads of transmission mounting bolts and tighten to 80-120 in.-lbs. (9-13 N·m). Adjust hydrostatic control linkage as previously outlined.

**OVERHAUL.** Model LT14H is equipped with a Hydro-Gear Model 210-1010S hydrostatic transaxle which uses a Hydro-Gear BDU-10L series hydrostatic transmission. Refer to the Hydro-Gear section in HYDROSTATIC TRANSMISSION SERVICE section for overhaul procedure.

# REDUCTION GEARS AND DIFFERENTIAL

## Model LT14H

**R&R AND OVERHAUL.** Model LT14H is equipped with a Hydro-Gear Model

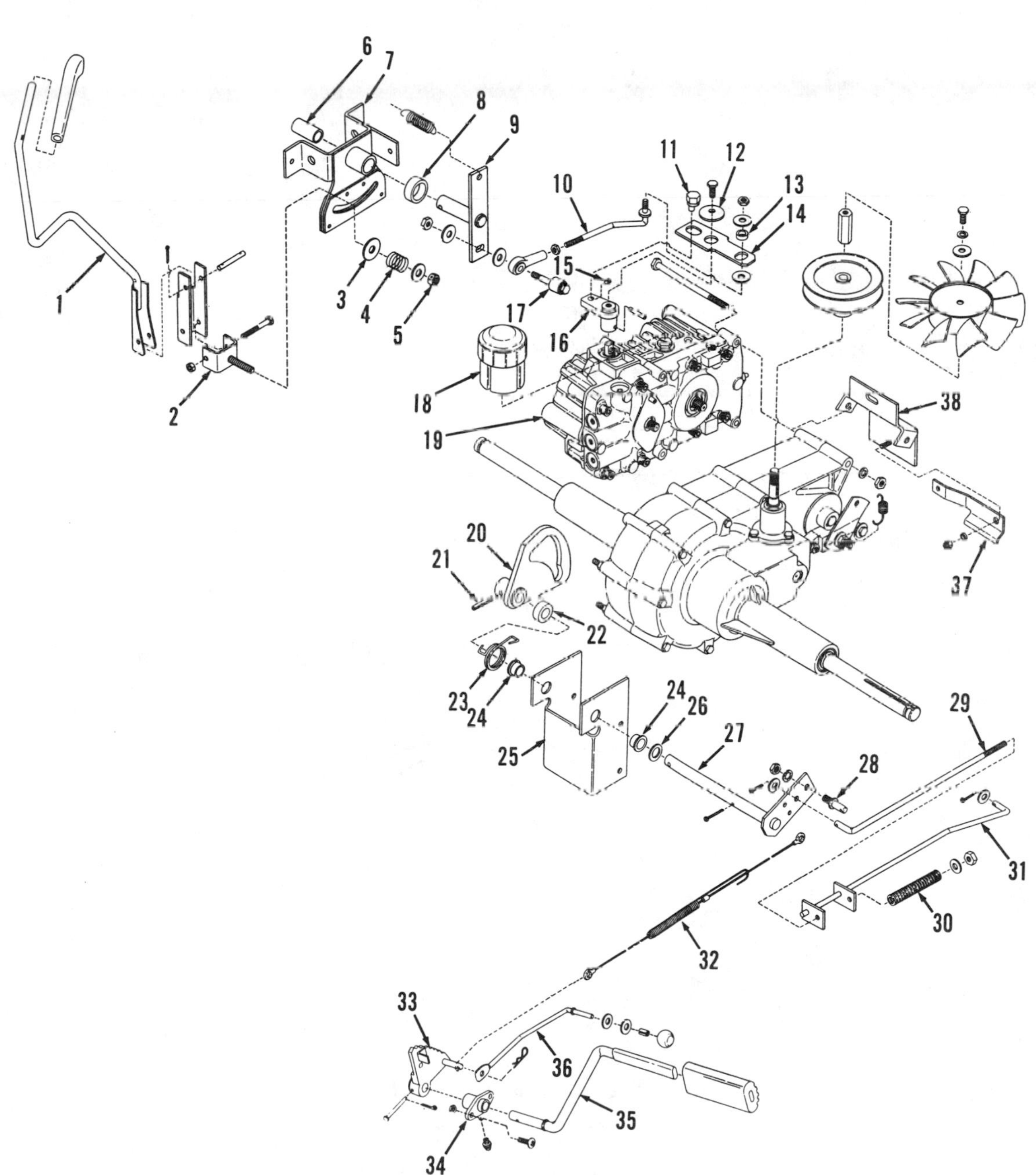

*Fig. SN30—Exploded view of hydrostatic transmission control linkage used on Model LT14H.*

1. Shift control lever
2. Control lever pivot
3. Friction washer
4. Tension spring
5. Friction adjusting nut
6. Pivot bearing
7. Shift pivot bracket
8. Spacer
9. Speed control lever
10. Speed control rod
11. Eccentric pin
12. Belleville washer
13. Roller
14. Speed control plate
15. Set screw
16. Speed control arm
17. Cam follower
18. Reservoir
19. Hydrostatic unit
20. Neutral return cam
21. Roll pin
22. Spacer
23. Torsion spring
24. Bushing
25. Neutral pivot bracket
26. Washer
27. Neutral return/ brake rod
28. Pivot stud
29. Brake spring rod
30. Brake spring
31. Brake rod
32. Neutral return/ brake cable
33. Pedal pivot bracket
34. Pivot bearing
35. Neutral return/ brake pedal
36. Park brake lever

Illustrations courtesy Snapper Power Equipment.

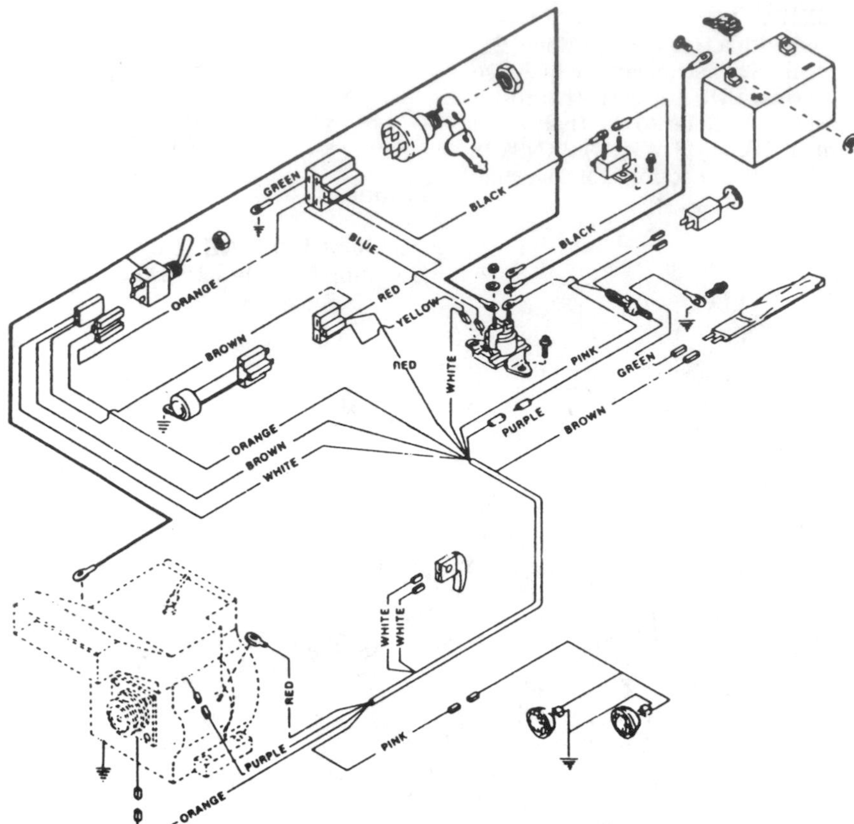


*Fig. SN31—Wiring diagram for Model LT11.*

210-1010S gear reduction and differential unit.

Removal and installation of gear reduction and differential unit is outlined in HYDROSTATIC DRIVE SYSTEM section. Refer to the Hydro-Gear section in REDUCTION GEAR AND DIFFERENTIAL SERVICE section for overhaul information.

# ELECTRICAL SYSTEM

## All Models

All tractors are equipped with a safety start interlock system which prevents starting of engine until the following conditions are met: The operator must be seated on the tractor seat, the pto control must be in "OFF" position and clutch/brake pedal must be fully depressed. The seat interlock switch also functions to shut off the engine if operator leaves the seat while tractor is in operation.

The engine is equipped with an electric starter motor and charging system. Refer to appropriate Briggs & Stratton or Kohler engine accessories section for service information.

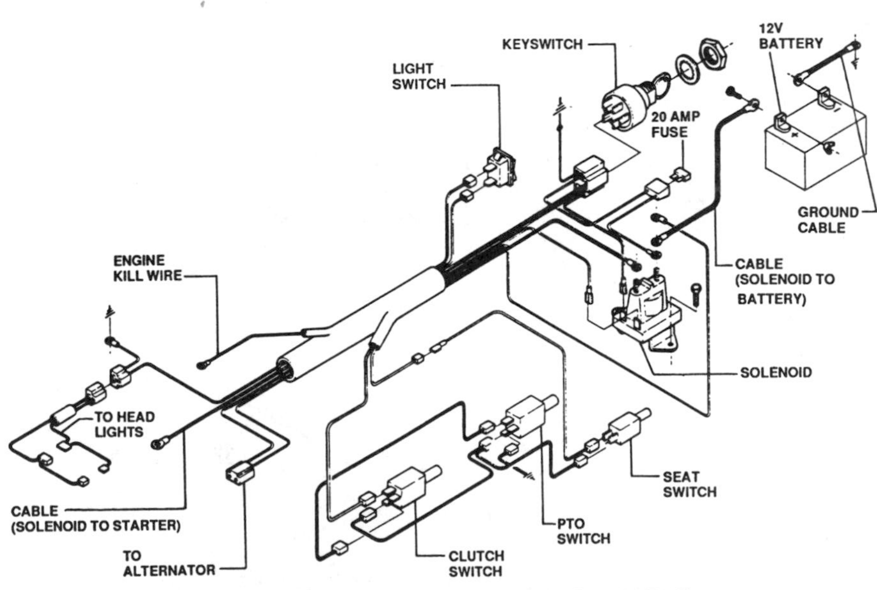


*Fig. SN32—Wiring diagram for Models LT12D and LT14H.*

# SPEEDEX

## CONDENSED SPECIFICATIONS

| | MODELS | | | |
|---|---|---|---|---|
| | **1240** | **1240M** | **1640** | **1640M** |
| Engine Make | Kohler | Kohler | Kohler | Kohler |
| Model | K301 | M12 | K341 | M16 |
| Bore | 3.375 in. (85.7 mm) | 3.375 in. (85.7 mm) | 3.75 in. (95.3 mm) | 3.75 in. (95.3 mm) |
| Stroke | 3.25 in. (95.3 mm) | 3.25 in. (95.3 mm) | 3.25 in. (95.3 mm) | 3.25 in. (95.3 mm) |
| Piston Displacement | 29.1 cu. in. (477 cc) | 29.1 cu. in. (477 cc) | 35.9 cu. in. (588 cc) | 35.9 cu. in. (588 cc) |
| Horsepower | 12 | 12 | 16 | 16 |
| Slow Idle Speed – Rpm | 1200 | 1200 | 1200 | 1200 |
| Full Load Speed – Rpm | 3600 | 3600 | 3600 | 3600 |
| Crankcase Oil Capacity | 4 pints (1.9 L) | 4 pints (1.9 L) | 4 pints (1.9 L) | 4 pints (1.9 L) |
| Weight | 10W-30 | | | |
| Transaxle Oil Capacity | 3 pints (1.4 L) | 3 pints (1.4 L) | 3 pints (1.4 L) | 3 pints (1.4 L) |
| Weight | SAE 90 EP | | | |

# FRONT AXLE AND STEERING SYSTEM

## AXLE MAIN MEMBER

### All Models

Axle main member (33 – Fig. SP10) is mounted on main frame and pivots on pivot pin. To remove axle assembly, raise and support front of tractor. Disconnect drag link end (30) at right spindle (27). Remove cotter pin (5) and washers (6). Carefully work pivot pin and axle assembly from main frame.

Reinstall by reversing removal procedure. Lubricate axle pivot pin during reassembly. Install washers (6) as required to allow axle to pivot freely with minimum axle end play.

## TIE ROD

### All Models

Tie rod (26 – Fig. SP10) used on all models is equipped with adjustable ends. To adjust toe-in, adjust length of tie rod to obtain $^1/_8$ inch (3 mm) toe-in.

## STEERING SPINDLES

To remove steering spindles, raise and support front of tractor. Remove wheel and tire assembly from side or sides to be serviced. On right side, disconnect drag link (32 – Fig. SP10) at spindle (27). Disconnect tie rod ends at spindles. Remove drive pins (20 and 28) and remove steering levers (25 and 29). Slip spindles down out of axle main member. Remove bushings (23 and 24) as required.

Reinstall by reversing removal procedure. Lubricate spindles with lithium base grease prior to installation. Install washers (19) as required to allow free wheel rotation with minimum wheel end play.

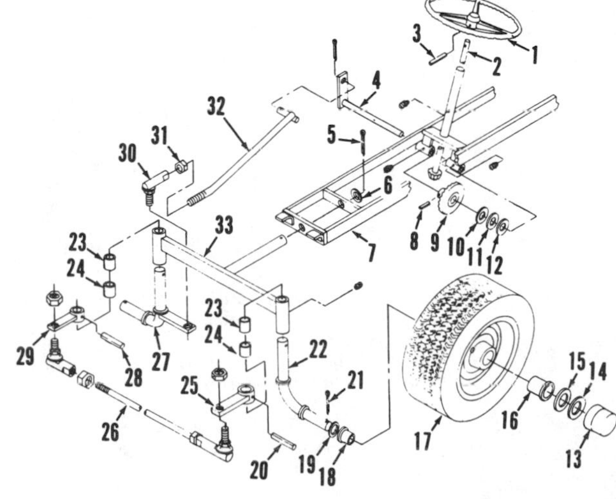

***Fig. SP10 – Exploded view of front axle assembly used on all models. Some models are equipped with an extended (wider) front axle main member (33).***

1. Steering wheel
2. Steering shaft & gear assy.
3. Drive pin
4. Steering arm
5. Cotter pin
6. Shim washer
7. Frame
8. Drive pin
9. Steering gear
10. Shim washer
11. Shim washer
12. Shim washer
13. Cap
14. Washer
15. Washer
16. Bushing
17. Tire & wheel assy.
18. Bushing
19. Washer
20. Drive pin
21. Cotter pin
22. Spindle
23. Bushing
24. Bushing
25. Steering lever
26. Tie rod
27. Spindle
28. Drive pin
29. Steering lever
30. Drag link end
31. Jam nut
32. Drag link
33. Axle main member

FRONT
Measurement "A"
REAR
Measurement "B"

***Fig. SP11 – Front wheels should toe-in about $^1/_8$ inch (3.0 mm). To check, subtract measurement "A" from measurement "B."***

Illustrations courtesy Speedex Tractor Co.

# STEERING GEAR

### REMOVE AND REINSTALL

#### All Models

To remove steering gear, remove drive pin (3–Fig. SP10) and steering wheel (1). Remove drive pin (8) and disconnect drag link (32) at steering arm (4). Remove shim washers (10, 11 and 12) and steering gear (9) as steering arm (4) is pulled from frame bushings. Pull steering shaft and gear assembly (2) down out of steering shaft frame tube.

Reinstall by reversing removal procedure. Lubricate steering shaft and steering arm during installation with lithium base grease. Install shim washers (10, 11 and 12) as required to allow steering wheel to turn smoothly with minimum free play.

# ENGINE

### REMOVE AND REINSTALL

#### All Models

To remove engine, remove hood and grille assembly. Remove traction drive belt and implement drive belt. Disconnect negative, then positive battery cables. Disconnect throttle cable, choke cable and all electrical connections at engine. Remove engine mounting bolts and lift engine frame.

To reinstall engine, reverse removal procedure.

### OVERHAUL

#### All Models

All models are equipped with Kohler engines. Refer to CONDENSED SPECIFICATIONS at the beginning of this section for engine model number and refer to the appropriate Kohler engine section in ENGINE SERVICE section for overhaul procedure.

# CLUTCH AND BRAKE

### ADJUSTMENT

#### All Models

All models are equipped with a combination clutch-brake pedal. Drive belt and brakes must be adjusted in the following sequence. Remove the right rear fender and rear inspection plate on belt guard. Fully depress clutch-brake pedal and lock in position. Adjust nut (1–Fig. SP12) to obtain 1 inch (25.4 mm) clearance between drive belt as shown in Fig. SP13. If clutch pedal hits foot plate when fully depressed, turn nut (A–Fig. SP14) at trunnion located under dash and behind engine on right side. With clutch-brake pedal fully depressed and locked in position, turn nut (B–Fig. SP15) to compress spring by one coil. Adjust nut (A) to obtain 1/16 inch (1.6 mm) clearance between nut and trunnion. Adjust all belt guides so there is 1/16 to 1/8 inch (1.6-3.0 mm) clearance between belt guides and belt. Reinstall rear inspection plate and fender.

### REMOVE AND REINSTALL BRAKE SHOE

#### All Models

To renew brake shoe, disconnect brake rod (12–Fig. SP17) at brake shoe band (7). Remove bolt (1) and washers. Slip brake band assembly from frame. Remove snap ring (8) to remove drum (9) from brake shaft.

Reinstall by reversing removal procedure. Adjust clutch brake as previously outlined.

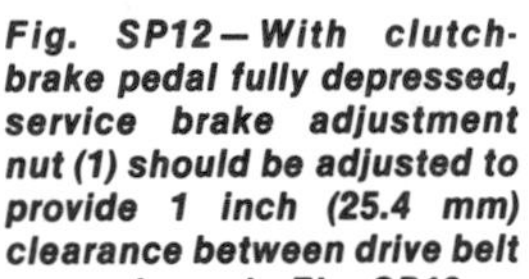

***Fig. SP12—With clutch-brake pedal fully depressed, service brake adjustment nut (1) should be adjusted to provide 1 inch (25.4 mm) clearance between drive belt as shown in Fig. SP13.***

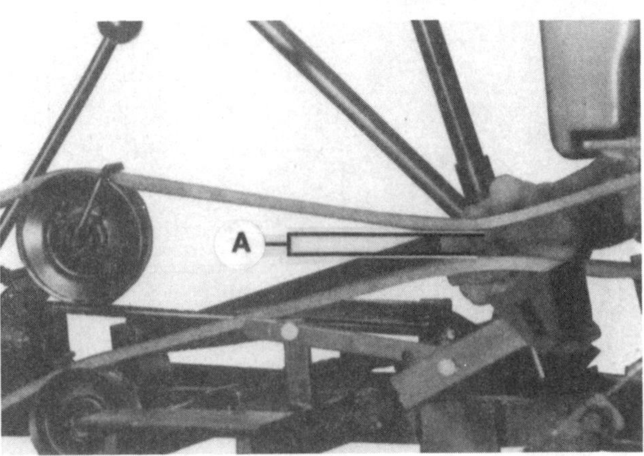


***Fig. SP13—With clutch-brake pedal fully depressed, traction drive belt should have 1 inch (25.4 mm) clearance measured at (A).***

***Fig. SP14—View of clutch adjustment nut located under dash and behind engine on right side.***

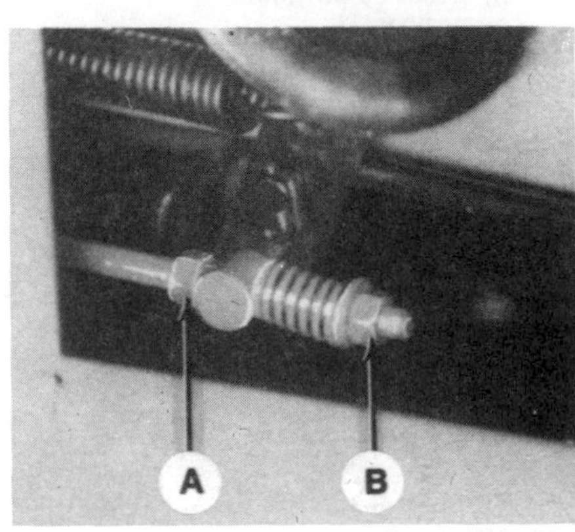


***Fig. SP15—View showing location of secondary brake adjustment nuts (A and B). Refer to text.***



Illustrations courtesy Speedex Tractor Co.

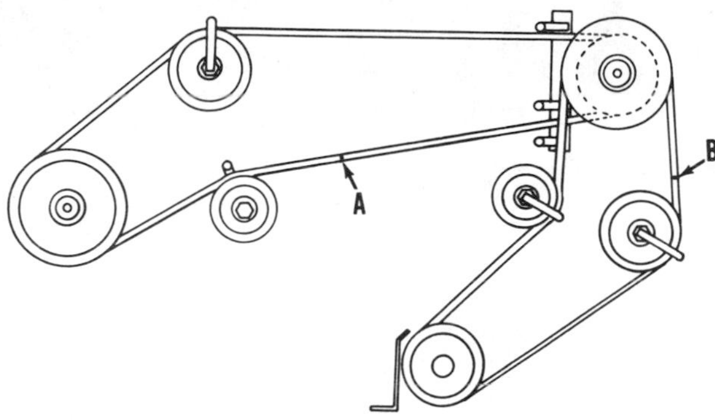


Fig. SP16—View of traction drive (A) and implement (B) drive belt routing.

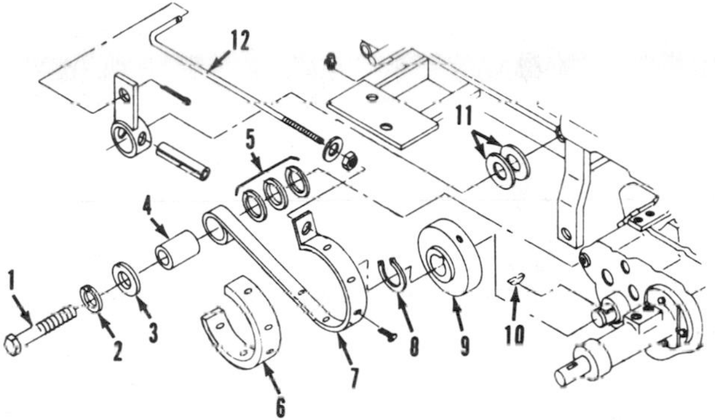


Fig. SP17—Exploded view of brake assembly used on all models.

1. Bolt
2. Washer
3. Washer
4. Pivot bushing
5. Shim washers
6. Brake lining
7. Brake band
8. Snap ring
9. Brake drum
10. Key
11. Washers
12. Brake rod

# DRIVE BELT

### ADJUSTMENT

#### All Models

Drive belt on all models must be adjusted during brake adjustment procedure. Refer to the ADJUSTMENT paragraphs in the previous CLUTCH AND BRAKE section.

### REMOVE AND REINSTALL

#### All Models

To renew drive belt, remove right rear fender and belt guard. Remove secondary brake. Loosen all belt guides and remove belt. Drive belt on all models is 5/8 inch x 83 inches.

Reinstall by reversing removal procedure and refer to Fig. SP16. Adjust as previously outlined under ADJUSTMENT.

# TRANSAXLE

### LUBRICATION

#### All Models

All models are equipped with a Peerless transaxle. Approximate transaxle fluid capacity is 3 pints (1.4 L) of SAE 90 EP gear oil. Gear oil is added through shift lever opening.

### REMOVE AND REINSTALL

#### All Models

Raise and support rear of tractor. Disconnect brake linkage and remove brake band. Remove shift lever. Remove traction drive belt. Remove all bolts retaining transaxle. Raise rear of tractor frame up off transaxle and roll transaxle assembly out from under tractor.

Reinstall by reversing removal procedure. Adjust traction drive belt and brake as previously outlined.

### OVERHAUL

#### All Models

All models are equipped with a Peerless 2300 series transaxle. Refer to Peerless Series 2300 in TRANSAXLE SERVICE section for overhaul procedure.

# IMPLEMENT DRIVE BELT AND CLUTCH

### ADJUSTMENT

#### All Models

To adjust tension on implement drive belt, loosen nut and bolt (2–Fig. SP18) and slide idler pulley as required to tighten or loosen belt. Belt retainers (3–Fig. SP19) should not touch belt. Idler pulleys should be approximately 1 inch (25.4 mm) apart when correctly adjusted.

### REMOVE AND REINSTALL

#### All Models

To renew implement drive belt, raise hood assembly. Loosen all belt guides and remove implement drive belt. Refer to Fig. SP16 for belt routing. Adjust belt guides so they are 1/16 to 1/8 inch (1.6-3.0 mm) from belt.

Fig. SP18—View showing location of implement drive idler pulley. Loosen nut and bolt (2) and slide idler pulley in bracket slot (1) to adjust tension on implement drive belt.

Fig. SP19—There should be a distance (4) of 1 inch (25.4 mm) between pulleys if correctly adjusted. Belt retainers (3) should not touch belt.

# WESTERN AUTO

## CONDENSED SPECIFICATIONS

| | WIZARD MODELS | | | | |
|---|---|---|---|---|---|
| | 5508, 7508 | 5510 | 5514 | 5520 | 5525 |
| Engine Make | B&S | B&S | B&S | B&S | B&S |
| Model | 190400 | 243434 | 320424 | 320424 | 320424 |
| Bore | 3 in. (76.2 mm) | 3-1/16 in. (77.8 mm) | 3-9/16 in. (90.5 mm) | 3-9/16 in. (90.5 mm) | 3-9/16 in. (90.5 mm) |
| Stroke | 2¾ in. (69.8 mm) | 3¼ in. (82.5 mm) | 3¼ in. (82.5 mm) | 3¼ in. (82.5 mm) | 3¼ in. (82.5 mm) |
| Piston Displacement | 19.44 cu. in. (319 cc) | 23.94 cu. in. (392 cc) | 32.4 cu. in. (531 cc) | 32.4 cu. in. (531 cc) | 32.4 cu. in. (531 cc) |
| Horsepower | 8 | 10 | 14 | 14 | 14 |
| Slow Idle Speed – Rpm | 1750 | 1000 | 1200 | 1200 | 1200 |
| High Idle Speed (No-Load) – Rpm | 3600 | 3600 | 3600 | 3600 | 3600 |
| Full Load Speed – Rpm | 3240 | 3240 | 3240 | 3240 | 3240 |
| Crankcase Oil Capacity | 2¾ pints (1.3 L) | 4 pints (1.9 L) | 4 pints (1.9 L) | 4 pints (1.9 L) | 4 pints (1.9 L) |
| Weight – | | | | | |
| Above 32°F (0°C) | | | SAE 30 | | |
| 0°F (–18°C) to 32°F (0°C) | | | SAE 10W | | |
| Below 0°F (–18°C) | | | SAE 5W-20 | | |
| Transmission Oil Capacity | 3 pints (1.4 L) | 4 pints (1.9 L) | 4 pints (1.9 L) | 4 pints (1.9 L) | 11 pints (5.2 L) |
| Weight | SAE 90 EP | SAE 90 EP | SAE 90 EP | SAE 90 EP | ATF "F" |
| Right Angle Drive Oil Capacity | .... | .... | .... | 6 oz. (177 mL) | .... |
| Weight | .... | .... | .... | EP Lithium Grease | .... |

| | WIZARD MODELS | | | | |
|---|---|---|---|---|---|
| | 7510 | 7520 | 7525 | 7600 | 7602 |
| Engine Make | B&S | B&S | B&S | B&S | B&S |
| Model | 243431 | 325431 | 325431 | 251417 | 252707 |
| Bore | 3-1/16 in. (77.8 mm) | 3-9/16 in. (90.5 mm) | 3-9/16 in. (90.5 mm) | 3-7/16 in. (87.3 mm) | 3-7/16 in. (87.3 mm) |
| Stroke | 3¼ in. (82.5 mm) | 3¼ in. (82.5 mm) | 3¼ in. (82.5 mm) | 2⅝ in. (66.7 mm) | 2⅝ in. (66.7 mm) |
| Piston Displacement | 23.94 cu. in. (392 cc) | 32.4 cu. in. (531 cc) | 32.4 cu. in. (531 cc) | 24.36 cu. in. (399 cc) | 24.36 cu. in. (399 cc) |
| Horsepower | 10 | 15 | 15 | 11 | 11 |
| Slow Idle Speed – Rpm | 1000 | 1200 | 1200 | 1800 | 1800 |
| High Idle Speed (No-Load) – Rpm | 3600 | 3600 | 3600 | 3600 | 3600 |
| Full Load Speed – Rpm | 3240 | 3240 | 3240 | 3200 | 3200 |
| Crankcase Oil Capacity | 4 pints (1.9 L) | 4 pints (1.9 L) | 4 pints (1.9 L) | 3 pints (1.4 L) | 3 pints (1.4 L) |
| Weight – | | | | | |
| Above 32°F (0°C) | | | SAE 30 | | |
| 0°F (–18°C) to 32°F (0°C) | | | SAE 10W | | |
| Below 0°F (–18°C) | | | SAE 5W-20 | | |
| Transmission Oil Capacity | 4 pints (1.9 L) | 4 pints (1.9 L) | 11 pints (5.2 L) | 3 pints (1.4 L) | 3 pints (1.4 L) |
| Weight | SAE 90 EP | SAE 90 EP | ATF "F" | SAE 90 EP | SAE 90 EP |
| Right Angle Drive Oil Capacity | 6 oz. (177 mL) | 6 oz. (177 mL) | .... | .... | .... |
| Weight | EP Lithium Grease | EP Lithium Grease | .... | .... | .... |

| | WIZARD MODELS | | | |
|---|---|---|---|---|
| | 7608 | 7610 | 7620 | 7625 |
| Engine Make | B&S | Tecumseh | B&S | B&S |
| Model | 190410 | HH100 | 326431 | 326431 |
| Bore | 3 in. (76.2 mm) | 3-5/16 in. (84.1 mm) | 3-9/16 in. (90.5 mm) | 3-9/16 in. (90.5 mm) |
| Stroke | 2¾ in. (69.8 mm) | 2¾ in. (69.8 mm) | 3¼ in. (82.5 mm) | 3¼ in. (82.5 mm) |
| Piston Displacment | 19.44 cu. in. (318 cc) | 23.75 cu. in. (389 cc) | 32.4 cu. in. (531 cc) | 32.4 cu. in. (531 cc) |
| Horsepower | 8 | 10 | 16 | 16 |
| Slow Idle Speed – Rpm | 1750 | 1200 | 1200 | 1200 |
| High Idle Speed (No-Load) – Rpm | 3600 | 3600 | 3600 | 3600 |
| Full Load Speed – Rpm | 3250 | 3240 | 3240 | 3240 |
| Crankcase Oil Capacity | 4 pints (1.9 L) | 2½ pints (1.2 L) | 4 pints (1.9 L) | 4 pints (1.9 L) |
| Weight – | | | | |
| Above 32°F (0°C) | SAE 30 | | | |
| 0°F (–18°C) to 32°F (0°C) | SAE 10W | | | |
| Below 0°F (–18°C) | SAE 5W-20 | | | |
| Transmission Oil Capacity | 3 pints (1.4 L) | 3 pints (1.4 L) | 4 pints (1.9 L) | 11 pints (5.2 L) |
| Weight | SAE 90 EP | SAE 90 EP | SAE 90 EP | Type "F" ATF |
| Right Angle Drive Oil Capacity | .... | .... | 6 oz. (177 mL) | .... |
| Weight | .... | .... | EP Lithium Grease | .... |

# FRONT AXLE AND STEERING SYSTEM

## AXLE MAIN MEMBER

### Model 5508

To remove axle main member (2–Fig. WA1), first disconnect tie rods (1) from steering spindles (3 and 4). Remove axle pivot bolt, then using a suitable jack under tractor main frame, raise front of tractor. Roll front axle assembly from tractor. Remove steering spindles and wheel assemblies.

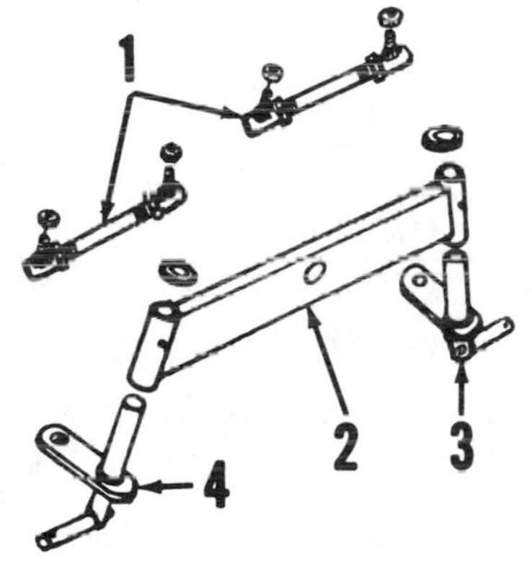


**Fig. WA1 – Exploded view of front axle assembly used on Model 5508.**

1. Tie rods
2. Axle main member
3. Steering spindle L.H.
4. Steering spindle R.H.

### Models 5510-5514

To remove axle member (2–Fig. WA2), first disconnect drag link from steering arm (3). Support front of tractor with a hoist or jack, then remove axle pivot bolt and stabilizer pivot bolt. Raise front of tractor and roll axle assembly from tractor. Unbolt stabilizer (1) from axle main member and remove steering spindles and front wheel assemblies. Inspect pivot bushings (4 and 8) and renew as necessary.

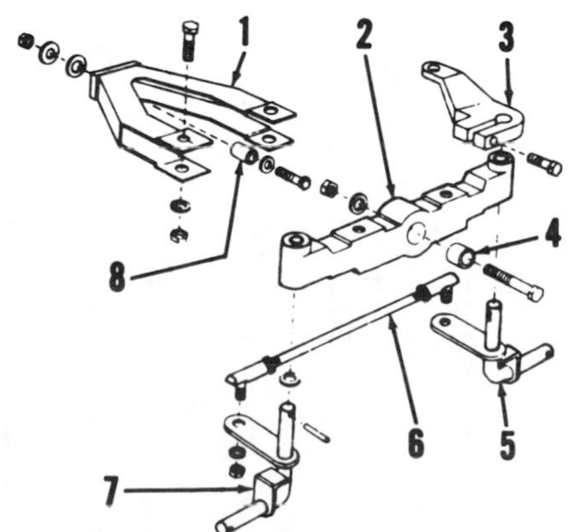


**Fig. WA2 – Exploded view of front axle assembly used on Models 5510 and 5514.**

1. Axle stabilizer
2. Axle main member
3. Steering arm
4. Pivot bushing
5. Steering spindle L.H.
6. Tie rod
7. Steering spindle R.H.
8. Spacer bushing

### Models 5520-5525-7510-7520-7525-7620-7625

To remove axle main member (5–Fig. WA3), disconnect drag link from left steering spindle (11). Remove axle pivot

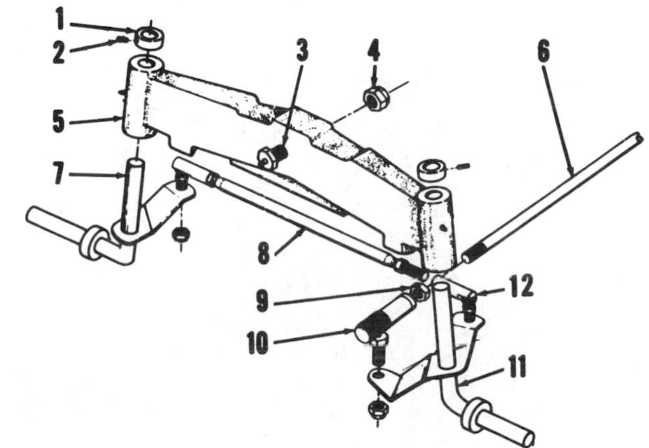


**Fig. WA3 – Exploded view of front axle assembly used on Models 5520, 5525, 7510, 7520, 7525, 7620 and 7625.**

1. Collar
2. Set screw
3. Pivot bolt
4. Nut
5. Axle main member
6. Drag link
7. Steering spindle R.H.
8. Tie rod
9. Locknut
10. Ball joint
11. Steering spindle L.H.
12. Ball joint

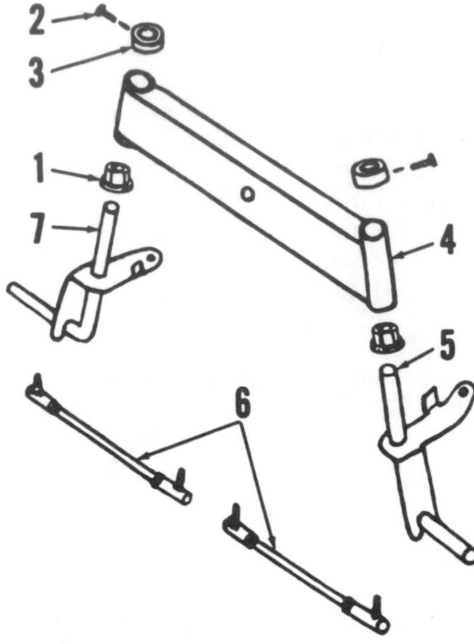


Fig. WA4 – Exploded view of front axle assembly used on Models 7508, 7600, 7608 and 7610.

1. Flange bushing (4 used)
2. Set screw
3. Collar
4. Axle main member
5. Steering spindle L.H.
6. Tie rods
7. Steering spindle R.H.

bolt (3) and raise tractor frame using a suitable jack or hoist. Roll front axle assembly from tractor. Remove steering spindles and front wheel assemblies.

## Models 7508-7600-7608-7610

To remove axle main member (4–Fig. WA4), disconnect tie rods (6) from steering spindles (5 and 7). Support tractor under main frame with a suitable jack. Remove axle pivot bolt, raise front of tractor and roll axle assembly from tractor. Loosen set screws (2), remove collars (3) and remove steering spindle and front wheel assemblies.

## Model 7602

To remove axle member (10–Fig. WA5), disconnect drag link from steering arm (15). Support front of tractor and remove axle pivot bolt and stabilizer bolts. Roll front axle assembly away from tractor. Remove tie bar (20), steering spindles (16 and 21) and front wheel assemblies. Inspect pivot bushings (22) and renew as necessary.

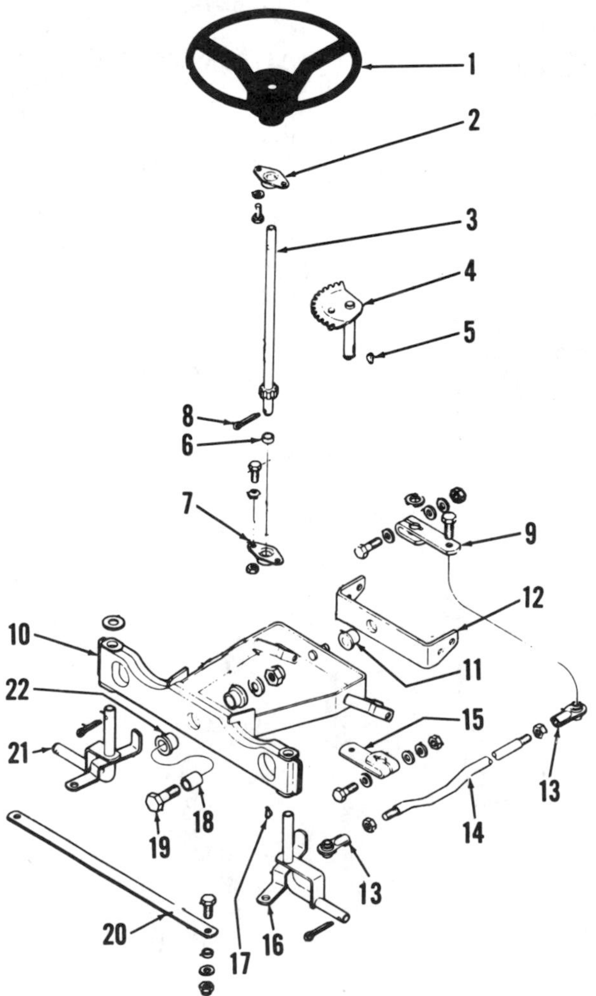

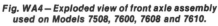

Fig. WA5 – Exploded view of front axle and steering gear assembly used on Model 7602.

1. Steering wheel
2. Bearing
3. Steering shaft assy.
4. Sector gear
5. Key
6. Spacer
7. Bearing
8. Cotter pin
9. Steering arm
10. Axle assy.
11. Bearing
12. Pivot bracket
13. Drag link end
14. Drag link
15. Steering arm
16. Steering spindle L.H.
17. Key
18. Sleeve
19. Pivot bolt
20. Tie rod bar
21. Steering spindle R.H.
22. Pivot bushing

## TIE RODS

## All Models

All models except Model 7602 are equipped with adjustable tie rod ends. To adjust front wheel toe-in, loosen locknuts on tie rod and disconnect ball joint end from steering spindle. Shorten or lengthen tie rod as necessary to obtain desired 1/8 inch (3 mm) toe-in. See Fig. WA6. On models with two tie rods, be sure to adjust both evenly. Renew ball joints that are excessively worn.

## STEERING SPINDLES

## Model 5508

To remove steering spindles (3 and 4–Fig. WA1), first raise front of tractor and remove front wheels. Disconnect tie rods (1) from steering spindle arms. Loosen set screws in retaining collars and lower steering spindles out of axle main member.

## Models 5510-5514

To remove steering spindles (5 and 7–Fig. WA2), support front of tractor and remove front wheels. Disconnect tie rod (6) from steering spindle arms. Loosen clamp bolt, remove steering arm (3) and remove left steering spindle (5). Drive out roll pin and remove right steering spindle (7).

## Models 5520-5525-7510-7520-7525-7620-7625

To remove steering spindles (7 and 11–Fig. WA3), support front of tractor and remove wheels and hubs. Disconnect tie rod ends from steering spindle arms. Disconnect drag link from left steering spindle. Loosen set screws in retaining collars and lower steering spindles out of axle main member.

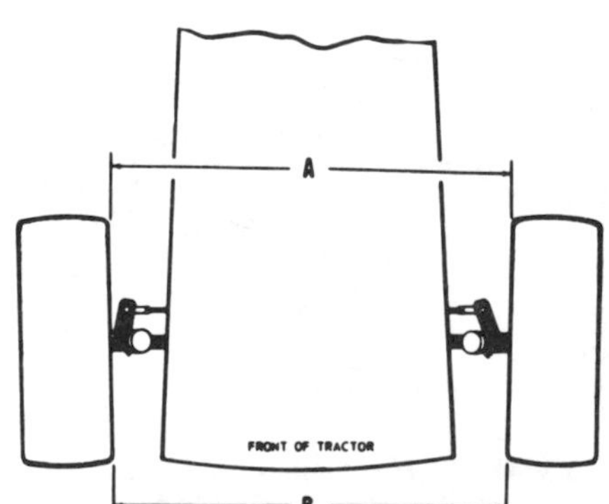


Fig. WA6 – Toe-in is correct when distance "B" is 1/8 inch (3 mm) less than distance "A" with both measurements taken at hub height.

### Models 7508-7600-7608-7610

To remove steering spindles (5 and 7–Fig. WA4), support front of tractor and remove front wheels. Disconnect outer tie rod ends from arms of steering spindles. Loosen set screws (2), remove collars (3) and lower steering spindles from axle main member. Inspect spindle bushings (1) and renew as necessary.

### Model 7602

To remove steering spindles (16 and 21–Fig. WA5), support front of tractor and remove front wheels. Disconnect tie bar (20) and drag link. Loosen clamp bolt, remove steering arm (15) and remove left steering spindle. Remove cotter key and remove right steering spindle.

## STEERING GEAR

### Models 5508-7508-7600-7608-7610

To remove steering gear, first disconnect tie rods from steering quadrant (13–Fig. WA7). Remove cap screw and washers from spacer (11) and the nut and Belleville washer from pivot bolt on bracket (12). Remove steering quadrant from tractor. Drive out roll pin (7), withdraw steering wheel and steering shaft assembly and remove pinion (9). Unbolt and remove bracket (10) with bushing (8). Remove cap (1), nut (2) and washer (3) on late models or drive out retaining pin on early models and remove steering wheel (4) from steering shaft (6).

Reassemble by reversing disassembly procedure. Before bolting steering quadrant (13) in position, make certain steering wheel and front wheels are in straight ahead position. To adjust steering gear free play, loosen the two mounting bolts in bracket (10). Move bracket forward to decrease free play, then tighten bracket mounting bolts.

Lubricate steering shaft bushings with SAE 30 oil and pinion gear and quadrant with multi-purpose grease.

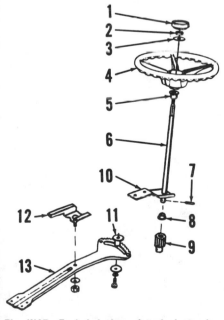

*Fig. WA7—Exploded view of typical steering gear assembly used on Models 7508, 7600, 7608 and 7610. Model 5508 is similar.*

1. Cap
2. Nut
3. Wave washer
4. Steering wheel
5. Flange bushing
6. Steering shaft
7. Roll pin
8. Flange bushing
9. Pinion
10. Bracket
11. Spacer
12. Pivot bracket
13. Steering quadrant

### Models 5510-5514

To remove steering gear, disconnect drag link (10–Fig. WA8) from quadrant shaft (9). Drive out roll pin (8), unscrew nut and remove quadrant gear (7). Drive out roll pin (5) and remove pinion gear (11). Withdraw steering wheel and shaft assembly, drive out roll pin (3) and remove steering wheel (1) from steering shaft (4).

To reassemble steering gear, reverse disassembly procedure. Pinion gear (11) and quadrant gear (7) should be positioned so front wheels and steering wheel are in straight ahead position. Lubricate with multi-purpose grease.

### Models 5520-5525-7510-7520-7525-7620-7625

To remove steering gear, disconnect drag link from quadrant gear arm. Loosen set screw in quadrant gear (10–Fig. WA9) and remove gear shaft (9) and quadrant gear. Drive out roll pin (7) and remove pinion gear (8). Remove steering wheel and shaft, drive out roll pin (2) and separate steering wheel (1) from steering shaft.

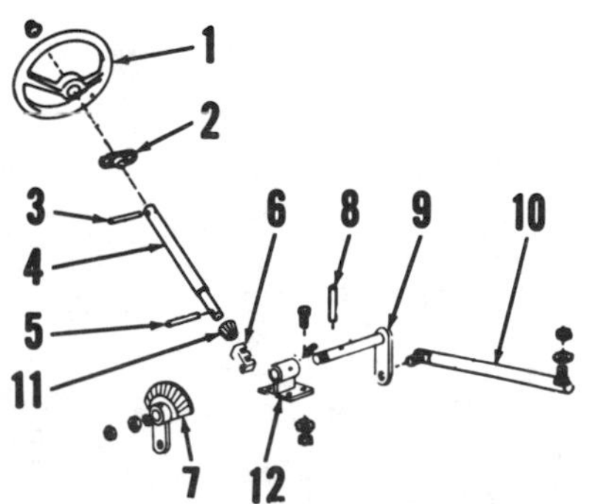


*Fig. WA8—Exploded view of steering gear used on Models 5510 and 5514.*

1. Steering wheel
2. Flange bearing
3. Roll pin
4. Steering shaft
5. Roll pin
6. Support
7. Quadrant gear
8. Roll pin
9. Gear shaft
10. Drag link
11. Pinion gear
12. Bracket

Reassemble by reversing disassembly procedure. Lubricate steering shaft bushings with SAE 30 oil and pinion gear and quadrant gear with multi-purpose grease.

### Model 7602

To remove steering gear, disconnect steering arm (9–Fig. WA5) from sector gear (4). Remove cotter pin (8) from steering shaft assembly. Unbolt upper shaft bearing (2) and withdraw shaft assembly. Remove steering gear assembly. Inspect bushings, bearings and gears for wear and renew as necessary. Reassemble by reversing disassembly procedure. Lubricate steering shaft bearings, bushing and gears with multi-purpose grease.

If excessive play develops, adjust flange bearing (7–Fig. WA5) as follows: Loosen the two mounting bolts on flange bearing. Slide flange bearing toward sector gear (4) carefully. When gears mesh smoothly and evenly, tighten mounting bolts.

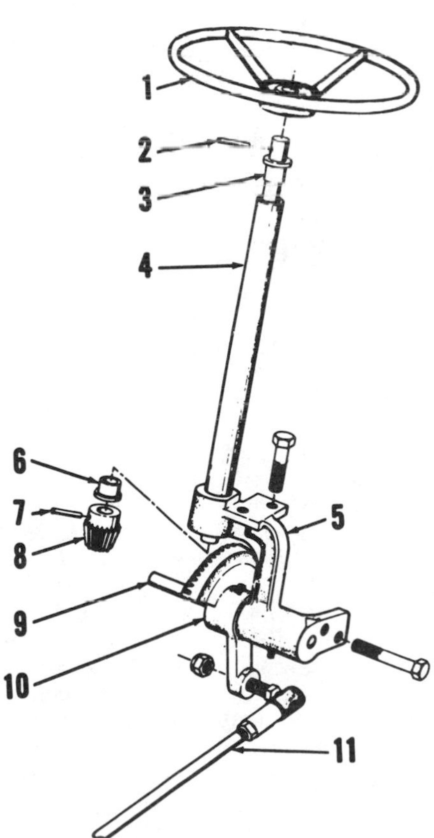


*Fig. WA9—Exploded view of steering gear used on Models 7510, 7520, 7525, 7620 and 7625. Models 5520 and 5525 are similar.*

1. Steering wheel
2. Pin
3. Bushing & shaft
4. Steering column
5. Steering support
6. Bushing
7. Pin
8. Pinion gear
9. Gear shaft
10. Quadrant gear
11. Drag link

# ENGINE

## REMOVE AND REINSTALL

### Model 5508

To remove engine assembly, loosen hood locks and tilt hood forward. On battery start models, disconnect battery cables and remove battery. On models equipped with 110-volt starter, unbolt starter switch and plug assembly. Then, on all models, disconnect throttle-choke control cable. Unbolt and remove belt guard from right side of engine. Depress clutch-brake pedal and tighten brake lock. Remove drive belt from engine drive pulley. Remove engine mounting bolts and lift engine from tractor.

Reinstall engine by reversing removal procedure, then adjust drive belt and brake as necessary.

### Models 5510-5514

To remove engine assembly, unlatch hood and tilt hood forward. Disconnect battery cables and remove battery. Disconnect wires from starter-generator and ignition coil. Disconnect throttle and choke control cables. Unbolt and remove belt guard from right side of engine. Remove engine draw bolt from front of tractor, then remove engine mounting bolts. Remove engine drive belts and lift engine from tractor.

Reinstall engine by reversing removal procedure. Adjust engine drive belts as follows: Tighten engine draw bolt and move engine forward to tighten engine drive belts. Make certain engine drive pulley and pulley on jackshaft are aligned, then tighten engine mounting bolts.

### Models 5520-7510-7520-7620

To remove engine assembly, remove hood and hood brace and disconnect battery cables. Remove cap screws securing right angle drive unit to frame. Move right angle drive and clutch assembly back from engine and remove pto drive belts. Disconnect starter-generator wires, shut off fuel valve and disconnect fuel line. Disconnect throttle and choke control cables. Remove engine mounting bolts and lift engine from tractor.

To install engine, reverse removal procedure. Adjust clutch and drive belt as necessary.

### Models 5525-7525-7625

To remove engine assembly, remove hood, grille brace and grille. Disconnect battery cables, starter-generator wires and connector on wiring harness. Disconnect fuel line and remove fuel tank and support bracket. Disconnect choke and throttle control cables. Loosen set screw in universal joint attached to engine crankshaft and drive out roll pin in opposite end of universal joint. Slide universal joint back on drive shaft. Remove lower pto belt guard and remove pto drive belts. Remove engine mounting bolts and lift engine from tractor.

Reinstall engine by reversing removal procedure.

### Models 7508-7600-7608-7610

To remove engine assembly, unlatch rear of hood, then tilt hood and grille assembly forward. Disconnect battery cables and electrical wiring from engine. Disconnect throttle and choke control cable. Shut off fuel valve and disconnect fuel line. Remove brace from top of engine and muffler and belt guard from right side of engine. Remove belts from engine drive pulley. Remove engine mounting cap screws and lift engine from tractor.

To reinstall engine, reverse removal procedure. Adjust drive belts as required.

### Model 7602

To remove engine assembly, remove hood assembly and disconnect battery cables. Lift fender and seat support and turn nut on top of frame counterclockwise ½ to 1½ turns. Remove main drive belt and crankshaft pulley. Disconnect electrical wiring, throttle and choke cables. Shut off fuel valve and disconnect fuel line. Remove engine mounting bolts and lift engine from tractor.

To reinstall engine, reverse removal procedure. Adjust drive belts as required.

## OVERHAUL

### All Models

Engine make and model are listed at the beginning of this section. To overhaul engine components and accessories, refer to Briggs & Stratton and Tecumseh sections of this manual.

# CLUTCH AND BRAKE

### Models 5508-7508-7600-7608-7610

**ADJUSTMENT.** The clutch idler is spring loaded and requires no adjustment. However, the angle of clutch-brake pedals (1 – Fig. WA10) can be adjusted as follows: Remove cotter pin from lower end of clutch rod (2). Turn clutch rod in or out of ferrule as required until desired pedal angle is obtained.

Adjust brake by turning adjusting nut (7) until top of spring tension idler is in disengaged position shown in Fig. WA11 when brake is applied.

**R&R DRIVE BELT.** To remove drive belt, first unbolt and remove belt guard from right side of engine. Remove

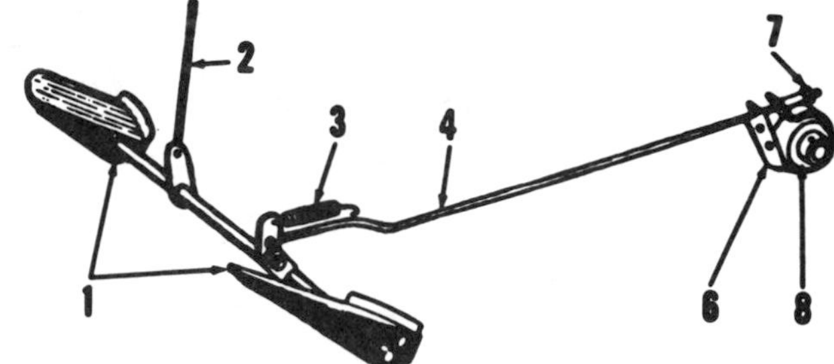


*Fig. WA10 – View showing brake assembly used on Models 5508, 7508, 7600, 7608 and 7610.*
1. Clutch-brake pedals
2. Clutch rod
3. Spring
4. Brake rod
6. Brake band
7. Adjusting nut
8. Brake drum

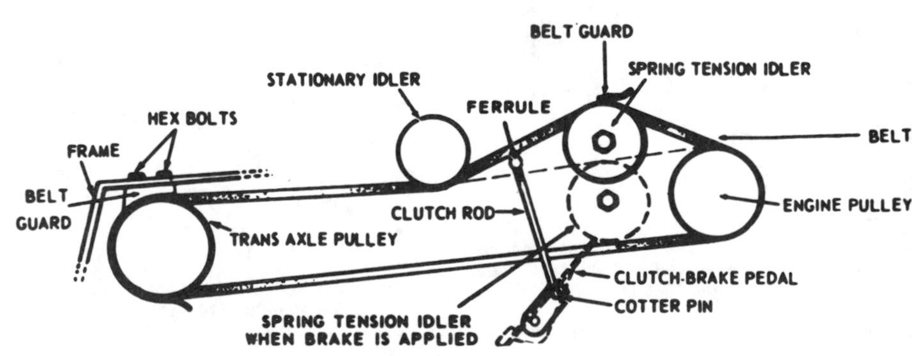


*Fig. WA11 – Remove cotter pin and adjust length of clutch rod to clutch-brake pedals to desired angle on Models 5508, 7508, 7600, 7608 and 7610. Adjust brake linkage until spring tension idler is at disengaged position shown when brake is applied.*

pto drive belt if so equipped. Loosen bolt in center of spring tension idler (Fig. WA11) and remove cap screw securing engine pulley to crankshaft. Slide pulleys out and remove drive belt from pulleys. Remove shoulder bolt or belt guard near transaxle input pulley and remove drive belt from tractor. Install new belt by reversing removal procedure. Adjust pedal angle and brake as required.

## Models 5510-5514

**ADJUSTMENT.** The clutch idler is spring loaded and requires no adjustment. The clutch-brake pedal (23–Fig. WA12) can be adjusted by loosening bolt (21) and moving pedal on adjusting plate (22). When desired pedal position is obtained, tighten bolt (21).

Adjust brake by turning adjusting nut (4) on rear of brake rod (15). Depress clutch-brake pedal and check to see that brake band (5) does not tighten on brake drum (3) until clutch idler tension is removed from transaxle drive belts.

**R&R DRIVE BELTS.** To remove transaxle drive belts (1–Fig. WA12), first unbolt and remove belt guide from around transaxle input pulley (2). Remove cotter pin from left end of shaft (16). Remove bolt (14), then lift out idler (12) with spacer (13) and bushing (11). Slide shaft (16) to the left. Unbolt bracket (35) from tractor frame. Remove belts over the end of shaft assemblies.

The transaxle drive belts are serviced only as a matched set and both belts should be renewed at the same time. Install new belts by reversing removal procedure. Check brake adjustment and adjust if necessary.

## Models 5520-7510-7520-7620

**ADJUSTMENT.** The clutch is adjusted by turning adjusting nut (15–Fig. WA13) at end of rod and chain (19). With clutch engaged, turn nut (15) until slack is removed from chain (19) and there is approximately 1/32 inch (1 mm) clearance between clutch arm (9) and bearing cover (10).

The brake is a disc and caliper type with renewable brake pads. To adjust brake, turn nut (13–Fig. WA14) so actuating pin (5) is in center of valley on cam lever (7) when brake pedal is in up (brake disengaged) position. Remove cotter pin (14) and adjust nut (9) so brake will stop tractor when pedal is fully depressed. Brake should not engage before clutch is disengaged.

To adjust tension of transaxle drive belt, loosen locknut on belt idler leveler screw shown in Fig. WA15. Unscrewing

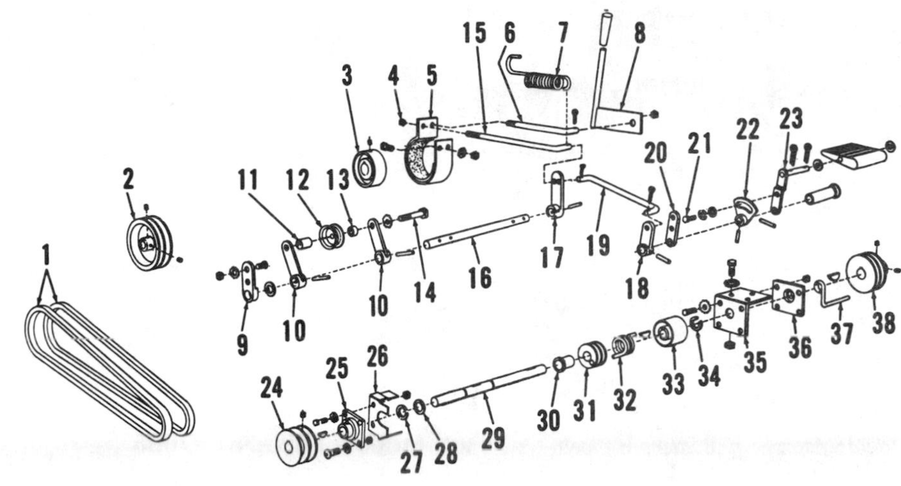

***Fig. WA12—Exploded view of clutch-brake system used on Models 5510 and 5514.***

1. Drive belts
2. Transaxle input pulley
3. Brake drum
4. Adjusting nut
5. Brake band
6. Park brake rod
7. Clutch spring
8. Park brake lever
9. Bracket
10. Idler arms
11. Bushing
12. Idler pulley
13. Spacer
14. Bolt
15. Brake rod
16. Shaft
17. Clutch-brake lever
18. Arm
19. Clutch-brake rod
20. Bracket
21. Bolt
22. Adjusting plate
23. Clutch-brake pedal
24. Jackshaft input pulley
25. Bearing assy.
26. Belt guide
27. Snap ring
28. Washer
29. Jackshaft
30. Bearing
31. Clutch drive pulley
32. Torsion spring
33. Spring drive sleeve
34. Snap ring
35. Bracket
36. Bearing assy.
37. Belt guide
38. Pto pulley

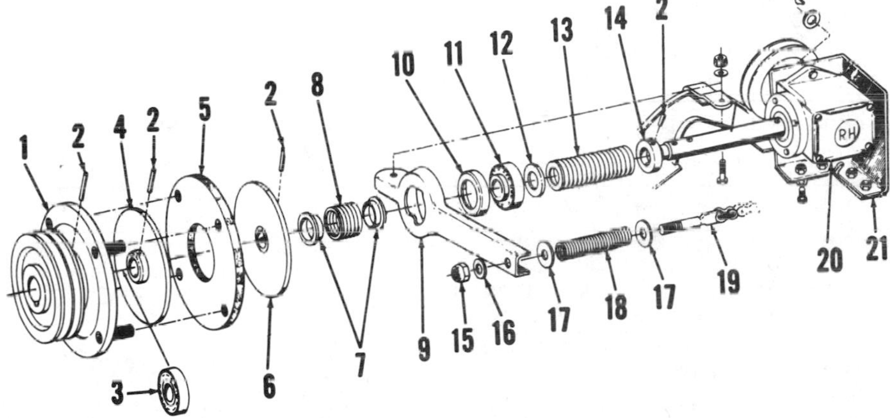

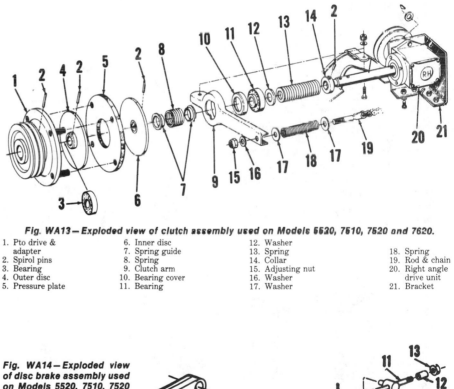

***Fig. WA13—Exploded view of clutch assembly used on Models 5520, 7510, 7520 and 7620.***

1. Pto drive & adapter
2. Spirol pins
3. Bearing
4. Outer disc
5. Pressure plate
6. Inner disc
7. Spring guide
8. Spring
9. Clutch arm
10. Bearing cover
11. Bearing
12. Washer
13. Spring
14. Collar
15. Adjusting nut
16. Washer
17. Washer
18. Spring
19. Rod & chain
20. Right angle drive unit
21. Bracket

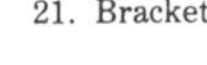

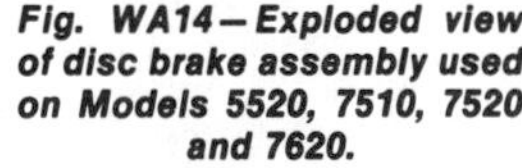

***Fig. WA14—Exploded view of disc brake assembly used on Models 5520, 7510, 7520 and 7620.***

1. Caliper & pad (inner)
2. Friction pad
3. Back-up disc
4. Caliper (outer)
5. Actuating pin
6. Spring
7. Cam lever
8. Washer
9. Nut
10. Spring
11. Brake rod
12. Spacer
13. Nut
14. Cotter pin

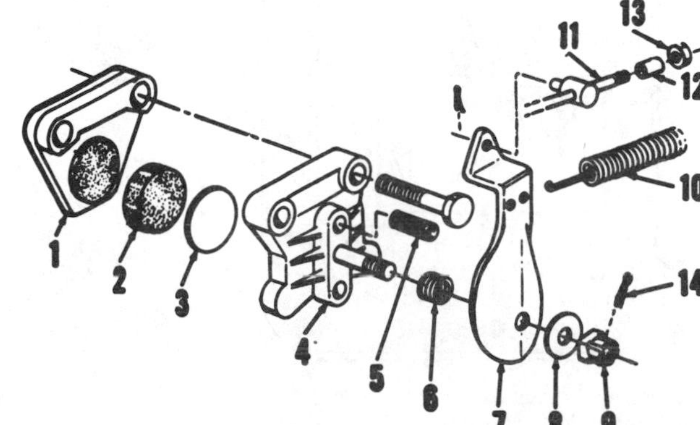

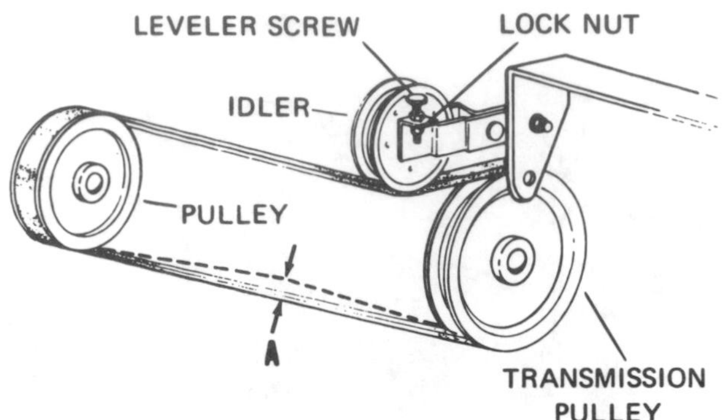


*Fig. WA15—Adjust tension of transmission drive belt on Models 5520, 7510, 7520 and 7620 by turning leveler screw. Belt should deflect ½ inch (13 mm) at (A) with 10 pounds (4.5 kg) force applied.*

leveler screw will increase belt tension. Belt deflection (A) should be ½ inch (13 mm) when 10 pounds (4.5 kg) of force is applied midway between transaxle input pulley and right angle drive pulley.

**R&R AND OVERHAUL CLUTCH.** To remove clutch assembly, disconnect clutch actuating rod and chain (19–Fig. WA13) from clutch arm (9). Remove clutch arm anchor bolt, then unbolt right angle drive bracket from frame. Move right angle drive and clutch assembly rearward and remove transaxle drive belt from right angle drive pulley. Lift right angle drive and clutch assembly from tractor. Place right angle drive bracket in a vise and place a pair of "C" clamps as shown in Fig. WA16. Tighten clamps so pressure is relieved from upper pin (2), then drive out pin. Slowly release "C" clamps to relieve spring pressure. Remainder of disassembly is evident after examination of unit and reference to Fig. WA13.

Reassemble and reinstall clutch and right angle drive assembly. Adjust clutch and drive belt as outlined in preceding paragraphs.

## Models 5525-7525-7625

**ADJUSTMENT.** To adjust disc brake, refer to Fig. WA17 and proceed as follows: With brake pedal in released (up) position, adjust nut (12) until actuating pins (18) are in center of valley in brake cam lever. Adjust nut (15) so brake will stop tractor when pedal is fully depressed.

Refer to HYDROSTATIC TRANSMISSION paragraphs for neutral return linkage adjustment.

## Model 7602

**ADJUSTMENT.** To adjust main drive belt, lift fender and seat support assembly. Loosen locknut on underside of frame (Fig. WA18). Turn nut on top of frame clockwise to tighten or counterclockwise to loosen. Retighten nut under frame and check belt tension. At approximately mid-point of belt, press down on belt. The belt should move about 1 inch (25 mm).

The final drive belt requires no adjustment. The belt is adjusted by a spring loaded idler pulley. Check idler arm to be sure it pivots freely and provides tension.

To adjust brake, remove cotter pin from castellated nut. Turn nut clockwise to tighten brake pad and compensate for wear. Slight drag is permitted.

**R&R DRIVE BELTS.** To remove main drive belt, lift fender and seat support. Loosen nut on top of frame (Fig. WA18). **Do not remove.** Remove engine pulley belt cover. Work belt off inner jackshaft pulley and engine pulley. Install new belt by reversing procedure.

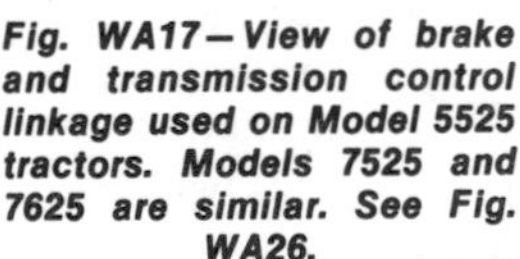

*Fig. WA17—View of brake and transmission control linkage used on Model 5525 tractors. Models 7525 and 7625 are similar. See Fig. WA26.*

1. Transmission control rod
2. Drive shaft & "U" joint
3. Control plate
4. Neutral return link
5. Control arm
6. Reduction drive
7. Brake pad (inner)
8. Brake disc
9. Brake pad (outer)
10. Bracket
11. Nut
12. Adjusting nut
13. Spacer
14. Ferrule
15. Adjusting nut
16. Washer
17. Spring
18. Pins (2)
19. Brake rod

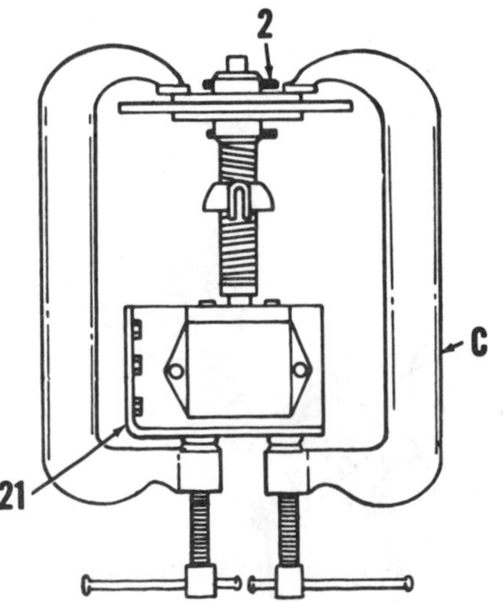

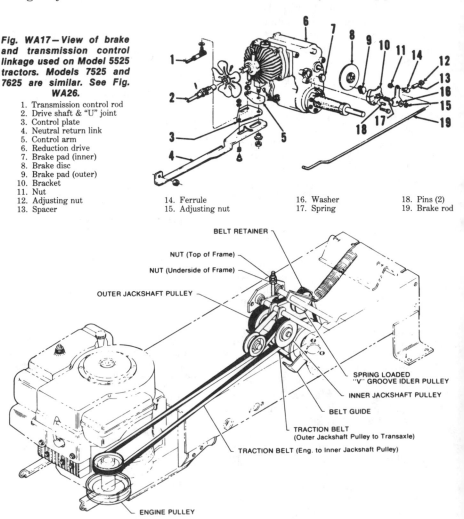

*Fig. WA16—To remove spirol pin (2), tighten "C" clamps against outer disc and right angle drive bracket (21).*

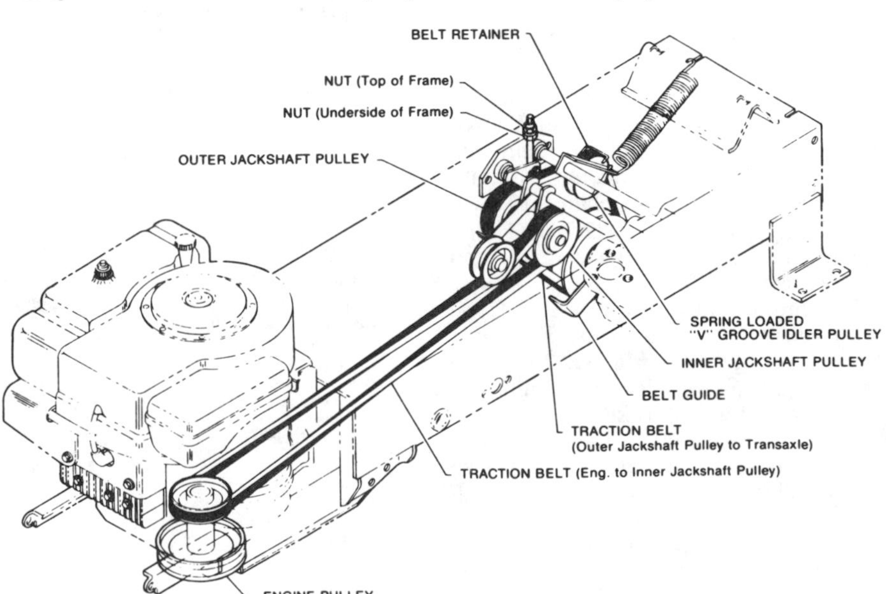


*Fig. WA18—Cross-sectional view of drive belt system used on Model 7602.*

To remove final drive belt, depress foot pedal and set parking brake. Loosen "V" groove idler pulley and remove belt. Reassembly by reversing disassembly procedure and adjust belt retainer. With belt engaged, there must be 1/16 to 3/8 inch (1.5-3 mm) clearance betwen retainer and belt.

# RIGHT ANGLE DRIVE UNIT

### Models 5520-7510-7520-7620

**R&R AND OVERHAUL.** To remove right angle drive unit, remove clutch assembly as outlined in previous paragraph and separate clutch from right angle drive assembly. Remove pulley and mounting bracket from drive unit.

To disassemble right angle drive unit, remove cover (1–Fig. WA19), gasket (2) and lubricant. Unbolt and remove seal retainer (13) with oil seal (14) and gasket (12). Unseat snap ring (18) from its groove in input shaft (10). Withdraw input shaft and bearing (11) and remove snap ring (18) and gear (9) through cover opening of case. Remove oil seal (17) and snap ring (16), then drive output shaft (6) with bearing (5) and gear (4) out through cover opening of case. Bearings (8 and 15) can now be removed from case. Remove snap ring (3), output gear (4) and bearing (5) from output shaft. Remove bearing (11) from input shaft.

Clean and inspect all parts and renew any showing excessive wear or other damage. Reassemble by reversing disassembly procedure and fill unit with 6 ounces (177 mL) of EP lithium grease.

# TRANSAXLE

## LUBRICATION

### All Models

All models are equipped with Peerless transaxle units. Refer to the CONDENSED SPECIFICATIONS tables at the beginning of this section for transaxle fluid capacities and recommended fluid type for specific model being serviced.

## REMOVE AND REINSTALL

### Models 5508-7508-7600-7602-7608-7610

To remove transaxle assembly, unbolt and remove rear frame cover. Remove shoulder bolt or belt guard near transaxle input pulley. Remove pulley retaining nut, depress clutch-brake pedal and slide belt and pulley from transaxle input shaft. Disconnect brake linkage and support tractor main frame. Remove transaxle mounting bolts, raise rear of tractor and roll transaxle assembly rearward from tractor.

Reinstall transaxle by reversing removal procedure. Adjust pedal angle and brake as necessary.

### Models 5510-5514

To remove transaxle assembly, first unbolt and remove belt guide from around transaxle input pulley. Depress clutch-brake pedal and remove drive belts from transaxle input pulley. Disconnect brake linkage. Block up under transaxle to prevent unit from tilting forward. Unbolt transaxle from tractor frame. Using a suitable jack or hoist, raise rear of frame and roll transaxle assembly rearward from tractor.

When reinstalling transaxle assembly, reverse removal procedure and adjust brake linkage as required.

### Models 5520-7510-7520-7620

To remove transaxle assembly, loosen locknut and turn idler lever screw (Fig. WA15) inward until drive belt can be removed from transaxle input pulley. Disconnect brake linkage and remove gear shift knob. Support tractor under main frame. Unbolt transaxle from tractor frame, raise rear of tractor and roll transaxle rearward from tractor.

Reinstall transaxle by reversing removal procedure. Adjust brake and drive belt tension as required.

## OVERHAUL

### All Models

Models 5508, 5510, 7608 and 7610 are equipped with a Peerless 1200 series

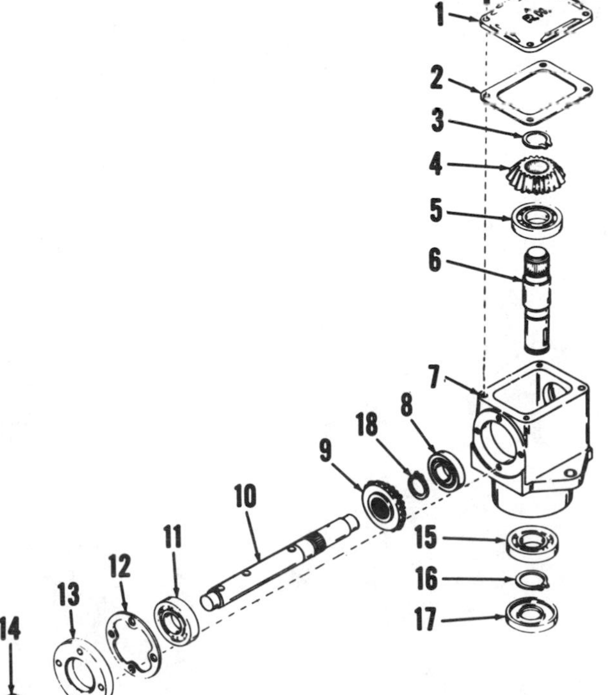

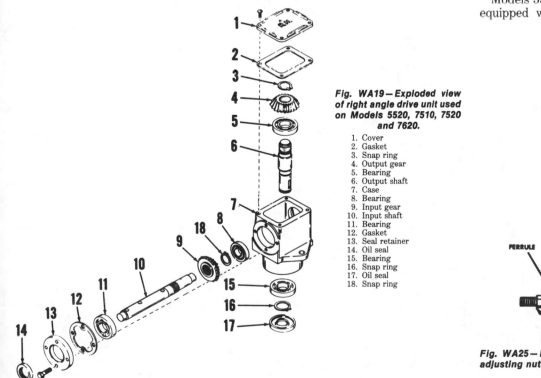

***Fig. WA19—Exploded view of right angle drive unit used on Models 5520, 7510, 7520 and 7620.***

1. Cover
2. Gasket
3. Snap ring
4. Output gear
5. Bearing
6. Output shaft
7. Case
8. Bearing
9. Input gear
10. Input shaft
11. Bearing
12. Gasket
13. Seal retainer
14. Oil seal
15. Bearing
16. Snap ring
17. Oil seal
18. Snap ring

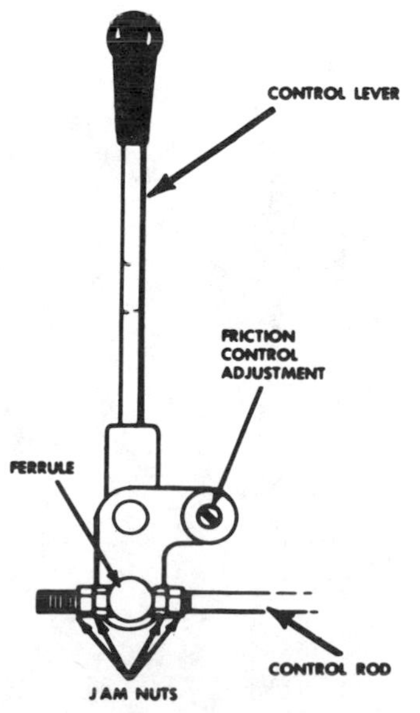


***Fig. WA25—Hydrostatic control lever position adjusting nuts. Note location of friction control adjustment screw.***

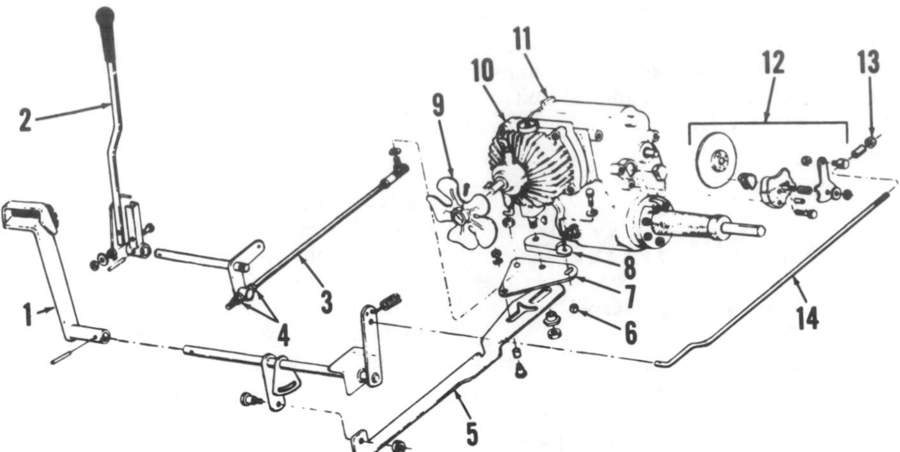

*Fig. WA26—Exploded view of hydrostatic control linkage, neutral return linkage and brake linkage used on Model 7525 and 7625 tractors. Model 5525 is similar.*

1. Brake pedal
2. Control lever
3. Control rod
4. Lever position adjusting nuts
5. Neutral return link
6. Adjusting nut
7. Control plate
8. Control arm
9. Cooling fan
10. Hydrostatic transmission
11. 2-speed reduction drive & differential assy.
12. Disc brake assy.
13. Adjusting nut
14. Brake rod

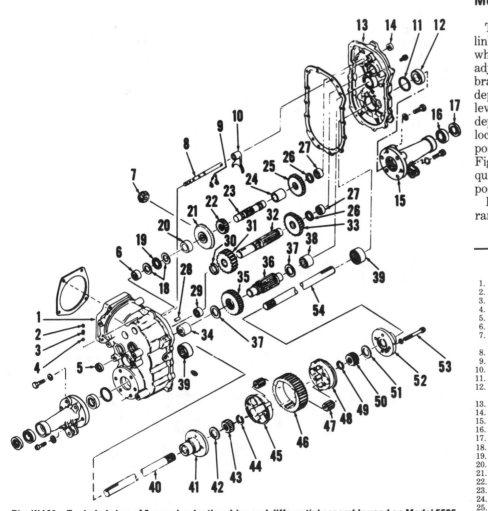

*Fig. WA30—Exploded view of 2-speed reduction drive and differential assembly used on Model 5525, 7525 and 7625 tractors.*

1. Case
2. Set screw
3. Spring
4. Ball
5. Seal
6. Needle bearing
7. Transmission output gear
8. Shift rail
9. Snap rings
10. Shift fork
11. Quad ring
12. Tapered roller bearing
13. Cover
14. Seal
15. Axle housing
16. Ball bearing
17. Oil seal
18. Thrust washers
19. Thrust bearing
20. Spacer
21. Bevel gear
22. Gear (16T)
23. Shaft
24. Spacer
25. Gear (23T)
26. Thrust washer
27. Needle bearing
28. Dowel pin
29. Needle bearing
30. Spacer
31. Gear
32. Brake shaft
33. Sliding gear
34. Needle bearing
35. Output gear
36. Output shaft
37. Thrust washer
38. Needle bearing
39. Needle bearing
40. Axle (L.H.)
41. Differential carrier (L.H.)
42. Thrust washer
43. Axle gear
44. Snap ring
45. Body core
46. Ring gear
47. Pinion gears (8)
48. Body core
49. Snap ring
50. Axle gear
51. Thrust washer
52. Differential carrier (R.H.)
53. Cap screw
54. Axle (R.H.)

transaxle and all other models are equipped with a Peerless 2300 series transaxle. Refer to the appropriate Peerless section in TRANSAXLE SERVICE section for overhaul procedure.

# HYDROSTATIC TRANSMISSION

## LUBRICATION

### Models 5525-7525-7625

The reduction drive and differential housing is the reservoir for hydrostatic transmission. Maintain oil level at flat area on dipstick which is located at top rear on reduction drive housing. Change oil filter and transmission oil every 200 hours of operation or once each year. Use Fram PH-16 filter or equivalent and fill unit with Type "F" automatic transmission fluid. Capacity is approximately 11 pints (5.2 L).

## LINKAGE ADJUSTMENT

### Models 5525-7525-7625

To adjust transmission control linkage, support rear of tractor so rear wheels are free to rotate. Loosen brake adjusting nut (13–Fig. WA26) until brake is ineffective when pedal is fully depressed. Start engine, move control lever to forward position, then fully depress brake pedal and engage brake lock. Control lever should be in neutral position. If not, stop engine, refer to Fig. WA25 and adjust jam nuts as required until control lever is in neutral position on quadrant.

Place 2-speed reduction drive in low range, start engine and with brake pedal released, move transmission control lever to forward drive position. Fully depress brake pedal, then release. Both rear wheels should stop and remain stationary. If rear wheels creep in either direction, refer to Fig. WA26 and loosen nut (6). Hold control plate (7) stationary and move control arm (8) until rear wheels stop turning.

**CAUTION: Use extreme care not to get hands in cooling fan during adjustment.**

Tighten nut (6) and recheck adjustment. When neutral adjustment is complete, adjust brake linkage as required.

### REMOVE AND REINSTALL

### Models 5525-7525-7625

To remove hydrostatic transmission, remove fenders, seat and rear frame cover. Disconnect hydraulic hoses and plug or cap openings to prevent dirt from entering system. Drive out roll pin in rear universal joint and loosen set screw in cooling fan hub. Push universal joint forward on drive shaft and remove fan. Disconnect transmission control rod and neutral linkage from transmission. Unbolt and lift out unit.

### OVERHAUL

### Models 5525-7525-7625

All models are equipped with an Eaton Model 10 hydrostatic transmission. Refer to Eaton Model 10 in HYDROSTATIC TRANSMISSION SERVICE section for overhaul procedure.

# REDUCTION DRIVE AND DIFFERENTIAL

### R&R AND OVERHAUL

### Models 5525-7525-7625

To remove 2-speed reduction drive and differential assembly, remove fenders, seat and rear frame cover. Disconnect hydraulic hoses and plug or cap openings to prevent dirt from entering system. Drive out roll pin in rear universal joint and loosen set screw in cooling fan. Push universal joint forward on drive shaft and remove cooling fan. Disconnect transmission control rod and neutral linkage from hydrostatic transmission, then disconnect brake rod. Support tractor frame, unbolt reduction drive and differential assembly from tractor, raise rear of frame and roll assembly rearward from tractor. Clean exterior of assembly, drain fluid and remove hydrostatic transmission. Remove disc brake assembly and rear wheel and hub assemblies.

To disassemble reduction drive and differential, remove axle housings (15–Fig. WA30). Postion unit with cover (13) facing up, then unbolt and remove cover. Lift out differential and axle assembly (40 through 54). Remove output shaft (36), gear (35) and thrust washers (37). Unscrew set screw (2) and remove spring (3) and ball (4). Remove brake shaft (32), sliding gear (33), shift fork (10) and shift rail (8). Remove input shaft and gear components (18 through 26).

To disassemble differential, remove cap screws (53) and separate differential carriers (41 and 52) and axles from ring gear assembly. Remove snap rings (44 and 49) and separate axle gears (43 and 50), thrust washers (42 and 51) and axle shafts (40 and 54). Remove pinions (47) and separate body cores (45 and 48) from ring gear (46).

Inspect components for damage or excessive wear. To reassemble, reverse disassembly procedure. Check movement of shift rail when tightening set screw (2). Install gears (22 and 25) so bevels on gear teeth face together as shown in Fig. WA31. Install carrier cap screws (53–Fig. WA30) so heads of cap screws are on side of shorter carrier (52). Do not rotate axle housings after housing have been pressed tight against seals (11) as seals might be cut.

Install unit in tractor by reversing removal procedure. Fill with Type "F" automatic transmission fluid and adjust linkage as outlined in previous paragraphs.

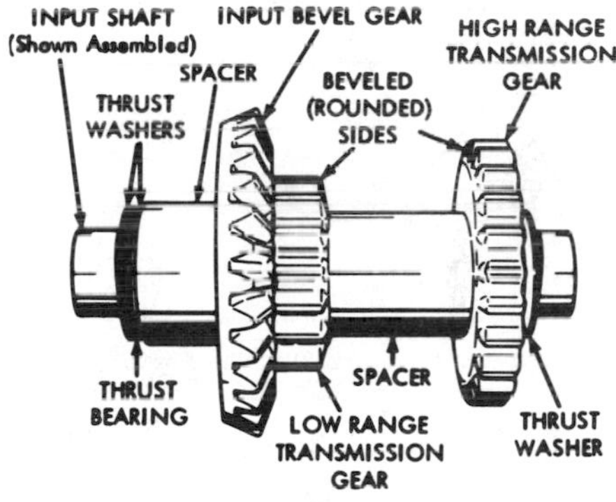


*Fig. WA31 – View of input shaft and gears. Note positions of bevels on gears.*

# WHEEL HORSE

## (Gear Drive)

## CONDENSED SPECIFICATIONS

| | MODELS | | | | |
|---|---|---|---|---|---|
| | CG7E, CG 7R | Workhorse 700 | 800 Special, A-90 Special | Workhorse 800 | Lawn Ranger (8E) |
| Engine Make | Tecumseh | Tecumseh | B&S | Tecumseh | Tecumseh |
| Model | V70 | H70 | 190434 | HH80 | V80 |
| Bore | 2¾ in. (69.8 mm) | 2¾ in. (69.8 mm) | 3 in. (76.2 mm) | 3-5/16 in. (84.1 mm) | 3-1/16 in. (77.8 mm) |
| Stroke | 2-17/32 in. (64.3 mm) | 2¾ in. (69.8 mm) | 2¾ in. (69.8 mm) | 2¾ in. (69.8 mm) | 2-17/32 in. (64.3 mm) |
| Piston Displacement | 15.0 cu. in. (246 cc) | 15.0 cu. in. (246 cc) | 19.44 cu. in. (319 cc) | 23.75 cu. in. (389 cc) | 18.65 cu. in. (306 cc) |
| Horsepower | 7 | 7 | 8 | 8 | 8 |
| Slow Idle Speed – Rpm | 1800 | 1800 | 1750 | 1200 | 1800 |
| High Idle Speed (No-Load) – Rpm | 3750 | 3750 | 3600 | 3600 | 3750 |
| Crankcase Oil Capacity | 1¾ pints (0.8 L) | 1½ pints (0.7 L) | 2¾ pints (1.3 L) | 3 pints (1.4 L) | 2 pints (0.9 L) |
| Weight – | | | | | |
| Above 32°F (0°C) | | | SAE 30 | | |
| 0°F (–18°C) to 32°F (0°C) | | | SAE 10W | | |
| Below 0°F (–18°C) | | | SAE 5W-20 | | |
| Transmission Oil Capacity | 4 pints (1.9 L) | 3 pints (1.4 L) | 2 pints (0.9 L) | 3 pints (1.4 L) | 2 pints (0.9 L) |
| Weight | SAE 90/140 | SAE 90 | SAE 90 | SAE 140 | SAE 90 |
| Grade | EP/GL-5 | EP | EP | GL-5 | EP |

---

| | MODELS | | | | |
|---|---|---|---|---|---|
| | 8 HP– 4 Speed | Commando 800, 8 HP–4 Speed, B-80 | Ranger (A-800) | B-81, B-82, B-85* | B-112 |
| Engine Make | Tecumseh | Kohler | Tecumseh | B&S | B&S |
| Model | V80 | K181S | VM80 | 191707 | 252707 |
| Bore | 3-1/16 in. (77.8 mm) | 2-15/16 in. (74.6 mm) | 3-1/16 in. (77.8 mm) | 3 in. (76.2 mm) | 3-7/16 in. (87.3 mm) |
| Stroke | 2-17/32 in. (64.3 mm) | 2¾ in. (69.8 mm) | 2-17/32 in. (64.3 mm) | 2¾ in. (69.8 mm) | 2⅝ in. (66.7 mm) |
| Piston Displacement | 18.65 cu. in. (306 cc) | 18.6 cu. in. (305 cc) | 18.65 cu. in. (306 cc) | 19.44 cu. in. (319 cc) | 24.36 cu. in. (399 cc) |
| Horsepower | 8 | 8 | 8 | 8 | 11 |
| Slow Idle Speed – Rpm | 1800 | 1200 | 1800 | 1750 | 1750 |
| High Idle Speed (No-Load) – Rpm | 3750 | 3600 | 3750 | 3300 | 3300 |
| Crankcase Oil Capacity | 2 pints (0.9 L) | 2½ pints (1.2 L) | 2 pints (0.9 L) | 2½ pints (1.2 L) | 3 pints (1.4 L) |
| Weight – | | | | | |
| Above 32°F (0°C) | | | SAE 30 | | |
| 0°F (–18°C) to 32°F (0°C) | | | SAE 10W | | |
| Below 0°F (–18°C) | | | SAE 5W-20 | | |
| Transmission Oil Capacity | 4 pints (1.9 L) | 4 pints (1.9 L) | 2 pints (0.9 L) | 3 pints (1.4 L) | 3 pints (1.4 L) |
| Weight | SAE 140 | SAE 90/140 | SAE 90 | SAE 90 | SAE 90 |
| Grade | GL-5 | EP/GL-5 | EP | EP | EP |

*B-85 is equipped with 5-speed Peerless transaxle.

| | | | MODELS | | |
|---|---|---|---|---|---|
| | B-111*, B-115 | C-81, C-85, Raider 8, 8HP-8 Speed | C-100, C-101, C-105, Raider 10, 10HP-8 Speed | C-120, C-121, C-125, Raider 12, 12HP-8 Speed | Raider 14, 14HP-8 Speed |
| Engine Make | B&S | Kohler | Kohler | Kohler | Kohler |
| Model | 252707 | K181S | K241S | K301S | K321S |
| Bore | 3-7/16 in. (87.3 mm) | 2-15/16 in. (74.6 mm) | 3¼ in. (82.5 mm) | 3⅜ in. (85.7 mm) | 3½ in. (88.9 mm) |
| Stroke | 2⅝ in. (66.7 mm) | 2¾ in. (69.8 mm) | 2⅞ in. (73.0 mm) | 3½ in. (88.9 mm) | 3¼ in. (82.5 mm) |
| Piston Displacement | 24.36 cu. in. (399 cc) | 18.6 cu. in. (305 cc) | 23.9 cu. in. (392 cc) | 29.07 cu. in. (476 cc) | 31.27 cu. in. (512 cc) |
| Horsepower | 11 | 8 | 10 | 12 | 14 |
| Slow Idle Speed – Rpm | 1750 | 1900 | 2100 | 2100 | 1200 |
| High Idle Speed (No-Load) – Rpm | 3300 | 3500 | 3400 | 3400 | 3600 |
| Crankcase Oil Capacity | 3 pints (1.4 L) | 2½ pints (1.2 L) | 3 pints (1.4 L) | 3 pints (1.4 L) | 4 pints (1.9 L) |
| Weight – | | | | | |
| Above 32°F (0°C) | | | SAE 30 | | |
| 0°F (–18°C) to 32°F (0°C) | | | SAE 10W | | |
| Below 0°F (–18°C) | | | SAE 5W-20 | | |
| Transmission Oil Capacity | 24 oz. (710 mL) | 4 pints (1.9 L) | 4 pints (1.9 L) | 4 pints (1.9 L) | 4 pints (1.9 L) |
| Weight | Lithium Grease | | SAE 140 | | |
| Grade | EP | | EP/GL-5 | | |

*Early B-111 is equipped with 6-speed Foote transmission. Late B-111 and B-115 are equipped with 5-speed Peerless transmission.

| | | | MODELS | | |
|---|---|---|---|---|---|
| | C-141, C-145 | C-160, 8 Speed (1-0385) | C-160, 8 Speed (1-0380) | C-161, C-165 | LT-832 |
| Engine Make | Kohler | Tecumseh | Kohler | Kohler | B&S |
| Model | K321AS | HH160 | K341S | K341AS | 191707 |
| Bore | 3½ in. (88.9 mm) | 3½ in. (88.9 mm) | 3¾ in. (95.2 mm) | 3¾ in. (95.2 mm) | 3 in. (76.2 mm) |
| Stroke | 3¼ in. (82.5 mm) | 2⅞ in. (73.0 mm) | 3¼ in. (82.5 mm) | 3¼ in. (82.5 mm) | 2¾ in. (69.8 mm) |
| Piston Displacement | 31.27 cu. in. (512 cc) | 27.66 cu. in. (453 cc) | 35.89 cu. in. (588 cc) | 34.89 cu. in. (588 cc) | 19.44 cu. in. (318 cc) |
| Horsepower | 14 | 16 | 16 | 16 | 8 |
| Slow Idle Speed – Rpm | 2100 | 1200 | 1200 | 2100 | 1750 |
| High Idle Speed (No-Load) – Rpm | 3400 | 3600 | 3600 | 3400 | 3300 |
| Crankcase Oil Capacity | 3 pints (1.4 L) | 4 pints (1.9 L) | 3 pints (1.4 L) | 3 pints (1.4 L) | 3 pints (1.4 L) |
| Weight – | | | | | |
| Above 32°F (0°C) | | | SAE 30 | | |
| 0°F (–18°C) to 32°F (0°C) | | | SAE 10W | | |
| Below 0°F (–18°C) | | | SAE 5W-20 | | |
| Transmission Oil Capacity | 4 pints (1.9 L) | 4 pints (1.9 L) | 4 pints (1.9 L) | 4 pints (1.9 L) | 1½ pints (0.7 L) |
| Weight | SAE 90 | SAE 90 | SAE 90 | SAE 90 | SAE 90 |
| Grade | EP | EP | EP | EP | EP |

| | | | MODELS | | |
|---|---|---|---|---|---|
| | LT-1032 | SB-371, LT-1136, LT-1137 | SB-421, GT-1142 | GT-2500 | SK-486 |
| Engine Make | Tecumseh | B&S | B&S | B&S | Kohler |
| Model | TVM220 | 252707 | 252417 | 252417 | K341AS |
| Bore | 3-5/16 in. (84.1 mm) | 3-7/16 in. (87.3 mm) | 3-7/16 in. (87.3 mm) | 3-7/16 in. (87.3 mm) | 3¾ in. (95.2 mm) |
| Stroke | 1-17/32 in. (64.3 mm) | 2⅝ in. (66.7 mm) | 2⅝ in. (66.7 mm) | 2⅝ in. (66.7 mm) | 3¼ in. (82.5 mm) |
| Piston Displacement | 21.82 cu. in. (357 cc) | 24.36 cu. in. (399 cc) | 24.36 cu. in. (399 cc) | 24.36 cu. in. (399 cc) | 35.89 cu. in. (588 cc) |
| Horsepower | 10 | 11 | 11 | 11 | 16 |
| Slow Idle Speed – Rpm | 1750 | 1750 | 1750 | 1750 | 2100 |

| | MODELS (Cont.) | | | | |
|---|---|---|---|---|---|
| | LT-1032 | SB-371, LT-1136, LT-1137 | SB-421, GT-1142 | GT-2500 | SK-486 |
| High Idle Speed (No-Load) – Rpm | 3300 | 3300 | 3300 | 3300 | 3400 |
| Crankcase Oil Capacity | 2 pints (0.9 L) | 3 pints (1.4 L) | 3 pints (1.4 L) | 3 pints (1.4 L) | 3 pints (1.4 L) |
| Weight – | | | | | |
| Above 32°F (0°C) | SAE 30 | | | | |
| 0°F (–18°C) to 32°F (0°C) | SAE 10W | | | | |
| Below 0°F (–18°C) | SAE 5W-20 | | | | |
| Transmission Oil Capacity | 1½ pints (0.7 L) | 1½ pints (0.7 L) | 4 pints (1.9 L) | 4 pints (1.9 L) | 4 pints (1.9 L) |
| Weight | SAE 90 | SAE 90 | SAE 140 | SAE 140 | SAE 140 |
| Grade | EP | EP | GL-5 | GL-5 | GL-5 |

| | MODELS | | | |
|---|---|---|---|---|
| | 208-4 | 211-4 | 211-5 | 212-6 |
| Engine Make | B&S | B&S | B&S | Kawasaki |
| Model | 191707 | 252707 | 253707 | FB460V |
| Bore | 3 in. (76.2 mm) | 3-7/16 in. (87.3 mm) | 3-7/16 in. (87.3 mm) | 3-1/2 in. (89.0 mm) |
| Stroke | 2-3/4 in. (69.8 mm) | 2⅝ in. (66.7 mm) | 2⅝ in. (66.7 mm) | 2.91 in. (74.0 mm) |
| Piston Displacement | 19.44 cu. in. (319 cc) | 24.36 cu. in. (399 cc) | 24.36 cu. in. (399 cc) | 28.1 cu. in. (460 cc) |
| Horsepower | 8 | 11 | 11 | 12.5 |
| Slow Idle Speed – Rpm | 1750 | 1750 | 1750 | 1750 |
| Full Load Speed – Rpm | 3500 | 3500 | 3500 | 3500 |
| Crankcase Oil Capacity | 2¾ pints (1.3 L) | 3 pints (1.4 L) | 3 pints (1.4 L) | 3 pints (1.4 L) |
| Weight – | | | | |
| Above 32°F (0°C) | SAE 30 | | | |
| 0°F (–18°C) to 32°F (0°C) | SAE 10W | | | |
| Below 0°F (–18°C) | SAE 5W-20 | | | |
| Transmission Oil Capacity | 26 oz. (769 mL) | 26 oz. (769 mL) | 30 oz. (888 mL) | 30 oz. (888 mL) |
| Weight | Bentonite Grease | | | |

| | MODELS | | | | |
|---|---|---|---|---|---|
| | 308-8 | 310-8 | 312-8 | 414-8 | 416-8 |
| Engine Make | Kohler | Kohler | Kohler | Kohler | Kohler |
| Model | M8 | M10 | M12 | M14 | 16 |
| Bore | 2.94 in. (74.6 mm) | 3.25 in. (82.6 mm) | 3.38 in. (85.7 mm) | 3.50 in. (88.9 mm) | 3.75 in. (95.3 mm) |
| Stroke | 2.75 in. (69.9 mm) | 2.88 in. (73.0 mm) | 3.25 in. (82.6 mm) | 3.25 in. (82.6 mm) | 3.25 in. (82.6 mm) |
| Piston Displacement | 18.6 cu. in. (305 cc) | 23.9 cu. in. (391 cc) | 29.1 cu. in. (477 cc) | 31.3 cu. in. (512 cc) | 35.9 cu. in. (588 cc) |
| Horsepower | 8 | 10 | 12 | 14 | 16 |
| Slow Idle Speed-Rpm | 1750 | 1750 | 1750 | 1750 | 1750 |
| Full Load Speed-Rpm | 3500 | 3500 | 3500 | 3500 | 3500 |
| Crankcase Oil Capacity | 1¼ quarts (1.2 L) | 2 quarts (1.9 L) | | | |
| Weight – | | | | | |
| Above 32°F (0°C) | SAE 30 | | | | |
| 0°F (–18°C) to 32°F (0°C) | SAE 10W | | | | |
| Below 0°F (–18C) | SAE 5W-20 | | | | |
| Transmission Oil Capacity | 2 quarts (1.9 L) | | | | |
| Weight | SAE 90 | | | | |
| Grade | EP | | | | |

# FRONT AXLE AND STEERING SYSTEM

## AXLE MAIN MEMBER

### Lawn Ranger Models

Axle main member pivots on a bolt (14–Fig. WH1) which also serves to secure front axle to tractor frame. Remove axle main member assembly by disconnecting drag link (10) from steering arm of left steering spindle (19). Raise tractor and support frame with suitable stands or solid blocking. Remove pivot bolt (14) and roll front axle assembly from under tractor.

### All Models Except Lawn Ranger And 200 Series

Refer to Figs. WH2, WH3, WH4 and WH5 and note the two tie rods are attached by ball joints to a bellcrank plate which is integral with lower steering shaft (7). To remove front axle assembly, tie rods (12) may be disconnected at both steering spindles (16) or from lower steering shaft (7) or completely removed. When front axle assembly is so disconnected from steering controls, raise and block tractor frame, then remove pivot pin so entire front axle can be rolled forward from under tractor.

To reinstall axle assembly, reverse removal procedure. Lubricate pivot with multi-purpose lithium base grease.

### All 200 Series Models

Axle main member pivots on a pin mounted on a front axle support. Remove axle main member by disconnecting drag link (10–Fig. WH5A) at steering spindle (5). Remove snap ring at outer end of pivot pin and remove all bolts retaining front of pivot pin plate. Support front of frame and carefully roll axle main member forward off of pivot pin.

To reinstall axle assembly, reverse removal procedure. Lubricate pivot pin with lithium base grease prior to reassembly.

## TIE RODS

### All Models

Lawn Ranger and 200 series models are furnished with a single tie rod which extends from steering spindle to steering spindle. Other models are fitted with two nonadjustable tubular tie rods which extend from bellcrank arm of lower steering shaft to each steering spindle arm. Removal and installation procedure will be apparent upon examination of unit. Fig. WH4, which pertains only to vertical crankshaft engine models, shows a toe-in adjustment applicable to these models only. Rotation of cam plate (16) after loosening nuts on ball joints at inner ends of tie rods and on pivot bolt at center of cam (16) will alter toe-in of front wheels. Turning cam plate (16) clockwise (facing forward) will draw tie rod ends inward and cause toe-out to increase. Turn cam counterclockwise to set toe-in to specification and tighten all three nuts securely. A setting of zero to 1/8 inch (0-3 mm) toe-in is recommended.

## STEERING SPINDLES

### All Models

To remove steering spindles, check Figs. WH1 through WH5A, raise and block up tractor securely, and remove front wheels. On Lawn Ranger style front axle shown in Fig. WH1, unbolt and remove tie rod (12) and drag link

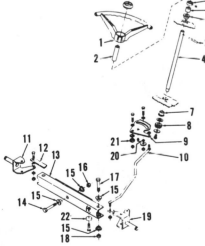

*Fig. WH1 – Exploded view of Lawn Ranger front axle and steering gear assemblies.*

1. Steering wheel
2. Steering tube
3. Pin
4. Steering shaft
5. Set collar
6. Spacer
7. Flange bearing
8. Pinion
9. Quadrant gear
10. Drag link
11. Steering spindle
12. Tie rod
13. Axle assy.
14. Pivot bolt
15. Flange bearing
16. Nut
17. Pivot bolt
18. Nut
19. Steering spindle
20. Spacer roller
21. Adjusting cam
22. Steering stop

*Fig. WH2 – Exploded view of typical steering gear and front axle as used on earlier models of 7 and 8 HP tractors.*

1. Insert
2. Steering wheel
3. Nylon bushing
4. Collar
5. Upper steering shaft
6. Steering support
7. Steering shaft
8. Roll pin
9. Bushing
10. Shim washers
11. "E" ring
12. Tie rod
13. Pivot pin
14. Axle
15. "E" ring
16. Steering spindle

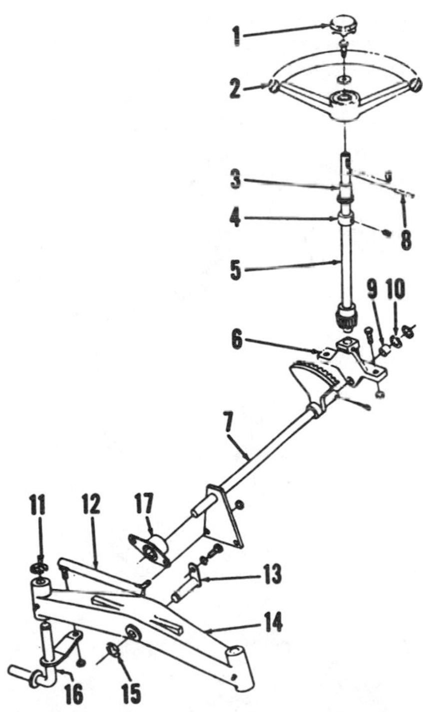

*Fig. WH3 – Exploded view of steering gear and front axle typical for 10, 12 and 14HP models, "C" and "GT" models, SB-421 and SK-486 tractors, Workhorse 800, 800 Special 300 series models and 400 series models; all equipped with horizontal crankshaft engines.*

1. Insert
2. Steering wheel
3. Nylon bushing
4. Collar
5. Upper steering shaft
6. Steering support
7. Lower steering shaft
8. Roll pin
9. Bushing
10. Shim washers
11. "E" ring
12. Tie rod
13. Pivot pin
14. Axle
15. "E" ring
16. Steering spindle
17. Flange bearing

(10), then unscrew pivot bolts (17) so steering spindles can be removed from ends of axle. Same procedure is followed for other models (Fig. WH2 through WH5A). On these other models, steering spindle is retained by "E" ring (11 – Figs. WH2, WH3, WH4 and WH5) or retaining ring (11 – Fig. WH5A) which must be removed before lowering spindle assembly from axle bore.

Reinstall steering spindles by reversing removal procedure. Lubricate with multi-purpose lithium base grease.

## STEERING GEAR

### Lawn Ranger Models

Adjustment is limited to elimination of excessive backlash between steering shaft pinion (8 – Fig. WH1) and spur gear portion of quadrant (9). To perform this adjustment, loosen pivot bolt of quadrant and turn steering adjustment cam (21) so eccentric will bring quadrant into tighter mesh with pinion to reduce backlash.

To remove steering gear, disconnect drag link (10) from quadrant gear (9). Remove pivot bolt and adjusting cam (21), then guide bolt and spacer (20) from curved slot in quadrant. Drive spirol pin (3) from steering wheel hub so wheel can be lifted off steering shaft (4). After pin (3) is removed, steering shaft can be lowered out at bottom. Worn or defective parts including bushings (7) can now be renewed.

When reassembling, lubricate bushings with SAE 30 oil and pinion gear and quadrant gear with multi-purpose grease.

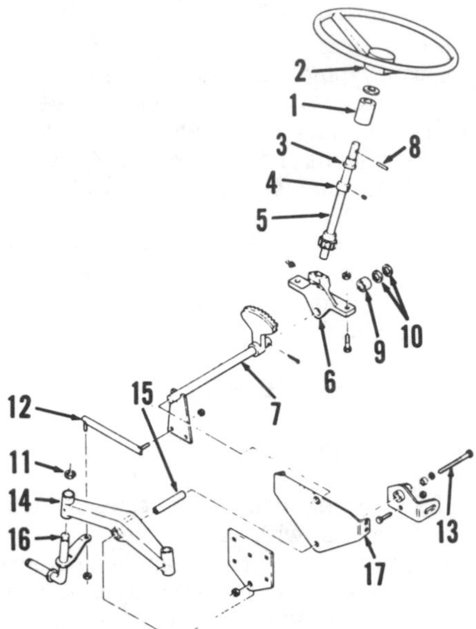


***Fig. WH5 – Exploded view of steering gear and front axle typical of "B" and "LT" models and SB-371 tractors. Later models do not use spacer (15) or pivot bolt (13).***

1. Insert
2. Steering wheel
3. Nylon bushing
4. Collar
5. Upper steering shaft
6. Steering support
7. Lower steering shaft
8. Roll pin
9. Bushing
10. Slim washers
11. "E" ring
12. Tie rod
13. Pivot pin
14. Axle
15. Spacer
16. Steering spindle
17. Steering & axle support

### All 200 Series Models

To adjust steering gear tooth mesh and backlash, first remove fuel tank and battery. Make certain front wheels are pointing straight ahead and steering wheel spokes are centered. Loosen nut (15 – Fig. WH5A) through opening in top of frame. Tighten nut (15) until there is a slight amount of tension on eccentric washer (14). Turn eccentric washer (14) clockwise until no clearance is obtained between ends of gear teeth on steering gear plate (13) and gear teeth on steering shaft gear (18). Tighten nut (15) to 25-35 ft.-lbs. (34-48 N•m). Steering wheel should turn smoothly to full left and full right.

### All Other Models

Range of adjustments for other models is also very limited. Serious malfunctions in steering system are usually best corrected by renewal of defective parts. Note in Fig. WH2 through WH5 that overall design of steering gear is similar for all models. Mesh of pinion on steering shaft (5) with gear sector quadrant of lower steering shaft (7) is adjustable by means of shims (10). Use these shims to correct excessive backlash in gear set.

To remove steering gear, first remove steering wheel. Note that some models have steering wheel attached to shaft by roll pin while others are retained by a Woodruff key and a center bolt through wheel hub. When steering wheel is removed, loosen set screw in collar (4) and

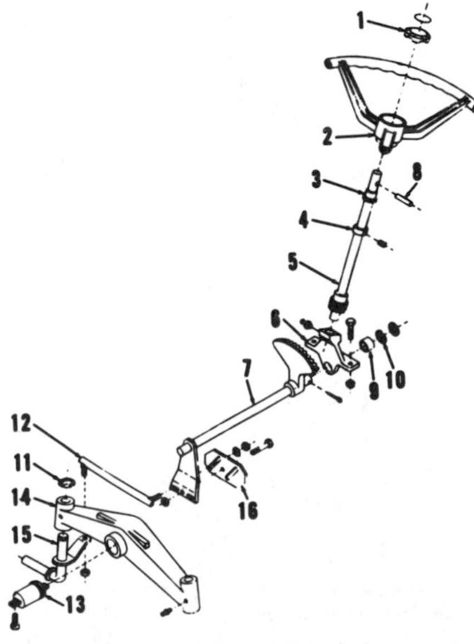


***Fig. WH4-Steering gear and front axle assembly used on A-800 Ranger and 8 HP 4-Speed, CG-7 and late Commando tractors with vertical crankshaft engines.***

1. Insert
2. Steering wheel
3. Bushing
4. Collar
5. Upper steering shaft
6. Support
7. Lower shaft
8. Roll pin
9. Bushing
10. Shims
11. "E" ring
12. Tie rod
13. Pivot
14. Axle
15. Steering spindle
16. Cam plate

***Fig. WH5A – Exploded view of front axle assembly used on Models 208-4, 211-4, 211-5 and 212-6.***

1. Spindle
2. Grease fittings
3. Axle main member
4. Tie rod
5. Spindle
6. Carriage bolt
7. Steering gear bracket
8. Retainer
9. Bolt
10. Drag link
11. Retaining ring
12. Washer
13. Steering gear plate
14. Eccentric washer
15. Nut
16. Bushing
17. Shim washer
18. Steering shaft & gear
19. Drive pin
20. Steering wheel

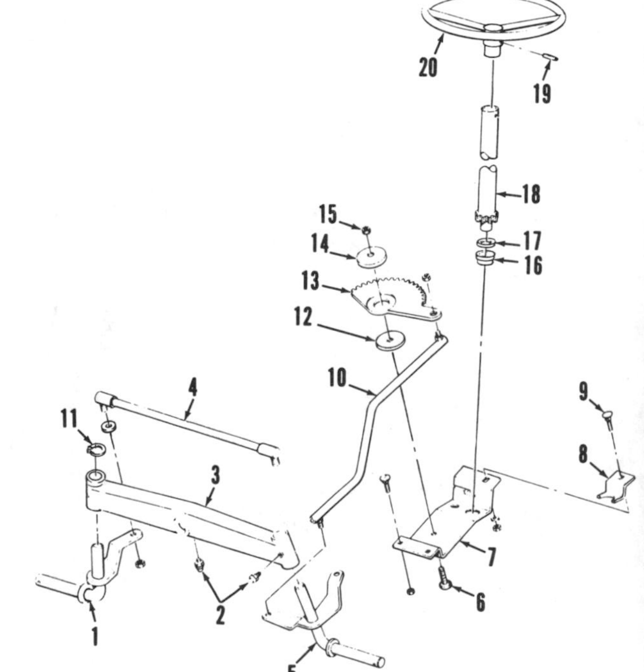

lift upper steering shaft (5) clear of support (6). Then disconnect inner ends of tie rods (12) from arm (bellcrank) of steering shaft (7). Remove cotter pin, washers and shims (10) from rear of shaft and unbolt and remove support (6). Shaft and gear assemblies (5 and 7) can now be removed from underside of tractor. If defective, flange bearing (17–Fig. WH3) on models so equipped, can be unbolted for renewal at this time.

To reassemble, reverse removal procedure. Lubricate with multi-purpose grease.

# ENGINE

## REMOVE AND REINSTALL

### Models Late Lawn Ranger – CG-7 – A-800 – 8 HP 4-Speed (1-0276, 1-0277)

To remove engine, disconnect battery cables and ignition wires. Disconnect fuel line and throttle and choke control cables. Detach exhaust header pipe from muffler if tractor is equipped with separate, frame-mounted muffler. Remove drive belt and engine drive pulley. Remove hood and front grille assembly. Unscrew engine mounting cap screws and lift engine out of tractor.

To reinstall engine, reverse removal procedure.

### Models B-81 – B-82 – B-85 – B-111 – B-112 – B-115

To remove engine, disconnect battery cables and all engine wiring. Disconnect fuel line, choke and throttle cables. Disconnect and remove pto linkage, pto brake adjustment screw and bracket. Remove pto clutch cone assembly, crankshaft bolt and bearing race. Depress clutch pedal and remove pto clutch housing. Remove engine mounting bolts and lift engine out.

Reinstall engine by reversing removal procedure.

### Models C-81 – C-85 – C-101 – C-105 – C-121 – C-125 – C-141 – C-145 – C-161 – C-165

To remove engine, disconnect battery cables and all engine wiring. Disconnect fuel line, choke cable and throttle cable. Remove engine pulley belt guard. Remove cotter pin from pto clutch rod and remove pto brake. Depress clutch pedal and slip drive belt off engine pulley. Remove isomount bolts and lift engine out of frame.

To reinstall engine, reverse removal procedure.

### All Other Models

To remove engine, raise and secure hood or unbolt at hinge if complete removal is more convenient. Some tractors may have a crankcase drain extension pipe which could interfere with engine removal. If so, drain engine oil and remove pipe nipple so engine can clear frame. Disconnect battery cables. Identify and disconnect engine wiring as necessary.

Close fuel valve at tank and remove fuel hose from carburetor inlet, then disconnect choke and throttle controls at carburetor. Release muffler clamp from engine exhaust pipe for muffler removal.

On tractors fitted with manual pto clutch, disconnect control linkage so housing rod can be unbolted at upper end and removed from its bracket on tractor frame. Unbolt and remove belt guard (cover) from right side of tractor for access to clutch idler and belt. Release and remove drive belts from engine pulleys.

Check for possible interference of other parts in engine compartment area, unbolt engine from base plate and lift out of tractor frame.

Reverse sequence of these steps to reinstall engine.

## OVERHAUL

### All Models

Engine make and model are listed at the beginning of this section. To overhaul engine components and accessories, refer to Briggs & Stratton, Kawasaki, Tecumseh and Kohler sections of this manual.

# CLUTCH AND BRAKE

The clutch used on most models, is a belt idler operated by clutch-brake pedal on left side of tractor. This pedal also operates the band on drum brake located on transmission. Some models are equipped with a separate brake pedal and a disc brake.

## ADJUSTMENT

### Models CG-7 – 8 HP 4-Speed (1-0276)

Clutch belt idler is spring loaded and does not require adjustment. To remove clutch-brake pedal free play, release clutch-brake pedal so it is in full up position. Loosen set screw (12–Fig. WH6) and move collar on rod (11) so collar is snug against clutch idler arm (8). To adjust brake, turn adjusting nut (15).

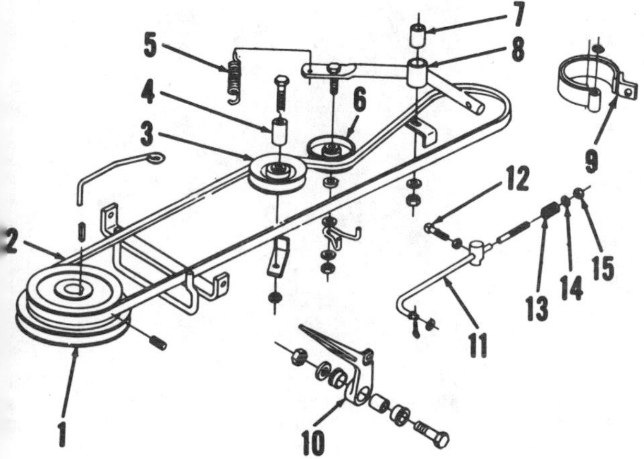

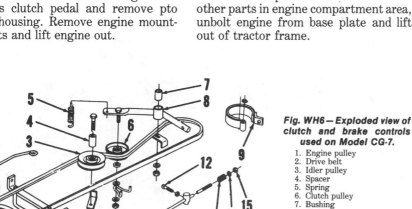

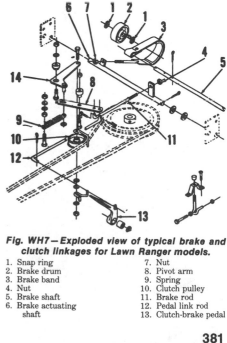

*Fig. WH6 – Exploded view of clutch and brake controls used on Model CG-7.*

1. Engine pulley
2. Drive belt
3. Idler pulley
4. Spacer
5. Spring
6. Clutch pulley
7. Bushing
8. Clutch arm
9. Brake band
10. Pedal
11. Brake rod
12. Set screw
13. Spring
14. Washer
15. Nut

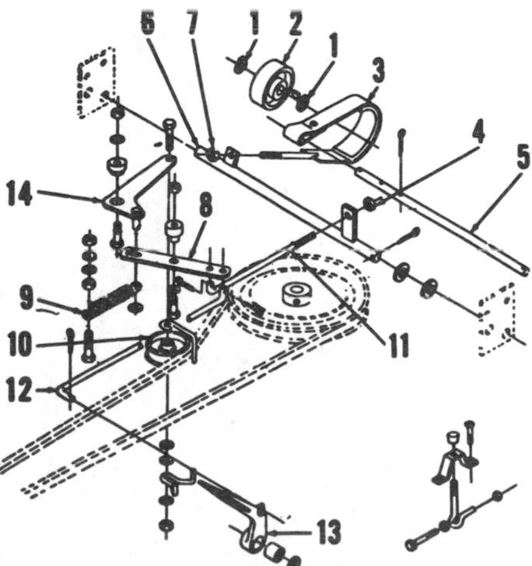

*Fig. WH7 – Exploded view of typical brake and clutch linkages for Lawn Ranger models.*

1. Snap ring
2. Brake drum
3. Brake band
4. Nut
5. Brake shaft
6. Brake actuating shaft
7. Nut
8. Pivot arm
9. Spring
10. Clutch pulley
11. Brake rod
12. Pedal link rod
13. Clutch-brake pedal

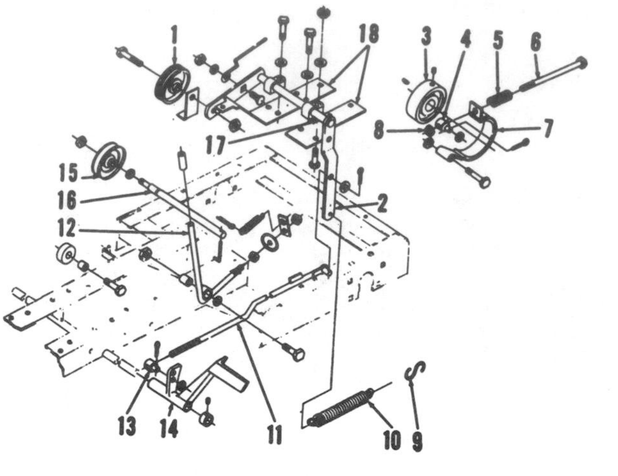

*Fig. WH8—Exploded view of clutch and brake assemblies used on 800 Special.*

1. Clutch pulley
2. Clutch arm
3. Brake drum
4. Adjuster
5. Spring
6. Bolt
7. Brake band
8. Nut
9. Hook
10. Spring
11. Clutch-brake rod
12. Park brake lever
13. Adjuster
14. Pedal
15. Idler pulley
16. Shaft
17. Shaft
18. Mounting brackets

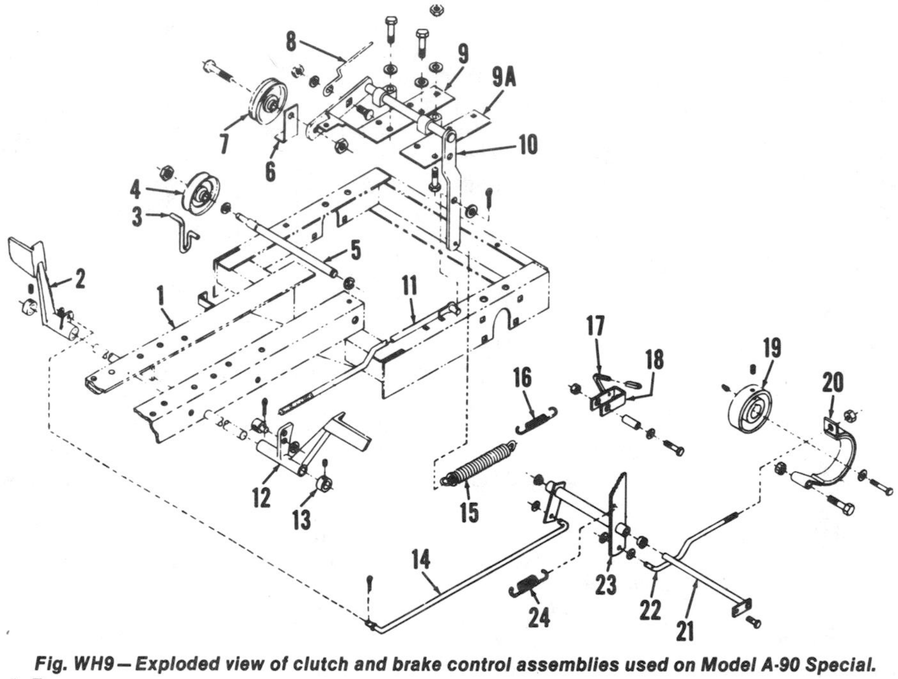

*Fig. WH9—Exploded view of clutch and brake control assemblies used on Model A-90 Special.*

1. Frame
2. Brake pedal
3. Belt guide
4. Idler pulley
5. Idler shaft
6. Belt guide
7. Idler pulley
8. Guide stop
9. Torque bar
9A. Support
10. Idler arm assy.
11. Clutch rod
12. Clutch pedal
13. Retainer collar
14. Brake link rod
15. Clutch spring
16. Pawl return spring
17. Pawl lever
18. Park brake pawl
19. Brake drum
20. Brake band
21. Pivot rod assy.
22. Brake rod
23. Bellcrank assy.
24. Brake return spring

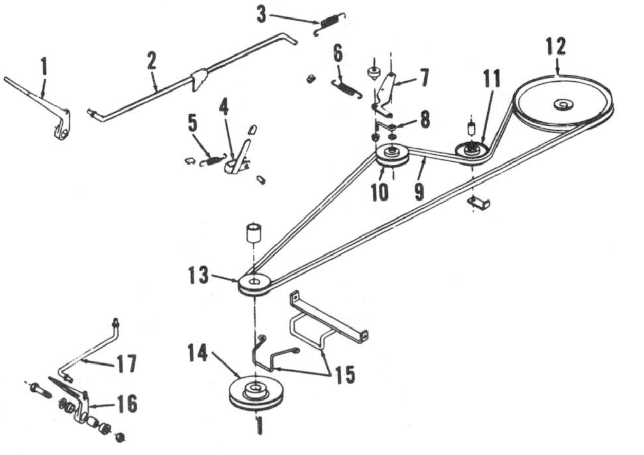

*Fig. WH10—Exploded view of clutch and brake controls used on Model A-800 tractors. "B" series and "LT" series tractors and Model SB-371 are similar.*

1. Brake pedal
2. Brake rod
3. Retractor spring
4. Park lock
5. Return spring
6. Clutch spring
7. Clutch lever
8. Belt retainer
9. Drive belt
10. Clutch pulley
11. Idler pulley
12. Transaxle pulley
13. Engine pulley
14. Pto drive pulley
15. Belt guides
16. Clutch pedal
17. Clutch rod

Brake should not engage before clutch is disengaged.

## Lawn Ranger Models

Clutch idler pulley is spring loaded and no adjustment is required. Proceed as follows to set brake engagement correctly: Tighten brake band adjusting nut (7–Fig. WH7) after setting parking brake with transmission in neutral until rear wheels are locked. When wheels skid when tractor is pushed by hand, tighten nut (7) another half turn. Release parking brake. Now, adjust nut (4) on brake rod (11) so there will be 3/8 inch (9.5 mm) clearance between nut (4) and arm of brake actuator shaft (6). This will ensure brakes are not applied before clutch is disengaged.

## Model 800 Special

The clutch idler is spring loaded on 800 Special and does not require adjustment, however, belt guide beneath engine pulley should clear drive belt by no more than 1/8 inch (3 mm). Bend guide if necessary. To adjust brake, loosen locknut (8–Fig. WH8) and turn adjuster (4). Brake should not engage before clutch is disengaged.

## Model A-90 Special

As with other models, clutch idler pulley is spring-loaded (15–Fig. WH9) and no adjustment is necessary, however, Model A-90 Special does have a safety interlock switch wired in series with starter solenoid which will not allow current to pass to starting motor unless clutch pedal is fully depressed. To make proper adjustment, remove drive belt cover so clutch pulley is in sight and adjust threaded trunnion on pedal end of clutch rod (11) so pedal boss closes interlock switch just as clutch idler pulley

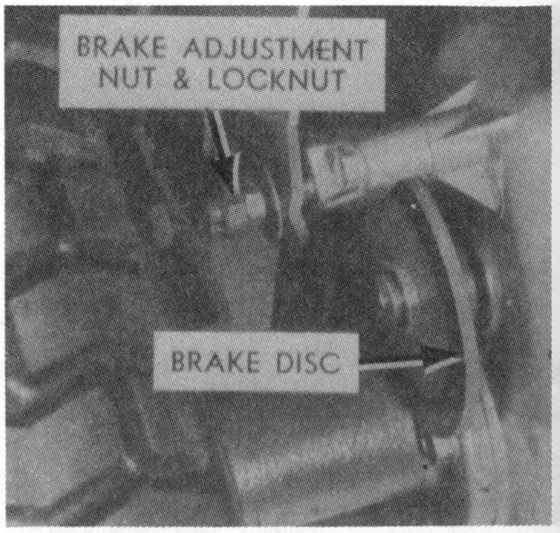


*Fig. WH11—View of disc brake adjustment for Model A-800. "B" series, "LT" series tractors equipped with 3-speed transaxle and all 200 series models are similar.*

arm (10) contacts its stop bolt.

Note brake pedal is separate on this model. Adjust in this sequence: Push down on brake pedal and engage parking brake lever (17) so pawl (18) is seated in topmost notch of parking brake arm of bellcrank (23). Now, tighten brake band adjuster nut at threaded end of rod (22) until drive wheels skid when tractor is pushed. Tighten nut another half turn. Operate tractor and observe braking.

### Models A-800 Ranger – B-81 – B-82 – B-85 – B-111 – B-112 – B-115 – LT-832 – LT-1032 – LT-1136 – LT-1137 – SB-371

These models have a separate brake pedal which operates a disc brake mounted on right side of transaxle. The clutch idler pulley (10 – Fig. WH10) is spring loaded and requires no adjustment.

To adjust disc brake, release brake pedal and loosen locknut at brake caliper as shown in Fig. WH11 or WH12. Turn adjusting nut until brake disc is locked, then back off adjusting nut just enough to permit brake disc to turn freely. Tighten locknut. On late models, check brake rod spring adjustment (Fig. WH12) after adjusting brake. Turn adjusting nut as required to obtain 2-11/16 to 2¾ inch (68-70 mm) measurement between inside of nut and washer on brake rod as shown.

A safety interlock switch, operated by clutch pedal, is used on these tractors. Be sure switch is actuated when foot pedal is depressed.

### Other Models With 3- and 6-Speed Transmissions: Raider 8, 10, 12, 14 – 8, 10, 12, 14 HP 8-Speed – Commando 800 – 8 HP 4-Speed – Workhorse 800 – 300 Series – 400 Series

Clutch idler pulley (13 – Fig. WH13) is spring loaded and not adjustable. For operator convenience, pedal height may be adjusted on these models by disconnecting clutch rod (9) at end attached to pedal (10) and turning threaded end of rod in or out to obtain desired pedal height.

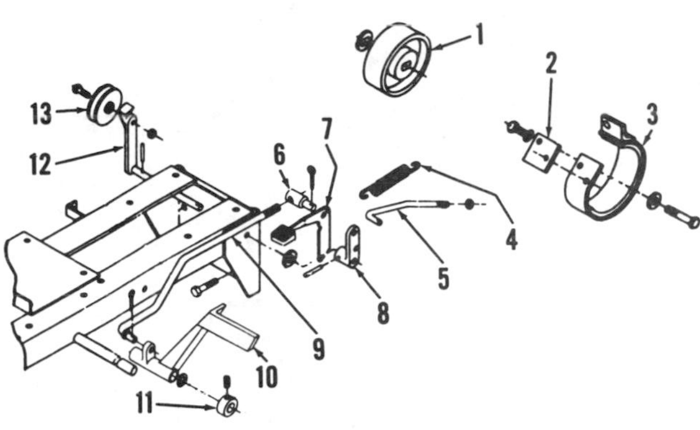


***Fig. WH13 – Exploded view of clutch and brake linkage typical of 3- and 6-speed models: Commando 800, 8 HP 4-speed, 8-10-12-14 HP 8-speed. Raider models, Workhorse 800, 300 series models and 400 series models.***

1. Brake drum
2. Stop plate
3. Brake band
4. Return spring
5. Brake rod
6. Clutch stud
7. Park brake lever
8. Clutch arm
9. Clutch rod
10. Clutch-brake pedal
11. Collar
12. Idler arm
13. Idler pulley

To adjust service brake, apply pedal (10) and engage park brake lever (7). Refer to Fig. WH14 for view of typical brake adjustment and tighten brake rod nut gradually against flange of brake band until both rear wheels of tractor will skid when tractor is pushed by hand. Tighten nut another half turn and service and parking brake are in proper adjustment. Release parking brake to check operation. Clutch must disengage before brake is applied.

### Models B-80 – C-81 – C-85 – C-100 – C-101 – C-105 – C-120 – C-121 – C-125 – C-141 – C-145 – C-160 – C-161 – C-165 – GT-1142 – GT-2500 – SB-421 – SK-486

These models have a separate brake and clutch pedal. A set of safety interlock switches is used on all 1974 and later models. If starting motor will not operate when ignition key is turned, check should be immediately made to make sure these switches are closed when pto clutch is disengaged and tractor drive clutch is fully disengaged. Perform proper adjustments. Do not short-circuit or bypass.

Refer to Fig. WH14 to identify brake and clutch adjustment points. Adjust clutch pedal so safety interlock switch is depressed by boss on clutch pedal when clutch idler arm (14 – Fig. WH15) contacts its stop bolt. Adjust at clutch trunnion at rear of clutch rod.

To adjust brakes, apply service brake and set parking brake lever so topmost notch of parking brake arm (5) is engaged. Adjust nut at end of brake rod (6) until brake band is tight enough to skid rear wheels when tractor is pushed. Tighten another half turn and check brake and clutch operation.

### All 200 Series Models

Brake adjustment is made at brake caliper located on left side of transaxle. With clutch-brake pedal released, tighten adjustment nut (Fig. WH11) until brake disc is no longer free to turn. Back off adjustment nut just enough to permit disc to turn freely. With clutch-brake pedal depressed, brake should be fully engaged when front edge of parking brake lever is even with rear edge of parking brake locking slot in frame. To adjust, rotate eccentric on idler arm underneath tractor.

To adjust clutch, perform brake adjustment as previously outlined. With clutch-brake pedal released, loosen nut on idler pulley and slide idler pulley in or

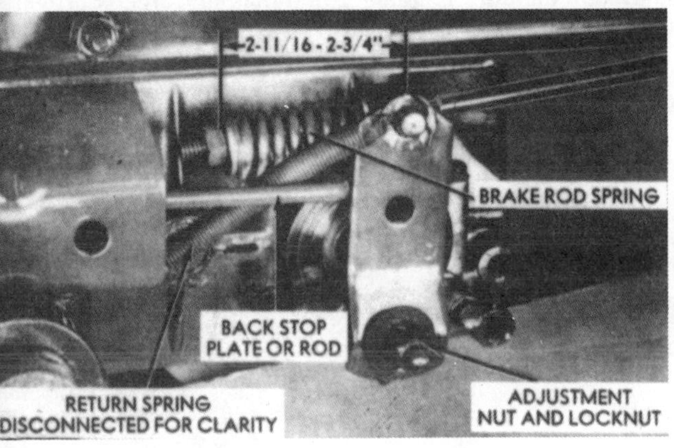


***Fig. WH12 – View of disc brake adjustment on late Model "B" series tractors and "LT" series tractors with 5-speed transaxle.***

***Fig. WH14 – View of clutch and brake adjustment points on Model B-80, "C" models, GT-1142, GT-2500, SB-421 and SK-486. Refer to text.***

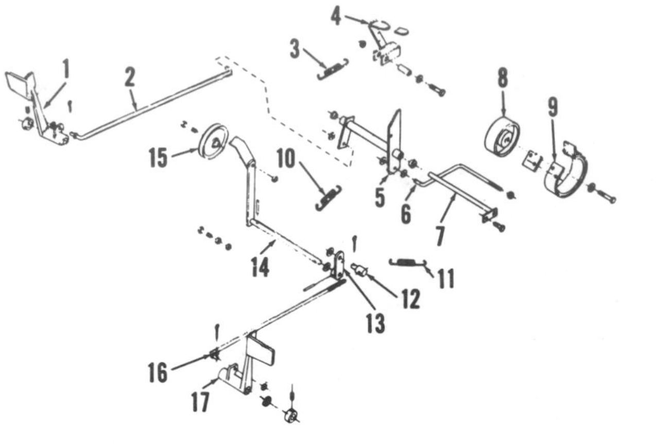


*Fig. WH15—Exploded view of clutch and brake control linkage typical of Model B-80, "C" models, GT-1142, GT-2500, SB-421 and SK-486.*

1. Brake pedal
2. Brake rod
3. Spring
4. Park lock
5. Bellcrank
6. Brake link
7. Pivot rod
8. Brake drum
9. Brake band
10. Return spring
11. Clutch spring
12. Swivel stud
13. Clutch arm
14. Idler arm assy.
15. Clutch pulley
16. Clutch rod
17. Clutch pedal

out of slot on bellcrank until parking brake lever is 3/8 inch (9.5 mm) from end of slot. Tighten nut on idler pulley.

# ELECTRIC PTO CLUTCH

## All Models So Equipped

Some models are equipped with an electro-magnetic pto clutch of design shown in Fig. WH16.

Should clutch fail, determination should be made of cause for failure. First step is a check of tractor electrical system for blown fuse, defective clutch switch, bad or corroded connections or for broken wires. Best procedure calls for use of an ohmmeter or test light to locate any possible break in continuity.

If no fault is found in service wiring to clutch body, a voltage check should be made across clutch leads (from switch wire to ground lug) with switch "ON". If voltmeter reading is ZERO, recheck wiring for open circuit or bad ground. If reading is over 8 volts, then use an ohmmeter to check resistance in clutch coil by connecting ohmmeter across connector terminals. Normal resistance reading should fall between 2.75 and 3.6 ohms. If reading is lower or higher, then coil winding is defective and renewal is called for.

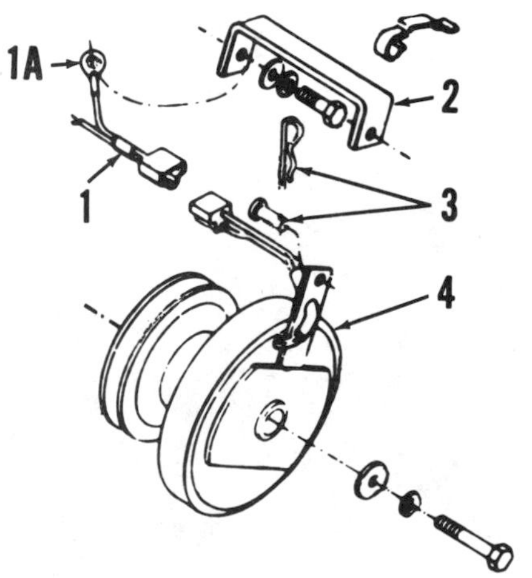


*Fig. WH16—Electro-magnetic pto clutch is used on some models.*

1. Cable connector
1A. Ground lug
2. Bracket
3. Pin assy.
4. Clutch unit

Earlier manufacturer policy required entire clutch assembly be renewed in case of failure. This has been changed as follows:

Based on current service bulletins, clutch unit breaks down into two components, a housing and pulley assembly and a field winding and bearing assembly. In case of failure, field and bearing assembly is more likely to be at fault and may be renewed separately.

**R&R ELECTRIC PTO CLUTCH.** Refer to Fig. WH16 and uncouple connector for electrical leads (1). Remove pin (3), wiring clips, and unbolt bracket (2) for removal. Back out center bolt from clutch hub. After center bolt and washer are removed, a puller bolt (jack screw) is threaded into clutch hub counterbore to pull unit from end of crankshaft. On clutches with part number 7915, 8278 or 9656 (earlier production) a 1 inch 8 thread bolt, five inches long is needed.

**NOTE: On clutch number 7915 only, a snap ring must first be removed. If clutch assembly is numbered 101470, 101472 or 101473, (later production) a 5/8 inch NC (1 thread) bolt four inches long is required for use as a puller.**

After clutch is removed from end of crankshaft, leave puller bolt threaded in place and field and bearing assembly can be removed from housing by striking bolt head a sharp blow on a solid surface. After bearing and field coil assembly is so loosened and separated, a new assembly can be pressed into housing bore until snug against retaining shoulder. Use an arbor which contacts only inner race of new bearing when pressing assemblies together. Reassembly is then completed by replacing all parts in reverse of removal order. After control wires are reconnected, test operation.

# MANUAL PTO CLUTCH

## All Models So Equipped

**ADJUSTMENT.** Some Wheel Horse tractors designed primarily for operation with belly-slung rotary mowers use only a spring-loaded idler pulley which is engaged by movement of a remote handle to transfer drive belt motion to mower deck. Such controls are basically simple though design may vary. Adjustments to be considered are limited to positioning of belt guides and keepers and maintenance of full spring tension on clutch pulley by ensuring slight free play at pulley ends of clutch rods. Usual adjustment means provided is by shim washers at pulley lever or by threaded rod ends.

Pto units which operate directly from engine crankshafts are considered here. Current examples are shown in exploded view in Figs. WH17, WH18 and WH19.

Older style pto clutch used on some models is shown in exploded view in Fig. WH17. This clutch has no pressure spring or over-center feature. All engagement and holding force is provided by control rod (1–Fig. WH17) which is

*Fig. WH17—Exploded view of manual pto clutch used in some earlier production tractors.*

1. Control handle
2. Instruction decal
3. Bracket
4. Clutch shaft
5. Snap ring (3/4 inch)
6. Snap ring (1 3/4 inch)
7. Ball bearing
8. Clutch housing
9. Bearing
10. Seal
11. Bearing race
12. Lockplates
13. Clutch plate
14. Fulcrum plate

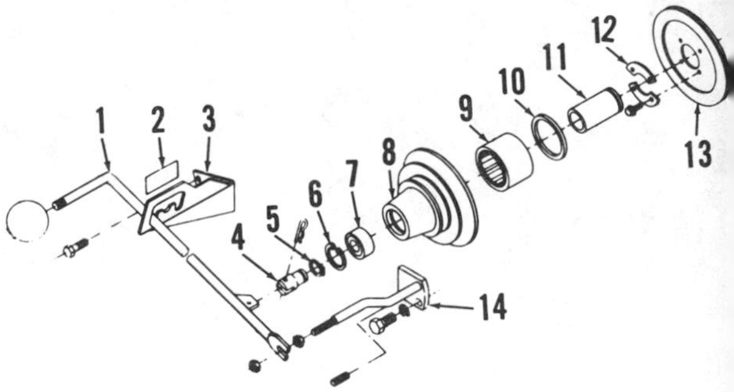

ully applied when placed in innermost otch of bracket plate (3). Clutch adjustnent is made by setting of two nuts on hreaded portion of rod (14) to control ivot position of forked end of control od (1). Adjust these nuts so clutch is ust disengaged with rod in shallow enter notch of bracket (3). This will provide full engagement when rod (1) is set nto inner notch of bracket and complete isengagement in outer notch. All parts re renewable including facings and ivets for clutch plate (13) if clutch peration becomes unsatisfactory.

To adjust pto shown in Fig. WH20, ngage pto clutch and turn adjusting olt to obtain 0.010 inch (0.254 mm) learance between brake pad and clutch ulley face. There should be 3/8 inch (9.5 nm) gap between threaded spacer on lutch rod and clutch brake bracket as hown. If not, loosen locknut and turn hreaded spacer as required to obtain /8 inch (9.5 mm) gap. Recheck brake pad djustment.

To adjust pto shown in Fig. WH21, urn trunnion towards rear of operating od (one turn at a time) until clutch slipage is eliminated. To adjust pto brake, oosen adjusting bolts and engage pto. Move brake pad bracket to obtain 0.012 nch (0.305 mm) clearance between rake pad and pulley face, then tighten djusting bolts.

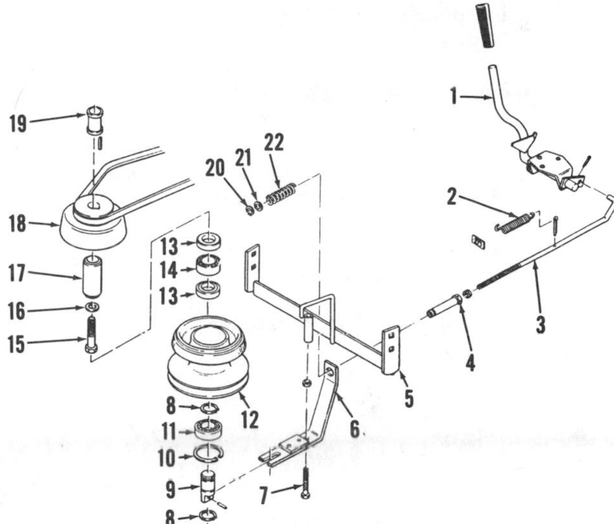


*Fig. WH19—Exploded view of pto clutch and operating linkage used on "B" series, "LT" series and SB-371 tractors.*

1. Control lever
2. Spring
3. Clutch rod
4. Threaded spacer
5. Clutch mounting bracket
6. Brake bracket
7. Adjusting bolt
8. Snap ring
9. Clutch shaft
10. Snap ring
11. Ball bearing
12. Pto pulley & clutch cone
13. Seals
14. Needle bearing
15. Bolt
16. Special washer
17. Bearing race
18. Engine pulley & clutch housing
19. Spacer tube
20. Snap ring
21. Special washer
22. Spring

**REMOVE AND REINSTALL.** To remove pto clutch unit shown in Fig. WH18, disconnect clutch rod trunnion (9) from shift plate (10). Remove yoke pin (12) and swing shift plate (10) and yoke (14) out of the way. Remove pto brake. With belts removed, slide pto clutch housing (19) off shaft. Remove four bolts securing lockplates (23) onto clutch plate (24). Slide bearing race (22) off shaft and remove clutch plate and facing. Renew worn parts as necessary and reinstall in reverse order of removal.

To remove pto clutch unit shown in Fig. WH19, remove adjusting bolt (7) and brake bracket (6). Withdraw pto pulley and clutch cone (12). Remove crankshaft bolt (15) and bearing race (17). Depress clutch pedal and slip drive belt off engine pulley (18), then remove pulley from crankshaft. Renew worn parts as necessary and reinstall by reversing removal steps.

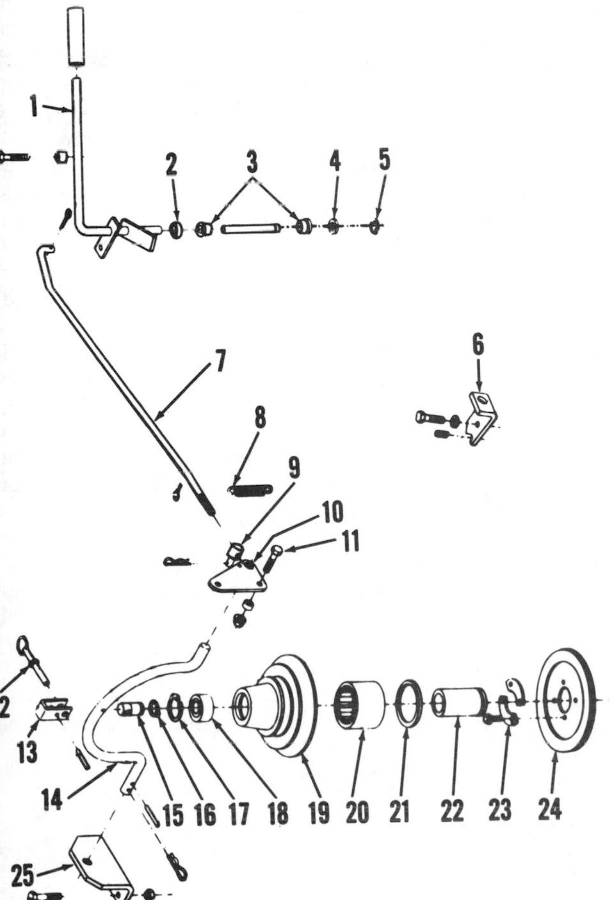


*Fig. WH18—Exploded view of manual pto clutch and operating linkage typical of "C" series and "GT" series tractors, 8-10-12-14 HP 8-speed models, SB-421, SK-486, 300 series and 400 series tractors.*

1. Lever assy
2. Spacer
3. Bushing (2)
4. Shim washer
5. "E" ring
6. Engine bracket
7. Clutch rod
8. Spring (rod-plate)
9. Adjuster trunnion
10. Shift plate
11. Pivot bolt
12. Clevis pin
13. Clevis
14. Yoke (housing rod)
15. Clutch shaft
16. Snap ring (3/4 inch)
17. Snap ring (1 3/4 inch)
18. Ball bearing
19. Clutch housing
20. Bearing
21. Seal
22. Bearing race
23. Lockplates
24. Clutch plate
25. Lower support

# TRANSAXLE

## LUBRICATION

### All Models

A variety of transaxles manufactured by Wheel Horse, Foote and Peerless have been used. Refer to the CONDENSED SPECIFICATIONS tables at the beginning of this section for transaxle fluid capacities and fluid type.

## REMOVE AND REINSTALL

### Models CG-7—8 HP 4-Speed

To remove transaxle, first remove fenders and seat from frame. Disconnect brake rod from brake band. Depress clutch-brake pedal and slip drive belt off transaxle pulley. Place shift lever in neutral position. Block up under rear of tractor, remove transaxle mounting screws and roll assembly away from tractor.

To reinstall transaxle, reverse removal procedure. Adjust brake as outlined in preceding CLUTCH AND BRAKE adjustment paragraph.

### Models Late Lawn Ranger–A-800 Ranger

To remove transaxle, depress clutch-brake pedal and remove drive belt from transaxle pulley. Remove brake band assembly. Place shift lever in neutral position. Block up under rear of tractor, unscrew axle retaining bolts and roll transaxle assembly away from tractor.

To reinstall transaxle, reverse removal procedure. Adjust brake as outlined in preceding CLUTCH AND BRAKE paragraphs which apply.

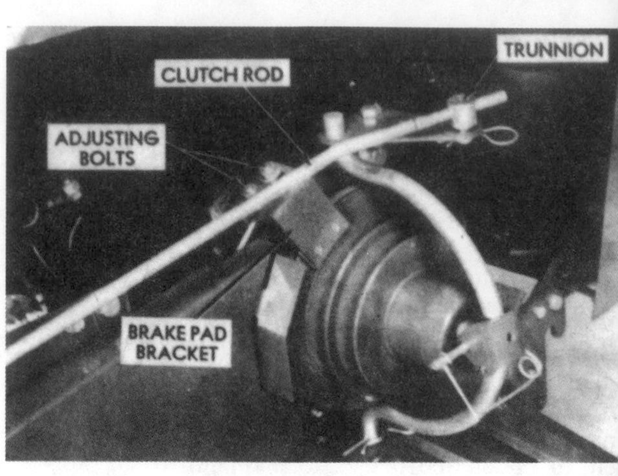


*Fig. WH21—View of pto adjustment points on "C" series and "GT" series tractors, 8-10-12-14 HP 8-speed models, SB-421, SK-486, 300 series and 400 series tractors.*

### Models 800 Special–A-90 Special

To remove transaxle, first remove seat and fender assembly. Remove drive belt guard, depress clutch or clutch-brake pedal and slip drive belt off transaxle pulley. Disconnect brake return spring and remove brake band assembly. Remove transaxle mounting cap screws and clutch shaft mount plates (18–Fig. WH8) or (9-9A–Fig. WH9). Block up under rear of tractor and remove rear wheels and hubs. Unbolt side plates attached to frame. Unbolt axle retaining bolts and remove transaxle from tractor.

To reinstall transaxle, reverse removal procedure. Adjust brake as outlined in appropriate preceding paragraph.

### All 200 Series Models

To remove transaxle, disconnect brake linkage at brake caliper. Disconnect shift linkage at transaxle. Remove transaxle drive belt. Remove all torque straps. Support rear of tractor, then remove transaxle retaining bolts and raise tractor off of transaxle. Roll transaxle from under tractor.

Reinstall by reversing removal procedure.

### Other Models: Commando 800–Workhorse–8, 10, 12, 14 HP 4- and 8-Speed Models–All Raiders–"B" Series–"C" Series–"GT" Series–"LT" Series–SB-371–SB-421–SK-486

To remove transaxle unit, first unbolt and remove belt guard from right side of tractor. Depress clutch pedal and remove drive belt at transaxle pulley. Disconnect brake rod from clutch linkage on models which have a common brake-clutch pedal and on models with separate brake pedal, disconnect and remove brake linkage rod at transaxle. Do not overlook retracting springs used on some tractors. Remove lever knobs from gear shift and range selector (if so equipped) so cover plates can be removed or transaxle may be lowered without interference from console deck. Raise and support tractor frame securely at side points just forward of transaxle, then remove transaxle mounting cap screws and lower and remove entire unit from tractor.

To reinstall, reverse removal procedure. Refer to appropriate preceding paragraph for brake adjustment procedure for model being serviced after transaxle is reinstalled.

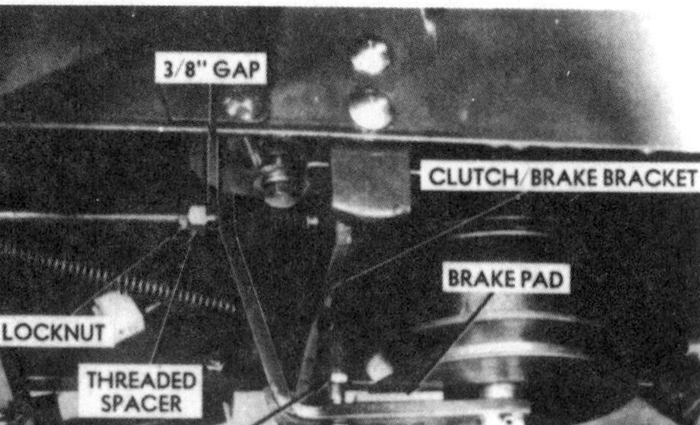


*Fig. WH20—View of pto adjustment points on "B" series, "LT" series and SB-371 tractors.*

## OVERHAUL

### All Models

Models CG-7 and 8 HP 4-Speed are equipped with a 4-speed transaxle manufactured by Wheel Horse. Models Lawn Ranger, A-800, 3-speed "B" series, 3-speed "LT" series and SB371 are equipped with a Peerless 600 series transaxle. Early Model B-111 is equipped with a Foote 4000-5 transaxle. Models B-85, late B-111, B-115 and 5-speed "LT" are equipped with a Peerless 800 series transaxle. Models 800 Special and A-90 Special are equipped with a Peerless 1200 series transaxle. Models 208-4, 211-4, 211-5 and 212-6 are equipped with a 4, 5 or 6-speed Peerless 900 series transaxle.

All models equipped with 3-speed and 4-speed transaxles except Models CG-7, 8 HP 4-Speed, Lawn Ranger, A-800, 3-speed "B" series, 3-speed "LT" series and SB371 are equipped with a three (four) speed transaxle manufactured by Wheel Horse.

All models equipped with 6-speed or 8-speed transaxles except Model 212-6 are equipped with a six (eight) speed transaxle manufactured by Wheel Horse.

Refer to the appropriate Wheel Horse, Foote or Peerless section in TRANSAXLE SERVICE section for overhaul procedure.

# WHEEL HORSE

## CONDENSED SPECIFICATIONS (Hydrostatic Drive)

| | MODELS | | | | |
|---|---|---|---|---|---|
| | 800 Automatic | Charger 10, 10HP-Automatic, B-100 | B-115 | Charger 12, 12HP-Automatic, C-120 | CG-8 |
| Engine Make | B&S | Kohler | B&S | Kohler | Tecumseh |
| Model | 190434 | K241S | 253707 | K301S | VH80 |
| Bore | 3 in. (76.2 mm) | 3¼ in. (82.5 mm) | 3-7/16 in. (87.3 mm) | 3⅜ in. (85.7 mm) | 3-5/16 in. (84.1 mm) |
| Stroke | 2¾ in. (69.8 mm) | 2⅞ in. (73.0 mm) | 2⅝ in. (66.7 mm) | 3¼ in. (82.5 mm) | 2¾ in. (69.8 mm) |
| Piston Displacement | 19.44 cu. in. (318 cc) | 23.9 cu. in. (392 cc) | 24.36 cu. in. (399 cc) | 29.07 cu. in. (476 cc) | 23.75 cu. in. (389 cc) |
| Horsepower | 8 | 10 | 11 | 12 | 8 |
| Slow Idle Speed – Rpm | 1750 | 1200 | 1750 | 1200 | 1200 |
| High Idle Speed (No Load) – Rpm | 3600 | 3600 | 3300 | 3600 | 3600 |
| Crankcase Oil Capacity | 2¾ pints (1.3L) | 4 pints (1.9L) | 3 pints (1.4L) | 4 pints (1.9L) | 3⅛ pints (1.5L) |
| Weight – | | | | | |
| Above 32°F (0°C) | SAE 30 | | | | |
| 0°F (−18°C) to 32°F (0°C) | SAE 10W | | | | |
| Below 0°F (−18°C) | SAE 5W-20 | | | | |
| Transmission Oil Capacity | 1½ pints (0.7L) | ** | 1½ pints (0.7L) | ** | 2⅔ pints (1.2L) |
| Weight | Type "F" | ** | SAE 20 | ** | Type "F" |
| Differential Oil Capacity | 2¾ pints (1.3L) | .... | 2¾ pints (1.3L) | .... | 2 pints (0.9L) |
| Weight | SAE 90 EP | .... | SAE 90 EP | .... | SAE 140 |

**Refer to table in HYDROSTATIC TRANSMISSION section.

| | MODELS | | | | | |
|---|---|---|---|---|---|---|
| | C-121, C-125 | GT-14, Bronco 14, 14HP-Automatic | C-141, C-145 | C-160 | C-161, C-165 | 16HP-Automatic |
| Engine Make | Kohler | Kohler | Kohler | Kohler | Kohler | Kohler |
| Model | K301AS | K321S | K321AS | K341S | K341AS | K341S |
| Bore | 3⅜ in. (85.7 mm) | 3½ in. (88.9 mm) | 3½ in. (88.9 mm) | 3¾ in. (95.2 mm) | 3¾ in. (95.2 mm) | 3¾ in. (95.2 mm) |
| Stroke | 3¼ in. (82.5 mm) | 3¼ in. (82.5 mm) | 3¼ in. (82.5 mm) | 3¼ in. (82.5 mm) | 3¼ in. (82.5 mm) | 3¼ in. (82.5 mm) |
| Piston Displacement | 29.07 cu. in. (476 cc) | 31.27 cu. in. (512 cc) | 31.27 cu. in. (512 cc) | 35.89 cu. in. (588 cc) | 35.89 cu. in. (588 cc) | 35.89 cu. in. (588 cc) |
| Horsepower | 12 | 14 | 14 | 16 | 16 | 16 |
| Slow Idle Speed – Rpm | 2100 | 1200 | 2100 | 1200 | 2100 | 1200 |
| High Idle Speed (No Load) – Rpm | 3400 | 3600 | 3400 | 3600 | 3400 | 3600 |
| Crankcase Oil Capacity | 3 pints (1.4L) | 4 pints (1.9L) | 3 pints (1.4L) | 4 pints (1.9L) | 3 pints (1.4L) | 4 pints (1.9L) |
| Weight – | | | | | | |
| Above 32°F (0°C) | SAE 30 | | | | | |
| 0°F (−18°C) to 32°F (0°C) | SAE 10W | | | | | |
| Below 0°F (−18°C) | SAE 5W-20 | | | | | |
| Transmission Oil Capacity | ** | | | | | |
| Weight | ** | | | | | |

**Refer to table in HYDROSTATIC TRANSMISSION section.

# FRONT AXLE AND STEERING SYSTEM

## AXLE MAIN MEMBER

### Model GT-14

To remove front axle from Model GT-14, refer to Fig. WH41 and disconnect ball joint at forward end of drag link (11) from arm of bellcrank (15). Raise and support tractor frame securely, then remove pin (13) so complete axle can be lowered and rolled forward away from tractor.

Reinstall axle by reversing removal procedure. Lubricate pivot with multi-purpose grease.

### All Other Models

Rigid axle main member is mounted to tractor main frame, center-pivoted on its mounting pin. To remove front axle assembly, tie rods (12–Fig. WH42, WH43 or WH44) may be disconnected at both steering spindles (16) or completely removed by disconnecting from bellcrank of lower steering shaft (7) as well. When axle is so disconnected from steering controls, raise and block tractor frame securely, remove pivot pin and entire front axle can be rolled from under tractor.

To reinstall axle assembly, reverse removal procedure. Lubricate pivot with multi-purpose grease.

## TIE RODS

### Model GT-14

Model GT-14 tractors are equipped with an adjustable tie rod (14–Fig. WH41). Renewable ball joint ends (12) are counter-threaded (right and left) to accommodate toe-in adjustment. Specified toe-in is 1/16 to 1/8-inch (1.5-3 mm).

### All Other Models

These tractors have two tubular tie rods with permanently fitted ball joint assemblies at each end. For all horizontal crankshaft engine equipped models, there is no adjustment. However, cam plate (16–Fig. WH43) does provide for minor toe-in adjustment for Model CG-8. To make this adjustment, loosen locknuts at inner ends of tie rods (12) and pivot bolt at center of cam (16). If cam plate is turned clockwise, as viewed from rear, tie rod ends will be drawn inward causing toe-out to increase. Turn cam counter-clockwise to set toe-in to specification and tighten all three nuts securely. A setting of zero to 1/8-inch (0-3 mm) toe-in is suggested.

## STEERING SPINDLES

### Model GT-14

To remove steering spindles, block up axle main member so wheels are clear. Disconnect tie rod ends and forward end of drag link from right and left steering arms. Remove wheels from spindles, drive out roll pins which retain steering arms then steering spindles can be lowered out of axle main member.

Renew worn parts as necessary. Lubricate with multi-purpose grease.

### All Other Models

For removal of steering spindles, refer to Figs. WH42, WH43 and WH44. Jack up tractor, block securely and remove front wheels. Disconnect tie rods (12) from steering arm portion of each steering spindle, remove "E" ring retainers (11) and lower steering spindles out of bores in axle.

To reinstall steering spindles, reverse removal procedure. Lubricate with multi-purpose grease.

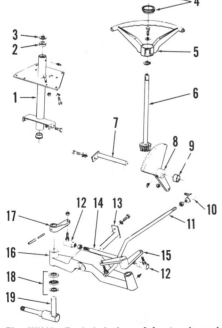

***Fig. WH41—Exploded view of front axle and steering assembly used on Model GT-14.***

1. Steering support
2. Bushing (2)
3. Washer
4. Insert
5. Steering wheel
6. Steering shaft
7. Shaft & plate assy.
8. Steering sector
9. Spacer
10. Ball joint
11. Drag link
12. Ball joint (2)
13. Pin/plate assy.
14. Tie rod
15. Bellcrank
16. Axle
17. Steering arm
18. Thrust bearing set
19. Steering spindle

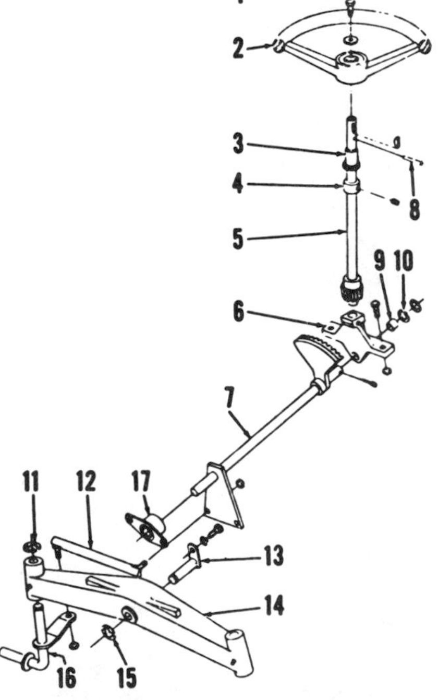

***Fig. WH42—Exploded view of front axle and steering gear typical of that used on models with horizontal crankshaft engines.***

1. Insert
2. Steering wheel
3. Nylon bushing
4. Collar
5. Upper steering shaft
6. Steering support
7. Lower steering shaft
8. Roll pin
9. Bushing
10. Shim washers
11. "E" ring
12. Tie rod
13. Pivot pin
14. Axle
15. "E" ring
16. Steering spindle
17. Flange bearing

***Fig. WH43—Exploded view of steering gear and front axle used on Model CG-8 which has a vertical crankshaft engine. See text.***

1. Insert
2. Steering wheel
3. Bushing
4. Collar
5. Steering shaft
6. Support
7. Lower shaft
8. Roll pin
9. Bushing
10. Shims
11. "E" ring
12. Tie rod
13. Pivot
14. Axle
15. Steering spindle
16. Cam plate

## STEERING GEAR

### Model GT-14

In order to remove steering gear from this model, first remove belt guard from right side of tractor. Disconnect ball joint (10–Fig. WH41) from arm of steering sector (8) and swing drag link (11) aside. Remove retaining cap screw from sector support shaft (7) and withdraw shaft at right side of tractor frame. Sector and shims will be freed for removal as shaft is pulled out. Remove insert and back out cap screw so steering wheel can be pulled. Remove Woodruff key, then pull steering shaft (6) down and out of steering support tube (1).

Reinstall steering gears by reversing removal procedure. Lubricate steering gears with multi-purpose grease.

### All Other Models

Minor adjustment can be made in mesh of pinion at lower end of steering shaft (5–Figs. WH42, WH43 or WH44) with gear sector quadrant (7) by means of shims (10). Use sufficient shims to eliminate backlash between gears when found to be excessive as well as to prevent binding.

First step in removal of steering gear is removal of steering wheel. Some steering wheels are attached to shaft by a roll pin while others are fitted over a Woodruff key and retained by a cap screw through wheel hub. When steering wheel has been removed, loosen set screw in collar (4) and lift steering shaft (5) clear of support (6). Disconnect inner ends of tie rods (12) from arm (bellcrank) of steering shaft (7), remove cotter pin, washers and shims (10) from rear of shaft and unbolt and remove support (6). Shaft and gear assemblies (5 and 7) can now be removed from underside of tractor. If defective flange bearing (17–Fig. WH42) should be unbolted for renewal at this time.

To reinstall, reverse removal procedure, Lubricate with multi-purpose grease.

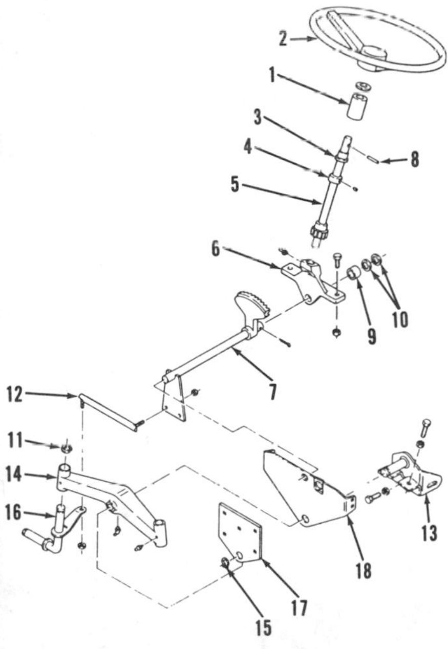


*Fig. WH44–Exploded view of steering gear and front axle assembly used on Model B-115.*

1. Spacer
2. Steering wheel
3. Bushing
4. Collar
5. Upper steering shaft
6. Support
7. Lower steering shaft
8. Roll pin
9. Bushing
10. Shims
11. "E" ring
12. Tie rod
13. Pivot bracket
14. Axle
15. Retaining ring
16. Steering spindle
17. Front plate
18. Axle support

# ENGINE

## REMOVE AND REINSTALL

### Model CG-8

To remove engine, disconnect battery cables and ignition wires. Disconnect fuel line and throttle and choke control cables. Detach exhaust header pipe from muffler. Remove drive belt and engine drive pulley. Remove hood and front grille assembly. Unscrew engine mounting cap screws and lift engine out of tractor.

To reinstall engine, reverse removal procedure.

### All Other Models

To remove engine, raise and secure hood or unbolt at hinge if complete removal is more convenient. Some tractors may have a crankcase drain extension pipe which could interfere with engine removal. If so, drain engine oil and remove pipe nipple so engine can clear frame. Disconnect battery cables. Identify and disconnect engine wiring as necessary.

Close fuel valve at tank and remove fuel hose from carburetor inlet, then disconnect choke and throttle controls at carburetor. Release muffler clamp from engine exhaust pipe for muffler removal.

On tractors fitted with manual pto clutch, disconnect control linkage so housing rod can be unbolted at upper end and removed from its bracket on tractor frame. Unbolt and remove belt guard (cover) from right side of tractor for access to clutch idler and belt. Release and remove drive belts from engine pulleys.

Check for possible interference of other parts in engine compartment area, unbolt engine from base plate and lift out of tractor frame.

To reinstall engine, reverse removal procedure.

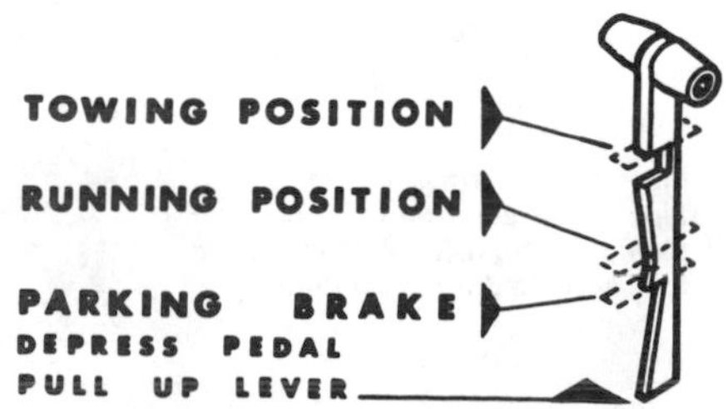


*Fig. WH45–Operating positions of parking brake lever used on CG-8 models. See text for details.*

## OVERHAUL

### All Models

Engine make and model are listed at the beginning of this section. To overhaul engine components and accessories, refer to Briggs & Stratton, Tecumseh and Kohler sections of this manual.

# CLUTCH AND BRAKE

### Model CG-8

Clutch used on this model is belt idler type. Clutch is disengaged by depressing parking brake lever all the way down and pulling back on lever so notch is engaged. By placing parking brake lever in this position and moving speed control lever as far forward as possible, tractor may be towed. With parking brake lever pulled up and locked, parking brake is engaged. See Fig. WH45 for parking brake diagram. To adjust parking brake and clutch, place parking brake lever in full up position and lock in place. Turn adjusting nut (7–Fig. WH46) until brake band is tight against brake drum. Place brake lever in "RUNNING POSITION." Loosen jam nuts (5), then turn inner nut until dimension shown in Fig. WH47 is obtained. Retighten nuts.

To make transmission neutral adjustments, refer to paragraph which applies in HYDROSTATIC TRANSMISSION section.

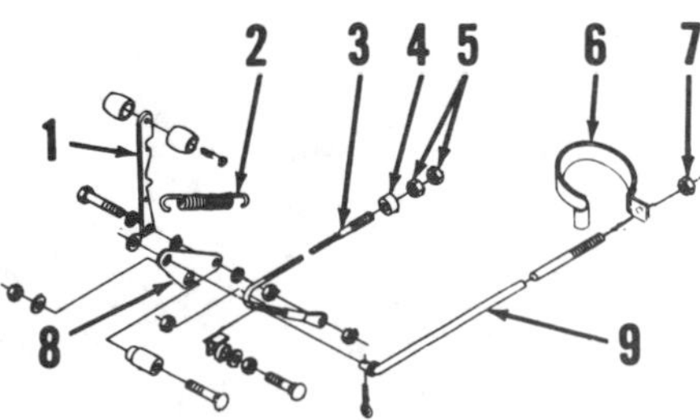


*Fig. WH46–Exploded view of operating parts of brake used on CG-8 tractors.*

1. Lever
2. Return spring
3. Clutch cable
4. Spacer
5. Adjusting nuts
6. Brake band
7. Adjusting nut
8. Brake pivot
9. Brake rod

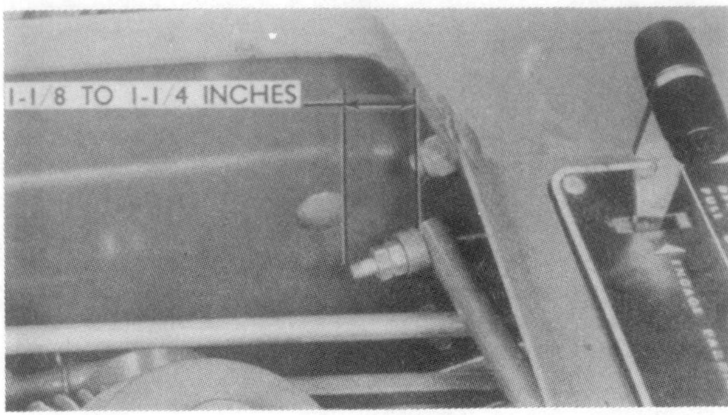


Fig. WH47—When brake (Fig. WH46) is adjusted as described in text, distance from inside edge of spacer to end of clutch cable adjuster threads should be 1⅛ to 1¼ inches (28-32 mm) as shown.

## Model 800 Automatic

A belt idler type clutch is used on 800 Automatic tractors. To disengage clutch, move parking brake lever to the rear which will also engage parking brake. Moving parking brake lever forward engages clutch and disengages parking brake. There is no adjustment for clutch or parking brake. Dynamic tractor braking is provided by hydrostatic transmission. Movement of speed control lever will increase or decrease tractor speed. Depressing brake-neutral pedal on left side of tractor returns transmission to neutral providing dynamic braking. To make transmission neutral adjustments, refer to applicable paragraph in HYDROSTATIC TRANSMISSION section.

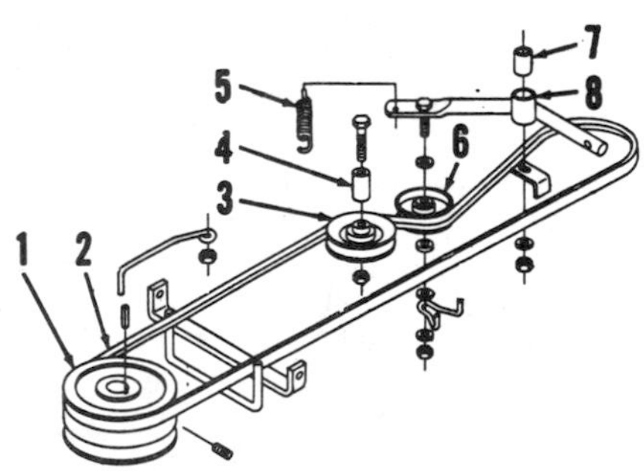


Fig. WH48—Exploded view of drive belt and clutch assembly used on CG-8 models.

1. Engine pulley
2. Drive belt
3. Idler pulley
4. Spacer
5. Spring
6. Clutch pulley
7. Bushing
8. Clutch arm

## Model B-115

Clutch used on this model is belt idler type. Clutch idler is spring loaded and does not require adjustment. The clutch is operated by moving clutch hand lever. Depressing brake-neutral pedal on left side of tractor returns hydrostatic transmission to neutral and provides dynamic tractor braking. When pedal is fully depressed, a mechanical disc brake is also applied for additional braking action.

To adjust disc brake, proceed as follows: Distance ("D"–Fig. WH49) between spring side (front) of nut and end of brake rod (1) should be ⅞-inch (22 mm). Adjust nut as required. With pedal released, loosen locknut and turn adjusting nut (3) on brake caliper until disc is locked. Then, loosen adjusting nut so brake rod (1) travels ⅜ to ¾-inch (9.5-19 mm) before brake pads contact disc. Tighten locknut.

To make transmission neutral adjustment, refer to appropriate paragraph in HYDROSTATIC TRANSMISSION section.

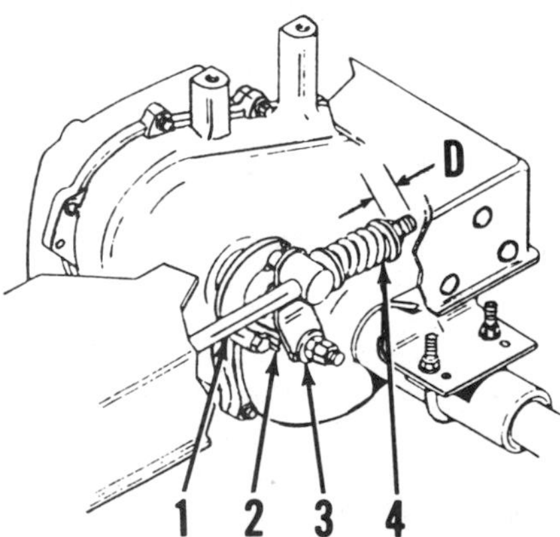


Fig. WH49—Brake adjustment points on Model B-115. Dimension "D" should be ⅞-inch (22 mm). Refer to text.

1. Brake rod
2. Disc brake assy.
3. Adjusting nut
4. Spring

Fig. WH50—View of band brake adjustment point typical of brake used on early "C" series tractors.

## Models C-121 – C-125 – C-141 – C-145 – C-161 – C-165

A hand operated, belt idler type clutch is used on these models. Clutch idler is spring loaded and does not require adjustment. Depressing brake-neutral pedal on left side of tractor returns hydrostatic transmission to neutral which provides dynamic tractor braking. When pedal is fully depressed, a mechanical band and drum type brake is applied for additional braking action.

To adjust brake, first remove left side cover. Depress brake pedal and latch parking brake lever in first notch in control cam. On early models, adjust nut (Fig. WH50) on end of brake rod until both rear wheels can not be turned, then tighten nut additional ½-turn. On later models, tighten nut on brake linkage bolt (Fig. WH51) until coils of spring are fully compressed, then back off nut ½-turn. On all models, be sure brake band does not drag when pedal is released.

To make transmission neutral adjustment, refer to appropriate paragraph in HYDROSTATIC TRANSMISSION section.

## All Other Models

These tractors are equipped with a belt idler type clutch. The clutch is spring loaded and does not require adjustment. Depressing neutral pedal on left side of tractor returns hydrostatic

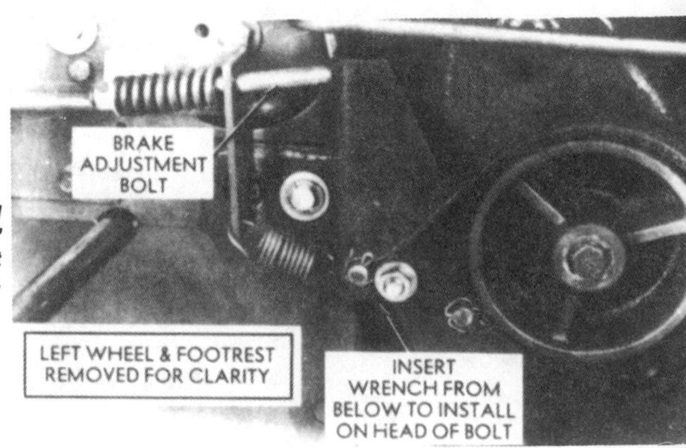


Fig. WH51—View of band type brake used on late "C" series tractors. Refer to text for adjustment procedure.

transmission to neutral which provides dynamic tractor braking. A mechanical brake is not used. Refer to HYDROSTATIC TRANSMISSION section for neutral linkage adjustment procedure.

# ELECTRIC PTO CLUTCH

## All Models So Equipped

Some models are equipped with an electro-magnetic pto clutch of design shown in Fig. WH52.

Should clutch fail, determination should be made of cause for failure. First check tractor electrical system for blown fuse, defective clutch switch, bad or corroded connections or broken wires. Best procedure calls for use of an ohmmeter or test light to locate any possible break in continuity.

If no fault is found in wiring to clutch body, a voltage check should be made across clutch leads (from switch wire to ground lug) with switch "ON". If voltmeter reading is ZERO, recheck wiring for open circuit or bad ground. If reading is over 8 volts, then use an ohm meter to check resistance in clutch coil by connecting ohmmeter across connector terminals. Normal resistance reading should fall between 2.75 and 3.6 ohms. If reading is lower or higher, then coil winding is defective and renewal is called for.

Earlier manufacturer policy required entire clutch assembly be renewed in case of failure. This has been changed as follows:

Based on current service bulletins, clutch unit breaks down into two components, a housing and pulley assembly and a field winding and bearing assembly. In case of failure, field and bearing assembly is more likely to be at fault and may be renewed separately.

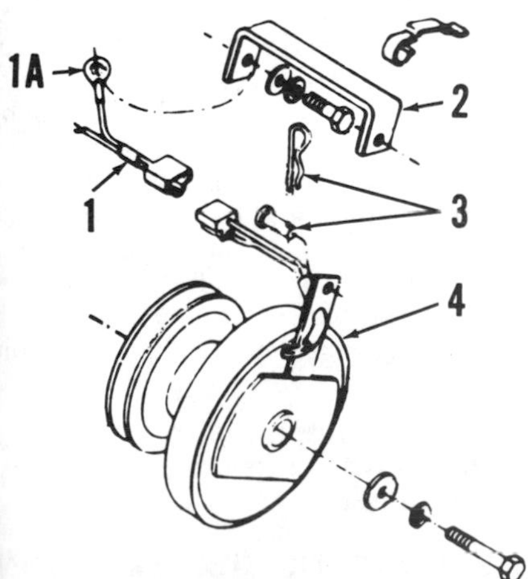


*Fig. WH52—Typical electric pto clutch used on some tractors.*

1. Cable & connector
1A. Ground lug
2. Mounting bracket
3. Clevis pin & cotter
4. Clutch assy.

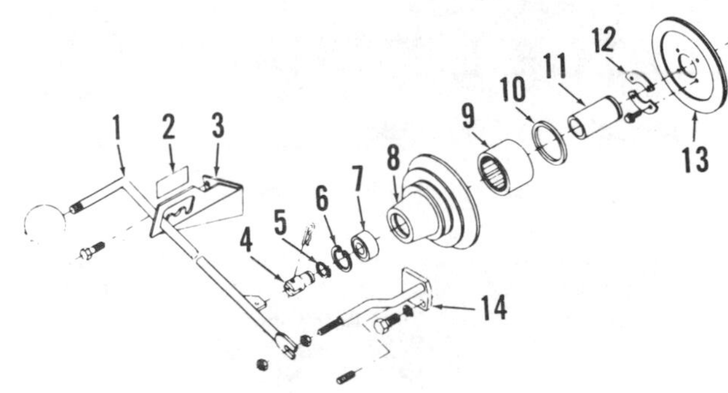


*Fig. WH53—Exploded view of early style manual pto clutch used on some models.*

1. Clutch control rod
2. Adjustment decal
3. Bracket
4. Clutch shaft
5. Snap ring (¾-inch)
6. Snap ring (1¾ inch)
7. Ball bearing
8. Pulley & housing
9. Bearing
10. Seal
11. Bearing race
12. Bearing race retainer (2)
13. Clutch plate
14. Rod & plate assy.

**R&R ELECTRIC PTO CLUTCH.** Refer to Fig. WH52 and uncouple connector for electrical leads (1). Remove pin (3), wiring clips, and unbolt bracket (2) for removal. Back out center bolt from clutch hub. After center bolt and washer are removed, a puller bolt (jack screw) is threaded into clutch hub counterbore to pull unit from end of crankshaft. On clutches with part number 7915, 8278 or 9656 (earlier production) a 1 inch 8 thread bolt, five inches long is needed.

**NOTE: On clutch number 7915 only, a snap ring must first be removed. If clutch assembly is numbered 101470, 101472 or 101473, (later production) a ⅝-inch NC (11 thread) bolt four inches long is required for use as a puller.**

After clutch is removed from end of crankshaft, leave puller bolt threaded in place and field and bearing assembly can be removed from housing by striking bolt head a sharp blow on a solid surface. After bearing and field coil assembly is so loosened and separated, a new assembly can be pressed into housing bore until snug against retaining shoulder. Use an arbor which contacts only inner race of new bearing when pressing assemblies together. Reassembly is then completed by replacing all parts in reverse of removal order. After control wires are reconnected, test operation.

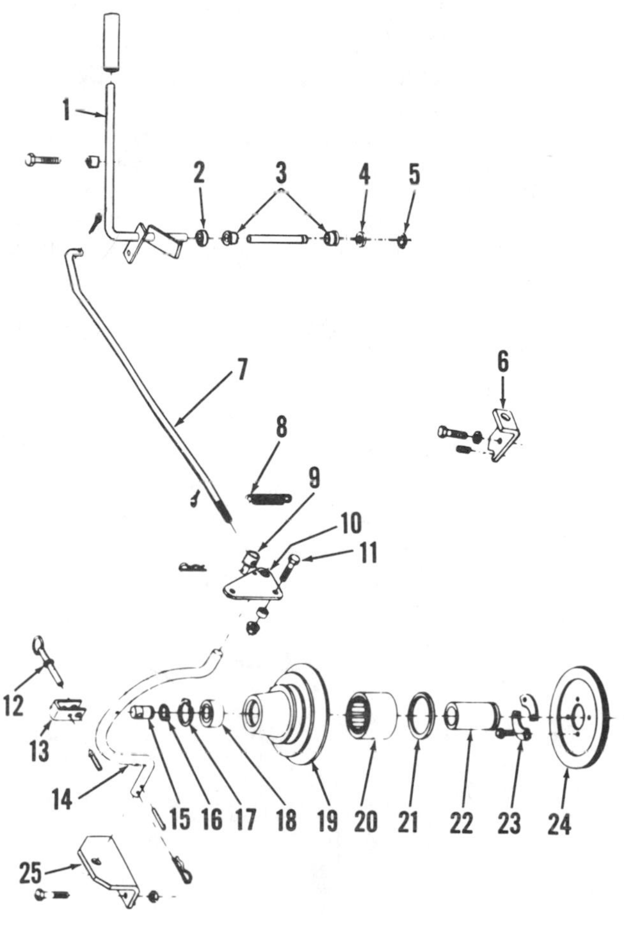

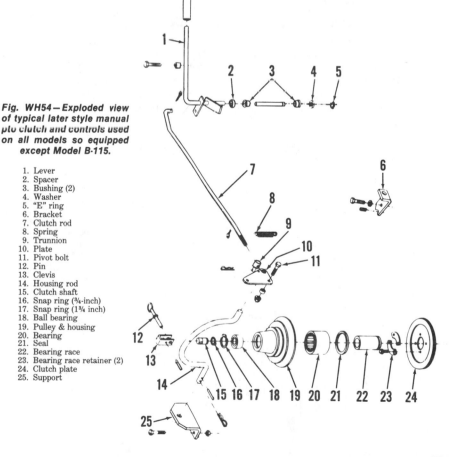

*Fig. WH54—Exploded view of typical later style manual pto clutch and controls used on all models so equipped except Model B-115.*

1. Lever
2. Spacer
3. Bushing (2)
4. Washer
5. "E" ring
6. Bracket
7. Clutch rod
8. Spring
9. Trunnion
10. Plate
11. Pivot bolt
12. Pin
13. Clevis
14. Housing rod
15. Clutch shaft
16. Snap ring (¾-inch)
17. Snap ring (1¾ inch)
18. Ball bearing
19. Pulley & housing
20. Bearing
21. Seal
22. Bearing race
23. Bearing race retainer (2)
24. Clutch plate
25. Support

# MANUAL PTO CLUTCH

## All Models So Equipped

Older style pto clutch used on some models is shown in exploded view in Fig. WH53. This clutch has no pressure spring or over-center feature. All engagement and holding force is provided by control rod (1–Fig. WH53) which is fully applied when placed in innermost notch of bracket plate (3). Clutch adjustment is made by setting of two nuts on threaded portion of rod (14) to control pivot position of forked end of control rod (1). Adjust these nuts so clutch is just disengaged with rod in shallow center notch of bracket (3). This will provide full engagement when rod (1) is set into inner notch of bracket and complete disengagement in outer notch. All parts are renewable including facings and rivets for clutch plate (13) if clutch operation becomes unsatisfactory.

Newer style pto clutch is shown in Fig. WH54. If clutch slips during normal operation, turn trunnion (Fig. WH56) towards rear of operating rod (one turn at a time) until clutch slippage is eliminated. To adjust pto brake, loosen adjusting bolts and engage pto clutch. Move brake pad bracket to obtain 0.012 inch (0.305 mm) clearance between brake pad and pulley face, then tighten adjusting bolts.

Pto clutch assembly shown in Fig. WH55 is used on Model B-115.

To adjust, engage clutch and turn brake adjustment bolt (Fig. WH57) to obtain 0.010 inch (0.254 mm) clearance between brake pad and clutch pulley face. There should be a 3/8 inch (9.5 mm) gap between threaded spacer and clutch brake bracket as shown. If not, loosen locknut and turn threaded spacer as required to obtain 3/8 inch (9.5 mm) gap. Recheck brake pad adjustment.

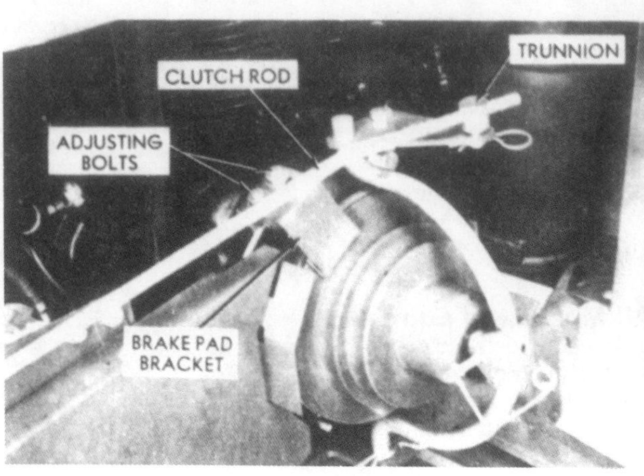


*Fig. WH56—View of current style pto clutch used on models so equipped.*

**REMOVE AND REINSTALL.** To remove pto clutch unit shown in Fig. WH54, disconnect clutch rod trunnion (9) from shift plate (10). Remove yoke pin (12) and swing shift plate (10) and yoke (14) out of the way. Remove pto brake. With belts removed, slide pto clutch housing (19) off shaft. Remove four bolts securing retainer plates (23) onto clutch plate (24). Slide bearing race (22) off shaft and remove clutch plate and facing. Renew worn parts as necessary and reinstall in reverse order of removal. Adjust as previously outlined.

To remove pto clutch unit shown in Fig. WH55, remove adjusting bolt (7) and brake bracket (6). Withdraw pto pulley and clutch cone (12). Remove crankshaft bolt (15) and bearing race (17). Depress clutch pedal and slip drive belt off engine pulley (18), then remove pulley from crankshaft. Renew worn parts as necessary and reinstall by reversing removal procedure. Adjust as previously outlined.

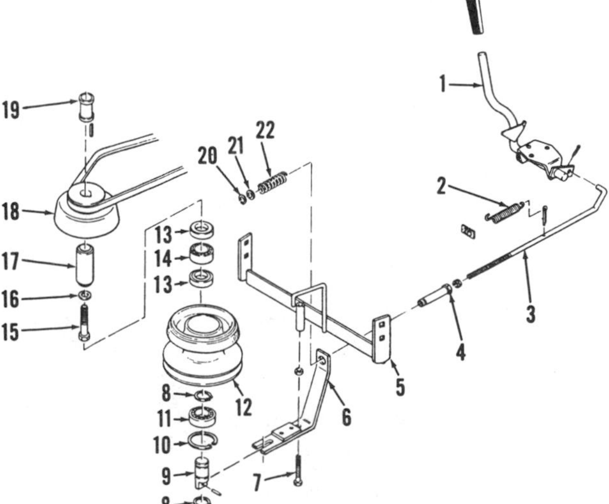


*Fig. WH55—Exploded view of manual pto clutch and operating linkage used on Model B-115.*

1. Control lever
2. Spring
3. Clutch rod
4. Threaded spacer
5. Clutch mounting bracket
6. Brake bracket
7. Adjusting bolt
8. Snap ring
9. Clutch shaft
10. Snap ring
11. Ball bearing
12. Pto pulley & clutch cone
13. Seals
14. Needle bearing
15. Bolt
16. Special washer
17. Bearing race
18. Engine pulley & clutch housing
19. Spacer tube
20. Snap ring
21. Special washer
22. Spring

# HYDROSTATIC TRANSMISSION

## LUBRICATION

### Models Equipped With Eaton Hydrostatic Transmission

#### HYDROSTATIC TRANSMISSION CAPACITIES

| Tractor Model | Capacity | Type |
|---|---|---|
| CG-8 | 2⅔ pints (1.2 L) | "F" |
| 800 Automatic | 1½ pints (0.7 L) | "F" |
| B-115 | 1½ pints (0.7 L) | SAE 20 |
| C-125 (Late) | 10 pints (4.7 L) | 10W-30/40 |
| C-145 (Late) | 10 pints (4.7 L) | 10W-30/40 |
| C-165 (Late) | 10 pints (4.7 L) | 10W-30/40 |

Where Type "F" is specified, "Dexron", Wheel Horse No. 8827 or Texaco Transhydral No. 2209 may be used. Premium engine oil is specified for units calling for SAE 20, SAE 10W-30 or 10W-40. On "C" series tractors, manufacturer recommends renewing transmission oil and oil filter every 100 hours of operation or once a year, whichever occurs first. On all other models periodic renewal of transmission oil is not necessary unless oil becomes contaminated.

### Models Equipped with Sundstrand Hydrostatic Transmission

#### HYDROSTATIC TRANSMISSION CAPACITIES

| Tractor Model | Capacity | Type |
|---|---|---|
| Charger 10 | 10 pints (4.7 L) | "F" |

| | | |
|---|---|---|
| 10HP-Automatic | 10 pints (4.7 L) | "F" |
| B-100 | 12 pints (5.7 L) | 10W-30/40 |
| Charger 12 | 10 pints (4.7 L) | "F" |
| 12HP-Automatic | 10 pints (4.7 L) | "F" |
| C-120 | 12 pints (5.7 L) | 10W-30/40 |
| C-121 | 11 pints (5.2 L) | 10W-30/40 |
| C-125 (Early) | 11 pints (5.2 L) | 10W-30/40 |
| GT-4 | 10 pints (4.7 L) | "F" |
| Bronco 14 | 10 pints (4.7 L) | "F" |
| 14HP-Automatic | 10 pints (4.7 L) | "F" |
| C-141 | 11 pints (5.2 L) | 10W-30/40 |
| C-145 (Early) | 11 pints (5.2 L) | 10W-30/40 |
| C-160 | 12 pints (5.7 L) | 10W-30/40 |
| C-161 | 11 pints (5.2 L) | 10W-30/40 |
| C-165 (Early) | 11 pints (5.2 L) | 10W-30/40 |
| 16HP-Automatic | 10 pints (4.7 L) | "F" |

Where Type "F" is specified, "Dexron," Wheel Horse No. 8827 or Texaco Transhydral No. 2209 may be used. Premium engine oil is specified for hydrostatic units calling for SAE 10W-30 or 10W-40. Fluid used also serves as lubricant for reduction gear sets in final drives. Main fluid reservoir is the differential case.

Manufacturer recommends renewing transmission oil and oil filter after every 100 hours of operation or once a year, whichever occurs first.

## LINKAGE ADJUSTMENT

### Model CG-8

Tractor should not creep with speed control lever in neutral position. To make adjustment, block up under tractor so rear wheels do not contact ground. Lift off seat and fender assembly and remove transmission fan from input pulley. Refer to Fig. WH58 and loosen set screw so adjusting screw will turn. Start engine and depress and release neutral pedal. Turn adjusting screw in or out until rear wheels stop rotating. Stop engine and tighten set screw. Recheck adjustment by moving speed control lever to forward and reverse positions and depressing and releasing neutral pedal. Speed control lever should return to neutral and wheels should not rotate with engine running.

**CAUTION: Do not run transmission longer than necessary without fan attached.**

To adjust freedom of movement of speed control lever, turn friction adjusting nut shown in Fig. WH58. Approximately 8-10 pounds (35.6-44.5 N) of force at grip should be required to move speed control lever.

### Model 800 Automatic

Tractor should not creep when speed control lever is in neutral position. To make adjustment, block up under tractor so rear wheels do not contact ground. Remove instruction plate on console. Depress and release neutral pedal. Loosen set screw shown in Fig. WH60 until neutral adjusting screw shown in Fig. WH61 can be turned. Start engine and move parking brake lever forward to engage clutch. Turn neutral adjusting screw in or out until rear wheels do not rotate. Stop engine and tighten set screw. Recheck adjust-

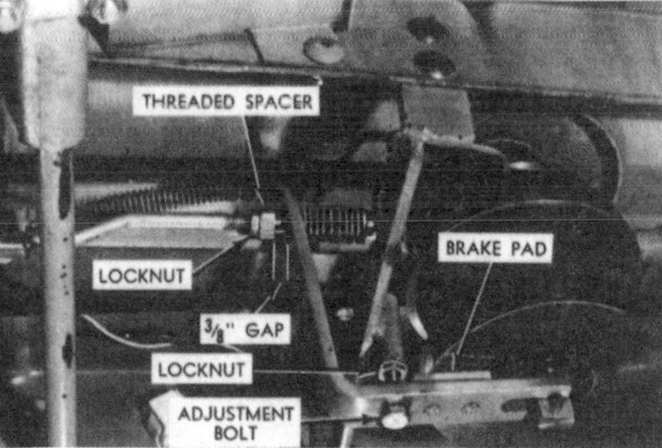


*Fig. WH57—View of pto clutch used on Model B-115 tractors.*

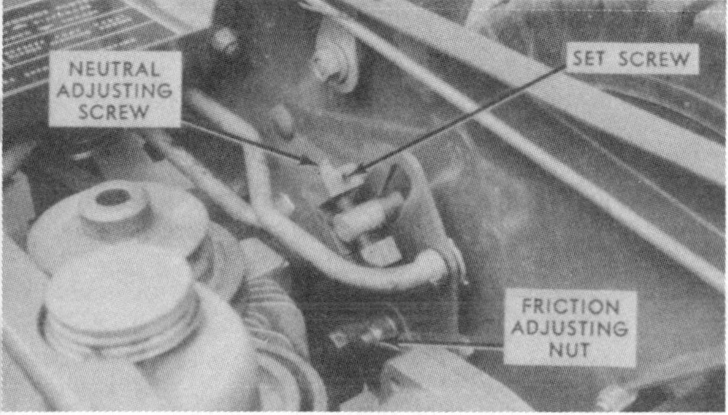


*Fig. WH58—Neutral adjustment point for CG-8 tractors. Refer to text.*

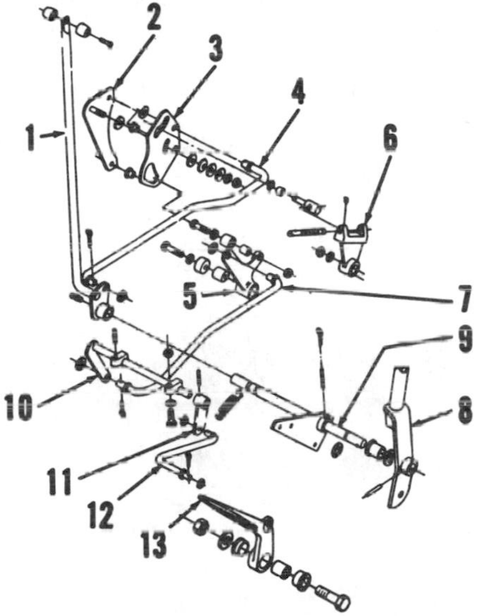


*Fig. WH59—Transmission control linkage for Model CG-8.*

1. Speed control lever
2. Mounting plate
3. Speed control cam
4. Speed control rod
5. Neutral return lever
6. Transmission control lever
7. Neutral return rod
8. Lift lever
9. Lever shaft
10. Lever & shaft
11. Neutral arm
12. Neutral return rod
13. Pedal

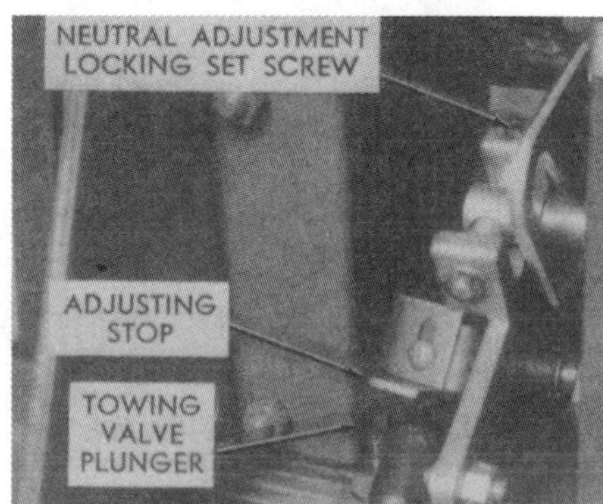


*Fig. WH60—View of towing valve plunger and control linkage for Model 800 Automatic.*

ment by moving speed control lever to forward and reverse positions and depress and release neutral pedal. Rear wheels should not rotate when engine is running. Set adjusting stop (Fig. WH60) for 1/16 inch (1.5 mm) clearance from plunger with towing valve lever in DRIVE position.

To adjust freedom of movement of speed control lever, turn friction adjusting nut shown in Fig. WH61. Approximately 8-10 pounds (35.6-44.5 N) of force at grip should be required to move speed control lever.

## Model B-115 – Late Models C-125 – C-145 – C-165

Tractor should not creep in either direction when speed control lever is returned to neutral position. To adjust linkage, first remove seat and rear fender on Models C-125, C-145 and C-165. On all models, raise and support rear of tractor so both wheels are free to turn. With transmission at normal operating temperature, operate engine at full throttle. Depress brake-neutral pedal fully, then release pedal. Loosen lockbolt (Fig. WH63) and turn eccentric until wheels stop turning. Tighten lockbolt and retest for neutral from both directions.

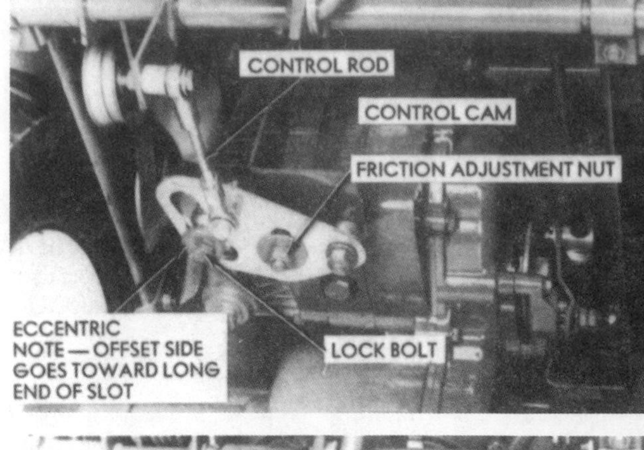


*Fig. WH63—View of control linkage used on Model B-115. Models C-125, C-145 and C-165 are similar. Refer to text.*

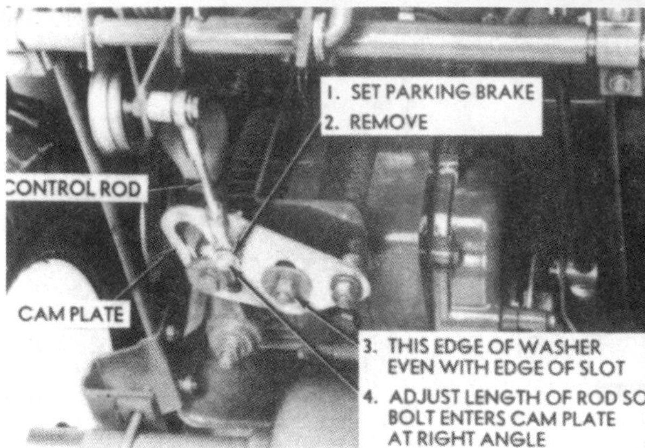


*Fig. WH64—View of control linkage adjustment points on B-115 tractor. Adjustment on Models C-125, C-145 and C-165 is similar. Refer to text.*

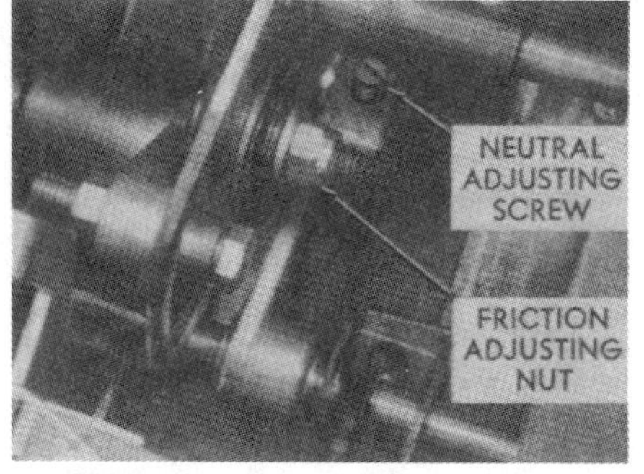


*Fig. WH61—Transmission linkage adjustment points for Model 800 Automatic. Refer to text.*

**CAUTION: Keep hands away from cooling fan and other moving parts.**

If tractor cannot be neutralized with eccentric, length of control rod must be adjusted. Refer to Fig. WH64 and disconnect control rod from cam plate. Adjust position of cam plate so rear edge of friction washer is even with rear end of cam plate slot. Adjust length of control rod so bolt enters cam plate at a right angle. Recheck neutral adjustment as previously outlined.

To adjust freedom of movement of speed control lever, turn friction adjusting nut (Fig. WH63) until approximately six pounds (26.7 N) of force at grip is required to move speed control lever.

On Models C-125, C-145 and C-165, be sure control lever is centered in detent spring notch after making neutral adjustment. Spring is provided with slotted mounting holes for adjustment. Belt cover and control plate cover in front of seat must be removed for access to spring.

## All Other Models

If tractor should creep while control handle is in neutral position, transmission neutral setting must be adjusted. To make neutral adjustment, block rear wheels off ground and remove instruction plate located in front of seat. Loosen set screw in arm with Allen wrench as shown in Fig. WH65. With engine operating, park brake disengaged and foot pedal depressed, insert a short screwdriver through hole in nylon cam and rotate eccentric cam pin until wheels stop rotating. Tighten set screw in arm and reinstall instruction plate.

**NOTE: Lobe on eccentric pin must be upward for proper operation.**

The control handle is friction loaded so it will hold any desired speed. If handle does not stay where set during operation, friction can be increased on early models by tightening the two screws

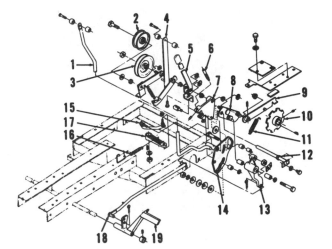

*Fig. WH62—Brake and transmission linkage for Model 800 Automatic shown in exploded view.*

1. Speed control lever
2. Idler pulley
3. Belt tension pulley
4. Park brake handle
5. Towing valve lever
6. Neutral adjusting screw
7. Cam follower lever
8. Bracket
9. Brake arm
10. Brake disc
11. Spring
12. Cam rod & bushing
13. Pivot arm
14. Speed control cam
15. Control rod
16. Spring
17. Control arm
18. Rod
19. Pedal

(Fig. WH65) that maintain pressure on nylon cam. On later models, loosen locknut shown in Fig. WH66 and turn friction adjustment screw. Approximately 6 pounds (26.7 N) of force at grip should be required to move speed control lever.

Later models have an adjustable detent spring which helps to hold control lever in neutral. This flat spring is behind belt guard, bolted to hood stand. Adjust in slotted mounting holes to hold lever firmly in neutral.

## REMOVE AND REINSTALL

### Model CG-8

To remove transmission, remove seat and fender assembly. Drain lubricant from differential. Disconnect control linkage at transmission. Remove transmission fan, position parking brake in towing position so drive belt will be loose and slip drive belt off transmission pulley. Disconnect oil line from reservoir to transmission. Remove transmission mounting screws and lift transmission out of tractor.

To reinstall transmission, reverse removal procedure. Adjust transmission linkage as outlined in preceding paragraphs. Refill differential to level of fill plug with SAE 90 EP gear oil. Hydrostatic transmission reservoir should be filled with Type "F" automatic transmission fluid.

### Model 800 Automatic

To remove transmission, remove seat and fender assembly and drive belt. Disconnect linkage from transmission. Raise and support rear of tractor. Unscrew retaining cap screws on differential and remove rear drive assembly. Transmission may now be separated from differential.

To reinstall transmission, reverse removal procedure. Adjust transmission linkage as outlined in preceding section. Fill transmission reservoir with Type "F" automatic transmission fluid to correct mark.

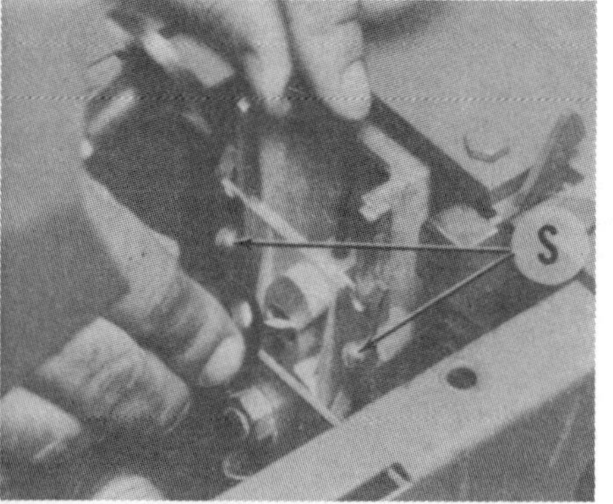


*Fig. WH65—View to show neutral adjustment procedure on models with Sundstrand transmissions. Screws (S) are used to adjust control handle friction on earlier models.*

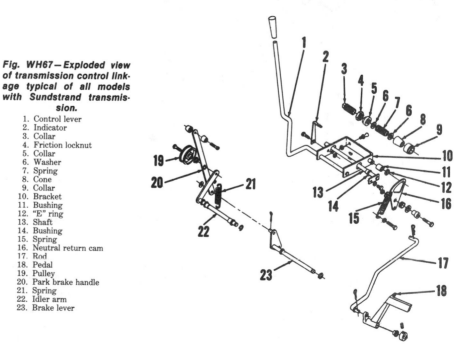

### Model B-115

To remove transmission, first depress clutch pedal and slip drive belt off transmission input pulley. Disconnect transmission control rod. Unbolt and remove actuating lever and pins from disc brake. Support transaxle with suitable stands or jack. Unbolt and remove transaxle mounting "U" bolts. Raise rear of frame with a hoist and roll front of tractor away from transaxle. Tip transaxle onto left wheel and remove right wheel. Remove four retaining bolts and withdraw transmission from transaxle housing.

Remove input pulley, cooling fan and output gear. Use a suitable puller to remove control arm. Do not attempt to hammer or pry off arm as internal damage to transmission may result.

To reinstall transmission, reverse removal steps. Be sure side of cooling fan with manufacturer's name faces transmission. Adjust control linkage and brake linkage as previously outlined.

### Models (Late) C-125 – C-145 – C-165

To remove transmission, first remove seat, rear fender and control cover plate. Support rear of tractor with stands under footrest rear cross rods. Drain oil from transaxle. Remove rear wheels. Shut off fuel and disconnect fuel hose. Unbolt oil filter base from seat

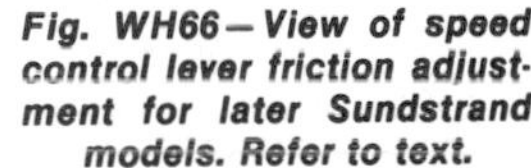

*Fig. WH66—View of speed control lever friction adjustment for later Sundstrand models. Refer to text.*

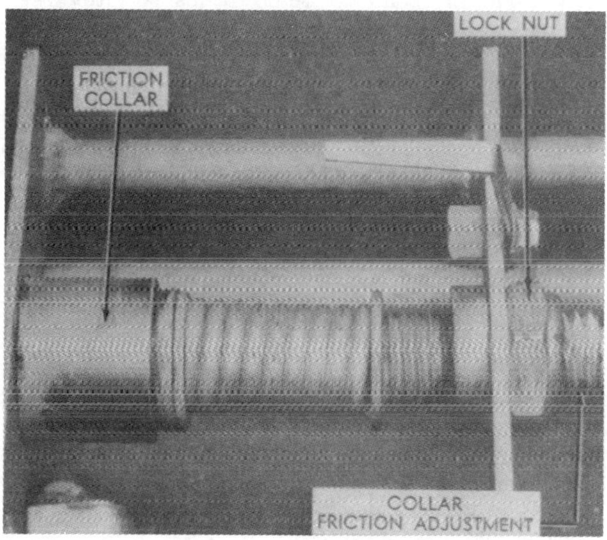


*Fig. WH67—Exploded view of transmission control linkage typical of all models with Sundstrand transmission.*

1. Control lever
2. Indicator
3. Collar
4. Friction locknut
5. Collar
6. Washer
7. Spring
8. Cone
9. Collar
10. Bracket
11. Bushing
12. "E" ring
13. Shaft
14. Bushing
15. Spring
16. Neutral return cam
17. Rod
18. Pedal
19. Pulley
20. Park brake handle
21. Spring
22. Idler arm
23. Brake lever

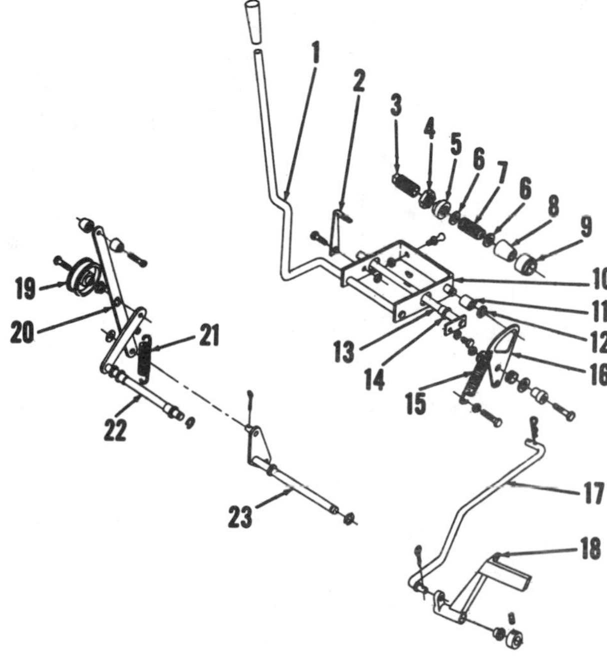

support. Remove two bolts, bracket and lift tube from top of transaxle. Remove two bolts securing seat support bracket and withdraw fuel tank and seat support as an assembly. Remove cooling fan and slip drive belt off input pulley. Disconnect speed control rod from cam plate. Disconnect all hydraulic hoses.

**NOTE: A 11/16 inch crow foot wrench will be needed to disconnect oil line (coming from oil filter) at front of transmission.**

Unbolt and remove transmission from transaxle housing. Remove input pulley, output gear and control arm from transmission. Do not attempt to hammer or pry control arm off control shaft as transmission internal damage may result.

Reinstall transmission by reversing removal procedure. Tighten transmission mounting bolts to 30-35 ft.-lbs. (41-47 N·m). Reinstall cooling fan making sure side with manufacturer's name faces out. Adjust control linkage and brake linkage as necessary.

### Models C-121 – C-141 – C-160 – Early Models C-125 – C-145 – C-165

To remove hydrostatic transmission, drain transaxle and remove control cover plate. Remove drive belt and seat assembly. Disconnect tail light wires and remove seat pan. Close fuel valve and disconnect fuel line at tank. Remove seat support brackets and fuel tank. Disconnect motion control lever and brake rod. On models equipped with hydraulic lift, disconnect two hydraulic lines at pump and mark for reinstallation. Support frame and remove left rear wheel. Remove four mounting bolts and withdraw hydrostatic unit from transaxle housing.

Reverse removal procedure to reinstall and refill with oil. Perform neutral adjustment and brake adjustment as outlined in previous paragraphs.

### All Other Models

To remove hydrostatic unit from tractor, first drain transaxle and raise and block rear of tractor frame. Remove left rear wheel. Remove seat, fender and tool box. It may be necessary to remove foot rest on some models. Remove cooling fan guard (early models) and drive belt guard, then release and remove belt from transmission pulley. Remove cooling fan and remove pulley from input shaft. Disconnect hydraulic hoses from hydrostatic unit and move hoses out of the way. Remove access plate and unbolt hydrostatic unit from transaxle housing. Slip unit rearward to disengage cam block pin from cam block and withdraw from transaxle.

To reinstall transmission, reverse removal steps. Refill with recommended transmission oil. Adjust transmission control linkage and brakes as outlined in previous paragraphs.

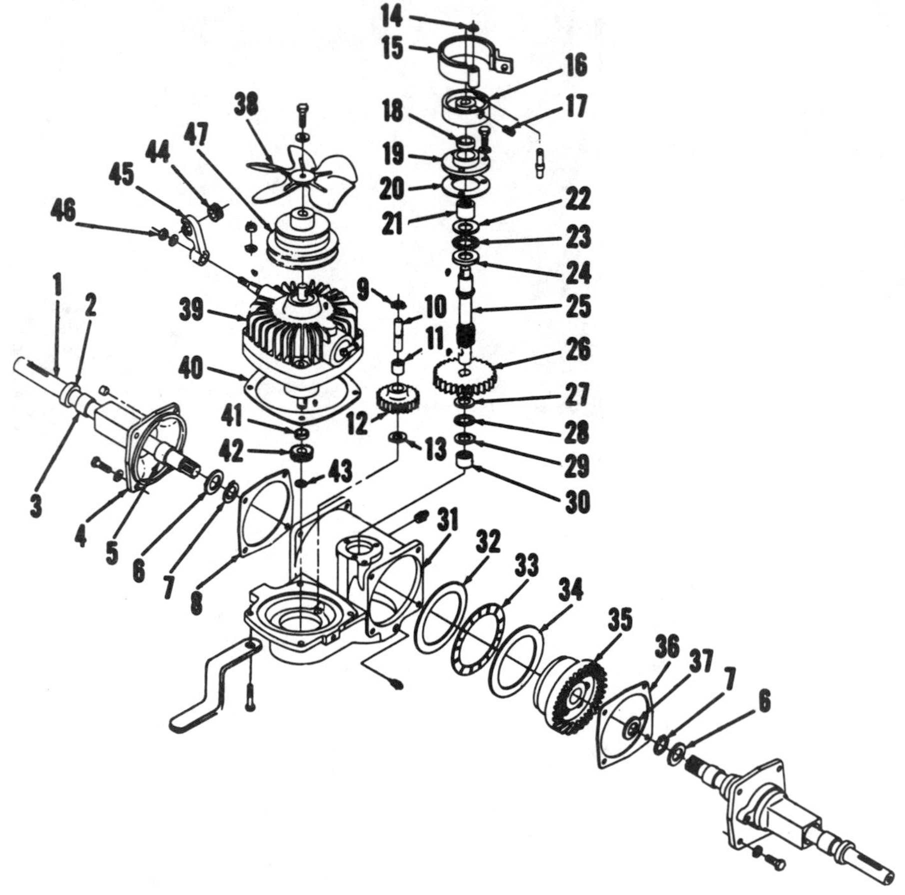

*Fig. WH91 – Exploded view of final drive assembly for CG-8 models. See Fig. WH92 for parts view of differential (35).*

1. Axle
2. Seal
3. Needle bearing
4. Axle housing
5. Needle bearing
6. Thrust race
7. Snap ring
8. Housing gasket
9. Snap ring
10. Idler shaft
11. Needle bearing
12. Idler gear
13. Thrust race
14. Snap ring
15. Brake band
16. Brake drum
17. Set screw
18. Seal
19. End cap (old style)
20. Gasket
21. Needle bearing
22. Thrust washer
23. Thrust bearing
24. Thrust washer
25. Pinion shaft
26. Drive gear
27. Thrust washer
28. Thrust bearing
29. Thrust washer
30. Needle bearing
31. Housing
32. Thrust race
33. Thrust bearing
34. Thrust race
35. Differential
36. Gasket
37. Washer (special)
38. Fan
39. Hydrostatic unit
40. Gasket
41. Spacer
42. Pinion
43. Snap ring
44. Adjuster nut
45. Lever (old style)
46. Shaft nut
47. Transmission pulley

## OVERHAUL

### All Models

Models CG-8, 800 Automatic and B115 are equipped with an Eaton Model 6 hydrostatic transmission. Late Model C-125 and Models C-145 and C-165 are equipped with an Eaton Model 11 hydrostatic transmission. All other models are equipped with either a Sundstrand "Hydrogear" model or Sundstrand "Piston-To-Piston" model hydrostatic transmission. Refer to the appropriate Eaton or Sundstrand section in HYDROSTATIC TRANSMISSION SERVICE section for overhaul procedure.

# REDUCTION GEARS AND DIFFERENTIAL

### Model CG-8

**R&R AND OVERHAUL.** To remove reduction gear and differential unit, disconnect control linkage at transmission. Remove transmission fan, position parking brake in towing position so drive belt will be loose and slip drive belt off transmission pulley. Disconnect oil line from transmission to oil reservoir. Disconnect brake linkage at brake. Drain lubricant from differential. Block up under rear of tractor and unscrew retaining cap screws at axle housings. Roll transmission and differential unit from tractor. Remove wheels and hubs and remove brake assembly. Separate transmission from differential.

To disassemble reduction gear and differential unit, position unit so bottom cover is up and remove cover and gasket. Remove idler gear assembly (9 through 13–Fig. WH91). Remove pinion drive gear (26), thrust washers (27 and 29) and thrust bearing (28). Place assembly on end so rear of unit is down. Unscrew end cap (19) cap screws and withdraw pinion drive gear assembly (18 through 25). Unscrew left axle housing retaining cap screws and remove left axle assembly. Remove differential assembly (35) and thrust washers (32 and 34) and thrust bearing (33). Unscrew right axle housing retaining cap screws and remove right axle assembly.

Inspect all components for damage or excessive wear. Axle gears and differential assembly shown in Fig. WH92 are available only as a unit assembly. To reassemble reduction gear and differential unit, reverse disassembly procedure and observe the following points: Install right axle assembly so breather plug is towards top of differential housing. Sharp edge of snap rings (7–Fig. WH91) should be towards axle splines. Splines of left axle thrust washer (5–Fig. WH92) must be adjacent to differential axle gear (4). Concave surface of washer (37–Fig. WH91) must be next to thrust washer (5–Fig. WH92). Thin washer (22–Fig. WH91) is above thrust bearing (23) while thick washer (24) is below thrust bearing. When installing end cap (19) and pinion gear shaft assembly in case, oil slot in end cap must align with relief in case (Fig. WH93). When assembly is completed, fill differential to level of fill plug with SAE 90 EP gear oil.

**Fig. WH92 – View of differential unit (35 – Fig. WH91). Assemble splined thrust washer (5) with splines against axle gear (4).**

1. Differential unit
2. Axle gear (R.H.)
3. Spacer
4. Axle gear (L.H.)
5. Thrust washer

**Fig. WH93 – Align oil slot in end cap with oil relief slot (R) in housing during reassembly. See text.**

## Models 800 Automatic – B-115

**R&R AND OVERHAUL.** To remove transaxle assembly, remove seat and fender assembly on Model 800 Automatic. On Model B-115, remove brake adjusting nuts and slide brake actuating lever off disc brake assembly. On all models, disconnect control linkage from transmission. Depress clutch pedal and slip drive belt off transmission pulley. Support transaxle with suitable stands, then unbolt transaxle from frame. Raise rear of frame and roll tractor forward from transaxle.

Remove wheels and hubs and drain lubricant from differential. Separate transmission from differential unit. Remove brake disc from brake shaft. Clean axle shafts and remove any burrs on shafts. Unscrew cap screws and drive out dowel pins in cover (29–Fig. WH94). Lift cover off case and axle shaft. Withdraw brake shaft (5), input gear (4) and thrust washers (3 and 6) from case. Remove output shaft (11), output gear (10), spacer (9), thrust washer (8) and differential assembly from case. Axle shaft housings (20 and 22) must be pressed from case and cover.

To disassemble differential, unscrew four cap screws and separate axle shaft and carriage assemblies from ring gear (28). Drive blocks (25), bevel pinon gears (26) and drive pin (27) can now be removed from ring gear. Remove snap rings (12) and slide axle shafts (18 and 23) from axle gears (13) and carriers (16 and 24).

Clean and inspect all parts and renew any parts damaged or excessively worn. When installing needle bearings, press bearings in from inside of case or cover until bearings are 0.015-0.020 inch (0.381-0.508 mm) below thrust surfaces. Be sure heads of differential cap screws and right axle shaft (18) are installed in right carrier (16). Right axle shaft is installed through case (1). Tighten differential cap screws to 7 ft.-lbs. (9 N·m) and cover cap screws to 10 ft.-lbs. (14 N·m). Differential assembly and output shaft (11) must be installed in case at same time. Remainder of assembly is reverse of disassembly procedure.

Reinstall transaxle by reversing removal steps. Fill unit with 2¾ pints (1.3L) of SAE 90 EP gear oil. Adjust linkage as necessary.

**Fig. WH94 – Exploded view of Peerless reduction gear and differential used on 800 Automatic tractors. Peerless Model 1320 transaxle used on B-115 hydrostatic drive tractors is similar.**

1. Case
2. Gasket
3. Washer
4. Idler gear
5. Brake shaft
6. Washer
7. Bearing
8. Washer
9. Spacer
10. Output gear
11. Output shaft
12. Snap ring
13. Bevel gear
14. Thrust washers
15. Thrust bearing
16. Differential carrier
18. Axle (R.H.)
19. Bushing
20. Axle housing
21. Oil seal
22. Axle housing
23. Axle (L.H.)
24. Differential carrier
25. Drive block
26. Pinion
27. Pinion shaft
28. Ring gear
29. Cover

## Models (Late) C-125 – C-145 – C-165

**R&R AND OVERHAUL.** To remove transaxle assembly, first remove seat, fenders and control cover plate. Support rear of tractor with suitable stands. Shut off fuel and disconnect fuel hose. Remove lift tube and bracket from top of transaxle. Unbolt oil filter base from seat support, then unbolt and remove seat support and fuel tank as an assembly. Remove cooling fan and slip drive

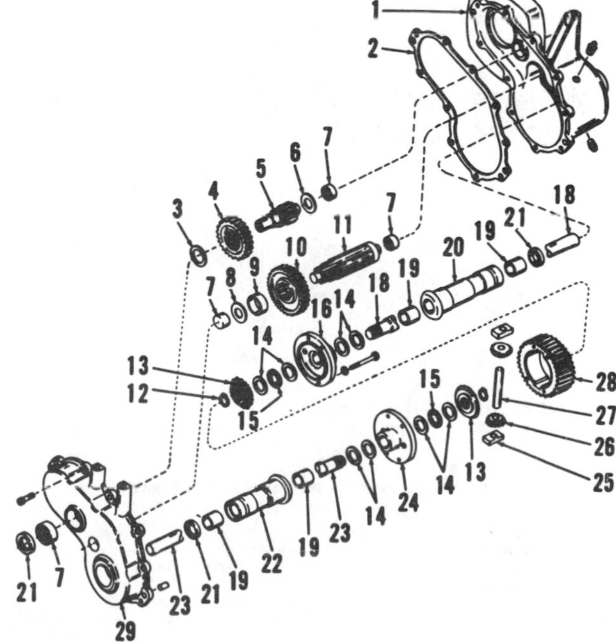

belt off input pulley. Disconnect transmission control linkage and brake linkage. Disconnect hydraulic hoses from transmission.

**NOTE: An 11/16 inch crow foot wrench is needed to disconnect line (coming from oil cooler) at front of transmission.**

Support transaxle with a floor jack, remove bolts securing transaxle to frame and roll assembly rearward from tractor. Drain fluid from transaxle housing and thoroughly clean exterior of housing. Separate hydrostatic unit from housing.

To disassemble transaxle, remove rear wheels and hubs. Remove burrs and corrosion from axle shafts. Remove brake drum and remove burrs and corrosion from brake shaft. Remove eight retaining bolts and lift off left case half. A soft mallet may be used to break gasket seal.

**NOTE: Some early models used two gaskets. Be sure to use two new gaskets when reassembling these units.**

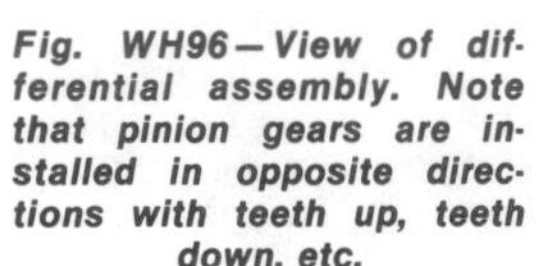

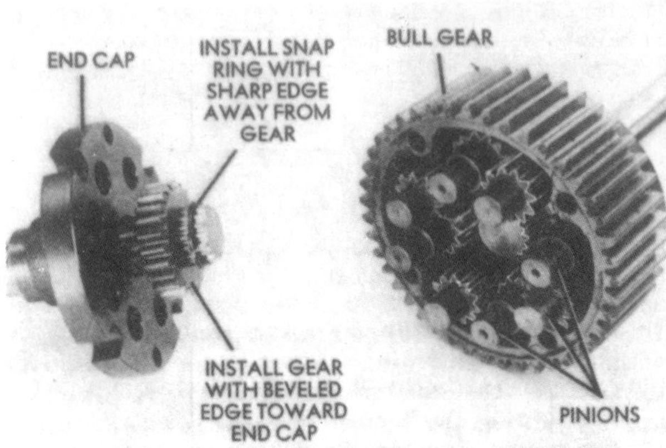


***Fig. WH96—View of differential assembly. Note that pinion gears are installed in opposite directions with teeth up, teeth down, etc.***

Withdraw pinion shaft (17–Fig. WH95) and reduction gear (16); brake shaft (6) and gears (4 and 5); and differential assembly from right case half (2). Remove axle seals (8) and brake shaft seal (10). New seals are not installed until after transaxle is reassembled.

Inspect bearings in case halves and renew as necessary. Axle needle bearings (9) can be driven out from inside case. All other bearings should be driven out from outside case. To remove upper bearing in right hand case, use a ¼ inch punch through small opening behind bearing.

Axle needle bearings (9) should be pressed in from outside. All other bearings are pressed in from inside case. All bearings should be flush with machined surface on inside of case.

To disassemble differential, remove four bolts and separate case halves (19). Remove pinion gears (21) and ring gear (22). Remove snap rings (24) and separate axles (18 and 23) from end caps (19) and gears (20).

Clean and inspect all parts and renew as necessary. Reduction gear (16) is a press fit on pinion shaft (17).

To reassemble, reverse disassembly procedure. Be sure differential pinions (21) are installed in opposite directions (teeth up, teeth down, teeth up, etc.). Be sure beveled edge of axle gears (Fig. WH96) face pinion gears. Use new high-tensile nuts and grade 8 bolts when reassembling differential, making sure hardened washers are under bolt heads and nuts are on same side as long axle. Tighten bolts to 30-35 ft.-lbs. (41-47 N·m). Tighten case retaining bolts to 30-35 ft.-lbs. (41-47 N·m). After assembling case, install new oil seals. Lubricate seals and protect from nicks; use suitable seal driver to install seals flush with outside of case.

Reinstall transaxle by reversing removal steps. Tighten wheel hub set screw to 28-32 ft.-lbs. (38-43 N·m). Adjust brake and transmission linkage as necessary.

## All Other Models

**R&R AND OVERHAUL.** To remove transaxle assembly, first unbolt and remove seat, fender and tool box. Remove transmission fan shield, belt guard and drive belt. Disconnect brake linkage (models so equipped). Disconnect control linkage and hydraulic hoses from transmission. Use a rolling floor jack to

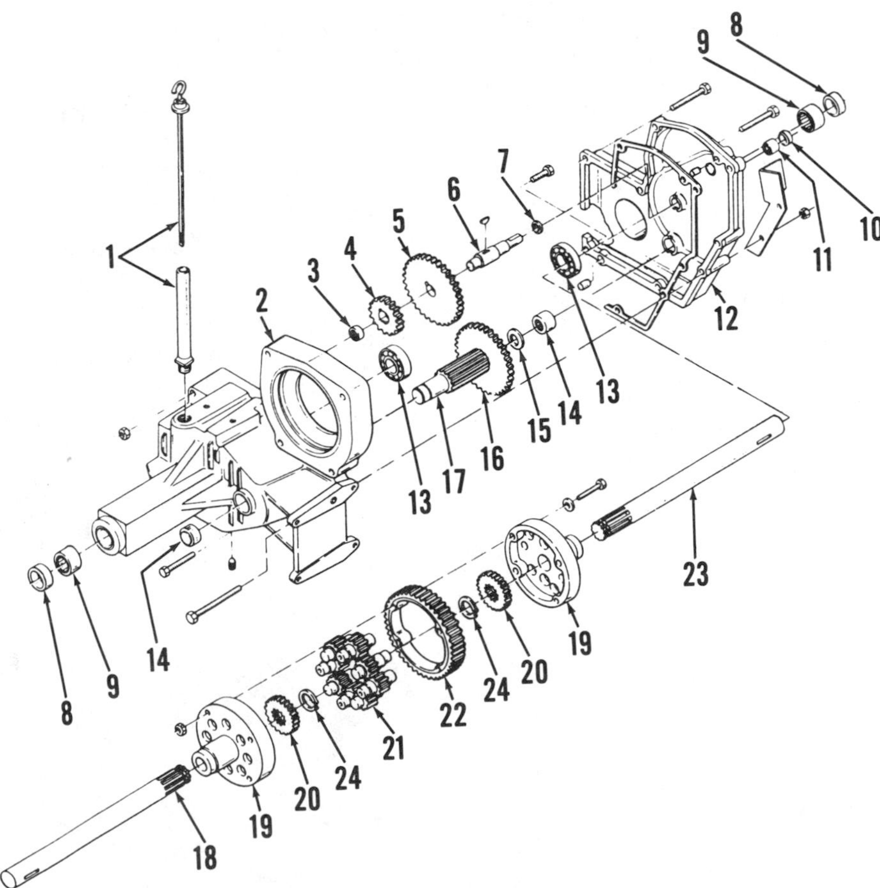

***Fig. WH95—Exploded view of Wheel Horse transaxle used on late Models C-125, C-145 and C-165 equipped with Eaton Model 11 hydrostatic unit.***

1. Dipstick & filler tube
2. Case half (R.H.)
3. Needle bearing
4. Gear (22T)
5. Gear (44T)
6. Brake shaft
7. Thrust washer
8. Axle seal
9. Needle bearing
10. Seal
11. Needle bearing
12. Case half (L.H.)
13. Ball bearing
14. Needle bearing
15. Thrust washer
16. Reduction gear
17. Pinion gear
18. Axle (R.H.) (13⅛ inches)
19. End caps
20. Axle gears
21. Pinion gears
22. Ring gear
23. Axle (L.H.) (10⅛ inches)
24. Snap rings

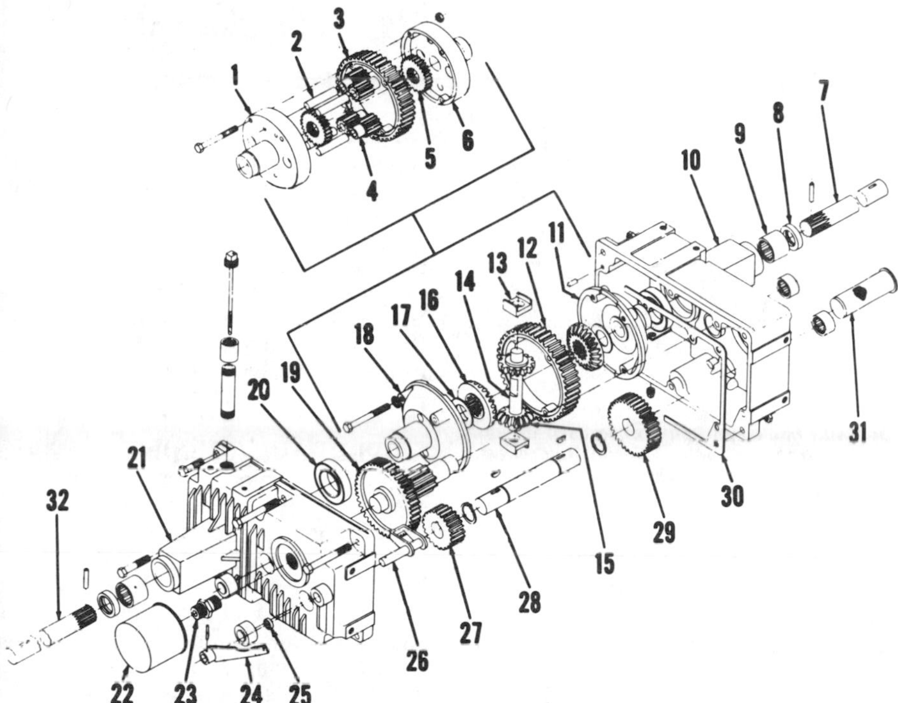

Fig. WH97 – Exploded view of Wheel Horse reduction gear and differential assembly used on models equipped with Sundstrand hydrostatic units. Bevel gear differential (out of production) is shown. See inset and adjacent figures for other differential types.

1. Carrier (R.H.)
2. Pinion shaft
3. Ring gear
4. Pinion
5. Axle gear
6. Carrier (L.H.)
7. Axle shaft (L.H.)
8. Oil seal
9. Bearing
10. Case half (L.H.)
11. Carrier (L.H.)
12. Ring gear
13. Drive block
14. Pinion shaft
15. Pinion gear
16. Axle gear (R.H.)
17. Thrust washer
18. Carrier (R.H.)
19. Output gear
20. Carrier bearing
21. Case half (R.H.)
22. Filter
23. Fitting
24. Parking lever
25. Oil seal
26. Park paw/shaft
27. Reduction gear
28. Countershaft
29. Input gear
30. Gasket
31. Strainer
32. Axle shaft (R.H.)

support transaxle and position stands under frame of tractor. Remove both rear wheel and tire assemblies. Unbolt transaxle from frame, lower transaxle and remove from tractor.

Drain unit, then unbolt and remove hydrostatic drive assembly. Remove strainer (31 – Fig. WH97) and filter (22). Remove rear wheel and hub assemblies. then place reduction gear and differential assembly in a vise or on a bench with right axle shaft (32) pointing downward. Unbolt and remove case half (10). Withdraw differential and axle shaft assembly and lay aside for later disassembly. Remove reduction shaft (28) with input gear (29) and reduction gear (27). Lift out output gear (19).

To disassemble differential, unbolt carrier (1 and 6) from ring gear (3). Differential pinion gears (4) and shafts (2) can now be removed. Remove snap ring from axle shafts and withdraw axle shafts from axle gears (5) and carriers.

On models having bevel gear differentials remove the four cap screws securing carriers (11 and 18) to ring gear (12), then separate carriers from ring gear. Drive blocks (13), differential pinions (15) and shaft (14) can now be removed from ring gear. Drive out roll pins and withdraw axle shafts (7 and 32) from axle gears (16), thrust washers (17) and carriers.

Some models are equipped with a limited slip differential. To disassemble differential, refer to Fig. WH98 and remove the five cap screws and separate axle assemblies from body cores (9). Using suitable snap ring pliers, remove cylindrical spring (13). Pinion gears (6) can now be removed from body cores. Separate body cores from ring gear (10). Remove snap ring (7) at end of axles and disassemble axle assemblies. Also see Fig. WH99 for other designs.

Clean and inspect all parts and renew any components showing excessive wear or damage. To reassemble limited slip type differential, install body cores (9 – Fig. WH98) in ring gear (10) so gear pockets in one core are out of alignment with gear pockets in other core. Reassemble axle assemblies. Install pinion gears (6) in one body core, then hold pinion gears in core by installing differential carrier and axle assembly and turn differential over. Be sure pinion gears mesh with side gear. Install pinion gears in other body core being sure gears mesh with previously installed pinion gears. Install cylindrical spring (13) making sure it bottoms against side gear. Spring should be in contact with most of the ten pinion gears. Install axle assembly and differential retaining bolts. To complete remainder of assembly, reverse disassembly procedure.

To assemble other gear reduction and differential units, reverse disassembly procedure. On all models, renew filter (22 – Fig. WH97). Refer to lubrication table in HYDROSTATIC TRANSMISSION section and fill unit with correct type of transmission fluid to level on dipstick.

# HYDRAULIC LIFT

## All Models So Equipped

**OPERATION.** Hydraulic pressure for lift system is provided by hydrostatic transmission charge pump. Normal working pressure is 500-700 psi (3448-4827 kPa). On models equipped with

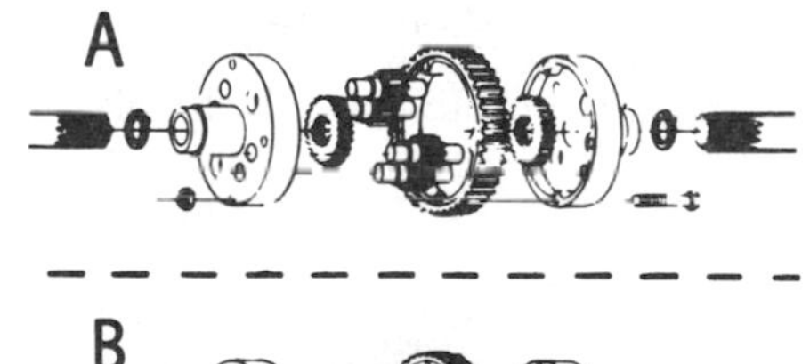

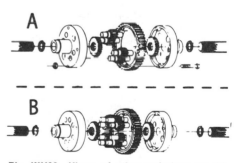

Fig. WH99 – Views of other variations on differential shown in Fig. WH97. View A shows 4-pinion spur gear type and view B shows 8-pinion design used on some tractor models.

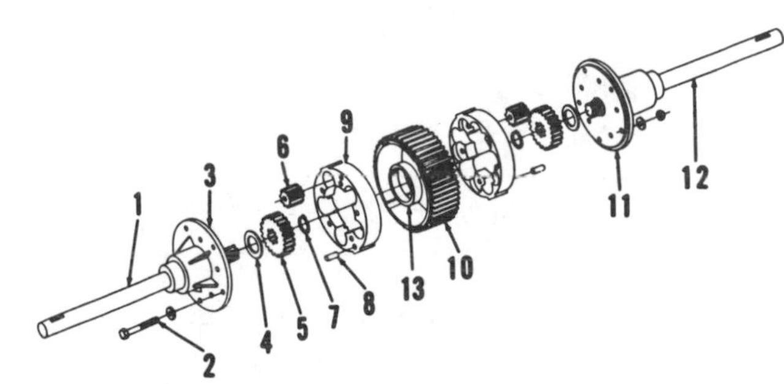

Fig. WH98 – Exploded view of limited slip differential used on some models.

1. Axle shaft (R.H.)
2. Bolt
3. Carrier (R.H.)
4. Washer
5. Axle (side) gear
6. Pinions (10)
7. Snap ring
8. Dowel
9. Body core
10. Ring gear
11. Carrier (L.H.)
12. Axle shaft (L.H.)
13. Cylindrical spring

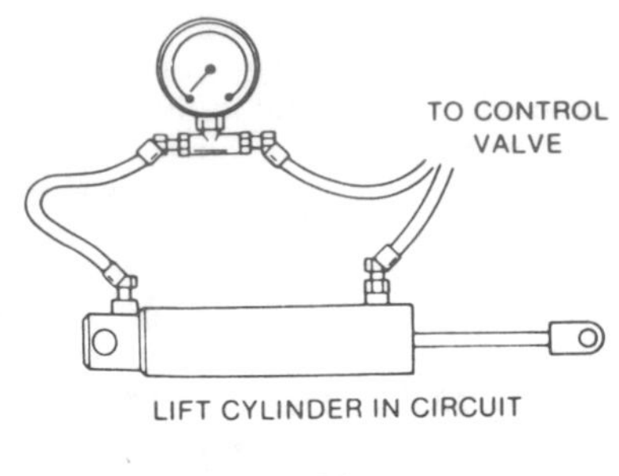


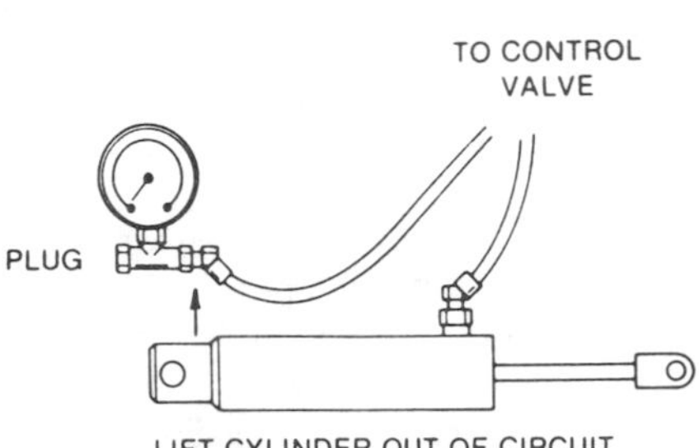


***Fig. WH100 — Connect a 0-1000 psi (0-7000 kPa) pressure gage to lift cylinder front hose as shown in check implement lift system pressure.***

Sundstrand transmission, implement relief valve is located in hydrostatic control valve section. On models equipped with Eaton transmission, implement relief valve is located in hydraulic control valve body.

**CAUTION: If relief valve adjustment is necessary, do not exceed 700 psi (4827 kPa) setting; serious transmission damage may result if pressure is incorrectly set.**

The open-center hydraulic control valves are made up of one or two spool valves and bodies. Control valves direct fluid to a double-acting hydraulic cylinder. Overhaul repair kits are available for valves and hydraulic cylinder.

**TESTING.** When checking relief valve pressure setting, hydraulic fluid should be at normal operating temperature. Connect a 0-1000 psi (0-7000 kPa) pressure gage to lift cylinder front hose

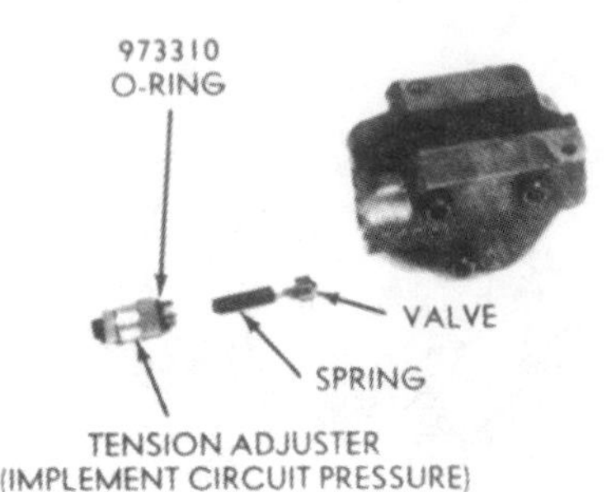


***Fig. WH102 — View of OMCO control valve equipped with implement relief valve used on early model tractors using Eaton hydrostatic transmission.***

as shown in Fig. WH100. With engine speed at high idle, hold lift control valve in "Down" direction and observe pressure reading. Normal pressure is approximately 700 psi (4827 kPa).

If pressure is not within specifications, remove implement relief valve and inspect from broken or weak spring or defective seat. Renew parts as necessary. Relief valve setting is adjusted on Sundstrand models by adding or removing shims behind relief valve spring. On Eaton models, implement relief valve is adjusted with shims or by turning adjusting screw, depending on style of hydraulic control valve used.

**CAUTION: If relief valve adjustment is necessary, do not exceed 700 psi (4827 kPa) setting; serious transmission damage may result if pressure is incorrectly set.**

## CONTROL VALVE

### All Models So Equipped

Three different manufacturers have supplied control valves for these tractors. An OMCO valve was used on tractors equipped with Sundstrand transmission and early Eaton equipped tractors. On 1983 and later "C" series tractors with Eaton transmission, either a VICTOR or AICO valve may be used. Before removing control valve, be sure to identify hose connections for correct reassembly.

**OVERHAUL (OMCO).** To disassemble valve, remove through-bolts and separate valve sections. Note location and quantity of mylar shims, located around bolt holes if used, for reassembly. Disconnect control valve handle and remove spool end cap (Fig. WH101). Remove screw from end of spool and withdraw spring and retainers, detent assembly (if so equipped) and spacer block. Push spool out of cap end of valve body.

**NOTE: Spool is select fit to valve body. When servicing two spool valves, identify parts so spool will be returned to original body.**

If valve is equipped with relief valve (Fig. WH102), remove it for cleaning and inspection. Remove and discard all "O" rings. If spool or valve body bore is deeply scratched or scored, complete valve must be renewed.

Reassemble valve in reverse order of disassembly. Lubricate all parts with

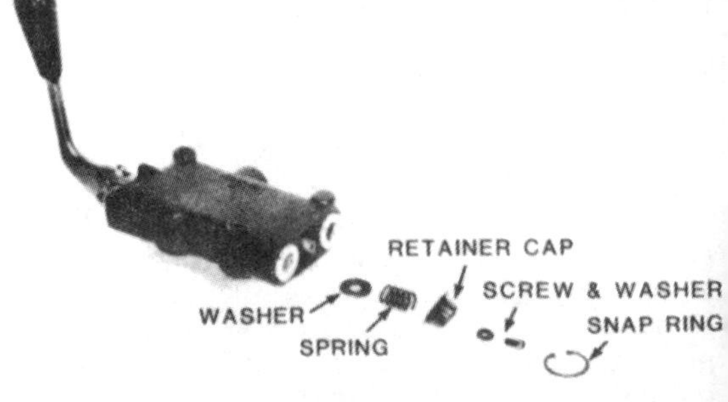


***Fig. WH103 — View of partially disassembled VICTOR control valve used on some late model tractors equipped with Eaton hydrostatic transmission.***

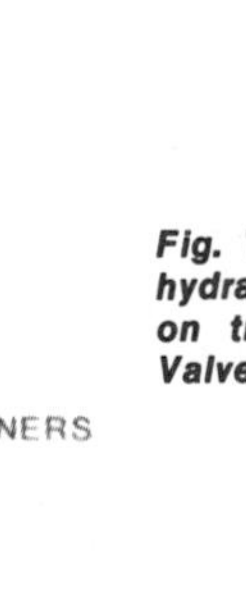

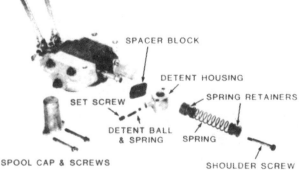

***Fig. WH101-View of OMCO hydraulic control valve used on tractors prior to 1983. Valve shown is equipped with float detent.***

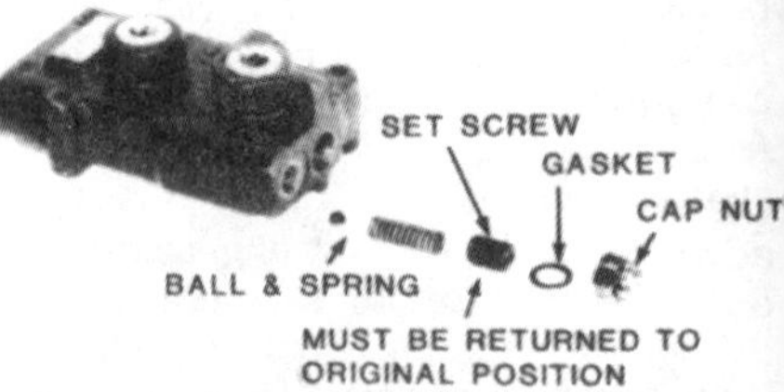

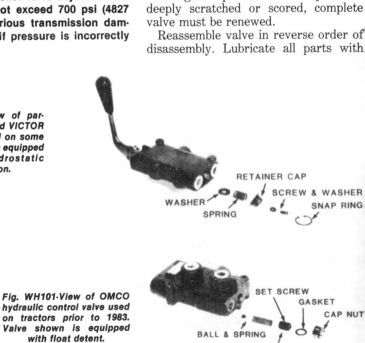

***Fig. WH104 — View of implement relief valve assembly used on VICTOR control valve. Pressure setting is adjusted by position of set screw. Refer to text.***

*Fig. WH105—AICO control valve is used on some late model tractors equipped with Eaton transmission. On models equipped with float detent, be careful not to lose detent spring and balls when removing spool cap.*

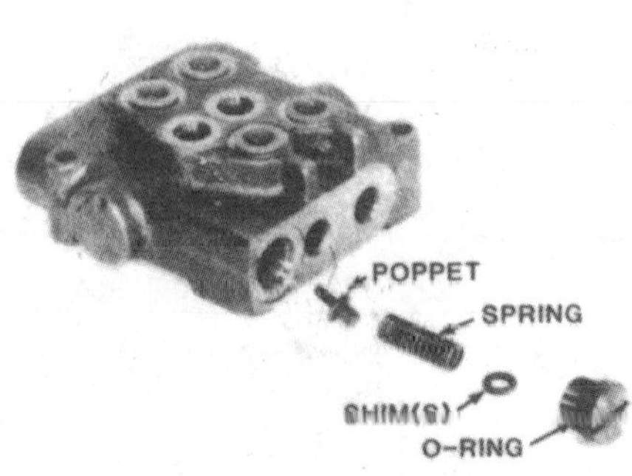


*Fig. WH106—Implement relief valve assembly used on AICO control valve is adjusted by adding or removing shims.*

clean oil prior to assembly. Tighten through-bolts evenly to 72-75 in.-lbs. (8-8.5 N•m). On valves equipped with float detent, adjust set screw (Fig. WH101) so spool will lock into float position when engaged, but release easily when light pressure is applied to handle. Adjust relief valve setting (if so equipped) as outlined in TESTING paragraph.

**OVERHAUL (VICTOR).** To disassemble valve, remove snap ring (Fig. WH103) from valve body. Remove retainer screw, cap, spring and washer. Remove handle from spool and pull spool out of valve body. Remove and discard all "O" rings. Remove relief valve assembly (Fig. WH104) for cleaning and inspection. If valve spool or body bore is deeply scratched or scored, renew complete valve.

Reassemble valve in reverse order of disassembly. Lubricate all parts with clean oil prior to assembly. Check and adjust relief valve pressure setting as outlined in TESTING paragraph.

**OVERHAUL (AICO).** To disassemble valve, first remove valve handle. Unscrew and remove spool end cap. On valves equipped with float detent, catch detent balls and spring as end cap is removed. Push spool out cap end of valve body. See Fig. WH105.

**NOTE: Spool is select fit to body bore. On two spool valves, identify spools so they can be returned to original bores.**

Unscrew spool stem and separate centering spring assembly from spool. Remove relief valve assembly (Fig. WH106) for cleaning and inspection. Remove and discard all "O" rings. If valve spool or body bore is deeply scratched or scored, renew complete valve.

Reassemble valve by reversing disassembly steps. Coat all parts with clean oil prior to assembly. Assemble detent spool cap (if so equipped) to spool before installing spool into body. Coat detent spring and balls with grease and be sure to work balls past detent ridge in cap before reinstalling. Check and adjust relief valve setting as outlined in TESTING paragraph.

## LIFT CYLINDER

### All Models So Equipped

**OVERHAUL.** To disassemble cylinder, refer to Fig. WH107 and remove snap ring (2A) or wire retaining ring (2B) from cylinder tube. Withdraw cylinder tube from piston and rod assembly. On "A" style cylinder, unscrew retaining nut (11) and withdraw piston (7) and guide (6). On "B" style cylinders, piston is threaded to rod and lightly staked. To remove piston, use a strap wrench or drill two holes 1/4 inch (6 mm) deep in end of piston for spanner wrench or pins as shown in Fig. WH108. Be careful not to mar piston or piston rod. Remove and discard all "O" rings and seals.

Reassemble cylinder in reverse order of disassembly. Coat all parts with clean oil prior to assembly. Be careful not to cut "O" rings during installation. Be sure rod guide bushing is seated against retaining ring.

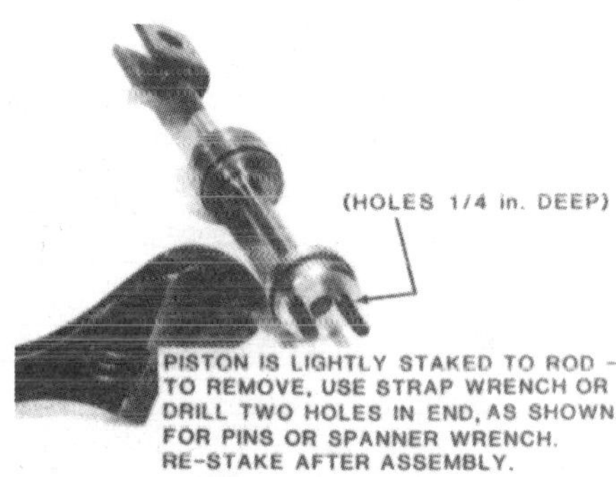

(HOLES 1/4 in. DEEP)
PISTON IS LIGHTLY STAKED TO ROD - TO REMOVE, USE STRAP WRENCH OR DRILL TWO HOLES IN END, AS SHOWN, FOR PINS OR SPANNER WRENCH. RE-STAKE AFTER ASSEMBLY.


*Fig. WH108—On "B" style cylinder (Fig. WH107), remove piston as shown. Be careful not to mar piston or rod surfaces.*

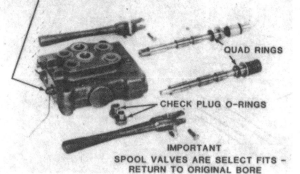

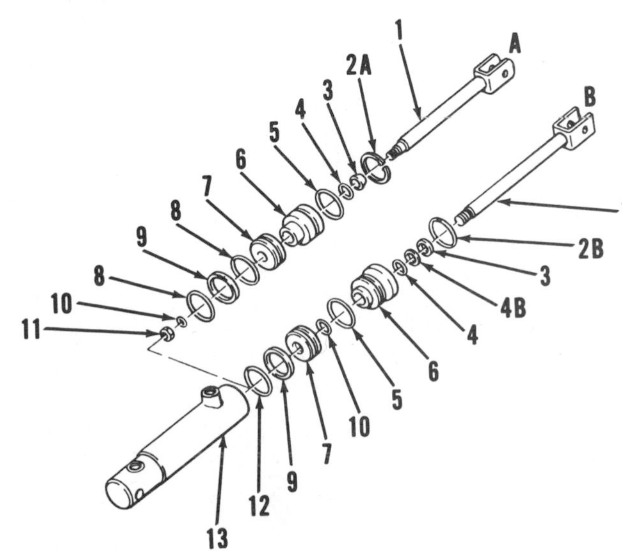

*Fig. WH107—Exploded view of two styles of lift cylinders used on tractors so equipped.*

1. Piston rod
2A. Snap ring
2B. Wire retaining ring
3. Wiper
4. "O" ring
4B. Back-up ring
5. "O" ring
6. Rod guide bushing
7. Piston
8. Back-up rings
9. Seal ring
10. "O" ring
11. Retaining ring
12. "O" ring
13. Cylinder tube

# WHITE

## CONDENSED SPECIFICATIONS

| | MODELS | | | | | |
|---|---|---|---|---|---|---|
| | T80, T82 | T85 | T100 (Early) | T100 (Late) | T110 | T112 |
| Engine Make | B&S | B&S | B&S | B&S | B&S | B&S |
| Model | 190707 | 190707 | 251707 | 252707 | 252707 | 252707 |
| Bore | 3 in. (76.2 mm) | 3 in. (76.2 mm) | 3-7/16 in. (87.3 mm) | 3-7/16 in. (87.3 mm) | 3-7/16 in. (87.3 mm) | 3-7/16 in. (87.3 mm) |
| Stroke | 2¾ in. (69.8 mm) | 2¾ in. (69.8 mm) | 2⅝ in. (66.7 mm) | 2⅝ in. (66.7 mm) | 2⅝ in. (66.7 mm) | 2⅝ in. (66.7 mm) |
| Piston Displacement | 19.44 cu. in. (319 cc) | 19.44 cu. in. (319 cc) | 24.36 cu. in. (399 cc) | 24.36 cu. in. (399 cc) | 24.36 cu. in. (399 cc) | 24.36 cu. in. (399 cc) |
| Horsepower | 8 | 8 | 10 | 11 | 11 | 11 |
| Slow Idle Speed – Rpm | 1750 | 1750 | 1750 | 1750 | 1750 | 1750 |
| High Idle Speed (No Load) – Rpm | 3600 | 3600 | 3600 | 3600 | 3600 | 3600 |
| Full Load Speed – Rpm | 3250 | 3250 | 3250 | 3250 | 3250 | 3250 |
| Crankcase Oil Capacity | 2¼ pints (1L) | | | | | |
| Weight – | | | | | | |
| Above 32°F (0°C) | SAE 30 | | | | | |
| 0°F (–18°C) to 32°F (0°C) | SAE 10W | | | | | |
| Below 0°F (–18°C) | SAE 5W-20 | | | | | |
| Transmission Oil Capacity | 12 oz. (355mL) | 5 oz. (148mL) | 1½ pints (0.7L) | 1½ pints (0.7L) | 3 pints (1.4L) | 24 oz. (710mL) |
| Weight | EP Lithium Grease | EP Lithium Grease | SAE 90 EP | SAE 90 EP | SAE 90 EP | EP Lithium Grease |
| Differential Oil Capacity | 1 oz. (30mL) | 1 oz. (30mL) | ...... | ...... | ...... | ...... |
| Weight | EP Lithium Grease | EP Lithium Grease | ...... | ...... | ...... | ...... |

| | MODELS | | | | |
|---|---|---|---|---|---|
| | LT84 | LT110, LT111 | GT1000 | GT1020 | GT1050 |
| Engine Make | B&S | B&S | B&S | B&S | B&S |
| Model | 190707 | 252707 | 251417 | 251417 | 243431 |
| Bore | 3 in. (76.2 mm) | 3-7/16 in. (87.3 mm) | 3-7/16 in. (87.3 mm) | 3-7/16 in. (87.3 mm) | 3-1/16 in. (77.8 mm) |
| Stroke | 2¾ in. (69.8 mm) | 2⅝ in. (66.7 mm) | 2⅝ in. (66.7 mm) | 2⅝ in. (66.7 mm) | 3¼ in. (82.5 mm) |
| Piston Displacement | 19.44 cu. in. (319 cc) | 24.36 cu. in. (399 cc) | 24.36 cu. in. (399 cc) | 24.36 cu. in. (399 cc) | 23.94 cu. in. (392 cc) |
| Horsepower | 8 | 11 | 10 | 10 | 10 |
| Slow Idle Speed – Rpm | 1750 | 1750 | 1750 | 1750 | 1200 |
| High Idle Speed (No Load) – Rpm | 3600 | 3600 | 3600 | 3600 | 3600 |
| Full Load Speed – Rpm | 3250 | 3250 | 3250 | 3250 | 3250 |
| Crankcase Oil Capacity | 2¼ pints (1L) | 2¼ pints (1L) | 2¾ pints (1.3L) | 3 pints (1.4L) | 4 pints (1.9L) |
| Weight – | | | | | |
| Above 32°F (0°C) | SAE 30 | | | | |
| 0°F (–18°C) to 32°F (0°C) | SAE 10W | | | | |
| Below 0°F (–18°C) | SAE 5W-20 | | | | |
| Transmission Oil Capacity | 24 oz. (710mL) | 24 oz. (710mL) | 3 pints (1.4L) | 4 pints (1.9L) | 4 pints (1.9L) |
| Weight | EP Lithium Grease | EP Lithium Grease | SAE 90 EP | SAE 90 EP | SAE 90 EP |
| Right Angle Drive Oil Capacity | ...... | ...... | ...... | ...... | 6 oz. (177mL) |
| Weight | ...... | ...... | ...... | ...... | EP Lithium Grease |

| | MODELS | | | | |
|---|---|---|---|---|---|
| | LGT1100 | GT1110, LGT1110 | GT1120 | LGT1155 | GT1600 (Early) |
| Engine Make | B&S | B&S | B&S | B&S | B&S |
| Model | 252707 | 252707 | 253417 | 252707 | 326431 |
| Bore | 3-7/16 in. (87.3 mm) | 3-7/16 in. (87.3 mm) | 3-7/16 in. (87.3 mm) | 3-7/16 in. (87.3 mm) | 3-9/16 in. (90.5 mm) |
| Stroke | 2⅝ in. (66.7 mm) | 2⅝ in. (66.7 mm) | 2⅝ in. (66.7 mm) | 2⅝ in. (66.7 mm) | 3¼ in. (82.5 mm) |
| Piston Displacement | 24.36 cu. in. (399 cc) | 24.36 cu. in. (399 cc) | 24.36 cu. in. (399 cc) | 24.36 cu. in. (399 cc) | 32.4 cu. in. (531 cc) |
| Horsepower | 11 | 11 | 11 | 11 | 16 |
| Slow Idle Speed – Rpm | 1750 | 1750 | 1750 | 1750 | 1200 |
| High Idle Speed (No Load) – Rpm | 3600 | 3600 | 3600 | 3600 | 3600 |
| Full Load Speed – Rpm | 3250 | 3250 | 3250 | 3250 | 3250 |
| Crankcase Oil Capacity | 3½ pints (1.6L) | 3 pints (1.4L) | 3 pints (1.4L) | 3 pints (1.4L) | 4 pints (1.9L) |
| Weight – | | | | | |
| Above 32°F (0°C) | SAE 30 | | | | |
| 0°F (−18°C) to 32°F (0°C) | SAE 10W | | | | |
| Below 0°F (−18°C) | SAE 5W-20 | | | | |
| Transmission Oil Capacity | 24 oz. (710mL) | 4 pints (1.9L) | 4 pints (1.9L) | * | 4 pints (1.9L) |
| Weight | EP Lithium Grease | SAE 90 EP | SAE 90 EP | SAE 20 | SAE 90 EP |
| Right Angle Drive Oil Capacity | ...... | ...... | ...... | ...... | 6 oz. (177mL) |
| Weight | ...... | ...... | ...... | ...... | EP Lithium Grease |
| Differential Oil Capacity | ...... | ...... | ...... | 2¾ pints 1.3L | ...... |
| Weight | ...... | ...... | ...... | SAE 90 EP | ...... |

*Refer to HYDROSTATIC TRANSMISSION section.

| | MODELS | | |
|---|---|---|---|
| | L-12 | LT-12 | LT-125 |
| Engine Make | B&S | B&S | B&S |
| Model | 281707 | 286707 | 286707 |
| Bore | 3-7/16 in. (87.3 mm) | 3-7/16 in. (87.3 mm) | 3-7/16 in. (87.3 mm) |
| Stroke | 3-1/16 in. (77.7 mm) | 3-1/16 in. (77.7 mm) | 3-1/16 in. (77.7 mm) |
| Piston Displacement | 28.4 cu. in. (465 cc) | 28.4 cu. in. (465 cc) | 28.4 cu. in. (465 cc) |
| Horsepower | 12 (9.0 kW) | 12.5 (9.3 kW) | 12.5 (9.3 kW) |
| Slow Idle Speed—Rpm | 1750 | 1750 | 1750 |
| High Idle Speed (No-Load) Rpm | 3600 | 3600 | 3600 |
| Crankcase Oil Capacity | 3 pints (1.4 L) | 3 pints (1.4 L) | 3 pints (1.4 L) |
| Transmission Oil Capacity | 10 ounces (295 mL) | 10 ounces (295 mL) | * |
| Weight | Grease | Grease | |
| Differential Oil Capacity | .... | .... | 16 ounces (475 mL) |
| Weight | .... | .... | Grease |

*Refer to HYDROSTATIC TRANSMISSION section.

# FRONT AXLE AND STEERING SYSTEM

## AXLE MAIN MEMBER

### Models T80-T82-T85-T100-T110-T112

**REMOVE AND REINSTALL.** To remove axle main member (4–Fig. W1, W2 or W3), disconnect drag link end from steering spindle arm. Support tractor under main frame with a suitable jack. Remove axle pivot bolt, raise front of tractor and roll front axle assembly from tractor. Remove tie rod. Loosen set screws (2) and remove collars (3), then withdraw steering spindle and wheel assemblies from axle.

Inspect for excessive wear and renew as necessary. To reinstall, reverse removal procedure. Lubricate bushings and pivot bolt with SAE 30 oil.

### Models LT84-LT110-LT111-L12-LT12-LT125

**REMOVE AND REINSTALL.** To remove axle main member (16–Fig. W4), raise and support front of tractor and remove front wheels. Disconnect tie rod (14) from spindles (15). Unbolt steering arm (17) from left spindle and remove push cap (10) from right spindle, then withdraw spindles and bushings (11) from axle ends. Unbolt and separate axle from frame.

Reassemble by reversing removal procedure. Lubricate all bushings with SAE 30 oil.

### Model GT1000

**REMOVE AND REINSTALL.** To remove axle main member (4–Fig. W5), disconnect tie rods (6) from steering spindles (5 and 7). Support tractor under main frame with a suitable jack. Remove axle pivot bolt, raise front of tractor and roll axle assembly from tractor. Loosen set screws (2), remove collars (3) and remove steering spindle and wheel assemblies.

### Models GT1020-GT1120

**REMOVE AND REINSTALL.** To remove front axle main member (5–Fig. W6), disconnect drag link (7) from steering spindle (6). Support tractor under frame using a suitable jack. Remove axle bolts (14). Unbolt front pivot bracket (4) and roll axle assembly away from tractor. Disconnect tie rod (8) from spindles. Remove dust covers and cotter pins, then withdraw steering spindle and wheel assemblies.

Reinstall axle by reversing removal procedure. Lubricate with multipurpose grease.

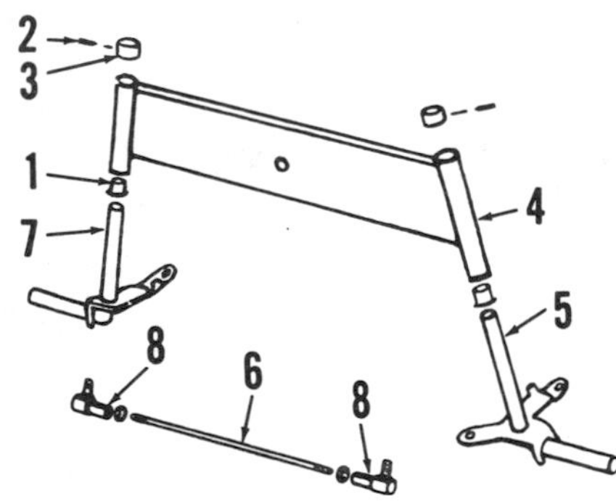


*Fig. W2–Exploded view of front axle assembly used on Model T85 and early Model T100.*

1. Flange bushing (4 used)
2. Set screw
3. Collar
4. Axle main member
5. Steering spindle L.H.
6. Tie rod
7. Steering spindle R.H.
8. Tie rod ends

### Models GT1050-GT1600

**REMOVE AND REINSTALL.** To remove axle main member (5–Fig. W7), disconnect drag link end (10) from left steering spindle (11). Support tractor under main frame with a suitable jack. Remove axle pivot bolt (3), raise front of tractor and roll axle assembly from tractor. Remove tie rod assembly (8). Loosen set screws (2), remove collars (1), then remove steering spindle and wheel assemblies.

Reinstall by reversing removal procedure. Lubricate with multi-purpose grease.

### Models LGT1100-LGT1110-LGT1155

**REMOVE AND REINSTALL.** To remove front axle assembly, (18–Fig. W8), disconnect drag link from steering spindle. Support tractor under frame with a suitable jack. Remove pivot bolt, raise tractor and roll axle assembly from tractor. Disconnect tie rod (16) from spindle arms. Remove dust cover, cotter pin and flat washer, then remove steering spindle and wheel assemblies.

Reinstall by reversing removal procedure. Spindle bushings (13) do not require lubrication.

## TIE RODS

### Model T80

Tie rod (6–Fig. W1) on Model T80 tractors is non-adjustable and removal is evident after examination of unit.

### All Other Models

All models are equipped with adjustable tie rods. If ball joint ends are excessively worn, renew as required.

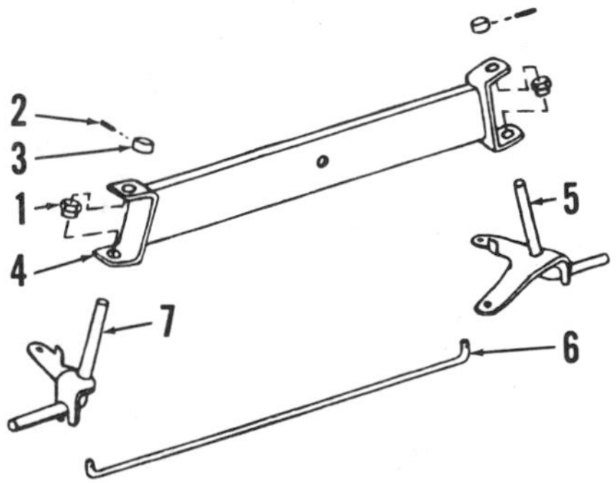


*Fig. W1–Exploded view of front axle assembly used on Model T80.*

1. Hex bushing (4 used)
2. Set screw
3. Collar
4. Axle main member
5. Steering spindle L.H.
6. Tie rod
7. Steering spindle R.H.

*Fig. W3–Exploded view of front axle assembly used on Models T82, late T100, T110 and T112.*

1. Collar
2. Set screw
3. Flange bearing
4. Axle
5. Drag link
6. Steering spindle R.H.
7. Tie rod ends
8. Tie rod
9. Steering spindle L.H.

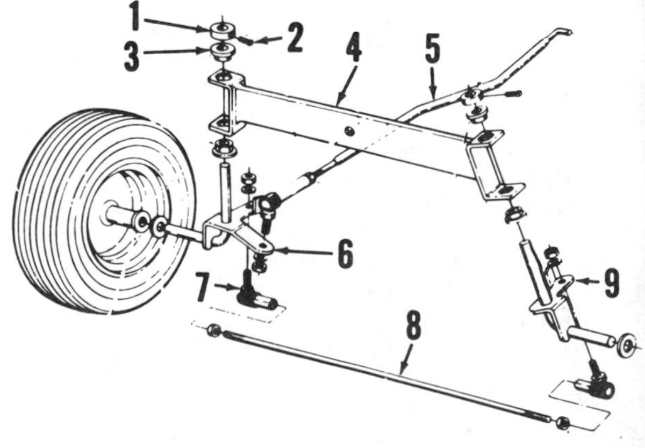




Illustrations courtesy White Outdoor Products.

To adjust toe-in, disconnect tie rod ends from steering spindle arms, loosen locknuts and turn ball joint in or out as required. Toe-in should be ⅛-inch (3 mm), measured as shown in Fig. W9. On models with two tie rods, be sure to adjust both tie rods evenly.

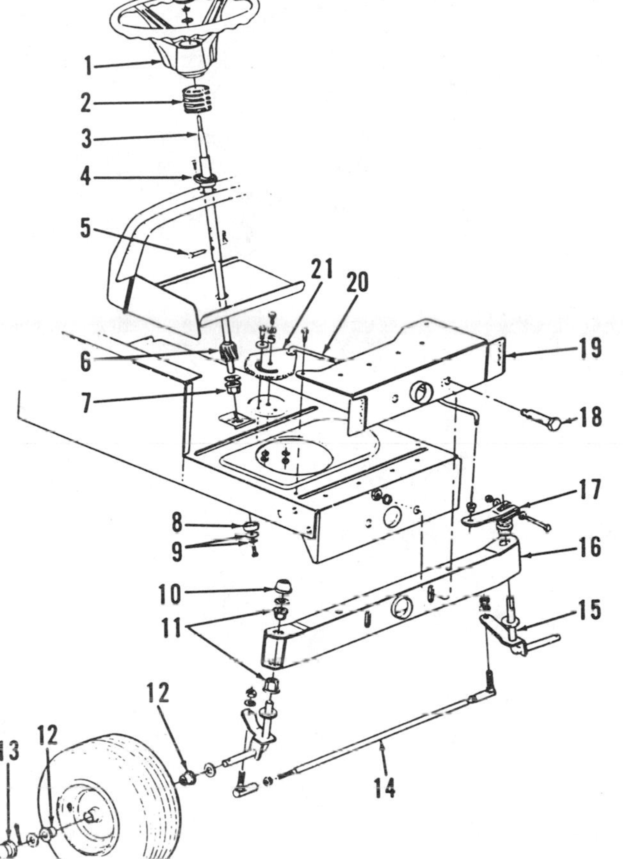


*Fig. W4—Exploded view of front axle and steering system used on Models LT84, LT110, LT111, L12, LT12 and LT125.*

1. Steering wheel
2. Bellow
3. Steering shaft extension
4. Bushing
5. Clevis pin
6. Steering shaft & gear
7. Bushing
8. Spacer
9. Washers
10. Push cap
11. Spindle bushings
12. Wheel bushings
13. Hub cap
14. Tie rod
15. Steering spindle
16. Axle
17. Steering arm
18. Shoulder bolt
19. Pivot bracket
20. Drag link
21. Gear segment

## STEERING SPINDLES

### Models T80-T82-T85-T100-T110-T112

**REMOVE AND REINSTALL.** To remove steering spindles (5 and 7–Fig. W1 or W2) or (6 and 9–Fig. W3), first raise and support front of tractor and remove front wheels. Disconnect drag link and tie rod from steering spindle arms. Loosen set screw (2), remove collars (3–Figs. W1 or W2) or (1–Fig. W3) and lower spindles out of axle main member.

Inspect spindle bushings and spindles and renew if necessary. Lubricate with SAE 30 oil.

### Models LT84-LT110-LT111-L12-LT12-LT125

**REMOVE AND REINSTALL.** To remove steering spindles, support front of tractor and remove front wheels. Disconnect drag link (20–Fig. W4) and tie rod (14) from spindles. Remove push cap (10) from right spindle and steering arm (17) from left spindle, then withdraw spindles from axle.

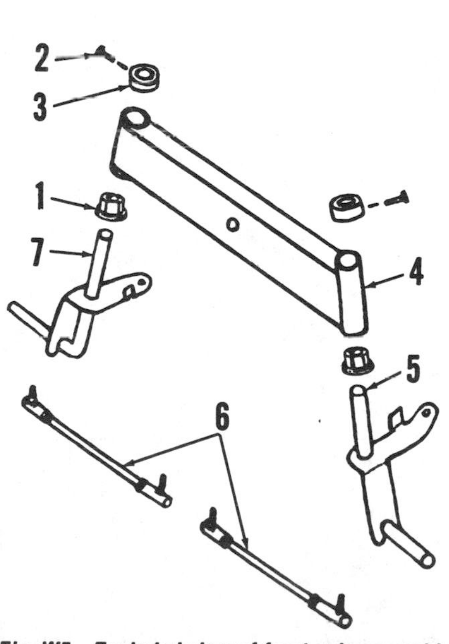


*Fig. W5—Exploded view of front axle assembly used on Model GT1000.*

1. Flange bearing (4 used)
2. Set screw
3. Collar
4. Axle main member
5. Steering spindle L.H.
6. Tie rods
7. Steering spindle R.H.

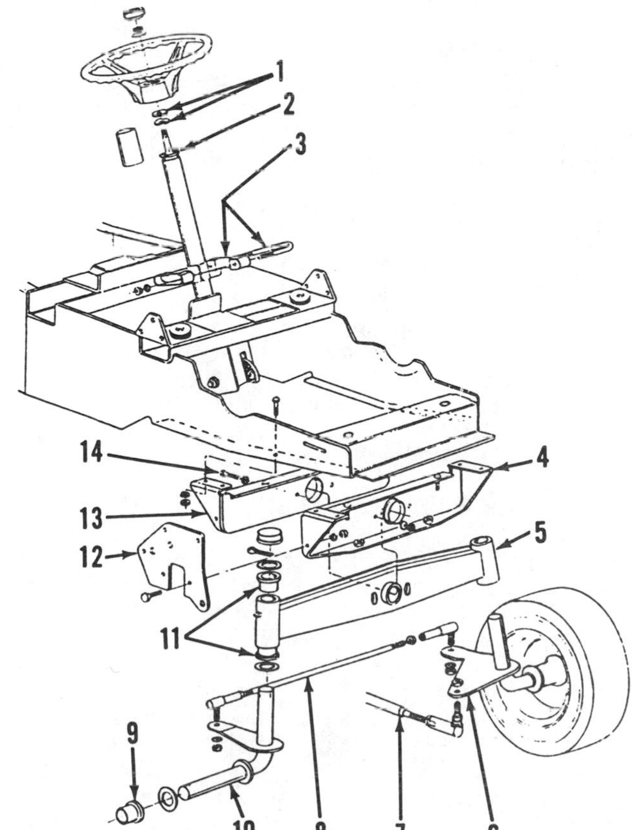


*Fig. W6—Exploded view of front axle assembly used on Models GT1020 and GT1120.*

1. Washers
2. Ball bearing
3. "U" clamp
4. Front pivot bracket
5. Axle main member
6. Steering spindle L.H.
7. Drag link
8. Tie rod
9. Flange bushing
10. Steering spindle R.H.
11. Spindle bushings
12. Side plate
13. Rear pivot bracket
14. Axle bolts

Illustrations courtesy White Outdoor Products.

Inspect spindles and bushings for wear and renew as needed. Reinstall by reversing removal procedure and lubricate with SAE 30 oil.

### Model GT1000

**REMOVE AND REINSTALL.** To remove steering spindles (5 and 7–Fig. W5), support front of tractor and remove front wheels. Disconnect outer tie rod ends from arms on steering spindles. Loosen set screws (2), remove collars (3) and lower steering spindles from axle main member.

Inspect spindles and bushings and renew as necessary. Spindle bushings require no lubrication.

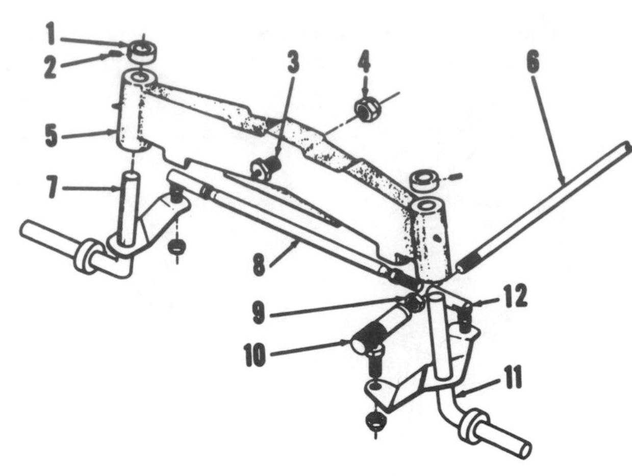


*Fig. W7–Exploded view of front axle assembly used on Models GT1050 and GT1600.*

1. Collar
2. Set screw
3. Pivot bolt
4. Nut
5. Axle main member
6. Drag link
7. Steering spindle R.H.
8. Tie rod
9. Locknut
10. Drag link end
11. Steering spindle L.H.
12. Tie rod end

### Models GT1050-GT1600

**REMOVE AND REINSTALL.** To remove steering spindles (7 and 11–Fig. W7), first disconnect drag link end (10) from arm on left steering spindle and tie rod ends from both steering spindles. Support front of tractor and remove front wheels. Loosen set screws (2), remove collars (1) and lower steering spindles from axle main member.

To reinstall spindles, reverse removal procedure. Lubricate with multi-purpose grease.

### Models GT1020-GT1120-LGT1100-LGT1110-LGT1155

**REMOVE AND REINSTALL.** To remove steering spindles (6 and 10–Fig. W6) or (15 and 17–Fig. W8), support front of tractor and remove front wheels. Disconnect drag link and tie rod ends from spindle arms. Remove dust covers and cotter pins, then lower spindles from axle.

Inspect bushings and spindles and renew as necessary. On Models GT1020 and GT1120, lubicate spindle bushings with multi-purpose grease. Bushings used on Models LGT1100, LGT1110 and LGT1155 do not require lubrication.

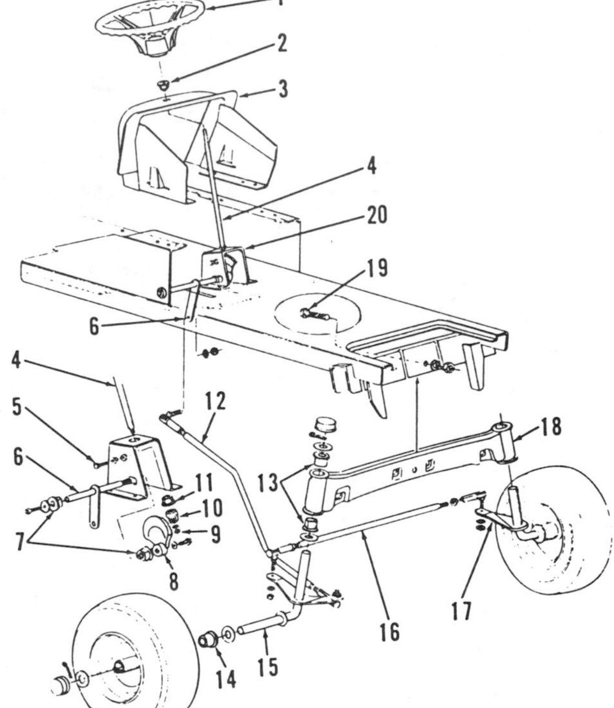


*Fig. W8–Exploded view of front axle and steering system used on Models LGT1100, LGT1110 and LGT1155.*

1. Steering wheel
2. Bushing
3. Dash
4. Steering shaft
5. Adjusting screw
6. Steering arm
7. Bushings
8. Sector gear
9. Retaining nut
10. Pinion gear
11. Bushing
12. Drag link
13. Spindle bushings
14. Bushing
15. Steering spindle R.H.
16. Tie rod
17. Steering spindle L.H.
18. Axle main member
19. Pivot bolt
20. Steering gear housing

## STEERING GEAR

### Models T80-T85-Early T100

**REMOVE AND REINSTALL.** To remove steering gear, unbolt bracket (13–Fig. W10) and disconnect drag link from steering rack (12). Drive roll pin (9) from pinion (8). Withdraw steering shaft (7) with steering wheel (4) and remove pinion. Unbolt and remove housing assembly (11) from frame. Withdraw two-piece rack (12) from housing. Remove cap (1), nut (2) and washer (3), then remove steering wheel (4) from shaft (7).

When reassembling, oil steering shaft bushings with SAE 30 oil and lubricate pinion (8) and rack (12) with multi-purpose grease.

### Models T82-Late T100-T110-T112-LGT1100-LGT1110-LGT1155

**REMOVE AND REINSTALL.** To remove steering gear, disconnect and remove battery and battery plate. Disconnect drag link from steering arm (6–Fig. W11). Remove pivot bolt (4), washer and bushing (5). Remove four mounting bolts from steering support. Lift and rotate support assembly to gain

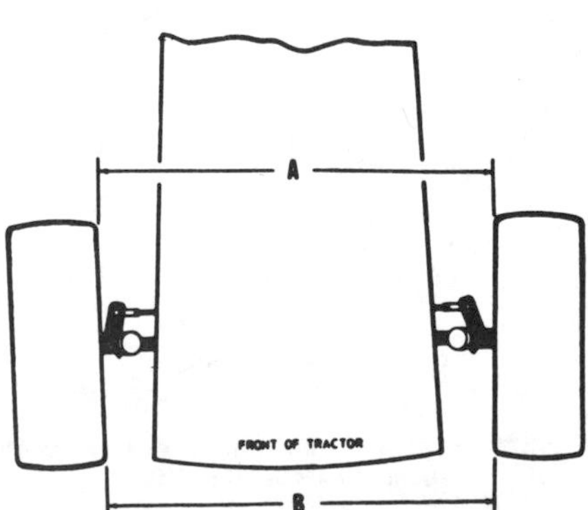


*Fig. W9–Toe-in is correct when distance "B" is ⅛-inch (3 mm) less than distance "A" with both measurements taken at hub height.*



Illustrations courtesy White Outdoor Products.

access to pinion gear. Remove pinion gear nut and withdraw steering shaft. Unbolt and withdraw sector gear (10), bushing (9) and shaft (6).

Reassemble by reversing disassembly procedure. Lubricate bushings (5) with SAE 30 oil and pinion and sector gear with a multi-purpose grease.

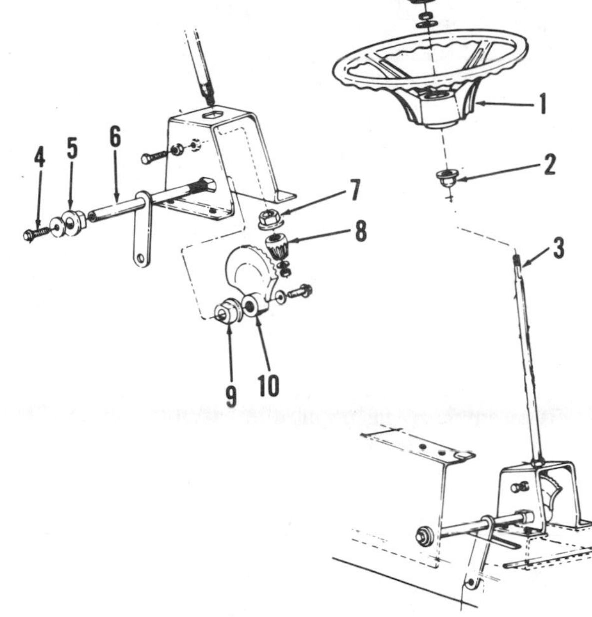


***Fig. W11—Exploded view of steering gear assembly used on Models T82, T100 (late), T110, T112, LGT1100, LGT1110 and LGT1155.***

1. Steering wheel
2. Flange bushing
3. Steering shaft
4. Bolt
5. Flange bushing
6. Steering arm shaft assy.
7. Bearing
8. Pinion gear
9. Flange bushing
10. Sector gear

### Models LT84-LT110-LT111-L12-LT12-LT125

**REMOVE AND REINSTALL.** To remove steering gears, remove steering wheel cap, retaining nut and washer, then lift off steering wheel (1–Fig. W4) and bellow (2). Disconnect battery cables. Remove clevis pin (5) and unbolt bushing (4), then withdraw shaft extension (3) and bushing. Disconnect drag link (20), then unbolt and remove gear segment (21). Remove retaining bolt from bottom of steering shaft (6) and withdraw washers (9), spacer (8), flange bushing (7) and steering shaft (6).

Inspect all parts for excessive wear or other damage and renew as needed. Reassemble by reversing removal procedure. Lubricate steering gears with multi-purpose grease and bushings with SAE 30 oil.

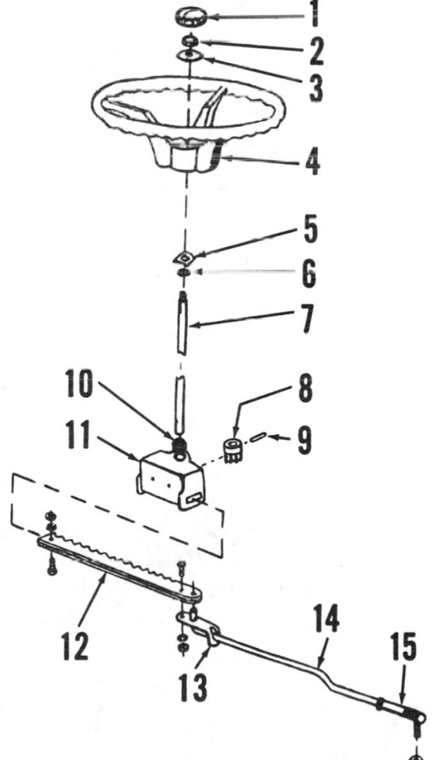


***Fig. W10—Exploded view of steering gear used on Models T80, T85 and early Model T100.***

1. Cap
2. Nut
3. Belleville washer
4. Steering wheel
5. Retainer
6. Washer
7. Steering shaft
8. Pinion
9. Roll pin
10. Bushing
11. Housing
12. Steering rack
13. Bracket
14. Drag link
15. Drag link end

### Model GT1000

**REMOVE AND REINSTALL.** To remove steering gear, first disconnect tie rods from steering quadrant (13–Fig. W12). Remove cap screw and washers from spacer (11) and the nut and Belleville washer from pivot bolt on bracket (12). Remove steering quadrant from tractor. Drive out roll pin (7), withdraw steering wheel and steering shaft assembly and remove pinion (9). Unbolt and remove bracket (10) with bushing (8). Remove cap (1), nut (2) and washer (3), then remove steering wheel (4) from shaft (6).

Reassemble by reversing disassembly procedure. Before bolting steering quadrant (13) in position, make certain steering wheel and front wheels are in straight ahead position. To adjust steering gear free play, loosen the two mounting bolts in bracket (10). Move bracket forward to decrease free play, then tighten bracket mounting bolts.

Lubricate steering shaft bushings with SAE 30 oil and pinion gear and quadrant with multi-purpose grease.

### Models GT1020-GT1120

**REMOVE AND REINSTALL.** To remove steering gear, disconnect drag link at steering arm (14–Fig. W13). Remove pinion gear nut and withdraw steering shaft and steering wheel assembly. Rotate sector gear (13) until steering arm contacts housing. Remove nut (8) and push shaft towards right side of tractor. Remove flange bearing (16) and steering arm. Sector gear is a light interference fit and must be carefully tapped off with a hammer. Further disassembly is evident from inspection.

Clean and inspect bearings and renew as necessary. Reassemble steering gear by reversing disassembly procedure. Lubricate bearings with SAE 30 oil and

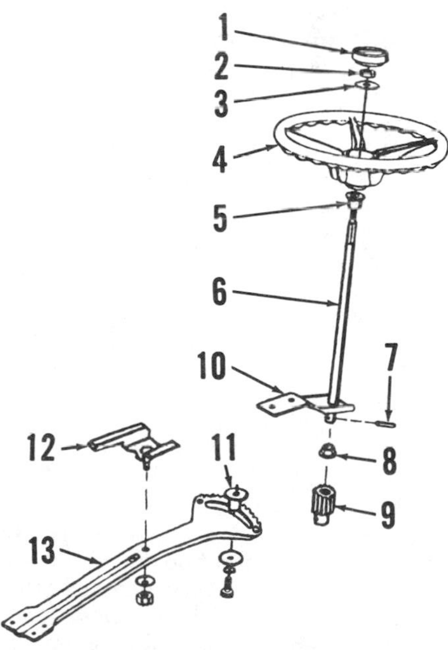


***Fig. W12—Exploded view of steering gear used on Model GT1000.***

1. Cap
2. Nut
3. Wave washer
4. Steering wheel
5. Flange bushing
6. Steering shaft
7. Roll pin
8. Flange bushing
9. Pinion
10. Bracket
11. Spacer
12. Pivot bracket
13. Steering quadrant

pinion and sector gears with a multipurpose grease.

### Models GT1050-GT1600

**REMOVE AND REINSTALL.** To remove steering gear, disconnect drag link (11–Fig. W14) from quadrant arm. Loosen set screw in quadrant gear (10) and remove gear shaft (9) and quadrant gear. Drive out roll pin (7) and remove pinion gear (8). Withdraw steering wheel and steering shaft assembly. Drive out roll pin (2) and separate steering wheel (1) from shaft (4).

Reassemble by reversing disassembly procedure. Lubricate steering shaft bushings (3 and 6) with SAE 30 oil and pinion gear and quadrant with multipurpose grease.

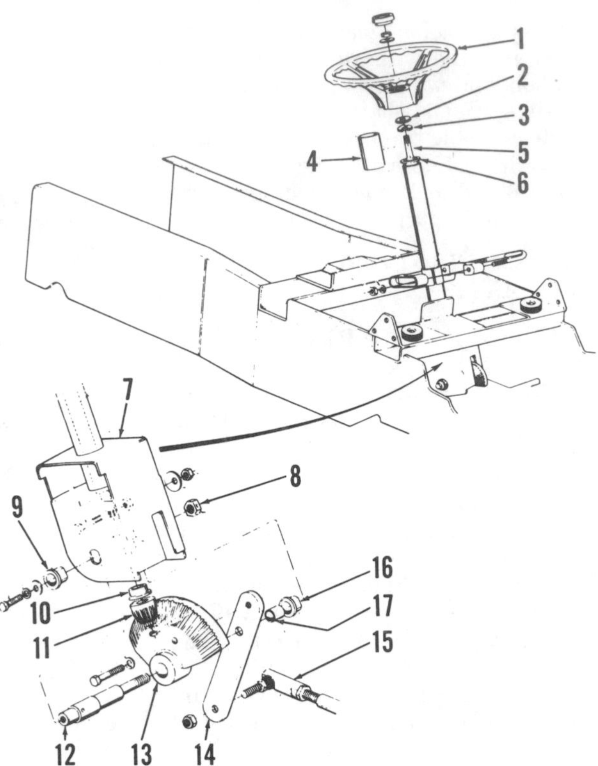

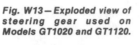

*Fig. W13 – Exploded view of steering gear used on Models GT1020 and GT1120.*

1. Steering wheel
2. "D" washer
3. Wave washer
4. Tube
5. Steering shaft
6. Bearing
7. Housing
8. Nut
9. Flange bearing
10. Flange bearing
11. Pinion gear
12. Steering gear shaft
13. Sector gear
14. Steering arm
15. Drag link end
16. Flange bearing
17. Spacer

# ENGINE

## REMOVE AND REINSTALL

### Models T80-T82-T85-T100-T110-T112

To remove engine assembly, unlatch rear of hood, then tilt hood and grille assembly forward. Disconnect battery cables and electrical wiring from engine. Disconnect throttle and choke control cable. Unbolt and remove belt guard in front of engine drive pulley. Remove drive belts from engine pulley, then unbolt and remove pulley. Remove remaining engine mounting bolts and lift engine from tractor.

Reinstall by reversing removal procedure.

### Models LT84-LT110-LT111

To remove engine assembly, remove hood and grille support rods. Disconnect battery cables and electrical wiring from engine. Disconnect throttle and choke control cable. Disconnect fuel line. Remove engine pulley belt guard, then remove drive belt from pulley. Remove engine mounting cap screws and lift engine from tractor.

To reinstall engine, reverse removal procedure.

### Model GT1000

To remove engine assembly, unlatch rear of hood, then tilt hood and grille assembly forward. Disconnect battery cables and starter cable, then unplug alternator and ignition wires at connector. Shut off fuel valve and disconnect fuel line. Remove brace from top of engine and muffler and belt guard from right side of engine. Remove belts from engine drive pulley. Remove engine mounting cap screws and lift engine from tractor.

To reinstall engine, reverse removal procedure. Adjust drive belts as necessary.

### Models GT1020-GT1120

To remove engine assembly, remove hood and disconnect battery. Disconnect all engine wiring, throttle cable and choke cable. Close fuel shut off valve and disconnect fuel line. Remove muffler and drive belt guard. Remove drive belts and crankshaft pulley. Remove heat shields and belt guard mounting plate. Remove engine mounting bolts and lift engine from tractor.

To reinstall engine, reverse removal procedures. Adjust drive belts as necessary.

### Models GT1050-GT1600

To remove engine assembly, remove hood and grille brace and disconnect battery cables. Unbolt right angle drive unit from frame, then move clutch and right angle drive assembly back from engine. Remove pto drive belts. Disconnect starter-generator wires, shut off fuel valve and disconnect fuel line. Disconnect throttle and choke control cables and remove muffler. Remove engine mounting bolts and lift engine from tractor.

To reinstall engine, reverse removal procedure. Adjust clutch as necessary.

### Models LGT1100-LGT1110-LGT1155

To remove engine assembly, remove hood and grille braces. Disconnect battery cables and engine wiring harness.

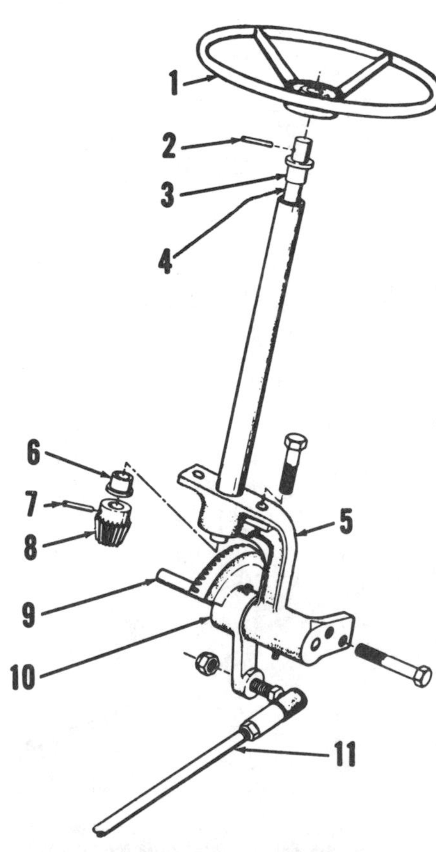


*Fig. W14 – Steering gear used on Model GT1050 and GT1600 tractors.*

1. Steering wheel
2. Roll pin
3. Bushing
4. Steering shaft
5. Steering support
6. Flange bushing
7. Roll pin
8. Pinion
9. Shaft
10. Quadrant gear
11. Drag link

Close fuel shut off valve and disconnect fuel line. Disconnect throttle and choke cables. Remove drive belts from crankshaft pulley. Remove engine mounting bolts and lift engine from tractor.

Reinstall engine by reversing removal procedure.

### Models L12-LT12-LT125

To remove engine, first remove mower deck from underneath tractor. Remove hood and side panels. Disconnect battery cables and starter cable, then unplug alternator and ignition wires at connectors. Shut off fuel and disconnect fuel line from engine. Disconnect throttle and choke control cables. Remove drive belt from engine pulley. Remove engine mounting bolts and lift engine from tractor.

To reinstall engine, reverse removal procedure.

## OVERHAUL

### All Models

Engine make and model are listed at the beginning of this section. To overhaul engine components and accessories, refer to Briggs & Stratton section of this manual.

# CLUTCH AND DRIVE BELTS

### Models T80-T82-Late T100-Late T110-T112

A belt idler type clutch is used on all models. The clutch idler is spring loaded and does not require adjustment. If drive belt slips during normal operation due to excessive belt wear or stretching, renew drive belt.

**R&R DRIVE BELT.** To remove drive belt (2 – Fig. W15), first unbolt and remove engine pulley belt guard. Remove belt keepers as necessary. Depress clutch pedal (9) and retain pedal in disengaged position with clutch lock (11). Remove belt from transmission input pulley (1) and from engine drive pulley (8). Unbolt drag link bracket (13 – Fig. W10) on Models T80 and T82 and separate drag link from steering rack (12). Remove drive belt. Install new drive belt by reversing removal procedure.

### Model T85

The variable speed pulley (2 – Fig. W16) is also used as a belt idler type clutch on Model T85. The pulley is spring loaded and does not require adjustment. Lubricate pulley sleeve (17) with dry type lubricant to ensure free movement of sheave (15).

**R&R DRIVE BELTS.** To remove drive belts (11 and 13 – Fig. W16) from Model T85 tractors, place variable drive lever in full forward position. Push variable speed pulley (2) towards transmission input pulley (1) and remove rear drive belt (13). Unbolt and remove engine pulley belt guard. Lower movable sheave half (15) and remove front drive belt (11). Install new belts by reversing removal procedure.

### Models (Early) T100-T110

A belt idler type clutch is used on early Models T100 and T110. See Fig. W17.

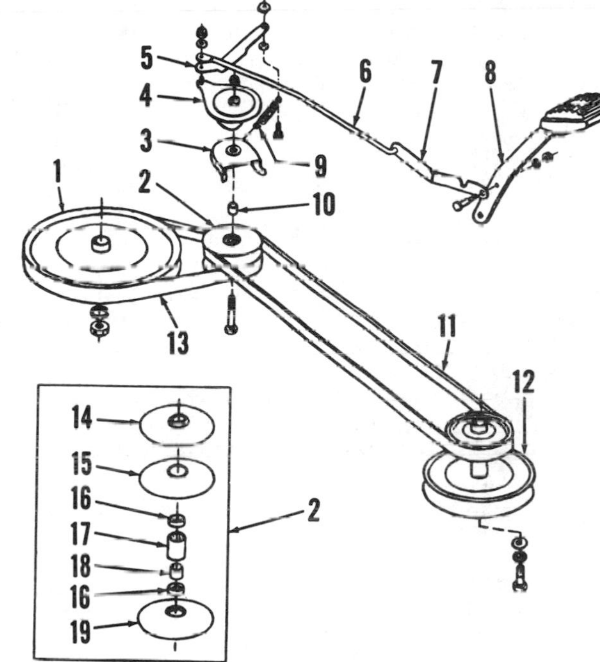

*Fig. W16 – Exploded view of clutch and variable speed drive belt assembly used on Model T85 tractors.*

1. Transmission pulley
2. Clutch & variable speed pulley
3. Belt guard
4. Clutch bracket
5. Variable speed link
6. Clutch rod
7. Clutch link
8. Clutch pedal
9. Spring
10. Spacer
11. Drive belt (front)
12. Engine drive pulley
13. Drive belt (rear)
14. Sheave half (top)
15. Movable sheave half
16. Ball bearing
17. Sleeve
18. Spacer
19. Sheave half (bottom)

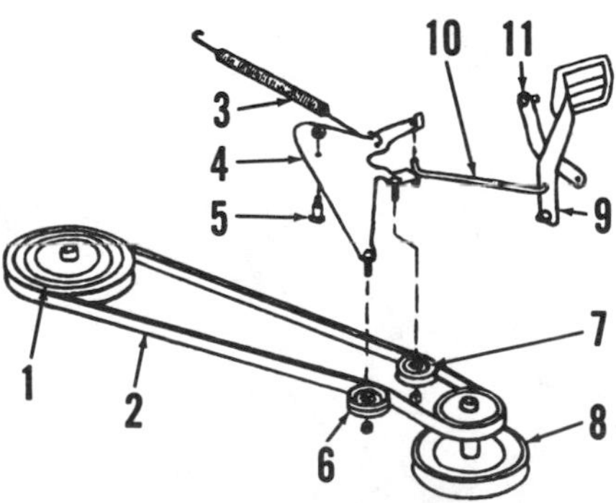

*Fig. W15 – Exploded view of clutch idler system used on Models T80 and T82. Late Models T100 and T110 and Model T112 are similar.*

1. Transmission input pulley
2. Drive belt
3. Clutch spring
4. Idler bracket
5. Pivot bolt
6. Flat idler
7. Vee idler
8. Engine drive pulley
9. Clutch pedal
10. Clutch rod
11. Clutch lock

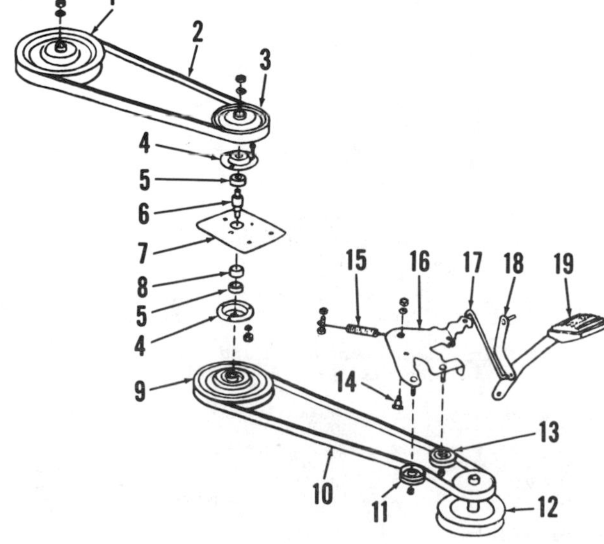

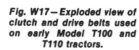

*Fig. W17 – Exploded view of clutch and drive belts used on early Model T100 and T110 tractors.*

1. Transmission pulley
2. Drive belt (rear)
3. Jackshaft pulley (upper)
4. Bearing retainer
5. Ball bearing
6. Jackshaft
7. Plate
8. Spacer
9. Jackshaft pulley (lower)
10. Drive belt (front)
11. Flat idler
12. Engine drive pulley
13. Vee idler
14. Pivot bolt
15. Clutch spring
16. Clutch bracket
17. Clutch rod
18. Clutch lock
19. Clutch pedal

Illustrations courtesy White Outdoor Products.

The clutch idler is spring loaded and does not require adjustment.

**R&R DRIVE BELTS.** To remove drive belts (2 and 10–Fig. W17) from early Models T100 and T110, unbolt and remove engine drive pulley belt guard. Depress clutch pedal (19) and retain pedal in disengaged position with clutch lock (18). Unbolt drag link bracket (13–Fig. W10) and separate drag link from steering rack (12). Remove front drive belt (10–Fig. W17). Move seat rearward and remove upper frame cover. Loosen transaxle mounting bolts and two adjusting nuts at rear of main frame. Move transaxle assembly forward and remove rear drive belt (2). Install new belts by reversing removal procedure. Adjust rear drive belt (2) by tightening adjusting nuts evenly until belt will deflect about ½-inch (13 mm) when 10 pounds (44.5 N) pressure is applied midway between pulleys (1 and 3). Tighten transaxle mounting bolts.

## Models LT84-LT110-LT111

A belt idler type clutch is used on these models. The clutch idler is spring loaded and requires no adjustment. If drive belt slips during normal operation due to excessive belt wear or stretching, renew drive belt.

**R&R DRIVE BELT.** To remove drive belt (7–Fig. W18), remove belt keepers and engine pulley belt guard (5). Disconnect clutch idler tension spring (4) and unbolt and remove idler pulley (6). Unbolt transaxle pulley belt guard and slide guard rearward. Unbolt and remove transaxle shift lever. Remove belt from engine pulley, then lift belt up and over transaxle pulley.

Install new belt by reversing removal procedure. Be sure back of belt is against idler pulley and belt is inside belt keepers.

## Model GT1000

**ADJUSTMENT.** A belt idler type clutch is used on Model GT1000 tractors. The clutch idler is spring loaded and does not require adjustment. However, angle of clutch-brake pedals (1–Fig. W19) can be adjusted as follows: Remove cotter pin from lower end of clutch rod (2). Turn clutch rod in or out of the ferrule as required until desired pedal angle is obtained.

**R&R DRIVE BELT.** To remove drive belt, first unbolt and remove belt guard from right side of engine. Remove pto drive belt if so equipped. Loosen bolt in center of spring tension idler and remove cap screw securing engine pulley to crankshaft. Slide pulleys out and remove drive belt from the pulleys. Remove shoulder bolt near transaxle pulley and remove drive belt from tractor. Install new belt by reversing removal procedure.

## Models GT1020-GT1120

**ADJUSTMENT.** A spring loaded belt idler type clutch is used on Models GT1020 and GT1120 with variable speed drive. If belts slip with speed in lowest position or if maximum speed is not reached with speed control in highest position, brake-clutch rod needs to be adjusted.

To adjust rod, place speed control in lowest position with engine running. Depress clutch pedal and release it. Check to see if engine drive belt (5–Fig. W21) is 1/16-inch (1.5 mm) below edge of variable speed pulley (4). If belt is too low, loosen locknut on brake-clutch rod (7) and screw rod in or out until clearance is obtained. Final drive belt (3) is spring loaded and requires no adjustment.

**R&R DRIVE BELTS.** To remove drive belts, remove pto belt from engine pulley. Unbolt and remove engine pulley. Place speed control lever in forward position and pull down on lower pulley on rear belt. Work rear belt from variable speed pulley and idler pulleys. Move speed control to low position and slide center section of variable speed pulley towards right side of tractor. Remove front belt. Install new belts by reversing removal procedure.

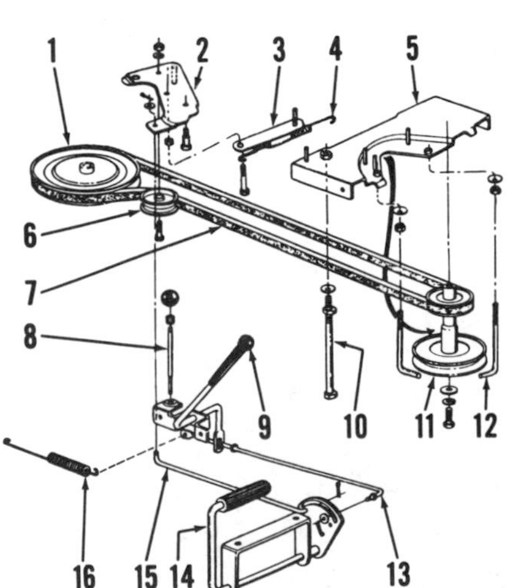


*Fig. W18–Exploded view of clutch and drive belt used on Models LT84, LT110 and LT111.*

1. Transaxle pulley
2. Clutch idler bracket
3. Belt guard
4. Idler tension spring
5. Belt guard
6. Idler pulley
7. Drive belt
8. Park brake lever
9. Hand brake lever
10. Belt guide
11. Engine pulley
12. Belt keeper
13. Brake rod
14. Clutch-brake pedal
15. Clutch rod
16. Brake linkage spring

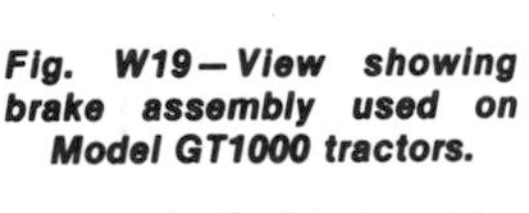

*Fig. W19–View showing brake assembly used on Model GT1000 tractors.*

1. Clutch-brake pedals.
2. Clutch rod
3. Spring
4. Brake rod
6. Brake band
7. Adjusting nut
8. Brake drum

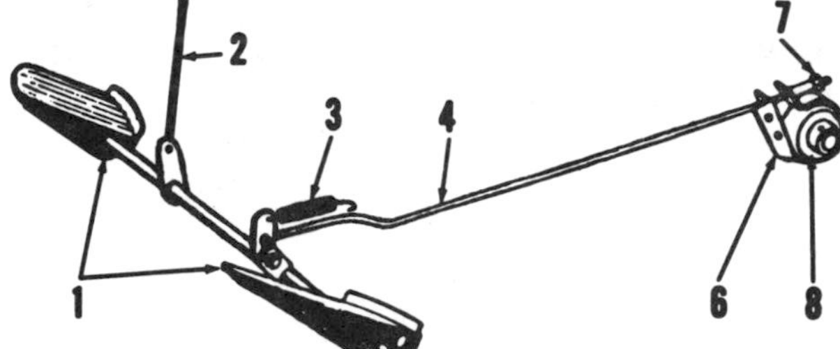


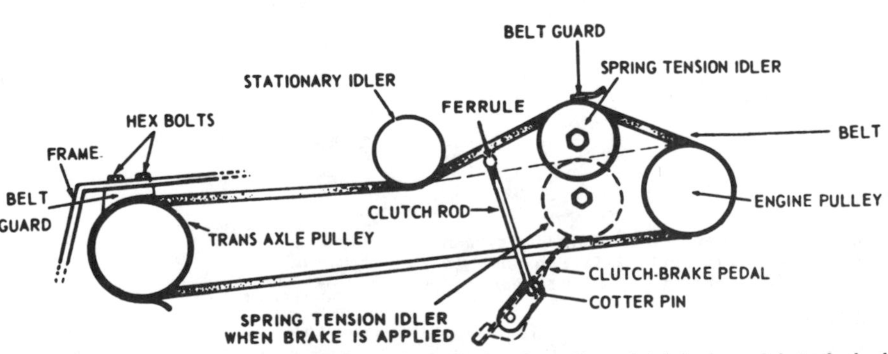


*Fig. W20–Remove cotter pin and adjust length of clutch rod to adjust clutch-brake pedals to desired angle on Model GT1000. Adjust brake linkage until spring tension idler is at disengaged position shown when brake is applied.*



Illustrations courtesy White Outdoor Products.

## Models GT1050-GT1600

**ADJUSTMENT.** The clutch used on Model GT1050 and GT1600 tractors is a spring loaded, double disc type and is operated by the clutch pedal on left side of tractor. The clutch is adjusted by turning adjusting nut (15 – Fig. W22) at end of actuating chain (19). With clutch engaged, turn nut (15) until slack is removed from chain (19) and there is approximately 1/32-inch (1 mm) clearance between clutch arm (9) and bearing cover (10).

To adjust tension of transmission drive belt, loosen locknut on belt idler leveler screw shown in Fig. W24. Unscrewing leveler screw will increase belt tension. Belt deflection (A) should be ½-inch (13 mm) with 10 pounds (44.5 N) of force applied midway between transmission input pulley and right angle drive pulley.

**R&R AND OVERHAUL CLUTCH.** To remove clutch assembly, disconnect clutch actuating rod and chain (19 – Fig. W22) from clutch arm (9). Remove clutch arm anchor bolt, then unbolt right angle drive bracket from frame. Move right angle drive and clutch assembly rearward and remove transmission drive belt from right angle drive pulley. Lift right angle drive and clutch assembly from tractor. Place right angle drive bracket in a vise and place a pair of "C" clamps as shown in Fig. W23. Tighten clamps until pressure is relieved from upper pin (2), then drive out pin. Slowly release "C" clamps to relieve spring pressure. Remainder of disassembly is evident.

To reassemble clutch, reverse disassembly procedure. Adjust clutch and drive belt as outlined in preceding paragraph.

## Models GT1110-LGT1110-LGT1155

The clutch used on these tractors is spring loaded and does not require adjustment. If drive belts slip during normal operation due to excessive belt wear or stretching, renew drive belts. See Fig. W25.

**R&R DRIVE BELTS.** To remove front drive belt, raise and block front of tractor. Observe the way belt is twisted. If new belt is installed with wrong twist, tractor will run backwards. Unscrew engine pulley belt guard and swing guard towards front of tractor. Use a bar to pry pulley assembly (Fig. W26) forward and unhook belt. When installing new belt, twist belt to the left before attaching it to pulley assembly.

To remove rear belt, depress clutch-brake pedal and set parking brake. Remove belt guard pins on pulley assembly (Fig. W27). Remove idler pulley by removing center bolt. On Models GT1110 and LGT1110, remove transaxle pulley center bolt and slide pulley and belt off. On Model LGT1155, remove hydrostatic pulley belt guard and loosen rear axle mounting bolts. Pry frame away from hydrostatic unit about ¼-inch (6 mm) and remove belt. Reverse procedure to reassemble.

## Model LGT1100

A belt idler type clutch is used on Model LGT1100. Clutch idler is spring loaded and does not require adjustment. If drive belt slips during normal operation, check for broken clutch tension

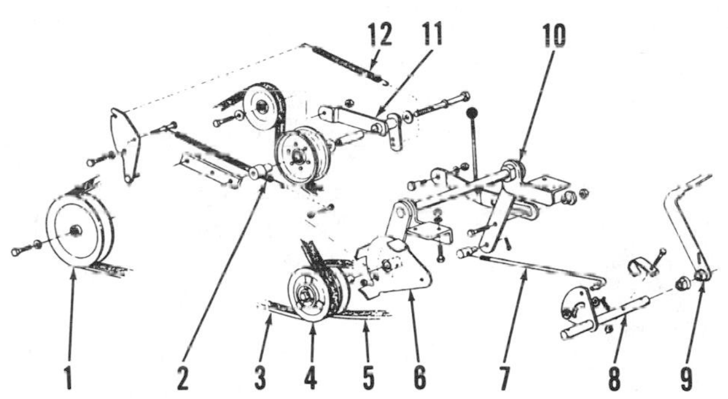

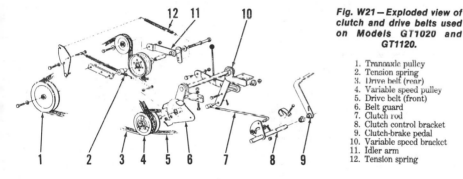

***Fig. W21 — Exploded view of clutch and drive belts used on Models GT1020 and GT1120.***

1. Transaxle pulley
2. Tension spring
3. Drive belt (rear)
4. Variable speed pulley
5. Drive belt (front)
6. Belt guard
7. Clutch rod
8. Clutch control bracket
9. Clutch-brake pedal
10. Variable speed bracket
11. Idler arm
12. Tension spring

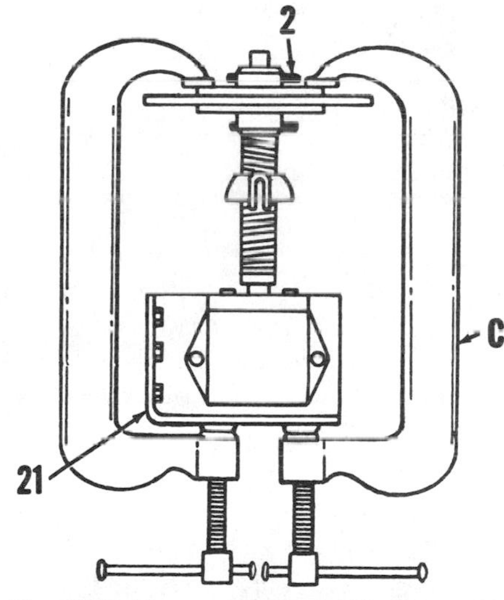


***Fig. W23 — To remove roll pin (2), tighten "C" clamps against outer disc and right angle drive bracket (21), then drive out pin.***

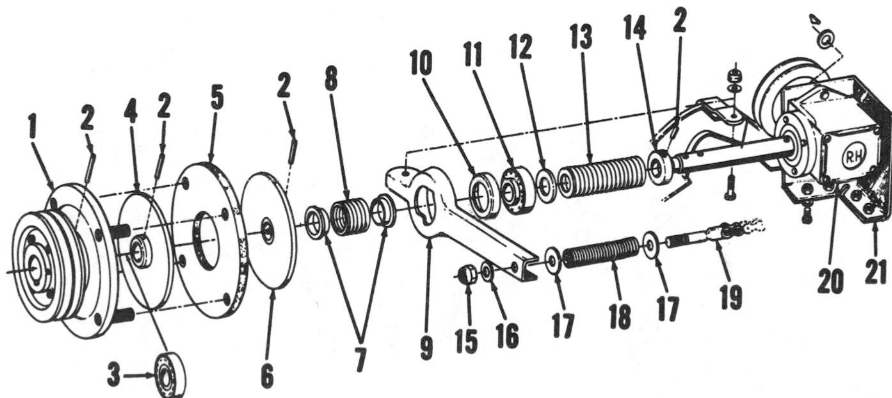


***Fig. W22 — Exploded view of clutch assembly used on Model GT1050 and GT1600 tractors.***

1. Pto drive & adapter assy.
2. Roll pins
3. Bearing
4. Outer disc
5. Drive plate
6. Inner disc
7. Spring guides
8. Spring
9. Clutch arm
10. Bearing cover
11. Bearing
12. Washer
13. Clutch spring
14. Collar
15. Adjusting nut
16. Washer
17. Washers
18. Spring
19. Rod & chain
20. Right angle drive unit
21. Bracket

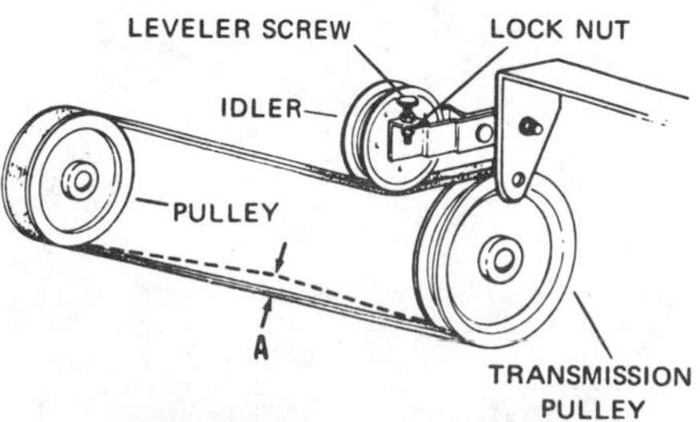


***Fig. W24 — Adjust tension of transmission drive belt on Models GT1050 and GT1600 by turning leveler screw. Belt should deflect ½-inch (13 mm) at (A) with 10 pounds (44.5 N) force applied.***

Illustrations courtesy White Outdoor Products.

spring (2–Fig. W28) or worn drive belt (12).

**R&R DRIVE BELT.** To remove drive belt, depress clutch-brake pedal and engage parking brake. Remove transaxle pulley belt guard and slip belt off pulley (1–Fig. W28). Unhook idler spring and unbolt and remove upper idler (5) and lower idler (10). Disconnect clutch-brake rod (3), remove outer cotter pin from clutch shaft (9) and pull shaft out of frame bracket (7). Disconnect transaxle shift rod from shifter bracket. Remove drive belt from engine pulley. Install new belt in reverse order of removal.

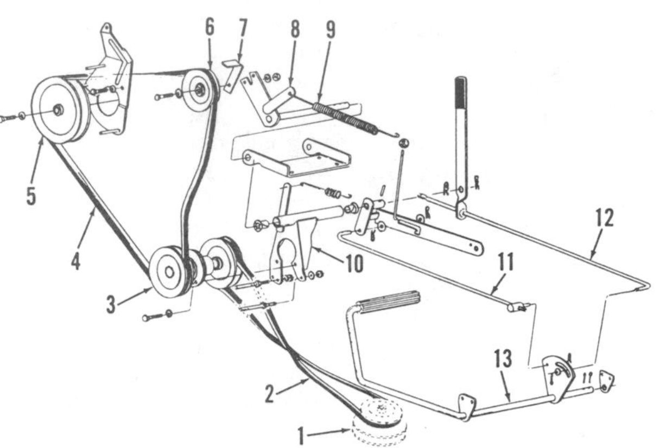

*Fig. W25—Exploded view of clutch and drive belts used on Models GT1110 and LGT1110. Model LGT1155 is similar.*

1. Engine pulley
2. Drive belt (front)
3. Jackshaft assy.
4. Drive belt (rear)
5. Transaxle pulley
6. Clutch idler pulley
7. Belt guard
8. Clutch bracket
9. Tension spring
10. Jackshaft bracket
11. Clutch rod
12. Brake rod
13. Clutch-brake pedal

*Fig. W26—To remove front drive belt, use a bar to pry pulley assembly forward and unhook belt from pulley.*

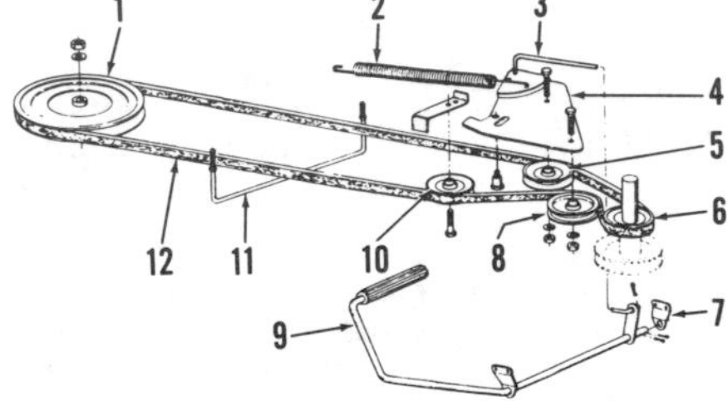

*Fig. W28—Exploded view of clutch and drive belt used on Model LGT1100.*

1. Transaxle pulley
2. Tension spring
3. Clutch rod
4. Idler bracket
5. Idler (upper)
6. Engine pulley
7. Bracket
8. Clutch idler
9. Clutch-brake pedal shaft
10. Idler (lower)
11. Belt guide
12. Drive belt

*Fig. W27—To remove rear clutch belt, remove belt guard pins and depress clutch-brake pedal.*

## Models L12-LT12

A continuously variable drive pulley is used on these models. Depressing the clutch-brake pedal part way disengages the clutch. Depressing pedal all the way down disengages the clutch and engages the disc brake.

To adjust clutch and speed control linkage, first adjust speed control lever linkage as follows: Push clutch-brake pedal forward until stop on brake rod (Fig. W29) contacts frame and hold in this position. Position speed control shift lever in parking brake position. Remove hairpin clip from speed control rod ferrule and adjust ferrule on rod so ferrule contacts rear end of slot in speed selector lever cam. Reinstall hairpin clip.

Adjust speed control link (Fig. W29) to obtain correct neutral adjustment as follows: Place transaxle shift lever in neutral position and start engine. Move speed control lever to full speed position. Release clutch-brake pedal completely, then fully depress pedal and hold in this position. Shut off engine, and after engine completely stops, release clutch-brake pedal. Move speed control lever to second position. Disconnect speed control link from variable

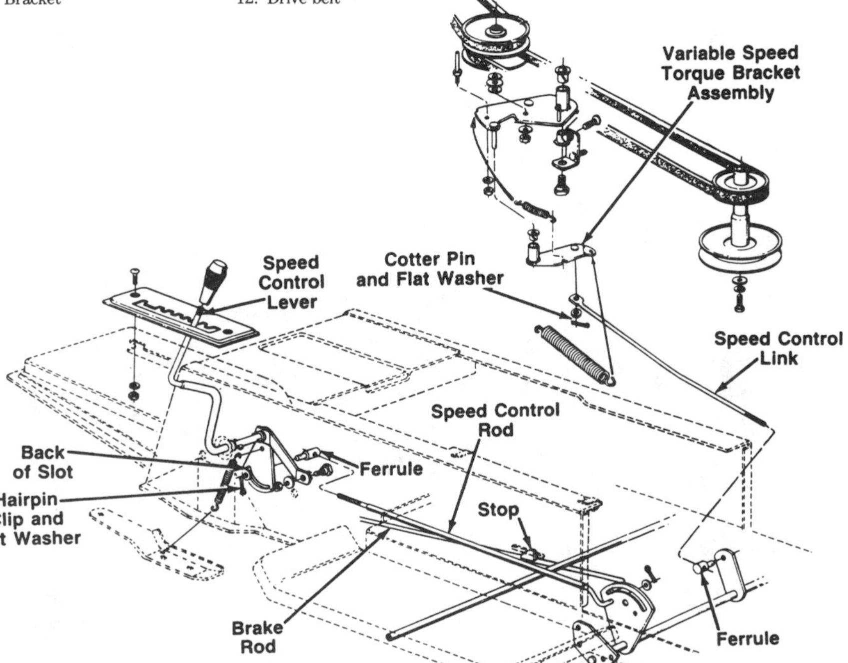


*Fig. W29—View of variable speed control linkage used on Models L12 and LT12.*

speed torque bracket. Move clutch-brake pedal as far up as it will go. While holding pedal in this position, thread speed control link in or out of ferrule until rod slips easily onto pin on torque bracket. Install cotter pin to secure speed control link to torque bracket.

**R&R DRIVE BELTS.** To remove secondary (rear) drive belt (7—Fig. W30), remove knob from transmission shift lever. Remove screws attaching transmission cover plate to frame, disconnect safety start switch wire and remove transmission cover. Push belt idler (5) to relieve tension on belt and work belt off variable pulley (8). Remove bolts attaching transmission shift lever bracket to frame and move bracket out of the way. Slip belt between shift lever bracket and frame and remove from transmission pulley. To install belt, reverse the removal procedure.

To remove primary (front) drive belt (13—Fig. W30), first remove secondary (rear) drive belt from idler pulley and variable speed pulley as outlined above. Remove belt guides (11) from engine pulley (12). Place mower lift lever in disengaged position, then work mower drive belt from engine pulley. Unbolt and remove engine pulley guard (10). Push clutch-brake pedal all the way down and hold in this position. Push forward on variable drive pulley and remove drive belt from engine pulley. Release clutch-brake pedal, lift belt off variable pulley and remove through top opening in frame. To install belt, reverse the removal procedure.

### Model LT125

A spring loaded belt idler is used on Model LT125 and no adjustment is required. If drive belt slips during normal operation due to excessive belt wear or stretching, renew drive belt.

**R&R DRIVE BELT.** To remove drive belt (Fig. W31), first remove mower deck from underneath tractor. Depress clutch-brake pedal and set park brake. Raise and support front of tractor. Remove transmission cover panel from tractor frame. Disconnect spring from rear idler pulley. Unbolt and remove belt keeper plate from engine pulley. Remove belt from idler pulleys. Work belt off engine pulley. If equipped with cold weather starting kit, remove belt guard at transmission pulley. On all tractors, remove belt from transmission pulley and remove from tractor. To install belt, reverse the removal procedure.

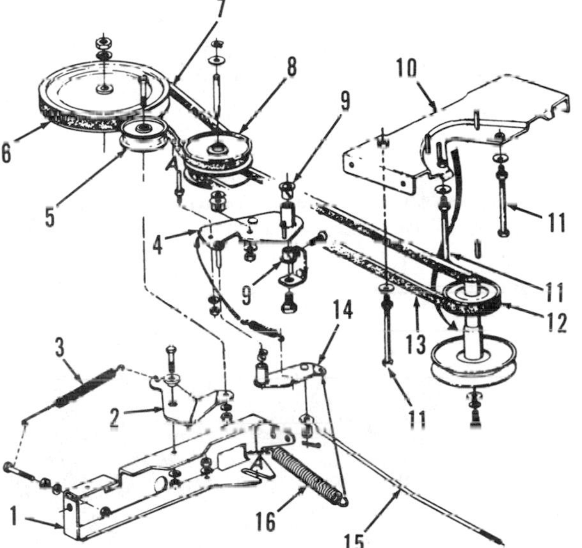


*Fig. W30—Exploded view of traction drive belts and pulleys used on Models L12 and LT12.*

1. Transaxle support bracket
2. Idler bracket
3. Spring
4. Variable speed bracket
5. Idler pulley
6. Transaxle pulley
7. Secondary drive belt
8. Variable speed pulley assy.
9. Bushings
10. Belt guard bracket
11. Belt guides
12. Engine pulley
13. Primary drive belt
14. Variable speed torque bracket
15. Speed control link
16. Spring

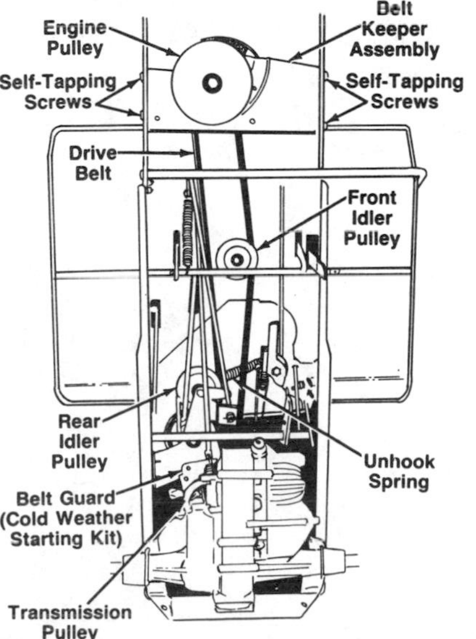


*Fig. W31—Underside view of traction drive belt on Model LT125.*

## BRAKE

### Models T80-T85

**ADJUSTMENT.** A disc type brake is used on these tractor. See Fig. W33. To adjust brake, move pedal forward by hand until a slight resistance is noted. This is the point where brake pedal spring begins to stretch. If adjustment is correct, parking brake lock will have moved approximately $^1/_4$ inch (6 mm) as shown in Fig. W32. If not, tighten or loosen adjusting nut (11—Fig. W33) until correct dimension is obtained.

**R&R AND OVERHAUL.** To remove disc brake, disconnect brake rod from

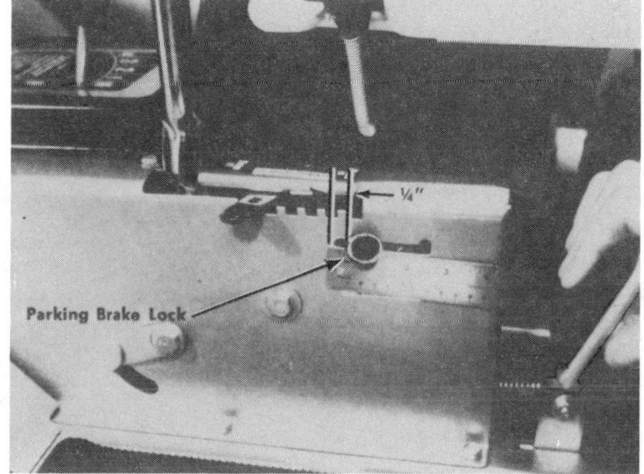


*Fig. W32—On Models T80, T82, T85, T100 and T110, move brake pedal forward until a slight resistance is noted. At this time, parking brake lock should have moved 1/4 inch (6 mm) as shown. Refer to text for adjustment procedure.*

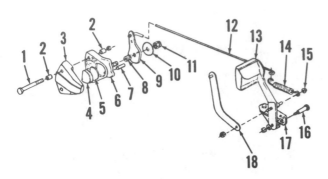

*Fig. W33—Exploded view of disc brake assembly used on Models T80 and T85.*

1. Cap screw
2. Spacers
3. Carrier & friction pad
4. Friction pad
5. Back-up disc
6. Carrier
7. Actuating pin
8. Spring
9. Actuating cam
10. Washer
11. Adjusting nut
12. Brake rod
13. Brake pedal
14. Linkage spring
15. Spring retainer
16. Shoulder bolt
17. Pedal bracket
18. Parking brake lever

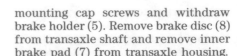

actuating cam lever (9—Fig. W33). Remove brake mounting cap screws and separate brake carriers (3 and 6).

Inspect all parts for excessive wear and renew as necessary. When reassembling brake, be sure round end of actuating pin (7) is toward actuating cam (9). Rear axle sprocket is the disc for brake assembly; be sure that axle sprocket is free of grease or oil. Adjust brake as previously outlined.

## Models T100-T110-LT84-LT110-LGT1100

**ADJUSTMENT.** The brake is a disc type (Fig. W34) located on right side of transaxle. To adjust brake, tighten adjusting nut (10) until brake disc is locked. Then, loosen nut one turn. Make sure disc turns freely when pedal is released.

**NOTE: When inside of cam lever (9—Fig. W34) contacts brake housing (5), brake pads (1 and 3) must be renewed.**

**R&R AND OVERHAUL.** To remove brake, disconnect brake linkage from cam lever (9—Fig. W34). Unbolt and remove brake pad holder (5). Withdraw brake disc from transaxle brake shaft and remove inner brake pad (1).

Inspect all parts for excessive wear and renew as necessary. Adjust brake as previously outlined.

## Models L12-LT12-LT125

**ADJUSTMENT.** The brake is a disc type located on right side of transaxle. To adjust brake, remove cotter pin from castle nut (2—Fig. W35). Turn nut until brake just starts to engage when brake lever (3) is $^{1}/_{4}$ to $^{5}/_{16}$ inch (6.5-8 mm) away from axle housing. Install cotter pin and test brakes. Repeat adjustment as necessary.

**R&R AND OVERHAUL.** To remove brake, disconnect brake linkage from brake lever (3—Fig. W35). Remove mounting cap screws and withdraw brake holder (5). Remove brake disc (8) from transaxle shaft and remove inner brake pad (7) from transaxle housing.

Inspect all parts for excessive wear and renew as necessary. When installing brake, be sure back-up plate (6) is in place between brake holder (5) and brake pad (7). Be sure round end of actuator pins (4) is toward brake lever (3). Be sure brake disc is free of grease or oil.

## Models T82-GT1110-LGT1110-LGT1155

**ADJUSTMENT.** A disc type brake is used on these models. To adjust brake, loosen locknut and turn center bolt all the way in (Fig. W36). Unscrew center bolt one complete turn. Tighten locknut and test brakes. Repeat adjustment as necessary.

**R&R AND OVERHAUL.** To remove brake, disconnect brake linkage from cam lever. Remove mounting cap screws and separate carriers (2 and 6—Fig. W37).

Inspect parts and renew as necessary. When assembling brake, be sure round end of actuator pin (3) is toward cam lever. Be sure brake disc is free of grease or oil.

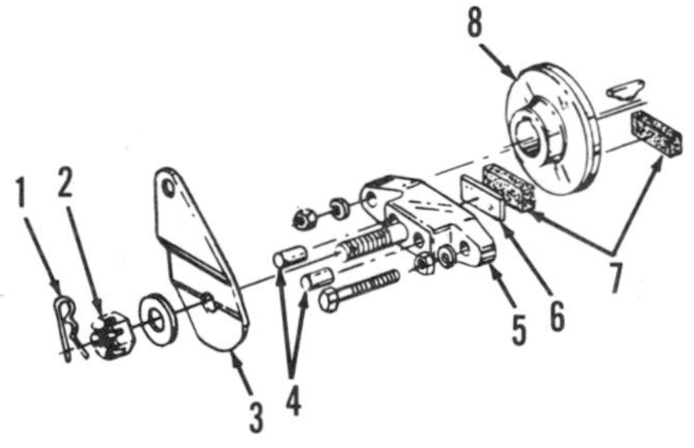

*Fig. W35—Exploded view of disc brake assembly used on Models L12, LT12 and LT125.*

1. Cotter pin
2. Adjusting nut
3. Brake cam lever
4. Actuating pins
5. Brake pad holder
6. Back-up plate
7. Brake pads
8. Brake disc

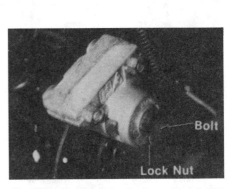

*Fig. W36—To adjust disc brake on Models T82, GT1110, LGT1110 and LGT1155, loosen locknut and turn center bolt all the way in. Then back bolt off one complete turn.*

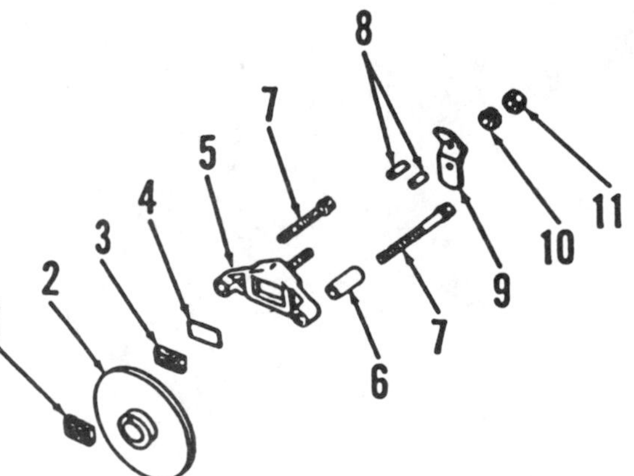

*Fig. W34—Exploded view of typical disc brake used on Models T100, T110, LT84, LT110, LT111 and LGT1100.*

1. Brake pad (inner)
2. Brake disc
3. Brake pad (outer)
4. Back-up plate
5. Pad holder
6. Spacer
7. Cap screw
8. Dowel pins
9. Cam lever
10. Adjusting nut
11. Jam nut

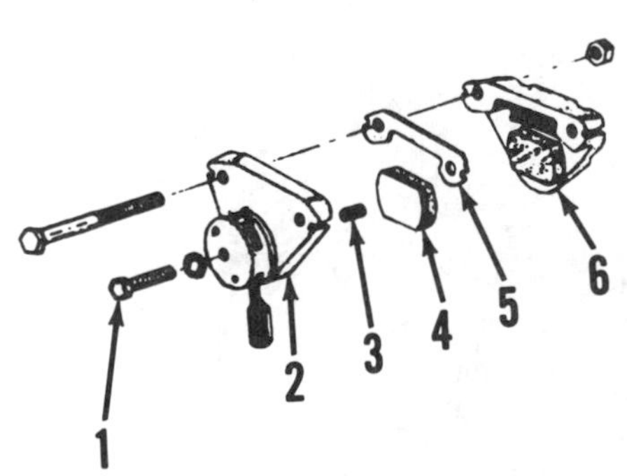

*Fig. W37—Exploded view of disc brake assembly used on Models T82, GT1110, LGT1110 and LGT1155. Spacer (5) is used on Model T82 only.*

## Model T112

**ADJUSTMENT.** A disc type brake is used on T112 tractors. Check and adjust air gap between brake pad (1—Fig. W38) and disc (3) with brake pedal in released (up) position. The air gap should be 0.010-0.020 inch (0.25-0.50 mm) and is adjusted by turning set screw (5) in center of brake jaw (4) or by placing shims under shoulder bolt (7).

**R&R AND OVERHAUL.** To remove brake, disconnect brake linkage from actuating lever (6—Fig. W38). Remove shoulder bolt (7) and withdraw brake jaw (4), disc (3) and pads (1) from transaxle.

Renew all worn or damaged parts and reassemble by reversing removal procedure. Adjust brake as previously outlined.

## Model GT1000

**ADJUSTMENT.** A band type brake, located on left side of transaxle, is used on Model GT1000. To adjust brake, turn adjusting nut (7—Fig. W19) until top of spring tension idler (Fig. W20) is in disengaged position as shown when brake is applied.

Service to brake normally consists of renewing brake band.

## Models GT1020-GT1050-GT1120-GT1600

**ADJUSTMENT.** The disc type brake is located on left side of transaxle. To adjust brake, tighten adjusting nut (9—Fig. W39) until brake is locked. Then, loosen nut one turn and recheck brake action. Be sure brake disc turns freely when pedal is released.

**R&R AND OVERHAUL.** Disconnect brake linkage from cam lever (7—Fig. W39). Remove mounting cap screws and separate brake calipers (1 and 4).

Renew all excessively worn parts. When reassembling brake, be sure rounded end of pin (5) is toward cam lever. Adjust as previously outlined.

# RIGHT ANGLE DRIVE UNIT

## Models GT1050-GT1600

**R&R AND OVERHAUL.** To remove right angle drive unit, remove clutch assembly as previously outlined and separate clutch from right angle drive assembly. Remove pulley and mounting bracket from drive unit.

To disassemble right angle drive unit, remove cover (1—Fig. W40) and drain lubricant. Unbolt and remove seal retainer (13) with oil seal (14) and gasket (12). Unseat snap ring (18) from its groove in input shaft (10). Withdraw input shaft and bearing (11) and remove snap ring (18) and gear (9) through cover opening of case. Remove oil seal (17) and snap ring (16), then drive output shaft (6) with bearing (5) and gear (4) out through cover opening of case. Remove snap ring (3), output gear (4) and bearing (5) from output shaft. Remove bearing (11) from input shaft.

Clean and inspect all parts and renew any showing excessive wear or other damage. Reassemble by reversing disassembly procedure and fill unit with 6 ounces (177 mL) of EP lithium base grease.

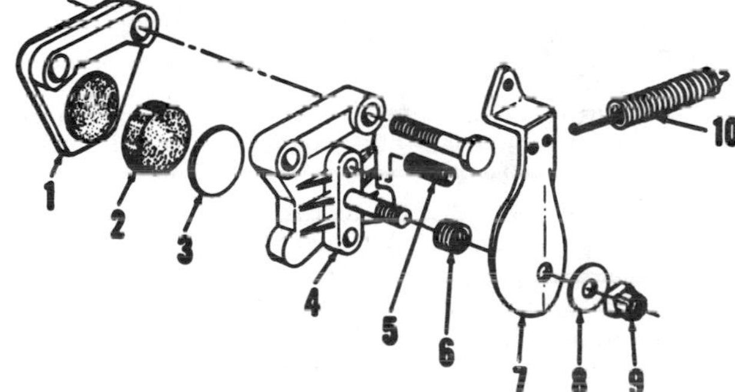


*Fig. W39—Exploded view of disc brake assembly used on Models GT1050 and GT1600. Brake used on Models GT1020 and GT1120 is similar.*

1. Caliper & pad (inner)
2. Friction pad
3. Back-up disc
4. Caliper (outer)
5. Actuating pin
6. Spring
7. Cam lever
8. Washer
9. Adjusting nut
10. Spring (2 used)

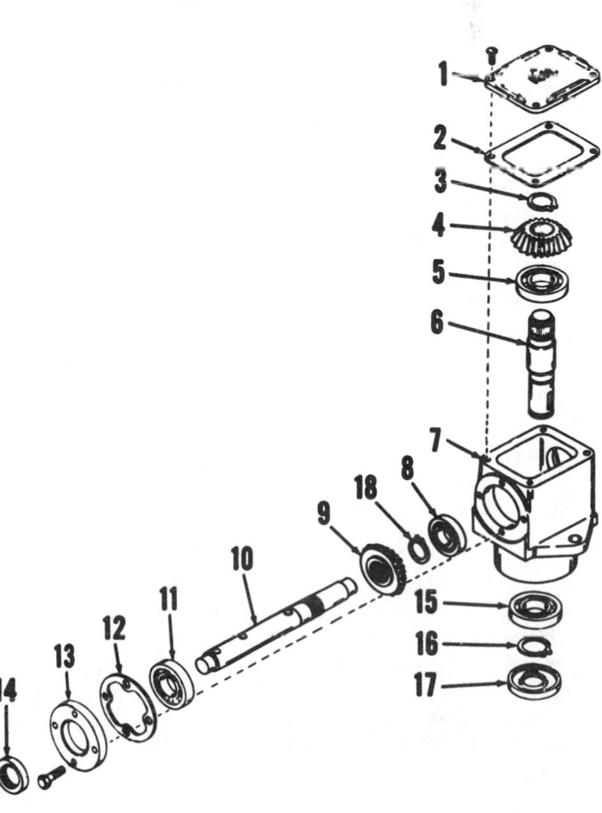


*Fig. W40—Exploded view of right angle drive unit used on Model GT1050 and GT1600 tractors.*

1. Cover
2. Gasket
3. Snap ring
4. Output gear
5. Bearing
6. Output shaft
7. Case
8. Bearing
9. Input gear
10. Input shaft
11. Bearing
12. Gasket
13. Seal retainer
14. Oil seal
15. Bearing
16. Snap ring
17. Oil seal
18. Snap ring

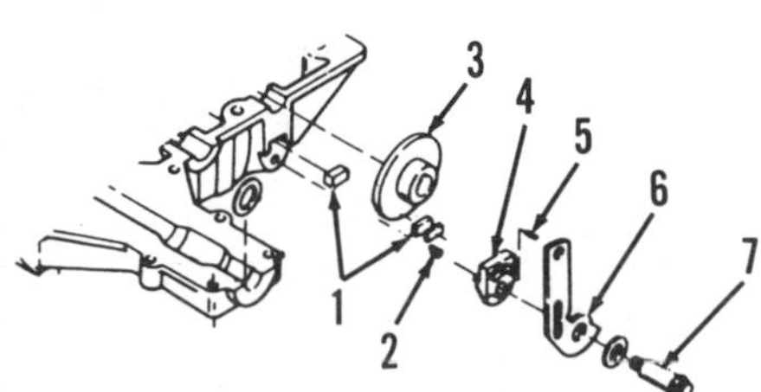


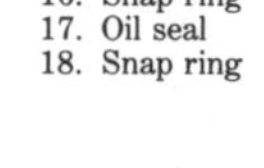

*Fig. W38—Exploded view of disc brake assembly used on Model T112.*

1. Brake pads
2. Spring
3. Brake disc
4. Brake jaw
5. Set screw
6. Brake lever
7. Shoulder bolt

# GEAR TRANSMISSION

## LUBRICATION

### Models T80-T82

Models T80 and T82 are equipped with a Peerless Model 500 gear transmission with four forward gears and one reverse. Transmission is packed at the factory with 12 ounces (355 mL) of lithium base grease.

Model T85 is equipped with a Foote single speed, forward-reverse gear transmission. Transmission is packed at the factory with 5 ounces (148 mL) of lithium base grease.

## REMOVE AND REINSTALL

### Models T80-T82

To remove transmission, depress clutch pedal and retain pedal in disengaged position. Remove nut and washer from transmission input pulley, then remove pulley and drive belt from transmission. Unbolt and remove upper frame cover. Loosen the two locking nuts on each end of rear axle mounting bracket and loosen the two adjusting nuts at rear of frame until drive chain can be removed from transmission output sprocket. Unbolt transmission from main frame and remove transmission assembly from tractor.

Reinstall transmission by reversing removal procedure. Adjust differential drive chain tension by tightening the two adjusting nuts at rear of frame. Drive chain should deflect about ½ inch (13 mm) when a force of 10 pounds (44.5 N) is applied midway between sprockets. When proper chain tension is obtained, tighten locking nuts on rear axle mounting bracket.

### Model T85

To remove forward-reverse transmission, place variable drive lever in full rearward position. Push variable speed pulley towards transmission input pulley and remove gear drive belt. Remove nut, washers and pulley from transmission input shaft. Unbolt and remove upper frame cover. Loosen locknuts on each end of rear axle mounting bracket and loosen the two adjusting nuts at rear of frame until drive chain can be removed from transmission output sprocket. Unbolt transmission from main frame, then lift transmission from tractor.

Reinstall in reverse order of removal. After transmission is reinstalled, adjust differential drive chain tension by tightening the two adjusting nuts at rear of frame. Drive chain should deflect about ½ inch (13 mm) when a force of 10 pounds (44.5 N) is applied midway between sprockets. When proper chain tension is obtained, tighten locknuts on rear axle mounting bracket.

## OVERHAUL

### Models T80-T82-T85

Models T80 and T82 are equipped with a Peerless 500 series gear transmission and Model T85 is equipped with a Foote Model 35-3500, single speed, forward-reverse, gear transmission. Refer to the appropriate Peerless or Foote section in GEAR TRANSMISSION SERVICE section for overhaul procedure.

# TRANSAXLE

## LUBRICATION

### All Models

Transaxle, on models so equipped, may be manufactured by Peerless or Foote. A variety of transaxle models and series have been used. Refer to the CONDENSED SPECIFICATIONS tables at the beginning of this section for transaxle fluid capacity and fluid type.

## REMOVE AND REINSTALL

### Models T100-T110

To remove transaxle assembly, move seat rearward and remove upper frame cover. Support tractor under main frame. Remove transaxle mounting bolts and the two adjusting nuts (early models) at rear of frame. Disconnect brake linkage, then remove drive belt and transaxle input pulley. Raise rear of tractor and roll transaxle assembly rearward from tractor. Unbolt and remove disc brake assembly and transaxle mounting brackets. Drive out roll pins and remove rear wheel and hub assemblies.

Reinstall transaxle assembly by reversing removal procedure. On early models, adjust rear belt tension by tightening the two adjusting nuts at rear of frame until belt will deflect about ½ inch (13 mm) when 10 pounds (44.5 N) pressure is applied midway between pulleys. When correct belt tension is obtained, tighten transaxle mounting bolts. Adjust brake linkage as required.

### Model T112

To remove transaxle assembly, support tractor under main frame. Disconnect brake linkage and Hi-Lo shifter. Remove gear shift knob and drive belt. Remove transaxle mounting bolts and roll assembly away from tractor. Unbolt and remove disc brake assembly and rear wheel assemblies.

Reinstall transaxle assembly by reversing removal procedure.

### Models LT84-LT110-LT111-LGT1100

To remove transaxle assembly, unbolt and remove seat plate and rear fenders. Support tractor main frame and remove transaxle belt keeper assembly. Depress clutch-brake pedal and work drive belt off transaxle pulley. Disconnect shift linkage and brake linkage. Unbolt transaxle from support brackets and braces and roll transaxle rearward away from tractor. Unbolt and remove brake pad holder and brake disc. Remove rear wheel and hub assemblies.

Reinstall transaxle assembly by reversing removal procedure.

### Model GT1000

To remove transaxle assembly, unbolt and remove rear frame cover. Remove shoulder bolt below transaxle input pulley. Remove pulley retaining nut, depress clutch-brake pedal and slide belt and pulley from transaxle input shaft. Disconnect brake linkage and support tractor main frame. Remove transaxle mounting bolts, raise rear of tractor and roll transaxle assembly rearward from tractor. Unbolt and remove brake band and brake drum. Remove cotter pins, washers, spacer sleeves and wheel and hub assemblies.

Reinstall transaxle by reversing removal procedure and fill transaxle housing to level plug opening on front of unit with SAE 90 EP gear oil. Capacity is approximately 3 pints (1.4 L). Adjust brake linkage as required.

### Models GT1020-GT1120-GT1110-LGT1110

To remove transaxle, remove rear drive belt, disconnect brake linkage and remove shift knob. Support tractor, then unbolt transaxle and roll transaxle away from tractor. Unbolt and remove disc brake assembly, input pulley and rear wheel assemblies.

Reinstall transaxle by reversing removal procedure and fill transaxle unit to level plug opening with SAE 90 EP gear oil. Capacity is approximately 4 pints (1.9 L).

### Models GT1050-GT1600

To remove transaxle assembly, loosen locknut and turn idler leveler screw inward until drive belt can be removed from transaxle pulley. Disconnect brake linkage and remove gear shift knob. Support tractor under main frame. Unbolt transaxle from tractor frame, raise rear of tractor and roll transaxle assembly rearward from tractor. Unbolt and remove disc brake assembly, transaxle input pulley and rear wheel and hub assemblies.

Reinstall transaxle by reversing removal procedure and fill transaxle unit to level plug opening with SAE 90 EP gear oil. Capacity is approximately 4 pints (1.9 L).

### Models L12-LT12

To remove transaxle assembly, unbolt and remove transmission cover plate from top of frame. Disconnect brake control linkage and shift control linkage. Remove bolts attaching transmission shift lever bracket to frame. Push idler pulley to relieve tension on drive belt idler and remove drive belt from transaxle pulley. Remove bolts securing transaxle housing to transaxle support bracket and rear of frame, raise rear of tractor and roll transaxle rearward from tractor.

Reinstall transaxle assembly by reversing removal procedure. Adjust shift control linkage and brake linkage as required.

## OVERHAUL

### All Models

Model T112 is equipped with a Spicer (Foote) 4000-5 transaxle. Models T100 and T110 are equipped with a Peerless 600 series transaxle. Models L12 and LT12 are equipped with a single speed MTD transaxle. Models LT110, LT111, LGT1100 and LT84 are equipped with a Peerless 800 series transaxle. Model GT1000 is equipped with a Peerless 1200 series transaxle. Models GT1020, GT1050, GT1110, GT1120, GT1600 and LGT1110 are equipped with a Peerless 2300 series transaxle. Refer to the appropriate Spicer (Foote), MTD or Peerless section in TRANSAXLE SERVICE section for overhaul procedure.

# HYDROSTATIC TRANSMISSION

## LUBRICATION

### Model LGT1155

The hydrostatic transmission is equipped with an integral reservoir. Recommended transmission fluid is SAE 20 high detergent oil with SF rating.

If natural color of transmission fluid has changed (black or milky), fluid should be drained and renewed. To drain hydrostatic transmission, remove hex plug on bottom of transmission housing and vent plug on top of housing. When refilling transmission, add oil to reservoir tank until oil overflows out vent hole in housing. Then, reinstall vent plug and continue to fill reservoir tank to COLD mark on tank.

### Model LT-125

The hydrostatic transmission is equipped with an integral reservoir. To check transmission fluid level, remove transmission cover plate located in front of the seat. Fluid level (oil cold) should be maintained at the LOWER mark on expansion tank (Fig. W41). Recommended fluid is SAE 10W-30 engine oil rated SF.

If natural color of transmission fluid has changed (black or milky), fluid should be drained and renewed. To drain hydrostatic transmission, remove plug from bottom of transmission housing. When refilling transmission, add oil to reservoir until level reaches LOWER mark on expansion tank. Start engine and run at slow idle for several minutes to purge air from system. Check fluid level and add oil as necessary.

## LINKAGE ADJUSTMENT

### Model LGT1155

Linkage adjustment is correct when tractor does not move with engine running, clutch disengaged and control lever in neutral. If tractor creeps either forward or backward with control lever in neutral, adjust linkage as follows:

Raise and block rear of tractor so both rear wheels are free to rotate. Block front tires to prevent tractor from rolling. Loosen locknuts on hydrostatic control rod (Fig. W42) and adjust length of control rod as required. Start engine and recheck adjustment.

**CAUTION: Do not attempt to adjust linkage with engine running.**

### Model LT125

The hydrostatic control linkage is in correct adjustment when tractor does not move with engine running, clutch disengaged and hydrostatic control lever in neutral position. If tractor creeps either forward or backward with control lever in neutral, adjust linkage as follows:

Raise and block rear of tractor so both rear wheels are free to rotate. Block front tires to prevent tractor from rolling.

Remove access panel located in front of the seat. Loosen cap screw that secures pintle arm extension (Fig. W43) to pintle arm. Start engine, fully depress clutch-brake pedal and set parking brake.

**CAUTION: Exercise caution when working around spinning wheels and drive components.**

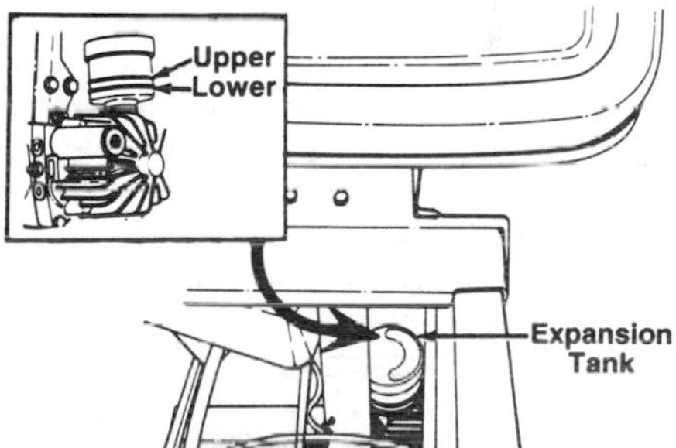


*Fig. W41—Hydrostatic transmission oil level should be checked when oil is cold. Level should be maintained at lower mark of expansion tank.*

*Fig. W42—View of hydrostatic transmission linkage adjustment point on Model LGT1155. Refer to text for adjustment procedure.*

Move hydrostatic control lever to move pintle arm until rear wheels do not rotate in either direction. Shut off engine, then tighten cap screw securing pintle arm extension to pintle arm. Release clutch-brake pedal, start engine and recheck for correct neutral adjustment.

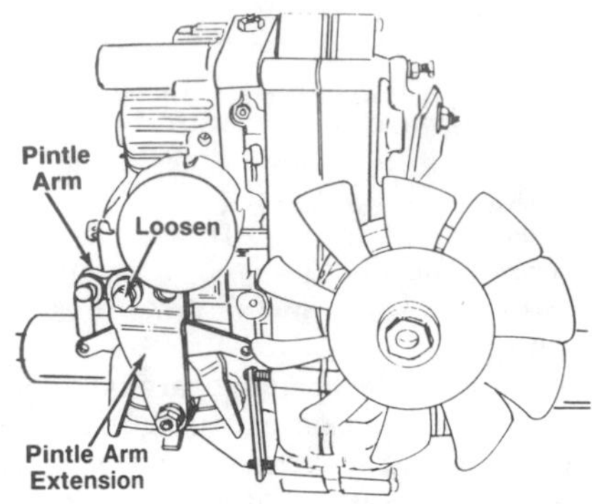


*Fig. W43—Top view of hydrostatic linkage adjustment point on Model LT125. Refer to text for adjustment procedure.*

Hydrostatic control lever (1—Fig. W44) should return to the Neutral notch in speed control quadrant when clutch-brake pedal is fully depressed. If lever does not return to neutral position, depress clutch-brake pedal and set parking brake. Loosen bolt securing hydrostatic control lever arm (1) to ball joint bracket (2). Position control lever in neutral notch, then tighten bolt attaching control lever arm to ball joint bracket.

If hydrostatic control lever is too hard to move or will not stay in set position during operation, turn adjusting nut (29—Fig. W44) as necessary to reduce or increase friction on control linkage.

## REMOVE AND REINSTALL

### Model LGT1155

To remove hydrostatic transmission, disconnect hydrostatic control linkage

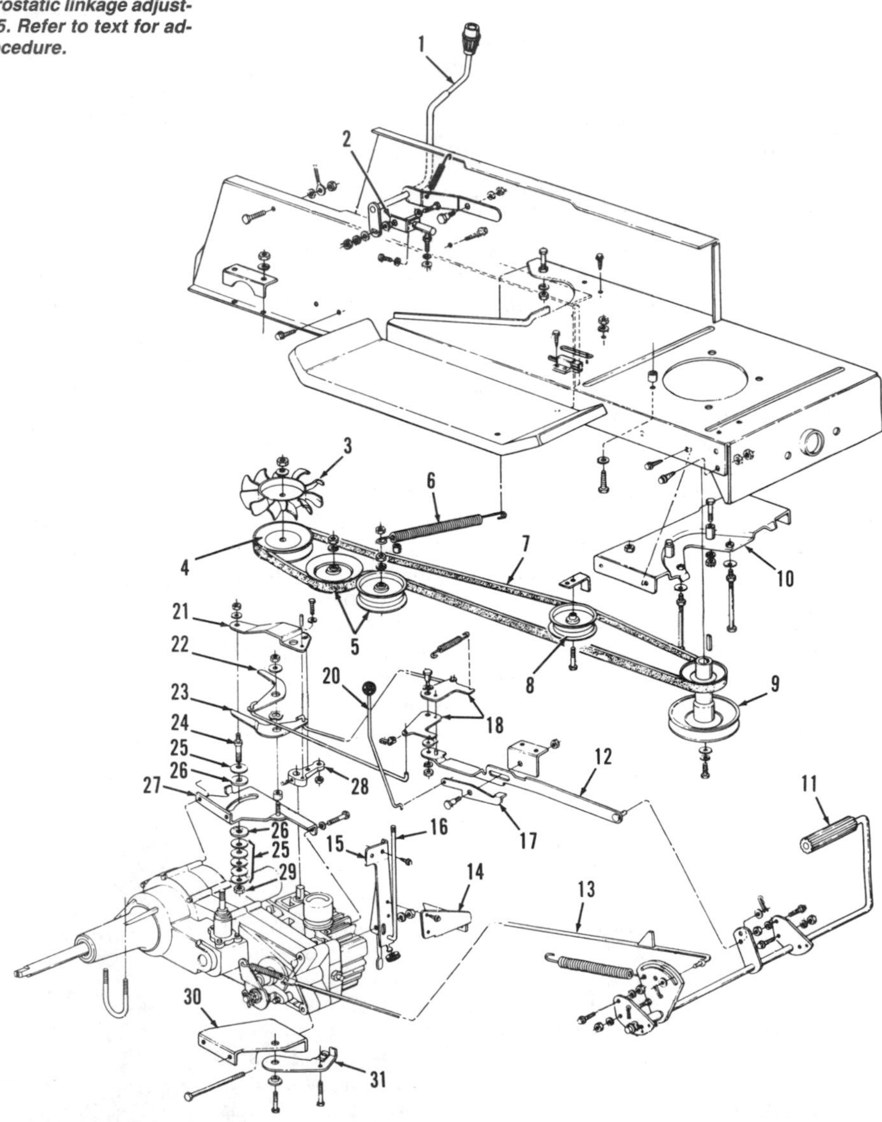

*Fig. W44—Exploded view of hydrostatic control linkage used on Model LT125.*

1. Speed selector lever
2. Ball joint bracket
3. Fan
4. Transmission pulley
5. Idler pulleys
6. Belt tension spring
7. Drive belt
8. Idler
9. Engine pulley
10. Belt guard
11. Clutch-brake pedal
12. Neutral return rod
13. Brake rod
14. Reinforcement plate
15. Transmission torque bracket
16. Release valve rod
17. Park brake lock bracket
18. Balancer brackets
20. Park brake rod
21. Pintle arm extension plate
22. Forward arm
23. Reverse arm
24. Special bolt
25. Belleville washers
26. Friction washers
27. Mounting bracket
28. Pintle shift arm
29. Nut
30. Idler plate
31. Idler bracket

from hydrostatic unit and brake control linkage from transaxle. Remove hydrostatic pulley belt guard. Remove rear axle mounting bolts. Raise rear of tractor and work drive belt off hydrostatic transmission pulley. Roll transmission and transaxle assembly rearward from tractor. Unbolt and remove hydrostatic unit from transaxle housing.

To reinstall, reverse removal procedure. Adjust transmission control linkage and brake linkage as previously outlined.

### Model LT125

To remove hydrostatic transmission, remove access plate located in front of the seat. Disconnect hydrostatic speed control lever linkage and neutral return linkage from hydrostatic unit. Disconnect brake control rod from disc brake. Remove drive belt from transmission pulley. Remove bolt securing transmission to torque bracket (15—Fig. W44). Remove axle housing U-bolts, raise rear of tractor and roll transmission and transaxle assemble from tractor. Unbolt and remove hydrostatic transmission from transaxle housing. Note that drive couplings are secured to hydrostatic transmission input and output shafts with Loctite. Removal of couplings may require use of a puller and heating couplings.

To reinstall transmission, reverse the removal procedure. Install drive couplings on transmission input and output shafts using Loctite 609 retaining compound. Apply Loctite 242 to threads of transmission mounting bolts and tighten to 80-120 in.-lbs. (9-13 N·m).

## OVERHAUL

### Models LGT1155-LT125

Model LGT1155 is equipped with an Eaton Model 6 hydrostatic transmission. Model LT125 is equipped with a Hydro-Gear Model BDU-10 hydrostatic transmission. Refer to Eaton or Hydro-Gear section in HYDROSTATIC TRANSMISSION SERVICE section for overhaul procedure.

# REDUCTION GEARS AND DIFFERENTIAL

### Models LGT1155-LT125

Model LGT1155 is equipped with a Peerless 1300 series gear reduction and differential unit. Model LT125 is equipped with a Hydro-Gear Model 210-1010S gear reduction and differential unit.

Removal and installation of gear reduction and differential unit is outlined in HYDROSTATIC TRANSMISSION remove and reinstall section. Refer to Peerless or Hydro-Gear section in REDUCTION GEAR AND DIFFERENTIAL SERVICE section for overhaul information.

# YARD-MAN

## CONDENSED SPECIFICATIONS

<table>
<tr><th></th><th colspan="5">MODELS</th></tr>
<tr><th></th><th>3260-3,<br>3260-4,<br>3260-5</th><th>3380-1,<br>3380-3,<br>3600-0</th><th>3380-2,<br>3600-1,<br>3950</th><th>3390-1,<br>3390-3</th><th>3390-2,<br>3610-0</th></tr>
<tr><td>Engine Make</td><td>B&S</td><td>B&S</td><td>B&S</td><td>B&S</td><td>B&S</td></tr>
<tr><td>Model</td><td>190707</td><td>170702</td><td>190702</td><td>170707</td><td>190707</td></tr>
<tr><td>Bore</td><td>3 in.<br>(76.2 mm)</td><td>3 in.<br>(76.2 mm)</td><td>3 in.<br>(76.2 mm)</td><td>3 in.<br>(76.2 mm)</td><td>3 in.<br>(76.2 mm)</td></tr>
<tr><td>Stroke</td><td>2¾ in.<br>(69.8 mm)</td><td>2⅜ in.<br>(60.3 mm)</td><td>2¾ in.<br>(69.8 mm)</td><td>2⅜ in.<br>(60.3 mm)</td><td>2¾ in.<br>(69.8 mm)</td></tr>
<tr><td>Piston Displacement</td><td>19.44 cu. in.<br>(319 cc)</td><td>16.79 cu. in.<br>(275 cc)</td><td>19.44 cu. in.<br>(319 cc)</td><td>16.79 cu. in.<br>(275 cc)</td><td>19.44 cu. in.<br>(319 cc)</td></tr>
<tr><td>Horsepower</td><td>8</td><td>7</td><td>8</td><td>7</td><td>8</td></tr>
<tr><td>Slow Idle Speed – Rpm</td><td>1750</td><td>1750</td><td>1750</td><td>1750</td><td>1750</td></tr>
<tr><td>High Idle Speed (No Load) – Rpm</td><td>4000</td><td>4000</td><td>4000</td><td>4000</td><td>4000</td></tr>
<tr><td>Full Load Speed – Rpm</td><td>3600</td><td>3600</td><td>3600</td><td>3600</td><td>3600</td></tr>
<tr><td>Crankcase Oil Capacity</td><td colspan="5">2¼ pints (1L)</td></tr>
<tr><td>Weight –</td><td colspan="5"></td></tr>
<tr><td>Above 32°F (0°C)</td><td colspan="5">SAE 30</td></tr>
<tr><td>0°F (–18°C) to 32°F (0°C)</td><td colspan="5">SAE 10W</td></tr>
<tr><td>Below 0°F (–18°C)</td><td colspan="5">SAE 5W-20</td></tr>
<tr><td>Transmission Oil Capacity</td><td>1½ pints<br>(0.7L)</td><td colspan="4">12 oz.<br>(355mL)</td></tr>
<tr><td>Weight</td><td>SAE 90 EP</td><td colspan="4">EP Lithium Grease</td></tr>
</table>

<table>
<tr><th></th><th colspan="5">MODELS</th></tr>
<tr><th></th><th>3400-1,<br>3400-2,<br>3400-3</th><th>3480-0,<br>3620-0</th><th>3630-0,<br>3810-0</th><th>3640-0</th><th>3960,<br>13885<br>(Early)</th></tr>
<tr><td>Engine Make</td><td>B&S</td><td>B&S</td><td>B&S</td><td>Tecumseh</td><td>B&S</td></tr>
<tr><td>Model</td><td>190707</td><td>190707</td><td>190707</td><td>VH100</td><td>252707</td></tr>
<tr><td>Bore</td><td>3 in.<br>(76.2 mm)</td><td>3 in.<br>(76.2 mm)</td><td>3 in.<br>(76.2 mm)</td><td>3-5/16 in.<br>(84.1 mm)</td><td>3-7/16 in.<br>(87.3 mm)</td></tr>
<tr><td>Stroke</td><td>2¾ in.<br>(69.8 mm)</td><td>2¾ in.<br>(69.8 mm)</td><td>2¾ in.<br>(69.8 mm)</td><td>2¾ in.<br>(69.8 mm)</td><td>2⅝ in.<br>(66.7 mm)</td></tr>
<tr><td>Piston Displacement</td><td>19.44 cu. in.<br>(319 cc)</td><td>19.44 cu. in.<br>(319 cc)</td><td>19.44 cu. in.<br>(319 cc)</td><td>23.75 cu. in.<br>(389 cc)</td><td>24.36 cu. in.<br>(399 cc)</td></tr>
<tr><td>Horsepower</td><td>8</td><td>8</td><td>8</td><td>10</td><td>10</td></tr>
<tr><td>Slow Idle Speed – Rpm</td><td>1750</td><td>1750</td><td>1750</td><td>1750</td><td>1800</td></tr>
<tr><td>High Idle Speed (No Load) – Rpm</td><td>4000</td><td>4000</td><td>4000</td><td>3750</td><td>3600</td></tr>
<tr><td>Full Load Speed – Rpm</td><td>3600</td><td>3600</td><td>3600</td><td>3600</td><td>3250</td></tr>
<tr><td>Crankcase Oil Capacity</td><td>2¼ pints<br>(1L)</td><td>2¼ pints<br>(1L)</td><td>2¼ pints<br>(1L)</td><td>2½ pints<br>(1.2L)</td><td>3 pints<br>(1.4L)</td></tr>
<tr><td>Weight –</td><td colspan="5"></td></tr>
<tr><td>Above 32°F (0°C)</td><td colspan="5">SAE 30</td></tr>
<tr><td>0°F (–18°C) to 32°F (0°C)</td><td colspan="5">SAE 10W</td></tr>
<tr><td>Below 0°F (–18°C)</td><td colspan="5">SAE 5W-20</td></tr>
<tr><td>Transmission Oil Capacity</td><td>*</td><td>*</td><td>1½ pints<br>(0.7L)</td><td>1½ pints<br>(0.7L)</td><td>1½ pints<br>(0.7L)</td></tr>
<tr><td>Weight</td><td>ATF "A"</td><td>ATF "A"</td><td>SAE 90 EP</td><td>SAE 90 EP</td><td>SAE 90 EP</td></tr>
<tr><td>Differential Oil Capacity</td><td>2¾ pints<br>(1.3L)</td><td>1 oz.<br>(30mL)</td><td>......</td><td>......</td><td>......</td></tr>
<tr><td>Weight</td><td>SAE 90 EP</td><td>EP Lithium<br>Grease</td><td>......</td><td>......</td><td>......</td></tr>
</table>

*Refer to HYDROSTATIC TRANSMISSION section.

| | MODELS | | | | |
|---|---|---|---|---|---|
| | 13720 | 13760 | 13875 | 13885 (Late) | 14910, 14912 |
| Engine Make | B&S | B&S | B&S | B&S | B&S |
| Model | 253417 | 253417 | 190707 | 253417 | 253417 |
| Bore | 3-7/16 in. (87.3 mm) | 3-7/16 in. (87.3 mm) | 3 in. (76.2 mm) | 3-7/16 in. (87.3 mm) | 3-7/16 in. (87.3 mm) |
| Stroke | 2⅝ in. (66.7 mm) | 2⅝ in. (66.7 mm) | 2¾ in. (69.8 mm) | 2⅝ in. (66.7 mm) | 2⅝ in. (66.7 mm) |
| Piston Displacement | 24.36 cu. in. (399 cc) | 24.36 cu. in. (399 cc) | 19.44 cu. in. (319 cc) | 24.36 cu. in. (399 cc) | 24.36 cu. in. (399 cc) |
| Horsepower | 11 | 11 | 8 | 11 | 11 |
| Slow Idle Speed – Rpm | 1800 | 1800 | 1750 | 1800 | 1800 |
| High Idle Speed (No Load) – Rpm | 3600 | 3600 | 4000 | 3600 | 3600 |
| Full Load Speed – Rpm | 3250 | 3250 | 3600 | 3250 | 3250 |
| Crankcase Oil Capacity | 3 pints (1.4L) | 3 pints (1.4L) | 2¼ pints (1L) | 3 pints (1.4L) | 3 pints (1.4L) |
| Weight – | | | | | |
| Above 32°F (0°C) | | | SAE 30 | | |
| 0°F (–18°C) to 32°F (0°C) | | | SAE 10W | | |
| Below 0°F (–18°C) | | | SAE 5W-20 | | |
| Transmission Oil Capacity | 24 oz. (710mL) | * | 1½ pints (0.7L) | 1½ pints (0.7L) | 4 pints (1.9L) |
| Weight | EP Lithium Grease | ATF "A" | SAE 90 EP | SAE 90 EP | SAE 90 EP |
| Differential Oil Capacity | ...... | 2¾ pints (1.3L) | ...... | ...... | ...... |
| Weight | ...... | SAE 90 EP | ...... | ...... | ...... |

*Refer to HYDROSTATIC TRANSMISSION section.

# FRONT AXLE AND STEERING SYSTEM

## AXLE MAIN MEMBER

### Models 13720-13760

**REMOVE AND REINSTALL.** To remove axle main member (18–Fig. Y1), raise and support front of tractor. Disconnect drag link (12) from steering spindle (15). Remove axle pivot bolt (19) and lower axle from frame. Disconnect tie rod (16) from steering spindles. Remove dust cap and cotter pin from spindles, then remove steering spindles and wheels.

Reinstall axle by reversing removal procedure. Lubricate bushings with SAE 30 oil.

### Models 14910-14912

**REMOVE AND REINSTALL.** To remove front axle main member (5–Fig. Y2), disconnect drag link (7) from steering spindle (6). Support tractor under frame using a suitable jack. Remove axle bolts (14). Unbolt front pivot bracket (4) and roll axle assembly away from tractor. Disconnect tie rod (8) from spindles. Remove dust covers

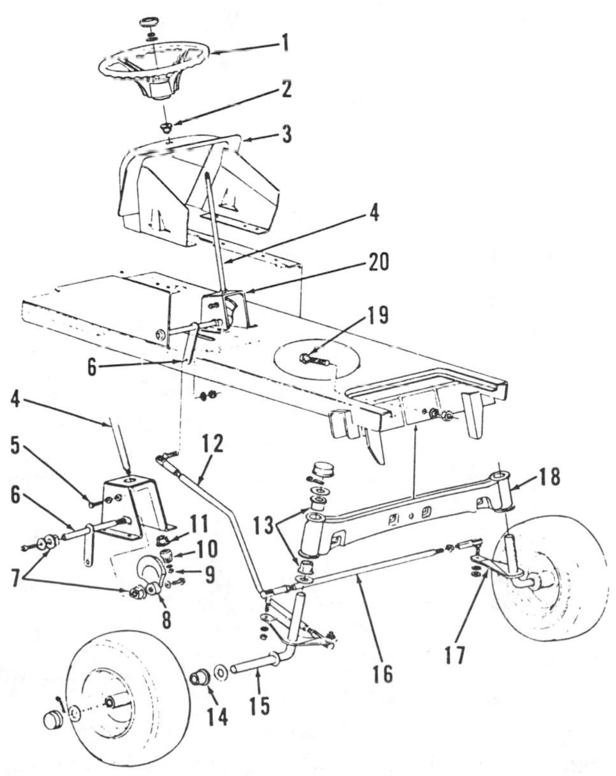


***Fig. Y1—Exploded view of front axle assembly and steering gears used on Models 13720 and 13760.***

1. Steering wheel
2. Bushing
3. Dash
4. Steering shaft
5. Adjusting screw
6. Steering arm
7. Bushings
8. Sector gear
9. Retaining nut
10. Pinion gear
11. Bushing
12. Drag link
13. Spindle bushings
14. Bushing
15. Spindle R.H.
16. Tie rod
17. Spindle L.H.
18. Axle main member
19. Pivot bolt
20. Steering gear housing

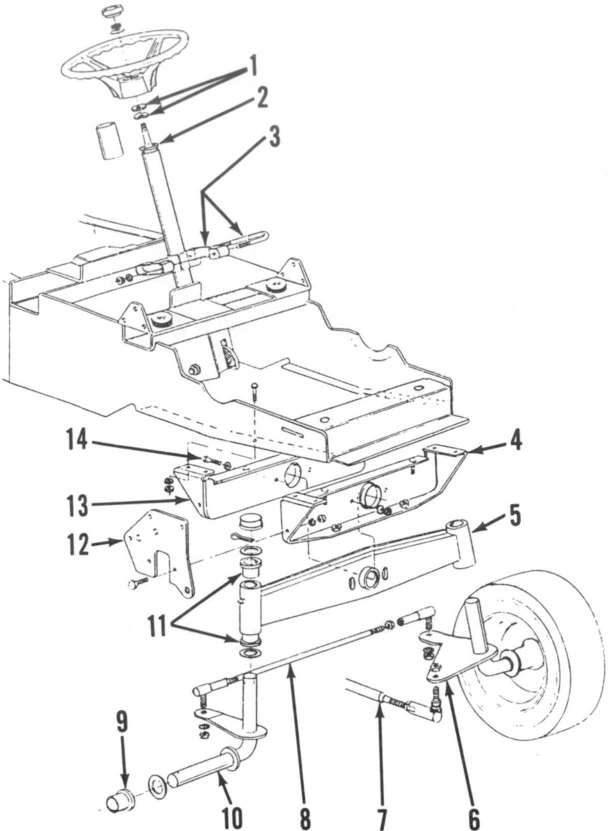

*Fig. Y2—Exploded view of front axle assembly used on Models 14910 and 14912.*

1. Washers
2. Ball bearing
3. "U" clamp
4. Front pivot bracket
5. Axle main member
6. Steering spindle L.H.
7. Drag link
8. Tie rod
9. Flange bushing
10. Steering spindle R.H.
11. Spindle bushings
12. Side plate
13. Rear pivot bracket
14. Axle bolts

and cotter pins, then withdraw steering spindle and wheel assemblies.

Reinstall axle by reversing removal procedure. Lubricate with multi-purpose grease.

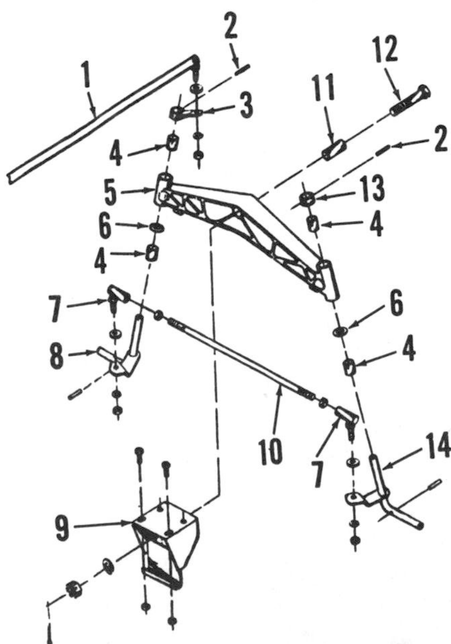

*Fig. Y3—Exploded view of typical front axle assembly used on all models except 13720, 13760, 14910 and 14912.*

1. Drag link
2. Roll pin
3. Steering arm
4. Bushing
5. Axle main member
6. Washer
7. Tie rod end
8. Steering spindle L.H.
9. Support
10. Tie rod
11. Bushing
12. Pivot bolt
13. Collar
14. Steering spindle R.H.

## All Other Models

**REMOVE AND REINSTALL.** The axle main member (5–Fig. Y3) is mounted to main frame and pivots on bolt (12). To remove axle main member, first disconnect drag link (1) from steering arm (3). Using a suitable jack under main frame, raise front of tractor until weight is removed from front wheels. Remove pivot bolt (12), then roll front axle assembly forward from tractor. Pivot bushing (11) can now be inspected and renewed if necessary. Disconnect tie rod (10), drive out roll pins (2) and withdraw spindle and wheel assemblies.

To reinstall axle, reverse removal procedure. Lubricate with SAE 30 oil.

## TIE RODS

### All Models

All models are equipped with adjustable tie rods. If ball joint ends are excessively worn, renew as required.

To adjust toe-in, disconnect tie rod ends from steering spindle arms, loosen locknuts and turn ball joints in or out as required. Toe-in should be 1/8-inch (3 mm), measured as shown in Fig. Y4.

## STEERING SPINDLES

### Models 13720-13760-14910-14912

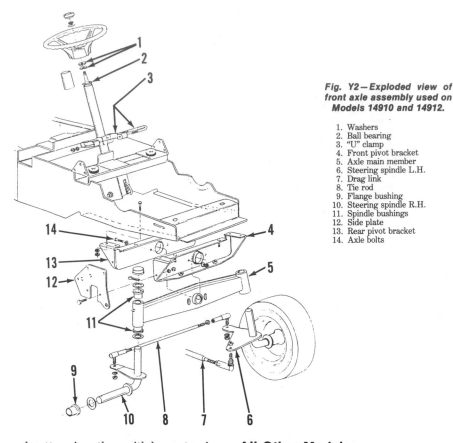

**REMOVE AND REINSTALL.** To remove steering spindles (15 and 17–Fig. Y1 or 6 and 10–Fig. Y2), support front of tractor and remove front wheels. Disconnect drag link and tie rod from spindle arms. Remove dust covers and cotter pins, then lower spindles from axle. Inspect bushings and renew as necessary.

### All Other Models

**REMOVE AND REINSTALL.** To remove steering spindles (8 and 14–Fig. Y3), support front of tractor and remove front wheels. Disconnect drag link (1) from steering arm (3) and tie rod (10) from spindle arms. Drive out pins (2) and lower steering spindles out of axle. Inspect spindle bushings (4) and renew as required.

## STEERING GEAR

### Models 13720-13760

**REMOVE AND REINSTALL.** To remove steering gears, disconnect and remove battery and battery plate. Remove steering wheel and upper bushing (2–Fig. Y1). Disconnect drag link (12) from steering arm (6). Remove pivot bolt, washer and flange bushing (7) from steering shaft (6). Remove four mounting bolts from steering support (20). Lift and rotate support to gain access to pinion gear (10). Remove pinion gear nut (9) and withdraw steering shaft (4). Unbolt and remove sector gear (8) from steering arm and shaft (6).

Reassemble by reversing removal procedure. Lubricate steering gears with light coat of multi-purpose grease and flange bushings with SAE 30 oil. Adjust backlash between steering gears by turning adjusting bolt (5) in or out, then tighten jam nut.

### Models 14910-14912

**REMOVE AND REINSTALL.** To remove steering gear, disconnect drag

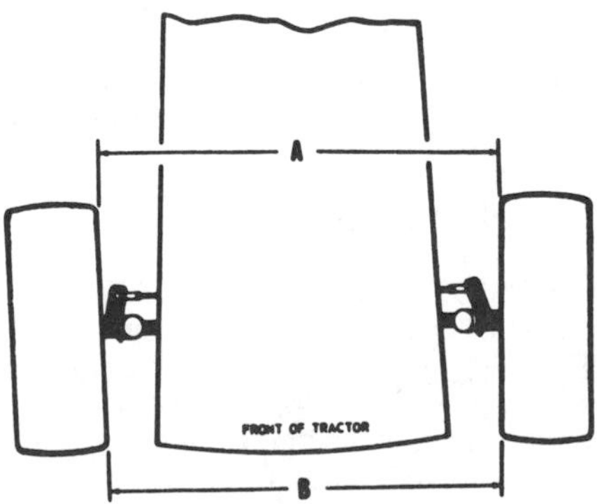


*Fig. Y4—Toe-in is correct when distance "B" is 1/8-inch (3 mm) less than distance "A" with both measurements taken at hub height.*

link at steering arm (14–Fig. Y5). Remove pinion gear (11) and withdraw steering shaft with steering wheel. Rotate sector gear (13) until steering arm contacts housing. Remove nut (8) and push shaft towards right side of tractor. Remove spacer (17) and steering arm (14). Sector gear is a light interference fit and must be carefully tapped off with a hammer. Further disassembly is evident after inspection.

Clean and inspect bearings and renew as necessary. Reassemble steering gear by reversing disassembly procedures. Lubricate bearings with SAE 30 oil and pinion and sector gears with multi-purpose grease.

### All Other Models

**REMOVE AND REINSTALL.** To remove steering gear, disconnect drag link (10–Fig. Y6) from quadrant arm (12) or (14). Remove quadrant arm retaining bolt and remove quadrant gear assembly. Drive pin (9) out of pinion gear (8) and remove pinion gear (8) from steering shaft (6). Remove steering shaft assembly and separate steering wheel from shaft by driving out pin (3).

Clean and inspect bearings and gears and renew as necessary. Reassemble by reversing removal procedure. Lubricate bearings with SAE 30 oil and pinion and quadrant gears with multi-purpose grease.

# ENGINE

## REMOVE AND REINSTALL

### Models 14910-14912

To remove engine assembly, remove hood and disconnect battery. Disconnect all engine wiring, throttle cable and choke cable. Close fuel shut off valve and disconnect fuel line. Remove muffler and drive belt guard. Remove drive belts and crankshaft pulley. Remove heat shields and belt guard mounting plate. Remove engine mounting bolts and lift engine from tractor.

To reinstall engine, reverse removal procedures. Adjust drive belts as necessary.

### All Other Models

To remove engine, detach hood locking knobs and tilt hood and grille assembly forward on Models 3260-3, 3260-4, 3260-5, 3400-1, 3400-2, 3400-3, 3630-0 and 3640-0. On all other models, unbolt and remove hood and grille assembly. Disconnect throttle control cable. Disconnect fuel line. Unscrew retaining bolt from engine drive pulley, loosen set screw and remove pulley. On models with recoil rope through instrument panel, remove handle from recoil starter rope. Prevent rope from coiling in starter housing and pull end of rope through dash. Knot end of rope at starter so rope cannot enter recoil starter. On electric start models, disconnect battery cables, engine wiring and headlight wires. Remove battery on models with battery mounted forward. Unscrew engine mounting bolts on all models and lift engine and mounting base out of tractor.

To reinstall engine, reverse removal procedure.

## OVERHAUL

### All Models

Engine make and model are listed at the beginning of this section. To overhaul engine components and accessories, refer to Briggs & Stratton and Tecumseh sections of this manual.

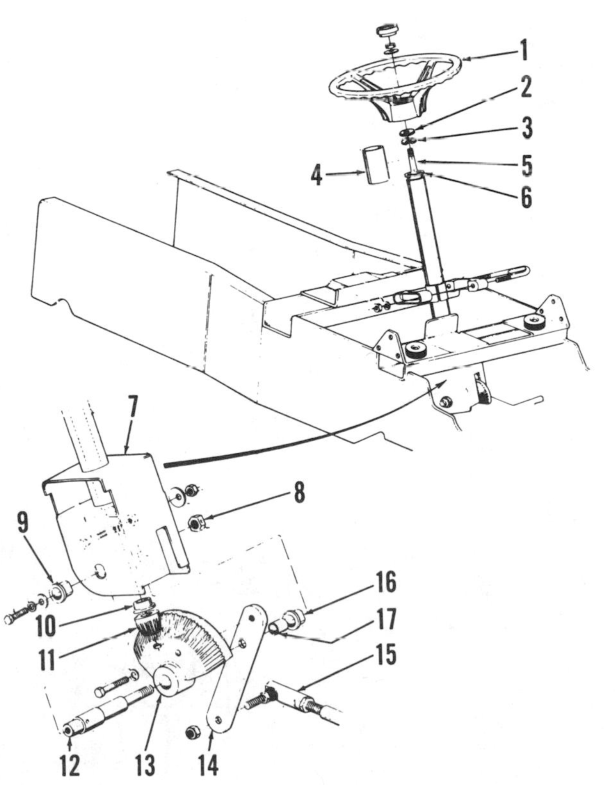


*Fig. Y5—Exploded view of steering gear used on Models 14910 and 14912.*

1. Steering wheel
2. "D" washer
3. Wave washer
4. Tube
5. Steering shaft
6. Bearing
7. Housing
8. Nut
9. Bearing
10. Flange bearing
11. Pinion gear
12. Steering gear shaft
13. Sector gear
14. Steering arm
15. Drag link end
16. Flange bearing
17. Spacer

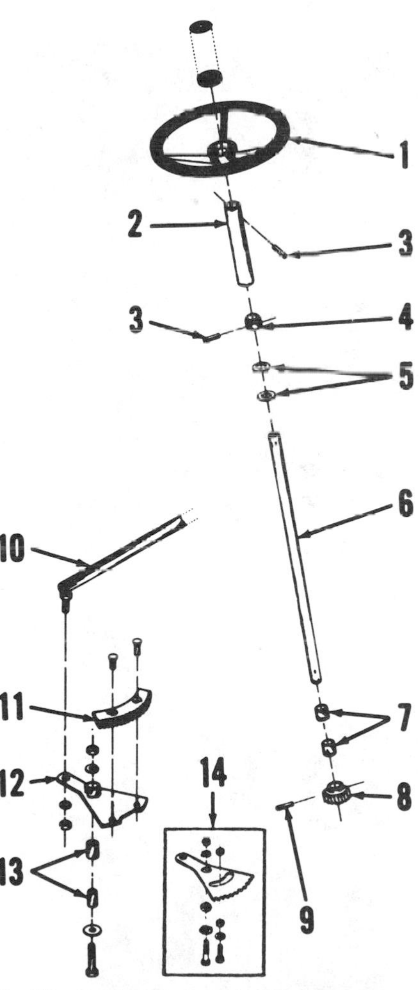


*Fig. Y6—Exploded view of typical steering assembly used on all models except Models 13720, 13760, 14910 and 14912. Some models are equipped with one-piece quadrant gear (14) in place of two-piece quadrant arm and gear (11 and 12).*

1. Steering wheel
2. Steering column
3. Pin
4. Collar
5. Washers
6. Steering shaft
7. Bushings
8. Pinion gear
9. Pin
10. Drag link
11. Quadrant gear
12. Quadrant arm
13. Bushing
14. Quadrant gear

# CLUTCH AND BRAKE

## Model 13760

**ADJUSTMENT.** The clutch used on Model 13760 is spring loaded and does not require adjustment.

To adjust disc brake, loosen locknut (Fig. Y7) and turn adjusting bolt all the way in, then unscrew bolt one turn. Tighten locknut and check brake operation.

**R&R AND OVERHAUL BRAKE.** Disconnect tension spring and return spring from actuating lever. Unbolt and remove disc brake assembly from transaxle. Separate housings and remove brake pads.

Reinstall by reversing removal procedure and adjust brake as previously outlined.

**R&R DRIVE BELT.** To remove front drive belt, depress clutch-brake pedal and engage pedal lock. Unscrew belt guard retainer and swing guard towards front of tractor.

**NOTE: Observe twist in front belt. If new belt is installed backwards, tractor will run backwards.**

Loosen stop bolt behind jackshaft pulley (Fig. Y8) and pry pulley forward while slipping front belt off jackshaft pulley and engine pulley. Reverse procedure to install new belt.

To remove rear drive belt (4–Fig. Y9), depress clutch-brake pedal and engage pedal lock. Remove jackshaft belt guard pins. Remove idler pulley (6) by removing center bolt. Remove hydrostatic pulley belt guard and loosen rear axle mounting bolts. Pry frame away from hydrostatic unit about ¼-inch (6 mm) and remove belt from pulleys. Reverse procedure to install new belt.

## Models 14910-14912

**ADJUSTMENT.** A spring loaded belt idler type clutch is used on these tractors. Model 14912 is equipped with variable speed drive. If variable speed belt slips with speed control in lowest position or if maximum speed is not reached with speed control in highest position, clutch control rod should be adjusted.

To adjust rod, place speed control in lowest position with engine running. Depress clutch pedal and release it. Check to see if engine drive belt is 1/16-inch (1.5 mm) below edge of variable speed pulley. If belt is too low, loosen locknut on brake-clutch rod and screw rod in or out until clearance is obtained. Final drive belt is spring loaded and requires no adjustment.

The brake is a disc type (Fig. Y10). To adjust brake, tighten nut (9) until brake locks with pedal released. Loosen nut one complete turn. Make sure disc turns freely when pedal is released.

**R&R AND OVERHAUL BRAKE.** Disconnect tension spring and return spring from cam lever (7–Fig. Y10). Unbolt and remove disc brake assembly from transaxle. Separate housings and remove brake pads.

Reinstall by reversing removal procedure, and adjust brake as previously outlined.

**R&R DRIVE BELTS.** To remove drive belts, remove pto belt from engine pulley. Unbolt and remove engine pulley. Place speed control lever in for-

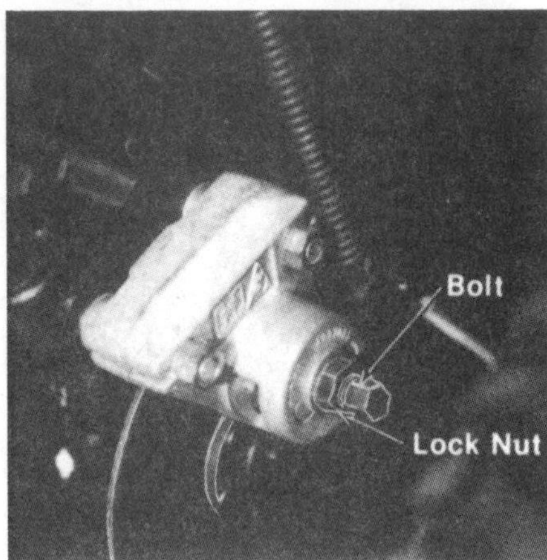


*Fig. Y7—To adjust disc brake on Model 13760, loosen locknut and turn center bolt all the way in. Then back bolt out one complete turn.*

*Fig. Y8—To remove front drive belt on Model 13760, use a bar to pry pulley assembly forward and slip belt out of pulley. Note twist in belt for correct reassembly.*

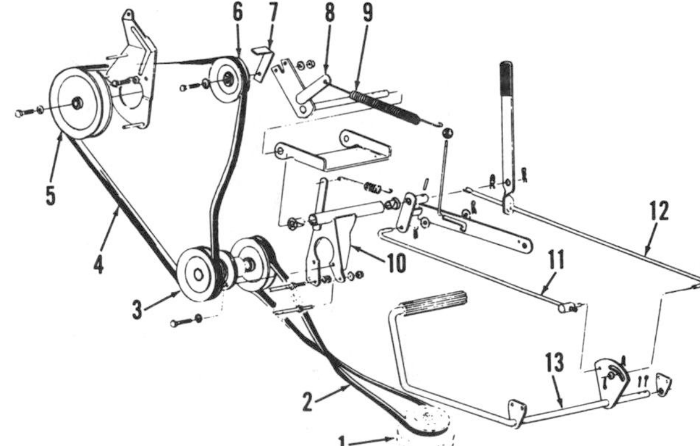


*Fig. Y9—Exploded view of traction drive clutch, drive belts and jackshaft assembly used on Model 13760.*

1. Engine pulley
2. Primary drive belt
3. Jackshaft
4. Secondary belt
5. Transmission pulley
6. Clutch idler pulley
7. Belt guard
8. Clutch arm
9. Idler spring
10. Jackshaft bracket
11. Brake cam rod
12. Clutch-brake rod
13. Clutch-brake pedal

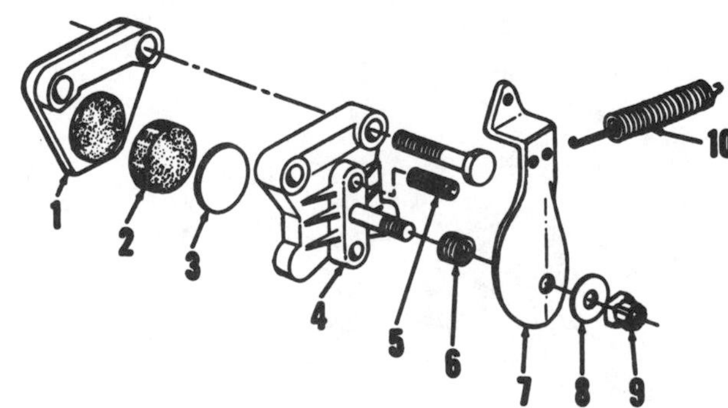


*Fig. Y10—Exploded view of Models 14910 and 14912 brake assembly.*

1. Caliper & pad (inner)
2. Friction pad
3. Back-up disc
4. Caliper (outer)
5. Actuating pin
6. Spring
7. Cam lever
8. Washer
9. Adjusting nut
10. Spring (2 used)

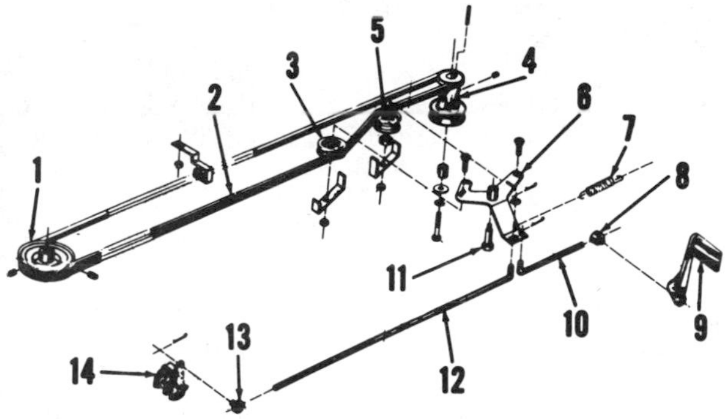


*Fig. Y11—Exploded view of typical clutch and brake assemblies used on some gear drive models. Disc brake and clutch linkage is similar on hydrostatic drive models.*

1. Transmission pulley
2. Drive belt
3. Clutch idler pulley
4. Engine pulley
5. Idler pulley
6. Clutch arm
7. Spring
8. Adjusting nut
9. Clutch-brake pedal
10. Clutch rod
11. Pivot bolt
12. Brake rod
13. Adjusting nut
14. Brake unit

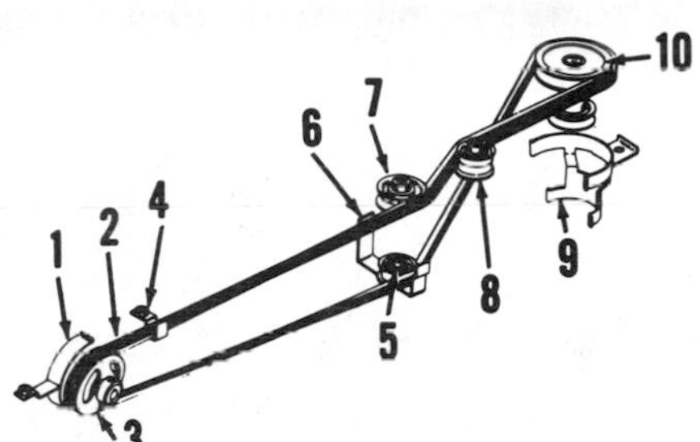


*Fig. Y12—View showing drive belt and clutch idler used on some models equipped with hydrostatic transmission. Disc brake and clutch linkage is similar to that shown in Fig. Y11.*

1. Belt guard
2. Drive belt
3. Transmission input pulley
4. Belt guide
5. Flat idler
6. Belt guide
7. "V" idler
8. Flat clutch idler
9. Belt guard
10. Engine pulley

ward position and pull down on lower pulley on rear belt. Work rear belt from variable speed pulley and idler pulleys. Move speed control to low position and slide center section of variable speed pulley towards right side of tractor. Remove front belt. install new belts by reversing removal procedure.

### All Other Models

**ADJUSTMENT.** The clutch used is the belt idler type while the brake is a disc type. The pedal on right side of tractor actuates clutch and brake mechanisms. The clutch idler pulley is spring loaded and does not require adjustment. Clutch-brake pedal can be adjusted by disconnecting pedal control rod (10–Fig. Y11) and turning adjuster (8). Be sure there is sufficient pedal travel to engage and disengage clutch.

To adjust brake, disconnect brake control rod (12) and turn adjuster (13). With clutch-brake pedal in normal drive (up) position, and with brake rod held rearward toward brake, a clearance of 3/8 inch (9.5 mm) should exist between brake rod and front of slot in clutch idler arm. For further brake adjustment, turn adjusting nut (10–Fig. Y13) on brake lever (9) of brake. Check to be sure brake does not engage before clutch is disengaged.

**R&R AND OVERHAUL BRAKE.** Disconnect brake rod from brake lever (9–Fig. Y13). Unbolt and remove brake pad holder (5). Remove brake disc (2) and inner brake pad (1).

Inspect for wear and renew as required. Adjust brake as previously outlined.

**R&R DRIVE BELT.** To remove drive belt (2–Fig. Y11 or Y12), disconnect battery cable on electric start models, and disconnect spark plug cable on all models. On Models 3260-3, 3260-4, 3260-5, 3630-0, 3640-0 and 3810-0, remove shift lever knob, then unbolt and remove shift lever position panel. On all models, loosen or remove belt guards as necessary. Depress clutch brake pedal and remove belt from engine pulley. Disconnect mower drive idler spring and idler connecting rod. Remove drive belt from clutch idler and transmission input pulley. On Models 3260-3, 3260-4, 3260-5, 3630-0, 3640-0 and 3810-0, thread belt over transmission shift lever. Remove belt from tractor.

To reinstall belt on all models, reverse removal procedure. Be sure when installing belt that flat idlers are on outside of belt and "V" idler is on inside of belt as shown in Figs. Y11 and Y12. If necessary, readjust brake as outlined in previous paragraph.

# GEAR TRANSMISSION

## LUBRICATION

### All Models So Equipped

Models 3380-1, 3380-2, 3380-3, 3390-1, 3390-2 and 3390-3 are equipped with a Peerless 353 3-speed gear transmission. Models 3950, 3600-0, 3600-1 and 3610-0 are equipped with a Peerless 506 4-speed gear transmission. All models have transmission case packed with 12 ounces (355 mL) of EP lithium base grease at the factory.

## REMOVE AND REINSTALL

### Models 3380-1 – 3380-2 – 3380-3 – 3390-1 – 3390-2 – 3390-3

To remove transmission, first remove fender and seat assembly over transmission. Disconnect and remove chain from transmission output sprocket. Remove drive belt from transmission pulley by depressing clutch-brake pedal and slipping belt from pulley. Remove snap ring and remove pulley from transmission input shaft. Unscrew transmission mounting screws and remove transmission from tractor.

To reinstall transmission, reverse removal procedure.

### Models 3600-0 – 3600-1 – 3610-0 – 3950

To remove transmission, first disconnect battery cables and remove battery on electric start models. Disconnect

*Fig. Y13—Exploded view of typical disc brake assembly used on some tractors.*

1. Brake pad (inner)
2. Brake disc
3. Brake pad (outer)
4. Back-up plate
5. Carrier
6. Spacer
7. Cap screws
8. Adjusting pins
9. Cam lever
10. Adjusting nut
11. Jam nut

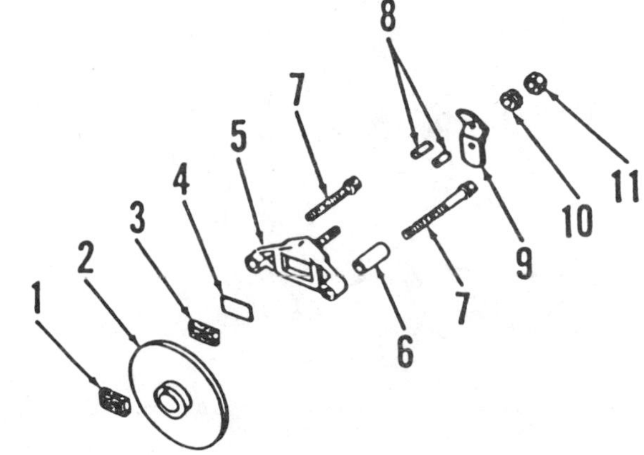

transmission shift linkage, then unbolt and remove seat and rear frame cover assembly. Remove transmission input pulley retaining ring, depress clutch-brake pedal and slide pulley and drive belt off transmission input shaft. Loosen chain idler, remove snap ring at end of output shaft and slide output sprocket and chain from output shaft. Unbolt transmission and lift assembly from tractor.

Reinstall transmission by reversing until all slack is removed from chain, then tighten idler bolt securely.

## OVERHAUL

### All Models So Equipped

Models 3380-1, 3380-2, 3380-3, 3390-1, 3390-2 and 3390-3 are equipped with a Peerless 353 3-speed gear transmission. Models 3950, 3600-0, 3600-1 and 3610-0 are equipped with a Peerless 506 4-speed gear transmission. Refer to the appropriate Peerless section in GEAR TRANSMISSION SERVICE section for overhaul procedure.

# TRANSAXLE

## LUBRICATION

### All Models So Equipped

Models 3260-3, 3260-4, 3260-5, 3630-0, 3640-0, 3810-0, 3960, 13875 and 13885 are equipped with a Peerless 600 series transaxle. Transaxle fluid capacity is 1½ pints (0.7 L) of SAE 90 EP gear oil.

Model 13720 is equipped with a Peerless 800 series transaxle. Transaxle fluid capacity is 24 ounces (710 mL) of lithium base grease.

Models 14910 and 14912 are equipped with a Peerless 2300 series transaxle. Transaxle fluid capacity is 4 pints (1.9 L) of SAE 90 EP gear oil.

## REMOVE AND REINSTALL

### Models 3260-3 – 3260-4 – 3260-5 – 3630-3 – 3640-0 – 3810-0 – 3960 – 13875 – 13885

To remove transaxle, remove shift lever knob, then unbolt and remove shift lever position panel. On electric start models with rear mounted battery, disconnect cables and remove battery. Disconnect brake linkage and remove rear belt guard. Depress clutch-brake pedal and remove belt from transmission input pulley. Support tractor under frame and unbolt transaxle from frame. Raise rear of tractor and roll transaxle assembly away from tractor.

To reinstall transaxle, reverse removal procedure and adjust brake linkage as necessary.

### Model 13720

To remove transaxle assembly, unbolt and remove seat plate and rear fenders. Support tractor main frame. Remove transaxle belt keeper assembly, then depress clutch-brake pedal and work drive belt off transaxle pulley. Disconnect shift linkage and brake linkage. Unbolt transaxle from support brackets and roll transaxle rearward away from tractor. Unbolt and remove brake pad holder and brake disc. Remove rear wheel and hub assemblies.

Reinstall transaxle by reversing removal procedure. Adjust brake linkage as required.

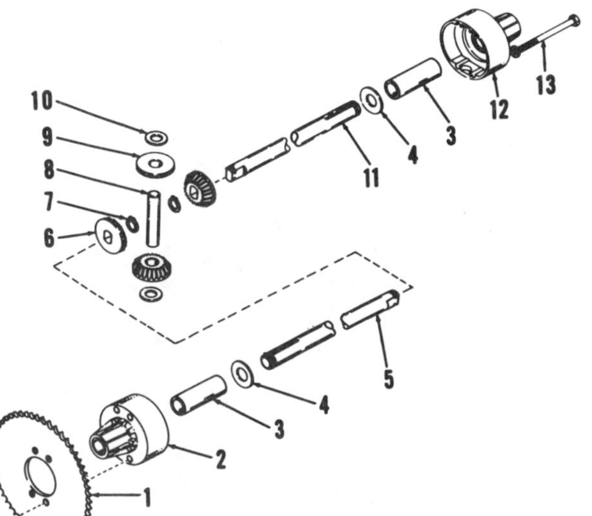

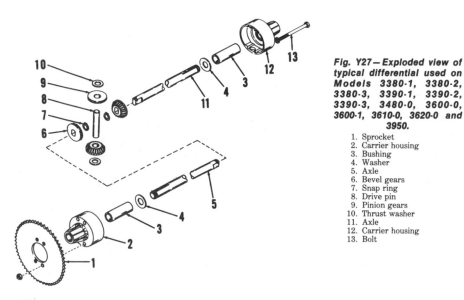

***Fig. Y27—Exploded view of typical differential used on Models 3380-1, 3380-2, 3380-3, 3390-1, 3390-2, 3390-3, 3480-0, 3600-0, 3600-1, 3610-0, 3620-0 and 3950.***

1. Sprocket
2. Carrier housing
3. Bushing
4. Washer
5. Axle
6. Bevel gears
7. Snap ring
8. Drive pin
9. Pinion gears
10. Thrust washer
11. Axle
12. Carrier housing
13. Bolt

### Models 14910-14912

To remove transaxle, remove rear drive belt. Disconnect brake linkage and remove gear shift knob. Support rear of tractor, unbolt transaxle and roll transaxle assembly away from tractor. Unbolt and remove disc brake assembly, input pulley and rear wheel and hub assemblies.

## OVERHAUL

### All Models So Equipped

Models 3260-3, 3260-4, 3260-5, 3630-0, 3640-0, 3810-0, 3960, 13875 and 13885 are equipped with a Peerless 600 series transaxle. Model 13720 is equipped with a Peerless 800 series transaxle. Models 14910 and 14912 are equipped with a Peerless 2300 series transaxle. Refer to the appropriate Peerless section in TRANSAXLE SERVICE section for overhaul procedure.

# HYDROSTATIC TRANSMISSION

## LUBRICATION

### Models 3400-1 – 3400-2 – 3400-3 – 3480-0 – 3620-0 – 13760

The hydrostatic transmission is equipped with an integral reservoir. Recommended transmission fluid is Type "A" automatic transmission fluid.

If contamination is observed in reservior tank or natural color of transmission fluid has changed (black or milky), fluid should be drained and renewed. When refilling transmission, remove vent plug and add oil until fluid overflows out vent hole in body. Then, reinstall vent plug and fill reservoir tank to COLD mark on tank.

## LINKAGE ADJUSTMENT

### Models 3400-1 – 3400-2 – 3400-3 – 3480-0 – 3620-0 – 13760

If tractor moves when hydrostatic control lever is in neutral position, control linkage adjustment is needed. To adjust linkage, raise and block rear of tractor so both rear wheels are free to rotate. On Model 13760, loosen locknuts and adjust length of control rod as required. On all other models, turn adjusting nuts at end of control cable as required. Start engine and recheck linkage adjustment.

**CAUTION: Do not attempt to adjust linkage with engine operating.**

### OVERHAUL

**Models 3400-1 – 3400-2 – 3400-3 – 3480-0 – 3620-0 – 13760**

All models are equipped with an Eaton Model 6 hydrostatic transmission. Refer to Eaton Model 6 in HYDROSTATIC TRANSMISSION SERVICE section for overhaul procedure.

## DIFFERENTIAL

**Models 3380-1 – 3380-2 – 3380-3 – 3390-1 – 3390-2 – 3390-3 – 3480-0 – 3600-0 – 3600-1 – 3610-0 – 3620-0**

**R&R AND OVERHAUL.** To remove differential, disconnect drive chain and block up under rear of tractor. Unbolt rear axle mounting plates from frame and roll differential and wheel assemblies from tractor. Remove wheels, mounting plates and support bearings from ends of both axle shafts. Clean axles and remove any burrs. Unscrew carrier bolts (13–Fig. Y27) and separate differential carrier housings. Remove drive pin (8), pinion gears (9) and thrust washers (10). Remove snap rings (7), bevel gears (6) and remove axle shaft from carrier housings. Renew bushings (3) if necessary.

To reassemble differential, reverse disassembly procedure. Tighten housing cap screws (13) to 15 ft.-lbs. (20 N•m). Fill differential with 1 ounce (30 mL) of EP lithium base grease.

Reinstall assembly and adjust chain idler to remove all slack from chain, then tighten idler bolt securely.

## REDUCTION GEARS AND DIFFERENTIAL

**Models 3400-1 – 3400-2 – 3400-3 – 13760**

**R&R AND OVERHAUL.** To remove reduction drive and differential assembly, first disconnect battery cables on all models and remove battery on Model 3400-3. On Model 13760, remove seat and fender assemblies and on all other models remove rear frame cover. On all models, unbolt and remove fan screen, cooling fan and rear belt guard. Depress clutch-brake pedal and remove drive belt from transmission input pulley. Disconnect transmission control linkage and brake linkage. Support tractor under frame, unbolt reduction gear and differential assembly, then raise rear of tractor and roll assembly from tractor.

Clean exterior of unit and drain lubricant from reduction gear and differential housing. Unbolt and separate hydrostatic drive unit from reduction drive and differential assembly. Remove wheel and hub assemblies from axles. Remove brake disc from brake shaft. Clean axle shafts and remove any burrs on shafts. Unscrew cap screws and drive out dowel pins in cover (29–Fig. Y28). Lift cover off case and axle shaft. Withdraw brake shaft (5), input gear (4) and thrust washers (3 and 6) from case. Remove output shaft (11), output gear (10), spacer (9), thrust washer (8) and differential assembly from case. Axle shaft housings (20 and 22) must be pressed from case and cover.

To disassemble differential, remove four cap screws and separate axle shaft and carrier assemblies from ring gear (28). Drive blocks (25), bevel pinion gears (26) and drive pin (27) can now be removed from ring gear. Remove snap rings (12) and slide axle shafts (18 and 23) from axle gears (13) and carriers (16 and 24).

Clean and inspect all parts and renew any parts damaged or excessively worn. When installing needle bearings, press bearings in from inside of case or cover until bearings are 0.015-0.020 inch (0.381-0.508 mm) below thrust surfaces. Be sure heads of differential cap screws and right axle shaft (18) are installed in right carrier housing (16). Right axle shaft is installed through case (1). Tighten differential cap screws to 7 ft.-lbs. (9 N•m) and cover cap screws to 10 ft.-lbs. (14 N•m). Differential assembly and output shaft (11) must be installed in case at same time. Remainder of assembly is reverse of disassembly procedure.

Reinstall hydrostatic transmission, reduction drive and differential assembly by reversing removal procedure. Fill expansion reservoir on hydrostatic transmission with Type "A" automatic transmission fluid until fluid is level with COLD mark on reservoir. Fill reduction drive and differential housing to level plug opening with SAE 90 EP gear oil. Capacity is approximately 2¾ pints (1.3L). Adjust transmission linkage and brake linkage as required.

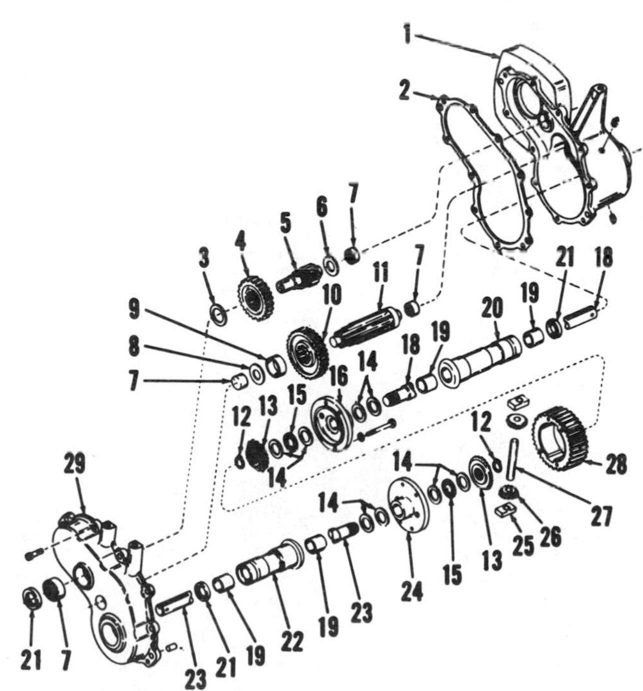

*Fig. Y28—Exploded view of Peerless 1303 gear reduction and differential unit used on Models 3400-1, 3400-2 and 3400-3. Peerless Model 1341, used on Model 13760, is similar.*

1. Case
2. Gasket
3. Washer
4. Idler gear
5. Brake shaft
6. Washer
7. Bearing
8. Washer
9. Spacer
10. Output gear
11. Output shaft
12. Snap ring
13. Bevel gear
14. Thrust washers
15. Thrust bearing
16. Differential carrier
18. Axle shaft R.H.
19. Bushing
20. Axle housing
21. Oil seal
22. Axle housing
23. Axle shaft L.H.
24. Differential carrier
25. Drive block
26. Drive pinion
27. Drive pin
28. Ring gear
29. Cover

# TRANSAXLE SERVICE

## KANZAKI

### Tuff Torq

**OVERHAUL.** To disassemble transaxle, drain oil from housing. Unbolt and remove brake components from transaxle shift shaft. Drive out roll pin (2—Fig. KZ1) and remove shift interlock arm (1). Remove cap screws securing housing halves and separate housing. Note the location of all thrust washers and shims as gears and shafts are removed from housing halves.

Drive out pins (16 and 17—Fig. KZ1) and remove shift arm (18) and shift lever (24). Drive out roll pin (12) and remove detent spring (9) and ball (10). Remove snap rings (15) and withdraw shift fork (19) from shift shaft (20).

Separate gears from reduction shaft (15—Fig. KZ2) and shift shaft (34). Remove shift collar assembly (3 through

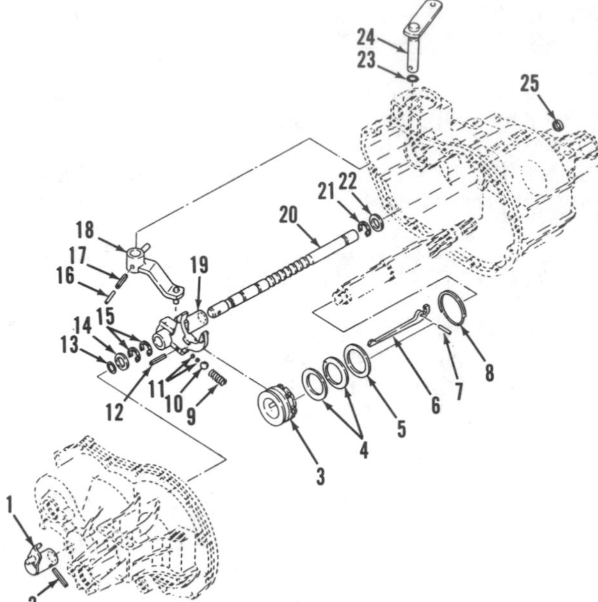

*Fig. KZ1—Exploded view of TUFF TORQ transaxle shift components.*

1. Shift interlock
2. Roll pin
3. Shift collar
4. Spring washers
5. Thrust washer
6. Shift key
7. Pin
8. Spring ring
9. Detent spring
10. Ball
11. Balls
12. Roll pin
13. "O" ring
14. Washer
15. Retainer rings
16. Pin
17. Pin
18. Shift arm
19. Shift fork
20. Shift shaft
21. Retainer ring
22. Washer
23. "O" ring
24. Shift lever
25. Plug

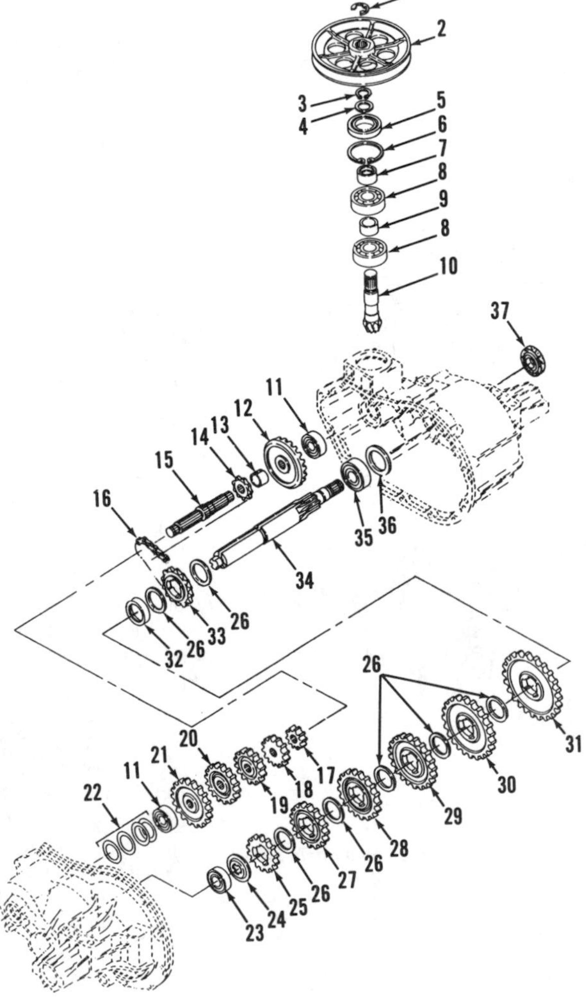

*Fig. KZ2—Exploded view of TUFF TORQ transaxle assembly.*

1. "E" ring
2. Pulley
3. Snap ring
4. Washer
5. Oil seal
6. Snap ring
7. Sleeve
8. Bearings
9. Spacer
10. Input shaft
11. Bearing
12. Bevel gear
13. Bushing
14. Sprocket
15. Reduction shaft
16. Drive chain
17. Gear (14 T)
18. Gear (18 T)
19. Gear (23 T)
20. Gear (26 T)
21. Gear (32 T)
22. Shims
23. Bearing
24. Washer
25. Gear (24 T)
26. Thrust washers
27. Gear (30 T)
28. Gear (34 T)
29. Gear (38 T)
30. Gear (49 T)
31. Gear (62 T)
32. Collar
33. Sprocket
34. Shift shaft
35. Bearing
36. Washer
37. Oil seal

8—Fig. KZ1) from shift shaft. Remove spring ring (8) and drive out pins (7) to disassemble shift collar assembly.

Remove "E" ring (1—Fig. KZ2), pulley (2), snap ring (3) and washer (4) from input shaft (10). Carefully pry oil seal (5) from housing bore, then remove snap ring (6) and tap input shaft with bearings out of housing.

Remove snap rings (7—Fig. KZ3) and press axle shafts (1 and 17) and needle bearings (4) out of housing halves. Remove mounting bolts from differential case halves and separate ring gear (8) and differential components. Note that bearing (9) must be pressed outward from case half (10) if renewal is necessary.

Inspect all parts for wear or damage and renew as necessary. Refer to the following specifications:

Shift arm OD . . . . . . . . 16.96-17.00 mm (0.668-0.669 in.)

Shift fork shaft OD . . . 16.96-17.00 mm (0.668-0.669 in.)

Transaxle housing shifter bore ID . . . . . 17.02-17.04 mm (0.670-0.671 in.)

Shift collar groove width . . . . . . . . . . 6.1-6.2 mm (0.240-0.244 in.)

Shift fork thickness . . . . . . . . . . . . . 5.7-5.9 mm (0.224-0.232 in.)

Differential thrust washer thickness— min. . . . . . . . . . . . . . . . . . . . 0.5 mm (0.020 in.)

Differential pinion gear ID . . . . . . . . . . . 14.02-14.03 mm (0.552-0.553 in.)

Differential pinion shaft OD . . . . . . . . . . 13.97-13.98 mm (0.550-0.551 in.)

Pinion shaft-to-gear clearance— Wear limit . . . . . . . . . . . . . . 0.4 mm (0.016 in.)

Axle shaft thrust washer thickness Wear limit . . . . . . . . . . . . . . 1.5 mm (0.059 in.)

To check tension of shift keys (6—Fig. KZ1), hold two keys all the way into grooves in shift shaft. Use a belt tension gage to measure pressure required to push third key into shaft groove. It should take a minimum of 2.7 kg (6 lbs.) to push key into groove. Repeat check with all three keys. Renew keys if tension is less than specified.

To reassemble transaxle, reverse the disassembly procedure while noting the following special instructions: When assembling shift collar components, be sure that spring washers (4—Fig. KZ1) are installed with outside edges away from each other. Install thrust washers (26—Fig. KZ2), sprocket (33) and collar (32) on shifter assembly with largest inside diameter of collar (32) facing sprocket (33). When installing dished tooth washer (24) on shift shaft (34), outer edge of washer should contact last shift shaft gear (25). Bearings (11) are a press fit on reduction shaft (15). When installing new axle shaft needle bearings (4—Fig. KZ3), press bearings into housings with printed side of bearing facing outward. Apply grease to lip of oil seals (2) before installing.

When assembling differential, align notch in pinion shaft (15—Fig. KZ3) with offset inside differential housing (16). Note that two holes in ring gear (8) and housing (10) are larger for installation of the two shoulder bolts. Clean threads of differential housing bolts and apply Loctite 242 to bolts, then tighten to 51 N·m (38 ft.-lbs.).

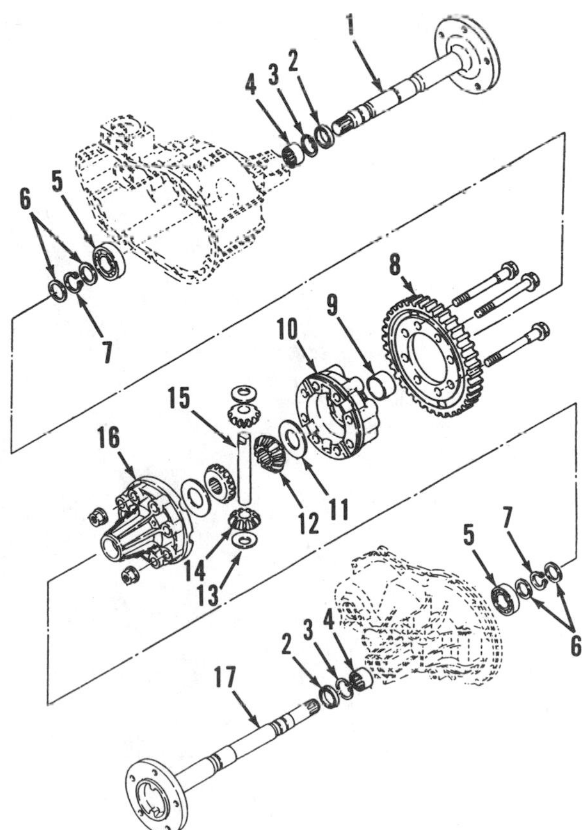

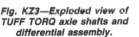

***Fig. KZ3—Exploded view of TUFF TORQ axle shafts and differential assembly.***

1. Axle R.H.
2. Oil seal
3. Snap ring
4. Needle bearing
5. Ball bearing
6. Washers
7. Snap ring
8. Ring gear
9. Bushing
10. Differential case half
11. Thrust washer
12. Differential side gear
13. Thrust washer
14. Differential pinion gear
15. Pinion shaft
16. Differential case half
17. Axle L.H.

Install inner detent ball (11—Fig. KZ1) and shift fork (19) on shift shaft (20) first, then install remainder of shifter components. Make sure that slot in roll pin (12) faces away from spring (9) when installing roll pin. Shift lever (24) must be pointing toward right-hand axle when installing shift arm (18).

Assemble gears and shafts in housings and tighten housing mounting screws to 29 N·m (22 ft.-lbs.) if new housing is used, or 24 N·m (18 ft.-lbs.) if original housing is reused. Use a dial indicator to measure end play of reduction shaft as shown in Fig. KZ4. Install shims (22—Fig. KZ2) between left housing half and reduction shaft bearing until end play is less than 0.1 mm (0.004 in.).

To check backlash between input shaft bevel gear and reduction shaft gear, position dial indicator against side of input shaft splines as shown in Fig. KZ5. Pull out and hold reduction shaft while rotating input shaft back and forth to measure backlash. Specified backlash is 0.20-0.35 mm (0.008-0.014 in.). Add or remove reduction shaft shims (22—Fig. KZ2) as necessary to obtain desired backlash.

Apply suitable gasket maker compound to mating surfaces of transaxle housing. Tighten housing cap screws to 29 N·m (22 ft.-lbs.) if new housing is used, or 24 N·m (18 ft.-lbs.) if original housing is reused. Lubricate lip of input shaft oil seal (5—Fig. KZ2) with grease, then install seal in housing bore. Install transaxle pulley and secure with "E" ring (1). Install shift interlock arm (1—Fig. KZ1) on shift shaft (20). Make certain that gears can be shifted.

*Fig. KZ4—Use a dial indicator to measure reduction shaft end play. Refer to text for adjustment procedure.*

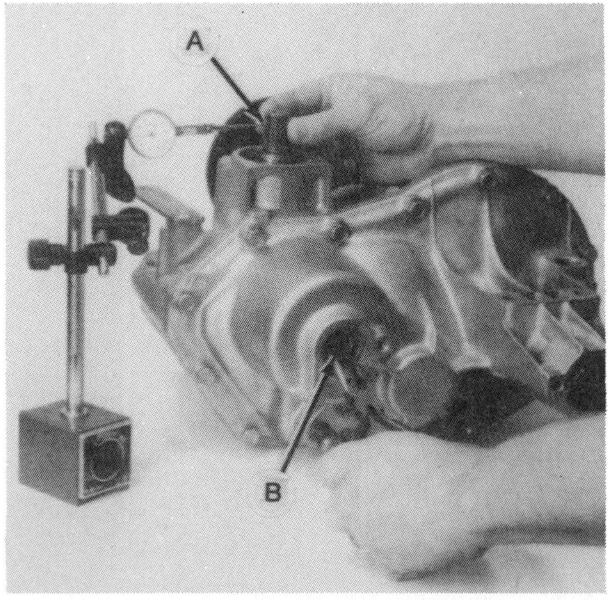


*Fig. KZ5—Use a dial indicator to measure backlash between reduction gear and input shaft bevel gear. Refer to text for adjustment procedure.*

# MTD

## Model 717-0750A

**OVERHAUL.** Thoroughly clean exterior of transaxle case. Remove input pulley and key (1–Fig. MT100). Remove brake caliper assembly, brake disc (27) and key (26). Remove all cap screws retaining upper case half (5) to lower case half (45). Carefully separate upper case half from lower case half. Remove snap rings (2 and 11), washers (3 and 4), gear (10), thrust washer (9) and square seal (8). Remove input shaft (7) and bearings (6) as required. Remove shifter assembly (14). Lift drive/brake shaft (17) and gear assembly out as an assembly and disassemble as required. Lift axle shafts (28) and differential as required. Lift axle shafts (28) and differential assembly out as an assembly. Remove the cap screws retaining differential housing (39) to differential gear (33). Remove snap rings (42), cross shaft (41) and spider gears (34). Remove nuts (36 and 37) and remove axle gears (35). Pull axles out of housing and gear assembly.

Reassemble by reversing disassembly procedure. Before installing upper case half, pack transaxle housing with 10 ounces (296 mL) of lithium base grease.

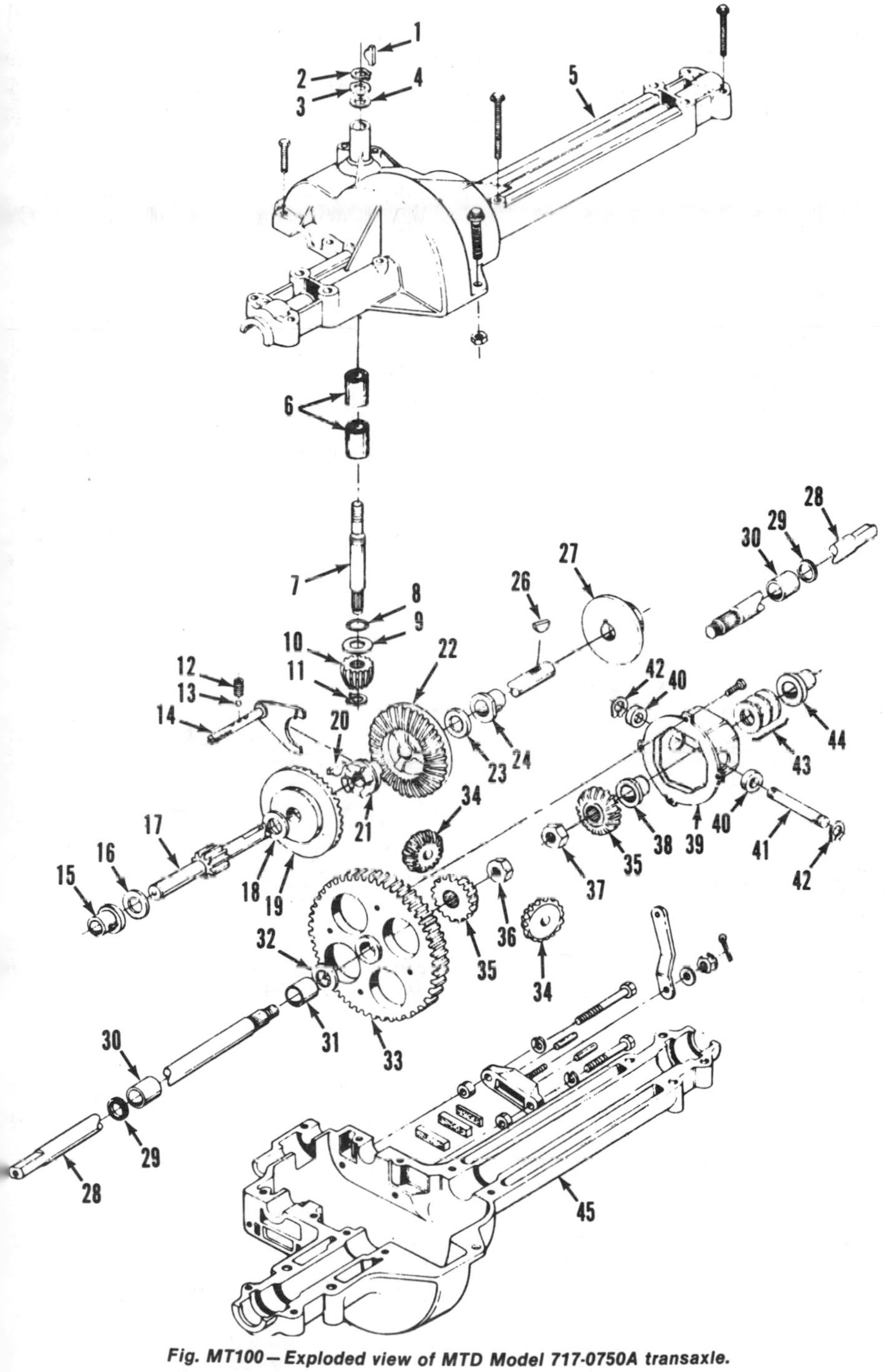

*Fig. MT100—Exploded view of MTD Model 717-0750A transaxle.*

1. Key
2. Snap ring
3. Washer (0.040 in)
4. Washer (0.030 in.)
5. Upper case half
6. Bearings
7. Input shaft
8. Square seal
9. Thrust washer
10. Gear
11. Snap ring
12. Spring detent
13. Detent ball
14. Shifter
15. Flange bearing
16. Washer
17. Drive/brake shaft
18. Washer
19. Bevel gear
20. Key
21. Clutch collar
22. Bevel gear
23. Washer
24. Flange bearing
26. Key
27. Brake disc
28. Axle shaft
29. Seal
30. Sleeve bearing
31. Sleeve bearing
32. Washer
33. Differential gear
34. Spider gear
35. Axle gear
36. Nut
37. Nut
38. Flange bearing
39. Housing
40. Thrust bearing
41. Cross shaft
42. Snap ring
43. Washers
44. Flange bearing
45. Lower case half

# PEERLESS

## Series 600

The Peerless 600 series transaxle is a lightweight unit which has a vertical input shaft at the top of the case. There are two basic types of 600 series transaxles. The 600 series is the standard model and the 601 series is a slow speed transaxle. Model number and series number will be located on a metal tag or stamped in case as indicated by (I–Fig. PT19). Variations in model number (603, 603A, 609, etc.) indicate differences in shift lever shape, axle lengths, axle machining for wheel hub attachment, axle housing variations or size of the brake shaft. Overhaul procedure is similar for all 600 series transaxles.

**OVERHAUL.** To disassemble the transaxle, remove drain plug and drain lubricant. Remove brake assembly, input pulley and rear wheel assemblies. Remove all keys from keyways and

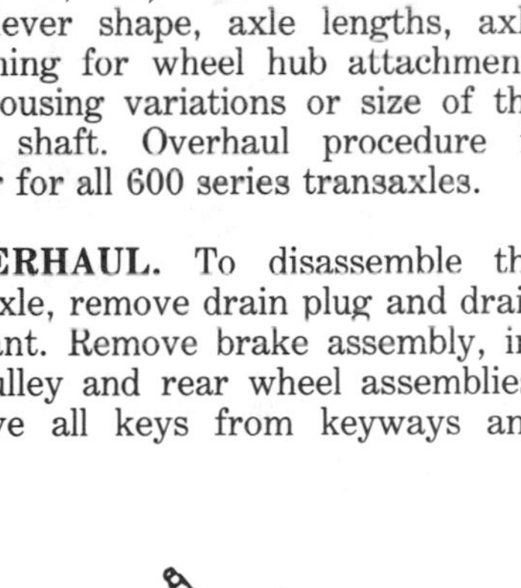

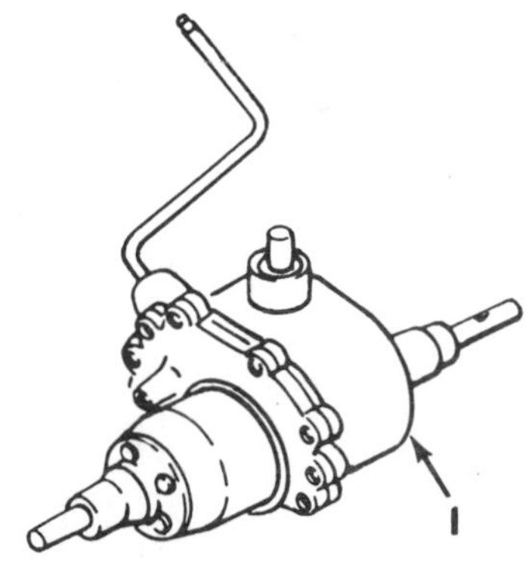


*Fig. PT19—Model and series numbers will be stamped into case or on a metal tag attached to case at location (I).*

polish any burrs or rust from exposed shafts. Place shift lever in neutral position, then unbolt and remove shift lever and housing assembly. Unbolt and remove axle housings (16 and 52 – Fig. PT20). Place unit in a vise so heads of socket head cap screws are pointing upward. Drive dowel pins out of case and cover. Unscrew socket head cap screws and lift off cover (55). Install two or three socket head screws into case to hold center plate (76) down while removing the differential assembly. Pull differential assembly straight up out of case. It may be necessary to gently bump lower axle shaft to loosen differential assembly. Remove center plate (76). Hold shifter rods (19) together and lift out shifter rods, forks (20), shifter stop (23), shaft (27), sliding gears (25 and 26) and spur gear (24) as an assembly. On early model transaxle, remove idler shaft (29) and gear (30) as individual parts. On late model transaxle, remove idler shaft and gear as a one-piece assembly as shown in (29A – Fig. PT21). On all models, remove reverse idler shaft (79 – Fig. PT20), spacer (80) and gear (81). On early model transaxle, with reference to Fig. PT20, remove cluster gears (35, 3 and 37) on sleeve (41) and thrust washe (42). On late model transaxle, wit reference to Fig. PT21, remove cluste gears (35, 36 and 37), spacers (S) o countershaft (C) and thrust washer (42) On all 600 series standard models remove bevel gear (31 – Fig. PT20) washers (32 and 34) and thrust bearing (33). On 601 series slow speed models remove bevel gear (31) and the singl thrust washer (32). On all models excep Model 612, remove input shaft oil sea (9), snap ring (10), input shaft (48) an gear (49). Washers (45 and 47) an thrust bearing (46) are removed with input shaft. Model 612 is equipped with a ball bearing in place of seal (9). To remove Model 612 input shaft, remove snap ring in case, ball bearing, snap ring (10), input shaft (48) and gear (49) Washers (45 and 47) and thrust bearing (46) are removed with input shaft. On al models, remove bearing (11) an bushing (12).

To disassemble cluster gear assembly press gears and key from sleeve (41) Bushings (38 and 40) are renewable i sleeve (41).

To disassemble the differential, driv roll pin (71) out of drive pin (74). Remov

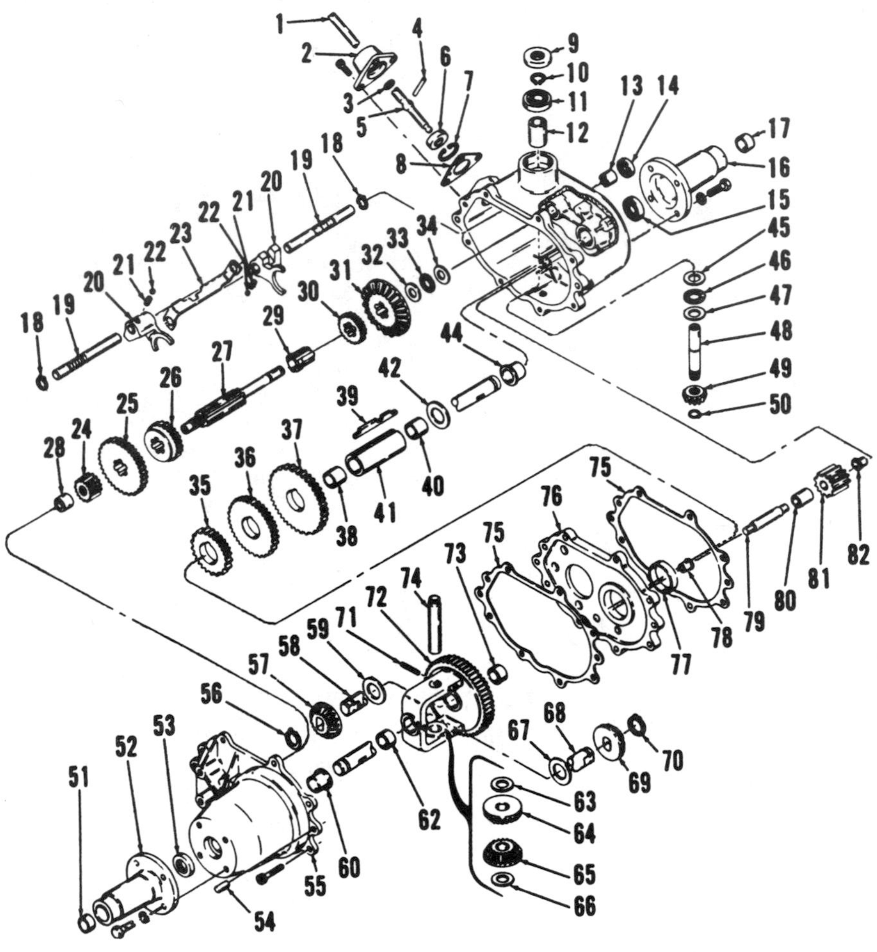

**Fig. PT20 – Exploded view of an early Peerless 600 series transaxle. Late model is similar, refer to Fig. PT21 for internal parts differences. On Model 601, slow speed transaxle, bevel gear (31) and input shaft assembly are not interchangeable with the 600 series parts.**

1. Shift lever
2. Lever housing
3. Quad ring
4. Roll pin
5. Shift lever
6. Retainer
7. Snap ring
8. Gasket
9. Oil seal
10. Snap ring
11. Ball bearing
12. Bushing
13. Needle bearing
14. Oil seal
15. Oil seal
16. Axle housing
17. Bushing
18. Snap ring
19. Shift rod
20. Shift fork
21. Spring
22. Detent ball
23. Shifter stop
24. Spur gear
25. Sliding gear (1st & reverse)
26. Sliding gear (2nd & 3rd)
27. Shift & brake shaft
28. Needle bearing
29. Idler shaft
30. Gear
31. Bevel gear
32. Washer
33. Thrust bearing
34. Washer
35. Gear
36. Gear
37. Gear
38. Bushing
39. Key
40. Bushing
41. Sleeve
42. Thrust washer
44. Bushing
45. Washer
46. Thrust bearing
47. Washer
48. Input shaft
49. Pinion gear
50. Snap ring
51. Bushing
52. Axle housing
53. Oil seal
54. Dowel pin
55. Cover
56. Snap ring
57. Side gear
58. Axle shaft
59. Thrust washer
60. Bushing
62. Bushing
63. Thrust washer
64. Bevel pinion gear
65. Bevel pinion gear
66. Thrust washer
67. Thrust washer
68. Axle shaft
69. Side gear
70. Snap ring
71. Roll pin
72. Differential carrier & gear
73. Bushing
74. Drive pin
75. Gasket
76. Center plate
77. Bushing
78. Bushing
79. Reverse idler shaft
80. Spacer
81. Reverse idler gear
82. Bushing

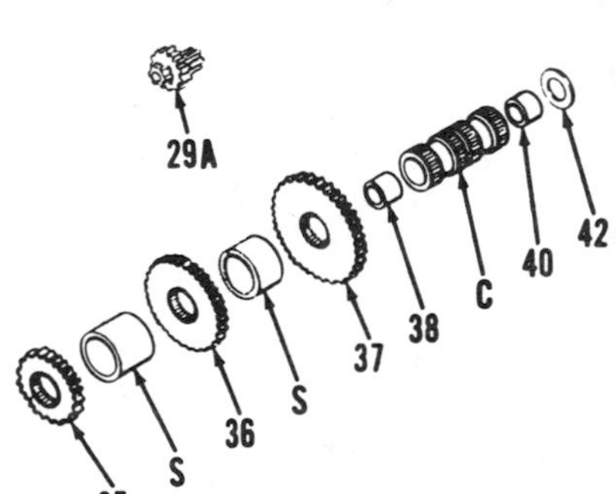

**Fig. PT21 – Exploded view showing late style countershaft assembly and one-piece idler shaft and gear assembly used on late 600 series transaxles.**

C. Countershaft
S. Spacer
29A. Idler shaft & gear assy.
35. Gear
36. Gear
37. Gear
38. Bushing
40. Bushing
42. Thrust washer

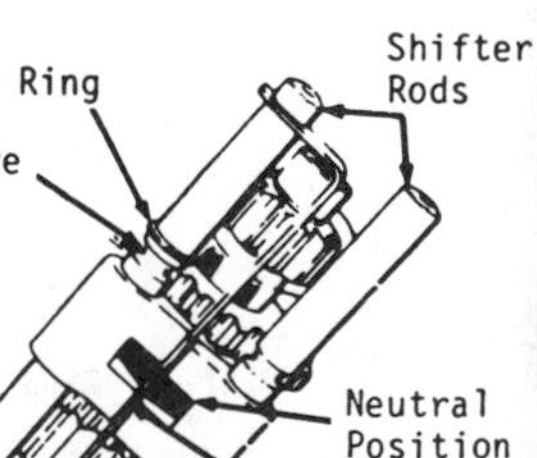

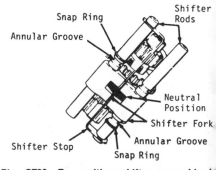

**Fig. PT22 – To position shifter assembly in neutral for reassembly, align notches in shifter forks with notch in shifter stop.**

drive pin, thrust washers (63 and 66) and bevel pinion gears (64 and 65). Remove snap rings (56 and 70) and withdraw axle shafts from side gears (57 and 69). Remove side gears.

Clean and inspect components for excessive wear or other damage. Renew all seals and gaskets. Check for binding of shift forks on shift rods. When reassembling, position shift forks in neutral position by aligning notches on shift rods with notch in shifter stop. See Fig. PT22. Install input shaft assembly by reversing the removal procedure. Position case so open side is up. Install needle bearing (13–Fig. PT20) and oil seal (14). On early model, install idler shaft (29) and gear (30). On late model transaxle, install one-piece idler shaft and gear (29A–Fig. PT21). On all models, install bevel gear (31–Fig. PT20), washers (32 and 34) and thrust bearing (33). Be sure thrust bearing is positioned between washers. Reverse idler shaft (79) may be used to temporarily hold idler gear assembly in position. On early model transaxle, place cluster gear (35, 36 and 37) on key (39) so bevel on gears (35 and 36) is toward large gear (37) and short section of key (39) is between middle gear (36) and large gear (37) as shown in Fig. PT23. Press gears and key on sleeve (41–PT20). On late model transaxle, install thrust washer (42–PT21), countershaft (C), cluster gears (35, 36 and 37) and spacers (S). On all models, install shifter assembly (18 through 27–Fig. PT20) in case, making certain that shifter rods are properly seated. Install reverse idler shaft (79), gear (81) and spacer (80). Beveled edge of gear should be up. Install gasket (75) and center plate (76), then second gasket (75) on case. Assemble differential by reversing disassembly procedure. Install differential assembly in case with longer axle pointing downward. Install locating dowel pins and secure cover (55) to case. Install oil seals (15 and 53) in axle housings (16 and 52). Transaxle housing should be filled through shifter opening with SAE 90 EP gear lubricant. Capacity will vary according to specific model numbers (603, 603A, 609, etc.) or mounting position on unit. Refer to CONDENSED SPECIFICATIONS or TRANSAXLE LUBRICATION paragraphs under appropriate TRACTOR SERVICE SECTION for specific model being serviced. Install shift lever assembly (1 through 8).

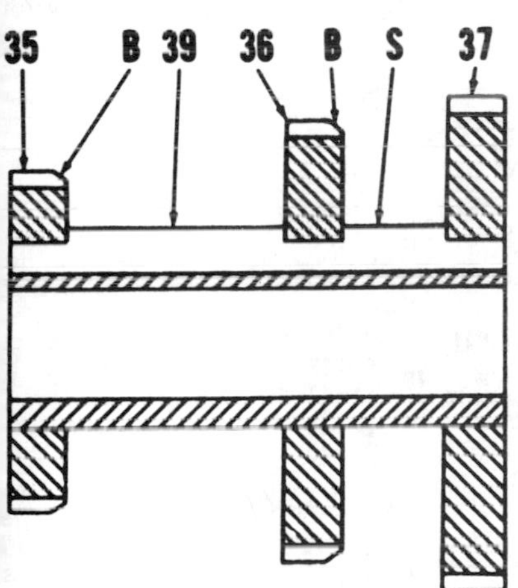


*Fig. PT23–On early model transaxle, note positions of bevels (B) on cluster gears and short section (S) of key (39) between gears (36 and 37).*

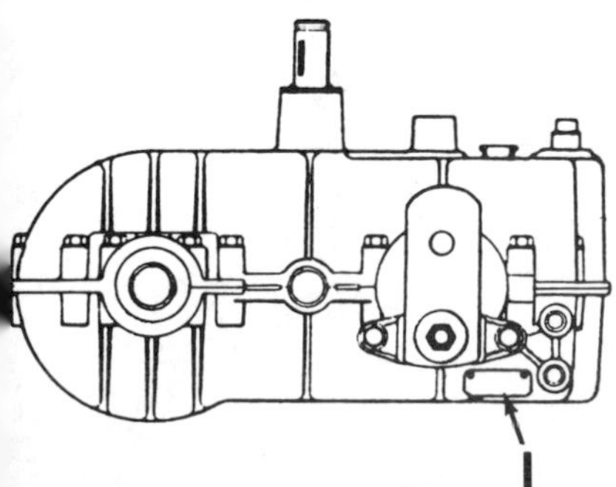


*Fig. PT30–Model and series numbers are located on a metal tag attached on transaxle case at location (I).*

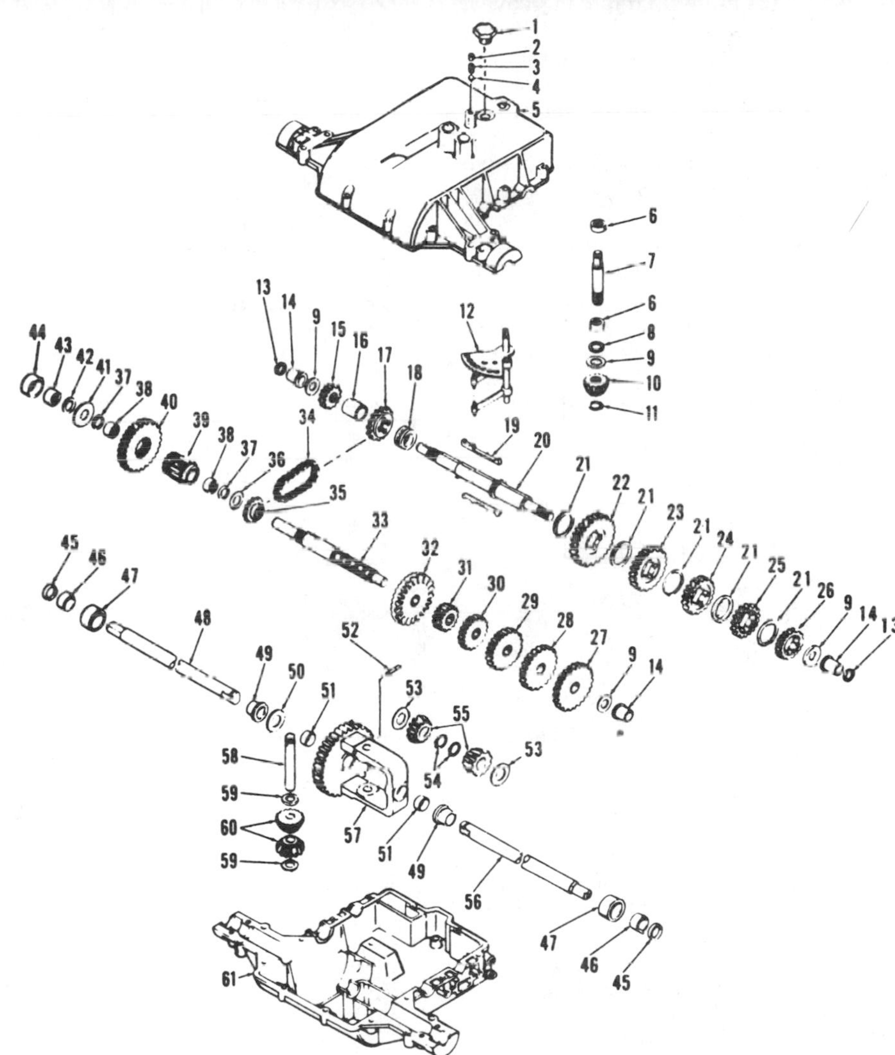

*Fig. PT31–Exploded view of Peerless 800 series transaxle.*

1. Plug
2. Set screw
3. Spring
4. Ball
5. Cover
6. Needle bearing
7. Input shaft
8. Square cut ring
9. Thrust washer
10. Input pinion
11. Snap ring
12. Shift fork assy.
13. Square cut ring
14. Bushing
15. Spur gear (12 or 15 tooth)
16. Spacer
17. Sprocket (18 tooth)
18. Shift collar
19. Key
20. Brake shaft
21. Thrust washer
22. Spur gear (35 tooth)
23. Spur gear (30 tooth)
24. Spur gear (25 tooth)
25. Spur gear (22 tooth)
26. Spur gear (20 tooth)
27. Gear (30 tooth)
28. Gear (28 tooth)
29. Gear (25 tooth)
30. Gear (20 tooth)
31. Spur gear (12 or 15 tooth)
32. Bevel gear (42 tooth)
33. Countershaft
34. Drive chain
35. Sprocket (9 tooth)
36. Flat washer
37. Square cut ring
38. Needle bearing
39. Output pinion
40. Output gear
41. Flat washer
42. Square cut seal
43. Needle bearing
44. Spacer
45. Oil seal
46. Needle bearing
47. Spacer
48. Axle shaft (short)
49. Bushing
50. Washer
51. Bushing
52. Pin
53. Thrust washer
54. Snap rings
55. Bevel side gears
56. Axle shaft (long)
57. Differential gear assy
58. Drive pin
59. Thrust washer
60. Bevel pinion gears
61. Case

Illustrations courtesy Tecumseh Products Co.

## Series 800

The 800 series transaxle may have 4 or 5 forward speeds and a single reverse speed. Bearings are oil impregnated bushings with needle bearings or ball bearings on axles, input and output shaft. The model number will be found on a tag located at (I – Fig. PT30).

**OVERHAUL.** To disassemble the transaxle, first remove drain plug and drain lubricant. Place shift lever in neutral and remove shift lever. Remove set screw (2 – Fig. PT31), spring (3) and index ball (4). Remove the 17 cap screws retaining cover (5). Push shift fork assembly (12) in while removing cover. Before removing gear shaft assemblies, shift fork (12) should be removed. It will be difficult to keep parts from falling off. Note position of parts before removal. Remove gear and shaft assemblies from case taking care not to disturb drive chain (34). Remove needle bearing (43), flat washer (41), square cut seals (42), output gear (40) and output pinion (39) from the countershaft. Angle the two shafts together (Fig. PT32). Mark the position of chain on sprocket collars and remove chain. Remove sprocket (35 – Fig. PT31), bevel gear (32), gears (27, 28, 29, 30), spur gear (31), thrust washer (9) and flange bushing (14). All gears are splined to the countershaft. Disassembly of brake shaft (20) is self-evident from observation. Remove snap ring (11), input pinion (10) and pull input shaft (7) through cover.

To disassemble the differential, drive roll pin out of drive pin (58) and remove drive pin. Remove pinion gears (60) by rotating gears in opposite directions. Remove snap rings (54), side gears (55), thrust washers (53) and slide axles out.

Clean and inspect all parts and renew any showing excessive wear or other damage. When installing new inner input shaft needle bearings, press bearing in to a depth of 0.135-0.150 inches (3.43-3.81 mm) below flush. When installing thrust washers and shifting gears on brake shaft, the 45 degree chamfer on inside diameter of thrust washers must face shoulder on brake shaft (Fig. PT33). The flat side of gears must face shoulder on shaft. Before upper cover (5 – Fig. PT31) is joined with case (61), pack 24 ounces (0.7 L) of EP lithium base grease into case. Complete reassembly and tighten case to cover cap screws to 80-100 in.-lbs. (9-11 N•m).

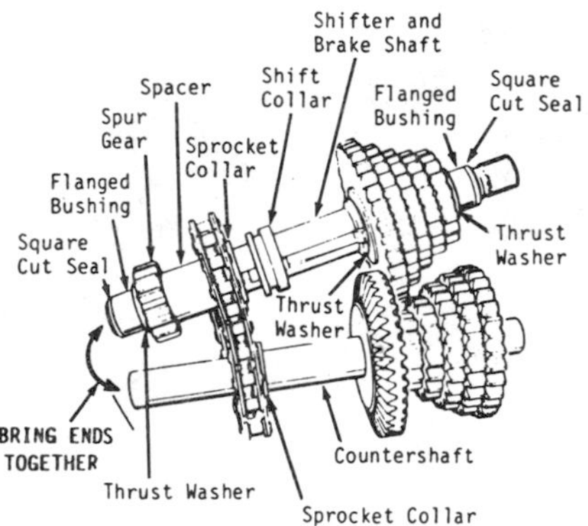


***Fig. PT32 — Mark position of chain on sprocket collars, angle shafts together and remove chain.***

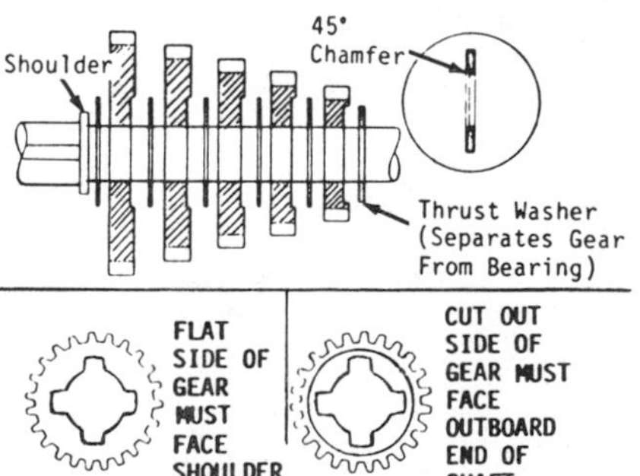


***Fig. PT 33 — When installing thrust washers and gears on brake shaft, 45 degree chamfer on inside diameter of thrust washers must face shoulder on brake shaft.***

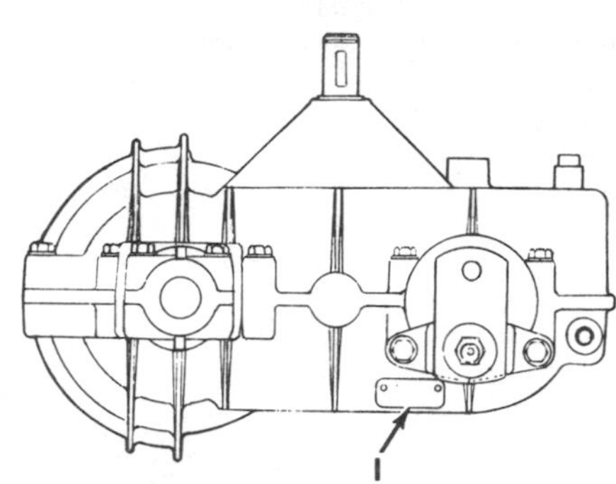


***Fig. PT35 — Transaxle identification tag is located at (I).***

## Series 900

The 900 series transaxle may have 1, 2, 3 or 4 speeds forward and a single reverse speed. Bearings are oil impregnated bushings with needle bearings or ball bearings on axles, input

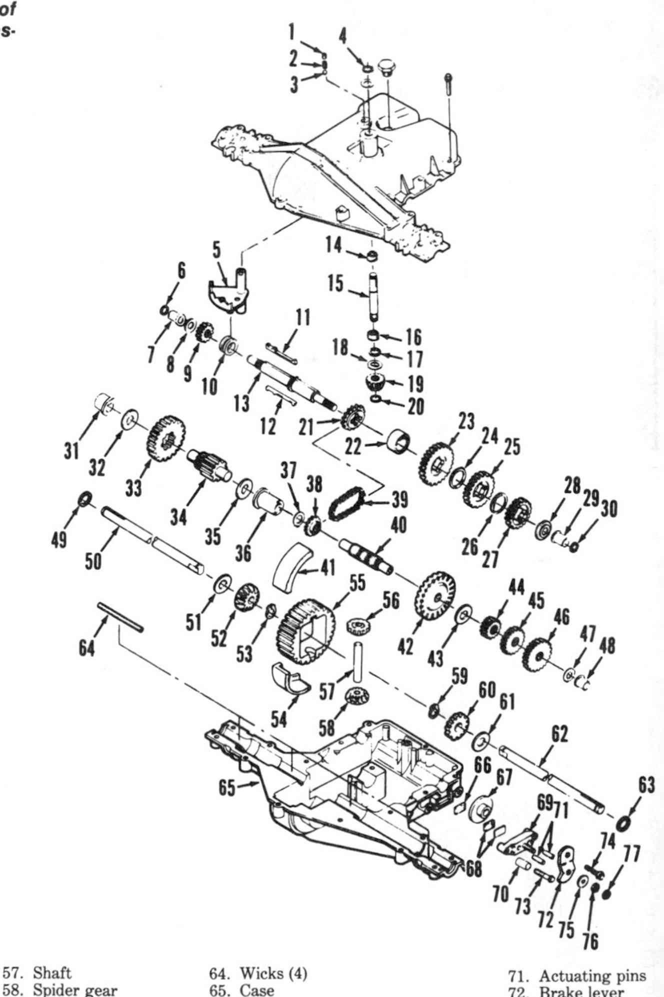

***Fig. PT36 — Exploded view of Peerless 900 series transaxle.***

1. Set screw
2. Spring
3. Detent ball
4. Retaining ring
5. Shifter
6. "O" ring
7. Bushing
8. Thrust washer
9. Gear
10. Collar
11. Key
12. Key
13. Shifter/brake shaft
14. Needle bearing
15. Input shaft
16. Needle bearing
17. Square cut seal
18. Thrust washer
19. Bevel gear
20. Retaining ring
21. Reverse gear (thick collar toward gears)
22. Neutral spacer
23. Gear
24. Washer (chamfered)
25. Gear
26. Washer (chamfered)
27. Gear
28. Thrust washer
29. Bushing
30. "O" ring
31. Large bushing
32. Thrust washer
33. Output gear
34. Output pinion
35. Thrust washer
36. Bushing
37. Thrust washer
38. Reverse gear (thick collar toward gears)
39. Chain
40. Countershaft
41. Bearing block
42. Gear (bevel installed toward sprocket)
43. Thrust washer
44. Spur gear
45. Spur gear
46. Spur gear
47. Thrust washer
48. Bushing
49. Washer
50. Axle shaft
51. Washer
52. Axle gear
53. Snap ring
54. Bearing block
55. Differential gear
56. Spider gear
57. Shaft
58. Spider gear
59. Snap ring
60. Axle gear
61. Washer
62. Axle shaft
63. Washer
64. Wicks (4)
65. Case
66. Inner brake pad
67. Disc
68. Outer brake pad & plate
69. Caliper
70. Spacer
71. Actuating pins
72. Brake lever
73. Cap screw
74. Cap screw
75. Washer
76. Adjustment nut
77. Jam nut



Illustrations courtesy Tecumseh Products Co.

shaft and output shaft. The model number will be found on a tag located at I—Fig. PT35.

**OVERHAUL.** To disassemble the transaxle, first remove drain plug and drain lubricant. Place shift lever in neutral position. Remove set screw (1–Fig. PT36), spring (2) and detent ball (3). Remove neutral start switch (as equipped). Remove cap screws and separate cover from case. It will be necessary to push shift lever rod in while pulling cover off of case. Remove brake caliper cap screws (73 and 74) and remove brake assembly, brake disc (67) and inner brake pad (66). Remove grease from unit as unit is disassembled. Remove shifter assembly (5). Note how "V" notches on flange bushings fit into recess "V" of case (Fig. PT37), then remove gear and shaft assemblies. Pull countershaft, output pinion and shaft assembly apart. To disassemble countershaft, remove the two thrust washers, sprocket bevel gear, spur gears and flanged bushing. Sprocket and spur gears are splined to the countershaft. To disassemble the output pinion and shaft, remove the large brass bushing, large washer, large output gear, washer and bushing. The shaft is pressed into the output pinion gear and is available as an assembly only. To disassemble the shifter shaft, remove the two square cut "O" rings and the two flanged bushings, the two thrust washers on shaft ends, shift collar with keys, sprocket, spacer, shifter gears and thrust washers.

The differential assembly is held together by its position in the case. Differential assembly is disassembled as unit is removed from case. Remove all flat washers on axle ends.

To disassemble input shaft, remove the retaining ring on bevel gear end of input shaft, remove bevel gear and pull shaft through case. The square cut "O" ring must be renewed if removed.

Clean and inspect all parts. Lubricate all parts during reassembly. Needle bearing (14–Fig. PT36) is pressed into bearing bore just far enough to allow installation of upper thrust washer and retaining ring (4). Needle bearing (16) is pressed into bearing bore of cover 0.135-0.150 inch (3.4-3.8 mm) below flush. Install input shaft and bevel gear in cover. Slide keys and collar on shifter and brake shaft. Assemble shifter/brake shaft and countershaft at the same time. Install reverse chain on reverse sprockets. Collars of reverse sprockets should be on the same side of the chain. Slide larger sprocket onto shifter/brake shaft with collar away from shifting keys and shoulder on shifter/brake shaft. Slide keys through gear and install the neutral collar over ends of shifting keys and pull back until gears touch shoulder of the shaft. Insert splined countershaft into smaller reverse sprocket. Place the large beveled gear on countershaft with beveled side of gear towards reverse sprocket. If unit is a 1, 2 or 3 speed unit, place a washer over the shaft and next to the backside of the large bevel gear. If the unit is a 4 speed unit, there will not be a washer in this location. Install spur gears onto the countershaft, alternating with mating gear on the shifter/brake shaft. Install largest shifting gears with the flat side of gear next to the neutral collar. On older models, install thrust washer with 45 degree chamfer on inside diameter of washer next to gear. Chamfer must face towards shifting keys. On newer models, thrust washer will have rounded sides and rounded side must face towards shifting keys. Older chamfered thrust washer and newer rounded thrust washer are interchangeable. Install thrust washer on each end of countershaft and a bushing next to the last spur gear on countershaft. Install larger thrust washer next to the smallest shifting gear, then install bronze bushing and "O" ring. Some units will use a stepped thrust washer; install washer onto shaft so the step is facing away from the shifting gears. The end of the shifter/brake shaft (opposite shifting gears) has a spline. Install spur gear that drives output gear onto this spline. Install thrust washer, bushing and "O" ring.

To assemble output shaft, install bronze bushing with collar, flat down, next to pinion. Install output gear over pinion with a washer on the outside of gear. After assembly of both shafts, install correct size flanged bushing on each end.

To assemble differential, assemble unit and hold in position while unit is installed in case. Axles and gears must be on center line of ring gear. Bearing block in case must have flange to the left-hand side. Block in cover must have flange to the right-hand side. Prior to differential installation in case, insert the four felt wicks with bosses and tabs to hold bearing blocks in position. Apply Bentonite grease to these bearing areas after wicks have been installed.

Install shifter assembly and pack 24 ounces (710 mL) of Bentonite grease around bearings and gears. Install cover on case and tighten cap screws to 90-100 in.-lbs. (10-11 N•m). Install detent ball, spring and set screw. Tighten set screw one turn below flush. Install neutral safety switch and brake unit.

## Series 920 and Series 930

The 920 series and 930 series transaxle is available with 5, 6 or 7 speeds forward and one reverse speed. The transaxle model number will be found on a tag located on right side of transaxle housing just below the brake assembly.

**OVERHAUL.** To disassemble transaxle, place shift lever in neutral position. Remove snap ring and drive pulley. Remove neutral start switch. Remove set screw (1—Fig. PT40), spring and detent ball (2). Remove mounting screws and separate cover (6) from case (63). Unbolt and remove disc brake assembly from case. Remove gear shifter assembly (13). Remove top bearing block on differential gear, then lift out axles and differential assembly. Remove countershaft (45) assembly, output shaft (39) assembly and shifter/brake shaft (20) assembly from case as complete units if possible. Remove snap ring (12) securing bevel gear (11) on input shaft (8), then pull input shaft out of case.

As parts are removed from shafts, clean grease from each part and arrange in order of removal to make reassembly easier. Inspect all parts for wear or damage and renew as necessary.

Lubricate all parts with grease during reassembly. Input shaft upper needle bearing is pressed flush with housing and lower needle bearing is pressed into housing 0.135-0.150 inch (3.4-3.8 mm ) below flush as shown in Fig. PT41. Square cut seal ring must be renewed whenever input shaft is removed. Lubricate needle bearings (7—Fig. PT40) with grease before installing input shaft (8).

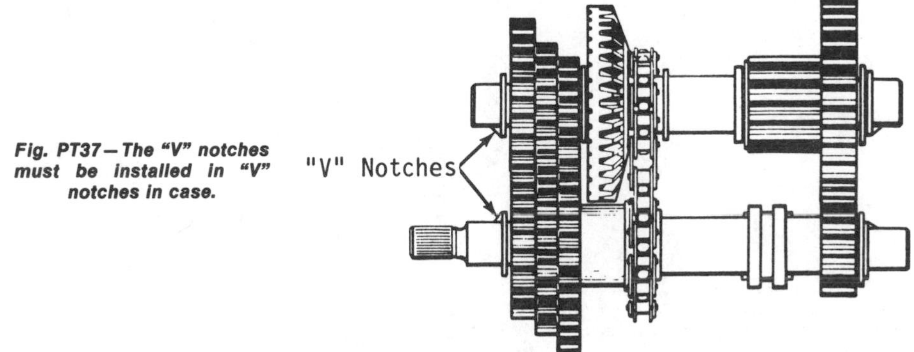


*Fig. PT37—The "V" notches must be installed in "V" notches in case.*

Assemble shifter/brake shaft and countershaft at the same time. Lubricate keyways of shifter/brake shaft, then slide keys (19) and shift collar (18) on shaft. Install chain (25) on reverse sprockets (23 and 44), making sure that hub side of both sprockets faces the same direction. Slide larger sprocket (23) onto shifter/brake shaft with hub side of sprocket facing away from shifting keys and shoulder on the shaft. Slide keys through the sprocket and install neutral collar (24) over ends of keys and pull collar and sprocket against shoulder of shaft. Insert splined countershaft (45) into smaller reverse sprocket (44). Install thrust washer (46) next to smaller reverse sprocket, then install bevel gear (47) with bevel toward reverse sprocket. Install another thrust washer (46) on other side of bevel gear. Install spur gears (48 through 52) on countershaft, alternating with mating gears (26 through 31) on shifter/brake shaft. Note that largest shifting gear (26) is installed

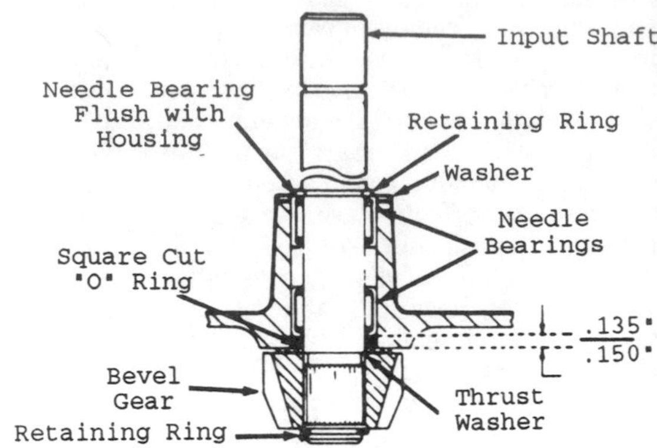


*Fig. PT41—Cross-sectional view of transaxle input shaft used on Peerless 920 series and 930 series transaxles showing correct installation of needle bearings.*

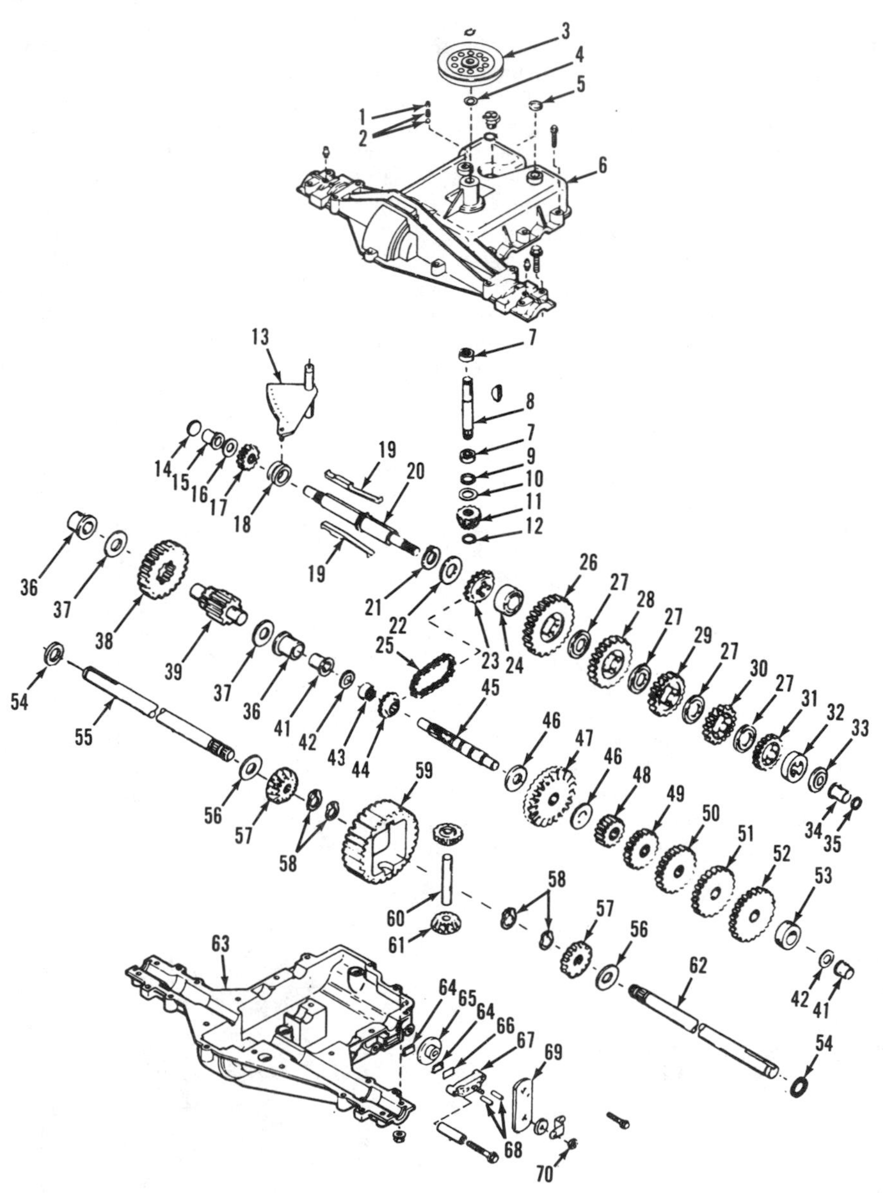

1. Set screw
2. Detent ball & spring
3. Pulley
4. Thrust washer
5. Seal ring
6. Cover
7. Needle bearings
8. Input shaft
9. Seal ring
10. Thrust washer
11. Bevel pinion gear
12. Snap ring
13. Shifter assy.
14. Plug
15. Flanged bushing
16. Thrust washer
17. Gear
18. Shift collar
19. Shift keys
20. Shifter/brake shaft
21. Snap ring
22. Thrust washer
23. Reverse sprocket
24. Neutral collar
25. Chain
26. Gear
27. Washers (curved)
28. Gear
29. Gear
30. Gear
31. Gear
32. Spacer
33. Thrust washer (thick)
34. Flanged bushing
35. Square cut ring
36. Flanged bushing
37. Thrust washer
38. Output gear
39. Output shaft
41. Flanged bushing
42. Thrust washer
43. Spacer
44. Reverse sprocket
45. Countershaft
46. Thrust washer
47. Bevel gear
48. Gear
49. Gear
50. Gear
51. Gear
52. Gear
53. Spacer
54. Seal
55. Axle L.H.
56. Thrust washer
57. Axle gear
58. Snap rings
59. Ring gear
60. Pinion shaft
61. Pinion gear
62. Axle R.H.
63. Case
64. Brake pads
65. Brake disc
66. Back-up plate
67. Brake pad holder
68. Actuating pins
69. Brake lever
70. Adjusting nut

*Fig. PT40—Exploded view of 930 series transaxle.*

first on shifter/brake shaft and that flat side of gears must face shoulder of shaft (Fig. PT42). Install shifting washers (27) on shifter/brake shaft with rounded side of washers toward shifting keys. Install spacers (43 and 53—Fig. PT40), thrust washers (42) and bronze bushings (41) on countershaft. Install spacer (32), larger thrust washer (33), bronze bushing (34) and "O" ring (35) on end of shifter/brake shaft. Install spur gear (17), thrust washer (16) and bronze bushing (15) on other end of shifter/brake shaft. Assembly of countershaft and shifter/brake shaft is complete.

Install output gear (38) on stepped end of output pinion (39). Position thrust washers (37) and flange bushings (36) on output pinion. Lubricate flange bearing mounting surfaces with grease. Assemble output shaft, countershaft and shifter/brake shaft assemblies in transaxle case. Make sure that the tabs of all flange bushings fit into "V" notches of case. Position seal plug (14) in case at end of shifter/brake shaft opposite the brake assembly. Install shifter fork.

Before installing differential into the case, insert four felt wicks in case and lubricate wicks and flange bearing surfaces with grease. Insert lower bearing block into the case. Assemble differential and axles and hold in position while the assembly is installed in case.

Pack 30 ounces (887 mL) of Bentonite grease in case. Install cover and tighten mounting cap screws to 90-100 in.-lbs. (10.2-11.3 N·m). Reinstall brake assembly making sure that brake pads and disc are free of oil and grease.

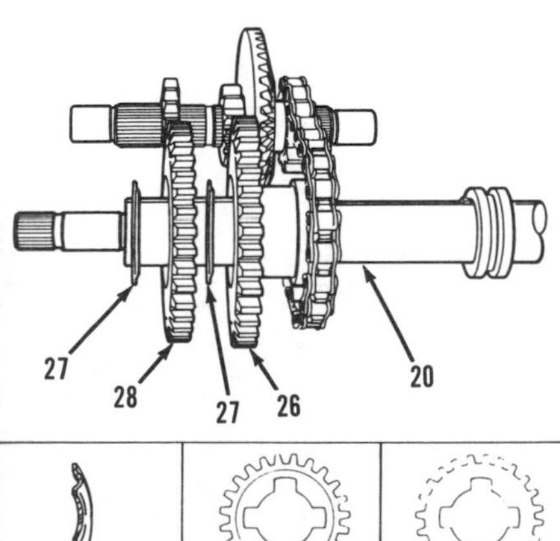


*Fig. PT42—When assembling shifter/brake shaft, install curved washers (27) so rounded side is toward shaft shoulder. Flat side of gears also must face shoulder on output shaft.*

## Series 1200 And Series 1400

The 1200 series and 1400 series transaxle has three forward speeds and one reverse speed. The 1200 series and 1400 series transaxle are equipped with axle support housings which are pressed from the inside of the case to the outside. Entire transaxle must be disassembled before axle housings can be removed. Variations in model numbers, within the series, indicate shift lever shape, axle lengths, axle machining for wheel hub attachment, axle housing variations, size of the brake shaft or the placement of the input shaft on the left-hand or right-hand side of the transaxle. Series and model numbers may be stamped into case or on a metal tag attached to case at locations indicated at (I–Fig. PT50).

**OVERHAUL.** Remove brake components and input pulley. Remove all keys from keyways and polish any burrs or rust from exposed shafts. Place shift lever in neutral position, unscrew shift housing cap screws and withdraw shift assembly from case. Place transaxle in a vise with longer axle pointing downward. Unscrew case cap screws and drive out dowel pins. Separate cover from case and lift cover upward off axle shaft. Brake shaft (30–Fig. PT51) and idler gear (29) will be removed with cover. Remove output shaft (41) with output gear (40), spacer (39) and washer (38). Withdraw differential and axle shaft assembly and lay aside for later disassembly. Hold upper ends of shifter rods together and lift out shifter rods, forks, shifter stop, shifter shaft (20) and sliding gears (22 and 23) as an assembly. Remove reverse idler gear (27), idler shaft (28) and spacer (26), then remove idler shaft (32) along with idler gears (33, 35 and 37) and spacers (34 and 36). Withdraw input shaft (24) and gear (25) from case. To remove brake shaft (30) and idler gear (29) from cover, block up under idler gear (29) and press brake shaft (30) out of gear while being careful pressure is not applied on cover during operation. Renew seals and bushings in axle housing (51 and 60) as required.

To disassemble differential, unscrew four cap screws and separate axle shaft and carriage assemblies from ring gear (68). Drive blocks (65), bevel pinion gears (66) and drive pin (67) can now be removed from ring gear. Remove snap rings (43) and slide axle shafts (45 and 57) from bevel gears (44) and carriers (48 and 62).

Clean and inspect all parts for damage or excessive wear and renew as required. When installing needle bearings, press bearings into case and cover from inside until bearings are 0.015-0.020 inches (0.381-0.508 mm) below thrust surfaces. Renew all seals and gaskets and reassemble transaxle assembly by reversing disassembly procedure. Install reverse idler gear (27) into case so rounded edge of gear teeth and spacer (26) will be towards cover. When installing idler shaft (32), place short spacer (36) between gears (35 and 37) and long spacer (34) between gears (33 and 35). Bevels on gear teeth of gears (33 and 35) must be on side of gear nearest large gear (37). Before installing shifter assembly, fill transaxle housing with SAE 90 EP gear lubricant. Capacity for Models 1203, 1204, 1204-A and 1205 through 1208 is 3 pints (1.4 L). Capacity for all other models is 2 pints (0.9 L). When installing shifter assembly, position shifter rods in neutral position as shown in Fig. PT52. Differential cap screws are tightened to 7 ft.-lbs. (9 N·m). Tighten case-to-cover and shift lever housing cap screws to 10 ft.-lbs. (14 N·m) and axle housing cap screws to 13 ft.-lbs. (18 N·m).

## Series 1700 And Series 2000

The Peerless 1700 series and 2000 series transaxle are similar to the 1200 series transaxle except that the axle housings bolt to the outside of the transaxle case disassembly. Model and series numbers are at the same locations as those for 1200 series transaxles (Fig. PT50).

**OVERHAUL.** Clean exterior of unit. Remove drain plug and drain lubricant. Remove brake band, brake drum and input pulley. Loosen set screws and remove rear wheel and hub assemblies. Place shift lever in neutral position, remove the three cap screws from shift lever housing, then withdraw shift lever assembly. Remove cap screws securing transaxle cover (59–Fig. PT61) to case (14). Place unit on the edge of a bench or in a vise with right axle pointing downward. Drive dowel pins out of

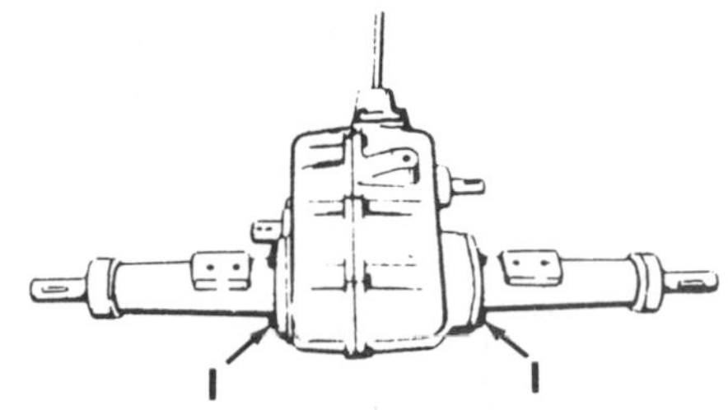


*Fig. PT50—Model and series numbers are either stamped into case or located on a metal tag attached on transaxle case at locations (I).*

cover. Remove all rust, paint or burrs from outer ends of axle shafts. Separate cover from case and lift cover upward off axle shaft. Brake shaft (33) and idler gear (32) will be removed with cover. Remove output shaft (45) with output gear (44), spacer (43) and washer (42). Withdraw differential and axle shaft assembly and lay aside for later disassembly. Hold upper ends of shifter rods together and lift out shifter rods, forks, shifter stop, shifter shaft (26) and sliding gears (28 and 29) as an assembly. Remove reverse idler gear (17), shaft (15) and spacer (18), then remove idler shaft (34) with idler gears (35, 37 and 39) and spacers (36 and 38). Input shaft (30) and input gear (31) can now be removed from case. To remove brake shaft (33) and idler gear (32) from cover, block up under idler gear (32) and press brake shaft (33) out of gear while being careful pressure is not applied on cover during operation.

To disassemble differential, unbolt and separate axle shaft and carriage assemblies from ring gear (49). Drive blocks (52), bevel pinion gears (51) and drive pin (50) can now be removed from ring gear. Remove snap rings (53) and slide axle shafts (47 and 55) from axle gears (54) and carriages (48 and 58).

Unbolt axle housings (12 and 64) and renew bushings (13 and 65) and seals (11 and 63) as required.

Clean and inspect all parts and renew any showing excessive wear or other damage. When installing needle bearings, press bearings in from inside of case and cover until bearings are 0.015-0.020 inch (0.381-0.508 mm) below thrust surfaces. Renew all seals and gaskets and reassemble by reversing removal procedure. Install reverse idler gear (17) into case so the rounded edge of the gear teeth and spacer (18) will be to the top. When installing idler shaft (34) and idler gears, position gears and spacers as follows: idler gear (39) with raised hub up, short spacer (38), idler gear (37) with rounded teeth edge down, long spacer (36) and idler gear (35) with rounded teeth edge down. Tighten differential cap screws to 7 ft.-lbs. (9 N•m). Tighten case-to-cover and shift lever housing cap screws to 10 ft.-lbs. (14 N•m) and axle housing cap screws to 13 ft.-lbs. (18 N•m). Fill transaxle housing to level plug opening with SAE 90 EP gear lubricant. Approximate capacity is 2 pints (0.9 L).

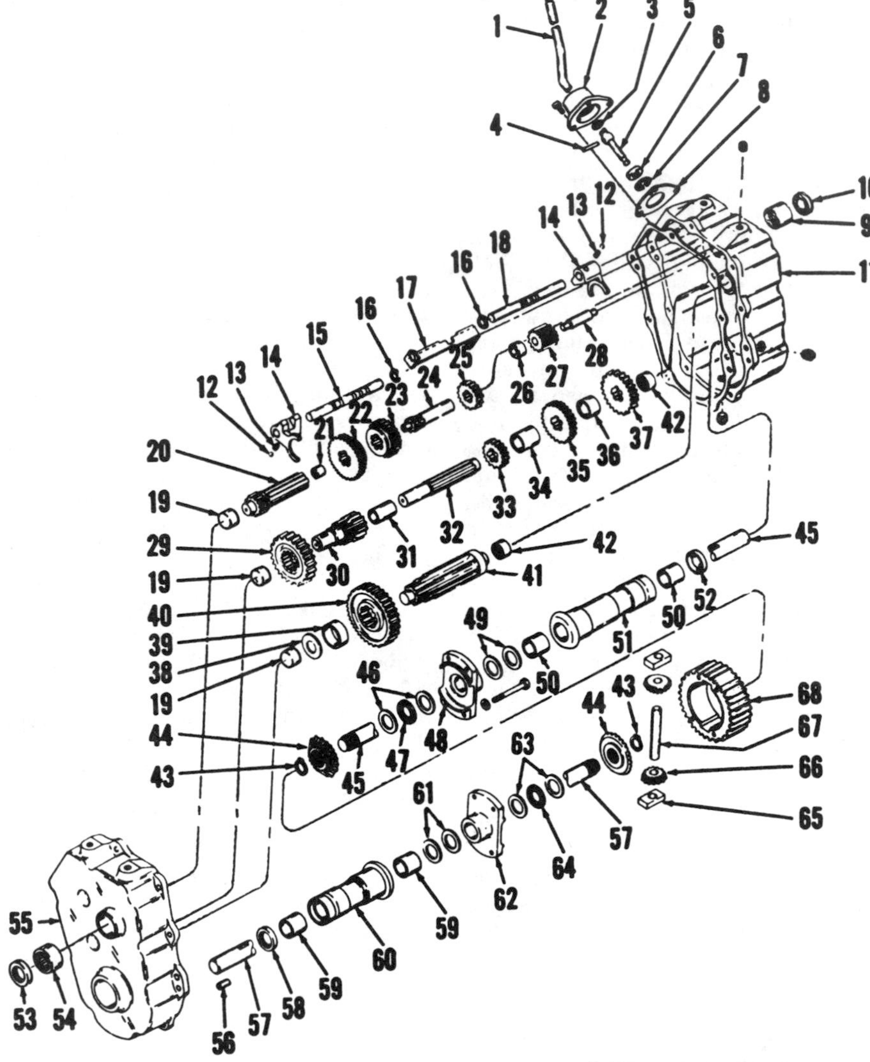

*Fig. PT51 — Exploded view of Peerless 1200 series and 1400 series transaxle.*

1. Shift lever
2. Shift housing
3. Quad ring
4. Roll pin
5. Shift lever
6. Keeper
7. Snap ring
8. Gasket
9. Bearing
10. Oil seal
11. Case
12. Steel ball
13. Spring
14. Shifter fork
15. Shifter rod
16. Snap ring
17. Shifter stop
18. Shifter rod
19. Bearing
20. Shifter shaft
21. Bearing
22. Sliding gear (1st & reverse)
23. Sliding gear (2nd & 3rd)
24. Input shaft
25. Gear
26. Spacer
27. Reverse idler gear
28. Reverse idler shaft
29. Idler gear
30. Brake shaft
31. Spacer
32. Idler shaft
33. Gear
34. Spacer
35. Gear
36. Spacer
37. Gear
38. Washer
39. Spacer
40. Output gear
41. Output shaft
42. Bearing
43. Snap ring
44. Bevel gear
45. Axle shaft
46. Thrust bearings
47. Thrust bearing
48. Differential carrier
49. Thrust washers
50. Bushing
51. Axle housing
52. Oil seal
53. Oil seal
54. Bearing
55. Cover
56. Dowel pin
57. Axle shaft
58. Oil seal
59. Bushing
60. Axle housing
61. Thrust washers
62. Differential carrier
63. Thrust washers
64. Thrust bearing
65. Drive blocks
66. Bevel pinion gear
67. Drive pin
68. Ring gear

## Series 2300

The Peerless 2300 series transaxle is a heavy-duty transaxle with four forward speeds and one reverse speed. The 2300 series transaxle is designed for small tractors which can be equipped with ground engaging attachments. The transaxle case is cast iron. The series and model numbers are stamped into the case or on a metal tag attached on the case in either location shown at (I – Fig. PT80).

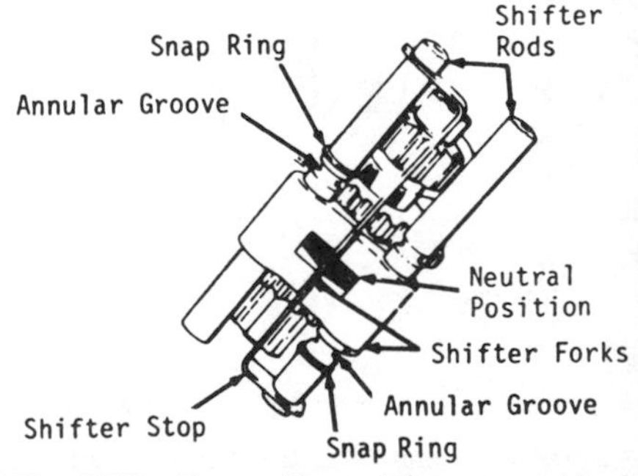


*Fig. PT52 — To position shifter assembly in neutral for reassembly, align notches in shifter forks with notch in shifter stop.*



Illustrations courtesy Tecumseh Products Co.

**OVERHAUL.** Clean exterior of unit. Remove drain plug and drain lubricant. Loosen set screws, remove snap rings, then remove rear wheel and hub assemblies. Remove brake assembly and input pulley. Place shift lever (1–Fig. PT81) in neutral position, then unbolt and remove shift lever assembly. Remove axle housings (14 and 64) and remove seal retainers (11) with oil seals (12) and "O" rings (13) by pulling each axle shaft out of case and cover as far as possible. Place transaxle unit on the edge of a bench with left axle shaft pointing downward. Remove cap screws securing case (16) to cover (66) and drive aligning dowel pins out of case. Lift case (16) up 1½ to 2 inches (40-50 mm), tilt case about 45 degrees, rotate case clockwise and remove from assembly. Input shaft (32) and input gear (33) will be removed with case. Withdraw differential and axle shaft assembly and lay aside for later disassembly. Remove 3-cluster gear (44) with its thrust washer (46) and spacer (42). Lift out reverse idler gear (25), spacer (24) and reverse idler shaft (23). Hold upper ends of shifter rods together and lift out shifter rods, forks, shifter stop (21), sliding gears (30 and 31) and shifter shaft (28) as an assembly. Remove low reduction gear (57), low reduction shaft (56) and thrust washer (55), then remove 2-cluster gear (40) from brake shaft. Lift out the output gear (50), output shaft (51) and thrust washers (49 and 52). To remove brake and cluster shaft (39) and idler gear (38) from cover (66), block up under idler gear and press shaft (39) out of gear. Do not allow cover or low reduction gear bearing boss to support any part of the pressure required to press brake and cluster shaft (39) from idler gear (38). Remove input shaft (32) with input gear (33) and thrust washer (34) from case (16).

To disassemble standard differential, remove four cap screws and separate axle shaft and carriage assemblies from ring gear (79). Drive blocks (78), bevel pinion gears (77) and drive pin (76) can now be removed from ring gear. Remove snap rings (59) and withdraw axle shafts (63 and 67) from axle gears (61) and carriages (62 and 72).

To disassemble limited-slip differential, remove the four cap screws (5–Fig. PT82) and separate axle assemblies from body cores (10 and 13). Remove snap rings (8 and 15) and remove side gears (7 and 16), carriers (6 and 17) and all thrust washers and bearings. Remove spring (11) on older models so equipped. On all models, remove pinion gears (9 and 14). To reassemble limited-slip differential, install body cores in ring gear so gear pockets in one core are out of alignment with gear pockets in the other core. Reassemble axle assemblies making certain flanged side of thrust washers (2 and 20) are installed toward carriers. Install pinion gears in one body core, then hold pinion gears in core by installing differential carrier and axle assembly. Turn differential over. Be sure pinion gears mesh with side

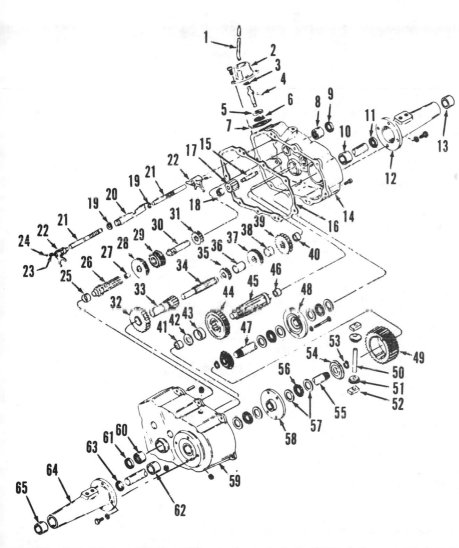

***Fig. PT61 — Exploded view of Peerless 1700 series transaxle. Series 2000 is similar except sealed ball bearings are used in place of bushings (13 and 65).***

1. Shift lever
2. Shift lever housing
3. Seal ring
4. Roll pin
5. Retainer
6. Snap ring
7. Gasket
8. Needle bearing
9. Oil seal
10. Bushing
11. Oil seal
12. Axle housing
13. Bushing
14. Transaxle case
15. Reverse idler shaft
16. Gasket
17. Reverse idler gear
18. Spacer
19. Snap ring
20. Shifter stop
21. Shifter rod
22. Shifter fork
23. Spring
24. Detent ball
25. Needle bearing
26. Shifter shaft
27. Center bearing
28. Gear (1st & reverse)
29. Gear (2nd & 3rd)
30. Input shaft
31. Input gear
32. Idler gear
33. Brake shaft
34. Idler shaft
35. Idler gear
36. Long spacer
37. Idler gear
38. Short spacer
39. Idler gear
40. Needle bearing
41. Needle bearing
42. Washer
43. Spacer
44. Output gear
45. Output shaft
46. Needle bearing
47. Axle shaft
48. Axle carriage (plain holes)
49. Ring gear
50. Drive pin
51. Bevel pinion gear
52. Drive block
53. Snap ring
54. Bevel axle gear
55. Axle shaft
56. Thrust bearing
57. Thrust washers
58. Axle carriage (tapped holes)
59. Transaxle cover
60. Needle bearing
61. Oil seal
62. Bushing
63. Oil seal
64. Axle housing
65. Bushing

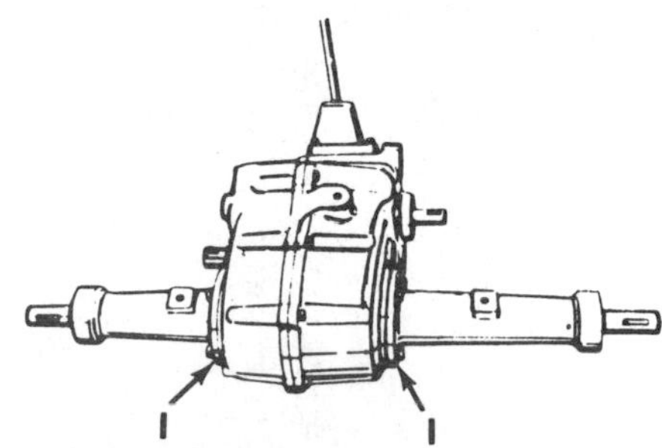

***Fig. PT80 — On 2300 series transaxle, model and series numbers are stamped into the transaxle case or are on a metal tag attached on the case in either location (I).***

Illustrations courtesy Tecumseh Products Co.

gear. Install pinion gears in remaining body core being sure gears mesh with previously installed pinion gears. Install cylindrical spring (as equipped) so spring bottoms against side gear. Spring (if so equipped) should be in contact with most of the ten pinion gears. Install remaining axle assembly and differential retaining bolts and tighten bolts to 7-10 ft.-lbs. (9-14 N·m).

Clean and inspect all transaxle parts and renew any showing excessive wear or other damage. When installing new needle bearings, press bearing (29 – Fig. PT81) into shifter shaft (28) to a depth of 0.010 inch (0.254 mm) below end of shaft and low reduction shaft bearings (54 and 58) 0.010 inch (0.254 mm) below thrust surfaces of bearing bosses. Carrier bearings (10) should be pressed in from inside of case and cover until bearings are

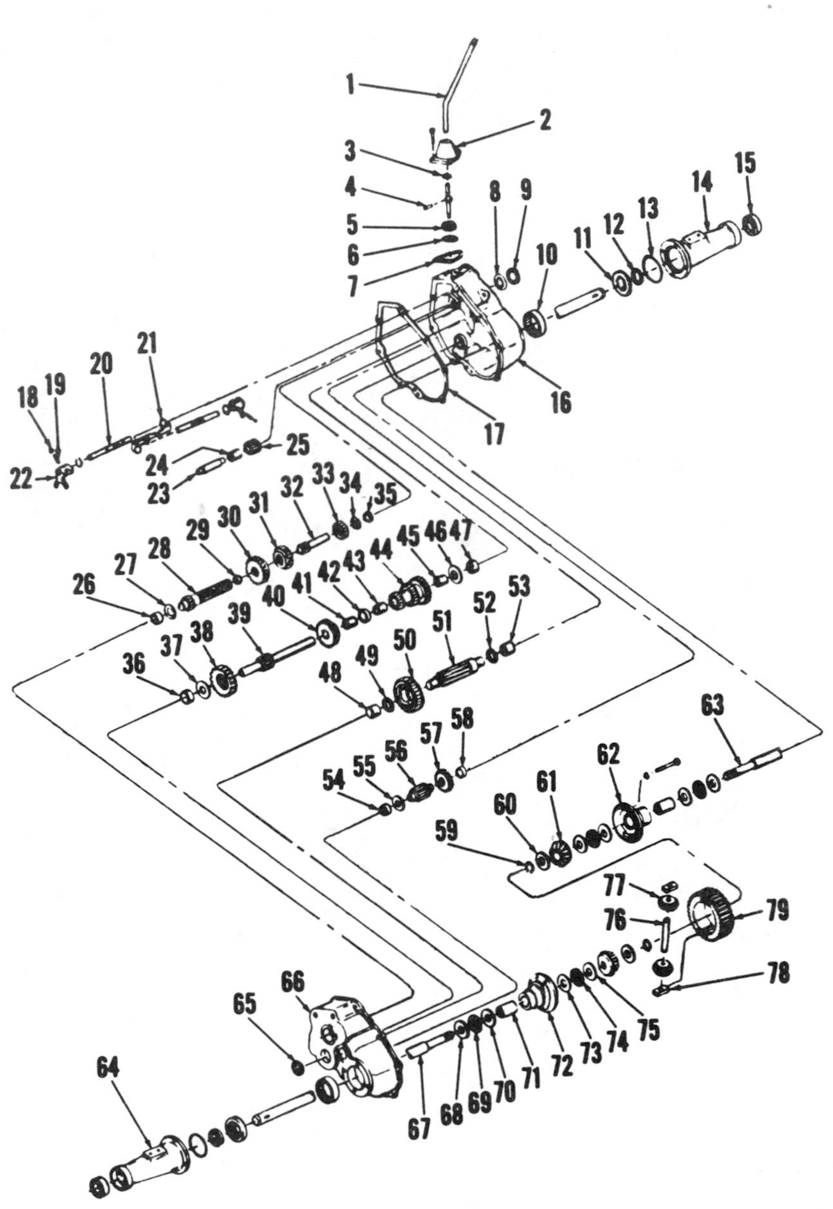

*Fig. PT81 – Exploded view of Peerless 2300 series transaxle.*

1. Shift lever
2. Shift lever housing
3. Seal ring
4. Roll pin
5. Retainer
6. Snap ring
7. Gasket
8. Ball bearing
9. Oil seal
10. Carrier bearing
11. Seal retainer
12. Oil seal
13. "O" ring
14. Axle housing
15. Axle outer bearing
16. Transaxle case
17. Gasket
18. Detent ball
19. Spring
20. Shifter rod
21. Shifter stop
22. Shifter fork
23. Reverse idler shaft
24. Spacer
25. Reverse idler gear
26. Needle bearing
27. Thrust washer
28. Shifter shaft
29. Needle bearing
30. Gear (1st, 2nd & reverse)
31. Gear (3rd & 4th)
32. Input shaft
33. Input gear
34. Thrust washer
35. Needle bearing
36. Needle bearing
37. Thrust washer
38. Idler gear
39. Brake & cluster shaft
40. 2-cluster gear
41. Bushing
42. Spacer
43. Bushing
44. 3-cluster gear
45. Bushing
46. Thrust washer
47. Needle bearing
48. Needle bearing
49. Thrust washer
50. Output gear
51. Output shaft
52. Thrust washer
53. Needle bearing
54. Needle bearing
55. Thrust washer
56. Low reduction shaft
57. Low reduction gear
58. Needle bearing
59. Snap ring
60. Thrust washer
61. Axle gear
62. Axle carriage (plain holes)
63. Axle shaft
64. Axle housing
65. Oil seal
66. Transaxle cover
67. Axle shaft
68. Thrust washer
69. Thrust bearing
70. Thrust washer
71. Bushing
72. Axle carriage (tapped holes)
73. Thrust washer
74. Thrust bearing
75. Thrust washer
76. Drive pin
77. Bevel pinion gear
78. Drive block
79. Ring gear



Illustrations courtesy Tecumseh Products Co.

0.290 inch (7.37 mm) below face of axle housing mounting surface. All other needle bearings are to be pressed in from inside of case and cover to a depth of 0.015-0.020 inch (0.381-0.508 mm) below thrust surfaces.

Renew all seals and gaskets and reassemble by reversing disassembly procedure. Install brake and cluster shaft (39) and idler gear (38) with beveled edge of gear teeth up away from cover. Install reverse idler shaft (23), spacer (24) and reverse idler gear (25) with rounded end of gear teeth facing spacer. Install input gear (33) and shaft (32) so chamfered side of input gear is facing case (16). Before installing shifter, fill transaxle housing through shifter opening with 4 pints (1.9 L) of SAE 90 EP gear lubricant. Tighten differential cap screws to 7 ft.-lbs. (9 N•m). Tighten case-to-cover and shift lever housing cap screws to 10 ft.-lbs. (14 N•m) and axle housing cap screws to 13 ft.-lbs. (14 N•m).

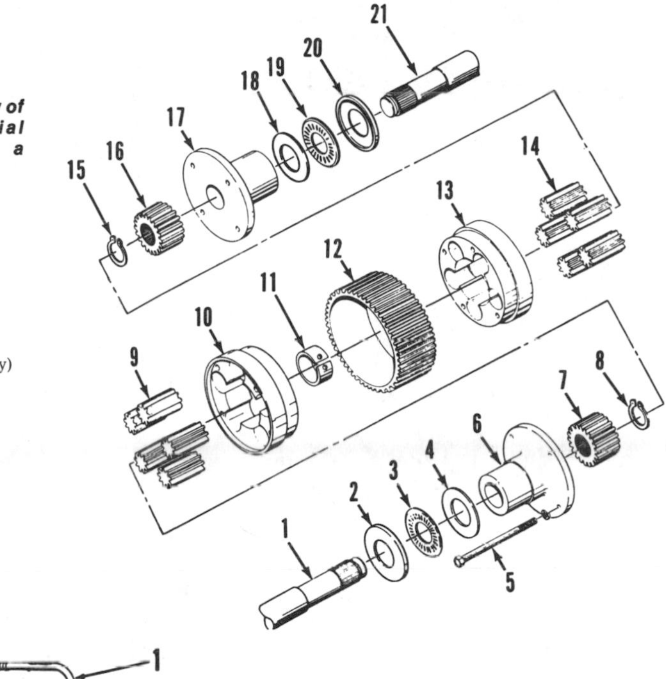


**Fig. PT82 — Exploded view of limited-slip differential assembly available as a transaxle option.**

1. Axle
2. Thrust washer
3. Thrust bearing
4. Thrust washer
5. Cap screw
6. Carrier
7. Side gear
8. Snap ring
9. Pinion gears
10. Body core
11. Spring (early models only)
12. Ring gear
13. Body core
14. Pinion gears
15. Snap ring
16. Side gear
17. Carrier
18. Thrust washer
19. Thrust bearing
20. Flanged thrust washer
21. Axle

# SIMPLICITY

## 2-Speed And 3-Speed

**OVERHAUL.** To overhaul transaxle, remove pins and slide off rear wheel and hub assemblies. Loosen set screws and slide brake drum off brake shaft (35 – Fig. S50). Drive alignment roll pins out of cover, remove cap screws from cover and pry cover off. Left axle shaft (38) will be removed with cover (10). Align spider gear teeth and withdraw right axle shaft (39). Lift out drive gear and differential assembly. Remove brake shaft (35), cluster gear (36) and low reduction gear and shaft. Remove nuts from shift rails (17 and 20) and reverse pinion shaft (23). Remove shift fork (21), shift rail (20), sliding gear (30) and pulley shaft (31). Shift fork (13), shift rail (17), reverse gear (24) and shaft (23) can now be removed. The balance of disassembly is evident after examination of unit.

When reassembling transaxle, tighten differential bolts to 20 ft.-lbs. (27 N•m) and nuts securing reverse shaft and shift rails to the case to 50 ft.-lbs. (68 N•m). Refill transmission with SAE 90 EP gear oil.

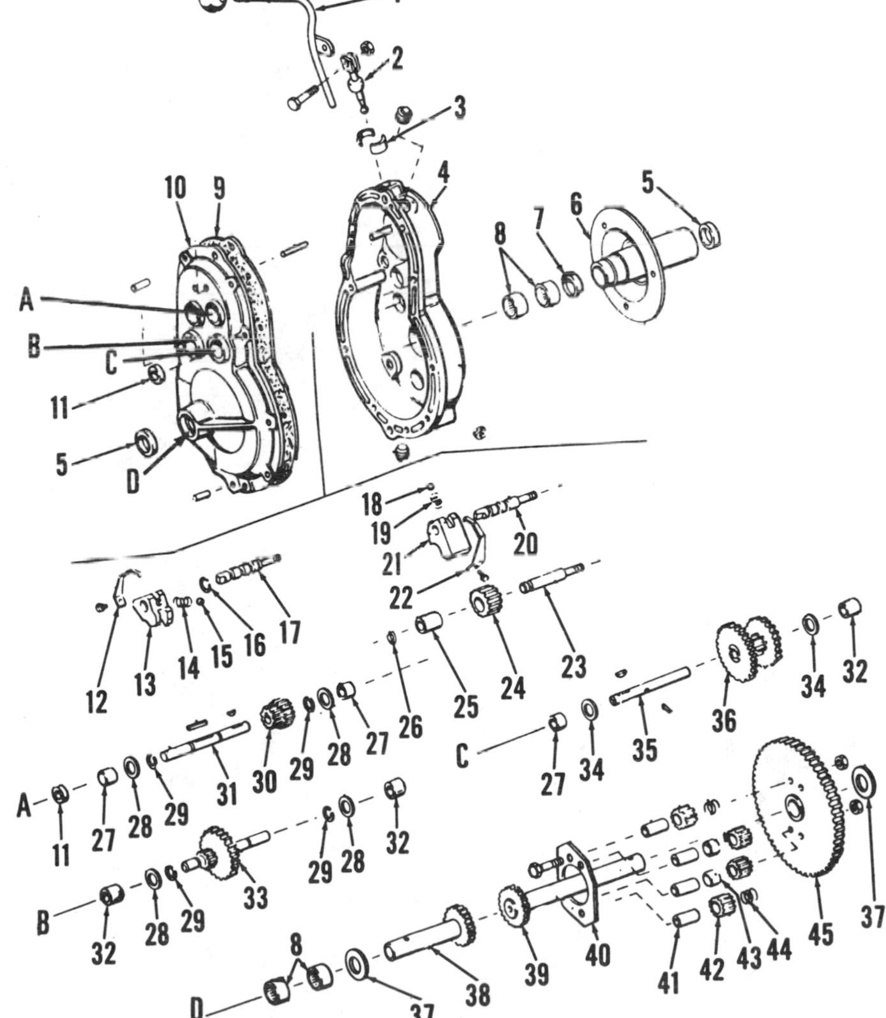


**Fig. S50 — Exploded view of Simplicity 3-speed transaxle. Gear and shaft assembly (33) is not used on 2-speed model.**

1. Shift lever assy.
2. Shift rod
3. Bushing
4. Gearcase
5. Seal
6. Axle housing
7. Seal
8. Roller bearings
9. Gasket
10. Gearcase cover
11. Seal
12. Spring
13. Shift fork
14. Shift lock spring
15. Shift lock ball
16. Retaining ring
17. Shift rail
18. Ball
19. Shift lock spring
20. Shift rail
21. Shift fork
22. Spring
23. Pinion shaft
24. Reverse pinion gear
25. Roller bearing
26. "O" ring
27. Roller bearing
28. Washer
29. Retaining ring
30. Hi & Lo gear pinion
31. Pto pulley shaft
32. Bearing
33. Gear & shaft assy.
34. Washer
35. Brake shaft
36. Cluster gear
37. Washer
38. Axle shaft
39. Axle shaft
40. Differential plate
41. Spindle
42. Differential pinion
43. Spacer
44. Spring
45. Drive gear assy.

# SPICER (Formerly Foote)

## Series 4000

The Spicer (Foote) Series 4000 transaxle may be equipped with two, three or six forward gears and one reverse gear.

**OVERHAUL.** Clean exterior of transaxle. Remove drive pulley from input shaft. Remove shoulder bolt (76—Fig. FT10) from brake assembly and remove brake jaw (72), brake pads (69), brake disc (68) and Woodruff key from intermediate shaft. Place shift lever in neutral, then unbolt and remove shift lever assembly. Remove the two set screws (3) from case, then turn transmission over and catch detent springs and balls (4).

With transmission upside down, remove case mounting screws and lift lower housing straight up to separate case halves. Lift drive shaft (53) with gears as an assembly from case. All parts on drive shaft are a slip fit.

**NOTE: It is recommended that all parts be kept in proper sequence when disassembling to aid reassembly. Correct placement of spacers and washers is critical.**

Lift intermediate shaft (36) with gears out of case. Remove "E" ring (23) from one end and slide parts off shaft, being careful to keep parts in order. Push axles (54 and 66) toward center of differential and lift the assembly from case. Disassemble each part from

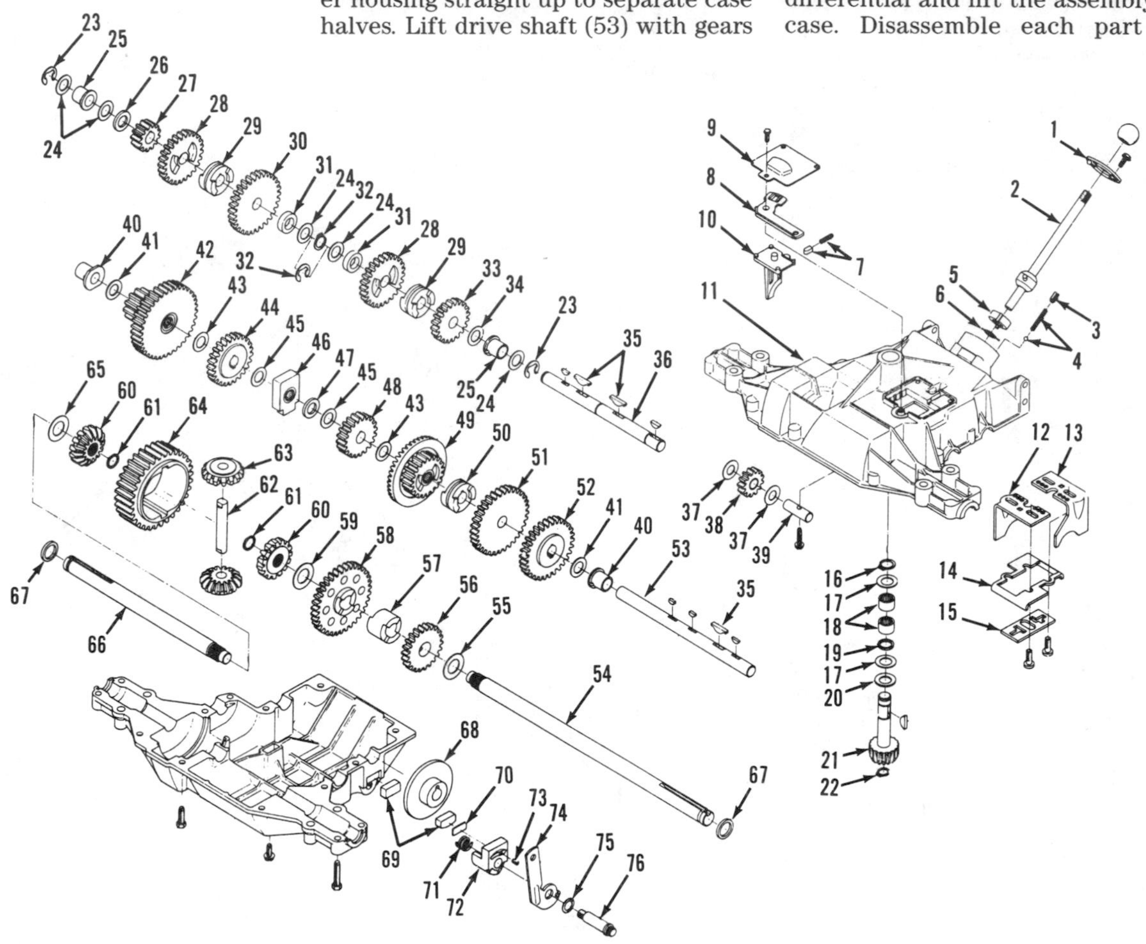

*Fig. FT10—Exploded view of Spicer (Foote) 4000 series transaxle. Size of washers is listed in parenthesis as their correct placement on shafts is critical. Shim washers are installed as required to adjust end play.*

1. Nylon cover
2. Shift lever
3. Set screw
4. Detent spring & ball
5. Nylon insert
6. Wave washer
7. Detent spring & pin
8. Hi-Lo shift lever
9. Cover
10. Hi-Lo shift fork
11. Upper housing
12. Shifter fork
13. Shifter fork
14. Support plate
15. Lock-out plate
16. Snap ring
17. Shim washer
18. Needle bearings
19. "O" ring
20. Washer (.040)
21. Input shaft & pinion gear
22. Snap ring
23. "E" ring
24. Shim washer
25. Flange bearing
26. Spacer (1.0x.630x.110)
27. Gear (13T)
28. Gear (25T)
29. Shift collar
30. Gear (30T)
31. Spacer (1.0x.630x.260)
32. Snap ring
33. Gear (20T)
34. Washer (.010)
35. Hi-pro key
36. Intermediate shaft
37. Washers (1.0x.505x.020)
38. Idler gear
39. Idler shaft
40. Flange bearing
41. Shim washer
42. Gear assy. (12T & 37T)
43. Washer (.045)
44. Gear (25T)
45. Washer (.025)
46. Shaft support
47. Spacer (1.0x.630x.110)
48. Gear (20T)
49. Bevel gear assy.
50. Shift collar
51. Gear (33T)
52. Gear (30T)
53. Drive shaft
54. Axle R.H.
55. Washer (1.25x.755x.031)
56. Gear (22T)
57. Gear lock
58. Gear (35T)
59. Washer (1.25x.755x.031)
60. Axle gear
61. Retaining ring
62. Cross shaft
63. Bevel gear
64. Differential gear
65. Shim washer
66. Axle L.H.
67. Felt seal
68. Brake disc
69. Brake pads
70. Back-up plate
71. Spring
72. Brake jaw
73. Set screw
74. Brake lever
75. Washer
76. Shoulder bolt



Illustration courtesy Spicer.

differential unit as necessary. Remove self-tapping screw from idler shaft (39) and remove shaft, gear (38) and thrust washers (37). Remove retaining ring (22) and press input shaft (21) out of housing. Press out needle bearings (18), being careful not to damage bore of housing. Remove shifter fork mounting screws and remove shifter forks (12 and 13), support plate (14) and lock-out plate (15). Unbolt and remove cover plate (9), Hi-Lo shift lever (8) and Hi-Lo shift fork (10).

Clean and inspect all parts and renew any showing excessive wear or damage.

To reassemble input shaft, press one needle bearing in from outside of housing until flush with outer surface of housing. Press the other needle bearing in from inside housing until bearing is recessed 0.093 inch (2.36 mm) below housing surface. Insert "O" ring (19) and original shim washers (17). Pack needle bearings with grease and install input shaft into housing from the inside. Install snap rings (16 and 22), then check shaft end play. Add or remove shim washers (17) as necessary to obtain recommended end play of 0.005-0.015 inch (0.13-0.38 mm).

Install Hi-Lo shifter mechanism and gear shift mechanism in case. Be sure that flared ends of fork support plate (14) face upward, and raised tab of shifter fork engages "T" slot of lock-out plate (15). Turn four shifter plate mounting screws clockwise as far as possible, then turn screws counterclockwise 1/4 turn to ensure free movement of shifter forks. There should be a maximum of 0.012 inch (0.3 mm) clearance between head of bolts and fork support plate. Install detent balls and springs (4) and tighten set screws (3) until heads are flush to 0.030 inch (0.76 mm) below top of case.

Install idler gear (38), thrust washers (37) and shaft (39). Tighten shaft retaining screw to 80-90 in.-lbs. (9.0-10.1 N·m). Assemble differential and axles and install in case.

Assemble gears (28, 30 and 33), shift collars (29), spacers and washers on intermediate shaft (36). Be sure that lug cavities in gears face the shift collars. Install intermediate shaft assembly in housing, making sure that legs of shift forks engage grooves of shift collars. Use a feeler gage to check end play of gears on intermediate shaft. End play should be 0.005-0.015 inch (0.13-0.38 mm) and is adjusted by changing thickness of shims (24).

Assemble components on drive shaft (53) in order shown in Fig. FT10. Note that gear (44) has two different width keyways; use the narrow keyway during this assembly. Hub side of gear (44) must face away from spur gear (42). Install shaft support (46) with stepped side facing hub side of gear (44). Be sure gears (49 and 51) are installed with lug cavities toward shift collar (50). Install gear (52) with large hub side facing outward. Install drive shaft assembly in housing, making sure that leg of Hi-Lo shift fork engages shift collar groove. Tabs on flange bearings must engage notches in housing, and shaft support (46) must be positioned upward. Use a feeler gage to measure gear end play on drive shaft. End play should be 0.005-0.015 inch (0.13-0.38 mm) and is adjusted by changing thickness of shims (41).

Pack housing with 30 ounces (887 mL) of Shell Darina "O" grease or equivalent. Tighten case mounting screws to 80-90 in.-lbs. (9.0-10.1 N·m). Tighten shaft support screw in center of case to 100-110 in.-lbs. (11.3-12.4 N·m).

# SPICER (Formerly Foote)

## Series 4360

**OVERHAUL.** Clean exterior of transaxle. Remove drive pulley and Woodruff key from input shaft. Remove cap screws from brake holder (64—Fig. SP20) and remove disc brake assembly. Place shift fork in neutral position. Remove the two set screws (2) from case, then turn transmission over and catch detent springs and balls (3).

With transmission upside down, remove case mounting screws and lift lower housing straight up to separate case halves. Lift intermediate shaft (21) with gears and drive shaft (43) with gears as an assembly from case. Remove chain (22) from sprockets. All parts on intermediate shaft and drive shaft are a slip fit.

**NOTE: It is recommended that all parts be kept in proper sequence when disassembling to aid reassembly.**

Lift out idler shaft (37) and gear (35) assembly. Push axles (53 and 59) toward center of differential and lift the assembly from case. Remove retaining ring (15) and press input shaft (13) out of housing. Press out needle bearings (10), being careful not to damage bore of housing.

Clean and inspect all parts and renew any showing excessive wear or damage.

To reassemble, reverse the disassembly procedure. Before installing input shaft assembly, pack needle bearings (10) with grease. Install input shaft using original shim washers (5 and 11), then check shaft end play. Add or remove shim washers (5 and 11) as necessary to obtain recommended shaft end play of 0.005-0.015 inch (0.13-0.38 mm) and bevel gear-to-pinion gear backlash of 0.005-0.015 inch (0.13-0.38 mm). Intermediate shaft and drive shaft end play should be 0-0.015 inch (0-0.38 mm). Adjust by changing thickness of shims (17 and 36).

Pack housing with 15 ounces (445 mL) of Shell Darina "O" grease or equivalent. Mate upper and lower case halves and tighten mounting bolts evenly to 80-90 in.-lbs. (9.0-10.1 N·m). Tighten brake holder mounting bolts to 200-250 in.-lbs. (22.6-28.2 N·m).

## Series 4450

**OVERHAUL.** To disassemble transaxle, remove mounting screws and separate the case halves. Lift drive shaft (35—Fig. SP25) and axles (19 and 26) with gears from case. All parts are a slip fit on shafts. Remove cap screw (49) retaining idler shaft (48) and remove shaft, gear (47) and thrust washers (46). Remove snap ring (10) and press input shaft (8) out of upper case.

Inspect all parts for wear or damage and renew as necessary. To reassemble, reverse the disassembly procedure. Before installing input shaft assembly, pack needle bearings (6) with grease. Install input shaft using original shim washers (5), then check shaft end play. Recommended end play is 0.005-0.015 inch (0.13-0.38 mm). End play is adjusted by changing thickness of shim washer (5). Recommended drive shaft end play is 0.005-0.015 inch (0.13-0.38 mm). Adjust by changing thickness of shims (28).

Pack housing with 14 ounces (414 mL) of Shell Darina "O" grease or equivalent. Join the housing halves and tighten mounting cap screws to 80-90 in.-lbs. (9.0-10.1 N·m).

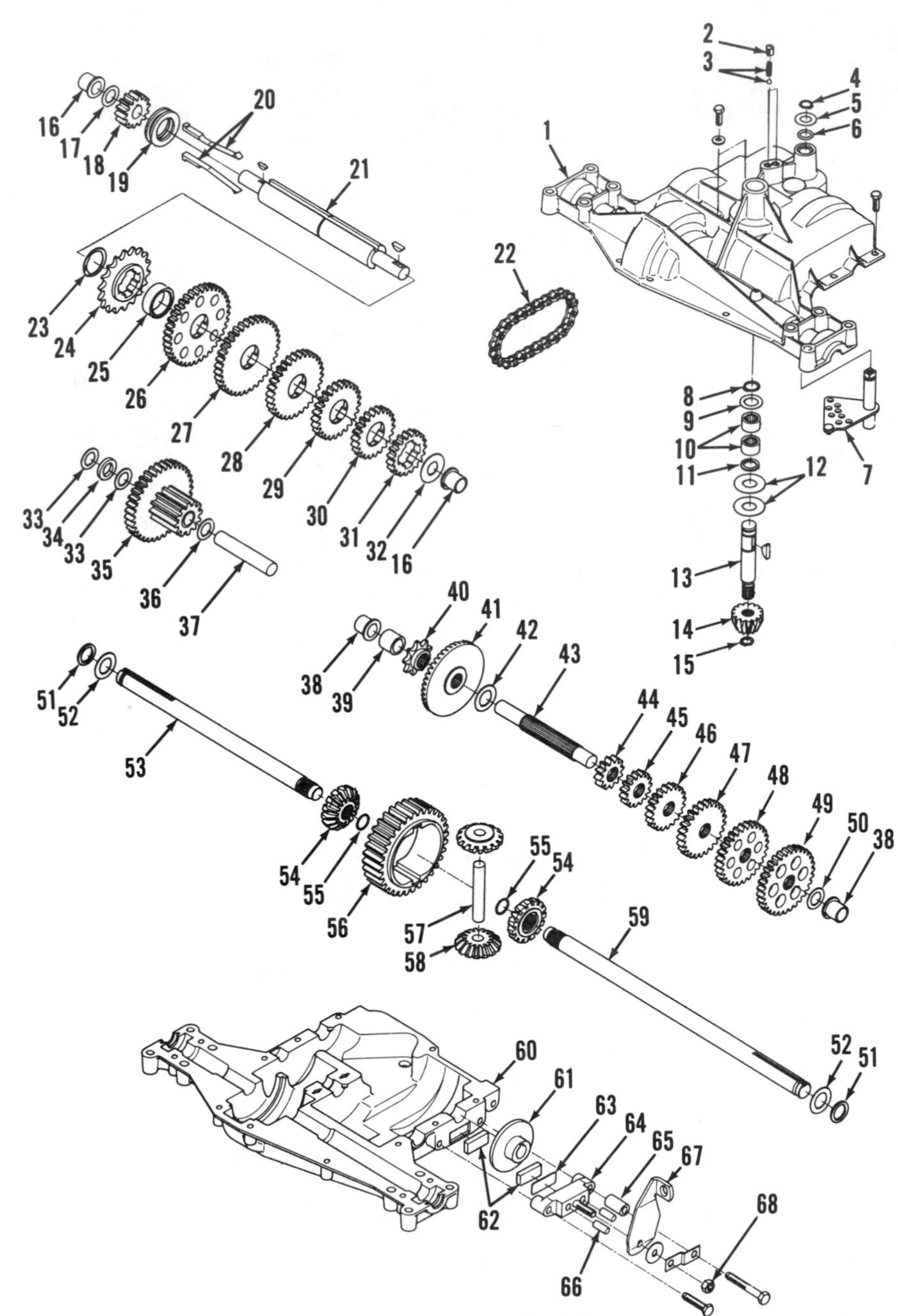

*Fig. SP20—Exploded view of Spicer Series 4360 transaxle. Unit shown has six forward speeds and one reverse speed.*

1. Upper housing
2. Set screw
3. Detent spring & ball
4. Snap ring
5. Shim washer
6. "O" ring
7. Shifter
8. Snap ring
9. Shim
10. Needle bearings
11. "O" ring
12. Washers
13. Input shaft
14. Bevel pinion
15. Snap ring
16. Flange bearing
17. Shim
18. Gear (14T)
19. Shift collar
20. Shift keys
21. Intermediate shaft
22. Chain
23. Snap ring
24. Sprocket
25. Spacer
26. Gear (37T)
27. Gear (35T)
28. Gear (30T)
29. Gear (25T)
30. Gear (22T)
31. Gear (19T)
32. Washer
33. Washers
34. Spacer
35. Gear assy.
36. Shim
37. Idler shaft
38. Flange bearing
39. Spacer
40. Sprocket
41. Bevel gear
42. Shim washer
43. Drive shaft
44. Gear (12T)
45. Gear (15T)
46. Gear (20T)
47. Gear (25T)
48. Gear (28T)
49. Gear (31T)
50. Washer
51. Felt seal
52. Shim washer
53. Axle L.H.
54. Axle gear
55. Retaining ring
56. Differential gear
57. Cross shaft
58. Differential pinion
59. Axle R.H.
60. Lower housing
61. Brake disc
62. Brake pads
63. Back-up plate
64. Brake holder
65. Spacer
66. Actuating pins
67. Actuating lever
68. Adjusting nut

Illustration courtesy Spicer.

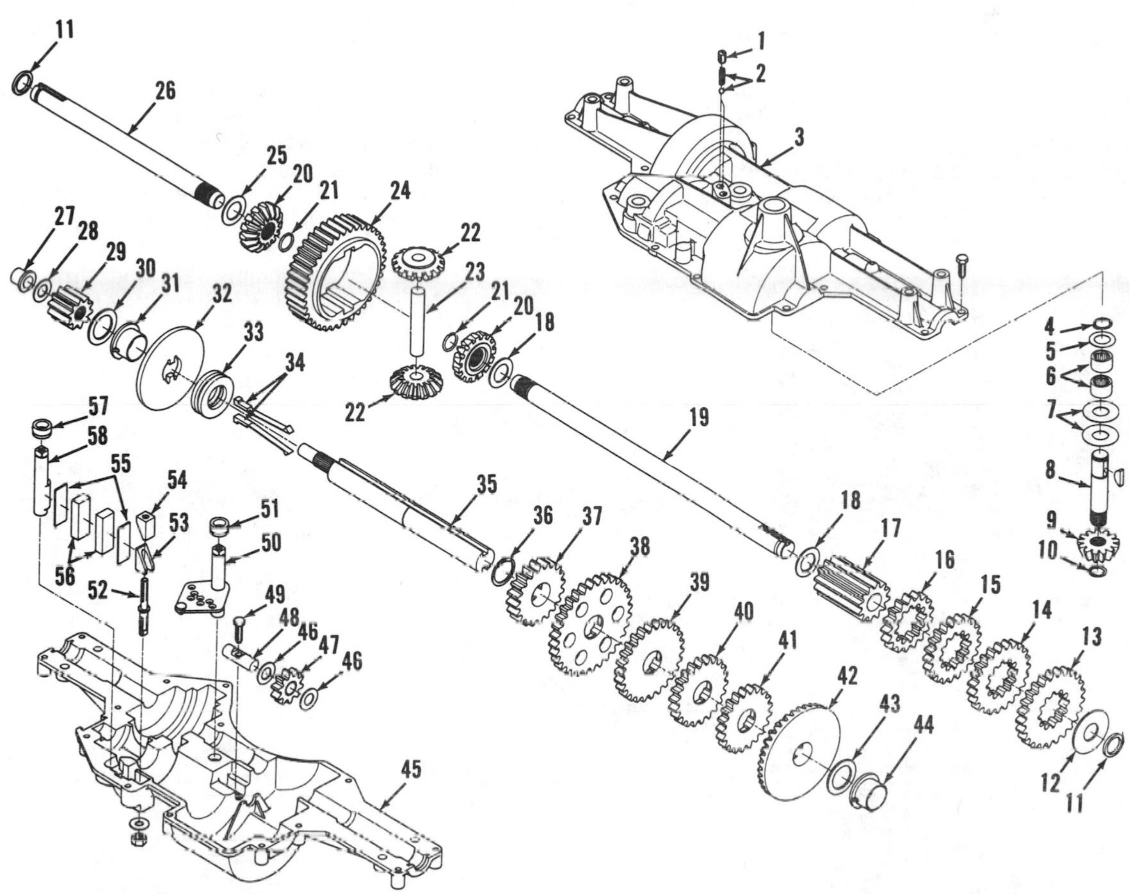


*Fig. SP25—Exploded view of Spicer Series 4450 transaxle. Unit shown has five forward speeds and one reverse speed.*

1. Set screw
2. Detent spring & ball
3. Upper housing
4. Snap ring
5. Shim
6. Needle bearings
7. Washers
8. Input shaft
9. Bevel pinion
10. Snap ring
11. Felt seal
12. Washer
13. Gear (25T)
14. Gear (23T)
15. Gear (21T)
16. Gear (17T)
17. Gear (12T)
18. Washer
19. Axle R.H.
20. Axle gear
21. Retaining ring
22. Differential pinions
23. Cross shaft
24. Differential gear
25. Shim washer
26. Axle L.H.
27. Flange bearing
28. Shim washer
29. Gear (10T)
30. Shim washer
31. Flange bearing
32. Brake disc
33. Shift collar
34. Shift keys
35. Drive shaft
36. Retaining ring
37. Gear (20T)
38. Gear (32T)
39. Gear (26)
40. Gear (22T)
41. Gear (21T)
42. Bevel gear
43. Washer
44. Flange bearing
45. Lower housing
46. Thrust washer
47. Idler gear
48. Idler shaft
49. Cap screw
50. Shifter
51. Seal
52. Brake adjustment stud
53. Adjustment cam
54. Brake cam
55. Spacers
56. Brake pads
57. Seal
58. Brake shaft

Illustration courtesy Spicer.

# WHEEL HORSE

## 4-Speed

**OVERHAUL.** To overhaul transaxle, first remove and thoroughly clean unit. Loosen retaining set screw and remove shift lever. Remove input pulley and brake assembly. Remove keys from input shaft and brake shaft. Remove wheel assemblies.

Position transaxle so bottom cover (72–Fig. WH125) is up and remove cover and gasket. Remove thrust bearing (36), washers (35 and 37) and pinion drive gear (34). Remove idler gear (54) with thrust washers (52 and 55). Withdraw reverse idler gear shaft (43) with gear (40). Place shift forks in neutral position as shown in Fig. WH126 and withdraw splined shaft (60–Fig. WH125) and gear (64). Remove first and reverse sliding gear (62) from shift fork. Remove and disassemble cluster gear assembly (45 through 51). Remove second and high speed sliding gear (61) from shift fork. To remove shift forks, remove plug (29) and carefully pull second and high speed shift fork and shaft (70) out of case. Be careful not to lose detent ball (26) which will be released when shift fork shaft is withdrawn. Remove shift ball assembly (26 through 28). Remove low and reverse shift fork and shaft (69). Stand transmission on end and tap on end of input shaft (58) and remove shaft. Unscrew end cap (17) retaining cap screws and remove end cap with pinion gear shaft (33). Reposition transaxle case with bottom down. Remove left axle assembly from case and disassemble if necessary. Remove differential assembly (23) and thrust bearing (22) and washers (21) from case. Remove

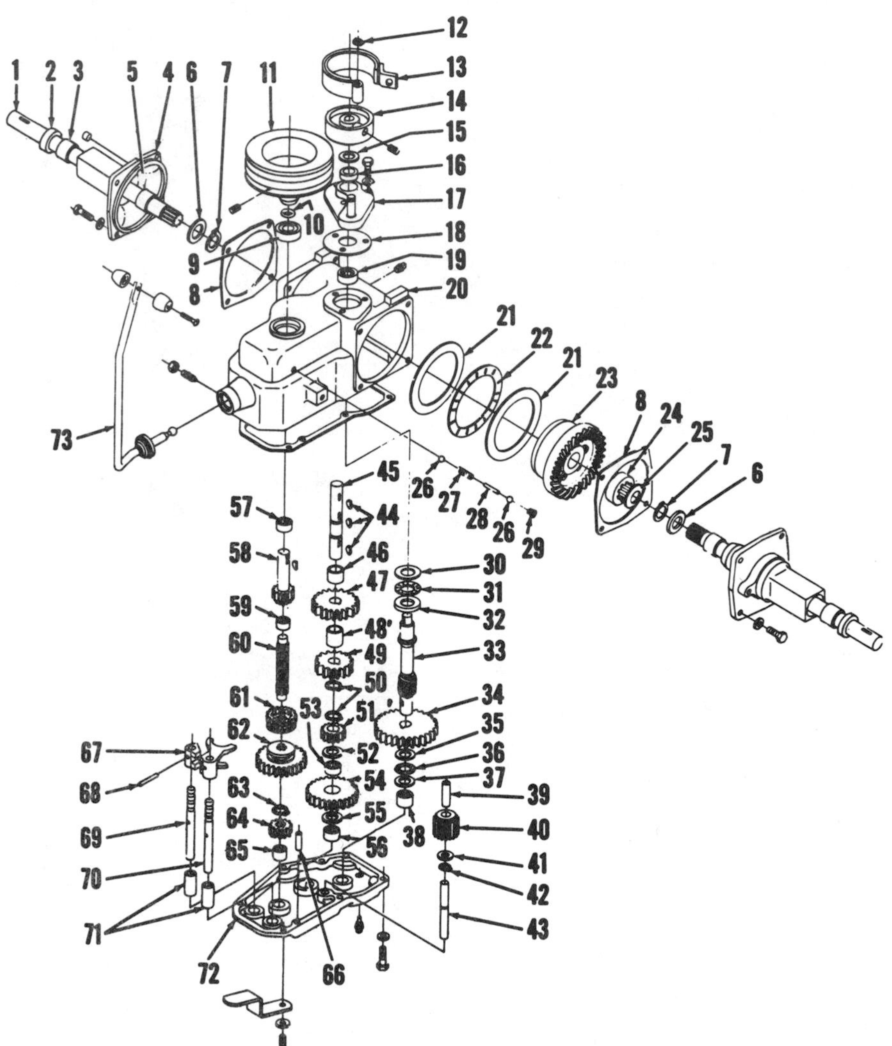

Fig. WH125—Exploded view of Wheel Horse 4-speed transaxle.

1. Axle shaft
2. Oil seal
3. Bearing
4. Axle housing
5. Bearing
6. Thrust washer
7. Snap ring
8. Gasket
9. Bearing
10. "O" ring
11. Input pulley
12. Snap ring
13. Brake band
14. Brake drum
15. Thrust washer
16. Oil seal
17. End cap
18. Gasket
19. Bearing
20. Case
21. Thrust washer
22. Thrust bearing
23. Differential assy.
24. Axle bearing
25. Spring washer
26. Ball
27. Spring
28. Shift stop pin
29. Plug
30. Thrust washer
31. Thrust bearing
32. Thrust washer
33. Pinion shaft
34. Drive gear
35. Thrust washer
36. Thrust bearing
37. Thrust washer
38. Bearing
39. Bushing
40. Reverse idler gear
41. Washer
42. Snap ring
43. Shaft
44. Key
45. Cluster gear shaft
46. Bearing
47. Gear
48. Spacer
49. Second speed gear
50. Snap ring
51. First speed gear
52. Thrust washer
53. Bearing
54. Idler gear
55. Thrust washer
56. Bearing
57. Bearing
58. Input shaft & gear
59. Bearing
60. Splined shaft
61. Sliding gear (2nd & 3rd)
62. Sliding gear (1st & reverse)
63. Snap ring
64. Gear
65. Bearing
66. Dowel pin
67. Shift forks
68. Pin
69. Shift shaft (1st & reverse)
70. Shift shaft (2nd & third)
71. Bushing
72. Cover
73. Shift lever/seal boot

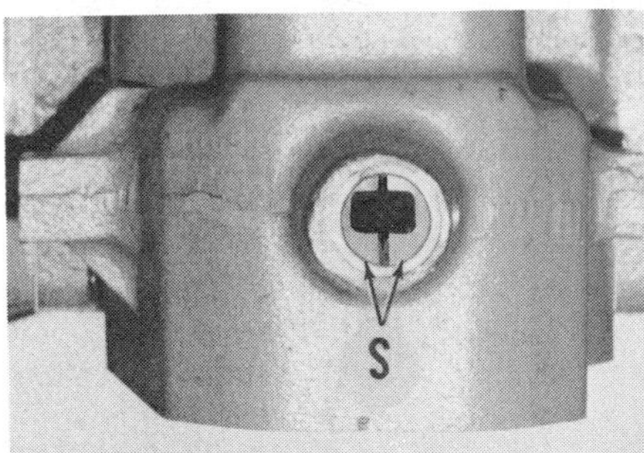



Fig. WH126—Align shift fork notches (S) as shown to set transmission gears in neutral.

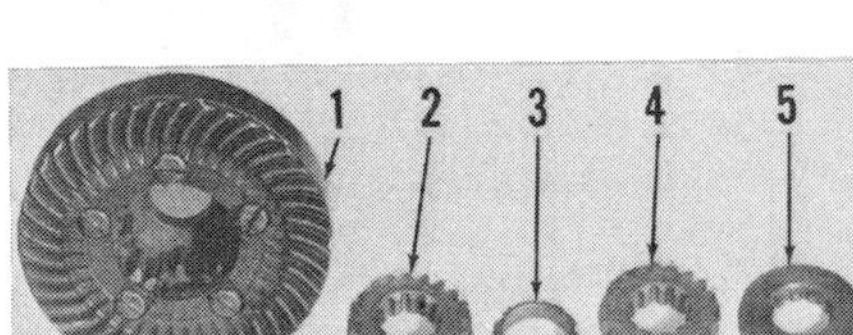



Fig. WH127—View of differential assembly (23–Fig. WH125). Unit (1) must be renewed as an assembly.

1. Differential unit
2. Axle gear (R.H.)
3. Spacer
4. Axle gear (L.H.)
5. Thrust washer

Fig. WH128—Oil slots in end cap (17–Fig. WH125) must align as shown with relief (R) in case.

right axle assembly and disassemble if necessary.

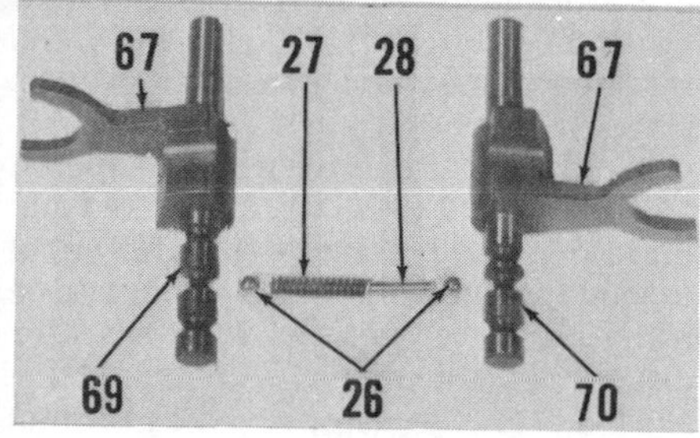


**Fig. WH129—Note difference in detents of shift shaft for first and reverse (69) from those of second and third shift shaft (70). Do not interchange. Identify parts by reference to Fig. WH125.**

Inspect all components for damage or excessive wear. Axle gears and differential assembly shown in Fig. WH127 are available only as a unit assembly. To reassemble transaxle, reverse disassembly procedure and observe the following points: Install right axle assembly so breather plug is towards top of transaxle. Sharp edge of snap rings (7–Fig. WH125) should be towards axle splines. Splines of left axle thrust washer (5–Fig. WH127) must be adjacent to differential axle gear (4). Concave surface of washer (25–Fig. WH125) must be next to axle bearing (24). Note position of thin washer (30) and thick washer (32). When installing end cap (17) and pinion gear shaft assembly in transaxle case, oil slot in end cap must align with relief in case (Fig. WH128). Identify shift forks as shown in Fig. WH129. Do not interchange shift shafts as detents will be incorrectly positioned.

**Fig. WH130—Install reverse idler gear on shaft so gear hub (H) is opposite washer (W) and snap ring (S).**

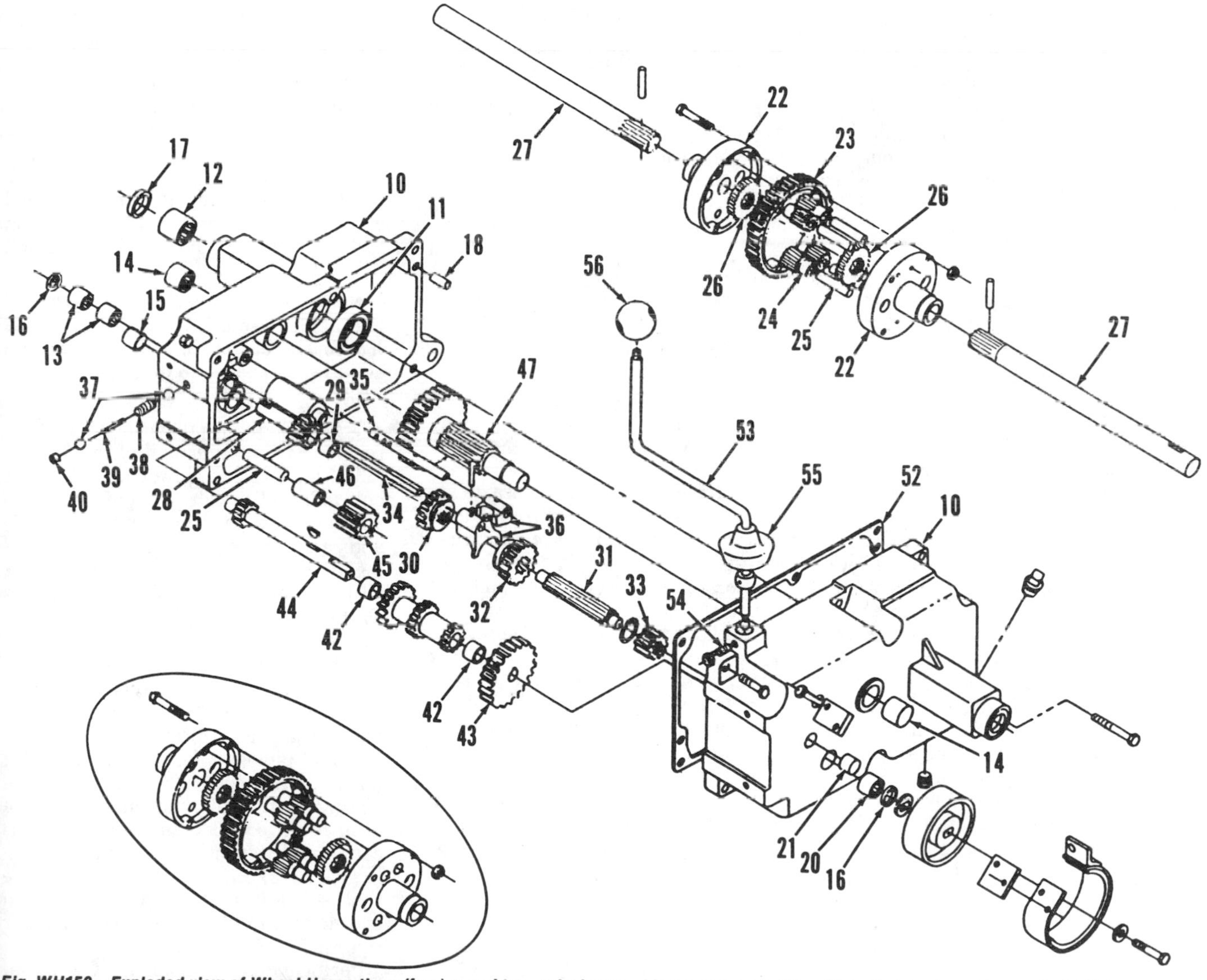

**Fig. WH150—Exploded view of Wheel Horse three (four) speed transmission used in current production. Note that design of input shaft (28) is modified from earlier models. Brake drum, formerly mounted on output shaft (47), is now fitted to cluster gear shaft (44) as shown. Differential pinions are now integral with pinion shafts as shown in inset view. Also see Fig. WH151.**

10. Case half
11. Ball bearing
12. Needle bearing
13. Needle bearing
14. Needle bearing
15. Needle bearing
16. Oil seal
17. Oil seal
18. Dowel pin
20. Needle bearing
21. Needle bearing
22. Differential case
23. Bull gear
24. Pinion gear
25. Pinion shaft
26. Axle gear
27. Axle shaft
28. Input gear/shaft
29. Needle bearing
30. Second high gear
31. Spline shaft
32. Low reverse gear
33. Pinion
34. Shift rail
35. Shift rail
36. Shift fork
37. Shift stop ball
38. Stop spring
39. Pin
40. Plug
41. Cluster gear
42. Bronze bushing
43. Reduction gear
44. Brake/cluster shaft
45. Reverse idler
46. Bronze bushing
47. Drive gear set
52. Gasket
53. Shift lever
54. Set screw
55. Boot
56. Knob

To install shift mechanism, install low and reverse shift shaft (69–Fig. WH125) with shift fork in case. Install shift balls, spring and pin in passage of case and hold in position with a punch. Move shift shaft up or down until shift ball moves into detent on shift shaft. Carefully install second and high shift shaft into case while removing punch. Allow shift shaft to move down only until first detent is engaged by ball. This is second gear position and second and high sliding gear can now be installed. Grooves of sliding gears will be next to each other if gears are properly installed.

Snap rings (63) should be installed on splined shaft so sharp edge of snap ring is nearest short end of shaft. Hub end of reverse idler gear (40) must be opposite washer (41) as shown in Fig. WH130. Position shift forks in neutral position as shown in Fig. WH126 before installing transaxle cover and shift lever. To install shift lever, tighten retaining set screw until snug, then back out set screw 1/8 turn and tighten locknut. After assembly is completed, fill transaxle to level of fill plug with SAE 90 EP gear oil.

## Three (Four) Speed

To overhaul transaxle, first remove and thoroughly clean unit.

**OVERHAUL.** To disassemble transaxle, drain lubricant and remove wheel and hub assemblies. Set transaxle up in a vise or holding fixture so right hand axle shaft points downward. Back out set screw (54–Fig. WH150) and lift out shift lever assembly (53). Remove lockbolt from extension of brake/cluster shaft (44) and pull brake drum from shaft. On older production models, brake drum was mounted on shaft (47) and retained on shaft end by a snap ring. At this point, transmission case half (10) can be unbolted and lifted off. Be sure axle shafts are cleaned and burrs are removed, especially near keyways. Now lift out differential assembly with axles for later attention. Pull out spline shaft (31) from hubs of sliding gears (30 and 32) and remove sliding gears and reverse idler gear (45). Cluster gear shaft (44) with cluster and reduction gear (43) can now be lifted out. Output drive gear set (47) is next in order for removal. Front shift fork and rail (34) should now be removed, taking care shift stop balls (37) are not dropped and lost when released from detents in shift rail during removal. Cover opening in case with free hand and watch for spring (38) and pin (39) as well. Remove second and high gear fork and rail (35) next. Remove input pulley from shaft end and lift out input/shaft (28).

Disassembly of differential unit requires through-bolts be removed so differential case halves (22) can be separated from bull gear (23) giving access to pinions (24). In later production, pinions and pinion shafts are integral as shown in inset. Finish disassembly by driving out roll pins and removing axle gears (26) from splined ends of axle shafts (27).

All parts should be thoroughly cleaned and inspected. Renew any parts which are severely worn or damaged beyond service limits. Pay particular attention to condition of needle bearings fitted into bosses in case halves. Upon completion, reassemble transaxle by reversing disassembly sequence. Refill unit with approximately 4 pints (1.9 L) of SAE 140 gear oil meeting GL-5 specifications.

## Six (Eight) Speed

**OVERHAUL.** After transaxle and axle assembly is removed from tractor, drain lubricant and remove rear wheels and hub assemblies. Thoroughly clean exterior of unit. For easier and more convenient disassembly, set transaxle up in a holding jig or large shop vise so right hand axle is pointed down. Back out set screw (80–WH152) so gear shift lever (79) can be removed. Remove anchor bolts (66) if removal of brake band (65) is desired, then remove lockbolt (63) at outer end of cluster/brake shaft (55) so brake drum can be pulled. Watch for special double "D" washer (61). Be sure exposed ends of axles are clean and burrs are removed, especially near edges of keyways.

Older models of this transaxle have brake drums fitted on shaft end of gear drive set (60) over a Woodruff key and retained at outer shaft end by a snap ring.

Interior of transaxle will be exposed when left-hand case half is unbolted and lifted off over left axle. Differential assembly and both axles can now be lifted out to set aside for later disassembly or repair. Pull out spline shaft (33) and then low-reverse gear (45) and second-high gear (44). Lift out cluster/brake shaft (55) with cluster gear (52) and reduction gear (54). For an easy grip on shaft (55), insert bolt (63) by a few threads to serve as a handle. Now, remove reverse idler gear (57) and idler shaft (59). First and reverse gear shift rail (46) and its shift fork should be removed using caution so stop balls (39) are not dropped and lost when out of engagement with shift rail detents. Balls, as well as spring (40) and guide pin (50) may be caught by holding free hand over case opening. Remove second and third gear (rear) shift rail (47) and fork. Remove output gear drive set (60).

**NOTE: When servicing transaxles of late model tractors, refer to Fig. WH153 for design change in output gear and shaft which applies to these models.**

Transaxle input pulley should next be removed from outer end of input shaft (29–Fig. WH152). Now, back out detent bolt (42) and withdraw input shaft (29) which carries input gear and spline (31) and range sliding gear (34). When moving these gears, watch for stop spring (40) and detent ball (39) when range shifter fork (38) is dislodged. Remove range cluster gear (35) and its shaft.

Disassemble limited slip differential assembly by unbolting through-bolts (23) so end caps (14 and 15) can be separated from ring gear (16). Next, remove differential pinions (18), cylindrical spring (22) and drive bodies (20) from each side of ring gear. After snap rings (28) have been removed, axle shafts (26 and 27) can be pulled from internal splines of axle gears (17) and out of end caps. Note that some models are furnished with spur gear differential as shown in upper right inset of Fig. WH152.

Perform detailed clean-up of all disassembled parts and carefully inspect each for damage or undue wear. Renew individual parts as needed and reassemble transaxle by reversal of disassembly procedure. Refill unit to check plug (70) opening with approximately 4 pints (1.9 L) of SAE 140 gear oil of specification GL-5.

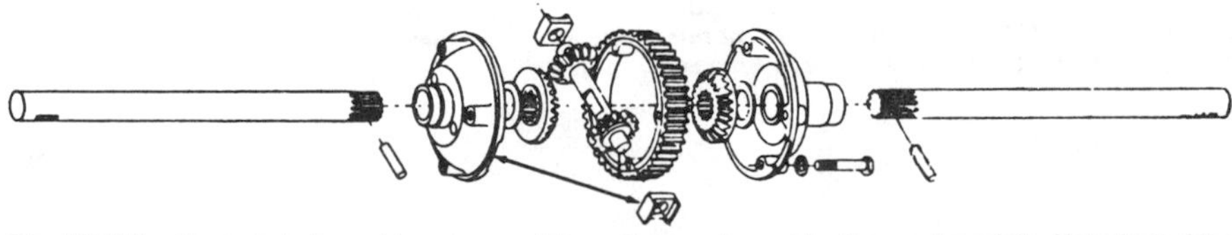

*Fig. WH151 – Exploded view of bevel gear differential used on older 3-speed models. Note how drive blocks fit recesses in differential case halves.*

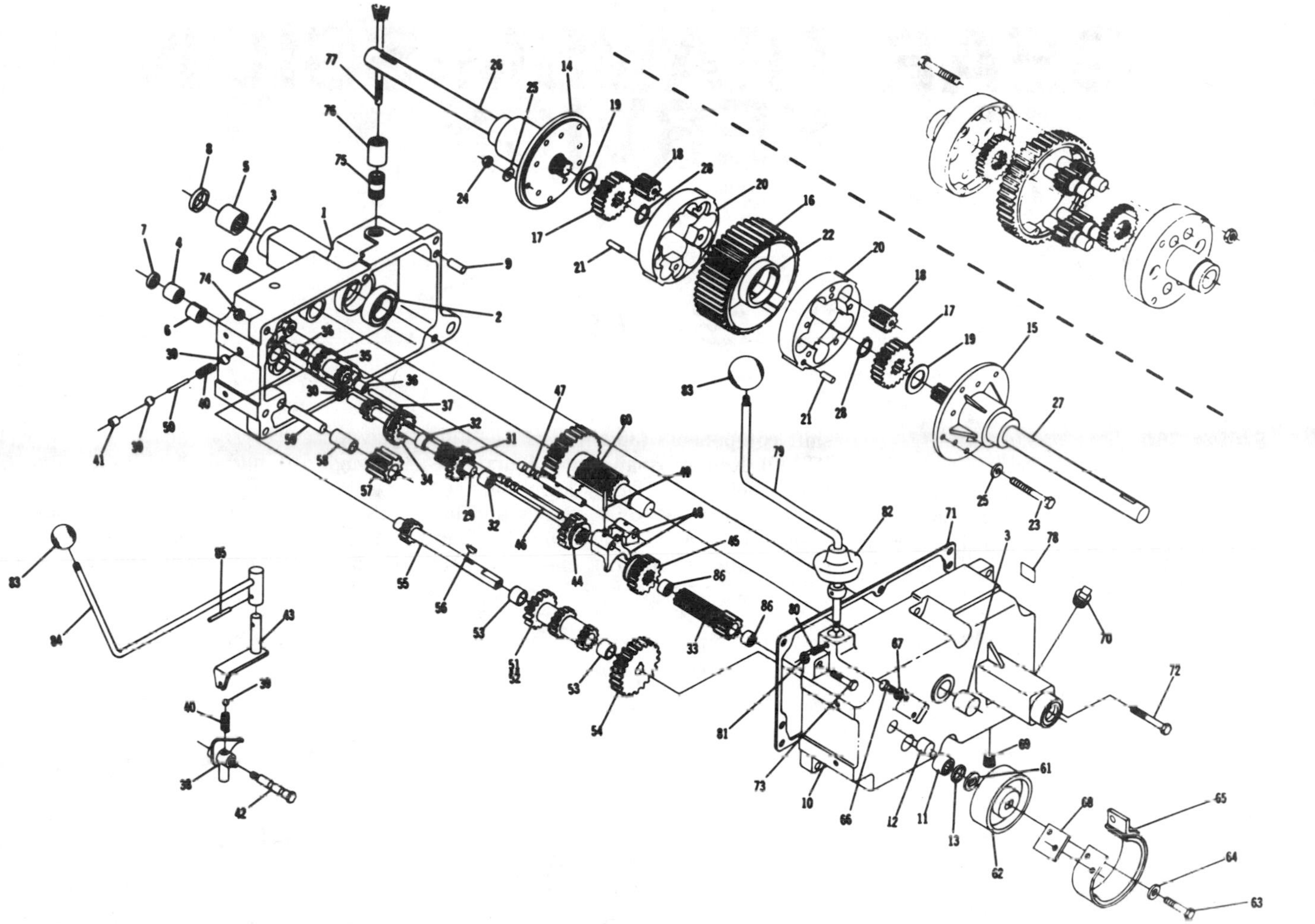

*Fig. WH152—Exploded view of Wheel Horse six (eight) speed transaxle used in current production tractors. See Fig. WH153 for recent change in drive gear (60). Differential spur gear pinion set shown in upper right inset is used on late models while limited slip design shown is used on some earlier models. Brake drum was mounted on shaft (60) in earlier models.*

1. Case (R.H.)
2. Ball bearing
3. Needle bearing
4. Needle bearing
5. Needle bearing
6. Needle bearing
7. Oil seal
8. Oil seal
9. Dowel pin
10. Case (L.H.)
11. Needle bearing
12. Needle bearing
13. Brake shaft seal
14. End cap (R.H.)
15. End cap (L.H.)
16. Ring gear
17. Axle gear
18. Pinion gear
19. Thrust washer
20. Differential body
21. Roll pin
22. Cylindrical spring
23. Through-bolt
24. Self-locking nut
25. Washer
26. Axle (R.H.)
27. Axle (L.H.)
28. Snap ring
29. Input shaft
30. Thrust washer
31. Input gear/spline
32. Needle bearing
33. Input pinion/spline
34. Sliding gear
35. Reduction gear
36. Needle bearing
37. Reduction gear shaft
38. Shift fork
39. Stop ball
40. Stop spring
41. Plug
42. Detent bolt
43. Shift lever
44. Second high gear
45. Low reverse gear
46. Shift rail
47. Shift rail
48. Shift fork
49. Roll pin
50. Shift stop pin
51. Gear/bearing assy.
52. Cluster gear
53. Bronze bearing
54. Reduction gear
55. Cluster/brake shaft
56. Woodruff key
57. Reverse idler
58. Bronze bushing
59. Idler shaft
60. Drive gear set
61. Double "D" washer
62. Brake drum
63. Lockbolt
64. Washer (special)
65. Brake band
66. Anchor bolt
67. Lockwasher
68. Stop plate
69. Drain plug
70. Check plug
71. Case gasket
72. Assembly bolt
73. Assembly bolt
74. Locking nut
75. Nipple 1/2 inch pipe
76. Coupling
77. Dipstick
78. Decal
79. Gear selector
80. Set screw
81. Locknut
82. Boot
83. Knob
84. Range selector
85. Roll pin
86. Bronze bushings

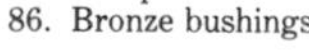

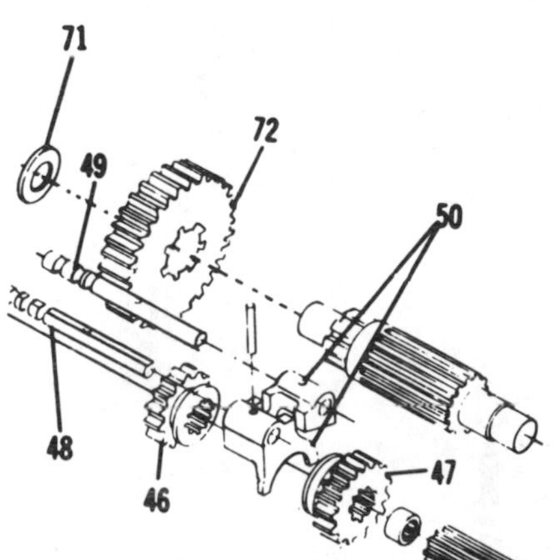


*Fig. WH153—Supplemental view showing change made in drive gear (60—Fig. WH152) on late model transaxles. Note that gear (72) is separated from splined shaft.*

46. Second high gear
47. Low reverse gear
48. Front shift rail
49. Rear shift rail
50. Shift forks
71. Thrust washer
72. Gear (44T)

# GEAR TRANSMISSION SERVICE

## PEERLESS

### Series 350

**OVERHAUL.** To overhaul transmission, first clean exterior of transmission. Shift transmission into neutral, unscrew shift lever housing screws and remove shift components (36 through 41–Fig. PT100). Remove snap ring (44) and output sprocket (43). Drive dowel pins out of case, unscrew cover screws and lift cover (45) from case (29). Lift out reverse idler shaft (12), idler gear (13) and spacer (14). Lift shifter assembly (1 through 10) and shaft (42) out of case. Remove output shaft (16) and attached gears (32, 17 and 18) and thrust washers (19 and 31). Remove bevel gear (27) from case. Remove snap ring (22), pinion

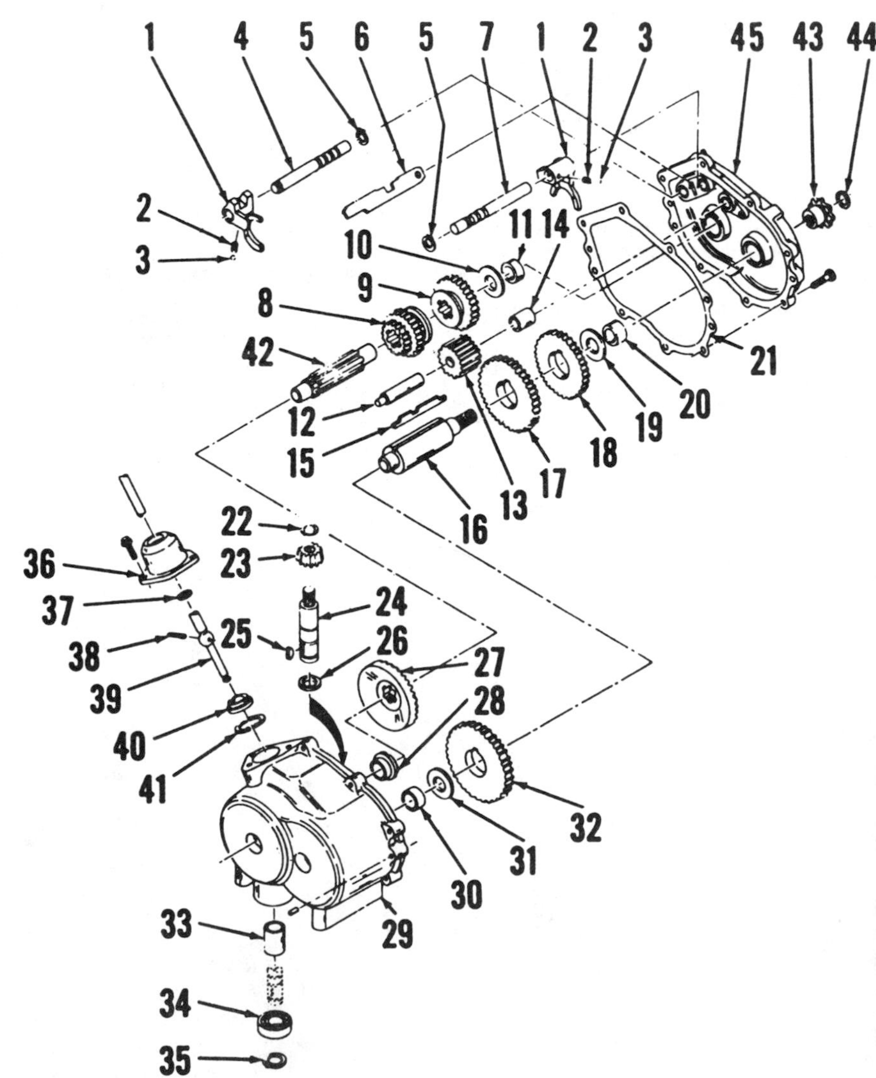


*Fig. PT100—Exploded view of Peerless Series 350 gear transmission.*

1. Shifter fork
2. Spring
3. Ball
4. Shifter rod
5. Snap ring
6. Shifter stop
7. Shifter rod
8. First & second gear
9. Third & reverse gear
10. Washer
11. Bushing
12. Reverse idler shaft
13. Reverse idler gear
14. Spacer
15. Key
16. Output shaft
17. Medium idler gear
18. Small idler gear
19. Washer
20. Bushing
21. Gasket
22. Snap ring
23. Pinion gear
24. Input shaft
25. Key
26. Thrust bearing
27. Bevel gear
28. Bushing
29. Case
30. Bushing
31. Washer
32. Large idler gear
33. Bushing
34. Bearing
35. Snap ring
36. Shift housing
37. Quad ring
38. Pin
39. Shift lever
40. Shift lever keeper
41. Snap ring
42. Shaft
43. Sprocket
44. Snap ring
45. Cover



Illustrations courtesy Tecumseh Products Co.

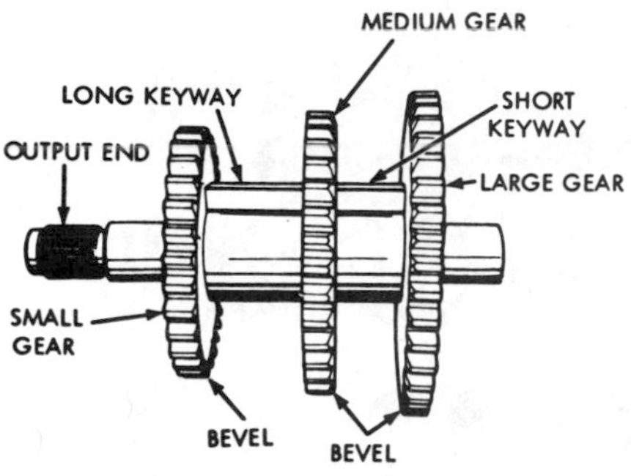


***Fig. PT101 – When assembling transmission, be sure idler gears are installed on shaft as shown above.***

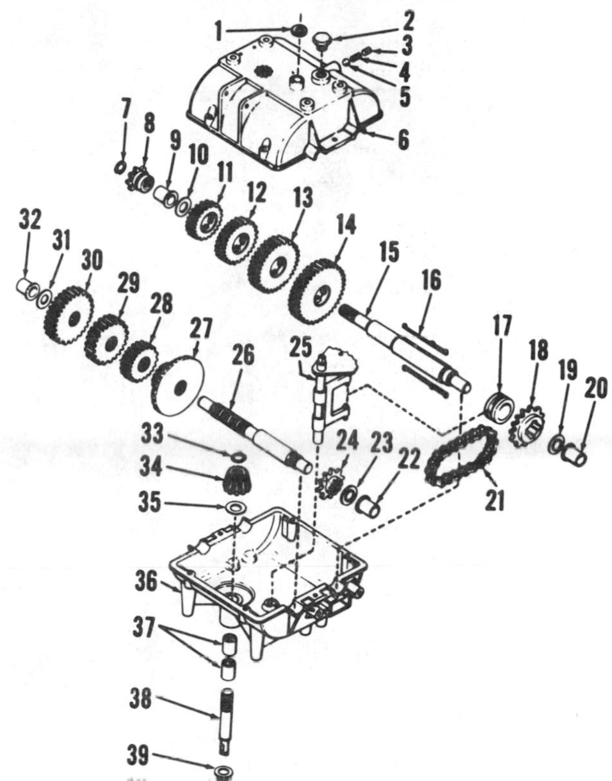

***Fig. PT105—Exploded view of Peerless Series 500 and Series 700 4-speed gear transmission.***

1. Washer
2. Plug
3. Set screw
4. Detent spring
5. Detent ball
6. Transmission cover
7. Snap ring
8. Output sprocket
9. Flange bushing
10. Thrust washer
11. Fourth speed gear
12. Third speed gear
13. Second speed gear
14. First speed gear
15. Output shaft
16. Shifter keys
17. Shift collar
18. Reverse sprocket
19. Thrust washer
20. Flange bushing
21. Reverse chain
22. Flange bushing
23. Thrust washer
24. Reverse drive sprocket
25. Shift rod & fork assy.
26. Countershaft
27. Bevel & first drive gear
28. Second drive gear
29. Third drive gear
30. Fourth drive gear
31. Thrust washer
32. Flange bushing
33. Snap ring
34. Bevel pinion
35. Thrust washer
36. Transmission case
37. Needle bearings
38. Input shaft
39. Thrust washer
40. Snap ring

gear (23) and pull input shaft (24) out bottom of case. Remove snap ring (35) and bearing (34) from shaft. Bushing (33) may now be removed from case.

Inspect components for excessive wear or damage. To reassemble, reverse disassembly procedure. Install gears (32, 17 and 18) on output shaft as shown in Fig. PT101. Note that bevel on small and middle sized gears face toward case, while bevel of large gear faces towards cover. Install reverse idler gear (13–Fig. PT100) so bevel of gear faces towards case. Pack housing with 12 ounces (355 mL) of EP lithium base grease. Tighen case-to-cover cap screws to 90-110 in.-lbs. (10-12 N·m). Do not force cover to close on case. If cover will not fit correctly, use needlenose pliers to reposition shifter components.

### Series 500 and Series 700

**OVERHAUL.** Clean outside of removed transmission, place shift lever in neutral position, then unbolt and remove shift lever assembly. Refer to Fig. PT105 and remove set screw (3), detent spring (4) and detent ball (5). Remove six cap screws and lift off cover (6). Remove shift rod and fork assembly (25). Lift output shaft and countershaft as an assembly from case (36) and place assembly on a bench. Remove flange bushings and thrust washers from ends of both shafts. Note collar side of reverse sprockets (18 and 24), then remove sprockets with chain (21) from shafts. Note position of bevel gear and spur gears (27 through 30) and remove gears from countershaft (26). Remove gears (11 through 14) from output shaft (15), then slide shift collar (17) and shifter keys (16) from shaft. Remove snap ring (33), bevel pinion (34) and thrust washer (35) and withdraw input shaft (38) with snap ring (40) and thrust washer (39). Needle bearings (37) can now be pressed out of case if necessary.

Clean and inspect all parts and renew any showing excessive wear or other damage. Input shaft needle bearings (37) should be installed flush to 0.005 inch (0.127 mm) below case inner and outer thrust surfaces at bearing bore. Using Fig. PT105 as a guide, reassemble transmission by reversing disassembly procedure. Make certain drive lug side of gears (11 through 14) are facing away from shift collar. Fill transmission case with 12 ounces (355 mL) of EP lithium base grease. Tighten cover-to-case cap screws to 90-100 in.-lbs. (10-11 N·m). Install detent ball (5), spring (4) and set screw (3). Tighten set screw two full turns below flush.

# SIMPLICITY

### 3-Speed And 4-Speed With Shuttle Drive

The gear transmission used on tractors equipped with forward-reverse shuttle drive, is equipped with four forward gears. Reverse gear is not required in this transmission since reverse drive, in any gear, is provided by forward-reverse shuttle drive unit. Transmission used on other models has three forward gears and one reverse. The differential is located at right rear wheel hub on all models.

**OVERHAUL.** To disassemble transmission, first drain gear oil from unit, then remove brake drum. remove cap screws from transmission cover and drive locating dowel pins into transmission case holes. Using a screwdriver, pry cover loose and remove from case. Remove gear (41–Fig. S51), then withdraw axle tube and output gear assembly (65 through 71). Remove second intermediate shaft and gears (44 through 51) and third intermediate shaft and gears (54 through 59). Place shift fork (6) in neutral position and pull shift fork (6A) out of case until input shaft (23) and sliding gears (24 and 75–Fig.

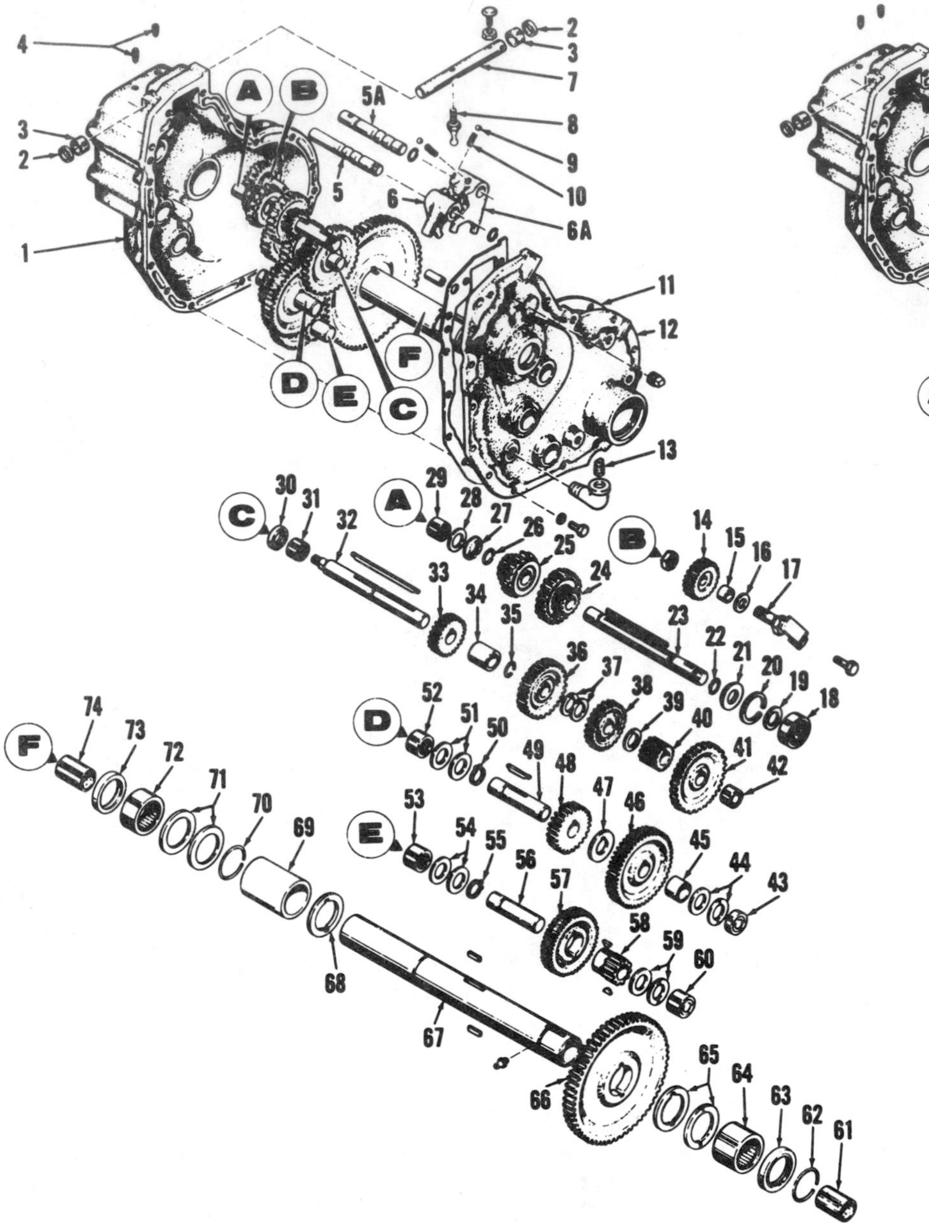

***Fig. S51—Exploded view of Simplicity 3-speed gear transmission. The 4-speed gear transmission used on shuttle reverse tractors is similar (refer to Fig. S52).***

1. Transmission case
2. Oil seal
3. Spacer
4. Set screws
5. Shift rail (2nd & reverse)
5A. Shift rail (1st & 3rd)
6. Shift fork (2nd & reverse)
6A. Shift fork (1st & 3rd)
7. Shift rod
8. Shifter stem
9. Ball
10. Poppet string
11. Gasket
12. Transmission cover
13. Oil level plug
14. Reverse idler gear
15. Spacer
16. Washer
17. Reverse idler shaft
18. Ball bearing
19. Washer
20. Retaining ring
21. Special washer
22. Snap ring
23. Input shaft
24. Sliding gear (1st & 3rd)
25. Sliding gear (2nd & reverse)
26. Snap ring
27. Special washer
28. Washer
29. Needle bearing
30. Oil seal
31. Needle bearing
32. Brake shaft
33. Reverse gear
34. Spacer
35. Snap ring
36. Second gear
37. Washers
38. Third gear
39. Washer
40. First intermediate pinion
41. First gear
42. Needle bearing
43. Needle bearing
44. Washers
45. Spacer
46. Second intermediate gear
47. Washer
48. Second intermediate pinion
49. Second intermediate shaft
50. Snap ring
51. Washers
52. Needle bearing
53. Needle bearing
54. Washers
55. Snap ring
56. Third intermediate shaft
57. Third intermediate gear
58. Third intermediate pinion
59. Washers
60. Needle bearing
61. Bushing
62. Snap ring
63. Oil seal
64. Needle bearing
65. Washers
66. Output gear
67. Axle tube
68. Washer
69. Spacer
70. Snap ring
71. Washers
72. Needle bearing
73. Oil seal
74. Bushing

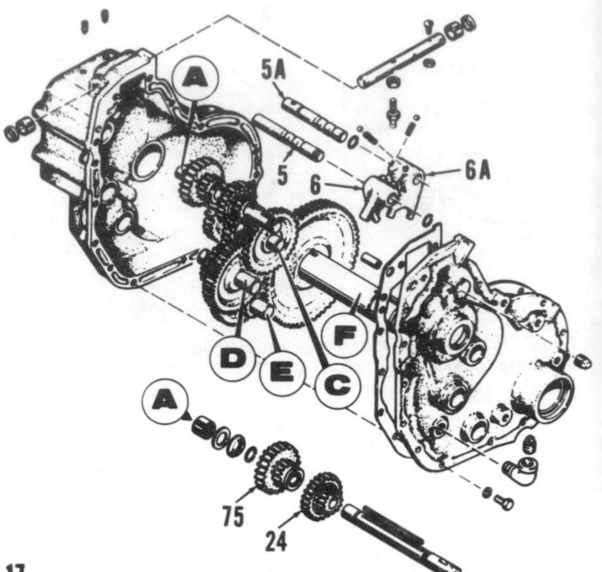

***Fig. S52—The 4-speed transmission used on shuttle reverse equipped tractors are equipped with a second and fourth sliding gear (75) in place of second and fourth gear (25—Fig. S51). Reverse idler gear and shaft (14 through 17—Fig. S51) are not used in this 4-speed transmission. All other parts are similar to the 3-speed transmission.***

5. Shift rail (2nd & 4th)
5A. Shift rail (1st & 3rd)
6. Shift fork (2nd & 4th)
6A. Shift fork (1st & 3rd)
24. Sliding gear (1st & 3rd)
75. Sliding gear (2nd & 4th)

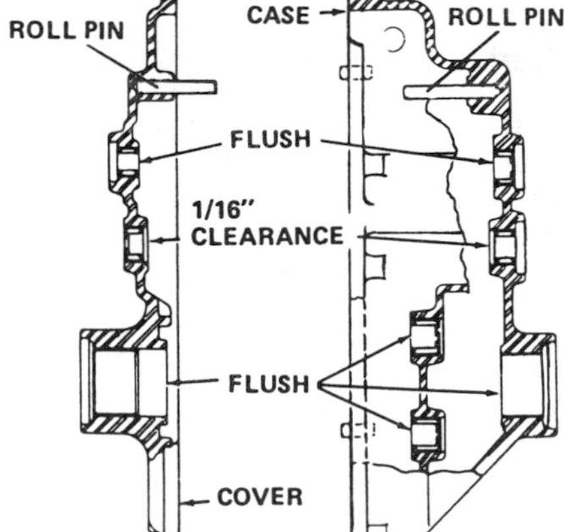


***Fig. S53—When renewing bearings, press into transmission case or cover to dimensions shown.***

S52) on 4-speed models or (24 and 25–Fig. S51) on 3-speed models, can be removed. Brake shaft (32) with gears (33, 36, 38 and 40) can now be withdrawn. On models so equipped, remove reverse idler gear (14) and shaft (17). Loosen set screws (4) and slide out shift fork and rail assemblies. Remove shifter stem (8) and withdraw shift rod (7) from case. Bearings and oil seals can now be removed from case and cover as required.

Clean and inspect all parts and renew any showing excessive wear or other damage. Using Figs. S51 and S52 as a guide, reassemble transmission by reversing disassembly procedure. When renewing bearings, press new bearings into case or cover until positioned as shown in Fig. S53. The shifter stem used on some models is adjustable and must be adjusted to 5/8 inch (16 mm) dimension shown in Fig. S54. The two roll pins ("A" and "B"–Fig. S55) which limit shifter stem movement, must be installed to proper height as shown. Check pins even if renewal was not necessary. After unit is reinstalled, fill transmission to level plug opening with recommended lubricant as listed in the CONDENSED SPECIFICATIONS table under appropriate TRACTOR SERVICE SECTION for model being serviced.

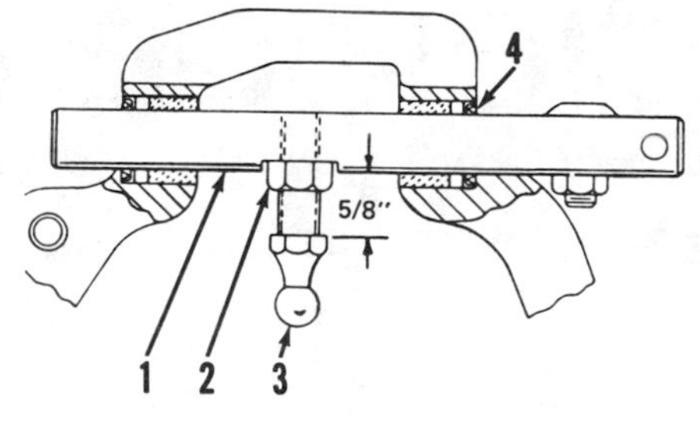


*Fig. S54—On models so equipped, adjust shifter stem (3) to 5/8 inch (16 mm) distance as shown. New style shift stem is nonadjustable. Lubricate seals (4) and shaft (1) prior to installation.*

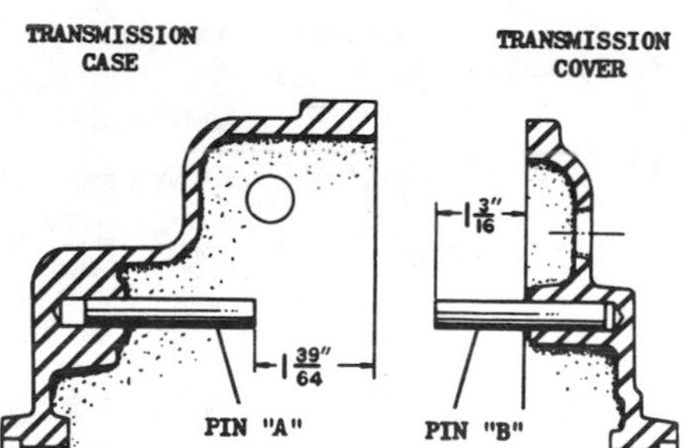


*Fig. S55—Roll pins (A & B) limit shifter stem movement and must be set to proper height as shown.*

# SPICER (Formerly Foote)

## Model 35-3500

**OVERHAUL.** To disassemble transmission, first unbolt and remove shift lever. Place unit in a vise so sprocket end of output shaft (15–Fig. SP1) is pointing upward. Remove snap ring (12), output sprocket (13) and key (14). Unbolt and remove cover (11) from case (5). Slide forward drive gear (9) from output shaft (15). Lift input and drive pinion assembly (17 through 22) from case (5). Carefully withdraw clutch collar (8) and shift fork (7) from shaft and case, taking care not to lose detent ball (4) and spring (3). Remove key (16), reverse drive gear (19), snap ring (1) and flat washer (2) from output shaft (15), then withdraw shaft from case. Remove snap ring (17), bevel pinion (18) and flange bushings (20) from input shaft (22). Flange bushings (6 and 10) can be removed from case (5) and cover (11) if necessary.

Clean all parts and renew any showing excessive wear or other damage. Reassemble by reversing disassembly procedure and fill case with 5 ounces (148 mL) of EP lithium base grease.

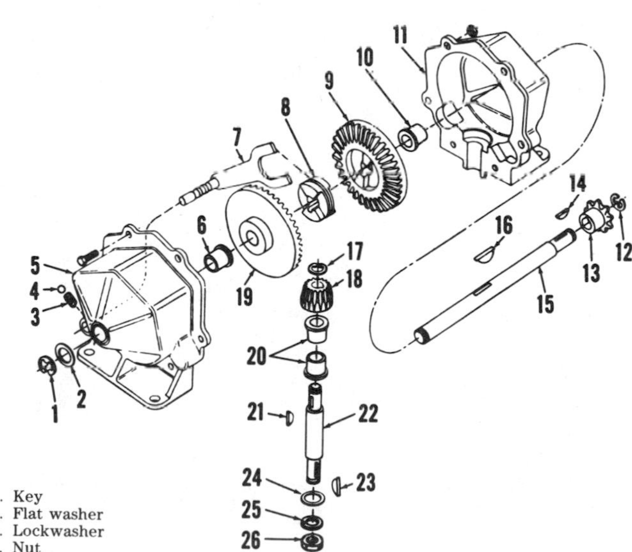


*Fig. SP1—Exploded view of Spicer (Foote) Model 35-3500 single-speed, forward-reverse gear transmission.*

1. Snap ring
2. Flat washer
3. Spring
4. Detent ball
5. Transmission case
6. Flange bushing
7. Shift fork
8. Clutch collar
9. Forward drive gear
10. Flange bushing
11. Transmission cover
12. Snap ring
13. Output sprocket
14. Key
15. Output shaft
16. Key
17. Snap ring
18. Bevel pinion
19. Reverse drive gear
20. Flange bushings
21. Key
22. Input shaft
23. Key
24. Flat washer
25. Lockwasher
26. Nut

Illustration courtesy Spicer.

# REDUCTION GEAR AND DIFFERENTIAL SERVICE

## HYDRO-GEAR

### Series 210-1010

**OVERHAUL.** Separate hydrostatic unit from transaxle housing. Note that hydrostatic input and output shafts are coupled to transaxle shafts with two sets of couplers (44—Fig. HG1) which are retained on the shafts with Loctite. It may be necessary to heat couplers and use a suitable puller to remove couplers from shafts.

Remove wheel and hub assemblies from axles. Remove park brake assembly from brake shaft (22—Fig. HG1). Clean axle shafts (10 and 36) and remove any burrs from shafts. Remove input pulley and fan from input shaft (3). Remove screws securing input shaft housing (5) and remove input shaft assembly. Remove case screws while noting length and location of screws. Separate case halves (9 and 37); it may be necessary to tap against end of drive shaft (18).

Clean grease from internal components and remove reduction gears (33 and 39), differential and axle shafts,

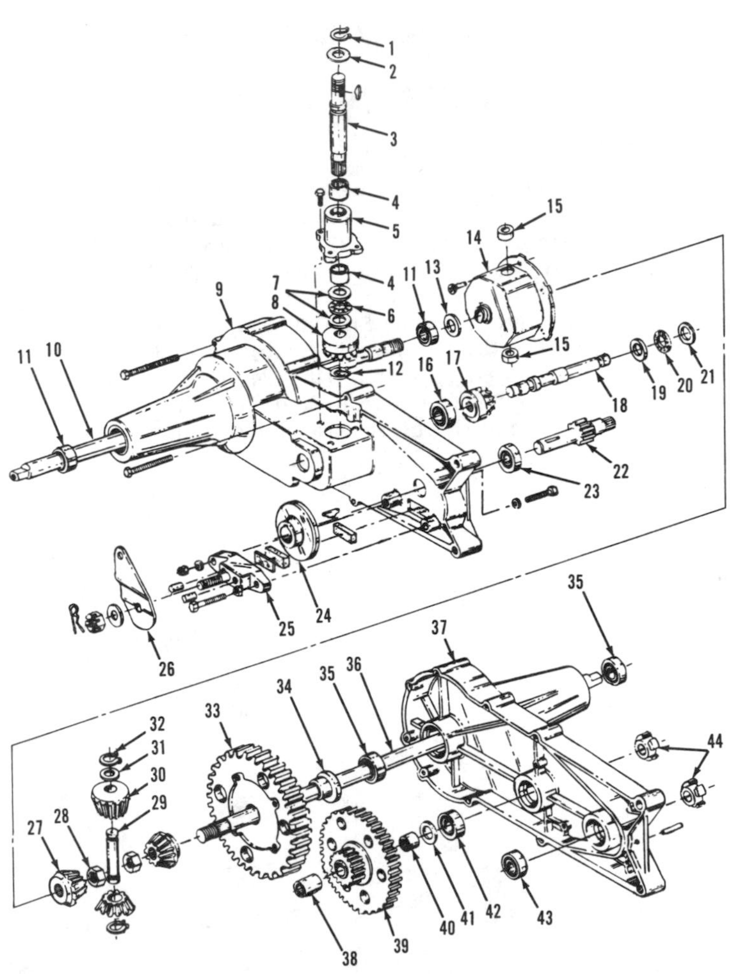

*Fig. HG1—Exploded view of Hydro-Gear 210-1010 series reduction gear and differential assembly. Some units use a single needle bearing in reduction gear (39) in place of two bearings (38 and 40) shown.*

1. Snap ring
2. Washer
3. Input shaft
4. Needle bearings
5. Input shaft housing
6. Thrust bearing
7. Thrust washers
8. Input pinion gear
9. Housing half R.H.
10. Axle shaft
11. Ball bearings
12. Snap ring
13. Thrust washer
14. Differential housing
15. Thrust bearings
16. Ball bearing
17. Drive pinion gear
18. Drive shaft
19. Washer (thick)
20. Thrust bearing
21. Washer (thin)
22. Brake shaft
23. Ball bearing
24. Brake disc
25. Brake caliper
26. Brake actuator arm
27. Differential side gear
28. Nut
29. Shaft
30. Differential pinion gear
31. Thrust washer
32. Snap ring
33. Differential gear
34. Flange bearing
35. Ball bearings
36. Axle shaft
37. Housing half L.H.
38. Needle bearing (long)
39. Reduction gear
40. Needle bearing (short)
41. Washer
42. Ball bearing
43. Ball bearing
44. Couplers

drive shaft (18), brake shaft (22) and bearings from housing halves. Remove snap rings (1 and 12) and pull pinion gear (8), thrust bearing (6 and 7) and input shaft (3) from housing (5). Unbolt and remove differential housing (14) from reduction gear (33) and remove side gears (27), snap rings (32), pinion gears (30) and pinion shaft (29). Discard snap rings (32) and differential housing bolts. Use a suitable puller to remove ball bearings from housings if bearing renewal is necessary.

Lubricate all components with type "O" grease when reassembling transaxle. Apply Loctite 242 to all retaining nuts and bolts. Install new ball bearings in housings using Loctite 609 Retaining Compound.

Install new snap rings (32) when assembling differential assembly. Tighten axle shaft nuts (28) to 40-55 ft.-lbs. (55-74 N·m). Install new locking bolts attaching differential housing (14) to differential gear (33) and tighten to 180-205 in.-lbs. (20.3-23.1 N·m).

When installing new needle bearing in reduction gear (39), note that numbered side of bearing is installed toward 60 tooth side of reduction gear assembly and that bearing must be 0.005-0.015 inch (0.13-0.38 mm) below the face of 17 tooth side of gear assembly. If a new reduction gear (39) is being installed, correct thickness washer (19) must be selected to obtain recommended running clearance. To select correct thickness washer, first install 0.050 inch (1.27 mm) thick washer and thrust bearing (20) on drive shaft (18) and assemble shaft in reduction gear. Position reduction gear and drive shaft assembly in housing. Place a straightedge across housing surface and measure distance between face of reduction gear (39) and straightedge (S—Fig. HG2). Subtract 0.019 inch (0.74 mm) from measured distance, the result must be within range of 0.015-0.030 inch (0.38-0.76 mm). If gap is within this range, 0.050 inch (1.27 mm) thick washer is correct size. If gap is too narrow, remove reduction gear and replace the 0.050 inch (1.27 mm) washer with a 0.040 inch (1.0 mm) thick washer (19—Fig. HG1).

Fill unit with 10 ounces (300 mL) of Shell Darina #0 type grease. Tighten screws securing case halves together to 80-120 in.-lbs. (9.0-13.6 N·m). After housings are bolted together, check for 0.015 to 0.030 inch (0.38-0.76 mm) minimum clearance between thrust race and thrust bearing using a feeler gage inserted through opening in housing for input shaft as shown in Fig. HG3. If clearance is not within specified range, repeat thrust washer selection procedure.

When installing new needle bearings (4—Fig. HG1) in input housing (5), press bearings in until flush with both ends of housing. Pack bearings with grease before installing input shaft (3). Input shaft end play is adjusted by installing correct thickness washer (2). Maximum allowable end play is 0.010 inch (0.25 mm). Pack five ounces (150 mL) of Shell Darina #0 type grease on input gear. Mount input shaft assembly in housing. Apply Loctite 242 to threads of input housing retaining screws and tighten screws to 80-120 in.-lbs. (9.0-13.6 N·m).

Reinstall couplings (44—Fig. HG1) using Loctite 609 to bond couplings to shafts. Allow Loctite to cure for 24 hours before operating unit. Assemble hydrostatic unit on reduction gear housing and tighten mounting bolts to 80-120 in.-lbs. (9.0-13.6 N·m).

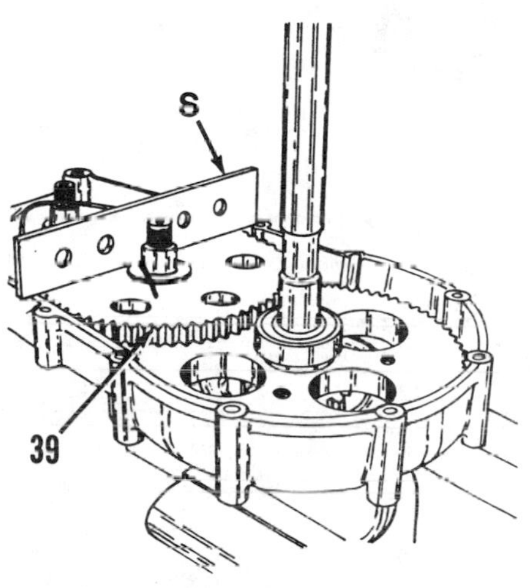


*Fig. HG2—Place straightedge (S) across housing as shown and measure distance between hub of reduction gear (39) and straightedge. Use this measurement to select correct thickness washer to obtain desired gear end play. Refer to text for details.*

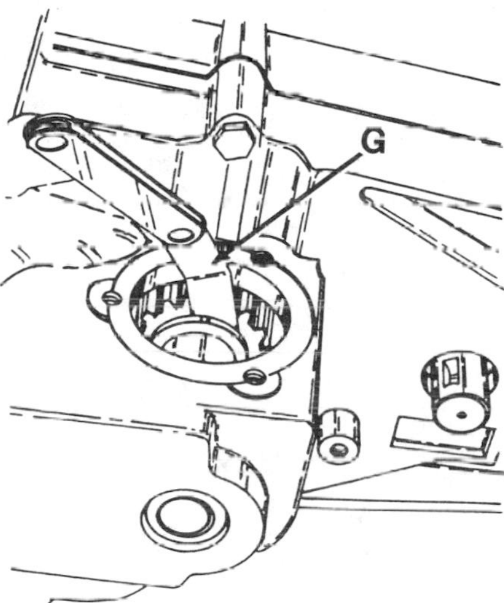


*Fig. HG3—After reduction gear housing halves are bolted together, use a feeler gage (G) to check for 0.015 to 0.030 inch (0.38-0.76 mm) clearance between thrust race and thrust bearing.*

# KANZAKI

## Tuff Torq

**OVERHAUL.** To disassemble gear reduction and differential unit, first remove wheels and brake components. Refer to Fig. KZ20 for an exploded view of reduction gear and differential assembly. Remove screws securing housings together. Separate housings while noting location of all washers and shims. Use a suitable press to remove axles. Refer to Fig. KZ20 and disassemble unit.

Minimum allowable thickness of washers (14) is 0.5 mm (0.020 in.). Minimum allowable thickness of washers (28 and 31) is 2.16 mm (0.085 in.). Pinion gear (18) inside diameter should be 14.02-14.03 mm (0.5520-0.5524 in.) and pinion shaft diameter should be 13.97-13.98 mm (0.5500-0.5504 in.). Maximum allowable clearance between pinion gears and shaft is 0.4 mm (0.016 in.). Minimum allowable thickness of washers (11) is 1.5 mm (0.060 in.).

Press bearings (8) into housings so printed side is out. Insert axles into housings and press bearings (10) onto axles so bearing is 4-5 mm (0.16-0.20 in.) below snap ring groove on axle. Place washer and snap ring on axle then tap inner (splined) end of axle until snap ring forces washer against bearing. Bearing (3) must be pressed onto pinion (4). Bearings (23 and 33) must be pressed onto gear shaft (32). Install gear (26) on shaft (25) and press bearings (24) onto shaft. Washers (28 and 31) must be installed on shaft (27) with oil grooves toward bearing (29).

Be sure differential pinion shaft (17) is properly centered within ring gear (16) when assembling differential housing components. Apply Loctite 242 to differential housing bolts and tighten to 27 N·m (20 ft.-lbs.). Assemble components in right housing (9) and tap idler shaft (27) to seat in housing. Install shims and washers in left housing using grease to hold them in place. Apply sealer to housing mating surface. Tighten housing screws to 26 N·m (19 ft.-lbs.) if original housing is being reused. If new housing with untapped holes is being installed, tighten screws to 30 N·m (22 ft.-lbs.).

Measure backlash of pinion (4) while pulling outward on splined, brake end of shaft (32). Backlash should be 0.06-0.24 mm (0.002-0.009 in.). Add or delete shims (34) as needed to obtain desired backlash.

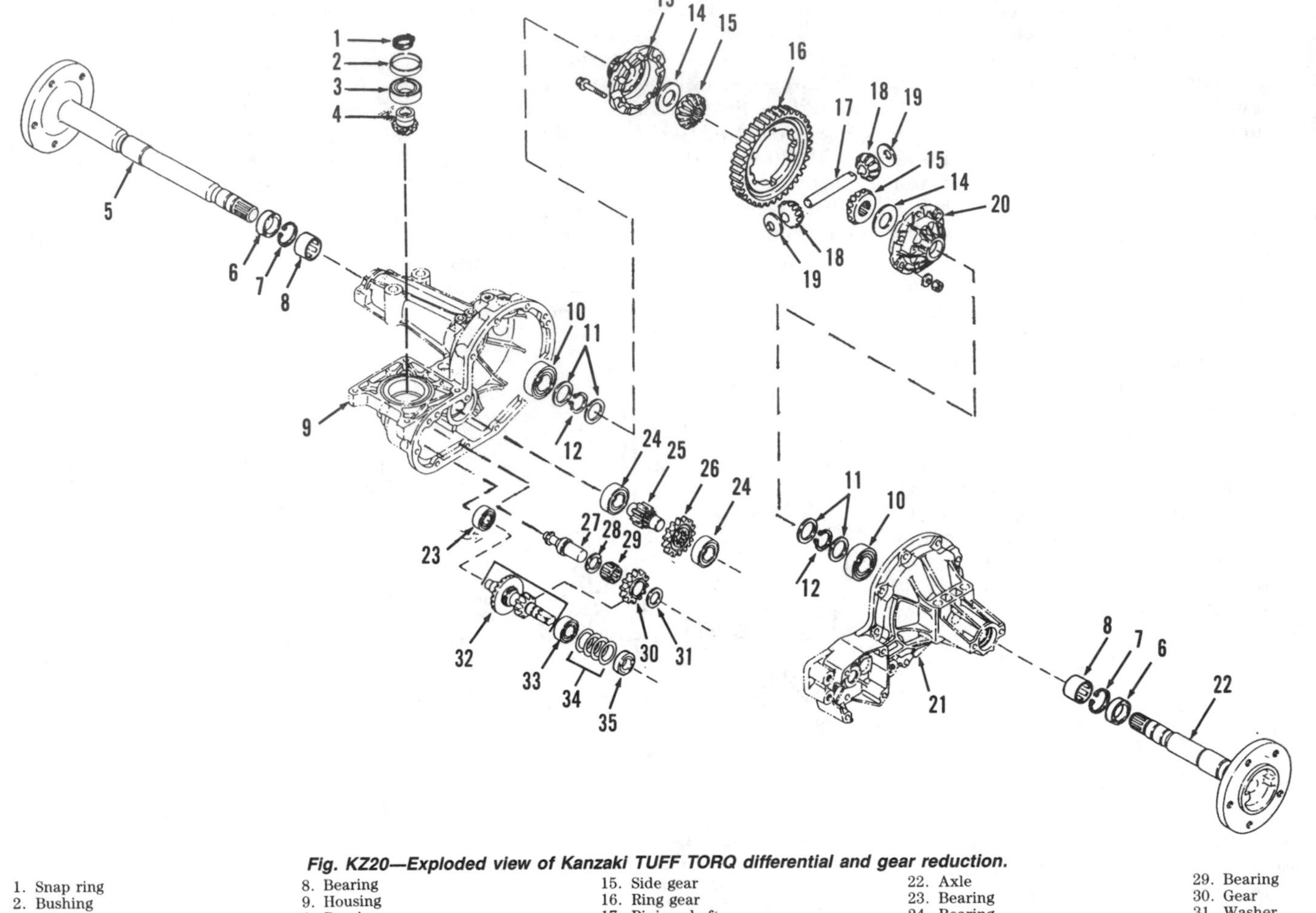


*Fig. KZ20—Exploded view of Kanzaki TUFF TORQ differential and gear reduction.*

1. Snap ring
2. Bushing
3. Bearing
4. Pinion
5. Axle
6. Seal
7. Snap ring
8. Bearing
9. Housing
10. Bearing
11. Washers
12. Snap ring
13. Carrier half
14. Washer
15. Side gear
16. Ring gear
17. Pinion shaft
18. Pinion
19. Washer
20. Carrier half
21. Housing
22. Axle
23. Bearing
24. Bearing
25. Gear
26. Gear
27. Shaft
28. Washer
29. Bearing
30. Gear
31. Washer
32. Brake shaft
33. Bearing
34. Shims
35. Seal

# PEERLESS

## Series 1300

**OVERHAUL.** Clean exterior of unit and drain lubricant. Separate hydrostatic transmission from gear reduction housing. Remove park brake disc from brake shaft. Clean axle shafts and remove any burrs from shafts. Unscrew housing cap screws and drive dowel pins out of cover (29—Fig. PL1). Lift cover off case and axle shaft. Withdraw brake shaft (5), idler gear (4) and thrust washers (3 and 6) from case. Remove output shaft (11), output gear (10), spacer (9), thrust washer (8) and differential assembly from case. Axle shaft housings (20 and 22) must be pressed from case and cover.

To disassemble differential, unscrew four cap screws (17) and separate axle shaft and carrier assemblies form ring gear (28). Drive blocks (25), bevel pinion gears (26) and drive pin (27) can now be removed from ring gear. Remove snap rings (12) and slide axle shafts (18 and 23) from axle gears (13) and carriers (16 and 24).

Clean and inspect all parts and renew any parts that are damaged or excessively worn. When installing new needle bearings, press bearings in from inside of case or cover until bearings are 0.015-0.020 inch (0.38-0.50 mm) below thrust surfaces. When installing axle supports (20 and 22), press supports into case or cover until flanges contact case or cover.

To reassemble, reverse disassembly procedure. Install differential assembly and output shaft into case at the same time. Align case and cover by tapping dowel pins into cover and tighten mounting cap screws to 10 ft.-lbs. (14 N·m). Install new axle shaft oil seals and brake shaft oil seal using suitable driver. Refill differential unit with 2¾ pints (1.3 L) of SAE 90 EP gear oil before reinstalling hydrostatic transmission.

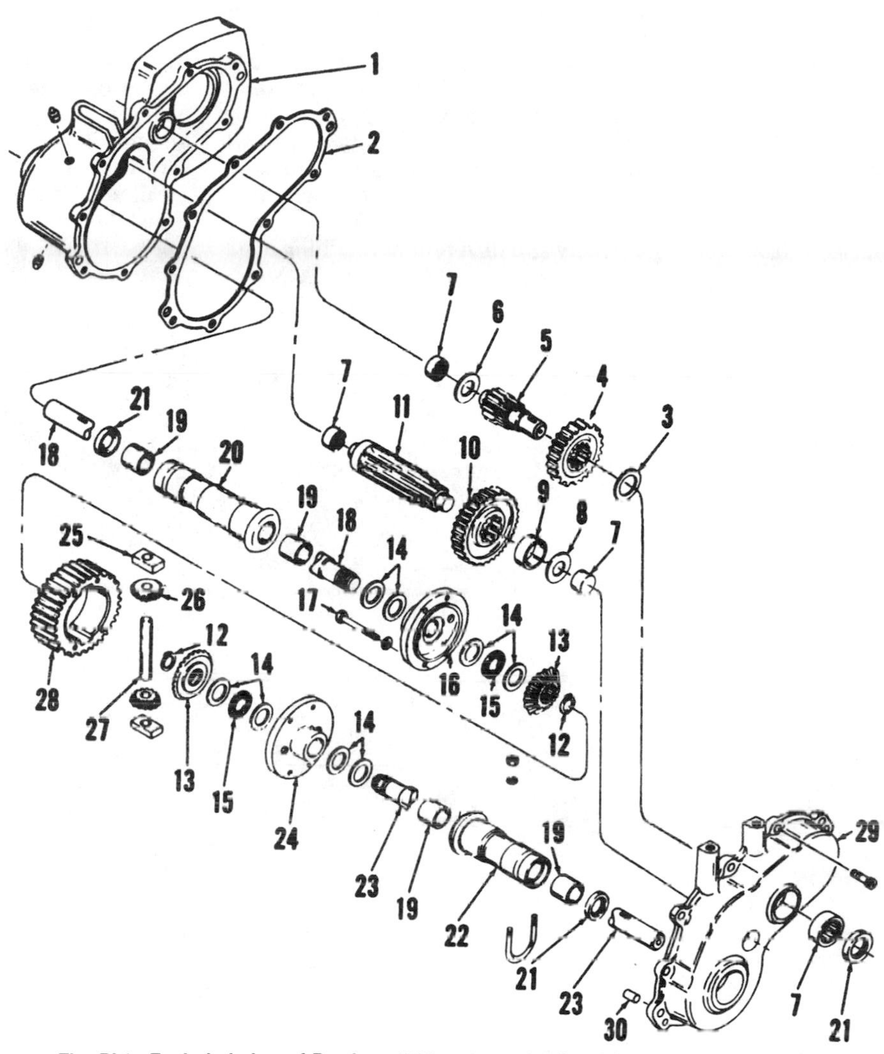

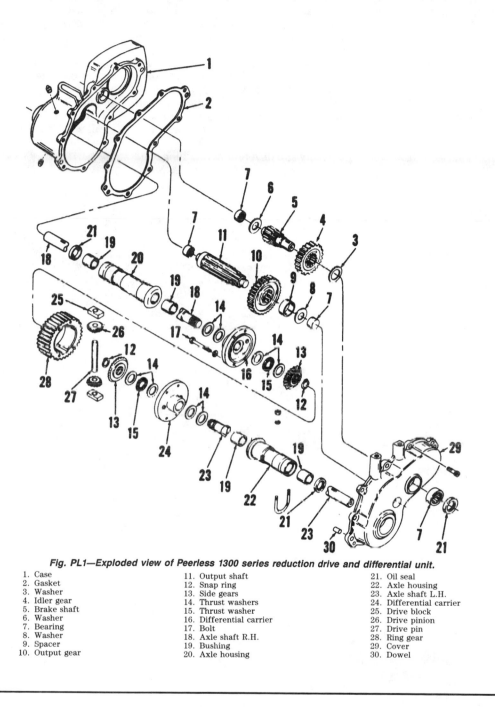

*Fig. PL1—Exploded view of Peerless 1300 series reduction drive and differential unit.*

1. Case
2. Gasket
3. Washer
4. Idler gear
5. Brake shaft
6. Washer
7. Bearing
8. Washer
9. Spacer
10. Output gear
11. Output shaft
12. Snap ring
13. Side gears
14. Thrust washers
15. Thrust washer
16. Differential carrier
17. Bolt
18. Axle shaft R.H.
19. Bushing
20. Axle housing
21. Oil seal
22. Axle housing
23. Axle shaft L.H.
24. Differential carrier
25. Drive block
26. Drive pinion
27. Drive pin
28. Ring gear
29. Cover
30. Dowel

## Series 2400

**OVERHAUL.** To disassemble, first clean exterior of unit and drain lubricant. Unbolt and remove hydrostatic transmission from transaxle housing. Remove coupling (8—Fig. PL11) from input shaft. Clean axles of burrs, rust or dirt. Scribe match marks on axle housings (14 and 37) and differential case halves (9 and 39) to aid reassembly, then unbolt and remove axle housings. Remove seal retainers (11) with oil seals (12) and "O" rings by pulling each axle shaft out of case and cover as far as possible. Place unit on the edge of a bench with left axle shaft (40) pointing downward. Remove cap screws securing cover (9) to case (39). Drive aligning dowels out of cover, then lift cover from case. Withdraw differential and axle assembly and lay aside for later disassembly. Remove output gear and shaft (24 and 25) with thrust washers (23 and 26). Remove input shaft (3) with thrust washers (2 and 4), then withdraw idler gear and shaft (17 and 18) with spacer (19) and thrust washers (16 and 20).

To disassemble differential, remove four cap screws and separate axle assemblies from body cores (41). Using suitable snap ring pliers, remove cylindrical spring (43). Pinion gears (28) can now be removed from body cores. Separate body cores from ring gear (42). Remove snap ring (29) at end of axle and disassemble axle assembly.

Clean and inspect all parts and renew any showing excessive wear or other damage. When installing new needle bearings, press carrier bearings (10) in from inside of case and cover until bearings are 0.290 inch (7.36 mm) below face of axle housing mounting surface. All other needle bearings are to be pressed in from inside of case and cover to a depth of 0.015-0.020 inch (0.38-0.50 mm) below thrust washer surface.

To reassemble differential, install body cores (41) in ring gear (42) so gear pockets in one core are out of alignment with gear pockets in other core. Reassemble axle assemblies. Install pinion gears (28) in one body core, then hold pinion gears in core by installing differential carrier and axle assembly and turn differential cover. Be sure that pinion gears mesh with side gear. Install pinion gears in other body core being sure gears mesh with previously installed pinion gears. Install cylindrical spring (43) so it bottoms against side gear. Spring should be in contact with most of the ten pinion gears. Install axle assembly and differential retaining bolts and tighten to 7-10 ft.-lbs. (9-14 N·m).

Reassemble remainder of unit by reversing disassembly procedure. Make certain that all thrust washers are properly installed on brake shaft (18), input shaft (3) and output shaft (25). Renew gasket (6), "O" rings (13) and oil seals (12) during reassembly. Install new oil seals (7 and 38) after unit is assembled. Tighten cover to case cap screws to 10 ft.-lbs. (14 N·m). Be sure match marks on axle housings and case and cover made prior to disassembly are aligned, then tighten axle housing cap screws to 13 ft.-lbs. (18 N·m).

Fill reduction gear housing, after unit is installed on tractor, to level plug opening with SAE 90 EP gear oil.

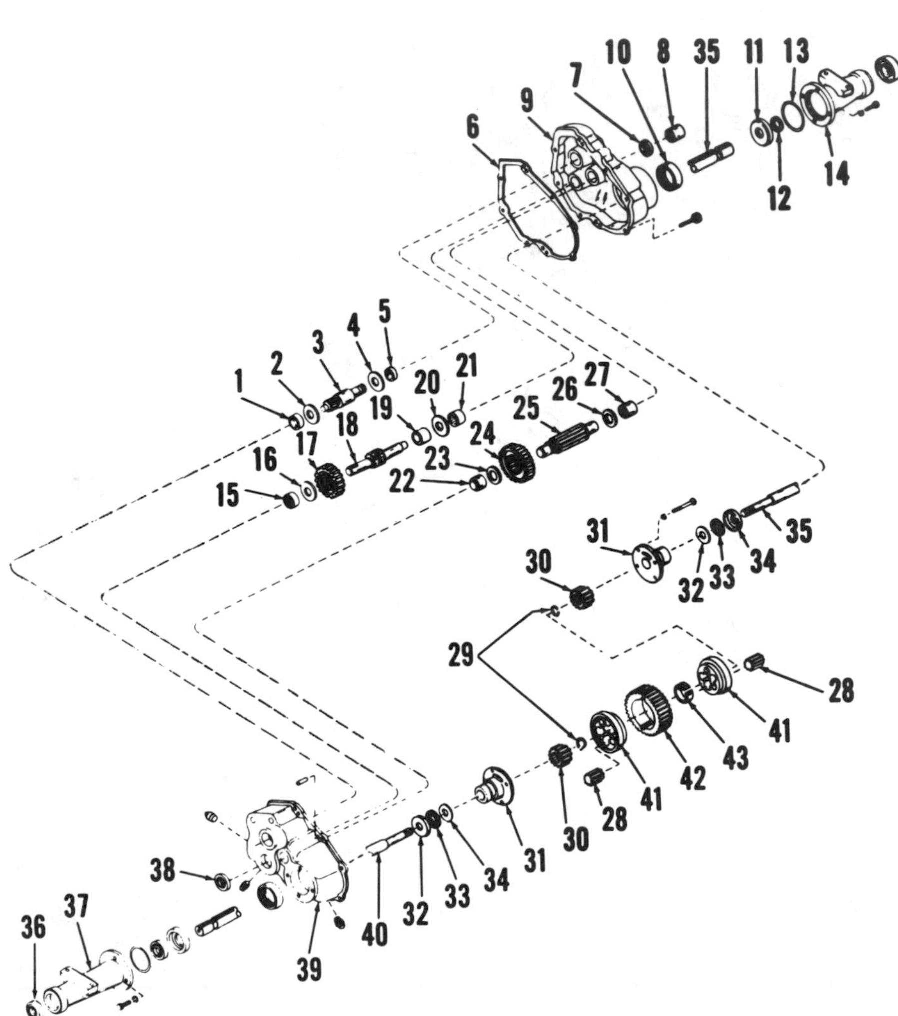


***Fig. PL11—Exploded view of Peerless 2400 series reduction drive and differential assembly.***

1. Needle bearing
2. Thrust washer
3. Input shaft
4. Thrust washer
5. Needle bearing
6. Gasket
7. Oil seal
8. Coupling
9. Cover
10. Carrier bearing
11. Seal retainer
12. Oil seal
13. "O" ring
14. Axle housing R.H.
15. Needle bearing
16. Thrust washer
17. Idler gear
18. Brake shaft
19. Spacer
20. Thrust washer
21. Needle bearing
22. Needle bearing
23. Thrust washer
24. Output gear
25. Output shaft
26. Thrust washer
27. Needle bearing
28. Pinion gear
29. Snap ring
30. Side gear
31. Differential carrier
32. Thrust washer
33. Thrust washer
34. Thrust washer
35. Axle shaft R.H.
36. Axle ball bearing
37. Axle housing L.H.
38. Oil seal
39. Case
40. Axle shaft L.H.
41. Body core
42. Ring gear
43. Cylindrical spring

## Series 2500

**OVERHAUL.** Clean exterior of unit, drain lubricant and remove hydrostatic transmission. Unbolt and remove disc brake assembly.

To disassemble, first scribe alignment marks on axle housings (15—Fig. PL21) and case (1) and cover (13) to aid reassembly. Remove burrs, rust and dirt from axle shafts. Unbolt and remove axle housings. Position unit with cover (13) facing up, then unbolt and remove cover. Lift out differential and axle assembly (40 through 54). Remove output shaft (36), gear (35) and thrust washers (37). Unscrew set screw (2) and remove spring (3) and ball (4). Remove brake shaft (32), sliding gear (33), shift fork (10) and shift rail (8). Remove input shaft and gear components (18 through 26).

To disassemble differential, remove cap screws (53) and separate differential carriers (41 and 52) and axles from ring gear assembly. Remove snap rings (44 and 49) and separate axle gears (43 and 50), thrust washers (42 and 51) and axle shafts (40 and 54). Remove pinions (47) and separate body cores (45 and 48) from ring gear (46).

Inspect components for damage or excessive wear. To reassemble, reverse disassembly procedure. Apply Loctite 242 to threads of differential bolts (53). Install differential bolts so heads of bolts are on side of shorter carrier (52) and tighten bolts to 7 ft.-lbs. (9 N·m). Check movement of shift rail (8) when tightening set screw (2). Install gears (22 and 25) so bevels on gear teeth face together as shown in Fig. PL22. Install axle housings (15—Fig. PL21), aligning match marks made prior to disassembly. Do not rotate axle housings after the housings have been pressed tight against seals (11) as seals might be cut.

Install unit in tractor, then refill with recommended transmission fluid.

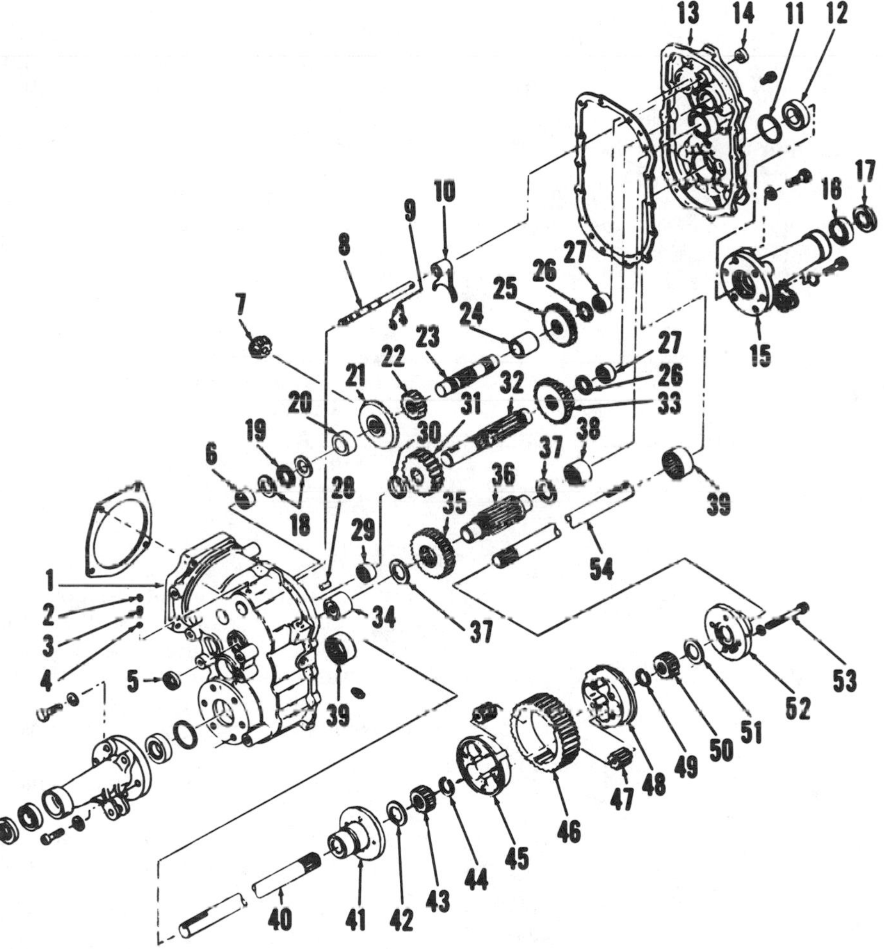

Fig. PL21—Exploded view of Peerless 2500 series two-speed reduction drive and differential assembly.

1. Case
2. Set screw
3. Spring
4. Ball
5. Seal
6. Needle bearing
7. Transmission output gear
8. Shift rail
9. Snap ring
10. Shift fork
11. Quad ring
12. Tapered roller bearing
13. Cover
14. Seal
15. Axle housing
16. Ball bearing
17. Oil seal
18. Thrust washers
19. Thrust bearing
20. Spacer
21. Bevel gear
22. Gear (16T)
23. Shaft
24. Spacer
25. Gear (23T)
26. Thrust washer
27. Needle bearing
28. Dowel pin
29. Needle bearing
30. Spacer
31. Gear
32. Brake shaft
33. Sliding gear
34. Needle bearing
35. Output gear
36. Output shaft
37. Thrust washer
38. Needle bearing
39. Needle bearing
40. Axle L.H.
41. Differential carrier L.H.
42. Thrust washer
43. Axle gear
44. Snap ring
45. Body core
46. Ring gear
47. Pinion gears (8)
48. Body core
49. Snap ring
50. Axle gear
51. Thrust washer
52. Differential carrier R.H.
53. Cap screw
54. Axle R.H.

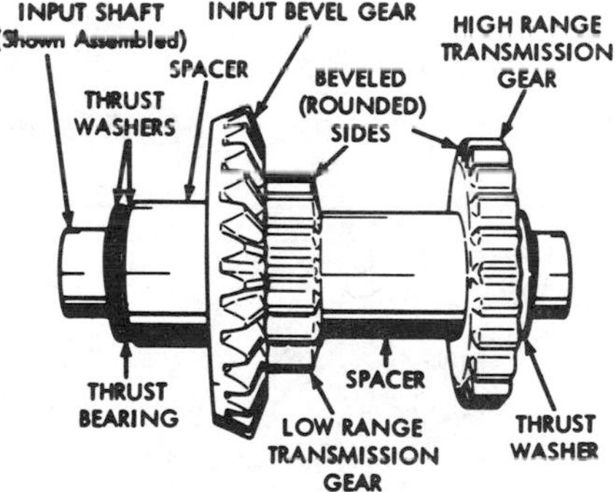


Fig. PL22—View of input shaft and gears. Note that beveled sides of gears face each other.

# HYDROSTATIC TRANSMISSION SERVICE

## EATON

### Model 6

**OPERATION.** The Eaton Model 6 hydrostatic transmission is composed of three major parts: A variable displacement, reversible flow, radial ball piston pump; a fixed displacement, ball piston motor; and a system of valves located between pump and motor. Tractor ground speed is regulated by changing amount of oil delivered by the variable displacement pump. Moving speed control lever in forward direction will control forward ground speed range of 0-4.16 mph at full engine rpm. When speed control lever is moved rearward from neutral position, a reverse range of 0-2.6 mph is achieved.

The pressurized oil from pump (high pressure oil in Fig. EA10) forces directional check valve (A) closed and directs flow to motor. The return oil flow from motor completes the closed loop circuit. Any oil lost due to internal leakage in the motor reduces the volume of oil in return line. This reduced volume (resulting in low pressure) allows directional check valve (B) to open and oil from reservoir will replace oil lost from circuit. When control lever is moved for opposite direction, hydraulic circuits are reversed.

**TROUBLE-SHOOTING.** Some problems which might occur during operation of hydrostatic transmission and their possible causes are as follows:

A. No output power in either direction. Could be caused by:
   1. Broken control shaft dowel pin.
   2. Low oil level.

B. Loss of output power under continuous load. Could be caused by:
   1. Internal leakage due to excessive wear.
   2. Water in transmission fluid.

C. No output power in one direction. Could be caused by:
   1. One of the directional valves is stuck.
   2. Loose control shaft dowel pin.

D. External oil leakage. Could be caused by:
   1. Fluid level too high.
   2. Defective input or control shaft seal.
   3. Reservoir loose or defective.
   4. Loose venting plug in body.

E. Excessive noise and violent action at control shaft. Could be caused by:
   1. Directional check ball stuck.
   2. Loose control linkage.
   3. Excessive motor rotor to pintle clearance.
   4. Water in fluid.
   5. Air in system.

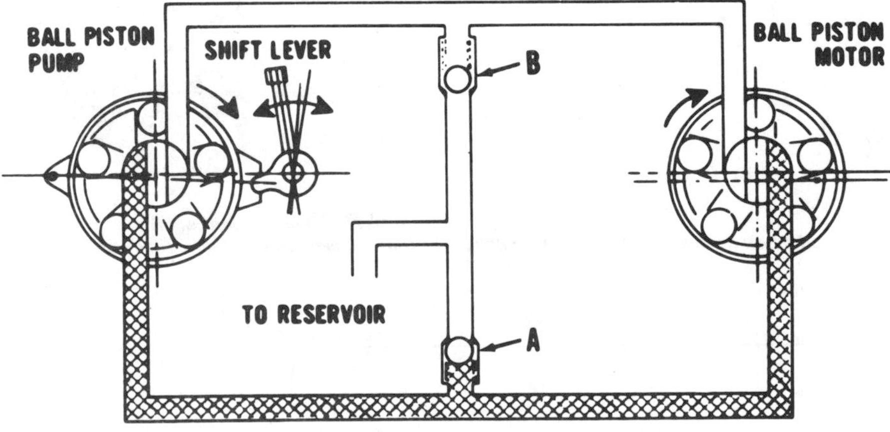


*Fig. EA10—Flow diagram of an Eaton Model 6 hydrostatic transmission. "A" and "B" are directional check valves.*

**OVERHAUL.** Before disassembling transmission, thoroughly clean exterior of unit. Remove venting plug (31–Fig. EA11), invert assembly and drain fluid from unit. Remove reservoir (3) or adapter by rotating clockwise (L.H. threads). Remove two cap screws (29) and place transmission (output shaft downward) in a holding fixture similar to one shown in Fig. EA12. Remove aluminum housing (5–Fig. EA11) with control shaft and input shaft assemblies.

**CAUTION: Do not allow pump and cam ring assemblies (16 through 20) to lift with housing. If pump rotor is raised with housing, ball pistons may fall out of rotor.**

The ball pistons (17) are selective fitted to rotor bores to a clearance of 0.0002-0.0006 inch (0.0051-0.0152 mm) and are not interchangeable. A wide rubber band can be used to prevent ball pistons from falling out. Remove cam ring (20) and pump race (19), then carefully remove pump assembly. Hold downward on motor rotor (49) and remove pintle assembly (46). Place a wide rubber band around motor rotor (49) to prevent balls (41) and springs (40) from falling out of rotor. Remove motor assembly and motor race (33).

Remove snap ring (22), gear (23), spacer (24), retainer (25), snap ring (26) and key (35). Support body (30) and press output shaft (34) out of bearing (27) and oil seal (28) can now be removed from body (30).

Remove retainer (9) and withdraw ball bearing (7) and input shaft (14). Bearing can be pressed from input shaft after removal of snap ring (8). Oil seal (6) can be removed from outside of housing. To remove control shaft (38), drill a 11/32 inch hole through aluminum housing (5) directly in line with center line of dowel pin (10). Press dowel pin from control shaft, remove snap ring (12) and washer (11) and withdraw control shaft. Remove oil seal (39). Thread drilled hole with a 1/8 inch pipe tap.



Illustrations courtesy Eaton Corp.

To remove directional check valves from pintle (46), drill through pintle with a drill bit that will pass freely through roll pins (47). Redrill holes from opposite side with a ¼ inch drill bit. Press roll pins from pintle. Using a 5/16-18 tap, thread inside of check valve bodies (43) and remove valve bodies using a draw bolt or a slide hammer puller. Remove check valve balls (44) and snap rings (45). Do not remove plugs (48).

Number piston bores (1 through 5) on pump rotor and on motor rotor. Use a plastic ice cube tray or equivalent and mark cavities 1P through 5P for pump and 1M through 5M for motor. Remove ball pistons (17) one at a time from pump rotor and place each ball in correct cavity in tray. Remove ball pistons (41) and springs (40) from motor rotor in same manner.

Clean and inspect all parts and renew any showing excessive wear or other damage. Ball pistons are selective fitted to 0.0002-0.0006 inch (0.0051-0.0152 mm) clearance and must be reinstalled in their original bores. If rotor bushings (18 and 37) are scored or badly worn 0.002 inch (0.051 mm) or more clearance on pintle journals, renew pump rotor or motor rotor assemblies. Install ball pistons (17) in pump rotor (16) and ball pistons (41) and springs (40) in motor rotor (49) and use wide rubber bands to hold pistons in their bores. Install snap rings (45), check valve balls (44) and valve bodies (43) in pintle (46) and secure with new roll pins (47). If plugs (48) are loose, install new plugs. Use "Loctite" grade 635 and tighten plugs to a torque of 12 in.-lbs. (1.4 N·m). Renew oil seals (6 and 39) and reinstall control shaft and input shaft in housing (5) by reversing removal procedure. When installing oil seals (6, 39 or 28), apply a thin coat of "Loctite" grade 635 to seal outer diameter. Press dowel pin (10) into control shaft until end of dowel pin extends $1^1/_8$ inches (28.6 mm) from control shaft. Apply "Loctite" grade 635 to a $^1/_8$ inch plug and install plug in drilled and tapped disassembly hole. Tighten plug until snug. Do not overtighten. Renew oil seal (28) and reinstall output shaft (34), bearing (27), snap rings, retainer, spacer and gear in body (30).

All components must be clean and dry before assembly. Place aluminum housing assembly in holding fixture with input shaft (14) pointing downward. Install pump cam ring (20) and race (19) on pivot pin (13) and dowel pin (10). Insert (21) must be installed in cam ring with hole to outside. If insert is installed upside down, it will contact housing and interfere with assembly. Cam ring must move freely from stop to stop. Install pump rotor assembly and remove rubber band used to retain pistons. Install pintle assembly (46) over cam pivot pin and into pump rotor. Place new "O" ring (15) in position on housing. Lay housing assembly on its side on a clean surface. Place body assembly in holding fixture with output shaft pointing downward. Install motor race (33) in body, then install motor rotor assembly aligning rotor slot with drive pin (36) on output shaft. Remove rubber band used to retain pistons in rotor. Place body and motor assembly on its side on bench so motor rotor is facing pintle in housing assembly. Slide assemblies together and align the two assembly bolt holes. Install two assembly cap screws (29) and tighten them to a torque of 15 ft.-lbs. (20 N·m). Rotate input shaft and output shaft. Both shafts should rotate freely. If not, disassemble unit and correct problem.

Place unit in a holding fixture with reservoir opening and venting plug opening facing upward. Install reservoir or reservoir adapter. Fill unit with specified lubricant until fluid overflows out of venting plug hole. Rotate input shaft and output shaft to purge any trapped air from unit. Install venting plugs (31) and gasket (32). Torque plug to 2-5 ft.-lbs. (3-7 N·m).

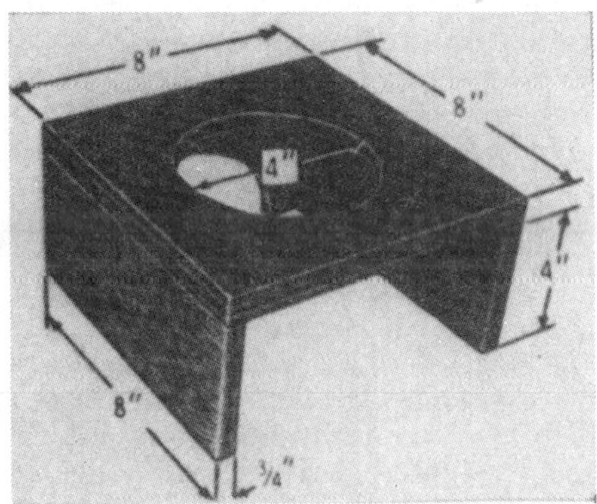


*Fig. EA12 – View showing dimensions of wooden stand used when disassembling and reassembling Eaton Model 6 hydrostatic transmission.*

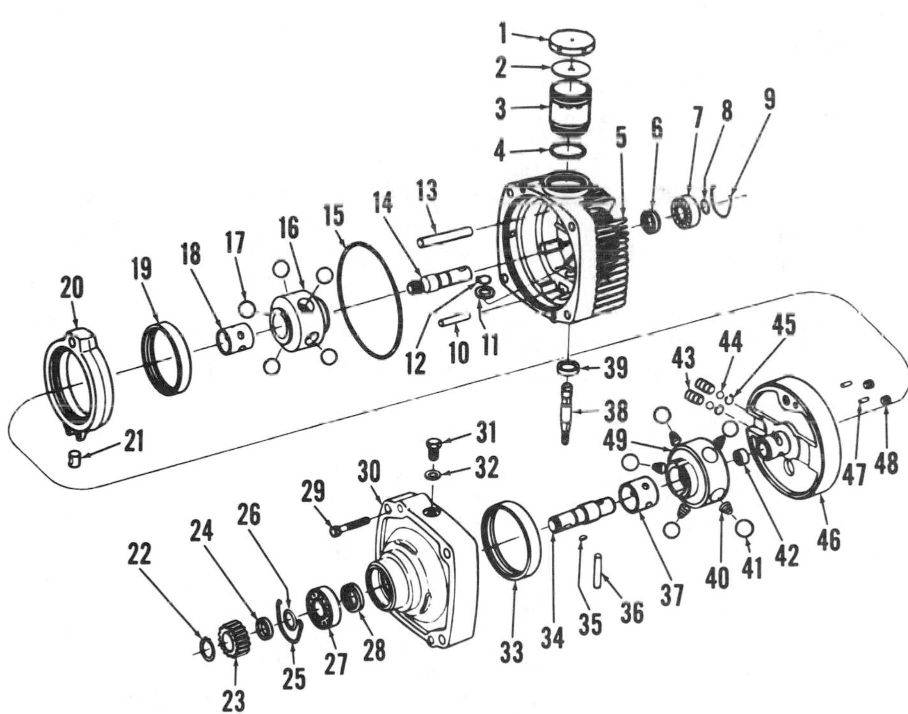


*Fig. EA11 – Exploded view of a typical Eaton Model 6 hydrostatic transmission. Oil expansion reservoir (3) may be mounted separately.*

1. Cover
2. Gasket
3. Reservoir
4. Gasket
5. Housing
6. Oil seal
7. Ball bearing
8. Snap ring
9. Retainer
10. Dowel pin
11. Washer
12. Snap ring
13. Cam pivot pin
14. Input shaft
15. "O" ring
16. Pump rotor
17. Pump ball pistons
18. Rotor bushing
19. Pump race
20. Pump cam ring
21. Insert
22. Snap ring
23. Output gear
24. Spacer
25. Retainer
26. Snap ring
27. Ball bearing
28. Oil seal
29. Cap screw
30. Body
31. Venting plug
32. Gasket
33. Motor race
34. Output shaft
35. Key
36. Drive pin
37. Rotor bushing
38. Control shaft
39. Oil seal
40. Springs
41. Motor ball pistons
42. Needle bearing
43. Directional check valve body
44. Check valve ball
45. Snap ring
46. Pintle
47. Roll pin
48. Plug
49. Motor rotor

## Model 7

**OVERHAUL.** Place transmission in a holding fixture with input shaft pointing up. Remove dust shield (1–Fig. EA15) and snap ring (3). Remove cap screws from charge pump body (7). One cap screw is ½ inch (12.7 mm) longer than the others and must be installed in original position. Remove charge pump body (7) with ball bearing (4). Ball bearing and oil seal (6) can be removed after removing retaining ring (2). Remove snap rings (5 and 8) and charge pump rotor assembly. Remove "O" rings (10) and pump plate (11). Turn hydrostatic unit over in fixture and remove output gear. Unscrew the two cap screws until two threads are engaged. Raise body (42) until it contacts cap screw heads. Insert a special fork tool (Fig. EA16) between motor rotor (39–Fig. EA15) and pintle (28). Remove cap screws, lift off body and motor assembly with fork tool and place assembly on a bench or in a holding fixture with output shaft pointing down. Remove fork and place a wider rubber band around motor rotor to hold ball pistons (38) in their bores. Carefully remove motor rotor assembly and lay aside for later disassembly. Remove motor race (41) and output shaft (40). Remove retainer (45), bearing (44) and oil seal (43). With housing assembly (12) resting in holding fixture, remove pintle assembly (28).

**CAUTION: Do not allow pump to raise with pintle as ball pistons (22) may fall out of rotor (21). Hold pump in position by inserting a finger through hole in pintle.**

Remove plug (37), spring (36) and charge relief ball (35). To remove directional check valves, it may be necessary to drill through pintle with a drill bit that will pass freely through roll pins. Redrill holes from opposite side with a ¼ inch drill bit. Press roll pin from pintle. Newer units are drilled at factory. Using a 5/16-18 tap, thread inside of valve bodies (34) then remove valve bodies using a draw bolt or slide hammer puller. Remove check valve balls (33) and retaining ring (32). To remove acceleration valves, remove retaining pin, insert a 3/16 inch (5 mm) rod 8 inches (203 mm) long through passage in pintle and carefully drive out spring (29), body (30) and ball (31). To remove dampening pistons (26), carefully tap outside edge of pintle on work bench to jar pistons free.

**NOTE: If pintle journal is damaged, pintle must be renewed.**

Remove pump cam ring (24) and pump race (23). Place a wide rubber band around pump rotor to prevent ball pistons (22) from falling out. Carefully remove pump assembly and input shaft (15).

To remove control shaft (19), drill a 11/32 inch hole through aluminum housing (12) directly in line with center line of dowel pin. Press dowel pin from control shaft, then withdraw control shaft. Remove oil seal (18). Thread drilled hole in housing with a ⅛ inch pipe tap. Apply a light coat of "Loctite" 635 to a ⅛ inch pipe plug, install plug and tighten until snug. Do no overtighten.

Number piston bores (1 through 5) on pump rotor and on motor rotor. Use a plastic ice cube tray or equivalent and mark cavities 1P through 5P for pump ball pistons and 1M through 5M for motor ball pistons. Remove ball pistons (22) one at a time, from pump rotor and place each ball in the correct cavity in tray. Remove ball pistons (38) and springs from motor rotor in the same manner.

Clean and inspect all parts and renew any showing excessive wear or other damage. Renew all gaskets, seals and "O" rings. Ball pistons are a select fit to 0.0002-0.0006 inch (0.0050-0.0152 mm) clearance in rotor bores and must be reinstalled in their original bores. If rotor bushing to pintle journal clearance is 0.002 inch (0.051 mm) or more, bushing wear or scoring is excessive and pump rotor or motor rotor must be renewed. Check clearance between input shaft (15) and housing bushing. Normal clearance is 0.0013-0.0033 inch

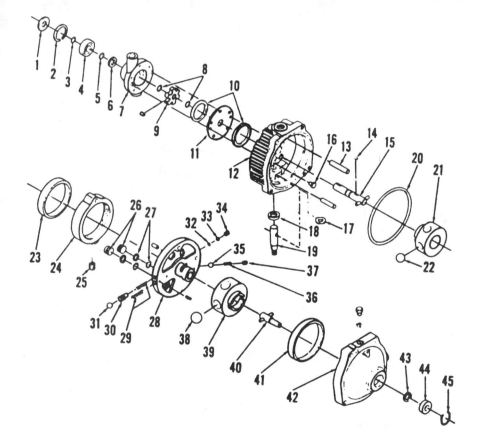

*Fig. EA15 – Exploded view of Eaton Model 7 hydrostatic transmission.*

1. Dust shield
2. Retaining ring
3. Snap ring
4. Ball bearing
5. Snap ring
6. Oil seal
7. Charge pump body
8. Snap ring
9. Charge pump rotor assy.
10. Square cut seals
11. Pump plate
12. Housing
13. Cam pivot pin
14. Key
15. Input shaft
16. Neutral spring cap
17. Washer
18. Oil seal
19. Control shaft
20. "O" ring
21. Pump rotor
22. Pump ball pistons
23. Pump race
24. Pump cam ring
25. Cam ring insert
26. Dampening pistons
27. "O" ring
28. Pintle
29. Spring
30. Acceleration valve body
31. Acceleration valve ball
32. Retaining ring
33. Check valve ball
34. Check valve body
35. Charge relief ball
36. Spring
37. Relief valve plug
38. Motor ball piston
39. Motor rotor
40. Output shaft
41. Motor race
42. Body
43. Oil seal
44. Ball bearing
45. Retainer

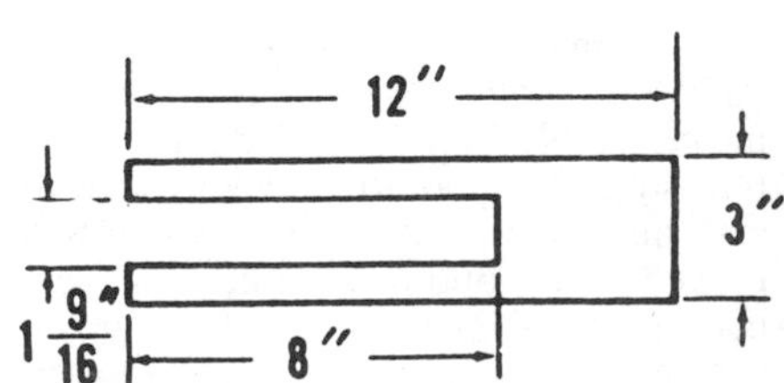


*Fig. EA16 – Special fork tool fabricated from a piece of ⅛ inch (3 mm) flat stock, used in disassembly and reassembly of hydrostatic transmission.*



Illustrations courtesy Eaton Corp.

(0.033-0.0838 mm). If clearance is excessive, renew input shaft and/or housing assembly.

Install ball pistons (22) in pump rotor (21) and ball pistons (38) and springs in motor rotor (39), then use wide rubber bands to hold pistons in their bores.

Install charge relief valve ball (35) and spring (36) in pintle. Screw plug (37) into pintle until just below outer surface of pintle. Install acceleration valve springs (29) and bodies (30) making sure valves move freely. Tap balls (31) into pintle until roll pins will go into place. Install snap rings (32), check valve balls (33) and valve bodies (34) in pintle and secure with new roll pins.

**NOTE: When installing oil seal (6, 18 or 43), apply a light coat of "Loctite" grade 635 to seal outer diameter.**

Renew oil seal (18) and install control shaft (19) in housing. Install special washer (17), then press dowel pin through control shaft until 1¼ inches (32 mm) of pin extends from control shaft. Renew oil seal (43) and reinstall output shaft (40), bearing (44), retainer (45), output gear and snap ring.

Insert input shaft (15) in housing (12). Install snap ring (8) in its groove on input shaft. Place "O" ring (10), pump plate (11) and "O" ring in housing, then install charge pump drive key (14). Apply light grease or "Vaseline" to pump rollers and place rollers in rotor slots. Install oil seal (6) and pump race in charge pump body (7), then install body assembly. Secure with the five cap screws, making certain long cap screw is installed in its original location (in heavy section of pump body). Tighten cap screws to 28-30 ft.-lbs. (38-41 N•m). Install snap ring (5), bearing (4), retaining ring (2), snap ring (3) and dust shield (1).

Place charge pump and housing assembly in a holding fixture with input shaft pointing downward. Install pump race (23) and insert (25) in cam ring (24), then install cam ring assembly over cam pivot pin (13) and control shaft dowel pin. Turn control shaft (19) back and forth and check movement of cam ring. Cam ring must move freely from stop to stop. If not, check installation of insert (25) in cam ring.

Install pump rotor assembly and remove rubber band used to retain pistons. Install pintle assembly (28) over cam pivot pin (13) and into pump rotor. Place "O" ring (20) in position on housing.

Place body assembly (42) in a holding fixture with output gear down. Install motor race (41) in body, then install motor rotor assembly and remove rubber band used to retain pistons in rotor.

Using special fork tool (Fig. EA16) to retain motor assembly in body, carefully install body and motor assembly over pintle journal. Remove fork tool, align bolt holes and install the two cap screws. Tighten cap screws to 15 ft.-lbs. (20 N•m).

Place hydrostatic unit on holding fixture with reservoir adapter opening and venting plug opening facing upward. Fill unit with recommened fluid until fluid flows from fitting hole in body. Plug all openings to prevent dirt or other foreign material from entering hydrostatic unit.

## Model 10 And Model 11

**OPERATION.** The Eaton Model 10 and Model 11 hydrostatic transmissions are composed of four major parts: A reversible flow, variable displacement, ball piston pump; a fixed displacement, ball piston motor; a system of valves located between pump and motor and a charge and auxiliary hydraulic supply pump. Tractor ground speed is regulated by changing amount of oil delivered by variable displacement pump. Moving speed control pedal in a forward direction will control forward ground speed range of 0-8 mph at full engine rpm. When speed control pedal is moved in reverse direction (depressed with heel), a reverse range of 0-4 mph is achieved.

The system operates as a closed loop type and any internal loss of oil from loop is replaced by oil from the charge pump. See Fig. EA20. This oil is forced into loop circuit through one of the directional check valves, depending on direction of travel. As more oil is pumped by charge pump than is needed to make up losses, all excess oil must pass through charge pressure relief valve and back into reservoir.

**OVERHAUL.** Before disassembling hydrostatic transmission, thoroughly clean exterior of unit. If so equipped, remove venting plug (59–Fig. EA21) and reservoir adapter (18 through 21), invert assembly and drain fluid from unit. Place unit in a holding fixture similar to one shown in Fig. EA22 so input shaft is pointing upward.

To disassemble, remove dust shield (1–Fig. EA21) and snap ring (3). Place an identifying mark across joining edges of each section to aid in correct placement and alignment during reassembly. Remove five cap screws from charge pump body (7). One cap screw is ½ inch longer than the others and must be reinstalled in original location (heavy section of pump body). Remove charge pump body (7) with ball bearing (4). Ball bearing and oil seal (6) can be removed from body (7) after first removing retaining ring (2). Remove six charge pump rollers (12), snap rings (5, 9 and 11) and charge pump rotor (10). Remove "O" rings (14 and 16) and pump plate (15). Invert drive unit in holding fixture so output shaft is pointing upward. Remove snap ring (65) and output gear (64). Unscrew two cap screws (60), then turn them in until two threads are engaged. Raise body (57) until it contacts heads of cap screws (60). Insert a fork tool between motor rotor (53) and pintle (48) until tool extends beyond opposite side. The

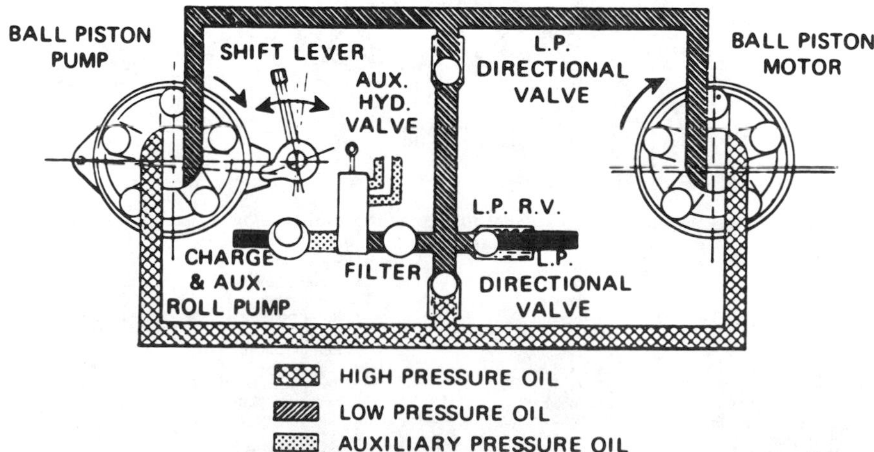


*Fig. EA20–Flow diagram for Eaton Model 10 hydrostatic transmission. Eaton Model 11 hydrostatic transmission is similar.*

special fork tool can be fabricated from a piece of 1/8 inch (3 mm) flat stock approximately 3 inches (76.2 mm) wide and 12 inches (304.8 mm) long. Cut a slot 1-9/16 inches (39.4 mm) wide and 8 inches (203.2 mm) long as shown in Fig. EA23. Taper ends of the prongs. Remove cap screws (60 – Fig. EA21) and by raising ends of forked tool, lift off body and motor assembly. Place removed assembly on a bench or in a holding fixture with output shaft pointing downward. Remove special fork tool and place a wide rubber band around motor rotor to hold ball pistons (51) and springs (52) in their bores. Carefully remove motor rotor assembly and lay aside for later disassembly. Remove motor race (56) and output shaft (55). **Remove retainer (63), bearing (62) and oil seal (61).**

With housing assembly (22) resting in holding fixture (input shaft pointing downward), remove pintle assembly (48).

**CAUTION: Do not allow pump to raise with pintle as ball pistons (35) may fall out of rotor (36).**

Hold pump in position by inserting a finger through hole in pintle. Remove plug (45), spring (46) and charge pump relief ball (47). To remove directional check valves from pintle (48), drill through pintle with a drill bit that will pass freely through roll pins (41). Redrill holes from opposite side with a 1/4 inch drill bit. Drive or press roll pins from pintle. Using a 5/16-18 tap, thread inside of valve bodies (44), then remove valve bodies using a draw bolt or a slide hammer puller. Remove check valve balls (43) and snap rings (42). Do not remove plugs (40).

Remove pump cam ring (39) and pump race (38). Place a wide rubber band around pump rotor to prevent ball pistons (35) from falling out. Carefully remove pump assembly and input shaft (33).

To remove control shaft (25), drill a 11/32 inch hole through aluminum housing (22) directly in line with center line of dowel pin (27). Press dowel pin from control shaft, then withdraw control shaft. Remove oil seal (24). Thread drilled hole in housing with a 1/8 inch pipe tap. Apply a light coat of "Loctite" grade 635 to a 1/8 inch pipe plug, install plug and tighten it until snug.

Number piston bores (1 through 5) on pump rotor and on motor rotor. Use a plastic ice cube tray or equivalent and mark cavities 1P through 5P for pump ball pistons and 1M through 5M for motor ball pistons. Remove ball pistons (35) one at a time, from pump rotor and place each ball in correct cavity in tray. Remove ball pistons (51) and springs (52) from motor rotor in same manner.

Clean and inspect all parts and renew any showing excessive wear or other damage. Ball pistons are selective fitted to 0.0002-0.0006 inch (0.0051-0.0152 mm) clearance in rotor bores and must be reinstalled in their original bores. If rotor bushings (37 or 50) are scored or badly worn (0.002 inch [0.051 mm] or more clearance on pintle journals), renew pump rotor or motor rotor assemblies. Check clearance between input shaft (33) and housing bushing (17). Normal clearance is 0.0013-0.0033 inch

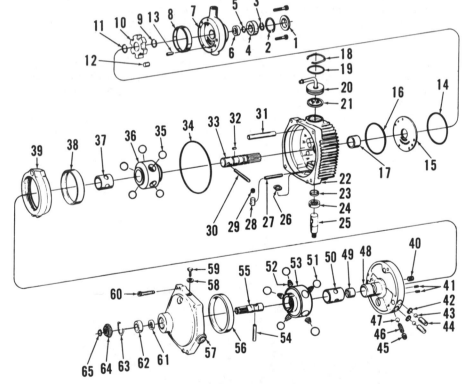

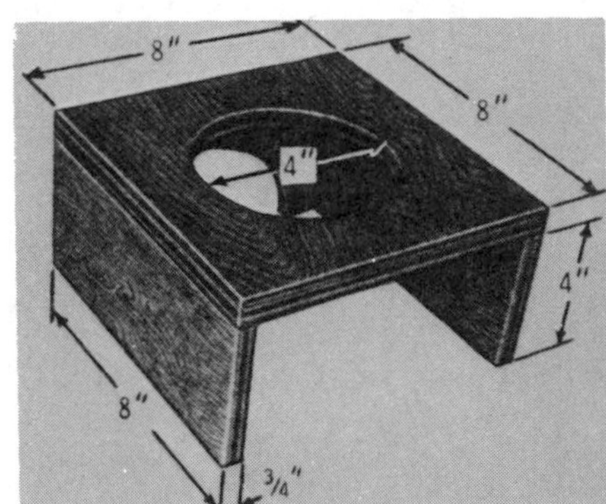


***Fig. EA22 – View showing dimensions of wooden stand used when disassembling and reassembling Eaton Model 10 or Model 11 hydrostatic transmission.***

***Fig. EA21 – Exploded view of Eaton Model 10 hydrostatic transmission. Eaton Model 11 hydrostatic transmission is similar.***

1. Dust shield
2. Retaining ring
3. Snap ring
4. Ball bearing
5. Snap ring
6. Oil seal
7. Charge pump body
8. Charge pump race
9. Snap ring
10. Charge pump rotor
11. Snap ring
12. Pump roller (6 used)
13. Dowel pin
14. "O" ring
15. Pump plate
16. "O" ring
17. Bushing
18. Retainer
19. "O" ring
20. Reservoir adapter
21. Screen
22. Housing
23. Bushing
24. Oil seal
25. Control shaft
26. Washer
27. Dowel pin
28. Insert
29. Insert cap
30. Drive pin
31. Cam pivot pin
32. Charge pump drive key
33. Input shaft
34. "O" ring
35. Pump ball pistons
36. Pump rotor
37. Rotor housing
38. Pump race
39. Pump cam ring
40. Plug (2 used)
41. Roll pins
42. Snap ring (2 used)
43. Check valve ball (2 used)
44. Directional check valve body (2 used)
45. Plug
46. Relief spring
47. Charge relief ball
48. Pintle
49. Needle bearing
50. Rotor bushing
51. Motor ball pistons
52. Springs
53. Motor rotor
54. Drive pin
55. Output shaft
56. Motor race
57. Body
58. Gasket
59. Venting plug
60. Cap screw
61. Oil seal
62. Ball bearing
63. Retainer
64. Output gear
65. Snap ring

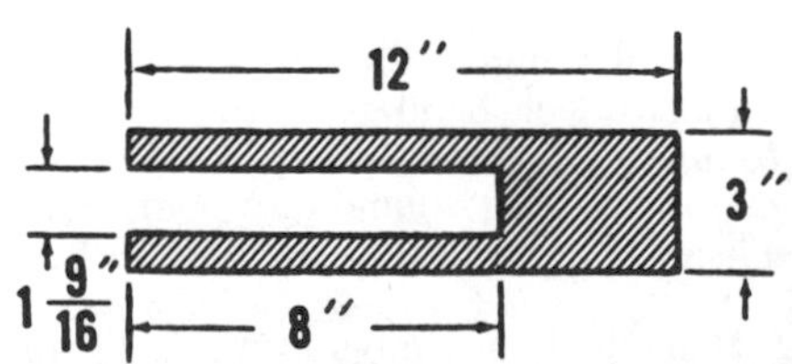


***Fig. EA23 – A special fork tool for disassembly and reassembly of Eaton Model 10 or Model 11 hydrostatic transmission can be made from a piece of 1/8 inch (3 mm) flat bar stock using dimensions shown.***



Illustrations courtesy Eaton Corp.

(0.0330-0.0838 mm). If clearance is excessive, renew input shaft and/or housing assembly.

Install ball pistons (35) in pump rotor (36) and ball pistons (51) and springs (52) in motor rotor (53), then use wide rubber bands to hold pistons in their bores. Install snap rings (42), check valve balls (43) and valve bodies (44) in pintle (48) and secure with new roll pins (41). Install charge pump relief valve ball (47), spring (46) and plug (45). When installing oil seals (6, 24 or 61), apply a light coat of "Loctite" grade 635 to seal outer diameter. Renew oil seal (24) and install control shaft (25) in housing. Install special washer (26), then press dowel pin (27) into control shaft until end of dowel pin extends 1¼ inches (28.5 mm) from control shaft. Renew oil seal (61) and reinstall output shaft (55) with drive pin (54), bearing (62), retainer (63), output gear (64) and snap ring (65) in body (57).

Insert input shaft (33) with drive pin (30) through bushing (17) in housing. Install snap ring (11) in its groove on input shaft. Place "O" ring (16), pump plate (15) and "O" ring (14) in housing, then install charge pump drive key (32), charge pump rotor (10) and snap ring (9). Apply light grease or Vaseline to pump rollers (12) and place rollers in rotor slots. Install oil seal (6) and pump race (8) in charge pump body (7), then install body assembly. Secure with five cap screws, making certain long cap screw is installed in its original location (in heavy section of pump body). Tighten cap screws to a torque of 28-30 ft.-lbs. (38-41 N•m). Install snap ring (5), bearing (4), retaining ring (2), snap ring (3) and dust shield (1).

Place charge pump and housing assembly in a holding fixture with input shaft pointing downward. Install pump race (38), insert cap (29) and insert (28) in cam ring (39), then install cam ring assembly over cam pivot pin (31) and control shaft dowel pin (27). Turn control shaft (25) back and forth and check movement of cam ring. Cam ring must move freely from stop to stop. If not, check installation of insert (28) and insert cap (29) in cam ring.

Install pump rotor assembly and remove rubber band used to retain pistons. Install pintle assembly (48) over cam pivot pin (31) and into pump rotor. Place "O" ring (34) in piston on housing.

Place body assembly (57) in a holding fixture with gear (64) downward. Install motor race (56) in body, then install motor rotor assembly and remove rubber band used to retain pistons in rotor.

Using special fork tool (Fig. EA23) to retain motor assembly in body, carefully install body and motor assembly over pintle journal. Remove fork tool, align bolt holes and install two cap screws (60–Fig. EA21). Tighten cap screws to 15 ft.-lbs. (20 N•m).

Place hydrostatic unit on holding fixture with reservoir adapter opening and venting plug opening facing upward. Fill unit with hydraulic oil or Type "A" automatic transmission fluid until fluid flows from fitting hole in body. Install venting plug (59) with gasket (58), then install reservoir adapter (20), screen (21), "O" ring (19) and retainer (18). Plug all openings to prevent dirt or other foreign material from entering hydrostatic unit.

## Model 12

**OPERATION.** The Eaton Model 12 hydrostatic transmission has four major parts: A reversible flow, variable displacement, radial piston pump; a fixed displacement, gear motor; a system of valves located between pump and motor; and a charge and auxiliary hydraulic supply pump. Tractor ground speed is regulated by changing oil delivery of variable displacement pump. Moving speed control pedal in a forward direction will control forward ground speed range of 0-8 mph at full engine rpm. When speed control pedal is moved in reverse direction (depressed with heel), a reverse range of 0-4 mph is achieved.

The system operates as a closed loop type and any internal loss of oil from loop is replaced by oil from the charge pump. See Fig. EA25. This oil is forced into loop circuit through one of the directional check valves, depending on direction of travel. As more oil is pumped by the charge pump than is needed to make up losses, all excess oil must pass through charge pressure relief valve and back into reservoir.

The system is protected by a high pressure relief valve located in the circuit after high pressure directional valve. Since a pressure operated directional valve is used, high pressure relief valve will protect circuit whether it is operating in forward or reverse direction.

An unloading valve actuated by a selector lever is used to achieve a neutral or free-wheeling position and oil from gear motor is dumped back into reservoir. This makes it possible to move the tractor when in NEUTRAL while engine is not operating. With selector valve in PARK, unloading valve is also open. However, tractor cannot be moved in this position as parking pawl is engaged. When selector lever is in DRIVE, unloading valve is closed completing closed loop circuit.

**OVERHAUL.** The Eaton Model 12 hydrostatic transmission was serviced as a direct exchange package only. No detailed service procedures have been released for publication. Operation of this hydrostatic transmission and its flow diagram (Fig. EA25) are covered in preceding OPERATION section. Any attempt to overhaul this model hydrostatic transmission is discouraged, mainly due to limited parts service, even to such basic items as gaskets and seals.

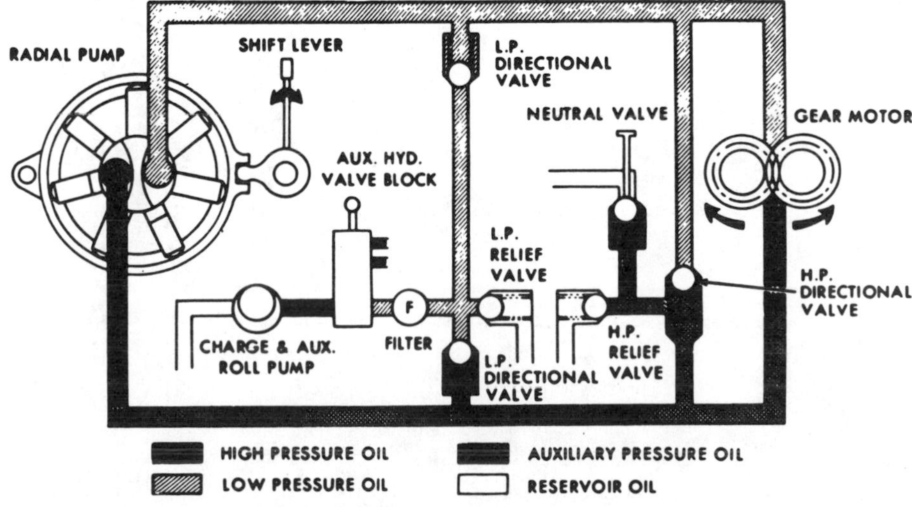

*Fig. EA25—Flow diagram of Eaton Model 12 hydrostatic transmission.*

## Models 750 and 850

**OPERATION.** The Eaton Models 750 and 850 hydrostatic transmissions use a variable displacement, reversible flow, ball piston pump and two fixed displacement, ball piston motors to provide infinite speed and torque output. The Model 850 is also equipped with a charge pump and an oil filter.

On both models, tractor ground speed is regulated by changing the oil delivery of the variable displacement pump. This is accomplished by changing the position of the cam ring in which the pump ball pistons operate. The system operates as a closed loop type. Any oil that is lost from the closed loop is replaced by oil from the reservoir. On Model 750, the hydrostatic pump draws oil directly into suction side of the loop from the reservoir through one of the directional check valves located in each side of the loop. On Model 850, the charge pump forces oil into suction side of the loop through one of the directional check valves, depending on direction of rotation.

**TROUBLE-SHOOTING.** The following problems and possible causes should be used as an aid in locating and correcting transmission problems.

1. Loss of power or transmission will not operate in either direction. Could be caused by:
   a. Drive belt slipping or broken.
   b. Speed control linkage broken.
   c. Transmission oil level low.
   d. Wrong type of transmission oil or oil contaminated with water.
   e. Transmission oil temperature too hot.
   f. Transmission roll release valve in wrong position.
   g. Oil filter plugged.
   h. Charge pump or charge pressure relief valve faulty.
   i. Transmission pump and/or motor worn or damaged.
   j. Drive pulley slipping on transmission input shaft.
   k. Internal damage to reduction gear assembly.

2. Transmission operating too hot. Could be caused by:
   a. Transmission oil level low.
   b. Wrong type of oil in transmission.
   c. Cooling fan defective.
   d. Transmission cooling fins blocked.
   e. Roll release valve faulty.
   f. Tractor is being overloaded.
   g. Transmission pump and/or motor worn.

3. Transmission jerks when starting or operates in one direction only. Could be caused by:
   a. Faulty speed control linkage.
   b. Faulty charge check valve.

4. Tractor creeps when in neutral. Could be caused by:
   a. Worn or misadjusted control linkage.

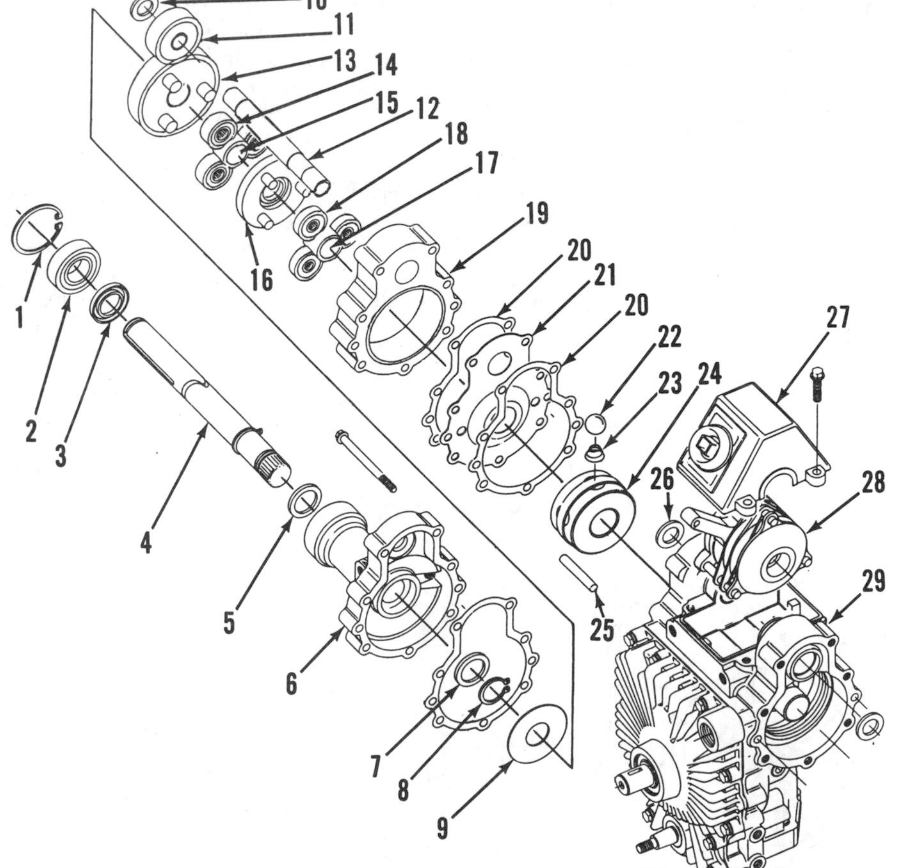


*Fig. EA30—Exploded view of Eaton 850 hydrostatic transaxle assembly. Model 750 is similar.*

1. Snap ring
2. Bearing
3. Seal
4. Axle shaft
5. Thrust washer
6. Axle housing
7. Thrust washer
8. Snap ring
9. Thrust washer
10. Spacer
11. Brake gear
12. Brake shaft
13. Planetary carrier
14. Planetary gear (second)
15. Sun gear (second)
16. Planetary carrier
17. Sun gear (first)
18. Planetary gear (first)
19. Ring gear
20. Gaskets
21. Wear plate
22. Ball piston
23. Spring
24. Motor rotor
25. Dowel
26. Seal
27. Brake cover
28. Parking brake assy.
29. Transmission housing

**OVERHAUL.** Disassembly of Model 750 and Model 850 transmissions is similar except that oil filter assembly and charge pump are not used on Model 750. Prior to disassembly, remove fan, pulley, and all external brackets, levers and fittings. Thoroughly clean outside of unit. Drain oil from unit, and if equipped, remove oil filter and detach oil filter base. During disassembly, mark components so they may be returned to their original position.

The axle housing assemblies must be removed to gain access to the hydrostatic motors (24—Fig. EA30). Service procedure is the same for either axle housing assembly. Remove cap screws securing axle housing (6) and withdraw axle housing and planetary assembly (components 1 through 21) from hydrostatic housing (29).

**CAUTION: Be very careful not to dislodge hydrostatic motor assembly. The spring-loaded balls (22) are a selective fit in motor rotor (24) and must be installed in matching bore in rotor if removed.**

To disassemble axle assembly, remove wear plate (21), first planetary assembly (16, 17 and 18), ring gear (19), brake gear (11) and second planetary assembly (13, 14 and 15). Remove large thrust washer (9), snap ring (8) and small thrust washer (7) from axle shaft. Remove outer snap ring (1), then remove axle shaft (4), oil seal (3) and bearing (2) from axle housing (6) by tapping on splined end of shaft with a soft hammer.

Detach brake housing (27) and remove parking brake assembly (28) being careful not to move brake lever. The brake is self-adjusting and moving lever will expand brake assembly making installation more difficult. Brake assembly is available only as a unit and should not be disassembled.

To remove hydrostatic motors, place a large rubber band or similar device around the motor rotor (24) to hold spring-loaded ball pistons (22) in their bores. Carefully withdraw motor assembly. Due to selective fit, if balls are removed they must be returned to original rotor bore.

To disassemble hydrostatic pump, unbolt and remove oil filter base (53—Fig. EA31) from housing on Model 850. On all models, unscrew fasteners retaining pump cover (35) to housing (47). Note that there is a screw located in the drain hole. Separate cover from housing and remove snap ring (30). Tap or press input shaft (32) and bearing (31) out of cover by forcing shaft towards outside of cover. Shaft and bearing assembly is available only as a unit assembly. Drive input shaft seal (33) out of cover bore. Remove charge pressure relief valve spring (45) and ball (46). Remove buttons (36), control shaft (37) and cam ring insert (38) from cam ring (40). Remove pump rotor drive ring (41). Place a wide rubber band or similar device around pump rotor (42) to hold the ball pistons (43) in their bores. The balls are a selective fit in rotor and must be installed in their matching bore if removed from rotor. Carefully lift pump rotor from housing.

Dump valve bracket (51) can be removed from housing after removing nut (48). Check valves (Fig. EA32) should be flushed with suitable solvent, but not removed, and are available only with housing. Removal of dampening pistons (39—Fig. EA31) is also not recommended.

On Model 850, charge pump assembly (1—Fig. EA33) may be removed from housing for inspection after removing pump plate (2). Charge pump components are available only with the housing (47) as an assembly.

Inspect components for excessive wear and damage. When removing ball pistons from pump and motor rotors, number rotor bores and place balls in a plastic ice cube tray or egg carton with cavities numbered to correspond to rotor bores. Piston balls and rotor bores must be smooth and free of any irregularities. Pump and motor rotors and balls are unit assemblies as balls are selectively fitted to rotor bores.

Assemble by referring to appropriate exploded view and reversing disassembly procedure while noting the following: Lubricate all assemblies with clean transmission oil. Install dump valve spring (52—Fig. EA31) so right angle bend points toward "O" ring (50). Tighten dump valve nut (48) to 150 in.-lbs. (17 N·m). Install charge pump cover (Model 850) so arrow (A—Fig. EA33) points toward "CW" on housing. Do not tight-

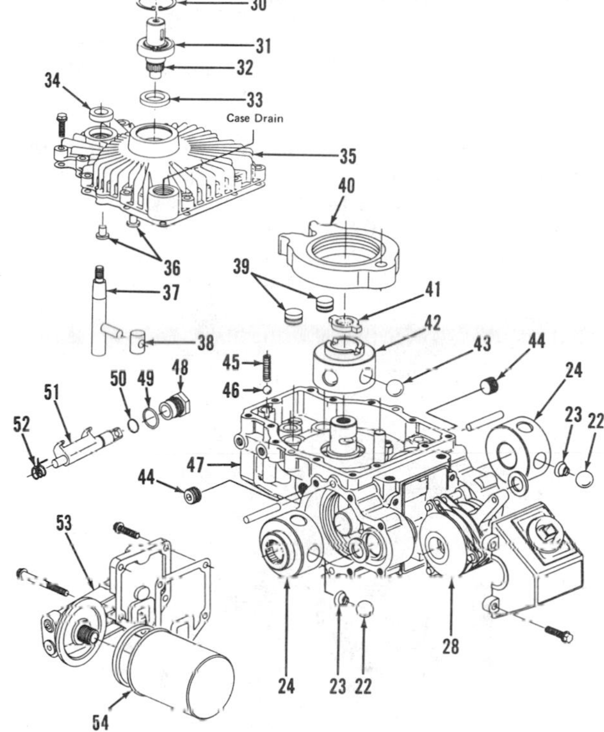

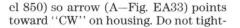

*Fig. EA31—Exploded view of pump and housing components on Eaton 850 hydrostatic transmission. Filter assembly (53 and 54) and charge pressure relief valve (45 and 46) are not used on Model 750 transmission.*

22. Ball piston
23. Spring
24. Motor rotor
28. Brake assy.
30. Snap ring
31. Bearing
32. Input shaft assy.
33. Oil seal
34. Oil seal
35. Cover
36. Buttons
37. Control shaft
38. Insert
39. Dampening pistons
40. Cam ring
41. Drive ring
42. Pump rotor
43. Ball piston
44. Plugs
45. Charge relief valve spring
46. Charge relief valve ball
47. Housing
48. Plug
49. "O" ring
50. "O" ring
51. Dump valve bracket
52. Spring
53. Oil filter base
54. Oil filter

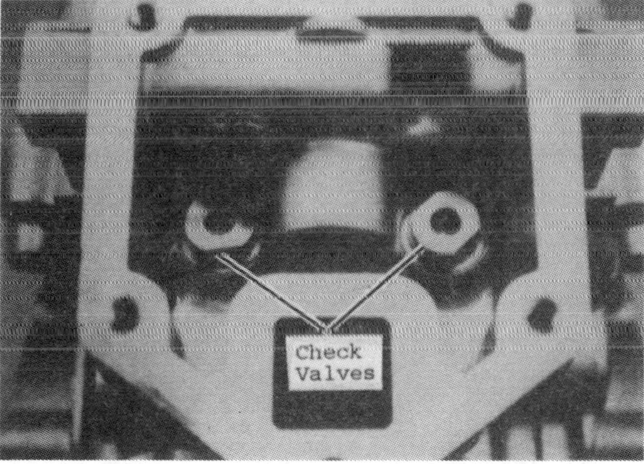


*Fig. EA32—Check valves are available only with hydrostatic housing and should be flushed, but not removed.*

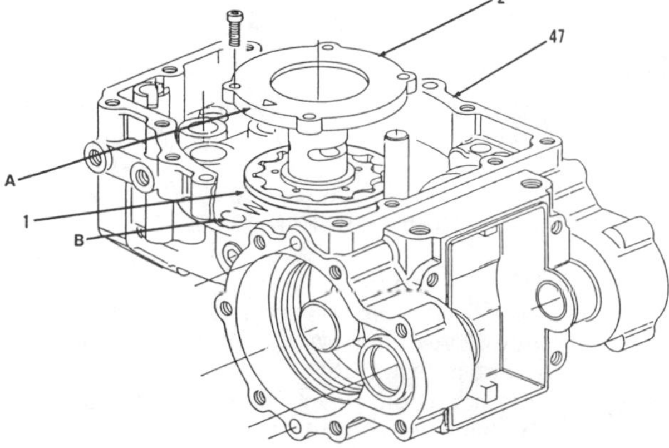


*Fig. EA33—On Model 850, install charge pump cover (2) so arrow (A) points toward "CW" on housing.*

en cover screws until pump rotor is installed. Note that pins on bottom of pump rotor (42—Fig. EA31) must engage holes in charge pump inner rotor. Rotate pump rotor clockwise to center pump cover then tighten cover screws in a crossing pattern to 44 in.-lbs. (5.0 N·m). Install cam ring (40) so flush side is out. Install seals (33 and 34) so lip is to inside of cover. Be sure snap ring (30) is firmly seated in cover after installing input shaft assembly (32). Hold buttons (36) in place with petroleum jelly. Be sure charge relief valve ball (46) is not dislodged when installing cover assembly on housing. Splines on input shaft must engage splines of drive ring (41); do not force cover onto housing. Tighten cover screws to 105 in.-lbs. (11.9 N·m) using pattern shown in Fig. EA34. Carefully install motor rotors in housing and remove rubber band used to retain ball pistons in rotors.

Install brake assembly (28—Fig. EA30) so lever is toward cover side of housing. Note that axle housings and sides of transaxle housing are identified with an "A" or "B" as shown in Fig. EA35. The "B" side of transaxle should be assembled first. Note that "B" side brake shaft (12—Fig. EA30) is longer than the "A" side shaft. Insert the "B" side brake shaft into the brake assembly and rotate so the splines are engaged. Install "A" side brake shaft. When both shafts are properly installed, the shafts will rotate independently.

Install axle components while noting the following: Inner sun gear (17—Fig. EA30) is taller than outer sun gear (15). Install ring gear (19) so side with needle bearing mates with axle housing (6). Install outer sun gear (15) so convex (pointed) end is towards inner sun gear (17). Install axle housing seal (3) so lip points inward. Install wear plate (21) so bowed side is facing motor rotor. Tighten axle housing screws to 125 in.-lbs. (14 N·m). Tighten oil filter base screws to 125 in.-lbs. (14 N·m).

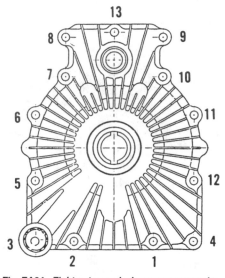

*Fig. EA34—Tighten transmission cover screws to 105 in.-lbs. (11.9 N·m) using sequence shown above.*

*Fig. EA35—Note that axle housings and sides of transaxle housing are identified with an "A" or "B" as shown above. Refer to text.*

# HYDRO-GEAR

## Series BDU-10

**OPERATION.** The hydrostatic transmission consists of a variable volume, reversible swashplate, axial piston pump connected in a closed loop to a fixed displacement, axial piston motor. The hydrostatic pump is driven by the engine, and the motor is connected to the gear reduction and differential assembly.

The hydrostatic pump inlet is connected to the reservoir (transmission housing), allowing the pump to make-up any oil that is lost from the closed loop system during operation. Make-up oil is drawn from the reservoir through an oil filter screen that is mounted in the hydrostatic transmission housing.

Hydrostatic motor speed is controlled by hydrostatic pump rpm and the angle of pump swashplate. As the angle of pump swashplate is increased from the zero degree (neutral) position, the length of each pump piston stroke increases and more oil is pumped to the motor. Since the motor is a fixed displacement unit, it must turn faster in order to accept the increased flow from the pump. When pump swashplate angle decreases, the opposite effect takes place and motor speed decreases.

The hydrostatic pump turns in the same direction all the time. The hydrostatic motor is capable of turning in both directions. Motor direction of rotation is reversed by reversing pump swashplate angle which reverses the flow of oil being pumped to the motor. When control lever is in neutral position, there is no pump swashplate tilt and no pump piston stroke.

**TROUBLE-SHOOTING.** When trouble-shooting the hydrostatic drive system, always check the easiest and most obvious items first. Some problems which may occur during operation of hydrostatic transmission and their possible causes are as follows:



Illustrations courtesy Eaton Corp.

A. Lack of drive or limited speed in both directions. Could be caused by:

1. Broken or misadjusted control linkage.
2. Transmission drive belt (if used) slipping or broken.
3. Bypass valve stuck open or leaking.
4. Low oil level.
5. Oil filter screen plugged.
6. Internal leakage of high pressure fluid due to excessive wear of pump and/or motor.
7. Failure of reduction drive or differential components.

B. Lack of drive or limited speed in one direction. Could be caused by:

1. Movement of pump swashplate being restricted in one direction.
2. Charge check valve not seating.

**OVERHAUL.** To disassemble transmission, remove transmission control arm. Unscrew (left-hand threads) oil reservoir (16—Fig. HG49) and drain oil from transmission housing. Unbolt and separate end cover (32) from housing (17), being careful not to damage machined surfaces of end cover and pump and motor cylinder blocks. Remove check valves (26) and bypass valve (29) from end cover. Pry out oil seals (30 and 31).

Position housing (17) on its side and slide out pump cylinder block (34) with pistons and motor cylinder block (27) with pistons. The motor shaft (23)

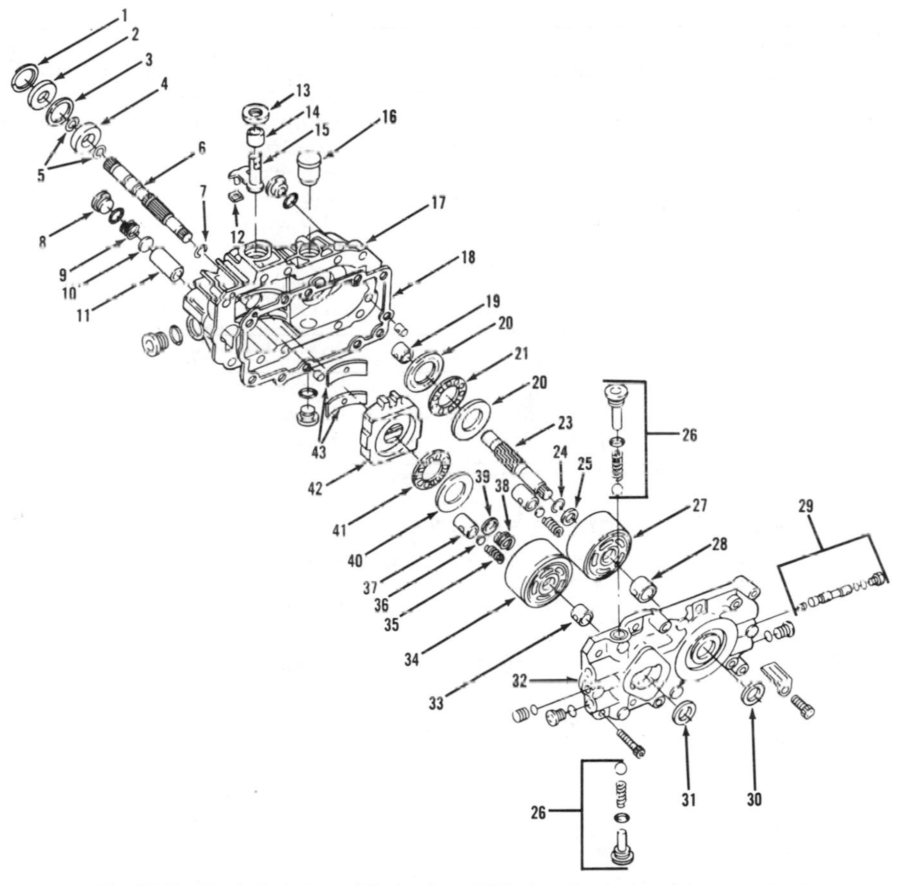


*Fig. HG49—Exploded view of Hydro-Gear BDU-10 series hydrostatic transmission.*

1. Retaining ring
2. Oil seal
3. Spacer
4. Ball bearing
5. Retaining rings
6. Pump shaft
7. Retaining ring
8. Plug
9. Spring
10. Washer
11. Filter
12. Slot guide
13. Oil seal
14. Bearing
15. Trunnion arm
16. Reservoir
17. Transmission housing
18. Gasket
19. Bearing
20. Thrust washers
21. Thrust bearing
23. Motor shaft
24. Retaining ring
25. Washer
26. Check valves
27. Motor cylinder block
28. Bearing
29. Bypass valve assy.
30. Oil seal
31. Oil seal
32. End cover
33. Bearing
34. Pump cylinder block
35. Spring
36. Seat
37. Piston
38. Spring
39. Washer
40. Thrust washer
41. Thrust bearing
42. Swashplate
43. Bearings

should slide out with the motor cylinder block. Remove motor thrust plates (20) and bearing (21). Remove spring (38), washer (39) and pump swashplate (42) with thrust plate (40) and bearing (41).

Remove slot guide (12) and the cradle bearings (43). Remove filter screen (11), washer (10) and spring (9). Remove retaining ring (1) and pry out oil seal (2), taking care not to damage pump shaft or housing. Tap inner end of pump shaft (6) with a soft hammer to remove shaft and bearing (4) from housing. Withdraw trunnion arm (15) and pry oil seal (13) from housing.

Inspect pistons and cylinder bores for excessive wear, scoring or other damage. Pump and motor cylinder blocks are serviced as complete assemblies. Check polished surfaces of end cover (32) and cylinder blocks for wear, scoring or scratches. End cover and cylinder blocks must be renewed if wear exceeds 0.0004 inch (0.01 mm). Inspect check valve balls and their seats for damage or wear and renew as necessary. Renew all "O" rings and oil seals.

Coat parts with oil during reassembly. To reassemble, reverse the disassembly procedure. Be sure that pistons are returned to their original bores in cylinder blocks and that they slide freely in cylinder block. Tighten end cover mounting screws evenly to 140-165 in.-lbs. (15.7-18.6 N·m).

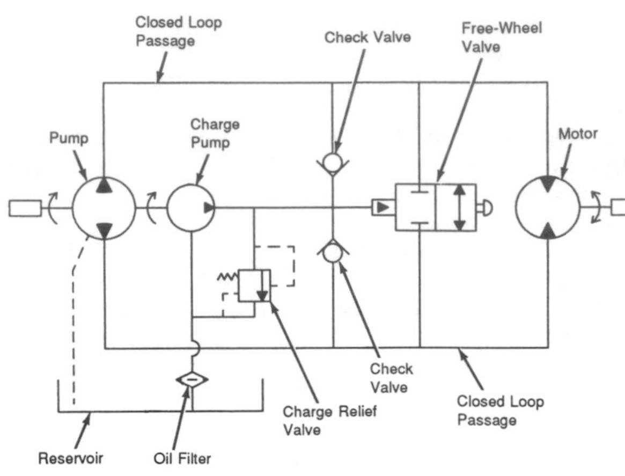


*Fig. HG50—Circuit diagram of Hydro-Gear Series BDU-21 hydrostatic transmission.*

## Series BDU-21

**OPERATION.** The hydrostatic transmission consists of a variable volume, reversible swashplate, axial piston pump connected in a closed loop to a fixed displacement, axial piston motor. Any oil lost internally from closed loop system is replaced by oil from the charge pump. See Fig. HG50. This make-up oil is drawn from the reservoir through an oil filter and is pumped through the check valve on low pressure side of hydrostatic loop. All excess charge oil passes through charge pressure regulator valve and is relieved to suction side of charge pump.

Hydrostatic motor speed is controlled by hydrostatic pump rpm and the angle of pump swashplate. As the angle of pump swashplate is increased from the zero degree (neutral) position, the length of each pump piston stroke increases and more oil is pumped to the motor. Since the motor is a fixed displacement unit, it must turn faster in order to accept the increased flow from the pump. When pump swashplate angle decreases, the opposite effect takes place and motor speed decreases.

The hydrostatic pump turns in the same direction all the time. The hydrostatic motor is capable of turning in both directions. Motor direction of rotation is reversed by reversing pump swashplate angle which reverses the flow of oil being pumped to the motor. When control lever is in neutral position, there is no pump swashplate tilt and no pump piston stroke.

A free-wheeling valve is included in the system to allow oil to bypass the pump when unit is moved without the engine running. The free-wheeling valve connects both sides of the closed loop together so there will not be a pressure build-up from the motor as it is turned by the differential.

**TROUBLE-SHOOTING.** When trouble-shooting the hydrostatic drive system, always check the easiest and most obvious items first. Some problems which may occur during operation of hydrostatic transmission and their possible causes are as follows:

A. Lack of drive or limited speed in both directions. Could be caused by:

1. Broken or misadjusted control linkage.
2. Transmission drive belt (if used) slipping or broken.
3. Free-wheeling valve stuck open or leaking.
4. Low oil level.
5. Oil filter plugged.
6. Charge pump or charge relief valve faulty.
7. Internal leakage of high pressure fluid due to excessive wear of pump and/or motor.
8. Failure of reduction drive or differential components.

B. Lack of drive or limited speed in one direction. Could be caused by:

1. Movement of pump swashplate being restricted in one direction.
2. Charge check valve not seating.

**OVERHAUL.** Before disassembling transmission, thoroughly clean exterior of unit. Scribe a line on charge pump housing (1—Fig. HG51) and center section (54) to ensure correct reassembly.

Unbolt and remove charge pump housing (1). Remove pump rotors (3), charge relief valve (4) and drive pin (39). Remove screws securing center section (54) and separate center section from housing (48). Remove check valves (12 through 15), free-wheeling valve (8 through 10) and plugs (7) as shown in Fig. HG51, being careful not to interchange parts or lose shims.

Position housing (48) on its side. Remove pump cylinder block (17) and piston assembly. Remove motor cylinder block (31) and piston assembly and shaft. Lay cylinder block assemblies aside for later disassembly.

**NOTE: Pump and motor pistons (21) must be identified prior to removal so they can be reinstalled in original cylinder bore. Do not lose ball (20) in each piston.**

Remove thrust washer (24), thrust bearing (25), thrust washer (26), swashplate (28) and bearings (29). Remove snap ring (45) and extract input shaft (40) assembly. Remove control arm (49).

Inspect components for damage and excessive wear. Inspect pistons and cylinder bores for scoring and scratches. Inspect mating surfaces of center section and pump and motor cylinder blocks for scratches or excessive wear. If scratches or wear can be detected by moving your fingernail or a soft lead pencil across the mating surfaces, components should be renewed. Inspect check valves for nicks and scratches. Maximum allowable clearance between tip of charge pump inner rotor and lobe of outer rotor is 0.13 mm (0.005 in.). See

Fig. HG52. Use straightedge and feeler gage to check end clearance between rotors (3—Fig. HG51) and pump housing (1). Maximum allowable rotor end clearance is 0.05 mm (0.002 in.). Inspect charge pump rotors and face of center section (54) for scoring and scratches.

Coat parts with transmission oil during assembly. Be sure pistons are returned to original bore in cylinders. Note that thrust washer (26) is thinner than thrust washer (24). Press bearing (16) into cover (54) so bearing is bottomed. Press bearing (30) into cover until flush with seal seat. Bottom seal (5) in housing. Install charge pump cover so flat edge (F—Fig. HG52) of cover is toward control arm side of transmission. Tighten charge pump housing screws to 11 N·m (97 in.-lbs.).

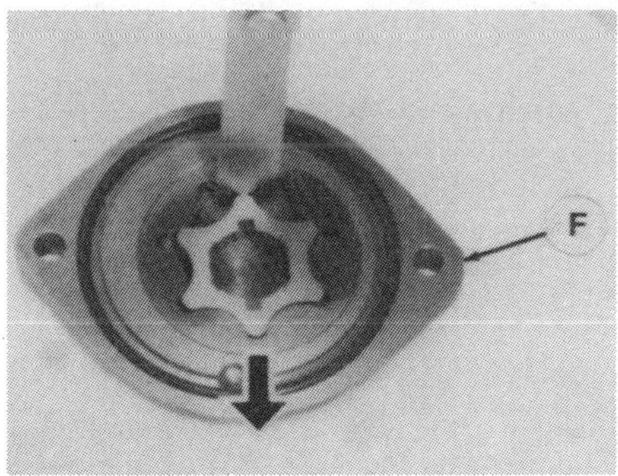


*Fig. HG52—Check clearance between tip of inner rotor and lobe of outer rotor, and between surface of pump housing and face of rotors. Refer to text for specifications. Install charge pump housing so flat edge (F) is toward control arm side of transmission.*

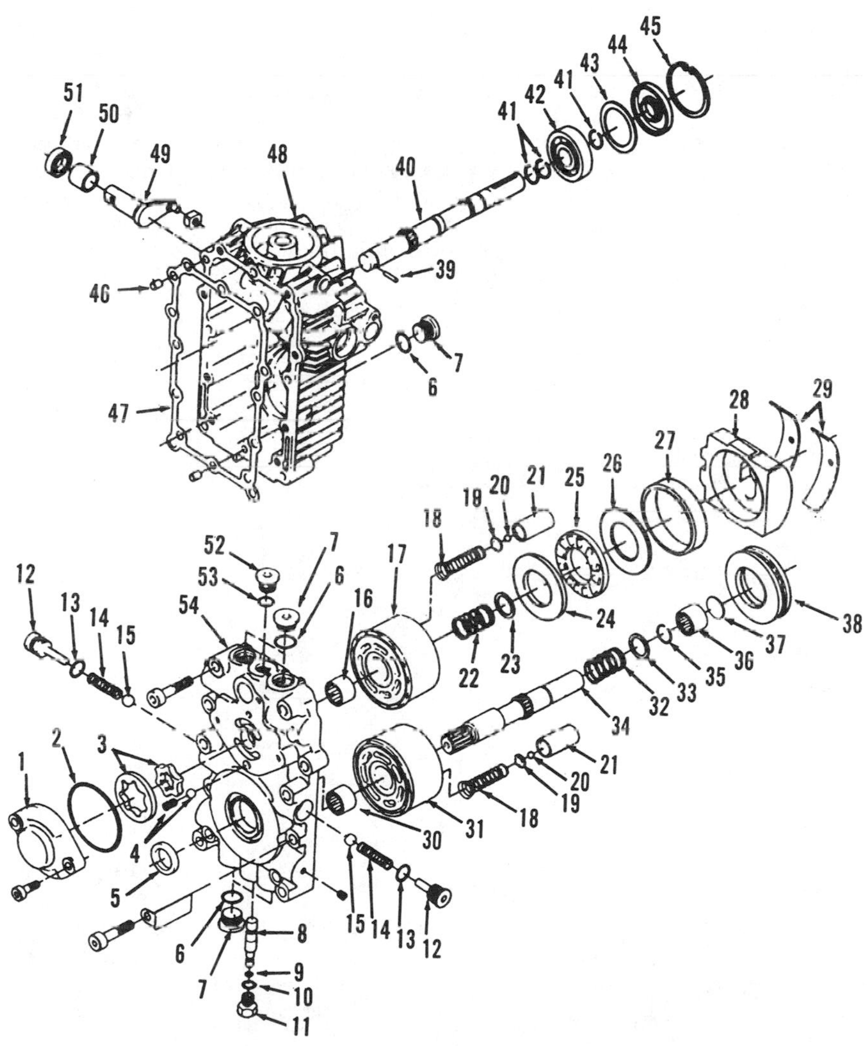


*Fig. HG51—Exploded view of Hydro-Gear BDU-21 hydrostatic transmission.*

1. Charge pump housing
2. "O" ring
3. Pump rotors
4. Charge relief valve
5. Seal
6. "O" ring
7. Plug
8. Free-wheeling valve
9. "O" ring
10. "O" ring
11. Plug
12. Plug
13. "O" ring
14. Spring
15. Check valve
16. Bearing
17. Cylinder block
18. Spring
19. Spring seat
20. Ball
21. Piston
22. Spring
23. Washer
24. Thrust washer (thick)
25. Thrust bearing
26. Thrust washer (thin)
27. Sleeve
28. Swashplate
29. Bearing
30. Bearing
31. Cylinder block
32. Spring
33. Washer
34. Motor shaft
35. Snap ring
36. Bearing
37. Thrust washer
38. Bearing
39. Pin
40. Pump shaft
41. Snap rings
42. Bearing
43. Spacer
44. Seal
45. Snap ring
46. Dowel
47. Gasket
48. Housing
49. Control arm
50. Bushing
51. Seal
52. Plug
53. "O" ring
54. Center section

# SUNDSTRAND

## Hydrogear Model

**OPERATION.** The hydrostatic transmission consists of three main components: A variable displacement, reversible swashplate, axial piston type pump; a fixed displacement, gear motor; a center section which houses a charge pump and a valve system.

When control handle is in neutral position, pump pistons are all in the same plane, no oil is being pumped and tractor does not move. When control handle is moved forward, pump swashplate is tilted and piston stroke is set for controlled volume of oil and flow direction. Refer to Fig. SU10. Oil is pumped through high pressure circuit (A) to gear motor. As oil passes through gear motor, tractor moves forward. The oil then becomes low pressure circuit (B) and flows directly back to the variable pump. When control handle is moved from forward towards neutral, swashplate tilt is reduced. This reduces piston stroke which in turn lowers volume of oil pumped into circuit (A). Since gear motor has a fixed displacement per revolution, lower volume of oil results in a slower forward ground speed.

When control handle is moved in reverse position, swashplate tilt is reversed and oil is pumped into circuit (B). Circuit (B) is now high pressure circuit and (A) becomes low pressure circuit. This rotates gear motor in reverse and tractor moves backward.

The circuits (A and B) are referred to as a closed loop circuit. However, any oil lost internally from loop circuit is replaced by low pressure charge pump through circuit (C). This oil is drawn from reservoir through circuit (S) by charge pump. The oil is then pumpd into circuit (C) and portion needed for make up oil is forced into loop circuit through check valve in low pressure side of circuit. The oil pressure in circuit (C) is maintained at 75-110 psi (517-758 kPa) by charge relief valve. All excess oil in circuit (C) passes through charge relief valve into circuit (R). Circuit (R) circulates oil through variable pump housing, cooling and lubricating pump, and then delivers the oil through a renewable filter to reservoir.

The acceleration control and relief valves, located between circuits (A and B), protect circuits from excessive pressure when control handle is moved quickly to any position. They also prevent all jerking motion or lurch, when control handle is shifted, by diverting part of high pressure oil into low pressure circuit for one or two seconds. Then, as new ground speed is established, valve closes and directs all oil to gear motor. At this time, valve operates as a high pressure relief valve for high pressure circuit.

The drive-no drive valve is a manually operated bypass valve located between circuits (A and B). When valve is in no drive (open) position, oil is allowed to recirculate through gear motor without passing through variable pump. Tractor can be pushed manually in this position. The valve must be in drive (closed) position for normal tractor operation.

**OVERHAUL.** "Hydrogear" type hydrostatic transmissions were manufactured in an inline and a right-angle configuration. Service procedures are similar.

To disassemble hydrostatic drive unit, first thoroughly clean exterior of unit, then remove control arm, input pulley and cooling fan. Drain unit, then unbolt and remove cover (1–Fig. SU11), spring (2) and filter (3). Remove three Allen head screws securing reservoir (4) to pump housing (11) and lift off reservoir and suction tube (6). Position transmission on a bench so pump input shaft is in horizontal position. Unbolt pump housing from center section. If necessary, tap sides of finned housing with a plastic hammer to break gasket seal loose. As pump is being removed, insert fingers between housing and valve plate to prevent block and piston assembly from falling out. The block (20) and valve plate (22) mating faces are lapped surfaces and extreme caution should be exercised to prevent damage to these parts. Carefully remove block and piston assembly and thrust plate (17). Remove pistons (18) from block by lifting upward on slipper retainer (19).

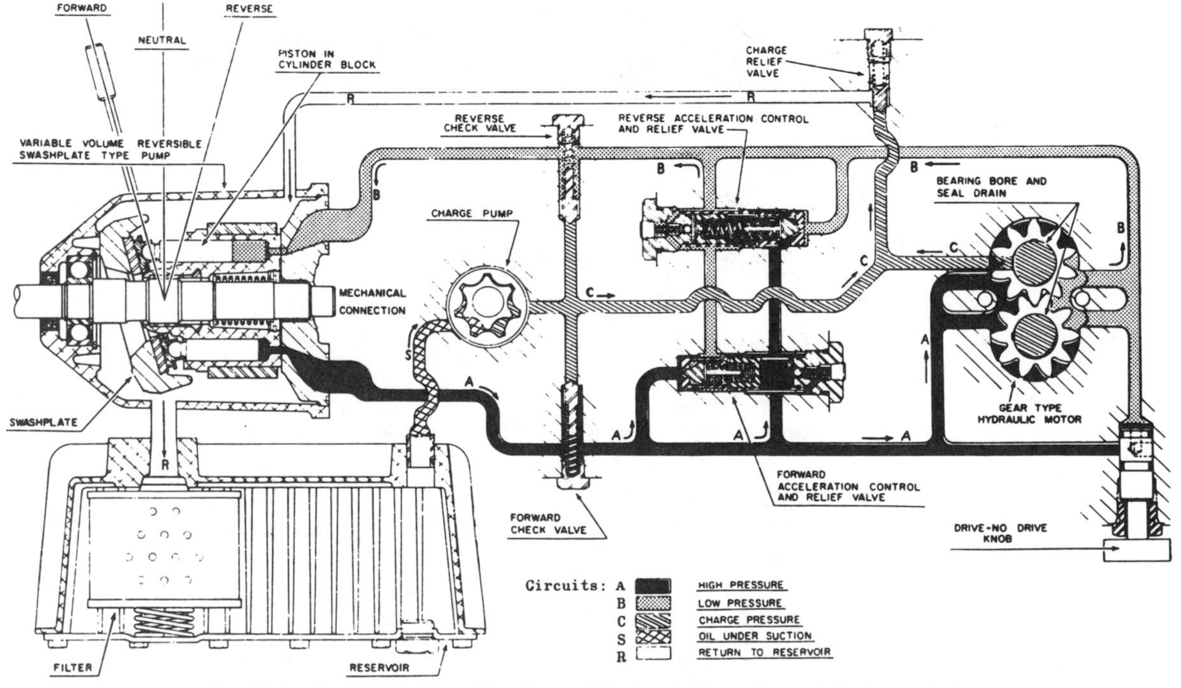


*Fig. SU10—Circuit diagram of Sundstrand "Hydrogear" type hydrostatic transmission.*



Illustrations courtesy Sundstrand.

**NOTE: Pistons are interchangeable; however, on units with long service, it is advisable to mark and return each piston to its respective bore.**

Support housing (11) and drive roll pins down into swashplate (16) until pins bottom on pump housing. Unbolt and remove control detent plate (13), taking care not to lose neutral detent ball and spring. Withdraw control shaft (14), drive hollow stub shaft (10) to inside and lift out swashplate. Remove retaining ring and remove input shaft (5) with bearing (7). Front oil seal (12) can now be removed.

Remove four cap screws securing valve plate (22) to center section (35) and carefully remove valve plate with charge pump gerotor set.

Place a scribe mark across gear motor sections to aid in reassembly. Unbolt end cap (31) and tap firmly with a plastic hammer to separate motor sections. Remove motor gears and shafts and lay removed motor parts aside for later inspection.

Remove acceleration valves (36 through 46), charge relief valve (27), check valves (28) and drive-no drive valve (26). After first removing retaining ring, remove motor output shaft pilot ring, oil seal, "O" ring and retainer. Remove all port plugs to facilitate cleaning of all internal passages in center section.

Thoroughly clean and inspect all parts and reassemble as follows: When renewing bearing (30), press bearings into location 0.095-0.140 inch (2.413-3.556 mm) below lapped face of end cap or center section. The mating surfaces between all motor sections are lapped surfaces flat within 0.0001 inch (0.0025 mm). Motor gears are lapped 0.0012-0.0014 inch (0.0305-0.0356 mm) thinner than spacer plate (34) to allow clearance for gear lubrication. If ex-

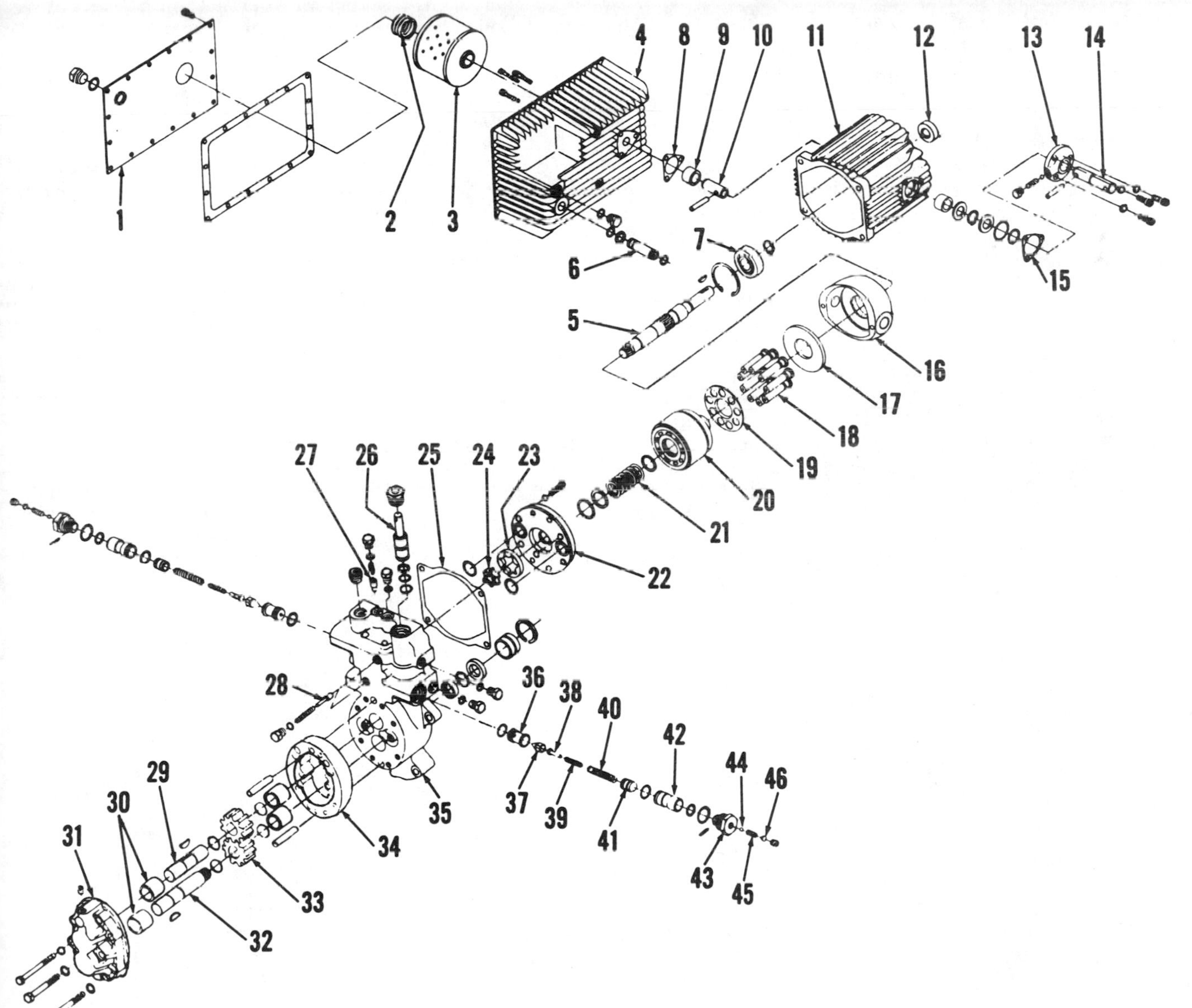


*Fig. SU11 – Exploded view of Sundstrand "Hydrogear" in-line type hydrostatic transmission. Gear pump components are positioned perpendicular to pump housing on right-angle type hydrostatic transmissions.*

1. Cover
2. Filter spring
3. Filter
4. Reservoir
5. Pump shaft
6. Suction tube
7. Ball bearing
8. Gasket
9. Needle bearing
10. Stub shaft
11. Pump housing
12. Oil seal
13. Neutral detent plate
14. Control shaft
15. Shim
16. Swashplate
17. Thrust plate
18. Pistons (9)
19. Slipper retainer
20. Pump cylinder block
21. Spring
22. Valve plate
23. Driven rotor
24. Driving rotor
25. Shim gasket
26. Drive-no drive valve
27. Charge relief valve
28. Check valve (2)
29. Motor idler shaft
30. Bearing
31. End cap
32. Motor output shaft
33. Gear set
34. Spacer plate
35. Center section
36. Seat
37. Cone
38. Spring guide
39. Spring (inner)
40. Spring (outer)
41. Piston
42. Sleeve
43. Metering plug
44. Ball
45. Spring
46. Spring seat

Illustrations courtesy Sundstrand.

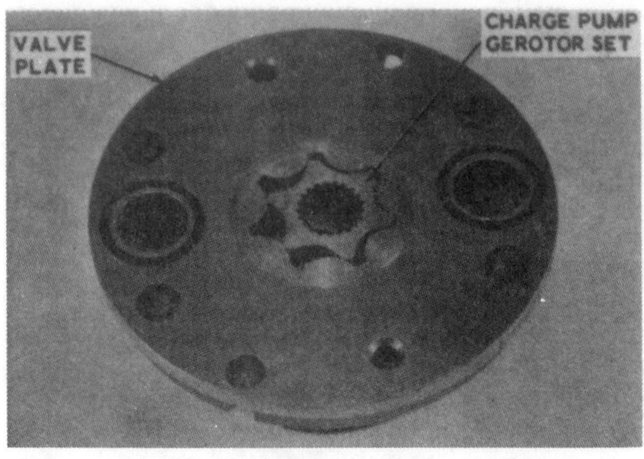


Fig. SU12—View showing valve plate and charge pump gerotor set used on Sundstrand "Hydrogear" type hydrostatic transmission.

cessive gear wear or severe scoring is evident on end cap or center section motor surface, renew end cap and spacer plate with matched gear set. Center section should be machine lapped to clean up surface if necessary. The maximum amount of stock which may be removed from center section face is 0.010 inch (0.254 mm). Install new output shaft seal and install gear and shaft assemblies. Lightly coat spacer plate with a mixture of shellac and alcohol, approximately 1/4 inch (6 mm) wide at outer edge of mating surfaces. Do not allow mixture to enter drain grooves in faces. Align scribe mark and install spacer plate. Lubricate gears and install end cap. Secure end cap by first tightening two tie bolts in center of end cap to a torque of 13-17 ft.-lbs. (18-23 N•m). Tighten remaining cap screws to a torque of 28-32 ft.-lbs. (38-43 N•m) using a cross tightening sequence. A rolling torque test of output shaft at this time should produce a reading of no more than 3 ft.-lbs. (4 N•m). A higher reading would indicate lack of proper clearance or excess shellac mixture extruded into the gears. The motor must be disassembled and difficulty corrected before proceeding with center section assembly.

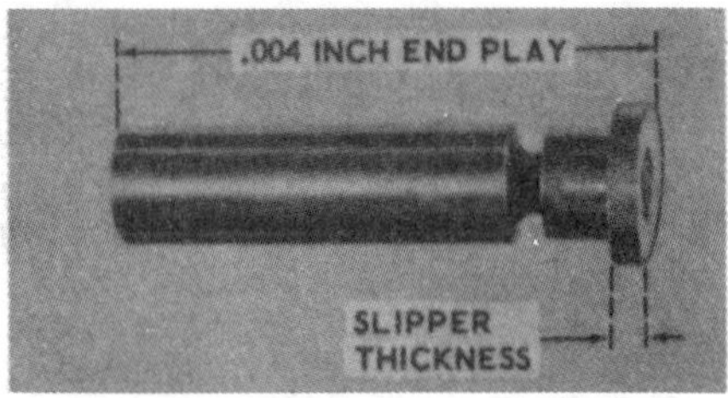


Fig. SU13—Slipper thickness should not vary more than 0.002 inch (0.051) for all nine pistons. Slipper should be free on piston with a maximum of 0.004 inch (0.102 mm) end play.

Install charge relief valve assembly (27) in its bore and tighten plug to a torque of 22-26 ft.-lbs. (30-35 N•m).

**NOTE: Use all new "O" rings when reassembling unit.**

Install two check valves (28) and torque both plugs to 22-26 ft.-lbs. (30-35 N•m). Insert drive-no drive valve (26) and tighten shoulder nut securely. When installing acceleration valves, pay particular attention to metering plug portion. Any blocking of metering plug orifice formed by small orifice ball will cause loss of power and slow response. Tighten 1-3/16 inch metering plugs (43) to a torque of 65-70 ft.-lbs. (88-95 N•m). Install all other plugs previously removed for cleaning.

Inspect valve plate (22) and charge pump gerotor set for excessive wear or scratches and renew if necessary. Superficial scratches on charge pump side of valve plate (Fig. SU12) may be removed by hand lapping. On kidney side of valve plate, machine lapping or valve plate renewal is indicated if 0.005 inch (0.127 mm) or more stock must be removed to clean up surface.

**NOTE: Do not install valve plate assembly at this time. The valve plate must be used to determine pump mounting shim gasket thickness.**

Inspect pump cylinder block (20–Fig. SU11), pistons (18) and thrust plate (17) for wear or damage and renew or rework as follows: The thrust plate may be lapped to remove scratches or light wear pattern. However, a maximum of 0.010 inch (0.254 mm) stock removal may be allowed for rework. The slippers are the bronze bonnets crimped to pistons. All slippers should be touch lapped by hand to remove superficial scratches. Piston assemblies should be renewed if slipper surface damage is deeper than 0.005 inch (0.127 mm). A lapping plate with

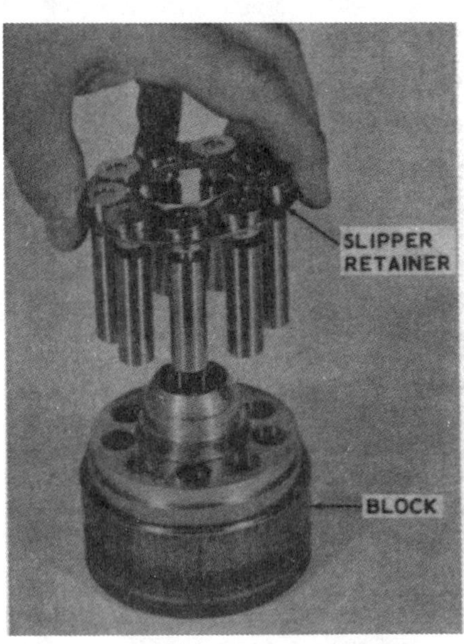


Fig. SU14—View showing pistons in slipper retainer being installed in pump cylinder block.

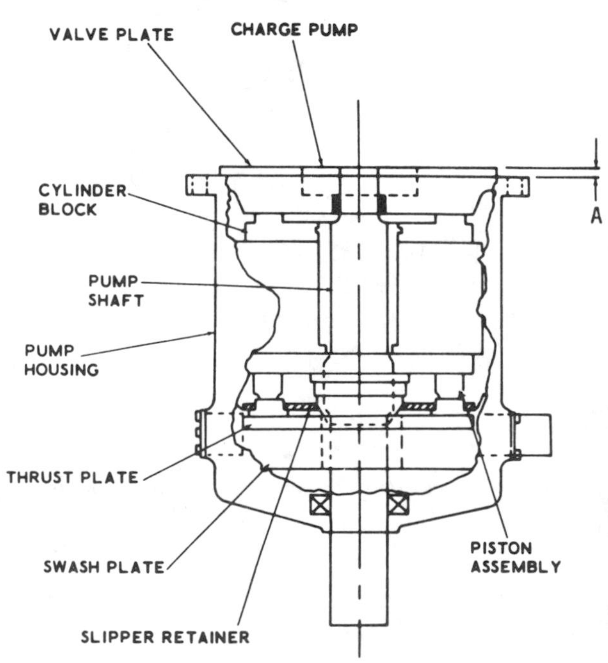


Fig. SU15—Dimension (A) must be measured with block spring removed and parts assembled as shown.



Illustrations courtesy Sundstrand.

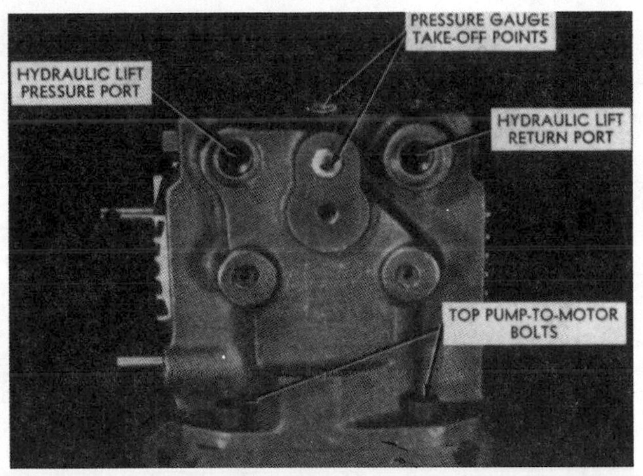


*Fig. SU20—View of "piston-to-piston" pump end cap to show location of pressure test ports. Charge pressure and hydraulic lift pressure can be checked at either port.*

1500 grit compound or 4/0 grit emery paper should be used for lapping slippers. After lapping, slipper thickness should not vary over 0.002 inch (0.051 mm) for all nine pistons. See Fig. SU13. Slipper should be free on piston with a maximum of 0.004 inch (0.102 mm) end play. When slippers are properly lapped, they should have equal chamfer between slipper face and edges. The block should be renewed if bores show excessive wear or scratches (0.002 inch [0.051 mm] or deeper). The block face (balance land end) is a lapped surface. Light scratches can be removed by hand lapping. Blocks which indicate removal of 0.005 inch (0.127 mm) or more stock to remove severe scratches should be renewed or machine lapped. In no case should more than 0.015 inch (0.381 mm) be removed from block face.

After all parts have been reworked, install new pump shaft seal, pump shaft with bearing, swashplate and shafts in pump housing by reversing disassembly procedure. Install "O" rings, shim and neutral detent plate, making certain detent ball and spring are in position. Compress spring inside of block, remove retaining ring and withdraw spring and washers from block. Install pistons in slipper retainer and insert pistons in block. See Sig. SU14. Make certain lip on slipper retainer and angle of ball hub of block match. Install thrust plate in swashplate and cylinder block assembly on pump drive shaft. Place valve plate on pump as shown in Fig. SU15. Measure dimension (A) as shown (distance surface of valve plate is above housing). Dimension (A) plus 0.003 divided by 0.6 will give nominal shim gasket thickness to be used when installing pump. Shim gaskets are available in 0.010, 0.015, 0.021 and 0.031 inch thickness. If nominal shim thickness is between shim thickness listed, use next larger size. If surface of valve plate is flush to 0.009 inch below pump housing, use one 0.010 inch shim gasket. If valve plate surface is more than 0.009 inch below face of pump housing, valve plate and/or block must be renewed.

After shim gasket thickness is determined, remove valve plate and block assembly from pump housing. Remove pistons from block and reinstall tension spring, washers and retaining ring. Lubricate pistons and reinstall them in cylinder block. Reinstall block and piston assembly in pump housing and set pump assembly aside.

Install valve plate and charge pump assembly on center section. Make certain new "O" rings are in proper location on valve plate. Install four cap screws with new copper washers and tighten cap screws to a torque of 36-38 ft.-lbs. (49-52 N·m).

Place previously determined shim gasket on center section. Lubricate mating surfaces of valve plate and cylinder block with clean transmission oil. Lay center section on its side and slide pump housing into position, making sure drive shaft enters bushing in valve plate. Rotate pump shaft until spline enters charge pump rotor. When properly positioned, gap between housing and center section will be 1/8 to 1/4 inch (3-6 mm) and housing will be spring loaded with respect to center section. Install and tighten pump mounting cap screws to a torque of 20-22 ft.-lbs (27-30 N·m). Check turning torque of pump shaft. A torque reading greater than 3 ft.-lbs. (4 N·m) is excessive and unit should be rechecked for proper shimming.

Install reservoir and suction tube, using new gasket and "O" rings. Tighten Allen head screws to 10 ft.-lbs. (14 N·m)

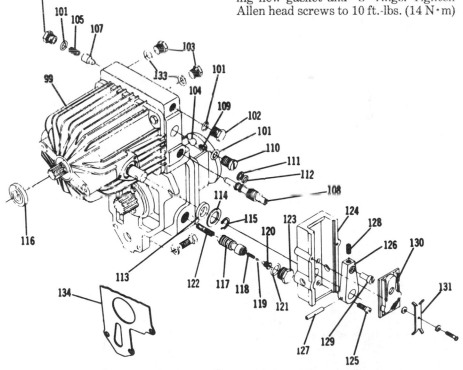

*Fig. SU21—Exploded view of typical Sundstrand "piston-to-piston" center section and control cam parts. On models equipped with hydraulic lift, charge relief valve (107) is opposite side of center section and lift relief valve is located in its place.*

99. Pump housing
101. "O" ring
102. Plug
103. Plug
104. Check valve ball
105. Charge relief spring
106. Charge relief plug
107. Charge relief cone
108. Bypass valve
109. Check valve spring
110. Check valve plug
111. "O" ring
112. Back-up ring
113. Control shaft seal
114. Trunnion washer
115. Retainer ring
116. Input shaft seal
117. Sleeve
118. Spring
119. Ball
120. Valve
121. "O" ring
122. Acceleration valve spring
123. Plug
124. Cam block support
125. Socket head screw (3)
126. Cam follower arm
127. Roll pin
128. Set screw
129. Cam follower pin
130. Cam
131. Tension plate (2)
133. "O" ring
134. Gasket

Illustrations courtesy Sundstrand.

torque. Install new filter and gasket, then install filter spring and cover. Cover retaining cap screws should be tightened to a torque of 10 ft.-lbs. (14 N•m).

## Piston-To-Piston Model

**PRESSURE TEST.** If tractor appears to lose power during operation with no deterioration of engine performance, hydrostatic transmission can be checked for hydraulic pressure loss. Such check can help to determine if transmission has internal deterioration due to long term use or simply has a malfunctioning control valve or faulty adjustment. Proceed as follows:

Raise and block up tractor drive axle clear of surface. Connect pressure test gage (0 to 1000 psi [0-7000 kPa] range) after removing ¼ inch pipe plug at either point shown in Fig. SU20. Start engine and run at near full throttle; engage transmission in either forward or reverse. Alternate between forward and reverse for comparison. Note gage reading when transmission is cold, then again after normal operating temperature has been reached. A large drop in pressure as warm-up proceeds indicates internal leakage due to worn parts.

Charge pressure reading should range from 70 to 150 psi (482-1034 kPa). It should never drop below 50 psi (345 kPa).

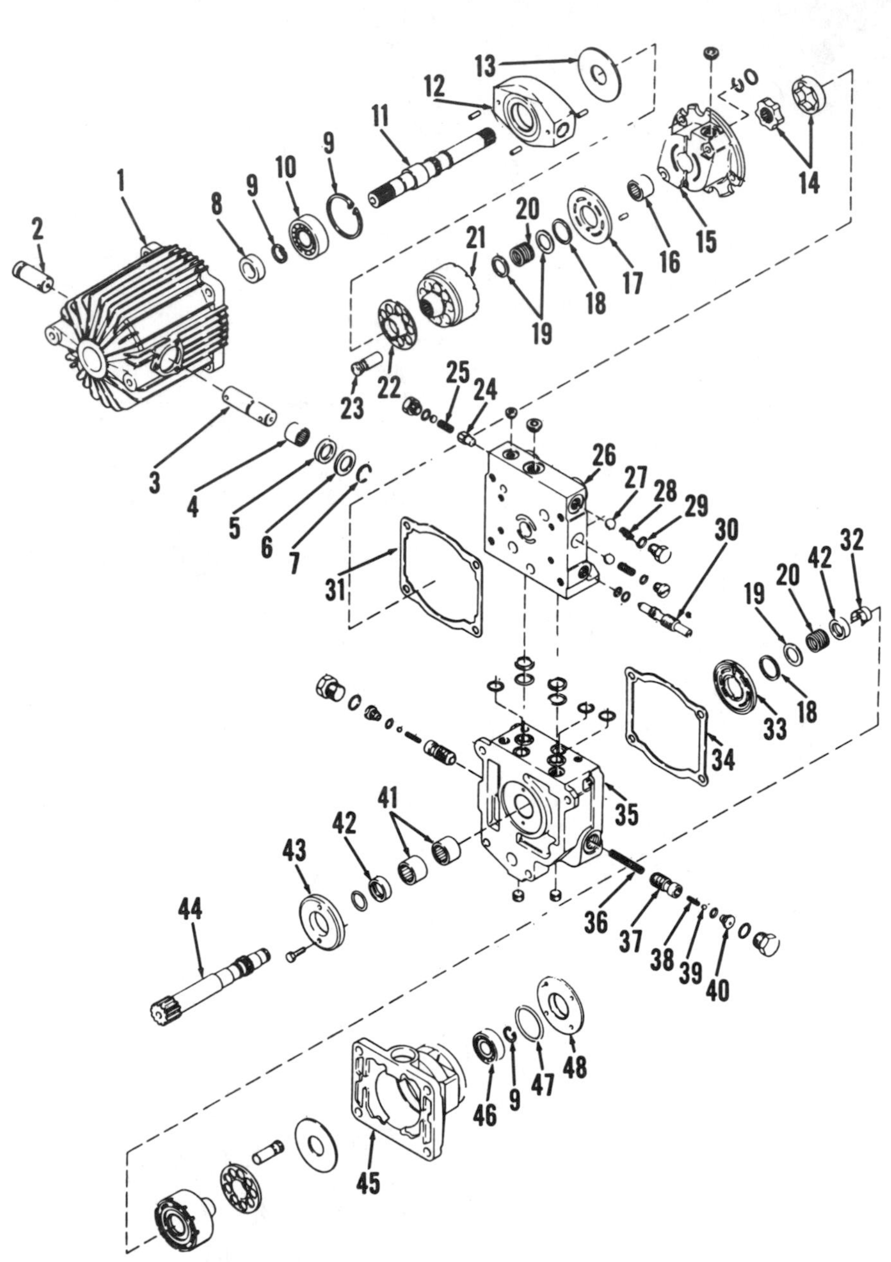

*Fig. SU22—Exploded view of late type "piston-to-piston" hydrostatic transmission.*

1. Pump housing
2. Stub shaft
3. Control shaft
4. Needle bearing
5. Seal
6. Washer
7. Retainer ring
8. Pump shaft seal
9. Snap ring
10. Bearing
11. Pump shaft
12. Variable swashplate
13. Thrust plate
14. Gerotor assy.
15. Charge pump housing
16. Needle bearing
17. Valve plate
18. Retainer ring
19. Washer
20. Spring
21. Cylinder block
22. Slipper retainer
23. Piston
24. Implement relief valve
25. Spring
26. Pump end cap
27. Charge relief valve
28. Spring
29. "O" ring
30. Free-wheeling valve
31. Gasket
32. Retainer clip
33. Valve plate
34. Gasket
35. Motor end cap
36. Spring
37. Acceleration valve body
38. Spring
39. Ball
40. Metering plug
41. Needle bearings
42. Retainer
43. Centering ring
44. Motor shaft
45. Motor housing
46. Ball bearing
47. "O" ring
48. Cover plate

**OVERHAUL.** Prior to disassembling hydrostatic unit, thoroughly clean outside of housing. If not previously removed, remove cooling fan and input pulley. Refer to Fig. SU21 and remove control arm asssembly. Separate pump and motor by removing four Allen head screws.

To disassemble pump, unbolt pump housing (1–Fig. SU22) from pump end cap (26). If necessary, tap sides of housing with a plastic hammer to break gasket loose. Make sure as pump housing and end cap separate that cylinder block assembly (21) stays with input shaft. Carefully slide cylinder block assembly off shaft and place on a lint free towel to prevent damage.

**NOTE: If any of the pistons (23) slip out, return them to their original bores.**

To remove variable swashplate (12), and input shaft, remove thrust plate (13). Use a sharp awl and remove pump shaft seal and retainer. Remove snap ring from shaft and tap lightly on input end. Use a 3/16 inch punch to drive trunnion shaft roll pins out (Fig. SU23). One roll pin is used in short stub shaft and two pins are used in control shaft. Remove trunnion shaft retaining rings (7–Fig. SU22) and drive stub shaft (2) inward. Drive control shaft out from inside. Remove swashplate (12) and trunnion seals (5). Press needle bearing out of housing from inside.

Remove valve plate (17) from charge pump housing. Remove charge pump housing mounting bolts and carefully remove pump assembly. If needle bearing (16) in charge pump housing is damaged, remove gerotor assembly (14) and press bearing out. Install new bearing with identification number showing from valve plate side. Press bearing until 0.100 inch (2.54 mm) is left out of the bore.

To disassemble motor, remove cover plate (48) and snap ring (9). Mark motor housing (45) and end cap (35) to aid in reassembly. Remove cap screws and separate housing and end cap. Remove thrust plate and ball bearing (46). Remove centering ring (43) and place motor end cap on press with cylinder



Illustrations courtesy Sundstrand.

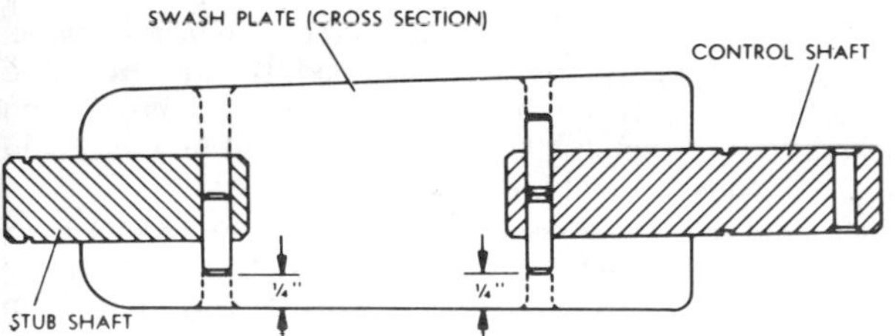


Fig. SU23—Cross-sectional view of variable swashplate, stub shaft and control shaft. Two roll pins are used to retain control shaft.

block assembly up. Press motor shaft until retaining spring clip (32) pops loose.

**CAUTION: Operation requires moving shaft only a short distance. DO NOT press shaft through cylinder block.**

Slide cylinder block assembly and retaining clip from motor shaft. Remove valve plate (33) and withdraw shaft. If motor end cap bearings are rough or damaged, press seal retainer and both needle bearings out the cylinder block side. When reinstalling bearings, press output side bearing in first with lettered end out. Press seal retainer insert (42) in with bearing until flush with end cap. Install second bearing from cylinder block side and press bearing (lettered end outward) until 0.100 inch (2.54 mm) is protruding from face of end cap.

Remove acceleration valves (36 through 40) from opposite sides of motor end cap (35), implement relief valve (24), charge relief valve (27) and free-wheeling valve (30). Remove all port plugs to facilitate cleaning of all internal passages.

Clean and inspect all components for damage or excessive wear and reassemble as follows: Install relief valve assembly (24) in its bore and tighten plug to a torque of 22-26 ft.-lbs. (30-35 N•m). Use all new "O" rings when reassembling unit. Install charge relief valve (27) and check valve assembly, then torque plugs to 22-26 ft.-lbs. (30-35 N•m). Insert free-wheeling valve. When installing acceleration valves, pay close attention to metering plug. Any blockage of metering plug orifice formed by the small orifice ball will cause loss of power and slow response. Tighten metering plug to a torque of 65-70 ft.-lbs. (88-95 N•m) and install other plugs.

Inspect pump housing end cap (26) and charge pump gerotor set for excessive wear or deep scratches and renew as necessary. See Fig. SU24. Superficial scratches on pump end cap may be removed by hand lapping. Check bronze side of valve plate (Fig. SU25) for scratches and wear. This surface must be smooth and free of scratches. If wear can be felt with fingernail, renew plate. Pump and motor valve plates are not interchangeable. Bronze side of valve plates must face pump or motor cylinder block.

Inspect cylinder blocks (21–Fig. SU22), pistons (23) and thrust plates (13) for wear or damage. Thrust plates must be checked for flatness, scoring and imbedded material and renewed as required. The slippers are bronze bonnets crimped to the pistons. Piston assemblies should be renewed if slipper surface damage is deeper than 0.005 inch (0.127 mm). A lapping plate with 1500 grit compound or 4/0 grit emery paper should be used for lapping slippers. After lapping, slipper thickness should not vary over 0.002 inch (0.051 mm) for all pistons. See Fig. SU26. Slipper should be free on piston with a maximum end play of 0.004 inch (0.102 mm). Cylinder block should be renewed if bores show excessive wear or severe scratches. Block face (balance land end) is a lapped surface. Light scratches can be removed by hand lapping. Renew blocks that require removal of 0.005 inch (0.127 mm) or more stock to remove scratches.

After all parts have been reworked, install new seals and "O" rings applying a light coat of SAE 10W-30 oil to each one. Lubricate mating surfaces of valve plate, cylinder block and bearing surfaces with SAE 10W-30 oil. Reassemble unit by reversing disassembly procedures. Reinstall control cam, input pulley and cooling fan, then install unit on differential assembly.

## Series 15 "In-Line" Type

**OPERATION.** Sundstrand Series 15 "In-Line" hydrostatic transmission consist of three main working components: A variable displacement, reversible swashplate, axial piston type pump

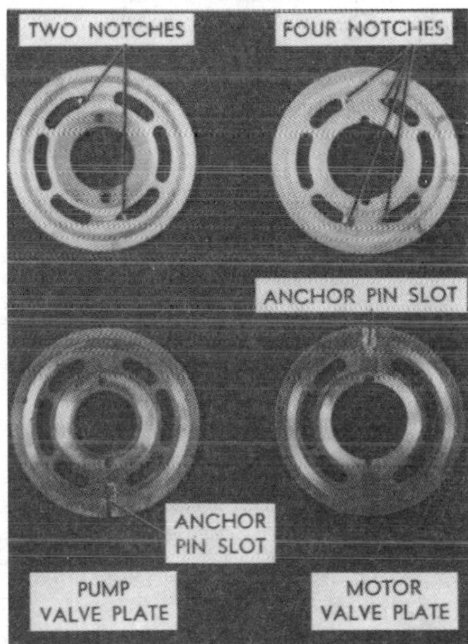


Fig. SU25—Views of pump and motor valve plates to show differences. Plates are not interchangeable.

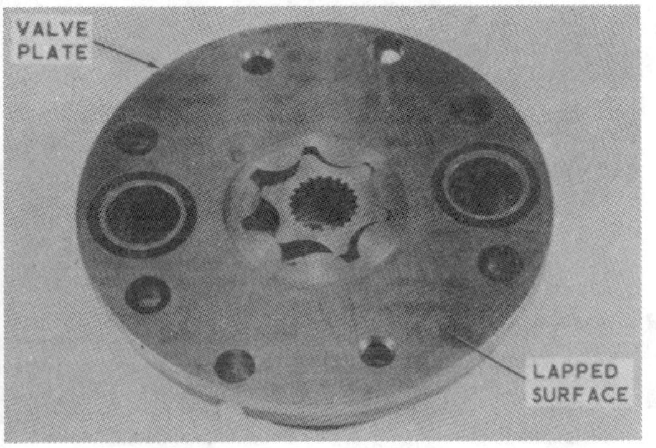


Fig. SU24—View of gerotor charge pump and valve plate assembly.

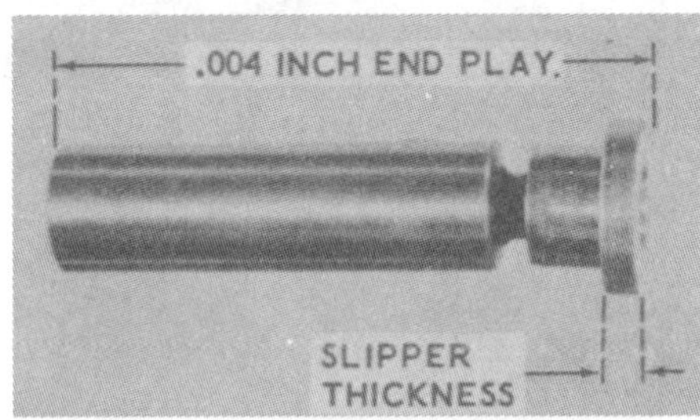


Fig. SU26—Thickness of slipper should not vary by more than 0.002 inch (0.051 mm) for all nine pistons. Slipper must move freely on piston with maximum end play of 0.004 inch (0.102 mm).

Illustrations courtesy Sundstrand.

which develops hydraulic pressure needed for motive power. A center or control section which contains a gear-type charge (or make-up) pump and a calibrated, functional set of automatic valves to control and direct oil flow and ensure smooth, shock-free operation. A hydraulic motor, which in "piston-to-piston" design is a fixed displacement, stationary swashplate motor very similar to the pump. Besides necessary external controls, system is complete with a hydraulic fluid reservoir, filter and a reduction gear to differential final drive.

Hydraulic pump is shaft-driven by tractor engine and entire hydrostatic unit is mounted on final drive housing at rear of tractor. Hydrostatic flow diagram of piston-to-piston unit is shown in Fig. SU30.

In operation, with control pedal set in neutral position, movable swashplate of pump is held vertical and all pistons revolve in a plane which is at a right angle to axis of rotating pump shaft. There is no piston stroke, thus no pumping action and no flow of oil. When control shaft is moved, swashplate is tilted, and pistons move in and out in their cylinder bores to develop oil flow and pressure from the pump. Variable tilt angle of pump swashplate controls oil volume and direction of its flow. In Fig. SU30, control is set in forward. Note that oil is pumped at high pressure to piston motor to force motor and its output shaft to turn, imparting forward motion to tractor drive. Oil is returned to pump through opposite side of circuit at lowered pressure as shown in flow diagram.

When control shaft is tilted only slightly from neutral, so swashplate is tilted very little, stroke of pump pistons will be short and a limited volume of oil will be set in motion toward hydraulic motor. Since piston motor has a fixed displacement for each revolution, a lesser volume of oil being delivered by pump will result in a slower ground speed than if a larger flow is being passed. Speed of tractor is thus controlled by degree of tilt given to swashplate of pump as control shaft is moved by pedal pressure.

When control shaft is shifted from forward to reverse, high pressure will be switched to opposite side of pump to motor circuit and motor will reverse direction of rotation so tractor will back up. A study of flow diagram will show that forward high pressure line will become a return line when swashplate angle is so shifted.

Pump to motor flow pattern is referred to as a closed loop circuit. Any losses of oil due to leakage in pressure circuit are replenished from fluid reservoir by operation of continuous-running charge pump. The amount of oil needed to replenish such loss is forced into the loop circuit through whichever of the two check valves is functioning in low pressure side, determined by flow direction from reversible primary pump. Oil pressure in charge pump (make-up) line is maintained at 70-150 (483-1034 kPa) by charge relief (make-up) valve. Excess oil released is passed to hydraulic system for implement control, when tractor is so equipped, then is circulated through swashplate pump housing and motor housing to cool and lubricate and finally, to unit reservoir.

Acceleration control and relief valves shown located in high and low pressure circuits serve to protect system from damaging surges of excess pressure due to sudden application of control pedal. They prevent jerking motion and lurch when control is shifted by diverting high pressure oil momentarily into low pressure side of system – a matter of a second or two. As ground speed changes and pressure normalizes, this automatic valve closes and all oil flow is directed to hydraulic motor. In effect, it serves as a pressure relief valve for whichever side of loop circuit is working under high pressure.

Hydrostatic unit is furnished with a "free-wheeling" valve to serve as a bypass valve between circuits; when manually opened, oil will circulate through motor only and tractor can be pushed by hand. This valve must be closed for normal operation.

**TESTING.** Refer to Fig. SU31 for proper installation of pressure test gages in hydrostatic unit. Gage used must be equipped with a male 1/8 inch pipe thread adapter to fit test ports. A 0-5000 psi (0-35000 kPa) range is recommended for gage used to check system pressure (A) and a 0-1000 psi (0-7000 kPa) range capacity gage for testing charge pressure (B). It is advised that a snubber or needle valve be set into

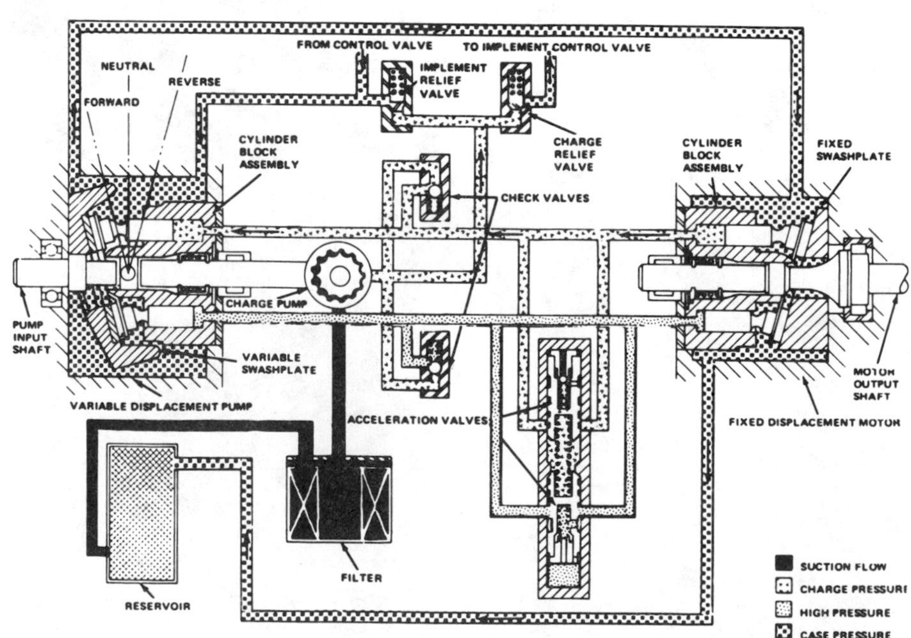


*Fig. SU30 – Hydraulic flow diagram of Sundstrand Series 15 "In-Line" type hydrostatic transmission.*

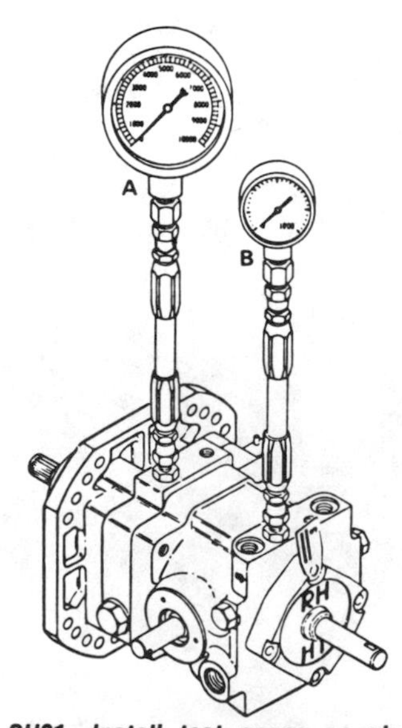


*Fig. SU31 – Install test gages as shown for pressure tests. Install in center section (A) for system pressure check or at (B) for testing charge pressure. Gages must fit 1/8 inch female pipe thread in test ports.*



Illustrations courtesy Sundstrand.

gage line hose to dampen fluid pulsation for protection of gages.

Test procedure is as follows:

Remove 1/8 inch socket-head pipe plug from either charge pressure testing port. If no fluid flows (port is dry), turn input shaft slowly (hand crank), until fluid appears, then install gage (B). Start engine and operate at low speed. Observe gage. Normal charge pressure should develop to a steady reading between 70-150 psi (483-1034 kPa). As unit warms up, increase engine speed to full operating rpm and note if charge pressure is maintained. **Charge pressure may increase, but not decrease.** If pressure falls off, shut down system and determine cause. If charge pressure falls below 50 psi (345 kPa), complete overhaul is indicated. If unit is equipped with hydraulic implement circuit, operate implement control valve slowly through a cycle or two and note if pressure is held between 550 and 700 psi (3792 and 4826 kPa), which is normal. Comparison of charge pump pressure reading with implement pressure reading may help in locating a problem. For example, if charge pump pressure holds above 70 psi (483 kPa) and implement pressure falls to 500 psi (3448 kPa), there may be a leak in hydraulic lift system. If this is the case, repair before proceeding. If no leak appears, it is likely implement relief valve is defective. Remove plug (12–Fig. SU32) followed by implement relief valve components (8, 9 and 10) for inspection and cleaning. If valve condition is satisfactory, pressure may be increased in steps of 50 psi (345 kPa) by adding 0.012 inch shims (10) as needed.

Install gage (A–Fig. SU31) in center section of hydrostatic unit for checking system pressure. Maximum acceptable reading is 300 psi (2070 kPa). Actual working pressure may vary widely, dependent upon throttle setting, tractor load and control position; however, a consistent low reading, especially if supported by other evidence such as marginal or sluggish performance calls for a check of acceleration valves (22–Fig. SU32).

**NOTE: Check valves in center section are not accessible unless hydrostatic unit is removed and disassembled.**

Keep in mind that whenever it is planned to remove valves from housing, exterior of unit should be thoroughly cleaned to eliminate chance of dirt entry into system. Removal of valves for cleaning and inspection may often be a solution for erratic or unsatisfactory operation especially if a particular valve or valves appear to be a cause for malfunction based on test procedures.

**OVERHAUL.** Before disassembling hydrostatic drive unit, thoroughly clean outside of housing; then scribe a mark at joining edges of each section for aid in reassembly. To overhaul unit, proceed in following sequence.

CHARGE PUMP. Place unit, output gear (motor) side down, in an appropriate holding fixture. Inspect exposed position of input shaft (26–Fig. SU33) for burrs or sharp keyway edges which might damage lips of seal (52). Remove four cap screws (54) and lift off housing (51) noting that left hand marking is upward. Charge pump "O" ring (47), drive pin (48), gerotor assembly (49), bearing (50) and seal (52) should now be inspected carefully to determine if renewal is needed. Scoring, imbedded foreign material or excessive wear in machined and lapped friction surfaces, especially those of gerotor are a reason for new parts.

**NOTE: Though there may be no apparent damage or defect, pump may be worn to such extent that minimum 70 psi (483 kPa) required working pressure cannot be maintained. Refer to TESTING.**

PUMP SECTION. With pump end placed downward on a smooth, clean surface with a center hole to accommodate protruding input shaft, separate pump, motor and center sections by removal of four long cap screws (1–Fig. SU33) which hold unit assembled.

**NOTE: Sections are lightly spring-loaded; separate with care.**

With pump section set aside on clean butcher paper or lint-free shop cloths, disassemble as follows:

Remove cylinder block assembly (6) from pump housing (32) followed by thrust plate (4). To remove variable tilt swashplate (28) from housing (32), place housing with input shaft down through hole in a holding fixture so three roll pins (27) can be lightly tapped from bores in control shaft (33) and trunnion shaft (38). Push shafts out of swashplate and remove swashplate from housing. Inspect needle bearings (34) and side seals (35). If condition is defective, or even doubtful, press from housing for renewal. To remove input shaft (26), remove snap rings (29 and 31) and shaft with bearing (30) can be lightly tapped from housing bore. If bearing is worn, rough or noisy, press off shaft in a shop press for renewal.

CYLINDER BLOCK ASSEMBLIES. Pump and motor cylinders, pistons and slipper retainers are identical, however,

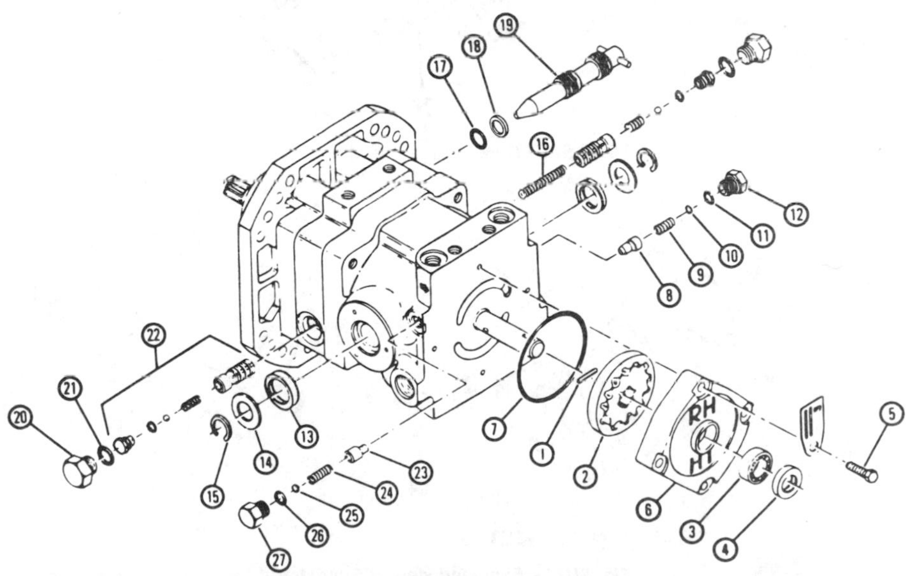


***Fig. SU32 — View of Sundstrand hydrostatic unit with charge pump, control shaft, and external valves removed to show their location in housing. These items may be serviced without removing or disassembling unit. Transmission must be disassembled to renew lip seals (4 and 13).***

1. Drive pin
2. Pump (gerotor set)
3. Needle bearing
4. Lip seal
5. Cap screw (4)
6. Charge pump housing
7. "O" ring
8. Relief valve cone (implement)
9. Implement relief spring
10. Shim pack
11. "O" ring
12. Plug
13. Lip seal (2)
14. Washer (2)
15. Retainer ring
16. Acceleration valve spring
17. "O" ring
18. Back-up ring
19. Free-wheeling valve
20. Acceleration valve plug (2)
21. "O" ring (2)
22. Acceleration valve (2)
23. Charge relief cone
24. Charge relief spring
25. Shims
26. "O" ring
27. Charge relief plug

due to extremely tight manufacturing tolerances, components are not interchangeable. Individual pistons must always be returned to same cylinder bores when removed for inspection or cleaning. Before removing pistons from cylinder block bores by lifting slipper retainer, it is advisable to index pistons to their correct bores by use of match marks. A felt-tipped pen will mark suitably when surfaces are clean and dry.

All parts must be thoroughly cleaned for inspection and to eliminate any chance of scoring from dirt or particles of foreign material. Be sure lube hole in center of slipper face is completely clear. If slight scratches are noted on slipper face, remove them by careful lapping; not to exceed 0.005 inch (0.127 mm). Polish with crocus cloth, nothing coarser.

Entire cylinder block assembly must be renewed under these conditions:

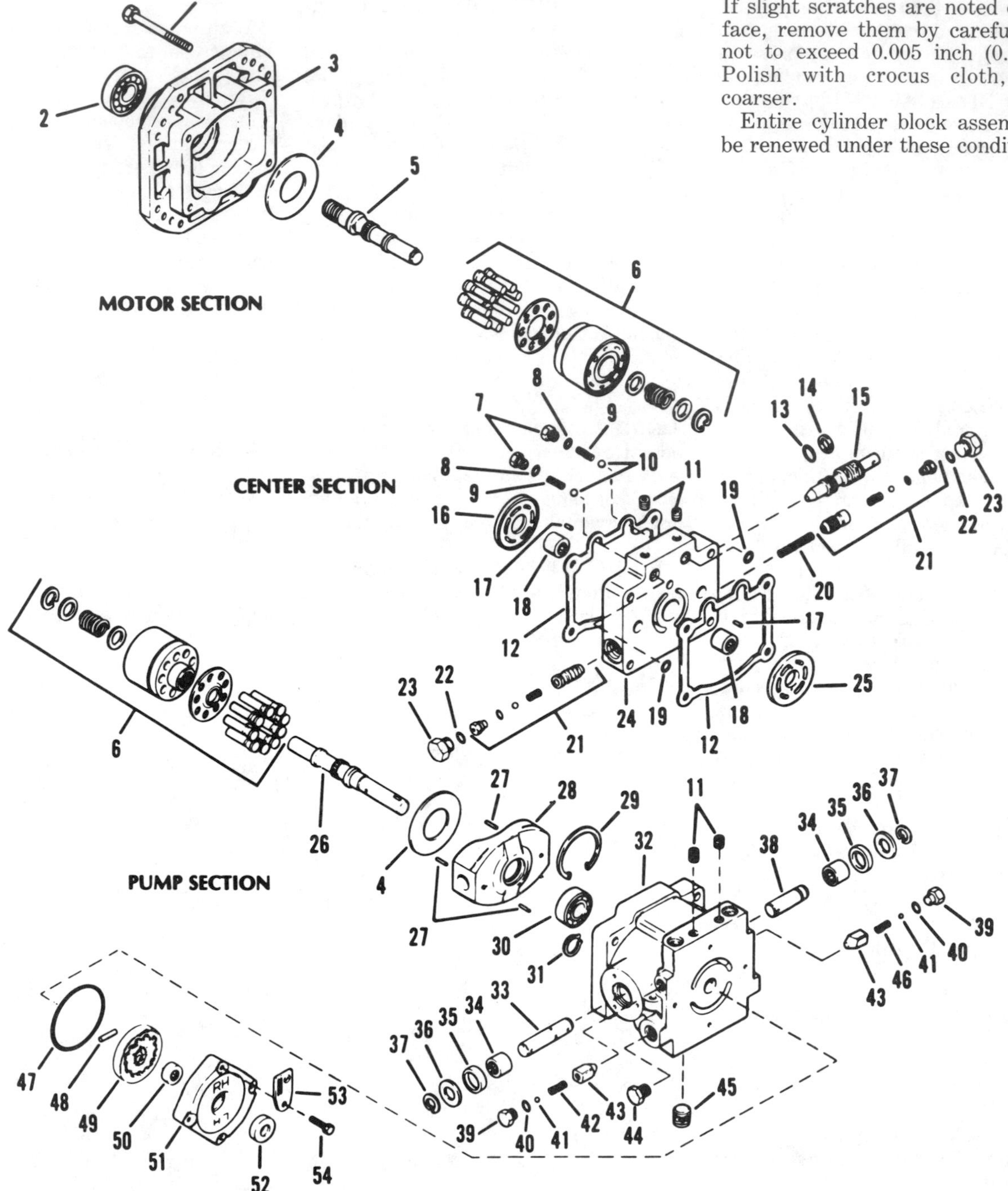


*Fig. SU33—Exploded view of Sundstrand Series 15 "In-Line" type hydrostatic transmission.*

1. Assembly cap screw (4)
2. Ball bearing
3. Motor housing
4. Motor thrust plate
5. Motor (output) shaft
6. Cylinder block assy. (2)
7. Check valve cap (2)
8. "O" ring (2)
9. Valve spring (2)
10. Ball (2)
11. Pipe plugs (1/8 inch)
12. Gaskets (2)
13. "O" ring
14. Back-up ring
15. Free-wheeling valve
16. Motor valve plate
17. Locator pin (2)
18. Needle bearing (2)
19. "O" ring
20. Acceleration valve spring
21. Acceleration valves
22. "O" ring
23. Plug (2)
24. Center section
25. Pump valve plate
26. Pump (output) shaft
27. Roll pins (3)
28. Pump swashplate
29. Snap ring
30. Ball bearing
31. Snap ring
32. Pump housing
33. Control shaft
34. Needle bearing
35. Lip seal
36. Washer
37. Retaining ring
38. Trunnion shaft
39. Plug (2)
40. "O" ring (2)
41. Shim pack (2)
42. Charge relief valve spring
43. Relief valve (2)
44. Plug
45. Filter stud tube
46. Implement relief valve spring
47. "O" ring
48. Drive pin
49. Gerotor set (pump)
50. Needle bearing
51. Charge pump body
52. Lip seal
53. Tag
54. Cap screw (4)

**Cylinder bores scored or out-of-round.**

**Valve plate face of cylinder worn, scratched or scored.**

**Piston barrels scratched or scored.**

**Slipper edges (contact with thrust plate) worn round in excess of 1/32 inch (0.8 mm).**

**Thickness of slippers (measure each with micrometer) varies by more than 0.002 inch (0.051 mm).**

**Slipper retainer must be perfectly flat.**

Be sure to remove snap ring retainer from valve plate end of cylinder block; see parts group (6 – Fig. SU33), and also remove internal spring and washers for cleaning. Swab out center bore carefully and blow dry. Reassemble.

Cylinder block assemblies should be set aside after inspection and cleaning in readiness for reinstallation in pump and motor during reassembly of hydrostatic unit.

MOTOR SECTION. Disassemble separated motor section by first removing cylinder block assembly (6 – Fig. SU33), then lift out motor thrust plate (4). To remove output shaft (5) and its bearing (2) from motor housing (3), tap lightly on inner end of shaft, and when bearing (2) is separated from its bore in rear of motor housing, set up shaft and bearing in a shop press for removal of bearing from shaft if renewal is needed. Thoroughly clean all parts in solvent and be sure to inspect motor thrust plate (4) for condition. Renew thrust plate if scratched or scored or if there is a distinct wear track from contact with motor piston slippers. After thorough cleaning and evaluation, reassemble motor section and set aside for final installation in overhauled drive unit.

*Fig. SU35 – Remove cap "A" from body "B" of acceleration valve for thorough cleaning and inspection. Do not intermix parts.*

CENTER SECTION. When center section is isolated by removal of pump and motor sections, detailed disassembly for inspection and thorough cleaning should be performed in this order:

Remove pump valve plate (19 – Fig. SU34) and motor valve plate (10) with their locator pins (11). Carefully, so as not to gouge or scratch joining surfaces, remove gaskets (6) from each side of center section housing (18). Remove check valve "O" rings (13) from pump side of housing and both check valves (complete) from motor side – items 1, 2, 3 and 4.

**IMPORTANT: Lay out all small parts of valve assemblies in proper sequence and maintain order without intermixing during inspection and cleaning process.**

Remove 7/8 inch hex plugs (17) and their "O" rings (16) to withdraw and push out forward and reverse acceleration valve assemblies (15) and their common centering spring (14). Take care not to drop valve bodies during removal and do not intermix parts. Clean inside of each valve body very carefully after its metering plug, spring and ball are removed. See Fig. SU35. Since these valves are a key to smooth, trouble free operation of tractor, care and attention at this point will ensure success of overhaul. Keep the following points in mind when servicing acceleration valves:

Be sure all small orifices are open and clear. Use compressed air to clean.

Renew **all** "O" rings.

Set valve ball carefully in its recess in metering plug; assemble against spring making sure it stays in place when plug is screwed back into valve body.

Reassembled valve bodies, coated with clean ATF, are returned to their bores when housing is ready with spring (14 – Fig. SU34) centered between them. Four or five internal threads should show at each open end when valve bodies are inserted so installer will know spring (14) is properly fitted into spring cavity of each valve body. Reinstall plugs (17) with new "O" rings (16) and tighten to 18-20 ft.-lbs. (24-30 N·m).

Press bearings (12) from housing and remove socket-head type 1/8 inch pipe plugs (5) from top. Back out free-wheeling valve (9) with "O" rings (7) and back-up rings (8).

When center section housing (18) has been cleaned with solvent and blown dry with particular attention to threaded portions and all internal passages, reinstall all removed parts with defective items renewed. Note that new bearings (12) are pressed in at each side (printed end of bearing cage outward) so 0.100 inch (2.54 mm) protrudes above polished surface to serve as a center pilot for valve plates. A convenient procedure is to use a number 39 drill (0.0995 inch) as a stop gage for press arbor when pressing these bearings into bores.

When check valves are reinstalled on motor side of housing, be sure to torque check valve caps (1) to 10 ft.-lbs. (14 N·m).

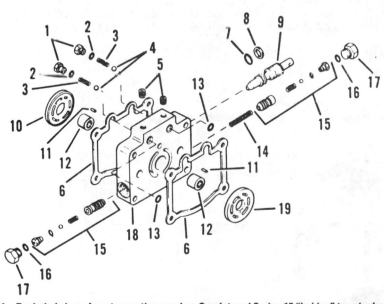

*Fig. SU34 – Exploded view of center section used on Sundstrand Series 15 "In-Line" type hydrostatic transmission. Center section is isolated for convenience of identification when overhauling.*

1. Check valve cap (2)
2. "O" ring (2)
3. Valve spring (2)
4. Ball (2)
5. Test plugs (1/8 inch pipe thread)
6. Gaskets (2)
7. "O" ring
8. Back-up ring
9. Free-wheeling valve
10. Motor valve plate
11. Locator pin (2)
12. Needle bearing (2)
13. "O" ring (2)
14. Acceleration valve spring
15. Acceleration valve assy. (2)
16. "O" ring (2)
17. Plug (2)
18. Center section body
19. Pump valve plate

Illustrations courtesy Sundstrand.

Condition of pump and motor valve plates (Fig. SU36) is critical. Sides of plates with anchor pin slots are steel-faced. Friction side, toward pump or motor cylinder, is bronze-finished. Check pin slots for wear as well as condition of pins. If valve plates are pitted or scored or if a wear track can be detected on bronze (friction) surface by contact with a finger nail, then valve plate must be renewed.

Service technician must be especially careful to properly identify valve plates during disassembly for overhaul. Note in Fig. SU36 that pump valve plate shown is for left hand rotation. The two notches (lead-ins) must be matched exactly on a renewal valve plate. If placement of these chamfers is opposite to that shown, then plate is for right hand rotation. Because motor rotates either way (changes direction), four chamfers are used at ends of fluid slots in motor plate. These parts must be correct and must be properly installed for normal operation of tractor.

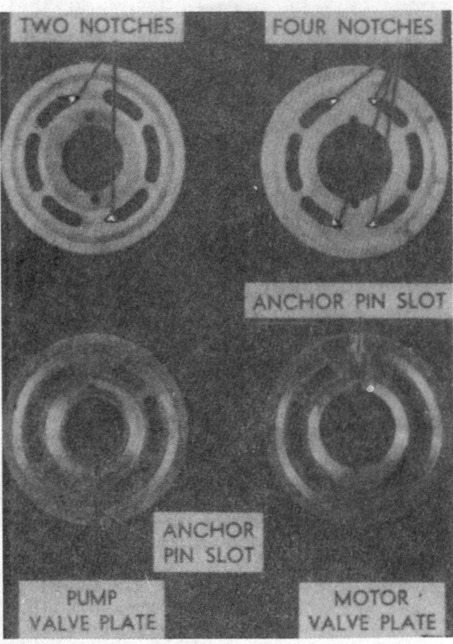


*Fig. SU36—View of both sides of pump and motor valve plates. Note four lead-in chamfers (notches) of motor valve plate for rotation in either direction. Refer to text.*

Renew gaskets (6–Fig. SU34) at each side of center section in preparation for final reassembly of hydrostatic unit.

With all sections reassembled individually and with all friction surfaces and bearings lubricated by a coating of ATF, pump and motor sections should be assembled on center section by alignment on four long cap screws (1–Fig. SU33) which are fitted through motor section, center section and into pump housing. Draw screws up evenly in alternating sequence to pull sections together gradually overcoming spring pressure as pump and motor cylinder block assemblies are compressed. Tighten cap screw heads at motor section end to 35 ft.-lbs. (47 N·m).

Carefully reinstall charge pump with a new input shaft seal (52) and new housing "O" ring (47) and such other new parts as may be called for. Tighten cap screws (54) to 20 ft.-lbs. (27 N·m).

At this point, test all three exposed shaft ends, input, output and control, by fitting a torque wrench or spring scale to determine that rolling torque of each shaft does not require effort of more than 25 in.-lbs. (2.8 N·m). If this value is exceeded, disassemble unit to locate and eliminate binding condition. Reinstall bevel output gear on motor shaft end, using a new snap ring if necessary, then complete installation of hydrostatic unit on reduction drive housing as outlined at beginning of this section.

## Series 15 "U" Type

**OPERATION.** The hydrostatic transmission consists of a variable volume, reversible swashplate, axial piston pump; a fixed displacement, axial piston motor; a gerotor charge pump; two check valves; a charge pressure regulator valve and an oil filter. The system operates as a closed loop type. See Fig. SU40. However, any oil lost internally from closed loop circuit is replaced by oil from the charge pump. This make up oil is drawn from the reservoir (differential case) through the oil filter and is pumped into the loop through the check valve on low pressure side at 70-120 psi (483-827 kPa). All excess charge oil passes through charge pressure regulator valve and is dumped on pump and motor; cooling and lubricating the units.

Motor speed is controlled by pump rpm and swashplate angle. Motor direction of rotation is reversed by reversing pump swashplate angle. During normal operation of tractor, operating pressure range is 750-1500 psi (5171-10342 kPa). When control lever is in neutral position, there is no pump swashplate tilt and no pump piston stroke. With no oil flowing through pump, a dynamic braking action takes place and tractor motion is halted. Although braking is normally accomplished by use of the control lever, a foot brake is also provided.

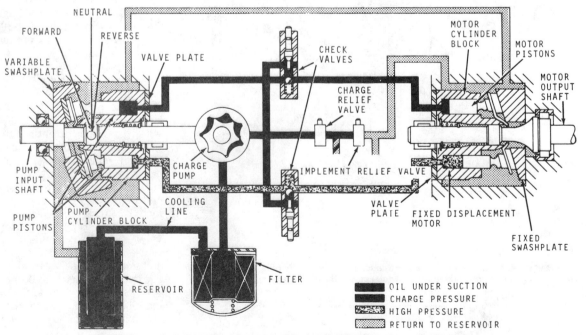

*Fig. SU40—Circuit diagram of Sundstrand Series 15 "U" type hydrostatic transmission.*



Illustrations courtesy Sundstrand

A free-wheeling valve knob is located beneath seat. When valve knob is turned clockwise, both check valves are held open and oil is allowed to recirculate through hydraulic motor while bypassing the pump. This allows manual movement of tractor. Free-wheeling valve knob must be turned fully counterclockwise for full power to be transmitted to rear wheels.

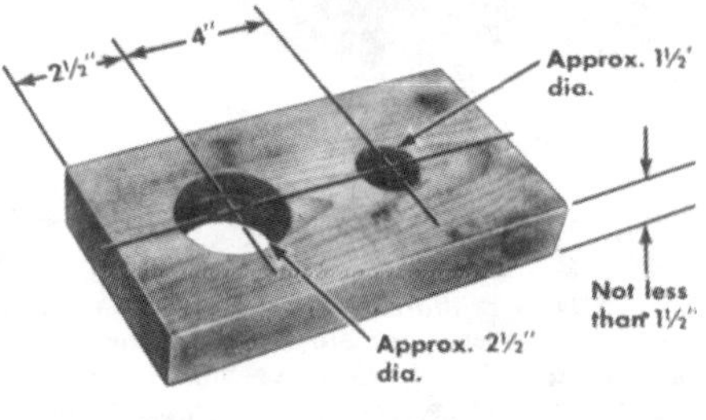


*Fig. SU41—View showing dimensions of holding fixture used in disassembly and reassembly of Sundstrand Series 15 "U" type hydrostatic transmission.*

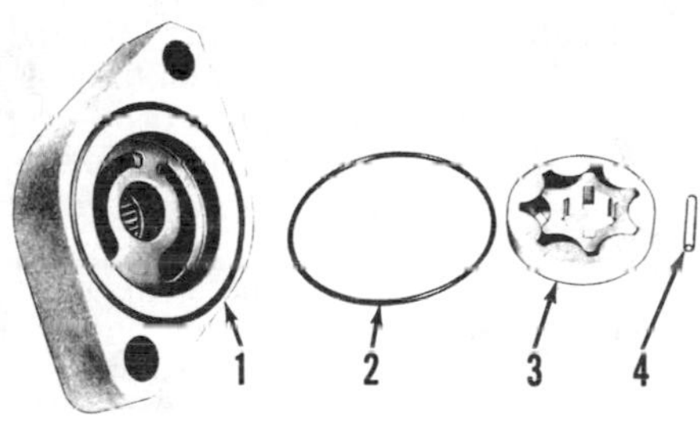

*Fig. SU42—Exploded view of charge pump used on Sundstrand Series 15 "U" type hydrostatic transmission.*

1. Pump housing
2. "O" ring
3. Rotor assy.
4. Drive pin

**OVERHAUL.** To disassemble hydrostatic unit, is it suggested that a wooden holding fixture be made from a piece of lumber 2 inches (50.8 mm) thick, 6 inches (152.4 mm) wide and 12 inches (304.8 mm) long as shown in Fig. SU41. Thoroughly clean exterior of unit, then place unit in holding fixture with charge pump facing upward. Scribe a mark on charge pump housing and center section to ensure correct reassembly.

Unbolt and remove charge pump assembly. See Fig. SU42. Pry oil seal (29–Fig. SU43) from housing (28), then press needle bearing (30) out front of housing. Remove check valves (20) and relief valves (24 and 34). Unbolt and lift off center section (33).

**CAUTION: Valve plates (18 and 36) may stick to center housing. Be careful not to drop them. Remove and indentify valve plates. Pump valve plate has two relief notches and motor valve plate has four notches. See Fig. SU44.**

Tilt housing (7–Fig. SU43) on its side, identify and remove cylinder block and piston assemblies from pump and motor shafts. Lay cylinder block assemblies aside for later assembly.

To remove pump swashplate (12), tilt and hold swashplate in full forward position while driving pins (13) out of shafts (2 and 8). Be careful not to damage housing when driving out pins. When pins are free of shafts, withdraw shafts and swashplate. Withdraw pump shaft (11) and bearing (10). Remove cap screws securing motor swashplate (40) to housing, then lift out swashplate and motor shaft (41). Bearings (5 and 6) and oil seals (4 and 9) can now be removed from housing. Remove needle bearings (35) from center section (33).

**NOTE: Pump cylinder block and pistons are identical to motor cylinder block and pistons and complete assemblies are interchangeable. However, since pistons or cylinder blocks are not serviced separately, it is advisable to keep each piston set with its original cylinder block.**

Carefully remove slipper retainer (16) with pistons (15) from pump cylinder block (17) as shown in Fig. SU45. Check cylinder block valve face and piston bores for scratches or other damage. Inspect pistons for excessive wear or scoring. Check piston slippers for excessive wear, scratches or embedded material. Make certain center oil passage is open in pistons. If excessive wear or other damage is noted on cylinder block or pistons, install a new cylinder block kit which includes pistons, slipper retainer and new cylinder block assembly. If original parts are serviceable, thoroughly clean parts, reassemble and wrap cylinder block assembly in clean paper. Repeat operation on motor cylinder block assembly (37 through 39–Fig.

1. Retaining ring (2)
2. Control shaft
3. Washer (2)
4. Seal (2)
5. Bearing (2)
6. Bearing
7. Housing
8. Trunnion shaft
9. Seal
10. Bearing
11. Pump shaft
12. Swashplate (pump)
13. Spring pins
14. Thrust plate
15. Pump pistons
16. Slipper retainer
17. Cylinder block (pump)
18. Valve plate
19. Dowel pin (2)
20. Check valves
21. Back-up washer
22. "O" ring
23. "O" ring
24. Implement lift relief valve
25. "O" ring
26. Rotor assy.
27. Drive pin
28. Charge pump housing
29. Seal
30. Bearing
31. Oil filter
32. Filter fitting
33. Center section
34. Charge relief valve
35. Bearing (2)
36. Valve plate
37. Cylinder block (motor)
38. Slipper retainer
39. Motor pistons
40. Swashplate (motor)
41. Motor shaft
42. Gasket

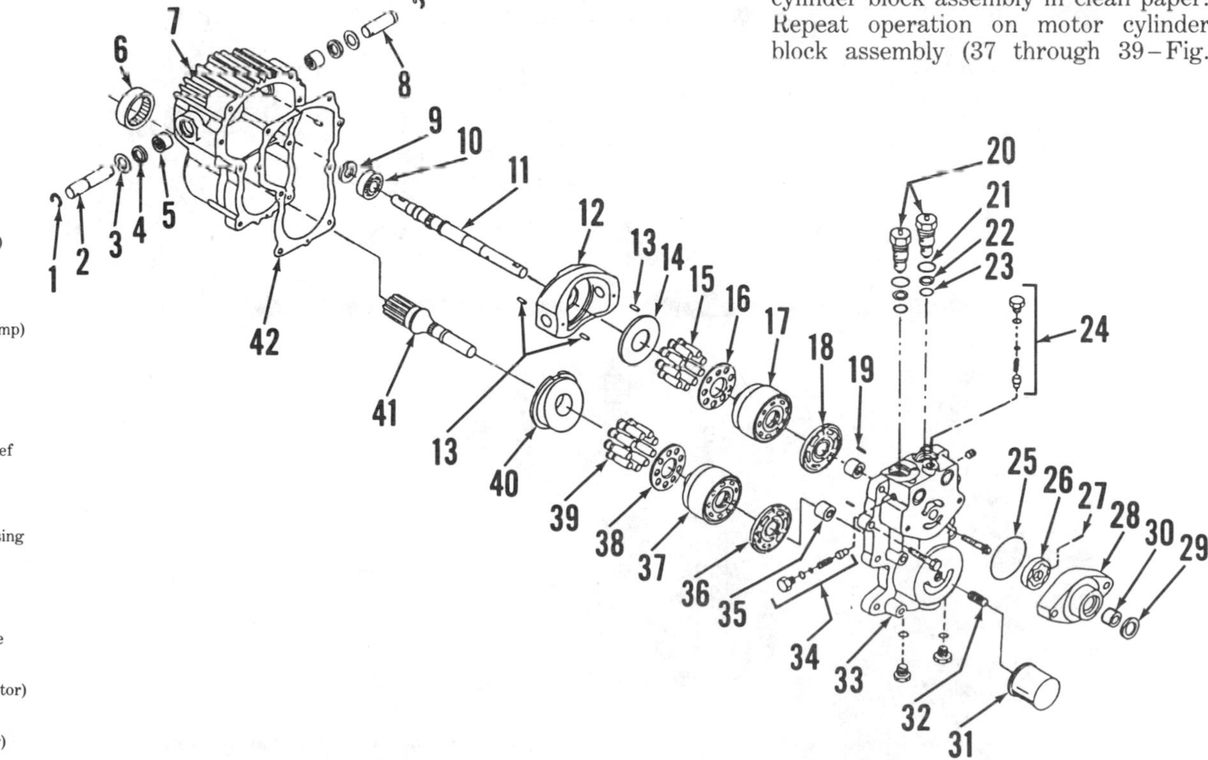

*Fig. SU43—Exploded view of Sundstrand Series 15 "U" type hydrostatic transmission.*

Illustrations courtesy Sundstrand.

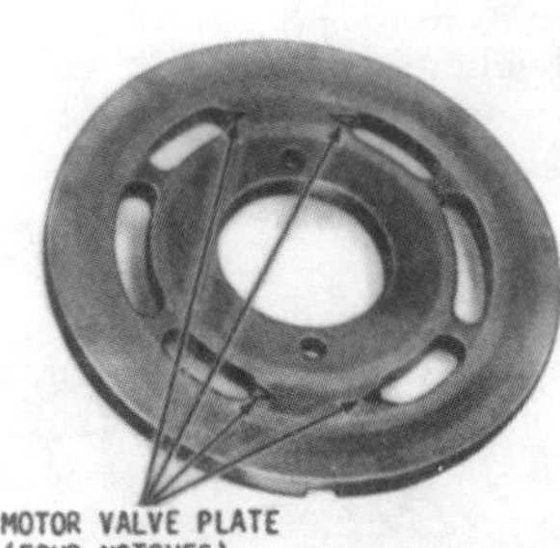


*Fig. SU44—View of valve plates used in Sundstrand Series 15 "U" type hydrostatic transmission. Note that pump valve plate has two notches and motor valve plate has four notches.*

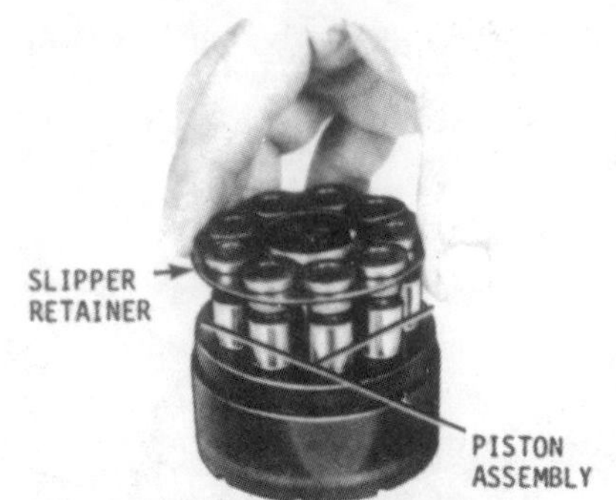


*Fig. SU45—Withdraw slipper retainer with pistons from cylinder block. Pump and motor piston and cylinder block assemblies are identical and must be renewed as complete units.*

SU43) using same checks as used on pump cylinder block assembly.

Check pump valve plate (18) and motor valve plate (36) for excessive wear or other damage and renew as necessary. Inspect motor swashplate (40) and pump swashplate thrust plate (14) for wear, embedded material or scoring and renew as required.

Check charge pump housing (28) and rotor assembly (26) for excessive wear, scoring or other damage and renew as necessary. Charge pump relief valve cone should be free of nicks and scratches.

The check valves (20) are interchangeable and are serviced only as assemblies. Wash check valves in clean solvent and air dry. Thoroughly lubricate check valve assemblies with clean oil before installation.

Renew all "O" rings, gaskets and seals and reassemble by reversing removal procedure, keeping the following points in mind: Lubricate all parts with clean oil. When installing new bearings (35), press bearings in until they are 0.100 inch (2.54 mm) above machined surface of the center housing. Pump swashplate (12) must be installed with thin stop pad towards top of transmission. Be sure control shaft (2) is installed on correct side. Drive new pins (13) into pump swashplate and shafts, using two pins on control shaft (2). Pins should be driven in until 1/4 inch (6 mm) below surface of swashplate. Tighten motor swashplate cap screws to 67 in.-lbs. (7.5 N·m) torque. Be sure pump and motor valve plates (18 and 36) are installed correctly and located on needle bearing (35) and pin (19). Tighten center section to housing cap screws to 30 ft.-lbs. (41 N·m) torque. Rotate pump and motor shafts while tightening these screws to check for proper internal assembly.

Reinstall unit and prime with oil as previously outlined.

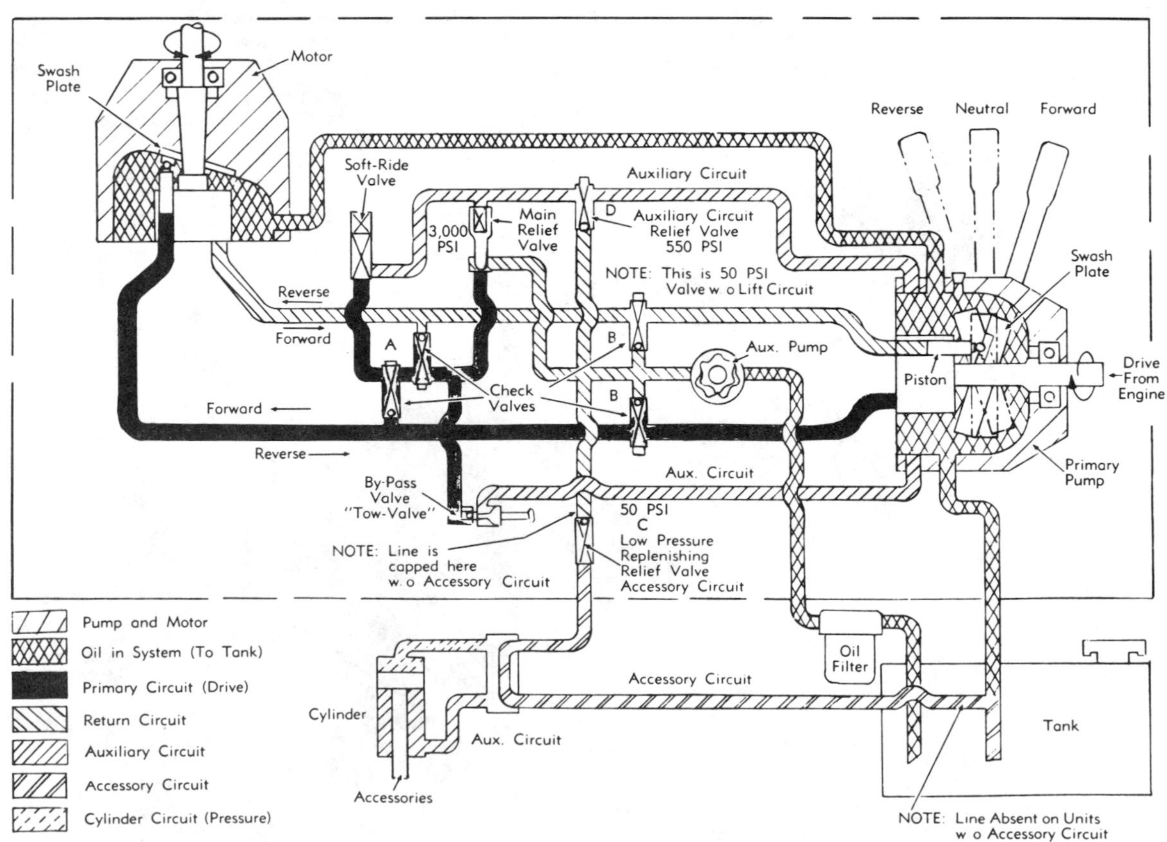


*Fig. V10—Hydraulic circuit diagram of Vickers T66 hydrostatic transmission and auxiliary hydraulic system.*



Illustrations courtesy Sundstrand.

# VICKERS

## Model T66

**OPERATION.** The Vickers T66 hydrostatic transmission consists of a variable displacement, reversible swashplate, axial piston pump; a fixed displacement, axial piston motor; a gerotor charge pump; two charge pressure check valves and a charge pump relief valve. The system is a closed loop type and reduction drive and differential housing is used as a common reservoir. Oil is directed through an oil filter installed between gear reduction unit and hydrostatic transmission pump. Refer to Fig. V10 for a schematic circuit diagram of hydrostatic transmission and auxiliary hydraulic system.

Motor speed is controlled by pump swashplate angle and by pump rpm. Reversing pump swashplate angle will reverse motor rotation. Moving control lever varies ground speed from 0-5.5 mph forward or 0-3 mph in reverse. Dynamic braking of tractor is accomplished by moving hydrostatic control lever to neutral position. In neutral, pump swashplate is not tilted resulting in no pump piston stroke. Since there is no oil flow to transmission motor, the motor ceases to turn and rear wheel rotation is stopped. The transmission is equipped with a release valve which will (when in release position) allow oil to circulate within the motor. This allows motor to turn and tractor can be moved manually. During normal operation, release valve must be in down position.

**OVERHAUL.** To overhaul removed hydrostatic transmission, first thoroughly clean outside of unit, then refer to Fig. V11 and proceed as follows: Drain fluid from transmission. Remove cap screws and separate motor valve plate (101) and motor assembly (73 through 90) from transfer block (100). Remove valve plate cap screws and

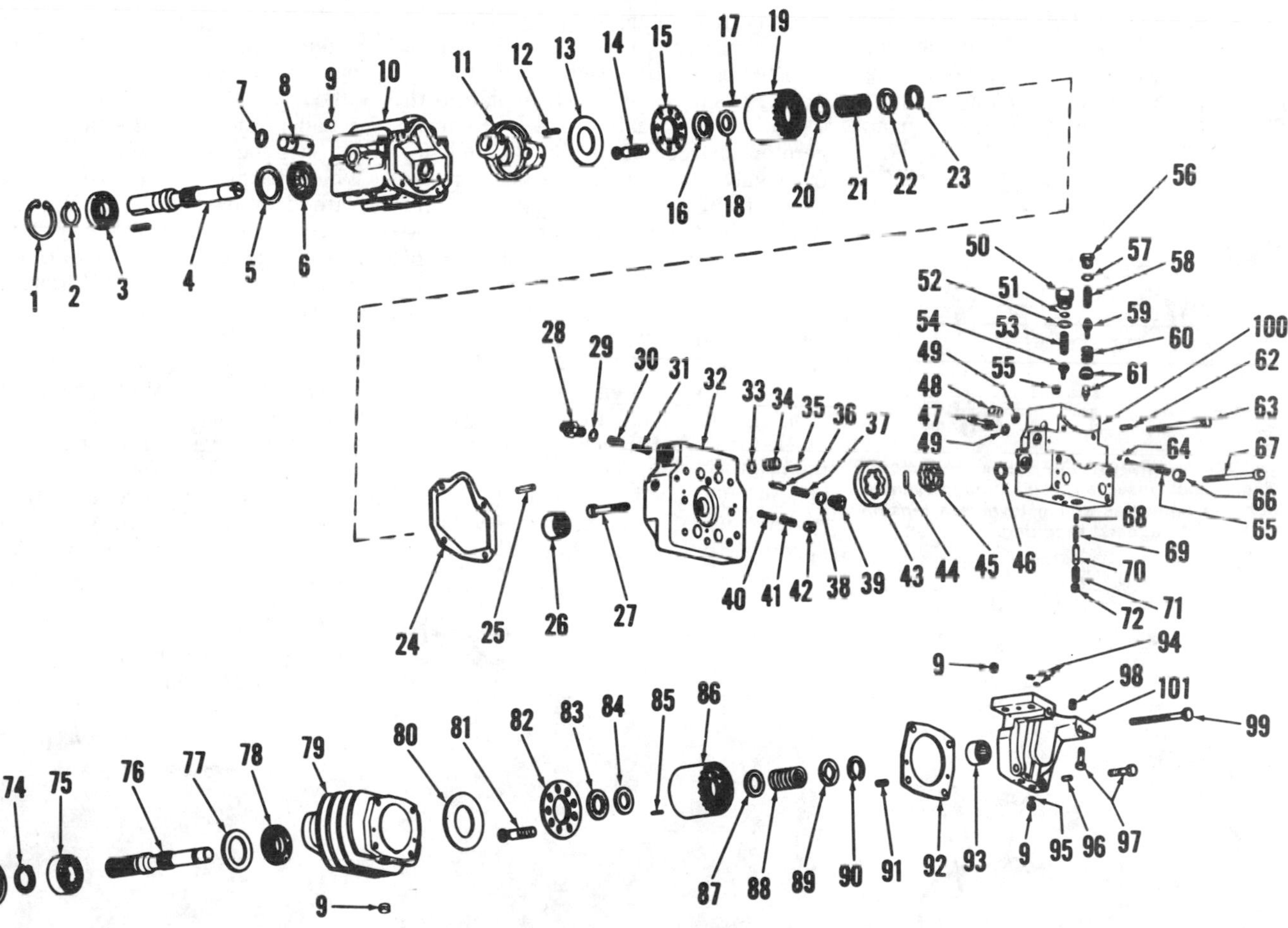

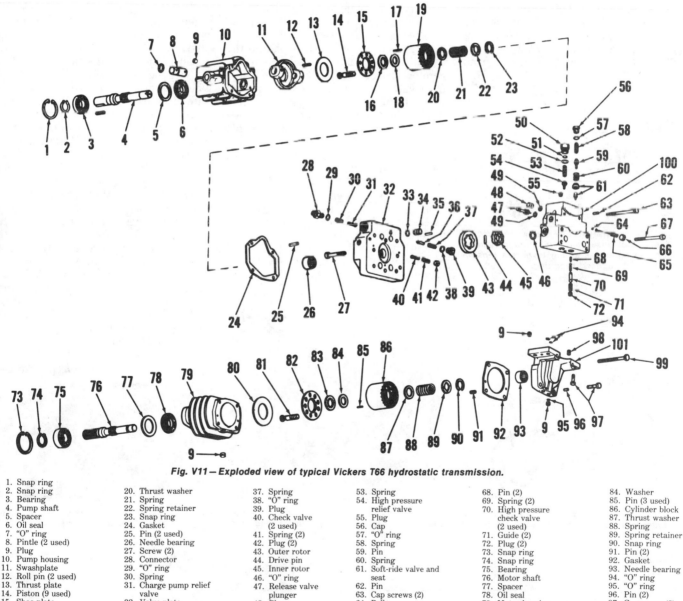

*Fig. V11—Exploded view of typical Vickers T66 hydrostatic transmission.*

1. Snap ring
2. Snap ring
3. Bearing
4. Pump shaft
5. Spacer
6. Oil seal
7. "O" ring
8. Pintle (2 used)
9. Plug
10. Pump housing
11. Swashplate
12. Roll pin (2 used)
13. Thrust plate
14. Piston (9 used)
15. Shoe plate
16. Spherical washer
17. Pin (3 used)
18. Washer
19. Cylinder block
20. Thrust washer
21. Spring
22. Spring retainer
23. Snap ring
24. Gasket
25. Pin (2 used)
26. Needle bearing
27. Screw (2)
28. Connector
29. "O" ring
30. Spring
31. Charge pump relief valve
32. Valve plate
33. "O" ring
34. Plug
35. Pin (2)
36. Lift relief valve
37. Spring
38. "O" ring
39. Plug
40. Check valve (2 used)
41. Spring (2)
42. Plug (2)
43. Outer rotor
44. Drive pin
45. Inner rotor
46. "O" ring
47. Release valve plunger
48. Plug
49. "O" rings
50. Plug
51. "O" ring
52. Shim
53. Spring
54. High pressure relief valve
55. Plug
56. Cap
57. "O" ring
58. Spring
59. Pin
60. Spring
61. Soft-ride valve and seat
62. Pin
63. Cap screws (2)
64. Ball
65. Spring
66. Plug
67. Allen head cap screw (2)
68. Pin (2)
69. Spring (2)
70. High pressure check valve (2 used)
71. Guide (2)
72. Plug (2)
73. Snap ring
74. Snap ring
75. Bearing
76. Motor shaft
77. Spacer
78. Oil seal
79. Motor housing
80. Thrust plate
81. Piston (9 used)
82. Shoe plate
83. Spherical washer
84. Washer
85. Pin (3 used)
86. Cylinder block
87. Thrust washer
88. Spring
89. Spring retainer
90. Snap ring
91. Pin (2)
92. Gasket
93. Needle bearing
94. "O" ring
95. "O" ring
96. Pin (2)
97. Cap screw (2)
98. Pin (2)
99. Cap screw (2)
100. Transfer block
101. Motor valve plate

separate valve plate and motor housing. It may be necessary to tap on valve plate with a leather or plastic mallet to separate valve plate from motor. Remove motor piston and cylinder block assembly with thrust plate (80 through 90) from motor housing. Remove thrust plate (80) and lift piston assembly (81 through 84) out of cylinder block (86). Pistons can now be removed for inspection and renewal if required. To remove cylinder block spring (88), insert a 3/8 inch bolt that is 2½ inches long with a 1 inch OD flat washer through bore of cylinder block as shown in Fig. V12. Place a 1 inch flat washer and a nut on bolt and tighten nut until spring tension is relieved from snap ring (90–Fig. V11). Remove snap ring and loosen nut. Remove spring retainer (89), spring (88) and washer (87). Remove snap ring (73) and tap on inner end of motor shaft (76) to remove shaft, bearing (75) and spacer (77) from housing. Remove snap ring (74) and press bearing from motor shaft. Oil seal (78) can now be removed from housing.

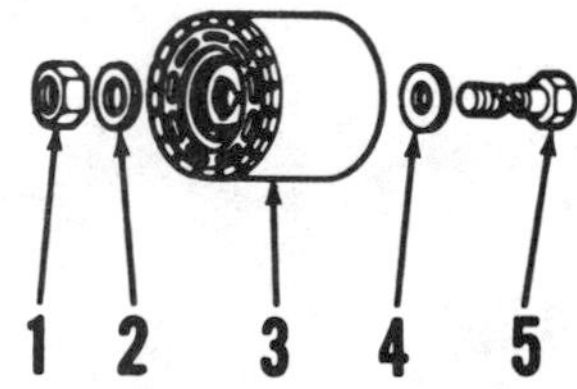


***Fig. V12—To disassemble pump and motor cylinder block, insert a bolt (5) through cylinder block and compress spring to relieve tension against snap ring.***

1. Nut
2. Washer
3. Cylinder assy.
4. Washer
5. Bolt (3/8 x 3½ in.)

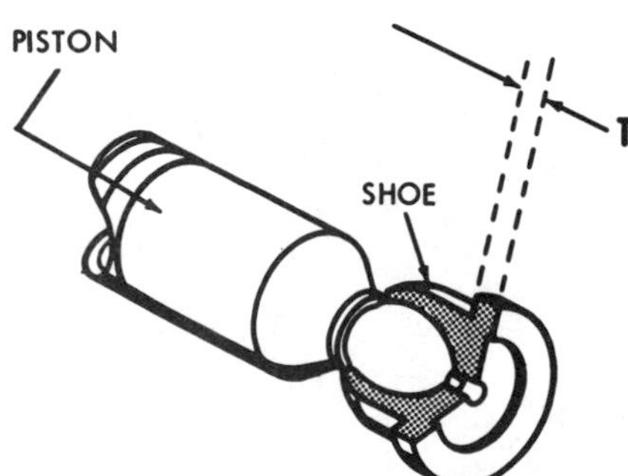


***Fig. V13—Shoe thickness (T) of all pistons in a cylinder must be within 0.001 inch (0.025 mm) of each other.***

To disassemble hydrostatic drive pump, remove Allen head cap screws (67) recessed in transfer block and hex head cap screws (63), then separate pump valve plate (32) and transfer block (100) from pump housing (10). Remove piston and cylinder block assembly (14 through 23) from pump housing. Remove shoe plate (15), pistons (14) and washers (16 and 18) from pump cylinder block. To remove spring (21), refer to preceding motor disassembly procedure as units are identical. Remove thrust plate (13) from swashplate (11). Remove snap ring (1) and tap on inner end of pump shaft (4) and remove pump shaft, bearing (3) and spacer (5). Remove snap ring (2) and press pump shaft from bearing. Drive roll pins (12) out of swashplate (11), remove pintles (8), then remove swashplate. Oil seal (6) can now be removed from pump housing.

To separate valve plate (32) from transfer block (100), remove Allen head cap screws (27) and tap valve plate with a leather or plastic mallet. Remove gerotor charge pump (43, 44 and 45) from valve plate. Remove and inspect valves from pump valve plate (32) and transfer block (100). Do not interchange valve components. Needle bearings (26 and 93) can be pulled from their respective valve plates.

Clean and inspect all parts for excessive wear or other damage. Inspect cylinder block bores and pistons for scoring and valve plate end of cylinder blocks for scratches or imbedded material. If minor defects in valve plate end of cylinder blocks cannot be removed by light tapping, renew block assembly. Piston shoe thickness (T–Fig. V13) must not vary more than 0.001 inch (0.025 mm) for all nine pistons in each cylinder block. New pistons should not have more than 0.003 inch (0.076 mm) end play; end play on used pistons must not exceed 0.008 inch (0.203 mm). Pistons and cylinder block should be renewed as a complete assembly. Remove minor scratches from face of thrust plates (13 and 80–Fig. V11) and valve plates (32 and 101) by light lapping, but renew parts if extensive wear or deep scratches are noted. Inspect faces of inner and outer rotors of gerotor charge pump and remove minor defects by light lapping.

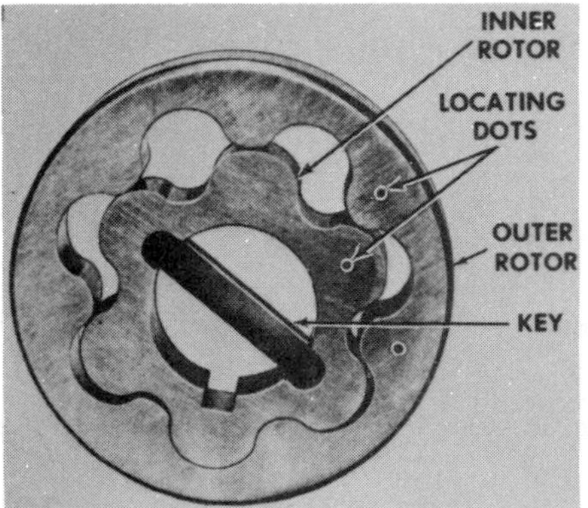


***Fig. V14—Assemble inner rotor of gerotor charge pump in outer rotor with locating dots positioned as shown.***

Renew all seals, "O" rings and gaskets and reassemble by reversing disassembly procedure, keeping the following points in mind: Lubricate all parts with new Type "A" automatic transmission fluid. Apply a sealant such as P&OB Sealing Compound Grade No. 4 approximately 3/8 inch (10 mm) wide around outside of valve plate and transfer block. Install gerotor charge pump rotors so dots are located as shown in Fig. V14. When charge pump is installed in valve plate, dots are not visible. When installing high pressure check valves, be sure valve guides (17–Fig. V11) are installed with open end outward. Tighten plugs (72) to a torque of 30-35 ft.-lbs. (41-47 N·m). Install pintles (8) with pintle end closest to "O" ring groove positioned in swashplate (11). Install roll pins (12) until they are 0.100 inch (2.54 mm) from surface of swashplate. Tighten valve plate to transfer block cap screws (27) to 30 ft.-lbs. (41 N·m) torque. Install thrust plates (13 and 80) so beveled edge is away from pistons as shown in Fig. V15. Tighten transfer block to pump housing Allen head cap screws to a torque of 25-30 ft.-lbs. (34-41 N·m). Tighten all other cap screws to a torque of 17-21 ft.-lbs. (23-28 N·m).

***Fig. V15—Install thrust plates so beveled edge is away from pistons as shown.***

# BRIGGS & STRATTON

| Model | No. Cyls. | Bore | Stroke | Displacement | Horsepower |
|---|---|---|---|---|---|
| 19 & 19D | 1 | 3 in. (76.2 mm) | 2-5/8 in. (66.7 mm) | 18.56 cu. in. (304 cc) | 7.25 (5.4 kW) |
| 23 & 23D | 1 | 3 in. (76.2 mm) | 3-1/4 in. (82.5 mm) | 22.97 cu. in. (376 cc) | 9 (6.7 kW) |

Engines covered in this Briggs & Stratton section have cast iron cylinder blocks.

## MAINTENANCE

**SPARK PLUG.** Recommended spark plug is Champion J-8, Autolite A-71, AC-GC46 or equivalent. Electrode gap is 0.030 inch (0.762 mm).

**CARBURETOR.** Float type carburetors are equipped with adjusting needles for both idle and power fuel mixtures. Counter-clockwise rotation of adjusting needles, as shown in Fig. B&S1, richens fuel mixtures. Initial adjustment is 3/4 turn open on idle needle valve and 1½ turns open on power needle valve. This will allow engine to start and run, but final adjustment should be made with engine running and hot. Run engine under full load at operating speed and turn power needle valve counter-clockwise until engine begins to run unevenly. Then, turn power needle valve clockwise slowly until engine runs smoothly. Return engine to idle and adjust idle speed regulating screw so engine is running at 1200 rpm. Adjust idle needle valve until engine runs smoothly. Readjust idle speed regulating screw if necessary.

After making above adjustments, engine should accelerate from idle speed to full speed without sputtering or hesitation. If it does not accelerate properly, turn power needle slightly counterclockwise to provide a richer fuel mixture.

Correct float setting is shown in Fig. B&S2. Bend tang on float that contacts float valve to bring float setting within specification shown.

Throttle shaft and bushings should be checked for wear and if a diametral clearance of 0.010 inch (0.254 mm) or more can be found, installation of a new shaft and/or bushings is required. Check upper body for being warped with a 0.002 inch (0.051 mm) feeler gage. If gage can be inserted between upper and lower bodies as shown in Fig. B&S3, a new upper body should be installed. Install new inlet float valve and seat if any wear is visible.

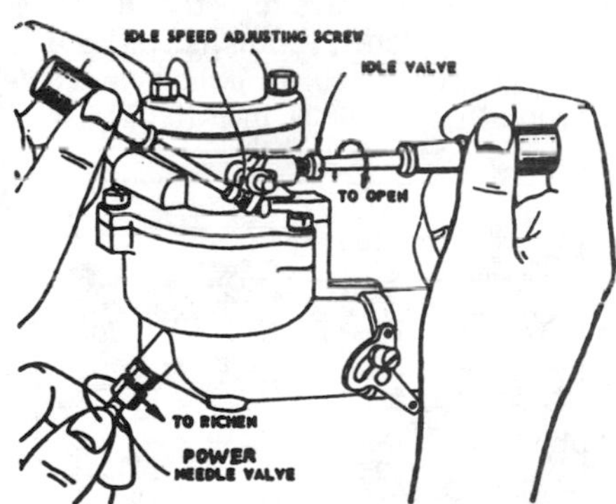


*Fig. B&S1—View showing fuel mixture adjustments and idle speed regulating screw.*

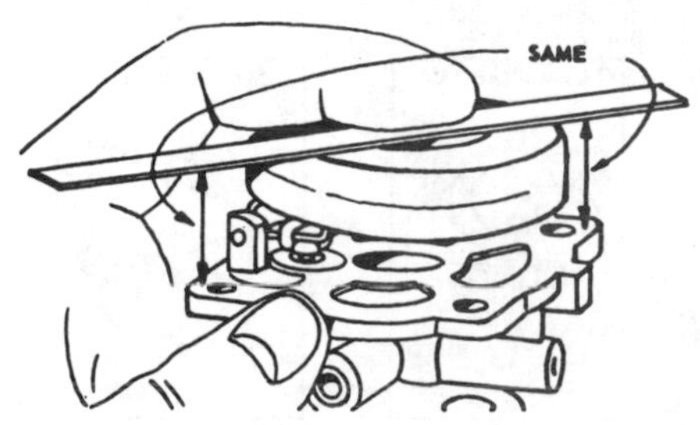


*Fig. B&S2—View showing correct float adjustment.*

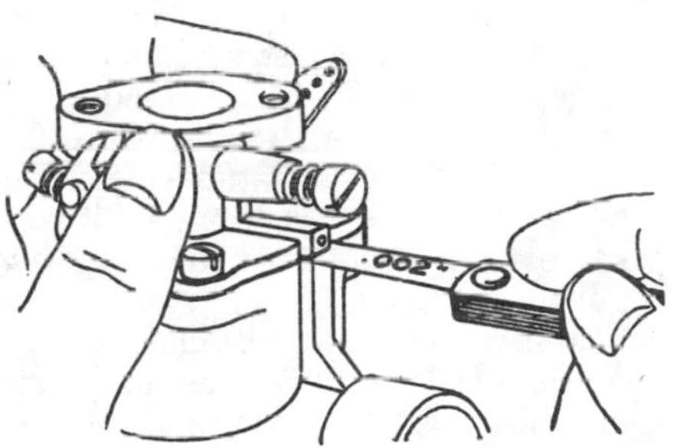


*Fig. B&S3—Checking upper body for warpage with a 0.002 inch (0.051 mm) feeler gage.*

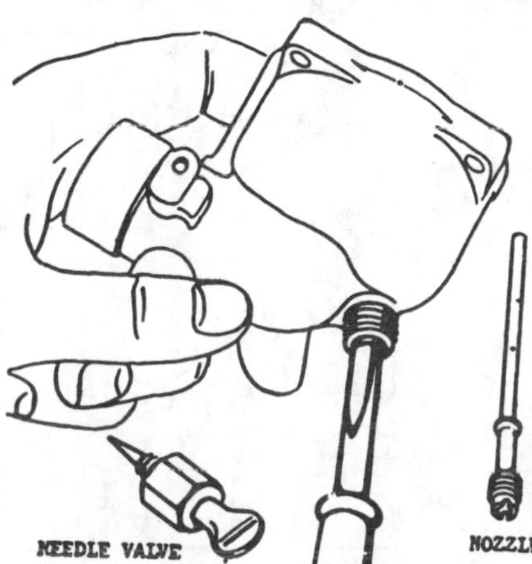


*Fig. B&S4—Remove main nozzle before separating upper and lower carburetor bodies.*

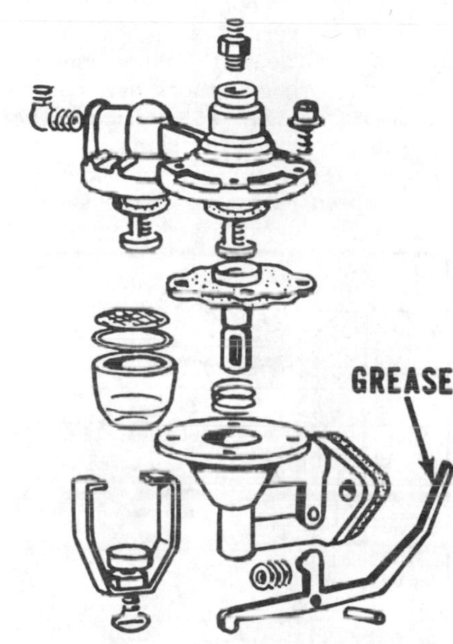


*Fig. B&S5—Exploded view of fuel pump used on some engines.*

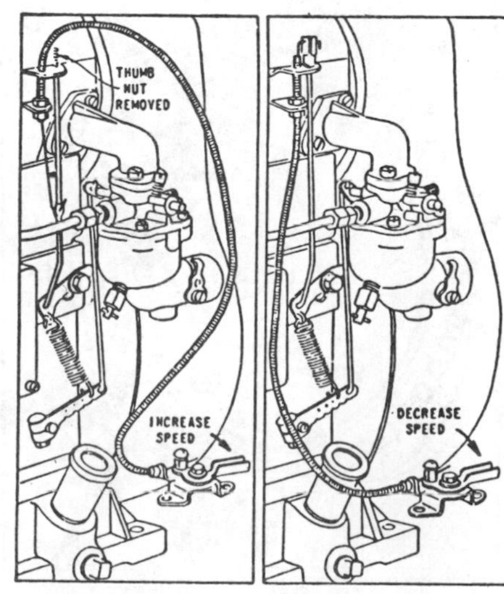


*Fig. B&S6—View showing mechanical governor linkage and remote governor controls.*

Illustrations courtesy Briggs & Stratton Corp.

**CAUTION: The upper and lower bodies are locked together by the main nozzle. Be sure to remove power needle valve and main nozzle before attempting to separate upper body from lower body. See Fig. B&S4.**

The fuel pump used on some engines is actuated by a lever which rides in a groove on the crankshaft. The lever should be greased at point shown in Fig. B&S5 before fuel pump is installed. The fuel pump diaphragm can be renewed.

**GOVERNOR.** The governor used is the gear driven mechanical type, with linkage as shown in Fig. B&S6. All slack due to wear must be removed from governor linkage to prevent "Hunting" or unsteady running. To adjust carburetor to governor linkage, loosen clamp on governor lever so lever will turn on governor shaft. Move carburetor throttle shaft to wide open position and turn governor shaft counterclockwise as far as possible. Then, tighten governor lever clamp.

Briggs & Stratton recommended operating speed range for those models is

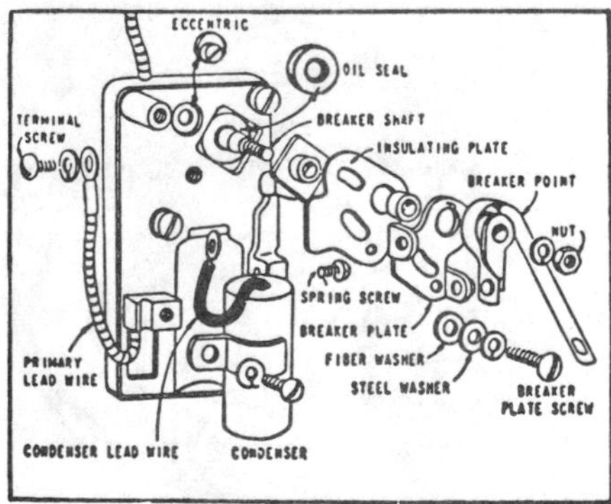


*Fig. B&S7—Exploded view of breaker box. Oil seal is installed with metal side out. See Fig. B&S15 also.*

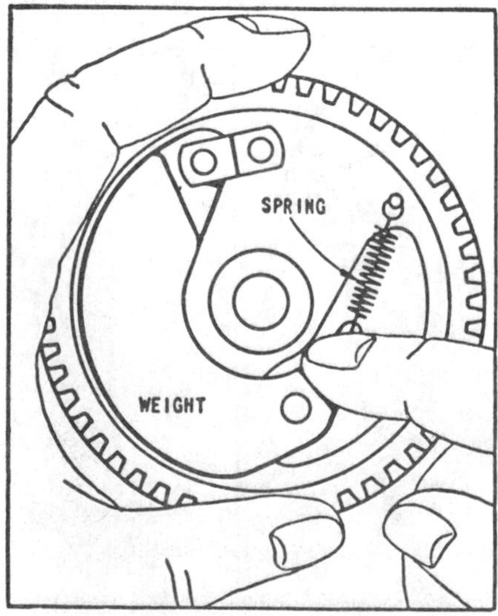


*Fig. B&S8—Method of checking advance weight action. Refer to text.*

1800-3600 rpm. However, engine rpm may differ slightly depending on equipment in which engines are used. Equipment manufacturers recommendations should be followed in all cases.

**MAGNETO.** The breaker contact gap is 0.020 inch (0.508 mm) and condenser capacity is .18 to .24 mfd. The breaker mechanism (Fig. B&S7) is located externally on carburetor side of engine. The armature, coil and magnetic rotor are enclosed by the flywheel. This ignition system is called "Magnamatic Ignition." This system includes a centrifugal unit mounted on face of camshaft gear which provides automatic advance of ignition timing. To check freeness of advance weight action, place camshaft gear in position shown in Fig. B&S8 and press weight down. When weight is released, spring should return weight to its original position without binding. If weight does not return to its original position, renew and recheck as before.

Static timing of ignition is controlled by the position of magneto armature on magneto back plate. To adjust timing, first remove flywheel and breaker box cover. Adjust breaker contact gap to 0.020 inch (0.508 mm). Turn crankshaft in normal direction of rotation until breaker contacts just start to open. At this point, arrow on armature (X–Fig. B&S9) should register with arrow on rotor marked with model number of engine. If arrow on armature does not register with correct arrow on rotor, loosen the three armature mounting screws and rotate armature until correct register is obtained, then tighten screws. The armature air gap is nonadjustable, but when installing an armature, make certain it is as concentric as possible with magnetic rotor.

**LUBRICATION.** Crankcase capacity is 3 pints (1.4L) for Models 19 and 19D and 4 pints (1.9L) for Models 23 and 23D. Use SAE 30 oil when operating in

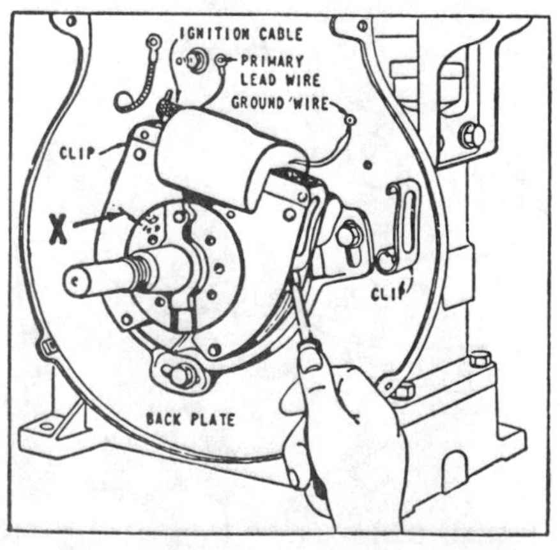


*Fig. B&S9—Arrow (X) on armature must align with appropriate number (as "19" for Model 19 engines, etc.) when points just start to open.*

temperatures above 32°F (0°C) and SAE 10W oil when operating in temperatures below 32°F (0°C). Use high quality detergent oil having API classification SE, SF or SG. These engines are splash lubricated by a connecting rod dipper.

The engines are equipped with crankcase breathers with a sucker valve in breather body. The valve fiber disc or complete valve should be renewed if it does not operate properly.

## REPAIRS

**NOTE: When checking compression on models with "Easy Spin" starting, turn engine opposite normal direction of engine rotation. See CAMSHAFT paragraph.**

**CYLINDER HEAD.** When removing cylinder head, be sure to note the position from which different length screws were removed. If they are not used in the same position when installing cylinder head, it will result in some screws bottoming in holes and not enough thread engagement on others. Install all screws finger tight, then tighten them with wrench in sequence shown in Fig. B&S10 to a torque of 190 in.-lbs. (21.5 N·m). Run engine about five minutes to allow it to warm up and retighten screws in same sequence.

**CONNECTING ROD.** Rod and piston assembly are removed from cylinder head end of block. The aluminum alloy connecting rod rides directly on the induction hardened crankpin. The rod should be rejected if crankpin hole is out-of-round over 0.0007 inch (0.0178 mm)

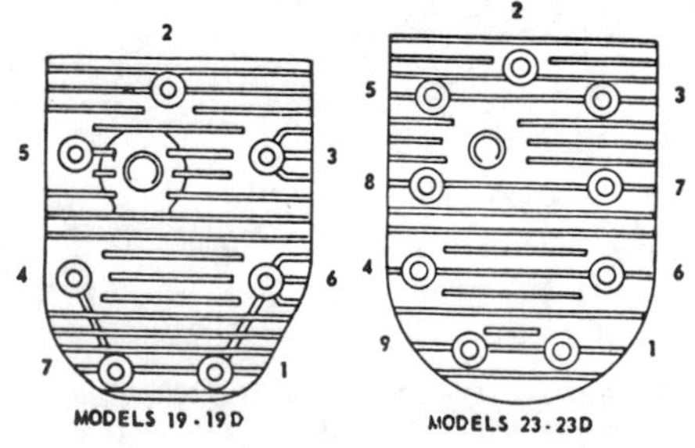

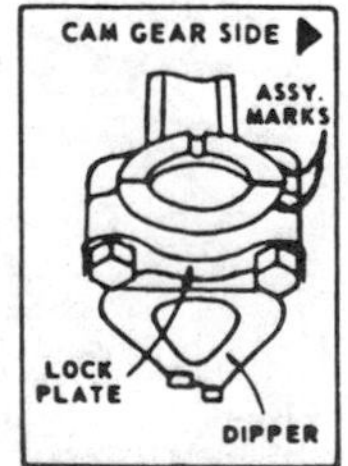


*Fig. B&S11—View showing connecting rod as assembly index marks and oil dippers.*

or piston pin hole is out-of-round over 0.0005 inch (0.0127 mm). The rod should also be rejected if either hole is scored or worn to rejection size of 1.001 inches (25.425 mm) on 19 and 19D or 1.189 inches (30.200 mm) on 23 and 23D for crankpin hole or 0.6735 inch (17.107 mm) on 19 and 19D or 0.736 inch (18.694 mm) on 23 and 23D for piston pin hole. Piston pins are available in 0.005 inch (0.127 mm) oversize.

Recommended clearance of rod to crankpin is 0.0015-0.0045 inch (0.0381-0.1143 mm) and rod to piston pin is 0.0015-0.002 inch (0.0381-0.051 mm). Tighten connecting rod bolts to a torque of 175-200 in.-lbs. (20-22 N•m). Refer to Fig. B&S11 for rod assembly index marks.

**PISTON, PIN AND RINGS.** Pistons in these models are aluminum alloy. If piston shows signs of wear, scoring or scuffing, it should be rejected. It should also be rejected if, after cleaning top ring groove, side clearance of a new ring installed in top groove exceeds 0.007 inch (0.178 mm).

Check piston pin by taking several measurements to find point of greatest wear. If a piston pin is 0.0005 inch (0.0127 mm) or more out-of-round, or is worn to rejection size of 0.6713 inch (17.051 mm) on 19 and 19D or 0.7338 inch (18.6385 mm) on 23 and 23D install a new pin. When piston pin holes in piston and connecting rod are worn beyond rejection size, are scored or are out-of-round over 0.0005 inch (0.0127 mm), the 0.005 inch (0.127 mm) oversize piston pin may be used if reaming piston and rod to 0.005 inch (0.127 mm) oversize cleans up worn or scored surfaces.

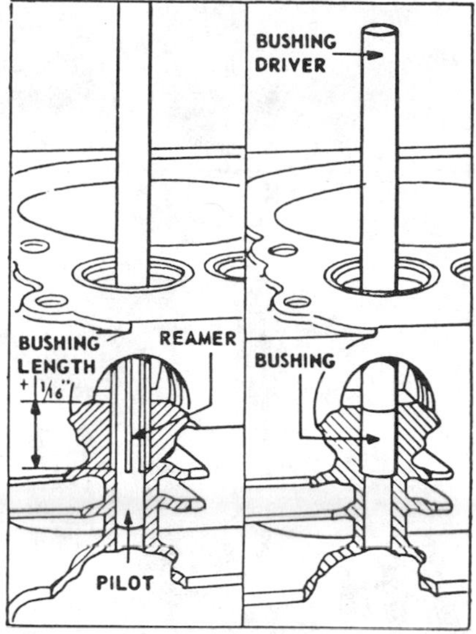


*Fig. B&S14—View showing valve guide being reamed and valve guide bushing installed.*

Reject piston rings having more than 0.030 inch (0.762 mm) end gap. End gap on new rings should be 0.010-0.018 inch (0.254-0.457 mm). If end gap on new rings exceeds 0.018 inch (0.457 mm), it is an indication cylinder should be rebored. Install rings on piston as shown in Fig. B&S12 and stagger ring end gaps 90 degrees apart around piston.

If cylinder is more than 0.003 inch (0.076 mm) oversize or 0.0015 inch (0.0381 mm) out-of-round, it will be necessary to rebore it. Pistons and rings are available in standard size and oversizes. The standard bore size for these engines is 2.999-3.000 inches (76.175-76.2 mm).

**CRANKSHAFT.** The crankshaft is carried in two main bearings which may be either bushing or ball bearing type, or be one bushing and one ball bearing.

On engines having a bushing type main bearings, running clearance should be not less than 0.0015 inch (0.0381 mm) and not more than 0.0045 inch (0.1143 mm). Wear on both crankshaft and bushings will determine running clearance; therefore, both crankshaft and bushings must be checked. Renew crankshaft if worn to the following rejection sizes: Models 19 and 19D crankpin journal 0.9974 inch (25.334 mm), main bearing journal 1.180 inches (29.972 mm); Models 23 and 23D crankpin journal 1.1854 inches (30.109 mm), main bearing journal 1.3769 inches (34.973 mm). Maximum allowable out-of-round on journals is 0.0007 inch (0.0178 mm). If main bearing bushings are rough, scored or out-of-round 0.0007 inch (0.0178 mm) or more, renew main

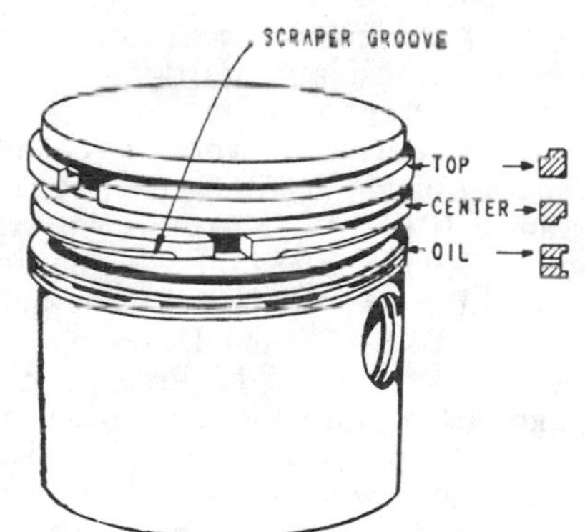


*Fig. B&S12—Install piston rings on piston as shown and stagger ring end gaps 90 degrees apart around piston.*

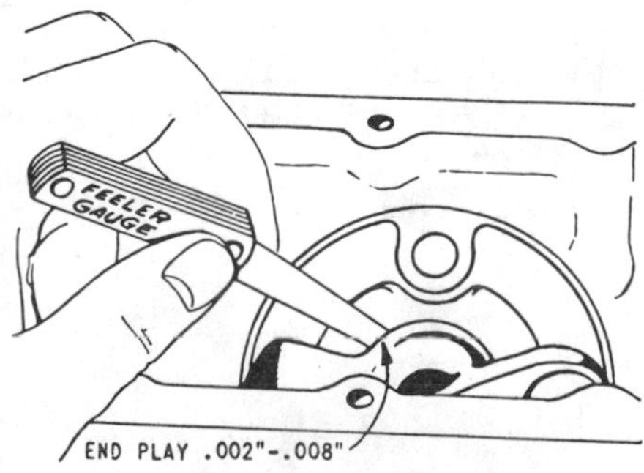


*Fig. B&S13—Checking end play between bearing plate and crankshaft thrust face.*

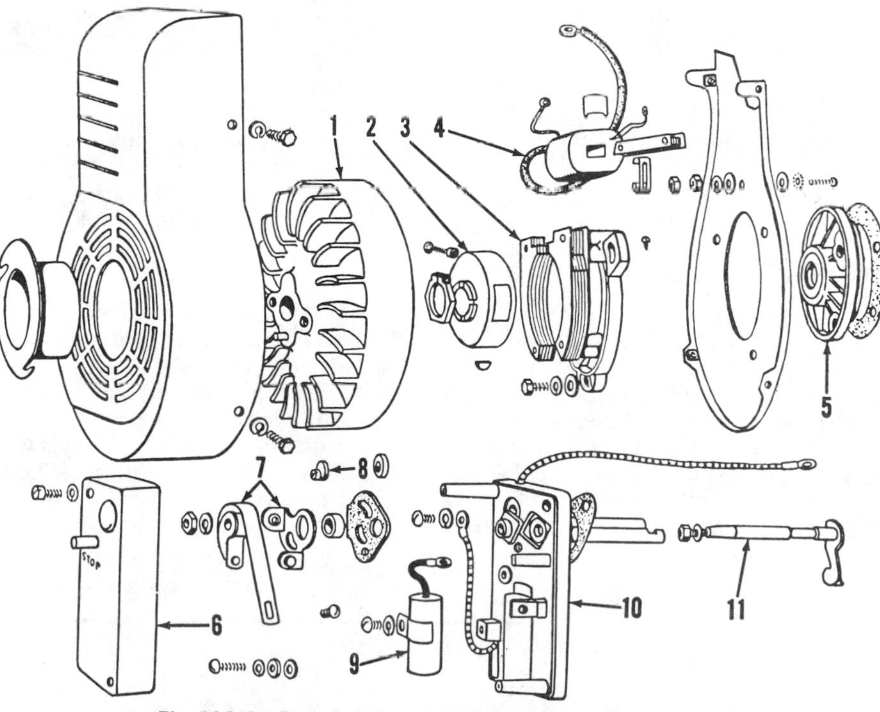


*Fig. B&S15—Exploded view of "Magna-matic" ignition system.*

1. Engine flywheel
2. Magneto rotor
3. Magneto armature
4. Coil assy.
5. Bearing plate
6. Breaker box cover
7. Breaker points
8. Point gap adjusting cam
9. Condenser
10. Breaker base
11. Breaker shaft

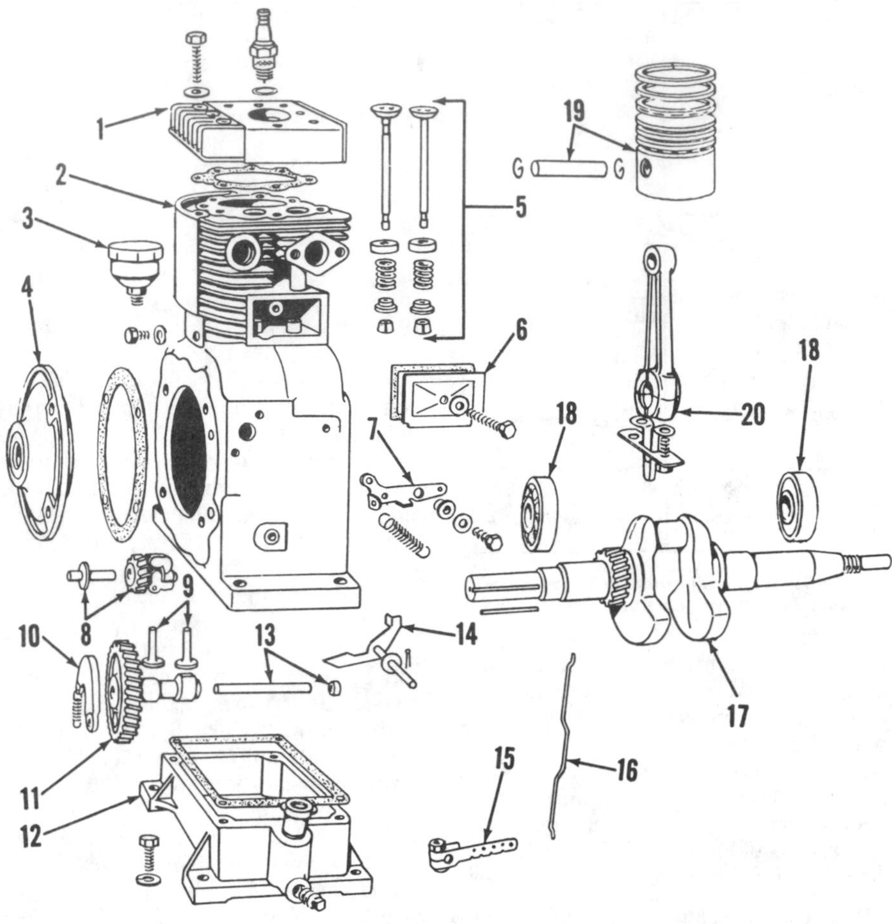


*Fig. B&S16–Exploded view of main engine components.*

1. Cylinder head
2. Cylinder assembly
3. Crankcase breather
4. Bearing plate
5. Valves, springs, and keepers
6. Tappet cover plate
7. Governor control lever
8. Governor shaft and weight assembly
9. Valve tappets
10. Spark advance weight and spring
11. Cam gear
12. Engine base
13. Camshaft and plug
14. Governor crank assembly
15. Governor lever
16. Throttle link
17. Crankshaft
18. Ball type main bearings
19. Piston, ring and pin assembly
20. Connecting rod with oil slinger

bearing support plates with factory reamed bushings. Main bearing bushing rejection sizes are as follows: 1.1843 inches (30.081 mm) for Models 19 and 19D and 1.3813 inches (35.085 mm) for Models 23 and 23D.

The recommended crankshaft end play is 0.002-0.008 inch (0.051-0.203 mm) and is measured as shown in Fig. B&S13. End play is controlled by use of different thickness gaskets between bearing plate and crankcase.

On engines equipped with ball bearing mains, check ball bearings for wear or roughness. When renewing ball bearing mains, press crankshaft out of old bearings. Expand new bearings by heating them in oil. Slide heated bearing in place with sealed side towards crankpin journal.

**CAMSHAFT.** On all models, camshaft and timing gear are an integral part and are referred to as the "cam gear". The cam gear turns on a stationary shaft which is referred to as the "camshaft." Reject camshaft if it is worn to a diameter of 0.49675 inch (12.6917 mm). Reject cam gear if lobes are worn to the following reject sizes: Models 19 and 19D, 1.115 inches (28.321 mm); Models 23 and 23D, 1.184 inches (30.073 mm).

On models equipped with "Easy Spin" starting, intake cam lobe is designed to hold intake valve slightly open on a part of compression stroke. Therefore, to check compression, engine must be turned backwards.

**NOTE: On engines equipped with either a wind-up or rewind starter, blower housing must be removed in order to turn engine in reverse direction.**

"Easy Spin" cam gears are identified by two holes drilled in web of the gear. Where part number of an older cam gear and an "Easy Spin" cam gear are the same (except for an "E" following "Easy Spin" part), gears may be interchanged. Align timing marks on cam gear and crankshaft gear on assembly.

**VALVE SYSTEM.** Always set valve clearance when engine is cold. Proper valve clearance is as follows: Models 19 and 19D intake valve 0.008 inch (0.203 mm) and exhaust valve 0.015 inch (0.381 mm); Models 23 and 23D intake valve 0.008 inch (0.203 mm) and exhaust valve 0.018 inch (0.457 mm). Valve clearance is adjusted by grinding end of valve stem squarely. Valves have a seat angle of 45 degrees and a seat width of 3/64 to 5/64-inch (1.2-2.0 mm).

Renewal of exhaust valve seat insert requires the use of special equipment which is available from Briggs & Stratton.

If valve guides are worn, they can be rebushed in the following manner. Use reamer (B&S #19183) to ream worn guide. See Fig. B&S14. Ream only 1/16 inch (1.6 mm) deeper than valve guide bushing (B&S #230655). Do not ream all the way through guide. Press in valve guide bushing until top end of bushing is flush with top end of valve guide. Use a soft metal driver so top end of bushing is not peened over. Valve guide bushings used in these engines are finish reamed to size at the factory so no further reaming is necessary and a standard valve can be used.

**VALVE TIMING.** When reinstalling cam gear, align timing mark on cam gear with timing mark on crankshaft gear. Valve to piston timing will then be correct.



Illustrations courtesy Briggs & Stratton Corp.

# BRIGGS & STRATTON

| Model | No. Cyls. | Bore | Stroke | Displacement | Horsepower |
|---|---|---|---|---|---|
| 130000 Series | 1 | 2-9/16 in. (65.1 mm) | 2-7/16 in. (61.9 mm) | 12.57 cu. in. (206 cc) | 5 (3.7 kW) |
| 140000 Series | 1 | 2-3/4 in. (69.8 mm) | 2-3/8 in. (60.3 mm) | 14.1 cu. in. (231 cc) | 6 (4.5 kW) |
| 170000 Series | 1 | 3 in. (76.2 mm) | 2-3/8 in. (60.3 mm) | 16.79 cu. in. (275 cc) | 7 (5.2 kW) |
| 171000 Series | 1 | 3 in. (76.2 mm) | 2-3/8 in. (60.3 mm) | 16.79 cu. in. (275 cc) | 7 (5.2 kW) |
| 190000 Series | 1 | 3 in. (76.2 mm) | 2-3/4 in. (69.8 mm) | 19.44 cu. in. (318 cc) | 8 (6.0 kW) |
| 191000 Series | 1 | 3 in. (76.2 mm) | 2-3/4 in. (64.8 mm) | 19.44 cu. in. (318 cc) | 8 (6.0 kW) |
| 251000 Series | 1 | 3-7/16 in. (87.3 mm) | 2-5/8 in. (66.7 mm) | 24.36 cu. in. (399 cc) | 10 (7.5 kW) |
| 252000 Series | 1 | 3-7/16 in. (87.3 mm) | 2-5/8 in. (66.7 mm) | 24.36 cu. in. (399 cc) | 11 (8.2 kW) |
| 253000 Series | 1 | 3-7/16 in. (87.3 mm) | 2-5/8 in. (66.7 mm) | 24.36 cu. in. (399 cc) | 11 (8.2 kW) |

All engines in this section have aluminum cylinder blocks with aluminum cylinder bores.

## MAINTENANCE

**SPARK PLUG.** Recommended spark plug for all models is a Champion J-8, Autolite A-71 or an AC GC46. Set electrode gap to 0.030 inch (0.762 mm) for all models.

**NOTE: If a resistor type plug is necessary to reduce radio interference, use Champion XJ-8 or equivalent. Briggs & Stratton Corporation does not recommend cleaning spark plugs by abrasive blasting method as this may introduce some abrasive material into the engine which could cause extensive damage.**

**FLO-JET CARBURETORS.** Two different float type carburetors are used. They are called a "two-piece" (Fig. B&S20) or a "one-piece" (Fig. B&S21) carburetor depending upon type of construction.

Float type carburetors are equipped with adjusting needle for both idle and power fuel mixtures. Refer to Fig. B&S22. Counter-clockwise rotation of adjusting needles richens the mixture. For initial starting adjustment, open idle mixture needle valve ½ to ¾ turn and main needle valve (power fuel mixture) 1⅛ turns on two-piece carburetor. On one-piece carburetor, open both needle valves 1⅛ turns. Start engine and when it is warm, make final adjustments as follows: Set engine control for desired operating speed, turn main needle clockwise until engine misses, and then turn it counter-clockwise just past smooth operating point until engine begins to run unevenly. Return speed control to idle position and adjust idle speed stop screw until engine idles at 1750 rpm. Then adjust idle needle valve until engine runs smoothly. Reset idle speed stop screw if necessary. The engine should then accelerate without

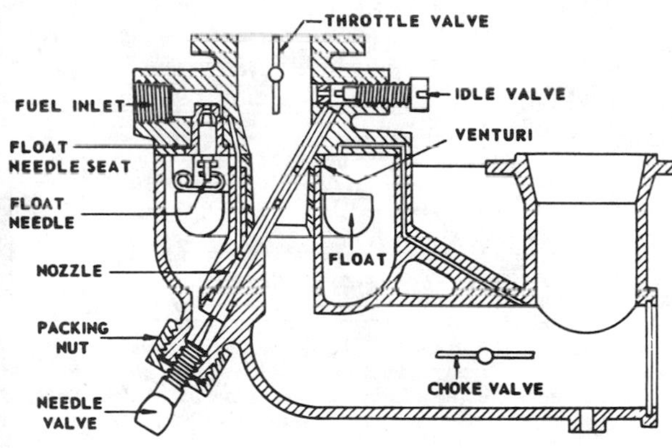


*Fig. B&S20 — Cross-sectional view of typical B&S "two-piece" carburetor. Before separating upper and lower body sections, remove packing nut and power needle valve as a unit. Then, using special screwdriver, remove nozzle.*

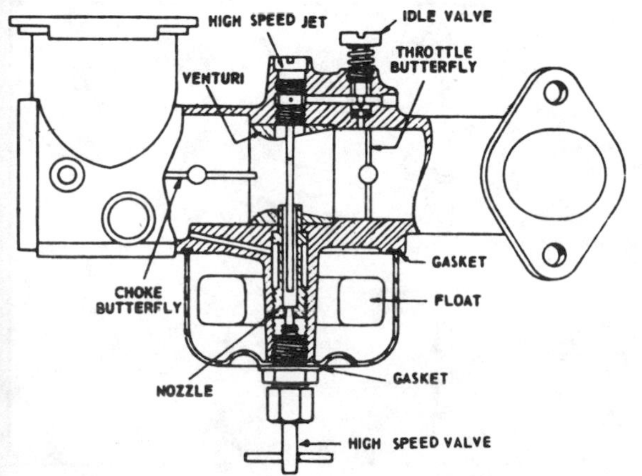


*Fig. B&S21 — Cross-sectional view of typical B&S "one-piece" carburetor.*

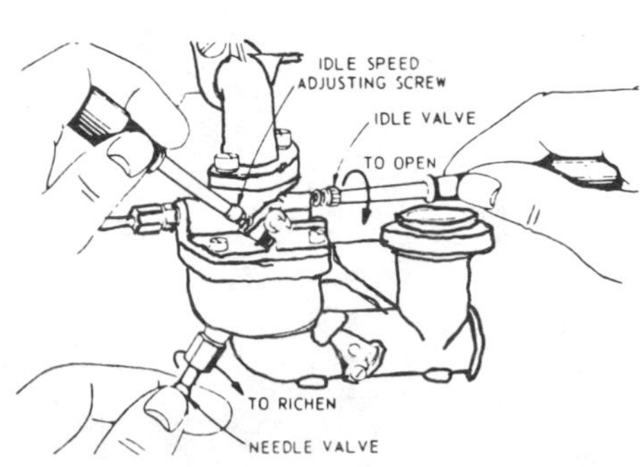


*Fig. B&S22 — Adjustment points for typical B&S carburetor. Refer to text for adjustment procedure.*

Illustrations courtesy Briggs & Stratton Corp.

hesitation or sputtering. If it does not accelerate properly, turn main needle valve counter-clockwise slightly to provide a richer fuel mixture.

**NOTE: The upper and lower bodies of two-piece float type carburetor are locked together by the main nozzle. Refer to cross-sectional view of carburetor in Fig. B&S20. Before attempting to separate upper body from lower body, loosen packing nut and unscrew nut and needle valve. Then, using special screwdriver (B&S tool #19061 or #19062), remove nozzle.**

If a 0.002 inch (0.051 mm) feeler gage can be inserted between upper and lower bodies of two-piece carburetor as shown in Fig. B&S23, upper body is warped and should be renewed.

The float level on both float type carburetors should be within dimensions shown in Figs. B&S24. If not, bend tang on float as shown in Fig. B&S25 to adjust float level. If any wear is visible on inlet valve or inlet valve seat, install a new valve and seat assembly. On one-piece carburetors, inlet valve seat is machined in carburetor body and is not renewable.

Check throttle shaft for wear on all float type carburetors. If 0.010 inch (0.254 mm) or more free play (shaft to bushing clearance) is noted, install new throttle shaft and/or throttle shaft bushings. To remove worn bushings, turn a ¼-inch x 20 tap into bushing and pull bushing from body casting with a tap. Press new bushings into casting by using a vise and, if necessary, ream bushings with a 7/32-inch (5.5 mm) drill bit.

**PUMP TYPE (PULSA-JET) CARBURETOR.** The pump type (Pulsa-Jet) carburetor is basically a suction type carburetor incorporating a fuel pump to fill a constant level fuel sump in top of fuel tank. Refer to schematic view in Fig. B&S26. This makes a constant fuel-air mixture available to engine regardless of fuel level in tank.

Carburetor adjustment is accomplished by turning fuel mixture needle. Turning needle clockwise leans fuel-air mixture. To adjust carburetor, engine should be warm and running at approximately 3000 rpm at no-load. Turn needle valve clockwise until engine begins to lose speed; then, turn needle slowly counter-clockwise until engine begins to run unevenly from excessively rich fuel-air mixture. This should result in a correct adjustment for full load operation. Adjust idle speed to 1750 rpm.

To remove pump type carburetor, first remove carburetor and fuel tank as an assembly; then, remove carburetor from fuel tank. When reinstalling carburetor on fuel tank, use a new gasket or pump diaphragm as required and tighten retaining screws evenly. Fig. B&S27 shows an exploded view of pump unit.

The pump type carburetor has two fuel feed pipes; the long pipe feeds fuel into pump portion of carburetor from which fuel then flows to constant level fuel sump. The short pipe extends into constant level sump and feeds fuel into carburetor venturi via fuel mixture needle valve. Check valves are incorporated in the pump diaphragm. The pipe or screen housing can be renewed if fuel screen in lower end of pipe is broken or clogged and cannot be cleaned. If pipe is made of nylon, unscrew old pipe and install new pipe with a wrench. Be careful not to overtighten new pipe. If pipe is made of brass, clamp pipe lightly in a

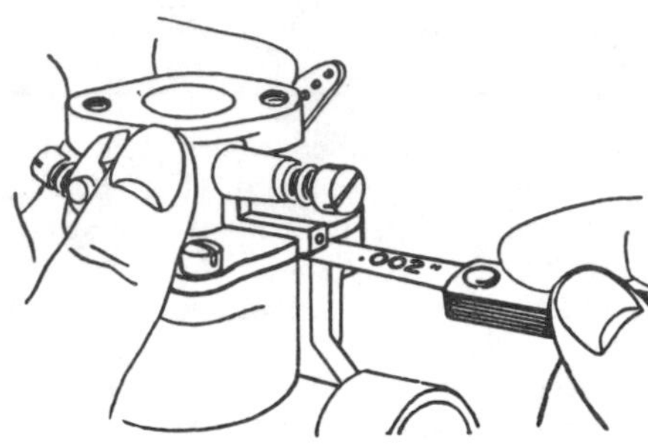

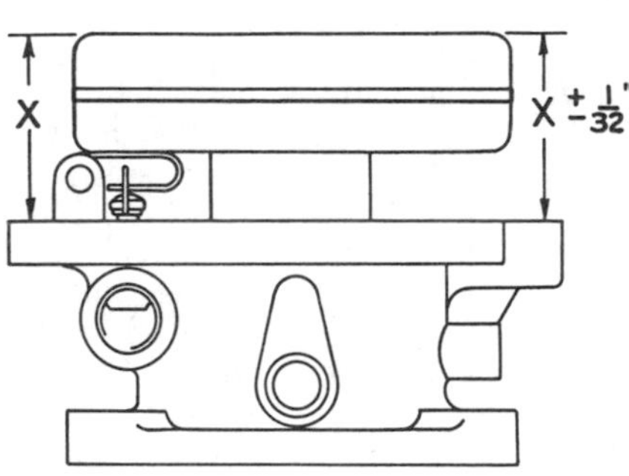


*Fig. B&S24—Float setting on both type carburetors should be within specifications as shown. Refer to Fig. B&S25 for adjustment.*

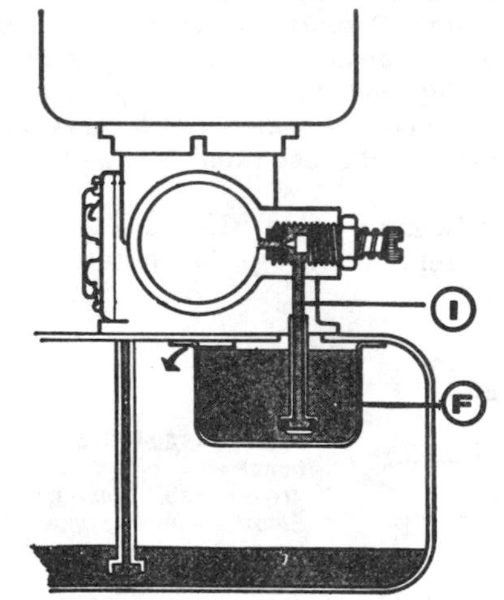


*Fig. B&S26—Fuel flow in Pulsa-Jet carburetor. Fuel pump incorporated in carburetor fills constant level sump below carburetor (F) and excess fuel flows back into tank. Fuel is drawn from sump through inlet (I) past fuel mixture adjusting needle by vacuum in carburetor.*

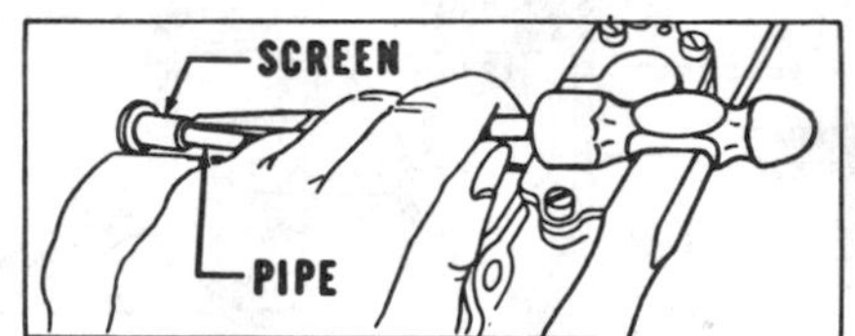


*Fig. B&S28—To renew screen housing on pump type carburetors with brass feed pipes, drive old screen housing from pipe as shown. To hold pipe, clamp lightly in a vise.*

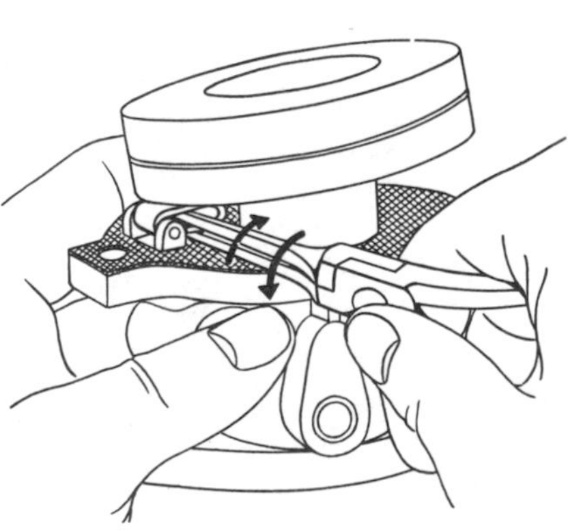

*Fig. B&S25—Bend tang with needle nose pliers to adjust float setting.*

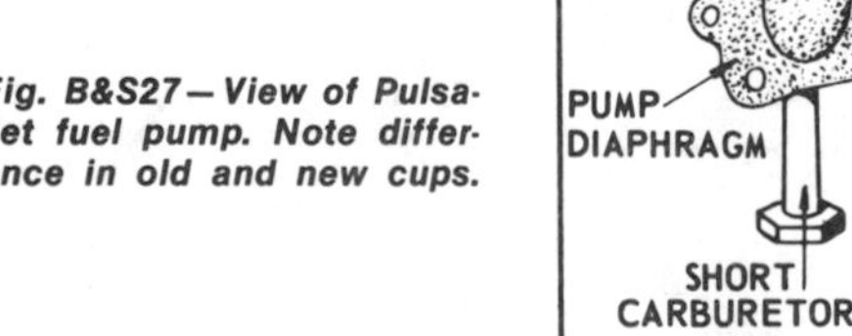

*Fig. B&S27—View of Pulsa-Jet fuel pump. Note difference in old and new cups.*

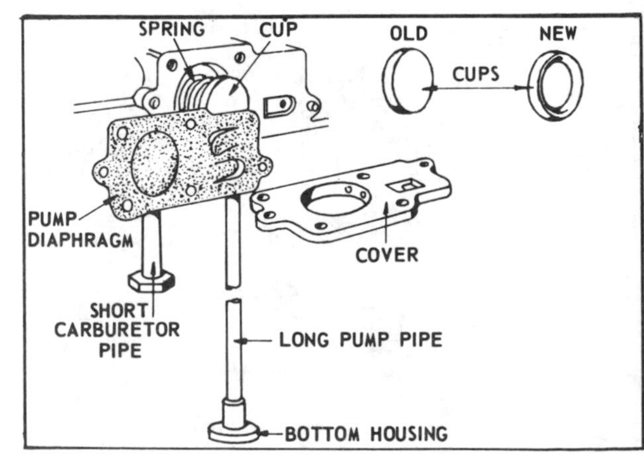




Illustrations courtesy Briggs & Stratton Corp.

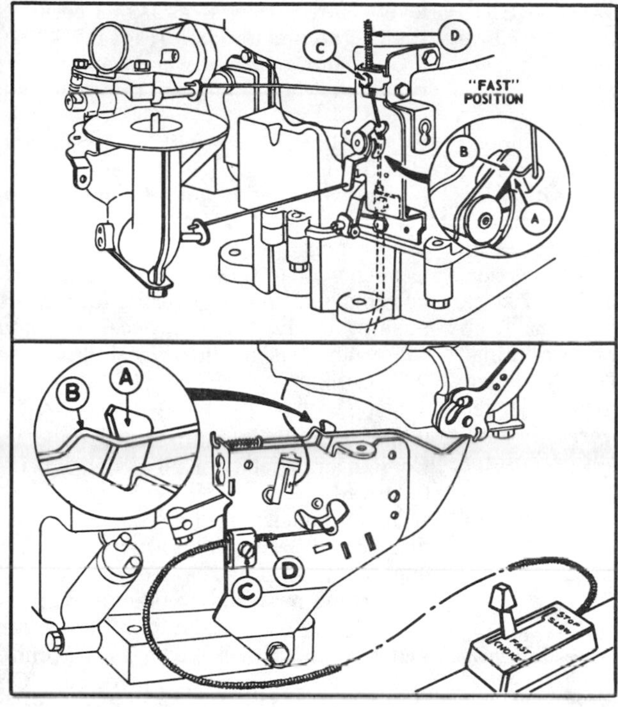


Fig. B&S29—On Choke-A-Matic controls shown, choke actuating lever (A) should just contact choke link or shaft (B) when control is at "FAST" position. If not, loosen screw (C) and move control wire housing (D) as required.

vise and drive old screen housing from pipe with a small chisel as shown in Fig. B&S28. Drive a new screen housing onto pipe with a soft faced hammer.

**NOTE: If soaking carburetor in cleaner for more than one-half hour, be sure to remove all nylon parts and "O" ring, if used, before placing carburetor in cleaning solvent.**

**CHOKE-A-MATIC CARBURETOR CONTROLS.** Engines may be equipped with a control unit with which carburetor choke and throttle and magneto grounding switch are operated from a single lever (Choke-A-Matic carburetors).

To check operation of Choke-A-Matic carburetor controls, move control lever to "CHOKE" position; carburetor choke slide or plate must be completely closed. Then, move control lever to "STOP" position; magneto grounding switch should be making contact. With control lever in "RUN", "FAST", or "SLOW" position, carburetor choke should be completely open. On units with remote controls, synchronize movement of remote lever to carburetor control lever by loosening screw (C–Fig. B&S29) and moving control wire housing (D) as required; then, tighten screw to clamp the housing securely. Refer to Fig. B&S30 to check remote control wire movement.

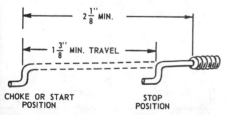

**AUTOMATIC CHOKE (THERMOSTAT TYPE).** A thermostat operated choke is used on some models equipped with two-piece carburetor. To adjust choke linkage, hold choke shaft so thermostat lever is free. At room temperature, stop screw in thermostat collar should be located midway between thermostat stops. If not, loosen stop screw, adjust collar and tighten stop screw. Loosen set screw (S–Fig. B&S31) on thermostat lever. Then, slide lever on shaft to insure free movement of choke unit. Turn thermostat shaft clockwise until stop screw contacts thermostat stop. While holding shaft in this position, move shaft lever until choke is open exactly 1/8-inch (3 mm) and tighten lever set screw. Turn thermostat shaft counter-clockwise until stop screw contacts thermostat stop as shown in Fig. B&S32. Manually open choke valve until it stops against top of choke link opening. At this time, choke valve should be open at least 3/32-inch (2 mm), but not more than 5/32-inch (4 mm). Hold choke valve in wide open position and check position of counterweight lever. Lever should be in a horizontal position with free end towards right.

**FUEL PUMP.** A fuel pump is available as optional equipment on some

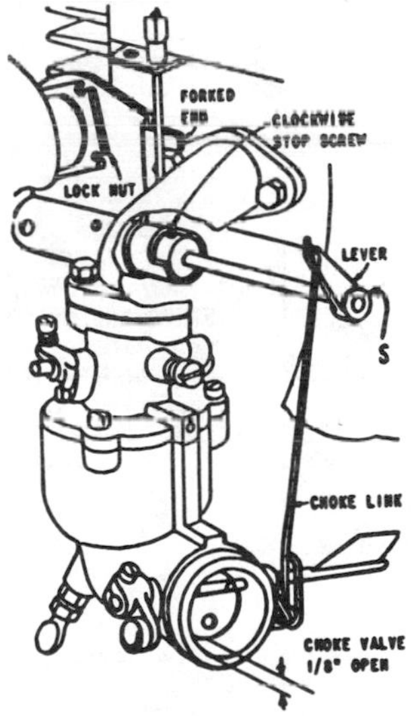


Fig. B&S31—Automatic choke used on some models equipped with two-piece Flo-Jet carburetor showing unit in "Hot" position.

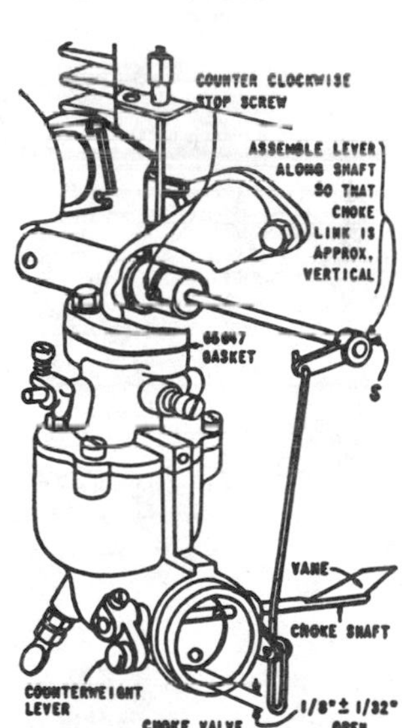


Fig. B&S32—Automatic choke on two-piece Flo-Jet carburetor in "Cold" position.

$2\frac{1}{8}$" MIN.
$1\frac{3}{8}$" MIN. TRAVEL
CHOKE OR START POSITION
STOP POSITION

Fig. B&S30—For proper operation of Choke-A-Matic controls, remote control wire must extend to dimension shown and have a minimum travel of 1⅜ inches (35 mm).

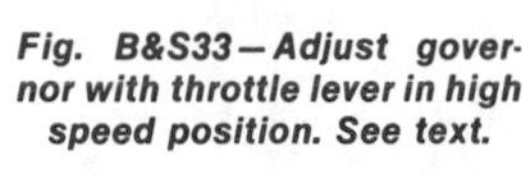

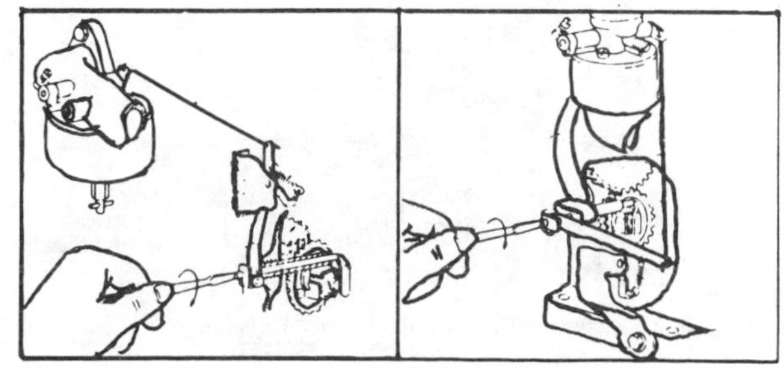

Fig. B&S33—Adjust governor with throttle lever in high speed position. See text.

Illustrations courtesy Briggs & Stratton Corp.

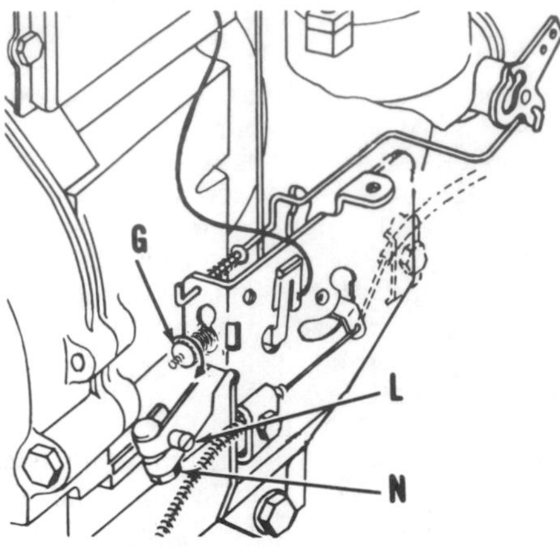

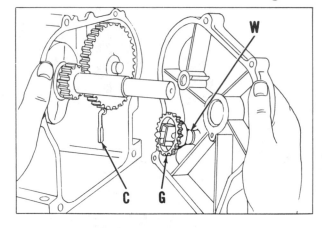

Fig. B&S34—View of governor linkage used on horizontal crankshaft engines; refer to text for adjustment procedure.

models. Refer to SERVICING BRIGGS & STRATTON ACCESSORIES section in this manual for fuel pump servicing information.

**GOVERNOR.** Engines are equipped with a gear driven mechanical governor. The governor unit is enclosed within the engine and is driven from camshaft gear. Governor unit and lubrication oil slinger are integral on all vertical crankshaft engines. All binding or slack due to wear must be removed from governor linkage to prevent "hunting" or unsteady operation. To adjust carburetor to governor linkage, loosen clamp bolt on governor lever. Move link end of governor lever until carburetor throttle shaft is in wide open position. Using a screwdriver, rotate governor lever shaft clockwise as far as possible, then tighten clamp bolt (Fig. B&S33).

Governor gear and weight unit can be removed when engine is disassembled. Refer to exploded views of engines in Figs. B&S48, B&S49, B&S50 and B&S51. Remove governor lever, cotter pin and washer from outer end of governor lever shaft. Slide governor lever out of bushing towards inside of engine. Governor gear and weight unit can now be removed. Renew governor lever shaft bushing in crankcase, if necessary, and ream new bushing after installation to 0.2385-0.239 inch (6.058-6.070 mm).

**MAGNETO.** The breaker point gap is 0.020 inch (0.508 mm) on all models. Condenser capacity on all models is 0.18-0.24 mfd.

On all models, breaker points and condenser are accessible after removing engine flywheel and breaker cover.

On some models, one breaker point is an integral part of ignition condenser and breaker arm is pivoted on a knife edge retained in a slot in pivot post. On these models, breaker contact gap is adjusted by moving condenser as shown in Fig. B&S37. On other models, breaker contact gap is adjusted by relocating position of breaker contact bracket; refer to Fig. B&S38.

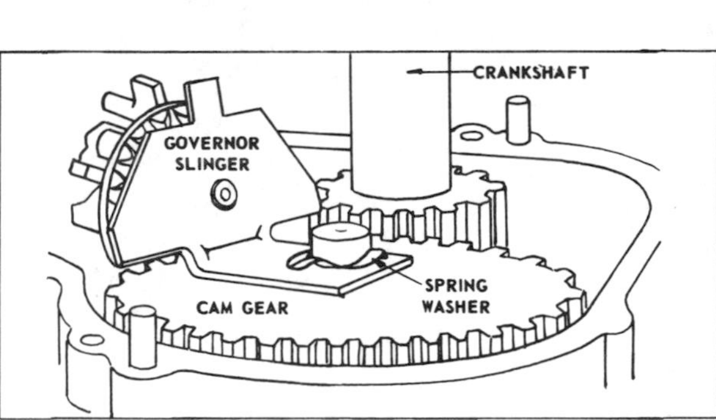

Fig. B&S35—Installing crankcase cover on horizontal crankshaft Series 170000, 190000 and late 140000 with mechanical governor. Governor on Series 251000, 252000 and 253000 is similar. Governor crank (C) must be in position shown. A thrust washer (W) is placed between governor (G) and crankcase cover.

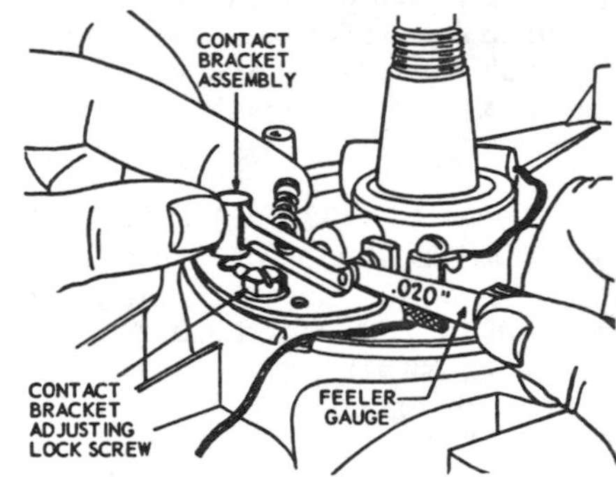

Fig. B&S38—Adjusting breaker point gap on models having breaker points separate from condenser.

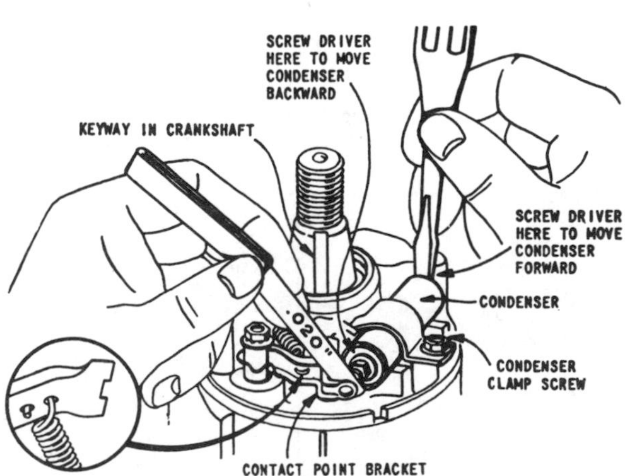

Fig. B&S36—View showing Series 140000, 170000, 171000, 190000, 191000, 251000 and 252000 vertical crankshaft mechanical governor unit. Drawing is of lower side of engine with oil sump (engine base) removed.


Fig. B&S37—View showing breaker point adjustment on models having breaker point integral with condenser. Move condenser to adjust point gap.

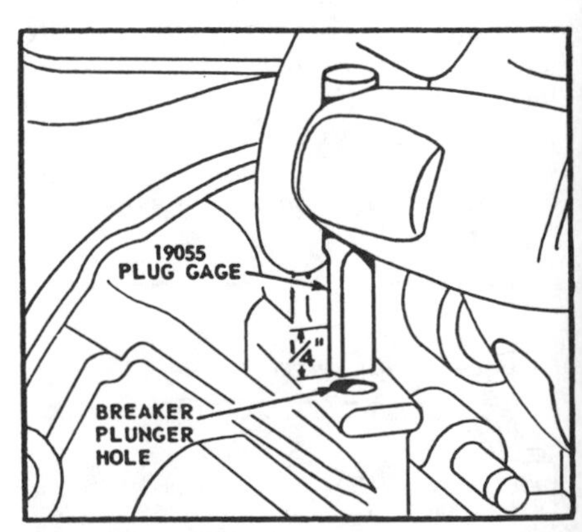

Fig. B&S39—If B&S plug gage #19055 can be inserted in breaker plunger bore a distance of 1/4-inch (6 mm) or more, bore is worn and must be rebushed.



Illustrations courtesy Briggs & Stratton Corp.

On all models, breaker contact arm is actuated by a plunger held in a bore in engine crankcase and riding against a cam on engine crankshaft. Plunger can be removed after removing breaker points. Renew plunger if worn to a length of 0.870 inch (22.098 mm) or less. If breaker point plunger bore in crankcase is worn, oil will leak past plunger. Check bore with B&S plug gage #19055; if plug gage will enter bore ¼-inch (6 mm) or more, bore should be reamed and a bushing installed. Refer to Fig. B&S39 for method of checking bore and to Fig. B&S40 for steps in reaming bore and installing bushing if bore is worn. To ream bore and install bushing, it is necessary that breaker points, armature and ignition coil and crankshaft be removed.

When reassembling, adjust breaker point gap to 0.020 inch (0.508 mm) and set armature to flywheel air gap at 0.010-0.014 inch (0.254-0.356 mm) on two-leg armature or 0.016-0.019 inch (0.406-0.483 mm) on three-leg armature. Ignition timing is non-adjustable on these models.

**LUBRICATION.** Vertical crankshaft engines are lubricated by an oil slinger wheel on governor gear which is driven by camshaft gear (See 15–Fig. B&S48 or B&S49.)

Horizontal crankshaft engines have a splash lubrication system provided by an oil dipper attached to connecting rod. Refer to Fig. B&S41 for view of various types of dippers used.

Use oils labeled "For Service SF or SG." SAE-30 or 10W-30 oil is recommended for temperatures above 40°F (4°C), SAE 10W oil in temperatures between 40°F (4°C) and 0°F (–18°C) and SAE 5W-20 (or 10W oil diluted with 10% kerosene) for below 0°F (–18°C).

For engine crankcase oil capacity, refer to condensed specifications for tractor model.

**CRANKCASE BREATHER.** The crankcase breather is built into engine valve cover. A partial vacuum must be maintained in crankcase to prevent oil from being forced out through oil seals and gaskets or past breaker plunger and piston rings. Air can flow out of crankcase through the breather, but the one-way valve blocks return flow, maintaining the necessary vacuum. Breather mounting holes are offset one way. A vent tube connects breather to carburetor air horn for extra protection against dusty conditions.

## REPAIRS

**NOTE: When checking compression on models with "Easy-Spin" starting, turn engine opposite the direction of normal rotation. See CAMSHAFT paragraph.**

**CYLINDER HEAD.** When removing cylinder head, be sure to note position from which each of the different length screws were removed. If they are not used in the same holes when reinstalling cylinder head, it will result in screws bottoming in some holes and not enough thread contact in others. Lubricate cylinder head screws with graphite grease before installation. Do not use sealer on head gasket. When installing cylinder head, tighten all screws lightly and then retighten them in sequence shown in Fig. B&S42 or B&S43 to a torque of 165 in. lbs. (18.6 N·m). Note early models use eight cap screws to retain cylinder head while later models use nine cap screws. Run engine for 2 to 5 minutes to allow it to warm up and retighten head screws again following sequence and torque values mentioned above.

**CONNECTING ROD.** The connecting rod and piston are removed from cylinder head end of block as an assembly. The aluminum alloy connecting rod rides directly on the induction hardened crankpin. The rod should be rejected if crankpin hole is scored or out-of-round over 0.0007 inch (0.0178 mm) or if piston pin hole is scored or out-of-round over 0.0005 inch (0.0127 mm). Wear limit sizes are given in the following chart. Reject connecting rod if either crankpin or piston pin hole is worn to or larger than sizes given in the chart.

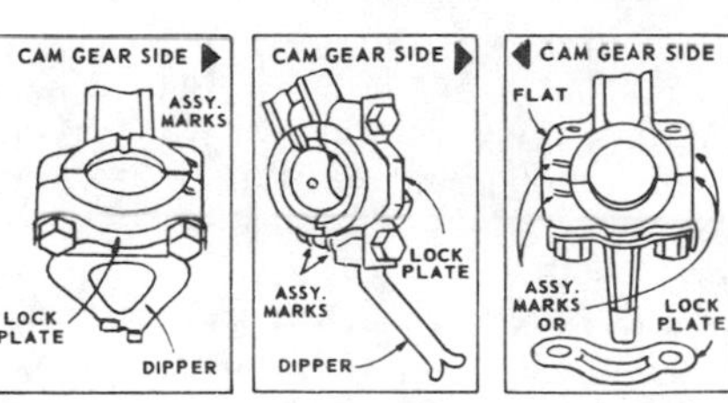

*Fig. B&S41 – View of various types of lubricating oil dippers used on horizontal crankshaft engines.*

**REJECT SIZES FOR CONNECTING ROD**

| Basic Model | Crankpin Hole | *Piston Pin Hole |
|---|---|---|
| 140000 | 1.0949 in. (27.8105 mm) | 0.674 in. (17.1196 mm) |
| 170000, 171000 | 1.0949 in. (27.8105 mm) | 0.674 in. (17.1196 mm) |
| 190000, 191000 | 1.1265 in. (28.6131 mm) | 0.674 in. (17.1196 mm) |
| All Other Models | (1.2520 in. (31.8008 mm) | (0.802 in.) (20.3708 mm) |

***NOTE: Piston pins of 0.005 inch (0.127 mm) oversize are available for service. Piston pin hole in rod can be reamed to this size if crankpin hole is O.K.**

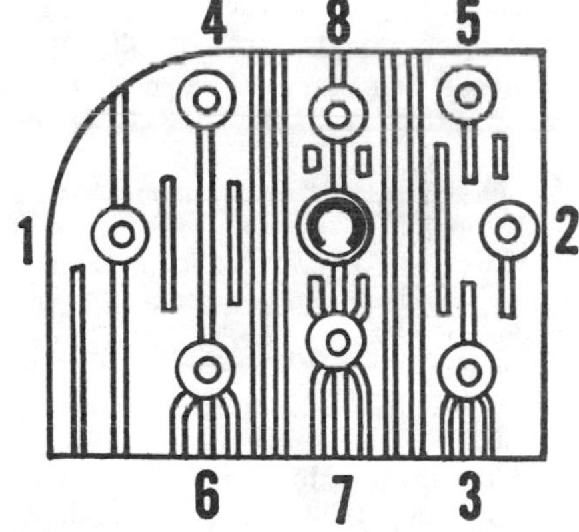

*Fig. B&S42 – Tightening sequence on models with eight cylinder head cap screws. Long screws are used in positions 2, 3 and 7.*

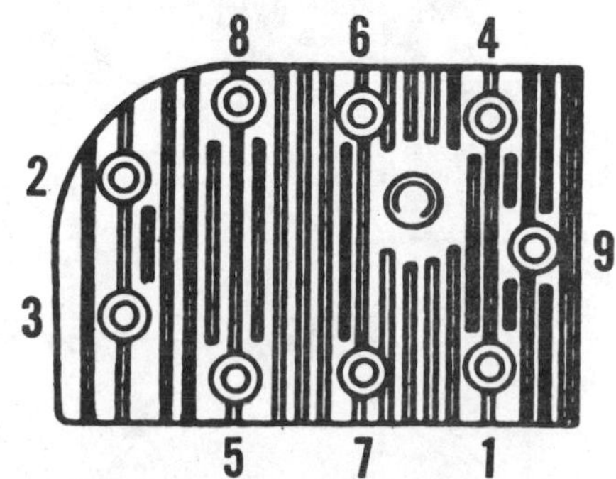

*Fig. B&S43 – Tightening sequence on models with nine cylinder head cap screws. Long screws are used in positions 1, 7 and 9.*

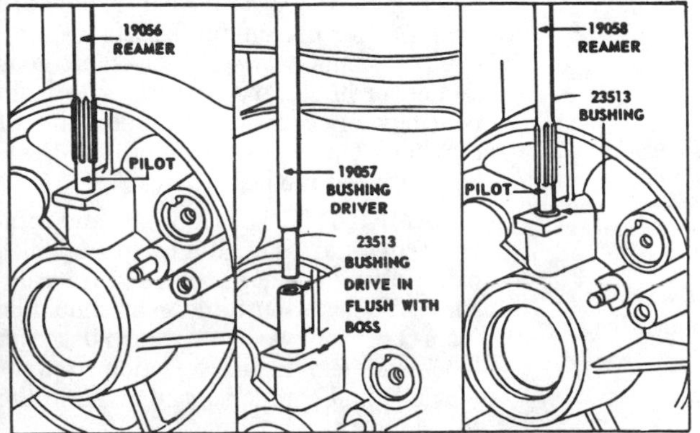

*Fig. B&S40 – Views showing reaming plunger bore to accept bushing (left view), installing bushing (center) and finish reaming bore of bushing (right).*

Tighten connecting rod cap screws to a torque of 165 in.-lbs. (18.6 N•m) on Models 140000, 170000, 171000, 190000 and 191000 and to 190 in.-lbs. (21.5 N•m) on all other models.

**PISTON, PIN AND RINGS.** Piston used in aluminum bore ("Kool-Bore") engine is not marked on top of piston. This chrome plated piston does not use an expander with the oil ring. Reject pistons showing visible signs of wear, scoring or scuffing. If, after cleaning carbon from top ring groove, a new top ring has a side clearance of 0.007 inch (0.178 mm) or more, reject the piston. Reject piston or hone piston pin hole to 0.005 inch (0.127 mm) oversize if pin hole is 0.0005 inch (0.0127 mm) or more out-of-round, or exceeds standard pin hole size.

Reject piston pin if pin is 0.0005 inch (0.0127 mm) or more out-of-round or if pin is worn to a diameter of 0.671 inch (17.043 mm) or smaller on Models 140000, 170000, 171000, 190000 and 191000 or to a diameter of 0.799 inch (20.294 mm) or smaller on all other models.

The piston ring end gap for new rings should be 0.010-0.025 inch (0.254-0.635 mm). Reject compression rings having an end gap of 0.035 inch (0.889 mm) or more and reject oil rings having an end gap of 0.045 inch (1.016 mm) or more.

Pistons and rings are available in standard size and oversizes.

A chrome ring set is available for slightly worn standard bore cylinders. Refer to note in CYLINDER paragraph.

**CYLINDER.** If cylinder bore wear is 0.003 inch (0.076 mm) or more or is 0.0025 inch (0.0635 mm) or more out-of-round, cylinder must be rebored to next larger oversize.

Standard bore size is 2.749-2.750 inches (69.825-69.850 mm) on Model 14000, 2.999-3.000 inches (76.175-76.200 mm) for Models 170000, 171000, 190000 and 191000 and 3.4365-3.4375 inches (87.287-87.312 mm) for all other models.

It is recommended that a hone be used for resizing cylinders. Operate hone at 300-700 rpm and with an up and down movement that will produce a 45 degree cross-hatch pattern. Clean cylinder after honing with oil or soap suds. Aproved hones are as follows: For aluminum bore, use Ammco No. 3956 for rough and finishing or Sunnen No. AN200 for rough and Sunnen AN500 for finishing.

A chrome piston ring set is available for slightly worn standard bore cylinders. No honing or cylinder deglazing is required for these rings. The cylinder bore can be a maximum of 0.005 inch (0.127 mm) oversize when using chrome rings.

**CRANKSHAFT AND MAIN BEARINGS.** Except where equipped with ball bearings, the main bearings are an integral part of crankcase and cover or sump. The bearings are renewable by reaming out crankcase and cover or sump bearing bores and installing service bushings. The tools for reaming crankcase and cover or sump, and for installing service bushings are available from Briggs & Stratton. If bearings are scored, out-of-round 0.007 inch (0.178 mm) or more, or are worn to or larger than reject sizes given below, ream bearings and install service bushings.

**MAIN BEARING REJECT SIZES**

| Basic Model | Bearing Magneto | Bearing Drive |
|---|---|---|
| 140000, 170000, 190000 | 1.006 in. (25.552mm) | 1.185 in. (30.099 mm) |
| 171000, 191000–Synchro Balanced | 1.185 in. (30.099 mm) | 1.185 in (30.099 mm) |
| All Other Models | 1.383 in. (35.128 mm) | 1.383 in. (35.128 mm) |

Rejection sizes for crankshaft bearing journals are given in the following chart. Figures given for main bearing journals would apply to plain bearing applications only.

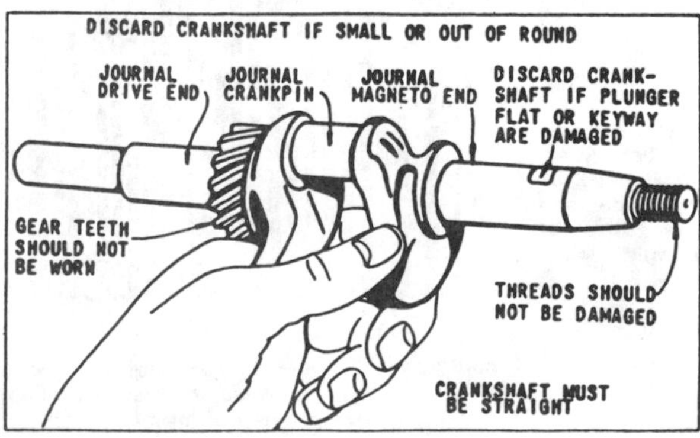


*Fig. B&S44—Inspection points on typical crankshaft.*

**CRANKSHAFT REJECTION SIZES**

| | |
|---|---|
| **Magneto Journal** | |
| 140000, 170000 | 0.0075 in. (25.3365 mm) |
| 190000 | 0.9975 in. (25.3365 mm) |
| 171000 Synchro Balanced | 1.179 in. (29.946 mm) |
| 191000 Synchro Balanced | 1.179 in. (29.946 mm) |
| All Other Models | 1.376 in. (34.950 mm) |
| **Crankpin Journal** | |
| 140000, 170000 | 1.090 in. (27.686 mm) |
| 190000 | 1.122 in. (28.499 mm) |
| 171000 Synchro Balanced | 1.090 in. (27.686 mm) |
| 191000 Synchro Balanced | 1.122 in. (28.499 mm) |
| All Other Models | 1.247 in. (31.674 mm) |
| **Drive End Journal** | |
| 140000, 170000 | 1.179 in. (29.946 mm) |
| 190000 | 1.179 in. (29.946 mm) |
| 171000 Synchro Balanced | 1.179 in. (29.946 mm) |
| 191000 Synchro Balanced | 1.179 in. (29.946 mm) |
| All Other Models | 1.376 in. (34.950 mm) |

Ball bearing mains are a press fit on crankshaft and must be removed by pressing crankshaft out of bearing. Reject ball bearing if worn or rough. Expand new bearing by heating it in oil and install it on crankshaft with shield side towards crankpin journal.

Crankshaft end play should be 0.002-0.008 inch (0.051-0.203 mm). At least one 0.015 inch cover or sump gasket must be used. Additional cover gaskets of 0.005 and 0.009 inch thicknesses are available if end play is less than 0.002 inch (0.051 mm). If end play is over 0.008 inch (0.203 mm) metal shims are available for use on crankshaft.

Place shims between crankshaft gear and cover or sump on models with plain bearings or between magneto end of crankshaft and crankcase on ball bearing equipped models.

**CAMSHAFT.** The camshaft and camshaft gear are an integral part which rides in journals at each end of the camshaft. The camshaft and gear should be inspected for wear on journals, cam lobes and gear teeth. Rejection sizes for journals and cam lobes are given in the following chart.



Illustrations courtesy Briggs & Stratton Corp.

### CAMSHAFT REJECTION SIZES

| Basic Model | Journal Reject Size | Lobe Reject Size |
|---|---|---|
| 140000, 170000, 171000 | 0.4985 in. (12.662 mm) | 0.977 in. (24.816 mm) |
| 190000, 191000 | 0.4985 in. (12.662 mm) | 0.977 in. (24.816 mm) |
| All Other Models | 0.498 in. (12.649 mm) | 1.184 in. (30.073 mm) |

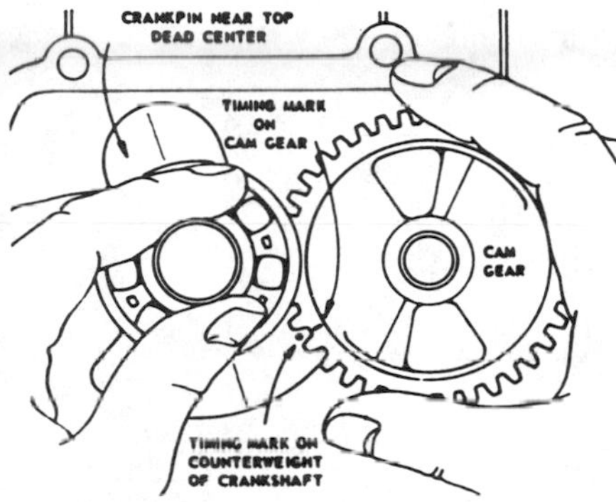


Fig. B&S45 Align timing marks on cam gear with mark on crankshaft counterweight on ball bearing equipped engines.

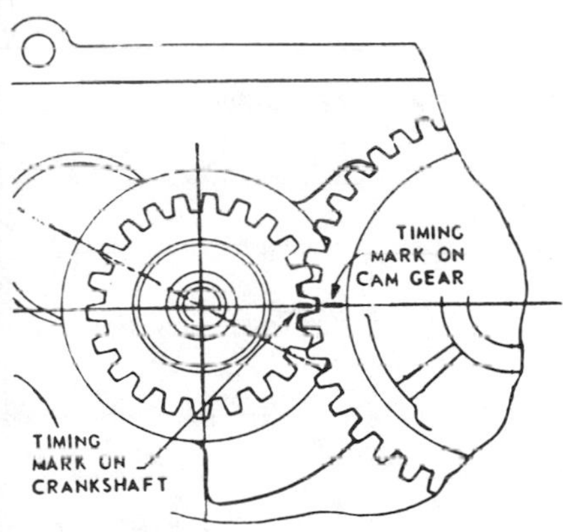


Fig. B&S46 – Align timing marks on cam gear and crankshaft gear on plain bearing models.

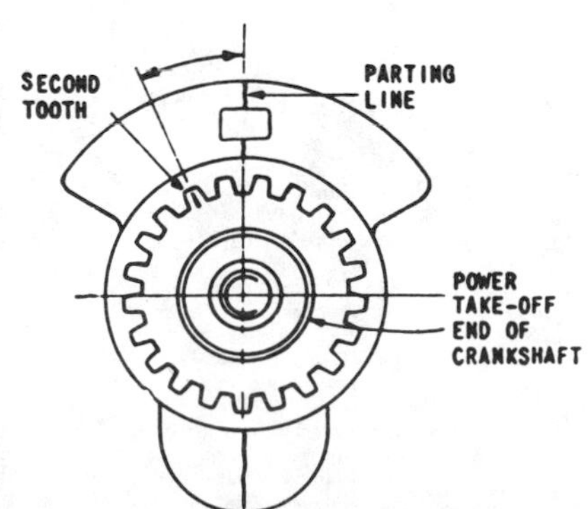


Fig. B&S47 – Location of tooth to align with timing mark on cam gear if mark is not visible on crankshaft gear.

On models with "Easy-Spin" starting, intake cam lobe is designed to hold intake valve slightly open on a part of compression stroke. Therefore, to check compression, engine must be turned backwards.

"Easy-Spin" camshafts (cam gears) can be identified by two holes drilled in web of the gear. Where part number of an older cam gear and an "Easy-Spin" cam gear are the same (except for an "E" following "Easy-Spin" part number), the gears are interchangeable.

**VALVE SYSTEM.** Intake valve clearance is 0.005-0.007 inch (0.127-0.178 mm) and exhaust valve clearance is 0.009-0.011 inch (0.229-0.279 mm) when engine is cold. The valve seat angle is 45 degrees. Regrind or renew valve seat insert if seat width is 5/64-inch (2 mm) or wider. Regrind to width of 3/64 to 1/16-inch (1.2-1.6 mm). Obtain specified valve clearance by grinding end of valve stem squarely. Renew valve if margin is 1/64-inch (0.4 mm) or less after refacing.

The valve guides on all engines with aluminum blocks are an integral part of cylinder block. If flat end of valve guide plug gage can be inserted into valve guide for a distance of 5/16-inch (8 mm), guide is worn and should be reamed and a bushing installed. Reamers and

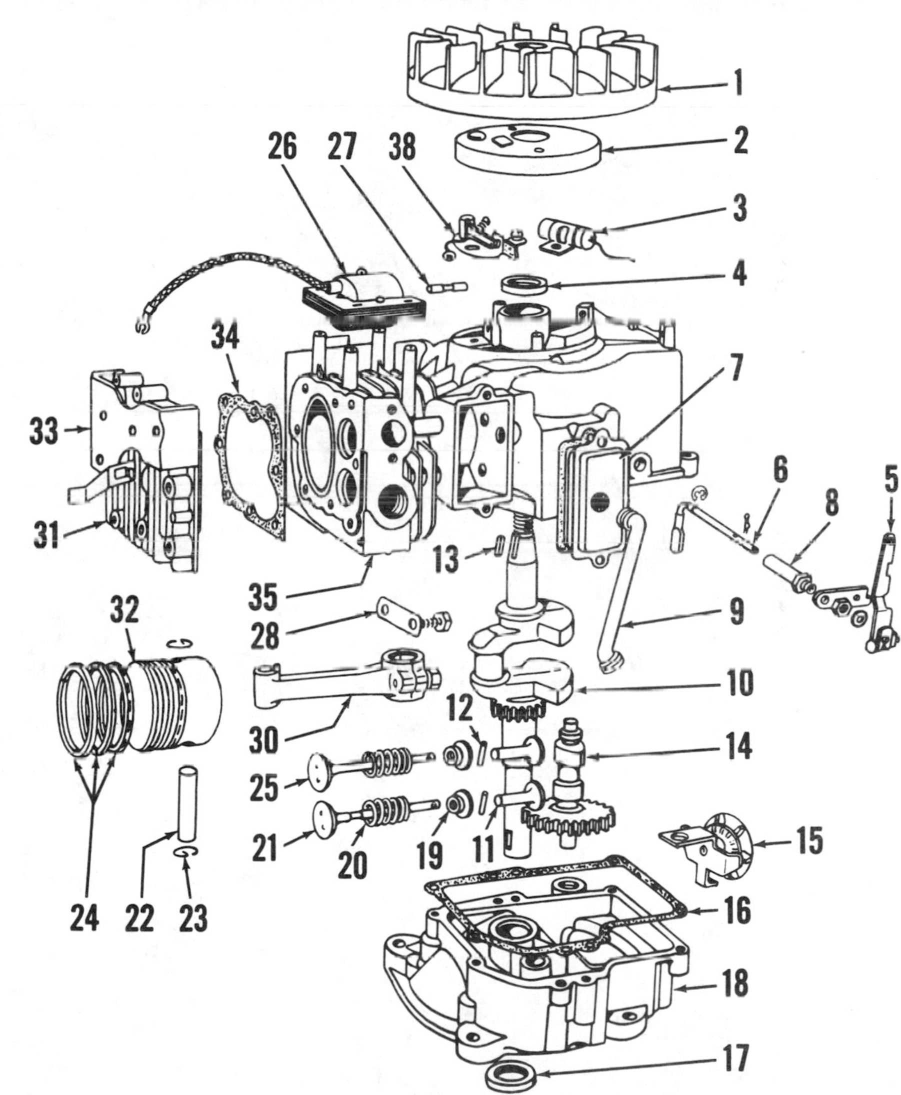

Fig. B&S48 – Exploded view of typical vertical crankshaft engine assembly not equipped with Synchro-Balancer.

1. Flywheel
2. Breaker point cover
3. Condenser
4. Oil seal
5. Governor lever
6. Governor crank
7. Breather & valve cover
8. Bushing
9. Breather vent tube
10. Crankshaft
11. Tappets (cam followers)
12. Valve retaining pins
13. Flywheel key
14. Cam shaft & gear
15. Governor oil slinger assy.
16. Gasket (0.005, 0.009 or 0.015 in.)
17. Oil seal
18. Oil sump (engine base)
19. Valve spring retainer or "Rotocoil"
20. Valve spring
21. Exhaust valve
22. Piston pin
23. Retaining rings
24. Piston rings
25. Intake valve
26. Armature & coil assy.
27. Breaker plunger
28. Rod bolt lock
30. Connecting rod
31. Cylinder head
32. Piston
33. Air baffle
34. Head gasket
35. Cylinder block
38. Breaker points

Illustrations courtesy Briggs & Stratton Corp.

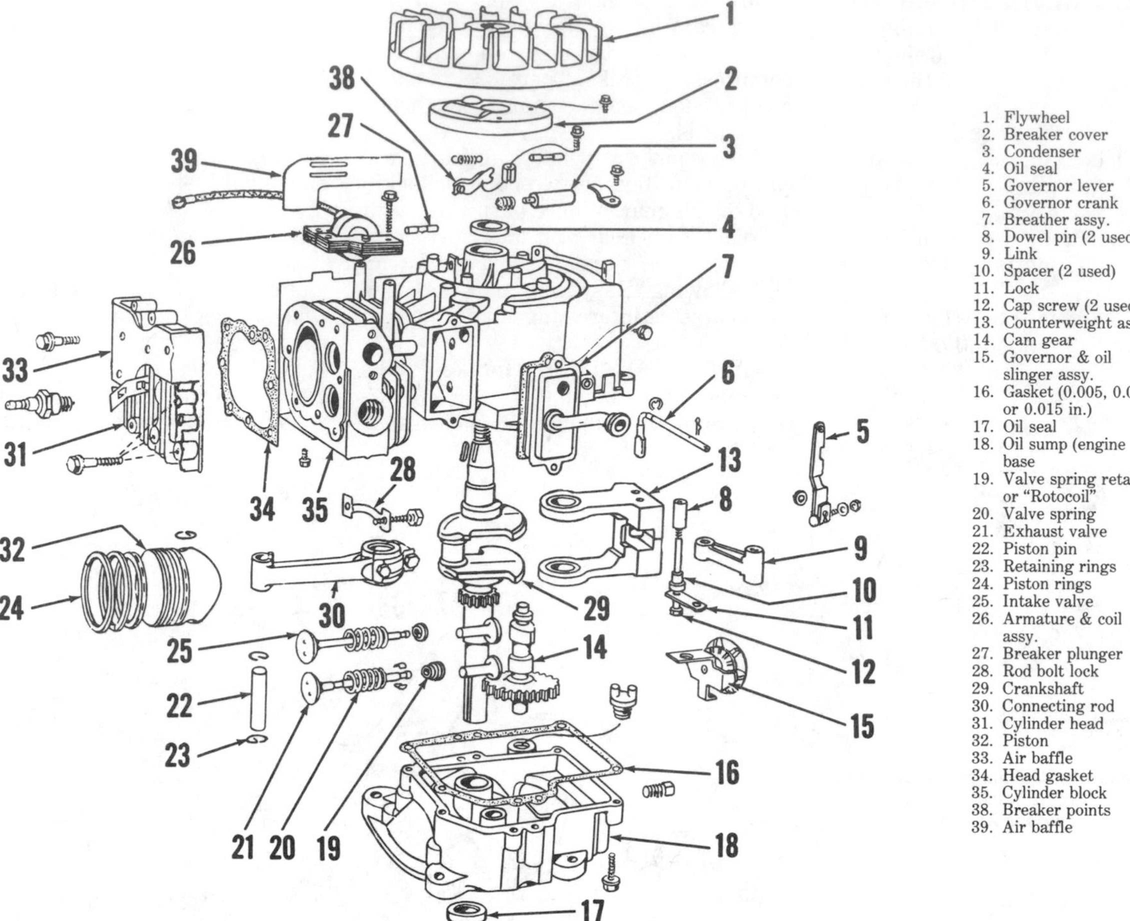

1. Flywheel
2. Breaker cover
3. Condenser
4. Oil seal
5. Governor lever
6. Governor crank
7. Breather assy.
8. Dowel pin (2 used)
9. Link
10. Spacer (2 used)
11. Lock
12. Cap screw (2 used)
13. Counterweight assy.
14. Cam gear
15. Governor & oil slinger assy.
16. Gasket (0.005, 0.009 or 0.015 in.)
17. Oil seal
18. Oil sump (engine base
19. Valve spring retainer or "Rotocoil"
20. Valve spring
21. Exhaust valve
22. Piston pin
23. Retaining rings
24. Piston rings
25. Intake valve
26. Armature & coil assy.
27. Breaker plunger
28. Rod bolt lock
29. Crankshaft
30. Connecting rod
31. Cylinder head
32. Piston
33. Air baffle
34. Head gasket
35. Cylinder block
38. Breaker points
39. Air baffle

*Fig. B&S49—Exploded view of Series 171000, 251000 or 252000 Synchro-Balanced vertical crankshaft engine assembly.*

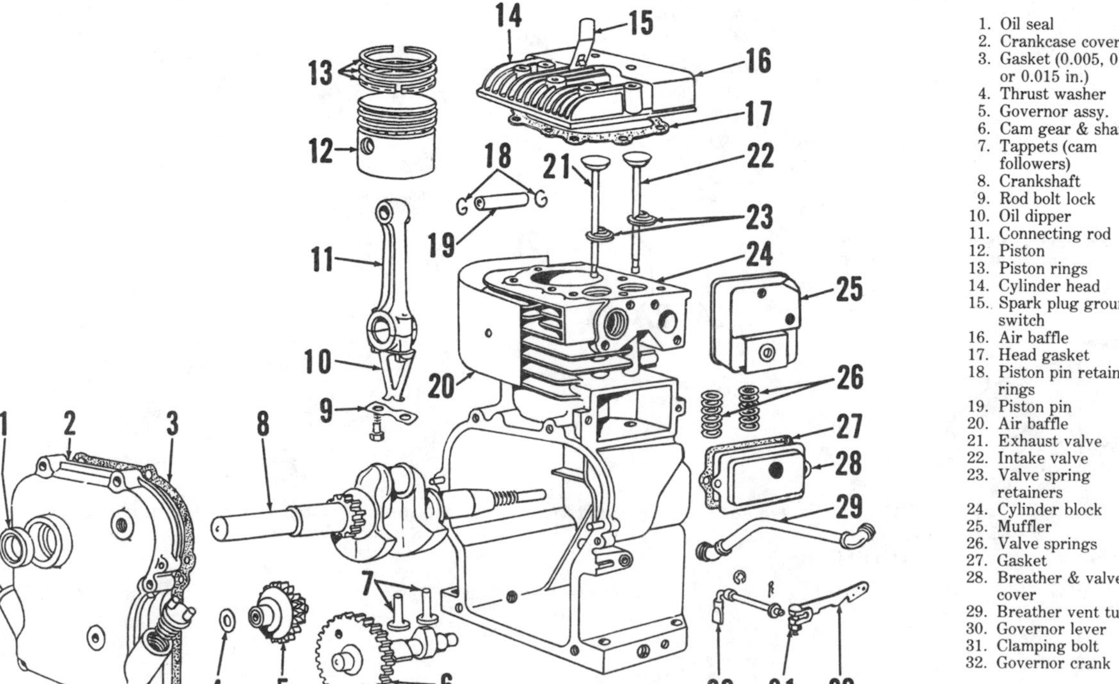

1. Oil seal
2. Crankcase cover
3. Gasket (0.005, 0.009 or 0.015 in.)
4. Thrust washer
5. Governor assy.
6. Cam gear & shaft
7. Tappets (cam followers)
8. Crankshaft
9. Rod bolt lock
10. Oil dipper
11. Connecting rod
12. Piston
13. Piston rings
14. Cylinder head
15. Spark plug ground switch
16. Air baffle
17. Head gasket
18. Piston pin retaining rings
19. Piston pin
20. Air baffle
21. Exhaust valve
22. Intake valve
23. Valve spring retainers
24. Cylinder block
25. Muffler
26. Valve springs
27. Gasket
28. Breather & valve cover
29. Breather vent tube
30. Governor lever
31. Clamping bolt
32. Governor crank

*Fig. B&S50—Exploded view of typical horizontal crankshaft engine assembly not equipped with Synchro-Balancer.*



Illustrations courtesy Briggs & Stratton Corp.

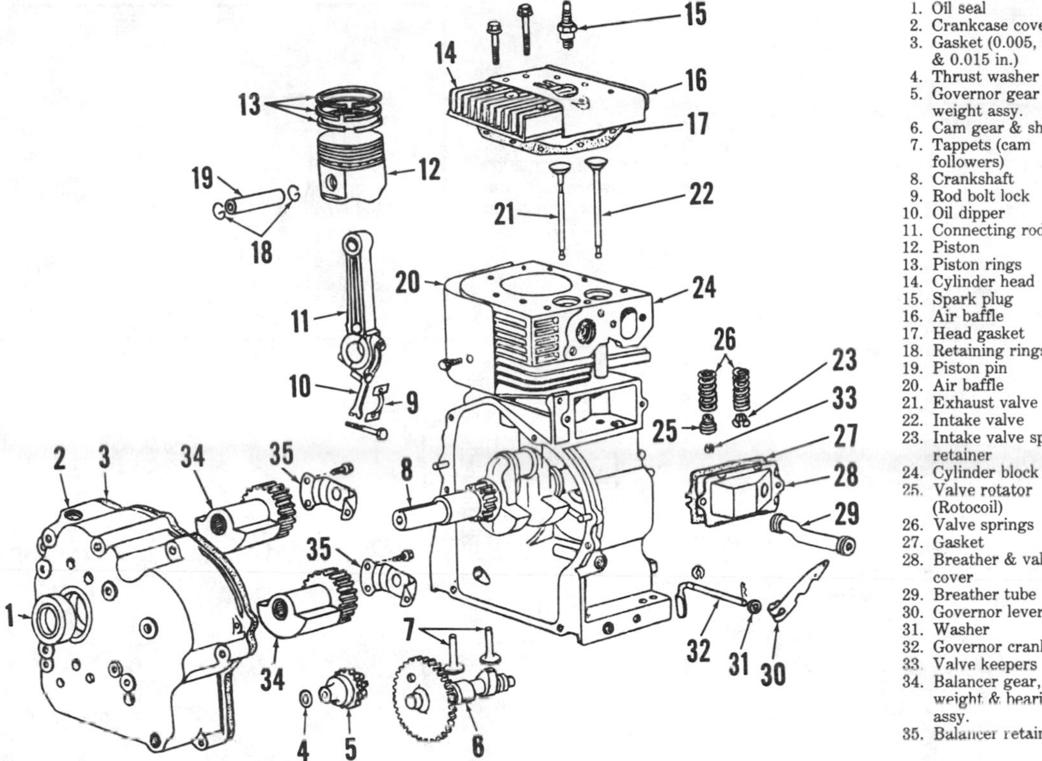

1. Oil seal
2. Crankcase cover
3. Gasket (0.005, 0.009 & 0.015 in.)
4. Thrust washer
5. Governor gear & weight assy.
6. Cam gear & shaft
7. Tappets (cam followers)
8. Crankshaft
9. Rod bolt lock
10. Oil dipper
11. Connecting rod
12. Piston
13. Piston rings
14. Cylinder head
15. Spark plug
16. Air baffle
17. Head gasket
18. Retaining rings
19. Piston pin
20. Air baffle
21. Exhaust valve
22. Intake valve
23. Intake valve spring retainer
24. Cylinder block
25. Valve rotator (Rotocoil)
26. Valve springs
27. Gasket
28. Breather & valve cover
29. Breather tube
30. Governor lever
31. Washer
32. Governor crank
33. Valve keepers
34. Balancer gear, weight & bearing assy.
35. Balancer retainers

*Fig. B&S51 – Exploded view of 251000, 252000 or 253000 Synchro-Balanced horizontal crankshaft engines.*

bushings are available from Briggs & Stratton. The part numbers are as follows:

Reamer No. . . . . . . . . . . . . . . . . . 19183
Bushing Part No. . . . . . . . . . . . . . 230655
Valve Guide Plug Gage No. . . . . . . 19151

Ream to only 1/16-inch (1.6 mm) deeper than length of valve guide bushing. Do not ream completely through valve guide. Press in bushing with soft driver as bushing is finish reamed at factory.

**VALVE TIMING.** On engines equipped with ball bearing mains, align timing mark on cam gear with timing mark on crankshaft counterweight as shown in Fig. B&S45. On engines with plain bearings, align timing marks on camshaft gear with timing mark on crankshaft gear (Fig. B&S46). If timing mark is not visible on crankshaft gear, align timing mark on camshaft gear with second tooth to the left of crankshaft counterweight parting line as in Fig. B&S47.

**SYNCHRO-BALANCER (OSCILLATING).** Some vertical crankshaft engines may be equipped with an oscillating Synchro-balancer. The balance weight assembly rides on eccentric journals on crankshaft and moves in opposite direction of piston. Refer to Fig. B&S52.

To disassemble balancer unit, first remove flywheel, engine base, cam gear, cylinder head and connecting rod and piston assembly. Carefully pry off crankshaft gear and key. Remove the two cap screws holding halves of counterweight together. Separate weights and remove link, dowel pins and spacers. Slide weights from crankshaft. See Fig. B&S53.

To reassemble, install magneto side weight on magneto end of crankshaft. Place crankshaft (pto end up) in a vise as

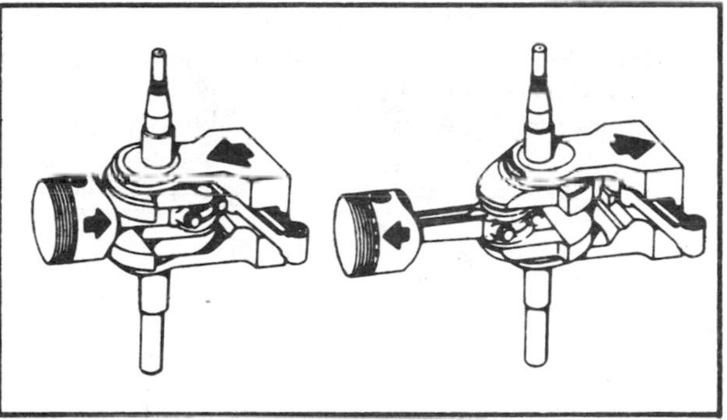

*Fig. B&S52 – View showing operating principle of Synchro-Balancer used on Series 171000, 191000, 251000 and 252000 vertical crankshaft engines. Counterweight oscillates in opposite direction of piston.*

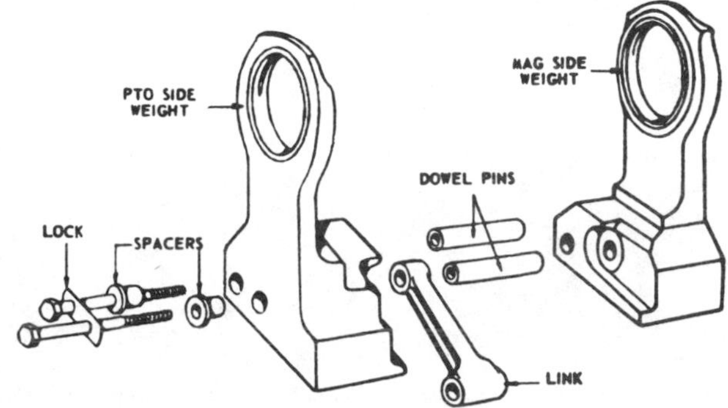


*Fig. B&S53 – Exploded view of Synchro-Balancer assembly used on Series 171000, 191000, 251000 and 252000 vertical crankshaft engines. Counterweights ride on eccentric journals on crankshaft.*

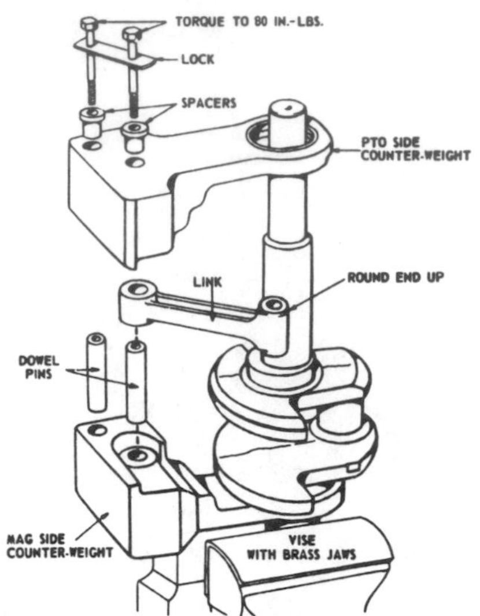


***Fig. B&S54—Assemble balance units on crankshaft as shown. Install link with rounded edge on free end toward pto end of crankshaft.***

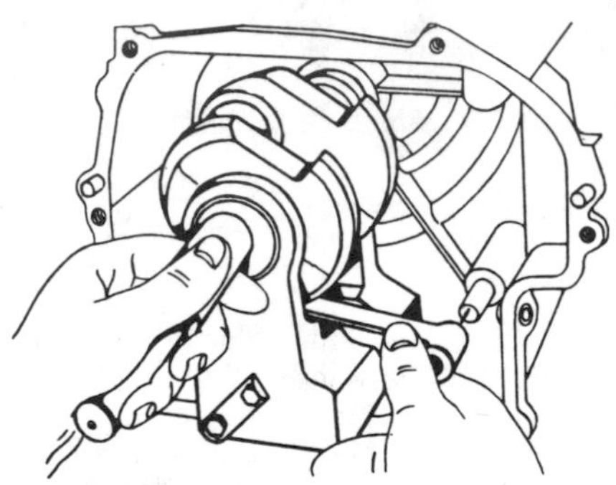

***Fig. B&S55—When installing crankshaft and balancer assembly, place free end of link on anchor pin in crankcase.***

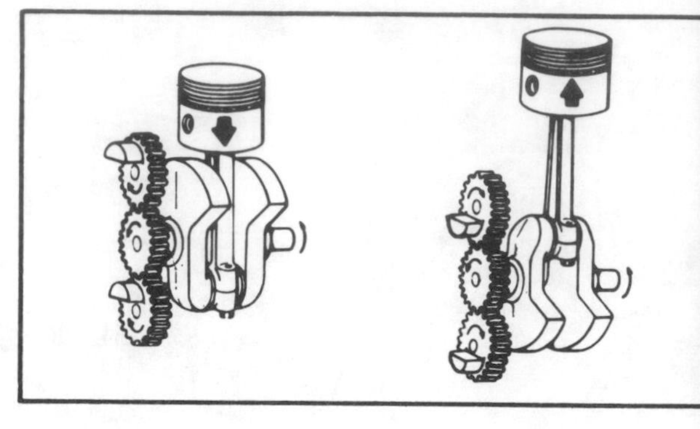

***Fig. B&S56—View showing operating principle of Synchro-Balancer used on 251000, 252000 and 253000 horizontal crankshaft engines. Balancers rotate in opposite direction of crankshaft rotation.***

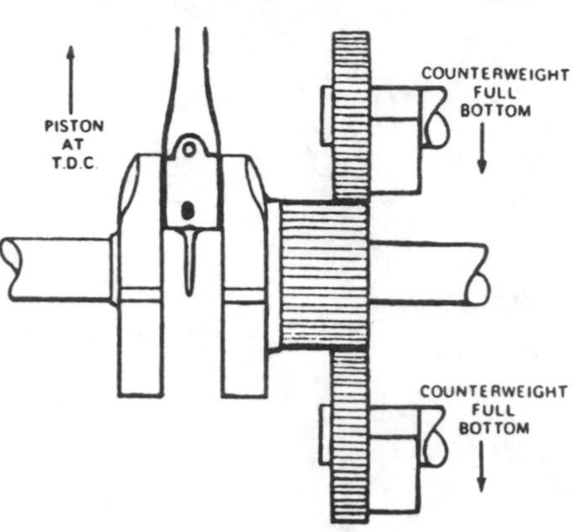


***Fig. B&S57—View showing correct position of crankshaft and counterweights when timing balancers to crankshaft gear. Refer to text.***

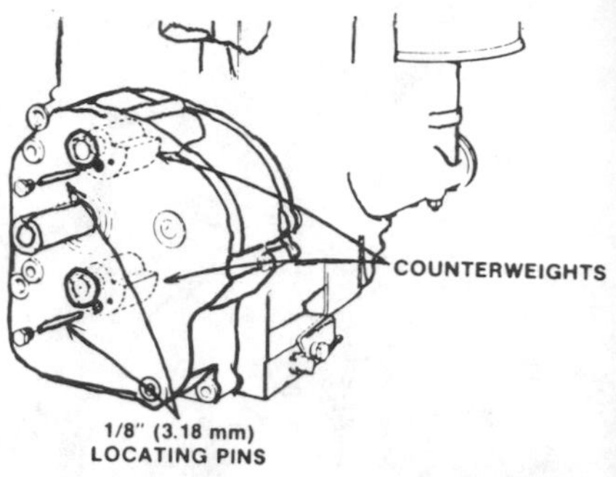


***Fig. B&S58—To properly align counterweights remove two small screws from crankcase cover and insert 1/8-inch (3 mm) diameter locating pins***

shown in Fig. B&S54. Install both dowel pins and place link on pin as shown. Note rounded edge on free end of link must be up. Install pto side weight, spacers, lock and cap screws. Tighten cap screws to 80 in.-lbs. (9 N·m) and bend up bolt lock ends. Install key and crankshaft gear with chamfer on inside of gear facing shoulder on crankshaft.

Install crankshaft and balancer assembly in crankcase, sliding free end of link on anchor pin as shown in Fig. B&S55. Reassemble engine.

**SYNCHRO-BALANCER (ROTATING).** Some horizontal crankshaft engines may be equipped with two gear driven counterweights in constant mesh with crankshaft gear. The gears, mounted in crankcase cover, rotate in opposite direction of crankshaft. See Fig. B&S56.

To properly align counterweights when installing cover, remove two small screws from cover and insert 1/8-inch (3 mm) diameter locating pins through holes and into holes in counterweights as shown in Fig. B&S58.

With piston at TDC, install cover assembly. Remove locating pins, coat threads of timing hole screws with non-hardening sealer and install screws with fiber sealing washers.

**NOTE: If counterweights are removed from crankcase cover, exercise care in handling or cleaning to prevent losing needle bearings.**



Illustrations courtesy Briggs & Stratton Corp.

# BRIGGS & STRATTON

| Model | No. Cyls. | Bore | Stroke | Displacement | Horsepower |
|---|---|---|---|---|---|
| 243000 Series | 1 | 3-1/16 in. (77.8 mm) | 3-1/4 in. (82.5 mm) | 23.94 cu. in. (392 cc) | 10 (7.5 kW) |
| 300000 Series | 1 | 3-7/16 in. (87.3 mm) | 3-1/4 in. (82.5 mm) | 30.16 cu. in. (494 cc) | 12 (8.9 kW) |
| 302000 Series | 1 | 3-7/16 in. (87.3 mm) | 3-1/4 in. (82.5 mm) | 30.16 cu. in. (494 cc) | 13 (9.7 kW) |
| 320000 Series | 1 | 3-9/16 in. (90.5 mm) | 3-1/4 in. (82.5 mm) | 32.4 cu. in. (531 cc) | 14 (10.4 kW) |
| 325000 Series | 1 | 3-9/16 in. (90.5 mm) | 3-1/4 in. (82.5 mm) | 32.4 cu. in. (531 cc) | 15 (11.2 kW) |
| 326000 Series | 1 | 3-9/16 in. (90.5 mm) | 3-1/4 in. (82.5 mm) | 32.4 cu. in. (531 cc) | 16 (11.9 kW) |

All Briggs & Stratton engines covered in this section are of cast iron construction.

## MAINTENANCE

**SPARK PLUG.** Recommended spark plug for all models is a Champion J-8, Autolite A-71 or an AC GC46. Set electrode gap to 0.030 inch (0.762 mm) for all models.

**NOTE: If a resistor type plug is necessary to reduce ratio interference, use Champion XJ-8 or equivalent. Briggs & Stratton Corporation does not recommend cleaning spark plugs by abrasive blasting method as this may introduce some abrasive material into the engine which could cause extensive damage.**

**CARBURETOR.** All models are equipped with Briggs & Stratton two-piece float type carburetors. Refer to Fig. B&S60 for cross-sectional view of typical unit.

Counter-clockwise rotation of both idle valve and needle valve will richen fuel mixture. For initial adjustment, open idle valve 3/4 turn and open needle valve 1½ turns. Make final adjustment with engine running at normal operating temperature. Turn needle valve in until engine misses from lean mixture, then out past smooth operating point until engine runs unevenly due to rich mixture. Final adjustment should be midway between lean and rich adjustment points. After adjusting needle valve (main fuel adjustment), hold throttle at slow idle position and adjust idle stop screw so engine is running at 1200 rpm. While holding throttle against stop screw, adjust idle valve for smoothest idle performance. Then, if necessary, readjust idle stop screw to obtain 1200 rpm.

Before disassembling carburetor, check for warped body as follows: If a 0.002 inch (0.051 mm) feeler gage can be inserted as shown in Fig. B&S61, upper body is warped and should be renewed. If diametral play of throttle shaft in bushings exceeds 0.010 inch (0.254 mm), upper body should be rebushed and/or throttle shaft renewed.

To disassemble carburetor, proceed as follows: Remove idle mixture valve. Loosen power needle valve packing nut, then screw needle valve and packing nut out together. Using a narrow blunt screwdriver (B&S special tool #19061 or #19062), carefully remove nozzle taking care not to damage threads in lower carburetor body. Remainder of carburetor disassembly is evident after examination of unit.

If necessary to renew throttle shaft bushings, they can be removed by threading a 1/4 inch x 20 tap into bushing, then pulling bushing from upper body. Press new bushings in with vise and ream with a 7/32-inch (5.5 mm) drill if throttle shaft binds. Check float level as shown in Fig. B&S62 and reassemble carburetor by reversing disassembly procedure.

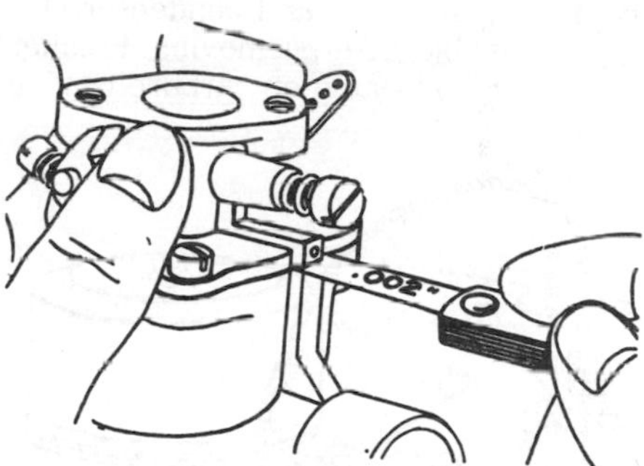


*Fig. B&S61—Checking carburetor for warped upper body. If a 0.002 inch (0.051 mm) feeler gage can be inserted between upper and lower bodies as shown, renew upper body.*

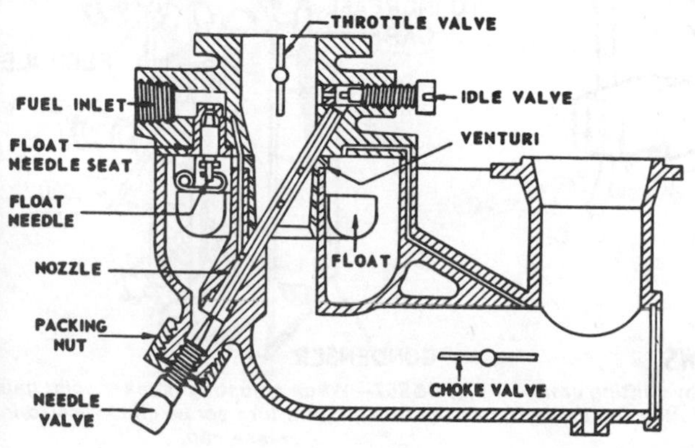


*Fig. B&S60—Cross-sectional view of typical float type carburetor. Before separating upper and lower carburetor bodies, loosen packing nut and unscrew needle valve and packing nut. Then, using special screwdriver, remove nozzle.*

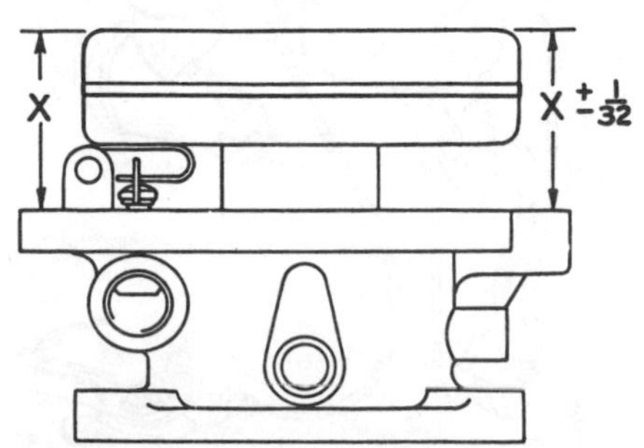


*Fig. B&S62—Check carburetor float level as shown. Bend tang if necessary to adjust float level.*

**GOVERNOR.** Engines are equipped with a gear driven mechanical governor. The governor unit is enclosed within the engine and is driven from camshaft gear. All binding or slack due to wear must be removed from governor linkage to prevent "hunting" or unsteady operation. To adjust carburetor to governor linkage, loosen clamp bolt on governor lever. Move link end of governor lever upward until carburetor throttle shaft is in wide open position. Using a screwdriver, rotate governor lever shaft counter-clockwise as far as possible, then tighten clamp bolt.

Briggs & Stratton recommended operating speed range for these models is 1200 rpm idle to 3800 rpm maximum. However, engine rpm may differ slightly depending on tractors in which engines are used. Tractor manufacturers recommendations should be followed in all cases.

Governor gear and weight unit can be removed when engine is disassembled. Remove governor lever, cotter pin and washer from outer end of governor lever shaft. Slide governor lever out of bushing towards inside of engine. Governor gear and weight unit can now be removed. Renew governor lever shaft bushing in crankcase, if necessary, and ream new bushing after installation to 0.2385-0.239 inch (6.058-6.070 mm).

**MAGNETO.** An exploded view of magneto is shown in Fig. B&S64. Breaker points (11) and condenser (10) are accessible after removing breaker box cover (8) located on carburetor side of engine. Adjust breaker point gap to 0.020 inch (0.508 mm). Condenser capacity is 0.18-0.24 mfd.

Installation of new breaker points is made easier by turning engine so points are open to their widest gap before removing old points. For method of adjusting breaker point gap, refer to Fig. B&S 67.

**NOTE: When installing points, apply Permatex or other sealer to retaining screw threads to prevent engine oil from leaking into breaker box.**

Breaker points are actuated by plunger that rides against breaker cam on engine cam gear. The plunger and plunger bushing are renewable after removing engine cam gear and breaker points.

Magneto armature and ignition coil are mounted outside the engine flywheel. Adjust armature air gap to 0.010-0.014 inch (0.254-0.356 mm). If armature mounting bracket (15–Fig. B&S64) has been loosened or removed, magneto edge gap (armature timing) must be adjusted as follows: First, be sure breaker point gap is adjusted to 0.020 inch (0.508 mm). Remove armature ignition coil assembly from mounting bracket and if available, con-

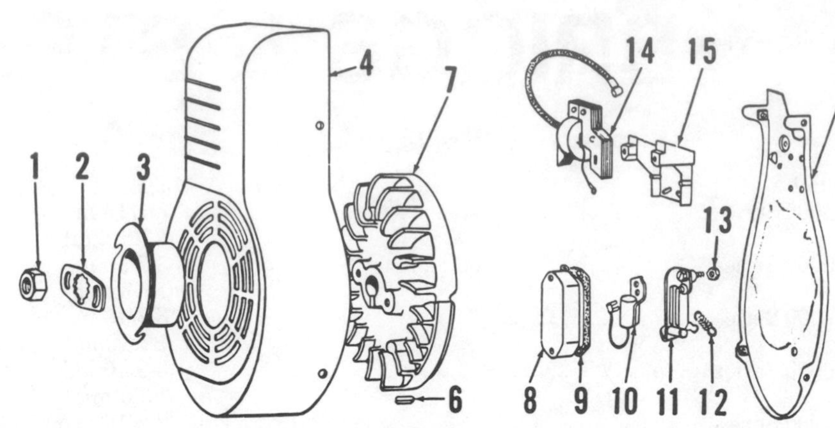


*Fig. B&S64 – Exploded view of typical magneto ignition system. Position of armature is adjustable to time magneto armature with magneto rotor (flywheel) by moving armature mounting bracket (15) in slotted mounting holes. Refer to text and Figs. B&S65 and B&S66.*

1. Flywheel nut
2. Retainer
3. Pulley
4. Blower housing
6. Flywheel key
7. Flywheel
8. Breaker box cover
9. Gasket
10. Condenser
11. Breaker points
12. Breaker spring
13. Locknut
14. Coil & armature assy.
15. Armature bracket
16. Backplate

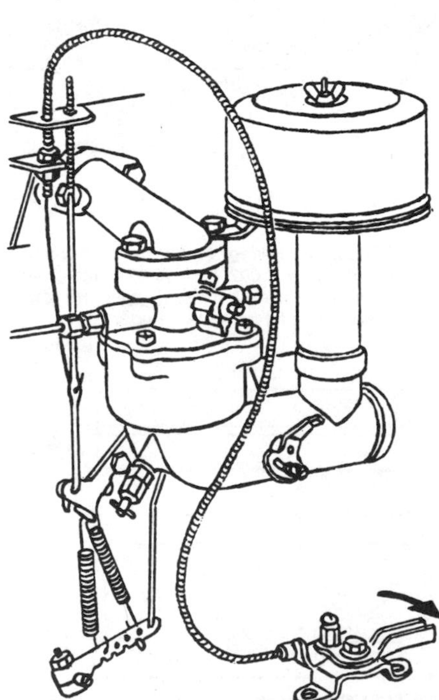

*Fig. B&S63 – View showing typical governor remote control and carburetor to governor linkage.*

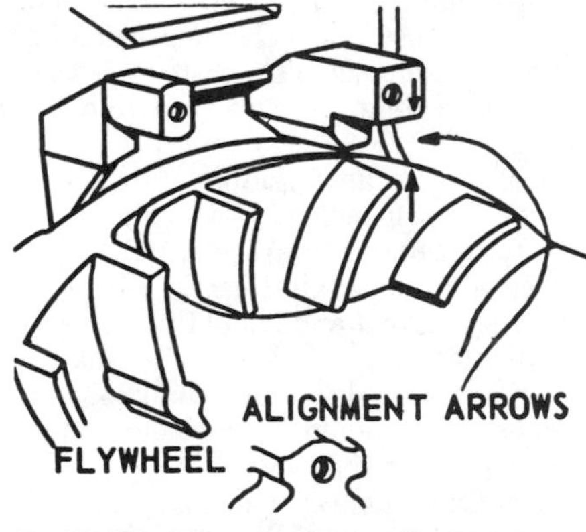


*Fig. B&S65 – Time magneto by aligning arrow on armature core support with arrow on flywheel when breaker points are just starting to open.*

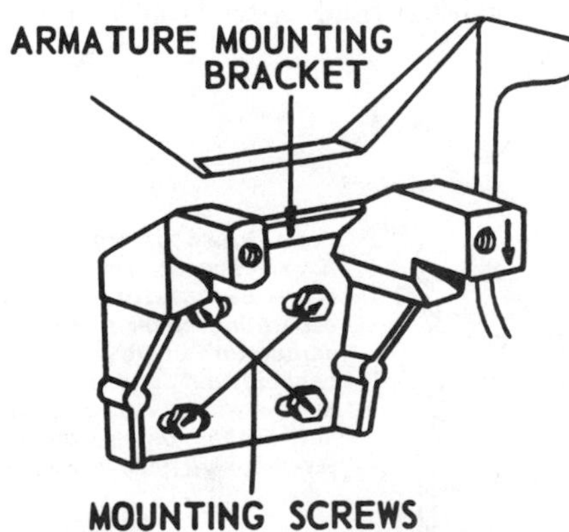


*Fig. B&S66 – Magneto is timed by shifting armature mounting bracket on slotted mounting holes.*

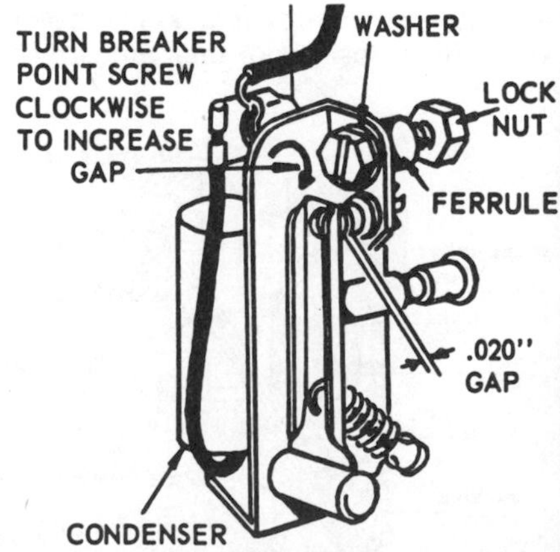


*Fig. B&S67 – When adjusting breaker point gap, loosen locknut and turn screw clockwise to increase gap.*



Illustrations courtesy Briggs & Stratton Corp.

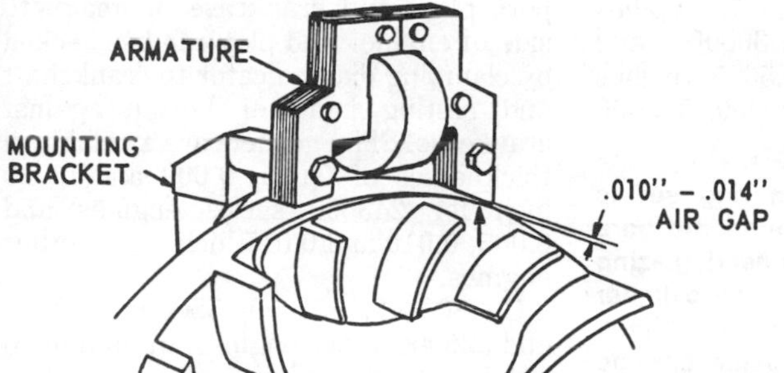


Fig. B&S68—After armature mounting bracket is properly installed, install armature and coil assembly so there is a 0.010-0.014 inch (0.254-0.356 mm) air gap between armature and flywheel.

nect a static timing light across breaker points after disconnecting coil primary wire. Slowly turn flywheel in a clockwise direction until breaker points just start to open (timing light goes out). The arrow on flywheel should then be exactly aligned with arrow on armature mounting bracket; refer to Fig. B&S65. If not mark position of bracket, remove flywheel and shift bracket on slotted mounting holes (Fig. B&S66) to bring arrows into alignment.

**NOTE: To simplify alignment of arrows, proceed as follows: Loosen, but do not remove engine flywheel; then, be sure engine is turned so breaker points are just starting to open and carefully slip flywheel off of crankshaft. Loosen mounting bracket retaining cap screws so bracket will slide on slotted mounting holes and carefully place flywheel back on crankshaft and drive key. Slide bracket to align timing arrow, carefully remove flywheel to avoid moving bracket and tighten bracket cap screws.**

Reinstall flywheel and tighten flywheel nut to a torque of 144 ft.-lbs. (195 N•m). Reinstall armature and ignition coil and adjust armature air gap to 0.010-0.014 inch (0.254-0.356 mm). See Fig. B&S68.

**LUBRICATION.** All models are splash lubricated by oil dipper attached to lower end of connecting rod.

Use oils labeled "For Service SF or SG." SAE-30 or 10W-30 oil is recommended for temperatures above 40°F (4°C), SAE 10W oil in temperatures between 40°F (4°C) and 0°F (−18°C) and SAE 5W-20 (or 10W oil diluted with 10% kerosene) for below 0°F (−18°C).

For engine crankcase oil capacity, refer to condensed specifications for tractor model.

## REPAIRS

**CYLINDER HEAD.** When removing cylinder head, be sure to note position from which different length screws were removed. If they are not used in the same position when reinstalling cylinder head, it will result in some screws bottoming in holes and not enough thread engagement on others. When installing cylinder head, tighten all screws lightly and then retighten them in sequence shown in Fig. B&S69 to a torque of 190 in.-lbs. (21.5 N•m).

Run engine about five minutes to allow it to warm up and retighten screws to 190 in.-lbs. (21.5 N•m using same sequence.

**CONNECTING ROD.** Rod and piston assembly are removed from cylinder head end of block. The aluminum alloy connecting rod rides directly on the induction hardened crankpin. The rod should be rejected if crankpin hole is out-of-round over 0.0007 inch (0.0178 mm) or piston pin hole is out-of-round over 0.0005 inch (0.0127 mm). The rod should also be rejected if either hole is scored or worn to rejection size of 1.314 inches (33.375 mm) for crankpin hole or 0.6735 inch (17.107 mm) (243000 series) or 0.8015 inch (20.358 mm) (all other models) for piston pin hole.

**NOTE: If rod is otherwise serviceable except for piston pin hole, rod and piston can be reamed and a 0.005 inch (0.127 mm) oversize piston pin installed.**

On 243000 series, install connecting rod with clearance flat (Fig. B&S70) toward cam gear side of crankcase. Tighten connecting rod cap screws to a torque of 190 in.-lbs. (21.5 N•m).

When assembling piston to connecting rod on 300000, 302000, 320000, 325000 and 326000 series, notch on top of piston and stamped letter "F" must be on same side as assembly marks on rod. See Fig. B&S71. Install assembly in cylinder with assembly marks to flywheel side of crankcase. Tighten connecting rod cap screws to a torque of 190 in.-lbs. (21.5 N•m).

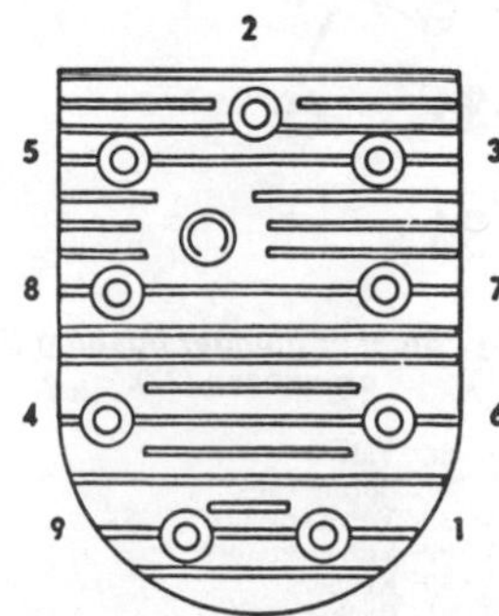


Fig. B&S69—View showing cylinder head cap screw tightening sequence.

Fig. B&S70—Drawing of lower end of 243000 series connecting rod showing clearance flat and assembly marks.

**PISTON, PIN AND RINGS.** Piston is of aluminum alloy and is fitted with two compression rings and one oil ring. If piston shows visible signs of wear, scoring or scuffing, it should be renewed. Also, renew piston if side clearance of new ring in top ring groove exceeds 0.007 inch (0.178 mm). Reject piston or hone piston pin hole to 0.005 inch (0.127 mm) oversize if pin hole is 0.0005 inch (0.0127 mm) or more out-of-round or worn to a diameter of 0.673 inch (17.094 mm) on 243000 series or 0.801 inch (20.345 mm) on all other models.

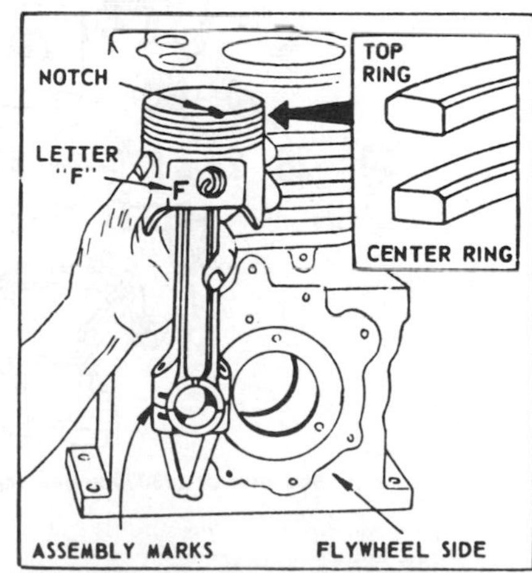


Fig. B&S71—Assemble piston to connecting rod, on 300000, 302000, 320000, 325000 and 326000 series, with notch and stamped letter "F" on piston to the same side as assembly marks on rod. Install assembly in cylinder with assembly marks to flywheel side of crankcase.

Illustrations courtesy Briggs & Stratton Corp.

Renew piston pin if 0.0005 inch (0.0127 mm) or more out-of-round or if worn to a diameter of 0.671 inch (17.043 mm) on 243000 series or 0.799 inch (20.294 mm) on all other models. A 0.005 inch (0.127 mm) oversize piston pin is available for service.

Reject piston rings having an end gap of 0.030 inch (0.762 mm) for compression rings and 0.035 inch (0.889 mm) for oil ring. If top ring has groove on inside, install with groove up. If second compression ring has groove on outside, install with groove down. Oil ring may be installed either side up. Piston and rings are available in standard size and oversizes. A chrome ring set is available for slightly worn standard bore cylinders. Refer to note in CYLINDER paragraph.

**CYLINDER.** Cylinder and crankcase are an integral iron casting. If cylinder is worn more than 0.003 inch, or is more than 0.0015 inch out-of-round, it should be rebored and next larger oversize piston and ring set installed.

The standard cylinder bore is 3.0615-3.0625 inches (77.762-77.787 mm) on 243000 series; 3.4365-3.4375 inches (87.287-87.312 mm) on 300000 and 302000 series; 3.5615-3.5625 inches (90.462-90.487 mm) on 320000, 325000 and 326000 series engines.

**NOTE: A chrome piston ring set is available for slightly worn standard bore cylinders. No honing or cylinder deglazing is required for these rings. The cylinder bore can be a maximum of 0.005 inch (0.127 mm) oversize when using chrome rings.**

**CRANKSHAFT.** The crankshaft is supported in two ball bearing mains. Check ball bearings for wear or roughness. If bearing is loose or noisy, renew the bearing. When renewing ball bearings, press crankshaft out of old bearings. Expand new bearings by heating them in oil to a maximum temperature of 325°F (160°C). Slide heated bearing in place with shield side towards crankpin journal.

Crankshaft end play should be 0.002-0.008 inch (0.051-0.203 mm). End play is controlled by use of different thickness shim gaskets between main bearing support plate and crankcase on magneto side of engine. End play can be checked by clamping dial indicator to crankshaft and resting indicator button against crankcase. Shim gaskets are available in thicknesses of 0.005, 0.009 and 0.020 inch for 243000 series engines and 0.005, 0.010 and 0.015 inch for all other engines.

On 300000, 302000, 320000, 325000 and 326000 series engines, tighten main bearing support plate cap screws to a torque of 85 in.-lbs. (9.6 N·m) on magneto end and 185 in.-lbs. (20.9 N·m) on pto end.

Renew crankshaft if crankpin is 0.0007 inch (0.0178 mm) or more out-of-round or if crankpin is worn to a diameter of 1.3094 inches (33.2587 mm).

**CAM GEAR.** The cam gear and lobes are an integral part. Renew cam gear if gear teeth are damaged or if cam lobes are worn to rejection point of 1.184 inches (30.073 mm) on 243000, 300000 and 302000 series engines. On 320000, 325000 and 326000 series engines, cam lobe rejection point is 1.215 inches

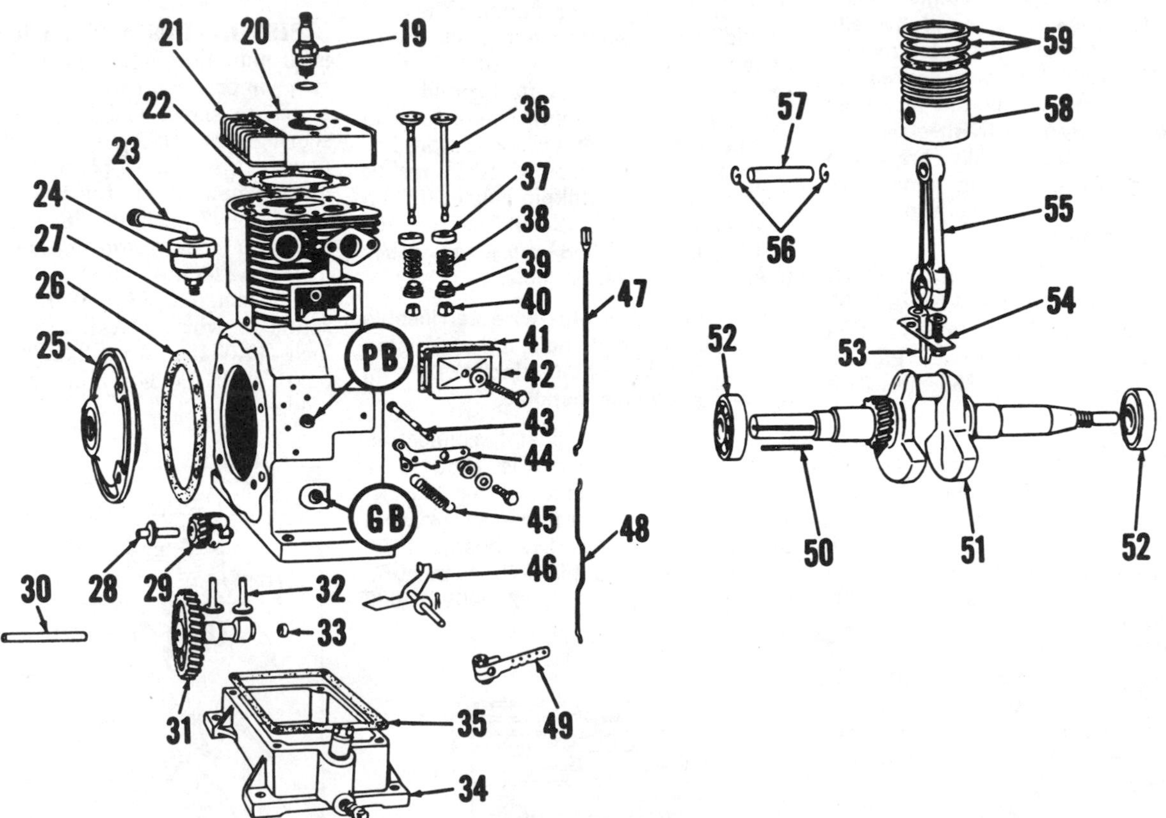


***Fig. B&S72—Exploded view of 243000 series engine assembly. Breaker plunger bushing (PB) and governor shaft bushing (GB) are renewable in engine crankcase (27).***

19. Spark plug
20. Air baffle
21. Cylinder head
22. Head gasket
23. Breather tube
24. Breather
25. Bearing plate
26. Gasket
27. Cylinder block
28. Governor shaft
29. Governor assy.
30. Camshaft
31. Cam gear
32. Valve lifters
33. Camshaft plug
34. Engine base
35. Gasket
36. Valves
37. Spring caps
38. Valve springs
39. Valve rotators
40. Keepers
41. Gasket
42. Valve spring cover
43. Breaker point plunger
44. Governor control lever
45. Governor spring
46. Governor lever shaft
47. Control rod
48. Link
49. Governor lever
50. Key
51. Crankshaft
52. Ball bearings
53. Oil dipper
54. Rod bolt lock
55. Connecting rod
56. Retaining rings
57. Piston pin
58. Piston
59. Piston rings



Illustrations courtesy Briggs & Stratton Corp.

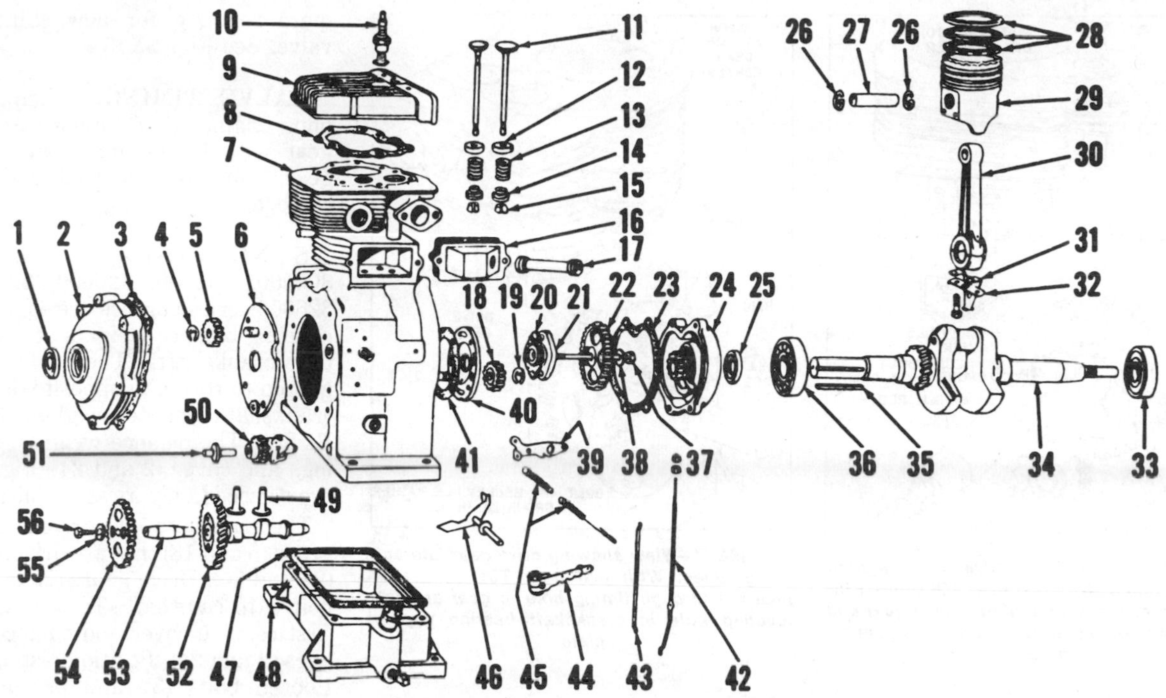

Fig. B&S73—Exploded view of typical 300000, 302000, 320000, 325000 and 326000 series engine assembly.

1. Oil seal
2. Cover & balance assy. (pto end)
3. Gasket
4. "E" ring
5. Idler gear
6. Bearing support
7. Cylinder block
8. Head gasket
9. Cylinder head
10. Spark plug
11. Valves
12. Spring caps
13. Valve springs
14. Valve rotators
15. Keepers
16. Breather assy.
17. Breather tube
18. Idler gear
19. "E" ring
20. Shim (0.005, 0.007 and 0.009 in.)
21. Cam bearing
22. Balance drive gear
23. Gasket
24. Cover & balance assy. (magneto end)
25. Oil seal
26. Retaining rings
27. Piston pin
28. Piston rings
29. Piston
30. Connecting rod
31. Oil dipper
32. Rod bolt lock
33. Ball bearing
34. Crankshaft
35. Key
36. Ball bearing
37. Drive gear bolt
38. Belleville washer
39. Governor control lever
40. Bearing support
41. Shim (0.005, 0.010 and 0.015 in.)
42. Control rod
43. Link
44. Governor lever
45. Governor springs
46. Governor lever shaft
47. Gasket
48. Engine base
49. Valve lifters
50. Governor assy.
51. Governor shaft
52. Cam gear
53. Camshaft
54. Balance drive gear
55. Belleville washer
56. Drive gear bolt

(30.861 mm). Also, renew cam gear if journals are worn to a diameter of 0.4968 inch (12.6187 mm) on 243000 series engines. On all other engines, renew cam gear if journals are worn to diameter of 0.8105 inch (20.5867 mm) on magneto end or 0.6145 inch (15.6083 mm) on pto end.

On 300000, 302000, 320000, 325000 and 326000 series, cam gear end play should be 0.002-0.008 inch (0.051-0.203 mm). End play is controlled by use of different thickness shims (20–Fig. B&S73) between cam bearing (21) and crankcase. Shims are available in thicknesses of 0.005, 0.007 and 0.009 inch. Tighten cam gear bearing cap screws to a torque of 85 in.-lbs. (9.6 N·m).

Align timing marks on crankshaft gear and cam gear when reassembling engine.

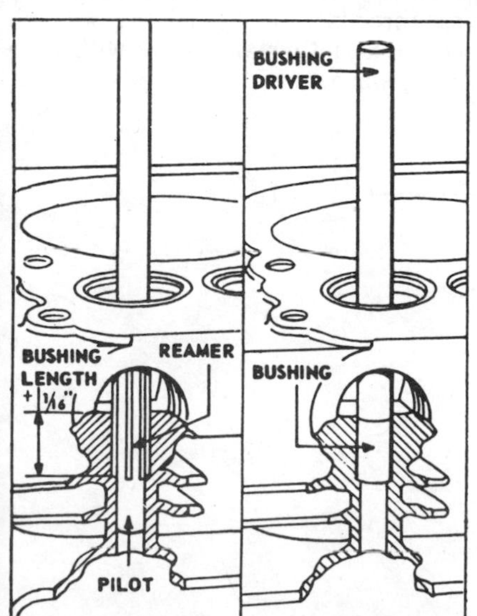


Fig. B&S74—View showing valve guide being reamed and valve guide bushing installed.

**VALVE SYSTEM.** Valve clearance is adjusted by grinding end of valve stems squarely. Check clearance with engine cold. Intake valve clearance should be 0.007-0.009 inch (0.0178-0.229 mm) and exhaust valve clearance should be 0.017-0.019 inch (0.432-0.483 mm).

Valve face and seat angle is 45 degrees. Desired seat width is 3/64 to 1/16-inch (1.2-1.6 mm). Renew valve if margin is 1/64-inch (0.4 mm) or less after refacing.

Engines are equipped with an exhaust valve seat insert and an intake valve seat is available for service. Renewal of

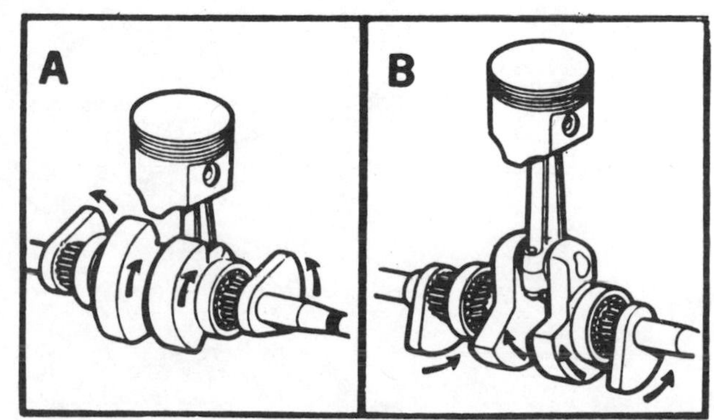


Fig. B&S75—Synchro-Balance weights rotate in opposite direction of crankshaft counterweights on 300000, 302000, 320000, 325000 and 326000 series engines.

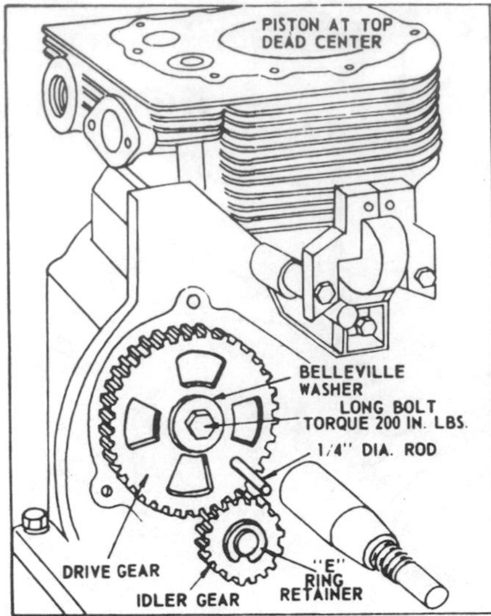


*Fig. B&S76—View showing drive gear (magneto end) being timed. With piston at TDC, insert 1/4-inch (6 mm) rod through timing hole in gear and into locating hole in crankshaft bearing support plate.*

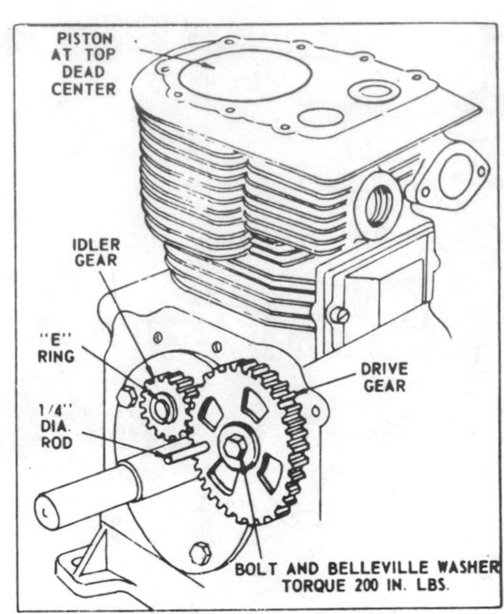


*Fig. B&S77—View showing drive gear (pto end) being timed. With piston at TDC, insert 1/4-inch rod through timing hole in gear and into locating hole in crankshaft bearing support plate.*

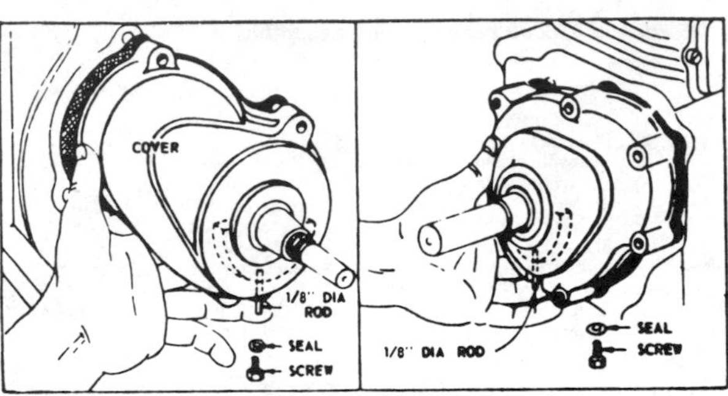


*Fig. B&S78—Insert 1/8-inch (3 mm) rod through timing hole in covers and into hole in balance weights when installing cover assemblies. Piston must be at TDC.*

exhaust valve seat insert and installation of intake valve service seat requires the use of special equipment which is available from Briggs & Stratton.

If Briggs & Stratton plug gage #19151 can be inserted a distance of 5/16-inch (8 mm) or more into valve guide, guide should be rebushed with a service housing, Briggs & Stratton part #230655, as follows: Ream guide a depth of 1/16-inch (1.6 mm) longer than bushing with Briggs & Stratton reamer #19183; then, press bushing in flush with top of guide. Bushing is pre-sized and should not require reaming for new standard size valve. See Fig. B&S74.

**VALVE TIMING.** When reassembling engine, align timing mark on cam gear with timing mark on crankshaft gear. Valve to piston timing will then be correct.

**SYNCHRO-BALANCER.** The 300000, 302000, 320000, 325000 and 326000 series engines are equipped with rotating balance weights at each end of the crankshaft. The balancers are geared to rotate in opposite direction of crankshaft counterweights. See Fig. B&S75. The balance weights, ball bearings and cover (2 and 24–Fig. B&S73) are serviced only as assemblies.

The balancers are driven from idler gears (5 and 18) that are driven by gears (22 and 54). Drive gears (22 and 54) are bolted to camshaft. To time balancers, first remove cover and balancer assemblies (2 and 24). Position piston at TDC. Loosen bolts (37 and 56) until drive gears will rotate on cam gear and camshaft. Insert a 1/4-inch (6 mm) rod through timing hole in each drive gear and into locating holes in main bearing support plates as shown in Figs. B&S76 and B&S77. With piston at TDC and 1/4-inch (6 mm) rods in place, tighten drive gear bolts to a torque of 200 in.-lbs. (22.6 N·m). Remove the 1/4-inch (6 mm) rods. Remove timing hole screws (Fig. B&S78) and insert 1/8-inch (3 mm) rods through timing holes and into hole in balance weights. Then, with piston at TDC, carefully slide cover assemblies into position.

Tighten cap screws in pto end cover to a torque of 200 in.-lbs. (22.6 N·m) and magneto end cover to 120 in.-lbs. (13.5 N·m). Remove the 1/8-inch (3 mm) rods. Coat threads of timing hole screws with Permatex and install screws with fibre sealing washers.

---

# BRIGGS & STRATTON

## SERVICING BRIGGS & STRATTON ACCESSORIES

### REWIND STARTER

**OVERHAUL.** To renew broken rewind spring, proceed as follows: Grasp free outer end of spring (S–Fig. B&S80) and pull broken end from starter housing. With blower housing removed, remove tangs (T) and remove starter pulley from housing. Untie knot in rope (R) and remove rope and inner end of broken spring from pulley. Apply a small amount of grease on inner face of pulley, thread inner end of new spring through notch in starter housing, engage inner end of spring in pulley hub and place pulley in housing. Insert a ¾-inch square bar in pulley hub and turn pulley approximately 13½ turns in a counter-clockwise direction as shown in Fig. B&S81. Tie wrench to blower housing with wire to hold pulley so hole (H) in pulley is aligned with rope guide (G) in housing as shown in Fig. B&S82. Hook a wire in inner end of rope and thread rope through guide and hole in pulley; then, tie a knot in rope and release pulley allowing spring to wind rope into pulley groove.

To renew starter rope only, it is not generally necessary to remove starter pulley and spring. Wind up spring and install new rope as outlined in preceding paragraph.

Two different types of starter clutches have been used; refer to exploded view of early production unit in Fig. B&S83 and exploded view of late production unit in Fig. B&S84. The outer end of late production ratchet (refer to cutaway view in Fig. B&S85) is sealed with a felt and a retaining plug and a rubber ring is used to seal ratchet to ratchet cover.

To disassemble early type starter clutch unit, refer to Fig. B&S83 and proceed as follows: Remove snap ring (3) and lift ratchet (5) and cover (4) from starter housing (7) and crankshaft. Be careful not to lose steel balls (6). Starter housing (7) is also flywheel retaining nut; to remove housing, first remove screen (2) and using Briggs & Stratton flywheel wrench #19114, unscrew housing from crankshaft in counter-clockwise direction. When reinstalling housing, be sure spring washer (8) is placed

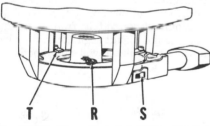

*Fig. B&S80 – View of rewind starter showing rope (R), spring end (S) and retaining tangs (T).*

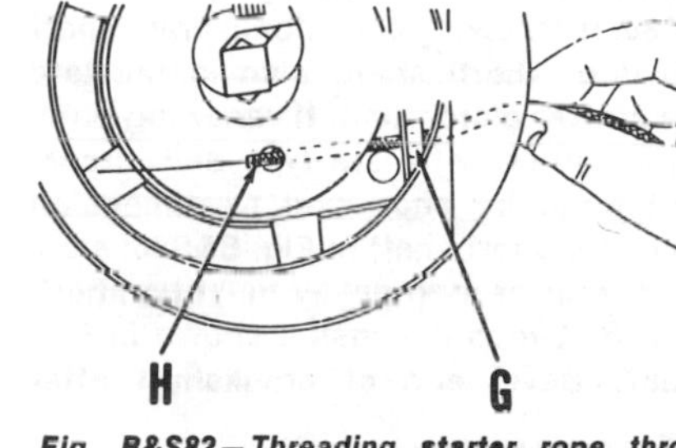

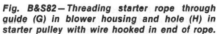

*Fig. B&S82 – Threading starter rope through guide (G) in blower housing and hole (H) in starter pulley with wire hooked in end of rope.*

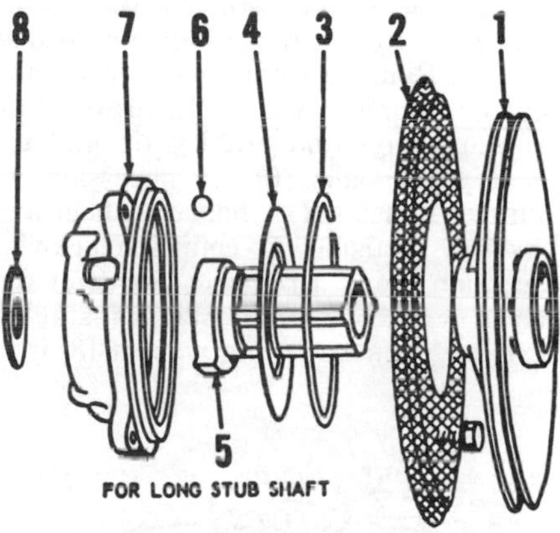


*Fig. B&S84 – View of late production sealed starter clutch unit. Late unit can be used with "short stub shaft" only; refer to Fig. B&S86. Refer to Fig. B&S85 for cut-away view of ratchet (5).*

1. Starter rope pulley
2. Rotating screen
3. Rubber seal
4. Ratchet cover
5. Starter ratchet
6. Steel balls
7. Clutch housing (flywheel nut)
8. Spring washer

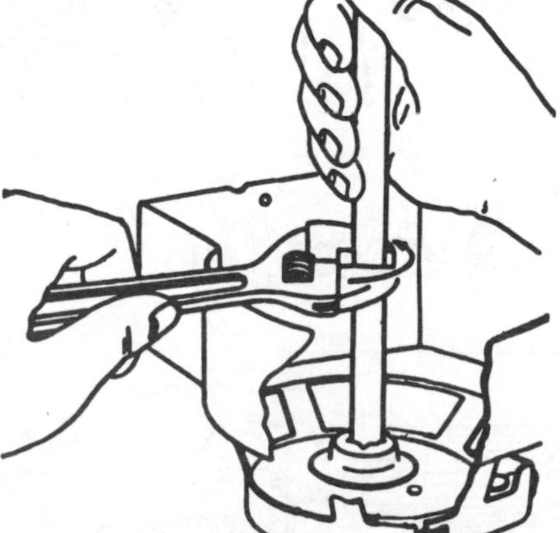

*Fig. B&S81 – Using square shaft and wrench to wind up rewind starter spring. Refer to text.*

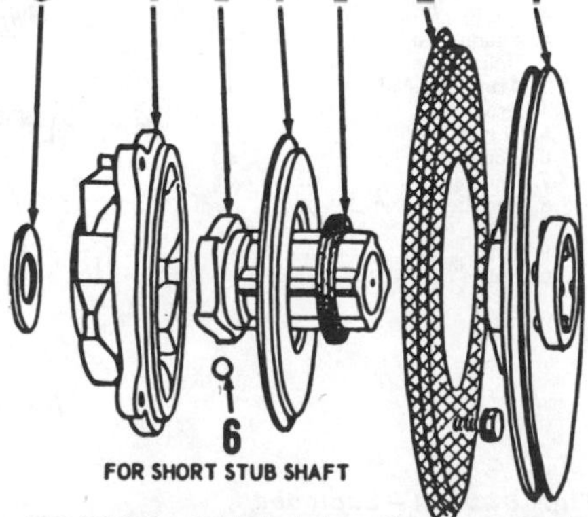


*Fig. B&S83 – Exploded view of early production starter clutch unit; refer to Fig. B&S86 for view of "long stub shaft." A late type unit (Fig. B&S85) should be installed when renewing "long" crankshaft with "short" (late production) shaft.*

1. Starter rope pulley
2. Rotating screen
3. Snap ring
4. Ratchet cover
5. Starter ratchet
6. Steel balls
7. Clutch housing (flywheel nut)
8. Spring washer

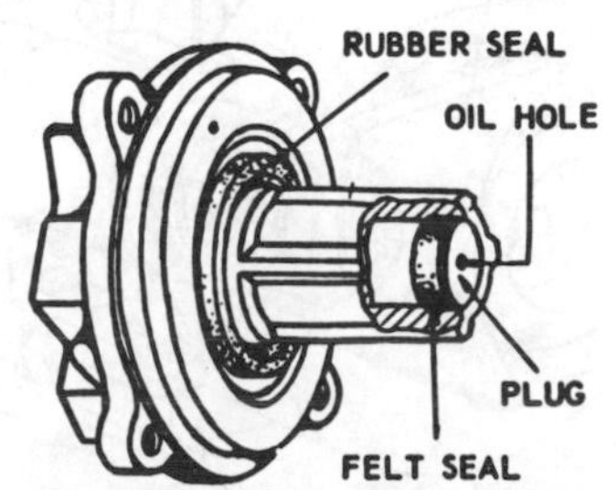


*B&S85 – Cut-away view showing felt seal plug in end of late production starter ratchet (5 – Fig. B&S84).*

Illustrations courtesy Briggs & Stratton Corp.

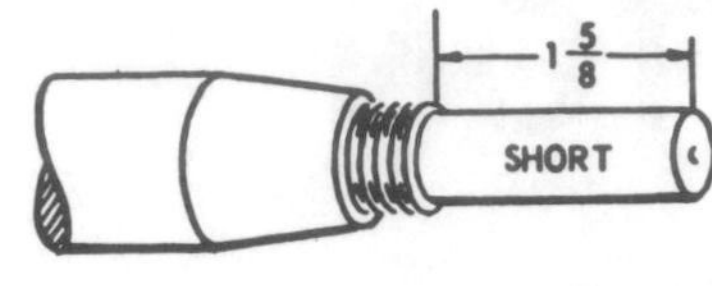


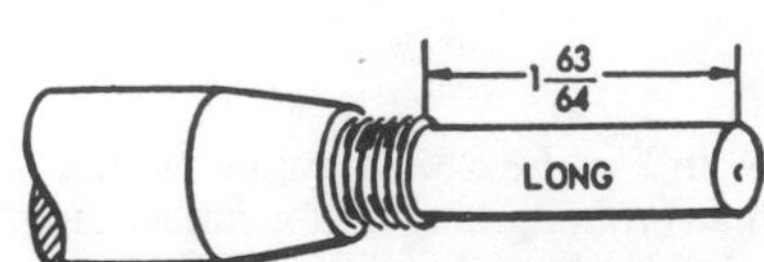


*Fig. B&S86—Crankshaft with short stub (top view) must be used with late production starter clutch assembly. Early crankshaft (bottom view) can be modified by cutting off stub end to dimension shown in top view and beveling end of shaft to allow installation of late type clutch unit.*

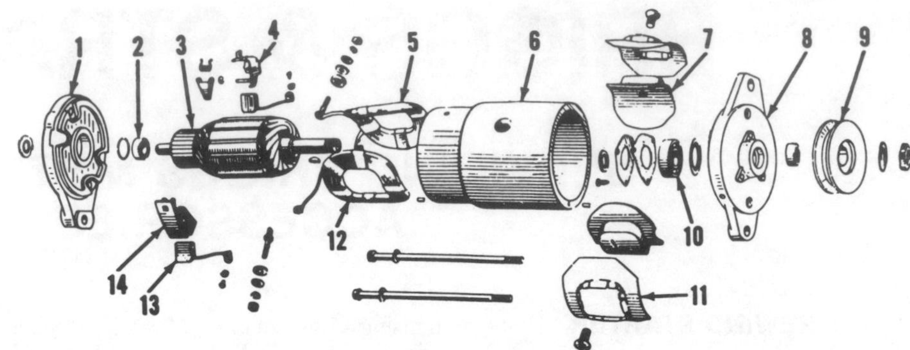


*Fig. B&S89—Exploded view of Delco-Remy starter-generator unit used on some B&S engines.*

1. Commutator end frame
2. Bearing
3. Armature
4. Ground brush holder
5. Field coil L.H.
6. Frame
7. Pole shoe
8. Drive end frame
9. Pulley
10. Bearing
11. Field coil insulator
12. Field coil R.H.
13. Brush
14. Insulated brush holder

on crankshaft with cup (hollow) side toward flywheel, then install starter housing and tighten securely. Reinstall rotating screen. Place ratchet on crankshaft and into housing and insert steel balls. Reinstall cover and retaining snap ring.

To disassemble late starter clutch unit, refer to Fig. B&S84 and proceed as follows: Remove rotating screen (2) and starter ratchet cover (4). Lift ratchet (5) from housing and crankshaft and extract steel balls (6). If necessary to remove housing (7), hold flywheel and unscrew housing in counter-clockwise direction using Briggs & Stratton flywheel wrench #19114. When installing housing, be sure spring washer (8) is in place on crankshaft with cup (hollow) side toward flywheel, then tighten housing securely. Inspect felt seal and plug in outer end of ratchet; renew ratchet if seal or plug are damaged as these parts are not serviced separately. Lubricate felt with oil and place ratchet on crankshaft. Insert steel balls and install ratchet cover, rubber seal and rotating screen.

**NOTE: Crankshafts used with early and late starter clutches differ; refer to Fig. B&S86. If renewing early (long) crankshaft with late (short) shaft, also install late type starter clutch unit. If renewing early starter clutch with late type unit, crankshaft must be shortened to dimension shown for short shaft in Fig. B&S86; also, hub of starter rope pulley must be shortened to ½-inch dimension shown in Fig. B&S87. Bevel end of crankshaft after removing the approximate ⅜-inch from shaft.**

When installing blower housing and starter assembly, turn starter ratchet so word "TOP" on ratchet is toward engine cylinder head.

## 12-VOLT STARTER-GENERATOR UNITS

The combination starter-generator functions as a cranking motor when starting switch is closed. When engine is operating and with starting switch open, unit operates as a generator. Generator output and circuit voltage for battery and various operating requirements are controlled by a current-voltage regulator. On units where voltage regulator is mounted separately from generator unit, do not mount regulator with cover down as regulator will not function in

*Fig. B&S87—When installing a late type starter clutch unit as replacement for early type, either install new starter rope pulley or cut hub of old pulley to dimension shown.*

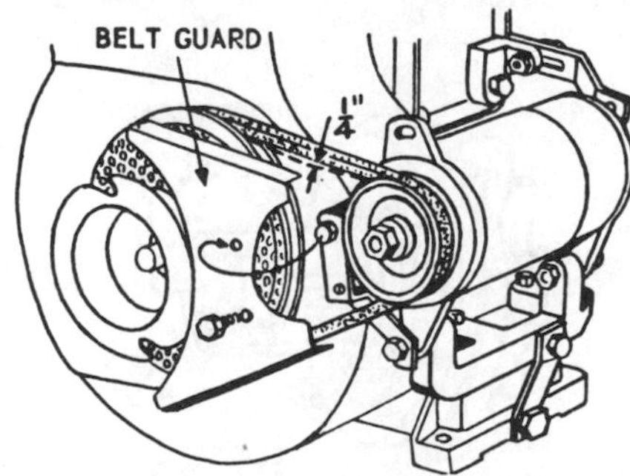


*Fig. B&S88—View showing starter-generator belt adjustment on models so equipped. Refer to text.*

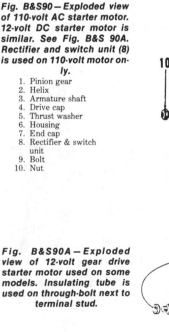

*Fig. B&S90—Exploded view of 110-volt AC starter motor. 12-volt DC starter motor is similar. See Fig. B&S 90A. Rectifier and switch unit (8) is used on 110-volt motor only.*

1. Pinion gear
2. Helix
3. Armature shaft
4. Drive cap
5. Thrust washer
6. Housing
7. End cap
8. Rectifier & switch unit
9. Bolt
10. Nut

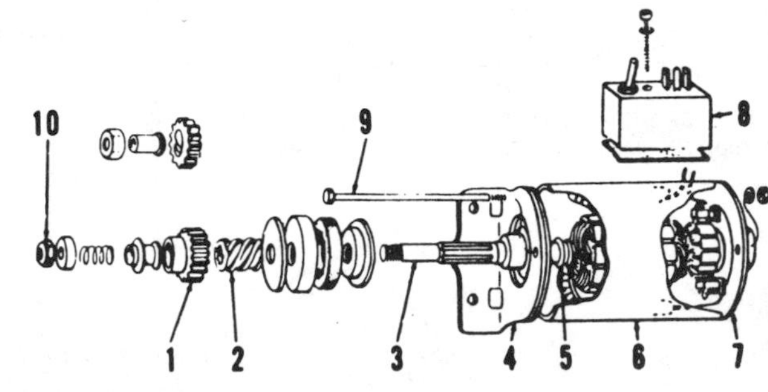


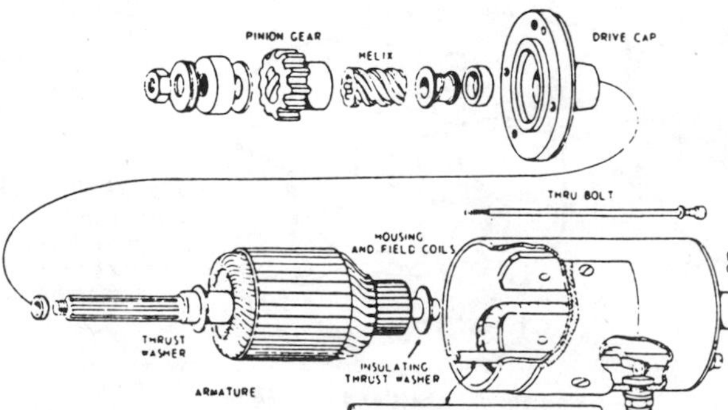


*Fig. B&S90A—Exploded view of 12-volt gear drive starter motor used on some models. Insulating tube is used on through-bolt next to terminal stud.*



Illustrations courtesy Briggs & Stratton Corp.

this position. To adjust belt tension, apply approximately 30 pounds (14 kg) pull on generator adjusting flange and tighten mounting bolts. Belt tension is correct when a pressure of 10 pounds (44.5N) applied midway between pulleys will deflect belt 1/4-inch (6 mm). See Fig. B&S88. On units equipped with two drive belts, always renew belts in pairs. A 50 amp-hour capacity battery is recommended Starter-generator units are intended for use in temperatures above 0°F (−18°C). Refer to Fig. B&S89 for exploded view of starter-generator. Parts and service on starter-generator are available at authorized Delco-Remy service stations.

## GEAR-DRIVE STARTERS

Two types of gear drive starters may be used, a 110-volt AC starter or a 12-volt DC starter. Refer to Fig. B&S90 or B&S90A for an exploded view of starter motors. A properly grounded receptacle should be used with power cord connected to 110-volt AC starter motor. A 32 amp-hour capacity battery is recommended for use with 12-volt DC starter motor.

To renew a worn or damaged flywheel ring gear, drill out retaining rivets using a 3/16-inch (4.7 mm) drill. Attach new ring gear using screws provided with new ring gear.

To check for correct operation of 110-volt AC starter motor, remove starter motor from engine and place motor in a vise or other holding fixture. Install a 0-5 amp ammeter in power cord to 110-volt AC starter motor. On 12-volt DC motor, connect a 12-volt battery to motor with a 0-50 amp ammeter in series with positive line from battery to starter motor. Connect a tachometer to drive end of starter. With starter activated on 110-volt motor, starter motor should turn at 5200 rpm minimum with a maximum current draw of 3½ amps. The 12-volt motor should turn at 6200 rpm minimum with a current draw of 16 amps maximum. If starter motor does not operate satisfactorily, check operation of rectifier or starter switch. if rectifier and starter switch are good, disassemble and inspect starter motor.

To check rectifier used on 110-volt AC starter motor, remove rectifier unit from starter motor. Solder a 10,000 ohm 1 watt resistor to DC internal terminals of rectifier as shown in Fig. B&S91. Connect a 0-100 range DC voltmeter to resistor leads. Measure voltage of AC outlet to be used. With starter switch in "OFF" position, a zero reading should be shown on DC voltmeter. With starter switch in "ON" position, the DC voltmeter should show a reading that is 0-14-volts lower than AC line voltage measured previously. If voltage drop exceeds 14-volts, renew rectifier unit.

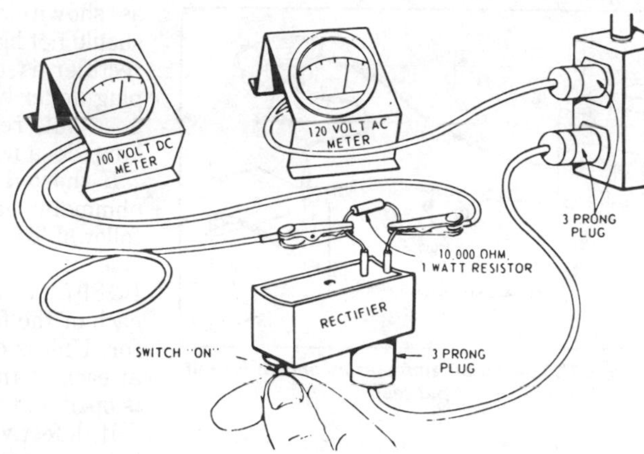


***Fig. B&S91—View of test connections for 110-volt rectifier. Refer to text for procedure.***

Disassembly of starter motor is self-evident after inspection of unit and referral to Fig. B&S90 or B&S 90A. Note position of through-bolts during disassembly so they can be installed in their original positions during reassembly. When reassembling motor, lubricate end cap bearings with SAE 20 oil. Be sure to match drive cap keyway to stamped key in housing when sliding armature into motor housing. Brushes may be held in their holders during installation by making a brush spreader tool from a piece of metal as shown in Fig. B&S92. Splined end of helix (2–Fig. B&S90) must be towards end of armature shaft as shown in Fig. B&S93. Tighten armature shaft nut to 170 in.-lbs. (19 N·m).

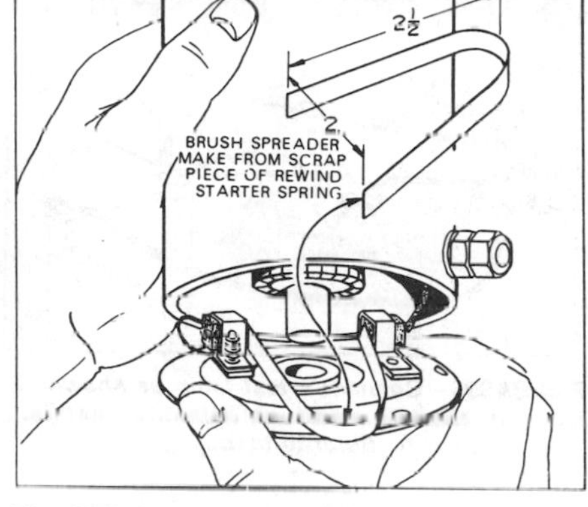


***Fig. B&S92—Tool shown may be fabricated to hold brushes when installing motor end cap.***

## FLYWHEEL ALTERNATORS

### 4 Amp Non-Regulated Alternator

Some engines are equipped with 4 amp non-regulated flywheel alternator shown in Fig. B&S94. A solid state rectifier and 7½ amp fuse is used with this alternator.

If battery is run down and no output from alternator is suspected, first check 7½ amp fuse. If fuse is good, clean and tighten all connections. Disconnect charging lead and connect an ammeter as shown in Fig. B&S95. Start engine and check for alternator output. If ammeter shows no charge, stop engine, remove ammeter and install a test lamp

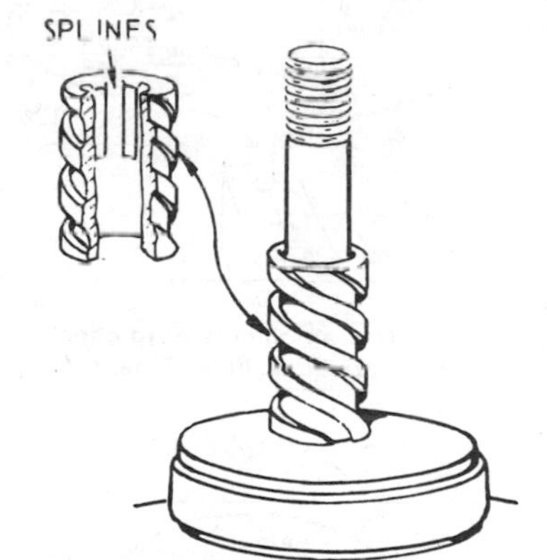


***Fig. B&S93—Install helix on armature so splines of helix are to top as shown above.***

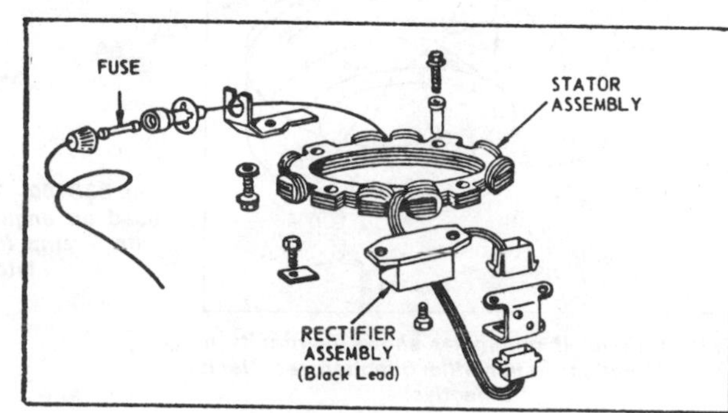


***Fig. B&S94—Stator and rectifier assemblies used on 4 amp non-regulated flywheel alternator. Fuse is 7½ amp AGC or 3AG.***

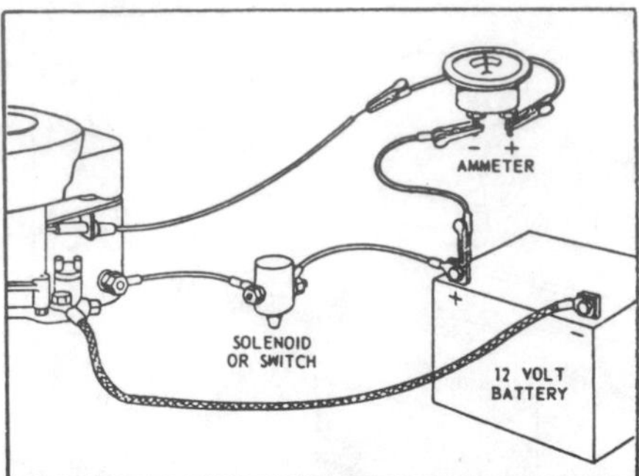


Fig. B&S95—Install ammeter as shown for output test.

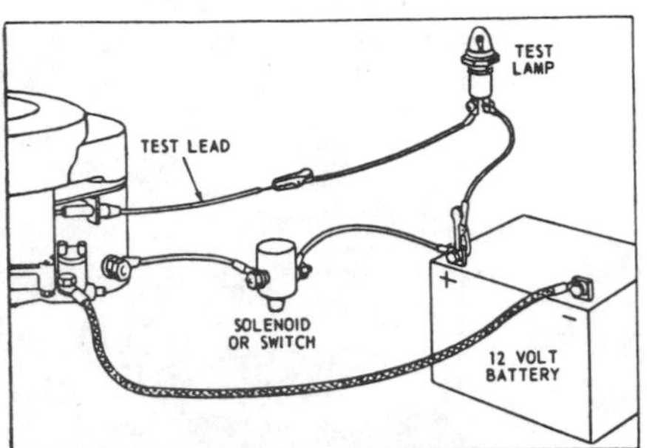


Fig. B&S96—Connect a test lamp as shown to test for shorted stator or defective rectifier. Refer to text.

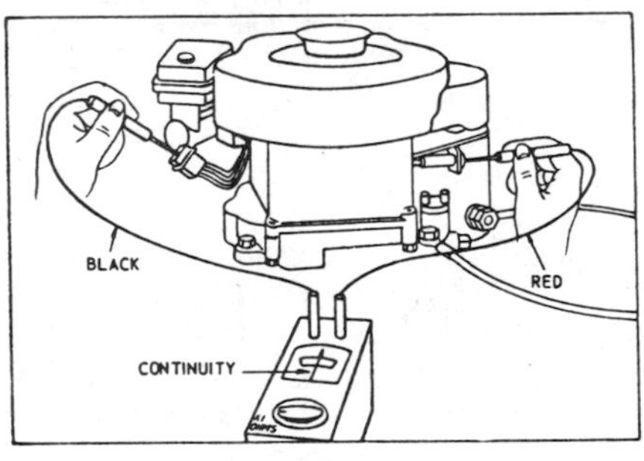


Fig. B&S97—Use an ohmmeter to check condition of stator. Refer to text.

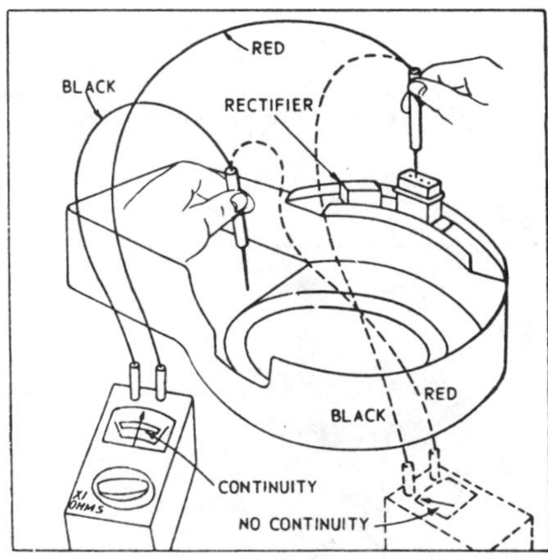


Fig. B&S98—If ohmmeter shows continuity in both directions or in neither direction, rectifier is defective.

as shown in Fig. B&S96. Test lamp should not light. If it does light, stator or rectifier is defective. Unplug rectifier plug under blower housing. If test lamp goes out, rectifier is defective. If test lamp does not go out, stator is shorted.

If shorted stator is indicated, use an ohmmeter and check continuity as follows: Touch one test lead to lead inside of fuse holder as shown in Fig. B&S97. Touch the other test lead to each of the four pins in rectifier connector. Unless ohmmeter shows continuity at each of the four pins, stator winding is open and stator must be renewed.

If defective rectifier is indicated, unbolt and remove flywheel blower housing with rectifier. Connect one ohmmeter test lead to blower housing and other test lead to single pin connector in rectifier connector. See Fig. B&S98. Check for continuity, then reverse leads and again test for continuity. If tests show no continuity in either direction or continuity in both directions, rectifier is faulty and must be renewed.

## 7 Amp Regulated Alternator

A 7 amp regulated flywheel alternator is used with 12-volt gear drive starter motor on some models. The alternator is equipped with a solid state rectifier and regulator. An isolation diode is also used on most models.

If engine will not start, using electric start system, and trouble is not in starting motor, install an ammeter in circuit as shown in Fig. B&S100. Start engine manually. Ammeter should indicate charge. If ammeter does not show battery charging taking place, check for defective wiring and if necessary proceed with troubleshooting.

If battery charging occurs with engine running, but battery does not retain charge, then isolation diode may be defective. The isolation diode is used to prevent battery drain if alternator circuit malfunctions. After troubleshooting diode, remainder of circuit should be inspected to find reason for excessive battery drain. To check operation of diode, disconnect white lead of diode from fuse holder and connect a test lamp from diode white lead to negative terminal of battery. Test lamp should not light. If test lamp lights, diode is defective. Disconnect test lamp and disconnect red lead of diode. Test continuity of diode with ohmmeter by connecting leads of ohmmeter to leads of diode then reverse lead connections. The ohmmeter should show continuity in one direction and an open circuit in the other direction. If readings are incorrect then diode is defective and must be renewed.

To troubleshoot alternator assembly, proceed as follows: Disconnect white lead of isolation diode from fuse holder and connect a test lamp between positive terminal of battery and fuse holder on engine. Engine must not be started. With connections made, test lamp should not light. If test lamp does light, stator, regulator or rectifier is defective. Unplug rectifier-regulator plug under blower housing. If lamp remains lighted, stator is grounded. If lamp goes out, regulator or rectifier is shorted.

If previous test indicated stator is grounded, check stator leads for defects and repair if necessary. If shorted leads

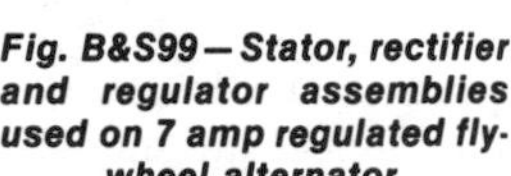

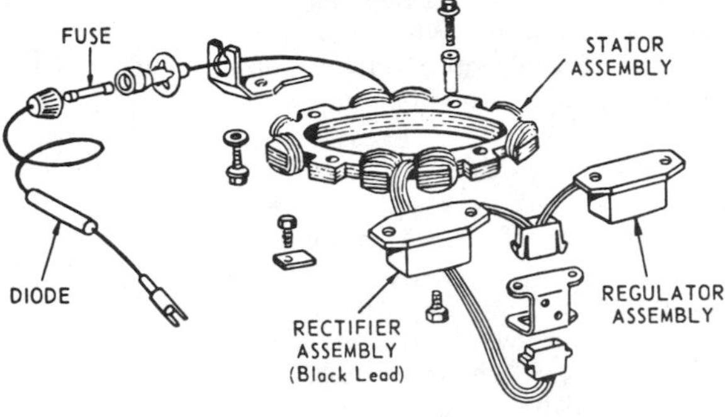


Fig. B&S99—Stator, rectifier and regulator assemblies used on 7 amp regulated flywheel alternator.

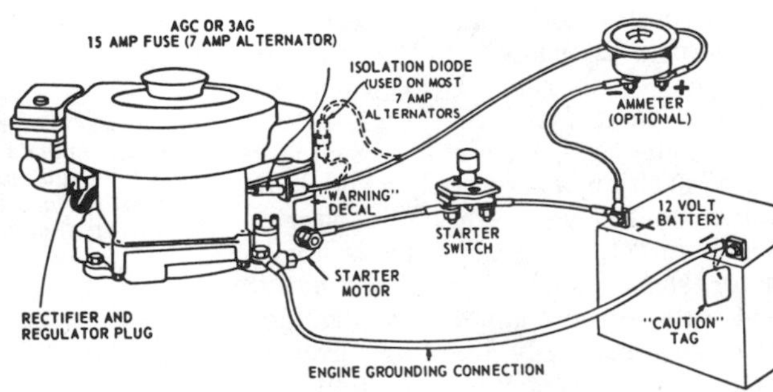


Fig. B&S100—Typical wiring used on engines equipped with 7 amp flywheel regulator.

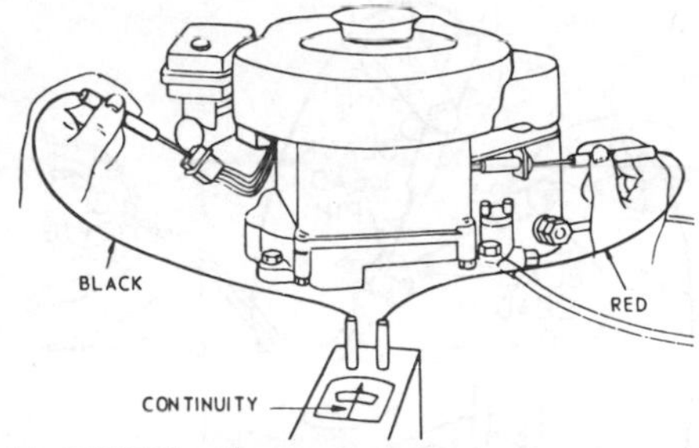


*Fig. B&S101 — Use an ohmmeter to check condition of stator. Refer to text.*

are not found, renew stator. Check stator for an open circuit as follows: Using an ohmmeter, connect red lead to fuse holder as shown in Fig. B&S101 and black lead to one of the pins in rectifier and regulator connector. Check each of the four pins in the connector. The ohmmeter should show continuity at each pin, if not, then there is an open in stator and stator must be renewed.

To test rectifier, unplug rectifier and regulator connector plug and remove blower housing from engine. Using an ohmmeter check for continuity between connector pins connected to black wires and blower housing as shown in Fig. B&S102. Be sure good contact is made with metal of blower housing. Reverse ohmmeter leads and check continuity again. The ohmmeter should show a continuity reading for one direction only on each pin. If either pin shows a continuity reading for both directions, or if either pin shows no continuity for either direction, then rectifier must be renewed.

To test regulator unit, repeat procedure used to test rectifier unit except connect ohmmeter lead to pins connected to red wire and white wire. If ohmmeter shows continuity in either direction for red lead pin, regulator is defective and must be renewed. White lead pin should read as an open on ohmmeter in one direction and a weak reading in the other direction. Otherwise, regulator is defective and must be renewed.

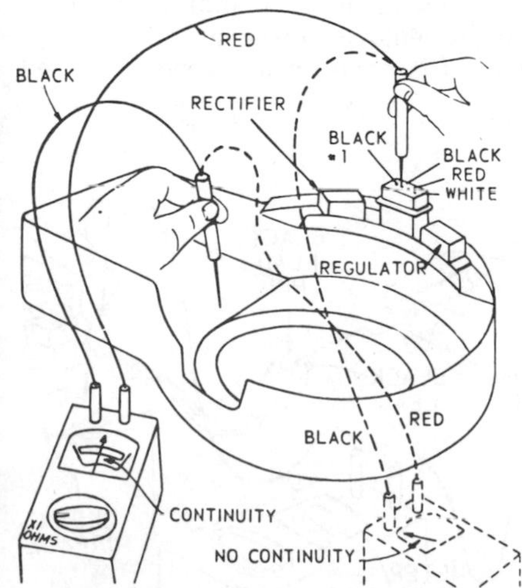


*Fig. B&S102 — Be sure good contact is made between ohmmeter test lead and metal cover when checking rectifier and regulator.*

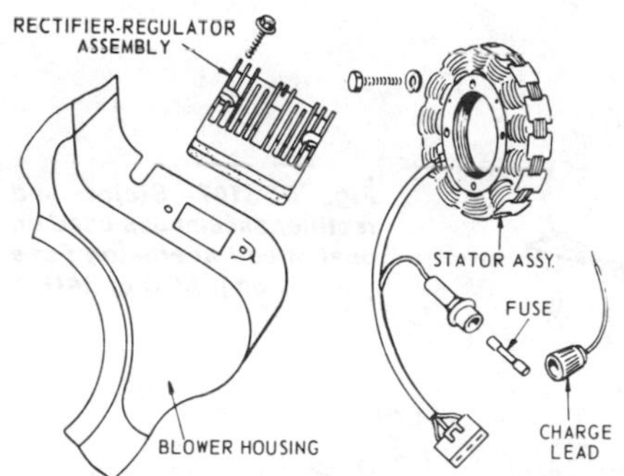


*Fig. B&S103 — View of 10 amp flywheel alternator stator and rectifier-regulator used on some engines.*

## 10 Amp Regulated Alternator

Engines may be equipped with a 10 amp flywheel alternator and a solid state rectifier-regulator. To check charging system, disconnect charging lead from battery. Connect a DC voltmeter between charging lead and ground as shown in Fig. B&S104. Start engine and operate at 3600 rpm. A voltmeter reading of 12 volts or above indicates alternator is functioning. If reading is less than 14 volts, stator or rectifier-regulator is defective.

To test stator, disconnect stator plug from rectifier-regulator. Operate engine at 3600 rpm and connect AC voltmeter leads to AC terminals in stator plug as shown in Fig. B&S105. Voltmeter reading above 20 volts indicates stator is good. A reading less than 20 volts indicates stator is defective.

To test rectifier-regulator, make certain charging lead is connected to battery and stator plug is connected to rectifier-regulator. Check voltage across battery terminals with DC voltmeter (Fig. B&S106). If voltmeter reading is 13.8 volts or higher, reduce battery voltage by connecting a 12 volt load lamp across battery terminals. When battery voltage is below 13.5 volts, start engine and operate at 3600 rpm. Voltmeter reading should rise. If battery is fully charged, reading should rise above 13.8 volts. If voltage does not increase or if voltage reading rises above 14.7 volts, rectifier-regulator is defective and must be renewed.

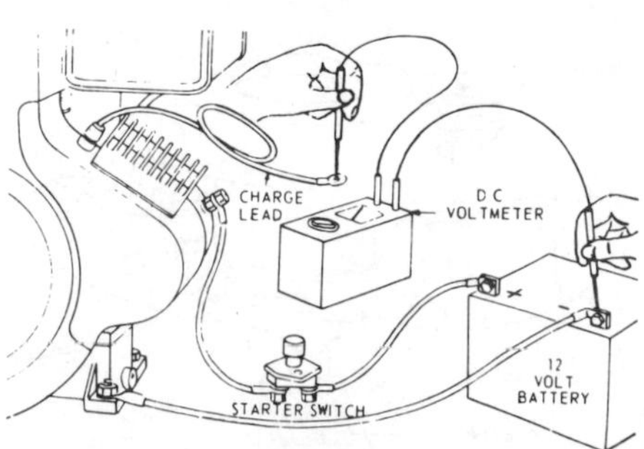


*Fig. B&S104 — DC voltmeter is used to determine if alternator is functioning. Refer to text.*

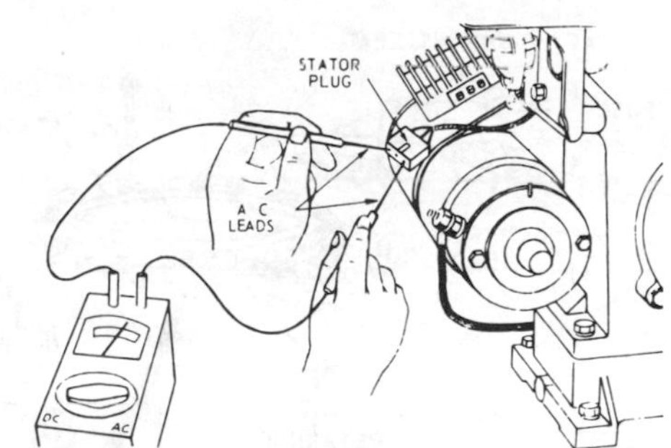


*Fig. B&S105 — AC voltmeter is used to test stator.*

## Dual Circuit Alternator

A dual circuit alternator is used on some models. This system operates as two separate alternators. See Fig. B&S107. A single ring of magnets inside flywheel supplies magnetic field for both sets of windings on the stator. One alternator uses a solid state rectifier and provides 2 amps at 2400 rpm or 3 amps at 3600 rpm for battery charging current. The other alternator feeds alternating current directly to the lights. Since the two are electrically independent, use of the lights does not reduce charge going into battery.

Current for the lights is available only when engine is operating. Twelve volt lights with a total rating of 60 to 100 watts may be used. With a rating of 70 watts, voltage rises from 8 volts at 2400 rpm to 12 volts at 3600 rpm. Since output depends on engine speed, brightness of lights changes with engine speed.

The battery charging current connection is made through a 7½ amp fuse mounted in fuse holder. See Fig. B&S108. Current for lights is available at plastic connector below fuse holder. The 7½ amp fuse protects 3 amp charging alternator and rectifier from burnout due to reverse polarity battery connections. The 5 amp lighting alternator does not require a fuse.

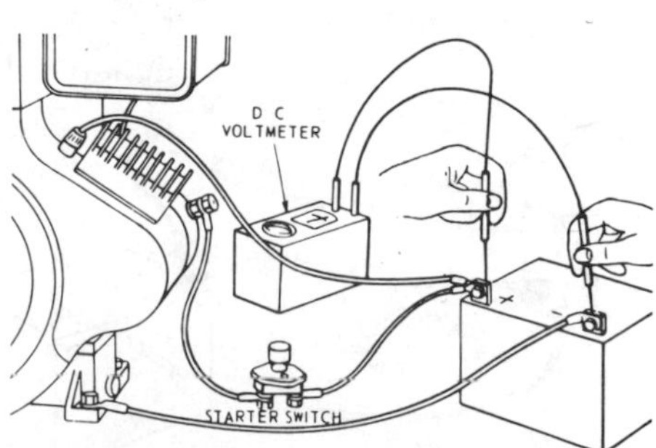


*Fig. B&S106 — Check battery voltage with DC voltmeter. Refer to text for rectifier-regulator test.*

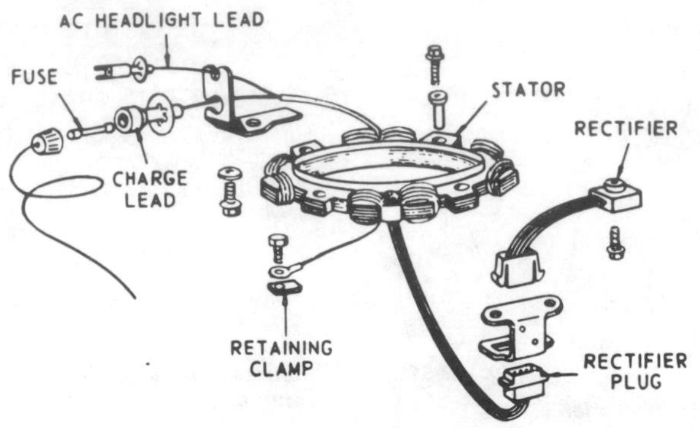


*Fig. B&S107—Stator and rectifier assemblies used on dual circuit alternator. Fuse is 7½ amp AGC or 3AG.*

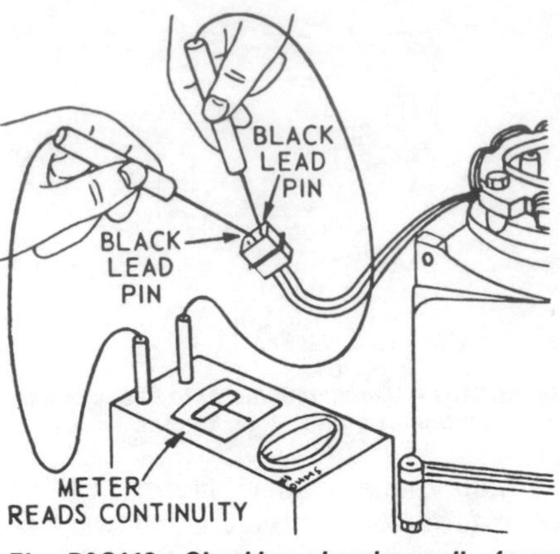


*Fig. B&S112—Checking charging coils for an "open". Meter should show continuity.*

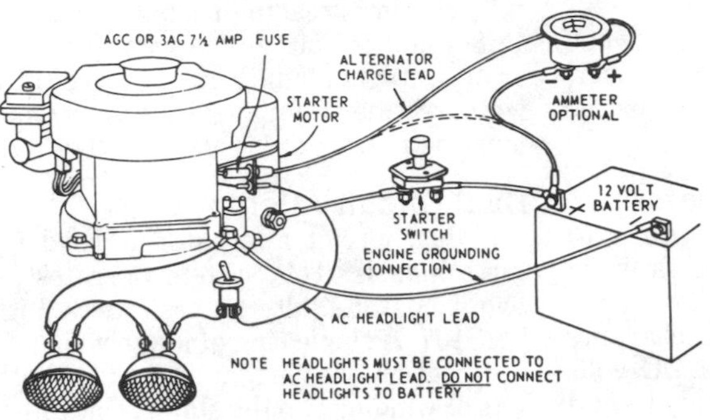


*Fig. B&S108—Typical wiring used on engines equipped with the dual circuit flywheel alternator.*

To check charging alternator output, install ammeter in circuit as shown in Fig. B&S109. Start engine and allow it to operate at a speed of 3000 rpm. Ammeter should indicate charge. If not, and fuse is known to be good, test for short in stator or rectifier as follows: Disconnect charging lead from battery and connect a small test lamp between battery positive terminal and fuse cap as shown in Fig. B&S110. DO NOT start engine. Test lamp should not light. If it does light, stator's charging lead is grounded or rectifier is defective. Unplug rectifier plug under blower housing. If test lamp goes out, rectifier is defective. If test lamp does not go out, stator charging lead is grounded.

If test indicates stator charging lead is grounded, remove blower housing, flywheel, starter motor and retaining clamp, then examine length of red lead for damaged insulation or obvious shorts in lead. If bare spots are found, repair with electrical tape and shellac. If short cannot be repaired, renew stator. Charging lead should also be checked for continuity as follows: Touch one lead of ohmmeter to lead at fuse holder and other ohmmeter lead to red lead pin in connector as shown in Fig. B&S111. If ohmmeter does not show continuity, charging lead is open and stator must be renewed. The charging coils should be checked for continuity as follows: Touch ohmmeter test leads to the two black lead pins as shown in Fig. B&S112. If ohmmeter does not show continuity, charging coils are defective and stator must be renewed. Test for grounded charging coils by touching one test lead of ohmmeter to a clean ground surface on engine and the other test lead to each of the black lead pins as shown in Fig. B&S113. If ohmmeter shows continuity, charging coils are grounded and stator must be renewed.

To test rectifier, use an ohmmeter and check for continuity between each of the three lead pin sockets and blower housing. See Fig. B&S114. Reverse ohmmeter leads and check continuity again. Ohmmeter should show a continuity reading for one direction only on each lead socket. If any pin socket shows continuity reading in both directions or neither direction, rectifier is defective and must be renewed.

To test AC lighting alternator circuit, connect a load lamp to AC output plug and ground as shown in Fig. B&S115. Load lamp should light at full brillance at medium engine speed. If lamp does not light or is very dim at medium speeds, remove blower housing and flywheel. Disconnect ground end of AC coil

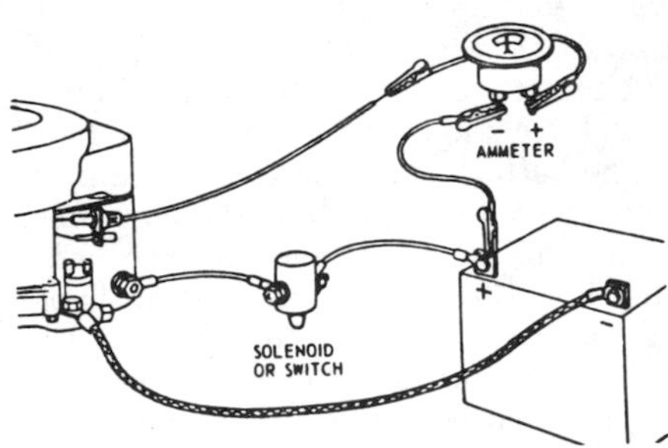


*Fig. B&S109—Install ammeter as shown for charging output test.*

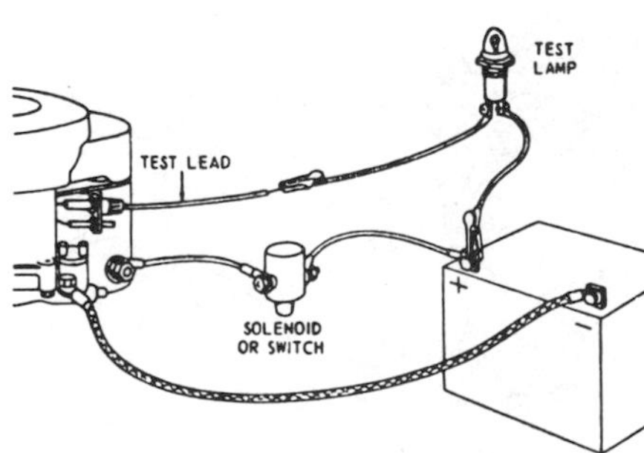


*Fig. B&S110—Connect a test lamp as shown to test for short in stator or rectifier.*

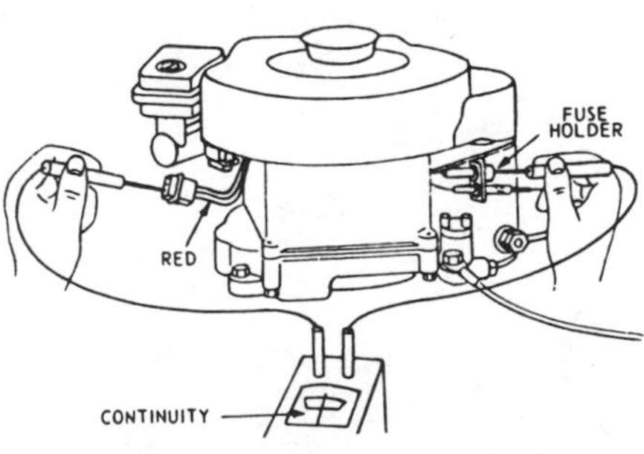


*Fig. B&S111—Use an ohmmeter to check charging lead for continuity. Refer to text.*

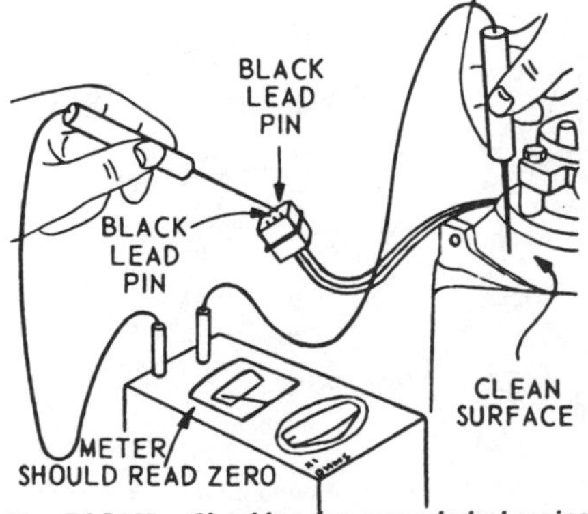


*Fig. B&S113—Checking for grounded charging coils. Refer to text.*



Illustrations courtesy Briggs & Stratton Corp.

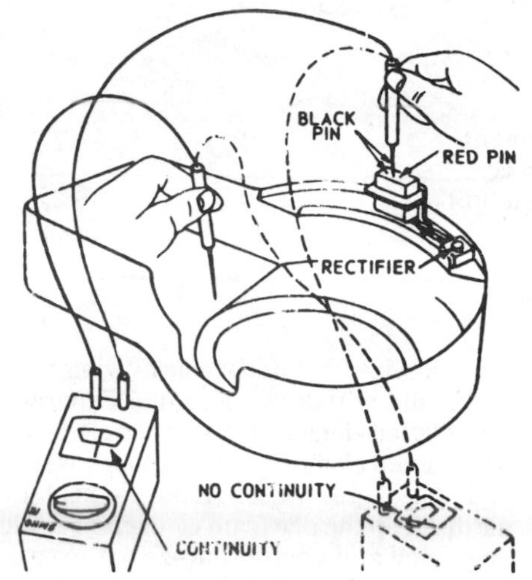

Fig. B&S114—If ohmmeter shows continuity in both directions or neither direction, rectifier is defective.

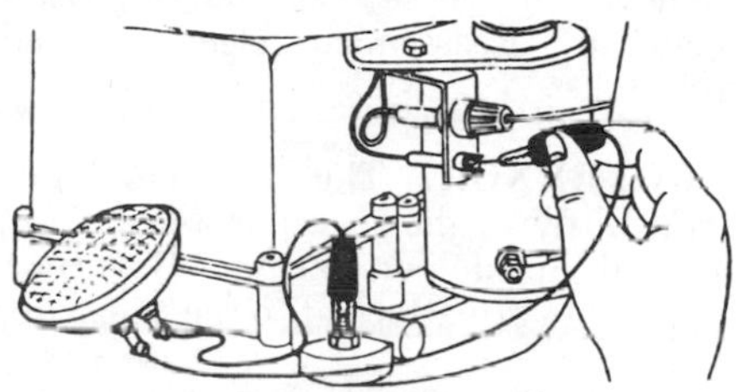
Fig. B&S115—Load lamp (GE #4001 or equivalent is used to test AC lighting circuit output.

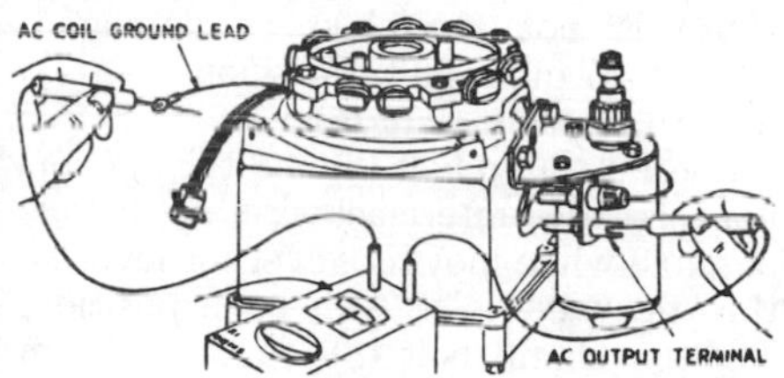

Fig. B&S116—Checking AC lighting circuit for continuity. Refer to text.

from retaining clamp screw (Fig. B&S107). Connect ohmmeter between ground lead of AC coil and AC output terminal as shown in Fig. B&S116. Ohmmeter should show continuity. If not, stator must be renewed. Be sure AC ground lead is not touching a grounded surface, then check continuity from AC output terminal to engine ground. If ohmmeter indicates continuity, lighting coils are grounded and stator must be renewed.

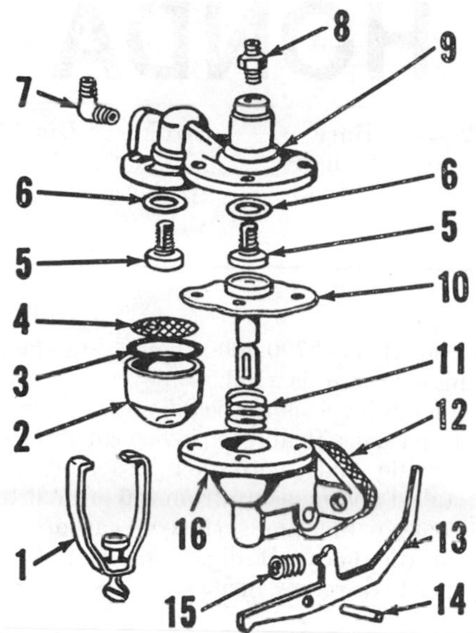

Fig. B&S117—Exploded view of diaphragm type fuel pump used on some B&S engines.

1. Yoke assy.
2. Filter bowl
3. Gasket
4. Filter screen
5. Pump valves
6. Gaskets
7. Elbow fitting
8. Connector
9. Fuel pump head
10. Pump diaphragm
11. Diaphragm spring
12. Gasket
13. Pump lever
14. Lever pin
15. Lever spring
16. Fuel pump body

## FUEL PUMP

A diaphragm type fuel pump is used on some models. Refer to Fig. B&S117 for exploded view of pump.

To disassemble pump, refer to Figs. B&S117 and B&S118; then, proceed as follows: Remove clamp (1), fuel bowl (2), gasket (3) and screen (4). Remove screws retaining upper body (9) to lower body (16). Pump valves (5) and gaskets (6) can now be removed. Drive pin (14) out to either side of body (16), then press diaphragm (10) against spring (11) as shown in view A, Fig. B&S118, and remove lever (13). Diaphragm and spring (11–Fig. B&S117) can now be removed.

To reassemble, place diaphragm spring in lower body and place diaphragm on spring, being sure spring enters cup on bottom side of diaphragm and slot in shaft is at right angle to pump lever. Then, compressing diaphragm against spring as in view A, Fig. B&S118, insert hooked end of lever into slot in shaft. Align hole in lever with hole in lower body and drive pin into place. Then, insert lever spring (15) into body and push outer end of spring into place over hook on arm of lever as shown in view B. Hold lever downward as shown in view C while tightening screws holding upper body to lower body. When installing pump on engine, apply a liberal amount of grease on lever (13) at point where it contacts groove in crankshaft.

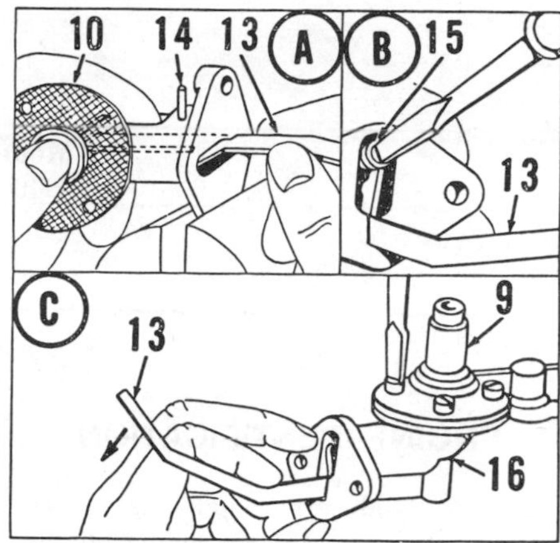

Fig. B&S118—Views showing disassembly and reassembly of diaphragm type fuel pump. Refer to text for procedure and to Fig. B&S117 for exploded view of pump and for legend.

# HONDA

| Model | Bore | Stroke | Displacement |
|---|---|---|---|
| G400 | 86 mm (3.4 in.) | 70 mm (2.8 in.) | 406 cc (24.8 cu. in.) |

## ENGINE IDENTIFICATION

Honda G400 series engine is a four-stroke, air-cooled, single-cylinder engine. Valves are located in cylinder block and crankcase casting. Model G400 engine develops 7.5 kW (10) horsepower at 3600 rpm. The "G" prefix indicates horizontal crankshaft model.

Engine model number decal is located on engine cooling shroud just above or beside rewind starter. Engine serial number is located as shown in Fig. HN1. Always furnish engine model and serial number when ordering service parts.

## MAINTENANCE

**SPARK PLUG.** Recommended spark plug is Champion L92C.

Spark plug should be removed and cleaned at 100 hour intervals. Set electrode gap at 0.6-0.7 mm (0.024-0.028 in.).

**NOTE: Caution should be exercised if abrasive type spark plug cleaner is used. Inadequate cleaning procedure may allow the abrasive cleaner to be deposited in engine cylinder causing rapid wear and premature failure of engine components.**

**CARBURETOR.** Model G400 engine is equipped with a float type side draft carburetor (Fig. HN2). Idle fuel mixture is controlled by adjusting a pilot screw and high speed fuel mixture is controlled by a fixed main jet. Initial adjustment of pilot screw is two turns open from a lightly seated position. Recommended engine idle speed (tractor application) is 2200 rpm and maximum engine speed (unloaded) is 3700-4000 rpm. Standard main jet size is #102.

*Fig. HN1—View showing location of engine serial number (A).*

Float level should be 8.6 mm (0.34 in.). To measure float level, invert carburetor throttle body with float assembly installed and measure from top of float to float bowl mating surface on carburetor throttle body. If dimension is not as specified, renew float.

**FUEL FILTER.** A fuel filter screen is located in sediment bowl below fuel shut-off valve. To remove sediment bowl, first shut off fuel. Unscrew threaded ring and remove ring, sediment bowl and gasket. Make certain gasket is in place during reassembly. To clean screen, fuel shut-off valve must be disconnected from the fuel line and unscrewed from fuel tank.

**AIR FILTER.** Engine is equipped with a dual element type air filter. Air filter should be removed and serviced at 20 hour intervals.

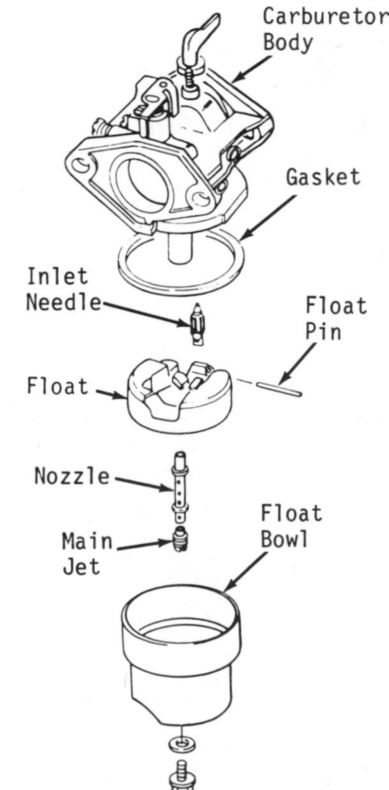


*Fig. HN2—Exploded view of carburetor used on Honda G400 engine.*

To service air filter, remove wing nut, cover and withdraw elements. Separate foam outer element from paper element. Wash foam element in warm soapy water and thoroughly rinse. Allow element to air dry. Dip the dry foam element in clean engine oil and gently squeeze out excess oil.

Direct low air pressure from inside paper element toward the outside to remove all loose dirt and foreign material. Reassemble elements and reinstall.

**GOVERNOR.** The internal centrifugal flyweight governor assembly is located inside crankcase. Governor flyweights are attached to the camshaft gear.

To adjust governor, first stop engine and make certain all linkage is in good condition and tension spring (2–Fig. HN4) is not stretched or damaged. Spring (4) must pull governor lever (3) toward throttle pivot (6).

Loosen clamp bolt (8) and turn governor shaft counterclockwise as far as possible while moving governor lever so throttle valve is at wide-open position. Tighten clamp bolt (8). Start and run engine until it reaches operating temperature. Adjust maximum speed screw (9) to obtain 3700-4000 rpm.

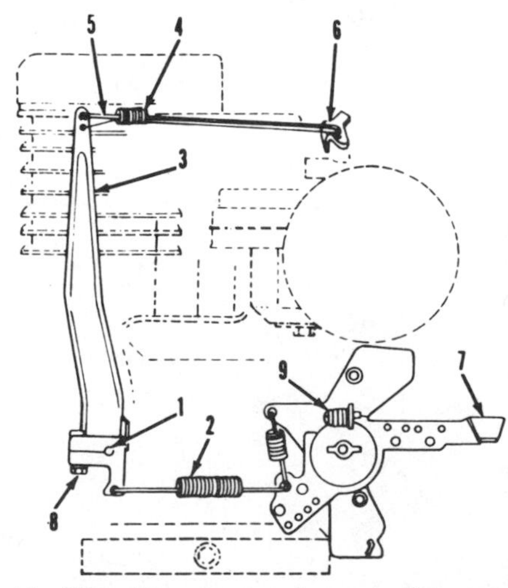


*Fig. HN4—View of external governor linkage.*

1. Governor shaft
2. Tension spring
3. Governor lever
4. Spring
5. Carburetor-to-governor lever rod
6. Throttle pivot
7. Throttle lever
8. Clamp bolt
9. Maximum speed screw

**IGNITION SYSTEM.** Engines may be equipped with a breaker point ignition system or a transistorized ignition system. Refer to appropriate paragraph for ignition system being serviced.

**Breaker Point Ignition System.** Breaker point set and ignition coil are located behind the flywheel on all models. Breaker points should be checked at 300 hour intervals. Initial breaker point gap should be 0.3-0.4 mm (0.012-0.016 in.) and point gap should be varied to obtain 20 degrees BTDC timing setting.

**NOTE: Timing tool 07974-8830001 is available from Honda Motor Company to allow timing adjustment with flywheel removed.**

To check ignition timing, connect positive ohmmeter lead to engine stop switch wire and connect negative ohmmeter lead to engine ground. Rotate flywheel until ohmmeter just does register. "F" mark on flywheel should align with index mark on crankcase (Fig. HN5). If marks do not align, remove flywheel and adjust point gap opening. Reinstall flywheel or use special tool 07974-8830001 and repeat previous procedure to verify correct timing setting is obtained.

To check ignition coil, connect positive ohmmeter lead to spark plug wire and negative ohmmeter lead to coil laminations. Ohmmeter should register 6.6 ohms. When installing ignition coil, make certain coil is positioned correctly on locating pins.

**Transistorized Ignition System.** The transistorized ignition system coil is mounted on engine block. Air gap between ignition coil and outer edge of flywheel should be 0.2-0.6 mm (0.008-0.024 in.).

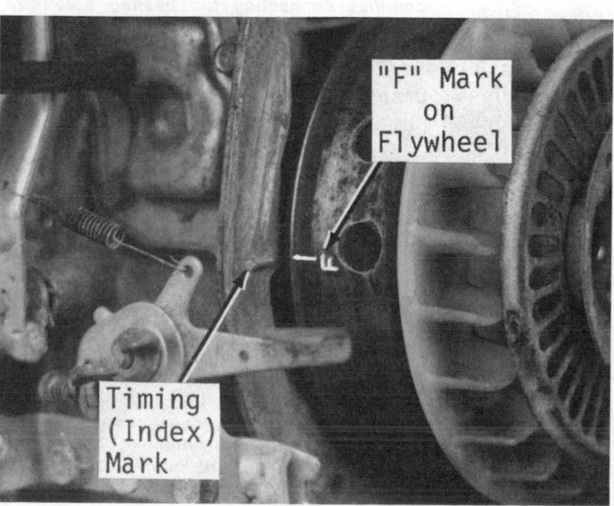


*Fig. HN5—"F" mark on flywheel should align with timing mark on crankcase when breaker points just begin to open. Honda timing tool 07974-8830001 is used to adjust timing with flywheel removed.*

To test primary side of transistorized ignition coil, attach one ohmmeter test lead to coil laminations. Connect remaining ohmmeter test lead to the primary (thin black) coil lead wire. Refer to Fig. HN6. Resistance reading should be 0.7-0.9 ohms.

To test the secondary side of transistorized ignition coil, remove spark plug boot and attach one ohmmeter test lead to coil laminations. Connect remaining ohmmeter test lead to the terminal end of spark plug lead. Refer to Fig. HN7. Resistance reading should be 6300-7700 ohms.

**VALVE ADJUSTMENT.** Valves and seats should be refaced and stem clearance adjusted at 300 hour intervals. Refer to VALVE SYSTEM paragraphs in REPAIRS section for service procedure and specifications.

**CYLINDER HEAD AND COMBUSTION CHAMBER.** Cylinder head, combustion chamber and piston should be cleaned and carbon and lead deposits removed at 300 hour intervals. Refer to CYLINDER HEAD paragraphs in REPAIRS section for service procedure.

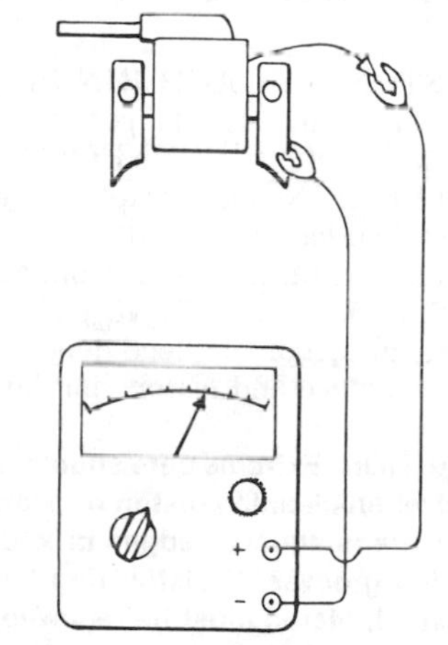

*Fig. HN6—Check resistance on ignition coil primary side using an ohmmeter as shown. Refer to text.*

**LUBRICATION.** Engine is splash lubricated and engine oil should be checked prior to each operating interval. Oil level should be maintained between reference marks on dipstick with dipstick just touching first threads. Do not screw dipstick in to check oil level.

Manufacturer recommends oil with an API service classification of SE or SF. Use SAE 10W-40 motor oil.

Oil should be changed after the first 20 hours of operation and at 100 hour intervals thereafter. Crankcase capacity is 1.2 L (1.27 qt.).

**GENERAL MAINTENANCE.** Check and tighten all loose bolts, nuts or clamps daily. Check for fuel or oil leakage and repair as necessary.

Clean dust, dirt, grease or any foreign material from cylinder head and cylinder block cooling fins at 100 hour intervals or more frequent if needed. Inspect fins for damage and repair as necessary.

## REPAIRS

**TIGHTENING TORQUES.** Recommended tightening torque specifications are as follows:

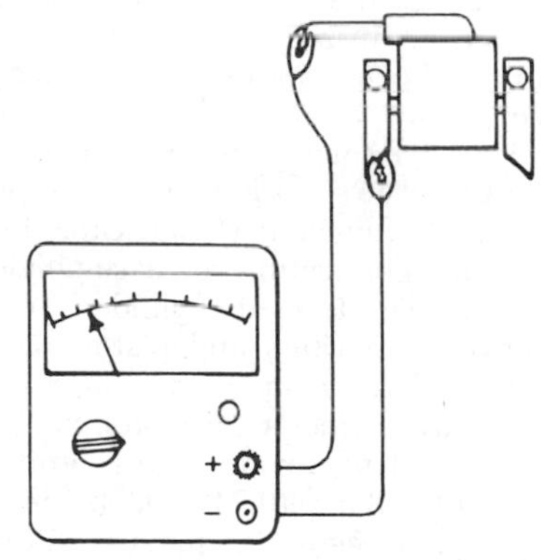

*Fig. HN7—Check resistance on ignition coil secondary side using an ohmmeter as shown. Refer to text.*

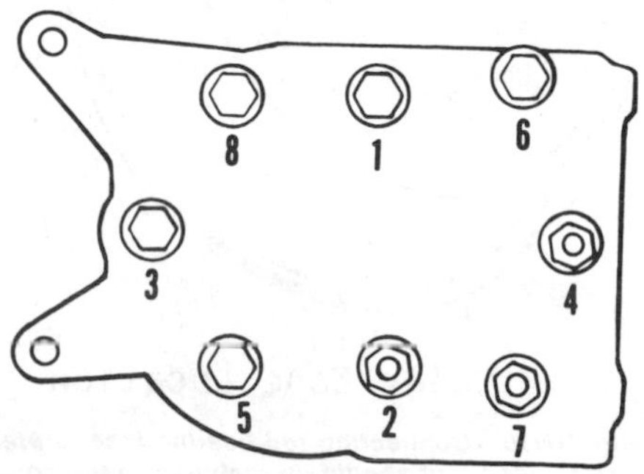


*Fig. HN8—Loosen or tighten cylinder head bolts in sequence shown.*

Spark plug . . . . . . . . . . . . . . . 10-15 N•m (7-11 ft.-lbs.)
Flywheel nut . . . . . . . . . . . 108-118 N•m (80-87 ft.-lbs.)
Cylinder head . . . . . . . . . . . . . 31-37 N•m (23-27 ft.-lbs.)
Tappet cover . . . . . . . . . . . . . . 8-12 N•m (6-9 ft.-lbs.)
Crankcase cover . . . . . . . . . . 20-23 N•m (15-17 ft.-lbs.)
Connecting rod . . . . . . . . . . . 23-27 N•m (17-20 ft.-lbs.)

**CYLINDER HEAD.** To remove cylinder head, first remove cooling shrouds. Clean engine to prevent entrance of foreign material. Loosen cylinder head cap screws in ¼-turn increments in sequence shown in Fig. HN8 until all cap screws are loose enough to remove by hand. Remove cylinder head.

Remove spark plug and clean carbon and lead deposits from cylinder head.

Reinstall cylinder head and new gasket. Tighten cylinder head cap screws to 31-37 N•m (23-27 ft.-lbs.) in sequence shown in Fig. HN8. Compression should be checked after cylinder head has been installed. Compression should be 588 kPa (85 psi).

**CONNECTING ROD AND BEARING.** Connecting rod is equipped with renewable type connecting rod bearing inserts. Piston and connecting rods are removed as an assembly after cylinder head has been removed and crankcase cover has been separated from crankcase. Remove the two connecting rod cap screws, lock plate, oil dipper plate and connecting rod cap. Push piston and connecting rod assembly out through the top of cylinder block. Remove snap rings and piston pin to separate piston from connecting rod.

Standard diameter for piston pin bore in connecting rod small end is 19.010-19.028 mm (0.7484-0.7491 in.). If dimension exceeds 19.8 mm (0.7512 in.), renew connecting rod.

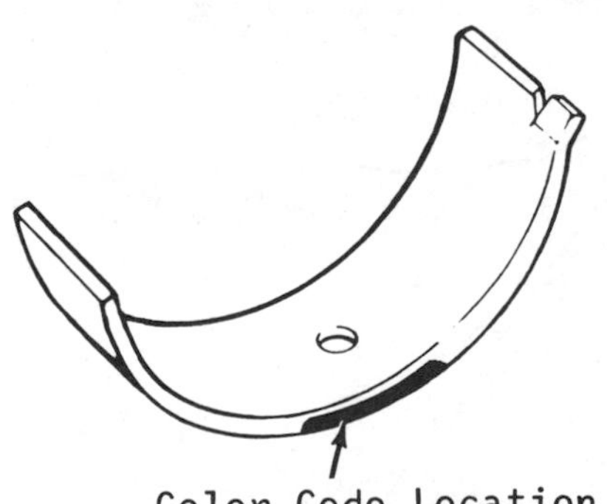


***Fig. HN10—Connecting rod bearing inserts are color coded and should be matched to the connecting rod and crankshaft identification numbers. Refer to text.***

Standard connecting rod side play on crankpin journal is 0.15-0.40 mm (0.0059-0.0159 in.). If side play exceeds 1.0 mm (0.0394 in.), renew connecting rod.

Connecting rod bearing inserts are color coded (Fig. HN10) and connecting rod and crankshaft are stamped with an identification number (Figs. HN11 and HN12) which identify different connecting rod bearing bore sizes or crankshaft connecting rod journal sizes. Bearing inserts, connecting rod and crankshaft must be matched by referring to the CRANKSHAFT, MAIN BEARINGS AND SEALS paragraphs.

Assemble piston to connecting rod with the arrow mark on top of piston toward ribbed side of connecting rod. Install piston pin retaining rings with gaps opposite notch in piston pin bore of piston. Align connecting rod and cap match marks and install connecting rod so ribbed side is toward crankcase cover. Arrow stamped on piston top should be toward valve side of engine after installation. Install oil dipper and lock plate. Tighten connecting rod cap screws to 23-27 N•m (17-20 ft.-lbs.).

**PISTON, PIN AND RINGS.** Piston and connecting rod are removed as an assembly. Refer to CONNECTING ROD AND BEARING paragraphs for removal and installation procedure.

After separating piston from connecting rod, carefully remove piston rings and clean carbon and lead deposits from piston surface and piston ring lands.

**CAUTION: Extreme care should be exercised when cleaning piston ring lands. Do not damage squared edges or widen piston ring grooves. If piston ring lands are damaged, piston must be renewed.**

Measure piston diameter on piston thrust surface, 90 degrees from piston pin. Standard piston diameter is 85.97 mm (3.385 in.). If piston diameter is less than 85.85 mm (3.380 in.), renew piston.

Before installing piston rings, install piston in cylinder bore and use a suitable feeler gage to measure clearance between piston and cylinder bore. Standard clearance is 0.05 mm (0.002 in.). If clearance exceeds 0.25 mm (0.010 in.), renew piston and/or recondition cylinder bore.

Standard piston pin bore diameter is 19.002-19.008 mm (0.7481-0.7483 in.). If diameter exceeds 19.046 mm (0.7498 in.), renew piston.

Standard piston pin outside diameter is 18.994-19.000 mm (0.7478-0.7480 in.). If diameter is less than 18.97 mm (0.7469 in.), renew piston pin.

Standard piston ring-to-piston groove side clearance is 0.020-0.060 mm (0.0008-0.0024 in.) for top ring and 0.010-0.050 mm (0.0004-0.0020 in.) for second ring. If clearance exceeds 0.15 mm (0.0059 in.) on both rings, then renew rings and/or piston.

Standard ring end gap for top or second piston ring is 0.2-0.4 mm (0.0079-0.0157 in.) with ring squarely installed in cylinder bore. If end gap exceeds 0.6 mm (0.023 in.), renew ring and/or recondition cylinder bore.

Standard ring end gap for the oil control ring is 0.2-0.3 mm (0.0079-0.0118 in.). If ring end gap exceeds 0.5 mm (0.020 in.), renew ring and/or recondition cylinder bore.

Install piston rings which are marked with marked side toward top of piston and stagger ring end gaps equally around circumference of piston.

**CYLINDER AND CRANKCASE.** Cylinder and crankcase are an integral casting. Standard cylinder bore diameter is 86.02 mm (3.387 in.). If bore diameter exceeds 86.10 mm (3.3898 in.) at any point, recondition cylinder bore.

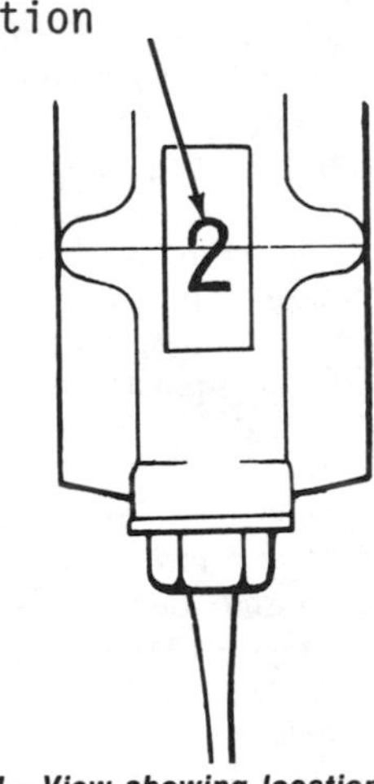


***Fig. HN11—View showing location of the connecting rod identification number. The number identifies connecting rod bearing bore size. Refer to text.***

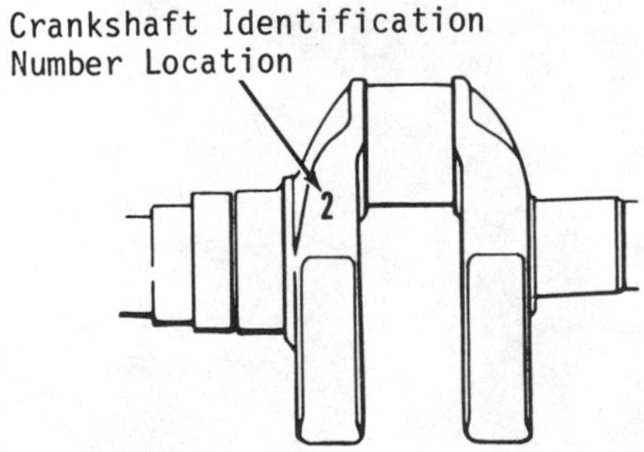

Crankshaft Identification Number Location

2

***Fig. HN12—View showing location of the crankshaft identification number. The number identifies connecting rod journal size. Refer to text.***

**CRANKSHAFT, MAIN BEARINGS AND SEALS.** Crankshaft is supported by ball bearing type main bearings on each end. To remove crankshaft, remove all cooling shrouds, flywheel, cylinder head and crankcase cover. Remove piston and connecting rod assembly. Carefully remove crankshaft and camshaft. Remove main bearings and crankshaft oil seals as necessary.

Crankshaft connecting rod journal diameters for G400 engines with serial number 1200001 to 1286491 is 36.968-36.976 mm (1.4554-1.4557 in.) for a crankshaft with "1" as the identification mark and 36.960-36.968 mm (1.4551-1.4554 in.) for a crankshaft with "2" as the identification number and 36.952-36.960 mm (1.4548-1.4551 in.) for crankshaft with "3" as the identification number. Crankshaft connecting rod journal diameters for G400 engines with serial number 1286492 and above are 36.976-36.984 mm (1.4557-1.4560 in.) for crankshaft with "O" as the identification mark, 36.968-36.976 mm (1.4554-1.4557 in.) for crankshaft with "1" as the identification mark and 36.960-36.968 mm (1.4551-1.4554 in.) for crankshaft with "2" as the identification mark.

Determine crankshaft and connecting rod identification numbers and refer to the chart shown in Fig. HN13 for engines with serial number 1200001 to 1286491 and to Fig. HN14 for engines with serial number 128492 and above to determine correct bearing insert by color code. For example, an engine with a serial number between 1200001 and 1286491 would use a bearing insert with a brown color code when installing a crankshaft with an identification number of "2" in conjunction with a connecting rod with an identification number of "3."

Main bearings are a light press fit on crankshaft and in bearing bores of crankcase and crankcase cover. It may be necessary to slightly heat crankcase or crankcase cover to reinstall bearings.

If main bearings are rough, loose, or loose fit on crankshaft journals or in crankcase or crankcase cover, renew bearings.

If crankshaft oil seals have been removed, use a suitable seal driver to install new seals. Seals should be pressed in evenly until slightly below seal bore surface.

Make certain crankshaft gear and camshaft gear timing marks are aligned as shown in Fig. HN15 during crankshaft installation.

BEARING COLOR CODE

| CRANKSHAFT IDENTIFICATION \ CONNECTING ROD IDENTIFICATION | 1 | 2 | 3 |
|---|---|---|---|
| 1 | Pink | Yellow | Green |
| 2 | Yellow | Green | Brown |
| 3 | Green | Brown | Black |

*Fig. HN13—On G400 engines with serial number 1200001 to 1286491, locate crankshaft and connecting rod identification numbers and use the appropriate color-coded bearing inserts. Refer to text.*

BEARING COLOR CODE

| CRANKSHAFT IDENTIFICATION \ CONNECTING ROD IDENTIFICATION | 1 | 2 | 3 |
|---|---|---|---|
| 0 | Pink | Yellow | Green |
| 1 | Yellow | Green | Brown |
| 2 | Green | Brown | |

*Fig. HN14—On G400 engines with serial number 1286492 and above, locate crankshaft and connecting rod identification numbers and use the appropriate color-coded bearing inserts. Refer to text.*

*Fig. HN15—When installing crankshaft or camshaft, make certain timing marks on gears are aligned as shown.*

**CAMSHAFT.** Camshaft is supported at each end by bearings which are an integral part of crankcase or crankcase cover casting. Refer to CRANKSHAFT, MAIN BEARINGS AND SEALS paragraphs for camshaft removal procedure.

Standard camshaft lobe height is 38.46-38.72 mm (1.5142-1.5244 in.) for intake lobe and 38.49-38.75 mm (1.5154-1.5256 in.) for exhaust lobe. If intake or exhaust lobe is less than 38.3 mm (1.5079 in.), renew camshaft.

Standard camshaft bearing journal diameter is 17.766-17.784 mm (0.6994-0.7002 in.). If diameter is less than 17.716 mm (0.6975 in.), renew camshaft.

Make certain camshaft gear and crankshaft gear timing marks are aligned as shown in Fig. HN15 during installation.

**ENGINE BALANCER.** The engine balancer (Fig. HN16) is mounted on a stub shaft located in crankcase cover and is driven by an auxiliary gear pressed onto crankshaft. Bearing is pressed into balancer counterweight to a depth of 1.0 mm (0.4 in.) using Honda bearing driver 07945-8910000 (Fig. HN17).

To install engine balance weight and crankcase cover, position piston at TDC. Remove the 8 mm plug from crankcase cover and secure balancer by inserting

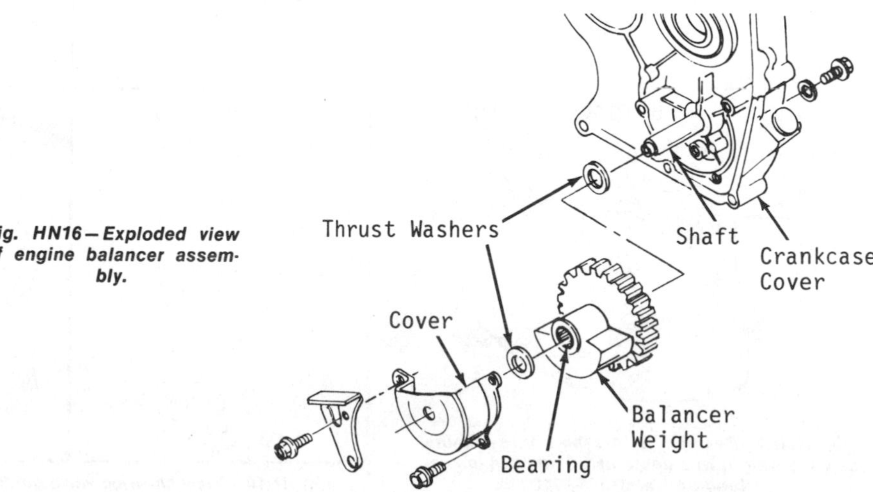


*Fig. HN16—Exploded view of engine balancer assembly.*

locating dowel rod as shown in Fig. HN18. Remove locating dowel rod after crankcase cover bolts are tightened to specified torque and install the 8 mm plug.

**GOVERNOR.** The internal centrifugal flyweight governor is located on camshaft gear. Refer to GOVERNOR paragraphs in MAINTENANCE section for external governor adjustments.

To remove governor assembly, remove external linkage, metal cooling shrouds and crankcase cover. The governor flyweight assembly is on camshaft gear.

When reassembling, make certain governor sliding sleeve and internal governor linkage is correctly positioned.

**VALVE SYSTEM.** Clearance between valve stem and valve tappet (cold) should be 0.08-0.16 mm (0.0031-0.0063 in.) for intake valve and 0.11-0.19 mm (0.0043-0.0075 in.) for exhaust valve.

On all models, valve clearance is adjusted by removing valve and grinding off end of stem to increase clearance or by renewing valve and/or grinding valve seat deeper to decrease clearance.

Valve face and seat angle is 45 degrees and standard valve seat width is 1.06 mm (0.0417 in.) for the intake valve and 1.414 mm (0.0557 in.) for the exhaust valve. If intake or exhaust valve seat width exceeds 2.0 mm (0.0787 in.), valve seat must be narrowed.

Standard valve spring free length for intake and exhaust valve springs is 42.7 mm (1.6811 in.). If spring length is 41.0 mm (1.6142 in.) or less, renew spring.

Standard valve stem diameter is 6.995-6.970 mm (0.2738-0.2744 in.) for intake valve stem and 6.910-6.925 mm (0.2720-0.2726 in.) for exhaust valve stem. If intake valve stem diameter is less than 6.91 mm (0.272 in.) or exhaust valve stem diameter is less than 6.89 mm (0.271 in.), renew valve.

Standard valve guide inside diameter is 7.000-7.015 mm (0.2756-0.2762 in.). If inside diameter of guide exceeds 7.07 mm (0.278 in.), guides must be renewed.

To remove and install valve guides, use the following procedure and refer to the sequence of illustrations in Fig. HN19. Cover tappet opening to prevent fragments from entering crankcase and use Honda driver 07942-8230000 to slightly drive valve guide down into valve chamber (A). Use a suitable cold chisel to fracture guide adjacent to guide bore (B). Drive remaining piece of guide into valve chamber (C) and remove from chamber. Place new guide on driver and start guide into guide bore (D). Alternate between driving guide into bore and measuring guide depth below cylinder head surface (E). Depth "X" in procedure (F) should be 32 mm (1.3 in.) for intake guide and 30 mm (1.2 in.) for exhaust valve. Finish ream intake and exhaust guides using Honda reamer 07984-6890100.

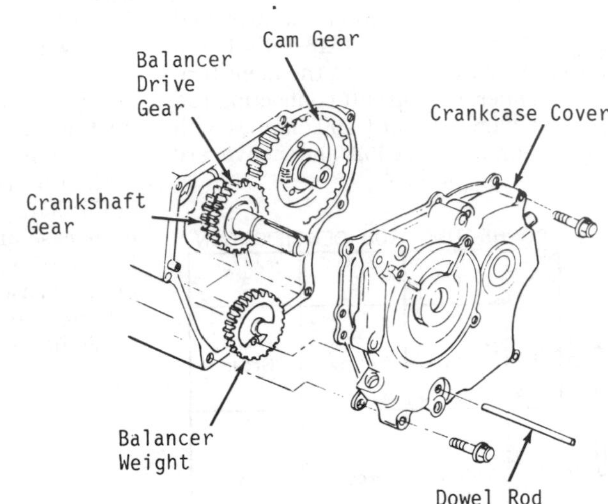


*Fig. HN18—When installing crankcase cover and balance gear assembly, a guide dowel rod must be used. Refer to text.*

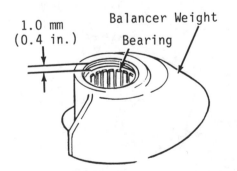

1.0 mm (0.4 in.)
Balancer Weight
Bearing

*Fig. HN17—Bearing is pressed into engine balance weight to a depth of 1.0 mm (0.4 in.) using Honda driver 07945-8910000.*

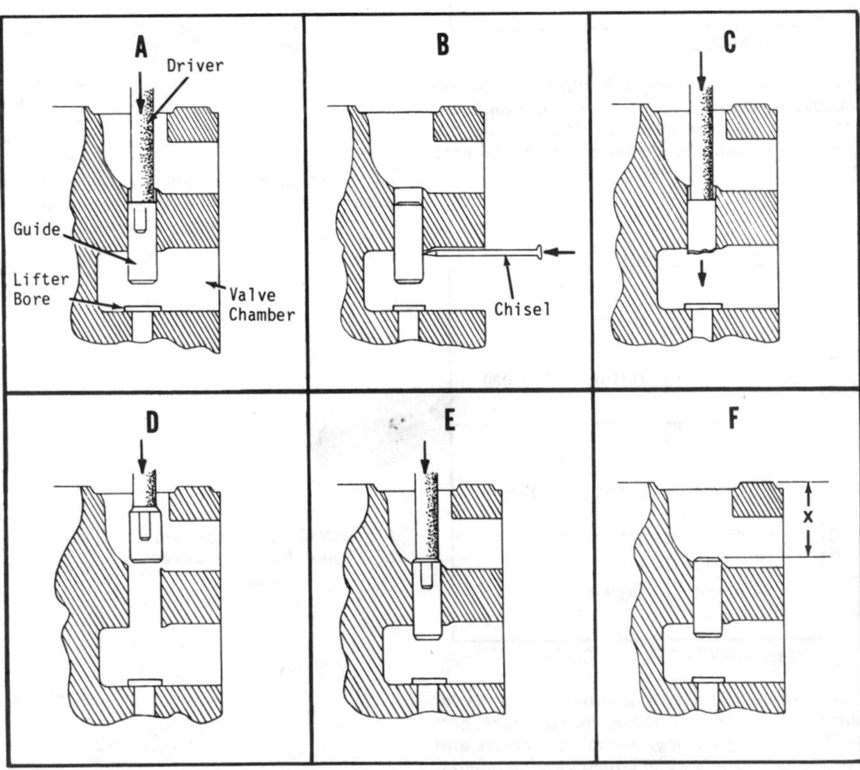


*Fig. HN19—View showing valve guide removal and installation sequence. Refer to text.*

# KAWASAKI

| Model | Bore | Stroke | Displacement | Horsepower |
|---|---|---|---|---|
| FB460V-AS, FB460V-BS | 89 mm (3.5 in.) | 74 mm (2.9 in.) | 460 cc (28.1 cu. in.) | 12.5 (9.3 kW) |

## ENGINE IDENTIFICATION

Model FB460V is a four-stroke, single-cylinder, air-cooled engine with a vertical crankshaft, pressurized lubrication and reciprocating balancer. Engine develops 12.5 horsepower (9.3 kW) at 3600 rpm.

## MAINTENANCE

**SPARK PLUG.** Recommended spark plug is NGK BMR-4A or Champion RCJ-8.

Spark plug should be removed, cleaned and electrode gap set to 0.6-0.7 mm (0.024-0.028 in.) after every 100 hours of operation. Renew spark plug if electrode is severely burnt or damaged.

**NOTE: Caution should be exercised if abrasive type spark plug cleaner is used. Inadequate cleaning procedure may allow the abrasive cleaner to be deposited in engine cylinder causing rapid wear and premature failure of engine components.**

**CARBURETOR.** All models are equipped with a float type side draft carburetor. Carburetor adjustment should be checked after every 50 hours of operation or whenever poor or erratic performance is noted.

Engine indle speed (no-load rpm) is 1350-1450 rpm. Adjust idle speed by turning throttle stop screw (1–Fig. KW110) clockwise to increase idle speed or counterclockwise to decrease idle speed. Initial adjustment of pilot screw (2) from a lightly seated position is 1⅛ turns open.

Make final adjustment with engine at operating temperature and running. Adjust pilot screw (2) to obtain maximum engine rpm, then turn pilot screw out (counterclockwise) ¼ turn more. Adjust throttle stop screw (1) so engine idles at 1350-1450 rpm. Main fuel mixture is controlled by a fixed jet.

Standard pilot jet (3) size is number 47.5 for all models. Standard main fuel jet (13) is number 112.5 for Model FB460V-AS and number 115 for Model FB460V-BS.

Float should be parallel to carburetor float bowl mating surface when float tab just touches inlet needle valve. Carefully bend float tab to adjust.

**AIR FILTER.** The air filter element should be removed and cleaned after the first 10 hours of operation and every 25 hours of operation thereafter. Paper element (5–Fig. KW111) should be renewed after 300 hours of operation.

To remove filter elements (4 and 5), remove the two wing bolts (1) and washers (2). Remove cover (3) and elements (4 and 5). Separate foam element (4) from paper element (5). Clean foam element in nonflammable solvent, then squeeze out excess solvent and allow to air dry. Soak element in SAE 30 motor oil and squeeze out excess oil. Clean paper element (5) by tapping element gently to remove dust. DO NOT use compressed air to clean element. Reinstall by reversing removal procedure.

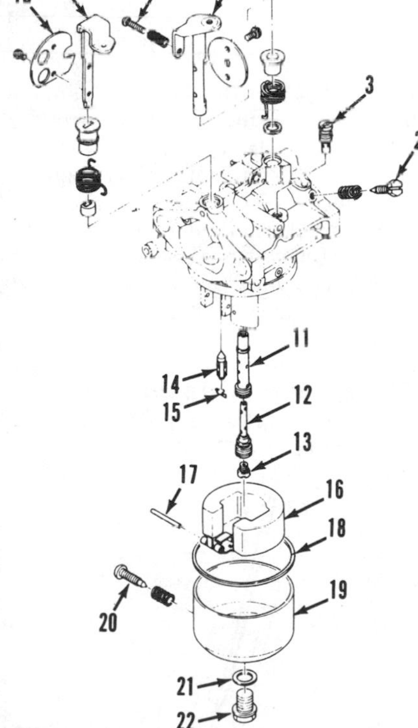

***Fig. KW110—Exploded view of the float type carburetor used on all models.***

1. Throttle stop screw
2. Pilot screw
3. Pilot jet
4. Throttle plate shaft
5. Choke plate shaft
10. Choke plate
11. Main nozzle
12. Bleed pipe
13. Main jet
14. Fuel inlet needle
15. Clip
16. Float
17. Float pin
18. Gasket
19. Float bowl
20. Drain screw
21. Washer
22. Bolt

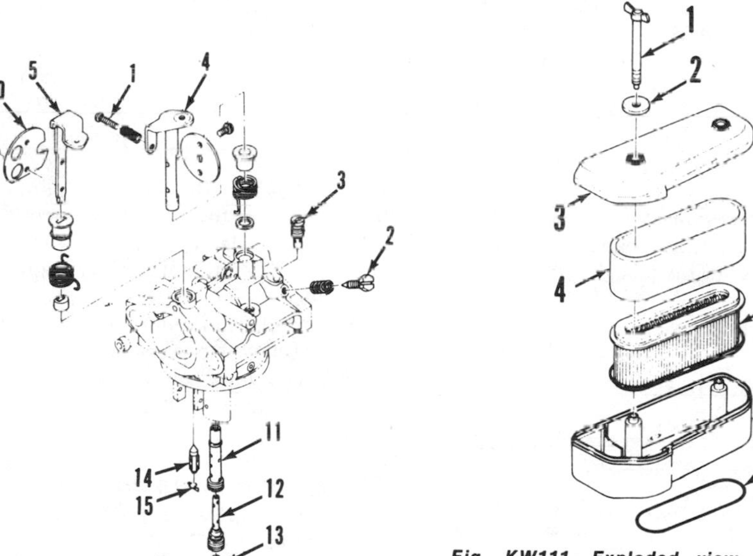

***Fig. KW111—Exploded view of air filter assembly.***

1. Wing bolt
2. Washer
3. Cover
4. Foam element
5. Paper element
6. Housing
7. "O" ring

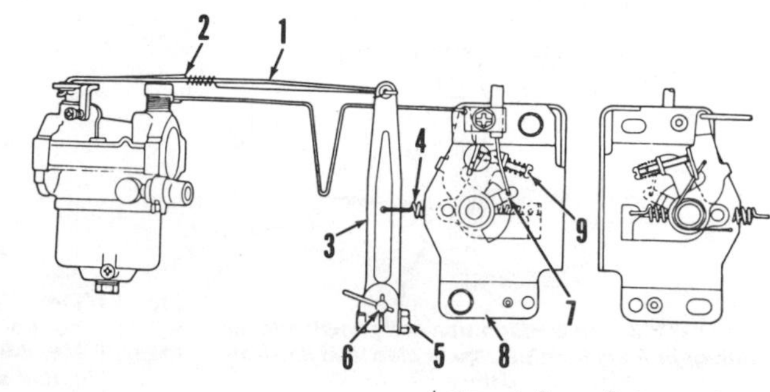


***Fig. KW112—View of external governor linkage used on all models.***

1. Governor-to-carburetor rod
2. Spring
3. Governor lever
4. Tension spring
5. Clamp bolt
6. Governor shaft
7. Speed control lever
8. Control plate
9. Choke setting screw

**GOVERNOR.** A gear driven flyweight governor assembly is located inside engine crankcase. To adjust external linkage, place engine throttle control in "FAST" position. Make certain all linkage is in good condition and that tension spring (4–Fig. KW112) is not stretched. Spring (2) around governor-to-carburetor rod must pull governor lever (3) and throttle lever toward each other. Loosen clamp bolt (5) nut on governor lever (3). Turn governor shaft (6) clockwise as far as possible. Tighten clamp bolt (5) nut. Speed control lever (7) should be at wide open position, but choke should not be activated. Adjusting choke setting screw (9) controls choke action.

**IGNITION SYSTEM.** All models are equipped with a transistor ignition system and regular maintenance is not required. Ignition timing is nonadjustable. Ignition coil is located outside flywheel. Ignition coil edge air gap should be 0.3 mm (0.01 in.).

To test ignition coil, remove cooling shrouds and ignition coil and refer to Fig. KW113. Connect one ohmmeter lead to coil core and remaining lead to high tension (spark plug) terminal. Secondary coil resistance should be 10,000-18,000 ohms. Remove the lead connected to high tension (spark plug) terminal and connect lead to primary terminal. Primary coil resistance should be 0.4-0.5 ohms. If readings are not as specified, renew ignition coil.

To test control unit, refer to Fig. KW114 and disconnect all electrical leads. Connect positive ohmmeter lead to terminal (T) and negative ohmmeter lead to ground lead or control unit case (G) according to model being serviced. Ohmmeter reading should be 10-40 ohms. Reverse leads. Ohmmeter reading should be 3-4 ohms. If ohmmeter readings are not as specified, renew control unit.

**VALVE ADJUSTMENT.** Valves and seats should be refaced and stem clearance adjusted after every 300 hours of operation. Refer to VALVE SYSTEM in REPAIRS section for service procedure and specifications.

**CYLINDER HEAD AND COMBUSTION CHAMBER.** Standard compression reading should be 380 kPa (55 psi). Excessive carbon build up on piston and cylinder head are indicated by higher than standard compression reading. A leaking cylinder head gasket, worn piston rings and cylinder bore or poorly seated valves are indicated by lower than standard compression reading. Cylinder head, combustion chamber and piston should be cleaned and carbon and other deposits removed after every 300 hours of operation. Refer to CYLINDER HEAD in REPAIRS section for service procedure.

**LUBRICATION.** Engine oil level should be checked prior to each operating interval. Oil should be maintained between reference marks on dipstick with dipstick just touching first threads. Do not screw dipstick in to check oil level (Fig. KW115).

Manufacturer recommends oil with an API service classification SF, SE/CC, SE or SD. Use SAE 5W-20 oil when temperature is below 0° C (32° F) and SAE 30 or 10W-30 oil when temperature is above 0°C (32°F).

Oil should be changed after 25 hours of operation if engine is not equipped with an oil filter or after 50 hours of operation if engine is equipped with an oil filter. Crankcase capacity is 1.4 L (2.96 pt.) for all models.

Oil pressure is regulated by an oil pressure relief valve located inside crankcase beside oil pump. Oil pressure should be 29.4 kPa (4.26 psi) at 3000 rpm. Oil pressure sensor (as equipped) should light when oil pressure falls below 29.4 kPa (4.26 psi).

**GENERAL MAINTENANCE.** Check and tighten all loose bolts, nuts or clamps prior to each day of operation. Check for fuel or oil leakage and repair if necessary.

Clean dust, dirt, grease or any foreign material from cylinder head and cylinder block cooling fins after every 100 hours of operation. Inspect fins for damage and repair if necessary.

## REPAIRS

**TIGHTENING TORQUES.** Recommended tightening torques are as follows:

| | |
|---|---|
| Spark plug | 28 N·m (20 ft.-lbs.) |
| Head bolts | 34-39 N·m (25-29 ft.-lbs.) |
| Connecting rod bolts | 19-20 N·m (14-15 ft.-lbs.) |
| Crankcase cover bolts | 17-23 N·m (12-17 ft.-lbs.) |
| Oil pump cover | 17-23 N·m (12-17 ft.-lbs.) |
| Flywheel | 83-88 N·m (62-65 ft.-lbs.) |

**CYLINDER HEAD.** To remove cylinder head, first remove cylinder head shroud. Clean engine to prevent entrance of foreign material. Loosen the six cylinder head bolts and the three cylinder head stud nuts in ¼-turn increments following sequence shown in Fig. KW116 until all bolts are loose enough to remove by hand.

Primary Terminal
Spark Plug Lead
Core

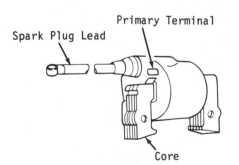

Fig. KW113—View of ignition coil showing location of primary terminal, spark plug lead and iron core.

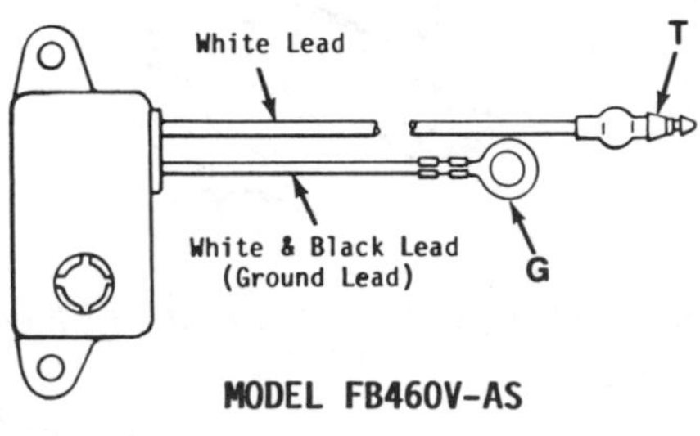


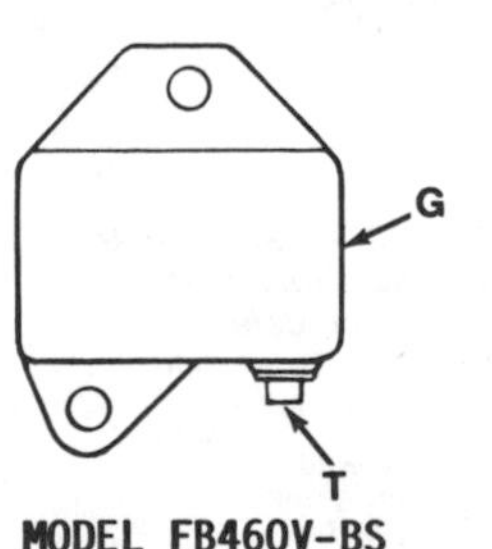


Fig. KW114—Model FB450V-AS is equipped with the control unit shown in upper view and Model FB460V-BS is equipped with the control unit shown in lower view.

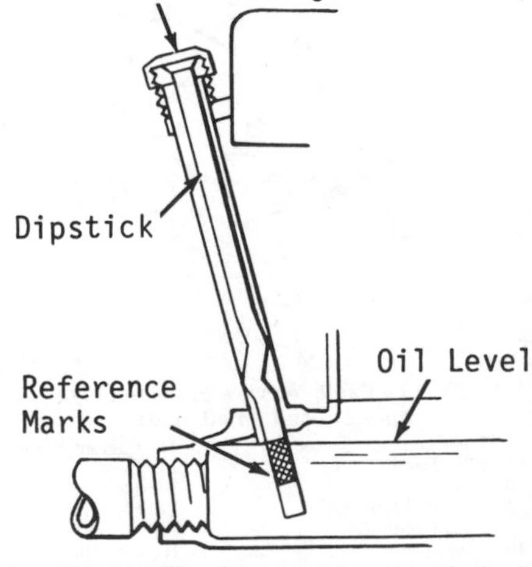


Fig. KW115—View showing procedure to check crankcase oil level. Refer to text.

Remove spark plug and clean carbon and other deposits from cylinder head. Place cylinder head on a flat surface and check entire sealing surface for warpage. If warpage exceeds 0.4 mm (0.015 in.), cylinder head must be renewed. Slight warpage may be repaired by lapping cylinder head. In a figure-eight pattern, lap head on a flat surface against 200 grit and then 400 grit emery paper.

Reinstall cylinder head and tighten bolts and nuts evenly to specified torque following sequence shown in Fig. KW116.

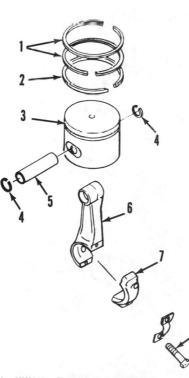

**CONNECTING ROD.** Connecting rod rides directly on crankshaft journal. Piston and connecting rod are removed as an assembly after removing cylinder head and splitting crankcase. Remove the two connecting rod bolts (8–Fig. KW117) and connecting rod cap (7). Push piston and connecting rod assembly out through the top cylinder block. Remove retaining rings (4) and push piston pin (5) out of piston to separate piston (3) from connecting rod (6). Use new retaining rings (4) during reassembly.

Maximum inside diameter for connecting rod small end is 21.039 mm (0.8283 in.) and maximum inside diameter for standard connecting rod big end bearing surface is 37.066 mm (1.4593 in.) A connecting rod is available for an undersize crankshaft journal. Inside diameter for undersize connecting rod big end bearing surface should be 36.5 mm (1.437 in.). Refer to CRANKSHAFT AND BALANCER section.

**PISTON, PIN AND RINGS.** Piston and connecting rod are removed as an assembly. Refer to CONNECTING ROD section for removal and installation procedure.

After separating piston and connecting rod, carefully remove piston rings and clean carbon and other deposits from piston surface and piston ring lands.

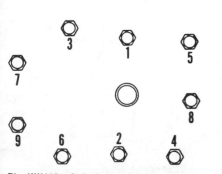

*Fig. KW116—Cylinder head bolts and nuts must be tightened evenly to the recommended torque following the sequence shown.*

**CAUTION: Extreme care should be exercised when cleaning piston ring lands. Do not damage squared edges or widen piston ring grooves. If piston ring lands are damaged, piston must be renewed.**

If piston pin bore in piston exceeds 21.028 mm (0.8279 in.), renew piston. Piston pin outside diameter should be 20.978 mm (0.8259 in.). If piston pin diameter is less than specified, renew piston pin.

If ring groove exceeds 2.120 mm (0.0835 in.) for top ring groove, 2.095 mm (0.0825 in.) for second ring groove or 4.055 mm (0.1596 in.) for oil ring groove, renew piston.

Piston ring thickness is 1.945 mm (0.0766 in.) for top ring and 1.941 mm (0.0764 in.) for second ring. Renew piston ring if thickness is less than specified.

Piston ring end gap is measured by placing piston ring into cylinder bore and using the top of the piston to press piston ring squarely into cylinder bore. Piston ring end gap should be 0.7 mm (0.028 in.) for top and second ring. If piston ring gap is greater than specified, check cylinder bore for wear. If cylinder bore is within limits, then renew piston ring.

During reassembly, install piston on connecting rod so arrow on top of piston is toward the "MADE IN JAPAN" side of connecting rod. Install piston in cylinder so arrow on top of piston is toward flywheel side of engine.

*Fig. KW117—Exploded view of piston and connecting rod assembly.*

1. Compression rings
2. Oil control ring
3. Piston
4. Retaining rings
5. Piston pin
6. Connecting rod
7. Connecting rod cap
8. Connecting rod bolts

Oversize pistons are available in 0.25 mm (0.010 in.), 0.50 mm (0.020 in.) and 0.75 mm (0.030 in.) sizes and cylinder can be bored or honed to 89.230-89.250 mm (3.51299-3.51378 in.) for the 0.25 mm (0.010 in.) oversize piston, 89.480-89.500 mm (3.52283-3.52362 in.) for the 0.50 mm (0.020 in.) oversize piston and to 89.730-89.750 mm (3.53268-3.53346 in.) for the 0.75 mm (0.030 in.) oversize piston.

**CYLINDER, CRANKCASE, MAIN BEARINGS AND SEALS.** Cylinder and crankcase are an integral casting. Standard cylinder bore diameter is 88.980-89.000 mm (3.5031-3.5039 in.). Maximum bore out-of-round is 0.063 mm (0.0025 in.). Cylinder may be bored or honed to fit oversize pistons.

The main bearing on pto side is an integral part of cylinder and crankcase assembly. Main bearing on flywheel side is a ball bearing. Inside diameter for the integral bearing on pto side is 35.061 mm (1.3804 in.). Ball bearing on flywheel side should be a press fit on crankshaft and in bearing bore of crankcase cover.

Renew crankcase seals if removed. Pack seals with high temperature grease prior to installation. Press flywheel side crankshaft oil seal into seal bore in crankcase cover until flush with housing. Press pto side crankshaft oil seal into cylinder and crankcase assembly seal bore so outside edge of seal is 0.5 mm (0.02 in.) below seal bore surface.

When installing crankcase cover, tighten crankcase cover bolts to specified torque following sequence shown in Fig. KW118.

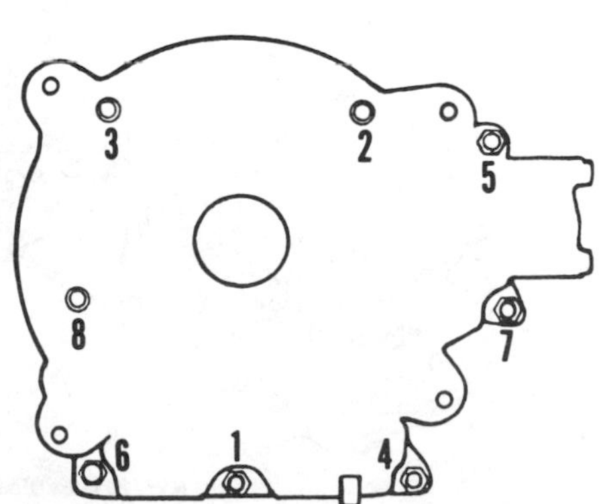


*Fig. KW118—Crankcase cover bolts must be tightened evenly to the recommended torque following the sequence shown.*

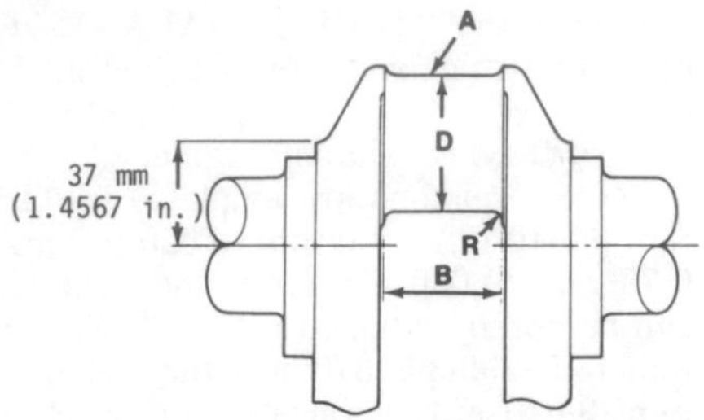


*Fig. KW119—Crankshaft connecting rod journal (A) may be reground to the dimensions shown and a special undersized connecting rod must be used.*

B. 32.3 mm (1.272 in.)
D. 36.467-36.480 mm (1.4357-1.4362 in.)
R. 2.30-2.70 mm (0.09-0.11 in.)

**CRANKSHAFT AND BALANCER.** Crankshaft is supported on flywheel side by a ball bearing type main bearing and on pto side by a plain type bearing which is an integral casting with cylinder and crankcase assembly. To remove crankshaft, remove all metal shrouds, flywheel, fan housing and cylinder head. Remove crankcase cover. Remove piston and connecting rod assembly. Remove governor shaft retaining pin and remove governor shaft. Rotate crankshaft until timing marks on crankshaft gear and camshaft gear are aligned. Remove camshaft. Mark locations and remove valve tappets. Rotate crankshaft carefully until crankpin is down toward balancer weight. Remove balancer guide (16–Fig. KW120). Remove crankshaft and balancer weight.

Clean and inspect crankshaft and balancer link rods. Crankshaft main journal diameter on flywheel side should be 34.945 mm (1.3757 in.). Crankshaft main journal diameter on pto side should be 34.914 mm (1.3746 in.),

Standard connecting rod bearing journal diameter should be 36.934 mm (1.4541 in.). Connecting rod bearing journal may be reground to a diameter of 36.467-36.480 mm (1.4357-1.4362 in.) and a special undersize connecting rod must be used. Refer to Fig. KW119 and CONNECTING ROD section.

Diameter of crankshaft balancer link rod journals should be 53.951 mm (2.12406 in.). Maximum inside diameters of balancer link rod big end bushings is 54.121 mm (2.13074 in.). If diameters are greater than specified, press old bushings out of balancer link rods and press new bushings in until bushings are 0.5 mm (0.02 in.) below flange surface of balancer link rods. Maximum small end inside diameter of balancer link rods is 12.059 mm (0.4748 in.). If diameters are greater than specified, balancer link rods must be renewed.

Balancer weight bushing inside diameter should be 26.097 mm (1.02744 in.). If bushing diameter is greater than specified, press old bushing out, align oil hole in new bushing with oil hole in balancer weight and press new bushing into bushing bore until 0.5 mm (0.02 in.)

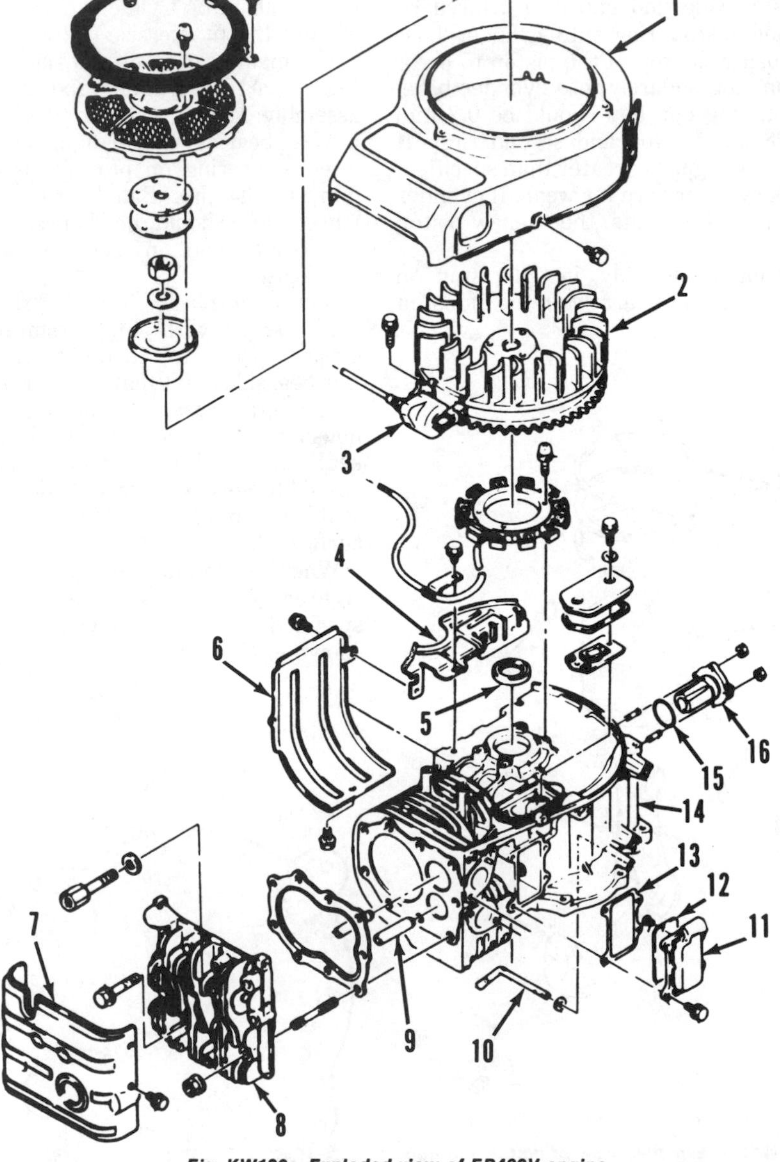


*Fig. KW120—Exploded view of FB460V engine.*

1. Blower housing
2. Flywheel
3. Coil
4. Shroud
5. Oil seal
6. Cooling shroud
7. Cooling shroud
8. Cylinder head
9. Valve guide
10. Governor shaft
11. Valve chamber cover
12. Cover
13. Gasket
14. Cylinder block & crankcase
15. "O" ring
16. Balancer guide

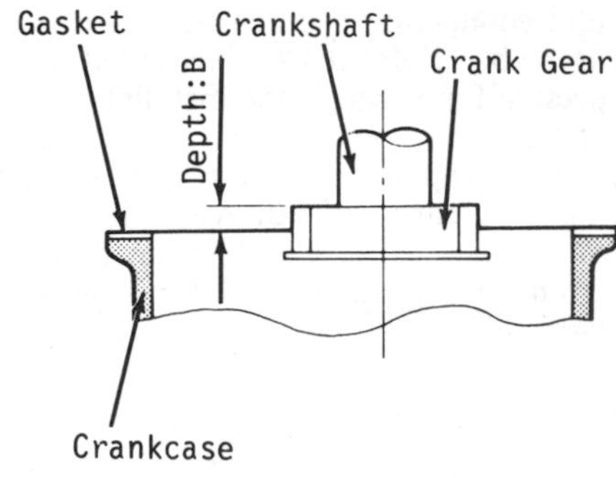


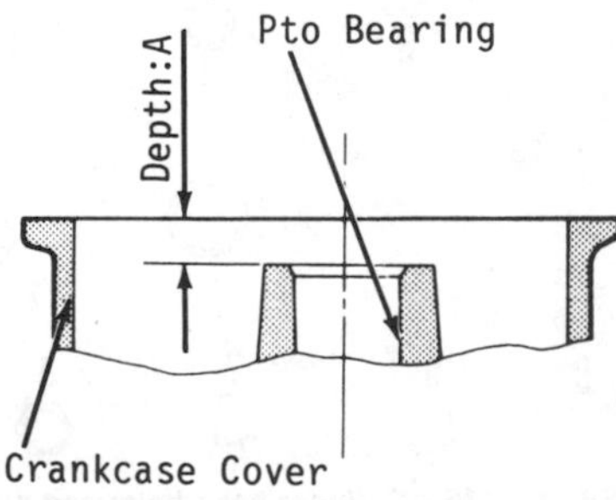


*Fig. KW121—Refer to text to determine shim thickness for correct crankshaft end play.*

below balancer weight. Make certain oil holes are aligned.

Balancer guide (16 – Fig. KW120) outside diameter should be 25.927 mm (1.0208 in.). If diameter is less than specified, renew balancer guide.

To reinstall crankshaft, install link rods, collars, gear, bearing and balancer weight. Oil grooves in link rods must face toward connecting rod after installation and oil hole in balancer weight must face flywheel side of engine. Install crankshaft with connecting rod journal at bottom dead center (BDC). Align center hole of balancer weight and support shaft hole in crankcase. Install "O" ring (15 – Fig. KW120) on balancer guide (16) and install balancer guide. Install piston and connecting rod assembly making certain the arrow on top of piston is toward flywheel side of engine. Install connecting rod cap with match marks aligned and tighten connecting rod bolts to specified torque. Install valve tappets in the tappet bores from which they were removed. Install governor shaft (10). Carefully rotate crankshaft until piston is at top dead center (TDC).

Align crankshaft and camshaft gear timing marks and install camshaft. Measure distance from crankcase cover mounting surface to pto shaft bearing edge as shown at (A – Fig. KW121) and note dimension. Measure distance from crank gear end of crankshaft to crankcase gasket surface (with gasket installed) as shown at (B) and note dimension. Subtract dimension (B) from dimension (A) and refer to chart shown in Fig. KW122 to determine shim thickness needed to provide 0.09-0.2 mm (0.0035-0.0078 in.) crankshaft end play after assembly. Make certain governor weights are closed, align oil pump shaft convex with camshaft end groove, align governor gear teeth with cam gear teeth and install crankcase cover. Tighten crankcase cover to specified torque following sequence shown in Fig. KW118.

**CAMSHAFT AND BEARINGS.** Camshaft is supported at each end in bearings which are integral part of crankcase or oil pump cover. Refer to CRANKSHAFT AND BALANCER section for camshaft removal. Camshaft lobe height for intake and exhaust lobes should be 35.40 mm (1.3937 in.). Outside diameter of camshaft bearing journal on pto side should be 19.907 mm (0.7837 in.). Outside diameter of camshaft bearing journal on flywheel side is 15.907 mm (0.6263 in.). If bearing diameters are less than specified, camshaft must be renewed. Inside diameter of camshaft bearing in crankcase should be 16.068 mm (0.6326 in.). Inside diameter of camshaft bearing in oil pump cover should be 20.071 mm (0.7902 in.). If diameters are greater than specified, renew crankcase or oil pump cover as required.

**GOVERNOR.** The internal centrifugal flyweight governor is gear driven off of the camshaft gear. Refer to GOVERNOR paragraph in MAINTENANCE section for external governor adjustments.

To remove governor assembly, remove external linkage, metal cooling shrouds, flywheel and crankcase cover. Use two screwdrivers to snap governor gear and flyweight assembly off governor stud shaft. Remove the thrust washer located between governor stud shaft. Remove the thrust washer located between governor gear assembly and crankcase cover. To reinstall, place thrust washer over governor stud shaft. Place governor gear and flyweight assembly over governor stud shaft and push down on governor assembly to snap into place.

**LOW OIL SENSOR.** The low oil sensor is located as shown in Fig. KW123. Oil sensor activates low oil pressure warning light if oil pressure falls below 29.4 kPa (4.26 psi).

**OIL PUMP AND RELIEF VALVE.** The trochoid type oil pump mounted on crankcase cover draws oil through a filtering screen and inlet into pump chamber. Pressurized oil is pumped to the pto main journal, into and through crankshaft to lubricate connecting rod bearing, lower balancer link rods and crankpins. Oil at the crankpin is passed through metered orifice in the connecting rod and is sprayed onto the piston to cool the piston and prevent ring sticking. Return oil mists and then lubricates the flywheel side ball bearing and all other bearings.

To remove oil pump, remove crankcase cover. Refer to CAMSHAFT AND BEARINGS section and check camshaft bearing diameter in oil pump cover. Remove oil pump cover and inspect oil screen. Inspect seating of ball in relief valve. Inspect relief valve spring free length. Free length is 19.5 mm (0.768 in.). If spring free length is

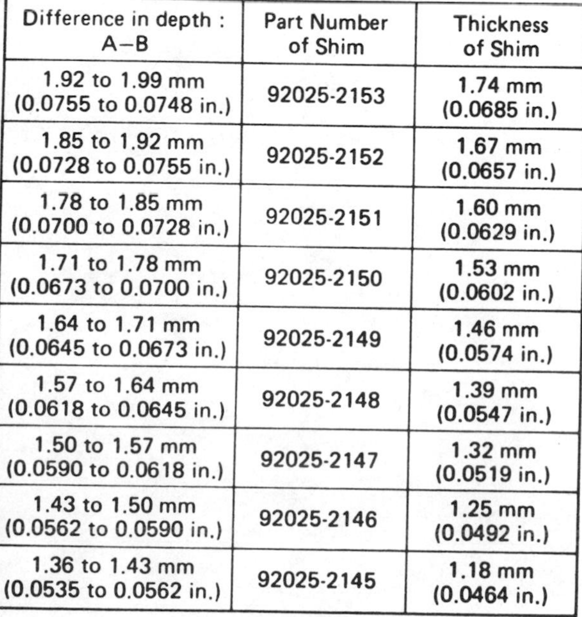

| Difference in depth : A–B | Part Number of Shim | Thickness of Shim |
|---|---|---|
| 1.92 to 1.99 mm (0.0755 to 0.0748 in.) | 92025-2153 | 1.74 mm (0.0685 in.) |
| 1.85 to 1.92 mm (0.0728 to 0.0755 in.) | 92025-2152 | 1.67 mm (0.0657 in.) |
| 1.78 to 1.85 mm (0.0700 to 0.0728 in.) | 92025-2151 | 1.60 mm (0.0629 in.) |
| 1.71 to 1.78 mm (0.0673 to 0.0700 in.) | 92025-2150 | 1.53 mm (0.0602 in.) |
| 1.64 to 1.71 mm (0.0645 to 0.0673 in.) | 92025-2149 | 1.46 mm (0.0574 in.) |
| 1.57 to 1.64 mm (0.0618 to 0.0645 in.) | 92025-2148 | 1.39 mm (0.0547 in.) |
| 1.50 to 1.57 mm (0.0590 to 0.0618 in.) | 92025-2147 | 1.32 mm (0.0519 in.) |
| 1.43 to 1.50 mm (0.0562 to 0.0590 in.) | 92025-2146 | 1.25 mm (0.0492 in.) |
| 1.36 to 1.43 mm (0.0535 to 0.0562 in.) | 92025-2145 | 1.18 mm (0.0464 in.) |

*Fig. KW122 – Chart showing recommended shim for correct crankshaft end play.*

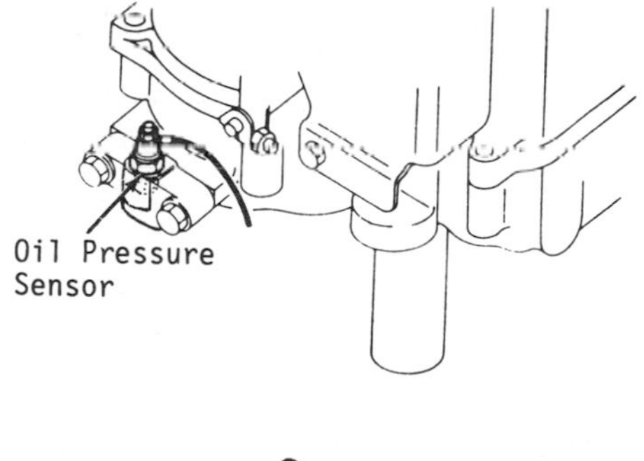


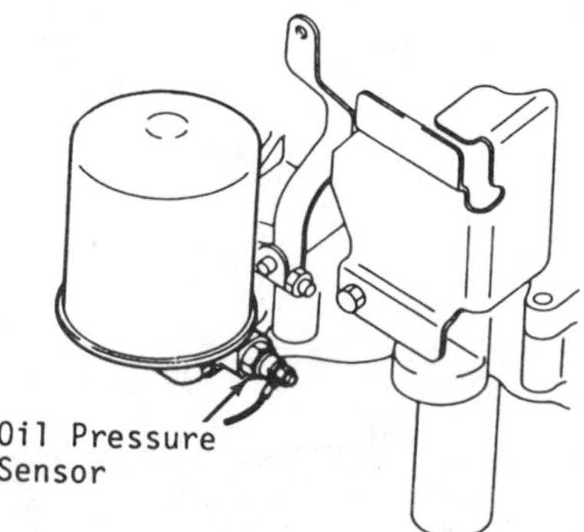


*Fig. KW123 – View showing locations of the low oil pressure sensing unit.*

less than specified, renew spring. Cap screws retaining oil pressure relief valve cover and oil induction guide plate are treated with thread locking compound. Remove only as required.

Reinstall by reversing removal procedure. Tighten oil pump cover to specified torque. Tighten crankcase cover to specified torque following sequence shown in Fig. KW118.

**VALVE SYSTEM.** Clearance between valve stem and valve tappet (cold) should be 0.10-0.16 mm (0.0039-0.0063 in.) for intake and exhaust valves. If clearance is not as specified, valves must be removed and end of stems ground off to increase clearance or seats ground deeper to reduce clearance.

Valve face and seat angles are 45 degrees and maximum valve seat width is 1.0-1.6 mm (0.039-0.063 in.). Minimum valve margin is 0.6 mm (0.02 in.).

Minimum valve stem diameter is 7.912 mm (0.3115 in.) for intake valve and 7.919 mm (0.3118 in.) for exhaust valve. Maximum valve stem bend is 0.03 mm (0.0012 in.). If valve stem bend exceeds specification, renew valve.

Valve spring free length should be 43.3 mm (1.705 in.) for intake valve spring and 39.0 mm (1.535 in.) for exhaust valve spring.

Maximum valve guide inside diameter for the renewable type valve guides is 8.062 mm (0.3174 in.). If guide inside diameter is greater than specified, use a suitable valve guide puller to remove guide. Press new guides into guide bore until top surface of guide is 30 mm (1.18 in.) from cylinder head mating surface on cylinder.

---

# KAWASAKI

| Model | Bore | Stroke | Displacement | Horsepower |
|---|---|---|---|---|
| FC420V | 89 mm (3.5 in.) | 68 mm (2.68 in.) | 423 cc (25.8 cu. in.) | 14 (10.4 kW) |
| FC540V | 89 mm (3.5 in.) | 86 mm (3.39 in.) | 535 cc (32.6 cu. in.) | 17 (12.7 kW) |

## ENGINE IDENTIFICATION

All models are four-stroke, single-cylinder, air cooled engines with a vertical crankshaft and pressurized lubrication. Engine serial number plate is located on the flywheel blower housing.

## MAINTENANCE

**SPARK PLUG.** Recommended spark plug is NGK BMR-4A or Champion RCJ-8.

Spark plug should be removed, cleaned and electrode gap set to 0.7 mm (0.028 in.) after every 100 hours of operation. Renew spark plug if electrode is severely burnt or damaged.

**NOTE: Caution should be exercised if abrasive type spark plug cleaner is used. Inadequate cleaning procedure may allow the abrasive cleaning material to be deposited in engine cylinder causing rapid wear and premature failure of engine components.**

**CARBURETOR.** All models are equipped with a float type side draft carburetor. Carburetor should be checked whenever poor or erratic performance is noted.

Recommended engine idle speed is 1350-1450 rpm. Adjust idle speed by turning throttle stop screw (10—Fig. KW150) clockwise to increase idle speed or counterclockwise to decrease idle speed.

Initial adjustment of pilot air screw (9) is $1^1/_2$ turns open from a lightly seated position. Make final adjustment with engine at operating temperature and running. Adjust pilot screw to obtain maximum engine idle speed, then turn pilot screw out (counterclockwise) an additional $^1/_4$ turn. Adjust throttle stop screw (10) so engine idles at 1350-1450 rpm.

Main fuel mixture is controlled by a fixed jet (29). Different size main jets are available for high altitude operation.

Disassembly of carburetor is self-evident upon examination of unit and reference to Fig. KW150. Note that pilot jet (7) is pressed into carburetor body on some FC540V engines.

Clean carburetor parts (except plastic components) using suitable carburetor cleaner. Do not clean jets or passages with drill bits or wire as enlargement of passages could affect calibration of carburetor. Rinse parts in warm water to neutralize corrosive action of carburetor cleaner and dry with compressed air.

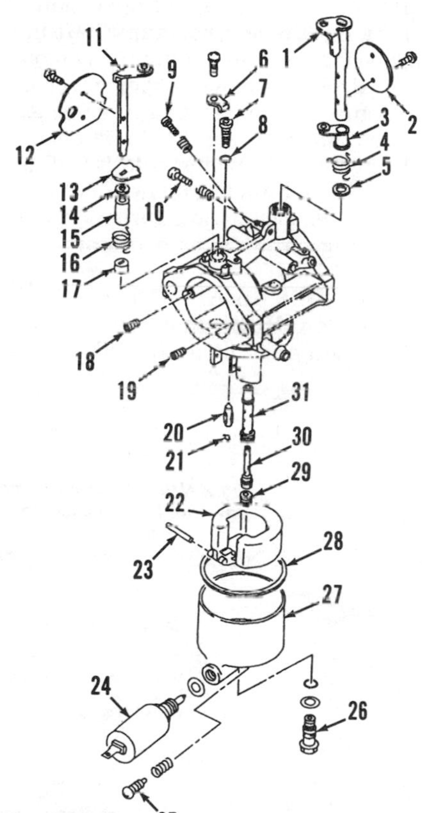


*Fig. KW150—Exploded view of typical float type carburetor used on all models. Fuel shut-off solenoid (24) is not used on some engines.*

1. Throttle shaft
2. Throttle plate
3. Ring
4. Spring
5. Seal
6. Retainer plate
7. Pilot jet
8. "O" ring
9. Pilot screw
10. Idle speed screw
11. Choke shaft
12. Choke plate
13. Plate
14. Seal
15. Ring
16. Spring
17. Ring
18. Pilot air jet
19. Main air jet
20. Fuel inlet needle
21. Clip
22. Float
23. Pin
24. Fuel shut-off solenoid
25. Drain screw
26. Special bolt
27. Float bowl
28. Gasket
29. Main jet
30. Bleed pipe
31. Main nozzle

With carburetor upside down, float should be parallel to carburetor float bowl mating surface. Carefully bend float tab to adjust float level. Be careful not to push on inlet needle valve when adjusting float level.

**AIR FILTER.** The air filter element should be removed and cleaned after every 25 hours of operation, or more often if operating in extremely dusty conditions. Paper element (5—Fig. KW151) should be renewed after every 300 hours of operation. Element should also be renewed if it is very dirty or if it is damaged in any way.

To remove filter elements (4 and 5), remove the two wing bolts (1) and washers (2). Remove cover (3), foam precleaner element and paper element. Clean foam element in solution of warm water and liquid detergent, then squeeze out excess water and allow to air dry. DO NOT wash paper element. Apply light coat of engine oil to foam element and squeeze out excess oil. Clean paper element by tapping gently

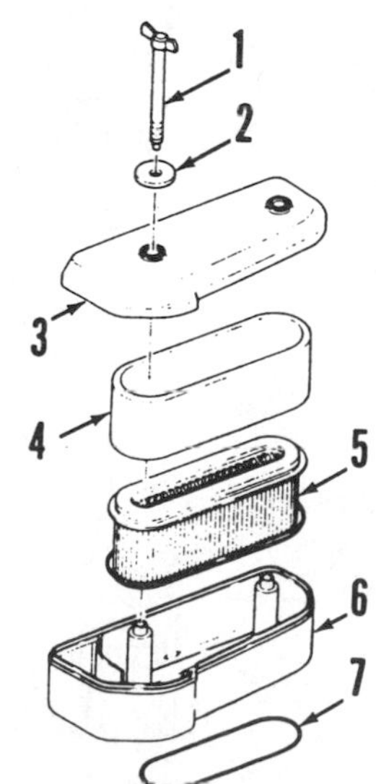


*Fig. KW151—Exploded view of air filter assembly.*

1. Wing bolt
2. Washer
3. Cover
4. Foam element
5. Paper element
6. Housing
7. "O" ring

to remove dust. DO NOT use compressed air to clean element. Inspect paper element for holes or other damage. Reinstall by reversing removal procedure.

**GOVERNOR.** A gear driven flyweight type governor is located inside engine crankcase. Before adjusting governor linkage, make certain all linkage is in good condition and that tension spring (4—Fig. KW152) is not stretched.

To adjust external linkage, place engine throttle control in "FAST" position. Spring (2) around governor-to-carburetor rod must pull governor lever (3) and throttle lever toward each other. Loosen governor lever clamp bolt (5) and turn governor shaft (6) clockwise as far as possible. Tighten clamp bolt nut. Speed control lever (7) should be at wide open position, but choke should not be activated. Adjusting choke setting screw (9) controls choke action.

**IGNITION SYSTEM.** All models are equipped with a transistor ignition system and regular maintenance is not required. Ignition timing is not adjustable. Ignition coil is located outside flywheel. Air gap between ignition coil and flywheel should be 0.30 mm (0.012 in.).

To test ignition coil, remove cooling shrouds and disconnect spark plug cable and primary lead wire (Fig. KW153). Connect ohmmeter test leads between coil core (ground) and high tension (spark plug) terminal. Secondary coil resistance should be 10.9-16.3 K ohms. Remove test lead connected to high tension terminal and connect lead to coil primary terminal. Primary coil resistance should be 0.48-0.72 ohms. If readings vary significantly from specifications, renew ignition coil.

To test ignition control unit, disconnect ignition module connector. Connect positive ohmmeter lead to control unit terminal and negative ohmmeter lead to control unit case (ground). Observe meter reading, then reverse ohmmeter test lead connections and again note meter reading. Ohmmeter readings should be 400-600 ohms in one direction and 60-100 ohms in opposite direction. If ohmmeter readings vary significantly from specifications, renew control unit.

**VALVE ADJUSTMENT.** Clearance between valve stem ends and rocker arms should be checked and adjusted after every 300 hours of operation. To check clearance, turn crankshaft until piston is at top dead center on compression stroke. Remove rocker cover and measure clearance using a feeler gage (G) as shown in Fig. KW154. Specified clearance with engine cold is 0.15 mm (0.006 in.) for intake and exhaust. To adjust, loosen locknut and turn rocker arm adjusting screw (S) as necessary.

**CYLINDER HEAD AND COMBUSTION CHAMBER.** Standard compression reading should be 483 kPa (71 psi).

**NOTE: When checking compression pressure, spark plug high tension lead must be grounded or electronic ignition could be damaged.**

Excessive carbon build-up on piston and cylinder head are indicated by higher than standard compression reading. A leaking cylinder head gasket, worn piston rings and cylinder bore or poorly seated valves are indicated by lower than standard compression reading.

**LUBRICATION.** Engine oil level should be checked prior to each operating interval. Oil should be maintained between reference marks on dipstick with dipstick just touching first threads. Do not screw dipstick in to check oil level (Fig. KW155).

Manufacturer recommends using oil with an API service classification of SF or SE. Use oil of suitable viscosity for the expected air temperature range during the period between oil changes. Re-

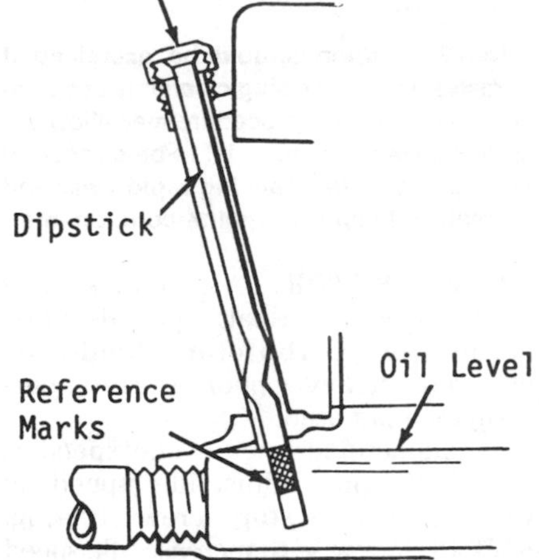


*Fig. KW155—View showing procedure to check crankcase oil level. Refer to text.*

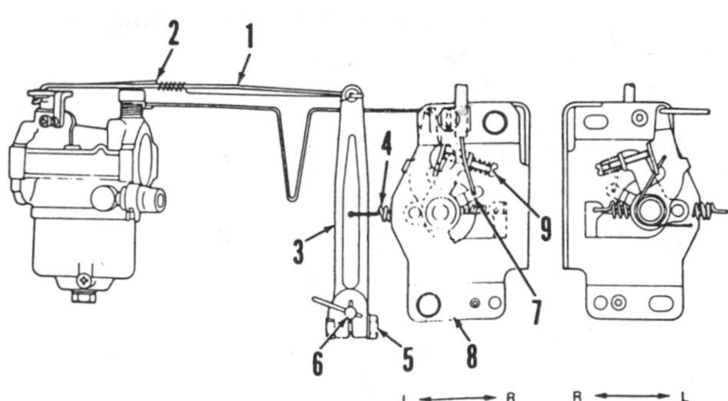


*Fig. KW152—View of external governor linkage used on all models.*

1. Governor-to-carburetor rod
2. Spring
3. Governor lever
4. Tension spring
5. Clamp bolt
6. Governor shaft
7. Speed control lever
8. Control plate
9. Choke setting screw

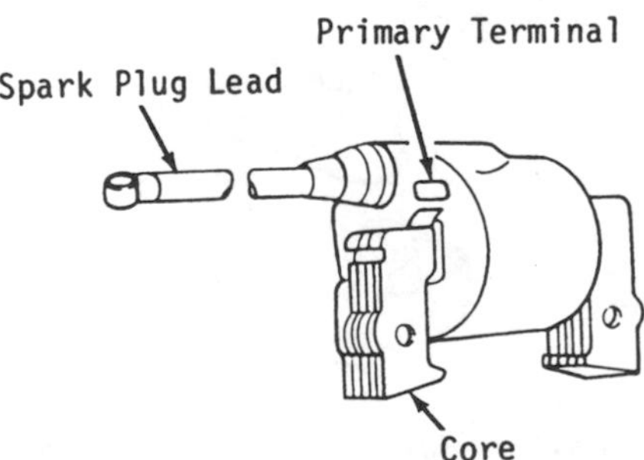


*Fig. KW153—View of ignition coil showing location of primary terminal, spark plug lead and iron core.*

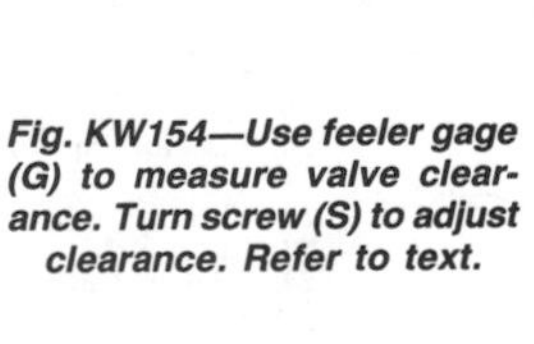

*Fig. KW154—Use feeler gage (G) to measure valve clearance. Turn screw (S) to adjust clearance. Refer to text.*

fer to temperature/viscosity chart shown in Fig. KW156.

On models without an oil filter, engine oil should be changed after every 50 hours of operation or yearly, whichever comes first. On models equipped with an oil filter, oil and filter should be changed after every 100 hours of operation or yearly, whichever comes first. Oil should be drained while engine is warm. Crankcase oil capacity for FC420V is approximately 1.3 L (2.75 pts.) without filter and 1.5 L (3.17 pts.) with filter. Crankcase oil capacity for FC540V is approximately 1.6 L (3.4 pts.) without filter and 1.9 L (4.0 pts.) with filter.

## REPAIRS

**TIGHTENING TORQUES.** Recommended tightening torques are as follows:

Connecting rod bolts . . . . . . . . 20 N·m (15 ft.-lbs.)
Crankcase cover bolts—
FC420V . . . . . . . . . . . . . . . . . . 26 N·m (19 ft.-lbs.)
FC540V . . . . . . . . . . . . . . . . . . 20 N·m (15 ft.-lbs.)
Cylinder head bolts . . . . . . . . . 52 N·m (38 ft.-lbs.)
Flywheel—
FC420V . . . . . . . . . . . . . . . . . 137 N·m (100 ft.-lbs.)
FC540V . . . . . . . . . . . . . . . . . 172 N·m (127 ft.-lbs.)
Spark plug . . . . . . . . . . . . . . . . 20 N·m (15 ft.-lbs.)

**CYLINDER HEAD.** To remove cylinder head, remove cylinder head shroud and blower housing. Remove carburetor and muffler. Remove rocker arm cover, loosen cylinder head mounting bolts evenly and remove cylinder head and gasket.

Remove carbon deposits from combustion chamber being careful not to damage gasket sealing surface. Inspect cylinder head for cracks, nicks or other damage. Place cylinder head on a flat surface and check entire sealing surface for distortion using a feeler gage. Renew cylinder head if sealing surface is warped more than 0.05 mm (0.002 in.).

To reinstall cylinder head, reverse removal procedure. Surfaces of cylinder head gasket are coated with a sealant and do not require additional sealant. Push rods should be installed in their original positions. Tighten cylinder head screws in sequence shown in Fig. KW157 to initial torque of 32 N·m (24 ft.-lbs.). Then, tighten screws 7 N·m (5 ft.-lbs.) at a time following sequence in Fig. KW157 until final torque of 52 N·m (38 ft.-lbs.) is reached. Adjust valve clearance as outlined in MAINTENANCE section.

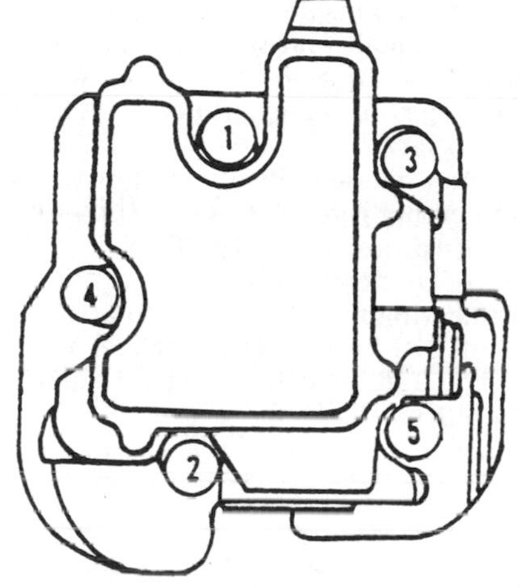


*Fig. KW157—Tighten cylinder head bolts in sequence shown.*

**VALVE SYSTEM.** Remove cylinder head as outlined above. Remove rocker arm shaft (21—Fig. KW158) and rocker arms (6 and 7). Use suitable valve spring compressor to compress valve springs and remove collet halves (8). Remove retainers (9), springs (10) and valves (19 and 20). Remove valve stem seals (11) from top of valve guides.

**NOTE: Removal of valve stem seal will damage the seal. Renew seals whenever they are removed.**

Check all parts for wear or damage. Refer to the following specifications:

Rocker arm shaft OD—
Wear limit . . . . . . . . . . . . . 12.94 mm (0.509 in.)
Rocker arm ID—
Wear limit . . . . . . . . . . . . . 13.07 mm (0.515 in.)
Valve spring free length—
Minimum allowable . . . . . . 37.50 mm (1.476 in.)
Valve guide ID—
Wear limit . . . . . . . . . . . . . . 7.07 mm (0.278 in.)

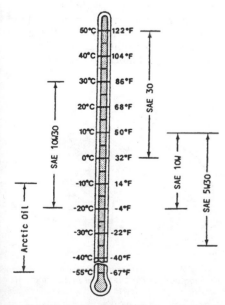

50°C 122°F
40°C 104°F
30°C 86°F
20°C 68°F
10°C 50°F
0°C 32°F
-10°C 14°F
-20°C -4°F
-30°C -22°F
-40°C -40°F
-55°C -67°F
Arctic Oil
SAE 10W30
SAE 30
SAE 10W
SAE 5W30

*Fig. KW156—Engine oil viscosity should be based on expected air temperature as indicated in chart above.*

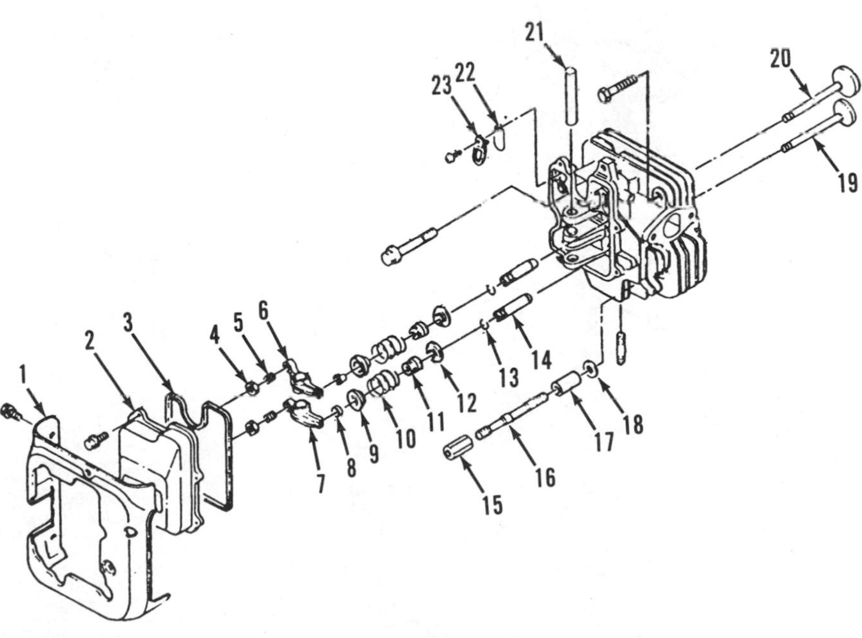


*Fig. KW158—Exploded view of cylinder head assembly.*

1. Shroud
2. Rocker arm cover
3. Gasket
4. Locknut
5. Adjusting screw
6. Rocker arm, intake
7. Rocker arm, exhaust
8. Retainer
9. Retainer
10. Valve spring
11. Seal
12. Plate
13. Snap ring
14. Valve guide
15. Nut
16. Stud
17. Bushing
18. Washer
19. Exhaust valve
20. Intake valve
21. Rocker arm shaft
22. Breather valve
23. Retainer plate

Renew valves if stem is warped more than 0.03 mm (0.001 in.) or if valve margin is less than 0.60 mm (0.020 in.). Valve stem ends should be ground square. Valve face and seat angle is 45 degrees for intake and exhaust.

**NOTE: Grinding face of exhaust valve is not recommended as life of valve will be shortened.**

Valve seating surface should be 1.00-1.46 mm (0.039-0.057 in.) for Model FC420V and 1.20 mm (0.048 in.) for Model FC540V. Seats may be narrowed using a 30 degree stone or cutter. Valves should be lapped into the seats to ensure proper contact. Seats should contact center of valve face.

Valve guides (14) can be renewed using suitable valve guide driver. Guides should be pressed into cylinder head until snap ring (13) just seats against cylinder head. Ream new guides with a 7 mm valve guide reamer. Valve guide finished inside diameter should be 7.0-7.02 mm (0.2756-0.2763 in.).

**CONNECTING ROD.** Connecting rod (16—Fig. KW159) and piston are removed as an assembly after removing cylinder head and crankcase cover. Remove carbon and ring ridge (if present) from top of cylinder before removing piston. Remove connecting rod bolts and connecting rod cap, then push connecting rod and piston out through top of cylinder. Remove retaining rings (18) and push piston pin (17) out of piston to separate piston from connecting rod.

Connecting rod rides directly on crankshaft journal. Maximum allowable inside diameter for connecting rod big end bearing surface is 41.07 mm (1.617 in.). Maximum connecting rod-to-crankpin clearance is 0.14 mm (0.006 in.). A connecting rod is available with 0.50 mm (0.020 in.) undersize big end for use with undersize crankshaft crankpin. Refer to CRANKSHAFT AND BALANCER section.

Maximum inside diameter of connecting rod small end is 22.06 mm (0.868 in.). Maximum allowable connecting rod-to-piston pin clearance is 0.08 mm (0.003 in.).

When reassembling, install piston on connecting rod so arrow on top of piston is toward the "MADE IN JAPAN" side of connecting rod. Install piston and connecting rod in cylinder so arrow on top of piston is toward flywheel side of engine. Tighten connecting rod cap bolts to 20 N·m (15 ft.-lbs.).

**PISTON, PIN AND RINGS.** Piston and connecting rod are removed as an assembly after removing cylinder head and crankcase cover. Refer to CONNECTING ROD section for removal and installation procedure.

After separating piston and connecting rod, carefully remove piston rings and clean carbon and other deposits from piston surface and piston ring lands.

**CAUTION: Extreme care should be exercised when cleaning piston rings lands. Do not damage squared edges or widen piston ring grooves. If piston ring lands are damaged, piston must be renewed.**

Maximum inside diameter of pin bore in piston is 22.04 mm (0.868 in.). Minimum piston pin outside diameter is 21.98 mm (0.827 in.). Maximum piston-to-pin clearance is 0.06 mm (0.002 in.).

To check piston ring grooves for wear, insert a new ring in ring groove and use a feeler gage to measure ring side clearance in groove. Renew piston if side clearance exceeds 0.17 mm (0.007 in.) for top ring, 0.15 mm (0.006 in.) for second ring or 0.20 mm (0.008 in.) for oil ring.

Insert each ring squarely in cylinder bore about 25 mm (1 in.) below top of cylinder and use a feeler gage to measure ring end gap. Maximum allowable end gap is 0.90 mm (0.035 in.) for compression rings and 1.30 mm (0.051 in.) for oil control ring. If piston ring gap is greater than specified, check cylinder bore for wear.

During reassembly, install piston on connecting rod so arrow on top of piston is toward "MADE IN JAPAN" side of connecting rod. Use new snap rings to retain piston pin in piston. Install oil ring spacer (3—Fig. KW160) first, then install side rails (4). Position side rail end gaps 180 degrees apart. Install second ring (2) and first ring (1) on piston with "N" or "NPR" mark on ring facing up.

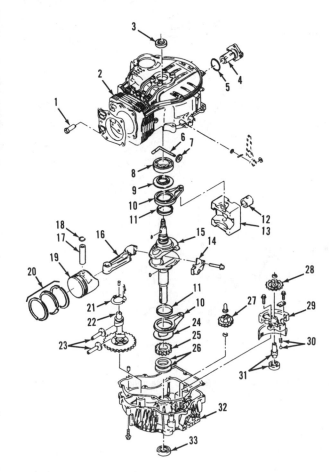

*Fig. KW159—Exploded view of engine.*

1. Check valve
2. Cylinder block & crankcase
3. Oil seal
4. Counterweight support shaft
5. "O" ring
6. Governor shaft
7. Washer
8. Main bearing
9. Spacer
10. Link rod
11. Bushing
12. Bushing
13. Balancer counterweight
14. Rod cap
15. Crankshaft
16. Connecting rod
17. Piston pin
18. Snap ring
19. Piston
20. Piston rings
21. Compression release mechanism
22. Camshaft assy.
23. Valve tappets
24. Spacer
25. Gear
26. Shims
27. Governor flyweight assy.
28. Gear
29. Oil pump housing
30. Oil pressure relief valve
31. Oil pump rotors
32. Crankcase cover
33. Oil seal

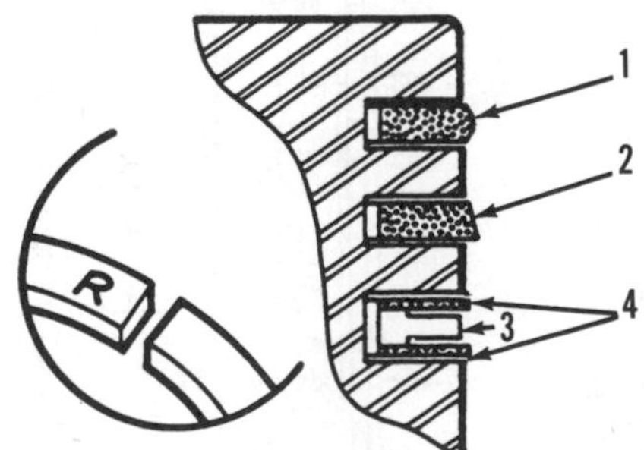


*Fig. KW160—Cross-sectional view of piston showing correct installation of piston rings. Refer to text.*

1. Top ring
2. Second ring
3. Spacer
4. Side rails

Stagger piston ring end gaps 180 degrees apart, but do not align with side rail end gaps. Lubricate piston and cylinder with engine oil. Use a suitable ring compressor to compress rings when installing piston in cylinder. Be sure that arrow on top of piston faces flywheel side of engine.

**CYLINDER, CRANKCASE, MAIN BEARINGS AND SEALS.** Cylinder and crankcase are an integral casting. Standard cylinder bore diameter is 88.90-89.00 mm (3.500-3.504 in.) for all models. Cylinder bore wear limit is 89.08 mm (3.507 in.) for FC420V and 89.06 mm (3.506 in.) for FC540V. Cylinder may be bored or honed to fit oversize pistons. Pistons are available in 0.25, 0.50 and 0.75 mm (0.010, 0.020 and 0.030 in.) oversizes.

The main bearing on pto side is an integral part of cylinder and crankcase assembly. Main bearing on flywheel side is a ball bearing. Maximum inside diameter for integral bearing bore in crankcase cover is 35.07 mm (1.381 in.) for FC420V and 38.06 mm (1.498 in.) for FC540V. Bearing on flywheel side should be a press fit on crankshaft and in bearing bore of crankcase.

Renew crankshaft seals (3 and 33—Fig. KW159) if worn or damaged. Pack seals with lithium base grease prior to installation. Install seals with lip facing inside of engine, and press in until flush with crankcase and crankcase cover (Model FC420V). On Model FC540V, press seal into crankcase cover until 0.50 mm (0.020 in.) below crankcase cover flange surface.

When installing crankcase cover, tighten cover mounting screws to 26 N·m (19 ft.-lbs.) on Model FC420V and 20 N·m (15 ft.-lbs.) on Model FC540V. On all models, tighten mounting screws in sequence shown in Fig. KW161.

**CRANKSHAFT AND BALANCER.** The crankshaft is supported on flywheel side by a ball type main bearing and on pto side by a plain type bearing which is an integral casting with crankcase cover. A reciprocating balancer is used on all models.

To remove crankshaft, remove shrouds, fan housing, flywheel, cylinder head and crankcase cover. Rotate crankshaft until timing marks on camshaft gear and crankshaft gear are aligned, then remove camshaft and gear. Remove valve tappets (23—Fig. KW159); identify tappets so they can be reinstalled in original position. Remove connecting rod and piston. Unbolt and remove counterweight support shaft (4—Fig. KW159). Remove crankshaft and balancer assembly from crankcase.

To disassemble balancer, remove collar (9), gear (25), spacer (24) and link rods (10) from crankshaft (15) and balancer (13) wrist pins.

Clean and inspect all parts for wear or damage. Crankshaft main journal minimum diameter on pto side is 34.91 mm (1.374 in.) for Model FC420V and 37.90 mm (1.492 in.) for Model FC540V. Main journals cannot be resized. Refer to CYLINDER, CRANKCASE, MAIN BEARINGS AND SEALS section for main bearing dimensions. Measure crankshaft runout at the main journals. Crankshaft should be renewed if runout exceeds 0.05 mm (0.002 in.). Crankshaft cannot be straightened.

Crankpin journal minimum diameter is 40.93 mm (1.611 in.) for all models. Crankpin may be reground to accept undersize connecting rod. Refer to CONNECTING ROD section.

Measure outside diameter of crankshaft balancer link rod journals (A—Fig. KW162), inside diameter of big end and small end of balancer link rods (B), inside diameter of support shaft bushing (D) and outside diameter of support shaft (E). Refer to the following table for wear limit specifications and renew parts as necessary.

| | |
|---|---|
| Link rod journal OD— | |
| FC420V | 53.95 mm (2.124 in.) |
| FC540V | 57.94 mm (2.281 in.) |
| Link rod big end ID— | |
| FC420V | 54.12 mm (2.132 in.) |
| FC540V | 58.19 mm (2.291 in.) |
| Link rod small end ID— | |
| All models | 12.06 mm (0.475 in.) |
| Support shaft bushing ID— | |
| All models | 26.10 mm (1.027 in.) |
| Support shaft OD— | |
| All models | 25.93 mm (1.021 in.) |

Balancer link rod bushing (11—Fig. KW159) and support shaft bushing (12) are renewable. When installing new link rod bushing, press bushing into link rod from side opposite oil grooves (G—Fig. KW163). Position seam (S) of bushing 90 degrees from centerline (C) of link rod. Install bushing so depth (D) below machined surface of rod is 0.50 mm (0.020 in.) for FC420V engine or 1.0 mm (0.040 in.) for FC540V engine. When installing new support shaft bushing, make sure that oil hole in bushing is aligned with oil passage in balancer. On FC420V engine, install support shaft bushing flush with surface of balancer. On FC540V engine, install bushing so it is 0.50 mm (0.020 in.) below surface of balancer.

To assemble crankshaft and balancer, install balance weight (W—Fig. KW162) with oil hole (O) toward flywheel side of crankshaft. Install link rods (B) with oil grooves facing away from crankwebs. Install spacer (24—Fig. KW159) with chamfered face toward link rod. Install balancer assembly with crankshaft in crankcase being careful not to damage crankshaft oil seal. Align balancer weight with hole in crankcase and insert support shaft (4). Install connecting rod and piston. Rotate crankshaft until piston is at top dead center.

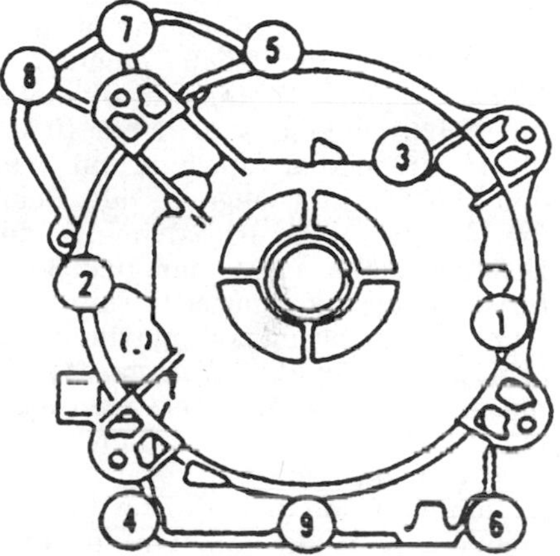


*Fig. KW161—Crankcase cover screws must be tightened evenly to specified torque following sequence shown.*

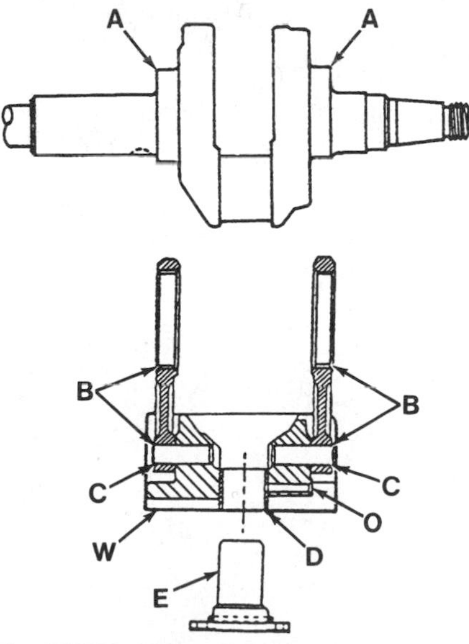


*Fig. KW162—View of crankshaft and engine balancer wear check points. Refer to text.*

A. Crankshaft journals
B. Link rod bearings
C. Wrist pins
D. Support shaft bushing
E. Support shaft

Install valve tappets in their original bores. Align timing marks on crankshaft gear and camshaft gear and install camshaft. Install crankcase cover with original shims (26), then use a dial indicator to measure crankshaft end play. Add or remove shims as necessary to obtain specified end play of 0.09-0.22 mm (0.004-0.009 in.).

**CAMSHAFT AND BEARINGS.** Camshaft is supported at each end in bearings which are integral part of crankcase and crankcase cover. Refer to CRANKSHAFT AND BALANCER section for camshaft and valve tappet removal. Mark tappets so they can be installed in their original guides if reused.

Camshaft minimum lobe height for intake and exhaust lobes is 36.75 mm (1.446 in.) for FC420V engine or 37.10 mm (1.461 in.) for FC540V engine.

Bearing journal minimum diameter for FC420V engine is 20.91 mm (0.823 in.) for pto side of camshaft and 19.91 mm (0.784 in.) for magneto side. Bearing journal minimum diameter for FC540V engine is 20.91 mm (0.823 in.) for both sides of camshaft.

Camshaft bearing bore maximum inside diameter for FC420V engine is 21.08 mm (0.830 in.) for crankcase cover bearing and 20.08 mm (0.790 in.) for crankcase bearing. Camshaft bearing bore maximum inside diameter for FC540V engine is 21.08 mm (0.830 in.) for both crankcase and crankcase cover bearings.

When reinstalling camshaft and tappets, be sure that tappets are installed in their original position. If camshaft is renewed, tappets should also be renewed. Make sure that timing marks on camshaft gear and crankshaft gear are aligned.

**GOVERNOR.** The internal centrifugal flyweight governor (27—Fig. KW159) is mounted in crankcase cover and gear driven off the camshaft gear.

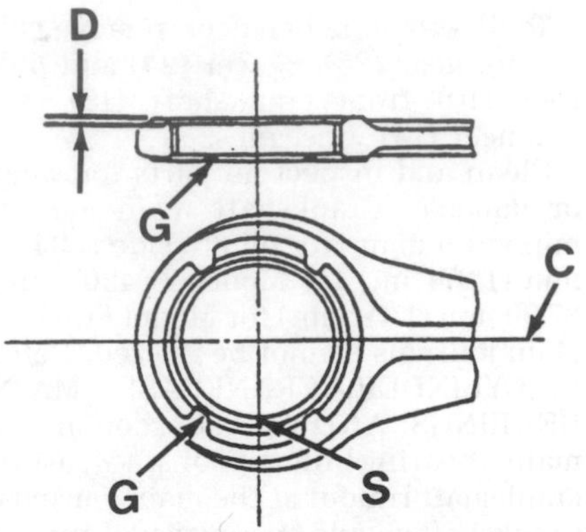


*Fig. KW163—Bushing in big end of balancer link rod is renewable. Refer to text for special installation instructions.*

C. Link rod centerline
D. Bushing depth
G. Oil grooves
S. Bushing seam

To remove governor assembly, split crankcase cover from crankcase. Use two screwdrivers to snap governor gear and flyweight assembly off governor stub shaft. Governor unit will be damaged when removed and must be renewed if removed.

Refer to MAINTENANCE section for external governor linkage adjustment.

**OIL PUMP AND RELIEF VALVE.** The trochoid type oil pump (Fig. KW164) is mounted on crankcase cover (11). To remove oil pump, first separate crankcase cover from cylinder block. Remove pump drive gear (2). Remove pump housing mounting cap screws and withdraw pump housing (4) and inner rotor shaft (6) together from crankcase cover. Remove retainer plate (3) and relief valve ball and spring (5).

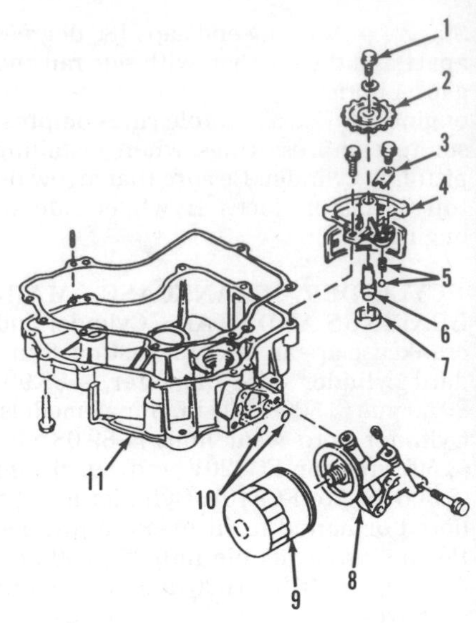


*Fig. KW164—Exploded view of engine oil pump assembly.*

1. Cap screw
2. Drive gear
3. Retainer plate
4. Pump housing
5. Pressure relief valve assy.
6. Pump inner rotor
7. Pump outer rotor
8. Filter base
9. Oil filter
10. "O" rings
11. Crankcase cover

Inspect seating of relief valve ball. Measure relief valve spring free length. Renew spring if free length is less than 19.00 mm (0.750 in.) on Model FC420V or 19.50 mm (0.770 in.) on Model FC540V.

Measure diameter of outer rotor shaft (6); wear limit is 12.63 mm (0.497 in.). Measure inside diameter of rotor shaft bearing surface in pump housing; wear limit is 12.76 mm (0.502 in.). Measure inside diameter of outer rotor bearing surface in crankcase cover; wear limit is 29.20 mm (1.149 in.) for Model FC420V or 40.77 mm (1.605 in.) for Model FC540V.

To reinstall pump, reverse removal procedure. Lubricate parts with engine oil.

# KOHLER

## KOHLER COMPANY
## Kohler, Wisconsin 53044

| Model | No. Cyls. | Bore | Stroke | Displacement | Power Rating |
|---|---|---|---|---|---|
| K-141* | 1 | 2.875 in. (73.025 mm) | 2.5 in. (63.5 mm) | 16.22 cu. in. (266 cc) | 6.25 hp. (4.7 kW) |
| K-141** | 1 | 2.9375 in. (74.613 mm) | 2.5 in. (63.5 mm) | 16.9 cu. in. (277.7 cc) | 6.25 hp. (4.7 kW) |
| K-160 | 1 | 2.875 in. (73.025 mm) | 2.5 in. (63.5 mm) | 16.22 cu. in. (266 cc) | 7 hp. (5.2 kW) |
| K-161* | 1 | 2.875 in. (73.025 mm) | 2.5 in. (63.5 mm) | 16.22 cu. in. (266 cc) | 7 hp. (5.2 kW) |
| K-161** | 1 | 2.9375 in. (74.613 mm) | 2.5 in. (63.5 mm) | 16.9 cu. in. (277.7 cc) | 7 hp. (5.2 kW) |
| K-181 | 1 | 2.9375 in. (74.613 mm) | 2.75 in. (69.85 mm) | 18.6 cu. in. (305.4 cc) | 8 hp. (6 kW) |
| KV-181 | 1 | 2.9375 in. (74.613 mm) | 2.75 in. (69.85 mm) | 18.6 cu. in. (305.4 cc) | 8 hp. (6 kW) |
| K-241 | 1 | 3.25 in. (82.55 mm) | 2.875 in. (73.025 mm) | 23.9 cu. in. (390.8 cc) | 10 hp. (7.5 kW) |
| K-301 | 1 | 3.375 in. (85.725 mm) | 3.25 in. (82.55 mm) | 29.07 cu. in. (476.5 cc) | 12 hp. (8.9 kW) |
| K-321 | 1 | 3.5 in. (88.9 mm) | 3.25 in. (82.55 mm) | 31.27 cu. in. (512.4 cc) | 14 hp. (10.4 kW) |
| K-341 | 1 | 3.75 in. (95.25 mm) | 3.25 in. (82.55 mm) | 35.89 cu. in. (588.2 mm) | 16 hp. (11.9 kW) |

* Designates early production (before 1970) engines.

** Designates late production (after 1970) engines.

All engines in this section are one cylinder, four-stroke engines. All models except KV-181 have horizontal crankshafts. Model KV-181 has a vertical crankshaft.

Model K-141 has a ball bearing main at pto end of crankshaft and a bushing type main bearing at flywheel end. Model KV-181 has a ball bearing main at pto end of crankshaft and a needle roller bearing main at flywheel end. All remaining models have ball bearing mains at each end of crankshaft.

Connecting rod on all models rides directly on crankpin journal. All models except KV-181 are splash lubricated. Model KV-181 has an oil circulating system which lubricates upper main bearing and crankpin.

Various models may be equipped with either a battery type ignition system, a magneto type system, each with externally mounted breaker points or a solid state breakerless ignition system.

Either a side draft or an updraft carburetor is used depending on model and application.

Special engine accessories or equipment is noted by a suffix letter on the engine model number. Key to suffix letters is as follows:

C – Over-center lever operated clutch.
P – Crankcase and crankshaft machined for direct drive applications.
R – Reduction drive unit.
S – Starter-generator unit or gear drive.
T – Rewind starter.

## MAINTENANCE

**SPARK PLUG.** Recommended spark plug for K-241, K-301, K-321 and K-341 engines is Champion H10 or equivalent. All other models use Champion J8C or equivalent. Spark plug gap should be 0.025 inch (0.635 mm) for all models.

If radio noise reduction is needed use Champion RH10 or equivalent for Model K-241, K-301, K-321 and K-341 engines and Champion RJ8C or equivalent in remaining models. Spark plug gap should be 0.020 inch (0.508 mm) for all models.

**CARBURETOR.** Model K-141 engines are equipped with a Tillotson "E" series updraft carburetor. Early production K-161, K-181, K-241 and K-301 engines are equipped with Carter "N" model side draft carburetors. Late production K-161, K-181, K-241 and K-301 and all KV-181, K-321 and K-341 engines are equipped with Kohler side draft carburetors. Refer to appropriate paragraph for carburetor service information.

CARTER CARBURETOR. Refer to Fig. KO1 for exploded view of typical "N" model Carter carburetor.

For initial adjustment, open idle fuel needle 1½ turns and open main fuel needle 2 turns. Make final adjustment with engine at normal operating temperature and running. Place engine under load and adjust main fuel needle for leanest setting that will allow satisfactory acceleration and steady governor operation. Set engine at idle speed, no load and adjust idle mixture screw to obtain smoothest idle operation.

As each adjustment affects the other, adjustment procedure may have to be repeated.

To check float level, invert carburetor throttle body and float assembly. There should be 13/64-inch (5.159 mm) clearance between free side of float and machined surface of body casting. Carefully bend float lever tang that contacts inlet valve as necessary to provide correct measurement.

KOHLER CARBURETOR. Refer to Fig. KO2 for exploded view of Kohler carburetor. For initial adjustment, open main fuel needle 2 turns and open idle fuel needle 1¼ turns. Make final adjustment with engine at normal operating temperature and running. Place engine under load and adjust main fuel needle to leanest mixture that will allow satisfactory acceleration and steady governor operation.

Adjust idle speed stop screw to maintain an idle speed of 1000 rpm, then adjust idle fuel needle for smoothest idle operation. As each adjustment affects the other, adjustment procedure may have to be repeated.

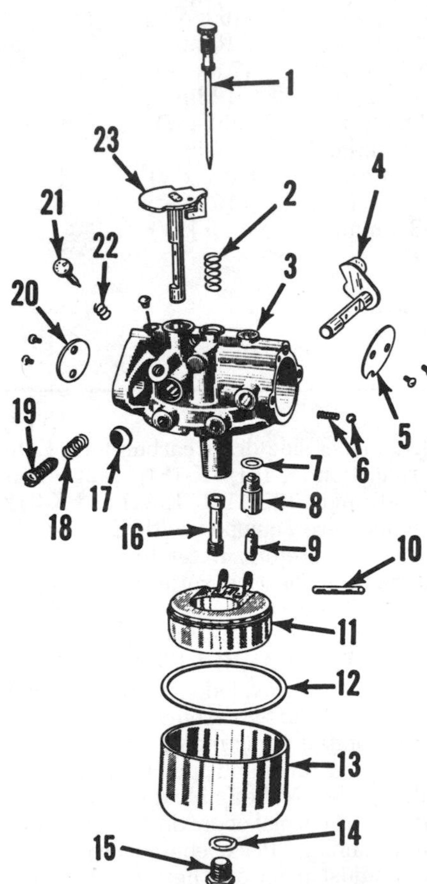


***Fig. KO1—Exploded view of typical Carter "N" model carburetor used on early production K-160, K-161, K-181, K-241 and K-301 engines.***

1. Main fuel needle
2. Spring
3. Carburetor body
4. Choke shaft
5. Choke disc
6. Choke detent
7. Sealing washer
8. Inlet valve seat
9. Inlet valve
10. Float pin
11. Float
12. Gasket
13. Float bowl
14. Sealing washer
15. Retainer
16. Main jet
17. Plug
18. Spring
19. Idle stop screw
20. Throttle disc
21. Idle fuel needle
22. Spring
23. Throttle shaft

To check float level, invert carburetor body and float assembly. There should be 11/64-inch (4.366 mm) clearance between machined surface of body casting and free end of float. Carefully bend float lever tang that contacts inlet valve as necessary to provide correct measurement.

TILLOTSON CARBURETOR. Refer to Fig. KO3 for exploded view of Tillotson "E" series carburetor similar to that used on Model K-141 engine. Design of choke shaft lever will differ from that shown in exploded view.

For initial adjustment, open idle fuel mixture needle ¾-turn and open main fuel mixture needle 1 turn. Make final adjustment with engine at normal operating temperature and running. Place engine under load and adjust main fuel needle to leanest mixture that will allow satisfactory acceleration and steady governor operation. Slow engine to idle speed and adjust idle mixture screw to obtain smoothest idle operation. As each adjustment affects the other, adjustment procedure may have to be repeated.

To check float level, invert carburetor cover and float assembly. There should be 1-5/64 inches (27.384 mm) clearance between free side of float and machined surface of cover. See Fig. KO4. Carefully bend float lever tang that contacts inlet valve as necessary to provide correct measurement.

**AUTOMATIC CHOKE.** Some models equipped with Kohler or Carter carburetors are also equipped with an automatic choke. "Thermostatic" type shown in Fig. KO5 may be used on either electric start or manual start models. "Electric-Thermostatic" type shown in Fig. KO6 can be used only on electric start models. Automatic choke adjustment should be made with engine cold.

THERMOSTATIC TYPE. To adjust "Thermostatic" type, loosen lock screw (Fig. KO5) and rotate adjustment bracket as necessary to obtain correct amount of choking. Tighten lock screw. In cold temperature, choke should be closed. At 70° F. (21° C) choke should be partially open and choke lever should be in vertical position. Start engine and allow it to run until normal operating temperature is reached. Choke should be fully open when engine is at normal operating temperature.

ELECTRIC-THERMOSTATIC TYPE. To adjust "Electric-Thermostatic" type, refer to Fig. KO6 and move choke lever arm until hole in brass cross shaft is aligned with slot in bearings. Insert a No. 43 (0.089 inch) drill through shaft until drill is engaged in notch in base of choke. Loosen clamp bolt on lever arm and move link end of lever arm upward until choke disc is closed to desired position. Tighten clamp bolt while holding lever arm in this position. Remove drill. Choke should be fully closed when starting a cold engine and should be fully open when engine is running at normal operating temperature.

**GOVERNOR.** All models are equipped with a gear driven flyweight governor that is located inside engine crankcase. Maximum recommended governed engine speed is 3800 rpm on KV-181 engines and 3600 rpm for all other engines. Recommended idle speed of 1000 rpm is controlled by adjustment of throttle stop screw on carburetor.

Before attempting to adjust engine governed speed, synchronize governor linkage as follows: On Models K-141,

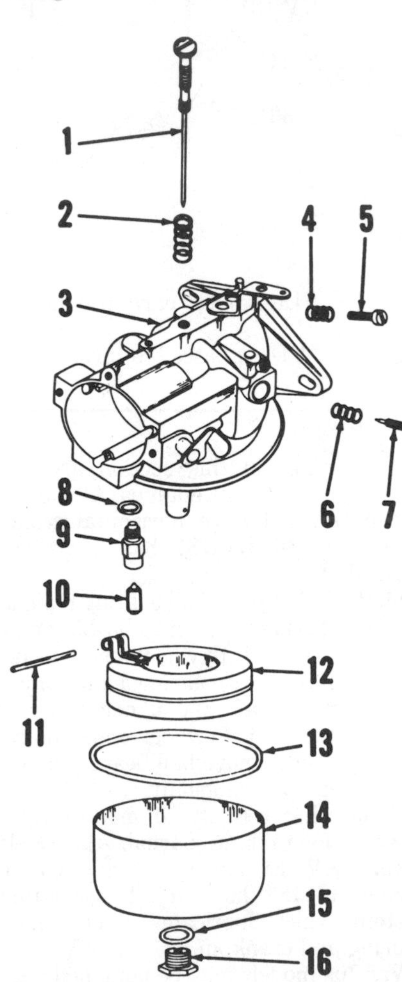


***Fig. KO2—Exploded view of Kohler carburetor used on late production K-161, K-181, K-241 and K-301 and all KV-181, K-321 and K-341 engines.***

1. Main fuel needle
2. Spring
3. Carburetor body assy.
4. Spring
5. Idle speed stop screw
6. Spring
7. Idle fuel needle
8. Sealing washer
9. Inlet valve seat
10. Inlet valve
11. Float pin
12. Float
13. Gasket
14. Float bowl
15. Gasket
16. Bowl retainer



Illustrations courtesy Kohler Co.

K-160, K-161 and K-181, loosen bolt clamping governor arm (G–Fig. KO7) to governor cross shaft (F) and turn governor cross shaft counter-clockwise as far as possible. While holding cross shaft in this position, move governor arm away from carburetor to limit of linkage travel and tighten clamping bolt.

To synchronize governor linkage on KV-181, follow procedure for K-141, K-160, K-161 and K-181 and refer to Fig. KO9.

On Models K-241, K-301, K-321 and K-341, refer to Fig. KO10 and loosen governor arm hex nut. Rotate governor cross shaft counter-clockwise as far as possible, move governor arm away from carburetor to limit of linkage travel, then tighten hex nut on arm.

To adjust maximum governed speed on Models K-241, K-301, K-321 and K-341, adjust position of stop so speed control lever contacts stop at desired engine speed. On Models K-141, K-160, K-161 and K-181, loosen governor shaft bushing nut (C-Fig. KO7) and move throttle bracket (E) to increase or decrease governed speed. See Fig. KO8 for direction of movement. Model KV-181 governed speed is adjusted by loosening set screw in speed control bracket and moving high speed stop shown in Fig. KO9. Adjust throttle cable so control handle is in full throttle position when drive pin in throttle is contacting bracket.

On Models K-241, K-301, K-321 and K-341, governor sensitivity is adjusted by moving governor spring to alternate holes in governor arm and speed lever.

Governor unit is accessible after removing engine crankshaft and camshaft. Governor gear and flyweight assembly turns on a stub shaft pressed into engine crankcase. Renew gear and weight assembly if gear teeth or any part of assembly is excessively worn. Desired clearance of governor gear to stud shaft is 0.0025-0.0055 inch (0.0635-0.1397 mm) for Models K-141, K-160, K-161 and K-181 and

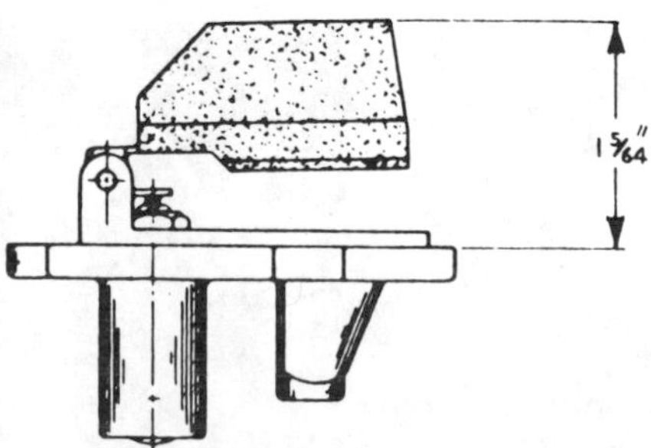


***Fig. KO4—Check float setting on Tillotson carburetor by inverting throttle body and float assembly and measuring distance from free end of float to edge of cover as shown. Float setting is correct if distance is 1-5/64 inch (27.384 mm).***

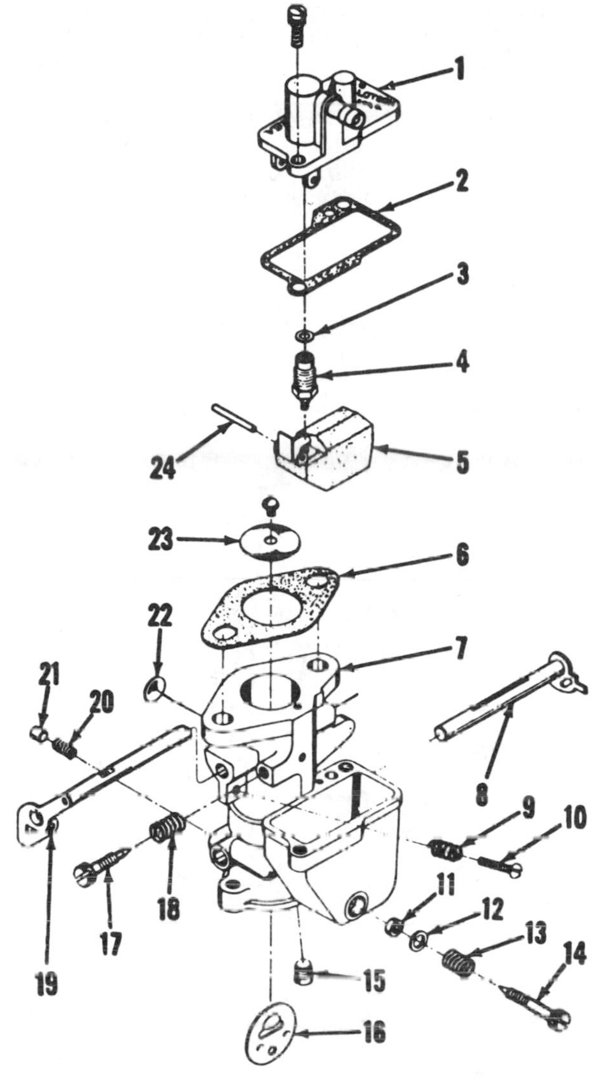

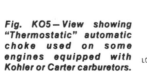

***Fig. KO3—Exploded view of Tillotson "E" series carburetor used on K-141 engine: Refer to Fig. KO4 for method of checking float level.***

1. Float bowl cover
2. Gasket
3. Gasket
4. Inlet valve assy.
5. Float
6. Gasket
7. Carburetor body
8. Choke shaft
9. Spring
10. Idle speed stop screw
11. Packing
12. Washer
13. Spring
14. Main fuel needle
15. Screw plug
16. Choke disc
17. Idle fuel needle
18. Spring
19. Throttle shaft
20. Spring
21. Choke shaft detent
22. Plug
23. Throttle disc
24. Float pin

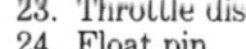
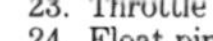

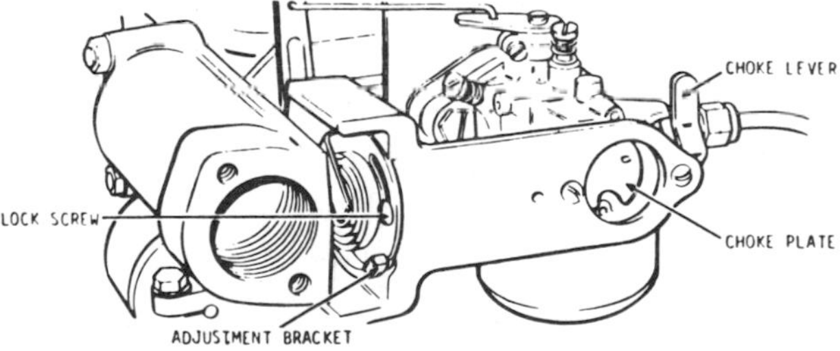


***Fig. KO5—View showing "Thermostatic" automatic choke used on some engines equipped with Kohler or Carter carburetors.***

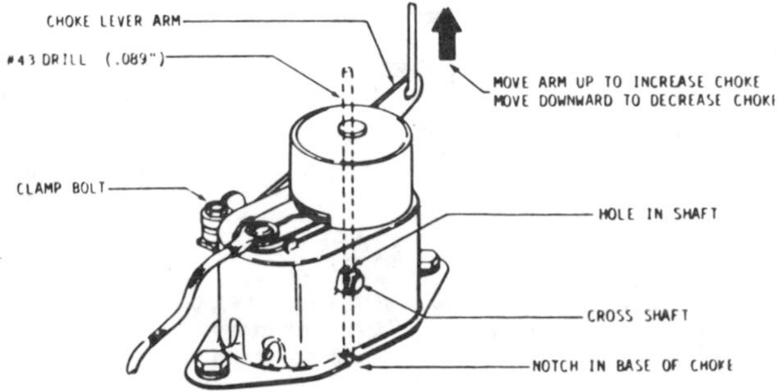


***Fig. KO6—View of "Electric-Thermostatic" automatic choke used on some engines equipped with Kohler or Carter carburetor.***

0.0005-0.002 inch (0.0127-0.0508 mm) for Models KV-181, K-241, K-301, K-321 and K-341.

**IGNITION AND TIMING.** Three types of ignition systems used are as follows: Battery ignition, flywheel magneto ignition and solid state breakerless ignition. Refer to appropriate paragraphs for timing and service procedures.

BATTERY AND MAGNETO IGNITION. On engines equipped with either battery or magneto ignition systems, breaker points are located externally on engine crankcase as shown in Fig. KO11. Breaker points are actuated by a cam through a push rod.

On early models, breaker cam is driven by camshaft gear through an automatic advance mechanism as shown in Fig. KO12. At cranking speed, ignition occurs at 3° BTDC on Models K-141, K-160, K-161 and K-181 or 3° ATDC on Models K-241 and K-301. At operating speeds, centrifugal force of the advance weights overcomes spring

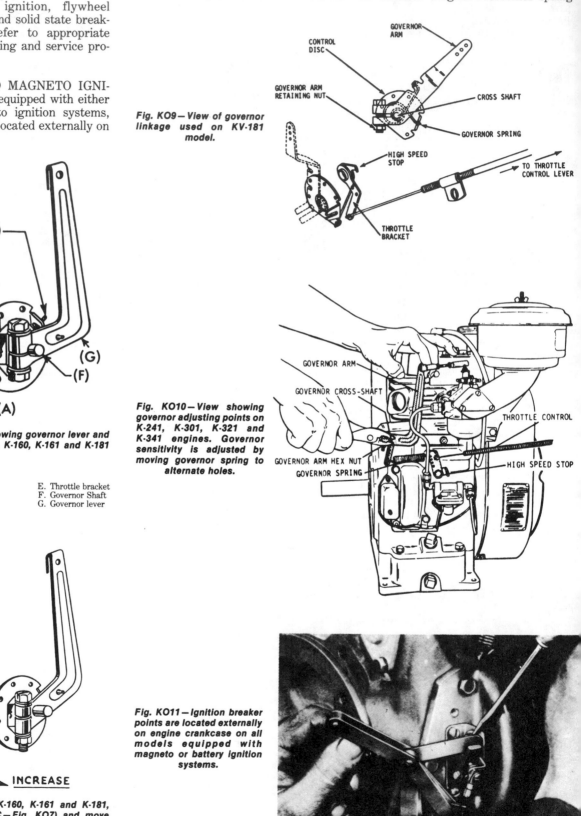

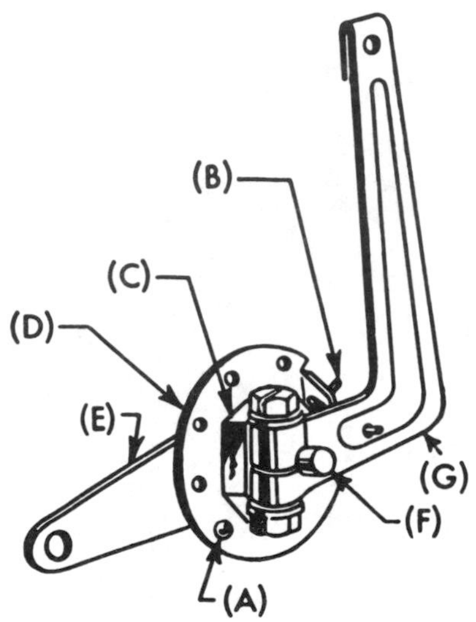


*Fig. KO7—Drawing showing governor lever and related parts on K-141, K-160, K-161 and K-181 models.*

A. Drive pin
B. Governor spring
C. Bushing nut
D. Speed control disc
E. Throttle bracket
F. Governor Shaft
G. Governor lever

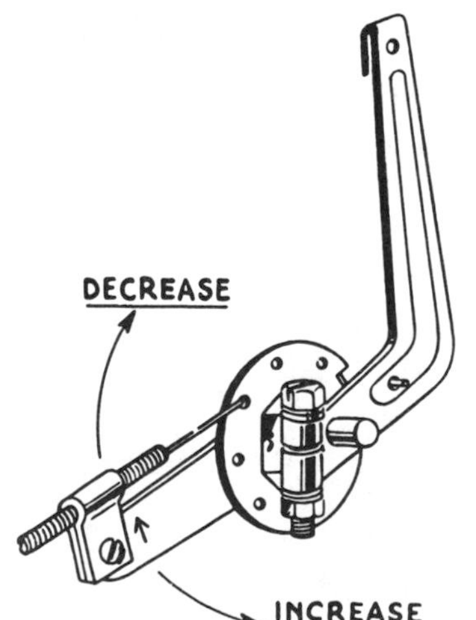


*Fig. KO8—On K-141, K-160, K-161 and K-181, loosen bushing nut (C—Fig. KO7) and move throttle bracket as shown to change governed speed of engine.*

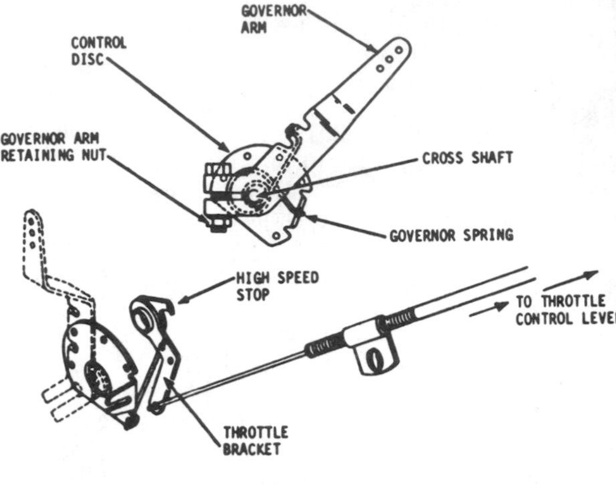


*Fig. KO9—View of governor linkage used on KV-181 model.*

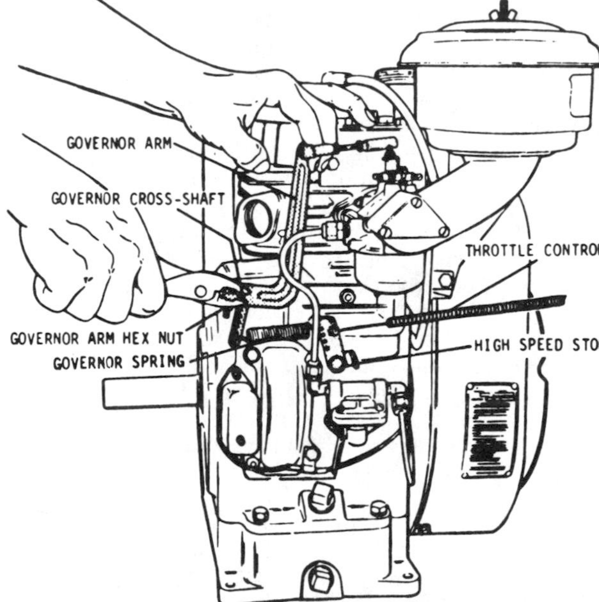


*Fig. KO10—View showing governor adjusting points on K-241, K-301, K-321 and K-341 engines. Governor sensitivity is adjusted by moving governor spring to alternate holes.*

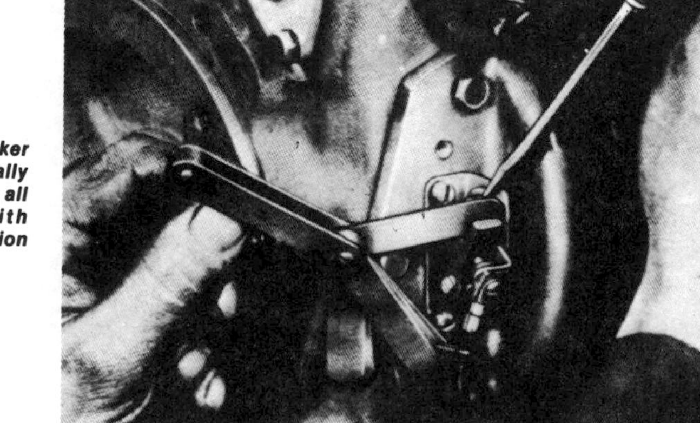

*Fig. KO11—Ignition breaker points are located externally on engine crankcase on all models equipped with magneto or battery ignition systems.*



Illustrations courtesy Kohler Co.

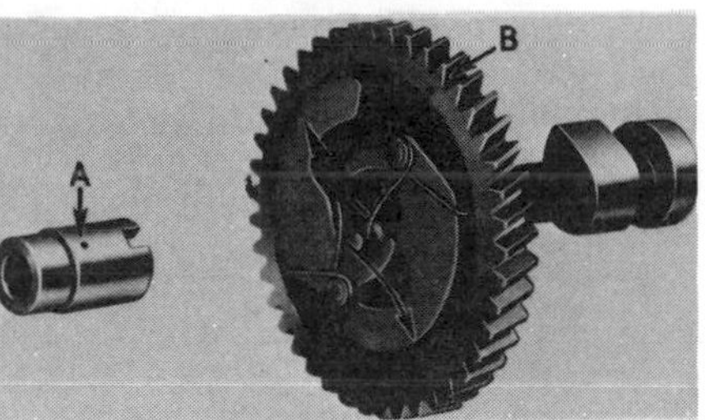


*Fig. KO12—View showing alignment marks on ignition breaker cam and camshaft gear on early models equipped with automatic timing advance.*

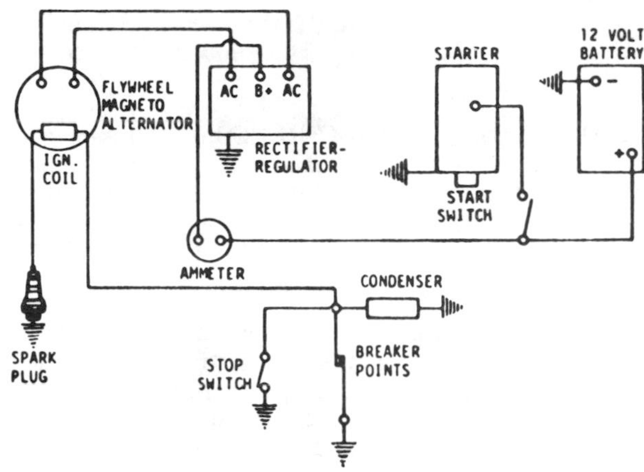

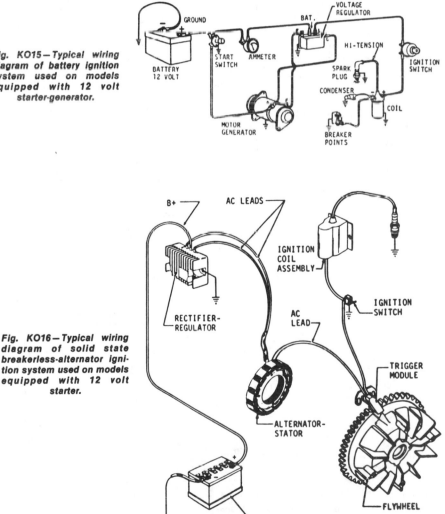

*Fig. KO14—Typical wiring diagram of magneto-alternator ignition system used on models equipped with 12 volt starter.*

tension and advances timing of breaker cam so ignition occurs at 20° BTDC on all models.

Late Model K-141, K-160, K-161, K-181, K-241 and K-301 and all Models K-321 and K-341 engines are equipped with an automatic compression release (see **CAMSHAFT** paragraph) and do not have an automatic timing advance. Ignition occurs at 20° BTDC at all engine speeds.

Initial breaker point gap on Model KV-181 is 0.015 inch (0.3810 mm) and is 0.020 inch (0.508 mm) for all remaining models. Breaker point gap should be varied to obtain exact ignition timing as follows: With a static timing light, disconnect coil and condenser leads from breaker point terminal and attach one timing light lead to terminal and ground remaining lead. Remove button plug from timing sight hole and turn engine so piston has just completed its compression stroke and "DC" mark (models with automatic compression release) on flywheel appears in sight hole. Loosen breaker point adjustment screw and adjust points to closed position (timing light will be on); slowly move breaker point base towards engine until timing light goes out. Tighten adjustment screw and check point setting by turning engine in normal direction of rotation until timing light goes on. Continue to turn engine very slowly until timing light goes out. "DC" mark (models with automatic timing advance) or "SP" mark (models with automatic compression release) should now be in register with sight hole. Disconnect timing light leads, connect leads from coil and condenser to breaker point terminal and install breaker cover.

If a power timing light is available, more accurate timing can be obtained by adjusting points with engine running. Breaker point gap should be adjusted so light flash causes "SP" timing mark (20° BTDC) to appear centered in sight hole when engine is running above 1500 rpm, when checking breaker point setting with a power timing light on models with automatic timing advance.

Typical wiring diagrams of magneto ignition systems are shown in Figs.

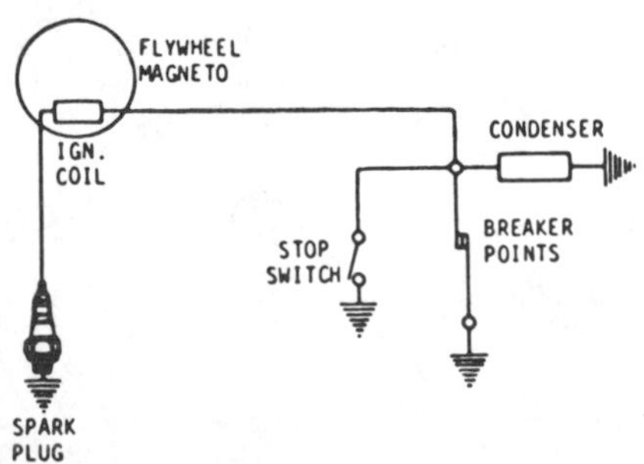


*Fig. KO13—Typical wiring diagram of magneto ignition system used on manual start engines.*

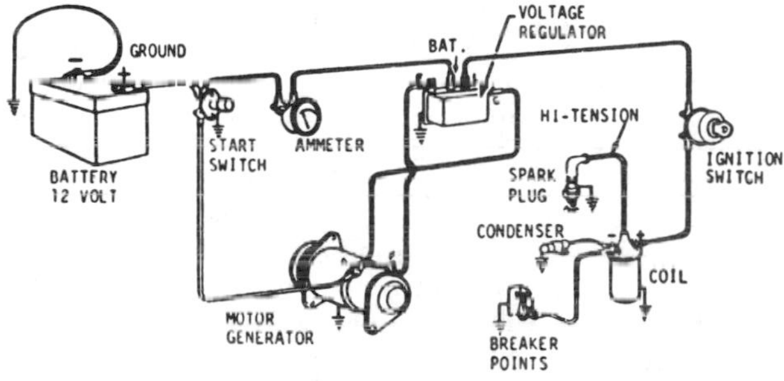


*Fig. KO15—Typical wiring diagram of battery ignition system used on models equipped with 12 volt starter-generator.*

*Fig. KO16—Typical wiring diagram of solid state breakerless-alternator ignition system used on models equipped with 12 volt starter.*

KO13 and KO14. Fig. KO15 is typical wiring diagram of battery ignition system.

SOLID STATE BREAKERLESS IGNITION. Breakerless-alternator ignition system uses solid state devices which eliminate need for mechanically operated breaker points. Ignition timing is non-adjustable. The only adjustment is trigger module to flywheel trigger projection air gap. To adjust air gap, rotate flywheel until projection is adjacent to trigger module. Loosen trigger retaining screws and move trigger until an air gap of 0.005-0.010 inch (0.127-0.254 mm) is obtained. Make certain flat surfaces on trigger and projection are parallel, then tighten retaining screws. Refer to Fig. KO16 for typical wiring diagram of breakerless ignition system.

The four main components of a breakerless ignition system are ignition winding (on alternator stator), trigger module, ignition coil assembly and special flywheel with trigger projection. System also includes a conventional spark plug, high tension lead and ignition switch. Ignition winding is separate from battery charging AC windings on alternator stator.

Trigger module includes three diodes, a resistor, a sensing coil and magnet plus the SCR (electronic switch). Trigger module has two clip-on type terminals. See Fig. KO17. Terminal marked "A" must be connected to ignition winding on alternator stator. "I" terminal must be connected to ignition switch. Improper connection will cause damage to electronic devices.

Ignition coil assembly includes capacitor and a pulse transformer arrangement similar to a conventional high tension coil. Flywheel has a special projection for triggering ignition.

If ignition trouble exists and spark plug is known to be good, the following tests should be made to determine which component is at fault. A flashlight type continuity tester can be used to test ignition coil assembly and trigger module.

To test coil assembly, remove high tension lead (spark plug wire) from coil. Insert one tester lead in coil terminal and remaining tester lead to coil mounting bracket. Tester light should be on. Connect one tester lead to coil mounting bracket and remaining tester lead to ignition switch wire of coil. Tester light should be out. Renew ignition coil if either test shows wrong results.

To test trigger module, connect one tester lead to AC inlet (A–Fig. KO17) and remaining lead to ignition lead terminal (I). Check for continuity. Reverse tester leads and again check for continuity. Test light must be on in one test only. The second test is made by connecting one tester lead to trigger module mounting bracket and other lead to AC inlet (A). Check for continuity. Reverse tester leads and again check for continuity. Again, test light must be on in one test only. The third test is made by connecting POSITIVE lead of tester to (I) terminal of trigger and connect remaining tester lead to trigger module mounting bracket. Test light should be off. Rotate flywheel in normal direction of rotation. When trigger projection on flywheel passes trigger module, test light should turn on. Renew trigger module if any of the three tests show wrong results.

If ignition trouble still exists after ignition coil assembly and trigger module tests show they are good, ignition winding on alternator stator is faulty. In this event, renew stator.

**LUBRICATION.** All models are splash lubricated except Model KV-181 which has an oil circulating system. See Fig. KO18. This vertical crankshaft engine has two oil sumps. Outer sump (7) is oil reservoir and inner sump (13) is a low level oil drain back sump. Oil is drawn from outer sump (7) through main gallery (6), oil passage (5) in crankcase and passage (4) in bearing plate. After lubricating upper main bearing (3), oil flows through thrust bearing (2) which acts as a centrifugal oil pump and is forced through tapered hole in crankpin (9) to lubricate connecting rod. Throw-off oil lubricates piston, camshaft, gears and lower main bearing (14). This drain back oil is then taken from inner sump (13) through oil pick-up assembly (10) and reed valve (11) and returned via gallery (12) to outer sump (7).

Maintain crankcase oil level at full mark on dipstick, but do not overfill. High quality detergent oil having API classification "SF" is recommended.

Use SAE 30 oil in temperatures above 32° F. (0° C), SAE 10W-30 oil in temperatures between 32° F (0° C) and 0° F (-18° C) and SAE 5W-20 oil in temperatures below 0° F (-18° C).

**CRANKCASE BREATHER.** Refer to Figs. KO19 and KO20. A reed valve assembly is located in valve spring compartment to maintain a partial vacuum in crankcase and thus reduce leakage of oil at bearing seals. If a slight amount of crankcase vacuum (5-10 inches water or ½-1 inch mercury) is not present, reed valve is faulty or engine has excessive blow-by past rings and/or valves or worn oil seals.

**AIR CLEANER.** Engine may be

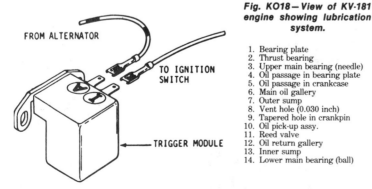

FROM ALTERNATOR
TO IGNITION SWITCH
TRIGGER MODULE

*Fig. KO17—Wires must be connected to trigger module as shown. Reversing connections will damage electronic devices.*

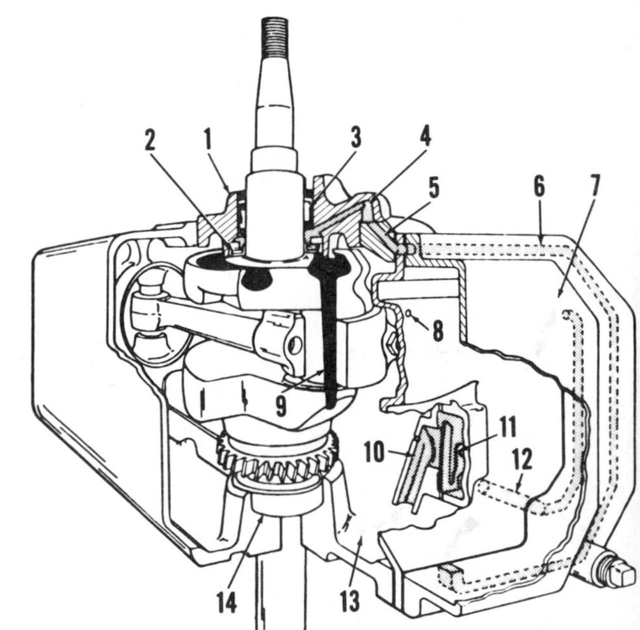


*Fig. KO18—View of KV-181 engine showing lubrication system.*

1. Bearing plate
2. Thrust bearing
3. Upper main bearing (needle)
4. Oil passage in bearing plate
5. Oil passage in crankcase
6. Main oil gallery
7. Outer sump
8. Vent hole (0.030 inch)
9. Tapered hole in crankpin
10. Oil pick-up assy.
11. Reed valve
12. Oil return gallery
13. Inner sump
14. Lower main bearing (ball)

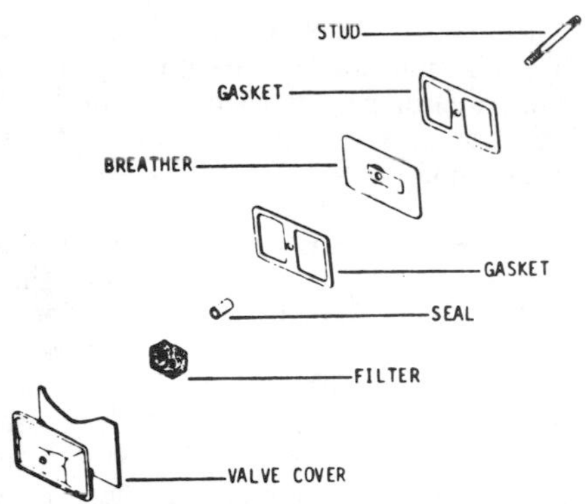


*Fig. KO19—Exploded view of crankcase breather assembly used on K-141, K-160, K-161, K-181 and KV-181 models.*

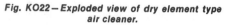

equipped with either an oil bath type air cleaner shown in Fig. KO21 or a dry element type shown in Fig. KO22.

Oil bath air cleaner should be serviced every 25 hours of normal operation or more often if operating in extremely dusty conditions. To service oil bath type, remove complete cleaner assembly from engine. Remove cover and element from bowl. Empty used oil from bowl, then clean cover and bowl in solvent. Clean element in solvent and allow to drip dry. Lightly re-oil element. Fill bowl to oil level marked on bowl using same grade and weight oil as used in engine crankcase. Renew gaskets as necessary when reassembling and reinstalling unit.

Dry element type air cleaner should be cleaned every 100 hours of normal operation or more frequently if operating in dusty conditions. Remove dry element and tap element lightly on a flat surface to remove surface dirt. Do not wash element or attempt to clean element with compressed air. Renew element if extremely dirty or if it is bent, crushed or otherwise damaged. Make certain sealing surfaces of element seal effectively against back plate and cover.

## REPAIRS

**TIGHTENING TORQUES.** Recommended tightening torques are as follows:

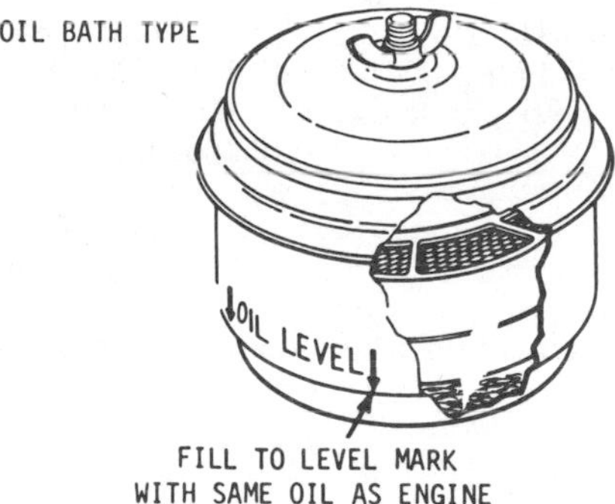


*Fig. KO21-View of oil bath type air cleaner.*

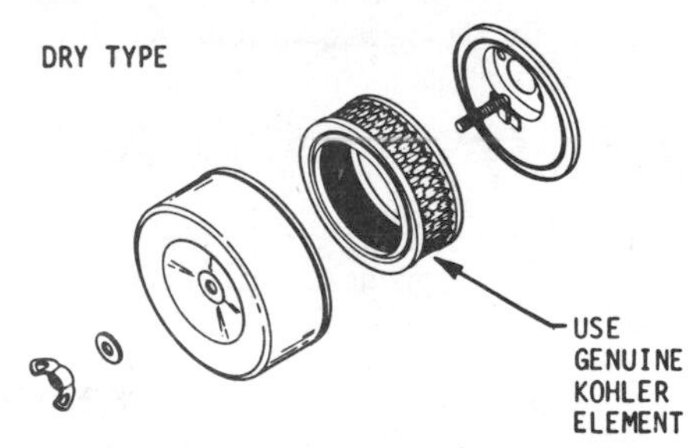


*Fig. KO22—Exploded view of dry element type air cleaner.*

Spark plug . . . . . . . . 22 ft.-lbs. (30 N·m)

Connecting rod cap screws* . . . . . See CONNECTING ROD section

Cylinder head cap screws*
- K-141, K-160, K-161, K-181, KV-181 . . . . . . . . 20 ft.-lbs. (27 N·m)
- K-241, K-301, K-321, K-341 . . . . . . . . 30 ft.-lbs. (41 N·m)

Flywheel retaining nut
- Models with 5/8-inch nut . . . . 60 ft.-lbs. (81 N·m)
- Models with 3/4-inch nut . . . 100 ft.-lbs. (136 N·m)

*With threads lubricated.

**CONNECTING ROD.** Connecting rod and piston unit is removed after removing oil pan and cylinder head. Aluminum alloy connecting rod rides directly on crankpin. Connecting rod with 0.010 inch (0.254 mm) undersize crankpin bore is available for reground crankshaft. Oversize piston pins are available on some models. Desired running clearances are as follows:

Connecting rod to crankpin . . . . . . . . 0.001-0.002 in. (0.0254-0.0508 mm)

Connecting rod to piston pin,
- K-141, K-160, K-161, K-181, KV-181 . . . . . . . . 0.0006-0.0011 in. (0.0152-0.0279 mm)
- K-241, K-301, K-321, K-341 . . . . . . . . 0.0003-0.0008 in. (0.0076-0.0203 mm)

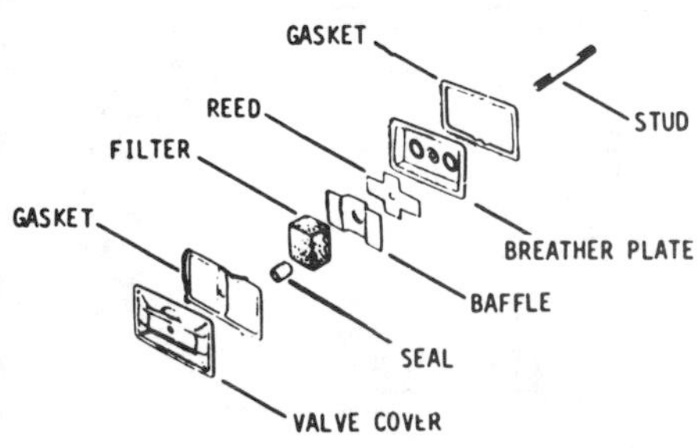


*Fig. KO20—Exploded view of crankcase breather assembly used on K-241, K-301, K-321 and K-341 models.*

Rod side play on crankpin
- K-141, K-160, K-161, K-181, KV-181 . . . . . . . . 0.005-0.016 in. (0.1270-0.4064 mm)
- K-241, K-301, K-321, K-341 . . . . . . . . 0.007-0.016 in. (0.1778-0.4064 mm)

Standard crankpin diameter is 1.1855-1.1860 inches (30.1117-30.1244 mm) on Models K-141, K-160, K-161, K-181 and KV-181 and 1.4995-1.5000 inches (38.0873-38.1000 mm) on Models K-241, K-301, K-321 and K-341.

Assemble piston to rod so arrow on piston (when so marked) faces away from valves and match marks (Fig. KO23) on rod and cap are aligned and towards camshaft side of engine. Always use new retainer rings to secure piston pin in piston.

Kohler recommends connecting rod cap screws be overtorqued to one specification, loosened, then tightened

*Fig. KO23—When installing connecting rod and piston unit, be sure marks on rod and cap are aligned and are facing toward flywheel side of engine.*

to correct torque specification. Tightening specifications are as follows:

K-141,
K-160,
K-161,
K-181,
KV-181 (Overtorque) . . . . . . . . 20 ft.-lbs. (27 N·m)
(Final torque) . . . . . . . . . . . . . . 17 ft.-lbs. (23 N·m)
K-241,
K-301,
K-321,
K-341 (Overtorque) . . . . . . . . . 28 ft.-lbs. (38 N·m)
(Final torque) . . . . . . . . . . . . . . 24 ft.-lbs. (32 N·m)

**NOTE: Torque specifications for connecting rod cap screws are with lubricated threads.**

**PISTON, PIN AND RINGS.** Aluminum alloy piston is fitted with two compression rings and one oil control ring. Renew piston if scored or if side clearance of new ring in piston top groove exceeds 0.005 inch (0.1270 mm). Pistons and rings are available in oversizes of 0.010, 0.020 and 0.030 inch (0.254, 0.508 and 0.762 mm) as well as standard sizes.

Piston pin fit in piston bore should be from 0.0001 inch (0.0025 mm) interference to 0.0003 inch (0.0076 mm) loose on Models K-141, K-160, K-161, K-181 and KV-181 and 0.0002-0.0003 inch (0.0051-0.0076 mm) loose on Models K-241, K-301, K-321 and K-341. Standard piston pin diameter is 0.6248 inch (15.8699 mm) on Models K-141, K-160, K-161, K-181 and KV-181, 0.8592 inch (21.8237 mm) on Model K-241 and 0.8753 inch (22.2326 mm) on Models K-301, K-321 and K-341. Piston pins are available in oversize of 0.005 inch (0.127 mm) on some models. Always renew piston pin retaining rings.

Recommended piston to cylinder bore clearance measured at thrust side at bottom of skirt is as follows:

K-141, K-160,
K-161, K-181,
KV-181 . . . . . . . . . . . . . 0.0045-0.0065 in. (0.1143-0.1651 mm)
K-241, K-301 . . . . . . . . . . 0.003-0.004 in. (0.0762-0.1016 mm)
K-321, K-341 . . . . . . . . 0.0035-0.0045 in. (0.0889-0.1143 mm)

Recommended piston to cylinder bore clearance measured at thrust side just below oil ring is as follows:

K-141, K-160,
K-161, K-181,
KV-181 . . . . . . . . . . . . . . 0.006-0.0075 in. (0.1524-0.1905 mm)
K-241 . . . . . . . . . . . . . . 0.0075-0.0085 in. (0.1905-0.2159 mm)
K-301 . . . . . . . . . . . . . . 0.0065-0.0095 in. (0.1651-0.2413 mm)
K-321,
K-341 . . . . . . . . . . . . . . . . 0.007-0.010 in. (0.1778-0.254 mm)

Minimum piston diameters measured just below oil ring 90° from piston pin are as follows:

K-141*
K-160
K-161* . . . . . . . . . . . . . . . . . . . 2.866 in. (72.7964 mm)
K-181
K-141**
K-161**
KV-181 . . . . . . . . . . . . . . . . . . 2.9275 in. (74.3585 mm)
K-241 . . . . . . . . . . . . . . . . . . . 3.2400 in. (82.296 mm)
K-301 . . . . . . . . . . . . . . . . . . . 3.3640 in. (85.4456 mm)
K-321 . . . . . . . . . . . . . . . . . . . 3.4885 in. (88.6079 mm)
K-341 . . . . . . . . . . . . . . . . . . . 3.7385 in. (94.9579 mm)

*Designates early production (before 1970) engines.

**Designates late production (after 1970) engines.

Renew any piston which does not meet specifications.

Kohler recommends piston rings always be renewed whenever they are removed. Piston ring specifications are as follows:

Ring end gap,
K-141, K-160,
K-161, K-181,
KV-181 . . . . . . . . . . . . . 0.007-0.017 in. (0.1778-0.4318 mm)
K-241, K-301,
K-321, K-341 . . . . . . . . 0.010-0.020 in. (0.254-0.508 mm)
Ring side clearance (compression rings),
K-141, K-160,
K-161, K-181,
KV-181 . . . . . . . . . . . . 0.0025-0.004 in. (0.0635-0.1016 mm)
Ring side clearance (oil control ring),
K-141, K-160,
K-161, K-181,
KV-181 . . . . . . . . . . . . 0.001-0.0025 in. (0.0254-0.0635 mm)
K-241, K-301,
K-321, K-341 . . . . . . . . 0.001-0.003 in. (0.0254-0.0762 mm)

If compression ring has a groove or bevel on outside surface, install ring with groove or bevel down. If groove or bevel is on inside surface of compression ring, install ring with groove or bevel up. Oil control ring can be installed either side up.

**CYLINDER BLOCK.** If cylinder wall is scored or bore is tapered more than 0.0025 inch (0.0635 mm) on Models K-141, K-160, K-161, K-181 and KV-181 or 0.0015 inch (0.0381 mm) on Models K-241, K-301, K-321 and K-341, or out-of-round more than 0.005 inch (0.1270 mm), cylinder should be honed to nearest suitable oversize of 0.010, 0.020 or 0.030 inch (0.254, 0.508 or 0.762 mm) for which piston and rings are available.

Standard cylinder bore diameters are as follows:

K-141*
K-160
K-161* . . . . . . . . . . . . . . . . . . . . 2.875 in. (73.025 mm)
K-141**
K-161**
K-181
KV-181 . . . . . . . . . . . . . . . . . . 2.9375 in. (74.613 mm)
K-241 . . . . . . . . . . . . . . . . . . . . 3.251 in. (82.58 mm)
K-301 . . . . . . . . . . . . . . . . . . . . 3.375 in. (85.725 mm)
K-321 . . . . . . . . . . . . . . . . . . . . 3.500 in. (88.90 mm)
K-341 . . . . . . . . . . . . . . . . . . . . 3.750 in. (95.725 mm)

*Designates early production (before 1970) engines.
**Designates late production (after 1970) engines.

**CYLINDER HEAD.** Always use a new gasket when installing cylinder head. Cylinder head should be checked for warpage by placing cleaned head on flat surface. If clearance between head and plate exceeds 0.003 inch (0.0762 mm) when checked with feeler gage, renew head. Tighten cylinder head cap screws evenly and in steps using correct sequence shown in Fig. KO24, KO25 or KO25A.

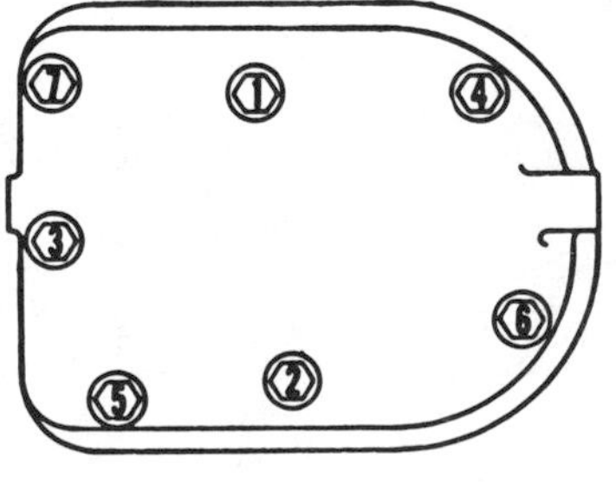


*Fig. KO24—On K-141, K-160, K-161, K-181 and KV-181 models, tighten cylinder head cap screws evenly, in sequence shown, to 15-20 ft.-lbs. (20-27 N·m) torque.*



Illustrations courtesy Kohler Co.

**CRANKSHAFT.** Crankshaft on standard K-141 engine is supported by ball bearing in crankcase at pto end of shaft and a bushing type bearing in bearing plate at flywheel end. Model KV-181 has a roller bearing at flywheel end of crankshaft and a ball bearing at opposite end. Crankshaft on all other models is supported in two ball bearings.

On Model K-141 engine with bushing type main bearing, renew crankshaft and/or bearing plate if crankshaft journal and bearing are excessively worn or scored. Recommended crankshaft journal to bushing running clearance is 0.001-0.0025 inch (0.0254-0.0635 mm).

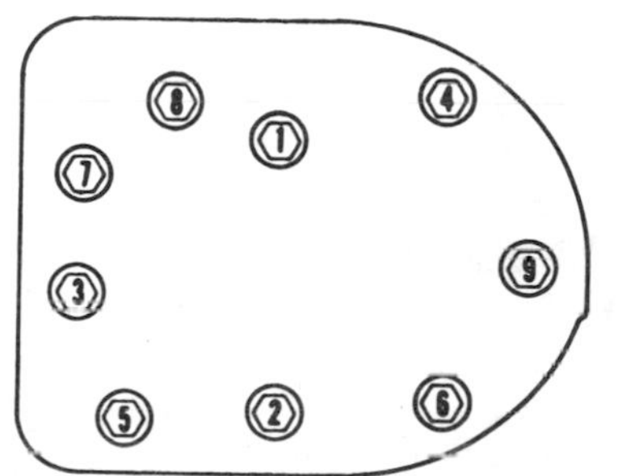

Fig. KO25—On K-241, K-301 and K-321 models, tighten cylinder head cap screws evenly, in sequence shown, to 25-30 ft.-lbs. (34-41 N·m) torque.

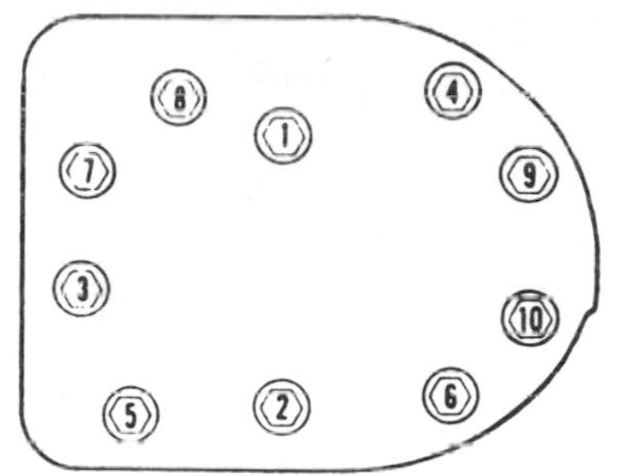

Fig. KO25A—On K-341 models, tighten cylinder head cap screws evenly, in sequence shown, to 25-30 ft.-lbs. (34-41 N·m) torque.

On all models, renew ball bearing type mains if excessively loose or rough. Crankshaft end play should be 0.003-0.028 inch (0.0762-0.7112 mm) on KV-181 models, 0.003-0.020 inch (0.0762-0.508 mm) on K-241, K-301, K-321 and K-341 models, and 0.002-0.023 inch (0.0508-0.5842 mm) on all other models. End play is controlled by thickness of bearing plate gaskets. Gaskets are available in thicknesses of 0.010 and 0.020 inch. Install ball bearing mains with sealed side towards crankpin.

Crankpin journal may be reground to 0.010 inch (0.254 mm) undersize for use of undersize connecting rod if journal is scored or out-of-round. Standard crankpin diameter is 1.1855-1.1860 inch (30.1117-30.1244 mm) on Models K-141, K-160, K-161, K-181 and KV-181 and 1.4995-1.500 inch (38.0873-38.10 mm) on Models K-241, K-301, K-321 and K-341.

When installing crankshaft, align timing marks on crankshaft and camshaft gear as shown in Fig. KO26.

**NOTE: On Models K-241, K-301, K-321 and K-341 equipped with dynamic balancer, refer to DYNAMIC BALANCER paragraph for installation and timing of balancer gears.**

On all models, Kohler recommends crankshaft seals be installed in crankcase and bearing plate after crankshaft and bearing plate are installed. Carefully work oil seals over crankshaft and drive seals into place with hollow driver that contacts outer edge of seals.

**CAMSHAFT.** The hollow camshaft and integral camshaft gear turn on a pin that is a slip fit in flywheel side of crankcase and a drive fit in closed side of crankcase. Remove and install pin from open side (bearing plate side) of crankcase. Desired camshaft to pin running clearance is 0.0005-0.003 inch (0.0127-0.0762 mm) on Models K-141, K-160, K-161, K-181 and KV-181 and 0.001-0.0035 inch (0.0254-0.0889 mm) on all other models. Desired camshaft end play of 0.005-0.010 inch (0.1270-0.254 mm) is controlled by use of 0.005 and 0.010 inch thick spacer washers between camshaft and cylinder block at bearing plate side of crankcase.

On early models, ignition spark advance weights, springs and weight pivot pins are renewable separately from camshaft gear. When reinstalling camshaft in engine, be sure breaker cam is cor-

Fig. KO27—Views showing operation of camshaft with automatic compression release. In view 1, spring (C) has moved control lever (D) which moves cam lever (B) upward so tang (T) is above exhaust cam lobe. This tang holds exhaust valve open slightly on a portion of compression stroke to relieve compression while cranking engine. At engine speeds of 650 rpm or more, centrifugal force moves control lever (D) outward allowing tang (T) to move below lobe surface as shown in view 2.

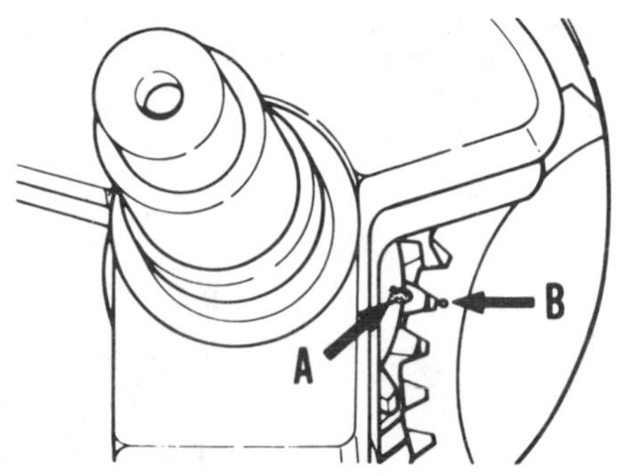



Fig. KO26—When installing crankshaft, make certain timing mark (A) on crankshaft is aligned with timing mark (B) on camshaft gear.

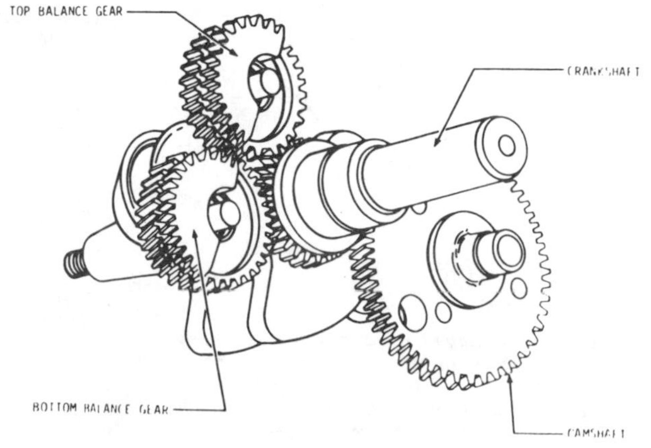



Fig. KO28—View showing components of dynamic balancer system used on all K-321 and K-341 models and some K-241 and K-301 models.

rectly installed. Spread springs as shown in Fig. KO12 and install breaker cam on tangs of flyweights with timing mark on cam and camshaft gear aligned.

Late production camshafts do not have automatic timing advance mechanism shown in Fig. KO12, but are equipped with automatic compression release mechanism shown in Fig. KO27. The automatic compression release mechanism holds exhaust valve slightly open during first part of compression stroke, reducing compression pressure and allowing easier cranking of engine. Refer to Fig. KO27 for operational details. At speeds above 650 engine rpm, compression release mechanism is inactive. Service procedures remain the same as for early production camshaft units except for the difference in timing advance and compression release mechanisms. Service kits are available for adding automatic compression release to early production engines.

To check compression on engine equipped with automatic compression release, engine must be cranked at 650 rpm or higher to overcome compression release action. A reading can also be obtained by rotating flywheel in reverse direction with throttle wide open. Compression reading should be 110-120 psi (758-827kPa) on an engine in top mechanical condition. When compression reading falls below 100 psi (689 kPa), it indicates leaking rings or valves.

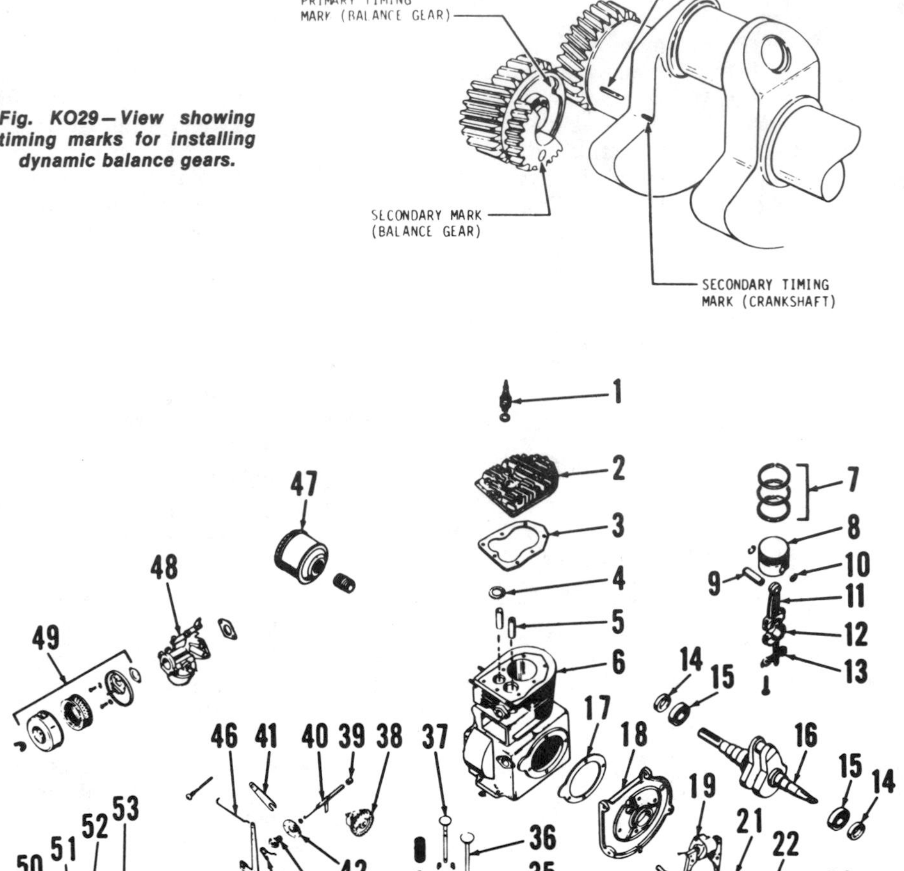

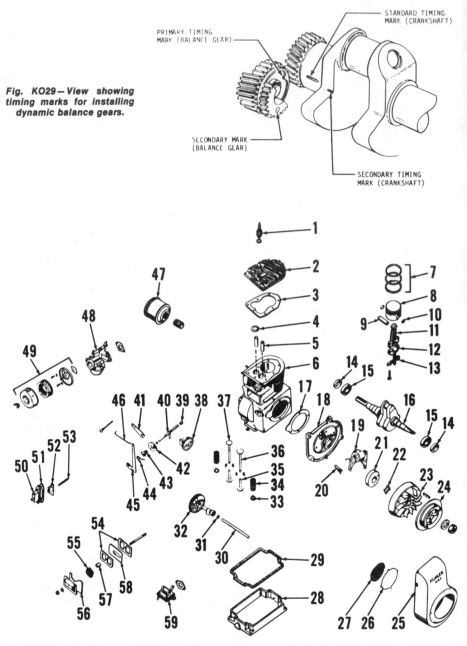

**Fig. KO29—View showing timing marks for installing dynamic balance gears.**

11/16" NOMINAL - PRESS DEPTH .735"
STUB SHAFT
ABOVE MAIN BEARING BOSS
STUB SHAFT BOSS
7/16"
IF SHAFT PROTRUDES ABOUT 11/16" ABOVE STUB SHAFT BOSS, DO NOT USE 3/8" SPACER

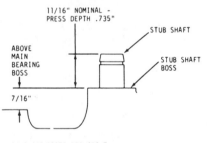

**Fig. KO28A—If stub shaft boss is approximately 7/16-inch (10.113 mm) above main bearing boss, press new shaft in until it is 0.735 inch (18.669 mm) above stub shaft boss.**

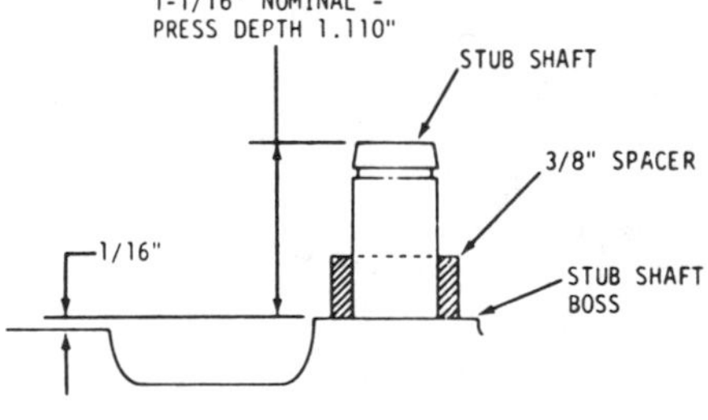


**Fig. KO28B—If stub shaft boss is approximately 1/16-inch (1.588 mm) above main bearing boss, press new shaft in until it is 1.110 inch (28.194 mm) above stub shaft boss and use a 3/8-inch spacer between block and gear.**

**Fig. KO30—Exploded view of K-181 model basic engine assembly. Models K-141, K-160 and K-161 are similar. Standard K-141 engine is equipped with a bushing type main bearing in bearing plate (18).**

1. Spark plug
2. Cylinder head
3. Head gasket
4. Exhaust valve seat
5. Valve guide
6. Cylinder block
7. Piston rings
8. Piston
9. Piston pin
10. Retaining rings
11. Connecting rod
12. Rod cap
13. Rod bolt lock
14. Oil seal
15. Ball bearing
16. Crankshaft
17. Gasket
18. Bearing plate
19. Magneto
20. Condenser
21. Magneto rotor
22. Wave washer
23. Flywheel
24. Pulley
25. Shroud
26. Screen retainer
27. Screen
28. Oil pan
29. Gasket
30. Camshaft pin
31. Shim washer
32. Camshaft
33. Spring retainer
34. Valve spring
35. Valve tappet
36. Intake valve
37. Exhaust valve
38. Governor gear & weight assy.
39. Needle bearing
40. Governor shaft
41. Bracket
42. Speed disc
43. Bushing
44. Governor spring
45. Governor lever
46. Link
47. Muffler
48. Carburetor
49. Air cleaner assy.
50. Breaker cover
51. Gasket
52. Breaker points
53. Push rod
54. Gaskets
55. Filter
56. Valve cover
57. Breather seal
58. Reed plate
59. Fuel pump



Illustrations courtesy Kohler Co.

**VALVE SYSTEM.** Valve tappet gap (cold) is as follows:

Models K-241, K-301, K-321 and K-341
- Intake . . . . . . . . . . . . . 0.008-0.010 in. (0.2032-0.254 mm)
- Exhaust . . . . . . . . . . . 0.017-0.020 in. (0.4318-0.508 mm)

Models K-141, K-160, K-161, K-181 and KV-181
- Intake . . . . . . . . . . . . . 0.006-0.008 in. (0.1524-0.2032 mm)
- Exhaust . . . . . . . . . . . 0.015-0.017 in. (0.3810-0.4318 mm)

Correct valve tappet gap is obtained by grinding ends of valve stems on Models K-141, K-160, K-161, K-181 and KV-181. Be sure to grind end square and remove all burrs from end of stem after grinding. Models K-241, K-301, K-321 and K-341 have adjustable tappets.

The exhaust valve seats on a renewable seat inset on all models. Intake valve seats directly on a machined seat in cylinder block on some models. On all Models K-321 and K-341 engines and some other models, a renewable intake valve seat insert is used. Valve face and seat angle is 45°. Desired seat width is 1/32 to 1/16-inch (0.794 to 1.588 mm).

Renewable valve guides are used on all models. Intake valve stem to guide clearance should be 0.001-0.0025 inch (0.0254-0.0635 mm) and exhaust valve stem to guide clearance should be 0.0025-0.004 inch (0.0635-0.1016 mm) on all models. Ream valve guides after installation to obtain correct inside diameter of 0.312-0.313 inch (7.9248-7.9502 mm).

**DYNAMIC BALANCER.** A dynamic balance system (Fig. KO28) is used on some K-241 and K-301 engines and on all K-321 and K-341 engines. The two balance gears, equipped with needle bearings, rotate on two stub shafts which are pressed into bosses on pto side of crankcase. Snap rings secure gears on stub shafts and shim spacers are used to control gear end play. Balance gears are driven by crankshaft in opposite direction of crankshaft rotation. Use following procedure to install and time dynamic balancer components.

To renew stub shafts, press old shafts out and discard. If stub shaft boss is approximately 7/16-inch (10.113 mm) above main bearing boss (see Fig. KO28A), press new shaft in until it is 0.735 inch (18.669 mm) above stub shaft boss. On blocks where stub shaft boss is approximately 1/16-inch (1.588 mm) above main bearing boss (Fig. KO28B), press new shaft in until it is 1.110 inch (27.19 mm) above stub shaft boss and use a 3/8-inch (9.525 mm) spacer between block and gear.

To install top balance gear-bearing assembly, first place one 0.010 inch shim on stub shaft, install top gear assembly on shaft making certain timing marks are facing flywheel side of crankcase. Install one 0.005 inch, one 0.010 inch and one 0.020 inch shim spacers in this order and install snap ring. Using a feeler gage, check gear end play. Proper end play of balance gear is 0.005-0.010 inch.

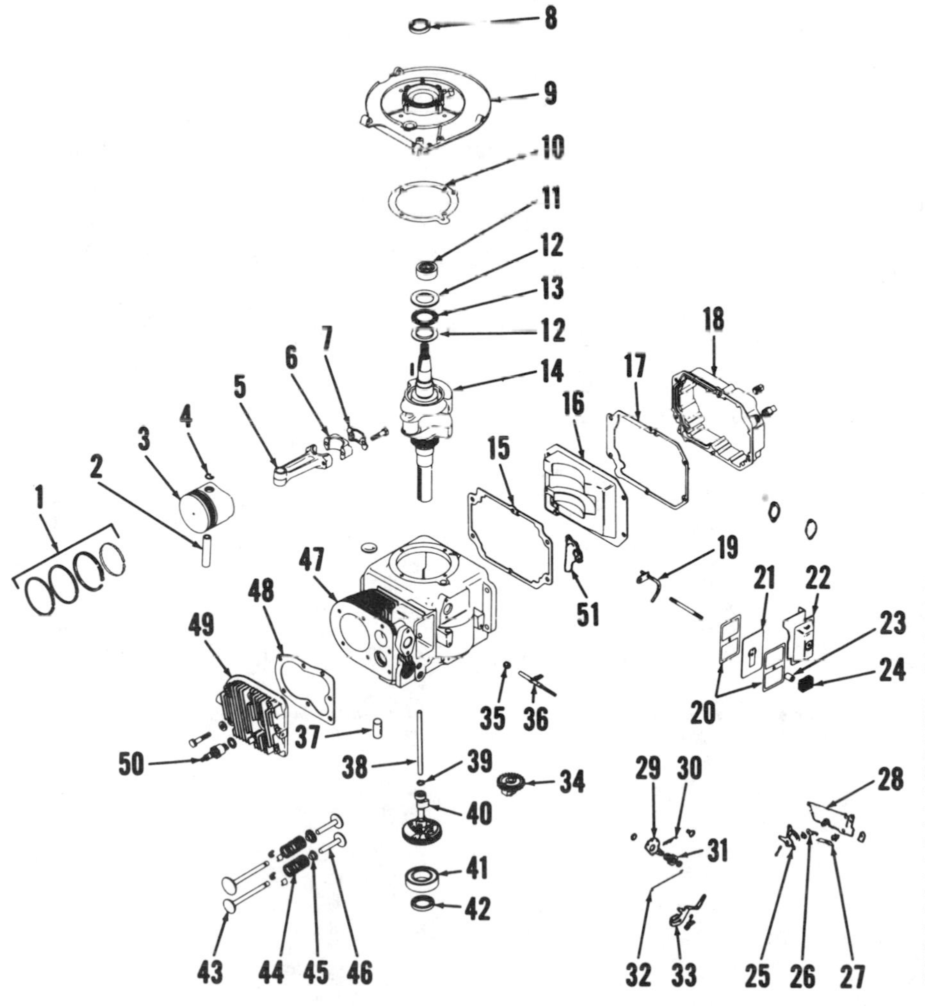

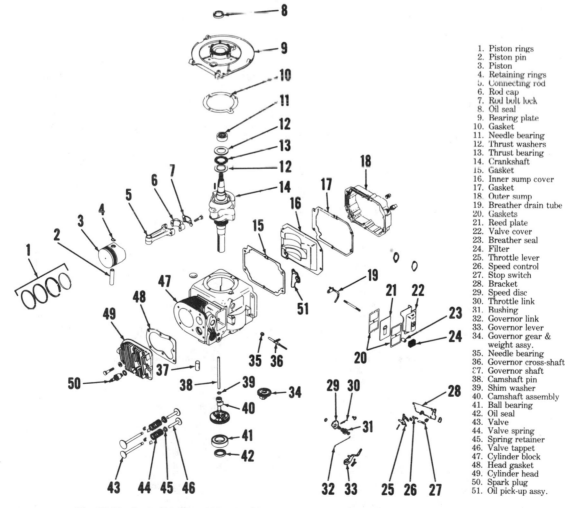

1. Piston rings
2. Piston pin
3. Piston
4. Retaining rings
5. Connecting rod
6. Rod cap
7. Rod bolt lock
8. Oil seal
9. Bearing plate
10. Gasket
11. Needle bearing
12. Thrust washers
13. Thrust bearing
14. Crankshaft
15. Gasket
16. Inner sump cover
17. Gasket
18. Outer sump
19. Breather drain tube
20. Gaskets
21. Reed plate
22. Valve cover
23. Breather seal
24. Filter
25. Throttle lever
26. Speed control
27. Stop switch
28. Bracket
29. Speed disc
30. Throttle link
31. Bushing
32. Governor link
33. Governor lever
34. Governor gear & weight assy.
35. Needle bearing
36. Governor cross-shaft
37. Governor shaft
38. Camshaft pin
39. Shim washer
40. Camshaft assembly
41. Ball bearing
42. Oil seal
43. Valve
44. Valve spring
45. Spring retainer
46. Valve tappet
47. Cylinder block
48. Head gasket
49. Cylinder head
50. Spark plug
51. Oil pick-up assy.

*Fig. KO31 – Exploded view of KV-181 model basic engine assembly.*

Illustrations courtesy Kohler Co.

Add or remove 0.005 inch thick spacers as necessary to obtain correct end play.

**NOTE: Always install the 0.020 inch thick spacer next to snap ring.**

Install crankshaft in crankcase and align primary timing mark on top balance gear with standard timing mark on crankshaft. See Fig. KO29. With primary timing marks aligned, engage crankshaft gear 1/16-inch into narrow section of top balance gear and rotate crankshaft to align timing marks on camshaft gear and crankshaft as shown in Fig. KO26. Press crankshaft into crankcase until it is seated firmly into ball bearing main.

Rotate crankshaft until crankpin is approximately 15° past bottom dead center. Install one 0.010 inch shim on stub shaft, align secondary timing mark on bottom balance gear with secondary timing mark on crankshaft counterweight. See Fig. KO29. Install gear assembly onto stub shaft. If properly timed, secondary timing mark on bottom balance gear will be aligned with standard timing mark on crankshaft after gear is fully on stub shaft. Install one 0.005 inch and one 0.020 inch shim, then install snap ring. Check bottom balance gear end play and add or remove 0.005 inch thick spacers as required to obtain proper end play of 0.005-0.010 inch. Make certain the 0.020 inch shim is used against the snap ring.

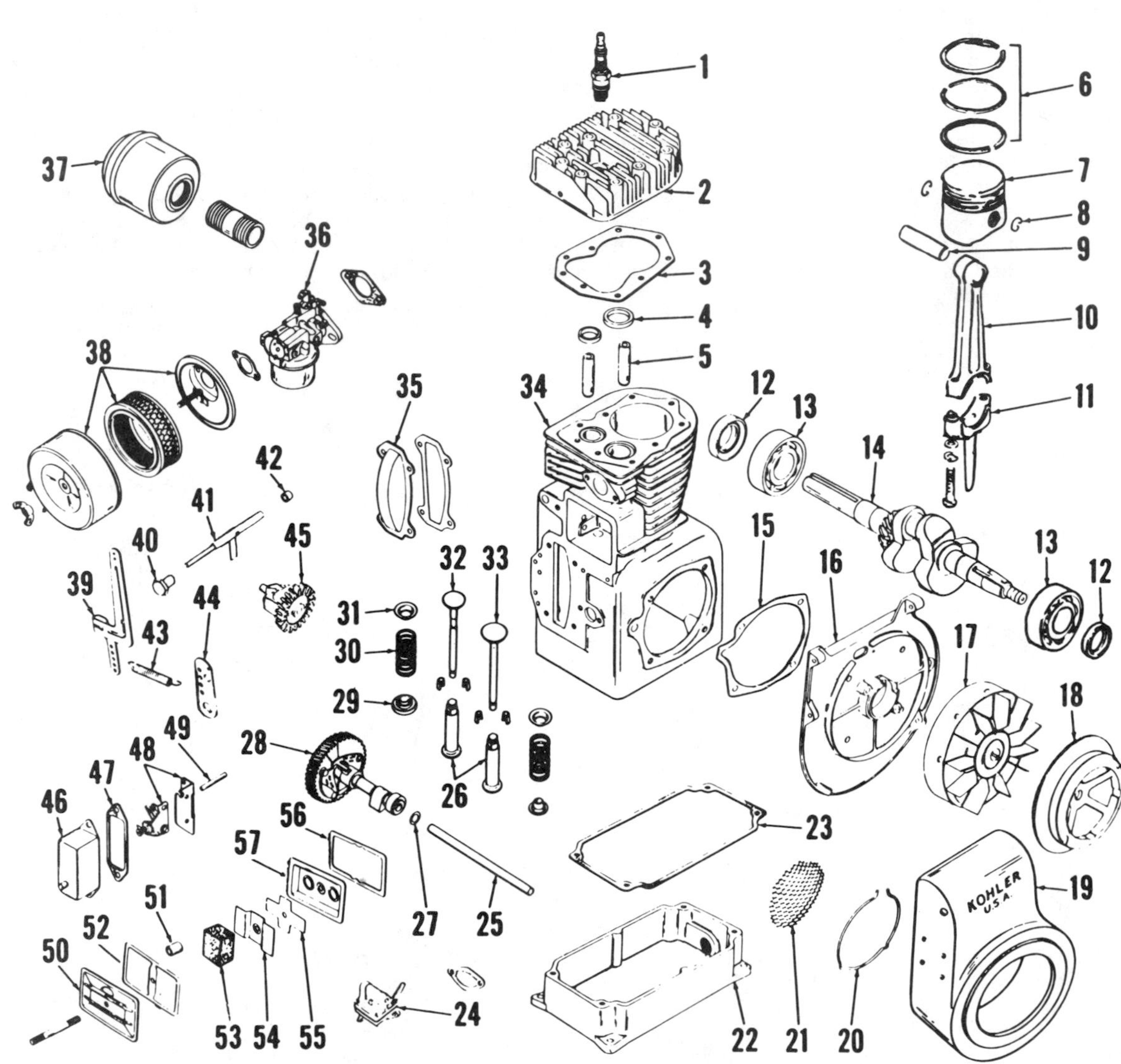


*Fig. KO32 – Exploded view of K-241 or K-301 basic engine assembly. Models K-321 and K-341 are similar. Refer to Fig. KO28 for dynamic balancer used on all K-321 and K-301 models.*

1. Spark plug
2. Cylinder head
3. Head gasket
4. Valve seat insert
5. Valve guide
6. Piston rings
7. Piston
8. Retaining rings
9. Piston pin
10. Connecting rod
11. Rod cap
12. Oil seal
13. Ball bearing
14. Crankshaft
15. Gasket
16. Bearing plate
17. Flywheel
18. Pulley
19. Shroud
20. Screen retainer
21. Screen
22. Oil pan
23. Gasket
24. Fuel pump
25. Camshaft pin
26. Valve tappets
27. Shim washer
28. Camshaft
29. Valve rotator
30. Valve spring
31. Spring retainer
32. Exhaust valve
33. Intake valve
34. Cylinder block
35. Camshaft cover
36. Carburetor
37. Muffler
38. Air cleaner assy.
39. Governor lever
40. Bushing
41. Governor shaft
42. Needle bearing
43. Governor spring
44. Speed lever
45. Governor gear & weight unit
46. Breaker cover
47. Gasket
48. Breaker point assy.
49. Push rod
50. Valve cover
51. Breather seal
52. Gasket
53. Filter
54. Baffle
55. Reed
56. Gasket
57. Breather plate

# KOHLER

**KOHLER COMPANY**
**Kohler, Wisconsin 53044**

| Model | No. Cyls | Bore | Stroke | Displacement | Power Rating |
|---|---|---|---|---|---|
| K-330, K-331 | 1 | 3.625 in. (92.08 mm) | 3.25 in. (82.55 mm) | 33.6 cu. in. (549.7 cc) | 12.5 hp (9.32 kW) |

Model K-330 and K-331 are one cylinder, four-stroke, horizontal shaft engines in which crankshaft is supported by ball bearing type main bearings.

Connecting rod bearings are renewable insert type and lubrication is provided by a full pressure system with a gear type oil pump.

Either a battery or a magneto ignition system with externally located points and automatic spark advance is used.

Fuel is supplied by a diaphragm type pump which is driven off of a lobe on camshaft. Carter side draft type carburetor is used on both models.

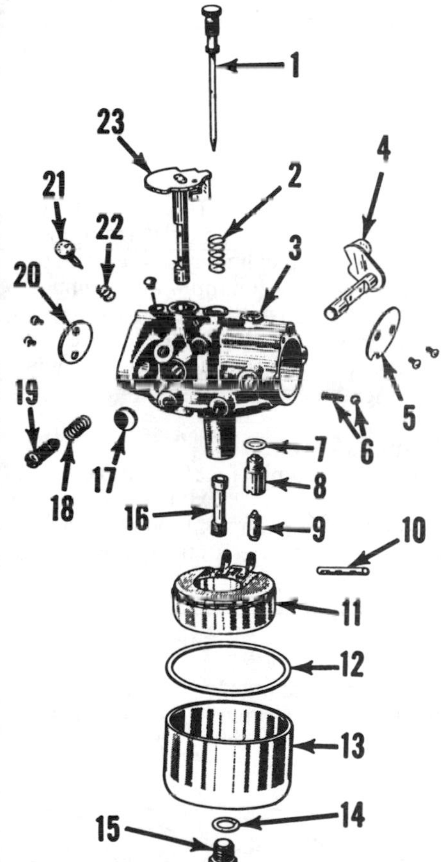


*Fig. KO35 – Exploded view of typical Carter "N" model carburetor. Refer to Fig. KO36 for location of idle fuel adjustment needle on K-330 and K-331 models.*

1. Main fuel needle
2. Spring
3. Carburetor body
4. Choke shaft
5. Choke disc
6. Choke detent
7. Sealing washer
8. Inlet valve seat
9. Inlet valve
10. Float pin
11. Float
12. Gasket
13. Float bowl
14. Sealing washer
15. Bowl retainer
16. Main jet
17. Plug
18. Spring
19. Idle stop screw
20. Throttle disc
21. Idle fuel needle
22. Spring
23. Throttle shaft

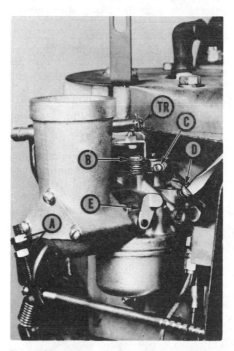

## MAINTENANCE

**SPARK PLUG.** Recommended spark plug is Champion J8C or equivalent. Electrode gap should be 0.025 inch (0.635 mm).

**CARBURETOR.** Refer to Fig. KO35 for exploded view of Carter "N" model carburetor similar to that used on Model K-330 and K-331 engines.

For initial adjustment, open idle fuel needle 1-1/2 turns and open main fuel needle 2 turns. Make final adjustment with engine running and at operating temperature. Place engine under load and adjust main fuel needle for leanest setting that will allow satisfactory acceleration and steady governor operation. Set engine at idle speed, no load and adjust idle mixture screw for smoothest idle operation. As each adjustment affects the other, adjustment procedure may have to be repeated.

*Fig. KO36 – View of carburetor adjustment points and variable speed governor linkage.*

A. Sensitivity adjustment
B. Main fuel needle
C. Idle stop screw
D. Idle fuel needle
E. Choke lever
TR. Throttle rod

To check float level, invert carburetor casting and float assembly. There should be 13/64-inch (5.159 mm) clearance between free side of float and machined surface of body casting. If not, carefully bend float lever tang that contacts inlet valve to provide correct float level measurement.

**GOVERNOR.** Maximum no-load speed is 3600 rpm. The governed speed is controlled by throttle position, but length of carburetor throttle rod (TR-Fig. KO36) must be such that it matches travel of governor arm to which it is attached at one end. Excessive speed drop or surging is controlled by nuts (A).

Engine speed governor weights are mounted on a separate governor gear as shown in Fig. KO37. Governor gear has a 0.0005-0.0015 inch (0.0127-0.0381 mm) interference fit on governor shaft.

**MAGNETO AND TIMING.** Either a Bendix-Scintilla crankshaft type magneto or a flywheel type Phelon (Repco) magneto is used.

The externally located breaker contacts (Fig. KO38) are operated by a push rod actuated by a removable cam located in and driven by separate flyweight governor in gear end of camshaft as

*Fig. KO37 – View showing governor gear and flyweight assembly (B) removed from engine. Governor yoke is shown at (A).*

Illustrations courtesy Kohler Co.

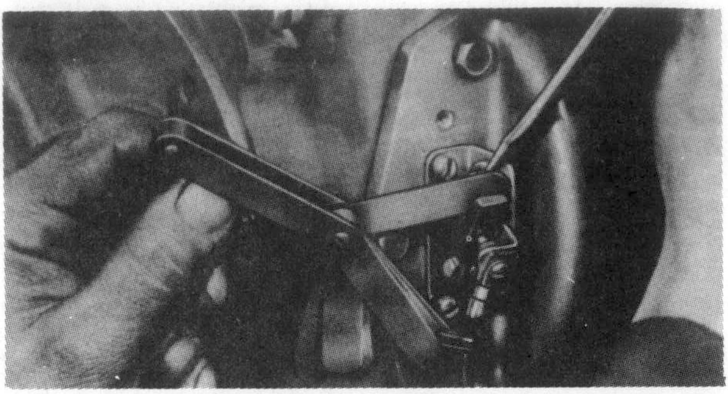

Fig. KO38—Ignition breaker points are located externally on engine crankcase for either magneto or battery ignition.

shown in Fig. KO39. This governor varies angular position of breaker cam in accordance with engine speed to provide automatic advance of ignition timing. Note assembly marks "A" and "B" must be in register when assembling breaker cam to governor.

A timing inspection port is provided in bearing plate and there are two timing marks on flywheel. Satisfactory timing is obtained by adjusting breaker contact gap to 0.018-0.020 inch (0.457-0.508 mm). For precision timing, use a timing light and adjust breaker gap until the first or "SP" timing mark is centered in inspection port with engine running at high idle speed.

**BATTERY IGNITION.** Battery ignition is generally used on electric starting engines. An automotive type Delco-Remy coil and condenser are used with this system. However, since breaker points and adjustments are the same as magneto ignition, refer to previous paragraph for adjustment procedure.

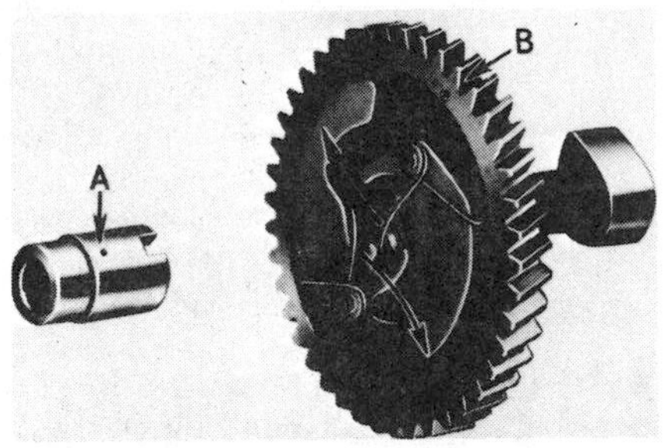


Fig. KO39—View showing alignment marks on ignition breaker cam and camshaft gear. Spread springs as indicated by arrows and insert cam on drive tangs of weights.

**LUBRICATION.** Engine is pressure lubricated by a gear type oil pump. High quality detergent type oil having API classification "SF" or "SG" should be used. Use SAE 30 oil in temperatures above 32° F (0° C), SAE 10W oil in temperatures between 32° F (0° C) and 0°F (-18°C) and SAE 5W oil in below 0°F (-18°C) temperatures. Maintain oil level at full mark on dipstick, but do not overfill.

**CRANKCASE BREATHER.** A reed valve assembly is located in valve spring compartment to maintain a partial vacuum in crankcase and thus reduce leakage of oil at bearing seals. If a slight amount of crankcase vacuum is not present, reed valve is faulty or engine has excessive blow-by past rings and/or valves.

**AIR CLEANER.** Engines may be equipped with either an oil bath type air cleaner shown in Fig. KO40 or a dry element type shown in Fig. KO41.

Oil bath air cleaner should be serviced every 25 hours of normal operation or more often if operating in extremely dusty conditions. To service oil bath type, remove complete cleaner assembly from engine. Remove cover and element from bowl. Empty used oil from bowl, then clean cover and bowl in solvent. Clean element in solvent and allow to drip dry. Lightly re-oil element. Fill bowl using same grade and weight oil as used in engine crankcase. Renew gaskets as necessary when reassembling and reinstalling unit.

Dry element type air cleaner should be cleaned every 100 hours of normal operation or more frequently if operating in dusty conditions. Remove dry element and tap element lightly on a flat surface to remove surface dirt. Do not wash element or attempt to clean element with compressed air. Renew element if extremely dirty or if it is bent, crushed or otherwise damaged. Make certain sealing surfaces of element seal effectively against back plate and cover.

## REPAIRS

**TIGHTENING TORQUES.** Recommended tightening torque values with threads lightly lubricated are as follows:

| | |
|---|---|
| Spark plug | 22 ft.-lbs. (30 N·m) |
| Connecting rod | See CONNECTING ROD paragraph |
| Cylinder head | 40 ft.-lbs. (54 N·m) |
| Flywheel nut | 100 ft.-lbs. (136 N·m) |

**CONNECTING ROD.** Connecting rod and piston unit is removed from above after removing cylinder head and oil pan (engine base). Aluminum alloy connecting rod is fitted with renewable crankpin bearing inserts, but rides directly on piston pin. Refer to the following specifications:

Desired clearances–

| | |
|---|---|
| Rod to crankpin | 0.0003-0.0023 in. (0.0076-0.0584 mm) |
| Rod to piston pin | 0.0003-0.0008 in. (0.0076-0.0203 mm) |
| Rod side play on crankpin | 0.007-0.011 in. (0.178-0.279 mm) |

Crankpin diameter is 1.873 inches (47.68 mm). Crankpin bearing inserts

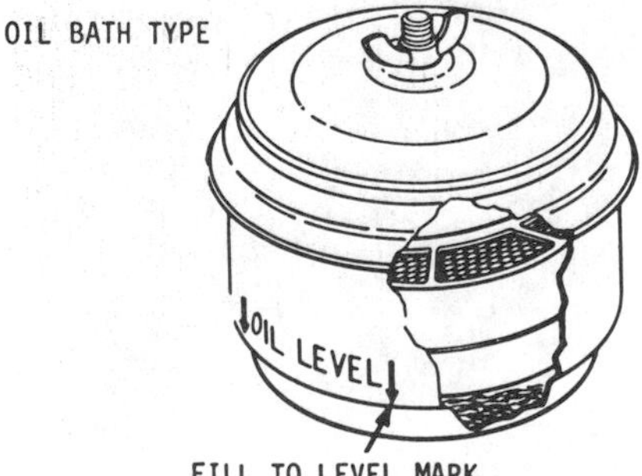


Fig. KO40—View of oil bath type air cleaner.

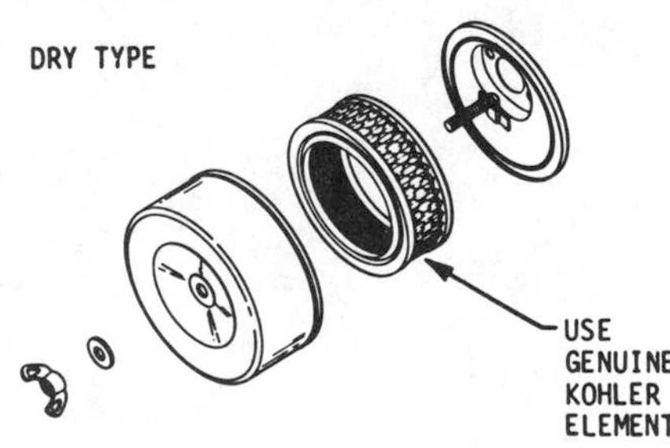


Fig. KO41—Exploded view of dry element type air cleaner.

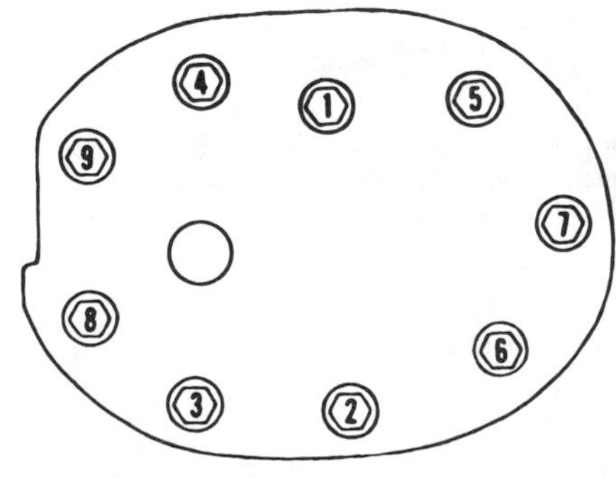


Fig. KO42—Tighten cylinder head cap screws evenly to 40 ft.-lbs. (54 N·m) torque using sequence shown.



Illustrations courtesy Kohler Co.

for connecting rod are available for 0.002, 0.010 and 0.020 inch (0.0508, 0.0254 and 0.508 mm) undersize crankshaft as well as standard size. If crankpin is only moderately worn, 0.002 inch (0.0508 mm) oversize bearing inserts can be installed. If crankpin is excessively worn, out-of-round or scored, crankpin can be reground for use with 0.010 or 0.020 inch (0.254 or 0.508 mm) oversize bearing inserts. Piston pin is available in standard size and 0.005 inch (0.127 mm) oversize.

When reinstalling piston and connecting rod assembly, piston may be installed either way on connecting rod; but match marks on connecting rod and cap must be aligned and be installed towards flywheel side of engine. Tighten connecting rod cap screws to a torque of 40 ft.-lbs. (54 N·m), then loosen cap screws and re-tighten to a torque of 35 ft.-lbs. (48 N·m).

**PISTON, PIN AND RINGS.** Two 3/32-inch (2.381 mm) compression rings and one 3/16-inch (4.763 mm) oil control ring are fitted with end gap limits of 0.007-0.017 inch (0.178-0.432 mm). Side clearance of compression rings in grooves should be 0.0025-0.0045 inch (0.0635-0.1143 mm); side clearance of oil ring 0.002-0.0035 inch (0.0508-0.0889 mm). Rings of 0.010, 0.020 and 0.030 inch (0.254, 0.508 and 0.762 mm) oversize are available.

The floating piston pin is retained in piston by a snap ring at each end. Recommended clearance of pin in unbushed aluminum rod is 0.0003-0.0008 inch (0.0076-0.0203 mm); in piston bosses, 0.0001-0.0003 inch (0.0025-0.0076 mm). Oversize pin is available.

Aluminum alloy piston should have a clearance of 0.0005-0.0015 inch (0.0127-0.0381 mm) in cylinder bore measured at top of skirt thrust face below oil ring. Reject piston if a new piston ring has 0.005 inch (0.127 mm) or more side clearance in top ring groove. Pistons of 0.010, 0.020 and 0.030 inch (0.254, 0.508 and 0.762 mm) oversize as well as standard size are available.

**CYLINDER HEAD.** Always use new head gasket when installing cylinder head. Tighten cylinder head cap screws evenly to a torque of 40 ft.-lbs. (54 N·m) using sequence shown in Fig. KO42.

**CYLINDER BLOCK.** If walls are scored or bore is tapered or out-of-round more than 0.005 inch (0.127 mm), cylinder should be resized to nearest suitable oversize of 0.010, 0.020 or 0.030 inch (0.254, 0.508 or 0.762 mm). Standard cylinder bore diameter is 3.625 inches (92.075 mm).

**CAMSHAFT ASSEMBLY.** Camshaft and gear assembly should have 0.001-0.0025 inch (0.0254-0.0635 mm) running clearance on camshaft support pin. Similar clearance should exist between breaker cam and camshaft pin. Desired camshaft end play of 0.005-0.010 inch (0.127-0.254 mm) is controlled by spacer washers (44-Fig. KO44) which are available in a variety of thicknesses. Ignition advance cam weights are mounted on face of cam gear. Check weights to make sure they work freely through their full travel. Ignition breaker cam should be installed with mark (A-Fig. KO39) in register with mark (B) on cam gear.

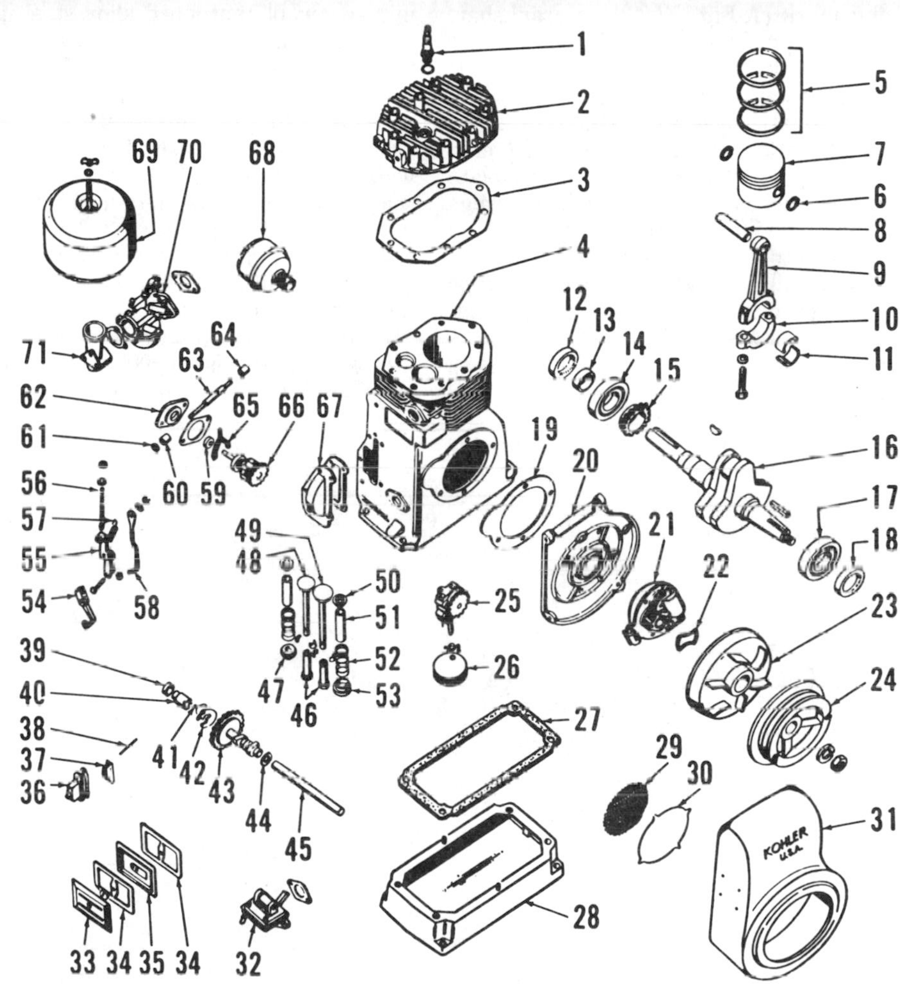

*Fig. KO44—Exploded view of K-330 or K-331 basic engine assembly.*

1. Spark plug
2. Cylinder head
3. Head gasket
4. Cylinder block
5. Piston rings
6. Retaining rings
7. Piston
8. Piston pin
9. Connecting rod
10. Rod cap
11. Rod bearing
12. Oil seal
13. Oil transfer tube
14. Ball bearing
15. Crankshaft gear
16. Crankshaft
17. Ball bearing
18. Oil seal
19. Gasket
20. Bearing plate
21. Magneto
22. Wave washer
23. Flywheel
24. Pulley
25. Oil pump
26. Oil strainer
27. Gasket
28. Oil pan
29. Screen
30. Screen retainer
31. Shroud
32. Fuel pump
33. Valve cover
34. Gaskets
35. Breather plate
36. Breaker cover
37. Breaker points
38. Push rod
39. Spacer
40. Breaker cam
41. Advance spring
42. Advance weight
43. Camshaft
44. Shim spacer
45. Camshaft pin
46. Valve tappets
47. Valve rotator
48. Exhaust valve
49. Intake valve
50. Spring seat
51. Valve guide
52. Valve spring
53. Spring retainer
54. Throttle arm
55. Control arm
56. Link
57. Governor spring
58. Throttle extension
59. Bushing
60. Needle bearing
61. Oil seal
62. Governor cover
63. Governor shaft
64. Needle bearing
65. Yoke
66. Governor gear & weight unit
67. Camshaft cover
68. Muffler
69. Air cleaner
70. Carburetor
71. Air intake elbow

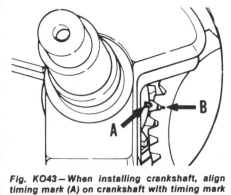

*Fig. KO43—When installing crankshaft, align timing mark (A) on crankshaft with timing mark (B) on camshaft gear.*

Illustrations courtesy Kohler Co.

Camshaft pin is a slip fit in open (flywheel) side of crankcase and a press fit in closed (pto) side of crankcase. Remove and install pin from open side of crankcase.

**CRANKSHAFT.** Crankshaft is supported in two ball bearing mains. Crankshaft end play should be 0.003-0.008 inch (0.076-0.203 mm) on pump models and 0.005-0.011 inch (0.127-0.279 mm) on other engines. End play is controlled by thickness of gasket used between crankcase and bearing plate (closure plate). Gaskets are available in a variety of thicknesses.

When installing crankshaft, align timing mark (A-Fig. KO43) on crankshaft with mark (B) on camshaft gear.

Crankshaft gear (15-Fig. KO44) should have an interference fit of 0.001-0.0015 inch (0.0254-0.0381 mm) on crankshaft. Install crankshaft main bearings in crankcase and bearing plate with shielded side of ball bearings toward inside of crankcase. Install oil seals with lips to inside of crankcase. Use a tapered protective sleeve or tape over crankshaft keyways to prevent damage to seals.

Oil transfer sleeve (13-Fig. KO44) is a press fit in crankcase between oil seal (12) and main bearing (14) at pto end of crankshaft. Oil clearance between transfer sleeve and crankshaft should be 0.001-0.0035 inch (0.0254-0.0889 mm). Oil holes in sleeve must be aligned with oil passage in crankcase. Purpose of transfer sleeve is to conduct oil to drilled passage in crankshaft for lubrication of crankpin bearing.

**VALVE SYSTEM.** Valve tappet gap (cold) is 0.008 inch (0.2032 mm) for intake valve and 0.020 inch (0.508 mm) for exhaust valve. Adjustable tappets are used.

The exhaust valve on all engines is equipped with a valve rotator and seats in a renewable hardened alloy steel insert. On some engines, a renewable intake valve seat insert is used although usually the intake valve seats directly on machined surface in crankcase and cylinder casting. Desired valve seat width is 1/32-inch (0.794 mm). If valve seat width exceeds 1/16-inch (1.588 mm), narrow the seat using 30° and 60° cutters or stones; then renew seating surface with 45° cutter or stone. Valve face and seat angle is 45°.

Desired clearance for intake valve stem in guide is 0.0005-0.002 inch (0.0127-0.0508 mm) and for exhaust valve stem in guide is 0.002-0.0035 inch (0.0508-0.0889 mm). Renew valve guides if clearance of new valve stem in guide is excessive. Clearance of tappets in bores of crankcase should be 0.0008-0.0023 inch (0.0203-0.0584 mm).

Free length of intake valve spring should be 2-1/4 inches (57.15 mm) and free length of exhaust valve spring should be 1-13/16 inches (46.038 mm). Renew spring if free length is not approximately equal to specified free length.

**OIL PUMP.** A gear type oil pump is used to supply lubricating oil under pressure to connecting rod. A sudden drop in oil pressure may be caused by dirt or foreign particles in the oil pump. Sometimes it is possible to disconnect oil line to oil pressure gage and dislodge foreign material by forcing compressed air into pump. Pump pressure is adjusted at factory. Should it be necessary to readjust oil pressure, turn screw in pump body to left to decrease pressure or to right to increase pressure. Seal screw with permatex or equivalent sealer when adjustment is completed.

When installing pump assembly, check pump drive gear for backlash and alignment with camshaft gear.

---

# KOHLER

## KOHLER COMPANY
## Kohler, Wisconsin 503044

| Model | No. Cyls. | Bore | Stroke | Displacement | Power Rating |
|---|---|---|---|---|---|
| K-361 | 1 | 3.75 in. (95.25 mm) | 3.25 in. (82.55 mm) | 35.89 cu. in. (588.2 cc) | 18 hp (13.4 kW) |

Model K-361 is a one cylinder, four-stroke, horizontal crankshaft engine in which crankshaft is supported by ball bearing type main bearings.

Connecting rod rides directly on crankpin journal and is lubricated by oil splash system.

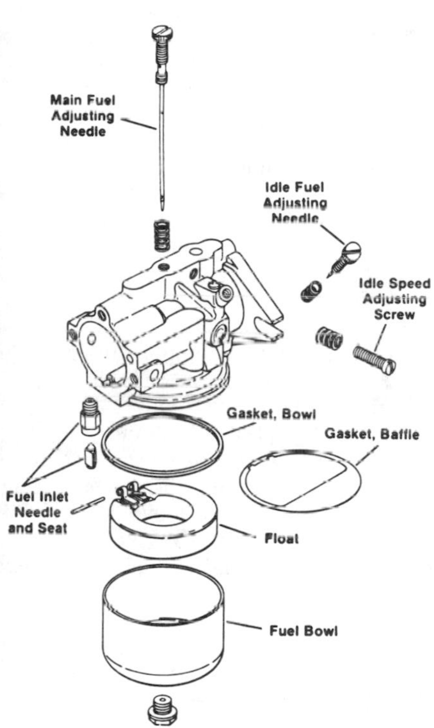


*Fig. KO45—Exploded view of Kohler side draft carburetor used on K-361 engines.*

A battery type ignition system with externally mounted breaker points is used.

Engines are equipped with Kohler side draft carburetors.

Special engine accessories or equipment is noted by a suffix letter on engine model number. Key to suffix letters is as follows:

A–Oil pan type
C–Clutch model
P–Pump model
Q–Quiet model
S–Electric start
T–Retractable start

## MAINTENANCE

**SPARK PLUG.** Recommended spark plug is Champion H10 or equivalent and for radio noise reduction, Champion RH10 or equivalent. Electrode gap is 0.035 inch (0.889 mm).

**CARBURETOR.** Refer to Fig. KO45 for exploded view of Kohler side draft carburetor. For initial adjustment, open main fuel needle 2-1/2 turns and open idle fuel needle 3/4-1 turn. Make final adjustment with engine at operating temperature and running. Place engine under load and adjust main fuel needle to leanest mixture that will allow satisfactory acceleration and steady governor operation.

Adjust idle speed stop screw so engine idles at 1725-1875 rpm, then adjust idle fuel needle for smoothest idle operation. As each adjustment affects the other, adjustment procedure may have to be repeated.

To check float level, invert carburetor body and float assembly. There should be 11/64-inch. (4.366 mm) clearance plus or minus 1/32-inch (0.794 mm) between machined surface of body casting and free end of float. Adjust float by bending float lever tang that contacts inlet valve. See Fig. KO46.

**AUTOMATIC CHOKE.** Some models are equipped with a Thermo-Electric automatic choke and fuel shutdown solenoid (Fig. KO47).

When installing or adjusting choke unit, position unit leaving mounting screw slightly loose. Hold choke plate wide open and rotate choke unit clockwise with slight pressure until it can no longer be rotated. Hold choke unit and

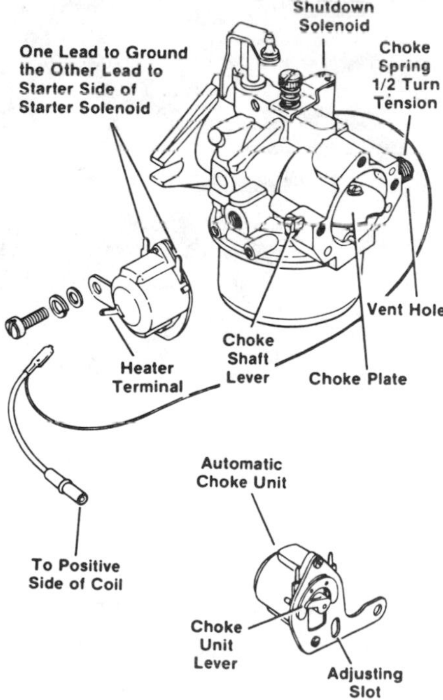

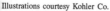

*Fig. KO47—Typical carburetor with Thermo-Electric automatic choke and shutdown control. Refer to text for details.*

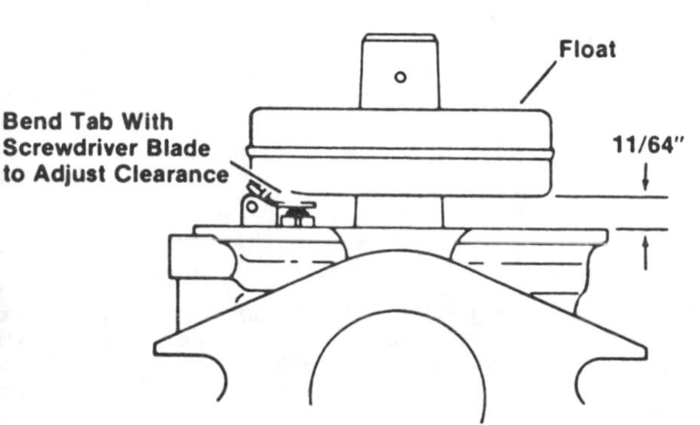


*Fig. KO46—Check float setting by inverting carburetor throttle body and float assembly and measuring distance from free end of float to machined surface of casting. Correct clearance is 11/64-inch (4.366 mm).*

Illustrations courtesy Kohler Co.

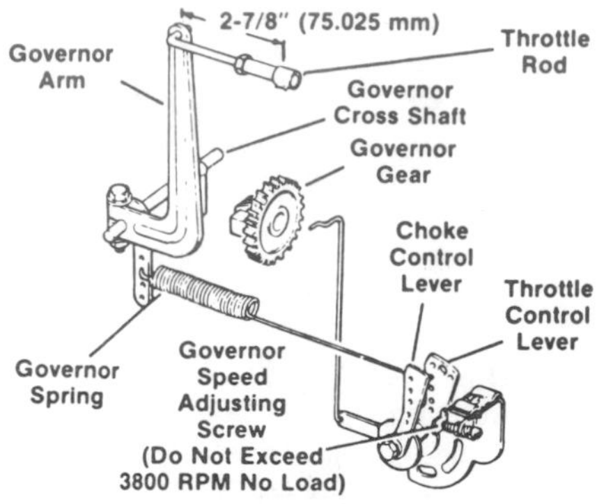


*Fig. KO48—View of typical governor linkage used on K-361 model.*

tighten mounting screws. Choke valve should close 5°-10° at 75°F (23.8°C).

With ignition on, shutdown solenoid plunger raises and opens float bowl vent to air horn. With ignition off, solenoid plunger closes vent and stops fuel flow. To check solenoid, remove solenoid and plunger from carburetor body. With lead wire connected, pull plunger approximately 1/4-inch from solenoid and ground casing to engine surface. Turn ignition switch on. Renew solenoid unit if solenoid does not draw plunger in. After renewing solenoid, reset main fuel adjusting screw.

**GOVERNOR.** Model K-361 is equipped with a centrifugal flyweight mechanical governor. Governor flyweight mechanism is mounted within crankcase and driven by camshaft. Maximum no-load speed is 3800 rpm.

Governor sensitivity can be adjusted by repositioning governor spring in governor arm and throttle control lever. If too sensitive, surging will occur with change of load. If a big drop in speed occurs when normal load is applied, sensitivity should be increased. Normal spring position is in third hole from bottom on governor arm and second hole from top on throttle control lever. To increase sensitivity, move spring end upward on governor arm. Refer to Fig. KO48.

Governor unit is accessible after removing crankshaft and camshaft. Gear and flyweight assembly turn on a stub shaft pressed into crankcase. To remove gear assembly, unscrew governor stop pin and slide gear off stub shaft. Remove governor cross-shaft by unscrewing governor bushing nut and removing shaft from inside. Renew gear assembly, cross-shaft or stub shaft if excessively worn or broken. If stub shaft must be renewed, press new shaft into block until it protrudes 3/8-inch (9.525 mm) above boss. Governor gear to stub shaft clearance is 0.0005-0.002 inch (0.0127-0.0508 mm).

**IGNITION TIMING.** A battery ignition system with externally mounted breaker points (Fig. KO49) is actuated by camshaft through a push rod. System is equipped with an automatic compression release located on camshaft and does not have an automatic timing advance. Ignition occurs at 20° BTDC at all engine speeds.

Initial breaker point gap is 0.020 inch (0.508 mm) but should be varied to obtain exact ignition timing as follows:

For static timing, disconnect spark plug lead from coil to prevent engine starting. Remove breaker point cover and rotate engine, by hand, in normal direction of rotation (clockwise, from flywheel side). Points should just begin to open when "S" mark appears in center of timing sight hole. Continue rotating engine until points are fully open. Check gap with a feeler gage. Gap setting can vary from 0.017-0.022 inch (0.4318-0.5588 mm), set to achieve smoothest running.

To set timing, using a power timing light, connect light to spark plug and with engine running at 1200-1800 rpm adjust points so "S" mark on flywheel is centered in timing sight hole.

**LUBRICATION.** A splash lubrication system is used. Oils approved by manufacturer must meet requirements of API service classification SE, SF or SG.

For operation in temperatures above 32°F (0°C), use SAE 30 or SAE 10W-30 oil. For temperatures below 32°F (0°C) use SAE 5W-20 or 5W-30 oil.

It is recommended oil be changed at 25 hour intervals under normal operating conditions. Maintain oil level at "FULL" mark on dipstick but **DO NOT** overfill. Oil capacity of K-361 model is 2 quarts

*Fig. KO49—Ignition breaker points are located externally on engine crankcase on all models equipped with magneto or battery ignition systems.*

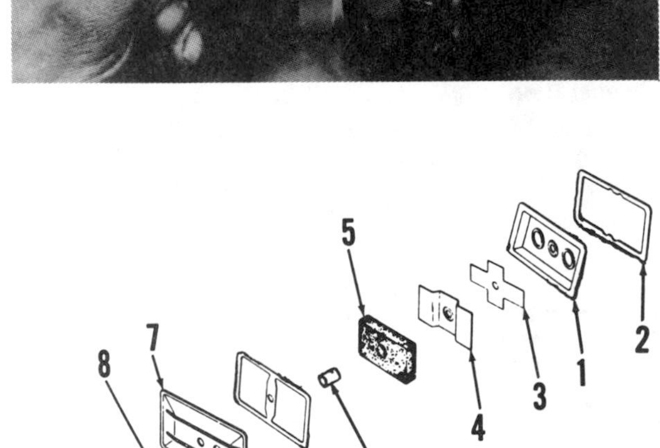


*Fig. KO50—Exploded view of crankcase breather assembly.*

1. Breather plate
2. Gasket
3. Reed
4. Baffle
5. Filter
6. Seal
7. Valve cover
8. Breather hose

*Fig. KO51—When installing connecting rod and piston unit, be sure marks on rod and cap are aligned and are facing toward flywheel side of engine.*

(1.9 L), K-361A model capacity is 1.5 quarts (1.4 L).

**AIR CLEANER.** Dry element type air cleaner should be cleaned every 50 hours of normal operation or more frequently if operating in dusty conditions. Remove dry element and tap element lightly on a flat surface to remove surface dirt. Do not wash element or attempt to clean element with compressed air. Renew element if extremely dirty or if it is bent, crushed or otherwise damaged. Make certain sealing surfaces of element seal effectively against back plate and cover.

## REPAIRS

**TIGHTENING TORQUES.** Recommended tightening torques, with lightly lubricated threads, are as follows:

Spark plug . . . . . . . . . . . . . . 18-22 ft.-lbs. (24-30 N·m)

Connecting rod cap screws . . . . . . . . . . . . . . . 25 ft.-lbs. (34 N·m)

Cylinder head cap screws . . . . . . . . . . . 30-35 ft.-lbs. (40-48 N·m)

Flywheel retainer nut . . . . . . . . . . . 60-70 ft.-lbs. (81-95 N·m)

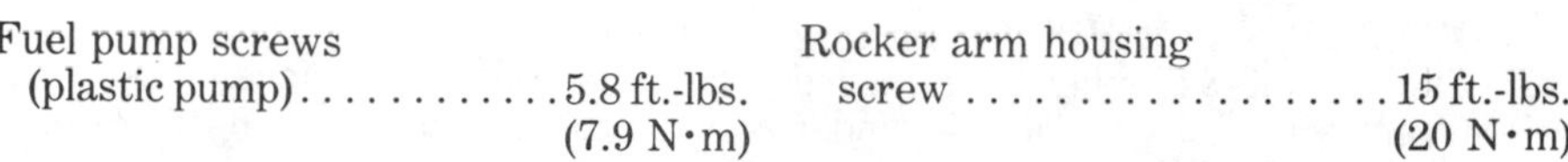

Fuel pump screws (plastic pump) . . . . . . . . . . . . 5.8 ft.-lbs. (7.9 N·m)

Rocker arm housing screw . . . . . . . . . . . . . . . . . . . 15 ft.-lbs. (20 N·m)

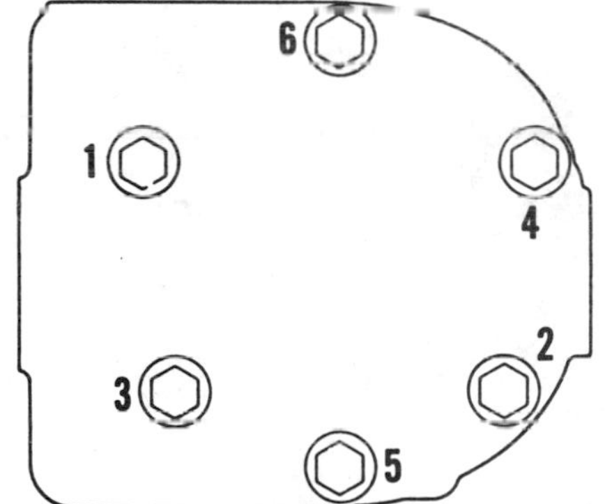


*Fig. KO52 – Tighten cylinder head cap screws evenly, in sequence shown, to 30-35 ft.-lbs. (40-48 N·m) torque.*

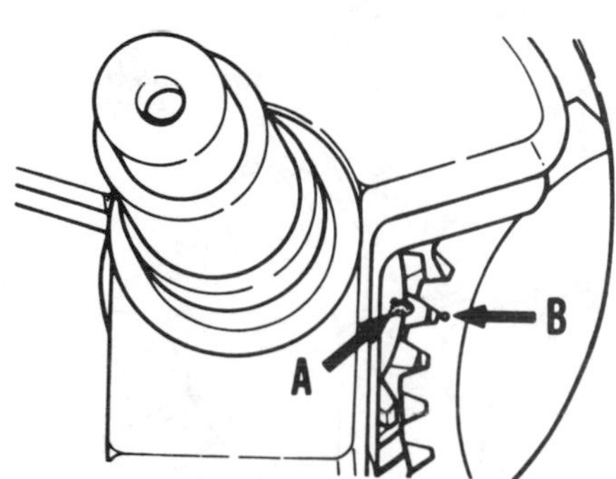


*Fig. KO53 – When installing crankshaft, make certain timing mark (A) on crankshaft is aligned with timing mark (B) on camshaft gear.*

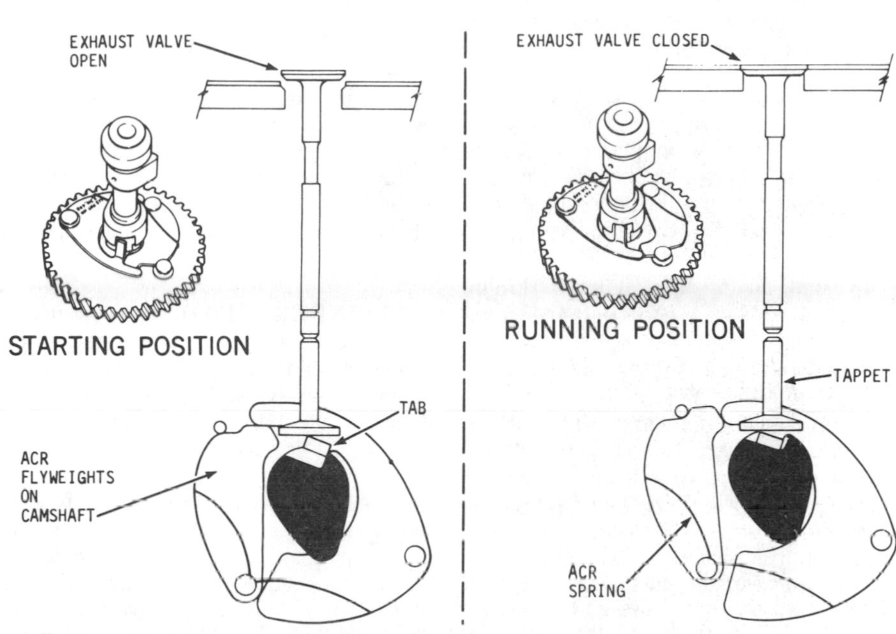


*Fig. KO54 – Views showing operation of camshaft with automatic compression release. In starting position, spring has moved control lever which moves cam lever upward so tang is above exhaust cam lobe. This tang holds exhaust valve open slightly on a portion of the compression stroke to relieve compression while cranking engine. At engine speeds of 650 rpm or more, centrifugal force moves control lever outward allowing tang to move below lobe surface.*

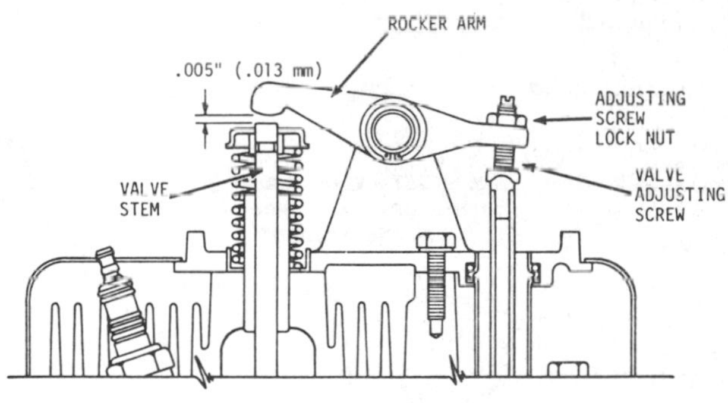


*Fig. KO55 – View of adjusting points on K-361 valve systems. Both intake and exhaust valve tappet clearance should be adjusted cold, to 0.005 inch (0.127 mm).*

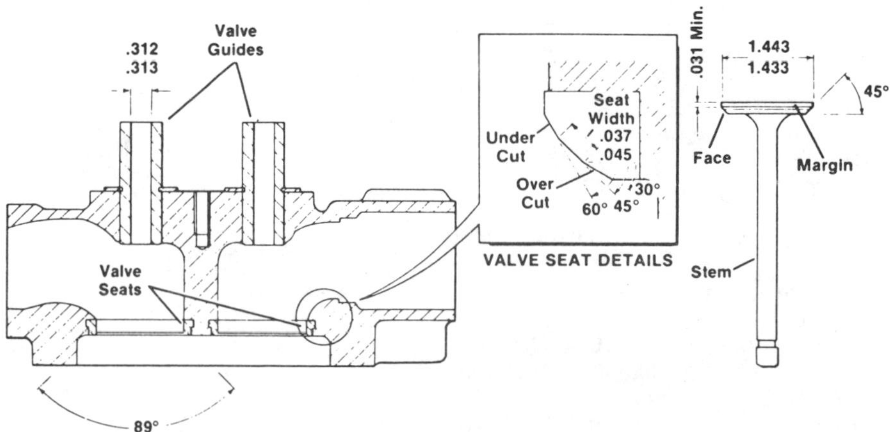


*Fig. KO56 – Principal valve service specifications illustrated. Refer to text for further details.*

**CONNECTING ROD.** Connecting rod and piston assembly is removed after removing oil pan and cylinder head. Aluminum alloy connecting rod rides directly on crankpin. Connecting rods are available in standard size as well as one for 0.010 inch (0.254 mm) undersize crankshafts. Desired running clearances are as follows:

Connecting rod to
crankpin . . . . . . . . . . . . 0.001-0.002 in.
(0.0254-0.0508 mm)

Connecting rod to
piston pin . . . . . . . . . 0.0003-0.0008 in.
(0.0076-0.0203 mm)

Rod side play
on crankpin . . . . . . . . . 0.007-0.0175 in.
(0.1778-0.4445 mm)

Standard crankpin diameter is 1.4995-1.500 inch (38.09-38.10 mm).

When reinstalling connecting rod and piston assembly, piston can be installed either way on rod, but make certain match marks (Fig. KO51) on rod and cap are aligned and are towards flywheel side of engine. Kohler recommends connecting rod cap screws be torqued to 30 ft.-lbs. (40 N•m), loosened and retorqued to 25 ft.-lbs (34 N•m). Cap screw threads should be lightly lubricated before installation.

**PISTON, PIN AND RINGS.** Aluminum alloy piston is fitted with two 0.093 inch (2.3622 mm) wide compression rings and one 0.187 inch (4.7498 mm) wide oil control ring. Renew piston if scored or if side clearance of new ring in piston top groove exceeds 0.005 inch (0.127 mm). Pistons and rings are available in oversizes of 0.010, 0.020 and 0.030 inch (0.254, 0.508 and 0.762 mm) as well as standard size. Piston pin fit in piston bore should be from 0.0001 inch (0.0025 mm) interference to 0.0003 inch (0.0076 mm) loose. Standard piston pin diameter is 0.8753 inch (22.23 mm).

Recommended piston to cylinder bore clearance measured at thrust side at bottom of skirt is 0.003-0.0045 inch (0.0762-0.1143 mm). Recommended clearance when measured at thrust side just below oil ring is 0.007-0.0095 inch (0.1778-0.2413 mm).

Kohler recommends piston rings always be renewed if they are removed.

Piston ring specifications are as follows:

Ring end gap . . . . . . . . . . 0.010-0.020 in.
(0.254-0.508 mm)

Ring side clearance –
Compression
ring . . . . . . . . . . . . . . . . 0.002-0.004 in.
(0.0508-0.1016 mm)

Oil control
ring . . . . . . . . . . . . . . . . 0.001-0.003 in.
(0.0254-0.0762 mm)

If compression ring has a groove or bevel on outside surface, install ring with groove or bevel down. If groove or bevel is on inside surface of compression ring, install ring with groove or bevel up. Oil control ring can be installed either side up.

**CYLINDER BLOCK.** If cylinder wall is scored or bore is tapered more than 0.0015 inch (0.0381 mm) or out-of-round more than 0.005 inch (0.127 mm), cylinder should be bored to nearest suitable oversize of 0.010, 0.020 or 0.030 inch (0.254, 0.508 or 0.762 mm). Standard cylinder bore is 3.750 inches (95.25 mm).

**CYLINDER HEAD.** Always use a new head gasket when installing cylinder head. Lightly lubricate cylinder head cap screws and tighten them evenly and in equal steps using sequence shown in Fig. KO52.

**CRANKSHAFT.** Crankshaft is supported by two ball bearings. Bearings have an interference fit with cylinder block of 0.0006-0.0022 inch (0.0152-0.0559 mm) and with bearing plate of 0.0012-0.0028 inch (0.0305-0.0711 mm). Ball bearing to crankshaft clearance is 0.0004 inch (0.0102 mm) interference to 0.0005 inch (0.0127 mm) loose.

Renew ball bearings if excessively loose or rough. Crankshaft end play should be 0.003-0.020 inch (0.0762-0.508 mm) and is controlled by varying thickness of bearing plate gaskets. Bearing plate gaskets are available in a variety of thicknesses.

Standard crankpin journal diameter is 1.4995-1.500 inches (38.09-38.10 mm) and may be reground to 0.010 inch (0.254 mm) undersize.

When installing crankshaft, align timing marks on crankshaft and camshaft gears as shown in Fig. KO53. Refer to **DYNAMIC BALANCER** paragraph for installation and timing of balancer gears.

Kohler recommends crankshaft seals be installed in crankcase and bearing plate after crankshaft and bearing plate are installed. Carefully work oil seals over crankshaft and drive seals into place with hollow driver that contacts outer edge of seals.

**CAMSHAFT.** The hollow camshaft and integral camshaft gear turn on a pin that is a slip fit in flywheel side of crankcase and a drive fit in closed side of crankcase. Remove and install pin from open side (bearing plate side) of crankcase. Desired camshaft to pin running clearance is 0.001-0.0035 inch (0.0254-0.0889 mm). Desired camshaft

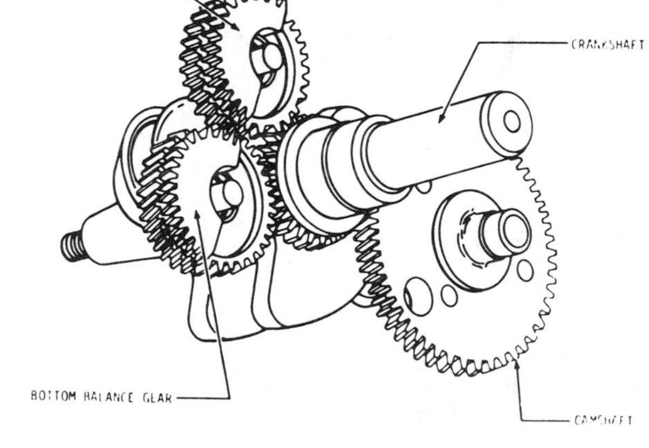


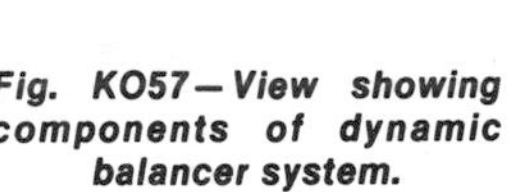
*Fig. KO57—View showing components of dynamic balancer system.*

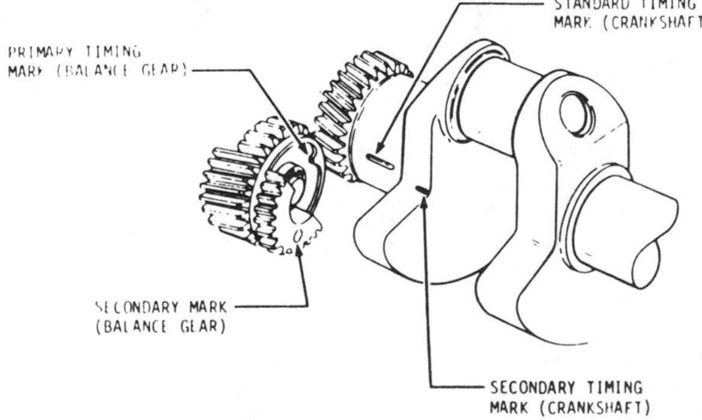


*Fig. KO58—View showing timing marks for installing dynamic balance gears.*



Illustrations courtesy Kohler Co.

end play of 0.005-0.010 inch (0.127-0.254 mm) is controlled by use of 0.005 and 0.010 inch (0.127 and 0.254 mm) thick spacer washers between camshaft and cylinder block at bearing plate side of crankcase.

Camshaft is equipped with automatic compression release shown in Fig. KO54. Automatic compression release mechanism holds exhaust valve open during first part of compression stroke, reducing compression pressure and allowing easier cranking. Refer to Fig. KO54 for operational details. At speeds above 650 rpm, release mechanism is inactive. Release mechanism weights and weight pivot pins are not renewable separately from camshaft gear, but weight spring is available for service.

To check compression on engine equipped with automatic compression release, engine must be cranked at 650 rpm or higher to overcome release mechanism. A reading can also be obtained by rotating flywheel in reverse directon with throttle wide open. Compression reading for engine in good condition should be 110-120 psi (758-827 kPa). When reading falls below 100 psi (690 kPa), it indicates leaking rings or valves.

**VALVE SYSTEM.** Valve seats are hardened steel inserts cast into head. If seats become worn or damaged entire cylinder head must be renewed. Refer to Fig. KO56 for valve seat and guide details.

Valve stem to guide operating clearance should be 0.0029-0.0056 inch (0.0762-0.1422 mm) for exhaust valve and 0.001-0.0027 inch (0.0254-0.0686 mm) for intake valve.

Intake and exhaust valve clearance should be adjusted to 0.005 inch (0.127

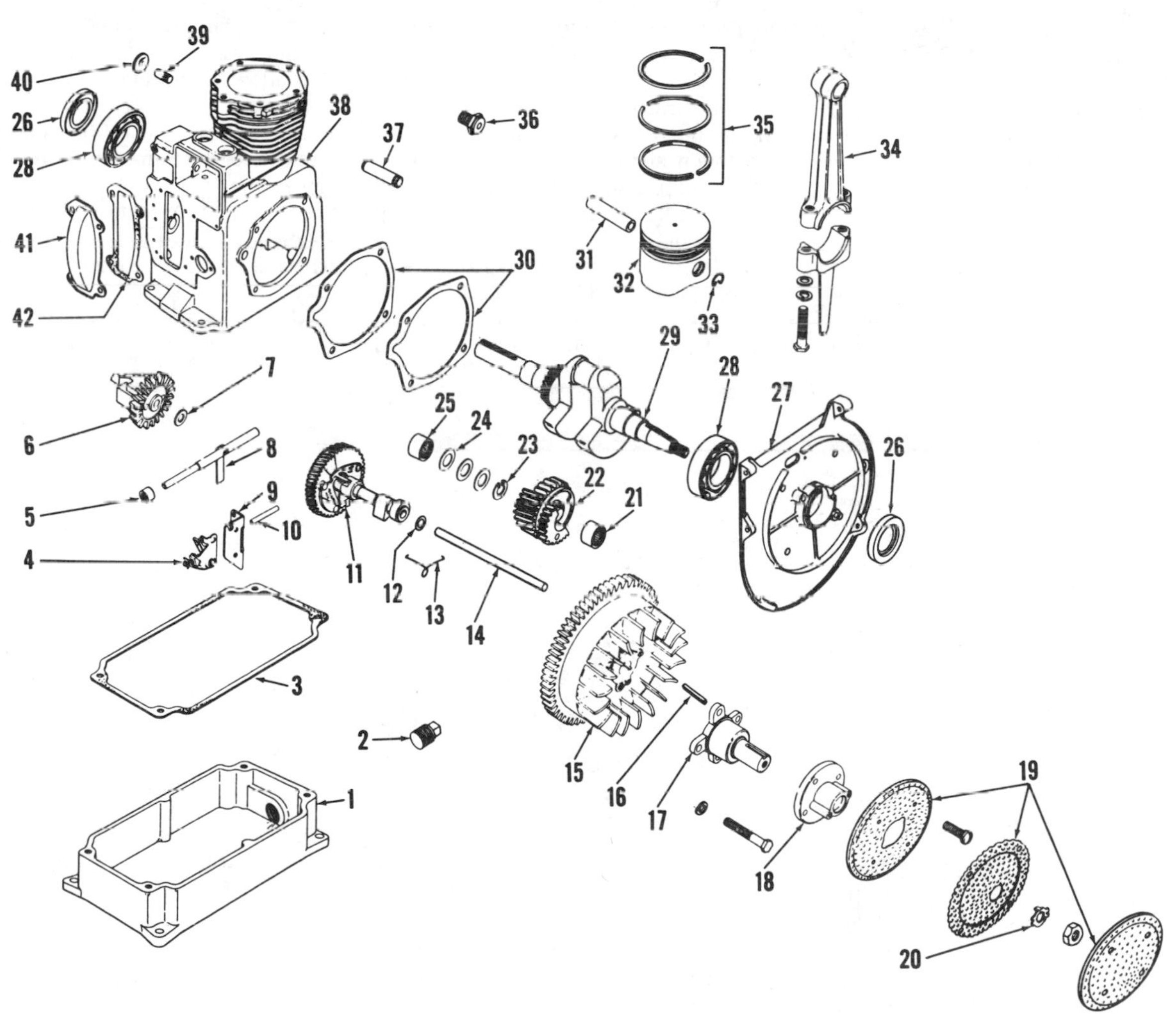


*Fig. KO59 — Exploded view of K-361 basic engine assembly.*

1. Oil pan
2. Oil drain plug
3. Oil pan gasket
4. Breaker points
5. Spacer
6. Governor gear
7. Thrust washer
8. Governor cross-shaft
9. Breaker plate
10. Breaker rod
11. Camshaft
12. Spacer
13. Actuating spring
14. Camshaft pin
15. Flywheel assy.
16. Key
17. Front drive shaft
18. Front drive adapter
19. Grass screen
20. Flywheel washer
21. Needle bearing
22. Balancer gear (2 used)
23. Retainer
24. Spacer
25. Needle bearing
26. Oil seal
27. Bearing plate
28. Main ball bearing
29. Crankshaft
30. Gasket
31. Piston pin
32. Piston
33. Retainer
34. Connecting rod assy.
35. Piston rings
36. Bushing
37. Shaft
38. Cylinder block assy.
39. Governor shaft
40. Expansion plug
41. Camshaft cover
42. Camshaft cover gasket

Illustrations courtesy Kohler Co.

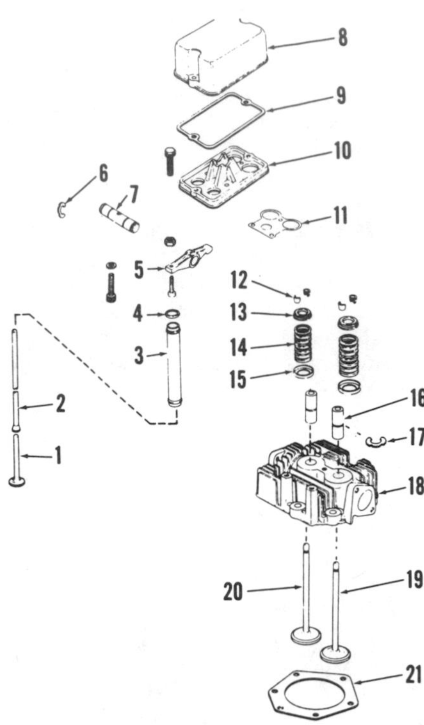


*Fig. KO60—Exploded view of overhead valve system used on K-361 engines.*

1. Tappet
2. Push rod
3. Push rod tube
4. "O" rings
5. Rocker arm
6. Retainer ring
7. Rocker arm shaft
8. Valve cover
9. Gasket
10. Rocker arm housing
11. Housing gasket
12. Valve keepers
13. Valve rotators
14. Valve springs
15. Spring retainers
16. Valve guides
17. Retainer ring
18. Cylinder head
19. Intake valve
20. Exhaust valve
21. Head gasket

mm) while cold. To adjust, disconnect spark plug wire and rotate engine by hand until both valves are seated and piston is at TDC. Loosen adjusting screw locknut (Fig. KO55) and turn adjusting screw in or out to obtain correct clearance. Tighten locknuts and recheck clearance.

**DYNAMIC BALANCER.** A dynamic balance system (Fig. KO57) is used on all K-361 engines. The two balance gears, equipped with needle bearings, rotate on two stub shafts which are pressed into bosses on pto side of crankcase. Snap rings secure gears on stub shafts and shim spacers are used to control gear end play. Balancer gears are driven by crankshaft in opposite direction of crankshaft rotation. Use following procedure to install and time dynamic balancer components.

To install new stub shafts, press shafts into special bosses in crankcase until they protrude 1.110 inches (28.194 mm) above thrust surface of bosses.

To install top balance gear-bearing assembly first place one 3/8-inch spacer and one 0.010 inch shim spacer on stub shaft, then slide top gear assembly on shaft. Timing marks must face flywheel side of crankcase. Install one 0.005, one 0.010 and one 0.020 inch shim spacers in this order, then install snap ring. Using a feeler gage, check gear end play. Correct end play of balance gear is 0.002-0.010 inch (0.0508-0.254 mm). Add or remove 0.005 inch thick spacers as necessary to obtain correct end play. Always make certain a 0.020 inch thick spacer is next to snap ring.

Install crankshaft in crankcase and align primary timing mark on top balance gear with standard timing mark on crankshaft. See Fig. KO58. With primary timing marks aligned, engage crankshaft gear 1/16-inch (1.588 mm) into narrow section of top balancer gear. Rotate crankshaft to align timing marks on camshaft gear and crankshaft as shown in Fig. KO53. Press crankshaft into crankcase until it is seated firmly into ball bearing main.

Rotate crankshaft until crankpin is approximately 15° past bottom dead center. Install one 3/8-inch spacer and one 0.010 inch shim spacer on stub shaft. Align secondary timing mark on bottom balance gear with secondary timing mark on crankshaft. See Fig. KO58. Slide gear assembly into position on stub shaft. If properly timed, secondary timing mark on bottom balance gear will be aligned with standard timing mark on crankshaft after gear is fully on stub shaft. Install one 0.005 inch and one 0.020 inch shim spacer, then install snap ring. Check bottom balance gear end play and add or remove 0.005 inch thick spacers as required to obtain proper end play of 0.002-0.010 inch (0.0508-0.254 mm).

Always make certain a 0.020 inch thick spacer is next to snap ring.

# KOHLER

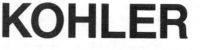

| Model | Bore | Stroke | Displacement | Rated Power |
|---|---|---|---|---|
| CV12.5 | 87 mm (3.43 in.) | 67 mm (2.64 in.) | 398 cc (24.3 cu. in.) | 9.33 kW (12.5 hp) |
| CV14 | 87 mm (3.43 in.) | 67 mm (2.64 in.) | 398 cc (24.3 cu. in.) | 10.5 kW (14 hp) |

**NOTE: Metric fasteners are used throughout engine.**

The Kohler CV12.5 and CV14 engines are four-stroke, air-cooled engines using an overhead valve system. Engine identification numbers are located on a decal affixed to flywheel fan shroud. Refer to preceding Kohler section for engine identification information.

## MAINTENANCE

**LUBRICATION.** Periodically check oil level; do not overfill. Oil dipstick should be resting on tube to check oil level; do not screw in dipstick. Change oil after first 5 hours of operation. Thereafter change oil after every 100 hours of operation. Oil should be drained while engine is warm. Oil capacity is approximately 1.9 liters (2.0 quarts). It is recommended that a new oil filter be installed at each oil change.

Manufacturer recommends using oil with an API service classification of SF or SG. Use 10W-30 or 10W-40 oil for temperatures above 0°F (-18°C). When operating in temperatures below 32°F (0°C), SAE 5W-20 or 5W-30 may be used. Manufacturer recommends use of SAE 10W-30 API SF oil for first 5 hours of operation of overhauled engines or new short blocks, then change oil according to ambient temperature requirements.

The engine may be equipped with a low-oil sensor. The sensor circuit may be designed to stop engine or trigger a warning device if oil level is low.

**AIR FILTER.** The engine is equipped with a foam precleaner element and paper type air filter. Service the precleaner after every 25 hours of operation and the air filter after every 100 hours of operation. Service more frequently if engine is operated in severe conditions.

Clean precleaner element by washing in soapy water. Allow to dry, then apply clean engine oil. Squeeze out excess oil.

The air filter should be renewed rather than cleaned. Do not wash or direct pressurized air at filter.

**FUEL FILTER.** If so equipped, periodically inspect fuel filter. If dirty or damaged, renew filter.

**CRANKCASE BREATHER.** A breather valve is attached to the top of the cylinder head under the rocker cover. A tube connects valve cover to the air cleaner base to allow crankcase vapors to be burned by the engine. Inspect and clean breather valve as needed to prevent or remove restrictions.

**SPARK PLUG.** Recommended spark plug is Champion RC12YC or equivalent. Specified electrode gap is 1.0 mm (0.040 in.). Tighten spark plug to 38-43 N·m (28-32 ft.-lbs.).

**NOTE: Manufacturer does not recommend spark plug cleaning using abrasive grit as grit may enter engine.**

**CARBURETOR.** Initial setting of idle mixture screw (Fig. KO70) is one turn out from lightly seated. Final adjustment of idle mixture screw should be made with engine at normal operating temperature. Adjust idle speed screw so engine idles at 1200 rpm, or at speed specified by equipment manufacturer. Turn idle mixture screw counterclockwise until engine rpm decreases and note screw position. Turn screw clockwise until engine rpm decreases again and note screw position. Turn screw to midpoint between the two noted positions. Reset idle speed screw if necessary to obtain idle speed of 1200 rpm, or to equipment manufacturer's specification.

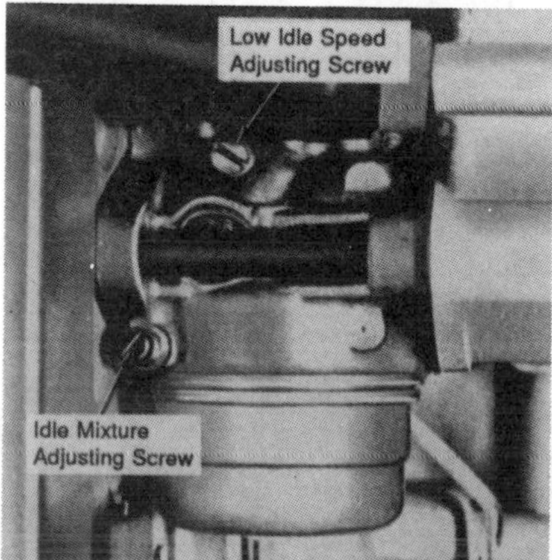


*Fig. KO70—View of carburetor showing adjustment points.*

High speed mixture is controlled by a fixed main jet. No optional jets are offered, although a high altitude kit is available.

To disassemble carburetor, refer to Fig. KO71. The edges of throttle and choke plates (3 and 8) are beveled and must be reinstalled in their original positions.

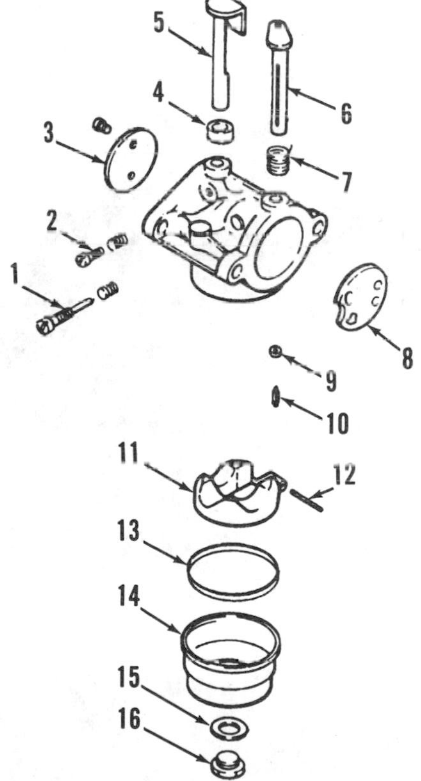


*Fig. KO71—Exploded view of float-type carburetor used on all engines. Some engines may be equipped with an electric fuel shut-off solenoid located in bottom of float bowl in place of retaining screw (16).*

1. Low idle fuel mixture screw
2. Low idle speed screw
3. Throttle plate
4. Throttle shaft dust seal
5. Throttle shaft
6. Choke shaft
7. Return spring
8. Choke plate
9. Fuel inlet seat
10. Fuel inlet needle
11. Float
12. Float shaft
13. Gasket
14. Fuel bowl
15. Gasket
16. Retaining screw

Mark choke and throttle plates before removal to ensure correct reassembly. Use a suitably sized screw to pull out the fuel inlet seat if seat is to be renewed. Do not reinstall a seat that has been removed. Use a sharp punch to pierce Welch plug and pry plug from carburetor body. Be careful to prevent punch from contacting and damaging carburetor body.

Clean all parts in suitable carburetor cleaner and blow out all passages with compressed air. Be careful not to enlarge any fuel passages or jets as calibration of carburetor may be altered.

Press new fuel inlet seat into carburetor body so seat is bottomed. Apply Loctite 609 to throttle plate retaining screw. Be sure throttle plate is properly seated against carburetor bore before tightening screw. Be sure choke shaft properly engages detent spring on carburetor. Locking tabs on choke plate must straddle choke shaft. Use a suitable sealant on Welch plug.

**IGNITION.** The engine is equipped with a breakerless, electronic magneto ignition system. The electronic ignition module is mounted outside the flywheel. The ignition switch grounds the module to stop the engine. There is no periodic maintenance or adjustment required with this ignition system.

Air gap between module and flywheel should be 0.20-0.30 mm (0.008-0.012 in.). Loosen module retaining screws and position module to obtain desired gap. Tighten screws to 4 N·m (35 in.-lbs.) for used engines or to 6.2 N·m (55 in.-lbs.) on a new engine cylinder block.

If ignition module fails to produce a spark, check for faulty kill switch or grounded wires. Measure resistance of ignition module secondary using suitable ohmmeter. Connect one test lead to spark plug terminal of high tension wire and other test lead to module core laminations. Resistance should be 7900-10850 ohms. If resistance is low or infinite, renew module.

**GOVERNOR.** A flyweight type governor is located in the crankcase. The governor gear is driven by the camshaft gear. Refer to REPAIRS section for overhaul information.

To adjust governor linkage, proceed as follows: Loosen governor lever clamp nut (Fig. KO72) and push governor lever so throttle is wide open. Turn governor cross shaft counterclockwise as far as possible and tighten clamp nut.

The recommended maximum high idle (no-load) setting is 3750 rpm. The actual high speed setting depends on the application. Use a tachometer to check engine speed.

To adjust high idle speed setting, first loosen throttle control cable clamp (Fig. KO73). Move the equipment speed control lever to "Fast" position. Align the hole in throttle lever with hole in speed control bracket by inserting a pencil or drill bit through the holes. Pull up on throttle control cable shield to remove slack and tighten cable clamp. Start engine and allow to reach operating temperature. Align hole in throttle lever with hole in speed control bracket as previously outlined. Loosen speed control bracket mounting screws and move bracket up (toward flywheel) to decrease high idle speed or down (toward pto) to increase high idle speed. When desired speed is obtained, tighten control bracket screws to 10.7 N·m (95 in.-lbs.) on a new short block or to 7.3 N·m (65 in.-lbs.) on all other engines.

Governor sensitivity is adjusted by positioning governor spring in different holes in governor lever arm. It is recommended that spring be installed in the hole closest to governor shaft if high idle speed is 3600 rpm or less. If high idle speed is greater than 3600 rpm, use the second hole which is farthest from governor cross shaft.

**VALVE CLEARANCE.** The CV12.5 and CV14 engines are equipped with hydraulic valve lifters which automatically maintain proper valve clearance. No periodic adjustment is required.

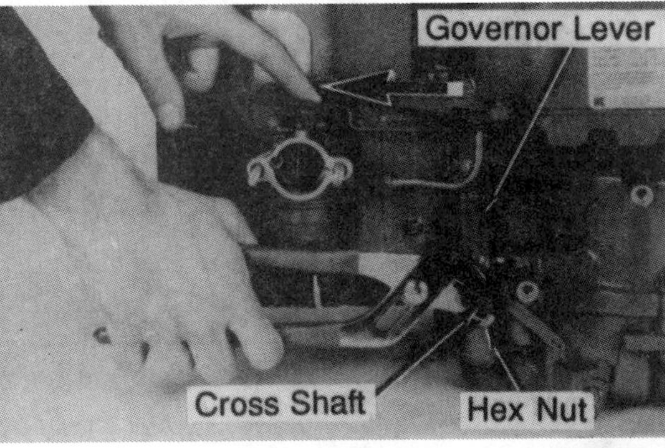


*Fig. KO72—View of governor external linkage. Refer to text for adjustment procedure.*

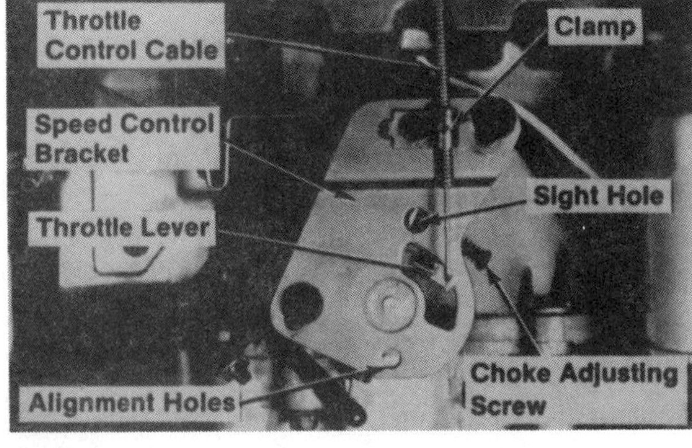


*Fig. KO73—View of typical speed control linkage. Refer to text for adjustment procedure.*

## REPAIRS

**TIGHTENING TORQUES.** Recommended tightening torques are as follows:

| | |
|---|---|
| Connecting rod | 22.6 N·m (200 in.-lbs.) |
| Cylinder head | 41 N·m (30 ft.-lbs.) |
| Flywheel | 66 N·m (49 ft.-lbs.) |
| Spark plug | 38-43 N·m (28-32 ft.-lbs.) |

**FUEL PUMP.** Some engines may be equipped with a mechanically operated diaphragm type fuel pump. The fuel pump is actuated by an eccentric on engine camshaft. Individual components are not available; pump must be renewed as a unit assembly.

When installing fuel pump assembly, make certain that fuel pump lever is positioned to the right side of camshaft. Damage to fuel pump and engine may result if lever is positioned on left side of camshaft. Tighten fuel pump mounting screws to 9.0 N·m (80 in.-lbs.) for first time installation on new short block. On all other engines, tighten mounting screws to 7.3 N·m (65 in.-lbs.).

**CYLINDER HEAD.** To remove cylinder head, remove air cleaner assembly and base. Detach speed control linkage and fuel line. Unbolt and remove carburetor and muffler. Remove recoil starter, blower housing and cylinder head air baffles and shields. Remove rocker arm cover. Rotate crankshaft so piston is at top dead center on compression stroke. Push rods and rocker arms should be marked so they can be reinstalled in their original position. Unscrew cylinder head bolts and remove cylinder head and gasket.

To disassemble, remove spark plug. Remove breather retainer (14—Fig. KO74) and reed (15). Push rocker shaft (13) out breather side of rocker arm bridge (12) and remove rocker arms (11). Use a valve spring compressor tool to compress valve springs. Remove split retainers (2), release spring tension and remove valves from cylinder head.

Clean combustion deposits from cylinder head and inspect for cracks or other damage. Maximum allowable warpage of head surface is 0.076 mm (0.003 in.).

To reassemble cylinder head components, reverse disassembly procedure. Be sure rocker pedestal (12) is installed with small counterbored hole toward exhaust port side of cylinder head. Tighten rocker pedestal mounting screws to 9.9 N·m (88 in.-lbs.). Install a new stem seal (6) on intake valve; do not reuse old seal.

Reverse removal procedure to reinstall head. Tighten cylinder head screws in increments of 14 N·m (10 ft.-lbs.) following sequence shown in Fig. KO75 until final torque of 41 N·m (30 ft.-lbs.) is reached. Install push rods in their original position, compress valve springs and snap push rods underneath rocker arms. Silicone sealant is used as a gasket between valve cover and cylinder head. GE Silmate type RTV-1473 or RTV-108 sealant (or equivalent) is recommended. The use of a silicone removing solvent is recommended to remove old silicone gasket, as scrapping the mating surfaces may damage them and could cause leaks. Apply a 1.5 mm (1/16 in.) bead of sealant to gasket surface of cylinder head. Follow tightening sequence shown in Fig. KO76 and tighten valve cover screws to 10.7 N·m (95 in.-lbs.) if a new cylinder head is installed, or to 7.3 N·m (65 in.-lbs.) if original head is installed.

**VALVE SYSTEM.** Clean valve heads and stems with a wire brush. Inspect each valve for warped or burned head, pitting or worn stem and renew as required.

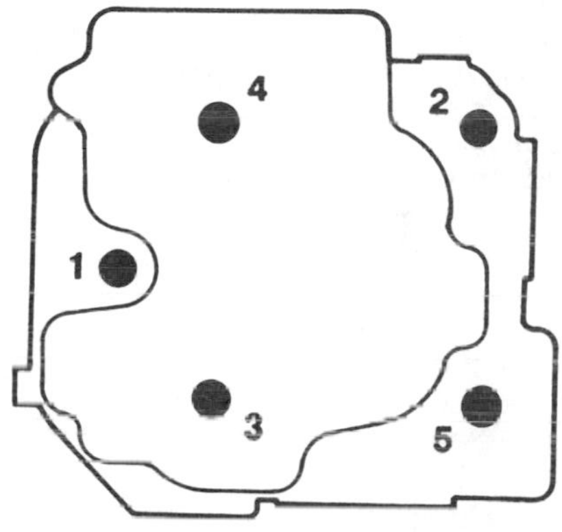


*Fig. KO75—Follow sequence shown when tightening cylinder head bolts. Refer to text.*

Valve face and seat angles are 45 degrees for intake and exhaust. Renew valve if valve margin is less than 1.5 mm (0.060 in.) after grinding valve face.

Specified valve stem-to-guide clearance is 0.03-0.076 mm (0.0015-0.0030 in.) for intake valve and 0.050-0.088 mm (0.0020-0.0035 in.) for exhaust valve. Specified new valve stem diameter is 6.982-7.000 mm (0.2749-0.2756 in.) for intake and 6.970-6.988 mm (0.2744-0.2751 in.) for exhaust. Specified new valve guide inside diameter for either valve is 7.033-7.058 mm (0.2769-0.2779 in.). Maximum allowable valve guide inside diameter is 7.134 mm (0.2809 in.) for intake guide and 7.159 mm (0.2819 in.) for exhaust guide. Valve guides are not renewable, however, guides may be reamed to accept valves with 0.25 mm oversize stem.

On late production engines, starting with S.N. 1933503554, the exhaust valve rotator (7—Fig. KO74) has been eliminated and a new spring seat with different length valve spring is used in its place. Free length of the new valve spring is 55.8 mm (2.197 in.), and spring is color coded green for identification. Free length of early production exhaust valve spring is 48.69 mm (1.917 in.).

**CONNECTING ROD.** The connecting rod and piston are removed as an assembly. Remove cylinder head as previously outlined. Remove oil pan (crankcase cover) mounting screws, then pry oil pan from crankcase using large screwdriver at splitting notches located in oil pan. Rotate crankshaft so timing marks on crankshaft and camshaft gears are aligned. Remove camshaft from crankcase. Identify hydraulic lifters so they can be returned to original position, then remove lifters from crankcase. Remove balance shaft from crankcase. Remove carbon deposits and ring ridge (if present) from top of cylinder before

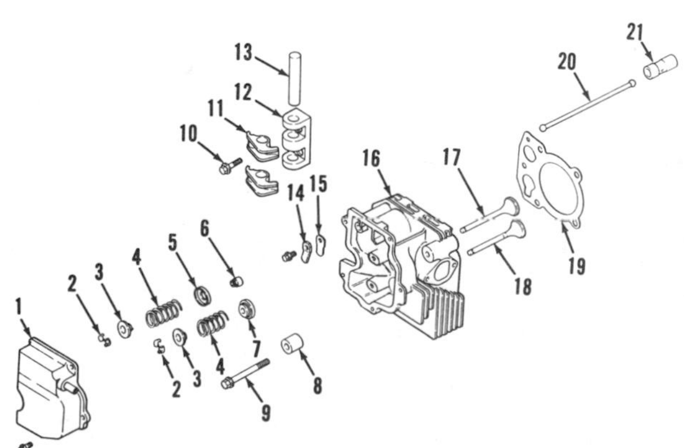


*Fig. KO74—Exploded view of cylinder head and valve components. Exhaust valve rotator (7) is used on early production engines, before S.N. 1933593554.*

1. Valve cover
2. Split retainer
3. Spring retainer
4. Valve spring
5. Spring seat
6. Valve seal (intake)
7. Valve rotator (exhaust)
8. Spacer
9. Head bolt
10. Screw
11. Rocker arm
12. Rocker bridge
13. Rocker shaft
14. Retainer plate
15. Breather reed
16. Cylinder head
17. Intake valve
18. Exhaust valve
19. Head gasket
20. Push rod
21. Valve lifter

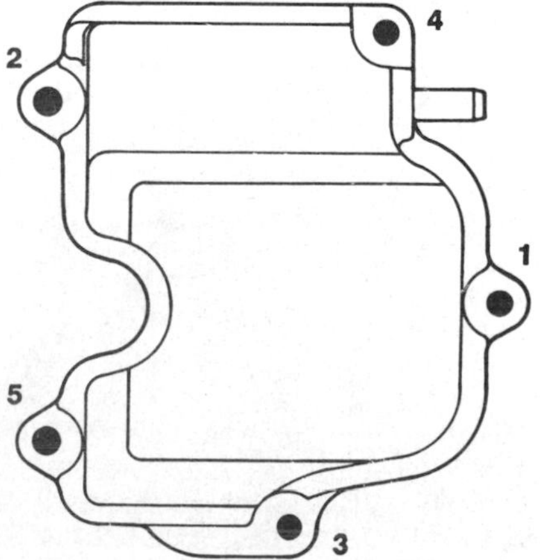


*Fig. KO76—Follow sequence shown when tightening valve cover mounting screws. Refer to text.*

Illustrations courtesy Kohler Co.

removing piston and rod assembly. Remove connecting rod cap and push connecting rod and piston out of cylinder. Remove piston pin retaining rings and separate piston and rod.

Renew connecting rod if bearing surfaces are scored or excessively worn. Specified connecting rod small end diameter is 19.015-19.023 mm (0.7486-0.7489 in.), and wear limit is 19.036 mm (0.7495 in.). Specified connecting rod-to-piston pin running clearance is 0.015-0.028 mm (0.0006-0.0011 in.).

Specified connecting rod-to-crankpin bearing clearance is 0.030-0.055 mm (0.0011-0.0022 in.), and maximum allowable clearance is 0.07 mm (0.0025 in.). A connecting rod with 0.25 mm (0.010 in.) undersize big end is available. The undersized rod can be identified by the drilled hole located in lower end of the rod.

Specified rod side clearance on crankpin is 0.18-0.41 mm (0.007-0.016 in.).

To reinstall connecting rod and piston assembly, reverse the removal procedure. Be sure that arrow mark on top of piston is toward flywheel side of crankcase (Fig. KO77). Tighten connecting rod cap bolts evenly to 22.6 N·m (200 in.-lbs.). Install balance shaft, camshaft and valve lifters and oil pan as outlined in appropriate sections.

**PISTON, PIN AND RINGS.** Piston and connecting rod are removed as an assembly as outlined in CONNECTING ROD section. Remove piston pin retaining rings (13—Fig. KO78) and separate piston and rod.

To determine piston clearance in cylinder, measure piston skirt diameter at a point 6 mm (0.24 in.) from bottom of skirt and perpendicular to piston pin bore. Measure cylinder bore inside diameter at point of greatest wear, approximately 63 mm (2.5 in.) below top of cylinder and perpendicular to piston pin. The difference between the two measurements is piston clearance in bore, which should be 0.041-0.044 mm (0.0016-0.0017 in.).

Piston and rings are available in standard size and oversizes of 0.25 and 0.50 mm (0.010 and 0.020 in.). Standard piston skirt diameter is 86.941-86.959 mm (3.4229-3.4236 in.), and wear limit is 86.814 mm (3.418 in.).

Specified piston pin bore is 19.006-19.012 mm (0.7483-0.7485 in.), and wear limit is 19.025 mm (0.749 in.). Specified piston pin diameter 18.995-19.000 mm (0.7478-0.7480 in.), and wear limit is 18.994 mm (0.7478 in.). Piston pin-to-piston clearance should be 0.006-0.017 mm (0.0002-0.0007 in.).

Insert new rings in piston ring grooves and measure ring side clearance using a feeler gage. Piston ring side clearance should be 0.040-0.105 mm (0.0016-0.0041 in.) for top compression ring; 0.040-0.072 mm (0.0016-0.0028 in.) for second compression ring; 0.551-0.675 mm (0.0217-0.0266 in.) for oil control ring. Renew piston if side clearance is excessive.

Specified piston ring end gap for compression rings is 0.30-0.50 mm (0.012-0.020 in.). Maximum allowable ring end gap in a used cylinder is 0.77 mm (0.030 in.).

When assembling piston rings on piston, install oil control ring expander (Fig. KO79) first and then the side rails. Install compression rings so side marked with "pip" mark is toward piston crown and stripe on face of ring is to the left of end gap. Second compression ring has a bevel on inside of ring and has a pink stripe on face of ring. Top compression ring has a barrel face and has a blue stripe on face of ring. Stagger ring end gaps evenly around the piston.

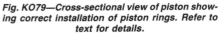

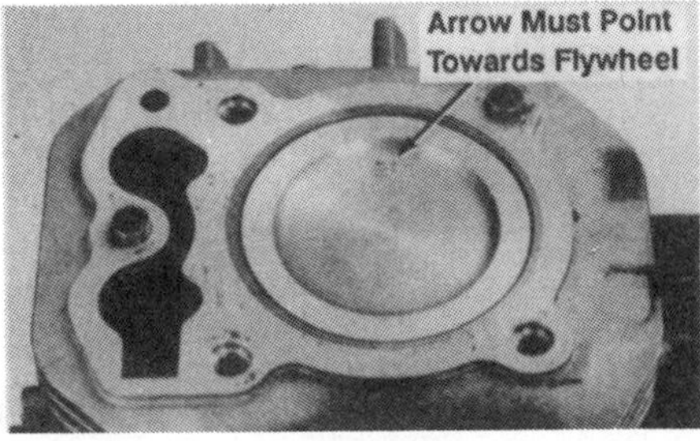


*Fig. KO77—Piston must be installed with arrow pointing toward flywheel side of engine.*

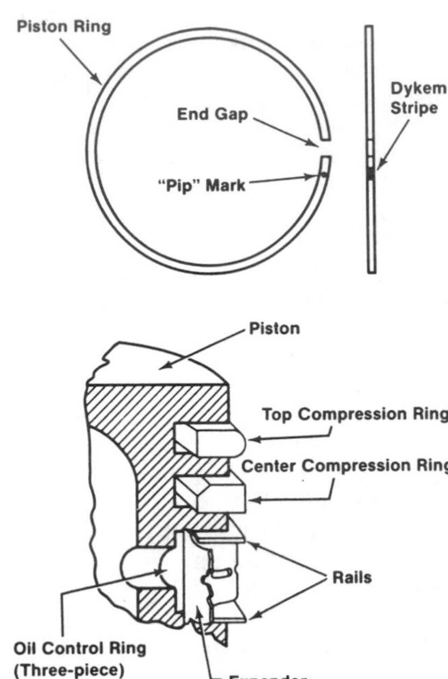


*Fig. KO79—Cross-sectional view of piston showing correct installation of piston rings. Refer to text for details.*

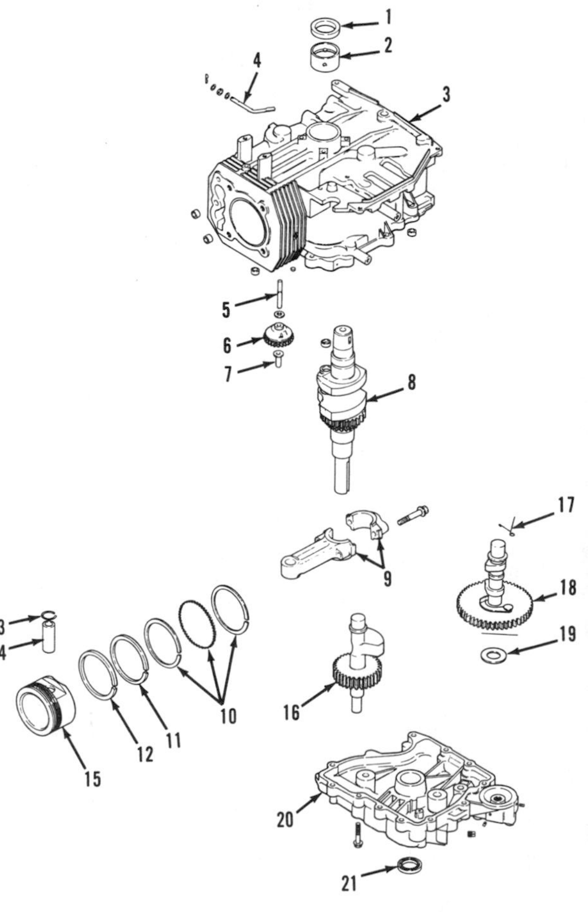


*Fig. KO78—Exploded view of crankcase/cylinder block assembly.*

1. Oil seal
2. Main bearing
3. Crankcase/cylinder block
4. Governor cross shaft
5. Governor gear shaft
6. Governor gear assy.
7. Governor pin
8. Crankshaft
9. Connecting rod
10. Oil control ring
11. Second compression ring
12. Top compression ring
13. Snap ring
14. Piston pin
15. Piston
16. Balance shaft & gear assy.
17. Compression release spring
18. Camshaft & gear assy.
19. Shim
20. Oil pan
21. Oil seal



Illustrations courtesy Kohler Co.

Lubricate piston and cylinder with oil, then use suitable ring compressor tool to install piston and rod. Be sure that arrow on piston crown is toward flywheel side of crankcase as shown in Fig. KO77. Refer to CONNECTING ROD section and reverse removal procedure to install remainder of components.

**CAMSHAFT AND HYDRAULIC LIFTERS.** To remove camshaft, first rotate crankshaft so piston is at top dead center on compression stroke. Remove rocker cover, compress valve springs and disengage push rods from rocker arms. Remove push rods while marking them so they can be returned to original position. Unbolt and remove oil pan, then withdraw camshaft from crankcase. Identify the valve lifters as either intake or exhaust so they can be returned to original position, then remove lifters from crankcase.

The camshaft is equipped with a compression reduction device to aid starting. The lever and weight mechanism on the camshaft gear moves a pin inside the exhaust cam lobe. During starting the pin protrudes above the cam lobe and forces the exhaust valve to stay open longer thereby reducing compression. At running speeds the pin remains below the surface of the cam lobe. Inspect mechanism for proper operation.

Inspect camshaft and lifters for scoring, pitting and excessive wear. Minimum cam lobe height is 8.96 mm (0.353 in.) for intake lobe and 9.14 mm (0.360 in.) for exhaust lobe. If camshaft is renewed, new valve lifters should also be installed.

If the hydraulic valve lifters are noisy after engine has run for several minutes and reached operating temperature, it is probably an indication that contamination is preventing the lifter check ball from seating or there is internal wear in the lifter. Individual parts are not available for the hydraulic lifters. Lifters should be renewed if faulty.

Before reassembling engine, the hydraulic lifters should be primed as follows: Use a lever operated oil can filled with SAE 10W-30 oil. Insert oil can nozzle into oil feed hole in side of lifter body as shown in Fig. KO80. Pump oil into lifter until body is full and oil is level with top of lifter body. Use a push rod to push down on lifter socket; lifter should feel solid. If socket can be pushed down into lifter body, repeat priming procedure and retest. If lifter will not become solid (pump up), renew lifter assembly.

Lubricate lifter bores with oil and install hydraulic lifters in their original position. The exhaust lifter bore is closest to crankcase gasket surface.

Install camshaft, aligning timing marks (Fig. KO81) on crankshaft and camshaft gears as shown. Camshaft end play is adjusted with shims (19—Fig. KO78), which are installed between camshaft and oil pan. To determine camshaft end play, install camshaft with original thickness shim in crankcase. Attach end play checking tool KO-1031 to crankcase and use a feeler gage to measure clearance between the shim and checking tool. Camshaft end play should be 0.076-0.127 mm (0.003-0.005 in.). Install different thickness shim as necessary to obtain desired end play.

No gasket is used with crankcase oil pan; apply silicone gasket compound to mating surface of pan. Tighten crankcase cover screws to 24.4 N·m (216 in.-lbs.) using sequence shown in Fig. KO84.

**CAUTION: Hydraulic lifter high pressure cavity will be filled with oil and lifter extended to maximum open position during the priming procedure. A waiting period is required after assembling engine before starting the engine. This allows valve spring pressure to return the hydraulic lifter socket to its proper position and seat the valve. Failure to wait may result in bent push rods or other engine damage.**

After completing assembly of engine, wait ten minutes before attempting to start engine. Then, rotate engine slowly and check for compression. If there is compression, valves are seating and engine may be started.

**GOVERNOR.** The engine is equipped with a flyweight mechanism mounted on governor gear (6—Fig. KO78). Remove oil pan (20) for access to governor gear. Inspect gear assembly for excess wear and damage. The governor gear is held onto governor shaft (5) by molded tabs on the gear. When gear is removed, the tabs are damaged and replacement of governor gear will be required. Gear and flyweight assembly are available only as a unit assembly. If governor gear shaft (5) requires renewal, tap new shaft into crankcase so it protrudes 32.64-32.84 mm (1.285-1.293 in.) above crankcase boss. Remove cotter pin to remove governor lever shaft (4). Inspect shaft oil seal in crankcase bore and renew if necessary.

No gasket is used with oil pan; apply silicone gasket compound to mating surface of oil pan. Tighten crankcase cover screws to 24.4 N·m (216 in.-lbs.) following sequence shown in Fig. KO84. Adjust governor as previously outlined in MAINTENANCE section.

**CRANKSHAFT.** To remove crankshaft, remove starter and flywheel. Remove crankcase oil pan, piston, connecting rod and camshaft as previously outlined. Remove balance shaft. Remove crankshaft from crankcase. The crankshaft rides in a renewable bushing (2—Fig. KO78) in the crankcase and in an integral bearing in the oil pan.

Specified main journal diameter at flywheel end is 44.913-44.935 mm (1.7682-1.7691 in.), and wear limit is 44.84 mm (1.765 in.). Bearing inside diameter at flywheel end is 44.965-45.003 mm (1.7703-1.7718 in.), and wear limit is 45.016 mm (1.7723 in.). Crankshaft-to-bearing running clearance should be 0.03-0.09 mm (0.0012-0.0035 in.). When renewing main bearing, make certain that oil hole in bearing aligns with oil passage in crankcase.

Specified main journal diameter at pto end is 41.915-41.935 mm (1.6502-1.6510 in.), and wear limit is 41.86 mm (1.648 in.). Crankshaft-to-oil pan bore running clearance should be 0.03-0.09 mm (0.0012-0.0035 in.).

Maximum allowable main journal taper is 0.020 mm (0.0008 in.) and maximum allowable out-of-round is 0.025 mm (0.0010 in.). Main journals cannot be machined undersize.

Specified standard crankpin diameter is 38.958-38.970 mm (1.5338-1.5343 in.). Minimum allowable crankpin diameter is 38.94 mm (1.533 in.). Maximum allowable crankpin taper is 0.012 mm (0.0005 in.) and maximum allowable out-of-round is 0.025 mm (0.0010 in.). Crankpin may be ground to accept a connect-

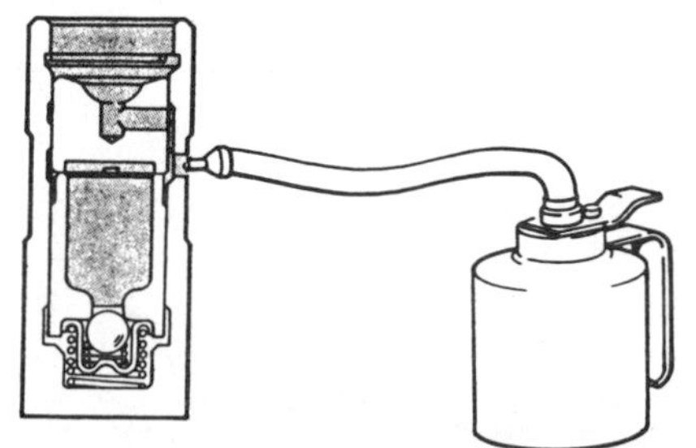

*Fig. KO80—Whenever hydraulic lifters are removed, they should be primed with oil prior to reassembly. Refer to text.*

*Fig. KO81—Align timing mark on small crankshaft gear with timing mark on camshaft gear.*

ing rod that is 0.25 mm (0.010 in.) undersize. Maximum allowable crankshaft runout is 0.10 mm (0.004 in.).

To install crankshaft, reverse the removal procedure. Install balance shaft, aligning timing marks on large crankshaft gear and balance shaft gear as shown in Fig. KO82. Install camshaft, aligning timing marks on small crankshaft gear and camshaft gear as shown in Fig. KO81. Apply silicone gasket compound to mating surface of oil pan. Tighten crankcase cover screws to 24.4 N·m (216 in.-lbs.) following sequence shown in Fig. KO84. Tighten flywheel retaining nut to 66 N·m (90 ft.-lbs.).

**CYLINDER/CRANKCASE.** Cylinder bore standard diameter is 87.000-87.025 (3.4252-3.4262 in.), and wear limit is 87.063 mm (3.4277 in.). Maximum bore out-of-round is 0.12 mm (0.005 in.). Maximum bore taper is 0.05 mm (0.002 in.). Cylinder may be bored to accept an oversize piston.

Install crankshaft oil seals in crankcase and oil pan using seal driver KO-1036. Force seal into crankcase or oil pan until tool bottoms.

**OIL PAN AND OIL PUMP.** A gerotor type oil pump is located in engine oil pan. The oil pump is driven by the engine balance shaft. Oil pump rotors (9—Fig. KO83) can be removed for inspection after removing pump cover (11) from bottom of oil pan. To remove oil pick-up screen (2) or oil pressure regulator valve (5 through 7), oil pan must be removed from crankcase.

Check oil pump rotors and oil pan cavity for scoring or excessive wear. Pressure relief valve body (7) and piston (6) must be free of scratches or burrs. Relief valve spring (5) free length should be approximately 25.20 mm (0.992 in.).

Lubricate oil pan cavity and pump rotors with oil during reassembly. Install new "O" ring (10) in groove in oil pan. Install pump cover (11) and tighten mounting screws to 6.2 N·m (55 in.-lbs.) on a new oil pan or 4.0 N·m (35 in.-lbs.) on a used oil pan.

RTV silicone sealant is used as a gasket between oil pan and crankcase. Note that scraping the mounting surface to remove old sealant is not recommended as surface may be damaged, resulting in leaks. The use of silicone removing solvent is recommended for removing old sealant material. Apply a 1.5 mm (1/16 in.) bead of silicone gasket compound to mating surface of oil pan. GE Silmate type RTV-1473 or RTV-108 silicone sealant (or equivalent) is recommended. Tighten crankcase cover screws in sequence shown in Fig. KO84 to 24.4 N·m (216 in.-lbs.).

*Fig. KO82—When assembling engine, align timing mark on large crankshaft gear with timing mark on balance shaft gear.*

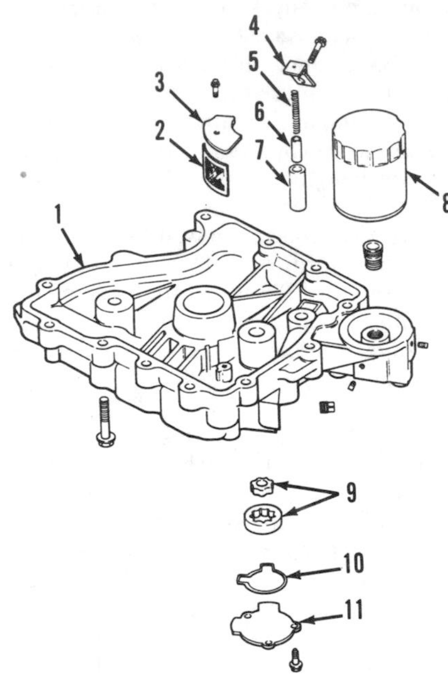


*Fig. KO83—Gerotor type engine oil pump is mounted in oil pan.*

1. Oil pan
2. Oil pick-up screen
3. Cover
4. Relief valve bracket
5. Relief valve spring
6. Relief valve piston
7. Relief valve body
8. Oil filter
9. Inner & outer rotors
10. "O" ring
11. Pump cover

**OIL SENSOR.** Some engines are equipped with an Oil Sentry oil pressure monitor. The system uses a pressure switch installed in one of the main oil galleries of the oil pan. The pressure switch is designed to break contact as oil pressure increases to normal pressure, and to make contact when oil pressure decreases within the range of 20-35 kPa (3-5 psi). When switch contacts close, either the engine will stop or a "Low Oil" warning light will be activated, depending on engine application.

To check sensor pressure switch, a regulated supply of compressed air and a continuity tester are required. With zero pressure applied to switch, tester should indicate continuity across switch terminal and ground. When pressure is increased through range of 20-35 kPa (3-5 psi), switch should open and tester should indicate no continuity. If switch fails test, install new switch.

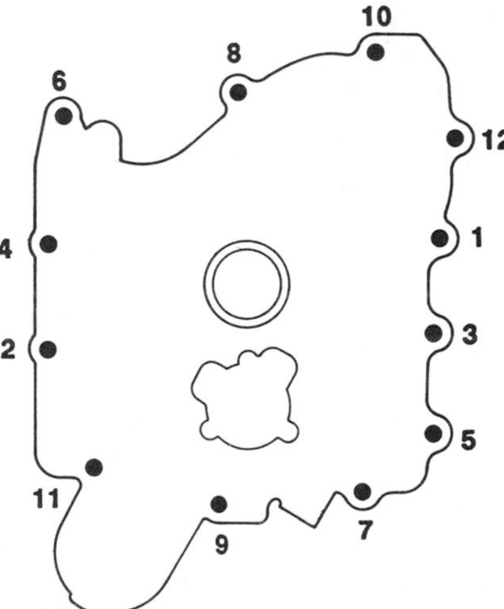


*Fig. KO84—Follow sequence shown when tightening oil pan mounting screws.*



Illustrations courtesy Kohler Co.

# KOHLER

**KOHLER COMPANY**
**Kohler, Wisconsin 53044**

| Model | No. Cyls. | Bore | Stroke | Displacement | Power Rating |
|---|---|---|---|---|---|
| M8 | 1 | 2.94 in. (74.6 mm) | 2.75 in. (69.9 mm) | 18.64 cu. in. (305 cc) | 8 hp. (6.0 kW) |
| M10 | 1 | 3.25 in. (82.5 mm) | 2.88 in. (73.0 mm) | 23.85 cu. in. (392 cc) | 10 hp. (7.5 kW) |
| M12 | 1 | 3.38 in. (85.7 mm) | 3.25 in. (82.5 mm) | 29.07 cu. in. (476 cc) | 12 hp. (8.9 kW) |
| M14 | 1 | 3.50 in. (88.9 mm) | 3.25 in. (82.5 mm) | 31.27 cu. in. (512 cc) | 14 hp (10.4 kW) |
| M16 | 1 | 3.75 in. (95.2 mm) | 3.25 in. (82.5 mm) | 35.90 cu. in. (588 cc) | 16 hp. (11.9 kW) |

## ENGINE IDENTIFICATION

All models are four-stroke, single cylinder, horizontal crankshaft type engines. All engines are equipped with ball bearing mains at each end of crankshaft and are splash lubricated. A side draft carburetor is used on all engines. Engine model, specification and serial numbers are located on a tag on carburetor side of the rewind starter and cooling fan housing. Always furnish engine model, specification and serial number when ordering parts.

An automotive diaphragm type fuel pump is used on some models. This pump is equipped with a priming lever. A fuel pump repair kit is available.

## MAINTENANCE

**SPARK PLUG.** Recommended spark plug for Model M8 is a Champion J-8. Recommended spark plug for Models M10, M12, M14 and M16 is a Champion H-10. Recommended electrode gap is 0.25 inch (6.35 mm) for all models.

**CARBURETOR.** All models are equipped with a Kohler side-draft carburetor. For initial adjustment, open idle mixture screw (7–Fig. KO100) 1¼ turns and main mixture screw (1) 2 turns from a lightly seated position on Model M8. For Models M10 and M12, open idle mixture screw (7) 2½ turns and main mixture screw (1) 1½ turns from a lightly seated position. For Models M14 and M16, open idle and main mixture screws 2½ turns from a lightly seated position.

Make final adjustments on all models with engine at operating temperature and running. Place engine under load and adjust main mixture screw (1) to leanest mixture that will allow satisfactory acceleration and steady governor operation. If engine misses and backfires under load, mixture is too lean. If engine shows a sooty exhaust and is sluggish under load, mixture is too rich. Adjust idle speed stop screw (5) to maintain an idle speed of 1200 rpm. Then, adjust idle mixture screw (7) for smoothest idle operation.

Main and idle mixture adjustments have some effect on each other. Recheck engine operation and readjust mixture screws as necessary for smoothest operation.

To check float level, invert carburetor body and float assembly. There should be 11/64 inch (4 mm) clearance between machined surface of body casting and free end of float as shown in upper view of Fig. KO101. Adjust as necessary by bending float lever tang that contacts inlet valve. Turn carburetor over and measure float drop. Float drop should be

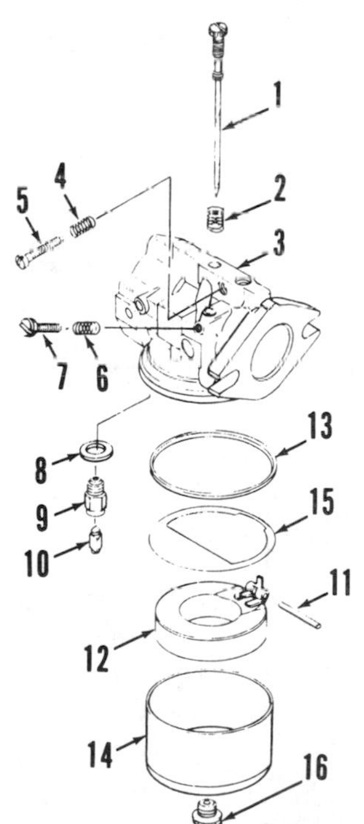


**Fig. KO100 – Exploded view of Kohler side draft carburetor.**

1. Main mixture screw
2. Spring
3. Carburetor body
4. Spring
5. Idle speed stop screw
6. Spring
7. Idle mixture screw
8. Sealing washer
9. Inlet valve seat
10. Inlet valve
11. Float pin
12. Float
13. Gasket
14. Float bowl
15. Baffle gasket
16. Bowl retainer

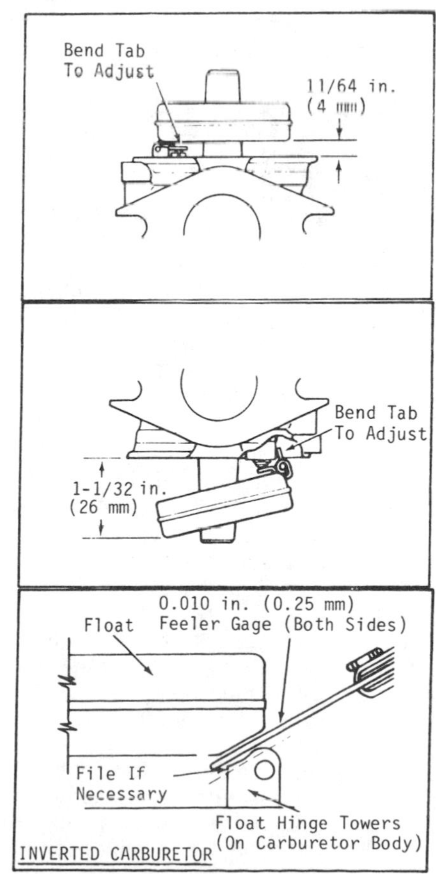


**Fig. KO101 – View showing float adjustment procedure. Refer to text.**

1-1/32 inches (26 mm) between the machined surface of body and the bottom of the free end of float as shown in middle view of Fig. KO101. Bend the float tab to adjust. Float-to-float hinge tower clearance should be 0.010 inch (0.25 mm) as shown in lower view of Fig. KO101. File float hinge tower as needed to obtain recommended clearance.

**AIR FILTER.** All models are equipped with a foam type precleaner and a paper air filter element. Foam precleaner should be serviced after every 25 hours of operation and paper element should be cleaned after every 100 hours of operation and renewed after every 300 hours of operation.

To service foam precleaner, remove precleaner and wash in a solution of warm water and detergent. Rinse thoroughly with clean water until all traces of detergent are eliminated. Squeeze out excess water and allow foam element to air dry. Saturate foam element in clean engine oil and squeeze out excess oil.

To clean paper element, remove foam precleaner and paper element. Remove foam precleaner element from paper element and gently tap paper element to dislodge dirt. Do not wash paper element or use compressed air to clean.

**GOVERNOR.** All models are equipped with a gear driven flyweight governor that is located inside engine crankcase. Maximum recommended governed engine speed is 3600 rpm. Recommended idle speed of 1200 rpm is controlled by adjustment of throttle stop screw on carburetor.

For initial adjustment of governor linkage, loosen governor lever clamp bolt nut and pull governor lever away from carburetor as far as it will go. Then, turn governor shaft counterclockwise as far as it will go while holding governor lever. Tighten clamp bolt nut. On Model M8, make certain there is at least 1/16 inch (1.6 mm) clearance between governor lever and cross shaft bushing nut (Fig. KO102). On Models M10, M12, M14 and M16, make certain there is at least 1/16 inch (1.6 mm) clearance between governor lever and upper left cam gear cover bolt (Fig. KO103).

High speed setting depends on engine application. Maximum allowable speed is 3600 rpm. Maximum speed is adjusted by loosening jam nut on high speed adjusting screw and turning screw until desired speed is obtained. Governor sensitivity is adjusted by repositioning governor spring in the holes in governor lever (KO104). Standard spring position on Model M8 is the third hole from the cross shaft. Standard spring position on Models M10, M12, M14 and M16 is the sixth hole from the cross shaft. To increase sensitivity, move spring toward cross shaft and to decrease sensitivity, move spring away from cross shaft.

**IGNITION SYSTEM.** All models are equipped with an electronic magneto ignition system consisting of a magnet cast into the flywheel, an electronic magneto ignition module mounted on the engine bearing plate outside of flywheel and an ignition switch which grounds ignition module to stop engine.

Air gap between flywheel and ignition module should be 0.012-0.016 inch (0.30-0.41 mm).

Ignition system is considered satisfactory if system will produce a spark that will jump a test plug gap of 0.035 inch (0.89 mm). To test the primary side of ignition module using an ohmmeter, connect the positive ohmmeter lead to ignition module laminations (A–Fig. KO105) and the negative ohmmeter lead to kill terminal (B). Ohmmeter reading should be 1.0-1.3 ohms. To test the secondary side of ignition module using an ohmmeter, connect the positive ohmmeter lead to ignition module laminations (A) and the negative ohmmeter lead to high tension lead (C). Ohmmeter reading should be 7,900-10,850 ohms. If ohmmeter readings are not as specified, renew ignition module.

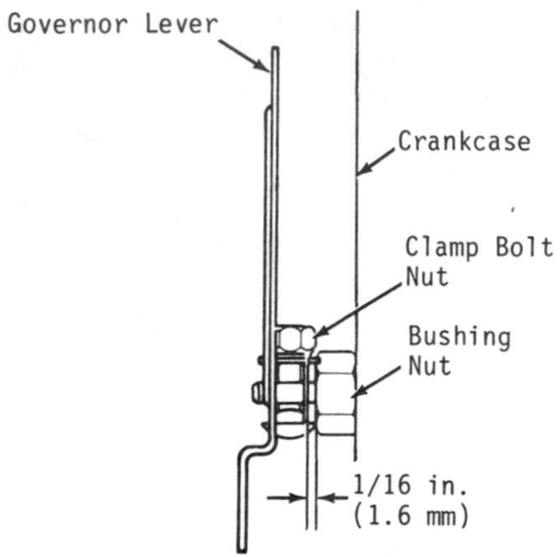


*Fig. KO102—View of Model M8 governor linkage. Refer to text for adjustment procedure.*

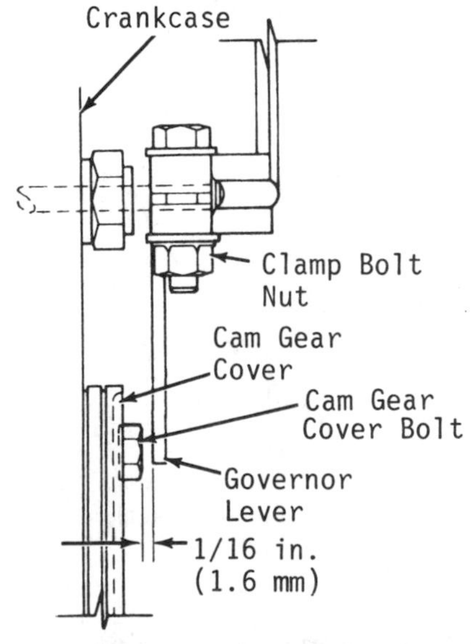


*Fig. KO103—View of Models M10, M12, M14 and M16 governor linkage. Refer to text for adjustment procedure.*

**VALVE ADJUSTMENT.** Valve stem clearance should be checked after every 500 hours of operation. Valve stem clearance for Model M8 should be 0.006-0.008 inch (0.15-0.20 mm) for intake valve and 0.017-0.019 inch (0.43-0.48 mm) for exhaust valve. Valve stem clearance for Models M10, M12, M14 and M16 should be 0.008-0.010 inch (0.20-0.25 mm) for intake valve and 0.017-0.019 inch (0.43-0.48 mm) for exhaust valve. If clearance is not as specified, refer to VALVE SYSTEM under REPAIR section for valve service procedure.

**CYLINDER HEAD AND COMBUSTION CHAMBER.** Cylinder head should be removed and carbon and lead deposits cleaned after every 500 hours of operation. Refer to CYLINDER HEAD under REPAIR section for cylinder head removal procedure.

**LUBRICATION.** Engine oil should be checked daily and oil level maintained between the "F" and "L" mark on dipstick. Push dipstick all the way down in tube to obtain reading.

Manufacturer recommends oil having API service classification of SC, SD, SE or SF. Use SAE 5W-30 oil for temperatures below 32° F (0° C) and SAE 30 oil for temperatures above 32° F (0° C).

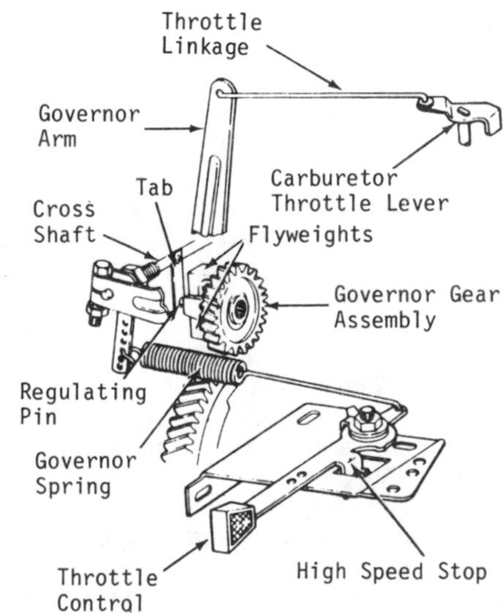


*Fig. KO104—View showing typical governor linkage arrangement used on most models.*

Illustrations courtesy Kohler Co.

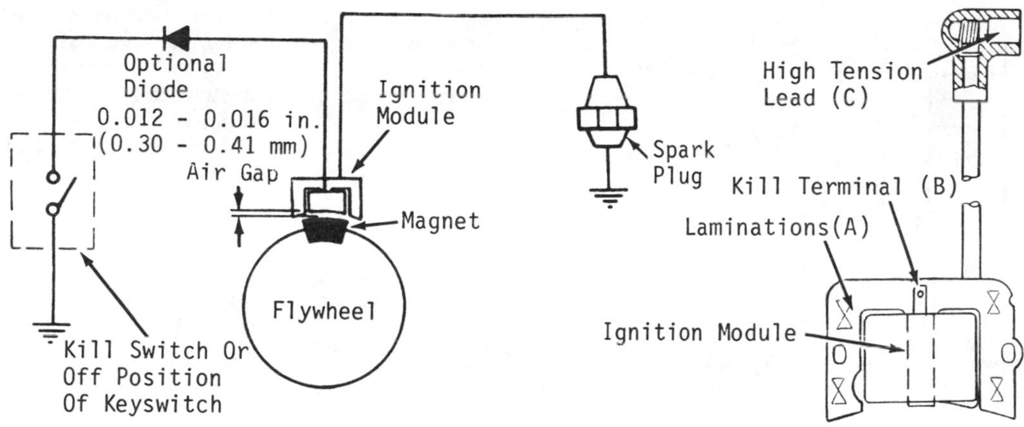


*Fig. KO105—Typical wiring diagram for all models.*

Oil should be changed after the first 5 hours of operation and at 25 hour intervals thereafter. Crankcase oil capacity is 1 quart (0.95 L) for Model M8 and 2 quarts (1.9 L) for Models M10, M12, M14 and M16.

**GENERAL MAINTENANCE.** Check and tighten all loose bolts, nuts and clamps daily. Check for fuel and oil leakage and repair if necessary. Clean cooling fins and external surfaces at 50 hour intervals.

## REPAIR

**TIGHTENING TORQUES.** Recommended tightening torque specifications are as follows:

Spark plug . . . . . . . . . . . . . 18-22 ft.-lbs.) (24-29 N·m)

Cylinder head:

Model M8. . . . . . . . . . . . . 15-20 ft.-lbs.) (20-27 N·m)

Models M10, M12, M14, M16 . . . . . . . . . . . . . . . . . 25-30 ft.-lbs.) (34-40 N·m)

Flywheel:

Model M8. . . . . . . . . . . . . 85-90 ft.-lbs.) (115-122 N·m)

Models M10, M12, M14, M16 (plastic fan) . . . . . . . 35-40 ft.-lbs.) (48-54 N·m)

Models M10, M12, M14, M16 (iron fins) . . . . . . . . . 22-27 ft.-lbs.) (29-37 N·m)

Connecting rod:

Model M8 (New) . . . . . . . . . . 12 ft.-lbs.) (16 N·m)

Model M8 (Used) . . . . . . . . . . 8 ft.-lbs.) (11 N·m)

Models M10, M12, M14, M16 (New) . . . . . . . . . . . . . . 22 ft.-lbs.) (29 N·m)

Models M10, M12, M14, M16 (Used) . . . . . . . . . . . . . . 17 ft.-lbs.) (23 N·m)

Engine base . . . . . . . . . . . . . . . . 7 ft.-lbs.) (10 N·m)

**CYLINDER HEAD.** To remove cylinder head, first remove all necessary metal shrouds. Clean engine to prevent entrance of foreign material and remove cylinder head retaining bolts.

Always use a new head gasket when installing cylinder head. Tighten cylinder head bolts evenly and in graduated steps using the sequence shown in Fig. KO106 for the model being serviced. Tighten bolts to specified torque.

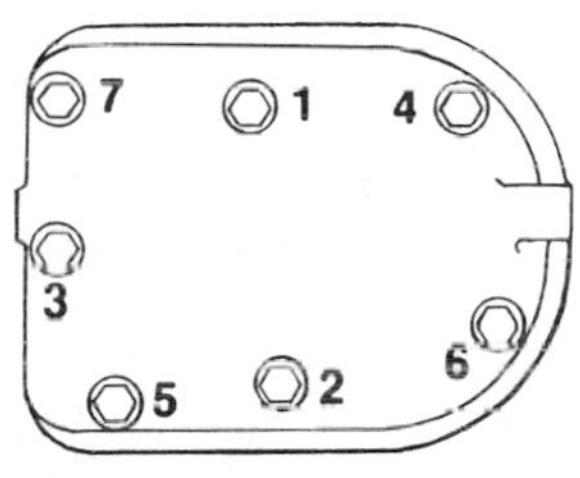


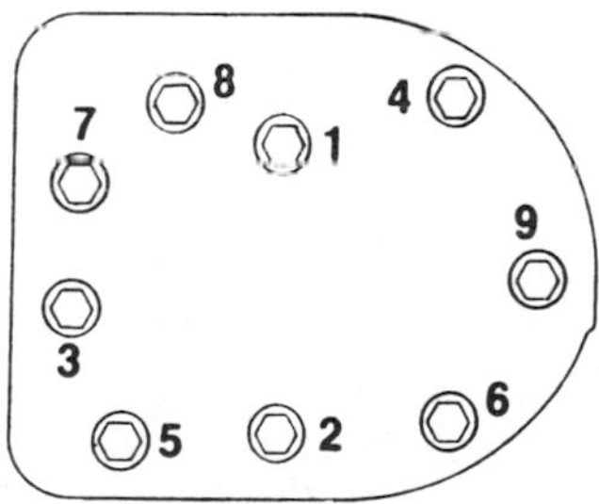


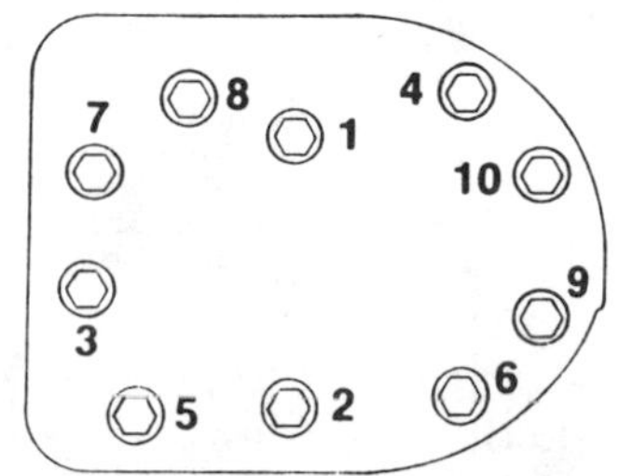


*Fig. KO106—Cylinder head bolts must be tightened in the sequence shown. Upper view is for Model M8, middle view is for Models M10, M12 and M14 and lower view is for Model M16.*

**CONNECTING ROD.** The aluminum alloy connecting rod rides directly on the crankpin journal. Model M8 engines are equipped with a narrow connecting rod for engines equipped with style "D" piston or a wider connecting rod for engines equipped with style "A" piston. Refer to following PISTON, PIN AND RINGS and upper view of Fig. KO107. Connecting rod and piston are removed as an assembly after cylinder head and engine base have been removed. Remove the two connecting rod bolts and connecting rod cap and push piston and rod assembly out top of block. Remove snap rings retaining piston pin and push pin out of piston and connecting rod.

Inside diameter for piston pin hole in connecting rod should be 0.6255-0.6258 inch (15.888-15.895 mm) for Model M8, 0.8596-0.8599 inch (21.834-21.842 mm) for Model M10 and 0.8757-0.8760 inch (22.243-22.250 mm) for Models M12, M14 and M16. Piston pin-to-connecting rod running clearance should be 0.0006-0.0011 inch (0.015-0.028 mm) for Model M8 and 0.0003-0.0008 inch (0.008-0.020 mm) for Models M10, M12, M14 and M16.

Connecting rod side play on crankpin should be 0.005-0.016 inch (0.13-0.41 mm) for Model M8 and 0.007-0.016 inch (0.18-0.41 mm) for Models M10, M12, M14 and M16.

Connecting rod-to-crankpin running clearance should be 0.001-0.002 inch (0.025-0.50 mm) for all models. If running clearance is 0.0025 inch (0.064 mm) or greater, renew connecting rod and/or recondition crankshaft journal. A 0.010 inch (0.25 mm) undersize connecting rod is available. Undersize connecting rod is identified by a drilled hole in connecting rod just above crankpin bearing end as shown in lower view of Fig. KO107.

Reinstall connecting rod and piston assembly with match marks on connecting rod and cap and the word "FLY" stamped on piston top toward flywheel

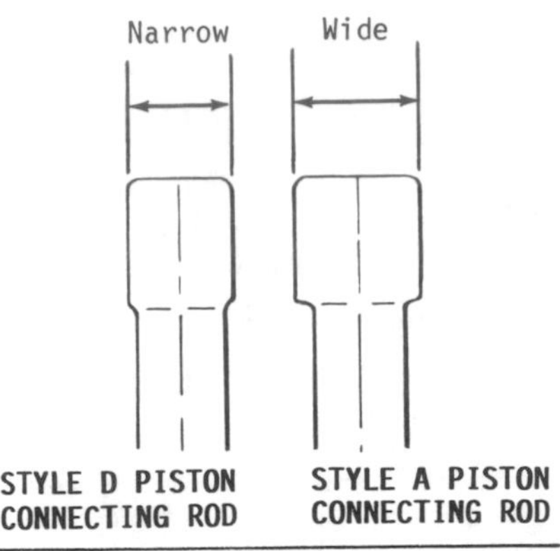


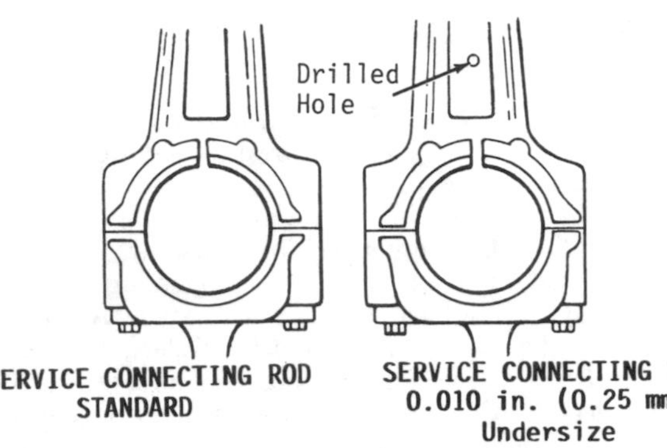


***Fig. KO107 — Style "D" piston must be mounted on narrow connecting rod. Style "A" piston must be mounted on wide connecting rod. Lower view shows location of drilled hole used to identify connecting rod used on 0.010 inch (0.25 mm) undersize crankpin journal.***

side of engine. Tighten connecting rod nuts to specified torque.

**PISTON, PIN AND RINGS.** The aluminum alloy piston is fitted with two compression rings and one oil control ring. Piston pin outside diameter should be 0.6247-0.6249 inch (15.867-15.873 mm) for Model M8 and 0.8752-0.8754 inch (22.230-22.235 mm) for Models M10, M12, M14 and M16. Model M8 can be equipped with either a style "A" or "C" piston (Fig. KO108), Models M10, M12 and M14 will be equipped with style "A" piston and Model M16 can be equipped with either style "C" or "D" piston. Refer to the following paragraphs for style "A," "C" and "D" piston specifications.

On all models, piston must be installed on connecting rod so the match marks on connecting rod and cap and the word "FLY" stamped on piston top are toward flywheel side of engine after installation.

**Style "A" Piston.** Diameter of piston is measured just below oil control ring groove as shown in upper view of Fig. KO108.

Piston diameter should be 2.9281-2.9297 inches (74.374-74.414 mm) for Model M8, 3.2413-3.2432 inches (82.329-82.377 mm) for Model M10, 3.365-3.368 inches (85.47-85.55 mm) for Model M12 and 3.4925-3.4941 inches (88.710-88.754 mm) for Model M14. If piston diameter is 2.925 inches (74.295 mm) or less for Model M8, 3.238 inches (82.245 mm) or less for Model M10, 3.363 inches (85.420 mm) or less for Model M12 or 3.491 inches (88.671 mm) or less for Model M14, renew piston.

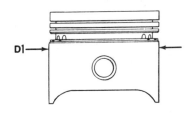

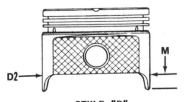

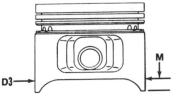

***Fig. KO108 — View showing differences between style "A," "C" and "D" pistons. Measure diameter of piston at location identified by (D1, D2 or D3). Dimension (M) is ½ inch (12.7 mm). Refer to text.***

Piston-to-cylinder clearance for Models M8, M10, M12 and M14 should be 0.007-0.010 inch (0.18-0.25 mm). Piston ring side clearance for Models M8, M10, M12 and M14 should be 0.006 inch (0.15 mm). Piston ring end gap for new rings should be 0.007-0.017 inch (0.18-0.37 mm) for Model M8 and 0.010-0.020 inch (0.25-0.51 mm) for Models M10, M12 and M14. Piston ring end gap for used rings should be 0.027 inch (0.69 mm) for Model M8 and 0.030 inch (0.76 mm) for Models M10, M12 and M14. If dimensions are not as specified, renew piston and/or rings.

**Styles "C" and "D" Piston.** Diameter of piston is measured ½ inch (12.7 mm) up from bottom of skirt as shown in middle and lower view of Fig. KO108. Piston diameter should be 2.9329-2.9336 inches (74.496-74.513 mm) for Model M8 and 3.7455-3.7465 inches (95.136-95.161 mm) for Model M16. If piston diameter is 2.9312 inches (74.453 mm) or less for Model M8, or 3.7435 inches (95.085 mm) or less for Model M16, renew piston. Piston-to-cylinder clearance should be 0.0034-0.0051 inch (0.086-0.130 mm) for Model M8 and 0.0030-0.0050 inch (0.076-0.127 mm) for Model M16.

Piston ring side clearance should be 0.006 inch (0.15 mm) for Models M8 and M16. Piston ring end gap for new rings should be 0.010-0.023 inch (0.25-0.58 mm) for Model M8 and 0.010-0.020 inch (0.25-0.51 mm) for Model M16. Piston ring end gap for used rings should be 0.032 inch (0.81 mm) for Model M8 and 0.030 inch (0.76 mm) for Model M16. If dimensions are not as specified, renew piston and/or rings.

**CYLINDER AND CRANKCASE.** Cylinder and crankcase are integral castings. Cylinder bore diameter should be 2.9370-2.9380 inches (74.5998-74.6252 mm) for Model M8, 3.2505-3.2515 inches (82.5627-82.5881 mm) for Model M10, 3.3745-3.3755 inches (85.7123-85.7377 mm) for Model M12, 3.4995-3.5005 inches (88.8873-88.9127 mm) for Model M14 and 3.7495-3.7505 inches (95.2373-95.2627 mm) for Model M16. If cylinder bore diameter is 2.941 inches (74.679 mm) or more for Model M8, 3.254 inches (82.652 mm) or more for Model M10, 3.378 inches (85.801 mm) or more for Model M12, 3.503 inches (88.976 mm) or more for Model M14 or 3.753 inches (95.326 mm) or more for Model M16, recondition cylinder bore.

If cylinder bore is out-of-round more than 0.005 inch (0.13 mm), recondition cylinder bore. If cylinder bore taper exceeds 0.003 inch (0.08 mm) for Model M8 or 0.002 inch (0.05 mm) for Models M10, M12, M14 or M16, recondition cylinder bore.

**CRANKSHAFT, MAIN BEARINGS AND SEALS.** The crankshaft is supported at each end by a ball bearing type main bearing. Renew bearings (13–Fig. KO109) if excessively rough or loose. Crankshaft end play should be 0.002-0.023 inch (0.05-0.58 mm) for Model M8 and 0.003-0.020 inch (0.08-0.51 mm) for Models M10, M12, M14 and M16.

Standard crankpin journal diameter is 1.1855-1.1860 inches (30.112-30.124 mm) for Model M8, 1.5745-1.5749 inches (39.99-40.00 mm) for Models M10, M12, M14 and M16. If crankpin journal is out-of-round 0.0005 inch (0.013 mm) or more, recondition crankpin journal. If crankpin journal taper is 0.001 inch (0.025 mm) or more, recondition crankpin journal.

Main bearings should be a light press fit on crankshaft journals and in crankcase and bearing plate bores. If not, renew bearings and/or crankshaft or crankcase and bearing plate.

Front oil seal should be pressed into bearing plate seal bore so seal is 1/32 inch (0.8 mm) below seal bore surface. Rear oil seal should be pressed into crankcase bearing bore so seal is 1/8 inch (3 mm) below seal bore surface.

When installing crankshaft, align timing marks on crankshaft and camshaft gears as shown in Fig. KO110.

**NOTE: On models equipped with dynamic balancer, refer to following DYNAMIC BALANCER for installation and timing of balancer gears.**

**CAMSHAFT.** The hollow camshaft and integral camshaft gear turn on a pin that is a slip fit in flywheel side of crankcase and a drive fit in closed side of crankcase. Remove and install pin from open side (bearing plate side) of crankcase. Drive camshaft pin into pto side of crankcase until pin is 0.275-0.285 inch (6.99-7.24 mm) from machined bearing plate gasket surface (Fig. KO111). Apply chemical locking compound on cup plug and install into bore in bearing plate mounting surface to a depth of 0.055-0.065 inch (1.4-1.7 mm) (Fig. KO111). Camshaft end play should be 0.005-0.010 inch (0.127-0.254 mm) and is controlled by use of 0.005 and 0.010 inch thick spacer washers between camshaft and cylinder block at bearing plate side of crankcase.

All models are equipped with automatic compression release mechanism. The automatic compression release mechanism holds exhaust valve slightly open during first part of compression stroke, reducing compression pressure and allowing easier cranking of engine. At engine speeds above 650 rpm, compression release mechanism is inactive. To check cylinder compression, engine must be cranked at 650 rpm or higher to overcome compression release action. A reading can also be obtained by rotating flywheel in reverse direction with throttle in wide open position. Compression reading should be 110-120 psi (758-827 kPa) for an engine in top mechanical condition. When compression reading falls below 100 psi (689 kPa), engine should be disassembled as needed and worn or damaged component or components renewed.

**VALVE SYSTEM.** Valve tappet gap (cold) should be 0.006-0.008 inch (0.15-0.20 mm) for intake valve and 0.017-0.019 inch (0.43-0.48 mm) for exhaust valve on Model M8 and 0.008-0.010 inch (0.20-0.25 mm) for intake valve and 0.017-0.019 inch (0.43-0.48 mm) for exhaust valve on Models M10, M12, M14 and M16.

Correct valve tappet gap is obtained on Model M8 by grinding ends of valve stem

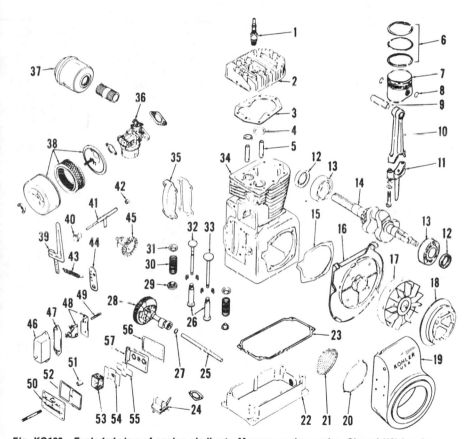

*Fig. KO109—Exploded view of engine similar to Magnum series engine. Shroud (19) has been replaced with a new design and cooling fins may be cast with flywheel (17) on some models or be a bolt-on plastic assembly on others.*

1. Spark plug
2. Cylinder head
3. Head gasket
4. Valve seat insert
5. Valve guide
6. Piston rings
7. Piston
8. Retaining ring
9. Piston pin
10. Connecting rod
11. Rod cap
12. Oil seal
13. Ball bearing
14. Crankshaft
15. Gasket
16. Bearing plate
17. Flywheel
18. Pulley
19. Shroud
20. Screen retainer
21. Screen
22. Oil pan
23. Gasket
24. Fuel pump
25. Camshaft pin
26. Valve tappets
27. Shim washer
28. Camshaft
29. Valve rotator
30. Valve spring
31. Spring retainer
32. Exhaust valve
33. Intake valve
34. Cylinder block
35. Camshaft cover
36. Carburetor
37. Muffler
38. Air cleaner assy.
39. Governor lever
40. Bushing
41. Governor shaft
42. Needle bearing
43. Governor spring
44. Speed lever
45. Governor gear & weight unit
46. Breaker cover (not used on M series)
47. Gasket
48. Breaker assy. (not used on M series)
49. Push rod
50. Valve cover
51. Breather seal
52. Gasket
53. Filter
54. Baffle
55. Reed
56. Gasket
57. Breather plate

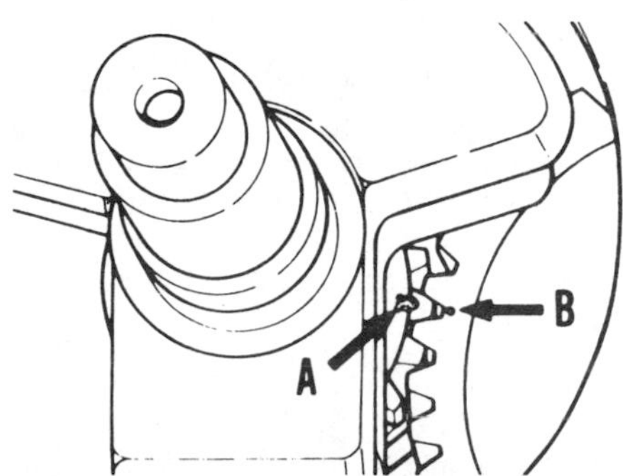


*Fig. KO110—Crankshaft gear and camshaft gear timing marks (A & B) must be aligned as shown during installation.*

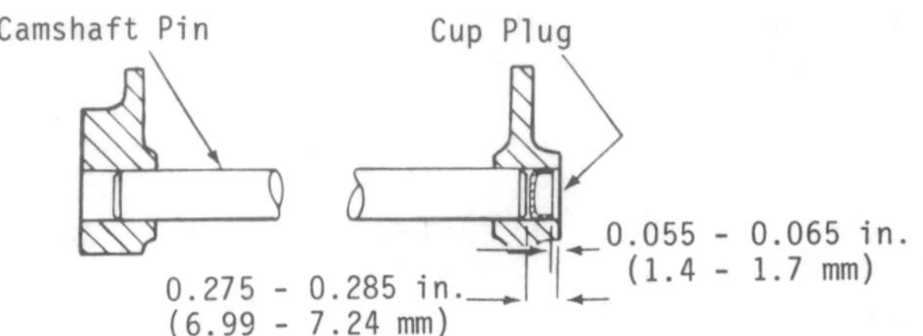


*Fig. KO111—View showing dimensions for camshaft pin installation.*

to increase clearance or by grinding seat or face of valve to decrease clearance. Models M10, M12, M14 and M16 are equipped with adjustable tappets.

Valve face and seat should be ground at a 45 degree angle for intake and exhaust valves. Standard seat width should be 1/32 to 1/16 inch (0.794-1.588 mm).

Renewable valve guides are used on all models. Intake valve stem to guide clearance should be 0.001-0.0025 inch (0.025-0.064 mm) and exhaust valve stem-to-guide clearance should be 0.0025-0.004 inch (0.064-0.102 mm) on all models. Ream valve guides after installation to obtain correct inside diameter of 0.312-0.313 inch (7.93-7.95 mm). Diameter of intake valve stem should be 0.3103 inch (7.88 mm) for all models. Exhaust valve stem on all models is slightly tapered. Exhaust valve stem diameter should be 0.3074 inch (7.81 mm) at upper valve stem area which enters valve guide.

**DYNAMIC BALANCER.** Some models may be equipped with a dynamic balancer system (Fig. KO112). The two balancer gears, equipped with needle bearings, rotate on two stub shafts which are pressed into bosses on pto side of crankcase. Snap rings secure gears on stub shafts and shim spacers are used to control gear end play. Balancer gears are driven by crankshaft in opposite direction of crankshaft rotation.

To renew stub shafts, press old shafts out and discard. Press new shaft in until it is 1.087-1.097 inches (25.598-25.601 mm) above stub shaft boss and use the 3/8 inch (9.525 mm) spacer between block and gear (Fig. KO113).

To install top balancer gear and bearing assembly, first place one 0.010 inch shim on stub shaft, install top gear assembly on shaft making certain timing marks are facing flywheel side of crankcase. In the following order, install one 0.005 inch shim, one 0.010 inch shim and one 0.020 inch shim on stub shaft and retain with snap ring. Using a feeler gage, check gear end play. Correct end play of balancer gear is 0.005-0.010 inch (0.13-0.25 mm). Add or remove shims in 0.005 inch increments as necessary to obtain correct end play.

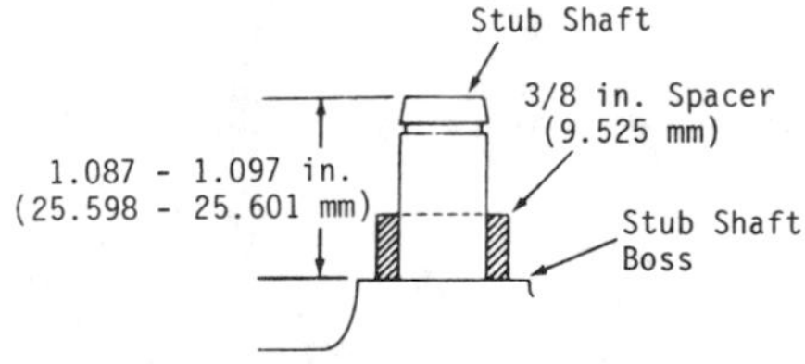


*Fig. KO113—View showing balancer gear stub shaft installation. Refer to text.*

**NOTE: Always install the 0.020 inch thick shim next to snap ring.**

Install crankshaft in crankcase and align primary timing mark on top balance gear with standard timing mark on crankshaft. See Fig. KO114. With primary timing marks aligned, engage crankshaft gear 1/16 inch (1.59 mm) into narrow section of top balancer gear and rotate crankshaft to align timing marks on camshaft gear and crankshaft as shown in Fig. KO110. Press crankshaft into crankcase until it is seated firmly in ball type main bearing.

Rotate crankshaft until crankpin is approximately 15 degrees past bottom dead center. Install one 0.010 inch shim on stub shaft, align secondary timing mark on bottom balancer gear with secondary timing mark on crankshaft counterweight. See Fig. KO114. Install gear assembly onto stub shaft. If properly timed, secondary timing mark on bottom balancer gear will be aligned with standard timing mark on crankshaft after gear is fully on stub shaft. Install one 0.005 inch shim and one 0.020 inch shim, then install snap ring. Check bottom balancer gear end play and add or remove shims in 0.005 inch increments as required to obtain proper end play of 0.005-0.010 inch (0.13-0.25 mm). Make certain the 0.020 inch shim is positioned against the snap ring.

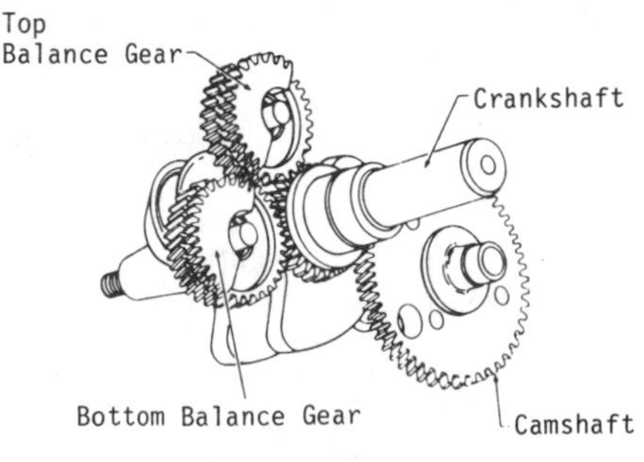


*Fig. KO112—View showing components of dynamic balancer system used on all models equipped with dynamic balancer.*

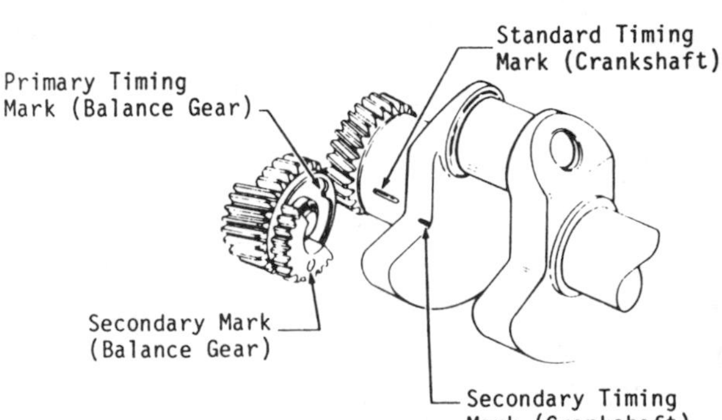


*Fig. KO114—View showing timing marks for installing dynamic balancer gears.*

# KOHLER

## SERVICING KOHLER ACCESSORIES

### RETRACTABLE STARTERS

Fairbanks-Morse or Eaton retractable starters are used on some Kohler engines. When servicing starters, refer to appropriate following paragraph.

### Fairbanks-Morse

**OVERHAUL.** To disassemble starter, remove retainer ring, retainer washer, brake spring, friction washer, friction shoe assembly and second friction washer as shown in Fig. KO160. Hold rope handle in one hand and cover in the other and allow rotor to rotate to unwind recoil spring preload. Lift rotor from cover, shaft and recoil spring. Note winding direction of recoil spring and rope for aid in reassembly. Remove recoil spring from cover and unwind rope from rotor.

When reassembling unit, lubricate recoil spring, cover shaft and its bore in rotor with "Lubriplate" or equivalent. Install rope on rotor and rotor to shaft, then engage recoil spring inner end hook. Preload recoil spring four turns, then install middle flange and mounting flange. Check friction shoe sharp ends and renew if necessary. Install friction washers, friction shoe assembly, brake spring, retainer washer and retainer ring. Make certain friction shoe assembly is installed properly for correct starter rotation. If properly installed, sharp ends of friction shoe plates will extend when rope is pulled.

Starter operation can be reversed by winding rope and recoil spring in opposite direction and turning friction shoe assembly upside down. See Fig. KO161 for counterclockwise assembly.

### Eaton

**OVERHAUL.** To disassemble starter, first release tension of rewind spring as follows: Hold starter assembly with pulley facing up. Pull starter rope until notch in pulley is aligned with rope hole in cover. Use thumb pressure to prevent pulley from rotating. Engage rope in notch of pulley and slowly release thumb pressure to allow spring to unwind until all tension is released.

When removing rope pulley, use extreme care to keep starter spring confined in housing. Check starter spring for breaks, cracks or distortion. If starter spring is to be renewed, carefully remove it from housing, noting direction of rotation of spring before removing. Exploded view of clockwise starter is shown in Fig. KO162.

Check pawl, brake, spring, retainer and hub for wear and renew as necessary. If starter rope is worn or frayed, remove from pulley, noting

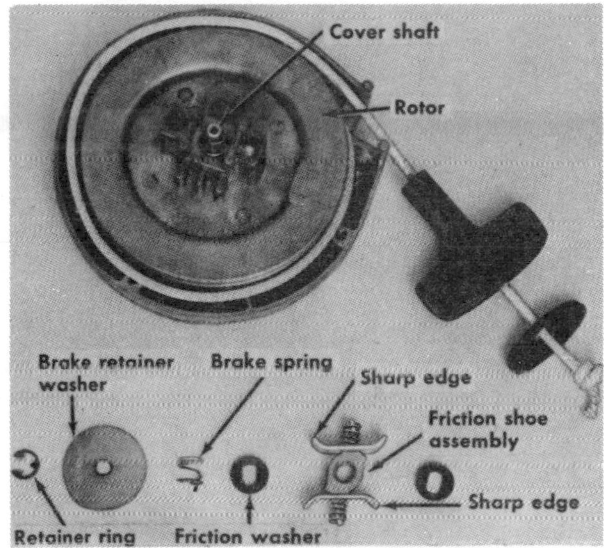


*Fig. KO160—Fairbanks-Morse retractable starter with friction shoe assembly removed.*

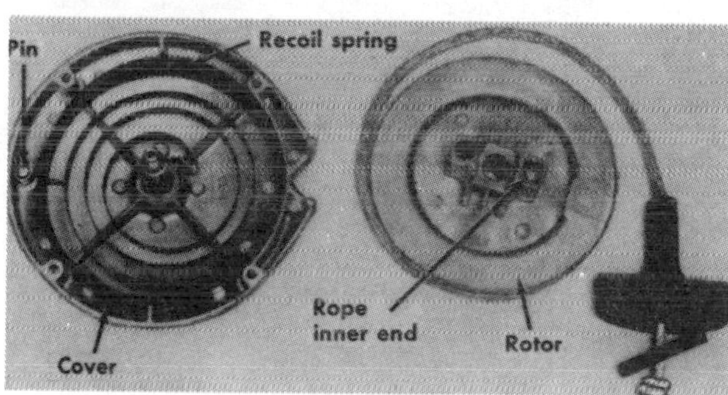


*Fig. KO161—View showing recoil spring and rope installed for counterclockwise starter operation.*

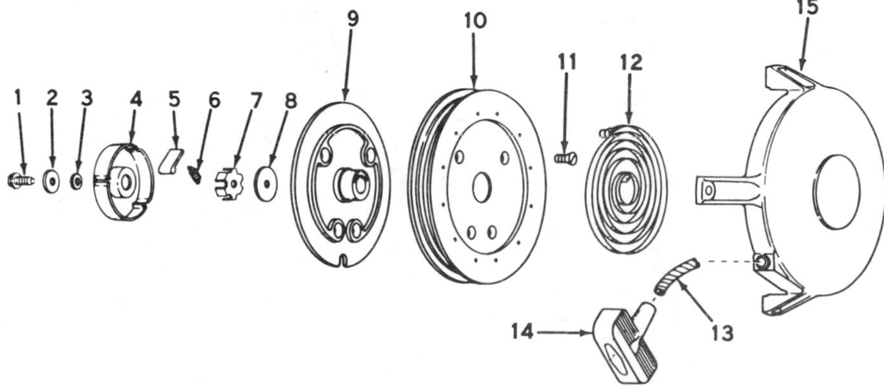


*Fig. KO162—Exploded view of Eaton retractable starter assembly.*

1. Retainer screw
2. Brake washer
3. Spacer
4. Retainer
5. Pawl
6. Spring
7. Brake
8. Thrust washer
9. Pulley hub
10. Pulley
11. Screw
12. Recoil spring
13. Rope
14. Handle
15. Starter housing

Illustrations courtesy Kohler Co.

direction it is wrapped on pulley. Renew rope and install pulley in housing, aligning notch in pulley assembly in housing, align notch in pulley hub with hook in end of spring. Use a wire bent to form a hook to aid in positioning spring in hub.

After securing pulley assembly in housing, engage rope in notch and rotate pulley at least two full turns in same direction it is pulled to properly preload starter spring. Pull rope to fully extended position. Release handle and if spring is properly preloaded, rope will fully rewind.

Before installing starter on engine, check teeth in starter driven hub (165-Fig. KO163) for wear and renew hub if necessary.

## 12-VOLT STARTER-GENERATOR

A combination 12-volt starter-generator manufactured by Delco-Remy is used on some Kohler engines. Starter-generator functions as a cranking motor when starting switch is closed. When engine is operating and with starting switch open, unit operates as a generator. Generator output and circuit voltage for battery and various operating requirements are controlled by a current-voltage regulator.

Kohler recommends starter-generator belt tension be adjusted until about 10 pounds pulling pressure (4.5 kg) applied midway between pulleys will deflect belt ½-inch (12.7 mm).

To determine cause of abnormal operation starter-generator should be given a "no-load" test or a "generator output" test. Generator output test can be performed with starter-generator on or off engine. No-load test must be made with starter-generator removed from engine. Refer to Fig. KO164 for exploded view of starter-generator assembly. Parts are available from Kohler as well as authorized Delco-Remy service stations.

Starter-generator brush spring tension for all models should be 24-32 oz. (0.68-0.91 kg).

Starter-generator and regulator service test specifications are as follows:

### Starter-Generators 1101940, 1101970, 1101973 & 1101980.

Field draw–
Amperes ...............1.52-1.62
Volts ........................12
Cold output–
Amperes ......................12
Volts ........................12
Rpm ........................4950
No-load test–
Volts ........................11
Amperes (max.) ...............18
Rpm (min.) .................2500
Rpm (max.) .................2900

### Starter-Generators 1101932, 1101948, 1101968, 1101972 & 1101974.

Field draw–
Amperes ...............1.45-1.57
Volts ........................12
Cold output–
Amperes ......................10
Volts ........................14
Rpm ........................5450
No-load test–
Volts ........................11
Amperes (max.) ...............17
Rpm (min.) .................2500
Rpm (max.) .................2900

### Starter-Generator 1101951 & 1101967.

Field draw–
Amperes ...............1.52-1.62
Volts ........................12
Cold output–
Amperes ......................15
Volts ........................14
Rpm ........................3400
No-load test–
Volts ........................11
Amperes (max.) ...............14
Rpm (min.) .................1650
Rpm (max.) .................1950

### Starter-Generator 1101996.

Field draw–
Amperes ...............1.52-1.62
Volts ........................12
Cold output–
Amperes ......................12
Volts ........................14
Rpm ........................4950
No-load test–
Volts ........................11
Amperes (max.) ...............18
Rpm (min.) .................2500
Rpm (max.) .................2900

### Regulators 1118984, 1118988 &1118999.

Ground polarity ............Negative
Cut-out relay–
Air gap ..................0.020 in. (0.508 mm)
Point gap.................0.020 in. (0.508 mm)
Closing voltage, range ..................11.8-14.0
Adjust to ....................12.8
Voltage regulator–
Air gap ..................0.075 in. (1.905 mm)
Setting voltage, range..................13.6-14.5
Adjust to ....................14.0

### Regulator 1118985.

Ground polarity .............Positive
Cut-out relay–
Air gap ..................0.020 in. (0.508 mm)
Point gap.................0.020 in. (0.508 mm)
Closing voltage, range..................11.8-14.0
Adjust to.....................12.8
Voltage regulator–
Air gap ..................0.075 in. (1.905 mm)
Setting voltage, range..................13.6-14.5
Adjust to.....................14.0

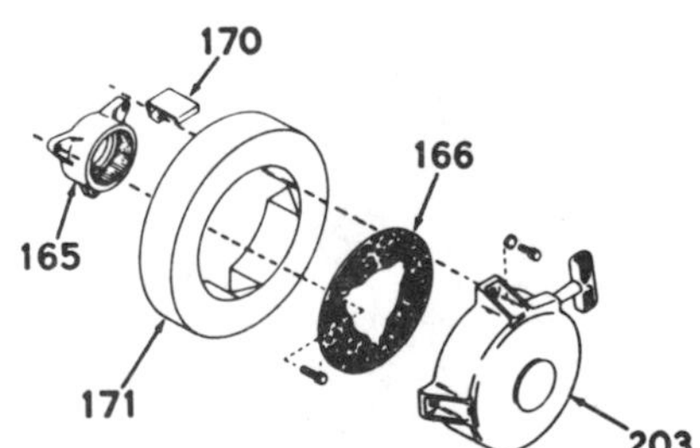


***Fig. KO163—View showing retractable starter and starter hub.***

165. Starter hub
166. Screen
170. Bracket
171. Air director
203. Retractable starter assy.

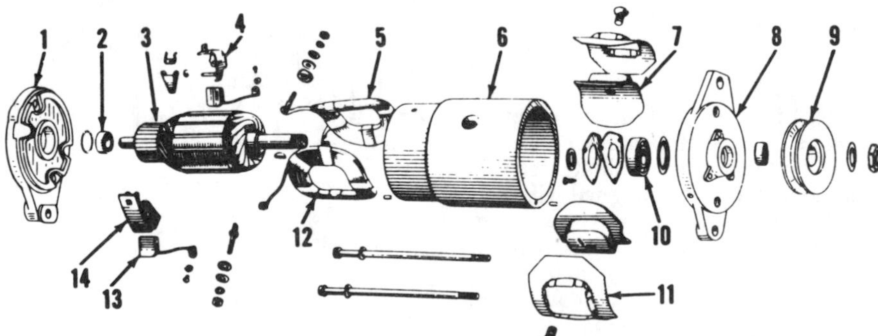


***Fig. KO164—Exploded view of typical Delco-Remy starter generator assembly.***

1. Commutator end frame
2. Bearing
3. Armature
4. Ground brush holder
5. Field coil (L.H.)
6. Frame
7. Pole shoe
8. Drive end frame
9. Pulley
10. Bearing
11. Field coil insulator
12. Field coil (L.H.)
13. Brush
14. Insulated brush holder



Illustrations courtesy Kohler Co.

## 12-VOLT GEAR DRIVE STARTERS

Four types of gear drive starters are used on Kohler engines. Refer to Figs. KO165, KO166, KO167 and KO168 for exploded view of starter motors and drives.

**TWO BRUSH COMPACT TYPE.** To disassemble starting motor, clamp mounting bracket in a vise. Remove through-bolts (H–Fig. KO165) and slide commutator end plate (J) and frame assemble (A) off armature. Clamp steel armature core in a vise and remove Bendix drive (E), drive end plate (F), thrust washer (D) and spacer (C) from armature (B).

Renew brushes if unevenly worn or worn to a length of 5/16-inch (7.938 mm) or less. To renew ground brush (K), drill out rivet, then rivet new brush lead to end plate. Field brush (P) is soldered to field coil lead.

Reassemble by reversing disassembly procedure. Lubricate bushings with a light coat of SAE 10 oil. Inspect Bendix drive pinion and splined sleeve for damage. If Bendix is in good condition, wipe clean and install completely dry. Tighten Bendix drive retaining nut to a torque of 130-150 in.-lbs. (15-18 N·m). Tighten through-bolts (H) to a torque of 40-55 in.-lbs. (4-7 N·m).

**PERMANENT MAGNET TYPE.** To disassemble starting motor, clamp mounting bracket in a vise and remove through-bolts (19 – Fig. KO166). Carefully slide end cap (10) and frame (11) off armature. Clamp steel armature core in a vise and remove nut (18), spacer (17), anti-drift spring (16), drive assembly (15), end plate (14) and thrust washer (13) from armature (12).

The two input brushes are part of terminal stud (6). Remaining two brushes (9) are secured with cap screws. When reassembling, lubricate bushings with American Bosch lubricant #LU3001 or equivalent. Do not lubricate starter drive. Use rubber band to hold brushes in position until started in commutator, then cut and remove rubber band. Tighten through-bolts to a torque of 80-95 in.-lbs. (8-10 N·m) and nut (18) to a torque of 90-110 in.-lbs. (11-12 N·m).

**FOUR BRUSH BENDIX DRIVE TYPE.** To disassemble starting motor, remove screws securing drive end plate (K–Fig. KO167) to frame (I). Carefully withdraw armature and drive assembly from frame assembly. Clamp steel armature core in a vise and remove Bendix drive retaining nut, then remove drive unit (A), end plate (K) and thrust washer from armature (J). Remove cover (H) and screws securing end plate (E) to frame. Pull field brushes (C) from brush holders and remove end plate assembly.

The two ground brush leads are secured to end plate (E) and the two field brush leads are soldered to field coils. Renew brush set if excessively worn.

Inspect bushing (L) in end plate (K) and renew bushing if necessary. When reassembling, lubricate bushings with light coat of SAE 10 oil. Do not lubricate Bendix drive assembly.

Note starter may be reinstalled with Bendix in engaged or disengaged posi-

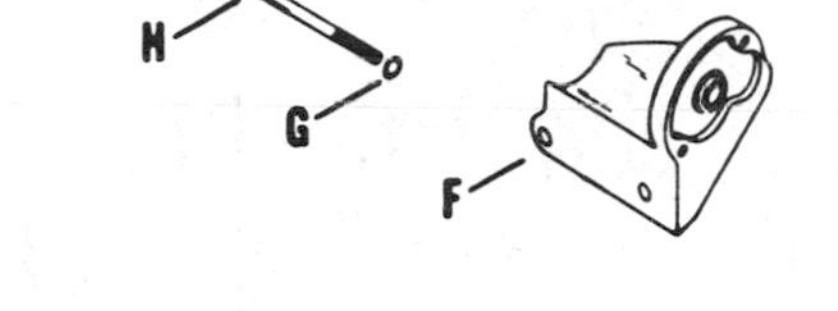

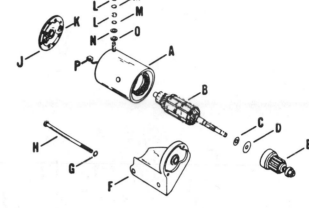

*Fig. KO165—Exploded view of two brush compact gear drive starting motor.*

A. Frame & field coil assy.
B. Armature
C. Spacer
D. Thrust washer
E. Bendix drive assy.
F. Drive end plate & mounting bracket
G. Lockwasher
H. Through bolt
J. Commutator end plate
K. Ground brush
L. Terminal nuts
M. Lockwashers
N. Flat washer
O. Insulating washer
P. Field brush

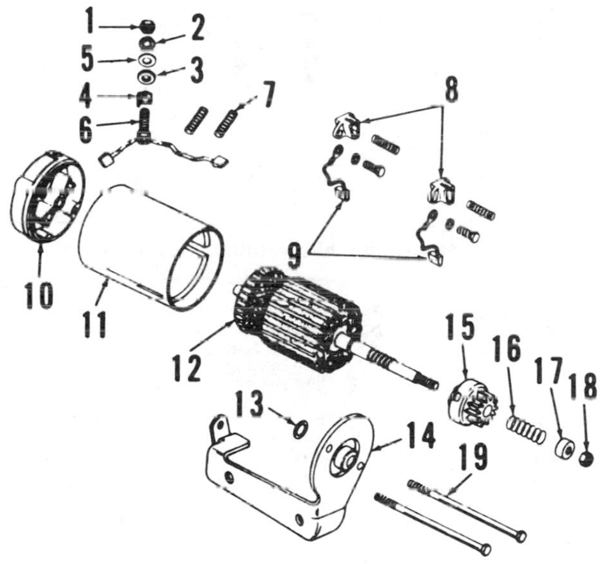


*Fig. KO166—Exploded view of permanent magnet type starting motor.*

1. Terminal nut
2. Lockwasher
3. Insulating washer
4. Terminal insulator
5. Flat washer
6. Terminal stud & input brushes
7. Brush springs (4 used)
8. Brush holders
9. Brushes
10. Commutator end cap
11. Frame & permanent magnets
12. Armature
13. Thrust washer
14. Drive end plate & mounting bracket
15. Drive assy.
16. Anti-drift spring
17. Spacer
18. Nut
19. Through-bolts

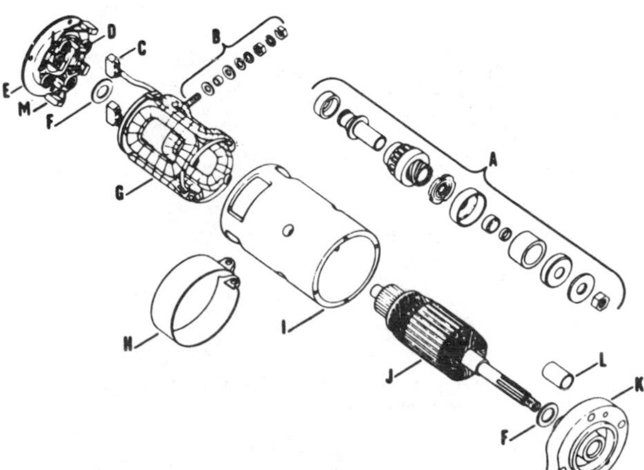


*Fig. KO167—Exploded view of conventional four brush starting motor with Bendix drive.*

A. Bendix drive assy.
B. Terminal stud set
C. Field brushes
D. Brush springs
E. Commutator end plate
F. Thrust washers
G. Field coils
H. Cover
I. Frame
J. Armature
K. Drive end plate
L. Bushing
M. Ground brushes

Illustrations courtesy Kohler Co.

tion. Do not attempt to disengage Bendix if it is in the engaged position.

**FOUR BRUSH SOLENOID SHIFT TYPE.** To disassemble starting motor, refer to Fig. KO168; then unbolt and remove solenoid switch assembly (items 1 through 6). Remove through-bolts (23), end plate (24) and frame (30) with brushes (26), brush holders (27 and 29) and field coil assembly (33). Remove screws retaining center bearing (21) to drive housing (12), remove shift lever pivot bolt, raise shift lever (9) and carefully withdraw armature and drive assembly. Drive unit (16) and center bearing (21) can be removed from armature (22) after snap ring (14) and retainer (15) are removed. Drive out shift lever pin and separate plunger (7), seal (8) and shift lever (9) from drive housing. Any further disassembly is obvious after examination of unit. Refer to Fig. KO168. Renew brushes (26), center bearing (21) and bushings in end plate (24) and drive housing (12) as necessary.

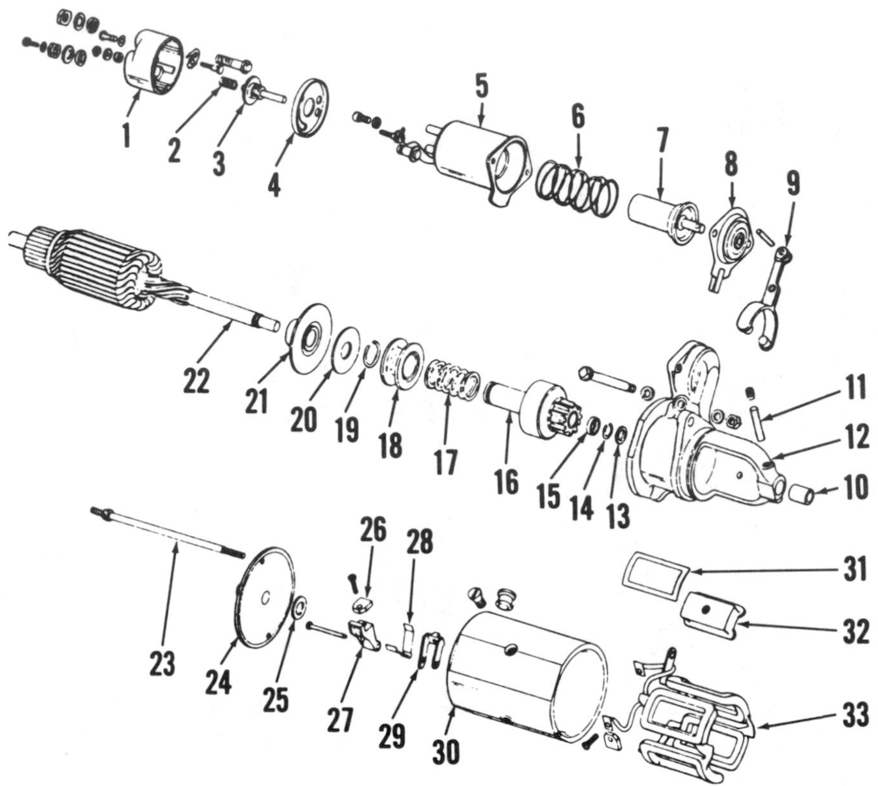


*Fig. KO168—Exploded view of conventional four brush starting motor with solenoid shift engagement.*

1. Switch cover
2. Spring
3. Contact disc
4. Gasket
5. Coil assy.
6. Return spring
7. Plunger
8. Seal
9. Shift lever
10. Bushing
11. Lubrication wick
12. Drive housing
13. Drive end thrust washer
14. Snap ring
15. Retainer
16. Drive unit
17. Spring
18. Shift collar
19. Snap ring
20. Brake washer
21. Center bearing
22. Armature
23. Through-bolt
24. End plate
25. Thrust washer
26. Brush (4 used)
27. Insulated brush holder
28. Brush spring
29. Ground brush
30. Frame
31. Field coil insulator
32. Pole shoe
33. Field coil assy.

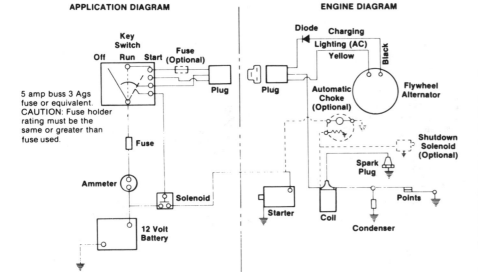

*Fig. KO169—Typical electrical wiring diagram for engines equipped with 3 amp alternator.*

## FLYWHEEL ALTERNATORS

**3 AMP ALTERNATOR.** The 3 amp alternator consists of a permanent magnet ring with five or six magnets on flywheel rim, a stator assembly attached to crankcase and a diode in charging output lead. See Fig. KO169.

To avoid possible damage to charging system, the following precautions must be observed:

1. Negative post of battery must be connected to engine ground and correct battery polarity must be observed at all times.
2. Prevent alternator leads (AC) from touching or shorting.
3. Remove battery or disconnect battery cables when recharging battery with battery charger.
4. Do not operate engine for any length of time without a battery in system.
5. Disconnect plug before electric welding is done on equipment powered by and in common ground with engine.

TROUBLESHOOTING. Defective conditions and possible causes are as follows:

1. No output. Could be caused by:
   A. Faulty windings in stator.
   B. Defective diode.
   C. Broken lead wire.
2. No lighting. Could be caused by:
   A. Shorted stator wiring.
   B. Broken lead.

If "no output" condition is the trouble, run following tests:

1. Connect ammeter in series with charging lead. Start engine and run at 2400 rpm. Ammeter should register 2 amp charge. Run engine at 3600 rpm. Ammeter should register 3 amp charge.
2. Disconnect battery charge lead from battery, measure resistance of lead to ground with an ohmmeter. Reverse ohmmeter leads and take another reading. One reading should be about mid-scale with meter set at R x 1. If both readings are high, diode or stator is open.
3. Expose diode connections on battery charge lead. Check resistance on stator side to ground. Reading should be



Illustrations courtesy Kohler Co.

1 ohm. If 0 ohms, winding is shorted. If infinity ohms, stator winding is open or lead wire is broken.

If "no lighting" condition is the trouble, use an AC voltmeter and measure open circuit voltage from lighting lead to ground with engine running at 3000 rpm. If 15 volts, wiring may be shorted.

Check resistance of lighting lead to ground. If 0.5 ohms, stator is good, 0 ohms indicates shorted stator and a reading of infinity indicates stator is open or lead is broken.

**3/6 AMP ALTERNATOR.** The 3/6 amp alternator consists of a permanent magnet ring with six magnets on flywheel rim, a stator assembly attached to crankcase and two diodes located in battery charging lead and auxiliary load lead. See Fig. KO170.

To avoid possible damage to charging system, the following precautions must be observed.

1. Negative post of battery must be connected to engine ground and correct battery polarity must be observed at all times.
2. Prevent alternator leads (AC) from touching or shorting.
3. Do not operate for any length of time without a battery in system.
4. Remove battery or disconnect battery cables when recharging battery with battery charger.
5. Disconnect plug before electric welding is done on equipment powered by and in common ground with engine.

TROUBLESHOOTING. Defective conditions and possible causes are as follows:

1. No output. Could be caused by:
   A. Faulty windings in stator.
   B. Defective diode.
   C. Broken lead.
2. No lighting. Could be caused by:
   A. Shorted stator wiring.
   B. Broken lead.

If "no output" condition is the trouble, run the following tests:

1. Disconnect auxiliary load lead and measure voltage from lead to ground with engine running 3000 rpm. If 17 volts or more, stator is good.
2. Disconnect battery charging lead from battery. Measure voltage from charging lead to ground with engine running at 3000 rpm. If 17 volts or more, stator is good.
3. Disconnect battery charge lead from battery and auxiliary load lead from switch. Measure resistance of both leads to ground. Reverse ohmmeter leads and take readings again. One reading should be infinity and the other reading should be about mid-scale with meter set at R x 1. If both readings are low, diode is shorted. If both readings are high, diode or stator is open.
4. Expose diode connections on battery charging lead and auxiliary load lead. Check resistance on stator side of diodes to ground. Readings should be 0.5 ohms. If reading is 0 ohms, winding is shorted. If infinity ohms, stator winding is open or lead wire is broken.

If "no lighting" condition is the trouble, disconnect lighting lead and measure open circuit voltage with AC voltmeter from lighting lead to ground with engine running at 3000 rpm. If 22 volts or more, stator is good. If less than 22 volts, wiring may be shorted.

Check resistance of lighting lead to ground. If 0.5 ohms, stator is good, 0 ohms reading indicates shorted stator and an infinity reading indicates an open stator winding or broken lead wire.

**10 AND 15 AMP ALTERNATOR.** Either a 10 or 15 amp alternator is used on some engines. Alternator output is controlled by a solid state rectifier-regulator.

To avoid possible damage to charging system, the following precautions must be observed:

1. Negative post of battery must be connected to engine ground and correct battery polarity must be observed at all times.
2. Rectifier-regulator must be con-

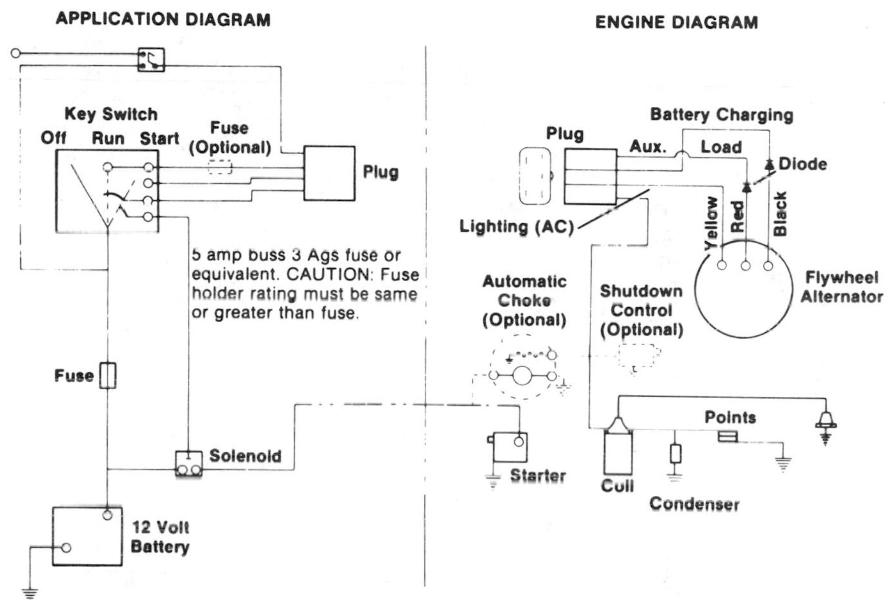


*Fig. KO170—Typical electrical wiring diagram for engines equipped with 3/6 amp alternator.*

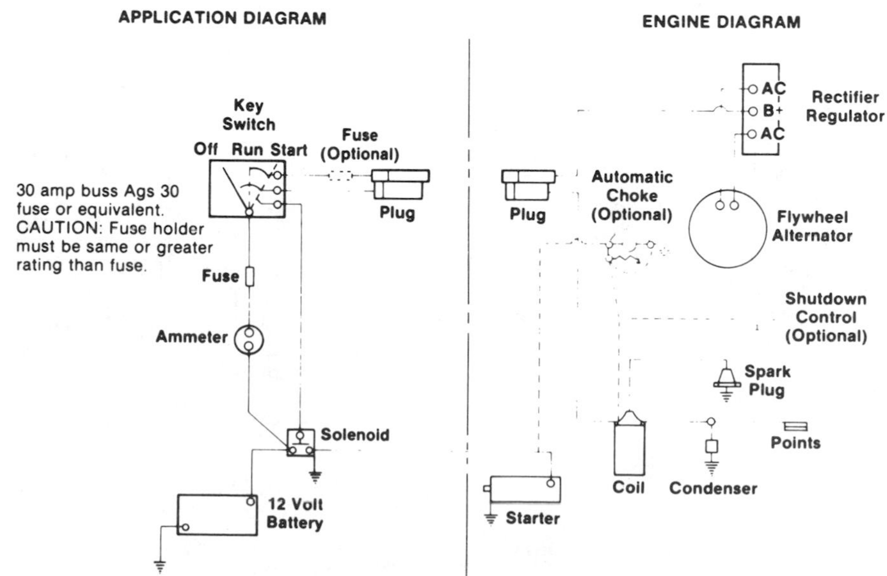


*Fig. KO171—Typical electrical wiring diagram for engines equipped with 15 amp alternator and breaker point ignition. The 10 amp alternator is similar.*

nected in common ground with engine and battery.

3. Disconnect leads at rectifier-regulator if electric welding is to be done on equipment in common ground with engine.

4. Remove battery or disconnect battery cables when recharging battery with battery charger.

5. Do not operate engine with battery disconnected.

6. Make certain AC leads are prevented from being grounded at all times.

OPERATION. Alternating current (AC) produced by alternator is changed to direct current (DC) in rectifier-regulator. See Fig. KO172. Current regulation is provided by electronic devices which "sense" counter-voltage created by battery to control or limit charging rate. No adjustments are possible on alternator charging system. Faulty components must be renewed. Refer to the following troubleshooting paragraph to help locate possible defective parts.

TROUBLESHOOTING. Defective conditions and possible causes are as follows:

1. No output. Could be caused by:
   A. Faulty windings in stator.
   B. Defective diode(s) in rectifier.
   C. Rectifier-regulator not properly grounded.
2. Full charge-no regulation. Could be caused by:
   A. Defective rectifier-regulator.
   B. Defective battery.

If "no output" condition is the trouble, disconnect B+ cable from rectifier-regulator. Connect a DC voltmeter between B+ terminal on rectifier-regulator and engine ground. Start engine and operate at 3600 rpm. DC voltage should be above 14 volts. If reading is above 0 volts but less than 14 volts, check for defective rectifier-regulator. If reading is 0 volts, check for defective rectifier-regulator or defective stator by disconnecting AC leads from rectifier-regulator and connecting an AC voltmeter to the two AC leads. Check AC voltage with engine running at 3600 rpm. If reading is less than 20 volts (10 amp alternator) or 28 volts (15 amp alternator), stator is defective. If reading is more than 20 volts (10 amp alternator) or 28 volts (15 amp alternator), rectifier-regulator is defective.

If "full charge-no regulation" is the condition, use a DC voltmeter and check B+ to ground with engine operating at 3600 rpm. If reading is over 14.7 volts, rectifier-regulator is defective. If reading is under 14.7 volts but over 14.0 volts, alternator and rectifier-regulator are satisfactory and battery is probably defective (unable to hold a charge).

**30 AMP ALTERNATOR.** A 30 amp flywheel alternator consisting of a permanent field magnet ring (on flywheel) and an alternator stator (on bearing plate on single cylinder engines or gear cover on two cylinder engines) is used on some models. Alternator output is controlled by a solid state rectifier-regulator.

To avoid possible damage to charging system, the following precautions must be observed:

1. Negative post of battery must be connected to engine ground and correct battery polarity must be observed at all times.

2. Rectifier-regulator must be connected in common ground with engine and battery.

3. Disconnect wire from rectifier-regulator terminal marked "BATT. NEG." if electric welding is to be done on equipment in common ground with engine.

4. Remove battery or disconnect battery cables when recharging battery with battery charger.

5. Do not operate engine with battery disconnected.

6. Make certain AC leads are prevented from being grounded at all times.

OPERATION. Alternating current (AC) produced by alternator is carried by two black wires to full wave bridge rectifier where it is changed to direct current (DC). Two red stator wires serve to complete a circuit from regulator to secondary winding in stator. A zener diode is used to sense battery voltage and it controls a Silicon Controlled Rectifier (SCR). SCR functions as a switch to allow current to flow in secondary winding in stator when battery voltage gets above a specific level.

An increase in battery voltage increases current flow in secondary winding in stator. This increased current flow in secondary winding brings about a corresponding decrease in AC current in primary winding, thus controlling output.

When battery voltage decreases, zener diode shuts off SCR and no current flows to secondary winding. At this time, maximum AC current is produced by primary winding.

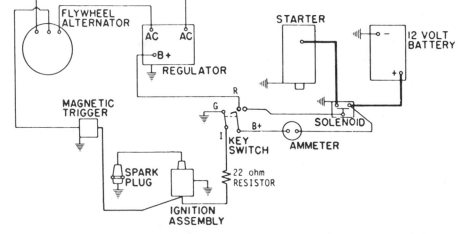

*Fig. KO172—Typical electrical wiring diagram for engine equipped with 15 amp flywheel alternator and breakerless ignition system. The 10 amp alternator is similar.*

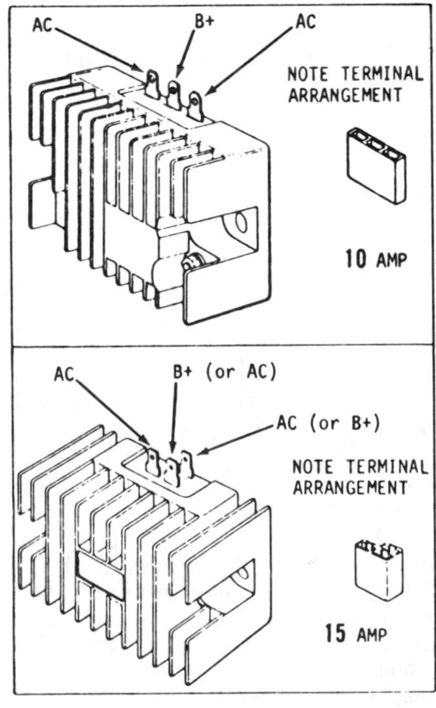


*Fig. KO173—Rectifier-regulators used with 10 amp and 15 amp alternators. Although similar in appearance, units must not be interchanged.*



Illustrations courtesy Kohler Co.

TROUBLESHOOTING. Defective conditions and possible causes are as follows:

1. No output. Could be caused by:
   A. Faulty windings in stator.
   B. Defective diode(s) in rectifier.
2. No charge (when normal load is applied to battery). Could be caused by:
   A. Faulty secondary winding in stator.
3. Full charge-no regulation. Could be caused by:
   A. Faulty secondary winding in stator.
   B. Defective regulator.

If "no output" condition is the trouble, check stator windings by disconnecting all four stator wires from rectifier-regulator. Check resistance on R x 1 scale of ohmmeter. Connect ohmmeter leads to the two red stator wires. About 2.0 ohms should be noted. Connect ohmmeter leads to the two black stator wires. Approximately 0.1 ohm should be noted. If readings are not at test values, renew stator. If ohmmeter readings are correct, stator is good and trouble is in rectifier-regulator. Renew rectifier-regulator.

If "no charge when normal load is applied to battery" is the trouble, check stator secondary winding by disconnecting red wire from "REG" terminal on rectifier-regulator. Operate engine at 3600 rpm. Alternator should now charge at full output. If full output of at least 30 amps is not attained, renew stator.

If "full charge-no regulation" is the trouble, check stator secondary winding by removing both red wires from rectifier-regulator and connecting ends of these two wires together. Operate engine at 3600 rpm. A maximum 4 amp charge should be noted. If not, stator secondary winding is faulty. Renew stator. If maximum 4 amp charge is noted, stator is good and trouble is in rectifier-regulator. Renew rectifier-regulator.

Refer to Fig. KO174 and KO175 for correct rectifier-regulator wiring connections.

**CLUTCH.** Some models are equipped with either a dry disc clutch (Fig. KO176) or a wet type clutch (Fig. KO178). Both type clutches are lever operated. Refer to the following paragraphs for adjustment procedure.

DRY DISC TYPE. A firm pressure should be required to engage over-center linkage. If clutch is slipping, remove nameplate (Fig. KO176) and locate adjustment lock by turning flywheel. Release clutch, back out adjusting lock screw, then turn adjusting spider clockwise until approximately 20 pounds (9 kg) pull is required to snap clutch over-center. Tighten adjusting lock screw. Every 50 hours, lubricate clutch bearing collar through inspection cover opening.

WET TYPE CLUTCH. To adjust wet type clutch, remove nameplate and use a screwdriver to turn adjusting ring (Fig.

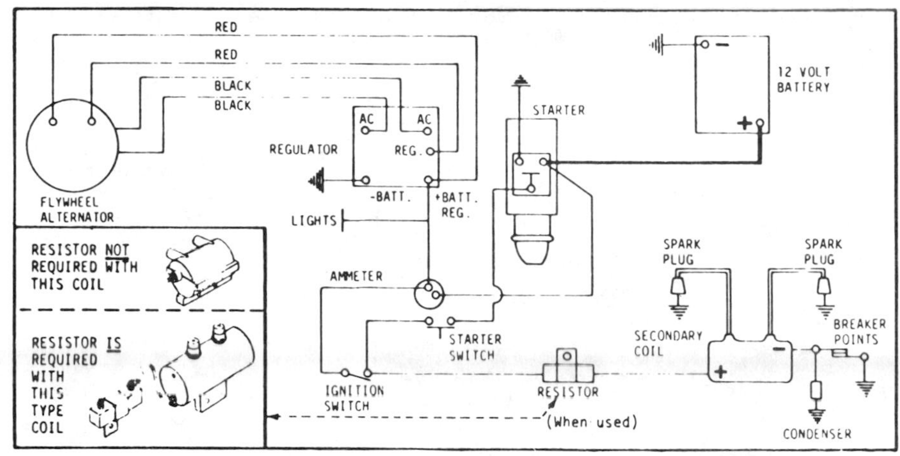


*Fig. KO174—Typical electrical wiring diagram of two cylinder engine equipped with 30 amp alternator charging system. The 30 amp alternator on single cylinder engines is similar.*

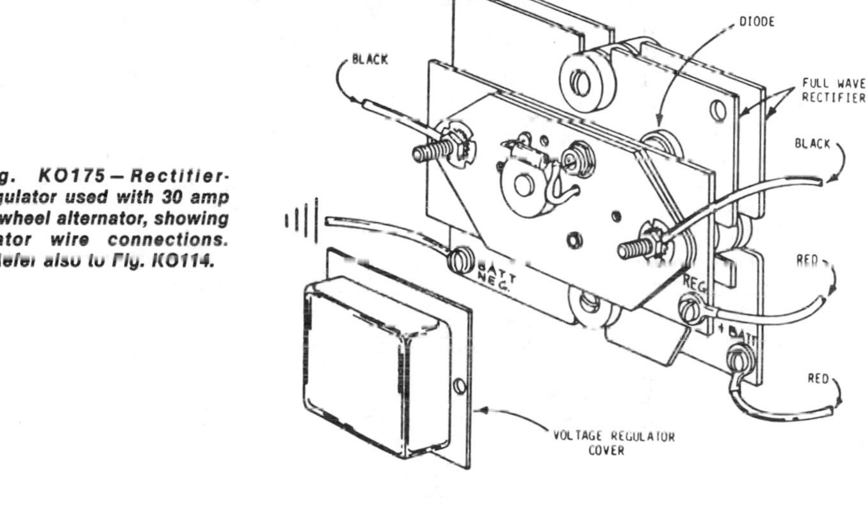

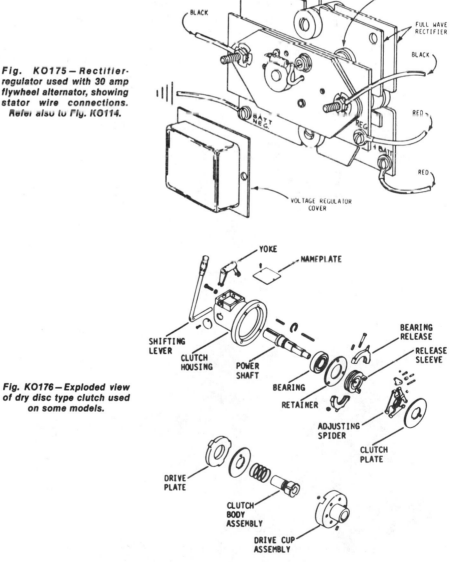

*Fig. KO175—Rectifier-regulator used with 30 amp flywheel alternator, showing stator wire connections. Refer also to Fig. KO114.*

*Fig. KO176—Exploded view of dry disc type clutch used on some models.*

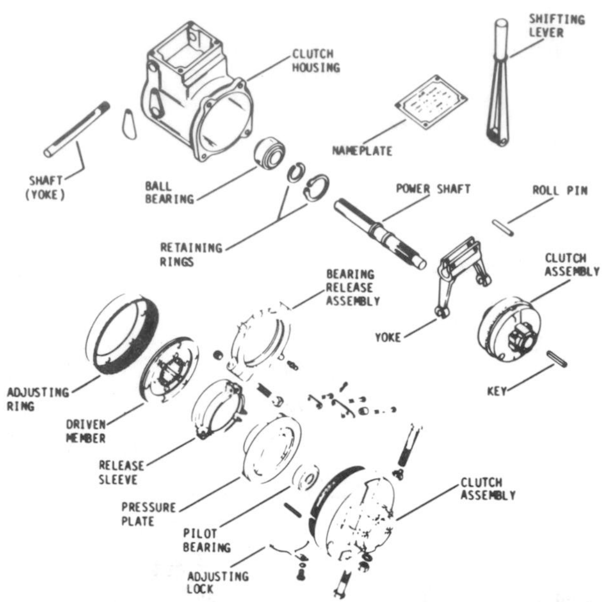


*Fig. KO178 – Exploded view of wet type clutch used on some models.*

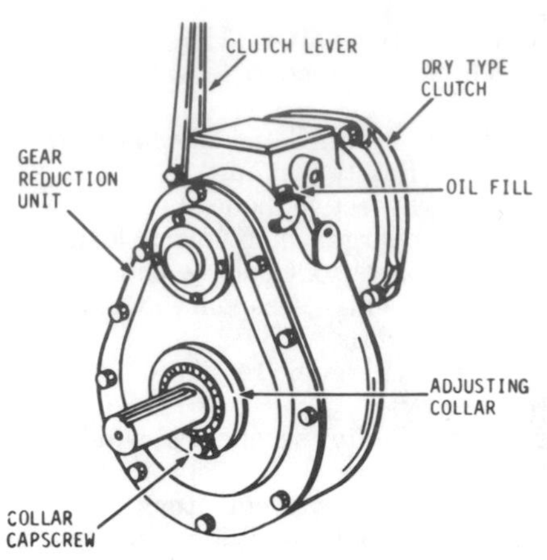


*Fig. KO181 – Output shaft end play on combination clutch and reduction drive must be adjusted to 0.0015-0.003 inch (0.0381-0.0762 mm). To adjust end play, loosen cap screw and rotate adjusting collar.*

KO178) in clockwise direction until a pull of 40-50 pounds (18-23 kg) at hand grip lever is required to snap clutch over-center.

**NOTE: Do not pry adjusting lock away from adjusting ring as spring type lock prevents adjusting ring from backing off during operation.**

Change oil after each 100 hours of normal operation. Fill housing to level plug opening with non-detergent oil. Use SAE 30 oil in temperatures above 50° F (10° C), SAE 20 oil in temperatures 50° F (10° C) to freezing and SAE 10 oil in temperatures below freezing.

**REDUCTION DRIVE (GEAR TYPE).** The 6:1 ratio reduction gear unit (Fig. KO179) is used on some models. To remove unit, first drain lubricating oil, then unbolt cover from housing. Remove cover and reduction gear. Unbolt and remove gear housing from engine. Separate reduction gear, shaft and thrust washer from cover. Renew oil seals and needle bearings (bronze bushings on early units) as necessary.

When reassembling, wrap tape around gear on crankshaft to protect oil seal and install gear housing. Use new copper washers on two cap screws on inside of housing. Wrap tape on shaft to prevent keyway from damaging cover oil seal and install thrust washer, shaft and reduction gear in cover. Install cover and gear assembly using new gaskets as required to provide a shaft end play of 0.001-0.006 inch (0.0254-0.1524 mm). Gaskets are available in a variety of thicknesses. Fill unit to oil check plug opening with same grade oil as used in engine.

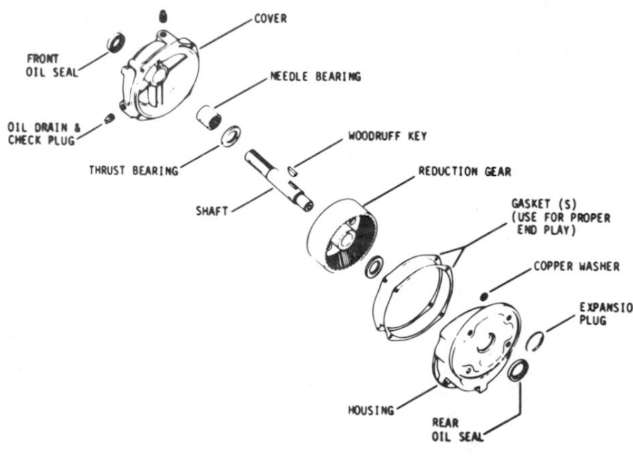


*Fig. KO179 – Exploded view of gear reduction drive used on some models.*

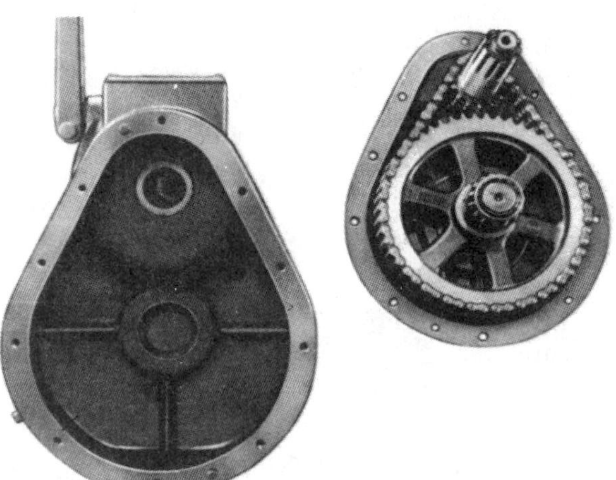

*Fig. KO180 – Combination clutch and chain type reduction drive used on some models.*

**CLUTCH AND REDUCTION DRIVE (CHAIN TYPE).** Some models are equipped with a combination clutch and reduction drive unit. Clutch is a dry type and method of adjustment is the same as for clutch shown in Fig. KO176. Clutch release collar should be lubricated each 50 hours of normal operation. Remove clutch cover for access to lubrication fitting. Reduction drive unit is a chain and sprocket type. See Fig. KO180. Fill reduction housing to level hole with same grade oil as used in engine. Capacity is 3 pints (1.4 L) and should be changed each 50 hours of normal operation. The tapered roller bearings on output shaft should be adjusted to provide 0.0015-0.003 inch (0.0381-0.0762 mm) shaft end play. Adjustment is by means of a collar which is locked in position by a 5/16-inch cap screw. See Fig. KO181.



Illustrations courtesy Kohler Co.

# ONAN

| Model | No. Cyls. | Bore | Stroke | Displacement |
|---|---|---|---|---|
| NB .................................. | 1 | 3-9/16 in. (90.5 mm) | 3 in. (76.2 mm) | 30 cu. in. (492 cc) |

Model NB is a single-cylinder, air-cooled, engine of "L"-head configuration. Cylinder bore is vertical and crankshaft is horizontal. This model develops 6.5 horsepower at 1800 rpm and 12.0 horsepower at 3600 rpm. Compression ratio is 7:1 and engine is splash-lubricated from a two quart oil sump.

## MAINTENANCE

**SPARK PLUG.** This engine calls for a 14 mm Champion H-8 spark plug or equivalent. Required plug electrode gap is 0.025 inch (0.635 mm).

**CARBURETOR.** Refer to Fig. O1 for details of carburetor construction. Set inlet valve of disassembled carburetor as shown in Fig. O2. A 1/16-inch (1.6 mm) drill is useful for measurement of float setting. To adjust carburetor, back main and idle fuel mixture needles out 1 to 1½ turns. Start engine and run until normal operating temperature is reached before making final adjustments. Idle mixture screw should be adjusted for smooth running at recommended idle speed which should be set using throttle stop screw. Main fuel mixture should be set with engine running under load. Turn screw inward until engine loses speed, then back out again until engine handles load without laboring. If it is difficult or impractical to operate engine under load, set main fuel mixture for even acceleration from idle speed to rated rpm. Use a tachometer or revolution counter for exact setting of rpm recommendations set forth in CONDENSED SPECIFICATIONS at beginning of section covering tractor to be serviced.

**FUEL PUMP.** NB engines are equipped with mechanical fuel pumps of styles shown in Fig. O3 or O4, dependent upon whether engine is of early or recent production. All internal parts of these fuel pumps are separately serviced. Performance check of fuel pump is routinely checked by disconnecting fuel delivery line at carburetor and observing for adequate flow and pressure at open end of line while turning engine over by hand or with starting motor. Because engines mounted on tractors are frequently exposed to dusty operating conditions, it is advisable to check condition of fuel line from tank to pump as well. Be sure lines and any in-line filters used are in good condition.

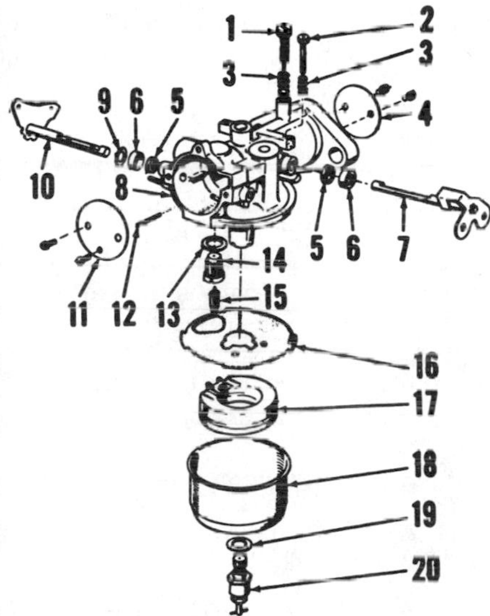


*Fig. O1—Exploded view of carburetor used on NB model engine.*

1. Idle mixture needle
2. Throttle stop screw
3. Spring
4. Throttle plate
5. Seal
6. Seal retainer
7. Throttle shaft
8. Body
9. Washer
10. Choke shaft
11. Choke plate
12. Float pin
13. Washer
14. Fuel inlet valve
15. Needle valve
16. Gasket
17. Float
18. Float bowl
19. Washer
20. Main jet

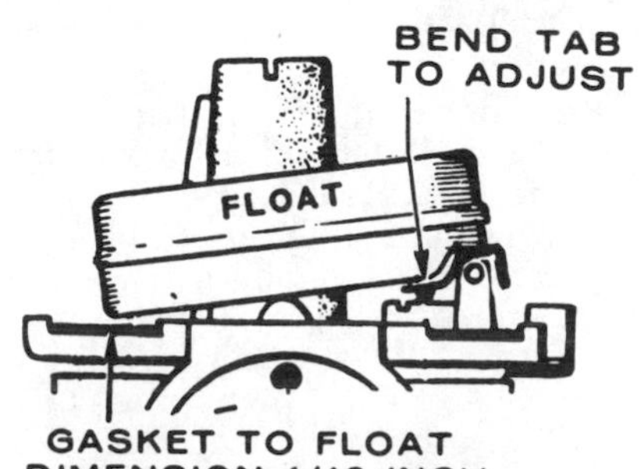


*Fig. O2—Float level on Model NB carburetor should be 1/16-inch (1.6 mm) measured from gasket.*

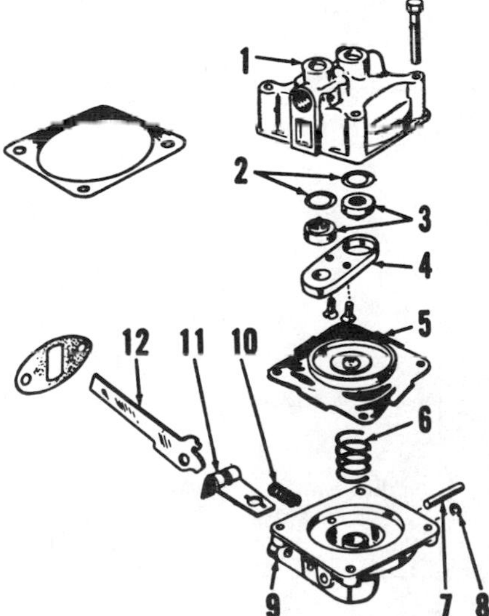


*Fig. O3—Exploded view of early fuel pump used on Model NB engines.*

1. Upper body
2. Gaskets
3. Valves
4. Valve retainer
5. Diaphragm
6. Spring
7. Pin
8. Snap ring
9. Lower body
10. Spring
11. Spring
12. Lever

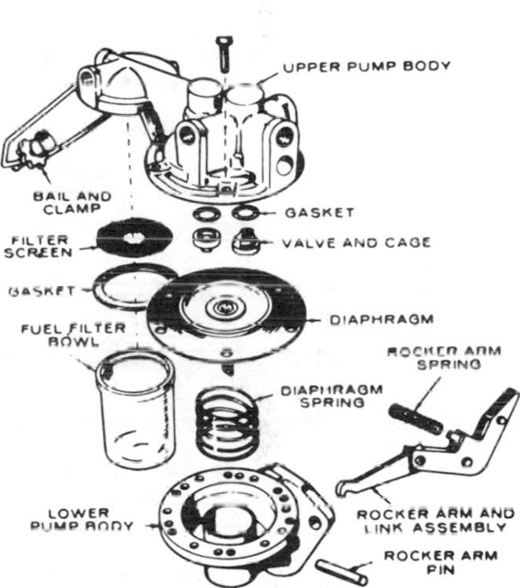


*Fig. O4—Exploded view of new style mechanical fuel pump on current NB models.*

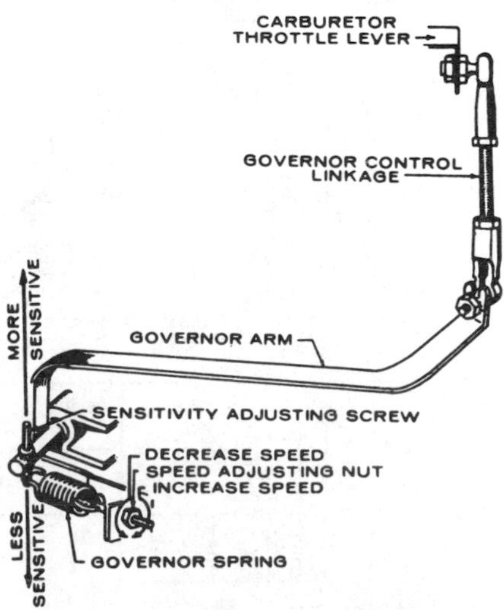


*Fig. O5—Governor controls for Model NB. Refer to text for adjustment procedure.*

Illustrations courtesy Onan Corp.

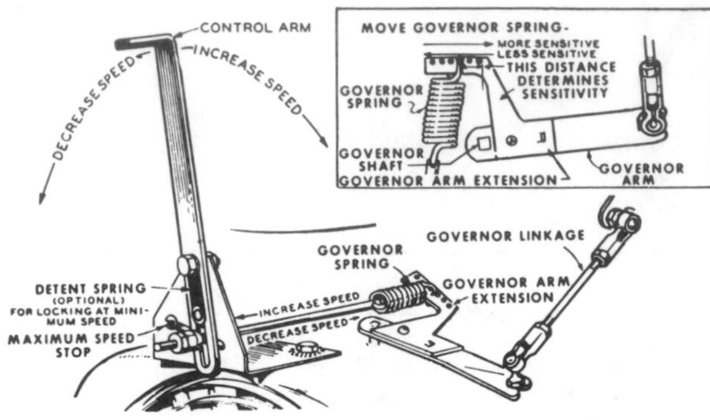


*Fig. O6—ONAN variable speed governor. Note adjustment points and refer to text.*

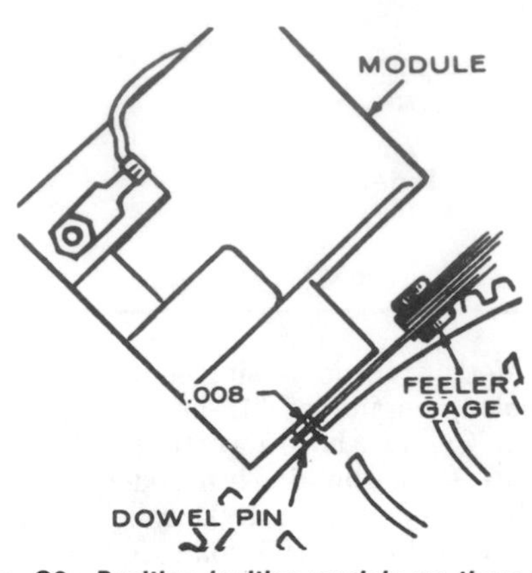


*Fig. O8—Position ignition module so there is 0.008 inch (0.203 mm) gap between trigger pin and module pin.*

**GOVERNOR.** Occasional adjustment of tractor engine governors is required to maintain idle and high operating speed within acceptable limits. Worn parts, binding linkages, dirt and improper connections can all contribute to unsatisfactory operation.

Certain general principles apply to all mechanical governor service:

When engine is halted, throttle plate is held wide open. Engine is restarted at wide open throttle.

Control linkage is adjusted by turning threaded ball joint on rod to shorten or lengthen link from governor arm to throttle lever. See Fig. O5.

Engine rpm under load is dependent upon tension of governor spring. See adjusting nut on governor spring stud as shown in Fig. O5 to make corrections.

Governor sensitivity is actual rapidity of response to changes in load or power demand. Sensitivity (or quickness of response) is increased as spring is moved closer to governor arm pivot point and decreased as spring is moved farther away. Note sensitivity adjustment screw function in Fig. O5. When governor is over-sensitive, engine will surge or "hunt". The opposite condition results in an unresponsive, sluggish engine. See Figs. O5 and O6 for applications.

Perform actual adjustment as follows:

Be sure carburetor and ignition system are adjusted to specifications. Refer to Fig. O16 in REPAIRS section, following and be sure governor drive assembly on camshaft and compression relief are fully operational.

Now, in sequence, disconnect throttle linkage at carburetor end (Fig. O5 or O6). Place throttle control in full speed position and hold throttle lever in wide open position. Adjust length of control linkage by turning threaded rod so link stud will fit easily in its hole in throttle lever. Reattach linkage.

Carefully check for binding, then proceed to adjust sensitivity, slow idle rpm and specified high idle and full load rpm after engine is running and warmed up. See REPAIRS section if governor drive does not operate normally.

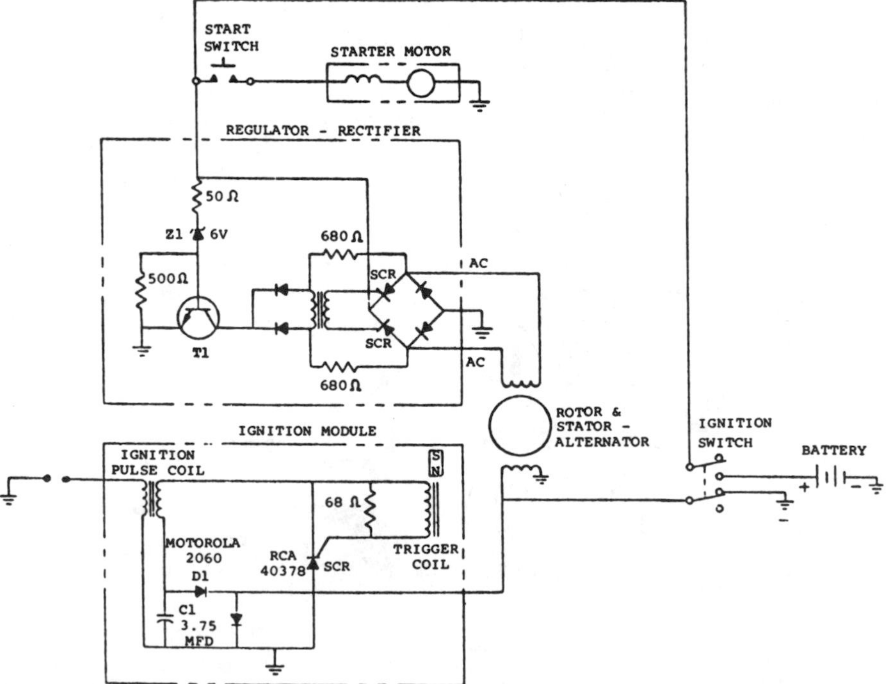


*Fig. O7—Schematic of solid state alternator and ignition system used on some Model NB engines.*

**IGNITION.** All types of ignition used on Model NB engines are considered. Refer to appropriate following paragraph.

SOLID STATE BREAKERLESS IGNITION. Some tractors are equipped with a capacitor discharge ignition system and a solid state regulator-rectifier. Only moving part is the revolving flywheel with its charging magnets and a trigger pin on its circumference. See Fig. O7 for system circuit diagram.

Operation of capacitive discharge system is as follows: Current generated by coil at flywheel passes through diode (D1–Fig. O7) and is stored in capacitor (C1). As trigger pin of flywheel passes trigger coil in module, SCR (silicon controlled rectifier) is energized through its gate and capacitor (C1) will discharge through the ignition coil to generate a high voltage spark at the spark plug.

Ignition timing is non-adjustable. To properly energize trigger coil, gap between trigger pin on flywheel and pin of ignition module should be set at 0.008 inch (0.203 mm) as shown in Fig. O8. To adjust, loosen module mounting bolts and position module so correct gap is obtained. Recheck gap after tightening module.

Regulator-rectifier operation is as follows: When battery (Fig. O7) is not up to full charge, SCR's in bridge rectifier circuit shown in Fig. O7 are turned on allowing rectifying of alternating current from alternator to provide DC to charge the battery. When battery reaches full charge, zener diode (Z1) passes current to allow transistor to operate. When transistor (T1) passes current by its switching action, gate voltage is removed from SCR's of bridge rectifier and charging current ceases to flow to



Illustrations courtesy Onan Corp.

battery. When battery voltage decreases due to use such as cranking engine, zener diode (Z1) will stop passing current, transistor (T1) will cease to operate and current will be switched back through bridge rectifier to battery as SCR's turn on.

In order to check regulator-rectifier output, orange wire must be disconnected from its terminal on rectifier and a DC voltmeter connected between this open terminal and ground. With engine running at high rpm, voltage should be 14.5 volts or more. If voltage is less than 14.5, alternator output must be checked. To do so, disconnect green wires from regulator-rectifier and connect an AC voltmeter across open ends of these wires. At high engine rpm, AC voltage should reach or exceed 20 volts. If voltage is less, alternator stator is defective and should be renewed. If alternator voltage is correct and regulator-rectifier voltage is deficient, regulator-rectifier is defective. It is normal to renew regulator-rectifier as a unit, however, in some cases individual parts may be serviced. Parts sources should be checked.

MAGNETO IGNITION. Breaker point gap for magneto equipped NB engines is 0.020 inch (0.508 mm). Adjust gap after turning engine by hand about ¼ turn past TDC when points are fully open. Be sure points are in serviceable condition with mating surfaces in proper alignment. Renew if defective. Ignition timing is set for 22° BTDC against flywheel index mark on compression stroke. Most accurate procedure is to connect a continuity test lamp between external breaker box terminal and a good ground on engine to determine exactly when points open. Shift breaker box upward to retard spark timing or downward to advance. Tighten breaker box mounting screws securely after adjustment. See Fig. O9 for wiring layout for magneto ignition. Fig. O10 provides a view of breaker box. Note that magneto coil assembly of this system is **grounded.**

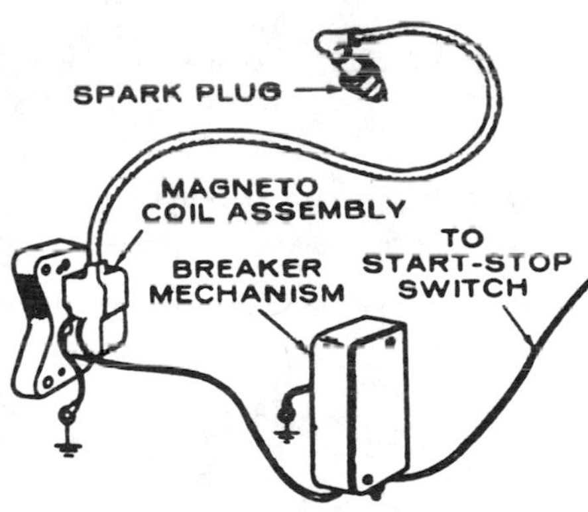


*Fig. O9—External wiring for magneto ignition system used on Model NB.*

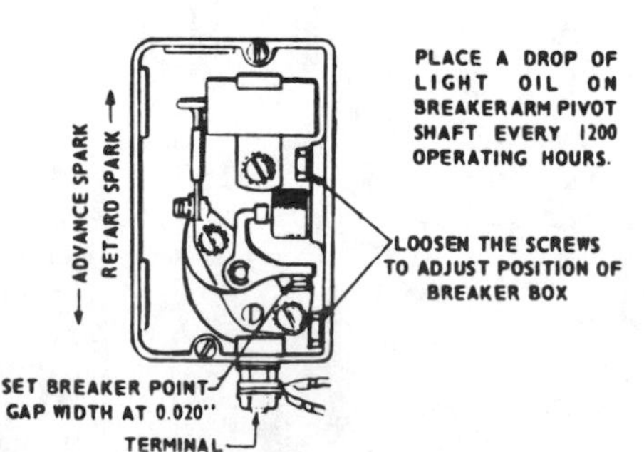


*Fig. O10—View of ignition breaker box used on Model NB. Timing and point adjustment procedure is typical.*

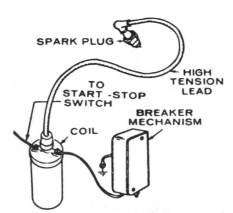

BATTERY IGNITION. Ignition timing and breaker point service for this system is identical to that used for magneto system which precedes. Check differences between Fig. O9 and Fig. O11 and note that in battery ignition system, coil is not grounded. Refer to FLYWHEEL ALTERNATOR section following for service to optional 20 amp alternator system.

**LUBRICATION.** Engine lubricating oils approved by manufacturer for this model must meet requirements of API service classification SE or SE/CC. Manufacturer specifies that DS (CD) oils not be used. Oil change interval should be shortened when unit is operated in extremely dusty conditions. Crankcase breathers should be serviced and cleaned regularly for continuous engine protection. Crankcase capacity is 2 quarts (1.9L).

Some NB engines were fitted with gear type oil pumps. Pump parts are not serviced, so in the unlikely event of failure, entire pump must be renewed.

## REPAIRS

**TIGHTENING TORQUES.** Recommended torque values for fastening bolts in these engines are as follows:

Cylinder head . . . . . . . . . . . 29-31 ft.-lbs. (39.3-42 N·m)
Rear bearing plate . . . . . . . 30-35 ft.-lbs. (40.7-47.4 N·m)
Connecting rod
  Aluminum . . . . . . . . . . . . 24-26 ft.-lbs. (32.5-35.2 N·m)
  Forged . . . . . . . . . . . . . . 27-29 ft.-lbs. (36.6-39.2 N·m)
Flywheel
  Zinc or aluminum . . . . . . . 30-35 ft.-lbs. (40.7-47.4 N·m)
  Cast iron . . . . . . . . . . . . . 40-45 ft.-lbs. (54.2-61 N·m)
Oil base . . . . . . . . . . . . . . . 38-43 ft.-lbs. (51.5-58.2 N·m)
Gearcase cover . . . . . . . . . . 14-18 ft.-lbs. (19-24.3 N·m)
Spark plug . . . . . . . . . . . . . . 15-20 ft.-lbs. (20.3-27 N·m)
Starter mounting . . . . . . . . 25-30 ft.-lbs. (33.9-40.6 N·m)

**CYLINDER HEAD.** Removable cylinder head should be torqued down in 5-10 ft.-lbs. (7-13 N·m) steps to value shown in table preceding, when engine is cold. Use tightening sequence shown in Fig. O12 and re-torque when engine has been run-in.

**CONNECTING ROD.** Rod and piston are removed together from top end of cylinder bore. Use a ridge reamer first if ridge at top of bore is prominent. Aluminum connecting rod used on some NB models is fitted directly to crankpin journal. Forged connecting rods have precision bearing inserts. Crankpin diameter is 1.6252-1.6260 inch (41.280-41.300 mm). Connecting rod bearing clearance is 0.0020-0.0033 inch (0.051-0.0838 mm) with rod bearing inserts available on 0.002, 0.010, 0.020 and 0.030 inch undersizes. Aluminum connecting rods are available in undersizes of 0.010, 0.020 and 0.030 inch. Bearing side clearance required is from 0.002 to 0.016 inch (0.051-0.406 mm).

*Fig. O11—External wiring of Model NB battery ignition. Note differences from Fig. O9.*

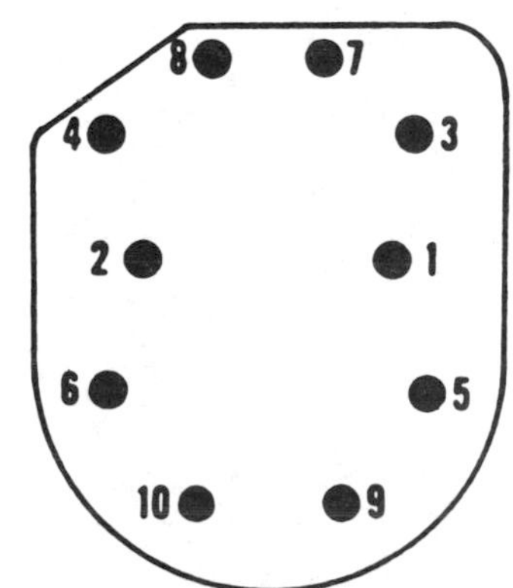


*Fig. O12—Tighten Model NB cylinder head cap screws to 29-31 ft.-lbs. (39-42 N·m) in sequence shown above.*

Illustrations courtesy Onan Corp.

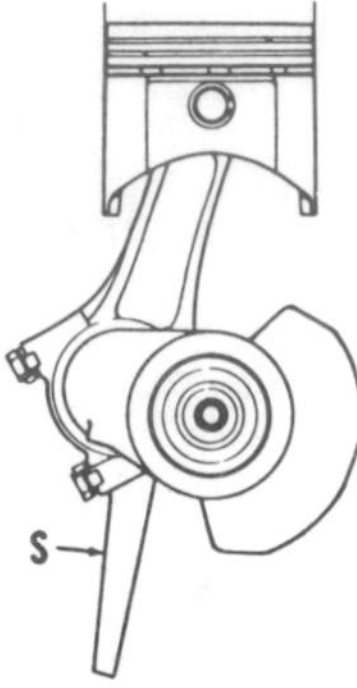


*Fig. O13—Be sure oil slinger (S) is installed in position shown on Model NB.*

Correct fitting of renewed rods or bearings calls for use of plastigage for accurate measurement. Witness marks on rods and caps should be matched and installed facing toward camshaft. In some cases, witness marks may be substituted for by numbers. If so, these should be installed to face camshaft.

**PISTON, PIN AND RINGS.** Two compression rings and one oil control ring are used. Required piston ring end gap is 0.010-0.020 inch (0.254-0.508 mm). Standard honed cylinder bore is 3.5625-3.5635 inches (90.4875-90.5129 mm) with a standard piston diameter of 3.56000-3.5610 inches (90.424-90.449 mm). Clearance of piston in cylinder bore, measured at right angles to piston pin just below oil ring groove is 0.0015-0.0035 inch (0.0381-0.0889 mm). Oversize pistons and rings for rebored cylinders are available at 0.010, 0.020, 0.030 and 0.040 inch for this engine.

Side clearance of new piston rings in grooves should be from 0.002 to 0.008 inch (0.051-0.203 mm). Renew piston if larger figure is exceeded. Both compression ring grooves are 0.0955-0.0965 inch (2.426-2.451 mm) wide and oil control ring groove measures 0.1880-0.1890 inch (4.775-4.800 mm) in new piston. Compression rings in renewal sets are installed with legend "TOP" (or other mark to indicate taper of ring) toward head of piston. Oil rings are furnished with a ribbon type expander only. No side rails are used. Stagger ring end gaps by one-third circumference from one another before refitting piston in engine bore.

Piston pins, 0.7500-0.7502 inch (19.050-19.055 mm) diameter, are a light push fit into bores of piston bosses. Piston pins, oversized by 0.002 inch are available, and should be installed if standard pin drops through dry bore of used piston of its own weight. Refit snap rings at opposite ends of piston pin bore to retain.

If cylinder requires boring, it should be honed to about 0.002 inch (0.05 mm) under finish bore diameter using 100-grit stones and finish-honed to final diameter with 300-grit stones. Be sure honing leaves a cross-hatch pattern distinctly visible in finished cylinder bore. Iron liners which are precision-cast into aluminum cylinder blocks are not renewable.

**CRANKSHAFT, BEARINGS AND SEALS.** Two renewable sleeve-type main bearings are used to support crankshaft in this engine. See Fig. O14 for details. These are precision bearings, not to be line-reamed. Main bearing journal diameter of crankshaft is 1.9992-2.0000 inches (50.7797-50.8 mm), and specified bearing clearance is 0.0025-0.0038 inch (0.0635-0.0965 mm). Undersize bearings are available with diameters reduced by 0.002, 0.010, 0.020 and 0.030 inch. Recommended crankshaft end play is 0.006-0.012 inch (0.152-0.305 mm). Crankshaft end play is checked by feeler gage measurement between crank shoulder and thrust washer after rear main bearing plate is reinstalled and torqued to specifications. Shims are fitted between bearing plate and thrust washer to make this adjustment. It is accepted as good practice to turn crankshaft during bearing plate installation to ensure free movement.

For easier fitting of renewal main bearings, best procedure is to heat crankcase and rear bearing plate to expand bearing bores and to chill-shrink new bearing sleeves before insertion. Be sure oil holes in bearings are aligned with oil supply holes in bores in which they are fitted.

Renewal of front oil seal requires removal of timing gear cover. Bearing plate must be removed for removal of rear crankshaft oil seal. Lip of seal is installed facing inward. Seal must be pressed into bottom against shoulder of bearing plate bore. Two types of gear cover oil seals have been used, one being thicker than the other. Be sure to determine which is furnished from parts stock. Older style (thicker) seal is pressed in so seal is 31/32-inch (24.6 mm) from gear cover mounting surface. Newer type seal is pressed in so seal is 1-7/64 inch (28.2 mm) from gear cover mounting surface. Use a seal protector or shim stock to prevent seal damage when installing gear cover and bearing plate.

**CAMSHAFT AND GOVERNOR.** Camshaft drive gear is a press fit on

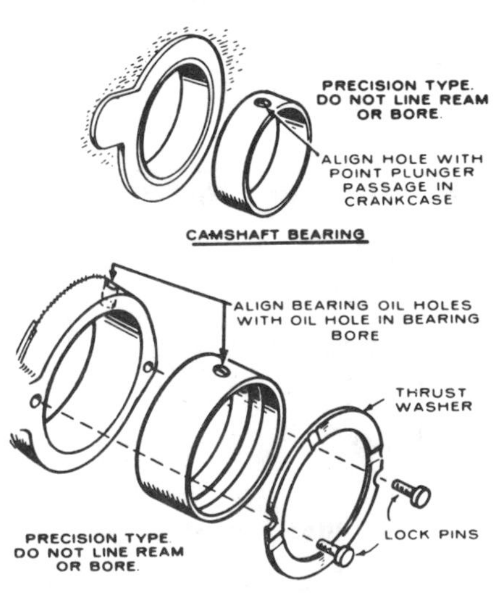


*Fig. O14—Precision main and camshaft bearings used on Model NB engine. See text.*

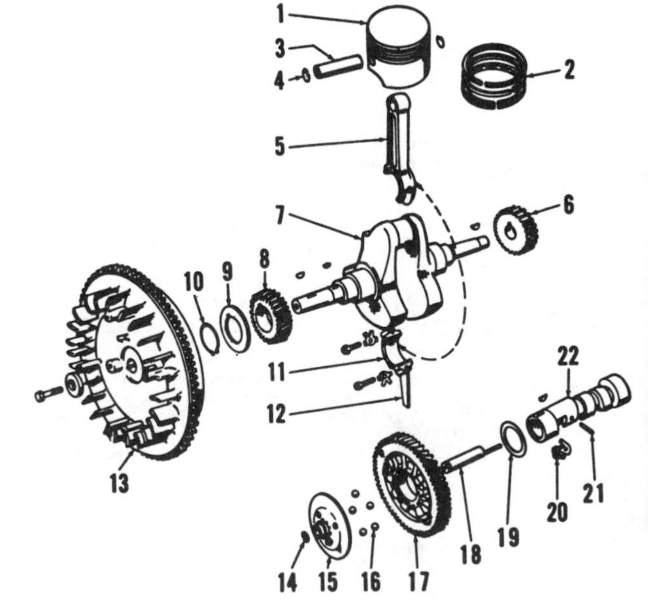

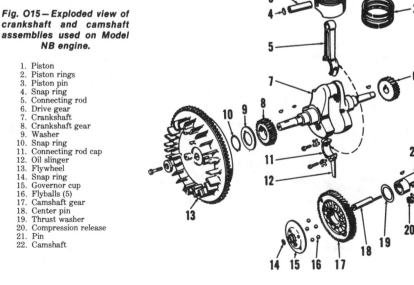

*Fig. O15—Exploded view of crankshaft and camshaft assemblies used on Model NB engine.*

1. Piston
2. Piston rings
3. Piston pin
4. Snap ring
5. Connecting rod
6. Drive gear
7. Crankshaft
8. Crankshaft gear
9. Washer
10. Snap ring
11. Connecting rod cap
12. Oil slinger
13. Flywheel
14. Snap ring
15. Governor cup
16. Flyballs (5)
17. Camshaft gear
18. Center pin
19. Thrust washer
20. Compression release
21. Pin
22. Camshaft

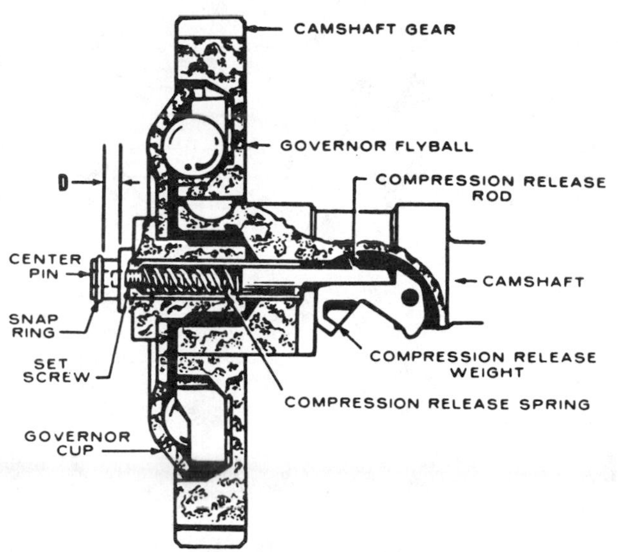


*Fig. O16 — View of camshaft, governor and compression release on Model NB. Distance (D) should be 7/32-inch (5.5 mm) as outlined in text.*

camshaft. To remove gear, camshaft must first be completely removed from engine block. To do so, first remove cylinder head, timing gear cover, fuel pump, valves and tappets and large washer (9 – Fig. O15) fitted outside crankshaft gear (8) after removing snap ring (10). Sleeve type precision bearings (see Fig. O14) and fitted into block bores at opposite ends of camshaft. No reaming is required if these bearings are renewed. Only standard sizes are available and clearance to camshaft journal should be 0.0015 to 0.0030 inch (0.0381-0.076 mm). Front (gear) end bearing is pressed in flush with outer surface of block. Rear bearing is pressed in flush with bottom of counterbore. This counterbore serves as a recess for a soft plug which seals rear of block.

Refer to Fig. O16 for view of governor weight unit assembly which fits into face of camshaft gear. Distance (D) is measured from outer face of governor cup to inner side of snap ring when cup is held in snug against governor flyballs. This distance must be 7/32-inch (5.5 mm). This is total outward travel which governor cup is allowed under pressure of flyballs when engine is running; it is critical to correct operation of governor. If this distance exceeds 7/32-inch (5.5 mm), camshaft center pin may be carefully pressed further into its bore in camshaft. If distance is less than 7/32-inch (5.5 mm), carefully grind off face of center bushing or flyball cup retainer.

In case camshaft has been completely disassembled and center pin pulled out, a new center pin must be installed. This new center pin must be pressed into camshaft so pin end extends **EXACTLY ¾-INCH** (19 mm) from end of camshaft. If center pin is installed correctly, flyball and governor movement will be correct. Check for specified 7/32-inch (5.5 mm) travel after completing assembly. Governors may have five or ten flyballs. Tractor engines, which require a wider speed range usually have five.

**IMPORTANT: When reinstalling gear cover, check length of roll pin which engages bushed hole in governor cup. This pin must extend exactly 25/32-inch (19.8 mm) from gear cover mating surface. Be sure tip of pin engages governor cup when installed.**

COMPRESSION RELEASE. Fig. O16 also shows compression release mechanism used in NB engines. Additional assembly detail is shown in Fig. O15. Function of compression release is to hold exhaust valve open by about 0.020 inch (0.508 mm) during starting. Release lever retracts as centrifugal force throws weight outward, valve becomes properly seated and functions normally as engine runs. No adjustment of compression release is required.

**TIMING GEARS.** Engine timing gears must be renewed as a set, even if only one is damaged or defective. Removal of camshaft gear is covered in CAMSHAFT AND GOVERNOR paragraph preceding. When removing cam gear from camshaft, take care not to disturb center pin. Fit a hollow tool over pin and carefully press camshaft out of gear bore. If ¾-inch (19 mm) depth setting of camshaft center pin is altered, pin must be pulled out of camshaft and renewed. Crankshaft gear may be removed by use of a conventional gear puller or by threading a pair of jack screws into tapped holes in gear to press against crank shoulder.

When new gears have been pressed on camshaft and crankshaft, be sure "O" marks on gear faces are in register to insure correct valve timing. See Fig. O17.

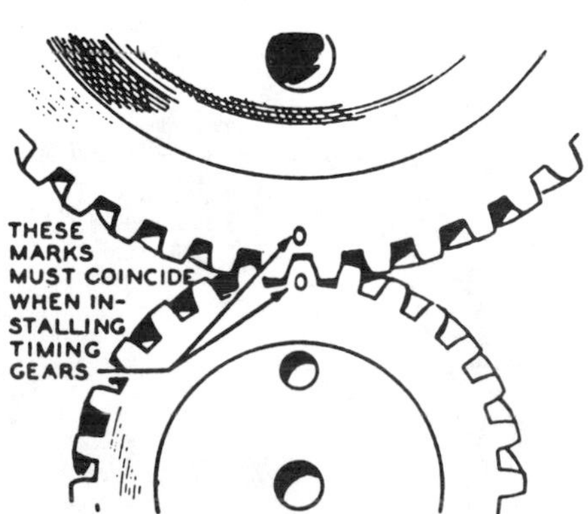


*Fig. O17 — View of camshaft and crankshaft timing marks.*

**VALVE SYSTEM.** "L"-head valve configuration is used. Valve tappet clearances are set by self-locking adjustment screws after removal of valve compartment cover. A 7/16-inch open end wrench will fit adjustment screw while a 9/16-inch wrench holds tappet from turning. Renew tappet if threads do not hold firm. Engine should be cold when valves are adjusted.

Set intake valve to 0.010 inch (0.254 mm) and exhaust valve to 0.014 inch (0.356 mm) with both valves closed and mark on flywheel aligned with "TC" mark on gear cover. Because of compression release feature of this engine, set exhaust valve clearance to 0.020 inch (0.508 mm) when making compression test, then reset to specified 0.014 inch (0.356 mm).

Face angle of valves is 44 degrees and valve seats are ground to 45 degrees to provide an interference angle of 1 degrees. Use of lapping compound is not recommended as it is likely to destroy sharp, clean edge between valve and seat furnished by this interference angle.

Renewable stellite seat is used for exhaust valve. Special ONAN tools are available for removal of these hardened seats. Best procedure for installing new exhaust inserts after recess in block is cleared is to heat block uniformly to about 300°F (150°C) and to chill-shrink new insert for fitting. New seats are available in standard size and in oversizes.

Minimum valve margin is 1/32-inch (0.8 mm). When this margin is lost by repeated machining, valve should be renewed or heat will not be adequately transferred. Valve seat width after grinding should be 1/32 to 3/64-inch (0.8-1.2 mm). Remove only enough metal when machining to eliminate pits from valve face and seat and to assure proper seating.

Stem clearance in valve guides is 0.0010-0.0025 inch (0.025-0.0635 mm) for intake valves and 0.0025-0.0040 inch (0.0635-0.102 mm) for exhaust valves.

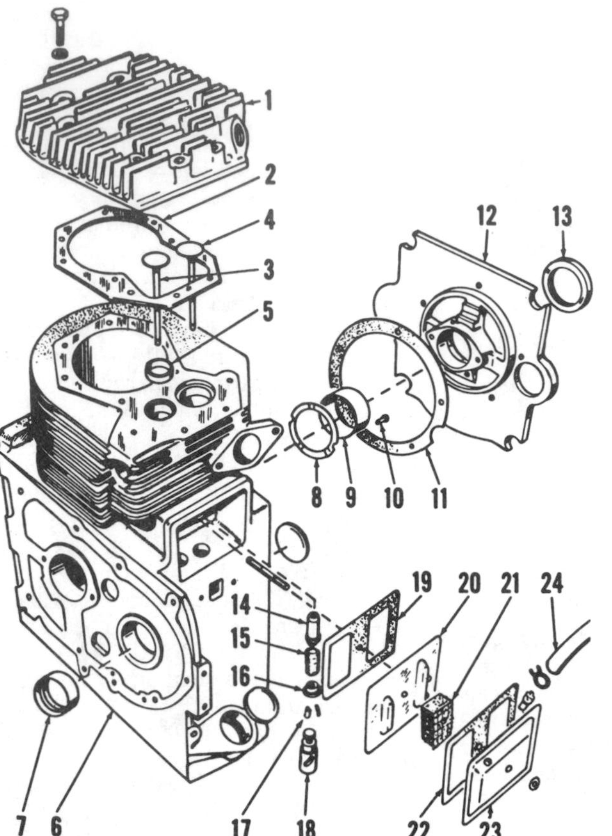

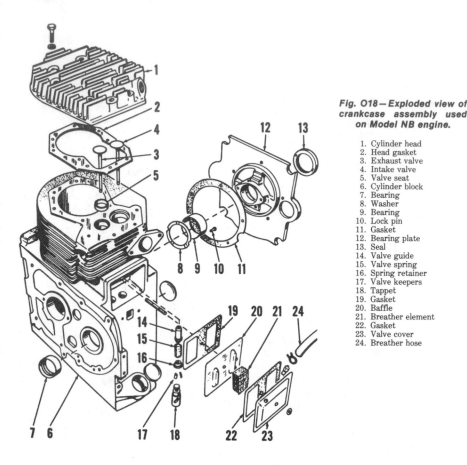

*Fig. O18—Exploded view of crankcase assembly used on Model NB engine.*

1. Cylinder head
2. Head gasket
3. Exhaust valve
4. Intake valve
5. Valve seat
6. Cylinder block
7. Bearing
8. Washer
9. Bearing
10. Lock pin
11. Gasket
12. Bearing plate
13. Seal
14. Valve guide
15. Valve spring
16. Spring retainer
17. Valve keepers
18. Tappet
19. Gasket
20. Baffle
21. Breather element
22. Gasket
23. Valve cover
24. Breather hose

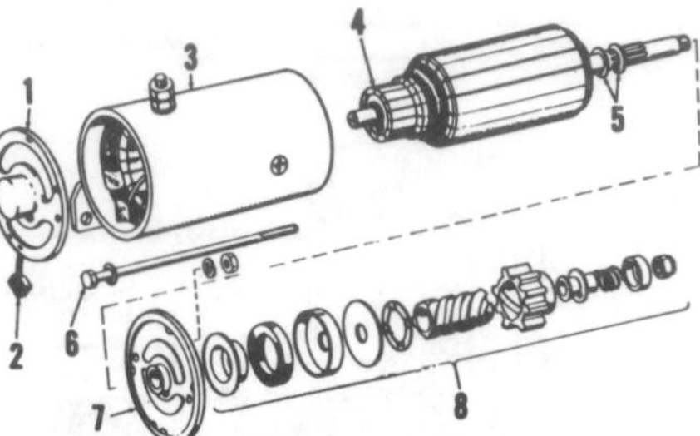

*Fig. O20—Exploded view of electric starter used on Model NB engine.*

1. End cap
2. Brush
3. Housing
4. Armature
5. Spacers
6. Bolt
7. Drive end cap
8. Drive assy.

Renewal valves and valve guides are offered only in standard size. Valve stem guides are removed and installed from within valve chamber. Press or drive with care.

Valve springs should be checked for squareness, free height and tension under compression. Do not re-use springs which are apparently distorted or damaged or which do not measure 1.662 inches (42.215 mm) in free height or which register less than 71-79 pounds (316-351N) pressure when compressed to 1-3/8 inch (35 mm) height.

Condition of valve rotators (5A–Fig. O19) used on exhaust valves in place of conventional valve spring retainers should be checked whenever cylinder head is removed. To do so, turn engine over slowly by hand observing if valve head rotates a slight amount every time valve is lifted from seat. When held open, valve should rotate freely in one direction only. Renew defective rotators.

**STARTER.** 12-volt electric starter used with this engine is shown in Fig. O20. Some useful service details: Armature end play should be 0.005-0.015 inch (0.127-0.381 mm). Adjust by use of spacers (5–Fig. O20). Tighten through-bolts (6) to a torque value of 35-44 in.-lbs. (4-5 N·m), armature end nut to 170-220 in.-lbs. (19-25 N·m). Brush spring tension should be 17-25 ounces (482-709 g).

No-load test specifications:

| | |
|---|---|
| Volts | 11.8 |
| Amperes | 25 |
| Rpm | 8000 |

**FLYWHEEL ALTERNATOR.** Some NB engines may be equipped with an op-

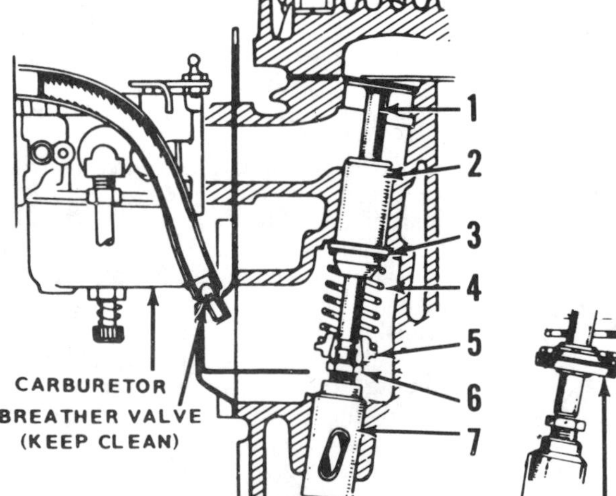


*Fig. O19—Arrangement of valve train components on Model NB engine.*

1. Valve
2. Valve guide
3. Gasket (intake only)
4. Valve spring
5. Spring retainer
5A. Rotator (exhaust only)
6. Adjuster
7. Tappet

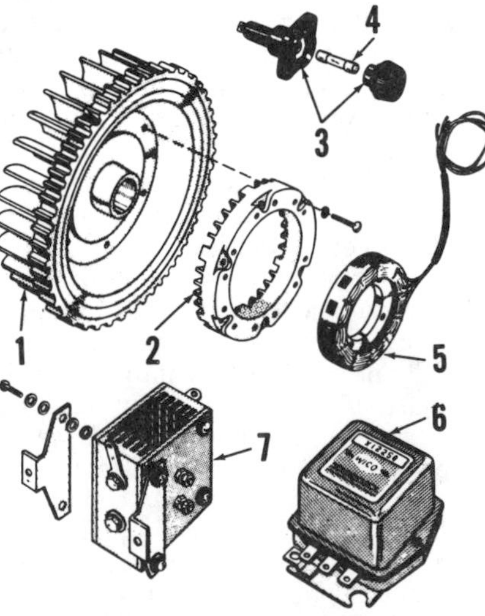

*Fig. O21—Typical flywheel alternator. Appearance of stator (5) may differ and on some models, regulator (6) and rectifier (7) are combined in one unit.*

1. Flywheel
2. Rotor
3. Fuse holder
4. Fuse
5. Stator & leads
6. Regulator
7. Rectifier assy.

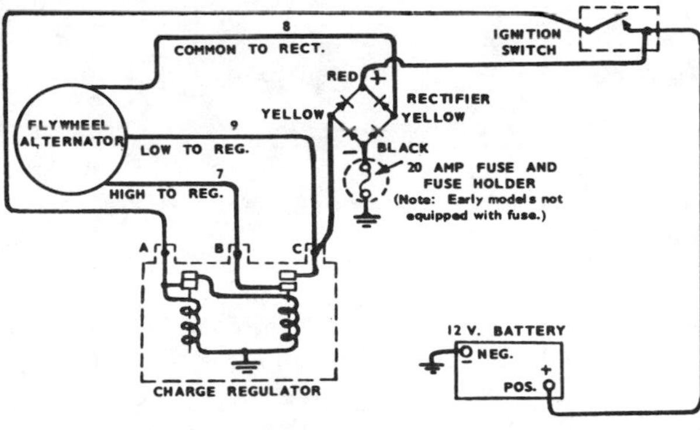


*Fig. O22—Schematic of flywheel alternator circuits for location of test and check points. Refer to text for procedures.*

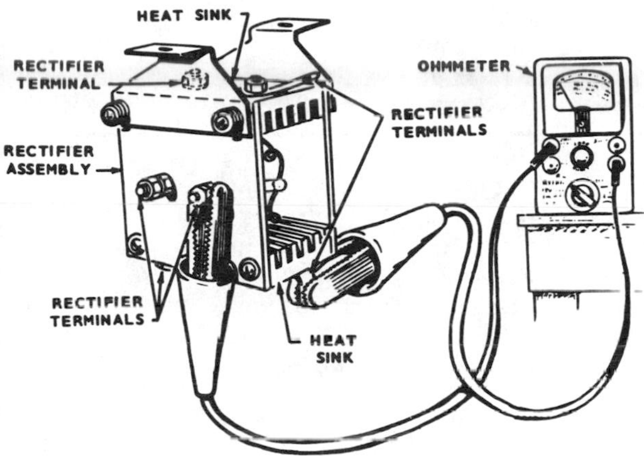


*Fig. O23—Test each of four diodes in rectifier using Volt-Ohmmeter hook-up as shown. See text for procedure.*

tional flywheel alternator. Flywheel-mounted permanent magnet rotor provides a rotating magnetic field to induce AC voltage in fixed stator coils. Current is then routed through a two-step mechanical regulator to a full-wave rectifier which converts this regulated alternating current to direct current for battery charging. Later models are equipped with a fuse between negative (−) side of rectifier and ground to protect rectifier from accidental reversal of battery polarity. See schematic, Fig. O22. Maintenance services are limited to keeping components clean and insuring that wire connections are secure.

TESTING. Check alternator output by connecting an ammeter in series between positive (+), red terminal of rectifier and ignition switch. Refer to Fig. O22. At 1800 engine rpm, a discharged battery should cause about 8 amps to register on a meter so connected. As battery charge builds up, current should decrease. Regulator will switch from high charge to low charge at about 14½ volts with low charge current of about 2 amps. Switch from low charge to high charge occurs at about 13 volts. If output is inadequate, test as follows:

Check rotor magnetism with a piece of steel. Attraction should be strong.

Check stator for grounds after disconnecting by grounding each of the three leads through a 12-volt test lamp. If grounding is indicated by lighted test lamp, renew stator assembly.

To check stator for shorts or open circuits, use an ohmmeter of proper scale connected across open leads to check for correct resistance values. Identify leads by reference to schematic.

From lead 7 to lead 8. . . . . . . . 0.25 ohms
From lead 8 to lead 9. . . . . . . . 0.95 ohms
From lead 9 to lead 7. . . . . . . . 1.10 ohms

Variance by over 25% from these values calls for renewal of stator.

RECTIFIER TESTS. Use an ohmmeter connected across a pair of terminals as shown in Fig. O23. All rectifier leads should be disconnected when testing. Check directional resistance through each of the four diodes by comparing resistance reading when test leads are reversed. One reading should be much higher than the other.

**NOTE: Forward-backward ratio of a diode is on the order of several hundred ohms.**

If a 12-volt test lamp is used instead of an ohmmeter, bulb should light, but dimly. Full bright or no light at all indicates that diode being tested is defective.

Voltage regulator may be checked for high charge rate by installing a jumper lead across regulator terminals (B and C–Fig. O22). With engine running, battery charge rate should be about 8 amps. If charge rate is low, then alternator or its wiring is defective.

If charge rate is correct (near 8 amps), defective regulator or its power circuit is indicated. To check, use a 12-volt test lamp to check input at regulator terminal (A). If lamp lights, showing adequate input, regulator is defective and should be renewed.

Engine should not be run with battery disconnected; however, this alternator system will not be damaged if battery terminal should be accidentally separated from binding post.

Illustrations courtesy Onan Corp.

# TECUMSEH

## MEDIUM FRAME MODELS

| Model | No. Cyls. | Bore | Stroke | Displacement | Horsepower |
|---|---|---|---|---|---|
| VM70 | 1 | 2-15/16 in. | 2-17/32 in. | 17.16 cu. in. | 7 |
| | | (74.6 mm) | (64.3 mm) | (281 cc) | (5.2 kW) |
| VM80 | 1 | 3-1/16 in. | 2-17/32 in. | 18.65 cu. in. | 8 |
| | | (77.8 mm) | (64.3 mm) | (305 cc) | (5.9 kW) |
| VM100 | 1 | 3-3/16 in. | 2-17/32 in. | 20.2 cu. in. | 10 |
| | | (80.9 mm) | (64.3 mm) | (331 cc) | (7.5 kW) |
| HM70 | 1 | 2-15/16 in. | 2-17/32 in. | 17.16 cu. in. | 7 |
| | | (74.6 mm) | (64.3 mm) | (281 cc) | (5.2 kW) |
| HM80 | 1 | 3-1/16 in. | 2-17/32 in. | 18.65 cu. in. | 8 |
| | | (77.8 mm) | (64.3 mm) | (305 cc) | (5.9 kW) |
| HM100 | 1 | 3-3/16 in. | 2-17/32 in. | 20.2 cu. in. | 10 |
| | | (80.9 mm) | (64.3 mm) | (331 cc) | (7.5 kW) |

## HEAVY FRAME MODELS

| Model | No. Cyls. | Bore | Stroke | Displacement | Horsepower |
|---|---|---|---|---|---|
| VH70 | 1 | 2-¾ in. | 2-17/32 in. | 15.0 cu. in. | 7 |
| | | (69.8 mm) | (64.3 mm) | (246 cc) | (5.2 kW) |
| VH80 | 1 | 3-5/16 in. | 2-¾ in. | 23.75 cu. in. | 8 |
| | | (84.1 mm) | (69.8 mm) | (389 cc) | (5.9 kW) |
| VH100 | 1 | 3-5/16 in. | 2-¾ in. | 23.75 cu. in. | 10 |
| | | (84.1 mm) | (69.8 mm) | (389 cc) | (7.5 kW) |
| HH70 | 1 | 2-¾ in. | 2-17/32 in. | 15.0 cu. in. | 7 |
| | | (69.8 mm) | (64.3 mm) | (246 cc) | (5.2 kW) |
| HH80 | 1 | 3-5/16 in. | 2-¾ in. | 23.75 cu. in. | 8 |
| | | (84.1 mm) | (69.8 mm) | (389 cc) | (5.9 kW) |
| HH100 | 1 | 3-5/16 in. | 2-¾ in. | 23.75 cu. in. | 10 |
| | | (84.1 mm) | (69.8 mm) | (389 cc) | (7.5 kW) |
| HH120 | 1 | 3-½ in. | 2-⅞ in. | 27.66 cu. in. | 12 |
| | | (88.9 mm) | (73 mm) | (453 cc) | (8.9 kW) |

Engines must be identified by complete model number, including specification number in order to obtain correct repair parts. Numbers on early models are located on a name plate or tag. Numbers on later models are stamped in blower housing. It is important to transfer ID tags from original engine to replacement short block so unit can be identified later.

Medium frame engines have aluminum blocks with cast iron sleeves. Heavy frame engines have cast iron cylinder and block assemblies. Early VH70 and HH70 engines were identified as V70 and H70. Models VH and VM are vertical crankshaft engines and HM and HH models have horizontal crankshafts.

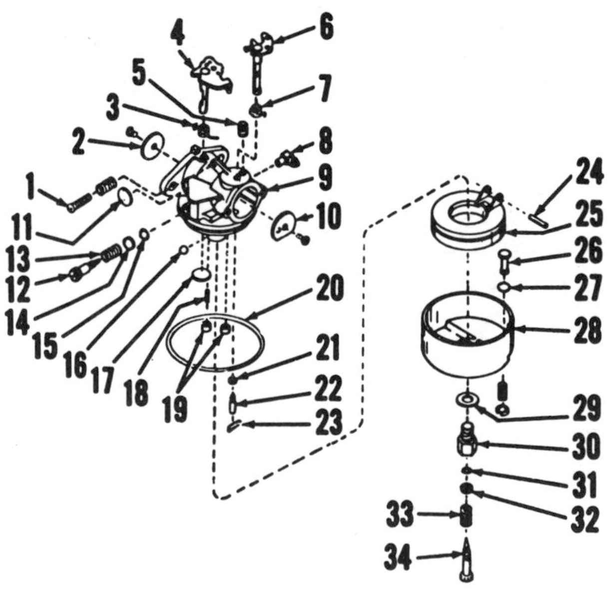

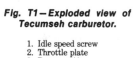

*Fig. T1—Exploded view of Tecumseh carburetor.*

1. Idle speed screw
2. Throttle plate
3. Return spring
4. Throttle shaft
5. Choke stop spring
6. Choke shaft
7. Return spring
8. Fuel inlet fitting
9. Carburetor body
10. Choke plate
11. Welch plug
12. Idle mixture needle
13. Spring
14. Washer
15. "O" ring
16. Ball plug
17. Welch plug
18. Pin
19. Cup plugs
20. Bowl gasket
21. Inlet needle seat
22. Inlet needle
23. Clip
24. Float shaft
25. Float
26. Drain stem
27. Gasket
28. Bowl
29. Gasket
30. Bowl retainer
31. "O" ring
32. Washer
33. Spring
34. Main fuel needle

## MAINTENANCE

**SPARK PLUG.** Recommended spark plug is Champion J-8 or equivalent. Set electrode gap to 0.030 inch (0.762 mm). Spark plug should be removed, cleaned and adjusted periodically. Renew plug if electrodes are burned and pitted or if porcelain is cracked. If frequent plug fouling is experienced, check for following conditions:

a. Carburetor setting too rich
b. Partially closed choke
c. Clogged air filter
d. Incorrect spark plug
e. Poor grade of gasoline
f. Too much oil or crankcase breather clogged

**CARBURETOR.** Tecumseh or Walbro float type carburetors may be used. Adjustment and service procedures for each type carburetor is outlined in the following paragraphs.

TECUMSEH CARBURETOR. Clockwise rotation of idle mixture needle (12–Fig. T1) and main fuel adjusting needle (34) leans the mixture. Initial adjustment of both needles is 1 turn open. Final adjustment is made with engine running at normal operating temperature. Adjust main fuel needle for smoothest operation at high speed. Then, adjust idle mixture needle for smoothest engine idle. Adjust idle speed stop screw (1) for engine idle speed of 1800 rpm.

When overhauling, check adjusting needles for excessive wear or other damage. Inlet fuel needle (22) seats against a Viton rubber seat (21) which is pressed into carburetor body. Remove rubber seat before cleaning carburetor in a commercial cleaning solvent. The seat should be installed grooved side first. See Fig. T2.

**NOTE: Some later models have a Viton tipped inlet needle (Fig. T3) and a brass seat.**

Install throttle plate (2–Fig. T1) with the two stamped lines facing out and at 12 and 3 o'clock position. The 12 o'clock line should be parallel to throttle shaft and to top of carburetor. Install choke plate (10) with flat side towards bottom of carburetor. Float setting should be 7/32-inch (5.5 mm), measured with body and float assembly in inverted position, between free end of float and rim on carburetor body. Fuel fitting (8) is pressed into body. When installing fuel inlet fitting, start fitting into bore; then, apply a light coat of Loctite 271 to shank and press fitting into position.

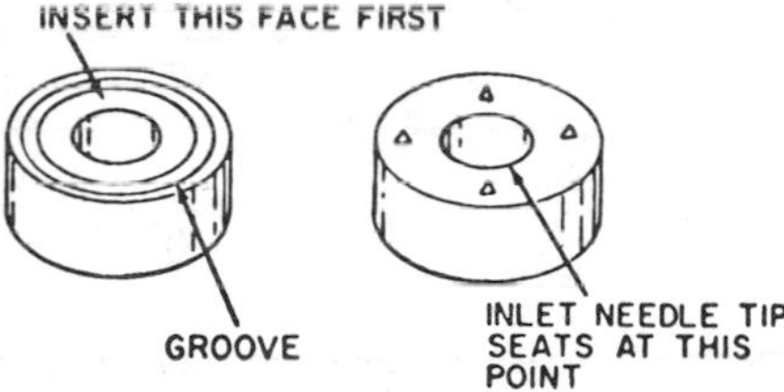


***Fig. T2—The Viton seat used on some Tecumseh carburetors must be installed correctly to operate properly. All metal needle is used with seat shown.***

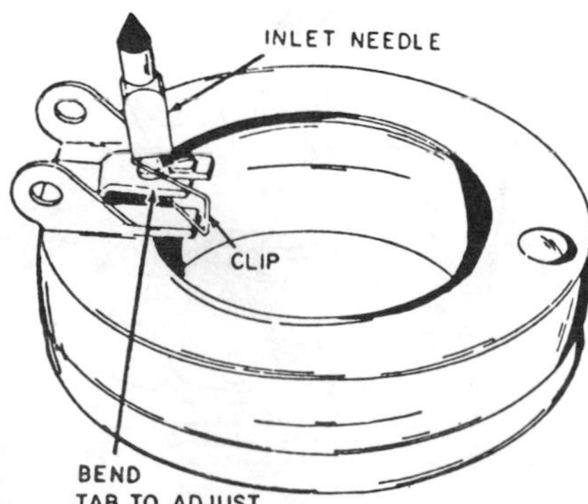


***Fig. T3—View of float and fuel inlet valve needle. The valve needle shown is equipped with resilient tip and a clip. Bend tab shown to adjust float height.***

WALBRO CARBURETOR. To adjust, refer to Fig. T4 and proceed as follows: Turn both fuel adjusting needles (9 and 33) in finger tight, then back idle mixture needle (9) out 1¾ turns and main fuel needle (33) out 2 turns. Make final adjustment with engine warm and running. Adjust main fuel needle until engine runs smoothly at normal operating speed. Back out idle speed stop screw (7), hold throttle to slowest idle speed possible without stalling and adjust idle mixture needle for smoothest idle performance. Readjust idle speed screw so engine idle speed is 1800 rpm.

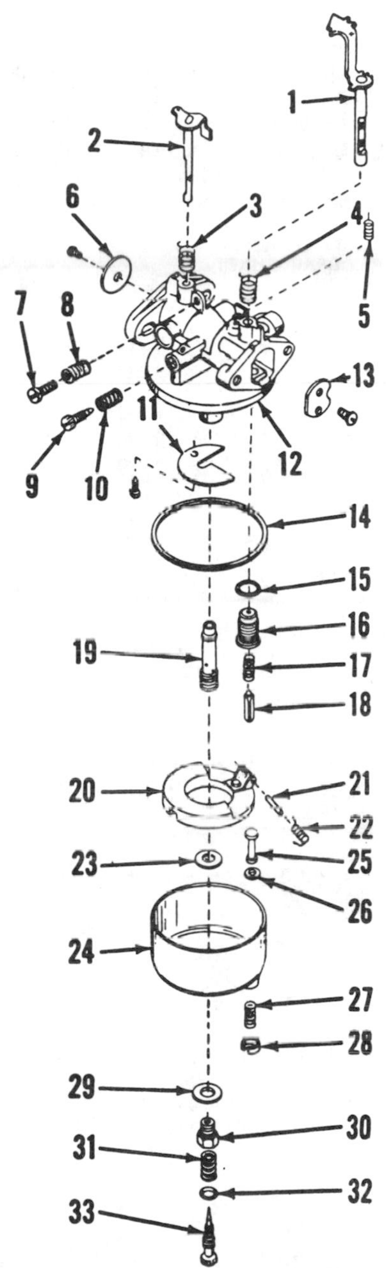


***Fig. T4—Exploded view of Walbro carburetor.***

1. Choke shaft
2. Throttle shaft
3. Throttle return spring
4. Choke return spring
5. Choke stop spring
6. Throttle plate
7. Idle speed stop screw
8. Spring
9. Idle mixture needle
10. Spring
11. Baffle
12. Carburetor body
13. Choke plate
14. Bowl gasket
15. Gasket
16. Inlet valve seat
17. Spring
18. Inlet valve
19. Main nozzle
20. Float
21. Float shaft
22. Spring
23. Gasket
24. Bowl
25. Drain stem
26. Gasket
27. Spring
28. Retainer
29. Gasket
30. Bowl retainer
31. Spring
32. "O" ring
33. Main fuel adjusting needle

Float setting for Walbro carburetors is ⅛-inch (3 mm) on horizontal crankshaft engines and 3/32-inch (2.4 mm) on vertical crankshaft engines when measured with carburetor in inverted position, between free side of float and body casting rim. See H–Fig. T5. Float travel should be 9/16-inch (14 mm) as measured at free end of float. Bend lip of float tang to adjust float level.

**NOTE: If carburetor has been disassembled and main nozzle (19–Fig. T4) removed, do not reinstall nozzle; obtain and install a new service nozzle. Refer to Fig. T6.**

**GOVERNOR.** A mechanical flyweight type governor is used on all models. Governor weight and gear assembly is

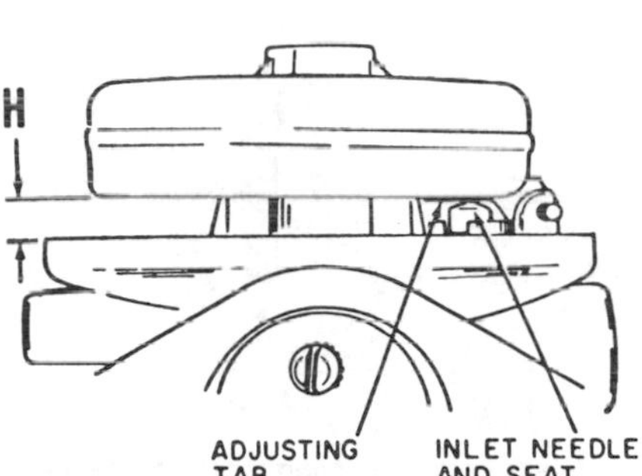


***Fig. T5—Float height (H) should be measured as shown on Walbro float carburetors. Bend adjusting tab to adjust height.***

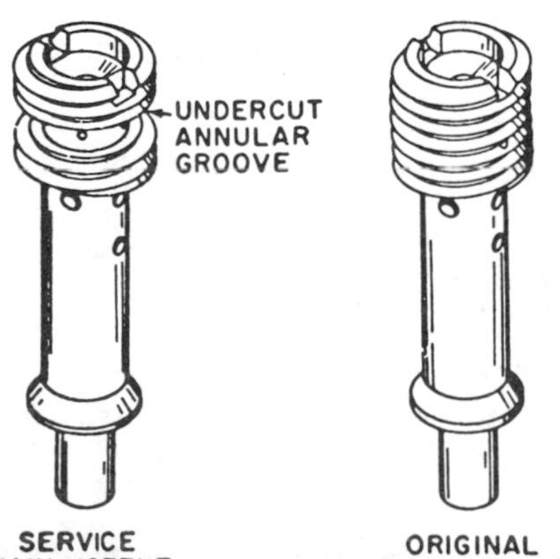


***Fig. T6—The main nozzle originally installed is drilled after installation through hole in body. Service main nozzles are grooved so alignment is not necessary.***

driven by camshaft gear and rides on a renewable shaft which is pressed into engine crankcase or crankcase cover. Press governor shaft in until shaft end is located as shown in Fig. T7, T8, T9 or T10.

To adjust governor lever position on vertical crankshaft models, refer to Fig. T11. Loosen clamp screw on governor lever. Rotate governor lever shaft counter-clockwise as far as possible. Move governor lever to the left until throttle is fully open, then tighten clamp screw.

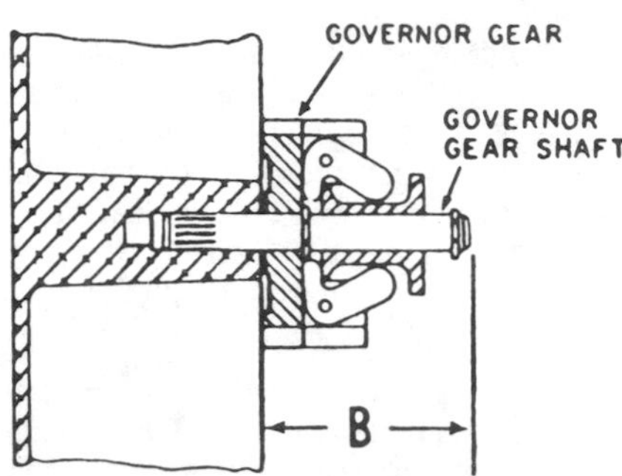


**Fig. T7—View showing installation of governor shaft and governor gear and weight assembly on Models HH80, HH100 and HH120. Dimension (B) is 1 inch (25.4 mm).**

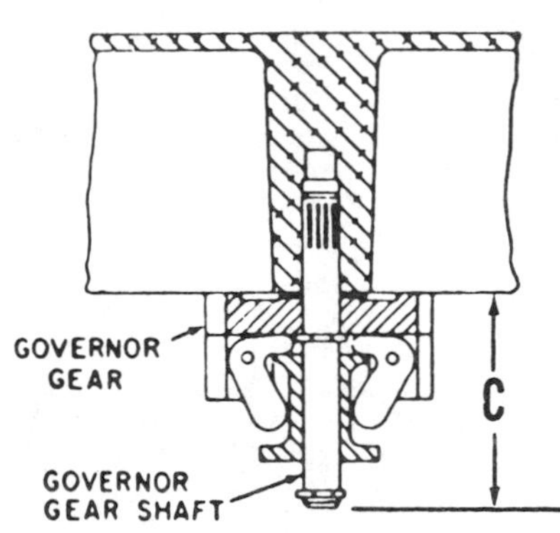


**Fig. T8—Governor gear and shaft installation on Models VH80 and VH100. Dimension (C) is 1 inch (25.4 mm).**

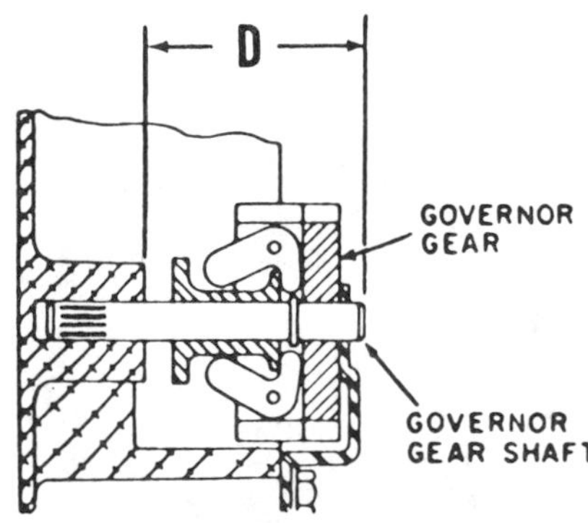


**Fig. T9—Correct installation of governor shaft and gear and weight assembly on Models HH70, HM70, HM80 and HM100. Dimension (D) is 1-3/8 inches (34.9 mm) on Models HM70, HM80 and HM100 or 1-17/64 inches (32.1 mm) on Models HH70.**

On horizontal crankshaft models, loosen clamp screw on lever, rotate governor lever shaft clockwise as far as possible. See Fig. T12. Move governor lever clockwise until throttle is wide open, tighten clamp screw.

For external linkage adjustments, refer to Figs. T13 and T14. Loosen screw (A), turn plate (B) counter-clockwise as far as possible and move lever (C) to the left until throttle is fully open. Tighten screw (A). Governor spring must be hooked in hole (D) as shown. Adjusting screws on bracket shown in Figs. T13 and T14 are used to adjust fixed or variable speed settings.

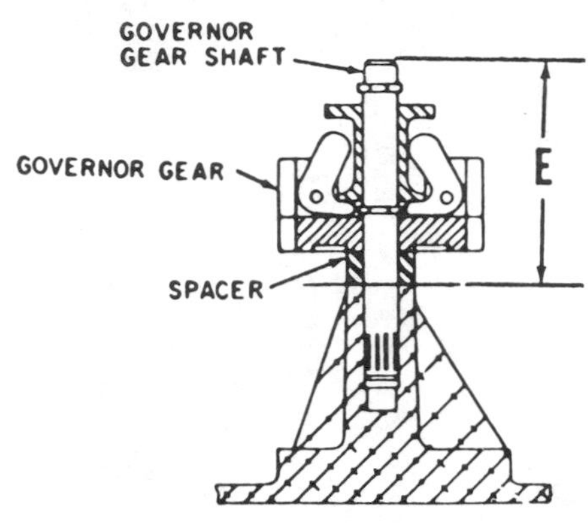


**Fig. T10—Governor gear and shaft installation on Models VH70, VM70, VM80 and VM100. Dimension (E) is 1-19/32 inches (40.5 mm).**

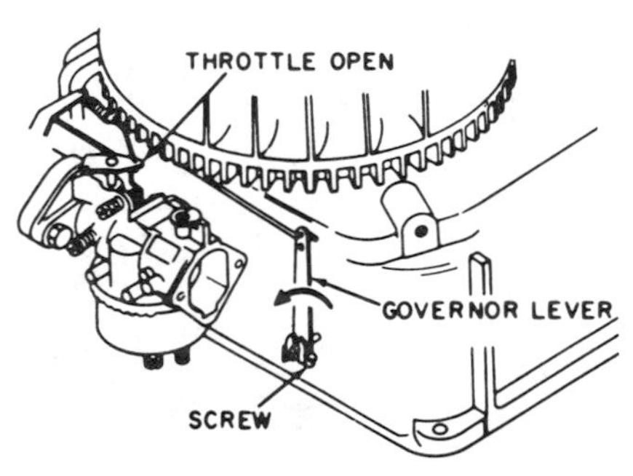


**Fig. T11—When adjusting governor linkage on Models VH70, VM70, VM80 or VM100, loosen clamp screw and rotate governor lever shaft and lever counter-clockwise as far as possible.**

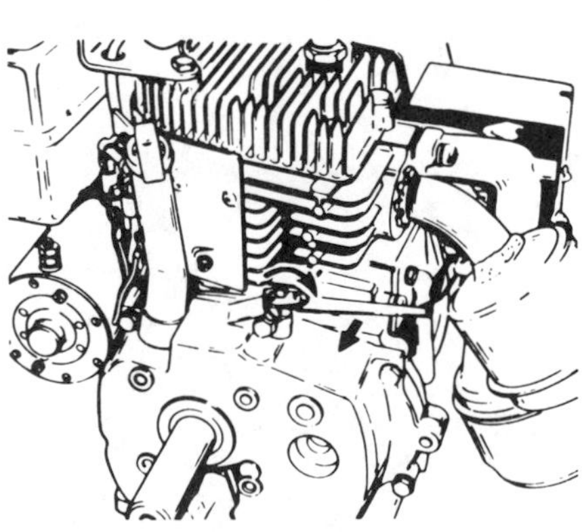

**Fig. T12—On Models HH70, HM70, HM80 and HM100, rotate governor lever shaft and lever clockwise when adjusting linkage.**

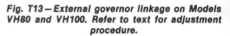

**MAGNETO IGNITION.** Tecumseh flywheel type magnetos are used on some models. On Models VM70, HM70, VM80, HM80, VM100, HM100, HH70 and VH70, breaker points are enclosed

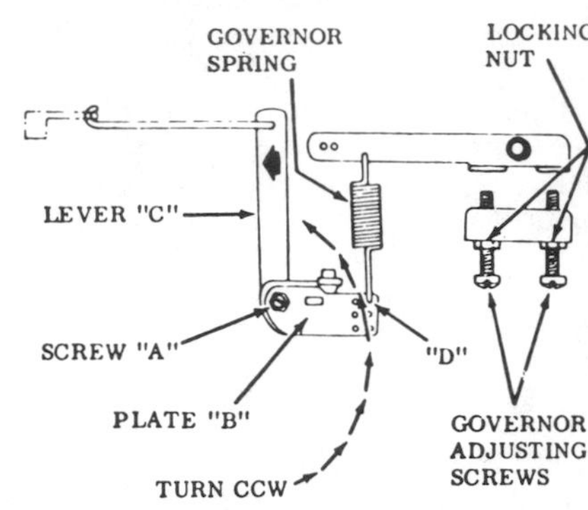


**Fig. T13—External governor linkage on Models VH80 and VH100. Refer to text for adjustment procedure.**

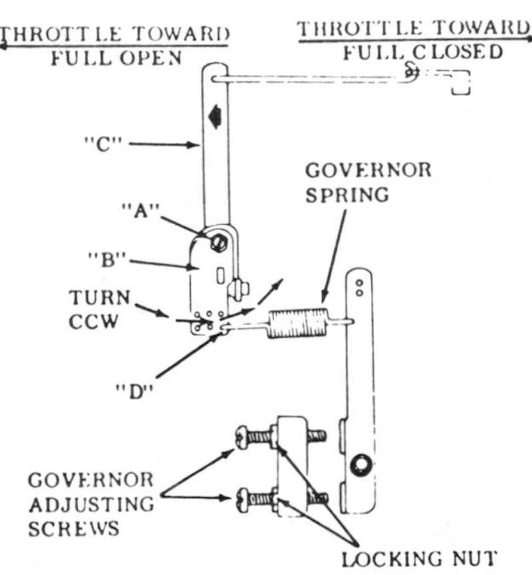


**Fig. T14—External governor linkage on Models HH80, HH100 and HH120. Refer to text for adjustment procedure.**

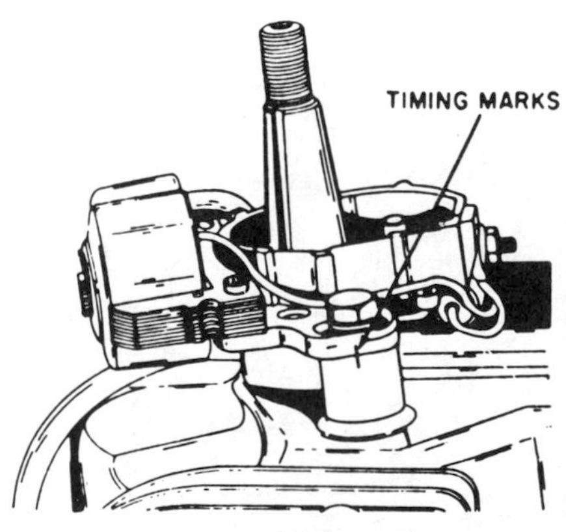


**Fig. T15—On Models VM70, VH70, HM70, HH70, VM80, HM80, VM100 and HM100 equipped with magneto ignition, adjust breaker point gap to 0.020 inch (0.508 mm) and align timing marks as shown.**



Illustrations courtesy Tecumseh Products Co.

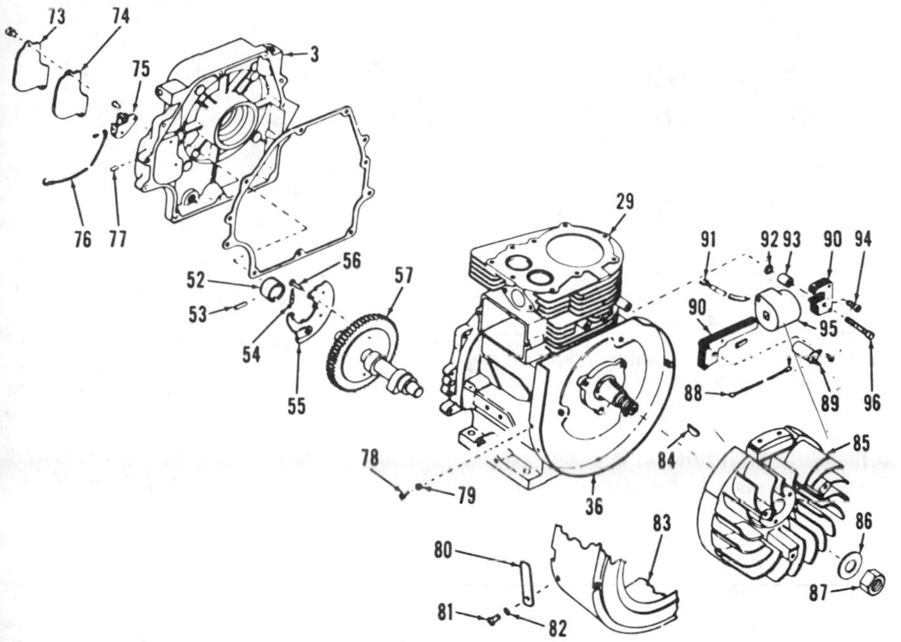

*Fig. T16—Exploded view of magneto ignition components used on Models HH80, HH100 and HH120. Timing advance and breaker points used on engines equipped with battery ignition are identical.*

3. Crankcase cover
29. Cylinder block
36. Blower air baffle
52. Breaker cam
53. Push rod
54. Spring
55. Timing advance weight
56. Rivet
57. Camshaft assy.
73. Breaker box cover
74. Gasket
75. Breaker points
76. Ignition wire
77. Pin
78. Screw
79. Clip
80. Ground switch
81. Screw
82. Washer
83. Blower housing
84. Flywheel key
85. Flywheel
86. Washer
87. Nut
88. Condenser wire
89. Condenser
90. Armature core
91. High tension lead
92. Washer
93. Spacer
94. Screw
95. Coil
96. Screw

by the flywheel. Breaker point gap must be adjusted to 0.020 inch (0.508 mm). Timing is correct when timing mark on stator plate is in line with mark on bearing plate as shown in Fig. T15. If timing marks are defaced, points should start to open when piston is 0.085-0.095 inch (2.159-2.413 mm) BTDC.

Breaker points on Models HH80, VH80, HH100, VH100 and HH120 are located in crankcase cover as shown in Fig. T16. Timing should be correct when points are adjusted to 0.020 inch (0.508 mm) gap. To check timing with a continuity light, refer to Fig. T17. Remove "pop" rivets securing identification plates to blower housing. Remove plate to expose timing port hole. Connect continuity light to terminal screw (78–Fig. T16) and suitable engine ground. Rotate engine clockwise until piston is on compression stroke and timing mark is just below stator laminations as shown in Fig. T17. At this time, points should be ready to open and continuity light should be on. Rotate flywheel until mark just passes under edge of laminations. Points should open and light should be out. If not, adjust points slightly until light goes out. The points are actuated by push rod (53–Fig. T16) which rides against breaker cam (52). Breaker cam is driven by a tang on advance weight (55). When cranking, spring (54) holds advance weight in retarded position (TDC). At operating speeds, centrifugal force overcomes spring pressure and weight moves cam to advance ignition so spark occurs when piston is at 0.095 inch (2.413 mm) BTDC.

An air gap of 0.006-0.010 inch (0.152-0.254 mm) should be between flywheel and stator laminations. To adjust gap, turn flywheel magnet into position under coil core. Loosen holding screws and place shim stock or feeler gage between coil and magnet. Press coil against gage and tighten screws.

**BATTERY IGNITION.** Models HH80, HH100 and HH120 may be equipped with a battery ignition. Delco-Remy 1115222 coil and 1965489 condenser are externally mounted while points are located in crankcase cover. See Fig. T18. Points should be adjusted to 0.020 inch (0.508 mm) gap. To check timing, disconnect primary wire between coil and points and follow same procedure as described in MAGNETO IGNITION section.

**SOLID STATE IGNITION (WITHOUT ALTERNATOR).** The Tecumseh solid state ignition system shown in Fig. T19 may be used on some models not equipped with flywheel alternator. This system does not use ignition breaker points. The only moving part of the system is the rotating flywheel with charging magnets. As flywheel magnet passes

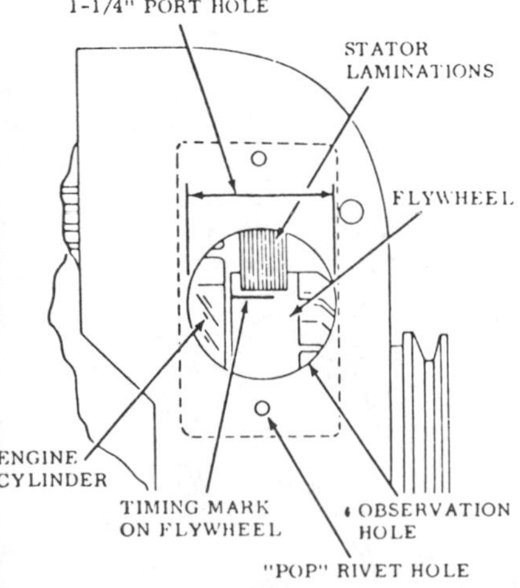


*Fig. T17—On Models HH80, HH100 and HH120, remove identification plate to observe timing mark on flywheel through port hole in blower housing.*

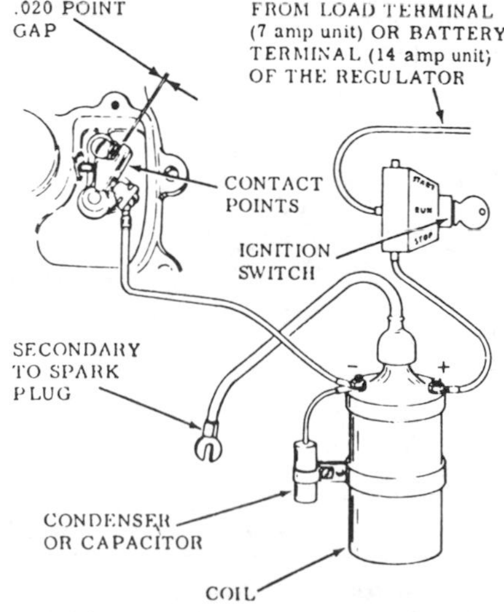


*Fig. T18—Typical battery ignition wiring diagram used on some HH80, HH100 and HH120 engines.*

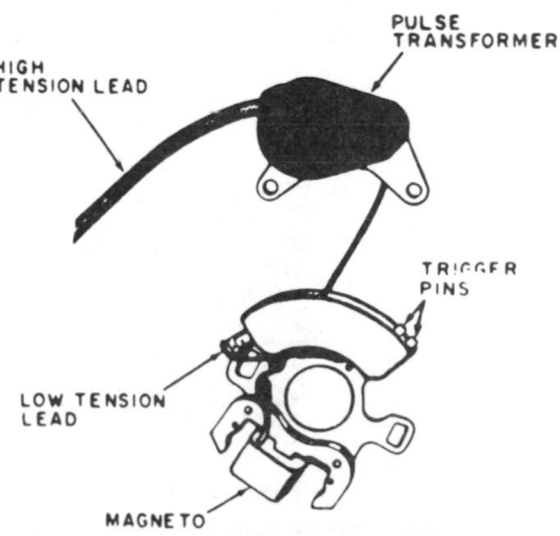


*Fig. T19—View of solid state ignition system used on some models not equipped with flywheel alternator.*

Illustrations courtesy Tecumseh Products Co.

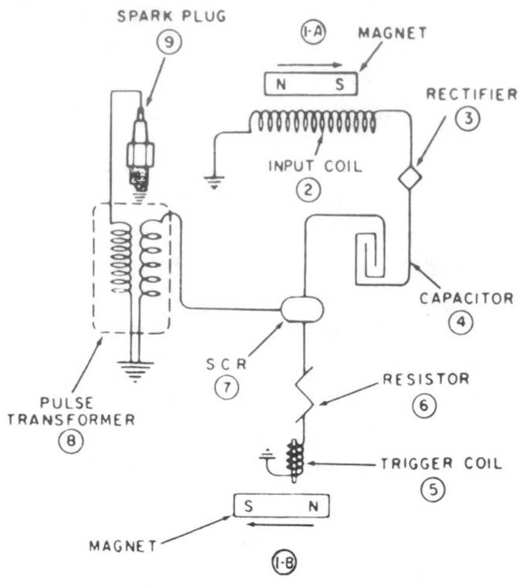


*Fig. T20—Diagram of solid state ignition system used on some models.*

position (1A–Fig. T20), a low voltage AC current is induced into input coil (2). Current passes through rectifier (3) converting this current to DC. It then travels to capacitor (4) where it is stored. The flywheel rotates approximately 180 degrees to position (1B). As it passes trigger coil (5), it induces a very small electric charge into the coil. This charge passes through resistor (6) and turns on the SCR (silicon controlled rectifier) switch (7). With SCR switch closed, low voltage current stored in capacitor (4) travels to pulse transformer (8). Voltage is stepped up instantaneously and current is discharged across electrodes of spark plug (9), producing a spark before top dead center.

Some units are equipped with a second trigger coil and resistor set to turn SCR switch on at a lower rpm. This second trigger pin is closer to the flywheel and produces a spark at TDC for easier starting. As engine rpm increases, the first (shorter) trigger pin picks up the small electric charge and turns SCR switch on, firing spark plug BTDC.

If system fails to produce a spark to spark plug, first check high tension lead Fig. T19. If condition of high tension lead is questionable, renew pulse transformer and high tension lead assembly. Check low tension lead and renew if insulation is faulty. The magneto charging coil, electronic triggering system and mounting plate are available only as an assembly. If necessary to renew this assembly, place unit in position on engine. Start retaining screws, turn mounting plate counter-clockwise as far as possible, then tighten retaining screw to a torque of 5-7 ft.-lbs. (7-9.5 N·m).

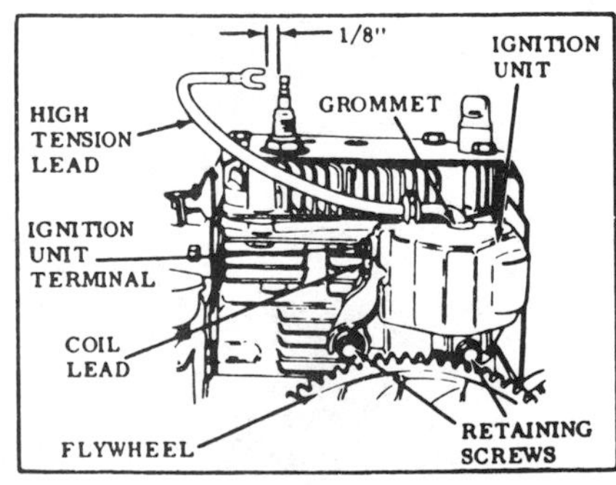


*Fig. T21—View of solid state ignition unit used on some models equipped with flywheel alternator. System should produce a good blue spark 1/8-inch (3 mm) long at cranking speed.*

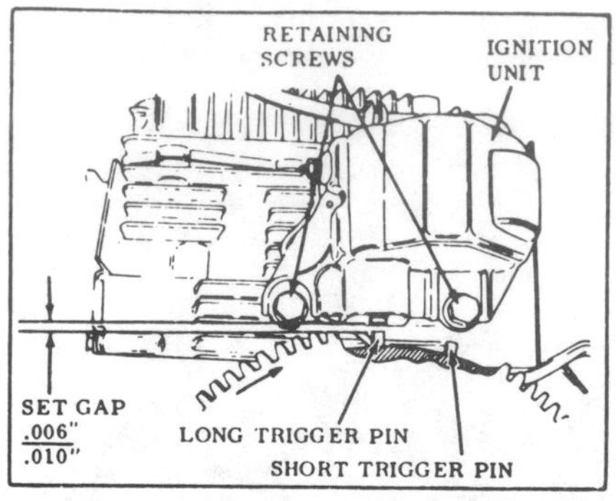


*Fig. T22—Adjust air gap between long trigger pin and ignition unit to 0.006-0.010 inch (0.152-0.254 mm).*

**SOLID STATE IGNITION (WITH ALTERNATOR).** The Tecumseh solid state ignition system used on some models equipped with flywheel alternator does not use ignition breaker points. The only moving part of the system is the rotating flywheel with charging magnets and trigger pins. Other components of system are ignition generator coil and stator assembly, spark plug and ignition unit.

The long trigger pin induces a small charge of current to close the SCR (silicon controlled rectifier) switch at engine cranking speed and produces a spark at TDC for starting. As engine rpm increases, the first (shorter) trigger pin induces the current which produces a spark when piston is 0.095 inch (2.413 mm) BTDC.

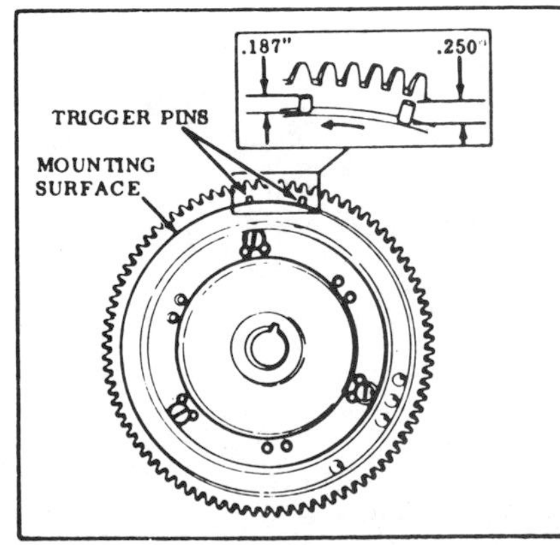


*Fig. T23—Remove flywheel and drive trigger pins in or out as necessary until long pin is extended 0.250 inch (6.35 mm) and short pin is extended 0.187 inch (4.75 mm) above mounting surface.*

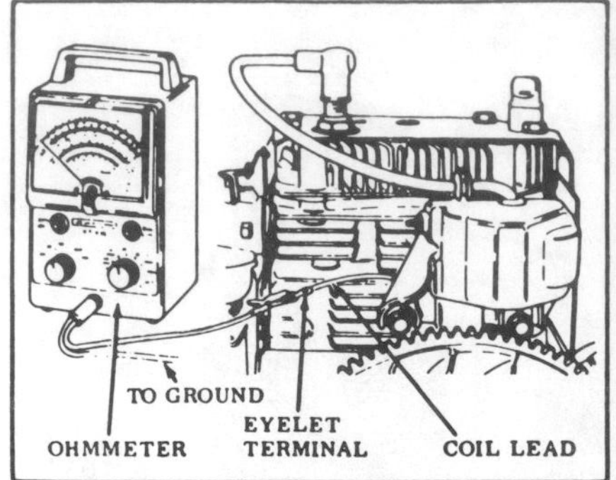


*Fig. T24—View showing an ohmmeter connected for resistance test of ignition generator coil.*

Test ignition system as follows: Hold high tension lead 1/8-inch (3 mm) from spark plug (Fig. T21), crank engine and check for a good blue spark. If no spark is present, check high tension lead and coil lead for loose connections or faulty insulation. Check air gap between long trigger pin and ignition unit as shown in Fig. T22. Air gap should be 0.006-0.010 inch (0.152-0.254 mm). To adjust air gap, loosen the two retaining screws and move ignition unit as necessary, then tighten retaining screws.

**NOTE: The long trigger pin should extend 0.250 inch (6.35 mm) and the short trigger pin should extend 0.187 inch (4.75 mm), measured as shown in Fig. T23. If not, remove flywheel and drive pins in or out as required.**

Remove coil lead from ignition terminal and connect an ohmmeter as shown in Fig. T24. If series resistance test of ignition generator coil is below 400 ohms, renew stator and coil assembly (Fig. T25). If resistance is above 400 ohms, renew ignition unit.

**LUBRICATION.** On Models VH70, VM70, VM80 and VM100, a barrel and plunger type oil pump (Fig. T26 or T27) driven by an eccentric on camshaft, pressure lubricates upper main bearing and connecting rod journal. When installing early type pump (Fig. T26), chamfered side of drive collar must be

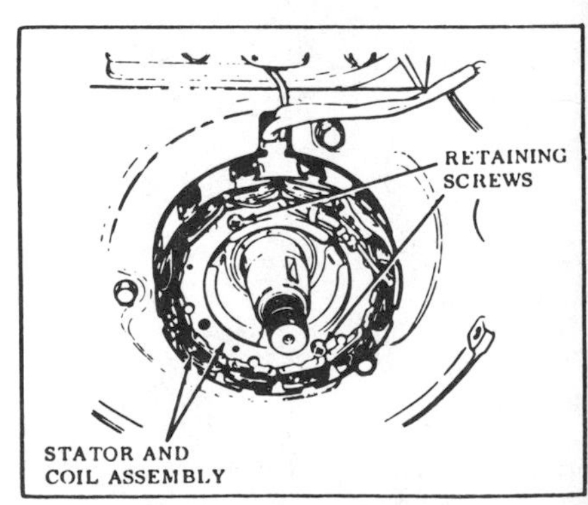


*Fig. T25—Ignition generator coil and stator serviced only as an assembly.*

against thrust bearing surface on camshaft gear. When installing late type pump, place side of drive collar with large flat surface shown in Fig. T27 away from camshaft gear.

An oil slinger (59–Fig. T28), installed on crankshaft between gear and lower bearing is used to direct oil upward for complete engine lubrication on Models VH80 and VH100. A tang on slinger hub, when inserted in slot in crankshaft gear, correctly positions slinger on crankshaft as shown in Fig. T28.

Splash lubrication system on all other models is provided by use of an oil dipper on connecting rod. See Figs. T30 and T31.

Use only high quality, detergent motor oil having API classification SE, SF or SG. SAE 30 oil is recommended for operating in temperatures above 32°F (0°C) and SAE 10W for operating in temperatures below 32°F (0°C).

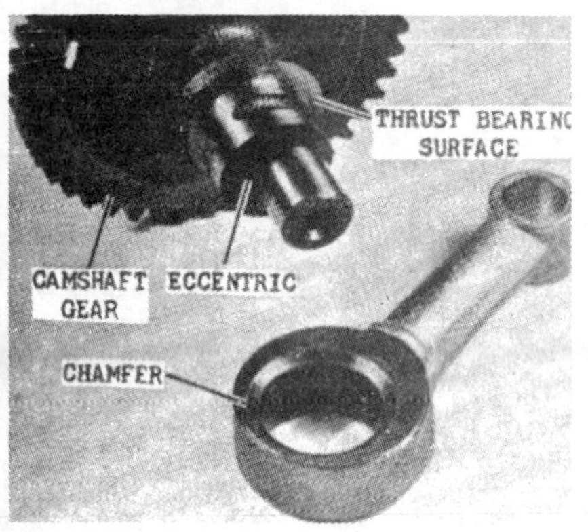


*Fig. T26–View of early type oil pump used on Models VH70, VM70 and VM80. Chamfered face of drive collar should be towards camshaft gear.*

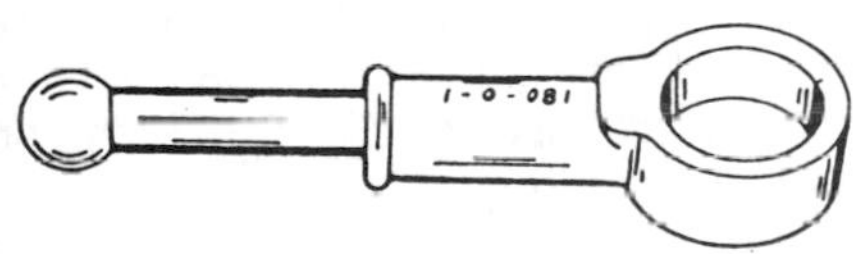

*Fig. T27–Install late type oil pump so large flat surface on drive collar is away from camshaft gear.*

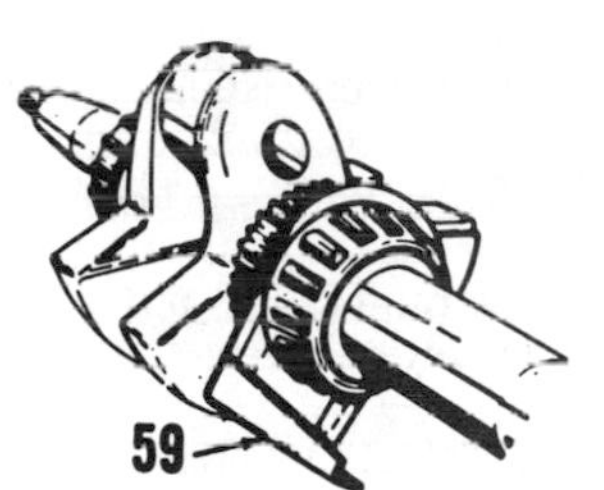


*Fig. T28–Oil slinger (59) on Models VH80 and VH100 must be installed on crankshaft as shown.*

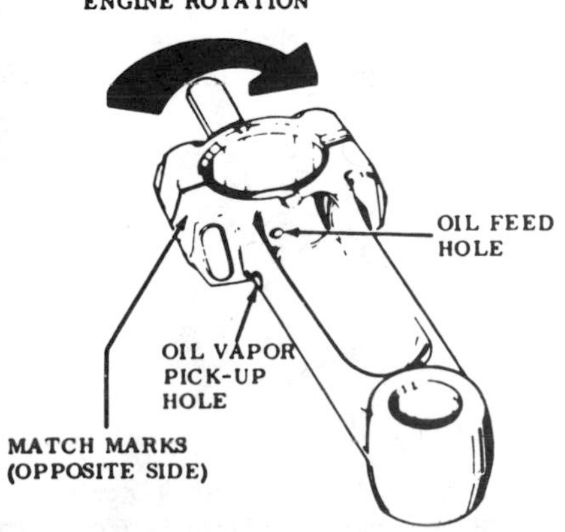


*Fig. T29–Connecting rods used on Models VH80 and VH100 have two oil holes.*

## REPAIRS

**TIGHTENING TORQUE.** Recommended tightening torques are as follows:

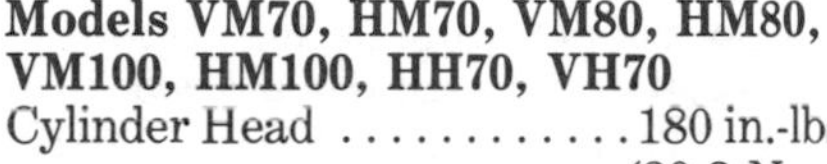

**Models VM70, HM70, VM80, HM80, VM100, HM100, HH70, VH70**

| | |
|---|---|
| Cylinder Head | 180 in.-lbs. (20.3 N·m) |
| Connecting Rod | 120 in.-lbs. (13.5 N·m) |
| Crankcase Cover | 110 in.-lbs. (12.4 N·m) |
| Ball Bearing Retainer Nut | 20 in.-lbs. (2.3 N·m) |

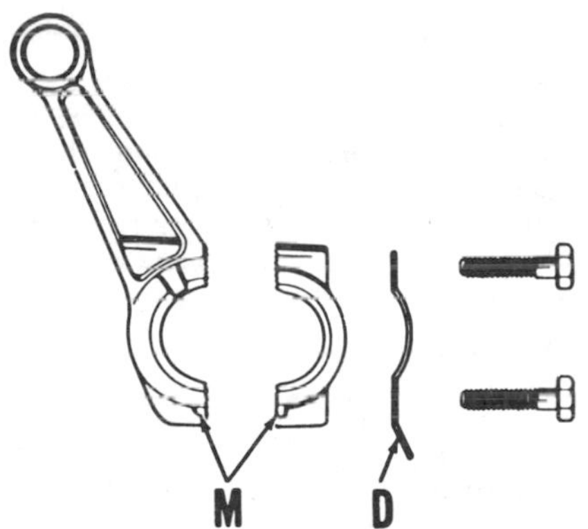


*Fig. T30–Connecting rod assembly used on Models VH70, VM70, VM80, VM100, HH70, HM70, HM80 and HM100. Note position of oil dipper (D) and match marks (M).*

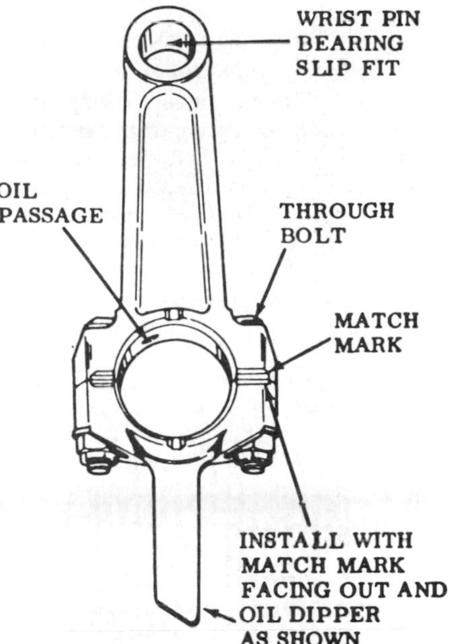


*Fig. T31–Connecting rod assembly used on Models HH80, HH100 and HH120.*

| | |
|---|---|
| Flywheel Nut | 440 in.-lbs. (49.7 N·m) |
| Spark Plug | 250 in.-lbs. (28.2 N·m) |
| Magneto Stator Mounting | 75 in.-lbs. (8.5 N·m) |
| Carburetor Mounting | 60 in.-lbs. (6.8 N·m) |

**Models HH80, VH80, HH100, VH100, HH120**

| | |
|---|---|
| Cylinder Head | 200 in.-lbs. (22.6 N·m) |
| Connecting Rod | 110 in.-lbs. (12.4 N·m) |
| Crankcase Cover | 110 in.-lbs. (12.4 N·m) |
| Bearing Retainer | 110 in.-lbs. (12.4 N·m) |
| Flywheel Nut | 650 in.-lbs. (73.5 N·m) |
| Spark Plug | 250 in.-lbs. (28.3 N·m) |
| Magneto Stator Mounting | 85 in.-lbs. (9.6 N·m) |
| Carburetor Mounting | 85 in.-lbs. (9.6 N·m) |

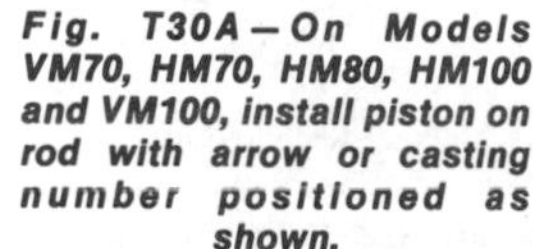

*Fig. T30A–On Models VM70, HM70, HM80, HM100 and VM100, install piston on rod with arrow or casting number positioned as shown.*

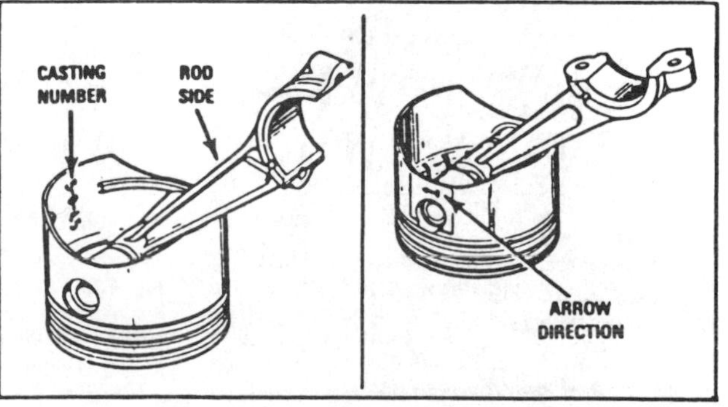

**CONNECTING ROD.** Piston and connecting rod assembly is removed from cylinder head end of engine. The aluminum alloy rod rides directly on the crankshaft. Running clearance is not adjustable. Crankpin diameter is 1.1865-1.1870 inches (30.137-30.150 mm) on Models VM70, HM70, VM80, HM80, VM100, HM100, HH70 and VH70 and 1.3750-1.3755 inches (34.925-34.938 mm) on all other models.

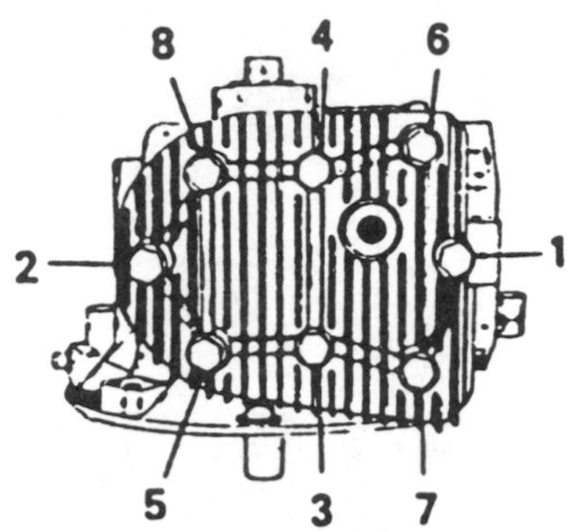


*Fig. T32—On Models VM70, HM70, VH70 and HH70, tighten cylinder head cap screws evenly to a torque of 180 in.-lbs. (20 N·m) using tightening sequence shown.*

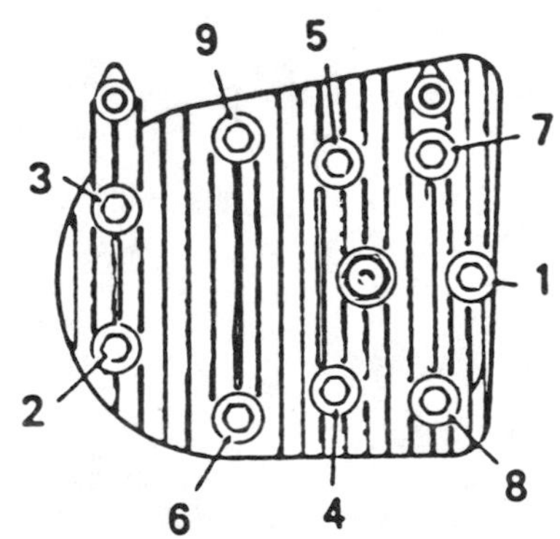


*Fig. T33—Tighten cylinder head cap screws on Models HM80, VM80, HM100 and VM100 in sequence shown to a torque of 180 in.-lbs. (20 N·m).*

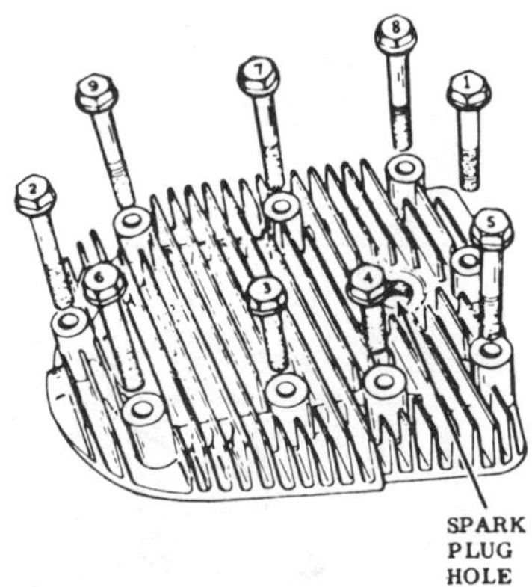


*Fig. T34—View showing cylinder head cap screw tightening sequence used on early HH80, HH100 and HH120 engines. Tighten cap screws to a torque of 200 in.-lbs. (22.6 N·m). Note type and length of cap screws.*

Connecting rods are equipped with match marks and on some models pistons are marked for correct assembly. See Figs. T29, T30, T30A and T31. Install rod on all models so marks are toward pto end of crankshaft. Use new self-locking nuts or rod bolt lock each time rod is installed.

**CYLINDER HEAD.** When removing cylinder head, be sure to note location of different length cap screws for aid in correct assembly. Always install new head gasket and tighten cap screws evenly in sequence shown in Figs. T32, T33, T34 or T35. Refer to TIGHTENING TORQUE section for correct torque values.

**PISTON, PIN AND RINGS.** Aluminum alloy piston is fitted with two compression rings and one oil control ring. Ring end gap on all models should be 0.010-0.020 inch (0.254-0.508 mm). Side clearance of new rings in ring grooves of a new piston should be 0.002-0.0035 inch (0.051-0.0889 mm) on Models HH80, HH100, HH120; 0.0025-0.003 inch (0.0635-0.076 mm) on Models VH80 and VH100; 0.002-0.003 inch (0.051-0.076 mm) on Models VM70, HM70, HM80, VM80, HH70, VH70; 0.002-0.005 inch (0.051-0.127 mm) on Models VM100 and HM100. Piston rings and pistons are available in standard size and oversizes of 0.010 and 0.020 inch for Models VM70, HM70, VM80, HM80, VM100, HM100, HH70 and VH70 or in standard size and oversizes of 0.010, 0.020, 0.030 and 0.040 inch for all other models.

The top compression ring must be installed with inside chamfer to top of piston. If second compression ring has a notch on outside of ring, install ring with notch towards bottom of piston skirt. Oil

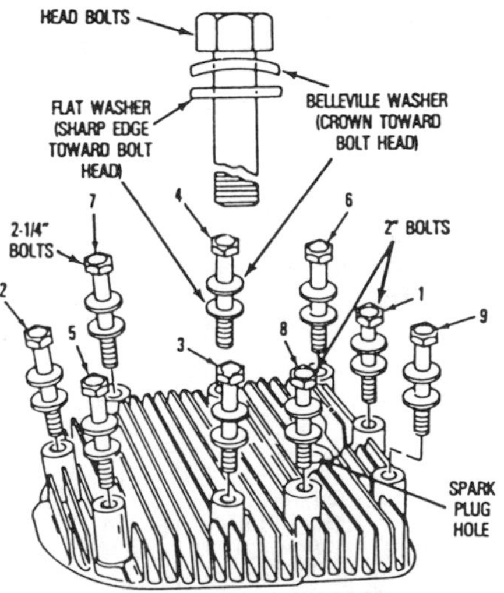


*Fig. T35—Flat washers and Belleville washers are used on cylinder head cap screws on late HH80, HH100 and HH120 and all VH80 and VH100 engines. Tighten cap screws in sequence shown to a torque of 200 in.-lbs. (22.6 N·m).*

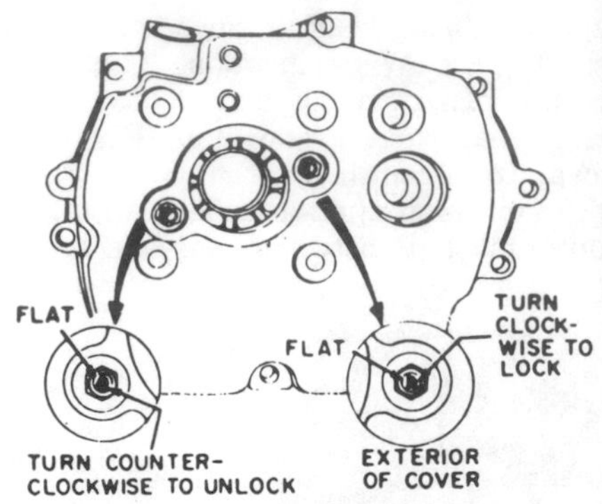


*Fig. T36—View showing bearing locks on Models HM70, HH70, HM80 and HM100 equipped with ball bearing main. Locks must be released before removing crankcase cover. Refer to Fig. T37 for interior view of cover and locks.*

ring can be installed either side up. Stagger ring gaps about 90 degrees around piston.

Piston skirt clearance in cylinder, measured at thrust side of piston just below oil ring, should be 0.010-0.012 inch (0.254-0.305 mm) on Model HH120; 0.006-0.008 inch (0.152-0.203 mm) on HH80 and HH100; 0.003-0.004 inch (0.076-0.203 mm) on VH80 and VH100; 0.0045-0.006 inch (0.1143-0.152 mm) on all other models.

Piston pin diameter is 0.6248-0.6250 inch (15.870-15.875 mm) on Models VM70, HM70, VM80, HM80, VM100, HM100, HH70 and VH70 or 0.6873-0.6875 inch (17.457-17.462) on all other models. Piston pin clearance should be 0.0001-0.0008 inch (0.0025-0.0203 mm) in rod and 0.0002-0.0005 inch (0.0051-0.0127 mm) in piston. If excessive clearance exists, both piston and pin must be renewed as pin is not available separately.

**CYLINDER.** If cylinder is scored or if taper or out-of-round exceeds 0.005 inch (0.127 mm), cylinder should be rebored to next suitable oversize. Standard cylinder bore is 2.9375-2.9385 inches (74.6125-74.6379 mm) on Models VM70 and HM70; 3.062-3.063 inches (77.775-77.800 mm) on early Models VM80 and HM80; 3.125-3.126 inches (79.375-

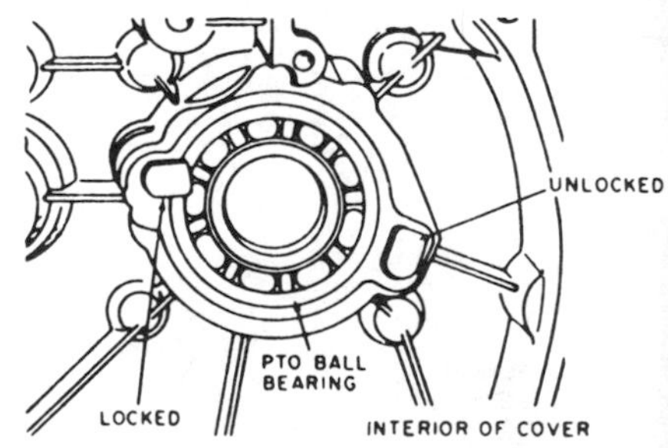


*Fig. T37—Interior view of crankcase cover and ball bearing locks used on Models HM70, HH70, HM80 and HM100.*

79.400 mm) on late Models VM80 and HM80; 3.187-3.188 inches (80.950-80.975 mm) on Models VM100 and HM100; 2.750-2.751 inches (69.850-69.875 mm) on Models HH70 and VH70; 3.312-3.313 inches (84.125-84.150 mm) on Models HH80, VH80, HH100 and VH100; 3.500-3.501 inches (88.900-88.925 mm) on Model HH120.

**CRANKSHAFT.** Crankshaft main journals ride directly in aluminum alloy bearings in crankcase and mounting flange (engine base) on vertical crankshaft engines or in two renewable steel backed bronze bushings. On some horizontal crankshaft engines, crankshaft rides in a renewable sleeve bushing at flywheel end and a ball bearing or bushing at pto end. Models HH80, VH80, HH100, VH100 and HH120 are equipped with taper roller bearings at both ends of crankshaft.

Normal running clearance of crankshaft journals in aluminum bearings or bronze bushings is 0.0015-0.0025 inch (0.0381-0.0635 mm). Renew crankshaft if main journals are more than 0.001 inch (0.025 mm) out-of-round or if crankpin is more than 0.0005 inch (0.0127 mm) out-of-round.

Check crankshaft gear for wear, broken tooth or loose fit on crankshaft. If gear is damaged, remove from crankshaft with an arbor press. Renew gear pin and press new gear on shaft making certain timing mark is facing pto end of shaft.

On models equipped with ball bearing at pto end of shaft, refer to Figs. T36 and T37 before attempting to remove crankcase cover. Loosen locknuts and rotate protruding ends of lock pins counter-clockwise to release bearing and remove cover. Ball bearing will remain on crankshaft. When reassembling, turn lock pins clockwise until flats on pins face each other, then tighten locknuts to 20 in.-lbs. (2.3 N·m).

Crankshaft end play on Models VM70, HM70, VM80, HM80, VM100, HM100, HH70 and VH70 should be 0.0005-0.027 inch (0.127-0.686 mm), and is controlled by washers (25 and 27 – Fig. T40) or (35 and 37 – Fig. T41).

To remove tapered roller bearings (30 and 51 – Fig. T42 or T43) from crankshaft on Models HH80, VH80, HH100, VH100 and HH120, use a suitable puller. Bearings will be damaged during removal and new bearings must be installed. Heat bearings in oil to approxi-

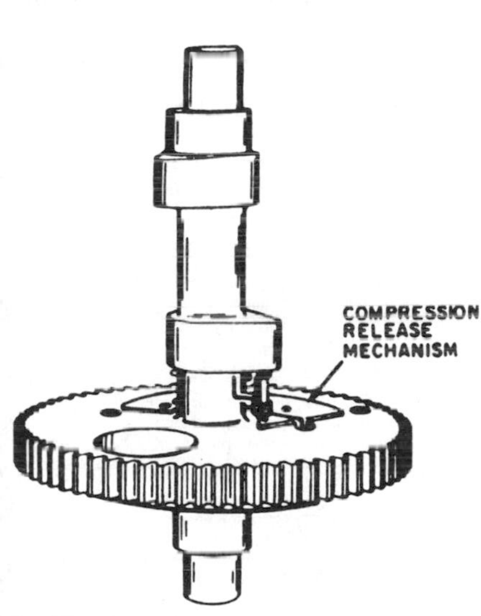


*Fig. T38 – View of Insta-matic Ezee-Start compression release camshaft assembly used on all models except HH80, HH100 and HH120.*

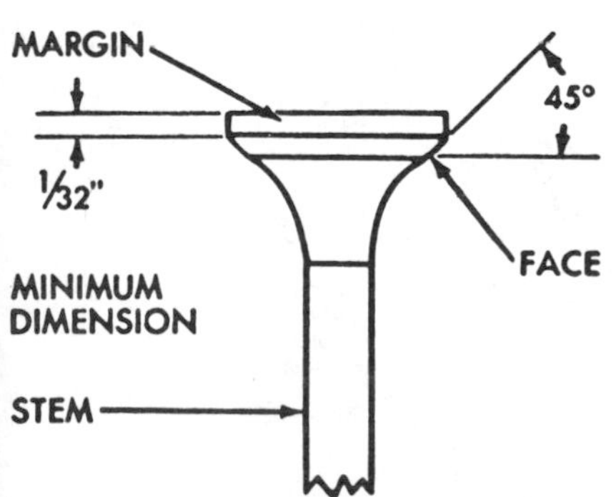


*Fig. T39 – Valve face angle should be 45 degrees. Minimum valve head margin is 1/32-inch (0.8 mm).*

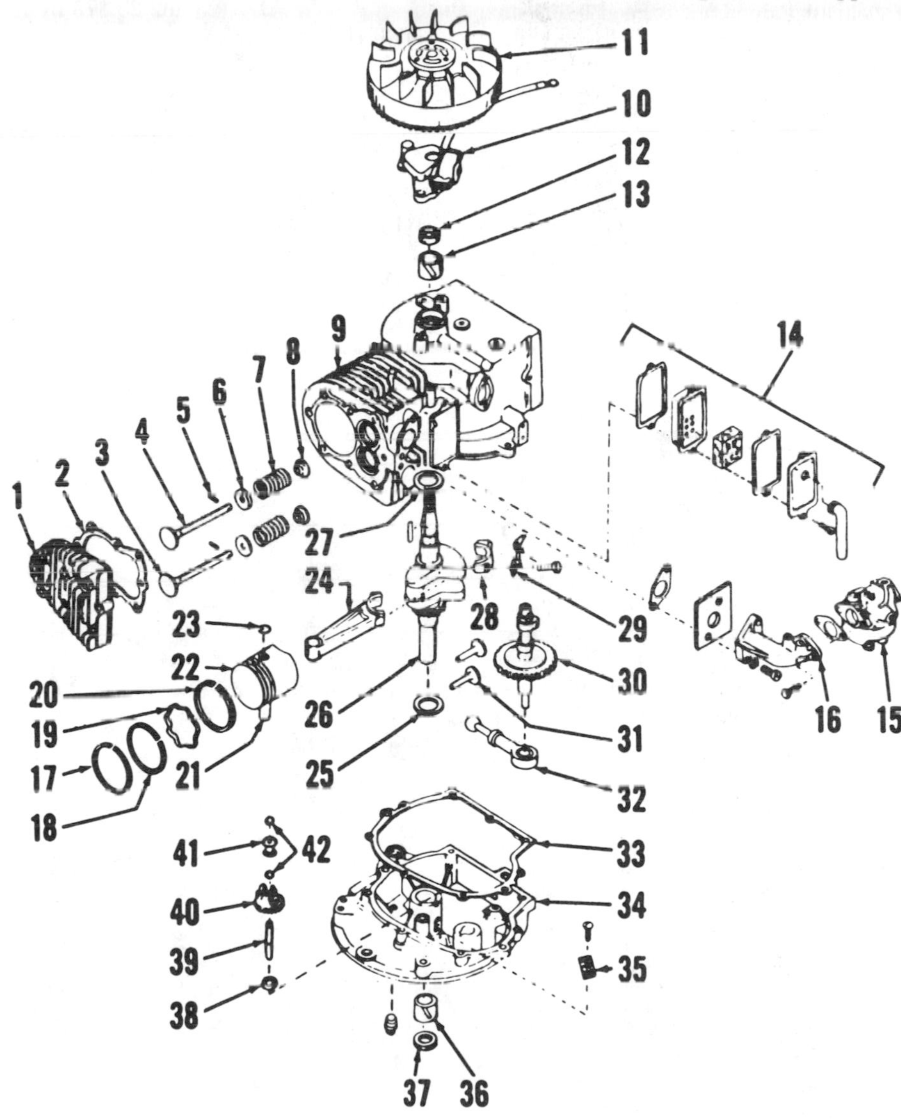


*Fig. T40 – Exploded view of vertical crankshaft engine typical of Models VH70, VM70, VM80 and VM100. Renewable bushings (13 and 36) are not used on Models VM70, VM80 and VM100.*

1. Cylinder head
2. Head gasket
3. Exhaust valve
4. Intake valve
5. Pin
6. Spring cap
7. Valve spring
8. Spring cap
9. Cylinder block
10. Magneto
11. Flywheel
12. Oil seal
13. Crankshaft bushing
14. Breather assy.
15. Carburetor
16. Intake pipe
17. Top compression ring
18. Second compression ring
19. Oil ring expander
20. Oil control ring
21. Piston pin
22. Piston
23. Retaining ring
24. Connecting rod
25. Thrust washer
26. Crankshaft
27. Thrust washer
28. Rod cap
29. Rod bolt lock
30. Camshaft assy.
31. Valve lifters
32. Oil pump
33. Gasket
34. Mounting flange (engine base)
35. Oil screen
36. Crankshaft bushing
37. Oil seal
38. Spacer
39. Governor shaft
40. Governor gear assy.
41. Spool
42. Retaining rings

Illustrations courtesy Tecumseh Products Co.

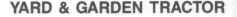

mately 300°F (150°C), then quickly slide bearings into position. Bearing cup (12) is a press fit in crankcase cover or engine base. Bearing cup (31) is a slip fit in block (29). To adjust crankshaft bearings, first assemble crankshaft assembly, piston and rod and crankcase cover or engine base. Tighten all bolts to correct torque value. Install bearing retaining cap (35) without shim gaskets (32), steel washers (33) or "O" ring (58). Tighten screws finger tight. Use a feeler gage to measure gap between bearing retainer flange and block. If no measurable clearance exists, install 0.010 inch steel washer between bearing retainer and cup until such clearance is obtained. If clearance does not exceed 0.007 inch (0.178 mm), no shim gasket (32) will be required and when retainer cap screws are tightened to correct torque, bearing preload will be 0.001-0.007 inch (0.025-0.178 mm). If clearance measures more than 0.007 inch (0.178 mm), subtract 0.001 inch (0.025 mm) from measurement to allow for preload; this will give actual distance to be shimmed. Since shim gaskets compress approximately 1/3 their thickness, shim pack should be 1½ times actual distance. Shim gaskets are available in thicknesses of 0.003-0.004, 0.004-0.005 and 0.005-0.007 inch. Remove bearing retainer, install "O" ring (58) and desired shim gaskets and reinstall retainer. Tighten cap screws to 110 in.-lbs. (12 N·m). Crankshaft seal should be installed to 0.025 inch (0.635 mm) below surface.

Crankshaft dimensions are as follows:

**Main Journal Diameter**

VH70, HH70
Flywheel and pto ends . . . . . 0.9985-0.9990 in. (25.362-25.375 mm)

VM70, HM70, VM80, HM80, VM100, HM100
Flywheel end . . . . . 0.9985-0.9990 in. (25.362-25.375 mm)
Pto end . . . . . 1.1870-1.1875 in. (30.150-30.162 mm)

HH80, VH80, HH100, VH100, HH120
Flywheel and pto ends . . . . . 1.1865-1.870 in. (30.137-30.150 mm)

**Crankpin Journal Diameter**

HH80, VH80, HH100, VH100, HH120 . . . . . 1.3750-1.3755 in. (34.925-34.938 mm)

All other models . . . . . 1.1860-1.1865 in. (30.124-30.137 mm)

**CAMSHAFT.** The camshaft and camshaft gear are an integral part which rides on journals at each end of shaft. Renew camshaft if gear teeth are worn or if bearing surfaces are worn or scored. Cam lobe nose to heel diameter should be 1.3045-1.3085 inches (33.134-33.236 mm) on Models HH80, VH80, HH100 and HH120 or 1.263-1.267 inches (32.080-32.182 mm) on all other models. Camshaft journal diameter is 0.6235-0.6240 inch (15.837-15.850 mm). Maximum allowable clearance between camshaft journal and bearing is 0.003 inch (0.076 mm).

Medium frame engines and Models VH70 and VH80 are equipped with Insta-matic Ezee-Start compression release camshaft (Fig. T38). Check compression release parts for binding, or excessive wear or other damage. If any parts are damaged or worn, renew com-

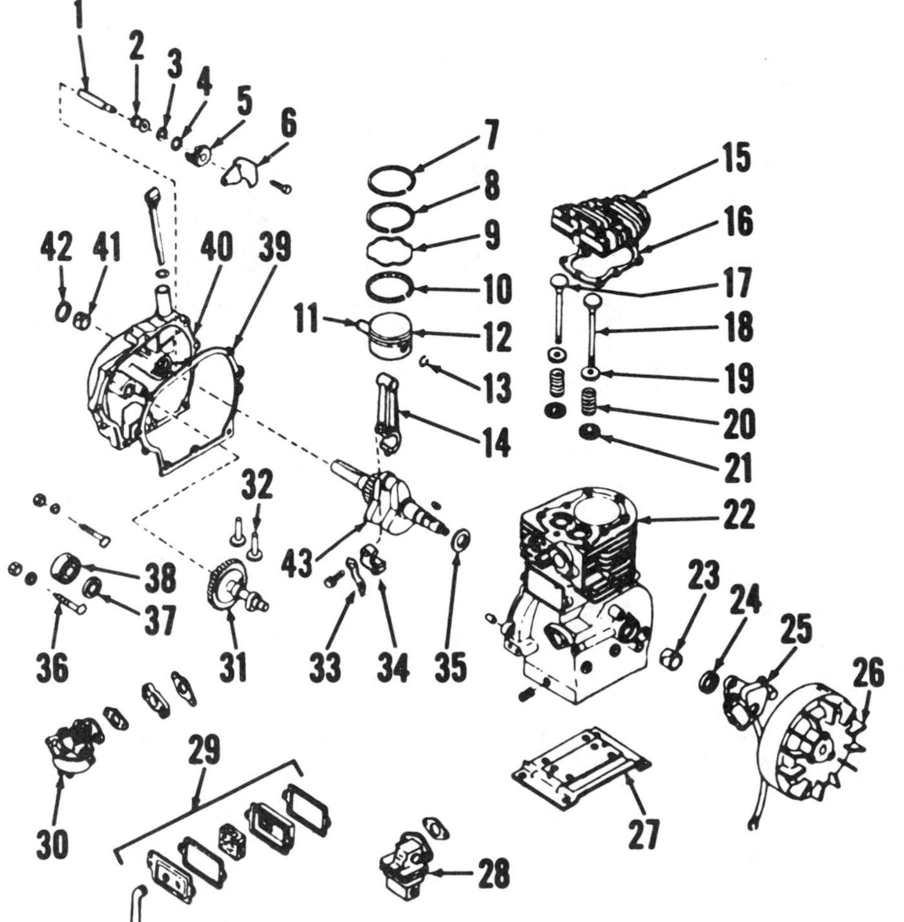


1. Governor shaft
2. Spool
3. Washer
4. Retaining ring
5. Gear & flyweight assy.
6. Bracket
7. Top compression ring
8. Second compression ring
9. Oil ring expander
10. Oil control ring
11. Piston pin
12. Piston
13. Retaining ring
14. Connecting rod
15. Cylinder head
16. Head gasket
17. Exhaust valve
18. Intake valve
19. Spring cap
20. Valve spring
21. Spring retainer
22. Cylinder block
23. Crankshaft bushing
24. Oil seal
25. Magneto
26. Flywheel
27. Mounting plate
28. Fuel pump
29. Breather assy.
30. Carburetor
31. Camshaft assy.
32. Valve lifter
33. Rod bolt lock
34. Rod cap
35. Thrust washer
36. Bearing lock pin
37. Thrust washer
38. Ball bearing
39. Gasket
40. Crankcase cover
41. Bushing
42. Oil seal
43. Crankshaft

*Fig. T41—Exploded view of horizontal crankshaft engine typical of Models HH70, HM70, HM80 and HM100. Engines may be equipped with crankshaft bushing (41) or ball bearing (38) at pto end of shaft.*



Illustrations courtesy Tecumseh Products Co.

plete camshaft assembly. Compression release parts are not serviced separately.

On Models HH80, HH100 and HH120, timing advance unit should be inspected and any worn or damaged parts renewed. Refer to Fig. T43 for exploded view of timing advance (52 through 56).

On all models, when installing camshaft, align timing mark on cam gear with mark on crankshaft gear. Timing mark on crankshaft gear is a chamfered tooth.

**VALVE SYSTEM.** On Models HH80, VH80, HH100, VH100 and HH120, valve tappet gap with engine cold is 0.010 inch (0.254 mm) for intake and 0.020 inch (0.508 mm) for exhaust. Valve tappet gap on all other models with engine cold is 0.010 inch (0.254 mm) for both valves. To obtain correct gap, grind valve stem end off squarely. Valve seat angle width is 3/64-inch (1.2 mm) on all models. When valve head margin is less than 1/32-inch (0.8 mm), renew valve. See Fig. T39.

Valve guides are non-renewable on all models. If excessive clearance exists, valve guide should be reamed and a new valve with oversize stem installed. Ream guide to 0.344-0.345 inch (8.738-8.763 mm) on Models HH80, VH80, HH100, VH100 and HH120 and to 0.3432-0.3442 inch (8.717-8.743 mm) on all other models.

Valve spring free length should be 1.885 inches (47.88 mm) on Models HH80, VH80, HH100, VH100 and HH120. Valve spring free length should be 1.562 inches (39.67 mm) on all other models.

**DYNA-STATIC BALANCER.** The Dyna-Static engine balancer operates by means of a pair of counterweighted gears driven by crankshaft to counteract the unbalance caused by counterweights on crankshaft. The balancer used on medium frame engine is similar to those used on heavy frame models. On medium frame models, balancer gears are held in position on the shafts by a bracket bolted to crankcase or engine base (Fig. T44). Snap rings are used on heavy frame models to retain balancer gears on shafts.

The renewable balancer gear shafts are pressed into crankcase cover or engine base. On medium frame models,

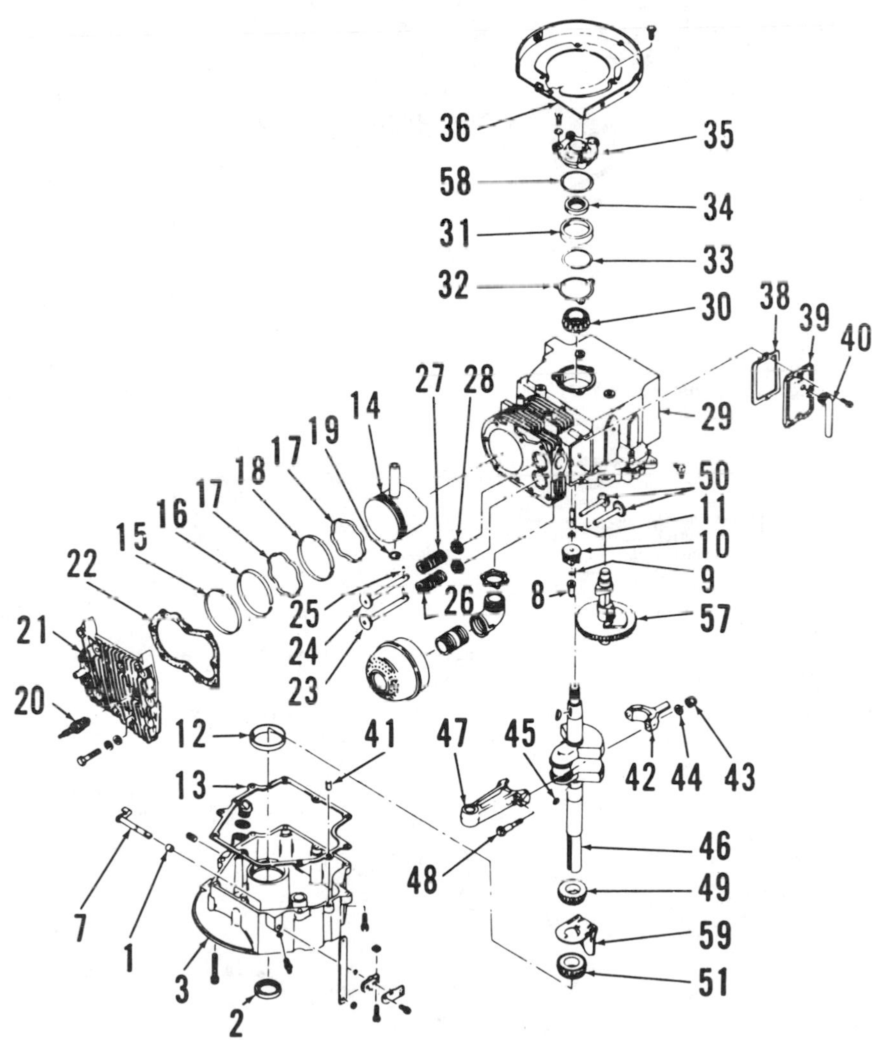


*Fig. T42—Exploded view of Model VH80 or VH100 vertical crankshaft engine.*

1. Governor arm bushing
2. Oil seal
3. Mounting flange (engine base)
7. Governor arm
8. Thrust spool
9. Snap ring
10. Governor gear & weight assy.
11. Governor shaft
12. Bearing cup
13. Gasket
14. Piston & pin assy.
15. Top compression ring
16. Second compression ring
17. Ring expanders
18. Oil control ring
19. Retaining ring
20. Spark plug
21. Cylinder head
22. Head gasket
23. Exhaust valve
24. Intake valve
25. Pin
26. Exhaust valve spring
27. Intake valve spring
28. Spring cap
29. Cylinder block
30. Bearing cone
31. Bearing cup
32. Shim gasket
33. Steel washer (0.010 in.)
34. Oil seal
35. Bearing retainer cap
36. Blower air baffle
38. Gasket
39. Breather
40. Breather tube
42. Rod cap
43. Self-locking nut
44. Washer
45. Crankshaft gear pin
46. Crankshaft
47. Connecting rod
48. Rod bolt
49. Crankshaft gear
50. Valve lifters
51. Bearing cone
57. Camshaft assy.
58. "O" ring
59. Oil slinger

Illustrations courtesy Tecumseh Products Co.

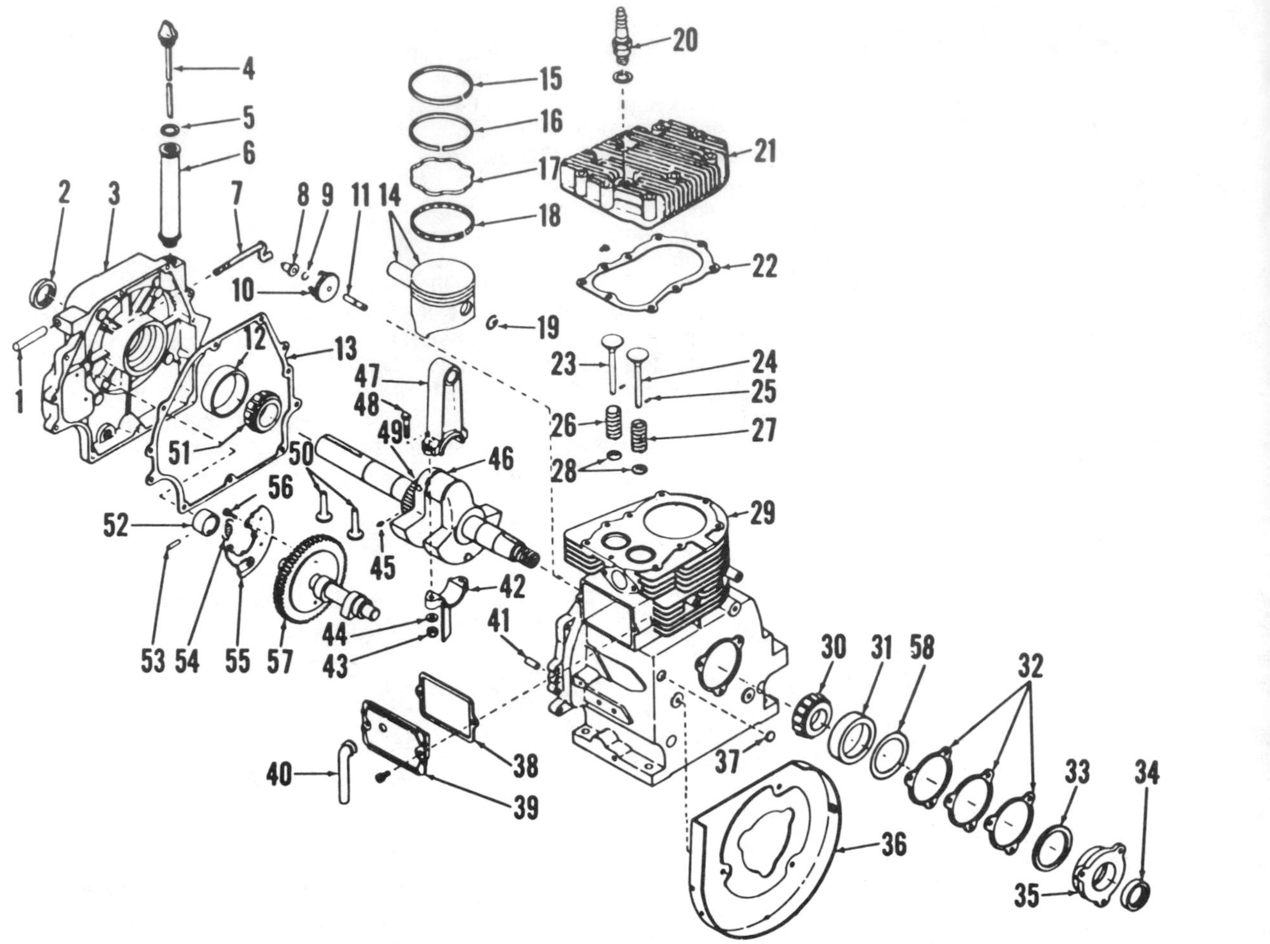

Fig. T43—Exploded view of Model HH80, HH100 or HH120 horizontal crankshaft engine.

1. Governor arm bushing
2. Oil seal
3. Crankcase cover
4. Dipstick
5. Gasket
6. Oil filler tube
7. Governor arm
8. Thrust spool
9. Snap ring
10. Governor gear & weight assy.
11. Governor shaft
12. Bearing cup
13. Gasket
14. Piston & pin assy.
15. Top compression ring
16. Second compression ring
17. Oil ring expander
18. Oil control ring
19. Retaining ring
20. Spark plug
21. Cylinder head
22. Head gasket
23. Exhaust valve
24. Intake valve
25. Pin
26. Exhaust valve spring
27. Intake valve spring
28. Spring cap
29. Cylinder block
30. Bearing cone
31. Bearing cup
32. Shim gaskets
33. Steel washer (0.010 in.)
34. Oil seal
35. Bearing retainer cap
36. Blower air baffle
37. Plug
38. Gasket
39. Breather assy.
40. Breather tube
41. Dowel pin
42. Rod cap
43. Self-locking nut
44. Washer
45. Crankshaft gear pin
46. Crankshaft
47. Connecting rod
48. Rod bolt
49. Crankshaft gear
50. Valve lifters
51. Bearing cone
52. Breaker cam
53. Push rod
54. Spring
55. Timing advance weight
56. Rivet
57. Camshaft assy.
58. "O" ring

press shaft into cover or engine base until a distance of 1.757-1.763 inches (44.628-44.780 mm) exists between shaft bore boss and edge of step cut on shafts as shown in Fig. T46. Heavy frame model shafts should be pressed until a distance of 1.7135-1.7185 inches (43.523-43.650 mm) exists between cover boss and the outer edge of snap ring groove as shown in Fig. T47.

All balancer gears are equipped with renewable cage needle bearings. See Figs. T48 and T49. Using tool #670210, press new bearings into gears until cage is flush to 0.015 inch (0.381 mm) below edge of bore.

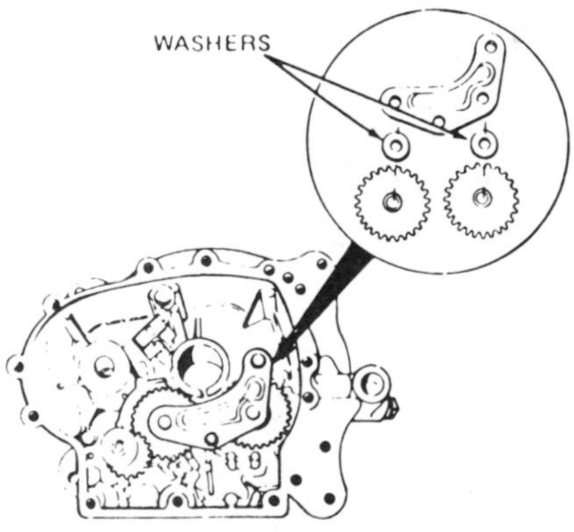

Fig. T44—View showing Dyna-Static balancer gears installed in Model VM80 or VM100 engine base. Balancer gears are identically located in Model HM80 or HM100 crankcase cover. Note location of washers between gears retaining bracket.

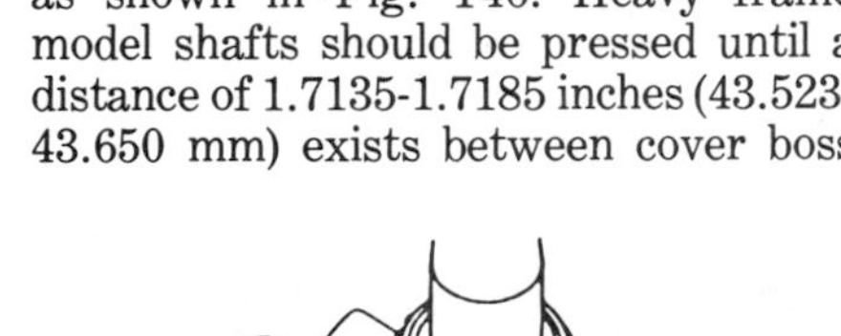

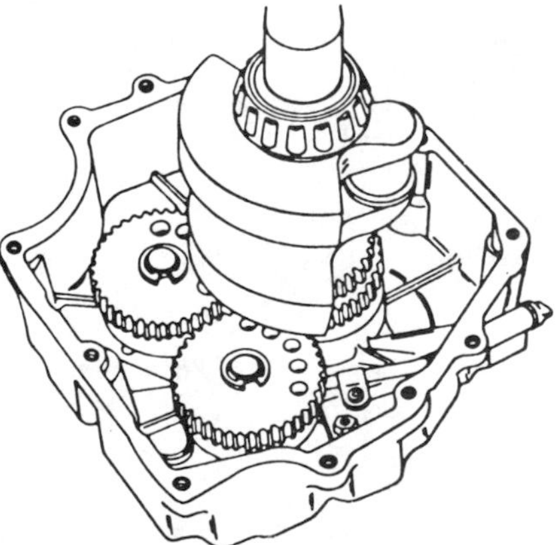

Fig. T45—View showing Dyna-Static balancer gears installed in Model HH80, HH100 or HH120 crankcase cover. Note gear retaining snap rings.

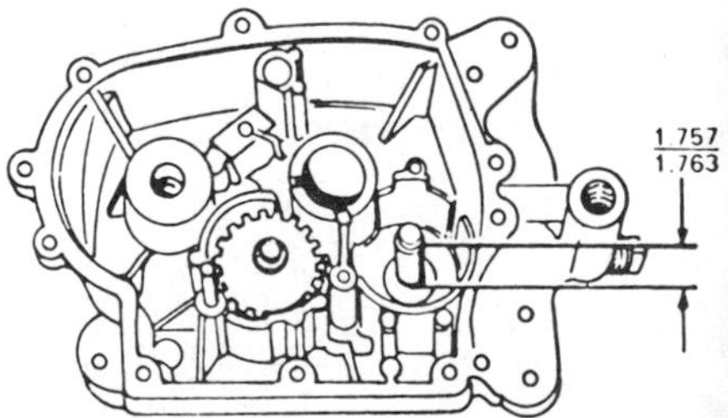


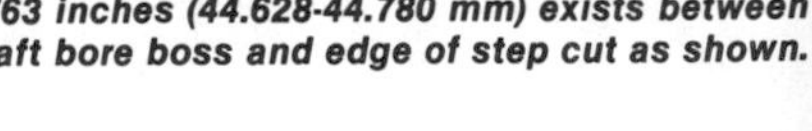

Fig. T46—On Models HM80, VM80, HM100 and VM100, balancer gear shafts must be pressed into cover or engine base so a distance of 1.757-1.763 inches (44.628-44.780 mm) exists between shaft bore boss and edge of step cut as shown.

Fig. T47—On Models HH80, HH100 and HH120, press balancer gear shafts into cover to dimension shown.

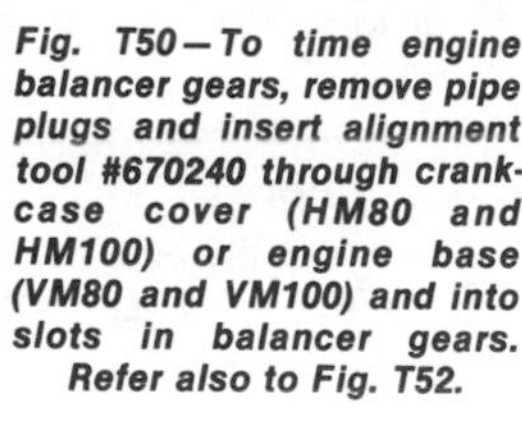

Fig. T50—To time engine balancer gears, remove pipe plugs and insert alignment tool #670240 through crankcase cover (HM80 and HM100) or engine base (VM80 and VM100) and into slots in balancer gears. Refer also to Fig. T52.

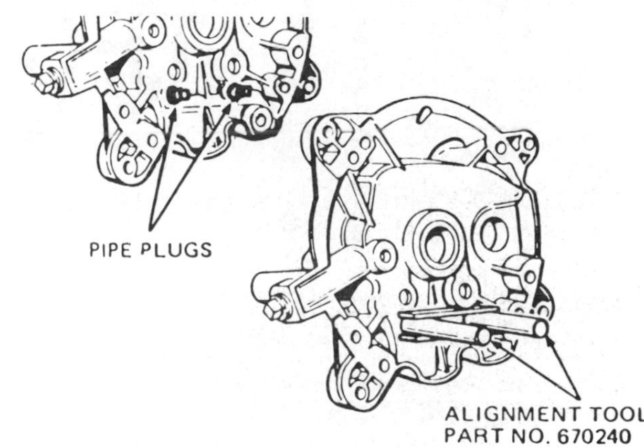


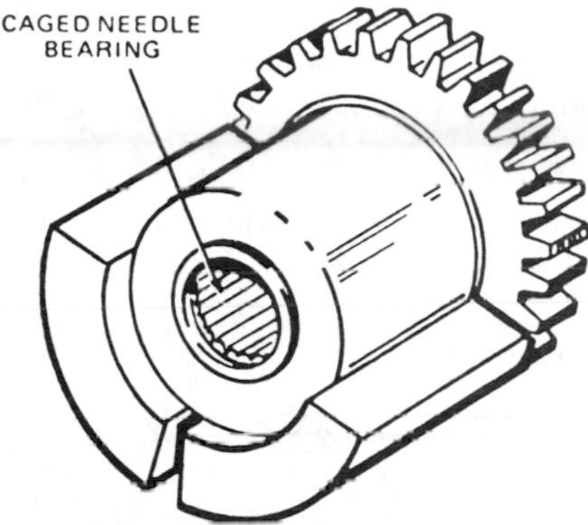


Fig. T48—Using tool #670210, press new needle bearings into Model HM80, VM80, HM100 or VM100 balancer gears until bearing cage is flush to 0.015 inch (0.381 mm) below edge of bore.

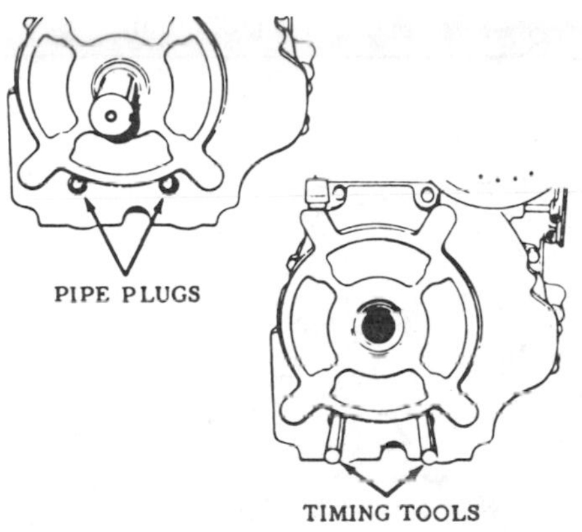


Fig. T51—To time balancer gears on Models HH80, HH100 and HH120, remove pipe plugs and insert timing tools #670239 through crankcase cover and into timing slots in balancer gears. Refer also to Fig. T53.

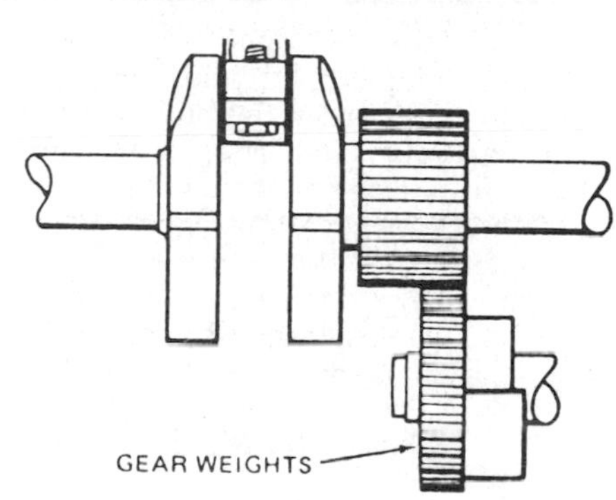


Fig. T52—View showing correct balancer gear timing to crankshaft gear on Models HM80, VM80, HM100 and VM100. With piston at TDC, weights should be directly opposite.

Fig. T49—On Models HH80, HH100 and HH120, needle bearings are installed flush to 0.015 inch (0.381 mm) below edge of bore. Note tool alignment notch at lower side of balancer.

When reassembling engine, balancer gears must be timed with crankshaft for correct operation. Refer to Figs. T50 and T51 and remove pipe plugs. Insert alignment tool #670240 through crankcase cover of Models HM80 and HM100 or engine base of Models VM80 and VM100 and into timing slots in balancer gears. On Models HH80, HH100 and HH120, insert timing tool #670239 through cover and into balancer gears. Then, on all models, turn crankshaft to place piston at TDC and carefully install engine base or cover with balancer gears. When correctly assembled, piston should be on TDC and weights on balancer gears should be in directly opposite position. See Figs. T52 and T53.

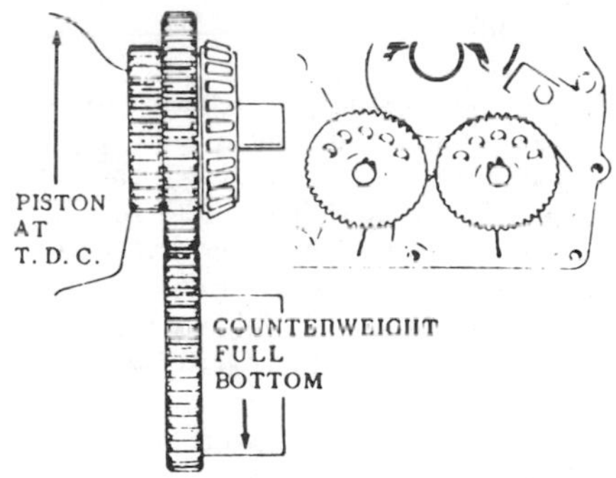


Fig. T53—On Models HH80, HH100 and HH120, balancer gears are correctly timed to crankshaft when piston is at TDC and weights are at full bottom position.

# TECUMSEH

| Model | No. Cyls. | Bore | Stroke | Displacement | Horsepower |
|---|---|---|---|---|---|
| OH120 | 1 | 3-1/8 in. (79.4 mm) | 2-3/4 in. (69.8 mm) | 21.1 cu. in. (346 cc) | 12 (8.9 kW) |
| OH140 | 1 | 3-5/16 in. (84.1 mm) | 2-3/4 in. (69.8 mm) | 23.75 cu. in. (389 cc) | 14 (10.4 kW) |
| OH160 | 1 | 3-1/2 in. (88.9 mm) | 2-7/8 in. (73.0 mm) | 27.66 cu. in. (453 cc) | 16 (11.9 kW) |
| HH140 | 1 | 3-5/16 in. (84.1 mm) | 2-3/4 in. (69.8 mm) | 23.75 cu. in. (389 cc) | 14 (10.4 kW) |
| HH150 | 1 | 3-1/2 in. (88.9 mm) | 2-7/8 in. (73.0 mm) | 27.66 cu. in. (453 cc) | 15 (11.2 kW) |
| HH160 | 1 | 3-1/2 in. (88.9 mm) | 2-7/8 in. (73.0 mm) | 27.66 cu. in. (453 cc) | 16 (11.9 kW) |

Engines must be identified by complete model number, including specification number in order to obtain correct repair parts. It is important to transfer ID tags from original engine to replacement short block so unit can be identified later.

All models in this section are heavy frame cast iron engines and are valve-in-head, horizontal crankshaft type.

## MAINTENANCE

**SPARK PLUG.** A Champion L-7 or equivalent spark plug is used. Set electrode gap to 0.030 inch (0.762 mm). Spark plug should be removed, cleaned and adjusted periodically. Renew plug if electrodes are burned and pitted or if porcelain is cracked.

**CARBURETOR.** A Walbro Model LM float type carburetor is used. To adjust carburetor, refer to Fig. T55 and proceed as follows: Turn idle mixture screw (9) clockwise until lightly seated, then back out 1¾ turns. Turn main fuel adjusting needle (27) clockwise until lightly seated, then back out 2¾ turns. Start and operate engine until normal operating temperature is reached. Then, readjust main fuel needle, if necessary, until engine runs smoothly and evenly under operating conditions.

Adjust idle speed screw (8) until engine idle speed of 1200 rpm is obtained. Readjust idle mixture needle (9), if necessary, until engine idles smoothly.

To check float setting, hold carburetor and float assembly in inverted position. A distance of 0.275-0.315 inch (7.0-8.0 mm) should exist between float and center boss measured as shown in Fig. T56. Carefully bend adjusting tab on float to adjust float setting. A Viton seat (12 – Fig. T55) is used with fuel inlet valve (13). The renewable seat must be installed grooved side first in bore so inlet valve will seat at smooth side. See Fig. T57.

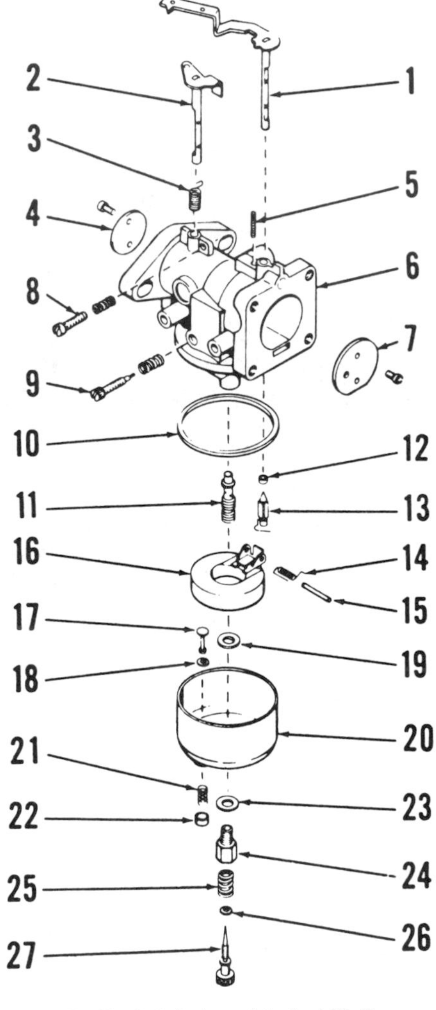

*Fig. T55 – Exploded view of typical Walbro carburetor used on all models.*

1. Choke shaft
2. Throttle shaft
3. Throttle return spring
4. Throttle plate
5. Choke stop spring
6. Carburetor body
7. Choke plate
8. Idle speed stop screw
9. Idle mixture needle
10. Bowl gasket
11. Main nozzle
12. Inlet valve seat
13. Inlet valve
14. Float spring
15. Float shaft
16. Float
17. Drain stem
18. Gasket
19. Gasket
20. Bowl
21. Spring
22. Retainer
23. Gasket
24. Bowl retainer
25. Spring
26. "O" ring
27. Main fuel adjusting needle

If main nozzle (11 – Fig. T55) is removed and is the original type (Fig. T58), obtain and install a new service

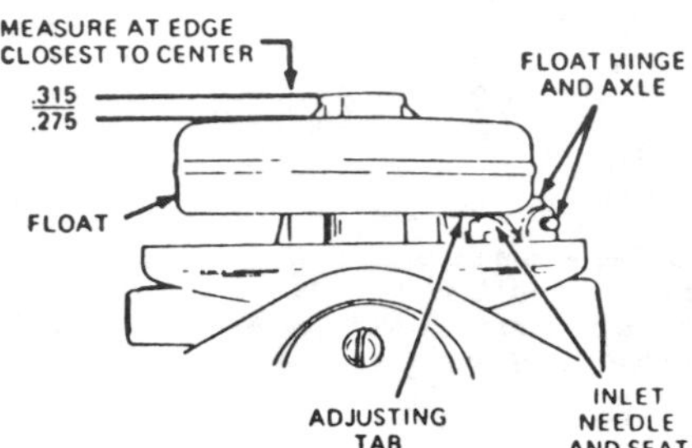


*Fig. T56 – Float setting should be measured as shown. Bend adjusting tab to adjust float setting.*

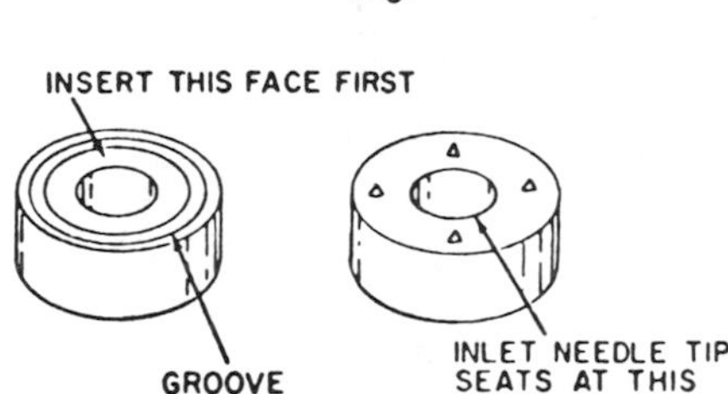


*Fig. T57 – The Viton inlet fuel valve seat must be installed grooved side first.*

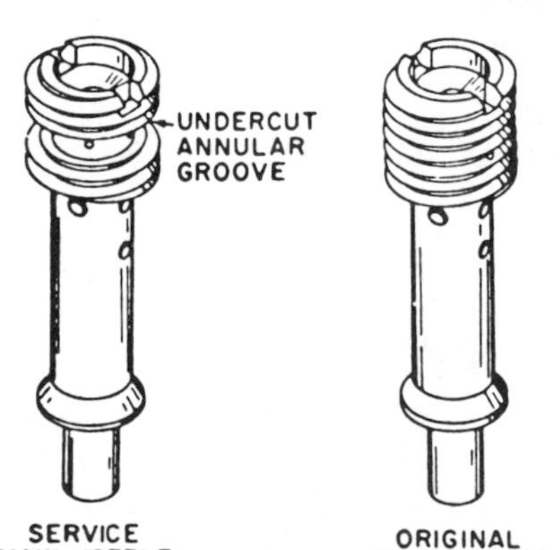


*Fig. T58 – The main nozzle originally installed is drilled after installation through hole in body. Service main nozzles are grooved so alignment is not necessary.*



Illustrations courtesy Tecumseh Products Co

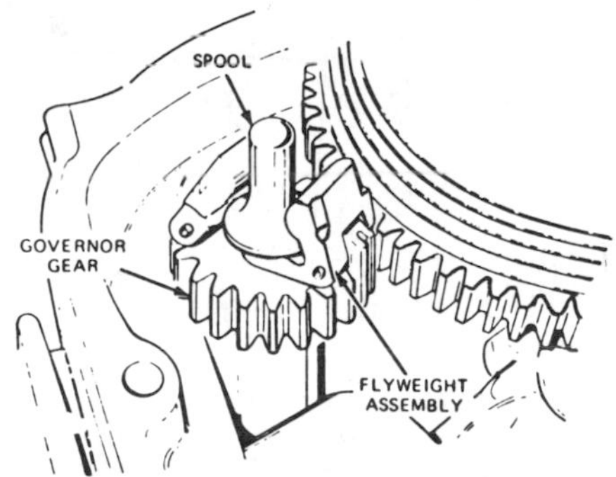


*Fig. T59—View showing governor assembly installed in crankcase. Governor gear is driven by camshaft gear.*

nozzle. The service nozzle will have an undercut annular groove in threaded area as shown in Fig. T58.

**GOVERNOR.** A mechanical flyweight type governor is used on all models. Governor gear, flyweights and shaft are serviced only as an assembly. Refer to Fig. T59 for view showing governor assembly installed in crankcase. Governor gear is driven by camshaft gear.

To adjust external governor linkage, refer to Fig. T60 and proceed as follows: Loosen screw (A), turn plate (B) counter-clockwise as far as possible and move governor lever (C) to the left until throttle is in wide open position. Tighten screw (A). Governor spring must be hooked in hole (D) as shown. Adjusting screws on bracket are used to adjust fixed or variable speed settings. Engine high idle speed should not exceed 3600 rpm.

**SOLID STATE IGNITION (WITHOUT ALTERNATOR).** The Tecumseh solid state ignition system shown in Fig. T61 is used on engines not equipped with flywheel alternator. This system does not use ignition breaker points. The only moving part of the system is the

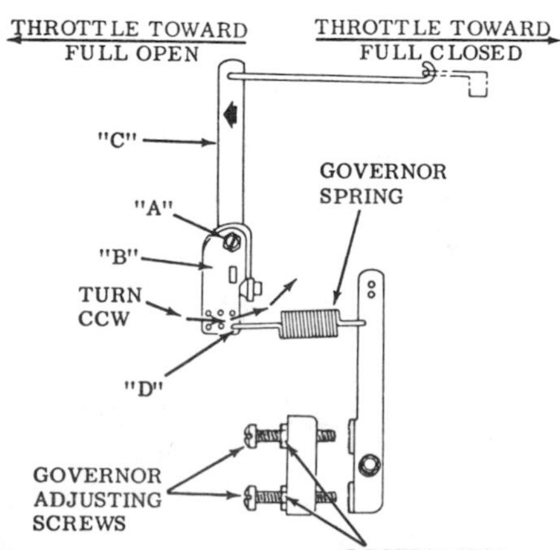


*Fig. T60—Typical external governor linkage. Refer to text for adjustment procedures.*

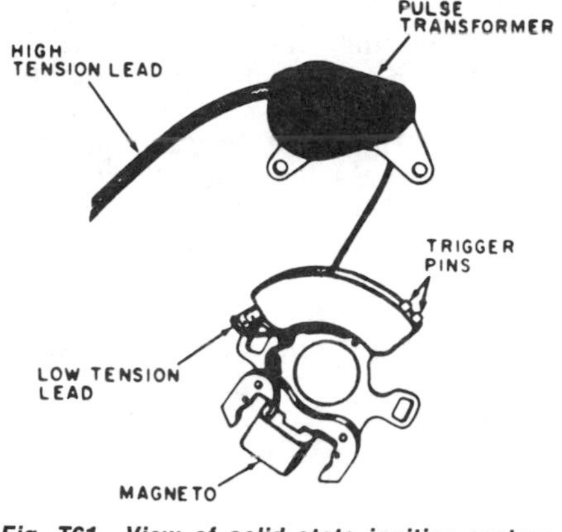


*Fig. T61—View of solid state ignition system used on engine not equipped with flywheel alternator.*

rotating flywheel with charging magnets. As flywheel magnet passes position (1A–Fig. T62), a low voltage AC current is induced into input coil (2). Current passes through rectifier (3) converting this current to DC. It then travels to capacitor (4) where it is stored. The flywheel rotates approximately 180 degrees to position (1B). As it passes trigger coil (5), it induces a very small electric charge into the coil. This charge passes through resistor (6) and turns on the SCR (silicon controlled rectifier) switch (7). With SCR switch closed, low voltage current stored in capacitor (4) travels to pulse transformer (8). Voltage is stepped up instantaneously and current is discharged across electrodes of spark plug (9), producing a spark before top dead center.

Units may be equipped with a second trigger coil and resistor set to turn SCR switch on at a lower rpm. This second trigger pin is closer to flywheel and produces a spark at TDC for easier starting. As engine rpm increases, the first (shorter) trigger pin picks up the small electric charge and turns SCR switch on, firing spark plug BTDC.

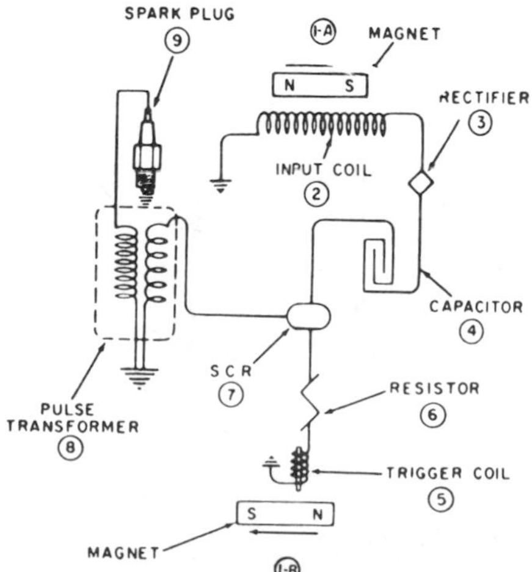


*Fig. T62—Operational diagram of solid state ignition system.*

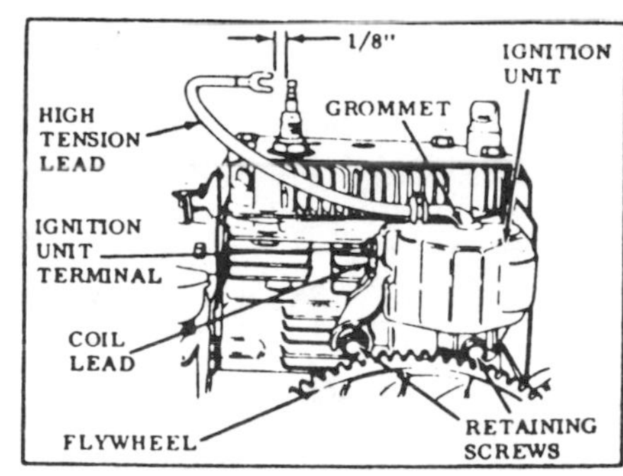


*Fig. T63—View of solid state ignition unit used on engine equipped with flywheel alternator. System should produce a good blue spark ⅛-inch (3 mm) long at cranking speed.*

If system fails to produce a spark to spark plug, first check high tension lead (Fig. T61). If condition of high tension lead is questionable, renew pulse transformer and high tension lead assembly. Check low tension lead and renew if insulation is faulty. The magneto charging coil, electronic triggering system and mounting plate are available only as an assembly. If necessary to renew this assembly, place unit in position on engine. Start retaining screws, turn mounting plate counter-clockwise as far as possible, then tighten retaining screws to a torque of 5-7 ft.-lbs. (7-9 N·m).

**SOLID STATE IGNITION (WITH ALTERNATOR).** The Tecumseh solid state ignition system used on engines equipped with flywheel alternator does not use ignition points. The only moving part of the system is the rotating flywheel with charging magnets and trigger pins. Other components of the system are ignition generator coil and stator assembly, spark plug and ignition unit.

The long trigger pin induces a small charge of current to close SCR (silicon controlled rectifier) switch at engine cranking speed and produces a spark at TDC for starting. As engine rpm increases, the first (shorter) trigger pin induces the current which produces a spark when piston is BTDC.

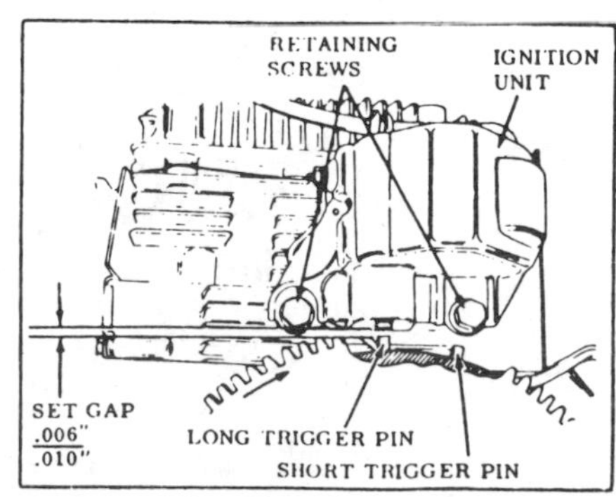


*Fig. T64—Adjust air gap between long trigger pin and ignition unit to 0.006-0.010 inch (0.152-0.254 mm).*

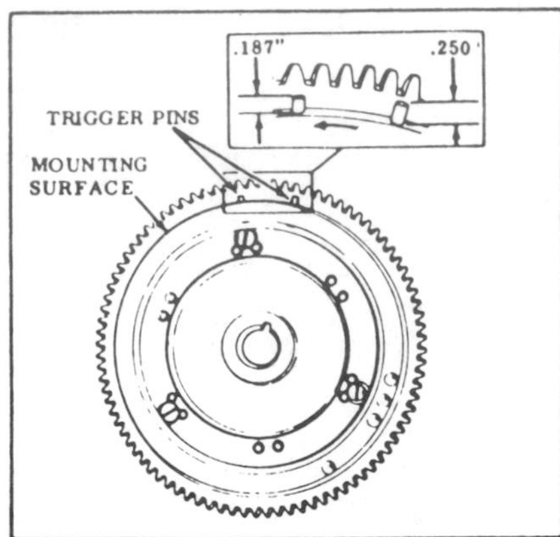


*Fig. T65—Remove flywheel and drive trigger pins in or out as necessary until long pin is extended 0.250 (6.35 mm) inch and short pin is extended 0.187 inch (4.75 mm) above mounting surface.*

Test ignition system as follows: Hold high tension lead 1/8-inch (3 mm) from spark plug (Fig. T63), crank engine and check for a good blue spark. If no spark is present, check high tension lead and coil lead for loose connections or faulty insulation. Check air gap between long trigger pin and ignition unit as shown in Fig. T64. Air gap should be 0.006-0.010 inch (0.152-0.254 mm). To adjust air gap, loosen the two retaining screws and move ignition unit as necessary, then tighten retaining screws.

**NOTE: The long trigger pin should extend 0.250 inch (6.35 mm) and the short trigger pin should extend 0.187 inch (4.75 mm), measured as shown in Fig. T65. If not, remove flywheel and drive pins in or out as required.**

Remove coil lead from ignition terminal and connect an ohmmeter as shown in Fig. T66. If series resistance test of ignition generator coil is below 400 ohms, renew stator and coil assembly (Fig. T67). If resistance is above 400 ohms, renew ignition unit.

**LUBRICATION.** Splash lubrication is provided by use of an oil dipper on connecting rod cap. See Fig. T68.

Use only high quality, detergent motor oil having API classification SE, SF or SG. SAE 30 oil is recommended for operating in temperatures above 32°F (0°C) and SAE 10W for operating in temperatures below 32°F (0°C).

## REPAIRS

**TIGHTENING TORQUES.** Recommended tightening torques are as follows:

Cylinder head . . . . . . . . . . . . 220 in.-lbs. (24.8 N·m)
Connecting rod . . . . . . . . . . . 110 in.-lbs. (12.4 N·m)
Crankcase cover . . . . . . . . 65-110 in.-lbs. (7.3-12.4 N·m)
Bearing retainer . . . . . . . . 65-110 in.-lbs. (7.3-12.4 N·m)
Flywheel nut . . . . . . . . . . 600-660 in.-lbs. (67.8-74.6 N·m)
Spark plug . . . . . . . . . . . 270-360 in.-lbs. (30.5-40.7 N·m)
Stator mounting . . . . . . . . . 60-84 in.-lbs. (6.8-9.5 N·m)
Carburetor to inlet pipe . . . . . . . . . . . . 48-72 in.-lbs. (5.4-8.1 N·m)
Inlet pipe to head . . . . . . . . 72-96 in.-lbs. (8.1-10.8 N·m)
Rocker arm housing to head . . . . . . . . . . . . . . 80-90 in.-lbs. (9.0-10.1 N·m)
Rocker arm shaft screw . 180-220 in.-lbs. (20.3-24.8 N·m)
Rocker arm cover . . . . . . . . 15-20 in.-lbs. (1.7-2.2 N·m)

**CONNECTING ROD.** The aluminum alloy connecting rod rides directly on the crankpin. Piston and connecting rod assembly is removed from above after removing rocker arm housing, cylinder head, crankcase cover and connecting rod cap.

Crankpin diameter is 1.3750-1.3755 inches (34.925-34.938 mm) and running clearance of connecting rod to crankpin should be 0.001-0.0015 inch (0.025-0.381 mm). Renew connecting rod if clearance is excessive. If crankpin is scored, out-

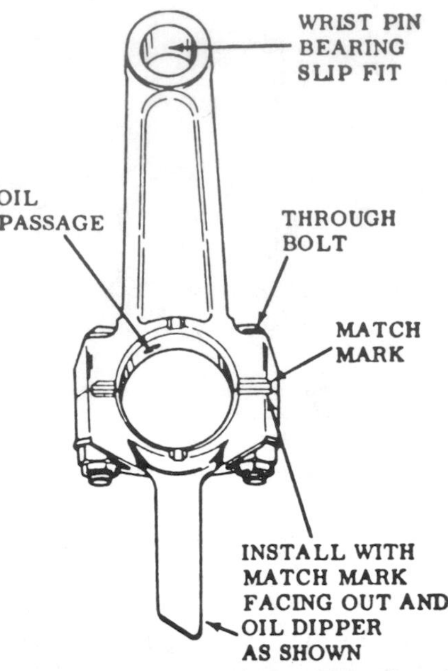


*Fig. T68—Connecting rod assembly used on all models. Note oil dipper on rod cap and match marks.*

of-round or excessively worn, crankshaft must be renewed. Connecting rod is available in standard size only. Standard diameter of piston pin hole in connecting rod is 0.6876-0.6881 inch (17.465-17.478 mm). Renew connecting rod if piston pin hole is excessively worn.

When installing piston and connecting rod assembly, make certain match marks on connecting rod and rod cap (Fig. T68) are aligned and marks are facing pto end of shaft. Always renew self-locking nuts on connecting rod bolts and tighten nuts to a torque of 110 in.-lbs. (12 N·m).

**CYLINDER HEAD AND VALVE SYSTEM.** To remove cylinder head and/or valves, first unbolt and remove blower housing and valve cover and breather assembly. Turn crankshaft until piston is at top dead center of compression stroke. Refer to Fig. T69,

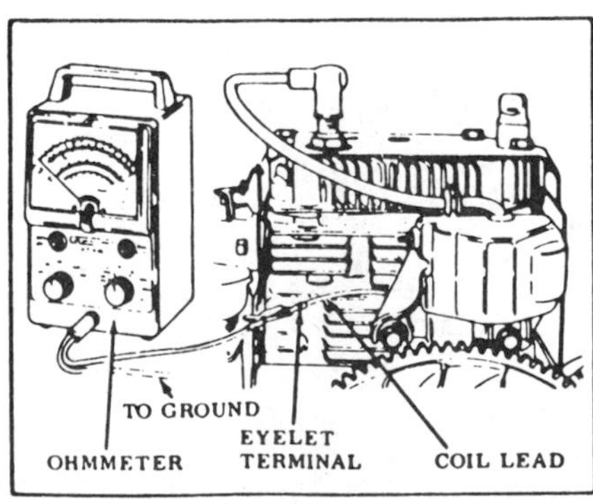


*Fig. T66—View showing ohmmeter connected for resistance test of ignition generator coil.*

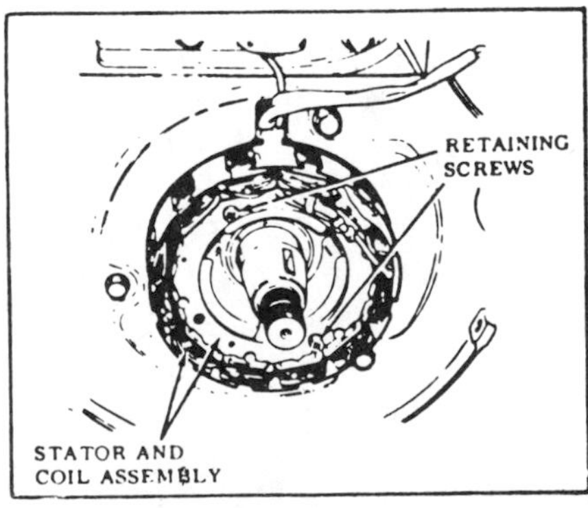


*Fig. T67—Ignition generator coil and stator is serviced only as an assembly.*

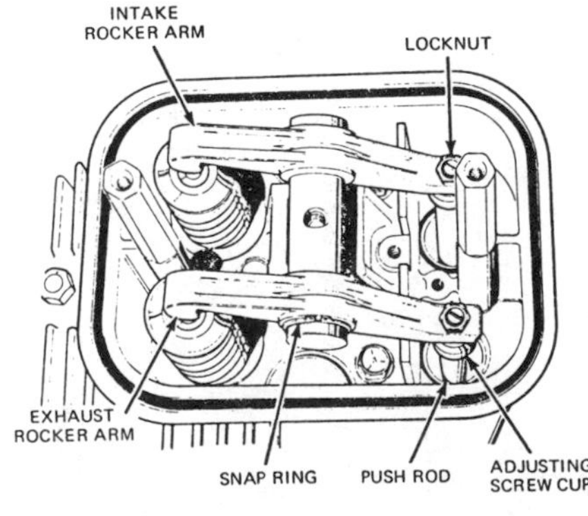


*Fig. T69—View showing rocker arms used on all models. Slotted adjusting screws were used on early production engines. Later engines have adjusting nut on screw below rocker arm.*



Illustrations courtesy Tecumseh Products Co.

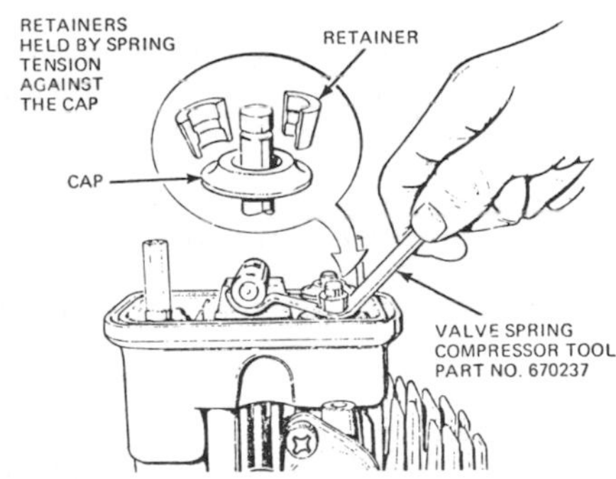


*Fig. T70—Use tool #670237 to compress valve springs while removing retainers.*

loosen locknuts on rocker arms and back off adjusting screws. Remove snap rings from rocker shaft and remove rocker arms. Using valve spring compressor tool #670237 as shown in Fig. T70, remove valve retainers. Then, remove upper spring cap, valve spring, lower spring cap and "O" ring from each valve. Remove the three cap screws, washers and "O" rings from inside rocker arm housing and carefully lift off housing. Push rods and push rod tubes can now be withdrawn. Unbolt and remove carburetor and inlet pipe assembly from cylinder head. Remove cylinder head cap screws and lift off cylinder head, taking care not to drop intake and exhaust valves.

Standard inside diameter of both guides is 0.312-0.313 inch (7.925-7.950 mm). If excessive clearance exists between valve stem and guide, ream guide to 0.343-0.344 inch (8.712-8.737 mm) and install 1/32-inch (0.8 mm) oversize valve, or renew valve guides. To renew valve guides, remove and submerge head in large pan of oil. Heat on a hot plate until oil begins to smoke, about 15-20 minutes. Remove head from pan and place head on arbor press with valve seats facing up. Use a drift punch ½-inch (13 mm) in diameter to press guides out.

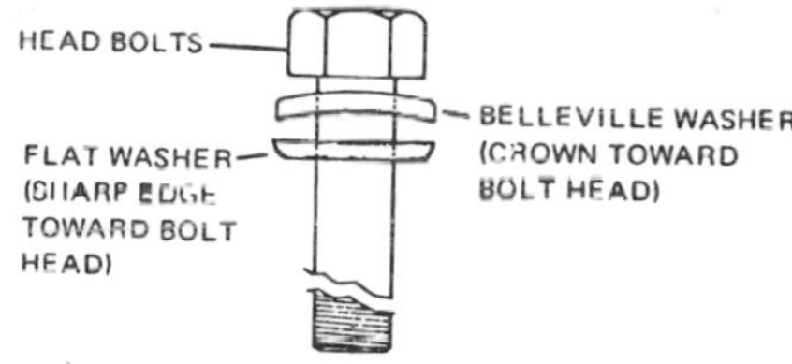


*Fig. T71—Install Belleville washer and flat washer on cylinder head cap screws as shown.*

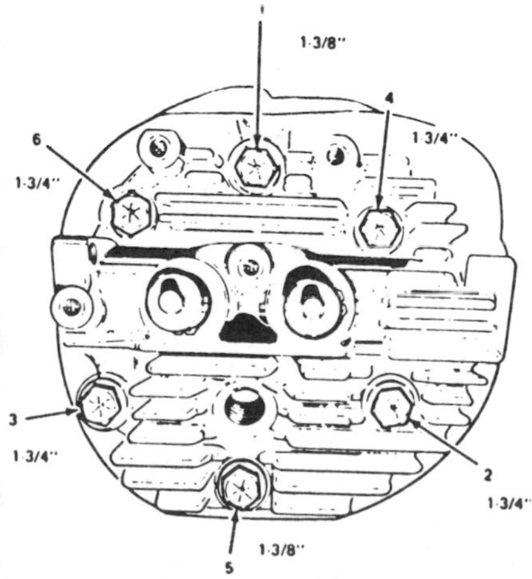


*Fig. T72—Tighten cylinder head cap screws evenly to a torque of 220 in.-lbs. (24.8 N·m) using tightening sequence shown. Note location of different length cap screws.*

**CAUTION: Be sure to center punch. DO NOT allow punch to contact head when pressing guides out.**

To install new guides, place guides in freezer or on ice for 30 minutes prior to installation. Submerge head in pan of oil. Heat on hot plate until oil begins to smoke, about 15-20 minutes. Remove head and place, gasket surface down, on a 6 x 12 inch piece of wood. Using snap rings to locate both guides, insert silver colored guide in intake side and brass colored guide in exhaust side. It may be necessary to use a rubber or rawhide mallet to fully seat snap rings. DO NOT use a metal hammer or guide damage will result. Allow head to cool and reface both valve seats.

Valve spring free length should be 1.915 inches (48.64 mm) and springs should test 25.6-28.6 pounds (113.9-127.2 N) when compressed to a length of 1.550 inches (39.37 mm). Renew springs if coils are rusted, pitted or cracked, or if springs fail to meet specifications.

Valves seat directly in cylinder head. Valve seat angle is 46 degrees and valve face angle is 45 degrees. Valve seat width should be 0.042-0.052 inch (1.07-1.32 mm). Renew valve when valve head margin is less than 0.060 inch (1.52 mm) after valve is refaced.

Use new head gasket and reinstall cylinder head and valves. Make certain Belleville washer and flat washer are installed on cylinder head cap screws as shown in Fig. T71 and the two short cap screws, 1-3/8 inches (35 mm), are installed in correct holes as shown in Fig. T72. Tighten cylinder head cap screws evenly to a torque of 220 in.-lbs. (24.8 N·m) using sequence shown in Fig. T72.

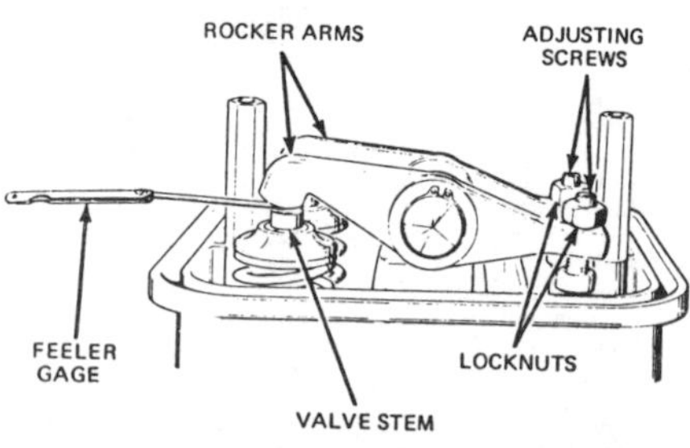


*Fig. T73—Use a feeler gage when adjusting valve clearance. Refer to text for adjustment procedure.*

Place new "O" rings on push rod tubes and install push rods and tubes. Install rocker arm housing and using new "O" rings on the three mounting cap screws, tighten cap screws to a torque of 80-90 in.-lbs. (9.0-10.1 N·m). Install new "O" ring, lower spring cap, valve spring and upper spring cap on each valve. Using tool #670237, compress valve spring and install retainers. Install rocker arms and secure them with snap rings.

To adjust valve clearance, make certain piston is positioned at TDC of compression stroke and proceed as follows: Refer to Fig. T73 and with locknuts loosened, turn adjusting screws until correct valve clearance is measured with feeler gage as shown. Valve clearance (cold) should be 0.005 inch (0.127 mm) for intake valve and 0.010 inch (0.254 mm) for exhaust valve. Tighten locknuts to secure adjusting screws.

**NOTE: Slotted adjusting screws were used on early production engines, while later engines have adjusting nut on screw below rocker arm. Locknuts are above rocker arms on all models.**

Reinstall valve cover and breather assembly, carburetor and inlet pipe assembly and blower housing.

**PISTON, PIN AND RINGS.** Aluminum alloy piston is fitted with two compression rings and one oil control ring. Recommended end gap for all rings is 0.010-0.020 inch (0.254-0.508 mm). Side clearance of new rings in ring grooves of new piston is 0.0015-0.0035 inch (0.038-0.089 mm). Maximum allowable (wear limit) piston ring side clearance is 0.006 inch (0.152 mm). Compression ring groove width of new piston is 0.095-0.096 inch (2.413-2.438 mm) and oil ring groove width (new) is 0.188-0.189 inch (4.775-4.800 mm). Piston rings and piston are available in standard size and oversizes.

The top compression ring must be installed with inside chamfer to top of piston. If second compression ring has a

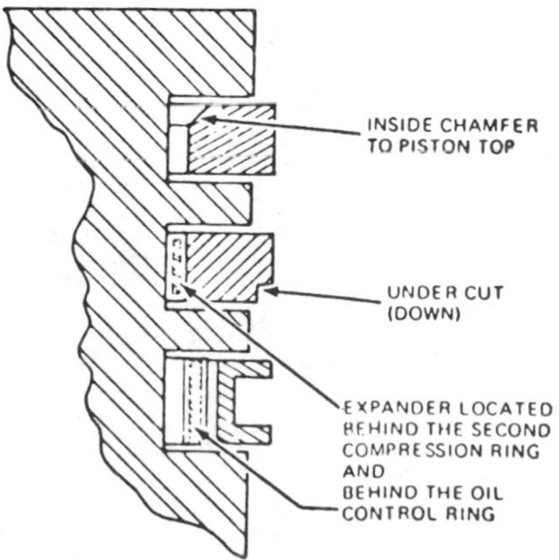


*Fig. T74—Cross-sectional view showing correct installation of piston rings.*

notch on outside of ring, install ring with notch toward bottom end of piston. Oil ring can be installed either side up. See Fig. T74. Stagger ring end gaps about 90 degrees around piston.

Piston skirt clearance in cylinder, measured at thrust side of piston just below oil ring should be 0.010-0.012 inch (0.254-0.305 mm).

Piston pin diameter is 0.6873-0.6875 inch (17.457-17.462 mm). Piston pin clearance should be 0.0001-0.0008 inch (0.0025-0.0203 mm) in rod and 0.0002-0.0005 inch (0.0051-0.0127 mm) in piston. If clearance is excessive, both piston and pin must be renewed as pin is not serviced separately.

**CYLINDER.** If cylinder is scored or if taper or out-of-round exceeds 0.005 inch (0.127 mm), cylinder should be rebored to next suitable oversize. Standard cylinder bore is 3.125-3.126 inches (79.375-79.400 mm) on Model OH120, 3.312-3.313 inches (84.125-84.150 mm) on Models HH140 and OH140 and 3.500-3.501 inches (88.900-88.925 mm) on all other models. Pistons and rings are available in standard size and oversizes.

**CAMSHAFT.** The camshaft and camshaft gear are an integral part which rides on journals at each end of camshaft. The camshaft is equipped with a compression release mechanism. See Fig. T75. Check compression release parts for binding, excessive wear or other damage. If any parts are excessively worn or damaged, renew complete camshaft assembly. Parts are not serviced separately for compression release mechanism.

Renew camshaft if gear teeth are excessively worn or if bearing surfaces or lobes are worn or scored. Camshaft lobe nose-to-heel diameter should be 1.3117-1.3167 inches (33.3172-33.4442 mm). Diameter of camshaft journals is 0.6235-0.6240 inch (15.8369-15.8496 mm). Maximum allowable clearance between camshaft journal and bearing bore is 0.003 inch (0.076 mm).

When installing camshaft, align timing mark on camshaft gear with timing mark (chamfered tooth) on crankshaft gear. This will provide correct valve timing.

**CRANKSHAFT.** The crankshaft is supported by tapered roller bearings (20 and 54 – Fig. T76). Use a suitable puller to remove bearings. Bearings will be damaged during removal and new bearings must be installed when reassembling. Heat bearings in oil to approximately 300°F (150°C), then quickly slide bearings into position on crankshaft. Bearing cup (55) in a press fit in crankcase cover (62) and must be pressed in against shoulder. Bearing cup (19) is a slip fit in cylinder block (21). To adjust crankshaft bearings, assemble engine to the point where cylinder block, crankshaft assembly, piston and connecting rod assembly and crankcase cover are assembled and all bolts are tightened to correct torque values given in TIGHTENING TORQUES paragraph. With bearing cup (19) installed in cylinder block, install bearing retainer cap (15) without shim gaskets (17), steel washers (16) or "O" ring (18). Tighten cap screws finger tight. Using a feeler gage, measure gap between bearing retainer flange and cylinder block. If no measurable clearance exists, install 0.010 inch steel washers (as required) between bearing retainer (15) and bearing cup (19) until such clearance is obtained. If measured

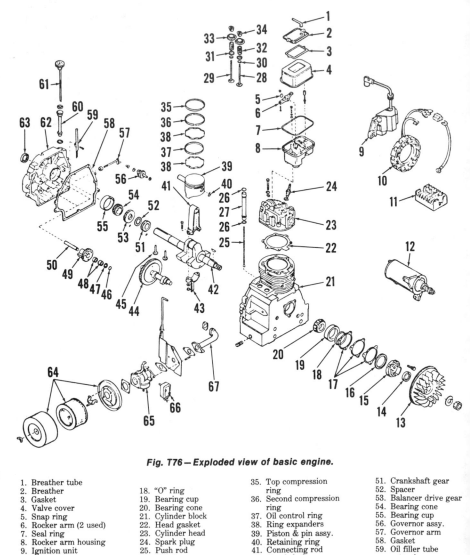

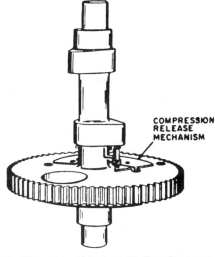

COMPRESSION RELEASE MECHANISM

*Fig. T75 – View of Insta-matic Ezee-Start compression release camshaft assembly.*

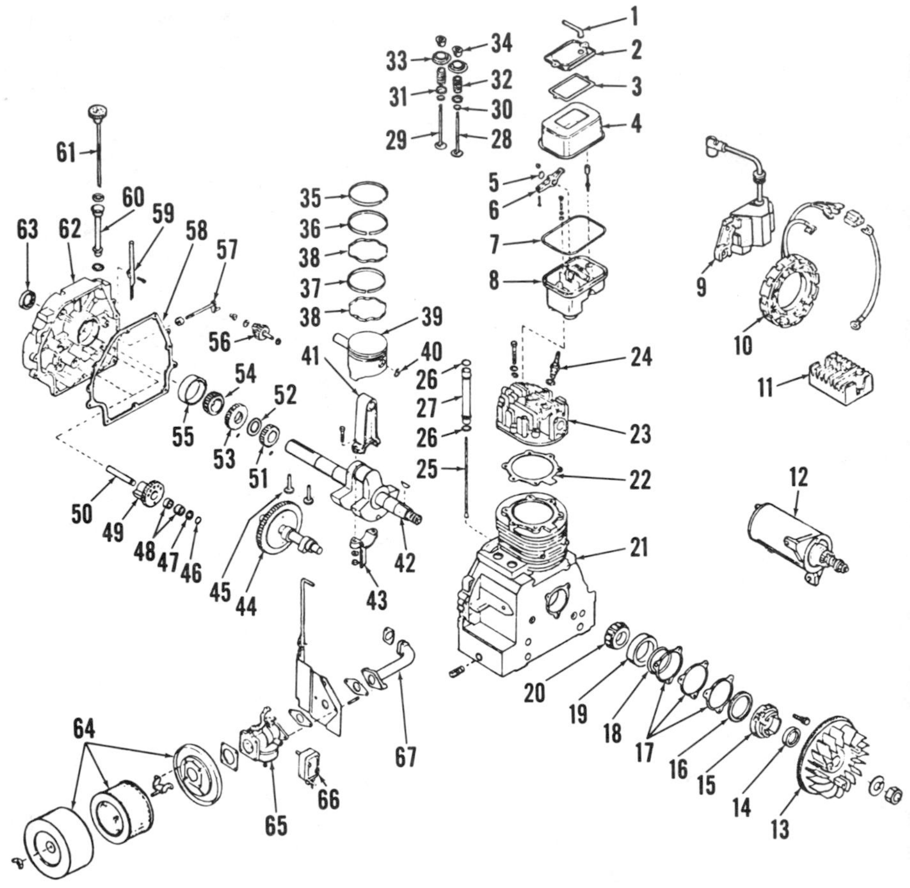

*Fig. T76 – Exploded view of basic engine.*

1. Breather tube
2. Breather
3. Gasket
4. Valve cover
5. Snap ring
6. Rocker arm (2 used)
7. Seal ring
8. Rocker arm housing
9. Ignition unit
10. Stator assy.
11. Regulator-rectifier
12. Starter motor
13. Flywheel
14. Oil seal
15. Bearing retainer cap
16. Steel washer (0.010 in.)
17. Shim gaskets
18. "O" ring
19. Bearing cup
20. Bearing cone
21. Cylinder block
22. Head gasket
23. Cylinder head
24. Spark plug
25. Push rod
26. "O" ring
27. Push rod tube
28. Intake valve
29. Exhaust valve
30. "O" ring
31. Lower spring cap
32. Valve spring
33. Upper valve cap
34. Valve retainers
35. Top compression ring
36. Second compression ring
37. Oil control ring
38. Ring expanders
39. Piston & pin assy.
40. Retaining ring
41. Connecting rod
42. Crankshaft
43. Rod cap
44. Camshaft assy.
45. Valve lifters
46. Snap ring
47. Thrust washer
48. Needle bearings
49. Dyna-Static balancer
50. Balancer shaft
51. Crankshaft gear
52. Spacer
53. Balancer drive gear
54. Bearing cone
55. Bearing cup
56. Governor assy.
57. Governor arm
58. Gasket
59. Oil filler tube extension
60. Oil filler tube
61. Dipstick
62. Crankcase cover
63. Oil seal
64. Air cleaner assy.
65. Carburetor
66. Fuel pump
67. Inlet pipe

Illustrations courtesy Tecumseh Products Co.

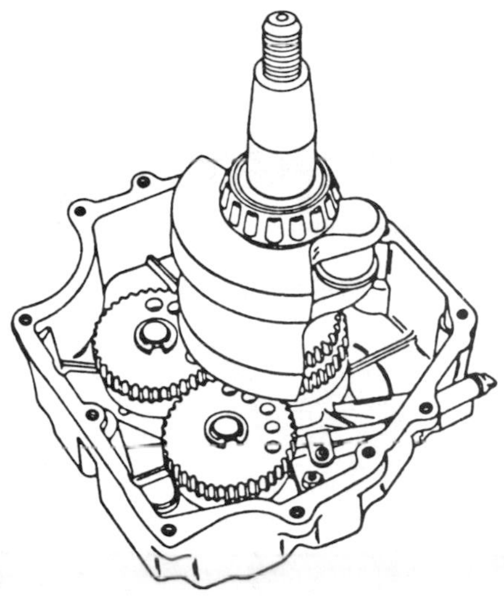

Fig. T77—View showing Dyna-Static balancer gears installed in crankcase cover. Note gear retaining snap rings.

Fig. T78—Press balancer gear shafts into crankcase cover to dimension shown.

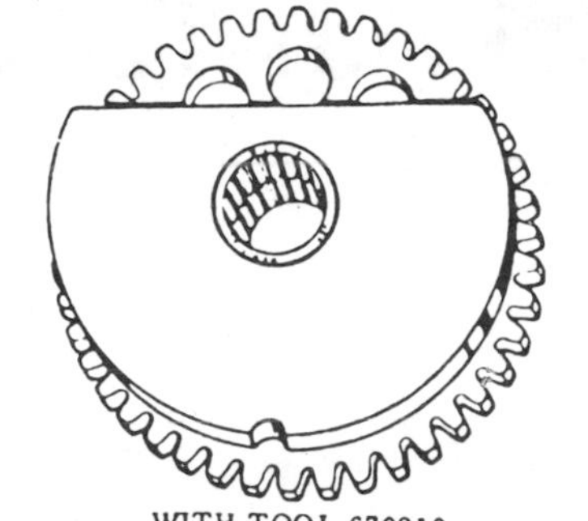


Fig. T79—Using tool #670210, press new needle bearings into balancer gears until bearing cage is flush to 0.015 inch (0.381 mm) below edge of bore. Note tool alignment notch at lower side of balancer.

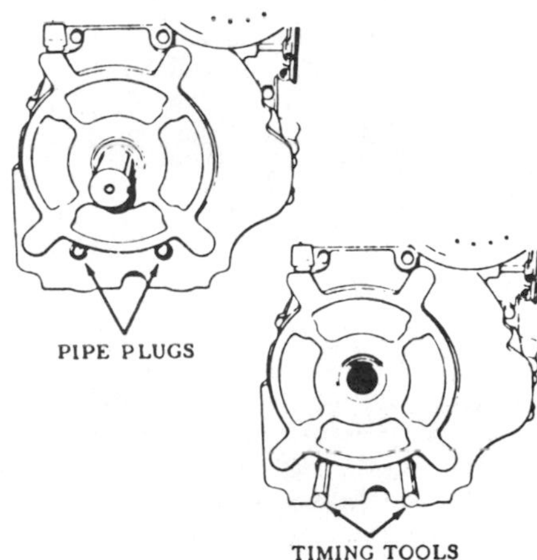


Fig. T80—To time engine balancer gears, remove pipe plugs and insert timing tools #670239 through crankcase cover and into slots in balancer gears. Refer also to Fig. T81.

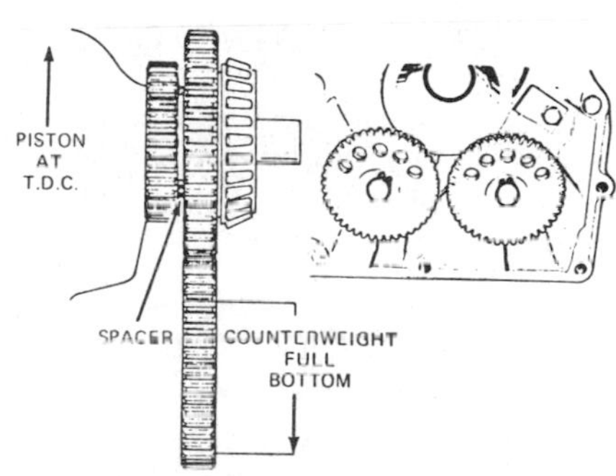


Fig. T81—Balancer gears are correctly timed to crankshaft when piston is at TDC and weights are at full bottom position.

clearance does not exceed 0.007 inch (0.178 mm) no shim gasket (17) will be required. When retainer cap screws are tightened to correct torque, bearing preload will be within recommended range of 0.001-0.007 inch (0.025-0.178 mm). If clearance measures more than 0.007 inch (0.178 mm), subtract 0.001 inch (0.025 mm) from measured clearance to allow for preload. This will give actual distance to be shimmed. However, since shim gaskets will compress approximately ⅓ of their thickness, shim pack thickness to be installed should be 1½ times actual distance. Shim gaskets are available in thickness of 0.003-0.004, 0.004-0.005 and 0.005-0.007 inch. Remove bearing cap, install "O" ring and thickness of shim gaskets previously determined and reinstall bearing retainer cap. Tighten cap screws to a torque of 65-110 in.-lbs. (7.3-12.4 N·m).

Crankshaft seat diameter for roller bearings is 1.1865-1.1870 inches (30.1371-30.1498 mm). Crankpin journal diameter is 1.3750-1.3755 inches (34.9250-34.9377 mm). Renew crankshaft if crankpin is scored or is tapered or worn over 0.002 inch (0.051 mm) or is out-of-round more than 0.0005 inch (0.0127 mm).

When installing crankshaft, align timing mark on crankshaft gear (chamfered tooth) with timing mark on camshaft gear.

Crankshaft oil seals should be installed flush to 0.025 inch (0.635 mm) below surface, with lips on seals facing inward.

**DYNA-STATIC BALANCER.** The Dyna-Static engine balancer operates by means of a pair of counterweighted gears driven by the crankshaft to counteract unbalance caused by counterweights on crankshaft. The balancer gears are held in position on balancer shafts by snap rings. See Fig. T77. The renewable balancer shafts are pressed into crankcase cover. Press shafts into cover until a distance of 1.7135-1.7185 inches (43.523-43.650 mm) exists between boss on cover and outer edge of snap ring groove on shafts as shown in Fig. T78.

Balancer gears are equipped with renewable caged needle bearings. See Fig. T79. Using tool #670210, press new bearings into balancer gears until bearing cage is flush to 0.015 inch (0.381 mm) below edge of bore.

When reassembling engine, balancer gears must be timed with crankshaft for correct operation. To time balancer gears, refer to Fig. T80 and remove pipe plugs. Insert timing tools #670239 through crankcase cover and into timing slots in balancer gears. Then, turn crankshaft to place piston at TDC position and carefully install crankcase cover with balancer gears. When correctly assembled, piston should be exactly at TDC and weights should be at full bottom position. See Fig. T81.

# TECUMSEH

| Model | No. Cyls. | Bore | Stroke | Displacement | Power Rating |
|---|---|---|---|---|---|
| OVM120 | 1 | 3.31 in. (84.2 mm) | 2.53 in. (64.3 mm) | 21.82 cu. in. (357 cc) | 12 hp (8.9 kW) |
| OVXL120 | 1 | 3.31 in. (84.2 mm) | 2.53 in. (64.3 mm) | 21.82 cu. in. (357 cc) | 12 hp (8.9 kW) |
| OVXL125, OVXL/C125 | 1 | 3.31 in. (84.2 mm) | 2.53 in. (64.3 mm) | 21.82 cu. in. (357 cc) | 12.5 hp (9.3 kW) |

## ENGINE IDENTIFICATION

All models are four-stroke, overhead valve, single-cylinder, vertical crankshaft gasoline engines. Aluminum alloy cylinder and crankcase assembly is equipped with a cast iron cylinder sleeve which is an integral part of the cylinder. Pressurized lubrication to bearing areas is provided by a plunger type oil pump.

Engine model number, serial number and specification number are stamped into the cooling shroud just above the rocker arm cover. Always furnish correct engine model, serial and specification numbers when ordering parts.

## MAINTENANCE

**SPARK PLUG.** Recommended spark plug is a Champion L86C or equivalent. Recommended electrode gap is 0.030 in. (0.76 mm).

**CARBURETOR.** All models are equipped with a float type carburetor. Some models are equipped with a carburetor with both an idle and a high speed fuel mixture adjustment screw. However, some models are equipped with just an idle speed fuel mixture screw; the high speed mixture is controlled by a fixed main jet. Other than adjustment, service procedure is similar for either type carburetor.

Initial adjustment of idle mixture screw (2—Fig. TC1) for all models is one turn open from a lightly seated position. Initial adjustment of high speed adjustment screw (3), if so equipped, is one turn open for Model OVM120 and 1½ turns open for Models OVXL120 and OVXL125 from a lightly seated position.

Make final adjustments on all models with engine at normal operating temperature. On models with high speed adjustment screw, set engine speed at full throttle and turn adjusting screw to find the lean drop-off point and the rich drop-off point. Then, set adjusting screw midway between the two extremes. When correctly set, engine should accelerate smoothly and run under load with steady governor operation. On all models, turn idle speed adjustment screw (1) to obtain desired idle speed as specified by the equipment manufacturer. Adjust idle mixture adjustment screw (2) to obtain smoothest idle operation using the same procedure as outlined for high speed adjustment screw.

As each adjustment affects the other, adjustment procedure may have to be repeated.

To clean carburetor, disassemble and clean all metallic parts with solvent or carburetor cleaner. Welch plugs should be removed from carburetor body to expose drilled passages to thoroughly clean carburetor. Use a small, sharp pointed chisel to pierce the Welch plug and pry plug out of carburetor body. When installing new plugs, use a flat punch equal, or greater in size than the plug and just flatten the plug. Do not drive the center of plug below surface of carburetor body.

**NOTE: Brass or ball plugs should not be removed from carburetor body. Do not remove main nozzle tube (11—Fig. TC2). Tube is installed to a predetermined depth, and altering its position in carburetor body will affect metering characteristics of the carburetor.**

Use compressed air and solvent to clean drilled passages and jets. Do not use drill bits or wire to clean jets or passages as carburetor calibration may be affected if openings are enlarged.

There are two different types of bowl nuts (24—Fig. TC2) that are used on carburetors equipped with adjustable main jets. One type has one fuel inlet port at bottom of the nut, and the other type has two fuel inlet ports at bottom of the nut (Fig. TC3). The difference between the nuts has to do with calibration changes of the carburetor, depending on engine application. DO NOT interchange bowl nuts. Fuel inlet port(s) and idle fuel transfer port, located in annular groove at top of nut, must be open and free of any debris to ensure proper fuel flow to high and low speed circuits.

When reassembling carburetor, it is important that throttle plate is installed with line on the plate facing outward and positioned at the 3 o'clock position. Choke plate must be installed with cutout section facing downward. Be sure that throttle and choke plates open and close without binding.

Fuel inlet needle (13—Fig. TC2) and seat (12) are renewable. If needle tip or seat is worn or deformed, new needle and seat should be installed. Make cer-

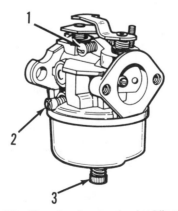

*Fig. TC1—View of carburetor showing idle speed screw (1), idle mixture adjusting screw (2) and high speed fuel mixture adjusting screw (3). Some models may not be equipped with adjustable high speed fuel mixture screw (3).*



Illustrations courtesy Tecumseh Products Co.

tain when installing new seat that grooved side of seat is installed in bore first so the inlet needle will seat against the smooth side of seat (Fig. TC4).

Assemble choke, inlet needle and needle clip as shown in Fig. TC5. To prevent binding, the long end of clip should face choke end of carburetor body.

To check float height, invert carburetor body and use float setting tool No. 670253A as shown in Fig. TC6. Float height is correct if float does not touch step portion of tool (1) and contacts step (2) as tool is pulled toward float hinge pin as shown. If tool is not available, measure distance from top of main nozzle boss to surface of float. Distance should be 0.275-0.315 inch (7-8 mm). If adjustment is required, bend float tab that contacts fuel inlet needle being careful not to force inlet needle onto its seat.

**GOVERNOR.** All models are equipped with a mechanical flyweight type governor located inside the crankcase. Governor gear, flyweights and shaft are serviced only as an assembly. If governor gear shaft is renewed, new shaft should be pressed into crankcase cover boss until exposed shaft length is 1²³/₆₄ inches (34.5 mm).

To adjust external governor linkage, stop engine and loosen the screw securing governor lever (1—Fig. TC7 or Fig. TC8) and governor clamp (2). Push governor lever to fully open carburetor throttle, then turn governor clamp counterclockwise as far as it will go. While holding clamp and lever in this position, tighten screw.

On 1985 and later production OVM120 and OVXL120 engines, a governor override system is used. Linkage is shown in Fig. TC8. On these engines, high speed setting is adjusted by turning top screw

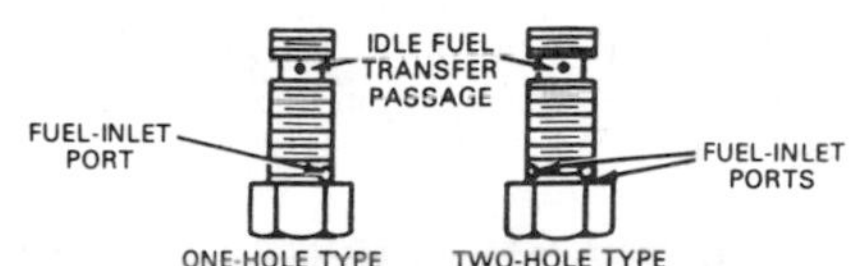


*Fig. TC3—Two different types of fuel bowl retaining nuts are used on adjustable main jet type carburetors. Different type nuts must not be interchanged. Refer to text.*

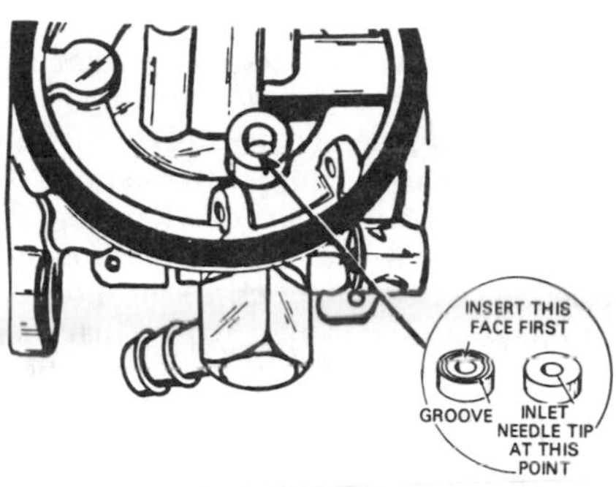


*Fig. TC4—Fuel inlet needle seat must be installed with grooved side against carburetor body. Refer to text.*

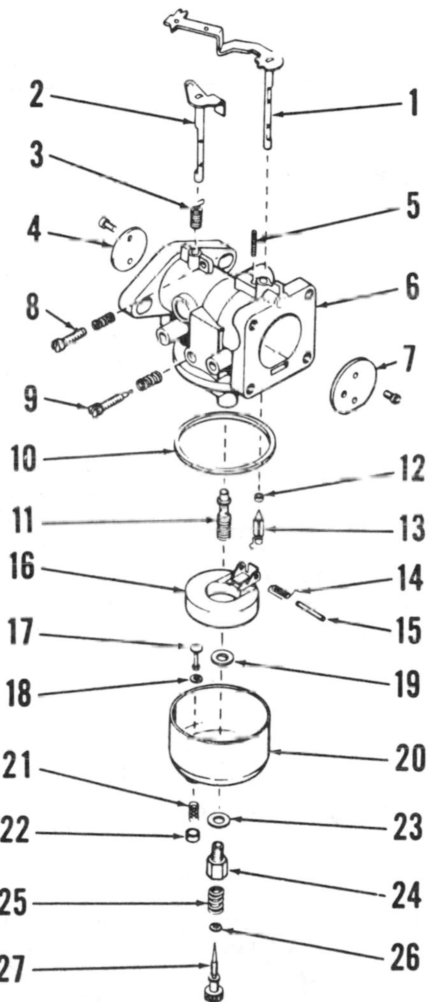

*Fig. TC2—Exploded view of carburetor.*

1. Choke shaft
2. Throttle shaft
3. Throttle return spring
4. Throttle plate
5. Choke stop spring
6. Carburetor body
7. Choke plate
8. Idle speed stop screw
9. Idle mixture needle
10. Bowl gasket
11. Main nozzle
12. Inlet valve seat
13. Inlet valve
14. Float spring
15. Float shaft
16. Float
17. Drain stem
18. Gasket
19. Gasket
20. Bowl
21. Spring
22. Retainer
23. Gasket
24. Bowl retainer
25. Spring
26. "O" ring
27. Main fuel adjusting needle

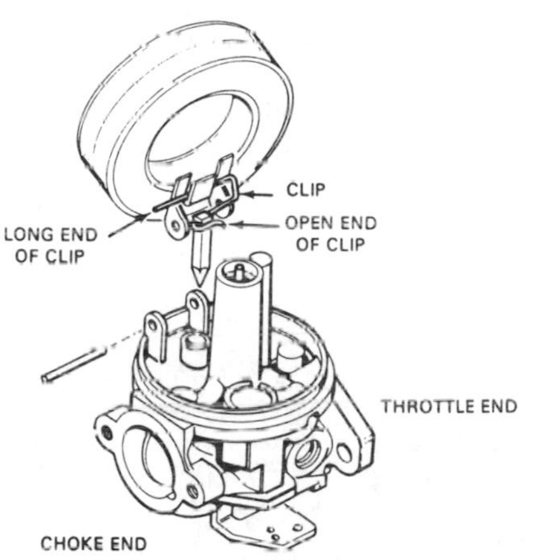


*Fig. TC5—View of carburetor float assembly showing correct installation of fuel inlet needle clip.*

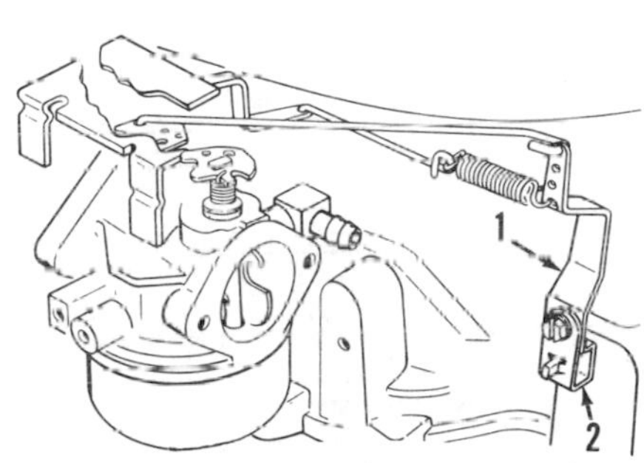


*Fig. TC7—Drawing of governor external linkage typical of standard engines without governor override system. Refer to text for adjustment procedure.*

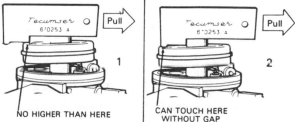

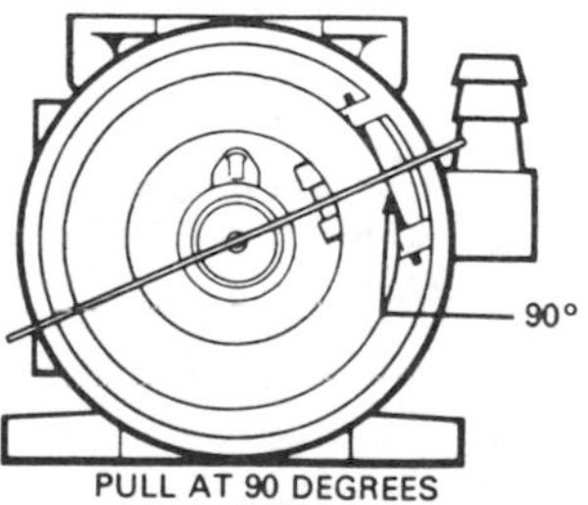


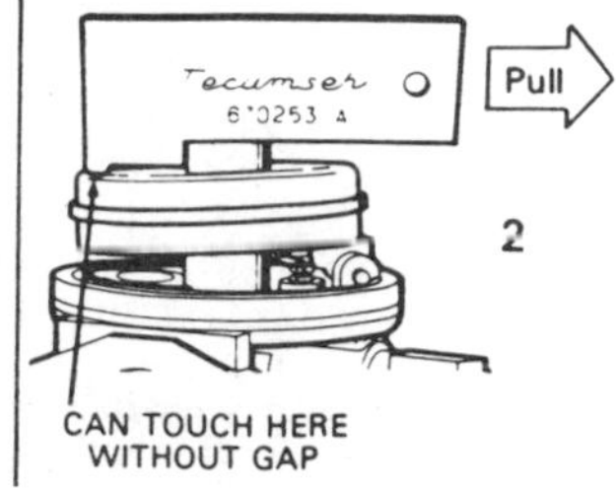


*Fig. TC6—Float height may be adjusted using float setting tool, No. 670253A.*

(H) of override lever and low idle speed is adjusted by turning bottom screw (L).

Various types of speed controls are used. A typical panel used with remote control lever is shown in Fig. TC9. To adjust speed control panel, loosen panel mounting screws. Move speed control lever to full speed position and insert a wire through hole in panel, hole in choke actuating lever and hole in choke shaft arm. With components aligned in this manner, tighten panel mounting screws. Move control linkage to choke position, and check for 0.040-0.070 inch (1.0-1.8 mm) gap at control lever as shown in Fig. TC9. Bend choke adjusting tab if necessary. Engine idle speed may be set by turning idle speed adjusting screw. Maximum governed speed is adjusted by bending high speed adjusting lever. Bend lever away from panel to increase speed and the opposite direction to decrease speed.

**IGNITION SYSTEM.** A solid-state ignition system is used on all models. Ignition system has no moving parts and is considered satisfactory if a spark will jump a 1/8 inch (3.2 mm) air gap when engine is cranked at 125 rpm.

Ignition module is mounted on outside of flywheel. Air gap setting between ignition module and flywheel magnets is 0.0125 inch (0.32 mm). To set air gap, loosen module mounting screws, move module as necessary and retighten screws.

**VALVE ADJUSTMENT.** Clearance between rocker arms and valve stem ends should be checked and adjusted with engine cold. Specified clearance is 0.002 inch (0.05 mm) for intake valve and 0.004 inch (0.10 mm) for exhaust valve.

To adjust valves, remove rocker arm cover and rotate crankshaft to position piston at top dead center (TDC) of compression stroke. Both valves should be closed and the push rods loose at this point. Use a feeler gage to measure clearance between rocker arm and valve stem as shown in Fig. TC10. Turn rocker arm locking/adjusting nut to obtain specified clearance.

**LUBRICATION.** A positive displacement plunger type oil pump is located in the bottom of crankcase cover. An eccentric on camshaft works the oil pump plunger back and forth in the barrel to force oil up the center of the camshaft. The pressurized oil lubricates top main bearing and top camshaft bearing. Oil is sprayed out of a hole between camshaft and main bearings to lubricate connecting rod and other internal parts.

Oil level should be checked before initial start-up and at five hour intervals. Maintain oil level at "FULL" mark on dipstick.

Recommended oil change interval is every 25 hours of normal operation. Oil should be drained when engine is warm. Manufacturer recommends using oil with API service classification SE, SF or SG. Use SAE 30 oil for temperatures above 32°F (0°C) and SAE 5W-20 or 10W-30 for temperatures below 32°F (0°C).

## REPAIRS

**TIGHTENING TORQUES.** Recommended tightening torques are as follows:

Connecting rod bolts . . . . . . . . . . . . . . 200-220 in.-lbs. (22.6-24.8 N·m)
Crankcase cover . . . . . . 100-130 in.-lbs. (11.3-14.7 N·m)
Cylinder head bolts . . . 180-240 in.-lbs. (20.4-27.1 N·m)
Flywheel nut . . . . . . . . . . 50-55 ft.-lbs. (68-74 N·m)
Intake pipe . . . . . . . . . . . . 72-96 in.-lbs. (8.2-10.8 N·m)
Rocker arm studs . . . . . 170-210 in.-lbs. (19.2-23.7 N·m)
Rocker cover . . . . . . . . . . 15-20 in.-lbs. (1.7-2.2 N·m)
Spark plug . . . . . . . . . . 220-280 in.-lbs. (24.9-31.6 N·m)

**CYLINDER HEAD.** Always allow engine to cool completely before loosening cylinder head bolts. To remove cylinder head, first locate piston at top dead center of compression stroke. Remove rocker arm adjusting nuts (1—Fig. TC11), bearing (2) and rocker arms (3).

*Fig. TC8—Drawing of governor external linkage typical of engines equipped with governor override system. Refer to text for adjustment procedure.*

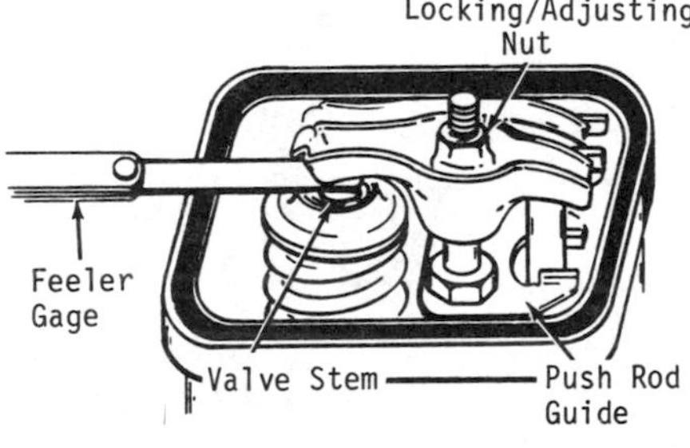


*Fig. TC10—Use a feeler gage to correctly set valve clearance.*

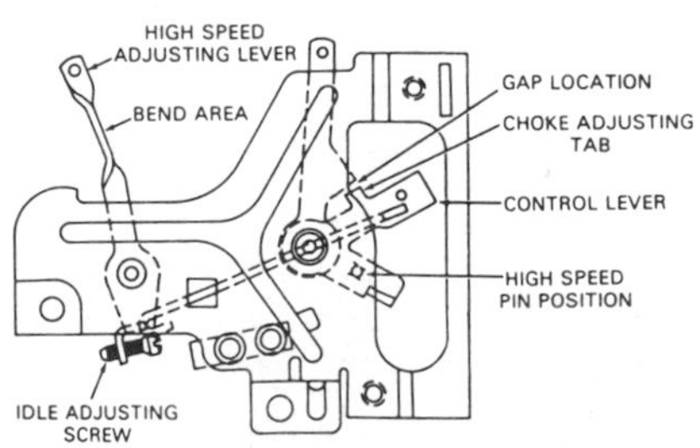


*Fig. TC9—Drawing of typical speed control plate used on engines equipped with remote control linkage.*

*Fig. TC11—Exploded view of cylinder head assembly.*

1. Adjusting nut
2. Rocker arm bearing
3. Rocker arm
4. Rocker arm stud
5. Push rod guide
6. "O" ring
7. Rocker arm housing
8. "O" ring
9. Push rod tube
10. Cap screw
11. Washer
12. "O" ring
13. Split retainers
14. Spring cap
15. Valve springs
16. Spring seats
17. "O" ring (white)
18. "O" ring (black)
19. Snap rings
20. Valve guide (intake)
21. Valve guide (exhaust)
22. Cylinder head
23. Head bolt
24. Belleville washer
25. Flat washer

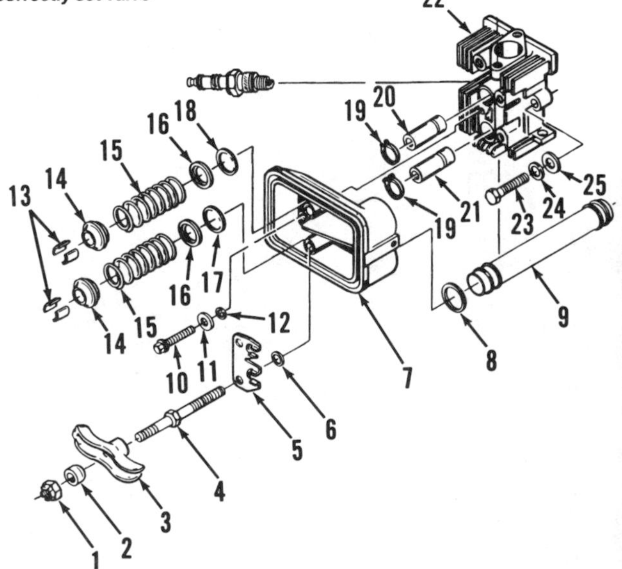



Illustrations courtesy Tecumseh Products Co.

Depress valve spring caps (14) and remove split retainers (13), caps, springs (15), spring seats (16) and "O" rings (17) and (18). Note that a white Teflon "O" ring (17) is used on exhaust valve guide and a black rubber "O" ring (18) is used on intake valve guide. Remove rocker arm studs (4), push rod guide (5) and rocker arm housing retaining screw (10) and withdraw rocker arm housing (7). Remove cylinder head mounting bolts and remove cylinder head (22) and valves. Remove valves from cylinder head.

Thoroughly clean cylinder head and inspect for cracks or other damage. Position cylinder head on a flat plate and use a feeler gage to check flatness of head gasket sealing surface. Renew cylinder head if necessary.

Use a new head gasket when installing cylinder head. Install Belleville washer on cylinder head bolt with crown up toward bolt head, then install flat washer (Fig. TC12). The two 1³/₈ inch (34.9 mm) long head bolts go in positions marked "1" and "5" in Fig. TC13. Tighten head bolts in 60 in.-lbs. (6.8 N·m) increments following sequence shown in Fig. TC13 until specified torque is obtained.

When installing valve guide seals, be sure that white Teflon "O" ring (17—Fig. TC11) is installed on exhaust valve guide (guide is bronze in color) and black "O" ring (18) is installed on intake valve guide (guide is silver in color). Switching the position of "O" rings may result in improper sealing and possible engine damage. Be sure to install new "O" rings on push rod tube (9) and underneath push rod guide (5) and retaining screw (10).

To install valve springs, valves must be raised and held on their seats. One way to do this is to insert a piece of rubber fuel line through intake and exhaust ports and wedge each end of the hose on opposite sides of the valve stem. Install valve springs with dampening coils (coils closer together) toward cylinder head. Place spring retainer on spring, use suitable tool to compress valve spring and install split retainer.

**NOTE: Anytime rocker arm housing assembly is removed from engine, new rocker arm locking/adjusting nuts and rocker arm cover screws should be installed.**

Tighten rocker arm studs (4) to 170-210 in.-lbs. (19.2-23.7 N·m). Install rocker arms and adjust valve clearance as outlined in MAINTENANCE section.

**VALVE SYSTEM.** Valve seats are machined directly in the cylinder head. Seats should be cut at a 46 degree angle and valve faces cut or ground at a 45 degree angle. Valve seat width should be ³/₆₄ inch (1.2 mm). The recommended procedure to cut the valve seats is as follows: First, use a 60 degree cutter to narrow seat from bottom toward the center. Second, use a 30 degree cutter to narrow seat from top toward the center. Then, use 46 degree cutter to cut seat to desired width.

Clean all combustion deposits from valves. Renew valves that are burned, excessively pitted, warped or if valve head margin after grinding is less than ¹/₃₂ inch (0.8 mm). Valves should be lapped to their seats using fine lapping compound.

Valve spring free length should be 1.980 inches (50.29 mm). It is recommended that valve springs be renewed when engine is overhauled. The valve spring dampening coils are coils wound closer together at one end than the other. The end with closer coils should be installed against cylinder head.

Standard valve guide inside diameter is 0.312-0.313 inch (7.93-7.95 mm). Guides may be reamed to 0.343-0.344 inch (8.71-8.74 mm) for use with oversize valve stems.

To renew valve guides, submerge cylinder head in a large pan of oil. Heat on a hot plate to temperature of 375°-400°F (190°-205°C) for about 20 minutes. Remove cylinder head from the oil and use an arbor press and ¹/₂ inch (13 mm) driver to push valve guides out top side of cylinder head. Make certain that driver does not contact and damage head as guide is removed.

To install new guides, place replacement guides in a freezer or on ice for minimum of 30 minutes prior to installation. Heat head in a pan of oil as previously outlined. Install locating snap rings on new guides, then press guides into cylinder head from the top until snap rings contact surface of head. Make certain that silver colored guide is installed in intake side and brass colored guide is installed in exhaust side. Allow cylinder head to cool, then reface both valve seats to ensure that they are concentric with valve guides.

**CONNECTING ROD.** Piston and connecting rod are removed as an assembly as follows: Remove all cooling shrouds. Remove rocker arm cover and cylinder head as previously outlined. Drain oil and remove oil pan (crankcase base). Remove connecting rod cap. Remove carbon or ring ridge (if present) from top of cylinder before removing piston. Push the connecting rod and piston out top of cylinder.

Connecting rod rides directly on crankshaft crankpin. Inside diameter of connecting rod bearing bore at crankshaft end should be 1.3760-1.3765 inches (34.950-34.963 mm) on Model OVM120 and 1.3775-1.3780 inches (34.989-35.001 mm) on Models OVXL120, OVXL125 and OVXL/C125.

Piston must be assembled on connecting rod so arrow on top of piston will be pointing toward push rod side of engine and match marks on connecting rod and cap will face outward when installed in engine. Tighten connecting rod cap bolts evenly to specified torque.

**PISTON, PIN AND RINGS.** Piston and connecting rod are removed as an assembly. Refer to CONNECTING ROD section for removal procedure.

Standard piston skirt diameter, measured at bottom of skirt 90 degrees from piston pin bore, is 3.309-3.311 inches (84.05-84.09 mm) for all models. Specified clearance between piston skirt and cylinder wall is 0.0012-0.0032 inch (0.031-0.081 mm). Oversize pistons are available. Oversize piston size should be stamped on top of piston.

To check piston ring grooves for wear, clean carbon from ring grooves and install new rings in grooves. Use a feeler gage to measure side clearance between ring land and ring. Specified side clearance is 0.0015-0.0035 inch (0.038-0.089 mm) for compression rings and 0.001-0.004 inch (0.025-0.102 mm) for oil control ring. Renew piston if ring side clearance is excessive.

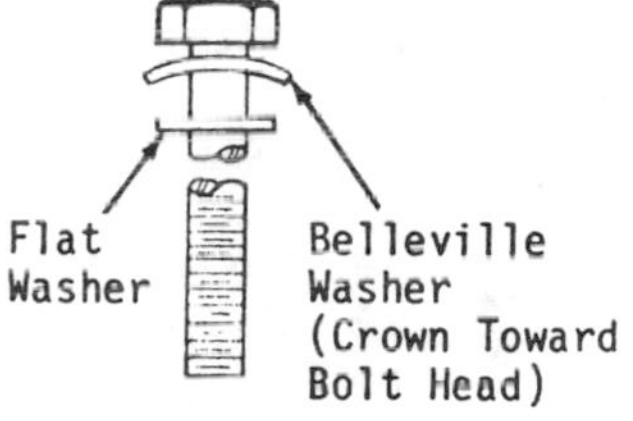


*Fig. TC12—Belleville washer is installed on head bolt with crown toward bolt head, then install flat washer with sharp edge toward bolt head.*

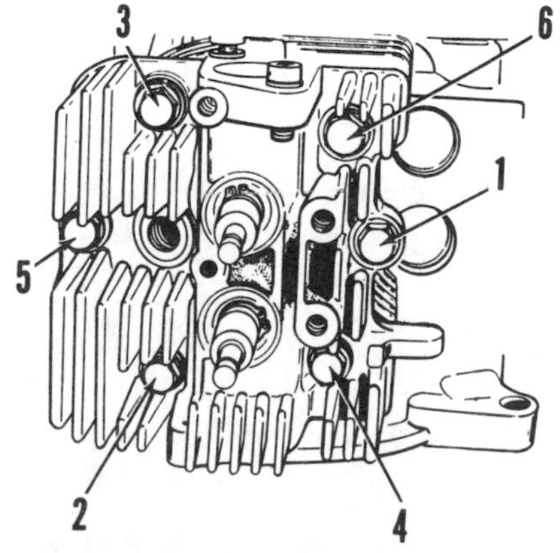


*Fig. TC13—Cylinder head bolts should be loosened and tightened following the sequence shown. The two 1-3/8 inch (34.9 mm) long bolts are installed in positions "1" and "5."*

Ring end gap should be 0.010-0.020 inch (0.25-0.51 mm) for all rings.

Rings must be installed on piston as shown in Fig. TC14. Stagger ring end gaps around piston. Lubricate piston and cylinder with engine oil prior to installing piston. Be sure that arrow on top of piston points toward push rod side of engine and match marks on connecting rod and cap are toward open side of crankcase after installation.

**CYLINDER AND CRANKCASE.** A cast iron liner is permanently cast into the aluminum alloy cylinder and crankcase assembly. Standard piston bore inside diameter is 3.312-3.313 inches (84.125-84.150 mm). If cylinder taper or out-of-round exceeds 0.004 inch (0.10 mm), cylinder should be bored to nearest oversize for which piston and rings are available.

**CRANKSHAFT, MAIN BEARINGS AND SEALS.** To remove crankshaft, first remove all shrouds. Remove flywheel. Remove connecting rod and piston as previously outlined. Remove balancer gear and shaft assembly. Remove balancer drive gear from crankshaft. Position engine so tappets fall away from camshaft, then withdraw camshaft from cylinder block and remove crankshaft.

Crankshaft is supported at each end in renewable steel backed bronze bushing type main bearings on Models OVM120, OVXL125 and OVXL/C125. On other models, main bearings are integral part of crankcase and crankcase base plate. On all models, main bearing inside diameter should be 1.3765-1.3770 inches (34.963-34.976 mm).

Standard crankshaft main journal diameter is 1.3745-1.3750 inches (34.912-34.925 mm) for each end. Standard crankpin journal diameter is 1.3740-1.3745 inches (34.900-34.912 mm).

Crankshaft end play should be 0.001-0.004 inch (0.025-0.10 mm) and is controlled by varying thickness of thrust washers between crankshaft and crankcase base plate (oil pan).

When renewing crankshaft oil seals, note if old seal is raised or flush with outer surface of crankcase or crankcase base and install new seal to same dimension. Attempting to install seal too far into casting bore may damage seal or engine. Use suitable installing tool to install new seal until it is lightly seated in casting bore.

When installing crankshaft, align timing mark on crankshaft gear with timing mark on camshaft gear to ensure correct valve timing. See Fig. TC15. With piston at top dead center, install counterbalance gear assembly and crankshaft balancer drive gear with timing marks (arrow) on gears facing each other as shown in Fig. TC16. Install oil pump and crankcase base plate. Apply Loctite 242 to threads of base plate cap screws and tighten to 100-130 in.-lbs. (11.3-14.7 N·m).

**ULTRA-BALANCE SYSTEM.** All models are equipped with Tecumseh's Ultra-Balance system which consists of a single counterbalance shaft driven by a gear on the crankshaft (Fig. TC17).

To correctly time the balancer shaft and the crankshaft during installation, position piston at top dead center and insert the counterbalance shaft into its boss in the crankcase with arrow on counterbalance gear pointing toward crankshaft. Slide drive gear onto the crankshaft, making certain the drive gear is secured in its keyway and that the arrow on the drive gear is aligned with the arrow on counterbalance shaft gear (Fig. TC16).

**CAMSHAFT.** Camshaft and camshaft gear are an integral part which may be removed from engine after removing the rocker arms, push rods and crankcase base plate (oil pan). Identify position of tappets as they are removed so they can be reinstalled in original position if reused.

Camshaft bearings are an integral part of crankcase and crankcase plate. Camshaft journal diameter should be 0.6235-0.6240 inch (15.84-15.85 mm). Camshaft bearing inside diameter should be 0.6245-0.6255 inch (15.86-15.89 mm). Clearance between camshaft journal and camshaft bearing should not exceed 0.003 inch (0.08 mm). Inspect camshaft lobes for pitting, scratches or excessive wear and renew as necessary. Tappets should be renewed whenever a new camshaft is installed.

Camshaft is equipped with a compression release mechanism (Fig. TC18) to aid starting. Compression release mechanism parts should work freely with no binding or sticking. Parts are not serviced separately from camshaft.

When installing camshaft, be sure that timing marks on camshaft gear and crankshaft gear are aligned as shown in Fig. TC15.

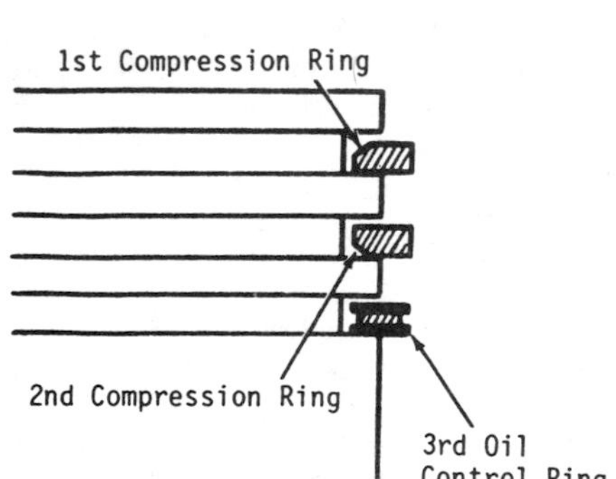


*Fig. TC14—Piston rings must be installed on piston so chamfered edge of top ring is facing up and chamfered edge of second ring is facing down.*

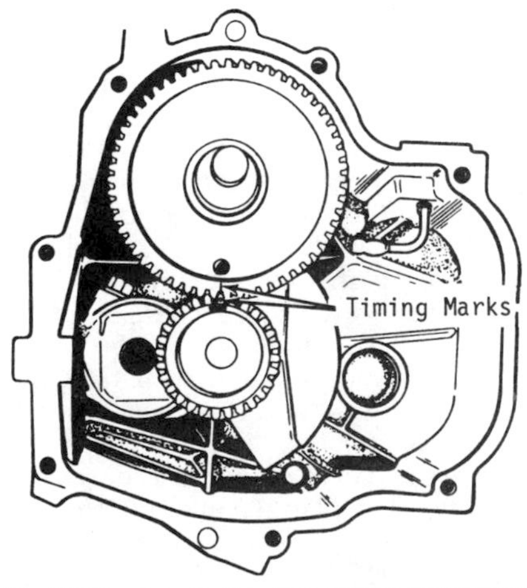


*Fig. TC15—Camshaft and crankshaft timing marks must be aligned after installation for proper valve timing.*

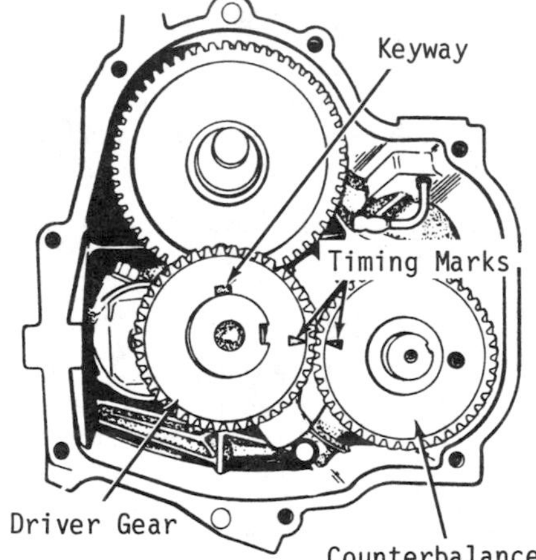


*Fig. TC16—Counterbalance gear and drive gear timing marks must be aligned after installation.*

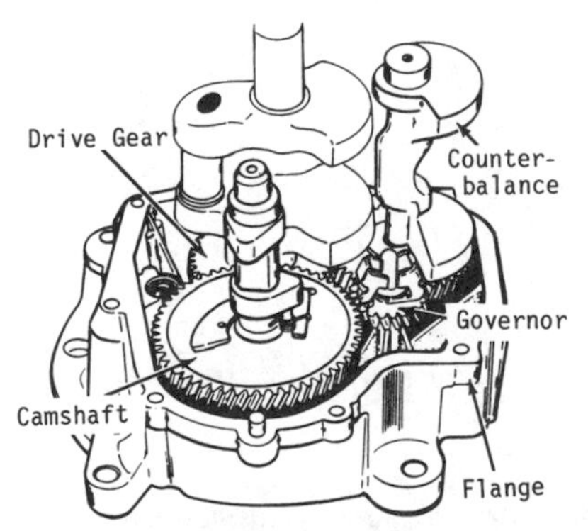


*Fig. TC17—View of relative position of camshaft, crankshaft and counterbalance shaft in crankcase base plate (oil pan).*



Illustrations courtesy Tecumseh Products Co.

**OIL PUMP.** All models are equipped with a positive displacement oil pump. Oil pump is located in crankcase base plate (oil pan) and is driven by an eccentric on camshaft.

When installing oil pump, be sure that chamfered side of pump faces the camshaft, and that plunger ball seats in recess in base plate.

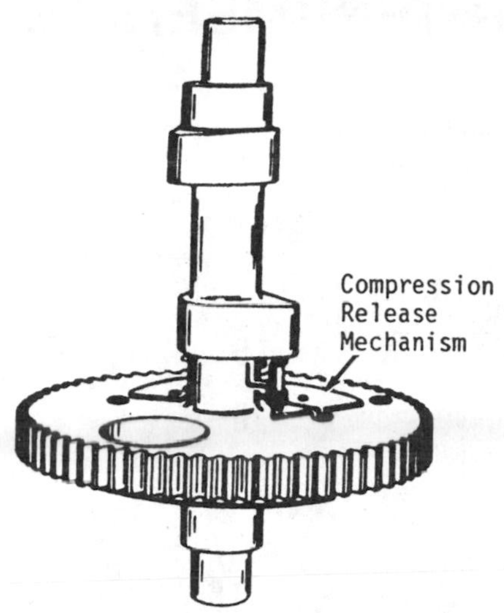


*Fig. TC18—Camshaft is equipped with a compression release mechanism.*

# TECUMSEH

## SERVICING TECUMSEH ACCESSORIES

### 12 VOLT STARTING AND CHARGING SYSTEMS

Some Tecumseh engines may be equipped with 12-volt electrical systems.

Refer to the following paragraphs for servicing Tecumseh electrical units and 12-volt Delco-Remy starter-generator used on some models.

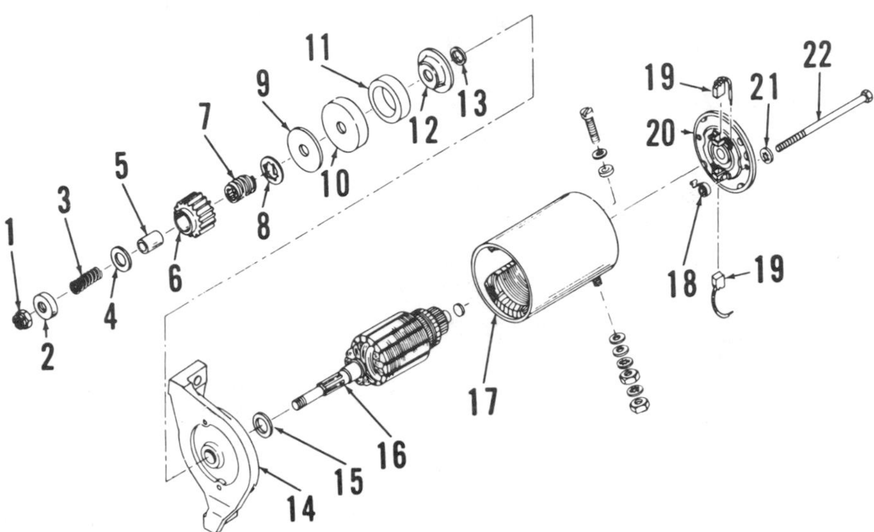

Fig. T85 – Exploded view of 12-volt starter motor Model No. 32817. Other starter motors are similar except as shown in Fig. T86. Spacer (15) is available in different thicknesses to adjust armature end play.

1. Nut
2. Pinion stop
3. Spring
4. Washer
5. Anti-drift sleeve
6. Pinion gear
7. Screw shaft
8. Stop washer
9. Thrust washer
10. Cushion cup
11. Rubber cushion
12. Thrust washer
13. Thrust bushing
14. Drive end cap
15. Spacer washer
16. Armature
17. Frame & field coil assy.
18. Brush spring
19. Brushes
20. End cap
21. Washer
22. Bolt

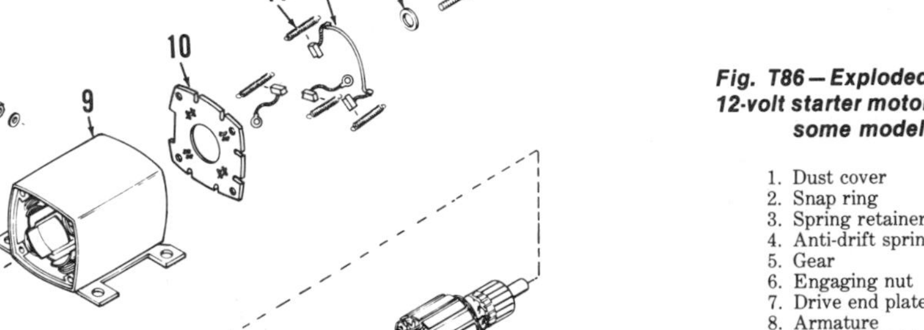

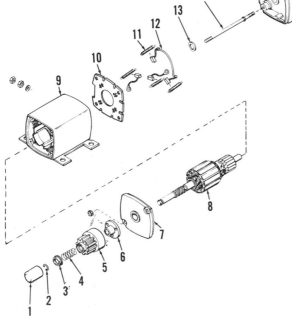

Fig. T86 – Exploded view of 12-volt starter motor used on some models.

1. Dust cover
2. Snap ring
3. Spring retainer
4. Anti-drift spring
5. Gear
6. Engaging nut
7. Drive end plate
8. Armature
9. Frame & field coil assy.
10. Brush card
11. Brush spring
12. Brushes
13. Thrust washer
14. Through-bolts
15. Commutator end plate

**12-VOLT STARTER MOTOR (BENDIX DRIVE TYPE).** Refer to Fig. T85 or T86 for exploded view of 12-volt starter motor and Bendix drive unit used on some engines. To identify starter, refer to service number stamped on end cap.

When assembling starter motor in Fig. T85, use spacers (15) of varying thicknesses to obtain an armature end play of 0.005-0.015 inch (0.127-0.381 mm). Tighten armature nut (1) to 100 in.-lbs. (11.3 N·m) on motor numbers 29965, 32468, 32468A, 32468B and 33202, to 130-150 in.-lbs. (14.7-16.9 N·m) on motor number 32510 and to 170-220 in.-lbs. (19.2-24.8 N·m) on motor number 32817. Tighten through-bolts to 30-35 in.-lbs. (3.4-3.9 N·m) on motor numbers 29965, 32468 and 32468A, to 35-44 in.-lbs. (3.9-5.0 N·m) on motor number 32817 and to 45-50 in.-lbs. (5.0-5.6 N·m) on motor number 32510.

To perform no-load test for starter motors 29965, 32468 and 32468A, use a fully charged 6-volt battery. Maximum current draw should not exceed 25 amps at 6 volts. Minimum rpm is 6500.

No-load test for Models 32468B and 33202 requires a fully charged 12-volt battery. Maximum current draw should not exceed 25 amps at 11.8 volts. Minimum rpm is 8000.

No-load test for starter motors 32510 and 32817 must be performed with a 12-volt battery. Maximum current draw should not exceed 25 amps at 11.5 volts. Minimum rpm is 8000.

Disassembly and reassembly of starter motors 33605, 33606 and 33835 is evident after inspection of unit and referral to Fig. T86. Note that stops on through-bolts (14) are used to secure brush card (10) in housing (9).

Through-bolts must be installed with stops toward end cover (15).

Maximum current draw with starter on engine should not exceed 55 amps at a minimum of 850 rpm for starters 33605 and 33606 or 70 amps at a minimum of 600 rpm for starter 33835. Cranking test should not exceed 10 seconds.

**ALTERNATOR CHARGING SYSTEMS.** Flywheel alternators are used on some engines for the charging system. The generated alternating current is converted to direct current by two rectifiers on rectifier panel (Figs. T87 and T88) or regulator-rectifier (Fig. T89).

The system shown in Fig. T87 has a maximum charging output of about 3 amps at 3600 rpm. No current regulator is used on this low output system. The rectifier panel includes two diodes (rectifiers) and a 6 amp fuse for overload protection.

The system shown in Fig. T88 has a maximum output of 7 amps. To prevent overcharging battery, a double pole switch is used in low output position to reduce output to 3 amps for charging battery. Move switch to high output position (7 amps) when using accessories.

The system shown in Fig. T89 has a maximum output of 7 amps on engine of 7 hp; 10 or 20 amps on engines of 8 hp and larger. This system uses a solid state regulator-rectifier which converts generated alternating current to direct current for charging the battery. The regulator-rectifier also allows only required amount of current flow for existing battery conditions. When battery is fully charged, current output is decreased to prevent overcharging battery.

TESTING. On models equipped with rectifier panel (Figs. T87 or T88), remove rectifiers and test them with either a continuity light or an ohmmeter. Rectifiers should show current flow in one direction only. Alternator output can be checked using an induction ampere meter over positive lead wire to battery.

On models equipped with regulator-rectifier (Fig. T89), check system as follows: Disconnect B+ lead and connect a DC voltmeter as shown in Fig. T90. With engine running near full throttle, voltage should be 14.0-14.7. If voltage is above 14.7 or below 14.0 but above 0, regulator-rectifier is defective. If voltmeter reading is 0, regulator-rectifier or alternator coils may be defective. To test alternator coils, connect an AC voltmeter to AC leads as shown in Fig. T91. With engine running at near full throttle, check AC voltage.

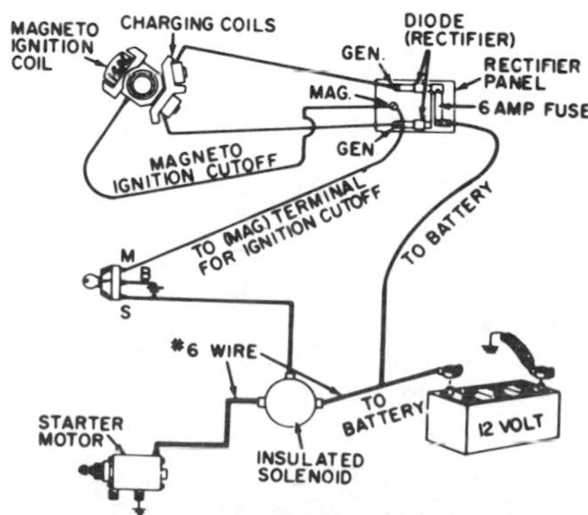


Fig. T87 — Wiring diagram of typical 3 amp alternator and rectifier panel charging system.

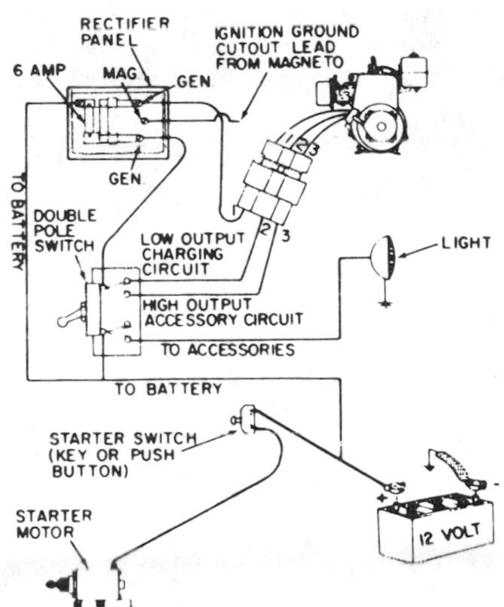


Fig. T88 — Wiring diagram of typical 7 amp alternator and rectifier panel charging system. The double pole switch in one position reduces output to 3 amps for charging or increases output to 7 amps in other position to operate accessories.

If voltage is less than 20.0 volts, alternator is defective.

**MOTOR-GENERATOR.** The combination motor-generator (Fig. T92) functions as a cranking motor when starting switch is closed. When engine is operating and starting switch is open, unit operates as a generator. Generator output and circuit voltage for battery and various accessories are controlled by current-voltage regulator.

To determine cause of abnormal operation, motor-generator should be given a "no-load" test or a "generator output" test. The generator output test can be performed with a motor-generator on or off the engine. The no-load test must be made with motor-generator removed from engine.

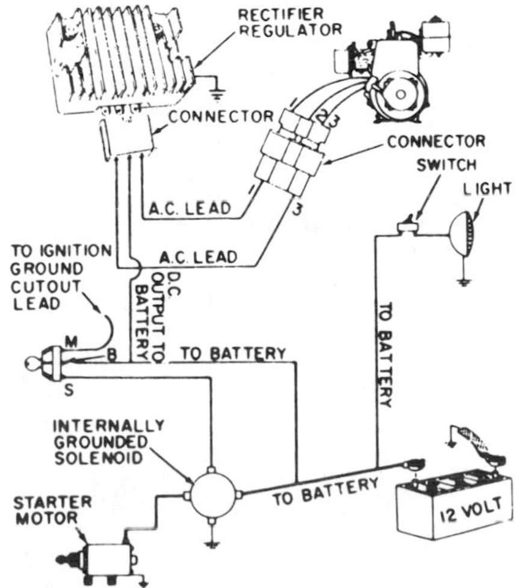


Fig. T89 — Wiring diagram of typical 7, 10 or 20 amp alternator and regulator-rectifier charging system.

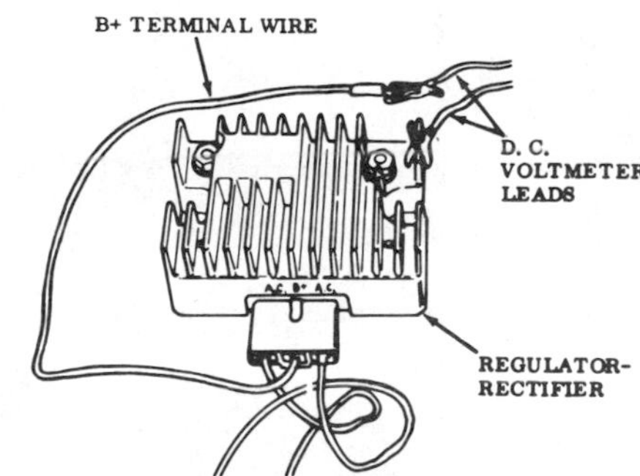


Fig. T90 — Connect DC voltmeter as shown when checking regulator-rectifier.

Motor-generator test specifications are as follows:

**Motor-Generator Delco-Remy No. 1101980**

Brush spring tension . . . . . . . . . 24-32 oz. (680-900g)
Field draw,
Amperes . . . . . . . . . . . . . . . . 1.52-1.62
Volts . . . . . . . . . . . . . . . . . . . . . . . . 12
Cold output,
Amperes . . . . . . . . . . . . . . . . . . . . . 12
Volts . . . . . . . . . . . . . . . . . . . . . . . . 14
Rpm . . . . . . . . . . . . . . . . . . . . . . . 4950
No-load test,
Amperes (max.) . . . . . . . . . . . . . . . 18
Volts . . . . . . . . . . . . . . . . . . . . . . . . 11
Rpm (min.) . . . . . . . . . . . . . . . . . 2500
Rpm (max.) . . . . . . . . . . . . . . . . . 2900

**CURRENT-VOLTAGE REGULATORS.** Two types of current-voltage regulators are used with motor-generator system. One is a low output unit which delivers a maximum of 7 amps. The high output unit delivers a maximum of 14 amps.

The low output (7 amp) unit is identified by its four connecting terminals (three on one side of unit and one on underside of regulator). The battery ignition coil has a 3 amp draw. This leaves a maximum load of 4 amps which may be used on accessory lead.

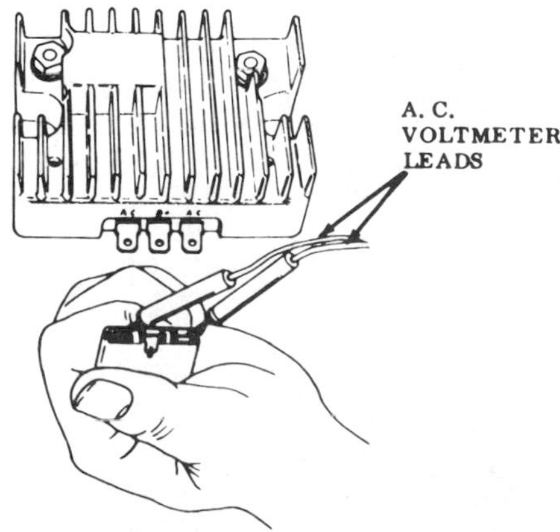


Fig. T91 — Connect AC voltmeter to AC leads as shown when checking alternator coils.

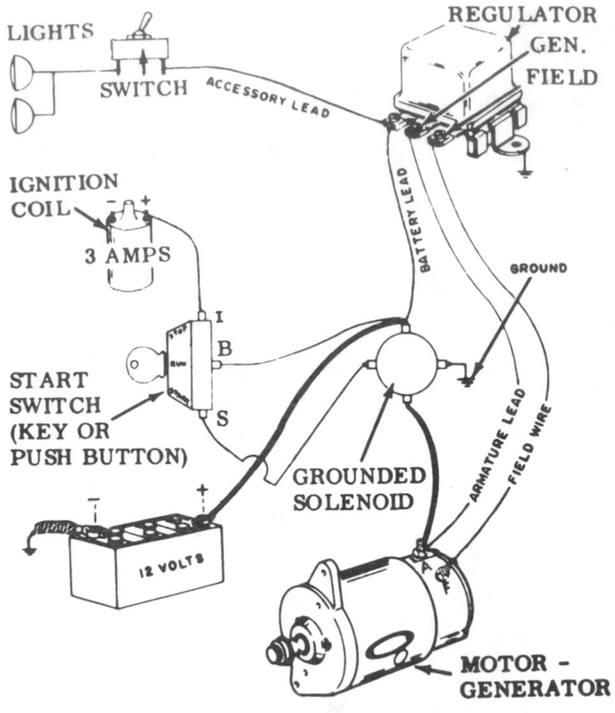


*Fig. T92—Wiring diagram of typical 14 amp output current-regulator and motor-generator system. The 7 amp output system is similar.*

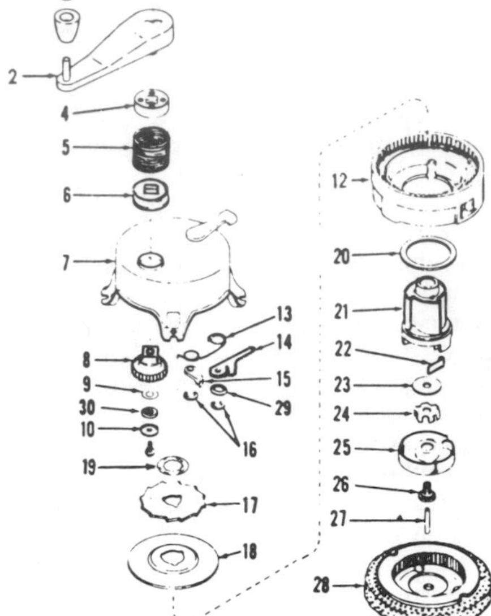

*Fig. T93—Exploded view of ratchet starter used on some engines.*

2. Handle
4. Clutch
5. Clutch spring
6. Bearing
7. Housing
8. Wind gear
9. Wave washer
10. Clutch washer
12. Spring & housing
13. Release dog spring
14. Release dog
15. Lock dog
16. Dog pivot retainers
17. Release gear
18. Spring cover
19. Retaining ring
20. Hub washer
21. Starter hub
22. Starter dog
23. Brake washer
24. Brake
25. Retainer
26. Screw (left hand thread)
27. Centering pin
28. Hub & screen
29. Spacer washers
30. Lockwasher

The high output (14 amp) unit has only three connecting terminals (all on side of unit). So with a 3 amp draw for battery ignition coil, a maximum of 11 amps can be used for accessories.

Regulator service test specifications are as follows:

**Regulator Delco-Remy No. 1118988 (7 amp)**

Ground polarity ............Negative
Cut-out relay,
  Air gap...........0.020 in. (0.5 mm)
  Point gap.........0.020 in. (0.5 mm)
  Closing voltage, range .....11.8-14.0
  Adjust to ...................12.8
Voltage regulator,
  Air gap...........0.075 in. (1.9 mm)
  Setting volts, range........13.6-14.5
  Adjust to ...................14.0

**Regulator Delco-Remy No. 1119207 (14 amp)**

Ground polarity ............Negative
Cut-out relay,
  Air gap...........0.020 in. (0.5 mm)
  Point gap.........0.020 in. (0.5 mm)
  Closing voltage, range .....11.8-13.5
  Adjust to ...................12.8
Voltage regulator,
  Air gap...........0.075 in. (1.9 mm)
  Voltage setting @ degrees F.
  14.4-15.4 @ 65°
  14.2-15.2 @ 85°
  14.0-14.9 @ 105°
  13.8-14.7 @ 125°
  13.5-14.3 @ 145°
  13.1-13.9 @ 165°
Current regulator,
  Air gap...........0.075 in. (1.9 mm)
  Current setting ..............13-15

## WIND-UP STARTER

**RATCHET STARTER.** On models equipped with ratchet starter, refer to Fig. T93 and proceed as follows: Move release lever to "RELEASE" position to remove tension from main spring. Remove starter assembly from engine. Remove left hand thread screw (26), retainer hub (25), brake (24), washer (23) and six starter dogs (22). Note position of starter dogs in hub (21). Remove hub (21), washer (20), spring and housing (12), spring cover (18), release gear (17) and retaining ring (19) as an assembly. Remove retaining ring, then carefully separate these parts.

**CAUTION: Do not remove main spring from housing (12). The spring and housing are serviced only as an assembly.**

Remove snap rings (16), spacer washers (29), release dog (14), lock dog (15) and spring (13). Winding gear (8), clutch (4), clutch spring (5), bearing (6) and crank handle (2) can be removed after first removing retaining screw and washers (10, 30 and 9).

Reassembly procedure is reverse of disassembly. Centering pin (27) must align screw (26) with crankshaft center hole.

## REWIND STARTERS

**FRICTION SHOE TYPE.** To disassemble starter, refer to Fig. T94 and proceed as follows: Hold starter rotor (12) securely with thumb and remove the four screws securing flanges (1 and 2) to cover (15). Remove flanges and release thumb pressure enough to allow spring to rotate pulley until spring (13) is un-

*Fig. T94—Exploded view of typical friction shoe rewind starter assembly.*

1. Mounting flange
2. Flange
3. Retaining ring
4. Washer
5. Spring
6. Slotted washer
7. Fibre washer
8. Spring retainer
9. Spring
10. Friction shoe
11. Actuating lever
12. Rotor
13. Rewind spring
14. Centering pin
15. Cover
16. Rope
17. Roller

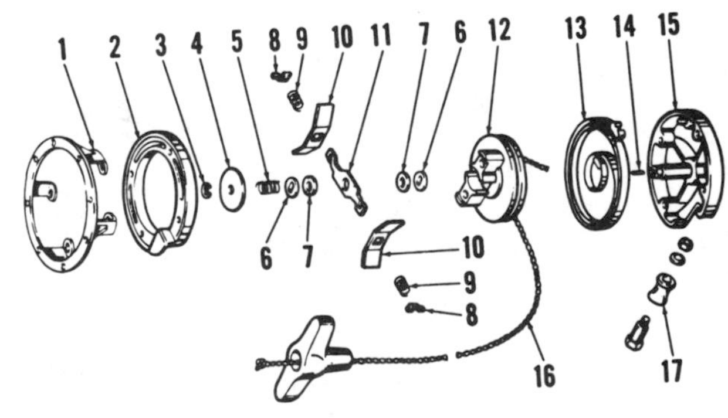



Illustrations courtesy Tecumseh Products Co.

wound. Remove retaining ring (3), washer (4), spring (5), slotted washer (6) and fibre washer (7). Lift out friction shoe assembly (8, 9, 10 and 11), then remove second fibre washer and slotted washer. Withdraw rotor (12) with rope from cover and spring. Remove rewind spring from cover and unwind rope from rotor.

When reassembling, lubricate rewind spring, cover shaft and center bore in rotor with a light coat of "Lubriplate" or equivalent. Install rewind spring so windings are in same direction as removed spring. Install rope on rotor, then place rotor on cover shaft. Make certain inner and outer ends of spring are correctly hooked on cover and rotor. Preload rewind spring by rotating rotor two full turns. Hold rotor in preload position and install flanges (1 and 2). Check sharp end of friction shoes (10) and sharpen or renew as necessary. Install washers (6 and 7), friction shoe assembly, spring (5), washer (4) and retaining ring (3). Make certain friction shoe assembly is installed properly for correct starter rotation. If properly installed, sharp ends of friction shoes will extend when rope is pulled.

Remove brass centering pin (14) from cover shaft, straighten pin if necessary, then reinsert pin 1/3 of its length into cover shaft. When installing starter on engine, centering pin will align starter with center hole in end of crankshaft.

**DOG TYPE.** Two dog type starters may be used as shown in Fig. T95 and Fig. T96. Disassembly and assembly of both types is similar. To disassemble starter shown in Fig. T95, remove starter from engine and while holding pulley remove rope handle. Allow recoil spring to unwind. Remove starter components in order shown in Fig. T95 noting position of dog (6) and direction spring (3) is wound. Be careful when removing recoil spring (3). Reassemble by reversing disassembly procedure. Turn pulley six turns before passing rope through cover so spring (3), is preloaded. Tighten retainer screw (9) to 45-55 in.-lbs. (5.08-6.21 N·m).

To disassemble starter shown in Fig. T96, pull starter rope until notch in pulley half (5) is aligned with rope hole in cover (1). Hold pulley and prevent from rotating. Engage rope in notch and allow pulley to slowly rotate so recoil spring will unwind. Remove components as shown in Fig. T96. Note direction recoil spring is wound being careful when removing spring from cover. Reassemble by reversing disassembly procedure. Preload recoil spring by turning pulley two turns with rope.

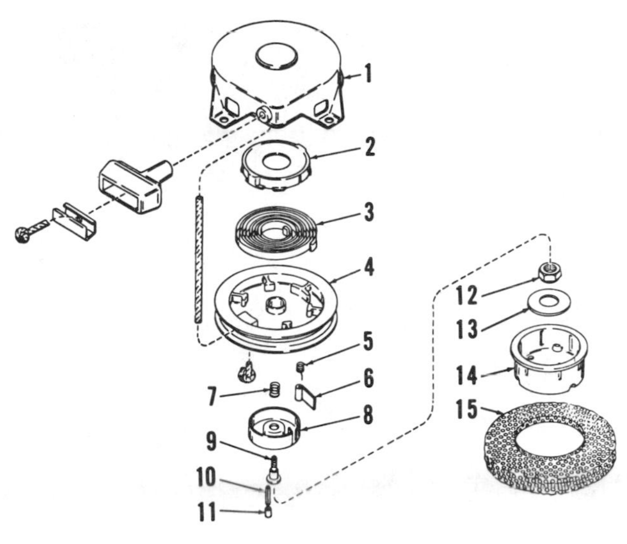

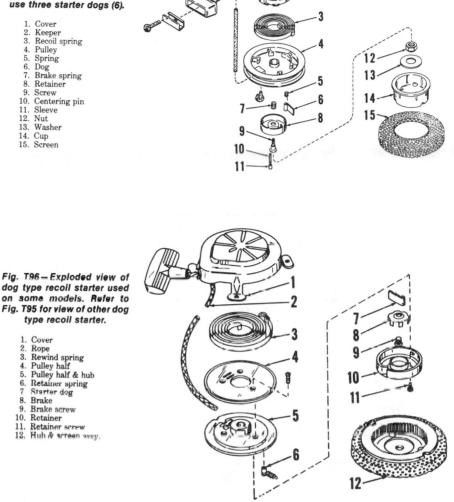

***Fig. T95—Exploded view of typical dog type recoil starter assembly. Some units of similar construction use three starter dogs (6).***

1. Cover
2. Keeper
3. Recoil spring
4. Pulley
5. Spring
6. Dog
7. Brake spring
8. Retainer
9. Screw
10. Centering pin
11. Sleeve
12. Nut
13. Washer
14. Cup
15. Screen

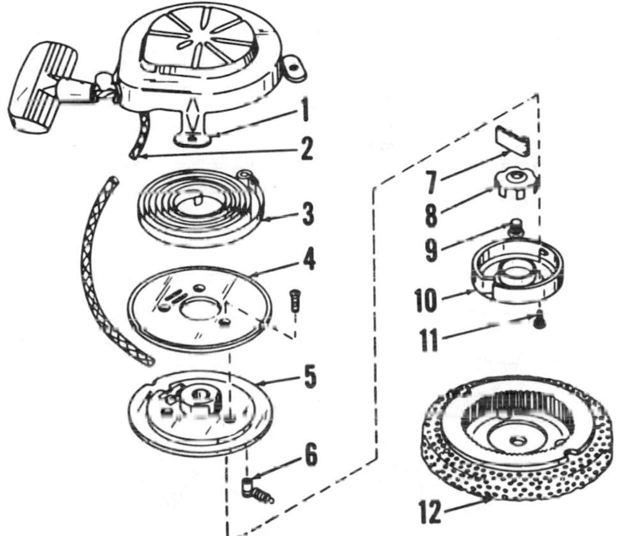


***Fig. T96—Exploded view of dog type recoil starter used on some models. Refer to Fig. T95 for view of other dog type recoil starter.***

1. Cover
2. Rope
3. Rewind spring
4. Pulley half
5. Pulley half & hub
6. Retainer spring
7. Starter dog
8. Brake
9. Brake screw
10. Retainer
11. Retainer screw
12. Hub & screen assy.

# WISCONSIN

| Model | No. Cyls. | Bore | Stroke | Displacement | Horsepower |
|---|---|---|---|---|---|
| TR-10D | 1 | 3-1/8 in. (79.4 mm) | 2-5/8 in. (66.7 mm) | 20.2 cu. in. (331 cc) | 10 (7.5 kW) |
| TRA-10D | 1 | 3-1/8 in. (79.4 mm) | 2-5/8 in. (66.7 mm) | 20.2 cu. in. (331 cc) | 10 (7.5 kW) |
| TRA-12D | 1 | 3-1/2 in. (88.9 mm) | 2-7/8 in. (73.0 mm) | 27.66 cu. in. (453 cc) | 12 (8.9 kW) |
| S-10D | 1 | 3-1/4 in. (82.5 mm) | 3 in. (76.2 mm) | 24.89 cu. in. (408 cc) | 10.5 (7.8 kW) |
| S-12D | 1 | 3-1/2 in. (88.9 mm) | 3 in. (76.2 mm) | 28.86 cu. in. (473 cc) | 12.5 (9.3 kW) |
| S-14D | 1 | 3-3/4 in. (95.2 mm) | 3 in. (76.2 mm) | 33.1 cu. in. (542 cc) | 14 (10.4 kW) |

## MAINTENANCE

**SPARK PLUG.** Recommended spark plug is a Champion D-16J, AC C86 or equivalent. Set electrode gap at 0.030 inch (0.762 mm). Tighten spark plug to a torque of 28-30 ft.-lbs. (38-41 N·m).

**CARBURETOR.** Zenith Model 68-7 carburetor is used on engine Models TR-10D and TRA-10D. See Fig. W1 for exploded view, Fig. W2 for cross-sectional view and Fig. W3 for location of adjustment points on carburetor.

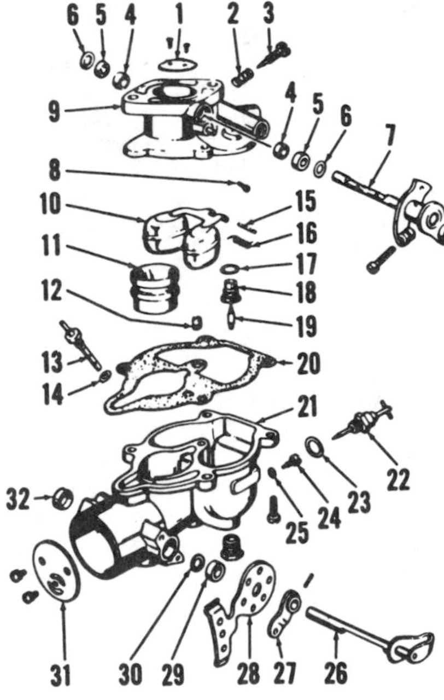

*Fig. W1—Zenith 68-7 carburetor is used on Model TR-10D and TRA-10D engines.*

1. Throttle plate
2. Spring
3. Idle mixture needle
4. Bushing
5. Seal
6. Retainer
7. Throttle shaft
8. Idle jet
9. Throttle body
10. Float
11. Venturi
12. Well vent
13. Discharge nozzle
14. Gasket
15. Float shaft
16. Float spring
17. Gasket
18. Inlet valve seat
19. Inlet valve
20. Gasket
21. Fuel bowl
22. Main fuel needle
23. Gasket
24. Main jet
25. Gasket
26. Choke shaft
27. Choke lever
28. Bracket
29. Retainer
30. Seal
31. Choke plate
32. Plug

TRA-12D engine is fitted with a Walbro LME-35 carburetor shown in exploded view in Fig. W4. Engine Models S-10D, S-12D and S-14D use a Zenith Model 1408 carburetor as shown in Fig. W5.

Float setting procedures for these carburetors varies. Measure float level of Zenith 68-7 carburetor as shown in Fig. W6. Bend float arm to obtain required height of 1-5/32 inches (29.4 mm).

See Fig. W7 for proper setting of float level of Walbro LME-35 carburetor. Space between free end of float and gasket surface should be 5/32-inch (4.0 mm).

Fig. W8 shows proper measurement procedure for checking float level of Zenith Model 1408 carburetors. Use a narrow blade depth gage as shown and be sure no pressure is on needle pin. Remove float when bending tab to make adjustment; do not try to adjust with float in place. Correct dimension is 7/8-inch (22.2 mm) as shown.

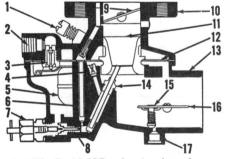

*Fig. W2—Zenith 68-7 carburetor shown in cross-section.*

1. Idle mixture needle
2. Fuel inlet
3. Float needle valve
4. Fuel well vent
5. Float
6. Idle fuel passage
7. Main jet adjusting needle
8. Main jet
9. Throttle plate
10. Throttle body
11. Venturi
12. Gasket
13. Fuel bowl
14. Main discharge jet
15. Poppet valve
16. Choke plate
17. Intake drain

Refer to Fig. W3 for adjustment points of Model 68-7 carburetor and for initial setting, open both idle and main mixture needles by 1¼ turns each. Make final and trim adjustments after engine is warm. Use this same procedure to set Walbro carburetor. Idle mixture needle is shown at (9–Fig. W4) with idle speed screw (7) and main fuel needle (33).

Model 1408 carburetor calls for initial setting of idle mixture at 1½ turns open (5–Fig. W9) and 2¼ turns open of main jet (18). Set idle speed (7) for 1000-1200 rpm.

**FUEL PUMP.** See Fig. W10 for exploded view of fuel pump used on some models. Repair kit (Wisconsin #LQ-28) is available from parts outlets and provides all parts marked (*) for service when renewal is needed.

**GOVERNOR.** All models are equipped with a mechanical governor of centrifugal flyweight design. Governor gear and weight assembly is driven by the

*Fig. W3—View of Zenith 68-7 carburetor to show adjustment point locations.*

IN. Idle mixture needle
IS. Idle speed adjustment
MJ. Main jet adjustment



Illustrations courtesy Teledyne Total Power.

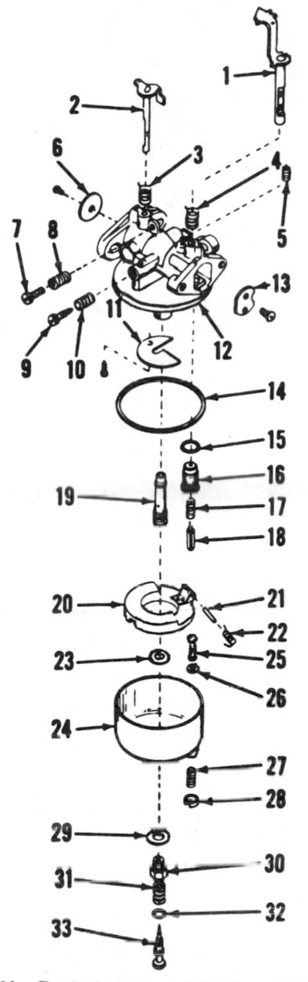

*Fig. W4—Exploded view of Walbro LME-35 carburetor used on TRA-12D engine.*

1. Choke shaft
2. Throttle shaft
3. Throttle spring
4. Choke spring
5. Choke stop spring
6. Throttle plate
7. Idle speed screw
8. Spring
9. Idle mixture needle
10. Spring
11. Baffle
12. Carburetor body
13. Choke plate
14. Bowl gasket
15. Gasket
16. Inlet valve seat
17. Spring
18. Inlet valve
19. Main nozzle
20. Float
21. Float shaft
22. Spring
23. Gasket
24. Bowl
25. Drain stem
26. Gasket
27. Spring
28. Retainer
29. Gasket
30. Bowl retainer
31. Spring
32. "O" ring
33. Main fuel needle

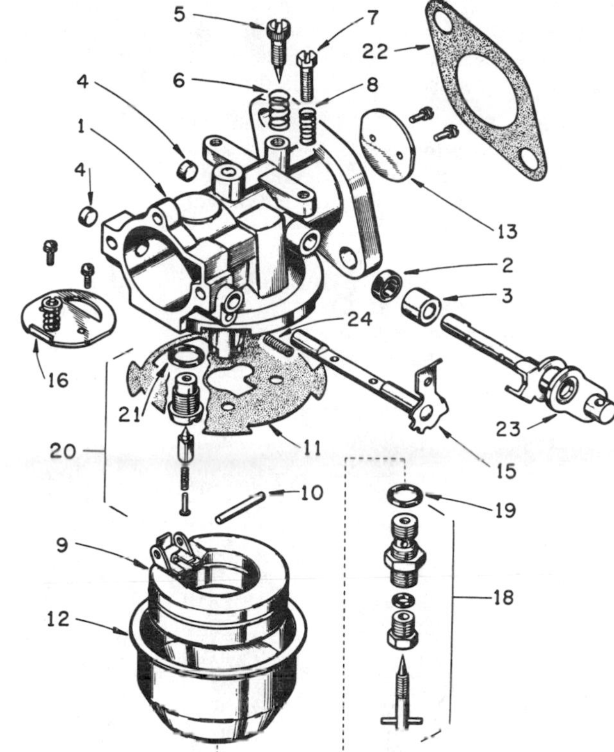

*Fig. W5—Exploded view of Zenith 1408 carburetor as used on engine Models S-10D, S-12D and S-14D.*

1. Carburetor body
2. Throttle shaft seal
3. Seal retainer
4. Cup plugs
5. Idle fuel needle
6. Spring
7. Idle speed stop screw
8. Spring
9. Float assy.
10. Float pin
11. Gasket
12. Fuel bowl
13. Throttle disc
15. Choke shaft
16. Choke disc
18. Main jet needle assy.
19. Washer
20. Inlet valve & seat assy.
21. Gasket
22. Gasket
23. Throttle shaft
24. Choke lever friction spring

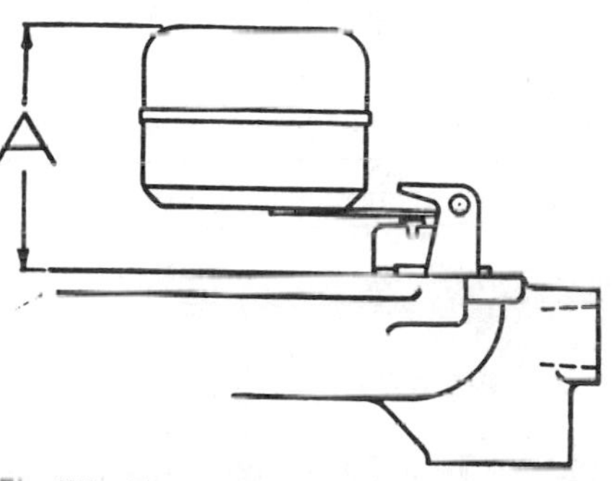


*Fig. W6—To measure float level of Zenith 68-7 carburetor, dimension "A" should be 1-5/32 inches (29.4 mm). Carefully bend float arm to adjust.*

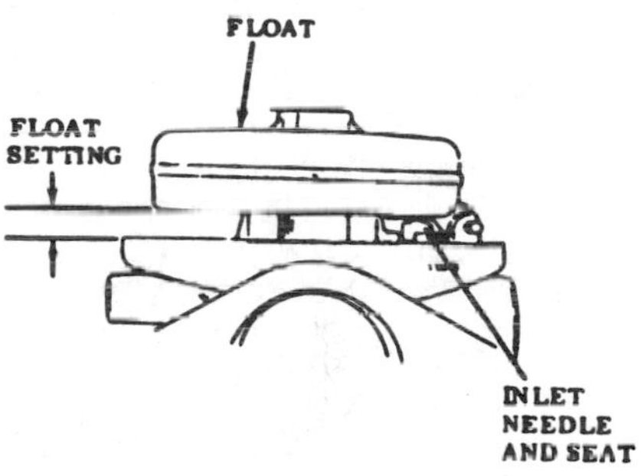


*Fig. W7—Float setting of Walbro carburetor calls for 5/32-inch (4 mm) space between free end of float and gasket surface as shown.*

camshaft gear. Figs. W11 and W12 show operating parts of each type used and identify models which pertain.

Note thrust of governor weights in governor style shown in Fig. W11 is transmitted through a sliding pin to a vane which imparts rotary motion to governor shaft and lever. Governor shown in Fig. W12 has a movable thrust sleeve which transmits flyweight pressure to governor cross shaft so as to rotate governor lever. See Fig. W13 for typical linkage.

In order to correctly set governed speeds, use of a tachometer or revolution counter to accurately measure crankshaft rpm is necessary. Refer to appropriate table (I or II) corresponding to engine model being serviced to determine proper governor lever hole for attaching governor spring to set required speed.

Be sure correct parts are used in governor linkages. It will be noted in tables that for full range of adjustment, different lengths of adjusting screws are specified. TR and TRA models (Table I)

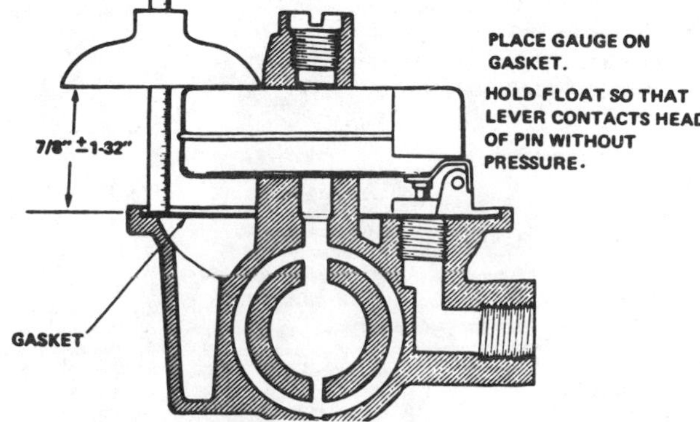


*Fig. W8—Measure for 7/8-inch (22 mm) float setting of Zenith 1408 carburetor as shown. See text.*

Illustrations courtesy Teledyne Total Power.

also may call for different governor springs for setting higher or lower governed speeds. Authorized WISCONSIN parts service should be consulted.

**Special Note: All TR-10D engines manufactured prior to S.N. 3909152 were set for full throttle operation. With governor lever in hole number 2, no-load rpm of 3800 will provide 3450 rpm under load.**

**Table I—Models TRA-10D, TRA-12D, TR10D**
**Use Lever Spring Hole Number and Set No-Load Rpm:**

| Desired Rpm Under Load | TRA-10D** | | TRA-12D | |
|---|---|---|---|---|
| 2000 | 1 | 2520 | 3 | 2230 |
| 2100 | 1 | 2580 | 4 | 2430 |
| 2200 | 1 | 2610 | 4 | 2515 |
| 2300 | 1 | 2690 | 4 | 2590 |
| 2400 | 1 | 2740 | 4 | 2660 |
| 2500 | 1 | 2800 | 4 | 2750 |
| 2600 | 1 | 2890 | 4 | 2810 |
| 2700 | 1 | 2935 | 5 | 3020 |
| 2800 | 2 | 3065 | 5 | 3100 |
| 2900 | 2 | 3160 | 5 | 3180 |
| *3000 | 3 | 3230 | 5 | 3260 |
| *3100 | 3 | 3300 | 5 | 3325 |
| *3200 | 3 | 3380 | 6 | 3535 |
| *3300 | 3 | 3460 | 6 | 3620 |
| *3400 | 4 | 3615 | 6 | 3700 |
| *3500 | 4 | 3690 | 6 | 3790 |
| *3600 | 5 | 3850 | 6 | 3860 |

**Applies to TR-10 engines S.N.3909152 and after.

2000-2900 rpm, TRA-10D uses 3-5/8 inch adjusting screw; TRA-12D uses 5-5/8 inch adjusting screw.

3000 rpm (*) and higher, TRA-10D uses 5 inch adjusting screw; TRA-12D uses 5-1/4 inch adjusting screw.

**Table II—Models S-10D, S-12D, S-14D**

| Desired Rpm Under Load | Hole Number | Adjust No-Load Rpm To: |
|---|---|---|
| 1600 | 1 | 1760 |
| 1800 | 2 | 1975 |
| 1900 | 2 | 2040 |
| 2000 | 2 | 2120 |
| 2100 | 3 | 2260 |
| 2200 | 3 | 2340 |
| 2300 | 3 | 2400 |
| 2400 | 4 | 2580 |
| 2500 | 4 | 2650 |
| *2600 | 4 | 2720 |
| *2700 | 4 | 2810 |
| *2800 | 5 | 2910 |
| *2900 | 5 | 3010 |
| *3000 | 6 | 3150 |
| *3100 | 6 | 3230 |
| *3200 | 7 | 3360 |
| *3300 | 7 | 3455 |
| *3400 | 7 | 3520 |
| *3500 | 7 | 3590 |
| *3600 | 7 | 3680 |

1600-2500 rpm, use 3-15/16 inch adjusting screw.

2600 rpm (*) and higher, use 3-5/8 inch adjusting screws.

GOVERNOR SETTING. (MODELS TR-10D AND TRA-12D). Refer to Fig. W11 and to table I. Position governor lever (4–Fig. W11) on governor (fulcrum) shaft (7) with control rod connected between governor lever and throttle lever and with governor spring attached in correct hole of governor lever as specified in table. Then, with carburetor throttle held wide open, loosen governor lever clamp so fulcrum shaft (7) can be turned independently of governor lever (4). Rotate fulcrum shaft counter-clockwise until internal governor vane (8) is in contact with flyweight thrust pin. Tighten clamp screw on governor lever (4), and on Model TR-10D engine, install idle return spring from breather tube to governor lever. Check no-load rpm using a tachometer. Regulate governor spring tension by means of the adjusting screw until required no-load rpm is set.

(MODELS S-10D, S-12D and S-14D). Refer to Fig. W12 and to Table II. Loosen locknut (1–Fig. W12) and remove lower end of throttle rod (2) from governor lever (6). Hold throttle in wide open position and turn governor lever (6) as far clockwise as possible. Adjust length of rod (2) by turning its threaded end in or out of carburetor throttle lever until lower end will enter hole in governor lever. Reinstall retainer clip (14) and retighten nut (1). Use a tachometer to check no-load rpm.

If governor appears over-sensitive or if not responsive under load, check for correct spring and linkage components and be sure parts are not binding and are properly assembled.

Fig. W13 shows typical governor control linkage. That illustrated is used on Models S-10D, S-12D and S-14D. Variable speed control may take the form of a control handle attached to control disc (CD–Fig. W13) or a remote control assembly which consists of a throttle

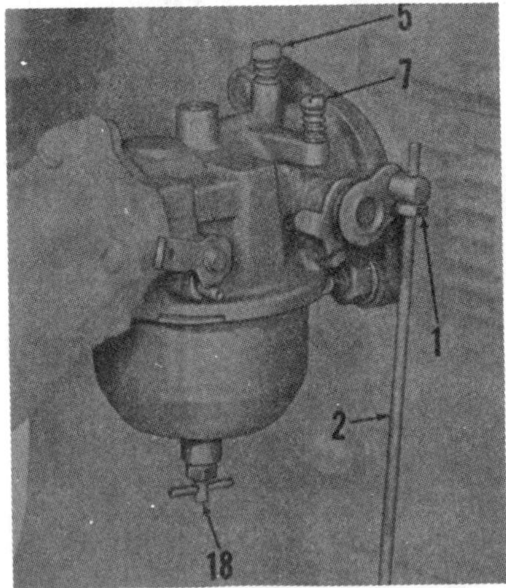


***Fig. W9—View of carburetor adjustment points and throttle linkage of Model 1408 carburetor. See Text for procedure.***

1. Nut
2. Throttle rod
5. Idle fuel needle
7. Idle speed adjustment screw
18. Main fuel needle

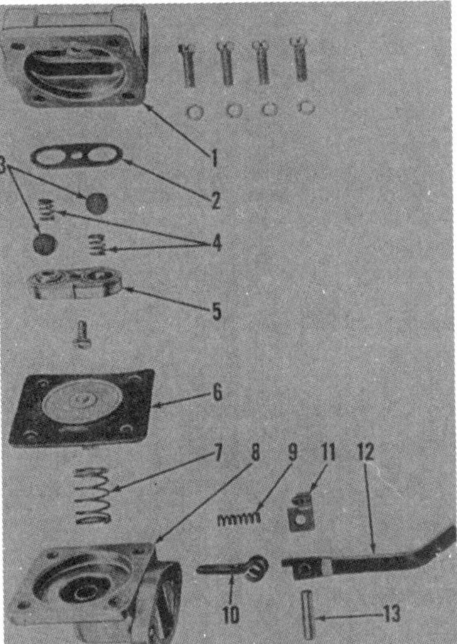


***Fig. W10—Exploded view of fuel pump used on these Wisconsin engines. Renewable service parts are marked (*).***

1. Pump head
2. Valve gasket*
3. Valve (2)*
4. Springs (2)*
5. Valve plate & seats
6. Diaphragm*
7. Spring*
8. Mounting bracket
9. Rocker arm spring
10. Linkage
11. Spring clip
12. Rocker arm
13. Rocker arm pin

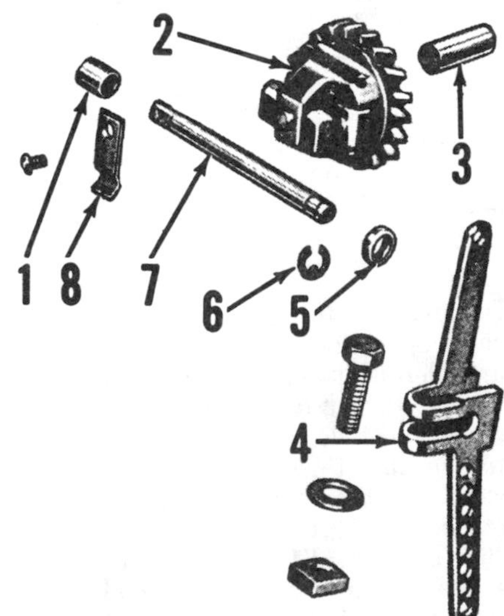


***Fig. W11—Exploded view of governor assembly typical of that used on Models TR-10D, TRA-10D and TRA-12D.***

1. Spacer
2. Gear/flyweight assy.
3. Governor shaft
4. Governor lever
5. Oil seal
6. Retaining ring
7. Fulcrum shaft
8. Vane

lever, conveniently mounted, which is connected by a Bowden cable to the control disc. If engine is equipped with variable speed controls, be sure they do not over-ride or cause binding in governor linkages.

**MAGNETO IGNITION.** Either Fairbanks-Morse or Wico flywheel magnetos are used. The breaker box is an integral part of the crankcase and points and condenser contained therein are interchangeable for either Wico or Fairbanks-Morse magnetos. However, should service replacement of flywheel or stator plate become necessary, both parts must be of the same manufacture.

See Fig. W14 for typical magneto ignition wiring diagram. Refer to IGNITION TIMING paragraph for breaker point adjustment.

**BATTERY IGNITION.** Engines equipped with battery ignition system use a conventional 12-volt ignition coil. Breaker points are the same as used with magneto ignition and are located in breaker box on crankcase. See Fig. W15 for typical battery ignition wiring diagram. Refer to IGNITION TIMING paragraph for point adjustment.

**IGNITION TIMING.** Ignition timing for engines equipped with either magneto ignition or battery ignition is as follows:

Breaker points and condenser are accessible when breaker box cover is removed. See Figs. W17 and W18. Models TR-10D and TRA-10D call for a point gap setting of 0.020 inch (0.508 mm). Models S-10D, S-12D and S-14D with conventional (magneto or battery) ignition require that points be set to 0.023 inch (0.584 mm). Model TRA-12D has breakerless (CD) ignition as standard; it is optional on Models S-10D, S-12D and S-14D. Fixed running spark advance is 18° BTDC on all models. Because this advance is regulated by point opening, a slight variation in breaker point setting may be necessary to obtain accurate spark advance.

Accuracy of spark timing can be checked by use of a neon timing light with engine running at operating speed. Placement of timing marks is shown for all models in Figs. W17 and W18. If it is not convenient to check timing with engine running, or if engine is being reassembled after other service, use the following static timing procedure.

Remove breaker box cover and disconnect coil primary wire from terminal stud at breaker box. Remove spark plug and place thumb over plug hole in cylinder head, then rotate flywheel clockwise by turning starting sheave until cylinder compression is felt against thumb. Continue to turn until timing

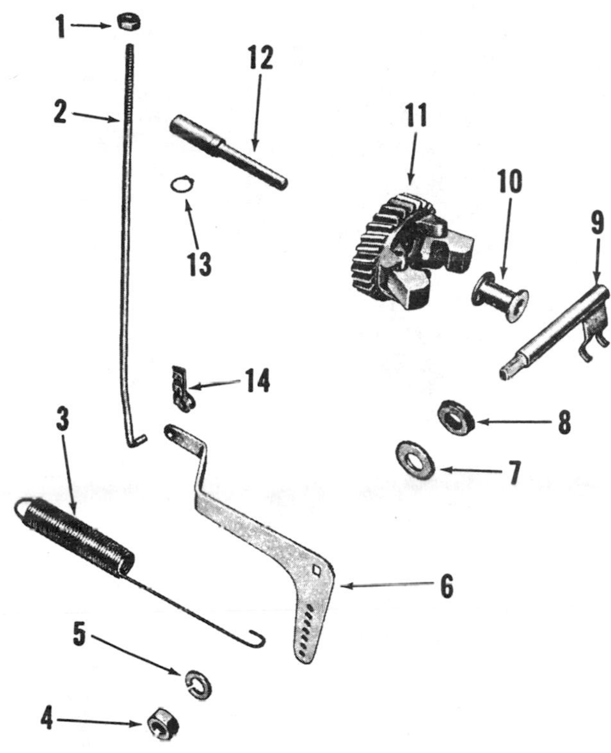

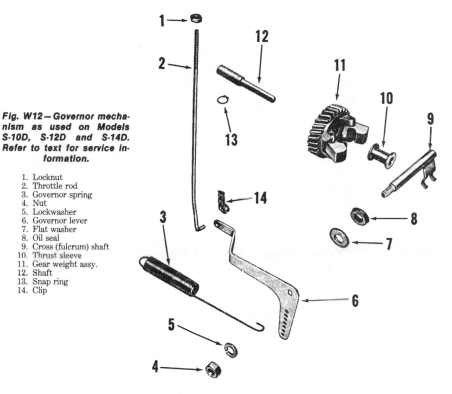

*Fig. W12—Governor mechanism as used on Models S-10D, S-12D and S-14D. Refer to text for service information.*

1. Locknut
2. Throttle rod
3. Governor spring
4. Nut
5. Lockwasher
6. Governor lever
7. Flat washer
8. Oil seal
9. Cross (fulcrum) shaft
10. Thrust sleeve
11. Gear weight assy.
12. Shaft
13. Snap ring
14. Clip

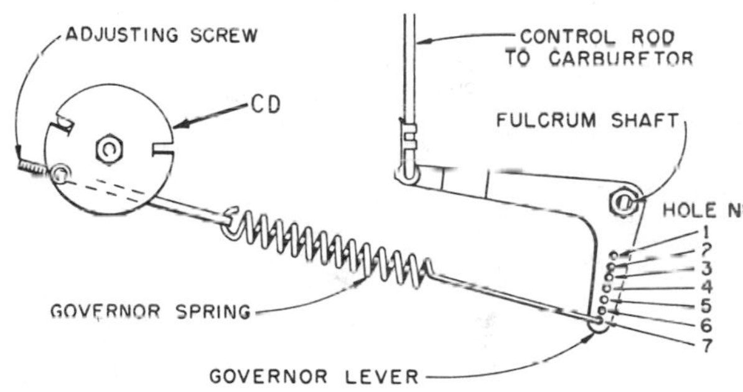


*Fig. W13—Typical governor adjustment and controls. Major speed changes are made by shifting holes in governor lever and minor adjustments on speed adjusting screw. In some cases, a control handle or remote control cable may be attached to control disc (CD) for variable speed control. See text and speed chart.*

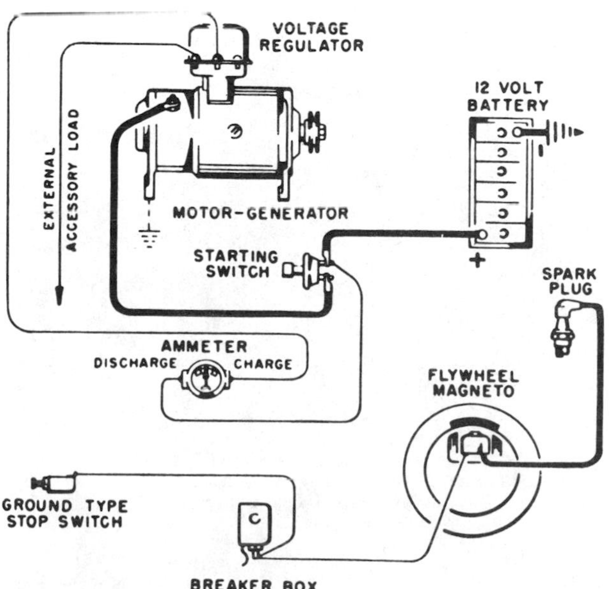


*Fig. W14—Typical magneto ignition wiring layout. Motor-generator for electric starting with battery and charging circuit also shown. Refer to text.*

Illustrations courtesy Teledyne Total Power.

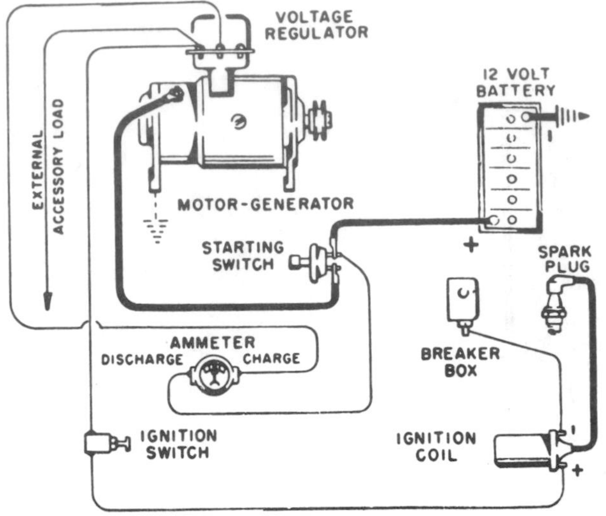


*Fig. W15—Typical battery ignition wiring diagram. Note by comparison with Fig. W14 how ignition system is tied in with motor-generator and battery circuits. See text.*

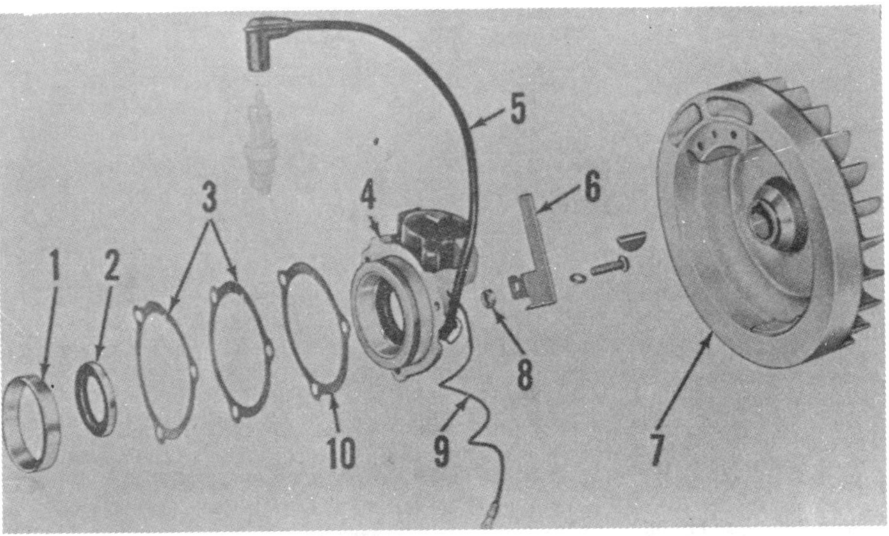

*Fig. W16—Typical flywheel magneto assembly. Note that crankshaft end play is adjusted by shims (3) which are offered in thickness of 0.005, 0.010, 0.015 and 0.20 inch. Flywheel must be pulled for access to magneto stator plate.*

1. Bearing cup
2. Oil seal
3. Shims
4. Stator plate assy.
5. Spark plug lead
6. Wire clip
7. Flywheel
8. Spacer
9. Breaker point lead
10. Stator plate gasket

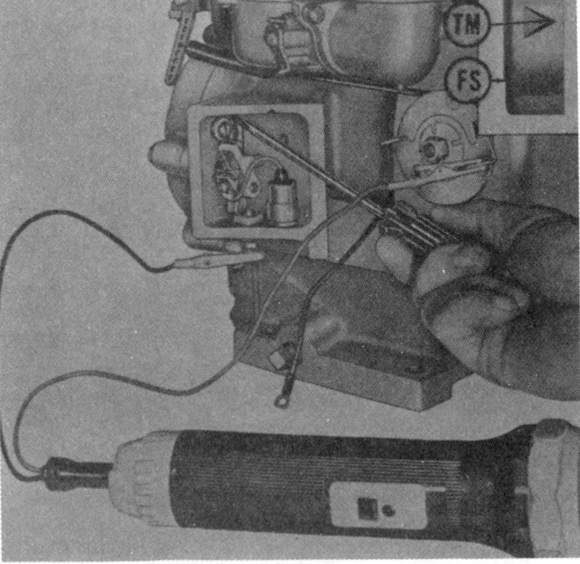


*Fig. W17—On Models TR-10D and TRA-10D, timing mark (TM) should be aligned with timing pointer on flywheel shroud (FS) as light goes out. Refer to text for static timing technique.*

marks are aligned. Connect a continuity timing light, Wisconsin Motor part #DF-81-S1, or equivalent, as shown in Figs. W17 or W18. Then loosen lockscrew of ignition points baseplate just enough so plate can be moved. Fit a screwdriver into adjusting slots and turn to close points so light will come on, then back off until light just goes off. Tighten lockscrew securely. Make a final check by turning flywheel counter-clockwise until light goes on, then rotate flywheel clockwise and stop immediately when light goes out. At this point, advance timing mark on flywheel should line up with pointer or hole in shroud.

Disconnect and remove timing light and reconnect coil primary lead to breaker box stud. Reinstall cover.

**SOLID STATE IGNITION (Models TRA-12D, S-10D, S-12D and S-14D).** Breakerless capacitive-discharge (CD) ignition is offered on these models (standard on TRA-12D) for ease of starting and simplified maintenance. No adjustments are required. Only three parts assemblies are used: A magnet ring (fitted to and part of flywheel), a stator (containing trigger coil, rectifier diode and a silicon-controlled rectifier) mounted on bearing plate at flywheel end of engine and a special ignition coil.

In operation, an alternating current (AC) is generated in wire-wound coil poles of stator by passage of rotating flywheel magnets. Resulting AC passes to diode rectifier in stator which converts AC to DC. This direct current is then stored in a capacitor where it remains until further rotation of flywheel passes a permanent magnet over trigger coil section of stator which will generate a minute current to "trigger" or activate silicon-controlled rectifier (SCR) to switch the much heavier current stored in the capacitor into primary windings of the ignition coil. Now, by induction, this voltage is multiplied in secondary windings and discharged across spark plug electrode gap to ignite a fuel mixture charge in the engine combustion chamber. Elimination of electrical arcing at breaker points and wear of parts due to friction provides greatly increased service life in such a system when compared to conventional battery or magneto ignition.

TIMING CHECK-BREAKERLESS IGNITION. Design of this system does not allow for adjustment or alteration of spark timing, however, timing should be checked to determine if automatic advance is operating properly or to establish possible cause of ignition malfunction. Note in Fig. W20 that mounted positions of magnet ring in flywheel and stator on bearing plate assembly are fixed so as to be non-adjustable.



Illustrations courtesy Teledyne Total Power.

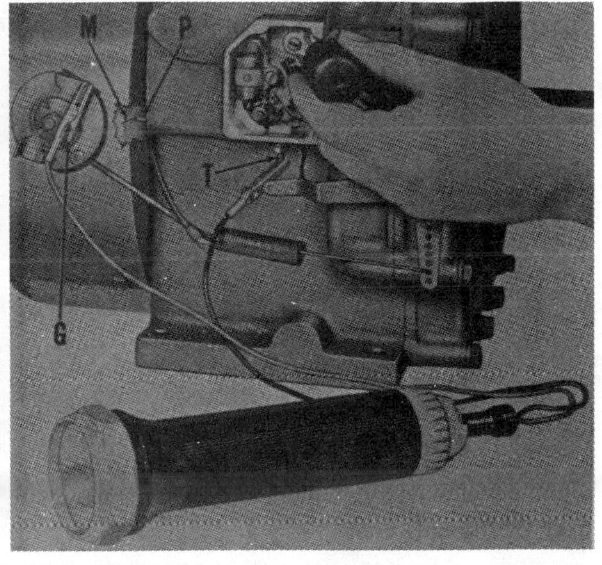


*Fig. W18—Use same static timing procedure on Models S-10D, S-12D and S-14D when equipped with magneto ignition. Be sure coil primary lead is disconnected from breaker terminal (T). Same breaker box is used on battery ignition models. See text.*

G. Ground connection
M. Timing mark
P. Timing pointer
T. Breaker terminals

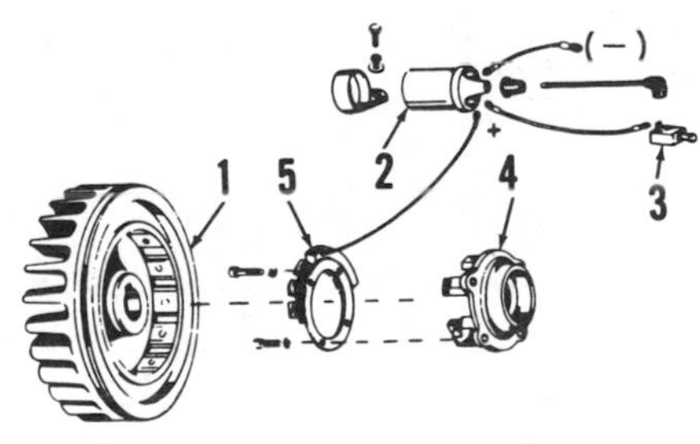


*Fig. W20—Exploded view of WISCONSIN solid state breakerless ignition system to show relationship of service parts.*

1. Flywheel & magnet ring
2. Ignition coil
3. Ignition switch assy.
4. Bearing plate assy.
5. Stator & trigger coil assy.

To check timing, a conventional neon timing light will serve. During cranking, spark is retarded to 10-12° BTDC and will advance to line up 18° BTDC mark on flywheel rim with timing pointer when engine is running at 1000 rpm. When checking running advance, which is 20° BTDC at 2500 rpm, timing mark will appear about 1/8 inch (3 mm) above pointer.

TROUBLESHOOTING. If cause for poor or no performance appears to be in ignition system, proceed as follows:

Inspect wiring, both primary and secondary leads, for grounding or for loose or dirty connections. A test light or ohmmeter continuity check will show if high resistance or broken conductors are the problem.

Remove, inspect condition, and if convenient, test spark plug. Be sure to measure electrode gap if plug is reinstalled.

To test for system output, fit a short section of bare wire into spark plug lead boot and hold exposed tip of this wire about 1/8-inch (3 mm) from cylinder head while cranking engine. Observe spark for condition. A weak spark (thin and yellow) or no spark indicates a defective stator. Since stator is without external test terminals, no electrical tests are feasible and evaluation is entirely based upon performance.

Failure of other system components, ignition coil or switch, is a remote possibility. If doubtful, these items may be isolated by disconnecting wire leads and tested with an ohmmeter. Resistance from coil secondary socket to case (ground) should be 4000-6000 ohms. Coil primary winding resistance is too low for significant measurement, however, this winding should be tested for continuity. Switch should make and break circuit sharp and clean without high resistance in closed position.

If parts are available, substitution of new units, spark plug, coil or stator, followed by performance check is most reliable.

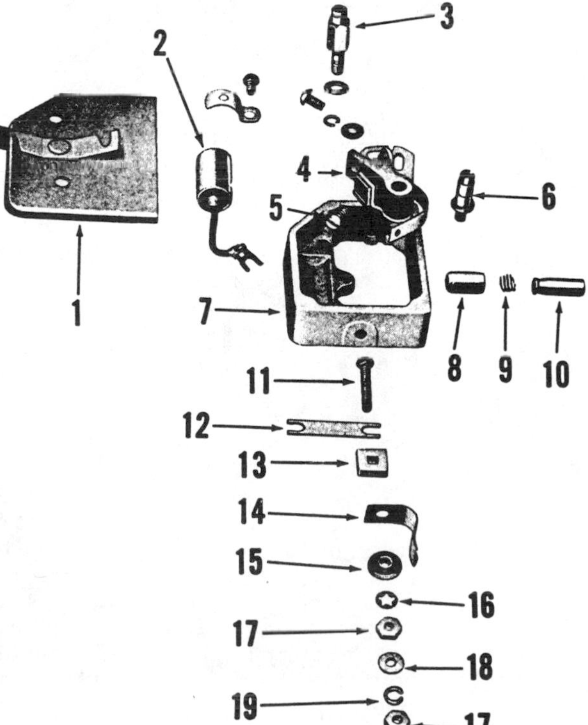


*Fig. W19—Exploded view of breaker box assembly used on magneto and battery ignition models of S-10D, S-12D and S-14D engines.*

1. Box cover
2. Condenser
3. Mounting stud
4. Breaker points
5. Terminal screw
6. Breaker pivot
7. Breaker box
8. Bushing
9. Spring
10. Push pin
11. Terminal stud
12. Terminal strip
13. Insulator
14. Ground strip
15. Insulator
16. Lockwasher
17. Nuts
18. Flat washer
19. Lockwasher

**LUBRICATION.** An oil dipper on connecting rod provides a splash lubrication system on all models. Use high quality detergent engine oil with a minimum API classification of "SD" or "SE". As seasonal temperatures vary, observe the following: Between 40°F (4°C) and 120°F (49°C), use SAE 30 weight oil. From 15°F (−9°C) to 40°F (4°C), use SAE 20W. From 0°F (−18°C) to 15°F (−9°C), use SAE 10W. Below 0°F (−18°C), use SAE 5W-20. Oil level should be checked for every eight hours of operation and changed every fifty hours. Crankcase capacity is one quart (0.9L) for Models TR-10D, TRA-10D and TRA-12D. Use two quarts (1.9L) in Models S-10D, S-12D and S-14D. When dipstick reads at "low" mark, add approximately 1/2-pint (0.2L) to restore proper oil level.

**CRANKCASE BREATHER.** A reed type breather valve is located at valve spring compartment. This one-way valve maintains a slight vacuum in the crankcase and helps prevent oil leakage of breaker point push rod and crankshaft oil seals. If a slight amount of crankcase vacuum is not present when engine is operating, clean and inspect breather valve. If breather valve is in satisfactory condition, check engine for

Illustrations courtesy Teledyne Total Power.

excessive blow-by past piston rings and/or valves.

## REPAIRS

**TIGHTENING TORQUES.** Recommended tightening torques are as follows:

**Models TR-10D, TRA-10D, TRA-12D**

Gear Cover . . . . . . . . . . . . . . . . . 8 ft.-lbs. (11 N•m)
Stator Plate . . . . . . . . . . . . . . . . 8 ft.-lbs. (11 N•m)
Connecting Rod Cap . . . . . . . . 22 ft.-lbs. (30 N•m)
Spark Plug . . . . . . . . . . . . . . 28-30 ft.-lbs. (38-41 N•m)
Flywheel Nut . . . . . . . . . . . . 50-55 ft.-lbs. (68-75 N•m)
Cylinder Head (see CYLINDER HEAD paragraph)

**Models S-10D, S-12D, S-14D**

Gear Cover . . . . . . . . . . . . . . . . 18 ft.-lbs. (24 N•m)
Stator Plate . . . . . . . . . . . . . . . 18 ft.-lbs. (24 N•m)
Connecting Rod Cap . . . . . . . . 22 ft.-lbs. (30 N•m)
Spark Plug . . . . . . . . . . . . . . 28-30 ft.-lbs. (38-41 N•m)
Flywheel Nut . . . . . . . . . . . . 50-55 ft.-lbs. (68-75 N•m)
Cylinder Block Nuts . . . . . . 42-50 ft.-lbs. (57-68 N•m)
Compartment Cap Screw (see Fig. W34) . . . . . . . . . . . . . . . 32 ft.-lbs. (43 N•m)
Cylinder Head (see CYLINDER HEAD paragraph)

Fig. W21 – Piston (P) is removed from top. Oil dipper (D) provides lubrication for horizontal crankshaft engines. Note placement of connecting rod index arrow at (A), location of governor shaft (GS) and that camshaft gear is fitted with a compression release (CR), typical of "TR" and "TRA" models.

**CYLINDER HEAD.** Always install a new head gasket when installing cylinder head. Be sure to note different lengths and styles of studs and cap screws for correct reinstallation. Lubricate threads.

Cylinder heads should be torqued in three stages: On Models TR-10D, TRA-10D and TRA-12D, torque first to 10 ft.-lbs. (14 N•m), then to 14 ft.-lbs. (19 N•m) and finally to 18 ft.-lbs. (24 N•m). On Models S-10D, S-12D and S-14D, stages for tightening are 16 ft.-lbs. (22 N•m), 24 ft.-lbs. (33 N•m) and 32 ft.-lbs. (43 N•m). A criss-cross pattern for tightening is preferred over a rotation pattern around circumference of cylinder head.

**CONNECTING ROD.** Connecting rod is removed along with piston from top end of cylinder bore as shown in Fig. W21 or W22. Models TR-10D, TRA-10D and TRA-12D have a crankpin diameter of 1.3755-1.3760 inches (34.938-34.950 mm). Rod bearing clearance for all TR and TRA models is 0.0005-0.0015 inch (0.0127-0.0381 mm) and side clearance is 0.009-0.016 inch (0.229-0.406 mm). Crankpin diameter for Models S-10D, S-12D and S-14D is 1.4984-1.4990 inches (38.059-38.075 mm) and clearance of insert type rod bearing is 0.0005-0.0015 inch (0.0127-0.0381 mm). Side clearance on "S" model engines is 0.004-0.013 inch (0.102-0.330 mm). New rods with crankpin bearing end of 0.010, 0.020 and 0.030 inch undersize are available for all TR and TRA models. Bearing inserts (shells) for S-10D, S-12D and S-14D are available in undersizes as well as standard size.

Fig. W22 – Open view of typical S-10D, S-12D or S-14D engine. Compare to Fig. W21, and note difference in placement of governor shaft, style of oil dipper and that cylinder and crankcase are separate castings. Flywheel should be left in place to balance crankshaft when gear cover is removed.

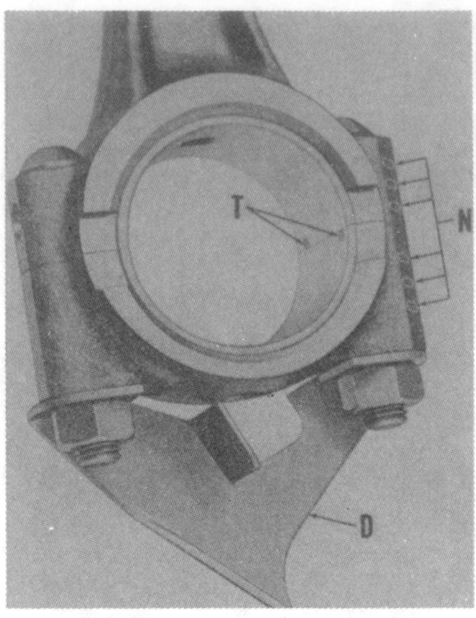


Fig. W23 – Install connecting rod cap (S-10D, S-12D and S-14D) so tangs (T) of bearing inserts are on same side. Numbers (N) on rod end and cap should also be aligned and installed toward gear cover side of crankcase. Oil dipper (D) open side also faces outward. See text.

Piston pin to connecting rod clearance

Fig. W24 – Section view showing proper arrangement of piston rings. In this typical view, top ring may not be chamfered inside as shown, however, all rings are marked with "TOP" or pit mark for correct installation. See text.

Fig. W25 – Location of cylinder-crankcase specification number on all "TR" and "TRA" models.



Illustrations courtesy Teledyne Total Power.

is 0.0002-0.0008 inch (0.0051-0.0203 mm) on all models except S-10D, S-12D and S-14D which are fitted with renewable bushings calling for clearance of 0.0005-0.0011 inch (0.0127-0.0279 mm). Oversize piston pins are available for some engines.

When installing piston and connecting rod assembly on models which are not equipped with renewable bearing inserts, TR-10D, TRA-10D and TRA-12D, align index arrows (A – Fig. W21) on rod end and cap. Arrows must face toward open end of crankcase. On all engines which are furnished with separate oil dipper (Fig. W22), install dipper so connecting rod cap screws are accessible from open end of crankcase. Refer to Fig. W23 when assembling cap to connecting rod on Models S-10D, S-12D and S-14D and be sure fitting tangs (T) are on same side as shown. Stamped numbers (N) and oil dipper (D) should face open side of crankcase.

*Fig. W26 – Dial indicator set up for checking crankshaft end play. Refer to text. Correct reading should be 0.001-0.004 inch (0.025-0.102 mm) measured with engine cold.*

**PISTON, PIN AND RINGS.** All engines are fitted with one chrome faced compression ring, one scraper ring and an oil control ring. Typical ring arrangement is shown in Fig. W24. Top side of all rings is marked "TOP" or bears a pit mark for correct installation. Ring end gaps should be spaced at 120 degree intervals from each other during reassembly.

When fitting pistons, clearance between skirt of cam ground piston and cylinder wall should be measured at right angle to piston pin. Required clearance for Models TR-10D and TRA-10D is 0.004-0.0045 inch (0.102-0.1143 mm) and for Models TRA-12D, S-10D and S-12D it is 0.0025-0.003 inch (0.0635-0.076 mm). Clearance for Model S-14D should be 0.0025-0.004 inch (0.0635-0.102 mm).

Ring end gaps of all models should measure 0.010-0.020 inch (0.254-0.508 mm). Side clearance of piston rings in grooves is as follows: For Models TR-10D, TRA-10D and TRA-12D, top (compression) ring should have a clearance of 0.002-0.0035 inch (0.051-0.0889 mm), second (scraper) ring calls for 0.001-0.0025 inch (0.025-0.0635 mm) and oil ring clearance is 0.002-0.0035 inch (0.051-0.0889 mm). For Models S-10D, S-12D and S-14D, top ring requires 0.002-0.004 inch (0.051-0.102 mm), second ring 0.002-0.004 inch (0.051-0.102 mm) and oil ring 0.0015-0.0035 inch (0.0381-0.0889 mm).

Renewal pistons and rings are available in oversize as well as standard. Tri-Chrome ring sets may also be used, and for long-term heavy duty service, are recommended.

Floating type piston pin is retained in bores by snap rings. Fit, for all models, should be from zero to 0.0008 inch (0.0203 mm) tight. See CONNECTING ROD paragraph for fit of piston pin to small end of connecting rod. Renewal piston pins for Models S-10D, S-12D and S-14D are available in standard and 0.005 and 0.010 inch oversize. Larger oversizes of 0.020 inch and 0.030 inch are offered for other models.

**CYLINDER.** Cylinder and crankcase are a one-piece casting for Models TR-10D, TRA-10D and TRA-12D. See Fig. W25. When cylinder bores of these models are worn to exceed 0.005 inch (0.127 mm), they should be rebored to accept next available oversize piston. Be sure to check parts availability at this point of overhaul process. Other models, S-10D, S-12D and S-14D, have separate castings for cylinder and crankcase as can be seen in Fig. W22. Cylinder assembly should be removed and rebored when wear exceeds 0.005 inch (0.127 mm). If entire cylinder block must be renewed due to extensive damage, new valves, seats, guides, springs, retainers and rotators are all furnished as part of complete assembly. When reassembling cylinder to crankcase, use a new gasket and tighten retaining stud nuts to a torque value of 42-50 ft.-lbs. (57-68 N·m). A cap screw is concealed within valve spring compartment. See Fig. W34 and tighten this cap screw to 32 ft.-lbs. (43 N·m). Refer to PISTON, PIN AND RINGS paragraph for information relating to oversize renewal parts.

*Fig. W27 – Locate timing mark (A) on camshaft gear between two marked teeth (B) of crankshaft gear. View is typical of all "TR" and "TRA" series.*

**CRANKSHAFT.** On all models, crankshaft rides in two tapered roller

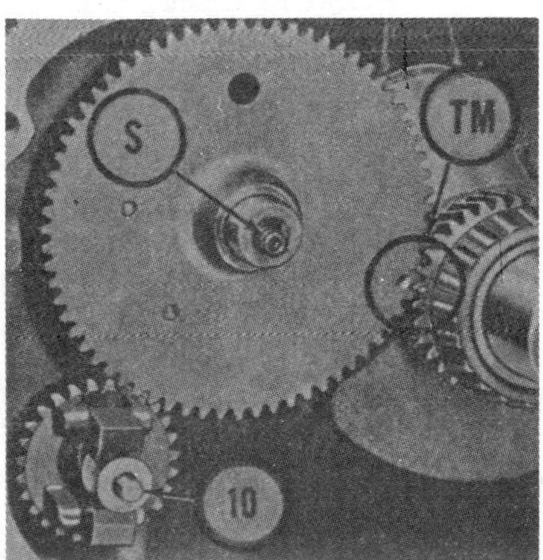


*Fig. W28 – View of timing marks lined up in Models S-10D, S-12D and S-14D. In current production, camshaft gear will support a compression release as shown in Fig. W31. Camshaft thrust spring (S) and governor thrust sleeve (10) must be in place before replacement of gear cover. Use heavy grease to hold camshaft thrust ball in cover hole during installation.*

Illustrations courtesy Teledyne Total Power.

bearings. Removal of crankshaft is from gear cover end of crankcase.

**CAUTION: When crankshaft removal is planned, be sure to loosen and remove flywheel nut from crankshaft and loosen flywheel from crankshaft tapered end before removing gear cover and its bearing from opposite end so crankshaft will be fully supported from heavy shock during flywheel removal. Leave flywheel loose on tapered shaft end to balance crankshaft during removal of gear cover.**

Crankshaft end play on all models is 0.001-0.004 inch (0.025-0.102 mm) with engine cold. Adjustment is made by varying number of shims in shim pack between crankcase and stator plate (main bearing support) at flywheel end of crankshaft. To check, use a dial indicator mounted as shown in Fig. W26. If new tapered roller main bearings have been installed, it will be necessary to firmly bump crankshaft ends with a heavy soft hammer to insure that bearings are fully seated before adjusting end play. Be sure camshaft and crankshaft timing marks are in proper register as shown in Figs. W27 and W28 and check tightening torque values for gear cover at beginning of the REPAIRS section. Figs. W29 and W30 show seal protectors which should be used and are identified by model.

In case of severe wear or scoring of crankpin journal, regrind to fit next undersize connecting rod or for proper undersize connecting rod bearing inserts, depending upon model. Refer to CONNECTING ROD paragraph. Should it be necessary to renew crankshaft, part number will be found stamped in counterweight toward tapered shaft end.

**GOVERNOR GEAR AND WEIGHT ASSEMBLY.** Governor gear and weight assemblies rotate on a shaft which is a press fit in a bore of crankcase. Exploded views are shown in Figs. W11 and W12. On Models TR-10D, TRA-10D and TRA-12D, shaft (3 – Fig. W11) has had its depth in block held by a snap ring beginning with production serial number 3909152. Models S-10D, S-12D and S-14D require end play of 0.003-0.005 inch (0.076-0.127 mm) be maintained on governor gear shaft between gear and its snap ring retainer. See Fig. W32 for measurement technique to be used on these models. Press-fitted shaft is driven in or out of bore to make adjustment. On models with straight governor lever and governor gear mounted above cam gear, note in Fig. W33 that upper end of governor lever must tilt toward engine so governor vane will not be fouled or interfere with flyweights as gear cover is installed. On Models S-10D, S-12D and S-14D, governor thrust sleeve must be in place as shown in Fig. W34 when gear cover is placed in position.

**CAMSHAFT AND TAPPETS.** Camshafts, all models, ride in unbushed bores in crankcase and gear cover. Camshaft end play is controlled by a thrust spring (See Figs. W33 and W34) fitted into shaft hub which centers upon a steel ball fitted into a socket in gear cover; during assembly, this ball is easily held in place by a coating of heavy grease. Cam followers (valve tappets) are removed downward from their bores in block after camshaft has been removed. During removal or installation of camshaft, place block on its side as shown in Fig. W35 to prevent tappets from dropping out.

Models TR-10D, TRA-10D and TRA-12D have a tappet body diameter of 0.309-0.310 inch (7.848-7.874 mm) with a clearance of 0.002-0.006 inch (0.051-0.152 mm) in block bores. Tappet diameter for Models S-10D, S-12D and S-14D is 0.6235-0.6245 inch (15.837-15.862 mm) with clearance of 0.0005-0.0025 inch (0.0127-0.0635 mm) required. These larger tappets in "S"

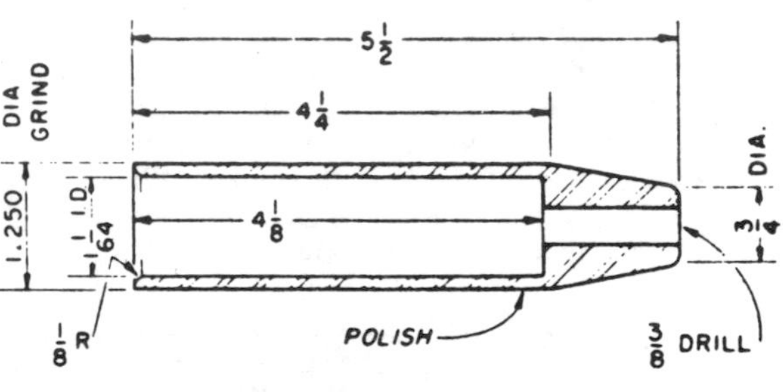

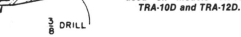

*Fig. W29 – Dimensions of seal protector sleeve to be used on Models TR-10D, TRA-10D and TRA-12D.*

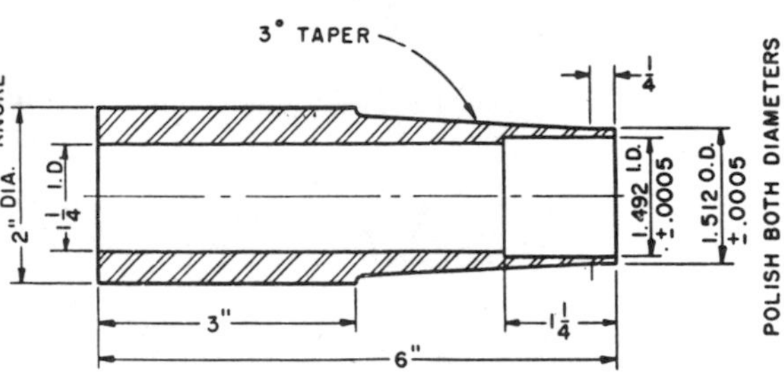


*Fig. W30 – Seal protector sleeve to be used on Models S-10D, S-12D and S-14D is fabricated to dimensions shown.*

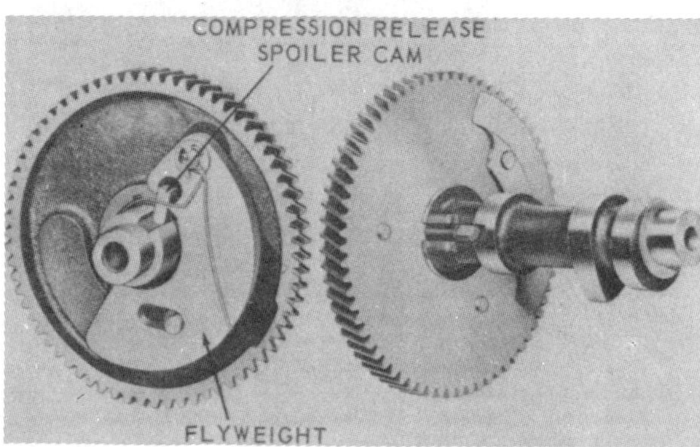


*Fig. W31 – View of both sides of camshaft gear to show compression release assembly installed. See text.*

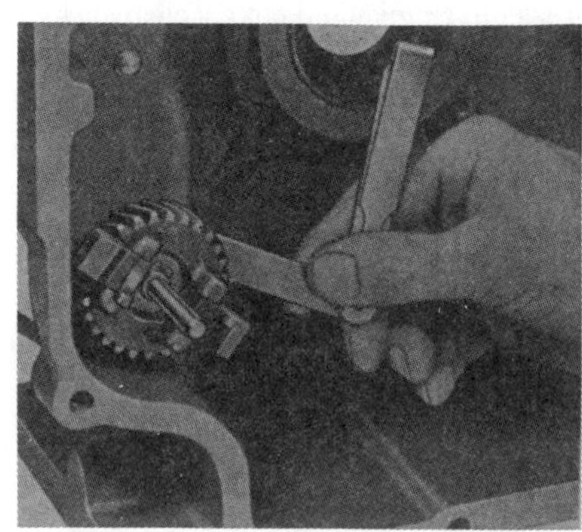

*Fig. W32 – Use of feeler gage to measure end play of governor gear on shaft; snap ring must be correctly seated. See text.*



Illustrations courtesy Teledyne Total Power.

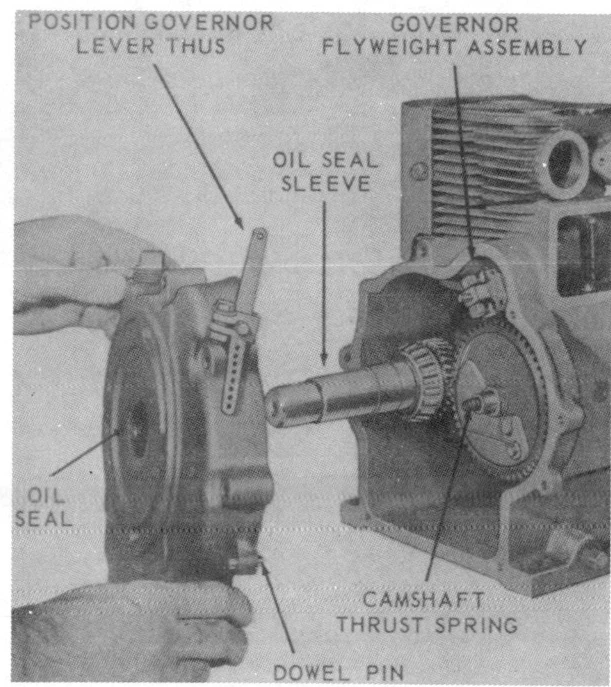


*Fig. W33—Replacement of gear cover on TR-10D, TRA-10D and TRA-12D engines, all integral cylinder-crankcase models. Note that governor flyweight assembly, camshaft thrust spring and oil seal protector are in place. Be sure governor lever is tilted as shown. Governor thrust ball is greased in place in its cover recess.*

*Fig. W35—Place engine on its side as shown to prevent tappets dropping from block bores when camshaft is removed.*

series engines are threaded, adjustable type.

On models equipped with a compression release type camshaft (Fig. W31), a spoiler cam holds exhaust valve slightly open during part of compression stroke while cranking. Reduced compression pressure allows for faster cranking speed at lower effort. When crankshaft reaches about 650 rpm during cranking, centrifugal force swings flyweight on front of cam gear to turn spoiler cam to inoperative position allowing exhaust valve to seat and restore full compression. Whenever camshaft is removed, compression release mechanism should be checked for damage to spring or excessive wear on spoiler cam. Flyweight and spoiler cam must move easily with no binding.

See Figs. W27 and W28 to set timing marks in register during reassembly.

**VALVE SYSTEM.** For all models, valve face and seat angle is 45 degrees for both valves. As indicated by letter "D" suffix to model numbers, all engines in this section are furnished with renewable stellite exhaust valve seat inserts and stellite-faced exhaust valves. Models S-10D, S-12D and S-14D also have renewable insert-type intake valve seats (not stellite) while others have their intake valves seated directly in cylinder block. Valve rotators are installed on all exhaust valves.

All valves are fitted in renewable guides pressed into cylinder block. Press or drive down (toward valve spring chamber) for both removal and installation. Tool #DF-72 guide driver is available from WISCONSIN. Internal chamfered end of guide is installed DOWN. Inside diameter of all valve guides is 0.312-0.313 inch (7.925-7.950 mm).

Diameter of valve stems is 0.310-0.311 inch (7.874-7.899 mm) for all intake valves and 0.309-0.310 inch (7.848-7.874 mm) for exhaust valves except for Models S-10D, S-12D and S-14D whose exhaust valve stems measure 0.308-0.309 inch (7.823-7.848 mm). Maximum allowable stem clearance in valve guides is 0.006 inch (0.152 mm) for all models except S-10D, S-12D and S-14D for which 0.005 inch (0.127 mm) clearance for intake and 0.007 inch (0.178 mm) for exhaust valves is specified.

Valve tappet clearance is adjusted by a

*Fig. W36—Reed-type breather valve located in valve spring compartment of Models TR-10D, TRA-10D and TRA-12D.*

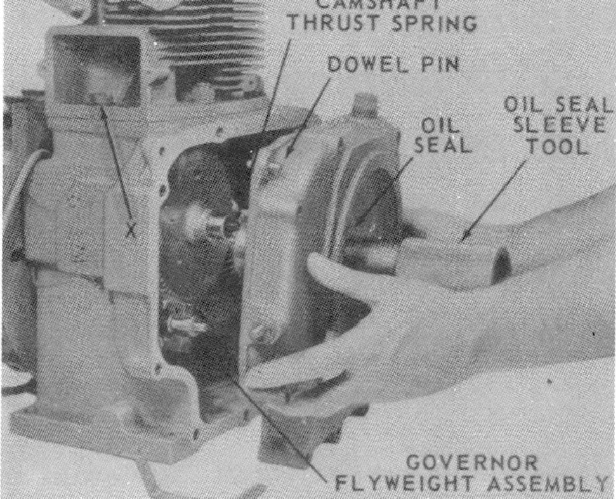


*Fig. W34—Installation of gear cover on S-10D, S-12D and S-14D engines. Note cap screw (X) in valve compartment, referred to in text. Protect cover oil seal with sleeve tool as shown and be sure thrust sleeve is in place on governor shaft. See TIGHTENING TORQUES.*

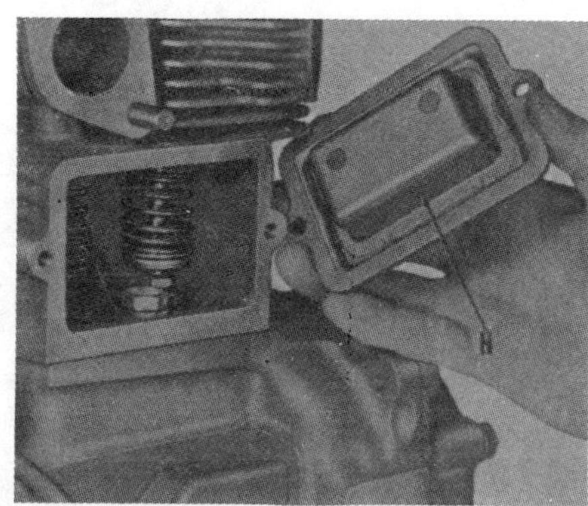


*Fig. W37—Breather valve for models S-10D, S-12D and S-14D is located in valve spring compartment cover. Drain hole (H) must be kept open.*

Illustrations courtesy Teledyne Total Power.

self-locking cap screw in tappet body of Models S-10D, S-12D and S-14D. Setting for these models, engine cold, is 0.007 inch (0.178 mm) for intake valves and 0.016 inch (0.406 mm) for exhaust valves.

Tappet clearance for all other engine models is adjusted by careful grinding of valve stems. Cold clearance is 0.006 inch (0.152 mm) for intake valves and 0.012 inch (0.305 mm) for exhaust valves except for exhaust valve of Model TRA-12D which calls for a clearance of 0.015 inch (0.381 mm).

Manufacturer specifies that all reground valves be lapped in for proper seating.

Valve spring compartments have reed-type breather valves of types shown in Figs. W36 and W37. Action of these valves during engine operation maintains a partial vacuum in engine crankcase to prevent internal pressure build-up which could cause oil leaks at seals and gaskets. If oil fouling occurs in ignition breaker box, condition of breather valve should be checked as a highly possible cause. These reed valve assemblies should be kept clean and renewed whenever found to be inoperable.

# WISCONSIN

## SERVICING WISCONSIN ACCESSORIES

### 12-VOLT STARTER-GENERATOR

The combination 12-volt starter-generator manufactured by Delco-Remy is used on some Wisconsin engines. The starter-generator functions as a cranking motor when starting switch is closed. When engine is operating and with starting switch open, unit operates as a generator. Generator output and circuit voltage for battery and various operating requirements are controlled by a current-voltage regulator.

To determine cause of abnormal operation, starter-generator should be given a "no-load" test or a "generator output" test. Generator output test can be performed with starter-generator on or off the engine. The no-load test must be made with starter-generator removed from engine. Refer to Fig. W38 for exploded view of starter-generator assembly. Parts are available from Wisconsin as well as authorized Delco-Remy service stations.

Starter-generator and regulator service test specifications are as follows:

**Starter-Generator 1101696**

Brush spring tension . . . . . 22-26 oz. (624-737 g)
Field draw:
- Amperes . . . . . 1.43-1.54
- Volts . . . . . 12

Cold output:
- Amperes . . . . . 10
- Volts . . . . . 14
- Rpm . . . . . 5750

No-load test:
- Volts . . . . . 11
- Amperes, max . . . . . 17
- Rpm, min . . . . . 2350
- Rpm, max . . . . . 2850

**Starter-Generator 1101870**

Brush spring tension . . . . . 22-26 oz. (624-737 g)
Field draw:
- Amperes . . . . . 1.52-1.62
- Volts . . . . . 12

Cold output:
- Amperes . . . . . 12
- Volts . . . . . 14
- Rpm . . . . . 4950

No-load test:
- Volts . . . . . 11
- Amperes, max . . . . . 18
- Rpm, min . . . . . 2500
- Rpm, max . . . . . 2900

**Starter-Generators 1101871 & 1101972**

Brush spring tension . . . . . 24-32 oz. (624-737 g)
Field draw:
- Amperes . . . . . 1.43-1.54
- Volts . . . . . 12

Cold output:
- Amperes . . . . . 10
- Volts . . . . . 14
- Rpm . . . . . 5450

No load test:
- Volts . . . . . 11
- Amperes, max . . . . . 17
- Rpm, min . . . . . 2500
- Rpm, max . . . . . 3000

**Regulators 1118791 & 1118985**

Ground polarity . . . . . Positive
Cut-out relay:
- Air gap . . . . . 0.020 in. (0.5 mm)
- Point gap . . . . . 0.020 in. (0.5 mm)
- Closing voltage, range . . . . . 11.8-14.0
- Adjust to . . . . . 12.8

Voltage regulator:
- Air gap . . . . . 0.075 in. (1.9 mm)
- Setting voltage, range . . . . . 13.6-14.5
- Adjust to . . . . . 14.0

**Regulators 1118983 & 1118984**

Ground polarity . . . . . Negative
Cut-out relay:
- Air gap . . . . . 0.020 in. (0.5 mm)
- Point gap . . . . . 0.020 in. (0.5 mm)
- Closing voltage, range . . . . . 11.8-14.0
- Adjust to . . . . . 12.8

Voltage regulator:
- Air gap . . . . . 0.075 (1.9 mm)
- Setting voltage, range . . . . . 13.6-14.5
- Adjust to . . . . . 14.0

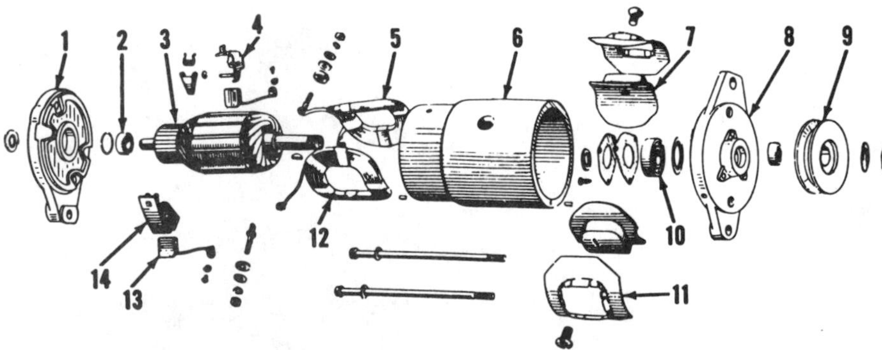


*Fig. W38—Exploded view of typical Delco-Remy starter-generator.*

1. Commutator end frame
2. Bearing
3. Armature
4. Ground brush holder
5. Field coil L.H.
6. Frame
7. Pole shoe
8. Drive end frame
9. Pulley
10. Bearing
11. Field coil insulator
12. Field coil R.H.
13. Brush
14. Insulated brush holder



Illustrations courtesy Teledyne Total Power.

## 12-VOLT GEAR DRIVE STARTER

Some einges may be equipped with a 12-volt gear drive starting motor manufactured by Prestolite. Test specifications are as follows:

**Prestolite MGD4102A**

Volts . . . . . . . . . . . . . . . . . . . . . . . . . .12
Brush spring tension . . . . . . . . .42-66 oz. (1190-1870g)
No-load test
Volts . . . . . . . . . . . . . . . . . . . . . . . .10
Amperes . . . . . . . . . . . . . . . . . . . . .38
Rpm . . . . . . . . . . . . . . . . . . . . . .10000

Refer to Fig. W39 for exploded view of starting motor and drive. Bendix drive (15) is available only as an assembly. Thrust washers (7, 8, 9, 12 and 13) are available in a service package.

To disassemble starting motor, remove the two through-bolts and commutator end cover (1). Remove brushes and springs from brush holder and remove holder assembly (3). Carefully withdraw frame and field coil assembly (6) from armature. Clamp steel core of armature in vise and remove Bendix drive retaining nut (16). Remove Bendix drive assembly (15), drive end plate (14) and thrust washers from armature (10).

Renew brush springs if heat damage is evident and renew brushes if excessively worn. Input brush (4) is integral with terminal stud and field brush (5) lead is soldered to field coil.

When reassembling, apply a light coat of oil to bushings. Do not lubricate Bendix drive assembly. Parts are available from Wisconsin as well as authorized Prestolite service stations.

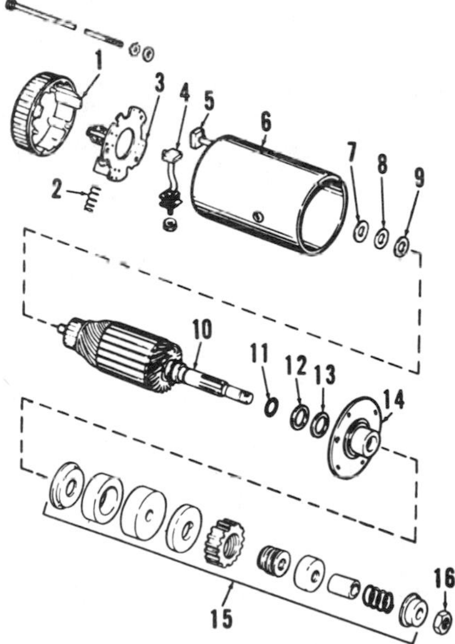


*Fig. W39—Exploded view of typical Prestolite gear drive starting motor.*

1. Commutator end cover
2. Brush spring (2 used)
3. Brush holder assy.
4. Input brush
5. Field brush
6. Frame & field coil assy.
7. Washer (0.031 in.)
8. Washer (0.23 in)
9. Washer (0.045 in.)
10. Armature
11. "O" ring
12. Washer (0.042 in.)
13. Washer (0.031 in.)
14. Drive end plate
15. Bendix drive assy.
16. Nut

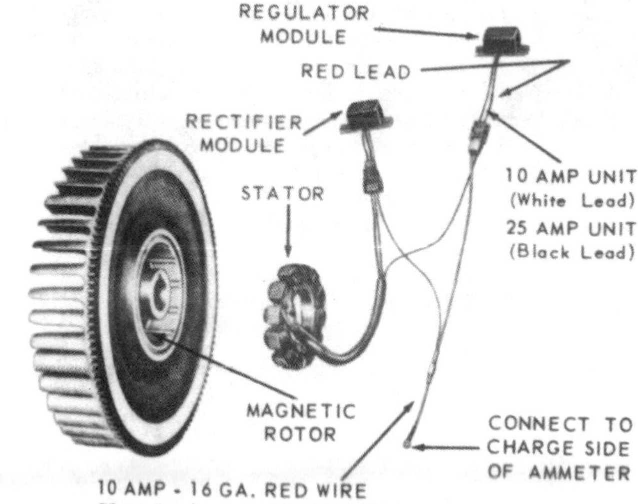


*Fig. W40—View of 10 or 25 amp flywheel alternator charging system used on some engines.*

## FLYWHEEL ALTERNATOR

Some engines may be equipped with either a 10 amp or 25 amp flywheel alternator. See Fig. W40. To avoid possible damage to alternator system, the following precautions must be observed:

1. Negative post of battery must be connected to ground on engine.
2. Connect booster battery properly (positive to positive and negative to negative.)
3. Do not attempt to polarize alternator.
4. Do not ground any wires from stator or modules which terminate at connectors.
5. Do not operate engine with battery disconnected.
6. Disconnect battery cables when charging battery with a battery charger.

**OPERATION.** Alternating current (AC) produced by the alternator is changed to direct current (DC) in the rectifier module. See Fig. W41. Current regulation is provided by the regulator module which "senses" counter-voltage created by the battery to control or limit charging rate. No adjustments are possible on alternator charging system. Faulty components must be renewed. Refer to following troubleshooting paragraph to help pin point faulty component.

**TROUBLESHOOTING.** Trouble conditions and their possible causes are as follows:

1. Full charge—no regulation. Could be caused by:
   a. Faulty regulator module
   b. Defective battery

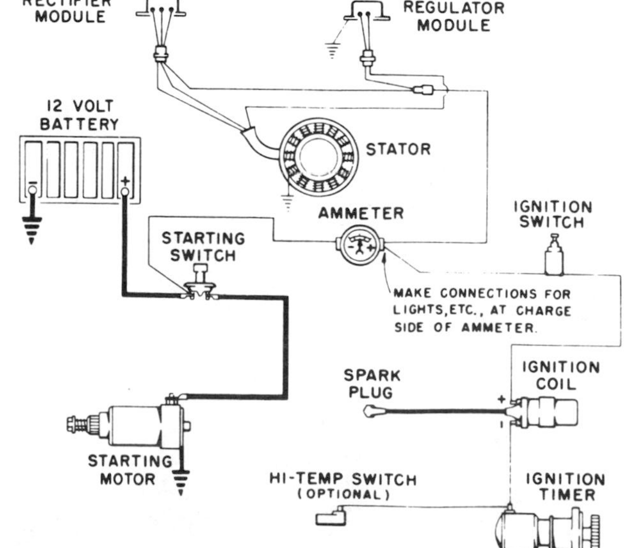


*Fig. W41—Typical wiring diagram for ignition, starting and alternator charging systems used on some engines.*

Illustrations courtesy Teledyne Total Power.

2. Low or no charge. Could be caused by:
   a. Faulty windings in stator
   b. Faulty rectifier module
   c. Regulator module not properly grounded or regulator module defective.

If "full-charge – no regulation" is the trouble, use a DC voltmeter and check battery voltage with engine operating at full rpm. If battery voltage is over 15.0 volts, regulator module is not functioning properly. If battery voltage is under 15.0 volts and over 14.0 volts, alternator, rectifier and regulator are satisfactory and battery is probably defective (unable to hold charge).

If "low" or "no charge" is the trouble, check battery voltage with engine operating at full rpm. If battery voltage is more than 14.0 volts, place a load on battery to reduce voltage to below 14.0 volts. If charge rate increases, alternator charging system is functioning properly and battery was fully charged. If charge rate does not increase, plug in a new rectifier module and retest. If charge increases, permanently install new rectifier module. If charge rate does not increase, stop engine and unplug all connectors between modules and stator. Start engine and operate at 2400 rpm. Using an AC voltmeter, check voltage between each of the black stator leads and ground. If either of the two voltage readings is zero or there is more than 10% difference between readings, the stator is faulty and should be renewed.

---

# METRIC CONVERSION TABLE

| INCHES | | MM |
|---|---|---|
| FRACT. | DECIMALS | |
| | .000 04 | .001 |
| | .000 39 | .01 |
| | .001 | .025 |
| | .000 78 | .02 |
| | .001 18 | .03 |
| | .001 57 | .04 |
| | .001 97 | .05 |
| | .002 | .051 |
| | .002 36 | .06 |
| | .002 5 | .0635 |
| | .002 76 | .07 |
| | .002 95 | .075 |
| | .003 | .0762 |
| | .003 15 | .08 |
| | .003 54 | .09 |
| | .003 94 | .1 |
| | .004 | .1016 |
| | .005 | .1270 |
| | .007 87 | .2 |
| | .009 84 | .25 |
| | .01 | .254 |
| | .011 81 | .3 |
| 1/64 | .015 63 | .3969 |
| | .015 75 | .4 |
| | .019 69 | .5 |
| | .02 | .508 |
| | .023 62 | .6 |
| | .025 | .635 |
| | .027 56 | .7 |
| | .029 5 | .75 |
| | .03 | .762 |
| 1/32 | .031 25 | .7938 |
| | .031 5 | .8 |
| | .035 43 | .9 |
| | .039 37 | 1.0 |
| | .04 | 1.016 |
| | .043 31 | 1.1 |
| 3/64 | .046 87 | 1.191 |
| | .047 24 | 1.2 |
| | .049 21 | 1.25 |
| | .05 | 1.27 |
| | .051 18 | 1.3 |
| | .055 12 | 1.4 |
| | .059 06 | 1.5 |

| INCHES | | MM |
|---|---|---|
| FRACT. | DECIMALS | |
| | .06 | 1.524 |
| 1/16 | .062 5 | 1.5875 |
| | .062 99 | 1.6 |
| | .066 93 | 1.7 |
| | .07 | 1.778 |
| | .07087 | 1.8 |
| | .075 | 1.905 |
| 5/64 | .078 13 | 1.9844 |
| | .078 74 | 2.0 |
| | .08 | 2.032 |
| | .082 68 | 2.1 |
| | .086 61 | 2.2 |
| | .088 58 | 2.25 |
| | .09 | 2.286 |
| | .090 55 | 2.3 |
| 3/32 | .093 75 | 2.3812 |
| | .094 49 | 2.4 |
| | .098 43 | 2.5 |
| | .1 | 2.54 |
| | .102 36 | **2.6** |
| | .106 30 | 2.7 |
| | .108 27 | 2.75 |
| 7/64 | .109 37 | 2.7781 |
| | .11 | 2.794 |
| | .110 24 | 2.8 |
| | .114 17 | 2.9 |
| | .118 11 | **3.0** |
| | .12 | 3.048 |
| | .12 05 | 3.1 |
| 1/8 | .125 | 3.175 |
| | .125 98 | 3.2 |
| | .127 96 | 3.25 |
| | .129 92 | 3.3 |
| | .13 | 3.302 |
| | .133 86 | 3.4 |
| | .137 80 | **3.5** |
| | .14 | 3.556 |
| 9/64 | .140 63 | 3.5719 |
| | .141 73 | 3.6 |
| | .145 67 | 3.7 |
| | .149 61 | 3.8 |
| | .15 | 3.810 |
| | .153 54 | 3.9 |

| INCHES | | MM |
|---|---|---|
| FRACT. | DECIMALS | |
| 5/32 | .156 25 | 3.9688 |
| | .157 48 | **4.0** |
| | .16 | 4.064 |
| | .161 42 | 4.1 |
| | .165 35 | 4.2 |
| | .169 29 | 4.3 |
| | .17 | 4.318 |
| 11/64 | .171 88 | 4.3656 |
| | .173 23 | 4.4 |
| | .177 17 | 4.5 |
| | .18 | 4.572 |
| | .181 10 | 4.6 |
| | .185 04 | 4.7 |
| 3/16 | .187 5 | 4.7625 |
| | .188 98 | 4.8 |
| | .19 | 4.826 |
| | .192 91 | 4.9 |
| | .196 85 | **5.0** |
| | .2 | 5.08 |
| | .200 79 | 5.1 |
| 13/64 | .203 13 | 5.1594 |
| | .204 72 | 5.2 |
| | .208 66 | 5.3 |
| | .21 | 5.334 |
| | .216 60 | 5.4 |
| | .216 54 | 5.5 |
| 7/32 | .21875 | 5.5562 |
| | .22 | 5.588 |
| | .220 47 | 5.6 |
| | .224 41 | 5.7 |
| | .228 35 | 5.8 |
| | .23 | 5.842 |
| | .232 28 | 5.9 |
| 15/64 | .234 38 | 5.9531 |
| | .236 22 | **6.0** |
| | .24 | 6.096 |
| | .240 16 | 6.1 |
| | .244 09 | 6.2 |
| | .248 03 | 6.3 |
| 1/4 | .25 | 6.35 |
| | .251 97 | 6.4 |
| | .255 91 | 6.5 |
| | .259 84 | 6.6 |
| | .26 | 6.604 |

| INCHES | | MM |
|---|---|---|
| FRACT. | DECIMALS | |
| | .263 78 | 6.7 |
| 17/64 | .265 63 | 6.7469 |
| | .267 72 | 6.8 |
| | .27 | 6.858 |
| | .271 65 | 6.9 |
| | .275 59 | 7.0 |
| | .279 53 | 7.1 |
| | .28 | 7.112 |
| 9/32 | .281 25 | 7.1438 |
| | .283 46 | 7.2 |
| | .287 40 | 7.3 |
| | .29 | 7.366 |
| | .291 34 | 7.4 |
| | .295 28 | 7.5 |
| 19/64 | .296 88 | 7.5406 |
| | .299 21 | 7.6 |
| | .30 | 7.62 |
| | .303 15 | 7.7 |
| | .307 09 | 7.8 |
| | .31 | 7.874 |
| | .311 02 | 7.9 |
| 5/16 | .312 5 | 7.9375 |
| | .314 96 | **8.0** |
| | .318 90 | 8.1 |
| | .32 | 8.128 |
| | .322 83 | 8.2 |
| | .326 77 | 8.3 |
| 21/64 | .328 13 | 8.3344 |
| | .33 | 8.382 |
| | .330 71 | 8.4 |
| | .334 65 | 8.5 |
| | .338 58 | 8.6 |
| | .34 | 8.636 |
| | .342 52 | 8.7 |
| 11/32 | .343 75 | 8.7312 |
| | .346 46 | 8.8 |
| | .35 | 8.89 |
| | .350 39 | 8.9 |
| | .354 33 | 9.0 |
| | .358 27 | 9.1 |
| 23/64 | .359 38 | 9.1281 |
| | .36 | 9.144 |
| | .362 20 | 9.2 |
| | .366 14 | 9.3 |

| INCHES | | MM |
|---|---|---|
| FRACT. | DECIMALS | |
| | .37 | 9.398 |
| | .370 08 | 9.4 |
| | .374 02 | 9.5 |
| 3/8 | .375 | 9.525 |
| | .377 95 | 9.6 |
| | .38 | 9.652 |
| | .381 89 | 9.7 |
| | .385 83 | 9.8 |
| | .389 76 | 9.9 |
| | .39 | 9.906 |
| 25/64 | .390 63 | 9.9219 |
| | .393 70 | **10.0** |
| | .397 64 | 10.1 |
| | .40 | 10.16 |
| | .401 57 | 10.2 |
| | .405 51 | 10.3 |
| 13/32 | .406 25 | 10.3188 |
| | .409 45 | 10.4 |
| | .41 | 10.414 |
| | .413 39 | 10.5 |
| | .417 32 | 10.6 |
| | .42 | 10.668 |
| | .421 26 | 10.7 |
| 27/64 | .421 88 | 10.7156 |
| | .425 20 | 10.8 |
| | .429 13 | 10.9 |
| | .43 | 10.992 |
| | .433 07 | 11.0 |
| | .437 01 | 11.1 |
| 7/16 | .437 5 | 11.1125 |
| | .44 | 11.176 |
| | .440 94 | 11.2 |
| | .444 88 | 11.3 |
| | .488 82 | 11.4 |
| | .45 | 11.430 |
| | .452 76 | 11.5 |
| 29/64 | .453 13 | 11.5094 |
| | .456 69 | 11.6 |
| | .46 | 11.684 |
| | .450 63 | 11.7 |
| | .464 57 | 11.8 |
| | .468 50 | 11.9 |
| 15/32 | .468 75 | 11.9062 |
| | .47 | 11.938 |
| | .472 44 | **12.0** |
| | .476 38 | 12.1 |
| | .48 | 12.192 |
| | .480 31 | 12.2 |
| | .484 25 | 12.3 |
| 31/64 | .484 38 | 12.3031 |
| | .488 19 | 12.4 |
| | .49 | 12.446 |
| | .492 13 | 12.5 |
| | .496 06 | 12.6 |
| 1/2 | .50 | 12.7 |
| | .503 94 | 12.8 |
| | .507 87 | 12.9 |
| | .51 | 12.954 |
| | .511 81 | 13.0 |
| 33/64 | .515 63 | 13.0969 |
| | .515 75 | 13.1 |
| | .519 68 | 13.2 |
| | .52 | 13.208 |
| | .523 62 | 13.3 |
| | .527 56 | 13.4 |
| | .53 | 13.462 |
| 17/32 | .531 25 | 13.4938 |
| | .531 50 | 13.5 |
| | .535 43 | 13.6 |
| | .539 37 | 13.7 |

| INCHES | | MM |
|---|---|---|
| FRACT. | DECIMALS | |
| | .54 | 13.716 |
| | .543 31 | 13.8 |
| 35/64 | .546 88 | 13.8906 |
| | .547 24 | 13.9 |
| | .55 | 13.970 |
| | .551 18 | **14.0** |
| | .555 12 | 14.1 |
| | .559 05 | 14.2 |
| | .56 | 14.224 |
| 9/16 | .562 50 | 14.2875 |
| | .562 99 | 14.3 |
| | .566 93 | 14.4 |
| | .57 | 14.478 |
| | .570 87 | 14.5 |
| | .574 80 | 14.6 |
| 37/64 | .578 13 | 14.6844 |
| | .578 74 | 14.7 |
| | .58 | 14.732 |
| | .582 68 | 14.8 |
| | .586 61 | 14.9 |
| | .59 | 14.986 |
| | .590 55 | 15.0 |
| 19/32 | .593 75 | 15.0812 |
| | .594 49 | 15.1 |
| | .598 42 | 15.2 |
| | .60 | 15.24 |
| | .602 36 | 15.3 |
| | .606 30 | 15.4 |
| 39/64 | .609 38 | 15.4781 |
| | .61 | 15.494 |
| | .610 24 | 15.5 |
| | .614 17 | 15.6 |
| | .61811 | 15.7 |
| | .62 | 15.748 |
| | .622 05 | 15.8 |
| 5/8 | .625 | 15.875 |
| | .625 98 | 15.9 |
| | .629 92 | **16.0** |
| | .63 | 16.002 |
| | .633 86 | 16.1 |
| | .637 79 | 16.2 |
| | .64 | 16.256 |
| 41/64 | .640 63 | 16.2719 |
| | .641 73 | 16.3 |
| | .645 67 | 16.4 |
| | .649 61 | 16.5 |
| | .65 | 16.510 |
| | .653 54 | 16.6 |
| 21/32 | .656 25 | 16.6688 |
| | .657 48 | 16.7 |
| | .66 | 16.764 |
| | .661 42 | 16.8 |
| | .665 35 | 16.9 |
| | .669 29 | 17.0 |
| | .67 | 17.018 |
| 43/64 | .671 88 | 17.0656 |
| | .673 23 | 17.1 |
| | .677 16 | 17.2 |
| | .68 | 17.272 |
| | .681 10 | 17.3 |
| | .685 04 | 17.4 |
| 11/16 | .687 50 | 17.4625 |
| | .688 98 | 17.5 |
| | .69 | 17.526 |
| | .692 91 | 17.6 |
| | .696 85 | 17.7 |
| | .70 | 17.78 |
| | .700 79 | 17.8 |
| 45/64 | .703 13 | 17.8594 |
| | .704 72 | 17.9 |

| INCHES | | MM |
|---|---|---|
| FRACT. | DECIMALS | |
| | .708 66 | **18.0** |
| | .71 | 18.034 |
| | .712 60 | 18.1 |
| | .716 53 | 18.2 |
| 23/32 | .718 75 | 18.2562 |
| | .72 | 18.288 |
| | .72047 | 18.3 |
| | .724 41 | 18.4 |
| | .728 35 | 18.5 |
| | .73 | 18.542 |
| | .732 28 | 18.6 |
| 47/64 | .734 38 | 18.6531 |
| | .736 22 | 18.7 |
| | .74 | 18.796 |
| | .740 16 | 18.8 |
| | .744 09 | 18.9 |
| | .748 03 | 19.0 |
| 3/4 | .75 | 19.050 |
| | .751 97 | 19.1 |
| | .755 90 | 19.2 |
| | .759 84 | 19.3 |
| | .76 | 19.304 |
| | .763 78 | 19.4 |
| 49/64 | .765 63 | 19.4469 |
| | .767 72 | 19.5 |
| | .77 | 19.558 |
| | .771 65 | 19.6 |
| | .775 59 | 19.7 |
| | .779 53 | 19.8 |
| | .78 | 19.812 |
| 25/32 | .781 25 | 19.8438 |
| | .783 46 | 19.9 |
| | .787 40 | **20.0** |
| | .79 | 20.066 |
| | .791 34 | 20.1 |
| | .795 27 | 20.2 |
| 51/64 | .796 88 | 20.2406 |
| | .799 21 | 20.3 |
| | .80 | 20.320 |
| | .803 15 | 20.4 |
| | .807 09 | 20.5 |
| | .81 | 20.574 |
| | .811 02 | 20.6 |
| 13/16 | .812 50 | 20.6375 |
| | .81496 | 20.7 |
| | .818 90 | 20.8 |
| | .82 | 20.828 |
| | .822 83 | 20.9 |
| | .826 77 | 21.0 |
| 53/64 | .828 13 | 21.0344 |
| | .83 | 21.082 |
| | .830 71 | 21.1 |
| | .834 64 | 21.2 |
| | .838 58 | 21.3 |
| | .84 | 21.336 |
| | .842 52 | 21.4 |
| 27/32 | .843 75 | 21.4312 |
| | .846 46 | 21.5 |
| | .85 | 21.590 |
| | .850 39 | 21.6 |
| | .854 33 | 21.7 |
| | .858 27 | 21.8 |
| 55/64 | .859 38 | 21.8281 |
| | .86 | 21.844 |
| | .862 20 | 21.9 |
| | .866 14 | 22.0 |
| | .87 | 22.098 |
| | .870 08 | 22.1 |
| | .874 01 | 22.2 |
| 7/8 | .875 | 22.225 |

| INCHES | | MM |
|---|---|---|
| FRACT. | DECIMALS | |
| | .877 95 | 22.3 |
| | .88 | 22.352 |
| | .881 89 | 22.4 |
| | .885 83 | 22.5 |
| | .889 76 | 22.6 |
| | .89 | 22.606 |
| 57/64 | .890 63 | 22.6219 |
| | .893 70 | 22.7 |
| | .897 64 | 22.8 |
| | .90 | 22.860 |
| | .901 57 | 22.9 |
| | .905 51 | 23.0 |
| 29/32 | .906 25 | 23.0188 |
| | .909 49 | 23.1 |
| | .91 | 23.114 |
| | .913 38 | 23.2 |
| | .917 32 | 23.3 |
| | .92 | 23.368 |
| | .921 26 | 23.4 |
| 59/64 | .921 88 | 23.4156 |
| | .925 20 | 23.5 |
| | .929 13 | 23.6 |
| | .93 | 23.622 |
| | .933 07 | 23.7 |
| | .937 01 | 23.8 |
| 15/16 | .937 50 | 23.8125 |
| | .94 | 23.876 |
| | .940 94 | 23.9 |
| | .944 88 | **24.0** |
| | .948 82 | 24.1 |
| | .95 | 24.130 |
| | .952 75 | 24.2 |
| 61/64 | .953 13 | 24.2094 |
| | .956 69 | 24.3 |
| | .96 | 24.384 |
| | .960 63 | 24.4 |
| | .964 57 | 24.5 |
| | .968 50 | 24.6 |
| 31/32 | .968 75 | 24.6062 |
| | .97 | 24.638 |
| | .972 44 | 24.7 |
| | .976 38 | 24.8 |
| | .98 | 24.892 |
| | .980 31 | 24.9 |
| | .984 25 | 25.0 |
| 63/64 | .984 38 | 25.0031 |
| | .988 19 | 25.1 |
| | .99 | 25.146 |
| | .922 12 | 25.2 |
| | .996 06 | 25.3 |
| 1″ | 1.000 00 | 25.4000 |
| 1-1/4 | 1.25 | 31.75 |
| 1-1/2 | 1.50 | 38.1 |
| 1-3/4 | 1.75 | 44.45 |
| 2″ | 2.000 | 50.8 |
| 2-1/2 | 2.5 | 63.5 |
| 3″ | 3.000 | 76.2 |
| 3-1/2 | 3.5 | 88.9 |
| | 3.937 | 100.00 |
| 4″ | 4.000 | 101.6 |
| 4-1/2 | 4.5 | 114.3 |
| 5″ | 5.000 | 127.0 |
| 6″ | 6.000 | 152.4 |
| 7″ | 7.000 | 177.8 |
| 8″ | 8.000 | 203.2 |
| 8-1/2 | 8.5 | 215.9 |
| 9″ | 9.000 | 228.6 |
| 10″ | 10.000 | 254.00 |
| 11″ | 11.000 | 279.4 |
| 12″ | 12.000 | 304.8 |

## TRACTOR MANUFACTURERS' ADDRESSES

**ALLIS-CHALMERS**
See Deutz-Allis

**ARIENS**
Ariens Company
655 West Ryan Street
Billion, WI 54110
(414) 756-2141

**BARON**
See Simplicity

**BOLENS**
Bolens
102nd Street & 9th Avenue
Troy, NY 12180
(518) 235-6010

**BROADMOOR**
See Simplicity

**CASE/INGERSOLL**
Ingersoll Equipment Co., Inc.
122 South 4th Street
Winneconne, WI 54986
(414) 582-7001

**CHARGER**
See Wheel Horse

**COMMANDO**
See Wheel Horse

**CUB CADET**
Cub Cadet Corp.
P.O. Box 360930
Cleveland, OH 44136
(216) 273-4550

**DEUTZ-ALLIS**
Deutz-Allis Lawn & Garden Equip.
500 North Spring Street
Port Washington, WI 53074
(414) 284-8669

**ENGINEERING PRODUCTS**
Engineering Products Co.
P.O. Box 1510
Waukesha, WI 53187
(414) 785-0786

**INTERNATIONAL HARVESTER**
See Cub Cadet

**JACOBSEN**
Jacobsen, Division of Textron, Inc.
1721 Packard Avenue
Racine, WI 53403
(414) 637-6711

**JIM DANDY**
See Engineering Products

**KUBOTA**
Kubota Tractor Corp.
550 W. Artesia Blvd.
Compton, CA 90220
(213) 537-2531

**JOHN DEERE**
Deere & Company
John Deere Road
Moline, IL 61265
(309) 765-4899

**FORD**
Ford New Holland, Inc.
500 Diller Avenue
New Holland, PA 17557
(717) 354-1112

**GILSON**
Lawn-Boy, Inc.
P.O. Box 152
Plymouth, WI 53073
(414) 893-1011

**GRAVELY**
Gravely International, Inc.
One Gravely Lane
Clemmons, NC 27012
(919) 766-7545

**HOMESTEADER**
See Deutz-Allis

**HONDA**
American Honda Motor Co., Inc.
4475 River Green Parkway
P.O. Box 100020
Duluth, GA 30136
(404) 497-6000

**LANDLORD**
See Simplicity

**LAWN RANGER**
See Wheel Horse

**MTD**
MTD Products, Inc.
P.O. Box 360900
Cleveland, OH 44136
(216) 225-0896

**MURRAY**
Murray Ohio Mfg. Co.
P.O. Box 268
Brentwood, TN 37027
(615) 373-6500

**POWER KING**
See Engineering Products

**RAIDER**
See Wheel Horse

**RANGER**
See Wheel Horse

**SERF**
See Simplicity

**SIMPLICITY**
Simplicity Manufacturing Co.
500 North Spring Street
Port Washington, WI 53074
(414) 284-8669

**SNAPPER**
Snapper
535 Macon Highway
McDonough, GA 30253
(404) 957-9141

**SOVEREIGN**
See Simplicity

**SPECIAL**
See Engineering Products

**SPEEDEX**
Speedex Tractor Co.
367 North Freedom Street
Ravenna, OH 44266
(216) 297-1484

**WESTERN AUTO**
Western Auto
2107 Grand
Kansas City, MO 64108
(816) 346-4000

**WHEEL HORSE**
Toro and Wheel Horse
8111 Lyndale Avenue South
Minneapolis, MN 55420
(612) 888-8801

**WHITE**
White Outdoor Products
P.O. Box 361131
Cleveland, OH 44136
(216) 273-5272

**WIZARD**
See Western Auto

**WORK HORSE**
See Wheel Horse

**YARD-MAN**
See MTD

**YEOMAN**
See Simplicity

## ENGINE MANUFACTURERS' ADDRESSES

**BRIGGS & STRATTON**
Briggs & Stratton Corp.
P.O. Box 702
Milwaukee, WI 53201
(414) 259-5333

**HONDA**
See Honda Under Tractor Manufacturers' Addresses

**KAWASAKI**
Kawasaki Motors Corp.
USA Engine Division
P.O. Box 504, 650 Industrial Circle
Station
Shakopee, MN 55379
(612) 445-6060

**KOHLER**
Kohler Co., Engine Div.
444 Highland Drive
Kohler, WI 53044
(414) 457-4441

**KUBOTA**
Kubota Engine Div.
1300 Remington Road
Schaumburg, IL 60173
(708) 884-0212

**ONAN**
Onan Corp.
1400 73rd Ave. N.E.
Minneapolis, MN 55432
(612) 574-5000

**TECUMSEH**
Tecumseh Products Co.,
Engine & Transmission Group
900 North Street
Grafton, WI 53024
(414) 377-4485

**WISCONSIN**
Teledyne Total Power
3409 Democrat Road
Memphis, TN 38181
(901) 365-3600

## TRANSMISSION MANUFACTURERS' ADDRESSES

**EATON**
Eaton Corp.
15151 Highway 5
Eden Prairie, MN 55344
(612) 937-7131

**HYDRO-GEAR**
Hydro-Gear, Inc.
P.O. Box 530
Sullivan, IL 61951
(217) 728-7665

**KANZAKI**
Tuff Torq Corp.
5943 Commerce Blvd.
Morristown, TN 37814
(615) 585-2000

**MTD**
See MTD Under Tractor
Manufacturers' Addresses

**PEERLESS**
Tecumseh Products Co.,
Engine & Transmission Group
900 North Street
Grafton, WI 53024
(414) 377-4485

**SIMPLICITY**
See Simplicity Under Tractor
Manufacturers' Addresses

**SPICER (FOOTE)**
Spicer Off-Highway Axle,
Division of Dana
P.O. Box 2424
Fort Wayne, IN 46801

**SUNDSTRAND**
Sauer-Sundstrand
2800 E. 13th Street
Ames, IA 50010
(515) 239-6000

**WHEEL HORSE**
See Wheel Horse Under Tractor
Manufacturers' Addresses

# NOTES

# NOTES

## NOTES

## Technical Information

Technical information is available from John Deere. Some of this information is available in electronic as well as printed form. Order from your John Deere dealer or call **1-800-522-7448**. Please have available the model number, serial number, and name of the product.

Available information includes:

- PARTS CATALOGS list service parts available for your machine with exploded view illustrations to help you identify the correct parts. It is also useful in assembling and disassembling.
- OPERATOR'S MANUALS providing safety, operating, maintenance, and service information. These manuals and safety signs on your machine may also be available in other languages.
- OPERATOR'S VIDEO TAPES showing highlights of safety, operating, maintenance, and service information. These tapes may be available in multiple languages and formats.
- TECHNICAL MANUALS outlining service information for your machine. Included are specifications, illustrated assembly and disassembly procedures, hydraulic oil flow diagrams, and wiring diagrams. Some products have separate manuals for repair and diagnostic information. Some components, such as engines, are available in separate component technical manuals
- FUNDAMENTAL MANUALS detailing basic information regardless of manufacturer:
  - Agricultural Primer series covers technology in farming and ranching, featuring subjects like computers, the Internet, and precision farming.
  - Farm Business Management series examines "real-world" problems and offers practical solutions in the areas of marketing, financing, equipment selection, and compliance.
  - Fundamentals of Services manuals show you how to repair and maintain off-road equipment.
  - Fundamentals of Machine Operation manuals explain machine capacities and adjustments, how to improve machine performance, and how to eliminate unnecessary field operations.

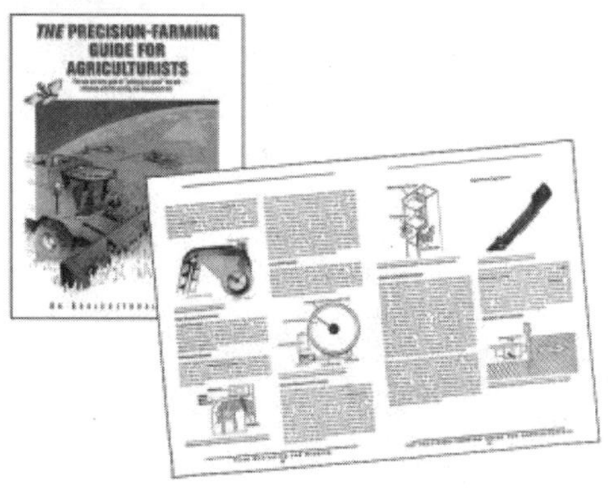